Drawn by D. Roberts. Printed by G. R. French. Engraved by J. H. Hills.

ROME-THE FORUM.

ROM. I. 7.
ACTS XXVIII. 14, 15, 30.

Hagar and Ishmael.

*And God opened her eyes, & she saw
a well of water; & she went & filled
the bottle with water, & gave the lad drink.*

GENESIS XXI. 19.

BRATTLEBORO'.

Published by Fessenden & Co.

ILLUSTRATIONS

OF THE

HOLY SCRIPTURES,

DERIVED PRINCIPALLY FROM THE

MANNERS, CUSTOMS, RITES, TRADITIONS, FORMS OF SPEECH ANTIQUITIES CLIMATE, AND WORKS OF ART AND LITERATURE,

OF THE

EASTERN NATIONS;

EMBODYING ALL THAT IS VALUABLE IN THE WORKS OF

HARMER, BURDER, PAXTON, AND ROBERTS,

AND THE MOST

CELEBRATED ORIENTAL TRAVELLERS;

EMBRACING ALSO THE SUBJECT OF THE

FULFILMENT OF PROPHECY

AS EXHIBITED BY KEITH AND OTHERS;

WITH DESCRIPTIONS OF THE

PRESENT STATE OF COUNTRIES AND PLACES MENTIONED IN THE SACRED WRITINGS, ILLUSTRATE BY NUMEROUS LANDSCAPE ENGRAVINGS, FROM SKETCHES TAKEN ON THE SPOT.

EDITED BY

REV. GEORGE BUSH,

PROFESSOR OF HEBREW AND ORIENTAL LITERATURE IN THE NEW YORK CITY UNIVERSITY.

PHILADELPHIA:

LIPPINCOTT, GRAMBO & CO.

1854.

PREFACE.

NEXT in worth and importance to the possession, is doubtless to be estimated the correct interpretation of the sacred volume. Indeed, it is the latter which gives its value to the former. A revelation not understood, or not intelligible, is no revelation, as far as its recipients are concerned. The position, therefore, that the meaning of the Bible *is* the Bible, we consider as unquestionably true, and consequently any new accession of light, which goes to clear up its obscurities, and cause its genuine sense to stand forth in bolder relief upon the inspired page, is in reality enriching us with a larger amount of its treasures, and virtually bestowing upon us added communications of the Divine will. In this view, the progressive elucidation of the scriptures, whether by the expository labours of critics, the researches of travellers, or the fulfilments of prophecy, may be compared to the gradual rolling away of the morning mist from a splendid landscape. As the sun advances, the shades retire, and new and interesting features of the scenery are continually opening upon the delighted eye of the spectator. Or, it may be said to resemble the slow, but momentous process of unfolding the ancient papyri, which the ravages of time and fire have spared among the ruins of Pompeii and Herculaneum. Here, as every successive word and letter, which can be redeemed from the crisp and crumbling texture of the blackened parchment, is noted down with the most scrupulous care, as forming a part of the continuous record, and going to make out its entire sense; so the sense of the sacred volume is gradually elicited, item by item, and needs only to be collected and treasured up with equal solicitude, in order to constitute a possession of infinitely more value than the choicest literary relics of antiquity. Perhaps it may be safely affirmed, that the materials are at this moment in existence, for the satisfactory solution of nearly every doubtful passage of holy writ; but the great desideratum is to have them brought together—to collect them from their wide dispersion over a countless multitude of writings, in various languages, which the great majority of Christians can neither procure nor understand. It is only in this way that they can be made really available to the great end which they are calculated to subserve; and far from idle are the claims of any one who professes to bring from scattered sources a new quota to the general stock of biblical illustration.

As the Bible, in its structure, spirit, and costume, is essentially an Eastern book, it is obvious that the natural phenomena, and the moral condition of the East, should be made largely tributary to its elucidation. In order to appreciate fully the truth of its descriptions, and the accuracy, force, and beauty of its various allusions, it is indispensable that the reader, as far as possible, separate himself from his ordinary associations, and put himself, by a kind of mental transmigration, into the very circumstances of the writers. He must set himself down in the midst of oriental scenery—gaze upon the sun, sky, mountains, and rivers of Asia—go forth with the nomade tribes of the desert—follow their flocks—travel with their caravans—rest in their tents—lodge in their khans—load and unload their camels—drink at their watering-places—pause during the heat of the day under the shade of their palms—cultivate the fields with their own rude implements—gather in or glean after their harvests—beat out and ventilate the grain in their open thrashing-floors—dress in their costume—note their proverbial or idiomatic forms of speech, and listen to the strain of song or story, with which they beguile the vacant hours. In a word, he must surround himself with, and transfuse himself into, all the forms, habitudes, and usages of oriental life. In this way only can he catch the sources of their imagery, or enter into full communion with the genius of the sacred penmen.

While, therefore, we readily concede the very high importance of critical and philological research in dissipating the obscurities of the scriptures, and fixing their exact sense, we cannot, at the same time, but think that the collateral illustrations derived from this source, are deserving of at least equal attention from the student of revelation. The truth is, the providence of God, which is never more worthily employed than about his Word, seems now to be directing the eyes of his servants, as with pointed finger, to the immense stores of elucidation constantly accumulating from this quarter. The tide of travel within a few years, has turned remarkably to the East. Animated either by the noble spirit of missionary enterprise, of commercial speculation, of military adventure, or laudable curiosity, men of intelligence and observation have made their way into every region on which the light of revelation originally shone; exploring its antiquities, mingling with its inhabitants, detailing its manners and customs, and displaying its physical, moral, and political circumstances. From these expeditions they have returned laden with the rich results of their industry, and the labours of the pen and the pencil have made thousands partakers of the benefit. Somewhat more than half a century ago, when the justly celebrated Observations of Harmer were given to the public, the range of materials to which he had access was comparatively limited. The travels of Chardin, Pococke, Shaw, Maundrell, Pitts, D'Arvieux, with Russel's Natural History of Aleppo, were his principal authorities—authorities, it is true, which have not yet been wholly superseded. But since his time, what an immense accession has the department of oriental travels received! The names of Volney, Niebuhr, Mariti, Clarke, Chateaubriand, Porter, Burckhardt, Buckingham, Morier, Seetzen, De Lamartine, Laborde, exhaust but a small part of the list of eastern tourists, whose labours have gone to make us familiarly acquainted with the land of patriarchs, prophets, and apostles. How desirable that the scattered gleams of illustrative light, which shine in their works, should be concentrated into one focus of illumination! This is the task which we have essayed in the present volume.

In entering upon and advancing in this task, we have been more and more impressed with the remarkable fact of the permanence of eastern usages. True to the traditions of their ancestors, and impenetrable thus far to the spirit of innovation, their manners and customs, opinions and institutions, retain all the fixedness of their mountains, and flow on as unvarying as the course of their streams. To the question, therefore, whether the state of things in the East, as described by modern travellers, really coincides with that which existed at the time the scriptures were written, so that one may be cited as conveying a correct idea of the other; we may reply, in the words of Sir John Chardin, one of the most respectable and authentic of the number:—"I have written nothing," says he, "of the Indies, because I lived but five years there, and understood only the vulgar languages, which are the Indian and Persian, without the knowledge of that of the Brahmins; but, nevertheless, I did not spend my time there in idleness: on the contrary, as the winters in that country will not permit one to travel, I employed that time in a work which I had long in my thoughts, and which I may call my *favourite design*, by the pleasure wherewith I laboured in it, and the profit which I hope the public will receive thereby; which is certain notes upon very many passages of holy scripture, whereof the explication depends on the knowledge of the customs of the eastern countries; for the East is the scene of all the historical facts mentioned in the Bible. The language of that divine book (especially of the Old Testament) being oriental, and very often figurative and hyperbolical, those parts of scripture which are written in verse, and in the prophecies, are full of figures and hyperboles, which, as it is manifest, cann'ot be well understood without a knowledge of things from whence such figures are taken, which are natural properties and particular manners of the countries to which they refer. I discerned this in my first voyage to the Indies: for I *gradually found a greater sense and beauty in divers passages of scripture than I had before*, by having in my view the things, either natural or moral, which explained them to me; and in perusing the different translations which the greatest part of the translators of the Bible had made, I observed that every one of them (to render the expositions, as they thought, more intelligible) used such expressions as would accommodate the phrase to the places where they writ; and which did not only many times pervert the text, but often rendered the sense obscure, and sometimes absurd also. In fine, consulting the commentators upon such kind of passages, I found very strange mistakes in them, and that they had long guessed at the sense, and did but grope (as in the dark) in search of it. And from these reflections I took a resolution to make my remarks upon many passages of the scriptures; persuading myself that they would be equally agreeable and profitable for use. And the learned, to whom I communicated my design, encouraged me very much, by their commendations, to proceed in it; and more especially when I informed them, that *it is not in Asia, as in our Europe, where there are frequent changes, more or less, in the form of things, as the habits, buildings, gardens, and the like.* IN THE EAST THEY ARE CONSTANT IN ALL THINGS; *the habits are at this day in the same manner as in the precedent ages;* so that one may reasonably believe, that in that part of the world, the exterior form of things (as their manners and customs) are the same now as they were two thousand years since, except in such changes as have been introduced by religion, which are, nevertheless, very inconsiderable."—(Preface to Travels in Persia, p. 6.) Morier, an eastern traveller, says, "The manners of the East, amid all the changes of government and religion, *are still the same;* they are living impressions from an original mould; and at every step, some object, some idiom, some dress, or some custom of common life, reminds the traveller of ancient times, *and confirms, above all, the beauty, the accuracy, and the propriety of the language and the history of the Bible.*"

This very striking testimony to the conformity, or rather identity, of the modern with the ancient usages of the East, is abundantly confirmed from other sources, as scarcely a traveller has set foot upon oriental soil, without professing himself to be at once struck with the remarkable coincidence between the picture of ancient manners, as drawn in the sacred writings, and the state of things which actually meets his eye. This steadfast resistance to the spirit of innovation and change, which thus remarkably distinguishes the nations of the East, will probably, in the providence of God, remain unsubdued, till it shall have answered all the important purposes of biblical elucidation, when it will give way to the all-pervading, all-regenerating influence of the Bible itself, borne upon the bosom of a new tide of civilization and improvement, which shall, ere long, set in upon the East from the nations of Europe, and the great continent of the West. "By a wonderful provision of Providence," says De Lamartine, "who never creates wants without at the same time creating the means of satisfying them, it happens, that at the moment when the great crisis of civilization takes place in Europe, and when the new necessities resulting from it are revealing themselves, both to governments and people, a great crisis of an inverse order takes place in the East, and a vast void is there offered for the redundancy of European population and faculties. The excess of life which is overflowing here, may and must find an outlet in that part of the world; the excess of force which overstrains us, may and must find employment in those countries, where the human powers are in a state of exhaustion and torpidity, where the stream of population is stagnant or drying up, where the vitality of the human race is expiring."

In the mean time, while the inevitable doom of revolution and transformation that awaits the East, lingers, it behooves us to make the most, for useful purposes, of that state of society which still exists, but which, ere long, will have passed away. With this view, we have endeavoured to imbody in the present volume a large mass of oriental illustration. The work is strictly of an eclectic character. Postponing the claims of originality to those of practical utility, the Editor, after arraying before him the amplest store of materials which he could command, set himself to the task of selecting and arranging the most valuable portions which he could bring within the limits of his plan. The kindred works of Harmer, Burder, Paxton, Taylor's edition of Calmet, scarcely any of which are in common accessible to the majority of biblical students, have been diligently gleaned, and all their important contents transferred to our pages. As these works are not likely ever to be reprinted in this country, there appeared no other way to arrest their progress to oblivion, and to secure a larger and wider circulation to the valuable matter which they contain.

But the range of selection has been by no means confined to the works now mentioned. So prolific has been the press within the last twenty or thirty years, of books of eastern travels, illustrative of manners, customs, and religion, that our resources in this department have been almost indefinitely multiplied. But to one work in particular—Roberts' Oriental

Illustrations of the Sacred Scriptures, collected during a residence of nearly fourteen years among the Hindoos—the Editor desires, as an act of justice, to which he is sure the reader will most heartily respond, to express his very deep obligations. He considers himself peculiarly fortunate in meeting with this work just as he was entering upon his own undertaking, so that he has been able to incorporate it nearly entire in the present volume. Though abounding chiefly in illustrations drawn from the parabolical, idiomatical, and proverbial phraseolgy common in the East, yet his notes are so pointed and pertinent in their scope, so felicitous and graphic in their turn of expression, and so remarkable for the vividness with which the leading idea is exhibited, that we doubt not the reader will find in this part alone an ample equivalent for the cost of the whole volume. The Rev. T. H. Horne says he feels himself "justified in recommending Mr. Roberts' 'Illustrations,' as supplying an important desideratum in biblical literature. They furnish to very many difficult or obscure passages satisfactory explanations, which are not more original than they are entertaining and instructive." "Mr. Roberts' work," says the British Critic, "is replete with interesting matter, and, in a condensed form, contains more illustrations of Holy Writ than any other book we know of. He richly deserves our thanks, and the thanks especially of those who are not able to possess many volumes illustrative of the oriental rites and customs to be found in the Bible. We have only to add, that this volume is worth all the twopenny trash which the last half dozen years have given birth to."

As the present work is designed to be marked by somewhat of the same *Comprehensive* character which distinguishes the other biblical works lately issued from the press of the Publishers, the illustrations bear upon numerous other points than those relating to manners and customs. Every thing of a purely doctrinal character, about which the different denominations of Christians might be supposed to disagree, has been studiously excluded; at least such has been the Editor's intention, and if any thing should be met with that seems to gainsay this declaration, he begs it may be set down to the account of a momentary inadvertence, rather than of a determinate purpose. But with this exception, he has given himself as much latitude in the selection of matter, as was consistent with a *prevailing* unity of design in the structure of the whole.

The subject of the Fulfilment of Prophecy, cannot well be lost sight of by any one conversant at once with the scriptures and the reports of modern travellers. The topographical descriptions of many of the most noted places of scripture, a department to which particular attention has been given in the ensuing pages, suggests at once the divine predictions bearing upon their future doom. The researches of tourists, both skeptics and Christians, have poured a flood of light upon this subject. It is perfectly astonishing, to one who has never examined the subject, to find how *literally* and *minutely* the prophetic declarations of scripture have been fulfilled, so that even infidel travellers and historians, as Volney and Gibbon, in their accounts of nations and countries, have unwittingly used for *description*, almost the words of scripture in which the events are foretold. Volney, particularly, (one of the bitterest opposers of Christianity,) in his published travels in the East, has afforded, unwillingly and unthinkingly, a wonderful attestation to the truth of the Bible, in the relation of facts which came under his own eye. There needs no better witness. Indeed, it is impossible for the most determined infidel carefully to examine and weigh this subject, and not be forced to feel that the Bible is divine; or, in the words of Bishop Newton, "he is reduced to the necessity, either to renounce his senses, deny what he reads in the Bible, and what he sees and observes in the world, or acknowledge the truth of prophecy, and consequently, of divine revelation." The researches of travellers in Palestine have been abundant, and the prophecies thereby verified are numerous and distinct, so that the facts may be related literally in the language of the prophecy. To use the words of a late writer in the London Quarterly Review, "we confess that we have felt more surprise, delight, and conviction, in examining the accounts which the travels of Burckhardt, Mangles, Irby, Leigh, and Laborde, have so recently given of Judea, Edom, &c. than we have ever derived from any similar inquiry. It seems like a miracle in our own times. Twenty years ago we read certain portions of the prophetic scriptures, with a belief that they were true, because other similar passages had, in the course of ages, been proved to be so, and we had an indistinct notion, that all these (to us) obscure and indefinite denunciations had been—we knew not very well when or how—accomplished: but to have graphic descriptions, ground plans, and elevations, showing the actual existence of all the heretofore vague and shadowy denunciations of God against Edom, does, we confess, excite our feelings, and exalt our confidence in prophecy, to a height that no *external* evidence has hitherto done. . . . . Here we have—bursting upon our age of incredulity, by the labours of accidental, impartial, and sometimes incredulous" (infidel) "witnesses—the certainty of existing facts, which fulfil what were considered hitherto the most vague and least intelligible of the prophecies. The value of one such contemporaneous proof is immense." Indeed, it would seem that in regard to such places as Babylon, Nineveh, Tyre, Moab, Edom, and others, the providence of God was no less conspicuous in bringing to light, in these latter ages, the *evidence* of the accomplishment of those prophecies, than formerly in working the *accomplishment itself*. The valuable labours of Keith in this department, arranged in accordance with our general plan, so as to exhibit the commentary under its appropriate text, will be found to have added much to the interest and profit of the reader in perusing our pages.

The numerous highly finished engravings, executed by distinguished artists, from sketches taken on the spot, and accompanied, for the most part, with letter-press descriptions by the Rev. T. H. Horne, originally published in Finden's Landscape Illustrations, will go also greatly to enhance the value of this portion of the illustrations.

A critical note is occasionally thrown in, where the point of a passage seemed capable of a happy explication, especially from a more exact analysis of the import of the original terms. Those bearing the signature of the Editor will perhaps usually be found of this character, and for any seeming infraction in this of his general plan, he solicits the indulgence not unreasonably claimed for a favourite mode of scripture exposition. They are, however, for the most part, "few and far between."

As a prominent object aimed at throughout has been, not only to increase the facilities for a complete understanding of the inspired volume, but also to multiply the evidences, and vindicate the claims of its divine original, a portion of our pages has been allotted to the direct consideration of infidel objections and cavils. The most important extracts of this description have been taken from the valuable and now rare "Life of David," by Chandler, in which the insinuations of Bayle against the character of David, are canvassed and refuted with distinguished ability, though perhaps somewhat more verbosely than is consistent with the taste either of modern writers or readers.

The original and acute remarks of Michaelis, on many points of the Mosaic laws and ritual, though sometimes bordering upon the fanciful, disclose a profound acquaintance with the genius of the East, and are generally entitled to deep attention.

As the authorities employed in the preparation of the ensuing pages are usually quoted in a very general way—for the most part merely by citing the writer's name—it will probably be rendering an important service to many of our readers, to give a more ample view of the sources upon which we have drawn for materials. The list is by no means complete, nor, as many have served us at second hand, is it perhaps practicable or necessary that it should be; but the most important and valuable will be found here grouped together, and ordinarily, by turning to this catalogue, the entire title, including edition and date, of any work cited in the ensuing pages simply by the author's name, will be found. Such a catalogue may be of service for other purposes than those connected with the present volume.

Harmer's *Observations on Various Passages of Scripture, with additions by Adam Clarke, LL. D.*, 4 vols. 8vo. Charlestown, 1811.
Paxton's *Illustrations*, 3 vols. 8vo. Edinburgh, 1825.
Burder's *Oriental Customs*, 2 vols. 8vo. London, 1816.
" *Oriental Literature, with Rosenmuller's Additions*, 2 vols. 8vo. London, 1822.
Roberts' *Oriental Illustrations*, 8vo. London, 1835.
Calmet's *Dictionary*, Taylor's Edition, 5 vols. 4to. London, 1829.
Shaw's *Travels through Barbary and the Levant*, folio. Lon. 1738.
Maundrell's *Journey from Aleppo to Jerusalem*, 8vo. Oxford, 1749.
Volney's *Travels through Egypt and Syria*, 8vo. New York, 1798.
Mariti's *Travels through Cyprus, Syria, and Palestine*, 2 vols. 8vo. Dublin, 1793.
Baron De Tott's *Memoirs on the Turks and Tartars*, 3 vols. 12mo. Dublin, 1785.
Russell's *Natural history of Aleppo*, 2 vols. 4to. London, 1794.
Clarke's *Travels in the Holy Land*, 12mo. Philadelphia, 1817.
Tournefort's *Voyage to the Levant*, 3 vols. 8vo. London, 1741.
Buckingham's *Travels in Mesopotamia*, 2 vols. 8vo. London, 1827.
" *Travels among the Arab Tribes*, 4to. London, 1825.
Burckhardt's *Travels in Arabia*, 4to. London, 1829.
" *Travels in Nubia and Egypt*, 4to. London, 1822.
Madden's *Travels in Turkey, Egypt, and Palestine*, 2 vols. 12mo. Philadelphia, 1830.
Madox's *Excursions in the Holy Land, Egypt, Nubia, Syria, &c.*, 2 vols. 8vo. London, 1834.
Callaway's *Oriental Observations*, 12mo. London, 1825.
Campbell's *African Light*, 12mo. London, 1835.
Anderson's *Tour through Greece*, 12mo. Boston, 1831.
Hardy's *Notices of the Holy Land*, 12mo. London, 1835.
Chateaubriand's *Travels*, 8vo. New York, 1814.
Keppel's *Narrative of a Journey from India to England*, 8vo. Philadelphia, 1827.
Morier's *Journey through Persia*, 8vo. Philadelphia, 1816.
Smith and Dwight's *Researches in Armenia*, 2 vols. 12mo. Boston, 1833.
Jowett's *Christian Researches in Syria and the Holy Land*, 8vo. London, 1825.
Modern Traveller, *Palestine, Syria, and Asia Minor*, 3 vols. 12mo. Boston, 1830.
Heeren's *Asiatic Nations*, 3 vols. 8vo. Oxford, 1833.
Waddington's *Travels in Ethiopia*, 4to. London, 1827.
Hoskins' *Travels in Ethiopia*, 4to. London, 1835.
Burnes's *Travels in Bokhara*, 2 vols. 12mo. Philadelphia, 1835.
Munroe's *Summer Ramble in Syria*, 2 vols. 8vo. London, 1835.
Hogg's *Visit to Alexandria, Damascus, and Jerusalem*, 2 vols. 12mo. London, 1835.
Wilkinson's *Thebes, and General View of Egypt*, 8vo. London, 1835.
Arundell's *Discoveries in Asia Minor*, 2 vols. 8vo. London, 1834.
De Lamartine's *Pilgrimage to the Holy Land*, 2 vols. 12mo. Philadelphia, 1835.
Stackhouse's *History of the Bible*, 2 vols. folio. London, 1755.
Chandler's *Life of David*, 2 vols. 8vo. London, 1766.
Michaelis's *Commentaries on the Laws of Moses*, 4 vols. 8vo. London, 1814.
Gleig's *History of the Bible*, 3 vols. 12mo. New York, 1831
Horsley's *Sermons*, 8vo. London, 1830.
Pococke's *Theological Works*, 2 vols. folio. London, 1740.
Newcome's *Minor Prophets*, 8vo. Pontefract, 1809.
Keith's *Evidence of Prophecy*, 12mo. New York. 1833.
Good's *Translation of Job*, 8vo. London, 1812.
Finden's *Landscape Illustrations*. London, 1835.

The importance of the present work must be obvious, and being altogether *illustrative*, without reference to doctrines, or other points in which Christians differ, it is hoped it will meet with favour from all who love the sacred volume, and that it will be sufficiently interesting and attractive to recommend itself, not only to professed Christians of *all* denominations, but also to the general reader. The arrangement of the texts illustrated with the notes, in the order of the chapters and verses of the authorized version of the Bible, will render it convenient for reference to particular passages, while the *copious* Index at the end, will at once enable the reader to turn to every subject discussed in the volume.

It only remains for the Editor to remark, that he would by no means be held responsible for the truth or justice of every sentiment advanced by way of interpretation or illustration in the present work. He hopes not to be considered as adopting himself all the various explications of scripture which he has yet felt it his duty to propound. Many of them are proposed by their authors themselves merely as conjectures, and though he may occasionally have entertained doubts of their correctness, yet, as they involved only points of minor importance, he has seldom felt himself called upon to turn aside to question or confute them. A very large mass of obviously true or highly probable illustration, is here presented to the reader. As to the pertinency or verisimilitude of particular portions, he will of course exercise a due discrimination; he cannot be expected to forego his own judgment, nor will he find it necessary to presume upon that of him who has thus endeavoured, however feebly, to minister, by so great a variety of provision, to his instruction and pleasure.

G. B.

New York, May 1st, 1836.

ILLUSTRATIONS

OF THE

HOLY SCRIPTURES.

GENESIS.

CHAP. 1. Ver. 1. In the beginning God created the heavens and the earth.

Notwithstanding the industrious attempts of many skeptical writers to array the evidence deducible from geological discoveries against the Mosaic account of the creation, nothing has yet been advanced to invalidate the testimony of the inspired record, as nothing has yet been brought to show that its statements, *when rightly understood*, are at all at variance with any of the clear and undoubted results of scientific research. We say, *when rightly understood;* for that the conclusions of the geologist, even the most legitimate and demonstrable, may be inconsistent with the *popular interpretation* of the sacred narrative, we by no means deny; but it is obvious that such interpretation *may* be erroneous, and that all that is requisite to bring the two departments into perfect harmony, may be the fixing of the *genuine sense* of the writer by a purely philological process. Until, therefore, it is established beyond controversy that the language of Moses cannot, by any possibility of fair construction, be made to tally with, or at least not to contradict, the admitted truths of geological science, it is vain to charge revelation with uttering oracles at variance with the irrefragable teachings of nature. But this, it is to be remembered, never has been, and we are confident never will be, done. The material fabric of the universe and the book of inspiration are the works of the same author, and we may be sure that the *truths* pertaining to the one cannot be at war with those belonging to the other. The following remarks of the Rev. Bartholomew Lloyd, Provost of Trinity College, Dublin, on the drift of the sacred penman in the first chapter of Genesis, cannot but commend themselves to every enlightened reader: "The sacred writer prefaces his history of God's government over his chosen people, by informing us, that 'in the beginning God created the heavens and the earth,' and it seems equally certain that he here speaks of the original creation of all things out of nothing. This, indeed, is a great subject, and though nothing circumstantial is here revealed to us concerning it, yet the sacred importance of the truth, assured to us by this simple expression, is every way suitable to the prominent place assigned to it; for it is nothing less than the authoritative statement of the first and fundamental article of all true religious faith. By it we are taught that self-existence is an attribute of the one supreme Being, and that all things besides owe their existence to His unlimited power. How necessary it was to mankind to have an authoritative declaration on this subject, we may readily convince ourselves by adverting to the errors into which the most celebrated men of all antiquity had fallen, who presumed to speculate on these matters, so far beyond the reach of human reason, without other guidances. Among these erroneous opinions, or rather among those wild conjectures, we find the following:—that matter was eternal; that the Deity was the soul of the world; agreeably to which, the material frame of nature was to be regarded as his body, and not as his work. Now, in this his first sentence, the inspired writer settles definitively what we are to believe on this subject, by stating the primary relation which all things in common bear to the supreme Being; and with this information he forbears from mixing up any other matter. For it will be perceived that the statement is made without any specification of time or other circumstance; seemingly, because no addition of this kind could be of use in aiding our conceptions of a truth purely religious, or in strengthening our faith in the authority on which it was proposed; but chiefly because it was the sole object of the writer, in this first sentence, to claim for God the creation of all things whatsoever, and that this claim must remain unshaken, however we may decide on other questions which may be raised about the creation; such as that relative to the time when it occurred; how long before the origin of the human race; whether all the parts of the universe were brought into existence simultaneously, or at different and widely distant epochs. It is plain, then, that in this place the sacred writer furnishes no helps for the decision of such questions. Let us look to what follows. In proceeding to those arrangements by which the earth was to be fitted for the residence and support of man, and the other inferior tribes by which it was then to be tenanted, we find him describing its preceding condition; informing us that it was then 'without form and void,' and that 'darkness was upon the face of the deep.' Now, I confess that this always seemed to me very like the description of a ruined world: and if such was the earth at that time, it would be difficult to suppose that it had not existed long before. But this is not all. When he does come to the work of the six days, we find the description of each day's work introduced by an expression of a particular form, and concluded by another, by which it appears that the original work of creation, spoken of in the first verse, is excluded from the series of performances belonging to those days;—and, if excluded, then, perhaps, removed to an indefinite distance; for had it immediately preceded, we might naturally expect to find it spoken of, either as the work of the first of a series of seven days, or as part of the work of the first of the six days. This, then, would seem to remove the work of the original creation far beyond that of the reconstruction of the globe. It is true, that nothing is exhibited to our imaginations to mark the interval between these performances; but to deny that there was such an interval, and for that reason, would be to conclude about as wisely as the peasant, who supposes the clouds to be contiguous to the stars, because when looking up he discerns nothing between them."

Dr. Chalmers, in his treatise on the Evidences of Christianity, speaks to the same effect. "Does Moses ever say, that when God created the heavens and the earth, he did more, at the time alluded to, than transform them out of previously existing materials? Or does he ever say, that there was not an interval of many ages between the first act of creation, described in the first verse of the book of Genesis, and said to have been performed in the beginning, and those more detailed operations, the account of which commences at the second verse, and which are described to us as having been performed in so many days? Or, finally, does he ever make us understand, that the generations of man went further than to fix the antiquity of the species, and of consequence that they left the antiquity of the globe a free subject for the speculations of philosophers?"

"We do not know," says Sharon Turner, "and we have no means of knowing, at what point of the ever-flowing eternity of that which is alone eternal—the Divine subsistence—the creation of our earth, or of any part of the universe began, nor in what section of it we are living now. All that we can learn explicitly from revelation is, that nearly 6000 years have passed since our first parent began to be. Our chronology, that of Scripture, is dated from the period of his creation; and almost 6000 years have elapsed since he moved and breathed a full-formed man. But what series of time had preceded his formation, or in what portion of the anteceding succession of time this was effected, has not been disclosed, and cannot by any effort of human ingenuity be now explored.—Creation must have begun at some early part of anteceding eternity; and our earth may have had its commencement in such a primeval era, as well as in a later one."

Professor Hitchcock, in an elaborate and very able essay on the connexion between Geology and the Mosaic History, (Biblic. Reposit. Oct. 1835,) undertakes to establish, and we think with entire success, the following positions, which we give in his own words:—"In the first place, we maintain that between geology and revelation there are several unexpected and remarkable coincidences, such as could have resulted only from veracity on the part of the sacred historian; and that the points of agreement are far more numerous than the points of apparent collision; and, therefore, even geology alone furnishes a strong presumptive evidence in favour of the truth of the Mosaic history. We maintain, secondly, that the first chapter of Genesis is a portion of Scripture that has always occasioned much difficulty in its interpretation, apart from geology, and that those portions of it about which commentators have differed most, are the very ones with which geology is supposed to come into collision; so that in fact scarcely any new interpretation has been proposed to meet the geological difficulty. We admit, thirdly, that the geological difficulty is real; that is, the established facts of geology do teach us that the earth has existed through a vastly longer period, anterior to the creation of man, than the common interpretation of Genesis allows. We maintain, fourthly, that most of the methods that have been proposed to avoid or reconcile the geological difficulty are entirely inadequate, and irreconcilably at variance either with geology or revelation. We maintain, fifthly, that at least one or two of these proposed modes of reconciling geology and Scripture, although not free from objections, are yet so probable, that without any auxiliary considerations, they would be sufficient, in the view of every reasonable man, to vindicate the Mosaic history from the charge of collision with the principles of geology. And finally, we maintain, that though all these modes of reconciliation should be unsatisfactory, it would be premature and unreasonable to infer that there exists any real discrepance: first, because we are by no means certain that we fully understand every part of the Mosaic account of the creation; secondly, because geology is so recent a science, and is making so rapid advances, that we may expect from its future discoveries that some more light will be thrown upon cosmogony: and thirdly, because, as geology has been more and more thoroughly understood, the apparent discrepances between it and revelation have become less numerous."—B.

Ver. 9. And God said, Let the waters under the heaven be gathered together unto one place, and let the dry *land* appear: and it was so.

We have before remarked, that, during the first and second days of the creation, the earth must have presented to the view, (had any human eye existed to look upon it,) a solid globe of spheroidal form, covered with a thin coat of aqueous fluid, and already revolving on its axis as a member of the solar system. We are fully authorized in coming to this latter conclusion, from the distinct mention made in the record, of the *days*, comprising, like our present days, the *evening* and the *morning*, with the darkness and the light following each other in regular succession. The sun, it is true, had not yet been made visibly to appear, or to shine through the, as yet, cloudy atmosphere. It was now the will of the Creator that the earth should no longer be "*invisible*" under its watery covering; and, accordingly, the command was given, that "the waters should be gathered together unto one place," that the "dry land" might appear. In considering this great event, it becomes a natural and fair question, as it has been left open to us by the record, as to *the mode* or means by which it must have taken place. The well-poised earth had already begun to revolve upon its axis; and the laws of gravitation and of fluids had consequently begun to act in our system. By these laws, it was impossible that the waters could have been gathered together by accumulation, or above the general level, as the *solids* of the earth might have been. We can, therefore, come to no other conclusion than that to which we are also led by various parts of the inspired writings, viz. that God did "rend the depths by his intelligence," and formed a depression, or hollow, on a part of the solid globe, within which, by the appointed laws of fluids, the "depths" were "gathered together." The following beautiful reflections on this part of our subject are from the enlightened mind of Mr. Granville Penn, who may, indeed, be called the first great advocate for the Mosaic Geology, among the men of science of our day. "The briefness of this clause, (Genesis i. 9,) and the nature of the subject, have caused it to be little contemplated in proportion to its importance, and to the fulness of the instruction which it conveys; and, therefore, it has not been observed that the same sublimity which is universally perceived in the clause, 'Let there be light, and there *was* light,' subsists equally in this clause; 'Let the waters be gathered together unto one place, and let the dry land be seen, and it was so.' The sentiment of sublimity in the former clause, results from the contemplation of an instantaneous transition of the universe from the profoundest darkness to the most splendid light, at the command of God. All men familiarly apprehend the *sadness* of the *former*, and the *delight* of the *latter;* and they are, therefore, instantly sensible of the glorious nature of the change which was then so suddenly produced. But the nature of the change which must necessarily have taken place, in *suddenly rendering visible* a part of a solid globe, the universal surface of which had been overflowed and concealed by a flood of waters, is not so familiarly or so instantly apprehended; the mind, therefore, does not care to dwell upon it, but is contented with receiving the general information *that the sea was formed.* Hence, both commentators and geologists have equally failed to draw the immediate and necessary inference from the revelation of *that great and undeniable geological fact.*"—FAIRHOLME'S GEOLOGY, p. 51—54.

Ver. 14. And God said, Let there be lights in the firmament of the heaven, to divide the day from the night; and let them be for signs, and for seasons, and for days, and years: 15. And let them be for lights in the firmament of the heaven, to give light upon the earth: and it was so. 16. And God made two great lights; the greater light to rule the day, and the lesser light to rule the night: *he made* the stars also. 17. And God set them in the firmament of the heaven, to give light upon the earth.

It is admitted that the Scriptures generally describe the phenomena of the natural world *as they appear*, rather than according to strict scientific truth. Thus the sun and moon are said to rise and set,—the stars to fall,—and the moon to be turned into blood. Consequently, if this history of the creation were designed to describe the effects of the six days' work *as they would have appeared to a spectator, had one been present*,—a supposition rendered probable from its being said, "Let the dry land appear," (Heb. be seen,) when as yet there was no eye to see it,—then we may reasonably conclude that the sun was formed on the first day, or perhaps had been created even *before* our earth, and was in fact the cause of the vicissitudes of the three first days and nights. But as the globe of the earth was during that time surrounded by a dense mass of mingled air and water, the rays of the sun would be intercepted; only a dim glimmering light, even in the daytime, would appear; and the bodies of the heavenly luminaries would be entirely hidden, just as they now are in a very cloudy day. Let it be supposed then that on the fourth day the clouds, mists, and vapours were all cleared away, and the atmosphere made pure and serene; the sun of course would shine forth in all his splendour, and to the eye of our imagined spectator would seem to have been just created; and so at night of the moon and stars. This effect of the Divine power, according to the usual analogy of the Scriptures, is described from its appearance, and the language employed,—"let there be lights in the firmament,"—and—"he made two great lights, and set them in the firmament"—is to be interpreted on the principle above stated. They might then be said to be "made," because they then first began to be visible, and to perform the office for which they were designed. The original word for "made" is not the same as that which is rendered "create." It is a term frequently employed to signify *constituted, appointed, set for a particular purpose or use.* Thus it is said that God "*made* Joseph a father to Pharaoh"—"*made* him lord of Egypt"—"*made* the Jordan a border between the tribes"—"*made* David the head of the heathen;" and so in innumerable other instances. As, therefore, the rainbow was *made* or *constituted* a sign, though it might have existed before, so the sun, moon, and stars may be said to have been *made* and *set* as lights in the firmament, on the fourth day, though actually called into existence on the first, or previously.—BUSH.

CHAP. 2. ver. 18. And the LORD God said, *It is* not good that the man should be alone; I will make him a help-meet for him.

This is the polite way of speaking of a wife in the East, though it must be confessed that they associate with this term too much of the idea of a servant. Does an aged person advise a young friend to get married; he will not say, "Seek for a wife," but "Try to procure a *thunive*, a help-meet." A man who repines at his single state, says, "I have not any female *help* in my house." A widower says, "Ah! my children, I have now no female *help*." A man, wishing to say something to his wife, will address her as follows: "My *help-meet*, hear what I am going to say." It is worthy of observation, that the margin has for *help-meet*, "as before him;" and this gives a proper view of her condition, for she literally has to *stand before* her husband to serve him on all occasions, and especially when he takes his food; she being then his servant. Say to a woman, "Leave thy husband!" she will reply, "No, no; I will *stand before* him."—ROBERTS.

Ver. 19. And whatsoever Adam called every living creature, that *was* the name thereof.

The verb *was* is not in the original text; and, therefore, the sentence may run in the present, with equal propriety as in the past; and, indeed, according to the genius of the language, with more propriety in the present—that *is* the name thereof. Hence the names by which the lower animals were known in the days of Moses, were those which Adam gave them in Paradise; and as these are pure Hebrew, the legitimate conclusion is, that Hebrew was the language spoken by Adam before the fall.

This argument receives an accession of strength from the ideal character of the Hebrew language. It is admitted, that all languages participate more or less of the ideal character; but it is one of the most remarkable circumstances by which the Hebrew is distinguished. A number of its words, as in other languages, are mere arbitrary signs of ideas; but, in general, they derive their origin from a very few terms, or roots, that are commonly expressive of some idea borrowed from external objects; from the human constitution; from our senses or our feelings. The names of men, and of the lower animals, and the names of many places, particularly in the remoter ages, allude to some remarkable character in the creature named; or, in reference to place, to some uncommon circumstance or event. Scarcely a proper name can be mentioned, which alludes not to something of this kind. To give a few examples: Korè, the partridge, received its name from the verb Kara, to call, in imitation of the note which that bird uses in calling its young. The camel is in Hebrew, Gamal, from a verb of the same form, which signifies to recompense, because that creature is remarkable for remembering and revenging an injury. The Hebrews call the scorpion Akrab, from two words which signify to kill one's father; now, both Pliny and Aristotle inform us, that it is the character of that creature to destroy its own parents.—PAXTON.

Ver. 20. And Adam gave names to all cattle, and to the fowl of the air, and to every beast of the field: but for Adam there was not found a help-meet for him.

With respect to the original language which Moses describes our first parents as making use of, from their very first creation, we are nowhere informed in what manner they first acquired it, nor how it was communicated to them. It is, indeed, probable that the inspired historian addressed himself to those who were much less skeptical on such subjects than ourselves; and that this remarkable endowment, peculiar to the human race, and by which they so far excel all other created beings, was never, in early times, doubted as having been directly communicated from the same wise and provident source from whence the human race itself had arisen; and the researches of the wisest and most learned men of all ages have invariably led them to the same natural conclusion.

We have no direct means of positive knowledge as to what relation the *primitive language* of the earth may have had with existing tongues; but, in the absence of such evidence, we may form some conjectures on the subject, which are certainly marked with the highest probability. In the first place, we must consider that the numbers of the antediluvian human race, and their consequent divisions into nations, could not have been nearly so great as in the present day, from the comparatively short period they had existed, and from the comparatively unrefined condition natural to a primitive race of beings, on whom the gift of reason was obviously bestowed by the Creator for the purposes of exertion, and of gradual cultivation and improvement. We must not here suppose, however, with too many advocates of an erring philosophy, that man was, at first, naturally *savage*, or in the state we now find the wild and uncultivated natives of savage countries; or that religion and knowledge were, in the first days, in the debased condition we now too often find them in the remote corners of the earth.

The savage state is not natural to man; but, on the contrary, is brought on by erring from the true path of knowledge, in which both Adam and Noah must have brought up their first descendants; and which, in both instances, was communicated in a direct manner, from the unerring source of every good which mankind now enjoys. In considering the progressive stages of society, we are too apt to content ourselves with merely looking *back*, from our own times, into the darker ages of barbarism, and thus to form our ideas on the false supposition, that the primitive nature of man is one of perfect ignorance, and such as we now find among the savages of Africa or America: whereas, if we trace the progress of society, in its proper and natural course, by *descending from the creation, and from the deluge,* instead of *ascending* from our own times, we shall find that the primitive state of mankind, even immediately after the creation, was one of *intelligence* and *understanding*, if not in arts and sciences, at least on the leading point of religion, which is, of all others, that in which the savage falls most short of the civilized man. It pleased his Creator to bestow upon primitive man a full and perfect conception of the relation in which he stood towards the Supreme Being; and it was in order to preserve a knowledge of the true religion among men, that a certain family and race were afterward expressly chosen; we find, accordingly, that to whatever state of idolatrous ignorance, or savage barbarity, the various ancient nations of the earth were, from time to time, reduced, there was always some portion of the world, and especially of the Jewish race, which adhered to the true faith, and which was, consequently, preserved from that state of unnatural debasement from which man has a constant tendency and desire to emancipate himself. It is, therefore, highly probable that, as we hear of no diversity of language on the earth until after the deluge, the whole primitive race was "of one language, and of one speech," and that that language must, consequently, have been the same spoken by those few individuals who were preserved from the flood.

Now, when we consider the great scheme of the Almighty, foretold from time to time, from the days of Adam to those of Abraham, and continued from thence, in a well-defined course of history, to our own times; when we consider the wonderful and miraculous events that were *foretold*, and were afterward so literally *fulfilled*, in the line of the chosen people of God;—that, through them, and through their language, the Inspired Writings of the early times were to be for ever handed down to the generations of men; that, of all the languages of the earth, the Hebrew tongue, like the Hebrew people, has hitherto withstood every change and every calamity; and been, like them, miraculously preserved by the Almighty will for a great and beneficent end; and when we further consider the strong analogy and filiation, so easily traced, in all the languages of the earth, to the Hebrew, as the most probable *postdiluvian* original tongue;—when all these considerations are combined, is it unreasonable to conclude to the high probability of the original language of the Sacred Scriptures being the pure and original tongue first communicated to man by his Maker? In considering, then, the language of the Hebrews as the most probable source from whence all other tongues have been derived; and when we trace in all these other tongues the gradual varieties that have arisen, and are still now proceeding in the dialects of the earth, by the *secondary causes*, and, seemingly, trivial accidents, by which the different shades of language are brought about, are we not justified in drawing a comparison betweeen the miraculously preserved *primitive language*, and the no less miraculously preserved chosen people, who are the constant *living miracle*, bearing *unwilling witness* to the truth of Inspiration, to all the generations of mankind? We are reminded, that it was repeatedly foretold in prophecy, that the Hebrew nation should be dispersed into all countries; yet that they should not be swallowed up and lost among their conquerors, but should subsist, to the latest times, a distinct people; that, "though God would make an end of the nations, their oppressors, He would not make an end of them."—FAIRHOLME.

The names which men and things received at the beginning of time, are so strikingly similar to those which they bore when the Hebrew was certainly a living language, that its claim to the honour of being the primeval speech of the human family, can scarcely be rejected. It is ever reckoned a proof of similar origin, when many words in any two languages have the same form, the same sound, meaning, and reason. But the names of the first generations of men, like those of the lower animals, are as pure Hebrew as the names of Peleg, Abraham, Isaac, and Jacob, or those of David and Solomon, or Malachi. They have the Hebrew form, are constructed according to Hebrew rules, are founded on certain reasons, like Hebrew names; and, in fine, are not to be distinguished in any one respect from pure Hebrew.

It deserves also to be remarked, that the reason assigned for these names will not correspond with any other language. The garden of Paradise was called Eden; because among the Hebrews it signifies pleasure or delight. The place of Cain's exile was for this reason called the land of Nod, from a root which signifies to wander. Adam received his name because he was taken out of the ground; but if the term for ground in the first language had been terra, or γη, or earth, there had been no propriety in the designation. Eve was called by this name, because she was the mother of all living; but it is derived from a pure Hebrew verb which signifies to live; and to this relation the name owes all its propriety and significance. Cain was named from the Hebrew verb Kana, to possess, because his mother had got him from the Lord; and in this instance also, the name is inseparably connected with the Hebrew root. The proper name Seth is derived from the Hebrew verb Shooth, to appoint; because, said our first mother, God hath appointed me another seed instead of Abel, whom Cain slew. The same mode of reasoning might be carried through all the names of the Adamitic age; but these instances are sufficient to show the near affinity, if not the positive identity, of the language which Adam spoke, with the Hebrew of the Old Testament.

The names ascribed by the inspired writer to the founders of our race, are not interpretations of primitive terms; for he declares they are the very names which were given at first; and as they are derivatives from pure Hebrew verbs, the language then spoken must have been the same in substance and structure. Had they been translations, we have reason to think the same method would have been followed as in several instances in the New Testament, where the original term is used, and the interpretation avowedly subjoined. But Moses gives not a single hint of his translating these terms; he asserts, on the contrary, that they are the original words employed; and the truth of his assertion is rendered indubitable by the reasons assigned for their imposition, which are inseparably connected with the Hebrew language. Nor does Moses, in the whole course of his history, when speaking of the names of persons and places, utter a single word from which we can infer the existence of an earlier language.

When the minute and extensive acquaintance with the natural character and temper of the numerous animals to which our first father gave names in Paradise, which he certainly had not time to acquire by his own industry, and which we have no reason to believe he owed to intuition, is considered, we must admit, that the language in which he conversed was not his own contrivance, but the immediate gift of Heaven. When Jehovah breathed into Adam and Eve the breath of life, he inspired them in the same moment with the knowledge of the tongue in which they were to express their thoughts. A similar favour was bestowed at the beginning of the New Testament dispensation, on the apostles and other ministers of the gospel; who were inspired in a moment with the perfect knowledge of many different languages.—PAXTON.

CHAP. 4. ver. 3. And in process of time it came to pass, that Cain brought of the fruit of the ground an offering unto the LORD.

The margin* reads, "at the end of days;" and this is truly Oriental. "When the days are ended, I will fulfil my promise." "After those days are ended, I shall have peace." "When the days come round, (in their circle,) I will do that for you."—ROBERTS.

Ver. 7. If thou doest well, shalt thou not be accepted? and if thou doest not well, sin lieth at the door. And unto thee *shall be* his desire, and thou shalt rule over him.

D'Oyly and Mant interpret this, "Your sin will find you out." "Thy punishment is not far off." They also say sin may be rendered SIN-OFFERING; and several other commentators take the same view, and think this is its true and only meaning. The victim proper for a sin-offering was lying at the door, and therefore was within his reach.

There are some who affect to smile at the idea of SIN lying at the door: it is, however, an Eastern figure. Ask a man who is unacquainted with Scripture, what he understands by sin lying at the threshold of the door; he will immediately speak of it as the guilt of some great crime which the owner had committed. A man accused of having murdered a child, would be accosted in the following language:—"If you have done this, think not to escape; no! for sin will ever lie at your door: it will descend from generation to generation." To a man accused of having committed any other dreadful crime, it would be said, "Ah! if I had done it, do I not know sin would ever lie at my door?" The idea is sin personified in the shape of some fierce animal crouched at the door. Its criminality and punishment remain.

If Cain had done well, would there not have been "the excellency?" (see margin;) but if not well, then sin, like a monster, was crouching at his door. Taking the other view of it, *seems* to amount to this; now, Cain, if thou doest well, that will be thy excellency, thou shalt be accepted: but if thou doest not well, it is a matter of no very great consequence, because there is a sin-offering at thy door.

* I would here observe, once for all, that I have gone regularly through the marginal readings, and have found, with few exceptions, that they literally agree with Eastern language in idiom and figure. In the course of this work, most of them will be illustrated; and I think few readers will doubt that they are the correct translations.

MOUNT ARARAT.—Gen. 8: 4.

SYRIAN DOVE.—Gen. 8: 8, 9. GOPHER WOOD. (*Cupressus Sempervirens.*) Gen. 6: 14. OLIVE. (*Olea Europea.*) Gen. 8: 11.

Dove. The nearest approximation to truth will be, perhaps, to consider the original word *Yonah* as a counterpart to *Columba*, the generic term for all the various kinds of dove. The fondness which these birds exhibit for home is well known, and for this reason, probably, the patriarch made choice of the dove for the purpose alluded to in the sacred narrative.

Gopher Wood. The cypress possessed unrivalled durability and compactness, rendering it peculiarly adapted to sacred purposes. The Athenians used it for coffins, and the Egyptians for mummy cases. The straight, elegant tree of the cut seems best entitled to have furnished the wood for the ark.

Olive. A very long lived tree. See, also, quite a full description of it, and a view of those very ancient olives at Gethsemane, in *Dr. Jenks's Comprehensive Commentary*, vol. ii. This is one of those trees, as the terebinth, &c. to whose roots, at least, naturalists accord a life of three or even four thousand years.

God's design appears to have been to induce Cain to do well, by speaking of the reward of righteousness, and to make him afraid of doing evil, by showing him the punishment of sin.—ROBERTS.

Ver. 13. And Cain said unto the LORD, My punishment *is* greater than I can bear.

The margin has, "Mine iniquity is greater than——— be forgiven." This form of speech is very common. Has a person committed a great crime; he will go to the offended individual, and piteously plead for mercy; and at intervals keep crying, "Ah! my guilt is too great to be forgiven. My hopes are gone."—ROBERTS.

Ver. 14. And it shall come to pass, *that* every one that findeth me shall slay me.

It has been tauntingly asked, How could every one slay Cain? Has a man escaped from prison; the people say, "Ah! *all* men will catch and bring that fellow back." Has a man committed murder; "Ah! *all* men will kill that murderer." This means, the feeling will be universal; all will desire to have that individual punished.—ROBERTS.

CHAP. 7. ver. 11. The same day were all the fountains of the great deep broken up, and the windows of heaven were opened.

The margin has, the "flood-gates of heaven were opened." In the East, when the rain falls in torrents, the people say, "the heavens are broken."—ROBERTS.

Ver. 21. And all flesh died that moved upon the earth, both of fowl, and of cattle, and of beast, and of every creeping thing that creepeth upon the earth, and every man.

We have some reason to doubt, from the fossil remains of animals now discovered, which have not yet been found alive upon the present earth, whether *every living creature* was included in this strong expression; and though, from the remarkable circumstance of the similarity of all languages in certain common expressions, and in the universal tradition of the deluge found among the most distant and savage nations, we feel assured that the whole existing race of *man* on the whole earth, has sprung from Noah and his family; we have no evidence to lead us to the same conclusion with respect to quadrupeds, or birds. It appears probable, that we ought to consider the strong expression used in the record, "*of every living thing of all flesh*," in the same sense as we find it in various other parts of Scripture; and, indeed, as such expressions are often used in our own, and in other languages, that is, not as literally meaning every *created being* over the whole globe, but merely *a great number*.—FAIRHOLME.

Ver. 22. All in whose nostrils was the breath of life, of all that was in the dry land, died.

What a scene of terrific and awful desolation does this narrative of the Bible convey! If the reader be affected as the writer was, when he first contemplated the Scriptural character of this sad transaction, he will literally tremble when he meditates on the dread catastrophe. He will, moreover, discover how inadequate, how puerile, and infinitely below the facts of the real case, are all those representations of the deluge to which we have been accustomed; and those comments which exhibit animals and men as *escaping* to the highest grounds and hills, as the flood advanced. Even Mr. Buckland supposes that animals, when the waters began to enter their caves under ground, might have rushed out and fled for safety to hills. The impossibility of any such escape may be immediately seen. Neither man nor beast, under such circumstances, could either advance or flee to any distance. Any animal found in the plain when the flood began, would thus be merged in water seven or eight feet deep in a quarter of an hour! independent of the overwhelming torrents, dashing upon his head. And were he to attempt advancing up the rising grounds, a cataract or sheet of water, several feet deep, would be gushing all the way in his face, besides impending water from the "flood-gates" of heaven, momentarily rushing over him; he would instantly become a prey to those mighty waters.—SCRIP. GEOLOGY, Lond. 1828.

CHAP. 8. ver. 4. And the ark rested in the seventh month, on the seventeenth day of the month, upon the mountains of Ararat.

We walked into the fields to gaze upon Mount Ararat, and reflect upon the time when Noah in this very valley builded an altar unto the Lord, and offered that acceptable sacrifice of a sweet savour, which procured for himself and his posterity a divine title to the earth and its productions, and the solemn covenant that "while the earth remaineth, seed-time and harvest, and cold and heat, and summer and winter, and day and night, shall not cease." We first saw that mountain the morning we entered Nakhchevân, and during the three weeks we were in the valley of the Aras, nothing but cloudy weather during a few days obscured it from our sight. It was nearer at any point between here and Erivân, but perhaps nowhere did we have a better view of it than from this place. The natives know it under no other name than *Mâsis* in Armenian, and *Aghurdagh* (heavy mountain) in Turkish. The name of *Ararat*, by which it is called among Europeans, is applied in Scripture only to a *country*, which is in one instance called a kingdom. The similar name of *Ararâd* was given by the Armenians, long before they had received the Scripture account of the flood by their conversion to Christianity, to the central, largest, and most fertile province of their country, the one which, with the doubtful exception of some 230 years, was the residence of their kings or governors from the commencement to the termination of their political existence, and nearly in the centre of which this mountain stands. The singular coincidence, considering the ease with which so distinguished a province might be named by foreigners for the kingdom itself, argues much for the identity of the Ararat of Scripture with the Ararâd of Armenia. It was on the mountains of Ararat that the ark rested after the flood; and certainly not among the mountains of Ararâd, or of Armenia generally, or of any part of the world, have I seen one, the majesty of whose appearance could plead half so powerfully as this, a claim to the honour of having once been the stepping-stone between the old world and the new. It lies N. 57° W. of Nakhchevân and S. 25° W. of Erivân, on the opposite side of the Aras; and from almost every point between the two places, the traveller has only to look across the valley, to take into one distinct field of vision, without a single intervening obstacle, the mighty mass from its base to its summit. At Erivân it presents two peaks, one much lower than the other, and appears to be connected with a range of mountains extending towards the northwest, which, though really elevated, are in comparison so low, as only to give distinctness to the impression of its lonely majesty. From Nakhchevân, not far from a hundred miles distant, and also from our present point of observation, it appears like an immense isolated cone of extreme regularity, rising out of the low valley of the Aras; and the absence of all intervening objects to show its distance or its size, leaves the spectator at liberty to indulge the most sublime conceptions his imagination may form of its vastness. At all seasons of the year, it is covered far below its summit with snow and ice, which occasionally form avalanches, that are precipitated down its sides with the sound of an earthquake, and, with the steepness of its declivities, have allowed none of the posterity of Noah to ascend it. It was now white to its very base with the same hoary covering; and in gazing upon it, we gave ourselves up to the impression, that on its top were once congregated the only inhabitants of the earth, and that, while travelling in the valley beneath, we were paying a visit to the second cradle of the human race.

Two objections are made to the supposition that Scripture refers to this mountain when it speaks of "the mountains of Ararat." One is, that there are now no olive-trees in its vicinity, from which Noah's dove could have plucked her leaf. And it is true, so far as we could learn, that that tree exists neither in the valley of the Koor nor of the Aras, nor on the coast of the Caspian, nor anywhere nearer than Batoom and other parts of the eastern coast of the Black sea, a distance of seven days journey of a caravan, or about 130 miles in the circuitous route that would thus be taken. But might not a dove make this journey in a day? Or might not the climate then have been warmer than it is now? The second objection is drawn from the fact that some of the old versions and paraphrases, particularly the Chaldee and the Syriac, refer "the mountains of Ararat" to the mountains of Kürdistán, where there is, not far from Jezeereh, a high mountain called Joody, on which the moslems suppose the ark to have rested. But if the ark rested on that, the posterity of Noah would, most likely, have descended at once into Mesopotamia, and have reached Shinar from the north; while, from the valley of the Aras, they would naturally have kept along on the eastern side of the mountains of Media, until they reached the neighbourhood of Hamadán or Kermansháh, which is nearly east of Babylon. Such is the route now taken every day by all the caravans from this region to Bagdád. The Armenians believe, not only that this is the mountain on which the ark rested after the flood, but that the ark still exists upon its top; though, rather from supernatural than from physical obstacles, no one has yet been able to visit it. A devout vartabéd, their legends relate, once attempted, for this purpose, to ascend the mountain. While yet far from the top, drowsiness came upon him, and he awoke at the bottom, in the very spot whence he had started. Another attempt resulted only in the same miraculous failure. He then betook himself more fervently to prayer, and started the third time. Again he slept, and awoke at the bottom; but now an angel stood before him with a fragment of the ark, as a token that his pious purpose was approved and his prayer answered, though he could never be allowed to reach the summit of the mountain. The precious gift was thankfully received, and is to this day carefully preserved, as a sacred relic, in the convent of Echmiádzin.—SMITH & DWIGHT.

Ararat forms the angle of an immense chain of mountains, on the loftiest pinnacles of which the natives of the country believe that part of the ark yet remains. It is a most sublime and stupendous object, which excites in the mind of the beholder the mingled emotions of admiration and terror. One of the great features of this mountain is the immense chasm which extends nearly half-way down, over which impends a cliff, discernible at a great distance, whose enormous masses of ice are from time to time precipitated into the abyss with a noise resembling the loudest thunder. "Nothing," says Mr. Morier, "can be more beautiful than its shape; more awful than its height. Compared with it, all the other mountains sink into insignificance. It is perfect in all its parts: no hard rugged features: no unnatural prominences; every thing is in harmony; and all combines to render it one of the most sublime objects in nature. Spreading originally from an immense base, its slope towards the summit is gradual, until it reaches the regions of the snows, when it becomes more abrupt. The cone is surmounted with a crown of ice, which glitters in the sun with a peculiar and dazzling brightness. As a foil to this stupendous work, a smaller hill rises from the same base, near the original mass, similar to it in shape and proportion, and in any other situation entitled to rank among the high mountains. The mountain is divided into three regions of different breadths. The first, composed of a short and slippery grass, or sand as troublesome as the quicksands of Africa, is occupied by the shepherds; the second, by tigers and crows: the remainder, which is half the mountain, is covered with snow which has been accumulating ever since the ark rested upon it; and these snows are concealed during one half of the year in very dense clouds." This stupendous mountain, Mr. Morier and his party endeavoured to scale; and after excessive fatigue arrived on the margin of eternal snow. But they found it impossible to proceed and penetrate the highest region; and not easy to go back. At length, utterly exhausted, they reached the bottom, and gave thanks to God for their safe return.—PAXTON.

[The remarkable achievement of the ascent of Mount Ararat, has at length, it appears, been accomplished by Professor Parrot of England. Taking with him Mr. Behagel as mineralogist, Messrs. Hehn and Schiemann, medical students of Moscow, and Mr. Federow, astronomer of St. Petersburg, he commenced his journey on the 20th of March, 1829, and arrived at Tiflis on the 6th of June. Owing to peculiar circumstances they were unable to leave Tiflis till the first of September, the distance to Mount Ararat being by the road about 280 wasts (say 200 miles.) The following account of the ascent, extracted from a work recently published by Professor Parrot, at Berlin, is from the Foreign Quarterly Review for June, 1835.]

At seven o'clock in the morning of the 12th September, I set out on my journey, [from the Convent of St. James near the foot of the mountain,] accompanied by Mr. Schiemann. We took with us one of our Cossacks and a peasant of Arguri, who was a good huntsman, and our route was first in the bottom of the valley, then up its right acclivity towards the spot where there are two small stone houses standing close to each other; the one formerly a chapel, and the other built as a protection for a spring which is considered sacred.

From the chapel we crossed the grassy elevation, which forms the right declivity of the cleft: we suffered so much from the heat of the day, that our Cossack, who would probably have much rather been seated on horseback and galloping about on the steppes for three days than scrambling over the rocks for a couple of hours, was ready to sink from fatigue, and we were obliged to send him back. At about six o'clock in the evening, when we also were much tired, and had almost reached the snowy region, we chose our night's lodgings in the clefts of the rocks. We had attained a height of 11,675 Paris feet; in the sheltered places about us lay some new-fallen snow, and the temperature of the air was at the freezing point. Mr. Schiemann and I had provided ourselves tolerably well for such an undertaking; besides, the pleasure of the expedition warmed us; but our athletic Jagar, Schak of Arguri, (Isaac,) was quite dejected from the cold, for he had nothing but his summer clothing; his whole neck and also his legs, from the knee to the sandal, were quite bare, and his head was only covered with an old handkerchief. I had neglected to think about his wardrobe before setting out, and, therefore, it was my duty to help him as well as I could: but as neither of us had much clothing to spare, I wrapped up his neck and his bare limbs in sheets of blotting-paper which I had taken with me for drying plants, and this was a great relief to him. At daybreak we pursued our journey towards the eastern side of the mountain, and soon reached the declivity which runs immediately from the summit; it consists entirely of pointed rocky ridges coming down from above, and leaving between them ravines of considerable depth, in which the icy mantle of the summit loses itself, and glaciers of great extent. There were several of these rocky ridges and clefts of ice lying between us and the side of the mountain which we were endeavouring to reach. When we had happily surmounted the first crest and the adjoining beautiful glacier, and reached the second crest, Schak had no courage to proceed. His benumbed limbs had not yet recovered their warmth, and the icy region towards which he saw us hastening, did not hold out much prospect of relief; thus one remained behind from heat and the other from cold—only Mr. Schiemann, though unaccustomed to these hardships, did not for an instant lose his courage or his desire to accompany me, but shared with alacrity and perseverance all the difficulties and dangers we had to encounter. Leaving the Jager behind us, we crossed the second glacier, and gained the third rocky ridge. Then immediately turning off in an oblique direction, we reached the lower edge of the icy crest, at a height of 13,180 Paris feet, and which from this place runs without interruption to the summit. We had now to ascend this declivity covered with perpetual snow. Though the inclination was barely 30 deg., this was a sheer impossibility for two men to accomplish in a direct line. We therefore determined to advance diagonally towards a long pointed ridge which runs far up towards the summit. We succeeded in this by making with our ice-poles deep holes in the ice of the glacier, which was covered with a thin layer of new-fallen snow, too slight to afford the requisite firmness to our steps. We thus reached the ridge, and advanced directly towards the summit by a track where the new snow was rather deeper. Though we might by great exertions have this time reached the goal of our wishes, yet the fatigue of the day had been considerable, and as it was already three o'clock in the afternoon, we were obliged to think of providing a lodging for the approaching night. We had attained the extreme upper ridge of the rocky crest, an elevation of 14,560 Paris feet above the level of the sea, (the height of the top of Mount Blanc,) and yet the summit of Ararat lay far above us. I do not think that any insurmountable obstacle could have impeded our farther progress, but to spend the few remaining hours of day light in reaching this point would have been worse than madness, as we had not seen any rock on the summit which could have afforded us protection during the night; independently of which, our stock of provisions was not calculated to last so long. Having made our barometrical observations, we turned back, satisfied from the result that the mountain on this side was not inaccessible. In descending, however, we met with a danger which we had not anticipated; for if in the descent of every mountain you tread less safely than in going up, it is still more difficult to tread firmly, when you look down upon such a surface of ice and snow as that over which we had to pass for more than a werst, and where, if we slipped and fell, there was nothing to stop us but the sharp-pointed masses of stone in which the region of eternal ice loses itself. The danger here is perhaps rather in the want of habit than in real difficulties. My young friend, whose courage had probably been proof against severer trials, lost his presence of mind here—his foot slipped, and he fell; but, as he was about twenty paces behind me, I had time to thrust my pole firmly in the ice, to take a sure footing in my capital snow-shoes, and while I held the pole in my right hand, to catch him in passing with my left. My position was well chosen, but the straps which fastened my ice-shoes broke, and, instead of being able to stop my friend, I was carried with him in his fall. He was so fortunate as to be stopped by some stones, but I rolled on for half a werst, till I reached some fragments of lava near the lower glacier. The tube of my barometer was dashed to pieces—my chronometer burst open, and covered with blood—every thing had fallen out of my pockets, but I escaped without severe injury. As soon as we had recovered from our fright, and thanked God for our providential escape, we collected the most important of our effects, and continued our journey. We were soon afterward delighted to hear the voice of our good Schak, who had very prudently waited for our return. Having made a fire, we passed the night in the grassy region, and on the third day reached the convent, where we were regaled with an excellent breakfast. We however took care not to tell the Armenians any thing about our accident, as they would certainly not have failed to ascribe it to a judgment from Heaven for our presumptuous attempt to reach the summit, which they say has been prohibited to mortals by a divine decree since the time of Noah. All the Armenians are firmly persuaded that Noah's ark exists to the present day on the summit of Mount Ararat, and that, in order to preserve it, no person is permitted to approach it. We learn the grounds of this tradition from the Armenian chronicles in the legend of a monk of the name of James, who was afterward Patriarch of Nissibus, and a contemporary and relative of St. Gregory. It is said that this monk, in order to settle the disputes which had arisen respecting the credibility of the sacred books, especially with reference to their account of Noah, resolved to ascend to the top of Ararat to convince himself of the existence of the ark. At the declivity of the mountain, however, he had several times fallen asleep from exhaustion, and found on awaking that he had been unconsciously carried down to the point from which he first set out. God at length had compassion on his unwearied though fruitless exertions, and during his sleep sent an angel with the message, that his exertions were unavailing, as the summit was inaccessible; but as a reward for his indefatigable zeal, he sent him a piece of the ark, the very same which is now preserved as the most valuable relic in the cathedral of Etschmaidsin. The belief in the impossibility of ascending Mount Ararat has, in consequence of this tradition, which is sanctioned by the church, almost become an article of faith, which an Armenian would not renounce even if he were placed in his own proper person upon the summit of the mountain.

[After recovering in some measure from the effects of his fall and an attack of fever which ensued, the professor set out on the 18th September to make a second attempt to gain the summit, taking with him a cross ten feet high, which it was proposed to set up on the top of the mountain, with an inscription in honour of Field Marshal Count Paskewitsch, by whose victories the Russian dominions had been extended to this point. They chose this time the northeast side of the mountain, by which the way was much longer, but not so steep. But as this second attempt also failed, we pass over the account of it, and proceed without further preface to the third, which succeeded. They however erected the cross on an almost horizontal surface covered with snow, at the height of 15,138 Paris feet above the level of the Euxine, or about 350 feet higher than the summit of Mount Blanc.]

In the meantime the sky cleared up, the air became serene and calm, the mountain too was more quiet, the noise occasioned by the falling of the masses of ice and snow grew less frequent—in short, every thing seemed to indicate that a favourable turn was about to take place in the weather, and I hastened to embrace it for a third attempt to ascend the mountain. On the 25th September I sent to ask Stepan whether he would join us, but he declined, saying that he had suffered too much from the former excursion to venture again so soon; he however promised to send us four stout peasants with three oxen and a driver. Early the next morning, four peasants made their appearance at the camp to join our expedition, and soon after a fifth, who offered himself voluntarily. To them I added two of our soldiers. The deacon again accompanied us, as well as Mr. Hehn, who wished to explore the vegetation at a greater elevation; but he did not intend to proceed beyond the line of snow. The experience of the preceding attempt had convinced me that every thing depended on our passing the first night as closely as possible to this boundary, in order to be able to ascend and return from the summit in one day, and to confine our baggage to what was absolutely necessary. We therefore took with us only three oxen, laden with the clothing, wood, and provisions. I also took a cross carved in oak. . . . . We chose our route towards the same side as before, and, in order to spare ourselves, Abowiam and I rode on horseback, wherever the rocky nature of the soil permitted it, as far as the grassy plain Kip-Giholl, whence we sent the horses back. Here Mr. Hehn parted from us. It was scarcely twelve o'clock when we reached this point, and, after taking our breakfast, we proceeded in a direction rather more oblique than on our former attempt. The cattle were, however, unable to follow us so quickly. We therefore halted at some rocks which it would be impossible for them to pass—took each our own share of clothing and wood, and sent back the oxen. At half-past five in the evening we were not far from the snow line, and considerably higher than the place where we passed the night on our previous excursion. The elevation at this point was 13,036 Paris feet above the level of the sea, and the large masses of rock determined me to take up our quarters here. A fire was soon made, and a warm supper prepared. I had some onion broth, a dish which I would recommend to all mountain travellers in preference to meat broth, as being extremely warm and invigorating. This being a fast-day, poor Abowiam was not able to enjoy it. The other Armenians, who strictly adhered to their rules of fasting, contented themselves with bread and the brandy which I distributed among them in a limited quantity, as this cordial must be taken with great caution, especially where the strength has been previously much tried, as it otherwise produces a sense of exhaustion and inclination to sleep. It was a magnificent evening, and, with my eyes fixed on the clear sky, and the lofty summit which projected against it, and then again on the dark night which was gathering far below and around me, I experienced all those delightful sensations of tranquillity, love, and devotion, that silent reminiscence of the past, that subdued glance into the future, which a traveller never fails to experience when on lofty elevations, and under pleasing circumstances. I laid myself down under an overhanging rock of lava, the temperature of the air at 4 1-2 degrees, which was tolerably warm, considering our great height.

At daybreak we rose, and began our journey at half past six. We crossed the last broken declivities in half an hour, and entered the boundary of eternal snow nearly at the same place as in our preceding ascent. In consequence of the increased warmth of the weather, the new-fallen snow, which had facilitated our progress on our previous ascent, had melted away, and again frozen, so that, in spite of the still inconsiderable slope, we were compelled to cut steps in the ice. This very much embarrassed our advance, and added greatly to our fatigue. One of the peasants had remained behind in our resting-place, as he felt unwell; two others became exhausted in ascending the side of the glacier. They at first lay down, but soon retreated to our quarters. Without being disheartened by these difficulties, we proceeded, and soon reached the great cleft which marks the upper edge of the declivity of the large glacier, and at ten o'clock we arrived at the great plain of snow which marks the first break on the icy head of Ararat. At the distance of a werst, we saw the cross which we had reared on the 19th of September, but it appeared to me so extremely small, probably on account of its black colour, that I almost doubted whether I should be able to find it again with an ordinary telescope from the plain of the Araxes. In the direction towards the summit, a shorter but at the same time a steeper declivity than the one we had passed lay before us; and between this and the extreme summit there appeared to be only one small hill. After a short repose we passed the first precipice, which was the steepest of all, by hewing out steps in the rock, and after this the next elevation. But here, instead of seeing the ultimate goal of all our difficulties, immediately before us appeared a series of hills, which even concealed the summit from our sight. This rather abated our courage, which had never yielded for a moment so long as we had all our difficulties in view, and our strength, exhausted by the labour of hewing the rock, seemed scarcely commensurate with the attainment of the now invisible object of our wishes. But a review of what had been already accomplished, and of that which might still remain to be done, the proximity of the series of projecting elevations, and a glance at my brave companions, banished my fears, and we boldly advanced. We crossed two more hills, and the cold air of the summit blew towards us. I stepped from behind one of the glaciers, and the extreme cone of Ararat lay distinctly before my enraptured eyes. But one more effort was necessary. Only one other icy plain was to be ascended, and at a quarter past three on the 27th of September, O. S., 1829, we stood on the summit of Mount Ararat! [Having thus happily accomplished his fatiguing and perilous enterprise, says the Review, our author's first wish and enjoyment was repose; he spread his cloak on the ground, and sitting down, contemplated the boundless but desolate prospect around him. He was on a slight convex, almost circular, platform, about 200 Paris feet in diameter, which at the extremity declines pretty steeply on all sides, particularly towards the S. E. and N. E.; it was the silver crest of Ararat, composed of eternal ice, unbroken by a rock or stone. Towards the east, the summit declined more gently than in any other direction, and was connected by a hollow, likewise covered with perpetual ice, with another rather lower summit, which by Mr. Federow's trigonometrical measurement was found to be 187 toises distant from the principal summit. On account of the immense distances nothing could be seen distinctly. The whole valley of the Araxes was covered with a gray mist, through which Erivan and Sardarabad appeared as small dark spots; to the south were seen more distinctly the hills behind which lies Bayazeed; to the N. W. the ragged top of Alaghes, covered with vast masses of snow, probably an inaccessible summit; near to Ararat, especially to the S. E. and at a great distance towards the west, are numerous small conical hills, which look like extinct volcanoes; to the E. S. E. was little Ararat, whose head did not appear like a cone, as it does from the plain, but like the top of a square truncated pyramid, with larger and smaller rocky elevations on the edges and in the middle; but what very much surprised Professor Parrot was to see a large portion of Lake Goktschai, which appeared in the N. E. like a beautiful shining dark blue patch, behind the lofty chain of mountains which encloses it on the south, and which is so high that he never could have believed that he should have been able from the top of Ararat to see over its summit into the lake behind it. Mr. Parrot, having allowed himself time to enjoy this prospect, proceeded to observe his barometer, which he placed precisely in the middle of the summit. The mercury was no higher than 15 inches 3 4 of a line Paris measure, the temperature being 3 7-10ths below the freezing point of the centrigrade thermometer. By comparing this observation with that which Mr. Federow made at the same time at the convent of St. James, the elevation of the summit appears to be 10,272 Paris feet above the convent, and, adding to that the height of the latter, the top of Ararat is 16,254 Paris feet, nearly five wersts, above the level of the sea. While the professor was engaged in his observations, the deacon planted the cross, not precisely on the summit, where it could not have been seen from the plain, as it was only five feet high, but on the N. E. edge, about thirty feet lower than the centre of the summit. The professor and his five companions, viz. the deacon, two Russian soldiers, and two Armenian peasants, having remained three quarters of an hour on the summit, commenced their descent, which was very fatiguing; but they hastened, as the sun was going down, and before they reached the place where the great cross was erected, it had already sunk below the horizon.]

It was a glorious sight to behold the dark shadows which the mountains in the west cast upon the plain, and then the profound darkness which covered all the valleys, and gradually rose higher and higher on the sides of Ararat, whose icy summit was still illuminated by the beams of the setting sun. But the shadows soon passed over that also, and would have covered our path with a gloom that would have rendered our descent dangerous, had not the sacred lamp of night, opportunely rising above the eastern horizon, cheered us with its welcome beams.

[Having passed the night on the same spot as on their ascent, where they found their companions, they arrived the next day at noon, at the Convent of St. James, and on the following day, Sunday, the 28th of September, O. S., they offered their grateful thanksgiving to Heaven for the success of their arduous enterprise, perhaps not far from the spot where "Noah built an altar to the Lord."]

Ver. 11. And the dove came in to him in the evening, and, lo, in her mouth *was* an olive leaf plucked off. So Noah knew that the waters were abated from off the earth.

The olive may be justly considered as one of the most valuable gifts which the beneficent Creator has bestowed on the human family. The oil which it yields, forms an important article of food; it imparts a greater degree of pliancy to the limbs, and agility to the whole body; it assuages the agonizing pain, and promotes, by its sanative influence, the cure of wounds; it alleviates the internal sufferings produced by disease; it illumines, at once, the cottage and the palace; it cheers, by the splendour of its combustion, the festive meeting; it serves to expel the deadly poison of venomous reptiles; it was used in consecrating a thing to the service of God; and it mingled, perhaps, from the first of time, by the command of Heaven, with many of the bloodless oblations which the worshipper presented at his altar. In these various and important uses, we may, perhaps, discover the true reason that the dove of Noah was directed, by God himself, to select the olive leaf from the countless variety which floated on the subsiding waters of the deluge, or bestrewed the slimy tops and declivities of Ararat, as the chosen symbol of returning peace and favour. From the creation of the world, the fatness of this tree signally displayed the divine goodness and benignity; and since the fall of man, it symbolizes the grace and kindness of our heavenly Father, and the precious influences of the Holy Ghost, in healing the spiritual diseases of our degenerate race, and in counteracting the deadly poison of moral corruption. Hence, the people of Israel were commanded to construct their booths, at the feast of tabernacles, partly with branches of olive; and all the nations of the civilized world were secretly directed, by the overruling providence of Heaven, to bear them in their hands as emblems of peace and amity. The olive is mentioned as the sign of peace, by both Livy and Virgil, in several parts of their works, but one instance from the latter shall suffice.

> "Tum pater Æneas puppi sic fatur ab alta
> Paciferæque manu ramum pretendit olivæ."
>
> *Æn.* b. viii. l. 116.

The celebrated navigator, Captain Cook, found that green branches, carried in the hands, or stuck in the ground, were the emblems of peace, universally employed and understood by the numerous and untutored inhabitants of the South Sea islands. The origin of a custom, thus received and religiously observed, by nations dwelling on opposite sides of the globe, who never had the smallest intercourse with one another, must be sought for near the beginning of time, when the inhabitants of our earth, forming but one family, lived under the gentle sway of their common parent. Dr. Chandler, indeed, is of opinion, that the idea of reconciliation and peace was not associated with the olive branch till ages long posterior to the deluge. The olive groves, he argues, are the usual resort of doves, and other birds, that repair to them for food; and thus endeavours to find a natural connexion between the dove of Noah and the olive leaf. The olive might, he thinks, be the only tree which had raised its head above the subsiding waters, near the place where the ark was floating, although it is only of a middling height; but if the dove saw a great number of other trees above the water, the habits of the bird naturally led it to the olive plantation for shelter and food, in preference to all others. But the greater part of this reasoning avowedly rests upon mere assumption; and although the olive grove may be the favourite retreat of the dove, how are we to account for the olive branch being chosen by almost every nation, from the remotest times, for the symbol of reconciliation and peace? It is far more probable, that the dove was directed by the finger of God to prefer the olive leaf, or a sprig of olive leaves, as being the symbol of peace with which Noah was already acquainted, or that it might, in future, be the token of reconciliation between God and his offending creatures, and between one nation and another.—Paxton.

Chap. 9. ver. 4. But flesh, with the life thereof, *which is* the blood thereof, shall ye not eat.

Mr. *Bruce* has given a very extraordinary account of the practice of eating blood in Abyssinia. This custom, so prevalent in several places, is forbidden in the scriptures. A recital of the narrative will probably suggest to the reader the reasons of the prohibition. Mr. *Bruce* tells us, that, "not long after our losing sight of the ruins of this ancient capital of Abyssinia, we overtook three travellers driving a cow before them: they had black goatskins upon their shoulders, and lances and shields in their hands; in other respects they were but thinly clothed; they appeared to be soldiers. The cow did not seem to be fattened for killing, and it occurred to us all, that it had been stolen. This, however, was not our business, nor was such an occurrence at all remarkable in a country so long engaged in war. We saw that our attendants attached themselves, in a particular manner, to the three soldiers that were driving the cow, and held a short conversation with them. Soon after, we arrived at the hithermost bank of the river, where I thought we were to pitch our tent: the drivers suddenly tripped up the cow, and gave the poor animal a very rude fall upon the ground, which was but the beginning of her sufferings. One of them sat across her neck, holding down her head by the horns, the other twisted the halter about her fore feet, while the third, who had a knife in his hand, to my very great surprise, in place of taking her by the throat, got astride upon her belly, before her hind legs, and gave her a very deep wound in the upper part of the buttock. From the time I had seen them throw the beast upon the ground, I had rejoiced, thinking that when three people were killing a cow, they must have agreed to sell part of her to us; and I was much disappointed upon hearing the Abyssinians say, that we were to pass the river to the other side, and not encamp where I intended. Upon my proposing they should bargain for part of the cow, my men answered, what they had already learned in conversation, that they were not then to kill her: that she was not wholly theirs, and they could not sell her. This awakened my curiosity; I let my people go forward, and stayed myself, till I saw, with the utmost astonishment, two pieces, thicker and longer than our ordinary beef steaks, cut out of the higher part of the buttock of the beast: how it was done I cannot positively say, because, judging the cow was to be killed from the moment I saw the knife drawn, I was not anxious to view that catastrophe, which was by no means an object of curiosity: whatever way it was done, it surely was adroitly, and the two pieces were spread upon the outside of one of their shields. One of them still continued holding the head, while the other two were busy in curing the wound. This, too, was done not in an ordinary manner. The skin, which had covered the flesh that was taken away, was left entire, and flapped over the wound, and was fastened to the corresponding part by two or more small skewers or pins. Whether they had put any thing under the skin, between that and the wounded flesh, I know not; but, at the river-side where they were, they had prepared a cataplasm of clay, with which they covered the wound; they then forced the animal to rise, and drove it on before them, to furnish them with a fuller meal when they should meet their companions in the evening." (*Travels*, vol. iii. p. 142.) "We have an instance, in the life of Saul, that shows the propensity of the Israelites to this crime: Saul's army, after a battle, *flew*, that is, fell voraciously upon the cattle they had taken, and threw them upon the ground to cut off their flesh, and eat them raw; so that the army was defiled by eating blood, or living animals. 1 Sam. xiv. 33. To prevent this, Saul caused to be rolled to him a great stone, and ordered those that killed their oxen, to cut their throats upon that stone. This was the only lawful way of killing animals for food; the tying of the ox, and throwing it upon the ground, were not permitted as equivalent. The Israelites did probably, in that case, as the Abyssinians do at this day; they cut a part of its throat, so that blood might be seen on the ground, but nothing mortal to the animal followed from that wound: but, after laying his head upon a large stone, and cutting his throat, the blood fell from on high, or was poured on the ground like water, and sufficient evidence appeared that the creature was dead, before it was attempted to eat it. We have seen that the Abyssinians came from Palestine a very few years after this, and we are not to doubt, that they then carried with them this, with many other Jewish customs, which they have continued to this day." (Bruce's *Travels*, vol. iii. p. 299.) To corroborate the account given by Mr. *Bruce*, in these extracts, it may be satisfactory to affix what Mr. *Antes* has said upon the subject, in his Observations on the Manners and Customs of the Egyptians, p. 17. "When Mr. *Bruce* returned from Abyssinia, I was at Grand Cairo. I had the pleasure of his company for three months almost every day, and having, at that time, myself an idea of penetrating into Abyssinia, I was very inquisitive about that country, on hearing many things from him which seemed almost incredible to me; I used to ask his Greek servant Michael, (a simple fellow, incapable of any invention,) about the same circumstance, and must say, that he commonly agreed with his master, as to the chief points. The description Mr. *Bruce* makes concerning the bloody banquet of live oxen among the natives, he happened never to mention to me, else I could have made the same inquiry; but I heard not only this servant, but many eyewitnesses, often speak of the Abyssinians eating raw meat."

On the general veracity of Bruce as a traveller, Madden observes, "Whatever have been the petty jealousy and egotism of Bruce, he was an enterprising and intelligent traveller; and his general descriptions are better entitled to credit than those of the travellers who have reviled him. Mr. Coffin has just arrived here after a residence of eighteen years in Abyssinia: this gentleman assures me, that those points in his travels which are most disputed in England, are the points which are most correct: he showed me how the flesh was taken from the glutæi muscles of the living bullock, dissected out without wounding the bloodvessels. Mr. Coffin performed this operation here upon the living animal, in presence of Lord Prudhoe, and Mr. Burton, one of our most intelligent travellers."—Madden's Travels.

Ver. 29. And all the days of Noah were nine hundred and fifty years: and he died.

In asking the age of a child or a man, the inquiry is not how many years, but, "Days how many?"—In speaking of a man who will die soon—"Ah! in five years his *days* will be gone. That young man has gray hairs; to him how many days? he has seen twenty-six years."—Roberts.

Chap. 11. ver. 1. And the whole earth was of one language, and of one speech.

See on ver. 4, and on chap. 2. 20.

Ver. 3. And they said one to another, Go to, let us make brick, and burn them thoroughly. And they had brick for stone, and slime had they for mortar.

The soil of ancient Assyria and Babylonia consists of a fine clay, mixed with sand, with which, as the waters of the river retire, the shores are covered. This compost, when dried by the heat of the sun, becomes a hard and solid mass, and forms the finest material for the beautiful bricks for which Babylon was so celebrated. We all put to the test the adaptation of this mud for pottery, by taking some of it while wet from the bank of the river, and then moulding it into any form we pleased. Having been exposed to the sun for half an hour, it became as hard as stone. These remarks are important, as the indications of buildings throughout this region are different from those of other countries, the universal substitution of brick for stone being observable in all the numerous ruins we visited, including those of the great cities of Seleucia, Ctesiphon, and of the mighty Babylon herself, for which we have the authority of Scripture, that her builders "had brick for stone, and slime had they for mortar." In consequence of this circumstance, the ruins now before us, which our guide called Mumliheh, instead of showing fragments of pillars, or any marks by which we might conjecture the order of architecture, exhibit an accumulation of mounds, which, on a dead flat, soon attract the eye of a traveller, and have at first sight the appearance of sandy hillocks. On a nearer inspection they prove to be square masses of brick, facing the cardinal points, and, though sometimes much worn by the weather, built with much regularity; the neighbourhood of these large mounds is strewed with fragments of tile, broken pottery, and manufactured vitreous substances. Coins, the incontestible proofs of former population, are generally to be found. In this place, they are so abundant, that many persons come from Bagdad in the dry season to search for them. Aboo Nasir told us, that some time ago he found a pot full of coins, and Mr. Hart picked up two, with apparently Cufic inscriptions, but their characters were not very decipherable. Near the place where they were found, was the fragment of a vessel which had possibly contained them.—KEPPEL.

Ver. 4. And they said, Go to, let us build us a city, and a tower, whose top *may reach* unto heaven; and let us make us a name, lest we be scattered abroad upon the face of the whole earth.

The words in which they couched their daring resolution, "Let us build us a city, and a tower, whose top may reach unto heaven," mean no more than a tower of extraordinary height. Such phrases may be found in every language; and their meaning can scarcely be misunderstood. When the messengers whom Moses employed to examine the land of Canaan, returned and made their report, they described the cities which they had visited, as great and walled up to heaven: and Moses himself, in his farewell address to the congregation, repeats it; "Hear, O Israel, thou art to pass over Jordan this day, to go in to possess nations greater and mightier than thyself, cities great and fenced up to heaven." The meaning of these phrases plainly is, that the walls of those cities were uncommonly strong and lofty. That the builders of Babel meant no more, is further evident from the words of Jehovah, recorded by Moses. "Now nothing will be restrained from them which they have imagined to do." It is here plainly admitted, that the design was practicable, and had been accomplished, if God had not thought proper to interrupt their operations. But to build a tower, the top of which should actually reach unto heaven, is beyond the power of mortals. The opinion of Josephus is not much more reasonable; that their design was to raise a tower higher far than the summits of the highest mountains, to defend them from the waters of a second flood, of which they were afraid. Had this been their design, they would not have commenced their operations on the level plain, but on the top of Ararat, where the ark rested. They had the solemn promise of Jehovah, that he would no more destroy the earth by water; and beheld the ratification of it in the radiant bow of heaven, placed in the cloud to quiet the fears of guilty mortals. If the Noachidæ had distrusted the promise and sign of heaven, they had not descended from the mountains, where only they could hope for safety from the strength and height of their tower, into the plains of Babylonia, and fixed their abode between two mighty rivers, to whose frequent inundations that province is exposed. Nor could they be so infatuated as to imagine, that a tower constructed of bricks, whether hardened in the sun, or burnt in the fire, could resist the waters of a general deluge, whose impetuous assault, as they must have well known, the strong barriers of nature could hardly endure. Equally inadmissible is the notion, that they constructed this tower to defend them from the general conflagration, of which they are supposed to have received some obscure and imperfect notices; for in the destruction of the world, who could hope to find safety in the recesses of a tower, or on the summit of the mountains? they would rather seek for refuge from the devouring element, in the profound caverns of the earth.

But it is vain to indulge in conjectures, when the true reason is clearly stated in the page of inspiration: "Let us build us a city, and a tower, whose top may reach unto heaven; and let us make us a name, lest we be scattered abroad upon the face of the whole earth." These words clearly show, that their object in building the tower was, to transmit a name illustrious for sublime conception and bold undertaking, to succeeding generations. In this sense, the phrase, to make one's self a name, is used in other parts of Scripture. Thus, "David gat him a name when he returned from smiting of the Syrians in the valley of salt;" and the prophet informs us, that the God of Israel "led them by the right hand of Moses, with his glorious arm dividing the waters before them, to make himself an everlasting name." They seem also to have intended it as a beacon or rallying point, to their increasing and naturally diverging families, to prevent them from separating in the boundless wilderness into independent and hostile societies. This may be inferred from these words, in which they further explain the motive of their undertaking: 'lest we be scattered abroad on the face of the whole earth.' They seem to have anticipated the necessity, and dreaded the consequences of dispersion; and, like all who seek to avert evil by unlawful means, they hastened, by the rash and impious measure which they adopted, the very mischief they sought to avoid. To build a city and a tower was certainly no crime; but to do this with a view merely to transmit an illustrious name to posterity, or to thwart the counsels of heaven, was both foolish and wicked, and justly excited the displeasure of the supreme Judge, who requires his rational creatures to acknowledge and to glorify him in all their undertakings.

It is by no means improbable that this tower was also intended for idolatrous purposes. The worship of fire began in a very remote age, and most probably under the direction and among the rebellious followers of Nimrod. This idea receives no small confirmation from the numerous fire towers which in succeeding ages were built in Chaldea, where the sacred fire was kept, and the religious rites in honour of the sun were celebrated. If this conjecture be well founded, it accounts in the most satisfactory manner, for the sudden and effectual dispersion of the builders, visibly and strongly marking the first combined act of idolatry after the flood, of which we have any notice, with the displeasure of the true God. Guilty of the same crime which procured the sudden dispersion of the first settlers at Babel, was the restorer of that great city, when he proudly boasted, "Is not this great Babylon which I have builded for the house of the kingdom, by the might of my power, and for the honour of my majesty:" and he was instantly visited with a similar punishment, but proportioned to the greater enormity of his transgression; for the place should have reminded him of the sin and punishment of his forefathers, and taught him to guard against the pride and vanity of his heart. Nebuchadnezzar was, for his wickedness, driven from his throne and kingdom, to dwell with the beasts of the field, and eat grass like oxen, "till seven times passed over him;" till the sun had seven times passed over his appointed circuit, and he had learned "that the most High ruleth in the kingdom of men, and giveth it to whomsoever he will." But his irreligious ancestors were punished with dispersion, by confounding their language. Till this memorable event, the inspired writer assures us, the whole earth was of one language and one speech. When Jehovah came down to see the tower which the Babylonians were building, he said, "Behold, the people is one, and they have all one language." They formed one great society, and conversed in the tongue which they had learned from those who lived before the flood; and which was the only language spoken on earth from the beginning of the world: for no hint of any confusion of language, or even material diversity of speech, before the building of Babel, is given in the sacred volume. It is exceedingly natural to suppose, that the devout Seth, and his religious descendants, would preserve with care the family tongue in which God conversed with their renowned father; in which the first promise was given to sinners, and many subsequent revelations were made. The language of our fathers is not easily changed, if we were so disposed; but no man is willing to change it; and a religious man will be yet more averse to relinquish a language which contains the only grounds of his hope, and that of the whole human race. We may therefore conclude, that since this language had so many claims on the affectionate care of Seth, he would certainly hand it down, with the gospel it contained, to his children, that they might teach it to succeeding generations, till it was received by his celebrated descendant Noah, the second father of our family. For the same reasons, which were daily receiving additional strength, Shem would preserve with pious care the sacred deposit, till he delivered it into the hands of Abraham, with whom he lived about two hundred years. The line of descent, by which the primitive language might be transmitted from Adam to Abraham, and from this patriarch to Moses, is short and straight; for between Adam and Noah were only eight persons, and the father of Noah was fifty-six years old when Adam died. The only interruption is the confusion of tongues, which happened after the flood. But though God confounded the speech of mankind at Babel, it is not said he extinguished the general language; nor that he confounded the speech of any but the colony at Babel. These only were in the transgression, and, therefore, these only were liable to the punishment. Noah, and the rest of his family, persevering in their dutiful obedience to God, undoubtedly retained their language, together with their ancient habitations. It may be urged that, by the testimony of Moses, the Lord confounded at Babel, "the language of all the earth." But the plain of Shinar could, with no propriety, be called the whole earth; nor could the inhabitants of Shinar, by any figure of speech, be entitled to that name. If mankind were in possession of a great part of the globe when the tower was built, by what rule of justice could they be punished for a crime in which they had no share, and of which multitudes of the distant settlers could not even have heard? "Shall not the Judge of all the earth do right?" The truth of this history depends upon two terms, which admit of different senses. In the first verse of the eleventh chapter of Genesis, the sacred historian says, The whole earth was of one language and of one speech. The word (כל) Col, signifies *the whole*, and also *every;* by (ארץ) Arets, is often meant the *earth*, it also signifies a *land* or *province;* and occurs frequently in this latter acceptation. In this very chapter, the region of Shinar is called Arets Shinar, the land or province of Shinar; and the land of Canaan, Arets Canaan, the country of Canaan. The psalmist uses both terms in precisely the same sense: "Their sound is gone out into every land," Col Arets. The words of Moses, then, ought to be rendered, Therefore is the name of it called Babel; because the Lord did there confound the language of the whole land. If this view of the text be just, the dispersion was a partial event, and related chiefly to the sons of Cush, whose intention was to found a great, if not a universal empire; but by this judgment their purpose was defeated. The language of the whole country, Mr. Bryant thinks, was confounded, by causing a labial failure, so that the people could not articulate. It was not an aberration, in words or language, but a failure and incapacity in labial utterance; for God said, "Go to, let us go down and confound, שפה, their lip, that they may not understand one another's speech." By this, their speech was confounded, but not altered; for, as soon as they separated, they recovered the true tenor of pronunciation; and the language of the earth continued, for some ages, nearly the same. This appears, from many interviews between the Hebrews, and other nations, in which they spoke without an interpreter. Thus, when Abraham left his native country to sojourn in the land of promise, he conversed with the natives in their own language, without difficulty, though they were the descendants of Canaan, who, for his transgression at Babel, was driven, by the divine judgments, from the chosen residence of his family. The Hebrew language, indeed, seems to have been the vernacular tongue of all the nations in those parts of the world; for the patriarchs, and their descendants, so late as the days of Moses and Joshua, conversed familiarly with the inhabitants of Midian and Canaan, without the help of interpreters.—PAXTON.

CHAP. 13. ver. 3. And he went on his journeys from the south even to Beth-el, unto the place where his tent had been at the beginning, between Beth-el and Hai.

Abraham, and the other patriarchs, led a wandering shepherd's life in tents, such as the Arabs, Turcomans, and numerous tribes of eastern Asia, lead to this day in the same countries. Divided into tribes, they traverse immense tracts with their numerous herds, consisting of camels, oxen, and especially sheep and goats; and when the pasture of a district is exhausted, the tents are taken down, and the whole family, or the whole tribe, removes to another spot. "Each of these tribes," says *Volney*, "of the Bedouin Arabs appropriates to itself a certain tract, which it considers as its property. They differ from agricultural nations only so far, as such tracts must be far more extensive to procure subsistence for their flocks all the year round. One man's camps distributed over such a tract, form a tribe; they traverse the whole in succession, as they have consumed with their flocks the pastures in one place." The following account by PARSONS (Travels from Aleppo to Bagdad, p. 109) of the movement of an Arab horde, is illustrative of the manners of the old patriarchs. "It was entertaining enough to see the horde of Arabs decamp, as nothing could be more regular. First went the sheep and goatherds, each with their flocks in divisions, according as the chief of each family directed; then followed the camels and asses, loaded with the tents, furniture, and kitchen utensils; these were followed by the old men, women, boys, and girls, on foot. The children that cannot walk are carried on the backs of the young women, or the boys and girls; and the smallest of the lambs and kids are carried under the arms of the children. To each tent belong many dogs, among which are some greyhounds; some tents have from ten to fourteen dogs, and from twenty to thirty men, women, and children, belonging to it. The procession is closed by the chief of the tribe, whom they call emir and father, (emir means prince,) mounted on the very best horse, and surrounded by the heads of each family, all on horses, with many servants on foot. Between each family is a division or space of one hundred yards, or more, when they migrate; and such great regularity is observed, that neither camels, asses, sheep, nor dogs, mix, but each keeps to the division to which it belongs, without the least trouble. They had been here eight days, and were going four hours journey to the north-west, to another spring of water. This tribe consisted of about eight hundred and fifty men, women, and children. Their flocks of sheep and goats were about five thousand, besides a great number of camels, horses, and asses. Horses and greyhounds they breed and train up for sale: they neither kill nor sell their ewe lambs. At set times a chapter in the Koran is read by the chief of each family, either in or near each tent, the whole family being gathered round, and very attentive."

The Compte de FERRIERES SAUVEBOEUF describes the manner of an Arab horde moving to a fresh pasturage. "Their wandering life, without ambition, brings to the mind of the traveller that of the ancient patriarchs. Nothing is more interesting than their manner of changing their abode. Numerous flocks, which precede the caravan, express by their bleating, their joy at returning to their old pastures. Some beasts of burden, guided by the young men, bear the little ones just dropped, and not able to travel; then come the camels carrying the baggage, and the old or sick women. The rest go on foot, carrying their infants on their backs or in their arms; and the men, mounted on the horses, armed with lances, ride round, or bring up the march of the cattle, which loiter behind, browsing too long a time. In this manner the Arabs journey, and find their homes, their hearths, and their country, in every lace."—BURDER.

Ver. 7. And there was a strife between the herdmen of Abram's cattle and the herdmen of Lot's cattle.

How often have I been reminded of the strife of the herdmen of the scriptures, by seeing, on a distant plain, a number of shepherds or husbandmen struggling together respecting some of the same causes which promoted strife in the patriarchal age. The fields are not, as in England, enclosed by fences; there is simply a *ridge* which divides one from another. Hence the cattle belonging to one person find no difficulty in straying into the field of another, and the shepherds themselves have so little principle, that they gladly take advantage of it. Nothing is more common than for a man, when the sun has gone down, thus to injure his neighbour. The time when most disputes take place, is when the paddy, or rice, has been newly cut, as the grass left among the stubble is then long and green. The herdmen at that time become very tenacious, and wo to the ox, if within reach of stick or stone, until he shall get into his own field. Then the men of the other party start up on seeing their cattle beaten, and begin to swear and declare how often the others have done the same thing. They now approach each other, vociferating the most opprobrious epithets: the hands swiftly move about in every direction; one pretends to take up a stone, or spits on the ground in token of contempt; and then comes the contest —the long hair is soon dishevelled, and the weaker fall beneath their antagonists. Then begins the beating, biting, and scratching, till in their cruel rage they have nearly destroyed some of the party. The next business is with the magistrate: all are clamorous for justice; and great must be his patience, and great his discernment, to find out the truth.

Another common cause of strife is that which took place between the herdmen of Gerar and those of Isaac. Water is at all times very precious in the East, but especially in the *dry season;* as the tanks are then nearly exhausted, and what remains is scarcely fit for use. At that time recourse must be had to the wells; which are often made at the expense or labour of five, ten, or twenty people. Here, then, is the cause of contention. One man has numerous herds; he gets there *first*, and almost exhausts the well; the others come, and, seeing what is done, begin the affray. But the most common cause of quarrel is when the owners of the well have to irrigate their lands from the same source. To prevent these contests, they have generally each an appointed time for watering their lands; or, it may be, that those who get there first, shall have the privilege: but where there is so little integrity, it is no wonder there should be so much strife.—ROBERTS.

Ver. 10. And Lot lifted up his eyes, and beheld all the plain of Jordan, that it *was* well watered every where, before the LORD destroyed Sodom and Gomorrah, *even* as the garden of the LORD, like the land of Egypt, as thou comest unto Zoar.

The Jordan flows from the Lake of Genesareth to the Dead Sea, between two ridges of moderately high mountains, in a valley that may be about twelve miles in breadth. This valley opens at Jericho, and encloses within it the Dead Sea, which is surrounded by a circle of mountains. Before the destruction of Sodom and Gomorrah there was, however, no lake here; but all this was a valley, which Moses calls the vale of Siddim. It is probable, that even at that time there was a lake under this valley, in which the Jordan discharged itself, which otherwise could have had no vent. This subterraneous lake was covered with a thick coat of earth, on which, besides Sodom and Gomorrah, other cities stood. This being the nature of the ground, it could never be deficient in the requisite moisture, and besides it was doubtless watered by canals supplied from the Jordan. In this view Moses compares it with Egypt, which was watered by innumerable canals led from the Nile, and cultivated like a garden.—BURDER.

CHAP. 14. ver. 3. All these were joined together in the vale of Siddim, which is the salt sea.

The lake Asphaltites, or the Dead Sea, is enclosed on the east and west with exceeding high mountains; on the north it is bounded with the plain of Jericho, on which side it receives the waters of the Jordan; on the south it is open, and extends beyond the reach of the eye. It is said to be twenty-four leagues long, and six or seven broad; and is fringed with a kind of coppice of bushes and reeds. In the midst of this border, not a furlong from the sea, rises a fountain of brackish water, which was pointed out to Maundrell by his Arab conductor; a sure proof that the soil is not equally impregnated with saline particles. The ground, to the distance of half an hour from the sea, is uneven and broken into hillocks, which Mr. Maundrell compares to ruinous lime-kilns; but whether these might be the pits at which the kings of Sodom and Gomorrah were overthrown by the four kings who invaded their country, he could not determine.—PAXTON.

As it has no outlet, Reland, Pococke, and other travellers, have supposed that it must throw off its superfluous waters by some subterraneous channel; but, although it has been calculated that the Jordan daily discharges into it 6,090,000 tons of water, besides what it receives from the Arnon and several smaller streams, it is now known, that the loss by evaporation is adequate to explain the absorption of the waters. Its occasional rise and fall at certain seasons, is doubtless owing to the greater or less volume which the Jordan and the other streams bring down from the mountains.—MODERN TRAVELLER.

The water of the lake is intensely salt, extremely bitter and nauseous, and so heavy, that the most impetuous winds can scarcely ruffle its surface. It is called by common writers the Dead Sea, because it nourishes neither animal nor vegetable life. No verdure is to be seen on its banks, nor fish to be found within its waters; but it is not true that its exhalations are so pestiferous as to kill birds that attempt to fly over it. Mr. Maundrell saw several birds flying about, and skimming the surface of its waters, without any visible harm. The same fact is attested by Volney, who states it as no uncommon thing to see swallows dipping for the water necessary to build their nests. The true cause that deprives it of vegetables and animals, is the extreme saltness of the water, which is vastly stronger than that of the sea. The soil around it, impregnated also with salt, produces no plants; and the air itself, which becomes loaded with saline particles from evaporation, and which receives also the sulphureous and bituminous vapours, cannot be favourable to vegetation: hence the deadly aspect which reigns around this lake. The ground about it, however, is not marshy, and its waters are limpid and incorruptible, as must be the case with a dissolution of salt. Mr. Maundrell questions the truth of the common tradition, which is admitted by Volney in all its extent, that the waters of the Dead Sea are destructive to animal existence, having observed among the pebbles on the shore two or three shells of fish, resembling oyster-shells. [Mr. Madden, however, says, Travels, vol. 2, p. 210, "I found several fresh water shells on the beach, such as I before noticed on the Lake of Tiberias; and also the putrid remains of two small fish, of the size of mullet; which no doubt had been carried down from the Jordan, as well as the shells; for I am well convinced, both from my own observation and from the accounts of the Arabs, that no living creature is to be found in the Dead Sea."] That respectable traveller, willing to make an experiment of its strength, went into it, and found it bore up his body in swimming, with an uncommon force; but the relation of some authors, that men wading in it are buoyed up to the top as soon as the water reaches to the middle, he found upon experiment untrue. Pococke, however, says: "I was much pleased with what I observed of this extraordinary water, and stayed in it near a quarter of an hour. I found I could lay on it in any posture, without motion, and without sinking. It bore me up in such a manner, that, when I struck in swimming, my legs were above the water, and I found it difficult to recover my feet. I did not care to venture where it was deep, though these effects would probably have been more remarkable farther in. They have a notion that if any one attempted to swim over, it would burn up the body; and they say the same of boats, for there are none on the lake." Van Egmont and Heyman state, that on swimming to some distance from the shore, they found themselves, to their great surprise, lifted up by the water. "When I had swam to some distance, I endeavoured to sink perpendicularly to the bottom, but could not; for the water kept me continually up, and would certainly have thrown me upon my face, had I not put forth all the strength I was master of, to keep myself in a perpendicular posture; so that I walked in the sea as if I had trod on firm ground, without having occasion to make any of the motions necessary in treading fresh water; and when I was swimming, I was obliged to keep my legs the greatest part of the time out of the water. My fellow-traveller was agreeably surprised to find that he could swim here, having never learned. But his case and mine proceeded from the gravity of the water, as this certainly does from the extraordinary quantity of salt in it." —MODERN TRAVELLER.

About six in the morning, says Mr. Madden, I reached the shore, and much against the advice of my excellent guide, I resolved on having a bath. I was desirous of ascertaining the truth of the assertion, that "nothing sinks in the Dead Sea." I swam a considerable distance from the shore; and about four yards from the beach I was beyond my depth: the water was the coldest I ever felt, and the taste of it most detestable; it was that of a solution of nitre, mixed with an infusion of quassia. Its buoyancy I found to be far greater than that of any sea I ever swam in, not excepting the Euxine, which is extremely salt. I could lie like a log of wood on the surface, without stirring hand or foot, as long as I chose; but with a good deal of exertion I could just dive sufficiently deep to cover all my body, but I was again thrown on the surface, in spite of my endeavours to descend lower. On coming out, the wounds in my feet pained me excessively; the poisonous quality of the waters irritated the abraded skin, and ultimately made an ulcer of every wound, which confined me fifteen days in Jerusalem; and became so troublesome in Alexandria, that my medical attendant was apprehensive of gangrene.—MADDEN.

The question of its specific gravity, indeed, has been set to rest by the chymical analysis of the waters made by Dr. Marcet, and published in the London Philosophical Transactions for 1807. In 1778, Messrs. Lavoisier, Macquer, and Le Sage, had concluded, by experiment, that a hundred pounds of the water contain forty-five pounds six ounces of salt; that is, six pounds four ounces of common marine salt, and thirty-eight pounds two ounces of marine salt with an earthy base. But Dr. Marcet's more accurate analysis has determined the specific gravity to be 1,211, (that of the fresh water being 1000,) a degree of density not to be met with in any other natural water; and it holds in solution the following salts, in the stated proportions to 100 grains of the water:—

Muriate of lime	3,920 grains.
Muriate of magnesia	10,246
Muriate of soda	10,360
Sulphate of lime	0,054
	24,580

So that the water of the lake contains about one fourth of its weight of salts, supposed in a state of perfect desiccation; or if they be desiccated at the temperature of 180° on Fahrenheit's scale, they will amount to forty-one per cent. of the water. Its other general properties are, that, 1. As stated by all travellers, it is perfectly transparent. 2. Its taste is extremely bitter, saline, and pungent. 3. Reagents demonstrate in it the presence of the marine and sulphuric acids. 4. It contains no alumine. 5. It is not saturated with common salt. 6. It did not change the colours of the infusions commonly used to ascertain the prevalence of an acid or an alkali, such as litmus, violet, and tumeric.

Mr. Maundrell neither saw nor heard of the apples of Sodom, so frequently mentioned by the ancients; nor did he discover any tree near the lake, from which a fruit of that kind might be expected. It is a production which exists only in the imagination and song of the poet; and has perhaps been kept up so long, because it furnished him with a good allusion, or helped him to a beautiful simile. Several travellers, however, claim the honour of having discovered that far-famed apple. Hasselquist says, the apple of Sodom is not the fruit either of a tree or of a shrub, but the production of the solanum melongena of Linnæus. It is found in great abundance round Jericho, in the vales near the Jordan, and in the neighbourhood of the Dead Sea. Its apples are sometimes full of dust; but this appears only when the fruit is attacked by an insect, which converts the whole of the inside into dust, leaving nothing but the rind entire, without causing it to lose any of its colour. M. Seetzen supposes it is the fruit of a tree which grows on the plain of El Gor, near the southern extremity of the Dead Sea. The tree resembles a fig-tree, and the fruit is like the pomegranate: it struck him, that this fruit, which has no pulp or flesh in the inside, but only a species of cotton resembling silk, and is unknown in the rest of Palestine, might be the celebrated apple of Sodom. Chateaubriand imagines that he has made the interesting discovery. The shrub which bears, in his opinion, the true apple of Sodom, grows two or three leagues from the mouth of the Jordan; it is thorny, and has small taper leaves; its fruit is exactly like the little Egyptian lemon, both in size and colour: before it is ripe, it is filled with a corrosive and saline juice; when dried, it yields a blackish seed, which may be compared to ashes, and which resembles bitter pepper in taste. He gathered half a dozen of these fruits, but has no name for them, either popular or botanical. Next comes Mr. Jolliffe. He found in a thicket of brushwood, about half a mile from the plain of Jericho, a shrub of five or six feet high, on which grew clusters of fruit, about the size of a small apricot, of a bright yellow colour, "which, contrasting with the delicate verdure of the foliage, seemed like the union of gold and emeralds. *Possibly*, when ripe, they may crumble into dust upon any violent pressure." Those which this gentleman gathered did not crumble, nor even retain the slightest mark of indenture from the touch; they would seem to want, therefore, the most essential characteristic of the fruit in question. But they were not ripe. This shrub is probably the same as that described by Chateaubriand. Lastly, Captains Irby and Mangles have no doubt that they have discovered it in the oskar plant, which they noticed on the shores of the Dead Sea, grown to the stature of a tree; its trunk measuring, in many instances, two feet or more in circumference, and the boughs at least fifteen feet high. The filaments enclosed in the fruit, somewhat resemble the down of a thistle, and are used by the natives as a stuffing for their cushions; "they likewise twist them, like thin rope, into matches for their guns, which, they assured us, required no application of sulphur to render them combustible." This is probably the same tree that M. Seetzen refers to. But still, the correspondence to the ancient description is by no means perfect; there being little resemblance between cotton and thistle-down, and ashes or dust. M. Chateaubriand's golden fruit, full of bitter seed, comes the nearest to what is told us of the deceitful apple. If it be any thing more than a fable, it must have been a production peculiar to this part of Palestine, or it would not have excited such general attention. On this account, the oskar and the solanum seem alike unentitled to the distinction; and for the same reason, the pomegranate must altogether be excluded from consideration. The fruit of the *solanum melongena*, which belongs to the same genus as the common potato, is white, resembling a large egg, and is said to impart an agreeable acid flavour to soups and sauces, for the sake of which it is cultivated in the south of Europe. This could hardly be what Tacitus and Josephus referred to. It is possible, indeed, that what they describe, may have originated, like the oak-galls in this country, in the work of some insect: for these remarkable productions sometimes acquire a considerable size and beauty of colour. Future travellers will be inexcusable if they leave this question undecided. —MODERN TRAVELLER.

The far-famed fruit of the tree of Sodom, "which tempts the eye and turns to ashes on the lips," is nowhere to be found on the western shore; and Burckhardt appears to favour the opinion of its having only an imaginary existence: but it does exist in the vicinity of *El Ghor*. I saw one of the apples at Mar Saba; and, perhaps, the only plant in Egypt producing this fruit I discovered at *Koum*

Ombos, in Upper Egypt, growing in a corner of the small temple of Isis, facing the Nile; the plant was not quite the height of the Palma Christi, the fruit was the size of the pomegranate; indeed, from the similarity of the fruit and leaves, I consider the Dead Sea apple as a spurious pomegranate. It was, indeed, tempting to the eye, but deceitful to the sense; on opening it, it was quite empty, the surface of the rind having only a light floculent sort of cotton attached to it, which was destroyed by the lightest touch; this was the true Dead Sea apple which I saw in Egypt, and which I also found in Mar Saba; albeit Shaw and Pococke doubt its existence.—MADDEN.

The extreme saltness of this lake, has been ascribed by Volney to mines of fossil salt in the side of the mountains, which extend along the western shore, and from time immemorial have supplied the Arabs in the neighbourhood, and even the city of Jerusalem. He does not attempt to invalidate the credit of the Mosaic narrative; but only insinuates, that these saline depositions were either coeval with the mountains in which they are found, or entered into their original conformation. The extraordinary fruitfulness of the vale of Siddim, before the destruction of Sodom and Gomorrah, is asserted by Moses in terms so clear and precise, that the veracity of the sacred writer must be overthrown, before a reasonable doubt can be entertained of the fact. No disproportionate quantity of saline matter, could then have been present, either in the soil or in the surrounding mountains. That it abounded with bitumen, some have inferred from the assertion of Moses, that the vale of Siddim was full of slime pits: where the Hebrew word chemar, which we render slime, others, and particularly the Seventy interpreters, render bitumen. But *gophrith*, and not *chemar*, is the word that Moses employs to denote brimstone, in his account of the judgment which overwhelmed the cities of the plain; and by consequence, brimstone is not meant, when *chemar* is used, but bitumen, a very different substance. Hence the brimstone which now impregnates the soil of the salt sea, and banishes almost every kind of vegetation from its shores, must be regarded, not as an original, but an accidental ingredient, remaining from the destruction of the vale by fire and brimstone from heaven. The same remark applies to the mines of fossil salt, on the surrounding mountains; the saline matter was deposited in the cavities which it now occupies at the same time, else the vale of Siddim, instead of verdant pastures, and abundant harvests, had exhibited the same frightful sterility from the beginning, for which it is so remarkable in modern times. Bitumen, if the Hebrew word chemar denotes that substance, abounds in the richest soils; for in the vale of Shinar, whose soil, by the agreement of all writers, is fertile in the highest degree, the builders of the tower of Babel used it for mortar. The ark of bulrushes in which Moses was embarked on the Nile, was in like manner daubed with bitumen (chemar) and pitch; but the mother of Moses, considering the poverty of her house, cannot be supposed to have procured it from a distance, nor at any great expense: she must therefore have found it in the soil of Egypt, near the Nile, on whose borders she lived. It is therefore reasonable to suppose, that bitumen abounded in Goshen, a region famed for the richness of its pastures. Hence it may be fairly concluded, that the vale of Siddim, before its destruction, in respect of natural fertility, resembled the plain of Shinar, and the land of Egypt along the Nile. But it is well known, that wherever brimstone and saline matter abound, there sterility and desolation reign. Is it not then reasonable to infer, that the sulphureous and saline matters, discovered in the waters and on the shores of the Asphaltites, are the relics of the divine vengeance executed on the cities of the plain, and not original ingredients in the soil. If we listen to the testimony of the sacred writers, what was reasonable hypothesis rises into absolute certainty. Moses expressly ascribes the brimstone, the salt, and the burning in the overthrow of Sodom, to the immediate vengeance of Heaven; "When they see the plagues of that land, . . . that the whole land is brimstone, and salt, and burning; that it is not sown, nor beareth, nor any grass groweth thereon, (like the overthrow of Sodom and Gomorrah, Admah and Zeboim, which the Lord overthrew in his anger, and in his wrath;) even all nations shall say, Wherefore has the Lord done thus unto this land? What meaneth the heat of this great anger?" In this passage, the brimstone, salt, and burning, are mentioned as true and proper effects of the divine wrath; and since this fearful destruction is compared to the overthrow of Sodom and Gomorrah, the brimstone and salt into which the vale of Siddim was turned, must also be the true and proper effects of divine anger. This, indeed, Moses asserts in the plainest terms: "Then the Lord rained upon Sodom, and upon Gomorrah, brimstone and fire from the Lord out of heaven; and he overthrew those cities, and all the plain, and all the inhabitants of the cities, and that which grew upon the ground." But since the brimstone and the fire were rained from heaven, so must the salt, with which they are connected in the former quotation: and this is the opinion received by the Jewish doctors. The frightful sterility which followed the brimstone, salt, and burning, in the first quotation, is in the same manner represented as an effect of the divine judgment upon the vale of Siddim; "it is not sown, nor beareth, nor any grass groweth thereon."—PAXTON.

Chateaubriand says: "Several travellers, and, among others, Troilo and d'Arvieux, assert, that they remarked fragments of walls and palaces in the Dead Sea. This statement seems to be confirmed by Maundrell and Father Nau. The ancients speak more positively on this subject. Josephus, employing a poetic expression, says, that he perceived on the banks of the lake, the shades of the overwhelming cities. Strabo gives a circumference of sixty *stadia* to the ruins of Sodom, which are mentioned also by Tacitus. I know not whether they still exist; but, as the lake rises and falls at certain seasons, it is possible that it may alternately cover and expose the skeletons of the reprobate cities." Mr. Jolliffe mentions the same story. "We have even," he says, "heard it asserted with confidence, that broken columns and other architectural ruins are visible at certain seasons, when the water is much retired below its usual level; but of this statement our informers, when closely pressed, could not adduce any satisfactory confirmation." We are afraid that, notwithstanding the authority of Strabo, we must class this legend with the dreams of imagination; or perhaps its origin may be referred to some such optical delusion as led to the mistake respecting the supposed island. In the travels of Egmont and Heyman, however, there is a statement which may throw some light on the subject. They say: "We also saw here a kind of jutty or prominence, which appears to have been a heap of stones from time to time thrown up by the sea; but it is a current opinion here, that they are part of the ruins of one of the towns which are buried under it." The bare possibility, that any wreck of the guilty cities should be brought to light, is sufficient to excite an intense curiosity to explore this mysterious flood, which, so far as appears from any records, no bark has ever ploughed, no plummet ever sounded. Should permission ever be obtained from the Turks, to launch a vessel on the lake, its navigation, if practicable, would probably lead to some interesting results.—MODERN TRAVELLER.

Ver. 10. And the vale of Siddim *was full of* slime-pits; and the kings of Sodom and Gomorrah fled, and fell there: and they that remained fled to the mountain.

People retired to the *mountains* anciently when defeated in war: they do so still. Dr. Shaw indeed seems to suppose, that there was no greater safety in the hills than in the plains of this country: that there were few or no places of difficult access; and that both of them lay equally exposed to the insults and outrages of an enemy. But in this point this ingenious writer seems to be mistaken; since, as we find that those that remained of the armies of the kings of Sodom and Gomorrah fled to the mountains, in the days of Abraham, Gen. xiv. 10; so d'Arvieux tells us, that the rebel peasants of the Holy Land, who were defeated while they were in that country by the Arabs, in the plain of Gonin, fled towards the mountains, whither the Arabs could not pursue them at that time So, in like manner, the Archbishop of Tyre tells us, that Baldwin IV. of the croisade kings of Jerusalem, ravaging a place called the valley of Bacar, a country remarkably fruitful, the inhabitants fled to the mountains, whither our troops could not easily follow them. This flying to hills and mountains for safety, is frequently alluded to in Scripture.—HARMER.

Ver. 14. And when Abram heard that his brother was taken captive, he armed his trained *servants* born in his own house, three hundred and eighteen, and pursued *them* unto Dan.

If we should turn our thoughts to the strength of an Arab emir, or the number of men they command, we shall find it is not very great, and that were Abraham now alive, and possessed of the same degree of strength that he had in his time, he would still be considered as a prince among them, and might, perhaps, even be called a mighty prince, he having three hundred and eighteen servants able to bear arms, Gen. xiv. 14, especially in the Eastern complimental style: for this is much like the strength of those Arab emirs of Palestine d'Arvieux visited. There were, according to him, eighteen emirs or princes that governed the Arabs of Mount Carmel; the grand emir, or chief of these princes, encamped in the middle, the rest round about him, at one or two leagues distance from him, and from each other; each of these emirs had a number of Arabs particularly attached to him, who called themselves his servants, and were properly the troops each emir commanded when they fought; and when all these divisions were united, they made up between four and five thousand fighting men. Had each of these emirs been equal in strength to Abraham, their number of fighting men must have been near six thousand, for three hundred and eighteen, the number of his servants, multiplied by eighteen, the number of those emirs, make five thousand seven hundred and twenty-four; but they were but between four and five thousand, so that they had but about two hundred and fifty each, upon an average. Abraham then was superior in force to one of these emirs. But though Abraham was a man of power, and did upon occasion make war, yet I hope a remark I before made concerning him will be remembered here, that is, that he was a pacific emir notwithstanding, at least, that he by no means resembled the modern Arabs in their acts of depredation and violence. —HARMER.

Ver. 15. And he divided himself against them, he and his servants, by night, and smote them, and pursued them unto Hobah, which *is* on the left hand of Damascus.

The manner in which the Arabs harass the caravans of the East, is described in the same page. Chardin tells us, "that the manner of their making war, and pillaging the caravans, is, to keep by the side of them, or to follow them in the rear, nearer or farther off, according to their forces, which it is very easy to do in Arabia, which is one great plain, and in the night they silently fall upon the camp, and carry off one part of it before the rest are got under arms." He supposes that Abraham fell upon the camp of the four kings, that had carried away Lot, precisely in the same Arab manner, and by that means, with unequal forces, accomplished his design, and rescued Lot. Gen. xiv. 15, he thinks, shows this; and he adds, that it is to be remembered, that the combats of the age of Abraham more resembled a fight among the mob, than the bloody and destructive wars of Europe.—HARMER.

Ver. 17. And the king of Sodom went out to meet him.

The conduct of this king, of Abraham, of Lot, of Saul, of the father of the prodigal, and of many others, is beautifully illustrated by the manners of the East, at this day. Not to *meet* a friend, or an expected guest, would be considered as rude in the extreme. So soon as the host hears of the approach of his visitant, he and his attendants go forth in courtly style; and when they *meet* him, the host addresses him, "Ah! this is a happy day for me; by your favour I am found in health." He will then, perhaps, put his arm round his waist, or gently tap him on the shoulder, as they proceed towards the house. When at the door, he again makes his bow, and politely ushers him in; and the rest joyfully follow, congratulating each other on the happy meeting.—ROBERTS.

Ver. 22. And Abram said to the king of Sodom, I have lifted up my hand unto the LORD, the most high God, the possessor of heaven and earth, 23. That I will not *take* from a thread even to a shoe-latchet, and that I will not take any thing that *is* thine, lest thou shouldest say, I have made Abram rich.

The use of shoes may be traced to the patriarchal age; Abraham protested to the king of Sodom, after his victory over Amraphel and his associates, "I have lifted up mine hand unto the Lord, the most high God, the possessor of heaven and earth, that I will not take from a thread even to a shoe-latchet." And when the Lord appeared to Moses in the bush, he commanded him to put off his shoes from his feet, for the place on which he stood was holy ground. In imitation of this memorable example, the priests officiated in the temple barefoot; and all the orientals, under the guidance of tradition, put off their shoes when they enter their holy places. The learned Bochart is of opinion, that the Israelites used no shoes in Egypt; but being to take a long journey, through a rough and barren wilderness, God commanded them to eat the passover with shoes on their feet; and those very shoes which they put on at that festival, when they were ready to march, he suffered not to decay during the whole forty years they traversed the desert; and to increase the miracle, Grotius adopts the idle conceit of some Jewish writers, that their clothes enlarged as they grew up to maturity, and their shoes also underwent a similar enlargement. This was not impossible with Jehovah, but it seems to have been quite unnecessary, for the clothes and shoes of those that died, might serve their children when they grew up; and it was sufficiently wonderful, without such an addition, that their clothes should not decay, nor their shoes wear, nor their feet swell, by travelling over hot and sandy deserts for the long period of forty years. It only remains to be observed, on this part of the subject, that no covering for the foot can exclude the dust in those parched regions; and by consequence, the custom of washing and anointing the feet, which is, perhaps, coeval with the existence of the human race, is not to be ascribed to the use of sandals. Whatever covering for the foot may be used, Chardin declares, it is still necessary to wash and anoint the feet after a journey. It is also the custom everywhere among the Asiatics, to carry a staff in their hand, and a handkerchief to wipe the sweat from their face. The handkerchiefs are wrought with a needle; and to embroider and adorn them, is one of the elegant amusements of the other sex.—PAXTON.

To lift up the right hand with the fingers towards heaven is equivalent to an oath. Hence Dr. Boothroyd has rendered the passage, "I *swear* to Jehovah." To lift up the hand in confirmation of any thing is considered a most sacred way of swearing. In Isaiah lxii. 8. it is written, "The Lord hath sworn by his *right* hand." It is an interesting fact, that many of the images of the gods of the heathen have the *right* hand lifted up, which to the understanding of the people, says, "*I am God; I am truth; I myself; I am. Fear not.*" Does a man make a solemn promise, and should the person to whom it is made express a doubt; he will say, "*Lift up your hand;*" which means, swear that you will perform it.—ROBERTS.

Ver. 23. That I will not *take* from a thread even to a shoe-latchet, and that I will not take any thing that *is* thine, lest thou shouldest say, I have made Abram rich.

This may refer to the red *thread* worn round the neck or the arm, and which binds on the amulet; or the *string* with which females tie up their hair. The latchet I suppose to mean the *thong* of the sandal, which goes over the top of the foot, and betwixt the great and little toes. It is proverbial to say, should a man be accused of taking away some valuable article, which belongs to another, "I have not taken away even a piece of the *thong* of your worn-out sandals."—ROBERTS.

CHAP. 15. ver. 3. And Abram said, Behold, to me thou hast given no seed: and, lo, one born in my house is mine heir.

Though the slaves in the oriental regions were treated with more severity than hired servants, their condition was by no means reckoned so degrading as in modern times, among the civilized nations of the west. The slave-master in the East, when he has no son to inherit his wealth, and even when the fortune he has to bequeath is very considerable, frequently gives his daughter to one of his slaves. The wealthy people of Barbary, when they have no children, purchase young slaves, educate them in their own faith, and sometimes adopt them for their own children. This custom, so strange and unnatural, according to our modes of thinking, may be traced to a very remote antiquity; it seems to have prevailed so early as the days of Abraham, who says of one of his slaves, "One born in mine house is mine heir:" although Lot, his brother's son, resided in his neighbourhood, and he had besides many relations in Mesopotamia. In the courts of eastern monarchs, it is well known, that slaves frequently rise to the highest honours of the state. The greatest men in the Turkish empire are originally slaves, reared and educated in the seraglio. When Maillet was in Egypt, there was a eunuch who had raised three of his slaves to the rank of princes; and he mentions a Bey who exalted five or six of his slaves to the same office with himself. With these facts before us, we have no reason to question the veracity of the inspired writers, who record the extraordinary advancement of Joseph in the house of Pharaoh, and of Daniel, under the monarch of Babylon. These sudden elevations, from the lowest stations in society, from the abject condition of a slave, or the horrors of a dungeon, to the highest and most honourable offices of state, are quite consistent with the established manners and customs of those countries.—Paxton.

Ver. 17. And it came to pass, that, when the sun went down, and it was dark, behold a smoking furnace, and a burning lamp that passed between those pieces.

Several eminent critics believe the *lamp of fire* was an emblem of the Divine presence, and that it *ratified* the covenant with Abram. It is an interesting fact that the burning *lamp* or *fire* is still used in the East in *confirmation* of a covenant. Should a person in the evening make a solemn promise to perform something for another, and should the latter doubt his word, the former will say, pointing to the *flame* of the lamp, "That is the *witness.*" On occasions of greater importance, when two or more join in a covenant, should the fidelity of any be questioned, they will say, "We invoke the lamp of the Temple" (as a witness.) When an agreement of this kind has been broken, it will be said, "Who would have thought this? for the *lamp* of the Temple was invoked." That *fire* was a symbol of the Divine presence, no one acquainted with the sacred scriptures can deny; and in the literature and customs of the East, the same thing is still asserted. In the ancient writings, where the marriages of the gods and demigods are described, it is always said the ceremony was performed in the presence of the god of *fire.* He was the witness. But it is also a general practice, at the celebration of respectable marriages at this day, to have a *fire* as a *witness* of the transaction. It is made of the wood of the *Mango*-tree, or the *Aal* or *Arasu*, or *Panne* or *Palāsu.* The fire being kindled in the centre of the room, the young couple sit on stools; but when the Brahmin begins to repeat the incantations, they arise, and the bridegroom puts the little finger of his left hand round the little finger of the right hand of the bride, and they walk round the fire three times from left to right. "*Fire* is the witness of their covenant; and if they break it, *fire* will be their *destruction.*" In the Scanda Purāna, the father of the virgin who was to be married to the son of the Rishi, said to him, "Call your son, that I may give him to my daughter in the presence of the *god of fire*, that he may be the witness;" that being done, "Usteyār gave his daughter Verunte in marriage, the *fire* being the *witness.*"—Roberts.

Chap. 16. ver 2. I pray thee, go in unto my maid; it may be that I may obtain children by her.

The Hebrew has, "Be builded by her." When a wife has been for some time considered steril, should she have a child, she is said to be making her house new, or rather, she has caused the house to be newly *built.* When a man marries, "he is making a *new house.*"—Roberts.

Ver. 12. And he will be a wild man; his hand *will be* against every man, and every man's hand against him: and he shall dwell in the presence of all his brethren.

The phrase, "a wild man," it is well known, is in the original text, "a wild ass man," that is, a man like a wild ass in temper and manners. The comparison seems to refer, first to Ishmael himself, and to intimate certain leading traits in his character; and then to his offspring in every succeeding age. The troops of *onagers*, are conducted by a leading stallion, that prefers the most arid deserts of the mountains, keeps watch while his companions repose, and gives the signal at the appearance of an enemy. The Nomades of Asia report of these animals, that the first of a troop which sees a serpent or a beast of prey, makes a certain cry, which brings, in a moment, the whole herd around him, when each of them strives to destroy it instantly. Such were the character and manners of Ishmael. He was the first prince of his family, the founder of a powerful nation, of a rough, wild, and untractable disposition. Nor was this all: ambitious of supreme authority, he loved to place himself at the head of his rising community, to regulate its affairs, and direct its operations; and, like the high-spirited leader of the *onagers*, he could brook no rival. He discovered his ruling passion, when he was but a stripling in the house of his father. Determined to maintain his prerogatives as the elder son, and provoked to see a younger, and a child of a different mother, preferred before him, he gave vent to his indignation, by deriding his brother, and the feast which was made on his account. Expelled for his imprudence from his father's house, he made choice of the sandy desert for his permanent residence, and required the heads of all the families around him, either to acknowledge his supremacy, and treat him with the highest respect, or be driven from his station and neighbourhood. Wherever he pitched his tent, he expected, according to a custom of great antiquity, all the tents to be turned with their faces towards it, in token of submission; that the band might have their eye always upon their master's lodging, and be in readiness to assist him if he were attacked. In this manner did Ishmael dwell "in the presence,"—"before," (על) or, "over against the faces of all his brethren." But the prediction embraced also the character and circumstances of his descendants. The manners and customs of the Arabians, except in the article of religion, have suffered almost no alteration, during the long period of three thousand years. They have occupied the same country, and followed the same mode of life, from the days of their great ancestor, down to the present times, and range the wide extent of burning sands which separate them from all the surrounding nations, as rude, and savage, and untractable as the wild ass himself. Claiming the barren plains of Arabia, as the patrimonial domain assigned by God to the founder of their nation, they consider themselves entitled to seize, and appropriate to their own use, whatever they can find there. Impatient of restraint, and jealous of their liberty, they form no connexion with the neighbouring states; they admit of little or no friendly intercourse, but live in a state of continual hostility with the rest of the world. The tent is their dwelling, and the circular camp their city; the spontaneous produce of the soil, to which they sometimes add a little patch of corn, furnishes them with means of subsistence, amply sufficient for their moderate desires; and the liberty of ranging at pleasure their interminable wilds, fully compensates in their opinion for the want of all other accommodations. Mounted on their favourite horses, they scour the waste in search of plunder, with a velocity surpassed only by the wild ass. They levy contributions on every person that happens to fall in their way; and frequently rob their own countrymen, with as little ceremony as they do a stranger or an enemy; their hand is still against every man, and every man's hand against them. But they do not always confine their predatory excursions to the desert. When booty is scarce at home, they make incursions into the territories of their neighbours, and having robbed the solitary traveller, or plundered the caravan.

immediately retire into the deserts far beyond the reach of their pursuers. Their character, drawn by the pen of inspiration, exactly corresponds with this view of their dispositions and conduct: "Behold, as wild asses in the desert, go they forth to their work, rising betimes for a prey: the wilderness yieldeth food for them and for their children." Savage and stubborn as the wild ass which inhabits the same wilderness, they go forth on the horse or the dromedary with inconceivable swiftness in quest of their prey. Initiated in the trade of a robber from their earliest years, they know no other employment; they choose it as the business of their life, and prosecute it with unwearied activity. They start before the dawn, to invade the village or the caravan; make their attack with desperate courage, and surprising rapidity; and, plunging instantly into the desert, escape from the vengeance of their enemies. Provoked by their continual insults, the nations of ancient and modern times have often invaded their country with powerful armies, determined to extirpate, or at least to subdue them to their yoke; but they always return baffled and disappointed. The savage freebooters, disdaining every idea of submission, with invincible patience and resolution, maintained their independence; and they have transmitted it unimpaired to the present times. In spite of all their enemies can do to restrain them, they continue to dwell in the presence of all their brethren, and to assert their right to insult and plunder every one they meet with on the borders, or within the limits of their domains.—PAXTON.

The fate of Ishmael is here identified with that of his descendants: and the same character is common to them both. The historical evidence of the fact, the universal tradition, and constant boast of the Arabs themselves, their language, and the preservation for many ages of an original rite, derived from him as their primogenitor,—confirm the truth of their descent from Ishmael. The fulfilment of the prediction is obvious. Even Gibbon, while he attempts, from the exceptions which he specifies, to evade the force of the fact that the Arabs have maintained a perpetual independence, acknowledges that these exceptions are temporary and local; that the body of the nation has escaped the yoke of the most powerful monarchies; and that "the arms of Sesostris and Cyrus, of Pompey and Trajan, could never achieve the conquest of Arabia." But even the exceptions which he specifies, though they were justly stated, and though not coupled with such admissions as invalidate them, would not detract from the truth of the prophecy. The independence of the Arabs was proverbial in ancient as well as in modern times; and the present existence, as a free and independent nation, of a people who derive their descent from so high antiquity, demonstrates that they had never been wholly subdued, as all the nations around them have unquestionably been; and that they have ever dwelt in the presence of their brethren. They not only subsist unconquered to this day, but the prophesied and primitive wildness of their race, and their hostility to all, remain unsubdued and unaltered. "*They are a wild people; their hand is against every man, and every man's hand is against them.*" In the words of Gibbon, which strikingly assimilate with those of the prophecy, they are "*armed against mankind.*" Plundering is their profession. Their alliance is never courted, and can never be obtained; and all that the Turks, or Persians, or any of their neighbours can stipulate for from them is a partial and purchased forbearance. Even the British, who have established a residence in almost every country, have entered the territories of the descendants of Ishmael to accomplish only the premeditated destruction of a fort, and to retire. It cannot be alleged, with truth, that their peculiar character and manner, and its uninterrupted permanency, is the necessary result of the nature of their country. They have continued wild or uncivilized, and have retained their habits of hostility towards all the rest of the human race, though they possessed for three hundred years countries the most opposite in their nature from the mountains of Arabia. The greatest part of the temperate zone was included within the limits of the Arabian conquests; and their empire extended from India to the Atlantic, and embraced a wider range of territory than ever was possessed by the Romans, those boasted masters of the world. The period of their conquest and dominion was sufficient, under such circumstances, to have changed the manners of any people; but whether in the land of Shinar or in the valleys of Spain, on the banks of the Tigris or the Tagus, in Araby the Blessed or Araby the Barren, the posterity of Ishmael have ever maintained their prophetic character: they have remained, under every change of condition, a wild people; their hand has still been against every man, and every man's hand against them. The natural reflection of a recent traveller, on examining the peculiarities of an Arab tribe, of which he was an eyewitness, may suffice, without any art of controversy, for the illustration of this prophecy:—"On the smallest computation, such must have been the manners of those people for more than three thousand years: thus in all things verifying the prediction given of Ishmael at his birth, that he, in his posterity, should be a wild man, and always continue to be so, though they shall dwell for ever in the presence of their brethren. And that an acute and active people, surrounded for ages by polished and luxuriant nations, should, from their earliest to their latest times, be still found a wild people, dwelling in the presence of all their brethren, (as we may call these nations,) unsubdued and unchangeable, is, indeed, a standing miracle—one of those mysterious facts which establish the truth of prophecy." (*Sir Robert K. Porter.*)—KEITH.

Ver. 14. Wherefore the well was called Beer-lahai-roi: behold, *it is* between Kadesh and Bered.

If in some places where there are wells, there are no conveniences to draw any water with, to refresh the fainting traveller, there are other places where the wells are furnished with troughs, and other contrivances, for the watering cattle that want to drink. Sir John Chardin tells us there are wells in Persia and in Arabia, in the driest places, and above all in the Indies, with troughs and basins of stone by the side of them. He supposes the well called Beer-lahai-roi, mentioned Gen. xvi. 14, was thus furnished. I do not remember any circumstance mentioned in that part of the patriarchal history that proves this; but it is sufficiently apparent there, that the well where Rebecca went to draw water, near the city of Nahor, had some convenience of this kind; as also had the Arabian well to which the daughters of Jethro resorted. Other wells, without doubt, had the like conveniences, though not distinctly mentioned. —HARMER.

CHAP. 18. ver. 1. And the LORD appeared unto him in the plains of Mamre: and he sat in the tent door in the heat of the day.

In the time of Chandler it was still the custom of eastern shepherds to sit at the door of their tents in the heat of the day. That traveller, "at ten minutes after ten in the morning," was entertained with the view of a plain full of booths, with the Turcomans sitting by their doors, under sheds resembling porticoes, or by shady trees, surrounded with flocks of goats. In the same situation the three angels found Abraham, when they came to destroy Sodom and Gomorrah, sitting under the portico, or skirts of his tent, near the door, to enjoy the refreshing breeze, and superintend his servants. It was not the hottest part of the day, when Chandler saw the Turcoman shepherds sitting at the doors of their booths; it was soon after ten in the morning; and when Abraham was sitting at his tent door, it might be nearly at the same hour. In the hottest part of the day, according to the practice of those countries, the patriarch had been retired to rest. The goats of the Turcomans were feeding around their huts; and if Abraham's cattle, which is extremely probable, were feeding around his tent in the same manner, it accounts for the expedition with which he ran and fetched a calf from the herd, in order to entertain his visitants.—PAXTON.

Often has my mind reverted to the scene of the good old patriarch sitting in the door of his tent in the heat of the day. When the sun is at the meridian, the wind often becomes softer, and the heat more oppressive; and then may be seen the people seated in the *doors* of their *huts*, to inhale the breezes, and to let them blow on their almost naked bodies.—ROBERTS.

Ver. 2. And he lifted up his eyes, and looked.

To *lift* up the eyes does not mean to look *upw*[illegible], but to look directly *at* an object, and that earnestly. A man coming from the jungle might say, "As I came this morning, I *lifted* up my eyes, and behold, I saw three elephants." "Have you seen any thing to-day in your travels?"—"I have not lifted up my eyes." "I do not see the thing you sent me for, sir."—"Just *lift* up your eyes, and you will soon find it."—ROBERTS.

Ver. 4. Let a little water, I pray you, be fetched, and wash your feet.

How often, in passing through a village, may we see this grateful office performed for the weary traveller! As the people neither wear shoes nor stockings, and as the sandal is principally for the defence of the *sole* of the foot, the upper part soon becomes dirty. Under these circumstances, to have the feet and ankles washed is very refreshing, and is considered a necessary part of Eastern hospitality. The service is always performed by servants. (John xiii. 14.)—ROBERTS.

Ver. 6. And Abraham hastened into the tent unto Sarah, and said, Make ready quickly three measures of fine meal, knead *it*, and make cakes upon the hearth. 7. And Abraham ran unto the herd, and fetched a calf tender and good, and gave *it* unto a young man; and he hasted to dress it. 8. And he took butter and milk, and the calf which he had dressed, and set *it* before them; and he stood by them under the tree, and they did eat.

In the cities and villages of Barbary, where public ovens are established, the bread is usually leavened; but among the Bedoweens and Kabyles, as soon as the dough is kneaded, it is made into thin cakes, either to be baked immediately upon the coals, or else in a shallow earthen vessel like a fryingpan, called Tajen. Such were the *unleavened cakes*, which we so frequently read of in Scripture, and those also which *Sarah made quickly upon the hearth.* These last are about an inch thick; and being commonly prepared in woody countries, are used all along the shores of the Black Sea, from the Palus-Mæotis to the Caspian, in Chaldea and in Mesopotamia, except in towns. A fire is made in the middle of the room; and when the bread is ready for baking, a corner of the hearth is swept, the bread is laid upon it, and covered with ashes and embers: in a quarter of an hour they turn it. Sometimes they use small convex plates of iron: which are most common in Persia, and among the nomadic tribes, as being the easiest way of baking, and done with the least expense; for the bread is extremely thin, and soon prepared. The oven is used in every part of Asia; it is made in the ground, four or five feet deep, and three in diameter, well plastered with mortar. When it is hot, they place the bread (which is commonly long, and not thicker than a finger) against the sides; it is baked in a moment. Ovens, Chardin apprehends, were not used in Canaan in the patriarchal age; all the bread of that time was baked upon a plate, or under the ashes; and he supposes, what is nearly self-evident, that the cakes which Sarah baked on the hearth, were of the last sort, and that the shew-bread was of the same kind. The Arabs about mount Carmel use a great stone pitcher, in which they kindle a fire; and when it is heated, they mix meal and water, which they apply with the hollow of their hands to the outside of the pitcher; and this extremely soft paste, spreading itself, is baked in an instant. The heat of the pitcher having dried up all the moisture, the bread comes off as thin as our wafers; and the operation is so speedily performed, that in a very little time a sufficient quantity is made. But their best sort of bread they bake, either by heating an oven, or a large pitcher half full of little smooth shining flints, upon which they lay the dough, spread out in the form of a thin broad cake. Sometimes they use a shallow earthen vessel, resembling a fryingpan, which seems to be the pan mentioned by Moses, in which the meat-offering was baked. This vessel, Dr. Shaw informs us, serves both for baking and frying; for the bagreah of the people of Barbary differs not much from our pancakes, only, instead of rubbing the pan in which they fry them with butter, they rub it with soap, to make them like a honeycomb. If these accounts of the Arab stone pitcher, the pan, and the iron hearth or copper plate, be attended to, it will not be difficult to understand the laws of Moses in the second chapter of Leviticus; they will be found to answer perfectly well to the description which he gives us of the different ways of preparing the meat-offerings. The precepts of Moses evidently bear a particular relation to the methods of preparing bread, used by those who live in tents, although they were sufficient for the direction of his people after their settlement in Canaan; and his mentioning cakes of bread baked in the oven, and wafers that were baked on the outside of these pitchers, in the fourth verse, with bread baked on a plate, and in a pan, in the fifth and seventh verses, inclines Mr. Harmer to think, the people of Israel prepared their meat-offerings in their tents, which they afterward presented at the national altar, rather than in the court of the tabernacle.—PAXTON.

While we were talking of the Turcomans, who had alarmed us on our way, a meal was preparing within; and soon afterward, warm cakes baked on the hearth, cream, honey, dried raisins, butter, lebben, and wheat boiled in milk, were served to the company. Neither the Sheikh himself nor any of his family partook with us, but stood around, to wait upon their guests, though among those who sat down to eat, were two Indian fakirs, or beggars, a Christian pilgrim from Jerusalem, and the slaves and servants of Hadjee Abd-el-Rakhmān, all dipping their fingers into the same dish. Coffee was served to us in gilded china cups, and silver stands or finjans, and the pipes of the Sheikh and his son were filled and offered to those who had none. If there could be traced a resemblance between the form of this tent, and that of the most ancient buildings of which we have any knowledge, our reception there no less exactly corresponded to the picture of the most ancient manners, of which we have any detail. When the three angels are said to have appeared to Abraham in the plains of Mamre, he is represented as sitting in the tent-door in the heat of the day. "And when he saw them, he ran to meet them from the tent-door, and bowed himself towards the ground." "And Abraham hastened *into* the tent, unto Sarah, and said, 'Make ready quickly three measures of fine meal, knead it, and make cakes upon the hearth.' And he took butter and milk, and the calf which he had dressed, and set it before them, and he *stood by them* under the tree, and they did eat." When inquiry was made after his wife, he replied, "Behold, she is *in* the tent." And when it was promised him, that Sarah should have a son, it is said, "And Sarah heard in the tent-door, which was *behind* him." The angels are represented, as merely passengers in their journey, like ourselves: for the rites of hospitality were shown to them, *before* they had made their mission known. At first sight they were desired to halt and repose, to wash their feet, as they had apparently walked, and rest beneath the tree, while bread should be brought them to comfort their hearts. "And after that," said the good old patriarch, "shall ye pass on, for *therefore* are ye come unto your servant;" so that the duty of hospitality to strangers seems to have been as well and as mutually understood in the earliest days, as it is in the same country at present. The form of Abraham's tent, as thus described, seems to have been exactly like the one in which we sit; for in both, there was a shaded open front, in which he could sit in the heat of the day, and yet be seen from afar off; and the apartment of the females, where Sarah was, when he stated her to be *within* the tent, was immediately *behind* this, wherein she prepared the meal for the guests, and from whence she listened to their prophetic declaration.—BUCKINGHAM.

CHAP. 19. ver. 19. Behold now, thy servant hath found grace in thy sight.

Nothing can be more common than this form of speech. Has a man been pleading with another and succeeded in his request, he will say, "Ah! since I have found favour in your sight, let me mention another thing." "My lord, had I not found favour in your sight, who would have helped me?" "Happy is the man who finds grace in your sight!"—ROBERTS.

Ver. 24. Then the LORD rained upon Sodom and upon Gomorrah brimstone and fire from the LORD out of heaven. 25. And he overthrew those cities, and all the plain, and all the inhabitants of the cities, and that which grew upon the ground.

With regard to the agents employed in this catastrophe, there might seem reason to suppose that volcanic phenomena had some share in producing it; but Chateaubriand's remark is deserving of attention. "I cannot," he says, "coincide in opinion with those who suppose the Dead Sea to be the crater of a volcano. I have seen Vesuvius, Solfatara, Monte Nuovo in the lake of Fusino, the peak of the Azores, the Mamalif opposite to Carthage, the extinguished volcanoes of Auvergne; and remarked in all of them the same characters; that is to say, mountains excavated in the form of a tunnel, lava, and ashes, which exhibited incontestible proofs of the agency of fire." After noticing the very different shape and position of the Dead Sea, he adds: "Bitumen, warm springs, and phosphoric stones, are found, it is true, in the mountains of Arabia; but then, the presence of hot springs, sulphur, and asphaltos, is not sufficient to attest the anterior existence of a volcano." The learned Frenchman inclines to adopt the idea of Professors Michaelis and Büsching, that Sodom and Gomorrah were built upon a mine of bitumen; that lightning kindled the combustible mass, and that the cities sank in the subterraneous conflagration. M. Malte Brun ingeniously suggests, that the cities might themselves have been built of bituminous stones, and thus have been set in flames by the fire of heaven. We learn from the Mosaic account, that the Vale of Siddim, which is now occupied by the Dead Sea, was full of "slime-pits," or pits of bitumen. Pococke says: "It is observed, that the bitumen floats on the water, and comes ashore after windy weather; the Arabs gather it up, and it serves as pitch for all uses, goes into the composition of medicines, and is thought to have been a very great ingredient in the bitumen used in embalming the bodies in Egypt: it has been much used for cerecloths, and has an ill smell when burnt. It is probable that there are subterraneous fires that throw up this bitumen at the bottom of the sea, where it may form itself into a mass, which may be broken by the motion of the water occasioned by high winds; and it is very remarkable, that the stone called the stone of Moses, found about two or three leagues from the sea, which burns like a coal, and turns only to a white stone, and not to ashes, has the same smell, when burnt, as this pitch; so that it is probable, a stratum of the stone under the Dead Sea is one part of the matter that feeds the subterraneous fires, and that this bitumen boils up out of it." To give force to this last conjecture, however, it would be requisite to ascertain, whether bitumen is capable of being detached from this stone, in a liquid state, by the action of fire. The stone in question is the black fetid limestone, used at Jerusalem in the manufacture of rosaries and amulets, and worn as a charm against the plague. The effluvia which it emits on friction, is owing to a strong impregnation of sulphureted hydrogen. If the buildings were constructed of materials of this description, with quarries of which the neighbouring mountains abound, they would be easily susceptible of ignition by lightning. The scriptural account, however, is explicit, that "the Lord rained upon Sodom and upon Gomorrah brimstone and fire from heaven;" which we may safely interpret as implying a shower of inflamed sulphur, or nitre. At the same time it is evident, that the whole plain underwent a simultaneous convulsion, which seems referible to the consequences of a bituminous explosion. In perfect accordance with this view of the catastrophe, we find the very materials, as it were, of this awful visitation still at hand in the neighbouring hills; from which they might have been poured down by the agency of a thunder-storm, without excluding a supernatural cause from the explanation of the phenomena. Captains Irby and Mangles collected on the southern coast lumps of nitre and fine sulphur, from the size of a nutmeg up to that of a small hen's egg, which, it was evident from their situation, had been brought down by the rain: their great deposite must be sought for," they say, "in the cliff." Dr. Shaw supposes that the bitumen, as it rises, is accompanied with sulphur, "inasmuch as both of them are found promiscuously upon the wash of the shore." But his conjecture is not founded on observation. The statement he gives, is founded on hearsay evidence; we cannot, therefore, admit him as (in this case) an original authority. "I was informed," he says, "that the bitumen, for which this lake hath been always remarkable, is raised, at certain times, from the bottom, in large hemispheres; which, as soon as they touch the surface, and so are acted upon by the external air, burst at once with great smoke and noise, like the *pulvis fulminans* of the chymists, and disperse themselves round about in a thousand pieces. But this happens only near the shore; for, in greater depths, the eruptions are supposed to discover themselves only in such columns of smoke as are now and then observed to arise from the lake." Chateaubriand speaks of the puffs of smoke "which announce or follow the emersion of asphaltos, and of fogs that are really unwholesome like all other fogs." These he considers as the supposed pestilential vapours said to arise from the bosom of the lake. But it admits of question, in the deficiency of more specific information, whether what has been taken for columns of smoke, may not be the effect of evaporation.—MODERN TRAVELLER.

Ver. 26. But his wife looked back from behind him, and she became a pillar of salt.

"From behind him." This *seems* to imply that she was following her husband, as is the custom at this day. When men, or women, leave their house, they never *look back*, as "it would be very unfortunate." Should a husband have left any thing which his wife knows he will require, she will not call on him to turn or look back; but will either take the article herself, or send it by another. Should a man have to *look back* on some great emergency, he will not then proceed on the business he was about to transact. When a person goes along the road, (especially in the evening,) he will take great care not to *look back*, "because the evil spirits would assuredly seize him." When they go on a journey, they will not look behind, though the palankeen, or bandy, should be close upon them; they step a little on one side, and then look at you. Should a person have to leave the house of a friend after sunset, he will be advised in going home not to *look back:* "as much as possible keep your eyes closed; *fear not.*" Has a person made an offering to the evil spirits, he must take particular care when he leaves the place not to *look back*. A female known to me is believed to have got her crooked neck by *looking back*. Such observations as the following may be often heard in private conversation. "Have you heard that *Comāran* is very ill?"—"No, what is the matter with him?"—"Matter! why he has *looked back*, and the evil spirit has caught him."—ROBERTS.

CHAP. 21. ver. 6. And Sarah said, God hath made me to laugh, *so that* all that hear will laugh with me.

A woman advanced in years, under the *same circumstances*, would make a similar observation: "I am made to *laugh*." But this figure of speech is also used on any *wonderful* occasion. Has a man gained any thing he did not expect, he will ask, "What is this? I am made to *laugh*." Has a person lost any thing which the moment before he had in his hand, he says, "I am made to laugh." Has he obtained health, or honour, or wealth, or a wife, or a *child*, it is said, "He is made to laugh." "Ah, his mouth is now full of *laughter;* his mouth cannot contain all that laughter." (Ps. cxxvi. 2.)—ROBERTS.

Ver. 8. And the child grew, and was weaned: and Abraham made a great feast the *same* day that Isaac was weaned.

When the time has come to wean a child, a *fortunate* day is looked for, and the event is accompanied with feasting and religious ceremonies. Rice is given to the child in a formal way, and the relations are invited to join in the *festivities*. For almost every event of life the Hindoos have a fixed rule from which they seldom deviate. They *wean* a female child within the year, "because, *if* they did not, it would become steril;" but boys are often allowed the breast till they are three years of age.—ROBERTS

Ver. 9. And Sarah saw the son of Hagar the Egyptian, which she had borne unto Abraham.

It is not uncommon for a man of property to keep a concubine in the *same* house with his wife; and, strange as it may appear, it is sometimes at the wife's *request.** Perhaps she has not had any children, or they may have died, and they both wish to have one, to perform their funeral ceremonies. By the laws of *Menu*, should a wife, during the first eight years of her marriage, prove unfruitful; or should the children she has borne be all dead in the tenth year after marriage; or should she have a daughter *only* in the eleventh year; he may, without her consent, put her away, and take a concubine into the house. He must, however, continue to support her.—ROBERTS.

Ver. 14. And Abraham rose up early in the morning, and took bread and a bottle of water, and gave *it* unto Hagar, (putting it on her shoulder,) and the child, and sent her away; and she departed, and wandered in the wilderness of Beer-sheba. 15. And the water was spent in the bottle, and she cast the child under one of the shrubs. 16. And she went, and sat her down over against *him* a good way off, as it were a bow-shot; for she said, Let me not see the death of the child. And she sat over against *him*, and lifted up her voice, and wept.

Chardin has given us, at large, an amusing account of these bottles, which, therefore, I would here set down. After observing that the bottle given to Hagar was a leather one, he goes on thus: "The Arabs, and all those that lead a wandering kind of life, keep their water, milk, and other kind of liquors in these bottles. They keep in them more fresh than otherwise they would do. These leather bottles are made of goat skins. When the animal is killed, they cut off its feet and its head, and they draw it in this manner out of the skin, without opening its belly. They afterward sew up the places where the legs were cut off, and the tail, and when it is filled, they tie it about the neck. These nations, and the country people of Persia, never go a journey without a small leather bottle of water hanging by their side like a scrip. The great leather bottles are made of the skin of a he-goat, and the small ones, that serve instead of a bottle of water on the road, are made of a kid's skin. Mons. Dandilly, for want of observing this, in his beautiful translation of Josephus, has put goat skin in the chapter of Hagar and Ishmael, instead of a kid's skin bottle, which, for the reasons assigned above, must have been meant." He reassumes the subject in another part of the same volume, in which he tells us, "that they put into these goat-skin and kid-skin vessels every thing which they want to carry to a distance in the East, whether dry or liquid, and very rarely make use of boxes and pots, unless it be to preserve such things as are liable to be broken. The reason is, their making use of beasts of carriage for conveying these things, who often fall down under their loading, or throw it down, and also because it is in pretty thin woollen sacks that they enclose what they carry. There is another advantage, too, in putting the necessaries of life in these skin vessels, they are preserved fresher; the ants and other insects cannot make their way to them; nor can the dust get in, of which there are such quantities in the hot countries of Asia, and so fine, that there is no such thing as a coffer impenetrable to it; therefore it is that butter, honey, cheese, and other like aliments, are enclosed in vessels made of the skins of this species of animals." According to this, the things that were carried to Joseph for a present, were probably enclosed in little vessels made of kid skins; not only the balm and the honey, which were somewhat liquid; but the nuts and the almonds too, that they might be preserved fresh, and the whole put into slight woollen sacks.—HARMER.

That Ishmael should, when just ready to faint, and unable to proceed onward in his journey, desire to lie down under some tree, where he might be in the shade, was quite natural: in such a situation Thevenot (Travels, p. 164) fell in with a poor Arab in this wilderness, just ready to expire. "Passing by the side of a bush," says this writer, "we heard a voice that called to us, and being come to the place, we found a poor languishing Arab, who told us that he had not eaten a bit for five days; we gave him some victuals and drink, with a provision of bread for two days more, and so went on our way." Ishmael was, without debate, fourteen years old when Isaac was born, (compare Gen. xvi. 16, with chap. xxi. 5,) and probably seventeen when Isaac was weaned, for it was anciently the custom in these countries to suckle children till they were three years old, and it still continues so; the translation then of the Septuagint is very amazing, for instead of representing Abraham as giving Hagar bread, and a skin bottle of water, and putting them upon Hagar's shoulder, that version represents Abraham as putting his son Ishmael on the shoulders of his mother. How droll the representation! Young children indeed are wont to be carried so; but how ridiculous to describe a youth of seventeen, or even fourteen, as riding upon his mother's shoulders, when sent upon a journey into the wilderness, and she loaded at the same time with the provisions. Yet unnatural and odd as this representation is, our version approaches too near to it, when it describes Hagar as *casting* the youth under one of the shrubs: which term agrees well enough with the getting rid of a half grown man from her shoulders, but by no means with the maternal affectionate letting go her hold of him, when she found he could go no farther, and desired to lie down and die under that bush: for that undoubtedly was the idea of the sacred writer; she left off supporting him, and let him gently drop on the ground, where he desired to lie. In a succeeding verse, the angel of the LORD bade her lift up Ishmael, and hold him in her hand, support him under his extreme weakness; she had doubtless done this before, and her quitting her hold, upon his lying down, is the meaning of the word (שלך) *shalak*, translated *casting*, that word sometimes, indeed, signifying a sudden and rather violent quitting hold of a thing, but at other times a parting with it in a gentle manner. It may also be wondered at, how Hagar came to give way to despair at that time, as she certainly did; for since there were several shrubs in that place, we may suppose it was a sure indication of water, and that therefore maternal anxiety would rather have engaged her to endeavour to find out the spring which gave this spot its verdure. But it is to be remembered, that though Irwin found many shrubs in that part of the wilderness through which he travelled, yet the fountains or wells there were by no means equal in number to the spots of ground covered with shrubs, a latent moisture in the earth favouring their growth, where there were no streams of water above ground: she might, therefore, having found her preceding searches vain, very naturally be supposed to have given up all hope of relief, when the angel made her observe where there was water to be found, upon drinking which Ishmael revived.—HARMER.

Ver. 16. And she went, and sat her down over against *him*, a good way off, as it were a bow-shot.

This is a common figure of speech in their ancient writings, "The distance of an *arrow*.—So far as the arrow flies." The common way of measuring a short distance is to say, "It is a *call* off," *i. e.* so far as a man's voice can reach. "How far is he off?" "O, not more than three *calls*," *i. e.* were three men stationed within the reach of each other's voices, the voice of the one farthest off would reach to that distance.—ROBERTS.

Ver. 19. And God opened her eyes, and she saw a well of water: and she went and filled the bottle with water, and gave the lad drink.

Few European readers are, probably, able to form an adequate idea of the horrors of such a situation as is here described. The following description may serve to paint to us the terrors of the desert, and the danger of perishing in it with thirst. "The desert of Mesopotamia now presents to our eyes its melancholy uniformity. It is a con-

* I knew a couple with whom this occurred, and the wife delights in nursing and bringing up the offspring of her husband's concubine.

tinuation, and, as it were, a branch of the Great Arabian desert on the other side of the Euphrates. Saline plants cover, at large intervals, the burning sand or the dry gypsum. Wormwood spreads here, as the furze in Europe, over immense tracts, from which it excludes every other plant. Agile herds of gazelles traverse those plains, where many wild asses formerly roved. The lion concealed in the rushes along the rivers lies in wait for these animals; but when he is unable to seize them, to appease his hunger, he sallies forth with fury, and his terrible roaring rolls like thunder from desert to desert. The water of the desert is, for the most part, bitter and brackish. The atmosphere, as is usual in Arabia, is pure and dry; frequently it is burning in the naked and sandy plains: the corrupt vapours of stagnant waters are diffused there; the exhalations of the sulphureous and salt lakes increase the pestilential matter. Whenever any interruption of equilibrium sets a column of such infected air into rapid motion, that poisonous wind arises, which is called Samum or Samyel, which is dreaded less in the interior of Arabia than on the frontiers, and especially in Syria and Mesopotamia. As soon as this dangerous wind arises, the air immediately loses its purity, the sun is covered with a bloody veil, all animals fall alarmed to the earth, to avoid this burning blast, which stifles every living being that is bold enough to expose itself to it. The caravans which convey goods backward and forward from Aleppo to Bagdad, and have to traverse these deserts, pay a tribute to the Arabs, who consider themselves as masters of these solitudes. They have also to dread the suffocating wind, the swarms of locusts, and the want of water, as soon as they leave the Euphrates." A French traveller affirms, that he was witness to a scene occasioned by the want of water, the most terrible that can be imagined for a man of feeling. It was between Anah and Dryjeh. The locusts, after they had devoured every thing, at last perished. The immense numbers of dead locusts corrupted the pools, from which, for want of springs, they were obliged to draw water. The traveller observed a Turk, who, with despair in his countenance, ran down a hill, and came towards him. "I am," cried he, "the most unfortunate man in the world! I have purchased, at a prodigious expense, two hundred girls, the most beautiful of Greece and Georgia. I have educated them with care; and now that they are marriageable, I am taking them to Bagdad to sell them to advantage. Ah! they perish in this desert for thirst, but I feel greater tortures than they." The traveller immediately ascended the hill; a dreadful spectacle here presented itself to him. In the midst of twelve eunuchs and about a hundred camels he saw these beautiful girls, of the age of twelve to fifteen, stretched upon the ground, exposed to the torments of a burning thirst and inevitable death. Some were already buried in a pit which had just been made; a great number had dropped down dead by the side of their leaders, who had no more strength to bury them. On all sides were heard the sighs of the dying; and the cries of those who, having still some breath remaining, demanded in vain a drop of water. The French traveller hastened to open his leathern bottle, in which there was a little water. He was already going to present it to one of these unhappy victims. "Madman!" cried his Arabian guide, "wouldst thou also have us die from thirst?" He immediately killed the girl with an arrow, seized the bottle, and threatened to kill any one who should venture to touch it. He advised the slave-merchant to go to Dryjeh, where he would find water. "No," replied the Turk, "at Dryjeh the robbers would take away all my slaves." The Arab dragged the traveller away. The moment they were retiring, these unhappy victims, seeing the last ray of hope vanish, raised a dreadful cry. The Arab was moved with compassion; he took one of them, poured a drop of water on her burning lips, and set her upon his camel, with the intention of making his wife a present of her. The poor girl fainted several times, when she passed the bodies of her companions, who had fallen down dead in the way. Our traveller's small stock of water was nearly exhausted, when they found a fine well of fresh and pure water; but the rope was so short, that the pail would not reach the surface of the water. They cut their cloaks in strips, tied them together, and drew up but little water at a time, because they trembled at the idea of breaking their weak rope, and leaving their pail in the well. After such dangers, they at last arrived at the first station in Syria.—BURDER.

Ver. 21. And he dwelt in the wilderness of Paran: and his mother took him a wife out of the land of Egypt.

When a father dies, the mother begins to look out for a wife for her son, though he may be very young; and her arrangements will generally be acceded to.—ROBERTS.

Ver. 28. And Abraham set seven ewe-lambs of the flocks by themselves. 29. And Abimelech said unto Abraham, What *mean* these seven ewe-lambs, which thou hast set by themselves? 30. And he said, For *these* seven ewe-lambs shalt thou take of my hand, that they may be a witness unto me that I have digged this well. 31. Wherefore he called that place Beer-sheba; because there they sware both of them.

Mr. BRUCE, (*Travels*, vol. i. p. 199,) relating the manner in which a compact was made between his party and some shepherds in Abyssinia, says, "Medicines and advice being given on my part, faith and protection pledged on theirs, two bushels of wheat and seven sheep were carried down to the boat."—BURDER.

CHAP. 22. ver. 3. And Abraham rose up early in the morning, and saddled his ass, and took two of his young men with him, and Isaac his son, and clave the wood for the burnt-offering, and rose up, and went unto the place of which God had told him.

There is no ground for supposing that the ancient eastern saddles were like our modern ones. Such were not known to the Greeks and Romans till many ages after the Hebrew judges. "No nation of antiquity knew the use of either saddles or stirrups," (GOGUET;) and even in our own times, *Hasselquist*, when at Alexandria, says, "I procured an equipage which I had never used before; it was an ass with an Arabian *saddle*, which consisted only of a cushion, on which I could sit, and a handsome bridle." But even the cushion seems an improvement upon the ancient eastern saddles, which were probably nothing more than a kind of rug girded to the beast.—BURDER.

CHAP. 23. ver. 2. And Sarah died in Kirjath-arba; the same *is* Hebron in the land of Canaan: and Abraham came to mourn for Sarah, and to weep for her.

The ancient Greeks were accustomed to lay out the body after it was shrouded in its grave-clothes; sometimes upon a bier, which they bedecked with various sorts of flowers. The place where the bodies were laid out, was near the door of the house: there the friends of the deceased attended them with loud lamentations; a custom which still continues to be observed among that people. Dr. Chandler, when travelling in Greece, saw a woman at Megara, sitting with the door of her cottage open, lamenting her dead husband aloud; and at Zante, a woman in a house with the door open, bewailing her little son, whose body lay by her dressed, the hair powdered, the face painted and bedecked with gold leaf. This custom of mourning for the dead, near the door of the house, was probably borrowed from the Syrians; and if so, it will serve to illustrate an obscure expression of Moses, relative to Abraham: "And Sarah died in Kirjath-arba; and Abraham came to mourn for Sarah, and to weep for her." He came out of his own separate tent, and seating himself on the ground near the door of her tent, where her corpse was placed, that he might perform those public solemn rites of mourning, that were required, as well by decency as affection, lamented with many tears the loss he had sustained.—PAXTON.

Ver. 7. And Abraham stood up, and bowed himself to the people of the land, *even* to the children of Heth.

The politeness of Abraham may be seen exemplified among the highest and the lowest of the people of the East: in this respect, nature seems to have done for them, what art has done for others. With what grace do all classes bow on receiving a favour, or in paying their respects to a superior! Sometimes they bow down *to the ground;* at other times they put their hands on their *bosoms,* and gently incline the head; they also put the right hand on the *face* in a longitudinal position; and sometimes give a long and graceful sweep with the *right hand,* from the *forehead* to the *ground.*—ROBERTS.

Ver. 9. That he may give me the cave of Machpelah, which he hath, which *is* in the end of his field: for as much money as it is worth he shall give it me, for a possession of a buryingplace among you.

This is the most ancient example of a family vault or an hereditary sepulchre in a cave. In the southern mountainous part of Palestine, there are many natural caves in the rocks, which may easily be formed into spacious buryingplaces. There are still found in Syria, Palestine, and Egypt, many such sepulchral caves, which have been frequently described by travellers who have visited those countries. These sepulchres are differently contrived. Sometimes they descend; only those which are made in the declivities of the mountains, often go horizontally into the rock. In Egypt, also, there are many open sepulchres, which run horizontally into the rock, but most of the mummy-pits are open perpendicularly, and you must let yourself down through this opening. In Palestine and Syria, on the contrary, the sepulchres which descend, are provided with steps, which are now for the most part covered with heaps of rubbish. Many of them consist in the inside of many chambers which are united by passages; in some of them the back chambers are deeper than the front ones, and you are obliged to descend some more steps to come to them. These chambers, as they are still found, are pretty spacious; in most of them recesses, six or seven feet long, are made in the walls all round, to receive the dead bodies; in others stone slabs of the same length are fixed against the walls; sometimes several, one above another, on which the dead bodies were laid; in some few there are stone-coffins, which are provided with a lid. It is nearly in this manner that the arrangement of graves is prescribed in the Talmud; only there is always to be an antechamber and recesses made in the walls of the square sepulchres, the number of which may be different.—BURDER.

Ver. 15. My lord, hearken unto me: the land *is worth* four hundred shekels of silver; what *is* that betwixt me and thee? bury therefore thy dead.

Respectable people are always saluted with the dignified title, "*My lord;*" hence English gentlemen on their arrival, are apt to suppose they are taken for those of very high rank. The man of whom Abraham offered to purchase Machpelah, affected to give the land. "Nay, my *lord,* hear me, the field I give thee." And this fully agrees with the conduct of those, who are requested to dispose of a thing to a person of superior rank. Let the latter go and ask the price, and the owner will say, "My *lord,* it will be a great favour if you will take it." "Ah, let me have that pleasure, my *lord.*" Should the possessor believe he will one day need a favour from the great man, nothing will induce him to sell the article, and he will take good care (through the servants or a friend) it shall soon be in his house. Should he, however, have no expectation of a favour in future, he will say as Ephron, "The thing is worth so much; your pleasure, my *lord.*"—ROBERTS.

CHAP. 24. ver. 2. And Abraham said unto his eldest servant of his house, that ruled over all that he had, Put, I pray thee, thy hand under my thigh: 3. And I will make thee swear by the LORD, the God of heaven, and the God of the earth, that thou shalt not take a wife unto my son of the daughters of the Canaanites, among whom I dwell.

The present mode of swearing among the Mohammedan Arabs, that live in tents as the patriarchs did, according to *de la Roque,* is by laying their hands on the Koran. They cause those who swear to wash their hands before they give them the book; they put their left hand underneath, and the right over it. Whether, among the patriarchs, one hand was under, and the other upon the thigh, is not certain; possibly Abraham's servant might swear with one hand under his master's thigh, and the other stretched out to Heaven. As the posterity of the patriarchs are described as coming out of the thigh, it has been supposed, this ceremony had some relation to their believing the promise of God, to bless all the nations of the earth, by means of one that was to descend from Abraham.—HARMER.

Ver. 11. And he made his camels to kneel down without the city by a well of water, at the time of the evening, *even* the time that women go out to draw *water.*

It is the work of *females* in the East to draw water both morning and evening; and they may be seen going in groups to the wells, with their vessels on the hip or the shoulder. In the morning they talk about the events of the past night, and in the evening about those of the day: many a time would the story of Abraham's servant and Rebecca, the daughter of Bethuel, be repeated by the women of Mesopotamia in their visits to the well.—ROBERTS.

The women among the orientals, are reduced to a state of great subjection. In Barbary they regard the civility and respect which the politer nations of Europe pay to the weaker sex, as extravagance, and so many infringements of that law of nature, which assigns to man the pre-eminence. The matrons of that country, though they are considered indeed as servants of better station, yet have the greatest share of toil and business upon their hands. While the lazy husband reposes under some neighbouring shade, and the young people of both sexes tend the flocks, the wives are occupied all the day long, either in toiling on their looms, or in grinding at the mill, or in preparing bread or other kind of farinaceous food. Nor is this all; for to finish the day, "at the time of evening," to use the words of the sacred historian, "even at the time that women go out to draw water," they must equip themselves with a pitcher or goat's skin, and tying their sucking children behind them, trudge out in this manner, two or three miles, to fetch water.—PAXTON.

Ver. 16. And the damsel *was* very fair to look upon, a virgin; neither had any man known her: and she went down to the well, and filled her pitcher and came up.

The vessel that the Eastern women frequently make use of, for the purpose of carrying water, is described as like our jars, and is, it seems, of earth. Bishop Pococke, in his journey from Acre to Nazareth, observed a well, where oxen were drawing up water, from whence women carried water up a hill, in earthen jars, to water some plantations of tobacco. In the next page he mentions the same thing in general, and speaks of their carrying the jars on their heads. There is no reason to suppose this kind of vessel was appropriated to the carrying water for the purposes of agriculture, it might do equally well when they carried it for domestic uses. Such seems to have been the sort of vessels in which the women of ancient times fetched water, for it is called a *kad* in the history of Rebecca, Gen. xxiv. 14, &c. and I have elsewhere shown, that the word signifies a jar of considerable size, in which they keep their corn, and in which, at least sometimes, they fetched their water.

Since the above was written, I have observed a passage

in Dr. Chandler's Travels in Asia Minor, that confirms and illustrates the preceding account: "The women," says the Doctor, "resort to the fountains by their houses, each with a large two-handled earthen jar, on the back, or thrown over the shoulder, for water." This account of the jars made use of by the Greek women of the island of Tenedos may, very naturally, be understood to be a modern, but accurate comment on what is said concerning Rebecca's fetching water. The Eastern women, according to Dr. Pococke, sometimes carry their jars upon their heads; but Rebecca's was carried on her shoulder. In such a case, the jar is not to be supposed to have been placed upright on the shoulder, but held by one of the handles, with the hand over the shoulder, and suspended in this manner on the back. Held, I should imagine, by the right hand over the left shoulder. Consequently, when it was to be presented to Abraham's servant, that he might drink out of it, it was to be gently moved over the left arm, and being suspended by one hand, while the other, probably, was placed under the bottom of the jar, it was in that position presented to Abraham's servant, and his attendants, to drink out of. *She said, Drink, my lord: and she hasted, and let down her pitcher upon her hand, and gave him drink.* Ver. 18.—HARMER.

Ver. 18. And she said, Drink, my lord: and she hasted, and let down her pitcher upon her hand, and gave him drink.

We met on this road (from Orfa to Bir) with several wells, at which the young women of the neighbouring villages, or of the tribes of the Curds and Turkomans, who were wandering in these parts, watered their flocks. They were not veiled like those in the towns. They were well made and beautiful, though tanned by the sun. As soon as we accosted them, and alighted from our horses, they brought us water to drink, and likewise watered our horses. Similar civilities had indeed been shown to me in other parts. But here it appeared to me particularly remarkable, because Rebecca, who was certainly brought up in these parts, showed herself equally obliging to travellers. Perhaps I have even drank at the same well from which she drew water. For Haran, now a small place, two days' journey to the south-south-east of Orfa, which is still visited by Jews, was probably the town which Abraham left to remove to the land of Canaan, and his brother Nahor's family probably remained in these parts. LEONARD RAUWOLF, a German traveller, who visited these countries about two hundred years before, observes, in his *Travels*, (part i. p. 259,) "This town (Orfa) is supposed by some to have been formerly called Haran, from which the holy patriarch Abraham, with Sarah, and Lot, his brother's son, removed by the command of God; so that the abundant well is still called Abraham's well, at which his servant first recognised Rebecca, when she gave him and his camels water to drink from it. The water of this well has more of a whitish colour than others, and also, as I drank it from the well in the middle of the great Khan, had a peculiar yet sweet and pleasant taste."—BURDER.

Ver. 22. And it came to pass, as the camels had done drinking, that the man took a golden ear-ring of half a shekel weight, and two bracelets for her hands of ten *shekels* weight of gold.

The weight of the ornaments that the servant of Abraham put upon Rebecca appears to us rather extraordinary. Sir J. Chardin assures us as heavy, and even heavier, were worn by the women of the East when he was there. The ear-ring, or jewel for the face, weighed half a shekel, and the bracelets for her hands ten shekels, Gen. xxiv. 22, which, as he justly observes, is about five ounces. Upon which he tells us, "the women wear rings and bracelets of as great weight as this, through all Asia, and even much heavier. They are rather manacles than bracelets. There are some as large as the finger. The women wear several of them, one above the other, in such a manner as sometimes to have the arm covered with them from the wrist to the elbow. Poor people wear as many of glass or horn. They hardly ever take them off: they are their riches."—HARMER.

Ver. 43. Behold, I stand by the well of water; and it shall come to pass, that when the virgin cometh forth to draw *water*, and I say to her, Give me, I pray thee, a little water of thy pitcher to drink.

It is still the proper business of the females to supply the family with water. From this drudgery, however, the married women are exempted, unless when single women are wanting. The proper time for drawing water in those burning climates, is in the morning, or when the sun is going down; then they go forth to perform that humble office, adorned with their trinkets, some of which are often of great value. Agreeably to this custom, Rebecca went instead of her mother to fetch water from the well, and the servant of Abraham expected to meet an unmarried female there who might prove a suitable match for his master's son. In the East Indies, the women also draw water at the public wells, as Rebecca did, on that occasion, for travellers, their servants and their cattle; and women of no mean rank literally illustrate the conduct of an unfortunate princess in the Jewish History, by performing the services of a menial. The young women of Guzerat daily draw water from the wells, and carry the jars upon the head; but those of high rank carry them upon the shoulder. In the same way Rebecca carried her pitcher; and probably for the same reason, because she was the daughter of an eastern prince.—PAXTON.

Ver. 47. And I put the ear-ring upon her face, and the bracelets upon her hand.

Nothing is more common than for heathen females to have a ring in the nose; and this has led some to suppose, that the jewel here alluded to was put into that member, and not on the face. "I put a jewel on thy *forehead*;" Ez. xv. 11. The margin has, for forehead, "nose." It does not appear to be generally known, that there is an ornament which is worn by females in the East on the *forehead*. It is made of thin gold, and is studded with precious stones, and called *Pattam*, which signifies dignity. Thus, to tie on the *Pattam*, is to "invest with high dignity." *Patta-Istere*, "is the name of the first lawful wife of the king." In the Sathur-Agaraathe, this ornament is called "*the ornament of the forehead.*" Tyerman and Bennet say of a bride they saw in China, "Her headdress sparkled with jewels, and was most elegantly beaded with rows of pearls encircling it like a coronet; from which a brilliant angular ornament hung over her forehead, and between her eyebrows."—ROBERTS.

Ver. 57. And they said, We will call the damsel, and inquire at her mouth.

Do people wish to know the truth of any thing which has been reported of another, they say, "Let us go and inquire of his *mouth*."—"Let us hear the *birth* of his *mouth*." Do servants ask a favour of their mistress, she will say, "I know not what will be the birth of the master's *mouth*; I will *inquire* at his *mouth*." So the mother and brother of Rebecca inquired at the *mouth* of the damsel, whether she felt willing to go with the man. "And she said, I will go."—ROBERTS.

Ver. 59. And they sent away Rebecca their sister, and her nurse, and Abraham's servant, and his men.

How often have scenes like this led my mind to the patriarchal age! The daughter is about for the *first time* to leave the paternal roof: the servants are all in confusion; each refers to things long gone by, each wishes to do something to attract the attention of his young mistress. One says, "Ah! do not forget him who nursed you when an infant:" another, "How often did I bring you the beautiful lotus from the distant tank! Did I not always conceal your faults?" The mother comes to take leave. She weeps, and tenderly embraces her, saying, "My daughter, I shall see you no more;—Forget not your mother." The brother infolds his sister in his arms, and promises soon to come and see her. The father is absorbed in thought, and is only aroused by the sobs of the party. He then affectionately embraces his daughter, and tells her not to fear. The female domestics must each *smell* of the poor girl, and the men touch her feet. As Rebecca had her *nurse* to accompany her, so, at *this* day, the *Aya* (the *nurse*) who has from infancy brought up the bride, goes with her to the new scene. She is her adviser, her assistant, and friend; and to her will she tell all her hopes, and all her fears.—ROBERTS.

Ver. 60. And they blessed Rebecca, and said unto her, Thou *art* our sister; be thou *the mother* of thousands of millions.

From the numerous instances which are recorded in the scriptures, of those who were aged, or holy, giving their *blessing*, may be seen the importance which was attached to such benedictions. Has a son, or a daughter, to leave a father, an aged friend, or a priest, a *blessing* is always given. To be the mother of a numerous progeny is considered a great honour. Hence parents often say to their daughters, "Be thou the mother of *thousands*." Beggars, also, when relieved, say to the mistress of the house, "Ah! madam, *millions* will come from you."—ROBERTS.

Ver 64. And Rebecca lifted up her eyes; and when she saw Isaac, she lighted off the camel.

It was always customary, in all the East, on perceiving a superior, to alight from the animal upon which they were riding. ANDERSON and IVERSON relate, that "when the governor of Mossul and his suite passed our caravan, we were obliged to alight from our horses, mules, and asses, and lead the animals till they had gone by." Even now, women show this mark of respect to men. NIEBUHR says, "that an Arabian lady who met them in a broad valley in the desert of Mount Sinai, retired from the road, and let her servant lead the camel till they had passed."—BURDER.

Ver. 65. For she *had* said unto the servant, What man *is* this that walketh in the field to meet us? And the servant *had* said, It *is* my master: therefore she took a veil, and covered herself.

Rebecca's covering herself with a veil, when Isaac came to meet her, which is mentioned Gen. xxiv. 65, is to be considered rather as a part of the ceremonial belonging to the presenting a bride to her intended husband, than an effect either of female delicacy, or desire to appear in the most attractive form. The eastern brides are wont to be veiled in a particular manner, when presented to the bridegroom. Those that give us an account of their customs, at such times, take notice of their being veiled all over. Dr. Russell gives us this circumstance in his account of a Maronite wedding, which, he says, may serve as a specimen of all the rest, there being nothing materially different in the ceremonies of the different sects.—HARMER.

CHAP. 25. ver. 21. And Isaac entreated the LORD for his wife, because she *was* barren.

Under *similar* circumstances, the husband and the wife *fast* and *pray*, and make a vow before the temple, that, should their *desire* be granted, they will make certain gifts, (specifying their kind,) or they will repair the walls, or add a new wing to the temple; or that the child shall be dedicated to the deity of the place, and be called by the same name. Or they go to a distant temple which has obtained notoriety by granting the favours they require. I have heard of husbands and wives remaining for a *year* together at such sacred places, to gain the *desire* of their hearts!—ROBERTS.

Ver. 28. And Isaac loved Esau, because he did eat of *his* venison; but Rebecca loved Jacob.

Margin, "Venison was in his mouth." Has a man been supported by another, and is it asked, "Why does Kandan love Muttoo?" the reply is, "Because Muttoo's rice *is in his mouth*." "Why have you such a regard for that man?" "Is not his rice *in my mouth?*"—ROBERTS.

Ver. 30. And Esau said to Jacob, Feed me, I pray thee, with that same red *pottage*.

The people of the East are exceedingly fond of *pottage*, which they call *Kool*. It is something like gruel, and is made of various kinds of grain, which are first beaten in a mortar. The red pottage is made of *Kurakan*, and other grains, but is not superior to the other. For such a contemptible mess, then, did Esau sell his birthright. When a man has sold his fields or gardens for an insignificant sum, the people say, "The fellow has sold his land for *pottage*." Does a father give his daughter in marriage to a low caste man, it is observed, "He has given her for *pottage*." Does a person by base means seek for some paltry enjoyment, it is said, "For one leaf* of *pottage*, he will do nine days' work." Has a learned man stooped to any thing which was not expected from him, it is said, "The learned one has fallen into the *pottage pot*." Has he given instruction or advice to others—"The Lizard, which gave warning to the people, has fallen into the *pottage pot*." Of a man in great poverty, it is remarked, "Alas! he cannot get *pottage*." A beggar asks, "Sir, will you give me a little *pottage?*" Does a man seek to acquire great things by small means—"He is trying to procure rubies by *pottage*." When a person greatly flatters another, it is common to say, "He praises him only for his *pottage*." Does a king greatly oppress his subjects, it is said, "He only governs for the *pottage*." Has an individual lost much money by trade—"The speculation has broken his *pottage pot*." Does a rich man threaten to ruin a poor man, the latter will ask, "Will the lightning strike my *pottage pot?*"—ROBERTS.

Ver. 41. And Esau said in his heart, The days of mourning for my father are at hand.

When the father (or the mother) has become aged, the children say, "The day for the *lamentation* of our father is at hand." "The *sorrowful* time for our mother is fast approaching." If requested to go to another part of the country, the son will ask, "How can I go? the day of sorrow for my father is fast approaching." When the aged parents are seriously ill, it is said, "Ah! the days of *mourning* have come."—ROBERTS.

CHAP. 26. ver. 15. For all the wells which his father's servants had digged in the days of Abraham his father, the Philistines had stopped them, and filled them with earth.

To stop the wells, is justly reckoned an act of hostility. The Canaanites, envying the prosperity of Abraham and Isaac, and fearing their power, endeavoured to drive them out of the country, by stopping "up all the wells which their servants had digged, and filling them with earth." The same mode of taking vengeance on enemies, mentioned in this passage, has been practised in more recent times. The Turkish emperors give annually to every Arab tribe near the road, by which the Mohammedan pilgrims travel to Mecca, a certain sum of money, and a certain number of vestments, to keep them from destroying the wells which lie on that route, and to escort the pilgrims across their country. D'Herbelot records an incident exactly in point, which seems to be quite common among the Arabs. Gianabi, a famous rebel in the tenth century, gathered a number of people together, seized on Bassorah, and Caufa; and afterward insulted the reigning caliph, by presenting himself boldly before Bagdad, his capital; after which he retired by little and little, filling up all the pits with sand, which had been dug on the road to Mecca, for the benefit of the pilgrims. Near the fountains and wells, the robber and assassin commonly took his station; and in time of war, the enemy placed their ambush, because the flocks and herds, in which the wealth of the country chiefly consisted, were twice every day collected to those places, and might be seized with less danger when the shepherds were busily engaged in drawing water. This circumstance, which must have been familiar to the inhabitants of those countries, is mentioned by Deborah in her triumphal song: "They

* It is common to fold a large leaf so as to hold the pottage.

hat are delivered from the noise of archers in the place of the drawing of water, there shall they rehearse the righteous acts of the Lord." But a still more perfect comment on these words is furnished by an historian of the croisades, who complains, that during the siege of Jerusalem by the Christian armies, numbers of their men were daily cut off, and their cattle driven away by the Saracens, who lay in ambush for this purpose near all the fountains and watering places.—PAXTON.

Ver. 18. And Isaac digged again the wells of water which they had digged in the days of Abraham his father; for the Philistines had stopped them after the death of Abraham: and he called their names after the names by which his father had called them.

This would appear a trifle among us, because water is so abundant, that it is scarcely valued, and nobody thinks of perpetuating his name in the name of a well. But in those deserts, where water is so scarce, and wells and springs are valued more, and as they are there the general permanent monuments of geography, it is also an honour to have given them names.—BURDER.

Ver. 20. And the herdmen of Gerar did strive with Isaac's herdmen.

See on chap. 13. 7.

Ver. 31. And they rose up betimes in the morning, and sware one to another: and Isaac sent them away, and they departed from them in peace.

In the same manner, family alliances are frequent among the Arabian shepherds, and indeed rendered necessary, by the state of continual warfare in which they live with the neighbouring tribes. The eighteen Arab emirs of the family which d'Arvieux visited, kept near one another, encamping at no greater distance from their chief than a league or two, and all removing together every month, sometimes every fortnight, as their cattle wanted fresh pasture, that they might be able to assemble with ease. But while Abraham and Isaac cultivated the friendship of their neighbours, entered into treaties of peace and amity with the kings and princes of Canaan, and entertained them in their tents,—Ishmael, animated by different principles and views, commenced a course of action, after leaving his father's house, so new and unprecedented, that it was made the subject of a distinct prediction. Standing on the verge of a burning desert, which he claimed as his proper inheritance, he assumed from the beginning a hostile attitude, spurned the ties of peace and friendship, and laid all the surrounding tribes under contribution. When he drew upon himself and his adherents the resentment of the fixed inhabitants, and was afraid to risk their attack, he withdrew into the depths of the great wilderness, where none could follow him with hopes of success. In the same manner have his descendants lived; when threatened with an unequal contest, they will strike their tents upon less than two hours' warning, and retire immediately, with all their effects, into the deserts, with whose wells and forage they only are acquainted. Within those impenetrable barriers, which are for ever guarded by hunger and thirst, the Arabians regard with utter contempt, the warlike array of the most powerful nations.—PAXTON.

CHAP. 27. ver. 4. And make me savoury meat, such as I love, and bring *it* to me, that I may eat; that my soul may bless thee before I die.

Our version of Gen. xxvii. 4, 7, 9, 14, 17, 31, may be presumed to have given us the true sense there of the word translated *savoury*, though it is undoubtedly of a more large and less determinate signification. That it is of a more large signification, is evident from hence, that a kindred word expresses the tasting of *honey*, 1 Sam. xiv. 43; and the taste of *manna*, which tasted like *fresh oil*, Numb. xi. 8, and like wafers made with *honey*, Exod. xvi. 31. These two last passages are easily reconciled, though honey and fresh oil are by no means like each other in taste, when we consider the cakes of the ancients were frequently a composition of honey, and oil, and flour; consequently, in tasting like one of these wafers or thin cakes, it might be said to resemble the taste of both, of oil mingled with honey. The word מטעמים *matâmmeem*, then, translated *savoury* in a confined sense, signifies generally whatever is gustful, or pleasing to the taste, whether by being salt and spicy, which the English word *savoury* means, or pleasant by its *sweetness;* or by being *acidulated.* However, it is very probable, that in this account of what Isaac desired, it means *savoury*, properly speaking, since though one might imagine, that in so hot a climate, and among people wont to observe so much abstemiousness in their diet, food highly seasoned should not be in request; yet the contrary is known to be fact. Almost all the dishes of the people of Aleppo, Dr. Russell informs us, "are either greasy with fat, or butter, pretty high-seasoned with salt and spices; many of them made sour with verjuice, pomegranate, or lemon juice; and onions and garlic often complete the seasoning." As it was something of the venison kind Isaac desired, it is very probable, the dish he wished for was of the savoury sort. Some of their dishes of meat, however, are of a sweet nature. "A whole lamb, stuffed with rice, almonds, raisins, pistaches, &c. and stewed, is a favourite dish with them." It was very just then, in our translators, to render this word by a more extensive term in Prov. xxiii. 3, "When thou sittest to eat with a ruler, consider diligently what is before thee," v. 1. "Be not desirous of his dainties, for they are deceitful meat," v. 3. It is translated in much the same manner in v. 6, dainty meats. I would observe further, as to this subject, that there is a great propriety in Solomon's describing these dainty meats as very much appropriated to the tables of rulers, or a few others of the great, since the food of the common people of Aleppo, a large and rich commercial city, is very simple and plain; for Russell tells us, "*bread, dibbs,* the juice of grapes thickened to the consistence of honey, *leban,* coagulated sour milk, butter, rice, and a very little mutton, make the chief of their food in winter; as rice, bread, cheese, and fruits, do in the summer." De la Roque gives much the same account of the manner of living of the Arabs, whose way of life very much resembles that of the patriarchs; "roast meat being almost peculiar to the tables of their emirs or princes, and lambs or kids stewed whole, and stuffed with bread, flour, mutton fat, raisins, salt, pepper, saffron, mint, and other aromatic herbs." I would only add further, with respect to the meat Isaac desired, that perhaps his desiring Esau to take his bow and arrows, and to kill him some venison,—an antelope, or some such wild animal, when a kid from his own flock would, as appears from the event, have done as well,—might as much arise from the sparingness natural to those that live this kind of life, together with the pleasure he proposed to himself from this testimony of filial affection from a beloved son, as from the recollection of some peculiar poignant flavour he had formerly perceived in eating the flesh of wild animals, though now his organs of taste were so much impaired as not to perceive the difference. So Dr. Shaw observes, that "the Arabs rarely diminish their flocks, by using them for food, but live chiefly upon bread, milk, butter, dates, or what they receive in exchange for their wool."—HARMER.

Ver. 19. And Jacob said unto his father, I *am* Esau thy first-born; I have done according as thou badest me: arise, I pray thee, sit and eat of my venison, that thy soul may bless me.

The ancient Greeks and Romans sat at meals. Homer's heroes were ranged on separate seats along the wall, with a small table before each, on which the meat and drink were placed. This custom is still observed in China, and perhaps some other parts of the greater Asia. When Ulysses arrived at the palace of Alcinous, the king displaced his son Laodamas, in order to seat Ulysses in a magnificent chair. The same posture was preferred by the Egyptians and the ancient Israelites. But, afterward, when men became soft and effeminate, they exchanged their seats for beds, in order to drink with more ease; yet even then, the heroes who drank sitting were still thought entitled to praise; and those who accustomed themselves to a primitive and severe way of living, retained the ancient posture. The custom of reclining was introduced from the nations of the east, and particularly from Persia, where it seems to have been adopted at a very remote period. The Old Testament scriptures allude to both customs: but they furnish undeniable proofs of the sitting posture, long before common authors took notice of the other. It was the custom in Isaac's family to sit at meat; for Jacob thus addressed his aged father: "Arise, I pray thee, sit and eat of my venison, that thy soul may bless me." At the entertainment which Joseph gave his brethren, on their return to Egypt, they seem to have followed the custom of their fathers; for "they sat before him, the first-born according to his birthright, and the youngest according to his youth." In the court of Saul, many ages after this, Abner sat at table by his master's side; and David also had his place allotted to him, which is emphatically called his seat. As this is undoubtedly the most natural and dignified posture, so it seems to have been universally adopted by the first generations of men; and it was not till after the lapse of many ages, and degenerate man had lost much of the firmness of his primitive character, that he began to lie flat upon his belly.—Paxton.

Ver. 27. And he came near, and kissed him: and he smelled the smell of his raiment, and blessed him, and said, See, the smell of my son *is* as the smell of a field which the Lord hath blessed.

The Orientals endeavour to perfume their clothes in various ways. They sprinkle them with sweet-scented oils, extracted from spices, they fumigate them with the most valuable incense or scented wood, and also sew the wood of the aloe in their clothes. By some of these means, Jacob's clothes were perfumed. Pliny observes, (*Nat. Hist.* b. xvii. chap. 5,) "that the land, after a long drought, moistened by the rain, exhales a delightful odour, with which nothing can be compared:" and soon after, he adds, "that it is a sign of a fruitful soil, when it emits an agreeable smell, when it has been ploughed."—Burder.

The natives are universally fond of having their garments strongly perfumed: so much so, that Europeans can scarcely bear the smell. They use camphor, civet, sandal wood or sandal oil, and a great variety of strongly scented waters. It is not common to *salute* as in England: they simply *smell* each other; and it is said that some people know their children by the smell. It is common for a mother or father to say, "Ah! child, thy *smell* is like the Sen-Paga-Poo." The crown of the head is the principal place for *smelling*. Of an amiable man, it is said, "How sweet is the *smell* of that man! the *smell* of his goodness is universal."—Roberts.

Chap. 28. ver. 18. And Jacob rose up early in the morning, and took the stone that he had put *for* his pillows, and set it up *for* a pillar, and poured oil upon the top of it.

One of the idols in the pagoda of Juggernaut is described by Captain Hamilton as a *huge black stone*, of a pyramidal form, and the *sommona codom* among the Siamese is of the same complexion. The *ayeen Akbery* mentions an octagonal pillar of black stone fifty cubits high. Tavernier observed an idol of black stone in the pagoda of Benares, and that the statue of Creeshna, in his celebrated temple of Mathura, is of black marble. It is very remarkable, that one of the principal ceremonies incumbent upon the priests of these stone deities, according to Tavernier, is to anoint them daily with odoriferous oils: a circumstance which immediately brings to our remembrance the similar practice of Jacob, who, after the famous vision of the celestial ladder, *took the stone which he had put for his pillow, and set it up for a pillar, and poured oil upon the top of it.* It is added, that he called the name of that place Beth-el, that is, the house of God. This passage evinces of how great antiquity is the custom of considering stones in a sacred light, as well as the anointing them with consecrated oil. From this conduct of Jacob, and this Hebrew appellative, the learned Bochart, with great ingenuity and reason, insists that the name and veneration of the sacred stones, called *baetyli*, so celebrated in all pagan antiquity, were derived. These *baetyli* were stones of a round form; they were supposed to be animated, by means of magical incantations, with a portion of the deity: they were consulted on occasions of great and pressing emergency, as a kind of divine oracles, and were suspended, either round the neck, or some other part of the body. Thus the setting up of a stone by this holy person, in grateful memory of the celestial vision, probably became the occasion of the idolatry in succeeding ages, to these shapeless masses of unhewn stone, of which so many astonishing remains are scattered up and down the Asiatic and the European world.—Burder.

Chap. 29. ver. 1. Then Jacob went on his journey, and came into the land of the people of the east.

The margin has, "lifted up his feet;" which, in Eastern language, signifies to walk quickly—to reach out—to be in good earnest—not to hesitate. Thus Jacob journeyed to the East, he lifted up his feet, and stretched forth in good earnest, having been greatly encouraged by the vision of the ladder, and the promise, "Thy seed shall be as the dust of the earth."—Roberts.

Ver. 2. And he looked, and behold, a well in the field, and lo, there *were* three flocks of sheep lying by it; for out of that well they watered the flocks: and a great stone *was* upon the well's mouth.

In Arabia, and in other places, they are wont to close and cover up their wells of water, lest the sand, which is put into motion by the winds there, like the water of a pond, should fill them, and quite stop them up. This is the account Sir J. Chardin gives us in a note on Ps. lxix. 15. I very much question the applicableness of this custom to that passage, but it will serve to explain, I think, extremely well, the view of keeping that well covered with a stone, from which Laban's sheep were wont to be watered; and their care not to leave it open any time, but to stay till the flocks were all gathered together, before they opened it, and then, having drawn as much water as was requisite, to cover it up again immediately, Gen. xxix. 2, 8. Bishop Patrick supposes it was done to keep the water clean and cool. Few people, I imagine, will long hesitate in determining which most probably was the view in keeping the well covered with so much care. All this care of their water is certainly very requisite, since they have so little, that Chardin supposes, "that the strife between Abraham's herdmen and Lot's was rather about water, than pasturage;" and immediately after observes, "that when they are forced to draw the water for very large flocks, out of one well, or two, it must take up a great deal of time."—Harmer.

Ver. 2. And he looked, and behold, a well in the field, and lo, there *were* three flocks of sheep lying by it; for out of that well they watered the flocks: and a great stone *was* upon the well's mouth. 3. And thither were all the flocks gathered: and they rolled the stone from the well's mouth, and watered the sheep, and put the stone again upon the well's mouth in his place.

To prevent the sand, which is raised from the parched surface of the ground by the winds, from filling up their wells, they were obliged to cover them with a stone. In this manner the well was covered, from which the flocks of Laban were commonly watered: and the shepherds, careful not to leave them open at any time, patiently waited till all the flocks were gathered together, before they removed the covering, and then having drawn a sufficient quantity of water, they replaced the stone immediately. The extreme scarcity of water in these arid regions, entirely justifies such vigilant and parsimonious care in the management of this precious fluid; and accounts for the fierce contentions about the possession of a well, which so frequently happened between the shepherds of different masters. But after the question of right, or of possession, was decided, it would seem the shepherds were often detected in fraudulently watering their flocks and herds from their neighbour's well. To prevent this, they secured the cover with a lock, which continued in use so late as the days of Chardin, who frequently saw such precautions used in different parts of Asia, on account of the real scarcity of water there. According to that intelligent traveller, when the wells and cisterns were not locked up, some person was so far the proprietor, that no one dared to open a well, or a cistern, but in his presence. This was probably the reason, that the shepherds of Padanaram declined the invitation of Jacob to water the flocks, before they were all assembled; either they had not the key of the lock which secured the stone, or if they had, they durst not open it, but in the presence of Rachel, to whose father the well belonged. It is ridiculous to suppose the stone was so heavy that the united strength of several Mesopotamian shepherds could not roll it from the mouth of the well, when Jacob had strength, or address, to remove it alone; or, that though a stranger, he ventured to break a standing rule for watering the flocks, which the natives did not dare to do, and that without opposition. The oriental shepherds were not on other occasions so passive; as the violent conduct of the men of Gerar sufficiently proves.—Paxton.

Ver. 7. And he said, Lo, *it is* yet high day.

Heb. "Yet the day is great." Are people travelling through places where are wild beasts, those who are timid will keep troubling the party by saying, "Let us seek for a place of safety:" but the others reply, "Not yet;" for "the day is *great*." "Why should I be in such haste? the day is yet *great*." When tired of working, it is remarked, "Why, the day is yet *great*."—"Yes, yes, you manage to leave off while the day is yet *great*."—Roberts.

Ver. 10. And it came to pass, when Jacob saw Rachel, the daughter of Laban his mother's brother, and the sheep of Laban his mother's brother, that Jacob went near, and rolled the stone from the well's mouth, and watered the flock of Laban his mother's brother.

Twice in the day they led their flocks to the wells; at noon, and when the sun was going down. To water the flocks, was an operation of much labour, and occupied a considerable space of time. It was, therefore, an office of great kindness with which Jacob introduced himself to the notice of his relations, to roll back the stone which lay upon the mouth of the well, and draw water for the flocks which Rachel tended. Some of these wells are furnished with troughs and flights of steps down to the water, and other contrivances, to facilitate the labour of watering the cattle. It is evident the well to which Rebecca went to draw water, near the city of Nahor, had some convenience of this kind; for it is written, "Rebecca hastened and emptied her pitcher into the trough, and ran again unto the well to draw water, and drew for all his camels." A trough was also placed by the well, from which the daughters of Jethro watered his flocks; and if we may judge from circumstances, was a usual contrivance in every part of the east. In modern times, Mr. Park found a trough near the well, from which the Moors watered their cattle, in the sandy deserts of Sahara. As the wells are often very deep, from a hundred and sixty to a hundred and seventy feet, the water is drawn up with small leathern buckets, and a cord, which travellers are often obliged to carry along with them, in their journey, because they meet with more cisterns and wells than springs. Dr. Richardson saw one of these buckets lying beside a deep well near a Christian church in Egypt to draw water for the congregation. And Buckingham found a party of twelve or fifteen Arabs drawing water in leathern buckets by cords and pulleys. To this custom, which they are forced to submit to by the scantiness of the population in those regions, the woman of Samaria refers in her answer to our Lord: "Sir, thou hast nothing to draw with;" thou hast no bucket and cord, as travellers commonly have; "and the well is deep; from whence then hast thou that living water?"—Paxton.

Ver. 18. And Jacob loved Rachel; and said, I will serve thee seven years for Rachel thy younger daughter.

Because he had no money or other goods which he could give to the father for his daughter. For among many people of the East, in ancient and modern times, we find it customary, not for the bride to bring a dowry to the bridegroom, but the bridegroom must, in a manner, purchase the girl whom he intends to marry, from the father. Therefore Shechem says, (ch. xxxiv. 12,) to Dinah's father and brothers, "Ask me never so much dowry and gift, and I will give according as ye shall say unto me: but give me the damsel to wife." In the same manner Tacitus relates, that among the ancient Germans, the wife did not bring the dowry to the man, but the man to the woman. "The parents and relations are present, who examine the gifts, and choose, not such as are adapted to female dress, or to adorn the bride, but oxen, and a harnessed horse, a shield, and a sword. In return for these presents he receives the wife." This custom still prevails among the Bedouins. "When a young man meets with a girl to his taste, he asks her of her father through one of his relations: they now treat about the number of camels, sheep, or horses, that the son-in-law will give to the father for his daughter; for the Bedouins never save any money, and their wealth consists only in cattle. A man that marries must therefore literally purchase his wife, and the fathers are most fortunate who have many daughters. They are the principal riches of the family. When, therefore, a young man negotiates with the father whose daughter he intends to marry, he says, 'Will you give me your daughter for fifty sheep, six camels, or twelve cows?' If he is not rich enough to give so much, he offers a mare or foal. The qualities of the girl, the family, and the fortune of him that intends to marry her, are the principal considerations in making the bargain." (*Customs of the Bedouin Arabs, by D'Arvieux*, p. 119.) This is confirmed by Seetzen, in his account of the Arab tribes whom he visited in 1808. The ceremonies at the marriage of a wandering Arab are remarkable; a young Arab knows a girl who pleases him; he goes to her father, and makes his wishes known to him. The latter speaks to his daughter. "Daughter," says he, "there is one who asks you for his wife: the man is good, and it depends upon yourself if you will become his wife; you have my consent." If the girl refuses, there is an end of the matter; if she is contented, the father returns to his guest, and informs him of the happy intelligence. "But," he adds, "I demand the price of the girl." This consists of five camels; but generally, by the intervention of others, a couple more are added, and those given are frequently miserable enough.—Burder.

Ver. 19. And Laban said, *It is* better that I give her to thee, than that I should give her to another man: abide with me.

So said Laban, in reference to his daughter Rachel; and so say fathers in the East, under *similar* circumstances. The whole affair is managed in a *business-like way*, without any thing like a consultation with the maiden. Her likes and dislikes are out of the question. The father understands the matter perfectly, and the mother is very knowing; therefore they manage the transaction. This system, however, is the fruitful source of that *general* absence of domestic happiness which prevails there. She has, perhaps, never seen the man with whom she is to spend her days. He may be young; he may be aged; he may be repulsive or attractive. The whole is a lottery to her. Have the servants or others whispered to her something about the match? she will make her inquiries; but the result will never alter the arrangements: for though her soul abhor the thoughts of meeting him, yet it must be done.—Roberts.

Ver. 23. And it came to pass, in the evening, that he took Leah his daughter, and brought her to him; and he went in unto her.

This deceit of giving Leah to Jacob instead of Rachel was the more easy, because the bride was introduced veiled to the bridegroom. The following passage from Olearius (*Travels in Persia*) is particularly applicable here. "If they are people of any consideration, they bring up their daughters, locked up in their chambers, to hide them from view, and they cannot be seen by the bridegroom till they are received in the chamber. In this manner many a one is deceived, and receives, instead of a handsome, a deformed and ugly girl, nay, instead of the daughter, some other relation, or even a maid. Also, when the bridegroom has sat down, the bride is seated by his side veiled, and magnificently dressed, and that neither may see the other, a piece of red silk is drawn between them, which is held by two boys."—ROSENMULLER.

Ver. 24. And Laban gave unto his daughter Leah, Zilpah his maid *for* a handmaid.

Chardin observes, that none but very poor people marry a daughter in the East, without giving her a female slave for a handmaid, there being no hired servants there as in Europe. So Solomon supposes they were extremely poor that had not a servant. *Prov.* xii. 9.—HARMER.

Ver. 26. And Laban said, It must not be so done in our country, to give the younger before the first-born.

The existence of this rule, and its application to practice, in those parts of the world, is confirmed by the Hindoo law, which makes it criminal to give the younger daughter in marriage before the elder; or for a younger son to marry while his elder brother remains unmarried.—PAXTON.

It has been said, (and with much truth,) that could Alexander revisit India, he would find the same customs and manners that prevailed in his day. From age to age the fashions and usages are carefully and reverently adhered to. When the eldest daughter is deformed, or blind, or deaf, or dumb, *then the younger* may be given first: but under other circumstances it would be disgraceful in the extreme. Should any one wish to *alter* the order of things, the answer of Laban is given. Should a father, however, have a very advantageous offer for a younger daughter, he will exert all his powers to get off the elder; but until this can be accomplished, the younger will *not* be married. Younger *brothers* are sometimes married first, but even this takes place but very seldom.—ROBERTS.

Ver. 30. And he went in also unto Rachel, and he loved also Rachel more than Leah, and served with him yet seven other years.

Polygamy was productive of many evils; and particularly gave occasion for jealousy and contention. It required, indeed, the utmost exertion of prudence on the part of the husband so to conduct himself towards his wives, as to prevent continual strife and discord. Wherever the practice obtains, the same care will always be requisite. Thus a late traveller, (Sir R. K. Porter's Travels in Persia, vol. ii. p. 8,) speaking of the number of wives a Persian keeps, says, "To preserve amity between these ladies, which had so excited my admiration, our communicative host told me, that himself, in common with all husbands, who preferred peace to passion, adhered to a certain rule, of each wife claiming, in regular rotation, the connubial attentions of her spouse: something of this kind is intimated in the domestic history of the ancient Jewish patriarchs, as a prevailing usage in the East, after men fell from the order of nature and of God, into the vice of polygamy."—BURDER.

Ver. 35. And she conceived again, and bare a son; and she said, Now will I praise the LORD: therefore she called his name Judah, and left bearing.

Margin, "She called his name Praise,"—"and left bearing." Heb. "stood from bearing." Scriptural names have generally a meaning. Thus, Didymus, means a twin; Boanerges, a son of thunder; and Peter, a stone. The names of the Orientals have always a distinct meaning. Thus, Ani Muttoo, the precious pearl; Pun Amma, the golden lady; Perrya Amma, the great lady; Chinny Tamby, the little friend; Kanneyar, the gentleman for the eye. Vast numbers of their children are named after their gods. "Stood from bearing." When a mother has ceased to bear children, should a person say it is not so, others will reply, "*She stood* from bearing at such a time."—ROBERTS.

CHAP. 30. ver. 14. And Reuben went, in the days of wheat-harvest, and found mandrakes in the field, and brought them unto his mother Leah. Then Rachel said to Leah, Give me, I pray thee, of thy son's mandrakes.

This plant is a species of melon, of which there are two sorts, the male and the female. The female mandrake is black, and puts out leaves resembling lettuce, though smaller and narrower, which spread on the ground, and have a disagreeable scent. It bears berries something like services, pale and of a strong smell, having kernels within like those of pears. It has two or three very large roots, twisted together, white within, black without, and covered with a thick rind. The male mandrake is called Morion, or folly, because it suspends the senses. It produces berries twice as large as those of the female, of a good scent, and of a colour approaching towards saffron. Pliny says, the colour is white. Its leaves are large, white, broad, and smooth, like the leaves of the beech-tree. The root resembles that of the female, but is thicker and bigger, descending six or eight feet into the ground. Both the smell and the taste are pleasant; but it stupifies those that use it, and often produces phrensy, vertigo, and lethargy, which, if timely assistance is not given, terminate in convulsions and death. It is said to be a provocative, and is used in the east as filters. The Orientals cultivate this plant in their gardens, for the sake of its smell; but those which Reuben found were in the field, in some small copse of wood perhaps, or shade, where they had come to maturity before they were found. If they resemble those of Persia rather than those of Egypt, which are of a very inferior quality, then we see their value, their superiority, and perhaps their rarity, which induced Rachel to purchase them from the son of Leah.—PAXTON.

Ver. 20. And Leah said, God hath endowed me *with* a good dowry; now will my husband dwell with me, because I have borne him six sons.

Should it be reported of a husband, that he is going to forsake his wife, *after* she has borne him children, people will say, "She has borne him *sons;* he will never, never leave her." To have children is a powerful tie upon a husband. Should she, however, not have any, he is almost certain to forsake her.—ROBERTS.

Ver. 30. And the LORD hath blessed thee since my coming.

Heb. "at my foot." By the labour of Jacob's *foot*, the cattle of Laban had increased to a multitude. Of a man who has become rich by his own industry, it is said, "Ah! by the labour of his *feet* these treasures have been acquired." "How have you gained this prosperity?" "By the favour of the gods, and the labour of my *feet.*" "How is it the king is so prosperous?" "By the labour of the *feet* of his ministers."—ROBERTS.

CHAP. 31. ver. 2. And Jacob beheld the countenance of Laban, and, behold, it *was* not towards him as before.

Heb. "as yesterday and the day before." See also marginal reading of Isa. xxx. 33. Of old, "from yesterday." The latter form of speech is truly Oriental, and means time gone by. Has a person lost the friendship of another, he will say to him, "Thy face is not to me as yesterday and the day before." Is a man reduced in his circumstances, he says, "The face of God is not upon me as *yesterday and the day before.*" The future is spoken of as *to-day and to-morrow;* "His face will be upon me *to-day and to-morrow.*" which means, *always.* "I will love thee to-day and to-morrow." "Do you think of me?"—"Yes, to-day and to-morrow." "Modeliar, have you heard that Tamban is trying to injure you?"—"Yes; and go and tell him that neither to-day nor to-morrow will he succeed." Our Saviour says, "Behold, I cast out devils, and I do cures to-day and to-morrow." A messenger came to inform him Herod would kill him; but this was his reply, intimating that the power could never be taken from him. Jacob said to Laban, "My righteousness answers for me in time to come;" but the Hebrew has for this, "*to-morrow;*" his righteousness would be perpetual. In Eastern language, therefore, "yesterday and the day before" signify time *past;* but "to-day and to-morrow" time to *come.* (See Ex. xiii. 14. Jos. iv. 6., also xxii. 24. margin.)—ROBERTS.

Ver. 4. And Jacob sent and called Rachel and Leah to the field unto his flock.

Besides those that live wholly in tents, numbers of the Eastern people spend part of the year in them. I have observed it particularly in the accounts of Mesopotamia. In that country Bishop Pococke tells us, he fell in with a summer village of country people, whose huts were made of loose stones covered with reeds and boughs; their winter village being on the side of a hill at some distance, consisting of very low houses; and that they chose this place for the convenience of being with their cattle, and out of the high road. Five pages after, he observes, that many of the Curdeens live honestly in Mesopotamia as well as Syria, removing in summer to some places at a distance from their village, where they live under tents, generally in places retired from the road, to avoid the injuries of the soldiery, and of the people of the pacha. May not this circumstance serve to explain a passage of the Old Testament, relating to this country? In Gen. xxxi. it is said, that Jacob sent and called Rachel and Leah to his flock, that he there told them of his design of returning from Mesopotamia to his native country, and that upon their consenting to go with him, he set out upon this journey so silently, that Laban had no notice of it, until the third day after; yet it appears, that he had all his effects with him, and tents for the accommodation of his family; and that Laban, who pursued him, had tents also for his company. Here one is surprised to find both parties so suddenly equipped with tents for their accommodation in travelling, and is naturally led to inquire, why Jacob sent for his wives to his flock? Bishop Patrick's account of the last circumstance, that it was for greater secrecy, and perhaps to avoid the danger of being seized upon by Laban and his sons, will hardly be thought satisfactory. Could not a husband speak to his wives with sufficient privacy in Laban's house? Were matters come to such an extremity, that Jacob durst not venture himself within the doors of his uncle's house, for fear of being seized upon, and made a prisoner? And in fact Jacob seems actually to have communicated his intention to Rachel in her father's house: for when he sent for his wives, she brought her father's teraphim with her, which she would by no means have done, had she been unapprized of the design. The case seems to have been thus. While Laban and his daughters dwelt in a house, they that tended the flocks had *tents* for their accommodation. Laban's flocks were in two parcels, one under the care of Jacob, the other committed to the care of Laban's sons, three days' journey off; Jacob's own afterward were also, for the same reason, probably at an equal distance. At the time of shearing sheep, it is reasonable to suppose, that more and better tents were erected for the reception and entertainment of their friends, it being a time of great feasting, 1 Sam. xxv. 4, 8, 36; to which they were wont to invite their friends, 2 Sam. xiii. 25; and the feasts being held at a distance from their own houses, in the places where the sheep were fed, as appears from the passage last cited, and also from Gen. xxxviii. 12. Laban went then with his relations at the time of sheep-shearing to his flocks; Jacob at the same time shore his own sheep, and sent to his wives to come to the entertainment, with all those utensils that they had with them of his, which would be wanted, having before communicated his intention to Rachel his beloved wife. This was a fair pretence for the having all his household stuff brought to him, which according to the present Eastern mode, we may believe was very portable, beds not excepted; and having told Leah then his views, in the company of Rachel, and both consenting to go with him, he had every thing ready for his journey, and could decamp immediately, taking his flocks and herds along with him. Somebody, upon this, went to inform Laban of Jacob's departure, who being at a considerable distance, did not receive the news till the third day. This accounts at once, in the most simple and natural way, for Jacob's sending for his wives to his flock; for his being able to get his goods together without jealousy; and for his and his father-in-law's being furnished with tents for the journey.—HARMER.

Ver. 7. And your father hath deceived me, and changed my wages ten times: but God suffered him not to hurt me. 8. If he said thus, The speckled shall be thy wages; then all the cattle bare speckled: and if he said thus, The ring-streaked shall be thy hire; then bare all the cattle ring-streaked.

The flocks which ranged the fertile pastures of Mesopotamia, seem also to have generally produced twins every year. Laban, who lived in that country, is said to have changed the wages of Jacob ten times in the space of six years; but since the wages of Jacob consisted of the lambs and the kids, they could not have been changed more than six times in six years, if his flock had brought forth only one a-year. Should it be thought that, according to this rule, the wages of Jacob must have been changed twelve times, let it be remembered, that the flocks of Laban had brought forth their first lambs before the bargain was concluded between him and Jacob, and by consequence, the latter had only the lambs of one yeaning that year; and again, the flocks had yeaned only once in the last year of his abode with Laban, because he was compelled to leave the service of his envious relative before the close of the season, and consequently, before the second yeaning. Thus the flocks yeaned only ten times from the date of their agreement, till the departure of Jacob to his own country. Or, we may consider the phrase "ten times," as a definite for an indefinite number; in which sense it is often used by the sacred writers. Thus, Jehovah complains of his ancient people whom he had brought out of Egypt, that they had tempted him "now these ten times," that is, many times, "and had not hearkened to his voice." Job uses it in the same sense: "These ten times have ye reproached me," that is, ye have often reproached me. In the same manner, when Jacob complained that Laban had changed his wages ten times, he might only mean that he had done so frequently. Had we therefore no stronger proof, that the sheep of Laban yeaned twice in the year, the fact might seem to rest merely on the state of the flocks in the adjacent regions, which, it cannot be doubted, generally yeaned twins, and for the most part twice in the year. A stronger proof, therefore, may be drawn from these words: "And it came to pass, whensoever the stronger cattle did conceive, that Jacob laid the rods before the eyes of the cattle in the gutters, that they might conceive among the rods. But when the cattle were feeble, he put them not in; so the feebler were Laban's, and the stronger Jacob's." Two yeanings are supposed to be suggested in this passage, by the terms stronger and feebler; the lambs of the first were always stronger than those of the second: and consequently, they fell to Jacob by the special bounty of Heaven, causing the cattle, not by any law of nature, but by an act of Almighty power, to conceive among the rods, the use of which was merely the test of Jacob's faith in the divine promise. This is evident, by the sense in which the Syriac interpreter, and the Chaldee Paraphrast understood the text; for, instead of the term "feebler," they use the word "later," rendering the clause, "so the later were Laban's." Jerome, Aquila, and other expositors, interpret the clause in the same manner. Kimchi and other Jewish writers often speak of the first and second yeanings; referring the former to the month Nisan, which corresponds to our March; and the latter to the month Tisri, which nearly corresponds to September; and they assert, that the lambs of the first yeaning are called קשורים, *keshorim*, or bound, because they had a more compact body; and those of the second, עטופים, *aetophim*, or deficient, because they were feebler. The autumnal lambs, however, were preferred by many before the vernal, and the winter before the summer lambs, as being more vigorous and healthy. But it must be confessed, that no certain trace of two yeanings in the year can be discovered in the sacred volume. The fact is attested by many common authors, and seems necessary to account for the rapid increase of oriental stock, and the prodigious numbers of which the Syrian flocks consisted. The words of Moses may refer, at least with equal probability, to the vigorous and healthy constitution of the ewes which Jacob selected for his purpose; and signify, that robust mothers produced robust lambs, and feeble mothers a weak and spiritless offspring. Aware of the advantages of a vigorous and healthy stock, especially with a long and perilous journey before him, "Jacob laid the rods before the eyes of the stronger ewes in the gutters, that they might conceive among the rods; but when the cattle were feeble, he put them not in; so the feebler were Laban's, and the stronger Jacob's." —PAXTON.

Ver. 27. Wherefore didst thou flee away secretly, and steal away from me, and didst not tell me, that I might have sent thee away with mirth, and with songs, and with tabret, and with harp?

The Easterns used to set out, at least on their longer journeys, with music. When the prefetto of Egypt was preparing for his journey, he complains of his being incommoded by the songs of his friends, who in this manner took leave of their relations and acquaintance. These valedictory songs were often extemporary. If we consider them, as they probably were used not on common but more solemn occasions, there appears peculiar propriety in the complaint of Laban.—HARMER.

Ver. 34. Now Rachel had taken the images, and put them in the camel's furniture, and sat upon them. And Laban searched all the tent, but found *them* not.

Mounted on this mild and persevering animal, (the camel,) the traveller pursues his journey over the sandy deserts of the east, with speed and safety. For his convenience, a sort of round basket is slung on each side with a cover, which holds all his necessaries, between which he is seated on the back of the animal. Sometimes two long chairs, like cradles, are hung on each side with a covering, in which he sits, or, stretched at his ease, resigns himself to sleep, without interrupting his journey. These covered baskets, or chairs, are the camel's furniture, where Rachel put the images which she stole from her father.—PAXTON.

Ver. 35. And she said to her father, Let it not displease my lord that I cannot rise up before thee; for the custom of women *is* upon me. And he searched, but found not the images.

In Persia, a son never sits in the presence of his father or his mother; even the king's son always stands before him; and is regarded only as the first of his servants. This is the reason that Rachel addressed her father in these words: "Let it not displease my lord, that I cannot rise up before thee."—PAXTON.

Ver. 38. This twenty years *have* I *been* with thee; thy ewes and thy she-goats have not cast their young, and the rams of thy flock have I not eaten. 39. That which was torn *of beasts* I brought not unto thee; I bare the loss of it: of my hand didst thou require it, *whether* stolen by day, or stolen by night.

The shepherds of the East were accountable for the flocks under their charge. Of this fact, the following extract from the Gentoo laws, furnishes a remarkable proof: "Cattle shall be delivered over to the cow-herd in the morning; the cow-herd shall tend them the whole day with grass and water; and in the evening, shall re-deliver them to the master, in the same manner as they were intrusted to him; if, by the fault of the cow-herd, any of the cattle be lost or stolen, that cow-herd shall make it good. When a cow-herd has led cattle to any distant place to feed, if any die of some distemper, notwithstanding the cow-herd applied the proper remedy, the cow-herd shall carry the head, the tail, the fore-foot, or some such convincing proof taken from that animal's body, to the owner of the cattle; having done this, he shall be no further answerable; if he neglects to act thus, he shall make good the loss." In this very situation was Jacob with Laban, his father-in-law, as we learn from his memorable expostulation, addressed to that deceitful and envious relation.—PAXTON.

Ver. 40. *Thus* I was; in the day the drought consumed me, and the frost by night; and my sleep departed from mine eyes.

See on Jeremiah 36. 30.

Does a master reprove his servant for being idle, he will ask, "What can I do? the heat eats me up by day, and the cold eats me up by night: how can I gain strength? I am like the trees of the field: the sun is on my head by day, and the dew by night."—ROBERTS.

In the midst of the burning deserts, where the heat is increased tenfold by the sandy surface on which it beats, the traveller encounters much inconvenience, and even distress, from the chilling cold of the night. Mr. Bruce, the justly celebrated Abyssinian traveller, lost all his camels in one night by the cold, in the deserts of Senaar. In the year 1779, the Bedouin Arabs plundered an English caravan in the desert, between Suez and Cairo. Seven of the Europeans, stripped entirely naked by their inhuman spoilers, in the hope of reaching Cairo, pushed forward into the desert. Fatigue, thirst, hunger, and the heat of the sun, destroyed one after another; one alone survived all these horrors. During three days and two nights, he wandered in this parched and sandy desert, frozen at night by the north wind, (it being in the month of January,) and burnt by the sun during the day, without any other shade but a single bush, into which he thrust his head among the thorns, or any drink but his own urine. At length, on the third day, he was descried by an Arab, who conducted him to his tent, and took care of him for three days, with the utmost humanity. At the expiration of that time, the merchants of Cairo, apprized of his situation, procured him a conveyance to that city, where he arrived in the most deplorable condition. From these important facts we may conclude, that even in those parched countries, a fire in the night, in the middle of May, might be very requisite, and highly acceptable. The hapless wanderer, whose affecting story Volney records, was frozen at night by the north wind, and burnt by the dreadful heat of the sun during the day; and the patriarch Jacob complains, that he was for many years exposed to similar hardships in the plains of Mesopotamia; "In the day the drought consumed me, and the frost by night." Nothing assuredly was remoter from the design of Volney, a proud and insolent enemy of revelation, than to confirm the truth of Scripture history; his statement clearly proves, that Jacob's complaint was not hastily made, but strictly agreeable to truth.—PAXTON.

Ver. 46. And Jacob said unto his brethren, Gather stones; and they took stones, and made a heap: and they did eat there upon the heap.

Our version of Genesis xxxi. 46, represents Jacob as sitting, with his relations and friends, when he held a solemn feast, *on a heap of stones:* one would be inclined to suspect the justness of the translation, as to this circumstance, of the manner in which he treated his friends; but it is made less incredible, by the account Niebuhr has given us, in the first volume of his travels, of the manner in which some of the nobles of the court of the Iman seated themselves, when he visited the prince at Sana of Arabia, his capital city. It is certain the particle על, *âl*, translated in this passage *upon*, sometimes signifies *near to*, or something of that sort; so it is twice used in this sense, Gen. xvi. "And the angel of the LORD found her *by* a fountain in the way to Shur." So Gen. xxiv. 13, "Behold, I stand here *by* the well of water, and the daughters of the men of the city come out to draw water." The same may be observed in many other places of the book of Genesis. Consequently the sitting of Jacob and Laban, with their relations and friends, might be understood to have been only near the heap of stones, which was collected together upon this occasion, and designed for a memorial of present reconciliation, and reciprocal engagement to preserve peace and amity in future times: but their actual sitting on this heap of stones may perhaps appear somewhat less improbable, after reading the following passage of Niebuhr's travels, relating to his being admitted to an audience of the Iman of Yemen. "I had gone from my lodgings indisposed, and by standing so long, found myself so faint, that I was obliged to ask permission to quit the room. I found near the door some of the principal officers of the court, who were sitting in a scattered manner, in the shade, *upon stones*, by the side of the wall. Among them was the nakib, the general, or rather master of the horse, Gheir Allah, with whom I had some acquaintance before. He immediately resigned his place to me, and applied himself to draw together stones into a heap, in order to build himself a new seat." This management to us appears very strange; it might possibly be owing to the extreme heat of that time of the year in that country, which made sitting on the ground very disagreeable; it can hardly however be supposed that they sat upon the heap of stones that had been gathered together on Mount Gilead, for this reason, since high grounds are cooler than those that lie low; since it was in spring time, when the heat is more moderate, for it was at the time of sheep-shearing: but it might be wet, and disagreeable sitting on the ground, especially as they were not furnished with sufficient number of carpets, pursuing after Jacob in a great hurry; and several countries furnishing stones so flat as to be capable of being formed into a pavement, or seat, not so uneasy as we may have imagined. Mount Gilead might be such a country. It might also be thought to tend more strongly to impress the mind, when this feast of reconciliation was eaten upon that very heap that was designed to be the lasting memorial of this renewed friendship. As for the making use of *heaps of stones* for a *memorial*, many are found to this day in these countries, and not merely by land, for they have been used for sea marks too: So Niebuhr, in the same volume, tells us of a heap of stones placed upon a rock in the Red Sea, which was designed to warn them that sailed there of the danger of the place, that they might be upon their guard.—HARMER.

Ver. 55. And early in the morning, Laban rose up, and kissed his sons and his daughters, and blessed them: and Laban departed, and returned unto his place.

Early rising is a universal custom. Thus, in every season of the year, the people may be seen at *sunrise*, strolling in all directions. At the time of the heavy dews, they bind a part of the robe round the head, which also falls on the shoulders. When a journey has to be taken, were they not to rise *early*, they would be unable to travel far before the sun had gained its meridian height. They therefore start a little before daylight, and rest under the shade during the heat of the day. Here also we have another instance of the interesting custom of *blessing* those who were about to be separated. A more pleasing scene than that of a father blessing his sons and daughters can scarcely be conceived. The fervour of the language, the expression of the countenance, and the affection of their embraces, all excite our strongest sympathy. "My child, may God keep thy hands and thy feet!" "May the beasts of the forest keep far from thee!" "May thy wife and thy children be preserved!" "May riches and happiness ever be thy portion!"—ROBERTS.

CHAP. 32. ver. 7. Then Jacob was greatly afraid, and distressed: and he divided the people that *was* with him, and the flocks, and herds, and the camels, into two bands.

This plan seems not to have been first invented by Jacob; but it may be conjectured that large caravans used at that time to take this precaution against hostile attacks. Sir H. Blount relates in his *Travels*, that he travelled with a caravan which had divided itself in like manner into two troops; one of which that went before, being attacked by robbers, had an action with them, and were plundered, whereas the other escaped uninjured.—ROSENMULLER.

Ver. 15. Thirty milch-camels with their colts, forty kine and ten bulls, twenty she-asses and ten foals.

Milch-camels, among the Arabs, constitute a principal part of their riches; the creature being every way so serviceable, that the providence of God appears peculiarly kind and wise in providing such a beast for those countries, where no other animal could be of equal use. Niebuhr relates, "that among other dishes presented to him by the Arabs at Menayre, there was also camels' milk. That it was indeed considered cooling and healthy in these hot countries, but that it was so clammy, that when a finger is dipped into it, and drawn up again, the milk hangs down from it like a thread." Host, in his *Account of Morocco and Fez*, says, "that the Moors also drink camels' milk; and when they have milked them for a short time, they suffer the young camels to suck, and then begin to milk again, partly to share it with the young camels, and partly to make the camels give the milk better." Pallas, in his *Russian Travels*, says, that it is customary among the Kirgise to milk the camels: "their milk is said to be bluish, thick, and of an agreeable taste. The Kirgise consider it to be very wholesome; and it is also said that a more intoxicating beverage is drawn from it than from mares' milk." In fact, the camel is of such multifarious use to the Orientals, and of such importance, that among the Bedouins, wealth is not estimated by money, but by the number of camels. These observations are confirmed by Seetzen, in his *Account of the Arab Tribes*. "No animal among the Arabs surpasses the camel in utility; besides the wholesome diet which his flesh, his milk, and their products, afford them, they turn every part of it to account. Out of its hair, they manufacture carpets, large strong sacks for corn, &c. Out of its skin, soles (serbul,) large water bottles (rawijch,) two of which are a load for a camel, and large leather sacks (karpha,) in which they transport and preserve butter, corn, and similar articles; they die them red on the outside; and two of these also are a load for a camel. They likewise cut straps out of the skin, and out of five or six such straps they prepare long, tough thongs, which they employ in drawing up water from deep wells. They also stitch the skin over a frame of bent sticks, and thus form large vessels, which they use to water the camels, and which are called Hhod. The two sinews of the neck of the camel (aelba) serve instead of ropes, and are extremely strong. Their dung is used for fuel. Even the urine of this animal is of utility: all the Arabs, Nomades of both sexes, and likewise many Arab peasants, wash the head every two or three days with the urine of the female camel, and consider this to be very healthy."—ROSENMULLER.

From the present which Jacob made to his brother Esau, consisting of five hundred and eighty head of different sorts, we may form some idea of the countless numbers of great and small cattle, which he had acquired in the service of Laban. In modern times, the numbers of cattle in the Turcoman flocks which feed on the fertile plains of Syria, are almost incredible. They sometimes occupy three or four days in passing from one part of the country to another. Chardin had an opportunity of seeing a clan of Turcoman shepherds on their march, about two days' distance from Aleppo. The whole country was covered with them. Many of their principal people, with whom he conversed on the road, assured him, that there were four hundred thousand beasts of carriage, camels, horses, oxen, cows, and asses, and three millions of sheep and goats. This astonishing account of Chardin, is confirmed by Dr. Shaw, who states that several Arabian tribes, who can bring no more than three or four hundred horses into the field, are possessed of more than so many thousand camels, and triple the number of sheep and black cattle. Russel, in his history of Aleppo, speaks of vast flocks which pass that city every year, of which many sheep are sold to supply the inhabitants. The flocks and herds which belonged to the Jewish patriarchs, were not more numerous.—PAXTON.

Ver. 19. And so commanded he the second, and the third, and all that followed the droves, saying, On this manner shall ye speak unto Esau, when ye find him.

I almost think I hear Jacob telling his servants what they were to say to Esau. He would repeat it many times over, and then ask, "What did I say?" until he had completely *schooled* them into the story. They would be most attentive; and at every interval, some of the most officious would be repeating the tale. The head servant, however, would be specially charged with the delivery of the message. When they went into the presence of Esau, they would be very particular in placing much stress on Jacob's saying, "the present is sent unto my *lord!*" and this would touch his feelings. Servants who see the earnestness of their master, imitate him in this when they stand before the person to whom they are sent. They repeat a number of little things respecting him; his great sorrow for his offence, his weeping, his throwing himself into the dust, and his fearful expressions. Should the occasion, however, be of a pleasing nature, they mention his great joy, and his anxiety for an interview. The dependants of Esau, also, would hear the story, and every now and then be making exclamations at the humility of Jacob, and the value of his present. They would also put their hands together in a supplicating posture, for Esau to attend to the request. He, feeling himself thus acknowledged as *lord*, seeing the servants of his brother before him, and knowing that all his people had witnessed the scene, would consider himself greatly honoured. In this way many a culprit in the East gains a pardon, when nothing else could purchase it. Should the offender be too poor to send a present, he simply despatches his wife and children to plead for him; and they seldom plead in vain.—ROBERTS.

CHAP. 33. ver. 3. And he passed over before them, and bowed himself to the ground seven times, until he came near to his brother.

There is something very touching, and, to an Eastern mind, very *natural*, in this action of Jacob's. His arrangements, also, may be seen to the life, at this day. His wives and children were placed behind him: they would be in a separate group, in order that Esau might the more easily see them. He would then walk forward, and cast himself on the earth, and rise again, till he had bowed seven times; after which, (as he would walk a short distance every time he arose,) he would be near to his brother. Esau could not bear it any longer, and ran to meet him, and fell on his neck, and kissed him, and wept. Then came the handmaids and their children, (I think I see them,) and bowed themselves before Esau; the wives, also, according to their age, and their children, prostrated themselves before him. What with the looks of the little ones, joined with those of the mothers, Esau could not help being moved.—ROBERTS.

Ver. 10. And Jacob said, Nay, I pray thee, if now I have found grace in thy sight, then receive my present at my hand.

It is the custom of the East, when one invites a superior, to make him a present after the repast, as an acknowledgment of his trouble. Frequently it is done before it, as it is no augmentation of honour to go to the house of an inferior. They make no presents to equals, or those who are below themselves.—BURDER.

Not to receive a present, is at once to show that the thing desired will not be granted. Hence, nothing can be more repulsive, nothing more distressing, than to return the gifts to the giver. Jacob evidently laboured under this impression, and therefore pressed his brother to receive the gifts, if he had found favour in his sight.—ROBERTS.

Ver. 13. And he said unto him, My lord knoweth that the children *are* tender, and the flocks and herds with young *are* with me; and if men should overdrive them one day, all the flock will die.

"Their flocks," says Chardin, speaking of those who now live in the East after the patriarchal manner, "feed down the places of their encampments so quick, by the great numbers which they have, that they are obliged to remove them too often, which is very destructive to their flocks, on account of the young ones, which have not strength enough to follow."—HARMER.

Ver. 14. Let my lord, I pray thee, pass over before his servant; and I will lead on softly, according as the cattle that goeth before me, and the children be able to endure, until I come unto my lord unto Seir.

People having taken a journey, say, "We came to this place according to the walking of our feet." "It was done according to the foot of the children;" which means, they did not come in a palankeen, or any other vehicle, but on foot. From this it appears, that the females, and the children, performed their journey on foot, and that, according to their strength.—ROBERTS.

Ver. 15. And Esau said, Let me now leave with thee *some* of the folk that *are* with me. And he said, What needeth it? let me find grace in the sight of my lord.

As Esau had received valuable gifts from his brother, he wished to make some present in return; and having received cattle, it would not have looked well to have given the same kind of gift that he had received; he therefore offered some of his people, (who were no doubt born in his house,) as a kind of recompense for what he had received, and as a proof of his attachment.—ROBERTS.

Ver. 19. And he bought a parcel of a field, where he had spread his tent, at the hand of the children of Hamor, Shechem's father, for a hundred pieces of money.

There is very great reason to believe that the earliest coins struck were used both as weights and money and indeed this circumstance is in part proved by the very names of certain of the Greek and Roman coins. Thus the Attic *mina* and the Roman *libra* equally signify a pound; and the στατηρ (*stater*) of the Greeks, so called from weighing, is decisive as to this point. The Jewish shekel, was also a weight as well as a coin: three thousand shekels, according to Arbuthnot, being equal in weight and value to one talent. This is the oldest coin of which we anywhere read, for it occurs *Gen.* xxiii. 16, and exhibits direct evidence against those who date the first coinage of money so low as the time of Crœsus or Darius, it being there expressly said, that Abraham weighed to Ephron four hundred shekels of silver, *current money with the merchant.* Having considered the origin and high antiquity of coined money, we proceed to consider the *stamp* or *impression* which the first money bore. The primitive race of men being shepherds, and their wealth consisting in their cattle, in which Abraham is said to have been rich, for greater convenience metals were substituted for the commodity itself. It was natural for the representative sign to bear impressed the object which it represented; and thus accordingly the earliest coins were stamped with the figure of an ox or a sheep: for proof that they actually did thus impress them, we can again appeal to the high authority of scripture: for there we are informed that *Jacob bought a parcel of a field for a hundred pieces of money.* The original Hebrew translated pieces of money, is *kesitoth*, which signifies lambs, with the figure of which the metal was doubtless stamped.—MAURICE'S *Indian Antiquities.*

CHAP. 34. ver. 1. And Dinah the daughter of Leah, which she bare unto Jacob, went out to see the daughters of the land. 2. And when Shechem the son of Hamor the Hivite, prince of the country, saw her, he took her, and lay with her, and defiled her.

Voltaire objects, in like manner, to the probability of the Old Testament history, in the account given us there of the dishonour done to Dinah, the daughter of Jacob, by a Hivite prince in Canaan, Gen. xxxiv. 1, 2, who he supposes was too young to have suffered such an injury, or to have excited the affections of Shechem. The two following citations will prove there was nothing incredible in it, and that an ardent young Eastern prince may be supposed to have been guilty of such a fact. The first citation shall be from Niebuhr's account of Arabia: "I have heard speak in Persia of one that was a mother at thirteen: they there marry girls at nine years of age; and I knew a man whose wife was no more than ten years old when the marriage was consummated." The other is from Dr. Shaw's Travels and observations. Speaking of the inhabitants of Barbary, he says, "The men, indeed, by wearing only the tiara, or a scull cap, are exposed so much to the sun, that they quickly attain the swarthiness of the Arab; but the women, keeping more at home, preserve their beauty until they are thirty: at which age they begin to be wrinkled, and are usually past childbearing. It sometimes happens that one of these girls is a mother at eleven, and a grandmother at two-and-twenty." If they become mothers at eleven, they might easily become the objects of attachment at ten, or thereabouts; and this cannot be supposed to be very extraordinary, when the daughter of such a one is supposed to become a mother too by eleven. It cannot then be incredible that Shechem should cast his eyes on Dinah at ten years of age, and should desire to marry her at that age; if human nature in the East then was similar, in that respect, to what it is now. But she might be considerably older than ten when this affair happened, for aught that is said in the book of Genesis relative to this matter.—HARMER.

Ver. 11. And Shechem said unto her father, and unto her brethren, Let me find grace in your eyes, and what ye shall say unto me I will give. 12. Ask me never so much dowry and gift, and I will give according as ye shall say unto me: but give me the damsel to wife.

In the remote ages of antiquity, women were literally purchased by their husbands; and the presents made to their parents or other relations were called their dowry. The practice still continues in the country of Shechem; for when a young Arab wishes to marry, he must purchase his wife; and for this reason, fathers, among the Arabs, are never more happy than when they have many daughters. They are reckoned the principal riches of a house. An Arabian suitor will offer fifty sheep, six camels, or a dozen of cows; if he be not rich enough to make such offers, he proposes to give a mare or a colt, considering in the offer, the merit of the young woman, the rank of her family, and his own circumstances. In the primitive times of Greece, a well-educated lady was valued at four oxen. When they agree on both sides, the contract is drawn up by him that acts as cadi or judge among these Arabs. In some parts of the East, a measure of corn is formally mentioned in contracts for their concubines, or temporary wives, besides the sum of money which is stipulated by way of dowry. This custom is probably as ancient as concubinage, with which it is connected; and if so, it will perhaps account for the prophet Hosea's purchasing a wife of this kind for fifteen pieces of silver, and for a homer of barley, and a half homer of barley.—PAXTON.

Ver. 21. These men *are* peaceable with us, therefore let them dwell in the land, and trade therein; for the land, behold, *it is* large enough for them: let us take their daughters to us for wives, and let us give them our daughters.

The shepherds of Syria and the East have, from the remotest antiquity, carried on a considerable trade with the circumjacent cities. The people of Aleppo are still supplied with the greater part of their butter, their cheese, and their cattle for slaughter, by the Arabs, Kushwans, or Turcomans, who travel about the country with their flocks and herds, as did the patriarchs of old. It was undoubtedly by trading with the ancient cities of Canaan in such articles of provision, that Abraham became so rich in silver and gold. The lucrative commerce which Jacob his grandson carried on with the inhabitants of Shechem, is mentioned by Hamor their prince, and urged as a reason of alliance and union: "these men are peaceable with us; therefore, let them dwell in the land, and trade therein; for the land, behold it is large enough for them." While the wealth of the country, where they tended their flocks and herds, flowed into the coffers of these shepherd princes, in a steady and copious stream, their simple and frugal manner of living, required but little expense for the support of their numerous households; and their nomadic state prevented them from contracting alliances, or forming connexions of an expensive nature. Hence, in a few years they amassed large quantities of the precious metals; they multiplied their flocks and their herds, till they covered the face of the country for many miles; they engaged a numerous train of servants from the surrounding towns and villages, and had servants born in their houses, of the slaves whom they had purchased, or taken prisoners in war. When Abraham heard that his brother Lot was taken captive by the king of Shinar and his confederates, he armed his trained servants born in his house, three hundred and eighteen, and pursued them unto Dan. The truth of the scripture accounts is verified by the present state of the Arabian chieftains in those very places where Abraham and his descendants formerly wandered. By the unimpeachable testimony of Russel, they are equally rich, and powerful, and independent, as were these renowned patriarchs; they are surrounded with servants and retainers, equally numerous, resolute, and faithful; they are, in fine, the modern patriarchs of the East. In Persia and in Turkey, where the country is full of Turcoman shepherds, their chiefs appear with a great train of servants, richly clothed and mounted. Chardin fell in with one of these pastoral chieftains between Parthia and Hyrcania, whose train filled him at once with surprise and alarm. The Turcoman had more than ten led horses, with harness all of solid gold and silver. He was accompanied by many shepherds on horseback, and well armed. They treated the traveller civilly, and answered all the questions his curiosity prompted him to put to them, upon their manner of life. The whole country, for ten leagues, was full of their flocks. An hour after, the chieftain's wives, and those of his principal attendants, passed along in a line: four of them rode in great square baskets, carried two upon a camel, which were not close covered. The rest were on camels, on asses, and on horseback; most of them with their faces unveiled, among whom were some very beautiful women. From this display of pastoral magnificence, which Chardin had an opportunity of contemplating, we are enabled to form a very clear idea of the splendour and elegance in which Abraham and other patriarchs lived; and of the beauty which the sacred historian ascribes to Sarah, Rebecca, and Rachel, who had very fair complexions.—PAXTON.

Ver. 24. When they were sore.

Circumcision in infants is easy and soon healed, and some have thought, that in adults, it was worst the third day; but Sir John Chardin says, that he had heard from divers renegadoes in the East, who had been circumcised, some at thirty and some at forty years of age, that the circumcision had occasioned them a great deal of pain, and that they were obliged to keep their bed at least twenty or twenty-two days, during which time they could not walk without feeling very severe pain; but that they applied nothing to the wound to make it cicatrize, except burnt paper. —BURDER.

Ver. 27. The sons of Jacob came upon the slain and spoiled the city, because they had defiled their sister.

Among the Bedouin Arabs, the brother finds himself more dishonoured by the seduction of his sister, than a man by the infidelity of his wife. As a reason, they allege, "that a wife is not of the family, and that they are obliged to keep a wife only as long as she is chaste; and if she is not she may be sent away, and is no longer a member of the family; but that a sister constantly remains a member of the family; and even if his sister became dissolute, and was defiled, nobody could hinder her from still being his sister." (D'Arvieux.) This is confirmed by Niebuhr. "I learnt at Basra, that a man is not allowed to kill his wife, even on account of adultery; but that her father, brother, or any of her relations, were suffered to do it without being punished, or at least paying a small sum as an atonement, because her relations had been dishonoured by her bad behaviour; but that after this satisfaction, nobody is permitted to reproach the family. They remembered examples of it in Basra and Bagdad; in this latter place, a rich merchant, a few years since, had found a young man with a relation of his, and not only hewed her in pieces on the spot, but also, by witnesses and money, caused the young man, who was the son of a respectable citizen, to be hanged the same night by the magistrates."—ROSENMULLER.

Ver. 30. And Jacob said to Simeon and Levi, Ye have troubled me, to make me to stink among the inhabitants of the land.

So said Jacob to Simeon and Levi. Of a man who has lost his honour, whose fame has entirely gone, it is said, "Ah! he has lost his smell—where is the sweet smell of former years?" "Alas!" says an old man, "my smell is for ever gone."—ROBERTS.

CHAP. 35. ver. 2. Then Jacob said unto his household, and to all that *were* with him, Put away the strange gods that *are* among you, and be clean, and change your garments.

The household of Jacob had strange gods among them, and he ordered them to put them away, and to make themselves clean, and to change their garments in token of their *purity*. When people have been to any unholy place, they always on returning wash their persons and change their garments. No man can go to the temple, wearing a dirty cloth: he must either put it on clean, or go himself to a tank and wash it; or put on one which is quite new. Hence, near temples, men may be seen washing their clothes, in order to prepare themselves for some ceremony. (Exodus xix. 10.)—ROBERTS.

Ver. 4. And they gave unto Jacob all the strange gods which *were* in their hand, and *all their* ear-rings which *were* in their ears; and Jacob hid them under the oak which *was* by Shechem.

The nose-jewel is another ornament peculiar to the East, which the Jewish females were accustomed to wear, and of which the Asiatic ladies are extremely fond. It is mentioned in several parts of scripture; thus the prophet Ezekiel: "And I put a jewel on thy forehead," or, as it should have been rendered, on thy nose. This ornament was one of the presents which the servant of Abraham gave to Rebecca, in the name of his master: "I put," said he, "the ear-ring upon her face;" more literally, I put the ring on her nose. They wore ear-rings besides; for the household of Jacob at his request, when they were preparing to go up to Bethel, gave him all the ear-rings which were in their ears, and he hid them under the oak which was by Shechem. The difference between these ornaments is clearly stated by the prophet: "I put a jewel on thy nose, and ear-rings in thine ears." The nose-jewel, therefore, was different from the ear-ring, and actually worn by the females as an ornament in the East. This is confirmed by the testimony of Sir John Chardin, who says, "It is the custom in almost all the East, for the women to wear rings in their noses, in the left nostril, which is bored low down in the middle. These rings are of gold, and have commonly two pearls and one ruby between them, placed in the ring; I never saw a girl or young woman in Arabia, or in all Persia, who did not wear a ring after this manner in her nostril." Some writers contend, that by the nose-jewel, we are to understand rings, which women attached to their forehead, and let them fall down upon their nose; but Chardin, who certainly was a diligent observer of Eastern customs, nowhere saw this frontal ring in the East, but everywhere the ring in the nose. His testimony is supported by Dr. Russel who describes the women in some of the villages about Aleppo, and all the Arabs and Chinganas, (a sort of gipsies,) as wearing a large ring of silver or gold, through the external cartilage of their right nostril. It is worn, by the testimony of Egmont, in the same manner by the women of Egypt. The difference in the statements of these travellers is of little importance, and may be reconciled by supposing, what is not improbable, that in some eastern countries they wear the ring in the left, and in others in the right nostril; all agree that it is worn in the nose, and not upon the forehead. Some remains of this custom have been discovered among the Indians in North America, where Clark and Lewis, in their travels to the sources of the Missouri, fell in with some tribes that wore a long tapering piece of shell, or bead, put through the cartilage of the nose.—PAXTON.

Ver. 8. But Deborah, Rebecca's nurse, died, and she was buried beneath Beth-el, under an oak: and the name of it was called Allon-bachuth.

Savary, speaking of the Egyptian women, and their manner of nursing their children, says, "When circumstances compel them to have recourse to a nurse, she is not looked upon as a stranger. She becomes part of the family, and passes the rest of her life in the midst of the children she has suckled. She is honoured and cherished like a second mother." So the Syrian nurse continued until her death with Rebecca, and was buried with great solemnity of mourning: since that oak was from that time distinguished by the name of the Oak of Weeping.—HARMER.

Ver. 19. And Rachel died, and was buried in the way to Ephrath, which *is* Beth-lehem. 20. And Jacob set a pillar upon her grave: that *is* the pillar of Rachel's grave unto this day.

The following account from the recent and valuable *Travels in Palestine*, by Mr. Buckingham, on the subject of Rachel's tomb, will be found highly interesting. "In the way, on the right, at a little distance from the road, is hewn the reputed tomb of Rachel, to which we turned off, to enter. This may be near the spot of Rachel's interment, as it is not far from Ephrath, and may correspond well enough with the place assigned for her sepulchre by Moses, who says, in describing her death in childbirth of Benjamin, 'and Rachel died, and was buried in the way to Ephrath, which is Bethlehem; and Jacob set a pillar upon her grave, that is the pillar of Rachel's grave unto this day.' Gen. xxxv. 19. Instead of a pillar, the spot is now covered by a Mohammedan building, resembling in its exterior the tombs of saints and scheiks in Arabia and Egypt, being small, square, and surmounted by a dome. We entered it on the south side by an aperture, through which it was difficult to crawl, as it has no doorway; and found on the inside a square mass of masonry in the centre, built up from the floor nearly to the roof, and of such a size as to leave barely a narrow passage for walking around it. It is plastered with white stucco on the outer surface, and is sufficiently large and high to enclose within it any ancient pillar that might have been found on the grave of Rachel. This central mass is certainly different from any thing that I have ever observed in Arabian tombs; and it struck me on the spot, as by no means improbable, that its intention might have originally been to enclose either a pillar, or fragment of one, which tradition had pointed out as the pillar of Rachel's grave; and that as the place is held in equal veneration by Jews, by Christians, and by Mohammedans, the last, as lords of the country, might have subsequently built the present structure over it in their own style, and plastered the high square pillar within. Around the interior face of the walls, is an arched recess on each side, and over every part of the stucco are written and engraved a profusion of names in Hebrew, Arabic, and Roman characters; the first executed in curious devices, as if a sort of abracadabra." P. 216. —BURDER. (*See Engraving.*)

CHAP. 36. ver. 6. And Esau took his wives, and his sons, and his daughters, and all the persons of his house.

The Margin has, for persons, "souls." Has a man gone to a distant place, it is said, "Viravan, and all the *souls* of his house, have gone to the far country." "Have you heard that the old man and thirty *souls* have gone on a pilgrimage?" "Sir, I can never get rich, because I have fifteen *souls* who daily look to me for their rice."—ROBERTS.

Ver. 24. And these *are* the children of Zibeon; both Ajah, and Anah: this *was that* Anah that found the mules in the wilderness, as he fed the asses of Zibeon his father.

The Hebrews ascribe the invention of mules to Anah, the son of Zibeon, whose daughter, Aholibamah, was given in marriage to Esau. "This was that Anah, that found the mules in the wilderness, as he fed the asses of Zibeon his father." In this text, Moses evidently censures the misguided and preposterous industry of Anah, who, not satisfied with the numerous flocks and herds which the bounty of Providence had bestowed on his family, or, perhaps, actuated by impure and licentious motives, contrived a new and spurious breed of animals unknown to nature, and contrary to the laws which regulate her operations. Whatever might be the motive, the conduct of this Horite prince was certainly criminal. We cannot, on any other supposition, account for the peculiar and emphatical phrase which Moses employs: "This was that Anah, that found the mules in the wilderness." In opposition to this idea, Bochart contends, that if Anah had found out the method of procreating mules, the sacred historian would not have said he found them; because the verb (מצא) *matsa*, among the Hebrews, does not signify to invent, but to find something already in existence. Nor to strengthen this conjecture, is it sufficient, that Anah is said at the time to have tended the asses of Zibeon his father; for mules are not procreated of asses only, but of an ass and a mare, or of a horse and a female ass. But of horses or wild asses, by whose union with the domestic ass a mule is generated, no mention is made in this passage. In addition to these arguments, our author insists on the improbability, that the method of generating mules was discovered in Idumea at that early period; because, the use of these animals does not seem to have become common in Judea, till the reign of David, about five hundred years after the death of Anah. No mention is made of mules in the flocks and herds of Abraham, of Isaac, of Job, and other shepherd princes of the East. In the various enumerations, horses, camels, asses, oxen, sheep, and goats, are expressly mentioned, but in relation to mules, the profoundest silence is uniformly observed; hence, Bochart argues, that the origin of mules is involved in great uncertainty. But the assertion of that celebrated writer, that the Hebrew verb (מצא) *matsa*, signifies only to find, not to invent, is incorrect. In Leigh's Critica Sacra, it signifies also to procure for himself by labour and industry; and in Parkhurst, the seventh sense is, to obtain, to procure. According to these respectable authors, the text may be rendered, This was that Anah, who, by labour and industry, procured for himself mules in the wilderness, which is quite consistent with the common exposition. If Anah did not invent the method of procreating mules, but only found them already existing, what can the sacred writer mean by the emphatical phrase, He, Anah; or, as in our version, This was that Anah? What was so remarkable or important in a person merely finding a knot of mules in the wilderness, that Moses should reckon it necessary to use such emphatical terms? And what reason can be given, that he takes not the smallest notice of those who found horses, or camels, or asses in the wilderness, although some individual must have found and reduced them to a state of servitude? Something unusual and peculiar is certainly intended in the phrase which Moses employs: and what can that be, but the invention of a new breed of animals. The want of mules in the numerous herds of the patriarchs, and the late period at which they came into general use among the Jews, will not prove that Anah was not the inventer of that spurious breed, but only, that it was not in much request till the reign of David. That the procreation of mules was actually discouraged among the holy people, we have the highest authority for asserting. The God of Israel, who is a God of order and not of confusion, enacted a law, which he introduces with more than usual solemnity, not indeed to prohibit the use of mules when procreated, but the rearing of them: "Ye shall keep my statutes. Thou shalt not let thy cattle gender with a diverse kind." The mules which David and the nobles of his kingdom rode, were therefore, in all probability, imported from other countries where they abounded, long before the time of that illustrious monarch. Bochart offers another interpretation, which he thinks ought to be preferred; that the original term which our translators render mules, is in reality the name of a people, probably the same as the gigantic Emim, mentioned in the fourteenth chapter of Genesis. The Samaritan Pentateuch, accordingly reads here, (האימים) the *Emim;* and the Targum in Genesis, renders the term by (גבליא) *giants;* and Aquila and Symmachus retain the Hebrew name, Emim; so, that the passage should be rendered: This is that Anah, who found, or lighted upon, the Emim in the desert. The verb (מצא) *matsa*, when spoken of enemies, is used for lighting upon them, or even attacking them suddenly: several examples of which, are quoted by Parkhurst. Thus, Anah is said to have found the Emim, or to have fallen upon them, or attacked them suddenly. By this daring exploit, which was greatly celebrated at the time it happened, whether he discomfited these gigantic enemies by his valour, or eluded the snare they had prepared for him by his address, he transmitted his fame to succeeding generations; and by this criterion the historian distinguishes him from others of the same name.—PAXTON.

[But for this interpretation there is no evidence in history, and we shall exhibit as more plausible, though by no means conclusive, the opinion of Mr. Bryant, (*Observations upon some Passages in Scripture*, p. 26.) There is reason to think, that the nature of these thirsty regions above mentioned is alluded to in the history of Anah, who was of the family of Seir the Horite, into which Esau had married. "And these are the children of Zibeon" (the son of Seir) "both Aiah and Anah: this was that Anah, who found mules in the wilderness, as he fed the asses of Zibeon, his father." Gen. chap. xxxvi. ver. 24. Why the word ימם, *Yamim*, is here rendered mules, I know not; and why in some other versions it is expressed giants. It manifestly denotes *waters;* and is so translated in the Syriac version; and by aquas calidas in the Vulgate. The translations of Aquila, Theodotion, and Symmachus, retain the original word, which they express in Greek characters *ιαμειν*, or *ιαμειμ*, as if it were a proper name. The word, I make no doubt, was in common use among the Edomites, and Horites of Mount Seir. It is the same as ימם of the scriptures, and as the word Hammim, by which baths and waters are denoted at this day by the Arabians, Persians, and other nations in the east. The account given in scripture is short, and was well understood by the persons to whom it is addressed, and undoubtedly related to water. The circumstance mentioned must have been of consequence, otherwise there would have been no necessity to specify the person, by whom it was effected. We should therefore read, that instead of *mules* Anah found out *water* in the wilderness: but to what does the history amount? Every known spring must have had somebody to have discovered it; so that Anah, if this be all, did no more than hundreds had done before. But to me there seems to be something of more importance in the account than at first appears; and for that reason the name of the person is recorded, as being of moment to those who lived in the vicinity of Edom, and were acquainted with the rites of Midian. It is to be observed, that the sacred writer, in speaking of Anah's first discovery of these waters, does not inform us, when, or where, he was feeding his father's asses; but only that the event took place, as he was feeding them. This may be found of some moment. I imagine, that the latent purport of the history is this. As Anah was attending these animals, in the desert, he observed that faculty with which they were endued, of snuffing the moisture of the air, and being by these means led to latent waters. Accordingly, either by the intimation of those which he fed, or by the traces of the wild brood, he was brought to the knowledge of those resources. And as those animals, which had been beneficial. were entitled in many countries to a particular regard, so these among others met with uncommon reverence among the Horites of Mount Hor, and the people of Seir: for they were looked upon as the instruments of Heaven, towards the finding out in those barren wilds the greatest blessing. Hence arose a town, and temple, where the divinity was worshipped under this emblem. They stood in a valley beneath Mount Hor, which was a part of the mountains Kiddim, upon the skirts of Edom. Thus, as I have before mentioned, what was natural sagacity, they looked upon as a supernatural impulse, an intimation from Heaven. And the animal, like the Apis and Mnevis in Egypt, was esteemed a living emblem of the Deity, and oracular. From the situation of Petora, which was very recluse, the place being almost surrounded by high mountains, we may suppose, that the water was first found out in the manner above: in consequence of which the animal was looked upon as an oracle, and accordingly reverenced. And when the false prophet proved disobedient, and was going to utter his curses against God's people, he was terrified by an angel, and rebuked by the beast he strode. Instead of that divine energy, which it was at times supposed to enjoy, and for which at Petora it was in an idolatrous manner reverenced, God gave the ass a human voice, a far superior and more surprising gift. Hence his power was shown above that of the gods of Edom and Midian; and the miracle was well calculated, in respect to the person on whose account it was exhibited. That the history did not relate either to mules, or to the Emims, but on the contrary, to water and fountains, may be seen in the name of the person. This was ענה, Anah, directly from עין, Ain, a fountain; and is analogous to Πηγαιος in Greek, and Fontanus, or Fonteius, in Latin. It is what the Greeks called a μετονομασια, and was bestowed in consequence of the discovery; and is applicable to nothing else.]—B.

CHAP. 37. ver. 3. Now Israel loved Joseph more than all his children, because he *was* the son of his old age: and he made him a coat of *many* colours.

Rauwolf says, "that Turks of rank at Aleppo dress their sons, when they are a little grown, and can walk, in loose coats of a fine texture, in which various colours are woven, and which look very handsome."—ROSENMULLER.

The margin has, instead of *colours*, "pieces;" and it is probable the coat was patch-work of different colours. For beautiful or favourite children, precisely the same thing is done at this day. Crimson, and purple, and other colours, are often tastefully sewed together. Sometimes children of the Mohammedans have their jackets embroidered with gold and silk of various colours. A child being clothed in a garment of many colours, it is believed that neither tongues nor evil spirits will injure him, because the attention is taken from the beauty of the person, to that of the garment. Children seldom wear them after they are eight years of age; though it must have been the custom among the ancients referred to in the Bible to wear them longer, as we read of Tamar having "a garment of divers colours upon her; for with such robes were the king's daughters that were virgins apparelled."—ROBERTS.

Ver. 10. Shall I, and thy mother, and thy brethren, indeed come to bow down ourselves to thee to the earth.

The Hebrew word here translated bow down, (by Luther, *anbelen, i. e.* worship,) means the manner customary in all Asia of testifying respect to kings and princes, by falling on the knee, and stooping till the forehead touches the ground. Ovington says, "The mark of respect which is paid to kings in the East approaches very near to adoration. The manner of saluting the Great Mogul is, to touch with the hand first the earth, then the breast, and then to lift it above, which is repeated three times in succession as you approach him."—BURDER.

Ver. 24. And they took him, and cast him into a pit: and the pit *was* empty, *there was* no water in it.

What is here meant by a pit is an empty cistern or reservoir dug in the ground, in which the rain-water is collected, of which there are many in the Arabian deserts. Rauwolf, in the account of his *Journey through the Desert of Mesopotamia*, says, "That the camels, besides other necessaries, were chiefly laden with water to refresh them selves and their cattle in the sultry heat of the sun, as they do not easily meet with springs or brooks in crossing the desert: though they may by chance meet with *pits or cisterns, which are for the most part without water*, which only runs into them from the rain."—ROSENMULLER.

Ver. 34. And Jacob rent his clothes.

This ceremony is very ancient, and is frequently mentioned in scripture. Levi (*Rites and Ceremonies of the Jews*, p. 174) says, it was performed in the following manner: "they take a knife, and holding the blade downward, do give the upper garment a cut on the right side, and then rend it a hand's-breadth. This is done for the five following relations, *brother, sister, son,* or *daughter*, or *wife;* but for *father* or *mother*, the rent is on the left side, and in all the garments, as coat, waistcoat, &c."—BURDER.

CHAP. 38. ver. 14. And she put her widow's garments off from her, and covered her with a veil, and wrapped herself, and sat in an open place, which *is* by the way to Timnath: for she saw that Shelah was grown, and she was not given unto him to wife.

The habit of eastern females was also suited to their station; and women of all ages and conditions, appeared in dresses of the same fashion; only a married woman wore a veil upon her head, in token of subjection; and a widow had a garment which indicated her widowed state. The daughters of a king, and ladies of high rank, who were virgins, wore a garment of many colours, reaching, as is supposed, to the heels or ankles, with long sleeves down to the wrists, which had a border at the bottom, and a facing at the hands, of a colour different from the garment: it was likewise embroidered with flowers, which in ancient times, was reckoned both splendid and beautiful. Before the Jews were carried captives to Babylon, their wives and daughters had arrived at the greatest degree of extravagance in dress. The prophet Isaiah gives a long list of the vestments, trinkets, and ornaments in use among the ladies of Israel, in that remote age; the greater part of which, it is extremely difficult to describe. A common prostitute among the Jews was known, as well by the peculiar vesture she wore, as by having no covering upon her head, and her eyebrows painted with stibium, which dilated the hair, and made the eyes look black and beautiful. In the days of Jacob, the harlot seemed to have been distinguished by her veil, and by wrapping herself in some peculiar manner; for these are the circumstances that induced Judah to consider Tamar his daughter-in-law as a woman of this character. When Judah saw her, he thought her to be a harlot, because she had covered her face. It may be justly inferred from this passage, that modest women did not constantly wear a veil in those days. Rebecca, indeed, put a veil upon her face when she met Isaac in the field: but it was a part of the marriage ceremony to deliver the bride covered with a veil, from head to foot; and Rebecca, in this instance, only followed the established custom of her country. Had it been the practice of modest women in that age to cover their faces, in the presence of the other sex, she would not have needed to veil herself when her future husband met her in the field. She seems to have had no veil when Abraham's servant accosted her at the well; nor, for any thing that can be discovered, was Rachel veiled at her first interview with Jacob; or if they did appear in veils, these prevented not a part of the face from being seen. The practice of wearing veils, except at the marriage ceremony, must, therefore, be referred to a later period, and was perhaps not introduced till after the lapse of several ages. These observations may serve to illustrate the address of Abimelech to Sarah: "Behold, he is to thee a *covering of the eyes*, unto all that are with thee; and with all other." Sarah, you have not been used to wear the veil constantly when at home, as a person of your beauty and accomplishments should do, and by that circumstance we were tempted; but now I insist that you wear a covering, which, by concealing your beautiful countenance, may prevent such desires; and henceforth be *correct*, (as the word may be rendered, that is, *circumspect*,) and do not show yourself; or, as in our translation, thus she was *corrected*, *reproved*, by a very handsome compliment paid to her beauty, and a very handsome present paid to her brother, as Abraham is sarcastically termed by Abimelech. —PAXTON.

Ver. 18. And he said, What pledge shall I give thee? and she said, Thy signet, and thy bracelets, and thy staff that *is* in thy hand: and he gave *it* her, and came in unto her: and she conceived by him.

The signet used by kings and persons of rank in the East was a ring which served all the purposes of sealing. All the Orientals, instead of signature by sign manual, use the impression of a seal on which their name and title (if they have one) is engraved. Among intriguing and malicious people, it is so easy to turn the possession of a man's seal to his disgrace, by making out false documents, that the loss of it always produces great concern. This shows how much Judah put himself in the power of Tamar, when he gave her his signet; and one reason of his anxiety, "Let her take it to her, lest we be ashamed," may therefore mean something beyond the mere discovery of the immoral action; "Lest by some undue advantage taken of the signet, I may be endangered." In an Indian court, the monarch still takes the ring from his finger, and affixes it to the decree, and orders the posts to be despatched to the provinces, as in the reign of Ahasuerus. When an eastern prince delivers the seal of empire to a royal guest, he treats him as a superior; but when he delivers it to a subject, it is only a sign of investiture with office. Thus the king of Egypt took off his ring from his hand and put it upon Joseph's hand, when he made him ruler over all his dominions; and the king of Persia took off the ring which he had taken from Haman and gave it unto Mordecai.—PAXTON.

CHAP. 39. ver. 6. And he left all that he had in Joseph's hand; and he knew not aught he had, save the bread which he did eat.

All respectable men have a head servant called a *Kanika-Pulli*, *i. e.* an accountant, in whose hands they often place all they possess. Such a man is more like a relation or a friend, than a servant; for, on all important subjects, he is regularly consulted, and his opinion will have great weight with the family. When a native gentleman has such a servant, it is common to say of him, "Ah! he has nothing—all is in the hand of his *Kanika-Pulli*."—"Yes, yes, he is the treasure pot." "He knows of nothing but the food he eats."—ROBERTS.

CHAP. 40. ver. 13. Yet within three days shall Pharaoh lift up thy head, and restore thee unto thy place: and thou shalt deliver Pharaoh's cup into his hand, after the former manner when thou wast his butler.

The ancients, in keeping their reckonings or accounts of time, or their list of domestic officers or servants, made use of tables with holes bored in them, in which they put a sort of pegs, or nails with broad heads, exhibiting the particulars, either number or name, or whatever it was. These nails or pegs the Jews call *heads*, and the sockets of the heads they call *bases*. The meaning therefore of Pharaoh's *lifting up his head is*, that Pharaoh would take out the peg, which had the cup-bearer's name on the top of it, to read it, *i. e.* would sit in judgment, and make examination into his accounts; for it seems very probable that both he and the baker had been either suspected or accused of having cheated the king, and that, when their accounts were examined and cast up, the one was acquitted, while the other was found guilty. And though Joseph uses the same expression in both cases, yet we may observe that, speaking to the baker, he adds, *that Pharaoh shall lift up thy head from off thee*, *i. e.* shall order thy name to be struck out of the list of his servants, by taking thy peg out of the socket.—BIBLIOTHECA BIBLICA, cited by STACKHOUSE.

CHAP. 41. ver. 40. Thou shalt be over my house, and according unto thy word shall all my people be ruled; only in the throne will I be greater than thou.

Pococke, when he describes the Egyptian compliments, tells us, that upon their taking any thing from the hand of a superior, or that is sent from such a one, they kiss it, and as the highest respect put it to their foreheads. This is not peculiar to those of that country: for the editor of the Ruins of Balbec observed, that the Arab governor of that city respectfully applied the firman of the Grand Seignior to his forehead, which was presented to him when he and his fellow-travellers first waited on him, and then kissed it, declaring himself the Sultan's slave's slave. Is not this what Pharaoh refers to in Gen. xli. 40? "Thou shalt be over my house, and according unto thy word," (or on account of thy word,) "shall all my people *kiss*," (for so it is in the original;) "only in the throne will I be greater than thou:" that is, I imagine, the orders of Joseph were to be received with the greatest respect by all, and kissed by the most illustrious of the princes of Egypt. Drusius might well deny the sense that Kimchi and Grotius put on these words, the appointing that all the people should kiss his mouth. That would certainly be reckoned in the West, in every part of the earth, as well as in the ceremonious East, so remarkable for keeping up dignity and state, a most strange way of commanding the second man in the kingdom to be honoured. It is very strange then that these commentators should propose such a thought; and the more so, as the Hebrew word פי *pee* is well known to signify *word*, or *commandment*, as well as *mouth*. As this is apparent from Gen. xlv. 21; so also that the preposition על *ăl*, often signifies *according to*, or *on account of*, is put out of the question by that passage, as well as by Sam. iv. 12, Ezra x. 9, &c. These are determinations that establish the exposition I have been giving. "Upon thy commandment," or when thou sendest out orders, "my people, from the highest to the lowest, shall *kiss*," receiving them with the profoundest respect and obedience.—HARMER.

In Psalm ii. 12, it is written, "Kiss the son, lest he be angry, and ye perish from the way." Bishop Patrick says on this, "Kiss the son; that is, *submit* to him, and obey him." Bishop Pococke says, "The Egyptians, on taking any thing from the hand of a superior, or that is sent from him, kiss it; and, as the highest respect, put it to their foreheads." It is therefore probable that Pharaoh meant, that all should *submit* to Joseph, that all should obey him, and pay him reverence, and that only on the throne he himself would be greatest. When a great man causes a gift to be handed to an inferior, the latter will take it, and put it on the right cheek, so as to cover the eyes; then on the left; after which he will kiss it. This is done to show the great superiority of the donor, and that he on whom the gift is bestowed is his dependant, and greatly reverences him. When a man of rank is angry with an inferior, the latter will be advised to go and kiss his feet; which he does by touching his feet with his hands, and then kissing them. When the Mohammedans meet each other after a long absence, the inferior will touch the hand of the superior, and then kiss it. All, then, were to *kiss* Joseph, and acknowledge him as their ruler.—ROBERTS.

Ver. 42. And Pharaoh took off his ring from his hand, and put it upon Joseph's hand.

That is, his signet. In the ring there is generally a seal, on which the name of the sovereign is engraved. This signet is dipped in a coloured matter, and impressed over the royal orders, instead of the king's title. Whoever is in possession of this seal, can issue commands in the name of the king. What is said in this text, would be expressed in modern language by, "Pharaoh raised Joseph to the dignity of grand vizier." The symbol of power and authority given to the grand vizier, is the seal of the sultan with his cipher, which is intrusted to his care. The signet was considered, in the East, from the most ancient times, as the sign of delegated power. That given to the grand vizier is so great, that no officer of state, no minister, dares to resist, or even to contradict his orders, without risking his head, because every one of his commands is obeyed, as if it had proceeded from the throne, or from the mouth of the sultan. He likewise receives almost royal honours; all about him bears the stamp of the highest honour, power, and splendour. Lüdecke, in his *Description of the Turkish Empire*, says, "The grand vizier is the principal of all the officers of state, and his dignity is similar to that with which Pharaoh invested Joseph. He is called Your Highness. The emperor scarcely differs from him except in name. There is nothing at the European courts similar to his dignity, and the *prêmiers ministres*, as they are called, are nothing to him. Being keeper of the imperial signet, he always has it suspended round his neck. The investing him with it, is the sign of his elevation to office, and the taking it off, of his discharge. Without further orders or responsibility, he issues all orders for the empire." In like manner, when Alexander the Great, on his death-bed, delivered his signet to Perdiccas, it was concluded that he had also given to him his royal powers, and intended him for his successor. (CURTIUS.)—The arraying of Joseph in fine linen, was probably a part of the ceremony of investing him with his high dignity. Thus the grand vizier on the day of his appointment is invested with a double golden caftan, or robe of honour.—ROSENMULLER.

This practice is still common, but was much more so in former times. "Aruchananan, a king, once became greatly enamoured with a princess called Alli, and desired to have her in marriage; but being in doubt whether he should be able to have her, he sent for a woman who was well skilled in *palmistry!* She looked carefully into his hand, and declared, 'You will marry a princess called Alli—you shall have her.' The king was so delighted, that *he took his ring off his finger, and put it upon that of the fortuneteller*." Should a rich man be greatly pleased with a performer at a comedy, he will call him to him, and take off the ring from his finger, and present it to him. Does a *poet* please a man of rank; he will take the ring off his finger, and put it on his. A father gives his son-in-law elect a ring from off his finger. When the bridegroom goes to the house of his bride, her brother meets him, and pours water on his feet; then the former takes a ring from off his finger, and puts it on that of the latter. Does one man send to another for any particular article, or to solicit a favour, and should he not have time to write, he will give his ring to the messenger, and say, "Show this in proof of my having sent you to make this request." Is a master at a distance, and does he wish to introduce a person to the notice of another; he says, "Take this ring, and you will be received." Pharaoh's ring carried with it the highest mark of favour towards Joseph, and was a proof of the authority conferred on him.—ROBERTS.

Ver. 43. And he made him to ride in the second chariot which he had; and they cried before him, Bow the knee: and he made him *ruler* over all the land of Egypt.

As to magnificent riding, chariots are not now made use of in the East, either by men, or even the fair sex. It may be difficult to say what this is owing to: whether to the difficulty of their roads, or to the clumsy and unmechanical manner of constructing their carriages; or to a junction of both causes. Certain it is, that they are not now used in these countries: and the magnificence of the furniture of their horses makes up the want of pompous chariots. Anciently, however, chariots were used by the great: they were thought most deadly machines of war; it was courage in war that in those ruder times gave dignity, and seems to have been chiefly looked at in conferring royal honours; it was natural then for their kings to ride in chariots, as their great warriors at that time in common did; which royal chariots were without doubt most highly ornamented. In the most magnificent of all that Pharaoh had, but one, Joseph was made to ride. But when chariots were laid aside in war, their princes laid aside the use of them by degrees, and betook themselves to horses, as upon the whole most agreeable, and they endeavoured to transfer the pomp of their chariots to them, and richly indeed they do adorn them.—HARMER.

The Hebrew has for *bow the knee*, "*Tender Father*," which I believe to be the true meaning. Dr. Adam Clarke says the word אברך *abrec*, which we translate *bow the knee*, might as well be translated any thing else. In chapter xlv. 8, Joseph says himself, "God hath made me a *father to Pharaoh*." A younger brother is called the *little father*; he being the next in authority. The king's minister (if a good man) is called the *little father*. There are *five* persons who have a right to this parental title. The father himself, a king, a priest, a gooroo or teacher, and a benefactor. Joseph was indeed the *father* of the Egyptians.—ROBERTS.

CHAP. 42. ver. 15. Hereby ye shall be proved: by the life of Pharaoh, ye shall not go forth hence, except your youngest brother come hither.

Extraordinary as the kind of oath which Joseph made use of may appear to us, it still continues in the East. Mr. Hanway says, the most sacred oath among the *Persians* is "by the king's head;" and among other instances of it we read in the Travels of the Ambassadors, that "there were but sixty horses for ninety-four persons. The *mehemander* (or conductor) swore *by the head of the king*, (which is the greatest oath among the Persians,) that he could not possibly find any more." And Thevenot says, "his subjects never look upon him but with fear and trembling; and they have such respect for him, and pay so blind an obedience to all his orders, that how unjust soever his commands might be, they perform them, though against the law both of God and nature. Nay, if they swear *by the king's head*, their oath is more authentic, and of greater credit, than if they swore by all that is most sacred in heaven and upon earth."—BURDER.

Ver. 37. And Reuben spake unto his father, saying, Slay my two sons, if I bring him not to thee: deliver him into my hand, and I will bring him to thee again.

Is a man placed in great difficulty, and does he make a solemn promise, in which another person is also involved; he will say, "Ah! if I do not this thing, then kill my children." "Yes, my lord, my children shall die if I do not accomplish this object." "Ah! my children, your lives are concerned in this matter."—ROBERTS.

CHAP. 43. ver. 3. And Judah spake unto him, saying, The man did solemnly protest unto us, saying, Ye shall not see my face, except your brother *be* with you.

See on 2 Sam. 14. 24.

Ver. 7. And we told him according to the tenor of these words.

The margin has, for words, "mouth." Send a messenger with a message to deliver, and ask him, on his return, what he said, he will reply, "*According to your mouth!*"—ROBERTS.

Ver. 18. Seek occasion against us, and fall upon us.

The margin has this, "Roll himself upon us." (Job xxx. 14. Psa. xxii. 8. xxxvii. 5. Prov. xvi. 3.) For to say a man rolls himself upon another, is the eastern way of saying he *falls* upon him. Is a person beaten or injured by another: he says of the other, "He *rolled* himself upon me." Of the individual who is always trying to live upon another, who is continually endeavouring to get something out of him, it is said, "That fellow is for ever rolling himself upon him." So, also, "I will not submit to his conduct any longer; I will beat him, and roll myself upon him." Has a man committed an offence, he is advised to go to the offended, and *roll* himself upon him. A person in great sorrow, who is almost destitute of friends, asks in his distress, "Upon whom shall I roll myself?" When men or women are in great misery, they wring their hands and *roll* themselves on the earth. Devotees *roll* themselves round the temple, or after the sacred car.—ROBERTS.

Ver. 19. And they came near to the steward of Joseph's house, and they communed with him at the door of the house.

Who, in India, has not seen similar scenes to this? When people come from a distance to do business, or to have an interview with a person, they do not (if it can be avoided) go to him at once, but try to find out the head servant, and after having made him some little present, try to ascertain the disposition of his master, what are his habits, his possessions, and his family. Every thing connected with the object of their visit is thoroughly *sifted*, so that when they have to meet the individual, they are completely prepared for him!—ROBERTS.

Ver. 25. And they made ready the present against Joseph came at noon: for they heard that they should eat bread there.

Presents are commonly sent, even to persons in private station, with great parade. The money which the bridegrooms of Syria pay for their brides, is laid out in furniture for a chamber, in clothes, jewels, and ornaments of gold for the bride, which are sent with great pomp to the bridegroom's house, three days before the wedding. In Egypt they are not less ostentatious; every article of furniture, dress, and ornament is displayed, and they never fail to load upon four or five horses, what might easily be carried by one: in like manner, they place in fifteen dishes, the jewels, trinkets, and other things of value, which a single plate would very well contain. The sacred writer seems to allude to some pompous arrangement of this kind, in the history of Joseph: "And they made ready the present against Joseph came at noon." They probably separated into distinct parcels, and committed to so many bearers, the balm, the honey, the spices, the myrrh, the nuts, and the almonds, of which their present consisted. —PAXTON.

Ver. 29. And he lifted up his eyes, and saw his brother Benjamin, his mother's son, and said, *Is* this your younger brother, of whom ye spake unto me? And he said, God be gracious unto thee, my son.

The forms of salutation in the East wear a much more serious and religious air than those in use among the nations of Europe. "God be gracious unto thee, my son," were the words which Joseph addressed to his brother Benjamin. In this country, it would be called a benediction; but Chardin asserts, that in Asia, it is a simple salutation, and used there instead of those offers and assurances of service which it is the custom to use in the West. The Orientals, indeed, are exceedingly eloquent in wishing good and the mercy of God on all occasions to one another, even to those they scarcely know; and yet their compliments are as hollow and deceitful as those of any other people. This appears from scripture, to have been always their character: "They bless with their mouths, but they curse inwardly." These benedictory forms explain the reason, why the sacred writers so frequently call the salutation and farewell of the East, by the name of blessing. —PAXTON.

"God be gracious unto thee, my son," was the address of Joseph to his brother Benjamin; and in this way do people of respectability or years address their inferiors or juniors. "*Son*, give me a little water." "The sun is very hot; I will rest under your shade, my *son*."—ROBERTS.

Ver. 32. And they set on for him by himself, and for them by themselves, and for the Egyptians, which did eat with him, by themselves: because the Egyptians might not eat bread with the Hebrews; for that *is* an abomination unto the Egyptians. 33. And they sat before him, the first-born according to his birthright, and the youngest according to his youth: and the men marvelled one at another. 34. And he took *and sent* messes unto them from before him: but Benjamin's mess was five times so much as any of theirs. And they drank, and were merry with him.

Public entertainments in the East, are not all conducted in the same way. At Aleppo, the several dishes are brought in one by one; and after the company has eaten a little of each, they are removed; but among the Arabs, the whole provisions are set on the table at once. In Persia, where the last custom is followed, the viands are distributed by a domestic, who takes portions of different kinds out of the large dishes in which they are served up, and lays four or five different kinds of meat in one smaller dish; these are set, furnished after this manner, before the company; one of these smaller dishes being placed before two persons only, or at most three. The same practice obtains at the royal table itself. It is not improbable that the ancient Egyptians treated their guests in a similar way; and in the entertainment given by Joseph to his brethren, we may discover many points of resemblance. The Persians were placed in a row on one side of the room, without any person before them; a distinct dish, with different kinds of food, was set before every guest; circumstances which entirely correspond with the arrangement of Joseph's entertainment.—PAXTON.

Ver. 34. And he took *and sent* messes unto them from before him: but Benjamin's mess was five times so much as any of theirs. And they drank, and were merry with him.

The manner of eating among the ancients was not for all the company to eat out of one and the same dish, but for every one to have one or more dishes to himself. The whole of these dishes were set before the master of the feast, and he distributed to every one his portion. As Joseph, however, is here said to have had a table to himself, we may suppose that he had a great variety of little dishes or plates set before him; and as it was a custom for great men to honour those who were in their favour, by sending such dishes to them as were first served up to themselves, Joseph showed that token of respect to his brethren; but to express a particular value for Benjamin, he sent him five dishes to their one, which disproportion could not but be marvellous and astonishing to them, if what *Herodotus* tells us be true, that the distinction in this case, even to Egyptian kings themselves, in all public feasts and banquets, was no more than a double mess.—STACKHOUSE.

CHAP. 44. ver. 1. And he commanded the steward of his house, saying, Fill the men's sacks *with* food, as much as they can carry, and put every man's money in his sack's mouth.

There are two sorts of sacks taken notice of in the history of Joseph, which ought not to be confounded; one for the corn, the other for the baggage. There are no wagons almost through all Asia as far as to the Indies; every thing is carried upon beasts of burden, in sacks of wool, covered in the middle with leather, the better to make resistance to water. Sacks of this sort are called tambellit; they enclose in them their things done up in large parcels. It is of this kind of sacks we are to understand what is said here and all through this history, and not of their sacks in which they carry their corn.—HARMER.

Ver. 18. Then Judah came near unto him, and said, O my lord, let thy servant, I pray thee, speak a word in my lord's ears, and let not thine anger burn against thy servant: for thou *art* even as Pharaoh.

A company of people have always some one among them, who is known and acknowledged to be the *chief speaker;* thus, should they fall into trouble, he will be the person to come forward and plead with the superior. He will say, "My *lord*, I am indeed a very ignorant person, and am not worthy to speak to you: were I of high caste, perhaps my lord would hear me. May I say two or three words?" (some of the party will then say, "Yes, yes, our lord will hear you.") He then proceeds,—"Ah, my lord, your mercy is known to all; great is your wisdom; you are even as a king to us: let, then, your servants find favour in your sight." He then, like Judah, relates the whole affair, forgetting no circumstance which has a tendency to exculpate him and his companions; and every thing which can *touch* the *feelings* of his judge will be gently brought before him. As he draws to a conclusion, his pathos increases, his companions put out their hands in a supplicating manner, accompanied by other gesticulations; their tears begin to flow, and with one voice they cry, "Forgive us, *this time*, and we will never offend you more."—ROBERTS.

Ver. 21. And thou saidst unto thy servant, Bring him down unto me, that I may set mine eyes upon him.

Has a beloved son been long absent, does the father anxiously desire to see him, he says, "Bring him, bring him, that the course of my eyes may be upon him." "Ah, my eyes, do you again see my son? Oh, my eyes, is not this pleasure for you?"—ROBERTS.

CHAP. 45. ver. 2. And he wept aloud: and the Egyptians and the house of Pharaoh heard.

Hebrew, "gave forth his voice in weeping." In this way do they speak of a person who thus conducts himself: "How loudly did he give forth his voice and weep." "That child is for ever giving forth its voice." The violence of their sorrow is very great, and their voice may be heard at a considerable distance.—ROBERTS.

"This," says Chardin, "is exactly the genius of the people of Asia, especially of the women. Their sentiments of joy or of grief are properly transports; and their transports are ungoverned, excessive, and truly outrageous. When any one returns from a long journey, or dies, his family burst into cries, that may be heard twenty doors off; and this is renewed at different times, and continues many days, according to the vigour of the passion. Especially are these cries long in the case of death, and frightful, for the mourning is right down despair, and an image of hell. I was lodged in the year 1676, at Ispahan, near the Royal square; the mistress of the next house to mine died at that time. The moment she expired, all the family, to the number of twenty-five or thirty people, set up such a furious cry, that I was quite startled, and was above two hours before I could recover myself. These cries continue a long time, then cease all at once; they begin again as suddenly, at daybreak, and in concert. It is this suddenness which is so terrifying, together with a greater shrillness and loudness than one could easily imagine. This enraged kind of mourning, if I may call it so, continued forty days; not equally violent, but with diminution from day to day. The longest and most violent acts were when they washed the body, when they perfumed it, when they carried it out to be interred, at making the inventory, and when they divided the effects. You are not to suppose that those that were ready to split their throats with crying out, wept as much; the greatest part of them did not shed a single tear through the whole tragedy." This is a very distinct description of eastern mourning for the dead: they cry out too, it seems, on other occasions; no wonder then *the house of Pharaoh heard*, when Joseph wept at making himself known to his brethren.—HARMER.

Ver. 14. And he fell upon his brother Benjamin's neck, and wept; and Benjamin wept upon his neck. 15. Moreover, he kissed all his brethren, and wept upon them; and after that his brethren talked with him.

When people meet, after long absence, they fall on each other's shoulder or neck, and kiss or smell the part. A husband, after long absence, kisses or smells the forehead, the eyes, the right and left cheeks, and the bosom, of his wife.—ROBERTS.

Ver. 17. And Pharaoh said unto Joseph, Say unto thy brethren, This do ye; lade your beasts.

Nearly all the merchandise, which goes by land, is carried by beasts of burden; and, no doubt, will continue to be so till regular roads are constructed. Hence may be seen hundreds of bullocks, or camels, carrying rice, salt, spices, and other wares, traversing the forests and deserts to distant countries. Some of the buffaloes carry immense burdens, and though they only make little progress, yet they are patient and regular in their pace. Bells are tied round the necks of some of the animals, the sound of which produces a pleasing effect on the feelings of a traveller, who now knows that he is not far from some of his fellows. The sound of the bells also keeps the cattle together, and frightens off the wild beasts.—ROBERTS.

CHAP. 46. ver. 4. I will go down with thee into Egypt; and I will also surely bring thee up *again:* and Joseph shall put his hand upon thine eyes.

A father, at the point of death, is always very desirous that his wife, children, and grandchildren should be with him. Should there be one at a distance, he will be immediately sent for, and until he arrives the father will mourn and complain, "My son, will you not come? I cannot die without you." When he arrives, he will take the hands of his son, and kiss them, and place them on his eyes, his face, and mouth, and say, "Now I die."—ROBERTS.

Ver. 6. And came into Egypt, Jacob, and all his seed with him.

In this way *descendants* are spoken of. Has a man been deceived by another, he will be asked, "How could you trust him? did you not know him to be bad (*veethe*) seed." "That fellow is of the *seed* of fiends." "The reason you see such good things in that youth is, that he is of good *seed*." "The old man and his *seed* have all left this village many years ago."—ROBERTS.

Ver. 24. For every shepherd *is* an abomination unto the Egyptians.

Cunæus, with great plausibility, ascribes this detestation on the part of the Egyptians, to the ferocious dispositions and rebellious conduct of the shepherds who tended their flocks in the plains and marshes of lower Egypt. "These," says that writer, "were active and able men, but execrable to all the Egyptians, because they would not suffer them to lead their idle course of life in security. These men often excited great commotions, and sometimes created kings for themselves. It was on this account, that the Romans, in succeeding times, when they easily held the rest of Egypt in obedience, placed a strong garrison in all these parts. When you have taken the most exact survey of all circumstances, you will find this was the reason that made the Egyptians, even from the first, so ill affected to shepherds; because these sedentary men and handicrafts could not endure their fierce and active spirits. Pharaoh himself, when he had determined to abate and depress the growing numbers of the Israelites, spake to his subjects in this manner: 'The Israelites are stronger than we; let us deal wisely, that they increase not, lest, when war arises, they join themselves to our enemies, and take up arms against us.' But this view does not account for the use of the term which is properly rendered abomination, and which indicates, not a ferocious and turbulent character, which is properly an object of dread and hatred, but a mean and despicable person, that excites the scorn and contempt of his neighbours. It is readily admitted, that the detestation in which shepherds were held in Egypt, could not arise from their employment in the breeding of cattle; for the king himself, in the days of Joseph, had very numerous flocks and herds, in the management of which he did not think it unbecoming his dignity to take a lively interest. This is proved by the command to his favourite minister; 'If thou knowest any men of activity among them, then make them rulers over my cattle.' Nor were his numerous subjects less attentive to this branch of industry; every one seems to have lived upon his paternal farm, part of which was converted into pasture. Hence, when money failed in the years of famine, 'all the Egyptians came to Joseph and said, Give us bread; for why should we die in thy presence? for the money faileth. And Joseph said, Give your cattle, and I will give you bread for your cattle, if money fail." But if Pharaoh and all his subjects, were themselves engaged in the rearing of stock, a shepherd could not be to them an object of general abhorrence. Besides, it was not unlawful in Egypt to deprive an ox or a sheep of life, and feast upon the flesh; for, in the temples, these animals were offered in sacrifice every day; and for what purpose did the Egyptians rear them on their farms, but to use them as food? The contempt in which this order of men were held, could not then be owing to the superstition of the nation in general. It may even be inferred from the command of Pharaoh to Joseph, requiring him to appoint the most active of his brethren rulers over his cattle, that the office of a shepherd was honourable among the Egyptians; for it could not be his design to degrade the brethren of his favourite minister. This idea is confirmed by Diodorus, who asserts that husbandmen and shepherds were held in very great estimation in that country. But that writer states a fact, which furnishes the true solution of the difficulty—that in some parts of Egypt, shepherds were not suffered. The contempt of shepherds seems, therefore, to have been confined to some parts of the kingdom: probably to the royal city, and the principal towns in Upper Egypt, where the luxury of a court, or the wealth and splendour of the inhabitants, taught them to look down with contempt and loathing upon those humble peasants. But the true reason seems to be stated by Herodotus, who informs us that those who worship in the temple of the Theban Jupiter, or belong to the district of Thebes, the ancient capital of Egypt, abstained from sheep and sacrificed goats. But sheep and oxen were the animals which the shepherds usually killed for general use. It was natural, therefore, for that superstitious people to regard with abhorrence those who were in the daily practice of slaughtering the objects of their religious veneration. But this custom was confined to the district of Thebes; for, according to the same writer, "in the temple of Mendes, and in the whole Mendesian district, goats were preserved and sheep sacrificed." Shepherds, therefore, might be abhorred in one part of Egypt and honoured in another. The sagacious prime minister of Egypt, desirous to remove his brethren from the fascinations of wealth and power, directed them to give such an account of themselves, that the counsellors of Pharaoh, from their dislike of the mean employment in which they had been educated, might grant their request, and suffer them to settle in Goshen, a land of shepherds, far removed from the dangerous blandishments of a court.—PAXTON.

CHAP. 47. ver. 29. And the time drew nigh that Israel must die: and he called his son Joseph, and said unto him, If now I have found grace in thy sight, put, I pray thee, thy hand under my thigh, and deal kindly and truly with me; bury me not, I pray thee, in Egypt.

See on chap. 24. 2, 3.

CHAP. 49. ver. 3. Reuben, thou *art* my first-born, my might, and the beginning of my strength, the excellency of dignity, and the excellency of power.

It is generally believed that the first-born son is the strongest, and he is always placed over his brethren. To him the others must give great honour, and they must not sit in his presence without his permission, and then only *behind* him. When the younger visits the elder, he goes with great respect, and the conversation is soon closed. Should there be any thing of a particular nature, on which he desires the sentiments of his elder brother, he sends a friend to converse with him. The younger brother will not enter the door at the same time with the elder; he must always *follow*. Should they be invited to a marriage, care will be taken that the oldest shall go in the first. The younger will never approach him with his wooden sandals on, he must take them off. He will not speak to the wife of the elder, except on some special occasion. When the father thinks his end is approaching, he calls his children, and, addressing himself to the elder, says, "My strength, my glory, my all is in thee." From this may be gained an idea of the importance which was attached to the "birthright."—ROBERTS.

Ver. 8. Judah, thou *art he* whom thy brethren shall praise; thy hand *shall be* in the neck of thine enemies.

The oriental conqueror often addressed his unfortunate captives in the most insulting language, of which the prophet Isaiah has left us a specimen: "But I will put it (the cup of Jehovah's fury) into the hand of them that afflict thee; which have said to thy soul, bow down that we may go over." And their actions were as harsh as their words were haughty; they made them bow down to the very ground, and put their feet upon their necks, and trampled them in the mire. This indignity the chosen people of God were obliged to suffer: "Thou hast laid thy body as the ground, and as the street to them that went over." Conquerors of a milder and more humane disposition put their hand upon the neck of their captives, as a mark of their superiority. This custom may be traced as high as the age in which Jacob flourished; for in his farewell blessing to Judah, he thus alludes to it: "Judah, thou art he whom thy brethren shall praise; thy hand shall be in the neck of thine enemies." This benediction, which at once foretold the victorious career of that warlike tribe, and suggested the propriety of treating their prisoners with moderation and kindness, was fulfilled in the person of David, and acknowledged by him: "Thou hast also given me the necks of mine enemies, that I might destroy them that hate me." Traces of this custom may be discovered in the manners of other nations. Among the Franks it was usual to put the arm round the neck, as a mark of superiority on the part of him by whom it was done. When Chrodin, declining the office of mayor of the palace, chose a young nobleman named Gogan, to fill that place, he immediately took the arm of the young man, and put it round his own neck, as a mark of his dependance on him, and that he acknowledged him for his general and chief.—PAXTON.

Ver. 9. Judah *is* a lion's whelp; from the prey, my son, thou art gone up: he stooped down, he couched as a lion, and as an old lion: who shall rouse him up?

The Hebrew words will be more accurately expressed by the following translation:—

A young lion is Judah,
From prey, my son, art thou become great;
He bends his feet under him and couches
Like a lion and like a lioness;
Who shall rouse him up?

Judah is compared to a young lion, which becomes great by prey, and which, when grown up and satiated with booty, is found reposing with his feet bent under his breast. The lion does this when he has eaten sufficiently; he then does not attack passengers, but if any one would venture to rouse him out of wantonness, he would repent of his temerity. The meaning of the image is, that the tribe of Judah would at first be very warlike and valiant, but in the sequel, satiated by conquests and victories, would cease to attack its neighbours, yet had made itself so terrible that nobody would venture to attack it. Among the eastern nations, the lion was always the emblem of warlike valour and might. —BURDER.

Ver. 11. Binding his foal unto the vine, and his ass's colt unto the choice vine.

One species of vine is not less distinguished by the luxuriance of its growth, than by the richness and delicacy of its fruit. This is the Sorek of the Hebrews, which the prophet Isaiah has chosen to represent the founders of his nation—men renowned for almost every virtue which can adorn the human character: "My well-beloved has a vineyard in a very fruitful hill, and he planted it with Sorek, or the choicest vine." It is to this valuable species that Jacob refers, in his prophetic benediction addressed to Judah; and the manner in which he speaks of it is remarkable: "Binding his foal unto the vine, and his ass's colt unto the choice vine." In some parts of Persia it was formerly the custom to turn their cattle into the vineyards after the vintage, to browse on the vines, some of which are so large, that a man can hardly compass their trunks in his arms. These facts clearly show, that agreeably to the prediction of Jacob, the ass might be securely bound to the vine, and without damaging the tree by browsing on its leaves and branches. The same custom appears, from the narratives of several travellers, to have generally prevailed in the Lesser Asia. Chandler observed, that in the vineyards around Smyrna, the leaves of the vines were decayed or stripped by the camels, or herds of goats, which are permitted to browse upon them after the vintage. When he left Smyrna on the thirtieth of September, the vineyards were already bare; but when he arrived at Phygela, on the fifth or sixth of October, he found its territory still green with vines; which is a proof, that the vineyards at Smyrna must have been stripped by the cattle, which delight to feed upon the foliage. This custom furnishes a satisfactory reason for a regulation in the laws of Moses, the meaning of which has been very imperfectly understood, which forbids a man to introduce his beast into the vineyard of his neighbour. It was destructive to the vineyard before the fruit was gathered; and after the vintage, it was still a serious injury, because it deprived the owner of the fodder, which was most grateful to his flocks and herds, and perhaps absolutely requisite for their subsistence during the winter. These things considered, we discern in this enactment, the justice, wisdom, and kindness of the great legislator: and the same traits of excellence might no doubt be discovered in the most obscure and minute regulation, could we detect the reason on which it is founded.—PAXTON.

Ver. 14. Issachar *is* a strong ass, couching down between two burdens: 15. And he saw that rest *was* good, and the land that *it was* pleasant; and bowed his shoulder to bear, and became a servant unto tribute.

The ass is not more remarkable for his power to sustain, than for his patience and tranquillity when oppressed by an unequal load. Like the camel, he quietly submits to the heaviest burden; he bears it peaceably, till he can proceed no farther; and when his strength fails him, instead of resisting or endeavouring to throw off the oppressive weight, he contentedly lies down, and rests himself under it, recruits his vigour with the provender that may be offered him, and then, at the call of his master, proceeds on his journey. To this trait in the character of that useful animal, the dying patriarch evidently refers, when, under the afflatus of inspiration, he predicts the future lot and conduct of Issachar and his descendants. "Issachar is a strong ass, couching down between two burdens. And he saw that rest was good, and the land that it was pleasant, and bowed his shoulder to bear, and became a servant unto tribute." This tribe, naturally dull and stupid, should, like the creature by which they were characterized, readily submit to the vilest master and the meanest service. Although, like the ass, possessed of ability, if properly exerted and rightly directed, to shake off the inglorious yoke of servitude, they would basely submit to the insults of the Phenicians on the one hand, and the Samaritans on the other. Issachar was a strong ass, "able," says a sprightly writer, "to refuse a load, as well as to bear it; but like the passive drudge which symbolized him, he preferred inglorious ease to the resolute vindication of his liberty; a burden of tribute, to the gains of a just and well-regulated freedom; and a yoke of bondage, to the doubtful issues of war."—PAXTON.

"Couching down between two burdens." The original word rendered "burdens," we believe, after careful investigation, properly signifies the double partition forming the sides of a stall for cattle or asses, or the bars and timbers of which they were made. A similar structure was erected about the dwellings of the Jews, in which their pots, kettles, and other kitchen utensils, were hung, and therefore rendered by Gusset, in Ps. 68. 14, "pot-ranges." This expression, as applied to a region of country, would naturally be supposed to imply two very marked and conspicuous limits, as for instance two ranges of mountains enclosing a valley, and by a very remarkable coincidence the tribe of Issachar received for its lot, in the distribution of the land, the fertile and delightful vale of Esdraelon, lying between ranges of hills, in the peaceful and industrious occupancy of which they might very justly be likened to an ass reposing between the sides of his stall. "Here, on this plain," says Dr. Clarke, "the most fertile part of all the land of Canaan, which, though a solitude, we found like one vast meadow covered with the richest pasture, the tribe of Issachar 'rejoiced in their tents.'" There is no authority whatever for rendering it "burdens," which seems to have been suggested solely by the words "couching between," as it was unnatural to suppose that if an ass couched between any two objects, it would of course be between two burdens. But as the blessings of several of the other sons have respect to the geographical features of their destined inheritance, it is natural to look for something of the same kind in that of Issachar, and viewed in this light the words yield a clear and striking sense, the appropriateness of which to the matter of fact is obvious to every eye. Chal. "Issachar rich in substance, and his possession shall be between the bounds;" Syr. "Issachar, a gigantic man, lying down between the paths;" Targ. Jon. "He shall lie down between the limits of his brethren;" Jerus. Targ. "and his boundary shall be situated between two limits."—"He saw that rest was good." Instead of interpreting this prediction with many commentators to the disparagement of Issachar, as though he were to be addicted to ignominious ease, we understand it in a sense directly the reverse, as intimating that he should have so high an esteem of the promised "rest" in another life, that he should give himself to unremitting labour in this; that he should be so intent upon "inheriting the earth" after the resurrection, the reversion of the saints, that he should willingly subject himself to toil, privation, and every species of endurance, with a view to secure the exceeding great reward. Thus his character would correspond with his name, the import of which is, "he shall bear or carry a reward."—BUSH.

Ver. 17. Dan shall be a serpent by the way, an adder in the path, that biteth the horse-heels, so that his rider shall fall backward.

The only allusion to this species of serpent, (the Cerastes, or horned snake,) in the sacred volume, occurs in the valedictory predictions of Jacob, where he describes the character and actions of Dan and his posterity: "Dan shall be a serpent by the way, an adder (שפיפן *sephiphon*) in the path, that biteth the horse's heels, so that his rider shall fall backward." It is indisputably clear, that the patriarch intended some kind of serpent; for the circumstances will not apply to a freebooter watching for his prey. It only remains to investigate the species to which it belongs. The principal care of the Jewish writers, is to ascertain the etymology of the name, about which their sentiments are much divided. The Arabian authors quoted by Bochart, inform us, that the Sephiphon is a most pernicious reptile, and very dangerous to man. It is of a sandy colour, variegated with black and white spots. The particulars in the character of Dan, however, agree better with the Cerastes, or horned snake, than with any other species of serpent. It lies in wait for passengers in the sand, or in the rut of the wheels on the highway. From its lurking-place, it treacherously bites the horse's heels, so that the rider falls backward, in consequence of the animal's hinder legs becoming almost immediately torpid by the dreadful activity of the poison. The Cerastes is equally formidable to man and the lower animals; and the more dangerous, because it is not easy to distinguish him from the sand in which he lies; and he never spares the helpless traveller who unwarily comes within his reach. "He moves," says Mr. Bruce, "with great rapidity, and in all directions, forward, backward, and sidewise. When he inclines to surprise any one who is too far from him, he creeps with his side towards the person, and his head averted, till, judging his distance, he turns round, springs upon him, and fastens upon the part next to him; for it is not true, what is said, that the Cerastes does not leap or spring. I saw one of them at Cairo, crawl up the side of a box, in which there were many, and there lie still as if hiding himself, till one of the people who brought them to us, came near him, and though in a very disadvantageous posture, sticking, as it were, perpendicular to the side of the box, he leaped near the distance of three feet, and fastened between the man's fore-finger and thumb, so as to bring the blood. The fellow showed no signs of either pain or fear: and we kept him with us full four hours, without applying any sort of remedy, or his seeming inclined to do so. To make myself assured that the animal was in its perfect state, I made the man hold him by the neck, so as to force him to open his mouth, and lacerate the thigh of a pelican, a bird I had tamed, as big as a swan. The bird died in about thirteen minutes, though it was apparently affected in fifty seconds; and we cannot think it was a fair trial, because a very few minutes before, it had bit, and so discharged a part of its virus, and it was made to scratch the pelican by force, without any irritation or action of its own." These serpents have always been considered as extremely cunning, both in escaping their enemies and seizing their prey: they have even been called insidious; a character which, from the preceding statement, they seem to deserve. The Orientals call him the *lier in ambush;* for, in this manner, both the Seventy and Samaritan render the text in Genesis; and this appellation well agrees with his habits. Pliny says, that the Cerastes hides its whole body in the sand, leaving only its horns exposed, which attract birds, who suppose them to be grains of barley, till they are undeceived, too late, by the darting of the serpent upon them. Ephraim, the Syrian, also mentions a kind of serpents whose heads only are seen above the ground. Like the Cerastes, Dan was to excel in cunning and in artifice, to prevail against his enemies, rather by his policy in the cabinet than by his valour in the field. But all the Jewish expositors refer the words of Jacob to Samson, who belonged to that tribe, and was undoubtedly the most illustrious personage of whom they could boast. This remarkable man, Jehovah raised up to deliver his chosen people, not so much by his valour, although his actions clearly showed, that he was by no means deficient in personal courage, as by his artful and unexpected stratagems. This interpretation has been adopted by several Christian expositors; while it has been opposed by others as a needless refinement. It is unnecessary, and perhaps improper, to restrict the prediction to Samson, when it can with equal propriety be applied to the whole tribe. Whether the words of Jacob, in this instance, were meant to express praise or blame, it may be difficult to determine; but, if the deceitful and dangerous character of the Cerastes, to which Dan is compared, be duly considered, the latter is more probable.—Paxton.

Ver. 22. Joseph *is* a fruitful bough, *even* a fruitful bough by a well, *whose* branches run over the wall.

To the northward and westward are several villages, interspersed with extensive orchards and vineyards, the latter of which are generally enclosed by high walls. The Persian vine-dressers do all in their power to make the vine run up the walls, and curl over on the other side, which they do by tying stones to the extremity of the tendril. The vine, particularly in Turkey and Greece, is frequently made to intwine on trellises, around a well, where, in the heat of the day, whole families collect themselves, and sit under the shade.—Morier.

All this falls very naturally on an eastern ear. Joseph was the fruitful bough of Jacob, and being planted near a *well*, his leaf would not wither, and he would bring forth his fruit in his season. Great delight is taken in all kinds of creepers, which bear edible fruits, and the natives allow them to run over the *walls* and *roofs* of their houses. The term "*branches*" in the verse is in the margin rendered "*daughters;*" and it is an interesting fact, (*and one which will throw light on some other passages,*) that the same term is used here to denote the same thing. "That man has only one *Chede*, *i. e.* branch, daughter." "The youngest *Chede* (branch) has got married this day." "Where are your branches?" "They are all married." "What a young branch to be in this state!—how soon it has given fruit!" When a mother has had a large family, "That branch has borne plenty of fruit." A husband will say to his wife, who is steril, "Of what use is a branch which bears not fruit?" The figure is much used in poetry.—Roberts.

The people of Israel, and other oriental nations of those days, appear to have bestowed particular attention on the cultivation of the vine. The site of the vineyard was carefully chosen in fields of a loose crumbling soil, on a rich plain, or on a sloping hill rising with a gentle ascent; or, where the acclivity was very steep, on terraces supported by masonry, and turned as much as possible from the setting sun. The plot was enclosed with a wall; the stones and other encumbrances were removed, and the choicest plants were selected to form the plantation. Within the vineyard, low walls were sometimes raised for the purpose of supporting the vines; a practice which seems to have been adopted before the days of Jacob; for in the blessing of Joseph, he speaks of it in a manner which shows that it was quite familiar to the vine-dresser: "Joseph is a fruitful bough, even a fruitful bough by a well; whose branches run over the wall." By this beautiful image then it appears, that while the dying patriarch justly appreciated and highly praised the admirable qualities of his beloved son, he intimated to his family in the most delicate but significant manner, their obligation to Joseph for the protection and comfort they enjoyed under his government.—Paxton.

Ver. 22. Joseph *is* a fruitful bough, *even* a fruitful bough by a well, *whose* branches run over the wall: 23. The archers have sorely grieved him, and shot *at him*, and hated him.

I have shown, in preceding observations, that vines in Judea sometimes grow against low stone walls; but I do not apprehend the ingenious Mr. Barrington can be right, when he supposes, in a paper of his on the patriarchal customs and manners, that Joseph is compared to a *vine growing against the wall*, Gen. xlix. 22. As vines are sometimes planted against a low wall, they might possibly be planted against a low wall surrounding a well: though it is difficult to guess, why a wall should be built round a well, in a vineyard, of such a height as to be proper for the support of a vine; and if it were, why archers direct their arrows against it, when it would be so easy to gather the fruit by hand, without injury. But I suppose this is not an exact representation. In the first place, a vine is not mentioned; it is only a *fruitful tree*, in general, to which Joseph is compared. Secondly, The being situated near water, is extremely conducive, in that dry and hot country, to the flourishing of vegetables in general; and trees among the rest. "We came," says Maundrell, "to the fountain of Elisha. Close by the fountain grows a large tree, spreading into boughs over the water, and here in the shade we took a collation." A tree, we find, planted near plenty of water, grows there to a large size. Thirdly, the wild Arabs of those countries are great plunderers of fruit. Maillet assigns that as the reason why the fruit of the land of Egypt, in these later times, is not better, namely, that they are wont to gather it before it is properly ripened, on account of the Arabs, who would otherwise rob them of it. Fourthly, It is very well known, that walls easily stop Arabs, who are continually on horseback in their roving about, and do not care to quit them, nor are used to climb walls. They had no better way then to get the fruit of those trees, whose luxuriant boughs ran over the walls of their enclosures, than by throwing their bludgeons at them, and gathering up the fruit that fell on the outside of the wall. To these things should be added, Fifthly, That the word translated *arrows*, means, not only those things that we are wont to call arrows, but such sticks as are thrown by the hand, as well as those missile weapons that are darted by means of a bow; for we find the word is made use of to express the staff of a spear, 1 Sam. xvii. 7, and consequently any piece of wood long in proportion to its diameter, especially if used as a missile instrument. The lords of arrows בעלי חצים *baalee chitseem*, for that is the Hebrew expression, conformable to an eastern mode of speech, which we translate *archers*, is a natural description of the wild Arabs, those lords of bludgeons, in committing their depredations on the eastern gardens and vineyards. But this manner of treating the vine would not be advantageous; bunches of grapes are by no means thus to be dislodged, and the fall would spoil the fruit. But there are other trees whose fruit might thus be gathered; among the rest, I suppose the pomegranate, whose fruit has so hard a shell, as neither to be injured by the fall, or destroyed by an accidental blow of the sticks they used for pelting the tree. The destroying a man is sometimes compared to the cutting down a tree: "I knew not," said the Prophet Jeremiah, "that they had devised devices against me, saying, Let us destroy the tree with the fruit thereof, and let us cut him off from the land of the living, that his name may be no more remembered," Jer. xi. 19. But the envious brethren of Joseph did not imbrue their hands in his blood, they did not destroy him as men destroy a tree when they cut it down, but they terribly distressed him; they sold him for a slave into Egypt: he had flourished in the favour of his father and of his GOD, like a tree by a reservoir of water; but they for a time dishonoured him, as a tree is disgraced by the breaking its boughs, and knocking off its leaves, by the wild Arabs, who want to derive some advantage from battering it after this manner, when they cannot come at it to destroy it.—HARMER.

Ver. 27. Benjamin shall raven *as* a wolf: in the morning he shall devour the prey, and at night he shall divide the spoil.

The wolf is weaker than the lion or the bear, and less courageous than the leopard; but he scarcely yields to them in cruelty and rapaciousness. So Benjamin, although not destitute of courage and address, nor disinclined to war, possessed neither the strength, nor the manly spirit of Judah, whose symbol was the lion's whelp; but yet he was greedy of blood, and delighted in rapine; and in the early periods of Jewish history, he distinguished himself by an active and restless spirit, which commonly, like the wolf among lambs and kids, spent itself in petty or inglorious warfare, although it sometimes blazed forth in deeds of heroic valour, and general utility. He had the honour of giving the second judge to the nation of Israel, who delivered them from the oppressive yoke of Moab; and the first king who sat on the throne of that chosen people, whose valour saved them from the iron sceptre of Ammon, and more than once revenged the barbarities of the uncircumcised Philistines upon their discomfited hosts. In the decline of the Jewish commonwealth, Esther and Mordecai, who were both of this tribe, successfully interposed with the King of Persia, for the deliverance of their brethren, and took their station in the first rank of public benefactors. But the tribe of Benjamin ravened like wolves, that are so ferocious as to devour one another, when they desperately espoused the cause of Gibeah, and in the dishonourable and bloody feud, reduced their own tribe to the very brink of ruin, and inflicted a deep wound on the other members of the state.—PAXTON.

CHAP. 50. ver. 10. And they came to the threshing-floor of Atad, which *is* beyond Jordan; and there they mourned with a great and very sore lamentation: and he made a mourning for his father seven days.

See on chap. 45. 2.

Ver. 26. So Joseph died, *being* a hundred and ten years old: and they embalmed him, and he was put in a coffin in Egypt.

The people of the East do not in general put their dead in a coffin; they simply fold up the corpse in a mat. When dying, the head is always placed towards the south, and in the grave also in the same direction. When a person is very ill, should another ask how he is, he will reply, "Ah! his head is towards the south;" meaning there is no hope. —ROBERTS.

When Joseph died, he was not only embalmed, but *put in a coffin*. This was an honour appropriated to persons of distinction, coffins not being universally used in Egypt. Maillet, speaking of the Egyptian repositories of the dead, having given an account of several niches that are found there, says, "it must not be imagined that the bodies deposited in these gloomy apartments were all enclosed in chests, and placed in niches; the greatest part were simply embalmed and swathed after that manner that every one hath some notion of; after which they laid them one by the side of another without any ceremony: some were even put into these tombs without any embalming at all, or such a slight one, that there remains nothing of them in the linen in which they were wrapped but the bones, and those half rotten." Antique coffins of stone, and sycamore wood, are still to be seen in Egypt. It is said that some were formerly made of a kind of pasteboard, formed by folding and gluing cloth together a great number of times; these were curiously plastered and painted with hieroglyphics.—THEVENOT.

EXODUS.

CHAP. 1. ver. 14. And they made their lives bitter with hard bondage, in mortar, and in brick, and in all manner of service in the field: all their service, wherein they made them serve, *was* with rigour.

Of a bad man it is said, in the East, "He makes the lives of his servants bitter." Also, "Ah! the fellow: the heart of his wife is made bitter." "My soul is bitter." "My heart is like the bitter tree."—ROBERTS.

Ver. 16. And he said, When ye do the office of a midwife to the Hebrew women, and see *them* upon the stools, if it *be* a son, then ye shall kill him; but if it *be* a daughter, then she shall live.

There have been great difficulties started in the nature and use of the instruments here rendered *stools*, (Heb. *stones*.) According to the rendering of the established version, it would seem that they were designed for procuring a more easy delivery for women in labour. But besides that stone seats were obviously very unfit for such a purpose, the Hebrew word plainly signifies a vessel of stone for holding water, (Ex. vii. 19.) A far more probable interpretation, we think, is made out by referring the pronoun *them*, not to the mothers, but to the children. The sense of the passage would then be this:—"When ye see the new-born children, for the purpose of being washed, laid in the troughs or vessels of stone for holding water, ye shall destroy the boys." A passage from Thevenot seems to confirm this construction. "The kings of Persia are so afraid of being deprived of that power which they abuse, and are so apprehensive of being dethroned, that they destroy the children of their female relations, *when they are brought to bed of boys, by putting them into an earthen trough*, where they suffer them to starve;" that is, probably, under pretence of preparing to wash them, they let them pine away or destroy them in the water.—B.

Ver. 19. And the midwives said unto Pharaoh, Because the Hebrew women *are* not as the Egyptian women; for they *are* lively, and are delivered ere the midwives come in unto them.

Oriental women suffer little from parturition; for those of better condition are frequently on foot the day after delivery, and out of all confinement on the third day. They seldom call midwives, and when they do, they are sometimes delivered before they come to their assistance; the poorer sort, while they are labouring or planting, go aside, deliver themselves, wash the child, lay it in a cloth, and return to work again. The same facility attended the Hebrew women in Egypt; and the assertion of the midwives seems to have been literally true.—PAXTON.

CHAP. 2. ver. 5. And the daughter of Pharaoh came down to wash *herself* at the river; and her maidens walked along by the river's side.

All this is very natural. Wherever there is a river, or a tank, which is known to be free from alligators, there females go in companies to some *retired* place to bathe. There are so many ceremonies, and so many causes for *defilement*, among the Hindoos, that the duty has often to be attended to. In the Scanda Purāna, the beautiful daughter of Mongaly is described as going to the river with her maidens to bathe.—ROBERTS.

CHAP. 3. ver. 5. And he said, Draw not nigh hither: put off thy shoes from off thy feet; for the place whereon thou standest *is* holy ground.

See on Gen. 14. 23.

No heathen would presume to go on holy ground, or enter a temple, or any other sacred place, without first taking off his sandals. Even native Christians, on entering a church or chapel, generally do the same thing. No respectable man would enter the house of another without having first taken off his sandals, which are generally left at the door, or taken inside by a servant.—ROBERTS.

CHAP. 7. ver. 1. And the LORD said unto Moses, See, I have made thee a god to Pharaoh; and Aaron thy brother shall be thy prophet.

A man who is afraid to go into the presence of a king, or a governor, or a great man, will seek an interview with the minister, or some principal character; and should he be much alarmed, it will be said, "Fear not, friend; I will make you *as a god* to the king." "What! are you afraid of the collector? fear not; you will be *as a god* to him." "Yes, yes, that upstart was once much afraid of the great ones; but now he is like a *god* among them."—ROBERTS.

Ver. 12. For they cast down every man his rod, and they became serpents: but Aaron's rod swallowed up their rods.

The rods of the magicians were hardly travelling staves, but doubtless such as they bore by virtue of their office as priests and servants of God. The Roman augurs were, in the like manner, accustomed to carry a staff called litures, which was crooked at the top, as described by Cicero (*on Divination*, b. i. chap. 17.) That these staves were a Roman invention, is improbable; they were derived, like others of their sacred customs, from the religion of older nations.—BURDER.

Ver. 18. And the fish that *is* in the river shall die, and the river shall stink; and the Egyptians shall loathe to drink of the water of the river.

There are few wells in Egypt, but their waters are not drank, being unpleasant and unwholesome; the water of the Nile is what they universally make use of in this country, which is looked upon to be extraordinarily wholesome, and at the same time, extremely delicious. "The water of Egypt," says the Abbè Mascrier, "is so delicious, that one would not wish the heat should be less, nor to be delivered from the sensation of thirst. The Turks find it so exquisitely charming, that they excite themselves to drink of it by eating salt. It is a common saying among them, that if Mohammed had drank of it, he would have begged of GOD not to have died, that he might always have done it. They add, that whoever has once drank of it, he ought to drink of it a second time. This is what the people of the country told me, when they saw me return from ten years' absence. When the Egyptians undertake the pilgrimage of Mecca, or go out of their country on any other account, they speak of nothing but the pleasure they shall find at their return in drinking the Nile water. There is nothing to be compared to this satisfaction; it surpasses in their esteem that of seeing their relations again, and their families. Agreeably to this, all those that have tasted of this water allow that they never met with the like in any other place. In truth, when one drinks of it the first time, it seems to be some water prepared by art. It has something in it inexpressibly agreeable and pleasing to the taste; and we ought to give it perhaps the same rank among waters, which champaigne has among wines. I must confess, however, it has, to my taste, too much sweetness. But its most valuable quality is, that it is infinitely salutary. Drink it in what quantities you will, it never in the least incommodes you. This is so true, that it is no uncommon thing to see some persons drink three buckets of it in a day, without finding the least inconvenience. . . When I give such encomiums to the water of Egypt, it is right to observe, that I speak only of that of the Nile, which indeed is the only water there which is drinkable. Well-water is detestable and unwholesome; fountains are so rare, that they are a kind of prodigy in that country; and as for the rain-water, it would be in vain to attempt preserving that, since scarce any falls in Egypt." The embellishments of a Frenchman may be seen here, but the fact, however, in general is indubitable. A person that never before heard of this delicacy of the water of the Nile, and the large quantities that on that account, are drank of it, will, I am very sure, find an energy in those words of Moses to Pharaoh, Exod. vii. 18, *The Egyptian shall loathe to drink of the water of the river*, which he never observed before. They will loathe to drink of that water which they used to prefer to all the waters of the universe, loathe to drink of that which they had been wont eagerly to long for; and will rather choose to drink of well-water, which is in their country so detestable. And as none of our commentators, that I know of, have observed this energy, my reader, I hope, will not be displeased that I have remarked it here. —Harmer.

Ver. 19. And *that* there may be blood throughout all the land of Egypt, both in *vessels of* wood, and in *vessels of* stone.

Perhaps these words do not signify, that the water that had been taken up into their vessels, was changed into blood. The water of the Nile is known to be very thick and muddy, and they purify it either by a paste made of almonds, or by filtrating it through certain pots of white earth, which is the preferable way, and therefore the possession of one of these pots is thought a great happiness. Now, may not the meaning of this passage be, that the water of the Nile should not only look red and nauseous, like blood in the river, but in their vessels too, when taken up in small quantities; and that no method whatever of purifying it should take place, but whether drank out of vessels of wood, or out of vessels of stone, by means of which they were wont to purge the Nile water, it should be the same, and should appear like blood? Some method must have been used in very early days to clarify the water of the Nile; the mere letting it stand to settle, hardly seems sufficient, especially if we consider the early elegance that obtained in Egypt. So simple an invention then as filtrating vessels may easily be supposed to be as ancient as the time of Moses; and to them therefore it seems natural to suppose the threatening refers.—Harmer.

The changing of the river into *blood*, in colour, I saw partially accomplished. For the first four or five days of the Nile's increase the waters are of a muddy red, owing to their being impregnated with a reddish coal in the upper country; as this is washed away, the river becomes of a greenish yellow for four or five days. When I first observed this, I perceived that the animalculæ in the water were more numerous than at any other period; even the Arabs would not drink the water without straining it through a rag: "And the river stank, and the Egyptians could not drink of the water of the river."—Madden.

Chap. 8. ver. 4. And the frogs shall come up, both on thee, and upon thy people, and upon all thy servants.

This loathsome plague extended to every place, and to every class of men. The frogs came up and covered the land of Egypt; they entered into their houses, and into their bed-chambers; they crawled upon their persons, upon their beds, and into their kitchen utensils. The whole country, their palaces, their temples, their persons—all was polluted and hateful. Nor was it in their power to wash away the nauseous filth with which they were tainted, for every stream and every lake was full of pollution. To a people who affected the most scrupulous purity in their persons, their habitations, and manner of living, nothing almost can be conceived more insufferable than this plague. The frog is, compared with many other reptiles, a harmless animal; it neither injures by its bite nor by its poison: but it must have excited on that occasion, a disgust which rendered life an almost insupportable burden. The eye was tormented with beholding the march of their impure legions, and the ear with hearing the harsh tones of their voices: the Egyptians could recline upon no bed where they were not compelled to admit their cold and filthy embrace; they tasted no food which was not infected by their touch; and they smelled no perfume, but the fœtid stench of their slime, or the putrid exhalations emitted from their dead carcasses. The insufferable annoyance of such insignificant creatures illustriously displayed the power of God, while it covered the haughty and unfeeling persecutors of his people with confusion, and filled them with utter dismay. How much the Egyptians endured from this visitation, is evident from the haste with which Pharaoh sent for Moses and Aaron, and begged the assistance of their prayers: "Entreat the Lord that he may take away the frogs from me and from my people; and I will let the people go that they may do sacrifice unto the Lord." Reduced to great extremity, and receiving no deliverance from the pretended miracles of his magicians, he had recourse to that God, concerning whom he had so proudly demanded, "Who is Jehovah, that I should obey his voice to let Israel go?" Subdued and instructed by adversity, he implores his compassion, and acknowledges the glory of his name; but, as the event proved, not with a sincere heart: "Then said Moses, Glory over me;" an obscure phrase, which is explained by the next clause, "when shall I entreat for thee?" that is, according to some writers, although it belongs not to thee, Pharaoh, to prescribe to me the time of thy deliverance, which entirely depends on the will and pleasure of God alone; yet I, who am a prophet, and the interpreter of his will, grant thee, in his name, the choosing of the time when this plague shall be removed. But this interpretation is more ingenious than solid. Moses intends rather to suggest an antithesis between the perverse boasting of the proud monarch, and the pious gloriation of the humbled penitent, who was now reduced to cry for mercy. Thus far, said Moses, thou hast trusted in thine own power; then, fascinated with the deceitful miracle of the magicians, thou hast perversely exalted thyself against the God of heaven; now rather glory that thou hast in me an intercessor with God, whose prayers for thy deliverance he will not refuse to hear: and in proof that he is the only true God, and that I bear his commission, fix thou the time of deliverance.

"And he said, To-morrow. And he said, Be it according to thy word: that thou mayst know, that there is none like unto the Lord our God." To-morrow, said Pharaoh: but why not to-day? It was to be expected, that the vexed and humbled monarch would ask for instant relief. It is probable, the king had called Moses and Aaron in the evening, and that he durst not ask the promised deliverance on the same day, because he thought it was not to be obtained without many prayers. Whatever might be the true reason of Pharaoh's procrastination, the renowned Calvin seems to have no ground for his opinion, that his only reason was, after obtaining his desire, to depart as formerly from his engagement to let the people go; and that Moses, content with his promise, retired to intercede with Jehovah in his favour. That great man was persuaded, that the plague was immediately removed, not suffered to continue till next day. It is better, however, to abide by the obvious meaning of the clear and precise terms used on that occasion, both by the king and the prophet: "and he said, To-morrow. And he said, Be it according to thy word." Moses and Aaron, it is true, "went out from Pharaoh, and immediately cried unto the Lord, because of the frogs which he had brought against Pharaoh." But it is not said, the Lord immediately removed the plague; but only, that he "did according to the word of Moses." Now, Moses had promised relief next day, in the clearest terms, and we have every reason to suppose, that his intercession proceeded upon his promise; therefore, when the Lord did according to the word of Moses, he removed the frogs on the next day. They were not, however, swept away, like the locusts which succeeded them, but destroyed, and left on the face of the ground. They were not annihilated, nor resolved into mud, nor marched back into the river, from whence they had come; but left dead upon the ground, to prove the truth of the miracle,—that they had not died by the hands of men, but by the power of God; that the great deliverance was not like the works of the magicians, a lying wonder, but a real interposition of almighty power, and an effect of divine goodness. The Egyptians were, therefore, reduced to the necessity of collecting them into heaps, which had the effect of more rapidly disengaging the putrid effluvia, and thus for a time, increasing the wretchedness of the country. Their destruction was probably followed by a pestilence, which cut off many of the people, in addition to those that died in consequence of the grievous vexations they endured from their loathsome adversaries; for, in one of the songs of Zion, it is said, "He sent frogs, which destroyed them;" laid waste their lands, and infected themselves with pestilential disorders. In another Psalm, the sweet singer of Israel brings the frogs which destroyed the Egyptians, from the land; whereas, Moses avers, they were produced by the river: "Their land brought forth frogs in abundance, in the chambers of their kings;" but the difference is only apparent, and may be easily reconciled; for the Psalmist may be understood as referring, not to any kind of land, but to the miry soil on the banks, or the mud in the bottom of the river. But the truth is, he uses a term, which signifies a region or country, comprehending both land and water. His true meaning then is, Their land or country, of which the Nile is a part, brought forth frogs: for the land of Egypt certainly produces whatever the Nile contains. Were it necessary to prove so clear a position, the words of Moses might be quoted, in which he reminds the people of Israel, that they came in the course of their journeyings to Jobath, a land of rivers; and the sublime ascription of Habakkuk: "Thou didst cleave the earth with rivers." The sea itself, belongs as it were to the neighbouring countries; for it is said, that Solomon constructed a fleet "in the land of Edom;" that is, in the sea which washed the shores of Edom.

It has been inquired, why David in the same passage says, the frogs penetrated into the chambers of their kings. The answer is easy: the plural is often used for the singular in Hebrew: thus the Psalmist himself: "We will go into his tabernacles;" although there was but one tabernacle where the people of Israel assembled for religious worship. The servants of Nebuchadnezzar accused the three children in these terms: "they do not worship thy gods," meaning only the golden image, which the king had set up in the plain of Dura. The language of David, therefore, in the text under consideration, meant no more than the king's palace. Some interpreters propose another solution: That the kingdom of Egypt was at that time divided into a number of small independent states, governed each by its own prince, and that all of them were equally subjected to the plague; but although it must be granted that this country was in succeeding ages, divided into a number of small principalities, no evidence has been adduced in support of such a state of things in the time of Moses; on the contrary, the whole tenor of his narrative leads to the opposite conclusion. Nor is it unreasonable to suppose, that the principal grandees of Egypt, many of whom were persons of great power and influence in the state, received from the royal Psalmist the title of kings; it is certainly not more incongruous, than to give the title of princes to the merchants of Tyre; or the title of kings to the princes of Assyria. The meaning of the passage then, is briefly this the potent monarch of Egypt, in the midst of his vassal princes, in the innermost recesses of his palace, could find no means of defence against the ceaseless intrusion of the impure vermin which covered the face of his dominions, and equally infested the palaces of the rich, and the cottages of the poor; the awful abode of the king, and the clay-built hovel of the mendicant.—PAXTON.

Ver. 9. And Moses said unto Pharaoh, Glory over me: when shall I entreat for thee, and for thy servants, and for thy people, to destroy the frogs from thee and thy houses, *that* they may remain in the river only?

The margin has, for "glory," "honour," and for "over me," "against me." Pharaoh had besought Moses to pray that the Lord might take away the frogs, and Moses wished the king to have the honour or glory (in preference to himself) of *appointing* a time when he should thus pray to the Lord to take them away. This was not only complimentary to Pharaoh, but it would have a strong tendency to convince him that the Lord had heard the prayer of Moses, because he himself had *appointed the time.* The Tamul translation* has this, "Let the honour be to you (or over me) to appoint a time when I shall pray."—ROBERTS.

Ver. 16. And the LORD said unto Moses, Say unto Aaron, Stretch out thy rod, and smite the dust of the land, that it may become lice throughout all the land of Egypt.

The learned have not been agreed in their opinion concerning the *third* of the plagues of Egypt: Exod. viii. 16, &c. Some of the ancients suppose that *gnats,* or some animals resembling them, were meant; whereas our translators, and many of the moderns, understand the original word כנים *kinneem,* as signifying *lice.* Bishop Patrick, in his commentary, supposes that Bochart has sufficiently proved, out of the text itself, that our version is right, since gnats are bred in fenny places, he might have said with truth, and with much greater energy of argument, in water, whereas the animals Moses here speaks of, were brought out of the dust of the earth. A passage I lately met with, in Vinisaur's account of the expedition of our King Richard the First into the Holy Land, may, perhaps, give a truer representation of this Egyptian plague, than those that suppose they were *gnats,* or those that suppose they were *lice,* that God used on that occasion, as the instrument of that third correction. Speaking of the marching of that army of Croisaders, from Cayphas to where the ancient Cæsarea stood, that writer informs us, that each night certain worms distressed them, commonly called *tarrentes,* which crept upon the ground, and occasioned a very burning heat by most painful punctures. They hurt nobody in the day time, but when night came on they extremely pestered them, being armed with stings, conveying a poison which quickly occasioned those that were wounded by them to swell, and was attended with the most acute pains.—HARMER.

CHAP. 9. ver. 8. And the LORD said unto Moses and unto Aaron, Take to you handfuls of ashes of the furnace, and let Moses sprinkle it towards the heaven in the sight of Pharaoh.

When the magicians pronounce an imprecation on an individual, a village, or a country, they take ashes of cow's dung, (or from a common fire,) and *throw them in the air,* saying to the objects of their displeasure, such a sickness, or such a curse, shall surely come upon you.—ROBERTS.

Ver. 25. And the hail smote throughout all the land of Egypt all that *was* in the field, both man and beast; and the hail smote every herb of the field, and brake every tree of the field.

I do not apprehend that it is at all necessary to suppose, that all the servants, and all the cattle of the Egyptians, that were abroad at the time the hail fell, which Moses threatened, and which was attended with thunder and lightning, died; it is sufficient to suppose they all felt the hailstones, and that several of them were killed. This was enough to justify the words of Moses, that it should be a "grievous hail, such as had not fallen before in Egypt from its foundation." For though it hails sometimes in Egypt as well as rains, as Dr. Pococke found it hailed at Fioume, when he was there in February; and thunders too, as Thevenot says it did one night in December, when he was at Cairo; yet fatal effects are not wont to follow in that country, as appears from what Thevenot says of this thunder, which, he tells us, killed a man in the castle there, though it had never been heard before that thunder had killed anybody at Cairo. For divers people then to have been killed by the lightning and the hail, besides cattle, was an event that Moses might well say *had never happened there before, from the time it began to be inhabited.* I will

* Which is made from the original; and the genius of the language is every way more suited to the Hebrew, than ours. And nearly all the orientalisms in the *marginal* references of the English Bible are inserted in *the text* of the Tamul translation.

only add, that Moses, by representing this as an extraordinary hail, supposed that it did sometimes hail there, as it is found in fact to do, though not as in other countries: the *not raining* in Egypt, it is well known, is to be understood in the same manner.—HARMER.

CHAP. 10. ver. 11. Not so: go now ye *that are* men, and serve the LORD; for that ye did desire. And they were driven out from Pharaoh's presence.

Among natives of rank, when a person is very importunate or troublesome, when he presses for something which the former are not willing to grant, he is told to begone. Should he still persist, the servants are called, and the order is given, "Drive that fellow out." He is then seized by the *neck*, or taken by the *hands*, and *dragged* from the premises; he all the time *screaming* and *bawling* as if they were taking his *life*. Thus to be driven out is the greatest indignity which can be offered, and nothing but the most violent rage will induce a superior to have recourse to it.—ROBERTS.

Ver. 19. And the LORD turned a mighty strong west wind, which took away the locusts, and cast them into the Red Sea; there remained not one locust in all the coasts of Egypt.

It was not the purpose of God to complete every punishment at once, but to carry on these judgments in a series, and by degrees to cut off all hopes, and every resource upon which the Egyptians depended. By the hail and thunder and fire mingled with rain, both the flax and barley were entirely ruined, and their pastures must have been greatly injured. The wheat and rye were not yet in ear; and such was the fertility of the soil in Egypt, that a very short time would have sufficed for the leaves of the trees, and the grass of the field, to have been recruited. To complete, therefore, these evils, it pleased God to send a host of locusts, to devour every leaf and blade of grass, which had been left in the former devastation, and whatever was beginning to vegetate. It is hard to conceive how wide the mischief extends, when a cloud of these insects comes upon a country. They devour to the very root and bark, so that it is a long time before vegetation can be renewed. How dreadful their inroads at all times were, may be known from a variety of authors, both ancient and modern. They describe them as being brought by one wind, and carried off by another. They swarm greatly in Asia and Africa. In respect to Europe, Thevenot tells us, that the region upon the Boristhenes, and particularly that inhabited by the Cossacks, is greatly infested with locusts, especially in a dry season. They come in vast clouds, which extend fifteen and sometimes eighteen miles, and are nine to twelve in breadth. The air, by their interposition, is rendered quite obscure, however bright the day may have been before. In two hours they devour all the corn, wherever they settle, and often a famine ensues. At night, when they repose upon the earth, the ground is covered with them four inches deep, or more: and if a carriage goes over them, and they are mashed under foot, the smell of them is scarcely to be borne, especially when they are reduced to a state of putrefaction. They come from Circassia, Mingrelia, and Tartary, on which account the natives rejoice in a north or northeast wind, which carries them into the Black Sea, where they perish. The vast region of Asia, especially the southern part, is liable to their depredations. China is particularly infested with them; and the natives use various means to obviate the evil, which is generally too powerful to be evaded. But the most fearful accounts are from Africa, where the heat of the climate, and the nature of the soil in many places, contribute to the production of these animals in astonishing numbers.—BURDER.

Ver. 21. And the LORD said unto Moses, Stretch out thy hand towards heaven, that there may be darkness over the land of Egypt, even darkness *which* may be felt.

When the magicians deliver their predictions, they *stretch forth* the *right hand* towards *heaven*, to show that they have power, and that God favours them. The Tamul translation has this, "darkness which *causeth* to feel;" *i. e.* so dark that a man is obliged to *feel* for his way, and until he shall have so felt, he cannot proceed. Thus the darkness was so great, that their eyes were not of any use; they were obliged to *grope* for their way.—ROBERTS.

[This is probably a correct view of the passage, as a darkness consisting of thick clammy fogs, of vapours and exhalations so condensed as to be perceived by the organs of touch, would have extinguished animal life in a few moments.]—B.

Ver. 28. And Pharaoh said unto him, Get thee from me, take heed to thyself, see my face no more: for in *that* day thou seest my face, thou shalt die.

Has a servant, an agent, or an officer, deeply offended his superior, he will say to him, "Take care never to see my face again; for on the day you do that, evil shall come upon you." "Begone, and in future never look in this *face*," pointing to his own.—ROBERTS.

CHAP. 11. ver. 2. Speak now in the ears of the people, and let every man borrow of his neighbour, and every woman of her neighbour, jewels of silver, and jewels of gold.

Dr. Boothroyd, instead of borrow, translates "ask." Dr. A. Clarke says, "request, demand, require." The Israelites wished to go three days' journey into the wilderness, that they might hold a feast unto the Lord. When the Orientals go to their sacred festivals, they always put on their *best jewels*. Not to appear before the gods in such a way, they consider would be disgraceful to themselves and displeasing to the deities. A person, whose clothes or jewels are indifferent, will BORROW of his richer neighbours; and nothing is more common than to see poor people standing before the temples, or engaged in sacred ceremonies, well adorned with jewels. The almost pauper bride or bridegroom at a marriage may often be seen decked with gems of the most costly kind, which have been BORROWED for the occasion. It fully accords, therefore, with the idea of what is due at a sacred or social feast, to be thus adorned in their best attire. Under these circumstances, it would be perfectly easy to BORROW of the Egyptians their jewels, as they themselves, in their festivals, would doubtless wear the same things. It is also recorded, the Lord gave them "favour in the sight of the Egyptians." It does not appear to have been *fully* known to the Hebrews, that they were going finally to leave Egypt: they might expect to return; and it is almost certain that, if their oppressors had known they were not to return, they would not have LENT them their jewels.

The Lord, however, did say to Moses, in chap. iii. 11., that He would "bring forth the children of Israel out of Egypt," and that they should worship Him upon that mountain; but whether Moses fully understood Him is not certain. But the Lord knew!—certainly He did. And as a father, or a master, who saw his children, or slaves, deprive each other of their rightful pay, (as the Egyptians did the Israelites,) had a right to give to the injured what they had been unjustly deprived of: so the Lord, in whose hands are all things, who daily takes from one, and gives to another; and who builds up, or destroys, the families of the earth; would have an undoubted right to give to the Hebrews that property of which the Egyptians had so unjustly and cruelly deprived them.—ROBERTS.

Ver. 5. And all the first-born in the land of Egypt shall die, from the first-born of Pharaoh that sitteth upon his throne, even unto the first-born of the maid-servant that *is* behind the mill; and all the first-born of beasts.

In the first ages, they parched or roasted their grain; a practice which the people of Israel, as we learn from the scriptures, long continued; afterward they pounded it in a mortar, to which Solomon thus alludes: "Though thou shouldst bray a fool in a mortar among wheat, with a pestle, yet will not his foolishness depart from him." This was succeeded by mills, similar to the handmills formerly used in this country; of which there were two sorts: the first were large, and turned by the strength of horses or asses: the second were smaller, and wrought by men, commonly by slaves condemned to this hard labour, as a punishment for their crimes. Chardin remarks in his manuscript, that the persons employed are generally female slaves, who are least regarded, or are least fit for any thing else: for the work is extremely laborious, and esteemed the lowest employment about the house. Most of their corn is ground by these little mills, although they sometimes make use of large mills, wrought by oxen or camels. Near Ispahan, and some of the other great cities of Persia, he saw water-mills; but he did not meet with a single windmill in the East. Almost every family grinds their wheat and barley at home, having two portable millstones for that purpose; of which the uppermost is turned round by a small handle of wood or iron, that is placed in the rim. When this stone is large, or expedition is required, a second person is called in to assist; and as it is usual for the women only to be concerned in this employment, who seat themselves over against each other, with the millstone between them, we may see the propriety of the expression in the declaration of Moses: "And all the first-born in the land of Egypt shall die, from the first-born of Pharaoh, that sitteth upon his throne, even unto the first-born of the maid-servant, that is behind the mill." The manner in which the hand-mills are worked, is well described by Dr. Clarke: "Scarcely had we reached the apartment prepared for our reception, when looking from the window, into the courtyard belonging to the house, we beheld two women grinding at the mill, in a manner most forcibly illustrating the saying of our Saviour: 'Two women shall be grinding at the mill, the one shall be taken and the other left.' They were preparing flour to make our bread, as it is always customary in the country when strangers arrive. The two women, seated upon the ground opposite to each other, held between them two round flat stones, such as are seen in Lapland, and such as in Scotland are called querns. In the centre of the upper stone was a cavity for pouring in the corn; and by the side of this, an upright wooden handle for moving the stone. As this operation began, one of the women opposite received it from her companion, who pushed it towards her, who again sent it to her companion; thus communicating a rotatory motion to the upper stone, their left hands being all the while employed in supplying fresh corn, as fast as the bran and flour escaped from the sides of the machine."—PAXTON.

CHAP. 12. ver. 11. And thus shall ye eat it; *with* your loins girded, your shoes on your feet, and your staff in your hand: and ye shall eat it in haste; it *is* the LORD's passover.

When people take a journey, they have always their *loins* well *girded*, as they believe that they can walk much faster and to a greater distance. Before the palankeen bearers take up their load, they assist each other to make tight a part of the sâli or robe round the loins. When men are about to enter into an arduous undertaking, bystanders say, "*Tie your loins well up.*" (Luke xii. 35. Eph. vi. 4. 1 Pet. i. 13.)—ROBERTS.

They that travel on foot are obliged to fasten their garments at a greater height from their feet than they are wont to do at other times. This is what some have understood to be meant by the girding their loins: not simply their having girdles about them, but the wearing their garments at a greater height than usual. There are two ways of doing this, Sir J. Chardin remarks, after having informed us that the dress of the eastern people is a long vest, reaching down the calf of the leg, more or less fitted to the body, and fastened upon the loins by a girdle, which goes three or four times round them. "This dress is fastened higher up two ways: the one, which is not much used, is to draw up the vest above the girdle, just as the monks do when they travel on foot; the other, which is the common way, is to tuck up the foreparts of their vest into the girdle, and so fasten them. All persons in the East that journey on foot always gather up their vest, by which they walk more commodiously, having the leg and knee unburdened and unembarrassed by the vest, which they are not when that hangs over them." And after this manner he supposes the Israelites were prepared for their going out of Egypt, when they ate the first passover, Exod. xii. 11. He takes notice, in the same passage, of the singularity of their having shoes on their feet at that repast. They in common, he observes, put off their shoes when they eat, for which he assigns two reasons: the one, that as they do not use tables and chairs in the East, as in Europe, but cover their floors with carpets, they might not soil those beautiful pieces of furniture; the other, because it would be troublesome to keep their shoes upon their feet, they sitting crosslegged on the floor, and having no hinder quarters to their shoes, which are made like slippers. He takes no notice in this note, of their having to eat this passover with a staff in their hand; but he elsewhere observes, that the eastern people very universally make use of a staff when they journey on foot; and this passage plainly supposes it.—HARMER.

Ver. 34. And the people took their dough before it was leavened, their kneading-troughs being bound up in their clothes upon their shoulders.

The dough, we are told, which the Israelites had prepared for baking, and on which it should seem they subsisted after they left Egypt for a month, was carried away by them in their kneading-troughs on their shoulders, Exod. xii. 34. Now, an honest thoughtful countryman, who knows how cumbersome our kneading-troughs are, and how much less important they are than many other utensils, may be ready to wonder at this, and find a difficulty in accounting for it. But this wonder perhaps may cease, when he comes to understand, that the vessels which the Arabs of that country make use of, for kneading the unleavened cakes they prepare for those that travel in this very desert, are only small wooden bowls; and that they seem to use no other in their own tents for that purpose, or any other, these bowls being used by them for kneading their bread, and afterward serving up their provisions when cooked: for then it will appear, that nothing could be more convenient than kneading-troughs of this sort for the Israelites, in their journey. I am, however, a little doubtful, whether these were the things that Moses meant by that word which our version renders *kneading-troughs*; since it seems to me, that the Israelites had made a provision of corn sufficient for their consumption for about a month, and that they were preparing to bake all this at once: now their own little wooden bowls, in which they were wont to knead the bread they wanted for a single day, could not contain all this dough, nor could they well carry a number of these things, borrowed of the Egyptians for the present occasion, with them. That they had furnished themselves with corn sufficient for a month, appears from their not wanting bread till they came into the wilderness of Sin; that the eastern people commonly bake their bread daily, as they want it, appears from an observation I have already made, and from the history of the patriarch Abraham; and that they were preparing to bake bread sufficient for this purpose at once, seems most probable, from the universal bustle they were in, and from the much greater conveniences for baking in Egypt than in the wilderness, which are such, that though Dr. Shaw's attendant sometimes baked in the desert, he thought fit, notwithstanding, to carry biscuit with him, and Thevenot the same. They could not well carry such a quantity of dough in those wooden bowls, which they used for kneading their bread in common. What is more, Dr. Pococke tells us, that the Arabs actually carry their dough in something else: for, after having spoken of their copper dishes put one within another, and their wooden bowls, in which they make their bread, and which make up all the kitchen furniture of an Arab, even where he is settled; he gives us a description of a round leather coverlet, which they lay on the ground, and serves them to eat off, which, he says, has rings round it, by which it is drawn together with a chain that has a hook to it to hang it by. This is drawn together, he says, and sometimes they carry in it their meal made into dough; and in this manner they bring it full of bread, and, when the repast is over, carry it away at once, with all that is left.

Whether this utensil is rather to be understood by the word משארת *misharoth*, translated *kneading-troughs*, than the Arab wooden bowl, I leave my reader to determine. I would only remark, that there is nothing, in the other three places, in which the word occurs, to contradict this explanation. These places are Exod. viii. 3, Deut. xxviii. 5, 17, in the two last of which places it is translated *store*. It is more than a little astonishing, to find Grotius, in his comment on Exod. xii. 39, explaining that verse as signifying, that they baked no bread in their departing from Egypt, but stayed till they came to Succoth, because they had not time to stay till it was leavened in Egypt; when it is certain that they were so hurried out of Egypt, as to be desired not to stay to bake unleavened bread; nor can we imagine they would stay till leaven put into it at Succoth, had produced its effect in their dough, since travellers now in that desert often eat unleavened bread, and the precepts of Moses, relating to their commemoration of their going out of Egypt, suppose they ate unleavened bread for some time. Succoth, the first station then of the Israelites, which Dr. Shaw supposes was nothing more than some considerable encampment of Arabs, must have been a place where there was a considerable quantity of broom, or other fuel, which is not to be found in that desert everywhere.—HARMER.

CHAP. 13. ver. 18. But God led the people about, *through* the way of the wilderness of the Red Sea: and the children of Israel went up harnessed out of the land of Egypt.

The margin of our translation remarks, that the word rendered *harnessed*, in Exodus xiii. 18, signifies *by fives*, but when it adds, five in a rank, it seems to limit the sense of the term very unnecessarily, as it may as well signify five men in a company, or their cattle tied one to another in strings of five each. If there were 600,000 footmen, besides children, and a mixed multitude, together with cattle, the marching of five only abreast, supposing only one yard for each rank to move in, would make the whole length of this enormous file of people more than sixty-eight miles. If we should suppose two such columns, and place the children, mixed multitude, and cattle between them, the length then of this body of people would be above thirty-four miles. At the same time we cannot conceive any reason for such a narrow front, on the one hand, in such a wide desert, nor, on the other, why they are described as marching five abreast, if there were many such columns. It would seem in such a case, to be a circumstance that required no particular notice. Pitts tells us, that in the march of the Mohammedan pilgrims from Egypt, through this very desert, they travel with their camels tied four in a parcel, one after the other, like so many teams. He says also that usually three or four of the pilgrims diet together. If we will allow that like circumstances naturally produce like effects, it will appear highly probable, that the meaning of the word used in the passage of Exodus is, that they went up out of Egypt with their cattle, *in strings of five each;* or that Moses ordered that five men with their families should form each a little company, that should keep together, and assist each other, in this difficult march. In either of these senses we may understand the term, in all the other places in which it appears; whereas it is not natural to suppose they all went out of Egypt properly armed for war, and it is idle to say, as some have done, that they were girded about the loins, that is always supposed to be done by the eastern people when they journey. Not to say that the kindred word continually signifies *five*, and this word should in course signify that they were, somehow or other, *formed into fives*, companies of five men each, or companies that had each *five beasts*, which carried their provisions and other necessaries, fastened to each other.—HARMER.

CHAP. 15. ver. 20. And Miriam the prophetess, the sister of Aaron, took a timbrel in her hand; and all the women went out after her with timbrels and with dances.

Lady M. W. Montague, speaking of the eastern dances, says, "Their manner is certainly the same that Diana is said to have danced on the banks of Eurotas. The great lady still leads the dance, and is followed by a troop of young girls, who imitate her steps, and if she sings, make up the chorus. The tunes are extremely gay and lively, yet with something in them wonderfully soft. Their steps are varied according to the pleasure of her that leads the dance, but always in exact time, and infinitely more agreeable than any of our dances." (*Letters*, vol. ii. p. 45.) This gives us a different apprehension of the meaning of these words than we should otherwise form. "Miriam the prophetess, the sister of Aaron, took a timbrel in her hand, and all the women went out after her, with timbrels and dances." She led the dance, and they imitated her steps, which were not conducted by a set well-known form, but extemporaneous. Probably David did not dance alone before the Lord when the ark was removed, but led the dance in the same authoritative kind of way. (2 Sam vi. 14. Judges xi. 34. 1 Sam. xviii. 6.)—BURDER.

Ver. 25. And he cried unto the LORD; and the LORD showed him a tree, *which* when he had cast into the waters, the waters were made sweet: there he made for them a statute and an ordinance, and there he proved them.

This water, which was bitter or brackish, (Dr. Shaw says the latter,) was thus made sweet by the casting in of the tree. Some suppose it was a bitter wood, such as *quassia*, which corrected the water. Water is often brackish in the neighbourhood of salt-pans or the sea, and the natives correct it by throwing in it the wood called *Perru-Nelli*, Phylanthus Emblica. Should the water be very bad, they line the well with planks cut out of this tree. In swampy grounds, or when there has not been rain for a long time, the water is often muddy, and very unwholesome. But Providence has again been bountiful by giving to the people the *Teatta Maram*, Strychnos Potatorum. All who live in the neighbourhood of such water, or who have to travel where it is, always carry a supply of the nuts of this tree. They grind one or two of them on the side of an earthen vessel: the water is then poured in, and the impurities soon subside.—ROBERTS.

"El-vah is a large village or town, thick planted with palm-trees; the Oasis Parva of the ancients, the last inhabited place to the west that is under the jurisdiction of Egypt; it yields senna and coloquintida. The Arabs call El-vah, a shrub or tree, not unlike our hawthorn, either in form or flower. It was of this wood, they say, that Moses' rod was made, when he sweetened the waters of Marah. With a rod of this wood too, they say, *Kaled Ibn el Waalid*, the great destroyer of Christians, sweetened these waters at El-vah, once bitter, and gave it the name from this miracle. A number of very fine springs burst from the earth at El-vah, which renders this small spot verdant and beautiful, though surrounded with dreary deserts on every quarter: it is situated like an island in the midst of the ocean." (BRUCE.)—Our colonists, who first peopled some parts of America, corrected the qualities of the water they found there, by infusing in it branches of sassafras; and it is understood that the first inducement of the Chinese to the general use of tea, was to correct the water of their rivers. That other water also stands in some need of correction, and that such correction is applied to it, appears from the custom of Egypt, in respect to the water of the Nile. "The water of the Nile," says Niebuhr, "is always somewhat muddy; but by rubbing with bitter almonds, prepared in a particular manner, the earthen jars in which it is kept, this water is rendered clear, light, and salutary."—BURDER.

We travelled, says Burckhardt, over uneven, hilly ground, gravelly and flinty. At one hour and three quarters, we passed the well of Howara, around which a few date-trees grow. Niebuhr travelled the same route, but his guides probably did not lead him to this well, which lies among hills about two hundred paces out of the road. The water of the well of Howara is so bitter, that men cannot drink it; and even camels, if not very thirsty, refuse to taste it. This well Burckhardt justly supposes to be the Marah of the Israelites; and in this opinion Mr. Leake, Gesenius, and Rosenmüller, concur. From Ayoun Mousa to the well of Howara we had travelled fifteen hours and a quarter. Referring to this distance, it appears probable that this is the desert of three days mentioned in the scriptures to have been crossed by the Israelites immediately after their passing the Red Sea; and at the end of which they arrived at Marah. In moving with a whole nation, the march may well be supposed to have occupied three days;

and the bitter well at Marah, which was sweetened by Moses, corresponds exactly to that at Howara. This is the usual route to Mount Sinai, and was probably, therefore, that which the Israelites took on their escape from Egypt, provided it be admitted that they crossed the sea at Suez, as Niebuhr, with good reason, conjectures. There is no other road of three days' march in the way from Suez towards Sinai, nor is there any other well absolutely bitter on the whole of this coast. The complaint of the bitterness of the water by the children of Israel, who had been accustomed to the sweet water of the Nile, are such as may be daily heard from the Egyptian servants and peasants who travel in Arabia. Accustomed from their youth to the excellent water of the Nile, there is nothing which they so much regret in countries distant from Egypt; nor is there any eastern people who feel so keenly the want of good water, as the present natives of Egypt. With respect to the means employed by Moses to render the waters of the well sweet, I have frequently inquired among the Bedouins in different parts of Arabia, whether they possessed any means of effecting such a change, by throwing wood into it, or by any other process; but I never could learn that such an art was known. At the end of three hours we reached Wady Gharendel, which extends to the northeast, and is almost a mile in breadth, and full of trees. The Arabs told me that it may be traced through the whole desert, and that it begins at no great distance from El Arysh, on the Mediterranean; but I had no means of ascertaining the truth of this statement. About half an hour from the place where we halted, in a southern direction, is a copious spring, with a small rivulet, which renders the valley the principal station on this route. The water is disagreeable, and if kept for a night in the water skins, it turns bitter and spoils, as I have myself experienced, having passed this way three times. If, now, we admit Bir Howara to be the Marah of Exodus, (xv. 23,) then Wady Gharendel is probably *Elim*, with its well and date-trees; an opinion entertained by Niebuhr, who, however, did not see the bitter well of Howara. The non-existence, at present, of twelve wells at Gharendel, must not be considered as evidence against the just-stated conjecture; for Niebuhr says, that his companions obtained water here by digging to a very small depth, and there was great plenty of it when I passed. Water, in fact, is readily found by digging, in every fertile valley in Arabia, and wells are thus easily formed, which are filled up again by the sands.

The Wady Gharendel contains date-trees, tamarisks, acacias of different species, and the thorny shrub *Gharkad*, the *Peganum retusum* of Forskal, which is extremely common in this peninsula, and is also met with in the sands of the Delta on the coast of the Mediterranean. Its small red berry, of the size of a grain of a pomegranate, is very juicy and refreshing, much resembling a ripe gooseberry in taste, but not so sweet. The Arabs are very fond of it. The shrub *Gharkad* delights in a sandy soil, and reaches its maturity in the height of summer, when the ground is parched up, exciting an agreeable surprise in the traveller, at finding so juicy a berry produced in the driest soil and season. Might not the berry of this shrub have been used by Moses to sweeten the waters of Marah? [The Hebrew in Ex. xv. 25, reads: "And the Lord showed him a tree, and he cast into the waters, and they became sweet." The Arabic translates, "and he cast of it into the waters," &c.] As this conjecture did not occur to me when I was on the spot, I did not inquire of the Bedouins, whether they ever sweetened the water with the juice of berries, which would probably effect this change in the same manner as the juice of pomegranate grains expressed into it.—CALMET.

CHAP. 16. ver. 13. And it came to pass, that at even the quails came up, and covered the camp; and in the morning the dew lay round about the host.

It is evident from the history of Moses, that the demands of Israel were twice supplied with quails by the miraculous interposition of divine providence. The first instance is recorded in the book of Exodus, and is described in these words; "I have heard the murmurings of the children of Israel: speak unto them, saying, At even ye shall eat flesh, and in the morning ye shall be filled with bread; and ye shall know that I am the Lord your God. And it came to pass, that at even the quails came up, and covered the camp." From these words it appears, that the quails were sent to supply the wants of the people, at the same time the manna began to be showered down from heaven, around their encampment in the desert of Sin; and it is clear, from the beginning of the chapter, that this event took place soon after their departure from Egypt, upon the fifteenth day of the second month, before they came to mount Sinai. This miracle was repeated at Kibroth-hattaavah, a place three days' journey beyond the desert of Sinai; but they struck their tents before Sinai, in the second year after their departure from Egypt, on the twentieth day of the second month; so that a whole year intervened between the first and second supply. In the first instance, the quails were scattered about the camp only for one day; but in the second, they came up from the sea for a whole month. They only covered the camp at their first appearance; but when they came the second time, they lay round about it to the distance of a day's journey. No signs of divine wrath attended the first miracle; but the second was no sooner wrought, than the vengeance of their offended God overtook these incorrigible sinners: "While the flesh was yet between their teeth, ere it was chewed, the wrath of the Lord was kindled against the people; and the Lord smote the people with a very great plague." Hence it is evident, that the sacred historian records two different events; of which, the one was more stupendous than the other, and seemed to Moses so extraordinary, that on receiving the divine promise, he could not refrain from objecting: "The people, among whom I am, are six hundred thousand footmen; and thou hast said, I will give them flesh, that they may eat a whole month. Shall the flocks and the herds be slain for them to suffice them? Or shall all the fish of the sea be gathered together for them to suffice them?" Moses had seen the power of Jehovah successfully exerted in feeding his people with flesh for one day; but he could scarcely imagine, from whence supplies of the same kind could be drawn for a whole month. That eminent servant of Jehovah, astonished at the greatness of the promised favour, seemed to forget for a moment, that with God all things are possible.

The quails were scattered around the camp of Israel, in the most astonishing numbers: "He rained flesh also upon them as dust, and feathered fowls like as the sand of the sea." The holy Psalmist had used the metaphorical word to rain, in relation to the manna, in a preceding verse, both to intimate its descent from heaven, and its prodigious abundance. And because a single metaphor is not sufficient to give us a just idea of the sudden and extraordinary supplies which descended on the tents of Israel, they are compared to the dust of the field, and to the sand of the sea, which cannot be numbered. To suggest at once the countless myriads of these birds, and the ease with which they are caught, it is added: "He let it fall in the midst of their camp round about their habitations." The account of Moses is still more striking. "And there went forth a wind from the Lord, and brought quails from the sea, and let them fall by the camp, as it were a day's journey on this side, and as it were a day's journey on the other side, round about the camp, and as it were two cubits high upon the face of the earth." Hence, these birds covered the whole camp and the surrounding waste, to the distance of a day's journey on every side. The only ambiguity lies in the phrase, "a day's journey;" whether it means the space over which an individual could travel in one day, in which case it would be much greater—or the whole army could traverse, which would be much less. If the journey of an individual is intended, it might be about thirty miles; but if the sacred historian refers to the whole army, a third part of this space is as much as they could march in one day in the sandy desert, under a vertical sun. In the opinion of Bochart, this immense cloud of quails covered a space of at least forty miles diameter; for a day's journey is at least twenty miles. Ludolf thinks, it ought to be reduced to sixteen miles; and others, to half that number, because, Moses refers to the march of Israel through the desert, encumbered with their women and children, their flocks and herds, and the baggage of the whole nation; which must have greatly retarded their movements, and rendered the short distance of eight miles more than sufficient for a journey of one day. It is equally doubtful, whether the distance mentioned by Moses, must be measured from the centre, or from the extremities of the encampment; it is certain, however, that he intends to state the countless numbers of these birds which fell around the tents of Israel.

Some interpreters have doubted, whether the next clause refer to the amazing multitude of these birds which strewed the desert, or to the facility with which they were caught; the wind let them fall by the camp—"as it were two cubits high upon the face of the earth." The Seventy, and after them the Vulgate, render it, They flew, as it were two cubits high above the earth. Others imagine, the quails were piled one above another over all that space, to the height of two cubits; while others suppose, that the heaps which were scattered on the desert with vacant spaces between, for the convenience of those that went forth to collect them, rose to the height of two cubits. The second opinion seems entitled to the preference; for the phrase "to rain," evidently refers to these birds after they had fallen to the ground, upon which they lay numerous as the drops of rain from the dense cloud. Besides, the people could scarcely have gathered ten homers a piece, in two days, if they had not found the quails lying upon the ground; for a homer is the largest measure among the Jews, and contains nearly six pints; according to some Hebrew writers, the load of an ass, from whose name the term is supposed to be derived.—Paxton.

Ver. 15. And when the children of Israel saw *it*, they said one to another, It *is* manna; for they wist not what it *was*. And Moses said unto them, This *is* the bread which the Lord hath given you to eat.

We cannot mistake in this description the natural production which is called, in all the European languages, manna. Manna is the common name for the thick, clammy, and sweet juice, which in the southern countries oozes from certain trees and shrubs, partly by the rays of the sun, partly by the puncture of some kinds of insects, and partly by artificial means. The manna common in our druggists' shops, comes from Calabria and Sicily, where it oozes out of a kind of ash-tree, from the end of June to the end of July, when the bicada appears, an insect at first sight resembling the locust, but is distinguished from it by a thorn under the belly, with which it punctures this tree. The juice issuing from this wound, is in the night fluid, and looks like dew, but in the morning it begins to harden. But the European manna is not so good as the oriental, which is gathered in particular in Syria, Arabia, and Persia; partly from the oriental oak, and partly from a shrub, which is called in Persia, Terengabin or Terendschabin. Rauwolf says, that the manna grains resemble coriander seeds, as mentioned in the Mosaic account; and this is confirmed by several modern travellers. Gmelin remarks, that the manna is as white as snow, and consists of grains like coriander seeds. The peasants about Ispahan gather it at sunrise, holding a sieve under the branch, into which the grains fall when the branches are struck with a stick; if the gathering it be put off till after sunrise, no manna can be obtained, because it melts.—Burder.

The Wady el Sheikh, the great valley of western Sinai, is in many parts thickly overgrown with the tamarisk or tarfa, (*Hedysarum Alhagi* of Linn.) It is the only valley in the peninsula of Sinai where this tree grows, at present, in any great quantity; though small bushes of it are here and here met with in other parts. It is from the tarfa that the manna is obtained. This substance is called by the Bedouins *mann*, and accurately resembles the description of manna given in the scriptures. In the month of June, it drops from the thorns of the tamarisk upon the fallen twigs, leaves, and thorns which always cover the ground beneath that tree in the natural state; the manna is collected before sunrise, when it is coagulated; but it dissolves as soon as the sun shines upon it. The Arabs clean away the leaves, dirt, etc. which adhere to it, boil it, strain it through a coarse piece of cloth, and put it in leathern skins: in this way they preserve it till the following year, and use it as they do honey, to pour over unleavened bread, or to dip their bread into. I could not learn that they ever made it into cakes or loaves. The manna is found only in years when copious rains have fallen; sometimes it is not produced at all. I saw none of it among the Arabs, but I obtained a small piece of the last year's produce, in the convent (of Mount Sinai,) where, having been kept in the cool shade and moderate temperature of that place, it had become quite solid, and formed a small cake; it became soft when kept some time in the hand; if placed in the sun for five minutes, it dissolved; but when restored to a cool place, it became solid again in a quarter of an hour. In the season at which the Arabs gather it, it never acquires that state of hardness which will allow of its being pounded, as the Israelites are said to have done, in Num. xi. 8. Its colour is a dirty yellow, and the piece which I saw was still mixed with bits of tamarisk leaves; its taste is agreeable, somewhat aromatic, and as sweet as honey. If eaten in any considerable quantity, it is said to be slightly purgative.

The quantity of manna collected at present, even in seasons when the most copious rains fall, is trifling, perhaps not amounting to more than five or six hundred pounds. It is entirely consumed among the Bedouins, who consider it the greatest dainty which their country affords. The harvest is usually in June, and lasts for about six weeks. In Nubia, and in every part of Arabia, the tamarisk is one of the most common trees; on the Euphrates, on the Astaboras, in all the valleys of the Hedjaz and the Bedja, it grows in great plenty. It is remarked by Niebuhr, that in Mesopotamia, manna is produced by several trees of the oak species; a similar fact was confirmed to me by the son of a Turkish lady, who had passed the greater part of his youth at Erzerum in Asia Minor; he told me that at Moush, a town three or four days distant from Erzerum, a substance is collected from the tree which produces the galls, exactly similar to the manna of the peninsula in taste and consistence, and that it is used by the inhabitants instead of honey. Burckhardt.

The notion, however, that any species of vegetable gum is the manna of the scriptures, appears so totally irreconcilable with the Mosaic narrative, that, notwithstanding the learned names which may be cited in support of the conjecture, it cannot be safely admitted as any explanation of the miracle. It is expressly said, that the manna was rained from heaven; that when the dew was exhaled, it appeared lying on the surface of the ground,—"a small, round thing, as small as the hoar-frost,"—"like coriander seed, and its colour like a pearl;" that it fell but six days in the week, and that a double quantity fell on the sixth day; that what was gathered on the first five days became offensive and bred worms if kept above one day, while that which was gathered on the sixth day kept sweet for two days; that the people had never seen it before, which could not possibly be the case with either wild-honey or gum-arabic; that it was a substance which admitted of being ground in a handmill or pounded in a mortar, of being made into cakes and baked, and that it tasted like wafers made with honey; lastly, that it continued falling for the forty years that the Israelites abode in the wilderness, but ceased on their arriving at the borders of Canaan. To perpetuate the remembrance of the miracle, a pot of the manna was to be laid up by the side of the ark, which clearly indicates the extraordinary nature of the production. In no one respect does it correspond to the modern manna. The latter does not fall from heaven, it is not deposited with the dew, but exudes from the trees when punctured, and is to be found only in the particular spots where those trees abound; it could not, therefore, have supplied the Israelites with food in the more arid parts of the desert, where they most required it. The gums, moreover, flow only for about a month in the year; they neither admit of being ground, pounded, or baked; they do not melt in the sun; they do not breed worms; and they are not peculiar to the Arabian wilderness. Others have supposed the manna to have been a fat and thick honey-dew, and that this was the wild-honey which John the Baptist lived upon,—a supposition worthy of being ranked with the monkish legend of St. John's bread, or the locust-tree, and equally showing an entire ignorance of the nature of the country. It requires the Israelites to have been constantly in the neighbourhood of trees, in the midst of a wilderness often bare of all vegetation. Whatever the manna was, it was clearly a substitute for bread, and it is expressly called meat, or food. The abundant supply, the periodical suspension of it, and the peculiarity attaching to the sixth day's supply, it must at all events be admitted, were preter natural facts, and facts not less extraordinary than that the substance also should be of an unknown and peculiar description. The credibility of the sacred narrative cannot receive the slightest addition of evidence from any attempt to explain the miracle by natural causes. That narrative would lead any plain reader to expect that the manna should no longer be found to exist, having ceased to fall upwards of 3,000 years. As to the fact that the Arabs give that name to the juice of the *tarfa*, the value of their authority may be estimated by the pulpit of Moses and the footstep of Mohammed's camel. The cause of Revelation has less to fear from the assaults of open infidels, than from such ill-judged attempts of skeptical philosophers, to square the sacred narrative by their notions of probability. The giving of the manna was either a miracle or a fable. The proposed explanation makes it a mixture of both. It admits the fact of a Divine interposition, yet insinuates that Moses gives an incorrect or embellished account of it. It requires us to believe, that the scripture history is at once true and a complete misrepresentation, and that the golden vase of manna was designed to perpetuate the simple fact, that the Israelites lived for forty years upon gum-arabic! The miracle, as related by Moses, is surely more credible than the explanation.—MODERN TRAVELLER.

Ver. 16. Gather of it every man according to his eating; an omer for every man, (Heb. a head,) *according to* the number of your persons; take ye every man for *them* which *are* in his tents.

A man, when offering money to the people to induce them to do something for him, says, "To every *head*, I will give one fanam." In time of sickness or sorrow, it is said, "Ah! to every *head* there is now trouble." "Alas! there is nothing left for any *head*." "Yes, yes, he is a good master: to every *head* he has given a cow." "What did you pay your coolies?"—"To every *head* one fanam."—ROBERTS.

CHAP. 17. ver. 1. And all the congregation of the children of Israel journeyed from the wilderness of Sin, after their journeys, according to the commandment of the LORD, and pitched in Rephidim: and *there was* no water for the people to drink.

At twenty minutes' walk from the convent of *El Erbayn*, a block of granite is shown as the rock out of which the water issued when struck by the rod of Moses. It is thus described by Burckhardt: "It lies quite insulated by the side of the path, which is about ten feet higher than the lower bottom of the valley. The rock is about twelve feet in height, of an irregular shape, approaching to a cube. There are some apertures upon its surface, through which the water is said to have burst out; they are about twenty in number, and lie nearly in a straight line round the three sides of the stone. They are for the most part ten or twelve inches long, two or three inches broad, and from one to two inches deep, but a few of them are as deep as four inches. Every observer must be convinced, on the slightest examination, that most of these fissures are the work of art; but three or four perhaps are natural, and these may have first drawn the attention of the monks to the stone, and have induced them to call it the rock of the miraculous supply of water. Besides the marks of art evident in the holes themselves, the spaces between them have been chiselled, so as to make it appear as if the stone had been worn in those parts by the action of the water; though it cannot be doubted, that if water had flowed from the fissures, it must generally have taken quite a different direction. One traveller saw on this stone twelve openings, answering to the number of the tribes of Israel; another describes the holes as a foot deep. They were probably told so by the monks, and believed what they heard, rather than what they saw. About 150 paces farther on in the valley, lies another piece of rock, upon which it seems that the work of deception was first begun, there being four or five apertures cut in it, similar to those on the other block, but in a less finished state. As it is somewhat smaller than the former, and lies in a less conspicuous part of the valley, removed from the public path, the monks thought proper, in process of time, to assign the miracle to the other. As the rock of Moses has been described by travellers of the fifteenth century the deception must have originated among the monks of an earlier period. As to the present inhabitants of the convent and of the peninsula, they must be acquitted of any fraud respecting it, for they conscientiously believe that it is the very rock from whence the water gushed forth. In this part of the peninsula, the Israelites could not have suffered from thirst. The upper Sinai is full of wells and springs, the greater part of which are perennial; and on whichever side the pretended rock of Moses is approached, copious sources are found within an hour of it." The fact, that this part of the peninsula abounds with perennial springs, which is attested by every traveller, proves decidedly that this cannot be the vale of Rephidim. It is astonishing to find such travellers as Shaw and Pococke credulously adopting this imbecile legend. "Here," says the former, "we *still* see that extraordinary antiquity, the rock of *Meribah*, which hath continued down to this day, without the least injury from time or accident. It is a block of granite marble, about six yards square, lying tottering as it were, and loose in the middle of the valley, and seems to have formerly belonged to Mount Sinai, which hangs in a variety of precipices all over this plain. The *waters which gushed out*, and *the stream which flowed*, (Psalm lxxviii. 20,) have hollowed, across one corner of this rock, a channel about two inches deep and twenty wide, appearing to be incrustated all over, like the inside of a teakettle that hath been long in use. Besides several mossy productions that are still preserved by the dew, we see all over this channel a great number of holes, some of them four or five inches deep, and one or two in diameter, the lively and demonstrative tokens of their having been formerly so many fountains. It likewise may be further observed, that art or chance could by no means be concerned in the contrivance, for every circumstance points out to us a miracle, and, in the same manner with the rent in the rock of Mount Calvary, at Jerusalem, never fails to produce a religious surprise in all who see it."

That this rock is as truly the Rock of Meribah, as the spot alluded to is *Mount* Calvary, may be freely admitted; but the surprise which they are adapted to awaken in an intelligent observer, is at the credulity of travellers. "These supernatural mouths," says Sir F. Henniker, "appear to me common crevices in the rock: they are only two inches in depth, and their length is not confined to the water-course. That the incrustation is the effect of water, I have not the slightest doubt, for the rocks close at hand, where water is still dripping, are marked in the same manner: and if a fragment of the cliff were to fall down, we should scarcely distinguish between the two. I therefore doubt the identity of the stone, and also the locality; for, in this place, the miracle would be that a mountain so lofty as Mount Sinai should be without water!"—MODERN TRAVELLER.

Ver. 16. For he said, Because the LORD hath sworn *that* the LORD *will have* war with Amalek from generation to generation.

Literally, "Because the hand of the Lord is upon the throne." These words are susceptible of a very different meaning, which has not escaped the notice of some valuable commentators: "For he said, Because his hand hath been *against* the throne of the Lord, therefore, will he have war with Amalek from generation to generation." The prophet is there giving a reason of the perpetual war which Jehovah had just proclaimed against that devoted race; their hand had been against the throne of the Lord, that is, they had attacked the people whom he had chosen, and among whom he had planted his throne; disregarding, or probably treating with contempt, the miraculous signs of the divine presence which led the way, and warranted the operations of Israel; they attempted to stop their progress, and defeat the promise of Heaven; therefore they dared to lift their hand against the throne of God himself, and were for their presumption, doomed to the destruction which they intended for others. Hence, the custom of laying the hand upon the gospels, as an appeal to God, if not the contrivance of modern superstition, is derived from the practice of some obscure Gentile nation, and has no claim whatever to a more reputable origin.—PAXTON.

CHAP. 19. ver. 1. In the third month, when the

children of Israel were gone forth out of the land of Egypt, the same day came they *into* the wilderness of Sinai.

We were near twelve hours in passing the many windings and difficult ways which lie betwixt the deserts of Sin and Sinai. The latter is a beautiful plain, more than a league in breadth, and nearly three in length, lying open towards the N.E., where we entered it, but is closed up to the southward by some of the lower eminences of Mount Sinai. In this direction, likewise, the higher parts of it make such encroachments on the plain, that they divide it into two, each of them capacious enough to receive the whole encampment of the Israelites. That which lieth to the eastward of the mount, may be the desert of Sinai, properly so called, where *Moses saw the angel of the Lord in the burning bush*, when he was guarding the flocks of Jethro. The convent of St. Catharine is built over the place of this divine appearance: it is near three hundred feet square, and more than forty in height, being partly built with stone, partly with mud only and mortar mixed together. The more immediate place of the Shekinah is honoured with a little chapel, which this old fraternity of St. Basil hath in such esteem and veneration, that, in imitation of Moses, they put off their shoes from off their feet, when they enter or approach it. This, with several other chapels, dedicated to particular saints, are included within the church, as they call it, of the Transfiguration, which is a large beautiful structure, covered with lead, and supported by two rows of marble columns. The floor is very elegantly laid out in a variety of devices in Mosaic work; of the same workmanship, likewise, are both the floor and the walls of the presbyterium, upon the latter whereof is represented the figure of the Emperor Justinian, together with the history of the transfiguration. On the partition, which separates the presbyterium from the body of the church, there is placed a small marble shrine, whereon are preserved the scull and one of the hands of St. Catharine. Mount Sinai hangs over this convent, being called by the Arabs, Jebbel Mousa, the mountain of Moses, and sometimes only, by way of eminence, El Tor, the mountain. St. Helena was at the expense of the stone staircase, that was formerly carried up entirely to the top of it; but, at present, as most of these steps are either removed, washed out of their places, or defaced, the ascent up to it is very fatiguing, and entirely imposed on their votaries as a severe penance. However, at certain distances, the fathers have erected, as so many breathing places, several little chapels, dedicated to one or other of their saints, who are always invoked on these occasions; and, after some small oblation, are engaged to lend their assistance. The summit of Mount Sinai is somewhat conical, and not very spacious, where the Mohammedans, as well as the Christians, have a small chapel for public worship. Here we were shown the place where Moses fasted forty days; where he received the law; where he hid himself from the face of God; where his hand was supported by Aaron and Hur, at the battle with Amalek. After we had descended, with no small difficulty, down the western side of this mountain, we came into the other plain formed by it, which is Rephidim.—SHAW.

The Arabs call Jebbel Musa, the mount of Moses, all that range of mountains at the exterior extremity of the valley of Paran; and to that part of the range on which the convent of St. Catharine stands, they give the name of Tur Sina. This similarity of name, owing most probably to tradition, affords ground for presuming, that the hill which we had now reached was the Sinai of the Jews, on which Moses received the law. It is, indeed, not easy to comprehend how such a multitude of people as the Jews, who accompanied Moses out of Egypt, could encamp in those narrow gullies, amid frightful and precipitous rocks. But, perhaps, there are plains on the other side of the mountain, that we know not of. Two German miles and a half up the mountain stands the convent of St. Catharine. The body of this monastery is a building one hundred and twenty feet in length, and almost as many in breadth. Before it stands another small building, in which is the only gate of the convent, which remains always shut, except when the bishop is here. At other times, whatever is introduced within the convent, whether men or provisions, is drawn up to the roof, in a basket, with a cord and a pulley. The whole building is of hewn stone, which, in such a desert, must have cost prodigious expense and pains. Next day our scheichs brought me an Arab, whom they qualified with the title of scheich of Mount Sinai. Under the conduct of this newly-created lord of Sinai, with our scheichs, I attempted to clamber to the summit of that mountain. It is so steep, that Moses cannot have ascended on the side which I viewed. The Greeks have cut a flight of steps up the rock. Pococke reckons three thousand of these steps to the top of the mountain, or, rather, bare-pointed rock. Five hundred steps above the convent we found a charming spring, which, by a little pains, might be improved into a very agreeable spot. A thousand steps higher, a chapel, dedicated to the Blessed Virgin; and five hundred above this, two other chapels, situated in a plain, which travellers enter by two small gates of mason work. Upon this plain are two trees, under which, at high festivals, the Arabs are regaled at the expense of the Greeks. My Mohammedan guides, imitating the practice which they had seen the pilgrims observe, kissed the images, and repeated their prayers in the chapels. They would accompany me no farther, but maintained this to be the highest accessible peak of the mountain; whereas, according to Pococke, I had yet a thousand steps to ascend. I was, therefore, obliged to return, and content myself with viewing the hill of St. Catharine at a distance.—NIEBUHR.

After reposing in the convent and its delightful garden, the first duty of a pilgrim is, to climb the summit of the *Djebel Mousa*, or mountain of Moses, the road to which begins to ascend immediately behind the walls of the convent. Regular steps (it is said, to the number of 15,000) have been cut all the way up; but they are now either entirely destroyed, or so much damaged by the winter torrents, as to be of very little use. They are ascribed to the munificence of the Empress Helena. "After ascending for about twenty-five minutes," says Burckhardt, "we breathed a short time under a large impending rock, close by which is a small well of water, as cold as ice. At the end of three quarters of an hour's steep ascent, we came to a small plain, the entrance to which from below is through a stone gateway, which in former times was probably closed: a little beneath it, stands, amid the rocks, a small church dedicated to the Virgin. On the plain is a larger building of rude construction, which bears the name of the convent of St. Elias: it was lately inhabited, but is now abandoned, the monks repairing here only at certain times of the year to read mass. Pilgrims usually halt on this spot, where a tall cypress-tree grows by the side of a stone tank, which receives the winter rains. On a large rock in the plain are several Arabic inscriptions, engraved by pilgrims three or four hundred years ago; I saw one also in the Syriac language. According to the Koran and Moslem traditions, it was in this part of the mountain, which is called Djebel Oreb, or Horeb, that Moses communicated with the Lord. From hence a still steeper ascent of half an hour, the steps of which are also in ruins, leads to the summit of Djebel Mousa, where stands the church which forms the principal object of the pilgrimage: it is built on the very peak of the mountain, the plane of which is at most sixty paces in circumference. The church, though strongly built with granite, is now greatly dilapidated by the unremitted attempts of the Arabs to destroy it; the door, roof, and walls are greatly injured.

Some ruins round the church indicate that a much larger and more solid building once stood here; and the rock appears to have been cut perpendicularly with great labour, to prevent any other approach to it than by the southern side. The view from this summit must be very grand, but a thick fog prevented me from seeing even the nearest mountains. About thirty paces from the church, on a somewhat lower peak, stands a poor mosque, without any ornaments, held in great veneration by the Moslems, and the place of their pilgrimage. It is frequently visited by the Bedouins, who slaughter sheep in honour of Moses, and who make vows to him, and entreat his intercession in heaven in their favour. There is a feast-day on which the Bedouins come hither in a mass, and offer their sacrifices. I was told that formerly they never approached the place without being dressed in the Ihram, or sacred mantle, with which the Moslems cover their naked bodies on visiting Mecca, and which then consisted only of a napkin tied round the middle; but this custom has been abandoned for the last forty years. Foreign Moslem pilgrims often repair

MOUNT SINAI AND MOUNT HOREB.—Exod. xxxi. 18. Deut. ix. 8, 9.

to the spot; and even Mohammed Ali Pasha, and his son Tousoun Pasha, gave notice that they intended to visit it, but they did not keep their promise. Close by the footpath, in the ascent from St. Elias to this summit, and at a small distance from it, a place is shown in the rock, which somewhat resembles the print of the forepart of the foot; it is stated to have been made by Mohammed's foot when he visited the mountain. We found the adjacent part of the rock sprinkled with blood, in consequence of an accident which happened a few days before to a Turkish lady of rank, who was on her way from Cairo to Mecca, with her son, and who had resided for some weeks in the convent, during which she had made the tour of the sacred places, barefooted, although she was old and decrepit. In attempting to kiss the mark of Mohammed's foot, she fell, and wounded her head, but not so severely as to prevent her from pursuing her pilgrimage. Somewhat below the mosque is a fine reservoir, cut very deep in the granite rock, for the reception of rain-water.

Mr. Fazakerley says, it is difficult to imagine a scene more desolate and terrific then that which is discovered from the summit of Sinai. A haze limited the prospect, and, except a glimpse of the sea in one direction, nothing was within sight but snow, and huge peaks and crags of naked granite. Sir F. Henniker describes it as a "sea of desolation." "It would seem," he says, "as if Arabia Petræa had once been an ocean of lava, and that while its waves were running literally mountains high, it was commanded suddenly to stand still." He did not ascend the *Djebel Katerin;* but the former traveller did, and speaks of it in the following terms: "The view from hence is of the same kind, only much more extensive than from the top of Sinai: it commands the two seas (gulfs) of Akaba and Suez; the island of Tiraan and the village of Tor were pointed out to us: Sinai was far below us; clouds prevented our seeing the high ground near Suez: all the rest, wherever the eye could reach, was a vast wilderness, and a confusion of granite mountains and valleys destitute of verdure." Burckhardt thus describes the country as seen from this same summit: "From this elevated peak, a very extensive view opened before us, and the direction of the different surrounding chains of mountains could be distinctly traced. The upper nucleus of the Sinai, composed almost entirely of granite, forms a rocky wilderness of an irregular circular shape, intersected by many narrow valleys, and from thirty to forty miles in diameter. It contains the highest mountains of the peninsula, whose shaggy and pointed peaks, and steep and shattered sides, render it clearly distinguishable from all the rest of the country in view. It is upon this highest region of the peninsula, that the fertile valleys are found, which produce fruit-trees: they are principally to the west and southwest of the convent, at three or four hours' distance. Water, too, is always found in plenty in this district, on which account it is the place of refuge of all the Bedouins, when the low country is parched up."—MODERN TRAVELLER.

Ver. 13. There shall not a hand touch it, but he shall surely be stoned, or shot through.

"To be stoned to death was a most grievous and terrible infliction. When the offender came within four cubits of the place of execution, he was stripped naked, only leaving a covering before, and his hands being bound, he was led up to the fatal place, which was an eminence twice a man's height. The first executioners of the sentence were the witnesses, who generally pulled off their clothes for the purpose: one of them threw him down with great violence upon his loins: if he rolled upon his breast, he was turned upon his loins again, and if he died by the fall there was an end; but if not, the other witness took a great stone, and dashed upon his breast, as he lay upon his back; and then, if he was not despatched, all the people that stood by threw stones at him till he died."—LEWIS's *Origines Hebrææ.*

CHAP. 20. ver. 5. Thou shalt not bow down thyself to them, nor serve them: for I the LORD thy God *am* a jealous God, visiting the iniquity of the fathers upon the children unto the third and fourth *generation* of them that hate me.

It is universally believed that children suffer for the iniquities of their ancestors, through many generations. "I wonder why Tamban's son was born a cripple?"—"You wonder! why, that is a strange thing; have you not heard what a vile man his grandfather was?" "Have you heard that Valen has had a son, and that he is born blind?"—"I did not hear of it, but this is another proof of the sins of a former birth." "What a wicked wretch that Venasi is! alas for his posterity, great will be their sufferings." "Evil one, why are you going on in this way; have you no pity for your seed?" "Alas! alas! I am now suffering for the sins of my fathers." When men enjoy many blessings, it is common to say of them, "Yes, yes, they are enjoying the good deeds of their fathers." "The prosperity of my house arises from the virtues of my forefathers." In the Scanda Purāna it is recorded, "The soul is subject to births, deaths, and sufferings. It may be born on the earth, or in the sea. It may also appear in ether, fire, or air. Souls may be born as men, as beasts or birds, as grass or trees, as mountains or gods." By these we are reminded of the question, "Who did sin, this man or his parents, that he was born blind?" "Jesus answered, Neither hath this man sinned, nor his parents."—ROBERTS.

Ver. 18. And all the people saw the thunderings, and the lightnings, and the noise of the trumpet, and the mountain smoking: and when the people saw *it,* they removed and stood afar off.

Large splinters of wood, either of a resinous nature in themselves, or perhaps prepared in some cases by art, are made use of in the Levant instead of flambeaux; and if they are in use in these times, in which great improvements have been made in all the arts of life, it is natural to suppose they were in use anciently, particularly among the peasants, shepherds, and travellers of the lower class. Dr. Richard Chandler found lighted brands made use of in Asia Minor, by some villagers, instead of torches, and he refers to Virgil, representing the Roman peasants as preparing, in his days, the same sort of flambeaux, in winter time, for their use. If they still continue in use in the East, there is reason to believe they were used anciently, and indeed, it seems to be a torch of this kind, that is meant by the Hebrew word לפיד *lappeed,* which our translators sometimes render firebrand, sometimes lamp, thus confounding things that are very distinct, and which are expressed by different words. I would remark further, that as this word is made use of, Exod. xx. 18, and a very different word is used to express lightning in the Hebrew, it is unfortunate that our version should render it lightning there, when it is to be understood, I apprehend, of the flaming of the trees on Mount Sinai, on that memorable occasion, whole trees flaming around the Divine presence, bearing some resemblance to the torches made of splinters of wood, which were made use of on less august occasions: "All the people saw the thunderings, and the trees flaming like so many torches, and the noise of the trumpet, and the mountain smoking; and when the people saw it, they removed and stood afar off." Lightning is understood here without doubt, and that the trees were set on fire by the lightning will hardly be contested; on the other hand, if the word directly meant lightning, still it is evidently supposed the trees and shrubs were fired by it; from whence else would have come the smoke? But as the word signifies torches, not flashes of lightning, it should not have been translated here lightning, differently from what it properly signifies. Agreeable to this account is the description given us, Exod. xix. 18, "And Mount Sinai was altogether on a smoke, because the LORD descended upon it in fire: and the smoke thereof ascended as the smoke of a furnace, and the whole mount quaked greatly."—HARMER.

CHAP. 21. ver. 10. If he take him another *wife;* her food, her raiment, and her duty of marriage, shall he not diminish.

Though *flesh meat* is not wont to be eaten by these nations so frequently as with us in the West, or in such quantities, yet people of rank, who often have it in their repasts, are fond of it, and even those in lower life, when it can be procured. Our translation then does not express the spirit of the Mosaic precept, relating to the superinducing a second wife in the lifetime of the first, Exod. xxi. 10. "Her food, her raiment, and her duty of marriage, shall he not diminish; in the original it is, *her flesh, her raiment*, &c. meaning that he should not only afford her a sufficient quantity of food as before, but of the same quality. The feeding her with bread, with herbs, with milk, &c. in quantities not only sufficient to maintain life, but as much as numbers of poor people contented themselves with, would not do, if he took away the *flesh*, and others of the more agreeable articles of food he had before been wont to allow her.—Harmer.

Ver. 20. And if a man smite his servant, or his maid, with a rod, and he die under his hand; he shall surely be punished. 21. Notwithstanding, if he continue a day or two, he shall not be punished: for he *is* his money.

The people of Israel, like all the nations of antiquity, had the power of life and death over their slaves; for slavery proceeded from the right of conquest, when the victors, instead of putting their enemies to death, chose rather to give them their lives, that they might have the benefit of their services. Hence it was supposed that the conqueror always reserved the power of taking away their lives, if they committed any thing worthy of death; and that he acquired the same power over their children, because they had never been born, if he had not spared the father, and transmitted it when he alienated his slave. Such is the foundation of the absolute power claimed by the Orientals over the unhappy persons whom they detained in slavery. It must be granted, that such reasons never can justify the exorbitant power of a slaveholder, or even his right to deprive his fellow-creature of his liberty, who has been guilty of no adequate crime. The claims of Israel rested upon different grounds, the positive grant of Jehovah himself, who certainly has a right to dispose of his creatures as he pleases. But among that people, the power of the master was limited by laws, which secured the safety and comfort of the slave, perhaps as much as that condition could possibly admit. Though the Israelitish master had the power of life and death, it has been alleged by some writers, that he seldom abused it; for his interest obliged him to preserve his slave, who made a part of his riches. This is the reason of the law, That he should not be punished who had smitten a servant, if he continued alive a day or two after. He is his money, says the lawgiver, to show that the loss of his property was deemed a sufficient punishment; and it may be presumed, in this case, that the master only intended his correction. But if the slave died under the strokes, it was to be supposed the master had a real design to kill him, for which the law commanded him to be punished. But considerations of interest are too feeble a barrier to resist the impulse of passions, inflamed by the consciousness and exercise of absolute power over a fellow-mortal. The wise and benevolent restraints imposed upon a master of slaves, by the law of Moses, clearly prove that he very often abused his power, or was in extreme danger of doing so; for laws are not made for the good, but for the evil-doer.—Paxton.

Chap. 22. ver. 5. If a man shall cause a field or vineyard to be eaten, and shall put in his beast, and shall feed in another man's field; of the best of his own field, and of the best of his own vineyard, shall he make restitution.

See on Gen. 49. 11.

Chandler observes, (*Travels in Asia Minor*,) that the tame cattle were very fond of *vine leaves*, and were permitted to eat them in the autumn. "We remarked," he says, "about Smyrna, the leaves were decayed, or stripped by the camels and herds of goats, which are admitted to browse after the vintage." If those animals are so fond of vine leaves, it is no wonder that Moses, by an express law, forbad *a man's causing another man's vineyard to be eaten by putting in his beast*. The turning any of them in before the fruit was gathered, must have occasioned much mischief; and even after it must have been an injury, as it would have been eating up another's feed.—Harmer.

Ver. 6. If fire break out, and catch in thorns, so that the stacks of corn, or the standing corn, or the field, be consumed *therewith*; he that kindleth the fire shall surely make restitution.

It is a common management in the East, to set the dry herbage on fire before the autumnal rains, which fires, for want of care, often do great damage. Moses has taken notice of fires of this kind, and by an express law has provided, that reparation shall be made for the damage done by those who either maliciously or negligently occasioned it. Chandler, speaking of the neighbourhood of Smyrna, says, "In the latter end of July, clouds began to appear from the south; the air was repeatedly cooled by showers which had fallen elsewhere, and it was easy to foretell the approaching rain. *This was the season for consuming the dry herbage and undergrowth on the mountains*: and we often saw the fire blazing in the wind, and spreading a thick smoke along their sides." He also relates an incident to which he was an eyewitness. Having been employed the latter end of August, in taking a plan at Troas, one day after dinner, says he, a Turk coming to us, "emptied the ashes from his pipe, and a spark of fire fell unobserved in the grass, which was long, parched by the sun, and inflammable like tinder. A brisk wind soon kindled a blaze, which withered in an instant the leaves of the bushes and trees in its way, seized the branches and roots, and devoured all before it with prodigious crackling and noise. We were much alarmed, as a general conflagration of the country seemed likely to ensue." After exerting themselves for an hour, they at length *extinguished* it. It is an impropriety worth correcting in this passage, where the word *stacks* of corn is used rather than *shocks*, which is more conformable to custom, as the *heaps* of the East are only the disposing of corn into a proper form to be immediately trodden out. The stacking of corn, in our agricultural language means, the collecting corn in the straw into heaps, larger or smaller as it happens, designed to continue for some considerable space of time. They are not wont to stack corn, in our sense of the word, in those countries. The term *shock*, by which the word גדיש *gadeesh* is translated in two other places, is less exceptionable, but not perfectly expressive of the original idea. We put together, or heap up our corn, not fully ripe, in parcels which are called shocks, that it may more perfectly ripen after being cut, but the original word גדיש *gadeesh*, means a heap of corn, fully ripe, see Job v. 26; means, in a word, the heaps of the eastern threshing-floors, ready to be trodden out.—Harmer.

Ver. 26. If thou at all take thy neighbour's raiment to pledge, thou shalt deliver it unto him by that the sun goeth down: 27. For that *is* his covering only; it *is* his raiment for his skin: wherein shall he sleep? and it shall come to pass, when he crieth unto me, that I will hear: for I *am* gracious.

The clothes which the Orientals wear by day, serve them as *bed-clothes* for the night. Does a man wish to retire to rest, he needs not to trouble himself about the curtains, he requires not the bed-steps, he does not examine whether his bolsters or pillows are in order, he is not very particular about the adjustment of his sheets and counterpane; he throws a mat on the floor, places his little travelling bag or turban for a pillow, takes off his cloth, (which is generally about nine yards long,) puts one end under him; then covers his feet, and folds the rest round his body, leaving the upper end to cover his face. Thus may be seen coolies in the morning, stretched side by side, having, during the night, defied all the stings of their foes, the moschetoes.—Roberts.

The upper garment of the Israelites was a large square cloth which folded round the whole body, and served the poor as a bed-covering during the night. Less alteration than could have been expected has taken place in the dress of the eastern people. This garment was still found by Shaw in the eighteenth century, among the Bedouin Arabs in the north of Africa, under the Arabian name of Hyke, *i. e.* texture, covering. In fair weather this cloth is therefore mostly worn on the shoulders, as

Niebuhr observes in his *Description of Arabia.* "It will not, perhaps, be imagined," says he, "that the above-mentioned little clothing constitutes the whole bedding of a common Arab. He spreads out his great girdle, and so he has a bed to lie down upon: with the cloth which he wears on his shoulders, he covers his whole body and face, and sleeps naked between these two cloths, quite happy and contented."—ROSENMULLER.

In all parts of Southern Africa, the skin cloak is the covering of males and females by day, and that in which they sleep by night: they have no other bed-clothes. The Hottentot cloak is composed of sheep skins, retaining the wool on the inside of it, in which he sleeps comfortably under a bush or tree wherever he goes. Deprive him of that covering, and he would find himself most uncomfortably placed. It would be a cruel act. The nations farther in the interior, have cloaks made from hides of oxen or cows, which they have a method of rendering soft and pliable, and use exactly for the same purposes as the others, viz. for clothing and for sleeping in. The Israelites sleeping in the wilderness in this simple manner, would be always ready to remove when the trumpet intimated the moving of the pillar of fire; like the dogs, when they shook themselves, they might be said to be dressed and ready to march. The God who gave such a humane, considerate law to the Israelites, might well be called a gracious God. —AFRICAN LIGHT.

CHAP. 23. ver. 4. If thou meet thine enemy's ox or his ass going astray, thou shalt surely bring it back to him again.

Among the Hindoos, malice often finds its victim in a dumb animal. If the wretch cannot revenge himself on the man, he will on his beast. The miscreant watches till the cattle go astray, or the owner shall be out of the way, when he pounces upon the innocent ox or cow, and cuts off the tail. Hence may be seen, in every village, cattle which thus proclaim the diabolical passions of man.—ROBERTS.

Ver. 17. Three times in the year all thy males shall appear before the LORD God.

To those that may wonder how Jerusalem could receive such multitudes, as were obliged by the Jewish law to attend there three times a-year, and as we know did sometimes actually appear in it, I would recite the account that Pitts gives of Mecca, the sacred city of the Mohammedans, and the number he found collected together there, for the celebration of their religious solemnities, in the close of the 17th century. This city, he tells us, he thought he might safely say, had not one thousand families in it of constant inhabitants, and the buildings very mean and ordinary. That four caravans arrive there every year, with great numbers of people in each, and the Mohammedans say, there meet not fewer than seventy thousand souls at these solemnities; and that though he could not think the number quite so large, yet that it is very great. How such numbers of people, with their beasts, could be lodged and entertained in such a little town as Mecca, is a question he thus answers. "As for house-room, the inhabitants do straiten themselves very much, in order at this time to make their market. As for such as come last, after the town is filled, they pitch their tents without the town, and there abide until they remove towards home. As for provision, they all bring sufficient with them, except it be of flesh, which they may have at Mecca; but all other provisions, as butter, honey, oil, olives, rice, biscuit, &c. they bring with them, as much as will last through the wilderness, forward and backward, as well as the time they stay at Mecca; and so for their camels they bring store of provender, &c. with them." The number of Jews that assembled at Jerusalem at their passover was much greater: but had not Jerusalem been a much larger city than Mecca is, as in truth it was, yet the present Mohammedan practice of abiding under tents, and carrying their provisions and bedding with them, will easily explain how they might be accommodated.—BURDER.

Ver. 19. Thou shalt not seethe a kid in his mother's milk.

The Jewish legislator three times forbids his people to "seethe a kid in his mother's milk." The meaning of this law has been greatly disputed, although the terms in which it is couched, are sufficiently clear and precise. It is the opinion of some writers, that the prohibition refers to a kid in the womb of its mother, which in that state is nourished only with milk; but the opinion of Clemens, that the people of Israel had been in the practice of eating the fœtus of a goat, which this precept was intended to prohibit, is supported by no proof. The disgusting custom of eating the fœtus of a sow, is indeed mentioned by Plutarch; but we have no proof that it was known to epicures in the times of Moses. Other expositors imagine, that the Jews were by this precept forbidden to take away the life of a kid, before it was eight days old, when, according to them, it may subsist without the aid of its mother's milk. This exposition is supposed to be confirmed by another precept: "When a bullock, or a sheep, or a goat is brought forth, then it shall be seven days under the dam; and from the eighth day, and thenceforth, it shall be accepted for an offering made by fire unto the Lord." But since the law, which prohibited the people of Israel to offer in sacrifice, "the young of the herd, or of the flock," before the eighth day, is immediately subjoined to the precept concerning the oblation of the first ripe fruits, and the first-born, in the twenty-second chapter of Exodus; so, in the twenty-third and thirty-fourth chapters, the law which forbids to seethe a kid in his mother's milk, follows the same precept; and by consequence, not only the sacred, but also the common use of the kid, is prohibited before the eighth day. Such is the opinion, and the reasoning by which it is supported; but it must be evident to every reader, that a kid is as much in his mother's milk all the time he is suckled, as during the first eight days; nor can any reason be imagined, why he may not be said to be in his mother's milk on the seventh day from his birth, rather than on the eighth or the ninth. Others are of opinion, that, according to this precept, a sucking kid was at no time to be slain, either for sacred or common use. The she-goat suckles her young about three months; and till this period, it was not to be subjected to the sacrificing knife. But it is very improbable, that the Jews were forbidden the use of a kid for so long a time; for that which the law permits to be offered in sacrifice to God, may surely be eaten by his people. Nor was any species of food prohibited by the law, but for ceremonial impurity. But that cannot be reckoned legally unclean, which the law permits to be offered in sacrifice at the altar. He permitted a sucking kid or lamb, to be offered on the eighth day; a sure proof they were not reckoned unclean, while they remained under the dam. The prophet Samuel offered a sucking lamb as a burnt-offering to the Lord on a day of public humiliation; and God condescended to give them a strong proof of his acceptance, in utterly discomfiting their enemies, by a furious tempest of thunder and lightning. If, therefore, a sucking kid might be offered in sacrifice to God, it might be used as food by his people. Nor is their opinion more tenable, who say, that by this law the dam and her suckling were not to be slain at the same time. To cherish kind and humane feelings among the chosen seed, Jehovah forbade them to kill a cow, a sheep, or a goat, on the same day with their young; but the precept under consideration cannot naturally bear such a meaning. Had this been the design of Moses, why did he not say in plain terms, Thou shalt not seethe a kid and his mother at the same time? He must, therefore, have meant what the words naturally suggest, that a kid is not to be seethed in the milk of his mother. The barbarous custom to which the lawgiver alludes, probably existed in some neighbouring countries, and particularly in Egypt, from whose iron yoke they had just been delivered; either because the flesh dressed in this manner was more tender and juicy, than when roasted with fire, or boiled in water; or, which is more probable, while at the feast of ingathering, they gave thanks to God for the mercies they had received, and expressed their dependance upon him for future blessings, they were not to expect his favour by imitating the superstitious rites of the heathens, among whom they had lived so long, who at the end of their harvest seethed a kid in his mother's milk, and sprinkled the broth in a magical way upon their gardens and fields, to render them more fruitful next season.—PAXTON.

CHAP. 24. ver. 28. And I will send hornets before thee, which shall drive out the Hivite, the Canaanite, and the Hittite, from before thee.

Another insect which Heaven has sometimes employed to avenge the quarrel of his covenant, is the hornet; which is a larger species of wasp. The irascible temper and poisonous sting of the wasp, are too well known to require description; they have been mentioned by the natural historians, and celebrated by the poets of every age and country. In three parallel places of scripture, the sacred writer mentions the hornet which Jehovah sent before his people, to expel the Canaanites from their habitations: "And I will send hornets before thee, which shall drive out the Hivite, the Canaanite, and the Hittite from before thee." This promise was afterward renewed a short time before that people passed the Jordan: "Moreover, the Lord thy God will send the hornet among them, till they that are left, and hide themselves from thee, be destroyed." Both these promises, we learn from Joshua, were punctually fulfilled: "And I sent the hornet before you, which drave them out from before you, even the two kings of the Amorites, but not with thy sword, nor with thy bow." At what particular time during the wars of Joshua, the Lord, in fulfilment of his promise, sent the hornet against the inhabitants of Canaan, and what impression its attack made upon the enemies of Israel, we are nowhere informed in scripture. On this account, several writers of great eminence consider the words of Moses as a metaphor, denoting the terror of the Lord, or some remarkable disease which he commissioned to lay waste the country before the armies of Israel. But neither the words of Moses nor Joshua, betray the smallest indication of metaphor: and in a plain narration, we are never, without the most obvious necessity, to depart from the literal sense. The inspired historian could not mean the terror of the Lord, as Augustine is inclined to suppose; for he had mentioned this in the verse immediately preceding: "I will send my fear before thee, and will destroy all the people to whom thou shalt come, and I will make all thine enemies turn their backs unto thee." Upon which it is added, "And I will send hornets before thee." Nor could any particular disease be intended; for no disease was ever called by this name. Junius gives a different version: I will send before thee fear or disease as a hornet; but the comparative particle *as*, is not in the text, and must not be supplied by the caprice of translators. The words of Joshua are express, without either metaphor or comparison: "I have sent the hornet before you." It is no valid objection to the literal sense, that the circumstances of time and place are not mentioned by the sacred writer, for this is by no means an unusual omission in the rapid narrative of an inspired historian. To mention but one example: the patriarch Jacob gave to his son Joseph a portion of land, which he took from the Amorite by force of arms; but when or in what place this battle was fought, we are not informed. The hornet, it is probable, marched before the armies of Israel, till the five nations that had been doomed for their numerous and long-continued crimes to destruction, were subdued; which rendered such a circumstantial detail unnecessary and improper. But who can believe, say they, that the hornets of Canaan were so vexatious to the inhabitants, that they were forced to abandon their dwellings, and seek for other habitations? The testimony of an inspired writer ought to silence all such objections; but, in reality, the same thing has not unfrequently happened in the history of the world. Both Athenæus and Eustatheus inform us, that the people about Pæonia and Dardania were compelled by frogs to forsake their native country, and fix their abode in a distant region. If Pliny may be credited, the ancient city of Troy was forced to open her gates, after a war of ten years, not so much by the victorious arms of the Greeks, as by an innumerable host of mice, which compelled the Trojans to desert their houses, and retire to the neighbouring mountains; and in Italy, whole nations were driven from their possession by the same destructive creature, which in immense numbers overran their fields, devoured every green thing, and, grubbing up the roots, converted some of the fairest regions of that country into an inhospitable waste. The Myusians, according to Pausanias, were forced, by swarms of gnats, to desert their city; and the Scythians beyond the Ister, are recorded to have been expelled from their country by countless myriads of bees. But, since the wasp is more vexatious than the bee, its sting more severe, and its hostility more virulent—it is by no means incredible, that many of the Canaanites were forced, by so formidable an enemy, to remove beyond the reach of their attack.—Paxton.

Chap. 25. ver. 5. And rams' skins died red, and badgers' skins, and shittim-wood.

To enter into the history of this animal is unnecessary, as it is mentioned in scripture only on account of its skin. This part of the animal seems to have been in great request among the people of Israel, for it is mentioned among the valuable articles which they were permitted to offer for the tabernacle: "Rams' skins died red, and badgers' skins." These last formed the exterior covering of that splendid structure, and of all the sacred utensils, which the Levites were commanded to spread over them during their march. Of these also the shoes of the mystical bride were formed, when, according to the representation of the prophet, she was richly adorned for the marriage. Jehovah had chosen Israel to be his peculiar people, and had bestowed upon them innumerable favours, but they had become ungrateful and perfidious, like a woman who proves inconstant and unfaithful to her husband, who had raised her from the meanest condition, to the greatest affluence and splendour: "Thou becamest mine. Then I washed thee with water; yes, I thoroughly washed away thy blood from thee, and I anointed thee with oil. I clothed thee also with broidered work, and shod thee with badgers' skin; and I girded thee about with fine linen, and I covered thee with silk." In this passage, badgers' skin is mentioned as a very precious and splendid substance, such as might be made into shoes for ladies of the highest rank, and worn on their marriage day; while, in the book of Exodus, it is represented as very coarse and homely, fit only to be made a covering for the tabernacle, and its furniture, during the journeys of the tribes. These very different representations cannot easily be reconciled, and involve the subject in doubt and uncertainty. And indeed the original word (תחש) *tahash*, which our translators render badgers' skins, is of very uncertain meaning. It is evident from scripture, that it was a kind of skin which, being capable of resisting rain, was manufactured by the people of Israel into coverings for the tabernacle and its furniture, and into shoes for persons of the highest rank in the state. But the inspired writers furnish no details from which it can be inferred, to what animal it originally belonged; it is even extremely doubtful, whether the word rendered badger, denotes an animal at all. The Seventy interpreters considered it merely as the name of a colour, and uniformly translate it hyacinth, or hyacinthine. In this opinion, they were followed by all the ancient translators of the scripture, without one exception; and the same idea has been adopted by the learned Bochart, and other eminent moderns. The reasons on which their interpretation is founded, seem to be quite conclusive. In the first place, no evidence can be found that the badger ever existed in Palestine, Arabia, or Egypt. Dr. Shaw made particular inquiry, but could hear of no such animal in Barbary. Harmer was unable to discover in modern travellers, the smallest traces of the badger in Egypt, or in any of the adjacent countries; Buffon represents it as unknown in that part of Asia. So little was the badger known to the ancients, that the Greeks had not a word in their language by which to express it; and the Latin term which is supposed to denote this animal, is extremely doubtful. But if the badger is not a native of the East, if it is not to be found in those countries, from whence could the people of Israel in the wilderness, procure its skin to cover the tabernacle? It is an animal of small size, and is nowhere found in great numbers; and, by consequence, its skin could not, in remote times, more than at present, constitute an article of commerce in the ports of Egypt, and come at last into the possession of that people. The exterior covering of the tabernacle, and its bulky utensils, must have required a greater number of skins than could be procured even in the native country of the badger; and therefore, it must have been formed of leather, fabricated from the skin of some other animal, which not only existed, but also abounded in Egypt, and the adjacent countries. The coarseness of the leather, fabricated of badgers' skin, which in the East is reluctantly employed for the meanest purposes of life, forbids us to consider it as the material of which the elegant shoes of an oriental lady are formed. When the prophet says in the name of the Lord, "I clothed thee also with broidered work, and shod thee with badgers' skin, and I girded thee about with fine linen, and I covered thee with silk," he certainly meant, that the shoes, corresponding to the other parts of the dress, were formed of costly materials. The Targum accordingly translates the passage, "I put precious shoes upon thy feet;" but this could be said with no propriety of shoes made of badgers' skins. Nor can it be supposed, that the skin of an animal, which the law of Moses pronounces unclean, strictly enjoins the people of Israel not to touch, or if they did happen to touch it, not to worship at the tabernacle, till the ceremonial pollution which they accidentally contracted was removed according to the precept,—would be employed to cover that sacred structure, and its consecrated utensils, and that the Levites should be obliged often to handle it in performing the duties of their office. The sacred implements of Jewish worship, certainly were defended from the injuries of the weather by the skins of clean beasts, which were easily procured, and that in sufficient numbers, even in the wilderness. This idea, so conformable to the spotless purity required in the ceremonial law, has been adopted and maintained by all the earlier Jewish writers, whose authority in matters of this kind is entitled to great respect. Many disputes indeed have been agitated among them, in relation to the particular animal employed; but none of them before the time of Jarchi, who flourished about the middle of the eleventh century, supposed that it was the skin of the badger. These considerations leave no room for doubt in the mind of the writer, that the original term denotes neither the badger, nor any other animal, but merely a colour. What particular colour is meant, it may not be easy to ascertain; but when it is considered, that the people of rank and fashion in the East, were accustomed to appear in purple shoes, it is extremely probable, that purple was the colour intended by the sacred writer. The Chaldee Paraphrast accordingly, expounds the words of the Song, "How beautiful are thy feet with shoes," how beautiful are the feet of Israel, when they go up to appear three times before the Lord in purple sandals! The Roman emperors, and the kings of Persia, reserved by a formal edict, shoes of a purple colour for their own use; and it is said, red shoes were among the insignia of the ancient kingdom of Bulgaria. Hence, Isaac Comnenus, the Roman emperor, deprived the patriarch of Constantinople of his dignity, because he presumed to put on shoes of a crimson colour, although these were formerly worn at Rome by persons of the senatorial order.—PAXTON.

Ver. 10. And they shall make an ark *of* shittim-wood: two cubits and a half *shall be* the length thereof, and a cubit and a half the breadth thereof, and a cubit and a half the height thereof.

Concerning the shitta tree, mentioned by the prophet Isaiah with the cedar and the myrtle, different opinions are entertained by commentators. The name is derived from the Hebrew verb *Shata, to decline or turn to and fro*, having for the plural *Shittim*. It is remarkable for being the wood of which the sacred vessels of the tabernacle were made. The Seventy interpreters generally render it by the term ασηπτα, incorruptible. Theodotion, and after him the Vulgate, translate it by Spina, a thorn. The shittim-wood, says Jerome, resembles the white thorn in its colour and leaves, but not in its size; for the tree is so large, that it affords very long planks. Hasselquist also says it grows in Upper Egypt, to the size of a large tree. The wood is hard, tough, smooth, without knots, and extremely beautiful. This kind of wood grows only in the deserts of Arabia; but in no other part of the Roman empire. In another place he remarks, it is of an admirable beauty, solidity, strength, and smoothness. It is thought he means the black acacia, the only tree found in the deserts of Arabia. This plant is so hard and solid, as to become almost incorruptible. Its wood has the colour of the Lotus tree; and so large, that it furnishes plank twelve cubits long. It is very thorny, and even its bark is covered with very sharp thorns; and hence it perhaps had the Hebrew name *Shata* from making animals decline or turn aside by the sharpness of its spines. The interpretation now given, seems to be confirmed by the following remark of Dr. Shaw: "The acacia being by much the largest and the most common tree of these deserts, we have some reason to conjecture, that the shittim-wood, of which the several utensils of the tabernacle were made, was the wood of the acacia. This tree abounds with flowers of a globular figure, and of an excellent smell; which is another proof of its being the shitta tree of the scriptures, which, in the prophecies of Isaiah, is joined with the myrtle and other sweet-smelling plants." Besides, we have no reason to conclude, that the people of Israel possessed any species of wood for making the utensils of the tabernacle, but what they could procure in the desert; but the desert produces none in the quantity required, except the acacia. In one place they found seventy-two palm-trees: but the sacred writer distinguishes them by their vulgar name; therefore they could not be the same tree; nor is the palm, which is a soft spongy wood, at all fit for the purpose,—for the nature of the utensils, as the ark of the testimony and the mercy-seat, required wood of a fibre the hardest, the most beautiful and durable which could be found, had it been in their power to make a choice; and these are the very characters of the acacia. To these important qualities may be added, the fragrant odour emitted by this wood, which to Orientals who delight in rich perfumes, must have been a powerful recommendation. But if the acacia was perfectly suited to the purpose of Moses, and if the desert produces no other, as Dr. Shaw declares, the shittim-wood mentioned in the scriptures must be the acacia of the natural historian.—PAXTON.

CHAP. 26. ver. 1. Moreover, thou shalt make the tabernacle *with* ten curtains *of* fine twined linen, and blue, and purple, and scarlet: *with* cherubims of cunning work shalt thou make them.

It seems that the tabernacle, as it was ordered in the plan given, might be called a tent or a house, because it had wooden walls or partitions like a house, and curtains and hangings like a tent; but as it *externally* resembled a *tent*, and that a common oblong tent, such as those of the Arabs, for the most part, now are, and the wooden walls were without a roof, and properly only supports for the many curtains and hangings which spread over them, it is better and more properly called a tent. Even the ordinary tents of the wandering tribes of the East have at least two main divisions; the innermost or hindmost is for the women; and, among the Orientals, it is in this sense *sacred, i. e.* parted off, inaccessible. The first space is divided from the innermost only by a curtain, and is for the men; what is found in the tents of the common people is found also, but far more rich and splendid, in the tents of the men of rank. The tent of an emir or prince has more conveniences; the innermost space is only accessible to himself, or to those whom he especially honours: into the first space, or outer tent, others may come. The furniture is costly, the floor is covered with a rich carpet, and a stand, with the censer and coals, on which incense is strewed. Here we have the simple idea after which this royal tent, this abode of God, who was at the same time king of the Hebrew people, was made. It was not to be a house or a palace, but a tent, and that with all the magnificence which the skill of the Hebrews in architecture could erect. The boards for the standing walls were covered with plates of gold; twenty boards, which served as pillars to the supporters, standing upright, joined together, each three feet broad and twenty high, made on each side the length, and eight the breadth, so that eight-and-forty such boards, twenty in the length on each side, and eight for the breadth of the back wall, (for the front side had only a curtain,) resting upon two silver sockets, formed the partition. This oblong quadrangle was separated into two parts or divisions; the innermost, or the most holy; and the front, or the holy. The innermost was properly the dwelling of the Lord, the front one was more for his service. The inner division was very considerable, sixty feet long, twenty feet broad, and twenty high; and, as over this extensive frame-work several covers were spread, which hung down on three sides, (that is, all round except at the entrance,) this also gave the tent a greater appearance, so that it was undoubtedly distinguished by its size. In the coverings of the tents, the Orientals, who are fond of magnificence, regard both the stuff and the colour: this royal tent was to be distinguished in both particulars. The curtain, which lay immediately under the beams, was the most beautiful and the most costly. On the finest linen stuff were embroidered cherubims of the most beautiful colours, dark blue, purple, and scarlet. Thus the tents of eastern princes, even in our days, are distinguished by most beautiful colours. Olearius, accompanying the ambassadors of Holstein Gottorf, who were invited by the Persian monarch to a hunting party, found in an Armenian village many tents, ready for the reception of the company, which afforded a pleasing sight on account of their manifold colours. Over the under curtain a covering of goats' hair was spread, which is the usual covering of the Arabian tents, commonly coarse, but here of the finest texture; and, that these coverings might not be injured by the sand or dust, two others, made of skins, were laid over them. The portable temple of the Israelites had, indeed, in its whole arrangement, a resemblance with the temples of other nations of antiquity. As they had spacious forecourts, so had the tabernacle an oblong quadrangular forecourt, two hundred feet long, and one hundred broad, which was formed by the hangings or curtains which hung on pillars. The tabernacle itself was divided into two parts, the holy and the most holy; in the latter was the ark of the covenant, with the symbols of the divine qualities, the cherubims; and no human being dared to enter this especially sanctified place, except the high-priest, once a year, (on the feast of reconciliation.) Thus, also, in many Grecian temples, the back part was not to be entered by anybody. (Lackemacher's Antiq. Græcor. Sacr.) This part, where, in the heathen temples, the statue of the deity was placed, was generally towards the west, and the entrance towards the east. (Spencer de Leg. Hebræor. Ritual.) In the same manner the entrance of the tabernacle was towards the east, and, consequently, the most holy place to the west. In the most holy, a solemn darkness reigned, as in most of the ancient temples. A richly-worked curtain divided the most holy from the holy, and thus, in the Egyptian temples, the back part, where the sacred animal to which the temple was dedicated, was kept, was divided from the front part by a curtain embroidered with gold.—ROSENMULLER.

Ver. 36. And thou shalt make a hanging for the door of the tent, *of* blue, and purple, and scarlet, and fine twined linen, wrought with needle-work.

We passed Lahar, close to a small valley, where we found several snug encampments of the Eelauts, at one of which we stopped to examine the tent of the chief of the *obah*, or family. It was composed of a wooden frame of circular laths, which were fixed on the ground, and then covered over with large felts, that were fastened down by a cord, ornamented by tassels of various colours. A curtain, curiously worked by the women, with coarse needle-work of various colours, was suspended over the door. In the king of Persia's tents, magnificent *perdahs*, or hangings of needle-work, are suspended, as well as on the doors of the great mosques in Turkey; and these circumstances combined, will, perhaps, illustrate *Exodus* xxvi. 36.—MORIER.

CHAP. 27. ver. 20. And thou shalt command the children of Israel, that they bring thee pure oil-olive beaten for the light, to cause the lamp to burn always.

By the expression *oil-olive*, this oil is distinguished from other kinds. The addition *beaten*, indicates that it is that oil obtained from olives pounded in a mortar, and not pressed from olives in the oil-mill. The oil obtained from pounded olives is, according to Columella's observation, much purer and better tasted, does not emit much smoke, and has no offensive smell.—BURDER.

CHAP. 28. ver. 33. And *beneath*, upon the hem of it, thou shalt make pomegranates *of* blue, and *of* purple, and *of* scarlet, round about the hem thereof; and bells of gold between them round about.

The bell seems to have been a sacred utensil of very ancient use in Asia. Golden bells formed a part of the ornaments of the pontifical robe of the Jewish high-priest, with which he invested himself upon those grand and peculiar festivals, when he entered into the sanctuary. That robe was very magnificent, it was ordained to be of sky-blue, and the border of it, at the bottom, was adorned with pomegranates and gold bells intermixed equally, and at equal distances. The use and intent of these bells is evident from these words: "And it shall be upon Aaron to minister, and his sound shall be heard when he goeth in unto the holy place before the Lord, and when he cometh out, that he die not." The sound of the numerous bells that covered the hem of his garment, gave notice to the assembled people that the most awful ceremony of their religion had commenced. When arrayed in this garb, he bore into the sanctuary the vessel of incense; it was the signal to prostrate themselves before the Deity, and to commence those fervent ejaculations which were to ascend with the column of that incense to the throne of heaven. "One indispensable ceremony in the Indian Pooja is the ringing of a small bell by the officiating brahmin. The women of the idol, or dancing girls of the pagoda, have little golden bells fastened to their feet, the soft harmonious tinkling of which vibrates in unison with the exquisite melody of their voices." (MAURICE's *Indian Antiquities.*) "The ancient kings of Persia, who, in fact, united in their own persons the regal and sacerdotal office, were accustomed to have the fringes of their robes adorned with pomegranates and golden bells. The Arabian courtesans, like the Indian women, have little golden bells fastened round their legs, neck, and elbows, to the scund of which they dance before the king. The Arabian princesses wear golden rings on their fingers, to which little bells are suspended, as well as in the flowing tresses of their hair, that their superior rank may be known, and they themselves, in passing, receive the homage due to their exalted station."—CALMET.

Ver. 41. And thou shalt put them upon Aaron thy brother, and his sons with him; and shalt anoint them, and consecrate them, and sanctify them, that they may minister unto me in the priest's office.

The Hebrew has for "consecrate," "fill their hands.' See also Judges xvii. 5, 12, and 1 Kings xiii. 33, and many other places where the word "consecrate" is in the margin rendered "*fill the hand.*" Is it not a remarkable fact that the word Kai-Reppi, which signifies, in Tamul, to *consecrate a priest*, also means to *fill the hand?* When a layman meets a priest, he puts his hands together as an act of reverence, and the priest stretches out his right hand, as if full of something, and says, "Blessings."—ROBERTS.

CHAP. 29. ver. 22. Also thou shalt take of the ram the fat and the rump.

Or the large tail of one species of the eastern sheep. Russell, (*Hist. of Aleppo*, p. 51,) after observing that they are in that country much more numerous than those with smaller tails, adds, "this tail is very broad and large, terminating in a small appendix that turns back upon it. It is of a substance between fat and marrow, and is not eaten separately, but mixed with the lean meat in many of their dishes, and also often used instead of butter. A common sheep of this sort, without the head, feet, skin, and entrails weighs about twelve or fourteen Aleppo rotoloes, of which the tail is usually three rotoloes or upwards; but such as are of the largest breed, and have been fattened, will sometimes weigh above thirty rotoloes, and the tail of these ten. These very large sheep, being about Aleppo kept up in yards, are in no danger of injuring their tails: but in some other places, where they feed in the fields, the shepherds are obliged to fix a piece of thin board to the under part of their tail, to prevent its being torn by bushes and thistles, as it is not covered underneath with thick wool like the upper part. Some have small wheels to facilitate the dragging of this board after them." A rotoloe of Aleppo is five pounds. With this agrees the account given by the Abbé Mariti, (*Travels through Cyprus.*) "The mutton is juicy and tender. The tails of some of the sheep, which are remarkably fine, weigh upwards of fifty pounds." This shows us the reason why, in the levitical sacrifices, the tail was always ordered to be consumed by fire.—BURDER.

Ver. 24. For I will cast out the nations before thee, and enlarge thy borders: neither shall any man desire thy land, when thou shalt go up to appear before the LORD thy God thrice in the year.

I find in Exod. xxxiv. 24, a very remarkable promise of God, which could hardly have been fulfilled in the common course of providence, and without a miracle, unless the Israelites and other neighbours had in their wars observed a certain law of truce, quite strange to us, and which I only know from the customs of the Arabs. Moses commands all the males of Israel to leave their homes thrice a year, and celebrate a festival for a week at the place where the tabernacle should be erected; assuring them, withal, that during this period, *no man should desire their land;* and that, therefore, however distant their abodes might be from the sanctuary, they might undertake this journey with perfect safety. According to the present course of things in the world, this is quite incomprehensible. Were all the males to leave certain parts of the country, and still more, the fortified cities, the greatest of all wonders would be, the enemy with whom the nation happened to be at war, refraining from seizing the opportunity to occupy the fortresses,—to plunder and burn the open country,—and to forage the corn-fields. And it is most obvious, that the danger of all this will be still greater among nations who do not maintain settled peace with each other; of which description were the marauding Arabs: or who carry on war rather by incursions than regular campaigns, and have no other object than to make booty in money, produce, women, and children. Shall we then venture so to expound the words of Moses, as if he had promised a periodical miracle from God, which should, for three weeks every year, convert all the enemies of the Israelites into statues? A promise so incredible, will, perhaps, not appear to be necessary, when, to illustrate this point, we call in the aid of the customs of the Arabs, who are Abraham's descendants, and the immediate brethren of the Israelites. In all their wars, and even amid their family feuds, during the holy month, in which they solemnized the festival at Mecca, they had a truce. Mohammed's greatest transgression is, that he is said to have broken this truce. Yet, in the Koran, he has commanded his followers to keep it only when their adversaries keep it; and he permits them to fight against the enemy during the holy month, only when he makes the first attack. Thus we see, in like manner, from 1 Kings xii. 27, that among the Israelites, during the high festivals, a suspension of arms took place; and the ten tribes who had revolted from the family of David, might, without hinderance, have kept the feast at Jerusalem, and would have done so, had not Jeroboam, for political reasons, endeavoured to prevent them. The Judahites, therefore, did not put any obstacle in their way; and they would *then* have been in as perfect security at Jerusalem, as, before Mohammed's time, every Arab during the holy month was at Mecca. It would appear, then, that the nations related to the Israelites, paid equal respect to the worship of God, and made a truce during war, whenever the people celebrated a festival. But probably the Canaanites were, both in religion and manners, so different from the Israelites, that they did not observe any such truce; for Moses expressly says on this occasion, that God would destroy the Canaanites; and *then*, no other people would conceive any desire to attack the land of Israel during the seasons of the festivals.

Now such a law of nations once introduced, God *might* fulfil his promise in the common course of providence, and without the aid of a miracle. This sacred truce, which is, however, quite unsuitable to the more connected operations of modern warfare, was likewise probably the cause, wherefore the commandment respecting the Sabbath could be given without any particular limitation. For on that day, all labour was prohibited. Moses does not, indeed, expressly specify fighting, marching, intrenching; but neither does he expressly except them. Now although, in a rational consideration of the matter, the justice of these exceptions, in cases of necessity, is manifest; this silence seems, nevertheless, to be a defect in the law; and a nation who in this point had even the smallest scruple of conscience, would make but a poor figure in war. We see in fact, that after the Babylonish captivity, when, as St Paul says, (Heb. viii. 7—13,) the law began to be useless from its antiquity, the observance of the Sabbath became very prejudicial to the Jews in their wars with the Syrians and Romans. For the former on the Sabbath attacked them, and burnt thousands of them in a cave, without their making any resistance: and the latter, in their first siege of Jerusalem under Pompey, carried on the works of investment undisturbed, and only guarded against attempting to storm the city, because against a storm the Jews defended themselves even on the Sabbath. But since, before the captivity, we never find, that in their numerous wars, the Sabbath had been detrimental to the Jews, or that any of their enemies availed himself of the advantage it gave him; the Israelites must either, from ancient and undoubted usage, have known that the commandment concerning the Sabbath did not extend to the operations of war; or else, betwixt them and all the neighbouring nations there must on this day have been a sacred truce. Among the latter, this day, which the Israelites dedicated to the Creator of the heavens and the earth, was probably sacred to *Saturn*, to whom the Phœnicians paid the highest veneration; because, before his being raised to divine honours, or numbered among the stars, he is said to have been king of their country. According to the testimony of Diodorus Siculus, they accounted him the chief of the planets; and the Arabians had, in like manner, dedicated to him their national temple, the Caaba at Mecca.—MICHAELIS.

CHAP. 38. ver. 8. And he made the laver *of* brass and the foot of it *of* brass, of the looking-glasses of *the women* assembling, which assembled *at* the door of the tabernacle of the congregation.

The eastern mirrors were made of *polished* steel, and for the most part *convex*. If they were thus made in the country of Elihu, the image made use of by him will appear very lively. "Hast thou with him spread out the sky, which is strong, and as a molten looking-glass?" (Job xxxvii. 18.) Shaw informs us, that "in the Levant looking-glasses are a part of female dress. The Moorish women in Barbary are so fond of their ornaments, and particularly of their looking-glasses, which they hang upon their breasts, that they will not lay them aside, even when, after the drudgery of the day, they are obliged to go two or three miles with a pitcher, or a goat's skin, to fetch water." The Israelitish women used to carry their mirrors with them, even to their most solemn place of worship. The word *mirror* should be used in the passages here referred to, rather than those which are inserted in the present translation of the Bible. To speak of looking *glasses* made of *steel*, and *glasses molten*, is palpably absurd; whereas the term *mirror* obviates every difficulty, and expresses the true meaning of the original.—BURDER.

LEVITICUS.

CHAPTER II.

Ver. 4. And if thou bring an oblation of a meat-offering baken in the oven, *it shall be* unleavened cakes of fine flour mingled with oil, or unleavened wafers anointed with oil.

What attracted our attention most this stormy day, was the apparatus for warming us. It was the species of oven called *tannoor*, common throughout Armenia and also in Syria, but converted here for purposes of warmth into what is called a *tandoor*. A cylindrical hole is sunk about three feet in the ground in some part of the room, with a flue entering it at the bottom to convey a current of air to the fire which heats it. For the emission of smoke no other provision is made than the open sky-light in the terrace. When used for baking bread, the dough, being flattened to the thickness of common pasteboard, perhaps a foot and a half long by a foot broad, is stuck to its smooth sides by means of a cushion, upon which it is first spread. It indicates, by cleaving off, when it is done, and being then packed down in the family chest, it lasts at least a month in the winter, and ten days in the summer. Such is the only bread known in the villages of Armenia; and even the cities of Erivân and Tebriz offer no other variety than a species perhaps only twice as thick, and so long that it might almost be sold by the yard. To bake it, the bottom of a large oven is covered with pebbles, (except one corner, where a fire is kept constantly burning,) and upon them when heated, the sheets of dough are spread. The convenience of such thin bread, where knives and forks are not used, and spoons are rare, is, that a piece of it doubled enables you to take hold of a mouthful of meat more delicately than with your bare fingers; or, when properly folded, helps you to convey a spoonful safely to your mouth, to be eaten with the spoon itself. When needed for purposes of warmth, the tannoor is easily transformed into a tandoor. A round stone is laid upon the mouth of the oven, when well heated, to stop the draught; a square frame, about a foot in height, is then placed above it; and a thick coverlet, spread over the whole, lies upon the ground around it, to confine the warmth. The family squat upon the floor, and warm themselves by extending their legs and hands into the heated air beneath it, while the frame holds, as occasion requires, their lamp or their food. Its economy is evidently great. So full of crevices are the houses, that an open fireplace must consume a great quantity of fuel, and then almost fail of warming even the air in its immediate vicinity. The tandoor heated once, or at the most twice in twenty-four hours, by a small quantity of fuel, keeps one spot continually warm for the relief of all numb fingers and frozen toes.

The house, apparently the best in the village, was built throughout, floor, walls, and terrace, of mud. Fortunately, as its owner had two wives, it had two rooms. The one assigned us, being the principal family apartment, was of course filled with every species of dirt, vermin, and litter; and withal, as they were in the midst of the process of baking, the insufferable smoke of the dried cow-dung which heated their *tannoor*, or cylindrical oven, detained us a long time before we could take possession. Persuaded at last by impatience that the bread must be done, I entered, and found our host and chief muleteer shaking their shirts in the oven, to dislodge the "crawling creatures" that inhabited them. Though new to us then, we afterward found reason to believe that this use of the tannoor is common, and for it alone we have known it to be heated. In such ovens was our bread baked, by being stuck upon their sides, and though we would fain have quieted our fastidiousness by imagining that they were purified by fire, the nature of the fuel of which that was almost invariably made, left little room upon which to found such a conception. And as for the loathsome company of which our host and muleteer had thus attempted to rid themselves, we found them too constantly affecting our senses to think of imagining them away; for the traveller can hardly journey a day here, or in any part of Turkey, without their annoying him, and his only relief is in a constant change of his linen. The apartment was finally cleared and swept, but the old man could give us neither carpet nor mat, and our own painted canvass and travelling carpets were all that covered the ground on which we sat and slept.—Smith and Dwight.

Mr. Jackson, in his Journey over land from India, gives an account of an eastern oven, equally instructive and amusing, as it confirms the statements of ancient travellers, and shows the surprising expertness of the Arabian women in baking their bread. "They have a small place built with clay, between two and three feet high, having a hole at the bottom for the convenience of drawing out the ashes, something similar to a lime-kiln." The oven, (which he thinks the most proper name for this place,) is usually about fifteen inches wide at top, and gradually widening to the bottom. It is heated with wood; and when sufficiently hot, and perfectly clear from the smoke, having nothing but clear embers at the bottom, which continue to reflect great heat, they prepare the dough in a large bowl, and mould the cakes to the desired size on a board, or stone, placed near the oven. After they have kneaded the cake to a proper consistence, they pat it a little, then toss it about with great dexterity in one hand, till it is as thin as they choose to make it. They then wet one side of it with water, at the same time wetting the hand and arm with which they put it into the oven. The side of the cake adheres fast to the side of the oven, till it is sufficiently baked, when, if not paid proper attention to, it would fall down among the embers. If they were not exceedingly quick at this work, the heat of the oven would burn their arms; but they perform it with such an amazing dexterity, that one woman will continue keeping three or four cakes in the oven at once, till she has done baking. This mode, he adds, requires not half the fuel that is consumed in Europe.—Paxton.

CHAPTER VII.

Ver. 9. And the meat-offering that is baken in the oven, and all that is dressed in the frying-pan, and in the pan, shall be the priest's that offereth it.

Our translation of this passage, presents a confusion more easily perceived than regulated by the general reader:—" And all the meat-offering that is baken in the oven, and all that is dressed in the fryingpan, and in the pan, shall be the priest's that offers it." It is evident that here are three terms used, implying three different manners of dressing food.—Do we understand them? The term, "meat-offering" is certainly unfortunate here, as it raises the idea of flesh-meat, without just reason, to say the least, especially as it stands connected with baking in the oven, תנור. Passing this, the following sentence, also, as it stands connected, expresses a meat-offering, dressed in a frying-pan, מרחשת; and then we have another kind of meat-offering, dressed in the pan, מחבת. Of what nature is this pan? To answer this question, we must dismiss the flesh-meat. Whether the following extract from Denon may contribute assistance on this subject, is submitted with great deference. It is his explanation of his plate LXXXV. "The manner of making macaroni, in Egypt.—The manufactory, and the shop for selling it, are both at once in the street;—an oven, over which a great plate of copper is heated; the maker sheds on it a thin and liquid paste, which is strained through the holes in a kind of cup which he passes up and down on the plate: after a few minutes, the threads of paste are hardened, dried, and baked, by a uniform degree of heat, maintained without intermission, by an equal quantity of branches of palm-tree, by which the oven is kept constantly heated. The same degree of heat is given in the same space of time to an equal quantity of macaroni; which is perpetually renewed on the plate, and sold directly as it is made."—TAYLOR IN CALMET.

Ver. 12. If he offer it for a thanksgiving, then he shall offer with the sacrifice of thanksgiving unleavened cakes mingled with oil, and unleavened wafers anointed with oil, and cakes mingled with oil, of fine flour, fried.

With the exception of two rare cases, oil was ordered to accompany every meal-offering, in order to its being therewith prepared, and baked into cakes. With this law, in so far as it is perhaps typical, and regards a holy ceremony, I have here nothing to do, because I consider it merely with respect to its political influence in the state; and *that*, among a people brought out of Egypt into Palestine, and still always hankering after Egypt, was important. It imperceptibly attached them to their new country, and served to render even the idea of a future residence in Egypt, irksome; while it also imperceptibly gave them an inclination to cultivate the olive-tree, for which nature seems to have pre-eminently adapted Palestine. In the greatest part of Egypt, according to Strabo, no olives were cultivated. It was only in the Heracleotic canton, that they came to such perfection as that oil could be made from them. In the gardens around Alexandria, (which, however, did not exist in the time of the ancient kings, that part of the country being an uncultivated waste till the reign of Alexander the Great,) there were olive-trees, but no oil was made. The consequence of this want of oil was, (as it still is,) that in Egypt they made use of butter, as we do, and also of honey, in their pastry: and even at this day, travellers, going from Egypt into Arabia, carry butter along with them; although, indeed, it is not very tempting to the appetite, because, in consequence of the great heat, it generally melts in the jars by the way. In those parts of Arabia likewise, which the Israelites traversed, and in which they might, perhaps, have thought of settling as wandering herdsmen, scarcely any olives were produced. The oil of Palestine, on the other hand, was not only most abundant, but also peculiarly excellent; and Hasselquist prefers it even to that of Provence. By this gift of nature, stony places and mountains, which would otherwise have been barren, became not only useful, but even more productive, than the best fields could be made. The only part of Palestine which Strabo, that much misquoted author, describes as unfruitful, is that about Jerusalem; and it really is so, in regard to the production of grain: but still the Jews say, that an acre about Jerusalem was formerly of much more value that in any other part of Palestine. This I should not believe on *their* word, if any degree of improbability attached to it; for Jewish accounts from hearsay and oral tradition, have little weight with me. But as long as Palestine was properly cultivated, an acre near Jerusalem, from its produce in wine and oil, must naturally have been more profitable, than as a cornfield. We need only call to mind the *Mount* of Olives, which lay to the east of the city. An acre planted with olives or vines, however rocky and arid the soil may be, will very easily be made worth ten times as much as an acre of the richest corn-land.—The account given by Abulfeda, in his Description of Syria, confirms this statement; for he says, that the country about Jerusalem is one of the most fertile in Palestine. Let us now represent to ourselves the effects of a law which enjoined, that the pastry of offerings should be baked with oil, (and, therefore, not with butter,) and that to every meal-offering so much oil should be added. The priests, who, among the Hebrews, were persons of distinction by birth, were accustomed to oil-pastry; and as their entertainments were generally offering-feasts, the people thus became acquainted with it. Now, what people have once tasted as a luxury at a feast, and found savoury, or heard of as eaten by the great, they begin first to imitate sparingly, and then, if they can, more and more frequently in their daily meals. This was an infallible means to accustom the Israelites to oil-pastry, with which, whoever is once acquainted, will always prefer it to that made with butter. For if the oil is fresh and good, it tastes much better; to which add, that as butter is very liable to spoil, it then communicates to pastry, and every other sort of meat, a disagreeable by-taste.—The worst faults in cookery arise from bad butter. This is a general maxim with our German housewives, particularly in Southern Germany. The natural consequences, then, of the use of oil-pastry, as now mentioned, were, in the first place, that the olive-tree, which formed so principal a source of the riches of the new country of the Israelites, came to be more carefully cultivated, and thus its natural treasures properly improved; and, in the next place, that the people at length lost their desire of returning back to Egypt. That in the time of Moses, they often thought of Egypt with regret, and were even inclined to return to their ancient bondage, we know from his own accounts. Indeed, their *penchant* for this their ancient country was so strong and permanent, that he found it necessary to introduce into the fundamental and unalterable laws of the government, as affecting the king, an express ordinance against all return to Egypt, Deut. xvii. 16. No sooner, however, would the Israelite become rightly acquainted with the chief of nature's gifts to his new country, and accustomed to the use of wine and oil, than his longing after a country, which produced neither, would totally cease. In fact, the object which the statutes, now considered, most probably had in view, was so completely attained, that,

1. Butter was entirely disused among the Israelites. In the whole Hebrew Bible, which contains so many other economical terms, we do not once find the word for butter; for חמאה, which in Job xx. 17. xxix. 6. Deut. xxxii. 14. Judg. v. 25. Isa. vii. 15, 16, 22, is commonly so translated, does not mean *butter*, but *thick milk*. It would therefore appear, that butter had been as rarely to be seen in Palestine, as it now is in Spain; and that the people had made use of nothing but oil in their cookery, as being more delicious. The reason why the LXX. have improperly rendered it *butter*, was this; that their Greek version was made by Egyptian Jews, who, from the want of oil in their new country, were accustomed to the use of butter only.

2. From the time of Joshua until the destruction of their government, the desire of returning to Egypt never once arose among the Israelites. It was only after Nebuchadnezzar had destroyed Jerusalem, and when the remnant of the people no longer thought themselves secure against similar disasters within Palestine, that, contrary to the divine prohibition, the Jews took refuge in Egypt, Jer. xlii. xliv.; and when the kingdom of the ten tribes was destroyed, and Samaria conquered by the Assyrians, many of the Israelites, as we must infer from Hosea, in like manner withdrew thither.—MICHAELIS.

Ver. 26. Moreover, ye shall eat no manner of blood, *whether it be* of fowl, or of beast, in any of your dwellings.

With the prohibition of fat, we find in *two* passages (Lev. iii. 17, and vii. 26, 27,) another prohibition joined, that of eating blood; which, however, occurs also in *five* other passages, (Lev. xvii. 10—14. xix. 26. Deut. xii. 16, 23, 24. xv. 23;) and was binding, not only on the Israelites themselves, but also on all foreigners living among them, under the penalty of death: Lev. xvii. 10. This unusually frequent recurrence of the prohibition, together with the punishment of extirpation from among the people, annexed to the transgression of it; and the denunciation of God's peculiar vengeance against every man who should eat blood, is quite sufficient to show, that the legislator must have been more interested in this, than in the other prohibitions relative to unclean meats, and likewise that the Israelites had had peculiar temptations to transgress it. These *we* really should not have, were blood forbidden to us; and one should think that the person who had not, from infancy, eaten blood, would rather have an antipathy at it. Bloodpuddings, it is true, (like goose and hare,) boiled black, we eat with great relish; but I cannot recollect to have found any person pre-eminently fond of them, but in the single case of their being quite fresh; and that would be the precise case, in which, to a person not previously accustomed to eat them, they would at first be most likely to cause sensations of abhorrence. Add to this, that blood-puddings of ox-blood are by no means so savoury, as ours made of swine's blood are; which cannot, however, be here in question. For they have something of a mealy taste; which, indeed, is very perceptible, when ox-blood is fraudulently mixed with swine's blood. The temptation, therefore, which the Israelites had had to violate this law, must have proceeded from another cause, than from an appetite for blood; and so much the more so, as the eating of blood would appear to have never been a custom of their ancestors; for even the Arabs, who are descended from Abraham, do not eat blood; and Mohammed (as we have seen,) has forbidden them to taste of idol-offerings and blood of beasts strangled, torn, or dead, and of swine's flesh. But before I proceed to state the cause of this so remarkably rigid prohibition of blood, I must observe, that it only extended to the blood of quadrupeds and birds; for the blood of fishes was, on the contrary, permitted to be eaten; Lev. vii. 26, xvii. 13. This point is so clear, that even our modern Jews, who in most things overstretch the law of Moses, make no conscience of eating carp stewed in their own blood. I now come to notice the reason of this prohibition, which we find so urgently repeated. It is connected with one of the grand objects, which the Hebrew legislator always had in view, namely, the exclusion of all manner of idolatry from among his people. Eating of blood, or rather drinking it, was quite customary among the pagan nations of Asia, in their sacrifices to idols, and in the taking of oaths. This, indeed, was so much an Asiatic, and in a particular manner, a Phœnician usage, that we find the Roman writers taking notice of it, as something outlandish at Rome, and peculiar to these nations; and as in the *Roman* persecutions, the Christians were compelled to burn incense, so were they, in the *Persian*, to eat blood. In the West the one, and in the East the other, was regarded as expressive of conversion to heathenism; because both were idolatrous practices. It was for this very reason, that Moses now prohibited blood so rigidly, and under the pain of death, not only among the Israelites themselves, but among all foreigners that lived within their land; and in order to render the prohibition the more sacred, and the more revered, by connecting with it a moral implication, God declared, (Lev. xvii. 11—14,) *That the Israelites, on account of the sins which they daily committed, and which could never be fully expiated by offerings on the altar, owed to him all the blood of the beasts which they slaughtered, and were not to eat of it, because it was destined as an atonement for their sins.* But for this very reason also, because it was an idolatrous usage among the neighbouring nations, were the Israelites in the greater danger of being led, by eating blood, into idolatry, from their great propensity to that universally-prevalent crime, and not from mere fondness for blood as a desirable article of food. In regard to many other heathenish customs, Moses acted quite otherwise, consecrating, instead of prohibiting them, by commanding that they should be kept up, under an altered signification, in honour of the true God; but it is not to be wondered that he should not have done so with regard to the drinking of blood in sacrifices and oaths, but rather have forbidden the use of it altogether. The *eating* of blood is a matter of indifference in a moral view, and, if not carried to excess, in a medical view also. It will not make a man cruel and pitiless; nor yet will it occasion disease and death. But *drinking* of blood is certainly not a becoming ceremony in religious worship. It is not a very refined custom, and if often repeated, it might probably habituate a people to cruelty, and make them unfeeling with regard to blood; and certainly religion should not give, nor even have the appearance of giving, any such direction to the manners of a nation. Add to this, that it is actually dangerous to drink blood; for if taken warm, and in large quantity, it may prove fatal; particularly ox-blood, which, by coagulating in the stomach, causes convulsions and sudden death, and was with this view given to criminals in Greece, as a poisoned draught. It is true, the blood of other animals may not always produce the same effects; but still, if it is not in very small quantity, its effects will be hurtful. At any rate, the custom of drinking blood in sacrifice, and in taking oaths, may, from imprudence, sometimes have the same effects which Valerius Maximus ascribes to it, in the case of Themistocles; only that he *purposely* drank as much during a sacrifice, as was sufficient to kill him; which others might also do from inadvertence, or from superstitious zeal. This was sufficient reason to keep Moses from making the drinking of blood a part of religious worship; and this being the case, it was, as a heathen rite, on his principles, necessarily prohibited in the strictest terms. Nor need we, after this, be surprised to find the eating of blood forbidden, not only in the Acts of the Apostles, (chap. xv. 20—29,) but also among the Arabs, and in the Koran, and classed with the offerings made to idols: for it actually was a part of idolatrous worship very common in the East.—MICHAELIS.

CHAPTER XI.

Ver. 2. Speak unto the children of Israel, saying, These *are* the beasts which ye shall eat among all the beasts that *are* on the earth.

Of the laws relative to clean and unclean beasts, which are recorded in Lev. xi. and Deut. xiv., the following may, perhaps, serve as an abstract, sufficient for a reader who has not to observe them, but means only to contemplate them philosophically.

In regard to *quadrupeds*, Moses reduces the previous customs of the Israelites, together with the additional ordinances which he found it necessary to make, into a very simple and natural system. According to him, *All beasts that have their feet completely cloven, above as well as below, and at the same time chew the cud, are clean.* Those which have neither, or indeed want one of these distinguishing marks, are unclean. That in so early an age of the world, we should find a systematic division of quadrupeds so excellent, as never yet, after all the improvements in natural history, to have become obsolete, but, on the contrary, to be still considered as useful by the greatest masters of the science, cannot but be looked upon as truly wonderful. In the case of certain quadrupeds, however, a doubt may arise, whether they *do* fully divide the hoof, or ruminate. For example, whether the hare ruminates or not, is so undecided, that if we put the question to any two sportsmen, we shall rarely receive the same answer. In such cases, to prevent difficulties, a legislator must authoritatively decide; by which I do not mean, that he is to prescribe to naturalists what their belief should be, but only to determine, for the sake of expounders or judges of the law, what animals are to be regarded as ruminating or parting the hoof. The camel ruminates, but whether it fully parts the hoof, is a question so undecided, that we do not, even in the *Memoirs of the Academy of Paris*, find a satisfactory answer to it on all points. The foot of the camel is actually divided into two toes, and the division even below is complete, so that the animal might be accounted clean; but then it does not extend the whole length of the foot, but only to the forepart; for behind it is not parted, and we find, besides, under it, and connected with it, a ball on which the camel goes. Now, in this dubious state of circumstances, Moses authoritatively declares, (Lev. xi. 4,) that the camel has *not* the hoof fully divided. It would appear as if he had meant that this animal, heretofore accounted clean by the Ishmaelites, Midianites, and all the rest of Abraham's Arabian descendants, should not be eaten by the Israelites; probably with a view to keep them, by this means, the more separate from these nations, with whom their connexion, and their coincidence in manners, was otherwise so close; and perhaps too, to prevent them from conceiving any desire to continue in Arabia, or to devote themselves again to their favourite occupation of wandering herdsmen. For in Arabia, a people will always be in an uncomfortable situation, if they dare not eat the flesh and drink the milk of the camel.

With regard to *fishes*, Moses has in like manner made a very simple systematic distinction. *All that have scales and fins are clean: all others unclean.*

Of *birds*, without founding on any systematic distinction, he merely specifies certain sorts as forbidden, thereby permitting all others to be eaten; but what the prohibited birds are, it is, from our ignorance of the language, in some instances impossible to ascertain; and the Jews, who still consider the Mosaic law as obligatory, are here placed in the awkward predicament of not understanding a statute which they have to observe, and of expounding it merely by guess.

Insects, serpents, worms, &c. are prohibited; and Moses

is especially careful to interdict the use of various sorts of lizards; which, of course, must have been eaten in some parts of Egypt, or by the people in the adjacent countries; but concerning which, I must admit, that I have not met with any account besides. There is, indeed, as we find from Hasselquist's Travels in Palestine, (under the class *Amphibia*, lvii.) one species of lizard in that country, viz. the *Gecko*, which is poisonous; so much so, that its poison kills when it happens to be among meat. This is not the case with the poison of serpents, which is only noxious in a wound, and may, as well as the animals themselves, which are edible, be safely taken into the stomach, if only the mouth be perfectly sound, and free from bloody spots. This *Lacerta Gecko* must certainly not have been eaten by any of the neighbouring nations, and Moses had therefore no occasion to prohibit it. With regard, however, to those winged insects, which besides *four* walking legs, (*Pedes saltatorii*,) Moses makes an exception, and under the denomination of *locusts*, declares them clean in all their four stages of existence, and under as many different degrees of hardness. In Palestine, Arabia, and the adjoining countries, locusts are one of the most common articles of food, and the people would be very ill off if they durst not eat them. For when a swarm of them desolates the fields, they prove, in some measure, themselves an antidote to the famine which they occasion; so much so, indeed, that poor people look forward with anxiety to the arrival of a swarm of locusts, as yielding them sustenance without any trouble. They are not only eaten fresh, immediately on their appearance; but the people collect them, and know a method of preserving them for a long time for food, after they have dried them in an oven.

The law further prohibited the touching the carcass of any unclean beast, Lev. xi. 8, 24, 25, 27, 31. This, however, does not mean that a carcass was, in a literal sense, *never* to be touched, (for then it must always have been in the way, and we shall see in the sequel that it was expressly ordered to be buried;) but only, that the person who touched it, was to be deemed unclean until the evening. To strangers who dwelt among the Israelites, unclean beasts were not forbidden: for certainly the legislator never thought of making his prohibition of certain meats a moral law, by which every man, of whatever nation, was to be bound to regulate his conduct. If his design in these statutes was to separate the Israelites from other nations, it must have been his wish and intention to prohibit the former from the use of those very meats which were eaten by the latter; and had the people in any of the surrounding countries deemed all such meats unclean, Moses would probably have given a set of laws on this subject quite different from those which he did give. When a commander gives his soldiers a cockade to distinguish them from other troops, he by no means wishes that everybody should indiscriminately wear it, but would rather have it taken from any foreigner who should mount it. The law relative to clean and unclean beasts was never, not even under the Old Testament, a precept of religion which every individual, to whatever nation he belonged, was bound to observe for the sake of his eternal salvation; it was only, if I may so term it, *a cockade* for the Israelites; but still one that they could not omit wearing without committing a trespass of a divine commandment; and indeed it was so firmly pinned upon them by their earliest education, that it must certainly have been difficult for them ever to lay it aside.—MICHAELIS.

Ver. 33. And every earthen vessel whereinto *any* of them falleth, whatsoever *is* in it shall be unclean; and ye shall break it.

This refers to any unclean or dead animal falling into or touching an earthen vessel. Most of the cooking utensils of the Hindoos are of earthen ware. Should an unclean, or dead animal, or insect, touch or fall into them, they must be broken. Nay, should a person of low caste get a look at the cooking vessels of a Brahmin, or one of the Saiva sect, they will immediately be broken; and no small portion of abuse be poured upon the offending individual. Should an unfortunate dog, in his prowlings, find his way into the kitchen, and begin to lick the vessels, wo be to him! for he will not only have hard words, but hard blows; and then follows the breaking of the vessels. On this account, the Brahmins, and others, conceal their earthen ware when not in use.—ROBERTS.

Ver. 35. And every *thing* whereupon *any part* of their carcass falleth shall be unclean; *whether it be* oven, or ranges for pots, they shall be broken down; *for* they *are* unclean, and shall be unclean unto you.

The scarcity of fuel in the East induces the people to be very frugal in using it. Rauwolff gives the following account of their management: "They make in their tents or houses a hole about a foot and a half deep, wherein they put their earthen pipkins or pots, with the meat in them, closed up, so that they are in the half above the middle. Three fourth parts thereof they lay about with stones, and the fourth part is left open, through which they fling in their dried dung, which burns immediately, and gives so great a heat that the pot groweth so hot as if it had stood in the middle of a lighted coal heap, so that they boil their meat with a little fire, quicker than we do ours with a great one on our hearths." As the Israelites must have had as much occasion to be sparing of their fuel as any people, and especially when journeying in the wilderness, Mr. Harmer considers this quotation as a more satisfactory commentary on this passage than any which has been given.—BURDER.

CHAPTER XIII.

Ver. 3. And the priest shall look on the plague in the skin of the flesh: and *when* the hair in the plague is turned white, and the plague in sight *be* deeper than the skin of his flesh, it *is* a plague of leprosy: and the priest shall look on him, and pronounce him unclean.

The leprosy, a contagious and dreadful disorder, which slowly consumes the human body, which is common, particularly in Egypt and Syria, but is also met with in other hot countries, generally manifests itself first in the manner described in the text. Peysonnel, a French physician, who was sent by his government, in the year 1756, to the island of Gaudaloupe, to examine the leprosy which had appeared there, writes in his report of 3d February, 1757, (in *Michaelis Mosaic Law*, part iv. p. 224:) "The commencement of the leprosy is imperceptible; there appear only a few dark reddish spots on the skin of the whites; in the blacks they are of a coppery red. These spots are at first not attended with pain, or any other symptom, but they cannot be removed by any means. The disease increases imperceptibly, and continues for some years to be more and more manifest. The spots become larger, and spread indiscriminately over the skin of the whole body: they are sometimes rather raised, though flat; when the disease increases, the upper part of the nose swells, the nostrils distend, and the nose itself becomes soft. Swellings appear on the jaw-bones, the eyebrows are elevated, the ears grow thick, the ends of the fingers, as well as the feet and toes, swell, the nails grow scaly, the joints on the hands and feet separate and die off; on the palms of the hands and the soles of the feet there are deep dry ulcers, which rapidly increase, and then vanish again. In short, when the disease reaches its last stage, the patient becomes horrible, and falls to pieces. All these circumstances come on very slowly, for many years are often required before they all occur; the patient has no severe pain, but he feels a kind of numbness in his hands and feet. These persons are not hindered, during the time, in any of the functions of nature, they eat and drink as usual, and even when some of their fingers and toes die off, the loss of the member is the only consequence, for the wound heals of itself without attention or medicine. But when the poor people reach this last period of the disease, they are horribly disfigured and most worthy of pity. It has been observed, that this disease has other dreadful properties, such, in fact, that it is hereditary, and, therefore, some families are more afflicted with it than others; secondly, that it is infectious, and that it is propagated by persons sleeping together, or even having long-continued intercourse; thirdly, that it is incurable, or, at least, that no means to cure it have been discovered.

A very well-grounded fear of being infected with this cruel disease, the difficulty of recognising the persons attacked with it, before the disorder has attained its height; the length of time that it remains secret, from the care of the patients to conceal it; the uncertainty of the symptoms at the beginning, which should distinguish it from other disorders, excited extraordinary claims among all the inhabitants of this island. They were suspicious of each, because virtue and rank were no protection against this cruel scourge. They called this disease the leprosy, and presented to the commander and governor several petitions, in which they represented all the above circumstances; the general food, the uneasiness caused in this newly-settled country; the inconveniences and the hatred which such inculpations produced among them; the laws which had been made against lepers, and their exclusion from civil society. They demanded a general inspection of all those who were suspected of having this disease, in order that those who were found to be infected might be removed into a particular hospital, or some separate place." All that these people required, and which was also granted them, we find to be prescribed in the laws relative to the leprosy, contained in the thirteenth chapter.—Rosenmuller.

Ver. 38. If a man also or a woman have in the skin of their flesh bright spots, *even* white bright spots; 39. Then the priest shall look: and, behold, *if* the bright spots in the skin of their flesh *be* darkish white; it *is* a freckled spot *that* groweth in the skin: he *is* clean.

The Hebrew word here translated "freckled spot," is *Bohak*, and the Arabs still use the same word to denote a kind of leprosy, of which Niebuhr says, "Bohak is neither contagious nor dangerous. A black boy at Mocha, who was affected with this eruption, had here and there on his body white spots. We were told that the use of sulphur had relieved this boy for a time, but had not entirely removed the disease." He adds, subsequently, from *Forskal's* papers, the following particulars: "On the 15th of May, 1765, I myself first saw the eruption called bohak in a Jew at Mocha. The spots of this eruption are of unequal size; they do not shine, are imperceptibly higher than the skin, and do not change the colour of the hair. Their colour is a dirty white, or rather reddish. The rest of the skin of the patient I saw was darker than the inhabitants of the country usually were, but the spots were not so white as the skin of a European when it is not tanned by the sun. The spots of this eruption do not appear on the hands or near the navel, but on the neck and face, yet not that part of the face where the hair grows thick. They spread gradually. Sometimes they remain only two months, sometimes one or two years, and go away by degrees of themselves. This disorder is neither contagious nor hereditary, and does not cause any bodily inconvenience." Hence it appears why a person affected with the bohak is declared in the above law not to be unclean.—Rosenmuller.

Ver. 45. And the leper in whom the plague *is*, his clothes shall be rent, and his head bare, and he shall put a covering upon his upper lip, and shall cry, Unclean, unclean.

The prophet Ezekiel, in reference to the death of his wife, was ordered not to "cry," neither to cover the lips; (the margin has, "upper lip.") The prophet Micah (iii. 7) describes the confusion and sorrow of those who had by their wickedness offended the Lord. "Then shall the seers be ashamed, and the diviners confounded: yea, they shall all cover their lips, for there is no answer of God." Margin again has, "upper lip." All these passages refer to the sorrow of those concerned. A person in deep distress puts his hand over his mouth, and hangs down his head, as if looking on the ground. When a man suddenly claps his hand on his mouth, it denotes great sorrow or surprise. To put the fingers in a line with the nose, conveys the idea of silence and submission. "Why is your hand on your mouth?"—"Not for joy." "But why?"—"My son, my son, my wicked son! He has gone with the evil ones to the distant country." "Ah, friend, why is your hand there?"—"Alas, the tigers got among my cattle last night, and great is the slaughter." "The king is angry with Râman—his hand is now on his mouth." "I may well put my hand on my mouth; I have been taken by the neck, and driven from the presence of my lord. My requests have all been denied." Job xxi. 5.—Roberts.

Ver. 47. The garment also that the plague of leprosy is in, *whether it be* a woollen garment, or a linen garment; 48. Whether *it be* in the the warp, or woof, of linen, or of woollen, whether in a skin, or in any thing made of skin; 49. And if the plague be greenish or reddish in the garment, or in the skin, either in the warp, or in the woof, or in any thing of skin; it *is* a plague of leprosy, and shall be showed unto the priest: 50. And the priest shall look upon the plague, and shut up *it that hath* the plague seven days.

The two statutes of Moses relative to the leprosy of clothes and houses, may appear to us at first view very strange, because in Europe we have never heard of any such leprosy, and the name immediately suggests to us the idea of something akin to human leprosy. Learned men who write upon the Bible in their closets, sometimes know nothing but books; being quite unacquainted with nature, and often with their own houses, in which, perhaps, the Mosaic leprosy may actually be; and they are too much wrapped up in themselves to think of asking the unlearned about such things. Perhaps the leprosy in question does not, properly speaking, fall to be treated under the present head, but under the statutes of police respecting buildings, manufactures, and clothes. Here, however, it will be looked for; and although it were not, I must nevertheless offer some general remarks on *both* the laws given by Moses respecting it, which would lose their effect, were I to separate the one from the other. In the *first* place then, when we hear of the leprosy of clothes and houses, we must not be so simple as to imagine it the very same disease which is termed leprosy in man. Men, clothes, and stones, have not the same sort of diseases; but the names of human diseases are, by analogy, or as the grammarian terms it, by a figure of speech, applied to the diseases of other things. In *Berne*, for instance, they speak of the *cancer of buildings*, but then that is not the distemper so called in the human body. The *cancer of buildings*, is with equal propriety a Swiss, as the *leprosy of buildings* is a Hebrew, expression. The late Dr. Forskal wrote me from Egypt, that two sorts of diseases of certain trees proceeding from insects, are there termed *leprosy;* but I do not print the words of his letter, because I am aware that a fuller account of this matter will be found in the Diary of his Travels, which is very soon to be published, and which I should not wish to anticipate. Hasselquist likewise, has, in p. 221 of his Travels in the Holy Land, spoken of a leprosy in the fig-trees.

In the *second* place, although Moses gives laws relative to the leprosy in clothes and houses, we must not imagine, considering that he lets not fall a single word on the subject, that any such leprosy could infect man. Of this Moses is so far from being afraid, that we find him, on the contrary, when a house lies under the suspicion of leprosy, commanding all the articles of furniture to be removed out of it, previous to its inspection, that the priest may not be obliged to pronounce them unclean. If there adhered to the walls any poisonous matter that could pass to human beings, and infect them with leprosy, this would be a very strange injunction indeed. Let us only conceive, in the case of a house infected with the plague, orders given to bring out every article within it previous to its being examined, that it might not be declared infected. What else would the consequence be, than the direct propagation of the infection? It would be the very same, though in a less degree, if the house-leprosy infected man. But will those who have already any knowledge of Moses as a legislator, suppose him capable of committing such an oversight?

The leprosy of clothes is described in Lev. xiii. 47—59, as consisting of green or reddish spots that remain in spite of washing, and still spread; and by which the cloth becomes bald, or bare, sometimes on the one side, sometimes on the other. This Moses terms *dropping or losing the hair;* that is, if we are to give the literal truth of the Hebrew text, in a passage which might have its difficulties to a man of learning, if he knew nothing of the manufacture of woollen. These symptoms too, of leprosy, are said to be found sometimes only in the *warp*, and at other times only in the *woof*. To a person who has nothing to do with the manufactures of woollen, linen, or leather, but with books only, this must doubtless be obscure; or, at most, he will be led to think of specks of rottenness, but still without being rightly satisfied. I have not been able to obtain complete information on this subject; but in regard to wool, and woollen stuffs, I have consulted the greatest manufacturer in the electorate of Hanover; and he informs me, that what he has read in my German Bible, at this passage, will be found to hold good, at any rate with regard to woollen articles; and that it proceeds from what is called *dead wool*, that is, the wool of sheep that have died by disease, not by the knife; that such wool, if the disease has been but of short duration, is not altogether useless, but in a sheep that has been long diseased, becomes extremely bad, and loses the points; and that, according to the established usage of honest manufacturers, it is unfair to manufacture dead wool into any article worn by man; because vermin are so apt to establish themselves in it, particularly when it is worn close to the body and warmed thereby. When I told him, that in the countries, with a view to which I questioned him, the people, for want of linen and from poverty, had always worn, and still wear, woollen stuffs next the skin, he stated it as his opinion that there the disagreeable effect just mentioned, must take place in a still higher degree than in countries where, according to our German fashion, which would there be a luxury, a linen shirt is worn between the woollen clothes and the body. He added, that dead wool was usually manufactured into sacks and horse-cloths; and he expressed his wish for a statute, in the style of Moses, which should discourage the use of dead wool, or inflict a punishment on those who either sold it, or knowingly manufactured it into human clothing.—I am likewise informed by Hamburghers, that in their neighbourhood, many frauds are committed with dead wool, from its being sold for good wool; in consequence of which, the stuffs made of it not only become very soon bare, but full first of little depressions, and then of holes.

These accounts serve to render this law pretty intelligible, as far as regards wool and woollen stuffs. We see how the disease may appear sometimes only in the warp, and sometimes only in the woof, from good wool being used for the one, and dead wool for the other. Whether this dead wool will, in process of time, infect good wool, I do not know; but to bring into complete discredit and disuse, stuffs, which so soon become threadbare, and burst out in holes, and at the same time so readily shelter vermin, although they cannot proceed from the wool itself, but only find it a very suitable breeding-place, unquestionably becomes the duty of legislative policy. How this end could be attained, without destroying stuffs thus manufactured contrary to law, our present system of police can scarcely conceive; and in that early age of the world, when every thing was yet in its infancy,—when merchants were not so knowing as now,—and when among the petty independent tribes, there was no police established for manufactures, nor any boards of inspection, the trick of using dead wool was probably more frequent than at present; while yet the cause of its effects was but imperfectly known; and these effects in those climates must have been still worse than with us, particularly in Egypt, which breeds such abundance of vermin. The best remedy was, in the language of Moses, to destroy the *leprous* article: for that would soon make every one careful to manufacture nothing either for himself, or for sale, that might be pronounced leprous; and people would soon observe where the fault lay, when they were losers, and found no sale for their goods, in consequence of former purchasers having suffered by them. The prohibition of dead wool, although the legislator be ever so fully satisfied that it is entirely to blame for the effects in question, is not sufficient of itself; for it will still be privately manufactured and then denied, particularly where there is no board of survey. But where the stuff, in which leprous symptoms make their appearance, is destroyed in spite of the owner, every one will become attentive to guard against such a loss. Moses therefore enjoined, *first*, that the place on which there were marks of leprosy that no washing could obliterate, should be torn out; and *then*, if the leprosy still recurred a second time, that the whole piece should be burnt. With regard to leather and linen, I can say nothing with historical certainty: because I know no great wholesale manufacturer or merchant in either line, and I do not choose to trouble my reader with conjectures, because they may occur to himself, just as well as to me. Perhaps, however, my book may find some readers better acquainted with such persons than I can be here in Gottingen, and who may hereafter communicate with me on the subject; for which purpose, I particularly request the attention of my readers in Holland, where I am inclined to think the best judges may be found. Now that the origin of the evil has been traced in wool, there will be no great difficulty in carrying on the investigation further. Only I must deprecate closet-accounts, and learned conjectures. It is only from those who are acquainted with the manufacture or sale of linen, leather, and furriery, on a large scale, that I look for any useful information.—Michaelis.

CHAPTER XIV.

Ver. 4. Then shall the priest command to take for him that is to be cleansed two birds alive *and* clean, and cedar-wood, and scarlet, and hyssop.

Interpreters have not been able to determine in what parts of scripture, the Hebrew term (צפור) *tsippor*, ought to be translated sparrow. Some suppose that Moses intends this bird in the law concerning the purification of the leprosy: "Then shall the priest command to take for him that is to be cleansed, two birds alive." One of these birds was to be killed over running water; and the living bird, after certain ceremonies described in the law, was ordered to be let loose into the open field. The same ceremonies were commanded to be observed in cleansing the leprous house. Jerome and many succeeding interpreters, render the word צפרים used in the law, sparrows. But it is evident from an attentive perusal of the fourth verse, that it signifies birds in general. "Then shall the priest command to take for him that is to be cleansed, two birds alive and clean." Now, if the sparrow was a clean bird, there could be no use in commanding a clean one to be taken, since every one of the species was ceremonially clean; but if it was unclean by law, then it could not be called clean. The term here must therefore signify birds in general, of which some were ceremonially clean, and some unclean; which rendered the specification in the command, proper and necessary. From the terms of the law it appears, that any species of clean birds might be taken on such occasions, domestic or wild; provided only they were clean, and the use of them conceded by the laws of Moses to the people. —Paxton.

Ver. 33. And the Lord spake unto Moses and unto Aaron, saying, 34. When ye be come into the land of Canaan, which I give to you for a possession, and I put the plague of leprosy in a house of the land of your possession; 35. And he that owneth the house shall come and tell the priest, saying, It seemeth to me *there is* as it were a plague in the house.

The house-leprosy is said in Lev. xiv. 33—57, to consist of greenish or reddish dimples, which appear on the walls, and continually spread wider and wider; and its nature would probably have been understood long ago, but for the prevalence of the notion of its being a disease communicable to man, which notion arose from taking the word *leprosy* in too literal a sense. The bare description of it given by Moses is so clear, that, I have known more than one example of children, who, shortly after reading it, having had occasion to go into the cellar, where, with terror, they thought they had observed it on the walls, on their return, described it distinctly or figuratively to their parents, and were laughed at for their pains. Laughed at they certainly ought not to have been, but instructed. Their acute vision had shown them what many a learned man has in vain sought to find out. In short, what we usually term the *Saltpetre*, that appears on walls, has much the same symptoms as the Mosaic house-leprosy, and is at the same time attended with such noxious effects as require the attention of a well-regulated police. I expressed this idea first in my 12th Question to the Arabian Travellers; but I did so very briefly, and as addressing men of sense and skill. I have not yet, however, received any answer, because *Forskal*, the person to whose province the question belonged, is dead, and his journal is not yet printed. The oftener, however, I consider the matter, I am the more impressed with the probability of this idea being the true one, and here is the place to expatiate more fully upon it. Our walls and houses are often attacked with something, that corrodes and consumes them, and which we commonly denominate *Saltpetre*. Its appearances are nearly as Moses describes them, only that we seldom find the spots greenish or reddish, although I think I have met with them of the latter colour. As, however, I cannot exactly recollect where, I must appeal to the testimony of Mr. Professor Bekmann, who, on my asking him, informed me that he had seen an instance of reddish ones at *Lubeck*. With us, this disease of walls is most frequently found in cellars, but it also ascends into the higher parts of buildings, particularly in the case of a privy being directly under the wall, or where any other sort of filth can affect it. In my native city, Halle, it is extremely common, because the soil of all the country around is full of what is called saltpetre; which is scraped off from the turf walls of the cottages, by people who make it their business to collect it. Properly speaking, it is not saltpetre, but it contains the acid from which saltpetre is prepared. Wherever any part of these walls, that is pregnant with this substance, is suffered to remain, it always effloresces anew; and such parts the collectors take care to leave, when they repair the cottages with new earth, that after a few years they may find a fresh crop on the walls. But I have never seen it to such a degree as at *Eisleben*, in the church in which Luther was baptized. In the year 1757, I observed, on the left side of the choir of that church, a gravestone, I think of marble, and dated in the present century, in which the inscription, though deeply cut, was in many places, by reason of numberless dimples, scarcely legible, while I read with perfect ease other two inscriptions, four times as old. On my asking the sexton the reason of this, he said, the saltpetre had come into the stone, and told me a great deal more about it, which I did not sufficiently attend to, because I had no idea of its ever being useful to me in explaining the Bible. In Bern, Mr. Apothecary Andreä heard the people complain of a disease that in an especial manner attacked sandstone, so as to make it exfoliate, and become as it were cancerous. They call it the *Gall*, and, in like manner, ascribe it to the saltpetre contained in the stone. The Society of Naturalists at Dantzig some time ago proposed a prize question on *the Causes of the Destructive Corrosion of Walls by Saltpetre, and on the Means, not only of preventing it in New Buildings, but of curing it in Old.* It was answered, among others, by Mr. Pastor Luther, who obtained the prize: but his essay, although, as the best, it might merit that distinction, has nevertheless given but little satisfaction to those who are versed in the subject, and particularly to Mr. Professor Bekmann, as we see from the third volume of his Physical and Œconomical Library, p. 574.

It is not, properly speaking, saltpetre that is in these walls and buildings, but an acid of nitre, from which, by the addition of a fixed alkali, we can make saltpetre. But the disease is likewise owing sometimes to other acids, to the acid of sea-salt, for instance, as Professor Bekmann informs me; and, from other experiments, Mr. Andreä has found the component parts of the efflorescence, to approach very near to those of Epsom salt, that is, vitriolic acid and magnesia.—See Bekmann's Biblioth. above quoted, vol. iv. p. 250. The detrimental effects of this efflorescence in walls, or, if I may use the common name, of this saltpetre, are the following:—

1. The walls become mouldy, and that to such a degree, as, in consequence of the corrosion spreading farther and farther, at least to occasion their tumbling down. Perhaps, however, this, at least in most parts of Germany, is the most tolerable evil attending the disease; for it is certain, that many houses affected with it last to a great age; only that the plaster of them requires very frequent repairing, because the lime with which they are coated, blisters, as it is called, that is, detaches itself from the wall, swells, and then falls off. I myself lived in a house at Halle, that was more than a hundred years old, and may probably stand a hundred years longer; in which, nevertheless, the saltpetre had on one side, at a period beyond all remembrance, penetrated as far as the second story. The walls, however, were from three to four feet thick, and really of excellent stone; for which, indeed, Halle is remarkable. In other places, this evil may no doubt be more serious; and I very much suspect, that such may have been the case in the damp parts of Egypt, where the Israelites dwelt. When I figure to myself those marshes, which the Greeks called *Bucolia*, at the mouth of the Nile, and the great quantity of saltpetre, or at any rate, of salt akin thereto, which Egypt produces, I cannot help thinking, that the saltpetre in buildings, must have been much more destructive there than with us. Only our travellers very seldom go into the marshy districts, but rather to Alexandria, Cairo, and along the Nile as far as Assouan, where the soil is quite different; and, of course, we can expect from them no information relative to the matter. Even the way along the coast, from Damietta to Alexandria, of which Abulfeda gives such a beautiful description, is, as far as I recollect, described by no other traveller. As my work has had the good fortune to find numerous readers in Holland, of whom, perhaps, some have it in their power to obtain more particular information concerning those parts, I have to request, that they will take some pains for that purpose, and have the goodness to communicate to me whatever accounts they may procure, that are authentic, and illustrative of the subject.

2. Many things that lie near walls affected with saltpetre, thereby suffer damage, and are spoiled. I have myself seen great piles of books nearly ruined from this cause, and it is the same with other articles that cannot bear dampness, and acids. The loss here may often be greater and more considerable, than by the slow decay of the building itself; for it shows itself very perceptibly in the course of a few years, by rendering such articles often perfectly useless.

3. If the saltpetre be strong in those apartments wherein people live, it is pernicious to health, particularly where they sleep close to the wall. Of this, I had long ago a general notion, at Halle, from observing that such apartments were not usually inhabited; but Professor Bekmann has just informed me of a remarkable case of a person, who, by occupying a room infected by saltpetre, was seized with (*Salzflüsse*) *saline defluctions*, which the physicians ascribed to the apartment alone. This unfortunate patient, who could not procure himself any better abode, he had often visited in company with a physician, whose attendance he had procured for him. Those people among us, who are in good circumstances, or not quite poor, may avoid the effects of the saltpetre corrosion, which seldom ascends higher than the lowest story, by living in the second floor, which is not so apt to be affected by it, and using the ground-floor for kitchen, waiting-parlour, &c. &c. But in a country where there was but little knowledge of architecture, and where they were obliged to be satisfied, in general, with houses of but one story, the pernicious effects of the house-leprosy could not be thus averted.

The consideration of these circumstances will render the Mosaic ordinances on this subject easily intelligible. Their object was to check the evil in the very bud; to extirpate it while it was yet extirpable, by making every one, from the loss to which it would subject him, careful, to prevent his house from becoming affected with leprosy, which he could easily be, where the houses had no damp stone cellars below ground; and thus also, to place not only himself in perfect security, but his neighbours also, who might very reasonably dread having their houses contaminated by the infection. For this purpose, Moses proceeded in the following manner:—

1. In the first place, he ordained that the owner of a house, when any suspicious spots or dimples appeared on the walls, should be bound to give notice of it, in order that the house might be inspected by a person of skill; and that person, as in the case of human leprosy, was to be the priest, whose duty it was to apply himself to the study of such things. Now this would serve to check the mischief in its very origin, and to make every one attentive to ob-

serve it. If we had any such regulations in our newly-founded cities, it is probable that the saltpetre would never acquire such a footing as it does. The cause of its establishment anywhere would soon be discovered and removed, instead of its being, as it now is, in our cities, suffered to increase to such a degree as to vitiate the whole atmosphere.

2. On notice being given, the priest was to inspect the house, but the occupant had liberty to remove every thing previously out of it; and that this might be done, the priest was empowered to order it *ex officio;* for whatever was found within a house declared unclean, became unclean along with it. Thus much is clear, that the legislator did not suppose that the furniture of an infected house could contaminate any other place, else would he not have allowed its removal, while the matter was doubtful; but here probably he yielded to the fears of the people, (as every legislator should do in such cases, instead of saying, *There can be no infection here, and ye must believe so;* for the dread of infection, whether well founded or not, is an evil against which we are fain to be secure; and if a legislator neglects to make us so, we will either take forcible measures to effect security, or else take fright, and shut ourselves up:) or perhaps he only meant to compel the possessor of a house, to a more honest intimation of the very first suspicious symptoms of the evil. For if he gave no such intimation, and his house, on being broke into, either at the request of a neighbour, or any other informer, interested in making a discovery, happened to be found unclean, its whole contents became unclean of course.

3. If, on the first inspection, the complaint did not appear wholly without foundation, but suspicious spots or dimples were actually to be seen, the house was to continue shut up for eight days, and then to be inspected anew. If, in this interval, the evil *did not* spread, it was considered as having been a circumstance merely accidental, and the house was not polluted; but if it *had* spread, it was not accounted a harmless accident, but the real house-leprosy; and the stones affected with it, were to be broken out of the wall, and carried to an unclean place without the city; and the walls of the whole house were scraped and plastered anew. These are the very same things that must be done at this day, if we want to clear a house of the saltpetre-evil. The stone or spot which produces it, must be absolutely removed: and the scraping, and fresh plastering, is also necessary; for it is in the very lime that the saltpetre, (or, to speak more properly, the acid of nitre,) establishes itself most firmly. In our large buildings, indeed, it is not just necessary to new-plaster the whole house; but the houses of the Hebrews were very small; and even the temple of Solomon itself, built some centuries posterior to the time of Moses, notwithstanding all the fame of its magnificence, was by no means nearly so large as many a house in Gottingen; although certainly we cannot boast of palaces, and have only good *bourgeois* houses.

4. If, after this, the leprosy broke out afresh, the whole house was to be pulled down, and the materials carried to an unclean place without the city. Moses, therefore, it would appear, never suffered a leprous house to stand. The injury which such houses might do to the health of the inhabitants, or to the articles they contained, was of more consequence in his estimation, than the buildings themselves. Those to whom this appears strange, and who lament the fate of a house pulled down by legal authority, probably think of large and magnificent houses like ours, of many stories high, which cost a great deal of money, and in the second story of which, the people are generally secure from all danger of the saltpetre; but I have already mentioned, that the houses of those days were low, and of very little value.

5. If, on the other hand, the house, being inspected a second time, was found clean, it was solemnly so declared, and an offering made on the occasion; in order that every one might know for certain, that it was not infected, and the public be freed from all fears on that score.

By this law many evils were actually prevented,—the spreading of the saltpetre-infection, and even its beginning; for the people would guard against those impurities whence it arose, from its being so strictly inquired into;—the danger of their allowing their property or their health to suffer in an infected house, from mere carelessness;—the difficulty of making (among the Hebrews it would have been, their slaves, but among us it would be) our hired servants, or perhaps our children's preceptor, occupy an infected apartment that was for no other use, and sleep close to an unwholesome wall. With such a law, no man can have any just ground of dissatisfaction; and we might at all events ask, why we have it not put in force in newly-built cities? It is certainly very singular, that in this country, or, at any rate, in some places of it, we have a law, which is a most complete counterpart to it. No doubt our house-leprosy is not attended with the same evils as it was among the Hebrews, by reason of the change of circumstances, and because the saltpetre, being necessary for the manufacture of gunpowder, is often scraped off; and herein we have a strong example of the diversity occasioned in legislative policy, by difference of time and climate. We have occasion for great quantities of saltpetre, in consequence of the invention of gunpowder; and, as in some parts of Germany where the soil abounds with it, such as the circle of the Saal, in the dutchy of Magdeburg, the cottages of the peasants have, from time immemorial, had their walls built only of earth, in which, by reason of that want of cleanliness, in many respects, which prevails in country villages, the saltpetre establishes itself, and effloresces; there is an ancient consuetudinary law, that the collectors of this substance may scrape it off; which they can do without any damage whatever to the houses; only they take care never to scrape it off to the very roots, nor dare the occupants of the houses extirpate it altogether. The walls are so thick, and so often cleaned by this operation, that, for my part at least, I never heard that the health of the people was affected by the saltpetre; and in the houses themselves, though inhabited by very substantial tenants, there is not much to spoil.—At the same time, I should be glad to be more fully informed by any physician of that country, whether he had ever traced any pernicious effects to the cause in question?—Michaelis.

CHAPTER XVI.

Ver. 10. But the goat on which the lot fell to be the scape-goat, shall be presented alive before the Lord, to make an atonement with him, *and* to let him go for a scape-goat.

When a person is sick he vows on his recovery to set a goat at liberty, in honour of his deity. Having selected a suitable one from his flocks, he makes a slit in the ear, or ties a yellow string round its neck, and lets it go whithersoever it pleases. Whoever sees the animal knows it to be a Nate-kadi, the vowed goat, and no person will molest it. Sometimes two goats are thus made sacred; but one of them will be offered *soon,* and the other kept for a *future* sacrifice. But it is not merely in time of sickness that they have recourse to this practice: for does a man wish to procure a situation, he makes a similar vow. Has a person heard that there are treasures concealed in any place, he vows to Virava (should he find the prize) to set a goat at liberty, in honour of his name. When a person has committed what he considers a great sin, he does the same thing; but in addition to other ceremonies, he sprinkles the animal with water, puts his hands upon it, and prays to be forgiven.—Roberts.

The *Aswamedha Jug* is an ancient Indian custom, in which a horse was brought and sacrificed, with some rites similar to those prescribed in the Mosaic law. "The horse so sacrificed is in place of the sacrificer, bears his sins with him into the wilderness, into which he is turned adrift, (for, from this particular instance, it seems that the sacrificing knife was not always employed,) and becomes the expiatory victim of those sins." Mr. Halhed observes, that this ceremony reminds us of the *scape-goat* of the Israelites; and indeed it is not the only one in which a particular coincidence between the Hindoo and Mosaic systems of theology may be traced. To this account may be subjoined a narrative in some measure similar from Mr. Bruce. "We found, that upon some dissension, the garrison and townsmen had been fighting for several days, in which disorders the greatest part of the ammunition in the town had been expended, but it had since been agreed on by the old men of both parties, that nobody had been to blame on either side, but the whole wrong was the work of *a camel. A camel,* therefore, was seized, and brought *without the town,* and there a number on both sides having met, they upbraided the *camel* with every thing that had been either said or done. The *camel* had killed men; *he* had threatened to set the town on fire; the camel had threatened to burn the aga's house and the castle; *he* had cursed the grand seignior and the sheriff of Mecca, the sovereigns of the two parties; and, the only thing the poor animal was interested in, he had threatened to destroy the wheat that was going to Mecca. After having spent great part of the afternoon in upbraiding the *camel*, whose measure of iniquity, it seems, was near full, each man thrust him through with a lance, devoting him *diis manibus et diris*, by a kind of prayer, and with a thousand curses upon his head, after which every man retired, fully satisfied as to the wrongs he had received from the *camel*!"—BURDER.

CHAPTER XVII.

Ver. 7. And they shall no more offer their sacrifices unto devils, after whom they have gone a-whoring. This shall be a statute for ever unto them throughout their generations.

The Hebrew word Seïrim, here translated devils, (field devils,) properly signifies *woolly*, *hairy*, in general; whence it is used as well for *he-goats*, as also for certain fabulous beings or *sylvan gods*, to whom, as to the satyrs, the popular belief ascribed the form of goats. But, in the above passage, he-goats are probably meant, which were objects of divine honour among the, Egyptians, under the name of *Mendes*, as emblems of the *fructifying power of nature*, or of the *fructifying power of the sun*. From this divinity, which the Greeks compared with their Pan, a province in Egypt had its name. Goats and he-goats, says Herodotus, are not slaughtered by the Egyptians whom we have mentioned, because they consider Pan as one of the oldest gods. But painters as well as statuaries represent this deity with the face and the legs of a goat, as the Greeks used to represent Pan. The Mandeseans pay divine honour to he-goats and she-goats; but more to the former than to the latter.—ROSENMULLER.

CHAPTER XVIII.

Ver. 6. None of you shall approach to any that is near of kin to him, (Heb. remnant of flesh,) to uncover *their* nakedness.

In his statutes relative to marriage, and sometimes, also, in other parts of his law, Moses expresses near relationship, either by the single word, שאר, (*Sheer*) *pars, scil. carnis*, or more fully by the two words, שאר בשר, *Sheer-basar*, *pars carnis*, (*part or remainder of flesh.*) The meaning of these terms has been the subject of much controversy. Some would translate them *flesh of flesh;* others, *remnant of flesh.* But those that say most of their etymology, are in general not so much oriental philologists, as divines and lawyers; and yet we should rather like to have an illustration of any obscure etymological question, from those who unite with the knowledge of Hebrew, an acquaintance with its kindred eastern languages. There are some also, who would make this distinction between *Sheer*, and *Sheer-basar*, that the former means only *persons immediately connected with us*, such as *children*, *parents*, *grandchildren*, *grandparents*, and *husbands or wives;* and the latter, those who are *related to us only mediately, but in the nearest degree*, such as, our *brothers and sisters*, who are, properly speaking, *our father's flesh.* Others again think, that *Sheer-basar* means nothing but *children* and *grandchildren.* These conjectures, however, are by no means consonant to the real usage of the language, in the Mosaic laws themselves; for in Levit. xxv. 48, 49, *Sheer-basar* follows as the name of a more remote relation, after brother, paternal uncle, or paternal uncle's son; and in Num. xxvii. 8—11, it is commanded, that "if a man die without sons, his inheritance shall be given to his daughters; if he have no daughters, it shall pass to his brothers, of whom, if he has none, then to his paternal uncles; and if these are also wanting, it shall then be given unto his nearest *Sheer* in his *family.*" It is manifest that, in this passage, *Sheer* includes those relations that follow in succession to a father's brother. If the reader wishes to know what these words etymologically signify, I shall here just state to him my opinion, but without repeating the grounds on which it rests. *Sheer* means, 1. *a remnant;* 2. *the remnant of a meal;* 3. *a piece of any thing eatable*, such as *flesh;* 4. *a piece of any thing in general.* Hence we find it subsequently transferred to relationship in the Arabic language; in which, though with a slight orthographical variation, that nearest relation is called *Taïr* or *Thsäir*, whom the Hebrews denominate *Goël.* In this way, *Sheer*, even by itself, would signify a relation.—*Basar*, commonly rendered *flesh*, is among the Hebrews equivalent to *body;* and may thence have been applied to signify relationship. Thus, *thou art my flesh, or body*, (Gen. xxix. 14,) means, *thou art my near kinsman.* When both words are put together, *Sheer-basar*, they may be rendered literally, *corporeal relation*, or by a half Hebrew phrase, *kinsman after the flesh.* In their derivation, there are no further mysteries concealed, nor any thing that can bring the point in question to a decision; and what marriages Moses has permitted or commanded, we cannot ascertain from *Sheer-basar*, frequent and extensive as is its use in his marriage-laws: but must determine, from his own ordinances, in which he distinctly mentions what *Sheer-basar*, that is, what relations, are forbidden to marry.—MICHAELIS.

Ver. 16. Thou shalt not uncover the nakedness of thy brother's wife: it *is* thy brother's nakedness. 18. Neither shalt thou take a wife to her sister, to vex *her*, to uncover her nakedness, besides the other in her life-*time*.

With regard to the marriages mentioned in this chapter, there arises the question, whether Moses only prohibits the marriages which he expressly mentions, or others besides, not mentioned, where the degree of relationship is the same? This question, which is of so great importance in the marriage laws of Christian nations, and which, from our imperfect knowledge of oriental customs, has been the subject of so much controversy, properly regards the following marriages never mentioned by Moses, viz.

1. With a brother's daughter.
2. With a sister's daughter.
3. With a maternal uncle's widow.
4. With a brother's son's widow.
5. With a sister's son's widow.
6. With a deceased wife's sister.

These marriages we may, perhaps, for brevity's sake, be allowed to denominate the *six marriages*, or the *consequential marriages.* They are as near as those mentioned in the foregoing article, and prohibited. Moses never mentions them in his marriage statutes; yet the ground of his prohibitions is nearness of relationship. The question, therefore, is, Are these marriages to be, or not to be, considered as prohibited, by just inference from the letter of his laws? In my opinion, *they are not;* and in proving this, I will most willingly concede to those of a contrary opinion, a multitude of objections against their consequences, as deduced from the letter of the Mosaic statutes; such, for instance, as this, that *according to the principle of judicial hermeneutics, prohibitions are not to be extended beyond the letter of the law;* for I readily acknowledge that this rule, how valid soever in our law, is nevertheless not universal and not always safely applicable to very ancient laws, if we wish to ascertain the true meaning and opinion of the lawgiver: Or this, again, that *in these marriages there is no violation of Respectus parentelæ;* for I have already admitted that that principle, to which the Roman lawyers appeal, was not the foundation of the Mosaic prohibitions. I will go yet one step further in courtesy, and promise to appeal on no occasion whatever to the common opinion of the Jews, or to those examples of ancient Jewish usage, whereby the marriages here mentioned are permitted; for all the Jewish expositors, and all the examples they can produce, are much too modern for me to found upon, where the question is concerning the true meaning of a law given some hundred, or rather thousand, years before them. So much generosity on my part, many readers would, perhaps, not have anticipated; but I owe nothing less to impartiality, and the love of truth. My reasons, then, for denying, and protesting against the conclusions in question, are as following:—

1. Moses does not appear to have framed or given his marriage laws with any view to our deducing, or acting

upon, conclusions which we might think fit to deduce from them: for if this was his view, he has made several repetitions in them, that are really very useless. What reason had he, for example, after forbidding marriage with a father's sister, to forbid it also with a mother's, if this second prohibition was included in the first, and if he meant, without saying a word on the subject, to be understood as speaking, not of particular marriages, but of degrees?

2. Moses has given his marriage laws in two different places of the Pentateuch, viz. in both the xviii. and xx. chapters of Leviticus; but in the latter of these passages we find only the very same cases specified, which had been specified in the former. Now, had they been meant merely as examples of degrees of relationship, it would have been more rational to have varied them; and if it had been said, for instance, on the first occasion, *Thou shalt not marry thy father's sister*, to have introduced, on the second, the converse case, and said, *Thou shalt not marry thy brother's daughter*. This, however, is not done by Moses, who, in the second enactment, just specifies *the father's sister*, as before; and seems, therefore, to have intended that he should be understood as having in his view no other marriages than those which he expressly names; unless we choose to interpret his laws in a manner foreign to his own meaning and design.

3. If, in opposition to this, the advocates of the contrary opinion urge, that the *six consequential marriages* are just as near as those expressly prohibited; my answer is, that though here they may seem to be in the right, there is yet, according to the customs of the Hebrews, so great a distinction between these two classes of marriages, that any conclusion drawn from the one to the other, is entirely nugatory. For,

(1.) In the *first* place, among the oriental nations, the niece was regarded as a more distant relation than the aunt. The latter, whether fathers' or mothers' sister, her nephew might see unveiled, in other words, had much nearer access to her; whereas the former, whether brothers' or sisters' daughter, could not be seen by her uncle without a veil. Now, this distinction refers to the very essence of the prohibitions; for it is not the natural degree of relationship, but the right of familiar intercourse, that constitutes the danger of corruption. If, therefore, these laws were given for the purpose of preventing early debauchery under the hope of marriage, with an aunt, and with a niece, they are by no means on the same footing; for to the former, by the law of relationship, an Israelite had a degree of access, which in the case of the latter was not permitted. Both stood in the same degree of affinity according to the genealogical tree, but not so by the intimacy of intercourse permitted with them.

(2.) In the *second* place, there was a difference equally great, or even greater, made between the paternal uncle's widow on the one hand, and the widow of the maternal uncle, or of the brother's or sister's son, on the other. For if by that ancient law, of which the Levirate-marriage may be a relic, the widow was regarded as part of the inheritance,—I, in the event of my father being dead, received *his* brother's widow by inheritance, but not my mother's brother's, because he belonged to a different family; nor yet could I thus receive the widow of my brother or sister's son, because inheritances do not usually ascend; or, at any rate, an inheritance of this kind; to make use of which, a man must necessarily not be old, if the person who has left it was young. In the case, therefore, of the prohibited marriages specified by Moses, there was by the ancient law an expectancy, and by the Levirate-law it become a duty, to marry the widow of a paternal uncle, who had died childless, and to raise up seed to him; but in the case of the marriages not prohibited by Moses, there could be no room for either. If, by reason of this distinction, there be, in regard to the brother's son's widow, as belonging to one family, the least doubt remaining in the mind of the reader, I hope to remove *it* likewise, into the bargain. Were I to receive her by inheritance, it must be presupposed that she would have first fallen naturally to my father, and only in consequence of his being no longer alive, have devolved upon me, one degree more distant. But any inheritance so abominable as that of a son's widow devolving to his father, we can scarcely figure to ourselves; although *Thamar*, from resentment and despair, conceived the idea of her having such a claim, and contrived by secret artifice to enforce it, Gen. xxxviii. Rather would she fall to her husband's brother, and were he not alive, naturally devolve to his son. It is therefore manifest, that the father's brother could never have had that expectancy of his brother's son's widow, which might be attended with such pernicious consequences as I have already remarked.

4. The strongest and most decisive argument against the *consequential system*, and the reckoning by degrees, is drawn from the case of marriage with a deceased wife's sister; The relationship here is as near as that of a brother's widow; and yet Moses prohibits the marriage of a brother's widow, and permits that of a deceased wife's sister, or rather (which makes the proof still stronger,) he presupposes it in his laws as permitted; and consequently, wished to be understood as forbidding only those marriages which he expressly specifies, and not others of the like proximity, though unnoticed. The reader who is not satisfied with these remarks, may consult the 7th chapter of my Treatise on the Marriage Laws, where he will find many particulars more fully detailed. But here I cannot say more, without dwelling too long on one part of my subject.—Michaelis.

CHAPTER XIX.

Ver. 9. And when ye reap the harvest of your land, thou shalt not wholly reap the corners of thy field, neither shalt thou gather the gleanings of thy harvest.

The right of the poor in Israel to glean after the reapers, was thus secured by a positive law. It is the opinion of some writers, that although the poor were allowed the liberty of gleaning, the Israelitish proprietors were not obliged to admit them immediately into the field, as soon as the reapers had cut down the corn, and bound it up in sheaves, but when it was carried off; they might choose also among the poor, whom they thought most deserving or most necessitous. These opinions receive some countenance, from the request which Ruth presented to the servant of Boaz, to permit her to glean "among the sheaves;" and from the charge of Boaz to his young men, "let her glean even among the sheaves;" a mode of speaking which seems to insinuate, that though they could not legally hinder Ruth from gleaning in the field, they had a right, if they chose to exercise it, to prohibit her from gleaning among the sheaves, or immediately after the reapers.—Paxton.

Ver. 28. Ye shall not make any cuttings in your flesh for the dead, nor print any marks upon you: I *am* the Lord.

The heathen print marks on their bodies, (by puncturing the skin,) so as to represent birds, trees, and the gods they serve. Some also, especially the *sacred* females of the temples, have representations on their arms of a highly offensive nature. All Hindoos have a black spot, or some other mark, on their foreheads. And the true followers of Siva rub holy ashes every morning on the knees, loins, navel, arms, shoulders, brow, and crown of the head.—Roberts.

Ver. 29. Do not prostitute thy daughter, to cause her to be a whore; lest the land fall to whoredom, and the land become full of wickedness.

Parents, in consequence of a vow or some other circumstance, often dedicate their daughters to the gods. They are sent to the temple, at the age of eight or ten years, to be initiated into the art of dancing before the deities, and of singing songs in honour of their exploits. From that period these dancing girls remain in some sacred building near the temple; and when they arrive at maturity, (the parents being made acquainted with the fact,) a feast is made, and the poor girl is given into the embraces of some influential man of the establishment. Practices of the most disgusting nature then take place, and the young victim becomes a prostitute for life.—Roberts.

CHAPTER XX.

Ver. 2. Again thou shalt say to the children of Israel, Whosoever *he be* of the children of Israel, or of the strangers that sojourn in Israel, that giveth *any* of his seed unto Molech, he shall surely be put to death: the people of the land shall stone him with stones.

One of the most common punishments in use among the Jews, was stoning, which appears to have been a most grievous and terrible infliction: "when the criminal arrived within four cubits of the place of execution, he was stripped naked, only leaving a covering before; and his hands being bound, he was led up to the fatal spot, which was an eminence about twice the height of a man. The first executioners of the sentence, were the witnesses, who generally pulled off their clothes for that purpose: one of them threw him down with great violence upon his loins; if he rolled upon his breast, he was turned upon his loins again: and if he died by the fall, the sentence of the law was executed; but if not, the other witness took a great stone and dashed it on his breast as he lay upon his back; and then, if he was not despatched, all the people that stood by, threw stones at him till he died."—LEWIS.

Ver. 25. Ye shall therefore put difference between clean beasts and unclean, and between unclean fowls and clean: and ye shall not make your souls abominable by beast, or by fowl, or by any manner of living thing that creepeth on the ground, which I have separated from you as unclean.

The Mosaic ordinances respecting clean and unclean beasts, other authors refer to the head of Ecclesiastical Laws; but as they relate, not to any ceremonies of religious worship, but merely to matters of a secular nature, I choose rather to treat of them under the head of Police Law, as one would naturally do in the case of any other laws, that prohibited the use of certain meats. And *first* of all, I must illustrate the terms *clean* and *unclean*, as applied to beasts; because we are apt to consider them as implying a division of animals with which *we* are entirely unacquainted, and then to wonder that Moses, as an historian, in describing the circumstances of the deluge, which took place many centuries before the era of his own laws, should mention clean and unclean beasts, and, by so doing, presuppose that there *was* such a distinction made at that early period. The fact however is, that we ourselves, and indeed almost all nations, make this very distinction, although we do not express it in these terms. *Clean and unclean beasts* is precisely tantamount to *beasts usual and not usual for food.* And how many animals are there not poisonous, but perfectly edible, which yet we do not eat, and at the flesh of which, many among us would feel a strong abhorrence, just because we have not been accustomed to it from infancy?

What Moses did in regard to this matter, was, in the main, nothing more than converting ancient national custom into positive law. The very same animals had, for the most part, previously been to the Israelites or their ancestors, clean or unclean, that is, usual or unusual for food; and we find that even in Joseph's time, the Egyptians, who had different customs with regard to meats, and observed them very rigidly, could not so much as eat at the same table with the Israelitish patriarchs, Gen. xliii. 32. These ancestorial usages Moses now prescribed as express laws; excluding, perhaps, some animals formerly made use of for food, and reducing the whole into what, upon the principles of physiology, was actually a very easy and natural system; concerning which, as I shall have to speak in the sequel, I only observe at present, that its limits were, perhaps, before trespassed, both on the side of prohibition and permission. As soon as we know what is the real meaning of *clean and unclean beasts*, many errors, some of them ludicrous, and from which, even men of great learning have not been wholly exempt, instantly vanish. The word *unclean*, applied to animals, is no epithet of degradation: of all animals, man was the *most unclean*, that is, human flesh was least of all things to be eaten; and such is the case, in every nation not reckoned among cannibals. The lion and the horse are unclean beasts, but were to the Hebrews just as little the objects of contempt as they are to us. It is another mistake to imagine that the Jews durst not have any unclean animals in their houses, nor have any thing to do with them; and hence has arisen our strange German proverb, *Like a sow in a Jew's house.* But let us only recollect the instances of the ass and camel, the common beasts of burden among the Hebrews, in addition to which, in later times, we have the horse. All the three species were unclean. Even the keeping of swine, as articles of trade, was as little forbidden to the Jews as dealing in horses, which they carried on very commonly.

The main design of Moses, in converting the ancient national customs of the Hebrews into immutable laws, might, no doubt, be, to keep them more perfectly separate from other nations. They were to continue a distinct people by themselves, to dwell altogether in Palestine, without spreading into other countries, or having too much intercourse with their inhabitants; in order to prevent their being infected, either with that idolatry, which was then the *sensus communis* of all mankind, or with the vices of the neighbouring nations, among whom the Canaanites were particularly specified. The *first* of these objects, the prevention of idolatry, and the maintenance of the worship of one only God, was the fundamental maxim of the Mosaic legislation, and the *second*, namely, the preservation of his people from the contagion of various vices, previously uncommon among them, such as bestiality, sodomy, incest, incestuous marriages, which are always destructive to the happiness of a country, divinations, human sacrifices, &c. &c.; together with the maintaining among them their present morals, if but tolerably good, must be an object of great importance with every legislator, if a profligate race, such as Moses and the Roman writers describe the Canaanites to have been, happen to live in their vicinity. And this Moses himself seems to point out as his object, in the xxth chapter of Leviticus, ver. 25, 26, and that too after warning the Israelites against imitating the Canaanites in the vices now mentioned: "Ye shall," says he, "distinguish beasts clean and unclean, and birds clean and unclean, from each other, and not defile yourselves by four-footed, flying, or creeping creatures, which I have separated as unclean; ye shall be holy to me, for I Jehovah am holy, and have separated you from other peoples, to be mine own."

The distinction of clean and unclean meats may be a very effectual means of separating one nation from another. Intimate friendships are, in most cases, formed at table; and with the man, with whom I can neither eat or drink, let our intercourse in business be what it may, I shall seldom become so familiar, as with him whose guest I am, and he mine. If we have, besides, from education, an abhorrence of the food which others eat, this forms a new obstacle to closer intimacy. Now, all the neighbours of the Israelites *did* make use of meats, which were forbidden to them from their infancy. The Egyptians differed most from them in this respect: for they had from immemorial ages, a still more rigorous system of national laws on this point, which restrained them even more strongly from intercourse with foreigners. Some of the animals which the Israelites ate, were among *them* not indeed unclean, but yet sacred, being so expressly consecrated to a deity, that they durst not be slaughtered; because, according to the Egyptian doctrine of the transmigration of souls, a man could not but be afraid of devouring his own forefathers, if he tasted the flesh of those beasts, in which the souls of the best of men usually resided. Even before the ancestors of the Israelites descended into Egypt, this had proceeded so far, that the Egyptians not only could not eat the same sort of food, but could not even so much as sit at the same table with Hebrews, Gen. xliii. 32; and these wandering herdsmen, who ate the flesh of goats, sheep, and oxen, which were all forbidden in one or other of the provinces of Egypt, were so obnoxious to them, that they would not allow them to live among them, but assigned them a separate part of the country for a residence, Gen. xlvi. 33, 34. An Egyptian durst not so much as use a vessel, in which a foreigner ate his impure victuals; still less durst he kiss a foreigner: although I will not venture to assert, that this last command was, in all cases, inviolably observed, where a tawny Egyptian found a fair Grecian alone, how impure soever her food rendered her.—We may therefore conjecture, that Moses here borrowed somewhat from the legislative policy of the Egyptians, and with a view to a more complete and permanent separation of the two peoples, made that a law among the Israelites, which before was nothing else than a custom of their fathers.

Besides this main object, there might, no doubt, in the case of certain animals, interfere dietetical considerations to influence Moses; only we are not to seek for them in *all* the prohibitions relative to unclean beasts. In regard to that respecting swine's flesh, they are pretty obvious; and every prudent legislator must endeavour either to divert by fair means a people in the circumstances and climate of the Israelites, from the use of that food, or else expressly interdict it. For whoever is affected with any cutaneous disease, were it but the common itch, if he wishes to be cured, must abstain from swine's flesh. It has likewise been long ago observed, that the use of this food produces a peculiar susceptibility of itchy disorders. Now, throughout the whole climate under which Palestine is situated, and for a certain extent both south and north, the leprosy is an endemic disease; and with this disease, which is pre-eminently an Egyptian one, the Israelites left Egypt so terribly overrun, that Moses found it necessary to enact a variety of laws respecting it; and that the contagion might be weakened, and the people tolerably guarded against its influence, it became requisite to prohibit them from eating swine's flesh altogether. This prohibition, however, is sufficiently distinguished, from all others of the kind, in these two respects; in the *first* place, the Arabs, who eat other sorts of food forbidden the Jews, yet hold swine's flesh to be unclean; and, in conformity with their ideas, Mohammed forbade the use of it in the Koran: in the *second* place, every physician will interdict a person labouring under any cutaneous disease, from eating pork; and it has been remarked of our Germany—a country otherwise in general pretty clear of them,—that such diseases are in a peculiar manner to be met with in those places where a great deal of pork is eaten.

Some have been inclined to discover moral reasons for the laws in question, and to ascribe to the eating of certain animals a specific influence on the moral temperament. Thus the camel is extremely revengeful; and it has been pretended, that it is their eating camels' flesh so frequently, that makes the Arabs so prone to revenge. But of this there is too little proof. Other nations in the south of Europe, charged with the same national passion, and who either, as in the case with the Italians, have a pleasure in revenge, even in secret revenge, or, like the Portuguese, are, by a strange point of honour, necessitated to the exercise of implacable revenge, neither eat the flesh nor drink the milk of camels. Perhaps the vindictive propensity of the Arabs is rather an effect of climate, or of their point of honour in regard to blood-avengement, than of eating camels' flesh. At the same time, I do not entirely deny the influence of food on the moral temperament; but I am by no means yet convinced, that the daily use of certain kinds of animal food will ever so far alter it, as to give a legislator reason to prohibit them; nor yet can I believe, that eating the flesh of any animal directly inspires us with the passions of that animal, although it may operate upon us in other respects.—MICHAELIS.

CHAPTER XXI.

Ver. 18. For whatsoever man *he be* that hath a blemish, he shall not approach; a blind man, or a lame, or he that hath a flat nose, or any thing superfluous.

Among the heathen, persons of the most respectable appearance were appointed to the priesthood; and the emperor, both among the Greeks and Romans, was both king and priest. Considering the object of religious worship, it is not possible that too much circumspection can be maintained in every part of it. If great men deem it reproachful to have things imperfect presented to them, it may most reasonably be supposed that such offerings would be rejected with anger by God. The general opinion was, that a priest who was defective in any member was to be avoided as ominous. At Elis, in Greece, the judges chose the finest looking man to carry the sacred vessels of the deity: he that was next him in beauty and elegance led the ox; and the third in personal beauty carried the garlands, ribands, wine, and the other things used in sacrifice. Among most nations of antiquity, persons who had bodily defects were excluded from the priesthood. Among the Greeks "it was required, that whoever was admitted to this office should be sound and perfect in all his members, it being thought a dishonour to the gods to be served by any one that was lame, maimed, or any other way imperfect; and therefore at Athens, before their consecration, they were ωφελεις, i. e. perfect and entire, neither having any defect, nor any thing superfluous." POTTER. Seneca says, "that Metellus, who had the misfortune to become blind, when he saved the Palladium from the flames, on the burning of the temple of Vesta, was obliged to lay down the priesthood:" and he adds, "Every priest whose body is not faultless, is to be avoided like a thing of bad omen." Sacerdos non integri corporis quasi mali ominis est vitandus est. M. Sergius, who lost his right hand in defence of his country, could not remain a priest for that reason. The bodily defects which disqualified a virgin from becoming a vestal are named by A. Gellius, *Noct. Att.* i. chap. 12. ROSENMULLER.

Even those of the seed of Aaron who had any *personal* defect, were not allowed to take a part in the offerings of the Lord. The priesthood among the Hindoos is hereditary, but a deformed person cannot perform a ceremony in the temple; he may, however, prepare the flowers, fruits, oils, and cakes, for the offerings, and also sprinkle the premises with holy water. The child of a priest being deformed at the birth will not be consecrated. A priest having lost an eye or a tooth, or being deficient in any member or organ, or who has not a wife, cannot perform the ceremony called Teevasam, for the manes of departed friends. Neither will his incantations, or prayers, or magical ceremonies, have any effect.—ROBERTS.

CHAPTER XXIII.

Ver. 22. And when ye reap the harvest of your land, thou shalt not make clean riddance of the corners of thy field when thou reapest, neither shalt thou gather any gleaning of thy harvest: thou shalt leave them unto the poor, and to the stranger: I *am* the LORD your God.

Fields in the East, instead of hedges, have *ridges*. In the *corners* they cannot easily work with the plough, and therefore prepare that part with a *man-vetty*, *i. e.* an earth-cutter, or large kind of hoe. The corn in these *corners* is seldom very productive, as the ridge for some time conceals it from the sun and other sources of nourishment, and the rice also, in the vicinity, soon springing up, injures it by the shade. Under these circumstances, the people think but little of the *corners*, and were a person to be very particular, he would have the name of a stingy fellow. From this view, it appears probable, that the command was given, in order to induce the owner to leave the little which was produced in the *corners* for the poor. No farmer will allow any of his family to *glean* in the fields, the pittance left is always considered the property of the poor. In carrying the sheaves, all that falls is taken up by the gleaners. ROBERTS.

CHAPTER XXIV.

Ver. 16. And he that blasphemeth the name of the LORD, he shall surely be put to death, *and* all the congregation shall certainly stone him; as well the stranger, as he that is born in the land, when he blasphemeth the name *of the LORD*, shall be put to death.

Among most nations blasphemy is regarded as one of the greatest crimes, and punished capitally. Whether in this they act rationally, and what force there is in the objection, that blasphemy does not hurt God, I shall not here stop to inquire; as, perhaps, some notice of these points will be taken in my proposed essay on the Intention of Punishments; and, therefore, I proceed to observe, that in the Mosaic polity, whereby God became both King and Lawgiver of the Israelites, and where, of course, blasphemy was a crime against the state, we find it, in like manner, considered as a capital crime, and the punishment of stoning annexed to it; Lev. xxiv. 10—14. Nor was the circumstance of the blasphemer being a foreigner, to make any difference in the punishment. Indeed, this was actually the case, on the occasion of the punishment of this crime being first settled. A man, whose father was an Egyptian, but his mother a woman of Israel, had, in a quarrel with an Israelite, blasphemed Jehovah. He was, after an inquiry into the mind of God, adjudged to be stoned; and the edict published on this occasion, concludes with these words, "One uniform law shall you all have, foreigners as well as natives; for I am Jehovah your God." Allowing that a foreigner does not believe in our God, although, indeed, with regard to the God of Israel this was not likely to happen, because paganism was *syncretistic*, and did not deny the divinity of other gods; and, besides, the Israelites believed in the God who created the world, and whom we know, and acknowledge from reason, without revelation; but allowing, I say, a foreigner to be an infidel, still he has no right to insult the people, under whose protection he lives, by blaspheming the object of their veneration, and whose name they hold supremely sacred.

It is with hesitation, and not without danger, that I venture to adopt a Jewish explanation, which has been commonly ridiculed as a piece of mere superstition, in regard to this law, in Lev. xxiv. 16, which declares, that whoever shall utter the name JEHOVAH shall die; the whole congregation shall stone him: foreigner as well as native shall die, if he utter the name JEHOVAH. Instead of *utter*, we may translate *curse*, for the Hebrew word *Nakab* (נקב) signifies both, and then we shall have the blasphemer spoken of a second time; but to this translation there seems to be this objection, that the 16th verse would thus be nothing but a needless repetition of the preceding one. Thus much is certain, that at a very ancient period, long before the birth of Christ, the Jews understood the law before us, as if it prohibited them from uttering the name *Jehovah*, which the true God had given himself as his *nomen proprium*, on any other than solemnly-sacred, or at any rate sacred, occasions; and, of course, from ever naming him at all in common life. The Greek version ascribed to the persons called the Seventy Interpreters, and which was made at least 250 years before Christ, here renders, "Whoever nameth the name of the LORD shall die;" and we see that, by this time, the Jews were accustomed, wherever they found the word *Jehovah* in the Bible, to pronounce, instead of it, the name *Adonai*, (אדני) or Lord: for, in place of *Jehovah*, (יהוה) the Seventy always put, ὁ Κυριος. *Philo*, who lived in the time of Christ, explains the passage, connecting it with the preceding verse, in the following terms, "Strange gods are not to be blasphemed, lest men should be accustomed to think meanly of the Deity. But if any one, (I do not say *blaspheme*, for that is not here in question, but) even so much as utter unseasonably the name of the Lord of men and gods, he shall die." We may, therefore, approve of this explanation, or not, as we please; but we must not look upon it as a piece of superstition originating with the Jews, who lived after the destruction of Jerusalem, and whose opinions, in regard to the Mosaic law, I do not, for the most part, so much as notice. This prohibition of uttering the name of God, whether it please us or not, does not, by any means, appear altogether improbable; for it is in conformity with the customs and legislative policy of the Egyptians, who had secret names for their gods, which it was lawful for the priests alone to pronounce; no man being permitted to do so in common life. And, in like manner, *Rhadamanthus*, who herein wished to imitate the Egyptians, would not, on occasions of taking oaths, allow the names of the gods to be mentioned, but only those of the animals consecrated to them, such as dogs, rams, geese, &c.

Nor would I be disposed to maintain, that no advantage could flow from such a prohibition. For in the *first* place, that name of the Deity, which was considered as his *proper name*, would be, at any rate, thereby guarded from profanations and misapplications, which sometimes leave behind them ludicrous and contemptuous impressions, that can never be effaced; and, in an age when polytheism was so prevalent, this was a matter of much more importance than at present; for then *God* was not, as with us in Germany, equivalent to a *nomen proprium*, but every god, whether true or false, had his own peculiar name; and hence we find Moses addressing the God who appeared to him, and who declared himself the "God of his fathers," and, of course, the creator of heaven and earth, and the only true God; and asking him what answer he should return to the Israelites, if they wished to know what was his name, Exod. iii. 13.

In the *second* place, a name of the deity, which is never mentioned in common life, will have something extremely solemn in it, particularly where it is so significant, as was the word *Jehovah*. It will, of course, in worship, in prayer, and in the case of an oath, make so much the deeper impression; and *that*, with respect to the last of these, may serve to prevent perjury, or, at least, to make it but rare: for whatever is unknown and uncommon, affects the human heart with terror and with awe. In fact, I myself believed that this law ought to be understood in this way, when I was translating the book of Leviticus, about three years ago; but since that time, the consideration of the great severity of the punishment has raised a doubt in my mind on this point. Moses prohibits naming the name *Jehovah*; but was that to be a capital crime? If so, where was there any gradation of punishments; stoning being thus the punishment of the blasphemer of God, and of the man also who but uttered his name?—But this doubt becomes still weightier, when we read *both* verses, namely, verses 15 and 16 of Lev. xxiv. together. And here I must acknowledge a mistake in my translation: for the words in ver. 15, "he shall bear his sin," I rendered periphrastically, "he shall atone for his crime;" because I adhered to the common opinion, that they related to the stoning, which was adjudged as the punishment of the blasphemer. If, however, I translate the passage quite literally thus, "Whoever blasphemeth his God, shall bear his sin. Whoever utters the name *Jehovah*, shall die; the whole congregation shall stone him;" it looks as if the utterer of the name was to be punished differently from, and more severely than, the blasphemer; as, indeed, Philo has remarked, though with quite another view. But then, it is to be considered, further, that the crime is not so much as distinctly expressed unless we explain the 16th verse by, and, in some measure, include it in, the one before it. The verb *Nakab* may as well mean *to write*, as *to utter*; and, therefore, even writing the name Jehovah, might seem to have been prohibited; and yet Moses has done that in every page of his writings. Let it, however, be rendered *utter*; was then all utterance of the name Jehovah forbidden? How then was it to be used, and for what purpose did God assume it? This law, then, is surely to be understood with some limitation? But with what limitation? Was the priest alone to utter the name, as the Jews think? or durst laymen also utter it, if they only did so in a holy manner? Durst it be mentioned in an oath, or in prayer? Was it permitted in instructing children? or was only the inconsiderate use of it prohibited? With regard to all this, we find nothing in this law, and yet it is the only one that treats on this subject; nor is it like other laws, illustrated by usage; for the name *Jehovah* was new, and it was Moses who first distinguished the God who sent him, by this philosophically sublime and expressive title. Here, then, we should have *some* crime, to which the punishment of death was annexed, and yet it was not rightly understood what it was, nor wherein it consisted.

These doubts have prompted me to connect the 16th verse more closely with the 15th; so that *to utter the name Jehovah*, becomes equivalent *to uttering it in blasphemy*; and this explanation is the more probable, because in the story which gave occasion to the law, we find, ver. 11, that the Egyptian *had uttered the name, and blasphemed.* The meaning then of the words, of which I shall first give a literal translation thus,—*A man, a man*, (that is, any man whatever, whether native or stranger,) *who blasphemeth his God, shall bear his sin, and whoever uttereth the name* JEHOVAH *shall die; the whole congregation shall stone him*—will be the following: "If any man blaspheme God, the God whom he deems *his* God, (the Israelite, the true, and the heathen a false God,) it is a heinous sin. It is a sin even in the heathen, to blaspheme what, according to his own opinion, is god. Such a person shall not escape his judge; although the magistrate has no right to interfere in the matter, but must leave it to the true or false God, that he may be his own judge. It is, besides, uncertain whom the man may have meant, when he cursed God, and here the law assumes the milder supposition. But if any one, in blaspheming, expressly mention the name *Jehovah*, so that no doubt can remain, whether he meant to blaspheme the true or a false God, *he* shall be stoned to death."

In this way the criminal law, with respect to blasphemers, would undergo a very material alteration; nor would it be *every* blaphemy, but only that which was distinguished by a certain specific aggravation, that incurred capital punishment; all other cases being left to the judgment of God, because the blasphemer cannot be *convicted* of having blasphemed the true God, and because God is certainly able to avenge himself, if he think fit, without having occasion for our aid; Judg. vi. 30, 31. And this appears quite suitable to the spirit of those times, and is a great mitigation of the rigour of the law. In our times, a legislator would, perhaps, grant to the blasphemer the *salvo* of not being in his right mind.—At any rate, blasphemy, inferred merely by deductions, or what is called blasphemous doctrine, could not be punished by the law. In later times, the Jews were extremely prone to construe every thing that did not please them, at once into blasphemy; and their *Zealots*, as they were called, arrogated to themselves the right of punishing on the spot, and without the smallest judicial inquiry, any supposed blasphemy; although perhaps they had stopped their ears against it, and were, therefore, but bad judges of its real nature. Both the one and the other of these measures are repugnant to the Mosaic statute. Even the utterer of aggravated blasphemy was not put to death on the spot, but taken into custody, until God could be consulted as to his fate. We must not, therefore, charge the Mosaic law with those illegal outrages, to which the zeal of the later Jews prompted them to resort.—MICHAELIS.

Ver. 19. And if a man cause a blemish in his neighbour; as he hath done, so shall it be done unto him; 20. Breach for breach, eye for eye, tooth for tooth: as he hath caused a blemish in a man, so shall it be done to him *again.*

In cases of corporal injuries done to *free persons*, (for the same rule did not extend to *servants*, they being less protected members of the community,) that far severer law of retaliation operated, whose language is, "Eye for eye, and tooth for tooth;" and upon that law I must here expatiate more fully, because it is so far removed from our laws, that it sometimes appears to us really barbarous, or, as others would say, *unchristian.* Barbarous, however, it was not; for those very nations of antiquity whom we look upon as most civilized, viz. the Athenians and Romans, had this law in the days of their freedom. But the singular circumstance respecting it, is, that it is, strictly speaking, only suited to a free people, and where the poorest citizen has equal rights with the greatest man that can injure him; although, no doubt, it may subsist under an aristocracy and a monarchy also, as long as no infringement is made on liberty, and on the equality of the lowest with the highest, in point of rights. Where, however, the eye of a nobleman is of more value than that of a peasant, it would be a very preposterous and inconvenient law; and where, for the benefit of the great, attempts might out of friendship be made to pervert justice, it is much more consonant to equity, in the case of such corporal injuries, to leave the determination of the punishment to the decision of the judge. It would seem that Moses retained the law of retaliation, from a more ancient, and a very natural, law of usage. It will be well worth our while to hear what he himself says on the subject of a law, so strange to us, and yet so common among ancient free nations. His *first* statute respecting it, clearly presupposes *retaliation* as consuetudinary, and only applies it to the very special case of a pregnant woman being pushed, by two men quarrelling with each other, and thereby receiving an injury; the man who pushed her, being adjudged to pay "life for life, eye for eye, tooth for tooth, hand for hand, foot for foot, brand for brand, wound for wound, bruise for bruise," Exod. xxi. 23—25. The *second* statute likewise occurs but incidentally; when, on occasion of blasphemy uttered by an Egyptian, it was ordained that both Israelites and strangers should have one and the same criminal law; and it is added, by way of example, "Whoever shall injure his neighbour in his person, shall receive even as he hath given: eye for eye, wound for wound, tooth for tooth; even as he hath injured another, so shall it be done to himself in return;" Lev. xxiv. 19, 20. What Moses then says (incidentally, in fact, and presupposing a more ancient law of usage) concerning the punishment of retaliation, I understand under the two following limitations:—

1. *When the injury is either deliberate, or at least in consequence of our fault;* (an instance of which last is that mentioned above, from Exod. xxi. 23, where a woman is hurt by two men fighting; an act of outrage of which they ought not to have been guilty;) but not where there is either no fault, or at any rate but an inadvertence; as where one man pushes out another's eye undesignedly. This limitation every one will admit, who remembers that Moses was so far from meaning to punish unpremeditated homicide by the law of retaliation, that he established an asylum for the unfortunate manslayer, to secure him from the fury of the *Goël.*

2. The person who suffered any personal injury, retained (for he is nowhere deprived of it) the natural right of abstaining, if he chose, from all complaint, and even of retracting a complaint already made, and remitting the punishment, if the other compounded with him for what we should call a *pecuniary indemnity*, or, to use the Hebrew expression, *a ransom.* Not to mention that this right is quite natural and obvious, and scarcely requires to be noticed in a penal statute, it may be observed, that among the Israelites such pecuniary expiations had been previously common, even in the case of deliberate murder, as they still are among the Orientals, and that in this case alone did Moses find it necessary to prohibit the acceptance of any such compensation; Numb. xxxv. 31. If it was customary in cases of deliberate murder, we may conclude with certainty, that it would frequently be accepted for the loss of a tooth or an eye; but as Moses did not prohibit this, we must suppose that the ancient usage still continued to prevail.

But is not the punishment of retaliation extremely rude? Does it not savour strongly of ancient barbarism? and must not every legislator, who out of philanthropy wishes the nobleman to preserve his own eyes, though he may previously have beaten out those of the worthless peasant, naturally keep at as great a distance here as possible from the brutal law of ancient times? And was not Moses then very much to blame, I will not say in *giving* such a law, for that cannot be laid to his charge, but in retaining it from ancient usage?

Let us listen with candour, to what may be said both for and against this species of punishment.

I. In *favour* of it, then, we may observe—

1. That it is the first punishment that will naturally occur to every legislator when left to himself; nor can any one justly complain, that that should happen to himself, which he has done to another: for he has certainly cause to be thankful, that he does not suffer more: since not only self-revenge, as authorized by the *jus naturæ*, but also punishments in civil society generally go much greater lengths, and retaliate for evils that have been suffered, perhaps tenfold.

2. That it has a more powerful effect than any other punishment in deterring from personal injuries; and is, indeed, almost the only adequate means of attaining this end of punishment. Pecuniary punishments will not be very formidable to the man of opulence, particularly if they are regulated by the rank of the person injured; nor will they, of course, do much to promote the security of the poor: nay, even though corporal punishments be legal, if they only rest *with the discretion of the judge*, (and here, that is a very alarming and despotically-sounding expression,) not only is not the security of the poor man thereby promoted, because the judge's discretion is generally pretty favourable to the great, but his humiliation becomes, in fact, only the greater. Should the nobleman, for instance, put out the eye of a peasant, and the judge estimate the loss at 1000 rix-dollars, which, though a sum pretty considerable in itself, can give the former but little concern; but the peasant, on the other hand, who puts out a nobleman's eye, be dragged to the gallows in a cart, though quite ready to pay him the same sum, which indeed many a peasant, in some countries, could very easily raise; such an inequality in the law would, to a man of spirit, who feels his hands, and who is both able and willing to defend his country with them, prove rather intolerable. Under such a law, can the

man in an humble station possibly have that security for sound limbs, that he must wish, and has a right to demand, from the community? When, on the contrary, the greatest and richest man in the land knows, that if he puts out the eye of a peasant, the latter has a right to insist that *his* eye be put out in return, that a sentence to that effect will actually be pronounced, and the said punishment inflicted, without the least respect to his rank, or his noble eye being considered as one whit better than the peasant's; and that he has no possible way of saving it, but by humbling himself before the other, as deeply as may be necessary to work upon his compassion, and make him relent, besides paying him as much money as he deems a satisfactory compensations for his loss; every one will be convinced (without my swearing to prove it) that the nobleman will bethink himself, before he put out any one's eye. The argument is precisely the same in the case of other injuries, down to the loss of a tooth; concerning which the ancient *jus talionis* came at last to teach so different a doctrine.

If here it be objected, (and no doubt the objection has weight,) that notwithstanding the exclusion of the *jus talionis*, from our law, and its superior mildness in all respects, we scarcely ever see an instance of an eye put out in deliberate malice; I beg leave to observe in answer, that this is, in fact, to be ascribed in a great measure, to the superior mildness and refinement of our manners: but such manners are not found in all nations; they certainly were not found in the ancient nations that approached nearer to the state of nature; nor yet do we find them among the people of southern countries; whose rage is more malicious, and loves to leave a lasting memorial behind it, in those on whom it is vented. By the gradually refined manners, therefore, of our more northerly regions, we can hardly expect that the ancient law of retaliation, should in southern nations have been regulated. Add to this, that among us, since the introduction of luxury and more effeminate education, or in consequence of hereditary disease, the nobleman has very seldom such bodily strength as to be a match for a peasant; and if it came to the driving out of teeth or eyes, would run the risk of losing two of either, before the latter lost one. There are, besides, to be taken into consideration several other fortunate circumstances, which though not, properly speaking, connected with our law, serve nevertheless to remedy its defects. For instance, most of the people of distinction among us are at the same time servants to the sovereign, and as such have both honour and revenues, and would sink into a sort of nothingness if they lost their posts; but such are the humane ideas of many sovereigns, that they would no longer retain in their service the person who had put out a poor man's eye, unless circumstances appeared that were highly alleviative of the outrage, or that he made a satisfactory compensation for it. But the advantage which *we* thus derive from our manners is not to be met with in every democracy or aristocracy; for there, as posts are conferred either by laws, or by votes, of which no individual is ashamed, so neither are they taken away without legal authority.

3. That in the state of nature every man has a right to take revenge at his own hand for any deliberate personal injury, such as the loss of an eye, &c. is perhaps undeniable. In fact, by the law of nature such revenge might be carried still further: but if it be confined within the limits of strict retaliation, the law of nature at any rate (for of morality I do not now speak) can certainly have nothing to object against it. Now, in the state of civil society, every man divests himself of the right in question; but then he justly expects, in return, that society will, after proper inquiry, duly exercise revenge in his room. Morality may say what it will to our revenge, (and certainly it does not absolutely condemn it,) but we are all naturally vindictive, and *that* to such a degree, that when we are grossly injured we feel a most irksome sort of disquietude and feverish heat, until we have gratified our revenge. Now, when creatures, thus constituted, are the citizens of any government, can we imagine that they will ever give up the prerogative of revenge, without looking for some equivalent in return? If the state means to withhold that equivalent, and yet prohibit the exercise of revenge, it must begin by regenerating human nature: or, if it be said, that God and his grace can alone effect such a change, and that whoever lays open his heart to grace, will never desire revenge, I can only say, that we must then figure to ourselves a state consisting of none but people all truly regenerated; but such a state the world has never yet seen.

4. If the law of *retaliation* were abrogated, nothing could be more natural, if the lower classes had not, by long constraint and oppression, become too much humbled, than for the poor man, who had received any personal injury, still to revenge it at his own hand, and more especially to lie in wait for his rich oppressor, at whom he could not come with open force, and put out *his* eye, with as little warning and ceremony as he had done his. And what could in such a case be done; were justice to be observed, and the poor man who only requited the injury he had received, to experience no severer punishment than he who set him the example? It might, no doubt, be said, that his conduct, in thus lying in wait, and in deliberately avenging his own quarrel, in contempt of a *legal* prohibition, aggravated his guilt in every respect; but where the injured person, aware that the laws gave him *no* reparation, only did *in instanti*, what every man of spirit would very naturally do, and what, if he did not go beyond blows, even our laws would excuse him for doing—if he only flew with all possible fury upon the person who had put out his eye, and tried to put out *his* in return; we should not, perhaps, think him deserving of so severe a punishment for having thus requited like for like, as the person who had begun the quarrel. Now this immediate self-revenge would, among a people who retained any feeling of their dignity, and their natural equality with even the most distinguished of their fellow-citizens, be the usual plan: and if no one attempts any such thing, we can scarcely impute it to the *refined* manners of the brawny peasantry, and even of the very lowest of the people, but rather to the melancholy circumstance, of their having become too tame, and having forgotten that they are not slaves, but, in point of rights, on a footing of equality with the rest of their countrymen.

5. Even our own laws admit the right of retaliation, and that too, in rather an equivocal case, and where an injury is not actually done, but only intended, and perhaps not even that. They allow us, in the case of having been calumniated, to sue the person who has falsely and maliciously charged us with any crime, for the same penalty, which the crime itself incurs according to the laws. No doubt, judgment is rarely pronounced in terms of our complaint, and much here depends on the discretion of the judge; but still it is clear, that the laws, in authorizing any such suit, presuppose the equity of the *jus talionis*.

II. The chief arguments *against* the law in question may, perhaps, be found comprehended under the following objections, which are usually urged against it.

1. There are many injuries, where it would be absurd to give the sufferer a right to retaliation: in the case of adultery, for instance, to permit the injured husband to sleep with the wife of the adulterer in return. In regard to this objection, however, some misconception seems to lie at bottom. It is not every description of injuries that we here speak of, but only of personal injuries: nor yet of any retaliation that the sufferer himself may choose to exact, such, for instance, as thrusting out another's eyes or teeth; but only of a punishment that depends upon, and is to be inflicted by the magistrate. Were any person to deduce *all* sorts of punishments from the *jus talionis*, this objection would hold: but it does not hold in the case of a legislator appointing the punishment of retaliation for *personal* injuries.

2. In many cases it is difficult to requite just as much, and no more, than has been suffered; for instance, where a man has thrust out one of another man's teeth, he may, in suffering retaliation, very easily lose *two* teeth by one stroke. In like manner, it would be difficult to inflict a wound of exactly the same size and depth with that given, and neither larger nor deeper. And what shall be done, where a man, having but one eye, happens to thrust out one of his neighbour's? Shall he lose his only eye by way of retaliation? This would be to make him suffer a much more serious injury than he had caused: for now he would be quite blind, whereas he had only made the other one-eyed, like himself. Here I will make much greater concessions than the opponents of the law of retaliation are wont to demand. For had they known human nature, they would have stated in addition, and I, for my own part, readily grant them, that punishment by retaliation is in almost every case, a much more sensible evil, than the original

injury: for every pain and every evil to which we look forward, is, by mere anticipation and fear, aggravated more than a hundred fold; the pang of a moment is extended to hours, days, weeks, &c.; and when it actually takes place, every individual part of the evil is felt in the utmost perfection, by both soul and body, in consequence of its being expected. The adversaries of the *lex talionis* were bad philosophers, when, with all their benevolence, this observation escaped them.—But after all, it would, even in conjunction with what went before, form no objection to the law in question; for this, in fact, is nothing more than what commonly takes place in all punishments, and in all the variety of revenge that we dread, even in the state of nature. If I had, in that state, beat out the eye of one of my neighbours, I should always be afraid that he, or his son, or his father, or his brother, or some other friend, or, perhaps some person hired for the purpose, might lie in wait for me, and beat out one of mine in return; and, under this unnecessary fear, I should really and truly be much more unhappy, than the man whose eye I beat out; in my very dreams, I should, who knows how often, lose an eye with pain and horror; and although, when I awoke again, I found myself possessed of it, I should, at first, be uncertain, perhaps, whether it had been a dream or not; and, stupified with fear, in the darkness of the night, I should be anxious to try whether it could see or not. Nay, not only should I be afraid of this, but well aware that revenge always studies to retaliate beyond what it suffers, I should anticipate a more serious injury than I had caused, the loss of an eye perhaps for a tooth, or even the loss of life itself, in short, every thing that is bad: and, under these continual apprehensions, I should be extremely miserable, even though the injured person might never actually retaliate the injury. Should he ever get me into his hands, and repay me merely according to the *jus talionis*, this would be a fresh addition to my misery; unless, indeed, it might be said, that I ought to look upon it as good luck, because I should no longer have to live in perpetual terror. Now these are nothing more than the terrors of conscience, that natural and awful avenger of all the crimes we commit, and, in the mythologies of the Greeks and Romans, represented under the image of the *Furies;* and thus, for wise ends, hath nature constituted our minds, to prevent us from injuring one another. Even in the case of murder, it is precisely the same. Whoever, in the state of nature, has perpetrated that crime, will continually be in fear of the son or friend of the deceased, as his *Goël;* will, while awake, fancy a hundred times that he sees him, and tremble at the thoughts of him, how distant soever he may be; and will be as often disturbed when asleep, by seeing him in his dreams, and thinking that he feels him giving him the fatal stab. In a word, he will, both sleeping and waking, die a thousand deaths. If he think this unjust, and too severe, let him blame God and nature, for having annexed such variety of wretchedness to the commission of guilt; and blame himself for being such a fool as to let such stuff come into his imagination.

If, again, it is committed by a member of civil society, and if (which is the mildest punishment of all those now in use) it costs him his head, he certainly, in suffering even this retaliation, suffers much more than the person whom he murdered; who had only a few minutes agony, which his rage, in self-defence, would scarcely let him feel; whereas *he*, in his prison, anticipates his death for weeks, and feels in imagination, which aggravates every evil, the sword of justice every moment on his neck; and at last, when he is actually brought out to execution, is so much overwhelmed by the previous feelings of death, that there have been instances of malefactors, who, having a pardon given them on the scaffold, were already so near death, that they could not be saved even by blood-letting, but died as thoroughly as if they had actually been beheaded. But thus to die of agony, is a much more terrible death than to die of mere wounds by the hand of a murderer. This objection, therefore, amounts to nothing at all; only there is another, which it is understood to imply, viz. *that the injurious party is under no obligation to suffer more evil than he has done;* and this was actually the reasoning of the philosopher *Favorinus*, whom *A. Gellius* introduces as speaking on this subject, in his *Noctes Atticæ*. But what ignorance doth such reasoning show of all the laws that have been introduced into all nations, and above all, that any man may, from his own feelings, know of the nature of revenge, if he pay but ever so little attention to what passes within him. The injurious party has no right to demand that the retaliation to which he subjects himself, shall not exceed the injury; for upon the same principle on which he did an injury to another, without any precedent or provocation, may the sufferer, following his example, requite him, in terms of his own law, with ten times, or ten thousand times, as great an injury. The relations between *nothing* and *something*, and between *something* and *infinity*, are alike: they both surpass all numeration. As to the morality of such a procedure, and whether God approves of evils being thus infinitely increased, I am not here concerned with deciding. The present question relates not to an evil infinitely augmented, but only of one requited with some addition. If, however, the injurious party have it requited him even in an infinite degree, he can have nothing more to say, than that as he had *done*, so had he *suffered*, wrong. But putting this infinity entirely out of the question; in all the circumstances wherein human beings can be placed together, proceeding from the rudest state of nature, and what is a relic of it, the consuetudinary law of duelling, through every stage of society, until we arrive at the best-regulated commonwealth, it holds as a fundamental principle, that the man who has caused evil to another, has no reason to complain if he should suffer a *greater* evil in return. In the state of nature, self-revenge goes certainly much beyond the offence, and would go infinite lengths, if not restrained at last by pity, or by contempt of its victim, or by the suggestions of magnanimity. In the old German proverb, which is strongly expressive of a national idea, it is said, (*Auf eine Maulschelle gehört ein Dolch,*) "Every blow has its dagger." The point of honour, in duelling, insists on revenge with the sword; and the whip, with the pistol; but where people's ideas are not so artificial, they find a satisfaction in, and plume themselves on, having given for *one* blow, *two* or more in return. —In the state of civil society, the design of punishment is to deter from crimes; for which purpose, a bare requital in kind will not be sufficient, because the criminal may hope to escape detection, or to escape from justice, and of course his fear of punishment is by its uncertainty materially lessened; and hence punishments are here much more severe, and by one example, many thousands are deterred from a repetition of the crime: so, that unless a man chooses to take the consequences, and to serve the public as an example *in terrorem*, he must abstain from injuring his neighbour. In the case of theft, restitution, with considerable additions, would not be accounted too severe, but on the contrary a very mild punishment for the crime; and yet here more is given back than was taken away.—But I here stop short, because I mean to offer some general remarks on the relation of punishments to crimes, in the *Essay* which I have already mentioned my intention of adding as an Appendix to this work. This observation only shall I yet offer in the meantime. The objection argues not only against the retaliation of personal injuries, now the subject of dispute, but against *all* punishments whatever, which consist of any evil that is at all a matter of feeling, or which, by fear and anticipation, may become aggravations of such evils; and many inferences flow from it, which to the objector himself must appear very strange, and would go at any rate to destroy all the security of human life. Assassination, for instance, and child-murder, would on this principle be mere trifles, and by no means worthy of being punished with death. The assassin might say, "The person, whom I murdered, did not know what befell him. *He* was no sooner stabbed than he fell; and he died, without knowing it, altogether unexpectedly, and in the midst of joy; and if I must die on his account, let my death be equally easy and unexpected. I only beg that people may not take it into their heads to declare me an outlaw, else shall I at every step be accompanied with the dread of death, and, in imagination, die a hundred thousand times instead of once."—The child-murderer, again, might say all this, and thus much more: "The child whom I despatched, knew nothing of the worth and enjoyment of life, and had been in a state of such obscure sensibilities, that his pain was next to nothing;" thus insinuating, that whenever he himself should happen to come into the same state, that is, to return to his mother's womb and be born again, by a sort of Pythagorean *Metempsychosis* he might *then* be punished for the crime in question; but that, till then, justice required his punishment to be delayed, because to make him die at present, would be doing him very great injustice.

3. The law of retaliation is barbarous. I do not see why it should be considered as more barbarous than hanging or beheading; and with the very same justice with which this assertion is made, it may in like manner be asserted, that to demand payment of a debt is base and avaricious, or that every punishment which is less severe than that of like for like, is fit only for a state where the people are oppressed and enslaved. The one assertion is just like the other, and neither of them proves any thing. The latter indeed would, in these times, manifest a stronger tone of sympathy, and perhaps more truth, than in former ages.

4. The sight of so many mutilated persons who, by the law of retaliation, had had an eye beat out, or a hand chopped off, or a nose bitten away, &c. &c., would be extremely disagreeable; and would not only be a punishment to the culprits themselves, but to every person of the least degree of sensibility, and especially to the fair sex at the time of conception, when they are afraid of having their imaginations affected by disgusting objects. This I readily grant; but I believe, at the same time, that where other circumstances, and the character of the people are the same, these are sights that will be much more rarely seen where the *lex talionis* is established, than where it is not. For every one will then be the more careful to avoid wounding or maiming his neighbour, in a quarrel, or in a passion; and certainly nobody will attempt any such thing after deliberate premeditation, when he knows that he must himself lose the same member of his body, of which he deprives his neighbour. Besides, it is certain that the law of retaliation will be but seldom enforced, and be chiefly confined to threatenings, and measures *in terrorem*. The man who has beat out the eye or tooth of another, or cut off his arm, will be at all possible pains to obtain his forgiveness, and a remission of the legal punishment. He will humble himself before him, and beg his pardon; not as *we* see sometimes done, with an air of proud contempt; but even the man of highest rank will heartily do so before the meanest of his dependants; will ever after honour him as his forgiver, and at the same time gladly make him any pecuniary recompense in his power. In such a case, the sufferer of the injury will be compassionate and generous, or, if not sufficiently either the one or the other, at any rate he will have as much love of money as, when the violence of his revenge has been a little mitigated by the humiliation and entreaties of his adversary, to accept the proffered peace-offering, and let self-interest settle the account between them. Men are naturally vindictive; but whenever we meet with humble apologies, and the injurious person throws himself on our mercy, we are in general sufficiently inclined to forget our wrongs; so much so, indeed, that to some people it is nothing less than intolerable punishment to hear such apologies, and they forget the injuries they have suffered, merely when they know that their author regrets them. Even those whose sentiments are not so refined, will still, when their fury is abated, yield to the power of gold. It was thus that at Rome the *lex talionis* came gradually into perfect desuetude, and gave place to a pecuniary compensation, depending on the discretion of the prætor; and *that*, though there had been nothing else, was *one* bad consequence of the change; for to a free man, the *discretion of a judge* is a term that sounds very suspiciously.

5. Sound morality cannot approve of that revenge, which nothing short of a repetition of the same injury will satisfy, and which insists on beating out the eye of another, if he has beaten out ours. This too I readily admit; but then morality and civil law are not one and the same thing; and the latter, as long as it has to do with people who are not all paragons of perfect virtue, must tolerate many things on account of hardness of heart, to avoid greater evils. Thus, for instance, as long as the greatest, or the greater part of the people are still prone to revenge, the law must give injured persons the means of obtaining satisfaction for their wrongs, else will the consequence be, that they will take revenge at their own hands; and thus, instead of authoritative punishments, none other will be known than that of personal revenge, which is always dangerous, by being carried beyond due bounds, and often affects the innocent, and provokes to fresh acts of vengeance. To this, however, we must add what has been already observed, that although those, who are in the least injured, will inexorably abide by the law of retaliation, they will still be satisfied with professions of repentance, with apologies, and with pecuniary compensations. The law does not peremptorily command an injured person to avail himself of the right of retaliation, without any alternative. It only fixes the punishment to which the author of an injury must submit, if he cannot compound matters with the injured party. It thus deters from outrages, because every one must be afraid, lest the sufferer insist upon his right, and in the case of personal mutilation, compel the person who has caused it, to agree to such terms of compensation, as he would otherwise have refused to offer.

6. Christ, in his sermon on the mount, condemns that revenge which requires *eye for eye, and tooth for tooth;* (Matt. v. 38, 39;) and consequently the law of retaliation is unchristian. This is, in fact, the same objection with the preceding, and therefore already answered. Christ does not find fault with the Mosaic statute of *eye for eye, and tooth for tooth;*—for he has throughout his whole sermon nothing to do with Moses, and neither expounds nor controverts his doctrines—he only condemns the bad morality of the Pharisees, which they thought fit to propound in his words. In the present instance, these expositors, confounded, as on many other occasions, civil law and morality together; and when the moral question was, How far may I be allowed to carry my resentment, and gratify my thirst for revenge? they answered in the words which Moses addressed, not to the *injured*, but to the *injuring* party, or to the judge, and said, *eye for eye, tooth for tooth.* That Christ has no intention of controverting, or censuring the laws of Moses, but merely the expositions of the Pharisees, is manifest, from comparing his own doctrine with that of Moses. Moses addresses the magistrate, or the delinquent who has mutilated his neighbour, and says, *Thou, delinquent, art bound to give eye for eye, tooth for tooth; and thou, judge, to pronounce sentence to that effect.* Christ, on the other hand, manifestly addresses the person injured, and forbids him to be vindictive; *Ye have heard, that it is said, eye for eye, tooth for tooth; but I command you not to requite evil; but whoever strikes you on the right cheek, offer to him also the left.* How this last clause is to be understood; whether it prohibits suing for revenge, and whether one should actually hold up the left cheek to the person who has slapped the right, it is not my business here to decide, because I am not explaining the sermon on the mount. But as long as a people is not composed of citizens, whose temper and conduct are altogether in conformity to the doctrine of the sermon on the mount, civil laws, which do not, as Christ himself says, permit many things, *on account of the hardness of the people's hearts*, and which presuppose such an exalted pitch of perfect virtue, will be improper and unwise. I am far from meaning, by what I have now said in defence of the *lex talionis*, to assert that it is the only proper punishment in the case of personal injuries, or that it ought to be introduced into every state, in which it is not yet in use; but only that where it already operates, and especially in the Mosaic policy, it does not merit censure. Here also it ought to be considered, that the same style of law is not equally suitable to every state. To southern countries the law of retaliation appears to be better adapted, and, in some respects, more necessary, than to northern; because in southern countries, such as Italy, Portugal, Palestine, and Arabia, the desire of revenge is generally more violent, and of longer duration, than with us in the 50th degree of latitude, who sooner forgive and forget injuries, and are really magnanimous in our revenge. Where it is once established, as where Moses found it already in force, it is dangerous to attempt its abrogation because the people accustomed to it might not be willing to give it up, and would, of course, enforce it themselves. But to introduce it among us would appear to be needless; because we hear of or see so few instances of personal injuries; for though we have people among us who want an eye, there are none who owe the loss of it to deliberate malice, nor is it by any means a *trait* of our national character, that we delight in inflicting permanent injuries on one another. A German is commonly too magnanimous to think of any such thing. Blows he will give, and show his superiority over his enemy; but even the peasant in the

utmost violence of rage, and though he hardly knows of any particular punishment for such an offence, will not, at any rate, willingly beat out his neighbour's eye, or think of giving him any such lasting mark of his revenge, as the inhabitant of a southern country, or that rare character among us, to whom, in lower Saxony, the epithet *glupisch* is applied, would exult in having left behind him. Except in cases of necessity, it is always a hazardous and doubtful experiment to alter laws, or to increase the severity of punishments; and with regard to uncommon crimes, a legislator will always decline taking any notice of them, or will, at any rate, make no new laws in relation to them, lest he should thus only make them known; he will think it better to let them quietly rest under the ancient national abhorrence, with which they are regarded. Thus as we are not accustomed to the law of retaliation, it would appear to us cruel, and no injured person would, for fear of the universal outcry it would raise against him, attempt commencing an action to enforce it: so that, as frequently happens in such cases, the increased severity of the punishment would prove nothing else than a sort of impunity to the person who had committed the crime. The more nearly that a people approaches to a state of nature, the more suitable to their circumstances is the law of retaliation: in like manner, it agrees better with a democracy, than with any of the other forms of government: although, no doubt, to these it can accommodate itself, and did subsist in Rome under a strong mixture of aristocracy. The following distinction, likewise, which has not, perhaps, been theoretically considered, is a very striking one. Where every citizen is a soldier, and defends his country with the strength of his arm, the law in question may answer well enough; but where there is one particular class of men, who follow the profession of arms, whether as hired soldiers, according to our present system, or, according to the feudal plan in the middle ages, as gentlemen, with land given them in fee instead of pay, there, at least, if crimes were very frequent, it could not be conveniently enforced without many exceptions. For if the soldier had an eye dug out, or his right arm, hand, or thumb, mutilated, he would not only be punished himself, but his country would also suffer, in his being rendered unfit for its defence. Here, therefore, there would require to be one law for the protectors, and another for the protected; at least, unless soldiers could be had in more than sufficient numbers. Many other dangers of the same kind would attend an alteration of the law; which is, in every case, a very hazardous experiment. At the same time, I readily own, that in cases of personal injury, I have no great partiality for the *pleasure* of the judge, but would infinitely prefer the decision of laws, that should place the high and the low on an equal footing, and estimate the tooth of a peasant at the same rate with that of a lord, particularly where the former must gnaw crusts, and the latter can have crumb if he chooses.—MICHAELIS.

CHAPTER XXV.

Ver. 23. The land shall not be sold for ever; for
the land *is* mine; for ye *are* strangers and sojourners with me. 24. And in all the land of
your possession, ye shall grant a redemption for
the land. 25. If thy brother be waxen poor,
and hath sold away *some* of his possession, and if
any of his kin come to redeem it, then shall he
redeem that which his brother sold. 26. And
if the man have none to redeem it, and himself
be able to redeem it; 27. Then let him count
the years of the sale thereof, and restore the
overplus unto the man to whom he sold it; that
he may return unto his possession. 28. But
if he be not able to restore *it* to him, then that
which is sold shall remain in the hand of him
that hath bought it until the year of jubilee:
and in the jubilee it shall go out, and he shall
return unto his possession.

Moses declared God, who honoured the Israelites by calling himself their king, the sole lord-proprietary of all the land of promise, in which he was about to settle them by his most special providence; while the people were to be merely his tenants, and without any right to alienate their possessions in perpetuity, Lev. xxv. 23. It was, indeed, allowable for a proprietor to sell his land for a certain period; but every fiftieth year, which Moses denominated the year of jubilee, it returned without any redemption to its ancient owner, or his heirs. Hence Moses very justly observes, that this was a sale, not of the land, but only of its crops, between the period of sale and the year of jubilee. It was reasonable that the value of a field should be estimated higher or lower, according as it came to sale at a longer or shorter period preceding that year; and Moses therefore admonished the Israelites, (Lev. xxv. 14—16,) against taking unjust advantage of the ignorant and simple in this particular on such occasions. This purchase of crops, however, must have been a very profitable speculation, because no man would lay out his money for such a length of time, and encounter all risks, (that of war not excepted,) as he was obliged to do, unless he purchased at a very cheap rate. It was not in his power to rid himself of those risks, by abandoning the bargain, as a lessee may his lease, and re-demanding the money expended, because at the year of jubilee all debts became instantly extinguished. He would, therefore, always take care to purchase on such terms, as, allowing for the very worst that could happen, might secure him from loss, and even yield him some profit—at least the interest of his money, prohibited as all usury was by the law. Hence, and as a consequence of the principle, that *the lands were to feed those to whose families they belonged*, there was established a law of redemption, or right of re-purchase, which put it in the power of a seller, if before the return of the year of jubilee his circumstances permitted him, to buy back the yet remaining crops, after deducting the amount of those already reaped by the purchaser, at the same price for which they were originally sold: and of this right, even the nearest relation of the seller, or, as the Hebrews termed him, his *Goël*, might likewise avail himself, if he had the means. Lev. xxv. 24—28.

The advantages of this law, if sacredly observed, would have been great. It served, in the *first* place, to perpetuate that equality among the citizens, which Moses at first established, and which was suitable to the spirit of the democracy, by putting it out of the power of any flourishing citizen to become, by the acquisition of exorbitant wealth, and the accumulation of extensive landed property, too formidable to the state, or in other words, a little prince, whose influence could carry every thing before it.—In the *second* place, it rendered it impossible that any Israelite could be born to absolute poverty, for every one had his hereditary land; and if that was sold, or he himself from poverty compelled to become a servant, at the coming of the year of jubilee he recovered his property. And hence, perhaps, Moses might have been able with some justice to say, what we read in most of the versions of Deut. xv. 4, *There will not be a poor man among you.* I doubt, however, whether that be the true meaning of the original words. For in the 11th verse of this same chapter, he assures them that *they should never be without poor;* to prevent which, indeed, is impossible for any legislator, because, in spite of every precaution that laws can take, some people will become poor, either by misfortunes or misconduct. But here, if a man happened to be reduced to poverty, before the expiry of fifty years, either he himself, or his descendants, had their circumstances repaired by the legal recovery of their landed property, which though indeed small, then became perfectly free and unincumbered. —In the *third* place, it served to prevent the strength of the country from being impaired, by cutting off one, and perhaps the greatest cause of emigration, viz. poverty. No Israelite needed to leave his home on that ground. Here, to be sure, the extraordinary case of any public calamity that might make the lands lose their value, must be excepted. But it was enough that in ordinary cases the law took away the chief inducement to emigration, by such a judicious provision as made it the interest of the people to remain contented at home.—In the *fourth* place, as every man had his hereditary land, this law, by its manifest tendency to encourage marriage, rather served to promote the population of the country, than to impair it.—In the *fifth* place, the land being divided into numerous small portions, each cultivated by the father of a family, acquainted with it from his infancy, and naturally attached to it as the inalienable property of his family, could not fail in consequence of this law, to be better managed, and more productive, than large estates in the hands of tenants and day-labourers could ever have been.—And, *lastly*, this institution served to attach every Israelite to his country in the strongest manner, by suggesting to him that, if he had to fight in its defence, he would at the same time be defending his own property, which it was, moreover, out of his power to convert into money, wherewith he might betake himself to a more peaceful habitation elsewhere.—Michaelis.

CHAPTER XXVI.

Ver. 33. And I will scatter you among the heathen, and will draw out a sword after you; and your land shall be desolate, and your cities waste.

By the concurring testimony of all travellers, Judea may now be called a field of ruins. Columns, the memorials of ancient magnificence, now covered with rubbish, and buried under ruins, may be found in all Syria. From Mount Tabor is beheld an immensity of plains, interspersed with hamlets, fortresses, and heaps of ruins. The buildings on that mountain were destroyed and laid waste by the Sultan of Egypt in 1290, and the accumulated vestiges of successive forts and ruins are now mingled in one common and extensive desolation. Of the celebrated cities Capernaum, Bethsaida, Gadara, Tarichea, and Chorazin, nothing remains but shapeless ruins. Some vestiges of Emmaus may still be seen. Cana is a very paltry village. The ruins of Tekoa present only the foundations of some considerable buildings. The city of Nain is now a hamlet. The ruins of the ancient Sapphura announce the previous existence of a large city, and its name is still preserved in the appellation of a miserable village called Sephoury. Loudd, the ancient Lydda and Diospolis, appears like a place lately ravaged by fire and sword, and is one continued heap of rubbish and ruins. Ramla, the ancient Arimathea, is in almost as ruinous a state. Nothing but rubbish is to be found within its boundaries. In the adjacent country there are found at every step dry wells, cisterns fallen in, and vast vaulted reservoirs, which prove that in ancient times this town must have been upwards of a league and a half in circumference. Cæsarea can no longer excite the envy of a conqueror, and has long been abandoned to silent desolation. The city of Tiberias is now almost abandoned, and its subsistence precarious; of the towns that bordered on its lake there are no traces left. Zabulon, once the rival of Tyre and Sidon, is a heap of ruins. A few shapeless stones, unworthy the attention of the traveller, mark the site of the Saffre. The ruins of Jericho, covering no less than a square mile, are surrounded with complete desolation; and there is not a tree of any description, either of palm or balsam, and scarcely any verdure or bushes to be seen about the site of this abandoned city. Bethel is not to be found. The ruins of Sarepta, and of several large cities in its vicinity, are now "mere rubbish, and are only distinguishable as the sites of towns by heaps of dilapidated stones and fragments of columns." But at Djerash, (supposed to be the ruins of Gerasa,) are the magnificent remains of a splendid city. The form of streets, once lined with a double row of columns, and covered with pavement still nearly entire, in which are the marks of the chariot-wheels, and on each side of which is an elevated pathway—two theatres and two grand temples, built of marble, and others of inferior note—baths—bridges—a cemetery with many sarcophagi, which surrounded the city—a triumphal arch—a large cistern—a picturesque tomb fronted with columns, and an aqueduct overgrown with wood—and upwards of two hundred and thirty columns still standing amid deserted ruins, without a city to adorn—all combine in presenting to the view of the traveller, in the estimation of those who were successively eyewitnesses of them both, "a much finer mass of ruins" than even that of the boasted Palmyra. But how marvellously are the predictions of their desolation verified, when in general nothing but ruined ruins form the most distinguished remnants of the cities of Israel; and when the multitude of its towns are almost all left, with many a vestige to testify of their number, but without a mark to tell their name.—Keith.

Ver. 34. Then shall the land enjoy her sabbaths, as long as it lieth desolate, and ye *be* in your enemies' land; *even* then shall the land rest, and enjoy her sabbaths.

A single reference to the Mosaic law respecting the Sabbatical year renders the full purport of this prediction perfectly intelligible and obvious. "But in the seventh year shall be a Sabbath of rest unto the land; thou shalt neither sow thy field nor prune thy vineyard." And the land of Judea hath even thus enjoyed its Sabbaths so long as it hath lain desolate. In that country, where every spot was cultivated like a garden by its patrimonial possessor, where every little hill rejoiced in its abundance, where every steep acclivity was terraced by the labour of man, and where the very rocks were covered thick with mould, and rendered fertile; even in that selfsame land, with a climate the same, and with a soil unchanged, save only by neglect, a dire contrast is now, and has for a lengthened period of time been displayed, by fields untilled and unsown, and by waste and desolated plains. Never since the expatriated descendants of Abraham were driven from its borders, has the land of Canaan been so "plenteous in goods," or so abundant in population, as once it was; never, as it did for ages unto them, has it vindicated to any other people a right to its possession, or its own title of the land of promise—it has rested from century to century; and while that marked, and stricken, and scattered race, who possess the recorded promise of the God of Israel, as their charter to its final and everlasting possession, still "*be in the land of their enemies, so long their land lieth desolate.*" There may thus almost be said to be the semblance of a sympathetic feeling between this bereaved country and banished people, as if the land of Israel felt the miseries of its absent children, awaited their return, and responded to the undying love they bear it by the refusal to yield to other possessors the rich harvest of those fruits, with which, in the days of their allegiance to the Most High, it abundantly blessed *them.* And striking and peculiar, without the shadow of even a semblance upon earth, as is this accordance between the fate of Judea and of the Jews, it assimilates as closely, and, may we not add, as miraculously, to those predictions respecting both, which Moses uttered and recorded ere the tribes of Israel had ever set a foot in Canaan. *The land shall be left of them, and shall enjoy her rest while she lieth desolate without them.*

To the desolate state of Judea every traveller bears witness. The prophetic malediction was addressed to the mountains and to the hills, to the rivers and to the valleys; and the beauty of them all has been blighted. Where the inhabitants once dwelt in peace, each under his own vine and under his own fig-tree, the tyranny of the Turks, and the perpetual incursions of the Arabs, the last of a long list of oppressors, have spread one wide field of almost unmingled desolation. The plain of Esdraelon, naturally most fertile, its soil consisting of "fine rich black mould," level like a lake, except where Mount Ephraim rises in its centre, bounded by Mount Hermon, Carmel, and Mount Tabor, and so extensive as to cover about three hundred square miles, is a solitude "almost entirely deserted; the country is a complete desert." Even the vale of Sharon is a waste. In the valley of Canaan, formerly a beautiful, delicious, and fertile valley, there is not a mark or vestige of cultivation. The country is continually overrun with rebel tribes; the Arabs pasture their cattle upon the spontaneous produce of the rich plains with which it abounds. Every ancient landmark is removed. Law there is none Lives and property are alike unprotected. The valleys are untilled, the mountains have lost their verdure, the rivers flow through a desert and cheerless land. All the beauty of Tabor that man could disfigure is defaced; immense ruins on the top of it are now the only remains of a once magnificent city; and Carmel is the habitation of wild beasts. "The art of cultivation," says Volney, "is in the most deplorable state, and the countryman must sow with the musket in his hand; and no more is sown than is necessary for subsistence." "Every day I found fields abandoned by the plough." In describing his journey through Galilee, Dr. Clarke remarks, that the earth was covered with such a variety of thistles, that a complete collection of them would be a valuable acquisition to botany. Six new species of that plant, so significant of wildness, were discovered by himself in a scanty selection. "From Kane-Leban to Beer, amid the ruins of cities, the country, as far as the eye of the traveller can reach, presents nothing to his view but naked rocks, mountains, and precipices, at the sight of which pilgrims are astonished, balked in their expectations, and almost startled in their faith." "From the centre of the neighbouring elevations (around Jerusalem) is seen a wild, rugged, and mountainous desert; no herds depasturing on the summit, no forests clothing the acclivities, no waters flowing through the valleys; but one rude scene of savage melancholy waste, in the midst of which the ancient glory of Judea bows her head in widowed desolation." It is needless to multiply quotations to prove the desolation of a country which the Turks have possessed, and which the Arabs have plundered for ages. Enough has been said to prove that *the land mourns and is laid waste, and has become as a desolate wilderness.*—KEITH.

CHAPTER XXVII.

Ver. 28. Notwithstanding, no devoted thing that a man shall devote unto the LORD, of all that he hath, *both* of man and beast, and of the field, of his possession, shall be sold or redeemed: every devoted thing *is* most holy unto the LORD.

Whatever has been devoted to the gods can never be sold, redeemed, or applied to any other purpose. In every village there are chroniclers of strange events, of the visitations of the gods on men who did not act fairly and truly with their *devoted* things. There is a story generally received of "a deranged man, who in a lucid interval made a vow that he would give his gold beads to the temple of Siva, and he became quite well. After this he refused to perform his vow, and he died." "Another person, who was very ill of a fever, devoted a goat to the gods, and immediately became well; but some time after he refused the gift, and his fever returned." When a child becomes sick, the parents forthwith inquire, "Have we given all the things we devoted to the gods?" The medical man also (when the disease baffles his skill) inquires, "Have you given all the things you devoted to the gods?"—ROBERTS.

NUMBERS.

CHAPTER II.

Ver. 31. All they that were numbered in the camp of Dan, *were* a hundred thousand and fifty and seven thousand and six hundred: they shall go hindmost with their standards. 34. And the children of Israel did according to all that the LORD commanded Moses: so they pitched by their standards, and so they set forward, every one after their families, according to the house of their fathers.

Mr. Harmer thinks the standards of the tribes were not flags, but little iron machines carried on the top of a pole, in which fires were lighted to direct their march by night, and so contrived, as sufficiently to distinguish them from one another. This is the kind of standard by which the Turkish caravans direct their march through the desert to Mecca, and seems to be very commonly used by travellers in the East. Dr. Pococke tells us, that the caravan with which he visited the river Jordan, set out from thence in the evening soon after it was dark for Jerusalem, being lighted by chips of deal full of turpentine, burning in a round iron frame, fixed to the end of a pole, and arrived at the city a little before daybreak. But he states also, that a short time before this, the pilgrims were called before the governor of the caravan, by means of a white standard that was displayed on an eminence near the camp, in order to enable him to ascertain his fees. In the Mecca caravans, they use nothing by day, but the same moveable beacons in which they burn those fires, which distinguish the different tribes in the night. From these circumstances, Harmer concludes, that, "since travelling in the night must in general be most desirable to a great multitude in that desert, and since we may believe that a compassionate God for the most part directed Israel to move in the night, the standards of the twelve tribes were moveable beacons, like those of the Mecca pilgrims, rather than flags or any thing of that kind." At night the camp was illuminated by large wood fires; and a bituminous substance secured in small cages or beacons, formed of iron hoops, stuck upon poles, threw a brilliant light upon the surrounding objects.—MUNROE'S SUMMER RAMBLE IN SYRIA.

CHAPTER V.

Ver. 2. Every one that hath an issue, and whosoever is defiled by the dead.

All who attend a funeral procession, or ceremony, become *unclean*, and before they return to their houses must wash their persons and their clothes. Neither those in the sacred office, nor of any other caste, can, under these circumstances, attend to any religious ceremonies. They cannot marry, nor be present at any festivity, nor touch a sacred book. A person on hearing of the death of a son, or other relative, immediately becomes unclean. The Brahmins are unclean twelve days; those of the royal family, sixteen days; the merchants, twenty-two; and all other castes, thirty-two days.—ROBERTS.

CHAPTER VI.

Ver. 26. The LORD lift up his countenance upon thee, and give thee peace.

"As I came along the road, I met Rāman, and he lifted up his face upon me; but I knew not the end;" which means, he looked pleasantly. Does a man complain of another who has ceased to look kindly upon him, he says, "Ah! my friend, you no longer lift up your countenance upon me."—ROBERTS.

CHAPTER X.

Ver. 7. But when the congregation is to be gathered together, ye shall blow, but ye shall not sound an alarm.

The form of the republic established by Moses was democratical. Its head admitted of change as to the name and nature of his office; and we find that, at certain times, it could subsist without a general head. If, therefore, we would fully understand its constitution, we must begin, not from above, but with the lowest description of persons that had a share in the government. From various passages of the Pentateuch, we find that Moses, at making known any laws, had to convene the whole congregation of Israel, (קהל or עדה;) and, in like manner, in the book of Joshua, we see, that when *Diets* were held, the whole congregation were assembled. If on such occasions every individual had had to give his vote, every thing would certainly have been democratic in the highest degree; but it is scarcely conceivable how, without very particular regulations made for the purpose, (which, however, we nowhere find,) order could have been preserved in an assembly of 600,000 men, their votes accurately numbered, and acts of violence prevented. If, however, we consider that, while Moses is said to have spoken to *the whole congregation*, he could not possibly be heard by 600,000 people, (for what human voice could be sufficiently strong to be so?) all our fears and difficulties will vanish; for this circumstance alone must convince any one that Moses could only have addressed himself to a certain number of persons deputed to represent the rest of the Israelites. Accordingly, in Numb. i. 16, we find mention made of such persons. In contradistinction to the common Israelites, they are there denominated *Kerüe Häeda*, (קרואי העדה) that is, "those wont to be called to the convention." In the xvi. chapter of the same book, ver. 2, they are styled, *Nesïe Eda Kerüe Moëd*, (נשיאי עדה קרואי מועד) that is, "chiefs of the community, that are called to the convention." I notice this passage particularly, because it appears from it, that 250 persons of this description, who rose up against Moses, became to him objects of extreme terror; which they could not have been, if *their* voices had not been, at the same time, the voices of their families and tribes. Still more explicit, and to the point, is the passage, Deut. xxix. 9, where Moses, in a speech to the whole people, says, "Ye stand this day all of you before the Lord your God, your heads, your tribes, (that is, chiefs of tribes,) your elders, your scribes, all Israel, infants, wives, strangers that are in your camp, from the hewer of wood to the drawer of water." Now as Moses could not possibly speak loud enough to be heard by two millions and a half of people, (for to so many did the Israelites amount, women and children included,) it must be manifest that the first-named persons *represented* the people, to whom they again repeated the word of Moses. Whether these representatives were on every occasion obliged to collect and lec are the sense of their constituents, or whether, like the members of the English House of Commons, they acted in the plenitude of their own power for the general good, without taking instructions from their constituents, I find nowhere expressly determined; but methinks, from a perusal of the Bible, I can scarcely doubt that the latter was the case.

Who these representatives were, may in some measure be understood from Josh. xxiii. 2., and xxiv. 1. They would seem to have been of two sorts. To *some*, their office as judges gave a right to appear in the assembly; and these were not necessarily of the same family in which they exercised that office. *Others*, again, had a seat and a voice in the Diet, as the heads of families.—MICHAELIS.

Ver. 31. And he said, Leave us not, I pray thee; forasmuch as thou knowest how we are to encamp in the wilderness, and thou mayest be to us instead of eyes.

An aged father says to his son, who wishes to go to some other village, "My son, leave me not in my old age; you are now my eyes." "You are on the look-out for me, your eyes are sharp." It is said of a good servant, "he is eyes to his master."—ROBERTS.

When Moses begged of Hobab not to leave Israel, because they were to encamp in the wilderness, and he might be to them instead of eyes, Numb. x. 31, he doubtless meant that he might be a guide to them in the difficult journeys they had to take in the wilderness: for so Job, when he would express his readiness to bring forward on their journey those that were enfeebled with sickness, or hurt by accidents, and to guide them in their way that were blind or ignorant of it, says, "I was eyes to the blind, and feet was I to the lame," Job xxix. 15. Everybody, accordingly, at all acquainted with the nature of such deserts as Israel had to pass through, must be sensible of the great importance of having some of the natives of that country for guides: they know where water is to be found, and can lead to places proper, on that account, for encampments. Without their help, travelling would be much more difficult in these deserts, and indeed often fatal. The importance of having these Arab guides appears, from such a number of passages in books of travels, that every one whose reading has at all turned this way, must be apprized of them; for which reason I shall cite none in particular. The application then of Moses to Hobab the Midianite, that is, to a principal Arab of the tribe of Midian, would have appeared perfectly just, had it not been for this thought, that the cloud of the Divine Presence went before Israel, and directed their marches; of what consequence then could Hobab's journeying with them be? A man would take more upon himself than he ought to do, that should affirm the attendance of such a one as Hobab was of no use to Israel, in their removing from station to station: it is very possible, the guidance of the cloud might not be so minute as absolutely to render his offices of no value. But I will mention another thing, that will put the propriety of this request of Moses quite out of dispute. The sacred history expressly mentions several journeys undertaken by parties of the Israelites, while the main body laid still: so in Numb. xiii. we read of a party that was sent out to reconnoitre the land of Canaan; in chap. xx. of the messengers sent from Kadesh unto the king of Edom; in chap. xxxi. of an expedition against the idolatrous Midianites; of some little expeditions, in the close of chap. xxx.; and more journeys of the like kind, were without doubt undertaken, which are not particularly recounted. Now Moses, foreseeing something of this, might well beg the company of Hobab, not as a single Arab, but as a prince of one of their clans, that he might be able to apply to him from time to time, for some of his people, to be conductors to those he should have occasion to send out to different places, while the body of the people, and the cloud of the LORD, continued unmoved.

Nor was their assistance only wanted in respect to water, when any party of them was sent out upon some expedition; but the whole congregation must have had frequent need of them, for directions where to find fuel. Manna continually, and sometimes water, were given them miraculously; their clothes also were exempted from decay while in the wilderness; but fuel was wanted to warm them some part of the year, at all times to bake and seethe the manna, according to Exod. xvi. 23, and was never obtained but in a natural way, that we know of: for this then they wanted assistance of such Arabs as were perfectly acquainted with that desert. So Thevenot, describing his travelling in this very desert, says, on the night of the 25th of January they rested in a place where was some broom, for that their guides never brought them to rest anywhere, willingly we are to suppose, but in places where they could find some fuel, not only to warm them, but to prepare their coffee and mafrouca. He complains also of their resting-place on the night of the 28th of January, on account of their not being able to find any wood there, not so much as to boil coffee. A like complaint he makes of the night between the eighth and ninth of February, when not being able to get into Suez, he was obliged to lie without the gates till it was day, suffering a great deal of cold, because they had no wood to make a fire. Moses hoped Hobab would be instead of eyes to the Israelites, both with respect to the guiding their parties to wells and springs in the desert, and the giving the people in general notice where they might find fuel: for though they frequently make use in this desert of camels' dung for fuel, this could not, we imagine, wholly supply their wants; and in fact, we find the Israelites sought about for other firing.—HARMER.

Ignorance is a kind of blindness often no less fatal than privation of sight; and partial, or deficient information, is little better than ignorance: so we find Moses saying to Hobab, "Leave us not, I pray thee; forasmuch as thou knowest how we ought to encamp in the wilderness, and thou mayest be to us instead of eyes," Numb. x. 31. The necessity and propriety of such a guide, will appear from considerations easily gathered from the following extract; and the description of a person of this character will be interesting, though it cannot be equally interesting to us who travel on hedge-bounded turnpike roads, as to an individual about to take his passage across the great desert. If it be said, in the case of Moses, the angel who conducted the camp might have appointed its stations without the assistance of Hobab; we answer, it might have been so; but, as it is now the usual course of Providence to act by means, even to accomplish the most certain events; and as no man who has neglected any mean, has now the smallest right to expect an interposition of Providence on his behalf, so we strongly *query*, whether it would not have been a failing, of presumption, in Moses, had he omitted this application to Hobab; or indeed, any other, suggested by his good sense and understanding.

"A *hybeer* is a guide, from the Arabic word *hubbar*, to inform, instruct, or direct, because they are used to do this office to the caravan travelling through the desert, in all its directions, whether to Egypt and back again, the coast of the Red Sea, or the countries of Sudan, and the western extremities of Africa. They are *men of great consideration*, knowing perfectly the situation and properties of all kinds of water, to be met on the route, the distances of wells, whether occupied by enemies or not, and if so, the way to avoid them with the least inconvenience. It is also necessary to them to know the places occupied by the simoom, and the seasons of their blowing in those parts of the desert; likewise those occupied by moving sands. He generally belongs to some powerful tribe of Arabs inhabiting these deserts, whose protection he makes use of, to assist his caravans, or protect them in time of danger; and handsome rewards are always in his power to distribute on such occasions; but now that the Arabs in these deserts are everywhere without government, the trade between Abyssinia and Cairo given over, that between Sudan and the metropolis much diminished, the importance of that office of *hybeer*, and its consideration, is fallen in proportion, and with these the safe conduct; and we shall see presently a caravan cut off by the treachery of the very *hybeers* that conducted them, the first instance of the kind that ever happened." (Bruce.)—TAYLOR IN CALMET.

CHAPTER XI.

Ver. 5. We remember the fish which we did eat in Egypt freely; the cucumbers, and the melons, and the leeks, and the onions, and the garlic.

To an Englishman the loss of these articles would not give much concern, and he is almost surprised at the Israelites repining at their loss, as at the loss of great delicacies. The people of the East do not in general eat flesh, nor even fish, so that when they can procure it they consider it a delicacy. Cucumbers are eaten in abundance in hot weather, and melons are most delicious and plentiful. I have never seen leeks in the East, and I am doubtful whether they are to be found; but whether or not, there is much difference of opinion as to the translation of the word. D'Oyly and Mant have a quotation to this effect:—"Whether the following word, rendered *leeks*, have that signification, may be doubted. Some think it was the *lotus*, which is a water plant, a kind of water-lily, which the Egyptians used to eat during the heats of summer." In the Universal History, (vol. i. p. 486,) it is said, that those "Egyptians who dwelt in the marshes, fed on several plants which annually grow, particularly the *lotus*, of which they made a sort of bread." Of the Arabs also, (in the same work,) it is recorded—"They make a drink of the Egyptian *lotus*, which is very good for inward heat." The Tamul name of the *lotus* is the Tamari. The Materia Medica, under the article Nelumbium Speciosum, says this plant is the true *lotus* of the Egyptians, and the Nymphea Nilufer of Sir William Jones. Its beautiful and fragrant flower is sacred to Lechimy, the goddess of Maga Vishnoo. It has a bulbous root, and is highly esteemed as an article of food. As it grows in *tanks*, it can *only* be had in the hottest weather, when the water is dried up; and, in this we see a most gracious provision in allowing it to be taken when most required. Its cooling qualities are celebrated all over India, and the Materia Medica says of it, "This is an excellent root, and is also prescribed medicinally, as cooling and demulcent." The natives eat it boiled, or in curry, or make it into flour for gruels. I am, therefore, of opinion, that it was the *lotus* of Egypt respecting which the Israelites were murmuring.—ROBERTS.

Whoever has tasted onions in Egypt must allow that none can be had better in any part of the universe. Here they are sweet, in other countries they are nauseous and strong; here they are soft, whereas in the north, and other parts, they are hard of digestion. Hence they cannot in any place be eaten with less prejudice and more satisfaction than in Egypt. They eat them roasted, cut into four pieces, with some bits of roasted meat, which the Turks in Egypt call *kobab*, and with this dish they are so delighted, that I have heard them wish they might enjoy it in paradise. They likewise make soup of them in Egypt, cutting the onions in small pieces; this I think one of the best dishes I ever eat.

By melons we are probably to understand the *water-melon*, which the Arabians call *batech*. It is cultivated on the banks of the Nile, in the rich clayey earth which subsides during the inundation. This serves the Egyptians for meat, drink, and physic. It is eaten in abundance during the season, even by the richer sort of people; but the common people, on whom providence has bestowed nothing but poverty and patience, scarcely eat any thing but these, and account this the best time of the year, as they are obliged to put up with worse fare at other seasons. This fruit likewise serves them for drink, the juice refreshing these poor creatures, and they have less occasion for water than if they were to live on more substantial food in this burning climate.—HASSELQUIST.

Among the different kinds of vegetables, which are of importance to supply the want of life, or to render it more agreeable, he tells us, is the *melons*, which, without dispute, is there one of the most salutary and common among them. All the species that they have in Europe, and in the seaports of the Mediterranean, are to be found in Egypt. Besides them, there is one, whose substance is green and very delicious. It grows round like a bowl, and is commonly of an admirable taste. There are also water-melons, extremely good. But above all the rest, at Cairo, and its neighbourhood, they boast of a species of melons, pointed at each end, and swelling out in the middle, which the people of the country call *abdelarins*. This is an Arabian word, which signifies the slave of sweetness. In fact, these melons are not to be eaten without sugar, as being insipid without it. Macrisi says, this last kind was formerly transported hither, by a man whose name they bear. They give it to the sick, to whom they refuse all other kinds of fruit. The rind is very beautifully wrought; its figure very singular; as well as the manner of ripening it, which is by applying a red-hot iron to one of its extremities. The people of the country eat it green as well as ripe, and in the same manner as we eat apples. These melons, of a foreign extraction, continue two whole months, and grow nowhere else in Egypt. They say the same species is found in Cyprus.—MAILLET.

Ver. 6. But now our soul *is* dried away; *there is* nothing at all, besides this manna, *before* our eyes.

In great hunger or thirst the people say, "Our soul is withered." "More than this, sir, I cannot do; my spirit is withered within me." "What! when a man's soul is withered, is he not to complain?"—ROBERTS.

Ver. 8. *And* the people went about, and gathered *it*, and ground *it* in mills, or beat *it* in a mortar, and baked *it* in pans, and made cakes of it: and the taste of it was as the taste of fresh oil.

The eastern mill consists of two circular stones, about eighteen inches in diameter, and three inches thick. The top stone has a handle in it, and works round a pivot, which has a hole connected with it to admit the corn. The *mortar* also is much used to make rice flour. It is a block of wood, about twenty inches high and ten inches in diameter, having a hole scooped out in the centre. The pestle is a stick of about four feet long, made of iron-wood, having an iron hoop fixed to the end.—ROBERTS.

Ver. 16. And the Lord said unto Moses, Gather unto me seventy men of the elders of Israel, whom thou knowest to be the elders of the people, and officers over them; and bring them unto the tabernacle of the congregation, that they may stand there with thee.

Moses established in the wilderness another institution, which has been commonly held to be of a judicial nature;

and under the name of *Sanhedrim* or *Synedrium*, much spoken of both by Jews and Christians, although it probably was not of long continuance. We have the account of its establishment in Num. xi.; and if we read the passage impartially, and without prejudice, we shall probably entertain an opinion of the Synedrium different from that generally received, which exalts it into a supreme college of justice, that was to endure for ever. A rebellion that arose among the Israelites distressed Moses exceedingly. In order to alleviate the weight of the burden that oppressed him, he chose from the twelve tribes collectively, a council of seventy persons to assist him. These, however, could hardly have been judges; for of *them*, the people already had between sixty and seventy thousand. Besides, of what use could seventy new judges, or a supreme court of appeal, have been in crushing a rebellion. It seems much more likely, that this selection was intended for a supreme senate to take a share with Moses in the government; and as it consisted of persons of respectability, either in point of family or merits, it would serve materially to support his power and influence among the people in general. By a mixture of aristocracy, it would moderate the monarchical appearance which the constitution must have assumed from Moses giving his laws by command of God, and it would unite a number of powerful families together, from their being all associated with Moses in the government. It is commonly supposed that this Synedrium continued permanent; but this I doubt. For in the whole period from the death of Moses to the Babylonish captivity, we find not the least mention of it in the Bible; and this silence, methinks, is decisive; for in the time of the judges, but particularly on those occasions when, according to the expression of the book of Judges, *there was neither king nor judge in Israel;* and again, during those great political revolutions, when David by degrees became king over all the tribes, and when the ten tribes afterward revolted from his grandson, Rehoboam; and lastly, under the tyrannical reigns of some of the subsequent kings; such a supreme council of seventy persons, if it had been in existence, must have made a conspicuous figure in the history; and yet we find not the least trace of it: so that it merely appears to have been a temporary council instituted by Moses for his personal service and security; and as he did not fill up the vacancies occasioned in it by deaths, it must have died out altogether in the wilderness. No doubt the Jews, after their return from the Babylonish captivity, *did* institute a sanhedrim at Jerusalem, of which frequent mention is made, not only in the New Testament, but also in Jewish writings. But this was merely an imitation of the ancient Mosaic Synedrium, with the nature of whose constitution the latter Jews were no longer acquainted; for they had indeed become ignorant of almost all the customs of their ancestors. The detail of this second sanhedrim established by the latter Jews belongs not to our present work, but to their history after the Babylonish captivity.—Michaelis.

Ver. 20. *But* even a whole month, until it come out of your nostrils, and it be loathsome unto you.

What does this mean? Is it not a figurative expression, to show that they were to eat till fully satisfied? Bishop Patrick says, "till you be glutted and cloyed with it." Is it not a striking illustration that this figure of speech is used at this day to convey the same meaning? A host says to his guests, "Now, friends, eat *mookamallam*, to the nose," literally, to eat till they are full up to the nose. "O, sir, how can I eat any more? I am full to the nose, I have no more room." Of a glutton, it is said, "That fellow always *fills up to the nose!*"—Roberts.

Ver. 21. And Moses said, the people, among whom I *am*, *are* six hundred thousand footmen; and thou hast said, I will give them flesh, that they may eat a whole month. 22. Shall the flocks and the herds be slain for them, to suffice them? or shall all the fish of the sea be gathered together for them, to suffice them?

When Moses mentioned Israel's being fed with fish, collected from the Red Sea, he seems to have supposed something of an extraordinary kind; but analogous to what had happened to several people, in small companies, not any thing miraculous. In answer to the divine declaration, Moses proposed a difficulty in accomplishing this promise, in the natural course of things, not as imagining it could not be done by a miracle; he could not but know, that he that rained down manna, could, by a miracle, gorge them with flesh; but in the common course of things, or in the natural, though more unusual operation of Providence, could it be brought about? That was what puzzled Moses. Some flocks, and a few oxen, they had with them for the solemnities of sacrifice; but could a part of them, with any addition that might be procured from the people on the skirts of the desert, be sufficient to support them a whole month? Fish might be obtained from the Red Sea, from which, it seems, they were not very distant, but could it be expected they would come in such numbers to the shore, within their reach, as fully to satisfy the cravings of their appetites, day after day, for a whole month? The ground of this inquiry, with respect to the flesh of quadrupeds, is visible to all: they had frequently tasted of their flesh in feasts, generally of a sacred nature, sometimes, perhaps, of a less devout kind. But how came Moses to think of *fish?* Irwin explains it, by observing, that a little lower down, toward the straits of Babelmandel, he found fish in abundance in the Red Sea; that the Arabs were very expert in catching them; and that great quantities were to be picked up, from time to time, on the sand-banks, which are extremely numerous in the Red Sea. There is no reason to believe, that Israel had not tasted fish in some of their encampments, of which some are expressly said to have been near the Red Sea, Numb. xxxiii. 10, 11; and others are known to have been on that coast, or not far from it, where no mention is made of that circumstance in the sacred writings. And there can be no reason to doubt, that since many of them found fish so grateful to their palates, but that they would endeavour to make use of that opportunity for gratifying themselves. Manna was an additional supply, only intended to make up a sufficiency of food; not designed to be exclusive of every other species of it. If the modern Arabs are so dexterous at catching fish now, the ancient Egyptians, we have reason to believe, were so in their time; and the low and oppressed state of Israel in that country, will not allow us to believe, that they did not exert themselves with equal assiduity, and in consequence of continual use, with equal success. *We remember the fish we did eat in Egypt freely*, was a part of their moan, Num. xi. 5. If Moses knew what the common people of Egypt now know, and which their sages in ancient days must, at least, have remarked, he could be no stranger to that change of place that may be observed as to fish, and their crowding together at certain times; and to some such a natural, but surprising and unknown occurrence, as to the inhabitants of this sea, the words of Moses seem to point: *Shall the flocks and herds be slain for them? . . . . or shall all the fish of the sea be gathered together*, by some natural impulse, to this place, for a month or more, which none of us have had any notion of, nor received any information about, to *suffice them?* Such is, I apprehend, the spirit of these words. —Harmer.

Ver. 31. And there went forth a wind from the Lord, and brought quails from the sea, and let *them* fall by the camp, as it were a day's journey on this side, and as it were a day's journey on the other side, round about the camp, and as it were two cubits *high* upon the face of the earth.

There are no birds of passage which arrive in greater and at the same time more unaccountable numbers, than quails. They assemble together on the sandy shore of Egypt, in very large flocks. It is difficult to imagine how a bird which, being so heavy in its flight, cannot fly to any distance, and which in our fields we see alight almost as soon as it has taken wing, should venture to traverse a pretty great extent of sea. The islands scattered over the Mediterranean, and the vessels sailing along its surface, serve them, indeed, for places of rest and shelter, when the winds become boisterous, or contrary to the direction of their route. But these asylums, which the quails have not always sufficient strength to reach, and the distance of which is frequently fatal to them, likewise prove to them places of destruction. Too much exhausted to fly, they suffer themselves to be caught without difficulty upon inhospitable shores: they are also easily taken by hand upon the rigging of ships; and when excess of fatigue prevents them from rising to that height, they strike with violence against the vessel's hull, fall back, stunned by the shock, and disappear in the waves. Whatever may be the danger of the long voyage to which these birds do not seem destined; whatever losses these bodies of feeble travellers may sustain in the course of the passage, there still arrives so great a multitude in the environs of Alexandria, that the number to be seen there is truly incredible. The Egyptian fowlers catch them in nets. During the first days of their arrival, such quantities are for sale in the markets of Alexandria, that three and sometimes four were to be purchased for a medine, or about fifteen or sixteen derniers.—SONNINI.

That quails really are used to migrate in countless flocks, is known, not only in Asia, but in the southern parts of Europe; for instance, in the kingdom of Naples, and especially in the beautiful islands in the bay of Naples. Yet the opinion of those commentators who think that they were not quails, but locusts, that the wind brought to the Israelites, may be worthy of attention, especially on account of the circumstance mentioned in the holy scriptures, that the Israelites "hung them up round the camp," (so Luther has it, and not "spread them abroad," as in the English translation,) as the Orientals still do with locusts, which they dry in the sun.—(Stollberg's Hist. of Religion.) The common opinion that they were quails which collected in such numbers round the camp of the Israelites, is, however, favoured by this circumstance, that these birds are still designated by the Arabic word, which is the same as the Hebrew *selav*.—ROSENMULLER.

Ver. 32. And the people stood up all that day, and all *that* night, and all the next day, and they gathered the quails: he that gathered least gathered ten homers; and they spread *them* all abroad for themselves round about the camp.

The surprising abundance of these birds may be inferred from the quantity which the tribes collected. The persons employed, were not a few of the people, but a great multitude that were not prevented by other domestic engagements or important reasons; and that discovered on this occasion, much alacrity and perseverance. Unwilling to lose so valuable an opportunity of gratifying their inordinate desires, and providing for their future wants, they continued their active exertions for several days; and that we may know the result of their diligence, and form some idea of the abundant supply with which divine providence had favoured them, the sacred historian states, "he that gathered least, gathered ten homers." This word (הומר) *homer*, is properly distinguished from (עמר) *omer*, a much smaller measure, and from (חמור) *hamor*, an ass, or the load which is commonly laid upon that animal. But some writers make it equal to the cor, which is more than double the weight, and is the common load of a camel. But it was not necessary that every one should gather ten camel loads of quails; for God had promised his people flesh for a month, and would have fulfilled his promise by bestowing on every individual the third part of a cor, or camel's burden. The truth of this assertion will appear, when it is considered, that every Israelite received for his daily subsistence, an omer of manna, which is the tenth part of an epha. But an epha is the tenth part of a cor; and by consequence, a cor contains a hundred omers. If then an omer is sufficient for one day, a cor must be sufficient for a hundred days, that is, for more than three months. Hence, if every Israelite gathered ten cors of quails, they collected thirty times more than God had promised. Bochart endeavours to remove this difficulty, by observing, that Moses, in this verse, speaks only of the heads of families, leaving out of his enumeration, the women, children, and slaves. But it is evident that Moses did not use the word people in this restricted sense; for he states, that the wrath of the Lord was kindled against the people that gathered the quails, "and the Lord smote them with a very great plague." And the people journeyed from Kibroth-hattaavah; but these things are surely said of the whole people. Dissatisfied with this solution, Bochart proposes another, with which he is better pleased: The ten homers are not ten cors, but ten heaps; for in this sense, the word is sometimes used. Thus, in the prophecies of Habakkuk, homer signifies a heap of many waters; and in the book of Exodus, a heap of frogs. Onkelos and other interpreters, accordingly render it in this passage ten heaps. If this be admitted, Moses has not determined the quantity of these birds which every one gathered; but only says, that every one at least gathered ten heaps, that is, by a familiar phrase among the Hebrews, a very great number; for ten is often used in scripture for many. This version ought to be preferred, both on account of what has been already stated, and because the cor is a measure of corn, not of flesh. The view now given is of some value; for if every Israelite gathered ten cors of quails, the number of these birds must have been so great as to exceed all belief. But it has been shown, that instead of ten cors, an Israelite did not collect and use the third part of one. It is not meant to limit the power of God; but surely no violence should be offered to human belief, by requiring more from it than God has revealed in his word.

The vast multitude of these birds, appears also from the long time that the many thousands of Israel subsisted upon them in the desert. Jehovah promises, with uncommon emphasis, "Ye shall not eat one day, nor two days, nor five days, neither ten days, nor twenty days; but even a whole month." The complete fulfilment of this promise, although not recorded by Moses, may be justly inferred from the great quantity which the people gathered and laid up in store, after drying them in the sun, for their subsistence. The Psalmist distinctly alludes to it in these words: "So they did eat and were filled; for he gave them their own desire." Thus were six hundred thousand footmen, besides women and children, supplied with quails for a whole month, by the power and goodness of Jehovah. In the colder regions of Europe, where the quail is less frequent, this could not have been done without a new creation; but in warm climates, the case is very different. There these birds are found in immense numbers. From Aristophanes it appears that no bird was more common in Greece; and Juvenal asserts, that none were of less value at Rome. Nor will that appear wonderful, when the assertion of some writers is considered, that, in the beginning of spring, within the space of five miles, a hundred thousand of these birds are sometimes caught in one day; and this astonishing number continues to be taken for nearly a whole month. Varro asserts, that turtles and quails return from their migrations into Italy, in immense numbers. Hence, their flight, when they approach the land, is alleged by Pliny, to be "attended with danger to mariners; for these birds, wearied with their journey, alight upon the sails, and this always in the night, and sink their frail vessels." The same fact is stated by Solinus, as quoted by Bochart: "When they come within sight of land, they rush forward in large bodies, and with so great impetuosity as often to endanger the safety of navigators; for they alight upon the sails in the night, and by their weight overset the vessels." Many places also have borne the name of Ortygia, from the multitude of quails which crowded their fields. Thus, Delus was called Ortygia; the island of Syracuse was known by the same name; also the city of Ephesus, as well as a grove very near it, and another in the vicinity of Miletus. For the same reason, the whole country of Libya, received from the ancients the name of Ortygia. But quails abounded nowhere in greater numbers than in Egypt, and the surrounding countries, whither they were allured by the intense heat of the climate, or the great fertility of the soil. Hence, the remark of Josephus, that the Arabic gulf is peculiarly favourable to the breeding of these birds. We have also heard the testimony of Diodorus, concerning the countless number of quails about Rhinocolura; and the ancients mention a species of quail peculiar to Egypt, which is so numerous at a certain season of the year, that the inhabitants, unable to consume them all, are compelled to salt them for future use. This was done in times when, according to Theocritus, the vale of Egypt contained more than thirty thousand cities; and by the testimony of Josephus, seven hundred and fifty myriads of people, without including the inhabitants of Alexandria. From this statement it must be evident, that in order to supply the many thousands of Israel with quails for a whole month, no act of creation was necessary; but only a strong breeze, to direct the flight of those innumerable flocks, which encumber the African continent, to the camp of Israel. We read that our Lord multiplied the loaves and the fishes, when he fed the attending multitudes; but no inspired writer insinuates, that Jehovah created or multiplied the quails with which he sustained his people in the wilderness. He had only to transport them on the wings of the wind, from the vale of Egypt, and the shores of the Red Sea. It was indeed a stupendous miracle, to collect such immense numbers, to bring them into the desert precisely at the time which he had appointed, and to let them fall about the camp, that they might be gathered by his people; but the provision itself existed already in the stores of common providence, and required only to be conveyed to the spot where it was needed.—PAXTON.

CHAPTER XII.

Ver. 14. And the LORD said unto Moses, If her father had but spit in her face, should she not be ashamed seven days? Let her be shut out from the camp seven days, and after that let her be received in *again*.

Miriam had greatly offended God, and, therefore, she was to be as a daughter, whose father had spit in her face. In Deuteronomy xxv. 9, the widow was to spit in the face of her late husband's brother, if he refused to marry her. And Job (xxx. 10) in his great misery says of his enemies, "they spare not to spit in my face;" and in reference to our Saviour, they did "spit in his face." The most contemptuous, the most exasperating and degrading action, which one man can do to another, is to *spit in his face*. A person receiving this insult is at once worked up to the highest pitch of anger, and nothing but the rank or power of the individual will prevent him from seeking instant revenge. Indeed, such is the enormity attached to this offence, that it is seldom had recourse to, except in extreme cases. A master, whose slave has deeply offended him, will not beat him, (for that would defile him,) but he spits in his face. When his anger is at the greatest height, he will not even condescend to do that, but order a fellow-servant, or some one near, to spit in his face. Is a person too respectable for this indignity; then the offended individual will spit upon the ground. Schoolmasters, also, when very angry with a scholar, do not, as in England, begin to beat him, but spit in his face, or order some one else to do it. To a person making use of offensive language, bystanders say, "*Spit in his face.*"—ROBERTS.

CHAPTER XIII.

Ver. 23. And they came unto the brook of Eshcol, and cut down from thence a branch with one cluster of grapes, and they bare it between two upon a staff; and *they brought* of the pomegranates, and of the figs.

It appears that the cultivation of the vine was never abandoned in this country. The grapes, which are white, and pretty large, are, however, not much superior in size to those of Europe. This peculiarity seems to be confined to those in this neighbourhood, for at the distance of only six miles to the south, is the rivulet and valley called Escohol, celebrated in scripture for its fertility, and for producing very large grapes. In other parts of Syria, also, I have seen grapes of such an extraordinary size, that a bunch of them would be a sufficient burden for one man. It is not at all surprising, therefore, that when the spies, sent by Moses to reconnoitre the promised land, returned to give him an account of its fertility, it required two of them to carry a bunch of grapes, which they brought with them suspended from a pole placed upon their shoulders. (Mariti.) Many eyewitnesses assure us, that in Palestine the vines, and bunches of grapes, are almost of an incredible size. Stephen Schultz relates, "At Beitdjin, a village near Ptolemais, we took our supper under a large vine, the stem of which was nearly a foot and a half in diameter, the height about thirty feet, and covered with its branches and shoots (for the shoots must be supported) a hut more than fifty feet long and broad. The bunches of these grapes are so large that they weigh from ten to twelve pounds, and the grapes may be compared to our plums. Such a bunch is cut off and laid on a board, round which they seat themselves, and each helps himself to as many as he pleases." Forster, in his Hebrew Dictionary, (under the word Eshcol,) says, "that he knew at Nurnburg, a monk of the name of Acacius, who had resided eight years in Palestine, and had also preached at Hebron, where he had seen bunches of grapes which were as much as two men could conveniently carry." Christopher Neitzschutz, who travelled through Palestine in the year 1634, speaking of his excursions on the Jewish mountains, says, "These mountains are pretty high on the right, and most beautifully situated; and I can say with truth, that I saw and ate of bunches of grapes which were each half an ell long, and the grapes two joints of a finger in length." Reland says, "that a merchant, who lived several years at Rama, assured him that he had there seen bunches of grapes which weighed ten pounds each." Vines and grapes of an extraordinary size are found in other parts of the East. Strabo says, "that in the Margiana, a country southwest of the Caspian sea, now called Ghilan, there are vines which two men can scarcely span, the bunches of which are of extraordinary length." *Olearius*, in 1637, saw in this part vines, the stem of which was as thick as a man's body. At Iran, he states, there is a kind of grapes called Enkuri ali deresi, which are of a brown red colour, and as large as Spanish plums. The carrying of a bunch of grapes between two men was not merely for its weight, but that it might be brought uninjured, and without being crushed, into the Israelite camp.—ROSENMULLER.

The pomegranate, the malus punica of the Romans, the ροα or ροια of the Greeks, and the Rimon of the Hebrews, is a kind of apple-tree, whose fruit is covered without, with a rind of a reddish colour, and which, opening lengthwise, shows red grains full of juice resembling wine, with little kernels. The Hebrew term Rimon, which expresses both the tree and the fruit, from Rama, to project, seems to have its name from the strong projection or reflection of light either from the fruit or from the starlike flower with six leaves, or rays, at the top of the apple. The Greek name ροα, which denotes the tree, and ροισκος, the fruit, by which the Seventy render the word Rimon, aim perhaps at the same thing, being derived from ρεω, to flow. We learn from Dr. Shaw, that August produces the first ripe pomegranates, some of which are three or four inches in diameter, and of a pound weight. The pomegranate, or malum punicum, as originally brought from Phœnicia, was formerly numbered among the most delicious fruits which the earth produces. That from Arabia is large, full of juice, and highly flavoured. The juice especially, when expressed from the seeds and interior film, by which the bitter flavour is avoided, is a delicate beverage: and one of those pomegranates will sometimes fill a small basin. The high estimation in which it was held by the people of Israel, may be inferred from its being one of the three kinds of fruit brought by the spies from Eshcol, to Moses and the congregation in the wilderness; and from its being specified by that rebellious people as one of the greatest luxuries they enjoyed in Egypt, the want of which they felt so severely in the sandy desert. The pomegranate, classed by Moses with wheat and barley, vines and figs, oil olive and honey, was, in his account, one principal recommendation of the promised land. But no circumstance more clearly proves the value which the Orientals put upon this fruit, than the choice which Solomon makes of it to represent certain graces of the church: "Thy temples are like a piece of pomegranate within thy locks;" and in the thirteenth verse, the children of God are compared to an orchard of pomegranates with pleasant fruits. Three sorts of pomegranates are used in Syria, the sour, the sweet, and another of an intermediate taste, for the purpose of giving a grateful acidity to their sauces or liquids. A very refreshing draught, such as the Syrians use in hot weather, composed of wine mixed with the juice of the pomegranate, it would seem, the spouse proposed to make for her beloved: "I would cause thee to drink of spiced wine of the juice of my pomegranate;" a delicious and cooling beverage to the parched inhabitant of the equatorial regions; or perhaps she means a species of wine made of pomegranate juice, which we learn from Chardin, is drank in considerable quantities in the East, and particularly in Persia. Which of these is really intended, it is not easy to determine. Liquors of this kind are still very common in the East. Sherbet, which is a syrup, chiefly that of lemons mixed with water, is used by persons of all ranks.

"I think," says Mr. Harmer in a note, "it is highly probable, that in the time of remote antiquity, pomegranate juice was used in those countries where lemon juice is now used, with their meat, and in their drinks; and, that it was not till afterward, that lemons came among them. I know not how else to account for the mention of pomegranates, in describing the fruitfulness of the Holy Land: they would not now, I think, occur in such descriptions; the juice of lemons and oranges have at present almost superseded the use of that of pomegranates." But the opinion of this respectable writer, is opposed by no less an authority than Dr. Russel, who spent many years in Syria, and wrote the natural history of that country. According to that able historian, lemons have by no means superseded the pomegranate; the latter is more easily preserved through the winter, and is often in cookery preferred to the lemon. In describing the fruitfulness of a country, the pomegranate would be mentioned; and it is diligently cultivated even where lemons are plenty. What Chardin calls Roubnar, he would not understand to be wine; Rab-al-nar is the inspissated juice of the pomegranate, or the juice of grapes preserved with sugar.—PAXTON.

Ver. 32. The land, through which we have gone to search it, *is* a land that eateth up the inhabitants thereof.

Of a very unhealthy place it is said, "That evil country eats up all the people." "We cannot remain in these parts, the land is eating us up." "*I* go to that place! never! it will eat me up." Of England it is said, in reference to her *victories*, "She has eaten up all countries."—ROBERTS.

CHAPTER XIV.

Ver. 9. Only rebel not ye against the LORD, neither fear ye the people of the land: for they *are* bread for us: their defence is departed from them, and the LORD *is* with us; fear them not.

Hebrew, "shadow." A poor man says of his rich friend, "He is my *shadow*;" *i. e.* he is my defence. "My shadow is gone;" meaning, he has lost his defence. "Alas! those poor people have lost their shadow."—ROBERTS.

Literally, *their shadow*, a metaphor highly expressive of protection and support in the sultry eastern countries. The Arabs and Persians have the same word to denote the same thing: using these expressions, "May the shadow of thy prosperity be extended." "May the shadow of thy prosperity be spread over the heads of thy well-wishers."

"May thy protection never be removed from my head;
May God extend thy shadow eternally."

At court, when mention is made of the sultan, the appellation of *alem-penah*, refuge of the world, is usually added to his title of *padisha*, or emperor. His loftiest title, and the most esteemed, because given to him by the kings of Persia, is *zil-ullah*, shadow of God.—BURDER.

CHAPTER XVII.

Ver. 6. And Moses spake unto the children of Israel, and every one of their princes gave him a rod apiece, for each prince one, according to their fathers' houses, *even* twelve rods: and the rod of Aaron *was* among their rods. 7. And Moses laid up the rods before the LORD in the tabernacle of witness. 8. And it came to pass, that on the morrow Moses went into the tabernacle of witness; and, behold, the rod of Aaron, for the house of Levi, was budded, and brought forth buds, and bloomed blossoms, and yielded almonds.

See on Jer. 1. 11, 12.

CHAPTER XVIII.

Ver. 16. And those that are to be redeemed, from a month old shalt thou redeem, according to thine estimation, for the money of five shekels, after the shekel of the sanctuary, which *is* twenty gerahs.

According to Leo of Modena, this was performed in the following manner. When the child is thirty days old, the father sends for one of the descendants of Aaron; several persons being assembled on the occasion, the father brings a cup, containing several pieces of gold and silver coin. The priest then takes the child into his arms, and addressing himself to the mother, says, "Is this thy son?" *Mother.* "Yes." *Priest.* "Hast thou never had another child, male or female, a miscarriage or untimely birth?" *Mother.* "No." *Priest.* "This being the case, this child, as first-born, belongs to me." Then turning to the father, he says, "If it be thy desire to have this child, thou must redeem it." *Father.* "I present thee with this gold and silver for this purpose." *Priest.* "Thou dost wish, therefore, to redeem the child?" *Father.* "I do wish so to do." The priest then turning himself to the assembly, says, "Very well: this child, as first-born, is mine, as it is written in Bemidbar, Numb. xviii. 16, *Thou shalt redeem the first-born of a month old for five shekels;* but I shall content myself with this in exchange." He then takes two gold crowns, or thereabouts, and returns the child to his parents.—BURDER.

Ver. 19. All the heave-offerings of the holy things, which the children of Israel offer unto the LORD, have I given thee, and thy sons and thy daughters with thee, by a statute for ever: it *is* a covenant of salt for ever before the LORD unto thee, and to thy seed with thee.

Among other descriptions of a covenant, there is one which demands explanation, Numb. xviii. 19, "The offerings I have given to thee, and thy sons and thy daughters with thee, by a statute for ever; it is *a covenant of salt, for ever*, before the Lord." 2 Chr. xiii. 5, "Ought you not to know that the Lord God of Israel gave the kingdom over Israel to David, for ever, to him, and to his sons, by *a covenant of salt?*" It is very properly, as we suppose, suggested, in answer to the inquiry, What means this covenant of salt? that salt preserves from decay and putrefaction; it maintains a firmness and durability. There is a kind of salt so hard, that it is used as money, and passes from hand to hand no more injured than a stone would be, says Mr. Bruce. Salt may therefore very properly be made an emblem of perpetuity.

But the *covenant of salt* seems to refer to an agreement made, in which salt was used as a token of confirmation. We shall give an instance from Baron du Tott. "He, (Moldovanji Pacha,) was desirous of an acquaintance with me, and seeming to regret that his business would not permit him to stay long, he departed, promising in a short time to return. I had already attended him half way down the staircase, when stopping, and turning briskly to one of my domestics who followed me, 'Bring me directly,' said he, 'some *bread and salt.*' I was not less surprised at this fancy, than at the haste which was made to obey him. What he requested was brought; when, taking a little *salt* between his fingers, and putting it with a mysterious air on a bit of bread, he ate it with a devout gravity, assuring me that I might now rely on him. I soon procured an explanation of this significant ceremony; but this same man, when become vizier, was tempted to violate this oath thus taken in my favour. Yet if this solemn contract be not *always* religiously observed, it serves, at least, to moderate the spirit of vengeance so natural to the Turks." The Baron adds in a note: "The Turks think it the blackest ingratitude, to forget the man from whom we have received food: which is signified by *the bread and salt* in this ceremony."—(Baron du Tott, part i. page 214.) The Baron alludes to this incident in part iii. page 36. Moldovanji Pacha, being ordered to obey the Baron, was not pleased at it. "I did not imagine I ought to put any great confidence in the mysterious COVENANT *of the bread and salt, by which this man had formerly vowed inviolable friendship to me.*" Yet he "dissembled his discontent," and "his peevishness only showed itself in his first letters to the Porte." It will now, we suppose, appear credible, that the phrase "a covenant of salt" alludes to some custom in ancient times; and without meaning to symbolize very deeply, we take the liberty of asking, whether the precept, Lev. ii. 13, "With all thine offerings thou shalt offer salt," may have any reference to ideas of a similar nature? Did the custom of feasting at a covenant-making include the same? according to the sentiment of the Turks hinted at in the Baron's note. We ought to notice the readiness of the Baron's domestics, in proof that they, knowing the usages of their country, well understood what was about to take place. Also, that this covenant is *usually* punctually observed, and where it is not punctually observed, yet it has a restraining influence on the party who has made it; and his non-observance of it disgraces him.

We proceed to give a remarkable instance of the power of this covenant of salt over the mind: it seems to imply a something attributed to salt, which it is very difficult for us completely to explain, but which is not the less real on that account: "Jacoub ben Laith, the founder of a dynasty of Persian princes called the Saffarides, rising, like many others of the ancestors of the princes of the East, from a very low state to royal power, being in his first setting out in the use of arms, no better than a freebooter or robber, is yet said to have maintained some regard to decency in his depredations, and never to have entirely stripped those that he robbed, always leaving them something to soften their affliction. Among other exploits that are recorded of him, he is said to have broken into the palace of the prince of that country, and having collected a very large booty, which he was on the point of carrying away, he found his foot kicked something which made him stumble; he imagined it might be something of value, and putting it to his mouth, the better to distinguish what it was, his tongue soon informed him it was a *lump of salt.* Upon this, according to the morality, or rather superstition, of the country, where the people considered salt as *a symbol and pledge of hospitality,* he was so touched, that he left all his booty, retiring without taking away any thing with him. The next morning, the risk they had run of losing many valuable things being perceived, great was the surprise, and strict the inquiry, what could be the occasion of their being left. At length Jacoub was found to be the person concerned; who having given an account, very sincerely, of the whole transaction to the prince, he gained his esteem so effectually, that it might be said, with truth, that it was his *regard for salt* that laid the foundation of his after fortune. The prince employing him as a man of courage and genius in many enterprises, and finding him successful in all of them, he raised him, by little and little, to the chief posts among his troops; so that, at that prince's death, he found himself possessed of the command in chief, and had such interest in their affections, that they preferred his interests to those of the children of the deceased prince, and he became *absolute master* of that province, from whence he afterward spread his conquests far and wide."—(D'Herbelot, Bibl. Orient. p. 466. Also, Harmer's Obs.)—TAYLOR IN CALMET.

CHAPTER XX.

Ver. 19. And the children of Israel said unto him, We will go by the highway; and if I and my cattle drink of thy water, then I will pay for it: I will only (without *doing* any thing *else*) go through on my feet.

The scarcity of water, and the great labour and expense of digging away so much earth, in order to reach it, render a well extremely valuable. As the water is often sold at a very high price, a number of good wells yield to the proprietor a large revenue. Pitts was obliged to purchase water at sixpence a gallon; a fact which illustrates the force of the offer made by Moses to Edom; "If I, and my cattle, drink of thy water, then will I pay for it." It is properly mentioned as a very aggravating circumstance in the overthrow of Jerusalem, that the ruthless conqueror forced the Jews to purchase with money, the water of their own wells and the wood of their own trees: "We have drunken our water for money; our wood is sold unto us." Even a cup of cold water cannot always be obtained in Syria, without paying a certain price. It is partly on this account our Lord promises, "Whosoever shall give to drink unto one of those little ones, a cup of cold water, in the name of a disciple, should in no wise lose his reward" —PAXTON.

How little do the people of England understand *feelingly* those passages of scripture which speak of want of water, of *paying* for that necessary fluid, and of the strife for such a valuable article as a well! So we read, "Abraham reproved Abimelech, because of a well of water, which Abimelech's servants had violently taken away." Gen. xxi. 25. So, chap. xxvi. 20: "The herdsmen of Gerar did strive with Isaac's herdsmen; and he called the well *Esek, contention.*"—To what extremities contention about a supply of water may proceed, we learn from the following extracts:—"Our course lay along shore, betwixt the mainland and a chain of little islands, with which, as likewise with rocks and shoals, the sea abounds in this part; and for that reason, it is the practice with all these vessels to anchor every evening: we generally brought up close to the shore, and the land-breeze springing up about midnight, wafted to us the perfumes of Arabia, with which it was strongly impregnated, and very fragrant; the latter part of it carried us off in the morning, and continued till eight, when it generally fell calm for two or three hours, and after that the northerly wind set in, after obliging us to anchor under the lee of the land by noon; it happened that one morning, when we had been driven by stress of weather into a small bay, called Birk Bay, the country around it being inhabited by the Budoes, [Bedoweens] the Noquedah sent his people on shore to *get water, for which it is always customary to pay.*"

This extract, especially illustrates the passage, Num. xx. 17, 19;—"We will not drink of the water of the wells:—if I, and my cattle, drink of thy water, then will I *pay for it.*"—This is always expected; and though Edom *might* in friendship have let his brother Israel drink *gratis*, had he recollected their consanguinity, yet Israel did not insist on such accommodation. How strange would it sound in England, if a person in travelling, should propose to pay for drinking water from the wells by the road-side! Nevertheless, still stronger is the expression, Lam. v. 4; "We have drank *our own water* for money:" we bought it of our foreign rulers; although we were the natural proprietors of the wells which furnished it.—TAYLOR IN CALMET.

Ver. 22. And the children of Israel, *even* the whole congregation, journeyed from Kadesh, and came unto mount Hor. 23. And the LORD spake unto Moses and Aaron in mount Hor, by the coast of the land of Edom, saying, 24. Aaron shall be gathered unto his people: for he shall not enter into the land which I have given unto the children of Israel, because ye rebelled against my word at the water of Meribah. 25. Take Aaron and Eleazar his son, and bring them up unto mount Hor: 26. And strip Aaron of his garments, and put them upon Eleazar his son; and Aaron shall be gathered *unto his people,* and shall die there. 27. And Moses did as the LORD commanded: and they went up into mount Hor in the sight of all the congregation. 28. And Moses stripped Aaron of his garments, and put them upon Eleazar his son; and Aaron died there in the top of the mount: and Moses and Eleazar came down from the mount.

The evidence already adduced leaves unquestionable the *possibility* that excavations in rocks may continue unimpaired for many ages. That monuments so extremely ancient as the days of Moses and Aaron should still bear their testimony to facts of other times, is too wonderful to be received without due circumspection.—If they were referred to buildings, to structures erected by human power, they would be something more than dubious: but this hesitation does not apply to chambers cut in rocks, or on the sides of rocky mountains: if the *identity* of such places can be established, their *antiquity* need occasion no difficulty; if the tomb of Aaron be not the tomb of any other person, it may be admitted to all the honours of the distant age to which it is ascribed. The rock and the mountain originated with the world, and will endure to the end of time. At least, it is proper that what is said of the tomb of Aaron, should find its place in a work like the present.

Our travellers left Petra, and taking a south-westerly direction, arrived at the foot of Mount Hor, by three o'clock in the afternoon. They climbed the rugged ascent, and found "a crippled Arab hermit, about eighty years of age, the one half of which time he had spent on the top of the mountain, living on the donations of the few Mohammedan pilgrims who resort thither, and the charity of the native shepherds, who supply him with water and milk. He conducted us into the small white building, crowned by a cupola, that contains the tomb of Aaron. The monument is of stone, about three feet high, and the venerable Arab, having lighted a lamp, led us down some steps to a chamber below, hewn out of the rock, but containing nothing extraordinary. Against the walls of the upper apartment, where stood the tomb, were suspended beads, bits of cloth and leather, votive offerings left by the devotees; on one side, let into the wall, we were shown a dark looking stone, that was reputed to possess considerable virtues in the cure of diseases, and to have formerly served as a seat to the prophet."—Taylor in Calmet.

CHAPTER XXI.

Ver. 6. And the Lord sent fiery serpents among the people, and they bit the people; and much people of Israel died.

The seraph, to a biblical student, is one of the most interesting creatures that has yet fallen under our notice. It bears the name of an order among the hosts of heaven, whom Isaiah beheld in vision, placed above the throne of Jehovah in the temple; the brazen figure of this serpent, is supposed to be a type of our blessed Redeemer, who was for our salvation lifted up upon the cross, as the serpent was elevated in the camp of Israel, for the preservation of that people. It is the only species of serpent which the almighty Creator has provided with wings, by means of which, instead of creeping or leaping, it rises from the ground, and, leaning upon the extremity of its tail, moves with great velocity. It is a native of Egypt, and the deserts of Arabia; and receives its name from the Hebrew verb saraph, which signifies to burn, in allusion to the violent inflammation which its poison produces, or rather its fiery colour, which the brazen serpent was intended to represent. Bochart is of opinion, that the seraph is the same as the hydrus, or, as Cicero calls it, the serpent of the waters. For, in the book of Isaiah, the land of Egypt is called the region from whence come the viper and flying seraph, or burning serpent. Ælian says, they come from the deserts of Libya and Arabia, to inhabit the streams of the Nile; and that they have the form of the hydrus.

The existence of winged serpents is attested by many writers of modern times. A kind of snakes were discovered among the Pyrenees, from whose sides proceeded cartilages in the form of wings; and Scaliger mentions a peasant who killed a serpent of the same species which attacked him, and presented it to the king of France. Le Blanc, as quoted by Bochart, says, at the head of the lake Chiamay, are extensive woods and vast marshes, which it is very dangerous to approach, because they are infested by very large serpents, which, raised from the ground on wings resembling those of bats, and leaning on the extremity of their tails, move with great rapidity. They exist, it is reported, about these places in so great numbers, that they have almost laid waste the neighbouring province. And, in the same work, Le Blanc affirms that he has seen some of them of immense size, which, when hungry, rushed impetuously on sheep and other tame animals. But the original term מעופף Moopheph, does not always signify flying with wings; it often expresses vibration, swinging backward and forward, a tremulous motion, a *fluttering;* and this is precisely the motion of a serpent, when he springs from one tree to another. Niebuhr mentions a sort of serpents at Bassorah, which they call *Heie thiare.* "They commonly keep upon the date trees; and as it would be laborious for them to come down from a very high tree, in order to ascend another, they twist themselves by the tail to a branch of the former, which making a spring by the motion they give it, throws them to the branches of the second. Hence it is, that the modern Arabs call them *flying serpents, Heie thiare.* Admiral Anson also speaks of the *flying serpents*, that he met with at the island of Quibo; but, which were *without wings.*" From this account it may be inferred, that the flying serpent mentioned in the prophet, was of that species of serpents which, from their swift darting motion, the Greeks call *Acontias*, and the Romans, *Jaculus.* The seraph is classed by the Hebrews, among those animals which emit an offensive odour; which corresponds with the character given of the hydrus by the poet: "graviter spirantibus hydris." This circumstance is confirmed by Ælian, who states, that in Corcyra, the hydræ turn upon their pursuers, and exhale from their lungs an air so noisome, that they are compelled to desist from the attack. It is an obvious objection to these arguments, that the hydræ are produced, and reared in marshy places; not in burning and thirsty deserts, where the people of Israel murmured because they could find no water. But, although that people might find no water to drink, it will not follow, that the desert contained no marshy place, or muddy pool, where the hydræ might lurk. Besides, it is well known, that when water fails, these serpents do not perish, but become chersydri, that is, seraphim or burners. Ælian says they live a long time in the parched wilderness, and lie in wait for all kinds of animals. These chersydri, it is extremely probable, were the serpents which bit the rebellious Israelites: and in this state they were more terrible instruments of divine vengeance; for, exasperated by the want of water, and the intense heat of the season, they injected a deadlier poison, and occasioned to the miserable sufferer more agonizing torments. The time of the year when Jehovah sent these serpents among his people, proves that this is no vain conjecture. According to Nicander, the hydræ become chersydri, and beset the path of the traveller about the dog days. Now, Aaron died on the first day of the fifth month, that is, the month Abib, which corresponds with the nineteenth day of July. The Israelites mourned for him thirty days; immediately after which, they fought a battle with Arad, the Canaanite, and destroyed his country: then recommencing their journey, they murmured for want of water, and the serpents were sent. This, then, must have happened about the end of August; the season when the hydræ become seraphim, and inflict the most cruel wounds. Nor is it a fact, that the frightful solitudes which Israel traversed, were totally destitute of water; for, in their fourth journey they came to the river Arnon; in the fifth, to Beer, a well greatly celebrated in scripture; and soon after the death of Aaron, they arrived at a region watered by numerous streams. In these irriguous places, which were at no great distance from the camp of Israel, the hydræ might be produced, and sent to chastise the rebellious tribes. The words of Moses also seem to countenance the idea, that the hydræ employed on this occasion, were not generated on the spot, but sent from a distance: "And the Lord sent fiery serpents, or seraphim, among the people." From these words it is natural to conclude, that they came from that "land of rivers," through which the congregation had lately passed. Nor will this be reckoned too long a journey, when it is recollected that they travelled from both the Libyan and Arabian deserts, to the streams of the Nile. They inflicted on this memorable occasion, an appropriate chastisement on the perverse tribes. That rebellious people had opened their mouth against the heavens; they had sharpened their tongues like serpents; and the poison of asps was under their lips: therefore they were made to suffer, by the burning poison of a creature which they so nearly resembled. —Paxton.

Ver. 18. The princes digged the well, the nobles of the people digged it, by *the direction of* the lawgiver, with their staves. And from the wilderness *they went* to Mattanah.

Michaelis observes on this passage, that Moses seems to have promised the Israelites that they would discover in this neighbourhood, and that by ordinary human industry and skill, a spring hitherto unknown; and that this promise was fulfilled. The discovery of springs, which often flow at a considerable depth below the surface of the earth, is of great importance to a country so poor in water as Arabia. Often a spot that is dry above has even subterraneous lakes, to reach which it is necessary to dig to some depth. We have a remarkable instance in a part of Africa which Shaw describes at the end of the eighth chapter of his geographical remarks on Algiers:—"The villages of Wadreag are supplied in a particular manner with water: they have, properly speaking, neither fountains nor rivulets; but by digging wells to the depth of a hundred, and sometimes two hundred fathoms, they never want a plentiful stream. In order, therefore, to obtain it, they dig through different layers of sand and gravel till they come to a flaky stone, like slate, which is known to lie immediately above the *bahar tâht el erd*, or the sea below the ground, as they call the abyss. This is easily broken through, and the flux of water, which follows the stroke, rises generally so suddenly, and in such abundance, that the person let down for this purpose has sometimes, though raised up with the greatest dexterity, been overtaken and suffocated by it." In some parts of Arabia, as at Faranard in the valley of Dschirondel, water is found, according to Niebuhr, on digging only a foot and a half deep.—Rosenmuller.

CHAPTER XXII.

Ver. 4. And Moab said unto the elders of Midian, Now shall this company lick up all *that are* round about us, as the ox licketh up the grass of the field.

A native gentleman, who has many people depending upon him, says, "Yes, they are all grazing upon me." "If I am not careful, they will soon graze up all I have." Of people who have got all they can out of one rich man, and who are seeking after another, "Yes, yes, they have done grazing there, and are now looking out for another place." "These bulls are grazing in every direction."—Roberts.

Ver. 6. Come now therefore, I pray thee, curse me this people; for they *are* too mighty for me: peradventure I shall prevail, *that* we may smite them, and *that* I may drive them out of the land: for I wot that he whom thou blessest *is* blessed, and he whom thou cursest *is* cursed.

The Orientals, in their wars, have always their magicians with them to curse their enemies, and to mutter incantations for their destruction. Sometimes they secretly convey a potent charm among the opposing troops, to cause their destruction. In our late war with the Burmese, the generals had several magicians, who were much engaged in cursing our troops; but, as they did not succeed, a number of witches were brought for the same purpose.—Roberts.

Ver. 21. And Balaam rose up in the morning, and saddled his ass, and went with the princes of Moab.

We learn from Niebuhr, that in Egypt the asses are very handsome, and are used for riding by the greater part of the Mohammedans, and by the most distinguished women of that country. The same variety serves for the saddle in Persia and Arabia; and must therefore have been common in Palestine. They are descended from tamed *onagers*, which are taken young, and sold for a high price to the nobles of Persia, and the adjacent countries, for their studs. They cost seventy-five ducats; and Tavernier says, that fine ones are sold in Persia dearer than horses, even to a hundred crowns each. He distinguishes them properly from the baser race of ordinary asses, which are employed in carrying loads. These saddle asses, the issue of *onagers*, are highly commended by all travellers into the Levant. Like the wild ass, they are extremely swift and rapid in their course; of a slender form, and animated gait. They have vigorous faculties, and can discern obstacles readily; at the sight of danger they emit a kind of cry; they are obstinate to excess, when beaten behind, or when they are put out of their way, or when attempts are made to control them against their will: they are also familiar and attached to their master. These particulars exactly correspond with several incidents in the history of Balaam's ass; from whence it may be inferred, that he rode one of the superior breed, and by consequence, was a person of considerable wealth and eminence in his own country. The high value which people of rank and fashion in the East set upon that noble race of asses, excludes them from the purchase of the commonalty, and restricts the possession of them to the great, or the affluent. This fact is confirmed by the manner in which the sacred writers express themselves on this subject.—Paxton.

CHAPTER XXIII.

Ver. 21. The Lord his God *is* with him, and the shout of a king *is* among them.

When people pass along the road, if they hear a great noise of joy or triumph, they say, "This is like the shout of a king." "What a noise there was in your village last evening! why, it was like the shout of a king."—Roberts.

CHAPTER XXIV.

Ver. 6. As the valleys are they spread forth, as gardens by the river's side; as the trees of lign-aloes which the Lord hath planted, *and* as cedar-trees beside the waters.

Gabriel Sionita, a learned Syrian Maronite, thus describes the cedars of Mount Lebanon, which he had examined on the spot. "The cedar-tree grows on the most elevated part of the mountain; is taller than the pine, and so thick, that five men together could scarce fathom one. It shoots out its branches at ten or twelve feet from the ground; they are large, and distant from each other, and are perpetually green. The cedar distils a kind of gum, to which different effects are attributed. The wood of it is of a brown colour, very solid, and incorruptible if preserved from wet; it bears a small apple, like that of the pine. De la Roque relates some curious particulars concerning this tree, which he learned from the Maronites of Mount Libanus: "The branches grow in parallel rows round the tree, but lessen gradually from the bottom to the top, shooting out parallel to the horizon, so that the tree is, in appearance, similar to a cone. As the snows, which fall in vast quantities on this mountain, must necessarily, by their weight on such a vast surface, break down these branches, nature, or rather the God of nature, has so ordered it, that at the approach of winter, and during the snowy season, the branches erect themselves, and cling close to the body of the tree, and thus prevent any body of snow from lodging on them." Maundrell, who visited Mount Libanus in 1697, gives the following description of the cedars still growing there: "These noble trees grow among the snow, near the highest part of Lebanon, and are remarkable, as well for their own age and largeness, as for those frequent allusions to them in the word of God. Some of them are very old, and of a prodigious bulk; others younger, and of a smaller size. Of the former I could reckon only sixteen, but the latter are very numerous. I measured one of the largest, and found it twelve yards and six inches in girth, and yet sound; and thirty-seven yards in the spread of its branches. At about five or six yards from the ground it was divided into five limbs, each of which was equal to a great tree."

The aloe-tree here meant is the aloe which grows in the East Indies, to the height of eight or ten feet, and (not to be confounded with the aloe-plant originally from America) its stem is the thickness of a thigh. At the top grows a tuft of jagged and thick leaves, which is broad at the bottom, but becomes gradually narrower towards the point, and is about four feet long; the blossom is red, intermingled with yellow, and double like cloves. From this blossom comes a red and white fruit, of the size of a pea. This tree has a very beautiful appearance, and the wood has so fine a smell, that it is used for perfume. The Indians consider this tree as sacred, and are used to fell it with various religious ceremonies. The Orientals consider this aloe as a tree of Paradise, on which account the Dutch call it the tree of Paradise. Therefore, Rabbi Solomon Jarchi explains the Hebrew word as 'myrrh and sanderswood, which God planted in the garden of Eden."—ROSENMULLER.

CHAPTER XXXI.

Ver. 50. We have therefore brought an oblation for the LORD, what every man hath gotten, of jewels of gold, chains, and bracelets, rings, ear-rings, and tablets, to make an atonement for our souls before the LORD.

There is not a man in a thousand who does not wear an ear-ring or a finger-ring, for without such an ornament a person would be classed among the most unfortunate of his race. Some time ago a large sacrifice was made for the purpose of removing the cholera morbus, when vast numbers came together with their *oblations*. The people seemed to take the greatest pleasure in presenting their *ear-rings*, *finger-rings*, *bracelets*, and *other ornaments*, because they were dearer to them than money, and consequently were believed to be more efficacious in appeasing the gods. When people are sick, they vow to give a valuable jewel to their god on being restored.—ROBERTS.

CHAPTER XXXII.

Ver. 55. Then it shall come to pass, that those which ye let remain of them *shall be* pricks in your eyes, and thorns in your sides, and shall vex you in the land wherein ye dwell.

People in the East, in consequence of their light clothing, of the exposed state of their feet, and the narrowness of the paths, have a great dread of thorns. Those who carry the palankeen, or who travel in groups, often cry aloud, *Mullu, mullu!* A thorn, a thorn! The sufferer soon throws himself on the earth, and some one, famous for his skill, extracts the thorn. Does a person see something of a distressing nature, he says, "That was a thorn in my eyes." A father says of his bad son, "He is to me as a thorn." "His vile expressions were like thorns in my body." A person going to live in an unhealthy place, or where there are quarrelsome people, is said to be going "to the thorny desert."—ROBERTS.

CHAPTER XXXV.

Ver. 19. The revenger of blood himself shall slay the murderer: when he meeteth him he shall slay him.

The interest of the common safety has for ages established a law among the Arabians, which decrees that the blood of every man who is slain must be avenged by that of his murderer. This vengeance is called *tar*, or retaliation, and the right of exacting it devolves on the nearest a-kin to the deceased. So nice are the Arabs on this point of honour, that if one neglects to seek his retaliation, he is disgraced for ever. He therefore watches every opportunity of revenge; if his enemy perish from any other cause, still he is not satisfied, and his vengeance is directed against the nearest relation. These animosities are transmitted as an inheritance from father to children, and never cease but by the extinction of one of the families: unless they agree to sacrifice the criminal, or purchase the blood for a stated price in money or in flocks. Without this satisfaction, there is neither peace, nor truce, nor alliance between them, nor sometimes even between whole tribes. There is blood between us, say they, on every occasion; and this expression is an insurmountable barrier.—VOLNEY.

"Among the Bedouin Arabs," says D'Arvieux, "the revenge of blood is implacable. If one man has killed another, the friendship between the two families and their descendants is dissolved. If an opportunity should occur to join in some common interest, or if one family propose a marriage to the other, they answer quite coolly, 'You know that there is blood between us, we cannot accept your proposal, and must consider our honour.' They do not forgive each other till they have had their revenge, with which, however, they are not in haste, but wait for time and opportunity." This is confirmed by Niebuhr, *Description of Arabia.* "The Arabs seldom wish to see the murderer put to death by the magistrates, or take his life themselves, because they would deliver his family from a bad member, and, consequently, from a great burden. The family of the person murdered generally reserve to themselves the right to declare war, as it were, against the murderer and his relations. But an honourable Arab must observe some equality of strength; it would be considered disgraceful if a strong person should attack one old or sick, or many, a single individual. They are, however, permitted to kill even the most distinguished, and, as it were, the support of the family: for they require that he in particular, who is considered as the chief, and who acknowledges himself as such, should have a watchful eye on the conduct of all the members. The murderer is, however, arrested by the magistrates, and released again, after paying a certain sum, for instance, two hundred dollars. This is, probably, the reason why the law is not abolished. After this, every member of both families must live in constant fear of anywhere meeting his enemy, till at length one of the family of the murderer is killed. There have been instances that similar family feuds have lasted fifty years, or more, because they do not challenge each other to single combat, but fight only when opportunity offers. A man of consequence at Loheia, who used to visit us frequently, besides the usual Arabian weapon, that is, a broad and sharp-pointed knife, always carried a small lance, which he hardly ever put out of his hands, even in the company of his friends. As we were not accustomed to see such a weapon in the hands of the other Arabs, and inquired about it, he complained that some years before he had had the misfortune to have one of his family killed. The injured family had then reserved to revenge themselves in single combat, of the murderer or his relations. One of his enemies, and the very one whom he principally feared, was also in this town. He once met him in our house also, armed with a lance. They might have terminated their quarrel immediately, but they did not speak one word to each other, and much less did any combat ensue. Our friend assured us, that if he should meet his enemy in the open country, he must necessarily fight him; but he owned at the same time, that he strove to avoid this opportunity, and that he could not sleep in peace for fear of being surprised." After the bombardment of Mocha by the French, and when peace was already concluded, the captain of a French ship was stabbed before his own door, where he sat asleep, by an Arab soldier, one of whose relations had been killed by a bomb.—ROSENMULLER.

I must now speak of a person quite unknown in our law, but very conspicuous in the Hebrew law, and in regard to whom Moses has left us, I might almost say, an inimitable, but, at any rate, an unexampled proof of legislative wisdom. In German, we may call him by the name which Luther so happily employs, in his version of the Bible, Der Bluträcher, the blood-avenger; and by this name we must here understand "the nearest relation of a person murdered, whose right and duty it was to seek after and kill the murderer with his own hand; so much so, indeed, that the neglect thereof drew after it the greatest possible infamy, and subjected the man who avenged not the death of his relation, to unceasing reproaches of cowardice or avarice." If, instead of this description, the reader prefers a short definition, it may be to this effect; "the nearest relation of a person murdered, whose right and duty it was to avenge the kinsman's death with his own hand." Among the Hebrews, this person was called גאל, *Goël*, according, at least, to the pronunciation adopted from the pointed Bibles. The etymology of this word, like most forensic terms, is as yet unknown. Yet we cannot but be curious to find out whence the Hebrews had derived the name, which they applied to a person so peculiar to their own law, and so totally unknown to ours. Unquestionably the verb גאל, *Gaal*, means to *buy off, ransom, redeem;* but this signification it has derived from the noun; for originally it meant *to pollute*, or *stain.* If I might here mention a conjecture of my own, *Goël of blood*, (for that is the term at full length,) implies *blood-stained;* and the nearest kinsman of a murdered person was considered as stained with his blood, until he had, as it were, washed away the stain and revenged the death of his relation. The name, therefore, indicated a person who continued in a state of dishonour, until he again rendered himself honourable, by the exercise and accomplishment of revenge; and in this very light do the Arabs regard the kinsman of a person murdered. It was no doubt afterward used in a more extensive sense, to signify the nearest relation in general, and although there was no murder in the case; just as in all languages, words are gradually extended far beyond their etymological meaning. Etymology may show the circumstances from which they may have received their signification; but it is by no means a definition suited to all their derivative meanings, else would it be prophetic. In Arabic, this personage is called *Taïr*, or according to another pronunciation, *Thsaïr*. Were this Arabic word to be written Hebraically, it would be שאר, (*Shaër*) that is, *the survivor.* It appears, therefore, according to its derivation, to be equivalent to *the surviving relation, who was bound to avenge the death of a murdered person.* The Latin word, *Superstes*, expresses this idea exactly. In Arabic writings, this word occurs ten times for once that we meet with *Goël* in Hebrew; for the Arabs, among whom the point of honour and heroic celebrity, consists entirely in the revenge of blood, have much more to say of their blood-avenger than the Hebrews; among whom, Moses, by the wisdom of his laws, brought this character in a great measure into oblivion. The Syrians have no proper name for the blood-avenger, and are of course obliged to make use of a circumlocution, when he is mentioned in the Bible. Hence they must either not have been acquainted with the office itself, or have lost their knowledge of it at an early period, during their long subjection to the Greeks, after the time of Alexander the Great.

If this character, with which the Hebrews and Arabs were so well acquainted, be unknown to us, this great dissimilarity is probably not to be ascribed to the effects of difference of climate, but rather to the great antiquity of these nations. Nations, how remote soever in their situation, yet resemble each other while in their infancy, much in the same way as children in every country have certain resemblances in figure and manners, proceeding from their age, by which we can distinguish them from adults and old people; and of this infancy of mankind, or, to speak more properly, of that state of nature, whence they soon pass into the state of civil society, the blood-avenger seems to me to be a relic. Let us figure to ourselves a people without magistrates, and where every father of a family is still his own master. In such a state, men's lives would of necessity be in the highest degree insecure, were there no such blood-avenger as we have above described. Magistrate, or public judicial tribunal, to punish murder, there is none; of course acts of murder might be daily perpetrated, were there no reason to dread punishment of another description. For their own security, the people would be forced to constitute the avengement of blood an indispensable duty, and not only to consider a murderer as an outlaw, but actually to endeavour to put him to death, and whithersoever he might flee, never to cease pursuing him, until he became the victim of vengeance. As, however, every one would not choose to undertake the dangerous office of thus avenging a murder, the nearest relations of the unfortunate sufferer would find it necessary to undertake it themselves. It would naturally be deemed a noble deed, and the neglect of it, of course, highly disgraceful, and justly productive of such infamy and reproach as blood alone could wash away. Nor would any one obstruct, but rather aid them, in the prosecution of their revenge, if he had a proper regard to his own security. Allowing, however, that the murderer's relations were to protect him against the blood-avenger, or to revenge his death by a fresh murder in their turn, this would still be a proof that they regarded such revenge as an honourable duty, and that they would have looked upon the family of the murdered person as despicable cowards, if they had left his death unrevenged. And this is in fact the language of nature among nations who have not even the most remote connexion with the Hebrews and Arabs. I remember to have read somewhere in *Labat's Voyages*, that the Caraibs practise the same sort of revenge, and that it gives rise to family contests of long duration, because the friends of the murderer take his part, and revenge his death on the relatives of the first victim. We can scarcely conceive the human race in a more perfect state of nature than immediately after the deluge, when only Noah and his three sons were on the face of the earth. Each of them was independent of the other; the father was too old to be able to enforce obedience, had any of them been refractory; and besides, a father is not expected to inflict capital punishment on his sons or grandsons. Add to this, that Noah's sons and their families were not to continue all together, and to form one commonwealth, but to spread themselves in perfect independence over the whole earth. In order, therefore, to secure their lives, God himself gave this command, Gen. ix. 5, 6: "Man's blood shall not remain unrevenged; but whoever killeth a man, be it man or beast, shall in his turn be put to death by other men." If the reader wishes to know more of this passage, which has been generally misunderstood, and held out as containing a precept still obligatory on magistrates, let him consult my *Commentationes ad leges divinas de pœna Homicidii*, in Part I. of my *Syntagma Commentationum.* Here, the only difference from the law now under consideration is, that God imposes this duty, not upon the nearest relation, but on mankind in general, as bound to provide for their common security, and that he gives every individual a right to put a murderer to death, although we have no connexion with the person murdered—a law which remained in force, until mankind introduced civil relations, made laws, nominated magistrates, and thus established a better security to the lives as well as the property of individuals.—MICHAELIS.

Ver. 25. And the congregation shall deliver the slayer out of the hand of the revenger of blood, and the congregation shall restore him to the city of his refuge, whither he was fled: and he shall abide in it unto the death of the high-priest, which was anointed with the holy oil.

Moses found the *Goël* already instituted, and speaks of him in his laws as a character perfectly known, and therefore unnecessary to be described; at the same time that he expresses his fear of his frequently shedding innocent blood. But long before he has occasion to mention him as the avenger of murder, he introduces his name in his laws relating to land, as in Lev. xxv. 25, 26, where he gives him the right of redeeming a mortgaged field; and also in the law relative to the restoration of any thing iniquitously acquired, Num. v. 8. The only book that is possibly more ancient than the Mosaic law, namely, the book of Job, compares God, who will re-demand our ashes from the earth, with the *Goël*, chap. xix. 25. From this term, the verb גאל, which otherwise signifies properly *to pollute*, had already acquired the signification of *redeeming, setting free, vindicating*, in which we find Moses often using it, before he ever speaks of the blood-avenger, as in Gen. xlviii. 15. Exod. vi. 6. Lev. xxv. 25, 30, 33. xxvii. 20, &c.; and even re-purchase itself is, in Lev. xxv. 31, 32, thence termed גאלה *geulla.* Derivatives in any language follow their primitives but very slowly: and when *verba denominativa* descend from terms of law, the law itself must be ancient. In the first statute given by Moses concerning the punishment of murder, immediately after the departure of the Israelites from Egypt, although he does not mention the *Goël* by name, he yet presupposes him as well known. For he says, *God will, for the man who has unintentionally killed another, appoint a place to which he may flee*, Exod. xxi. 12, 13. There must, of course, have been some one who pursued him, and who could only be stopped by the unhappy man reaching his asylum. At any rate, he needed not to flee from justice; and it was quite enough if the magistrate acquitted him, after finding him innocent. The first passage in which Moses expressly speaks of the *Goël*, as the avenger of blood, is in the xxxvth chapter of Numbers: but even there he certainly does not institute his office, but only appoints (and that too merely by-the-by, while he is fixing the inheritances of the Levites) certain *cities of refuge*, to serve as *asyla* from the pursuit of the blood-avenger, (ver. 12,) for which there was no necessity, had there been no such person. In the second statute, Deut. xix. 6, he manifests great anxiety lest the *Goël* should pursue the innocent slayer in a rage, and overtake him, when the place of refuge happened to be too far distant. Now these are evidently the ordinances of a legislator not instituting an office before unknown, but merely guarding against the danger of the person who happened to hold it, being led by the violence of prejudice or passion, to abuse its rights—that is, in the case in question, being hurried, by a false refinement of ideas on the score of honour, to shed the blood of an innocent man. I think I can discover one trace of the terrors which the *Goël* occasioned, as early as the history of the patriarchal families. When Rebecca learned that Esau was threatening to kill his brother Jacob, she endeavoured to send the latter out of the country, saying, "Why should I be bereft of you both in one day?" Gen. xxvii. 45. She could not be afraid of the magistrate punishing the murder; for the patriarchs were subject to no superior in Palestine; and Isaac was much too partial to Esau, for her to entertain any expectation, that *he* would condemn him to death for it. It would, therefore, appear, that she dreaded lest he should fall by the hand of the blood-avenger, perhaps of some Ishmaelite. Now to this *Goël* although Moses leaves his rights, of which indeed he would in vain have endeavoured to deprive him, considering that the desire of revenge forms a principal trait in the character of southern nations; he nevertheless avails himself of the aid of certain particulars of those rights, in order to bring the prevalent ideas of honour under the inspection of the magistrate, without hurting their energy, and to give an opportunity of investigating the circumstances of the crime meant to be avenged, before its punishment should be authorized.

We see that sacred places enjoyed the privileges of *asyla*: for Moses himself took it for granted, that the murderer would flee to the altar, and, therefore, he commanded that when the crime was deliberate and intentional, he should be torn even from the altar, and put to death, Exod. xxi. 14. Among the Arabs we find that revenge likewise ceased in sacred places, as for instance (long before Mohammed's time) in the country round about Mecca, particularly during the *holy month of concourse*. In such places, therefore, honour did not bind the avenger to put a murderer to death.—Now Moses appointed, as places of refuge, six cities, to which ideas of sanctity were attached, because they were inhabited by the priests, Numb. xxxv. 9—35. Deut. xix. 1—10. To these every murderer might flee, and they were bound to protect him, until the circumstances of the case should be investigated; and, in order that the *Goël* might not lie in wait for him, or obstruct his flight, it was enjoined, that the roads to these six cities should be kept in such a state, that the unfortunate man might meet with no impediment in his way, Deut. xix. 3. I do not by this understand, such a state of improvement as is necessary in our highways on account of carriages, but, 1. That the roads were not to make such circuits, as that the *Goël* could overtake the fugitive on foot, or catch him by lying in wait, before he reached an asylum; for, in fact, the Hebrew word (כונ) properly signifies *to make straight*; 2. That guide-posts were to be set up, to prevent him from mistaking the right way; and, 3. That the bridges were not to be defective;—in short, that nothing should retard his flight. If the *Goël* happened to find the fugitive before he reached an asylum, and put him to death, in that case Moses yielded to the established prejudices respecting the point of honour. It was considered as done in the ardour of becoming zeal, and subjected him to no inquisition, Deut. xix. 6. If he reached a place of refuge, he was immediately protected, and an inquiry was then made, as to his right to protection and asylum; that is, whether he had caused his neighbour's death undesignedly, or was a deliberate murderer. In the latter case he was judicially delivered to the *Goël*, who might put him to death in whatever way he chose, as we shall state at more length, under the head of capital punishments. Even although he had fled to the altar itself, which enjoyed the *jus asyli* in the highest degree, it could not save him, if he had committed real murder, Deut. xix. 14. If, however, the person was killed accidentally, and unintentionally, the author of his death continued in the place of refuge, and the fields belonging to it, which extended to the distance of 1,000 ells all around the walls of Levitical cities; and he was there secure, in consequence of the sanctity of the place, without any reflection upon the honour of the *Goël*, even in the opinion of the people. But further abroad he durst not venture; for if the *Goël* met with him without the limits of the asylum, Moses paid no respect to the popular *point d'honneur*; he might kill him without subjecting himself to any criminal accusation. The expression of Moses is, *It is no blood*, or blood-guilt, Numb. xxxv. 26, 27. This confinement to one place may, perhaps, be thought a hardship: but it was impossible in any other way to secure the safety of an innocent manslayer, without attacking the popular notions of honour; that is, without making a law which would have been as little kept as are our laws against duelling. But by this exile in a strange city, Moses had it besides in view, to punish that imprudence which had cost another man his life; and we shall, in the sequel, meet with more instances of the severity of his laws against such imprudences. Allowing that it was an accident purely blameless, still its disagreeable consequences could not fail to make people more on their guard against similar misfortunes; a matter to which, in many cases, our legislators, and our police-regulations, pay too little attention. For that very reason, Moses prohibited the fugitive from being permitted, by any payment of a fine, to return home to his own city before the appointed time, Numb. xxxv. 32. His exile in the city of refuge continued until the death of the high-priest. As soon as that event took place, the fugitive might leave his asylum, and return to his home in perfect security of his life, under the protection of the laws. It is probable that this regulation was founded on some ancient principle of honour attached to the office of the *Goël*; of which, however, I have not been able to find any trace remaining. It would seem as if the death of the priest, or principal person in the nation, had been made the period beyond which the avengement of blood was not to extend, in the view of thus preventing the perpetual endurance of family enmities and outrages. We shall perhaps hereafter find an opportunity of giving a more particular illustration of this point.

By these regulations, borrowed from those very notions of honour which influenced the *Goël*, Moses did not, it is true, effect the complete prevention of the shedding of *innocent blood*, (for so Moses terms it, in the case of the *Goël's* killing the innocent manslayer in his flight;) for civil laws cannot possibly prevent all moral evil; nor yet was he able to protect the man who had through mere inadvertence deprived another of his life, from all the vexatious consequences of such a misfortune: but thus much he certainly did effect, that the *Goël* could but very rarely kill an innocent man, and that a judicial inquiry always preceded the exercise of his revenge; and that inquiry, even when it terminated in condemnation, drew after it no fresh bloodshed on the part of the murderer's family, because every one knew that no injustice was done him. Of course, ten murders did not now proceed from one, as was the case when the *Goël's* procedure was altogether arbitrary, and subject to no restraint. It would appear that Moses had thus completely attained the object of his law. At least, in the history of the Israelitish nation, we find no examples of family enmities proceeding from the avengement of blood, or of murders either openly or treacherously perpetrated from that national idea of honour; and but one single instance of the abuse of *Goëlism*, or rather where it was used merely for a pretext, and the transaction carried on in complete opposition to the acknowledged principles of honour. This instance we find in the history of David, in which the three following particulars relative to this subject deserve notice.

1. David, in his elegy on the death of Saul and Jonathan, seems, in one of his expressions, to allude to the avengement of blood. The Arabs, in their poems, very commonly observe, that no dew falls on the place where a murder has been committed, until the blood has been avenged; and David thus exclaims, *Ye mountains of Gilboa, on you fall neither dew nor rain*, 2. Sam. i. 21; which was as much as saying, the Philistines may look for my avengement of the death of Saul and Jonathan. This, however, is merely a poetical allusion; for the law of *Goëlism* did not extend to those slain in battle.

2. Joab assassinated Abner under the pretext of revenge for his having killed Asahel *his* brother in battle, 2 Sam. iii. 19—23. iii. 22—27. This, however, was a mere pretext; for Joab's only object was to get that man put out of the way, whom David had appointed to the chief command of the war. He afterward acted in the same manner to Amasa, who had killed no brother of his, but had been only guilty of the same crime of getting himself made generalissimo to Absalom, 2 Sam. xvii. 25. xx. 10. David, when he lay on his death-bed, made this remark on Joab's conduct in these two instances, that blood shed in war was not,

according to the Hebrew ideas of honour, to be avenged in peace; and that he therefore regarded Joab as a wilful murderer: and he gave it in charge to Solomon his son to have him punished as such, 1 Kings ii. 5, 6.

3. When we take a connected view of the whole story related in 2 Sam. xiii. 37 to xiv. 20, we should almost suppose that David had for a time pursued his son Absalom, on account of his murdering his elder brother, not so much in discharge of his duty as a king, as in the capacity of *Goël*, and that the idea of his honour, as such, had prevented him from forgiving him. Absalom stayed out of the country with the king of Geshur, and yet David withdrew for a time in quest of him, chap. xiii. 39. This is properly not the business of a magistrate, who is not required to punish a murderer who has fled from the country, but of a *Goël*.

Allowing, however, that I were here in a mistake, thus much still is certain from chap. xiv. 10, 11, that there was yet a *Goël;* that to mothers he was an object of terror; and that David, on some occasions, took upon him to prohibit him by an arbitrary decree from pursuing an actual murderer, when there were any particular circumstances in the case. So much concerning the rights of the *Goël*, as modified by the Mosaic statute. There is yet to be noticed one additional circumstance relative to it, entirely conformable to oriental ideas of honour, and of great importance to the security of lives. Moses (Numb. xxxv. 31) positively prohibits the receiving of a sum of money from a murderer in the way of compensation. By the ancient Arabian manners, too, we have seen that this was deemed disgraceful. Here, therefore, Moses acted quite differently from Mohammed, and, as will be universally acknowledged, much more judiciously.—MICHAELIS.

Ver. 31. Moreover, ye shall take no satisfaction for the life of a murderer, which *is* guilty of death; but he shall be surely put to death.

Moses absolutely forbids the acceptance of any compensation for the life of a murderer. Through the influence of money it appears that punishment was often evaded in some countries, and probably till this time among the Jews. The Baron du Tott tells us, that in case of a duel, if one of the parties is killed, the other is tried for the offence, and if condemned, "the criminal is conducted to the place of punishment; he who performs the office of executioner takes on him likewise that of mediator, and negotiates till the last moment with the next of kin to the deceased, or his wife, who commonly follows, to be present at the execution. If the proposals are refused, the executioner performs the sentence; if they are accepted, he reconducts the criminal to the tribunal to receive his pardon."—BURDER.

CHAPTER XXXVI.

Ver. 8. And every daughter, that possesseth an inheritance in any tribe of the children of Israel, shall be wife unto one of the family of the tribe of her father, that the children of Israel may enjoy every man the inheritance of his fathers.

The assertion that no Israelite durst marry out of his tribe, and which we find repeated in a hundred books, is a silly fiction, directly confuted by the Mosaic writings. Even the high-priest himself was not obliged to confine himself to his own tribe; nothing more being enjoined him, than to look out for an Israelitish bride. It was only in the single case of a daughter being the heiress of her father's land, that she was prohibited from marrying out of her tribe, in order that the inheritance might not pass to another tribe, Num. xxxvi. From that law, it clearly follows, that any Israelitess that had brothers, and of course was not an heiress, might marry whomsoever she pleased, and to me it is incomprehensible how this chapter should ever have been quoted as a proof of the assertion, that the Israelites durst not marry out of their tribes. A strange oversight has been committed, in support of this erroneous opinion, which was devised for the purpose of proving (what scarcely required a proof) that Jesus was of the tribe of Judah; for, say its advocates, "Had not Mary his true mother been of the tribe of Judah, Joseph, a descendant of David's, could not have married her." Here, by the way, they might improve the proof, and make it still more subservient to their purpose, by adding that Mary must have been an heiress, and consequently, for that reason, durst not marry out of her tribe. But how surprising is it, that such incongruous blunders could possibly have been committed? Luke expressly says, chap. i. 36, that Mary and Elizabeth were relations, and Elizabeth's husband was a priest. Hence her connexion with Mary is a most manifest proof, that Israelites of one tribe might marry into another, and that a priest, for instance, might marry a virgin of the house of Judah, or a descendant of Judah marry the daughter of a Levite.

It was even in the power of an Israelite to marry a woman born a heathen: although this also is denied by those who press upon Moses a law of their own. The statute in Deut. xxi. 10—14, already illustrated, puts this liberty beyond a doubt: and he who disputes it, confounds two terms of very different import and extent, *heathen* and *Canaanite*. An Israelite might certainly marry a heathen woman, provided she no longer continued an idolatress; which, however, she could not, as a captive and slave within Palestine, have been even previously suffered to be; but all marriages with Canaanitish women was, by the statute Exod. xxxiv. 16, prohibited. In that statute, Moses had it particularly in view to prevent the Canaanites, who were both an idolatrous, and a very wicked race, from continuing to dwell in Palestine, and by intermarriages with Israelites, at last becoming one people with them: for he dreaded lest they should infect them with their vices and superstitions. Should I here be asked, "*Wherein then did Solomon sin, who, in* 1 Kings, xi. 1, 2, *is certainly censured for marrying heathens?*" my answer would be, (1.) that among the wives and concubines whom he took, there were Sidonians, who belonged to the race of Canaanites, and these were expressly forbidden; (2.) that, contrary to the positive prohibition of Moses, he kept a great seraglio; (3.) that he permitted his wives to practise idolatry; and, (4.) that he was himself led into it also: as we have only to read down to verse 8, to be convinced. I have only further to observe, what I remarked before, that the people of Israel must, in consequence of the toleration of polygamy, have been in a state of continual decrease, had not marriages with foreigners, and particularly with the captive daughters of the neighbouring people, been permitted.—MICHAELIS.

DEUTERONOMY.

CHAPTER I.

Ver. 19. And when we departed from Horeb, we went through all that great and terrible wilderness, which ye saw by the way of the mountain of the Amorites, as the Lord our God commanded us; and we came to Kadesh-barnea.

The divine blessing has not bestowed the same degree of fruitfulness on every part of Canaan. This fertile country is surrounded by deserts of immense extent, exhibiting a dreary waste of loose and barren sand, on which the skill and industry of man are able to make no impression. The only vegetable productions which occasionally meet the eye of the traveller in these frightful solitudes, are a coarse sickly grass, thinly sprinkled on the sand; a plot of senna, or other saline or bitter herb, or an acacia bush; even these but rarely present themselves to his notice, and afford him little satisfaction when they do, because they warn him that he is yet far distant from a place of abundance and repose. Moses, who knew these deserts well, calls them "great and terrible," "a desert land," "the waste howling wilderness." But the completest picture of the sandy desert is drawn by the pencil of Jeremiah, in which, with surprising force and brevity, he has exhibited every circumstance of terror, which the modern traveller details with so much pathos and minuteness; "Neither say they, Where is the Lord that brought us up out of the land of Egypt, that led us through the wilderness, through a land of deserts and of pits, through a land of drought, and of the shadow of death, through a land that no man passed through, and where no man dwelt?"—Paxton.

Ver. 44. And the Amorites, which dwelt in that mountain, came out against you, and chased you, as bees do, and destroyed you in Seir, *even* unto Hormah.

It is said of numerous armies, that they are like bees; and of a multitude, who go to chastise a few, "Yes, they came upon us as bees." To a person who has proved a man of numerous connexions, "Yes, you will have them as bees upon you." Of any thing which has come suddenly, and in great numbers, "Alas, these things come as bees upon us."—Roberts.

The bee is represented by the ancients, as a vexatious, and even a formidable adversary; and the experience of every person who turns his attention to the temper and habits of that valuable insect, attests the truth of their assertion. They were so troublesome in some districts of Crete, that, if we may believe Pliny, the inhabitants were actually compelled to forsake their habitations. And, according to Ælian, some places in Scythia, beyond the Ister, were formerly inaccessible, on account of the numerous swarms of bees by which they were infested. The statements of these ancient writers is confirmed by Mr. Park, in the second volume of his Travels. Some of his associates imprudently attempted to rob a numerous hive, which they found in their way. The exasperated little animals rushed out to defend their property, and attacked the spoilers with so much fury, that they quickly compelled the whole company, men, horses, and asses, to scamper off in all directions. The horses were never recovered, and a number of the asses were so severely stung that they died next day: and so great was the loss our intrepid traveller sustained in the engagement, that he despondingly concluded his journey was at an end. The allusion of Moses, therefore, to their fierce hostility, in the beginning of his last words to Israel, is both just and beautiful: "And the Amorites which dwelt in that mountain came out against you, and chased you as bees do, and destroyed you in Seir, even unto Hormah." The Amorites, it appears, were the most bitter adversaries to Israel, of all the nations of Canaan; like bees that are easily irritated, that attack with great fury, and increasing numbers, the person that dares to molest their hive, and persecute him in his flight, to a considerable distance—the incensed Amorites had collected their hostile bands, and chased, with considerable slaughter, the chosen tribes from their territory. The Psalmist also complains, that his enemies compassed him about like bees; fiercely attacking him on every side. The bee, when called to defend her hive, assails with fearless intrepidity the largest and the most ferocious animal; and the Psalmist found from experience, that neither the purity of his character, the splendour of his rank, nor the greatness of his power, were sufficient to shield him from the covered machinations, or open assaults, of his cruel and numerous enemies.—Paxton.

CHAPTER III.

Ver. 11. For only Og king of Bashan remained of the remnant of giants; behold, his bedstead *was* a bedstead of iron: *is* it not in Rabbath of the children of Ammon? nine cubits *was* the length thereof, and four cubits the breadth of it, after the cubit of a man.

This is a very curious account of a giant king: his bedstead was made of iron, and we are able to ascertain its exact length, nine cubits, *i. e.* "after the cubit of a man." This alludes to the eastern mode of measuring from the tip of the middle finger to the elbow, which will be found to be in general eighteen inches. Thus his bedstead was thirteen feet six inches in length, and six feet in breadth. The hawkers of cloth very seldom carry with them a yard wand; they simply measure from the *elbow* to the *tip* of the *middle finger*, counting two lengths of that for a yard.—Roberts.

Ver. 25. I pray thee, let me go over, and see the good land that *is* beyond Jordan, that goodly mountain, and Lebanon.

The beauties of Lebanon seem to have left a deeper impression in the mind of D'Arvieux. "After travelling six hours in pleasant valleys," says that writer, "and over mountains covered with different species of trees, we entered a small plain, on a fertile hill wholly covered with walnut-trees and olives, in the middle of which is the village of Eden.—In spite of my weariness, I could not but incessantly admire this beautiful country. It is truly an epitome of the terrestrial paradise, of which it bears the name. Eden is rather a hamlet than a village.. The houses are scattered, and separated from each other by gardens, which are enclosed by walls made of stones piled up without mortar. We quitted Eden about eight o'clock in the morning, and advanced to mountains so extremely high, that we seemed to be travelling in the middle regions of the atmosphere. Here the sky was clear and serene above us, while we saw below us thick clouds dissolving in rain, and watering the plains. After three hours of laborious travelling, we arrived at the famous cedars about eleven o'clock. We counted twenty-three of them. The circumference of these trees is thirty-six feet. The bark of the cedar resembles that of the pine; the leaves and cone also bear considerable resemblance. The stem is upright, the wood is hard, and has the reputation of being incorruptible. The leaves are long, narrow, rough, very green, ranged in tufts along the branches; they shoot in spring, and fall in the beginning of winter. Its flowers and fruit resemble those of the pine. From the full grown trees, a fluid trickles naturally, and without incision; this is clear, transparent, whitish, and after a time dries and hardens: it is supposed to possess great virtues.—The place where these great trees are stationed, is in a plain of nearly a league in circumference, on the summit of a mount which is environed on almost all sides by other mounts, so high that their summits are always covered with snow.' This plain is level, the air is pure, the heavens always serene. On one side of this plain is a frightful precipice, from whence flows a copious stream, which, descending into the valley, forms a considerable part of the Holy River, or *Nahar Kadisha.* The view along this valley is interesting; and the crevices of the rocks are filled with earth of so excellent a quality, that trees grow in them; and being continually refreshed with the vapours rising from the streams below, attain to considerable dimensions. Nor is the sense of smelling less gratified than that of sight, by the fragrance diffused from the odoriferous plants around." He afterward says, "the banks of the river appeared enchanted. This stream is principally formed by the source which issues below the cedars, but is continually augmented by a prodigious number of rills and fountains, which fall from the mountain, gliding along the clefts of the rocks, and forming many charming natural cascades, which communicate cooling breezes, and banish the idea of being in a country subject to extreme heat. If to these enjoyments we add that of the nightingale's song, it must be granted that these places are infinitely agreeable." The cedars which he visited, encircle the region of perpetual snow. Lebanon is in this part free from rocks, and only rises and falls with small easy unevennesses, but is perfectly barren and desolate. The ground, where not concealed by the snow, for several hours' riding appeared to be covered with a sort of white slate, thin and smooth. Yet these dreary summits are not without their use; they serve as a conservatory for abundance of snow, which, thawing in the heat of summer, furnishes ample supplies of water to the rivers and fountains in the valleys below. In the snow, he saw the prints of the feet of several wild beasts, which are the sole proprietors of these upper parts of the mountain. Maundrell found only sixteen cedars of large growth, and a natural plantation of smaller ones, which were very numerous. One of the largest was twelve yards six inches in girth, and thirty-seven yards in the spread of its boughs. At six yards from the ground, it was divided into five limbs, each equal to a great tree. Dr. Richardson visited them in 1818, and found a small clump of large and tall and beautiful trees, which he pronounces the most picturesque productions of the vegetable world that he had ever seen. In this clump are two generations of trees; the oldest are large and massy, rearing their heads to an enormous height, and spreading their branches to a great extent. He measured one, not the largest in the clump, and found it thirty-two feet in circumference. Seven of these trees appeared to be very old, the rest younger, though, for want of space, their branches are not so spreading. This statement sheds a clear and steady light on those passages of scripture which refer to Lebanon; and enables us to reconcile with ease several apparent contradictions. So famous was this stupendous mountain in the days of Moses, that to be permitted to see it, was the object of his earnest desires and repeated prayers; and as the strongest expression of his admiration, he connects it in his addresses to the throne of his God, with Zion, the future seat of the divine glory. "I pray thee, let me go over and see the good land that is beyond Jordan; that goodly mountain and Lebanon."—Paxton.

CHAPTER IV.

Ver. 20. But the Lord hath taken you, and brought you forth out of the iron furnace, *even* out of Egypt, to be unto him a people of inheritance, as *ye are* this day.

It has been observed by chymical writers, not only that iron melts slowly even in the most violent fire, but also that it ignites, or becomes red-hot, long before it fuses: and any one may observe the excessive brightness of iron when *red*, or rather *white hot.* Since, therefore, it requires the strongest fire of all metals to fuse it, there is a peculiar propriety in the expression, *a furnace for iron*, or an *iron furnace*, for *violent* and *sharp afflictions.*—Burder.

CHAPTER V.

Ver. 14. But the seventh day *is* the sabbath of the Lord thy God: *in it* thou shalt not do any work, thou, nor thy son, nor thy daughter, nor thy man-servant, nor thy maid-servant, nor thine ox, nor thine ass, nor any of thy cattle, nor thy stranger that *is* within thy gates; that thy man-servant and thy maid-servant may rest as well as thou.

In order to render the situation of slaves more tolerable, Moses made the three following decrees for their benefit.

1. On the sabbath day they were to be exempted from all manner of work. Of course every week they enjoyed one day of that rest which is so suitable to the nature of the human frame, and so requisite to the preservation of health and strength, Exod. xx. 10. Deut. v. 14, 15. In the latter of these passages it is expressly mentioned, that one design of the sabbath was to give a day of rest to slaves, and the Israelites are reminded of their own servitude in Egypt, when they longed in vain for days of repose.

2. The fruits growing spontaneously during the sabbatical year, and declared the property of none, were destined by Moses for the slaves and the indigent.

3. The Israelites were wont, at their high festivals, to make feasts of their tithes, firstlings, and sacrifices; indeed almost all the great entertainments were offering-feasts. To these, by the statutes of Deut. xii. 17, 18 and xvi. 11, the slaves were to be invited. Such occasions were therefore a sort of *saturnalia* to them: and we cannot but extol the clemency and humanity of that law, which procured them twice or thrice a-year a few days' enjoyment of those luxuries, which they would doubtless relish the more, the poorer their ordinary food might be.

It was a part of the good treatment due to domestic animals, that they were to be allowed to share the enjoyment of the sabbatical rest. On the people's own account this was no doubt necessary; because in general beasts can perform no work without man's assistance: but still Moses expressly declares that his commandment respecting the sabbath had a direct reference to the rest and refreshment of beasts as well as of man. His words are, "On the seventh day thou shalt rest from thy labour; that thine ox and thine ass may also rest, and thy servant and stranger may be refreshed," Exod. xxiii. 12. xx. 10. Deut. v. 14. In fact, some such alternation of labour and rest seems necessary to the preservation of beasts: for those that perform the same kind of work day after day, without any interruption, soon become stupid and useless. At least, we see this the case with horses: and the reader will not take it amiss, that a town-bred writer, having better access to observe the effects of labour on them, than on oxen, should prefer taking an example from the former. A horse that has to travel three German miles every day will not hold out long: but, with intervening days of rest, in the same time, he will be able to go over a much greater space without injury. He will, for example, in ten days travel thirty-five German miles, with three resting days, that is, at the rate of five miles each day of the other seven. This fact is so well known, that in riding schools, one or two days of rest, besides Sunday, are usually allowed to the horses, in order to preserve their spirit and activity; whereas the post-horses, which are constantly at work, soon become stiff and unserviceable. The case is probably the same with other beasts of burden, although they do not require so many intervals of rest as horses. And hence the good treatment of beasts enjoined in the Mosaic law, and the sabbatical rest ordained for their refreshment, was highly expedient, even in an economical point of view, and wisely suited to the circumstances of a people, whose cattle formed the principal part of their subsistence.—Michaelis.

CHAPTER VI.

Ver. 7. And thou shalt teach them diligently unto thy children.

If you inquire how a good schoolmaster teaches his pupils, the answer will be, very koormeyāna, *i. e.* "sharply, makes sharp, they are full of points." A man of a keen and cultivated mind, is said to be full of points. "He is well sharpened."—ROBERTS.

Ver. 8. And thou shalt bind them for a sign upon thy hand, and they shall be as frontlets between thine eyes.

I look upon the words in Deut. vi. 8, as not properly a law, but an admonition; because they merely occur in an harangue which Moses addressed to the people. The Orientals make great use of amulets;—a subject on which I cannot here expatiate, but of which I generally treat under Art. 26, of my Hebrew Antiquities. These amulets consist sometimes of jewels and other ornaments, and sometimes of certain sentences, or unintelligible lines, and *Abracadabra*, written on billets, or embroidered on pieces of linen. Some such things the Israelites, in those days, seem to have worn on their foreheads, and on their hands; and the Mohammedans do so still. For how often do we find on their breasts a passage from the *Koran*, which is said to make them invulnerable, or rather actually does so; for this I know for certain, that no Turk, wearing any such billet, was ever yet slain or wounded in battle, excepting in the single case (which, indeed, they themselves except) of his death-hour being come, according to the decree of God. It would appear, that with regard to these embroidered phylacteries, the Israelites, in the days of Moses, did not entertain such superstitious ideas, (else would he probably have forbidden them,) but only wore them as ornaments, and for fashion's sake. As Moses, therefore, wished to exhort the Israelites to maintain the remembrance of his laws in every possible way, and, in a particular manner, to impress it on the hearts of their children, he suggested to them a variety of expedients for the purpose; and this among others, that if they chose to wear any embroidered ornament on the hand or forehead, it should not consist of any thing useless, and still less of any superstitious nonsense, but rather of sentences out of the laws, which their children would thus be in the way of learning. If, however, the fashion changed, and embroidery was no more worn, the Israelites were no longer bound to wear embroidered linen, or billets inscribed with sentences from the Mosaic law; and that the Jews, during the time of prayer, still use them under the name of *Thefillin*, proceeds from a misconception of the statute in question. A further detail on this subject, with the proofs that the words of Moses in this passage are not to be understood as *only* figurative, I cannot here give: but I give it, as I have said, in my Hebrew Antiquities. To most of the readers of the present work, who may be desirous of having a philosophical glance at the ancient laws of mankind, researches merely antiquarian would not afford much gratification.—MICHAELIS.

Ver. 9. And thou shalt write them upon the posts of thy house, and on thy gates.

The observation made in the beginning of the preceding article is equally applicable to the subject of the present one. The words of Moses in Deut. vi. 9, immediately following those just illustrated, are in like manner to be understood, not as a positive injunction, but as an exhortation to inscribe his laws on the door-posts of their houses. In Syria and the adjacent countries, it is usual at this day to place inscriptions above the doors of the houses, not, as the vulgar among us do, in doggerel rhyme, but consisting of passages from the Koran, or from the best poets; and some of them, that are quoted in books of travels, are truly elegant. This must now be a very ancient practice, as it existed in the time of Moses. For when he exhorts the Israelites to take every opportunity in inculcating his laws on their children, we find him suggesting to them this as one means of doing so; "Write them on the doors of your houses, and on the gates of your cities." In these words we have not properly a statute; for if the Israelite did not choose to have an inscription over his door, he had no occasion to make one; but they are merely introduced in an exhortatory discourse to the people, as furnishing an instance of the means which they might take, to impress the laws upon the minds of their posterity in their earliest years. Among us, where, by the aid of printing, books are so abundantly multiplied, and may be put into the hands of every child, such measures would be quite superfluous; but if we would enter into the ideas of Moses, we must place ourselves in an age, when the book of the law could only come into the hands of a few opulent people.—MICHAELIS.

CHAPTER VII.

Ver. 20. Moreover, the LORD thy God will send the hornet among them, until they that are left, and hide themselves from thee, be destroyed.

To the people of England this may appear a puerile way of punishing men, but they should recollect that the natives of the East wear scarcely any clothes, having, generally speaking, only a piece of cloth round their loins. They are, therefore, much more exposed than we are to the sting of insects. The sting of the hornet and wasp of those regions is much more poisonous than in Europe, and the insect is larger in size. I have heard of several who died from having a single sting; and not many days ago, as a woman was going to the well "to draw water," a hornet stung her in the cheek, and she died the next day. I have many times seen the hornet attack and kill the tarantula. Under large verandahs the former may be seen flying near the roof, searching in every direction for his foe, and never will he leave them, till he has accomplished his destruction. Sometimes they both fall from the roof together, when the hornet may be seen thrusting his sting most furiously in the tarantula, and it is surprising to see with what dexterity the former eludes the bite of the latter. The people often curse each other by saying, Unsuttār-Aniverum-Kullive Kuttam, *i. e.* "May all around thee be stung by the hornet!" (meaning the person and his relations.) The toddy drawers use this imprecation more than other people, because the hornet's nest is generally found in the top of the palmirah or cocoa-nut tree, whence they procure the toddy. When they ascend, their hands and feet being engaged, they cannot defend themselves against their attacks. The god Siva is described as having destroyed many giants by hornets.—ROBERTS.

CHAPTER VIII.

Ver. 7. For the LORD thy God bringeth thee into a good land; a land of brooks of water, of fountains, and depths that spring out of valleys and hills.

The account which has been now given of the soil and productions of Canaan, will enable the reader to perceive with greater clearness, the force and justice of the promise made by Moses to his nation, a little before he died: "The Lord thy God bringeth thee into a good land; a land of brooks of water, of fountains and depths, that spring out of valleys and hills; a land of wheat and barley, and vines, and fig-trees, and pomegranates, a land of oil olive, and honey." If to the natural fertility of this highly-favoured country be added, the manner in which it was divided among the tribes of Israel, it will furnish an easy and satisfactory answer to the question which the infidel has often put: "How could so small a country as Canaan maintain so immense a population, as we find in the writings of the Old Testament?" That rich and fertile region was divided into small inheritances, on which the respective proprietors lived and reared their families. Necessity, not less than a spirit of industry, required that no part of the surface capable of cultivation should be suffered to lie waste. The husbandman carried his improvements up the sides of the steepest and most rugged mountains, to the very top; he converted every patch of earth into a vineyard, or olive plantation; he covered the bare rocks with soil, and thus turned them into fruitful fields; where the steep was too great to admit of an inclined plane, he cut away the face of the precipice, and built walls around the mountain to support the earth, and planted his terraces with the vine and the olive. These circles of excellent soil were seen rising gradually from the bottom to the top of the mountains, where the vine and the olive, shading the intermediate rocks with the liveliest verdure, and bending under the load of their valuable produce, amply rewarded the toils of the cultivator. The remains of those hanging gardens, those terrace plantations, after the lapse of so many centuries, the revolutions of empire, and the long decline of industry among the miserable slaves that now occupy that once highly-favoured land, may still be distinctly traced on the hills and mountains of Judea. Every spot of ground was in this manner brought into a state of cultivation; every particle of soil was rendered productive; and by turning a stream of water into every field where it was practicable, and leading the little rills into which they divide it, to every plantation, every tree, and every plant, they secured, for the most part, a constant succession of crops.

"Thus much is certain," says Volney, "and it is the advantage of hot over cold countries, that in the former, wherever there is water, vegetation may be perpetually maintained, and made to produce an uninterrupted succession of fruits to flowers, and flowers to fruits. In cold, nay even in temperate climates, on the contrary, nature, benumbed for several months, loses in a steril slumber the third part, or even half the year. The soil which has produced grain, has not time before the decline of summer heat to mature vegetables; a second crop is not to be expected; and the husbandman sees himself condemned to a long and fatal repose. Syria is exempt from these inconveniences; if, therefore, it so happens, that its productions are not such as its natural advantages would lead us to expect, *it is less owing to its physical than to its political state.*"—PAXTON.

Ver. 8. A land of wheat, and barley, and vines, and fig-trees, and pomegranates; a land of oil-olive, and honey.

If Palestine were now cultivated and inhabited as much as it was formerly, it would not be inferior in fertility and agreeableness to any other country. The situation and nature of the country favour agriculture, and amply reward the farmer. Between the 31st and 32d degrees of north latitude, it is sheltered towards the south by lofty mountains, which separate it from the sandy deserts of Arabia; breezes from the Mediterranean cool it from the west side; the high Mount Lebanon keeps off the north wind, and Mount Hermon the northeast. Mountains which decline into hills, are favourable for the cultivation of the vine and olive, and the breeding of cattle; the plains and valleys are watered by innumerable streams. The fame of the fertility of Palestine, and its former riches in corn, wine, and dates, is even immortalized by ancient coins which are still in existence. But since the land has been several times devastated, greatly depopulated, and come under the Turkish dominion, and the Arab tribes, who rove about it, not only make it insecure for natives and strangers, but also have continual feuds among each other, agriculture has decreased, and the country has acquired its present desert appearance, particularly near the roads; but the traces of its original fertility and beauty are not even now wholly obliterated. As a proof, we may adduce the following passage from D'Arvieux. "We left the road to avoid the Arabs, whom it is always disagreeable to meet with, and reached, by a side path, the summit of a mountain, where we found a beautiful plain. It must be confessed, that if one could live secure in this country, it would be the most agreeable residence in the world, partly on account of the pleasing diversity of mountains and valleys, partly on account of the salubrious air which we breathe there, and which is at all times filled with balsamic odours from the wild flowers of these valleys, and from the aromatic herbs on the hills. Most of the mountains are dry and arid, and more rock than mould adapted for cultivation; but the industry of its old inhabitants had triumphed over the defects of the soil. They had hewn these rocks from the foot to the summit into terraces, carried mould there, as on the coast of Genoa, planted on them the fig, olive, and vine; sowed corn and all kinds of pulse, which, favoured by the usual spring and autumnal rains, by the dew which never fails, by the warmth of the sun and the mild climate, produced the finest fruit, and most excellent corn. Here and there you still see such terraces, which the Arabs, who live in the neighbouring villages, keep up, and cultivate with industry. We then came through a valley about six hundred feet long; and, to judge from the fineness and fresh verdure of the grass, it appeared to be an excellent pasture; at the end of which we found a deeper, longer, broader, and by far more agreeable valley than the former, in which the soil was so rich and fertile, and so covered with plants and fruit-trees, that it seemed to be a garden cultivated by art." Remains of the practice of making terraces on the hills for the purpose of cultivation, were also found by Maundrell, as he states in the account of his journey from Aleppo to Jerusalem. The produce of Palestine is still considerable, not only serving for the supply of the inhabitants, but also affording an overplus for exportation. Corn and pulse are excellent in their kind, and much corn is annually sent from Jaffa to Constantinople. Though the Mohammedan religion does not favour the cultivation of the vine, there is no want of vineyards in Palestine. Besides the large quantities of grapes and raisins which are daily sent to the markets of Jerusalem and other neighbouring places, Hebron alone, in the first half of the eighteenth century, annually sent three hundred camel loads, that is, nearly three hundred thousand weight of grape-juice or honey of raisins to Egypt. The cotton which is grown on the plains of Ramle and Esdraelon, is superior to the Syrian, and is exported partly raw and partly spun. Numerous herds of oxen and sheep graze on the verdant hills of Galilee, and on the well-watered pastures of the northern valley of the Jordan. Countless swarms of wild bees collect honey in the trees and clefts of the rock; and it is still literally true that Palestine abounds in milk and honey.—ROSENMULLER.

It is, I think, highly probable, that in the time of the most remote antiquity, pomegranate juice was used, in those countries where lemon juice is now used, with their meat, and in their drinks, and that it was not till afterward, that lemons came among them: I know not how else to account for the mention of pomegranates in describing the fruitfulness of the Holy Land, Deut. viii. 7, 8; Numb. xx. 5. They would not now, I think, occur in such descriptions: the juice of lemons and oranges have, at present, almost superseded the use of that of pomegranates. Sir John Chardin supposes that this pomegranate wine means, wine made of that fruit; which he informs us is made use of in considerable quantities, in several places of the East, and particularly in Persia: his words are, On fait, en diverses parts de l'Orient, du vin de grenade, nommé roubnar, qu'on transporte par tout. Il y en a sur tout en Perse. My reader must determine for himself, whether pomegranate wine, or wine commonly so called mixed with pomegranate juice, was most probably meant here. The making the first of these was a fact unknown to me, till I saw this manuscript, I confess, though it seems it is made in such large quantities as to be transported.—HARMER.

Hasselquist, in the progress of his journey from Acre to Nazareth, tells us, that he found "great numbers of bees, bred thereabouts, to the great advantage of the inhabitants. They make their bee-hives, with little trouble, of clay, four feet long, and half a foot in diameter, as in Egypt. They lay ten or twelve of them, one on another, on the bare ground, and build over every ten a little roof." Mr. Maundrell, (observing also many bees in the Holy Land,) takes notice, "that by their means the most barren places of that country in other respects became useful, perceiving in many places of the great salt-plain near Jericho, a smell of honey and wax, as strong as if he had been in an apiary." Hasselquist also tells us, that he ate olives at Joppa, (upon his first arrival in the Holy Land,) which were said to grow on the Mount of Olives, near Jerusalem; and that, independent of their oiliness, they were of the best kind he had tasted in the Levant. As olives are frequently eaten in their repasts, the delicacy of this fruit in Judea ought not to be forgotten; the oil that is gotten from these trees much less, because still more often made use of. In the progress of his journey, he found several fine vales abounding with olive-trees. He saw also olive-trees in Galilee, but none farther, he says, than the mountain where it is supposed our Lord preached his sermon.—ROSENMULLER.

Ver. 9. A land wherein thou shalt eat bread without scarceness, thou shalt not lack any *thing* in it; a land whose stones *are* iron, and out of whose hills thou mayest dig brass.

Iron is the only mineral which abounds in these mountains, (Lebanon,) and is found in those of Kesraouan, and of the Druzes, in great abundance. Every summer the inhabitants work those mines, which are simply ochreous

Report says, there was anciently a copper-mine near Aleppo, which Volney thinks must have been long since abandoned: he was also informed by the Druzes, that in the declivity of the hill formerly mentioned, a mineral was discovered which produced both lead and silver; but as such a discovery would have proved the ruin of the whole district, by attracting the attention of the Turks, they quickly destroyed every vestige of it. These statements establish the accuracy of Moses, in the account which he gave his nation of the promised inheritance: "A land whose stones are iron, and out of whose mountains thou mayest dig brass." A different temperature prevails in different parts of these mountains; hence, the expression of the Arabian poets, That Lebanon bears winter on his head, spring upon his shoulders, and autumn in his bosom, while summer lies sleeping at his feet.—PAXTON.

Ver. 15. Who led thee through the great and terrible wilderness, *wherein were* fiery serpents, and scorpions, and drought; where *there was* no water; who brought thee forth water out of the rock of flint.

The sacred historian gives here a most accurate and luminous description of an African desert. It is not only descriptive of that desert at the north end of Africa, in which the Israelites sojourned for forty years, but equally so of those at the southern end, on its western side, the greater part of which, for about two thousand miles along the coast, is covered with deep sand. A desert is great when it is extensive; and such a desert may be called terrible, from the anxiety, dread, or fear, which it causes to the persons travelling in it, from what they experience, and from their doubts as to the result. He comes to pools, but he finds that they are like broken cisterns, which, though they once contained water, contain none now; it has sunk into the ground. He observes two rows of trees and bushes at a distance, which raises hope in his mind, expecting there to find a river. He hastens to the spot; but on reaching the banks, he finds the stream is dried up, not a drop of water is visible, for it only runs after rains. He then digs a few feet under the surface in the bed or channel of the river, in hopes of reaching some remnant of its waters, but finds his labour is fruitless; the water has either sunk beyond his reach, or has been exhaled into the heavens. He has no expectation of relief from a shower falling that evening, or week, or month, for it is a land of DROUGHT, as no rain has fallen for the preceding six, twelve, or eighteen months. Would it be surprising to hear the traveller's assistants express themselves thus—"This is indeed a great and terrible wilderness, a land of drought, where no water is!" There were also fiery serpents, and scorpions. It is believed in Africa that the most poisonous serpents were in the most arid parts, and where the heat was greatest. In such parts I uniformly found the scorpions most numerous. The knowledge of this being the case might render the wilderness through which the Israelites travelled, more terrible to them.—AFRICAN LIGHT.

CHAPTER XI.

Ver. 10. For the land whither thou goest in to possess it, *is* not as the land of Egypt, from whence ye came out, where thou sowedst thy seed, and wateredst *it* with thy foot, as a garden of herbs.

To water a large garden requires three men, one of whom stands on a lever near the well, (which has a rope and a bucket attached to it;) on this he moves backward or forward, as the bucket has to ascend or descend. Another person stands on the ground near the well, to pour the water into a basin. From this a channel, of about eight inches deep and nine broad, runs through the garden; and connected with it are smaller water-courses, which go to the different beds and shrubs. The business of the third person, then, is to convey the water to its destined place, which he does by stopping the mouth of each course (where sufficient water has been directed) with a little earth; so that it flows on to the next course, till the whole be watered. On those herbs or shrubs which require an extra quantity he *dashes the water plentifully with his foot!*—ROBERTS.

The custom of watering with the foot, Dr. Shaw thus explains, from the present practice of the Egyptians: "When their various sorts of pulse, safranon, musca, melons, sugar-canes, &c. (all of which are commonly planted in rills) require to be refreshed, they strike out the plugs that are fixed in the bottoms of the cisterns, [wherein they preserve the water of the Nile,] and then the water gushing out is conducted from one rill to another by the gardener, who is always ready as occasion requires, to stop and divert the torrent, by turning the earth against it *with his foot*, and opening at the same time, with his mattock, a new trench to receive it. This method of conveying moisture and nourishment to a land rarely or never refreshed with rain, is often alluded to in the holy scriptures; where also it is made the distinguishing quality betwixt *Egypt* and the land of *Canaan*, Deut. xi. 10, 11." Mr. Parkhurst is inclined to adopt another interpretation of the expression, *watering with the foot*. He says, "it seems more probable that Moses alluded to drawing up water with a machine which was worked *by the foot*. Such a one, *Grotius* long ago observed, that *Philo*, who lived in *Egypt*, has described as used by the peasants of that country in his time; and the ingenious and accurate *Niebuhr*, has lately given us a representation of a machine which the Egyptians make use of for watering the lands, and probably the same, says he, that Moses speaks of. They call it *sakki tdir beridsjel*, or *an hydraulic machine worked by the feet*."—BURDER.

In the gardens in Africa, into which they can lead water for irrigation, they have small trenches between each row of plants, made by a rake or hoe. The water being led into the first trench, runs along it until it reaches the other end, when a slave, WITH HIS FOOT, removes any mould which might have slid into the little trench, that it may have a free unobstructed course; then again clearing a way for it *with his foot* round the end of the second row of plants, the water freely runs into the next trench; and in this way I have seen a slave lead the little stream from one trench to another, zigzag, over the whole garden; which is much easier done with the foot than by stooping down and doing it with the hands. The first time I witnessed this operation, it cleared up, to my satisfaction, the meaning of the above text.—AFRICAN LIGHT.

Sometimes the drought of summer renders frequent waterings necessary even in Judea. On such occasions, the water is drawn up from the wells by oxen, and carried by the inhabitants in earthen jars, to refrigerate their plantations on the sides of the hills. The necessity to which the Jewish husbandman is occasionally reduced, to water his grounds in this manner, is not inconsistent with the words of Moses, which distinguish the Holy Land from Egypt, by its drinking rain from heaven, while the latter is watered by the foot. The inspired prophet alludes, in that passage, not to gardens of herbs, or other cultivated spots on the steep declivities of the hills and mountains, where, in so warm a climate as that of Canaan, the deficiency of rain must be supplied by art, but to their corn-fields; which, in Egypt, are watered by artificial canals, in the manner just described; in Canaan, by the rain of heaven. The lands of Egypt, it must be granted, are supplied with water by the overflowing of the Nile, and are so saturated with moisture, that they require no more watering for the producing of corn, and several other vegetables; while the gardens require fresh supplies every three or four days. But then it is to be remembered, that immense labour was requisite to conduct the waters of the river to many of their lands; and those works of the ancient kings of Egypt, by which they distributed the streams of the Nile through their whole country, are celebrated by Maillet, as the most magnificent and the most admirable of their undertakings; and those labours which they caused their subjects to undergo, doubtless were designed to prevent much heavier, to which they must otherwise have submitted. The words of Moses, addressed to the people of Israel, probably contained a significancy and force of which we can form but a very imperfect idea, and which has not of late been at all understood. Maillet was assured, that the large canal which filled the cisterns of Alexandria, and is at least fifteen leagues long, was entirely paved, and its sides were lined with brick, which were as perfect as in the days of the Romans. If bricks were used in the construction of their more ancient canals, a supposition extremely probable; and if those made by the people of Israel were designed for purposes of this kind,—they must have heard with a peculiar satisfaction, that the country to which they were going, required no canals to be dug, no bricks to be prepared for paving and lining them, in order to water it; labours which had so greatly imbittered their lives in Egypt. This idea is favoured by the account which Moses gives of their former servitude: hard bondage, in mortar and brick, is joined with other services of the field, among which may be numbered the digging and cleansing of their canals; and in this view, the mortar and brick are very naturally joined with those laborious and standing operations.—PAXTON.

Ver. 11. But the land, whither ye go to possess it, *is* a land of hills and valleys, *and* drinketh water of the rain of heaven.

The striking contrast, in this short but glowing description, between the land of Egypt, where the people of Israel had so long and cruelly suffered, and the inheritance promised to their fathers, where Jehovah reserved for them and their children every blessing that a nation can desire, must have made a deep impression upon their minds. In Egypt, the eye is fatigued with wandering over an immense flat plain, intersected with stagnant canals, and studded with mud-walled towns and cottages; seldom refreshed with a single shower; exhibiting, for three months, the singular spectacle of an extensive sheet of water, from which the towns and villages that are built upon the higher grounds, are seen like islands in the midst of the ocean—marshy and rank with vegetation for three others—and parched and dusty the remainder of the year. They had seen a population of naked and sun-burnt peasants, tending their buffaloes, or driving their camels, or sheltering themselves from the overwhelming heat beneath the shade of the thinly scattered date or sycamore trees; below, natural or artificial lakes, cultivated fields, and vacant grounds of considerable extent—overhead, a burning sun, darting his oppressive rays from an azure sky, almost invariably free from clouds. In that "weary land," they were compelled to water their corn-fields with the foot, a painful and laborious employment, rendered necessary by the want of rain. Those vegetable productions which require a greater quantity of moisture than is furnished by the periodical inundations of the Nile, they were obliged to refresh with water drawn out of the river by machinery, and lodged afterward in capacious cisterns. When the melons, sugar-canes, and other vegetables that are commonly disposed in rills, required to be refreshed, they struck out the plugs which are fixed in the bottom of the cisterns; and then the water gushing out, is conducted from one rill to another by the husbandman, who is always ready, as occasion requires, to stop and divert the torrent, by turning the earth against it with his foot, opening at the same time with his mattock a new trench to receive it. Such is the practice to which Moses alludes; and it continues to be observed without variation to this day. But from this fatiguing uniformity of surface, and toilsome method of watering their grounds, the people of Israel were now to be relieved; they were going to possess a land of hills and valleys, clothed with woods—beautiful and enriched with fountains of water—divided by rivers, streams, and brooks, flowing cool and pure from the summits of their mountains—and, with little attention from the cultivator, exciting the secret powers of vegetation, and scattering plenty wherever they came. The highlands, which are not cultivated by irrigation, are to this day more prized in the East than those which must be watered by means of dikes and canals; both because it requires no labour, which in the low country is necessary, to watch the progress of the water through the channels, in order to give it a proper direction, and because every elevation produces an agreeable change of temperature, where the hills display the loveliness of paradise, while the plains are burnt up with insufferable heat.—PAXTON.

Ver. 19. And ye shall teach them your children, speaking of them when thou sittest in thy house, and when thou walkest by the way, when thou liest down, and when thou risest up.

When a heathen sits down, he makes mention of the name of his god. Thus, the worshippers of Siva say, when they sit down, "Siva, Siva;" and when they arise, they repeat the same name. At night, when they retire to rest, also when they arise in the morning, or when they stumble in the way, they utter, "Siva, Siva." They have a proverb to the same purport, "When I stumble in the way, I know only to mention thy holy name."—ROBERTS.

CHAPTER XII.

Ver. 31. Thou shalt not do so unto the LORD thy God: for every abomination to the LORD which he hateth have they done unto their gods; for even their sons and their daughters they have burnt in the fire to their gods.

See on chap. 18. 10.

Some have doubted whether parents could be so cruel as to compel their offspring to pass through the fire, or to be burnt as a sacrifice to the gods; but we have only to look at modern India, at the numerous infants thrown into the sacred waters, and at the burning alive of widows on the funeral pile of their husbands, to see what human nature is capable of doing. There is reason to believe that, though the British legislature has covered itself with unfading honour in abolishing, by law, these fiendish practices, there are still those of a private nature. Not long ago there were two children offered to the cruel goddess Kāli; and one of the supposed perpetrators was arraigned and tried before the Supreme Court, but escaped for want of evidence.—ROBERTS.

CHAPTER XIII.

Ver. 5. And that prophet, or that dreamer of dreams, shall be put to death; because he hath spoken to turn *you* away from the LORD your God, which brought you out of the land of Egypt, and redeemed you out of the house of bondage, to thrust thee out of the way which the LORD thy God commanded thee to walk in: so shalt thou put the evil away from the midst of thee.

The Hindoos may be called a nation of *dreamers*; they are often elevated or depressed by the gay or sorrowful scenes of their sleeping hours. The *morning* is the time for the young and the old to tell their wondrous stories, and many a sage prognostication is then delivered to the attentive hearers. Men and women often take long journeys, perform arduous penances, and go through expensive ceremonies, from no other cause than a dream. The crafty Bramin finds this to be a powerful medium of access to the superstition and purses of the people. How many a splendid temple has been built or repaired; how many a rest-house erected; how many a costly present has been the result of a real or pretended dream! Mendicants, pandārams, priests, and devotees, have all had their profitable revelations from the gods. Does a needy impostor wish to have a good berth and a settled place of abode, he buries an idol in some lonely place, and at the expiration of about twelve months he has a dream, and a vision into the bargain, for the god actually appears to him when he is *not* asleep, and says, "Go to such a place, and you will find my image: there long, long has it been in disgrace; but now you must build a temple to my glory." The knave affects to be greatly excited, and relates the whole as a profound secret to a few of his select friends. The story soon gets abroad, and numbers of people beg of him to go to the sacred place in search of the deity. At last he consents; but expresses many a fear, as they proceed, that he has been deceived, or that his or their unbelief will hinder him from finding out the place. In approaching the scene of operation, he hesitates, thinks he cannot be far off—"the country had just such an appearance in his dream:" he then says, "Dig;" and numbers of the people fall to work in good earnest. After some time, he shakes his head, repeats his incantations, and says, "It is not here." He then points to the real spot, and again his gulled attendants commence their meritorious operations. At last the god is found, and the multitude make the welkin ring with their shouts of joy. They fall before the grave impostor, and worship at his feet. His object is gained; money and materials come in on every hand; and shortly after a temple and its goodly courts arise, in which he dwells for life.

The good or evil of dreams is minutely described in some of their scientific works; and it is not a little amusing to see that some of their notions agree with the English, and especially with those of the inhabitants of North Britain. Does a man dream about the sun, moon, the gods, a mountain, river, well, gold, precious stones, father, child, mother, elephant, horse, car, temple, Bramin, lotus, flesh of animals, flowers, fruits, swan, cow, fowl, toddy; or that he has his hands tied, or is travelling in a palanquin; that the gods are making ceremonies; that he sees a beautiful and fair woman, arrayed in white robes, coming into his house; that his house is on fire; that he sees a chank, or lamp, or full water-pot; that he roasts and eats his own flesh;—he will be a king: that he wears new cloth; that he plays in the mud; that he climbs trees; that swarms of ants creep over his body;—these are all good—"he will have great felicity." But to dream the gods laugh, dance, run, sing, weep, or clap their hands, is for the country very evil. That you see a crow, eagle, hawk, ass, black cobra capella, pig, monkey, jackal, or salt, curds, milk, sandals, butter, lime, cotton, mud, red flowers, firewood, a black dog, a devil, a giant, a water-melon, jack-fruit, pumpkin, a hare, an alligator, a bear, a tiger, a ghost; that you go to, or come from, the sea; that the teeth fall out; that the hand is broken; that you wear dirty clothes; that the walls of the temple fall; that you miss your way; that you travel towards the *south;* that you fall into a pit; or that you see a company of serpents;—these are all *evil* tokens. To avert the evil implied by those dreams, (and a thousand others not enumerated,) a person must make offerings to the Bramins, and give articles of food. Alms must be bestowed on the poor, and on the Pandārams and other religious mendicants, and the person must bathe in holy water. Let him also listen to the song of Pāratham, and all the malignity of his nightly visitations shall be removed. —ROBERTS.

Ver. 6. If thy brother, the son of thy mother, or thy son, or thy daughter, or the wife of thy bosom, or thy friend, which *is* as thine own soul, entice thee secretly, saying, Let us go and serve other gods, which thou hast not known, thou, nor thy fathers.

These, and many other passages, show how much the term *bosom* is used in the scriptures, and that it generally denotes something of great value or security, affection and happiness. Any thing which is valuable or dear to a person is said to be *madeyilla*, i. e. in his bosom. When a husband wishes to express himself affectionately to his wife, he says, "Come hither, thou wife of my bosom." Is she dead, "Ah! I have lost the wife of my bosom." In the Scanda Purāna, the goddess of Vishnoo is said to rest in the bosom of the god "Vishnoo, whose bosom is the abode of Lechimy." To a father it is said respecting a bad son, "Notwithstanding this, you press him to your bosom;"—and of a flatterer, "He would cause the child to fall from the bosom of its mother." (See on Luke xvi. 22.)—ROBERTS.

CHAPTER XIV.

Ver. 1. Ye *are* the children of the LORD your God. Ye shall not cut yourselves, nor make any baldness between your eyes for the dead.

Not only common readers, but even the learned themselves appear to be perplexed about the meaning of that prohibition of the law of Moses, contained in the latter part of the first verse of the 14th of Deuteronomy, *Ye shall not cut yourself, nor make any baldness between your eyes for the dead;* but it seems to be clearly explained by a passage of Sir John Chardin, as to its expressing sorrow, though it is probable the idolatrousness of the practice may, at this distance of time, be irrecoverably lost. Sir John tells us, "that black hair is most esteemed among the Persians, as well on the head, as on the eyebrows, and in the beard. That the largest and thickest eyebrows are the most beautiful, especially when they are of such a size as to touch one another. The Arab women have the most beautiful eyebrows of this sort. The Persian women, when they have them not of this colour, tinge them, and rub them with black, to make them the larger. They also make in the lower part of the forehead, a little below the eyebrows, a black spot, in form of a lozenge, not quite so large as the nail of the little finger." This is probably not of a lasting nature, but quickly wears off. These notions of beauty differ very much from those of the ladies of Europe. None of them, I think, are fond of having their eyebrows meet; but, on the contrary, take pains to keep the separation between them very distinct. But if the eastern people are of a different opinion, it is not at all surprising, that at the same time that they laid aside the hair of their heads, with their more artificial ornaments, in a time of mourning, they should make a space bald between their eyes too, since it was their pride to have them meet when in a joyful state, and even to join them with a black perishable spot, rather than have an interruption appear between the eyebrows. But as the sacred writers admitted the making their heads bald in mourning, while Moses forbids not only idolatrous cuttings of the flesh, but this making the space bald between the eyebrows, it appears there was something of idolatry in this too, as well as in those cuttings, though it is not easily made out. After this circumstance, relating to eastern beauty, is known, the addition to bishop Patrick's account of the heathens being wont to shave the eyebrows, in times of mourning, will, I presume, give no pleasure: "Or," says this worthy writer, "(which some think is the meaning of between the eyes,) the hair in the forepart of the head, or near the temples, as R. Solomon interprets it. Which seems to be the meaning of the Hierusalem Targum, which translates it, 'Ye shall not make any baldness in the house of your countenance.'"—HARMER.

Ver. 4. These *are* the beasts which ye shall eat; the ox, the sheep, and the goat.

See on Lev. 11. 2.

CHAPTER XV.

Ver. 6. For the LORD thy God blesseth thee, as he promised thee: and thou shalt lend unto many nations, but thou shalt not borrow; and thou shalt reign over many nations, but they shall not reign over thee.

From the numerous allusions in the sacred writings, to the subject of lending and of usury, it is easy to perceive that this was a very common practice among the ancients of the East. There are thousands at this day who live on the interest of a very small capital, and thousands who make immense fortunes by nothing but *lending*. So soon as a man has saved a small sum, instead of locking it up in his box, it goes out to interest at the rate of twelve, and sometimes twenty, per cent. People of great property, on account of their anxiety to put out every farthing, often leave themselves in considerable difficulty. Children are taught, in early life, the importance of this plan: hence, striplings may be heard to boast that they have such and such sums out at interest. This propensity often places government in circumstances of great loss in reference to their shroffs, or native treasurers. They lend out money from the chest to a great amount, merely to gain the interest. "Ah! you shall lend money to many people," is one of the blessings pronounced on a youthful pair. When a person acquires a new situation, when a man is prosperous, it is said, "He will lend to many people;" which means, he will be rich, and have much influence.—ROBERTS.

Ver. 8. But thou shalt open thy hand wide unto him, and shalt surely lend him sufficient for his need, *in that* which he wanteth.

Of a liberal man, it is said, "He has an *open* hand." "That man's hand is so open, all will soon be gone." When a poor man asks a favour of a rich man, in the presence of another, the bystanders will say, "Open your hand wide to him." A person who has been refused a favour, says, on his return, "Alas! he would not open his hand; no, not a little."—ROBERTS.

Ver. 16. And it shall be, if he say unto thee, I will not go away from thee, (because he loveth thee and thy house, because he is well with thee,) 17. Then thou shalt take an awl, and thrust *it* through his ear unto the door, and he shall be thy servant for ever: and also unto thy maid-servant thou shalt do likewise. 18. It shall not seem hard unto thee, when thou sendest him away free from thee; for he hath been worth a double hired servant *to thee*, in serving thee six years: and the LORD thy God shall bless thee in all that thou doest.

Moses specifies two periods, at which the Hebrew servant was to regain his freedom; the *seventh* year, Exod. xxi. and Deut. xv; and the *fiftieth*, or year of jubilee, Lev. xxv. How these periods are reconciled with each other, considering that the year of jubilee must always have immediately followed a sabbatical year, and that of course the servants must have been already free, before its arrival, deserves inquiry. Here then all depends upon the sense in which Moses understands *the seventh year;* whether as the sabbatical year, in which the land lay fallow, or as the seventh year from the time when the servant was bought? Maimonides was of the latter opinion, and to me also it appears the more probable. For Moses uniformly calls it *the seventh* year, without using the term *sabbatical* year. What then is more natural than to understand the seventh year of servitude? And besides, when he describes the sabbatical year in Lev. xxv. 1—7, we find not a word of the manumission of servants. The apparent inconsistency of the two laws thus ceases. The servant was regularly restored to freedom after *six* years' service; but supposing him bought in the forty-sixth year of the Jewish calculation, that is, *four* years before the jubilee, he did not, in that case, wait seven years, but received his freedom in the year of jubilee, and with it the land he might have sold. In this way Moses took care that too great a proportion of the people should not be slaves at one time, and thus the state, instead of free citizens to defend it with arms in their hands, have only the protection of a number of unarmed servants. There might still be other cases in which a slave only recovered his freedom in the fiftieth year. For instance, if a man was sold for debt, or for theft, and the sum which he had to pay exceeded what a servant sold for six years was worth, it is certainly conformable to reason that the said debtor or thief should have been sold for a longer period, at least for twice six years: but still, in that case, his servitude would cease on the coming of the jubilee, when every thing reverted to its former state. It has been generally supposed, that those servants who did not choose to accept their freedom in the seventh year, and of whom I shall immediately speak, became free at the year of jubilee. Here, however, a doubt has occurred to me, whether any such servant could, after he had become so much older, have ventured to accept freedom in the fiftieth year; and whether he would not rather wish and expect, that the master to whose service he had, from attachment, generously sacrificed his best days, should keep and maintain him in his old age? At the same time, it occurs to me to observe, on the other hand, that in the fiftieth year every Israelite received the land he had sold: so that the servant, who before refused his freedom, because he had nothing to live on, might now accept it with joy, when his paternal inheritance returned to him quite unincumbered.

Moses, as I have just remarked by the way, presupposes it a possible and probable case, that a servant, who had a good master, might wish to remain with him constantly during life, without seeking to be free; particularly if he had lived *in contubernio* with one of his master's female slaves, and had children by her, from whom, as well as from himself, he must separate, if he left his master's house. In such a case, he permits the servant to bind himself for ever to the service of the master, with whose disposition he had by six years' experience become acquainted. But, in order to guard against all abuse of this permission, it was necessary that the transaction should be gone about judicially, and that the magistrate should know of it. The servant was therefore brought before the magistrate, and had his ear bored at his master's door. It does not belong to my present subject, but to that of Hebrew antiquities, to enter into a particular illustration of this custom, which, in Asia, where men generally wear ear-rings, was not uncommon, and was, besides, among the other Asiatic nations a mark of slavery; and, therefore, I here merely remark, that it was the intention of Moses, that every Hebrew who wished to continue a servant for life, should, with the magistrate's previous knowledge, bear a given token thereof in his own body. He thus guarded against the risk of a master having it in his power either to pretend that his servant had promised to serve him during life, when he had not; or, by ill usage, during the period that he had him in his service, to extort any such promise from him. I may further observe, *en passant*, that the statute of Moses made boring the ears in some degree ignominious to a free man; because it became the sign whereby a perpetual slave was to be known. And if the Israelites had, for this reason, abandoned the practice, Moses would not have been displeased. Indeed, this was probably the very object which he had in view to get imperceptibly effected by his law; for in the wearing of ear-rings, superstition was deeply concerned. They were very frequently consecrated to some of the gods, and were thus considered as amulets to prevent the sounds of enchantment from entering the ear and proving hurtful. If, however, the servant was willing to accept his freedom, not only was it necessarily granted him, but Moses besides ordained in one of his latter laws, as an additional benefit, that the master, instead of sending him empty away, should make him a present of sheep, fruits, oil, and wine, to enable him to begin housekeeping anew, Deut. xv. 13—15. On this occasion he observes, that such a servant does his master twice as much service as a servant hired by the day; which I thus understand. If a man bought a servant for six years, he only paid half as much as a hireling would in that period have received besides his maintenance: because the purchase money was necessarily paid down on the spot, and the purchaser had to run the risk of his servant dying before the term of his service was expired. But when this risk was passed, and the servant had actually earned him his daily hire, his master was bound, in recompense of the advantages he thus brought him, to grant him some little gratification. At the same time, Moses reminds the Israelites that their forefathers had all been slaves in Egypt, and that therefore it was their duty to act with kindness towards those of their brethren, whose fate it was to feel the hardships of bondage. —MICHAELIS.

CHAPTER XVI.

Ver. 16. Three times in a year shall all thy males appear before the LORD thy God in the place which he shall choose; in the feast of unleavened bread, and in the feast of weeks, and in the feast of tabernacles: and they shall not appear before the LORD empty.

Moses instituted other festivals besides the Sabbath; and *three* of them, which we usually denominate *High Festivals*, were distinguished from the Sabbath and all other holydays, by this remarkable difference, that they lasted for *seven*, one of them, indeed, for *eight*, successive days; and that all the males in Israel were then obliged to assemble at the place where the sanctuary stood. That every people interested in the preservation of their religion, must set apart, I will not say a *day*, but certainly a specific *time* for divine worship, is obvious. This is a point, the proofs of which I willingly leave to theology, or even to philosophical ethics, from which I may here assume it as well understood. But besides this, (and here I must beg leave, as it is more agreeable to present usage, to employ the word *days* for *times*, without meaning, by *day*, either the precise period of 24 hours, or that from sunrise to sunset,) there is a necessity for days of rest and pleasure. By unintermitted labour, the body becomes weakened, loses that activity and vigour which the alternations of labour, rest, and amusement, produce, and grows soon old. Bodily labour otherwise, no doubt, increases strength; and the peasant who works with his hands, will always be a stronger man than the person who folds them across his breast, or only writes with them; but then it must not be unceasing labour, and without repose, or else it will have the contrary effect. The man who is obliged to toil day after day without intermission, and especially if he has done so from infancy, becomes in a manner cramped, stiff, and awkward, at all other bodily exercises; continues, as it were naturally, of small stature, and, like a horse daily hacked, is prematurely worn out. Alternation is the grand maxim of dietetics; which, indeed, holds good so universally, that the very best rules of diet prescribed by the ablest physician, will be found in most cases detrimental, if too strictly observed. Even the exercises which serve to strengthen and refresh us, if we constantly use any one of them without variation, such as walking or riding, will become irksome and hurtful, if we are obliged to take it every day without intermission. The daily runner, who knows no intervals of rest, will not, it is true, be affected with hypochondria, but will, nevertheless, feel his health otherwise impaired. The postillion, who rides every day, Sunday not excepted, commonly grows old before his time; and his whole figure shows, that he has not had a healthy occupation. We see this, even in countries where posts travel so intolerably slow, that the violence of the motion can certainly not be blamed for the injury which incessant riding occasions to their health. The trooper in the field, and the sportsman in the chase, ride perhaps more and harder, and *that* too in all weathers, but yet we do not remark in them the appearances of premature old age and decrepitude, visible in the postillion, who sits on horseback day after day, and must soon be discharged in consequence of his infirmities. Putting all this, however, out of the question, that man can have no enjoyment of life, who is obliged to toil perpetually, and in the same irksome uniformity of employment. Yet every man ought to have some enjoyment of life, were it only for a single day of recreation occasionally: wherefore else is he in the world? If he never tastes the pleasures of life, he soon dwindles into wrinkled insignificance. Nor is it merely rest from his daily toil that he ought, in justice, to enjoy on such occasions; but he should have it in his power to sport away the time in social enjoyment, in feasting, dancing, or whatever else is most agreeable to his taste, if not contrary to good morals. By this variety of pleasure, the mind is roused from its usual dull uniformity, enlivened, and restored; the powers of the body are renovated; and it becomes more supple, and fitted for greater exertion. In short, the common man throws off the slave, the porter, the hind, the tailor; and the man of learning the dull pedant. It were cruel to deprive even the slave of a share in such enjoyments, for they are, as it were, a recompense for the hardships of his life; and every man who lives, manifestly has a right to partake in them: and it were no less foolish than cruel; for his health, vivacity, and bodily vigour will suffer in consequence of such privations. It is, therefore, prudent to allow him seasons of recreation: although selfish and tyrannical masters, who only look to immediate advantages, are, from their ignorance of human nature, and the effects of unceasing labour, sometimes inclined to be of a different opinion.

In this way, the three annual festivals were, in fact, so many additional and prolonged seasons of pleasure, in which the people were to indulge themselves, exclusive of the weekly enjoyment of the Sabbath. Seven successive days spent in such a manner, serve as a recreation both to body and mind, and we think ourselves after them, as it were, regenerated. To bodily health, such relaxations undoubtedly contribute; for that man will always have more strength and activity, who, from his youth, has occasionally mingled in the cheerful dance, than the person who has been subjected to unvaried and uninterrupted labour. For that particular sort of labour, the latter may, no doubt, manifest great strength; but he will become stiff, and in all other applications of his bodily powers, awkward, and almost as if lamed. This is a dietetical remark, in regard to which, we find a coincidence of opinion, between learned physicians and those officers who have to enlist or select soldiers. And as to the mind, by festivities of this nature, *it* likewise becomes better humoured, and more cheerful: We return to our ordinary labours with more spirit and activity, after spending a whole week in the enjoyment of the pleasures of such extraordinary occasions; which, however, certainly must not be the constant business of our whole lives, but only that of festal seasons. Hence it seems to have been one of the great objects of the Mosaic polity, that every individual, without exception, should, along with the evils, occasionally taste also the pleasures of life; the legislator having taken care, that not even the poorest persons, not even the very slaves, should be excluded from sharing in these, during the festivals. The words which, without once thinking of any thing learned, or of the subject of the present work, I have, in the poem entitled *Moses*, and annexed to the second edition of my "Poetical Sketch of the Ecclesiastes of Solomon," put into the mouth of Moses, when he is entreating Pharaoh for a three-days festival to the Israelites, will, perhaps, be found to express, with tolerable accuracy, his real ideas on this point, as far as the tenor of his laws enables us to portray them.

> But three days rest they ask, to keep the feast
> Commanded by their God; through all the year, besides,
> Thy duteous slaves. They seek not to rebel
> Against thy sway; e'en though the sacred rest
> Of Sabbath, in thy house of bondage dire,
> They ne'er enjoy. And canst thou then withhold
> From these poor slaves, this respite from their toils?
> Or grudge, that they should taste the sweets of life
> For three short days, and then, as too much blest,
> Serve thee for ever?——

But without reference to this point, the institution of the three high festivals had, in many other respects, salutary influences on the community. The most important of these, and what the legislator, without doubt, had principally in his view, was, that the whole people would thus become more closely connected together, learn to regard each other as fellow-citizens and brethren, and not be so likely to be perpetually splitting into different petty states. They consisted, as has been already mentioned, of twelve tribes, of which each had its own common weal, and sometimes one was jealous of another. The consequences of this might have been, considering the narrow-minded patriotism of those ancient times, that they might have hated, and, in process of time, been completely alienated from each other. The yearly festivals had the greatest possible effect in preventing this misfortune. For while the Israelites thus frequently assembled all together for the purposes of religious worship and social enjoyment, they learnt to be more intimately acquainted with each other, and laid the foundations of firm friendships. That such friendships often have their origin in social intercourse of this kind, and that when people are met at the festive board, many little grudges are forgotten or removed, is an ancient and well-known observation. If, on a day of mirth and jollity, we experience pleasure in the society of others, we naturally wish for its frequent repetition; we seek fresh opportunities of intercourse with them, and thus form friendships before we are aware. It was, indeed, only specially commanded, that *males* should go to the Israelitish festivals; but fathers, no doubt, gratified their daughters, by taking them along with them to these solemnities, which consisted in dancing, and entertainments; and thus the men had an opportunity of seeing all the young beauties of the different tribes. This must naturally have occasioned intermarriages of one tribe with another, by which the interests of families belonging to different tribes would become more and more closely connected, and thus the twelve petty states, be not merely nominally, but really, and from social love, united into one great people. If any of the tribes happened to be jealous of each other, or, as was sometimes the case, involved in civil war, still their meeting together in one place for the purposes of religion and sociality, had a tendency to prevent their being completely alienated, and forming themselves into two or more unconnected states: and even though this had at any time happened, it gave them an opportunity of again cementing their differences and re-uniting. This is so correctly true, that the separation of the ten tribes from the tribe of Judah under Rehoboam and Jeroboam, could never have been permanent, had not the latter abrogated one part of the law of Moses relative to the festivals. In every case it is quite a sufficient recommendation of any measure of legislative policy, when experience has proved that the evil, which it was its object to prevent, could not possibly have taken place without an abrogation of the law; and that the destroyer or revolutionizer of the state, could not have effected his purpose, without annulling the statutes that regard religion; difficult though it always be to manage such an attempt without discomposing and exasperating the minds of the people. Now, Jeroboam immediately perceived, that the ten tribes would one day re-unite with the tribe of Judah, and subject themselves again to the rightful sovereign of the house of David, if they continued to frequent the high festivals at Jerusalem; which, by reason of the suspension of arms, at the holy place, would still have been quite in their power with perfect safety: and, therefore, in order to maintain his own authority, and to perpetuate the separation, he prohibited the annual pilgrimage to Jerusalem, and, contrary to the law of Moses, appointed *two* places for divine service, within his own territories, (1 Kings xii. 27—30;) in which, no doubt, the true God *was* worshipped, but, in order to gratify the propensity of the Israelites to idolatry, it was under the similitude of a golden calf. In order to make still surer of his point, he transferred the celebration of the feast of tabernacles, and probably of the other two festivals likewise, to a different season from that appointed by Moses; making it a month later, (1 Kings xii. 33;) in doing which, he very likely availed himself of the harvest and vintage being, in the tract adjacent to Lebanon, and which extended through the mountains, sometimes a little later than in the other parts of Palestine.

Another effect of these festivals regarded the internal commerce of the Israelites. I will not positively assert, that Moses had this effect in his view; but God, who instructed him as to the laws which he was to enact, certainly foresaw all the future uses of those laws; and it was an object in *his* view, though Moses might not have known it. From the annual conventions of the whole people of any country for religious purposes, there generally arise, without any direct intention on their part, annual fairs and internal commerce; for, even if it were for no other purpose, merchants, who are always on the watch to espy and embrace every favourable opportunity of a sale, will resort thither, in order to dispose of their commodities. That our yearly fairs in Germany originally arose in this manner, is evident from the name, which the principal ones bear, *Messen*, or Masses. In ancient Catholic times, masses were said on certain days in particular places, in memory of different saints; as, for instance, on the Wednesday after Easter, near *Querfurt*, in the place called the *Asses-meadow*, from the *Ass*, which is so much celebrated in the history of the church; and, as many people assembled for devotion on such occasions, merchants, who had various wares to sell, likewise made their appearance; and so from the masses then read by the Catholic priests, arose what we now, in mercantile language, denominate *Messen*. Our country, therefore, is indebted to religion, or rather to religious meetings, not indeed enjoined by God, but merely devised by men, for a great part of its trade and commerce; which still subsists, long after people destitute of education have ceased to know wherefore our great yearly fairs, that are of such importance, have been called *Messen*.

Among the Mohammedans similar festivals have had the very same effect; for, notwithstanding the difficulties of travelling through the deserts, and the dangers to which the caravans are exposed from *banditti*, and the great intolerance of Islamism, which is such, that no uncircumcised person dare approach Mecca, without the risk of circumcision; not to mention the perpetual variation of the time of the pilgrimage thither, in consequence of their strange mode of reckoning by lunar years;—circumstances which, anywhere else, would ruin the most flourishing fairs—still the annual pilgrimage of the Mohammedans to Mecca, has given birth to one of the greatest markets in the world, where people from the extremities of the East and of the West, meet for the purpose of trade and commerce. Now the very same effects, and to a still higher degree, must, without any effort on the part of the legislator, have resulted from the high festivals of the Israelites, to which the whole people were bound to assemble; and more particularly, as far as regards *internal* trade, which is always the most essential branch of commerce to any people. Let us only figure to ourselves, what would follow from such festivals being once set a-going. Every man would bring along with him every portable article which he could spare, and wished to turn into money; and, as several individuals would go from the same place, they would contrive various expedients to render their goods portable: for they would, for one thing, have to carry the *ipsa corpora* of their tithes, that were to be consumed during the festivals; not to mention other articles necessary to their accommodation, and which would require means of conveyance (or, as I might perhaps more properly term them, *voitures*) expensive in the regions of the East; for they consist, not as with us, of wagons and horses, but of asses and camels; beasts of burden which are highly serviceable in promoting the commerce of Arabia, and the neighbouring country of Palestine. There never could be any want of buyers, when the whole people were convened; and the wholesale merchants would soon find it for their advantage to attend and purchase the commodities offered to sale by individuals, especially manufactured articles; nor would the owners of goods, as they must require money to make good cheer on such occasions, hold them at unreasonable rates. Whoever wished to buy any particular articles, would wait the festivals, in order to have a choice; and this too would lead great merchants to attend with all manner of goods for sale, for which they could hope to find purchasers. That Moses was by no means anxious to engage the Israelites actively in foreign commerce, I have already admitted. The most important species of commerce, however—that whereby every man has it in his power to convert at a particular place whatever he can spare, that is at all portable, into money, and with that money to buy, at first hand, whatever he wants from any other quarter—must have been, by means of their festivals, much brisker among the Israelites, than we could ever hope to see it in Europe on such occasions. That people, having a national religion from God, and having God himself for their king, enjoyed, in this respect, an advantage, which no other people *can* enjoy: for if it is not God, but only the sovereign, who enjoins a pilgrimage to a festival, every one who can, will endeavour to get quit of the trouble of the journey, or, at best, to make it with reluctance; and if religious imposture is resorted to, in order to enforce attendance, the fraud will soon be discovered, and the political artifice thereby come to naught.—Michaelis.

Ver. 18. Judges and officers shalt thou make thee in all thy gates, which the Lord thy God giveth thee, throughout thy tribes: and they shall judge the people with just judgment.

Among the persons that appear in the Israelitish Diet, besides those already mentioned, we find the *Schoterim*, (שוטרים) or *scribes*. They were different from the judges; for Moses had expressly ordained (Deut. xvi. 18) that in every city there should be appointed, not only judges, but *Schoterim* likewise. It is very certain that Moses had not originally instituted these officers, but already found them among the people while in Egypt. For when the Israelites did not deliver the required tale of bricks, the Schoterim were called to account, and punished; Exod. v. 6—14. Now, as *satar* in Arabic, signifies *to write;* and its derivative, *Mastir, a person whose duty it is to keep accounts, and collect debts*, I am almost persuaded that these *Schoterim* must have been the officers who kept the genealogical tables of the Israelites, with a faithful record of births, marriages, and deaths; and, as they kept the rolls of families, had, moreover, the duty of apportioning the public burdens and services on the people individually. An office exactly similar, we have not in our governments, because they are not so genealogically regulated; at least we do not institute enumerations of the people by families. But among a people whose notions were completely clannish, and among whom all hereditary succession, and even all posthumous fame, depended on genealogical registers, this must have been an office fully as important as that of a judge. In Egypt, the Levites had not yet been consecrated and set apart from the rest of the tribes; there, of course, the *Schoterim* must have been chosen either out of every family, or, perhaps, merely according to the opinion entertained of their fitness for the office. In the time of the kings, however, we find them generally taken from the tribe of Levi; 1 Chron. xxiii. 4. 2 Chron. xix. 8—11. xxxiv. 13. This was a very rational procedure, as the Levites devoted themselves particularly to study; and among husbandmen and unlearned people, few were likely to be so expert at writing, as to be intrusted with the keeping of registers so important. Add to this, that in later times, the genealogical tables were kept in the temple. We find these *Schoterim* mentioned in many other passages besides those quoted above. In Numb. xi. 16, they are the persons of respectability from among whom the supreme senate of 70 is chosen. In Deut. i. 15, mention is made of *Schoterim* appointed by Moses in the wilderness, although the people had previously had such magistrates in Egypt; most probably he only filled the places of those who were dead. In Deut. xx. 5, we see them charged with orders to those of the people that were selected *to go to war;* which is perfectly suited to my explanation of the nature of their office. In Deut. xxix. 10, xxxi. 28, Josh. viii. 33, xxiii. 2, we find them as representatives of the people in the Diets, or when a covenant with God is entered into. In Josh. i. 10, they appear as the officers who communicated to the people the general's orders respecting military affairs; and this, again, corresponds to the province of muster-masters. In 2 Chron. xxvi. 11, we have the chief *Schoter*, under whose command the whole army stands after the general, if indeed he himself be not so. In 1 Chron. xxvii. 1, the name of the office alone is mentioned.—MICHAELIS.

CHAPTER XVII.

Ver. 16. But he shall not multiply horses to himself, nor cause the people to return to Egypt, to the end that he should multiply horses; forasmuch as the LORD hath said unto you, Ye shall henceforth return no more that way.

The king was not to keep a strong body of cavalry, nor an immoderate number of horses. As Palestine was a mountainous country, and on the more level side bounded by the Arabian deserts, in which an enemy's cavalry could not advance for want of forage, a powerful cavalry was almost unnecessary for its defence; and nothing but the spirit of conquest could prompt any king to violate the prohibition of Moses. But how little such a spirit accorded with the views of their divine lawgiver, we have already seen, in treating of the boundaries of the land. For agricultural purposes, the Israelites made no use of horses; but only (which in an economical point of view is far more profitable) of oxen and asses. The latter were also most commonly employed as beasts of burden in travelling; but the people made most of their journeys on foot. A king, therefore, could have no occasion for a great number of horses, unless he had it in view to carry on foreign wars.—MICHAELIS.

Ver. 17. Neither shall he multiply wives to himself, that his heart turn not away: neither shall he greatly multiply to himself silver and gold.

The king was not to take many wives, ver. 17. This law stands most in need of illustration; for as Moses did not forbid polygamy to the Israelites in general, it could not be his intention to confine the king within narrower limits, in this respect, than the citizen. Most probably, therefore, Moses had no objection to his having *four* wives, as seems to have been allowed to every Israelite. Even the high-priest, Jehoiada, of whom the Bible always gives a good character, gave *two* wives to King Joash: nor did he think that in this he was trespassing the Mosaic precept, of which he was by his office the authentic expounder; 2 Chron. xxiv. 3.—But the oriental seraglio now goes far beyond this moderate polygamy. There, more for state than for connubial purposes, great multitudes of women are brought together, and compelled to be miserable. Now it is only this excessive polygamy, this seraglio, as a part of royal state, that Moses appears to have forbidden. The nature of the thing itself shows, that it tends to make kings effeminate; and history confirms this to a much greater extent than could have been presupposed. That it exposes a reigning family to the danger of becoming extinct, we have at present a proof in the Turkish empire; for of the house of Othman there are so few heirs remaining, that now (1774) while I am adding this remark for the second edition, they are apprehensive of losing the very last of them in infancy.—The imitation of the practice too, by people of rank and opulence, carries polygamy to such a pitch, that, as contributing to the depopulation of a country, it is much more destructive than even the pestilence. To the Mosaic polity it was peculiarly unsuitable, for this special reason, that the most beautiful women of all nations are collected for a seraglio: and Moses, as he expressly mentions, was afraid lest such foreign beauties should win the heart of the king, and make him a proselyte to idolatry; and that his fears were not groundless, the example of Solomon is a striking proof. No law of Moses was less observed than this. It would appear that Saul had a seraglio, and *that* too belonging to him as king; for David (2 Sam. xii. 8) is said to have succeeded to it. David, before he was king, had, besides Michal, other two wives, Abigail and Ahinoam, 2 Sam. ii. 2. His first wife, Michal, had indeed been taken from him by his father-in-law; but he received her again while king of Judah. But after he had reigned some years in Hebron, we find him, besides these, in possession of four new wives, Maacha, Haggith, Abital, and Eglah, 2 Sam. iii. 2—8. This, however, was but a *moderate superabundance* for the king of a single tribe, considering, that seven years after, when he could less plead youth and passion in excuse, we find him, as king of all Israel, with still more wives and concubines, 2 Sam. v. 13; the latter, indeed, in such numbers, that on his flight from Absalom, he left *ten* of them to look after the palace, 2 Sam. xv. 16.—To what excess Solomon, the father of but one son, carried polygamy, is known to every one who has but heard of the Bible. It is difficult to believe that he could have *known* all the inmates of his seraglio; indeed it required a good memory to have been able to call them by their names. After his time, we have, in the books of the Chronicles, accounts of the polygamy of the kings, not indeed on such an immoderate and magnificent scale, but still far exceeding the degree permitted by Moses.—MICHAELIS.

CHAPTER XVIII.

Ver. 10. There shall not be found among you *any one* that maketh his son or his daughter to pass through the fire, *or* that useth divination, *or* an observer of times, or an enchanter, or a witch.

All idolatrous ceremonies, and even some which, though innocent in themselves, might excite suspicions of idolatry, were prohibited. Of these, human sacrifices are so conspicuous, as really the most abominable of all the crimes to which superstition is capable of hurrying its votaries, in defiance of the strongest feelings of humanity, that I must expatiate a little upon them. For this species of cruelty is so unnatural, that to many readers of the laws of Moses, it has appeared incredible. Against no other sort of idolatry, are the Mosaic prohibitions so rigorous, as against this; and yet we find that it continued among the Israelites to a very late period; for even the prophets Jeremiah and Ezekiel, who survived the ruin of the state, and wrote in the beginning of the Babylonish captivity, take notice of it, and describe it, not as an antiquated or obsolete abomination, but as what was actually in use but a little before, and even during their own times. For a father to see his children suffering, is in the highest degree painful; but that he should ever throw them to the flames, appears so utterly improbable, that we can hardly resist the temptation of declaring any narrative of such inhuman cruelty an absolute falsehood. But it is nevertheless an undoubted fact, that the imitation of the neighbouring nations, of which Moses expresses such anxious apprehensions in his laws, had, in spite of all the punishments denounced against it, kept up the abominable custom of offering children in sacrifice; and hence we see how necessary it was to enact the most rigorous laws against the idolatry, which required sacrifices of such a nature. The lives of children were to be secured against the fury of avaricious priests, and the fears of silly fools; and if the punishments of the law did not completely produce that effect, we can hardly avoid thinking, how much it is to be regretted that they were not more severe. To many, both Jewish and Christian expositors, it has appeared so incredible that the Israelites should have sacrificed their own children, that wherever, in the laws, or in the history, they find the expression, *making their sons pass through the fire to Moloch,* (for it was chiefly to that god that human sacrifices were offered,) they are fain to explain it on the more humane principle of their merely *dedicating* their sons to Moloch, and in token thereof, *making them pass between two sacrifice-fires.* In confirmation of this idea, the Vulgate version of Deut. xviii. 10, may be adduced; *Qui lustret filium suum aut filiam, ducens per ignem.* In this way, the incredible barbarity of human sacrifices would appear to have no foundation in truth; and I very readily admit, that of *some* other passages, such as Lev. xviii. 21. 2 Kings xxi. 6. xxiii. 10. Jer. xxxii. 35, an explanation on the same principle may be given with some show of truth.—More especially with regard to the first of these passages, I may remark, as *Le Clerc* has done before me, that we find a variety of lection which makes a material alteration of the sense; for instead of (העביר) *Haobir, to cause to pass through*, the Samaritan text, and the LXX., read (העביד) *Haabid, to cause to serve*, or, *to dedicate to the service of.* In my German version, I have, on account of this uncertainty, here made use of the general term *Weihem, to dedicate*, as the Vulgate had already set me the example, in rendering the clause, *De semine tuo non dabis, ut consecretur idolo Moloch.* I was the less inclined to employ the term *burn* here, because no mention is made of fire, *transire facere per ignem*, as in other passages; but it is merely said, *transire facere.* At the same time I really believe, from the strain of other passages to be mentioned immediately, that burning is here meant.—With regard, in like manner, to 2 Chron. xxviii. 3, where it is expressly said, that *Ahaz had, in imitation of the abominable practice of the nations whom Jehovah drove out before the Israelites*, burnt *his sons with fire*, the weighty objection may be made, that there is a various reading, and that, instead of (ויבער) *Veibor, he burnt*, almost all the ancient versions, such as the LXX., Syriac, Chaldee, and Vulgate, had read (ויעבר) *Veiober, he made to pass through*, by the mere transposition of the second radical into the place of the first. The following passages, however, are decisive of the reality of sacrificing their children.

1. Ezek. xvi. 21, (where we find the first-mentioned expression,) *Thou hast slain my sons, and given them, to cause them* pass through *to them.* Here it is evident that, *to pass through*, or *to cause to pass through the fire*, can be nothing else than *burning*, because the sons were previously slain.

2. The passages where the word (שרף) *Saraf, to burn*, is used; and where no suspicion of any various reading can take place; Deut. xii. 31. Jer. vii. 31. xix. 5.

3. Psalm cvi. 37, 38. "Their sons and daughters they sacrificed unto devils. They shed the innocent blood of their children, and offered it to the gods of Canaan, and the land was profaned with blood."

The punishment of those who offered human sacrifices was stoning; and *that*, as I think, so summarily, that the bystanders, when any one was caught in such an act, had a right to stone him to death on the spot, without any judicial inquiry whatever. *Whatever Israelite*, says Moses, in Lev. xx. 2, *or stranger dwelling among you, gives one of his children to Moloch, shall die; his neighbours shall stone him to death.* These are not the terms in which Moses usually speaks of the punishment of stoning judicially inflicted; but, *all the people shall stone him; the hands of the witnesses shall be the first upon him.* Besides, what follows a little after, in verses 4 and 5, does not appear to me as indicative of any thing like a matter of judicial procedure; *If the neighbours shut their eyes, and will not see him giving his children to Moloch, nor put him to death, God himself will be the avenger of his crime.* I am therefore of opinion, that in regard to this most extraordinary and most unnatural crime, which, however, could not be perpetrated in perfect secrecy, Moses meant to give an extraordinary injunction, and to let it be understood, that whenever a parent was about to sacrifice his child, the first person who observed him was to hasten to its help, and the people around were instantly to meet, and to stone the unnatural monster to death. In fact, no crime so justly authorizes extrajudicial vengeance, as this horrible cruelty perpetrated on a helpless child; in the discovery of which we are always sure to have either the lifeless victim as a proof, or else the living testimony of a witness who is beyond all suspicion; and where the *mania* of human sacrifices prevailed to such a pitch as among the Canaanites, and got so completely the better of all the feelings of nature, it was necessary to counteract its effects by a measure equally extraordinary and summary.—MICHAELIS.

Ver. 11. Or a charmer, or a consulter with familiar spirits, or a wizard, or a necromancer.

Sorcery is the fruitful source of numerous evils in the East. Charms and counter-charms call for the ingenuity, the property, the hopes, and fears of thousands. They are often used to effect the most diabolical purposes, and many a seduction is attributed to their supernatural power. The prophet Isaiah gives a description of the voice of a familiar spirit, and of its proceeding like a whisper from the dust. "Thou shalt be brought down, and shalt speak out of the ground, and thy speech shall be low out of the dust, and thy voice shall be as of one that hath a familiar spirit, out of the ground, and thy speech shall whisper out of the dust." Isa. xxix. 4. The margin has, for whisper, "peep or chirp." Lev. xix. 31. 1 Sam. xxviii. 7. The deluded Hindoos, in great emergencies, have recourse to familiar spirits, for the purpose of knowing how they may avoid the evil which is expected, or has in part already come. In the distraction of their minds, they run to the "consulter with familiar spirits," make known their desperate case, and entreat him to lend his assistance. Those "wizards that peep and that mutter," and who seek "for the living to the dead," Isa. viii. 19, are generally frightful in their persons, and disgusting in their manners. See the aged impostor, with a staff in his hand: his person bent by years; his wild, piercing, cat-like eye; a scowling, searching look; a clotted beard; a toothless mouth; dishevelled hair; a mumbling unearthly voice; his more than half-naked body, covered with ashes; a wild unsteady gait, joined with the other insignia of his office;—give a fearful influence to his infernal profession. A man who is in distress, and who has resolved to consult with a familiar spirit, sends for two magicians: the one is called the *Manthera-vāthe*, i. e. he who repeats the incantations; the other, the *Anjanam-Pārkeravan*, i. e. he who looks, and who answers to the questions of the former. His hand is rubbed with the Anjanam, which is made of the burnt bones of the sloth, and the scull of a virgin; and when the ceremonies have commenced, he looks steadily into his hand, and can never wink or take off his eyes till all shall be finished. On the ground are placed rice, cocoa-nuts, plantains, areca nuts, betel leaves, milk, camphire, and frankincense. The chief magician then, with a loud voice, begins to invoke the nine gods—Ammon, Pulliār, Scandan, Aiyenar, Iyaner, Veerapatteran, Anjana, Anuman, Viraver. He then falls to the earth (as do all present) nine times, and begins to whisper and "mutter," while his face is in the "dust," and he who looks in the hand "peeps" and stares for the beings who have to appear. All then stand up, and the first wizard asks the second, "What do you see?" He replies, "My hand is cracked, has opened, and I see on the ground." "What else do you see?"—"All around me is light—come, Pulliār, come." "He comes! he comes!" (His person, shape, and dress, are then described.) The other eight gods are now entreated to appear; and as they approach, the second person says, "They come! they come!" and they are invited to be seated in the places prepared for them. The first magician then inquires of the assembled gods, what is the cause of the affliction, adversity, or danger of the person, for whom the ceremonies have been instituted? He who "peeps" in the hand then replies, and mentions the name of the evil spirit, who has produced all the mischief. The malignant troubler is summoned to appear, and to depart; but should he refuse, he is bound, and carried off by the gods. Is it not probable that Saul, and the woman who had "a familiar spirit at Endor," were engaged in a similar way? Saul was in great distress, for the Lord would neither answer him "by dreams, nor by Urim, nor by prophets;" and being wound up to desperation, he determined to consult "with familiar spirits." He took "TWO men" with him, who were probably qualified like the TWO used by the Hindoos. From the fear which the woman showed, it is probable her incantations had not exactly answered her expectations, because "she cried with a loud voice" when she saw Samuel, proving that she did not expect to see him, and that, therefore, he was sent by some other power; Saul inquired, "What sawest thou?" which agrees with the question proposed by the first magician to his assistant, as to what he saw through the crack of his hand in the earth. The witch then replied to Saul, "I saw gods ascending out of the earth," which naturally reminds us of the nine gods which are believed to ascend after the incantations of the wizard. Saul then asked, "What form is he of?" and the witch said he was old, and covered with a mantle, which also finds a parallel in the description of "the shape and dress" given of Pulliār by the second magician. I am, therefore, of opinion, that God allowed Samuel to come to Saul, or sent him; and that the witch was confounded and terrified at the result of her incantations.—ROBERTS.

CHAPTER XIX.

Ver. 14. Thou shalt not remove thy neighbour's land-mark, which they of old time have set in thine inheritance, which thou shalt inherit in the land that the LORD thy God giveth thee to possess it.

When the sons of Israel had conquered the land of promise, it was, by the divine command, surveyed and divided by lot, first among the twelve tribes; and then the portion of each tribe was laid out in separate inheritances, according to the number of the families composing the tribe; and thus every man in the nation had his field, which he was directed to cultivate for the support of himself and his family. To prevent mistake and litigation, these fields were marked off by stones set up on the limits, which could not be removed without incurring the wrath of heaven. The divine command, in relation to this matter, runs in these terms: "Thou shalt not remove thy neighbour's land-mark, which they of old time have set in thine inheritance, which thou shalt inherit in the land which the Lord thy God giveth thee to possess." In Persia, land-marks are still used: in the journey from Arzroum to Amasia, Morier found the boundaries of each man's possession, here and there, marked by large stones. Land-marks were used in Greece long before the age of Homer; for when Minerva fought with Mars, she seized with her powerful hand, a piece of rock, lying in the plain, black, rugged and large, which ancient men had placed to mark the boundary of the field.—PAXTON.

CHAPTER XX.

Ver. 19. When thou shalt besiege a city a long time, in making war against it to take it, thou shalt not destroy the trees thereof by forcing an axe against them: for thou mayest eat of them, and thou shalt not cut them down, (for the tree of the field *is* man's *life*,) to employ *them* in the siege.

Can it be a matter of surprise that the Orientals have a great aversion to cut down any tree which bears fruit, when it is known that they principally live on vegetable productions? Ask a man to cut down a cocoa-nut or palmirah tree, and he will say, (except when in want, or to oblige a great person,) "What! destroy that which gives me food? from which I have thatch for my house to defend me from the sun and the rain? which gives me oil for my lamp, a ladle for my kitchen, and charcoal for my fire? from which I have sugar for my board, baskets for my fruits, a bucket for my well, a mat for my bed, a pouch for my betel leaf, leaves for my books, a fence for my yard, and a broom for my house? Destroy such a tree? Go to some needy wretch who has pledged his last jewel, and who is anxious to eat his last meal."—ROBERTS.

CHAPTER XXI.

Ver. 6. And all the elders of that city, *that are* next unto the slain *man*, shall wash their hands over the heifer that is beheaded in the valley.

When a great man refuses to grant a favour to a friend or relation, the latter asks, "What! are you going to wash your hands of me?" "Ah! he has washed his hands of all his relations;" which means, he will not have any thing more to do with them; he is entirely free, and will not be accountable for them. Hence the Tamul proverb, *Avon ellātilum kai kaluvi nitkerān*, i. e. "He has washed his hands of all."—ROBERTS.

Ver. 12. Then thou shalt bring her home to thy house, and she shall shave her head, and pare her nails; 13. And she shall put the raiment of her captivity from off her, and shall remain in thy house, and bewail her father and her mother a full month: and after that thou shalt go in unto her, and be her husband, and she shall be thy wife.

The margin has, instead of *pare her nails*, "OR SUFFER TO GROW;" which is, I doubt not, the true meaning. This woman was a prisoner of war, and was about to become the wife of the man who had taken her captive. Having thus been taken from her native land, having had to leave her earliest and dearest connexions, and now to become the wife of a foreigner, and an enemy, she would naturally be overwhelmed with grief. To acquire a better view of her state, let any woman consider herself in similar circumstances. She accompanies her husband, or father, to the battle; the enemy becomes victorious, and she is carried off by the hand of a ruthless stranger, and obliged to submit to his desires. Poignant indeed would be the sorrow of her mind. The poor captive was to "*shave her head*" in token of her distress, which is a custom in all parts of the East at this day. A son on the death of his father, or a woman on the decease of her husband, has the HEAD SHAVED in token of sorrow. To shave the head also, is a punishment inflicted on females for certain crimes. The fair captive, then, as a sign of her misery, was to shave her head, because her father or mother was among the slain, or in consequence of having become a prisoner of war. It showed her sorrow; and was a token of her submission. (See also Job i. 20. See on 2 Chronicles xvi. 14. Isa. vii. 20, and xviii. 2.) But this poor woman was to suffer her *nails to grow*, as an additional emblem of her distress. That it does not mean she was to PARE her nails, as the text has it, is established by the custom in the East, of allowing them to grow, when in sorrow. The marginal reading, therefore, would have been much better for the text. When people, either in the church or state, are performing penance, or are in captivity, or disgrace, or prison, or are devotees, they suffer their nails to grow; and some may be seen, as were those of the monarch of Babylon, in his sorrow, "like birds' claws," literally folding round the ends of the fingers, or shooting through the backs of their hands. But when men fast, which is sometimes done for one or two years, or when husbands fast during their wives' first pregnancy, they suffer their nails to grow; also a female, when in sorrow from other causes, does not "pare her nails" until she has performed the ceremony called Antherette.—ROBERTS.

There is a passage in Deuteronomy xxi. 12, about the sense of which our translators appear to have been extremely uncertain: translating one clause of the 12th verse, *and pare her nails*, in the text; and the margin giving the clause a quite opposite sense, "suffer to grow." So that, according to them, the words signify, that the captived woman should be obliged, in the case referred to by Moses, to *pare her nails*, or, to *suffer them to grow*, but they could not tell which of these two contradictory things the Jewish legislator required; the Jewish doctors are, in like manner, divided in their opinion on this subject. To me it seems very plain, that it was not a management of affliction and mourning that was enjoined; such an interpretation agrees not with the putting off the raiment of her captivity; but then I very much question whether the paring her nails takes in the whole of the intention of Moses. The precept of the law was, that she should *make her nails:* so the Hebrew words literally signify. Making her nails, signifies making her nails neat, beautifying them, making them pleasing to the sight, or something of that sort: *dressing* them is the word our translators have chosen, according to the margin. The 2 Sam. xix. 24, which the critics have cited on this occasion, plainly proves this: "Mephibosheth, the son of Saul, came down to meet the king, and had neither made his feet, nor made his beard, nor washed his clothes, from the day the king departed, until the day he came again in peace." It is the same word with that in the text, and our translators have rendered it in one clause dressed, in the margin of Deut. xxi. *dressed his feet;* and in the other trimmed, *nor trimmed his beard.* Making the feet, seems here to mean washing the feet, paring their nails, perhaps anointing, or otherwise perfuming them, as he was a prince; see Luke vii. 46. As making his beard may mean combing, curling, perfuming it; every thing, in a word, that those that were people of distinction, and in a state of joy, were wont to do. *Making her nails*, undoubtedly means paring them; but it must mean too every thing else relating to them, that was wont to be done for the beautifying them, and rendering them beautiful. We have scarcely any notion of any thing else but paring them; but the modern eastern women have; they stain them with the leaves of an odoriferous plant, which they call Al-henna, of a red, or, as others express it, a tawny saffron colour. But it may be thought, that is only a modern mode of adorning their nails: Hasselquist, however, assures us, it was an ancient oriental practice. "The Al-henna," he tells us, "grows in India, and in Upper and Lower Egypt, flowering from May to August. The leaves are pulverized, and made into a paste with water: they bind this paste on the nails of their hands and feet, and keep it on all night. This gives them a deep yellow, which is greatly admired by the eastern nations. The colour lasts for three or four weeks, before there is occasion to renew it. The custom is so ancient in Egypt, that I have seen the nails of mummies died in this manner. The powder is exported in large quantities yearly, and may be reckoned a valuable commodity." It appears by this to be a very ancient practice; and since mummies were before the time of Moses, this custom of dying the nails might be as ancient too; though we do not suppose the mummies Hasselquist saw, with their nails thus coloured, were so old as his time.

If it was practised in Egypt before the law was given, we may believe the Israelites adopted it, since it appears to be a most universal custom now in the eastern countries: Dr. Shaw observing that all the African ladies that can purchase it, make use of it, reckoning it a great beauty; as we learn from Rauwolff, it appears also to the Asiatic females. I cannot but think it most probable then, that making the nails, signifies *tinging* as well as paring them. *Paring* alone, one would imagine too trifling a circumstance to be intended here. No commentator, however, that I know of, has taken any notice of ornamenting the nails by colouring them. As for shaving the head, which is joined with making the nails, it was a rite of cleansing, as appears from Lev. xiv. 8, 9, and Num. vi. 9, and used by those who, after having been in an afflicted and squalid state, appeared before persons to whom they desired to render themselves acceptable, and who were also wont to change their raiment on the same occasion. See Gen. xli. 14.—Harmer.

Ver. 17. But he shall acknowledge the son of the hated *for* the first-born, by giving him a double portion of all that he hath: for he *is* the beginning of his strength; the right of the first-born *is* his.

Next to the father, the first-born of a family possessed the greatest rights. There were not, however, in a family as many first-born as mothers; in other words, to be so called, it was not enough that a man should be the first fruit of the mother, or, as the Hebrews term it, *Pheter Rechem*, (פטר רחם) but that he should, at the same time, be the first son of his father, who was called *Becor*, (בכור) and *the beginning of his strength*. The law of Deut. xxi. 15—17, places this beyond doubt, and the family history of Jacob confirms it. For though Jacob had four wives, and children by them all, yet he gave the birthright to one son only, 1 Chron. v. 1, 2. That right Reuben had forfeited by a great crime; but if he had not done so, *he* would certainly have been considered as the only first-born, as he alone is indeed called so in the history, Gen. xlix. 3. If, instead of this, the first son of every mother had been denominated the first-born, it would have been impossible that, among a people consisting of 600,000 adult males, and where there must have been at least 300,000 males above 20 years of age, there could be numbered no more than 22,000 first-born of a month old, and above it; because this would have required that every mother, one with another, had brought 40 (but because it is so incredible I will write the word at length, *forty*) children into the world. In my Dissertation, *De Censibus Hebræorum*, to which I here refer the reader, I have illustrated this point at greater length. How the matter was settled when a father had his first-born son by a widow, that had had children by her former marriage, I do not *historically* know; but this much is certain, that such son could not be called *Pheter Rechem*, the first-fruit of the mother; and, therefore, could be none of the first-born who, by the Levitical law, (Exod. xiii. 12. Numb. iii. 40—51,) were consecrated to the Lord; but still he probably enjoyed the rights of a first-born in relation to his brothers. This, however, was a case that could rarely occur, because it appears that the Hebrews seldom married widows who had been mothers; although I do find one example of such a marriage. Besides his double share of the inheritance, the first-born in patriarchal families had great privileges, and a sort of authority over his brethren; just as at present an Arab *emir* is, for the most part, only the *first-born of the first-born* of his family, and, as such, rules a horde, composed merely of his kinsmen. This was also the case under the Mosaic polity, though with some limitation in point of authority; and hence we find in the genealogies of the first book of Chronicles, the first-born is often likewise termed *the head* (הראש) of the family; and in chap. xxvi. 10, it is stated as a circumstance somewhat singular and unusual, that a father constituted one, who was *not* a first-born, *the head*. How much further these rights extended, I know not, excepting only in this particular, that the first-born was only the head of the lesser family.—Michaelis.

Ver. 19. Then shall his father and his mother lay hold on him, and bring him out unto the elders of the city, and unto the gate of his place.

The gates of cities, in these days, and for many ages after, were the places of judicature and common resort. Here the governors and elders of the city went to hear complaints, administer justice, make conveyances of titles and estates, and, in short, to transact all the public affairs of the place. And from hence is that passage in the Psalmist, "They shall not be ashamed when they speak to their enemies in the gate." (Ps. cxxvii. 5.) It is probable that the room, or hall, where the magistrates sat, was over the gate, because *Boaz* is said *to go up to the gate;* and the reason of having it built there, seems to have been for the convenience of the inhabitants, who, being all husbandmen, and forced to pass and repass every morning and evening as they went and came from their labour, might be more easily called, as they went by, whenever they were wanted to appear in any business.—Burder.

Ver. 23. His body shall not remain all night upon the tree, but thou shalt in anywise bury him that day.

An Englishman is astonished in the East, to see how soon after death the corpse is buried. Hence a new-comer, on hearing of the death of a servant, or native officer, who died in the morning, and who is to be interred in the evening, is almost disposed to interfere with what is to him apparently a barbarous practice. When the cholera prevails, it is truly appalling to see a man in one hour in health, and the next carried to his long-home. The reason assigned for this haste is the heat of the climate.—Roberts.

CHAPTER XXII.

Ver. 4. Thou shalt not see thy brother's ass or his ox fall down by the way, and hide thyself from them: thou shalt surely help him to lift *them* up again.

Whoever saw a beast tottering or lying under the weight of his burden, was bound to help him; and that with the same exertion and perseverance as the owner himself was doing, or would have done. Nor durst he (for this the words of Moses seem to imply) desist, but *with* the owner; that is, until the owner himself left the beast, seeing him past relief, Exod. xxiii. 5. Both these were incumbent duties even when the beast belonged to an enemy; and the passages above referred to, expressly mention the ox and ass of an enemy. This is reasonable; for we expect that even our enemy will be humane enough to foreget his enmity, and give us his aid in a time of need, or, at any rate, that he will not be so *little* as to extend his enmity to a beast quite innocent of our quarrel, and that lies in distress before his eyes. What we expect, we should do in our turn; and if we will not listen to the suggestions of moral obligation, still we must see, that among a nation of husbandmen and herdsmen, it was a matter of great importance to preserve the lives of work-beasts. And upon the same principle, we might perhaps be enjoined to extinguish, if need were, a fire in our enemy's house, as if it were our own. How humane soever this law of Moses may appear, we must at the same time recollect, that it was not given to a people like ourselves, but to a people among whom every individual generally had cattle; so that they could not but be influenced by the great duty of reciprocity, which among us, at least in towns, does not here hold, because but few have cattle.—Among the Israelites, none almost could be so unaccustomed to their management, or to their relief in distress, as our town's-people are. This last circumstance is peculiarly deserving of notice. I grant that such a law would, in Germany, be a very strange one, if accompanied with no limitation to certain classes of the community; for he who is not from his infancy conversant with beasts, seldom acquires the confidence or dexterity requisite for their aid when in danger, without hurting himself. He, perhaps, sits perfectly well on horseback, and can do all that belongs to a good rider, when mounted; but to help up with a horse fallen down under his load, or to stop one that has run off, would not be his *forte*.—Add to this, that among us, neither the ox, nor the ass, but the horse alone, is so honourable, that a gentleman could help up with him, without demeaning himself, and being laughed at. But among a nation of farmers, who ploughed with oxen and asses, and where there were no hereditary noblesse, such a foolish idea, which a legislator must have attended to, could have no place.

We shall find that Moses, throughout his laws, manifests even towards animals a spirit of justice and kindness, and inculcates the avoidance, not only of actual cruelty, but even of its appearance. A code of civil law does not, indeed, necessarily provide for the rights of animals, because they are not citizens; but still, the way in which animals are treated, so strongly influences the manners and sentiments of a people even towards their fellow-creatures, (for he who habitually acts with cruelty and want of feeling to beasts, will soon become cruel and hard-hearted to men,) that a legislator will sometimes find it necessary to attend to it, to prevent his people from becoming savage. —MICHAELIS.

Ver. 6. If a bird's-nest chance to be before thee in the way in any tree, or on the ground, *whether they be* young ones or eggs, and the dam sitting upon the young or upon the eggs, thou shalt not take the dam with the young.
7. *But* thou shalt in anywise let the dam go, and take the young to thee; that it may be well with thee, and *that* thou mayest prolong *thy* days.

It is the command of Moses, that if a person find a bird's-nest in the way, whether on a tree or on the ground, though he may take the eggs, or the young, he shall not take the mother, but always allow her to escape. It is clear that he here speaks, not of those birds which nestle upon people's property; in other words, that he does not, for instance, prohibit an Israelite from totally destroying a sparrow's or a swallow's nest, that might happen to be troublesome to him, or to extirpate to the utmost of his power the birds that infested his field or vineyard. He merely enjoins what one was to do on finding such nests *on the way*, that is, *without* one's property: thus guarding against either the utter extinction, or too great diminution of any species of bird indigenous to the country. And this in some countries is still, with respect to partridges, an established rule; which, without a special law, is observed by every real sportsman, and the breach of which subjects him to the reproaches of his brethren. Nor would any further illustration be necessary, if Moses spoke only of edible birds, and as if merely concerned for their preservation. But this is not the case. His expression is so general, that we must needs understand it of all birds whatever, even those that are most destructive, besides what are properly birds of prey. And here many readers may think it strange, that Moses should be represented as providing for the preservation of noxious birds; yet, in fact, nothing can be more conformable to legislative wisdom, especially on the introduction of colonies into a new country. To extirpate, or even to persecute, to too great an extent, any species of birds in such a country, from an idea, often too hastily entertained, of its being hostile to the interests of the inhabitants, is a measure of very doubtful policy. It ought, in general, to be considered as a part of Nature's bounty, bestowed for some important purpose; but what that is, we certainly discover too late, when it has been extirpated, and the evil consequences of that measure are begun to be felt. In this matter, the legislator should take a lesson from the naturalist. Linnæus, whom all will allow to be a perfect master in the science of natural history, has made the above remark in his Dissertation, entitled, *Historia Naturalis cui Bono?* and gives two remarkable examples to confirm it: the one, in the case of the *Little Crow of Virginia*, (*Gracula Quiscula*,) extirpated, at great expense, on account of its supposed destructive effects, and which the inhabitants would soon gladly have re-introduced at double expense; the other, in that of the *Egyptian Vulture*, or *Racham*, (*Vultur Percnopterus*, Linn.) In the city of Cairo, every place is so full of dead carcasses, that the stench of them would not fail to produce putrid diseases; and where the caravans travel, dead asses and camels are always lying. The *Racham*, which molests no living thing, consumes these carcasses, and clears the country of them; and it even follows the track of the caravan to Mecca, for the same purpose: and so grateful are the people for the service it thus does the country, that devout and opulent Mohammedans are wont to establish foundations for its support, by providing for the expense of a certain number of beasts to be daily killed, and given every morning and evening to the immense flocks of *Rachams* that resort to the place where criminals are executed, and rid the city, as it would seem, of *their* carcasses in like manner. These eleemosynary institutions, and the sacred regard shown to these birds by the Mohammedans, are likewise testified by Dr. Shaw, in his Travels. These examples serve pretty strongly to show, that in respect, at least, to birds, we ought to place as much confidence in the wisdom and kindness of Nature, as not rashly to extirpate any species which she has established in a country, as a great, and, perhaps, indispensable blessing. Limit its numbers we certainly may, if they incommode us; but still so as that the race shall not become extinct. Of quadrupeds and insects I say nothing, because, with regard to them, we have not such experience to guide us. No inconvenience has arisen in England, nor even in that populous part of Germany between the Weser and the Oder, from the loss of the wolves; although I cannot understand, but must leave it to naturalists to find out, how it should happen, that, in any country, *beasts* of prey can be extirpated with less inconvenience than *birds*; wild cats, for instance, and to bring that parallel closer, than owls, both of which live upon mice? There are yet *three* peculiar circumstances to be noted, which would naturally make the Israelitish legislator singularly attentive to the preservation of birds.

1. He was conducting a colony of people into a country with which they were unacquainted, and where they might very probably attempt to extirpate any species of bird that seemed troublesome, without adverting to its real importance; just as the Virginian colonists did, in the case of their crow.

2. Palestine is situated in a climate producing poisonous snakes and scorpions, and between deserts and mountains, from which it would be inundated with those snakes, if the birds that lived on them were extirpated.

3. From the same deserts too, it would be overwhelmed with immense multitudes of locusts and mice, if it were destitute of those birds, that resort thither to feed on them; not to mention the formidable swarms of flies in the East, and particularly in Palestine, of which I have taken notice in my Dissertation on this law.—MICHAELIS.

Ver. 8. When thou buildest a new house, then thou shalt make a battlement for thy roof, that thou bring not blood upon thy house, if any man fall from thence.

The roof is always flat, and often composed of branches of wood laid across rude beams, and to defend it from the injuries of the weather, to which it is peculiarly exposed in the rainy season, it is covered with a strong plaster of terrace. It is surrounded by a wall breast high, which forms the partition with the contiguous houses, and prevents one from falling into the street on the one side, or into the court on the other. This answers to the battlements which Moses commanded the people of Israel to make for the roof of their houses, for the same reason. "When thou buildest a new house, then thou shalt make a battlement (מעקה) for thy roof, that thou bring not blood upon thy house, if any man fall from thence." Instead of the parapet wall, some terraces are guarded, like the galleries, with balustrades only, or latticed work. Of the same kind, probably, was the lattice or net, as the term (שבכה *shebaca*) seems to import, through which Ahaziah, the king of Samaria, fell down into the court. This incident proves the necessity of the law which Jehovah graciously dictated from Sinai, and furnishes a beautiful example of his paternal care and goodness; for the terrace was a place where many offices of the family were performed, and business of no little importance was occasionally transacted. Rahab concealed the spies on the roof, with the stalks of flax which she had laid in order to dry; the king of Israel, according to the custom of his country, rose from his bed, and walked upon the roof of his house, to enjoy the refreshing breezes of the evening; upon the top of the house, the prophet conversed with Saul, about the gracious designs of God, respecting him and his family; to the same place, Peter retired to offer up his devotions; and in the feast of tabernacles, under the government of Nehemiah, booths were erected, as well upon the terraces of their houses, as in their courts, and in the streets of the city. In Judea, the inhabitants sleep upon the tops of their houses during the heats of summer, in arbours made of the branches of trees, or in tents of rushes. When Dr. Pococke was at Tiberias in Galilee, he was entertained by the sheik's steward, and with his company supped upon the top of the house for coolness, according to their custom, and lodged there likewise, in a sort of closet of about eight feet square, formed of wicker-work, plastered round towards the bottom, but without any door, each person having his cell. In like manner, the Persians take refuge during the day in subterraneous chambers, and pass the night on the flat roofs of their houses.—Paxton.

We have repeated intimations in scripture, of a custom which would be extremely inconvenient in England;—that of sleeping on the top of the house, exposed to the open air, and sky: so we read, "Samuel came to call Saul about the spring of the day, not *to*—but on—the top of the house; and communed with him on the house-top." So Solomon observes, "It is better to dwell in a corner on the house-top, than with a brawling woman in a wide street." The same idea may be noticed elsewhere. "It has ever been a custom with them, [the Arabs in the East,] equally connected with health and pleasure, to pass the nights in summer upon the house-tops, which for this very purpose are made flat, and divided from each other by walls. We found this way of sleeping extremely agreeable; as we thereby enjoyed the cool air, above the reach of gnats and vapours, without any other covering than the canopy of the heavens, which unavoidably presents itself in different pleasing forms, upon every interruption of rest, when silence and solitude strongly dispose the mind to contemplation." (Wood's Balbec, Introduction.) "I determined he should lodge in a kiosque, on the top of my house, where I kept him till his exaltation to the patriarchate, which, after a long negotiation, my wife's brother obtained, for a pretty large sum of money, to be paid in new sequins." (Baron du Tott.) The propriety of the Mosaic precept (Deut. xxii. 8,) which orders a kind of balustrade, or parapet, to surround the roof, lest any man should fall from thence, is strongly enforced by this relation; for, if we suppose a person to rise in the night, without being fully awake, he might easily kill himself by falling from the roof. Something of the kind appears in the history of Amaziah, 2 Kings i. 2. In several places scripture hints at grass growing on the house-tops, but which comes to nothing. The following quotation will show the nature of this: "In the morning the master of the house laid in a stock of earth; which was carried up, and spread evenly on the top of the house, which is flat. The whole roof is thus formed of mere earth, laid on, and rolled hard and flat. On the top of every house is a large stone roller, for the purpose of hardening and flattening this layer of made soil, so that the rain may not penetrate: but upon this surface, as may be supposed, grass and weeds grow freely. It is to such grass that the Psalmist alludes, as useless and bad." (Jowett's Christian Researches in Syria.) There is also mention of persons on the house-top hastily escaping from thence without entering the house to secure their property—as if hastily awaked out of sleep, or, &c. by the clamours of an invading enemy.—Taylor in Calmet.

Ver. 10. Thou shalt not plough with an ox and an ass together.

Le Clerc and some others think that this text is to be taken in a symbolical sense, and that intermarriages with pagans and unbelievers are forbidden by it. Maimonides and the Jewish rabbies are of opinion, that this prohibition was given in consequence of the ox being a clean, and the ass an unclean animal. But no other interpretation need be sought than that which arises from the humanity shown to animals in various parts of the Mosaic laws. The ass is lower than the ox, and when in a yoke together must bear the principal weight, and that in a very painful position of the neck; his steps are unequal, and his strength is inferior, which must occasion an irregular draught, and great oppression to both. The ass is a stubborn, refractory, and, in these countries, a spirited creature; the ox, on the contrary, is gentle, tractable, and patient: writers on agriculture, therefore, have given the same precept as Moses; and Calpurnius says generally, Ne pecora quidem jugo nisi paria succedant.—"Let no cattle be yoked together except they match." Cruel and unnatural as this practice is, we may suppose it was not uncommon; for we find it alluded to in the *Aulularia* of Plautus, act i. s. 4. Old Euclio, addressing himself to Megadorus, says, Nunc si filiam locassem meam tibi, in mentem venit. Te bovem esse, et me esse asellum, ubi tecum conjunctus sim. "If I were to give my daughter to you, it occurs to me, that when we had formed this alliance, I should be the ass, and you the ox."—Burder.

In the sandy fields of Syria and Egypt, where deep ploughing, by draining off the moisture necessary to vegetation, would be hurtful, a single ass is occasionally seen drawing the plough. The implement employed, is made to correspond with the strength of the animal; it is so light, "that a man of moderate strength," says Dr. Russel, "may easily carry it with one hand; a little cow, or at most two, and sometimes only an ass, is sufficient to draw it." But this is done only in very light soils; where the ground is stiffer, and a deeper furrow required, two beasts are yoked together in one plough. In Syria, where the distinction between clean and unclean beasts did not exist, and where unnatural associations were disregarded, they very often joined an ox and an ass in the same yoke. But the law of Moses prohibited, by an express statute, such incongruous mixtures: "Thou shalt not plough with an ox and an ass together." The chosen people might employ them both in tilling their ground; but, in every instance, they were to be joined only with those of their own species. This precept embraced at once, the benefit of the tribes, and the comfort of their cattle. The benevolent legislator would not have animals of unequal strength, and of discordant habits and dispositions, forced into a union to which they are naturally averse, and where the labour could not be equally divided. But Jehovah, whose care extends to the happiness even of an ox or an ass, had certainly a higher object in view. He meant, by this prohibition, to instruct his people to preserve, with solicitude, the unaffected simplicity of the patriarchal ages, in their manner of living; to avoid unnatural associations among themselves, and undue familiarity with the idolatrous nations around them, by contracting marriages with them, entering into alliances, or engaging in extensive mercantile transactions, still more, by joining in the impure rites of their worship. To this moral aspect of the law, the great apostle of the Gentiles evidently refers in his charge to the Corinthians: "Be ye not unequally yoked together with unbelievers; for what fellowship hath righteousness with unrighteousness? and what communion hath light with darkness."—Paxton.

CHAPTER XXIII.

Ver. 19. Thou shalt not lend upon usury to thy

brother; usury of money, usury of victuals,
usury of any thing that is lent upon usury.
20. Unto a stranger thou mayest lend upon
usury; but unto thy brother thou shalt not lend
upon usury: that the LORD thy God may bless
thee in all that thou settest thy hand to in the
land whither thou goest to possess it.

See on Lev. 25. 26.

Ver 24. When thou comest into thy neighbour's
vineyard, then thou mayest eat grapes thy fill,
at thine own pleasure; but thou shalt not put
any in thy vessel. 25. When thou comest
into the standing corn of thy neighbour, then
thou mayest pluck the ears with thy hand;
but thou shalt not move a sickle unto thy
neighbour's standing corn.

If a man was passing along another's field, he was allowed to pluck ears of corn to eat, but forbidden to use the sickle, Deut. xxiii. 25. This pretty much accords with what is common among ourselves; for no owner of a field, unless he wishes to render himself ridiculous by his niggardliness, will hinder a passenger from plucking his ears of corn, and eating them. But the liberty of the stranger, by the Mosaic law, perhaps extended still further: for if the poor man had plucked up whole handfuls of ears, and carried them off, I do not thence see how he could have been found punishable, or how it could have been prevented. I do not take upon me absolutely to decide the point, because the law is very briefly expressed. I only remark, that this very law, which among us would be very unjust and pernicious, had quite another aspect among a people consisting entirely of husbandmen: for where every citizen, or, in other words, every one belonging to the nation, has his own land, one will not be apt, from avarice, to tear up another's corn, because he must expect that his neighbour will retaliate in like manner upon his. It will, therefore, most probably be only as he travels along, that he will eat a few ears for pleasure, and that may readily be allowed him. In the verse immediately preceding, (Deut. xxiii. 24,) Moses has an ordinance respecting vineyards, which may to us appear more singular, and to bear harder on their owners. The stranger that came into another's vineyard, was authorized to eat as many grapes as he pleased, only he might not carry any off in his basket, or other such vessel. To my illustration of this law, I must premise, that I am not a native of a wine country; having been born at Halle, on the extreme verge of the wine district of Germany, and where vineyards are so rare, that under such a law they could not possibly exist. In such a climate, every individual bunch of grapes is not indeed a rarity, (for that I cannot say of my native country,) but, at any rate, an article of sale, and worth money. Perhaps, therefore, a native of a more southern region, where wine is produced in greater abundance, would be able to explain this part of the Mosaic law better, and would find it more agreeable to justice. But besides all that persons acquainted with wine countries could say, there is this additional circumstance here to be attended to, and which is quite inapplicable to all *our* wine countries, viz. that every Israelite had his paternal land; and if he lived in a district where wine was grown, (which was the case in most parts of Palestine, the country being mountainous,) he probably had a vineyard of his own, as well as his neighbour. The right, therefore, to eat one's fill in another's vineyard, was, in most cases, merely a *jus reciprocum:* and thus I might with freedom satisfy my appetite, wherever I saw grapes before me; single bunches being there no article of sale. This to travellers was a gratification always acceptable, and a piece of courtesy that cost the owners but little; and to those who had no land, that is, to the poor, it was a sort of alms, or, at least, a comfort, that they could thus satisfy their appetite without being chargeable with theft, or injustice. If the owner of a vineyard found them too assiduous, or their visits too frequently repeated, there was nothing in the law that hindered him from enclosing it, or turning them out. Only they could not be declared thieves, if they but plucked the grapes, and ate them within the vineyard. We shall frequently see, that the laws of Moses manifest a certain degree of indulgence and kindness to the cravings of nature; which, far from wishing to torture, they would not even have exposed to any temptation, that might lead a man to theft. This is a point of great importance to the preservation of the moral character of a people. Hunger, or appetite, often hurries a man of the most honourable principles to devour grapes and other eatables that are not watched; if his conscience make this theft, the great boundary that distinguishes the man of honour from the thief, is in a manner overstepped, and if this happen often, he will at last become a thief in a higher sense, having lost all conscience and regard to character. It is, therefore, certainly better, if it can be done without any material injury to property, to allow him the liberty of eating a little of such things, in order to keep him a conscientious, honourable man. Legislators sometimes attend but too little to moral niceties of this nature; and yet it is possible thereby to corrupt a whole people, and rob them of their honesty. Moses, on the other hand, would give no sanction to the practice of free pasturage, although he gave his laws to a people sprung from wandering herdsmen, to whose cattle, the whole country where they lived was a common; and herein he is a most perfect antipode to our laws of indiscriminate pasturage, which prove so great a misfortune to Germany. Whoever drove his cattle into another's field or vineyard, and fed therein, was obliged to pay a *grazing rent;* but whether for the whole year, or only for the precise time of occupation, I am uncertain, Exod. xxii. However favourable, therefore, he may have been to the poor, in authorizing them to pluck a few ears of corn, or to glean what was left in the fields, he by no means thought it just that, by any law of free pasturage, a man should be obstructed in using his field as his own property solely, and in turning it to the best account, even after harvest. Whoever has heard the complaints of economists against commons, which with us, without injustice to individuals, it is so difficult to abolish, while yet they so effectually obstruct the full improvement of the fields, will perceive the importance and the wisdom of this law, the enforcing of which was attended with no difficulty after the conquest of a new country.—MICHAELIS.

CHAPTER XXIV.

Ver. 10. When thou dost lend thy brother any
thing, thou shalt not go into his house to fetch
his pledge. 11. Thou shalt stand abroad, and
the man to whom thou dost lend shall bring out
the pledge abroad unto thee. 12. And if the
man *be* poor, thou shalt not sleep with his
pledge: 13. In any case thou shalt deliver him
the pledge again when the sun goeth down,
that he may sleep in his own raiment, and
bless thee: and it shall be righteousness unto
thee before the LORD thy God.

Among the Israelites in the time of Moses, it must have been very common to lend on pledge—and *that*, according to the meaning of the word, in natural law, which allows the creditor, in the case of non-payment, to appropriate the pledge to his own behoof, without any authoritative interposition of a magistrate, and to keep it just as rightfully as if it had been bought with the sum which has been lent for it, and which remains unpaid. But while pledges are under no judicial regulation, much extortion and villany may be practised, when the poor man who wishes to borrow is in straits, and must of course submit to all the terms imposed by the opulent lender. This we know from daily experience: the persons who lend money extrajudicially on pledge, being generally odious or contemptible usurers. Among a poor people, such as we must suppose every people to be in their infancy, the evils of pledging are still more oppressive. The poor man often finds himself under a far greater necessity of borrowing, than we can easily imagine, because there is nothing to be earned; and the husbandman, who has had a bad harvest, or his crop destroyed by hail, or locusts, must often borrow, not money, but bread, or else starve. In such cases, he will give in pledge, whatever the rich lender requires, however greatly it may be to his loss. Nor has he, like borrowers in our days, many articles which he can dispense with, and pledge; such as superfluous apparel, numerous shirts, and changes of linen, household furniture, and various little luxuries, that are become fashionable among our poorest people; but he must instantly surrender things of indispensable use and comfort, such as the clothes necessary to keep him warm, his implements of husbandry, his cattle, and (who could suppose it?) his very children. Here the avaricious lender on pledge cannot but be most heartily detested, and incur the universal execration of the people. And hence, in the book of Job, which gives us some views of Arabian manners, such as they were a little before the departure of the Israelites from Egypt, when the picture of a villain is drawn, the author does not forget, as one trait of his character, to represent him as a *lender upon pledge.* Thus in chap. xxii. 6, xxiv. 7. *He extorts pledges without having lent,* (an act of extreme injustice, which, however, may take place when the pledge is given, before the loan is paid down,) and *makes his debtors go naked;* probably because he has taken their most necessary clothes in pledge, and as unfeelingly as illegally detained them.—In chap. xxiv. 3. *He takes the widow's ox for a pledge;* so that she cannot plough her land, to gain the needful for clearing off the debt; and the ox, thus pledged perhaps for a trifle, if it cannot be redeemed on the day of payment, becomes the certain property of the greedy creditor. But the poor widow thus loses ten times as much as he unjustly gains, unless he yet think fit to repair the injury done to her land; for she can now no more cultivate it, and must be every day plunging deeper in debt and misery.—At ver. 9. *He takes even the infant of the needy for a pledge,* and, of course, if not duly redeemed, keeps it, for bond-service, however disproportioned to its value the loan may have been. Moses by no means attempts to abolish the practice of extrajudicial pledging, or to make such regulations, as we have in our laws, whereby the pledge, under what agreement soever given, may be sold to the highest bidder, while of the price the creditor can only receive the real amount of his debt. These are inventions to be found only in the more elaborate laws of nations further advanced in opulence and refinement; and which, in the present situation of the Israelites, would have been impracticable and unavailing. Indeed, among a people so poor, they must have proved detrimental, had it been possible to put them in practice: for no one would have been inclined to lend a trifle (and to a poor borrower even trifles are important) on pledge, under so many formalities, and when the way to arrive at payment, instead of being short and simple, was through the interference of a magistrate. In this way a needy person must always have found it difficult, if not impossible, to obtain a loan, particularly a small one: which, among a poor people, is just as great an evil, as can arise from fraudulent practices in pledging. It will not, therefore, be imputed to Moses as a fault, that his statutes contain not those legal refinements, which probably were not then invented, and which even yet may be said rather to be in record in *our* statute books, than to be in our practice. They would have been dangerous to his people, and peculiarly oppressive to the poor. He let *pledge* remain in its proper sense, *pledge;* and thus facilitated the obtaining of loans: satisfying himself with making laws against some of the chief abuses of pledging.—Michaelis.

Ver. 13. In any case thou shalt deliver him the pledge again when the sun goeth down, that he may sleep in his own raiment, and bless thee: and it shall be righteousness unto thee before the Lord thy God.

The Talmudists enumerate eighteen several garments, which belonged to the full dress of an ancient Jew. A woollen shirt was worn next the skin, although some had shirts of linen in which they slept, because these were more cleanly and wholesome. But this part of their dress is to be distinguished from the caffetan or shirt, which the bridegroom and the bride sent to each other; which they wore over their clothes at their solemn festivals; and in which they were at last buried. Next to it was the coat, which reached to their feet, and was accounted a modest and honourable article of dress. This greatly aggravated the indignity which the king of Ammon offered to the ambassadors of David, by cutting off their garments in the middle to their buttocks; he insulted them by spoiling the most esteemed part of their dress; he exposed them to shame, by uncovering their nakedness, as they seem to have worn no breeches under their upper garments. The tunic was the principal part of the Jewish dress; it was made nearly in the form of our present shirt. A round hole was cut at top, merely to permit the head to pass through. Sometimes it had long sleeves, which reached down to the wrists; at other times short sleeves, which reached to the elbow; some had very short sleeves, which reached only to the middle of the upper arm, and some had no sleeves at all. The tunic was nearly the same with the Roman stola; and was, in general, girded round the waist, or under the breast, with the zona or girdle. Descending to the ground, and floating round the feet, it was, in the days of our Lord, a distinguishing badge of the proud Pharisee: "Beware of the scribes," said he, "who love to walk in long robes," in tunics at full length, and reaching to the ground. These coats were collared at the neck, and fringed at the bottom. Over the tunic they wore a blanket, which the Arabs call a hyke, and is the very same with the plaid of the Scotch Highlanders. These hykes are of different sizes, and of different quality and fineness. They are commonly six yards long, and five or six feet broad; serving the Kabyle and Arab for a complete dress in the day; and "as they sleep in raiment," like the Israelites of old, it serves likewise for their bed and covering by night. It is a loose but troublesome garment, frequently discomposed, and falling upon the ground; so that the person who wears it, is every moment obliged to tuck it up, and fold it anew about his body. This shows the great use of a girdle whenever they are concerned in any active employment, and by consequence the force of the scripture injunction, alluding to that part of the dress, to have our loins girded, in order to set about it with any reasonable prospect of success. The method of wearing these garments, and the use they are put to at other times in serving as coverlets to their beds, should induce us to take the finer sorts of them, at least such as are worn by the ladies and persons of distinction, to be the *peplus* of primitive times. Ruth's veil, which held six measures of barley, might be of a similar fashion, and have served, upon extraordinary occasions, for the same use; as were also the clothes, or upper garments, worn by the Israelites, in which they folded up their kneading troughs, as the Arabs and others do to this day, things of similar burden and encumbrance, in their hykes. It is very probable, likewise, that the loose folding garment, the *toga* of the Romans, was of this kind; for if we may form our opinion from the drapery of their statues, this is no other than the dress of the Arabs, when they appear in their hykes.—Paxton.

CHAPTER XXV.

Ver. 4. Thou shalt not muzzle the ox when he treadeth out *the corn.*

The custom of thrashing corn by the trampling of bullocks, still prevails in the East. The floor is made in the open air, of cows' dung and clay. In its centre a post is driven into the ground, and the corn is placed in order around it; and the bullocks, being fastened to the post, begin to move in the circle, enjoying themselves, as they work, by eating the corn.—Roberts.

This statute, which has been seldom sufficiently understood, establishes, in the first place, certain rights, as belonging even to the beasts which man uses for the purpose of labour. We must not here think of our mode of thrashing, but on that used in the East, where the corn being laid on the thrashing-floor, is trodden out by oxen or asses, or by thrashing-wagons and thrashing-planks drawn over it by oxen. Here, then, Moses commands that no muzzle be put on the ox, but that he be allowed, as long as he is employed in thrashing, to eat both of the grain and straw. It appears that an ancient consuetudinary usage which Moses adopted in his written law, had established this as nothing more than equitable; for we find it still observed in places of the East, where the Mosaic law is not in force; as, for instance, according to Dr. Russel's testimony, at Aleppo, among the Arabs that dwell in that neighbourhood; and likewise, even among the inhabitants of the coast of Malabar. Russell, in his Natural History of Aleppo, says, that there beef is pretty good at all seasons, but particularly excellent in summer, because, to this day, the inhabitants sacredly adhere to the ancient custom of allowing the ox, while thrashing, to eat as much as he chooses. In the periodical accounts of the Malabar mission, we are told that they have a proverb to this effect, "What an ox thrashes, is his profit." The people of the most ancient ages, in general, gave the ox a high preference above other beasts, on account of his great and indispensable usefulness in agriculture, and conferred upon him, as man's assistant, many privileges, insomuch that mythology speaks of a time when it was unlawful to kill him. I believe, however, that the statute before us does not extend to oxen only, but includes also other beasts employed by man in thrashing; for Moses is wont to represent general principles, by particular and well-known examples. This point, however, is too inconsiderable to occupy more room in its illustration, else might I quote Isa. xxx. 24, in proof that the ass had the same right as the ox; for as to the horse, he was not then used in husbandry.

The origin of this benevolent law with regard to beasts, is seemingly deducible from certain moral feelings or sentiments prevalent among the people of the early ages. They thought it hard that a person should be employed in the collection and preparation of edible and savoury things, and have them continually before his eyes, without being once permitted to taste them; and there is in fact a degree of cruelty in placing a person in such a situation; for the sight of such dainties is tormenting, and the desire to partake of them increases with the risk of the prohibition. If any of my readers has a heart so devoid of sensibility towards the feelings of his inferiors, that he can form no idea of any thing torturous in such circumstances, let him endeavour to recollect from the heathen mythology, the representations which the Greek and Roman poets gave of the torments of hell; such as tables spread with the most costly dainties, and placed before the eyes of the damned, without their being permitted so much as to touch them; or again, the water in which thirsty Tantalus was immersed to his lips, and which fled from him whenever he bowed to taste it. Add to this, that by prohibitions of this nature, the moral character of servants and day-labourers, to the certain injury of their master's interest, seldom fails to become corrupted; for the provocation of appetite at the sight of forbidden gratification will, with the greater number, undoubtedly overpower all moral suggestions as to right and wrong. They will learn to help themselves without leave, that is, in other words, (for although not in civil, yet in moral law, it is theft,) they will learn to steal; and if the attempt is frequently repeated, the wall of partition between right and wrong, which was at first so formidable to conscience, is at length broken through: they soon learn to go greater and greater lengths, and thus in this school are bred arrant thieves. Our laws, it is true, pay no attention to such things; but still, the voice of nature, if we will but listen to it, will teach us, that in every country, servants imagine, that to steal eatables is no crime; or, as the saying is in Upper Saxony, that "what goes into the mouth, brings no sin with it." Here they are certainly quite in the wrong: and among a people that had already a taste for foreign and expensive luxuries, such a benevolent law as that now under consideration, could not be introduced, without the complete destruction of domestic economy; although indeed, after all, cooks and butlers cannot well be prohibited from tasting the dishes and the wine of which they have the charge. But without dwelling on what our modern luxury renders necessary in this matter, I only say, that to the people of the East, in those times of ancient simplicity, it appeared very cruel to debar a slave or a hireling from tasting of the food which he had under his hand. When Job wishes to describe a perfect monster of insensibility and hardheartedness, he says, "The hungry carry his sheaves; immured in workhouses they prepare his oil; they tread his wine-presses, and yet they thirst." Job xxiv. 10, 11. I seldom appeal to Jewish testimonies, or, to speak more accurately, to the Talmud and Rabbins, because they are too recent for illustration of the Mosaic statutes; but here I cannot altogether overlook the following Jewish doctrine, laid down in the *Baba Mezia*, fol. 83. "The workman may lawfully eat of what he works among; in the vintage he may eat of grapes; when gathering figs, he may partake of them; and in harvest he may eat of the ears of corn. Of gourds and dates he may eat the value of a denarius;" that is, of four groschen, or one fourth of a florin. The mention of this specific sum, which was, perhaps, rather too great an allowance, seems to have proceeded from the circumstance of the Jews reckoning a denarius the price of a day's labour, because it was introduced so lately before the destruction of Jerusalem. I quote the passage, however, not for proof, but merely as a relic of ancient manners among the Jews.

This kindness, then, the Hebrews and Arabs extended unto oxen, to which, by reason of their great utility in agriculture, they conceived that they were bound to manifest a certain degree of gratitude. And therefore when Moses, in terms of this benevolent custom ordained, that the ox was not to be muzzled while thrashing, it would seem that it was not merely his intention to provide for the welfare of that animal, but to enjoin with the greater force and effect, that a similar right should be allowed to human labourers, whether hirelings or slaves. He specified the ox, as the lowest example, and what held good in reference to him, was to be considered as so much the more obligatory in reference to man. That he wished to be understood in this way, we have the less reason to doubt, from this consideration, that in the sequel we shall meet with other statutes, in which he carries his attention to the calls of hunger so far, as to allow the eating of fruits and grapes in other people's gardens and vineyards, without restraint. It would appear, therefore, that not only servants, but also day-labourers, might eat of the fruits they gathered, and drink of the *must* which they pressed. The wages of the latter seems to have been given them over and above their meat, and, in consideration of this privilege, to have been so much the less; for with a labourer, who found his own victuals, and yet had the right of eating and drinking of whatever came under his hands, a master would have stood on a very disadvantageous footing. In fact, if they did not afford food to day-labourers, it would be impossible to understand how the value of a servant could be compared with the hire of a labourer, Deut. xv. 18, and found double; for that a master maintained his servants, is unquestionable. But if they likewise gave the labourer his victuals, the value of a servant, and the wages of a labourer, might be compared. —MICHAELIS.

Ver. 9. Then shall his brother's wife come unto him in the presence of the elders, and loose his shoe from off his foot, and spit in his face, and shall answer and say, So shall it be done unto that man that will not build up his brother's house.

The last mark of disrespect, which is by no means confined to the East, is to spit in the face of another. Chardin observes, that spitting before any one, or spitting upon the ground in speaking of any one's actions, is, through the East, an expression of extreme detestation. It is, therefore, prescribed by the law of Moses, as a mark of great disgrace to be fixed on the man who failed in his duty to the house of his brother. To such contemptuous treatment, it will be recollected, our blessed Redeemer submitted in the hall of the high-priest, for the sake of his people. The practice has descended to modern times; for in the year 1744, when a rebel prisoner was brought before Nadir Shah's general, the soldiers were ordered to spit in his face; which proves that the savage conduct of the Jews corresponded with a custom which had been long established over all the East.—PAXTON.

Ver. 13. Thou shalt not have in thy bag divers weights, a great and a small.

The prophet Micah also speaks of "the bag of deceitful weights." As in former times, so now, much of the business in the East is transacted by travelling merchants. Hence all kinds of spices, and other articles, are taken from one village to another by the Moors, who are in those regions, what the Jews are in the West. The pedler comes to your door, and vociferates the names of his wares; and, so soon as he catches your eye, begins to exhibit his very cheap, and valuable articles. Have you agreed as to the price, he then produces the BAG of "divers weights," and after fumbling some time in it, he draws forth the weight by which he has to *sell*; but, should he have to *purchase* any thing of you, he will select a *heavier* weight. The man who is not cheated by this trader, and his "bag of divers weights," must be blessed with more keenness than most of his fellows.—ROBERTS.

CHAPTER XXVII.

Ver. 2. And it shall be, on the day when you shall pass over Jordan unto the land which the LORD thy God giveth thee, that thou shalt set thee up great stones, and plaster them with plaster: 3. And thou shalt write upon them all the words of this law, when thou art passed over, that thou mayest go in unto the land which the LORD thy God giveth thee, a land that floweth with milk and honey; as the LORD God of thy fathers hath promised thee.

The book of the law, in order to render it the more sacred, was deposited beside the ark of the covenant, Deut. xxxi. 26; and we find the same procedure likewise observed afterward with regard to other laws, such as that which was made on the first establishment of regal authority, or, in other words, the compact between the king and the estates, 1 Sam. x. 26; but I cannot precisely determine whether *that* was kept in the holy of holies beside the ark, or only in the holy place. The guardians of the law, to whom was intrusted the duty of making faithful transcripts of it, were the priests, Deut. xxvii. 19. But Moses did not account even this precaution sufficient for the due preservation of his law in its original purity; for he commanded that it should besides be engraven on stones, and these stones kept on a mountain near Sichem, in order that a genuine exemplar of it might be transmitted even to the latest generations, Deut. xxvii. 1—8. In his ordinance for this purpose, there are one or two particulars that require illustration. He commanded that the stones should be coated with lime; but this command would have been quite absurd had his meaning only been, that the laws should be cut through this coating; for after this unnecessary trouble, they could by no means have been thus perpetuated with such certainty, nor have nearly so long resisted the effects of wind and weather, as if at once engraven in the stones themselves. Kennicott, in his *Second Dissertation on the printed Hebrew Text*, p. 77, supposes that they might have been cut out in black marble, with the letters raised, and the hollow intervals between the black letters filled up with a body of white lime, to render them more distinct and conspicuous. But even this would not have been a good plan for eternizing them: because lime cannot long withstand the weather, and whenever it began to fall off in any particular place, the raised characters would, by a variety of accidents, to which writing deeply engraved is not liable, soon be injured, and become illegible. No one that wishes to write any thing in stone, that shall descend to the most remote periods of time, will ever think of giving a preference to characters thus in relief. And besides, Moses, if this was his meaning, has expressed himself very indistinctly; for he says not a word of the colour of the stone, on which, however, the whole idea turns. I rather suppose, therefore, that Moses acted in this matter with the same view to future ages, as is related of Sostratus, the architect of the Pharos, who, while he cut the name of the then king of Egypt in the outer coat of lime, took care to engrave his own name secretly in the stone below, in order that it might come to light in after times, when the plaster with the king's name should have fallen off. In like manner, Moses, in my opinion, commanded that his laws should be cut in the stones themselves, and these coated with a thick crust of lime, that the engraving might continue for many ages secure from all the injuries of the weather and atmosphere, and then, when by the decay of its covering it should, after hundreds or thousands of years, first come to light, serve to show to the latest posterity whether they had suffered any change. And was not the idea of thus preserving an inscription, not merely for hundreds, but for thousands of years, a conception exceedingly sublime? It is by no means impossible that these stones, if again discovered, might be found still to contain the whole engraving perfectly legible. Let us only figure to ourselves what must have happened to them amid the successive devastations of the country in which they were erected. The lime would gradually become irregularly covered with moss and earth; and now, perhaps, the stones, by the soil increasing around and over them, many resemble a little mount; and were they accidentally disclosed to our view, and the lime cleared away, all that was inscribed on them 3500 years ago would at once become visible. Probably, however, this discovery, highly desirable though it would be both to literature and religion, being in the present state of things, and particularly of the Mosaic law, now so long abrogated, not indispensably necessary, it is reserved for some future age of the world. What Moses commanded, merely out of legislative prudence, and for the sake of his laws, *as* laws, God, who sent him, may have destined to answer likewise another purpose; and may choose to bring these stones to light at a time when the laws of Moses are no longer of any authority in any community whatever. Thus much is certain, that nowhere in the Bible, is any mention made of the discovery of these stones, nor indeed any further notice taken of them, than in Josh. viii. 30—35, where their erection is described; so that we may hope they will yet be one day discovered. Moses' whole procedure in this matter, is precisely in the style of ancient nations, who generally took the precaution, now rendered unnecessary by the invention of printing, to engrave their laws in stones; only that he studied, by a new contrivance, to give to his stony archives a higher degree of durability than was ever thought of by any other legislator. What was to be inscribed on the stones, whether the whole Pentateuch, or only the book of Deuteronomy, or but the blessings and curses pronounced in Deut. chap. xxvii, or merely the ten commandments alone, has been the subject of a controversy, for particulars concerning which, I again refer the reader to Kennicott's Second Dissertation. In my judgment, the expression, *all the words of this law*, implies, at least, that all the *statutory* part of the Mosaic books was to be engraved on the stones, which is far from being impossible, if we make but a distinction between the stones and the altar, which must, no doubt, have been too small for that purpose. It is well known that in very ancient times, nations were wont to engrave their laws in stones; and the Egyptians had recourse to stone pillars (στηλαις) for perpetuating their discoveries in science, and the history of their country. All these circumstances considered, together with this above all, that the Israelites had just come out of Egypt, where writing in stone was employed for so many *further* purposes, (although, indeed, hieroglyphic characters were used which Moses prohibited, because, when not understood, they might give a handle to idolatry,) I do not see why the phrase, *all the words of this law*, should not be left in its full force, nor what should oblige us to limit it, with Dr. Kennicott, merely to the decalogue.—MICHAELIS.

Ver. 15. Cursed *be* the man that maketh *any* graven or molten image, an abomination unto the LORD, the work of the hands of the craftsman, and putteth *it* in a secret *place*. And all the people shall answer and say, Amen.

The images of the Hindoos are generally made of copper or stone, but some are of silver or gold. It is not easy to find out the difference betwixt the *graven* and *molten* image, except the first mean that which has been produced by the chisel from stone, and the second that which has been cast in a mould by the action of fire. These images, however, have all of them to be graven, or filed, before they are consecrated.—ROBERTS.

Ver. 17. Cursed *be* he that removeth his neighbour's land-mark: and all the people shall say, Amen.

Fields in the East have not fences or hedges, as in England, but a ridge, a stone, or a post; and, consequently, it is not very difficult to encroach on the property of another Should a man not be very careful, his neighbour will take away a *little* every year, and keep pushing his ridge into the other's ground. Disputes of the most serious nature often occur on this account, and call for the greatest diligence and activity of the authorities. An injured man repeats to his aggressor the proverb, "The serpent shall bite him who steps over the ridge," *i. e.* he who goes beyond the landmark.—Roberts.

CHAPTER XXVIII.

Ver. 5. Blessed *shall be* thy basket and thy store.

Heb. "*dough or kneading-trough.*" Eastern farmers have large baskets made of Palmirah leaves, or other materials, for the purpose of keeping their grain: they will contain from one hundred to one hundred and fifty parrahs. These baskets, then, were to be blessed; they were not to be injured by animals, nor robbed by man. But corn is also kept in a store which is made of sticks and clay, in a circular form. This little building is always elevated, to keep the grain from the damp, and is situated near to the house. When beggars have been relieved, they often say, "Ah! may the place where you make ready your food ever be blessed." "May the rice-pot ever prosper." Thus, that which corresponds with the "kneading-trough" of the Hebrews, has also its benediction.—Roberts.

Hasselquist informs us, that baskets made of the leaves of the palm-tree are used by the people of the East on journeys, and in their houses. Harmer conjectures that such baskets are referred to in these words, and that the store signifies their leathern bags, in both which they used to carry things in travelling.—Burder.

Ver. 13. And the Lord shall make thee the head, and not the tail; and thou shalt be above only, and thou shalt not be beneath; if that thou hearken unto the commandments of the Lord thy God, which I command thee this day, to observe and to do *them.*

The prophet Isaiah, chap. ix. 14, says, "The Lord will cut off from Israel head and tail:" meaning, no doubt, those who were *high*, and those who were *low*. It is amusing to hear men of rank in the East speak of their dependants as *tails*. Has a servant not obeyed his master, the former asks, "Who are you? are you the head or tail?" Should a person begin to partake of food before those of high caste, it is asked, "What! is the tail to begin to wag before the head?" A husband, when angry with his wife, inquires, "What are you? are you the head or the tail?" —Roberts.

Ver. 24. The Lord shall make the rain of thy land powder and dust: from heaven shall it come down upon thee, until thou be destroyed.

It may be of use to inquire a little into the nature and properties of such a kind of rain; in which the following extracts may assist us. "Sometimes there [in India] the wind blows very high in those hot and dry seasons—raising up into the air a very great height, thick clouds of dust and sand. . . .These dry showers most grievously annoy all those among whom they fall; enough to smite them all with a present blindness; filling their eyes, ears, nostrils; and their mouths are not free, if they be not also well guarded: searching every place, as well within, as without, our tents or houses; so that, there is not a little keyhole of any trunk, or cabinet, if it be not covered, but receives some of that dust into it; the dust forced to find a lodging anywhere, everywhere, being so driven and forced as it is by the extreme violence of the wind." (Sir T. Roe's Embassy.) To the same purpose speaks Herbert. "And now the danger is past, let me tell you, most part of the last night we crossed over an inhospitable sandy desert, where here and there we beheld the ground covered with a loose and flying sand, which by the fury of the winter weather is accumulated into such heaps, as upon any great wind the track is lost; and passengers (too oft) overwhelmed and stifled; yea, camels, horses, mules, and other beasts, though strong, swift, and steady in their going, are not able to shift for themselves, but perish without recovery: those rolling sands, when agitated, by the winds, move and remove more like sea than land, and render the way very dreadful to passengers. Indeed in this place I thought that curse fulfilled, (Deut. xxviii. 24,) where the Lord, by Moses, threatens instead of rain to give showers of dust." These instances are in Persia: but such storms might be known to the Israelites; as, no doubt, they occur, also, on the sandy deserts of Arabia, east of Judea: and to this agrees Tournefort, who mentions the same thing—"At Ghetsci there arose a tempest of sand: *in the same manner as it happens sometimes in Arabia, and in* Egypt, especially in the spring. It was raised by a very hot south wind, which drove so much sand, that one of the gates of the Caravansary was half stopped up with it; and the way could not be found, being covered over, above a foot deep, the sand lying on all hands. This sand was extremely fine, and salt; and was very troublesome to our eyes, even in the Caravansary, where all our baggage was covered over with it. The storm lasted from noon to sunset; and it was so very hot the night following, without any wind, that one could hardly fetch breath, which in my opinion was partly occasioned by the reflection of the hot sand. Next day I felt a great pain in one eye, which made it smart, as if salt had been melted into it," &c. This may give us a lively idea of the penetrating powers of the dust of the land of Egypt; which (Exod. viii. 16) was converted into lice:—also, chap. ix. 8, of the effect of the ashes of the furnace, which Moses took, and sprinkled "up towards heaven, and it became a bile, breaking forth in blains upon man and beast."—Taylor in Calmet.

Ver. 27. The Lord will smite thee with the botch of Egypt, and with the emerods, and with the scab, and with the itch, whereof thou canst not be healed.

This is a complaint which is far more common, and more formidable in the East, than in England. Those who live on bad food, or reside in the vicinity of a swamp, are the most subject to it. See the poor object with a small piece of cloth round his loins, a staff in his hand, his body "from the sole of his foot unto his crown" literally covered with sores, an imploring piteous look, a weak tremulous voice, and bowing to the earth to excite your charity. —Roberts.

Ver. 39. Thou shalt plant vineyards, and dress *them*, but shalt neither drink *of* the wine, nor gather *the grapes;* for the worms shall eat them.

This threatening has often been fulfilled to the great disappointment and injury of the inhabitants of those countries where wine is produced or consumed. An insect, called the vine weevil, which is a small beautiful beetle, is extremely hurtful to the vines. The caterpillar, which mines or cuts the leaves of the vine, has no feet; and yet, by a singular expedient, can make a progressive motion in all positions, and even over the smoothest and most polished bodies. It advances its body out of its oval pod, (constructed of the two outer skins of a vine leaf,) forms a kind of hillock of silk, and, by means of a thread which attaches it to it, draws its pod or case to the hillock. It continually repeats the same operation, and in this (laborious) manner advances progressively. The traces of its progress are marked by hillocks of silk at the distance of half a line from each other. Its food is the parenchyma or pith of the vine leaf, between the two epidermes, of which it eats out its oval habitation or pod. When it is taken out of its habitation, it never attempts to make a new one: it writhes about very much, but can make no progressive motion; and after having overspread the place in which it is with threads of silk, in an irregular manner, it dies at the end of twenty-four hours.—Burder.

CHAPTER XXIX.

Ver. 23. *And that* the whole land thereof *is* brimstone, and salt, *and* burning.

When a place is noted for being unhealthy, or the land very unfruitful, it is called a *kenthaga poomy*, a place or country of brimstone. Tricomalee, and some other places, have gained this appellation on account of the heat and sterility of the soils.—ROBERTS.

The effect of salt, where it abounds, on vegetation, is described by burning. Thus Volney, speaking of the borders of the Asphaltic Lake, or Dead Sea, says, "the true cause of the absence of vegetables and animals, is the acrid saltness of its waters, which is infinitely greater than that of the sea. The land surrounding the lake being equally impregnated with that saltness, refuses to produce plants; the air itself, which is by evaporation loaded with it, and which moreover receives vapours of sulphur and bitumen, cannot suit vegetation; whence the dead appearance which reigns around the lake." Hence the ancient custom of sowing an enemy's city, when taken, with salt, in token of perpetual desolation. Judges ix. 45. And thus in aftertimes, the city of Milan was burnt, razed, sown with salt, and ploughed, by the exasperated emperor Frederick Barbarossa.—BURDER.

CHAPTER XXX.

Ver. 14. But the word *is* very nigh unto thee, in thy mouth, and in thy heart, that thou mayest do it.

Does a person pretend that he cannot understand another, that he must make additional inquiries, it will be said, "Do you not understand? In thy mouth are the words." Should a child at school be troublesome to the master, he will peevishly exclaim, In thy mouth are the words; meaning the inquiry was unnecessary, that the subject was well understood.—ROBERTS.

Ver. 19. I call heaven and earth to record this day against you, *that* I have set before you life and death, blessing and cursing: therefore choose life, that both thou and thy seed may live.

In solemn oaths, people point to the clouds, to the earth, to the grass, to the herbs, to the trees, as witnesses to the truth of what they have said. "O ye clouds above! have I not said the truth? Ah! well do you know it: speak to this, unbeliever." "Ah! these trees can bear testimony to my veracity." When mariners are at sea, they appeal to it, or to Varuna the god. In storms, they say to the water, "O mother! be calm."—ROBERTS.

CHAPTER XXXII.

Ver. 2. My doctrine shall drop as the rain, my speech shall distil as the dew; as the small rain upon the tender herb, and as the showers upon the grass.

Oriental writers often speak of beautiful language as dropping upon the hearers. The Hebrew has for "prophesy," in Micah ii. 6, "*drop.*" The same word is used for drops of rain, for tears, or for the dew dropping from flowers. When a man has received consolation from another, he says, "His words were like rain upon the scorched corn." Of a beautiful speaker, and an appropriate subject, "Ah! his speech is like the honey rain, upon the *pandal* bower of sugar."—ROBERTS.

Ver. 5. Their spot *is* not the *spot* of his children.

There may be here an allusion to the marks which the worshippers of particular idols had on different parts of their bodies, particularly on their foreheads. The different sects of idolaters in the East are distinguished by their sectarian marks, the stigma of their respective idols. These sectarian marks, particularly on the forehead, amount to nearly one hundred among the Hindoos, and especially among the two sects, the worshippers of Siva and the worshippers of Vishnoo. In many cases these marks are renewed daily; for they account it irreligious to perform any sacred rite to their god without his mark on the forehead. The marks are generally horizontal and perpendicular lines, crescents, circles, leaves, eyes, &c. in red, black, white, and yellow. It is pleasing to see the Hindoos every morning perform their ablutions in the sacred lakes, and offer an innocent sacrifice under the solemn grove. After having gone through their religious ceremonies, they are *sealed* by the officiating Bramin with the mark either of Vishnoo or Siva, the followers of whom respectively form the two great sects among the Hindoos. The mark is impressed on the forehead with a composition of sandal-wood dust and oil, or the ashes of cow-dung and turmeric: this is a holy ceremony, which has been adopted in all ages by the eastern nations, however differing in religious profession.—FORBES.

Ver. 10. He found him in a desert land, and in the waste howling wilderness; he led him about, he instructed him, he kept him as the apple of his eye.

Where the wild beasts are, is called the place of howling. Thus relations, when their friends are on a journey, say, "Ah! they are now in the place of howling." "My friend, go not through the howling desert." Precious things are spoken of as being the apple of the eye. Affectionate husbands say to their wives, "*En kan mulli,*" *i. e.* "apple of my eye." Of a beloved child, in relation to his parents, it is said, "He is the apple of their eye."—ROBERTS.

Ver. 11. As an eagle stirreth up her nest, fluttereth over her young, spreadeth abroad her wings, taketh them, beareth them on her wings.

It is pretended by some writers, that when the eaglets are somewhat grown, the mother kills the weakest or the most voracious of them; but were the fact admitted, it is no satisfactory proof that she is without natural affection. It is well known that several animals of the mildest dispositions forsake their young, when they find it impossible to provide for their subsistence. The parent eagles, says Buffon, not having sufficient for themselves, seek to reduce their family; and as soon as the young ones are strong enough to fly and provide for themselves, they chase them from the nest, and never permit them to return. The account of this celebrated naturalist so far agrees with the statement of the sacred writer; according to whom, the eagle stirreth up her nest, that is, rouses her young from their sloth and inactivity, and provokes them to try their wings by fluttering about her nest. When she sees them indifferent to her admonitions, or afraid to follow her example, "she spreadeth abroad her wings; taketh them, and beareth them upon her wings." The remarkable circumstance of bearing them upon her wings, is alluded to in another part of scripture: "Ye have seen," said Jehovah to Israel, "what I did unto Egypt, and how I bare you on eagles' wings, and brought you unto myself." Many passages in the writings of ancient authors countenance the idea, that the eagle actually takes up her timid young ones, and bears them on her wings till they venture to fly. Ælian says, that when Tilgamus, a Babylonian boy, fell from the top of a tower, before he reached the ground, an eagle received and bore him up on her back. A similar story is recorded in the writings of Pausanias, who tells us, that an eagle flew under Aristimenes, who was cast by the Lacedemonians from the top of a tower, and carried him on her wings till he reached the ground in safety. These stories, although the mere creatures of imagination, show that the idea of the eagle bearing a considerable weight on her wings, was familiar to the ancients. It is not to be supposed, that she wafts her unfledged young through the void of heaven, or to distant places; the meaning probably is, that she aids with her wings their feeble and imperfect attempts to fly, till, imboldened by her example, and their own success, they fearlessly commit themselves to the air. So did Jehovah for his chosen people: when they were slumbering in Goshen, or groaning in despair of recovering their freedom, he sent his servant Moses to rouse them from their inglorious sloth, to assert their liberty, and to break their chains upon the heads of their oppressors. He carried them out of Egypt, and led them through the wilderness into their promised inheritance. He taught them to know their strength: he instructed them in the art of war; he led them to battle, and by his almighty arm routed their enemies.—PAXTON.

Ver. 13. He made him ride on the high places of the earth, that he might eat the increase of the fields; and he made him to suck honey out of the rock, and oil out of the flinty rock.

This must mean the procuring of it from the olive-trees growing there. Maundrell, speaking of the ancient fertility and cultivation of Judea, says, "the most rocky parts of all, which could not well be adjusted for the production of corn, might yet serve for the plantation of vines and olive-trees, which delight to extract, the one its fatness, the other its sprightly juice, chiefly out of such dry and flinty places."—BURDER.

In Africa the bees deposite their honey on the trunks of trees and on rocks. Trees in some countries being scarce, the honey in most parts is found upon the front of rocks or cliffs, plastered on the outside, having a covering of wax to protect it from intruders. This outside coating, after a short exposure to the weather, assumes nearly the same colour as the rock, which, at a little distance, cannot easily be distinguished from the rock, so that a person making an incision with a knife, and putting his mouth to it to suck it, were a person a little way off to notice some of the honey dropping from his chin, would believe that he saw a man sucking honey from a rock; so that the scripture method of expressing it is very beautiful.—AFRICAN LIGHT.

Ver. 15. But Jeshurun waxed fat, and kicked: thou art waxen fat, thou art grown thick, thou art covered *with fatness;* then he forsook God *which* made him, and lightly esteemed the Rock of his salvation.

This does not appear to mean that Jeshurun had become fat in person, but fat or proud in spirit. Thus, of people who have risen from obscurity, and who conduct themselves proudly, it is said, "They have become *fat.*" To hear, "how fat that man is now," might lead a stranger to suppose it was meant so literally; whereas the individual alluded to may be as meagre as one of Pharaoh's lean cattle.—ROBERTS.

Ver. 25. Thy shoes *shall be* iron and brass.

The Hebrew word here translated *shoes,* signifies *bolts.* The proper translation of this word is, *thy bolts shall be iron and brass:* that is, thy cities must be strong and secure against your enemies. To understand the force of these words, we must know that in the East, and even in modern times, the locks and bolts of houses, and even of city gates, were of wood. "Their doors and houses," says Rauwolff, "are mostly closed with wooden bolts, which are hollow within; to open which they have wooden keys, which are a span long, and a thumb thick, and have on one side, 5, 6, 7, 8, 9, &c. short nails or strong wires, so placed as to catch in others that fit into them, and thus move the bolt backward and forward." Thevenot observes, "all their locks and keys are made of wood; they have none of iron, not even those of the city gates, which are, therefore, also opened without keys." He describes the keys like Rauwolff, and adds, that the door may be opened without the key, by smearing the finger with clay.—ROSENMULLER.

CHAPTER XXXIII.

Ver. 22. And of Dan he said, Dan *is* a lion's whelp; he shall leap from Bashan.

Although the lion fearlessly meets his antagonist in the open field, in this respect differing from leopards and some other beasts of prey, that never openly attack the fated victim, yet this bold and noble animal often descends to stratagem and ambuscade: "He couches in his den, and abides in the covert to lie in wait." He watches the approach of his victim with cautious attention, carefully avoiding the least noise, lest he should give warning of his presence and designs. Such has the glowing pencil of David painted the insidious conduct of the murderer: "He lieth in wait secretly as a lion in his den; he lieth in wait to catch the poor—he croucheth and humbleth himself, that the poor may fall by his strong ones." "Like as a lion that is greedy of his prey, and as it were a young lion lurking in secret places." From his lurking-place, he commonly leaps upon the victim at one spring. So, in the farewell prediction of Moses, it is foretold, "Dan is a lion's whelp, he shall leap from Bashan." This fact is attested by all the ancient historians: Aristotle asserts, that when the lion judges himself within reach, he throws himself upon his prey; Pliny says, he leaps with a bound; and Solinus, when he is in full pursuit, he springs forward upon the game. When he leaps on his prey, says Buffon, he makes a spring of twelve or fifteen feet. In the same manner acted Dan; proceeding, as it were, by a single bound, from the one extremity of Canaan to the other, he invaded the city of Laish, which, after its reduction, he called by his own name.—PAXTON.

Ver. 24. And of Asher he said, *Let* Asher *be* blessed with children; let him be acceptable to his brethren, and let him dip his foot in oil.

The juice of the grape, it is well known, is expressed in the East by treading, an operation which Dr. Chandler had an opportunity of seeing near Smyrna. Black grapes were spread on the ground in beds, and exposed to the sun to dry for raisins; while in another part, the juice was expressed for wine, a man with feet and legs bare, treading the fruit in a kind of cistern, with a hole or vent near the bottom, and a vessel beneath it to receive the liquor. When a few clusters of grapes are to be squeezed, it may be done commodiously enough by the hand; in this way, Pharaoh's butler supposed he took the grapes and pressed them into his master's cup. This, it is true, was only a visionary scene, but we must suppose it was agreeable to the custom of the country. But when a large quantity of juice was required, the grapes were subjected in the wine-press to the feet of a treader. Oil of olives was expressed in the same way, before the invention of mills. The existence of this practice in Palestine, is ascertained by that threatening in the prophecies of Micah: "Thou shalt sow, but thou shalt not reap; thou shalt tread the olives, but shalt not anoint thee with oil; and sweet wine, but shalt not drink wine." But unequivocal traces of it may be discovered in ages long anterior to the days of that prophet; for in the blessing of Asher, we find Moses praying: "Let Asher dip his foot in oil." Whether any preparation was used in those ancient times to facilitate the expression of the juice, we are not informed; but it is certain that mills are now used for pressing and grinding the olives which grow in the neighbourhood of Athens, and probably in other eastern countries. These mills are in the town, and not in the spot where the olives grow; and seem to be used in consequence of its being found, that the mere weight of the human body is insufficient for the purpose of effectually extracting the oil.—PAXTON.

CHAPTER XXXIV.

Ver. 1. And Moses went up from the plains of Moab unto the mountain of Nebo, to the top of Pisgah, that *is* over against Jericho: and the LORD showed him all the land of Gilead, unto Dan.

Mr. Buckingham, travelling through the mountains of Gilead, says, "We were now in a land of extraordinary richness, abounding with the most beautiful prospects, clothed with thick forests, varied with verdant slopes, and possessing extensive plains of a fine red soil, now covered with thistles as the best proof of its fertility, and yielding in nothing to the celebrated plains of Zabulon and Esdraelon, in Galilee and Samaria. We continued our way to the northeast, through a country, the beauty of which so surprised us, that we often asked each other, what were our sensations; as if to ascertain the reality of what we saw, and persuade each other, by mutual confession of our delight, that the picture before us was not an optical illusion. The landscape alone, which varied at every turn, and gave us new beauties from very different points of view, was, of itself, worth all the pains of an excursion to the eastward of Jordan to obtain a sight of; and the park-like scenes, that sometimes softened the romantic wildness of the general character as a whole, reminded us of similar spots in less neglected lands."

JOSHUA.

CHAPTER I.

Ver. 1. Now, after the death of Moses, the servant of the Lord, it came to pass, that the Lord spake unto Joshua the son of Nun, Moses' minister, saying, 2. Moses my servant is dead; now therefore arise, go over this Jordan, thou, and all this people, unto the land which I do give to them, *even* to the children of Israel.

The conquest of Canaan, by the Israelites, having so often been the subject of cavil among the enemies of revelation, and being adverted to in terms of approbation above, may properly be considered in this place. Their conduct in this affair is satisfactorily vindicated by Mr. Townsend, in his "Old Testament historically and chronologically arranged," from which we transcribe the following passages:—God, the great governor, who possesses all power over his creatures, and may justly punish those who violate his laws, in that manner which to his wisdom may seem most impressive and useful, commanded the Israelites to exterminate the Canaanites, as the just retribution for their crimes and idolatries. God might have destroyed them by famine, by earthquake, by pestilence: He might have drowned by a local deluge, or consumed them by fire from heaven; instead of these, he commissioned the people of Israel to root them out by the sword. In so doing, the Almighty not only demonstrated to the whole world his hatred of the corruptions and pollutions of superstition, but he more particularly enforced on the Israelites the purity of his law, the certainty of their own punishment if they apostatized, and the freedom from temporal evil which they should consequently enjoy if they persevered in their allegiance to him, their sovereign. Lest this invasion of Canaan by the Israelites, however, should be drawn into precedent by other nations, for ambition or religious persecution; they were assured by continued and powerful miracles, that their cause was just, that they should be successful, and that they were not subject at that period to the common laws of nations. The people of Israel was the sword of God, the great magistrate of earth, and they were no more to be condemned in thus acting in conformity to the commands of God, than the executioner can be who fulfils the last sentence of the law. Before, then, other nations invade the territory of their neighbours on the same supposed authority as the Israelites, the same commission from heaven must be given; and that commission must be authenticated by miracles equally evident, perpetual, and wonderful. Many, however, have not been satisfied with this argument; and would discard the doctrine of the peculiar providence, which regulated by a visible theocracy the conduct of the chosen people: they would defend the invasion of Palestine on other grounds. They would judge of the transactions of that period, (regardless of the peculiar circumstances under which they took place,) by modern ideas, and the present law of nations. Some suppose that the conduct of the Israelites was solely defensible, on the supposition that there had been a partition of the whole earth by the sons of Noah; and that Canaan had been allotted to Shem: the sons of Shem, therefore, were justified in claiming their ancient inheritance from the Canaanites, who were descended from Ham. Others have asserted that the Canaanites commenced the war by attacking the Israelites; an assertion that cannot be defended from the history. While others have affirmed, without any well-grounded arguments, that the Israelites, as a wandering people, having no certain home, were justified in forcibly invading, and taking possession of an adjoining territory. But Michaelis is of opinion that the right of the Israelites originated in their being actually the proprietors of Canaan, of which they had been unjustly dispossessed by the intruding and hostile Canaanites.

The laws of nations are always the same. If any nation, or tribe, or part of a tribe, take possession of an unknown, undiscovered, unoccupied, or uninhabited country, the right of property vests in them; they are its proprietors and owners. After the deluge, the world might be said to be in this state; and Michaelis has endeavoured to prove, that the ancestors of Abraham were the original occupiers of the pasture land of Canaan. Canaan, therefore, by the law of nations, as well as by the promises of God, was the lot of Abraham's inheritance, and the rightful land of his descendants. The Canaanite and the Perizzite had only just established themselves in Canaan when Abraham removed from Haran to that country; and were so weak and few in number, that they never interfered with the right of sovereignty assumed and exerted by Abraham. The Canaanites were merchants and adventurers who had been originally settled near the borders of the Indian Ocean; and who, having been dispossessed by the Cuthic Sidonians, had migrated westward, to form establishments on the seacoasts of Palestine, and carry on commerce with the herdsmen who traversed it. They were for some time contented with their factories on the seacoasts, but they gradually obtained possession of the inland country. The Perizzites, too, were a warlike tribe, who now first made their appearance in Canaan; they had originally inhabited the northeast of Babylonia. Whether they had been dispossessed of their settlements; whether they were seeking new establishments; or for whatever purpose they were now in Palestine, they gave no interruption to the progress of Abraham, although Abraham entered upon the Holy Land and continued his journeyings with a large retinue, and as a powerful prince. He took possession of Canaan as the territory of his ancestors; not indeed as a fixed habitation, but as a pasture land adapted to his numerous flocks and herds. He traversed the whole country as a proprietor, without a competitor. He had the power of arming three hundred and eighteen of his own servants, born in his own house; and it is most probable that he had others who are not enumerated. He declared war as an independent prince of this country against five neighbouring princes; and formed an alliance with Abimelech, as an equal and as a sovereign. It is true, he purchased land of the Canaanitish family of Heth, but this was because the Hittites had gradually made a more fixed settlement in that part of the country; their intrusion had not been at first prevented by the ancestors of Abraham; and by this sufferance they made that district their peculiar property. As Abraham thus traversed and possessed Canaan, with undisputed authority, so too did Isaac and Jacob in like manner. No one opposed their right. They exercised, as Abraham had done before them, sovereign power; they never resigned that power; nor gave up to others the property of that land, which now, by long prescription, as well as by the promise of God, had become entirely their own.

The ancestors, then, of the Israelites, Michaelis argues, were either the sole sovereigns, or the most powerful of those princes who possessed, in early ages, the Holy Land. By the famine which occurred in the days of Joseph, they were compelled to leave their own country, and take refuge in Egypt: yet they never lost sight of the sepulchre of their fathers. And though we do not read that acts of ownership were continued to maintain and perpetuate their right, we can have but little doubt, that something of the kind took place, for Jacob was taken from Egypt to be buried there; Joseph assured them that they should return; and the Egyptians, their oppressors, a kindred branch of the powerful tribes which had by this time entirely taken possession of Palestine, kept them in bondage, and refused to let them go, lest they should claim the inheritance of their fathers. If this claim of the Israelites can be proved to be well founded, they would have been entitled, by the law of nations, forcibly to take possession of the Holy Land; and it will be interesting to observe how the merciful providence of God afforded them the opportunity of successfully regaining their lawful inheritance, and at the same time accomplishing his own divine purposes, to the fulfilment of his prophecies, and to the happiness and security of his church. The Israelites may be considered as the servants and ministers of God, punishing the idolatry of the Canaanites, and instituting in its place, in the midst of an apostate world, the religion of the one true God. In every victory they obtained, they must have admired the faithfulness of that promise which had foretold their entire possession of this land; and they must have been persuaded, that if they served other gods, they would bring down upon themselves the punishments predicted by Moses.—Vide Michaelis, Comment. &c. vol. i. book ii. ch. iii. p. 155, &c.; Horæ Mosaicæ, vol. i. p. 458; Faber's Origin of Pag. Idol. vol. iii. p. 561, &c.—Townsend's Old Testament, vol. i. pp. 444—446.—Critica Biblica.

CHAPTER II.

Ver. 1. And Joshua the son of Nun sent out of Shittim two men to spy secretly, saying, Go view the land, even Jericho. And they went, and came into a harlot's house, named Rahab, and lodged there.

Most of the eastern cities contain one caravansary at least, for the reception of strangers; smaller places, called choultries, are erected by charitable persons, or munificent princes, in forests, plains, and deserts, for the accommodation of travellers. Near them is generally a well, and a cistern for the cattle: a bramin or faquir often resides there to furnish the pilgrim with food, and the few necessaries he may stand in need of. When benighted in a dreary solitude, travellers in India were thus certain, within a moderate distance, to find one of these buildings appropriated for their accommodation, and were often supplied with the necessaries of life gratis. (Forbes.) Dr. Franklin says, that among the Indians of North America, there is in every village a vacant dwelling, called the stranger's house. Hither the traveller is led by two old men, who procure him victuals, and skins to repose on, exacting nothing for the entertainment. Among the ancients, women generally kept houses of entertainment. "Among the Egyptians, the women carry on all commercial concerns, and keep taverns, while the men continue at home and weave." Herodotus asserts, that "the men were the slaves of the women in Egypt, and that it is stipulated in the marriage contract, that the woman shall be the ruler of her husband, and that he shall obey her in all things."—Burder.

CHAPTER III.

Ver. 15. And as they that bare the ark were come unto Jordan, and the feet of the priests that bare the ark were dipped in the brim of the water, (for Jordan overfloweth all his banks all the time of harvest.)

The largest and most celebrated stream in Palestine, is the Jordan. It is much larger, according to Dr. Shaw, than all the brooks and streams of the Holy Land united together; and, excepting the Nile, is by far the most considerable river, either of the coast of Syria or of Barbary. He computed it to be about thirty yards broad, and found it nine feet deep at the brink. This river, which divides the country into two unequal parts, has been commonly said to issue from two fountains, or to be formed by the junction of two rivulets, the Jor and the Dan; but the assertion seems to be totally destitute of any solid foundation. The Jewish historian, Josephus, on the contrary, places its source at Phiala, a fountain which rises about fifteen miles from Cesarea Philippi, a little on the right hand, and not much out of the way to Trachonitis. It is called Phiala, or the Vial, from its round figure; its water is always of the same depth, the basin being brimful, without either shrinking or overflowing. From Phiala to Panion, which was long considered as the real source of Jordan, the river flows under ground. The secret of its subterraneous course was first discovered by Philip, the tetrarch of Trachonitis, who cast straws into the fountain of Phiala, which came out again at Panion. Leaving the cave of Panion, it crosses the bogs and fens of the lake Semichonitis; and after a course of fifteen miles, passes under the city of Julias, the ancient Bethsaida; then expands into a beautiful sheet of water, named the lake of Gennesareth; and after flowing a long way through the desert, empties itself into the lake Asphaltites, or Dead Sea. As the cave Panion lies at the foot of mount Lebanon, in the northern extremity of Canaan, and the lake Asphaltites extends to the southern extremity, the river Jordan pursues it course through the whole extent of the country from north to south. It is evident also, from the history of Josephus, that a wilderness or desert of considerable extent, stretched along the river Jordan in the times of the New Testament; which was undoubtedly the wilderness mentioned by the evangelists, where John the Baptist came preaching and baptizing. The Jordan has a considerable depth of water. Chateaubriand makes it six or seven feet deep close at the shore, and about fifty paces in breadth a considerable distance from its entrance into the Dead Sea. According to the computation of Volney, it is hardly sixty paces wide at the mouth; but the author of Letters from Palestine, states that the stream, when it enters the lake Asphaltites, is deep and rapid, rolling a considerable volume of waters; the width appears from two to three hundred feet, and the current is so violent, that a Greek servant belonging to the author who attempted to cross it, though strong, active, and an excellent swimmer, found the undertaking impracticable. It may be said to have two banks, of which the inner marks the ordinary height of the stream; and the outer, its ancient elevation during the rainy season, or the melting of the snows on the summits of Lebanon. In the days of Joshua, and it is probable for many ages after his time, the harvest was one of the seasons when the Jordan overflowed his banks. This fact is distinctly recorded by the sacred historian: "And as they that bare the ark were come unto Jordan, and the feet of the priests that bare the ark were dipped in the brim of the water (for Jordan overfloweth all his banks all the time of harvest.") This happens in the first month of the Jewish year, which corresponds with March. But in modern times, (whether the rapidity of the current has worn the channel deeper than formerly, or whether its waters have taken some other direction,) the river seems to have forgotten his ancient greatness. When Maundrell visited Jordan on the thirtieth of March, the proper time for these inundations, he could discern no sign or probability of such overflowing; nay, so far was it from overflowing, that it ran, says our author, at least two yards below the brink of its channel. After having descended the outer bank, he went about a furlong upon the level strand, before he came to the immediate bank of the river. This inner bank was so thickly covered with bushes and trees, among which he observed the tamarisk, the willow, and the oleander, that he could see no water till he had made his way through them. In this entangled thicket, so conveniently planted near the cooling stream, and remote from the habitations of men, several kinds of wild beasts were accustomed to repose till the swelling of the river drove them from their retreats. This circumstance gave occasion to that beautiful allusion of the prophet: "He shall come up like a lion, from the swelling of Jordan, against the habitation of the strong." The figure is highly poetical and striking. It is not easy to present a more terrible image to the mind, than a lion roused from his den by the roar of the swelling river, and chafed and irritated by its rapid and successive encroachments on his chosen haunts, till forced to quit his last retreat, he ascends to the higher grounds and the open country, and turns the fierceness of his rage against the helpless sheep-cots, or the unsuspecting villages. A destroyer equally fierce, and cruel, and irresistible, the devoted Edomites were to find in Nebuchadnezzar and his armies. The water of the river, at the time of Mr. Maundrell's visit, was very turbid, and too rapid to allow a swimmer to stem its course. Its breadth might be about twenty yards; and in depth, it far exceeded his height. The rapidity and depth of the river, which are admitted by every traveller, although the volume of water seems now to be much diminished, illustrate those parts of scripture, which mention the fords and passages of Jordan. It no longer indeed rolls down into the Salt Sea so majestic a stream as in the days of Joshua, yet its ordinary depth is still about ten or twelve feet, so that it cannot even at present be passed but at certain places. Of this well-known circumstance, the men of Gilead took advantage in the civil war, which they were compelled to wage with their brethren: "The Gileadites took the passages of Jordan before the Ephraimites: . . . then they took him, and slew him at the passages of Jordan." The people of Israel, under the command of Ehud, availed themselves of the same advantage in the war with Moab: "And they went down after him, and took the fords of Jordan towards Moab, and suffered not a man to pass over." But although the state of this river in modern times, completely justifies the incidental remarks of the sacred writers, it is evident, that Maundrell was disconcerted by the shallowness of the stream, at the time of the year when he expected to see it overflowing all its banks; and his embarrassment seems to have increased, when he contemplated the double margin within which it flowed. This difficulty, which has perhaps occurred to some others, may be explained by a remark which Dr. Pococke has made on the river Euphrates. "The bed of the Euphrates," says that writer, "was measured by some English gentlemen at Beer, and found to be six hundred and thirty yards broad; but the river only two hundred and fourteen yards over; that they thought it to be nine or ten feet deep in the middle; and were informed, that it sometimes rises twelve feet perpendicularly. He observed that it had an inner and outer bank; but says, it rarely overflows the inner bank: that when it does, they sow watermelons and other fruits of that kind, as soon as the water retires, and have a great produce." From this passage, Mr. Harmer argues; "Might not the overflowings of the Jordan be like those of the Euphrates, not annual, but much more rare?" The difficulty, therefore, will be completely removed, by supposing that it does not, like the Nile, overflow every year, as some authors by mistake had supposed, but, like the Euphrates, only in some particular years; but when it does, it is in the time of harvest. If it did not in ancient times annually overflow its banks, the majesty of God in dividing its waters, to make way for Joshua and the armies of Israel, was certainly the more striking to the Canaanites; who, when they looked upon themselves as defended in an extraordinary manner by the casual swelling of the river, its breadth and rapidity being both so extremely increased, yet, found it in these circumstances part asunder, and leave a way on dry land for the people of Jehovah.

The casual overflowing of the river, in Mr. Harmer's opinion, seems to receive some confirmation from a passage in Josephus, where that writer informs his readers, that the Jordan was sometimes swelled in the spring, so as to be impassable in places where people were wont to go over in his time; for, speaking of a transaction on the fourth of the month Dystrus, which answers to our March, or, as others reckon, to February, he gives an account of great numbers of people who perished in this river, into which they were driven by their enemies; which, by the circumstances, appears to have happened in a few days after what was done on the fourth of Dystrus. But the solution offered by this respectable author is rather strained and unsatisfactory. The inspired writer of the book of Joshua uses language on that subject, which naturally suggests the idea of periodical inundations: "Jordan overfloweth all his banks all the time of harvest." The present time certainly indicates the general habit of the subject to which it refers, and in this case, what commonly happens to the river. It may be swelled in the spring occasionally; but it is not easy to discover a reason for the general remark of the sacred writer, if the inundations in the time of harvest were not annual. The causes of these inundations, the melting of the snows on the top of Lebanon, and the former and latter rain, uniformly take place at their appointed seasons; but a steady periodical cause will certainly produce a corresponding effect. But if this reasoning be just, why did not Maundrell see the effect when he visited the river at the appointed time? This question may be answered by another, Why do the inundations even of the Nile sometimes fail? The reason is obvious; the rains in Abyssinia are not every season equally copious. In the same manner, if the snows on Lebanon, and the periodical rains, are less abundant in some seasons, it will easily account for the state of the river when it was visited by Maundrell. Admitting the fact, that the volume of water in the Jordan is diminished, and that he never overflows his banks as in ancient times, that intelligent traveller himself has sufficiently accounted for the circumstance: some of the waters may be drained off by secret channels, which is not uncommon in those parts of the world; and if the rapidity of the current be so great that he could not swim against it, the depth of the channel must be greatly increased since the days of Joshua and the Judges. To these, some other causes of considerable power may be added; the present state of Lebanon, now for a long time deprived of its immense forests of cedar, which formerly exerted a powerful attraction on the humidity of the atmosphere, and served to accumulate the snows on the Sannin, while they screened from the burning rays of the sun, the fountains and rills that fed the Jordan and his tributary streams: and the great extent to which the declivities of that noble mountain have been subjected to the arts of cultivation, by the Maronites, and other nations, who have taken refuge in its sequestered retreats from the intolerable oppression of the Turks, by which its numerous streams have been still further diminished,—must, it is imagined, produce a very sensible difference in the volume of water which that river, once so celebrated for its full and majestic tide, now pours into the Salt Sea. Still, however, taking the mean depth of the stream during the whole year at nine feet, and admitting that it runs about two miles an hour, the Jordan will daily discharge into the Dead Sea, about 6,090,000 tons of water.

But although these causes must have produced a considerable diminution in the swellings of Jordan, we have the authority of a recent traveller for asserting, that they still take place at the appointed season, and exhibit a scene of no inconsiderable grandeur. In winter, the river overflows its narrow channel, which between the two principal lakes is not more than sixty or eighty feet broad, and, swelled by the rains, forms a sheet of water sometimes a quarter of a league in breadth. The time of its overflowing is generally in March, when the snows melt on the mountain of the Shaik; at which time, more than any other, its waters are troubled and of a yellow hue, and its course impetuous. The common receptacle into which the Jordan empties his waters, is the lake Asphaltites, from whence they are continually drained off by evaporation. Some writers, unable to find a discharge for the large body of water which is continually rushing into the lake, have been inclined to suspect, it had some communication with the Mediterranean; but, besides that we know of no such gulf, it has been demonstrated by accurate calculations, that evaporation is more than sufficient to carry off the waters of the river. It is in fact very considerable, and frequently becomes sensible to the eye, by the fogs with which the lake is covered at the rising of the sun, and which are afterward dispersed by the heat.

How large the common receptacle of the Jordan was, before the destruction of Sodom, cannot now be determined with certainty; but it was much smaller than at present; the whole vale of Siddim, which, before that awful catastrophe, was crowded with cities, or covered with rich and extensive pastures, and fields of corn, being now buried in the waters of the lake. The course of the stream, which is to the southward, seems clearly to indicate, that the original basin was in the southern part of the present sea. But, although the waters of the river at first presented a much less extended surface to the action of the sun and the atmosphere, still a secret communication between the lake and the Mediterranean, is not perhaps necessary to account for their discharge. By the admission of Volney, evaporation is *more* than sufficient to carry them off at present: and if to this be added, the great quantity of water consumed in the cities, and required by the cultivator, to refresh his plantations and corn-fields, under the burning rays of an oriental sun, it is presumed, a cause equal to the effect is provided. This is not a mere conjecture, unsupported by historical facts; for only a very small portion of the Barrady, the principal river of Damascus, escapes from the gardens that environ the city, through which it is conducted in a thousand clear and winding streams, to maintain their freshness and verdure.—Paxton.

CHAPTER V.

Ver. 15. And the captain of the LORD'S host said unto Joshua, Loose thy shoe from off thy foot; for the place whereon thou standest *is* holy. And Joshua did so.

Every person that approaches the royal presence in the East, is obliged to take off his shoes, because they consider as sacred the ground on which the king sits, whom they dignify with the title of the Shadow of God. Allusive to this custom, perhaps, is the command given to Joshua: "Loose thy shoe from off thy foot; for the place whereon thou standest is holy. And Joshua did so." And so strictly was this custom observed, that the Persians look upon the omission of it as the greatest indignity that can be offered to them. The king (says Morier) is never approached by his subjects without frequent inclinations of the body: and when the person introduced to his presence has reached a certain distance, he waits until the king orders him to proceed; upon which *he leaves his shoes*, and walks forward with a respectful step to a second spot, until his majesty again directs him to advance. The custom which is here referred to, not only constantly prevailed all over the East, from the earliest ages, but continues to this day. To pull off the *sandals*, or slippers, is used as a mark of respect, on entering a mosque or temple, or the room of any person of distinction; in which case they were either laid aside, or given to a servant to bear. Ives (*Travels*, p. 75) says, that, "at the doors of an Indian pagoda, are seen as many slippers and sandals as there are hats hanging up in our churches." The same custom prevails among the Turks. Maundrell describes exactly the ceremonials of a Turkish visit, on which (though a European and a stranger) he was obliged to comply with this custom.—BURDER.

CHAPTER VI.

Ver. 26. And Joshua adjured *them* at that time, saying, Cursed *be* the man before the LORD that riseth up and buildeth this city Jericho: he shall lay the foundation thereof in his firstborn, and in his youngest *son* shall he set up the gates of it.

It appears from the following passage from Strabo's *Geography of Troy*, (b. xiii. chap. 1. § 42,) that it was not unusual in remote antiquity to pronounce a curse upon those who should rebuild a destroyed city. "It is believed that those who might have afterward wished to rebuild Ilium, were deterred from building the city in the same place, either by what they had suffered there, or because Agamemnon had pronounced a curse against him that should rebuild it. For this was an ancient custom. Thus Crœsus, after he had destroyed Sidene, into which the tyrant Glaucias had thrown himself, uttered a curse upon him who should rebuild the walls of that place." Zonaras says, that the Romans pronounced a curse upon him who should rebuild Carthage. Joshua's curse on the rebuilder of Jericho, was fulfilled, according to 1 Kings xvi. 34, on one Hiel, who lost his eldest son, Abiram, when he laid the foundation, and his youngest son, Segub, when he built the gate.—ROSENMULLER.

CHAPTER VII.

Ver. 6. And Joshua rent his clothes, and fell to the earth upon his face before the ark of the LORD until the even-tide, he and the elders of Israel, and put dust upon their heads.

Joshua and the elders of Israel were in great distress, because they had been defeated by the men of Ai, and because they saw in that a token of the divine displeasure. They therefore fell prostrate before the ark of the Lord, and put dust on their heads as an emblem of their sorrow. (1 Sam. iv. 12. 2 Sam. i. 2. Neh. ix. 1.) How often is the mind affectingly thrown back on this ancient custom by similar scenes at this day! See the poor object bereft of wife, children, property, friends; or suffering under some deep affliction of body: he sits on the ground, with his eyes fixed thereon, a dirty rag round his loins, his arms folded, his jewels laid aside, his hair dishevelled and covered with *dust*, and bitterly bemoaning his condition, saying, *Iyo! iyo! iyo!*—"Alas! alas! alas!"—ROBERTS.

CHAPTER IX.

Ver. 4. They did work wilily, and went and made as if they had been ambassadors, and took old sacks upon their asses, and wine-bottles, old, and rent, and bound up.

Chardin informs us that the Arabs, and all those that lead a wandering life, keep their water, milk, and other liquors, in leathern bottles. "They keep in them more fresh than otherwise they would do. These leathern bottles are made of goat-skins. When the animal is killed, they cut off its feet and its head, and they draw it in this manner out of the skin, without opening its belly. They afterward sew up the places where the legs were cut off, and the tail, and when it is filled, they tie it about the neck. These nations, and the countrypeople of Persia, never go a journey without a small leathern bottle of water hanging by their side like a scrip. The great leathern bottles are made of the skin of a he-goat, and the small ones, that serve instead of a bottle of water on the road, are made of a kid's skin." These bottles are frequently rent, when old and much used, and are capable of being repaired by being bound up. This they do, Chardin says, "sometimes by setting in a piece; sometimes by gathering up the wounded place in the manner of a purse; sometimes they put in a round flat piece of wood, and by that means stop the hole." Maundrell gives an account exactly similar to the above. Speaking of the Greek convent at Bellmount, near Tripoli, in Syria, he says, "the same person whom we saw officiating at the altar in his embroidered sacerdotal robe, brought us the next day, on his own back, a kid and a goat-skin of wine, as a present from the convent." These bottles are still used in Spain, and called borrachas. Mr. Bruce gives a description of the girba, which seems to be a vessel of the same kind as those now mentioned, only of dimensions considerably larger. "A girba is an ox's skin, squared, and the edges sewed together very artificially, by a double seam, which does not let out water, much resembling that upon the best English cricket balls. An opening is left at the top of the girba, in the same manner as the bunghole of a cask; around this the skin is gathered to the size of a large handful, which, when the girba is full of water, is tied round with whip-cord. These girbas generally contain about sixty gallons each, and two of them are the load of a camel. They are then all besmeared on the outside with grease, as well to hinder the water from oozing through, as to prevent its being evaporated by the heat of the sun upon the girba, which, in fact, happened to us twice, so as to put us in imminent danger of perishing with thirst."—BURDER.

Ver. 23. Now therefore ye *are* cursed; and there shall none of you be freed from being bondmen, and hewers of wood, and drawers of water, for the house of my God.

In the kingdom of Algiers, the women and children are charged with the care of their flocks and their herds, with providing food for the family, cutting fuel, fetching water, and when their domestic affairs allow them, with tending their silk worms. The daughters of the Turcomans in Palestine, are employed in the same mean and laborious offices. In Homer, Andromache fed the horses of her heroic husband. It is probable, the cutting of wood was another female occupation. The very great antiquity of these customs, is confirmed by the prophet Jeremiah, who complains that the children were sent to gather wood for idolatrous purposes; and in his Lamentations, he bewails the oppressions which his people suffered from their enemies, in these terms: "They took the young men to grind, and the children fell under the wood." Hence the servile condition to which the Gibeonites were reduced by Joshua, for imposing upon him and the princes of the congregation, appears to have been much more severe than we are apt at first to suppose: "Now, therefore, ye are cursed, and there shall none of you be freed from being bondmen, and hewers of wood, and drawers of water, for the house of my God."

The bitterness of their doom did not consist in being subjected to a laborious service, for it was the usual employment of women and children; but in their being degraded from the characteristic employment of men, that of bearing arms, and condemned with their posterity for ever to the employment of females.—PAXTON.

CHAPTER X.

Ver. 6. And the LORD said unto Joshua, Be not afraid because of them; for to-morrow, about this time, will I deliver them up all slain before Israel: thou shalt hough their horses, and burn their chariots with fire.

With the enemy's horses, the Israelites had a different procedure from other booty. For their direction, indeed, on this point, they had no general and permanent law, prescribed them, but merely the order from God, issued by Joshua (x. 6) before the battle at the waters of Merom; according to which order, they were naturally led to regulate their conduct in aftertimes. In their wars before the reign of Solomon, they made no use of horses, though some of their enemies did; and this same cavalry of their enemies was wont to be very formidable, and sometimes gave them the superiority of the Israelites in the plains. At the same time, the event has often shown, that a brave, steady, close infantry, without the support of horse, will stand the shock of hostile cavalry without the smallest disorder; of which, although *our* cavalry is far more formidable by reason of their close charge, modern history furnishes examples. Indeed, on one occasion, besides more than 20,000 infantry, David took, I know not whether 1700, or 7000 cavalry, prisoners; their retreat across the Euphrates having been probably cut off, or that they were compelled to surrender for want of subsistence. But when the Israelites *did* get a booty of horses, they did not know what use to make of them. Their husbandry was carried on in the ancient way, and to much more advantage, with oxen, which are not so expensive to maintain; and to this their whole rural economy was directed. In war, they did not employ cavalry, and would have been bad horsemen; and for travelling, they commonly made use of the ass, to which whoever is accustomed from his youth, will not willingly venture to ride a mettled horse, particularly such a one as is employed in war. Horses, therefore, were to them quite a useless sort of plunder, unless they had sold them, which was not advisable, because their enemies, in a roundabout way, might have bought them again. It was far better policy for them to diminish as far as possible this race of animals, by means of which their enemies might, on some occasions, obtain a manifest advantage over them; just as the Romans put the elephants of their enemies to death, because they had no desire to make use of this foreign and dubious expedient to help them to victory, and yet saw that elephants might sometimes be dangerous to their troops. In the first engagement which the Israelites had with an enemy whose cavalry and war-chariots made him formidable, God commanded them to hough or hamstring, that is, to cut the thigh-sinew of the horses which they took; and they did so, Josh. x. 6—9. From ignorance of military affairs, most expositors have understood this command as if it meant, not that the horses should be killed, but merely lamed in the hind-legs, and then let go: and into this mistake, by following Bochart, as he had Kimchi, I was led in the first edition of this work.—I have never been in war, and know just as little of the veterinary art; nor have I ever seen a ham-strung horse. But a horse so treated, must, instead of running off, fall instantly backward, and writhe about miserably till he die, which generally happens from loss of blood, by the stroke of the sabre cutting the artery of the thigh. This is still, as military people have since informed me, the plan adopted to make those horses that are taken, but cannot be easily brought away, unserviceable to the enemy again. They ham-string them, which can be done in an instant; and they generally die of the wound, by bleeding to death; but though they should not, the wound never heals; so that if even the enemy recover them alive, he is forced to despatch them: and every compassionate friend of horses, who has ever seen one in that situation, will do so, in order to terminate his misery. There is, therefore, no foundation for Kimchi's opinion, that mere laming was enjoined, because it would be wrong to put an animal unnecessarily to death. For thus to lame a horse that would still live, in my opinion, would rather have been extreme cruelty; because, being then useless, nobody would be likely to give him any food. —MICHAELIS.

Ver. 11. And it came to pass, as they fled from before Israel, *and* were in the going down to Beth-horon, that the LORD cast down great stones from heaven upon them unto Azekah, and they died: *they were* more which died with hailstones, than *they* whom the children of Israel slew with the sword.

Some writers are of opinion that this was hail, larger and more violent than usual; others maintain that Joshua is to be understood literally, of a shower of stones. Such a circumstance, so far from being impossible, has several times occurred. The Romans, who looked upon showers of stones as very disastrous, have noticed many instances of them. Under the reign of Tullius Hostilius, when it was known to the people of Rome that a shower of *stones* had fallen on the mountain of Alba, at first it seemed incredible. They sent out proper persons to inquire into this prodigy, and it was found that stones had fallen after the same manner as a storm of hail driven by the wind. Some time after the battle at Cannæ, there was seen upon the same mountain of Alba a shower of stones, which continued for two days together. In 1538, near a village in Italy called Tripergola, after some shocks of an earthquake, there was seen a shower of stones and dust, which darkened the air for two days, after which they observed that a mountain had risen up in the midst of the Lucrine Lake.—BURDER.

A similar phenomenon in modern times is thus described in Com. Porter's Letters from Constantinople and its Environs, (vol. 1. p. 44,) as having occurred in the summer of 1831:—

"We had got perhaps a mile and a half on our way when a cloud rising in the west, gave indications of an approaching rain. In a few minutes we discovered something falling from the heavens with a heavy splash, and of a whitish appearance. I could not conceive what it was, but observing some gulls near, I supposed it to be them darting for fish; but soon after discovered that they were large balls of ice falling. Immediately we heard a sound like rumbling thunder, or ten thousand carriages rolling furiously over the pavement. The whole Bosphorus was in a foam, as though heaven's artillery had been discharged upon us and our frail machine. Our fate seemed inevitable, our umbrellas were raised to protect us; the lumps of ice stripped them into ribands. We fortunately had a bullock's hide in the boat, under which we crawled and saved ourselves from further injury. One man, of the three oarsmen, had his hand literally smashed; another much injured in the shoulder; Mr. H. received a severe blow in the leg; my right hand was somewhat disabled, and all more or less injured. A smaller kaick accompanied, with my two servants. They were both disabled, and are now in bed with their wounds; the kaick was terribly bruised. It was the most awful and terrific scene that I ever witnessed, and God forbid that I should be ever exposed to such another. Balls of ice as large as my two fists, fell into the boat, and some of them came with such violence as certainly to have broken an arm or leg, had they struck us in those parts. One of them struck the blade of an oar and split it. The scene lasted, may be, five minutes; but it was five minutes of the most awful feeling that I ever experienced. When it passed over, we found the surrounding hills covered with masses of ice, I cannot call it hail; the trees stripped of their leaves and limbs, and every thing looking desolate. We proceeded on our course, however, and arrived at our destination, drenched and awe-struck. The ruin had not extended so far as Candalie, and it was difficult to make them comprehend the cause of the nervous and agitated condition in which we arrived; the Reis Effendi asked me if I was ever so agitated when in action? I answered no, for then I had something to excite me, and human means only to oppose. He asked the minister if he ever was so affected in a gale of wind at sea? He answered no, for then he could exercise his skill to disarm or render

VALLEY OF AJALON.—*Joshua* x. 12.

harmless the elements. He asked him why he should be affected now? He replied, 'From the awful idea of being crushed to death by the hand of God with stones from heaven, when resistance would be vain, and where it would be impious to be brave.' He clasped his hands, raised his eyes to heaven, and exclaimed, 'God is great!'

"Up to this hour, late in the afternoon, I have not recovered my composure; my nerves are so affected as scarcely to be able to hold my pen, or communicate my ideas. The scene was awful beyond all description. I have witnessed repeated earthquakes; the lightning has played, as it were, about my head; the wind roared, and the waves have at one moment thrown me to the sky, and the next have sunk me into a deep abyss. I have been in action, and seen death and destruction around me in every shape of horror; but I never before had the feeling of awe which seized upon me on this occasion, and still haunts, and I feel will ever haunt me. I returned to the beautiful village of Buyucdere. The sun was out in all its splendour; at a distance all looked smiling and charming; but a nearer approach discovered roofs covered with workmen repairing the broken tiles; desolated vineyards, and shattered windows. My porter, the boldest of my family, who had ventured an instant from the door, had been knocked down by a hailstone, and had they not dragged him in by the heels, would have been battered to death. Of a flock of geese in front of our house, six were killed, and the rest dreadfully mangled. Two boatmen were killed in the upper part of the village, and I have heard of broken bones in abundance. Many of the thick brick tiles with which my roof is covered, are smashed to atoms, and my house was inundated by the rain that succeeded this visitation. It is impossible to convey an idea of what it was. Imagine to yourself, however, the heavens suddenly froze over, and as suddenly broken to pieces in irregular masses, of from half a pound to a pound weight, and precipitated to the earth. My own servants weighed several pieces of three quarters of a pound; and many were found by others of upwards of a pound. There were many which fell around the boat in which I was, that appeared to me to be as large as the swell of the large sized water decanter. You may think this romance. I refer to the bearer of this letter, who was with me, and witnessed the scene, for the truth of every word it contains."—LETTERS FROM CONSTANTINOPLE.

Ver. 12. Then spake Joshua to the LORD in the day when the LORD delivered up the Amorites before the children of Israel, and he said in the sight of Israel, Sun, stand thou still upon Gibeon; and thou, Moon, in the valley of Ajalon.

(*See Engraving.*)

Ver. 21. And all the people returned to the camp to Joshua at Makkedah in peace: none moved his tongue against any of the children of Israel.

When a person speaks of the fear to which his enemy is reduced, he says, "Ah! he dares not now to shake his tongue against me." "He hurt you! the fellow will not shake his tongue against you."—ROBERTS.

Ver. 24. And said unto the captains of the men of war which went with him, Come near, put your feet upon the necks of these kings. And they came near, and put their feet upon the necks of them.

See on 2 Sam. 44. 21.

This in the East is a favourite way of triumphing over a fallen foe. In the history of the battles of the gods, or giants, particular mention is made of the closing scene, how the conquerors went and trampled on their enemies. When people are disputing, should one be a little pressed, and the other begin to triumph, the former will say, "I will tread upon thy neck, and after that beat thee." A low-caste man insulting one who is high, is sure to hear some one say to the offended individual, "Put your feet on his neck." (See on Isa. xviii. 2, 7.)—ROBERTS.

CHAPTER XIV.

Ver. 12. Now therefore give me this mountain, whereof the LORD spake in that day; for thou heardest in that day how the Anakims *were* there, and *that* the cities *were* great *and* fenced; if so be the LORD *will be* with me, then I shall be able to drive them out, as the LORD said.

The mountainous parts of the Holy Land are so far from being inhospitable, unfruitful, or the refuse of the land of Canaan, that in the division of this country, the mountain of Hebron was granted to Caleb as a particular favour; "Now, therefore, give me this mountain of which the Lord spake in that day." In the time of Asa, the "hill country of Judah" mustered five hundred and eighty thousand men of valour; an argument beyond dispute, that the land was able to maintain them. Even in the present times, though cultivation and improvement are exceedingly neglected, while the plains and valleys, although as fruitful as ever, lie almost entirely desolate, every little hill is crowded with inhabitants. If this part of the Holy Land was composed, as some object, only of naked rocks and precipices, why is it better peopled than the plains of Esdraelon, Rama, Acre, or Zabulon, which are all of them extremely fertile and delightful? It cannot be urged that the inhabitants live with more safety on the hills and mountains, than on the plains, as there are neither walls nor fortifications to secure their villages and encampments; and except in the range of Lebanon, and some other mountains, few or no places of difficult access; so that both of them are equally exposed to the insults of an enemy. But the reason is obvious; they find among these mountainous rocks and precipices, sufficient convenience for themselves, and much greater for their cattle. Here they have bread to the full, while their flocks and their herds browse upon richer herbage, and both man and beast quench their thirst from springs of excellent water, which is but too much wanted, especially in the summer season, through all the plains of Syria. This fertility of Canaan is fully confirmed by writers of great reputation, whose impartiality cannot be justly suspected. Tacitus calls it a fruitful soil, uber solum; and Justin affirms, that in this country the purity of the air, and the fertility of the soil, are equally admirable: Sed non minor loci ejus apricitatis quam ubertatis admiratio est. The justice of these brief accounts, Dr. Shaw, and almost every modern traveller, fully verifies. When he travelled in Syria and Phenicia, in December and January, the whole country, he remarks, looked verdant and cheerful; and the woods particularly, which are chiefly planted with the gall-bearing oak, were everywhere bestrewed with a variety of anemonies, ranunculusses, colchicas, and mandrakes. Several pieces of ground near Tripoli were full of licorice; and at the mouth of a famous grotto he saw an elegant species of the blue lily, the same with Morrison's lilium Persicum florens. In the beginning of March, the plains, particularly between Jaffa and Rama, were everywhere planted with a beautiful variety of fritillaries, tulips of innumerable hues, and a profusion of the rarest and most beautiful flowers; while the hills and the mountains were covered with yellow pollium, and some varieties of thyme, sage, and rosemary. —PAXTON.

CHAPTER XVII.

Ver. 16. And all the Canaanites that dwell in the land of the valley have chariots of iron, *both they* who *are* of Bethshean and her towns, and *they* who *are* of the valley of Jezreel.

The warriors of primitive times were carried to the field in chariots, drawn for the most part by two horses. The custom of riding and fighting upon horses, was not introduced into Greece, and the regions of Asia bordering on the Hellespont, till some time after the Trojan war; for Homer, whose authority in such cases is indisputable, always conducts his heroes to battle in chariots, never on horseback. In what age the chariot was first used in battle, cannot now be ascertained; but by the help of the sacred volume, we can trace the practice to a very remote antiquity, for the aboriginal inhabitants of Canaan appear, from the number of armed chariots which they possessed, when Joshua invaded their country, to have been trained to that mode of warfare long before. "And the children of Joseph said, The hill is not enough for us; and all the Canaanites that dwell in the land of the valley have chariots of iron, both they who are of Bethshean and her towns, and they who are of the valley of Jezreel." This by no means intimates, that the chariots were made of iron, but only that they were armed with it. Such chariots were by the ancients called *currus falcati*, and in Greek δρεπανοφυραι. They had a kind of scythes, of about two cubits long, fastened to long axle-trees on both wheels; these being driven swiftly through a body of men, made great slaughter, mowing them down like grass or corn. The efficacious resistance which the Canaanites, from their chariots of iron, opposed to the arms of Israel, is emphatically remarked by the sacred historian: "And the Lord was with Judah, and they drave out the inhabitants of the mountain, but could not drive out the inhabitants of the valley, because they had chariots of iron." The native princes of Canaan, fully aware of the great advantages to be derived from this species of force, in combating the armies of Israel, which consisted, as has been already observed, entirely of infantry, continued to improve it with a care and diligence proportioned to its importance. In the time of the judges, not long after the death of Joshua, Jabin the king of Canaan, sent nine hundred chariots of iron into the field against the people of Israel: and in a succeeding war, between this people and their inveterate enemies the Philistines, the latter met them in the field with "thirty thousand chariots, and six thousand horsemen, and people as the sand which is on the seashore for multitude."—PAXTON.

CHAPTER XVIII.

Ver. 25. Gibeon, and Ramah, and Beeroth.

The oriental geographers speak of Ramah as the metropolis of Palestine; and every appearance of its ruins even now confirms the opinion of its having been once a considerable city. Its situation, as lying immediately in the high road from Jaffa to Jerusalem, made it necessarily a place of great resort; and from the fruitfulness of the country around it, it must have been equally important as a military station or a depot for supplies, and as a magazine for the collection of such articles of commerce as were exported from the coast. In its present state, the town of Ramah is about the size of Jaffa, in the extent actually occupied. The dwellings of this last, however, are crowded together around the sides of a hill, while those of Ramah are scattered widely over the face of the level plain on which it stands. The style of building here is that of high square houses, with flattened domes covering them; and some of the old terraced roofs are fenced around with raised walls, in which are seen pyramids of hollow earthenware pipes, as if to give air and light, without destroying the strength of the wall itself. The inhabitants are estimated at little more than five thousand persons, of whom about one third are Christians of the Greek and Catholic communion, and the remaining two thirds Mohammedans, chiefly Arabs; the men of power and the military being Turks, and no Jews residing there. The principal occupation of the people is husbandry, for which the surrounding country is highly favourable, and the staple commodities produced by them are corn, olives, oil, and cotton, with some soap and coarse cloth made in the town. There are still remains of some noble subterranean cisterns at Ramah, not inferior either in extent or execution to many of those at Alexandria: they were intended for the same purpose, namely, to serve in time of war as reservoirs of water."—BUCKINGHAM.

CHAPTER XXIII.

Ver. 7. But they shall be snares and traps unto you, and scourges in your sides, and thorns in your eyes, until ye perish from off this good land which the LORD your God hath given you.

"What!" says a wife to her angry husband, "am I a thorn in your eyes?" "Alas! alas! he has seen another; I am now a thorn in his eyes." "Were I not a thorn in his eyes, his anger would not burn so long." "My old friend Tamban never looks at my house now, because it gives thorns to his eyes."—ROBERTS.

CHAPTER XXIV.

Ver. 12. And I sent the hornet before you, which drave them out from before you, *even* the two kings of the Amorites; *but* not with thy sword, nor with thy bow.

See on Ex. 24. 28.

Ver. 32. And the bones of Joseph, which the children of Israel brought up out of Egypt, buried they in Shechem, in a parcel of ground which Jacob bought of the sons of Hamor, the father of Shechem, for a hundred pieces of silver: and it became the inheritance of the children of Joseph.

Joseph was not interred in Shechem, but, according to the ancient custom, in a field adjoining. Probably the other children of Jacob received the like honour, each tribe taking care to bury its ancestor, either at Machpelah, or elsewhere in the land of Canaan. Josephus asserts that it was so, upon the credit of an ancient tradition. St. Stephen confirms the relation. Acts vii. 16. Savages consider the tombs of their ancestors as titles to the possession of the lands which they inhabit. This country is ours, say they; the bones of our fathers are here laid to rest. When they are forced to quit it, they dig them up with tears, and carry them off with every token of respect. About thirty miles below the falls of St. Anthony, (says Carver,) in North America, several bands of the Naudowessie Indians have a burying-place, where these people, though they have no fixed residence, living in tents, and abiding but a few months on one spot, always contrive to deposite the bones of their dead. At the spring equinox these bands annually assemble here to hold a grand council with all the other bands; wherein they settle their operations for the ensuing year. At this time, in particular, they bring with them their dead, for interment, bound up in buffaloes' skins. If any of these people die in the summer, at a distance from the burying-ground, and they find it impossible to remove the body before it would putrify, they burn the flesh from the bones, and preserving the latter, bury them in the manner described.—BURDER.

JUDGES.

CHAPTER I.

Ver. 7. Threescore and ten kings, having their thumbs and their great toes cut off.

The Hebrew has this, "the thumbs of their hands and of their feet." The Hindoos call the thumb the *reria-viril*, the great finger of the hand, and the large toe is named the great finger of the foot. This punishment was exceedingly common in ancient times, and was inflicted principally on those who had committed some flagrant offence with their hands and their feet. Thus, those convicted of forgery, or numerous thefts, had their thumbs cut off. The practice is abolished, but its memory will remain, as it is now one of the scarecrows of the nursery and domestic life: "If you steal any more, I will cut off your thumbs." "Let me find out the thief, and I will soon have his thumbs."—ROBERTS.

CHAPTER III.

Ver. 17. And he brought the present unto Eglon king of Moab: and Eglon *was* a very fat man. 18. And when he had made an end to offer the present, he sent away the people that bare the present.

See on Gen. 43. 45.

There is often in the East a great deal of pomp and parade in presenting their gifts. "Through ostentation," says Maillet, "they never fail to load upon four or five horses what might easily be carried by one. In like manner as to jewels, trinkets, and other things of value, they place in fifteen dishes, what a single plate would very well hold." Something of this pomp seems to be referred to in this passage, where we read of *making an end of offering the present*, and of a number of people who conveyed it. This remark also illustrates 2 Kings viii. 9. *So Hazael went to meet him, and took a present with him, even of every good thing of Damascus, forty camels' burden.*—HARMER.

Ver. 19. But he himself turned again from the quarries that *were* by Gilgal, and said, I have a secret errand unto thee, O king: who said, Keep silence. And all that stood by him went out from him.

From a circumstance mentioned by Mr. Bruce, it appears that Ehud acted in strict conformity to the customs of the time and place, so that neither the suspicion of the king nor his attendants should be excited by his conduct. It was usual for the attendants to retire when secret messages were to be delivered. "I drank a dish of coffee, and told him, that I was a bearer of a confidential message from Ali Bey of Cairo, and wished to deliver it to him without witnesses, whenever he pleased. The room was accordingly cleared without delay, excepting his secretary, who was also going away, when I pulled him back by the clothes, saying, stay, if you please; we shall need you to write the answer."—BURDER.

Ver. 20. And Ehud came unto him; and he was sitting in a summer-parlour, which he had for himself alone.

Dr. Shaw tells us, their doors are large, and their chambers spacious; conveniences, as he observes, very well adapted to those hotter climates. But when Eglon is represented as receiving Ehud and Death, in a *parlour of cooling*, as it is called, in the margin of Judges iii. 20, or rather in a *chamber of cooling*, something more seems to be meant than merely its having a large door, or being spacious; at least there are *now* other contrivances in the East, to give coolness to particular rooms, which are very common; and though the time in which Eglon lived, is acknowledged to be of very remote antiquity, yet we are to remember he was a prince, and in the palaces of such these contrivances without doubt began. The doctor is silent upon this point, but Russell has given us the following account of one of their methods of cooling rooms. Their great houses at Aleppo are composed of apartments on each of the sides of a square court, all of stone; and consist of a ground door, which is generally arched, and an upper story, which is flat on the top, and either terraced with hard plaster, or paved stone; above-stairs is a colonnade, if not round the whole court, at least fronting the West, off from which are their rooms and kiosques; these latter are a sort of wooden divans, that project a little way from their other buildings, and hang over the street; they are raised about a foot and a half higher than the floor of the room, to which they are quite open, and by having windows in front and on each side, there is a great draught of air, which makes them cool in the summer, the advantage chiefly intended by them. They have another way of cooling their rooms in Egypt. It is done by openings at the top, which let the fresh air into them. Egmont and Heyman, as well as Maillet, make mention of them, but the last-mentioned author gives the most distinct account of these contrivances: they make, he tells us, their halls extremely large and lofty, with a dome at the top, which towards the North has several open windows; these are so constructed as to throw the north wind down into these rooms, and by this means, though the country is excessively hot, they can make the coolness of these apartments such as, oftentimes, not to be borne without being wrapped in furs. Egmont and Heyman speak of chambers cooled after this manner, as well as halls. Eglon's appears to have been a chamber, and what Shaw calls an *olee*, which gives a propriety to the mention that is made of Ehud's passing through the porch, which no interpreter before the doctor has, that I know of, remarked: but whether it was cooled by a kiosque, as they are called at Aleppo, or by an Egyptian dome, or by some contrivance distinct from both, is of no consequence to determine. That some contrivance to mitigate the extreme heat of that climate began early to obtain, in the palaces of princes, is natural to believe; that it began as early as the time of Eglon, this passage puts out of all doubt. It was the more necessary, as Eglon appears to have kept his court at Jericho, where the heat is so excessive, that it has proved fatal to some even in March.—HARMER.

Ver. 25. And they tarried till they were ashamed; and, behold, he opened not the doors of the parlour: therefore they took a key and opened *them;* and, behold, their lord *was* fallen down dead on the earth.

The wooden locks commonly used in Egypt, "consist of a long hollow piece of wood, fixed in the door, so as to slide backward and forward, which enters a hole made for it in the doorpost, and is there fastened by small bolts of iron wire, which fall from above into little orifices made for them in the top of the lock. The key is a long piece of wood, having at the end small pieces of iron wire of different lengths, irregularly fixed in, corresponding in number and direction with the bolts which fall into the lock; these it lifts upon being introduced into the lock, which it then pulls back. The bolts of wire differ in number from three to fourteen or fifteen, and it is impossible to guess at the number a lock contains, or at the direction in which they are placed."—TURNER'S *Journal of a Tour in the Levant.*

Ver. 31. And after him was Shamgar the son of Anath, which slew of the Philistines six hundred men with an ox-goad: and he also delivered Israel.

Mr. Maundrell has an observation which at once explains this transaction, and removes every difficulty from the passage. He says, "the countrypeople were now everywhere at plough in the fields, in order to sow cotton. It was observable, that in ploughing they used goads of an extraordinary size; upon measuring of several, I found them about eight feet long, and at the bigger end six inches in circumference. They were armed at the lesser end with a sharp prickle for driving the oxen, at the other end with a small spade, or paddle of iron, strong and massy, for cleansing the plough from the clay that encumbers it in working. May we not from hence conjecture, that it was with such a goad as one of these, that Shamgar made that prodigious slaughter related of him, Judges iii. 21. I am confident that whoever should see one of these instruments, would judge it to be a weapon not less fit, perhaps fitter, than a sword for such an execution. Goads of this sort I saw always used hereabouts, and also in Syria; and the reason is, because the same single person both drives the oxen, and also holds and manages the plough; which makes it necessary to use such a goad as is above described, to avoid the encumbrance of two instruments."—BURDER.

CHAPTER IV.

Ver. 6. And she sent and called Barak the son of Abinoam out of Kedesh-naphtali, and said unto him, Hath not the LORD God of Israel commanded, *saying*, Go, and draw towards Mount Tabor, and take with thee ten thousand men of the children of Naphtali, and of the children of Zebulun?

Arriving at the top, we found ourselves on an oval plain, of about a quarter of a mile in its greatest length, covered with a bed of fertile soil on the west, having at its eastern end a mass of ruins, seemingly the vestiges of churches, grottoes, strong walls, and fortifications, all decidedly of some antiquity, and a few appearing to be the works of a very remote age. First were pointed out to us three grottoes, two beside each other, and not far from two cisterns of excellent water; which grottoes are said to be the remains of the three tabernacles proposed to be erected by St. Peter, at the moment of the transfiguration, when Jesus, Elias, and Moses, were seen talking together. In one of these grottoes, which they call more particularly the Sanctuary, there is a square stone used as an altar; and on the sixth of August in every year, the friars of the convent come from Nazareth, with their banners and the host, to say mass here; at which period they are accompanied by all the Catholics of the neighbourhood, who pass the night in festivity, and light large bonfires, by a succession of which they have nearly bared the southern side of the mountain of all the wood that once clothed it. Besides these grottoes, no particular history is assigned to any other of the remains, though among them there seem to have been many large religious buildings. The whole of these appear to have been once enclosed with a strong wall, a large portion of which still remains entire on the north side, having its firm foundation on the solid rock. This appeared to me the most ancient part. Traditions here speak of a city built on the top, which sustained a five years' siege, drawing its supplies by skirmish from different parts of the fertile plains below, and being furnished with water from two excellent cisterns still above; but as no fixed period is assigned to this event, it may probably relate to the siege of Vespasian. As there still remained the fragments of a wall on the southeast angle, somewhat higher than the rest, we ascended it over heaps of fallen buildings, and enjoyed from thence a prospect truly magnificent, wanting only the verdure of spring to make it beautiful as well as grand. Placing my compass before me, we had on the northwest a view of the Mediterranean sea, whose blue surface filled up an open space left by a downward bend in the outline of the western hills: to west-northwest a smaller portion of its waters were seen: and on the west again the slender line of its distant horizon was just perceptible over a range of land near the seacoast. From west to south the plain of Esdraelon extended over a vast space, being bounded on the south by the range of hills, generally considered to be the Hermon, whose dews are poetically celebrated, Psalm cxxxiii. 3, and having in the same direction, nearer the foot of Tabor, the springs of Ain-el-Sherrar, which send a perceptible stream through its centre, and form the brook Kishon of antiquity. Psalm lxxxiii 9. From southeast to the east is the plain of Galilee, being almost a continuation of Esdraelon, and, like it, appearing to be highly cultivated, being now ploughed for seed throughout. Beneath the range of this supposed Hermon is seated Endor, famed for the witch who raised the ghost of Samuel, to the terror of the affrighted Saul; and Nain, equally celebrated as the place at which Jesus raised the only son of a widow from death to life, and restored him to his afflicted parent. The range which bounds the eastern view is thought to be the mountains of Gilboa, where the same Saul, setting an example of self-destruction to his armour-bearer and his three sons, fell on his own sword, rather than fall wounded into the hands of the uncircumcised, by whom he was defeated. The sea of Tiberias, or the Lake of Gennesareth, famed as the scene of many miracles, is seen on the northeast, filling the hollow of a deep valley, and contrasting its light blue waters with the dark brown shades of the barren hills by which it is hemmed around. Here, too, the steep is pointed out down which the herd of swine, who were possessed by the legion of devils, ran headlong into the sea. In the same direction, below, on the plain of Galilee, and about an hour's distance from the foot of Mount Tabor, there is a cluster of buildings, used as a bazar for cattle, frequented on Mondays only. Somewhat farther on is a rising ground, from which it is said that Christ delivered the long and excellent discourse called the Sermon on the Mount; and the whole view in this quarter is bounded by the high range of Gebel-el-Telj, or the Mountain of Snow, whose summit was at this moment clothed with one white sheet, without a perceptible breach or dark spot in it. The city of Saphet, supposed to be the ancient Bethulia, a city said to be seen far and near, and thought to be alluded to in the apophthegm which says, "a city set on a hill cannot be hid," is also pointed out in this direction: but though the day was clear, I could not distinguish it, its distance preventing its being defined from hence without a glass. To the north were the stony hills over which we had journeyed hither, and these completed this truly grand and interesting panoramic view. —BUCKINGHAM.

Van Egmont and Heyman give the following account of Tabor:—"This mountain, though somewhat rugged and difficult, we ascended on horseback, making several circuits round it, which took us about three quarters of an hour. It is one of the highest in the whole country, being thirty *stadia*, or about four English miles, a circumference that rendered it more famous. And it is the most beautiful I ever saw, with regard to verdure, being everywhere decorated with small oak-trees, and the ground universally enamelled with a variety of plants and flowers, except on the south side, where it is not so fully covered with verdure. On this mountain are great numbers of red partridges, and some wild-boars; and we were so fortunate as to see the Arabs hunting them. We left, but not without reluctance, this delightful place, and found at the bottom of it a mean village, called Deboura, or Tabour, a name said to be derived from the celebrated Deborah mentioned in Judges." Pococke notices this village, which stands on a rising ground at the foot of Mount Tabor westward; and the learned traveller thinks, that it may be the same as the Daberath, or Daberah, mentioned in the book of Joshua, as on the borders of Zebulun and Issachar. "Any one," he adds, "who examines the fourth chapter of Judges, may see that this is probably the spot where Barak and Deborah met at Mount Tabor with their forces and went to pursue Sisera; and on this account, it might have its name from that great prophetess, who then judged and governed Israel; for Josephus relates, that Deborah and Barak gathered the army together at this mountain." This point Josephus was not required to prove, as the sacred history contains explicit information on this head, to which the Jewish historian was incapable of adding a single particular. The name of the village seems, however, more probably to be derived from the mountain, than from the prophetess. Deborah, the name of the place where she dwelt, and to which the children of Israel came up to her for judgment, was between Ramah and Bethel in Mount Ephraim, and consequently much farther to the south. Whereas in Deboura, or Dabour, we have the very Dabor or Thaboor of the scriptures, with only that slight corruption which the Hebrew names receive, as pronounced by the Arabs. The mountain itself they call *Djebel Tour*.—MODERN TRAVELLER.

Ver. 10. And Barak called Zebulun and Naphtali to Kedesh; and he went up with ten thousand men at his feet: and Deborah went up with him.

The phrase "men at his feet," did not, I believe, refer to any particular class of soldiers, but applied to ALL, whether they fought in chariots, on horses, or on foot. This form of speech is used in eastern books to show how many *obey* or *serve* under the general. It may be taken from the action of a slave being prostrate at the feet of his master, denoting submission or obedience. In this way devotees, when addressing the gods, always speak of themselves as being at their feet. When the Orientals speak of his Majesty of Britain, they often allude to the millions who are at his feet. The governors, generals, or judges in the East, are said to have the people of such countries, or armies, or districts, at their feet. Nay, it is common for masters, and people of small possessions, to speak of their domestics as being at their feet. It is therefore heard every day, for "I will send my servants," *en-kāl-adiyila*, "those at my feet."—ROBERTS.

Ver. 18. And Jael went out to meet Sisera, and said unto him, Turn in, my lord, turn in to me; fear not. And when he had turned in unto her into the tent, she covered him with a mantle.

The Arabs are not so scrupulous as the Turks about their women; and though they have their harem, or women's apartment, in the tent, they readily introduce their acquaintances into it, or those strangers whom they take under their special protection. Pococke's conductor, in his journey to Jerusalem, led him two or three miles to his tent, where he sat with his wife and others round a fire. The faithful Arab kept him there for greater security, the wife being always with him; no stranger ever daring to come into the women's apartment unless introduced. We discover in this custom, the reason of Jael's invitation to Sisera, when he was defeated by Barak: "Turn in, my lord, turn in to me, fear not." She invited him to take refuge in her own division of the tent, into which no stranger might presume to enter; and where he naturally supposed himself in perfect safety.—PAXTON.

There is an apparent treachery in the conduct of Jael to Sisera; and it appears from the following account as if the inhabitants of that country were still actuated by the same principle of interested dissimulation. "It was about noon when we reached the small village of Deborah, where we alighted to refresh, not suspecting that the treachery for which it is traditionally infamous, both in holy and profane records, was still to be found here at so distant a period. We entered into this village, and, like the unfortunate Sisera, demanded only a little water to drink, for with every thing else our scrip was well provided. It was furnished to us, as we desired, with provender for our beasts, and the offer of all that the village possessed. While the animals were feeding, I was desirous of ascending to the summit of Mount Tabor, for the enjoyment of the extensive view which it commands. Our guide from the convent offering to accompany me, we took with us a man from the village, who promised to facilitate our ascent by directing us to the easiest paths; and taking our arms with us, while my servant and the muleteer remained below to take care of the beasts, we all three set out together; by forced exertions we reached the summit in about half an hour. In our descent from Mount Tabor we entered a grotto, in which there had formerly been a church, and had scarcely got within it, before we heard the rushing of persons before the outer part of the passage by which we had entered. On turning round to ascertain the cause of this noise, we observed five or six armed men, three of whom we recognised to be those who had made such offers of their hospitality in the village of Deborah below. They called out to us in a loud voice, that if we attempted the slightest resistance we should be murdered, but that if we submitted to be quietly stripped, no violence should be offered to our persons. There was no time for parley, though my companions at first cried for mercy, but as I rushed out with my musket cocked, and presented, they instantly followed me, and an unexpected discharge drove our assailants to seek shelter behind the masses of rock near the cave. A regular skirmish now commenced, in which we kept up a retreating fire, and often exposed ourselves to their shot, for the sake of getting to our mules at the foot of the hill. During a full hour of this kind of running fight, none of our party was hurt. From the first it seemed evident to us that we had been betrayed by our Deborah guide, and our notion was at length confirmed by his going over to the assailing party, and using his arms against us. Fortunately, and justly too, this man was himself wounded by a ball from my musket, and when he fell shrieking, on the side of the hill, his companions hastened to his relief, while we profited by the alarm of the moment to continue our retreat, and rejoin our mules below. Here we drew off at a short distance from the village of Deborah, and, with arms in our hands, being exhausted and fatigued, refreshed ourselves beneath a tree; but we had not yet remounted, when a large party, professing to be from the sheik of Deborah, a village consisting only of a few huts, came to sequester our beasts, for what they called the public service. We treated this with a proper degree of warmth, and threatened death to the first that should dare to lay hands on any thing belonging to us: so that the brave villagers kept aloof."—BUCKINGHAM.

Ver. 19. And he said unto her, Give me, I pray thee, a little water to drink; for I am thirsty. And she opened a bottle of milk, and gave him drink, and covered him.

The method of making butter in the East, illustrates the conduct of Jael, the wife of Heber, described in the book of Judges: "And Sisera said unto her, Give me, I pray thee, a little water to drink, for I am thirsty: and she opened a bottle of milk, and gave him drink, and covered him." In the song of Deborah, the statement is repeated: "He asked water, and she gave him milk, she brought forth butter in a lordly dish." The word (חמאה *hemah*) which our translators rendered butter, properly signifies cream; which is undoubtedly the meaning of it in this passage, for Sisera complained of thirst, and asked a little water to quench it, a purpose to which butter is but little adapted. Mr. Harmer indeed urges the same objection to cream, which, he contends, few people would think a very proper beverage for one that was extremely thirsty; and concludes, that it must have been buttermilk which Jael, who had just been churning, gave to Sisera. But the opinion of Dr. Russell is preferable, that the *hemah* of the scriptures, is probably the same as the *haymak* of the Arabs, which is not, as Harmer supposed, simple cream, but cream produced by simmering fresh sheeps' milk for some hours over a slow fire. It could not be butter newly churned, which Jael presented to Sisera, because the Arab butter is apt to be foul, and is commonly passed through a strainer before it is used; and Russell declares, he never saw butter offered to a stranger, but always *haymak:* nor did he ever observe the Orientals drink buttermilk, but always *leban*, which is coagulated sour milk, diluted with water. It was *leban*, therefore, which Pococke mistook for buttermilk, with which the Arabs treated him in the Holy Land. A similar conclusion may be drawn concerning the butter and milk which the wife of Heber presented to Sisera; they were forced cream or *haymak*, and *leban*, or coagulated sour milk diluted with water, which is a common and refreshing beverage in those sultry regions.—PAXTON.

Ver. 21. Then Jael Heber's wife took a nail of the tent, and took a hammer in her hand, and went softly unto him, and smote the nail into his temples, and fastened it into the ground: (for he was fast asleep and weary:) so he died.

Shaw, describing the tents of the Bedouin Arabs, says, "these tents are kept firm and steady, by bracing or stretching down their eaves with cords tied down to hooked wooden pins well pointed, which they drive into the ground with a mallet; one of these pins answering to the nail, as the mallet does to the hammer, which Jael used in fastening to the ground the temples of Sisera."—BURDER.

CHAPTER V.

Ver. 6. In the days of Shamgar the son of Anath, in the days of Jael, the highways were unoccupied, and the travellers walked through byways.

There are roads in these countries, but it is very easy to turn out of them, and go to a place by winding about over the lands, when that is thought safer. Dr. Shaw takes notice of this circumstance in Barbary, where, he says, they found no hedges, or mounds, or enclosures, to retard or molest them. To this Deborah doubtless refers, though the doctor does not apply this circumstance to that passage, when she says, "In the days of Shamgar, the son of Anath, in the days of Jael, the highways were unoccupied, and the travellers walked through byways," or crooked ways, according to the margin, Judges v. 6. The account Bishop Pococke gives of the manner in which that Arab, under whose care he had put himself, conducted him to Jerusalem, illustrates this with great liveliness, which his lordship tells us was by night, and not by the highroad, but through the fields; "and I observed," says he, "that he avoided as much as he could going near any village or encampment, and sometimes stood still, as I thought, to hearken." And just in that manner people were obliged to travel in Judea, in the days of Shamgar and Jael.—HARMER.

Ver. 10. Speak, ye that ride on white asses, ye that sit in judgment, and walk by the way.

The ancient Israelites preferred the young ass for the saddle. It is on this account, the sacred writers so frequently mention riding on young asses and on ass colts. They must have found them, from experience, like the young of all animals, more tractable, lively, and active, than their parents, and, by consequence, better adapted to this employment. Buffon remarked particularly of the young ass, that it is a gay, nimble, and gentle animal, "and therefore, to be preferred for riding to the same animal, when become lazy and stubborn through age." "Indeed the Hebrew name of the young ass, עיר," from a root which signifies to rouse or excite, "is expressive of its character for sprightliness and activity." On public and solemn occasions, they adorned the asses which they rode, with rich and splendid trappings. "In this manner," says an excellent writer of Essays on Sacred Zoology, "the magistrates in the time of the Judges, appear to have rode in state. They proceeded to the gate of their city, where they sat to hear causes, in slow procession, mounted on asses superbly caparisoned with white cloth, which covered the greater part of the animal's body. It is thus that we must interpret the words of Deborah: 'Speak, ye that ride on white asses,' on asses caparisoned with coverings made of white woollen cloth, 'ye that sit in judgment, and walk,' or march in state, 'by the way.' The colour is not that of the animal, but of his *hiran* or covering, for the ass is commonly dun, and not white." No doubt can be entertained in relation to the existence of the custom alluded to in this quotation. It prevails among the Arabs to the present day; but it appears rather unnatural, to ascribe the colour of a covering to the creature that wears it. We do not call a man white or black, because he happens to be dressed in vestments of white or black cloth; neither did the Hebrews. The expression naturally suggests the colour of the animal itself, not of its trappings; and the only point to be ascertained, is, whether the ass is found of a white colour. Buffon informs us, that the colour of the ass is not dun but flaxen, and the belly of a silvery white. In many instances the silvery white predominates; for Cartwright, who travelled into the East, affirms that he beheld on the banks of the Euphrates, great droves of wild beasts, among which were many wild asses all white. Oppian describes the wild asses, as having a coat of silvery white; and the one which professor Gmelin brought from Tartary, was of the same colour. White asses, according to Morier, come from Arabia; their scarcity makes them valuable, and gives them consequence. The men of the law count it a dignity, and suited to their character, to ride on asses of this colour. As the Hebrews always appeared in white garments at their public festivals and on days of rejoicing, or when the courts of justice were held; so, they naturally preferred white asses, because the colour suited the occasion, and because asses of this colour being more rare and costly, were more coveted by the great and wealthy. The same view is taken of this question by Lewis, who says, the asses in Judea "were commonly of a red colour; and therefore white asses were highly valued, and used by persons of superior note and quality." In this passage, he clearly speaks of the colour of the animals themselves, not of their coverings.—PAXTON.

Ver. 11. *They that are delivered* from the noise of archers in the places of drawing water.

Dr. Shaw mentions a beautiful rill in Barbary, which is received into a large basin, called *shrub we krub*, drink and away, there being great danger of meeting there with rogues and assassins. If such places are proper for the lurking of murderers in times of peace, they must be proper for the lying in ambush in times of war: a circumstance that Deborah takes notice of in her song, Judges v. 11. But the writer who is placed first in that collection, which is entitled Gesta Dei per Francos, gives a more perfect comment still on that passage: for, speaking of the want of water, which the Croisade army so severely felt, at the siege of Jerusalem, he complains, that besides their being forced to use water that stunk, and barley bread, their people were in continual danger from the Saracens, who, lying hid near all the fountains, and places of water, everywhere destroyed numbers of them, and carried off their cattle. To which may be added a story from William of Tyre, relating to Godfrey, Duke of Lorrain, afterward king of Jerusalem, who, stopping short of Antioch five or six miles, to which place he was returning, in order to take some refreshment in a pleasant grassy place near a fountain, was suddenly set upon by a number of horsemen of the enemy, who rushed out of a reedy fenny place near them, and attacked the duke and his people.—HARMER.

Ver. 17. Gilead abode beyond Jordan: and why did Dan remain in ships? Asher continued on the seashore, and abode in his breaches.

Though the coast of that part of Syria which is denominated Palestine, is not remarkable for the number of its ports, yet besides Joppa, St. John d'Acre, Caipha under Mount Carmel, and a few others that might be named, there are some creeks, and small convenient places, where little vessels, and such are those that are used for fishing, may shelter themselves, and land what they take, though there are very few rivers on all that coast. To these places Deborah seems to refer, when she says, *Asher continued on the seashore, and abode in his breaches*, or creeks, as it is translated in the margin.—HARMER.

Ver. 21. The river of Kishon swept them away, that ancient river, the river Kishon. O my soul, thou hast trodden down strength.

The Kishon, whose furious current swept away the routed legions of Sisera, though mentioned in scripture as a river, is only a small stream, except when swelled by the rain or melting snow. "That ancient river" pursues his course down the middle of the plain of Esdraelon, and then passing close by the side of Mount Carmel, falls into the sea at a place named Caipha. When Maundrell crossed this stream, on his way to Jerusalem, its waters were low and inconsiderable; but in passing along the side of the plain, he observed the tracts of many tributary rivulets falling down into it from the mountains, by which it must be greatly swelled in the rainy season. It was undoubtedly at the season when the Kishon, replenished by the streams of Lebanon, becomes a deep and impetuous torrent, that the bands of Sisera perished in its waters. The Kishon, like several other streams in Palestine, does not run with a full current into the sea, except in the time of the rains, but percolates through the sands which interpose between it and the Mediterranean. It has been immortalized in the song of Deborah and Barak: "The kings came and fought; then fought the kings of Canaan in Tanach by the waters of Megiddo; they took no gain of money. They fought from heaven; the stars in their courses fought against Sisera." The confederate kings took no gain for money; they were volunteers in the war, stimulated only by hatred and revenge. But they strove in vain; the hosts of heaven fought for Israel; the stars in their courses, against the powerful bands of Jabin. By the malignant influences of the heavenly bodies, by the storms of hail, thunder, and rain, produced, it is probable, by the power, and directed by the sagacity of holy angels, the confident hopes of Sisera were blasted, and a mark of eternal infamy stamped upon his name. From heaven, says the Chaldee Paraphrast, from heaven, the place where the stars go forth, war was commenced against Sisera; the God of heaven shot forth his arrows, and discomfited the hostile armies; and the river of Kishon, swelled over all its banks by the furious tempests, engaged also in the warfare, by the command of its sovereign Lord, and swept the fugitives away. For this stroke of vengeance, the Kishon was ordained of old: and this is the reason the inspired bard applies to it the distinguishing epithet in the text: "The river of Kishon swept them away; that *ancient* river, the river Kishon. O my soul, thou hast trodden down strength."—PAXTON.

Ver. 25. He asked water, *and* she gave *him* milk; she brought forth butter in a lordly dish.

Though the bowls and dishes of the vulgar Arabs are of wood, those of their emirs are, not unfrequently, of copper, tinned very neatly: La Roque takes notice of this circumstance in more places than one. I have met with a like account, I think, in other travellers. May we not believe that the vessel which Jael made use of, to present buttermilk to Sisera, and which Deborah in her hymn calls a *lordly* dish, or a dish of *nobles*, was of this sort? Her husband certainly was an Arab emir; the working of metals much more ancient than her time, Gen. iv. 22; and the mere size of the vessel hardly could be the thing intended. La Roque, indeed, tells us, that the fruits that were brought in at the collation, that the grand emir of the Arabs, whom he visited, treated him with, were placed in a large painted basin of wood; its being painted was, without doubt, a mark of honour set on this vessel of the grand emir, which distinguished it from the wooden bowls of the commonalty; but a painted wooden vessel would have been not so proper for buttermilk, as one of copper tinned, which therefore most probably was the sort Jael used.—HARMER.

Speaking of the hospitable manner in which he was received at a house in Tronyen in Norway, Dr. Clarke says, "If but a bit of butter be called for in one of these houses, a mass is brought forth weighing six or eight pounds; and so highly ornamented, being turned out of moulds, with the shape of cathedrals set off with Gothic spires, and various other devices, that, according to the language of our English farmers' wives, we should deem it almost a pity to cut it. Throughout this part of Norway, the family plate of butter seemed to be the state dish of the house: wherever we sat down to make a meal, this offering was first made, as in the tents of the primeval Arabs, when Jael, the wife of Heber the Kenite, brought forth butter in a lordly dish."—BURDER.

Ver. 30. Have they not sped? have they *not* divided the prey; to every man a damsel *or* two; to Sisera a prey of divers colours, a prey of divers colours of needle-work, of divers colours of needle-work on both sides, *meet* for the necks of *them that take* the spoil?

See on Is. 3. 18.

CHAPTER VI.

Ver. 19. And Gideon went in, and made ready a kid, and unleavened cakes of an ephah of flour: the flesh he put in a basket, and he put the broth in a pot, and brought *it* out unto him under the oak, and presented *it*.

All roasted meat is a delicacy among the Arabs, and rarely eaten by them, according to La Roque; *stewed meat* also is, according to him, only to be met with among them at feasts, and great tables, such as those of princes, and consequently a delicacy also; the common diet being only boiled meat, with rice pottage and pillaw. This is agreeable to Dr. Pococke's account of an elegant entertainment he met with at Baalbeck, where he tells us they had for supper a roasted fowl, pillaw, stewed meat, with the soup, &c.; and of a grand supper prepared for a great man of Egypt, where he was present, and which consisted, he tells us, of pillaw, a small sheep boiled whole, a lamb roasted in the same manner, roasted fowls, and many dishes of stewed meat in soup, &c. This soup, in which the stewed meat is brought to table, or something very much like it, was, we believe, the broth that Gideon presented to the angel, whom he took for a mere mortal messenger of GOD. Many a reader may have wondered why he should bring out his broth; they may have been ready to think it would have been better to have kept that within, and have given it to the poor after the supposed prophet, whom he desired to honour, should be withdrawn, but these passages explain it: the broth, as our translators express it, was, I imagine, the stewed savoury meat he had prepared, with such sort of liquor as the eastern people at this day bring their stewed meat in, to the most elegant and honourable tables. What then is meant by the flesh put into the basket, Judg. vi. 19? "And Gideon went in, and made ready a kid, and unleavened cakes of an ephah of flour; the flesh he put in a basket, and he put the broth in a pot, and brought it out to him under the oak, and presented it." The preceding quotations certainly do not decipher this perfectly; but I have been inclined to think, there is a passage in Dr. Shaw that entirely unravels this matter, and affords a perfect comment on this text. It is in his preface: "Besides a bowl of milk, and a basket of figs, raisins, or dates, which upon our arrival were presented to us, to stay our appetites, the master of the tent where we lodged, fetched us from his flock, according to the number of our company, a kid or a goat, a lamb or a sheep, half of which was immediately seethed by his wife, and served with cuscasoe; the rest was made kabab, i. e. cut into pieces and roasted; which we reserved for our breakfast or dinner next day." May we not imagine that Gideon presenting some slight refreshment to the supposed prophet, according to the present Arab mode, desired him to stay till he could provide something more substantial for him; that he immediately killed a kid, seethed part of it, made kabab of another part of it, and when it was ready, brought the stewed meat in a pot, with unleavened cakes of bread which he had baked; and kabab in a basket for his carrying away with him, and serving him for some after repast in his journey? Nothing can be more conformable to the present Arab customs, or a more easy explanation of the text; nothing more convenient for the carriage of the reserved meat than a light basket; so Thevenot informs us he carried his ready dressed meat with him in a maund. What others may think of the passage I know not, but I never could, till I met with these remarks, account for his bringing the meat out to the angel in a basket. As for Gideon's leaving the supposed prophet under a tree, while he was busied in his house, instead of introducing him into some apartment of his habitation, and bringing the repast out to him there, we have seen something of it under the last observation; I would here add, that not only Arabs that live in tents, and their dependants, practise it still, but those also that live in houses, as did Gideon. Dr. Pococke frequently observed it among the Maronites, and was so struck with this conformity of theirs to ancient customs, that he could not forbear taking particular notice of it: laymen of quality and ecclesiastics, the patriarchs and bishops, as well as poor obscure priests, thus treating their guests.—HARMER.

Ver. 37. Behold, I will put a fleece of wool in the floor; *and* if the dew be on the fleece only, and *it be* dry upon all the earth *besides*, then shall I know that thou wilt save Israel by my hand, as thou hast said.

In Palestine, as in Greece and Italy, the floor was for the most part in the open air. Thus the thrashing-floor of Gideon appears to have been an open uncovered space, upon which the dews of heaven fell without interruption. "I will put a fleece of wool in the floor, and if the dew be on the fleece only, and it be dry on all the earth besides, then shall I know that thou wilt save Israel by my hand as thou hast said." But a barn, or covered space, had been unfit for such an experiment. The thrashing-floor of Araunah the Jebusite, seems also to have been an open area, else it had not been a proper place for erecting an altar, and offering sacrifice. In the prophecies of Hosea, the idolaters of Israel are compared to the chaff that is driven with the whirlwind out of the floor. Hence it was designedly prepared in a place to which the wind had free access on all sides; and from this exposed situation it derived its name in Hebrew. In Greece, the same kind of situation was chosen; for Hesiod advises his farmer to thrash his corn in a place well exposed to the wind. From this statement, it appears that a thrashing-floor (rendered in our translation a void place) might well be formed near the gate of Samaria, which was built on the summit of a hill; and afforded a very convenient place for the kings of Israel and Judah giving audience to the prophets.—Paxton.

Ver. 38. And it was so: for he rose up early on the morrow, and thrust the fleece together, and wringed the dew out of the fleece, a bowl full of water.

It may seem a little improbable to us who inhabit these northern climates, where the dews are inconsiderable, how Gideon's fleece, in one night, should contract such a quantity, that when he came to wring it, a *bowl full of water* was produced. *Irwin*, in his voyage up the Red Sea, when on the Arabian shores, says, "difficult as we find it to keep ourselves cool in the daytime, it is no easy matter to defend our bodies from the damps of the night, when the wind is loaded with the heavest dews that ever fell; we lie exposed to the whole weight of the dews, and the cloaks in which we wrap ourselves, are as wet in the morning as if they had been immersed in the sea."—Burder.

Ver. 4. And the Lord said unto Gideon, The people *are* yet *too* many; bring them down unto the water, and I will try them for thee there; and it shall be, *that* of whom I say unto thee, This shall go with thee, the same shall go with thee; and of whomsoever I say unto thee, This shall not go with thee, the same shall not go. 5. So he brought down the people unto the water: and the Lord said unto Gideon, every one that lappeth of the water with his tongue, as a dog lappeth, him shalt thou set by himself; likewise every one that boweth down upon his knees to drink. 6. And the number of them that lapped, *putting* their hand to their mouth, were three hundred men: but all the rest of the people bowed down upon their knees to drink water.

The Arabs *lap their milk* and *pottage*, but not their *water*. On the contrary, D'Arvieux tells us, that after they have eaten, they rise from table, and go and drink large draughts out of a pitcher, or, for want of that, out of a leathern bottle, which they hand to one another round and round. Few of the Israelites, if they did in common sup their milk and pottage out of their hands, as the Arabs do, would have been disposed to lap water in the same manner, if they drank too as the Arabs now drink. Two considerations more will complete the illustration of this part of the history of Gideon. The one is, that the eastern people are not wont to drink *standing*. Busbequius, the imperial ambassador at Constantinople, in his celebrated letters concerning the eastern people, affirms this in a very particular manner; the other, that the lapping with their hands is a very expeditious way of taking in liquids. "They are not restrained in their choice," says Dr. Russell. "When they take water with the palms of their hands, they naturally place themselves on their hams to be nearer the water; but when they drink from a pitcher, or gourd, fresh filled, they do not sit down on purpose to drink, but drink standing, and very often put the sleeve of their shirt over the mouth of the vessel, by way of strainer, lest small leeches might have been taken up with the water. It is for the same reason they often prefer taking water with the palm of the hand, to the lapping it from the surface. D'Arvieux, in that accurate account of the Arabs of Mount Carmel, expressly takes notice of this, observing that this may be the reason why spoons are so universally neglected among the Arabs, as a man would eat upon very unequal terms with a spoon, among those that use the palms of their hands instead of them. Until I met with this passage of Busbequius, I could not tell what to make of that particular circumstance of the history of the Jewish judge, that all the rest of the people *bowed down upon their knees* to drink water. It appeared to me rather the putting themselves into an attitude to *lap water*, than any thing else: as I supposed the words signified that they kneeled down by the side of some water in order to drink. But the matter is now clear: three hundred men, immediately upon their coming to the water, drank of it in the quickest manner they could, in order to be ready without delay to follow Gideon; the rest took up water in pitchers, or leathern bottles, or some kind of vessel, and bending down so as to sit jointly upon their heels and knees, or with their knees placed upright before them, either of which might be called bowing their knees to drink, though the last is the posture Busbequius refers to, they handed these drinking vessels with ceremony and slowness from one to another, as they were wont to do in common, which occasioned their dismission. So two-and-twenty thousand of those that were faint-hearted were first sent away; then all the rest, excepting three hundred men of peculiar alacrity and despatch, the most proper for the business for which they were designed, but visibly unequa. to the task of opposing the Midianites; and without some miraculous interposition of God, absolutely unequal."—Harmer.

A dog lappeth by means of forming the end of his tongue into the shape of a shallow spoon, by which he laves or throws up the water into his mouth. The Hottentots have a curious custom, resembling the dog and the three hundred chosen men of Gideon's army. On a journey, immediately on coming to water, they stoop, but no farther than what is sufficient to allow their right hand to reach the water, by which they throw it up so dexterously, that their hand seldom approaches nearer to their mouth than a foot; yet I never observed any of the water to fall down upon their breasts. They perform it almost as quickly as the dog, and satisfy their thirst in half the time taken by another man. I frequently attempted to imitate this practice, but never succeeded, always spilling the water on my clothes, or throwing it against some other part of the face, instead of the mouth, which greatly amused the Hottentot spectators, who then, perhaps for the first time, perceived that there was some art in it.—African Light.

CHAPTER VII.

Ver. 12. And the Midianites, and the Amalekites, and all the children of the East, lay along in the valley like grasshoppers for multitude; and their camels *were* without number, as the sand by the seaside for multitude.

This animal remembers an injury long, and seizes with great keenness a proper opportunity of revenge. A camel's anger is, among the Arabians, a proverb for an irreconcilable enmity. They estimate their riches by the number of their camels. They can sustain great labour and fatigue upon the poorest means of subsistence; travelling four or five days without water, while half a gallon of beans and barley, or a few balls made of the flour, will sustain him for a whole day. Dr. Shaw says, that before drinking, they disturb the water with their feet, first of all thrusting their heads a great way above the nostrils into the water, and then, after the manner of pigeons, make several successive draughts. "Nature has furnished the camel with parts and qualities adapted to the office he is employed to discharge.

The driest thistle and the barest thorn is all the food this useful quadruped requires; and even these, to save time, he eats while advancing on his journey, without stopping, or occasioning a moment of delay. As it is his lot to cross immense deserts, where no water is found, and countries not even moistened with the dew of heaven, he is endued with the power, at one watering-place, to lay in a store, with which he supplies himself for thirty days to come. To contain this enormous quantity of fluid, nature has formed large cisterns within him, from which, once filled, he draws at pleasure the quantity he wants, and pours it into his stomach, with the same effect as if he then drew it from a spring; and with this he travels patiently and vigorously all day long; carrying a prodigious load upon him, through countries infected with poisonous winds, and glowing with parching and never-cooling sands." (Bruce.)—BURDER.

Ver. 13. And when Gideon was come, behold, *there was* a man that told a dream unto his fellow, and said, Behold, I dreamed a dream, and, lo, a cake of barley-bread tumbled into the host of Midian, and came unto a tent, and smote it that it fell, and overturned it, that the tent lay along.

Barley-bread is in some regions of Persia commonly used by the lower orders. It must not however be omitted, that in making bread, barley was used before any other sort of corn; for it is reported, says Artemidorus, that this was the first food which the gods imparted to mankind; and it was, according to Pliny, the most ancient sort of provision. But in more civilized ages, to use the words of the same author, barley-bread came to be the food of beasts only; yet it was still used by the poorer sort, who were not able to furnish their tables with better provisions; and in the Roman camp, as Vegetius and Livy inform us, soldiers who had been guilty of any offence, were fed with barley, instead of bread corn. An example of this punishment is recorded in the history of the second Punic war. The cohorts that lost their standards, had an allowance of barley assigned by Marcellus. And Augustus Cesar commonly punished the cohorts which gave way to the enemy, by a decimation, and allowing them no provision but barley. So mean and contemptible, in the estimation of the numerous and well-appointed armies of Midian, was Gideon, with his handful of undisciplined militia; but guided by the wisdom, and supported by the power of the living God, he inflicted a deserved and exemplary punishment on these proud oppressors. The meagre barley-cake was put into the hand of Midian by the God of armies, as a punishment for disobedience of orders, not to make a full end of his chosen people. "And when Gideon was come, behold, there was a man that told a dream unto his fellow, and said, Behold, I dreamed a dream, and lo, a cake of barley-bread tumbled into the host of Midian, and came unto a tent, and smote it that it fell, and overturned it, that the tent lay along. And his fellow answered and said, This is nothing else save the sword of Gideon, the son of Joash, a man of Israel; for into his hand hath God delivered Midian, and all the host."—PAXTON.

Ver. 16. And he divided the three hundred men *into* three companies, and he put a trumpet in every man's hand, with empty pitchers, and lamps within the pitchers.

Though it must, one would think, be much more convenient to carry water in skins or leathern bottles, when water must be carried, and accordingly, such we find are generally made use of in the East in travelling; yet, whatever the cause may be, they sometimes content themselves with earthen jars. Thus we find, in the beginning of Dr. Chandler's expeditions, in search of the antiquities of these countries, though he was equipped under the direction of a Jew of that country, of such eminence as to act as the British consul at the Dardanelles, and was attended at first by him, yet the vessel in which their water was to be carried, was an earthen jar, which not only served them in the wherry in which they coasted some of the nearer parts of Asia Minor, but was carried upon the ass of a poor peasant, along with other luggage, when they made an excursion from the seaside up into the country, to visit the great ruin at Troas. This may serve to remove our wonder that Gideon should be able to collect three hundred water-jars from among ten thousand men, for we have no reason to suppose the method he was to make use of, to surprise the Midianites, was not suggested to him before he dismissed all the army to the three hundred. In an army of ten thousand Israelitish peasants, collected together on a sudden, there might be many goat-skin vessels for water, but many might have nothing better than earthen jars, and three hundred water-jars, collected from the whole army, were sufficient to answer the views of divine Providence.—HARMER.

CHAPTER VIII.

Ver. 7. And Gideon said, Therefore, when the LORD hath delivered Zebah and Zalmunna into my hand, then I will tear your flesh with the thorns of the wilderness, and with briers.

Thus did Gideon threaten the inhabitants of Succoth; and thus do masters, fathers, and schoolmasters, swear they will punish those who have offended them. To see the force of the figure, it must be kept in mind that the people are almost in a state of nudity. To tear a man's naked body, therefore, with briers and thorns, would be no small punishment. See poor travellers sometimes, who, in consequence of a wild beast, or some other cause, have to rush into the thicket; before they can get out again, in consequence of thorns, they are literally covered with blood. There have been instances where a master, in his anger, has taken the jagged edge of the palmirah branch, to tear the naked body of his slave, and nothing can be more common than to threaten it shall be done to those who have given offence. People also often menace each other with the repetition of the old punishment of tying the naked body in a bundle of thorns, and rolling it on the ground.—ROBERTS.

This threat probably relates to a cruel method of torture used in those times for putting captives to death, by laying briers and thorns on their naked bodies, and then drawing over them some heavy implements of husbandry. Drusius thinks, that persons put to death in this manner were laid naked on thorns and briers, and then trampled on.—BURDER.

Ver. 18. As thou *art*, so *were* they; each one resembled the children of a king.

Of a person who is beautiful or of a fair complexion, who is courageous and stately in his gait, it is said in the East, "He is like the son of a king." "He is as the son of Manmathon (Cupid.") "He is the son of a god."—ROBERTS.

CHAPTER IX.

Ver. 8. The trees went forth *on a time* to anoint a king over them; and they said unto the olive-tree, Reign thou over us.

The people of the East are exceedingly addicted to apologues, and use them to convey instruction or reproof, which with them could scarcely be done so well in any other way. Has a man been told a secret, he says, in repeating it, for instance, "A tree told me this morning, that Kandan offered a large bribe to the Modeliar, to get Muttoo turned out of his situation." Does a man of low caste wish to unite his son in marriage to the daughter of one who is high, the latter will say, "Have you heard that the pumpkin wants to be married to the plantain tree?" Is a wife steril, "The cocoa-nut tree in Viraver's garden does not bear any fruit." Has a woman had children by improper intercourse, it is said of her husband's garden, "Ah, the palmirah-trees are now giving cocoa-nuts." Has a man given his daughter in marriage to another who uses her unkindly, he says, "I have planted the sugar-cane by the side of the *margossa* (bitter) tree."—ROBERTS.

Ver. 27. And they went out into the fields, and gathered their vineyards, and trode *the grapes*, and made merry, and went into the house of their god, and did eat and drink, and cursed Abimelech.

In the East they still tread their grapes after the ancient manner. "August 20, 1765, the vintage (near Smyrna) was now begun, the juice (of the grapes) was expressed for wine; a man, with his feet and legs bare, was treading the fruit in a kind of cistern, with a hole or vent near the bottom, and a vessel beneath to receive the liquor." (Chandler's Travels in Greece.)—BURDER.

Ver. 33. Then mayest thou do to them as thou shalt find occasion.

The Hebrew has, "As thy hand shall find." (1 Sam. x. 7, margin.) In asking a favour, it is common to say, "You must not deny me, sir; but as your hand finds opportunity, so you must assist me."—"Well, my friend, when I have the opportunity of the hand, I will assist you." "The man has assisted me according to the opportunity of his hand; what can he do more?"—ROBERTS.

Ver. 36. And when Gaal saw the people, he said to Zebul, Behold, there come people down from the top of the mountains. And Zebul said unto him, Thou seest the shadow of the mountains as *if they were* men.

Our translation of the book of Judges, from the Hebrew, represents Zebul as saying to Gaal, upon his being alarmed at seeing troops of men making to him, *Thou seest the shadows of the mountains as if they were men;* whereas, Josephus represents him as telling him, he mistook the shadow of the rocks for men. A commentator might be at a loss to account for this change, that had not read Doubdan's representation of some part of the Holy Land, in which he tells us, that in those places there are many detached rocks scattered up and down, some growing out of the ground, and others are fragments, broken off from rocky precipices, the shadow of which, it appears, Josephus thought might be most naturally imagined to look like troops of men at a distance, rather than the shadow of the mountains.—SHAW.

The dreariness of the far-stretching ruins was dismally increased by the shadowy hour of our approach; and being again in the region of the Bactriani descents, our own flitting shades, as we passed between old mouldering walls and the moonlight, sometimes bore an alarming interpretation. Our mehmander was ready to embattle every frowning heap with a murderous legend.—SIR R. K. PORTER.

CHAPTER X.

Ver. 4. And he had thirty sons that rode on thirty ass-colts, and they had thirty cities, which are called Havoth-jair unto this day, which *are* in the land of Gilead.

To ride upon an ass was, in the days of the Judges, a mark of distinction, to which it is probable the vulgar might not presume to aspire. This is evident from the brief notices which the inspired historian gives of the greatness and richness of Jair, the Gileadite, one of these judges: "he had thirty sons that rode on thirty ass-colts; and they had thirty cities, which are called Havoth-jair unto this day." Abdon the Pirathonite, another of these judges, "had forty sons and thirty nephews, that rode on threescore and ten ass-colts." It is reasonable to suppose, that the manners and customs of the chosen tribes underwent a change when the government became monarchical, and the fascinating pleasures of a court began to exert their usual influence; still, however, the ass kept his place in the service of the great. Mephibosheth, the grandson of Saul, rode on an ass; as did Ahithophel, the prime minister of David, and the greatest statesman of that age. Even so late as the reign of Jehoram, the son of Ahab, the services of this animal were required by the wealthy Israelite: the Shunamite, a person of high rank, saddled her ass, and rode to Carmel, the residence of Elisha, to announce the death of her son to the prophet, and to solicit his assistance.—PAXTON.

Ver. 8. And that year they vexed and oppressed the children of Israel eighteen years.

The Hebrew has, "crushed." Of a severe master it is said, "He crushes his servants." "Ah! my lord, crush me not." "When will the king cease to crush his people?"—ROBERTS.

CHAPTER XI.

Ver. 30. And Jephthah vowed a vow unto the LORD, and said, If thou shalt without fail deliver the children of Ammon into my hands,
31. Then it shall be, that whatsoever cometh forth of the doors of my house to meet me, when I return in peace from the children of Ammon, shall surely be the LORD'S, and I will offer it up for a burnt-offering.

One species of vow called *Cherem*, (for which, in German, we generally use the terms *Bann*, *Verbannen*, &c.; but in a thing altogether foreign to us, I rather choose to abide by the Hebrew word,) was, from ancient usage, more sacred and irremissible than all others. Moses nowhere mentions what Cherem was, nor by what solemnities or expressions it was distinguished from other vows; but presupposes all this as already well known. But from Lev. xxvii. 21, every one must see, that there was a difference between a Cherem and other vows; for if a man had vowed his field, and omitted to redeem it, it devolved unto God in the same way as the *field of Cherem*, for ever, and beyond the power of future redemption; and in ver. 28, 29, it is expressly ordained, that a Cherem can never be redeemed like other vows, but continues consecrated to God; and if it be a man, that he shall be put to death. I have already stated, that of the formalities which distinguished the Cherem from common vows, we know nothing; nor does the etymology of the term at all aid our conjectures, for the radical word in Arabic means, *to consecrate;* but every thing *vowed* or devoted, was consecrated. The species of Cherem with which we are best acquainted, was the previous devotement to God of hostile cities, against which they intended to proceed with extreme severity; and *that* with a view the more to inflame the minds of the people to war. In such cases, not only were all the inhabitants put to death, but also, according as the terms of the vow declared, no booty was made by any Israelite; the beasts were slain; what would not burn, as gold, silver, and other metals, was added to the treasure of the sanctuary; and every thing else, with the whole city, burnt, and an imprecation pronounced upon any attempt that should ever be made to rebuild it. Of this the history of Jericho (Josh. vi. 17—19, 21—24, and vii. 1, 12—26) furnishes the most remarkable example. In Moses' lifetime we find a similar vow against the king of Arad, Numb. xxi. 1—3. The meaning, however, as we see from the first-mentioned example, was not, that *houses* might *never* again be built on the accursed spot; for to *build a city*, here means *to fortify it.* Joshua himself seems to explain it thus; for in his curse he makes use of this expression, "Cursed be he who rebuilds this city Jericho; for his first-born son shall he found it, and for his latest, set up its gates." The *beginning*, therefore, of the building of a city, is to *found it;* which can hardly be to lay the foundation stone of a single house, (for who, whether Hebrew or not, ever called *that* founding a city?) but of the city walls; and its *conclusion*, is to set up its gates. The history still further confirms this, as the meaning of the term *to build;* Jericho was so advantageously situated for all manner of trade, because near the usual passage across the Jordan, that it could not long remain a place entirely desolate. In fact, as early as the time of the Judges, Jericho, or, as it was then called, *the city of palms*, appeared again as a town, subdued by the Moabites; (Judg. iii. 13, compared with Deut. xxxiv. 3;) and in David's time, we have unquestionable proof of the existence of a city of the name of Jericho. See 2 Sam. x. 5. But notwithstanding all this, Joshua's imprecation was not yet trespassed; but, at least 100 years after David's death, Jericho was first *rebuilt* (that is, fortified) by Hiel the Bethelite; and in laying its foundation he lost his first-born son, and in setting up the gates, his youngest, 1 Kings xvi. 34.

If an Israelitish city introduced the worship of strange gods, it was in like manner to be devoted, or consecrated to God, and to remain unrebuilt for ever; Deut. xiii. 16—18. In these cases, therefore, *consecrated*, or *devoted*, is nearly equivalent to the Latin phrase, *ejus caput Jovi sacrum esto*, or *sacer esto*. The consecration of the transgressor to God made the remission of his punishment impossible. It is easy to perceive, that this master-piece of legislative policy ought never to have its importance lessened by an injudicious application to common crimes, that do not affect the principles of the constitution: and therefore, so much the greater was the abuse which Saul made of the *Cherem*, when, in issuing an arbitrary inconsiderate order, he swore that whoever trespassed it should die; this was, in fact, making the offender against his whim, a *Cherem;* and accordingly we see, that the people did not mind the oath of their king, but insisted on saving Jonathan, whom, because he had eaten a little honey, his father had devoted to death. 1 Sam. xiv. 24—45. But a still grosser abuse of the *Cherem*, proceeding from imitation of foreign and heathenish practices, we shall probably find in the history of Jephthah, Judges, chap. xi. This brave barbarian, an illegitimate child, and without inheritance, who had from his youth been a robber, and was now, from being the leader of banditti, transformed into a general, had vowed, if he conquered the Ammonites, to make a burnt-offering to the Lord of whatever should first come out of his house to meet him, on his return. This vow was so absurd, and at the same time so contrary to the Mosaic law, that it could not possibly have been accepted of God, or obligatory. For, what if a dog, or an ass, had first met him? Could he have offered *it?* By the law of Moses no unclean beast could be brought to the altar; nor yet even all clean ones; but of quadrupeds, only oxen, sheep, and goats. Or, what if a man had first met him? Human sacrifices Moses had most rigidly prohibited, and described as the abomination of the Canaanites; of which we shall afterward say more, under criminal law; but Jephthah, who had early been driven from his home, and had grown up to manhood among banditti in the land of Tob, might not know much of the laws of Moses, and probably was but a bad lawyer, and just as bad a theologian. The neighbouring nations used human sacrifices: the Canaanites, especially, are by Moses and the other sacred writers often accused of this abominable idolatry, of which we find still more in the Greek and Latin authors; and possibly, therefore, Jephthah, when he made the vow, may have thought of being met, not merely by a beast, but by a slave, whom, of course, he would sacrifice, after the heathen fashion. His words are, "If thou givest the Ammonites into my hands, whatever first cometh forth from my house to meet me on my happy return from the Ammonites, shall be the Lord's, and I will bring it to him as a burnt-offering."—Most unfortunately, his only daughter first came out to congratulate him: and the ignorant barbarian, though extremely affected at the sight, was yet so superstitious, and so unacquainted with the religion and laws of his country, as to suppose he could not recall his vow. His daughter too was heroic enough to fulfil it, on her part; requesting only two months respite, for the romantic purpose of going with her companions into lonely dales, there to lament that she must die a virgin. Then, after two months' absence, this hapless maid, who, either from ambition or superstition, was a willing victim to her father's inconsiderate vow, actually returned; and Jephthah, it is said, *did with her as he had vowed;* which cannot well mean any thing else, than that he put her to death, and burnt her body as a burnt-offering. The greater number of expositors, indeed, would fain explain the passage differently, because they look upon Jephthah as a saint, who could not have done any thing so abominable. "Human sacrifices," say they, "are clearly contrary to the law of Moses."—Very true.—But how many things have ignorance and superstition done in the world, that expressly contradict the law of God! Have we not, among Christians, seen persecutions and massacres on account of religion, with various other atrocities, and abominable proceedings, that are just as directly repugnant to the gospel, as any human sacrifice could be to the laws of Moses?—"But would the high-priest have accepted such an offering, and brought it to the altar?"—I certainly believe not; but we find not a word spoken of the high-priest, but only of Jephthah. What if he had performed the sacrifice himself? This would certainly have been a transgression of the Levitical law; which enjoined that every offering should be made by the hand of the priest, and at the place where the tabernacle and altar stood. But that injunction had, on numberless occasions, been violated by the Israelites, and had, by the opposite usage, become almost abrogated. Jephthah, who, from superstitious ignorance, was, in the sacrifice of his daughter, after the Canaanitish fashion, about to perpetrate a most abominable act, forbidden not only by the law of his country, but also by the law of nature, might very well have been guilty of the lesser fault, now actually a very common one, of making his offering in the country beyond Jordan, of which he was himself master. Amid all the doubts that we start concerning this clearly-related story, we do not consider *who* Jephthah was; a fugitive from his country, who, in foreign lands, had collected and headed a band of robbers; nor yet *where* he now ruled,—beyond Jordan, in the land of Gilead. And a still more important circumstance mentioned in the chapter (xii.) immediately following our story, has been most inadvertently overlooked. Immediately after his victory over the Ammonites, Jephthah went to war with the tribe of Ephraim: but the tabernacle was at Shiloh, within the limits of that tribe; and the high-priest, therefore, could certainly have had no concern with an offering that *Jephthah* meant to make on account of his success, nor would it have been brought to the altar at Shiloh, but made in the land where Jephthah himself ruled. It is unaccountable, that not a single expositor should have attended to this war with the Ephraimites: but that the one half of them should be so simple as to deny, that Jephthah did offer up his daughter, because the high-priest would not have accepted the offering: and the other, in other respects more correct in their opinion, so obliging, as to obviate that objection, by presuming that the high-priest must have been deposed for making such an offering.—This, however, is a controversy into which I will not enter further, because it does not deserve it. That carelessness is too gross, which forgets the end of the eleventh chapter, at the beginning of the twelfth.—MICHAELIS.

CHAPTER XII.

Ver. 3. And when I saw that ye delivered *me* not, I put my life in my hands, and passed over against the children of Ammon.

The Ephraimites had found fault with Jephthah because he did not call them to war against the Ammonites, but he vindicated himself, and addressed them in the language of the verse, as a proof of his courage, and that he had been exposed to danger. The Hindoos use the same figure; and the idea appears to be taken from a man carrying something very precious in his hands, and that under circumstances of great danger. When a son who has been long absent returns home, his father says, "My son has returned from the far country with his life in his hand;" which means, he has passed through many dangers. "Last night, as I went home through the place of evil spirits, I put my life in my hands." "The other day, in passing through the forest, I put my life in my hands, for the beasts were near to me in every direction." "Danger! truly so; I put my life in my bosom." "O that divine doctor! my son was at the point of death, but he brought his life in his hand."—ROBERTS.

Ver. 14. And he had forty sons, and thirty nephews, that rode on threescore and ten ass-colts: and he judged Israel eight years.

To an Englishman, this may appear almost incredible, but we have a great number of similar cases. A man of property has as many wives as he thinks proper to support; and such is the state of morals, that he finds no difficulty in procuring them. I have known men who have had, in each of the neighbouring villages, a wife or concubine. Santherasega, Modeliar of Oodeputty, who has been dead about thirty years, had two wives and six concubines, who bare to him thirty children. The old man is described as being of large stature, and as having indulged in strong kinds of food.—A friend of mine in Manilla knew a man who was the father of forty children.—Lieutenant-colonel Johnson says (in his Travels through Persia) of the king, "The number of his children I could not exactly ascertain: it is generally agreed that he has at least sixty boys and sixty girls living; and many persons add, that there are an equal number deceased, so that their total number must have been two hundred and forty. He has already given in marriage twelve of his daughters; and about twenty-five of the elder of his sons are governors of the principal provinces and cities of the empire. Preparations of fireworks, &c. were at this time making at the palace to celebrate the nuptials of one of his sons, which were to take place in about three weeks."—ROBERTS.

CHAPTER XIII.

Ver. 5. For, lo, thou shalt conceive, and bear a son; and no razor shall come on his head: for the child shall be a Nazarite unto God from the womb.

This command was given to the wife of Manoah, the father of Samson, who had previously been steril. Hannah, the mother of Samuel, was also steril, "and she vowed a vow, and said, O Lord of hosts, if thou wilt indeed look on the affliction of thy handmaid, and remember me, and not forget thy handmaid, but will give unto thy handmaid a man-child, then I will give him unto the Lord all the days of his life, and there shall no razor come upon his head." (Numbers vi. 5. Acts xviii. 18.) All who are married in the East, have an intense desire for children. It is considered disgraceful, and a mark of the displeasure of the gods, to have a childless house. Under these circumstances, husbands and wives perform expensive ceremonies; and vow, that should the gods favour them with a son, "no razor shall come upon his head," (*i. e.* excepting "the corners,") until he shall be ten or twelve years of age. In all schools, boys may be seen with elf-locks of ten or twelve years standing, giving a testimony to the solicitude, superstition, and affection of the parents, and a memorial of the favour of their deities.—ROBERTS.

Ver. 19. So Manoah took a kid with a meat-offering, and offered *it* upon a rock unto the LORD: and *the angel* did wonderously; and Manoah and his wife looked on. 20. For it came to pass, when the flame went up towards heaven from off the altar, that the angel of the LORD ascended in the flame of the altar: and Manoah and his wife looked on *it*, and fell on their faces to the ground.

The circumstances in the histories of Gideon and Manoah are well illustrated, by some things mentioned occasionally by Doubdan, in the account of his journey to the Holy Land, for he speaks of many rocks which he found rising up out of the earth there, and some as parts of great rocks fallen down. Some of them are described in such a manner, as shows they resembled altar-tombs, or altars. Speaking of his return from a town called St. Samuel, to Jerusalem, by a way leading to the sepulchres of the judges of Israel, he tells us, (p. 98, 99,) that he found them in a great field planted with vines, in which were great rocks, which rose out of the earth; among them, one, near the wayside, was so large, as to be hollowed out into several rooms, in whose sides were long and narrow holes cut out, proper for placing the dead in, even with the floor. When he was at Joppa, waiting to embark, upon his return, he describes himself and his companion as placing themselves, after they had walked until they were tired, on the beach, viewing some Greek pilgrims, who were also waiting to take ship, and who amused themselves with dancing on the shore, as placing themselves in the shade of a great rock, newly fallen down from the mountains, (p. 455.) Rocks appear in this country: some in their original situation, rising out of the ground; others are fragments, that have been detached from rocky eminences, and have fallen down on the ground below. Of this considerable number of rocks, some were flat, or nearly flat, on the top, so as conveniently to be used for altars. There are some such now found in that country.—BURDER.

CHAPTER XIV.

Ver. 7. And he went down and talked with the woman; and she pleased Samson well. 8. And after a time he returned to take her.

Ten or twelve months commonly intervened between the ceremony of espousals, and the marriage; during this interval, the espoused wife continued with her parents, that she might provide herself with nuptial ornaments suitable to her station. This custom serves to explain a circumstance in Samson's marriage, which is involved in some obscurity: "He went down," says the historian, "and talked with the woman, (whom he had seen at Timnath,) and she pleased him well." These words seem to refer to the ceremony of espousals; the following to the subsequent marriage, "And after a time he returned to take her." Hence, a considerable time intervened between the espousals, and their actual union.—PAXTON.

Ver. 8. And, behold, *there was* a swarm of bees and honey in the carcass of the lion.

The bee is a gregarious insect, living in a state of society, and subject to a regular government. From this circumstance, its Hebrew name דברה, from a root which signifies to speak, to rule, to lead, is derived. It is an opinion commonly received among the ancients, that bees were propagated in two ways, either by those of their own species, or in the cavities of a dead carcass. Their opinion is beautifully stated by Virgil in these lines:

> "Hic vero subitum ac dictu mirabile monstrum
> Aspiciunt, liquefacta boum per viscera toto
> Stridere apes utero et ruptis effervere costis,
> Immensas que trahi nubes jamque arbore summa
> Confluere, et lentis uvam demittere ramis."

"But here they behold a sudden prodigy, and wondrous to relate, bees through all the belly, hum amid the putrid bowels of the cattle, pour forth with the fermenting juices from the burst sides, and in immense clouds roll along, then swarm together on the top of a tree, and hang down in a cluster from the bending boughs." This opinion, however, is directly contradicted by another, which was held by some writers of the greatest reputation in ancient times. Aristotle taught, that the bee will not light upon a dead carcass, nor taste the flesh. Varro asserts, that she never sits down in an unclean place, or upon any thing which emits an unpleasant smell. They are never seen, like flies, feeding on blood or flesh; while wasps and hornets all delight in such food, the bee never touches a dead body. So much they dislike an impure smell, that when one of them dies, the survivors immediately carry out the carcass from the hive, that they may not be annoyed by the effluvia. The discovery which Samson made, when he went down to Timnath, may seem to contradict the latter, and confirm the former opinion: "And after a time, he returned to take her, and he turned aside to see the carcass of the lion; and behold there was a swarm of bees, and honey in the carcass of the lion." But it is not said the swarm was generated there, but only that Samson found them in the carcass; nor is it said that the lion had been recently killed, and that the carcass was in a state of putrefaction: the contrary seems to be intimated by the phrase *after a time*, literally, after days, one of the most common expressions in scripture for a year. Hence the lion was killed a whole year before this visit to Timnath, when he discovered the swarm in the carcass. But the flesh of the carcass, which Samson left in the open field a whole year, the prey of wild beasts and ravenous birds, must have been entirely consumed long before his return, or so completely dried by the violent heat of the sun, that nothing but the skeleton, or exsiccated frame, remained. Within the bare, or withered enclosure of the bones, which had exhaled their last putrid effluvia, the swarm, in perfect consistency with their usual delicacy, might construct their cells and deposite their honey. This conjecture is confirmed by the testimony of Herodotus, who declares that bees have swarmed in dry bones.—PAXTON.

Ver. 12. And Samson said unto them, I will now put forth a riddle unto you: if ye can certainly declare it me within the seven days of the feast, and find *it* out, then I will give you thirty sheets and thirty change of garments.

It is customary for the Turks and Moors, according to Dr. Shaw, to wear shirts of linen, or cotton, or gauze, under their tunics; but the Arabs wear nothing but woollen. This is frequently the case also with the Arabs of Palestine, it seems, though D'Arvieux gives a contrary account of the Arabs of the camp of the grand emir whom he visited; for Egmont and Heyman assure us, that they saw several Arabian inhabitants of Jaffa going along almost naked, the greatest part of them without so much as a shirt or a pair of breeches, though some wore a kind of a mantle; as for the children there, they ran about almost as naked as they were born, though they had all little chains about their legs as an ornament, and some of silver.—HARMER.

Many of the Arabian inhabitants of Palestine and Barbary wear no shirts, but go almost entirely naked, or with only a cloth cast about their bodies, or a kind of mantle. It is not improbable, that the poorer inhabitants of Judea were clothed in much the same manner as the Arabs of those countries in modern times, having no shirts, but only a sort of mantle to cover their naked bodies. If this be just, it greatly illustrates the promise of Samson to give his companions thirty sheets, or, as it is more properly rendered in the margin of our Bibles, thirty shirts, if they could discover the meaning of his riddle. It cannot easily be imagined they were what we call sheets, for Samson might have slain thirty Philistines near Askelon, and not have found one sheet; or if he slew them who were carrying their beds with them on their travels, as they often do in present times, the slaughter of fifteen had been sufficient, for in the East, as in other countries, every bed is provided with two sheets; but he slew just thirty, in order to obtain thirty sedinim, or shirts. If this meaning of the term be admitted, the deed of Samson must have been very provoking to the Philistines; for since only people of more easy circumstances wore shirts, they were not thirty of the common people that he slew, but thirty persons of figure and consequence. The same word is used by the prophet Isaiah, in his description of the splendid and costly dress in which people of rank and fashion then delighted, rendered in our translation fine linen; which seems to place it beyond a doubt that they were persons of rank that fell by the hand of Samson on that occasion.

But it is by no means improbable, that these sheets were the hykes or blankets already described, which are worn by persons of all ranks in Asia. (See on Deut. 24. 13.) Pococke, who gives a description of this vestment, and of the way in which it is wrapped about the body, which does not materially differ from the account of it in a preceding section, particularly observed, that the young people, and the poorer sort about Faiume, had nothing on whatever, but this blanket; hence it is probable, that the young man was clothed in this manner who followed our Saviour when he was taken, having a linen cloth cast about his naked body. "When the young man," who came to apprehend Jesus, "laid hold of" him, "he left the linen cloth, and fled from them naked:" but this language by no means requires us to suppose that he was absolutely naked, but only that he chose rather to quit his hyke or plaid, than run the risk of being made a prisoner, although by doing so he became unduly exposed. This view is confirmed by the observations formerly made on the hyke and tunic; and by the state of the weather, which was so cold, that the servants of the high-priest were compelled to kindle a fire in the midst of the hall to warm themselves. It is very improbable, that he would go into the garden on such a night so thinly clothed; and we have no reason to think he was so poor, that this linen cloth was the only article of clothing in his possession. But Mr. Harmer, and other expositors, considering that the apostles were generally poor men, and that the poor in those countries had often no other covering than this blanket, rather suppose, that the terrified disciple fled away in a state of absolute nudity. But if it was the apostle John, where was he furnished with clothes to appear almost immediately after in the high-priest's hall? This difficulty Mr. Harmer endeavours to remove by supposing, that from the garden he might go to his usual place of residence in the city, and clothe himself anew before he went to the palace.—PAXTON.

Ver. 15. And it came to pass on the seventh day, that they said to Samson's wife, Entice thy husband, that he may declare unto us the riddle, lest we burn thee and thy father's house with fire: have ye called us to take that we have? *is it* not *so?*

The marriage feast was of old, frequently protracted to the length of seven days; for so long Samson entertained his friends at Timnath. To this festival, Laban is thought by many divines to refer, in his answer to Jacob's complaint, that he had imposed Leah upon him instead of Rachel; "Fulfil the week of the marriage, and we will give thee this also." This feast was called the nuptial joy, with which no other was to be intermixed; all labour ceased while it continued, and no sign of mourning or sorrow was permitted to appear. It may be only further observed, that even in modern times, none but very poor people give a daughter in marriage without a female slave for a handmaid, as hired servants are scarcely known in the oriental regions. Hence Laban, who was a man of considerable property in Mesopotamia, "gave unto his daughter Leah, Zilpah his maid, for a handmaid;" and "to Rachel his daughter, Bilhah his handmaid, to be her maid." In Greece also, the marriage solemnity lasted several days. On the third day, the bride presented her bridegroom with a robe; gifts were likewise made to the bride and bridegroom, by the bride's father and friends; these consisted of golden vessels, beds, couches, plates, and all sorts of necessaries for housekeeping, which were carried in great state to the house by women, preceded by a person carrying a basket, in the manner usual at processions, before whom went a boy in white vestments, with a torch in his hand. It was also customary for the bridegroom and his friends to give presents to the bride, after which, the bridegroom had leave to converse freely with her, and she was permitted to appear in public without her veil. The money, says Dr. Russell, which the bridegrooms of Aleppo pay for their brides, is laid out in furniture for a chamber, in clothes, jewels, or ornaments of gold, for the bride, whose father makes some addition, according to his circumstances: which things are sent with great pomp to the bridegroom's house three days before the wedding.—PAXTON.

Ver. 16. And he said unto her, Behold, I have not told *it* my father nor my mother, and shall I tell *it* thee?

In all parts of the world, I believe, people are pretty much alike as to their capability of keeping secrets. The Hindoos, however, improperly reflect upon the female sex in their proverb, "*To a woman tell not a secret.*" That secret must be great indeed which will prevent a son or daughter from telling it to the father or mother. The greatest proof of confidence is to say, "I have told you what I have not revealed to my father." In proof of the great affection one has for another, it is said, "He has told things to him that he would not have related to his parents." "My friend, do tell me the secret."—"Tell you? yes, when I have told my parents."—ROBERTS.

CHAPTER XV.

Ver. 4. And Samson went and caught three hundred foxes, and took firebrands, and turned tail to tail, and put a firebrand in the midst between two tails.

The book of Judges contains a singular anecdote, of the mischief which Samson did by means of this animal to the property of his enemies. He "went and caught three hundred foxes, and took firebrands, and turned tail to tail, and put a firebrand in the midst, between two tails; and when he had set the brands on fire, he let them go into the standing corn of the Philistines, and burnt up both the shocks, and also the standing corn, with the vineyards and olives." On reading this curious statement, the infidel asks with an air of triumph, How could Samson procure so many foxes in so short a time? To this question it may be answered, the concurring testimony of travellers clearly proves, that the land of promise abounded with foxes. The same fact is suggested by the prediction of David, that his enemies should become the prey of foxes; and by the invitation of Solomon already quoted from the Song. Some districts and cities in that country, take their name from the fox; a sure proof of their numbers in those parts: "Thus, the land of Shual, mentioned in the first book of Samuel, signifies the land of the fox;" and Hazarshual, the name of a city, belonging to the tribe of Judah, or Simeon, means the fox's habitation. Besides, the term foxes, in the opinion of Bochart, embraces the thoes, a species of wolf, which very much resemble the fox, and are extremely numerous in Judea, particularly about Cesarea. Bellonius asserts, that they may be seen in troops of two or three hundred, prowling about in quest of their prey; and Morizon, who travelled in Palestine, says, that foxes swarm in that country, and that very great numbers of them lurk in hedges and in ruinous buildings. To find so many of these animals, therefore, could be no great difficulty to a person accustomed to the chase, as this renowned Israelite may be reasonably supposed to have been. Nor is it said, that Samson caught all these foxes in one, or even in two days; a whole week, or even a month, might be spent in the capture, for any thing that appears to the contrary. Add to this, that, although Samson himself might be a most expert hunter, we have no reason to think he caught all these animals alone. So eminent a personage as the chief magistrate of Israel might employ as many people as he pleased, in accomplishing his purpose. When, for example, it is said, that Solomon built the temple at Jerusalem, no man supposes, that he executed the work with his own hands; he only caused the work to be done: and, in the same manner, Samson may be said to do what he only commanded to be done, or assisted in doing. Nor can it be reasonably denied, that the God who made the world, and by his special providence, watched over the prosperity of his ancient people, and intended, at this time, to deliver them from their enemies, could easily dispose matters, so as to facilitate or secure the capture of as many foxes, as the design of Samson required. In this singular stratagem, he is thought, by some writers, to have had two things in view; at once, to deliver his country from those noxious animals, and to do the greatest possible mischief to his enemies. No kind of animals could be more suited to his purpose, especially when coupled together in this manner; for they run long and swiftly, not in a direct line, but with many windings, so that, while they dragged in opposite directions, they spread the fire over all the fields of the Philistines with the greater rapidity and success, and were at the same time prevented from getting into the woods, or holes in the rocks, where the firebrands had been extinguished, and the stratagem rendered ineffectual.—PAXTON.

Ver. 18. And he was sore athirst, and called on the LORD, Thou hast given this great deliverance into the hand of thy servant: and now shall I die for thirst, and fall into the hand of the uncircumcised? 19. But God clave a hollow place that *was* in the jaw, and there came water thereout; and when he had drunk his spirit came again, and he revived: wherefore he called the name thereof En-hakkore, which *is* in Lehi unto this day.

The impression ordinarily received from this passage by the English reader, viz. that a fountain was opened in the jaw-bone, the instrument of Samson's victory, is probably erroneous. From a preceding verse in this chapter it appears that the Philistines had gone up, and pitched in Judah, and spread themselves *in Lehi*. But as it happens *Lehi* is the original word for *jaw*, or *jaw-bone*, and our translators, following some of the ancient versions, have confounded the name of the place with that of the object from which it was derived. There is no good reason to suppose that the hollow place was cloven *in the jaw itself*, for what can be understood by God's cleaving a cavity which was already in the bone? For if he clave a cavity previously existing, would not the water naturally run through it and empty itself upon the ground? But let the word *Lehi* stand untranslated, and all is plain. A certain cavity in the earth, in the place called *Lehi*, was miraculously cloven and opened, and a refreshing fountain of water gushed forth, which continued thenceforth to flow down to the time when the history was written. This was called, in memory of the circumstance which gave rise to it, "En-hakkore," i. e. *the well or fountain of him that cried*.—B.

All that this passage affirms is, that in the place where Samson then was, and which, from this transaction, he called *Lehi*, or the Jaw-bone, there was a *hollow place* which God clave, from whence a fountain flowed, which relieved Samson when ready to perish, and which continued to yield a considerable supply of water, at the time this sacred book was written, and possibly may flow to this day. Doubdan, in one single day, when he visited the country about Jerusalem, met with two such places. On Easter Monday, the first of April, 1652, he set out, he informs us, with about twenty in company, to visit the neighbourhood of Jerusalem. They went the same road the two disciples are supposed to have taken, when our Lord joined them, when he made their hearts burn within them. A convent was afterward built in the place where our Lord is imagined to have met them. Only some pieces of the walls of freestone are now remaining, with some walls and half-broken arches, and heaps of rubbish, together with a great cistern full of water, derived partly from rain, and partly from the springs in the mountain there, particularly from a most beautiful and transparent fountain, a little above it, which breaks out at the farther end of the grotto, naturally hollowed out in the hard rock, and which is overhung with small trees, where they made a considerable stop to refresh themselves. The water of this spring running by a channel into the cistern, and afterward turning a mill which was just by the cistern, and belonged to the monastery, and from thence flowed, as it still does, into the torrent-bed of that valley, from whence David collected the five smooth stones, of which one proved fatal to Goliath. Here we see a hollow place, a grotto, in which the God of nature had divided the rock for the passage of the water of a beautiful spring. It was a grotto in Lehi, in which God, on this occasion, made the water to gush out, and run in a stream into the adjoining country, where the exhausted warrior stood.—BURDER.

CHAPTER XVI.

Ver. 6. And Delilah said to Samson, Tell me, I pray thee, wherein thy great strength *lieth*, and wherewith thou mightest be bound to afflict thee. 7. And Samson said unto her, If they bind me with seven green withes that were never dried, then shall I be weak, and be as another man.

That is, any kind of pliant, tough wood, twisted in the form of a cord or rope. Such are used in many countries, formed out of osiers, hazle, &c. In Ireland, very long and strong ropes are made of the fibres of bog-wood, or the larger roots of the fir, which is often dug up in the bogs or mosses of that country. In some places, they take the skin of the horse, cut it lengthwise from the hide, into thongs about two inches broad; and after having laid them in salt for some time, take them out for use. This is frequently done in the country parts of Ireland; and is chiefly used for agricultural purposes, particularly for drawing the plough and the harrow, instead of iron chains.—BURDER.

Ver. 7. And Samson said unto her, If they bind me with seven green withes that were never dried, then shall I be weak, and be as another man.

People in England would be much surprised to see what powerful ropes are made from the withes of shrubs or trees. While they are in a green state, they are stronger than any other ropes that are made in the country. Wild elephants, or buffaloes just caught, generally have their legs bound with green withes.—ROBERTS.

Ver. 19. And she made him sleep upon her knees.

It is very amusing to see a full-grown son, or a husband, asleep on his mother's or wife's knees. The plan is as follows: the female sits cross-legged on the carpet or mat, and the man having laid himself down, puts his head in her lap, and she gently taps, strokes, sings, and sooths him to sleep.—ROBERTS.

Ver. 21. But the Philistines took him, and put out his eyes, and brought him down to Gaza, and bound him with fetters of brass; and he did grind in the prison-house.

With the Greeks and Asiatics, the way of putting out the eyes, or blinding, was not by pulling or cutting out the eyes, as some have imagined; but by drawing, or holding a red-hot iron before them. This method is still in use in Asia. According to Chardin, however, the pupils of the eyes were pierced and destroyed on such occasions. But Thevenot says, that "the eyes in these barbarous acts are taken out whole, with the point of a dagger, and carried to the king in a basin." He adds, that, "as the king sends whom he pleases to do that cruel office, some princes are so butchered by unskilful hands, that it costs them their lives." In Persia it is no unusual practice for the king to punish a rebellious city or province by exacting so many pounds of eyes; and his executioners accordingly go and scoop out from every one they meet, till they have the weight required.—BURDER.

The custom of daily grinding their corn for the family, shows the propriety of the law: "No man shall take the nether or the upper millstone to pledge, for he taketh a man's life to pledge;" because if he take either the upper or the nether millstone, he deprives him of his daily provision, which cannot be prepared without them, and, by consequence, exposes him and all his house to utter destruction. That complete and perpetual desolation which, by the just allotment of heaven, is ere long to overtake the mystical Babylon, is clearly signified by the same precept: "The sound of the millstone shall be heard no more at all in thee." The means of subsistence being entirely destroyed, no human creature shall ever occupy the ruined habitations more. In the book of Judges, the sacred historian alludes, with characteristic accuracy, to several circumstances implied in that custom, where he describes the fall of Abimelech. A woman of Thebez, driven to desperation by his furious attack on the tower, started up from the mill at which she was grinding, seized the upper millstone, (פלחרכב) and rushing to the top of the gate, cast it on his head, and fractured his skull. This was the feat of a woman, for the mill is worked only by females: it is not a piece of a millstone, but the *rider*, the distinguishing name of the upper millstone, which literally rides upon the other, and is a piece or *division* of the mill: it was a stone of "two feet broad," and therefore fully sufficient, when thrown from such a height, to produce the effect mentioned in the narrative. It displays also the vindictive contempt which suggested the punishment of Samson, the captive ruler of Israel. The Philistines, with barbarous contumely, compelled him to perform the meanest service of a female slave; they sent him to grind in the prison, but not for himself alone; this, although extremely mortifying to the hero, had been more tolerable; they made him grinder for the prison, while the vilest malefactor was permitted to look on and join in the cruel mockery of his tormentors. Samson, the ruler and avenger of Israel, labours, as Isaiah foretold the virgin daughter of Babylon should labour: "Come down, and sit in the dust, O virgin daughter of Babylon; there is no throne, (no seat for thee,) O daughter of the Chaldeans . . . Take the millstones and grind meal," but not with the wonted song: "Sit thou silent, and get thee into darkness," there to conceal thy vexation and disgrace.—PAXTON.

Ver. 25. And it came to pass, when their hearts were merry, that they said, Call for Samson, that he may make us sport.

"By this time all the kaavy in that house was exhausted, the drinkers therefore removed to another, and Staus, the prisoner, was told to follow; his legs were then tied together, and he was told to jump, while they laughed and shouted, See, our meat is jumping. He asked if this was the place where he was to die. No, his master replied; but these things were always done with foreign slaves. Having seen him dance, they now ordered him to sing; he sung a hymn; they bade him interpret it, and he said it was in praise of God. They then reviled his God; their blasphemies shocked him, and he admired in his heart the wonderful indulgence and long-suffering of God towards them." (Southdey's Brazil.) Don Gabriel de Cardenas gives an account nearly similiar of the treatment of prisoners by the Iroquois Indians. He describes the sufferings of Father Bresano, a Spanish priest, who had the misfortune to be captured by them. As soon as he arrived at the place of assembly, they inflicted many wounds, and treated him in the most cruel manner; as soon as the warriors appeared, he was commanded to sing like the other prisoners; he was also commanded to dance: in vain he excused himself on the plea of inability. Forced into the middle of the circle by these barbarians, he was by one ordered to sing, by another to dance; if he persisted in keeping silence, he was cruelly beaten, and when he attempted to comply with their requests, his treatment was nearly the same. For upward of a month during their revels, he endured the most exquisite sufferings, which were to have been terminated by his being burnt to death, had not one of the chiefs mitigated his sentence, and delivered him to an old woman in place of her grandson, who had been killed some years before.—BURDER.

Ver. 27. Now the house was full of men and women; and all the lords of the Philistines *were* there: and *there were* upon the roof about three thousand men and women, that beheld while Samson made sport.

The method of building in the East, may assist us in accounting for the particular structure of the temple or house of Dagon, and the great number of people that were buried in its ruins, by pulling down the two principal pillars upon which it rested. About three thousand persons crowded the roof, to behold while the captive champion of Israel made sport to his triumphant and unfeeling enemies. Samson, therefore, must have been in a court or area beneath; and consequently, the temple will be of the same kind with the ancient τεμενη, or sacred enclosures, which were only surrounded, either in part or on all sides, with some plain or cloistered buildings. Several palaces and *dou-wanas*, as the halls of justice are called in these countries, are built in this fashion, in whose courts, wrestlers exhibit for the amusement of the people, on their public festivals and rejoicings; while the roofs of these cloisters are crowded with spectators, that behold their feats of strength and agility. When Dr. Shaw was at Algiers, he frequently saw the inhabitants diverted in this manner, upon the roof of the dey's palace; which, like many more of the same quality and denomination, has an advanced cloister *over against the gate of the palace*, made in the form of a large pent-house, supported only by one or two contiguous pillars in the front, or else in the centre. In such open structures as these, the great officers of state distribute justice, and transact the public affairs of their provinces. Here, likewise, they have their public entertainments, as the lords of the Philistines had in the temple of their god. Supposing, therefore, that in the house of Dagon, was a cloistered building of this kind, the pulling down of the front or centre pillars which supported it, would alone be attended with the catastrophe which happened to the Philistines.—PAXTON.

CHAPTER XIX.

Ver. 8. And he arose early in the morning on the fifth day to depart; and the damsel's father said, Comfort thy heart, I pray thee. And they tarried until afternoon, and they did eat both of them.

"Until afternoon." Hebrew, "till the day declined." In this way also do the people of the East speak, when the sun has passed the meridian; "I shall not go till the sun decline;" "I must not go till the declining time."—ROBERTS.

Ver. 27. And her lord rose up in the morning,
and opened the doors of the house, and went
out to go his way; and, behold, the woman his
concubine was fallen down *at* the door of the
house, and her hands *were* upon the threshold.
28. And he said unto her, Up, and let us be
going: but none answered. Then the man
took her *up* upon an ass, and the man rose up,
and gat him unto his place. 29. And when
he was come into his house, he took a knife,
and laid hold on his concubine, and divided
her, *together* with her bones, into twelve pieces,
and sent her into all the coasts of Israel. 30. And
it was so, that all that saw it said, There was
no such deed done nor seen, from the day that
the children of Israel came up out of the land
of Egypt unto this day: consider of it, take advice, and speak *your minds.*

The interpreters say little or nothing of the real views of the Levite, in thus cutting to pieces the body of his concubine, and sending a part to each tribe of Israel. They only say that the Levite was induced to this seeming outrage, merely "to excite a general indignation against the authors of so black a crime; that he committed no sin in thus maltreating a dead body, though it was his own concubine's; as being so far from having any intention to offer it the least indignity, that he only considered the reparation of the ignominy with which his concubine had been treated: and that, after all, the success fully justified his action and conduct." It is certain that the Levite's motives were good and regular: he intended to unite the whole nation in vengeance of a crime in which it was interested, and which covered it with infamy; but it was not, as some have thought, the horror of the spectacle which the Levite held forth to the view of everybody, which produced this effect, and constrained their minds; that is, it was not the sight of these human limbs, thus cut and torn to pieces, which made the Jews conspire, and obliged them to take a striking vengeance of so black a crime.

The bare relation of an outrage so enormous, was sufficient to put the whole nation to the necessity of exacting punishment for an infamy of this nature: natural equity spoke for the Levite; the most sacred rights were violated to the utmost; never was adultery more glaringly committed, or more insolently countenanced: it had involved a whole tribe; a general and universal punishment, therefore, was indispensably necessary; the text of scripture is express in a hundred places; and the Israelites could not be ignorant. But they might be checked by the extent of the punishment; by the great number, the credit, the forces and power of the offenders; by the natural commiseration which is felt for those who are of the same blood; in a word, by an aversion to destroy a city, and to involve it utterly in the vengeance due to it. To oblige the nation to hear none of these reasons, the Levite sought and seized a method which might bind it, and by no means allow it to avoid his pursuits; which, in short, might put them to the indispensable necessity of espousing his and his concubine's interests, or to speak more properly, of taking up the cause of both. The only part, then, which he had to take, was to cut in pieces either the body of his wife, as he did, or else that of an ox, or other like animal, which had been either devoted, or offered in sacrifice, and to send a part of it to each tribe. In consequence of this, every tribe entered into a covenant and indissoluble engagement with them, to see justice done him, for the injury he had received. This is what the interpreters of scripture seem not to have known, and which it is necessary to explain. The ancients had several ways of uniting themselves together by the strictest ties, and these ties lasted for as long as the parties had stipulated. Among these, there were two principal; both admirably well described in the sacred books. The first is that sacrifice of Abraham, the circumstances of which are mentioned, Gen. xv. 9, &c. The second is as follows:—A bullock was offered in sacrifice, or devoted: it was cut in pieces and distributed; all who had a piece of this sacrificed or devoted bullock, were from thenceforward connected, and were to concur in the carrying on the affair which had given place to the sacrifice. But this sacrifice or devoting, and this division, was variously practised, which also produced engagements somewhat different. If he who was at the expense of the sacrifice or devoting, were a public person, in a high office—a king, for instance, a prince, or judge—that is to say, a chief magistrate, or had the principal authority in a city, or state; he sent, of his own accord, a piece of the victim or animal devoted, to all who were subject to him; and by this act they were obliged to enter into his views, to obey him, and to execute his orders without examination, or pretending difficulty or incapacity. If, on the contrary, the sacrifice were offered by a private person, those only who voluntarily took a piece of the sacrificed or devoted portions, entered into a strict engagement to espouse the interest of him who sacrificed or devoted, and to employ therein their fortunes and their persons. Connexions of this kind derived their force from the deities in honour of whom the sacrifice was offered, or the devotion made: from the true God, when the devotion was made by the Jews; from idols, when the sacrifice was offered by the gentiles. The devotion was adopted by the Jews, and the sacrifice by the pagans. This difference betwixt them, produced a second: the Jews were content to invoke and take to witness the Lord; whereas the pagans never failed to place in the midst of them, upon an altar of green turf, the deities who presided over their covenant; and these kind of deities were called common, because in fact they were the common deities of all who are thus united, and received in common the honours which they thought proper to pay them.

These facts place the Levite's intents in their full light. His cutting in pieces the body of his concubine, was an anathema, a devoting which he made to the Lord; and his sending a part of the pieces to each tribe, clearly signified that he considered all the tribes as subject to the same anathema. God authorized these kinds of consecrations. The scripture is full of examples, which represent sometimes persons, sometimes whole nations, whom he had himself smitten with a curse. He would have no sacrifices, however, of human victims; but he approved of devotions to death: and yet, to consider both in certain points of view, they amounted nearly to the same thing. Again, devotion to death was a much stronger obligation than the promise of a sacrifice. A sacrifice vowed might be dispensed with, and redeemed; whereas, so soon as the anathema was pronounced, the party was for ever bound, and there was no room for redemption, Lev. xxvii. 28, 29. It is certain that the Levite had a right to devote his wife to death, while she lived; much more reasonably, then, might he devote her body when dead. It is so much the more probable that he really did so, as there was no other method of devotion and anathema that could induce the whole nation to be bound to declare itself in his favour. This anathema, as has been already remarked, extended not only to the body of his wife, but also to the twelve tribes, whom he involved in it, in case they took not effectual means to avenge both the indignity which the Benjamites of Gibeah would have offered him, and the horrible outrages which they had committed upon his concubine. What confirms this opinion, is, that in fact the twelve tribes assembled subscribed to this devotion. First, by taking up arms, as they did. Secondly, by swearing before the ark, not to return to their tents or into their houses, till they had punished the offenders, Judges xx. 8, 9. Thirdly, by putting to the sword all that remained in the city of Gibeah, both man and beast, and burning all the cities and towns of Benjamin, Judges xx. 48. Fourthly, by swearing with an imprecation, not to give their daughters in marriage to the children of Benjamin, and by cursing him who should do so, ch. xxi. 1—18. Fifthly, and lastly, by engaging themselves by a terrible oath, to kill every Israelite who should not take arms against the Benjamites, ib. ver. 5.

These are all of them marks of anathema and devoting; and it would be to shut one's eyes to the light, not to discern in them the most express anathemas and devotions. Some, perhaps, will object, that a private individual, as was this Levite, could not, of his own authority, subject to the anathema his whole nation. It is true, this Levite could devote to death only his wives, his children, and his slaves, and submit to the anathema only his fields, vineyards, houses, household stuff, and, in short, his goods and what belonged to him. His authority extended no further. Only a judge of the Israelites, or their king, or perhaps the high-priest, could do this. So that the Levite had no intention to devote his whole nation, as he devoted the body of his concubine. He included his authority within its natural bounds; he contented himself with declaring, by the sending the flesh and limbs of his concubine, that the whole nation was subject to the anathema: this anathema was pronounced by God himself, and clearly declared in the law; if just measures were not taken to punish in a body the infamous crimes of the Benjamites, these crimes no way yielded to those of the inhabitants of Sodom and Gomorrah, so solemnly anathematized. A like fate, therefore, was to await them.

God had expressly forbidden adultery, and had placed it in the number of those crimes, of which the simple fact rendered the offenders accursed. They were not only to be put to death, (Lev. xx. 10; Deut. xxii. 22, &c.,) but also to perish from among God's people, Lev. 19; that is, they were to be cut off from the synagogue; they could no longer pretend to the promises of the covenant, or the prerogatives of true and faithful Israelites; in a word, they were to be excommunicated and anathematized. The nation, therefore, could not leave unpunished the crimes of the inhabitants of Gibeah, without charging themselves with the crime, and whatever was attached to it. The Levite, by announcing the crime, by declaring the obligation which there lay to punish, and by placing in full view the anathema which they incurred who should refuse to league, to contribute to the effectual punishment, did nothing more than he might do; nothing inconsistent with his condition, his rank, his quality, his dignity: he was even obliged to do so by his function of Levite: he explained the text of the law, 2 Esdras viii. 9. There was, properly speaking, no other method than that which he took, to specify the greatness of the crime of the inhabitants of Gibeah; and he confined himself to that. The whole nation instantly understood it as a universal anathema, without being informed of the nature of the crime which had incurred it. Thus, it is remarkable, that all the tribes expressly assembled at Mizpeh, to know of the Levite what was the matter. He answered, "That the Benjamites of Gibeah had threatened to kill him, unless he consented to their infamous passion; that, moreover, they had injured his concubine with so mad and incredible a brutality, that, in short, she had died of it." Judg. xx. 3—5. Upon this, every one was convinced of the reality of the anathema, and they not only all obliged themselves by oath not to return to their houses, without chastising the inhabitants of Gibeah, in a manner suitable to the extent and blackness of their crime, ver. 10; but also to treat, in like manner, all those of the nation who should not march with the army of the Lord against the Benjamites of Gibeah, ch. xxi. 5; which was, in fact, executed with regard to the inhabitants of Jabesh Gilead, who were all put to the sword, without regard to sex or age, ver. 10. Thus is the anathema sufficiently made out.—CRITICA BIBLICA.

CHAPTER XXI.

Ver. 19. Then they said, Behold, *there is* a feast of the LORD in Shiloh yearly, *in a place* which *is* on the north side of Beth-el, on the east side of the highway that goeth up from Beth-el to Shechem, and on the south of Lebonah.

"On the east side." The Hebrew has, "towards the sun-rising." Does a person ask the way to a place which lies towards the east, he will be told to go to the *rising place*, to the *rising sky*. If to the west, walk for the *departed place*, *the gone down place*.—ROBERTS.

RUTH.

CHAPTER I.

Ver. 11. *Are* there *any more* sons in my womb?

So said Naomi to the widows of her sons who were following her. When a mother has lost her son, should his widow only come occasionally to see her, the mother will be displeased, and affect to be greatly surprised when she does come. "Do I again see you!" "Is it possible!" "Are there any more sons in my womb?" But the mother-in-law also uses this form of expression when she does not wish to see the widow.—ROBERTS.

Ver. 17. Where thou diest, will I die, and there will I be buried: the LORD do so to me, and more also, *if aught* but death part thee and me.

The dreadful practice of widows burning themselves on the funeral pile with the dead bodies of their husbands, has made the declaration of the text familiar to the native mind. Hence a wife, when her husband is sick, should he be in danger, will say, "Ah! if he die, I also will die; I will go with him; yes, my body, thou also shalt be a corpse." A slave, also, to a good master, makes use of the same language. Husbands sometimes boast of the affection of their wives, and compare them to the eastern stork, which if it lose its mate in the night is said immediately to shriek and die.—ROBERTS.

CHAPTER II.

Ver. 2. And Ruth the Moabitess said unto Naomi, Let me now go to the field, and glean ears of corn after *him* in whose sight I shall find grace. And she said unto her, Go, my daughter.

The word *glean* comes from the French *glaner*, to gather ears or grains of corn. This was formerly a general custom in England and Ireland: the poor went into the fields, and collected the straggling ears of corn after the reapers; and it was long supposed that this was their right, and that the law recognised it: but although it has been an old custom, it is now settled by a solemn judgment of the Court of Common Pleas, that a right to glean in the harvest-field cannot be claimed by any person at common law. Any person may permit or prevent it in his own grounds. By certain acts of Henry VIII., gleaning and leasing are so restricted, as to be, in fact, prohibited in that part of the united kingdom.—BURDER.

Ver. 4. And, behold, Boaz came from Bethlehem, and said unto the reapers, The LORD *be* with you. And they answered him, The LORD bless thee.

He went into the field to see how his workmen performed their service, and to encourage them by his presence. Though he was both rich and great, he did not think it beneath him to go into his field, and personally inspect his servants. Thus Homer represents a king among his reapers, with his sceptre in his hand, and discovering great cheerfulness on the occasion.

> ———— *βασιλευς δ' εν τοισι σιωπη*
> *Σκηπτρον εχων εϛηκει επ' ογμου γηθοσυνος κηρ.*
> *Iliad*, xviii. *ver.* 556, 557.

> Amid them, staff in hand, the master stood
> Enjoying mute the order of the field,
> While, shaded by an oak, apart, his train,
> Prepared the banquet. (*Cowper.*)—Burder.

The reapers go to the field very early in the morning, and return home betimes in the afternoon. They carry provisions along with them, and leathern bottles, or dried bottle-gourds, filled with water. They are followed by their own children, or by others, who glean with much success; for a great quantity of corn is scattered in the reaping, and in their manner of carrying it. The greater part of these circumstances, are discernible in the manners of the ancient Israelites. Ruth had not proposed to Naomi, her mother-in-law, to go to the field, and glean after the reapers; nor had the servant of Boaz, to whom she applied for leave, so readily granted her request, if gleaning had not been a common practice in that country. When Boaz inquired who she was, his overseer, after informing him, observes, that she came out to the field in the morning; and that the reapers left the field early in the afternoon, as Dr. Russel states, is evident from this circumstance, that Ruth had time to beat out her gleanings before evening. They carried water and provisions with them; for Boaz invited her to come and drink of the water which the young men had drawn; and at meal-time, to eat of the bread, and dip her morsel in the vinegar. And so great was the simplicity of manners in that part of the world, and in those times, that Boaz himself, although a prince of high rank in Judah, sat down to dinner, in the field, with his reapers, and helped Ruth with his own hand. Nor ought we to pass over in silence, the mutual salutation of Boaz and his reapers, when he came to the field, as it strongly marks the state of religious feeling in Israel at the time, and furnishes another proof of the artless, the happy, and unsuspecting simplicity, which characterized the manners of that highly favoured people. "And, behold, Boaz came from Bethlehem, and said unto the reapers, The Lord be with you. And they answered him, The Lord bless thee." Such a mode of salutation continued among that people till the coming of Christ; for the angel saluted Mary in language of similar import: "Hail, highly favoured, the Lord is with thee; blessed art thou among women." It appears from the beautiful story of Ruth, that in Palestine, the women lent their assistance in cutting down and gathering in the harvest; for Boaz commands her to keep fast by his maidens:—the women in Syria shared also in the labours of the harvest; for Dr. Russel informs us, they sang the Ziraleet, or song of thanks, when the passing stranger accepted their present of a handful of corn, and made a suitable return.—Paxton.

Ver. 14. And Boaz said unto her, At meal-time come thou hither, and eat of the bread, and dip thy morsel in the vinegar.

When Boaz is represented as having provided vinegar for his reapers, into which they might dip their bread, and kindly invited Ruth to share with them in the repast, we are not to understand it of simple vinegar, but vinegar mingled with a small portion of oil, if modern managements in the Levant be allowed to be the most natural comment on those of antiquity. For even the Algerines indulge their miserable captives with a small portion of oil to the vinegar they allow them with their bread, according to the account Pitt gives of the treatment he and his companions received from them, of which he complains with some asperity. What the quality of the bread was, that the reapers of Boaz had, may be uncertain, but there is all imaginable reason to suppose the vinegar into which they dipped it, was made more grateful by the addition of oil.—Harmer.

Ver. 14. And she sat beside the reapers: and he reached her parched *corn*, and she did eat, and was sufficed, and left.

"To-day we crossed the valley of Elassar, and bathed in the hot-baths of Solomon, situated on the southern side, nearly at the bottom, near some corn-fields, where one of our Arabs plucked some green ears of corn, parched them for us, by putting them in the fire, and then, when roasted, rubbed out the grain in his hands." (Macmichel.) "After a ride of two hours from the valley of Zebulon," says Korte, "we came to a place where the disciples of the Lord are said to have plucked and eaten ears of corn on the sabbath day. The wheat in this country is not different from ours, only the grains are as hard as a stone from the heat, and therefore not so good to eat as with us. But in Egypt, in the Holy Land, and in all Syria, there grows a kind of beans, or peas, which are superior to our peas; the stalk grows almost like the lentil: in the pod, which is very thick, and mostly hangs in bunches, there is generally only one grain. This kind is eaten green in the country, and also in the towns, whither they are brought in bunches: when they are too old, they are roasted over coals, and so eaten, when they taste better. This is doubtless the parched corn mentioned in the book of Ruth, and several other places."—Rosenmuller.

They have other ways of preparing their corn for food, besides making it into bread. Burgle is very commonly used among the Christians of Aleppo; which is wheat boiled, then bruised in a mill so as to separate it from the husk, after which it is dried, and laid up for use. The drying of burgle, though mentioned by some writers as a modern operation, seems to throw light on a remarkable passage in the history of David; the concealment of his two spies in a well whose mouth was covered with corn. The custom of exposing corn in this way, must have been very common in Judea, else it had rather excited suspicion in the minds of the pursuers, than diverted their attention from the spot where the spies were concealed. That the well's mouth was covered on that occasion with burgle or boiled wheat, is exceedingly probable; for Dr. Russel observes, that in preparing it after it has been softened in warm water, it is commonly laid out in the courtyard to dry. It could not be flour or meal; for they grind it only in small quantities, and as they want it, and never are known to expose it in this way. Bishop Patrick supposes it was corn newly thrashed out, she pretended to dry; but if this was practised at all, of which we have no evidence, it was by no means common, and therefore calculated rather to betray, than to conceal the spies. Besides, the same word is used to signify corn beaten in a mortar with a pestle, not on the barn-floor with a thrashing instrument; now burgle is actually pounded in this manner. It was therefore burgle or boiled wheat, which D'Arvieux expressly says is dried in the sun; adding that they prepare a whole year's provision of it at once. Wheat and barley were prepared in the same way by the ancient Romans; which renders it very probable that the custom was universal among the civilized nations of antiquity. This is the reason that neither the exposure of the corn, nor the large quantity, produced the least suspicion; every circumstance accorded with the public usage of the country, and by consequence, the preparation of this species of food is as ancient as the days of David. Sawick is a different preparation, and consists of corn parched in the ear; it is made, as well of barley and rice, as of wheat. It is never called, in the inspired volume, parched flour or meal, but always parched corn; and consequently, seems to remain after the roasting, and to be eaten in the state of corn. In confirmation of this idea, we may quote a fact stated by Hasselquist, that in journeying from Acre to Sidon, he saw a shepherd eating his dinner, consisting of half-ripe ears of wheat roasted, which he ate, says the traveller, with as good an appetite as a Turk does his pillaw. The same kind of food, he says, is much used in Egypt by the poor; they roast the ears of Turkish wheat or millet; but it is in his account far inferior to bread. Dr. Shaw is of a different opinion; he supposes the kali, or parched corn of the scriptures, which he translates parched pulse, means parched cicers. But we frequently read in scripture of dried or parched corn; and the word used in those passages is most naturally to be understood of corn, and not of pulse. Besides, Rauwolf asserts that cicers are used in the East only as a part of the dessert after their meals. But it cannot be reasonably supposed, that Boaz would entertain his reapers with things of this kind; or that those fruits which in modern times are used only in desserts, formed the principal part of a reaper's meal, in the field of so wealthy a proprietor. This, however, the opinion of Dr. Shaw requires to be supposed; for it is said in the inspired record, "He reached Ruth parched corn, and she did eat, and was sufficed, and left."—PAXTON.

CHAPTER III.

Ver. 2. And now *is* not Boaz of our kindred, with whose maidens thou wast? Behold, he winnoweth barley to-night in the thrashing-floor.

In these regions much of the agricultural labour is performed in the night. The sun is so hot, and so pernicious, that the farmers endeavour, as much as possible, to avoid its power. Hence numbers plough and irrigate their fields and gardens long after the sun has gone down, or before it rises in the morning. The wind is also generally stronger in the night, which might induce Boaz to prefer that season. From the next two verses we learn that he took his supper there, and slept among the barley. Corn in the East is not kept in stacks, but after being reaped, is, in a few days, thrashed on the spot. The thrashing-floor is a circle of about forty feet in diameter, and consists generally of clay, and cowdung, without wall or fence. Under these circumstances, it is necessary for some of the people to sleep near the corn, till all shall have been thrashed and taken home.—ROBERTS.

Ver. 7. And when Boaz had eaten and drunk, and his heart was merry, he went to lie down at the end of a heap of corn: and she came softly, and uncovered his feet, and laid her down.

Margin to the fourth verse, "lift up the clothes that are on his feet." All inferiors, all servants, sleep at the feet of their master. It is no uncommon thing for those who have a great favour to procure, to go to the house of the rich, and sleep with the head at his door, or in the verandah. Thus, when he arises in the morning, he finds the suppliant at his door. Should a master wish to dismiss his servants, they often say, "My lord, turn us not away; how many years have we slept at your feet?"—ROBERTS.

Ver. 9. And he said, Who *art* thou? And she answered, I *am* Ruth thy handmaid: spread therefore thy skirt over thy handmaid; for thou *art* a near kinsman.

The prophet Ezekiel, in describing the Jewish church as an exposed infant, mentions the care of God in bringing her up with great tenderness, and then, at the proper time, marrying her; which is expressed in the same way as the request of Ruth: "I spread my skirt over thee"——"and thou becamest mine." Dr. A. Clarke says, "Even to the present day, when a Jew marries a woman, he throws the skirt or end of his talith over her, to signify that he has taken her under his protection." I have been delighted, at the marriage ceremonies of the Hindoos, to see among them the same interesting custom. The bride is seated on a throne, surrounded by matrons, having on her veil, her gayest robes, and most valuable jewels. After the thāli has been tied round her neck, the bridegroom approaches her with a silken skirt, (purchased by himself,) and folds it round her several times over the rest of her clothes. A common way of saying he has married her, is, "he has given her the *koori*," has spread the skirt over her. There are, however, those who throw a long robe over the shoulders of the bride, instead of putting on the skirt. An angry husband sometimes says to his wife, "Give me back my skirt," meaning, he wishes to have the marriage compact dissolved. So the mother-in-law, should the daughter not treat her respectfully, says, "My son gave this woman the koori, skirt, and has made her respectable, but she neglects me." The request of Ruth, therefore, amounted to nothing more than that Boaz should marry her.—ROBERTS.

CHAPTER IV.

Ver. 1. Then went Boaz up to the gate, and sat him down there: and, behold, the kinsman of whom Boaz spake came by; unto whom he said, Ho, such a one! turn aside, sit down here. And he turned aside, and sat down.

The word *gate* is often used in scripture, to denote the place of public assemblies where justice is administered.—This definition of the word gate, in its first sense, agrees exactly with the usages of the Hindoos. People, therefore, who understand it literally, as meaning always a gate fixed in the walls of the city, do not comprehend its meaning. At the entrance of every town or village, there is a public building, called a rest-house, where travellers remain, and where people assemble to hear the news, or talk over the affairs of the place. There may be seen many a Boaz asking for the advice of his relations and friends, and many an Abraham as he sat "at the gate of his city," bargaining "for the field," and "the cave of Machpelah," in which to bury his beloved Sarah.—ROBERTS.

Ver. 2. And he took ten men of the elders of the city, and said, Sit ye down here. And they sat down.

Among the Hebrews, and, before them, among the Canaanites, the purchase of any thing of consequence was concluded, and the price paid, publicly, at the gate of the city, as the place of judgment, before all that went out and in, Gen. xxiii. Ruth iv.—As those who wanted amusement, and to pass away the time, were wont to sit in the gates, purchases there made could always be testified by numerous witnesses. Their care to have them so attested, might, perhaps, be a relic of the custom of the times preceding the invention of the art of writing; (which, by the way, took place probably not very long before the days of Abraham;) and it did not even after that period cease to be useful, because among the Hebrews writing not being very common, the memory of witnesses had often to supply the place of a document of purchase. At the same time, it would seem that such documents were not altogether unusual. For the xxiii. chapter of Genesis is in its style so different from that of Moses on other occasions, and has so much of the appearance of the record of a solemn juridical procedure, that it almost seems to be a *deed of purchase.* From Ruth iv. 7, we learn another singular usage on occasions of purchase, cession, and exchange, viz. that the transference of alienable property had, in earlier times, been confirmed by the proprietor plucking off his shoe, and handing it over to the new owner. We see at the same time, that in the age of David this usage had become antiquated; for the writer introduces it as an unknown custom of former times, in the days of David's great-grandfather. I have not been able to find any further trace of it in the East; nor yet has the Danish travelling mission to Arabia, as Captain Niebuhr himself informs me. Bynæus, in his book, *De Calceis Hebræorum*, treats of it at great length; but, excepting the mere conjectures of modern literati, he gives no account of the origin of this strange symbol of the transfer of property. In the time of Moses it was so familiar, that *barefooted* was a term of reproach, and probably signified a man that had sold every thing, a spendthrift, and a bankrupt; and we see from Deut. xxv. 9, 10, that Moses allowed it to be applied to the person who would not marry his brother's widow. Could it have been an Egyptian custom, as we do not find it again in the East? The Egyptians, when they adored the Deity, had no shoes on; and of this the Pythagoreans gave the following explanation: "The philosopher, who came naked from his mother's womb, should appear naked before his Creator; for God hears those alone who are not burdened with any thing extrinsic."—Among the Egyptians too, *barefooted* was equivalent to *naked*, and *naked* synonymous with *having no property*, but one's self. This same custom of pulling off the shoe, and that at the gate before all who went out and in, was also usual in important cases of the exchange or resignation of property; as for instance, (to take the example just quoted from Ruth iv. 7, 9,) when the nearest kinsman abandoned his right of redemption to a distant relation; and we may, perhaps, thence conclude, that a similar form took place in cases of great donations, when not made on a sick-bed, but by persons in health.—MICHAELIS.

Ver. 7. Now this *was the manner* in former time in Israel, concerning redeeming, and concerning changing, for to confirm all things; a man plucked off his shoe, and gave *it* to his neighbour; and this *was* a testimony in Israel. 8. Therefore the kinsman said unto Boaz, Buy *it* for thee. So he drew off his shoe.

See on Matt. 22. 24.

The simple object, therefore, in taking off the shoe, was to confirm the bargain: it was the testimony or memorial of the compact. In Deuteronomy it is mentioned that the brother of a deceased husband shall marry the widow, but should he refuse, then the widow is to "go up to the gate unto the elders and say, My husband's brother refuseth to raise up unto his brother a name in Israel; he will not perform the duty of my husband's brother." Then the elders were to call the man, and if he persisted in his refusal, the woman was to come forward "and loose his shoe from off his foot, and spit in his face; was to answer and say, So shall it be done unto that man that will not build up his brother's house." From that time the man was disgraced, and whenever his person or establishment was spoken of, it was contemptuously called "the house of him that hath his shoe loosed." To be spit at in the face is the most degrading ceremony a man can submit to. This was done by the widow to her husband's brother, and she CONFIRMED his ignominy by taking off his shoe. But this taking off the SHOE (as we shall hereafter see) may also allude to the DEATH of her husband, whose SHOES were taken off and of no further use to him. And as she said, when she had taken off the SHOE from her husband's brother's foot, "thus shall it be done unto that man that will not build up his brother's house," may mean, he also shall soon follow his brother, and have his SHOES taken off his feet in death. When Ramar had to go to reside in the desert for fourteen years, his brother Parathan was very unwilling for him to go; and tried, in every possible way, to dissuade him from his purpose. But Ramar persisted in his resolution, having fully made up his mind to take his departure. When the brother, seeing that his entreaties were in vain, said, "Since you are determined to go, promise me faithfully to return." Then Ramar, having made the promise, gave his SHOES to Parathan as a CONFIRMATION of his vow. Does a priest, a father, or a respectable friend, resolve to go on a pilgrimage to some distant country; some one will perhaps say, "Ah! he will never return, he intends to remain in those holy places." Should he deny it, then they say, "Give us your SHOES as a witness of your promise," and having done so, never will he break it. An affectionate widow never parts with her late husband's SHOES: they are placed near her when she sleeps, she kisses and puts her head upon them, and nearly every time after BATHING, she goes to look at them. These, therefore, are the "TESTIMONY," the melancholy CONFIRMATION of her husband's death.—ROBERTS.

Ver. 10. Moreover, Ruth the Moabitess, the wife of Mahlon, have I purchased to be my wife, to raise up the name of the dead upon his inheritance, that the name of the dead be not cut off from among his brethren, and from the gate of his place: ye *are* witnesses this day.

I now proceed to the explanation of a singular law, which I must however preface, with entreating, in behalf of the lawgiver, that it may not be considered as an invention of his own; as it was in fact several centuries older than his laws, and as he very much limited and mitigated its operation. The law I mean, is what has been termed the Levirate law: in obedience to which, when a man died without issue, his brother was obliged to marry the widow he left, and *that* with this express view, that the first son produced from the marriage should be ascribed, not to the natural father, but to his deceased brother, and become his heir. This has been denominated Levirate-marriage, from the word *Levir*, which though it appears not in the ancient classic authors, but only in the Vulgate and the Pandects, is nevertheless really an old Latin word, and is explained by Festus to signify *a husband's brother*. The Hebrews had in like manner an ancient law term, which we meet not with elsewhere, (יבם *Jabam*,) of the very same import; whence come יבמת (*Jebemet*,) *a brother's wife*, and יבם (*Jebbem*,) *to marry such a person*. The Chaldee, Syriac, and Samaritan versions of the Bible do indeed retain this word, but it is not otherwise at all current in these languages, nor can we find in them the least trace of an etymology for it, and in the Arabic tongue it is altogether unknown. This is often the case with respect to the Hebrew law terms. The Hebrew language alone has them, and without all etymology, while in the kindred languages, they are either not to be found at all, or in quite a different sense. How that happens I am ignorant, with this exception, that I frequently remark, in like manner, among ourselves, ancient law terms, whose etymology is obscure, because old words have been retained in law, while the language has in other respects undergone alterations. The law which obliged a man to marry the widow of his childless brother, was much more ancient than the time of Moses; having been in use in Palestine among the Canaanites, and the ancestors of the Israelites, at least more than 250 years previous to the date of his law, and indeed with such rigour, as left a person no possible means of evading it, however irksome and odious compliance with it might appear to him. The law, however, was unquestionably attended with great inconveniences: for a man cannot but think it the most unpleasant of all necessities, if he *must* marry a woman whom he has not chosen himself. *Must*, in matters of love and marriage, is a fearful word, and almost quite enough to put love to flight, even where beauty excites it. We see, likewise, that the brother, in some instances, had no inclination for any such marriage, (Gen. xxxviii. Ruth iv.) and stumbled at this, that the first son produced from it could not belong to him. Whether a second son might follow, and continue in life, was very uncertain; and among a people who so highly prized genealogical immortality of name, it was a great hardship for a man to be obliged to procure it for a person already dead, and to run the risk, meanwhile, of losing it himself. Nor was this law very much in favour of the morals of the other sex; for not to speak of Tamar, who, in reference to it, conceived herself justified in having recourse to a most infamous action, I will here only observe, that what Ruth did, (chap. iii. 6—9,) in order to obtain, for a husband, the person whom she accounted as the nearest kinsman of her deceased husband, is, to say the least, by no means conformable to that modesty and delicacy which we look for in the other sex. A wise and good legislator could scarcely have been inclined to patronise any such law. But then it is not advisable directly to attack an inveterate point of honour; because in such a case, for the most part, nothing is gained; and in the present instance, as the point of honour placed immortality of name entirely in a man's leaving descendants behind him, it was so favourable to the increase of population, that it merited some degree of forbearance and tenderness. Moses, therefore, left the Israelites still in possession of their established right, but at the same time he studied as much as possible to guard against its rigour and evil effects, by limiting and moderating its operation in various respects.

In the *first* place, he expressly prohibited the marriage of a brother's widow, if there were children of his own alive. Before this time, brothers were probably in the practice of considering a brother's widow as part of the inheritance, and of appropriating her to themselves, if unable to buy a wife, as the Mongols do; so that this was a very necessary prohibition. For a *successor præsumptivus in thoro*, whom a wife can regard as her future husband, is rather a dangerous neighbour for her present one's honour; and if she happen to conceive any predilection for the younger brother, her husband, particularly in a southern climate, will hardly be secure from the risk of poison.

In the *second* place, he allowed, and indeed enjoined, the brother to marry the widow of his childless brother but if he was not disposed to do so, he did not absolutely compel him, but left him an easy means of riddance; for he had only to declare in court, that he had no inclination to marry her, and then he was at liberty. This, it is true;

subjected him to a punishment which at first appears sufficiently severe: the slighted widow had a right to revile* him in court as much as she pleased; and from his pulling off his shoe, and delivering it to the widow, he received the appellation of *Baresole*, which any body might apply to him without being liable to a prosecution. A little consideration, however, will show that this punishment was not so severe in reality as in appearance. For if *Baresole* is once understood, according to the usage of the language, to mean nothing more than *a man who has given a woman the refusal*, it is no longer felt as a term of great reproach, and any one will rather endure it, than have his *own* refusal talked of. To be once in his lifetime solemnly abused in a public court by a woman, is at any rate much easier to be borne, than the same treatment from a man, or extrajudicially; and if, besides, the cause is known, and that the court allows her this liberty, in order to give free vent to her passion, because the man will not marry her according to her wish; the more violent the emotions of her rage are, the more flattering to him must they prove; and he will go out of court with more pride than if she had excused him from marrying her, with much coolness, or without any emotion at all.—I have often heard vain fops mention in company, how many women in *other* places would gladly have married them, and were greatly enraged that they would not take them. On persons of this description, such a judicial punishment would indeed have been very justly bestowed. But it is at worst more flattering than even the very politest language with which a lady begs leave to decline an offer of marriage, or but distantly yields to it. A legislator, in ordaining a punishment of this nature, could hardly have had it in view to insist very particularly on the observance of a statute, that but ratified an old custom by way of a compliment. If it had been a point in which he was interested, he would have ordained a very different punishment.

3. The person whose duty it was to marry a childless widow, was the *brother* of her deceased husband, in the strict sense of the word, as the story in Gen. xxxviii. clearly shows. I would not have thought it necessary to make this remark, had not the contrary opinion been maintained in a Dissertation delivered here at Gottingen, in which it is asserted, that the word *brother*, in Deut. xxv. 5—10, is to be taken in a general sense, and means *a relation*, excluding the real brother. The law, however, only extended to a brother living in the same city or country, not to one residing at a greater distance. Nor did it affect a brother having already a wife of his own. At least, if it had its origin in this, that by reason of the dearness of young women, often only one brother could marry, and the others also wished to do the same, it could only affect such as were unmarried; and in the two instances that occur in Gen. xxxviii. and Ruth iv. we find the brother-in-law, whose duty it was to marry, apprehensive of its proving hurtful to himself and his inheritance, which could hardly have been the case, if he had previously had another wife, or (but that was at least expensive) could have taken one of his own choice. When there was no brother alive, or when he declined the duty, the Levirate-law, as we see from the book of Ruth, extended to the next nearest relation of the deceased husband, as for instance, to his paternal uncle, or nephew; so that at last, even pretty remote kinsmen, in default of nearer ones, might be obliged to undertake it. Boaz does not appear to have been very nearly related to Ruth, as he did not so much as know who she was, when he fell in love with her, while she gleaned in his fields. Nor did she know that he was any relation to her, until apprized of it by her mother-in-law. Among the Jews of these days, Levirate-marriages have entirely ceased; so much so, that in the marriage contracts of the very poorest people among them, it is generally stipulated, that the bridegroom's brothers abandon all those rights to the bride, to which they could lay claim by Deut. xxv.—MICHAELIS.

Ver. 11. And all the people that *were* in the gate, and the elders, said, *We* are witnesses. The LORD make the woman that is come into thy house like Rachel and like Leah, which two did build the house of Israel; and do thou worthily in Ephratah, and be famous in Bethlehem.

The marriage ceremony was commonly performed in a garden, or in the open air; the bride was placed under a canopy, supported by four youths, and adorned with jewels according to the rank of the married persons; all the company crying out with joyful acclamations, Blessed be he that cometh. It was anciently the custom, at the conclusion of the ceremony, for the father and mother, and kindred of the woman, to pray for a blessing upon the parties. Bethuel and Laban, and the other members of their family, pronounced a solemn benediction upon Rebecca before her departure: "And they blessed Rebecca, and said unto her, thou art our sister, be thou the mother of thousands of millions; and let thy seed possess the gate of those that hate them." And in times long posterior to the age of Isaac, when Ruth the Moabitess was espoused to Boaz, "All the people that were in the gate, and the elders, said, we are witnesses. The Lord make the woman that is come into thine house like Rachel and like Leah, which two did build the house of Israel; and do thou worthily in Ephratah, and be famous in Bethlehem." After the benedictions, the bride is conducted, with great pomp, to the house of her husband; this is usually done in the evening; and as the procession moved along, money, sweetmeats, flowers, and other articles, were thrown among the populace, which they caught in cloths made for such occasions, stretched in a particular manner upon frames.—PAXTON.

* The Hebrew expression in Deut. xxv. 9, וירקה בפניו, has been by some so understood, as if the widow had a right to spit in his face. And no doubt it may signify as much; but then that act in a public court is so indecent, that if any other interpretation is admissible, this one ought not to be adopted. Now there are two others: 1. *She shall spit before his face*. The Arabs, at this day, when they wish to affront any one, spit, and cry *Fi*; even people of rank do so, just as the common people do with us. This account we find even in lexicons; but I know it besides, from the information furnished both by Solomon Negri, a native Arab, and by travellers. 2. ירק may also mean *to revile*; properly *Bilem evomere*, which signification is familiar in Arabia; only that, according to the usual rule, the Hebrew *Jod* must be changed into *Vau*, and the word written *Varak*.

THE FIRST BOOK OF SAMUEL.

CHAPTER I.

Ver. 1. Now there was a certain man of Ramathaim-zophim, of mount Ephraim, and his name *was* Elkanah, the son of Jeroham, the son of Elihu, the son of Tohu, the son of Zuph, an Ephrathite: 2. And he had two wives; the name of the one *was* Hannah, and the name of the other Peninnah.

How much soever some may have denied it, nothing is more certain, than that by the civil laws of Moses a man was allowed to have more wives than one. No doubt, all the proofs of this fact, which it is usual to adduce, are not valid; and to the maintainers of the opposite opinion, it may be an easy matter to controvert such as are weak or inaccurate; but the following arguments appear to me to place the matter beyond all doubt.

1. It is certain that *before* the time of Moses, polygamy was in use among the ancestors of the Israelites, and that even Abraham and Jacob lived in it. It is also certain, that it continued in use *after* the time of Moses. I will not interrupt the text with a multitude of examples; but there are two of such weight as to merit particular notice.—One of them we find in 1 Chron. vii. 4, where not only the five fathers, named in the preceding verse, but also their descendants, forming a tribe of 36,000 men, had lived in polygamy, which also shows, by the way, that it must have been more common in some families than in others.—The other occurs in 2 Chron. xxv. 3, where we see the high-priest himself, who was of course the authentic expounder of the Mosaic statutes, taking for Joash, who clave to him as a son, *two wives*, which shows that he had not at any rate looked upon *bigamy* as prohibited by the law of Deut. xvii. 17. As then, Moses, adhering to established usage, nowhere prohibited a man's taking a second or a third wife, along with the first, it is clear that, as a civil right, it continued allowable; for what has hitherto been customary, and permitted, remains so, in a civil sense, as long as no positive law is enacted against it. Therefore, the objection here made, *that Moses nowhere authorizes polygamy, by an express statute*, amounts to nothing; more especially when it is considered, that, as we shall immediately see under Nos. 2, 3, 4, it is implied in *three* several texts, that he actually did authorize it. But although he had not done so, his silent acquiescence in, and non-prohibition of, the practice previously held lawful, is quite enough to sanction our opinion of his having left it still allowable as a civil right. And,

2. This proof becomes still stronger, when we remark how very common polygamy must have been at the very time when Moses lived and gave his laws. For, when Moses caused the Israelites to be numbered, he found 603,550 males above 20 years of age. Now, according to political calculations, the proportion of those under 20, to those above it, is in general reckoned as 12 to 20, or, at any rate, as 12 to 15; but admitting, in the present case, that it was but as 10 to 20, to the above number of adult males, we should thus have still to add a half more, or 301,775, for those under 20, besides 22,000 Levites that were reckoned separately; so that the whole number of males must have amounted to at least 927,325. Now among all this people, we find from Numb. iii. 43, that there were no more than 22,273 *first-born males, of a month old and upward;* that is, only *one* first-born among 42: so that, had the Israelites lived in monogamy, it would follow that every marriage had on an average given birth to 42 children, which, however, is hardly possible to be conceived; whereas if every Israelite had four or more wives, it was very possible that of every father on an average that number might have sprung, and, of course, of 42 Israelites, there would be but one first-born. At the same time, this being the case, polygamy must certainly have gone great lengths, and been very universally practised among them; and if it was so, and Moses forbade it by no law, it is obvious that it continued allowable as a civil right. If in this deduction there appear any thing dubious or obscure, I must refer the reader to my Dissertation, *De Censibus Hebræorum*, in paragraphs 4, 5, and 6 of which, I have considered this argument at greater length.

3. The law of Deut. xxi. 15—17, already explained, presupposes the case of a man having *two* wives, one of whom he peculiarly loves, while the other, whom he hates, is the mother of his first-born. Now this is the very case which occurs in Genesis, in the history of Jacob, and his wives Leah and Rachel; and this law ordains, that in such a case the husband was not to bestow the right of primogeniture upon the son of the favourite wife, but to acknowledge as his first-born the son that actually was so.

4. The law of Exod. xxi. 9, 10, in like manner already explained, expressly permits the father, who had given his son a slave for a wife, to give him, some years after, a second wife, of *freer* birth; and prescribes how the first was then to be treated. The son was bound to pay her matrimonial duty as often as she could have claimed it before his second marriage; and, therefore, if he did so, the marriage still subsisted. If he refused, the marriage immediately ceased, and the woman received her liberty. When Moses, in Lev. xviii. 18, prohibits a man from marrying the sister of his wife, to vex her while she lives, it manifestly supposes the liberty of taking another wife besides the first, and during her lifetime, provided only it was *not* her sister. But because the sense of this passage has been much disputed, and others, in opposition to the plain words of Moses, consider it as a general prohibition of polygamy; as I cannot with propriety expatiate fully on their explanation here, I must refer the reader to my Dissertation already quoted, *On the Mosaic Statutes prohibitory of Marriages betwixt Near Relations.*

It does not appear, however, that Moses permitted polygamy willingly, or as a matter of indifference in either a moral or a political view, but, as Christ expresses it, merely on account of the hardness of the people's hearts. In other words, he did not approve it, but found it advisable to tolerate it, as a point of civil expediency. His first book, which is entirely historical, includes many particulars that are by no means calculated to recommend polygamy. According to him, God, even at the very time when the rapid population of the earth was his great object, gave to the first man but *one* wife, although it is evident that with *four* wives, he could have procreated more children than with one; and when, in consequence of the flood, the earth was to be reduced anew to its original state in this respect, and God resolved to preserve alive only Noah and his three sons, we still find that each of them had but one wife with him. Now had God approved of polygamy, he would have commanded each of Noah's sons to marry as many wives as possible, and take them with him into the ark. From these two historical facts, the natural proportion between the sexes, which, where population is numerous, cannot be discovered without much trouble, becomes at once obvious; and this very proportion, considering that we actually find much about the same number of men as of women fit for the married state, is the strongest possible argument against polygamy; the lawfulness or unlawfulness of which, as Montesquieu very justly observes, resolves itself, properly speaking, into a question of arithmetic. Moses did not permit eunuchs to be made among the Israelites. Indeed he went so far as to prohibit even the castration of cattle, Lev. xxii. 24; and besides this, a eunuch that came from another country to reside among the Israelites, was by a special statute excluded from ever becoming one of the people of God, that is, was incapable of enjoying the privileges and rights of an Israelite, both sacred and civil, Deut. xxiii. 2. This was an ordinance highly unfavourable to polygamy. We commonly find polygamy and eunuchism going together; and in those countries in which the former prevails, such as Turkey, Persia, and China, there are thousands, and even millions of eunuchs. Where so many of the males that are born, can never become husbands and obtain wives, it is nothing less than merciful to place them beyond the temptation of longing for a wife; and, in early infancy, before they know what has befallen them, to assign them that intermediate state, in which, without properly belonging to either sex, they are to live, and earn their bread. Besides, where polygamy is carried to great lengths, there is in the nature of the case an imperious necessity for vigilant watchers of their chastity. In a word, without eunuchs, a great seraglio cannot be guarded; and of course, a law prohibiting castration imperceptibly counteracts polygamy. This is also an observation of M. de Premontval.

It would appear, that in the course of time, polygamy had very much decreased among the Israelites, and become rather uncommon. Solomon, in Prov. xxxi. 10—31, in his description of that wife whom he accounted a blessing to her husband, represents her entirely as a *mater-familias*, that is, the mistress and ruler of the whole household; which a wife in the state of polygamy can never be, being destined solely for her husband's bed, and having no permission to concern herself at all about domestic economy. It would therefore seem, that although Solomon himself lived in boundless polygamy, his subjects were contented with one wife. Besides, had polygamy continued as common as in the days of Moses, the price of wives would have advanced in proportion to the increased value of other commodities; but we find that in the time of the prophet Hosea, a wife was still the same as the medium rate in the time of Moses; for that was about 30 shekels; and Hosea (iii. 2) bought *his* for 15 shekels, and 15 ephahs of barley. Every thing else had risen in price, (as I have shown in my Dissertation, *De pretiis rerum apud Hebræos*, in the 3d Part of the *Commentaria* of the Gottingen Society of Sciences,) except wives; and consequently, polygamy, which makes *them* scarce and dear, must have been much diminished, or have ceased almost altogether among the Israelites. That it ceased entirely after the return of the Jews from the Babylonish captivity, is, indeed, certain; but with that fact we have here nothing to do, as it was neither an article nor an effect of the Mosaic law, but proceeded from other accidental causes.

But how came it to pass that Moses, who certainly did not approve of polgyamy, and counteracted its increase by various impediments, did not rather at once prohibit it altogether? This is indeed an important question, and has not hitherto received a satisfactory answer. Many of Montesquieu's readers will perhaps think, that nothing can be easier than to answer it fully in the following terms: "The lawfulness or unlawfulness of polygamy depends entirely on the proportion of females born to that of males, or is, as Montesquieu very properly terms it, a problem of arithmetic. Now in Asia there are many more females than males, and consequently, polygamy should be there permitted for the very same reason for which it is prohibited in Europe. Where the numbers of both sexes are equal, there both nature and arithmetic prescribe monogamy; but where the procedure of nature is different, and several girls are born for one boy, there she allows, or, I should rather say, there she authorizes polygamy." Here, however, and in what he says of Asia, Montesquieu is undoubtedly mistaken. For without very clear proofs, and without having accurate enumerations, and birth-lists, of all the Asiatic nations, who will believe either him or any other traveller, asserting that, in regard to the proportion of the sexes born, the procedure of nature in Asia, particularly in Turkey, Persia, China, and Japan, is altogether different from what we find it in Europe? It cannot be supposed that the circumstance of these countries lying more to the east than our European regions, can have any effect in this respect; for the difference of climate depends not on the easterly or westerly, but on the southerly or northerly position of a country; in other words, not on the degree of longitude, but of latitude. Now, Minorca lies under the 39th degree of latitude, and of course, some degrees more to the south than Constantinople, and the countries between the Black and Caspian Seas, whence the Turks and Persians purchase young women for their seraglios, but in the very same latitude with a great part of Turkey, Persia, China, and Japan; and yet this Island, according to Armstrong's account, in letter 15th, of his history of it, had, in the year 1742, exclusive of the English garrison, 15,000 male inhabitants, and but only 12,000 female. Now, how can we believe, after this, that under the very same climate, but farther eastward, nature should, on the contrary, produce more persons of the other sex than of ours, merely because there it is noon, when the sun but begins to rise on Minorca? The English colonies in America have, part of them at least, a still more southerly position; but even there, no other proportion of births, in the two sexes, has been remarked, than what is found in England itself. The whole mistake, into which even the venerable Montesquieu himself has been betrayed, proceeds from this, that in some of the great capitals of Asia, there are a great many more women than men, owing to the residence of monarchs and people of fortune, who keep great seraglios, for which girls are purchased in other places, and brought to the metropolis. It does not, however, thence follow, that in Asia there are more females born than males, but only that the former being *more* numerous in the rich cities, are in the provinces, whence they are bought, *less* so, in the very same proportion. Mr. Porter, the British ambassador at Constantinople, makes this remark in the Philosophical Transactions, vol. xlix. art. 21st; so that it is not matter of speculation, but of experience. But the conclusion drawn from the oriental capitals, to the state of whole countries, in regard to the proportion of the sexes, is much in the same style as would be that of the traveller, who on seeing a German army of 100,000 troops, and remarking that there was scarcely *one* woman with it to *ten* men, should go home and assert that he had discovered, that in Germany there were ten times as many males born as females. I am therefore of opinion, that with regard to the polygamy allowed among the Israelites, we can say nothing else than what Christ has said on the subject of divorce. Moses tolerated it *on account of their hardness of heart*, and because it would have been found a difficult matter to deprive them of a custom already so firmly established. The Egyptian monarchs endeavoured to prevent the multiplication of the Israelites, and for this purpose, went so far as to order all their male children, as soon as born, to be thrown into the Nile; and yet Moses found polygamy among them, which, of course, could not have been prohibited by the Egyptian government. A people, whose children a tyrant drowned to hinder their increase, while yet he dared not to check their polygamy, must have clung very closely to that privilege, and not have been likely to surrender it without rebelling.

Whether the climate may have, in any degree, contributed to produce *this hardness of heart*, I will neither confidently affirm nor deny, so long as we are destitute of what I would call a geographical history of polygamy and monogamy, which a person might survey at a short glance; for thus much is certain, that in the most *northerly* regions of Siberia and Tartary, there are nations that live in polygamy; and in the very warmest climates, on the contrary, we find Christians, and even nations, satisfied with monogamy. If the former is more prevalent towards the south, we must bear in mind, that in regard to laws, though *much* depends on climate, yet *every* thing does not, but still *more* on accidental circumstances; and that ancient usage, or religion, may have a very powerful influence on the nature of the law. But should even the climate actually cause a difference in the point in question, and make it more difficult to put a stop to polygamy, by law, among southern than northern nations, because they are naturally more addicted to it; still the cause thereof would not be referable to any inequality in the proportion of the sexes, but to the earlier puberty of southern nations, and the earlier violence of libidinous propensities therewith connected. The natural consequence of these early and strong feelings of love, are early marriages; the wife, in such a case, can hardly be more than two years younger, and the appropriated concubine is perhaps even older than the boy that becomes her husband: and when he has reached his 25th or 30th, and still more, his 37th year, which Aristotle fixed as the fittest time for a man to marry, his wife, or concubine, particularly if she has borne many children, has by that time become too old for him, and then he either meditates a divorce, or taking a younger wife in addition to the former. This last is indeed the least of the two evils for the unfortunate first wife; and the legislator who wishes that she, particularly if a slave, that can have no will of her own, may experience the least possible hardship or injustice, will in this view tolerate polygamy. Indeed if he were to prohibit it, it is probable the people would not submit to the privation without some disturbance.—If what I have now said, merely by way of conjecture, be correct, the consideration of climate might have had some influence with Moses in his toleration of polygamy, as a civil right; for Palestine is certainly to be numbered among southern climates, although indeed the Israelites, at the time when Moses may be said to have taken them under his protection, had been accustomed to a country somewhat farther south, and much warmer.

There is yet another circumstance to be taken into the account, which made polygamy in Palestine more tolerable in a political light, than among us, where it would soon depopulate a country, because we have not, as was then the case, any opportunity of purchasing, or of carrying off as captives, the young women of other nations. The laws of war, in those days, gave the victors a right to make slaves of young women, and these they might employ for the purposes of polygamy, without thereby depriving any Israelite of a wife born to him among his own people. No doubt this was a very severe war law, and detrimental to the general interests of mankind: but it was once established, and although the Israelites had not acted up to it, their neighbours would not therefore have lost any opportunity of doing so, which the fortune of war put into their power. It must also be considered that the Israelites lived in the vicinity of a poor people, whose daughters they could purchase: for nature has been so unkind to Arabia, that most of its inhabitants must always be in a state of indigence, with the exception of any particular family or city that may happen to be enriched by trade, or by singular good-fortune in rearing sheep. Mr. Wood in his *Essay on the original genius of Homer*, has given a very faithful description of the natural poverty of Arabia, which, after all the improvements it can receive from fortune and art, uniformly sinks back to its original state; and Mr. Niebuhr has orally given me an account of the poverty of the Arabs, which far exceeded even what I should have expected.

Although the Mosaic laws do not prohibit more than one wife, still they did not thereby authorize polygamy in the whole extent of the word, and that a man might have as many wives as he pleased. This is not perhaps altogether the consequence of those statutes, which enjoined the husband to perform the conjugal rites with every wife within stated periods; for Moses, (as we have already seen,) most expressly prohibited even the future king *from having many wives*, (Deut. xvii. 17:) and of course, that could not but be forbidden to the people at large. But if more than *one* wife was allowed, and *many* forbidden, the question comes to be, what is meant by many? And to that question I can only give what may be called a probable answer, and to this effect: that by *many* seems to be meant *more than four*, that number being permitted, but not more. This is the doctrine of the Talmud and the Rabbins, of which the reader will find a more detailed account in *Selden de Uxore Hebraica.* To their testimony and opinion I would indeed pay but little respect, in most points relating to the original Mosaic jurisprudence: but here they seem for once to be in the right. For Mohammed, who generally follows the ancient Arabian usages, in the fourth chapter of the Koran, also fixes *four* as the number of wives to be allowed, and commands that it be not exceeded: and before the time of Moses, there would seem to have likewise been an ancient usage, in the patriarchal families, which limited polygamy to this same number, and which may also have continued among the Jews and Arabs. We have reason to presume that this was the case from a passage in Gen. chap. xxxi. 50. Jacob had four wives, Leah, Rachel, and their two maids. Laban, his father-in-law, was so little an enemy to polygamy, that instead of *one* of his daughters, whom Jacob wished to have, he contrived by a piece of artifice, and contrary to Jacob's inclination, to force them *both* upon him. But notwithstanding this, we find him in this passage requiring Jacob to take an oath that he would not take any more wives. He seems to have thought with the poet,

Est modus in rebus, sunt certi denique fines:

and this *modus* was, in his opinion, what Jacob already had, *four wives.* Now as Moses does not explain what he calls *many*, he must, from such established custom, have presupposed it perfectly known.—Michaelis.

Marriage is evidently meant by scripture and reason, to be the union of one man with one woman. When God said, "It is not good that the man should be alone;" he promised him the help only of a single mate: "I will make him a help-meet for him." This gracious promise he soon performed in the formation of one woman; a clear intimation of his will that only one man and one woman should be joined in wedlock. This design Adam recognised, and acknowledged in express terms: and his declaration was certainly meant as a rule for his descendants in every succeeding age: "Therefore shall a man leave his father and his mother, and shall cleave unto his wife, and they shall be one flesh." These quotations, which are all couched in terms of the singular number, are inconsistent with the doctrine of polygamy. The original appointment was confirmed by our Lord in these words: "Have ye not read, that he which made them at the beginning, made them male and female; and said, for this cause, shall a man leave father and mother, and shall cleave to his wife; and they twain shall be one flesh? Wherefore they are no more twain, but one flesh." The apostle is not less decisive in his direction to the churches: "Nevertheless, to avoid fornication, let every man have his own wife; and let every woman have her own husband." But though the law is so decisive, it cánnot be doubted that polygamy was introduced soon after the creation; Lamech, one of the descendants of Cain, and only the sixth person from Adam, married two wives; he was probably the first who ventured, in this respect, to transgress the law of his Maker. This unwarrantable practice, derived from the antediluvian world, seems to have become very common soon after the flood; for it is mentioned as nothing remarkable that Sarah, when she despaired of having children, took her handmaid Hagar, and gave her to Abraham her husband, by whom she had a son. Both Esau and Jacob had a number of wives; and that is undoubtedly one of the practices which Moses suffered to remain among his people, because of the hardness of their hearts, prohibiting only the high-priest to have more than one wife.

Every transgression of the divine law is attended by its corresponding punishment. Polygamy has proved in all ages, and in all countries where it has been suffered, a teeming source of evil. The jealousy and bitter contentions in the family of Abraham, and of his grandson Jacob, which proceeded from that cause, are well known; and still more deplorable were the dissensions which convulsed the house, and shook the throne of David. Such mischiefs are the natural and necessary effects of the practice; for polygamy divides the affections of the husband, and by consequence, generates incurable jealousies and contentions among the unhappy victims of his licentious desires. To prevent his abode from becoming the scene of unceasing confusion and uproar, he is compelled to govern it, as the oriental polygamist still does, with despotic authority, which at once extinguishes all the rational and most endearing comforts of the conjugal state. The husband is a stern and unfeeling despot; his harem, a group of trembling slaves. The children espouse, with an ardour unknown to those who are placed in other circumstances, the cause of their own mother, and look upon the children of the other wives as strangers or enemies. They regard their common father with indifference or terror; while they cling to their own mother with the fondest affection, as the only parent in whom they feel any interest, or from whom they expect any suitable return of attention and kindness. This state of feeling and attachment, is attested by every writer on the manners of the East; and accounts for a way of speaking so common in the scriptures: "It is my brother, and the son of my mother." "They were my brethren," said Gideon, "the sons of my mother; as the Lord liveth, if ye had saved them alive, I would not slay you." It greatly aggravated the affliction of David, that he had become an alien to his mother's children; the enmity of his brethren, the children of his father's other wives, or his more distant relatives, gave him less concern; "I am become a stranger to my brethren, and an alien to my mother's children." The same allusion occurs in the complaint of the spouse: "Look not upon me, because I am black, because the sun hath looked upon me: my mother's children were angry with me; they made me the keeper of the vineyards." The children of one wife, scarcely looked upon the children of the other wives as their brothers and sisters at all; and they scarcely felt more regard for their father. An Oriental, in consequence of this unnatural practice, takes little notice of an insult offered to his father; but expresses the utmost indignation when a word is spoken to the disadvantage of his mother. To defame or to curse her, is the last insult which his enemy can offer; and one which he seldom or never forgives. "Strike," cried an incensed African to his antagonist, "but do not curse my mother."—PAXTON.

Ver. 2. And he had two wives; the name of the one *was* Hannah, and the name of the other Peninnah.

The names the eastern people give to women and slaves, appear to us to be oftentimes not a little odd; something of the same kind may, however, be remarked in the scriptures, though they are there more frequently of the devout kind. The author of the *History of Ali Bey* mentions a female, whose name, Laal, signified ruby. One of the wives of Elkanah, the father of the prophet Samuel, seems to have been named in the same way, for such was the meaning of the word Peninnah. The plural word peninim signifies rubies, or precious stones that are red. *Lam.* iv. 7. If both these ladies were called by names that in their respective languages signified a ruby, probably both one and the other were so denominated, either from the floridness of their complexion, or the contrary to a ruby teint: for it may be understood either way.—BURDER.

Ver. 11. And she vowed a vow, and said, O LORD of hosts, if thou wilt indeed look on the affliction of thy handmaid, and remember me, and not forget thy handmaid, but wilt give unto thy handmaid a man-child, then I will give him unto the LORD all the days of his life, and there shall no razor come upon his head.

Among these vows of abstinence, may be classed those of *Nazaritism*, although they have also something in common with the first species, and are, as it were, a mixture of both kinds. A Nazarite, during the continuance of his vow, durst drink no wine nor strong drink; nor eat of the fruit of the vine, either grapes or raisins; nor come near any dead body; or otherwise wittingly defile himself. He was also obliged to let his hair grow. At the termination of the period of his vow, he had to make certain offerings prescribed by Moses, and what other offerings he had vowed besides; as also to cut off his hair, and burn it on the altar, and then first drink wine again at the offering-feast. These ordinances, however, rather belong to the ceremonial law, than to the Mosaical jurisprudence, of which I here treat. It is only necessary to attend to this further circumstance, that vows of Nazaritism were not an original institution of Moses, but of more ancient, and probably of Egyptian, origin; and that, in his laws, he only gives certain injunctions concerning them, partly to establish the ceremonies and laws of such vows, and partly to prevent people from making them to, or letting their hair grow in honour of, any other than the true God. What typical views he may have had in the ceremonies he prescribed, it forms no part of my present subject, in which I merely consider the Mosaic laws on the principles of jurisprudence, but rather belongs to theology, to ascertain. But that before the Mosaic law was given there had been Nazarites among the Israelites, is manifest from the following circumstance: The ordinance of Moses concerning the Nazarites, which stands in chap. vi. of Numbers, was given in the *second* year after the departure from Egypt; but in an earlier law concerning the sabbatical year, which was made in the *first* year, Moses adopts a figurative expression from Nazaritism, calling the vines, which in that year were not to be pruned, *Nazarites*, Lev. xxv. 5. The thing itself must, therefore, have been already in use, and that for a long period; because such figurative expressions, particularly in agriculture, gardening, and rural economy, do not succeed to the proper signification even of the most familiar and best-known terms, till after a lapse of many years. The vow of Nazaritism was not necessarily, nor usually, of perpetual endurance; and hence Moses ordained what offerings should be made at its termination or discontinuance. In latter times, it is true, we have, in the case of Samson, an example of a person devoted by his parents to be a Nazarite for life; but even here, Nazaritism was not understood in its whole extent, as prescribed in the Mosaic law; for Samson plainly deviated from it, when he attacked and defeated the Philistines, from whose dead bodies a strict Nazarite must have fled, to avoid defilement. Of such perpetual Nazaritism, however, Moses does not at all treat in his laws; and, of course, does not say whether, like other vows, it could have been redeemed, had it proved a hardship to a son to abstain from wine all his life. According to the analogy of the other laws of Moses on this subject, it should have been redeemable.—MICHAELIS.

It frequently happens after the birth of a son, that if the parent be in distress, or the child sick, or that there be any other cause of grief, the mother makes a vow, that no razor shall come upon the child's head for a certain portion of time, and sometimes for all his life. 1 Sam. i. 11. If the child recovers, and the cause of grief be removed, and if the vow be but for a time, so that the mother's vow be fulfilled, then she shaves his head at the end of the time prescribed, makes a small entertainment, collects money and other things from her relations and friends, which are sent as *nezers* (offerings) to the mosque at Kerbelah, and are there consecrated. Numbers vi.—MORIER.

Ver. 12. And it came to pass, as she continued praying before the LORD, that Eli marked her mouth.

Hannah, the wife of Elkanah, was steril, but she had an intense desire to be the mother of a "man-child," and she went to the "temple of the Lord" to vow, if he would give her one, that she would "give him unto the Lord all the days of his life—there shall no razor come upon his head." How often do we witness a similar scene. See the afflicted wife prostrate in the dust before the temple of her god: she earnestly entreats the deity to give unto her a "male child." "Ah! then will my husband love me—then will my neighbours cease to reproach me—Ah! my god, a male child, a male child—he shall be called by thy name—and sacred shall be his hair."—ROBERTS.

CHAPTER II.

Ver. 1. And Hannah prayed, and said, My heart rejoiceth in the LORD; my horn is exalted in the LORD.

In this and many other parts of scripture, mention is made of the exaltation of the horn. Colonel Light thus describes the dress of the Druses. "The females of both Maronites and Druses appear in a coarse blue jacket and petticoat, without stockings, their hair platted, hanging down in long tails behind. On their heads they wore a tin or silver conical tube about twelve inches long, and perhaps twice the size of a common post-horn; over which was thrown a white piece of linen, that completely enveloped their body, and gives a most singular and ghost-like appearance. Upon Mount Lebanon the wife of the emir sometimes made her appearance in the costume of the country, adorned with a golden horn on her head, enriched with precious stones, instead of the ordinary one of the other women of the country."—BURDER.

"One of the most extraordinary parts of the attire of the female Druses is a silver horn, sometimes studded with jewels, worn on their heads in various positions, distinguishing their different conditions. A married woman has it affixed on the right side of the head, a widow on the left, and a virgin is pointed out by its being placed on the very crown; over this silver projection the long veil is thrown, with which they so completely conceal their faces, as rarely to leave more than one eye visible."—MACMICHEL.

This woman, who was a Christian, wore on her head a hollow silver horn, rearing itself upward obliquely from her forehead, being four or five inches in diameter at the root, and pointed at its extreme.—BUCKINGHAM.

About two years ago, some of our Indian ships brought over a number of *Sepoys*, who did duty as marines on the voyage; these were newly clothed in England, and presented to the king. Perhaps there were but few, possibly not one, who, having the opportunity of seeing these soldiers, made the same observations as the writer of this article, respecting the helmets worn on their heads. These helmets appeared to be made of stout leather, or other strong substance; they were oval and nearly flat, like the trencher caps worn at our universities: in the centre rose a head-piece, or crown, ornamented with feathers, &c. and on the front, *directly over the forehead*, was *a steel* HORN, rising as it were from a short stem, and then assuming the form of one of our extinguishers, used to extinguish the light of a candle.

It appeared, also, that the comparison of such a military horn to the horn of a reem, (the unicorn of our translators,) the rhinoceros, was extremely applicable: for having seen the great rhinoceros at the menagerie at Versailles, we recollected the resemblance perfectly. Whether we should be justified in referring this part of dress to the military *only*, may be questioned; because Hannah, for instance, says, "*My* horn is exalted." 1 Sam. ii. 1. But women, occasionally, might adopt, as parts of dress, ornaments not altogether unlike this horn, even if this form of speech were not derived originally from the soldiers' dress, and transferred to a notorious disposition of mind; or to other instances. This also diminishes the apparent strangeness of Zedekiah's conduct, 1 Kings xxii. 11, *who made himself* HORNS *of iron*, and said, "Thus saith the Lord, With these" military insignia, "shalt thou push the Syrians until thou hast consumed them." We are apt to conceive of these horns, as projecting, like bulls' horns, on each side of Zedekiah's head. How different from the real fact! Zedekiah, though he pretended to be a prophet, did not wish to be thought *mad*, to which imputation such an appearance would have subjected him: whereas, he only acted the hero,—the hero returning in military triumph: it was little more than a flourish with a *spontoon*. In corroboration of this idea, let us hear Mr. Bruce, who first elucidated this subject by actual observation:—

"One thing remarkable in this cavalcade, which I observed, was the headdress of the governors of provinces. A large broad fillet was bound upon their forehead, and tied behind their head. In the middle of this was *a* HORN, *or conical piece of silver, gilt, about four inches long, much in the shape of our common candle extinguishers.* This is called *kern* (קרן) or horn, and is only worn in reviews, or parades after victory. This I apprehend, like all other of their usages, is taken from the Hebrews, and the several allusions made in scripture to it, arises from this practice:—'I said to the wicked, Lift not up the horn,'—'Lift not up your horn on high; speak not with a stiff neck.'—'The horn of the righteous shall be exalted with honour.'"—TAYLOR IN CALMET.

Ver. 5. *They that were* full have hired out themselves for bread.

A man of high caste, or one who was once in affluence, will almost as soon die as work for food; and, generally speaking, such is the pity felt for those people, that there are always some who will give a trifle to supply their wants. It is a phrase indicative of great misery to say, "The once rich man is now hiring himself out for conjee," (gruel.)—ROBERTS.

Ver. 8. He raiseth up the poor out of the dust, *and* lifteth up the beggar from the dunghill, to set *them* among princes, and to make them inherit the throne of glory.

In preparing their victuals, the Orientals are, from the extreme scarcity of wood in many countries, reduced to use cowdung for fuel. At Aleppo, the inhabitants use wood and charcoal in their rooms, but heat their baths with cowdung, the parings of fruit, and other things of a similar kind, which they employ people to gather for that purpose. In Egypt, according to Pitts, the scarcity of wood is so great, that at Cairo they commonly heat their ovens with horse or cow dung, or dirt of the streets; what wood they have, being brought from the shores of the Black Sea, and sold by weight. Chardin attests the same fact: "The eastern people always used cowdung for baking, boiling a pot, and dressing all kinds of victuals that are easily cooked, especially in countries that have but little wood;" and Dr. Russel remarks, in a note, that "the Arabs carefully collect the dung of the sheep and camel, as well as that of the cow; and that the dung, offals, and other matters used in the bagnios, after having been new gathered in the streets, are carried out of the city, and laid in great heaps to dry, where they become very offensive. They are intolerably disagreeable, while drying, in the town adjoining to the bagnios; and are so at all times when it rains, though they be stacked, pressed hard together, and thatched at top." These statements exhibit, in a very strong light, the extreme misery of the Jews, who escaped from the devouring sword of Nebuchadnezzar: "They that fed delicately, are desolate in the streets; they that were brought up in scarlet, embrace dunghills." To embrace dunghills, is a species of wretchedness, perhaps unknown to us in the history of modern warfare; but it presents a dreadful and appalling image, when the circumstances to which it alludes are recollected. What can be imagined more distressing to those who lived delicately, than to wander without food in the streets? What more disgusting and terrible to those who had been clothed in rich and splendid garments, than to be forced by the destruction of their palaces, to seek shelter among stacks of dung, the filth and stench of which it is almost impossible to endure. The dunghill, it appears from holy writ, is one of the common retreats of the mendicant, which imparts an exquisite force and beauty to a passage in the song of Hannah: "He raiseth up the poor out of the dust, and lifteth the beggar from the dunghill, to set them among princes, and to make them inherit the throne of glory." The change in the circumstances of that excellent woman, she reckoned as great, (and it was to her not less unexpected,) as the elevation of a poor despised beggar, from a nauseous and polluting dunghill, rendered ten times more fœtid by the intense heat of an oriental sun, to one of the highest and most splendid stations on earth.—PAXTON.

Ver. 24. Nay, my sons; for *it is* no good report that I hear: ye make the LORD's people to transgress.

This affectionate form of speech may be heard in the mouth of every father. Thus, it is not common to mention the name, but my eldest, my youngest son, (or some other epithet to designate the one he wants.) "My sons, listen to the voice of your father." In passing through a village, a man or woman may be heard in every corner bawling out, "Maganea," *i. e.* O son, or "Magalea," O daughter, "come hither; I want you."—ROBERTS.

Ver. 31. Behold, the days come that I will cut off thine arm, and the arm of thy father's house, that there shall not be an old man in thy house.

People, in cursing each other, say, "In thy family may there never be an old man," meaning, may all die in youth. "Alas! alas! there has not been an old man in that family for many generations."—ROBERTS.

CHAPTER IV.

Ver. 12. And there ran a man of Benjamin out of the army, and came to Shiloh the same day, with his clothes rent, and with earth upon his head.

He indulged his grief to a violent degree, beating his breast, and, among his other exclamations, frequently made use of one, very illustrative of that ancient act of grief heaping ashes on the head. He said, *Ah cheh hak be ser-mun amed*, What earth has come on my head? repeating this with a constant intermixture of *Ah wahi*, which he would continue to repeat for above fifty times, in a whining piteous voice, lowering its tone till it became scarcely audible, and then continuing it *soto voce*, until he broke out again into a new exclamation.—MORIER.

Ver. 13. And when he came, lo, Eli sat upon a seat by the wayside watching: for his heart trembled for the ark of God. And when the man came into the city, and told *it*, all the city cried out.

Sitting on a cushion is, with the Orientals, an expression of honour, and the preparing a seat for a person of distinction seems to mean, laying things of this kind on a place where such a one is to sit. "It is the custom of Asia," Sir J. Chardin informs us, "for persons in common not to go into the shops of that country, which are mostly small, but there are wooden seats, on the outside, where people sit down, and if it happens to be a man of quality, they lay a cushion there." He also informs us, "that people of quality cause carpets and cushions to be carried everywhere, that they like, in order to repose themselves upon them more agreeably." When Job speaks of his preparing his seat, ch. xxix. 7, it is extremely natural to understand him of his sending his servants, to lay a cushion and a carpet on one of the public seats there, or something of that sort, as Sir John supposes; but I do not imagine a seat in the street, means a seat by a shop. Job is speaking evidently of his sitting there as a ruler among his people. Eli's seat by the wayside, was a seat adorned, we may believe, after the same manner. He did not sit in a manner unbecoming so dignified a personage.—HARMER.

CHAPTER VI.

Ver. 4. Then said they, What *shall be* the trespass-offering which we shall return to him? They answered, Five golden emerods, and five golden mice, *according to* the number of the lords of the Philistines: for one plague *was* on you all, and on your lords. 5. Wherefore ye shall make images of your emerods, and images of your mice that mar the land; and ye shall give glory unto the God of Israel: peradventure he will lighten his hand from off you, and from off your gods, and from off your land.

This animal (the mouse) is so very diminutive, that the Jewish naturalist places it among the reptiles, refusing it the honour of appearing among the quadrupeds. But, small and apparently insignificant as it is, in the oriental regions it often produces greater calamities than are experienced from all the beasts of prey with which they are infested. Formidable by its activity, its voraciousness, and its countless numbers, it lays waste the fields of Palestine and Syria, devours their harvests, and spreads famine and wretchedness among the helpless inhabitants. The extent and severity of the distress in which its ravages frequently involve the people of those countries, are sufficiently attested by the offering of five golden mice, from the lords of the Philistines, to appease the wrath of God, and avert the plague under which they had so greatly suffered. The account of this transaction is recorded in the first book of Samuel, and runs in these terms: "Then said they, what shall be the trespass-offering which we shall return to him? They answered, Five golden emerods, and five golden mice, according to the number of the lords of the Philistines: for one plague was on you all, and on your lords. Wherefore ye shall make images of your emerods, and of your mice that mar the land; and ye shall give glory unto the God of Israel: peradventure he will lighten his hand from off you, and from off your gods, and from off your land." These words undoubtedly intimate, that Palestine was very often visited by this scourge, and that the sufferings of its inhabitants were very severe. The devastations of this little destructive creature were so frequent, so extensive, and followed by consequences so dreadful, that even the unenlightened Philistines considered them as an immediate judgment from God himself. But this terrible scourge was not peculiar to Palestine: Strabo mentions that so vast a multitude of mice sometimes invaded Spain, as to produce a destructive pestilence; and in Cantabria, the Romans, by setting a price on a certain measure of these animals, escaped with difficulty from the same calamity. In other parts of Italy, the number of field-mice was so great, that some of the inhabitants were forced to leave the country. In Thrace, the frogs and mice sometimes united their hordes, and compelled the inhabitants to seek new settlements. In modern times, instances of the same calamity are not wanting. About the beginning of the twelfth century, innumerable swarms of locusts and mice, during four successive years, so completely ravaged that country, as to produce almost a total failure of the necessaries of life. So great and general was the distress of the people, that a kind of penitential council was held at Naplouse, in the year 1120, for the reformation of manners, and to invoke the mercy of the Almighty, who had been provoked by their sins to inflict upon them such terrible judgments.—PAXTON.

Ver. 5. Wherefore ye shall make images of your emerods, and images of your mice that mar the land; and ye shall give glory unto the God of Israel.

This command was given by the heathen priests and diviners to the Philistines, who were smitten with emerods, and whose land was nearly destroyed by the mice. It is a remarkable fact, that when the Hindoos are afflicted in any particular member, (or in the person generally,) they make an image to represent the afflicted part, and send it to the temple of Kanda Swamy, the Scandan of Bengal, in order to get relieved from their trouble. The temple of Kattaragam (sacred to Scandan) is famous, in ALL parts of the East, for the cures which have been performed by the deity there. Hence may be seen pilgrims at its shrine, suffering under every kind of disease, who have walked, or have been carried, from an immense distance. The images presented are generally made of silver, and I have seven of them in my possession, which are offerings in the famous temple already mentioned. The first represents a boy with a very large belly, which has probably been presented by the parents for their child labouring under that (very common) complaint. The second is that of an infant, probably sent by a mother who had a sick infant, or who, being herself in a state of pregnancy, had some fears respecting the future. The third is, I suppose, intended to represent an old man, who may have made a vow in his sickness, that he would present an image of silver to the temple, should he recover.—ROBERTS. (*See Engraving.*)

CHAPTER VII.

Ver. 5. And Samuel said, Gather all Israel to Mizpeh, and I will pray for you unto the LORD.

Aware of the dangers and calamities of war, ancient Israel were accustomed to perform very solemn devotions before they took the field: and it would seem, they had certain places particularly appropriated to this purpose. Samuel convened the people to Mizpeh, in order to prepare, by a solemn address to the throne of Jehovah, for the war which they meditated against the Philistines. "And Samuel said, Gather all Israel to Mizpeh, and I will pray for you unto the Lord." At other times, they asked counsel of God by the Urim and Thummim, or by a prophet of the Lord. Such a custom was common in Egypt, when Pococke visited that country. Near Cairo, says that traveller, beyond the mosque of Sheik Duisse, and in the neighbourhood of a burial-place of the sons of some pashas, on a hill, is a solid building of stone about three feet wide, built with ten steps, being at the top about three feet square, on which the sheik mounts to pray on an extraordinary occasion, as when all the people go out at the beginning of a war; and also when the Nile does not rise as they expect it should; and such a place, they have without all the towns of Turkey.—PAXTON.

Ver. 6. And they gathered together to Mizpeh, and drew water, and poured *it* out before the

LORD, and fasted on that day, and said there, We have sinned against the LORD.

Samuel had been reproving the people for their sins, and exhorting them to repent, and come to Mizpeh to fast and pray, and confess their sins. They complied with his directions, and in CONFIRMATION of the solemn vows, they poured out water before the Lord, to show that their words and promises had gone forth, and were "as water spilt on the ground, which cannot be gathered up again." To *pour water* on the ground is a very ancient way of taking a *solemn oath* in the East. When the god Vishnoo, in the disguise of a dwarf, requested the giant Mahā-Ville (Bāli) to grant him one step of his kingdom, the favour was conceded, and CONFIRMED by Mahā-Ville *pouring out water before the dwarf*. But in that ancient work, the Scanda Purāna, where the account is given of the marriage of the god Siva with Pārvati, it is said of the father, "He placed the hand of the goddess Pārvati, genitress of the world, in the hand of Parama Easuran, (Siva,) and, POURING OUT THE WATER, said, 'I give her with a joyful heart.'" This, therefore, was also done in CONFIRMATION of the compact. The children of Israel, in their misery, came before the Lord: they wept, they fasted, and prayed, and made their solemn vows; and, in CONFIRMATION of their promises, they "*poured out water before the Lord!*"—ROBERTS.

CHAPTER VIII.

Ver. 6. But the thing displeased Samuel, when they said, Give us a king to judge us. And Samuel prayed unto the LORD.

Hebrew, "was evil in the eyes of Samuel." When any thing gives displeasure to another, it is said to be evil in his eyes. "This thing is evil in his sight." "Alas! my lord, I am evil in your sight!"—ROBERTS.

CHAPTER IX.

Ver. 7. Then said Saul to his servant, but, behold, *if* we go, what shall we bring the man? for the bread is spent in our vessels, and *there is* not a present to bring to the man of God: what have we?

In no quarter of the world, is the difference of ranks in society maintained with more scrupulous exactness than in Asia. The intercourse among the various classes of mankind, which originate in the unequal distributions of creating wisdom, or providential arrangement, is regulated by laws, which, like those of the Medes and Persians, suffer almost no change from the lapse of time, or the fluctuation of human affairs. To these laws, which have extended their influence far beyond the limits of the East, the sacred writers make frequent allusions. No mark of esteem is more common through all the oriental regions, none more imperiously required by the rules of good breeding, than a present. When Mr. Maundrell and his party waited upon Ostan, the basha of Tripoli, he was obliged to send his present before him to secure a favourable reception. It is even reckoned uncivil in that country, to make a visit without an offering in the hand. The nobility, and officers of government, expect it as a kind of tribute due to their character and authority; and look upon themselves as affronted, and even defrauded, when this compliment is omitted. So common is the custom, that in familiar intercourse among persons of inferior station, they seldom neglect to bring a flower, an orange, a few dates or ..tsnes, or some such token of respect, to the person whom they visit. In Egypt the custom is equally prevalent: the visits of that people, which are very frequent in the course of the year, are always preceded by presents of various kinds, according to their station and property. So essential to human and civil intercourse are presents considered in the East, that, says Mr. Bruce, "whether it be dates or diamonds, they are so much a part of their manners, that without them an inferior will never be at peace in his own mind, or think that he has a hold of his superior for his favour or protection." Sir John Chardin affirms, that "the custom of making presents to the great, was universal in the East; and that every thing is received even by the great lords of the country, fruit, pullets, a lamb. Every one gives what is most at hand, and has a relation to his profession; and those who have no particular profession, give money. As it is accounted an honour to receive presents of this sort, they receive them in public; and even choose to do it when they have most company." "Throughout the East," says Du Tott, "gifts are always the mark of honour." This custom is, perhaps, one of the most ancient in the world. Solomon evidently alludes to it in that proverb: "A man's gift maketh room for him, and bringeth him before great men." We recognise it in the reply of Saul to his servant, when he proposed to consult the prophet Samuel about the object of their journey: "If we go, what shall we bring the man of God? for the bread is spent in our vessels, and there is not a present to bring to the man of God. What have we?" Saul was inclined at first to offer the seer, who was at the same time the chief magistrate in Israel, a piece of bread, till he recollected it was all spent, and then agreed to present him with "the fourth part of a shekel of silver," in value about a sixpence. It could not then be their design, by offering such a trifle, to purchase his services, but merely to show him that customary mark of respect to which he was entitled. Nor were the prophets of the Lord a set of mercenary pretenders to the knowledge of future events, who sold their services to the anxious inquirer for a large reward. Had they refused to accept of such presents, they would have been guilty of transgressing an established rule of good manners, and of insulting the persons by whom they were offered. When Elisha refused, with an oath, to accept of the present which Naaman the Syrian urged him to receive, it was not because he thought it either unlawful or improper to receive a gift, for he did not hesitate to accept of presents from his own people; nor was the prophet regardless of an established custom, which offended no precept of the divine law, or disposed to wound, without necessity, the feelings of the Syrian grandee; but because he would not put it in the power of Naaman to say he had enriched the prophet of Jehovah; and by this act of self-denial, it is probable he was desirous of recommending the character and service of the true God to that illustrious stranger.—PAXTON.

Such as are prejudiced against the sacred history, and unacquainted with eastern customs, may be ready, from the donations to the prophets, to imagine they were a mercenary set of people, and rudely to rank them with cunning men and fortunetellers, who will not from principles of benevolence reveal those secrets, or foretel those future events, of the knowledge of which they are supposed to be possessed; but demand of the anxious inquirer a large reward. This, however, will make impressions on none but those who know not the oriental usages, which Maundrell long since applied, with such clearness and force, to one of the most exceptionable passages of the Old Testament, that he has sufficiently satisfied the mind upon this point. As he has expressly applied it to a passage of scripture, it would not have been agreeable to my design to have mentioned this circumstance, had I not had some additional remarks to make upon this head, which possibly may not be ungrateful to the curious reader, and which therefore I shall here set down. I suppose my reader acquainted with Maundrell; but it will be proper, for the sake of perspicuity, first to recite at full length that passage in him I refer to.

"Thursday, March 11. This day we all dined at Consul Hastings's house; and after dinner went to wait upon Ostan, the basha of Tripoli, having first sent our present, as the manner is among the Turks, to procure a propitious reception. It is counted uncivil to visit in this country without an offering in hand. All great men expect it as a kind of tribute due to their character and authority; and look upon themselves as affronted, and indeed defrauded, when this compliment is omitted. Even in familiar visits, among inferior people, you shall seldom have them come without bringing a flower, or an orange, or some other such token of their respect to the person visited: the Turks in this point keeping up the ancient oriental customs hinted 1 Sam. ix. 7. *If we go*, says Saul, *what shall we bring the man of* GOD? *there is not a present*, &c. which words are questionless to be understood in conformity to this eastern custom, as relating to a token of respect, and not a price of divination."

Maundrell does not tell us what the present was which they made Ostan. It will be more entirely satisfying to the mind to observe, that in the East they not only universally send before them a present, or carry one with them, especially when they visit superiors, either civil or ecclesiastical; but that this present is frequently a piece of money, and that of no very great value. So Dr. Pococke tells us, that he presented an Arab sheik of an illustrious descent, on whom he waited, and who attended him to the ancient Hierapolis, with a piece of money, which he was told he expected; and that in Egypt an aga being dissatisfied with the present he made him, he sent for the doctor's servant, and told him, that he ought to have given him a piece of cloth, and, if he had none, two sequins, worth about a guinea, must be brought to him, otherwise he should see him no more, with which demand he complied. In one case a piece of money was expected, in the other two sequins demanded. A trifling present of money to a person of distinction among us would be an affront; it is not however, it seems, in the East. Agreeably to these accounts of Pococke, we are told in the travels of Egmont and Heyman, that the well of Joseph in the castle of Cairo is not to be seen without leave from the commandant; which having obtained, they, in return, presented him with a sequin. These instances are curious exemplifications of Mr. Maundrell's account of the nature of some of the eastern presents, and ought by no means to be omitted in collections of the kind I am now making. How much happier was the cultivation of Mr. Maundrell's genius than of St. Jerome's! Though this father lived so many years in the East, and might have advantageously applied the remains of their ancient customs to the elucidation of scripture, to which, if he was a stranger, he must have been an egregiously negligent observer; yet we find him, in his comment on Micah iii. 11, roundly declaring, that by a prophet's receiving money, his prophesying became divination. And when he afterward mentions this case of Saul's application to Samuel, as what he foresaw might be objected to him, he endeavours to avoid the difficulty, by saying, We do not find that Samuel accepted it, or that they even ventured to offer it; or if it must be supposed that he received it, that it was rather to be considered as money presented to the tabernacle, than the reward of prophesying. How embarrassed was the saint by a circumstance capable of the most clear explanation! Fond of allegorizing, he neglected the surest methods of interpretation, for which he had peculiar advantages; how different are the rewards of divination, which were to be earned, from the unconditional presents that were made to persons of figure upon being introduced into their presence! Before I quit this observation, I cannot forbear remarking, that there are other things presented in the East, besides money, which appear to us extremely low and mean, unworthy the quality of those that offer them, or of those to whom they are presented; and consequently that we must be extremely unqualified to judge of these oriental compliments. In what light might a European wit place the present of a governor of an Egyptian village, who sent to a British consul fifty eggs as a mark of respect, and that in a country where they are so cheap as to be sold at the rate of ten for a penny?—HARMER.

A present always precedes the man who is to ask a favour. Those who come on a complimentary visit, or to ask a favour, always present a lime, or a nosegay, with a graceful bow, to propitiate their benefactor.—ROBERTS.

Ver. 13. Now the LORD had told Samuel in his ear.

The priests have a remarkable custom of whispering something in the ear of those who are to be initiated. When a boy has reached the age of eight, he is eligible to have the Ubatheasum whispered in his right ear. The communication is generally made in the Grandam language, which, of course, is not understood: they do, however, sometimes speak in familiar speech; but it will never be repeated, for the priest assures him, should he do this, his head will split in two. This ceremony is believed to have the power of a charm, and to possess talismanic influence. It is sometimes very expensive, but the benefits are believed to be so great as to warrant the expense.—ROBERTS.

Ver. 23. And Samuel said unto the cook, Bring the portion which I gave thee, of which I said unto thee, Set it by thee. 24. And the cook took up the shoulder, and *that* which *was* upon it, and set *it* before Saul. And *Samuel* said, Behold that which is left! set *it* before thee, *and* eat: for unto this time hath it been kept for thee, since I said, I have invited the people. So Saul did eat with Samuel that day.

The shoulder of a lamb well roasted, and covered with butter and milk, is another delicacy, which the orientals greatly value. This explains the reason why Samuel ordered it to be set before his future sovereign, as well as what that was which was upon it, the butter and milk of which the sacred historian takes so particular notice.—This was by no means a contemptible dish for a royal entertainment, as some have alleged; but on the contrary, one of the most delicious which could be set before the future anointed of Jehovah. It appears from the accounts of travellers, that lamb is, in those parts of the world, extremely delicate. One, says Chardin, must have eaten of it in several places of Persia, Media, and Mesopotamia, and of their kids, to form a conception of the moisture, taste, delicacy, and fat of this animal; and as the eastern people are no friends of game, nor of fish, nor fowls, their most delicate food is the lamb and the kid. It is therefore not without reason, the sacred writers often speak of the lamb and the kid, as the most agreeable food in those countries; and that the holy Psalmist celebrates the blessings of salvation, and particularly the spiritual comforts of the heaven-born soul, under the figure of "marrow and fatness."—PAXTON.

Ver. 25. And when they were come down from the high place into the city, *Samuel* communed with Saul upon the top of the house. 26. And they arose early: and it came to pass, about the spring of the day, that Samuel called Saul to the top of the house, saying, Up, that I may send thee away. And Saul arose, and they went out both of them, he and Samuel, abroad.

Egmont and Heyman tell us, that at Caipha, at the foot of Mount Carmel, "the houses are small and flat-roofed, where, during the summer, the inhabitants sleep in arbours made of the boughs of trees." They mention also tents of rushes on the flat roofs of the houses at Tiberias, which are doubtless for the same purpose, though they do not say so. Dr. Pococke in like manner tells us, "that when he was at Tiberias in Galilee, he was entertained by the sheik's steward, the sheik himself having much company with him, but sending him provisions from his own kitchen, and that they supped on the top of the house for coolness, according to their custom, and lodged there likewise, in a sort of closet, about eight feet square, of a wicker-work, plastered round towards the bottom, but without any door, each person having his cell." In Galilee then we find they lodged a stranger, whom they treated with respect, on the top of the house, and even caused him to sup there. This was the latter end of May. This writer is more distinct than the others on this point, and I have recited his account at large, because it may perhaps lead to the true explanation of 1 Sam. ix. 25, 26, which verses tell us, that after they descended from the high place, Samuel conversed with Saul (על הגג *âl haggag*) on the house-top; and that at the spring of the day Samuel called Saul to the housetop; or, as it may be equally well translated, *on the housetop;* that is, Samuel conversed with him for coolness on the housetop in the evening, and in the morning called Saul, who had lodged there all night, and was not got up, saying, *Up, that I may send thee away*. The Septuagint seem to have understood it very much in this light, for they thus translate the passage, *And they spread a bed for Saul on the housetop, and he slept;* which shows how suitable this explanation is to those that are acquainted with eastern customs. As it is represented in our translation, Samuel called Saul *to* the housetop in the morning; but no account can be easily given for this; it does not appear to have been for secrecy, for he did not anoint then, but after he had left Samuel's house, for which transaction the prophet expressly required secrecy. "As they were going down to the end of the city, Samuel said to Saul, bid the servant pass on before us, and he passed on, but stand thou still awhile, that I may show thee the word of God." This sleeping on the terraces of their houses is only in summer-time. By this then we may determine, in the general, that this secret inauguration of Saul was in that part of the year.

Dr. Shaw has cited this passage concerning Samuel and Saul, when mentioning the various uses to which the people of the East put the flat roofs of their houses, though without explaining it; but he has not mentioned, among the other scriptures, that relating to Nebuchadnezzar, who is described by the prophet as walking on the roof of his palace, and taking a view of Babylon, when he fell, upon surveying that mighty city, into that haughty soliloquy which brought after it a dreadful humiliation. This is the more to be regretted, because though many have, all have not considered the passage in this light. Our own translation in particular has not, but renders the words, "He walked in the palace of the kingdom of Babylon," Dan. iv. 29, and has thrown the other reading "*upon* the palace," into the margin, as less preferable. But to those that are acquainted with eastern customs, who recollect the passage, which Dr. Shaw, it seems, did not, there cannot be any doubt how it is to be understood. "Sur la terrasse," says Sir J. Chardin, in his MS. note on this place, "pour le plaisir de la vue, pour de lá considerer la ville, et pour prendre la frais, et c'est ce que prouve, le verset suivant." That is, he walked upon the terrace, for the pleasure of the prospect, to take a view of the city, and to enjoy the fresh air, which the following verse proves. Nothing can be more natural than this interpretation.—HARMER.

CHAPTER X.

Ver. 5. When thou art come hither to the city, thou shalt meet a company of prophets coming down from the high place, with a psaltery, and a tabret, and a pipe, and a harp before them; and they shall prophesy.

The prophets in the ordinary modes of prophesying, were accustomed to compose their hymns to some musical instrument; and there could be but little difficulty in adapting their effusions to a measure which required, probably, no great restrictions in a language so free and uncontrolled as the Hebrew. The Jews conceived that music calmed the passions, and prepared the mind for the reception of the prophetic influence. It is probable, that the prophets on these occasions did not usually perform themselves on the musical instruments, but rather accompanied the strains of the minstrel with their voice.—(Lowth.) It has been the practice of all nations to adapt their religious worship to music, which the fabulous accounts of antiquity derived from heaven.—BURDER.

Ver. 27. But the children of Belial said, How shall this man save us? And they despised him, and brought him no presents: but he held his peace.

See on Ps. 76. 11.

CHAPTER XI.

Ver. 2. Then Nahash the Ammonite came up, and encamped against Jabesh-gilead: and all the men of Jabesh said unto Nahash, Make a covenant with us, and we will serve thee. 2. And Nahash the Ammonite answered them, On this *condition* will I make *a covenant* with you, that I may thrust out all your right eyes.

This cruel practice was very common, formerly, in the East, and even yet prevails in some places. Mr. Hanway gives several instances of it. "Mohammed Khan, (not long after I left Persia,) his eyes were cut out." Page 224. "The close of this hideous scene of punishment, was an order to cut out the eyes of this unhappy man: the soldiers were dragging him to this execution, while he begged, with bitter cries, that he might rather suffer death." Page 203. "Sadoc Aga had his beard cut off, his face was rubbed with dirt, and his eyes were cut out." Page 204. "As we approached Astrabad, we met several armed horsemen, carrying home the peasants whose eyes had been put out, the blood yet running down their faces." Page 201. Chardin relates an instance of a king of Imiretta, who lived in this condition. Page 160.—BURDER.

Ver. 4. Then came the messengers to Gibeah of Saul, and told the tidings in the ears of the people: and all the people lifted up their voices, and wept.

See on Jer. 6. 1.

CHAPTER XII.

Ver. 16. Now therefore stand and see this great thing which the LORD will do before your eyes. 17. *Is it* not wheat-harvest to-day? I will call unto the LORD, and he shall send thunder and rain; that ye may perceive and see that your wickedness *is* great, which ye have done in the sight of the LORD, in asking you a king.

Though the summer in Syria is commonly dry, the heavens are sometimes overcast, and a smart thunder-shower suddenly rushes down to refresh the parched soil. One of these fell at Aleppo in the night between the first and second of July, 1743; but it was regarded as a very uncommon occurrence at that season. It is probably still more extraordinary at Jerusalem; for Jerome, who lived long in Palestine, denies, in his commentary on Amos, that he had ever seen rain in those provinces, and especially in Judea, in the end of June, or in the month of July. It may, however, occasionally fall, though Jerome had never seen it, as it did at Aleppo, while Dr. Russel resided in that city. But such an occurrence by no means invalidates the proof which the prophet Samuel gave of his divine mission, when he called for thunder and rain from heaven in the time of wheat-harvest; since a very rare and unusual event immediately happening without any preceding appearance of it, upon the prediction of a person professing himself to be a prophet of the Lord, and giving it as an attestation of his sustaining that character, is a sufficient proof that his affirmation is true, although a similar event has sometimes happened without any such declared interposition of God, and therefore universally understood to be casual and without design. Nor should it be forgotten, that this thunderstorm in the book of Samuel, seems to have happened in the daytime, while the people of Israel were celebrating the accession of Saul to the throne; a circumstance which, from its singularity, added considerable energy to this event, and, perhaps, was to them a sufficient proof of the miraculous interference of Jehovah. Dr. Russel informs us, that the rains in those countries usually fall in the night, as did those extraordinary thunderstorms already mentioned, which happened in the month of July —PAXTON.

CHAPTER XIII.

Ver. 18. And another company turned the way *to* Beth-horon: and another company turned *to* the way of the border that looketh to the valley of Zeboim, towards the wilderness.

See on Jer. 12. 9.

CHAPTER XIV.

Ver. 25. And all *they of* the land came to a wood; and there was honey upon the ground.

See on Ps. 81. 16.

Ver. 26. And when the people were come into the wood, behold, the honey dropped.

Bees, in the East, are not, as in England, kept in hives: they are all in a wild state. The forests literally flow with honey; large combs may be seen hanging on the trees as you pass along, full of honey. Hence this article is cheap and plentiful, and is much used by the Vedahs to preserve the flesh of animals they catch in the chase. The ancient poets take great pleasure in speaking of the value of milk and honey.—ROBERTS.

CHAPTER XV.

Ver. 9. But Saul and the people spared Agag, and the best of the sheep, and of the oxen, and of the fatlings, and the lambs.

The margin has, instead of "fatlings," of the "*second sort.*" This curious way of designating the quality of animals finds an exact parallel among the Hindoos. They do not usually compare, as we do, by good, better, best; but first, second, or third sort. An animal of the finest proportions is said to be of the first sort; the next, of the second; and the last, the third. All the productions of art and nature are compared, as to their value, in the same way. They tell us there are three kinds of fruit they prefer to all others: first, gold; second, precious stones; and third, land.—ROBERTS.

Ver. 33. And Samuel said, As thy sword hath made women childless, so shall thy mother be childless among women. And Samuel hewed Agag in pieces before the LORD in Gilgal.

See on Ezra 4. 14.

Criminals were sometimes hewed in pieces, and their mangled bodies given as a prey to ravenous beasts. This punishment seems to have been extremely common in Abyssinia, when Mr. Bruce was there, and was probably handed down from the founders of that kingdom: "Coming across the market-place," says the traveller, "I had seen Za Mariam, the Ras's doorkeeper, with three men bound, one of whom he fell *a-hacking to pieces* in my presence; and upon seeing me running across the place, stopping my nose, he called me to stay till he should despatch the other two, for he wanted to speak with me, as if he had been engaged about ordinary business; that the soldiers, in consideration of his haste, immediately fell upon the other two, whose cries were still remaining in my ears; that the hyenas at night would scarcely let me pass in the streets, when I returned from the palace; and the dogs fled into my house, to eat pieces of human carcasses at their leisure." This account elucidates the mode of execution adopted by the prophet Samuel, in relation to Agag, the king of Amalek: "And Samuel said, (כאשר) As (or, in the same identical mode) thy sword hath made women childless, so shall thy mother be childless among women. And Samuel hewed Agag in pieces before the Lord in Gilgal." This was not a sudden and passionate act of vengeance, but a deliberate act of retributive justice. That savage chieftain had hewed many prisoners to death; and therefore, by the command of Jehovah, the judge of all the earth, he is visited with the same punishment which he had cruelly used towards others.—PAXTON.

In Light's *Travels*, we are informed, that "Djezzar had reason to suspect fraud in the conduct of some of the officers of the seraglio: and, as he could not discover the offenders, he had between fifty and sixty of them seized, stripped naked, and laid on the ground: and to each was placed a couple of janizaries, who were ordered to hew them in pieces with their swords."—BURDER.

CHAPTER XVII.

Ver. 6. And *he had* greaves of brass upon his legs, and a target of brass between his shoulders.

These were necessary to defend the legs and feet from the iron stakes placed in the way by the enemy, to gall and wound their opponents. They were a part of ancient military harness, and the artifices made use of by contending parties rendered the precaution important.—BURDER.

Ver. 7. And the staff of his spear *was* like a weaver's beam; and his spear's head *weighed* six hundred shekels of iron: and one bearing a shield went before him.

The oriental warrior had a person who went before him in the hour of danger, whose office it was to bear the great massy buckler, behind which he avoided the missile weapons of his enemy. Goliath had his armour-bearer carrying a shield before him, when he came up to defy the armies of Israel. When David went first to court, he was made armour-bearer to Saul; and Jonathan had a young man who bore his armour before him in the day of battle. Besides the large and ponderous buckler, the gigantic Philistine had another of smaller size called *cidon*, which we render target in one part of our version, and shield in another. It might either be held in the hand when the warrior had occasion to use it, or, at other times, be conveniently hung about his neck, and turned behind; and, therefore, the historian observes he had "a target of brass between his shoulders."—PAXTON.

Ver. 18. And carry these ten cheeses unto the captain of *their* thousand, and look how thy brethren fare.

The art of coagulating milk, and converting it into cheese, was known among the Syrian shepherds, from the remotest times. Instead of runnet, they turn the milk, especially in the summer season, with sour buttermilk, the flowers of the great-headed thistle, or wild artichoke; and, putting the curds afterward into small baskets made with rushes, or with the dwarf palm, they bind them up close, and press them. These cheeses are rarely above two or three pounds weight; and in shape and size, resemble our penny loaves. Oriental cheeses are sometimes of so very soft a consistence, after they are pressed, and even when they are set upon the table, that they bear a very near resemblance to curds, or to coagulated milk, which forms a very considerable part of eastern diet. But the ten cheeses which David carried to the camp of Saul, seem to have been fully formed, pressed, and sufficiently dried, to admit of their being removed from one place to another, without the frames in which they were made.—PAXTON.

The sons of Jesse were serving in the army of Saul; and as he probably had not heard from them for some time, he sent their brother David to take a present to the captain, to induce him to be kind to his sons; also to bring a pledge, or token, from his sons themselves, to assure him that they were well. A person in a distant country sends to those who are interested in his welfare a ring, a lock of hair, or a piece of his nail. This is his "*pledge*" of health and prosperity. A man who has returned from a far country, in calling upon an old friend (should he not be at home) will leave a handkerchief as a token, to testify that he had called.—ROBERTS.

The Vulgate illustrates this passage by translating the Hebrew words, decem formellas casei, ten little baskets of cheese, or, ten cheeses made in such baskets. To this day, in Barbary, "after turning the milk with the flowers of the great-headed thistle, or wild artichoke, they put the curds into small baskets, made with rushes or with the dwarf palm, and bind them up close and press them." (Shaw.) "Another offered me milk in baskets; a circumstance that astonished me. What, exclaimed I, milk in baskets! These baskets, he continues, are very pretty, and fabricated with reeds so closely interwoven, that they will hold water, and were afterwards of much service to me for that use." (Vaillant.) "In the evening they sent us in return some baskets of milk. These baskets were made from a species of cyperus, a strong reedy grass that grew in the springs of Zaure Veld. The workmanship was exceedingly clever and neat, and the texture so close that they were capable of containing the thinnest fluid." (Barrow.) "The girls also twist cotton yarn for fringes, and prepare canes, reeds, and palmetto leaves, as the boys also do, for basket making: but the making up the baskets is the men's work, who first die the materials of several curious lively colours, and then mix and weave them very prettily. They weave little baskets like cups also very neat, with the twigs wrought so very fine and close, as to hold any liquor without any more to do, having no lacker or varnish: and they as ordinarily drink out of these woven cups, as out of their calabashes, which they paint very curiously. They make baskets of several sizes for carrying their clothes, or other uses, with great variety of work; and so firm, that you may crush them, or throw them about how you will, almost with little or no damage to them."—BURDER.

Ver. 20. And David rose up early in the morning, and left the sheep with a keeper, and took, and went, as Jesse had commanded him: and he came to the trench as the host was going forth to the fight, and shouted for the battle.

After the introduction of trumpets into Greece, her armies generally began the attack at the sound of this warlike instrument; but the Lacedemonians were particularly remarkable for beginning their engagements with the soft tones of the flute, which were intended to render the combatants cool and sedate, and enable them to march with a firm and majestic step against their enemies. In the armies of Israel, the courage of the soldiers was roused and sustained by a concert of various instruments; in which were distinguished the martial sounds of the silver trumpet, and the gentler notes of the harp and the psaltery. In the beginning of their onset, they gave a general shout to encourage and animate one another, and strike terror into their enemies. This circumstance is distinctly stated in the first book of Samuel: "And David rose up early in the morning, and left the sheep with a keeper, and took, and went, as Jesse had commanded him; and he came to the trench, as the host was going forth to the fight, and shouted for the battle. For Israel and the Philistines had put the battle in array, army against army." This custom seems to have been used by almost every nation under heaven; and is mentioned by all writers, who treat of martial affairs. Homer compares the confused noise of two armies in the heat of battle, to the deafening roar of torrents rushing with impetuous force from the mountains into subjacent valleys.

In the wars which the Hebrews prosecuted in Canaan, and in the surrounding countries, the generals fought at the head of their armies, performing at once the part of a private soldier, and the various duties of a resolute captain. In the heroic ages, the Grecian generals exposed their persons in the same way. Homer, in all his battles, places the principal officers in the front, and calls them προμαχοι and προμοι, because they fought before their armies. Thus when he led up the Trojans, the godlike Paris fought at their head; and when Achilles sends out his soldiers to defend the Grecian ships, having allotted to the rest of his officers their several posts, he places Patroclus and Automedon, as chief commanders, before the front.—PAXTON.

Ver. 23. And as he talked with them, behold, there came up the champion (the Philistine of Gath, Goliath by name) out of the armies of the Philistines, and spake according to the same words: and David heard *them*. 24. And all the men of Israel, when they saw the man, fled from him, and were sore afraid.

The ancient Hebrews, like the nations around them, were wholly unacquainted with the refinements of modern warfare. From the age of Abraham, the renowned father of their tribes, they had little other business to employ their leisure hours, but feeding their flocks and herds, or tilling a few acres of land in the districts which they visited, except in Egypt, where their severe bondage was still more unfavourable to the cultivation of military habits. In such circumstances, the defence of their flocks and herds from the violence of roving hordes, which occasionally scoured the country in quest of spoil, generally produced the only wars in which they engaged. The rapid history of the patriarchs records a sufficient number of incidents, to show, that how rude and unpolished soever they may be deemed, they were by no means deficient in personal courage; and in the expedition of Abraham against the confederate kings, we can discern the rudiments of that military conduct, which has so often since his time filled the world with admiration or dismay. It will be readily admitted, that when the chosen people went up out of Egypt, where they had been long and cruelly oppressed, and in consequence of their miseries had contracted the abject and cowardly dispositions of the slave, they were quite incapable of warlike enterprises; but when their minds recovered that vigour and elevation which the freedom and hardships of the wilderness inspired, they discovered on many trying occasions, a boldness and resolution which were never surpassed by any of their antagonists. Till the reign of David, the armies of Israel were no better than a raw and undisciplined militia; and the simplicity of their behaviour sufficiently appears from the story of Goliath, who defied all the warriors that fought under the banners of Saul; and with a haughty look, and a few arrogant words, struck them with so great a terror that they fled before him. But the troops of the surrounding kingdoms were neither more courageous nor more skilful in the use of arms, which is evident from the history of David's captains, the first of whom engaged, single handed, three hundred men, and slew them at one time. And this is not the only instance of such daring and successful valour; he was one of three warriors who defended a plot of barley, after the people had fled, against the whole force of the Philistines, whom they routed with prodigious slaughter, after a desperate conflict. Nor is the sacred historian justly chargeable with transgressing the rules of probability in such relations, which, however strange and incredible they may appear to us, exactly accord with the manners of the times in which he wrote. Homer often introduces Achilles, Hector, and other heroes engaging, and, by the valour of their own arm, putting to flight whole squadrons of their enemies. Such feats are by no means uncommon in the history of the rude and unpolished nations, who, in the revolution of a few ages, became not less celebrated for their steady and disciplined heroism in the field, than for the sagacity of their measures in the cabinet. Under the banners of David, a prince of a truly heroic mind, the tribes of Israel often put to flight vast numbers of their enemies, and became a terror to all the circumjacent kingdoms.—PAXTON.

Ver. 34. And David said unto Saul, Thy servant kept his father's sheep, and there came a lion and a bear, and took a lamb out of the flock.

Although the lion is the terror of the forest, and has been known to scatter destruction over the fairest regions of the East; yet he is often compelled to yield to the superior prowess or address of man. When Samson, the champion of Israel, went down to Timnath, a city belonging to the tribe of Dan, situated in the valley of Sorek, so renowned for the excellence of its vines, a young lion roared against him; "and the spirit of the Lord came mightily upon him, and he rent him as he would have rent a kid, and he had nothing in his hand." In this instance, the lion was only giving the usual signal for the attack which he meditated, and consequently his kindling passions had not reached their highest excitement; but it appears from the authentic page of history, that the prey is sometimes rescued from his devouring jaws, when his fury is excited to the highest degree of intensity. To this circumstance, the prophet Amos refers, in that part of his prophecy where he describes the extreme difficulty with which a few of the meaner and poorer inhabitants of Samaria, should escape from the power of their enemies: "Thus saith the Lord, as the shepherd taketh out of the mouth of the lion, two legs or a piece of an ear, so shall the children of Israel be taken out that dwell in Samaria." The daring intrepidity, the admirable presence of mind, and great strength of David, when he tended his father's flocks in the wilderness, were subjected to a severe trial, by the attack of a lion, which he thus relates to Saul: "Thy servant kept his father's sheep; and there came a lion and a bear, and took a lamb out of the flock; and I went out after him, and smote him, and delivered it out of his mouth; and when he rose against me, I caught him by his beard, and smote him, and slew him: thy servant slew both the lion and the bear." In these words, the youthful shepherd indisputably details the particulars of two exploits performed on different occasions; for the lion and the bear never hunt in company. Like the greater part of other wild beasts, they prowl alone, rejecting the society of even one of their own species. "It is not therefore to be supposed, they will associate on such occasions with other animals. A careless reader might imagine that David encountered them both at the same time, and Castalio has been so inconsiderate as to make the text speak this language; for he translates it, There came a lion, *una cum*, together or in company with a bear. But are we to suppose, that these two animals, contrary to their nature, entered into partnership on this occasion, and that to seize upon one poor lamb, and divide it between them? Or if no miracle was wrought in the case, but the victory was achieved by the natural strength and resolution of David, aided by the good providence of God, how many hands must we suppose him to have had, in order at once to seize two such animals, to smite them both, and to rescue the lamb" from their jaws? How was it possible for a single youth, for at that time he was not more than twenty years of age, to encounter with success two of the strongest and fiercest beasts that range the forest? Or if David vanquished these terrible depredators, not by his own courage and address, but by the miraculous assistance of heaven, still the difficulty is not removed; for he could have no warrant from such a victory to encounter Goliath. It became him to enter the lists with the giant, depending upon the ordinary assistance of God, and the usual vigour of his own arm, not upon a miracle, which God had not promised. To avoid these inconveniences, it is necessary to admit, that David mentions two different rencounters, one with a lion, and another with a bear; in both which he succeeded in rescuing the prey from the devourer. This hypothesis has the advantage of being perfectly consistent with the text; for the particle rendered *and*, is often disjunctive, and ought to be translated *or*. Thus, in the law of the passover, it is commanded, "Ye shall take it out from the sheep or from the goats;" and in the precept for securing reverence to parents, "He that smiteth his father or his mother, shall surely be put to death;" "and he that curseth his father or his mother, shall surely be put to death;" in all which, the connecting particle is the same. But by the law of Moses, only one lamb, or one kid, was to be taken for each household, not two; and if a person smote, or cursed one of his parents, he was guilty of death; in these cases, therefore, the particle is properly rendered *or*; and by consequence, may be so rendered in the text under consideration. The words of David would then run thus: There came a lion or a bear, and took a lamb out of the flock. This version is also required by the verb, which, instead of being in the plural, as the conjunctive particle demands, is in the singular number, which clearly indicates a disjunctive sense. This is confirmed by the next verse, in which David speaks of them in the singular number: "And I went out after him, and smote him, and delivered it out of his mouth; and when he rose against me, I caught him by his beard, and smote him, and slew him." If these two animals had been in company, he could with no propriety have spoken of them in this manner. The meaning therefore is, there came a lion on one occasion, and on another a bear, and took each a lamb out of the flock; and he went out against each of them and rescued the lamb from his mouth. Thus, by the favour of Providence, did the future shepherd of Israel, on two different occasions, slay both the lion and the bear. Nor ought this to be reckoned an achievement beyond the power of a single combatant; for an ancient poet only admits it to be extremely dangerous, and almost beyond the powers of man, to deliver the prey from the mouth of a hungry lion, but does not venture to pronounce it impracticable:—

"Esurienti leoni ex ore exculpere prædam."

Nor is any mistake imputable to David, when he speaks of seizing a bear by the beard; for the original term sometimes denotes the chin; as in this precept of the ceremonial law: "If a man or woman have a plague upon the head or beard; then the priest shall see the plague." He, therefore, seized the lion by his beard, and the bear, that was not favoured with this ornament, by the chin; which entirely removes the difficulty.—PAXTON.

Ver. 38. And Saul armed David with his armour, and he put a helmet of brass upon his head; also he armed him with a coat of mail.

A principal piece of defensive armour entitled to our notice, is the helmet, which protected the head. This has been used from the remotest ages by almost every nation of a martial spirit. The champion of the Philistines had a helmet of brass upon his head, as had also the king of Israel, who commanded the armies of the living God. This martial cap was also worn by the Persians and Ethiopians in the day of battle. The Grecian helmets were very often made of the skins of beasts; but the helmet of the Jewish warrior seems to have been uniformly made of brass or iron; and to this sort of casque only, the sacred writer seems to refer. In allusion to this piece of defensive armour, Paul directs the believer to put on for a helmet the hope of salvation, which secures the head in every contest, till through him that loved him, he gain a complete victory over all his enemies. That well-grounded hope of eternal life, which is attended with ineffable satisfaction, and never disappoints the soul, like a helmet of brass shall guard it against fear and danger, enable it patiently to endure every hardship, and fortify it against the most furious and threatening attacks of Satan and all his confederates. Such adversaries, this solid hope is not less calculated to strike with dismay, than was the helmet of an ancient warrior in the day of battle his mortal foes, by its dazzling brightness, its horrific devices of Gorgons and Chimeras, and its nodding plumes which overlooked the dreadful cone.—PAXTON.

Ver. 43. And the Philistine said unto David, *Am* I a dog, that thou comest to me with staves? And the Philistine cursed David by his gods.

Men of high caste will not strike those who are of low caste with the hand, because the touch would defile them: they therefore beat them with a stick or some other weapon. Hence to offer to strike any person with a stick is very provoking, and the person so struck will ask, "Am I a dog?" When a man wishes to make another angry, he pretends to be looking for a stick, which will produce a similar question and feeling. Sometimes, however, they only repeat the proverb, "Take up a stick, and the dog will run off." As did the Philistines, so do these people curse each other by their gods. The imprecations are generally of such a kind as it would be improper to repeat. The extremes of filthiness, of sin and hell, are put under contribution, to furnish epithets and allusions for their execrations. —ROBERTS.

Ver. 44. And the Philistine said to David, Come to me, and I will give thy flesh unto the fowls of the air, and to the beasts of the field.

The rhodomontade of Goliath is still the favourite way of terrifying an enemy. "Begone, or I will give thy flesh to the jackals." "The crows shall soon have thy carcass." "Yes, the teeth of the dogs shall soon have hold of thee." "The eagles are ready."—ROBERTS.

Ver. 51. Therefore David ran, and stood upon the Philistine, and took his sword, and drew it out of the sheath thereof, and slew him, and cut off his head therewith. And when the Philistines saw their champion was dead, they fled.

The ancient Grecians frequently committed their cause to the issue of a single combat, and decided their quarrels by two or more champions on each side; and their kings and great commanders were so eager in the pursuit of glory, and so tender of the lives of their subjects, that they frequently sent challenges to their rivals, to end the quarrel by a single encounter, that by the death of one of them, the effusion of more blood might be prevented. Ancient history contains many remarkable instances of such combats; Xanthus, king of Bœotia, challenged the king of Attica, to terminate the dangerous war in which their states were engaged in this way, and lost his life in the contest; and Pittacus, the famous Mitylenian, killed Phryno the Athenian general, in a single combat. This custom was not unknown in Palestine and other eastern countries, for the champion of the Philistines challenged the armies of Israel, to give him a man to fight with him; and when he fell by the valour of David, his countrymen, struck with dismay, immediately deserted their standards, and endeavoured to save themselves by flight. The challenge given on those occasions, was generally couched in the most insolent language, and delivered with a very contemptuous air. Thus, Homer makes one chief address another in these terms: "Bold as thou art, too prodigal of ife, approach and enter the dark gates of death." But his is a tame spiritless defiance, compared with the proud and insulting terms which Goliath addressed to his young and inexperienced antagonist: "Come to me, and I will give thy flesh to the fowls of the air and the beasts of the field;" or the bold and manly, but devout reply of the youthful warrior: "Thou comest to me with a sword, and with a spear, and with a shield, but I come to thee in the name of the Lord of hosts, the God of the armies of Israel, whom thou hast defied. This day will the Lord deliver thee into my hand, and I will smite thee, and take thy head from thee, and I will give the carcasses of the hosts of the Philistines this day unto the fowls of the air, and to the wild beasts of the earth; that all the earth may know that there is a God in Israel." The Philistines no sooner saw their champion fallen, and his head severed from his body, than, seized with a panic fear, they fled, and the armies of Israel pursued with loud acclamations. Another instance of panic which struck the army of the Philistines, a short time before, when Jonathan and his armour-bearer fell upon their garrison and put them to flight, is described in these terms: "And there was trembling in the host, in the field, and among all the people; the garrison and the spoilers, they also trembled; and the earth quaked; so it was a very great trembling." In the Hebrew, it is a trembling of God; that is, a fear which God sent upon them, and consequently which the strongest mind could not reason down, nor the firmest heart resist. This fear, the Greeks and other heathen nations called a panic; because Pan, one of their gods, was believed to be the author of it. Bacchus, in his Indian expedition, led his army into some defiles, where he was surrounded by his enemies, and reduced to the last extremity. By the advice of Pan, his lieutenant-general, he made his army give a sudden shout, which struck the enemy with so great astonishment and terror, that they fled with the utmost precipitation. Hence, it was ever afterward called a panic, and supposed to come directly from heaven. It is thus expressed by Pindar: "When men are struck with divine terrors, even the children of the gods betake themselves to flight." The flight of the Syrians, in the reign of Jehoram, king of Israel, was produced by a panic, which so completely unmanned them, that, says the sacred historian, "all the way was full of garments and vessels, which the Syrians had cast away in their haste." The flight of Saladin's army, which was defeated by Baldwin IV. near Gaza, in the time of the crusades, was marked with similar circumstances of consternation and terror. To flee with greater expedition, they threw away their arms and clothes, their coats of mail, their greaves, and other pieces of armour, and abandoned their baggage, and fled from their pursuers, almost in a state of complete nudity.—PAXTON.

Ver. 55. And when Saul saw David go forth against the Philistine, he said unto Abner, the captain of the host, Abner, whose son *is* this youth? And Abner said, *As* thy soul liveth, O king, I cannot tell.

It is a favourite way of addressing a person by saying, "You are the son of such a person," or, "Is he not the son of such a man?" How Saul could have forgotten David, is impossible to account for. When a person has to ask a number of questions, though he know well the name of the individual he has to address, he often begins by asking, "Whose son are you?" Many people never go by their proper name: they are known by the son of such a person, as *Nellinäderin Maggan*, *i. e.* the son of *Nellinäder*.—ROBERTS.

Ver. 57. And as David returned from the slaughter of the Philistine, Abner took him, and brought him before Saul, with the head of the Philistine in his hand.

On some occasions the victor cut off the head of his enemy, and carried it in triumph on the point of a spear, and presented it, if a person of inferior rank, to his prince or the commander-in-chief. Barbarossa, the dey of Algiers, returned in triumph from the conquest of the kingdom of Cucco, with the head of the king, who had lost his life in the contest, carried before him on a lance. Mr. Harmer thinks it probable that the Philistines cut off the head of Saul, whom they found among the slain, on Gilboa, to carry it in triumph on the point of a spear to their principal city, according to the custom of those times; and that David, in a preceding war, severed the head of Goliath from his body, for the purpose of presenting it to Saul, in the same manner, on the point of a lance. The words of the inspired historian do not determine the mode in which it was presented; we must therefore endeavour to form our opinion from the general custom of the East. The words of the record are: "And as David returned from the slaughter of the Philistine, Abner took him and brought him before Saul, with the head of the Philistine in his hand." It is scarcely to be supposed that the youthful warrior was introduced with the sword in the one hand, and the head of his enemy in the other, like one of our executioners holding up the head of a traitor; it is more reasonable to imagine, says Mr. Harmer, that he appeared in a more graceful and warlike attitude, bearing on the point of a lance the head of his adversary. But it must be confessed that the other idea, after all that respectable writer has said, is more naturally suggested by the words of the inspired historian. It is a common practice in Turkey to cut off the heads of enemies slain in battle, and lay them in heaps before the residence of their emperor, or his principal officers. In Persia Mr. Hanway saw a pyramid of human heads at the entrance of Astrabad. They were the heads of Persians who had rebelled against their sovereign. This barbarous custom may be traced up to a very remote antiquity; and it was probably not seldom reduced to practice in the various governments of Asia. When Jehu conspired against Ahab, he commanded the heads of his master's children, seventy in number, to be cut off, and brought in baskets to Jezreel, and "laid in two heaps at the entering in of the gate until the morning." The renowned Xenophon says, in his Anabasis, that the same custom was practised by the Chalybes; and Herodotus makes the same remark in relation to the Scythians. —PAXTON.

CHAPTER XVIII.

Ver. 4. And Jonathan stripped himself of the robe that *was* upon him, and gave it to David, and his garments, even to his sword, and to his bow, and to his girdle.

See on Est. 6. 7, 8.

An ancient mode of ratifying an engagement, was by presenting the party with some article of their own dress; and if they were warriors, by exchanging their arms. The greatest honour which a king of Persia can bestow upon a subject, is to cause himself to be disrobed, and his habit given to the favoured individual. The custom was probably derived from the Jews; for when Jonathan made his covenant with David, "he stripped himself of the robe that was upon him, and gave it to David, and his garments; even to his sword, and to his bow, and to his girdle."—In a similar way, Julus, and the other Trojan chiefs, confirmed their solemn engagements to Nisus and Euryalus: "Thus weeping over him, he speaks; at the same time divests his shoulders of his gilded sword—On Nisus Mnestheus bestows the skin and spoil of a grim shaggy lion; trusty Alethes exchanges with him his helmet." This instance proves, that among the ancients, to part with one's girdle was a token of the greatest confidence and affection; in some cases it was considered as an act of adoption. The savage tribes of North America, that are certainly of Asiatic origin, ratify their covenants and leagues in the same way; in token of perfect reconciliation, they present a belt of wampum.—PAXTON.

Ver. 6. And it came to pass, as they came, when David was returned from the slaughter of the Philistine, that the women came out of all the cities of Israel, singing and dancing, to meet king Saul, with tabrets, with joy, and with instruments of music.

Has a long absent son returned, is a person coming who has performed some great exploit, are the bride and bridegroom with their attendants expected; then, those in the house go forth with tabrets and pipes to meet them, and greet them, and conduct them on the way. When a great man is expected, the people of the village always send the tabrets and pipes to meet him. It is amusing to see with what earnestness and vehemence they blow their instruments, or beat their tom-toms, and stamp along the road.—ROBERTS.

The dancing and playing on instruments of music, before persons of distinction, when they pass near the dwelling-places of such as are engaged in country business, still continue in the East. When the Baron de Tott was sent by the French government, to inspect the factories of that nation in the Levant, having proceeded from Egypt to the maritime cities of Syria, he went from them to Aleppo, and returning from thence to Alexandretta, in order to visit Cyprus, and some other places of which he has given an account in his memoirs, he tells us, that between Aleppo and Alexandretta, he saw, on a sudden, the troop the governor of Aleppo had sent with him, to escort him, turn back and ride towards him. "The commander of the detachment then showed me the tents of the Turcomen, pitched on the banks of the lake, near which we were to pass. It was no easy task to keep my company in good spirits, within sight of six or seven thousand Asiatics, whose peaceable intentions were at least doubtful." "I took care to cover my escort with my small troop of Europeans; and we continued to march on, in this order, which had no very hostile appearance, when we perceived a motion in the enemy's camp, from which several of the Turcomen advanced to meet us, and I soon had the musicians of the different hordes, playing and dancing before me all the time we were passing by the side of their camp." The translation does not determine, whether these musicians were of the male or female sex; but I doubt not but that it would appear, on consulting the original French, that they were women that played and danced before M. de Tott, the French inspector, while passing along the side of that large encampment. We cannot after this wonder at the account of the sacred historian, that when Saul and David were returning from the slaughter of Goliath, the great hero of the Philistines, *the women came out of all the cities of Israel, singing and dancing to meet King Saul, with tabrets, with joy, and with instruments of music*. That is, as I apprehend, the women of the several villages of Israel near which he passed, in returning to his settled abode, universally paid him the honour of singing and playing before him for some considerable way, while he passed along in the road near to them. All Israel were engaged in rural employments, as well as these Turcomen. De Tott ascribes the honours paid him by these Asiatics to the hope of a reward: "I took leave of them, by presenting them with that reward, the hope of which had brought them to attend us, and with which they were very civil to go away contented." I would remark, that the eastern princes sometimes cause money to be scattered in processions on joyful occasions, according to this very writer; however, the satisfaction that succeeded great terror, upon the death of Goliath, was enough to engage the Israelitish women universally to pay this honour to their own king, and an heroic youth of their own nation, who had been the instrument of effecting such a great salvation for their country, without any lucrative considerations whatever.—HARMER.

When leaving the city of Lattakoo, to visit the king of the Matslaroos, on the confines of the great southern Zahara desert, a party of men was returning from a distant expedition, after an absence of several months. The news of their approach had reached the town, and the women were hastening to meet them. On joining the party, they marched at their head, clapping their hands, and singing with all their might, till they arrived at their homes in the town. On witnessing this scene, my mind was carried back three thousand years, to the very occurrence recorded in the above passage. The occasion, no doubt, was a joyful one to the females, some of whom had their husbands, and others their fathers and brothers, in the expedition, for whose safety they were interested, and had been anxiously concerned. The same must have been the case with respect to the Israelitish women, while Saul's army were returning victorious from the Philistine war.—AFRICAN LIGHT.

Ver. 25. And Saul said, Thus shall ye say to David, The king desireth not any dowry, but a hundred foreskins of the Philistines, to be avenged of the king's enemies. But Saul thought to make David fall by the hand of the Philistines.

In the remote ages of antiquity, women were literally purchased by their husbands; and the presents made to their parents or other relations were called their dowry. The practice still continues in the country of Shechem; for when a young Arab wishes to marry, he must purchase his wife; and for this reason, fathers, among the Arabs, are never more happy than when they have many daughters. They are reckoned the principal riches of a house. An Arabian suiter will offer fifty sheep, six camels, or a dozen of cows; if he be not rich enough to make such offers, he proposes to give a mare or a colt; considering in the offer, the merit of the young woman, the rank of her family, and his own circumstances. In the primitive times of Greece, a well-educated lady was valued at four oxen. When they are agreed on both sides, the contract is drawn up by him that acts as cadi or judge among these Arabs. In some parts of the East, a measure of corn is formally mentioned in contracts for their concubines, or temporary wives, besides the sum of money which is stipulated by way of dowry. This custom is probably as ancient as concubinage, with which it is connected; and if so, it will perhaps account for the prophet Hosea's purchasing a wife of this kind, for fifteen pieces of silver, and for a homer of barley, and a half homer of barley. When the intended husband was not able to give a dowry, he offered an equivalent. The patriarch Jacob, who came to Laban with only his staff, offered to serve him seven years for Rachel; a proposal which Laban accepted. This custom has descended to modern times; for in Cabul, the young men who are unable to advance the required dowry, "live with their future father-in-law and earn their bride by their services, without ever seeing the object of their wishes." Saul, instead of a dowry, required David to bring him a hundred foreskins of the Philistines, under the pretence of avenging himself of his enemies. This custom has prevailed in latter times; for in some countries they give their daughters in marriage to the valiant men, or those who should bring them so many heads of the people with whom they happen to be at war. It is recorded of a nation in Caramania, that no man among them was permitted to marry, till he had first brought the head of an enemy to the king. Aristotle admits, that the ancient Grecians were accustomed to buy their wives; but they no sooner began to lay aside their barbarous manners, than this disgusting practice ceased, and the custom of giving portions to their sons-in-law, was substituted in its place. The Romans also, in the first ages of their history, purchased their wives; but afterward, they required the wife to bring a portion to the husband, that he might be able to bear the charges of the matrimonial state more easily.—PAXTON.

CHAPTER XIX.

Ver. 12. So Michal let David down through a
window; and he went, and fled, and escaped.
13. And Michal took an image, and laid *it* in
the bed, and put a pillow of goats' *hair* for his
bolster, and covered *it* with a cloth. 14. And
when Saul sent messengers to take David, she
said, He *is* sick. 15. And Saul sent the messengers *again* to see David, saying, Bring him
up to me in the bed, that I may slay him.
16. And when the messengers were come in
behold, *there was* an image in the bed, with a
pillow of goats' *hair* for his bolster. 17. And
Saul said unto Michal, Why hast thou deceived
me so, and sent away mine enemy, that he is
escaped? And Michal answered Saul, He said
unto me, Let me go; why should I kill thee?

An accident led me into a train of thought, relating to that piece of furniture the Romans called a *canopeum*, and which is said to denote a canopy or pavilion made of net-work, which hung about beds, and was designed to keep away gnats, which are sometimes insupportably troublesome to the more delicate. I recollected that it is at this time used in the East; and that if it may be supposed to have obtained so early there as the time of King Saul, it may very happily illustrate the above passage of scripture, of which our commentators have given a very unsatisfactory account. I should suppose a canopeum, or guard against gnats, is what is meant by the word translated a *pillow of goats' hair*. I cannot conceive what deception could arise from the pillow's being stuffed with goats' hair, or for making a truss of goats' hair serve for a pillow. This last must have been, on the contrary, very disagreeable to a sick man; especially one who, having married a princess, must be supposed to have been in possession of agreeable accommodations of life, such at least as were used at that time, and in that country. A piece of fine net-work to guard them from gnats, and other troublesome insects, that might disturb the repose of a sick man, was extremely natural, if the use of them was as early as the days of Saul. It is in one place translated a *thick cloth*, in another, a *sieve;* now a cloth of a nature fit to use for a sieve, is just such a thing as I am supposing, a fine net-work or gauze like cloth. Here it is translated *a pillow*, but for no other reason, but because it appeared to be something relating to the head; but a canopeum relates to the head as well as a pillow, being a canopy suspended over the whole bed, or at least so far as to surround the head, and such upper part of the body as might be uncovered. Modern canopies of this nature may be of other materials: they may be of silk or thread, but goats' hair was in great use in those earlier ages, and may be imagined to have been put to this use in those times, as our modern sieves still continue frequently to be made of the hair of animals.

After this preparatory remark, I would produce a proof, that this kind of defence against gnats is used in the East. "Among the hurtful animals that Egypt produces," says Maillet, "those that we call gnats ought not to be forgotten. If their size prevents all apprehensions of dangerous accidents from them, their multitudes make them insupportable. The Nile water, which remains in the canals and the lakes, into which it makes its way every year, produces such a prodigious quantity of these insects, that the air is often darkened by them. The nighttime is that in which people are most exposed to receive punctures from them; and it is with a view to guard themselves from them, that they sleep so much here on the tops of their houses, which are flat-roofed. These terraces are paved with square flat stones, very thin; and as in this country, they have no apprehensions from rain or fogs, they are wont to place their beds on these roofs every night, in order to enjoy their repose more undisturbedly and coolly, than they could anywhere else. Gnats seldom rise so high in the air. The agitation of the air at that height is too much for them; they cannot bear it. However, for greater precaution, persons of any thing of rank never fail to have a tent set up in these terraces, in the midst of which is suspended a pavilion of fine linen, or of gauze, which falls down to the ground, and encloses the mattress. Under the shelter of this pavilion, which the people of the country call *namousie*, from the word *namous*, which in their language signifies *fly*, or *gnat*, people are secured against these insects, not only on the terraces, but everywhere else. If they were to make use of them in Europe, I do not doubt but that people that sleep in the daytime, and above all the sick, would find the advantage of them; for it must be acknowledged, that in summer-time those small insects, which introduce themselves into all places, are insupportable to people that would take their repose, and much more so to those that are ill." No curious carved statue, which indeed one can hardly imagine was to be found in the house of David, was necessary; any thing formed in a tolerable resemblance of the body of a man was sufficient for this deception, covered over with the coverlet belonging to the mattress on which it was laid, and where the head should have been placed, being covered all over with a pavilion of goats' hair, through which the eye could not penetrate. A second visit, with a more exact scrutiny, discovered the artifice.

There is another passage in which the word occurs, and in the same sense. It is in the account the historian gives us of the real cause of the death of Benhadad, the king of Syria, 2 Kings viii. 15; "And it came to pass on the morrow, that he took a thick cloth, and dipped it in water, and spread it over his face, so that he died: and Hazael reigned in his stead." If Hazael stifled him, why all this parade? the drawing the pillow from under his head, and clapping it over his mouth, would have been sufficient. Why the procuring a thick cloth, according to our translators? why the dipping it in water? It is the same word (כביר *kebeer*) with that in Samuel, and, it is reasonable therefore to suppose, means the same thing, a gnat pavilion. The dipping it in water may well be supposed to be under the pretence of coolness and refreshment. So Pitts tells us, that the people of Mecca "do usually sleep on the tops of the houses for the air, or in the streets before their doors. Some lay the small bedding they have on a thin mat on the ground; others have a slight frame, made much like drink-stalls, on which we place barrels, standing on four legs, corded with palm cordage, on which they put their bedding. Before they bring out their bedding, they sweep the streets, and water them. As for my own part, I usually lay open without any bed-covering, on the top of the house; only I took a linen cloth, dipped in the water, and after I had wrung it, covered myself with it in the night: and when I awoke, if I should find it dry, then I would wet it again; and thus I did two or three times in a night." In like manner, Niebuhr tells us, in his description of Arabia, that "as it is excessively hot, in the summer-time, on the eastern shore of the Persian gulf, and they do not find that the dew there is unwholesome, they sleep commonly in the open air." He goes on, "in the island of Charedsj, I never enjoyed my repose better than when the dew moistened my bed in the night." Hazael then had a fair pretence to offer to moisten the gnat pavilion, if Benhadad did not himself desire it, on the account of his extreme heat, which might prove the occasion of his death, while the distemper itself was not mortal. Whether the moisture of that piece of furniture proved at that time destructive from the nature of the disease, or whether Hazael stifled him with it, we are not told by the historian, and therefore cannot pretend absolutely to determine. Conjecture is not likely to be very favourable to Hazael.—Harmer.

CHAPTER XX.

Ver. 30. Then Saul's anger was kindled against Jonathan, and he said unto him, Thou son of the perverse rebellious *woman*, do not I know that thou hast chosen the son of Jesse to thine own confusion, and unto the confusion of thy mother's nakedness.

In the East, when they are angry with a person, they abuse and vilify his parents. Saul thought of nothing but venting his anger against Jonathan, nor had any design to reproach his wife personally; the mention of her was only a vehicle by which, according to oriental modes, he was to convey his resentment against Jonathan into the minds of those about him.—Harmer.

CHAPTER XXI.

Ver. 9. And the priest said, The sword of Goliath the Philistine, whom thou slewest in the valley of Elah, behold, it *is here*, wrapped in a cloth behind the ephod: if thou wilt take that, take *it;* for *there is* no other save that here. And David said, *There is* none like that; give it me.

To the jewels of silver and gold, which the Hebrew soldier was accustomed to bring as a free-will offering into the treasury of his God, must be added the armour of some illustrious foe, which, in gratitude for his preservation, he suspended in the sanctuary. The sword of Goliath was wrapped up in a cloth, and deposited behind the ephod; and in a succeeding war, the Philistines proving victorious, took their revenge by depositing the armour of Saul in the temple of Ashtaroth. The custom of dedicating to the gods the spoils of a conquered enemy, and placing them in their temples as trophies of victory and testimonies of gratitude, is very ancient, and universally received in Asia and Greece. Hector promises to dedicate his enemy's armour in the temple of Apollo, if he would grant him the victory: "But if I shall prove victorious, and Apollo vouchsafe me the glory to strip off his armour, and carry it to sacred Troy, then will I suspend it in the temple of the far-darting Apollo." Virgil alludes to this custom in his description of the temple, where Latinus gives audience to the ambassadors of Æneas:

"Multaque præterea sacris in postibus arma," &c.
Æn. lib. vii. l. 183.

"Besides, on the sacred doorposts, many arms, captive chariots, and crooked cimeters are suspended, helmets, crested plumes, and massy bars of gates, and darts, and shields, and beaks torn from ships." Nor was it the custom only to dedicate to heaven the weapons taken from an enemy; when the soldier retired from the tumults of war to the bosom of his family, he frequently hung up his own arms in the temple, as a grateful acknowledgment of the protection he had received, and the victories he had won. In this custom, the Greeks and Romans imitated the Asiatic nations, and particularly the Hebrews; for when David resigned the command of his armies to his generals, he laid up his arms in the tabernacle, where they continued for several ages; and there is reason to believe his conduct in this respect, was followed by many of his companions in arms. When Joash, one of his descendants, was crowned, Jehoiada the high-priest, under whose care he had been educated, delivered to the captains of hundreds, spears, and bucklers, and shields, that had been King David's, which were in the house of God.—PAXTON.

CHAPTER XXII.

Ver. 6. When Saul heard that David was discovered, and the men that *were* with him, (now Saul abode in Gibeah under a tree in Ramah, having his spear in his hand, and all his servants *were* standing about him.)

Though mean people in travelling might make use of trees for shelter from the heat, we may perhaps think it almost incredible that kings should not imagine that either proper houses would be marked out for their reception; or if that could not be conveniently done in some of their routes, that at least they would have tents carried along with them, as persons of more than ordinary rank and condition are supposed by Dr. Shaw now to do. For these reasons we may possibly have been extremely surprised at that passage concerning Saul, 1 Sam. xxii. 6, *Now Saul abode in Gibeah, under a tree in Ramah*, or, according to the margin, *under a grove in a high place, having his spear in his hand, and all his servants were standing about him.* Yet strange as this may appear to us, it is natural enough according to the present customs of the East, where we know the solemnity and awfulness of superiority is kept up as high as ever. Thus when Dr. Pococke was travelling in the company of the governor of Faiume, who was treated with great respect as he passed along, they passed one night, he tells us, in a grove of palm-trees. The governor might, no doubt, had he pleased, have lodged in some village; but he rather chose a place which we think very odd for a person of figure. The position of Saul, which was on a high place according to the margin, reminds me of another passage of this author, where he gives us an account of the going out of the Caya, or lieutenant of the governor of Meloui, on a sort of Arab expedition, towards a place where there was an ancient temple, attended by many people with kettledrums and other music: the doctor visited that temple, and upon his return from it went to the caya, he says, "whose carpets and cushions were laid on a height, on which he sat with the standard by him, which is carried before him when he goes out in this manner. I sat down with him, and coffee was brought; the sadar himself, came after as incognito." Saul seems, by the description given, as well as by the following part of the history, to have been pursuing after David, and stopping, to have placed himself, according to the present oriental mode, in the posture of chief. Whether the spear in his hand, or at his hand, as it might be translated according to Noldius, and as appears by the use of that prefix in Ezek. x. 15, was the same thing to Saul's people that the standard was to those of the caya, I know not: if it was, there is a third thing in this text illustrated by the doctor's accounts, the *stopping under a tree or grove;* the *stopping on a high place;* and the sacred historian's remark, that *he had his spear by him.* It is certain, that when a long pike is carried before a company of Arabs, it is a mark that an Arab sheik, or prince, is there, which pike is carried before him; and when he alights, and the horses are fastened, the pike is fixed, as appears by a story in Norden.—HARMER.

Ver. 18. And the king said to Doeg, Turn thou, and fall upon the priests. And Doeg the Edomite turned, and he fell upon the priests, and slew on that day fourscore and five persons that did wear a linen ephod.

In ancient times, persons of the highest rank and station were employed to execute the sentence of the law. They had not then, as we have at present, public executioners; but the prince laid his commands on any of his courtiers whom he chose, and probably selected the person for whom he had the greatest favour. Gideon commanded Jether, his eldest son, to execute his sentence on the kings of Midian: the king of Israel ordered the footmen who stood around him, and were probably a chosen body of soldiers for the defence of his person, to put to death the priests of the Lord; and when they refused, Doeg, an Edomite, one of his principal officers. Long after the days of Saul, the reigning monarch commanded Beniah, the chief captain of his armies, to perform that duty. Sometimes the chief magistrate executed the sentence of the law with his own hands; for when Jether shrunk from the duty which his father required, Gideon, at that time the supreme magistrate in Israel, did not hesitate to do it himself. In these times such a command would be reckoned equally barbarous and unbecoming; but the ideas which were entertained in those primitive ages of honour and propriety, were in many respects extremely different from ours. In Homer, the exasperated Ulysses commanded his son Telemachus to put to death the suiters of Penelope, which was immediately done. The custom of employing persons of high rank to execute the sentence of the law, is still retained in the principality of Senaar, where the public executioner is one of the principal nobility; and, by virtue of his office, resides in the royal palace.—PAXTON.

CHAPTER XXIII.

Ver. 16. And Jonathan Saul's son arose, and went to David into the wood, and strengthened his hand in God.

A passage in the *Travels* of Pietro della Valle, which bears a strong resemblance to this part of David's history, considerably illustrates it. Speaking of his passing through a forest or wood in Mazanderan, a province of Persia, into which they entered on the 11th of February, and complaining of the moisture and heaviness of the roads there, he tells us, "We did at length master them, but with so much difficulty that we could not get forward above two leagues that day, and night overtook us before we got through the forest. We endeavoured to find some place of retreat in different parts, to which the barking of dogs, or noise made by other animals, seemed to guide us. But at last, finding no inhabited place near us, we passed the night in the same forest, among the trees, under which we made a kind of intrenchment with our baggage, in a place where we found many leaves that had fallen from the trees. These served us for a carpet and for bedding both, without any other tent than the branches of the great trees there, through which the moonshine reached us, and made a kind of pavilion of cloth of silver. There was no want of wood for the making a great fire, any more than of provisions for supper, which we sent for from the nearest village in the forest, seated by the highway-side, where, after some contest with the people, of a savage and suspicious temper, who were ready to come to blows with my messengers, without knowing any reason why they should; they, after coming to a right understanding with us, became very civil, would have lodged us, and made us presents: but on our refusal on account of the distance of the way, the chief person of the town, with other principal inhabitants, came of their own accord to our camp, laden with good meat, and other provisions, and spent the night with us with great gayety. They even brought us a country musician, who regaled us during supper, and all night long, with certain forest songs, in the language of the country, that is, of Mazanderan, where a coarse kind of Persian is spoken, sung to the sound of a miserable violin, which was sufficiently tiresome."—Harmer.

Ver. 19. Then came up the Ziphites to Saul to Gibeah, saying, Doth not David hide himself with us in strongholds in the wood, in the hill of Hachilah, which *is* on the south of Jeshimon?

The margin has, for *south*, "on the right hand." "The Hebrews express the east, west, north, and south, by words which signify before, behind, left, and right, according to the situation of a man with his face turned towards the south." In the same way do the Hindoos speak on this subject, the north is shown by the left, the south by the right hand, the face being considered to be towards the east. When the situation of any thing is spoken of, it is always mentioned in connexion with the cardinal points. Often, when people wish to give intelligence respecting any thing, they begin by asking a question which *conveys the information required.* Thus the situation of poor David was described by asking a question. "Have not the elephants been ravaging the fields of Tamban last night?" is a question asked when such a circumstance *has* taken place. —Roberts.

Ver. 29. And David went up from thence, and dwelt in strongholds at En-gedi.

The village of Engedi, situated in the neighbourhood of Jericho, derives its name from the Hebrew word (עין) *Ain*, a fountain, and (גדי) *a kid.* It is suggested by the situation among lofty rocks, which, overhanging the valleys, seem to threaten the traveller with immediate destruction. A fountain of pure water rises near the summit, which the inhabitants call Engedi, the fountain of the goat, because it is hardly accessible to any other creature.—Paxton.

CHAPTER XXIV.

Ver. 8. And when Saul looked behind him, David stooped with his face to the earth, and bowed himself.

"Some time after this, the ambassador had his public audience, when we saw the king in great splendour: he was decked in all his jewels, with his crown on his head, his bazubends or armlets on his arms, seated on his throne. We approached him, bowing after our own manner; but the Persians bowed as David did to Saul, who *stooped with his face to the earth, and bowed himself.* 1 Sam. xxiv. 8. That is, not touching the earth with the face, but bowing with their bodies at right angles, the hands placed on the knees, and the legs somewhat asunder. It is only on remarkable occasions that the prostration of the Rouee Zemeen, the face to the earth, is made, which must be the falling upon the face to the earth, and worshipping as Joshua did."—Morier.

Ver. 12. The Lord judge between me and thee, and the Lord avenge me of thee: but my hand shall not be upon thee.

The attitudes and expression of respect, which the rules of good-breeding require from the Oriental, are far more diversified and servile than ours; yet he uses a freedom with his equals, and even with persons of superior condition, which we are uniformly taught to regard as improper. It is reckoned among us a sure mark of vulgarity, in any person to mention his own name before that of his equal; and an instance of great arrogance to name himself before his superior; but in the East, it is quite customary for the speaker to name himself first. This was also the habitual practice in Israel, and quite consistent with their notions of good-breeding: for David, who had been long at the court of Saul, and could be no stranger to the rules of good manners, addressed his sovereign in these words: "The Lord judge between me and thee;" and this at a time too, when he treated that prince with great reverence; for "he stooped with his face to the earth, and bowed himself" immediately before. In the same manner, Ephron the Hittite replied to the patriarch Abraham, who was at least his equal, more probably his superior: "My lord, hearken unto me; the land is worth four hundred shekels of silver; what is that between me and thee?" Hence David was guilty of no rudeness to Saul, in naming himself first; his conduct was quite agreeable to the modern ceremonial of eastern courts, at least to that of Persia, which seems to have been established soon after the flood.—Paxton.

Ver. 14. After whom is the king of Israel come out? after whom dost thou pursue? after a dead dog, after a flea?

It is highly contemptible and provoking to compare a man to a dead dog. Has a servant offended his master; he will say, "Stand there and be like a dead dog to me." Does a creditor press much for his money; the debtor will say, "Bring your bond, and then he is a dead dog to me." "I care as much for that fellow as for a dead dog." "I will tell you what that fellow is worth; a dead dog!"—Roberts.

Ver. 16. And it came to pass, when David had made an end of speaking these words unto Saul, that Saul said, *Is* this thy voice, my son David? And Saul lifted up his voice and wept.

When a man in great sorrow is spoken of, it is said, "Ah, how he did lift up his voice and weep!" "Alas, how great is their trouble, they are all lifting up the voice." —Roberts.

CHAPTER XXV.

Ver. 1. And Samuel died; and all the Israelites were gathered together, and lamented him, and buried him in his house at Ramah. And David arose, and went down to the wilderness of Paran.

While walking out one evening, a few fields' distance from Deir el Kaner, with Hanna Doomani, the son of my host, to see a detached garden belonging to his father, he pointed out to me, near it, a small solid stone building, apparently a house; very solemnly adding, "*Kabbar beity,*" *the sepulchre of our family.* It had neither door nor window. He then directed my attention to a considerable number of similar buildings, at a distance; which to the eye are exactly like houses, but which are in fact family mansions for the dead. Perhaps this custom may have been of great antiquity; and may serve to explain some scripture phrases. The prophet Samuel was buried in his house at Ramah: it could hardly have been his dwellinghouse, compare 1 Kings ii. 34, Job xxx. 23. Possibly also the passages in Prov. ii. 18, 19, and vii. 27, and ix. 18, describing the house of a wanton woman, may have drawn their imagery from this custom.—Jowett.

Ver. 5. Go to Nabal, and greet him in my name. Job xxix. 8. The aged arose and stood up. Acts xxviii. 10. Who also honoured me with many honours.

In the Old and New Testaments we have some striking examples of what may be termed good-breeding. Look at the patriarchs and others in their renunciation of self, their anxiety to please, to show respect to the aged, and learned, the dignified, or those of the sacerdotal character; listen to their affecting eulogies and their touching appeals, and then say, have we not in them some of the most pleasing instances of gentility and good-breeding? On their great anniversary festivals, the Hindoos always send to "greet" each other. Has a son or daughter got married; has a "male child" been born; has prosperity attended the merchant in his pursuits; does a traveller pass through a town or village where some of his friends or acquaintances reside: then, those concerned send greeting expressive of their joy, and best wishes for future prosperity. See them on receiving company. A servant, or friend, stands at the gate to watch for the approach of the guests, and to give notice to the master of the house. When they approach the premises the host goes out to meet them, and bows and expresses his joy at seeing them; he then puts his arm over their shoulders, or takes them by the hand, and conducts them into the house. When they retire also, he always accompanies them to the gate, and expresses the great joy he has had in their company. Before people take their food they always wash their hands, feet, and mouth; and when they sit down, they take their places according to rank and seniority. Should any man presume to sit down "in the highest" place when he has not a title to it, he will be sure (as in the parable) to hear the master say to him, in respect to "a more honourable man," "Give this man place;" and then, "with shame," he will be compelled "to take the lowest" place. In supplying the guests, the chief person present is always served the first, and generally by the hands of the host himself. They are also particular as to the *order* of serving up their viands and condiments; to set on the table certain articles first would be there considered as much out of place as it is in England to set on the dessert before the more substantial dishes. Epicures at home would smile, and pout the lip, at the *vegetable* feast of a Saiva man. His first course consists of pulse, green gram, rice, and ghee, or butter; the second, of numerous curries, and pickles made of half-ripe fruits, vegetables, and spices: the third, an acid kind of broth; the fourth, curds, honey, and rice; the fifth, a rich supply of mellow fruits. From this humble repast the guests arise with more pleasure and at less expense of health, than the luxurious Englishman does from his half-medicated meal, to which science is now the footman, and a few French terms its fashionable vocabulary. When the visiters have taken what they require, the principal person arises from his seat, and all present follow his example.—ROBERTS.

Ver. 10. And Nabal answered David's servants, and said, Who *is* David? and who *is* the son of Jesse? There be many servants now-a-days that break away every man from his master.

When a man has gained some ascendency over others, or when he assumes authority which is offensive to some one present, it will be inquired, by way of contempt, as Nabal did, respecting David, "Who is he? and whose son is he?"—ROBERTS.

Ver. 16. They were a wall unto us, both by night and day, all the while we were with them keeping the sheep.

This was said of David and his men, who had been kind unto the servants of Nabal, and had probably been a defence to them while they had been in the wilderness tending their sheep. And the same figure is also used among us, in reference to those who have been a defence to others. "Ah! my friend; you have been a *mathil*, *i. e.* a wall, unto me." "Alas! my wall is fallen," means, the friend is dead, or become weak. "What care I for that jackal? I have a good wall before me."—ROBERTS.

Ver. 23. And when Abigail saw David, she hasted, and lighted off the ass, and fell before David on her face, and bowed herself to the ground.

A rider was expected to dismount, when he met a person of more elevated rank. Under the influence of this ancient custom, the Egyptians dismount from their asses, when they approach the tombs of their departed saints; and both Christians and Jews are obliged to submit to the same ceremony. Christians in that country must also dismount when they happen to meet with officers of the army. In Palestine, the Jews, who are not permitted to ride on horseback, are compelled to dismount from their asses and pass by a Mohammedan on foot. This explains the reason that Achsah, the daughter of Caleb, and Abigail the wife of Nabal, alighted from their asses; it was a mark of respect which the former owed to her father, and the latter to David, a person of high rank and growing renown. It was undoubtedly for the same reason, that Rebecca alighted from the camel on which she rode, when the servant informed her, that the stranger whom she descried at a distance in the field, was his master; and that Naaman, the Syrian grandee, alighted from his chariot, at the approach of Gehazi, the servant of Elisha.—PAXTON.

Ver. 29. Yet a man is risen to pursue thee, and to seek thy soul: but the soul of my lord shall be bound in the bundle of life with the LORD thy God; and the souls of thine enemies, them shall he sling out, *as out* of the middle of a sling.

Any thing which is important or valuable is called a *kattu*, *i. e.* "a bundle, a pack, a bale." A young man who is enamoured of a female, is said to be "bound up in the *kattu*, bundle, of love." Of a just judge the people say, "He is bound up in the bundle of justice." When a man is very strict in reference to his caste, "he is bound up in the bundle of high caste." When a person is spoken to respecting the vanities or impurities of his system, he often replies, "Talk not to me, I am bound up in the bundle of my religion." "Why do those people act so?—Because they are bound up in the bundle of desire." David, therefore, was to be bound up in the bundle of life—nothing was to harm him.—ROBERTS.

Ver. 35. So David received of her hand *that* which she had brought him, and said unto her, Go up in peace to thy house: see, I have hearkened to thy voice, and have accepted thy person.

Does a person ask a favour of his superior; it will not be, in general, said in reply, "I grant your request;" or, "You shall have your desire:" but, *Nan un muggatti parttain*, "I have seen thy face." Has a man greatly offended another, and does he plead for mercy; the person to whom offence has been given will say, "I have seen thy face;" which means, that he is pardoned. Should a friend inquire, "Well, what punishment do you intend to inflict on that fellow?" he will reply, "I have seen his face." In applying for help, should there be a denial, the applicant will ask, "In whose face shall I now look?" When a man has nearly lost all hope, he says, "For the sake of the face of God grant me my request."—ROBERTS.

Ver. 36. And Abigail came to Nabal; and, behold, he held a feast in his house, like the feast of a king: and Nabal's heart *was* merry within him, for he *was* very drunken: wherefore she told him nothing, less or more, until the morning light.

Sheep-shearing is an operation to which allusion is more frequently made in the sacred volume. The wool in very remote times was not shorn with an iron instrument, but plucked off with the hand. From the concurrent testimony of several writers, the time when it is performed in Palestine, falls in the month of March. If this be admitted, it fixes the time of the year when Jacob departed from Laban on his return to his father's house, for he left him at the time he went to shear his sheep. In like manner, the sheep of Nabal were shorn in the spring; for among the presents which Abigail made to David, five measures of parched corn are mentioned. But we know, from other passages of scripture, that they were accustomed to use parched corn when it was full grown, but not ripe; for the people of Israel were commanded in the law not to eat parched corn nor green ears, until the selfsame day they had made an offering to the Lord. This time seems to have been spent by the eastern swains, in more than usual hilarity. And it may be inferred from several hints in the scriptures, that the wealthier proprietors invited their friends and dependants to sumptuous entertainments. Nabal, on that joyous occasion, which the servants of David called a good, or festive day, although a churlish and niggardly man, "held a feast in his house, like the feast of a king;" and on a similar occasion, Absalom treated his friends and relations in the same magnificent style The modern Arabs are more frugal and parsimonious;

yet their hearts, so little accustomed to expand with joyous feelings, acknowledge the powerful influence of increasing wealth, and dispose them to indulge in greater jollity than usual. On these occasions, they perhaps kill a lamb, or a goat, and treat their relations and friends; and at once to testify their respect for their guests, and add to the luxury of the feast, crown the festive board with new cheese and milk, dates and honey.—Paxton.

Ver. 41. And she arose, and bowed herself on *her* face to the earth, and said, Behold, *let* thy handmaid *be* a servant to wash the feet of the servants of my lord.

The necessity for washing the feet in the East has been attributed to their wearing sandals; but it is very requisite, according to Sir John Chardin, let the covering of the feet be of what kind it will. "Those that travel in the hot countries of the East," he tells us, "such as Arabia is, begin, at their arriving at the end of their journey, with pulling off the coverings of their feet. The sweat and the dust, which penetrate all sorts of coverings for the feet, produce a filth there, which excites a very troublesome itching. And though the eastern people are extremely careful to preserve the body neat, it is more for refreshment than cleanliness, that they wash their feet at the close of their journey."

According to D'Arvieux, the little yellow morocco boots, worn by the Arabs, which are made very light, so as that they may walk in them afoot, and even run in them, are yet so tight as not to be penetrated by water; but none of the eastern coverings for the foot, it seems, can guard against the dust; consequently this custom of washing the feet is not to be merely ascribed to their use of sandals; a circumstance that has not, I think, been attended to, and which therefore claims our notice.—Harmer.

CHAPTER XXVI.

Ver. 5. And David rose, and came to the place where Saul had pitched; and David beheld the place where Saul lay, and Abner the son of Ner, the captain of his host: and Saul lay in the trench, and the people pitched round about him.

The encampments of Israel in Canaan seem to have been opened and unguarded on all sides. When David reconnoitred the camp of Saul, the king "lay in the trench, and all the people pitched round about him." The Hebrew term *magal* never signifies a ditch and rampart, as our translators seem to have understood it, but a chariot or wagon way, or highway, or the rut of a wheel in the ground. Nor is it to be understood of a ring of carriages, as the marginal reading seems to suppose, and as Buxtorf interprets the word; for it is not probable that Saul would encumber his army with baggage in so rapid a pursuit, nor that so mountainous a country was practicable for wagons. It seems then simply to mean, the circle these troops formed, in the midst of which, as being the place of honour, Saul reposed. An Arab camp is always circular, when the dispositions of the ground will permit, the chieftain being in the middle, and the troops at a respectable distance around him. Their lances are fixed near them in the ground, all the day long, ready for action. This was precisely the form and arrangement of Saul's camp, as described by the sacred historian. As it is a universal custom in the East to make the great meal at night, and consequently to fall into a deep sleep immediately after it, a handful of resolute men might easily beat up a camp of many thousands. This circumstance undoubtedly facilitated the decisive victory which Gideon obtained over the combined forces of Midian.—Paxton.

Ver. 11. The Lord forbid that I should stretch forth my hand against the Lord's anointed; but I pray thee, take thou now the spear that *is* at his bolster, and the cruse of water, and let us go.

Thus did Saul sleep, with his head on the bolster, and a vessel of water by his side; and in this way do all eastern travellers sleep at this day. The bolster is round, about eight inches in diameter, and twenty in length. In travelling, it is carried rolled up in the mat on which the owner sleeps. In a hot climate, a draught of water is very refreshing in the night; hence a vessel filled with water is always near where a person sleeps.—Roberts.

Ver. 13. Then David went over to the other side, and stood on the top of a hill afar off, a great space *being* between them: 14. And David cried to the people, and to Abner the son of Ner, saying, Answerest thou not, Abner? Then Abner answered and said, Who *art* thou *that* criest to the king?

The establishment of a colony of Jews in Abyssinia, is an event sufficiently vouched for by history; and among other things, it has had the effect of preserving in that country many usages of the Jews of Judea, traces of which we find in the historical books of scripture. The remote situation of this country, with our very imperfect knowledge of it, has rendered what evidence it furnishes obscure, and consequently feeble: nevertheless we find, occasionally, instances of such close conformity with scripture incidents, that their resemblance strikes even the least observant. This has been stated in strong terms by Mr. Salt, one of our latest travellers into Abyssinia; and has been found not less remarkable by Mr. Pearce, who resided there several years. It will be elucidated by the following extracts, which scarcely admit of additional remarks. "While the army remained encamped on this spot, Mr. Pearce went out on an excursion with Badjerund Tesfos and Shalaka Lafsgee, and others of the Ras's people, for the purpose of carrying off some cattle which were known to be secreted in the neighbourhood. In this object the party succeeded, getting possession of more than three hundred oxen; but this was effected with very considerable loss, owing to a stratagem put in practice by Guebra Guro, and about fourteen of his best marksmen, who had placed themselves in a recumbent position on the overhanging brow of a rock, which was completely inaccessible, whence they picked off every man that approached within musketshot. At one time Mr. Pearce was so near to this dangerous position, that he could understand every word said by Guebra Guro to his companions; and he distinctly heard him ordering his men not to shoot at either him (Mr. Pearce) or Ayto Tesfos, calling out to them at the same time with a strange sort of savage politeness, to keep out of the range of his matchlocks, as he was anxious that no harm should personally happen to them; addressing them very kindly by the appellation of friends. On Mr. Pearce's relating this incident to me, I was instantly struck with its similarity to some of the stories recorded in the Old Testament, particularly that of David, 'standing on the top of a hill afar off, and crying to the people and to Abner, at the mouth of the cave, Answerest thou not, Abner? and now see where the king's spear is, and the cruse of water at his bolster.' The reader conversant in scripture cannot fail, I conceive, to mark, in the course of this narrative, the general resemblance existing throughout, between the manners of this people and those of the Jews previously to the reign of Solomon; at which period the connexions entered into by the latter with foreign princes, and the luxuries consequently introduced, seem in a great measure to have altered the Jewish character. For my own part, I confess, that I was so much struck with the similarity between the two nations, during my stay in Abyssinia, that I could not help fancying at times that I was dwelling among the Israelites, and that I had fallen back some thousand years upon a period when the king himself was a shepherd, and the princes of the land went out, riding on mules, with spears and slings, to combat against the Philistines. It will be scarcely necessary for me to observe, that the feelings of the Abyssinians towards the Galla partake of the same inveterate spirit of animosity which appears to have influenced the Israelites with regard to their hostile neighbours." Taylor in Calmet.

Ver. 19. If the LORD have stirred thee up against me, let him accept an offering.

The Hebrew has, for accept, "smell." Valuable gifts are said to have a pleasant smell. A man, also, of great property, "has an agreeable smell." "Why are you taking this *small* present to the great man? it has not a good smell." "Alas! I have been with my gifts to the Modeliar, but he will not smell of them;" which means, he will not accept them.—ROBERTS.

Ver. 20. Now therefore, let not my blood fall to the earth before the face of the LORD: for the king of Israel is come out to seek a flea, as when one doth hunt a partridge in the mountains.

Thus did David compare himself to a flea, to show his insignificance before the king. When a man of rank devotes his time and talents to the acquirement of any thing which is not of much value, it is asked, "Why does he trouble himself so much about a flea?" In asking a favour, should it be denied, it will be said, "Ah! my lord, this is as a flea to you." "Our head man gave me this ring the other day, but now he wishes to have it again; what is this? it is but a flea." When poor relations are troublesome, the rich say, "As the flea bites the long-haired dog, so are you always biting me." Should an opulent man be reduced to poverty his FRIENDS forsake him, and the people say, "Yes, the same day the dog dies the fleas leave him."—ROBERTS.

We find only two allusions to the partridge in the holy scriptures. The first occurs in the history of David, where he expostulates with Saul concerning his unjust and foolish pursuit: "The king of Israel is come out to seek a flea, as when one doth hunt a partridge on the mountains." The other in the prophecies of Jeremiah: "As the partridge sitteth on eggs, and hatcheth them not; so he that getteth riches, and not by right, shall leave them in the midst of his days, and at his end shall be a fool." The Hebrew name for the partridge is (קורא) *kore*, from the verb *kara* to cry, a name suggested by the harsh note of that bird. Bochart indeed denies that *kore* signifies the partridge; he thinks the woodcock is intended, because the *kore* of which David speaks in the first quotation, is a mountain bird. But that excellent writer did not recollect that a species of partridge actually inhabits the mountains, and by consequence his argument is of no force. Nor is the opinion of others more tenable, that the *kore* hatches the eggs of a stranger, because Jeremiah observes, "she sitteth on eggs and hatcheth them not;" for the passage only means, that the partridge often fails in her attempts to bring forth her young. To such disappointments she is greatly exposed from the position of her nest in the ground, where her eggs are often spoiled by wet, or crushed by the foot. The manner in which the Arabs hunt the partridge and other birds, affords an excellent comment on the complaint of David to his cruel and unrelenting sovereign; for observing that they become languid and fatigued after they have been hastily put up two or three times, they immediately run in upon them and knock them down with their bludgeons. It was precisely in this manner that Saul hunted David; he came suddenly upon him, and from time to time drove him from his hiding-places, hoping at last to make him weary of life, and find an opportunity of effecting his destruction. When the prophet says the partridge sitteth on eggs, and hatcheth them not, the male seems to be understood; because both the verbs are masculine, and the verb *yalad* in the masculine gender cannot signify to lay eggs. The red partridges of France, says Buffon, appear to differ from the red partridges of Egypt; because the Egyptian priests chose for the emblem of a well-regulated family, two partridges, the one male, the other female, sitting or brooding together. And by the text in Jeremiah, it seems that in Judea the male partridge sat as well as the female. But while the incubation of other birds, which are by no means so attentive, is generally crowned with success, the hopes of the partridges are frequently disappointed by circumstances already noticed, which she can neither see nor prevent.—PAXTON.

CHAPTER XXVII.

Ver. 2. And David said to Achish, Surely thou shalt know what thy servant can do. And Achish said to David, Therefore will I make thee keeper of my head for ever.

The head is always spoken of as the principal part of the body, and when a man places great confidence in another, he says, "I will make him the keeper of my life or head." An injured man expostulating with another, to whom he has been kind, asks, "Why is this? have I not been the keeper of your life." A good brother is called, "the life-keeping brother." But any thing valuable also is spoken of as being on the head.—ROBERTS.

Ver. 10. And Achish said, Whither have ye made a road to-day? And David said, Against the south of Judah, and against the south of the Jerahmeelites, and against the south of the Kenites.

After the expedition was over, David returns to Achish, and upon being asked where he had made his incursion, David answers: Against the south of Judah, and against the south of the Jerahmeelites, and against the south of the Kenites. Mr. Bayle, not with extreme good manners, calls this A LIE. But, with his leave, the answer was literally true, but ambiguous; for all those people dwelt on the south of Judah, &c. Achish, through self-partiality, understood the answer to mean, that the incursion was made on the southern borders of Judah, the Jerahmeelites and Kenites themselves, though David asserted no such thing. David therefore was not guilty of any falsity; and if he was in any thing to blame, it was for giving an ambiguous answer to a question to which he was not obliged to give any direct reply. Mr. Bayle says, "This conduct was very unjustifiable, in that he deceived a king to whom he had obligations." But David's answer was not such as necessarily to impose on Achish, and therefore it may be as truly said, that Achish put a deceit upon himself, as that David deceived him. I allow he intended to conceal from Achish who the people were that he invaded, and this he did, not by a lie, but by an answer true in fact. The precise determined truth was, that he had made an incursion on the south of Judah and the Kenites. The Amalekites dwelt on the south of Judah, and the Kenites lived intermingled with them, till they removed by Saul's order, when he was sent to destroy the Amalekites, and probably returned to their former dwellings, after that expedition was over. It is certain at least, that they were much in the same situation as before; viz. on the south of Judah, and at no great distance from the country of the Amalekites; and therefore Achish might as reasonably have understood David's answer to mean, that he invaded the Amalekites and neighbouring hordes, who dwelt beyond the south parts of Judah, as that he invaded the southern parts of the very country of Judah. For the original words will equally bear this double version: against the country south of Judah, &c. and, against the south country of Judah. If Achish took David in a wrong sense, I do not see that David, in his circumstances, was obliged to undeceive him. For as he had done Achish no injury in the expedition against the Amalekites, &c. so neither did he, in permitting him quietly to impose on himself. Whereas, had he convinced Achish of his mistake, he would have endangered his own life, and the destruction of all his people. The greatest and best casuists have allowed, that ambiguous answers are not always criminal, but sometimes justifiable, and particularly in the critical situation in which David now was. Thus Grotius: "When any word, or sentence, admits of more significations than one, whether from common use, or the custom of art, or by any intelligible figure; and if the sense of one's own mind agrees to any one of these interpretations, it is no lie, though we should have reason to think, that he who hears us should take it in the other. Such a manner of speaking should not be used rashly; but it may be justified by antecedent causes; as when it is for the instruction of him who is committed to our care, or when it is to avoid an unjust interrogation; i. e. as Gronovius explains it, such an interrogation, which, if we gave a simple plain answer to, would hazard our own safety, or that of other innocent persons." Of this sentiment were Socrates, Plato, Xenophon, Cicero, the Stoics, Aristotle, Quintilian, and others mentioned by Grotius; and it may be reasonably expected, that those who condemn David for his ambiguous answers to Achish, should fairly prove, that they are in their nature, and therefore always, criminal; or in what circumstances they are so; or that there is somewhat in this answer of David that peculiarly renders it so. Mr. Bayle thinks he says something very considerable, when he says, "that he deceived a king to whom he had obligations; others charge him with ingratitude, because he deceived his patron and benefactor." This would be an objection of some weight, if it could be proved that he deceived him to his real injury or that of his country. But this, as hath been shown, cannot be proved. A man may lawfully conceal his sentiments, on some occasions, even from a real friend and benefactor, who asks him questions, which, if clearly answered, may be prejudicial to his interest.

But he had obligations to Achish, who was his patron and benefactor. What were these great obligations, and in what respects was Achish a benefactor to David? Why, he allowed him, and his followers, a safe retreat into his country from the persecutions of Saul, for about sixteen months; first, at Gath his capital, and soon after, upon David's request, at Ziglag. But with what view did Achish allow him this retreat? Not with the noble generous view of giving refuge to a brave man, ungratefully persecuted, and driven into exile by the unrelenting malice of an arbitrary prince; but merely from political mercenary considerations; to detach so great a general, and so brave a body of soldiers, from the interest of their country, and to prevent their joining with the Hebrew army in the defence of it, against that invasion which the Philistines were now meditating, and to engage him in actual hostilities with his own nation, that he might make him and them perpetual and irreconcilable enemies to each other. This appears from what Achish said, either to himself, or some of the Philistine princes, upon the invasion of the Geshurites, &c. He hath made his people Israel utterly to abhor him, therefore he shall be my servant for ever. Both Achish and David seem to have acted merely upon political principles in this affair, and their obligations to each other to be pretty equal. David fled for protection to Achish, but with no design to assist him against the Hebrews. Achish received David, not out of any love and friendship to him, but to serve himself, by engaging David and his forces against the Hebrews, and thereby to put him under a necessity of continuing in his service for ever. They both appear to act with great confidence in each other, without either letting the other into their secret and real views; and therefore as Achish was under no obligation to David for his retiring to Gath, David was really under as little to Achish for the reception he gave him; for as David would not have put himself under his protection, but to serve his own purposes; so neither would Achish have received him, had he not had his own views of advantage in doing it. David's deceiving Achish therefore received no aggravation from any ingratitude in David towards him; but the shelter Achish gave him was upon the mean, dishonourable, perfidious principle, of making David a detestable traitor to his king and country.—Chandler.

CHAPTER XXVIII.

Ver. 1. And it came to pass in those days, that the Philistines gathered their armies together for warfare, to fight with Israel. And Achish said unto David, Know thou assuredly, that thou shalt go out with me to battle, thou and thy men. 2. And David said to Achish, Surely thou shalt know what thy servant can do. And Achish said to David, Therefore will I make thee keeper of my head for ever.

Soon after these transactions, while David yet remained in the territories of the Philistines, they formed their army to invade the Hebrews, when Achish said to David: Know thou assuredly, that thou and thy men shall go with me to the camp; his troops being now increased by a party from the tribe of Manasseh. David answered him: Therefore thou shalt know what thy servant will do; i. e. as some interpret the words: Achish met with a cheerful compliance from David; and Mr. Bayle affirms, that it was not owing to David, that he did not fight under the standard of this Philistine prince, against the Israelites, in the unhappy war wherein Saul perished; or, as he further says, that when the Philistines had assembled their forces, David and his brave adventurers joined the army of Achish, and would have fought like lions against their brethren, if the suspicious Philistines had not forced Achish to dismiss them. I am extremely glad, however, that the princes of the Philistines, who may reasonably be supposed to know as much of David's dispositions and views as any modern writers can do, were of a quite different opinion from Mr. Bayle and his followers; who instead of believing with Achish and Mr. Bayle, that David would have been so very fierce against his own people, made no doubt but he would have fought like a lion, or a tiger, against Achish and the Philistines. And indeed David's answer to Achish implies nothing like a cheerful compliance with him, to engage with his forces against his own people. Achish did not directly ask this, and therefore David had no occasion to make the promise. The demand was only that he would go to the camp. And the answer was, that he would there make Achish witness to his conduct. But this was so far from promising that he would employ his men, as Achish promised himself, as that it seems rather to imply a kind of denial; and would appear, I believe, very unsatisfactory to most persons in like circumstances: "You shall see what I will do. I make no promise, but I will go with you to the camp, where you yourself will be judge of my conduct." An evidently cold and evasive answer.

Thus far there appears to be nothing blameable in David's conduct, and it is worthy of observation, that David's going to the camp was not his own forward officious proposal to Achish, but the order of Achish to him, which he was not then in circumstances to dispute, and which, in his situation, he was forced to obey; and therefore it is not true, that David voluntarily offered his assistance against Saul and the Hebrews, to the Philistine army. If he was in any thing to blame, it was for throwing himself in the power of the Philistines. But he thought that this was the only method left him for the preservation of his life from the power and malice of Saul, who was therefore in reality responsible for David's conduct in this instance, and the real cause of that embarrassment, in which he now unhappily found himself. His situation was undoubtedly very delicate and difficult, and it hath been thought impossible for him to have performed an honourable part, let him have acted how he would; and that in his circumstances, he would not have deserved a much better character, had he betrayed his benefactor for the sake of his country, than he would, had he betrayed his country for the sake of his benefactor. But it hath been shown, that David owed Achish little thanks for the refuge he gave him, and that his debt of gratitude on this account was too small, to prevent him from exerting himself in his country's service, whenever he had an opportunity. But supposing his obligations to Achish were real, yet surely the affection and duty he owed his country were infinitely superior to any demands of friendship and gratitude that Achish could have upon him. I will therefore suppose that David was reduced to the necessity of acting contrary to the gratitude he owed Achish, or the natural affection and duty he owed his country. And can there be a moment's doubt, whether private affection should not give place to public? Or, whether one particular accidental obligation to the avowed enemy of a man's country, and that greatly lessened by political views of interest in him who conferred it, should not yield to innumerable obligations, arising out of nature, constant and immutable, and which to counteract would argue the most detestable baseness, perfidy, and iniquity? Had David therefore been reduced to the hard necessity of fighting against Achish, or his country, though the alternative would have been grating to a generous mind; yet his preferring his duty, which he owed to his country, to his personal obligations to Achish, was right in itself, would have been truly heroic, and deserved immortal applause and commendation. Such was the virtue of the ancient Romans, that they would nave sacrificed the love of father, son, brother, the nearest relations by blood and affinity, the obligations of friendship, and even life itself, to their affection to their country. And would they have scrupled, or thought it dishonourable, to have sacrificed some personal obligations to an avowed enemy of it, when such sacrifice was necessary to its preservation and safety?

But it is possible, that if David had continued with the Philistine army, he might not have been reduced to the necessity of employing his arms against either his country, or the Philistines. May we not suppose, that before the engagement, David might have proposed terms of peace, in order to prevent it? Might he not have told Achish, that notwithstanding his personal obligations to him, he had none to the Philistines in general, and therefore could not stand still, and see his countrymen destroyed by the Philistine forces? That unless they would give over the expedition, he should think himself obliged to join the army of Saul, and do his utmost to prevent their destruction? And would not this have been acting like a man of honour, a lover of his country, and been consistent with any gratitude that he owed to Achish for his protection? This, I think, I may safely affirm, that it is in all views of policy impossible that, as Mr. Bayle asserts, he could have fought under the standard of the Philistine princes against the Israelites. For as he had in immediate view the throne of Israel, had he fought in the Philistine army against his own nation, it must have irritated all the tribes of Israel against him, and according as Achish wished, made all his people abhor him for ever; whereby he would have cut off every possible prospect of succeeding to the crown. But David was too prudent a man to take such a step, and if Achish endeavoured, by forcing him into his camp, to ensnare and ruin him with his own nation; as he well knew the intention of Achish, he had a right to guard against it, to counteract policy by policy, and though obliged to give an answer, to give him such a one, as should leave himself at liberty to act as prudence and duty should direct him. And finally, had he turned his arms against the Philistines, he might have shown his gratitude to Achish, without injuring his country, by affording him protection in his turn, and securing his person, and the lives of many of his people, had the Israelites been victorious in the engagement. However, Achish had such an opinion of his interest in David's friendship, that he took his answer in good part, and concluding that he was entirely gained over to his interest, and the more effectually to secure and encourage him, promises him: "I will make you keeper of my head for ever:" you shall be always near me, and have the charge of my person. David made no reply, but kept himself entirely upon the reserve, without disclosing the real sentiments of his mind. He followed Achish with his forces, who marched into the territories of the Hebrews, and encamped at Shunem, in the tribe of Naphtali; while Saul, with his army, pitched their tents on the famous mountains of Gilboa.—CHANDLER.

Ver. 7. Then said Saul unto his servants, Seek
me a woman that hath a familiar spirit, that I
may go to her, and inquire of her. And his
servants said to him, Behold, *there is* a woman
that hath a familiar spirit at En-dor. 8. And
Saul disguised himself, and put on other raiment, and he went, and two men with him, and
they came to the woman by night; and he said,
I pray thee, divine unto me by the familiar
spirit, and bring me *him* up whom I shall name
unto thee. 9. And the woman said unto him,
Behold, thou knowest what Saul hath done,
how he hath cut off those that have familiar
spirits, and the wizards, out of the land: wherefore then layest thou a snare for my life, to
cause me to die? 10. And Saul sware to her
by the LORD, saying, *As* the LORD liveth, there
shall no punishment happen to thee for this
thing. 11. Then said the woman, Whom shall
I bring up unto thee? And he said, Bring me
up Samuel. 12. And when the woman saw
Samuel, she cried with a loud voice: and the
woman spake to Saul, saying, Why hast thou
deceived me? for thou *art* Saul. 13. And the
king said unto her, Be not afraid: for what
sawest thou? And the woman said unto Saul,
I saw gods ascending out of the earth.

How long the profession of necromancy, or the art of raising up the dead, in order to pry into future events, or to be informed of the fate of the living, has obtained in the world, we have no indications from history. We perceive no footsteps of it in the ages before the flood, and yet it is strange that a people, abandoned to all kind of wickedness in a manner, could keep themselves clear of this; but our account of these times is very short. The first express mention that we meet with of magicians and sorcerers is almost in the beginning of the book of Exodus, where Moses is soliciting the deliverance of the children of Israel out of Egypt; and therefore Egypt, which affected to be the mother of most occult sciences, is supposed to have been the inventress of this. From Egypt it spread itself into the neighbouring countries, and soon infected all the East; for, as it undertook to gratify man's inquisitiveness and superstitious curiosity, it could not long want abetters. From Egypt, it is certain that the Israelites brought along with them no small inclination to these detestable practices, and were but too much addicted to them, notwithstanding all the care that the state had taken to suppress them, and the provision which God had made, by establishing a method of consulting him, to prevent their hankering after them. The injunction of the law is very express:—"When thou art come into the land which the Lord thy God giveth thee, thou shalt not learn to do after the abominations of those nations. There shall not be found among you any that useth divination, or an observer of times, or an enchanter, or a witch, or a charmer, or a consulter with familiar spirits, or a wizard, or a necromancer; for all that do these things are an abomination to the Lord." And therefore their punishment was this:—"A man or a woman that hath a familiar spirit, or that is a wizard, shall surely be put to death: they shall stone them with stones, their blood shall be upon them." Nor was it only the practisers of such vile arts, but those likewise that resorted to them upon any occasion, that were liable to the same punishment; for "the soul that turneth after such as have familiar spirits, and after wizards, to go a-whoring after them, I will even set my face against that soul, and will cut him off from among his people, saith the Lord." Such was the severity of the Jewish laws against those who either practised or encouraged any manner of magical arts; and it must be said in Saul's commendation, that he had put the laws in execution against such vile people; he had destroyed and drove away those that had familiar spirits, and the wizards out of the land; and yet, (observe the weakness as well as wickedness of the man!) when himself fell into distress, and had abundant reason to believe that God had forsaken him, he flees to one of these creatures for relief, and requests of her to raise up his old friend Samuel, as expecting, very probably, some advice from him: but, whether this was really done or not, or, if done, in what manner it was effected, are points that have so much exercised the heads and pens, both of ancient and modern, both of Jewish and Christian writers, that little or nothing new can be said upon them; and therefore all that I shall endeavour to do, will be, to reduce their several sentiments into as narrow a compass, and to state them in as fair a light, as I can, by inquiring into these three particulars:—

1. Whether there was a real apparition.
2. What this apparition (if real) was; and,
3. By what means, and for what purposes, it was effected.

1. It cannot be denied, indeed, but that those who explode the reality of the apparition, and make it to be all nothing but a cheat and juggle of the sorceress, have found out some arguments that, at first sight, make a tolerable appearance. They tell us that the sacred history never once makes mention of Saul's seeing Samuel with his own eyes It informs us, indeed, that Saul knew him by the description which the woman gave, and that he held, for some considerable time, a conversation with him; but since it is nowhere said that he really saw him, "why might not the

woman counterfeit a voice, say they, and pretend it was Samuel's? When Saul asked her to raise him up Samuel, *i. e.* to disturb the ghost of so great a prophet, she might think he was no common man; and when he swore unto her by the Lord, that he would defend her from all danger, he gave her intimation enough that he was the king. The crafty woman therefore having picked up the knowledge of this, might retire into her closet, and there, having her familiar, *i. e.* some cunning artful man, to make proper responses, in a different voice, might easily impose upon one who was distracted with anxious thoughts, and had already shown sufficient credulity, in thinking there was any efficacy in magical operations to evocate the dead. The controversy between Saul and David every one knew; nor was it now become a secret, that the crown was to devolve upon the latter; and therefore that part of the discourse, which passed between Saul and Samuel, any man of a common genius might have hit off, without much difficulty. Endor was not so far distant from Gilboa or Shunem, but that the condition of the two armies might easily be known, and that the Philistines were superior both in courage and numbers; and therefore his respondent, without all peradventure, might prognosticate Saul's defeat; and though there was some hazard in the last conjecture, viz. that he and his sons would die in battle; yet there was this advantage on the side of the guess, that they were all men of known and experienced valour, who would rather sacrifice their lives than turn their backs upon their enemies." Upon the whole, therefore, the maintainers of this system conclude, that as there is no reason, so there was no necessity, for any miraculous interposition in this affair, since this is no more than what any common gipsy, with another in confederacy to assist her, might do to any credulous person who came to consult her.

They who undertake to oppose this opinion lay it down for a good rule, in the interpretation of scripture, that we should, as far as we can, adhere to the primary sense of the words, and never have recourse to any foreign or singular explications, but where the literal is inconsistent, either with the dictates of right reason, or the analogy of faith. Let any indifferent person then, say they, take into his hand the account of Saul's consulting this sorceress, and upon the first reading it he must confess, that the notion which it conveys to his mind, is that of a real apparition; and since the passages that both precede and follow it, are confessedly to be taken in their most obvious meaning, why should a strange and forced construction be put upon this? Apparitions indeed are not very common things; but both sacred and profane history inform us, that they are realities, as the examples of Moses and Elias, conversing with our Saviour on the mount, and the several bodies of saints, which slept, coming out of their graves after his resurrection, and appearing unto many, do abundantly testify. It is owned, indeed, that according to the series of the narration, Saul did not see the spectre (be it what it will) so soon as the woman did, because, probably, the woman's body, or some other object, might interpose between him and the first appearance; or perhaps, because the vehicle which Samuel assumed upon this occasion, was not as yet condensed enough to be visible to Saul, though it was to the woman: but, that he did actually see him is manifest, because, when he perceived (which word in the original signifies seeing so as to be assured of our object) that it was Samuel, he stooped with his face to the ground, and bowed himself, which a man is not apt to do to bare ideas or imaginations.

Persons of this woman's character, who are under the displeasure of the government, generally affect obscurity, live privately, and are little acquainted with affairs of state; but suppose her to have been ever so great a politician, and ever so intimate with what had passed between Saul and Samuel heretofore, ever so well assured that God had rejected him, and elected David in his stead; yet how could she come to the knowledge of this, viz., that the battle should be fought the next day, the Israelites be routed, Saul and his sons slain, and their spoils fall into the enemy's hands; since each of these events (even in the present situation of Saul's affairs) were highly casual and uncertain? For might not this prince lose a battle without losing his life? Or if he himself fell in the action, why must his three sons be all cut off in the same day? Whatever demonstrations of innate bravery he had given in times past, after such severe menaces as he now received from the apparition, prudence, one would think, would have put him upon providing for his safety, either by chicaning with the enemy, or retiring from the field of battle, without going to expose himself, his sons, and his whole army, to certain and inevitable death. These are things which no human penetration could reach, and which only he who is the absolute and Almighty ruler of all causes and events, could either foresee or predict. But the truth is, those menacing predictions, how proper soever for a messenger sent from God to utter, were highly imprudent either in this witch's, or her accomplice's, mouth: for since they knew nothing of futurity, and were, at the best, but put to conjecture, it is much more reasonable to believe, that at such a juncture as this, they would have bethought themselves of flattering the king, and giving him comfort, and promising success, and not of thundering out such comminations against him as might probably incense him, but could do them no good. They could not but know that the temper of most kings is, to hate to hear shocking truths, and to receive with the utmost despite those that bring them ill news: and therefore it is natural to suppose, that had these threatening replies been of the woman's or her confederate's forming, they would have given them quite another turn, and not run the hazard of disobliging the king to no purpose, by laying an additional load of trouble upon him. The truth is, the woman, by her courteous entertainment of Saul, seems to be a person of no bad nature; and therefore, if she had an accomplice, who understood to make the most of his profession, his business, at this time, must have been to sooth and cajole the king, which would have both put money in his pocket, and saved the credit of his predictions. For, had he foretold him of success and victory, and a happy issue out of all his troubles, he and the woman had been sure of reputation, as well as further rewards, in case it had happened to prove so; and if it had not (since no one was privy to their communion) the falsehood of the prediction upon Saul's defeat and death, must, in course, have been buried with him.

From these reasons then we may infer, that the woman, in this transaction, did not impose upon Saul, since he had a plain sight of the apparition; what the apparition foretold him, was above human penetration; and (upon the supposition of a juggle) the witch and her confederate would have certainly acted clean contrary to what they did. And so the next,

2. Inquiry meets us, namely, What this apparition was? Some of the ancient doctors, both of the Jewish and Christian church, have made an evil angel the subject of this apparition, in pure regard to the honour of God. "God, say they, had sufficiently declared his hatred against necromancy, and all kinds of witchcraft, in the severe laws which he enacted against them; but it is certainly denying himself, and cancelling his own work, to seem in the least to countenance or abet them, as he necessarily must do, if, upon the evocation of an old hag, any messenger is permitted to go from him. Far be it from us therefore to have such conceptions of God. He is holy, and just, and uniform in all his ways; and therefore this coming at a call, and doing the witch's drudgery, must only appertain to some infernal spirit, who might possibly find his account in it at last. It was one of this wicked crew, that either assumed a phantom, or a real body, appeared in a mantle like Samuel, spake articulately, and held this conversation with Saul; which, considering his knowledge and foresight of things, he was well enough qualified to do, notwithstanding the sundry predictions relating to future contingencies, which are contained in it." How far the honour of God is concerned in this transaction, will more properly fall under our next inquiry: in the mean time, I cannot but observe, that whatever incongruity may be supposed in the real appearance of Samuel, it is not near so much, as to find one of the apostate spirits of hell expressing so much zeal for the service of the God of heaven, and upbraiding Saul with those very crimes which he himself tempted him to commit; as to find this wicked and impure spirit making use of the name of God (that sacred and tremendous name, whose very pronunciation was enough to make him quake and shiver) no less than six times, in this intercourse with Saul, without any manner of uneasiness or hesitation; as to find this angel of darkness and father of lies, prying into the womb of futurity, and determining the

most casual events positively and precisely. We do not indeed deny but that the devil's knowledge is vastly superior to that of the most accomplished human understanding; that his natural penetration, joined with his long experience, is such, that the greatest philosophers, the subtlest critics, and the most refined politicians, are mere novices in comparison of him; yet what genius, (however exacted and improved,) without a divine revelation, could (as we said before) be able to foretel things that were lodged in God's own breast, viz. the precise time of the two armies engaging, the success and consequence of the victory, and the very names of the persons that were to fall in battle. This is what the apparition plainly revealed to Saul: and yet this, we dare maintain, is more than any finite understanding, by its own mere capacity, could ever have been able to find out. But (without this multitude of arguments) if we are to take the scripture in its plain and literal sense, read we over the story of Saul and the witch of Endor ever so often, we shall not so much as once find the devil mentioned in it. And therefore it is somewhat wonderful that he should be brought upon the stage by many learned men, merely to solve a difficulty which, upon examination, appears to be none at all. But now on the other hand, it appears that through the whole narration, Samuel is the only thing that is mentioned. It is Samuel whom Saul desires to be called up; Samuel, who appeared to the woman; Samuel, whom the woman describes; Samuel, whom Saul perceives and bows himself to, with whom he converses so long, and, because of whose words, he was afterward so sore afraid. The scripture indeed speaks sometimes according to the appearance of things, and may call that by the name of Samuel, which was only the semblance or phantom of him: but that this cannot be the sense of the matter here, we have the testimony of the wise son of Sirach, (an excellent interpreter of canonical scriptures,) who tells us expressly, that Samuel, after his death, prophesied and showed the king his end; pursuant to what we read in the version of the Septuagint, viz. that Saul asked counsel of one that had a familiar spirit, and Samuel answered him. So that, upon the whole, we may be allowed to conclude, that it was the real soul of Samuel, clothed in some visible form, which, at this time, appeared to the king of Israel: but by what means, or for what purposes, it appeared, is the other question we are now to determine.

3. Several of the fathers of the Christian church were of opinion, that the devil had a certain limited power over the souls of the saints, before Jesus Christ descended into hell, and rescued them from the tyranny of that prince of darkness. St. Austin, in particular, thinks that there is no absurdity in saying, that the devil was as able to call up Samuel's soul, as he was to present himself among the sons of God, or set our Saviour on one of the pinnacles of the temple; and a learned Jewish doctor supposes that devils have such a power over human souls, for the space of a year after their departure, as to make them assume what bodies they please; and thereupon he concludes, (but very erroneously,) that it was not a year from the time of Samuel's death to his appearance. But these are such wild and extravagant fancies as deserve no serious confutation. It is absurd to say that the souls of saints (such as we are now speaking of) were ever in hell, and more absurd to say, that if they are in heaven it is in the power of any magical, nay, of any diabolical incantation, to call them down from thence. Great, without all doubt, is the power of apostate angels; but miserable, we may say, would the state of the blessed be, if the other had any license to disturb their happiness, when, and as long as they pleased: "For God forbid," says Tertullian, "that we should believe the soul of any holy man, much less of a prophet, should be so far under his disposal, as to be brought up at pleasure by the power of the devil." Since the devil then has no power to disturb the happiness of souls departed, this apparition of Samuel could not proceed from any magical enchantments of the sorceress, but must have been effected by the sole power and appointment of God, who is the sovereign Lord, both of the living and of the dead: and, accordingly, we may observe from the surprise which the woman discovered upon Samuel's sudden appearing, that the power of her magic was not concerned therein, but that it was the effect of some superior hand. The scripture relates the matter thus: "When the woman saw Samuel, she cried with a loud voice, and the woman spake unto Saul, saying, Why hast thou deceived me, for thou art Saul? And the king said unto her, Be not afraid, what sawest thou? And the woman said unto Saul, I saw gods ascending out of the earth." Now it is plain from this narration, that the woman saw something she was not accustomed to see. Her necromancy had ordinary power over demons only, or such wretched spirits as were submitted to the devil's tyranny; but, on this occasion, she saw an object so august, so terrible, so majestic, so contrary indeed to any thing she had ever raised before, and that coming upon her before she had begun her enchantments, that she could not forbear being frightened, and crying out with a loud voice, as being fully satisfied that the apparition came from God.

"But since the scripture assures us, that God had wholly withdrawn himself from Saul, and would answer him, neither by prophets nor by dreams; how can we imagine that he should, all on a sudden, become so kind as to send Samuel to him, or that Samuel should be in any disposition to come, when it was impossible for him to do any good by his coming?" Now there seems to be some analogy between God's dealing with Saul in this particular, and his former treatment of the prophet Balaam. Balaam was for disobeying the orders which God had given him to bless the Israelites; and was searching into magical secrets for what he could not obtain of God, viz. a power to change into curses the blessings which God pronounced by his mouth. In this case there was but small likelihood that God would continue to communicate himself to a person so unworthy of any extraordinary revelation; and yet he did it: but then, it was with a design to reveal to him those very miseries from which his mercenary mind was so desirous to rescue the Midianites. The application is easy: and it further suggests this reason why God appointed Samuel at this time to appear unto Saul, viz. that through him he might give him a meeting, where he least of all expected one; and might show him that the fate which his own disobedience had brought upon him was determined; that there was no reversing the decrees of heaven, no procuring aid against the Almighty's power, no fleeing (though it were to hell) from his presence, no hiding himself in darkness from his inspection; with whom darkness is no darkness at all, but the night is as clear as the day, and the darkness and light are both alike. That the souls of men departed have a capacity, and, no doubt, an inclination to be employed in the service of men alive, as having the same nature and affections, and being more sensible of our infirmities than any pure and abstracted spirits are, can hardly be contested; that in their absent state, they are imbodied with aerial, or ethereal vehicles, which they can condense or rarify at pleasure, and so appear, or not appear to human sight, is what some of the greatest men, both of the heathen and Christian religion, have maintained; and that frequent apparitions of this kind have happened since the world began, cannot be denied by any one that is conversant in its history: if therefore the wisdom of God (for reasons already assigned) thought proper to despatch a messenger to Saul upon this occasion, there may be some account given why the soul of Samuel (upon the supposition it was left to its option) should rather be desirous to be sent upon that errand. For, whatever may be said in diminution of Saul's religious character, it is certain that he was a brave prince and commander; had lived in strict intimacy with Samuel; professed a great esteem for him in all things; and was by Samuel not a little lamented, when he had fallen from his obedience to God. Upon these considerations we may imagine, that the soul of Samuel might have such a kindness for him as to be ready to appear to him in the depth of his distress, in order to settle his mind, by telling him the upshot of the whole matter, viz. that he should lose the battle, and he and his sons be slain; that so he might give a specimen (as the Jews love to speak in commendation of him) of the bravest valour that was ever achieved by any commander; fight boldly when he was sure to die; and sell his life at as dear a price as possible; that so, in his death, he might be commemorated with honour, and deserve the threnodia which his son-in-law made on him; "The beauty of Israel is slain upon the high places; how are the mighty fallen! From the blood of the slain, from the fat of the mighty, the bow of Jonathan turned not back, and the sword of Saul turned not empty. How are the mighty fallen in the midst of the battle!"—Stackhouse.

Ver. 14. And he said unto her, What form *is* he of? And she said, An old man cometh up; and he *is* covered with a mantle. And Saul perceived that it *was* Samuel, and he stooped with *his* face to the ground, and bowed himself.

In augury it seems to have been usual to represent those who were to be consulted, and whose oracular declarations were to be received, as covered with a mantle, or some garment. This certainly gave an appearance of mystery to such transactions. Thus it appears the Roman acted, according to what Plutarch says in his Life of Numa. "Taking with him the priests and augurs, he went up to the capitol, which the Romans at that time called the Tarpeian Rock. There the chief of the augurs covered the head of Numa, and turned his face towards the south." It appears from Livy that the augur covered his own head, not that of Numa. The augur always wrapped up his head, in a gown peculiar to his office, when he made his observations.—Burder.

Ver. 20. Then Saul fell straightway all along on the earth, and was sore afraid, because of the words of Samuel: and there was no strength in him; for he had eaten no bread all the day, nor all the night.

When people are under the influence of great sorrow or fear, they always do the same thing, and roll themselves along, making bitter lamentations. And when men have escaped great danger, they roll themselves on the earth to the distance of a quarter of a mile, after the car of the temple, in performance of their vow.—Roberts.

Ver. 23. But he refused, and said, I will not eat. But his servants, together with the woman, compelled him; and he hearkened unto their voice; so he arose from the earth, and sat upon the bed.

Saul, no doubt, on account of his sorrow and fear, refused to eat, as do others under similar circumstances at this day. But when people are angry also they decline taking their food. Should the wife not bring the dinner to her *lord!* at the proper time, or should it not be properly prepared, he declares he will not partake of it, and that he has made up his mind to die of hunger. She entreats him by the love she bears for him, she touches his feet with her hands, and strokes his chin, but no! he has made up his mind; die he will. "She shall have no more trouble." The afflicted woman then runs to call the mother or sisters of her inexorable lord, who has determined to commit suicide by starvation. They all come round him, but his eyes are fixed on the ground, and there are the viands just as left by his weeping wife. Then commence their tender entreaties, backed by the eloquence of tears; the mother, the sisters, the wife, all beseech him to take a little, and then the matron, from whose hand he has often been fed before, puts a little into his mouth, and it is merely to please them he begins to eat.—Roberts.

Ver. 24. And the woman had a fat calf in the house; and she hasted, and killed it, and took flour and kneaded *it*, and did bake unleavened bread thereof: 25. And she brought *it* before Saul, and before his servants; and they did eat. Then they rose up, and went away that night.

This calf was killed, dressed, cooked, and eaten in as short a time as possible; which might be called for from the necessity of the guest. But it is evident from other passages that it was a custom to kill, cook, and eat an animal in a very short time. The heat of the climate certainly prevents flesh from being kept many hours, but there is no need to put the animal on the fire while its flesh is still warm. The people affect to be disgusted with us for keeping fowls six or eight hours before they are cooked, and say we are fond of eating *chettareyche*, i. e. dead flesh. There are some Englishmen who become so accustomed to these things, that they have the chicken grilled, and on their table, which a quarter of an hour before was playing in their yard.—Roberts.

CHAPTER XXIX.

Ver. 1. Now the Philistines gathered together all their armies to Aphek: and the Israelites pitched by a fountain which *is* in Jezreel.

The Archbishop of Tyre tells us, (*Gesta dei,*) that the Christian kings of Jerusalem used to assemble their forces at a fountain between Nazareth and Sepphoris, which was greatly celebrated on that account. This being looked upon to be nearly the centre of their kingdom, they could from thence, consequently, march most commodiously to any place where their presence was wanted. He mentions also another fountain near a town called Little Gerinum, which, he says, was the ancient Jezreel; near this Saladin pitched his camp, for the benefit of its waters, while Baldwin, king of Jerusalem, had, as usual, assembled his army at the first-mentioned place.

Of the fountain Ain-el-Scanderoni, Buckingham remarks, "This is a modern work; the charitable gift, perhaps, of some pious Mussulman, being well built, with a cistern beneath an arch, whence issue two streams, and over which is an Arabic inscription of several lines. It has, besides, a square platform, walled in, for prayers, shelter, or refreshment, and a flight of steps ascending to it, with a dome of a sepulchre, now partly buried by the falling in of adjacent ruins."—Burder.

Ver. 2. And the lords of the Philistines passed on by hundreds and by thousands; but David and his men passed on in the rearward with Achish. 3. Then said the princes of the Philistines, What *do* these Hebrews *here?* And Achish said unto the princes of the Philistines, *Is* not this David, the servant of Saul the king of Israel, which hath been with me these days, or these years, and I have found no fault in him since he fell *unto me* unto this day?

The situation of Saul's mind, after this adventure, must have been very anxious and distressed, as he received no directions from Samuel how to behave in, or extricate himself out of, the difficulties in which he found himself involved. Nor were David's circumstances much easier, who had been pressed into the Philistine camp and service by Achish, whereby he was reduced to the greatest straits, and scarce knew how to behave himself, consistently with the confidence which that prince placed in him, the duty he owed to his own country, and his own interest and views, as an expectant of the crown and kingdom of Israel. But happily for David, providence extricated him from this embarrassment; for as the troops of the Philistines were passing in review before their principal officers, David also with his corps marched in the rear, under the command of Achish king of Gath. This gave great uneasiness to the Philistine princes, who immediately expostulated with Achish, and said, What business have these Hebrews in our army? Achish answered: Is not this the gallant David, formerly the servant and officer of Saul the king of Israel; who, to save himself from the persecution and cruelty of his ungrateful master, hath put himself under my protection, and of whose fidelity and attachment to my person and service, I have had long experience? For though he hath been with me now a considerable time, I have not had the least reason to suspect his integrity, or find fault with his conduct. But this was far from removing the jealousy of the Philistine officers, who, highly displeased with Achish for what they judged his ill-placed confidence in David, said in great anger to him: Command this man immediately to retire from the army, and to go back to Ziklag, the place thou hast appointed for his residence. We will not suffer him to go with us to the battle, lest in the engagement he should turn his forces against us. For what more effectual method can he take to reconcile himself to his former master, than by lending his assistance to defeat and destroy our army? Is not this that very David whose praises were publicly celebrated in songs and dances? And in honour of whom the Israelitish women cried out in triumph: Saul hath slain his thousands, and David his ten thousands. Such a man is too dangerous to trust in our present critical situation. Achish finding the princes peremptorily fixed in their resolution not to permit David and his forces to go with them to the engagement, immediately sent for him, and said, "By the life of Jehovah, I acknowledge thy integrity in the whole of thy conduct towards me, and there is nothing that I more entirely approve, or more sincerely wish, than thy continuance in the army, and joining with us in the engagement, for I have nothing to reproach thee with, from the time thou didst first put thyself under my protection, to the present day. But the lords of the Philistines have not that opinion of thy attachment to our interest and cause that I have, so that I am forced to dismiss thee from thy attendance. You must therefore return peaceably, and are allowed by them to do it in safety, to the town I have given you, because your longer continuance with us is disagreeable to them, and may be attended with very dangerous consequences." David, with seeming displeasure replied, "What have I done to incur their displeasure, or what hast thou found in thy servant, ever since I have been with thee, to forfeit thy confidence and favour? However, since it is their pleasure, I must submit, and will not, in obedience to their order, fight against the enemies of my lord the king." Achish told him, that "he was so far from entertaining any suspicion of him, that he esteemed him for his integrity and worth, and regarded him as an angel, or messenger from God, immediately sent to his assistance; but that as the princes of the Philistines had resolved that he should not go with them to the battle, he could not but order him to march away by daybreak with his master's servants to the place he had appointed for him and his followers." David accordingly returned with his troops into the territories of the Philistines, while their army penetrated farther into the dominions of Saul, and encamped at Jezreel.

It appears from the answer given by David to Achish, as I have rendered the words, that David was not in the least displeased at his being dismissed, but gladly took Achish at his word, and laid hold of the first opportunity of disengaging himself from the service in which that prince expected his assistance. However, if we take David's answer in that sense, which is given it in our version: "What have I done——that I may not go fight against the enemies of my lord the king?" it will appear to be a very prudent one, and such as became the circumstances in which he then found himself, by which he promised nothing, and laid himself under no manner of engagement. It was a general, ambiguous, and cautious one; in which he neither denies what the Philistines suspected, that he would fall off to Saul in the battle, nor makes the least mention of his readiness to fight with the Philistines against Saul and the Hebrew army. He only asks, why he should be refused to fight against the enemies of the king? If he had some obligations to him, to the Philistines he had none. Against the enemies of Achish he would have fought, where he could have done it with honour; where he could not, as a man of honour, he must have refused it. Against the enemies of the Philistines, neither his inclination, or duty, or interest, would have permitted him to fight; and the Philistines themselves did not think his personal obligations to Achish a sufficient security for his assisting them; and even Achish himself seems to have been at last in some doubt, whether or not he could depend on him, when he says to him: "Rise up early in the morning, with thy master's servants that are come with thee;" hereby more than intimating, that he could not but consider Saul as David's king and master, and all David's forces as servants to Saul; and actually urging this as a reason for their immediate departure from him. Had David made such a speech to Achish, previous to his dismission, or to the Philistine princes to prevent their dismissing him, it would have looked as though he had been uneasy at his not being suffered to assist them in the engagement. But as they had determined he should not go with them to battle, and Achish had peremptorily ordered him to march off; David, who could not but be highly pleased that he was now wholly extricated from the difficulties he was involved in, artfully chose to express himself to Achish in such terms, which, though they implied a real truth, yet might lead Achish to put a further meaning on them than David intended, in order to give Achish the highest opinion of his zeal for his service; by a general assurance, that he was always ready to assist him against his enemies, though he was now dismissed by the lords of the Philistines in a very reproachful and dishonourable manner. I would further observe, that if there is any thing wrong in David's ambiguous reply to Achish, we should make the proper allowances for the circumstances of the times, when morality was not carried to that noble height, as it is by the clearer light of the gospel revelation. It appears from many instances in the Old Testament, that the greatest men did not think these ambiguous evasive answers, in any degree, or, as I apprehend, at all criminal; especially when the preservation of life depended on it. Let it therefore be allowed, with all my heart, that David, in his equivocal answers, did what, according to our present sentiments of morality, in this very enlightened and conscientious age, was not so perfectly agreeable to the stricter rules of it; he might still be an excellent man for the times he lived in; when such equivocations were generally allowed of, almost universally practised, and by no means thought inconsistent with true religion and virtue, but rather in many cases necessary and commendable.—CHANDLER.

CHAPTER XXX.

Ver. 8. And David inquired at the LORD, saying, Shall I pursue after this troop? shall I overtake them? And he answered him, Pursue: for thou shalt surely overtake *them*, and without fail recover *all*.

The chosen people of Jehovah, not less eager than others to know the issue of their military expeditions, or if heaven regarded their undertakings with a favourable eye, had frequent recourse to the holy oracle; they consulted the prophet of the Lord; they offered sacrifices, and consulted with the high-priest who bore the Urim and Thummim in his breastplate, by means of which he discovered the will of the Deity; or, presenting himself at the altar of incense, received the desired response by an audible voice from the most holy place. The son of Jesse, in a time of great distress and perplexity, consulted the oracle by means of an ephod, a part of sacerdotal vestments: "And David said to Abiathar the priest, Abimelech's son, I pray thee, bring me hither the ephod; and Abiathar brought hither the ephod to David. And David inquired at the Lord, saying, Shall I pursue after this troop? shall I overtake them? And he answered him, Pursue; for thou shalt surely overtake them, and without fail recover all." Here was no brightening of arrows, after the custom of superstitious heathens; no consulting with images, nor inspecting of intestines, from which nothing but vague conjecture can result; but a devout and humble application to the throne of the true God: and the answer was in every respect worthy of his character; it was clear and precise, at once authorizing the pursuit, and promising complete success; or forbidding them, in plain terms, to prosecute their designs.—PAXTON.

Ver. 11. And they found an Egyptian in the field, and brought him to David, and gave him bread, and he did eat; and they made him drink water; 12. And they gave him a piece of a cake of figs, and two clusters of raisins: and when he had eaten, his spirit came again to him; for he had eaten no bread, nor drunk *any* water, three days and three nights.

Thevenot says, "At about five o'clock in the morning, when passing by the side of a bush, we heard a voice that called to us, and being come to the place, we found a poor languishing Arab, who told us, that he had not eaten a bit for five days: we gave him some victuals and drink, with a provision of bread for two days more." This was on the journey from Suez to Tor.—BURDER.

Ver. 16. And when he had brought him down, behold, *they were* spread abroad upon all the earth, eating and drinking, and dancing, because of all the great spoil that they had taken out of the land of the Philistines, and out of the land of Judah.

This is said of the Amalekites, after they had spoiled Ziklag. Parkhurst says, under חג on the above, also on 1 Kings xii. 32, "It plainly denotes dancing round in circles;" and he believes the word "is applied to the celebration of religious feasts, whether in honour of the true God, or of idols," and he cites several passages in support of his opinion. When the heathen worship their demon gods, they dance in circles round the sacrifices, throw themselves into the most violent contortions; the arms, head, and legs, appear as if they were in convulsions. They throw themselves suddenly on the ground, then jump up, and again join in the circular dance.—ROBERTS.

Ver. 17. And David smote them from the twilight even unto the evening of the next day; and there escaped not a man of them, save four hundred young men which rode upon camels, and fled.

There were two reasons, exclusive of all religious considerations, that fully justified David in this attack upon the Amalekites. He now resided among the Philistines, in whose country these Amalekites had made great depredations, while the Philistines themselves were engaged in war with the Hebrews, and incapable of defending their own frontiers. He was their ally, obliged to act in their favour, and behaved like a soldier of honour in avenging the injuries that had been done them. This insult of David therefore upon the Amalekites was not unprovoked, if we consider his connexion with the Philistines; much less, if we add to this, the loss he himself and his men sustained. For surely the burning of the city where he dwelt, the leading captive into slavery his own wives, and the wives and children of above six hundred persons, and the making a booty of all their substance, must have been the highest provocation to men, that had any feeling of natural affection. David and his soldiers thought it so; and if it be lawful to put to death incendiaries, women and children stealers, thieves, robbers, and vagabonds; David's executing this vengeance on the Amalekites for their treachery in making this invasion, and committing these unprovoked violences, while neither the Philistines nor Hebrews could defend their territories, was a deserved and necessary severity.—CHANDLER.

Ver. 21. And they went forth to meet David, and to meet the people that *were* with him; and when David came near to the people, he saluted them.

This was a usual mode of honouring persons of dignity. 'Before any person of rank enters a city, it is usual for him to be received by a deputation. If his rank is very considerable, the Peeshwaz is sent to a great distance. A thousand men were sent to meet the prince, halfway between Ispahan and Sheeraz, a hundred miles." (Waring's Tour to Sheeraz.) "At this place (Jerusalem) two Turkish officers, mounted on beautiful horses, sumptuously caparisoned, came to inform us, that the governor, having intelligence of our approach, had sent them to escort us into town." (Clarke's Travels.)—BURDER.

"Saluted them." Hebrew, "asked them how they did." It is in the East, as in England, a common mode of salutation to inquire after the health. They do not, however, answer in the same unhesitating way. When a man has perfectly recovered from a fit of sickness, he will not say, "I am quite well," because he would think that like boasting, and be afraid of a relapse; he would, therefore, say, "I am a little better—not quite so ill as I was:" sometimes, when the question is asked, he will reply, "Can you not see for yourself? what answer can I give?" To say you look well, or have become stout, is very annoying. A short time after my arrival in Ceylon, a very stout Bramin paid me a visit, and on my saying he looked remarkably well, he fell into a great rage and left the room. I explained to him afterward that I did not mean any offence, and he said it was very *unfortunate* to be addressed in such language.—ROBERTS.

Ver. 24. For who will hearken unto you in this matter? but as his part *is* that goeth down to the battle, so *shall* his part *be* that tarrieth by the stuff: they shall part alike.

In Greece, "the whole booty was brought to the general, who had the first choice, divided the remainder among those who had signalized themselves, according to their rank and merits, and allotted to the rest equal portions; thus in the Trojan war, when the captive ladies were to be chosen, Agamemnon, in the first place, took Astynome, the daughter of Chryses; next Achilles had Hippodamia, daughter to Brises; then Ajax chose Tecmessa, and so of the rest; Achilles therefore complains of Agamemnon, that he had always the best part of the booty, while himself, who sustained the burden of the war, was content with a small pittance." From the time of David, the Hebrew warriors, as well those who went to the field, as those who guarded the baggage, shared alike; the law is couched in these terms: "As his part is that goeth down to the battle, so shall his part be that tarrieth by the stuff." But a more satisfactory account of the mode in which the spoils of vanquished nations were divided among the Hebrews, is recorded in the book of Numbers. The whole booty taken from the Midianites, was brought before Moses, and Eliezer the priest, and the princes of the tribes; they, by the divine command, divided it into two parts, between the army and the congregation; of the army's half they took "one soul of five hundred, both of the persons, and of the beeves, and of the asses, and of the sheep, and gave it unto Eliezer the priest, for a heave-offering of the Lord;" and of the congregation's half they took "one portion of fifty, of the persons, of the beeves, of the asses, and of the flocks, of all manner of beasts, and gave them unto the Levites." This law probably continued in force till the captivity; and according to its provisions, were the spoils of succeeding wars distributed; for the regulation which David established, referred only to this question, whether the soldiers, who from weakness were obliged to remain with the baggage, should have an equal share of the booty, with their brethren in arms who had been engaged. Before the spoils were distributed, the Greeks considered themselves obliged to dedicate a part of them to the gods, to whose assistance they reckoned themselves indebted for them all. This custom, also, they borrowed from the Orientals; for the Hebrews, in dividing the spoils of Midian, separated a portion for the service of the tabernacle; and the practice, so reasonable in itself, being imitated by the surrounding nations, at last found its way into Greece and other countries of Europe. But besides the public offerings of the nation, the soldiers often of their own accord, consecrated a part of their spoils to the God of battles: they had several methods of doing this; at one time they collected them into a heap, and consumed them with fire; at another, they suspended their offerings in the temples. Pausanias, the Spartan, is reported to have consecrated out of the Persian spoils, a tripod to Delphian Apollo, and a statue of brass, seven cubits long, to Olympian Jupiter. The origin of these customs is easily discernible in the manners of the Hebrews. After the rich and various spoils of Midian were divided, the officers of the army, penetrated with gratitude that they had not lost a man in the contest, "presented an oblation to the Lord, jewels of gold, chains, and bracelets, rings, ear-rings, and tablets, to make atonement," as they piously expressed it, "for their souls before the Lord." But the city of Jericho and all its inhabitants, except Rahab and her family, were devoted to utter destruction, as an offering to the justice and holiness of God, whom they had incensed by their crimes; "And the city," said Joshua, "shall be accursed, even it, and all that are therein, to the Lord; only Rahab the harlot shall live, she and all that are with her in the house, because she hid the messengers that were sent. . . . But all the silver and gold, and vessels of brass and iron, are consecrated unto the Lord; they shall come into the treasury of the Lord. . . . And they burnt the city with fire, and all that was therein; only the silver, and the gold, and the vessels of brass and of iron, they put in the treasury of the house of the Lord." When the demands of religion were satisfied, the Grecian soldiers commonly reserved articles of extraordinary value which they had obtained, as a present to their general or commander of their party. To this mark of respect, Deborah perhaps alludes in the words which she puts into the mouth of Sisera's mother and her attendants: "Have they not sped? have they not divided the prey; to every man a damsel or two; to Sisera, a prey of divers colours, a prey of divers colours of needle-work, of divers colours of needle-work on both sides, meet for the necks of them that take the spoil." "It has been," says Malcom, "the invariable usage of all Asiatic conquerors, from the monarch who subdues kingdoms, to the chief that seizes a village, to claim some fair females as the reward of his conquest."—PAXTON.

CHAPTER XXXI.

Ver. 8. And it came to pass on the morrow, when the Philistines came to strip the slain, that they found Saul and his three sons fallen in Mount Gilboa. 9. And they cut off his head, and stripped off his armour, and sent into the land of the Philistines round about, to publish *it in* the house of their idols, and among the people.

It was the practice of ancient warriors to strip the dead bodies of their enemies on the field of battle, after the victory was secured, and the pursuit had ceased; and not satisfied with this, they often treated them in the most brutal manner, basely revenging the injuries which they had received from them while living, by disfiguring their remains, and exposing them to scorn and ignominy. When the Philistines came to strip the dead that fell in the battle on the mountains of Gilboah, they found Saul and his three sons among the slain. But instead of respecting his rank and valour, they "cut off his head, and stripped off his armour, which they put in the house of Ashtaroth; and they fastened his body, and the bodies of his sons, to the wall of Beth-shan." Capital offences were sometimes punished by throwing the criminal upon hooks, which were fixed in the wall below, where they frequently hung in the most exquisite tortures, thirty or forty hours before they expired. It is probable that the bodies of Saul and his sons were fixed to such hooks as were placed there for the execution of the vilest malefactors; but whatever be in this, it was certainly meant as one of the greatest indignities which they could offer to the remains of an enemy whom they both feared and detested.

The ancient Greeks treated the dead bodies of their enemies in a manner equally indecent and inhuman. They mangled, dismembered, dragged them about the field of battle, and suffered them to lie unburied for a long time, and even to become the prey of savage beasts and ravenous fowls. No instance of this kind is more remarkable than that of the brave, the generous, but unfortunate Hector, whose dead body suffered every indignity which the infuriate rage of Achilles, or the ferocious brutality of his myrmidons, could invent. Nay, the whole army joined in the brutish and barbarous insult; which shows that it was their constant practice, and regarded as quite consistent with virtue and honour. Tydeus is not treated with more respect in Statius; and in Virgil, the body of Mezentius is cruelly lacerated, for though he only received two wounds from Æneas, we find his breastplate afterward pierced through in twelve places. These instances, to which many others might be added, prove that it was the common practice of ancient warriors. In the heroic ages too, the conquerors compelled their enemies to pay a large sum of money for permission to bury their dead. Hector's body was redeemed from Achilles; and that of Achilles was redeemed from the Trojans for the same price he had received for Hector. And Virgil introduces Nisus dissuading his friend Euryalus from accompanying him into danger, lest, if he were slain, there should be no person to recover by fight, or redeem his body. These statements prove, that it was a common practice in the primitive ages, to redeem the dead body of a warrior; and if this was neglected or refused, it was frequently suffered to remain unburied. But, in succeeding times, it was considered as the greatest impiety, as the indubitable mark of a savage or ungenerous temper, to deny the rites of burial to an enemy. The more civilized Grecians reckoned it a sacred duty to bury the slain, a debt which they owed to nature; and they seldom or never neglected it, or refused their permission to pay it, except on extraordinary and unusual provocations. It was a very aggravating circumstance in the desolations of Jerusalem, so feelingly described by the pen of Asaph, that the dead bodies of her inhabitants remained unburied, and the terms in which he mentions it, prove that the Hebrews had the same acute feelings, relative to this subject, as the most refined nations of antiquity: "O God, the heathen are come into thine inheritance; thy holy temple have they defiled; they have laid Jerusalem on heaps. The dead bodies of thy servants have they given to be meat unto the fowls of the heaven, the flesh of thy saints unto the beasts of the earth. Their blood have they shed like water round about Jerusalem; and there was none to bury them."—PAXTON.

Ver. 10. And they put his armour in the house of Ashtaroth; and they fastened his body to the wall of Beth-shan.

Three Bakhtiarees had been condemned to death by the prince for robbery; one was beheaded, and the second blown up; the third was cut in half, and the two parts of his body hung on two of the most frequented gates of the city as a warning to other thieves. The horrid spectacle was displayed for three days. It illustrates, in some degree, an ancient custom exemplified in the case of Saul, 1 Sam. 31. 10, whose body was fastened to the wall of Beth-shan by the Philistines. *Shekch-kerden* is the technical name for this punishment, which consists in cutting the body in two lengthwise, with a sword, beginning between the legs, and terminating in the side of the neck above the shoulder.—MORIER.

Ver. 12. All the valiant men arose, and went all night, and took the body of Saul, and the bodies of his sons, from the wall of Beth-shan, and came to Jabesh, and burnt them there.

The Chaldee and other versions render the words, "and they burnt or kindled a light or lamp over them there, as they are accustomed to burn over kings." Upon which a rabbi observes, that this has reference to a custom, delivered down from their ancestors, of burning the beds and other utensils of the dead upon their graves, or to the burning of spices over them. See Jer. xxxiv. 5.—BURDER.

THE SECOND BOOK OF SAMUEL.

CHAPTER I.

Ver. 2. It came even to pass on the third day, that, behold, a man came out of the camp from Saul, with his clothes rent, and earth upon his head: and *so* it was, when he came to David, that he fell on the earth, and did obeisance.

In several passages of scripture mention is made of *dust* strewed on the head, as a token of mourning, or *earth*, or *ropes* carried on the head, as a token of submission. The following instance is remarkably analogous to these acts of humiliation: "He then descended the mountain, carrying, as is the custom of the country, for vanquished rebels, a stone upon his head, as confessing himself guilty of a capital crime." (Bruce.)—Burder.

Ver. 10. And I took the crown that *was* upon his head, and the bracelet that *was* on his arm, and have brought them hither unto my lord.

A bracelet is commonly worn by the oriental princes, as a badge of power and authority. When the calif Cayem Bemrillah granted the investiture of certain dominions to an eastern prince, he sent him letters patent, a crown, a chain, and bracelets. This was probably the reason that the Amalekite brought the bracelet which he found on Saul's arm, along with his crown, to David. It was a royal ornament, and belonged to the regalia of the kingdom. The bracelet, it must be acknowledged, was worn both by men and women of different ranks; but the original word, in the second book of Samuel, occurs only in two other places, and is quite different from the term, which is employed to express the more common ornament known by that name. And besides, this ornament was worn by kings and princes in a different manner from their subjects. It was fastened above the elbow; and was commonly of great value. The people of Israel found the bracelet among the spoils of Midian, when they destroyed that nation in the time of Moses; but it will be remembered, that they killed at the same time five of their kings. The prophet Isaiah, indeed mentions the kind of bracelet, which Mr. Harmer considers as the peculiar badge of kings, in his description of the wardrobe of a Jewish lady, which proves, that in the age when he flourished, it was not the exclusive decoration of regal personages, but had been assumed, and was often worn by persons of inferior rank; but it is by no means improbable, that the extravagance of the female sex in his time, which seems to have arisen to an unprecedented height, might have confounded, in some measure, the distinctions of rank, by inducing the nobility of Judah to affect the state and ornaments of their princes. Persons of distinction in various countries of the East, wore chains of silver and gold; and not satisfied with this, ostentatiously displayed their wealth and rank, by suspending chains of the same precious metals about the necks of their camels. Silver chains, according to Pococke, hung from the bridles of the seven military agas in Egypt, to the breastplates of their horses. The camels of the kings of Midian, whom Gideon discomfited, were, agreeably to this custom, adorned with chains of gold.—Paxton.

Margin, "My coat of mail, or my embroidered coat." The marginal reading here probably conveys the true meaning of the Hebrew. Saul, for his personal security, most likely wore a close coat, made of rings, or oilets, in the nature of a coat of mail. Montfaucon (*Supplement*, vol. iii. p. 397) thus represents a combat between a person on horseback and another on foot. "The horseman, represented on an Etruscan vase, of Cardinal Gualtieri's, is armed in such a singular manner, that I thought it necessary to give the figure here. This horseman is mounted on a naked horse, with only a bridle, though the horse seems to have something on his neck, which passes between his two ears, but it is impossible to distinguish what it is. The armour also of this horseman is as extraordinary as that of the Sarmatian horsemen on Trajan's pillar. His military habit is very close, and fitted to his body, and covers him even to his wrist, and below his ancles, so that his feet remain naked, which is very extraordinary. For, I think, both in the ancient and modern cavalry, the feet were a principal part which they guarded: excepting only the Moorish horse, who have for their whole dress only a short tunic, which reaches to the middle of the thigh: and the Numidians, who ride quite naked, upon a naked horse, except a short cloak which they have, fastened to their neck, and hanging loose behind them, in warm weather, and which they wrap about themselves in cold weather. Our Etruscan horseman here hath his feet naked, but he hath his head well covered, with a cap folded about it, and large slips of stuff hanging down from it. He wears a collar of round stones. The close-bodied coat he wears is wrought all over with zigzags, and large points, down to the girdle, which is broad, and tied round the middle of his body; the same flourishing is continued lower down his habit, quite to his ankle, and all over his arms, to his wrist." Something similar to this might be the military dress of Saul.—Burder.

Ver. 15. And David called one of the young men, and said, Go near, *and* fall upon him. And he smote him that he died.

Others were condemned to be slain with the sword, which was by decapitation, executed in the manner used in modern times. Such was the punishment which David inflicted on the Amalekite, for putting Saul to death. It seems also to be the usual punishment in Abyssinia, for taking away the life of a king: for Socinios, an Abyssinian monarch, being informed that one Mahardin, a Moor, had been the first to break through that respect due to a king, by wounding Za Denghel, his predecessor, at the battle of Bartcho, he ordered him to be brought at noonday before the gate of his palace, and his head to be then struck off with an axe, as a just atonement for violated majesty. The punishment of strangling, as described by the Jewish writers, resembled the Turkish punishment of the bowstring, rather than the present mode of executing by the gibbet. The offender was placed up to the loins in dung, and a napkin was twisted about his neck, and drawn hard by the witnesses, till he was dead. Those who had committed great and notorious offences, and who deserved to be made public examples, were hanged upon a tree after they had actually suffered the death to which they were condemned; which shows, that this punishment was not the same with the Roman crucifixion, in which the malefactors were nailed to the gibbet, and left to expire by slow and excruciating torments. The Hebrew custom was no more than hanging up their bodies after they were dead, and exposing them for some time to open shame. For this purpose, a piece of timber was fixed in the ground, out of which came a beam, to which the hands of the sufferer were tied, so that his body hung in the posture of a person on the cross. When the sun set, the body was taken down; for the law says, "He that is hanged on a tree, is accursed of God;" not that the criminal was accursed because he was hanged, but he was hanged because he was accursed.—Paxton.

Ver. 12. And they mourned and wept, and fasted until even for Saul, and for Jonathan his son and for the people of the Lord, and for the house of Israel; because they were fallen by the sword.

Thus did David, and those that were with him, weep and fast until the evening, because the "mighty were fallen," and because "the weapons of war" had perished. When a father or mother "falls on the ground," the children have stated periods when they weep and fast in memory of their dead. On the day of the full moon, those who have lost their mothers fast until the sun come to the meridian, and in the evening they take milk and fruit. For a father, the sons fast on the new moon in the same way as for the mother.—Roberts.

Ver. 18. (Also he bade them teach the children of Judah *the use* of the bow: behold, *it is* written in the book of Jasher.)

These words have been generally understood of Jonathan teaching the children of Judah the use of the bow. But a better interpretation of the passage, probably is, that the bow is the name of the lamentation which David uttered over Jonathan; and that it is so denominated, because he met his death from the bow. The following extract, describing a funeral procession of women, to commemorate the death of a merchant, named Mahomet, at Cosire, where he was murdered by two Arabs, who attacked him with swords, will illustrate this representation. Speaking of the murder of Mahomet, Mr. Irwin, (*Travels*, p. 254,) says, "The tragedy which was lately acted near Cosire, gave birth to a mournful procession of females, which passed through the different streets of Ginnah, and uttered dismal cries for the death of Mahomet. In the centre was a female of his family, who carried a naked sword in her hand, to intimate the weapon by which the deceased fell. At sundry places the procession stopped, and danced round the sword to the music of timbrels and tabours. They paused a long time before our house, and some of the women made threatening signs to one of our servants, which agrees with the caution we received to keep within doors. It would be dangerous enough to face this frantic company, whose constant clamour and extravagant gestures gave them all the appearance of the female bacchanals of Thrace, recorded of old." From this custom of carrying in the funeral procession the weapon by which the deceased met death, it seems likely that the lamentations of David over Jonathan might have been called *The Bow*, and sung by the men of Judah in funeral procession.—Burder.

Ver. 21. Ye mountains of Gilboa, *let there be* no dew, neither *let there be* rain upon you, nor fields of offerings: for there the shield of the mighty is vilely cast away.

The want of rain in the East is partly compensated by the copious dews which fall in the night, to restore and refresh the face of nature. The sacred writers were too much alive to the beauties of nature, too keen and accurate observers of the works and operations of their God, not to avail themselves of this part of the divine arrangements to give us a visible and lively conception of the purity and influence of his blessing. In the sublime benediction which the dying patriarch pronounced on the future inheritance of Joseph, the dew occupies a prominent place, clearly indicating its incalculable value in the mind of an Oriental: "And of Joseph he said, blessed of the Lord be his land, for the precious things of heaven, for the dew, and for the deep that coucheth beneath." When the holy Psalmist many ages afterward poured out the sorrows of his heart over the fallen house of Saul, he deprived the spot where the king and his sons fell, of the dew, the rain, and the fields of offerings, as the greatest curse which his lacerated feelings could devise: "Ye mountains of Gilboa, let there be no dew, neither let there be rain upon you, nor fields of offerings; for there the shield of the mighty is vilely cast away." So silent, irresistible, and swift, is the descent of the dew on every field and on every blade of grass, that Hushai, David's friend, selects it as the most appropriate phenomenon in nature to symbolize the sudden onset of an enemy; "We will light upon him as the dew falleth on the ground." When the chosen people were scattered among the rivers of Babylon, they resembled a field burnt up by the scorching sun; but the favour and blessing of heaven are promised to restore them to the high estate from which they had fallen. "For thy dew is as the dew of herbs, and the earth shall cast out the dead." Although they were dried and withered as the grass, yet he promises to revive, refresh, and strengthen them by the power of his spirit and the riches of his grace. The dewdrops of the morning are not more pure and insinuating, more lovely and ornamental, when they descend on the tender grass, than the doctrines of inspiration in the heart and conduct of a genuine Christian. This idea is beautifully expressed by Moses in his dying song; "My doctrine shall drop as the rain, my speech shall distil as the dew, as the small rain upon the tender herb, and as the showers upon the grass." The mutual regard which ought to animate the people of God is compared to the dew which moistens the hill of Hermon and clothes it with verdure. The drops of dew are countless and brilliant, glittering over all the field, cheering the heart of the husbandman, and stimulating his exertions; not less abundant, illustrious, and encouraging, were the first converts to the Christian faith, after the ascension of Christ. That splendid manifestation of almighty grace was celebrated many ages before in the songs of Zion: "Thy people shall be willing in the day of thy power, in the beauties of holiness from the womb of the morning: thou hast the dew of thy youth." But it too frequently happens that the glory of the church, as well as the attainments of her children, suffers a mournful decline, and passes rapidly away: and what emblem more appropriate can be chosen to indicate such a change than the sudden evaporation of the dews, by the kindling rays of a vertical sun? "O Ephraim, what shall I do unto thee? O Judah, what shall I do unto thee? for your goodness is as a morning cloud, and as the early dew it goeth away."

The shield was more highly valued by the ancients than all their other armour. It was their delight to adorn it with all kinds of figures, of birds and beasts, especially those of generous natures, as eagles and lions: they emblazoned upon its capacious circle the effigies of their gods, the forms of celestial bodies, and all the works of nature. They preserved it with the most jealous care; and to lose it in the day of battle was accounted one of the greatest calamities that could befall them, worse than defeat, or even than death itself; so great was their passion for what is termed military glory, and the estimation in which it was held, that they had a profound regard for all sorts of arms the instruments by which they attained it; and to leave them in the hands of their enemies, to give them for a pledge, or dispose of them in a dishonourable way, was an indelible disgrace both in Greece and at Rome, for which they could hardly ever atone. But these sentiments were not confined to Greece and Rome; among no people were they carried higher than among the Jews. To cast away the shield in the day of battle, they counted a national disgrace, and a fit subject for public mourning. This affecting circumstance was not omitted in the beautiful elegy which David, a brave and experienced soldier, composed on the death of Saul and the loss of his army: "The shield of the mighty was vilely cast away." On that fatal day, when Saul and the flower of Israel perished on the mountains of Gilboa, many of the Jewish soldiers who had behaved with great bravery in former battles, forgetful of their own reputation and their country's honour, threw away their shields, and fled from the field. The sweet singer of Israel adverts to that dishonourable conduct, with admirable and touching pathos: "Ye mountains of Gilboa, let there be no dew, neither let there be rain upon you, nor fields of offerings; for there the shield of the mighty is vilely cast away, the shield of Saul, as though he had not been anointed with oil." The apostle has availed himself of this general feeling in his epistle to the Hebrews, to encourage them in the profession of the gospel, and in a courageous, firm, and constant adherence to the truth: "Cast not away therefore your confidence." Abide without wavering in the profession of the faith, and in the firm belief of the truth; and aim at the full assurance of the grace of faith, which, as a spiritual shield, should be sought with unwearied diligence, and retained with jealous care.—Paxton.

Ver. 23. Saul and Jonathan *were* lovely and

pleasant in their lives, and in their death they were not divided: they were swifter than eagles, they were stronger than lions.

The military exercises of the Hebrews resembled those of other nations around them. Swiftness of foot was highly valued, as it gave the warrior a great advantage over his slower and more unwieldy antagonist. It is accordingly mentioned to the honour of Asahel, one of David's captains, that he was swifter of foot than a wild roe; and the sweet singer of Israel, in his poetical lamentation over those two great captains, Saul and Jonathan, takes particular notice of this warlike quality: "They were swifter than eagles, stronger than lions." Nor were the ancient Greeks less attentive to a qualification which the state of the military art in those days rendered so valuable. The footraces in the Olympic games were instituted by warlike chieftains, for the very purpose of inuring their subjects to the fatigues of war, and particularly of increasing their speed, which was regarded as an excellent qualification in a warrior, both because it served for a sudden attack and a nimble retreat. Homer, fully aware of its value in ancient warfare, says, that swiftness of foot is one of the most excellent endowments with which a man can be favoured. To invigorate the frame, on the strength and firmness of which the victory almost entirely depended in primitive times, the Hebrew captains are said to have exercised their soldiers in lifting great weights. After the defeat of Saul, which seems to have been chiefly effected by the skill and valour of the enemy's archers, David commanded his officers to instruct their troops in the use of the bow, which, though employed by the Hebrew warriors from the earliest times, appears to have been rather neglected till that terrible catastrophe taught them the necessity of forming a body of skilful archers, which might enable them to meet their enemies in the field on equal terms. The Hebrew youth were also taught to hurl the javelin, to handle the spear, and to use the sling, in which many of them greatly excelled.—PAXTON.

Ver. 26. I am distressed for thee, my brother Jonathan: very pleasant hast thou been unto me: thy love to me was wonderful, passing the love of women.

Than the love of women; or, as the word is frequently rendered, wives. This figure hath been censured, as not well chosen, and insinuations dropped highly to the dishonour of the two noble friends. But the expression gives no countenance to it. It appears to me, that there was somewhat in the conduct of Michal, David's wife, in too hastily consenting to be married to Phalti, that gave occasion to this comparison. It is certain from her behaviour to him, at the bringing the ark to Jerusalem, that she had not that high esteem and affection for him, that she ought to have had, as she took this opportunity so bitterly to reproach him. It is certain also, that her marriage to Phalti must have been preceded by a divorce from David; otherwise her second marriage would have been real adultery: and her consenting to a divorce, though by her father's order, showed great want of affection and fidelity to David. On this supposition, no comparison could be better chosen, nor more tenderly and delicately expressed. The brother's love to him, as a friend, was more generous and constant than the sister's, though a wife. The compliment to Jonathan was very high, and just; and the concealing the sister's name, was truly polite.

He who can read this excellent composure without admiration and pleasure, must be totally destitute of all true taste. The lamentation over the slain heroes of Israel, in the beginning, and several times repeated; the manner in which he expresses his anguish, at the thought of the defeats being published in the cities of the Philistines, and the triumphs of the daughters of the uncircumcised upon account of it; his passionately wishing that neither dews nor rains might ever fall on the mountains of Gilboa, and the fields surrounding them, in which the slaughter of the Israelites happened; his recounting the past victories of Saul and Jonathan, who never drew a bow, or brandished a sword, but it proved fatal to their enemies, to heighten the glory of their character, and set forth in a more lively manner the sad reverse of their condition; his comparing them, the one to an eagle for swiftness, the other to a lion for strength and valour; the honourable mention of their mutual affection while they lived, and dying bravely together in the field of battle; the exclamation to the daughters of Israel to mourn over Saul, and the reasons he gives for it; his celebrating the mutual tender friendship between himself and Jonathan: in a word, this elegy, in every part of it, both in sentiment and expression, hath all the charms with which the spirit of poetry can adorn it; shows the richness of David's genius, and will be a monument to his praise throughout all generations.—CHANDLER.

CHAPTER II.

Ver. 4. And the men of Judah came, and there they anointed David king over the house of Judah. And they told David, saying, *That* the men of Jabesh-gilead *were they* that buried Saul. 5. And David sent messengers unto the men of Jabesh-gilead, and said unto them, Blessed *be* ye of the LORD, that ye have showed this kindness unto your lord, *even* unto Saul, and have buried him. 6. And now the LORD show kindness and truth unto you: and I also will requite you this kindness, because ye have done this thing. 7. Therefore now let your hands be strengthened, and be ye valiant: for your master Saul is dead, and also the house of Judah have anointed me king over them. 8. But Abner the son of Ner, captain of Saul's host, took Ishbosheth the son of Saul, and brought him over to Mahanaim: 9. And he made him king over Gilead, and over the Ashurites, and over Jezreel, and over Ephraim, and over Benjamin, and over all Israel. 10. Ishbosheth, Saul's son, *was* forty years old when he began to reign over Israel, and reigned two years. But the house of Judah followed David. 11. And the time that David was king in Hebron, over the house of Judah, was seven years and six months.

David was now thirty years old; had in many instances shown his courage, fortitude, moderation, and patience; had been inured by a long persecution, and series of disappointments and distresses, to submission to God, and trust in his power and goodness; and had experienced the care of the Almighty, in the protection afforded him, under the innumerable dangers to which the jealousy and enmity of Saul had exposed him. As he had under all his difficulties strengthened himself in God, left his fate to the divine disposal, and was determined never to hasten his accession to the throne by any acts of treason and violence; God now began to reward his singular virtue, and from a fugitive and exile he was made king over the most powerful of all the tribes, by their unsolicited and voluntary consent; as an earnest of what God had in further reserve for him,—the kingdom over all his people. From hence it appears, how unreasonably it hath been alleged, that David had no pretension to the sovereignty, either by right of inheritance, which was claimed by Ishbosheth, a remaining son of Saul, nor by popular election, but by the clandestine appointment of an old Levite, which inspired him with hopes, of which by arms and intrigues he obtained the fruition. Mr. Bayle also censures the conduct of David in the measures he took to secure himself the crown. For he informs us, that David had gained the principal men of the tribe of Judah by presents; and that had not Abner prevented it, there is no doubt but he would have become king over all Israel, by the same method, viz. by gaining the principal persons by presents. It is acknowledged that David had no pretension to the sovereignty by right of inheritance; and in this respect Saul had no more right than David; nor Ishbosheth than either of them; the hereditary right, if any such there was, being vested in Mephibosheth,

Saul's grandson, by his eldest son Jonathan. And, thus, I doubt not, Mephibosheth himself thought; at least Saul's family certainly did. For when David asked Ziba where Mephibosheth was, Ziba answered: "He abideth at Jerusalem; for he said, to-day shall the house of Israel restore me the kingdom of my father." Whether this charge was true or false, it is evident that Mephibosheth, or his family, thought the right of succession to the kingdom of Israel belonged to him, as it most unquestionably did, if the succession had been made hereditary in Saul's family. Besides, if Saul himself, as some affirm, had only the show of a popular election, he had no real popular election at all, and therefore no right to the crown, and therefore Ishbosheth could derive no right from him to succeed him. Ishbosheth further doth not appear to have had, either the show or reality of a popular election; no, nor the clandestine appointment of the old Levite, which both Saul and David had. He was the mere creature of Abner, the captain of Saul's host; who, ambitious of retaining the power in his own hand, took Ishbosheth, and, by military force, made him king over Israel; without, as far as appears, the choice or consent of the eleven tribes, and in direct opposition to he choice and consent of the tribe of Judah, the most considerable and powerful of all, and the inclination of the whole body of the people. Ishbosheth therefore was a usurper in every respect, in prejudice of the right heir; and David, and every man in Israel, had a natural right to oppose him, and prevent his establishment in the kingdom. Mr. Bayle says, that David did not pretend that Ishbosheth reigned by usurpation; for he allowed him to be a righteous man, and therefore a lawful king. But this reasoning will not hold good, if Mr. Bayle's own account of David be true. He allows David to have been one of the greatest men in the world, commends him for his conspicuous piety, and extols him as a son of holiness in the church. And yet he tells us, that David acted like an infidel, and most ambitious prince; and that his policy and prudence were such, as he can never persuade himself to think that the strict laws of equity, and the severe morals of a good servant of God can possibly approve; and that his actions were not those of a saint. I therefore say, that according to Mr. Bayle, a person may have a general character for a saint and a righteous man, and yet, in some particular actions, may act contrary to the character of both; and that therefore it doth not follow, that because David allowed Ishbosheth to be a righteous man, therefore he allowed him to be a lawful king. Ishbosheth was undoubtedly a righteous man, with respect to his murderers, whom he had never injured; and probably in his private character he might be a man of virtue. But at the same time David could not but know, that he reigned in every view by usurpation, and that consequently he was in this respect a very unrighteous man. The right of David to the crown was indisputable, and the highest by which any man could claim it. When Saul was made king, the crown was not made hereditary in his family, and the same power that made him king, be that what it will, declared, that his kingdom should not stand, or be perpetuated in his family, but be transferred to his neighbour. Upon the death of Saul therefore, the throne became vacant, and the people were at full liberty, under the direction of God, to choose whom they pleased. The tribe of Judah unanimously chose David for their king, and it is highly probable, that the whole body of the nation would have fallen in with him, had they not been prevented by the influence of Abner. This Abner himself more than intimates, when in order to bring over the eleven tribes to David, he puts them in remembrance, saying: "Ye fought for David in times past to be king over you," viz. even in Saul's time, who was abhorred and detested by many of the principal men for his tyranny. Nay, we are expressly informed, that the princes, and captains of hundreds and thousands, and great parties from the Benjamites, Gibeonites, Gadites, the tribe of Judah and Manasseh revolted to him, even before the battle in which Saul was slain, day by day, till it was a great host, like the host of God. These were voluntary in the offer of the crown to David, and no kind of bribes or force employed by him to bring them to submission. The whole nation was in motion, and nothing prevented their unanimously declaring for him, but the opposition of Abner in favour of Ishbosheth.

But did not David gain in particular the tribe of Judah by bribes or presents? Mr. Bayle affirms he did: The whole tribe of Judah, of which he had gained the principal men by presents, acknowledged him for king. The history only says, that he once made presents to such of the elders of Judah, as were his friends, consisting of part of the spoil he took from the Amalekites, after the recovery of the prey they had taken from Ziklag; and probably that very part which the Amalekites had taken from Judah, the south o which they had just invaded. But if these elders of Judah were his friends, before he sent them this present, then he did not gain them by sending them these presents, and their making him king was not because he made them a present, but from the greatness of their affection for him before. When Mr. Bayle adds, there is no doubt, had not Abner prevented it, but he would have been king of all Israel, by the same method of presents; I think there is great reason to doubt of it; for David doth not appear to have been in circumstances to give such presents; nor did they seem to desire or want them, being led by their own inclinations and sense of interest and duty at last to submit to him. David was certainly a man of a generous disposition, and liberal in his favours; and this temper I never so much as suspected to be criminal, unworthy a great and good prince, or a real saint; and if by a prudent liberality he could secure his own rights, I think he acted much more like a saint, than if he had recovered them by force, without ever first attempting to do it by the gentler methods of liberality and goodness. The true reason of the tribe of Judah's falling in with him, and the readiness of the other tribes to acknowledge him as king, was his excellent character as a brave and generous soldier, under whom they themselves had formerly served; and especially his designation by God to the royal dignity, having been anointed king by Samuel, according to the express order of God. It was this latter consideration, that led him to ask the divine direction upon Saul's death, what measures he should take to secure his succession. The very question: "Shall I go up to any of the cities of Judah?" would have been highly indecent, had he not had the divine promise and assistance to depend on. His claim, by virtue of Samuel's unction, was his only claim, was universally known to the people of Israel, and the avowed reason why they at last advanced him to the throne. It was known to Jonathan his friend. Saul himself was no stranger to it. I know, says he, that thou shalt be surely king, and that the kingdom of Israel shall be established in thy hand. It was known even to private persons. Nabal's wife confesses this appointment of God. Abner terrified Ishbosheth by putting him in mind of it. "So do God to Abner, and more also, except, as the Lord hath sworn to David, even so I do to him, to translate the kingdom from the house of Saul, and to set up the throne of David over Israel." He declares the same in his message to the elders of Israel. The Lord hath spoken of David, saying, "By the hand of my servant David I will save my people Israel out of the hands of the Philistines, and out of the hand of all their enemies." And when they came to make him king, this was the grand inducement to it. "In time past, when Saul was king over us, thou wast he that leddest out and broughtest in Israel, and the Lord said to thee: Thou shalt feed my people Israel, and thou shalt be captain over Israel; and they anointed David king over Israel, according to the word of the Lord by Samuel." So that this was the foundation of his claim, was universally known, and justified his pretensions to, and contest for, the crown after the death of Saul.

To this contest David was forced, by Ishbosheth's usurpation, supported by the authority and influence of Abner, a near relation of Saul, and who had been his general. It lasted above seven years, and Mr. Bayle is extremely displeased with poor David, and censures him very severely on this account. He says, "That as Abner preserved by his fidelity eleven whole tribes for Ishbosheth, the same thing happened as would have happened between two infidel and most ambitious princes. David and Ishbosheth made incessant war on one another, to try which of the two could get the other's share, in order to enjoy the whole kingdom without division." But the real question, by which David's conduct is to be determined, is: Did the free election of the tribe of Judah, neither bought by bribes, nor forced by power, give David a right to be king over it; and did his appointment by God to succeed Saul, and rule over all Israel, give him a just claim to enjoy the whole kingdom, without division? I think in both cases he had an indisputable right, and consequent ly he might, consistently even with the character of a saint, defend and maintain his right. Ishbosheth therefore, by keeping David out of part of the kingdom, and endeavouring by arms to dispossess him of the whole, might well enough deserve Mr. Bayle's character of an infidel and ambitious prince; and David, endeavouring only to secure what he had, and to recover what he was unjustly kept out of, may still pass for a very good believer, and doth not seem to have had any more ambition in him, than what was honourable and virtuous. If wars are in their nature unlawful, David's character as a saint will greatly suffer by his carrying on the war with Ishbosheth. But if wars are in any case lawful, it must be when waged for supporting those just and important rights, which cannot be secured without them. Such were certainly the rights of David, and therefore his maintaining the war against Ishbosheth, was both his interest and duty, and doth not in the least diminish the glory of this son of holiness in the church. The promise of God to David, that he should be king of Israel, was not a promise to make him so by extraordinary and miraculous methods, but in the use of all prudential and proper ones; and if he actually employed arms when necessary to vindicate his just claims, and prudence and policy to turn every event to his advantage, it only shows that he was born for empire, worthy of a kingdom, and a man after God's own heart; or fit for the purposes for which God raised him to the throne. And though these methods should have been, to all appearance, like those which wicked men, or infidel and most ambitious princes, make use of to obtain their ends, they may for all that be very just and honourable. For infidel and wicked princes may sometimes pursue lawful ends, and be forced to maintain their rights by policy and arms. And therefore unless the means which David used were base and criminal, or employed for wicked and unjustifiable purposes, they may be allowed to be, to external appearance, the same with what wicked, ambitious, infidel princes use, and yet be agreeable to the rules of justice and honour.—CHANDLER.

Ver. 5. And David sent messengers unto the men of Jabesh-gilead, and said unto them, Blessed *be* ye of the LORD, that ye have showed this kindness unto your lord, *even* unto Saul, and have buried him.

The bodies of Saul and his sons were BURNT by the men of Jabesh-gilead. Two of the thirty-two charities of the Hindoos are, to burn the bodies of those whose relations cannot do it, and to pay for the beating of the tom-toms to the place of burning. It is therefore considered a work of great merit to perform the funeral rites for a respectable stranger, or for those whose relations are not able to meet the expenses. Hence may be seen the funerals of those who have lived in poverty, or who have seen better days, conducted with great pomp, because the reward is great to him who advances the money, and because he receives great praise from the people.—ROBERTS.

Ver. 9. And Joab said to Amasa, *Art* thou in health, my brother? And Joab took Amasa by the beard with the right hand to kiss him.

Dr. Shaw takes no notice of their taking hold of the beard in order to kiss, but Thevenot does, saying, that among the Turks it is a great affront to take one by the beard, unless it be to kiss him, in which case they often do it. Whether he means by kissing him, kissing his beard, or not I do not know; but Joab's taking Amasa by the beard to kiss him, 2 Sam. xx. 9, seems to be designed to express his taking his beard to kiss it; at least this is agreeable to the customs of those that now live in that country; for D'Arvieux, describing the assembling together of several of the petty Arab princes at an entertainment, tells us, that "All the emirs came just together a little time after, accompanied by their friends and attendants, and after the usual civilities, caresses, kissings of the beard, and of the hand, which every one gave and received according to his hand and dignity, they sat down upon mats." He elsewhere speaks of the women's kissing their husbands' beards, and children those of their fathers, and friends reciprocally saluting one another in this manner; but the doing it by their emirs more exactly answers this history of Joab and Amasa, and in this stooping posture he could much better see to direct the blow, than if he had only held his beard, and raised himself to kiss his face.—HARMER.

Ver. 18. And there were three sons of Zeruiah there, Joab, and Abishai, and Asahel: and Asahel *was as* light of foot as a wild roe.

The name of the antelope in the Hebrew scripture, is צבי (*tsebi;*) and in the version of the Seventy Δορκας, (*dorcas.*) In our version, the original term is translated roe and roe buck; but Dr. Shaw, and others, have proved by several conclusive arguments, that it is not the roe, but the antelope, which the sacred writers intend. The former is extremely rare in the oriental regions, while the latter is common in every part of the Levant. But is it to be supposed, that the sacred writers would borrow their figures from creatures which are either not known at all in Palestine and the surrounding countries, or but rarely seen; while they had not even a name for an animal, which, in large herds of several thousands, fed in their fields, and around their dwellings? Such a supposition would contradict some of the strongest laws which regulate the operations of the human mind, and is therefore quite inadmissible. It is equally absurd to suppose that the Jewish legislator, when he regulated by fixed laws the food of his people, would mention a creature which they probably had never seen, of which perhaps they had not even heard, which was not to be found in the deserts over which they had to travel, nor in the country they were to possess; while he omitted one of daily occurrence, which was found everywhere, in the wilderness and in the cultivated field, on the mountains and in the plains; whose flesh was greatly esteemed, and, by consequence, could not fail to become an important article of subsistence. These considerations are of themselves sufficient to establish the superior claims of the antelope to a place in the sacred volume. The arguments which have been drawn from the etymological meaning of the Hebrew terms צבא and צבי, and the authority of the Septuagint, although of inferior importance, are not destitute of weight. The first of these names suggests the idea of a very gregarious animal; but this is not the character of the roes, for, instead of associating in herds, they live in separate families; while the antelopes are commonly found in very large herds, sometimes to the number of two or three thousand together. The second term, צבי, primarily signifies beauty; and when put for the concrete, as in this instance, by a very common figure of speech in Hebrew, has the force of a superlative, and signifies a thing or animal of uncommon beauty. Thus the land of Canaan is, in the prophet, styled ארץ הצבי, the land of beauty; or, as it is rendered by our translators, the glory of all lands. The *tsebi*, therefore, is an animal that excels in beauty; which exactly corresponds with all the accounts that natural historians have given us of the antelope. Both the roe and the antelope, it must be admitted, are, in the general opinion of mankind, very beautiful animals; but the preference is commonly given to the latter. Buffon says, the figure of the small antelopes is elegant, and their members are finely proportioned to their size; and make prodigious bounds. The Septuagint uniformly translate the terms, צבא and צבי, by δορκας; and the correctness of their translation is attested by Luke, for he mentions "a certain disciple" who resided "at Joppa, named Tabitha, which, by interpretation, is called Dorcas." The name Tabitha is formed by a slight alteration from the Chaldee noun טביא (*Tabia,*) and this from the Hebrew term צבי (*tsebi.*) The Hebrew term signifies, as has been already observed, a creature of surpassing beauty; Dorcas, its divinely attested equivalent, limiting somewhat the general signification, denotes a creature remarkable for the fineness of its eyes; and from this last circumstance, it is conjectured that Tabitha received her name. But while the eyes of the roe have attracted no particular attention, so far as the writer has observed, the antelope has been celebrated for the fineness of its eyes in all the countries of the East. Their beauty, according to Dr. Shaw, is proverbial there to this day; and it is still the greatest compliment which, in these countries, can be paid to a fine woman, to say, "You have the eyes of an antelope." From Bochart, and other authors, we learn that it was equally celebrated by the ancients for the acuteness of its vision; its eyes, they pretend, never become bleared; it sees in the dark; it sleeps with both eyes open, or, as others will have it, with one eye open and another shut. These circumstances appear to be much more applicable to the antelope, which is a quadruped well known, than to the roe, which is either not known at all, or very rare, in those parts of the world. The natives of Syria make a distinction between the antelopes of the mountain, and those of the plain. Dr. Russel, who gives us this information, says, "the former is the most beautifully formed, its back and sides are of a dark brown colour, and it bounds with surprising agility; the latter is of a much lighter colour, its limbs are not so cleanly turned, and it is neither so strong, nor so active; both, however, are so fleet, that the greyhounds, though reckoned excellent, cannot, without the aid of the falcon, come up with them, except in soft deep ground." This is probably the reason, that the sacred writers frequently mention the "antelope upon the mountains," and not simply the antelope, when they allude to surpassing beauty of form, or amazing rapidity of motion. The swiftness of this beautiful creature, has been celebrated by writers of every age, in terms of high admiration. Its exquisite symmetry, its active form, and the delicate turn of its limbs, clearly show, that it is intended by its Maker to hold a distinguished place among the fleetest animals that scour the desert. Sir John Malcom says, it may be termed the fleetest of quadrupeds. It seems rather to vanish, than to run from the pursuer, and when closely pressed, bounds with so great agility, that it hardly seems to touch the ground in its career. Oppian calls it the swiftest species of goat; and according to Ælian, it equals the whirlwind in speed. He outruns the antelope, said the Arabians, when they wished to pay the highest compliment to the youthful warrior. To this trait in its character, the sacred writers often allude. The surprising agility which Asahel, the brother of Joab, displayed in his pursuit of Abner, drew this eulogium from the sacred historian: "And Asahel was light of foot, as one of the antelopes that are in the field." Another allusion to the amazing speed of that animal, occurs in the description of the warlike qualifications which distinguished a troop of Gadites in the service of David: "They were men of might, men of war, fit for the battle, that could handle shield and buckler, whose faces were like the faces of lions, and were as swift as the roes (the antelopes) upon the mountains."—PAXTON.

Ver. 28. So Joab blew a trumpet, and all the people stood still, and pursued after Israel no more, neither fought they any more.

See on 2 Sam. 18. 16.

CHAPTER III.

Ver. 12. And Abner sent messengers to David on his behalf, saying, Whose *is* the land? saying *also*, Make thy league with me, and, behold, my hand *shall be* with thee, to bring about all Israel unto thee.

Though Abner, with the eleven tribes, asserted Ishbosheth's cause for several years, yet he saw that his interest greatly declined, and that he should not long be able to support him, as his forces were worsted in every rencounter; while David prospered in all his affairs, his party was continually increasing, and every thing seemed to conspire to crown his wishes, and soon put him in possession of the kingdom over all Israel. This was the opportunity that Abner had waited for, to bring about that revolution in favour of David, which he had continually in his view, and was determined to effect, upon the first occasion that presented itself. He soon found one, that he immediately closed with. Saul had a concubine, whose name was Rispah, and Ishbosheth, having found out that Abner had been too intimate with her, took an opportunity to reproach him on that affair, and with an air of displeasure said to him: Why hast thou gone in unto my father's concubine? Abner, enraged to be thus called to an account, said to Ishbosheth with indignation: "What, am I to be used in so contemptuous and disagreeable a manner, as though I were as insignificant as a dog's head, and thus haughtily questioned, as though I had been guilty of a heinous crime, concerning this woman, which you reprove me for having been too free with! What, this to me, who, in opposition to the tribe of Judah, have advanced you to the throne, have been so firm and faithful a friend to the house of Saul thy father, his brethren, and adherents, and have not delivered thee, as I could easily have done, into the hands of David! Too long have I already resisted the appointment of God, and may I fall under his heaviest curse, except I perform to David, what the Lord hath sworn to David; even to translate the kingdom from the house of Saul, and to establish his throne over all Israel and Judah, from Dan even to Beersheba!" This threatening so terrified the unhappy prince, that he could not answer him a word, as he knew he was absolutely in Abner's power, and had too much reason to fear that he would put his threatening too soon in execution. He did it without delay, and sent private messengers to David to offer him his service, and say to him: "To whom doth the government over the country of Israel belong? Even to thyself. Enter therefore into an agreement with me, and I will lend thee my assistance, to bring over all the tribes of Israel to thy interest?" David, in return to his message, sent him word, he was willing to enter into a treaty; but would have no interview with him, but upon condition that he should bring Michal, Saul's daughter, with him, when he admitted him to an audience. He sent at the same time messengers to Ishbosheth, to demand that Michal, his wife, whom he purchased for a hundred foreskins of the Philistines; i. e. at the hazard of his life, should be immediately delivered to him; who had by force been taken from him, and married to Phaltiel, the son of Laish. Here David also falls under censure, as manifesting, in this instance, a too sensual disposition; and Mr. Bayle speaks of this affair in such a manner, as shows that he greatly disapproved it. For he says that Michal, Saul's daughter, was David's first wife, that she was taken from him during his disgrace, that he successively married several others, and yet demanded the first again; adding, to enhance David's offence, that to restore her to him, they were obliged to force her from a husband, who loved her greatly, and followed her as far as he could, weeping like a child. I confess I cannot help smiling at this last observation, nor perceive that it is to the purpose; for I can never imagine, that because one man loves another man's wife very dearly, that therefore the husband has no right to reclaim her; or should relinquish her, because the man cries like a child at parting with her. I think David was most certainly in the right to demand her; for whatever may be said as to his other wives, he had certainly the strongest claim to this; for he had purchased her for a hundred foreskins of the Philistines. And supposing there was nothing of a sensual disposition that influenced David in this instance, there might be other very substantial reasons to induce him to insist upon her being sent to him. He purchased her at the hazard of his life, and she was a living proof of his military valour and ability. She was his predecessor's daughter, and he did not probably choose to lose the honour and advantage of the alliance. It might conciliate some of Saul's family and tribe to his interest, when they saw one of his daughters owned and treated as David's wife, and that he did not pursue his resentment to Saul, to the injury or disgrace of any of the branches of his family. There was also a real generosity in the thing, both to her and Saul; in that he received her after she had been another man's; remembering probably how once he owed his life to her affection, and knowing that she was partly separated from him by her father's authority: whereas many princes, for much less provocations of a wife's father, would have turned off their consorts in revenge of them, and even put them to death for having been married to another. In consequence of this demand made to Abner and Ishbosheth, she was immediately put into Abner's hands: who, to prepare things for an accommodation with David, went and assembled all the elders of Israel, and said to them: "You have formerly oftentimes expressed your desire, that David might be king over you. You have now an opportunity to gratify your own inclinations in this respect; and what should engage you to advance him to the throne is, that God himself hath pointed out to you the man, as he hath declared: By the hand of my servant David I will save my people Israel out of the hand of the Philistines, and out of the hand of all their enemies;" intimating hereby the incapacity of Ishbosheth, and that it was both their interest and duty to transfer the kingdom and government to David; would be happy for themselves, and an instance of obedience to their God. He went also and applied himself particularly to the tribe of Benjamin, to which Saul's family belonged, and persuaded them, by the same kind of arguments, to fall in with the general sense of all the other tribes, and concur with them in advancing David to the throne.—CHANDLER.

Ver. 21. And Abner said unto David, I will arise and go, and will gather all Israel unto my lord the king, that they may make a league with thee, and that thou mayest reign over all that thy heart desireth. And David sent Abner away; and he went in peace.

Having settled this important point to his mind, he took Michal, and waited with her on David at Hebron, attended with twenty persons of rank in his retinue, whom David favourably received, and for whom he made a royal entertainment; and having fixed the terms of accommodation between them, Abner took his leave, and at parting told the king, "I will go and assemble all Israel together to my lord, whom I now acknowledge for my sovereign and king, that they may all of them submit to thine authority and government, upon such terms as shall be judged honourable on both sides, and that, according to the utmost wishes of thy heart, thou mayest reign over us all, and the kingdom may be established in thy house and family." Abner then took his leave, and went away pleased and happy, to bring about the revolution he had projected and promised. Here Mr. Bayle is out of all patience, and after having told us that Abner, being discontented with the king his master, resolved to dispossess him of his dominions, and deliver them up to David, adds: "David gives ear to the traitor, and is willing to gain a kingdom by intrigues of this nature. Can it be said that these are the actions of a saint? I own there is nothing in all this, but what is agreeable to the precepts of policy, and the methods of human prudence; but I shall never be persuaded, that the strict laws of equity, and the severe morals of a good servant of God, can approve such conduct." There are some persons whom it is extremely difficult to please. In a former note Mr. Bayle heavily censures David, that he had made incessant war on Ishbosheth, like a very ambitious and even infidel prince; and now, he ceases even to be a saint, and shows he is destitute of the severe morals of a good servant of God, because he took the first opportunity, and the only means that were in his power, to put a stop to the war, and prevent the further effusion of blood, by a general and solid peace. What, I wonder, would Mr. Bayle have had David to have done, when Abner sent his first proposals for an accommodation? Ought he to have immediately rejected them, reproached Abner as a traitor to his prince, told him he would enter into no terms of peace with him, nor his master, but reduce them both, with all the eleven tribes that adhered to them, by force of arms? Had David done this, would not all the world have reproached him for folly, thus to hazard, by continuing the war, what he could so certainly and easily obtain by the voluntary offer of Abner? Would he not have been justly censured for delighting in blood, for pursuing by the sword, what he could secure by treaty and accommodation? Or, would Mr. Bayle have had David sent to Ishbosheth, and informed him of Abner's treachery, and advised him to the proper methods of preventing it? This, perhaps, Mr. Bayle might have commended as an act of exceeding great generosity, and Ishbosheth might have thought himself greatly obliged to David for such an instance of friendship. But how would the tribe of Judah have stood affected to him? Would they not have concluded him unworthy to be their prince, who no better understood his own interest or theirs, by his rejecting a measure, which every prudential consideration, which humanity, and the love that he owed to his people, obliged him immediately and thankfully to embrace? David had no other choice left him, but either to fall in with Abner's offer, or prolong the calamities of the civil war; except Mr. Bayle thought he was obliged, upon discovering Abner's treachery, to have informed Ishbosheth of it, and sent him at the same time an offer of resigning the crown of Judah to him, and all his pretensions to be king over all Israel. It is plain David was not of this sentiment, but thought his own right was better than Ishbosheth's, and therefore made use of that method to secure it, which he was persuaded that the strict laws of equity, and the severe morals of a good servant of God, did not in the least prohibit and condemn. And I confess, I do not see any just reason for this censure of Mr. Bayle's, or in what David acted, by accepting Abner's proposals, contrary to the strictest laws of equity, or the severe morals of a good servant of God. To David belonged the throne by the appointment of God; and Abner, by advancing Ishbosheth, and beginning a civil war in the kingdom, acted contrary to his duty to God, the allegiance he owed David, the laws of hereditary succession, and the peace and happiness of his country. Here Abner was extremely criminal, and every moment he continued to support Ishbosheth, he supported an unnatural rebellion, and acted contrary to his own conviction, by keeping David out of the possession of the kingdom, which he knew and confessed God had sworn to give him. Through a regard to Saul's family, and more to his own ambition, he determined to defer David's possession as long as he could; till at length, finding that Ishbosheth was unworthy of the throne, and incapable of government; that David would finally prevail, probably tired out with the calamities of the civil war, and, I doubt not, willing to make some good terms for himself, he took hold of the first opportunity to break with Ishbosheth, and reconcile himself, and the whole nation, to David. In this Abner certainly acted as right a part, as he, who having supported a usurpation and real rebellion, at length returns to his duty, deserts the pretender, and submits himself to his lawful prince. Though the motives to such an alteration of conduct may not be altogether quite honourable, the conduct itself is certainly right; and the only possible means, by which such a person can atone for his past guilt, is to lay down his arms, and put an end to the usurpation, and thereby restore the public peace. Mr. Bayle, with great indignation, calls Abner the traitor But did ever any one imagine, that the deserting a usurper, and submitting to a man's lawful prince, really constituted him a traitor to his lawful prince? Rather, doth he not cease to be a traitor to him, when he declares for his rightful sovereign? Ishbosheth was Abner's king, as Mr. Bayle tells us; but it was a king he had treasonably made, and whom he had supported by violence, in opposition to the order of God, and without any pretence of right and justice. If therefore the making him king was wrong, the deserting him, and bringing over the tribes to David, was right. And the easy method by which Abner effected this revolution, and the cordial manner in which the whole nation submitted to David, is a demonstration that they approved Abner's change, and were glad to accept David for their king. For no sooner had Abner a conference with the elders of Israel, and put them in mind that they had formerly desired David for their king, and that the Lord had resolved to deliver them from the Philistines, and the hand of their enemies, by the hand of David; but instantly all the tribes came to Hebron, all the men of war, with a perfect heart, and all Israel with one heart, to make him king, and accordingly anointed him king over Israel. In this whole affair, David's conduct, to me, seems perfectly honourable. He received a rebel general to his favour upon his submission, agrees with him that he should bring in all the tribes to do what they desired to do, and were bound by the order of God to do, even to make him king over them, that hereby he might have the peaceable possession of the whole kingdom. Abner had openly told Ishbosheth of his design. Abner sent messengers to David, and not David to Abner, on the affair. It was Abner who conferred with the princes of Israel, and came openly to David at Hebron to agree upon proper measures. David carried on no secret intrigues to bring over Abner and the eleven tribes to his party. He only consented to a just proposal that was made him of recovering his own right, without invading the real right of a single person; and indeed it was the only method he could take, and he would not have acted like a saint, or a wise and just prince, had he not hereby put an end to the civil war, secured his own rights, and restored and established the peace and prosperity of his people.—CHANDLER.

Ver. 31. And David said to Joab, and to all the people that *were* with him, Rend your clothes, and gird you with sackcloth, and mourn before Abner. And King David *himself* followed the bier.

The word here translated the bier is in the original the bed: on these, persons of quality used to be carried forth to their graves, as common people were upon a bier. Kings were sometimes carried out upon beds very richly adorned; as Josephus tells us that Herod was; he says the bed was all gilded, set with precious stones, and that it had a purple cover curiously wrought.—PATRICK.

Ver. 33. And the king lamented over Abner, and said, Died Abner as a fool dieth? 34. Thy hands *were* not bound, nor thy feet put into fetters; as a man falleth before wicked men, *so* fellest thou. And all the people wept again over him.

See on Rev. 2. 17.

The feet as well as the hands of criminals are wont to be secured, some how or other, by the people of the East, when they are brought out to be punished, to which there seems to be a plain allusion in the Old Testament. Thus when Irwin was among the Arabs of Upper Egypt, where he was very ill used, but his wrongs afterward redressed by the great sheik there, who had been absent, and who, it seems, was a man of exemplary probity and virtue; he tells us, that upon that sheik's holding a great court of justice, about Irwin's affairs and those of his companions, the bastinado was given to one of those who had injured them, which he thus describes in a note, page 271: "The prisoner is placed upright on the ground, with his hands and feet bound together, while the executioner stands before him, and, with a short stick, strikes him with a smart motion on the outside of his knees. The pain which arises from these strokes is exquisitely severe, and which no constitution can support for any continuance." As the Arabs are extremely remarkable for their retaining old customs, we have just grounds of believing, that when malefactors in the East were punished, by beating, and perhaps with death by the sword, their hands were bound together, and also their feet. How impertinent, according to this, is the interpretation that Victorinus Strigelius gives of 2 Sam. iii. 34! as he is cited by Bishop Patrick in his Commentary on those words: "The king lamented over Abner, and said, Died Abner as a fool dieth? Thy hands were not bound, nor thy feet put into fetters; as a man falleth before wicked men, so fellest thou. And all the people wept again over him." "Strigelius," says the Bishop, "thinks that David, in these words, distinguishes him from those criminals, whose hands being tied behind them, are carried to execution; and from those idle soldiers, who being taken captive in war, have fetters clapped upon their legs, to keep them from running away. He was none of these; neither a notorious offender, nor a coward." Patrick adds, "The plain meaning seems to be, that if his enemy had set upon him openly, he had been able to make his part good with him." How impertinent the latter part of what Strigelius says! how foreign from the thought of David, not to say inconsistent with itself, the explanation of the English prelate! What is meant appears to be simply this: Died Abner as a fool, that is, as a bad man, as that word frequently signifies in the scriptures? Died he as one found on judgment to be criminal, dieth? No! Thy hands, O Abner! were not bound as being found such, nor thy feet confined; on the contrary, thou wert treated with honour by him whose business it was to judge thee, and thy attachment to the house of Saul esteemed rather generous than culpable; as the best of men may fall, so fellest thou, by he sword of treachery, not of justice!—HARMER.

CHAPTER IV.

Ver. 2. And Saul's son had two men *that were* captains of bands; the name of the one *was* Baanah, and the name of the other Rechab, the sons of Rimmon a Beerothite, of the children of Benjamin.

This is added to show us that these two regicides were not only officers in the king's army, but of the same tribe with Saul, and therefore had more ties than one upon them, to be honest and faithful to his family. For there is reason to believe that Saul, who lived in the borders of Benjamin, conferred more favours upon that tribe than any other, and might therefore justly expect, both to him and his, a greater esteem and fidelity from those of his own tribe than from others. This patronymic is therefore very properly prefixed to the names of Rechab and Baanah, to show what vile ungrateful villains they were, and how justly they deserved the severe and exemplary punishment which David inflicted on them.—STACKHOUSE.

Ver. 5. And the sons of Rimmon the Beerothite, Rechab and Baanah, went, and came about the heat of the day to the house of Ish-bosheth, who lay on a bed at noon. 6. And they came thither into the midst of the house, *as though* they would have fetched wheat; and they smote him under the fifth *rib:* and Rechab and Baanah his brother escaped.

The females engaged in this operation, endeavoured to beguile the lingering hours of toilsome exertion with a song. We learn from an expression of Aristophanes, preserved by Athenæus, that the Grecian maidens accompanied the sound of the millstones with their voices. This circumstance imparts an additional beauty and force to the description of the prophet: (Isa. xlvii. 1.) The light of a candle was no more to be seen in the evening; the sound of the millstones, the indication of plenty; and the song of the grinders, the natural expression of joy and happiness, were no more to be heard at the dawn. The grinding of corn at so early an hour, throws light on a passage of considerable obscurity: "And the sons of Rimmon the Beerothite, Rechab and Baanah, went and came about the heat of the day to the house of Ishbosheth, who lay on a bed at noon; and they came thither into the midst of the house, as though they would have fetched wheat, and they smote him under the fifth rib; and Rechab and Baanah his brother escaped." It is still a custom in the East, according to Dr. Perry, to allow their soldiers a certain quantity of corn, with other articles of provisions, together with some pay: and as it was the custom also to carry their corn to the mill at break of day, these two captains very naturally went to the palace the day before, to fetch wheat, in order to distribute it to the soldiers, that it might be sent to the mill at the accustomed hour in the morning. The princes of the East, in those days, as the history of David shows, lounged in their divan, or reposed on their couch, till the cool of the evening began to advance. Rechab and Baanah, therefore, came in the heat of the day, when they knew that Ishbosheth their master would be resting on his bed; and as it was necessary, for the reason just given, to have the corn the day before it was needed, their coming at that time, though it might be a little earlier than usual, created no suspicion, and attracted no notice.—PAXTON.

It is exceedingly common for people to recline on their couches in the heat of the day. Hence, often, when you call on a person at that time, the answer is, "The master is asleep." Captain Basil Hall speaks of the inhabitants of South America having the same custom. The old Romish missionaries in China used to take their siesta with a metal ball in the hand, which was allowed to project over the couch; beneath was a brass dish, so that as soon as the individual was asleep the fingers naturally relaxed their grasp, and let the ball fall, and the noise made awoke him from his slumbers.—ROBERTS.

Ver. 12. And David commanded his young men, and they slew them, and cut off their hands and their feet, and hanged *them* up over the pool in Hebron. But they took the head of Ish-bosheth, and buried *it* in the sepulchre of Abner in Hebron.

In times of tumult and disorder, they frequently cut off the hands and feet of people, and afterward exposed them, as well as the head. Lady M. W. Montague speaking of the Turkish ministers of state says, "if a minister displease the people, in three hours' time he is dragged even from his master's arms; they cut off his hands, head, and feet, and throw them before the palace gate, with all the respect in the world, while the sultan (to whom they all profess an unlimited adoration) sits trembling in his apartment." Thus were the sons of Rimmon served for slaying Ishbosheth.—Harmer.

CHAPTER V.

Ver. 3. So all the elders of Israel came to the
king to Hebron; and King David made a
league with them in Hebron before the Lord:
and they anointed David king over Israel.
4. David *was* thirty years old when he began
to reign, *and* he reigned forty years.

In the foregoing history we have seen the various steps, by which providence brought David to the quiet possession of the throne of Israel; an event that, to all human probability, seemed the most unlikely, as the family of Saul, his predecessor, was very numerous, all the forces of the kingdom under his command, and large bodies of them frequently employed by him to accomplish David's destruction. But God's purposes must stand, and he will do all his pleasure. He had assured Saul, by the mouth of Samuel his prophet, that he had sought him, a man after his own heart, and commanded him to be captain over his people. This character has been thought, by some writers, to denote the highest degree of moral purity, and that therefore it could not, with truth or justice, be ascribed to David, who was certainly guilty of some very great offences, and hath been plentifully loaded with others, which he was entirely free from the guilt of. Every one knows, that in a literal translation of words from one language to another, the original and the literal version may convey very different ideas; and should any one assert, that what the version properly imports is the genuine meaning of the original, he would betray his ignorance and want of learning, and all his reasonings from such an assertion would be inconclusive and false. *A good man*, upon the exchange of London, means, a responsible and wealthy man, who is able to answer his pecuniary obligations, and whose credit is every way unexceptionable, though his character for morals may be extremely bad. But this is not the meaning of the Greek word *αγαθος*, and but seldom, or ever, of the Latin word *bonus;* and should any one argue, that such a man was *αγαθος* or *bonus*, according to the common acceptation of those words in Greek and Latin, because in the English phrase he is called a good man, he would expose himself for his ignorance and simplicity. *A man after God's own heart*, in English, if we interpret the expression in the strictest and highest sense, undoubtedly denotes a character irreproachable and pure, without spot or blemish. But doth it follow that this is the meaning of the Hebrew expression, and that David, because he is so called, was intended to be represented as a man of the highest purity? This is presuming on a meaning, that the expression by no means necessarily conveys, and taking for granted what ought to be proved, and what every man, who understands the original language, knows to be mistaken. The immediate occasion of these words of Samuel to Saul was, Saul's disobedience in sacrificing, contrary to the express orders he had received from God by this great prophet, not to offer sacrifices till he should come, and give him the proper directions for his behaviour. The pretence was piety, but the real cause was impatience, pride, and contempt of the prophet; who not coming just at the time Saul expected, he thought it beneath him to wait any longer for him; and imagined, that as king, all the rites of religion, and the ministers of it, were to be subjected to his direction and pleasure. But when Samuel came, notwithstanding his plea of devotion, and the force he put upon himself, Samuel plainly tells him: Thou hast done foolishly, thou hast not kept the commandment of the Lord thy God, which he commanded thee; for now would the Lord have established thy kingdom upon Israel for ever. But now thy kingdom shall not continue. The Lord hath sought him, אש כלבבי, *a man after his own heart;* he shall be captain over his people, because thou hast not kept that which the Lord hath commanded thee. It is evident here, that the man after God's own heart stands in opposition to the character of Saul, who is described as acting foolishly, by breaking the commandment of God by his prophet, and rejected by him, i. e. deprived of the succession to the crown in his family, on account of his folly, presumption, and disobedience. And it therefore means one who should act prudently, and obey the commandments of God delivered him by his prophets, and whom therefore God would thus far approve and continue to favour. Thus the expression is actually interpreted by the Chaldee paraphrase: *The man who doth my will;* and by St. Paul to the Jews at Antioch, who says, that when God hath removed Saul, he raised them up David to be their king; to whom he gave testimony, and said: I have found David, the son of Jesse, a man after my own heart, who shall execute my will. There are therefore two senses, which are evidently implied in this character of the man after God's own heart; a man, who should faithfully execute the will of God according as he was commanded, and who on that account, and so far, should be the object of his approbation. And in one or other, or both these senses, we find the expression always used. Thus David, recounting the singular favours of God towards himself, says; For thy word's sake, כלבך, *according to thy heart*, i. e. thy will and pleasure, hast thou done all these great things. In another place God saith to the Jews: I will give you pastors, כלבי, *according to my heart:* pastors who shall answer the purposes for which I sent them, and act agreeable to their office, as the words immediately following explain it: Who shall feed you with knowledge and understanding. Thus also the Psalmist: The Lord grant thee *according to thy heart*, i. e. as the next words explain it: Fulfil all thy counsel; give thee thy wishes, and by his favour prosper all thy designs. In like manner, when Jonathan said to his armour-bearer: "Come, let us go over to the garrison of these uncircumcised," his armour-bearer said to him: Do all that is *in thy heart*. Do whatever thou desirest and approvest. Turn thee. Behold, I am with thee *according to thy heart;* in every thing in which thou canst desire, or command my concurrence. These remarks may be confirmed by some other forms of expression of the like nature. Thus God tells Eli: "I will raise me up a faithful priest, that shall do *according to what is in my heart and my soul*," i. e. what I command, and what I approve. When Jehu, king of Israel, had cut off the whole house and family of Ahab, whom God for his numerous crimes had doomed to destruction, God said to him: "Thou hast done well, in executing that which is right in my eyes, and hast done unto the house of Ahab, *according to all that was in my heart*," i. e. every thing I proposed, and commanded thee to do. And yet in the very next verse, Jehu is described as a very bad prince; for he took no heed to walk in the law of the Lord God of Israel with all his heart, nor departed from the sins of Jeroboam, who made Israel to sin. So Moses tells the people: "By this ye shall know, that the Lord hath said to me to do all these things, and that they are not *from my own heart;*" i. e. that I have not acted by my own suggestions, and according to my own pleasure; and he commands them: "Ye shall remember all the commandments of the Lord and do them, and not seek *after your own heart*, and your own eyes," what is agreeable to your passions, and pleasing to your vanity. Many more places might be mentioned to the same purpose; but from those already alleged, the reader will see, that David is characterized as *a man after God's own heart*, not to denote the utmost height of purity in his moral character, as a private man, which by no means enters into the meaning of the expression, and which in no one single instance is intended by it; but to represent him as one, who in his public character, as king of Israel, was fit for the purposes to which God advanced him, and who knew he would faithfully execute the commands he should give him by his prophets; and who on this account should be favoured and approved of God, and established, himself and family, on the throne of Israel. He was, I doubt not, upon the whole, a really virtuous and religious man, according to the dispensation he was under; and he certainly was a wise, a just, a munificent and prosperous prince; but yet he had his faults, and those great ones, in his private character; and these faults were not inconsistent with his character of being a man *according to God's heart;* for if he was such a prince as God intended him to be, faithfully executing his orders, and bringing to pass those great events, which he was raised up by God to be the instrument of accomplishing; he thus far acted *according to the heart,* i. e. the purpose and will of God, and thereby, in this respect, rendered himself well pleasing and acceptable to him. The particular purposes for which God advanced him to the throne were, that by his steady adherence to the one true God, and the religion which he was pleased to establish by Moses, he might be an illustrious example to all his posterity that should reign after him: and here he was absolutely without blemish, and a man, in the strictest sense of the expression, after God's own heart; as he never departed from his God, by introducing the deities of other nations, or permitting and encouraging the impious rites which they performed in honour of them. On this account his heart is said to be perfect with the Lord his God, because his heart was never turned away after other gods; and it is spoken to the honour of the good princes of his house, who reigned after him, that they did that which was right in the eyes of the Lord, as did David their father; and of the idolatrous princes, it is mentioned as the greatest reproach to them, that their hearts were not perfect with the Lord their God, as the heart of David their father. During the reign of Saul, little regard was shown by him to the institutions of religion, and he acted as though he was independent of the God of Israel, and therefore seldom or never inquired of him, how he was to act in the affairs of government, at the ark, from whence God, as peculiarly present in it, had promised to give the proper answers to those who rightly consulted him. As the ark itself had no fixed residence, and some of the principal services of religion could not, for that reason, be regularly and statedly performed, David was raised up to be king over God's people, that he might provide a rest for his ark, where it should perpetually continue, to which all the people might resort, where all the solemn festivals might be celebrated, and the whole worship of God might be constantly performed, according to the prescriptions of the law of Moses. David fully answered this purpose by fixing the ark at Jerusalem, settling all the necessary ceremonies and forms of worship for perpetual observance, and composing sacred hymns and psalms, that should be sung in honour of the true God, providing the expenses, and many of the costly materials, that were necessary to build and adorn the house of God, which he himself had proposed to erect, but which God reserved for his son and successor to raise up; and regulating the order, that was to be observed among all the various persons, that were to be employed in the daily services of the ark and temple; a full and ample account of which is transmitted to us in the first book of Chronicles. It must not be omitted also, that there was yet another end of providence, in David's appointment, to be king over Israel; that, according to God's promise concerning him, he might save his people Israel out of the hand of the Philistines, and out of the hand of all their enemies; and further, that by him he might accomplish the more ancient promises which God had made to Abraham, in their full extent, of giving to his seed the whole country, from the river of Egypt, unto the great river, the river Euphrates. Here also David answered the intentions of providence in his advancement, as he subdued the Philistines, and made them tributary to his crown; as he cleared his kingdom of all the remains of the nations that had formerly possessed it, or reduced them into entire subjection, or made them proselytes to his religion; and as the consequence of just and necessary wars, conquered all the neighbouring nations, garrisoned them by his victorious troops, and put it out of their power to disturb his people for many years, and left to his son and successor a forty years' peace, and dominion over all the kingdoms, from the river Euphrates, unto the land of the Philistines, and unto the border of Egypt, who brought presents and served Solomon all the days of his life. And finally, God raised him up to exalt the glory of his people Israel, and render them a flourishing and happy people, by the wisdom and justice of his government. He chose David his servant, to feed Jacob his people, and Israel his inheritance. So he fed them according to the integrity of his heart, and guided them by the skilfulness of his hands, i. e. he governed them with integrity, prudence and courage; for he reigned over all Israel, and executed judgment and justice among all his people. See here, reader, the true portrait of *the man after God's own heart,* who fulfilled all his pleasure, who amid all the idolatries of the nations around him, never wickedly apostatized from the worship of his God, and was an amiable example of a steady adherence to those forms of religion, which God had prescribed to all the princes his successors; who, though king, subjected himself to God the supreme king of Israel, and faithfully executed the commands he received from him; who made his people triumph in the numerous victories he obtained, by the directions, and under the conduct of God himself; who enlarged their dominions, and put them into possession of all the territories God had promised to their forefathers; and who amid all the successes that were granted him, the immense riches he had gathered from the spoils of his conquered enemies, and the sovereign power with which he was invested, never degenerated into despotism and tyranny, never oppressed his people; but governed them with integrity, ruled over them with moderation and prudence, impartially distributed justice, left an established durable peace, and fixed the whole administration, both civil and religious, upon the most substantial and durable foundation. In these instances he was the true vicegerent of God, on whose throne he sat, and all whose pleasure, in these great instances, he faithfully performed. If therefore David's private moral character was worse than it will be ever proved to be, he might be still a man after God's own heart, in the proper original sense of the expression; and the attempt to prove that he was not possessed of the height of moral purity, is an impertinent attempt to prove David not to be, what the sacred history never asserted him to be.—CHANDLER.

Ver. 6. And the king and his men went to Jerusalem unto the Jebusites, the inhabitants of the land; which spake unto David, saying, Except thou take away the blind and the lame, thou shalt not come in hither: thinking, David cannot come in hither. 7. Nevertheless David took the strong hold of Zion; the same *is* the city of David. 8. And David said on that day, Whosoever getteth up to the gutter, and smiteth the Jebusites, and the lame and the blind, *that are* hated of David's soul, *he shall be chief and captain.* Wherefore they said, The blind and the lame shall not come into the house.

1 CHRONICLES, CHAPTER XI.

Ver. 5. And the inhabitants of Jebus said to David, Thou shalt not come hither. Nevertheless David took the castle of Zion, which *is* the city of David. 6. And David said, Whosoever smiteth the Jebusites first shall be chief and captain. So Joab the son of Zeruiah went first up, and was chief.

The words *inhabitants of Jebus,* which are not in the original of Samuel, are not in the Vat. copy of the LXX. in Chronicles; but the Alexandrian translates regularly according to the present Hebrew text. In Samuel there is a clause or two in the speech of the Jebusites, which is omitted in Chronicles for brevity; as the history in Chronicles is regular, and the sense complete without it. But though the history be regular and very intelligible in Chronicles, yet the additional clauses in Samuel make the history there remarkably perplexed; and (as Dr. Delany observes) encumber it with more difficulties than are ordinarily to be met with. In full proportion to the difficulties has been the number of different interpretations; and yet there seems to be very sufficient room for offering another interpretation, in some material points differing from them all. The words in Samuel, so far as the text in Chronicles coincides, are clear and determinate in their meaning, "And the inhabitants of Jebus said to David, Thou shalt not come hither." But the succeeding words in Samuel are very difficult; or, at least, have been variously interpreted. The present English translation is, "Except thou take away the blind and the lame, thinking, David cannot come in hither." The chief difficulty here lies in determining who are *these blind and lame;* whether Jebusites, or the Jebusite *deities*, called *blind and lame* by way of derision. The latter opinion has been maintained by some considerable writers; but seems indefensible. For however David and the Israelites might be disposed to treat such idols with scorn and contempt, it is not at all likely the Jebusites should revile *their own* deities; and we must remember, that these deities are supposed to be here called *blind and lame* by the Jebusites themselves. But, admitting them to be idol deities, what meaning can there be in the Jebusites telling David, "he should not come into the citadel, unless he took away the deities upon the walls?" If he could scale the walls, so as to reach these guardian deities, he need not ask leave of the Jebusites to enter the citadel. But, (which is much more difficult to be answered,) what can possibly be the meaning of the last line, "Wherefore they said, the blind and the lame shall not come into the house?" For, who said? Did the Jebusites say, their own deities (before expressed by *the blind and the lame*) should not come into the house, should not (according to some) come where they were, or, should not (according to others) come into the house of the Lord?—Or, could these deities say, David and his men should not come into the house? The absurdity of attributing such a speech, or any speech, to these idols, is too clear to need illustration; and it is a known part of their real character, that they have mouths, but speak not. But, though these deities could not denounce these words, yet the Jebusites might; and it is possible (it has been said) that the *blind and the lame*, in this latter part of the sentence, may signify the Jebusites; not any particular Jebusites, so maimed; but the Jebusites in general, called *blind and lame*, for putting their trust in *blind and lame* idols. This seems too refined an interpretation; and we may safely conclude—that the same expression of the blind and lame means the same beings in the two different parts of the same sentence. It has been further observed, that these blind and lame are here spoken of as different from the Jebusites, "Whosoever smiteth the Jebusites, and the lame and the blind;" and if they were different, it requires no great skill at deduction to determine they were not the same. Perhaps then these *blind and lame* were, in fact, a few particular wretches, who laboured under these infirmities of blindness and lameness; and therefore were different from the general body of the Jebusites. But here will it not be demanded at once—how can we then account rationally for that bitterness with which David expresses himself here against these *blind and lame;* and how it was possible, for a man of David's humanity, to detest men for mere unblameable, and indeed pitiable, infirmities? And lastly, the authors of the Universal History, in their note on this transaction, mention the following, as the first plausible argument against the literal acceptation—"How could David distinguish the halt, or the lame, or the blind, from able men, when posted upon lofty walls; since those infirmities are not discernible but near at hand?" This, it must be allowed, would be a difficulty indeed, if David's information here had been only from his eyesight. But this objection immediately vanishes, when we reflect, that the Jebusites are said in the text to have told David—*the blind and the lame should keep them off:* for certainly David could easily conceive the men, who were placed upon the walls to insult him, were blind and lame; when he was told so by the Jebusites themselves; and told so, to render this insult of theirs the greater.

Having thus mentioned some of the present interpretations, it may be now proper to submit another to the judgment of the reader. I shall first give what seems to be the true interpretation of this passage; and then subjoin the several arguments in defence of it. "And the inhabitants of Jebus said to David, Thou shalt not come hither; for the blind and the lame shall keep thee off, by saying, David shall not come hither. But David took the strong hold of Sion, which is the city of David. And David said on that day, Whosoever (first) smiteth the Jebusites, and through the subterraneous passage reacheth the lame and the blind, that are hated of David's soul, because the blind and the lame continued to say, he shall not come into this house"—shall be chief captain. That the connected particles (כי אם *ki im*) rendered *except*, in Samuel, signify *for* in this place, is evident, because the words following are rather causal than objective; and we have several instances of this sense of the two particles given us by Noldius: thus Prov. xxiii. 18, they are rendered *for* in the English translation; and so in the English, Greek, Syriac, and Arabic versions of Lam. v. 22. That the verb (הסירך *esirek*) rendered *to take away*, is not here the infinitive, but the preter of Hiphil, is apparent from the sense; that it has been so considered, is certain from the Masoretic pointing, as De Dieu and other critics have observed: and we see it is translated as such by the LXX. in the plural number, αντεϛησαν. From this version, then, and from the plurality of the two nouns, which are necessarily the nominatives to this verb, we may infer, that it was originally הסירוך (*esiruk*) to keep off, the vau having been dropped here as in many other places. Enough having been said of the number, let us now consider the tense of this verb; which being preter, some have translated it by a word expressive of time past. But the sense necessarily requires it to be translated as future in other languages, though it be more expressive in the original in the preter tense, it being agreeable to the genius of the Hebrew language frequently to speak of events yet future, as having actually happened, when the speaker would strongly express the certainty of such event. This observation is peculiarly applicable to the case here. For this castle of mount Sion had never yet been taken by the Israelites, though they had dwelt in Canaan about four hundred years; as we learn from the sacred history, Josh. xv. 63; Judg. i. 21; xix. 10; and from Josephus, lib. vii. cap. 3. The Jebusites, then, absolutely depending on the advantage of their high situation and the strength of their fortification, (which had secured them against the Israelites so many hundred years,) looked upon this of David's as a vain attempt, which therefore they might safely treat with insolence and raillery. Full of this fond notion, they placed upon the walls of the citadel the few blind and lame that could be found among them, and told David, "He should not come thither; for the blind and lame" were sufficient to keep him off: which they (these weak defenders) should effectually do, only "by their shouting, David shall not come hither." That the blind and the lame were contemptuously placed upon the walls by the Jebusites, as before described, we are assured not only by the words of the sacred history before us, but also by the concurrent testimony of Josephus. Now that these blind and lame, who appear to have been placed upon the walls, were to insult and did insult David in the manner before mentioned, seems very evident from the words— *The blind and the lame shall keep thee off* BY SAYING, etc. and also from the impossibility of otherwise accounting for David's indignation against these (naturally pitiable) wretches. And the not attending to this remarkable circumstance seems one principal reason of the perplexity so visible among the various interpreters of this passage. It is very remarkable, that the sense before given to כי אם הסירך (*ki im esirek*,) "For the blind and the lame shall keep thee off," is confirmed by Josephus in the place just cited. And it is further remarkable that the same sense is given to these words in the English Bible of Coverdale, printed in 1535, in which they are rendered, **Thou shalt not come hither, but the blind and lame shal dryve the awaie.** This is one great instance to prove the credit due to some parts of this very old English version; as the sense of this passage seems to have been greatly mistaken both before and since. That it has been changed for the worse since that edition, is very evident; and that it was improperly rendered before appears from Wickliff's MS. version of 1383, where we read—**Thou shalt not entre hidur: no but thou do awey blynd men and lame**, etc. After this additional clause of Samuel, in the speech of the Jebusites, the two histories agree in saying, "David took the strong hold of Sion, which was afterward called the city of David." By this strong hold of Sion, or city of David, we are led by the words of the text to understand—not the fortress or citadel (which was not yet taken, as appears from the order of the history in both chapters)—but the town of the Jebusites, or city of David, which was spread over the wide hill of Sion: and is what Josephus means when he tells us—David first took the lower town, the town which lay beneath the citadel; after which he tells us, that the citadel remained yet to be taken, lib. vii. cap. 3. The two chapters having agreed in this circumstance of David's making himself master of the town or city, they now vary as before; and here also the history in Chronicles is regular, though it takes no notice of some further circumstances relating to the blind and the lame: and indeed the latter circumstances were to be omitted of course, as the historian chose, for brevity, to omit the former. But as to Samuel, there is in that book a deficiency of several words, which are necessary to complete the sense; which words are preserved in the text of Chronicles. And as the difficulty *here also* lies entirely in the text of Samuel, let us see whether it may not be cleared up to satisfaction. David having now possessed himself of the strong town of the Jebusites, situate upon the hill of Sion, proceeds, *the same day*, to attack the citadel or fortress; which was considered by the Jebusites as impregnable. And probably the Israelites would have thought so too, and David had retired from before it, like his forefathers, if he had not possessed himself by stratagem, when he found he could not storm or take it by open force. For this seems in fact to have been the case; and the history of this success may be properly introduced by a similar case or two. And first, Dr. Prideaux (in his Connexion, part i. book 2) tells us of the city of Babylon,—that when it was besieged by Cyrus, the inhabitants, thinking themselves secure in their walls and their stores, looked on the taking of the city by a siege as an impracticable thing; and therefore *from the top of their walls scoffed at Cyrus, and derided him or every thing he did towards it.* (A circumstance most exactly parallel to that of the history before us.) But yet, that Cyrus broke down the great bank or dam of the river, both where it ran into the city, and where it came out; and as soon as the channel of the river was drained, in the middle of the night, while Belshazzar was carousing at the conclusion of an annual festival, "the troops of Cyrus entered through these passages in two parties, and took the city by surprise." And there is a second remarkable case related by Polybius, which will further illustrate the present history; and was communicated to me by a learned friend. "Rabatamana," says Polybius, "a city of Arabia, could not be taken, till one of the prisoners showed the besiegers a subterraneous passage, through which the besieged came down for water." Now this fortress of the Jebusites seems to have been circumstanced like Rabatamana; in having also a subterraneous passage which is called in the original צנור (*tzenur*,) a word which occurs but once more in the Bible, and does not seem commonly understood in this place. The English version calls it the *gutter*—the Vulgate, *fistulas*—Vatablus, *canales*—Jun. and Trem. *emissarium*—Poole, *tubus aquæ*—and Bochart, *alveus*, &c. But not to multiply quotations, most interpreters agree in making the word signify something hollow, and applying it to water: just the case of the subterraneous passage, or great hollow, of Rabatamana, through which men could pass and repass for water. That this צנור (*tzenur*) in the text was such an underground passage might be strongly presumed from the text itself; but it is proved to have been so by Josephus. For, speaking of this very transaction, he calls them subterraneous cavities, putting this interpretation upon a very solid footing. That the preposition ב, rendered in, prefixed to צנור (*tzenur*,) sometimes signifies by, is evident from Noldius; and that it signifies so in this place is certain from the nature of the context, and the testimony of Josephus, who expresses it thus: the verb יאמרו (*iamru*,) rendered, they said, in this sentence is very properly future; as Hebrew verbs in that tense are known to be frequentative, or to express the continuance of doing any thing; and therefore that tense is with great propriety used here to express the frequent repetition of the insolent speech used by the blind and the lame upon the walls of the fortress. It only remains here to make an observation or two on the reward proposed by David, and the person who obtained it. The text of Chronicles tells us, "David said, Whosoever smiteth the Jebusites first, shall be chief and captain, or head and prince." We are to recollect, that Joab the son of Zeruiah (David's sister) had been general of his army, during the civil war, between the men of Judah under David, and the Israelites commanded by Abner, in favour of Ishbosheth the son of Saul: but that the Israelites, having now submitted to David, he was king over the whole twelve tribes. David, we know, frequently endeavoured to remove Joab from his command of the army, on account of his haughtiness, and for several murders; but complained, that this son of Zeruiah was too hard for him. One of these attempts of David seems to have been made at the time Israel came in to David, by the persuasion of Abner; when it is probable the condition on Abner's side was to have been made David's captain-general: and perhaps Joab suspected so much, and therefore murdered him. The next attempt seems to have been made at the taking this strong citadel of the Jebusites. For David proposes the reward absolutely to every officer of his army, "Whosoever smiteth the Jebusites first;" i. e. whosoever will ascend first, put himself at the head of a detachment, and march up through the subterraneous passage into the citadel, shall be head and captain. This proposal, we may observe, was general; and yet, how much soever David might wish Joab safely removed, it is reasonable to think that he made Joab the first offer. And, we find, that however dangerous and dreadful this enterprise appeared, yet Joab had prudence enough to undertake it, and courage enough to execute it: and Joab went up first, or at the head of a party, and was accordingly declared head, or chief captain, or (in the modern style) captain-general of the united armies of Israel and Judah. It is not unlikely that the men of Israel expected, that though Abner their general had been basely murdered by Joab, yet David's chief captain should be chosen from among *them;* or at least that they should have a chance for that first post of honour, as well as the men of Judah. And if they had declared any expectation of this kind, David seems to have taken the wisest step for determining so important a point—by declaring, that neither relation, nor fortune, nor friendship should recommend upon the occasion; but, as the bravest man and the best soldier ought to be commander-in-chief, so this honour should be the reward of the greatest merit; that there was now a fair opportunity of signalizing themselves in the taking this important fortress; and therefore his resolution was—that *Whosoever would head* a detachment up this subterraneous passage, and should first make himself master of the citadel, by that passage, or by scaling the walls, or by any other method, should be *head and captain*, i. e. captain-general. It is remarkable, that the text in Samuel is very incomplete in this place: David's proposal to the army is just begun, and a circumstance or two mentioned; but the reward proposed, and the person rewarded, are totally omitted. We may presume the text could not have been thus imperfect originally, since no ellipsis can supply what is here wanting; and therefore the words in the coinciding chapter in Chronicles, which regularly fill up this omission, were doubtless at first also in Samuel, and are therefore to be restored: the necessity of thus restoring the words not found in the present copies of Samuel is apparent.

And the English version of these texts, in Samuel is—"And they spoke unto David, saying, Thou shalt not come hither; for the blind and the lame shall keep thee off, by saying, David shall not come hither. But David took the strong hold of Sion, which is the city of David. And David said on that day, Whosoever (first) smiteth the Jebusites, and by the subterraneous passage reacheth the blind and the lame, which are hated of David's soul, (because the blind and the lame continued to say, He shall not come into this house)—shall be head and captain. So Joab the son of Zeruiah went up first, and was head—or captain-general." The English version, then, of these texts in Chronicles is—"And the inhabitants of Jebus said to David, Thou shalt not come hither. But David took the strong hold of Sion, which is the city of David. And David said, Whosoever first smiteth the Jebusites, shall be head and captain. So Joab the son of Zeruiah went up first, and was chief captain." (Kennicott.)—CRITICA BIBLICA.

Ver. 9. So David dwelt in the fort, and called it, The city of David: and David built round about, from Millo and inward.

The old city founded by the Jebusites before Abraham arrived in Canaan, is styled by some writers *the city of Melchizedek*, not because he was the founder, but because it was the seat of his government. This ancient city was so strongly fortified both by nature and art, that the people of Israel could not drive out the Jebusites, its original inhabitants, but were reduced to live with them at Jerusalem. The armies of Israel indeed seized the city; but the Jebusites kept possession of the strong fort which defended the town, till the reign of David, who took it by storm, and changed its name to the city of David, to signify the importance of the conquest, and to perpetuate the memory of the event. Having chosen Jerusalem for the place of his residence and the capital of his kingdom, he adorned the fortress with a royal palace for his own accommodation, and a variety of other buildings; which, from the continual additions made to them in succeeding reigns, increased to the size of a considerable city, and covered nearly the whole of mount Sion. The largeness of the city of David may be inferred from the expression of the sacred historian; "David built round about from Millo and inward." This passage, and particularly the word Millo, has greatly exercised the genius and divided the sentiments of commentators; and is therefore entitled to more particular notice. That Millo was situated in the city of David, the inspired historian expressly asserts: and by consequence, it must either have been upon mount Sion or in its immediate vicinity. It is worthy of notice, that the inspired writer of David's history could not allude to Millo itself, which was not then in existence, but to the place where it afterward stood; for Millo was not built till the succeeding reign. It seems to have been a public building, where the king and his princes met in council about affairs of state; for in the passage already quoted from the first book of Kings, it is connected with the house of the Lord and the royal palace. The words of the historian are; "And this is the reason of the levy (or tax) which king Solomon raised; for to build the house of the Lord and his own house, and Millo, and the wall of Jerusalem, and Hazor, and Megiddo, and Gezer." But every ground of hesitation is removed by the sacred writer of the second book of Kings, who calls it expressly "the house of Millo." That it was a public building, in one of whose apartments the council of state met to deliberate upon public affairs, is rendered extremely probable by one of the kings of Judah losing his life there by the hands of his princes; for we are told, that "the servants of king Joash arose and made a conspiracy, and slew him in the house of Millo," whither he had probably come to consult with his princes and other principal persons upon some affairs of state. This interpretation is greatly strengthened by a passage in the book of Judges, which informs us, that "all the men of Shechem gathered together, and all the house of Millo, and went and made Abimelech king." The city of Shechem then had also its house of Millo, and a great number of persons connected with it, whom the sacred writer distinguishes from the men of the city. Now since both were concerned in making Abimelech king, it is natural to conclude, that the men of the city were the inferior inhabitants, and the house of Millo the governors of the place: both of whom on this occasion met in the senate-house, to set the crown upon the head of their favourite.

The house of Millo upon mount Sion, appears to have been a place of great strength, and essentially connected with the defence of Jerusalem; for when Hezekiah discovered that Sennacherib meditated the reduction of his capital, "he strengthened himself, and built up all the wall that was broken, and raised it up to the towers, and another wall without, and repaired Millo in the city of David, and made darts and shields in abundance." From the intimate connexion between the repairing of Millo and the making of darts and other implements of war, it has been conjectured by some writers, that one part of that public building was occupied as an armory; in which there is nothing improbable. It is necessary, however, before leaving this part of the subject, to state another opinion that has been advanced concerning Millo, by several men of genius and learning. They suppose that Solomon filled up a deep valley or hollow, that separated the hill of Sion and the site of the ancient city from mount Moriah, upon whose summit he built the temple of Jehovah, and made a plain level road from the one to the other. The execution of this stupendous work, they contend, may be inferred from the root of the word Millo, which signifies "to fill up;" and from a passage in 2d Chronicles, where it is said, the king made terraces to the house of the Lord, and to the king's palace. The word which is here rendered terraces, may be translated as in the margin, stays or supports. But neither of these senses amounts to a sufficient proof, that the terraces were made by filling up the hollow between mount Sion and mount Moriah. That Solomon planned and executed a noble and magnificent way from the royal palace on mount Sion, to the temple on mount Moriah, which excited the admiration of all that saw it, is attested in plain terms by the sacred writer; "And when the queen of Sheba had seen all Solomon's wisdom, and the house which he had built, . . . and his ascent by which he went up unto the house of the Lord, there was no more spirit in her." This passage also proves, that although the declivity on each side was easy, the road was not perfectly level, for Solomon went up an ascent to the house of the Lord. The same circumstance is mentioned in another book, where the sacred writer speaks of "the causey of the going up." And we read, that Joash was slain in the house of Millo, which goes down to Silla. The term Silla, is thought by some learned commentators, to have the same meaning as Messilah, which signifies a causey or cast up way; and consequently, that between the two mounts Sion and Moriah, were two declivities, one towards the temple or mount Moriah, the other towards the palace or mount Sion. The last is supposed to be the descent of Silla, near which stood the house of Millo. From this statement it is clear, that the house of Millo stood on the east side of mount Sion, at the upper end of the causey which goes down to Silla, and the royal palace on the opposite side. When, therefore, the sacred historian says, David built round about from Millo and inward, or as the original word may be rendered, "to the house," he seems to intimate, that David built round about from the place where Millo was afterward erected by Solomon, or where more probably the senate-house, or Millo of the Jebusites, had stood, which was pulled down to make room for the more sumptuous edifice of Solomon, to his own house; so that David built from one part of mount Sion, quite round to the opposite point. Hence, the residence of David, even in the reign of that renowned monarch, began to assume the size and splendour of a city, and to be justly entitled to the appellation which it receives from the sacred historian.—Paxton.

Ver. 19. And David inquired of the Lord, saying, Shall I go up to the Philistines? wilt thou deliver them into my hand? And the Lord said unto David, Go up; for I will doubtless deliver the Philistines into thy hand.

I cannot here help observing, in honour of the Hebrew oracle, that its answers were such, as became the character of the true God, who hath all events at his disposal, and cannot be mistaken as to those which he expressly foretels. Let any one compare it with the heathen oracles, and he will be forced to acknowledge, that they were shuffling, ambiguous, and vague; and the answers they gave of so uncertain a nature, so equivocal and deceitful, as that they might be interpreted in two direct contrary senses, might be equally true of two contrary events, and evidently demonstrated, that they who gave them out knew no more of those events on which they were consulted, than they who inquired about them, who were often deceived in the application of them to their own destruction. Thus Crœsus was foretold by Apollo, that if he made war with the Persians, he should overturn a great empire; which Crœsus interpreting in his own favour, made war upon Cyrus, and thereby put an end to his own empire; after which, he severely reproached Apollo for deceiving him. And thus Pyrrhus, king of Epirus, who is said, upon the credit of an ambiguous oracle of the same Apollo, to have engaged in war with the Romans, was entirely defeated by them, and forced at last to retire with great disgrace and loss into his own dominions. Whereas, the answers of the Hebrew oracle had one plain obvious certain meaning, that needed no interpretation, that no one could possibly mistake the meaning of, and that was never found, in one single instance, to deceive or disappoint those who depended on, and directed themselves by the order of it. Do this, or, Do not this, was the peremptory form, in which they, who consulted it, were answered; which, in the judgment of Cicero, was the manner in which the oracles of God ought to be delivered.—Chandler.

CHAPTER VI.

Ver. 2. And David arose, and went with all the people that *were* with him from Baale of Judah, to bring up from thence the ark of God, whose name is called by the name of The LORD of Hosts, that dwelleth *between* the cherubims.

David being now at rest, in peace at home, and free from all foreign wars, applied himself to make some necessary regulations in religion, and a proper provision for the more stated performance of the solemnities of divine worship. The ark, which was the emblem of the divine presence, where God dwelt between the cherubim, was now at Kirjath-jearim, in the house of Abinidab on the hill; where it was placed, when the Philistines had sent it back, after they had taken it in the battle, in which Hophni and Phineas, the sons of Eli, perished, and great part of the Hebrew army were cut off. The time of its continuance here was about forty-six years, except when, on some particular occasions, it was removed, as once in Saul's time, when he fought his first battle against the Philistines. As David had now fixed his own residence at Jerusalem, and intended it for the capital of his whole kingdom, he was resolved to do every thing in his power, that could contribute to the splendour, dignity, and safety of it. His first care was to secure it the presence and protection of the God of Israel; and accordingly, he provided a proper habitation and residence for his ark, and pitched for it a tent, where it might continually remain throughout all future ages. The ark was a small chest, made of shittim-wood, two cubits and a half, or a yard and a half and one inch long, a cubit and a half, or two feet nine inches broad, and overlaid within and without, with pure gold. On the top of the ark was placed a seat, or cover, called כפרת, ἱλαστηριον, *the mercy-seat*, as we render the word, or, *the propitiatory cover*, because the blood of the propitiatory sacrifice was sprinkled on, and before it. In this ark were placed the two tables of stone, on which the ten commandments were engraven, called the testimony; because God testified and declared, these ten commandments were essential and unalterable laws of his kingdom. On this account the ark is called, The ark of the testimony. In the order to make it, God says: "Let them make me a sanctuary, that I may dwell among them." Here, God tells Moses: "I will meet with thee, and I will commune with thee, from above the mercy-seat, from between the two cherubims, of all things, which I will give thee in commandment, unto the children of Israel; and I will appear in the cloud upon the mercy-seat." Hence the ark was considered as the house, the sanctuary, and temple of God, where he resided; and God is described as dwelling between, or rather above the cherubim; not because the Hebrews were so stupid as to imagine any personal residence of God in the ark, or that he could be confined to any particular place, whom they well knew the heaven, even the heaven of heavens, could not contain; much less any house that could be erected for him by human hands; but because the cloud and glory, which appeared there, were the visible emblems of his gracious presence with them, and of his peculiar inspection and care over them; or, as Joshua tells them, whereby they should know, that the living God was among them, even the Lord of the whole earth; viz. to protect and prosper them. That the majesty of this ark or portable temple of God, might be preserved inviolable, God ordered a tabernacle to be prepared for its reception, and a veil to be placed before the ark, to separate the holy place, where the ark was fixed, from the other part of the tabernacle, where Aaron and his sons were to minister continually before God. Besides this, there was a spacious court prepared round about the tabernacle and the altar, where the congregation were allowed to enter, and present their offerings at the door of the tabernacle, before the Lord. At the door of the tabernacle of the congregation the daily burnt-offering was to be offered, where God promised to meet with the children of Israel, to sanctify it by his glory, and to dwell among the children of Israel, and be their God, i. e. their almighty guardian, and protector. Here also were to be brought all their various kinds of sacrifices, in reference to which the charge was so strict, as that God commanded, that whoever did not bring his sacrifice to the door of the tabernacle, there to offer it to the Lord, should be cut off from his people: the most effectual provision this, that could possibly be made against idolatry, as it struck at the root of all idol worship; and which, had they observed the command, must have prevented the introduction of any other god, in opposition to Jehovah, the true God, who dwelt in the ark, and on whose altar their sacrifices must have been offered by his priests, who resided in the tabernacle. Hither also, as to the temple of God, the religious Hebrews loved to resort, not only to present their sacrifices, but to join in the celebration of the divine praises, and the singing those sacred songs, that were composed in honour of the true God, to offer up their supplications to him, and to make and pay their vows before him; and their appearance at the tabernacle for these purposes, where the ark of the presence resided, was styled, appearing before God, coming before his presence, frequenting his courts, abiding in his house, and the like; because they saw there his power and glory, or the glorious manifestation of his power and majesty, which were frequently given, as the immediate token of God's accepting their sacrifices, thanksgivings, and prayers. From these observations it appears, that this ark of God was of the highest importance in the Hebrew republic, as it was a standing memorial for Jehovah, the one true God, the God of Israel, the centre of all the public solemnities of religion, the place where the whole nation was to pay their homage and adoration to him, where he appeared propitious and favourable to his people, where they were to inquire of him, and wait for his direction; and that the presence of it was essentially necessary, wherever the public solemnities of worship were to be performed; and that Jerusalem could never have been fixed on for these sacred services, nor the visible emblems of the divine Majesty and presence, in the cloud and glory, have ever been expected in it, unless this ark had been translated to, and settled there, as the place of its future and fixed residence. These were some of the considerations that induced David to remove it into the new city that he had built, but there were others also that the very law of Moses suggested to him. God had by him commanded the Hebrews, that "unto the place which the Lord their God had chosen out of all the tribes, to put his name there, even unto his habitation should they seek, and thither they should come, and thither should they bring their burnt offerings, their sacrifices, their tithes and heave offerings, their vows, their free-will offerings, and the firstlings of their herds and flocks, and that there they should eat before the Lord their God, and rejoice in all that they put their hand to, they and their household, wherein the Lord their God had blessed them." He further promised them, that after they had passed over Jordan, and dwelt in the land, which he had given them to inherit; then, "there should be a place, which the Lord their God would choose, to dwell there, and that there they should bring their burnt-offerings, and all their choice vows, and that there they should rejoice before the Lord their God, they, and their sons, and their daughters, and their men-servants, and their maid-servants, and the Levite that was with them in their gates, and do all that he commanded them;" and that here, and nowhere else, they should eat the passover, and appear three times in it every year, before the Lord their God; at the feast of unleavened bread, the feasts of weeks, and the feast of tabernacles; and that here they were to apply for determining their principal causes and controversies: in a word, that this very place, which the Lord should choose, should be the capital of the whole kingdom, the principal seat of all their public solemnities, and the perpetual residence of the supreme courts of justice and equity.

During all the preceding periods of the Hebrew republic, no such place had been chosen and appointed by God; the ark itself had no settled and fixed habitation, but removed from place to place, as convenience or necessity required; and the several judges and supreme officers, that presided over and judged the people, had their particular cities, where they resided, and administered justice to those who applied to them. In this unsettled state of the republic, many and great inconveniences must have necessarily arisen, and the most significant and important solemnities of the national religion were absolutely incapable of being performed, according to the prescription of the law of God by Moses.

The honour of making the necessary settlement in these things, and perfecting the civil polity, and the ceremonial of the Hebrew worship, was reserved for David; who when he had retaken Jerusalem from the Jebusites, had considered the strength and convenience of its situation, had enlarged it with new buildings, adorned it with palaces, erected a magnificent one for himself, had well fortified it with walls and bulwarks, and chosen it for his own residence; was in hope that this was the place God had now chosen to dwell in, and immediately formed the great design of translating the ark of God into it, and providing a suitable habitation for its future rest; that this emblem of God's immediate presence might be perpetually near him, where he himself might constantly worship in the courts of his tabernacle, where all the solemn sacrifices might be statedly offered, and the affairs in general of the whole kingdom, relating to religion and justice, for the future, be transacted with regularity, order, and dignity. In pursuance of this great design, he first gathered together all the chosen men of Israel, thirty thousand men, consisting of the captains of thousands, and hundreds, and all the princes; and said to them, thus assembled at Jerusalem: "If it seem good unto you, and it be approved of by the Lord our God, let us send abroad unto our brethren everywhere, that are left in all the land of Israel, and with them to the priests and Levites which are in their cities and suburbs, that they may gather themselves together unto us, and let us bring up to us the ark of God; at which we but seldom inquired in the days of Saul." To this proposal the congregation unanimously agreed. David accordingly sent messengers to Israel, throughout all his dominions, from Sichor, or the Egyptian Nile, the most southern boundary of his kingdom, to the entrance of Hemath, northward, near the rise of Jordan. When the assembly were met, David led them to Baalah, which is Kirjath-jearim, and which belonged to the tribe of Judah; and from thence they conveyed the ark of God, "where his name was invocated, even the name Jehovah Zebaoth, or Lord of hosts, who sits upon the cherubim, that were over the ark." They had prepared a new carriage, drawn by oxen, for the conveyance of it, which Uzzah and Ahio the sons of Abinidab drove to Abinidab's house; and then placing the ark upon it, they attended on it; Ahio marching before the ark, and Uzzah on one side of it. When the procession began, David, with all the house of Israel, gave the highest demonstrations of satisfaction and pleasure, playing before the Lord on all manner of instruments, made of fir-wood, even on harps, and on psalteries, and on timbrels, and on cornets, and on cymbals. But the joy of David and his people on this solemn occasion was soon interrupted. For when the procession was advanced as far as Nachon's thrashing-floor, the oxen stumbled, and thereby shook the ark; on which Uzzah, fearing probably it might be thrown off the carriage, very rashly laid hold of the ark of God with his hand, in order to support it; not considering, that as he was but a Levite, he was forbidden to touch it under penalty of death, and that, as it was the dwelling of God, and immediately under his protection, he could and would have preserved it from falling, without Uzzah's officious care to prevent it. For this violation of the law, Uzzah was immediately struck by the hand of God, and fell down dead by the ark.

God smote him, as the text says, for his error, or as we have it in the margin, for his rashness; and as this is the first instance that we have of the violation of this prohibition of the Levites, from touching any thing sacred under the penalty of death, the punishment of it shows that the prohibition was really divine, and that as the penalty of death was incurred, it was justly inflicted, as an example to others, and to preserve a due reverence for the *divine institutions*. Besides, God had particularly appointed the manner in which the ark should be removed from place to place; not upon a carriage drawn by oxen, but by ordering that the sons of Kohath should carry it on their shoulders, by the staves, that were put into the rings, on the sides of the ark; and their neglecting to do it on this solemn occasion, and consulting their ease more than their duty, by placing it on a carriage drawn by oxen, was an offence of no small aggravation, as it was an innovation contrary to the express order of the law. This David himself afterward acknowledges, and assigns it as the reason of the punishment inflicted upon Uzzah, and as he himself and the whole house of Israel were present at this solemnity, and it was impossible that the nature and cause of Uzzah's death could have been concealed. The history expressly says, that God smote him for his rashness, in laying hold of what he ought not to have touched; or for his error in thinking God was not able to protect and secure it; and David affirms, that the Lord had made a breach upon Uzzah, and in commemoration of it called the name of the place, Perez-uzzah, i. e. the breach of Uzzah: a plain evidence, that he knew his death to be extraordinary, and inflicted by the immediate hand of God; this is further evident from the terror David was in upon account of this extraordinary accident, and his desisting for this reason from the resolution he had formed of introducing the ark into Jerusalem. David "was afraid of the Lord that day, and said: How shall the ark of the Lord come to me?" I am at a loss what method to take to bring the ark, with safety to myself and people, into Jerusalem. Every circumstance in this transaction shows that Uzzah's death was a divine punishment, and had he died by any other hand, it must have been known to many that were present, as he died in open day light, and in the view of thousands who attended in this solemn procession.

Should it be said, that if the Lord would have saved the ark, because he could; it may be also urged, that he would have brought it to any place where he intended it to be, because he could have done it, and that therefore David was impertinently officious in removing it himself: the answer is; that as God had forbidden the ark to be touched, on any occasion, by the Levites, under penalty of death, it was an assurance, that in all its movements he would take it under his especial protection, and that as he was able to secure it against every hazard, without human assistance, so he certainly would do it. But God never promised to remove it himself from place to place, but expressly gave that service in charge to the Levites; and therefore it doth not follow, that because he himself could, therefore he would remove it, because he expressly ordered it to be done by others. But Uzzah's intention was certainly good, and therefore the alleged crime certainly pardonable; the seeming exigency precluding all reflection. But this seeming exigency was no real one, and his acting without reflection, an aggravation of his fault; especially as he committed this offence, in consequence of a former. Uzzah knew, or might have known, that the ark was never to be moved in any carriage, but on the shoulders of the Levites; and had it been thus removed, the accident would not have happened to the ark, and his rashness in touching, and the punishment he suffered for it, would have been both prevented. His good intention therefore here could be of no avail. It was no excuse for his ignorance, if he was really ignorant, because he might, and ought to have known better; nor for his presumption, and such it must have been, if he could not plead ignorance for his error, because this was in its nature a high aggravation of his fault. And light as this offence may seem, yet when it is considered in all its consequences, and what an encouragement it might have given for the introduction of other innovations, contrary to the institutions of the law of Moses, had this offence been passed by with impunity; it was no wonder that God should manifest his displeasure against it, by punishing with death, what he had forbidden under the penalty of it; thereby to prevent all future attempts to make any changes in that constitution which he had established. But "supposing that the ark had been overturned for want of this careful prevention, might not Uzzah, with greater plausibility, have been smote for his omission, than he was for his commission?" That is, might not God have more plausibly punished Uzzah for omitting what he had strictly forbidden him to do, under pain of death, and what therefore it could never be his duty to do; than for committing what it was unlawful by God's own command for him to commit, and which he had made the commission of a capital crime? What some critics may think of this, I know not; I cannot for my life conceive, how Uzzah could have been more plausibly, or reasonably punished for omitting what it was his duty to omit, than for committing what he was obliged never to commit. The very contrary seems to me to be true, because he who doth not commit an illegal action can never deserve punishment on that account; whereas he, who actually doth such an illegal action, becomes thereby guilty, and liable to the punishment denounced against it.

During the march, David, in order to render it more solemnly religious, sacrificed, at proper intervals, oxen and fatlings; and though the ark, with its proper furniture, must have been of a considerable weight, and the service of the Levites, in carrying it such a length of way on their shoulders, as from Obed-Edom's house to mount Sion, could not but be very difficult; yet the history observes, that God helped the Levites, by enabling them to bring it to its appointed place, and preserving them from every unhappy accident, till they had safely deposited it; in grateful acknowledgment of which they presented an offering unto God of seven bullocks and seven rams. As the procession was accompanied with vocal as well as instrumental music, David had prepared a proper psalm or ode (Ps. 68) to be sung by the chanters, the several parts of which were suited to the several divisions of the march, and the whole of it adapted to so sacred and joyful a solemnity; as will appear by a careful perusal and examination of it. I hope my reader will not be displeased, if I give him a short and easy paraphrase of this excellent composure.

When the Ark was taken up on the shoulders of the Levites.

Ver. 1. Arise, O God of Israel, and in thy just displeasure execute thy vengeance upon the enemies of thy people, and let all who hate them be put to flight, and never prevail against them.

2. Drive them before thee, and scatter them, as smoke is dispersed by the violence of the wind, and let all their power and strength die away and dissolve, as wax melts away before the fire.

3. But let thy righteous people be glad, exult in the presence and under the protection of thee their God, and in the triumph of their joy cry out:

4. "Sing psalms of thanksgivings to God. Celebrate his name and glory with songs of Praise. Prepare ye his way, and let all opposition cease before him, who rode through the deserts, and guided his people with the cloud by day, and the flame of fire by night. His name is Jah, the tremendous being. And O exult with joy before him.

5. "He is the orphan's father, who will protect and provide for him. He is the judge and avenger of the widow, will vindicate her cause, and redress her injuries, even that God, who is present with us in his holy sanctuary.

6. "He it is who increases the solitary and desolate into numerous families, and restores to liberty, and blesses with an abundance, those who are bound in chains, but makes those who are his refractory implacable enemies, dwell as in a dry and desert land, by destroying their families and fortunes, and utterly blasting their prosperity."

When the Procession began.

7. How favourably didst thou appear, O God, for thy people in ancient times! How powerful was that protection, which thou didst graciously afford them! when thou didst march before them at their coming out of Egypt, and guidedst them through the wilderness!

8. The earth shook, the very heavens dissolved at thy presence, even Sinai itself seemed to melt, the smoke of it ascending as the smoke of a furnace, when thou the God of Israel didst in thine awful majesty descend upon it.

9. Thou, O God, didst rain down, in the most liberal manner, during their passage through the desert, bread and flesh as from heaven, and didst thereby refresh, satisfy, and confirm thine inheritance, fatigued with their marches, and in the utmost distress for want of food.

10. Such was the abundance provided for them, that they dwelt in the midst of the manna and quails, in heaps surrounding them, on every side. Thy poor and distressed people were thus liberally supplied by thy wonderful and never-failing goodness.

11. And not only were they thus miraculously fed by thy benevolent hand, but made to triumph over all their enemies, who molested and opposed them. For thou gavest forth the order to attack. Thou didst assure them of success, leddest them forth against their adversaries, and their victories were celebrated by large numbers of matrons and virgins, who shouted aloud, and sang these joyful tidings:

12. "The kings of armies fled away. They fled away utterly discomfited, and they who abode with their families in their tents, received their shares in the spoils of their conquered enemies.

13. "Though when you were slaves to the Egyptians, employed in the servile drudgery of attending their pots and bricks, you appeared in the most sordid and reproachful habits, and took up your dwellings in the most wretched and miserable huts; yet now you are enriched with the gold and silver of your conquered enemies, possessed of their tents, and arrayed with garments shining and beautiful, you resemble the dove's feathers, in which the gold and silver colours mixed with each other, give a very pleasing and lovely appearance."

14. When the Lord thus scattered and overcame kings for the sake of his inheritance, how were thy people refreshed! How great was the joy thou gavest them in Salmon, where they obtained, beheld, and celebrated the victory!

When the Procession came in view of Mount Sion.

15. Is Bashan, that high hill Bashan, with its rough and craggy eminences, is this the hill of God, which he hath chosen for his residence, and where his sanctuary shall abide hereafter for ever?

16. Why look ye, O ye craggy hills, with an envious impatience? See, there is the hill, which God hath chosen and desired to dwell in. Assuredly the Lord will inherit it for ever.

17. The angels and chariots of God, who attend this solemnity, and encompass the ark of his presence, are not only, as at the giving of his law, ten thousand, but twice ten thousand, and thousands of thousands. God is in the midst of them, as formerly on thee, O Sinai, and will constantly reside in his sanctuary on mount Sion, and as the guardian of it, by his almighty power continue to defend it.

When the Ark ascended Sion, and was deposited in David's Tabernacle.

18. Thus hast thou now, O God, ascended the heights of Sion's hill, and taken possession of it, as thy future favourite dwelling, after having subdued our adversaries, and delivered our captive brethren from the power of their enslavers. Thou hast received gifts from men, even from our inveterate enemies, by enriching us with their spoil, subjecting them as tributaries to my crown, and enabling me by them to provide a habitation for our God, and in this joyful manner to attend thine entrance into it.

19. O blessed be Jehovah. From day to day he supports his people, and like a father bears them up, and protects them from all destructive evils.

20. He is that God to whom we owe all our past salvations, and from whom alone we can expect all we may hereafter need. For under his direction are all the outgoings of death, so that he is able to preserve his people from the approaches of it, when their inveterate enemies meditate and resolve their destruction.

21. But vain and impotent shall be their power and malice. God will avenge himself on their devoted heads, and their strength and craft shall not be able to protect them from his indignation, if they continue wickedly to disturb me in the possession of that kingdom, to which he hath advanced me.

22, 23. For this end, he raised me to the throne, and assured me that I should deliver his people from the Philistines, and from the hand of all their enemies. Let them therefore begin their hostilities when they please, God will appear for me, as he did in former times for our forefathers, and my victories over them shall be as signal and complete, as that over Pharaoh and his army, who were destroyed in the sea, through which he safely led his people; or as over Og the king of Bashan, the slaughter of whose army was so great, as that our victorious troops were forced to trample over their slaughtered and bloody bodies, and even our very dogs licked up their blood, and feasted on the carnage.

While the sacrifices were offering, which concluded the whole solemnity, they closed the anthem with the following verses.

24. Thy people have now, O God, seen thy marches, the triumphant marches of my God and king, present in his holy sanctuary, into the tabernacle prepared for it, amid the loudest acclamations of the whole assembly.

25. The procession was led by a chosen band of singers, the players on instruments came behind them, and in the midst of them a virgin train, who accompanied their timbrels with the harmony of their voices, and sung:

26. "O celebrate the praises of God in this united congregation of our tribes. Celebrate the praises of Jehovah, all you who are descended from Israel, your great and fruitful progenitor."

27. Even Benjamin himself was present, who, though the smallest of our tribes, had so far the pre-eminence over the rest, as to give the first king and ruler to the people; even he was present, and rejoiced to see the honour done to Jerusalem, and the crown established on my head. Here the princes of Judah attended, with the supreme council of that powerful tribe; with the princes of Zebulon, and those of Naphtali; who from their distant borders joined the procession; all unanimously consenting that Jerusalem should become the seat of worship, and capital of my kingdom.

28. It is thy God, O Israel, who hath thus advanced thee, as a nation, to thy present state of dignity and power. Strengthen, O God, the foundation of our happiness, and by thy favour render it perpetual.

29. As the ark of thy presence is now fixed in Jerusalem, protect it by thy power, and let the kings of the earth bring their gifts, present their offerings, and pay their adoration at thy altar.

30. O rebuke and break the power of the Egyptian crocodile, his princes and nobles, who pay homage to their bulls, and all his people, who stupidly worship their calves, and dance in honour of them to the tinkling sounds of instruments and bells. Trample under foot their silver-plated idols, and utterly disperse the people who delight in war.

31. Let the princes of Egypt come and worship at thy sanctuary, and the far-distant Ethiopia accustom herself to lift up her hands in adoration of thy majesty.

32. O may all the kingdoms of the earth celebrate, in sacred songs, the majesty of our God. Let all sing the praises of our Jehovah.

33. He is the omnipresent God, the proprietor and Lord of the heaven of heavens, which he spread out of old. He makes the clouds his chariot when he rides through the heavens, and storms and tempests, thunders and lightnings, the instruments of his vengeance against his enemies. When he sends forth his voice in the mighty thunder, how awful and astonishing that voice!

34. Ascribe to him that almighty strength which belongs to him. Though his empire is universal, his kingdom is peculiarly exalted over Israel, by whom alone he is acknowledged as the true God, and who manifests the greatness of his power in the clouds of heaven.

35. O God, the God of Israel, how terrible is thy majesty, when thou comest forth from thy heavenly and earthly sanctuaries, for the destruction of thine enemies, and the defence of thy people. It is he who inspires them with strength, and courage, and renders them a mighty and powerful nation. Eternal blessing and praise be ascribed unto our God.

I think the division I have made of this psalm, into its several parts, is natural and easy, which the subject matter of it points out, and which renders the whole of it a regular, well-connected, and elegant composure. Without this, or some such method, it appears to me broken, and its parts independent on each other; the expressions will be many of them unintelligible, and the occasion and propriety of them scarcely discernible. The very learned Michaelis acknowledges the difficulties attending this psalm, and I suspect my own strength, when I attempt to do what he thought above his much greater abilities. I have however done my best, and submit the whole to the candour of my readers.

I shall now conclude by making a few observations on the whole anthem. And I would first take notice of the great and glorious subject of this hymn. It is the God of the Hebrews, and designed to celebrate his praises, on account of the perfections of his nature, and the operations of his providence. And with what dignity is he described! How high and worthy the character given him, in every respect suitable to his infinite majesty, and the moral rectitude and purity of his nature! How grand are the descriptions of him as the omnipresent God, inhabiting his sanctuaries both in heaven and earth! as the original self-existing being, which his name Jehovah signifies; the tremendous being, worthy of all adoration and reverence, included in the name of Jah! as the almighty God, encompassed with thousands and ten thousands of angels, and innumerable chariots, that stand ready prepared in the armory of heaven! that rides through the heavens in his majesty, whose voice is in the thunder, who makes the clouds and vapours of heaven subservient to his pleasure, and at whose presence the earth, the heavens dissolve, and the highest hills seem to melt away like wax! Descriptions the most sublime in their nature, and that tend to strike the mind with a holy reverence and awe. And as to his moral character, and providential government of the world, he is represented as the righteous God, the hater and punisher of incorrigible wickedness, the father of the fatherless, the judge of the widow, that blesses men with numerous families, that breaks the prisoner's chains, and restores him to his liberty; the God and guardian of his people, the great disposer of victory, and giver of national prosperity; the supreme author of every kind of salvation, and as having death under his absolute command, and directing the outgoings of it by his sovereign will. This was the God of the ancient Hebrews. This is the God whom David worshipped, and whom all wise and good men must acknowledge and adore. Nor is there one circumstance or expression in this noble composure, derogatory to the majesty and honour of the supreme being, or that can convey a single sentiment to lessen our esteem and veneration for him. Let any one compare, with this psalm of David, the ancient hymns of the most celebrated poets on their deities, how infinitely short will they fall of the grandeur and sublimity which appear in every part of it. Strip the hymn of Callimachus on Jove of the poetry and language, and the sentiments of it will appear generally puerile and absurd, and it could not be read without the utmost contempt. Jove with him, that *αιεν αναξ, αει μεγας, δικασπολος ουρανιδησι*, that perpetual king, ever great, and lawgiver to the celestial deities, as he calls him, was born, he can't tell where, whether in Mount Ida, or Arcadia, washed on his birth in a river of water, to cleanse him from the defilements he brought into the world with him, had his navel string fall from him, sucked the dugs of a goat, and ate sweet honey, and so at last he grew up to be the supreme God. No despicable ballad can contain more execrable stuff than this, and some other like circumstances that he relates of him; circumstances that render utterly incredible what he says of him, as never dying, giving laws to the gods, obtaining heaven by his power and strength, governing kings and princes, and the inspector of their actions, the giver of riches and prosperity, wisdom and virtue, strength and power. That a mortal-born baby should grow up to become the one supreme and immortal God, or an infant nursed in Crete should rise to be the king of heaven, or one who gloried in his adulteries, should be constituted lawgiver to the celestial deities, or he whose character was stained with the vilest impurities, should be the giver of virtue; are absurdities, that one would think it was impossible for any one to digest. How free are the hymns of David from all such absurd, dishonourable, and impious descriptions of God! Every sentiment he conveys of him is excellent and grand, worthy a being of infinite perfection, and the supreme Lord and governor of the universe. It would be easy to enlarge on this subject. We may further take notice of the propriety of these historical incidents, that the Psalmist takes notice of in this sacred composure, and how the whole of it is calculated to promote the true spirit of piety and rational devotion. The ark, that was now translating to its fixed seat in Jerusalem, was the same ark that accompanied the Hebrews in the wilderness, where God was in a peculiar manner present, where Moses consulted God, where he received answers from him, and whence he received his directions; and who gave him manifest tokens of his special protection and favour, in the miraculous works he performed for them. Hence David puts them in mind of God's going before them in the wilderness, of the terror of his majesty on mount Sinai, of the manna and quails he rained down on them as from heaven, of the victories he gave them over their enemies, and his enriching them with the spoils of their conquered forces and countries; to excite in them a religious hope and trust, that God would protect Jerusalem, which was to be the future residence of the ark of his presence, and bless the whole nation with prosperity, if they continued firm in their allegiance to and worship of him. On this account the hymn is calculated to celebrate his praises for these ancient wonders of his power and goodness wrought in their favour, as well as for that present state of national grandeur and prosperity to which he had advanced them under David's government; and, on the other hand, to excite their fear of his displeasure, if they went on in their trespasses, and proved a corrupt and wicked people. Well might this grand assembly be glad and rejoice before their God, sing praises to his name, ascribe all power and dominion to him, whose excellency, whose majesty and government, were peculiarly over Israel on earth, and who rules in heaven, and manifests his power in the clouds thereof. I would just add, that the several ascriptions of glory to God, and the frequent exhortations to bless him, with which the psalm abounds, give an agreeable relief to the mind, are added with great propriety, and render the whole composure more pleasing and solemn. It was customary, as has been observed, among the gentiles, to celebrate the supposed advent of their gods, at particular times, and to particular places, with the greatest demonstrations of joy; but David had much nobler reasons for introducing the ark into the tabernacle he had prepared for it at Jerusalem, with all the pomp and splendour, and public festivity and joy, that could possibly be shown on the occasion. The whole procession was in honour of, and a national instance of homage paid to the true God. By the ark's being fixed at Jerusalem, that God, who honoured the ark with the tokens of his presence, made Jerusalem his perpetual habitation, became the immediate guardian and protector of the new-built city, and thereby peculiarly concerned for its prosperity and peace. This is represented as the language of God himself. "The Lord hath chosen Sion. He hath desired it for his habitation. This is my rest for ever. Here will I dwell, for I have desired it. I will abundantly bless her provisions. Her saints shall shout aloud for joy."—CHANDLER.

Ver. 3. And they set the ark of God upon a new cart, and brought it out of the house of Abinadab that *was* in Gibeah: and Uzzah and Ahio, the sons of Abinadab, drave the new cart.

The history of conveyance by means of vehicles, carried or drawn, is a subject too extensive to be treated of fully here. There can be no doubt, that after man had accustomed cattle to submit to the control of a rider, and to support the incumbent weight of a person, or persons, whether the animal were ox, camel, or horse, that the next step was to load such a creature, properly trained, with a litter, or portable conveyance; balanced, perhaps, on each side. This might be long before the mechanism of the wheel was employed, as it is still practised among pastoral people. Nevertheless, we find that wheel-carriages are of great antiquity; for we read of wagons so early as Gen. xlv. 19, and military carriages, perhaps, for chiefs and officers, first of all, in Exodus xiv. 25: "The Lord took off the chariot wheels of the Egyptians:" and as these were the fighting strength of Egypt, this agrees with those ancient writers, who report that Egypt was not, in its early state, intersected by canals, as in later ages; after the formation of which, wheel-carriages were laid aside, and little used, if at all. The first mention of chariots, we believe, occurs Genesis xli. 43: "Pharaoh caused Joseph to ride (*recab*) in the second chariot (*marecabeth*) that belonged to him." This, most likely, was a chariot of state, not an ordinary or travelling, but a handsome equipage, becoming the representative of the monarch's person and power. We find, as already hinted, Gen. xlv. 19, that Egypt had another kind of wheel-carriage, better adapted to the conveyance of burdens; "Take out of the land of Egypt (עגלות *ogeluth*) wagons, wheel-carriages, for conveyance of your little ones and your women:" these were family vehicles, for the use of the feeble; including, if need be, Jacob himself: accordingly, we read (verse 27) of the wagons which Joseph had sent to carry him, (Jacob,) and which perhaps the aged patriarch knew by their construction to be Egypt-built; for, so soon as he sees them, he believes the reports from that country, though he had doubted of them before when delivered to him by his sons. This kind of chariot deserves attention, as we find it afterward employed on various occasions in scripture, among which are the following: first, it was intended by the princes of Israel for carrying parts of the sacred utensils; Numb. vii. 3: "They brought their offering—six covered wagons (*ogeluth*) and twelve oxen;" —(two oxen to each wagon.) Here these wagons are expressly said to be covered; and it should appear that they were so generally; beyond question those sent by Joseph for the women of Jacob's family were so; among other purposes, for that of seclusion. Perhaps this is a radical idea in their name; as *gal* signifies *circle*, these wagons might be covered by circular headings, spread on hoops, like those of our own wagons; what we call a tilt. Considerable importance attaches to this heading, or tilt, in the history of the curiosity of the men of Bethshemesh, 1 Sam. vi. 7, where we read that the Philistines advised to make a new covered wagon, or cart (*ogeleh;*)—and the ark of the Lord was put into it—and, no doubt, was carefully covered over—concealed—secluded by those who sent it;—it came to Bethshemesh; and the men of that town who were reaping in the fields, perceiving the cart coming, went and examined what it contained: "and they saw the *very* (את) ark, and were joyful in seeing it." Those who first examined it, instead of carefully covering it up again, as a sacred utensil, suffered it to lie open to common inspection, which they encouraged, in order to triumph in the votive offerings it had acquired, and to gratify profane curiosity; the Lord, therefore, punished the people, (verse 19,) "because they had inspected—*pried into* (ב) the ark." This affords a clear view of the transgression of these Israelites, who had treated the ark with less reverence than the Philistines themselves; for those heathen conquerors had at least behaved to Jehovah with no less respect than they did to their own deities; and being accustomed to carry them in covered wagons, for privacy, they maintained the same privacy as a mark of honour to the God of Israel. The Levites seemed to have been equally culpable with the common people; they ought to have conformed to the law, and not to have suffered their triumph on this victorious occasion to beguile them into a transgression so contrary to the very first principles of the theocracy. That this word *ogeleh* describes a covered wagon, we learn from a third instance, that of Uzzah, 2 Sam. vi. 3, for we cannot suppose, that David could so far forget the dignity of the ark of the covenant, as to suffer it to be exposed, in a public procession, to the eyes of all Israel; especially after the punishment of the people of Bethshemesh. "They carried the ark of God, on a new *ogeleh*—covered cart" —and Uzzah put forth [his hand, or some catching instrument] to the ark of God, and laid hold of it, to stop its advancing any farther, but the oxen harnessed to the cart, going on, they drew the cart away from the ark, and the whole weight of the ark falling out of the cart unexpectedly, on Uzzah, crushed him to death —"and he died on the spot, with the ark of God" upon him. And David called the place "the breach of Uzzah"—that is, where Uzzah was broken—crushed to death. See now the proportionate severity of the punishments attending profanation of the ark. 1. The Philistines suffered by diseases, from which they were relieved after their oblations. 2. The Bethshemites also suffered, but not fatally, by diseases of a different nature, which, after a time, passed off. These were inadvertences. But, 3. Uzzah, who ought to have been fully instructed and correctly obedient, who conducted the procession, who was himself a Levite—this man was punished fatally for his remissness—his inattention to the law; which expressly directed that the ark should be carried on the shoulders of the priests, the Kohathites, Numb. iv. 4, 19, 20, distinct from those things carried in *ogeluth*—covered wagons, chap. vii. 9. That this kind of wagon was used for carrying considerable weights and even cumbersome goods, (and therefore was fairly analogous to our own wagons—tilted wagons,) we gather from the expression of the Psalmist, xlvi. 9:—

He maketh wars to cease to the end of the earth,
The bow he breaketh; and cutteth asunder the spear;
The chariots (*ogeluth*) he burneth in the fire.

The writer is mentioning the instruments of war—the bow—the spear; then, he says, the wagons (plural) which used to return home loaded with plunder, these share the fate of their companions, the bow and the spear; and are burned in the fire, the very idea of the classical allegory, peace burning the implements of war, introduced here with the happiest effect: not the general's *marecabeth;* but the plundering wagons. This is still more expressive, if these wagons carried captives; which we know they did in other instances, women and children. "The captive-carrying wagon is burnt." There can be no stronger description of the effect of peace; and it closes the period with peculiar emphasis.—TAYLOR IN CALMET.

Ver. 6. And when they came to Nachon's thrashing-floor, Uzzah put forth *his hand* to the ark of God, and took hold of it; for the oxen shook *it*. 7. And the anger of the LORD was kindled against Uzzah, and God smote him there for *his* error; and there he died by the ark of God.

Happy were it for us, if we could account for the operations of God, with the same facility that we can for the actions of his saints; but his counsels are a great deep, and his judgments (just though they be) are sometimes obscure, and past finding out. For what shall we say to the fate of Uzzah? or what tolerable cause can we assign for his sudden and untimely end? It was now near seventy years since the Israelites had carried the ark from place to place, and so long a disuse had made them forget the manner of doing it. In conformity to what they had heard of the Philistines, they put it into a new cart, or wagon, but this was against the express direction of the law, which ordered it to be borne upon men's shoulders. It is commonly supposed that Uzzah was a Levite, though there is no proof of it from scripture; but supposing he was, he had no right to attend upon the ark; that province, by the same law, was restrained to those Levites only who were of the house of Kohath: nay, put the case he had been a Kohathite by birth, yet he had violated another command, which prohibited even these Levites, (though they carried it by staves upon their shoulders,) upon pain of death, to touch it with their hands: so that here was a threefold transgression of the divine will in this method of proceeding. The ark, (as some say,) by Uzzah's direction, was placed in a cart; Uzzah, without any proper designation, adventures to attend it; when he thought it in danger of falling, officiously he put forth his hand, and laid hold on it, (all violating of the divine commands!) and this (as is supposed) not so much out of reverence to the sacred symbol of God's presence, as out of diffidence of his providence, as unable to preserve it from overturning. The truth is, this ark had so long continued in obscurity, that the people, in a manner, had almost lost all sense of a divine power residing in it, and therefore approached it with irreverence. This is implied in David's exhortation to Zadock and Abiathar, after this misfortune upon Uzzah. "Ye are the chief of the fathers of the Levites, sanctify yourselves therefore, both ye and your brethren, that you may bring up the ark of the Lord God of Israel, unto the place that I have prepared for it; for, *because ye did it not at the first*, the Lord our God made a breach upon us, for that we sought him not after the due order." What wonder then, if God, being minded to testify his immediate presence with the ark, to retrieve the ancient honour of that sacred vessel, and to curb all licentious profanations of it for the future, should single out one that was the most culpable of many, one who, in three instances, was then violating his commands, to be a monument of his displeasure against either a wilful ignorance or a rude contempt of his precepts, be they ever so seemingly small; that by such an example of terror, he might inspire both priests and people with a sacred dread of his majesty, and a profound veneration for his mysteries. —STACKHOUSE.

Ver. 13. And it was *so*, that when they that bare the ark of the LORD had gone six paces, he sacrificed oxen and fatlings.

From these words, some would infer, that David, having measured the ground between Obed-edom's house, and the place he had built for the reception of the ark, had altars raised, at the distance of every six paces, whereon he caused sacrifices to be offered as the ark passed by. But it is easy to imagine what a world of confusion this would create in the procession, and therefore the more rational construction is, that after those who carried the ark had advanced six paces, without any such token of divine wrath as Uzzah had undergone, then did they offer a sacrifice to God, which might consist of several living creatures, all sacrificed and offered up at once. But even supposing that, at set distances, there were sacrifices all along the way that they went; yet we are to know that it was no unusual thing for heathens to confer on their gods, nay, even upon their emperors, the same honours that we find David here bestowing upon the ark of the God of Israel. For in this manner (as Suetonius tells us) was Otho received—Cum per omne iter, dextra finistraque, oppidatim victimæ cæderentur: and the like he relates of Caligula—Ut a miseno movit, inter altaria, et victimas, ardentesque tædas, dencissimo ac lætissimo obviorum agmine incessit.—STACKHOUSE.

Ver. 14. And David danced before the LORD with all *his* might; and David *was* girded with a linen ephod.

In the oriental dances, in which the women engage by themselves, the lady of highest rank in the company takes the lead; and is followed by her companions, who imitate her steps, and if she sings, make up the chorus. The tunes are extremely gay and lively, yet with something in them wonderfully soft. The steps are varied according to the pleasure of her who leads the dance, but always in exact time. This statement may enable us to form a correct idea of the dance, which the women of Israel performed under the direction of Miriam, on the banks of the Red Sea. The prophetess, we are told, "took a timbrel in her hand, and all the women went out after her, with timbrels and dances." She led the dance, while they imitated her steps, which were not conducted according to a set, well-known form, as in this country, but extemporaneous. The conjecture of Mr. Harmer is extremely probable, that David did not dance alone before the Lord, when he brought up the ark, but as being the highest in rank, and more skilful than any of the people, he led the religious dance of the males. —PAXTON.

Ver. 16. And as the ark of the LORD came into the city of David, Michal, Saul's daughter, looked through a window, and saw King David leaping and dancing before the LORD; and she despised him in her heart. 17. And they brought in the ark of the LORD, and set it in his place, in the midst of the tabernacle that David had pitched for it: and David offered burnt-offerings and peace-offerings before the LORD. 18. And as soon as David had made an end of offering burnt-offerings and peace-offerings, he blessed the people in the name of the LORD of hosts. 19. And he dealt among all the people, *even* among the whole multitude of Israel, as well to the women as men, to every one a cake of bread, and a good piece *of flesh*, and a flagon *of wine*. So all the people departed every one to his house. 20. Then David returned to bless his household. And Michal, the daughter of Saul, came out to meet David, and said, How glorious was the king of Israel to-day, who uncovered himself to-day in the eyes of the handmaids of his servants, as one of the vain fellows shamelessly uncovereth himself!

When this public transaction of removing the ark was happily concluded, the pious prince retired to his palace, to bless his own family and household, and share with them the public joy. But an unexpected accident interrupted the pleasure he promised himself, and could not but greatly affect him, as it arose from one, from whom he had no reason to expect the contemptuous treatment that she gave him. As the ark of the Lord was just entered into the city of David, or mount Sion, Michal, Saul's daughter, looked through a window of the palace to behold the procession, saw David dancing with great spirit and earnestness, and viewed him with contempt; or, as the text says, she despised him in her heart; and when, after the solemnity,

David was returned to his habitation, she came out to meet him, and, with indignation and a sneer, said to him, "How glorious was the king of Israel to-day, who openly showed himself to-day to the eyes of the handmaids of his servants, as one of the vain persons openly shows himself!" David's answer to her was severe, but just. "Have I descended beneath the dignity of my character, as king of Israel, by divesting myself of my royal robes, appearing publicly among my people, and, like them, dancing and playing before the ark? It was before the Lord, who chose me before thy father, and before all his house, to appoint me ruler over the people of the Lord. Therefore will I play on my harp before the Lord; and if this be to make myself cheap and contemptible, I will be more so than this; and how high soever be my condition as king, I will always be humble in the judgment I form of myself; and as for those maid-servants of whom thou speakest, I shall be honoured among them; the very meanest of the people will respect me the more for my popularity, when they see me condescend to share in their sacred mirth, and express it in the same manner, by which they testify their own joy in the public solemnities." In this he acted as a wise and politic, as well as a religious prince; for in ancient times dancing itself was in use, as a religious ceremony, and in testimony of gratitude and joy, in public solemnities. Thus Miriam, the prophetess, took a timbrel in her hand, and all the women went out after her with timbrels and with dances, to celebrate their deliverance from Pharaoh, his destruction in the Red Sea, and their own safe passage through the waters of it. So also Jephthah's daughter met her father with timbrels and dances, to congratulate his victory over the Ammonites, and God's having taken vengeance for him of those enemies. Thus at the yearly feast of the Lord at Shiloh, the virgins of the place came out to dance in dances. It was used also frequently among the gentiles, by the greatest personages in honour of the gods, and recommended by the greatest philosophers, as a thing highly decent and becoming in itself.

But though David acted from a truly religious zeal, yet he had been very severely censured for his habit and behaviour on this occasion; being dressed, as it hath been represented, in a linen ephod, and "dancing before the Lord, in such a frantic indecent manner, that he exposed his nakedness to the bystanders." Mr. Bayle in the first part of his remarks, expresses himself in a more cautious and temperate manner, and doth not pass his judgment, whether David discovered his nakedness or not; but says, that "if he did discover it, his action might be deemed ill, morally speaking; but if he did no more than make himself contemptible by his postures, and by not keeping up the majesty of his character, it was but an imprudence at most, and not a crime." He adds, that "it ought to be considered, on what occasion it was that he danced. It was when the ark was carried to Jerusalem, and consequently the excess of his joy and of his leaping, testified his attachment and sensibility for sacred things." I shall just remark here, that if David did really discover his nakedness on this occasion, yet if it was merely accidental, and without any design, it could not be deemed ill, morally speaking, by any good judge of morality. I apprehend also that Mr. Bayle doth not know enough of David's manner of dancing, and the postures he made use of, to be sure that he rendered himself deservedly ridiculous by the use of them; because persons may dance in a very brisk and lively manner, without any postures that shall deserve contempt, and because there is no word in the original, that is made use of to express David's behaviour in this procession, that either implies, or will justify such a supposition.

The case which Mr. Bayle mentions from Ferrand of St. Francis of Assisi, is so perfectly different from that of David, as that it should not have been related by him in the article of David, at least without some mark of disapprobation. St. Francis voluntarily stripped himself stark naked, in the presence of many persons, met together to be witness to his absolute renunciation of his paternal inheritance. This was the downright madness of enthusiasm. David, on the contrary, divested himself only of his royal dress, and put on such a habit, as effectually preserved him from every thing of indecency and absurdity in his appearance. For he was clothed in a double garment; a robe of fine linen, with a linen ephod. These two garments are expressly distinguished in the account of the vestments of the high-priests: "Thou shalt take garments and put upon Aaron, (and as we well render it,) the ephod, and the robe of the ephod." And again: "These are the garments, which they shall make, the breastplate, and the ephod, and the robe." The fabric of them was different; the ephod being made of gold, blue, purple, and scarlet; but the robe formed all of blue. The shape of them was also different; the ephod reaching only to the knees, but the robe flowing down so as to cover the feet; called therefore by the LXX. ποδηρης, and the Vulgate version, stola. The robe also had no division in it throughout, but was made whole and round, with an opening in the middle of it, on the top, so that it was impossible that any part of the body could be seen through it; or that David, in dancing, could expose to view, what decency required him to conceal; especially as the ephod was, on this occasion, thrown over it, and certainly tied with a girdle, as the priest's ephod always was. With these linen garments David clothed himself on this solemnity, both out of reverence for God, and for conveniency; because they were cooler, and less cumbersome than his royal habit, and would not occasion that large perspiration, which the exercise of dancing would otherwise have produced. And however improper such a long flowing robe, girt round with a girdle, may be thought for a man dancing with all his might, yet it is certain that David did dance in such a one, and there is no reason to think it could be anywise inconvenient to him. For, though the robe was close, i. e. had no opening from the breast to the feet, and was girt round with the ephod, yet it was large and wide, and flowing at the lower end; and hanging down in various folds, gave room sufficient for the full exercise of the feet in dancing. And of this every one will have full conviction, who frequents any of our polite assemblies, in which he will see many fair ones dance, like the king of Israel, with all their might, without any great inconvenience from the flowing habits, which so greatly adorn them.

It may be further observed, that this robe was worn by kings, their children, priests, Levites, and prophets, when they appeared on very solemn occasions, which also covered over their other garments. Thus Samuel is represented as covered with a robe or mantle, as we render it. All the Levites, that bare the ark, and the singers, and Chenaniah, the master of the carriage, or of those who carried the ark, appeared in it on this very occasion. Kings' daughters were clothed in the same habit. The princes of the sea wore them. And even God himself is represented, clad with zeal, as with a robe. As David therefore dressed himself on this occasion, with a long flowing linen robe, instead of the robe of state, proper to him as king of Israel, which was made of different, and much richer materials; he was scornfully insulted by Saul's daughter, not for exposing his nakedness to the spectators, which he no more did, nor could do, than all the rest of the attendants, who wore the same habit, but for uncovering himself in the eyes of the handmaids of his servants, i. e. appearing openly before the meanest of the people, in a dress, wholly unworthy, as she thought, the character and majesty of the king of Israel. Nor was this all; for it appears, by part of David's answer to Michal, that she was particularly offended with his playing publicly on the harp; and, probably, she mimicked and ridiculed him, by the attitude in which she put herself on this occasion. For, in answer to her reproach, David says to her, "It was before the Lord that I uncovered myself . . . . therefore I will play before the Lord," i. e. look on it with what contempt you please, yet as I openly played on my harp in the presence, and in honour of God, I glory in it, and will continue to do it, when any fair opportunity presents itself. His particularly mentioning *playing before the Lord*, plainly shows, that there was somewhat, in the nature and manner of her reproach, that gave occasion to it.

Besides, it should be remarked, that the eastern princes, out of affectation, and to strike the people with greater reverence, seldom appeared in public, and whenever they did, not without great pomp and solemnity; as is the custom among them to this day. Michal therefore unquestionably thought, that David made himself too cheap, by thus discovering himself to public view, without any royal pomp, or marks of distinction, and familiarly mixing himself with the attendants on this solemnity, as though he had been one of them, and not the king of Israel. And the meaning of Michal's words in this view will be: How glorious was the king of Israel to-day, who uncovered, i. e. stripped himself of his majesty, and all the ensigns of his royal dignity, and openly exposed himself to the most public view of the meanest of the people, as a vain thoughtless person, who, without a proper habit, or regard to character, exposes himself to public ridicule and scorn!

Mr. Bayle seems to be pretty much of Michal's opinion, when he says, "It would be thought very strange, in any part of Europe, if, on a day of procession of the holy sacrament, the kings should dance in the streets with nothing but a small girdle on their bodies." It may be so, but the observation is nothing to the purpose, because David did not dance in the streets in this manner, as he insinuates. Besides, Mr. Bayle could not but know, that customs vary, and that the same customs may be thought very venerable and ridiculous, in different nations, and at different times. However solemn and sacred the procession of the sacrament might have seemed here, two or three centuries ago, and may at this day appear in popish countries, it would now seem a most contemptible and absurd farce in this nation. We should look with indignation and scorn, to see a crowned head holding the stirrup or bridle of a triple-mitred monk's horse, or humbly bending to kiss his toe; or emperors and princes carrying wax candles in their hands, in company of a set of shorn baldpated priests, or devoutly praying before a dead log of wood, or going in pilgrimage to consecrated statues, and kiss thresholds, and venerate the relics of dead bodies; and yet, despicable as these practices are in themselves, they have been used, and some of them continue in other nations to be used to this day; and have been, and are now, so far from being thought strange or ridiculous, as that they were, and are still esteemed very high and laudable instances of piety and devotion.

If we examine the words themselves, by which Michal reproached David, they can never be fairly so interpreted, as to mean that indecency, which some writers would be glad to find in them; and as to David's answer, it is utterly inconsistent with such a meaning. David said to Michal, "It was before the Lord." What was before the Lord? What, his discovering his nakedness? The very consideration of his being before the Lord would have prevented it, as he knew that such an indecency, in the solemnities of divine worship, was highly offensive to God, and prohibited under penalty of death. Again he says, "Therefore will I play before the Lord," i. e. play upon my harp; which must refer to her reproaching him, as appearing like a common harper; for it would be no answer to her, had she reproached him for that scandalous appearance, which some would make him guilty of. Further he adds: "And I will be more vile than this, and will be base in my own sight." I will not scruple to submit to lower services than this, in honour of God; and notwithstanding my regal dignity, will not think myself above any humiliations, how great soever they may be, that may testify my gratitude and submission to him;—expressions these which evidently show, that what she called David's uncovering himself, was what he had designedly done, and not an accidental involuntary thing, without design, and contrary to his intention. And had he designedly exposed his nakedness, or even without design, how could he have made himself more vile, or rendered himself more worthy of censure and reproach? Upon the whole, that David danced so, as to discover what he ought to have concealed, is an invidious surmise, that no man of learning or candour will affirm, and which has nothing in the grammatical sense of the expressions made use of to support it, and is in its nature impossible, from the make and form of the garments he was clothed with.

I shall only add, that when the scripture says, "Therefore Michal, Saul's daughter, had no child to the day of her death," it doth not seem to be remarked, as though it was a punishment on her for this contempt of David, unless he voluntarily left her bed, for so heinous and undeserved an insult; but as a reproach on herself for her barrenness, she having never had any children by David; barrenness being accounted as reproachful and dishonourable a circumstance, as could befall a married woman. So that she had little reason to reproach her husband, when she was liable to a much greater reproach herself.—Chandler.

Ver. 19. And he dealt among all the people, *even* among the whole multitude of Israel, as well to the women as men, to every one a cake of bread, and a good piece *of flesh*, and a flagon *of wine*. So all the people departed every one to his house.

The entertainer at a feast, occasionally dismissed his guests with costly presents. Lysimachus of Babylon having entertained Hemerus the tyrant of the Babylonians and Seleucians, with three hundred other guests, gave every man a silver cup, of four pounds weight. When Alexander made his marriage feast at Susa in Persia, he paid the debts of all his soldiers out of his own exchequer, and presented every one of his guests, who were not fewer than nine thousand, with golden cups. The master of the house among the Romans, used also to give the guests certain presents at their departure, or to send them after they were gone, to their respective habitations. It is probable that this custom, like many others which prevailed in Greece and Rome, was derived from the nations of Asia; for the sacred writers allude repeatedly to a similar custom, which closed the religious festivals or public entertainments among the chosen people of God. When David brought up the ark from the house of Obed-edom, into the place which he had prepared for it, he offered burnt-offerings and peace-offerings before the Lord. And as soon as the solemnity was finished, "he dealt among all the people, even among the whole multitude of Israel, as well to the women as men, to every one a cake of bread, and a flagon of wine."—Paxton.

Dr. Chandler and his associates, received presents from the Greeks of Athens, consisting of perfumed flowers, pomegranates, oranges, and lemons, pastry, and other articles. The presents made by David were no doubt very different. Leavened and unleavened bread, the flesh which remained from the peace-offerings, and some of the wine then presented. (Josephus.) The rabbins suppose that the word we translate, *a good piece of flesh*, signifies the sixth part of an animal. Without, however, admitting the propriety of this assertion, it may lead to the true explanation of the word. Maillet affirms, that a sheep, with a proper quantity of rice, which answers the purpose of bread very frequently in the East, will furnish a good repast for sixty people. If now the people of the Jewish army were divided into tens, as it seems they were, who might mess together, and lodge under one and the same tent, as it is highly probable, from every tenth man's being appointed to fetch or prepare provision for their fellow-soldiers, according to what we read, Judges xx. 10, then the sixth part of a sheep would be sufficient for the men at one repast, and be sufficient for one mess or tent of soldiers; and from this particular case it may come to signify, in general, a sufficient portion for each person, which, indeed, seems to be the meaning of our translators, when they render the word a *good piece of flesh*—enough for an ample repast. The other part of this royal and sacred donation was a *flagon* of wine, perhaps a *gourd* full of wine is meant. The shells of gourds are used to this day in the eastern parts of the world for holding quantities of wine for present spending, and particularly in sacred festivals. So when Dr. Richard Chandler was about leaving Athens, he tells us, he supped at the customhouse, where "the archon provided a gourd of choice wine, and one of the crew excelled on the lyre." And describing a panegyris, or general sacred assembly of the Greeks in the Lesser Asia, he informs us, "that the church was only stones piled up for walls, without a roof, and stuck on this solemnity with wax-candles lighted, and small tapers, and that after fulfilling their religious duties, it is the custom of the Greeks to indulge in festivity; at which time he found the multitude sitting under half-tents, with a store of melons and grapes, besides lambs and sheep to be killed, wine in gourds and skins, and other necessary provision." What the size of the gourds that anciently grew in that country was, or what that of those that are now found there, may not be quite certain. But a gourd full of wine, for each person, was abundantly sufficient for a joy that required attention to temperance.—Harmer.

CHAPTER VII.

Ver. 18. Then went King David in, and sat before the LORD, and he said, Who *am* I, O LORD God? and what *is* my house, that thou hast brought me hitherto?

Pococke has given the figure of a person half sitting and half kneeling, that is, kneeling so as to rest the most muscular part of his body on his heels. This, he observes, is the manner in which inferior persons sit at this day before great men, and is considered as a very humble posture. In this manner, probably, David sat before the Lord, when he went into the sanctuary, to bless him for his promise respecting his family.—HARMER.

CHAPTER VIII.

Ver. 2 And he smote Moab, and measured them with a line, casting them down to the ground; even with two lines measured he to put to death, and with one full line to keep alive: and *so* the Moabites became David's servants, *and* brought gifts.

See on 2 Sam. 12. 31.

David had scarce ended his wars with the Philistines, but he was engaged in another with the Moabites, of which the scripture history gives, as I understand it, the following account. "He also smote Moab, and he measured them by a line," i. e. in one tract of the country, to throw them down level with the ground. Then he measured out two tracts, one to put to death, and one full tract to preserve alive; and Moab became David's servants, bringing him gifts. When he had beat the Moabites, he ordered a general survey to be made of the whole country; in one part or tract of which he levelled Moab with the ground, i. e. razed so many of their towns and fortresses, as he thought necessary to secure his conquest. He then proceeded to animadvert on the inhabitants, measuring out two tracts, or parts of the country; one line or tract for death, and the fulness of a line, a very large tract of the country, to keep alive, i. e. to cut off the inhabitants of the one, those who had been most active in the war against him, and to preserve the far larger part of them alive; and thus made the whole nation tributary to his crown. Who was the aggressor in these two last actions, the scripture history doth not determine. Some authors seem inclined to give David the credit of it, though without any shadow of proof. I apprehend the contrary may be collected from what the Psalmist says: "That Edom, Moab, Ammon, Amalek, the Syrians under Hadadezer, and other nations, had consulted together with one consent to cut off Israel from being a nation; and that the name of Israel might be no more in remembrance. This seems plainly to refer to the history of the wars with these very nations, related in Samuel. Against such a cruel confederacy as this, David had a right to defend himself, and to take such a vengeance on his enemies, as was necessary to his own and his people's future safety. If this powerful league, to extirpate the Israelites, was a justifiable compact, because Israel was a common enemy, who ravaged ad libitum, not from the common misunderstanding of states, but from an insatiable appetite for blood and murder, as some writers choose to represent them; it will certainly follow, that there may be occasions that will justify this severe execution, in the utter excision of nations; and that if the Moabites, Amalekites, Philistines, and other nations, were common enemies to the Hebrews, and ravaged them, ad libitum, from an insatiable appetite for blood and murder, David had a right to extirpate them, whenever he could, without deserving the charge of barbarity, and a blood-thirsty spirit. This was certainly the character of many of the enemies of the Hebrew nation, but can never be applicable to the Hebrews themselves. It is allowed, that they were to maintain a perpetual hostility with, and extirpate, if they could, the seven nations, because God had proscribed them, and their own prosperity, and almost being, depended on it. But as to the Edomites, Moabites, and Ammonites, they were expressly forbid to meddle with them, and invade any of their territories, by beginning hostilities against them. And from the whole history of the Hebrew nation, from their first settlement in Canaan, to their destruction by Nebuchadnezzar, there is scarce one instance to be produced, of their invading the neighbouring nations, without being first attacked by them, or of their plundering them any further than as their victories over them, gained in their own defence, gave them a right to it, by the common usages and laws of war. During the period preceding the regal government, we read of nothing almost but their grievous oppressions by the Moabites, Ammonites, Amalekites, Midianites, Philistines, and other neighbouring nations, who forced them into dens, mountains, and strongholds, deprived them of all manner of arms for their defence, and destroyed the increase of their lands, so that there was no sustenance for Israel, neither sheep, nor ox, nor ass. But we have not a single intimation of the Hebrews invading, plundering, and destroying them. And indeed it was not possible that as a nation they could, during this long period, make any considerable invasions upon the neighbouring states. For they had no kings, no settled government, no generals and captains to lead them, nor standing armies to protect them; God, in a very extraordinary manner, and at particular seasons, being pleased to raise them up proper persons, to give them some temporary relief from those who enslaved and despoiled them; which made them at last resolve to have a king, who might be always ready to protect and defend them. They were in themselves an easy quiet people, never inured to war, employed in husbandry, and raising of cattle; and so far from being a common enemy to all the nations round them, as that they took every method to cultivate their friendship, taking their daughters to be their wives, and giving their daughters to their sons, forsaking their own God, and following after the gods of every neighbouring nation. And yet they were almost perpetually under oppression, and their too great fondness to be on good terms with their oppressors, was the very reason why God sold them into their enemies' hands, and suffered them so often to groan, by turns, under the yoke of every petty state, that had a mind to enslave them. And as for David, he had hitherto been engaged in no wars against any of his neighbours, except two defensive ones against the Philistines; who, upon his first accession to the throne of Israel, invaded his dominions, with an intention to deprive him of his kingdom, or render him and his people wholly dependant on their power. If therefore the Moabites joined in the confederacy with the Ammonites, Edomites, Philistines, and others, to extirpate the Hebrew nation, David treated them with comparative lenity and moderation, if he cut off even two thirds of them, whom he found in arms against him; and especially, if he put to the sword but one half of them, who intended his utter destruction, and the entire extirpation of his people. And as this is certain, that the Amalekites, Philistines, Moabites, and other nations, were perpetual and inveterate enemies to the Hebrews, and invaded them whenever they were able, the Hebrews had a right to make reprisals, to attack them on every occasion that offered, and to treat them with that severity, that was necessary to their own peace and safety for the future. I may add, what Bishop Patrick and others observe, that the Jewish writers affirm, that David exercised this severity on the Moabites, because they had slain his parents and brethren, whom he committed to the custody of the king of Moab, during his exile. But I lay no great stress on this tradition, as it is wholly unsupported by the scripture history; and because David's treatment of them is sufficiently justified by the ancient law of nations; as to which my reader will be abundantly satisfied by consulting Grotius.—CHANDLER.

The war laws of the Israelites are detailed by Moses in the twentieth chapter of Deuteronomy. I shall at present only take notice of those particulars that relate to the course they were to pursue towards foreign nations, and postpone those that regard levies, the division of plunder, &c. until I come to treat of private law. Of a declaration of war, before proceeding to hostilities, Moses says nothing; and, therefore, seems not to have deemed it so indispensably necessary as the Romans did. The disputes concerning its necessity are so well known, that I shall not trouble my readers with any remarks upon them. At present, we do not consider this solemnity as at all essential to the lawfulness of a war, but commence hostilities without any previous announcement of our intention, whenever we conceive that the injuries offered us require them. Moses appears (Numb. xxxi.) to have done the same; and to have attacked the Midianites, without giving them time to arm; and hence (ver. 49) he did not lose a single man, which would otherwise have been incomprehensible. The word צבא, so often repeated in that chapter, and probably wrong pointed by the Jews, signifies in Arabic, an *inroad*, or attack by surprise. On the other hand, it was the injunction of Moses, that a hostile city should be summoned before an attack, and if it surrendered without fighting, that its inhabitants should have their lives granted, upon the condition of becoming tributaries. If, however, a city should make resistance, then all the men in it were to be put to the sword; and the women and children to become captives to the Israelites. The former of these particulars, viz. massacring all the men, stamps *their* war law with a much greater degree of severity than is manifested in ours; for although we must take into the account, that among ancient nations all the males who *could* bear arms actually did so when it was necessary, and that there was no such distinction between soldier and citizen as among us; yet even in the case of a city being taken by storm, we are wont to give quarter; and no Frenchman will have any anxiety to be reminded that *bois-le-duc* forms a solitary exception to this practice. Still, however, it is not contrary to the law of nature, if we get the upper hand, to kill our enemy, who either himself bears arms in order to kill us, or hires others in his room for that purpose. The Israelites could not regulate their conduct by our more merciful law of nations, which is, by several thousand years, of later date; but they acted precisely as their vanquished foes would have done, had they been lucky enough to have been the conquerors; and they therefore merit the praise of magnanimity, if, to lessen the evils of war, we see them refraining in the smallest degree from insisting on requital of like for like to the utmost. The enemies with whom the Israelites had to do, were wont not merely to put the vanquished to death, but at the same time to exercise great cruelties upon them. The Bible is full of relations to this purport. Sometimes infants and sucklings were massacred, and their bodies collected into heaps; for which we find in Hebrew a particular term, רטש; sometimes pregnant women were ripped up, 2 Kings viii. 12. Amos i. 13; sometimes people were laid upon thorns, and put to death with thrashing wains, Judg. viii. 7—16. Amos i. 3. Sometimes even royal princes were burnt alive, 2 Kings iii. 27. I will not relate all the cruelties of those nations with whom the Israelites had to carry on war, and might, according to the law of nature, have repaid like for like. The law of nations, according to which the Israelites had to act, was made by those nations themselves; for this law is founded on the manners of nations, and on the permission which we have to treat others as they treat us. If we do not choose to confine our attention to the details given in scripture, we may resort to profane history, where we shall find the Romans (who behaved to their enemies much more harshly than we do) complaining of the barbarous conduct of the Carthaginians towards their prisoners; and these Carthaginians were the direct descendants of those Canaanites, and had an Asiatic law of nations. We need not, therefore, now wonder that David (2 Sam. viii. 2) should have made the vanquished Moabites lie down together on the ground, and with a measuring-line have marked off two thirds of them for death, and spared the remaining third, after being thus subjected to the fear of sharing the fate of their brethren. He acted here with more clemency than the Mosaic law prescribed, by which he would have been justified in putting them all to death. For as to the assertion of some writers, that the severe law of Moses on this point did not extend beyond the Canaanites, it is contrary to the clearest evidence; for Moses expressly says, (Deut. xx. 15, 16, compared with 13,) "Thus shalt thou do unto those cities which are far from thee, and not of the cities of these nations; but of those nations whose land Jehovah giveth thee, thou shalt let nothing that breatheth live." David acted with much greater severity (2 Sam. xii. 31) to the inhabitants of Rabbah, the Ammonitish capital. He put them all to death together, and that with most painful and exquisite tortures; which, however, were not unusual in other countries of the East. But we must consider how very different this war was from other wars. The Ammonites had not only resisted to the last extremity, (which alone by the Mosaic law was sufficient to justify the victors in putting them to death,) but they had, moreover, by their gross contempt of the ambassadors whom David had sent with the best intentions, been guilty of a most outrageous breach of the law of nations, and manifested their implacable hatred against the Israelites. They shaved half their beards, (an insult which, according to the account of D'Arvieux, the Arabs of the present day reckon as great an evil as death itself,) and then they cut off the lower half of their garments, and in this ignominious plight sent them back into their own country. Nor was this so much the particular act of the Ammonitish king, as of his principal subjects, who had incited him to it, (2 Sam. x. 3,) which so much the more clearly demonstrated their universal enmity against the Israelites; and a violation of the law of nations so very unusual justly provoked them to take severer revenge, than they were wont to exercise in common wars.

If we admit the maxim, that the law both of nature and nations allows me to treat my enemies as they, if victorious, would have treated me, the story in 1 Sam. xi. 2 furnishes a strong vindication of David's conduct. These same Ammonites had, in the beginning of his predecessor's reign, been so extremely cruel as to grant to the Israelitish city, Jabesh, which they had invested, and which was inclined to surrender without resistance, no other terms of capitulation than that, by way of insult to the Israelites in general, all its inhabitants should submit to have their right eyes put out. Now to an enemy of this description, and who at last seized their ambassadors, whose persons the laws both of nations and nature hold sacred, could any punishment in use in the East, have been too cruel?—We find, however, that the character of the Ammonites was the same in every age. The prophet Amos (i. 13) speaks of them as ripping up the bellies of women with child, not in the fury of a storm, but deliberately, in order to lessen the number of the Israelites, and thus to enlarge their own borders. If these acts of David, then, appear to us, I will not say *severe*, (for who will deny that? or who that lives in our days would not wish to have acted differently in *his* place?) but *unjust*, it is owing, either to our confounding the modern with the ancient law of nations, or with the law of nature itself; and thus judging of them by quite a different rule from that which we are wont to apply to similar actions, which we know from our youth. I may at any rate put this question, "Has a magistrate a right to proceed more severely against a band of robbers than one nation against another, that has behaved with as much hostility and cruelty as robbers can do?"—If it is answered, "Yes, for the robbers are subjects;"—then would robbers, particularly if natives of foreign lands, in order to escape painful deaths, have only to declare, that they wish to be considered not as subjects, but as enemies; since they do not generally desire the protection of the magistrate, but have their abode in the forests. But on such banditti we inflict, not merely capital punishment, but that punishment aggravated by torture; as, for instance, breaking on the wheel. Now, if this is not unjust, and if a robber, even though a foreigner, cannot with effect urge against it the plea of wishing to be treated as an enemy; certainly David's procedure towards the Ammonites, who had in fact been more cruel to the Israelites than most modern banditti are wont to be, should not be condemned as absolutely unjust; although, no doubt, it would have been much more laudable if he had displayed greater clemency and magnanimity. Further; as we in our childish years read the Roman authors, who think and write with great partiality for their countrymen, we are commonly impressed with very favourable ideas of the moderation and equity of the Roman people in war. But these ideas are by no means just; for the Romans, except when their own interest required the contrary, were a severe people; and with so much the worse reason, that their wars, in which they manifested such inexorable severity, were for the most part unjust. This people, of whose war laws we are apt to think so highly, for a long time, even to the days of Cæsar, massacred their prisoners in cold blood, whenever they survived the disgrace of the triumph; and they very frequently put to death the magistrates and citizens of conquered cities, after making them undergo a flagellation, which, perhaps, in point of physical pain, was not different from the punishments inflicted by David on the Ammonites. *Lacerare corpora virgis* is the phrase in which it is described by Livy, who remarks, that by reason of these inexorable severities, (of which we know nothing in our wars,) some cities defended themselves to the last extremity, rather than submit. Thus acted the Romans towards those nations that certainly were not Ammonites in cruelty, or in the malice of their injuries. And if, nevertheless, not contented with keeping silence on the subject, we re-echo the Latin writers in their phrases of Roman justice and mercy, why should David be called an oppressor and a barbarian, because to the very scum of cruel and inhuman enemies, who from universal national hatred had so grossly and unjustly violated the sacred rights of ambassadors, he acted with rigour, and put them to painful deaths? There seems here to be an unfairness in our way of judging, which David does not deserve, merely because he is an Oriental, and because on other occasions the Bible speaks so much in his praise. This severity has, nevertheless, always been a stigma on the character of David, with those who do not attend to the arbitrary and variable nature of the law of nations, and judge of it according to the very humane war laws of modern times. Hence some friends of religion have been at pains to represent his conduct in a more humane point of view than it is described in the Bible itself. The late Professor Dantz of Jena, published a Dissertation, *De mitigata Davidis in Ammonitas Crudelitate*, which experienced the highest approbation both in and out of Germany, because people could not imagine a war law so extremely different from modern manners, as that which the common interpretation of 2 Sam. xii. 31 implies. Of that passage he gives this explanation; that David merely condemned his Ammonitish captives to severe bodily labours; to hewing and sawing of wood; to burning of bricks, and working in iron mines. But how much soever this exposition may be approved, it has but little foundation: it does great violence to the Hebrew words, of which, as this is not the place to complain philologically, I must be satisfied with observing, that it takes them in a very unusual, and till then unknown, acceptation; and for this no other reason is assigned, than that David had previously repented of his sins of adultery and murder; and being in a state of grace, could not be supposed capable of such cruelties. But a proof like this, taken from the king's being in a state of regeneration, is quite indecisive. We must previously solve the question, whether, considering the times in which he lived, and the character of the enemy, who had given such proofs, to what atrocities their malignant dispositions towards the Israelites would have carried them, had they been the victors, the punishment he inflicted on them was too severe? or else from the piety of a king, I might in like manner demonstrate, in opposition to facts, that such and such malefactors were not broken on the wheel, but that they must only have gone to the wheel, in order to draw water. But allowing even that David carried severity of punishment too far, it is entirely to be ascribed to the rude manners of his age: as in the case of still more blameless characters, even of Abraham himself, we find that the customs of their times betrayed them into sins of ignorance, although some of their contemporaries questioned the lawfulness of the acts which involved those sins.

It is further to be remarked, that towards the most cruel foes of the Israelites, and who had besides done himself an injury altogether unparalleled, David would have been acting with more mildness than the Mosaic law authorized, even towards any common enemy, if he had only condemned the Ammonites to servile labours. And besides this, those labours which Dantz alleges, are, some of them at least, not at all suited to the circumstances of either the country or the people. Firewood, for instance, is so scarce in Palestine, that a whole people certainly could not have been converted into hewers and sawyers of wood. For the sanctuary and the altar, the Gibeonites had it already in charge to provide wood; while the common people throughout the country principally made use of straw, or dried dung, for fuel. When Solomon, many years after, made the timber required for the temple to be felled, it was by the heads of the remnant of the Canaanites; and therefore the Ammonites were not employed in it.—In Palestine, again, mines of different sorts were wrought. Now, of all mines, none are more wholesome to work in than those of iron; because that metal is very friendly to the human constitution, is actually mixed with our blood, (as experiments made with blood clearly show,) is often used in medicine, and is almost never hurtful to us, except when forged into edgetools and weapons. Hence it has been observed, that in iron-works and forges, we generally find the healthiest and longest-lived people. Other sorts of mines, on the contrary, by reason of the lead and arsenic which they contain, are very often unwholesome, and even fatal to life. Can it then be believed that David would have condemned a people that he wanted to punish, to labour in iron-works, wherein they were sure to enjoy a long life of health and activity, while, perhaps, his own native subjects had to labour in unwholesome mines for the more precious metals? A king who had mines in his dominions, and wished to use them for the purposes of punishment, would probably have heard what sorts of them were favourable, and what hostile to health, and not have gone so preposterously to work. The applause bestowed on this dissertation of Dantz, from the humanity it displayed, was probably what moved the late Wahner to write a dissertation of a similar tendency, which was published at Gottingen in the year 1738, under the following title, David *Moabitarum Victor crudelium numero eximitur*. But it could not obtain equal approbation, because in the conduct of David towards the Moabites, 2 Sam. viii. 2, there is less appearance of cruelty; inasmuch as he merely enforced the war law as prescribed by Moses, and indeed far less rigorously. Wahner gives three different and new explanations of the passage, according to which none of the vanquished Moabites were put to death; but they are all somewhat forced: and there was no necessity, by a different translation of the text, to free David from the charge of cruelty; for in putting but two thirds of them to death, he acted unquestionably with one third more clemency than the Mosaic law required.—The war which Saul carried on against the Amalekites, and in which to the utmost of his power he extirpated the whole people, sparing only their king, is yet blamed, not on account of its rigour, but for the conqueror's clemency to the king, 1 Sam. xv. But I will not by any means adduce this for an example; but merely appeal to the precepts of Moses, the rigour of which David so much relaxed, in the cases of the Moabites. —MICHAELIS.

Ver. 13. And David gat *him* a name when he returned from smiting of the Syrians in the Valley of Salt, *being* eighteen thousand *men*.

These great successes over the Syrians and Edomites greatly heightened the reputation and character of David; or, as the historian observes, he got himself a name when he returned from smiting the Syrians, and Edomites, in the Valley of Salt. He was regarded and celebrated by all the neighbouring princes and states, as a brave commander, and glorious prince and conqueror. To get a name, in the eastern style, doth not mean to be called by this or the other particular name, which is a ridiculous interpretation of the words, but to be spoken of with admiration and praise, as an excellent prince, and a fortunate victorious soldier. Thus it is joined with praise, "I will make you a name, and a praise among all people." It is said of God himself, upon account of the signs and wonders he wrought in Egypt. "Thou hast made thee a name at this day;" which our version in another place renders: "Thou hast gotten thee renown at this day." Thus David got himself a name, i. e. as God tells him by Nathan the prophet: "I was with thee wheresoever thou wentest, and have cut off all thine enemies out of thy sight, and have made thee a great name, like unto the name of the great men that are in the earth," i. e. made thee to be esteemed and reverenced in all countries round about, as a mighty prince and successful warrior; a name that he must have had even from the Syrians, and all his enemies whom he subdued by his conduct and valour.

There is some difficulty in this short history of the conquest of the Edomites. In the book of Chronicles, it is said, that Abishai, the son of Zeruiah, smote Edom in the Valley of Salt, eighteen thousand men. 1 Chron. xviii. 12 In the 60th Psalm, Title, that when Joab returned, he smote of Edom, in the Valley of Salt, twelve thousand men. In the book of Samuel, 2 Sam. viii. 13, that David got himself a name, when he returned from smiting the Syrians, in the Valley of Salt. Part of this difficulty is easily obviated, as the rout and slaughter of the Edomitish army, in which they lost six thousand of their men, was begun by David and Abishai. And as, after Joab's joining the army, twelve thousand more of the Edomites were cut off, the slaughter of those twelve thousand is ascribed to Joab, which, with six thousand cut off under David and Abishai, before Joab came up with his reinforcement, make up the number eighteen thousand; the whole eighteen thousand being ascribed to David, as they were cut off by his army, that fought under him; and to Abishai, who was chief commander under him in this action; so that what was done by the one, was done by the other also. But there is also another difficulty, how to reconcile the two different accounts; the one, that David smote the Syrians, the other, that he smote the Edomites, in the Valley of Salt. The altering the pointing of the words, as we have them in Samuel, and the repeating a single word, *απο κοινου*, from the first part of the account, will entirely remove this difficulty; and I render the passage thus: David got himself a name, when he returned from smiting the Syrians, in the Valley of Salt, by smiting eighteen thousand men. Or, he got himself a name in the Valley of Salt, by smiting eighteen thousand men, after he returned from smiting the Syrians. And without this repetition of the word מכה smiting, or בהכה by smiting, the construction and sense is quite imperfect. Le Clerc, F. Houbigant, and others, add this supplement, and this alone renders all the other emendations of the learned Father quite unnecessary. The version of the Vulg. Latin confirms the interpretation, which thus renders the place: *Fecit sibi quoque* David *nomen cum reverteretur capta* Syria, *in valle* Salinarum, *cæsis decem et octo millibus.* "David also got him a name when he returned from the capture of Syria, having slain eighteen thousand men."—CHANDLER.

Ver. 16. And Jehoshaphat, the son of Ahilud, *was* recorder.

That is, as is generally believed, remembrancer or writer of chronicles, an employment of no mean estimation in the eastern world, where it was customary with kings to keep daily registers of all the transactions of their reign: and a trust, which, whoever discharged to purpose, must be let into the true springs and secrets of action, and consequently must be received into the utmost confidence.—BURDER.

Ver. 18. And Benaiah, the son of Jehoiada, *was over* both the Cherethites and the Pelethites: and David's sons were chief rulers.

These guards are called in the text, the Cherethites and the Pelethites, but what they were is variously conjectured. That they were soldiers, is evident from their being mentioned as present at the proclamation of King Solomon against Adonijah, which could not evidently have been done without some armed force to protect the persons that proclaimed him: and that they were not common soldiers, but the constant guards of David's person, is manifest from the title of Σωματοφύλακες, *keepers of the body*, which Josephus gives them. Some are of opinion that they were men of gigantic stature; but we find no ground for that, though they were doubtless proper and robust men, (as we speak,) and of known fidelity to their prince, 2 Sam. xv. 18, and xx. 7. Others again think that they were Philistines; but it is hardly supposable, that David would have any of these hated, uncircumcised people to be his bodyguard; neither can we believe that Israelitish soldiers would have took it patiently to see foreigners of that nation put in such places of honour and trust. It is much more likely, then, that they were some select men of the tribe of Judah, which had their names from the families they sprung from, one of which is mentioned, 1 Sam. xxx. 14, and the other, 1 Chron. ii. 33, unless we will come into the notion of others, who, as they find that there were men of this denomination among the Philistines, think that these guards of David's, which were originally of his own tribe, had these *exotic* names given them from some notable exploit or signal victory gained over the Philistines of this name, as (in 1 Sam. xxx. 14) we have express mention of one action against them.—STACKHOUSE.

CHAPTER IX.

Ver. 11. Then said Ziba unto the king, According to all that my lord the king hath commanded his servant, so shall thy servant do. As for Mephibosheth, *said the king*, he shall eat at my table, as one of the king's sons.

See on 2 Kings 9. 11.

CHAPTER X.

Ver. 4. Wherefore Hanun took David's servants, and shaved off the one half of their beards, and cut off their garments in the middle, *even* to their buttocks, and sent them away.

This was one of the greatest indignities that the malice of man could invent in those countries, where all people thought their hair so great an ornament, that some would have rather submitted to die, than part with it. What a foul disgrace and heavy punishment this was accounted in ancient times, we may learn from Nicholaus Damascenus, as mentioned by Stobæus, (Tit. 42.) who says, that among the Indians the king commanded the greatest offenders to be shaven, as the heaviest punishment that he could inflict upon them; and, to the like purpose, Plutarch (in Egesil) tells us, that, whenever a soldier, among the Lacedemonians, was convicted of cowardice, he was obliged to go with one part of his upper lip shaved, and the other not. Nay, even at this day, no greater indignity can be offered to a man of Persia, than to cause his beard to be shaved; and therefore, Tavernier, in his travels, relates the story, that when the Sophi caused an ambassador of Aurengzeb's to be used in this manner, telling him that he was not worthy to wear a beard, the emperor (even in the manner as David here did) most highly resented the affront that was done to him in the person of his ambassador. And, as shaving David's ambassadors was deservedly accounted a grievous affront, so the cutting off half the beard (which made them look still more ridiculous) was a great addition to it, where beards were held in great veneration; and where long habits down to the heels were worn, especially by persons of distinction, without any breeches or drawers, the cutting their garments, even to the middle, thereby to expose their nakedness, was such a brutal and shameless insult, as would badly become a man of David's martial spirit, and just sentiments of honour, to have tamely passed by.—STACKHOUSE.

The customs of nations in respect to this part of the human countenance, have differed, and still do differ, so widely, that it is not easy, among us, who treat the beard as an encumbrance, to conceive properly of the importance which is attached to it in the East. The Levitical laws have noticed the beard, but the terms in which most of them are expressed, are somewhat obscure; i. e. they are obscure to us, by the very reason of their being familiar to the persons to whom they were addressed. Perhaps the following quotations may contribute to throw a light, at least upon some of them: "The first care of an Ottoman prince, when he comes to the throne, is, *to let his beard grow*, to which Sultan Mustapha added, the *dying of it black*, in order that it might be more apparent on the day of his first appearance, when he was to GIRD ON THE SABRE; a ceremony by which he takes possession of the throne, and answering the coronation among us." (Baron du Tott.) So, De la Motraye tells us, "that the new Sultan's beard had not been permitted to grow, but only since he had been proclaimed emperor: and was very short, it being customary to shave the Ottoman princes, as *a mark of their subjection* to the reigning emperor." "In the year 1764, Kerim Khan sent to demand payment of the tribute due for his possessions in Kermesir: but, Mir Mahenna maltreated the officer who was sent on the errand, and *caused his beard to be cut off.* Kerim Khan then sent a strong army against him, which conquered Bender Rigk, and all the territories of Mir Mahenna." (Niebuhr.) This will remind the reader of the insult offered to the ambassadors of David, by Hanun, (2 Sam. x.) which insult, however, seems to have had a peculiarity in it—of shaving one half of the beard; i. e. the beard on one side of the face. On this subject, we translate from Niebuhr (French edit.) the following remarks: "The Orientals have divers manners of letting the beard grow; the Jews, in Turkey, Arabia, and Persia, preserve their beard from their youth; and it differs from that of the Christians and Mohammedans, in that they do not shave it either at the aers, or the temples. The Arabs keep their whiskers very short; some cut them off entirely; but they never shave off the beard. In the mountains of Yemen, where strangers are seldom seen, *it is a disgrace to appear shaven;* they supposed our European servant, who had only whiskers, *had committed some crime, for which we had punished him, by cutting off his beard.* On the contrary, the Turks have commonly long whiskers; the beard among them is a mark of honour. The slaves and certain domestics of the great lords, are forced to cut it off, and dare not keep any part of it, but whiskers; the Persians have long whiskers, and clip their beard short with scissors, which has an unpleasant appearance to strangers. The Kurdes shave the beard, but leave the whiskers, and a band of hair on the cheeks." "The true Arabs have black beards, yet some old men die their white beards red; but this is thought to be to hide their age; and is rather blamed than praised. The Persians blacken their beards much more; and, probably, do so to extreme old age, in order to pass for younger than they really are. The Turks do the same in some cases. [How differently Solomon thought! Prov. xx. 29, 'The glory of young men is their strength, and the beauty of old men is the gray head.']—When the younger Turks, after having been shaven, let their beards grow, they recite a *fatha*, [or kind of prayer,] which is considered as a vow never to cut it off; and when any one cuts off his beard, he may be very severely punished, (at Basra, at least, to 300 blows with a stick.) He would also be the laughing-stock of those of his faith. A Mohammedan, at Basra, having shaved his beard when drunk, fled secretly to India, not daring to return, for fear of public scorn, and judicial punishment."

"Although the Hebrews took great care of their beards, to fashion them when they were not in mourning, and on the contrary, did not trim them when they were in mourning, yet I do not observe that their regard for them amounted to any veneration for their beard. On the contrary, the Arabians have so much respect for their beards, that they look on them as sacred ornaments given by God, to distinguish them from women. They never shave them: nothing can be more infamous than for a man to be shaved; they make the preservation of their beards a capital point of religion, because Mohammed never cut off his: it is likewise a mark of authority and liberty among them, as well as among the Turks; the Persians, who clip them, and shave above the jaw, are reputed heretics. The razor is never drawn over the grand seignior's face: they who serve in the seraglio, have their beard shaved, as a sign of servitude: they do not suffer it to grow till the sultan has set them at liberty, which is bestowed as a reward upon them, and is always accompanied with some employment. Unmarried young men may cut their beards; but when married, especially if parents, they forbear doing so, to show that they are become wiser, have renounced the vanities of youth, and think now of superior things. When they comb their beards, they hold a handkerchief on their knees, and gather carefully the hairs that fall: and when they have got together a proper quantity, they fold them up in paper, and carry them to the place where they bury the dead. Among them it is more infamous for any one to have his beard cut off, than among us to be publicly whipped, or branded with a hot iron. Many men in that country would prefer death to such a punishment. The wives kiss their husbands' beards, and children their fathers', when they come to salute them: the men kiss one another's beards reciprocally, when they salute in the streets, or come from a journey.—They say, that the beard is the perfection of the human face, which would be more disfigured by having this cut off, than by losing the nose.

"They admire and envy those, who have fine beards: 'Pray do but see,' they cry, 'that beard; the very sight of it would persuade any one, that he, to whom it belongs, is an honest man.' If anybody with a fine beard is guilty of an unbecoming action, 'What a disadvantage is this,' they say, 'to such a beard! How much such a beard is to be pitied!' If they would correct any one's mistakes, they will tell him, 'For shame of your beard! Does not the confusion that follows light on your beard?' If they entreat any one, or use oaths in affirming or denying any thing, they say, 'I conjure you by your beard,—by the life of your beard,—to grant me this,'—or, 'by your beard, this is, or is not, so.' They say further, in the way of acknowledgment, 'May God preserve your blessed beard! May God pour out his blessings on your beard!' And, in comparisons, 'This is more valuable than one's beard.'" Mœurs des Arabes, par M. D'Arvieux, chap. vii. These accounts may contribute to illustrate several passages of scripture.

The dishonour done by David to his beard, of letting his spittle fall on it, (1 Sam. xxi. 13,) seems at once to have convinced Achish of his being distempered: *q. d.* "No man in good health, of body and mind, would thus defile what we esteem so honourable as his beard." If the beard be thus venerated, we perceive the import of Mephibosheth's neglect, in his not trimming it, 2 Sam. xix. 24. We conceive, also, that after the information given us, as above, that men *kiss one another's beards*, when they salute in the streets, *or when one of them is lately come from a journey;* we may discover traces of deeper dissimulation in the behaviour of Joab to Amasa (2 Sam. xx. 9) than we have heretofore noticed: "And Joab held in his right hand the beard of Amasa, *that he might give it a kiss.*"—No wonder then, that while this act of friendship, of gratulation after long absence, occupied Amasa's attention, he did not perceive the sword that was in Joab's *left* hand. The action of Joab was, indeed, a high compliment, but neither suspicious nor unusual; and to this compliment Amasa paying attention, and, no doubt, returning it with answerable politeness, he could little expect the fatal event that Joab's perfidy produced. Was the behaviour of Judas to Jesus something like this behaviour of Joab to Amasa?—a worthy example worthily imitated!—With this idea in our minds, let us hear the Evangelists relate the story; Matt. xxvi. 49, "And coming directly to Jesus, he said, Hail [joy to thee] Rabbi! and kissed him:" so says Mark xiv. 45. But Luke seems to imply, that Judas observed a more respectful manner, in his salutation. Jesus, according to Matthew, before he received the kiss from Judas, had time to say, "Friend [in what manner] unto what purpose art thou come?" And while Judas was kissing him—suppose his beard—Jesus might easily, and very aptly express himself, as Luke relates, "Ah! Judas, betrayest thou the Son of Man by a kiss?" The cutting off the beard is mentioned (Isaiah xv. 2) as a token of mourning; and as such it appears to be very expressive, Jer. xli. 5: "Fourscore men came from Samaria, having their beards shaven, and their clothes rent."—See, also, chap. xlviii. 37. Is not this custom somewhat illustrated by the idea which the Arabs attached to the shaven servant of Niebuhr, *i. e.* as a kind of punishment suffered for guilt, expressed or implied?—TAYLOR IN CALMET.

While the Orientals had their emblems of honour, and tokens of regard, they had also peculiar customs expressive of contempt or dislike; of which the first I shall mention is cutting off the beard. Even to talk disrespectfully of a Persian's beard, is the greatest insult that can be offered to him, and an attempt to touch it would probably be followed by the instant death of the offender. Cutting off the beard is reckoned so great a mark of infamy among the Arabs, that many of them would prefer death to such a dishonour. They set the highest value upon this appurtenance of the male; for when they would express their value for a thing, they say it is worth more than his beard; they even beg for the sake of it, "By your beard, by the life of your beard, do."—PAXTON.

When Peter the Great attempted to civilize the Russians, and introduced the manners and fashions of the more refined parts of Europe, nothing met with more opposition than the cutting off their beards, and many of those who were obliged to comply with this command, testified such great veneration for their beards, as to order them to be buried with them. Irwin also, in his voyage up the Red Sea, says, that at signing a treaty of peace with the vizier of Yambo, they swore by their beards, the most solemn oath they can take. D'Arvieux gives a remarkable instance of an Arab, who, having received a wound in his jaw, chose to hazard his life rather than to suffer his surgeon to take off his beard.—BURDER.

This shows, according to the oriental mode of thinking, the magnitude of the affront which Hanan offered to the ambassadors of David, when he took them and shaved off the one half of their beards. It was still, in times comparatively modern, the greatest indignity that can be offered in Persia. Shah Abbas, king of that country, enraged that the emperor of Hindostan had inadvertently addressed him by a title far inferior to that of the great Shah-in-Shah, or king of kings, ordered the beards of the ambassadors to be shaved off, and sent them home to their master. This ignominious treatment discovers also the propriety and force of the type of hair in the prophecies of Ezekiel; where the inhabitants of Jerusalem are compared to the hair of his head and beard, to intimate that they had been as dear to God as the beard was to the Jews; yet for their wickedness they should be cut off and destroyed.—PAXTON.

Ver. 5. When they told *it* unto David, he sent to meet them, because the men were greatly ashamed: and the king said, Tarry at Jericho until your beards be grown, and *then* return.

It is customary to shave the Ottoman princes, as a mark of their subjection to the reigning emperor. In the mountains of Yemen, where strangers are seldom seen, it is a disgrace to appear shaven. The beard is a mark of authority and liberty among the Mohammedans, as well as among the Turks: the Persians, who clip the beard, and shave above the jaw, are reputed heretics. They who serve in the seraglio, have their beards shaven as a sign of servitude: they do not suffer it to grow till the sultan has set them at liberty. Among the Arabians it is more infamous for any one to have his beard cut off, than among us to be publicly whipped, or branded with a hot iron. Many in that country would prefer death to such a punishment.—(Niebuhr.) At length Ibrahim Bey suffered Ali, his page, to let his beard grow, that is to say, gave him his freedom; for, among the Turks, to want mustaches and a beard is thought only fit for slaves and women; and hence arises the unfavourable impression they receive on the first sight of a European. (Volney.)—BURDER.

Ver. 9. When Joab saw that the front of the battle was against him before and behind, he chose of all the choice *men* of Israel, and put *them* in array against the Syrians: 10. And the rest of the people he delivered into the hand of Abishai his brother, that he might put *them* in array against the children of Ammon.

Immediately before the signal was given, and sometimes in the heat of battle, the general of a Grecian army made an oration to his troops, in which he briefly stated the motives that ought to animate their bosoms; and exhorted them to exert their utmost force and vigour against the enemy. The success which sometimes attended these harangues was wonderful; the soldiers, animated with fresh life and courage, returned to the charge, retrieved in an instant their affairs, which were in a declining and almost desperate condition, and repulsed those very enemies by whom they had been often defeated. Several instances of this might be quoted from Roman and Grecian history, but few are more remarkable than that of Tyrtæus, the lame Athenian poet, to whom the command of the Spartan army was given in one of the Messenian wars. The Spartans had at that time suffered great losses in many encounters; and all their stratagems proved ineffectual, so that they began to despair almost of success, when the poet, by his lectures on honour and courage, delivered in moving verse to the army, ravished them to such a degree with the thoughts of dying for their country, that, rushing on with a furious transport to meet their enemies, they gave them an entire overthrow, and by one decisive battle brought the war to a happy conclusion. Such military harangues, especially in very trying circumstances, are perfectly natural, and may be found perhaps in the records of every nation. The history of Joab, the commander-in-chief of David's armies, furnishes a striking instance: "When Joab saw that the front of the battle was against him, before and behind, he chose of all the choice men of Israel, and put them in array against the Syrians; and the rest of the people he delivered into the hand of Abishai his brother, that he might put them in array against the children of Ammon. And he said, If the Syrians be too strong for me, then thou shalt help me; but if the children of Ammon be too strong for thee, then I will come and help thee. Be of good courage, and let us play the men for our people, and for the cities of our God; and the Lord do that which seemeth good in his sight." In a succeeding age, the king of Judah addressed his troops, before they marched against the confederate armies of Moab and Ammon, in terms becoming the chief magistrate of a holy nation, and calculated to make a deep impression on their minds: "And as they went forth, Jehoshaphat stood and said, Hear me, O Judah, and ye inhabitants of Jerusalem: Believe in the Lord your God, so shall ye be established; believe his prophets, so shall ye prosper." To express his own confidence in the protection of Jehovah, and to inspire his army with the same sentiments, after consulting with the people, he "appointed singers unto the Lord, and that should praise the beauty of holiness, as they went out before the army, and to say, Praise the Lord, for his mercy endureth for ever." This pious conduct obtained the approbation of the living and true God, who rewarded the cheerful reliance of his people with a complete victory over their enemies, unattended by loss or danger to them; for "when they began to praise, the Lord turned every man's sword against his fellow," in the camp of the confederates, till not one escaped. Animated with joy and gratitude for so great a deliverance, the pious king returned to Jerusalem at the head of his troops, preceded by a numerous band of music, celebrating the praises of the God of battles. A custom not unlike this, and perhaps derived from some imperfect tradition of it, long prevailed in the states of Greece. Before they joined battle, they sung a hymn to the god of war, called *παιαν εμβατηριος*; and when victory declared in their favour, they sung another to Apollo, termed *παιαν επινικιος*.—PAXTON.

CHAPTER XI.

Ver. 1. And it came to pass, after the year was expired, at the time when kings go forth *to battle*, that David sent Joab, and his servants with him, and all Israel.

The most usual time of commencing military operations was at the return of spring; the hardships of a winter campaign were then unknown. In the beginning of spring, says Josephus, David sent forth his commander-in-chief Joab, to make war with the Ammonites. In another part of his works, he says, that as soon as spring was begun, Adad levied and led forth his army against the Hebrews. Antiochus also prepared to invade Judea at the first appearance of spring; and Vespasian, earnest to put an end to the war in Judea, marched with his whole army to Antipatris, at the commencement of the same season. The sacred historian seems to suppose, that there was one particular time of the year to which the operations of war were commonly limited: "And it came to pass, after the year was expired, at the time kings go forth to battle, that David sent Joab and his servants and all Israel, and they destroyed the children of Ammon and besieged Rabbah." The kings and armies of the East, says Chardin, do not march but when there is grass, and when they can encamp, which time is April. But in modern times, this rule is disregarded, and the history of the crusades records expeditions and battles in every month of the year.—PAXTON.

Ver. 2. And it came to pass in an evening-tide, that David arose from off his bed, and walked upon the roof of the king's house: and from the roof he saw a woman washing herself; and the woman *was* very beautiful to look upon.

The place of greatest attraction to an oriental taste certainly was the summer bath. It seemed to comprise every thing of seclusion, elegance, and that luxurious enjoyment which has too often been the chief occupation of some Asiatic princes. This bath, saloon, or court, is circular, with a vast basin in its centre, of pure white marble, of the same shape, and about sixty or seventy feet in diameter. This is filled with the clearest water, sparkling in the sun, for its only canopy is the vault of heaven; but rose-trees, with other pendent shrubs, bearing flowers, cluster near it, and at times their waving branches throw a beautifully quivering shade over the excessive brightness of the water. Round the sides of the court are two ranges, one above the other, of little chambers, looking towards the bath, and furnished with every refinement of the harem. These are for the accommodation of the ladies who accompany the shah during his occasional sojourns at the Negauristan. They undress or repose in these before or after the delight of bathing: for so fond are they of this luxury, they remain in the water for hours; and sometimes, when the heat is very relaxing, come out more dead than alive. But in this delightful recess, the waters flow through the basin by a constant spring; thus renewing the body's vigour by their bracing coolness: and enchantingly refreshing the air, which the sun's influence, and the thousand flowers breathing around, might otherwise render oppressive with their incense. The royal master of this Hortus Adonidis, frequently takes his noonday repose in one of the upper chambers which encircle the saloons of the bath: and, if he be inclined, he has only to turn his eyes to the scene below, to see the loveliest objects of his tenderness, sporting like Naiads amidst the crystal streams, and glowing with all the bloom and brilliancy which belongs to Asiatic youth. In such a bath court it is probable that Bathsheba was seen by the enamoured king of Israel. As he was walking at evening-tide on the roof of his palace, he might undesignedly have strolled far enough to overlook the androon of his women, where the beautiful wife of Uriah, visiting the royal wives, might have joined them, as was often the custom in those countries, in the delights of the bath.—SIR R. K. PORTER.

The following history is, in some points, an accurate counterpart to that of David. "Nour Jehan signifies the light of the world; she was also called Nour Mahl, or the light of the seraglio: she was wife to one Sher Afkan Khan, of a Turcoman family, who came from Persia to Hindostan in very indifferent circumstances. As she was exquisitely beautiful, of great wit, and an elegant poetess, Jehanguire, the sultan, was resolved to take her to himself. He sent her husband, who was esteemed the bravest man in his service, with some troops, to command in Bengal, and afterward sent another with a greater force to cut him off. When he was killed, Nour Jehan was soon prevailed upon to become an empress. The coin struck in Jehanguire's reign, with the signs of the zodiac, were not, as is usually thought in Europe, done by his empress's order; nor did she reign one day, as the common opinion is, but she ruled the person who reigned for above twelve years." (Fraser.)—BURDER.

Ver. 4. And David sent messengers and took her: and she came in unto him, and he lay with her; (for she was purified from her uncleanness;) and she returned unto her house.

The kings of Israel appear to have taken their wives with very great ease. This is quite consistent with the account given in general of the manner in which eastern princes form matrimonial alliances. "The king, in his marriage, uses no other ceremony than this: he sends an azagi to the house where the lady lives, where the officer announces to her, it is the king's pleasure that she should remove instantly to the palace. She then dresses herself in the best manner, and immediately obeys. Thenceforward he assigns her an apartment in the palace, and gives her a house elsewhere in any part she chooses. Then when he makes her *iteghe*, it seems to be the nearest resemblance to marriage; for whether in the court or the camp, he orders one of the judges to pronounce in his presence, that he, the king, has chosen his handmaid, naming her, for his queen: upon which the crown is put on her head, but she is not anointed."—BURDER.

Ver. 25. Then David said unto the messenger, Thus shalt thou say unto Joab, Let not this thing displease thee, for the sword devoureth one as well as another: make thy battle more strong against the city, and overthrow it; and encourage thou him.

It has been asserted, of the portion of scripture before us, that it tells a tale of little else besides cruelties and crimes, many of them perpetrated by David himself; and it has been triumphantly demanded how a man stained with so many vices, can, without impiety, be styled a "man after God's own heart." We will endeavour to meet the objection, because under it is comprehended all that the infidel is justified in urging against the credibility of the narrative. The peculiar term, of which a use so unworthy is made, was applied, it will be recollected, to David, while that personage yet lived the life of a private man, and kept his father's sheep. It was employed, moreover, by God himself, as distinguishing the future from the present king of Israel, not in their individual characters, as members of the great family of mankind, but as the chief rulers of God's chosen people. To understand its real import, therefore, all that seems necessary is, to ascertain the particular duties of the kings of Israel; and no man who is aware that these monarchs filled, in the strictest sense of the phrase, the station of Jehovah's vicegerents, can for a moment be at a loss in effecting that discovery. The kings of Israel were placed upon the throne, for the purpose of administering the Divine law, as that had been given through Moses. In an especial degree, it was their duty to preserve the people pure from the guilt of idolatry; idolatry being, among the Hebrews, a crime equivalent to high-treason among us; while, on all occasions, whether of foreign war or domestic arrangements, they were bound to act in strict obedience to the will of God, as that might be from time to time revealed to them. Whether this should be done by Urim, by the voice of a prophet, or some palpable and immediate vision, the king of Israel was equally bound to obey; and as long as he did obey, literally, fully, and cheerfully, he was, in his public capacity, a man after God's own heart.

An ordinary attentive perusal of the preceding pages will show, that David, as compared with Saul, (and it is only with reference to such comparison, that the phrase under review ought to be regarded,) was strictly worthy of the honourable title bestowed upon him. Whatever his private vices might be, in all public matters his obedience to God's laws was complete; indeed, he never speaks of himself in any other language than as the servant or minister of Jehovah. No individual among all that reigned in Jerusalem ever exhibited greater zeal against idolatry; of the Mosaic code he was, in his official capacity, uniformly observant; and to every command of God, by whomsoever conveyed, he paid strict attention. Such was by no means the case with Saul, as his assumption of the priestly office, and his conduct towards the Amalekites, demonstrate; and it was simply to distinguish him from his predecessor, as one on whose steady devotion to Divine wishes reliance could be placed, that God spoke of him to Samuel, in the terms so frequently misinterpreted. If it be further urged that David's moral conduct was far from being perfect; that his treatment of Joab, after the murder of Abner, was weak; his behaviour to the captive Ammonites barbarous; his conduct in the case of Uriah, the Hittite, infamous; and his general treatment of his children without excuse; we have no wish, as we profess not to have the power, absolutely to deny the assertions. His receiving Joab into favour, while his hands were red with the blood of Abner, may be pronounced as an act of weakness; yet it was such an act as any other person, in his circumstances, would have been apt to perform. Joab was a distinguished soldier, highly esteemed by the troops, and possessed of great influence in the nation; it would have been the height of imprudence, had David, situated as he was, made such a man his enemy; but that he wholly disapproved of the treacherous deed which Joab had done, he took every conceivable means to demonstrate. He conferred a species of public funeral upon the murdered man, and attended it in person, as chief mourner. The treatment of the captive Ammonites was doubtless exceedingly cruel; yet its cruelty may admit of some extenuation, provided we take one or two matters, as they deserve to be taken, into consideration. In the first place, the age was a barbarous one, and from the influence of the times in which he lived, it would be folly to expect that David could be free. In the next place, the tortures inflicted upon the Ammonites are not to be understood as heaped indiscriminately upon the whole body of the people. The magistrates and principal men were alone "put under saws and harrows of iron, and made to pass through the brick-kiln." And these suffered a fate so horrible, only in retaliation for similar excesses committed by their order upon certain Hebrew prisoners. Besides, the gross and unprovoked indignities heaped upon David's ambassadors might well inflame his fury to the highest pitch; since then, even more conspicuously than now, the persons of envoys were considered sacred, especially in the East. Without, therefore, attempting to excuse such actions, as no enlightened person would now, under any provocation, perpetrate, we must nevertheless repeat, that David's treatment of the Ammonites was not absolutely devoid of extenuating circumstances; an assertion which cannot, we feel, be hazarded in reference to that monarch's behaviour towards Uriah the Hittite. Perhaps there is not recorded in any volume a series of crimes more gross or inexcusable than those of which we are now bound to take notice. Adultery and murder are terms too mild for them, inasmuch as the particular acts of adultery and murder implied other offences scarcely less heinous than themselves. The woman abused by David was the wife of a proselyte from a heathen nation, whom it was to the interest and honour of the true religion for the chosen head of God's nation to treat with marked delicacy. He was, moreover, a brave and faithful soldier; so brave and zealous in his master's service, that even when summoned by the king himself to the capital, he refused to indulge in its luxuries, while his comrades were exposed to the hardships of war. This man David would have vitally wronged, by introducing into his family a child of which the king himself was the father; and failing in the accomplishment of a design so iniquitous, he coolly devised his death. Again, that the deed might be done without bringing disgrace upon himself, he ordered his general to place this gallant soldier in a post of danger, and, deserting him there, to leave him to his fate; and when all had befallen as he wished, his observation was, that "the sword devoured one as well as another." These several occurrences, summed up, as they were, by the abrupt and shameless marriage of Bathsheba, combine to complete a concatenation of crimes, of which it is impossible to speak or think without horror; yet is there nothing connected with them, in the slightest degree, mischievous to the credibility or consistency of scripture. It cannot, with any truth, be asserted, that God either was, or is represented to have been, a party to these black deeds. So far is this from being the case, that we find a prophet sent expressly to the sinful monarch, to point out to him the enormity of his offences, and to assure him of a punishment, grievous in proportion to the degree of defilement which he had contracted. But as David's crimes had been committed in his private capacity, so his punishment was made to affect his private fortunes. His own children became the instruments of God's anger, and heavier domestic calamities than fell upon him, no man, perhaps has ever endured. His only daughter (and, as such, doubtless his favourite child) is ravished by her brother Amnon; the ravisher is murdered by his brother Absalom; Absalom revolts against his father, drives him from his capital, and is finally slain in battle fighting against him. If there be not in this enough to vindicate the honour of God, we know not where marks of Divine displeasure are to be looked for; and as to the credibility of the scriptural narrative, that appears to be strengthened, rather than weakened, by the detail of David's fall. No fictitious writer would have represented one whom he had already designated as "a man after God's own heart," and whom he evidently desires his readers to regard with peculiar reverence, as a murderer and adulterer. It is the province of a narrator of facts alone to speak of men as they were, by exposing the vices and follies even of his principal heroes; nor is the history without its effect as a great moral warning. It teaches the important lesson, that the commission of one crime seldom, if ever, fails to lead to the commission of others; while it furnishes a memorable example of the clemency which forbids any sinner to despair, or regard himself as beyond the pale of mercy. Of David's conduct towards his children, it seems to us little better than a waste of time to set up either an explanation or a defence. Extravagantly partial to them he doubtless was; so partial as to pass over in their behaviour crimes which, we can hardly believe, would have been passed by, had others besides the members of his own family committed them. It is indeed true, that the law of Moses, by which alone David professed to be guided, is not very explicit as to the punishment which ought to have been awarded to Amnon; but the truth we suspect to be, as Josephus has given it, that David abstained from bringing him to a public trial after his outrage to Tamar, because the feelings of the father prevailed over those of the magistrate. In like manner, his pardoning Absalom's crime, in defiance of the law, which expressly enjoins blood to be shed for blood, without redemption, is open to a similar charge; yet even here, there is more to be urged in the king's defence, than the mere operation of natural affection. Absalom took shelter at a foreign court immediately on the perpetration of the murder; it might not be in David's power to force his surrender, and hence the only alternative was, to leave him in exile, among heathen, at the manifest hazard of the corruption of his religious principles, or to permit his return to Jerusalem, and ultimately to receive him into favour. With respect, again, to his subsequent indulgence of that prince—an indulgence to which, in some degree, his insurrection deserves to be traced back—we see in it only one more proof of that amiable weakness which characterized all the monarch's dealings towards his family, his fondness for every member of which unquestionably led him into errors, if not of the heart, at all events of the head. Such errors, however, leave but trivial blots upon the general reputation of any man. They proceed from a good principle, even when carried to weakness, and will be sought for in vain among the utterly heartless, profligate, or selfish; and as David is not represented in scripture as either a perfect saint or a perfect hero, we see no reason why his strength of mind, more than his moral character, should be vindicated from all the charges which may be brought against it.—Gleig.

Ver. 25. Then David said unto the messenger,
Thus shalt thou say unto Joab, Let not this
thing displease thee, for the sword devoureth
one as well as another: make thy battle more
strong against the city, and overthrow it; and
encourage thou him. 26. And when the wife
of Uriah heard that Uriah her husband was
dead, she mourned for her husband. 27. And
when the mourning was passed, David sent
and fetched her to his house, and she became
his wife, and bare him a son. But the thing
that David had done displeased the Lord.

This is the account of David's fall, as related in scripture; a fall attended with numerous circumstances of heinous aggravation, and the attempt to vindicate his conduct, in any of the principal parts of this transaction, would be injurious to the laws of truth and virtue. But if there are any circumstances of alleviation, that can be fairly alleged, justice and candour require that they should be mentioned; as well as to own and admit others, that heighten his fault, and render him inexcusable. And I think there cannot be a greater pleasure, than what arises to a good mind, from being able, in some measure, to apologize for actions, in some particulars of them, which upon the whole are bad, and extenuate that guilt, where it can be fairly done, which, as far as real, ought neither to be concealed nor defended. There are some crimes peculiarly aggravated by previous deliberate steps that men take to commit them; when they lay schemes to gratify bad passions, and accomplish purposes they know to be injurious and dishonourable. David, in the beginning of this transaction, seems to be entirely free from every charge of this kind. He did not so much as know who she was, much less that she was a married woman, when he first casually saw her; and the passion he conceived for her, might, for any thing he then knew, be lawful, and such as he might, without any offence, allow himself in the gratification of. And this would have been the case, under the dispensation in which he lived, had she been a single person. David therefore, though very imprudently, and I think in some degree criminally, did not deliberate upon an affair, which he saw no immediate reason to prohibit him from pursuing; and thereby heightened that inclination, which he ought to have checked, as a good man, till he was sure he had a right to indulge it. By not doing this, it became too strong for his management; and when he had been informed who she was, yet fired with the imagination, that the beautiful object he beheld had raised in his mind, all other considerations at last gave way, and he immediately resolved to gratify his desires, at the expense of his conscience, honour, and duty. He instantly sends for Bathsheba, she immediately complied with him, and the whole affair seems to have been completed the very evening it was begun. Every one must see, that as David had but little time for deliberation, it was not very likely, that in the small interval, between the rise of his passion, and the gratifying it, one in his circumstances should be cool enough to use that deliberation, which was necessary to bring him to himself, and restrain him from the crime he was hurried on to commit; and that therefore his sin, thus far, had not that aggravation which it would have had, if there had been more time and leisure for him to reflect, and had he pursued his criminal inclinations, after having seriously and calmly weighed the nature and consequences of what he was about to do, and used, as too many others in like cases have done, fraud, perfidy, and force, to gratify them. To say there was no time for any deliberation, may be saying too much; for there is scarce any sin so suddenly committed, but there are some moments for reflection; but, in some circumstances, men may be so hurried away by a sudden gust of passion, as that they may be wholly incapacitated by it, rightly to improve those moments. David had no time to prevent the first rise of his passion. It was as instantaneous as the sight, and he might not think himself obliged to suppress it, till after he knew Bathsheba was Uriah's wife; so that all the interval he could have for reflection was only that between his knowing who she was, and his actually possessing her; an interval too entirely engrossed by imagination and desire, to leave room sufficient for the exercise of reason, or the influence of any good principles to restrain him. If David and Bathsheba had been casually together, a more sudden and violent gust of passion could not have hurried him away, without allowing him some time for deliberation, than what the attitude, in which he first saw her, would have naturally excited, and did actually excite; which swept away all consideration and reflection before it, and drove him down a precipice, that wellnigh proved his absolute destruction. I cannot help adding, that Bathsheba herself seems to have too easily yielded to the king's inclination, and thereby rendered it almost impossible for him to suppress it. For the history informs us, that David "sent messengers, and he received her, and she came in unto him, and he lay with her." Her compliance seems voluntary, unforced, immediate. But she went, met his passion, indulged it, without, as appears, any reluctance, without remonstrating against David's attempt upon her honour; and thereby prevented those reflections, that her denial and resistance might have occasioned in him, and that might have made him sensible of the enormity of the crime, and preserved him from the commission of it. And how great soever this sin was, David is not the only instance of men's being unhappily betrayed in an evil hour, by the power of a sudden and unexpected temptation. Too many instances may be produced, even of habitually good and virtuous persons being drawn aside, in some unguarded moment, and by the force of an unthought-of strong temptation, into the commission of those sins, which, in other circumstances, they would have trembled at, and abhorred the very mention and thought of.

The first crime thus committed, and the dreaded consequences of it appearing, the unhappy prince found himself involved in difficulties, out of which he knew not how to extricate himself. Conscious guilt, concern for his own character, regard for the honour of the fair partner of his crime, and even fear of his own, and her life; the punishment of their adultery being death; all united, to put him on forming some contrivances how to conceal and prevent the scandal of it from becoming public. Hence, all the little tricks and shifts he made use of to entice the injured husband to his wife's bed, and father the fruit of their adultery upon him. Who can help pitying a great, and I will venture to affirm, a hitherto virtuous prince, reduced to these wretched expedients, to prevent that public infamy, which he now apprehended to be near him, and dreaded the falling under? But even these failed him. What must he do? Where can a man stop, when once he is entangled in the toils of vice, and hath presumptuously ventured into the paths of guilt? Bathsheba must be preserved at any rate. His own honour was at stake to prevent her destruction, and he saw but one way to secure that end, which he thought himself obliged, at any hazard, to obtain. If Uriah lived, she must inevitably die. Uriah could have demanded the punishment, and seems to have been a soldier of that roughness of temper, and firmness of resolution, as that he would have prosecuted his vengeance against her to the utmost. The law was express and peremptory. Which of the two must be the victim? Cruel dilemma! It is at last determined that the husband should be sacrificed, to save the wife, whom David's passion had made a criminal; and had he forsaken her in this dreadful situation, and left her to her punishment, he would not only have pronounced sentence of death against himself, but been censured, I am persuaded, by almost every man, as a monster of perfidy, baseness, and ingratitude. But how was Uriah to be got rid of? Poison, assassination, or a false charge of treason, or some secret way of destruction, were methods which the eastern princes were well acquainted with. David was above them all, and had a kind of generosity in his very crimes. The man he was to destroy was a brave soldier, and he causes him to fall in the bed of honour, gloriously fighting against the enemies of his king and country; and if dying in the field of battle, by the sword of an enemy, and in a glorious action, be a more eligible and honourable death, than the being despatched by the stab of a stiletto, the tortures of poison, or as a criminal on a false accusation of treason; the causing an innocent person to die in the former manner, though this hath its great aggravation, yet is not so base and villanous an action, as destroying him by any one of the latter methods; and had David had recourse to any of them to get rid of a worthy man, whom he had criminally reduced himself to an almost absolute necessity of despatching, the crime would have been of a more horrid die, and justly excited a higher indignation and abhorrence. And though I am far from mentioning these particulars to excuse David's conduct, or palliate his aggravated offences; yet the circumstances I have mentioned excite my compassion, carry in the nature of the thing some alleviation of his crimes, and should ever be remembered to soften the pen that is employed in describing them. Having thus, by accumulated guilt, taken off the man that he dreaded should live, David, after Bathsheba had gone through the usual time of mourning, took her to his palace, and made her his wife, to screen her from a prosecution of adultery, to secure her against the penalty of death, and in some measure to repair the injury he had done her, by his criminal commerce with her, during her former husband's life; which, as a plurality of wives was not forbidden by that constitution and polity he lived under, was the least compensation that he could make, and which he was obliged in honour and justice to make her. One would have thought, that after such a complication of aggravated crimes, David, upon a review of his conduct, should have been struck with remorse, voluntarily confessed his sins to God, and humbly entreated from him the mercy and forgiveness he so much needed. But nothing of this appears from the history. He rather seems, on the contrary, to have been insensible and callous, and to have enjoyed his new-acquired pleasures, without any uneasiness at the dreadful expense by which he purchased them. The siege of Rabbah went on successfully, he saw no appearing proofs of the divine displeasure that threatened him, the affairs of government employed much of his time and thoughts, he esteemed himself happy in the preservation of Bathsheba, and at full liberty to gratify the ardent passion he had conceived for her; and probably might persuade himself, that as Uriah was a Hittite, the taking away his wife and life greatly lessened the aggravation of his sin; or, that as king of Israel, he was above the laws, and that however criminal such actions might have been in others, yet that the royal prerogative and power might render them lawful in him, or at least so extenuate the evil of them, as that they would pass unobserved by God, who had solemnly promised him the establishment of the throne and kingdom in his person and family.

But by whatever means he made himself easy, the history informs us, that "the thing which David had done displeased the Lord," who resolved to show his abhorrence of the crime, to execute on him a vengeance proportionable to the heinousness and guilt of it, and hereby to rouse his conscience, and bring him to those acknowledgments of his sin, as might prepare him for, and render him capable of that forgiveness, which, how much soever he needed it, he was greatly unworthy of. He was pleased to employ Nathan the prophet on this solemn occasion; who, by an artfully composed fable, brought the king to pronounce his own condemnation, even without suspecting or intending it. Bathsheba had just been delivered of a son, the fruit of her adulterous commerce with David, and who was, in the strictness of the letter, conceived by his mother in sin, and shapen in iniquity. David appears to have been fond of the child, and, in the midst of his joy on this account, Nathan demands an audience, and addresses him with the following complaint. There were two men, who lived in the same city, one of whom was rich, and the other poor. The rich man had flocks and herds in great abundance; but the poor man had not any thing, save only one little ewe-lamb, which he had brought, and nourished, so that it grew up together with him, and with his children. It did eat of his morsel, and drank of his cup, and lay in his bosom, and was to him as a daughter. And there came a certain traveller to the rich man, and he begrudged to take of his own flock and his own herd, to entertain his guest, but took the poor man's lamb, and provided for the traveller that came to him. David was extremely incensed against the man, and said to Nathan: "As the Lord lives, the man who has done this is worthy of death, and he shall restore the lamb fourfold, inasmuch as he hath done this thing, and because he had no compassion." "Then Nathan said to David: Thou art the man. Thus saith the Lord God of Israel: I have anointed thee to be king over Israel, and delivered thee from the hand of Saul. I gave thee also thy master's house, and the wives of thy master into thy bosom, and gave thee the house of Israel and of Judah; and if this be but a small matter, I have also added to thee this and the other thing, which thou well knowest. Why then hast thou despised the commandment of the Lord, to do this wickedness in his sight? Thou hast smote Uriah the Hittite with the sword, and hast taken his wife to be thy wife, and hast slain him by the sword of the children of Ammon. Now therefore the sword shall never depart from thy house, because thou hast despised me, and hast taken the wife of Uriah the Hittite to be thy wife. Thus saith the Lord: Behold, I will raise up evil against thee out of thine own house, and will take thy wives before thine eyes, and will give them to thy neighbour, and he shall lie with thy wives before the sun. Though thou hast done this secretly, yet I will do what I have now said, before all Israel, and before the sun." This dreadful sentence roused the conscience of David, and from the fullest conviction of the heinousness of his offence, he immediately made this acknowledgment to Nathan: "I have sinned against the Lord." Upon this ingenuous confession, Nathan immediately replies: "The Lord also hath put away thy sin. Thou shalt not die. However, since by this deed thou hast caused the enemies of the Lord contemptuously to reject him, the son also that is born unto thee shall surely die."

When Nathan had thus boldly and faithfully executed his commission, he left the king, and the lecture which he read him was worthy the dignity of a prophet's character and station, and such as became the majesty of him to whom it was given. It was grave, strong, affecting, insinuating, and polite. The parable, in which he conveyed to him his message from God, is dressed up with all the circumstances of art, tenderness, and delicacy, to move compassion, and, at the same time, to force from him that dreadful sentence: "As the Lord liveth, the man that hath done this thing shall surely die, because he did this thing, and because he had no compassion;" thus drawing from him the sentence of his own condemnation, even before he perceived it. But how home, how bold was the application, when Nathan said to the king: "Thou art the man .... Wherefore hast thou despised the commandment of the Lord to do evil in his sight? Thou hast killed Uriah the Hittite with the sword, and hast taken his wife." How dreadful also was the sentence pronounced against him by the order of God! Such as showed the height of his abhorrence of the crime, and his displeasure and indignation against him that committed it. But how did the unhappy offender receive this bold and severe remonstrance? Why, no sooner was the application made, but he falls under conviction, acknowledges his offence against God, and owns himself worthy of death; and the psalms he penned on this occasion show the deep sense he had of the guilt he had contracted, and will be a memorial of the sincerity of his repentance throughout all generations. But was not David's repentance all affectation and hypocrisy, and did he not bear the reproof, and humble himself, because he took care not to disagree with his best friends; or, in other words, to keep fair with the priests and Levites? But if the priests and Levites were such kind of men, as some have represented them; ready to support David in all his measures of iniquity, and when he projected any scheme, were never wanting in their assistance to him; why should any one of them give him any trouble in this affair? In what had he disobliged them, by killing a Hittite, and debauching his wife? Or why should they disagree with him about a transaction that no way related to them? I should rather think, they should have endeavoured to have made him compound with them for a round sum of money, or a good number of sheep and oxen for sacrifices, that they might have feasted themselves on the price of his forgiveness; especially, as we have been told, that this same prophet, "Nathan, was a great lover of this sort of food, and very angry when he was excluded from good cheer." But indeed the insinuation itself is wholly groundless; and let any man read through the reproof that Nathan gave him, and the direct charge of murder and adultery that he urged to his face, and, I think, he cannot but be convinced, that David's acknowledgment, "I have sinned against the Lord," could proceed from nothing but a real and deep sense of the greatness of his crime, and that he deserved to be cut off by the hand of God for that aggravated transgression. What further effectually refutes this suggestion is, that his bearing with the reproof, and humbling himself under it, did not at all reconcile Nathan to him, who left him with a threatening dreadful in its nature, enough to make his ears tingle, and his heart tremble within him. The only favourable thing Nathan said to him was: "Thou shalt not die;" but, at the same time, tells him, that the murder he had been guilty of should be revenged by the sword's never departing from his house, and his adultery retaliated in the most exemplary and public manner, upon his own wives; threatenings that were made him, before he owned his fault, and submitted himself; and therefore his submission could be with no view of reconciling himself to Nathan, because that prophet had already peremptorily pronounced his punishment, which David's after confession did not in the least mitigate or alter; for the punishment threatened was inflicted to the full; and the particular nature and circumstances of it were such, and the events on which it depended were so distant and various, as that no human wisdom and sagacity could foresee them, or secure their futurity; and therefore Nathan, who pronounced his doom, must have been immediately inspired by God, who foresaw and permitted the means, by which his threatenings should be punctually executed, and thus brought upon David all the evils that his prophet had foretold should certainly befall him. The nature of his repentance my reader will be the better enabled to judge of, if he carefully reads over the 51st psalm, which he certainly penned on this occasion.—Chandler.

No one can read this psalm, but must see all the characters of true repentance in the person who wrote it, and the marks of the deepest sorrow and humiliation for the sins of which he had been guilty. The heart appears in every line, and the bitter anguish of a wounded conscience discovers itself by the most natural and affecting symptoms. How earnestly does he plead for mercy, and thereby acknowledge his own unworthiness! How ingenuous are the confessions he makes of his offences, and how heavy was the load of that guilt that oppressed him! The smart of it pierced through his very bones and marrow, and the torture he felt was as though they had been broken, and utterly crushed to pieces. He owns his sins were of too deep a die for sacrifices to expiate the guilt of, and that he had nothing but a broken heart and contrite spirit to offer to that God, whom he had so grievously offended. How earnest are his prayers, that God would create in him a clean heart, and renew a right spirit within him! How doth he dread the being deserted of God! How earnestly deprecate the being deprived of his favour, the joy of his salvation, and the aids and comforts of his holy spirit! Let but this psalm be read without prejudice, and with a view only to collect the real sentiments expressed in it, and the disposition of heart that appears throughout the whole of it; and no man of candour, I am confident, will ever suspect that it was the dictate of hypocrisy, or could be penned from any other motive, but a strong conviction of the heinousness of his offence, and the earnest desire of God's forgiveness, and being restrained from the commission of the like transgressions for the future. And those who run riot upon David's character, on account of his conduct in the matter of Uriah, though they cannot too heartily detest the sin, and must severely censure the offender; yet surely may find some room in their hearts for compassion towards him, when they consider how he was surprised into the first crime, and how the fear and dread of a discovery, and his concern for the life of the woman he had seduced, led him on, step by step, to further degrees of deceit and wickedness, till he completed his guilt by the destruction of a great and worthy man; especially when they see him prostrate before God, confessing his sin, and supplicating forgiveness; and even exempted by God himself from the punishment of death he had incurred, upon his ingenuously confessing, "I have sinned against the Lord;" an evident proof that his repentance was sincere, as it secured him immediately forgiveness from God, whom he had offended.

I shall conclude this article by the remarks which Mr. Bayle makes on it. "His amour with the wife of Uriah, and the orders he gave to destroy her husband, are two most enormous crimes. But he was so grieved for them, and expiated them by so admirable a repentance, that this is not the passage in his life, wherein he contributes the least to the instruction and edification of the faithful. We therein learn the frailty of the saints, and it is a precept of vigilance. We therein learn in what manner we ought to lament for our sins, and it is an excellent model." Let me add, that the wisdom and equity of the law of Moses evidently appears, in that it appointed no sacrifices to atone for such crimes, the pardoning of which would have been inconsistent with the peace and safety of civil society; such as those which David laments in this psalm, murder and adultery. Here the punishment prescribed by the law was death, and David had no other way of escaping it, but by the undeserved mercy of God. This God was pleased to extend to him, to show how acceptable the sinner's unfeigned repentance will be, whatever be the nature and aggravations of his offences; and if we learn from hence, what the scripture calls "the deceitfulness of sin," to be cautious of the first beginnings of it, and not to indulge those sensual appetites, which, when given way to, draw men insensibly into crimes, they would have once trembled at the thoughts of committing; we shall make the best and wisest improvement of this melancholy part of David's history, and be real gainers by his sins and sorrows.—Chandler.

CHAPTER XII.

Ver. 11. Thus saith the Lord, Behold, I will raise up evil against thee out of thine own house, and I will take thy wives before thine eyes, and give *them* unto thy neighbour, and he shall lie with thy wives in the sight of this sun. 12. For thou didst *it* secretly; but I will do this thing before all Israel, and before the sun.

The words, I will raise up, I will take, I will do, do not denote any positive actions of God, as if he prompted wicked men to do the same things wherewith he threatens David, insomuch that, without such prompting, they would not have done them, but by it were necessitated to do them; such a construction as this is injurious to the divine attributes, and makes God the author of evil: but the true meaning is, that God, at that time, saw the perverse disposition of one of his sons, and the crafty wiliness of one of his counsellors, which, without his restraining them, would not fail to create David no small uneasiness; and therefore, because David had violated his law, and, to gratify his lust, had committed both adultery and murder, God would not interpose, but suffered the tempers of these two wicked persons to follow their own course, and have their natural swing; whereupon the one, being ambitious of a crown, endeavours to depose his father, and the other, willing to make the breach irreparable, advised the most detested thing he could think of. This indeed was the very thing that God had foretold, but, without any imputation upon his attributes, we may say, that God can so dispose and guide a train of circumstances, that the wickedness of any action shall happen in this manner, rather than another, though he do not infuse into any man the will to do wickedly. So that from such scripture phrases as these, we may not infer, that God either does, or can do evil, but only that he permits that evil to be done, which he foreknew would be done, but might have prevented, had he pleased; or, in other terms, that he suffers men, naturally wicked, to follow the bent of their tempers, without any interposition of his providence to restrain them.—Stackhouse.

Ver. 16. David therefore besought God for the child; and David fasted, and went in and lay all night upon the earth. 17. And the elders of his house arose, *and went* to him, to raise him up from the earth: but he would not, neither did he eat bread with them. 18. And it came to pass on the seventh day, that the child died. And the servants of David feared to tell him that the child was dead; for they said, Behold, while the child was yet alive, we spake unto him, and he would not hearken unto our voice; how will he then vex himself, if we tell him that the child is dead? 19. But when David saw that his servants whispered, David perceived that the child was dead: therefore David said unto his servants, Is the child dead? And they said, He is dead. 20. Then David arose from the earth, and washed, and anointed *himself*, and changed his apparel, and came into the house of the Lord, and worshipped: then he came to his own house; and, when he required, they set bread before him, and he did eat.

The account Sir John Chardin gives us of eastern mourning, in order to illustrate Ecclesiasticus xxxviii. 17, is as follows. "The practice of the East is to leave a relation of the deceased person to weep and mourn, till, on the third or fourth day at farthest, the relations and friends go to see him, cause him to eat, lead him to a bath, and cause him to put on new vestments, he having before thrown himself on the ground," &c. The surprise of David's servants then, who had seen his bitter anguish while the child was sick, arose apparently from this, that, when he found it was dead, he that so deeply lamented, arose of himself from the earth, without staying for his friends coming about him, and that presently; immediately bathed and anointed himself, instead of appearing as a mourner; and, after worshipping God with solemnity, returned to his wonted repasts without any interposition of others; which as now, so perhaps anciently, was made use of in the East. The extremity of his sorrows for the child's illness, and his not observing the common forms of grief afterward, was what surprised his servants. Every eye must see the general ground of astonishment; but this passage of Chardin gives great distinctness to our apprehensions of it.—Harmer.

Ver. 20. Then David arose from the earth, and washed, and anointed *himself*, and changed his apparel, and came into the house of the Lord and worshipped: then he came to his own house; and, when he required, they set bread before him, and he did eat. 21. Then said his servants unto him, What thing *is* this that thou hast done? thou didst fast and weep for the child *while it was* alive; but when the child was dead, thou didst rise and eat bread.

The oriental mourner was distinguished by the slovenliness of his dress. He suffered the hair of his head, if not cut or plucked off in the excess of his grief, to hang dishevelled upon the shoulders; he neither trimmed his beard, nor washed his feet, even in the hottest weather; he did not wash his shirt, nor any of the linen he wore. During the whole time of mourning, he refused to change his clothes. In this state of total negligence, it appears that David mourned for his infant son; for after he learned from his attendants that the child was dead, the inspired historian observes, "Then David arose from the earth, and washed and anointed himself, and changed his apparel."—PAXTON.

Ver. 29. And David gathered all the people together, and went to Rabbah, and fought against it, and took it. 30. And he took their king's crown from off his head, (the weight whereof *was* a talent of gold with the precious stones,) and it was *set* on David's head: and he brought forth the spoil of the city in great abundance. 31. And he brought forth the people that *were* therein, and put *them* under saws, and under harrows of iron, and under axes of iron, and made them pass through the brick-kiln: and thus did he unto all the cities of the children of Ammon. So David and all the people returned unto Jerusalem.

Josephus tells us, that the men were put to death by exquisite torments. And this hath been the sentiment of many learned commentators. Supposing this interpretation of the passage to be true, I cannot help observing, with Mr. Le Clerc, on the place, that if the punishments inflicted on this people were as severe as they are represented to be, they might be inflicted by way of reprisal. That learned commentator thinks that they were such as the Ammonites themselves used, and that when they were conquered by David, he used them in the same manner as they had treated their Hebrew prisoners. It is very certain that the Ammonites used them with great severity. Nahash, the father probably of this Hanun, in the wantonness of his cruelty, would not admit the inhabitants of Jabesh Gilead, under Saul's reign, to surrender themselves prisoners to him, but upon condition of their every one's consenting to have their right eye thrust out, that he might lay it as a reproach upon all Israel; to which, consistently enough, Josephus adds, that he treated his Hebrew captives with great barbarity, by putting out their right eye, to prevent their being further serviceable in defence of their country; because as the left eye was hid by the shield, they were rendered by the loss of the other incapable of all military duty. Besides, the Ammonites frequently used the Hebrews with excessive cruelty, and are represented by the prophet, as ripping up their women with child, that they might enlarge their border, i. e. prevent the Hebrews from having any posterity ever after, to inhabit the cities that had been taken from them. Casaubon also, in his notes upon Suetonius's life of Caligula, who cruelly used to saw men asunder, produces other examples of the same atrocious punishment, and thinks it was common among the eastern people. And if these severities were now exercised upon the Ammonites in retaliation for former cruelties of the like nature, they certainly had no right to complain; and it will greatly lessen the horror that may be conceived upon account of them, and, in some measure, justify David in using them. Retaliations of this kind have been practised by the most civilized nations. Thus the Romans revenged the death of the brave Regulus, by giving up the Carthaginian captives at Rome into the power of Marcia, the wife of Regulus, who caused them to be shut up, two and two, in great chests stuck with nails, there to suffer the same torments which her husband had endured at Carthage. If to this we add, that this execution, if made at all, which however is not so very certain as some are willing to believe, it was made in revenge for an infamous outrage on majesty, the violation of the law of nations, the bringing two powerful armies to invade his dominions, the great number of his subjects that must have been lost in these two battles, while the injuries were fresh in his mind, the persons who offered them present to his view, the whole nation engaged in an unrighteous war in vindication of the insult, and some severe animadversion was in justice due to the authors and abetters of such repeated acts of violence and injustice. The character of an ambassador was held sacred and inviolable among all nations, and any injuries offered to them were thought deserving the most exemplary punishments. The Roman history affords us many remarkable instances of this nature. When the Tarentines had affronted the Roman ambassador, Posthumius, one of them, whose robe a drunken Tarentine, in the wantonness of insolence, had defiled by urinating against it, said to the citizens, "It is not a little blood that must wash and purify this garment." And when the Romans were informed of this outrage, they immediately declared war against them, took their ships from them, dismantled the city, first made them tributaries, and at last massacred great numbers of the inhabitants, and sold thirty thousand, who escaped the carnage, for slaves to the best bidder. In like manner, when the Roman deputies were treated with insolent language only by the Achaians, though they offered no injury to their persons, yet the Romans revenged it by the total destruction of Corinth, putting all the men to the sword, selling the women and children for slaves, and burning the whole city to the ground.

Let me add here also, that the greatest generals, who have been remarkable for their humanity and mildness of disposition, have sometimes thought themselves obliged to use, in terrorem, great severity towards their prisoners. Fabius Maximus, desirous of softening and taming the fierce and turbulent dispositions of the people of Celtiberia, now Arragon, was forced to do violence to his nature, and act with an apparent cruelty, by cutting off the hands of all those who had fled from the Roman garrisons to the enemy; that, by being thus maimed, they might terrify others from revolting. So also Lucullus used the Thracians, destroying many of his prisoners, some by the sword, others by fire, and as to others, cutting off their hands, which the barbarians themselves looked on as an instance of great inhumanity, as hereby they were forced to outlive their very punishments. Many more instances of the like nature may be easily produced; and let David's conduct, as a general, be considered with the same candour and equity, as we would consider that of a Roman or Grecian commander, and those executions, which he may have been supposed to have ordered on particular occasions and offenders, and that appear to have the character of great severity and cruelty, will be found capable of such an apology, as will greatly lessen the blame that hath been so liberally thrown on them, and no more be considered as indications of a disposition naturally inhuman and barbarous.

I think the punishment of crucifixion is one of the most horrid and shocking that can be inflicted, in which the hands and feet are pierced through, and the whole body is upon the stretch and rack, and the person crucified dies a lingering and exquisitely painful death; a punishment this, equally cruel and inhuman, with David's supposed saws, and harrows, and brick-kilns. Now supposing that David, instead of those instruments of death, had crucified the Ammonites by thousands before the gates of Rabbah; or supposing, that when he took the city, he had condemned all above seventeen years old to mines, or distributed them by thousands and ten thousands, into the provinces of his kingdom, to be leisurely, and in cool blood, thrown to the beasts, or forced to murder each other on theatres, for the entertainment of his blood-thirsty people; would not Mr. Bayle and his followers have cried out: Bella, horrida bella! and censured David's conduct herein as unworthy a saint, and a man after God's own heart. And yet this was what the gentle, the benevolent Titus, did to the Jews, whom the Romans, by their cruelty and oppressions, forced to take up arms against them; and who may be truly said to have fought for their liberties, of which they had been unjustly deprived. Yet, during the siege, he ordered them to be scourged and crucified before the walls of Jerusalem, by hundreds at a time, and in such large numbers, as that they wanted room to place the crosses, and crosses for the bodies of those they condemned to crucifixion. And not only this, which perhaps may be thought to admit of some apology, as done in the heat and fury of the siege, but when the siege was over, and all instances of cruelty should have ceased, he murdered them wantonly, and in cool blood, for the diversion of the provinces. When he was at Cesarea, he threw great numbers of them to the beasts, and made others of them cut each other's throats. He celebrated his brother's birthday by destroying above two thousand five hundred of them by the same methods, and with the additional cruelty of burning many of them alive; and on his father's birthday he acted with the same barbarity towards a large number of his captives at Berytus. The whole of them amounted to 97,000; and yet, would one think it, Titus thought he was a man after God's own heart, or that he executed the divine pleasure and vengeance on the Jews; for when he viewed the city after his conquest, he publicly said: "We have carried on the war agreeable to God's will, or under his favour. It is God who pulled down the Jews from their fortresses, which were unconquerable by human arms and engines."

But we need not these examples to justify David's conduct; for the more carefully I consider the scripture account of his treatment of the Ammonites, I am the more fully convinced that he did not execute these severities upon them, and that the sacred history, fairly interpreted, will warrant no such charge; and I will now venture thus to render the original words, "He brought forth the inhabitants of it, and put them to the saw, to iron-mines, and to iron-axes, and transported them to the brick-kilns," or rather, to the brick frame and bed, to make and carry bricks. He reduced them to slavery, and put them to the most servile employments of sawing, making iron harrows, or rather working in the mines, to the hewing of stones, and making and carrying of bricks. To these drudgeries, some to one, and some to another, he condemned them, or by these means brought them into entire subjection, and put it out of their power to give him any further disturbance. This interpretation is so far from being forced, as that it is entirely agreeable to the proper sense and meaning of the original words, and fully vindicates David from that inhumanity, by which some have characterized the man after God's own heart. The bella, horrida bella, all here vanish in an instant. This account may also be confirmed by the parallel place in Chronicles, where the historian tells us, that David brought them forth, and, as I would render the words, divided or separated them to the saw, to the mines and axes; agreeable to what is said in Samuel, that he removed them from their former habitations to work in these servile employments. Or they may be rendered: "He made them to cut with the saw, the harrow, and the axe," i. e. condemned them to these slavish employments. Or finally, some interpreters give this version: "He ruled over them by the saw, the mine," &c. kept them in a state of subjection, by putting them to these hard labours.

It is a further confirmation of the foregoing representation, what the historian adds: "Thus did David unto all the cities of the children of Ammon." What did he do? What! put them to death throughout all their cities, by those exquisite methods of cruelty? The thing is impossible, for then he would have totally extirpated them, and we should never have heard of them again, as a nation, in history. And yet it is certain, that within a very few years after the taking of Raboah, this very city existed, and was inhabited, and had a tributary king or viceroy; even Shobi, the son of Nahash, and therefore probably the brother of Hanun, who offered this violence to David's ambassadors. For while David was at Mahanaim, on the other side Jordan, waiting the event of Absalom's rebellion, this Shobi, among other of David's friends, brought him very large supplies of all sorts of necessaries, beds, basins, earthen vessels, wheat, barley, flower, parched corn, beans, lentile, parched pulse, honey, butter, sheep, and cheese, for himself and people; for they said, the people are hungry and weary, and thirsty in the wilderness. So that the city and country were both inhabited, and the lands cultivated, abounding with plenty of all necessaries; and therefore there could be no general massacre, or very large destruction of the inhabitants, by David. Nor is it at all probable, that had David made those cruel executions among the Ammonites, which some ascribe to him, he would have found so much friendship from them in his distresses, while the barbarities he exercised on them were fresh in their memories; but rather, that they would have wished his destruction, and at least have waited the fortune of the war, that threatened David with entire ruin, and not have supplied him, for fear of their incurring the displeasure of Absalom, who aimed at his life, that he might usurp his throne, and would not have failed, had he been victorious, to have executed a severe revenge on them, for the assistance they gave him; especially as they might have urged a very plausible plea for their not assisting him; the scarcity of the inhabitants by the late executions, had that been really the case, and the impoverishment of their lands, for want of hands to cultivate them, and by the ravages committed on them, by David's army.

Besides, we read of these Ammonites, and the inhabitants of Seir, and the Moabites, all united, and bringing a very formidable army to invade the dominions of Jehoshaphat. And though this was many years after their being subdued by David, yet it is not to be wondered at, that we hear little of them during this interval, as they were kept in strict subjection, and curbed with garrisons by the successors of David; just as the Edomites, during the same period, who, together with the Moabites, endeavoured to shake off the yoke of the Hebrew kings, but were reduced by them to their former subjection. Now it is altogether incredible, that if David had thus utterly extirpated the inhabitants of these countries, as some represent his conduct, they could, in one hundred and forty years afterward, under Jehoshaphat, have brought such a multitude of men against him, as forced him to acknowledge, in his prayer to God, that "he had no might against that great company that came against him, and that he knew not what to do;" even when he had above a million of men, mighty men of valour, ready prepared for the war. When therefore the history says, "thus did David to all the cities of the children of Ammon," the meaning can only be, that he condemned to slavery, not the whole nation, but such of the people, in their several towns and cities, as he had done to the inhabitants of Rabbah, who had been the advisers of the outrage, or principally concerned in that unrighteous war, which they carried on against him in vindication of it. The rest he permitted to dwell in their towns, and cultivate their possessions, and appointed over them Shobi, the brother of Hanun, king, as a tributary to his crown; and I doubt not in grateful remembrance of the kindness he formerly received from Nahash, Shobi's father, which was also the real reason of the congratulatory message he sent to Hanun his eldest son, upon his accession to the throne.

I would further observe, that as David certainly had a great deal of generosity and goodness in his natural temper, the sacred writers, who have, with great freedom and impartiality, mentioned his faults, and who have transmitted to us this account of his treatment of the Ammonites, have passed no censure on him for having exceeded the bounds of humanity and justice, in the punishment he inflicted on them: and from hence we may, I apprehend, justly conclude, either that it was not so severe, as it hath been generally thought, or that there were some peculiar reasons which demanded it, and which, if we were particularly acquainted with them, would, in a great measure, alleviate the appearing rigour of it; or that the law of nations, and the jus belli, then subsisting, admitted such kinds of executions upon very extraordinary occasions; though I think there are scarce any that can fully justify them. But if the account which I have given of this affair be, as I think it is, the true one, the Ammonites were treated just as they deserved, and according to what was practised by the most civilized nations, and all exclamations against the man after God's own heart, will be unreasonable and unjust.

Mr. Bayle, among others, grievously complains on this article, "Can this method," says he, "of making war be denied to be blameworthy? Have not the Turks and Tartars a little more humanity? If a vast number of pamphlets daily complain of the military executions of our own time, which are really cruel, and highly to be blamed, though mild in comparison of David's; what would not the authors of those pamphlets say at this day, had they such usage to censure, as the saws, the harrows, and brick-kilns, of David?" It is a pity this learned and candid critic should form his notion of the cruelty of some military executions by a set of pamphleteers, a sort of authors not always of the best information and credit. But what if these same pamphlet writers, should complain of the cruelty of certain military executions, that had no foundation in fact, but only in their misinterpretation of some accounts of them, which they did not understand, or could not translate rightly from the language in which they were written?

Or what if some person, assuming the character of a critic, should take upon trust his account, from these very respectable pamphlet writers, of the cruelty of some military executions, and censure the authors of them, as worse than Turks and Tartars, without ever searching himself the original relaters of them, to know whether the account of the pamphleteers were genuine or not; what censure would he not deserve from the impartial world, for propagating such false and groundless stories? I am confident Mr. Bayle never critically examined, in the original language, the account of these military executions by David, for if he had, he would certainly have found reason, at least to have suspended his judgment, if not entirely to have altered it. I should be in no pain for David's character, if I could as well defend him, in what the truth of history obliges me now to relate, as I think he may be justified in the treatment of the Ammonites.—Chandler.

Ver. 31. And he brought forth the people that *were* therein, and put *them* under saws, and under harrows of iron, and under axes of iron, and made them pass through the brick-kiln: and thus did he unto all the cities of the children of Ammon.

It seems to have been the practice of eastern kings, to command their captives, taken in war, especially those that had, by the atrociousness of their crimes, or the stoutness of their resistance, greatly provoked their indignation, to lie down on the ground, and then put to death a certain part of them, which they measured with a line, or determined by lot. This custom was not perhaps commonly practised by the people of God, in their wars with the nations around them; one instance, however, is recorded in the life of David, who inflicted this punishment on the Moabites: "And he smote Moab, and measured them with a line, casting them down to the ground; even with two lines measured he to put to death, and with one full line to keep alive; and so the Moabites became David's servants, and brought gifts." The same warlike prince inflicted a still more terrible punishment on the inhabitants of Rabbah, the capital city of Ammon, whose ill-advised king had violated the law of nations, in offering one of the greatest possible indignities to his ambassadors: "He brought out the people that were therein, and put them under saws, and under harrows of iron, and under axes of iron, and made them pass through the brick-kiln; and thus did he unto all the cities of the children of Ammon." Some of them he sawed asunder; others he tore in pieces with harrows armed with great iron teeth; or lacerated their bodies with sharp sickles or sharp stones; or rather, he dragged them through the place where bricks were made, and grated their flesh upon the ragged sherds. This dreadful punishment was meant to operate upon the fears of other princes, and prevent them from violating the right of nations in the persons of their ambassadors. These were usually persons of great worth or eminent station, who, by their quality and deportment, might command respect and attention from their very enemies. Ambassadors were accordingly held sacred among all people, even when at war; and what injuries and affronts soever had been committed, heaven and earth were thought to be concerned to prosecute the injuries done to them, with the utmost vengeance. So deep is this impression engraved on the human mind, that the Lacedemonians, who had inhumanly murdered the Persian ambassadors, firmly believed their gods would accept none of their oblations and sacrifices, which were all found polluted with direful omens, till two noblemen of Sparta were sent as an expiatory sacrifice to Xerxes, to atone for the death of his ambassadors by their own. That emperor, indeed, gave them leave to return in safety, without any other ignominy than what they suffered by a severe reflection on the Spartan nation, whose barbarous cruelty he professed he would not imitate, though he had been so greatly provoked. The divine vengeance, however, suffered them not to go unpunished, but inflicted what those men had assumed to themselves, on their sons, who being sent on an embassy into Asia, were betrayed into the hands of the Athenians, who put them to death: which Herodotus, who relates the story, considered as a just revenge from heaven, for the cruelty of the Lacedemonians. The character of ambassadors has been invested with such inviolable sanctity, by the mutual hopes and fears of nations; for if persons of that character might be treated injuriously, the friendly relations between different states could not be maintained; and all hopes of peace and reconciliation among enemies, must be banished for ever out of the world. But these considerations, although they might justify David in demanding satisfaction, and inflicting condign punishment on the king of Rabbah, cannot be reckoned a sufficient excuse for such severities. They may therefore be considered as a proof, that he was then in the state of his impenitence, in consequence of his illicit connexion with Bathsheba, when the mild, and gentle, and humane spirit of the gospel in his bosom, had suffered a mournful decline, and he was become cruel and furious, as well as lustful and incontinent. The captives taken by Amaziah, in his war with Edom, were also treated with uncommon severity, for "he took ten thousand of them alive, and brought them to the top of a rock, and cast them down, so that they were all broken in pieces."—Paxton.

CHAPTER XIII.

Ver. 6. So Amnon lay down, and made himself sick.

The Asiatics are certainly the most expert creatures I have seen in feigning themselves sick. Thus, those who wish to get off work, or any duty, complain they have a pain here, and another there: they affect to pant for breath, roll their eyes, as if in agony; and, should you touch them, they shriek out, as if you were killing them. The sepoys, and those who are servants in the government offices, give great trouble to their superiors by ever and anon complaining they are sick; and it requires great discernment to find out whether they are so, or are merely affecting it. Their general object is either to attend a marriage, or some religious festival.—Roberts.

Ver. 8. So Tamar went to her brother Amnon's house, and he was laid down. And she took flour, and kneaded *it*, and made cakes in his sight, and did bake the cakes.

In the most considerable houses of Persia, they kindle their fires, not under a chimney, as is usual with us in fireplaces, but in a kind of oven, called tinnor, about two palms from the ground, formed of a vase of burnt clay, in which they place burning coals, charcoal, or other combustible matter. The smoke from the coals is conveyed by means of a pipe from the oven under ground; and by means of another, communicating with the grated bottom of the fire, it is supplied with air. Here they cook their meat, and can bake their cakes on a flat sheet of iron laid over the tinnor, in little more than an instant of time. When the oven is not thus used, they place a plank over it in the shape of a small table, which they cover entirely, spreading over it a large cloth which extends on all sides to the ground, over a part of the floor of the chamber. By this contrivance, the heat being prevented from diffusing itself all at once, it is communicated insensibly, and so pleasantly throughout the whole apartment, that it cannot be better compared than to the effect of a stove. Persons at their meals, or in conversation, and some even sleeping, lie on the carpets round this table, supporting themselves against the walls of the apartment on cushions kept for the purpose, which likewise serve for seats in this country, the tinnor being so placed as to be equally distant from the sides of the room. Thus circumstanced, those to whom the cold is not unpleasant, put their legs under the cloth: others, who feel it more sensibly, their hands and the rest of their body. By bringing their extremities thus towards the central fire, they receive thence a mild and penetrating warmth, which diffuses itself agreeably over their whole body, without any injury to the head.—Burder.

Let it not appear strange that a king's daughter in the reign of David, was employed in this menial service; for Dr. Russel says, the eastern ladies often prepare cakes and other things in their own apartments; and some few particular dishes are cooked by themselves, but not in their apartments; on such occasions they go to some room near the kitchen. The eastern bread is made in small, thin, moist cakes: it must be eaten new, and is unfit for use when kept longer than a day. Both Russel and Rauwolf, however, mention several kinds of bread and cakes; some which are done with yolks of eggs; some which are mixed with coriander and other seeds; and some which are strewed with them; and Pitts describes a kind of biscuits, which the Mohammedan pilgrims carry from Egypt to Mecca, and back again, perfectly fresh and good. The holy scriptures accord with the narratives of modern travellers, in representing the oriental loaves as very small, three of them being required for the repast of a single person: "Which of you shall have a friend, and shall go unto him at midnight, and say unto him, Friend, lend me three loaves: for a friend of mine in his journey is come to me, and I have nothing to set before him?" It appears also from the history of Abraham, and particularly from his entertaining the three angels, that they were generally eaten new, and baked as they were needed. Sometimes, however, they were made to keep several days; for the shew-bread might be eaten after it had stood a week before the Lord. The pretence of the Gibeonites, that their bread had become mouldy from the length of the road, although it was taken fresh from the oven when they left home, proves, that bread for a journey was made to keep a considerable time. In every one of those minute circumstances, the sacred volume perfectly corresponds with the statements of modern travellers.—Paxton.

Ver. 17. Then he called his servant that ministered unto him.

Eastern masters do not keep their servants at the distance usual in England. The affairs of the family, the news of the day, and the little incidents of life, are mutually discussed, as by equals. The difference between them, in reference to property, is sometimes not great; the master has, perhaps, his small family estate, or some business which produces a little profit, and the servant is content with his rice, and a scanty cloth for his loins. No native who can afford it is without his servant, and many who can scarcely procure food for themselves, talk very largely about their domestics. See my lord seated in his verandah, chewing his beetel, and cogitating his plans: hear him at every interval say to his attendant, "What think you of that?" "Shall I succeed?" "You must assist me; I know you have great sense: let this prosper, and you shall have rings for your ears, and a turban for your head. Good: pour water on me." They go to the well, and the servant bales about a hogshead of water on his master's head. They go to the house, and then the command is, "Rub my joints and limbs." "Ah! bring my rice and curry." That finished, "Bring water to wash my mouth; pour it on my hands: a shroot and fire bring; fetch my sandals, my turban, umbrella, and beetel-box. Let us depart." Then may be seen the master stepping out with a lordly air, and the domestic at his heels, giving advice, or listening to his master's tales.—Roberts.

Ver. 19. And Tamar put ashes on her head, and rent her garment of divers colours that *was* on her, and laid her hand on her head, and went on crying.

See on Mat. 11. 21.

Ver. 21. And when King David heard of all these things, he was very wroth.

Mr. Bayle, who takes every occasion to depreciate the character of David, says that "his indulgence to his children exceeded all reasonable bounds, and that had he punished, as the crime deserved, the infamous action of his son Amnon, he would not have had the shame and uneasiness, to see another person revenge the injury done to Tamar." I suppose he means, that he should have punished Amnon with death. But Amnon was David's eldest son, and heir apparent to his throne and kingdom, and he might not think it prudent, or that it would have been well taken by the nation, if he had put him to death without consulting them. And this would have been exposing, in the most public manner, the disgrace of his own family, which he thought it was best to conceal, as far as he was able. That David did not punish Amnon in some very exemplary manner, is more than Mr. Bayle could be sure of. There are some circumstances that make it very probable he did. The history assures us, that when David heard of the affair, he was very wroth. And it is very natural to suppose he made Amnon feel the effects of it. He seems to have put him under arrest and confinement, and allowed him to go nowhere without his express leave. For when Absalom invited the king and all his servants to go to his sheepshearing feast, and the king denied him, he particularly pressed him to let Amnon go with him; which shows, that, though all the other sons of David easily obtained leave to attend Absalom, yet that Amnon was under greater restraint than all the rest, otherwise there would have been no need for him particularly to have pressed David to grant Amnon leave to accompany him, or reason why David should with difficulty and reluctance grant it. This was two full years after Amnon's affair with Tamar. So long a confinement as this to a king's eldest son, was itself a very severe punishment, and probably attended with several circumstances, that rendered it peculiarly grievous. It is not however consistent with candour to accuse men of faults, which there is no real proof of, and especially when there are some intimations, that they never committed them; or to aggravate them beyond the real demerit. One cannot help observing here, how David's adultery with Bathsheba was punished by his son's incest with his sister Tamar; and as he now saw the threatenings of God by Nathan beginning to take place, he had too much reason to fear they should be all of them executed to the full. It was a circumstance also that must greatly affect him, that he had been, though unwillingly, a sort of accessary to Amnon's crime, by yielding so readily to Amnon's desire, of having his sister sent to him; the very proposal he made of her dressing and receiving his food from her, seeming enough to create some suspicion in David, that he had some design upon Tamar, which he ought to have been peculiarly careful to guard against. But probably Amnon had never offended him, nor given any occasion to suspect him capable of so heinous a crime, as he was now meditating, and therefore David more easily consented, that his sister should have the liberty of attending him.—Chandler.

Ver. 39. And *the soul of* King David longed to go forth unto Absalom: for he was comforted concerning Amnon, seeing he was dead.

The Hebrew has, for *longed*, "*was consumed.*" A person labouring under an intense desire for the possession of an object, says, "My soul is consumed for it," meaning that his spirit is wasting away by the intensity of his wishes. "My life is burning away through fear." "My spirit is consuming for his safety."—Roberts.

CHAPTER XIV.

Ver. 2. And Joab sent to Tekoah, and fetched thence a wise woman, and said unto her, I pray thee, feign thyself to be a mourner, and put on now mourning apparel, and anoint not thyself with oil, but be as a woman that had a long time mourned for the dead.

It is a curious fact, that the Hindoos do not put on what is called mourning at the death of their friends. The relations take off their ear-rings and other ornaments, and neglect the dressing of their hair. A woman, on the death of her husband, takes off the thali (equivalent to the marriage ring) from her neck; and formerly she used to shave her head; but in all other respects she dresses as before. Those who are sick, as they suppose, under the influence of Saturn, generally wear something black, or have marks of that colour on their clothes, as they believe the indisposition is in this way removed.—Roberts.

Ointments were in great esteem and constant use among the ancients, as the means of cleanliness, and to give a grateful odour to their bodies, as these ointments were mixed up with the richest perfumes. At their festivals, especially among the rich and prosperous, they used them for the refreshment of their guests, and to render the entertainment more acceptable and delightful. But as great affliction and distress naturally create negligence of person and dress, they forbore anointing themselves at such seasons, as inconsistent with the condition of mourners.—CHANDLER.

Ver. 7. And so they shall quench my coal which is left, and shall not leave to my husband *neither* name nor remainder upon the earth.

So said the woman of Tekoah, who went with a fictitious story to David, in order to induce him to recall Absalom. She affected to be a widow, and said that one of her sons had killed the other, and that now the family demanded his life as an atonement for that of his brother; and she said, that if they succeeded they would QUENCH her COAL. But the life is sometimes called the light, as in chap. xxi. 17, which in the margin is translated "candle, or lamp." Both the comparisons include the idea of fire. Formerly, and even now, it is not uncommon for travellers to have to *purchase* their fire before they can cook their victuals. Hence it is common, when neighbours ask for a light in the morning, to be answered, by way of pleasantry, "You want fire—well, where is your money?" Children in Ceylon are not called coals, but SPARKS. It is said of a man who has a large family, "He has plenty of *porrekal*, i. e. sparks." Those who are favoured with fine children, are said to have large sparks. Of those whose children are all dead, "Alas! their sparks are all quenched." To a person who is injuring an only child, it is said, "Ah! leave him alone, he is the only spark."—ROBERTS.

Ver. 17. Then thy handmaid said, The word of my lord the king shall now be comfortable: for as an angel of God, so *is* my lord the king, to discern good and bad; therefore the LORD thy God will be with thee.

Thus did the woman of Tekoah compliment David, and thus did Mephibosheth address him, when he had been slandered by Ziba. Great men are often compared to the messengers (the true meaning of angel) of the gods. Thus men of great wisdom or eloquence are said to be like the angels of the gods. "Ah! my lord, you know all things: you are one of the angels of the gods." Sometimes the person will not address you in a direct way, but speak as to a third person, loud enough for you to hear. "Ah! what wisdom he has; there is nothing concealed from him. Whence has he had his wisdom? from the gods—Yes, yes, all things are known to him." Then turning to you, they look humbly in your face, and say, "My lord, there are only two for me: God is the first; but you are the second."—ROBERTS.

The compliments which they addressed to their princes, and the manner in which they spoke of them, were not less hyperbolical. The address of the wise woman of Tekoah to David, furnishes a memorable example of the extravagant adulation in which they indulged, and which seems to have been received with entire satisfaction by one of the wisest and holiest of men: "As an angel of God, so is my lord the king, to discern good and bad;" and again, "My lord is wise according to the wisdom of an angel of God, to know all things that are in the earth." Equally hyperbolical was the reply of a Persian grandee to Chardin, who objected to the price which the king had set upon a pretty rich trinket: "Know that the kings of Persia have a general and full knowledge of matters, as sure as it is extensive; and that equally in the greatest and in the smallest things, there is nothing more just and sure than what they pronounce." This incident admirably shows the strong prepossession of these Asiatics in favour of their kings, or rather of their own slavery; and gives some plausibility to the remark of Mr. Harmer, that there may be more of real persuasion in such addresses than we are ready to apprehend. In the estimation of the Persian courtier, the knowledge of his prince was like that of an angel of God. If the ancient Egyptians supposed their princes were possessed of equal knowledge and sagacity, which is not improbable, the compliment of Judah to his brother Joseph was a very high one, and, at the same time, couched in the most artful terms: "Thou art even as Pharaoh;" knowing, and wise, and equitable as he. But it cannot be inferred, with any degree of certainty, from these customs, that either the Persian grandee, or the brother of Joseph, really believed such compliments were due. The former, most probably, thought it incumbent upon him to support the dignity of his master, especially in the presence of many of his nobles, or expressed himself in such extravagant terms, merely in compliance with the etiquette of the court; and as for Judah, it was his desire to sooth with good words and fair speeches the second ruler in Egypt, whose resentment he knew it was death to incur; and no compliment could be supposed more acceptable to an Egyptian grandee, than the one which he paid to his unknown brother. The same remark applies, with little variation, to the woman of Tekoah; her design was to sooth the mind of her sovereign, to mitigate, and, if possible, to extinguish his just resentment of the atrocious murder which Absalom had committed, and procure the restoration of the fratricide to his country, and the presence of his father.—PAXTON.

Ver. 24. And the king said, Let him turn to his own house, and let him not see my face. So Absalom returned to his own house, and saw not the king's face.

Few things are more offensive in the East than to refuse to show yourself to those who come to see you. Send your servant to say you are engaged, or that the individual may go, and he will be distressed, or enraged, and not hesitate to express his feelings. Should there, however, be any reason to hope, he will wait for hours at your door; nay, he will come day after day, till he shall have seen your face. They have an opinion, that if they once gain admission into your presence, a great point is attained, and so it is; for, what with their eloquence, and tears, and abject submissions, they seldom fail to make an impression. Even low people, who have no particular business, often call upon you that they may be able to say that they have seen your face. When a person says he has not seen the face of the great man, it means, that he has not gained his suit. See the high caste native passing along the road; an humble suppliant is there to attract his attention: and let him turn his face another way, and it is a dagger through the poor man's soul.—ROBERTS.

Ver. 26. And when he polled his head, (for it was at every year's end that he polled *it;* because *the hair* was heavy on him, therefore he polled it:) he weighed the hair of his head at two hundred shekels after the king's weight.

See on 1 Pet. 3. 3.

The eastern ladies are remarkable for the length, and the great number of the tresses of their hair: the men there, on the contrary, wear very little hair on their heads now, but they do not seem always to have done so. That the eastern women now are remarkable for the quantity of the hair of their heads, and their pride in adorning it, appears from the quotation from Dr. Shaw under a preceding observation. Lady Mary Wortley Montague abundantly confirms it: their "hair hangs at full length behind," she tells us, "divided into tresses, braided with pearl or riband, which is also in great quantity. I never saw in my life so many fine heads of hair. In one lady's I have counted a hundred and ten of these tresses, all natural; but it must be owned that every kind of beauty is more common here than with us." The men there, on the contrary, shave all the hair off their heads, excepting one lock; and those that wear their hair are thought effeminate. I have met with both these particulars in Sir J. Chardin. As to the last, he says in his note on 1 Cor. xi. 14, that what the Apostle mentions there is the custom of the East: the men are shaved, the women nourish their hair with great fondness, which they lengthen by tresses and tufts of silk, down to the heels. The young men who wear their hair, in the East, are looked upon as effeminate and infamous. It appears from this passage of the Corinthians, that in the days of St. Paul, the women wore their hair long, the men short, and that the Apostle thought this a natural distinction. It does not however appear it was always thought so, or, at least, that the wearing long hair by the men was thought infamous, since it was esteemed a beauty in Absalom, 2 Sam. xiv. 26. That passage is curious, and requires some consideration, as being attended with some difficulties; and, I am afraid, somewhat improperly explained.

The weight of the hair, which seems to be enormously great, is the first thing that occurs to the mind. Two hundred shekels, at two hundred and ninety grains each, make forty-three thousand and eight hundred grains. This is rather more than one hundred ounces avoirdupois, for four hundred and thirty-seven grains and a half are equal to such an ounce. It is a very good English head of hair, I am told, that weighs five ounces; if Absalom's then weighed one hundred ounces, it was very extraordinary. Some very learned men, I think, have believed a royal shekel was but half the weight of the sacred shekel; be it so; yet fifty ounces, ten times the weight of a good British head of hair, seems to be too great an allowance. To suppose, as some have done, that adventitious matters, united with the hair, are to be taken in to make up the weight, seems to me not a little idle: what proof would this have been of his possessing an extraordinary fine head of hair, since it would be possible to attach to the hair of a man half bald, substances that should weigh one hundred ounces? Commentators then should by no means talk of the oil, the fragrant substances, the gold dust, with which they suppose the hair might be powdered, as making up this weight; they might as well have added ornaments of gold, ribands, or what answered them, artificial tresses of hair, and all the matters that are now in different methods fastened to the hair: but would not this have been ridiculous? It is more reasonable to say, the present reading may be faulty, as in other cases there have frequently been mistakes in numbers; or that we were not sure what number of grains two hundred shekels, after the king's weight, was equal to; than to attempt to remove the difficulty by such an incompetent method. It was an uncommonly fine head of hair, of very unusual weight, which is all that we know with certainty about it.

The shaving off all this hair, for so the original word signifies, is a second thing that seems very strange. It was this thought, I should imagine, that led our translators to render the word by the English term polled, or cut short: for it seems very unaccountable, that a prince who prided himself so much in the quantity of his hair, should annually shave it off quite close; and for what purpose? would not the shortening of it have relieved him from its excessive weight? not to say, that the hair of one year's growth can, in the common course of things, be of no great length, or weigh very much. The word elsewhere signifies to shave off all the hair; is opposed to polling, or trimming the hair a little by shortening it; and was necessary in order to gain the knowledge of the true weight of the hair. Mourners shaved themselves, Job i. 20; and those that had been in a state of bitterness when they presented themselves before kings, as appears from what is related of Joseph, Gen. xli. 14; if then "from the end of days," which is the original expression, may be understood to mean at the end of the time of his returning to his own house, and not seeing the king's face, instead of at the end of the year, then the shaving himself may be thought to express one single action, and to describe, in part, the manner in which he presented himself before the king. This would make the prophetic account very natural. But then the word כבד *kabed*, translated *heavy*, must be understood in another sense, a sense in which it is sometimes used, if we have no regard to the Masoretic points, namely, as signifying in glory, or honour, or something of that sort. And so the general meaning of the passage will be, "And when he shaved his head, and it was in the end of the days, of the days of his disgrace, that is, at the time in which he was to shave, because it was a glory upon him, and he shaved himself and weighed the hair of his head, two hundred shekels after the king's weight." But does not St. Paul suppose, that nature teaches us, that if a man have long hair, it is shame unto him, 1 Cor. xi. 14? He certainly does; Absalom's hair however is evidently spoken of in the book of Samuel, as what was thought to be part of his beauty, 2 Sam. xiv. 25: whether it was that they had different notions on this point in the age of David; or that they thought it rather effeminate, but however a beauty.—HARMER.

CHAPTER XV.

Ver. 13. And there came a messenger to David,
saying, The hearts of the men of Israel are after
Absalom. 14. And David said unto all his ser
vants that *were* with him at Jerusalem, Arise, and
let us flee; for we shall not *else* escape from
Absalom: make speed to depart, lest he overtake us suddenly, and bring evil upon us, and
smite the city with the edge of the sword.

One cannot help being surprised, at first view, how so excellent a prince as David was, who had exalted the kingdom of Israel to so high a degree of glory and power, who had subdued and rendered tributary all the neighbouring nations, which had so often oppressed them, who had made the best and wisest regulations for the honourable performance of the solemnities of their public worship, who, in the whole course of his reign, had administered justice and judgment to all his people, and who certainly deserved to be loved and esteemed by all ranks and degrees of them, for the happiness they enjoyed under his government; I say, one cannot help wondering at the sudden revolution that was brought about in favour of an ungrateful and perfidious son, who was well known to have stained his hands with the blood of his elder brother. But there were many things that concurred to bring it about. By the death of Amnon he became heir-apparent to the crown, and being suspicious that the king his father might exclude him from the succession, upon the account of his character and crimes, he resolved to stick at no measures to obtain his ambitious views, and put it out of his father's power to set him aside. To accomplish this, being the handsomest man in Israel, he showed himself everywhere in public, to captivate with his person all that beheld him. He then set up a princely equipage to attract their admiration of his splendour and magnificence. He treated all that approached him with great condescension and affability; and as any were approaching the city from the other tribes of Israel, to have their causes heard before the king, he, in the most friendly manner, inquired of them, of what tribe they were, and hoped their cause was good; but reproached his father with remissness of government, and neglect of his people; telling them, that how just soever their cause was, they could have no audience, and that there was no man deputed of the king to hear them; wishing, for their sakes, that he was constituted a judge in the land, that every man, who had any suit or cause, might come to him, and have immediate justice done him; and thus persuaded them to return home, without making any application for a hearing, discontented with the king's government, and highly pleased with Absalom's condescension and goodness; greatly disposed to spread disaffection and sedition in the places to which they respectively belonged. And in order to secure the popularity he courted, whoever approached him to pay their respects to him, as the king's son, he familiarly took by the hand and embraced him. By these means he won the affections of great numbers among all the tribes; who, though probably at first they had no design of deposing the king, and advancing Absalom in his room, wished to see him intrusted with the principal administration of affairs under his father, and were willing to enter into any measures with him to obtain it, and to prevent his exclusion from the throne after his father. Besides this, he sent emissaries throughout all the tribes to strengthen his interest, and to secure a good body of men to join him, whenever his affairs required their assistance.

Absalom did not at first open his intentions of dethroning his father, but wished only to be a judge in the land; following herein the crafty counsel of Ahithophel, who was David's chief counsellor, and treated by him as his intimate friend, and who having been admitted to his secrets, probably informed Absalom of his father's design to exclude him from the succession, in favour of one of his younger brethren; advising him, what steps he should take in order to prevent it. His appearance to countenance the rebellion allured many to become partners in it, as he was esteemed the ablest politician in the kingdom. What added further strength to it was, Amasa, David's own nephew, joined the conspiracy, and putting himself at the head of the rebel army, who, by his relation to the king, was a man of great consequence, and an able soldier, and who therefore would be thought by many incapable of entering into a conspiracy against his uncle to dethrone him, without some very great and justifiable causes. It may be added, that Absalom's carrying off with him two hundred of the principal citizens of Jerusalem, and retaining them with his followers at Hebron, where the standard of the rebellion was first set up, added to the credit of the cause, and drew in many to abet and support it, who could not know but they engaged voluntarily in Absalom's party, and were not drawn in to espouse his interest by subtlety and force. Nor must it be forgot here, that the providence of God permitted the conspiracy to go on without discovery, and to arise to that height, as to drive David from his throne, and thus bring on him the punishments he had threatened him with by Nathan the prophet, for his sin in the matter of Bathsheba and Uriah. All these circumstances together considered, it is no wonder that Absalom should draw together a number of men sufficient to oppose and oppress his father, who suspected nothing of the conspiracy formed against him, and who appears to have had no part of his army with him, but some of his officers and ordinary guards, and which therefore made him take the resolution of retiring from Jerusalem, to prevent his being surprised by a superior force, that he knew himself unable to resist. But then it should be considered, that this sudden insurrection was not the effect of a general or national disaffection to his person and government. This is evident from many hints in the sacred history. The best part of the inhabitants of Jerusalem were firmly attached to him, and followed him in his retreat from the capital, and all the country through which he went, showed their affection to him by loud acclamations. The Cherethites and Pelethites, the Gittites, and the ablest of his officers, continued steadfast in their attachment to him, and followed his fortune. The tribes on the other side Jordan gladly received him, and the richest persons of that country supplied him and his forces with all necessary provisions, and he soon collected among them an army sufficient to check the rebels, and at one blow to crush the rebellion. And this was no sooner known, than the tribes in general were all in motion to show their loyalty to the king, and restore him to his throne and government. The truth is, that David was surprised unawares and unprovided, by a wicked and impious faction, who had, by their emissaries, drawn together a large body of men, wherever they could pick them up, among all the tribes; gaining over, probably, some well-minded persons, by lies, and slanderous reports of the king's government, and such others, as, in all nations, are always ready to enter into any measures of wickedness and violence, in hopes of making their advantage by the public confusion and calamity, by those methods which are constantly practised by profligate conspirators, in order to gratify their pride, ambition, and revenge, though at the expense of the religion, liberties, and prosperity of their country. And it is therefore no wonder, that this rebellion, which was evidently contrary to the general sense and inclination of the people, was so suddenly suppressed, and David's restoration to his throne and government was immediately resolved on by the unanimous consent of all the tribes of Israel; whereby God was graciously pleased to put an end to his troubles, bringing him in safety to his capital and palace, and preserving his life, till he happily settled the succession on Solomon his son, the wisest of princes, and the most prosperous monarch in the world.—Chandler.

Ver. 30. And David went up by the ascent of *mount* Olivet, and wept as he went up, and had his head covered, and he went barefoot.

Thus did David conduct himself in his sorrow, when Absalom had rebelled against him. But the Hindoos do not cover the head; they take a part of their robe and cover the face. In going to a funeral, the turban is generally taken off, and a part of the garment is held over the face. Nor is this merely common at funerals, for on all occasions of deep sorrow they observe the same thing. At such times, also, they always go "*barefoot.*"—Roberts.

This was an indication of great distress: for in ancient times the shoes of great and wealthy persons were made of very rich materials, and ornamented with jewels, gold, and silver. When any great calamity befell them, either public or private, they not only stripped themselves of these ornaments, but of their very shoes, and walked barefoot. In this manner, prisoners taken in war were forced to walk, both for punishment and disgrace.—Burder.

Ver. 32. And it came to pass, that *when* David was come to the top *of the mount*, where he worshipped God, behold, Hushai the Archite came to meet him with his coat rent, and earth upon his head: 33. Unto whom David said, If thou passest on with me, then thou shalt be a burden unto me: 34. But if thou return to the city, and say unto Absalom, I will be thy servant, O king; *as* I *have been* thy father's servant hitherto, so *will* I now also *be* thy servant: then mayest thou for me defeat the counsel of Ahithophel.

Mr. Bayle calls this "the most treacherous piece of villany that can be imagined." But he might have spared the reflection, for he could easily have produced instances of much greater villany than this, practised for the most criminal and execrable purposes. Hushai's treachery was to prevent the effects of the most detestable treachery, and an instance of loyalty and fidelity to his king and country. His villany was the dictate of public spirit and patriotism, and to counteract the plots of a most desperate and bloody villain, who advised the murder of a father, and incest with his wives, in support of an unnatural, ambitious, and desperate son. How far these policies of princes and great men, are reconcileable with the rules of those rigid casuists of which Mr. Bayle speaks, I pretend not to determine. This I know, that without these and the like stratagems, government cannot be frequently supported, and that the most nefarious attempts to destroy all that is valuable to mankind can never be defeated; and that they have been practised by the best and wisest of princes, who have been so far from being blamed on account of them, as that they have been recorded as the proofs of their wisdom, and regard to the honour and interest of their country. And this Mr. Bayle himself confesses, when he says, that "stratagems of this nature are undoubtedly very laudable, if we judge of things according to human prudence, and the politics of sovereigns." If David therefore acted in this affair, according to the rules of human prudence, and the constant policy of sovereigns, why should he be censured more than other great and excellent princes, who have acted like him? Especially as he had none of those rigid casuists about him, who judged this conduct unworthy a saint and an honest man. Supposing this conduct not quite reconcileable with the rules of rigid casuistry, yet, if David was not acquainted with them, he might possibly be a saint and an honest man, if he did not regard them. If Hushai had stabbed Absalom to the heart, under pretence of friendship, as Brutus did Cæsar, must not those who defend Brutus, defend Hushai too? But is it a more base and criminal part, by pretences of friendship, to betray a tyrant's, a usurper's, a parricide's counsels, than, in like circumstances, to assassinate him? I leave David's censurers fairly to state this important point of casuistry: Whether it be in itself absolutely unlawful to make use of stratagems, i. e. arts of deception, in the management of wars between princes and states: If not, in what instances they are lawful, and reconcileable with the rigid rules of morality and virtue. When these points are settled, we shall be the better able to determine concerning the morality and honesty of David and his friend Hushai in the instance before us; and, till this is done, Mr. Bayle's charges will appear to be uncandid and groundless. I have only to add, that David's character, as a man after God's own heart, in the scripture sense of it, by no means implies, that, as a prince, he should always act according to the rules of morality laid down by rigid casuists; or, that he should not, in the management of his wars, and defeating unnatural rebellions, act with the usual policy of wise and good princes, and make use of proper stratagems, when necessary to the defence of his country, and the safety of his person.

In Cicero's consulate, the conspiracy of Catiline broke out, and it was fully discovered by that great consul's vigilance, prudence, and policy. Ambassadors from the Allobroges, the ancient inhabitants of Savoy and Piedmont, were then at Rome to solicit the senate for the removal of their grievances. Umbrenius, one of the conspirators, attempted to bring over these ambassadors, to engage in the scheme that had been concerted for the destruction of Rome. In order to this he opened to them the nature of the conspiracy, named the principal persons concerned in it, and promised them every thing they desired, if they would engage their nation to join with them in support of it. The ambassadors, upon considering the affair, discovered the whole conspiracy to Fabius Sanga, as they had been informed of it by Umbrenius. Sanga immediately acquaints the consul with it, and introduced the ambassadors themselves to him. What doth he do? Why, like a very wicked and ungodly man, as the scrupulous and righteous Mr. Bayle to be sure thought him, bid them carry on the pretence, warmly favouring the conspiracy, go to as many of the conspirators as they could, make them fair promises, and use all their endeavours fully to discover them. The ambassadors, as Cicero ordered, met them, and demanded from the chief of them an oath, to be signed with their own hand, that their countrymen might be more easily induced, to give them that assistance which they desired of them. They all but one, without suspicion of any design, signed the oath. The ambassadors discovered all to Cicero, who immediately seized the principal conspirators, and greatly rejoiced, that as the conspiracy was discovered, the city was delivered from the danger that immediately threatened it. The senate thought that Cicero had acted a noble patriotic part, for they immediately decreed, that public thanks should be given to him in the most solemn manner, by whose virtue, counsel, and providence, the republic was delivered from the extremest dangers; and that a public thanksgiving should be rendered to the gods, in Cicero's name, for his having delivered the city from being laid in ashes, the citizens from a massacre, and Italy from a war. Now did Cicero act in this affair as a patriot and an honest man? Or did he, by this policy, damn himself, and damn the ambassadors? by causing them to feign, that they embraced the party of those men, they designed effectually to destroy? What censure would he not have undergone, had he suffered the conspiracy to take place, and his country to be ruined, by refusing to make use of that policy which was necessary to discover and defeat the conspiracy? Of two evils, it is an old maxim, a man must choose the least, when he is under the necessity of submitting to one. Thus were David and Cicero circumstanced. They both chose the patriotic part; and, as Cicero is justly celebrated as the Father and Saviour of his country, from the ruin that was intended, David will deserve the like commendation, for defeating, by like measures, the projects of impious conspirators, and delivering the nation from the destruction that threatened them.—CHANDLER.

CHAPTER XVI.

Ver. 1. And when David was a little past the top *of the hill*, behold, Ziba the servant of Mephibosheth met him, with a couple of asses saddled, and upon them two hundred *loaves* of bread, and a hundred bunches of raisins, and a hundred of summer fruits, and a bottle of wine.

See on 2 Kings 4. 8.

Ziba met David, according to the sacred historian, 2 Sam. xvi. 1, with a couple of asses, and upon them two hundred loaves of bread, a hundred bunches of raisins, a hundred of *summer fruits*, and a bottle of wine. These summer fruits the Septuagint supposes were *dates*, but the more common opinion is that they were figs, which it seems was that also of the Chaldee paraphrast. Grotius, however, supposes the original word signifies the fruits of trees in general. I cannot adopt any of these opinions. If the notes of distinction are not numerous enough, or sufficiently clear, to determine with precision what the fruit was, I believe they are sufficient to satisfy us that these authors were mistaken. We may gather three things relating to them: that they were of some considerable size, since their quantity was estimated by tale; that they came before the bean season was ended, for after this we find that the inhabitants of the country beyond Jordan sent to David, along with other provisions, quantities of beans, 2 Sam. xviii. 28, they being things, according to Dr. Shaw, that, after they are boiled and stewed with oil and garlic, constitute the principal food, in the spring, of persons of all distinctions; and they were thought by Ziba a suitable refreshment to those that were travelling in a wilderness, where it was to be supposed they would be thirsty as well as hungry. Nothing then could be more unhappy, or more strongly mark out the inattention of the translators of the Septuagint for it cannot be imagined they were ignorant of these matters, than the rendering this word, in this place, *dates*, which are neither produced in summer, nor suited to allay the heat of that season: Dr. Pococke observing that they are not ripe till November; and that they are esteemed of a hot nature, Providence seeming to have designed them, as they are warm food, to comfort the stomach, he thinks, during the cold season, in a country where it has not given wine, for he is there speaking concerning Egypt. When then I find that *watermelons* grow spontaneously in these hot countries, are made use of by the Arabs of the Holy Land in summer instead of water, to quench their thirst, and are purchased as of the greatest use to travellers in thirsty deserts; and that cucumbers are very much used still in that country to mitigate the heat: I am very much inclined to believe these summer fruits were not the produce of trees, but of this class of herbs, which creep along the ground, and produce fruits of a cooling moisture, and very large in proportion to the size of the plant. They could scarcely however be *watermelons*, I imagine, because they do not begin to gather them before June; but *cucumbers*, which come in May, and were actually eaten in Galilee the latter end of that month by Dr. Pococke, he having stopped at an Arab tent, where they prepared him eggs and sour milk, he tells us, cutting into it raw cucumbers as a cooling diet in that season, which he found very hot: cucumbers continued at Aleppo to the end of July, and are brought again to market in September and October, and consequently are contemporaries with grapes and olives, according to Jer. xl. 10—12, as well as with beans and lentils. Dr. Russel also tells us that the squash comes in towards the end of September, and continues all the year; but that the orange-shaped pumpion is more common in the summer months. Of one or other of these kinds of fruit, I should think the writer of 2 Sam. designed to be understood: they are all more or less of considerable size; they are contemporary with beans; and fit for them that have to travel through a dry wilderness, in the latter part of the spring, when the weather grows hot, as Pococke found it, about which time, from the circumstance of the beans and the lentils, it is plain that David fled from Absalom. If this be allowed, it will appear that they were called summer fruits, from their being eaten to allay the summer heats, not from their being dried in the summer, as Vatablus strangely imagines; nor from their being produced only that time of the year; for this passage shows that they were come to maturity before beans went out, and consequently before summer.—HARMER.

Ver. 3. And the king said, And where *is* thy master's son? And Ziba said unto the king behold he abideth at Jerusalem: for he said, to-day shall the house of Israel restore me the kingdom of my father. 4. Then said the king to Ziba, Behold, thine *are* all that *pertained* unto Mephibosheth. And Ziba said, I humbly beseech thee *that* I may find grace in thy sight, my lord, O king.

Not the least material exception that objectors make to David's conduct, in this period of time, is his making a grant of Mephibosheth's estate to a perfidious servant without ever giving the master a fair hearing. But, how could David have leisure to send for Mephibosheth from mount Olivet to Jerusalem, and inquire into the merits of the cause depending between him and his servant, when he was in so great a hurry, and under flight from the arms of his rebel son? Or how could he suppose that Ziba could have dared to have told him so notorious a lie, when it might in a short time be disproved? Every circumstance, in short, on Ziba's side, looked well, but none on his master's. To his master, David had been extremely kind, in restoring him to the forfeited estate of his grandfather Saul and in allowing him to eat at his own table, as one of the king's sons; and now, at the general rendezvous of his friends, David might well have expected that the person to whom he had extended so many favours, should not have been so negligent of his duty, as to absent himself, unless it had been upon some extraordinary business; and therefore, when Ziba acquaints him with the occasion of his absence, though it was a mere fiction, yet with David it might find a readier credence, because, at this time, he had reason to mistrust everybody; and seeing his own family disconcerted and broken; might think the crown liable to fall to any new claimant that could pretend to the same right of succession that Mephibosheth might. On the contrary, every thing appeared bright and plausible on Ziba's side. He, though but a servant, came to join the king, and instead of adhering to his master's pretended schemes of advancement, had expressed his duty to his rightful sovereign, in bringing him a considerable present, enough to engage his good opinion. The story that he told of his master likewise, though utterly false, was cunningly contrived, and fitly accommodated to the nature of the times; so that, in this situation of affairs, as wise a man as David might have been induced to believe the whole to be true, and upon the presumption of its being so, might have proceeded to pass a judgment of forfeiture (as in most eastern countries every crime against the state was always attended with such a forfeiture) upon Mephibosheth's estate, and to consign the possession of it to another. All that David can therefore be blamed for, in this whole transaction, is an error in judgment, even when he was imposed upon by the plausible tale of a sycophant, and had no opportunity of coming at the truth; but upon his return to Jerusalem, when Mephibosheth appears before him, and pleads his own cause, we find this the decision of it,—"Why speakest thou any more of thy matters? I have said, thou and Ziba divide the land:" which words must not be understood as if he appointed at the time an equal division of the estate between Mephibosheth and his servant, (for where would the justice of such a sentence be?) but rather, that he revoked the order he had given to Ziba, upon the supposed forfeiture of his master, and put things now upon the same establishment they were at first. "I have said," i. e. "My first grant shall stand, when I decreed that Mephibosheth should be lord of the whole estate, and Ziba his steward to manage it for him." Thus, though we are not obliged to vindicate David in every passage of his life, and think some of the crying sins he was guilty of utterly inexcusable, yet (if we except these) we cannot but think that, although he was a very tender and indulgent parent, yet he was no encourager of vice in his own family, or tame conniver at it in others, had he not been restrained, by reasons of state, sometimes from punishing it; that he was true to his promises, just in his distributions, and prudent, though not crafty, in his military transactions; "of a singular presence of mind, (as Josephus speaks of him,) to make the best of what was before him, and of as sharp a foresight for improving of all advantages, and obviating all difficulties, that were like to happen;" tender to all persons in distress, kind to his friends, forgiving to his enemies, and, when at any time he was forced to use severity, was only in retaliation of what other people had done to him.—STACKHOUSE.

Ver. 13. And as David and his men went by the way, Shimei went along on the hill's side over against him, and cursed as he went, and threw stones at him, and cast dust.

Who, in the East, has not often witnessed a similar scene? Listen to the maledictions: they are of such a nature that evil spirits only could have suggested them. Look at the enraged miscreant: he dares not come near for fear of punishment, but he stands at a distance, vociferates his imprecations, violently throws about his hands; then stoops to the ground, and takes up handfuls of dust, throws it in the air, and exclaims, "Soon shalt thou be as that—thy mouth shall soon be full of it—look, look, thou cursed one, as this dust, so shalt thou be."—ROBERTS.

In the East, the right of calling an offender to account is claimed either by the person who receives the injury, or his nearest relation; and the same person, with the permission or connivance of his people, sustains at once the character of party, judge, and executioner. In such a state of things, we are not to be surprised if the exercise of justice be often precipitate and tumultuary. The act of the Philistines, in burning the spouse of Samson and her father with fire, was entirely of this character; not the result of a regular sentence, but the summary vengeance of an incensed multitude. In the law of Moses, the right of the private avenger was distinctly recognised; but to prevent the dreadful effects of sudden and personal vengeance, cities of refuge were appointed at convenient distances through the land of promise, to which the manslayer might flee for safety, till he could be brought to a regular trial, before a court of justice. In almost every part of Asia, those who demand justice against a criminal throw dust upon him, signifying that he deserves to lose his life, and be cast into the grave; and that this is the true interpretation of the action, is evident from an imprecation in common use among the Turks and Persians, Be covered with earth; Earth be upon thy head. We have two remarkable instances of casting dust recorded in scripture; the first is that of Shimei, who gave vent to his secret hostility to David, when he fled before his rebellious son, by throwing stones at him, and casting dust. It was an ancient custom, in those warm and arid countries, to lay the dust before a person of distinction, and particularly before kings and princes, by sprinkling the ground with water. To throw dust into the air while a person was passing, was therefore an act of great disrespect; to do so before a sovereign prince, an indecent outrage. But it is clear from the explanation of the custom, that Shimei meant more than disrespect and outrage to an afflicted king, whose subject he was; he intended to signify by that action, that David was unfit to live, and that the time was at last arrived to offer him a sacrifice to the ambition and vengeance of the house of Saul.—PAXTON.

Ver. 20. Then said Absalom to Ahithophel, Give counsel among you what we shall do. 21. And Ahithophel said unto Absalom, Go in unto thy father's concubines, which he hath left to keep the house; and all Israel shall hear that thou art abhorred of thy father.

The wives of the conquered king were always the property of the conqueror: and, in possessing these, he appeared to possess the right to the kingdom. Herodotus, b. iii. cap. 68. informs us, that Smerdis having seized on the Persian throne, after the death of Cambyses, espoused all the wives of his predecessor.

The choosing or confirming of a new king in Guinea, seldom continues long in dispute; for the eldest son no sooner hears of the king's death, than he immediately makes his interest among his friends, to take possession of the late king's court and wives: and succeeding happily in these particulars, he need not doubt the remainder, for the commonalty will not easily consent that after that he shall be driven from the throne: this seems somewhat like Absalom's design on his father David. To accomplish this design, the younger brother's party are always careful enough that he is near at hand, in order to take possession of the court. (Bosman's Guinea.) The name of Quiteva is common to the sovereign lord of the country bordering on the river Sofala in Ethiopia. He maintains a number of wives, the chief of whom are his near relations, and are denominated his queens; the residue are regarded merely as concubines. As soon as the Quiteva ceases to live, a successor is chosen, capable of governing with wisdom and prudence; and, indeed, should he be deficient in this respect, it would be enough that a majority of the king's concubines should join in his favour, as on these the possession of the throne depends. He therefore repairs to the royal palace, where he meets with some of the concubines of the late king, and with their consent he seats himself on the throne prepared for him in the midst of a large hall; when seated here, a curtain is drawn before him and his wives: hence he issues orders for his proclamation through the streets; this is the signal for the people to flock to render him homage and swear obedience, a ceremony which is performed amid great rejoicings.—BURDER.

From the polygamy of the Israelitish monarchs, there arose a singular law, which I can only illustrate by examples from the Bible, without finding any thing similar in profane history; which, however, only makes these examples the clearer. It consisted in this, that the successor to the crown inherited the seraglio of his predecessor; and it was considered as a step to the throne, even to marry the mistresses of the deceased monarch. In this way, David succeeded to the concubines of Saul, although he was his father-in-law, 2 Sam. xii. 8. And after he had fled from Absalom, Ahithophel, who is described as a man of the greatest abilities, as well as the greatest wickedness, counselled this rebellious son to lie publicly with his father's ten concubines, to annihilate, in hesitating minds, all hope of a reconciliation between them; 2 Sam. xvi. 21—23. Now incest is such an abominable crime, and so expressly contrary to the Mosaic law, that such proceedings must have been followed by the most direful consequences, if these concubines had not been considered, not as David's, but as the king's; and as belonging to the state, not to the individual; so that sleeping with them formed part of the ceremony of taking possession of the throne.—After David's death, Bathsheba, the mother of his successor, Solomon, was entreated by his brother Adonijah, to obtain the royal permission to marry Abishag, the Shunamite. But Solomon so fully saw through his brother's designs, and what effect the acceding to his request would have among the people, that he answered his mother, "Rather ask the kingdom for him too," and immediately caused him to be put to death, 1 Kings ii. 13—25. Of the origin of this strange law I can find no traces in the great kingdoms of the East; and yet most certainly these kings of Israel, as yet but novices in royalty, must have derived it, not from Israelitish, but foreign usage. It could scarcely have arisen in an hereditary kingdom, in which such incestuous procedure would have become too notorious and disgusting. Most probably it first arose among the beggarly elective monarchies in the neighbourhood, where it was found too expensive to provide every new king with a new seraglio; perhaps in the kingdom of Edom, whose needy practices the Israelites were wont at first to adopt. After Solomon's time, I find no further traces of it.—MICHAELIS.

CHAPTER XVII.

Ver. 8. For, said Hushai, thou knowest thy father and his men, that they *be* mighty men, and they *be* chafed in their minds, as a bear robbed of her whelps in the field: and thy father *is* a man of war, and will not lodge with the people.

The Hindoos are as much afraid of bears as any other animal in the forest; hence, when the letter-carriers and others have to travel through districts infested by them, they are always armed with a crooked knife, in the shape of a sickle: thus, when the bear is preparing to give them a hug, one cut from the instrument will send it off. When the female is robbed of her whelps, she is said to be more fierce than any other animal: hence, many sayings refer to her rage, and are applied to the fury of violent men. "I will tear thee to pieces as a bear which has cubbed." "Begone, or I will jump upon thee as a bear." When a termagant goes with her children to scold, it is said, "There goes the she-bear and her whelps."—ROBERTS.

The furious passions of the female bear never mount so high, nor burn so fiercely, as when she is deprived of her young. When she returns to her den, and misses the object of her love and care, she becomes almost frantic with rage. Disregarding every consideration of danger to herself, she attacks with great ferocity every animal that comes in her way; and in the bitterness of her heart will dare to attack even a band of armed men. The Russians of Kamtschatka never venture to fire on a young bear when the mother is near: for if the cub drop, she becomes enraged to a degree little short of madness, and if she gets sight of the enemy, will only quit her revenge with her life. (Cook's Voyages.) A more desperate attempt can scarcely be performed than to carry off her young in her absence. Her scent enables her to track the plunderer; and unless he has reached some place of safety before the infuriated animal overtake him, his only safety is in dropping one of the cubs, and continuing to flee; for the mother, attentive to its safety, carries it home to her den before she renews the pursuit.—BURDER.

Ver. 12. So shall we come upon him in some place where he shall be found, and we will light upon him as the dew falleth on the ground.

This is very beautiful and expressive. The dew in Palestine, as in several other climates, falls fast and sudden, and is therefore no unapt emblem of an active, expeditious soldiery. It was, perhaps, for this reason that the Romans called their light-armed forces *Rorarii*. The dew falls upon every spot of the earth; not a blade of grass escapes it. A numerous army resembles it in this respect. It is able to search everywhere.—BURDER.

Ver. 13. Moreover, if he be gotten into a city, then shall all Israel bring ropes to that city, and we will draw it into the river, until there be not one small stone found there.

On advancing, the chopdars or heralds proclaimed the titles of this princely cow-keeper, Futty Sihng, in the usual hyperbolical style. One of the most insignificant looking men I ever saw, then became the destroyer of nations, the leveller of mountains, the exhauster of the ocean. After commanding every inferior mortal to make way for this exalted prince, the heralds called aloud to the animal creation, Retire, ye serpents; fly, ye locusts; approach not, guanas, lizards, and reptiles, while your lord and master condescends to set his foot on the earth! Arrogant as this language may appear, it is less so than the oriental pageantry in general. The sacred writings afford many instances of such hyperbole. None more so than Hushai's speech to Absalom.—FORBES.

Ver. 17. Now Jonathan and Ahimaaz stayed by En-rogel; (for they might not be seen to come into the city;) and a wench went and told them: and they went and told King David.

In the East, the washing of foul linen is performed by women by the sides of rivers and fountains. Dr. Chandler (*Travels in Asia Minor*, p. 21) says, that "the women resort to the fountains by the houses, each with a two-handled earthen jar on her back, or thrown over her shoulder, for water. They assemble at one without the village or town, if no river be near, to wash their linen, which is afterward spread on the ground or bushes to dry." May not this circumstance, says Mr. Harmer, serve to confirm the conjecture, that the young woman that was sent to En-rogel, went out of the city with a bundle of linen, as if she were going to wash it? Nothing was more natural, or better calculated to elude jealousy.—BURDER.

Ver. 19. And the woman took and spread a covering over the well's mouth, and spread ground corn thereon; and the thing was not known.

This was done to conceal Jonathan and Ahimaaz, who had gone down the well to escape from the servants of Absalom. Wells in the East have their mouths level with the ground, hence, nothing is more easy than to put a mat or covering over the opening to conceal them from the sight. Who has not seen corn or flour spread on mats in the sun to dry? The woman affected to have this object in view when she spread a covering over the well: her "ground corn" was spread thereon to dry in the sun. The men were in the well, and when Absalom's servants came, and inquired, "Where is Ahimaaz and Jonathan;" she said, "They be gone over the brook of water." In the Kandian war great numbers were required to follow the army as bearers, cooks, and messengers, and such was the aversion of the people to the duty, that government was obliged to use force to compel them to go. And it was no uncommon thing, when the officers were seen to approach a cottage, for the husband or sons to be concealed as were Ahimaaz and Jonathan.—ROBERTS.

Ver. 28. Brought beds, and basins, and earthen vessels, and wheat, and barley, and flour, and parched *corn*, and beans, and lentiles, and parched *pulse*.

Parched corn is a kind of food still retained in the East, as Hasselquist informs us: "On the road from Acre to Seide, we saw a herdsman eating his dinner, consisting of half-ripe ears of wheat, which he roasted and ate with as good an appetite as a Turk does his pillau. In Egypt such food is much eaten by the poor, being the ears of maize or Turkish wheat, and of their durra, which is a kind of millet. When this food was first invented, art was in a simple state; yet the custom is still continued in some nations, where the inhabitants have not even at this time learned to pamper nature." The flour of parched barley is the chief provision which the Moors of West Barbary make for travelling. It is indeed much used as a part of their diet at home. "What is most used by travellers is zumeet, tumeet, or flour of parched barley for limereece. They are all three made of parched barley-flour, which they carry in a leathern satchel. Zumeet is the flower mixed with honey, butter, and spice; tumeet is the same flour done up with origan oil; and limereece is only mixed with water, and so drank. This quenches thirst much better than water alone, satiates a hungry appetite, cools and refreshes tired and weary spirits, overcoming those ill effects which a hot sun and fatiguing journey might occasion." (Jones.) Mr. Harmer proposes this extract as an illustration of the passage now cited.—BURDER.

Ver. 29. And honey, and butter, and sheep, and cheese of kine, for David, and for the people.

This, perhaps, was flesh of kine, or beef, prepared in such a manner as we call potted, by beating and bruising. The eastern people in modern times prepare potted flesh for food on a march or journey. Thus Busbequius, speaking of the Turkish soldiers going on an expedition into Persia, says, "Some of them filled a leathern bag with beef dried, and reduced to a kind of meal, which they use with great advantage, as affording a strong nourishment." And Dr. Shaw mentions potted flesh as part of the provisions carried with him in his journey through the Arabian deserts.—BURDER.

CHAPTER XVIII.

Ver. 8. For the battle was there scattered over the face of all the country: and the wood devoured more people that day than the sword devoured.

The land of promise cannot boast, like many other countries, of extensive woods; but considerable thickets of trees and of reeds sometimes arise to diversify and adorn the scene. Between the Lake Samochonites and the sea of Tiberias, the river Jordan is almost concealed by shady trees from the view of the traveller. When the waters of the Jordan are low, the Lake Samochonites is only a marsh, for the most part dry and overgrown with shrubs and reeds. The lake of Tiberias is bordered with reeds; while the banks of the river on both sides, are shaded with planes, alders, poplars, tamarisks, and reeds of different kinds. In these thickets, among other ferocious animals, the wild boar seeks a covert from the burning rays of the sun. Large herds of them are sometimes to be seen on the banks of the river, near the sea of Tiberias, lying among the reeds, or feeding under the trees. Such moist and shady places are in all countries the favourite haunts of these fierce and dangerous animals. Those marshy coverts are styled woods in the sacred scriptures; for the wild boar of the wood is the name which that creature receives from the royal Psalmist: "The boar out of the wood doth waste it; and the wild beast of the field doth devour it." The wood of Ephraim, where the battle was fought between the forces of Absalom and the servants of David, was probably a place of the same kind; for the sacred historian observes, that the wood devoured more people that day, than the sword devoured. Some have supposed the meaning of this passage to be, that the soldiers of Absalom were destroyed by the wild beasts of the wood; but it can scarcely be supposed, that in the reign of David, when the land of promise was crowded with inhabitants, the wild beasts could be so numerous in one of the woods as to cause such a destruction. But if their numbers had been so great, we know that, unless they had been detained contrary to their natural dispositions by the miraculous interposition of Heaven, for the purpose of executing his righteous vengeance on the followers of Absalom, intimidated by the approach of two hostile armies, and still more by the tumult of the battle, they must have sought their safety in flight, rather than have stayed to devour the discomfited party. Besides, we do not hear that one of David's men perished by the wood: were they miraculously preserved; or, were the wild beasts able to distinguish between the routed army and the victors, and politic enough to side with the strongest? We are not without an express revelation, or at least without necessity, to suppose a miraculous interposition. The scene of the expeditions which the Turks undertook against Faccardine, the famous emir, in the fifteenth century, was chiefly in the woods of mount Lebanon, which all travellers agree furnish a retreat to numerous wild beasts, yet the historian says not one word of either Turk or Maronite being injured by them, in his whole narrative. Absalom himself was the only person who properly perished by the wood; being caught by the hair of his head, of which he had been so vain, in the branches of a large oak, where Joab found him, and thrust him through with a dart. But, supposing the wood of Ephraim to have been a morass covered with trees and bushes, like the haunts of the wild boar near the banks of Jordan, the difficulty is easily removed. It is certain that such a place has more than once proved fatal to contending armies, partly by suffocating those who in the hurry of flight inadvertently venture over places incapable of supporting them, and partly by retarding them till their pursuers come up and cut them to pieces. In this manner a greater number of men than fell in the heat of battle may be destroyed. The archbishop of Tyre informs us, that one of the Christian kings of Jerusalem lost some of his troops in a marshy vale of this country, from their ignorance of the paths which lead through it, although he had no enemy to molest his march. The number of those who died was small; but in what numbers would they have perished, may we suppose, had they been forced to flee, like the men of Absalom, before a victorious and exasperated enemy? Lewis II., king of Hungary, lost his life in a bog in his own kingdom, in the sixteenth century: and according to Zozimus, Decius the Roman emperor perished in a fen, with his whole army. It may, therefore, be justly concluded, that Absalom's army perished neither by the trees of the wood, like their guilty leader, nor by the wild beasts which occupied its recesses; but by the deceitful quagmires with which it abounded.—PAXTON.

Ver. 11. And Joab said unto the man that told him, And, behold, thou sawest *him;* and why didst thou not smite him there to the ground? and I would have given thee ten *shekels* of silver, and a girdle.

Among us, here in Europe, the distinction between honorary and pecuniary rewards is so great, that we oftentimes can hardly think of jumbling them together as an acknowledgment of public services; and the same person that would receive the first with emotions of great pleasure, would think himself affronted by one of a pecuniary kind; but it is otherwise in the East, and it was so anciently. De Tott did many great services to the Turkish empire, in the time of their late war with Russia, and the Turks were disposed to acknowledge them by marks of honour. "His highness," said the first minister, speaking of the grand seignior, "has ordered me to bestow on you this public mark of his esteem," and, at the same time, made a sign to the master of the ceremonies to invest me with the pelisse; while the hasnadar presented me with a purse of 200 sequins. The lively French officer was hurt by the offer of the sequins. "I directly turned towards those who had accompanied me, and showing them my pelisse, I have received, said I, with gratitude, this proof of the grand seignior's favour; do you return thanks to the vizier for this purse, it is his gift. This expedient, which I preferred to a discussion of our different customs, was a sufficient lesson to the vizier, at the same time that it disengaged me from the embarrassment of oriental politeness." He then in a note adds, "This Turkish custom of giving money occasioned the greatest mortification to M. De Bonneval, that a man, like him, could receive. The ambassador extraordinary, from the emperor, who in the Austrian army had been in an inferior station to the refugee, dined, as is customary, with the vizier. The Porte had chosen Kiathana, for the place of this entertainment. M. De Bonneval had orders to repair thither with the corps of bombardiers, of which he was commander. When the exercise was over, he was sent for by the vizier, who gave him a handful of sequins, which his situation obliged him to accept, with submission." Just thus we find Joab would have rewarded an Israelitish soldier of his army, in the days of King David, who saw Absalom hanging in a tree: "Why didst thou not smite him there to the ground, and I would have given thee ten shekels of silver, and a girdle?" 2 Sam. xviii. 11. The girdle would have been an honorary reward, like De Tott's ermined vest; the ten shekels, or half crowns, would have been a pecuniary recompense, like the 200 sequins De Tott disdained to receive. I may add, that a furred robe, in general, is no distinguishing badge of dignity, for it may be worn by wealthy people in private life, who can bear the expense; so that there is no ground to suppose Joab's giving a girdle to the soldier would have been conferring some military honour, somewhat like knighting him, as, if I remember right, some have imagined: it would have been simply a valuable present, and enabling him in after-time to appear with such a girdle as the rich wore, instead of the girdle of a peasant, but united with the consciousness and the reputation of its being acquired by doing some public service, and not the mere effect of being descended from a wealthy family. The apparatus which some of the eastern people make use of to gird themselves with is very mean. The common Arabs, according to De la Roque, use a girt adorned with leather; and their women make use of a cord, or strip of cloth: but some of the Arab girdles are very rich, according to this writer. The girdle Joab proposed to give was doubtless designed by him to be understood to be one of such value, as to be answerable to the supposed importance of the service he wished the man had performed, as well as his own dignity. So Symon Simeonis, an Irish traveller to the Holy Land, in the year 1322, tells us, "That the Saracens of Egypt rarely, if ever, girded themselves with any thing but a towel, on which they kneeled to say their prayers, except their people of figure, who wore girdles like those of ladies, very broad, all of silk, and superbly adorned with gold and silver, in which they extremely pride themselves." I cannot well finish this article without remarking, from what the French baron says concerning himself, what strong disagreeable impressions of an erroneous kind may be made upon the mind of a European at the offering some of the Asiatic presents, which are not only not affronting in *their* views, but designed to do those honour to whom they are presented, since De Tott could not get the better of it, though he perfectly knew the innocency of the intention, and had resided long enough, one would have thought, in the country, to have destroyed the impression.—HARMER.

To loose the girdle and give it to another, was among the Orientals, a token of great confidence and affection. Thus to ratify the covenant which Jonathan made with David, and to express his cordial regard for his friend, among other things he gave him his girdle. A girdle curiously and richly wrought was, among the ancient Hebrews, a mark of honour, and sometimes bestowed as a reward of merit; for this was the recompense which Joab declared he meant to bestow on the man who put Absalom to death: "Why didst thou not smite him there to the ground, and I would have given thee ten shekels of silver, and a girdle." The reward was certainly meant to correspond with the importance of the service which he expected him to perform, and the dignity of his own station as commander-in-chief: we may therefore suppose it was not a common one of leather, or plain worsted, but of costly materials and richly adorned; for people of rank and fashion in the East wear very broad girdles, all of silk, and superbly ornamented with gold and silver, and precious stones, of which they are extremely proud, regarding them as the tokens of their superior station, and the proof of their riches.—PAXTON.

Ver. 17. And they took Absalom, and cast him into a great pit in the wood, and laid a very great heap of stones upon him: and all Israel fled every one to his tent.

To mark the spot where the chiefs were buried, and to remain at the same time as a memorial of the battle in which they fell, their surviving friends raised over them a heap of stones. This practice may be traced to the primitive ages of the world; for when Absalom was defeated and slain, "they cast him into a great pit in the wood, and laid a very great heap of stones upon him." This monumental heap was not intended to indicate that Absalom deserved to be stoned as a rebellious son, but merely to mark, according to a very common and a very ancient custom, the grave of that ambitious and unnatural prince. It was usual in the East, indeed, to distinguish any remarkable place or event by a heap of stones. All the Mohammedans that go in pilgrimage to mount Sinai, visit a rock, on which the form of a camel's foot is imprinted, which they foolishly suppose to be the animal that Mohammed rode; and, therefore, in honour of their prophet, they bring every one a stone, till, by continual accumulation, a large heap has risen near the place. Jacob, and his family too, raised a heap of stones in commemoration of the covenant so happily concluded between him and Laban, on mount Gilead. That "heap of witness" informed every passenger that it was raised in memory of some interesting event; and every relation that brought a stone to the heap, made himself a witness to the agreement, as well as recommended it to the attention of others. The surviving warriors, too, might bring every man his stone, in token of their respect for the deceased, to raise a monumental heap over the body of the hero who had led them to battle and to victory, which should arrest the notice of the passing traveller, and bear witness to future times of their attachment and regret.—PAXTON.

Ver. 18. Now Absalom in his lifetime had taken and reared up for himself a pillar, which *is* in the king's dale: for he said, I have no son to keep my name in remembrance: and he called the pillar after his own name: and it is called unto this day Absalom's Place.

On the east, we came to the reputed tomb of Absalom, resembling nearly, in the size, form, and the decoration of its square base, that of Zacharias, before described; except that it is sculptured with the metopes and triglyphs of the Doric order. This is surmounted by a sharp conical dome, of the form used in our modern parasols, having large mouldings, resembling ropes running round its base, and on the summit something like an imitation of flame. The dome is of masonry, and on the eastern side there is a square aperture in it. It is probable that this monument really occupies the place of that mentioned to have been set up by him whose name it bears. 2 Sam. xviii. 18. Josephus, in relating the same circumstance, calls the pillar a marble one; he fixes its distance at two furlongs from Jerusalem, and says it was named Absalom's Hand.—BUCKINGHAM.

Ver. 24. And David sat between the two gates: and the watchman went up to the roof over the gate unto the wall, and lifted up his eyes, and looked, and behold a man running alone.

The watchman, in a time of danger, seems to have taken his station in a tower, which was built over the gate of the city. We may form a tolerably distinct idea of the ancient towers in Palestine, from the description which the sacred historian gives us of one, in the entrance of Mahanaim: "And David sat between the two gates, and the watchman went up to the roof over the gate unto the wall, and lifted up his eyes and looked, and behold a man running alone. The watchman cried and told the king; and the king said, If he is alone, there is tidings in his mouth. And the watchman saw another man running; and the watchman called unto the porter, and said, Behold, another man running alone; and the king said, He also bringeth tidings." When the tidings were announced, the historian observes, "the king was much moved, and went up to the chamber over the gate and wept." It is afterward added, "Then the king arose and sat in the gate; and they told unto all the people saying, Behold the king doth sit in the gate; and all the people came before the king, for Israel had fled every man to his tent." From this description it appears, that the tower in the entrance of Mahanaim, had two pair of gates, at some distance from each other; in a small room, which was often found by the side of these fortified gates, the door of which opened into the passage between them, sat the king, waiting, in fearful suspense, the issue of the contest, for it cannot be supposed he sat in the passage itself, which had been at once unbecoming his dignity, and incommodious to the passengers entering or leaving the city. We find a watchman stationed on the top of this tower, to which he went up by a staircase from the passage, which, like the roof of their dwellinghouses, was flat, for the purpose of descrying at a distance those that were approaching the place, or repelling the attacks of an enemy. The observations made by the watchman were not communicated by him immediately to the king, but by the intervention of a warder at the outer gate of the tower; and it appears, that a private staircase led from the lower room in which the king was sitting, to the upper room over the gateway; for by that communication he retired to give full vent to his sorrow. The only circumstance involved in any doubt, is in what part of this building he sat, (for it is evident he continued in some part of the gate,) when he returned his thanks to the army for their exertions in his favour; or in the language of the historian, "spake to the hearts of his servants," and received their congratulations. It is somewhat uncertain whether he gave audience to his people in the upper room, where he lamented in strains so affecting, the death of Absalom, or in the little chamber between the two gates, where he waited the arrival of the messengers, or in some other part of the building. The ancient custom of sitting in the gate on solemn occasions, rather favours the opinion, that David went down from the apartment above the gate, to the chamber in the side of the passage. This custom, which may be traced to the remotest antiquity, is still observed in the East; for when Pococke returned from viewing the town of ancient Byblus, the sheik and the elders were sitting in the gate of the city, after the manner of their ancestors.—Paxton.

Ver. 25. And the watchman cried, and told the king. And the king said, If he *be* alone, *there is* tidings in his mouth. And he came apace, and drew near.

This was said by David when the watchman told him that there was a man running alone. He proved to be Ahimaaz, who had escaped from the well, and had run to tell David, "All is well." Is a man seen to run fast, it is said, "Ah! there is news in his mouth." "Why have you come so fast?"—"In my mouth there is news." To a man in trouble it is often said, "Fear not, a man will soon come with tidings in his mouth."—Roberts.

Ver. 32. And the king said unto Cushi, *Is* the young man Absalom safe? And Cushi answered, The enemies of my lord the king, and all that rise against thee to do *thee* hurt, be as *that* young man *is*.

This was a delicate way of telling David that the rebel Absalom was dead. A person, in communicating, by letter, intelligence of the death of a friend, does not always say, in so many plain terms, "He is dead;" but, "Would that all our enemies were now as our friend Muttoo." "Ah! were they all as he, we should have peace in our village." A son, in writing to an uncle concerning the death of his father, says, "Ah! the children of your brother are now given unto the Lord." "Would that our enemies were now as our father; they will now rejoice over us."—Roberts.

CHAPTER XIX.

Ver. 13. And say ye to Amasa, *Art* thou not of my bone, and of my flesh? God do so to me, and more also, if thou be not captain of the host before me continually in the room of Joab. 14. And he bowed the heart of all the men of Judah, even as *the heart of* one man; so that they sent *this word* unto the king, Return thou, and all thy servants.

Mr. Le Clerc and others object, that David's resolution to remove Joab from the chief command of the army, was but an unthankful return for the victory which that officer had just gained him, and for his attachment to his interest all along, and therefore David's conduct in this instance was imprudent and unaccountable. What Joab's share in obtaining this victory was, the history doth not say. Abishai and Ittai, who each commanded a third part of the forces, might, as for any thing that appears, as much contribute to the victory over the rebels, as Joab. But be that as it will, the imprudence of David's conduct is effectually disproved by the event; and that it was not unaccountable is certain, because of the evident prudence of it; especially if it be true, and I think it certainly is true, that Joab had now lost the favour of his master, of which the murder of Abner, the killing of Absalom, in direct contradiction to David's order, and lastly, his want of sympathy, and his indelicacy in the present instance, were the undoubted causes. And surely it could be nothing unaccountable, nor argue any great ingratitude, to turn out an imperious general, even after he had helped to gain a victory, who had stained his laurels by the treasonable murder of the king's own son, in defiance of his most express command, and then instantly threatened him with a fresh rebellion, if he did not openly appear to justify and approve his crimes: crimes, that a successful battle few will think to be a sufficient atonement for, or a just reason to exempt him from disgrace, and the punishment he deserved. The ancient Roman discipline was much more severe and rigorous than this, and a victory obtained, if contrary to the general's orders, was punished with death. When T. Manlius, the son of Manlius the consul, upon a challenge of Metius, one of the generals of the Latins, with whom the Romans were then at war, had engaged him in single combat, slain him, taken his spoils, and presented them in triumph to his father, the consul immediately ordered him to be beheaded in sight of the whole army, because it was an express breach of his orders; telling his son, "If thou hast any thing of my blood in thee, thou thyself wilt not, I think, refuse to restore, by thy punishment, that military discipline, which hath been impaired by thy offence." In like manner, when Papirius, the Roman dictator, had commanded Fabius, the master of his horse, not to engage the enemy during his absence, Fabius being informed that the army of the Samnites were in a state of great disorder, attacked them with his forces, entirely routed them, and slew twenty thousand of them on the field of battle. The dictator, upon his return to the army, in a council of officers, ordered him to be beheaded, because in breach of the rules of war, and the ancient discipline, he had dared, contrary to his orders, to engage with the enemy. He was however at last saved by the intercession of the Roman people. David's removing Joab from his command was a much less punishment for much more aggravated crimes.

As to the promise to Amasa, of constituting him general in Joab's room, the prudence of this may be also easily vindicated. For Amasa stood in the same degree of consanguinity to David as Joab did, and the offer to him of making him captain-general must, as it has been well observed, have been influenced by the personal qualities of the man, the importance of gaining him over, he being a person of great power and authority, and a resentment against Joab for the murder of Abner and Absalom. Besides, I doubt not but that David thought he should now be able to break Joab's power, and bring him to an account for his repeated assassinations and treasons, as well as fix Amasa for ever in his interest, by placing so high a degree of confidence in him, as to give him the command of all the forces in his kingdom. This hath been frequently the method by which great men have endeav oured to gain over their enemies, and it argues a real generosity of soul, of which little minds are utterly incapable, to win an adversary to his duty, by such unexpected instances of confidence and friendship. When Cinna, the grandson of Pompey, and other great men, conspired against Augustus, he not only pardoned them, but nominated Cinna consul for the ensuing year; and Cæsar not only spared Brutus, after he had appeared in arms against him, but took him into favour as his intimate friend, and intrusted him with the government of Gaul.—CHANDLER.

Ver. 24. And Mephibosheth the son of Saul came down to meet the king, and had neither dressed his feet, nor trimmed his beard, nor washed his clothes, from the day the king departed until the day he came *again* in peace.

They almost universally die them black, by an operation not very pleasant, and necessary to be repeated generally once a fortnight. It is always performed in the hot bath, where the hair being well saturated, takes the colour better. A thick paste of khenna is first made, which is largely plastered over the beard, and which, after remaining an hour, is all completely washed off, and leaves the hair of a very strong orange colour, bordering upon that of brickdust. After this, as thick a paste is made of the leaf of the indigo, which previously has been pounded to a fine powder, and of this also a deep layer is put upon the beard; but this second process, to be taken well, requires full two hours. During all this operation the patient lies quietly flat upon his back; while the die (more particularly the indigo, which is a great astringent) contracts the features of his face in a very mournful manner, and causes all the lower parts of the visage to smart and burn. When the indigo is at last washed off, the beard is of a very dark bottle-green, and becomes a jet black only when it has met the air for twenty-four hours. Some, indeed, are content with the khenna or orange colour; others, more fastidious, prefer a beard quite blue. The people of Bokhara are famous for their blue beards.—MORIER.

Ver. 24. And Mephibosheth the son of Saul
came down to meet the king, and had neither
dressed his feet, nor trimmed his beard, nor
washed his clothes, from the day the king departed until the day he came *again* in peace.
25. And it came to pass, when he was come
to Jerusalem to meet the king, that the king
said unto him, Wherefore wentest not thou
with me, Mephibosheth? 26. And he answered, My lord, O king, my servant deceived
me: for thy servant said, I will saddle me an
ass, that I may ride thereon, and go to the king;
because thy servant *is* lame. 27. And he hath
slandered thy servant unto my lord the king;
but my lord the king *is* as an angel of God:
do therefore *what is* good in thine eyes.
28. For all *of* my father's house were but
dead men before my lord the king: yet didst
thou set thy servant among them that did eat
at thine own table. What right therefore have
I yet to cry any more unto the king? 29. And
the king said unto him, Why speakest thou any
more of thy matters? I have said, Thou and
Ziba divide the land. 30. And Mephibosheth
said unto the king, Yea, let him take all, forasmuch as my lord the king is come again in
peace unto his own house.

This conduct of David to Mephibosheth is objected against, as a very ungenerous and unjust action; in that, when Ziba's accusation against Mephibosheth was found to be false, instead of equitably punishing the asperser of innocence, and reinstating Mephibosheth in his former favour, he restored him but half the forfeiture for his supposed guilt, leaving the villain Ziba in the quiet possession of the other half, as the reward of his treachery. Supposing this account true, that Mephibosheth had but half his patrimony restored to him, there might be reasons of state, reasons of great prudence and equity, that might induce David, at that time, to give this check to the house of Saul; especially if David had any suspicion that Mephibosheth had really behaved ill, and as Shimei, one of Saul's family, had used him with peculiar marks of indignity, and discovered that they wanted only the opportunity to revenge themselves on him, and place one of Saul's house upon the throne of Israel. But I think there is great reason to question, whether the behaviour of Mephibosheth was so innocent as hath been asserted, during the progress of the rebellion. The late ingenious and learned Mr. Hallet and others, think he was guilty and deserved punishment; and after having reviewed his apology to David for not accompanying him in his flight from Jerusalem, with the utmost impartiality and care, that apology doth not seem to me sufficient wholly to exculpate him. For what is the apology he makes? Why, only this; that he said, "he would saddle him an ass, and go on it to the king, because he was lame, and could not go on foot." Why then, what hindered him from saddling his ass, and riding after his royal patron and benefactor? Surely there were more asses than one to be had at Jerusalem, and he had servants enough of his own to have saddled one, had he been disposed to go after David. For when that prince was restored, he found means to wait on him, without Ziba's assistance; and I suppose, the same means might have been found, if he had pleased, to have attended David when he fled, as well as to go to meet him when he returned. He pretends indeed that Ziba deceived him; but he doth not say how, nor offer any proof of it; nor could he deceive him about the getting him an ass, because he could have got one, whether Ziba would procure him one or not. So that his justification was as lame as his feet, and, as far as I can judge, is but a poor shuffling vindication of his innocence. He seems to me to have been very well pleased to stay at Jerusalem, and wait the issue of the rebellion, as not knowing, but that during the confusion of affairs, some fortunate circumstances might arise, by which, as heir to Saul's house, he might be advanced to the throne in the room both of David and his rebellious son. The only circumstance that can be alleged in his favour is, that he did not take the usual care of himself, as to his cleanliness and dress, but appeared in the squalid habit of a mourner. But this might be merely political, and would equally serve to excite compassion to himself among the people, to see Saul's heir reduced to this forlorn condition; and to provide some excuse for himself to David, should his affairs at last take a favourable turn, and to urge as an argument and proof of his affection and concern for him, during the continuance of his troubles. This was a well-known custom among the Romans, and other nations, for those who were accused of any crimes, to clothe themselves with a black garment, to let their beards and hair grow, and to appear in a negligent, dirty manner, in order to raise the public pity in their behalf. And not only thus, but the friends and patrons of such unhappy persons, appeared publicly in the same manner, as those whose cause they espoused. Thus Cicero tells us, that the whole senate, and all good men, did it to express their grief on his account, and the better to obtain his recall from banishment. Yea, this very art hath been made use of by a dethroned prince to obtain the recovery of his crown and kingdom. Thus Ptolemy Philometor, king of Egypt, being driven out of his kingdom by his brother Physcon, came attended only by a few servants to Rome, *squalore obsitus*, covered over with filth, to implore the assistance of the senate. And in this wretched condition he presented himself before them. They advised him, that *depositis sordibus*, laying aside his wretched habit, he should petition for an audience. So that this affectation of Mephibosheth, or appearing at Jerusalem with these external marks of grief, was really no proof of his affection to David, but might be with an artful intention to serve himself. Ziba's charge against him was direct and positive, and the only answer is, that Ziba had slandered him. So that here are two positive assertions contrary to one another. Ziba's charge had probability to support it; because it is natural to suppose, that Mephibosheth might think that he had, as heir to Saul, some claim to the crown, and would be glad of any occasion to recover it, that he might not be beholden to David's generosity, and live by courtesy at his table; and that he might mention it to Ziba, as he also was one of Saul's house and family. Mephibosheth's answer to the charge had nothing satisfactory in it, because he could never want an ass, or a servant to have conveyed him, had he desired or resolved to make use of them. Besides, as Ziba's carrying provisions to David plainly showed Ziba's belief and hope of David's restoration, he must know that if he had charged Mephibosheth falsely, the falsehood must have been discovered when David was resettled on the throne; and that being convicted of calumniating his master, he would, in all probability, have been so far from having Mephibosheth's whole estate confirmed to him, as that he would have lost his maintenance out of it for himself and family. And indeed David himself seems to me not to have been thoroughly satisfied with Mephibosheth's apology, by the answer he makes him: "Why speakest thou any more about thy matters?" Let me hear no more of thy affairs. I will neither regard Ziba's charge, nor your vindication; an answer that evidently carries an air of coldness, indifference, and displeasure, and of one who did not choose to make any strict inquiry into Mephibosheth's conduct, but to admit his excuse, though in itself insufficient and unsatisfactory; and he therefore only adds: Thou and Ziba divide the land. If this be the true state of the case, as it appears to me to be, David's annulling the grant to Ziba, so far as to reinstate Mephibosheth in the possession of even half the land, was a noble instance of David's generosity, and of the grateful remembrance he retained of Jonathan's affection and friendship for him. But I must question the truth of the account, that David restored to Mephibosheth but half of the estate. Ziba had been an old servant in Saul's family, who had fifteen sons, and twenty servants. To him David had said: "I have given thy master's son all that pertaineth to Saul, and to all his house. Thou therefore and thy sons and thy servants shall till the land for him, and bring in the fruits, that thy master's son may have food to eat, viz. for his household and family. As for Mephibosheth himself, he shall always eat at my table, as one of the king's sons." Ziba therefore was to take care of the estate, to account for the profits of it to Mephibosheth, and to be himself and his whole family maintained out of the annual produce, for his care in cultivating it. This was a proper division of it between Mephibosheth, as lord of the estate, and Ziba as the farmer and manager of it. What now is the determination of David, upon his restoration to the throne? Mephibosheth had been entirely ousted upon Ziba's complaint; but after he had made his apology, David said to him: "I have said, Thou and Ziba divide the land." But where and when did David ever say, "I give each of you a moiety of the estate?" He first gave the whole in property to Mephibosheth, and afterward to Ziba; but never divided it, share and share alike, between them. And yet, "I have said, Thou and Ziba divide the land," must refer to some former division of the estate by David's order. But no such determination or order is to be found, but in that original one, in which the estate was divided between Mephibosheth in property, and Ziba as husbandman, for his own and family's maintenance. So that this last determination of David was so far from taking away one half of the estate from Mephibosheth, that it was in reality confirming the original grant, and restoring him to the possession of the whole, upon the same terms on which that possession was originally granted him. So that if David was too hasty in giving away Mephibosheth's estate to Ziba, he was, upon better recollection, as hasty in restoring it to him; and it ought to be acknowledged as a proof of his inviolable regard to his oath to Jonathan, since he had reason for just suspicion, that his son had been wanting in that affection and fidelity which he owed him, as his generous protector and benefactor. And though by his confirming the original grant, he left Ziba and his family a maintenance out of the estate, it was not as the reward of his treachery, of which there is no proof, but out of respect even to Saul, of whose house Ziba was, and as a recompense for his faithful adherence to him in his distresses, and that seasonable and noble supply with which he furnished him and his followers, when he was forced to abandon his capital, by the unnatural rebellion of his son Absalom. Hereby David did more than full justice to Mephibosheth, and at the same time rewarded Ziba by continuing him on the estate, upon the former conditions of possessing it. Mr Bayle has a long article on this affair, in which he takes it for granted, that David restored Mephibosheth but one half of the estate, and says, "that some interpreters maintain, that Ziba's accusation was not unjust; or, at least, that it was founded on so many probabilities, that it might be credited without passing a wrong judgment;" but there are but few, says he, of that opinion; and he affirms, "that David found him a false accuser." But Mr. Bayle offers not a single proof for these assertions, and he who relates the different opinions of others concerning any fact, and declares on the unfavourable side of it, without giving his reasons for it, doth not act like a candid critic, but with the spirit of partiality and party. I must therefore leave these particulars to the judgment of the more candid and impartial reader, when he hath duly considered what hath been said above in order to obviate them; agreeing at the same time with him, that if Mephibosheth was unjustly treated, David's holiness could never make that sentence just, though Pope Gregory hath insisted upon it; and that to conclude the sentence was just, merely because David passed it, though it was unjust in itself, is to establish a very dangerous principle.—Chandler.

Ver. 29. And the king said unto him, Why speakest thou any more of thy matters? I have said, Thou and Ziba divide the land.

This form of speech is exceedingly common when a man wishes to confirm any thing, or when he wants to give weight to a promise. To show that all will be fulfilled, he says, *Năn-chon-nain-nea*, "Oh! I have said it."—Roberts.

CHAPTER XX.

Ver. 1. And there happened to be there a man of Belial, whose name *was* Sheba, the son of Bichri, a Benjamite; and he blew a trumpet, and said, We have no part in David, neither have we inheritance in the son of Jesse: every man to his tents, O Israel.

When slaves are liberated from their owners, they say, "We have no *pangu*, i. e. part, in them, nor they in us." It is also very common to mention the name of the person, and that of his father; and this sometimes implies disgrace, especially when the family has arisen from obscurity, and therefore to allude to its origin is to insult the descendants. —Roberts.

Ver. 1. And there happened to be there a man of Belial, whose name *was* Sheba, the son of Bichri, a Benjamite; and he blew a trumpet, and said, We have no part in David, neither have we inheritance in the son of Jesse: every man to his tents, O Israel. 2. So every man of Israel went up from after David, *and* followed Sheba the son of Bichri: but the men of Judah clave unto their king, from Jordan even to Jerusalem.

The blame of this new rebellion hath been charged on David, and he censured for thus inadvertently plunging himself into fresh troubles, by suffering himself to be conducted home by a deputation from the tribe of Judah. The learned authors of the Universal History, have made a like observation on this part of David's conduct, and say, that "the partiality, which he showed to his own tribe, in inviting it to come foremost to receive him, raised such a jealousy in the other ten, as ended at length in a new revolt." But where doth the history justify this reflection, that he was partial to his own tribe, in inviting it to come foremost to receive him? The truth is, that he did not invite them at all to come and receive him, till he had been informed by expresses from all the other tribes, that they were universally in motion to restore him, and his message to them only was: "Why are ye the last to bring back the king?" Not, why are ye not the foremost? And though the other tribes complained to that of Judah, "Why did ye despise us, that our advice should be first had in bringing back our king?" Yet the tribe of Judah was so far from coming to meet the king, out of any regard to, or contempt of, their brethren, that the very zeal and movements of those tribes, in David's favour, was the principal motives urged by him, to bring back the tribe of Judah to their duty, and their great inducement to return to their allegiance to him. This was paying a real deference to their judgment, and what they ought to have been pleased with, and highly applauded. It is true, that the tribes all concurred in their resolutions to restore him, and were taking the proper methods to effect it, yet that David continued at Mahanaim, till the deputies from Judah came to him there, with an invitation from the whole tribe to repair to Jerusalem, and to assure him, that they would receive him in a body at Gilgal, and prepare every thing necessary for his passage over Jordan. Nor could he indeed set out for Jerusalem, till he had received certain information, that the men of Judah, and Amasa, who was in possession of it, would quietly permit him to return to it, without endangering his own person, or hazarding the peace of the nation, should he attempt to reduce the city by force. But when he knew the city would open her gates to him, it is no wonder he should resolve immediately to begin his march to it, as he had now nothing to fear from that quarter, and imagined, that as all the tribes had declared for him, the sooner he acted agreeably to their desires, they would be the better pleased, and without the formality of any particular invitations, receive him with open arms, wherever he should meet them.

The pretence, that the men of Judah had stolen him away, was unreasonable and unjust. For while he was at Mahanaim, the tribes on that side Jordan all declared for him, and accompanied him to the passage of that river, and went over with him to join the rest of their brethren, who were come down to meet him; so that when they were all united at the passage of the river, there were actually present, by large deputations, the tribes of Judah, Benjamin, and five others, who waited on him in his march to Gilgal. The truth of the case seems to be, that the deputations from the more distant tribes, not being able to get farther than Gilgal, before the king's arrival there, envied the other tribes, and particularly that of Judah, which had the principal share in providing every thing necessary for the king's passage over Jordan, and laid hold of the first opportunity to express their resentment against them. This was heightened by the imprudent haughty answer, which the men of Judah made to their expostulation, that they had a peculiar right in the king, as he was near akin to them, because he was of their own tribe; and seeming to insinuate, that they came voluntarily, but that the other tribes came with an expectation of being provided for at the king's expense, and hoping some donative from him, as the reward of their submission to him. This, I think, is plainly implied, when they told them: "Have we eaten at all at the king's cost? Or hath he given us any gift?" Words which seem to carry a tacit insinuation, that other tribes expected both. This reflection, and the claim of a particular interest in the king, disgusted all the other tribes in general, and disposed them to enter into violent measures to revenge themselves. David, upon the whole, seems to me to be nowise blameable on account of Sheba's revolt, but that it was occasioned by misunderstandings between the tribes themselves, which it was not at that time in his power to prevent.—CHANDLER.

Ver. 3. And David came to his house at Jerusalem; and the king took the ten women *his* concubines, whom he had left to keep the house, and put them in ward, and fed them, but went not in unto them: so they were shut up unto the day of their death, living in widowhood.

In China, when an emperor dies, all his women are removed to an edifice called the Palace of Chastity, situated within the walls of the palace, in which they are shut up for the remainder of their lives.—BURDER.

Ver 9. And Joab said to Amasa, *Art* thou in health, my brother? And Joab took Amasa by the beard with the right hand to kiss him.

D'Arvieux was present at an Arabian entertainment, to which came all the emirs, a little while after his arrival, accompanied by their friends and attendants: and after the usual civilities, caresses, kissings of the beard, and of the hand, which every one gave and received according to his rank and dignity, sat down upon mats. It was in this way, perhaps, that Joab pretended to testify his respect for Amasa, his rival in the favour of the king; he took him by the beard to kiss him, or agreeably to the custom of these emirs, or Arabian chieftains, to kiss the beard itself; and in this stooping posture he could much better see to direct the blow, than if he had only held his beard, and raised himself to kiss his face; while Amasa, charmed by this high compliment, which was neither suspicious nor unusual, and undoubtedly returning it with corresponding politeness, paid no attention to the sword in the hand of his murderer. It is extremely probable that Judas betrayed his Lord in the same way, by kissing his beard. The evangelists Matthew and Mark say, that he came directly to Jesus, and said, Hail, Master, and kissed him; but Luke seems to hint, that Judas saluted him with more respect. Jesus, according to Matthew, had time to say, before he received the kiss from Judas, "Friend, wherefore art thou come?" and while Judas was kissing his beard, Jesus might express himself with great ease and propriety, as Luke relates, "Judas, betrayest thou the Son of man with a kiss?"—PAXTON.

Ver. 18. Then she spake, saying, They were wont to speak in old time, saying, They shall surely ask *counsel* at Abel: and so they ended *the matter*.

Intimating, that the city of Abel was very famous, in ancient times, for giving advice, and determining controversies. But of this there is no intimation except in this place, and the sense seems very forced and unnatural. I think R. S. Jarchi's exposition leads to the true interpretation, which our learned Bishop Patrick seems also to approve; who observes, that the word בראשנה refers, not to old time, but the beginning of the siege. As if she had said, When the people saw thee lay siege to the city, they said, surely they will ask us, if we will have peace, and then we shall soon come to an agreement, and make an end; putting Joab in mind of the rule in the law, Deut. xx. 10, which commands them to offer peace to the cities of other nations, when they came to besiege them, and therefore much more to a city of their own, as Abel was. This agrees well with what follows, that they were a peaceable people, and faithful to their prince, and therefore would not have refused to yield to him upon summons.—CHANDLER.

Ver. 23. Now Joab *was* over all the host of Israel: and Benaiah the son of Jehoiada *was* over the Cherethites and over the Pelethites.

This hath occasioned a very severe reflection on David's honour and justice, and he is reproached because Joab was continued in the command, and not a single syllable of any notice taken by David of the murder of Amasa, whom he himself had appointed general; as though David had acquiesced in the murder, and confirmed Joab in the command of the army, as the reward of it. But that David greatly resented this murder of Amasa, is evident from his last advice to Solomon, in which he nobly recommends, and gives it in charge to him, to do justice on that bloody assassin for the murders of Abner and Amasa. David was not now able himself to do it, and Joab was too powerful a subject to be brought to any account. We have seen that he had insolence enough, after Absalom's death, to threaten the king with a new revolt, if he did not do what he ordered him; and after the assassination of Amasa, he usurped, in defiance of his master's appointment, the command of all the forces. They seem to have had an affection for him as a brave and successful general; he had just now restored the quiet of the land, by entirely quelling the insurrection under Sheba, and returned to Jerusalem, without fear of the king, and in defiance of justice, as generalissimo of the army; and continued to assume this rank, not by David's order and inclination, but by his mere acquiescence in a measure that was contrary to his will, but which he was not able to set aside. It should be observed to David's honour, that when the rebellion under Absalom, and the insurrection by Sheba, were entirely suppressed, we read of no bloody executions for treason and rebellion. David resolved that no one should be put to death on that account. He was all mercy and forgiveness. The cursing Shimei was reprieved. The suspected Mephibosheth was restored, and the rebel general constituted captain of the forces of the kingdom. Had he been the Nero or the Turk he hath been figured out by Mr. Bayle and others, this occasion would have abundantly enabled him to gratify his revenge, and satiate himself with blood. Should it be said, that David's clemency was owing to his thinking it hazardous to make examples of any of them; and his not being able to do it, because the revolt was general; or, to his policy, considering the precariousness of his situation; the answer is obvious, that neither of these suppositions hath any probability to support it. There could be no possible hazard in executing Shimei, and such others as had been the principal incendiaries and promoters of the rebellion. This was now totally suppressed, his victorious army at his devotion, and his general ready to support him, and obey him even in the most sanguinary measures, as appears from his conduct in the affair of Uriah; so that there could be no hazard in his making proper examples of just indignation and vengeance. David knew this, and said to Abishai: "Do I not know that I am this day king over Israel? restored to my power and authority as king? and I will execute it at my pleasure." And in truth he could have none to control him in his present situation. The assertion that the revolt was general, is not true in fact, as hath been elsewhere proved. As to David's policy, that it induced him to resolve that no one should be put to death on account of the rebellion, I acknowledge that there might be somewhat in this; but then it could not arise from the precariousness of his situation, of which there is no appearance or proof; for he was restored by the almost unanimous consent of his people; but from the noble policy, which never influences tyrants, but is inspired by benevolence and humanity, that suppresses the vindictive spirit, and chooses the obedience which arises from affection and esteem, rather than that which flows from fear, and is enforced by severity. Charges of acting from criminal and unworthy motives, without facts to support them, deserve no regard from persons of integrity and honour. I shall only further observe, that from Nathan's threatening David, to the suppression of the rebellion under Sheba, by which the punishment, as far as it related personally to David, was accomplished, were, by the marginal chronology of our Bible, thirteen years; which shows how groundless the observation is that hath been made, as to this melancholy part of David's history, viz. that it would not be easy to select any period of any history more bloody, or abounding in wickedness of more various dies, than that which has been now mentioned. Instances succeed so quick, that the relation of one is scarce concluded, but fresh ones obtrude upon our notice. Supposing this observation true, how do the vices of other men, or the misfortunes of his own family, affect David, as a man after God's own heart? Or is he the first good man who hath been unhappy in some of his children? Or whose affection towards them hath been much more tender and passionate than they deserved? Insulting great and good men, and holding them up to public view, as objects of horror and detestation, from those crimes of their family which gave them the greatest anxiety, is what virtue abhors, and is shocking even to humanity. David had in all seventeen sons. Two of them were profligates, and perished by their crimes. As to the rest, they appear to be worthy men, and were employed by David in the principal departments of the administration; a circumstance that shows he took great care of their education, and that, upon the whole, he was very far from being unhappy in his family. The crimes committed by the two eldest, were Amnon's affair with his half-sister Tamar; Absalom's murder of Amnon for the injury done his sister; his impious rebellion against his father; and his public incest with his wives, to which Ahithophel advised and promoted him. These were the wickednesses of various dies complained of, to which may be added, the murder of Absalom by Joab, contrary to the king's express order. These instances, as related in the history, succeed so quick, as that the account of one is scarce concluded, but fresh ones obtrude upon our notice. But then the relation of these things is much quicker than the succession of years in which they happened, and many events intervened between the commission of the one and the other. Between Amnon's rape, and his murder by Absalom, were more than two years. From Absalom's banishment, to his being restored to the king's presence, were more than five years, and from this to his rebellion and death, three or four; in all eleven or twelve years. But are there no instances in history to be found of more numerous crimes, and as various dies, committed within a much shorter period of time? Will not our own history furnish us with such an instance?—From the year 1483 to 1485, i. e. in less than three years, one man, Richard duke of Gloucester, usurped the crown, actually murdered the king and his brother, both of them his nephews; poisoned his own queen, to make way for an incestuous marriage with his niece, imbrued his hands in the blood of many of the English nobility, was the author of a civil war in the kingdom, and was himself slain in an engagement with the duke of Richmond, afterward Henry VII. I refer the reader for another instance of implicated wickedness, still of a more terrible nature, in Xerxes the Persian emperor, related at large by Dr. Prideaux in his Connexion, v. i. p. 348, &c. and it would be easy to mention several others, both in the Roman and eastern histories, to show the rashness of this observation on which I have been remarking. —CHANDLER.

CHAPTER XXI.

Ver. 1. Then there was a famine in the days of
David three years, year after year; and David
inquired of the LORD. And the LORD answered,
It is for Saul, and for *his* bloody house, because
he slew the Gibeonites. 2. And the king
called the Gibeonites, and said unto them; (now
the Gibeonites *were* not of the children of Israel,
but of the remnant of the Amorites; and
the children of Israel had sworn unto them;
and Saul sought to slay them in his zeal to the
children of Israel and Judah;) 3. Wherefore
David said unto the Gibeonites, What shall I
do for you; and wherewith shall I make the
atonement, that ye may bless the inheritance of
the LORD? 4. And the Gibeonites said unto
him, We will have no silver nor gold of Saul,
nor of his house; neither for us shalt thou kill
any man in Israel. And he said, What you
shall say, *that* will I do for you.

We now enter upon a part of David's history and conduct, that hath been thought exceptionable by many persons of good sense and sober minds; and which others have represented as a masterpiece of wickedness, and for which they have censured him as the most accomplished hypocrite, and a perjured and profligate villain. It will therefore be necessary more particularly to consider it. I confess, for my own part, that I think it one of the most unexceptionable parts of his behaviour as a king, and an illustrious proof of the generosity of his temper, the regard he paid to his oath to Saul, and the friendship he owed to the memory and family of Jonathan. That the reader may the better judge of this, I shall give the history just as it is recorded in the Old Testament writings. The inhabitants of Gibeon, a large royal city, which, after the division of the country, was yielded to the tribe of Benjamin, were Amorites by birth and nation; and when the Hebrews, under Joshua, invaded the land of Canaan, the Gibeonites hearing what Joshua had done to Jericho and Ai, and fearing for their own safety, fraudulently persuaded the Hebrews to enter into a league with them; which was solemnly ratified by a public oath, so that they had the national faith for the security of their lives and properties; for which reason the children of Israel, when they came to their cities, and understood the fraud, murmured against the princes, because they had made a league with them. The princes, to appease them, said to them: "We have sworn unto them by the Lord God of Israel, therefore we may not touch them. We will even let them live, lest wrath be upon us, because of the oath which we sware to them;" and they were accordingly spared, but condemned to servitude, and made hewers of wood, and drawers of water, for the congregation, and for the altar of the Lord perpetually, in the place which he should choose; i. e. wherever the tabernacle or ark should reside. But Saul, in his zeal to the children of Israel and Judah, to ingratiate himself with them, under the specious pretence of public spirit, to enrich his servants and soldiers, and to appear warm and active for the public interest, "sought to slay them, and to destroy them from remaining in any of the coasts of Israel," and actually put many of them to death, employing those of his own house or family in the execution. This was a notorious violation of the public faith, laid the nation under the guilt of perjury and murder, and subjected them to the displeasure of God, who is the righteous avenger of these national crimes, but seems to have been regarded as an affair of no consequence, or rather acquiesced in as a useful and public-spirited measure. God, however, was pleased to make inquisition for the blood which had been thus unrighteously shed, and sent a famine upon the land, which lasted three years, in the third of which, David, moved by so extraordinary a calamity, inquired of the Lord the cause of it, and was answered by the oracle, that it was for Saul, and his bloody house, because he slew the Gibeonites. In consequence of this, David sent for some of the principal persons who had escaped the massacre, and said to them: "What shall I do for you, and wherewithal shall I make the atonement, that ye may bless the inheritance of the Lord?" What satisfaction do you require for the injuries that have been done you, that you may be induced to pray for the prosperity of my people? The Gibeonites answered him: "We will have no silver or gold of Saul, nor of his house; neither for us shalt thou kill any man in Israel." The king then bid them ask what they would have, and promised that he would do it for them. They replied: "The man that consumed us, and that devised against us, that we should be destroyed from remaining in any of the coasts of Israel; let seven of his sons be delivered unto us, and we will hang them up unto the Lord in Gibeah of Saul, who was chosen of the Lord." The king immediately replied: "I will give them;" and in consequence of it, sparing Mephibosheth, the son of Jonathan, and all the male line of Saul, who had any claim to, or were capable of contending with him for the crown, and disturbing him in the possession of it; he delivered to them the two bastard sons of Rizpah, Saul's concubine, and the five sons of Micah, his youngest daughter, by Adriel, the son of Barzillai, the Meholathite, not one of whom was capable of succeeding Saul, especially while any of the male line, and particularly those by the eldest son, were alive. Now, at this very time, Mephibosheth, Jonathan's eldest son, dwelt in David's family at Jerusalem; and though lame in his feet, yet he was sound enough to be the father of a son, named Micah, who had a numerous posterity, the descendants of whom continued down through many generations. In this account the reader will observe, that what gave rise to this execution in the family of Saul, was a three years' famine. The famine is not denied. The cause of it, some think, was the preceding intestine commotions. But this is highly improbable; for there is no intimation or probability, that the civil war continued so long as twelve months, as it was determined by a single battle, and as that battle was certainly fought not long after the rebellion broke out. For David continued in the plain of the wilderness, where he first retreated, and which was not far distant from Jerusalem, till he was informed what measures Absalom was determined to follow. These were fixed on soon after that rebel's entrance into Jerusalem, and as soon as the affair would admit, put in execution. Nay, so soon was the plan of operations fixed, that Hushai, David's friend, who continued with Absalom at Jerusalem, sent an express to David to acquaint him, that he had defeated the counsel of Ahithophel, but withal to advise him, not to lodge a single night more in the plains, but instantly to pass over Jordan, lest he and all his people should be swallowed up by a strong detachment from the rebel army. David immediately hastened to and passed the river, and could have but a few weeks or months to draw together his troops; for Absalom was soon after him, attacked his father, and his death put an end to the unnatural rebellion. Besides, the country in general must have been free from any great commotions; for, as David retreated beyond Jordan, collected his forces, and fought the rebels in the territories of the tribes on that side the river, the principal commotions must have happened there, and could not much affect the ten tribes, and occasion a three years' famine throughout that whole country.

The natural cause of that famine was the want of the usual rains, and the violent heat and drought of the seasons during that period; for it is observed of Rizpah, that as soon as her two sons were put to death, she spread herself a tent upon the rock where they were hung up from the beginning of harvest until water dropped on them out of heaven, i. e. till the rain came, which had been so long withheld, and it thereby appeared that the displeasure of God towards the nation was fully appeased. But though David could account for the natural cause of the famine, yet its long continuance was so unusual and extraordinary an event, as that he thought himself obliged to inquire of the Lord for the reasons of it, that he might prevent, if he could, the further continuance of it, by averting the displeasure of God, of which the famine seemed to be the immediate effect. Upon his inquiring, he was answered, that it was upon the account of "Saul, and his bloody house, because he slew the Gibeonites;" after which the historian immediately informs us, that "Saul sought to slay them in his zeal to the children of Israel and Judah;" and the Gibeonites themselves complained to David, that Saul was the man that "consumed them, and devised against them, that they should be destroyed from remaining in any of the coasts of Israel." And indeed the murder of these poor people was an action suitable to Saul's sanguinary temper; and if he was bloody enough to put to the sword, without any provocation, a whole city of his own subjects, what should hinder him from endeavouring to exterminate these Amorites out of the land, if he could hereby oblige his own people, by enriching them with their fields and vineyards, and thereby better establish himself and his family in the kingdom. Samuel indeed is not anywhere said to have charged Saul with any such slaughter. Probably that prophet was dead before this carnage of the Gibeonites happened, and therefore it was no wonder he never charged Saul with it. He lived long enough after Samuel's death to perpetrate this crime, when it would not be in Samuel's power to reproach him with it. If Samuel was alive, it is absolutely certain that he never visited Saul, and so could not reproach him for his barbarity. But to question the fact is to deny the history, which as peremptorily fastens it on Saul, as it does any other fact whatsoever. The deed itself was a perfidious and bloody one; the destruction of many of the Gibeonites, and a determined purpose wholly to extirpate the remainder of them out of the country, in violation of the public oath and faith that had been given them for their security, without any provocation or forfeiture of life on their part. He cut them off in cold blood, defenceless and unarmed, though they were serviceable to the nation, and many of them appropriated to the service of God and of his tabernacle, merely for secular and political views, and that he might serve himself, by gratifying some of the tribes among whom they lived, and who wanted to possess themselves of their cities and lands. It is probable his death prevented the full execution of this barbarous purpose, which therefore seems to have been begun but a very little while before it, in order to support his declining interest, and ingratiate himself with the children of Israel and Judah; with Judah particularly, of which tribe David was, and in whose territories some of the Gibeonitish towns were, to whom he thought the expulsion of that people might be agreeable, and so might be a means of retaining that powerful tribe in his interest. The crime therefore was enormous in itself, and aggravated with the most heinous circumstances; and which all civilized nations, almost in all ages, have looked upon with horror, and as highly deserving the divine displeasure and vengeance. Antiphon, one of the principal orators of Greece, pleading for the bringing a murderer to justice, against whom the evidence was not so full as was desired, but the circumstances exceedingly strong, urges this as a reason why the judges should not clear him; that it would be extremely dangerous to the public, to permit such an impure polluted wretch to enter into the temple of the gods and defile them, and to sit down at the tables of those who were innocent; because this would produce barren and unfruitful seasons, and render the public affairs unfortunate. Ælian also relates, that the Lacedemonians were punished with the entire ruin of Sparta by an earthquake, which left only five buildings in the city standing, for the murdering some of the Helotæ, who were slaves, and had fled into a temple for safety, after they had surrendered themselves on the promise of safety. When the noble Roman, Horatius, who, by his victory over the Curiatii, had established the supremacy of Rome over Alba, was accused by some of the principal citizens of Rome for having murdered his sister, who, upon his return from his victory had unseasonably and severely reproached him for killing her lover; they urged his being brought to justice, because he had violated the laws, and recounted several instances of the divine vengeance on cities who had suffered such atrocious crimes to go unpunished. But may it not be asked, that if God sought vengeance for a particular act of cruelty, perpetrated by Saul, when was vengeance demanded for David's massacre of the Geshurites, Gezrites, Amalekites, Moabites, Ammonites, Jebusites, and others, who at times became the objects of David's wrath? The answer is, it was never demanded, because there was no vengeance due, and the cases are by no means parallel. There was no violation of the national faith, no breach of oath, that David and his people had been guilty of in any of these instances. In most of them, the people mentioned were the aggressors; and, as to the rest of them, they were the inveterate enemies of the Jews, wandering clans, who lived upon robbery and plunder, and had been long before justly devoted to destruction. Besides, the Gibeonites were massacred in cold blood, in times of peace, unarmed, and incapable of any self-defence; and therefore every one must see the difference between these unhapppy people, whom Saul causelessly and treacherously destroyed, and those whom David cut off; who provoked their own ruin by unjustly making war on his subjects, whom he was in duty and honour bound to protect and defend, or who had been proscribed by God himself for the crimes of which they had been guilty.

The persons employed with Saul in perpetrating these murders, were those of his own house. The history here is express: "It is for Saul and his bloody house, because he," viz. by them as his instruments, "slew the Gibeonites;" for which reason they justly said to David, that they demanded satisfaction only of the man that had consumed them. He thought the destruction of the Gibeonites so popular a thing, as that he was resolved, himself and his family and relations, should have the whole credit and merit of the affair. Whether Jonathan and his brethren, who seem to have been brave men, were concerned in it, is not said. I think it probable they were not; for as they were good soldiers, they would be ashamed to massacre unarmed slaves, and of too generous a disposition to have any hand in so base and cruel an assassination. But if they every one refused to be employed in it, there were others of Saul's house, i. e. his family, who certainly were; who either in person, or by the soldiery, put many of these poor people to the sword; in which latter case they were equally guilty of the murder, as though they had killed every one of them with their own hands; just as Saul was guilty of the murder of the priests, and the massacre at Nob, though he employed Doeg in the first, and his soldiers in the latter execution. I think it probable from the choice which David made, that the very persons he gave up to the Gibeonites, were employed by Saul in his butchery, and that for this reason he delivered them up as sacrifices to public justice. These were the two bastard sons of Rizpah, Saul's concubine, and the five sons of Michal, the daughter of Saul, which she bare to Adriel, the son of Barzillai, the Meholathite. It appears to me, that Michal was married to this Adriel, before she was married to David, and had five children by him, which would be all of them of age sufficient to be employed in this unrighteous affair. Saul was about forty years old when he came to the crown; for his sons were all grown men, men of strength and valour, and his two daughters are spoken of as not being children at that time, but as women arrived at some maturity. From his being made king to David's marriage with Michal, was, by the chronology of our Bible, thirty-two years. Allow her therefore to be ten years of age on her father's advancement to the kingdom, she must be above forty years of age when David married her; a space of time, in which she might have had many more children than five by a former husband, that would be of age sufficient, in the latter part of Saul's reign, to act under his commission in the slaughter of the Gibeonites. It is not very probable that Saul's daughter should continue unmarried till she was forty years old and more, and the scripture is express, that she bare to Adriel, the son of Barzillai, the Meholathite, five children. It is indeed said, that Saul married his eldest daughter Merab, to Adriel, the Meholathite. But this Adriel might be a very different person from Adriel the son of Barzillai, who was the husband of Michal, who seems to have been thus particularly described, to distinguish him from the other Adriel, who, though a Meholathite, is nowhere said to be the son of Barzillai. If these remarks are just, we need no critical emendation of the text, and can defend the justice of David in giving up these persons to the vengeance of the Gibeonites. But supposing these sons of Michal, or Merab, were too young to have any hand in the guilt of this transaction, I do not see that an immediate command from God to deliver them up to death is anywise inconsistent with the rectitude of his nature, or the justice and equity of his moral providence. The judgment of Grotius on this affair is worthy our regard. "God," says that great man, "threatens in the law of Moses, that he would visit the iniquity of the fathers on their posterity. But then he hath an absolute dominion and right, not only over all we have, but over life itself; so that he can take away from any one his own gift whensoever he pleases, without assigning any reason for it. And therefore when he takes away the children of Achan, Saul, Jeroboam, and Achab, by an untimely and violent death, he exercises his right of dominion, not of punishment, over them; but, at the same time, he by this means more grievously punishes the parents of them. For whether the parents survive them, which the law principally supposes, the parents are certainly punished by seeing their children thus taken from them; or whether they do not live to see their children cut off, yet the fear that they may suffer for their crimes, is a very great punishment to the parents." He further observes, that "God does not make use of this extraordinary vengeance, except it be against crimes peculiarly dishonourable to him; such as idolatry, perjury, sacrilege, and the like."

The crime of Saul was a wilful breach of the laws of God and man, a perjurious violation of the national faith and honour, which it became God, the supreme governor of the Jewish nation, to manifest his resentment against. Suppose all who were actual perpetrators of this aggravated crime were dead, and out of the reach of vengeance. Yet some of their posterity were still remaining. But they were innocent. Allowed. Therefore. What? That God was unjust in taking away their lives? But what right had they to live longer? Does the gift of life convey an inalienable right to live for ever, or to any particular period of life? And that in bar of God's right to resume it when he pleases, and when there are valuable ends to be answered by his resuming it? The evident intention of God, in ordering the death of this part of Saul's family, was to be a public attestation of his abhorrence of Saul's perfidy and cruelty, to strike a terror into the princes his successors, and caution them against committing the like offences, as they would not have them avenged by the sufferings of their posterity, and especially to prevent all future attempts against the lives of the Gibeonites, whom God now declared to be under his protection, though they seem to have been looked on with a malignant eye by the Jewish nation; who probably would have in time completed the extirpation which Saul began, had it not been for this remarkable manifestation of God's displeasure against it. The death of these seven persons therefore, supposing them all innocent, was, in this view, no punishment at all inflicted on them by God, but an appointment of God in virtue of his sovereign right over the lives of all men, to teach princes moderation and equity, and prevent for the future the commission of those enormous crimes, which, if permitted to go with impunity, would be inconsistent with the peace and welfare, and even being, of civil government; and God did these innocent persons no more injustice, by ordering them to die by the hands of the Gibeonites, than if he had taken them away by any kind of natural death, which I presume no real Theist will deny his right to, because it is a right which he exercises in the daily dispensations of his providence. And as he intended their death should be subservient to promote the public virtue, welfare, and safety; the manner of their death, whatever it might be in the imagination of others, was to them much more honourable than if they had been cut off at the same age in the ordinary course of things, when no public utility could have been so perfectly answered by it.

That children do, and very frequently too, suffer and die for the sins of their parents, in which they have had no share, and even by the constitution of God himself, is evident from history, and the constant experience of all ages and nations. Thus God punished David by the death of his first child by Bathsheba, and Jeroboam, by the death of his eldest son, who was a religious and virtuous young prince; and for any thing that we can tell, the death of both might, instead of being a punishment, be a real blessing to them; and God ever hath it in his power to compensate those whom he deprives of life for the promoting any public good. Indeed this is a case that frequently happens, according to that divine threatening, of "visiting the iniquity of the fathers upon the children, unto the third and fourth generation of them that hate him;" i. e. by such punishments, the effects of which should continue, and be felt by their children to the third and fourth generation. And if this be a difficulty, it affects natural religion as well as revealed, since the fact itself is indisputable. How frequently do parents by their vices transmit to their innocent children a miserable corrupted constitution, and entail upon them distemper and death? In public calamities, such as pestilences, earthquakes, famines, and the like, by which God chastises the sins of nations, how frequently are the guilty and innocent, parents and their children, involved in one common destruction! Why then might not God, by an immediate command, appoint some of the innocent children of Saul's bloody family to be put to death for his sins, as well as command a pestilence or an earthquake to destroy children of other families for the crimes of their parents? It makes no difference in the nature of the thing, whether God takes away their lives by that course of nature which he established, or by a command immediately given for the purpose, since, in both cases, the lots of such children's lives is equally the appointment of God, who hath a right over life supreme and inalienable. Every one can see one wise intention of providence in this constitution of things, viz. to render children a sort of security for the good behaviour of the parents, as they are indeed in all human government, and that their affection for their families may be a powerful means to guard them against the practice of those crimes which tend to involve their children in misery and ruin; or that if they will not be restrained by these motives, the distresses of their families may teach others wisdom, and show them the necessity of a more regular and virtuous behaviour. It is indeed a constitution of the Mosaic law, and founded on natural equity, that the "fathers shall not be put to death for the children, neither shall the children be put to death for the fathers. Every one shall be put to death for his own sins." This constitution ought to take place in all human governments; because, as far as these are concerned, every one hath an inalienable right to keep his life, till he forfeits it to human justice; and for men to take away the life of one for the fault of another, is to take it away without forfeiture, and is therefore an act of evident injustice and cruelty. But because God forbids men, who have no sovereign right over the lives of any, to punish one person with death for the offences of another, doth he therefore lose his own right of taking away the lives of others, whensoever, and by what means soever he pleases? Or, is he guilty of injustice and cruelty, because he resumes his own gift, and what no one living hath any right to demand the continuance of from him, for one single moment longer than he is pleased to continue it, and what every man is bound willingly to lay down when God calls him to it, in order to promote any public good, and it is necessary to answer any valuable purpose in the moral providence and government of God? Besides we see, in the constant course of things, that infants, children, persons of every age and stage of life, are cut off by death, without any peculiar guilt or forfeiture of life, either to human or divine justice, and by various kinds of deaths, some of them extremely mortifying and affecting. Will any sensible Theist dare to arraign the justice of God in this constitution of things, or complain that God properly punishes those who are thus taken off in the common course of nature? As for myself, I cannot comprehend all the reasons of providence in this dispensation, nor do I think that I have a right to demand that God should acquaint me with those reasons. It must be right, because it is the constitution of God; and therefore he had an equal right to cut off these seven persons of Saul's family by the hands of the Gibeonites, as he hath to cut off any other persons in the common course of things, and, in taking them away, he no more properly punished them, if they were wholly innocent of the murder of the Gibeonites, than he punishes any of those, who may be esteemed innocent, and yet are every day taken off by distemper or accident; and Rizpah and Michal had no more reason to complain of the injustice of providence for the loss of their children, than any other tender mothers have, when providence bereaves them of any of the valuable branches of their family, by an untimely death.

It is evident from what hath been said on this article, that God's ordering these seven persons to be delivered up to the Gibeonites, is not in the least contrary to the Mosaic law, nor any true notion of justice and equity, nor making justice, when applied to God, one thing, and when applied to men, a quite different thing; for the rights of God and man over life are infinitely different. For life is his gift, given by him without claim or merit, given for that period only for which he intended it, and may therefore be justly resumed, as his gift, at any period he thinks proper to demand it, without doing any injustice to him from whom he takes it; because he violates no right that belongs to him, nor takes from him any property, which he hath a real claim to, as his proper inheritance. But, with regard to men, every one hath an inalienable claim to his life, and he who takes it from another without a just forfeiture of it, violates the most sacred rights of nature, and wickedly robs him of his most valuable treasure, which he can never restore to him, and for the loss of which he cannot make him any possible compensation. But then it may be asked, what equity there is in punishing a whole nation with a three years' famine, for the crimes of Saul and his bloody house? The equity of their punishment appears, because both Israel and Judah consented to and acquiesced in the massacre. This is plainly intimated in the history, which says, that Saul slew the Gibeonites in his zeal to the children of Israel and Judah, because he knew they would like it, and esteem it, as a proof of his desire and readiness to serve them. The Israelites, as Mr. Le Clerc on the place observes, seem, for some cause or other, to have envied the Gibeonites, so that by extirpating them Saul thought to oblige them. And from hence it is evident, that he did not destroy them because they had formerly deceived the Israelites, and that the slaughter of them was far from being displeasing to, or opposed by the people.

It hath been asked, how we are to account for the deferring the punishment of Saul's crime, for so many years after the fact was committed, and Saul's death. I do not think myself obliged to account for all the reasons by which God proceeds in the administrations of his moral providence, and am content to be ignorant, whenever those reasons of divine conduct are not somehow or other revealed to me. However, though Saul was dead, yet there were some of his bloody house still remaining, and the circumstance of Saul's death could be no reason against bringing to justice those of that bloody family, that had been employed by him as the instruments of his treachery and cruelty; or why providence should never express its disapprobation against such a notorious violation of the public faith and honour. If no satisfactory account could be given for the delay of this punishment for several years, it would by no means follow that there was none. Had we lived in those times, we might have been better able to solve this difficulty. Some things, however, offer themselves on this subject which deserve our regard. While Saul, the principal actor in this tragedy, was living, and was well known for his contempt of the prophets and the cruelty of his disposition, who was there to call him to an account, and execute the just vengeance on him and his bloody house? In the beginning of David's reign, his own unsettled condition for seven years and more, when Saul's family disputed the crown with him, and could none of them have been brought to justice by him; the many necessary wars he was afterward engaged in, and perhaps not thinking himself obliged to take notice of Saul's conduct during his reign, or his very tenderness for the family of his predecessor and father-in-law, might all concur to prevent any public inquisition into this cruel transaction, or calling any of the offenders to an account for it in the common course of justice. And God permitted things to take their natural course, and not to manifest his displeasure on this account, till it could be done in such a manner, as should make his justice, as the God and king of Israel, more conspicuous, and the execution of his vengeance more observable and awful, and as should, at the same time, most effectually prevent all future attempts to injure or extirpate that unhappy people.

Particular events may for a long while be delayed, and the very delay of them may, in concurrence with the operations of providence, be one means at last of bringing them to pass with greater observation, and more convincing evidence of the interposition of God in bringing them about, as is frequently the case in long-concealed murders. God therefore, in a time of profound peace, when David's government was settled, and there was nothing to interrupt the course of justice, punishes the people with a three years' famine, to let them feel his displeasure, to render them solicitous to know the cause of it, and take the proper methods to appease it. So that though no train of intervening and unavoidable circumstances can impede the operations of providence, or prevent what God is determined to bring to pass, yet such circumstances may, for a very considerable while, impede the operations of human justice; nevertheless, how long soever that justice may be delayed, it will certainly at last take place, when God judges it the proper season to execute it, and when such execution shall most effectually demonstrate his inspection, and tend to secure the purposes of his moral providence and government over mankind.

It is, I think, more than obscurely intimated, in those words of David to the Gibeonites, "What shall I do for you, and wherewithal shall I make the atonement, that ye may bless the inheritance of the Lord?" that they had loudly exclaimed against the violation of the public faith, and the perfidy and cruelty of Saul and his family, who had destroyed them; and demanded that some satisfaction should be made them, and had invocated the vengeance of God against their murderers. To demand satisfaction they had a right, as the *vindices sanguinis*, the avengers of blood, or the near relations of those whom Saul had cut off; and it is probable that they took occasion, from the continuance of the famine for three years, to renew their complaints for the injuries they had suffered, and to desire that justice might be done them. This must greatly embarrass David, as Saul and his sons were killed in battle, and no satisfaction possibly could be obtained from them; and therefore, in order to know the real cause of the famine, and whether any, or what satisfaction was to be made to the Gibeonites, he determined to inquire of the oracle, and govern himself by the directions of it. The answer he received was, that the famine was sent for Saul, for his bloody house, because he slew the Gibeonites.

It is true, that the oracular response did not in words dictate any act of expiation that was to be made to the Gibeonites, but only mentioned the cause of the famine. And the reason is plain, because when it was known that the famine was sent for the slaughter of these poor people by Saul and his bloody house, it was as well known they were to have some justice done them on that bloody family, for the outrages that had been committed on them; for David knew that, in the ordinary course of justice, the shedding of blood was only to be atoned for by the shedding of his or their blood on whom the murder was chargeable. So that the oracle did really dictate, though not in words, the necessity of an expiation, by pointing out the crime for which the famine was sent. And thus David understood it, when sending for the Gibeonites, he said to them: "What shall I do for you? Wherewith shall I make the atonement?" i. e. the atonement for the blood of your people, that hath been unrighteously shed. The Gibeonites replied: "We will have no silver or gold of Saul, neither for us shalt thou kill any man in Israel." No compensation could be made under the law, for wilful murder, by silver and gold; and indeed nothing could have argued a meaner and more sordid disposition in these people, than a demand of money, in satisfaction for the massacre committed on them; and though the nation might have been, and certainly was, in some respect criminal, for permitting Saul to cut them off, yet, as Saul was the contriver of the mischief, and his family the immediate agents who destroyed them, they did not desire that any one person in Israel should be put to death on their account, which was an argument of their great moderation and regard to justice. David then bid them name the satisfaction they demanded, and promised that he would give it them, acting herein in obedience to the prophet's direction, who, as Josephus rightly observes, ordered him to grant the Gibeonites whatsoever satisfaction they should demand of him. We have something of a like history in Herodotus, who tells us, that after the Pelasgi had murdered their Athenian wives, and the children had by them, they found that their lands became barren, their wives unfruitful, and their flocks failed of their usual increase. On this account they sent to the oracle at Delphos, to know by what means they might obtain deliverance from these calamities. The oracle ordered them to give the Athenians whatsoever satisfaction they should demand of them. The Athenians demanded, that they should deliver up their country to them, in the best condition they could. This the Pelasgi promised upon a certain condition, which they thought impossible. However, they were forced in virtue of this promise, many years after, to surrender it to Miltiades, some of them making no resistance to his forces, and those who did, were besieged and taken prisoners.—CHANDLER.

Ver. 5. And they answered the king, The man that consumed us, and that devised against us *that* we should be destroyed from remaining in any of the coasts of Israel, 6. Let seven men of his sons be delivered unto us, and we will hang them up unto the LORD in Gibeah of Saul, *whom* the LORD did choose. And the king said, I will give *them*.

It appears by this, that the demand of these seven persons, to be put to death, was by order of God, and the sacrifice that he appointed to be made to the public justice, to expiate the murders committed by Saul, for they were to be hung up to the Lord; i. e. in obedience to his will, and to appease his displeasure, because wilful murders are highly offensive to God, and are properly to be expiated by the death of those who have committed them; in which sense every offender who is guilty of capital offences, expiates his guilt by suffering the penalty of death, and thereby becomes a sacrifice to justice, human and divine. It deserves also to be remarked, that the Gibeonites did not intend to exterminate the family of Saul, in revenge for his intention to destroy them out of the coasts of Israel, but only demanded seven of his sons, and left the choice of these seven to David himself, hereby putting it out of their power to sacrifice the male line of Saul to their revenge, and giving David a glorious opportunity to show how religiously he remembered his covenant with his friend Jonathan, and that no policy of state should ever induce him to the violation of it. It appears from hence, that David could not instigate the Gibeonites to make this request, that seven of Saul's sons might be delivered to them, that they might kill them, to prevent its being said that he killed them for their sakes, and that the Gibeonites might hereby take the blame of their destruction upon themselves, and screen David from being charged with that murder which he himself had contrived, and by them perpetrated. For if the Gibeonites had acted with a determined purpose to cut off Saul's family, they would have named their men, and made sure work by a demand of Mephibosheth and his family. Or if David had the same view, he would have prompted the Gibeonites to have asked the delivery of the same persons; or, when the choice was left to himself, would readily have seized the opportunity of giving up those that he apprehended it was most for his interest to get rid of. Indeed nothing can be a more improbable absurd supposition than this of David's instigating the Gibeonites to demand seven of Saul's family to be delivered up to death, as an expiation for his having destroyed many of them. Whether there was, or was not, such a massacre of them by Saul, must be universally known to the people of Israel. For such an execution could not have been committed in a corner. If there was not, how could the Gibeonites demand satisfaction? For what could they demand it? Or how demand it from the house of Saul, if they, and all the people of Israel knew, that Saul and his house had never injured them? Or, how could David instigate them to ask satisfaction for a massacre, that he and all his people knew had never been committed on them? No man of common sense would openly pretend a reason for an act of cruelty and injustice, which had not the shadow of a reason in it, and which every one must know the absolute falsehood of; and it must have been much less exceptionable to all David's subjects, had he put Saul's family to death by an act of power, and openly avowed, that he did it to secure himself and his own family on the throne, than to cut them off by such a barefaced paltry contrivance, which every one must see through, and which could not diminish the guilt and horror of the fact, but only serve to heighten his own impudence and wickedness, and expose him for his perfidy, subornation, and cruelty, to the greater abhorrence of all his people. And indeed it is acknowledged that a more barefaced deceit was never exhibited; such indeed as could only have been attempted among the poor bigoted Jews. But I would observe, that as this transaction was carried on in an open public manner; as it was occasioned by a three years' famine; as the oracular response declared the famine was sent because that Saul and his bloody house had consumed the Gibeonites; as they demanded Saul's sons for an expiation; and David delivered them up for an atonement; stupid as the Jews were, it was too barefaced a deceit to pass even on them; for if there had been no massacre of the Gibeonites at all, nor a famine of three years' continuance, the oracle would have been convicted of an immediate lie, and could never have persuaded the people into the belief of facts, which they themselves were absolutely certain never existed. If David was so vile as to attempt this deceit, and the Jews so stupid as to be deluded by it, what must the Gibeonites be, who acted in this tragedy by David's instigation, charged Saul with consuming and destroying them, and demanded seven of his sons as victims? For what? Why, for nothing; for destroying and consuming them, when, in reality, they knew that he did not destroy and consume them, and all the nation knew that this charge against Saul was an imposture and a lie, and the demand of his sons for an expiation was the highest villany and impiety. There is, I believe, no man living who can really believe, that either David or the Gibeonites could be thus designedly, shamelessly, and without inducement wicked, since the Gibeonites were to have neither gold nor silver for the part they acted, and since David might have cut off Saul's family, had it been in his heart to have done it, and assigned reasons for it, that would have carried some appearance of necessity and justice. If Saul was in reality guilty of the murder of these Gibeonites, it became the providence of God, who was supreme king and judge in Israel, to make inquisition for the blood that was shed, and manifest his displeasure against such a notorious violation of the public faith and honour. Thus also will David be fully vindicated from the charge of instigating the request of the Gibeonites, and they from the iniquitous imputation of concerting with him so extremely childish, but wicked a scheme, of cutting off Saul's posterity.

It hath been suggested to the dishonour of David, that in consequence of this request of the Gibeonites, which he himself must have instigated, David, not withheld by any motives of gratitude towards the posterity of his unhappy father-in-law, in direct violation of his oath to Saul at the cave of Engedi, granted it; sparing only Mephibosheth, who luckily was so unfortunate as to be a cripple, and so much dependant on David, that he had no room for apprehension from him. He therefore reserved Mephibosheth, in memory of another oath between him and his father, Jonathan; for he was under obligations by two oaths, and forgot one, and remembered the other. But this charge is contrary to the most express account of the history, and David's conduct in this affair was worthy a man of probity and honour, and consistent with the strictest regard to his oaths both to Saul and Jonathan. That in granting the request to the Gibeonites, he directly violated his oath to Saul at the cave of Engedi; or cut off the remainder of Saul's family, in defiance of the solemn oath by which he engaged to spare that unhappy race, needs no other refutation than the oath itself. Saul asked David to swear by the Lord, "that thou wilt not cut off my seed after me, that thou wilt not destroy my name out of my father's house." David gave him his oath accordingly. I will not urge here, that had Saul's family committed crimes worthy of death, David's oath would have been no reason against punishing them according to their deserts; and such punishment, if deserved, had been no breach of his oath. But I shall only observe, that if David did not cut off his seed after him, so as to destroy his name out of his father's house, he did not violate his oath to Saul. Now David did not cut off one single person of Saul's family, whose death had the least tendency to destroy his name out of his father's house. The seed is always reckoned by the males, and not the females of a family, and the name in a father's house could only be preserved by the male descendants. But David gave up only the sons of Saul's concubine, who were not the legal seed of Saul, and those of his eldest daughter, who could only keep up Adriel's name, and not Saul's; and hereby conscientiously observed, without the least violation, his oath to Saul, or need of any mental reservation to help him out.

To this it is objected, that if the seed is always reckoned by the males, and not the females, then Jesus Christ could not be the son of David, because he did not descend from David, by the male line, but from the female. But it should be observed, that the son by a daughter is as really the son of the grandfather, as a son in the male succession, and that the only difference is, that the succession in a family is kept by the sons, and not by the females, who by marriage enter into other families, and therefore cannot keep up the names of the families from whence they sprang. Jesus Christ therefore was the son of David, though only so by the mother's side; and as he was not to keep up David's line according to the flesh, it was expressly predicted of him, by a double prophecy, that he should be of the female line. The one, that he should be the seed of the woman; the other, that his mother should be a virgin; so that he could not have been that son of David who was to be the Messiah, and to sit on his throne for ever and ever, had he been David's son by an earthly father. The same spirit of prophecy that declared he should be David's son, as expressly declared that he should be so by the mother; an exception that makes no alteration in the general rule of family successions, which were constantly among the Jews, and almost every nation in the world, in the male line, and not in the female. Nor is it true that he spared only Mephibosheth, and that he reserved only one cripple, from whom he could have no apprehensions, and who being the son of Jonathan, gave him the opportunity of making a merit of his gratitude. The history expressly contradicts this assertion, for Mephibosheth had a son, whom he called Micah, who was now old enough to have children, and had four sons, from whom descended a numerous posterity. See his line in the following table :—

Saul, Jonathan, Mephibosheth, or Merib-baal,
‖
Micah,
‖
Pithon, Melech, Tarea, Abaz,
‖
Jehoadah,
‖
Alemeth, Zimri, Asmaveth,
‖
Moza,
‖
Binea,
‖
Rapha,
‖
Eleasah,
‖
Azel,
‖
Azrikam Bocheru, Ishmael, Sheariah, Obadiah, Hanan,
‖
Eshek,
‖
Ulam, Jeush, Eliphelet,
‖
150 sons and grandsons.

O faithless David, thus to leave Saul only one poor cripple! and who, not withheld by any motives of gratitude, and in direct violation of his oath to Saul, did thus wickedly cut off all his seed after him, and wholly destroy his name, out of his father's house! It appears from what hath been said also, that when it is insinuated that David spared Mephibosheth, only because as a cripple, and dependant on David, he had no room for apprehension from him, it is mere suggestion, and inconsistent with the plainest appearance to the contrary. For as this could not be the reason for his saving Mephibosheth's son Micah, and his family, it is not likely he acted from it in sparing Mephibosheth himself, but from a more worthy motive towards both, out of regard to his oath, and the grateful remembrance he still preserved of his former obligations to, and friendship with Jonathan, Mephibosheth's father. This the scripture asserts; that the king spared Mephibosheth, the son of Saul, because of the Lord's oath that was between them, between David and Jonathan the son of Saul.

I have one remark more to make on this part of the history, which turns out to David's immortal honour. It is observed, that some certain contemplations, which are put into David's head, calling to his remembrance, that some of Saul's family were yet living, he concluded it expedient to cut them off, lest they should hereafter prove thorns in his side; and then whenever David projected any scheme, a religious pretence, and the assistance of the priests, were never wanting. But for this charge there is not any foundation. For Saul's bastard children, and the children by his daughter, could never be thorns in David's side, any more than other people, or the other branches of Saul's family, because incapable of the crown; especially, while there continued a lineal descent in the male line from Saul himself. David therefore could not be guilty of all this villany and folly with which he hath been charged, for the sake of cutting off Saul's family, lest they should be thorns in his side, because he cut off none but those who could be no thorns in his side, and suffered all those to live, who alone were capable of proving thorns in his side; and therefore David projected no such scheme as this of cutting off Saul's family; yea, his conduct in this affair was directly the reverse of what he must have done had he projected any such scheme; and therefore I must conclude, that as no such scheme was ever projected, there was, and could be, no occasion for a religious pretence, or the assistance of the priests, to sanctify and accomplish it. There have been, I acknowledge, commotions excited in states by illegitimate children, and by descendants in the female line. But I know of no instance, in ancient or modern history, of any prince, who remembering that some of his predecessor's family, who might dispute with him his crown by their descent, were living, and concluding it expedient to cut them off, lest they should hereafter prove thorns in his side, should, to answer this end, cut off only the bastard children, and those of the daughters, and leave the son and grandson of his predecessor alive to propagate their descendants, and in them claimants to his crown, and thorns in his side, to all generations. Suspicious and jealous tyrants love to make surer work; but David, under a necessity of delivering up some of his predecessor's family to justice, generously preserved the claimants to his crown alive, and delivered up those only from whom he could have nothing to fear, as having no kind of legal right to the government and kingdom.

Illustrious prince! Be thy name and memory ever revered, thy generosity ever spoken of with praise; who, when forced by providence to give up to justice some of the guilty family of thy persecutor and sworn enemy, didst from the greatness of thy mind, thy prevailing humanity, thy regard to thy oath to one who sought thy life, and thy pleasing remembrance of thy once loved friend; refuse to cut off the seed of him that persecuted thee, and to destroy his name out of his father's house, but didst nourish his seed in thy bosom, maintain it in thy family, suffer it to increase and prosper, and spread itself out into numerous branches, even when policy might have dictated other measures, and a wicked craft would certainly have pursued them. Fresh be thy laurels to the latest posterity, and thine unexampled generosity ever be remembered with the veneration and esteem, which it claims from all the benevolent and virtuous part of mankind. It should be further mentioned, on this occasion, to David's honour, that though he was necessitated to deliver up some of Saul's family to justice, to give satisfaction to the injured Gibeonites, yet that he took the first opportunity to pay the last tokens of respect that could be to Saul and his unhappy family. For as soon as ever it appeared, that the natural cause of the famine was over, by the return of the rains, David ordered the bones of Saul and Jonathan to be fetched from the men of Jabesh-gilead, who had recovered them from the Philistines, and took them, together with the bones of those that had been hanged up, and buried them honourably in the sepulchre of Kish, Saul's father; whereby he showed, that he had no inveterate enmity to Saul's family, but was pleased with the opportunity of showing respect to his name and memory. This whole account concludes with this observation of the historian: "They performed all that the king commanded, and after that God was entreated for the land." God approved his generosity to the family and remains of his enemy, and as the reward of it, sent prosperity to him and his people.—CHANDLER.

Ver. 10. And Rizpah the daughter of Aiah took sackcloth, and spread it for her upon the rock, from the beginning of harvest until water dropped upon them out of heaven, and suffered neither the birds of the air to rest on them by day, nor the beasts of the field by night.

Speaking of a great precipice near Bylan, Mr. Parsons says, "three loaded camels fell down the precipice, and were killed on the spot, in my remembrance; and what is very remarkable, in less than thirty hours after their loads were taken off, there was not left a piece of flesh, but all was devoured by the vultures in the day, and the beasts of prey, mostly jackals, in the night."—BURDER.

By a passage of La Roque, it appears, that if the usual rains have failed in the spring, it is of great benefit to have a copious shower, though very late: for he tells us, that when he arrived at Sidon, in the end of June, it had not rained there for many months, and that the earth was so extremely dry, that the cotton plants, and the mulberry-trees, which make the principal riches of that country, were in a sad condition, and all other things suffered in proportion, so that a famine was feared, which is generally followed with a pestilence. He then tells us, that all the sects of religion which lived there had, in their various ways, put up public prayers for rain, and that at length on the very day that the Mohammedans made a solemn procession out of the city, in the way of supplicating for mercy, all on a sudden the air thickened, and all the marks of an approaching storm appeared, and the rain descended in such abundance, that all those that attended the procession got back to the city with considerable difficulty, and in disorder. He adds, that the rain continued all that day, and part of the night, which perfected the revival of the plants, and the saving of the productions of the earth.

La Roque is evidently embarrassed with this fall of the rain just at the time the Mohammedans were presenting their supplications, when neither the solemn prayers of the Greek bishop, nor those of the Latin monks, nor even the exposing of the Host for many days, had been thus honoured: "At last," said he, "Heaven, which bestows its favours, when and how it pleases, and who causes it to rain on the unjust and the infidel, permitted so great an abundance of rain to fall," &c. But there certainly was no occasion for any such disquietude; there was no dispute which religion was most excellent involved in this transaction, nor does any thing more appear in it than this, that God, the universal parent, having at length been sought to by all, showered down his mercies upon all. But the intention of these papers leads me to remarks of a different kind. This author does not tell us when this rain fell, which is to be regretted, and the more so, as he is often exact in less important matters. However, it could not be before the end of June, N. S. for he did not arrive at Sidon until then; and it could not be so late as the usual time of the descent of the autumnal rains, for the cotton is ripe in September, until the middle of which month those rains seldom fall, often later, and this rain is supposed to have been of great service to the growing cotton; consequently, these general prayers for rain could not refer to autumnal showers, but a late spring rain, which probably happened soon after his arrival, or about the time that Dr. Russel tells us those severe thundershowers fell at Aleppo, which I have before taken notice of, that is, about the beginning of July, O. S. And though the harvest must have been over at Sidon by the time this gentleman arrived there, and they had, therefore, nothing then to hope or to fear for as to that, yet as the people of those countries depend so much on garden stuff, the inspissated juice of grapes, figs, olives, &c. they might be apprehensive of a scarcity as to these too, which they might hope to prevent by this late rain. For the like reason, such a rain must have been extremely acceptable in the days of David. And it must have been more so, if it came a good deal earlier, though we must believe it to have been after all expectations of it in the common way were over; and such a one, I suppose, was granted. Dr. Delany indeed, in his life of David, tells us, that the Rabbins suppose the descendants of Saul hanged from March, from the first days of the barley-harvest, to the following October, and he seems to approve their sentiments. Dr. Shaw mentions this affair only cursorily; however, he appears to have imagined that they hanged until the rainy season came in course. But surely we may much better suppose it was such a rain as La Roque speaks of, or one rather earlier. The ground Delany goes upon is a supposition, that the bodies that were hanged up before the Lord, hung until the flesh was wasted from the bones, which he thinks is affirmed in the 13th verse of that chapter; but, I must confess, no such thing appears to be affirmed there; the bodies of Saul and his sons, it is certain, hanged but a very little while on the wall of Bethshan before the men of Jabesh-gilead removed them, which yet are called bones;—"They took their bones and buried them," 1 Sam. xxxi. 13; the seven sons of Saul then might hang a very little time in the days of King David. And if it should be imagined that the flesh of Saul was consumed by fire, verse 12, and so the word bones came to be used in the account of their interment, can any reason be assigned why we should not suppose these bodies were treated after the same manner? But it appears that the word *bones* frequently means the same thing with *corpse*, which circumstance also totally invalidates this way of reasoning: so the embalmed body of Joseph is called his *bones*, Gen. l. 25, 26, and Exod. xiii. 19; so the lying prophet terms his body, just become breathless, his bones: "When I am dead, then bury me in the sepulchre wherein the man of God is buried, lay my bones beside his bones," 1 Kings xiii. 31. So Josephus tells us that Simon removed the bones of his brother Jonathan the high-priest, who was slain by Tryphon when he was departing out of that country, though Simon seems to have removed the body as soon as might be after Tryphon's retirement.

Such a late spring rain would have been attended, as the rain at Sidon was, with many advantages; and coming after all hope of common rain was over, and presently following the death of these persons on the other hand, would be a much more merciful management of Providence, and a much nobler proof that the execution was the appointment of God, and not a political stratagem of David, than the passing of six months over without any rain at all, and then its falling only in the common track of things. This explanation also throws light on the closing part of this story, "And after that God was entreated for the land." Dr. Delany seems to suppose that the performing these funeral rites was requisite to the appeasing God: but could that be the meaning of the clause? Were the ignominy of a death the law of Moses pronounced accursed, and the honour of a royal funeral, both necessary mediums of appeasing the Almighty? Is it not a much easier interpretation of this clause, The rain that dropped on these bodies was a great mercy to the country, and the return of the rains in due quantities afterward, in their season, proved that God had been entreated for the land?—HARMER.

Ver. 12. And David went and took the bones of Saul, and the bones of Jonathan his son, from the men of Jabesh-gilead, which had stolen them from the streets of Beth-shan, where the Philistines had hanged them, when the Philistines had slain Saul in Gilboa.

"Beth-shan." Calmet says on this, "House, or temple of the tooth, or of ivory; from (בית) beth, *a house*, and (שן) shen, *a tooth*. This title means, no doubt, simply the temple of the tooth, but we have no reason to conclude that a TOOTH only was worshipped in any temple in Canaan; it must have been the symbol of some deity." Calmet then proceeds to show that this may have been the god Ganesa of the East, who is represented with an elephant's head, and supposes the tusks are alluded to by the tooth. I am not aware, however, of any such distinction being made in that deity, and think it unlikely that his tusk would give the name to a temple. Is it not a curious fact, that the tooth of Buddha is the most SACRED and precious relic, in the opinion of the inhabitants of Siam, of the Burman empire, and of Ceylon? That TOOTH is kept in the temple of Kandy, the capital of Ceylon. Buddhism is the religion of China, and of those countries alluded to, and it was formerly the religion of multitudes in India.—ROBERTS.

CHAPTER XXII.

Ver. 6. The sorrows of hell compassed me about; the snares of death prevented me.

This is an allusion to the ancient manner of hunting, which is still practised in some countries, and was performed by surrounding a considerable tract of ground by a circle of nets, and afterward contracting the circle by degrees, till they had forced all the beasts of that quarter together into a narrow compass, and then it was that the slaughter began. This manner of hunting was used in Italy of old, as well as all over the eastern parts of the world, and it was from this custom that the poets sometimes represented death as surrounding persons with her nets, and as encompassing them on every side.—BURDER.

Ver. 35. He teacheth my hands to war; so that a bow of steel is broken by mine arms.

The bow is the first weapon mentioned in the holy scriptures, and seems to have been quite familiar to the immediate descendants of Abraham. "Take," said Isaac, "thy quiver and thy bow, and go out to the field, and take me some venison." Here indeed the reference is to hunting; but we learn from the remark of Jacob to his favourite son, that the weapon which was found so useful in his art, was soon turned against our species; and it still continues to maintain its place in some countries, among the instruments of human destruction.

We learn from Homer, that the Grecian bow was at first made of horn, and tipped with gold. But the material of which it was fabricated, seems for the most part to have been wood, which the workman frequently adorned with gold and silver. One of these ornamented weapons procured for Apollo, a celebrated Cretan, the significant name of Αργυροτοξος, the bearer of the silver-studded bow. But the Asiatic warrior often used a bow of steel or brass, which, on account of its great stiffness, he bent with his foot. Those that were made of horn or wood probably required to be bent in the same way; for the Hebrew always speaks of treading his bow, when he makes ready for the battle; and to tread and bend the bow are in all the writings of the Old Testament convertible phrases. The bow of steel is distinctly mentioned by the Hebrew bard: "He teaches my hand to war, so that a bow of steel is broken by mine arms." This was a proof of great strength, and of uncommon success in war, which he ascribes with equal piety and gratitude to the infinite power and goodness of Jehovah. To bend the bow, was frequently proposed as a trial of strength. After Ulysses had bent his bow, which all the suiters of Penelope had tried in vain, he boasted to his son Telemachus of the deed, because it was an undeniable proof that he had not lost his ancient vigour, in which he was accustomed to glory. Herodotus relates, that when Cambyses sent his spies into the territories of Ethiopia, the king of that country, well understanding the design of their visit, thus addressed them: When the Persians can easily draw bows of this largeness, then let them invade the Ethiopians. He then unstrung the bow, and gave it to them to carry to their master. The Persians themselves, according to Xenophon, carried bows three cubits in length. If these were made of steel or brass, which are both mentioned in the sacred volume, and of a thickness proportioned to their length, they must have been very dangerous weapons even in close fight; and as such they are represented by the prophet Isaiah: "Their bows also shall dash the young men in pieces; and they shall have no pity on the fruit of the womb; their eyes shall not spare children." In time of peace, or when not engaged with the enemy, the oriental warriors carried their bow in a case, sometimes of cloth, but more commonly of leather, hung to their girdles. When it was taken from the case, it was said, in the language of Habakkuk, to be "made quite naked."—PAXTON.

Ver. 41. Thou hast also given me the necks of mine enemies, that I might destroy them that hate me.

The neck is often used for the whole body, and in threatenings, it is the part mentioned. A proprietor of slaves is said to have their necks. To a person going among wicked or cruel people it is said, "Go not there, your *puddara*, i. e. neck, or nape, will be given to them." "Depend upon it, government will have it out of the necks of those smugglers." "Have you paid Chinnan the money?" "No, nor will I pay him." "Why?" "Because he has had it out of my neck." When two men have been fighting, the conqueror may be seen to seize the vanquished by the neck, and thrust him to the ground.—ROBERTS.

CHAPTER XXIII.

Ver. 16. And the three mighty men brake through the host of the Philistines, and drew water out of the well of Beth-lehem, that *was* by the gate, and took *it*, and brought *it* to David: nevertheless he would not drink thereof, but poured it out unto the LORD.

There is an account very similiar to this in Arrian's *Life of Alexander.* Tunc poculo pleno, sicut oblatum est reddito: non solus, inquit bibere sustineo, nec tam exiguum devidere omnibus possum. "When his army was greatly oppressed with heat and thirst, a soldier brought him a cup of water; he ordered it to be carried back, saying, I cannot bear to drink alone, while so many are in want: and this cup is too small to be divided among the whole. Give it to the children for whom you brought it." —BURDER.

CHAPTER XXIV.

Ver. 1. And again the anger of the LORD was kindled against Israel, and he moved David against them to say, Go, number Israel and Judah.

Here arises the question, If Moses presupposed the lawfulness of this measure, and did actually twice number the people, wherein consisted David's sin when he did the same? Yet the Bible says that he actually did sin in this matter, and was punished for it by God, with a pestilence, which lessened the sum of the people numbered, by 70,000. The history of this event is given in 2 Sam. xxiv. and 1 Chron. xxi.; and these passages I must beg the reader to peruse, if he wishes to understand what follows. The common opinion is, that David offended God by his pride, and his desire to gratify it, by knowing over how many subjects he was king. This is, perhaps, the worst explanation that can be given of the unlawfulness of his order. Were God to punish by pestilence every ambitious motion in the hearts of kings, and every sin they commit in thought, pestilences would never cease. It must, besides, appear very strange indeed, how such a man as Joab should have expressed so great an abhorrence at a sin that consisted merely in pride of heart, and have so earnestly dissuaded David from it. Yet he thus remonstrates with him, saying, "May God multiply the people a hundred-fold, that the king may see it; but wherefore will the king urge this measure?" Or, as we read in Chronicles, "May God multiply the people a hundred-fold! They are entirely devoted to the king's service. But why seeketh the king to do this? and why should guilt be brought upon Israel?" Notwithstanding this remonstrance, however, the king, we are told by both historians, repeated his command with so much rigour, that Joab found it necessary to carry it into execution. Now Joab was not, on other occasions, a man of narrow conscience. He had already deliberately planned, and, in cold blood, perpetrated, two murders, merely to rid himself of rivals. And when David gave him the hint to place Uriah in the post of danger, he was by no means squeamish, but immediately planned and commenced an attack, in which, besides Uriah, a great number of his bravest soldiers were slain. His conscience, therefore, could not be incommoded by a mandate relative to a matter in itself lawful, and where the sin, in whatever it consisted, lay altogether hid in the king's ambitious heart. If we think so, we must look upon him in the light of a court-chaplain, and a semi-pietist; and he certainly was neither. What he hesitated, therefore, about doing, must have appeared in his own eyes, something more serious than bare murder. Josephus, however, has hit upon an idea, which may, by some, be thought to account somewhat more probably, than the opinion now mentioned, for the guilt which David is said to have incurred on this occasion. "David," says he, "made the people be numbered, without exacting for the sanctuary, the half-shekel of polltax enjoined by the Mosaic law." But this idea loses all its weight, if I am right in my opinion, that Moses enjoined the exaction of the half-shekel, not upon *every* occasion of a *census*, but merely on the *first;* and even allowing me to be wrong in this, and the common exposition of the statute, in the time of Josephus, to be the more correct one, still the notion of Josephus is certainly inadmissible here. For neither in Samuel nor Chronicles do we find the least mention of the half-shekel; nor does David *forbid* the payment of it, but only orders the people to be numbered; so that every conscientious person had it in his power to pay it of himself, and the high-priest to demand it in virtue of his office. At any rate, David's *census* appears, in this respect, altogether as blameless as Moses' second one, in the account of which (Numb. xxvi.) not a word is said concerning the poll-tax. Nor do Joab and the other generals here represent to the king, that he ought to order the payment of the half-shekel, but only intreat him to desist from the *census* itself. And finally, David, who had amassed so many millions of shekels, (1 Chron. xxix.) and, to the manifest prejudice of his own family, destined so much for building a temple, must actually have been in the delirium of a hot fever, if, contrary to all his other views, he had not had a desire to grant for the future erection of that edifice, projected by himself, the half-shekel payable on the *census*, which was a mere trifle compared to his own donations, and came not out of his own purse.

But as far as I can understand the story, David caused the people to be numbered, neither out of that prudent solicitude which will always actuate a good king, nor yet out of mere curiosity, but that by means of such a *census* they might be enrolled for permanent military service, and to form a standing army; the many successful wars he had already carried on, having filled his mind with the spirit of conquest. We find at least, that the enumeration was ordered to be carried on, not as had before been usual, by the priests, but by Joab and the other generals; and the very term here used, *Safar*, (ספר) *numeravit, scripsit*, includes also in itself the idea of numbering for military service, and is, without any addition, equivalent to our German military term, *enrolliren*, to enrol, or muster. This, indeed, is so much the case, that *Hassofer*, (הספר) *the scribe*, is that general who keeps the muster-rolls, and marks those called on to serve. In like manner, the officers are termed (סופרים) *scribes.* David's sin, therefore, or rather (not to speak so theologically, but more in the language of politics) his injustice and tyranny towards a people who had subjected themselves to him on very different terms, and with the reservation of many liberties consisted in this. Hitherto, the ancient and natural rule of nations, *Quot cives, tot milites*, had certainly been so far valid, as that, in cases of necessity, every citizen was obliged to bear arms in defence of the state. Such emergences, however, occurred but very rarely; and at other times every Israelite was not obliged to become a soldier, and in peace, for instance, or even during a war not very urgent, subject himself to military discipline. David had made a regulation, that, exclusive of his lifeguards, called in the Bible, *Creti* and *Pleti*, 24,000 men should be on duty every month by turns; so that there were always 288,000 trained to arms within the year; which was certainly sufficient for the defence of the country, and for commanding respect from the neighbouring nations, especially considering the state of the times, and the advantages in point of situation, which David's dominions enjoyed. It would appear, however, that he did not think this enough. Agitated, in all probability, by the desire of conquest, he aspired at the establishment of a military government, such as was that of Rome in after-times, and at subjecting, with that view, the whole people to martial regulations; that so every man might be duly enrolled to serve under such and such generals and officers, and be obliged to perform military duty at stated periods, in order to acquire the use of arms.

Whether such a measure, if not absolutely necessary to the preservation of the state, be a hardship on the people, every man may judge from his own feelings, or even from the most recent history of certain nations. For even in a country where the government is purely monarchical, and the people extremely martial, and the frontiers of which, from the uncompactness of its territories, are not, like those of the Israelitish empire, surrounded and secured by mountains or deserts, the enrolment of every individual for military service, introduced 40 years ago, has been of late spontaneously abolished by a very warlike sovereign, because he found that it was too oppressive, and furnished a pretext for a multitude of extortions. Now if this was David's object, it is easy to conceive, that Joab, although in private life a very bad character, and twice guilty of murder, might yet have as much patriotism, or rather political sagacity, as to deprecate, in the most energetic terms, the execution of a royal mandate, the effect of which would have been to bring a free people under the worst military despotism. Very bad consequences were to be apprehended, if the subjects should not prove sufficiently patient to submit to such an innovation. The army, however, devoted as it was to David, and approved as was its valour in many campaigns, *may*, perhaps, have effected their patient submission; and, in fact, the expression, (2 Sam. xxiv. 5,) *And they*, viz. Joab, and the other generals to whom the task was committed, *encamped near Aroer*, appears to insinuate, that this enumeration, or rather this enrolment of the people, required the support of a military force.

What David intended, Uzziah, his successor, in the eighth generation, may perhaps have accomplished. The martial measures of that prince (2 Chron. xxvi. 11—14) are not commended; the prophet Isaiah (chap. ii. 5—8) seems rather to describe them in the language of censure. It is to be observed, however, that the enrolment of the whole people by David, and by Uzziah, is by no means one and the same thing. The former ruled over a powerful nation, wherein there were nearly a million and a half of people able to bear arms, and which had a compact and secure frontier, from the Euphrates to the Mediterranean: so that, for the safety of the state, no such oppressive measure was requisite. But Uzziah had under him only two tribes, consisting probably of about 300,000 men, and his territories were not rounded, nor the frontiers distinct and strong. Here, therefore, that measure might be necessary for self-defence, or, at any rate, admit of a sufficient apology, which, in David's time, was quite needless, and if strictly enforced, must have proved absolutely tyrannical. —MICHAELIS.

From several passages in the Old Testament, compared with each other, it appears that this *census*, or numbering of the people, was a sacred action; as the money was to be applied to the service of the temple. It was not like that in other nations, to know the strength of the government; for God was their king in a peculiar manner, and promised to protect them from all their enemies, and to multiply them as the stars of the sky, while they obeyed his laws.—David's crime, therefore, seems to have lain in converting a sacred action to a civil purpose. He was culpable both in the thing itself, and in the manner of doing it. For whereas by the rule given to Moses, in the passages referred to above, they were to number the males from twenty years old and upward; David gave orders, that all should be numbered, who were fit for war, though under that age. This must have been highly criminal in David, now in his old age, after so many instances of the Divine favour expressed towards him. And as to the people, their offence seems to have consisted in their compliance with that order. He was culpable in giving the order, and they in obeying it. And therefore Joab, who was sensible of this, and unwilling to execute the command, asks David, "Why he would be the cause of trespass in Israel?" For by that means, he reduced them to the difficulty of disobeying God, or himself, as their prince. It was doubtless their duty to have obeyed God; but we find, as it generally happens in such cases, that the majority, at least, chose to obey the king. However, it appears that Joab was weary of the office, and did not go through it. Probably he might find many of the people uneasy, and averse to submit to the order. Besides, it was expressly enjoined, that when the people were to be numbered from twenty years old and upward, the Levites should be excepted, as being appointed for the service of the tabernacle. And as they were not called out to war, so they had no share in the land of Canaan allotted to them, when it was conquered by the other tribes; who were therefore ordered to give them a number of cities, each tribe out of their portion, which was accordingly done. And Josephus assigns that reason for it, when he says:—"Moses, because the tribe of Levi were exempted from war and expeditions, being devoted to the service of God, lest being needy and destitute of the necessaries of life, they should neglect the care of their sacred function; ordered the Hebrews, that when by the will of God they possessed the land of Canaan, they should give to the Levites forty-eight large and handsome cities, with two thousand cubits of land round the walls." But David seems to have ordered them likewise to be mustered, with a military view; which, perhaps, was an aggravation. For, it is said, that when Joab, by his command, numbered the people, "they were eleven hundred thousand men that drew sword." And it is added: "But Levi and Benjamin counted he not among them, for the king's word was abominable to Joab." So that it looks as if his orders were to count them with the rest. Indeed, we find them once armed upon an extraordinary occasion, which was to guard the temple at the coronation of Joash, king of Judah. For, at that time, they were ordered "to encompass the king round about, every man with his weapons in his hand." But that was in the temple, where the rest of the people were not permitted to enter. And besides their religious function, they were sometimes employed in other civil offices. So David, when he was making preparations for building the temple, appointed six thousand of them for officers and judges. Grotius, indeed, observes, with regard to this fact of David, that he declared the people innocent: which he seems to have concluded from what David says, 1 Chron. xxi. 17. But it does not appear, from what has been said above, that they were altogether blameless, though not equally criminal with himself. And in such a case, the equity of a national punishment is acknowledged both by Philo and Josephus, in the passages cited from them by Grotius.—CRITICA BIBLICA.

These wars being thus happily ended, David enjoyed for some time a settled peace and prosperity, without any foreign invasions to call him into the field, or domestic troubles to interrupt him in the affairs of government; but being at length persuaded and prevailed on to number the people, he became the cause of trespass to Israel, and brought on them the severe punishment of a pestilence. The author of the books of Samuel, in relating this affair, says: "That the anger of the Lord was kindled against Israel," and he moved David against them to say, "Go, number Israel and Judah." The author of the Chronicles differently expresses it. "And Satan stood up against Israel, and provoked David to number Israel;" and this is objected against as an absurd thing, that David should be said to be moved both by God and Satan to number the people. But I apprehend this difficulty may be easily removed, by observing, that these two places are capable of a more favourable turn, so as to render them perfectly reconcileable with each other, according to the genius of the language, and the common forms of expression in it. The text in Samuel may be thus rendered: "And again the anger of the Lord was kindled against Israel; for he moved David," or "David was moved against them to say, Go, number Israel and Judah;" active verbs in the third person, being frequently to be rendered as impersonals, and not to be referred to the nouns immediately foregoing; and thus the text will be fully reconcileable with that in Chronicles, which says, that "Satan moved him to number the people." Or, it may reasonably be supposed, as the original words we render, "He moved David against them," are the same in Samuel and the Chronicles, that the word Satan hath been omitted by some careless transcriber in the text in Samuel, which is expressly mentioned in, and to be supplied from that of Chronicles; and then the version will be, that "The anger of the Lord was kindled against Israel, for Satan moved David to number the people:" and very probably, had we more ancient MSS., this omission in Samuel, if such, would be rectified by them. A candid critic will make some allowances, both for defects and redundancies in books of that great antiquity, which the Old Testament books confessedly are; and where several of those books treat of the same affairs, will have the good sense, as far as he can, to supply what is defective in one, by what appears complete in the other. If there needs a supplement in Kings it is actually found in Chronicles, and therefore should be inserted from thence. This would certainly be, in like instances, the case in other books, and it is injustice not to apply the same fair rules of criticism, to remove the difficulties that may occur in the writings of the Old Testament. But there is another way of rendering and understanding this passage, viz. "For he moved David," or, "David was moved against them," not, as in our version, To say, but לאמר, dicendo, by saying, "Go number Israel and Judah;" which last words will then be, not David's to his officers, which follow in the next verse, but his, who counselled David to this action. And thus David's numbering the people will be, neither by the instigation of God, or Satan, as that word means the Devil. It is certain, that God never instigated and said to David, "Go, number the people." For if God had commanded this, David's heart would never have smote him for it, nor would he have acknowledged to God, "I have sinned greatly in that I have done." Nor would Joab have remonstrated against it, nor have represented it to the king, as what would be a cause of trespass to Israel, if he had known that David had received such an order from God. Every circumstance in this account proves, that there was no hand or direction of God in this affair. And if the Devil had bid him do it, I suppose he might have seen the cloven foot, and would scarce have followed the measure for the sake of the adviser. And yet somebody actually said to him: "Go, number the people;" and this person seems to have been one of his courtiers, or attendants; who, to give David a higher notion of his grandeur, and of the number and strength of his forces, put it into his head, and persuaded him to take the account of them; who, in Chronicles, is therefore called Satan, or an adversary, either designedly or consequentially, both to David and his people. And this will exactly agree with what the author of the book of Chronicles says: "An adversary stood up against Israel, and provoked," or, as the word is rendered in Samuel, "moved him against them." Thus Mr. Le Clerc understands this passage, and I think the expressions made use of seem to countenance and warrant the explication. But it is said, that David's numbering the people is oddly enough imputed to him as a great sin in him to require; for he was but a passive instrument in the affair. But who doth not know, that a man may be hanged for a crime, to which his indictment says, "He was moved by the Devil;" and because the Devil moved him, is he therefore a passive instrument, and free from guilt? Or doth the being persuaded or moved by another to do a bad action, render the person so moved a passive instrument, or would it excuse him, in a court of justice, from the punishment due to his crimes?

It is further objected, that David was but the instrument of a purpose, confessedly overruled to the execution of that purpose by supernatural influence, and that to punish one in such circumstances, would be just as if we should convict a knife or pistol, and discharge the criminal. If David was the mere instrument of a purpose, and overruled by supernatural influence to execute it, the similitude may be allowed. But who ever confessed that David was overruled to do it by supernatural power? David himself did not, but confesses directly the contrary. David's heart smote him, and he said unto God, "Is it not I that commanded the people to be numbered? Am not I the person who alone is accountable for it? Even I it is that have sinned greatly, and done evil indeed, and very foolishly." David knew it was his own act, and that, whoever advised or instigated him to it, the blame was his own, and his punishment deserved. A confession that would have been absurd and false, if he knew that the influence he acted under, was really supernatural, or such as he could not resist, or overrule. But as David did not know this, it is impossible any one else should know it. There is nothing in the history to support the assertion. If it was really Satan that moved him, he moved him no otherwise than as he doth all other men to that which is wrong; not by influences which he could not resist, but by those undue passions and affections which he might and ought to have resisted. But if the measure was suggested by one of his own counsellors, as really seems to be the case, it was his duty to have overruled it, and hearkened to the better advice of Joab, who told him of the danger of it, and would fain have dissuaded him from executing it. The truth is, as I apprehend, that David's prosperity had too much elated him, and that being advised by some rash imprudent courtiers to take the number of his people, that he might better know his strength, and be fully acquainted with the power and grandeur of his kingdom, his vanity, in this respect, got the better of his duty; on which, God was pleased to check the rising presumption of his heart, by letting him see how vain his dependance on his forces was, and to punish him and them for their violation of a law, which he had ordered to be observed under the severest penalty. For, among other commands that were given by God to Moses, this was one: "When thou takest the sum of the children of Israel, after their number, then shall they give every man a ransom for his life, unto the Lord, when thou numberest them, that there be no plague among them, when thou numberest them. This shall they give; every one that passeth among them that are numbered, half a shekel shall be the offering of the Lord; every one that passeth among them that are numbered, from twenty years old, and above, shall give this offering to the Lord." David, either not thinking of this command, or thinking himself, as king of Israel, exempt from it, ordered the people to be numbered, without exacting the ransom from each of them. This was one of the highest stretches of authority, and claiming a despotic arbitrary power over the people, as seems plain from Joab's words to him: "Are they not all my lord's servants?" Why then this badge of slavery, to subject them to a census contrary to the law of Moses? It was indeed assuming a prerogative that God reserved to himself, and a violation of one of the standing laws of the kingdom, for the capitation tax that God had appointed to be taken, whenever they were numbered, was ordered to be paid for the service of the tabernacle, as a memorial, that God was their supreme governor and king. But God, to support the dignity of his own constitution, and to put David in mind, that though king, he was still to limit the exercise of his power by the precepts of the law, gives him by the prophet the option of three punishments, of which David chose the plague; recollecting probably, at last, that this was the very punishment threatened by God to the violation of this statute, concerning the numbering the people; as well as for the reason he himself alleges: "Let us fall now into the hands of the Lord, for his mercies are great."

It is evident from the history, that this action of David was looked upon as a very wrong step, even by Joab, who remonstrated against it, as apprehensive of the bad consequences that might attend it; for he says, "The Lord make his people a hundred times so many more as they be. But, my lord the king, are they not all my lord's servants? Why then doth my lord require this thing? Why will he be a cause of trespass to Israel?" And therefore Joab counted not Levi and Benjamin, because the king's word was abominable to him. Probably we do not understand all the circumstances of this affair; but Joab's censure of it, who was no scrupulous man, shows that David's conduct in it was extremely imprudent, and might subject his people to very great inconveniences. But is it not strange, that because David sinned in numbering the people, therefore the people should be punished; since of the three punishments propounded to David for his choice, one of them must necessarily fall upon his subjects? Possibly this difficulty may be eased, when I put my reader in mind, that kings are no otherwise to be punished in their regal capacities, nor oftentimes to be brought to correct the errors of their administration, but by public calamities; by famine, pestilence, foreign wars, domestic convulsions, or some other like distresses that affect their people. This David thought a punishment; and if it be right at all for God to animadvert on the conduct of princes, or to show his displeasure against them for the public errors of their administration, it must be right and fit for him to afflict their people; and indeed this is what continually happens in the common course of providence, and the observation that,

Quicquid delirant reges plectuntur Achivi,

is an old and a true one. And if this be a difficulty, it affects natural religion as well as revealed, and the same considerations that will obviate the difficulty in one case, will solve it also in the other. As to the thing itself, that kings are no otherwise to be punished in their regal capacities, but by public calamities which affect their people, it is, I apprehend, so self-evident and certain, as that it can need no proof. Whether princes profit more or less, or nothing, by the misfortunes of their subjects, is nothing to this argument. Some bad kings may not profit by it. All good kings will. The people's welfare, however, is necessary to the prince's prosperity, and secures the principal blessings of his reign, which can never be enjoyed without it. On the other hand, kings must be affected with, and deeply share in the misfortunes of their people; because a plague or a famine, or a hostile invasion, or any national calamity, tends to destroy the peace of government, or to subvert the foundations of it, lessens the revenues of princes, the number of their subjects, the profits of labour and industry, and interrupts the enjoyment of those advantages and pleasures, which regal power and plenty can otherwise secure to the possessors of them. David was most sensibly affected with his people's sufferings under that pestilence which his imprudence and their neglect had brought upon them. How tenderly, how affectionately doth he plead with God in their behalf! "Even I it is that have sinned. But as for these sheep, what have they done!" What a noble instance of public spirit, and generous concern for the safety of his people, doth that moving and pathetic expostulation manifest, which he made when he saw the angel of the Lord standing between heaven and earth, with a drawn sword in his hand, stretched out over Jerusalem, and fell down with his elders, all clothed in sackcloth, upon their faces, and thus affectionately interceded for them: "Let thy hand, I pray thee, O Lord my God, be on me and on my father's house, but not on thy people, that they should be plagued." Here is the real language and spirit of a genuine ποιμην λαων, a true shepherd of the people, devoting himself and family as a sacrifice to God for the salvation of his subjects.

Besides, in this case, the people were themselves very culpable; for the command was absolute: "When thou takest the sum of the children of Israel, then shall they give every man a ransom for his soul." And therefore, as they knew or might have known, that, upon being numbered, they were to pay the prescribed ransom, which yet they neglected or refused to do; as partners in the offence, they justly shared in the penalty inflicted. It is allowed, that the tax was not at this time demanded by David; and this was his sin, in setting aside a positive command of God, to gratify his own vanity and pride. The demanding this tax by his own authority might have created a national disturbance, and therefore should have prevented him from numbering his people. But they submitted to be numbered, and they were therefore bound to pay the tax, whether David demanded it of them or not, for the law did not exempt them from the payment, if he who numbered them did not demand it. They were to pay it as a ransom for their lives, and to exempt themselves from the plague; and were therefore punished with a plague for their neglect and disobedience. David indeed takes the guilt upon himself, and declares his people innocent of it: "As for these sheep, what have they done?" And it is true, that the order to number the people was David's, of which his people were wholly innocent. But they should have remonstrated against the thing, or voluntarily paid the capitation tax required of them; and as they did neither, David was, as Joab foretold him, a cause of trespass to Israel, and they could not plead innocence, as a reason for their exemption from punishment. And even supposing they were entirely free from all blame in this affair, were they so far entirely free from all other transgressions, as that it was injustice in God to visit them by a pestilence? If not, God did them no injustice by sending that pestilence; and therefore not by sending it at that time, and as an immediate punishment of David's sin. God, by virtue of his supreme authority over mankind, may resume life whenever he pleases. If there be no sin, the resumption of life will be no punishment; if there be, the resumption of it will not be unjust, though the immediate reason of that resumption may be for the punishment of another; especially, as all such instances have a real tendency to promote the public good, and to preserve alive, in the minds both of princes and people, that reverence for Deity, without which neither public nor private virtue can subsist, nor the prosperity of kingdoms ever be secured and established upon solid and lasting foundations.

Upon this solemn humiliation of David, and intercession with God for his people, the prophet Gad was sent to him the same day, with an order that he should rear up an altar unto the Lord, in the thrashing-floor of Araunah the Jebusite, the hill where Solomon's temple was afterward built. David accordingly purchased the ground, built an altar unto the Lord, offered burnt-offerings and peace-offerings, whereby the Lord was entreated for the land, and the plague, which had raged from Dan to Beersheba, was stayed from Israel, the city of Jerusalem being mercifully spared, and exempted from this dreadful calamity. After this, David, encouraged by the gracious token God had given him of his acceptance at this thrashing-floor of Araunah, by the fire from heaven that consumed his burnt-offering, continued to offer upon the altar he had erected in this place; and publicly declared, "This is the house of the Lord God, this is the altar of the burnt-offering for Israel;" hereby consecrating this place for the erection of the temple, and to be the seat and centre of the public worship for all the tribes of Israel. On the whole, if they who object, credit the history of the Old Testament in this part of it, and think it true, that one of these three plagues was offered to David, as the punishment of his offence; that he chose the pestilence, that it came accordingly, and was removed upon David's intercession; they are as much concerned to account for the difficulties of the affair, as I or any other person can be. If they do not believe this part of the history, as the sacred writings represent it, let them give us the account of it as it stands in their own imagination; and tell us, whether there was any plague at all, how, and why it came, and how it went and disappeared so all of a sudden. In their account, whatever it be, David will stand certainly clear of every imputation; and, according to the scripture narration, he will be an offender, but only against the statute law of the kingdom, as usurping an authority and dispensing power that did not belong to him, but not against any law of God, of original, intrinsic, and immutable obligation, as far as we can judge by the short and imperfect account that is left us of this transaction; and so may still be the "man after God's own heart."—CHANDLER.

Ver. 18. And Gad came that day to David, and said unto him, Go up, rear an altar unto the LORD in the thrashing-floor of Araunah the Jebusite.

Thrashing-floors, among the ancient Jews, were only, as they are to this day in the East, round level plots of ground in the open air, where the corn was trodden out by oxen, the *Libycæ areæ* of Horace, ode i. 1. 10. Thus Gideon's floor (*Judges* vi. 37) appears to have been in the open air; as was likewise that of Araunah the Jebusite; else it would not have been a proper place for erecting an altar and offering sacrifice. In Hosea xiii. 3, we read of *the chaff which is driven by the whirlwind* from the floor. This circumstance of the thrashing-floor's being exposed to the agitation of the wind, seems to be the principal reason of its Hebrew name; which may be further illustrated by the direction which Hesiod gives his husbandman, *to thrash his corn in a place well exposed to the wind.* From the above account it appears that a *thrashing-floor* (rendered in our textual translation a *void place*) might well be *near* the entrance of the gate of Samaria, and that it might afford no improper place for the kings of Israel and Judah to hear the prophets in.—BURDER.

CHAPTER XXV.

Ver. 23. And when David inquired of the LORD he said, Thou shalt not go up; *but* fetch a compass behind them, and come upon them over against the mulberry-trees. 24. And let it be, when thou hearest the sound of a going in the tops of the mulberry-trees, that then thou shalt bestir thyself: for then shall the LORD go out before thee, to smite the host of the Philistines.

It is doubtful whether the mulberry-tree is once mentioned in the scriptures. If Hasselquist may be credited, it scarcely ever grows in Judea, very little in Galilee, but abounds in Syria and mount Lebanon. Our translators have rendered the original term Baca, by mulberry, in two different passages: "And when David inquired of the Lord, he said, Thou shalt not go up, but fetch a compass behind them, and come upon them over against the mulberry-trees (Becaim;) and let it be, when thou hearest the sound of a going in the tops of the mulberry-trees, that then thou shalt bestir thyself." And the words, Who passing through the valley of Baca, make it a pool; the rain also filleth the pools,—are in the margin, Who passing through the valley of mulberry-trees. The Seventy, in Chronicles, render it pear-trees; in which they are followed by Aquila and the Vulgate. Some think Baca, in the eighty-fourth Psalm, is the name of a rivulet, which burst out of the earth, at the foot of a mountain, with a plaintive murmur, from which it derived its name. But it is more probable, that Baca is the name of some shrub or tree. Those who translate it the mulberry-tree, to illustrate the passage in the psalm, pretend it grows best in the dry ground; but this seems to be unfounded. Marinus imagines, that Baca signifies the mulberry-tree, because the fruit of the mulberry exudes a juice resembling tears. Parkhurst rather thinks that Baca means a kind of large shrub, which the Arabs likewise call Baca, and which probably was so named from its distilling an odoriferous gum. For Baca with an *aleph*, seems to be related to Baca with a *hay*, which signifies to ooze, to distil in small quantities, to weep or shed tears. This idea perfectly corresponds with the description which Celsius has given of this valley. It is not, according to him, a place abounding with fountains and pools of water, but rugged and embarrassed with bushes and stones, which could not be passed through without labour and suffering; a striking emblem of that vale of thorns and tears, through which all believers must pass to the heavenly Jerusalem. The great uncertainty among interpreters concerning the real meaning of the term Becaim, has induced Mr. Harmer to hazard a conjecture, that the tree meant in this passage is the weeping-willow. But this plant is not found in a dry sandy vale, where the thirsty traveller is compelled to dig for water, and to form cisterns in the earth, to receive the rain of heaven. In such a situation, we expect to find the pungent aromatic shrub distilling its fragrant gum; not the weeping-willow, the favourite situation of which is the watery plain, or the margin of the brook.—PAXTON.

THE FIRST BOOK OF KINGS.

CHAPTER I.

Ver. 2. Wherefore his servants said unto him, Let there be sought for my lord the king a young virgin; and let her stand before the king, and let her cherish him, and let her lie in thy bosom, that my lord the king may get heat.

This is by no means so uncommon a thing as people in England suppose. Men of seventy years of age and upwards often take a young virgin for the same purpose as David did, and no other. It is believed to be exceedingly healthful for an aged person thus to sleep. "In the hot season, he is kept cool, and in the cold season, warm, by sleeping with a young person; his withered body derives nourishment from the other." Thus, decrepit men may be seen having a young female in the house, (to whom, generally, they are not married,) and to whom they bequeath a considerable portion of their property.—ROBERTS.

Ver. 9. And Adonijah slew sheep, and oxen, and fat cattle, by the stone of Zoheleth, which *is* by En-rogel, and called all his brethren the king's sons, and all the men of Judah the king's servants.

The oriental banquet, in consequence of the intense heat, is often spread upon the verdant turf, beneath the shade of a tree, where the streaming rivulet supplies the company with wholesome water, and excites a gentle breeze to cool their burning temples. The vine and the fig, it appears from the faithful page of inspiration, are preferred on such joyous occasions: "In that day, saith the Lord of Hosts, shall ye call every man his neighbour under the vine and under the fig-tree." To fountains, or rivers, says Dr. Chandler, the Turks and the Greeks frequently repair for refreshment, especially the latter on their festivals, when whole families are seen sitting on the grass, and enjoying their early or evening repast, beneath the trees by the side of a rill. And we are assured by the same author, that in such grateful retreats they often give public entertainments. He visited an assembly of Greeks, who, after celebrating a religious festival, were sitting under half tents, with store of melons and grapes, besides lambs and sheep to be killed, wine in gourds and skins, and other necessary provisions. Such appears to have been the feast which Adonijah gave his friends at En-rogel. It was held near a well or fountain of water, and there "he slew sheep, and oxen, and fat cattle, and invited his brethren" and the principal people of the kingdom. En-rogel was not chosen for secrecy, for it was in the vicinity of the royal city, but for the beauty of the surrounding scenery. It was not a magnificent cold collation; the animals on which they feasted were, on the contrary, killed and dressed on the spot for this princely repast. In Hindostan feasts are "given in the open halls and gardens, where a variety of strangers are admitted, and much familiarity is allowed. This easily accounts for a circumstance in the history of Christ, which is attended with considerable difficulty; the penitent Mary coming into the apartment and anointing his feet with the ointment, and wiping them with the hair of her head. This familiarity is not only common, but far from being deemed either disrespectful or displeasing." More effectually to screen the company from the burning sunbeams, a large canopy was spread upon lofty pillars, and attached by cords of various colours: "Some of these awnings," says Forbes, "belonging to the Indian emperors, were very costly, and distinguished by various names. That which belonged to the emperor Akber was of such magnitude as to contain ten thousand persons; and the erecting of it employed one thousand men for a week, with the help of machines; one of these awnings, without any ornaments, cost ten thousand rupees." Similar to these were the splendid hangings under which Ahasuerus the king of Persia entertained his court. They "were white, green, and blue, fastened with cords of fine linen and purple, to silver rings and pillars of marble."—PAXTON.

Siloam was a fountain under the walls of Jerusalem, east, between the city and the brook Kedron; it is supposed to be the same as the fountain En-rogel, or the Fuller's fountain. "The spring issues from a rock, and runs in a silent stream, according to the testimony of Jeremiah. It has a kind of ebb and flood, sometimes discharging its current like the fountain of Vaucluse; at others, retaining and scarcely suffering it to run at all. The pool, or rather the two pools of the same name, are quite close to the spring. They are still used for washing linen as formerly. The water of the spring is brackish, and has a very disagreeable taste; people still bathe their eyes with it, in memory of the miracle performed on the man born blind." (Chateaubriand.)—BURDER.

Ver. 14. Behold, while thou yet talkest there with the king, I also will come in after thee, and confirm thy words.

The Hebrew has for *confirm*, "fill up." "I wish you to go and inform Tamban, that I will gladly go into court and *fill up* all his words." "My friend, do not believe that man's words."—"Not believe them! why, his words have been filled up by many people." "Well, you say you saw Muttoo turn his cattle last night into your rice-fields, what proof have you?"—"None, my lord, I was alone, and, therefore, have no one to fill up my words." "As Venāse was coming through the cinnamon gardens, that notorious robber Kalloway met him, took from him his ear-rings, finger-rings, and five gold mohurs; but, before he got off, several people came up, who knew him well, so that there will be plenty of witnesses to fill up his words."—ROBERTS.

Ver. 16. And Bath-sheba bowed, and did obeisance unto the king. And the king said, What wouldest thou?

When a husband goes on a journey, or when he returns, his wife, on seeing him, puts her hands together, and presents them to him as an act of obeisance. When she has an important request to make, she does the same thing; and it is surprising to see the weakness of him who pretends to be the stronger vessel, for, under such circumstances, she will gain almost any thing she wants. Hence, the force of their popular proverb, "The woman who regularly makes obeisance to her husband, can make it rain whenever she pleases." When Bathsheba made her obeisance to the king, he asked, "What wouldest thou?" but, the Hebrew has this, "What to thee?" This accords with the idiom of the Tamul language. Thus it will be asked of a person who stands with his hands presented to a great man, *ummak-enna*, "To thee what?" If speaking of a third person, *avanuk-enna*, "To him what?" or, literally, "Him to what?"—ROBERTS.

CHAPTER II.

Ver. 5. Moreover, thou knowest also what Joab the son of Zeruiah did to me, *and* what he did to the two captains of the hosts of Israel, unto Abner the son of Ner, and unto Amasa the son of Jether, whom he slew, and shed the blood of war in peace, and put the blood of war upon his girdle that *was* about his loins, and in his shoes that *were* on his feet. 6. Do therefore according to thy wisdom, and let not his hoar head go down to the grave in peace.

David having settled this great affair of Solomon's succession to his throne, but a little before his death sends for him, and gave him a particular charge, in reference to two state criminals, Joab and Shimei. That to Joab in these words: "Thou knowest also what Joab the son of Zeruiah did to me, and what he did to the two captains of the host of Israel, unto Abner the son of Ner, and unto Amasa the son of Jether, whom he slew, and shed the blood of war in peace, and put the blood of war upon his girdle that was upon his loins, and in his shoes that were upon his feet;" i. e. treacherously, and under pretence of peace and friendship, besprinkled his girdle and wet his shoes with the blood of these two generals, as though he had slain them in battle. "But do thou according to thy wisdom, and let not his hoar head go down to the grave in peace." Here are three murders David mentions to Solomon as the ground of this charge, not to let him die a natural death. The one intimated, "thou knowest what he did to me," viz. when he cruelly stabbed Absalom, contrary to my immediate orders; the two others expressly mentioned, those of Abner and Amasa; on these accounts he advises him to put him to death; and I allow David's dying advice, or rather order, in this instance, to be peremptory and absolute; and, if I understand any thing of justice and equity, it was an order worthy of a good king, and fit to be given in the last moments of his life. The reader will remember, that the facts are these. Upon Abner's reconciliation with David, and bringing over the people to his interest, Joab out of revenge for his brother Asahel's death, whom Abner, forced to it by Asahel's rashness, had unwillingly slain, and probably envying him the glory of settling David on the throne of Israel, and afraid of his being placed at the head of the Hebrew army, as the reward of so signal a service, under the pretence of a friendly salutation, in the most base and cowardly manner, stabbed him unexpectedly to the heart. David highly resented this murder, followed Abner's corpse to the grave, and to show what part he would have acted immediately, had it been in his power, says: "I am this day weak, though anointed king; and these men, the sons of Zeruiah, are too hard for me. The Lord shall reward the doer of evil according to his wickedness." After the rebellion under Absalom was ended, David thought this a proper opportunity to show his displeasure to Joab; and as he imagined it would be an acceptable thing to the people of Israel, who were now zealous to restore the king to his throne, he ordered it to be signified to Amasa, who had been their general in the rebellion, that he would constitute him captain-general of his armies in the room of Joab, and actually appointed him, as such, to assemble the forces of Judah, and suppress the new insurrection under Sheba. As Amasa was returning with his troops, Joab meets him, and with a compliment and a kiss, thrust his sword through his body, and laid him at a single blow dead at his feet; and immediately usurped the command of the army, quelled the insurrection, and returned to Jerusalem.

And now, reader, let me appeal to thy conscience. Were not these two execrable murders deserving of punishment? Was the cowardly base assassin worthy to live? If he was too powerful a subject for David to bring to justice, did not David do well, and act like a righteous prince, to give it in charge to his successor, to punish, as soon as ever he had power, such a villain, according to his desert? Mr. Bayle's judgment is, that David well knew that Joab deserved death, and that the suffering the assassinations, with which that man's hands were polluted, to go unpunished, was a flagrant injury done to the laws and to justice. With what truth then can it be said, that David delivered two murders in charge to his son Solomon; one of them to be executed on his old faithful general, Joab? Was it charging Solomon to murder a man, to order him to put to death a criminal, for having basely committed two most execrable murders? Or is the doing justice on murderers and assassins committing murder? Or is the representation just, that this order, viz. to murder Joab, was afterward fulfilled in the basest manner, by the administrator to this pious testament? Judge, reader, and be thyself a witness to the manner of Joab's execution, which is thus stigmatized with the epithet of basest. Solomon, in obedience to his father's directions, gives orders to Benaiah to put Joab to death in these words: "Fall on him, that thou mayest take away the innocent blood which Joab shed, from me, and from the house of my father; and the Lord shall return his blood upon his own head, who fell upon two men, more righteous and better than himself, and slew them with the sword, my father David knowing nothing thereof." Solomon was now king, firmly fixed on the throne, and had it in his power to execute justice on the greatest offenders; and rem[illegible]nbering, I doubt not, how Saul's house was punish[illegible] [illegible]r the innocent blood of the Gibeonites which he spilt, he [illegible]s willing to secure himself and family from a like venge[illegible]nce. He would have been in some measure chargeable with Joab's guilt, had he refused to punish it when it was in his power; and especially, as he had it in charge from his father to execute the vengeance on him that his crime deserved. But where shall we here fix the character of basest? What, on Solomon's command to take away the guilt of innocent blood from himself and his father's house; or on his ordering the execution of the man that shed it, the man that slew two men, more righteous and better than himself; or on God's returning his own blood upon his head; or, on his ordering Joab to be slain at the horns of the altar, and not permitting even the altar of God himself to be an asylum for murderers; or, on his appointing Benaiah, the captain of his host, to execute justice on this treacherous assassin? This was the manner in which Solomon performed his father's orders, in an open public manner, appealing to God for the reasons of his conduct, and by a hand too honourable for the wretch that fell by it. And is this, what it hath been termed, putting a man to death in the basest manner? Is not this condemning, as a piece of villany, a most exemplary instance of royal justice, and exhibited in such a manner as showed a regard to religion, conscience, honour, and the prosperity of his government and people?

But in order to show David's ingratitude to Joab in ordering Solomon to punish him for the murder of Abner, it hath been urged that it appears, that Joab, uniting his revenge with the dead, acted basely for David's service. Supposing it. Doth it follow, that David's ordering the execution of a base and treacherous assassin was baseness and ingratitude, because the assassination was intended for his service? I do not understand this morality. I should rather raise a panegyric upon a prince, who should order a treacherous assassin to execution, notwithstanding the pretence of the assassin's intending to serve him by the villany; than on one, who should protect a villain from the punishment of treachery and murder, because he intended to serve, or actually served him by these notorious crimes. But the supposition itself, that Joab murdered Abner for David's service is without any foundation, and contradicted by the whole history of that affair. For this asserts once and again, that Joab murdered Abner in revenge for his brother Asahel's death. And as to his expostulating with David on the imprudence of trusting Abner, saying, He came to deceive thee, and to know thy going out, and thy coming in, and all that thou dost; David had all the reason in the world to look on this charge against Abner as a mere calumny. For Abner, before ever he had waited on David, had brought the elders of Israel to a resolution to accept of David for their king, and he came to inform him of this transaction. Abner went also to speak in the ears of David all that seemed good to Israel, and that seemed good to the whole house of Benjamin; i. e. all that had been agreed on between Abner and the tribes in reference to David. So that Joab's charge of treachery against Abner was contrary to the strongest evidence of his integrity, and only a pretence to colour over that murder of him which he intended. Joab knew very well the intention of Abner's interview with David; for he was informed that he had been with the king, and that he had sent him away in peace; and he expostulated with the king for thus dismissing him, that he came only to deceive him. And therefore his murdering Abner could be with no intention to serve David, but to execute his own revenge and serve himself; for no transaction could have been at that time more directly contrary to David's interest, as the tribes would naturally resent so cruel a breach of faith, as the treacherous assassination of their own general and ambassador to David, sent by them to fix the terms on which they would receive him for their king; and it was a thousand to one, that, in their fury, they had not broke off all treaty with him, and with their united forces opposed his accession to the throne of Israel. What prevented this was, David's so solemnly and publicly clearing himself of having any hand in the murder, and showing, to the fullest satisfaction of the people, that it was wholly the contrivance of Joab, and perpetrated by him without his privity and consent.

Had Abner lived to have finished this great revolution in favour of David, and actually settled him on the throne of Israel, Abner ought in justice to have continued in the command of the army. This Joab could not be ignorant of, and therefore, uniting his revenge with his ambition, he assassinated Abner, to free himself from a rival in power and his prince's favour, and secure himself in the chief command. He acted just the same infamous part afterward, when he assassinated Amasa, because David had promised him to make him general of the army in Joab's room; and this strengthens the probability, or rather renders it certain, that he murdered Abner, not only out of revenge for his brother's death, but also from the same cause of jealousy, envy, and ambition. And indeed Josephus will not so much as allow, that even the revenging Asahel's death was any thing more than a pretence for Joab's murdering Abner, but says, that the true cause was, his being afraid of losing the generalship, the favour of his master, and being succeeded by Abner in both.

It is further objected, that Joab was really ill used in the affair of Amasa. But to me it appears, that he was used no otherwise than he deserved. It is true he gained the victory over the rebels; but the merit of this victory he destroyed by a base and infamous murder, contrary to the express command of his sovereign. For David charged Joab and Abishai, and all his officers, before the engagement: Deal gently, for my sake, with the young man, even with Absalom. Had Joab cut him off in the heat of the battle, he would have had somewhat to have alleged in his defence. But nothing could argue greater insolence and contempt of the king's order than Joab's conduct on this occasion. For when one of the army informed him he saw Absalom hanging by the hair in a tree, Joab replies: "Why didst thou not smite him there to the ground, and I would have given thee ten shekels of silver and a girdle?" The soldier answered him with a noble spirit of loyalty: "Though I should receive a thousand shekels of silver, I would not put forth my hand against the king's son: for, in our hearing, the king charged thee, and Abishai, and Ittai, saying, Beware, that none touch the young man Absalom; otherwise I should have wrought falsehood against my own life, and thou thyself would have set thyself against me." But what doth the loyal Joab do after this warning? He said: I may not tarry thus with thee. Tell me no more of the king's orders. I have something else to do; and immediately he took three darts in his hand, and thrust them through the body of Absalom, while he was hanging alive in the midst of the oak. Could there be a greater insult offered to the king than this? Or, a more treasonable violation of his orders? Or, a more deliberate and aggravated murder committed? Would any prince have endured this? Or, ought he to have pardoned even a victorious general, after such an audacious cruel instance of disobedience? But not content with this, he carries his insolence to the king further, and keeps no measures of decency with him. For, upon David's mourning over his rebel son, Joab imperiously reproaches him "Thou hast showed this day the faces of all thy servants which this day have saved thy life, and the lives of thy sons, and daughters, and wives; in that thou lovest thine enemies, and hatest thy friends. For thou hast declared this day, that thou regardest neither princes nor servants; for this day I perceive, that if Absalom had lived, and all we had died this day, then it had pleased thee well;" and then, to complete his audacious insolence, threatens with an oath to dethrone him, if he did not do as he ordered him. "Now therefore arise, go forth, and speak comfortably to thy servants; for I swear by the Lord, if thou go not forth, there shall not tarry one with thee this night; I will cause the whole army to revolt from thee before morning; and that will be worse unto thee than all the evil that befell thee from thy youth until now." I will appeal to all men, that know what duty or decency means, whether Joab, after such a behaviour to his sovereign, was fit to be continued general of the forces: and, whatever might be his merits in other respects, whether any prince, who consulted his own honour and safety, would not take the first opportunity to humble and break him? The opportunity came. Amasa, the general of the rebel army, brought Jerusalem and Judah back to their allegiance, and, according to David's promise, was constituted captain-general in the room of Joab. In defiance of this appointment, Joab, to get rid of his rival, like a coward and poltron, under pretence of peace, and a friendly salutation, ripped open Amasa's belly, and shed out his bowels upon the ground. But it is said, to extenuate Joab's guilt, that he confined his resentment to his rival.

What then? Is a cowardly murder to be pardoned, because committed on a rival? Do not the laws of God and man call for an exemplary punishment of such an atrocious offender? Are not such treacherous cruelties, though practised towards a rival, offences of a public nature, a breach of that allegiance which men owe to their princes, and a capital violation of the sacred laws of government? David, it is plain, thought so; and though Joab was too powerful a subject for him to call to an immediate account, yet to show that he had never forgiven it, he orders Solomon, agreeable to all the rules of honour and justice, to punish him as he deserved for his numerous treasons and murders. But we are told that "it will avail nothing to plead the private faults of the man. We are now to consider him as relative to David in his public capacity, as his old faithful general, who powerfully assisted him on all occasions, and who adhered to him in all his extremities; in which light we must loathe the master, who died meditating black ingratitude against so faithful, so useful a servant." I would ask: If David had had power, and had ordered the execution of Joab, immediately upon the assassination of Abner, or of Amasa, whether his master David ought to have been loathed on that account, because Joab had been an old faithful servant? If it should be said, that he ought to have been loathed for it, the doctrine advanced is this: that whatever person hath been an old faithful servant, or general, to any prince, and powerfully assisted him upon all occasions; and murders, presuming on his own power, and past services, through malice, revenge, or ambition, by a secret stab, and under the pretence of friendship, one or two of the principal officers of the kingdom; the prince, whom he serves, becomes an object of loathing and abhorrence, and is guilty of black ingratitude, if he resolves on his death, and actually executes him, as such a base and treacherous assassination deserves. No man, I believe, will coolly assert this. If it is said, that David ought not to have been loathed, but commended, if he had then ordered his execution; I think it cannot be true, that because Joab had been an old faithful general, &c., we ought to loathe David for ingratitude, for meditating Joab's punishment while he lived, and expressly ordering it just before his death; for whatever it was just for him to do, it was just for him to order to be done; inasmuch as he really did himself what Solomon did by his order; and because an act, that is just to-day, cannot become unjust merely by being deferred till to-morrow, or the most convenient opportunity of performing it. But it is said, that it will avail nothing to plead the private faults of Joab. What, were the murder of Abner, who had just brought over the eleven tribes to submit to David, and the assassination of Amasa, appointed general of the national forces, at the head of his troops, private faults? High treason, murder, and felony, private faults! What then can be public ones, and what faults can be aggravated with any more heinous circumstances than these?

But it avails nothing, it seems, to plead these private faults, in vindication of David's ordering him to be put to death by his successor; because we are to consider him as relative to David in his public capacity. Very right: David in his public capacity was king of Israel, and Joab in his public capacity stood related to him as his general, and assisted him, and adhered to him in all extremities. David therefore, in his public capacity, was obliged, by the laws of God and man, to punish assassinations and murders; and Joab, in his public capacity, as general, was an assassin and murderer; and therefore David, in his public capacity, as king, was obliged to punish Joab with death, in his public capacity, as general, assassin, and murderer. If Joab had been his faithful general, and frequently assisted David in his extremities, private obligations are in their nature inferior, and ought to give way to public ones; and the yielding up such an offender to public justice, when personal obligations might have been pleaded by the prince in his favour, was a nobler sacrifice in its nature, and renders David's merits, as a prince, the more illustrious, and himself more worthy the character of the man after God's own heart. And this Mr. Bayle thinks David ought to have done sooner, and says, that notwithstanding Joab deserved death, yet that he kept his place; he was brave, he served the king his master faithfully, and to good purpose, and dangerous discontents might be apprehended if he attempted to punish him. These were the political reasons which made the law give place to utility. But when David had no further use for that general, he gave orders that he should be put to death. So that Mr. Bayle blames David, not for ordering Joab to be put to death at last, but for deferring to do it so long, through reasons of policy, and ordering it only when those reasons of policy subsisted no longer. I would here just observe, that what Mr. Bayle calls political reasons were really reasons of necessity. For Joab was too powerful a subject to bring to justice. He attempted it twice, by turning him out from being general. But he restored himself to his command by murder and treason, in spite of David, who seized the very first opportunity, after Joab's power was broken, of ordering his execution.

It should be added also on this head, that whatever Joab's past services were to David, and however faithful he had formerly been to him, yet he had now been engaged in a treasonable conspiracy against him, to set aside the intended succession to the crown, and had actually proclaimed Adonijah king of Israel during his father's life; altogether without, and even contrary to his consent. And it is allowed, that David had on this account justifiable cause for chagrin. And it is certain, that Joab's treason, in endeavouring to depose the good old king, and advance an ambitious youth into his throne, was just reason for chagrin. And therefore as Joab added rebellion to murder, David did justly, in his last moments, to order his execution by his son and successor, and he would neither have been a wise or a righteous prince, had he forgotten or refused to do it. When it is said, that Joab had not appeared against him in actual hostility, and that his defection may admit of being interpreted into a patronisation of that particular plan for the succession, rather than into a rebellion against David, it is in part not true in fact. To proclaim any person king, in opposition to the reigning king, is an overt act of rebellion, and therefore of real hostility. This Joab did, and had not the design been seasonably prevented, by the loyalty and prudence of Nathan, further hostilities must have been immediately committed; David himself at least confined, and Solomon, his intended successor, actually put to death. The plan of the succession, concerted by Joab, in favour of Adonijah, was, in every view of it, a treasonable one. It was a plan formed without the consent of the nation, without the knowledge of David, and the appointment of God. David had, a considerable while before this, solemnly sworn to Bathsheba, that Solomon her son should reign after him, and sit upon his throne in his stead; and tells all the nobles and officers of his kingdom, that as the Lord God of Israel had chosen him, among the sons of his father, to be king over all Israel, so, of all his sons, God had chosen Solomon to sit upon the throne of the kingdom of the Lord over all Israel. To patronise therefore any other plan of succession, and actually to take measures to execute that plan, was breaking out into open rebellion; and the favourers, abetters, patrons, and aiders, in such a plan, were traitors to their king and country, and in all nations would have been punished as such; and should it be pleaded in excuse of such persons, that their defection to patronise such a plan of succession, was not a rebellion, it would be treated with the contempt it deserved; and as a defection from a prince is a revolt from him, and a revolt a rebellion, they would probably be told, that they should have the choice of being hanged for a defection, or rebellion, just as they pleased.

I shall only take notice further, on this head, that David, in his lamentation for Abner, had declared the Lord to be the rewarder of evil-doers; by this expression referring the punishment of Joab to the Lord. And the inference that hath been made from hence is, that David having enjoyed the benefit of Joab's services through his life, he having been his right hand all along, gratitude, after such an attachment, ought to have influenced David to have left him to the justice of God, and not have bequeathed him death, as a legacy for his long friendship. But David did not bequeath him death for his friendship, but for his repeated treasons and murders; which no just principle of gratitude will ever shelter; since no services, public or private, can be a compensation for these impious violations of the laws of God and man, and ought not to hinder the progress of justice in the execution of such notorious offenders; and were kings and princes to act according to this notion of gratitude, the peace, order, and safety of society, could not possibly be maintained. Besides, as David declared the Lord to be the rewarder of evil-doers, so he really left it to the providence of God to reward Joab, by not punishing him himself, but by waiting for the proper opportunity to give him his reward, when it could be done consistently with his own safety, and the peace of his kingdom. Joab's defection or rebellion in favour of Adonijah, and Solomon's establishment on the throne, furnished this opportunity, and the providence of God, by these means, brought on the punishment he had long deserved. Let Solomon explain his father's meaning in the very order he gives for Joab's execution. The king said to Benaiah: "Fall upon him . . . . that thou mayest take away the innocent blood which Joab shed, from me and the house of my father, and the Lord shall return his blood upon his own head, who fell upon two men more righteous and better than himself, and slew them with the sword." David therefore left Joab to the justice of God, and God executed justice on him by Solomon's order; and the hand of providence was very remarkable in this transaction; in that, had Joab's treason, in patronising Adonijah's usurpation, succeeded, Joab would have escaped with impunity; for Adonijah, no doubt, out of gratitude to Joab, would have forgiven him his murders, for the sake of his services. David's meaning, therefore, in declaring that the Lord would reward the evil-doers, could be no other than that in which Solomon understood it: That though Joab was too powerful for him, at that time, to punish, yet that God would not suffer him finally to escape; but that, sooner or later, in the course of his providence, he would bring the punishment on him which he so richly deserved. And this Joab experienced, since the very measures he took in the close of David's reign, to secure himself from it, fixed his doom, and proved his destruction. David's conduct therefore, in this instance, is no proof that his repentance for his sins was not sincere, nor any argument that he had not forgiven his enemies, as far as he ought to do it, and did not die in charity with all mankind, as far as that charity ought to be extended. If a prince's charity influences him, living or dying, to pardon repeated offences, inconsistent with the public safety and peace, such as assassinations and treasons, it is folly and weakness, and not virtuous charity; it is cruelty to his people, instead of real generosity and goodness. David had not this charity, and it heightens his character that he had not. His last charge to Solomon shows his inviolable regard to justice, by positively ordering the execution of a murderer, who was too powerful for himself to punish; and the order was executed by Solomon, in a manner worthy a wise, a just, and a great prince; or, worthy the son of such a father.—CHANDLER.

Ver. 7. But show kindness unto the sons of Barzillai the Gileadite, and let them be of those that eat at thy table: for so they came to me when I fled because of Absalom thy brother.

At public entertainments in the courts of eastern kings, many of their nobles have a right to a seat, others are admitted occasionally by special favour. In this sense Chardin understands the dying charge of David to his successor, to show kindness to the sons of Barzillai the Gileadite, and to let them be of those that should eat at his table. He means not that they should eat at his table at every meal, or on every day, but only on days of public festivity. In the same light, he views the conduct of the king of Babylon to the captive monarch of Judah: "Evil-Merodach spake kindly to Jehoiakim, and set his throne above the throne of the kings that were with him in Babylon; and changed his prison-garments, and he did eat bread continually before him all the days of his life." He received a daily allowance from the king suitable to his high station, and the value which Evil-Merodach had for him; besides this, he had a seat at all the public entertainments of the court. The eastern custom explains the reason that David was not expected at Saul's table, till the day of the new moon; he did not sit at the king's table every day, but according to established usage, he had a right, and was expected to be present in his allotted seat on the day of a public and solemn festival. In the same manner, though Mephibosheth was to sit at David's table on all public occasions, yet he wanted the produce of his lands for food at other times. It was therefore very proper to mention the circumstances to Ziba, that he might understand it would be necessary for him to bring the produce of the lands to Jerusalem, and in sufficient quantity to support Mephibosheth in a style suitable to the dignity of one who had a right, by the royal grant, to appear at court, and sit at the king's table on public occasions: "Thou, therefore, and thy sons, and thy servants, shall till the land for him; and thou shalt bring in the fruits, that thy master's son may have food to eat; but Mephibosheth thy master's son shall eat bread always at my table."—PAXTON.

Ver. 8. And, behold, *thou hast* with thee Shimei the son of Gera, a Benjamite of Bahurim, which cursed me with a grievous curse in the day when I went to Mahanaim: but he came down to meet me at Jordan, and I sware to him by the LORD, saying, I will not put thee to death with the sword. 9. Now therefore hold him not guiltless; for thou *art* a wise man, and knowest what thou oughtest to do unto him; but his hoar head bring thou down to the grave with blood.

After the charge to Solomon, to execute the due punishment on Joab, for his numerous and aggravated crimes, David gives him another, relative to Shimei the Benjamite, who, as hath been already observed, when the king was in his flight from Jerusalem, to prevent his falling into Absalom's hands, met him, railed at, and cursed David in his journey; and as he went on, had the further insolence to pelt him with stones, and dust him with dust, crying out to the king, "Come out, come out, thou bloody man, and thou man of Belial. The Lord hath returned upon thee all the blood of the house of Saul, in whose stead thou hast reigned; and the Lord hath delivered the kingdom into the hand of Absalom thy son; and behold thou art taken in thy mischief, because thou art a bloody man." This, as Mr. Bayle says, is a small specimen of the abuses to which David was exposed among the friends of Saul; they accused him of being a man of blood, and looked on the rebellion of Absalom as a just punishment for the mischiefs which they said David had done to Saul and his whole family. But surely an abuse and insult of a more atrocious and insolent nature was never offered to a prince; an insult the viler, as it had no foundation in reality or truth to support it. He twice styles him a bloody man; and tells him, that because he had reigned in the stead of Saul, the Lord had returned on him all the blood of the house of Saul. The reader will observe, that this transaction was before the affair of the Gibeonites; and therefore this circumstance could not enter into Shimei's thoughts, nor be any reason for his charging David with being a bloody man, and having the blood of Saul's house returned on him. Now, in what other respects could David be guilty of the blood of Saul's house? Saul's three eldest sons were slain with him in a battle with the Philistines, in which David was not present. The only remaining son that Saul had was Ishbosheth, whom Abner made king in Saul's room, in opposition to David, who was raised to the throne by the house of Judah. Ishbosheth was killed by two of his captains, whom David put to death for that treason and murder; and Mephibosheth, the son of Jonathan, the only remaining one, was restored to his patrimony, and, in all things, treated as one of David's own sons; and Saul's line by him, the eldest branch, continued down through many generations. The charge therefore that David was a bloody man, because the blood of the house of Saul was upon him, was a scandal and a lie, and uttered in the madness of the passion and malice of a man, who, being of Saul's house and family, was enraged to see that family rejected from the throne, and David advanced to it in their stead.

Mr. Bayle himself acknowledges, that the friends of Saul carried things too far in these reproaches against David. And yet, as though he had made too large a concession in his favour, he doth, in a manner, retract it, by adding: "It is true, that, by the testimony of God himself, David was a man of blood, for which reason God would not permit him to build the temple." But, by Mr. Bayle's good leave, David *was not a man of blood*, by any testimony of God himself; nor doth either of the places he cites in proof of it, prove any such thing. The expression which Shimei made use of to revile David was, איש דמים אתה, *Thou art a man of blood;* an expression always used, I think, in a bad sense, to denote a cruel bloody man. But God never gave this character to David. What God said of him was that he had been a man of wars, ודמים שפכת *and hast shed blood;* or, as it is elsewhere expressed: *Thou hast shed much blood, and hast made great wars.* Now the shedding of blood implies nothing criminal, except it be shed חנם *sine causa, without reason* or cause; *innocent blood*, as our version renders; and this very expression is used, in the same verse, in the criminal and in the good sense, to denote murder, and the justly putting the murderer to death. "Whoso sheddeth man's blood, by man shall his blood be shed." If then David's wars were just and necessary, the blood he shed in them was not his crime; and it is evident, that when David told his son, and afterward all the princes and officers of his kingdom, that the reason why God would not permit him to build his house, was because he had shed much blood in his wars; he did not mention it to them as a reproach, or any crime imputed to him by God. Indeed this could not be the case, because, immediately after God had assigned this reason why he would not permit him to do it, yet, without in the least blaming him, he graciously gave him a proof of his peculiar favour, by assuring him, that his son should build his house, should long enjoy prosperity and peace, and that the throne of his kingdom over Israel should be established for ever. Mr. Bayle urges it as a further reason of David's being a bloody man, or else he introduces it for no purpose at all, that, to appease the Gibeonites, he delivered up to them two sons, and five grandsons of Saul, who were all seven hanged. Had Mr. Bayle told, as he ought to have done, the reason of David's delivering them up, it would have been no proof of his delighting in blood. He did it not by choice, but by necessity, and a divine order. As therefore God never charged David with being a man of blood, this charge, as thrown on him by Shimei, was false and injurious; and the observation, that "here an opportunity may be taken to introduce a circumstance, which is so far material, as it serves to show, that the sanctity of David was not quite so universally assented to, as may be imagined, while he was living, and his actions not only fresh in memory, but more perfectly known, than was prudent to transmit to these distant ages," is quite groundless and injudicious. For how doth the being reviled and cursed by one interested and disappointed person, and charged with crimes for which there is no foundation, but many strong concurring circumstances to show the falsehood of the charge; how doth this, I say, serve to prove, that David's sanctity was not so universally assented to, as may be imagined? It is no proof that Shimei himself believed the truth of his own reproaches; nothing being more common than for men, in the extravagance and fury of passion, to vent many things, which they well know they have not any foundation for affirming: much less doth it serve to show that David deserved these reproaches; and, least of all, that others believed them just, and had as bad an opinion of him, as Shimei who reviled him. If this be argument, then I will, to the fullest conviction, demonstrate, that David's sanctity was, while he lived, thought as great as any body imagines. For, in the first place, Jonathan tells Saul; "He hath not sinned against thee, his works have been to thee ward very good." In the next place, Saul, his professed enemy, acknowledges David's innocence, and that he was a more righteous man than himself, and that in persecuting him, "he had played the fool, and erred exceedingly." Nay, Shimei himself, upon whose railing against David this notable observation I am remarking upon is grounded, retracts all he had said, owns himself a slanderer and a liar, and begs pardon for his abusive impudence. "Let not my lord impute iniquity unto me, nor remember what his servant did perversely; for thy servant doth know that I have sinned." From hence I argue: If Shimei's reproaching David shows his sanctity was not quite so universally assented to, as may be imagined, while he was living, therefore, a fortiori, Jonathan's, and Saul's, and Shimei's testimony, to David's innocence and righteousness, serves to show, that the sanctity of David was really as universally assented to, as hath been imagined, while he was living, and all his actions fresh in memory. I must beg leave also to add, that as Shimei owned himself to be a lying, slanderous, iniquitous varlet, and that the charge of David's being "a man of blood, and guilty of the blood of Saul's house," was an iniquitous, perverse calumny; that charge destroys its own credit and truth; and instead of serving to show that David's sanctity was not quite so universally assented to, as may be imagined, while he was yet living, rather serves to show that it was. For, as there are several unquestionable evidences to his integrity and virtue, of persons that knew him well, and were his contemporaries; as friends and enemies have given their united testimony in his favour, and there is but one evidence to the contrary, and that a lying one, upon record, who retracted his own charge publicly, and begged pardon for the falsehood of it; the sanctity of David's character in the opinion of the public, while he lived, stands unimpeached; and Shimei's infamous calumny against him, refuted and falsified by himself, can never, with justice, be pressed into the service against David to defame his reputation. As to the suspicion here thrown in, that David's "actions, when fresh in memory, and perfectly known, were worse than have been represented, or was prudent to transmit to these distant ages;" surely this must have been a very unreasonable one, if the actions that have been transmitted to these ages are such, as justify the charges brought against David, and the splendid character given him, of usurper, ungrateful, perfidious, perjured, whose conscience was his slave and his drudge, a tyrant, a Nero; in a word, a monster and a devil. Can he be painted in worse colours than these? Or do the enemies of David suspect the representations they have made of the actions recorded, as injurious and false, and want further materials to bespatter one of the greatest and best of princes? But they needed no further memoirs to assist them. For, in spite of Shimei, and though he had retracted all his curses and calumnies, yet the world is told, after reciting Shimei's blasphemies: "This is pathetic, and truly characteristic of the tyrant," to whom the speech was addressed. But David's real character was quite the reverse of a tyrant. He never oppressed his subjects; but when he reigned over Israel, executed justice and judgment among all his people; and, perhaps, there never was a prince of greater humanity and clemency, or that gave more shining and disinterested proofs of it, than David, though he hath been characterized as the vilest of men, and the worst of tyrants.

Shimei himself was one illustrious proof of this. For when David's officers would have effectually silenced his reproaches, by putting the brawler to death, as he really deserved, what saith this Nero of the Hebrews? See, reader, the lineaments of his blood-thirsty disposition, in his reply to Abishai: "Let him curse. For if the Lord hath said unto him, curse David, who shall then say, wherefore hast thou done so? Behold, my son, which came forth of my bowels, seeketh my life. How much more now may this Benjamite do it? Let him alone, and let him curse, if the Lord hath bidden him. It may be that the Lord will look on my affliction, and that the Lord will requite me good for his cursing this day." In this grievous calamity, David could not but see the hand of God, it was now falling heavy on him for his great sin in the affair of Uriah, and therefore ascribes the curses of Shimei to his immediate permission, and, in some measure, even to his appointment; as he was now reduced to that low condition, through the effect of his displeasure, as that this wretch dared to pour out these undeserved calumnies against him. This shows the moderation and great command of his temper, who would deny himself the vengeance due to such an outrageous insult on his person and character. Oh! how perfect a picture doth this exhibit to us of a Nero, and who can help discerning and admiring the happy resemblance!

But it was not, it seems, piety, or humanity and goodness of heart in David, but policy and prudence, that prompted him to preserve Shimei's life. For so we are told: "Some of his retinue were at the point of silencing this brawler with the ultima ratio regum; but David prevented it; wisely considering this was not a season for proceeding to extremities." Why, what was there in the season to prevent David from punishing a treasonable reviler and brawler as he deserved? What would David's cause and interest have suffered by permitting a single person to be put to death, for a crime that made him worthy of it? There is but one possible inconveniency that would have attended it, and that is, there would have been wanting one noble instance of his generous disposition, and the government of his passions; which is now recorded, to do honour to his memory, and heighten the glory of his truly illustrious character. But supposing that this was not a season for proceeding to extremities, yet when David recovered his throne, and had Shimei fully in his power, this surely was a season for David's coming to any just extremities that he pleased; and he did not want very powerful advisers to make use of them; for Abishai said to him: "Shall not Shimei be put to death for this, because he hath cursed the Lord's anointed?" And is there any one man in the world, that would not have applauded David's justice, in ordering to execution a wretch that had cursed and pelted him with stones in his adversity? It is true, Shimei owned his fault, and, as it is expressed, reflecting on David's vindictive temper, came to make his submission, and petition forgiveness. This persuasion, one would think, would certainly have kept Shimei from ever coming near him, and forced him to seek safety by flight. I should rather have imagined, that, reflecting on David's merciful and forgiving temper, and the experience he had lately of it, in David's not permitting his officers to cut him off, when he was actually cursing and stoning him, he made his submission, and petitioned for mercy. If David had been the vindictive Nero, which he hath been represented to be, Shimei's owning his fault would not have been his security, and he would have paid dearly for the scurrility of his abusive tongue; especially as he was one of Saul's family, whom, it is said, lest they should hereafter prove thorns in his side, he concluded it expedient to cut off. But notwithstanding this expediency, David accepted his acknowledgments, and told him with an oath: Thou shalt not die.

But what shall we think, it is said, when we see this Nero of the Hebrews die in a manner uniform and consistent with the whole course of his life? What will be our reflections, when we find him, with his last accents, delivering two murders in charge to his son Solomon? One against Joab, the other against Shimei, which we are now to consider. The charge that David gave to Solomon concerning him runs thus: "And behold thou hast with thee Shimei, the son of Gera, a Benjamite of Bahurim, which cursed me with a grievous curse, in the day when I went to Mahanaim; but I swore to him by the Lord, saying, I will not put thee to death with the sword. Now therefore hold him not guiltless, for thou art a wise man, and knowest what thou oughtest to do unto him; but his hoar head bring thou down to the grave with blood." This is the ground of the accusation brought against David; that when he lay on his death-bed, where all mankind resign their resentments and animosities, his latest breath was employed in dictating this posthumous murder to his son Solomon. My reader will not forget who Shimei was; of the house and family of Saul; that he was a person of great power and influence in the tribe of Benjamin, of whom he had a thousand in his train, when he made his submission to David upon his restoration; and that the manner in which he accosted David, when fleeing from Jerusalem, discovered the inward rancour of his heart, and his readiness to join in any measures to distress and disturb his government, and cause the crown to revert to the house of Saul. Therefore David puts Solomon in mind, that Shimei *cursed him with a grievous curse*, in the day that he went down to Mahanaim; that he was an implacable enemy to his person and family, one who was not to be trusted, and would not fail to show his hatred upon any proper occasion. It appears further by the expression: "Behold thou hast with thee Shimei;" that he was now in Jerusalem; and that therefore David thought this a proper opportunity of confining him, that he might not spread disaffection to Solomon's government, among those of his own tribe, or of any of the other tribes of Israel; a precaution the more necessary in the infancy of Solomon's reign, and as some of his brethren were inclined to dispute with him the succession to the crown; and therefore David said: "But now do not thou hold him guiltless;" i. e. though I forgave him, and swore to him that he should not die, do not thou let him go off, do not leave him at liberty, nor treat him as an innocent man, that is reconciled to my family, and thy succession in the throne of Israel. He is Shimei still, and wants nothing but a fair opportunity to declare it. He is now with thee. Hold him fast, keep him continually under thine eye to prevent his doing any mischief; and if thou findest him guilty of any malpractices, his hoar head bring thou down to the grave with blood; cut him off as an old offender, and dangerous enemy, to secure thy own peace, and the safety of thy government.

Further, David's telling Solomon that he sware to Shimei by the Lord, that he would not put him to death for his outrage and treason, is a demonstrative proof, that he did not advise Solomon to put him to death for the crime that he himself had solemnly forgiven him. For can any one imagine, that David should tell Solomon, that he had sworn by the Lord not to put Shimei to death, and, in the same breath, order him, in defiance of the oath, to be put to death by Solomon? Common decency and prudence would have made him conceal the circumstance of the oath, unless he intended to brand himself publicly for the grossest perfidy and perjury; or, what is the real truth, to prevent Solomon from putting Shimei to death, in resentment for a crime for which he had solemnly sworn he would never execute him; and therefore it may be allowed Mr. Bayle, that strictly speaking, a man, who promises his enemy his life, doth not acquit himself of that promise, when he orders him to be put to death by his will. But this doth not affect David's integrity, who either never promised him absolutely his life, or never gave any positive orders by his will to execute him. I add therefore, that the words themselves, when rightly rendered, imply no such order. The common rendering of them is: *His hoar head bring thou down to the grave with blood.* But it is a better interpretation, and supported by parallel passages, if we render them, *Bring down his gray hairs to the grave for blood*, or for being guilty of it. Shimei was *a man in blood*, intentionally of murdering the king, and who actually attempted it by stoning him; and, on that account, deserved to be put to death. Now, though David could not order Solomon to put him to death for this attempt, because he had forgiven him, yet he might justly urge it, as a reason why Solomon should keep a constant strict guard over him, in order to prevent him from any seditious practices, or put him to death, if he found him guilty of any. The authors of the critical remarks give another turn to the words, which may be justified also by many other places of like nature. They would have the middle words put into a parenthesis, and the negative particle A L repeated in the last clause from the first; thus: "Now therefore do not hold him guiltless (for thou art a wise man, and knowest what thou oughtest to do for him,) but do not bring down his hoary head with blood." I would propose a little alteration in the reading of the prefix *vaw*. "Do not hold him guiltless, (for thou art a wise man,) nor bring down his hoary head with blood." According to this translation, David's direction to Solomon will be: That he should not put Shimei to death for having cursed him, because he had forgiven him upon oath; but, at the same time, should not hold him guiltless; leaving it to Solomon's wisdom to inflict a proper punishment on him, provided it was not a capital one. If David had intended that Solomon should immediately put him to death, there would be no sense nor reason in what David adds: "Thou art a wise man, and knowest what thou oughtest to do to him;" which is evidently the same thing as saying: I give thee no particular directions about him, only observe him. Thou art a wise man, and knowest how to manage him, and to thy prudence and care I entirely leave him. This is the natural proper meaning of the expression, which cannot be construed into any other sense, without doing violence to the words. Now, to what purpose was it to tell Solomon, that he knew how to behave to Shimei, if David's command was immediately to cut him off, and Solomon understood him in this sense? The thing is absurd in its nature, and there can be no meaning in a charge of this kind, viz. giving any man an absolute order to put another to death for a crime, and, in the same breath, leaving him entirely to the management of his own wisdom and prudence, to put him to death or not. If he gave a positive order for his death, he did not leave him to Solomon's wisdom; and if he left him to Solomon's wisdom, as he certainly did, he did not give him any positive order for his death.

It is certain that Solomon did not understand his father in this sense, of putting Shimei to death for his treason at Mahanaim; but only that he should have a watchful eye over him, and prevent him from all seditious practices for the future. For what doth Solomon do after his father's death? What, instantly put Shimei to death? No, but as a wise man, who knew what he ought to do to him, orders him to build a house for himself at Jerusalem; where he confines him, that he might be perpetually under his inspection, and bound him by an oath never to go further out of it than to the brook Kidron; telling him, that whenever he passed it, he should surely die. This is further evident from the different manner in which Solomon treated Joab and Shimei. Joab he immediately, on his accession, put to death, because David could be understood in no other sense, in the charge he gave concerning him, but absolutely to cut him off; for he gives no intimation that he had pardoned him, or that he left it to his son's prudence to do with him as he should think proper; but says peremptorily, after recounting the two murders he had committed: Do thou according to thy wisdom. Do justice on him, and thereby show thyself a wise man, and let not his hoar head go down to the grave in peace. Now if the charge had been the same in reference to Shimei as it was to Joab, what should have prevented Solomon from immediately executing Shimei as well as Joab? Solomon had much less to apprehend from executing Shimei, than Joab. Joab had an interest in the army, and had David's sons, and the high-priest of his party, which Shimei could not have, as he was a powerful man of the house of Saul: a circumstance this, however, enough to incline a jealous prince to get rid of him if he fairly could do it. And if Solomon had David's positive order to do it, the regard to his father's command, and the rules of policy, would have engaged him to have immediately executed him. But this Solomon, in his wisdom, knew he could not do; for David told him that he had pardoned Shimei to prevent his execution, because his offence was personal, and David had a right to forgive it. But he had never pardoned Joab, nor in justice could do it; because he was guilty of death, for repeated murders, by the laws of God and man. Solomon therefore acted wisely and justly in putting Joab to death, and showed his prudence in reference to Shimei, by sparing him; but honourably confining him, that he might have the proper security for his future good behaviour. But to this it is objected, that the executing Joab, and sparing Shimei, was owing to a different cause from what I have now assigned. For Joab, by joining the party of Adonijah, had furnished the pretence for putting him to death, which Shimei doth not appear to have done. Joab therefore was assassinated, and Shimei watched. But this contradicts the history; for David, in his order to put Joab to death, mentions not one word about his being of Adonijah's party, but orders him to be cut off expressly for the treacherous assassination of Abner and Amasa. And when Solomon ordered his execution, not a word of Adonijah; but take away the innocent blood which Joab shed from me, and from the house of my father. So that, as the cause of Joab's execution was not his being of Adonijah's party, so the cause of Shimei's being spared, cannot be said to be, because he was not of Adonijah's party. The true reason of their treatment, was the different nature of their crimes, and the difference of the order relating to them. And as Joab was put to death for repeated murders, by the express order of the king, it is with great injustice that his death is censured as an assassination; especially as he was executed in the same manner as state criminals at that time generally were.

Besides, if, as hath been asserted, David had, without any condition, and by a positive injunction, ordered Shimei to be put to death, then his joining, or not joining Adonijah, had been a circumstance of no weight; for, whether the one, or the other, Solomon ought not to have ordered him to be watched, but instantly to have put him to death, as he did Joab. And if, because he was not of Adonijah's party, Solomon spared him, and ordered him only to be watched, then Solomon did not think his father's order to be an order to cut him off, but only to have a watchful eye over him. For David knew Shimei's circumstances as well as Solomon, and Solomon's conduct to Shimei is an abundant explication of the nature of his father's command, and how he himself understood it. This is the sentiment of F. Houbigant, who doth not so much as give a single intimation that Shimei was watched, and not put to death, because he was not of Adonijah's party; but absolutely denies that David gave any order at all to Solomon to put him to death for the crimes which he had pardoned him, but only to watch his conduct, till he should render himself guilty by some fresh transgression. And when upon breaking his oath, he was sent for by Solomon, the king reproached him for his perjury, for acting contrary to the condition of life, which he himself acknowledged to be just and equitable, and for the wickedness that his heart was privy to in his conduct to his father David; the mercy that had been shown him, in the pardon of that offence, aggravating his fresh crime in violating his oath, and in transgressing the king's command; a crime that showed he was of a restless spirit, and incapable of being restrained within due bounds by the most solemn oaths, or any sense of interest, gratitude, or duty, whatsoever. Solomon adds: "The Lord shall return thy wickedness on thine own head, and King Solomon shall be blessed: and the throne of David shall be established before the Lord for ever;" plainly intimating, that Solomon now cut him off, as an act of prudence and justice, because he knew him to be a turbulent implacable enemy to his person and government, and saw it necessary for establishing the throne of David before the Lord.

I would further add, that Shimei himself, sensible of Solomon's great kindness to him, approves the sentence pronounced on him, and therefore the charge that David gave him, promising him upon oath obedience to the condition, on which his life was afterward to depend. "The sentence is good. As my Lord the king hath said, so will thy servant do." It doth not appear that Solomon mentioned one word about Shimei's cursing David, when he ordered him to confine himself to Jerusalem, and that therefore this was not the immediate reason why he confined him, but as his father had forewarned him, because he thought it would be a dangerous thing to suffer a person of Shimei's family, tribe, interest, and known rancour to his crown and government, to be entirely at liberty. And, upon this supposition, Shimei could not but own the justice of the sentence, and Solomon's lenity in pronouncing it. But if Shimei had any apprehension that David had violated his oath of safety to him by the charge he gave Solomon concerning him, or that Solomon had broken it, by making his life depend on a new condition, which his father had never obliged him to come under; why did he not plead David's oath and promise, and that had no condition annexed to it, when he appeared before Solomon; that the annexing a new condition to it was actually reversing it, and therefore a breach of oath in David, if he directed it, or in Solomon, if it was his order only, and not David's? And though David, being dead, Shimei could not reproach him to his face, yet he might have reproached him, and Solomon himself to his own face, for this breach of oath, if there had been any. But Shimei urges nothing of all this in favour of himself, and instead of reproaching David or Solomon, acknowledges the king's moderation, and says: The sentence is good. It is most just and merciful. As my lord the king hath said, so will thy servant do. Shimei therefore knew, either that he had an absolute pardon from David, or that he had forfeited that pardon, or that, whatever was the purport of David's oath to him, no injustice had been done him, either by David's charge to Solomon, or by Solomon's executing it. The adversaries of David may choose which they please. David's honour, and Solomon's justice, will be abundantly vindicated.

Let me beg the candid reader's attention to another remark: That though it hath been positively affirmed, that David guarantied Shimei's pardon with a solemn oath, yet this is by no means certain from the history. For let it be observed, that after Shimei's confession of his fault, Abishai said to David: "Shall not Shimei be put to death, because he cursed the Lord's anointed?" Meaning, be put to death instantly, as appears by David's answer: "Shall there be any man put to death this day in Israel? Do I not know that I am this day king over Israel?" Therefore the king said to Shimei: "Thou shalt not die;" and the king swore to him, viz. that he should not then, or that day, or at that time, be put to the sword. And it is observable, that the Arabic version expressly mentions this circumstance: "Thou shalt not die אליום *this day.*" This was certainly all that the king declared to Abishai, that, as he was that day restored to the exercise of his regal power, no man should that day be put to death; and therefore he swore to Shimei, that he should not then die. So again, in David's direction to Solomon about Shimei, the same version hath the same word: "I sware to him by God: I will not put thee to the sword אליום *this day*." Thus also Josephus understands the words. He assured him, says he, that he should suffer nothing at that time. And indeed nothing further can be certainly collected from the words, as they stand connected, but that David reprieved Shimei from immediate execution, and left him at liberty to call him to an account, at any other time, for the outrage and treason that he had been guilty of. To this it is objected, that probity is greatly wounded by such excuses. By what excuses? What, by excusing David from breaking a promise that he never made; or, for putting a criminal to death whom he only reprieved, but never pardoned? The question is, whether David guarantied Shimei's pardon with a solemn oath? Or, sware that he should never be put to death for cursing and stoning him? The history makes it somewhat probable that David never swore this, but only that he should not be put to death at that time, as Joab and Abishai thought reasonable. If this was all that David promised, David broke no oath in afterward ordering him, for just reasons of state, for execution; and probity is not at all wounded by thus excusing David, because it is an excuse founded in truth. Instances enough may be produced, even in our own nation, of offenders being brought to justice, after a very considerable reprieve, perfectly consistent with the probity and equity of government.

And how is this inconsistent with piety, or the advice unworthy a just and religious prince on his death-bed? It is true, the forgiveness of enemies is a duty, provided they cease to become our enemies; but no man is obliged, by any law that I know of, so to forgive an enemy, continuing such, as not to take the proper methods to guard against the effects of his enmity, and bring him to justice, if no other method will prove effectual. Much less is a prince obliged so to forgive an implacable enemy to his crown and government, and one who is likely to disturb the settlement of the crown in his successor, as not to order his successor to be upon his guard against him, and punish him, when guilty, according to his demerits. Such a caution and order is what he owes to his people; and he may die, as a private person, in charity with all mankind, and forgive every private injury against himself; and yet, as a prince, advise what is necessary to the public good, and even the execution of particular persons, if, by abusing the lenity of government, and the respite they once obtained, they should become guilty of new and capital offences. David may therefore still be, the man after God's own heart. I shall only add, that it is a very uncharitable and groundless supposition of Mr. Bayle, that David only let him live, first to gain the glory of being a merciful prince, and afterward, on his death-bed, charged his son to put him to death, to avoid being reproached to his face of having broken his word. But surely David's resolution, that no man in Israel should be put to death who had been concerned in the rebellion, and the moderation and lenity of his whole reign over his people, were much nobler evidences of his being a merciful prince, than his sparing Shimei, whose execution, had it been immediately ordered, all the world would have commended as an exemplary act of justice, without the least impeachment of his goodness and mercy. Besides, if David was so false and unprincipled a wretch, as this supposes him, I cannot but think he would have little regarded such reproaches, if he had had an inclination, in his lifetime, out of revenge to have put him to death; and if he was so cautious of these reproaches while he lived, I can scarce think he would have given an order that should have blasted the glory of that character, and eternally stained his memory with the complicated guilt of hypocrisy, perfidy, and cruelty, and subjected his memory to them after death. Besides, whose reproaches would he have been afraid of? What, Shimei's? Surely he might have put him to death by the hands of his officers, without ever permitting Shimei to reproach him to his face; and I presume few of his courtiers would have cared, or dared, thus to reproach him. The truth of the case is—the charge concerning Shimei could not be given till David had established Solomon on his throne. It concerned Solomon only, and he gave him the caution, because necessary to the peace and security of his future reign; and it was of such a nature, as to deserve no reproach while he lived, and to expose him to no just reproach after his death. And if Mr. Bayle cannot prove, that David died immediately after this charge to Solomon concerning Shimei, he might have lived long enough to be reproached for it to his face; and therefore it could not be to avoid this reproach, that he gave this charge to Solomon towards the conclusion of his life. I cannot help therefore thinking, that the same reasons that led him to spare Shimei, when he cursed and stoned him, in his retreat from Jerusalem, induced him to spare him upon his return to it; viz. as Mr. Bayle himself expresses it—his acknowledging and adoring the hand of God, in the reproaches with which that furious Benjamite loaded him; and that as God had done what he scarce allowed himself to hope for, looked upon his affliction, and requited him with good for Shimei's cursing, he was resolved, in imitation of his God, to requite Shimei with good, and to bless the man who had reviled, cursed, and despitefully used him.—Chandler.

Another view of this charge to Solomon is given by Kennicott, whose remarks are well deserving attention. "David is here represented in our English version, as finishing his life with giving a command to Solomon to kill Shimei; and to kill him on account of that very crime, for which he had sworn to him by the Lord, he would not put him to death. The behaviour thus imputed to the king and prophet, should be examined very carefully, as to the ground it stands upon. When the passage is duly considered, it will appear highly probable that an injury has been done to this illustrious character. It is not uncommon in the Hebrew language to omit the negative in a second part of a sentence, and to consider it as repeated, when it has been once expressed, and is followed by the connecting particle. The necessity of so very considerable an alteration, as inserting the particle not, may be here confirmed by some other instances. Thus Psalm i. 5, 'The ungodly shall not stand in the judgment, nor (Heb. *and*, signifying *and not*) sinners in the congregation of the righteous.' (Psalm ix. 18. Psalm xxxviii. 1. Psalm lxxv. 5. Prov. xxiv. 12.) If then, there are in fact many such instances, the question is, whether the negative, here expressed in the former part of David's command, may not be understood as to be repeated in the latter part; and if this may be, a strong reason will be added why it should be so interpreted. The passage will run thus: 'Behold, thou hast with thee Shimei, who cursed me, but I sware to him by the Lord, saying, I will not put thee to death by the sword. Now therefore, hold him not guiltless, (for thou art a wise man, and knowest what thou oughtest to do unto him) but bring not down his hoary head to the grave with blood.' Now, if the language itself will admit this construction, the sense thus given to the sentence derives a very strong support from the context. For, how did Solomon understand this charge? did he kill Shimei in consequence of it? Certainly he did not. For, after he had immediately commanded Joab to be slain, in obedience to his father, he sends for Shimei, and knowing that Shimei ought to be well watched, confines him to a particular spot in Jerusalem for the remainder of his life."—B.

Ver. 16. And now I ask one petition of thee, deny me not. And she said unto him, Say on.

The Hebrew has for "deny me not," "turn not away my face." When a man has gained the attention of the person to whom he wishes to speak, he generally says *oru-kealve-mäte-ram*, i. e. *one* request only, to show he is not going to give him much trouble, and to ask for many things. Adonijah said to Bathsheba, "turn not away my face:" under similar circumstances it would be said here, "Ah! do not make my face ashamed—Do not put away my face—Reject not my face."—Roberts.

Ver. 19. Bath-sheba therefore went unto king Solomon, to speak unto him for Adonijah. And the king rose up to meet her, and bowed himself unto her, and sat down on his throne, and caused a seat to be set for the king's mother; and she sat on his right hand.

When visited by a superior, the Persian rises hastily, and

meets his guest nearly at the door of the apartment. On the entrance of an equal, he just raises himself from his seat, and stands nearly erect: but to an inferior he makes the motion only of rising.—MORIER.

Ver. 23. Then King Solomon sware by the LORD, saying, God do so to me, and more also, if Adonijah have not spoken this word against his own life. 24. Now therefore, *as* the LORD liveth, which hath established me, and set me on the throne of David my father, and who hath made me a house, as he promised, Adonijah shall be put to death this day. 25. And King Solomon sent by the hand of Benaiah, the son of Jehoiada; and he fell upon him that he died.

Far are we from vindicating Solomon in all his actions, any more than David in the matter of Uriah: his severity to his brother, for a seemingly small offence, looked like revenge, and as if he had taken the first opportunity to cut him off for his former attempt upon the kingdom; and yet we cannot but imagine, from Solomon's words to his mother, that there was some further conspiracy against him, though not mentioned in holy writ, of which he had got intelligence, and in which Joab and Abiathar were engaged; and that he looked upon this asking Abishag in marriage as the prelude to it, and the first overt act, as it were, of their treason. It is certain, that they thought to impose upon the king, as they had done upon his mother, and carry their point, without ever discovering the malevolent intent of it.

The wives of the late king (according to the customs of the East) belonged to his successor, and were never married to any under a *crowned* head. Abishag was, doubtless, a beautiful woman, and by her near relation to David might have a powerful interest at court; Adonijah might therefore hope, by this marriage, to strengthen his pretensions to the crown, or, at least, to lay the foundation for some future attempt, upon a proper opportunity, either if Solomon should die, and leave a young son, not able to contest the point with him, or if, at any time, he should happen to fall under the people's displeasure, as his father had done before him. This might be Adonijah's design, and Solomon, accordingly, might have information of it. But, supposing that his brother's design was entirely innocent, yet since his request, (according to the customs then prevailing,) was confessedly bold and presumptuous, and had in it all the appearance of treason, it was none of Solomon's business to make any further inquiry about it, or to interpret the thing in his brother's favour. It was sufficient for him that the action was in itself criminal, and of dangerous consequence to the state, for it is by their actions, and not intentions, that all offenders must be tried. Adonijah indeed, had he lived under our constitution, would have had a fair hearing before conviction. But we ought to remember, that in the kingdoms of the East the government was absolute, and the power of life or death entirely in the prince: so that Solomon, without the formality of any process, could pronounce his brother dead; and because he conceived that in cases of this nature delays were dangerous, might send immediately and have him despatched, though we cannot but say, that it had been much more to his commendation had he showed more clemency, and spared his life.—STACKHOUSE.

Ver. 26. And unto Abiathar the priest said the king, Get thee to Anathoth, unto thine own fields; for thou *art* worthy of death; but I will not at this time put thee to death, because thou barest the ark of the LORD God before David my father, and because thou hast been afflicted in all wherein my father was afflicted. 27. So Solomon thrust out Abiathar from being priest unto the LORD; that he might fulfil the word of the LORD, which he spake concerning the house of Eli in Shiloh.

How far the high-priest Abiathar was concerned in the plot against Solomon, the sacred history does not particularly inform us; but such was the reverence paid to the sacerdotal character, that Solomon would have hardly dared to have deposed such a one from his office, had not the constitution of the nation authorized him so to do. The kings in the East, indeed, soon found out ways to make themselves absolute; but it looks as if, at the first establishment, the king was at the head of the Hebrew republic, and the high-priest his subject, and, in all civil affairs, submitted to his correction: insomuch that, when any one abused the power of his office, to the prejudice of the commonweal, or endangering the king's person, the king might justly deprive him of his honours and titles, of his temporalities and emoluments, and even of life itself. And therefore, when Abiathar by his conspiracy had merited all this, whatever was dependant on the crown (as all the revenues of this place, as well as the liberty of officiating in it, were dependant) Solomon might lawfully take from him; but the sacerdotal character, which he received from God, and to which he was anointed, this he could not alienate: and therefore we may observe, that, after his deprivation, and even when Zadok was in possession of his place, he is nevertheless still mentioned under the style and title of the *priest.* The truth is, there is a great deal of difference between depriving a man of the dignity, and of the exercise of his function, in such a determinate place: between taking from him an authority that was given him by God, and the profits and emoluments arising from it, which were originally the gift of the crown. The former of these Solomon could not do, and the latter, it is probable, he was the rather incited to do, out of regard to the prophecy of Samuel, wherein he foretold Eli (from whom Abiathar was descended) that he would translate the priesthood from his to another family, as he did in the person of Zadok, who was of the house of Eleazar, even as Eli was of that of Ithamar; so that, by this means, the priesthood reverted to its ancient channel.—STACKHOUSE.

Ver. 34. So Benaiah the son of Jehoiada went up, and fell upon him, and slew him; and he was buried in his own house in the wilderness.

This refers to the interment of Joab, who was slain by the hands of Benaiah. It is probable that Joab had built this house for the purpose of being buried in it, as it is not reasonable to suppose that he would erect a house in such a place to be the habitation of the living. Children or parents often build a house in a retired place, over, or for the remains of their dead; and the rest of the family also when they die are buried there. In some of these places may be seen the funeral car, or palanquin, in which the corpse was taken to its long home, suspended from the roof. At the anniversary of the death of a father, mother, or any other near relation, the friends go thither to perform the annual rites for the benefit of their manes. Such a house, so long as the descendants of the dead interred there have the power to prevent it, will never be allowed to go to decay.—ROBERTS.

Ver. 38. And Shimei dwelt in Jerusalem many days.

Ask a man how long he has lived in the village, or a priest how long he has officiated in the temple, the answer is not a long time, or many years, but *veagu-nāl,* i. e. many days. "How long were they digging that tank?"—"Ah! many days." "Who built that temple?"—"Ah! my lord, how can I tell? it has been built many days." "I hear you were at the taking of Seringapatam, when the great Tippoo Saib was slain."—"Yes, I was." "How long is that since?"—"I cannot really tell, but many days."—ROBERTS.

CHAPTER III.

Ver. 4. And the king went to Gibeon to sacrifice there; for that *was* the great high place: a thousand burnt-offerings did Solomon offer upon that altar.

An exception has been taken to the account of the great quantity of sacrifices which he is said to have offered on one altar only; but without recurring to any miracle for this, or without supposing this fire, which originally came from heaven, was more strong and intense than any common fire, and therefore, after the return from the captivity, the altar (as some observe) was made larger, because there wanted this celestial flame: without any forced solution like this, we have no reason to think that all these sacrifices were offered in one day. The king, we may imagine, upon one of the great festivals, went in procession with his nobles, to pass his devotion at Gibeon, where was the tabernacle and the brazen altar, which Moses had made. Each of the great festivals lasted for seven days; but Solomon might stay much longer at Gibeon, until, by the daily oblations, a thousand burnt-offerings were consumed; and, at the conclusion of this course of devotion, he might offer up his ardent prayer to God for wisdom, and God, for the confirmation of his faith, might appear to him in a dream by night, and have that converse with him, that the scripture takes notice of.—STACKHOUSE.

Ver. 7. And now, O LORD my God, thou hast made thy servant king instead of David my father; and I *am but* a little child: I know not *how* to go out or come in.

So said Solomon when he came to the kingdom of his father; and so say men here, though they be advanced in years, when they wish to speak of their incapacity for any performance. "What can I do in this affair; I am but a boy of yesterday's birth?" When a man pleads for forgiveness, he says, "I am but a little child, it was my ignorance." Has a man insulted another by not bowing to him, or refusing to take off his sandals in his presence, or by the use of some improper expressions; those who go to intercede for him, say, "Forgive him, sir, he is but an infant of yesterday." A person wishing to compliment a holy or learned person, says, "I am but a little infant when compared with you."—ROBERTS.

Ver. 25. And the king said, Divide the living child in two, and give half to the one, and half to the other.

This was apparently a very strange decision; but Solomon saw that the only way to discover the real mother was by the affection and tenderness she would necessarily show to her offspring. The plan was tried, and succeeded; and it was a proof of his sound judgment, penetration, and acquaintance with the human heart, if not of his extraordinary and supernatural wisdom. There are several similar decisions recorded by heathen writers. Suetonius, in his Life of the Emperor Claudian, whom he celebrates for his wonderful sagacity and penetration, tells us, that this emperor discovered a woman to be the real mother of a young man, whom she refused to acknowledge, by commanding her to marry him, the proofs being doubtful on both sides; for, rather than commit incest, she confessed the truth. Diodorus Siculus also informs us, that Ariopharnes, king of Thrace, being appointed to decide between three young men, each of whom professed to be the son of the deceased king of the Cimmerians, and claimed the succession, discovered the real son, by ordering each to shoot an arrow into the dead body of the king: two of them did this without hesitation; but the real son of the deceased monarch refused.—GREENFIELD.

The great merit of the king in this matter was finding out the true mother. "A woman who was going to bathe left her child to play on the banks of the tank, when a female demon who was passing that way carried it off. They both appeared before the deity, and each declared the child was her own: the command was therefore given that each claimant was to seize the infant by a leg and an arm, and pull with all their might in opposite directions. No sooner had they commenced than the child began to scream, when the real mother, from pity, left off pulling, and resigned her claim to the other. The judge therefore decided, that as she only had shown affection, the child must be hers." The decision of a Hindoo *magistrate* in the case of some travellers is also in point. "Two travellers once went into a rest-house to sleep; the one had on beautiful earrings, the other had none. In the night the latter arose, and while the other slept, took off one of his rings and put in his own ear. In the morning the former finding one of his rings missing, looked at his companion and saw it in his ear. He immediately charged him with the theft, but the thief retorted, and charged him with having stolen one of his rings. They disputed for some time, and at last each determined to make his complaint before a magistrate: his worship patiently heard the case, but as each swore that the other was the thief, and as neither of them could produce a witness, he was at a loss how to decide. He then took one of them into a private apartment, and said, I cannot find out who is guilty, but as I perceive the rings are worth one hundred rupees, I will sell them; you shall each pay a fine of twenty-five rupees, and the remaining fifty you may divide betwixt yourselves. The man replied, 'I will not have the twenty-five rupees; they are my own rings, you can do as you please.' The magistrate then called the other man into the room, and proposed the same thing; he replied, 'What can I do, my lord, I must submit to your pleasure; I accept of the twenty-five rupees.' His worship saw that the man was much pleased with the prospect of getting the rupees, and therefore concluded that he was the thief. The ring was then given to the other man, who was the rightful owner."—ROBERTS.

Ver. 26. For her bowels yearned upon her son.

The Hebrew has for yearned, "were hot." A mother, in lamenting over her suffering child, says, "Ah! my bowels are *hot* over the child." "My bowels burn in his misery." "My heart is burnt to ashes."—ROBERTS.

CHAPTER IV.

Ver. 7. And Solomon had twelve officers over all Israel, which provided victuals for the king and his household: each man his month in a year made provision.

The eastern people to this day, it seems, support the expenses of government, in common, by paying such a proportion of the produce of their lands to their princes. These are their taxes. No wonder it was so in remoter ages. Chardin gives us this account: "The revenues of princes in the East are paid in the fruits and productions of the earth. There are no other taxes upon the peasants." The twelve officers of Solomon then, mentioned 1 Kings iv. 7—19, are to be considered as his general receivers. They furnished food for all that belonged to the king; and the having provisions for themselves and attendants, seems to have been, in those times of simplicity, all the ordinary gratification his ministers of state, as well as his meaner servants, received. Silver, gold, horses, armour, precious vestments, and other things of value, came to him from other quarters: partly a kind of tribute from the surrounding princes, partly from the merchants, whom he suffered to pass through his country to and from Egypt, or elsewhere, partly from his own commerce by the Red Sea. The horses and armour he seems to have distributed among the most populous towns, who were to find horsemen and people to drive chariots to such a number when called for; and out of the silver, and other precious things that came to him, he made presents upon extraordinary occasions to those that distinguished themselves in his service. And according to this plan of conducting the expenses of civil government, the history of Solomon is to be explained. Commentators have not always had this present to their minds when illustrating this part of scripture.—HARMER.

Ver. 23. Ten fat oxen, and twenty oxen out of the pastures, and a hundred sheep, besides harts, and roe-bucks, (antelopes,) and fallow-deer, and fatted fowl.

"Harts." Dr. Shaw (Trav. p. 414) understands the original איל *ayil* as the name of the genus, including all the species of the deer kind, whether they are distinguished by round horns, as the stag; or by flat ones, as the fallow-deer; or by the smallness of the branches, as the roe.

"Fallow-deer." The Hebrew יחמור *yachmur*, rendered *bubalus* by the Vulgate, probably denotes the *buffalo*; and though the "flesh of a buffalo does not seem so well tasted as beef, being harder and more coarse, yet in our times persons of distinction, as well as the common people, and even the European merchants, eat a good deal of it in countries where that animal abounds." (Niebuhr.)—GREENFIELD.

The flesh of the antelope is very grateful to the taste of an Oriental. It is, in the estimation of Arabian writers, the most delicious and wholesome of all venison. They pronounce its juices better than those of any other wild animal, and more adapted to the human constitution. The sentiments of these venerable ancients, are confirmed by the testimony of several intelligent modern authors. Dr. Shaw says, "it is in great esteem in the East for food, having a sweet musky taste, which is highly agreeable to their palates;" and according to Dr. Russel, "the antelope venison, during the winter, or sporting season, is well flavoured, but very lean, and in the spring is fat, and of a flavour which might vie with English venison." These statements account for its being daily served up on the sumptuous table of Solomon and other eastern princes. Besides, the antelope has all the marks which distinguished clean animals under the law; it both divides the hoof and chews the cud. An Israelite, therefore, might lawfully eat of its flesh, although he was not permitted to offer it in sacrifice. This creature belonged to the class of clean beasts, which the people of Israel, as well during their wanderings in the desert, as after their settlement in the land of promise, were permitted to kill wherever they could find them, and use for the subsistence of their families, although, at the time, they might be ceremonially unclean. But the ox, the sheep, and the goat, which some writers distinguished by the name of clean cattle, might both be lawfully eaten and offered in sacrifice; yet while the chosen people sojourned in the wilderness, they were forbidden to kill any of these animals, although intended merely for private use, except at the door of the tabernacle; and if ceremonially unclean, even to eat of their flesh. This regulation occasioned little inconvenience to the tribes in the desert, where they lived in one vast encampment, in the midst of which the sacred tent was pitched; but after their settlement in Canaan, their circumstances required either an alteration in the law, or that the greater part of the nation should abstain altogether from the use of flesh. The permission was accordingly enlarged; while they were still restricted to shed the blood of cattle intended for sacrifice, only before the national altar, they were permitted, when too far from the tabernacle, to kill those which they designed merely for common food, in any of their cities, or in their houses; even the ceremonial regulation was abolished, and in private clean and unclean fared alike. This permission, which is couched in very express terms, is repeated in the course of a few verses, lest the suspicious mind of an Israelite might suppose that Jehovah envied his people the enjoyment of what he had given them; and "in both instances it is illustrated by an example which must, from the use of it, have been familiar to the Israelites:" "The unclean and the clean may eat thereof, as of the (antelope,) and of the hart."—PAXTON.

The great number of beasts required daily in Solomon's kitchen, will by no means be found incredible, when we compare it with the accounts of the daily consumption of oriental courts in modern times, and the prodigious number of servants of an Asiatic prince. Thus Tavernier, in his description of the seraglio, says, that five hundred sheep and lambs were daily required for the persons belonging to the court of the sultan.—ROSENMULLER.

Ver. 25. And Judah and Israel dwelt safely, every man under his vine and under his fig-tree, from Dan even to Beer-sheba, all the days of Solomon.

Plantations of trees about houses are found very useful in hot countries, to give them an agreeable coolness. The ancient Israelites seem to have made use of the same means, and probably planted fruit trees rather than other kinds, to produce that effect. "It is their manner in many places," says Sir Thomas Row's chaplain, speaking of the country of the Great Mogul, "to plant about, and among their buildings, trees which grow high and broad, the shadow whereof keeps their houses by far more cool: this I observed in a special manner when we were ready to enter Amadavar; for it appeared to us, as if we had been entering a wood rather than a city." The expression in the Old Testament, of people *dwelling under their vines and their fig-trees*, seems strongly to intimate, that this method anciently obtained much in Judea; and that vines and fig-trees were what were commonly used in that country. Nor was this management at all to be wondered at; as the ancient patriarchs found it very agreeable to pitch their tents under the shade of some thick tree, their children might naturally be disposed to plant them about their houses. And as it was requisite for them to raise as many eatables as they could, in so very populous a country as that was, it is no wonder they planted fig-trees, whose shade was thickened by vines, about their houses, under which they might sit in the open air, and yet in the cool. This writer mentions another circumstance, in which there is an evident similarity between the ancient Jews and these more eastern people: "But for their houses in their *aldeas*, or villages, which stand very thick in that country, they are generally very poor and base. All those country dwellings are set up close together; for I never observed any house there to stand single, and alone."

The account the Baron De Tott gives of the Egyptian villages, shows they are shaded in much the same manner. "Wherever the inundation can reach, their habitations are erected on little hills, raised for that purpose, which serve for the common foundation of all the houses which stand together, and which are contrived to take up as little room as possible, that they may save all the ground they can for cultivation. This precaution is necessary, to prevent the water's washing away the walls, which are only of mud. The villages are always surrounded by an infinite number of pointed turrets, meant to invite thither the pigeons, in order to collect the dung. Every village has, likewise, a small wood of palm-trees near it, the property of which is common: these supply the inhabitants with dates for their consumption, and leaves for fabrication of baskets, mats, and other things of that kind. Little causeways, raised, in like manner, above the inundation, preserve a communication during the time it lasts." Palm-trees, according to this, are planted universally about the Egyptian villages; had they been as generally about the Jewish towns, Jericho would hardly have been called the *city of palm-trees*, by way of distinction from the rest. It appears to have been, in Judea, rather a peculiarity. But the Jewish towns and houses might be wont to be surrounded by other trees, proper for their use, which probably were vines and fig-trees, which furnished two great articles of food for their consumption, and the cuttings of their vines must have been useful to them for fuel. That plantations of some sort of trees were common about the Jewish towns, may be deduced even from the term כפר *kopher*, used in their language for a village, which is derived from a root that signifies to *cover* or *hide*.—HARMER.

Immediately on entering, I was ushered into the court-yard of the Aga, whom I found smoking under a vine, surrounded by horses, servants, and dogs, among which I distinguished an English pointer.—TURNER.

Ver. 28. Barley also and straw for the horses and dromedaries brought they unto the place where *the officers* were, every man according to his charge.

Besides provisions for themselves, the Orientals are obliged to carry food for the beasts on which they ride, or carry their goods. That food is of different kinds. They make little or no hay in these countries, and are therefore very careful of their straw, which they cut into small bits, by an instrument which at the same time thrashes out the corn; this chopped straw, with barley, beans, and balls made of bean and barley-meal, or of the pounded kernels of dates, are what they are wont to feed them with. The officers of Solomon are accordingly said to have brought, every man in his month, barley and straw for the horses and dromedaries, 1 Kings iv. 28. Not straw to litter them with, there is reason to think, for it is not now used in those countries for that purpose; but chopped straw for them to eat alone with their barley. The litter they use for them is their own dung, dried in the sun, and bruised between their hands, which they heap up again in the morning, sprinkling it in the summer with fresh water to keep it from corrupting. In some other places we read of provender and straw, not barley and straw: because it may be, other things were used for their food anciently, as well as now, besides barley and chopped straw. בליל *beleel*, one of the words translated provender, Is. xxx. 24, implies something of mixture, and the participle of the verb from which it is derived is used for the mingling of flour with oil; so the verb in Judges xix. 21, may be as well translated, "he mingled (food) for the asses," ויבל לחמורים *veyabal lechamoreem*, as, he gave them provender, signifying that he mixed some chopped straw and barley together for the asses. And thus also barley and chopped straw, as it lies just after reaping unseparated in the field, might naturally be expressed by the Hebrew word we translate provender, which signifies barley and straw that had been mingled together, and accordingly seems to be so, Job xxiv. 6, "They reap every one his corn in the field"—"Hebrew, mingled corn, or dredge," says the margin. What ideas are usually affixed to secondary translation, I do not know; but Job apparently alludes to the provender, or heap of chopped straw and corn lying mingled together in the field, after having passed under the thrashing instrument, to which he compares the spoils that were taken from the passengers, so early as his time, by those that lived somewhat after the present manner of the wild Arabs, which spoils are to them what the harvest and vintage were to others. To this agrees that other passage of Job where this word occurs, ch. vi. 5, "Will the ox low, in complaint, over his provender?" or fodder, as it is translated in our version; when he has not only straw enough, but mixed with barley.

The accurate Vitringa, in his commentary, has taken notice of that word's implying something of mixture which is translated provender in Is. xxx. 24, but for want of more nicely attending to eastern customs, though he has done it more than most commentators, he has been very unhappy in explaining the cause of it; for he supposes it signifies a mixture of straw, hay, and bran. I have nowhere observed in books of travels, that they give their labouring beasts bran in the East, and hay is not made there; the mixture that is meant, if we are to explain it by the present eastern usages, is chopped straw and barley. But the additional word there translated *clean*, and in the margin *leavened*, which, Vitringa observes, is the proper meaning of the word, may be supposed to make the passage difficult. The Septuagint seem to have thought the words signified nothing more than straw mingled with winnowed barley: and if the word translated provender, though originally intended to express mixture, might afterward come to signify uncompounded food, as Vitringa supposes, the passage is easily deciphered; for though the word translated *clean* does commonly signify *leavened*, or *made sour*, yet not always; signifying sometimes mere mixing, as in Is. lxiii. 1, where it is used for staining a garment with blood, and so it may signify here, as the Septuagint seem to have understood the passage, chopped straw, leavened or mixed with barley. But there is no necessity of supposing the word translated provender is used in a sense different from its common and ancient meaning, and signifying uncompounded meat for cattle; that single word may be understood to mean chopped straw mingled with barley, since we find that barley, when given to beasts of labour, is sometimes mingled, or, to express it poetically, leavened, with a few beans, to which therefore the prophet might refer. The wild Arabs, who are extremely nice in managing their horses, give them no food but very clean barley. The Israelites were not so scrupulous, as appears from the passage I cited relating to the provision made for Solomon's horses, but they may nevertheless think the cleanness of the provender a very great recommendation of it, and seem to have done so, since Isaiah, in the above-mentioned passage, speaks of leavened provender winnowed with the shovel and with the fan. It is not the more important to them, as a good deal of earth, sand, and gravel, are wont, notwithstanding all their precautions, to be taken up with the grain, in *their* way of thrashing. But though the Israelites were not so scrupulous as the Arabs, giving their beasts of burden straw as well as barley, yet it must have been much more commodious for them in their journeying to have carried barley alone, or balls of bean, or barley-meal, rather than a quantity of chopped straw, with a little other provender of a better kind; and accordingly we find no mention made by Dr. Shaw, of any chopped straw being carried with them to Mount Sinai, but only barley, with a few beans intermixed, or the flour of one or other of them, or both, made into balls with a little water. The Levite's mentioning therefore his having straw, along with other provender, rather conveys the idea of his being a person in mean circumstances, who was not able to feed his asses with pure barley, or those other sorts of provender that eastern travellers are wont to carry with them.—HARMER.

In the East, horses are still fed with barley. Hasselquist observes, that in the plain of Jericho, the Arabians had sown barley for their horses. They are very careful of their straw, which they cut into small bits, by an instrument which at the same time thrashes out the corn: this chopped straw, with barley, beans, and balls made of bean and barley-meal, or of the pounded kernels of dates, are what they usually feed their beasts with.—MAILLET.

CHAPTER V.

Ver. 6. Now therefore command thou that they hew me cedar-trees out of Lebanon; and my servants shall be with thy servants: and unto thee will I give hire for thy servants according to all that thou shalt appoint: for thou knowest that *there is* not among us any that can skill to hew timber like unto the Sidonians.

The Hebrew word ארז *aroz*, whence the Chaldee and Syriac ארזא *arzo*, and the Arabic and Ethiopic ארז *arz*, and Spanish *alerze*, unquestionably denotes the *cedar;* it is thus rendered by the Septuagint and other Greek versions κέδρος, and by the Vulgate *cedras;* and the inhabitants of mount Lebanon still call it *arz.* The cedar is a large and noble evergreen tree, and according to Tournefort makes a distinct genus of plants, but it is comprehended by Linnæus among the junipers.—GREENFIELD.

The cedar grows, it is true, on the mountains of Amanus and Taurus, in Asia Minor, but it does not there attain the height and strength it acquires on mount Lebanon, on which account the cedars of Lebanon have been renowned from the most ancient times. But the cedar woods, which formerly covered a part of this mountain, have long ago vanished. Only on the northeast side is a small wood, consisting of an inconsiderable number of small thick cedars, and eight or nine hundred younger ones. The oldest and largest cedars are distinguished from the younger ones chiefly by this, that the latter grow up straight, and their boughs branch out horizontally from the stem, but hang down a little; and in these two particulars, and in general in their whole form, entirely resemble our European pines and firs; whereas the old cedars have a short and very thick trunk, which divides not far from the root, into three, four, or five large arms, which grow straight up, and are very thick; some of them grow together for about ten feet. "These trees," says Rauwolf, "which remain green during the whole year, have large trunks, which may be some fathoms thick, and as high as our firs; but as they have larger arms, according to which the stem bends, this takes away so much of their perpendicular height. The branches spread out pretty far in such a beautiful equality, that they look as if they had been clipped above, and made even with particular care. It may easily be perceived before you get very near them, that there is a great difference between these and other resinous trees. Otherwise they nearly resemble larch-trees, especially in the leaves, which are small, narrow, and shoot out as close together."

The latest accounts of the cedars of Lebanon are given by Mr. John Henry Mayer, who visited this part in the summer of the year 1813. "I counted," says he, "nine principal cedar-trees, which were distinguished from all the others by their thickness and age, but not by their height, for younger ones exceed them in this respect. I measured the circumference of the trunk of one of the largest with a cord, about four feet from the ground, and found it ten French ells and a half. A single branch was thirty steps in length to the end, when it divided into small twigs. The trunk of five of the largest consists of three or four divisions, each of which equals in circumference the stem of our largest oaks. The cedar itself, probably, belongs to the class of trees with acerose leaves, but is neither a pine, nor a fir, nor a larch, though the young cedars are like the latter. The broken twigs almost resemble the elder, and the smell puts one in mind of the arbor vitæ. The greatest beauty of these trees consists in their stiff, strong, and far-spreading boughs; and, what no other kind of tree has, the brittleness of the wood, even of the smallest and tenderest twigs, which broke like glass, particularly the old ones. The whole wood, probably, does not contain above eight or nine hundred trees, large and small included. The young and middle-aged ones bore fruit of the size of an egg, which were bright green, with brown rings and spots, and stood upright on the small twigs. This peculiarity of the fruit of the cedar also distinguishes it from other trees of the same genus: in other respects, it has an affinity and resemblance to them, as well by its resinous quality as its form." Hardly any kind of wood unites so many good qualities for building as the cedar: its wood not only pleases the eye by its reddish stripes, and exhales an agreeable smell, but it is hard, and without knots, and is never eaten by worms, and lasts so long, that some persons consider it as imperishable. Hence it was used for rafters and boards, either to cover the houses or floors: it was also employed in building the principal wall; and combined with stones, so that, for instance, after three layers of stones, there followed one of cedar-wood. 1 Kings vi. 36. vii. 12. Ezra vi. 3, 4. Sometimes, too, each division of the wall was built alternately with cedar-wood and stones, so that first a course of wood, and then a course of stones, extended from one division to the other, and so each division nearly resembled a chess-board. The temple at Jerusalem, as well as the palace of Solomon, was built of cedar; and in the latter there was such a quantity of this wood, that it was called, 1 Kings vii. 2. x. 10, *The house of the forest of Lebanon.* (Rosenmuller.)—BURDER.

Ver. 9. My servants shall bring *them* down from Lebanon unto the sea; and I will convey them by sea in floats unto the place that thou shalt appoint me, and will cause them to be discharged there, and thou shalt receive *them:* and thou shalt accomplish my desire in giving food for my household.

Bishop Patrick supposes, "that they conveyed the pieces of timber from the high parts of the mountains to the river Adonis, or to the plain of Biblos." "By floats is probably meant that the pieces of timber were bound together, and so drawn through the rivers and the sea." In exactly the same way, timber is conveyed in all parts of the East. The trees are cut down before the rainy season, all the branches are lopped off, and the trunks are squared on the spot. Notches are then made in the logs, and they are tied together by ropes made of green withes gathered in the forests. If, however, the waters of the rainy season should not reach the spot where they are hewn down, they are dragged singly to the place where it is known that in the wet monsoon they will float. Thus, in passing through remote forests in the dry season, the inexperienced traveller, in seeing numerous trees felled in every direction, and then again, in another place, a large collection bound together like a raft, which is also fastened to trees that are still standing, (to prevent it from being lost when the floods come,) is at a loss to know how it can be got to the river, or to the sea; for he sees no track or path except that which is made by the wild beast: he knows no vehicle can approach the place, and is convinced that men cannot carry it. But let him go thither when the rains have fallen, and he will see in one place men in a little canoe winding through the forest, in another directing a float with some men on it moving gently along; and in the river he sees large rafts sweeping down the stream, with the dexterous steersmen making for some neighbouring town, or the more distant ocean; and then may be seen in the harbour immense collections of the finest timber, which have been brought thither "by sea in floats." Sometimes the rains come on earlier than expected; or the logs may not have been fastened to trees still standing; hence, when the floods come, they naturally move towards the river; and then may be seen noble trees whirling and tumbling along till they reach the sea, and are thus lost to man.—ROBERTS.

Two methods of conveying wood in floats appear to have been practised. The first by pushing single trunks of trees into the water, and suffering them to be carried along by the stream. This was commonly adopted as it regarded firewood. The other was ranging a number of planks close to each other in regular order, binding them together, and steering them down the current. This was probably the most ancient practice. The earliest ships or boats were nothing else than rafts, or a collection of deals and planks bound together. By the Greeks they were called *Schedai*, and by the Latins, *Rates.* The ancients ventured out to sea with them on piratical expeditions, as well as to carry on commerce: and after the invention of ships, they were still retained for the transportation of soldiers, and of heavy burdens. Pliny, lib. vi. cap. 56. Strabo, lib. xvi. Scheffer, *De Militia Navali Veterum*, lib. i. cap. 3. Pitisci, *Lexicon Antiquitat. Rom.* art. *Rates.* Solomon entered into a contract with Hiram, king of Tyre, by which the latter was to cause cedars for the use of the temple to be cut down on the western side of mount Lebanon, above Tripoli, and to be floated to Jaffa. At present no streams run from Lebanon to Jerusalem; and the Jordan, the only river in Palestine that could bear floats, is at a great distance from the cedar-forest. The wood, therefore, must have been brought along the coast by sea to Jaffa.—BURDER.

CHAPTER VI.

Ver. 7. And the house, when it was in building, was built of stone made ready before it was brought thither: so that there was neither hammer, nor ax, *nor* any tool of iron, heard in the house while it was in building.

This passage is illustrated by what D'Arvieux remarks of Alexandria in Egypt. "The city gates, which are still standing, have a magnificent appearance, and are so high and broad, that we may infer from them the ancient greatness and splendour of the place. They properly consist only of four square stones; one of which serves as the threshold, two are raised on the sides, and the fourth laid across and resting upon them. I need not say that they are of great antiquity; for it is well known, that for many centuries past such immense stones have not been used in building. It is a matter of surprise how the ancients could raise such heavy masses from the stone quarries, remove them, and set them up. Some are of opinion that these stones were *cast*, and, probably, only consisted of a heap of small stones, which were united by the finest cement; that at the place where they were wanted, wooden models or moulds were made, in which the cement and stones were mixed together, and when this mass became dry and sufficiently firm, the mould was taken off by degrees, and the stones then polished."—ROSENMULLER.

Ver. 18. And the cedar of the house within *was* carved with knobs and open flowers.

The people of the East are exceedingly profuse in their carved work. See a temple; it is almost from its foundation to its summit a complete mass of sculpture and carved work. Look at their sacred car in which their gods are drawn out in procession, and you are astonished at the labour, taste, and execution displayed by the workmen in carved work: nay, the roof and doors of private dwellings are all indebted to the chisel of the "cunning workman." The pillars that support the verandas, their chests, their couches, (as were those of Solomon,) the handles of different instruments, their ploughs, their vessels, (however rude in other respects,) must be adorned by the skill of the carver.—ROBERTS.

CHAPTER VII.

Ver. 7. Then he made a porch for the throne where he might judge, *even* the porch of judgment: and *it was* covered with cedar from one side of the floor to the other.

It deserves remark, that the eastern floors and ceilings are just the reverse of ours. Their ceilings are of wood; ours of plaster or stucco-work; their floors are of plaster or of painted tiles, ours of wood. This effectually detects a mistake of Kimchi and R. Solomon, who, according to Buxtorf, supposed the floor of the porch of judgment which Solomon built was all of cedar; whereas the sacred writer, 1 Kings vii. 7, undoubtedly meant its covering a-top, its ceiling, was of cedar. Indeed here in the West, where these Jewish Rabbis lived, such places are usually built after the eastern mode, which makes their mistake so much the more strange. Westminster Hall is, I think, paved with stone and ceiled with wood; and such without doubt was the ceiling and the pavement of the porch for judgment which Solomon built, and which was erected in a much hotter climate.—Harmer.

Ver. 10. And the foundation *was of* costly stones, *even* great stones, stones of ten cubits, and stones of eight cubits.

In the ruins of Balbec, stones of great magnitude are found. "But what is still more astonishing, is, the enormous stones which compose the sloping wall. To the west the second layer is formed of stones which are from twenty-eight to thirty-five feet long, by about nine in height. Over this layer, at the northwest angle, there are three stones, which alone occupy a space of one hundred and seventy-five feet and one half: viz. the first, fifty-eight feet seven inches; the second, fifty-eight feet eleven; and the third, exactly fifty-eight feet; and each of these are twelve feet thick. These stones are of a white granite, with large shining flakes, like gypse. There is a quarry of this kind of stone under the whole city, and in the adjoining mountains, which is open in several places: and, among others, on the right, as we approach the city, there is still lying there a stone, hewn on three sides, which is sixty-nine feet two inches long, twelve feet ten inches broad, and thirteen feet three in thickness." (Volney.)

"The city of Jerusalem is utterly unlike any other place I have ever seen. Its situation upon an immense rock, surrounded by valleys that seem cut out by the chisel; the contrast exhibited between the extremest degree of barrenness and the extremest degree of fertility, which border upon each other here almost every yard, without one shade of mitigated character on either side; the structure of the walls, many of the stones in which are fifteen or sixteen feet long, by four high and four deep, the very size mentioned of the hewn stones of Solomon, 1 Kings vii. 10; the houses, where almost every one is a fortress, and the streets, where almost every one is a covered way, altogether formed an appearance totally dissimilar from that of any other town I have met with either in Europe or Asia." (Carlyle.)—Burder.

CHAPTER VIII.

Ver. 31. If any man trespass against his neighbour, and an oath be laid upon him to cause him to swear, and the oath come before thine altar in this house.

Bishop Patrick alleges, that it was the custom of all nations to touch the altar when they made a solemn oath, calling God to witness the truth of what they said, and to punish them if they did not speak the truth: and he supposes, that Solomon alludes to this practice, in his prayer at the dedication of the temple: "If any man trespass against his neighbour, and an oath be laid upon him, to cause him to swear, and the oath come before thine altar in this house." But the royal suppliant says not one word about touching the altar; but clearly refers to the general practice of standing before it, for his words literally are: And the oath come (לפני מזבחך) before the face of thine altar. In imitation of God's ancient people, many of the surrounding nations, among whom Livy and other celebrated writers of antiquity mention the Athenians, the Carthaginians, and the Romans, were accustomed to stand before the altar when they made oath; but it does not appear they laid their hand upon it, and by consequence, no argument from the sacred text, nor even from the customs of these nations, can be drawn for the superstitious practice of laying the hand upon the gospels and kissing them, instead of the solemn form authorized by God himself, of lifting up the right hand to heaven.—Paxton.

Ver. 44. If thy people go out to battle against their enemy, whithersoever thou shalt send them, and shalt pray unto the Lord towards the city which thou hast chosen, and *towards* the house that I have built for thy name.

"By a decree passed in the eighteenth year of the Emperor Adrian, the Jews were forbidden not only to enter into the city of Jerusalem, (then called Œlia,) but even to turn their looks towards it; which most probably had a reference to this custom of turning their faces towards the Holy City at their prayers. I observed that Mecca, the country of their prophet, and from which, according to their idea, salvation was dispensed to them, is situated towards the south, and for this reason they pray with their faces turned towards that quarter." (Mariti.) "The Mexicans prayed generally upon their knees, with their faces turned towards the east, and, therefore, made their sanctuaries with the door to the west." (Cullen's Mexico.) In a description of the people of the Ganow hills, we find the same custom prevalent. "Their mode of swearing is very solemn: the oath is taken upon a stone, which they first salute, then, with their hands joined and uplifted, their eyes steadfastly fixed to the hills, they call on Mahadeva in the most solemn manner, telling him to witness what they declare, and that he knows whether they speak true or false. They then again touch the stone, with all the appearance of the utmost fear, and bow their heads to it, calling again upon Mahadeva. They also, during their relation, look steadfastly to the hills, and keep their right hand upon the stone. When the first person swore before me, the awe and reverence with which the man swore forcibly struck me: my Moherrir could hardly write, so much was he affected by the solemnity. I understand their general belief to be, that their god resides in the hills; and though this belief may seem inconsistent with an awful idea of the divinity, these people appeared to stand in the utmost awe of their deity, from the fear of his punishing them for any misconduct in their frequent excursions to the hills." (Asiatic Researches.) "An hour before sunrise, the coffeegee having prepared our coffee, retired into a corner of the room, and having, without the least reserve, performed the necessary ablutions, spread his garment on the ground, and began his prayers: he turned himself to the east, and though several persons entered and left the apartment during his devotions, he seemed quite absorbed, and rose, and knelt, and prostrated himself with as much appearance of piety as if he had been praying in the holy temple of Mecca itself." (Macmichel.) —Burder.

Ver. 66. On the eighth day he sent the people away: and they blessed the king, and went unto their tents joyful and glad of heart, for all the goodness that the Lord had done for David his servant, and for Israel his people.

The Hebrew has, for blessed, "thanked." The Tamul translation has, for blessed, "praised." So in Joshua xxii. 33, also in 2 Sam. xxii. 47, and in all other passages where the word occurs, (when used in reference to God,) it is rendered, "praise," or "praised." The word bless, among the Hindoos, is, I think, not used, as in English, to *praise*, to glorify, but *to confer happiness, to convey a benediction, or to show good-will.* St. Paul says, "Without all contradiction, the less is blessed of the greater;" and this I believe, joined with greatness, is the only idea the Orientals attach to those who bless others. Hence he who blesses another, must be a superior, either in years, rank, or sanctity. The heathen never *bless* their gods.—Roberts.

CHAPTER X.

Ver. 1. And when the queen of Sheba heard of the fame of Solomon concerning the name of the Lord, she came to prove him with hard questions.

The Septuagint has, for hard questions, *αινιγμασι*, enigmas, riddles. The Hindoos (especially their females) take great delight in riddles, apologues, and fables. By this method they convey pleasure, instruction, or reproof. See them in their marriage feasts, or in their "evenings at home;" how pleasantly they pass their time, in thus puzzling each other, and calling forth the talents of the young.—ROBERTS.

Ver. 4. And when the queen of Sheba had seen all Solomon's wisdom, and the house that he had built, 5. And the meat of his table, and the sitting of his servants, and the attendance of his ministers, and their apparel, and his cup-bearers, and his ascent by which he went up unto the house of the LORD; there was no more spirit in her.

By these words we may understand that this ascent was consecrated to the use of Solomon alone. Thus we are told by Sir George Staunton, in his account of the first presentation of the British embassy, that, "on his entrance into the tent, the emperor of China mounted immediately the throne by the front steps, consecrated to his use alone." He also informs us, that "one highway was reserved for the use of the emperor alone; this was rendered perfectly level, dry, and smooth: cisterns were contrived on the sides of the imperial road, to hold water for sprinkling it occasionally, in order to keep down the dust: parallel to the emperor's, was another road, not quite so broad, nor swept continually with so much care, but perfectly commodious and safe: this was intended for the attendants of his imperial majesty: and upon this the British embassy was allowed to pass. All other travellers were excluded from these two privileged roads, and obliged to make out a path wherever they were able."—BURDER.

Ver. 8. Happy *are* thy men, happy *are* these thy servants, which stand continually before thee, *and* that hear thy wisdom.

"When the king" (of Persia) "is seated in public, his sons, ministers, and courtiers, stand erect, with their hands crossed, and in the exact place of their rank. They watch the looks of the sovereign, and a glance is a mandate. If he speak to them, you hear a voice reply, and see their lips move, but not a motion nor gesture betrays that there is animation in any other part of their frame." When he places himself at the windows of his palace, his domestics take their station in the court before it, hard by the fountain which plays in the middle, to watch the looks of their lord. A principal part of the regal state in Persia consists in the number of the men who stand before the monarch; and we learn from the address of the queen of Sheba to Solomon, that he was not indifferent to this part of eastern splendour. It is reckoned an act of great humility in the king of Persia, or even in a person of high rank, to walk on foot, this being a part of the service exacted from servants. When a prince or great man goes abroad, he is mounted on a horse, and always attended by a multitude of servants on foot, one bearing his pipe, another his shoes, another his cloak, a fourth his saddle-cloth, and so on, the number increasing with the dignity of the master. These statements impart great force to the remark of the wise man: "I have seen servants upon horses, and princes walking as servants upon the earth."—PAXTON.

Ver. 16. And King Solomon made two hundred targets *of* beaten gold; six hundred *shekels* of gold went to one target.

The word צנה *tsinnah*, used for those martial ensigns of royal dignity, which were carried before King Solomon, and which our version renders *targets*, 1 Kings x. 16, was supposed by the Septuagint to signify spears or lances: and as the word is to be understood to signify some sharp-pointed weapon, it may be more natural to understand it of a *lance*, than of a defensive piece of armour with a short sharp-pointed umbo in the middle, considering that shields of gold were also carried before this prince, at solemn seasons. One can hardly find a disposition to admit, that two sorts of things so much alike as targets and shields, should be meant here; and if such similar defensive pieces of armour were hardly meant, the translation of the Septuagint is as natural as any, to say nothing of the authority of so ancient a version, in which, so far as appears by Lambert Bos, all the copies, which frequently disagree in other matters, concur. But whatever we may think of this way of translating the original word, we can hardly suppose such martial ensigns of honour were unknown in the time when this translation was made. It is certain they now appear in the Levant. Thus Windus, in his description of a pompous cavalcade of the emperor of Morocco, tells us, that after several parties of people were passed, "came Muley Mahomet Lariba, one of the emperor's sons; he is alcaid of the stables, or master of the horse: there attended him a guard of horse and foot, at the head of which he rode with a lance in his hand, the place where the blade joins to the wood covered with gold." Soon after which came the emperor himself.

The account of this lance seems to give a clear illustration, of what the Septuagint referred to in their translation of this passage; if not of the original of the Hebrew historian. A comparatively modern prince of Persia seems to have emulated this piece of grandeur of Solomon, and to have even surpassed it, though by means of a different kind of weapon from either of those I have been mentioning. According to d'Herbelot, he had two troops of horsemen, consisting of a thousand each; one troop carrying maces of gold, each of which weighed one thousand drachms, or thousand crowns of gold; the second, maces of silver of the same weight. These two brigades served him for his ordinary guard, and upon extraordinary ceremonies each of these horsemen carried his mace upon his shoulder. One tenth part of the number would have been extremely majestic.—HARMER.

Ver. 18. Moreover, the king made a great throne of ivory, and overlaid it with the best gold.

The throne of Solomon is described as having been extremely magnificent, (1 Kings x. 18,) having twelve lions; but on what part of it these ornamental animals were placed is not easy to determine, as we have no accurate idea of its form and construction. We shall therefore now merely extract a description of the mogul's throne, which we find had divers steps also, and, on the top of its ascent, four lions; wherein it seems to bear a partial resemblance to Solomon's stately seat of majesty. "And further, they told me, that he (the mogul) hath at Agra a most glorious throne within his palace, ascended by divers steps, which are covered with plates of silver; upon the top of which ascent stand four lions, upon pedestals of curious coloured marble; which lions are all made of massy silver, some part of them gilded with gold, and beset with precious stones. Those lions support a canopy of fine gold, under which the mogul sits when he appears in his greatest state and glory."—(Sir Thomas Roe's Voyage.)

Thrones were of different kinds; sometimes they resembled a stool, sometimes a chair, sometimes a sofa, and sometimes they were as large as a bed. One of the thrones of Tippoo Saib was the back of a very large royal tiger, made of gold, studded with precious stones; and that part of his back which was employed as a seat, was covered with fine chintses, &c. by way of cushions.—TAYLOR IN CALMET.

Ver. 20. And twelve lions stood there on the one side, and on the other, upon the six steps: there was not the like made in any kingdom.

In after ages we read of thrones very glorious and majestic. Athanæus says, that the throne of the Parthian kings was of gold, encompassed with four golden pillars, beset with precious stones. The Persian kings sat in judgment under a golden vine, (and other trees of gold,) the bunches of whose grapes were made of several sorts of precious stones. To this article may be very properly annexed the following account of the famous peacock throne of the Great Mogul. "The Great Mogul has seven thrones, some set all over with diamonds; others with rubies, emeralds, and pearls. But the largest throne is erected in the hall of the first court of the palace; it is, in form, like one of our field-beds, six feet long and four broad. I counted about a hundred and eight pale rubies in collets about that throne, the least whereof weighed a hundred carats; but there are some that weigh two hundred. Emeralds I counted about a hundred and forty, that weighed some threescore, some thirty carats. The underpart of the canopy is entirely embroidered with pearls and diamonds, with a fringe of pearls round the edge. Upon the top of the canopy, which is made like an arch with four panes, stands a peacock, with his tail spread, consisting entirely of sapphires, and other proper coloured stones: the body is of beaten gold, enchased with numerous jewels; and a great ruby adorns his breast, to which hangs a pearl that weighs fifty carats. On each side of the peacock stand two nosegays, as high as the bird, consisting of various sorts of flowers, all of beaten gold enamelled. When the king seats himself upon the throne, there is a transparent jewel, with a diamond appendant, of eighty or ninety carats weight, encompassed with rubies and emeralds, so suspended that it is always in his eye. The twelve pillars also that uphold the canopy are set round with rows of fair pearl, and of an excellent water, that weigh from six to ten carats a piece. At the distance of four feet, upon each side of the throne, are placed two umbrellas, the handles of which are about eight feet high, covered with diamonds; the umbrellas themselves being of crimson velvet, embroidered and fringed with pearl. This is the famous throne which Timur began, and Shah Johan finished, and is really reported to have cost a hundred and sixty millions and five hundred thousand livres of our money." (Tavernier.)—Burder.

Ver. 21. And all King Solomon's drinking vessels *were of* gold, and all the vessels of the house of the forest of Lebanon *were of* pure gold; none *were of* silver: it was nothing accounted of in the days of Solomon.

The magnificence of Solomon, particularly with respect to his drinking vessels, has not been exceeded by modern eastern princes. They were all of gold, and it should seem of the purest gold, 1 Kings x. 21. The gold plate of the kings of Persia has been extremely celebrated, and is mentioned in Sir J. Chardin's note on this passage of the sacred historian: he observes, that the plate of the king of Persia is of gold, and that very fine, exceeding the standard of ducats, and equal to those of Venice, which are of the purest gold. The vessels of gold, we are told in Olearius, were made by the order of Shah Abbas, esteemed the most glorious of the princes of the Sefi royal family, who died 1629. It seems that he caused seven thousand two hundred marks of gold to be melted upon this occasion; that his successors made use of it whenever they feasted strangers; and that it consisted chiefly of dishes, pots, flagons, and other vessels for drinking. A French mark is eight of their ounces, and is but four grains lighter than an English ounce troy. Abbas then melted on this occasion near thirty-six thousand English troy ounces of the purest gold, or almost forty-one three-fourths Jewish talents. Astonishing magnificence of Persia! Nor have we reason to think that of Solomon was inferior. We may believe, sure, his royal drinking vessels were of equal weight, when the two hundred targets Solomon made, 1 Kings x. 16, weighed but little less than the drinking vessels of Shah Abbas. Sir J. Chardin's way of comparing the glory of Solomon, with that of a most illustrious monarch of Persia of late ages, is perhaps one of the most efficacious methods of impressing the mind with an apprehension of the magnificence of this ancient Israelitish king, and, at the same time, appears to be perfectly just.—Harmer.

Ver. 22. For the king had at sea a navy of Tharshish with the navy of Hiram: once in three years came the navy of Tharshish, bringing gold and silver, ivory, and apes, and peacocks.

This beautiful bird, which is now familiarly known to perhaps every nation of Europe, does not seem to have found his way into Palestine before the reign of Solomon. That rich and powerful monarch, added to his unexampled wisdom, a taste for natural history; and every three years his fleets returned laden with the most curious and valuable products of distant regions. The elegant shape, the majestic mien, and the splendid plumage of the peacock, rendered him a present not unbefitting the greatest king the world had ever seen; and the servants of Solomon, stimulated probably not more by a sense of duty, than by the inclination to gratify their amiable sovereign, were forward to place it under his eye. "For the king had at sea a navy of Tharshish, with the navy of Hiram: once in three years came the navy of Tharshish, bringing gold and silver, ivory, and apes, and peacocks." The Hebrew name of this bird is (תכיים) *thochijim*, which the Greek interpreters, not understanding, left without explanation; but the Chaldee, the Syriac, and other translators, render it the peacock. The origin of the Hebrew name is unknown; and accordingly various are the conjectures in which the learned have indulged their imaginations, or critical acumen. Bochart imagines it is an exotic term; and changing the Hebrew (תכיים) *thochijim* by inversion into (כותיים) *cuthijim*, he traces it to a Cushite root, intended to denote the native country of the peacock. Nor is it uncommon for an animal to derive its proper name from the place of its original residence. The pheasant is indebted for her name to the Phasis, a river of Colchus, on the banks of which she first drew the attention of the postdiluvian tribes; and African and Numidian birds are so called from Africa or Numidia, the country where they were hatched, and where they commonly fixed their abode. On the same principle, the peacock himself is everywhere called by the ancients the bird of Media or Persia, in which the land of Cush, or Cuth, was situate, because he came originally from that region. Aristophanes calls the peacock the bird of Persia; Suidas, the bird of Media; and Clemens Pædagogus, the bird of India. Diodorus observes, that Babylonia produces a very great number of peacocks marked with colours of every kind. In the opinion of Bochart, India is the true native country of that bird; but it is frequently mentioned as a native of Persia and Media, because it was first imported from India into these countries, from whence it passed into Judea, Egypt, and Greece, and gradually found its way into the other parts of the globe. Hence the peacocks, which were imported in the fleet of Solomon, probably came from Persia; for in that long voyage of three years, in which they visited Taprobane, it is by no means probable they would always pursue a direct course; but along the various windings of the coast, search for any thing that suited their purpose. It is even probable that they sailed up the Persian gulf, and touched at the renowned isles of the Phœnicians, Tyrus or Tylus, and Aradus, at no great distance from Persia.

The elegance of the peacock's form, and the brilliancy of his plumage, seem to be the principal reasons which induced the mariners of Solomon to bring him into Palestine, and that the sacred historian so distinctly mentions the circumstance. Nature, according to the remark of Varro, has certainly assigned the palm of beauty to the peacock; but since the introduction of the ape into Palestine, an animal neither distinguished by the elegance of his form, nor the brilliancy of his colour, is mentioned at the same time, the historian might intend to direct the reader's attention, as well to the riches and splendour of Solomon, as to his taste for rare and curious articles of natural history. In the Lesser Asia, and in Greece, the peacock was long held in high estimation, and frequently purchased by the great and the wealthy, at a very great price. We learn from Plutarch, that in the age of Pericles, a person at Athens made a great fortune by rearing these birds, and showing them to the public, at a certain price, every new moon; and to this exhibition, the curious Greeks crowded from the remotest parts of the country. The keeper of these birds, the same author informs us, sold a male and female for a thousand drachms, about thirty-six pounds of our money. Peacocks were very rare in Greece, even in the time of Alexander, who, by the testimony of Ælian, was struck with astonishment at the sight of these birds on the banks of the Indus; and from admiration of their beauty, commanded every person that killed one of them, to be severely punished. At Rome, as the same historian relates, when Hortensius first killed one for supper, he was brought to trial, and condemned to pay a fine. Their eggs, according to Varro, were sold in his time at five denarii, or more than three shillings a piece; and the birds themselves commonly at about two pounds of our money. The same writer affirms, that M. Aufidius Luzco derived an yearly revenue of more than sixty thousand pieces of silver, which amounts to four hundred and sixty-eight pounds fifteen shillings sterling, from the sale of peacocks; for although their flesh is not better tasted than that of a domestic fowl, they were sold at a much greater price on account of the richness and brilliancy of their plumes. These statements prove, that the peacock was deemed, in remote ages, a present not unworthy of a king.—PAXTON.

The last word תכיים *tukkiyeem*, of those paragraphs which describe the imports of Solomon's navy from Tharshish, is dubious: some of the learned have thought it means *parrots*, the greatest number, *peacocks*. What led some of the curious to imagine parrots were meant, I do not well know; but there is a passage in Hasselquist, which strongly inclines me to adopt their sentiment: describing the commerce of the people of Ethiopia, he says, the Abyssinians make a journey every year to Cairo, to sell the products of their country, slaves, gold, elephants, drugs, monkeys, parrots, &c. As Solomon's navy is said to have brought gold and silver, elephants' teeth, and apes, and peacocks, and this by the way of the Red Sea, 1 Kings ix. 26, which washes the east of Abyssinia, one would imagine, as many of the other particulars tally with each other, that instead of *peacocks*, the true translation of the last word is *parrots*. Religion indeed is not at all concerned in this uncertainty; but it is a matter of curiosity, and as such may, with great propriety, be taken notice of in these papers.—HARMER.

Ver. 28. And Solomon had horses brought out of Egypt, and linen yarn: the king's merchants received the linen yarn at a price.

Horses were conducted to foreign markets in strings; a circumstance "favourable to those interpreters, who would refer the whole passage, 1 Kings x. 28, and 2 Chron. i. 16, to *horses*, instead of *linen yarn*, which seems rather to break the connexion of the verses." Some are therefore inclined to read, "And Solomon had horses brought out of Egypt, even *strings* of horses, (literally, *drawings out—prolongations:*) the king's merchants received the *strings*, *i. e.* of horses, *in commutation*, exchange, or barter. And a chariot, or set of chariot horses, (*i. e.* four,) came up from Egypt for six hundred shekels of silver, and a single horse for one hundred and fifty."—And these he sold again, at a great profit, to the neighbouring kings. As the whole context seems rather applicable to horses than to linen yarn, so this idea, while it strictly maintains the import of the words, preserves the unity of the passage. The Egyptian horses were held in great estimation in Syria and the neighbouring countries. The breed seems to have been introduced into Egypt at a very remote period; for the cavalry of Pharaoh was numerous and completely trained to war, when the people of Israel were delivered from his yoke: "But the Egyptians pursued after them, all the horses and chariots of Pharaoh, and his horsemen, and his army, and overtook them encamping by the sea." The dreadful overthrow which Pharaoh received at the Red Sea, did not prevent his successors from again directing their attention to the rearing of horses for the purpose of war: for the numerous and splendid studs of Solomon were chiefly formed of Egyptian horses; and in the fifth year of his son Rehoboam, Shishak, king of Egypt, invaded Canaan "with twelve hundred chariots, and threescore thousand horsemen." In times long posterior, the prophet Jeremiah addressed the forces of Pharaoh Neco, which the king of Babylon routed near the Euphrates, in these words: "Harness the horses; and get up, ye horsemen, and stand forth with your helmets.—Come up, ye horses; and rage, ye chariots; and let the mighty men come forth." From these passages, it may be certainly inferred, that the strength of the Egyptian armies chiefly consisted in cavalry and chariots of war. The Egyptian warrior adorned the neck of his charger with small bells, which were of great use when he had to engage with enemies mounted on camels, the noise of which these animals cannot endure. In allusion to this custom, which was probably adopted by Solomon, who delighted so much in pomp and show, it is promised, "upon the bells of the horses shall be written, Holiness to the Lord." The Egyptian horses appear to have been much stronger than the Syrian breed, and by consequence, much more useful in the field. On this account, the prophet Isaiah tells the people of Israel, that "the Egyptians were men, and not God, and their horses were flesh, and not spirit." The high estimation in which the Egyptian horses were held, and the eagerness with which the surrounding nations purchased them at exorbitant prices, might be one reason for enacting the law which forbade the chosen people to multiply horses, that they might not idly waste their substance, and especially, that they might not return again into Egypt, the scene of their grievous oppression, even for the purposes of commerce.—PAXTON.

CHAPTER XI.

Ver. 36. And unto his son will I give one tribe, that David my servant may have a light always before me in Jerusalem, the city which I have chosen me to put my name there.

The houses in the East were, from the remotest antiquity, lighted with lamps; and hence it is so common in scripture to call every thing which enlightens the body or mind, which guides or refreshes, by the name of a lamp. These lamps were sustained by a large candlestick set upon the ground. The houses of Egypt, in modern times, are never without lights; they burn lamps all the night long, and in every occupied apartment. So requisite to the comfort of a family is this custom reckoned, or so imperious is the power which it exercises, that the poorest people would rather retrench part of their food than neglect it. If this custom prevailed in Egypt and the adjacent regions of Arabia and Palestine in former times, it will impart a beauty and force to some passages of scripture, which have been little observed. Thus, in the language of Jeremiah, to extinguish the light in an apartment is a convertible phrase for total destruction; and if it was the practice in Judea, as in modern Egypt, which can scarcely be doubted, to keep a lamp continually burning in an occupied apartment, nothing can more properly and emphatically represent the total destruction of a city, than the extinction of the lights. "I will take from them the light of a candle; and this whole land shall be a desolation and an astonishment." Job describes the destruction of a family among the Arabs, and the desolation of their dwellings, in the very language of the prophet: "How oft is the candle of the wicked put out, and how oft cometh their destruction upon them!" Bildad expresses the same idea, in the following beautiful passage: "Yea, the light of the wicked shall be put out, and the spark of his fire shall not shine." "The light shall be dark in his tabernacle, and his candle shall be put out with him." A burning lamp is, on the other hand, the chosen symbol of prosperity, a beautiful instance of which occurs in the complaint of Job: "Oh that I were as in months past, as in the days when God preserved me, when his candle shined upon my head, and when by his light I walked through darkness." When the ten tribes were taken from Rehoboam, and given to his rival, Jehovah promised to reserve one tribe, and assigns this reason, "that David my servant may have a light always before me in Jerusalem."—PAXTON.

CHAPTER XII.

Ver. 11. And now whereas my father did lade you with a heavy yoke, I will add to your yoke: my father hath chastised you with whips, but I will chastise you with scorpions.

It is not easy to know which to admire most, the folly or the tyranny of Rehoboam, who in the very commencement of his reign, threatened to lay aside the whips with which his father had chastised the people of Israel, and rule them with scorpions; it was adding insult to cruelty. Nor is the injurious treatment much alleviated, although the idea of some interpreters were admitted, that the scorpion was the name of a kind of whip in use among the Jews, armed with points like the tail of that animal. The sting of the scorpion occasioned an excruciating pain, although death did not ensue. This is attested by John, in the book of Revelation: "And to them it was given that they should not kill them, but that they should be tormented five months; and their torment was as the torment of a scorpion, when he striketh a man." And so intolerable is the agony, that it is added, "In those days shall men seek death, and shall

33

not find it; and shall desire to die, and death shall flee from them." If the Jews used a whip which they called a scorpion, it must have been because it occasioned a similar torment. If these things are properly considered, we shall cease to wonder at the instantaneous revolt of the ten tribes; for it is not easy to conceive an address more calculated to rouse and exasperate the bitter passions of a high-spirited people, than the puerile and wicked speech of Rehoboam.—PAXTON.

CHAPTER XIII.

Ver. 2. And he cried against the altar in the word of the LORD, and said, O altar, altar, thus saith the LORD, Behold, a child shall be born unto the house of David, Josiah by name; and upon thee shall he offer the priests of the high places that burn incense upon thee, and men's bones shall be burnt upon thee.

These words were uttered in consequence of the profanation of the altar, and the wickedness of those concerned. Has a man brought or purchased a kid for sacrifice to his deity, and should it have been stolen, he goes to his god to tell his story, and then says, "O Swamy! may the bones and the body of him who stole the kid intended for you, be offered up to you as a sacrifice." Whoever walks upon the place where men's bones have been burnt, becomes impure.—ROBERTS.

Ver. 6. And the king answered and said unto the man of God, Entreat now the face of the LORD thy God, and pray for me, that my hand may be restored me again. And the man of God besought the LORD, and the king's hand was restored him again, and became as *it was* before.

This is said in reference to the hand of Jeroboam, which had become stiff in consequence of the violence he had offered to the prophet. The face of the Lord was to be entreated. Has a man injured another, he says, "Ah! my lord, forgive me for the sake of the FACE of your son." Or, does he wish another to intercede for him, he says, "Ah! go, and beseech his face for me." A man, whose name was *Veatha-Veyāthar*, was once asked by some prophet, "Who is the greatest god, Siva or Vishnoo?" The man then stretched forth his hand towards a temple of Vishnoo, and said, "He is the greatest." Immediately his arm became stiff and withered. The prophet, seeing this, then prayed to Siva, and his hand was restored.—ROBERTS.

Ver. 31. And it came to pass, after he had buried him, that he spake to his sons, saying, When I am dead, then bury me in the sepulchre wherein the man of God *is* buried; lay my bones beside his bones.

His object in making this request, was no doubt a selfish one; he believed the deceased was a good man, and felt a hope, that if his body were to rest near him it would be protected from insult, and that with him he would share the blessings of the resurrection. Wherever the body or the bones of Hindoo or Mohammedan saints are buried, there will others also wish to be interred. Often, when men think themselves near death, they say, "Take care that you bury me near the holy man. Ah! remember you are to put me near to the sacred place." The idea seems to be, that the spot being thus sanctified, neither devils nor evil spirits can injure them. Numbers are carried to a great distance to be thus interred.—ROBERTS.

Not far from this is another large mausoleum, built by Shah Suleiman, over the remains of a mussulman doctor of the name of Mollah Hossein, who was a native of Consori, a large town of Irak Ajem, three days' journey from Ispahan. Around these and such like monuments are, in general, to be seen collections of minor tombs; for it is a received opinion, that those who are buried in the vicinity of a holy personage will meet with his support at the day of resurrection.—MORIER.

Ver. 32. For the saying which he cried by the word of the LORD against the altar in Bethel, and against all the houses of the high places which *are* in the cities of Samaria, shall surely come to pass.

Leaving Nablous, the road lies along the narrow vale, and, in about three quarters of an hour, conducts the traveller to a copious spring of good water, called Beersheba. This, Dr. Richardson says, is the broadest and best cultivated part of the valley; he saw the natives busily engaged (May) in reaping a scanty crop of barley. Maundrell notices a village on the left of the road (going northward) called *Barseba*, deriving its name, no doubt, from this well; and, half an hour farther, another village, which he calls *Sherack*. After leaving Beersheba, Dr. Richardson's account makes the road ascend. "In about a quarter of an hour," he says, "we reached the top of the hill; and as we wound our way down the other side, had an excellent view of the delightfully situated Sebaste. In a few minutes we passed a ruined aqueduct of Roman architecture, and pitched our tents at the bottom of the hill, nearly opposite to its unworthy successor, a poor village of the same name; having travelled this day about nine hours." This makes the distance from Khan Leban about twenty-seven miles, but allowing for deviations from the direct track, twenty-four miles, and sixteen hours, or forty-eight miles from Jerusalem. Josephus, however, makes it but one day's journey from the capital. It is six miles beyond Napolose; and if the distance of the latter place is correctly given by our authorities, it cannot exceed forty miles. Sebaste is the name which Herod gave to the ancient Samaria, the imperial city of the ten tribes, in honour of Augustus (Sebastos) Cesar, when he rebuilt and fortified it, converting the greater part of it into a citadel, and erecting here a noble temple. "The situation," says Dr. Richardson, "is extremely beautiful, and strong by nature; more so, I think, than Jerusalem. It stands on a fine, large, insulated hill, compassed all around by a broad deep valley; and when fortified, as it is stated to have been by Herod, one would have imagined that, in the ancient system of warfare, nothing but famine could have reduced such a place. The valley is surrounded by four hills, one on each side, which are cultivated in terraces up to the top, sown with grain, and planted with fig and olive trees, as is also the valley. The hill of Samaria likewise rises in terraces to a height equal to any of the adjoining mountains. The present village is small and poor, and, after passing the valley, the ascent to it is very steep. Viewed from the station of our tents, it is extremely interesting, both from its natural situation, and from the picturesque remains of a ruined convent of good Gothic architecture.

"Having passed the village, towards the middle of the first terrace, there is a number of columns still standing. I counted twelve in one row, besides several that stood apart, the brotherless remains of other rows. The situation is extremely delightful, and my guide informed me, that they belonged to the serai, or palace. On the next terrace there are no remains of solid building, but heaps of stone, and lime, and rubbish, mixed with soil, in great profusion. Ascending to the third or highest terrace, the traces of former buildings were not so numerous, but we enjoyed a delightful view of the surrounding country. The eye passed over the deep valley that encompasses the hill of Sebaste, and rested on the mountains beyond, that retreated as they rose with a gentle slope, and met the view in every direction, like a book laid out for perusal on a reading-desk. This was the seat of the capital of the short-lived and wicked kingdom of Israel; and on the face of these mountains the eye surveys the scene of many bloody conflicts and many memorable events. Here those holy men of God, Elijah and Elisha, spoke their tremendous warnings in the ears of their incorrigible rulers, and wrought their miracles in the sight of all the people. From this lofty eminence we descended to the south side of the hill, where we saw the remains of a stately colonnade, that stretches along this beautiful exposure from west to east. Sixty columns are still standing in one row. The shafts are plain, and fragments of Ionic volutes, that lie scattered about, testify the order to which they belonged. These are probably the relics of some of the magnificent structures with which

Herod the Great adorned Samaria. None of the walls remain." Mr. Buckingham mentions a current tradition, that the avenue of columns formed a part of Herod's palace. According to his account there were eighty-three of these columns erect in 1816, besides others prostrate; all without capitals. Josephus states, that, about the middle of the city, Herod built "a sacred place, of a furlong and a half in circuit, and adorned it with all sorts of decorations; and therein erected a temple, illustrious for both its largeness and beauty." It is probable that these columns belonged to it. On the eastern side of the same summit are the remains, Mr. Buckingham states, of another building, "of which eight large and eight small columns are still standing, with many others fallen near them. These also are without capitals, and are of a smaller size, and of an inferior stone to the others." "In the walls of the humble dwellings forming the modern village, portions of sculptured blocks of stone are perceived, and even fragments of granite pillars have been worked into the masonry." The Gothic convent referred to by Dr. Richardson, is the ruined cathedral, attributed, like every thing else of the kind in Palestine, to the Empress Helena. It stands east and west, and is about one hundred feet in length, by fifty in breadth.—MODERN TRAVELLER.

CHAPTER XIV.

Ver. 3. And take with thee ten loaves, and cracknels, and a cruise of honey, and go to him: he shall tell thee what shall become of the child.

When they consulted a prophet, the eastern modes required a present; and they might think it was right rather to present him with eatables than other things, because it frequently happened that they were detained some time, waiting the answer of God, during which hospitality would require the prophet to ask them to take some repast with him. And as the prophet would naturally treat them with some regard to their quality, they doubtless did then, as the Egyptians do now, proportion their presents to their avowed rank and number of attendants. "This custom," (of making presents,) says Maillet, "is principally observed in the frequent visits which they make one another through the course of the year, which are always preceded by presents of fowls, sheep, rice, coffee, and other provisions of different kinds. These visits, which relations and friends make regularly to each other, were in use among the ancient Egyptians; and though they are often made without going out of the same city, yet they never fail of lasting three or four days, and sometimes eight. They carry all their family with them, if they have any; and the custom is, as I have just observed, to send presents beforehand, proportionable to their rank, and the number of their attendants." In other cases, the presents that anciently were, and of late have been made to personages eminent for study and piety, were large sums of money or vestments. Sums of money are presented also to others, by princes and great personages. Sir John Chardin observes, in his MS., on occasion of Joseph's being said to have given Benjamin three hundred pieces of silver, Gen. xlv. 22, that the kings of Asia almost always make presents of this kind to ambassadors, and other strangers of consideration who have brought them presents. So the Calif Mahadi, according to D'Herbelot, gave an Arab that had entertained him in the desert, a vest and a purse of silver: as to vestments, D'Herbelot tells us, that Bokhteri, an illustrious poet of Cufah, in the ninth century, had so many presents made him in the course of his life, that at his death he was found possessed of a hundred complete suits of clothes, two hundred shirts, and five hundred turbans.

D'Arvieux tells us, that when he waited on an Arab emir, his mother and sister, to gratify whose curiosity that visit was made, sent him, early in the morning after his arrival in their camp, a present of pastry, honey, fresh butter, with a basin of sweetmeats of Damascus. Sir John Chardin tells us, in his Travels, of an officer whose business it was to register the presents that were made to his master or mistress; and I have since found the same practice obtains at the Ottoman court: for Egmont and Heyman, speaking of the presents made there on the account of the circumcision of the grand seignior's children, tell us that all these donations, with the time when, and on what occasion given, were carefully registered in a book for that purpose. When Dr. Perry travelled in Egypt, and visited the temple at Luxor, he says, "We were entertained by the calif here with great marks of civility and favour; he sent us, in return of our presents, several sheep, a good quantity of eggs, bardacks," &c. These bardacks he had described a little before, in speaking of a town called Keene: "Its chief manufactory," he there tells us, "is in bardacks, to cool and refresh their water in, by means of which it drinks very cool and pleasant in the hottest seasons of the year. They make an inconceivable quantity of these, which they distribute to Cairo, and all other parts of Egypt. They send them down in great floats, consisting of many thousands, lashed together in such a manner as to bear the weight of several people upon them. We purchased a good many of them for the fancy, at so inconsiderable a price as twenty pence a hundred; and are really surprised how they could make them for it."—BURDER.

The presents made to the ancient prophets were not always of the same kind and value; an inhabitant of Baal-shalisha "brought the man of God bread of the first-fruits, twenty loaves of barley, and full ears of corn in the husk." The king of Israel sent a present by his wife to the prophet Ahijah, of ten loaves, and cracknels, and a cruise of honey; which, it appears from other statements, was not deemed unworthy of an eastern king. Some commentators are of opinion, that it was a present fit only for a peasant to make, and was designedly of so small value, to conceal the rank of the messenger. But this idea by no means corresponds with the custom of the East; for D'Arvieux informs us, that when he waited on an Arabian emir, his mother and sister sent him a present of pastry, honey, fresh butter, with a basin of sweetmeats, which differs very little from the present of Jeroboam. It was certainly the wish of the king, that his wife should not be recognised by the aged prophet; but the present she carried, though not intended to discover her, was, in the estimation of the Orientals, not unbecoming her rank and condition.—PAXTON.

Travellers agree that the eastern bread is made in small, thin moist cakes, must be eaten new, and is good for nothing when kept longer than a day. This, however, admits of exceptions. Dr. Russel of late, and Rauwolf formerly, assure us, that they have several sorts of bread and cakes. Some, Rauwolf tells us, done with yelk of eggs, some mixed with several sorts of seeds, as of sesamum, Romish coriander, and wild garden saffron, which are also strewed upon it: and he elsewhere supposes that they prepare biscuits for travelling. Russel also mentions this strewing of seeds on their cakes, and says they have a variety of rusks and biscuits. To these authors let me add Pitts, who tells us, the biscuits they carry with them from Egypt will last them to Mecca and back again. So the scripture supposes their loaves of bread were very small, three of them being requisite for the entertainment of a single person, Luke xi. 5; that they were generally eaten new, and baked as they wanted them, as appears from the case of Abraham; that sometimes, however, they were made so as to keep several days; so the shew-bread was fit food after having stood before the LORD a week. And that bread for travellers was wont to be made to keep some time, appears from the pretences of the Gibeonites, Josh. ix. 12; and the preparations Joseph made for Jacob's journey into Egypt, Gen. xlv. 23. In like manner, too, they seem to have had then a variety of eatables of this kind, as the Aleppines now have. In particular, some made like those on which seeds are strewed, as we may collect from that part of the present of Jeroboam's wife to the prophet Ahijah, which our translators have rendered *cracknels*, 1 Kings xiv. iii. Buxtorf indeed supposes the original word נקרים *nakkadeem*, signifies biscuits, called by this name either because they were formed into little buttons like some of our gingerbread, or because they were pricked full of holes after a particular manner. The last of these two conjectures, I imagine, was embraced by our translators of this passage, for *cracknels*, as they are all over England of the same form, are full of holes, being formed into a kind of flourish of lattice-work. I have seen some of the unleavened bread of our English Jews, made in like manner, in a net-work form. Nevertheless, I think it more natural to understand the word of biscuits spotted with seeds; for it is used elsewhere to signify works of gold spotted with studs of silver; and, as it should seem, bread spotted with mould, Josh. ix. 5—12; how much more natural then is it to understand the word of cakes spotted with seeds, which are so common, that not only Rauwolf and Russel speak of them at Aleppo, but Hanway tells us, too, that the cakes of bread that were presented to him at the house of a Persian of distinction, were in like manner sprinkled with the seeds of poppies and other things, than of cracknels, on account of their being full of holes. It is used for things that are *spotted* we know, never in any other place for a thing *full of holes.* Our translators then do not appear to have been very happy in the choice of the word *cracknels* here.—HARMER.

Ver. 6. And it was *so*, when Ahijah heard the sound of her feet, as she came in at the door, that he said, Come in, thou wife of Jeroboam; why feignest thou thyself *to be* another? for I *am* sent to thee *with* heavy *tidings*.

This woman disguised herself in order to deceive the prophet, and therefore he addressed her by name, to show that she was known to him. Married women are generally spoken to as the WIFE of such a person. Supposing a married female to be in a crowd, and a man on the outside wishes to speak to her, he will say, "Come hither, wife of Chinne Tamby;" literally, Chinne Tamby's wife, hither come. "O! Muttoo's wife, where are you?" Should a person have to speak to a female who is walking before him, he will not call her by name, but address her, "Such a one's wife, I wish to speak to you."—ROBERTS.

Ver. 10. Therefore, behold, I will bring evil upon the house of Jeroboam, and will cut off from Jeroboam him that pisseth against the wall, *and* him that is shut up, and left in Israel, and will take away the remnant of the house of Jeroboam, as a man taketh away dung, till it be all gone.

Sometimes, when a successful prince has endeavoured to extirpate the preceding royal family, some of them have escaped the slaughter, and secured themselves in a fortress or place of secrecy, while others have sought an asylum in foreign countries, from whence they have occasioned great anxiety to the usurper. The word *shut up*, strictly speaking, refers to the first of these cases; as in the preservation of Joash from Athaliah in a private apartment of the temple. Such appears also to have been the case in more modern times. "Though more than thirty years had elapsed since the death of the Sultan Achmet, father of the new emperor, he had not, in that interval, acquired any great information or improvement. *Shut up* during this long interval in the apartment assigned him, with some eunuchs to wait on him, the equality of his age with that of the princes who had a right to precede him, allowed him but little hope of reigning in his turn; and he had, besides, well-grounded reasons for a more serious uneasiness." (Baron De Tott.) But when David was in danger, he *kept himself close* in Ziklag, but not so as to prevent him from making frequent excursions. In latter times, in the East, persons of royal descent have been *left*, when the rest of a family have been cut off, if no danger was apprehended from them, on account of some mental or bodily disqualification. Blindness saved the life of Mohammed Khodabendeh, a Persian prince of the sixteenth century, when his brother Ismael put all the rest of his brethren to death.—HARMER.

We find divine anger threatening to "cut off from Jeroboam him who is *shut up* and left in Israel," 1 Kings xiv. 10. In chap. xxi. 21, the same threat is made against Ahab; *vide* also 2 Kings ix. 8. This *shutting up* of the royal family appears sufficiently strange to us; and the rather as we perceive that the sons of David the king enjoyed liberty sufficient, and more than sufficient. The following extracts will throw some light on this subject: "In one of them we find the royal family dwelling together on a mountain, which, though a place of confinement, yet had some extent. In the other, we find them in a palace, which only in name differed from a prison. The crown being hereditary in one family, but elective in the person, and polygamy being permitted, must have multiplied these heirs very much, and produced constant disputes; so that it was found necessary to provide a remedy for the anarchy and effusion of royal blood, which was otherwise inevitably to follow. The remedy was a humane and gentle one; they were confined in a good climate upon a high mountain, and maintained there at the public expense. They are there taught to read and write, but nothing else; 750 cloths for wrapping round them; 3000 ounces of gold, which is 30,000 dollars, or crowns, are allowed by the state for their maintenance. These princes are hardly used, and, in troublous times, often put to death upon the smallest misinformation. While I was at Abyssinia, their revenue was so grossly misapplied, that some of them were said to have died with hunger and of cold, by the avarice and hard-heartedness of Michael neglecting to furnish them necessaries. Nor had the king, as far as I could discern, that fellow-feeling one would have expected from a prince rescued from that very situation himself. Perhaps this was owing to his fear of Ras Michael.

"However that be, and however distressing the situation of those princes, we cannot but be satisfied with it, when we look to the neighbouring kingdom of Sennaar or Nubia. There no mountain is trusted with the confinement of their princes, but as soon as the father dies, the throats of all the collaterals, and all their descendants that can be laid hold of, are cut; and this is the case with all the black states in the desert west of Sennaar, Dar Four, Sele, and Bagirma." (Bruce.) We see now how Athaliah might destroy, not merely an individual, but all the seed royal, (2 Kings xi. 1,) because, if she found access to the palace to accomplish the slaughter of any one, she might easily cut off the whole. This also renders credible the slaughter of Ahab's sons, seventy young persons at one time. They were kept shut up, it seems, in Samaria, where their keepers became their destroyers. How far the same confinement might take place in the instance of the sons of Gideon, (Judges ix. 2, 5,) we cannot determine; but it should appear, that at least they were kept in one place of abode, whether that place were the mansion or the tower of their father.—TAYLOR IN CALMET.

CHAPTER XV.

Ver. 2. Three years reigned he in Jerusalem. And his mother's name *was* Maachah, the daughter of Abishalom.

It has been conjectured by Mr. Baruh, that the phrase, "and his mother's name was," &c. when expressed on a king's accession to the throne, at the beginning of his history, does not always refer to his natural mother, but that it is a title of honour and dignity, enjoyed by one of the royal family, denoting her to be the first in rank. This idea appears well founded from the following extracts: "The Oloo Kani is not governess of the Crimea. This title, the literal translation of which is, great queen, simply denotes a dignity in the harem, which the khan usually confers on one of his sisters; or if he has none, on one of his daughters, or relations. To this dignity are attached the revenues arising from several villages, and other rights." (Baron De Tott.) "On this occasion the king crowned his mother Malacotawit, conferring upon her the dignity and title of *iteghe*, i. e. as king's mother, regent and governess of the king when under age." (Bruce's Travels.)—BURDER.

Ver. 18. And King Asa sent them to Ben-hadad, the son of Tabrimon, the son of Hezion, king of Syria, that dwelt at Damascus, saying,
19. *There is* a league between me and thee, *and* between my father and thy father: behold, I have sent unto thee a present of silver and gold; come and break thy league with Baasha, king of Israel, that he may depart from me.

I will not push my remarks on the presents of the East any further here, excepting the making this single observation more, that the sending presents to princes to induce them to help the distressed, has been practised in these countries in late times, as well as in the days of Asa, of whom we read, that he "took all the silver and the gold that were left in the treasures of the house of the Lord, and the treasures of the king's house, and delivered them into the hand of his servants: and king Asa sent them to Benhadad the son of Tabrimon, the son of Hezion, king of Syria, that dwelt at Damascus, saying, There is a league between me and thee, and between my father and thy father: behold, I have sent unto thee a present of silver and gold; come and break thy league with Baasha, king of Israel, that he may depart from me." To us it appears strange, that a present should be thought capable of inducing one prince to break with another, and engage himself in war; but as it was anciently thought sufficient, so we find in the Gesta Dei per Francos, that an eastern nobleman, that had the custody of a castle called Hasarth, quarrelling with his master, the prince of Aleppo, and finding himself obliged to seek for foreign aid, *sent presents* to Godfrey of Bouillon, to induce him to assist him. What they were we are not told: but gold and silver, the things Asa sent Benhadad, were frequently sent in those times to the crusade princes, and might probably be sent on this occasion to Godfrey.—HARMER.

CHAPTER XVI.

Ver. 34. In his days did Hiel the Bethelite build Jericho: he laid the foundation thereof in Abiram his first-born, and set up the gates thereof in his youngest *son* Segub, according to the word of the LORD, which he spake by Joshua the son of Nun.

See on Judges 11. 30, 31.

CHAPTER XVII.

Ver. 1. And Elijah the Tishbite, *who was* of the inhabitants of Gilead, said unto Ahab, *As* the LORD God of Israel liveth, before whom I stand, there shall not be dew nor rain these years, but according to my word.

The latter rain falls in the middle or towards the end of April, from which, if there be three months to the harvest, as the prophet asserts, it must fall in the middle or towards the end of July. But at present in Syria, barley-harvest commences about the beginning of May, and that, as well as the wheat-harvest, is finished by the twentieth of the same month. In Judea the harvest is still more early. The rain, therefore, which God threatens to withhold from his people, must have commonly fallen in the first part of February. That a quantity of snow descends at Jerusalem at this time, which is of great importance to the succeeding harvest, by making the fountains to overflow a little afterward, is confirmed by the authority of Dr. Shaw. It is no real objection to this view, that the prophet threatens to withhold the rain; for the great difference of temperature in Palestine, may be the cause that it snows in the mountainous districts, while it rains in other parts of the same country. By the moderate quantity of rain or snow which falls in the month of February, the reservoirs of water on which the cities of Palestine chiefly depend, are filled, and the prospect of a fruitful and plentiful year is opened. Of so great importance to the subsistence and comfort of that people are these rains, that upon their descent, they make similar rejoicings with the Egyptians upon the cutting of the Nile. The prophet evidently refers to both these circumstances; to the succeeding harvest, in these words: "the piece or field upon which it rained not, withered;" to the state of the cisterns in these: "so two or three cities wandered into one city to drink water, but they were not satisfied." Hence, Mr. Harmer, who treats Jerome on this occasion with undue severity, is wrong in supposing that the inspired writer refers to the single circumstance of filling their cisterns with water. He refers to both, and this Jerome distinctly notices: "God suspended the rain," says that father, "not only to punish them with want of bread, but also with thirst; for in those countries in which they then resided, excepting a few fountains, they had only cistern-water; so that if the divine anger suspended the rains, there was more danger of perishing by thirst than by famine." Jerome certainly committed a mistake when he referred the words of Amos to the latter rain; but he understood as certainly the true extent of the threatening.

The former and the latter rains were, in the days of Elijah, suspended for three years and six months. But when the prophet said to Ahab, "As the Lord God of Israel liveth, before whom I stand, there shall not be dew nor rain these years, but according to my word;" he could not mean, there shall be no rain at all for three years; for long before their termination, the whole population of Israel must have miserably perished. It is not uncommon among the Orientals, to express a great deficiency by an absolute negative. Thus Philo affirms, that in Egypt they have no winter; by which, according to his own explanation, he meant no hail, no thunder, no violent storms of wind, which constitute an eastern winter. Pliny in like manner affirms there are no rains, no thunders, no earthquakes in that country; while Maillet, who quotes him, asserts that he had seen it rain there several times, and that there were two earthquakes in Egypt during his residence. His idea therefore, is very plausible, that Pliny meant only to state the rare occurrence of these phenomena; that it seldom feels the power of the earthquake, and when it does, suffers but little damage; that it very seldom rains or thunders, although on the seacoast the rains and thunders are often very violent; but it does not rain there as in other parts of the world. This account of the rain of Egypt is confirmed by the testimony of two English travellers. When Pitts was at Cairo, the rain descended in torrents, and the streets having no kennels to carry off the water, it reached above the ankles, and in some places much higher. In Upper Egypt it rained and hailed almost a whole morning, when Dr. Pococke was there in the month of February; and the following night it also rained very hard. These authentic statements unfold the true meaning of the prophet's assertion, "that Egypt has no rain;" he must be understood in the same qualified sense as Pliny and other writers. In the same manner, the words of Elijah to Ahab must be interpreted; they only mean, that the dew and the rain should not fall in the usual and necessary quantities. Such a suspension of rain and dew was sufficient to answer the corrective purposes of God, while an absolute drought of three years' continuance, must have converted the whole country into an uninhabitable waste. But such a destruction is not intimated in the scriptures; and, we may conclude from the inspired narrative, did not take place. That guilty people were certainly reduced in the righteous judgments of God to great straits; but still they were able to subsist until his fierce anger passed away, and mercy returned to bless their afflicted habitations.—PAXTON.

Ver. 4. And it shall be, *that* thou shalt drink of the brook; and I have commanded the ravens to feed thee there.

It is a singular circumstance, that the raven, an unclean bird, and one too of very gross and impure dispositions, was chosen by Jehovah to provide for his servant Elijah, when he concealed himself, by the divine command, from the fury of Ahab. So improbable is the story in the ear of reason, that morose and voracious ravens should become caterers for the prophet, that some interpreters have maintained that the original word denotes merchants or Arabians, or the inhabitants of the city Arbo: according to this interpretation, the promise would run, "I have commanded the Arabs, or the Orebim, to nourish thee." But it is easy to show that these opinions have no foundation in scripture and reason. The prophet Ezekiel indeed describes the merchants of Tyre by the phrase (ערבי מערבך) *arbi mearobeha*, "thy merchants who transact thy business;" but the word *orebim*, (ערבים) by itself, never signifies merchants. Nor had God said in general, I have commanded the merchants, but I have commanded the merchants of this or that place, to nourish thee. The situation of the place in which the miracle happened, refutes the other opinions; for in the neighbourhood of Jordan, where Elijah concealed himself, were no Arabs, no Orebim, and no city which bore the name of Arbo. Besides, the Arabs are not called in Hebrew (ערבים) *orebim*, but (ערבים) *arbim*, and the inhabitants of Arbo, if any city of that name existed, according to the genius of the Hebrew language, must have been called (ערבוים) *arabojim*, not *orebim*. Add to this, Elijah was commanded to hide himself there; but how could he hide himself, if the inhabitants of the city or encampment knew of his retreat, as they must have done, if his daily subsistence depended upon their bounty. The place of his retreat must have been discovered in a very short time to Ahab, who sought him with g eat industıy in every direction. The solemn declaration ɩf Obadiah to the prophet, when he went by the divine command to show himself to the king, proves how impossible it was for him to remain concealed in the inhabited part of the country: "As the Lord thy God liveth, there is no nation or kingdom whither my lord hath not sent to seek thee; and when they said, He is not there, he took an oath of the kingdom and nation, that they found thee not." Hence these *haırebim* were not merchants, nor human beings of any station or employment, but true ravens; and so the term has been rendered by the whole Christian church, and by many Jewish writers, particularly by their celebrated historian, Josephus.

These voracious and impure animals received a commandment from their Maker to provide for his prophet by the brook Cherith, near its confluence with the Jordan. The record is couched in these terms: "Get thee hence and turn thee eastward, and hide thyself by the brook Cherith, that is before Jordan: and it shall be that thou shalt drink of the brook; and I have commanded the ravens to feed thee there." In the history of providence, such commands are by no means uncommon; the locust, the serpent, and the fishes of the sea, have all in their turn received the charge to do the will of their Almighty Creator. Thus he promised to Solomon at the dedication of the temple: "If I command the locusts to devour the land —if my people, which are called by my name, shall humble themselves, and pray, and seek my face, and turn from their wickedness; then will I hear from heaven, and will forgive their sin, and will heal their land." The marine serpent that lurks in the deepest caverns of the ocean, in like manner hears his voice, and submits to his authority; for Jehovah directed the prophet to address his guilty countrymen in these memorable terms: "Though they be hid from my sight in the bottom of the sea, thence will I command the serpent, and he shall bite them." Nor was the great fish which he prepared to swallow up the refractory prophet, less prompt in its obedience: "And the Lord spake unto the fish, and it vomited out Jonah upon the dry land." His providence extends its powerful influence even to inanimate objects: "I, even my hands, have stretched out the heavens, and all their hosts have I commanded." And David, in the Spirit, complained of his ancestors, that "they believed not in God, and trusted not in his salvation: though he had commanded the clouds from above, and opened the doors of heaven." Even the furious billows of the sea dare not pass the line which his finger has traced, without his permission: "I made the cloud the garment thereof, and thick darkness a swaddling band for it, and brake up for it my decreed place, and set bars and doors, and said, Hitherto shalt thou come, but no farther; and here shall thy proud waves be stayed." The inanimate and irrational parts of creation, properly speaking, cannot receive and execute the commands of the Almighty; they are only passive instruments employed by him in his providential dispensations, to produce certain effects. To command the ravens then, is to make use of them in providing for the necessities of his servant; to impart for a time an instinctive care to supply him with food, to which they were by nature entire strangers, and which they ceased to feel when the end was accomplished. A command to sustain the destitute seer, after the brook of which he drank was dried up, was addressed in a very different manner to the widow of Zarephath. It was couched in words addressed to her understanding and heart, while the secret power of Jehovah inclined her to yield a prompt and efficacious obedience. On this occasion, a number of ravens were employed, because the service of one was not sufficient to supply the prophet with daily food. But the circumstance entirely accords with the native instincts of that bird; for the ravens go in quest of their prey in troops, and share in common the spoils of the chase. Following, therefore, the instincts of their nature, which received for a time a peculiar direction, by the miraculous interposition of Jehovah, a number of ravens associated together, in order to supply the wants of Elijah, whom his country had abandoned to the rage of an impious and cruel monarch: "And they brought him bread and flesh in the morning, and bread and flesh in the evening, and he drank of the brook." The Septuagint, in many copies, read the passage, "They brought bread in the morning, and flesh in the evening;" but the common reading is entitled to the preference. It gives a striking display of divine goodness, that when the whole resources of Israel were exhausted by a long and severe famine, the prophet of the Lord was miraculously and abundantly supplied with nutritious food twice every day. The ravens brought it in the evening and in the morning, which were the stated hours of repast among the Jews and other oriental nations.

The Hebrew writers eagerly inquire where the ravens found the provisions to supply the wants of Elijah; and, as may be supposed, very different are the opinions they advance; but on this question, which is of little importance, no certainty can be obtained. The scriptures are silent on the subject, and we have no other means of information. It was enough for the prophet, that his winged providers regularly supplied his necessities; and it is sufficient to excite our admiration of the power and goodness of God, and our confidence in his providential care, without attempting to discover what the divine wisdom has seen meet to conceal. On another occasion, an angel was sent from heaven to supply the exhausted prophet with bread and water in the desert; which, in the eye of reason, may seem to be a more becoming messenger of the King of glory, than a raven. But "the ways of God are not as our ways, nor his thoughts as our thoughts;" he did not think it beneath his dignity at this time, to employ the ravens in the same office; and he perhaps intended to teach us, that all creatures are equally subject to his authority, and fit for his purpose. When he gives the commandment, a raven is as successful in his service, according to the range of its faculties, as an angel; and we must not presume to refuse or slight his aid, how mean soever the agent he condescends to employ. The Jewish legislator placed the raven in the list of unclean birds, which imparted pollution to every thing they touched; but the same God who gave the law, had a right to repeal or suspend it; and that he did suspend it for a time in favour of his persecuted servant, cannot be reasonably denied. Nor was this a singular instance of divine clemency; for the observance of ceremonial institutions often yielded to urgent necessity. The Jews were forbidden to touch a dead carcass; but Samson was allowed, for a special purpose, to eat of the honey which he found in the dead lion. The priests only were permitted by the law to eat the shew-bread; yet David and his men were justified by our Lord himself in using the consecrated loaves, when no other could be procured.

Many are the reasons assigned by different writers, for the employment of ravens on this occasion; but they are so trifling, or so fanciful, that it is unnecessary to state them; the true reason perhaps was to convince the dejected prophet, that although his nation had forsaken him, the God whom he served continued to watch over him with unceasing care; and that he would employ the most unpromising means, and counteract the most powerful instincts, rather than suffer him to want the necessaries of life. And when he saw those voracious birds, the cravings of whose appetite are seldom entirely satisfied, part, of their own accord, with their favourite provision, morning and evening, for many days, and bring it themselves to the place of his retreat; he could not mistake or disregard the secret influence under which they acted. The brook Cherith, on whose border the miracle was wrought, is supposed to be the same as the river Kana, mentioned in the sixteenth and seventeenth chapters of Joshua, which watered the confines of Ephraim and Benjamin. This brook derived its name Kana, from the reeds, which, in great abundance, clothed its banks; among which the prophet found a secure retreat from the persecution of his enemies. Its other name, Cherith, may be traced to the verb Charah, which the Greek interpreters render to feed, because on its margin the prophet was fed by the ravens. Were this conjecture true, the name must have been given by anticipation; for which no satisfactory reason can be assigned. It is more natural to suppose, that, as the verb commonly signifies to dig, and sometimes to rush on with violence, the name Cherith alludes to the violent rapidity of the stream at certain seasons of the year, or to the deep pits which, like many other torrents in those regions, it excavates in its furious course. The particular situation of this brook is more distinctly marked by the sacred historian, who says, it "is before Jordan." This phrase seems to mean, that it flowed into the Jordan; and from the second clause of the verse we may infer, that its course lay on the west side of the river, because it is said by God to Elijah, "Get thee hence, and turn thee eastward, and hide thyself by the brook Cherith, that is before Jordan:" for Elijah must have been on the west side of Jordan, when he was commanded to go eastward to a stream that flowed [illegible] the Jordan on that side.—PAXTON.

Some suppose ravens to be a mistranslation, and that the promise referred to a people who were to feed the prophet. The following quotation from the Scanda Purāna does not negative the opinion, but it shows, in a remote period, that birds were supposed on some special occasions to depart from their usual habits. In the relation of the events of great antiquity among the heathen, much of fable must be expected, but there is often a glimmering ray of light in the obscurity, pointing to circumstances which assist the mind in its attainment of truth. In the town of Kanche (Conjeveram) it is said, "Of the birds, there is a sāthaka bird which takes food to the gods, a swan which gives precious stones, a parrot which repeats science, and a cock which crows not in time of trouble."—ROBERTS.

Ver. 12. And she said, *As* the LORD thy God liveth, I have not a cake, but a handful of meal in a barrel, and a little oil in a cruse: and, behold, I *am* gathering two sticks, that I may go in and dress it for me and my son, that we may eat it, and die.

So said the widow of Zarephath to the prophet Elijah. How often do we see females, just before the time of boiling their rice, strolling about in search of a few sticks to make it ready. All their fires are made of wood, (or dried cows' dung,) and in a country where there is so much jungle, and so little rain, they seldom trouble themselves before the moment they require it. But the widow said that she was gathering TWO sticks; and it is not a little singular to find that the Hindoos often use the same number when it refers to MANY things. "Well, Venāsi, what are you looking for?"—"I am looking for two sticks to prepare my rice." "Child, go fetch me *irendu-taddi*, two sticks, to make ready my curry." "Alas! I cannot find two sticks to make the water hot." "My lord, I only ask for two mouthfuls of rice." "Ah! sir, if you will allow me to repeat two words in your ear, I shall be satisfied." "Good, have you any thing more to say?" "No, sir." "Then I have not two words for that," (meaning, he does not object.) Any person who has been in the East, will recognise, in these quotations, a figure of speech he has heard a thousand times.—ROBERTS.

The corn which they reserve for daily use, they keep in long earthen jars; because, when kept in sacks or barrels, it is liable to be eaten by worms. This is confirmed by Norden, who tells us, that when he was travelling in Upper Egypt, one of the natives opened a great jar, in order to show him how they preserved their corn there. In some regions of the East Indies, the paddy, or rice in the husk, is also preserved in large earthen jars, that are kept in the house; or in small cylindrical stores, which the potters make of clay; the mouth is covered with an inverted pot; and the paddy is drawn out of a hole at the bottom, as it is wanted. It seems to have been in one of these earthen jars that the woman of Zarephath kept her corn, of which she had only enough left, when the prophet Elijah applied to her for a morsel of bread, to make a handful of meal. In our translation, the original term (כד) *chad* is rendered barrel; but a barrel, properly speaking, it could not be, because a vessel of that sort is never used for holding corn in those regions. Neither could it be a chest, although this is often used in the East for preserving corn; because the Hebrew term is quite different. In the second book of Kings it is stated, that "Jehoiada the priest took (ארון *aron*) a chest, and bored a hole in the lid of it, and set it beside the altar." The same word is employed by Moses, to denote a coffin; but most generally, to signify the chest, or ark of the testimony, on which the cherubim stood, in the holy of holies. This term, among the Hebrews, therefore, properly signified a chest made of wood; never a vessel for holding water. But (כד) *chad* they commonly used to signify a jar or pitcher for holding water; which was made of earth, never of wood. It is the same word in the original, which the sacred historian employs, to denote the vessels in which Gideon's army concealed their torches, and which they broke with a clashing terrific noise, when they blew with their trumpets. Both these circumstances suppose they were vessels of earth, which are employed in the East for the double purpose of preserving corn and holding water. The (כד) *chad* was also the vessel with which Rebecca went out to fetch water from the well; which, in our translation, is rendered pitcher. But the Orientals never carried a barrel to the fountain, nor drew water with a wooden vessel. Hence, the barrel in which the woman of Zarephath kept her corn, was in reality an earthen jar. The four barrels of water, then, which Elijah commanded his attendants to pour on the sacrifice, should have been translated four jars or pitchers; for the original word is the same in all these instances.—PAXTON.

CHAPTER XVIII.

Ver. 5. And Ahab said unto Obadiah, Go into the land, unto all fountains of water, and unto all brooks: peradventure we may find grass to save the horses and mules alive, that we lose not all the beasts. 6. So they divided the land between them, to pass throughout it: Ahab went one way by himself, and Obadiah went another way by himself.

See on Est. 8. 10.

Brooks were generally the most likely places to find grass in a time of drought, though far from being places where they might be certain of succeeding; for in such seasons, herbaceous animals generally stop near fountains of water, and feed in the vicinity, till all the grass be consumed. Thus travellers are often greatly disappointed, who naturally expect to find grass where they find water; but on reaching the spot they find that the game has consumed every blade of grass. However, as the cattle could not graze long where there was no water, it was the wisest method Ahab could pursue. The circumstance shows the simplicity of ancient manners, that a king and one of his principal governors should go at the head of such expeditions. It is the same in Africa at this present time; for no king there, nor any of his principal chiefs, would think they were at all lessening their dignity by engaging in an expedition either in search of water or grass. Indeed, it would be viewed by the people as one of the most important affairs in which their rulers could be engaged, and, did they succeed, few things would be likely to render them more popular.—AFRICAN LIGHT.

It appears there had not been rain for three years and six months, which must have had a fatal effect on vegetation. What would England (situated in a temperate climate) be under such circumstances? In droughts in the East, which have lasted from six to ten months, how often have we seen men, like Obadiah, going along in marshy places, or by the sides of tanks, in search of grass for their cattle? See the poor fellow with a basket, made of the leaves of the palmirah, on his back, a little instrument (which works like a Dutch hoe) in his hand; he strolls from fountain to brook, and no sooner does he see a green patch of verdure, than he runs with eagerness to the spot! Perhaps he meets another in search of the same thing, when each declares he had the first view. They set to work, snarling at each other, and dealing out all kinds of abuse, till they have cleared the place of every green blade. Wherever there is a stream or an artificial watercourse, there the eye is refreshed with delightful verdure; but look a few yards from the place, and you see the withered herbage, apparently gone beyond recovery, but which, in a few hours, would start into fresh life, if visited by showers. The effect of rain is like enchantment on the scene, and the English stranger is often reminded of the green fields of his own native land.—ROBERTS.

Ver. 9. And he said, What have I sinned, that thou wouldest deliver thy servant into the hand of Ahab, to slay me?

Obadiah asked this question of Elijah, when the prophet wished him to go and tell Ahab, his bitter enemy, "Behold, Elijah is here." Thus, a person requested to do any thing which implies danger or difficulty, asks, *Enna-pollāpposey-thane?* "What evil or sin have I done?" The question is also asked, when a man is visited with affliction, "What evil has he done?"—ROBERTS.

Ver. 10. *As* the LORD thy God liveth, there is no nation or kingdom whither my lord hath not sent to seek thee: and when they said, *He is* not *there*, he took an oath of the kingdom and nation, that they found thee not.

People in England would be astonished and appalled at the frequency and nature of the oaths of the heathen. A man's assertion or affirmation, in common conversation, is seldom believed. Thus, men may be heard in the streets, in the fields, or bazaars, and children in the schools or the play-grounds, say, "Swear you will do this; now take an oath you have not done it." Then they swear by the temple, or its lamp, by their parents, or children, and appeal to their deities for a confirmation of the assertion.—ROBERTS.

Ver. 19. Now therefore send, *and* gather to me all Israel unto Mount Carmel, and the prophets of Baal four hundred and fifty, and the prophets of the groves four hundred, which eat at Jezebel's table.

We are not, I apprehend, to suppose that these eight hundred and fifty prophets, or even the four hundred of the groves, ate at the royal table, where Jezebel herself took her refection; for though I am sensible it is not unusual in the East for servants to eat at the same table where their masters have eaten, after their masters have done; and that several hundreds eat in the palaces of the eastern princes; yet it could never be thought necessary by Jezebel to have four hundred chaplains in waiting at once at court. I should think the words mean, that these four hundred prophets of the groves fed daily at a common table, in or near the temple of that idol which they served, and which was provided for at the expense of Jezebel, living there in a kind of collegiate way, as the prophets of JEHOVAH appear to have done. Their business was, I suppose, to sing the praises of the idols they worshipped; and to watch from time to time in their temples, under the pretence of receiving oracular answers to the inquiries of those that came to consult them; and, it may be, to teach the worshippers in what form of words to address the deity they served.—HARMER.

Ver. 27. And it came to pass at noon, that Elijah mocked them, and said, Cry aloud; for he *is* a god: either he is talking, or he is pursuing, or he is in a journey, *or* peradventure he sleepeth, and must be awaked.

In the hottest part of the day the Orientals retire to rest on their bed, till the cool of the evening summons them again to active life. "The heathens," says Mr. Blunt, "assigned all the properties and habits of man to their gods, and among the number, that of reposing at midday. Hence was it unlawful to enter the temples at that hour, lest their slumbers should be disturbed. The goatherd ventured not to play upon his pipe at noon, for fear of awakening Pan. Hence, too, the peculiar force of the derision with which Elijah addressed the priests of Baal: 'And it came to pass at noon, that Elijah mocked them, and said, Cry aloud; for he is a god —— peradventure he sleepeth, and must be awaked.' Accordingly we read that these priests did not despair of rousing their god, and inducing him to declare himself, 'till the time of evening sacrifice.' At that hour the period allowed for repose had terminated: and when he still continued deaf to their cries, then, and not till then, their cause became altogether hopeless."—PAXTON.

The margin has, for "talking," "*meditateth*," and for "pursuing," "*hath a pursuit*." This keen and ingenious sarcasm relates, I doubt not, to their god, as having been accustomed sometimes to sleep, to talk, to go on a journey, or to join in the pursuit. That the Baal-peor of Assyria, and the Siva-lingam of India, are the same, is certain. And is it not interesting to know that those things which are attributed to Baal are also attributed to Siva? "Either he is talking." The margin has, for "talking," *meditateth*. Dr. A. Clarke says, "Perhaps the word should be interpreted as in the margin, he meditateth, he is in a profound revery, he is making some godlike projects, he is considering how he may keep up his credit in the nation." Siva was once absorbed in a profound meditation: to him the time appeared only as a moment, but to the world as ages. Universal nature, for want of his attention, was about to expire. Women had ceased to bear, and all things were out of course. The gods and men became alarmed, and their enemies began to oppress them. All were afraid to disturb him in his meditations, till Cama, the god of love, agreed to stand before him: when Siva, being aroused from his revery, sent fire from his frontal eye, which destroyed the intruder.

"Or he is pursuing." The Hebrew has this, "hath a pursuit:" on which Dr. A. Clarke says, "he may be taking his pleasure in hunting." Siva is described as taking great pleasure in the chase; and in the month of September, his image and that of Pārvati, his wife, are taken from the temple, put into a *kead-agam*, or car, and carried on men's shoulders to enjoy the pleasures of the chase!

"Or he is in a journey." Siva is represented as taking long journeys, and sometimes for very discreditable purposes.

"Peradventure he sleepeth." Siva often did this, especially when he took the form of a cooly; for, after he had performed his task, he fell asleep under the tree called the *Konda Maram*. Thus the prophet mentioned four things, in some of which their god was engaged, and consequently, could not attend to their requests. But it was manifestly improper, if he were thus occupied, for them to disturb him: yet Elijah said, "Cry aloud," let him hear you; he is no doubt a god.

When a holy person before the temple, or in any sacred place, is meditating, not one will presume to disturb him: how, then, could they interrupt their deity? When engaged in pleasure, whether of the chase or any other amusement, no one dares to interfere with the great man; and yet Baal was to be called from his pleasures. It is improper to interrupt those that are on a journey. They have an object in view, and that must first be accomplished. No one will disturb a person when he is asleep—to them it seems to be almost a sin to awake a man from his slumbers. Where is your master? "*Nittari*," asleep; and then you may walk off till another day. Yet, improper as it was to interfere with Baal in his engagements, the sarcastic prophet said, "Cry aloud." "And they cried aloud, and cut themselves—— with knives." Here, also, the devotees may be seen cutting themselves with knives till the blood stream from their bodies, or suspended with hooks in their flesh from a pole, or with their tongue cut out, or practising other cruelties on themselves, for the expiation of their sins, or the glory of their gods.—ROBERTS.

Ver. 28. And they cried aloud, and cut themselves, after their manner, with knives and lancets, till the blood gushed out upon them.

If we look into antiquity, we shall find that nothing was more common in the religious rites of several nations, than this barbarous custom. To this purpose we may observe, that (as Plutarch de Superstitione tells us) the priests of Bellona, when they sacrificed to that goddess, besmeared the victim with their own blood. The Persian *magi* used to appease tempests, and allay the winds, by making incisions in their flesh. They who carried about the Syrian goddess, cut and slashed themselves with knives, till the blood gushed out. This practice remains in many places at the present time, and frequent instances of it may be met with in modern voyages and travels.—BURDER.

There has been no little supposition and conjecture, for what reason the priests of Baal "cut themselves, after their manner, with knives, and with lancets, till the blood gushed out upon them." 1 Kings xviii. 28. This seems, by the story, to have been *after* Elijah had mocked them, (or, at least, while he was mocking them,) and had worked up their fervour and passions to the utmost height. Mr. Harmer has touched lightly on this, but has not set it in so clear a view as it seems to be capable of, nor has he given very cogent instances. It may be taken as an instance of earnest entreaty, of conjuration, by the most powerful marks of affection: *q. d.* "Dost thou not see, O Baal! with what passion we adore thee?—how we give thee most decisive tokens of our affection? We shrink at no pain, we decline no disfigurement, to demonstrate our love for thee; and yet thou answerest not! By every token of our regard, answer us! By the freely flowing blood we shed for thee, answer us!" &c. They certainly demonstrated their attachment to Baal; but Baal did not testify his reciprocal attachment to them, in proof of his divinity, which was the article in debate between them and Elijah. Observe, how readily these still bleeding cuttings would identify the priests of Baal at the subsequent slaughter; and how they tended to justify that slaughter; being contrary to the law that ought to have governed the Hebrew nation, as we shall see presently. As the demonstration of love, by cuttings made in the flesh, still maintains itself in the East, a few instances may be at least amusing to European lovers, without fear of its becoming *fashionable* among us. "But the most ridiculous and senseless method of expressing their affection, is their singing certain amorous and whining songs, composed on purpose for such mad occasions; between every line whereof they cut and slash their naked arms with daggers: each endeavouring, in their emulative madness, to exceed the other by the depth and number of the wounds he gives himself. [A lively picture this, of the singing, leaping, and self-slashing priests of Baal!] Some Turks, I have observed, when old, and past the follies which possessed their youth, show their arms, all gashed and scarred from wrist to elbow; and express a great concern, but greater wonder, at their past simplicity." The "oddness of the style invited me to render some of the above named songs into English:

> Could I, dear ray of heavenly light,
> Who now behind a cloud dost shine,
> Obtain the blessing of thy sight,
> And taste thy influence all divine;
>
> 'Thus would I shed my warm heart's blood,
> As now I gash my veiny arm:
> Wouldst thou, but like the sun, think good
> To draw it upward by some charm.'

Another runs thus:

> 'O, lovely charmer, pity me!
> See how my blood does from me fly!
> Yet were I sure to conquer thee,
> Witness it, Heaven! I'd gladly die.'"
> (AARON HILL'S *Travels.*)

This account is confirmed by De la Motraye, who gives a print of such a subject. Lest the reader should think that this love, and its tokens, are homages to the all-subduing and distracting power of beauty only, we add Pitts' account of the same procedure: "It is common for men there to fall in love with boys, as it is here in England to be in love with women; and I have seen many, when they have been drunk, give themselves *deep gashes on their arms, with a knife*, saying, 'It is for the love I bear to such a boy!' and I assure you, I have seen several, who have had their *arms full of great cuts*, as tokens of their love," &c. (Pitts' Account of Mohammedism.) This custom of cutting themselves is taken, in other places of scripture, as a mark of affection: so Jer. xlviii. 37, "Every head shall be bald, every beard clipped, *and upon all hands*, CUTTINGS; and upon the loins, sackcloth:" as tokens of excessive grief for the absence of those *thus regarded.* So, chap. xvi. ver. 6, "Both the great and the small shall die in the land: they shall not be buried, neither shall men lament for them, *nor cut themselves*," in proof of their affection, and expression of their loss; "nor make themselves bald for them," by tearing their hair, &c. as a token of grief. So, chap. xli. 5, "There came from Samaria fourscore men, having their beards shaven, and their clothes rent, and having *cut themselves*, with offerings to the house of the Lord." So, chap. xlvii. 5, "Baldness is come upon Gaza: Ashkelon is cut off, with the residue of her valleys; how long wilt thou *cut thyself?*" rather, perhaps, *how deep*, or to *what length* wilt thou *cut thyself?* All these places include the idea of painful absence of the party beloved. Cuttings for the dead had the same radical idea of privation. The law says, Lev. xix. 28, and Deut. xiv. 1, "Ye are the children of the Lord your God; ye shall not *cut yourselves*, nor make any baldness between your eyes, for the dead;" *i. e.* restrain such excessive tokens of grief; sorrow not as those without hope, if for a dead friend; but if for a dead idol, as Calmet always takes it, then it prohibits the idolatrous custom, of which it also manifests the antiquity. Mr. Harmer has anticipated us, in referring "the wounds in the hands" of the examined prophet, Zech. xiii. 6, to this custom;—the prophet denies that he gave himself these wounds in token of his affection to an idol; but admits that he had received them in token of affection to a person. It is usual to refer the expression of the apostle, Gal. vi. 17, "I bear in my body the marks (*stigmata*) of the Lord Jesus," to those imprinted on soldiers by their commanders; or to those imprinted on slaves by their masters; but would there be any *degradation* of the apostle, if we referred them to tokens of affection towards Jesus? *q. d.* "Let no man take upon him to [molest, fatigue,] trouble me by questioning my pretensions to the apostleship, or to the character of a true lover of Jesus Christ, as some among you Galatians have done; for I think my losses, my sufferings, my scars, received in the fulfilment of my duty to him, are tokens sufficiently visible to every man who considers them of my regard to him, for whose sake I have borne, and still bear them: I shall therefore write no more in vindication of my character, in that respect, however it may be impugned."—TAYLOR IN CALMET.

Ver. 33. And he put the wood in order, and cut the bullock in pieces, and laid *him* on the wood, and said, Fill four barrels with water, and pour *it* on the burnt-sacrifice, and on the wood.

See on 1 Kings 17. 12.

Ver. 41. And Elijah said unto Ahab, Get thee up, eat and drink; for *there is* a sound of abundance of rain.

It is as common in the East to say there is the *sound* of rain, as it is in England to say there is an appearance of rain. Sometimes this refers to thunder, as the precursor; and at other times to a blowing noise in the clouds, which indicates rain is at hand. In the vicinity of a hill or tall trees, the sound is the loudest; and it is worthy of notice, that Elijah was in the neighbourhood of Mount Carmel.—ROBERTS.

Ver. 42. So Ahab went up to eat and to drink. And Elijah went up to the top of Carmel; and he cast himself down upon the earth, and put his face between his knees.

David's posture, mentioned 1 Chron. xvii. 16, in all probability was not unlike that of Elijah, which was one of most earnest supplication. I remember being present in the supreme court at Matura, when the prisoners were brought up to receive their sentences; and when a Cingalese woman, on hearing her son's condemnation to suffer death, rushed through the crowd, and presenting herself before the bench, in the very posture ascribed to Elijah, entreated, in the most heart-rending manner, that his life might be spared.—CALLAWAY.

Who, in the East, has not seen the natives thus sitting on the earth, with their faces between their knees? *Those engaged in deep meditation, in a long train of reasoning, when revolving the past, or anticipating the future*, when in great sorrow or fatigue, as coolies after a journey, may be seen seated on the ground with the face between the knees. "This morning, as I passed the garden of Chinnan, I saw him on the ground with his face between his knees; I wonder what plans he was forming: it must have been something very important to cause him thus to meditate." "Kandan is sick or in trouble, for he has got his face between his knees." "The man threatens to trouble you." —"He trouble me! I shall never put my face between my knees on his account." "Alas! poor woman, she must have a cruel husband, for she has always her face between her knees." Elijah went "to the top of Carmel," *to meditate on the past and the future:* there he was, after the display of God's majesty in the fire from heaven, in the destruction of the priests, and in the certain anticipation of rain, with "*his face between his knees.*"—ROBERTS.

The devout posture of some people of the Levant greatly resembles that of Elijah. Just before the descent of the rain, "he cast himself down upon the earth, and put his face between his knees." Chardin relates that the dervises, especially those of the Indies, put themselves into this posture, in order to meditate, and also to repose themselves. They tie their knees against their belly with their girdle, and lay their heads on the top of them, and this, according to them, is the best posture for recollection.—Harmer.

Ver. 44. And it came to pass at the seventh time, that he said, Behold, there ariseth a little cloud out of the sea, like a man's hand, And he said, Go up, say unto Ahab, Prepare *thy chariot*, and get thee down, that the rain stop thee not.

That is, says Bp. Patrick, Elijah saw such abundance of rain coming as would cause floods, and render the way impassable, if Ahab did not make haste home: and accordingly, in a very short space of time that little cloud spread itself, and with a great thickness covered the face of the sky.

When Elijah's servant reported to his master, that he saw *a little cloud* arising out of the sea like a man's hand, he commanded him to *go up and say unto Ahab, prepare thy chariot, and get thee down, that the* rain *stop thee not.* This circumstance was justly considered as the sure indication of an approaching shower, *for it came to pass, in the mean while, that the heaven was black with clouds and wind, and there was a great rain.* Mr. Bruce has an observation, which greatly corroborates this relation. He says, "there are three remarkable appearances attending the inundation of the Nile: every morning, in Abyssinia, is clear, and the sun shines; about nine, a small cloud, not above four feet broad, appears in the east, whirling violently round as if upon an axis; but arrived near the zenith, it first abates its motion, then loses its form, and extends itself greatly, and seems to call up vapours from all opposite quarters. These clouds having attained nearly the same height, rush against each other with great violence, and put me always in mind of Elijah's foretelling rain on mount Carmel. The air, impelled before the heaviest mass, or swiftest mover, makes an impression of its own form in the collection of clouds opposite, and the moment it has taken possession of the space made to receive it, the most violent thunder possible instantly follows, with rain; and after some hours the sky again clears."—Burder.

Ver. 45. And it came to pass in the mean while, that the heaven was black with clouds and wind, and there was a great rain. And Ahab rode out, and went to Jezreel.

See on 2 Kings 3. 16, 17.

Ver. 46. And the hand of the Lord was on Elijah: and he girded up his loins, and ran before Ahab to the entrance of Jezreel.

See the man who has to run a race, or take a journey; he girds up his loins with a long robe or shawl. Elijah, therefore, thus prepared himself to run before the chariot of the king. Great persons have always men running before them, with an ensign of office in their hands. Elijah probably did this in consequence of the wonderful events that had taken place: fire having come from heaven, Baal's priests having been destroyed, the rain having descended, and the proud king his enemy having been reconciled, he ran before, as the priest of the Lord, to show from whom the blessings had come.—Roberts.

Hanway tells us, that Nadir Shah, when he removed his camp, was preceded by his running footmen, and these by his chanters, who were nine hundred in number, and frequently chanted moral sentences, and encomiums on the Shah, occasionally proclaiming his victories also.

The like practice obtained among the inhabitants of Mount Libanus, in the time of Pope Clement VIII. for Dandini, the pope's nuncio to the Maronites, says, "We were always accompanied with the better sort of people, who walked on foot before our mules, and out of the respect they bore to the pope, and in honour to us, they would sing certain songs, and spiritual airs, which they usually sung as they marched before the patriarch, and other persons of quality." It was not confined, according to this account, to mean persons; but persons of figure went before him in procession with songs.

We are willing to suppose, that Elijah's running before Ahab's chariot to the gates of Jezreel, was not unworthy his prophetic character; but as the idea of the mob's running before a royal coach will present itself to some minds, when they read this passage, so commentators are not very happy in explaining this piece of the history of Elijah. Bishop Patrick supposes he ran before Ahab like one of his footmen, in which he showed his readiness to do the king all imaginable honour, and that he was far from being his enemy: would it however have become Becket, the Archbishop of Canterbury, to have run before the horse of Henry II. to show he was not his enemy? or even Friar Peito before Henry VIII. to do him all imaginable honour? But if Ahab had chanters running before him, like Nadir Shah, it does not appear at all contrary to the rules of decorum, for one brought up to celebrate the divine praises, to put himself at the head of them, to direct them, in singing praise to him that was then giving them rain, and to intermingle due encomiums on the prince that had permitted the extermination of the priests of Baal; or if he had none such, yet if it had been practised in those times, and was thought graceful and becoming a prince, nothing forbade Elijah's doing it alone: and perhaps what is said concerning the singers of the contemporary king of Judah, 2 Chron. xx. 21, 22, may enable us to guess, whether or not it was a practice totally unknown at that time. The expression of the divine historian, that *the hand of the* Lord *was upon him*, perfectly agrees to this thought, for it appears, from 2 Kings iii. 15, that it signifies enabling a prophet to prophesy: and consequently we are rather to understand these words, of God's stirring him up to the composing, and singing, of some proper hymns on this occasion, than the mere enabling him to run with greater swiftness than his age would otherwise have permitted him to do, in which sense alone, I think, commentators have understood that clause.—Harmer.

CHAPTER XIX.

Ver. 4. But he himself went a day's journey into the wilderness, and came and sat down under a juniper-tree: and he requested for himself that he might die; and said, It is enough; now, O Lord, take away my life; for I *am* not better than my fathers.

The juniper is mentioned more than once in our translation of the scriptures; but the opinions of learned men are much divided, concerning the shrub or tree to which the inspired writers allude. The gadha or gadhat, a species of tree very like the tamarisk, which grows in the sandy deserts, resembles, in more than one instance, the juniper in our translation. It flourishes in the burning wild; its wood is extremely proper to burn into charcoal, which has the property of long retaining fire; on which account, it is carried into the cities and sold for fuel. The camel is very fond of its leaves, although they frequently affect him with pains in his bowels; and under its shade, the wolf so commonly lurks, that it has become a proverb among the Arabs, "The wolf is near the gadha." But from these circumstances it cannot be determined with certainty, whether the gadha of the roving Arab be the same with the juniper. The Hebrew word for the plant to which we give the name of juniper, is rothem, from the verb ratham, to bind or tie, on account of the toughness or tenacity of its twigs. In Parkhurst, it is the genista, or Spanish broom, which eminently possesses the character of tenacity. So great is their flexibility, that the Italians still weave them into baskets. The genista, it must be granted, affords but a poor shelter to the weary traveller from the intense heat of an oriental sky; while the prophet Elijah, exhausted with a long and precipitate flight, found a refreshing shade under the spreading branches of the rothem. But the remark applies with equal, if not greater force, to the juniper, which in this country never rises above the stature of an humble shrub. The words of the inspired writer are by no means inconsistent with this circumstance: "But Elijah went a day's journey into the wilderness, and came and sat down under a juniper-tree.—And as he lay and slept under the juniper-tree, behold, then an angel touched him and said unto him, Arise and eat." The passage seems to import that the prophet, unable to proceed, embraced the shelter of a *genista*, which, according to Bellonius, grows in the desert, for want of a better; as the prophet Jonah was glad to screen himself from the oppressive heat of the sun under the frail covert of a gourd. But in reality, the genista, in the oriental regions, interposed with considerable effect between the parched wanderer and the scorching sunbeam.

The roots of the rothem, or juniper, as we translate the term, were used in the days of Job for food, by the poorest of the people: "For want and famine they were solitary: fleeing into the wilderness, in former time desolate and waste. Who cut up mallows by the bushes, and juniper-roots, (ve shoresh rethamim,) for their meat." But this circumstance determines nothing; for neither the roots of juniper, nor of genista, nor of any other tree in those deserts, can afford a salutary nourishment to the human body: nor can any modern instance be found, of the roots of juniper or genista being used for food. Job only says that it was done in times of extreme want, when the famished poor were frequently compelled to prolong their miserable existence by the use of the most improper substances. It is certain that the shoots, the leaves, the bark, and the roots of other shrubs and trees, have been eaten among many nations, in times of scarcity and famine. Thus, for instance, Herodotus informs us, that when the routed army of Xerxes was fleeing from Greece, such of them as could not meet with better provision, were compelled by hunger to eat the bark and leaves, which they stripped off all kinds of trees. The hungry Laplander devours the tops and bark of the pine; and even in Sweden, the poor in many places are obliged to grind the bark of birch-trees to mix with their corn, to make bread in unfavourable seasons. The royal Psalmist mentions the coals of the rethamim as affording the fiercest fire of any combustible matter that he found in the desert, and therefore the fittest punishment for a deceitful tongue; "What shall be given unto thee, or what shall be done to thee, thou false tongue? Sharp arrows of the mighty, with coals of juniper:" the wrath of God, like a keen and barbed arrow from the bow of the mighty, shall pierce the strongest armour, and strike deep into the hardest heart, and like the fierce and protracted flame of the juniper, shall torment the liar with unutterable anguish. Now, if it be the property of juniper long to retain the fire, or to emit a vehement flame, it is not less the characteristic of genista: for according to Geierus, as quoted by Parkhurst, the Spanish genista, or rethama, *lignis aliis vehementius scintillet, ardeat, ac strideat*, sparkles, burns, and crackles more vehemently than any other wood. The people of Israel in their journeys through the wilderness, came to a place called Rithma, probably from the great quantity of rethamim growing there. In traversing the same inhospitable wilds, Thevenot and his fellow-travellers were compelled to gather broom for warming themselves and boiling their coffee. This greatly corroborates the opinion of Parkhurst, that the rothem of the Old Testament is not properly the juniper, but Spanish broom; but although his opinion is extremely probable, our imperfect acquaintance with the natural history of those remote countries, renders it impossible to reach a satisfactory conclusion.

The shade of rothem, (whether it be translated the juniper, or the genista,) is supposed by some writers of great eminence to be noxious. This circumstance is mentioned only for the purpose of vindicating the prophet Elijah, from the imputation of wishing to put an end to his existence, when he fled for his life into the wilderness. He went on that occasion a day's journey into the wilderness of Beersheba; and sitting down under a juniper-tree, fatigued with his journey, and oppressed with grief, he fell asleep, after having requested God that he might die.

Grotius imagines, that the prophet rested under the shade of the juniper, because he was now become careless of his health; and he cites a passage from Virgil, as a proof that the shadow of this tree is noxious.

"Solet esse gravis cantantibus umbra;
Juniperi gravis umbra; nocent et frugibus umbræ." *Ecl.* x. l. 75.

But his conclusion will not follow; because Virgil evidently means, that the shades of evening are hurtful; not the shade of the juniper, except by night, when the shade of every tree is thought by natural historians to be injurious to health. If the shade of the juniper were noxious, it would be noxious to every one, and not merely to singers. And how could it be hurtful to the fruits? They do not grow under it, and are therefore not exposed to its deleterious influence. It is easy to see how the shades of evening are hurtful to the fruits; but how the shade of the juniper should be noxious to them, is quite inconceivable. The poet, indeed, expressly mentions the danger of reposing under the shade of that tree; but the true reason seems to be this: the juniper being an evergreen, and its leaves growing very close, extends in the evening a more damp and chilly shade, than perhaps any other tree in that part of Italy. So little afraid were the Orientals of its noxious qualities, that some of their most magnificent cities were imbosomed in a grove of juniper-trees. This is an incontestible proof that they did not find their effluvia deadly, nor even injurious to health.

Another commentator of considerable celebrity, supposes, on the contrary, that Elijah reposed himself under the juniper-tree, for the more effectual preservation of his health; the shade of it being, according to him, a protection from serpents; and alleges, that it was the custom of the people in that part of the world, to guard themselves by such precautions against the bite of these venomous reptiles. But this opinion seems to be no less visionary than the allegation of Grotius. Travellers often recline beneath the shade of a spreading tree; but in all their narratives, the reason assigned by Peter Martyr is never once mentioned. According to Dioscorides, the glowing embers of juniper wood, not the shade of the living tree, possessed the power of driving away those unwelcome visitants. The most obvious reason is in this, as in most instances, the best: Elijah flying into the wilderness from the rage of Jezebel, became oppressed with the burning heat of the day, and the length of the road, and cast himself down under the shade of the first shrub that he found. Or, if it was in his power to make a choice, he preferred the juniper for the thickness of its covert, without any apprehension of its possessing either a deleterious quality, or the power of defending him from the bite of the serpent; he chose it merely for its shade, where, under the watchful and efficacious protection of Jehovah, his own God, and the God of his people, he sunk into quiet repose. To suppose that he repaired to the shade of the juniper with the view of ruining his health, and shortening his days, is quite inconsistent with every trait in the character, and every action in the life of that holy man. So far from harbouring the horrible idea of suicide, although certainly tired of life, he prayed to his God to remove him from the disgusting scene of idolatry and oppression, into his immediate presence; a sure proof he neither expected nor desired that favour from the noxious exhalations of the juniper. To this may be added, that the question is not yet decided, whether it was a juniper, or what particular species of tree it really was, under whose friendly covert the weary and afflicted prophet sought repose.—PAXTON.

Ver. 18. Yet I have left *me* seven thousand in Israel, all the knees which have not bowed unto Baal, and every mouth which hath not kissed him.

Things which have been sent to the temples to be presented to idols, are, when returned, kissed by the people. Should a priest give areca-nuts, beetel leaves, or cakes, which have been presented to the gods, the person receiving them kisses them. When a devotee has touched the feet of a priest, he kisses his hands.—ROBERTS.

Ver. 19. So he departed thence, and found Elisha the son of Shaphat, who *was* ploughing *with* twelve yoke *of oxen* before him, and he with the twelfth: and Elijah passed by him, and cast his mantle upon him.

The natives use the ox for the plough and all other agricultural purposes. It is no disgrace for a great man to follow the plough; and, generally speaking, the master is the first to commence the operations of the season. The first day is always settled by a soothsayer, or a book of fate. "Elijah passed by him, and cast his mantle upon him." By this act Elisha was invested with the sacred office; but it is probable there would be other ceremonies, and a more pointed address, and extended conversation than that recorded in the verse. When a Bramin is invested with the sacred office, both in the *first*, *second*, and *third* initiations, he is always covered with a yellow mantle, and in such a way as to prevent him from seeing any object. The sacred string also is put over his right shoulder, (and worn like a soldier's belt,) which indicates his office. Elisha said, "Let me, I pray thee, kiss my father and my mother, and then I will follow thee." And Elijah "said unto him, Go back again; for what have I done to thee?" The answer of Elijah is certainly not very easy to be understood. The Hebrew has, instead of "go back again," "go, return;" this makes good sense, especially when the conjunction is added, "GO, *and* RETURN." The Tamul version has it also in that way. The same translation has, instead of "for what have I done to thee?" "what I have done to thee THINK;" literally, "I to thee what have done, think." I have called thee according to the Divine command; now thou askest to take leave of thy father and mother: take care thou art not led aside from thy calling; "go, and return," THINK on what I have done to thee.—ROBERTS.

Among the Persians, the principal khalifas or teachers consider the sacred mantle as the symbol of their spiritual power. Though the khirka or mantle was in general only transferred to a beloved pupil, at the death of his master, some superior saints were deemed possessed of a power, even while living, to invest others with the sacred and mysterious garment. "When the khalifa or teacher of the sooffees dies, he bequeaths his patched garment, which is all his worldly wealth, to the disciple whom he esteems the most worthy to become his successor, and the moment the latter puts on the holy mantle, he is vested with the power of his predecessor." (Malcolm.)—BURDER.

Ver. 26. Therefore their inhabitants were of small power, they were dismayed and confounded; they were *as* the grass of the field, and *as* the green herb, *as* the grass on the house-tops and *as corn* blasted before it be grown up.

"The *sam* wind, as described to me by an old inhabitant of the Dashtistan, commits great ravages in this district, particularly at Dashtiarjan, hurtful to vegetation. It blows at night, from about midnight to sunrise, comes in a hot blast, and is afterward succeeded by a cold one. About six years ago there was a *sam* during the summer months, which so totally burnt up all the corn, then near its maturity, that no animal would eat a blade of it, or touch any of its grain. The image of corn blasted before it be grown up, was most probably taken from the circumstance now mentioned." (Morier.) Sir R. K. Porter however says, that the samiel, though hostile to human life, is so far from being prejudicial to the vegetable creation, that a continuance of it tends to ripen the fruits. These accounts may be reconciled by observing, that the former relates to the corn, and the latter to fruit, and that it may refer to its gradual approach rather than its sudden attack. If any unfortunate traveller, too far from shelter, meets the blast, he falls immediately, and in a few minutes his flesh becomes almost black, while both it and his bones at once arrive at so extreme a state of corruption, that the smallest movement of the body would separate the one from the other.—BURDER.

CHAPTER XX.

Ver. 7. And Isaiah said, Take a lump of figs: and they took and laid *it* on the bile, and he recovered.

Whatever the disorder was with which Hezekiah was afflicted, the remedy prescribed was a softening plaster, designed to ripen the bile, and to prepare it for receiving such assistance as to discharge it with ease and certainty. We have an instance of a similar proceeding, and with the same design, in regard to the plague, related by Pitts of himself. "The plague reigned among us;—soon after we got ashore at Algiers, I was seized with it, but, through the divine goodness, escaped death. It rose under my arm, and the bile which usually accompanies the plague, rose on my leg. After it was much swollen, I was desirous to have it lanced, but my patroon told me it was not soft enough. There was a neighbour, a Spaniard slave, who advised me to roast an onion, and apply a piece of it dipped in oil to the swelling, to mollify it; which accordingly I did. The next day it became soft, and then my patroon had it lanced, and, through the blessing of my good God, I recovered."—BURDER.

Ver. 10. And Ben-hadad sent unto him, and said, The gods do so unto me, and more also, if the dust of Samaria shall suffice for handfuls for all the people that follow me.

It is an interesting fact, that this figure of speech, in reference to the dust not being sufficient to fill the hands of the numerous hosts of Benhadad, is in common use at this day. In the story called *Asuvāmca-thaiya-kathi*, it was said by the inhabitants of certain countries, who were expecting an invasion from a king who had already conquered the "eight quarters,"—"We had better at once give up our possessions: why attempt to resist such hosts? the dust of the country will not be sufficient to furnish a handful for each of the soldiers. *Ovvoru-pud-de-man-kānumo?* i. e. for every one will there be a handful of dust?" The people of the village of Sandarippi ask, "Why do the inhabitants of Batticotta hate and despise us? If we all go against them, will their country afford a handful of earth for each of us?" The people of the two large villages of Batticotta and Sandarippi often meet to play at rude games, when the latter are generally the conquerors, which has led to great animosity. Hence the proverb, "Take up the stalk of a cocoa-nut leaf, and the Batticottians run;" and hence the saying respecting the handfuls of earth. Benhadad said, "The gods do so unto me, and more also." This form of imprecation or prayer is very common. "If I do not ruin that fellow, then the gods do so to me." "If I kill not that wretch, then may the gods kill me." If, therefore, the dust of Samaria be sufficient to fill the hands of each of my soldiers, then may my dominions be subject to the same fate.—ROBERTS.

Ver. 12. And it came to pass, when *Ben-hadad* heard this message, as he *was* drinking, he and the kings in the pavilions, that he said unto his servants, Set *yourselves in array:* and they set *themselves in array* against the city.

The word שפיר *shapheer*, which we translate *pavilion*, may, it is very likely, excite the notion of something superior to a common tent; so our translators use that term to express the superb tent of a king of Babylon, Jer. xliii. 10, "He (Nebuchadnezzar) shall spread his royal pavilion over them." A mere English reader will be surprised, perhaps, when he is told that the word סכות *succoth*, translated pavilions, 1 Kings xx. 12, 16, signifies nothing more than *booths;* and more still, if he is told that the sacred historian might, possibly, precisely design to be so understood, when describing the places in which kings were drinking. That the word signifies those slight temporary defences from the heat which are formed by the setting up the boughs of trees, is visible by what is said Jonah iv. 5, and Neh. viii. 16; and we know that the common people of the East frequently sit under them; but it may be thought incredible that princes should make use of such, as the term, precisely taken, seems to imply. "And it came to pass, when Benhadad heard this message, as he was drinking, he and the kings in the pavilions," 1 Kings xx. 12. "But Benhadad was drinking himself drunk in the pavilions, he and the kings, the thirty and two kings that helped him," v. 16. In the margin our translators have put the word *tents;* but that there is nothing incredible in the account, if we should understand the prophetic historian as meaning booths, properly speaking, will appear, if we consider the great simplicity of ancient times, and the great delight the people of the East take in verdure, and in eating and drinking under the shade of trees; especially after reading the following paragraph of Dr. Chandler's Travels in the Lesser Asia: "While we were employed on the theatre of Miletus, the Aga of Suki, son-in-law, by marriage, to Elez Oglu, crossed the plain towards us, attended by a considerable train of domestics and officers, their vests and their turbans of various and lively colours, mounted on long-tailed horses, with showy trappings and furniture. He returned after hawking to Miletus; and we went to visit him, with a present of coffee and sugar; but we were told that two favourite birds had flown away, and that he was vexed and tired. A couch was prepared for him beneath a shed, made against a cottage, and covered with green boughs, to keep off the sun. He entered as we were standing by, and fell down on it to sleep, without taking any notice of us." A very mean place, a European would think, to be prepared for the reception of an aga that made so respectable a figure, and in a town which, though ruinated, still had several cottages, inhabited by Turkish families. It does not appear incredible then, that Benhadad, and the thirty-two petty kings that attended him, might actually be drinking wine beneath such green sheds, as a Turkish aga, of considerable distinction, chose to sleep under, rather than in an adjoining cottage, or rather than under a tent, which he otherwise might have carried with him, to repose under when he chose to rest himself. Oriental manners are very different from those in the West.—HARMER.

Ver. 27. And the children of Israel were numbered, and were all present, and went against them: and the children of Israel pitched before them like two little flocks of kids; but the Syrians filled the country.

A flock of goats is fewer in number than a flock of sheep, because the former are given to wander and separate, while the latter, more gregarious in their temper, collect into one place. This is the reason, says Bochart, that the sacred writer compares the small army of the Israelites to a flock of goats rather than to a flock of sheep. While seven is always used by the Hebrews to denote a sufficient or complete number, two is constantly employed to signify a few, or very few. Thus the widow woman said to the prophet, "As the Lord thy God liveth, I have not a cake, but a handful of meal in a barrel, and a little oil in a cruise: and behold, I am gathering two sticks, that I may go in and dress it for me and my son, that we may eat it and die." The phrase is used in the same sense by the prophet concerning the reduced state of his people: "Yet gleaning grapes shall be left in it; as the shaking of an olive-tree, two or three berries in the top of the uppermost bough." Another prophet uses it in relation to the return of a small number of the captives to their own land: "I will take you; one of a city and two of a family, and I will bring you to Zion." And Hosea encourages his people to repentance with the promise, "After two days will he revive us: in the third day he will raise us up, and we shall live in his sight," or, within a very short time he will deliver them from their enemies. The sacred historian accordingly compares the armies of Israel opposed to the Syrians to "two little flocks of kids;" two, because they were few in number; little flocks, as goats from their roaming disposition always are; flocks of kids, feeble and timid, without resources and without hope. A more complete and glowing picture of national weakness, even the pen of inspiration never drew.—PAXTON.

Ver. 28. And there came a man of God, and spake unto the king of Israel, and said, Thus saith the LORD, Because the Syrians have said, The LORD *is* God of the hills, but he *is* not God of the valleys; therefore will I deliver all this great multitude into thy hand, *and* ye shall know that I *am* the LORD.

That there were many gods who had each their particular charge and jurisdiction, that some presided over whole countries, while others had but particular places under their tuition and government, and were some of them gods of the woods, others of the rivers, and others of the mountains, was plainly the doctrine of all heathen nations. Pan was reckoned the god of the mountains, for which reason he was styled Ὀρειβάτης, *mountain traverser;* and in like manner, the Syrians might have a conceit that the god of Israel was a god of the mountains, because Canaan, they saw, was a mountainous land; the Israelites delighted to sacrifice on high places; their law, they might have heard, was given on the top of a mountain; their temple stood upon a famous eminence, as did Samaria, where they had so lately received a signal defeat: for their further notion was, that the gods of the mountains had a power to inject a *panic* fear into any army, whenever they pleased. Nay, that they did not only assist with their influence, but actually engaged themselves in battle in behalf of their favourites, is a sentiment as old as Homer.—STACKHOUSE.

Ver. 30. But the rest fled to Aphek, into the city; and *there* a wall fell upon twenty and seven thousand of the men *that were* left. And Ben-hadad fled, and came into the city, into an inner chamber.

See on ch. 22. 25.

In regard to this passage, we are not to suppose that this wall, or castle, or fort, (as it may be rendered,) fell upon every individual one, much less that it had killed every man it fell on: it is sufficient to justify the expression, that it fell upon the main body of these seven and twenty thousand, and that it killed some and maimed others, (for the scripture does not say that it killed all,) as is usual in such cases. Let us suppose then, that these Syrians, after their defeat on the plains of Aphek, betook themselves to this fenced city, and despairing of any quarter, mounted the walls, or retired into some castle, with a resolution to defend themselves to the last; and that the Israelitish army coming upon them, plied the walls or the castle on every side so warmly with their batteries, that down they came at once, and killing some, wounding others, and making the rest disperse for fear, did all the execution that the text intends.

Thus we may account for this event in a natural way; but it is more reasonable to think that God, upon this occasion, wrought a miracle; and either by some sudden earthquake or violent storm of wind, overturned these walls, or this fortress, upon the Syrians. And indeed, if any time was proper for his almighty arm to interpose, it was at such a time as this, when these blasphemous people had denied his sovereign power and authority in the government of the world, and thereby in some measure obliged him, in vindication of his own honour, to give them a full demonstration of it, and to show that he was the God of the plains as well as of the mountains; that he could as effectually destroy them in strongholds as in the open field, and make the very walls, wherein they trusted for defence, the instruments of their ruin.

This Aphek, or Aphaca, (as it is called by profane authors,) was situated in Libanus, upon the river Adonis, between Heliopolis and Biblos, and in all probability is the same that Paul Lucas, in his voyage to the Levant, speaks of, as swallowed up in a lake of Mount Libanus, about nine miles in circumference, wherein there are several houses, all entire, to be seen under water. The soil about this place (as the ancients tell us) was very bituminous, which seems to confirm their opinion, who think that subterraneous fires consumed the solid substance of the earth, whereon the city stood, so that it was subdued and sunk at once, and a lake was soon formed in its place.—STACKHOUSE.

Ver. 31. And his servants said unto him, Behold now, we have heard that the kings of the house of Israel *are* merciful kings: let us, I pray thee, put sackcloth on our loins, and ropes upon our heads, and go out to the king of Israel; peradventure he will save thy life.

The vanquished foe, in testimony of his submission, hung his sword from his neck, when he came into the presence of his conqueror. When Bagdat was taken by the Turks, in the year 1638, the governor's lieutenant and principal officer was sent to the grand vizier, with a scarf about his neck, and his sword wreathed in it, which is accounted by them a mark of deep humiliation and perfect submission, to beg for mercy in his own and his master's name. His request being granted, the governor came and was introduced to the grand seignior, and obtained, not only a confirmation of the promise of life that had been made him, but also various presents of considerable value. These circumstances forcibly recall to our minds the message of Benhadad, after his signal defeat, to the king of Israel; the passage runs in these terms: "And his servants said unto him, Behold now, we have heard that the kings of the house of Israel are merciful kings; let us, I pray thee, put sackcloth on our loins, and ropes upon our heads, and go out to the king of Israel; peradventure he will save thy life. So they girded sackcloth on their loins, and put ropes on their heads, and came to the king of Israel, and said, Thy servant Benhadad saith, I pray thee, let me live. And he said, Is he yet alive? he is my brother." The servants of Benhadad succeeded in obtaining a verbal assurance that his life should be spared; but a surer pledge of protection was to deliver a banner into the hand of the suppliant. In the year 1099, when Jerusalem was taken by the crusaders, about three hundred Saracens got upon the roof of a very lofty building, and earnestly begged for quarter, but could not be induced by any promise of safety to come down, till they had received the banner of Tancred, one of the chiefs of the crusaders, as a pledge of life. This they reckoned a more powerful protection than the most solemn promise; although in this instance their confidence was entirely misplaced; for the faithless zealots who pretended to fight for the cross, put every man of them to the sword.—Paxton.

Ver. 34. And *Ben-hadad* said unto him, The cities which my father took from thy father I will restore; and thou shalt make streets for thee in Damascus, as my father made in Samaria. Then *said Ahab*, I will send thee away with this covenant. So he made a covenant with him, and sent him away.

When the king of Syria had obtained security for his life, and assurance of being restored in peace to his throne, he promised in return for such great and unexpected favours, to restore the cities which his father had taken from Israel, and to permit Ahab to make streets in Damascus for himself, as his father had made in Samaria. This extraordinary privilege of making streets in Damascus, has exceedingly puzzled commentators. Some of them suppose the word *houtsoth* signifies market-places, where commodities were sold, the duties on which should belong to Ahab; others imagine he meant courts of justice, where the king of Israel should have the prerogative of sitting in judgment, and exercising a jurisdiction over the Syrians; others think they were a sort of piazzas, of which he should receive the rents; one class of interpreters understand by the word, fortifications or citadels; another class attempt to prove, that palaces are meant, which Ahab should be permitted to build as a proof of his superiority. The privileges which we know, from the faithful page of history, were actually granted to the Venetians for their aid, by the states of the kingdom of Jerusalem, during the captivity of Baldwin II., may perhaps explain, in a more satisfactory manner, these words of Benhadad. The instrument by which these privileges were secured, is preserved in the history of William, bishop of Tyre, the historian of the crusades, from which it appears, they were accustomed to assign churches, and to give streets in their towns and cities, with very ample prerogatives in these streets, to the foreign nations who lent them the most effectual assistance. The Venetians had a street in Acre, with full jurisdiction in it; and in what this consisted, we learn from the deed of settlement just mentioned; they had a right to have in their streets an oven, a mill, a bath, weights, and measures for wine, oil, and honey; they had also a right to judge causes among themselves, together with as great a jurisdiction over all those who dwelt in their street, of what nation soever they might be, as the kings of Jerusalem had over others. The same historian informs us, that the Genoese also had a street in that city, with full jurisdiction in it, and a church, as a reward for their services, together with a third part of the dues of the port. In the treaty of peace granted by Bajazet, emperor of the Turks, to Emanuel, the Greek emperor, it was stipulated that the latter should grant free liberty to the Turks to dwell together in one street of Constantinople, with the free exercise of their own religion and laws, under a judge of their own nation. This humiliating condition the Greek emperor was obliged to accept; and a great number of Turks, with their families, were sent out of Bithynia to dwell in Constantinople, where a mosque was built for their accommodation. It is not improbable, that the same kind of privileges that were granted to the Venetians, the Genoese, and the Turks, had been granted to the father of Benhadad, by the king of Israel, and were now offered to Ahab in Damascus, in the distressed state of his affairs. The Syrian monarch promised to give his conqueror a number of streets in his capital city, for the use of his subjects, with peculiar rights and privileges, which enabled him to exercise the same jurisdiction there as in his own dominions.—Paxton.

Mr. Harmer has remarked, that "the proposal of Benhadad, as to the making and possession of *streets* in Damascus, was better relished by Ahab, than understood by commentators;" some of whom have guessed that this expression meant the erection of markets, or of courts of judicature, or of piazzas, or of citadels and fortifications, &c. Mr. Harmer then proceeds to narrate the privileges granted to the Venetians, in recompense for their aid, by the states of the kingdom of Jerusalem; and he observes, that it was customary to assign *churches*, and to give *streets*, in their towns, to foreign nations, &c. His instances, however, are rather instances of rewards for services performed, than proofs of such terms as conditions of peace: probably, therefore, it will not be disagreeable to the reader to see a passage still more applicable to the history of Benhadad, than any of those are which Mr. Harmer has produced; it occurs in Knolles's "History of the Turks," p. 206. "Baiazet having worthily relieued his besieged citie, returned againe to the siege of Constantinople, laying more hardly vnto it than before, building forts and bulwarks against it on the one side towards the land; and passing ouer the strait of Bosphorus, built a strong castle vpon that strait ouer against Constantinople, to impeach so much as was possible, all passage thereunto by sea. This streight siege (as most write) continued also two yeres, which I suppose by the circumstance of the historie, to haue been part of the aforesaid eight yeres. *Emanuel, the besieged Emperor, wearied with these long wars, sent an embassador to Baiazet, to intreat with him a peace;* which Baiazet was the more willing to hearken vnto, for that he heard newes, that Tamerlane, the great Tartarian Prince, intended shortly to warre upon him. *Yet could this peace not be obtained, but upon condition that the Emperor should grant free libertie for the Turks to dwell together in one* STREET *of Constantinople, with free exercise of their own religion and lawes, vnder a judge of their own nation;* and further, to pay vnto the Turkish king a yeerely tribute of ten thousand duckats. *Which dishonourable conditions the distressed Emperor was glad to accept of.* So was this long siege broken vp, and presently *a great sort of Turks with their families were sent out of Bithynia, to dwell in Constantinople, and a church there built for them:* which not long after was by the Emperor pulled downe to the ground, and the Turks againe driuen out of the citie, at such time as Baiazet was by the mighty Tamerlane ouerthrowne and taken prisoner." The circumstances of these two stories are so much alike, that it merely now remains to notice the propriety with which our translators have chosen the word *streets*, rather than any other proposed by commentators.—Taylor in Calmet.

CHAPTER XXI.

Ver. 2. And Ahab spake unto Naboth, saying, Give me thy vineyard, that I may have it for a garden of herbs, because it *is* near unto my house: and I will give thee for it a better vineyard than it; *or*, if it seem good to thee, I will give thee the worth of it in money.

Our first parents had for their residence a beautiful garden, which may have had some influence upon their immediate descendants, in giving them a predilection for such situations. People in England will scarcely be able to appreciate the value which the Orientals place on a garden. The food of many of them consists of vegetables, roots, and fruits; their medicines, also, being indigenous, are most of them produced in their gardens. Hence they have their fine fruit trees, and the constant shade; and here they have their wells and places for bathing. See the proprietor, in his undress walking around his little domain; his fence or wall is so high no one can overlook him: he strolls about to smoke his shroot, to pick up the fruit, and cull the flowers; he cares not for the world; his soul is satisfied with the scenes around him. Ahab wished to have Naboth's garden; but how could he part with "the inheritance" of his "fathers?" There was scarcely a tree which had not some pleasing associations connected with it: one was planted by the hand of a beloved ancestor, another in memory of some great event; the water he drank, and the fruit he ate, were from the same sources as those which refreshed his fathers. How then could he, in disobedience to God's command, and in violation of all those tender feelings, give up his garden to Ahab? To part with such a place is, to the people of the East, like parting with life itself.—Roberts.

Ver. 4. And he laid him down upon his bed, and turned away his face, and would eat no bread.

Thus acted the puissant monarch, because he could not get Naboth's garden. See the creature in the shape of a man pouting his lip, and throwing himself on his bed, and refusing to eat food, because he could not gain his wishes. The domestics brought refreshment, but their lord would not take it; and, therefore, they went to queen Jezebel, to communicate the sorrowful intelligence; and she immediately went to his majesty and inquired, "Why is thy spirit so sad, that thou eatest not bread?" and he told his mournful story. How often do we see full-grown men acting in a similar way, when disappointed in their wishes: go near them, and they avert their faces; offer them food, they will not eat; and, generally speaking, their friends are so weak as, at any expense, to gratify their wishes.—Roberts.

Ver. 7. And Jezebel's wife said unto him, Dost thou now govern the kingdom of Israel? arise, *and* eat bread, and let thy heart be merry: I will give thee the vineyard of Naboth the Jezreelite.

I do not find any statute that prohibited an Israelite from exchanging his inheritance; nor was there, indeed, in such exchange, unless when it transferred a person to a different tribe, any thing contrary to the intention of the law, which was to prevent his latest posterity from ever being altogether denuded of their land. Perhaps, therefore, it was a piece of mere crossness in Naboth to refuse, in such uncourtly terms, not only to sell, but even to exchange his vineyard with King Ahab, 1 Kings xxi. 7. At the same time, it is impossible to vindicate the despotic measure, to which the barbarous wife of this too obsequious monarch had recourse in order to obtain it; for certainly Naboth was not *obliged* to exchange his vineyard, unless he chose.—Michaelis.

Ver. 8. So she wrote letters in Ahab's name, and sealed *them* with his seal, and sent the letters unto the elders and to the nobles that *were* in his city dwelling with Naboth.

At this day, in the East, not a female in ten thousand is acquainted with the art of writing; and I think it probable that Ahab's affectionate queen did not write the letters with her own hand, but that she caused it to be done by others. It is not unlikely that the state of female education, in modern times, is precisely the same as that of antiquity; for I do not recollect any female in the scriptures, excepting Jezebel, who is mentioned as being concerned in the writing of letters. The talented Hindoo female, Aviyār, has left wonderful memorials of her cultivated mind; and I doubt not, when female education shall become general in the East, from them will be furnished many an Aviyār, to bless and adorn the future age.—Roberts.

The very ancient custom of sealing despatches with a seal or signet, set in a ring, is still retained in the East. Pococke says, "in Egypt they make the impression of their name with their seal, generally of cornelian, which they wear on their finger, and which is blacked when they have occasion to seal with it." Hanway remarks, that "the Persian ink serves not only for writing, but for subscribing with their seal; indeed, many of the Persians in high office could not write. In their rings they wear agates, which serve for a seal, on which is frequently engraved their name, and some verse from the Koran." Shaw also has a remark exactly to the same purpose.—Burder.

Ver. 10. And set two men, sons of Belial, before him, to bear witness against him, saying, Thou didst blaspheme God and the king.

Princes never want instruments to execute their pleasure; and yet it is strange, that among all these judges and great men, there should be none that abhorred such a villany. It must be considered, however, that for a long while they had cast off all fear and sense of God, and prostituted their consciences to please their king: nor dare they disobey Jezebel's commands, who had the full power and government of the king, (as they well knew,) and could easily have taken away their lives, had they refused to condemn Naboth.—Stackhouse.

Ask any judge, any gentleman in the civil service of India, whether men may not be had in any village to swear any thing for the fraction of a shilling? Jezebel would not find it difficult to procure agents to swear away the life of Naboth the Jezreelite.—Roberts.

Ver. 13. And I will stretch over Jerusalem the line of Samaria, and the plummet of the house of Ahab; and I will wipe Jerusalem as *a man* wipeth a dish, wiping *it*, and turning *it* upside down.

The Vulgate renders this clause, *Delebo Jerusalem, sicut deleri solent tabulæ:* I will blot out Jerusalem as tablets are wont to be blotted out. It is a metaphor taken from the ancient method of writing. They traced their letters with a stile on boards, thinly spread over with wax: for this purpose one end of the stile was sharp, the other end blunt and smooth; with this they could rub out what they had written, and so smooth the place, and spread back the wax, as to render it capable of receiving any other words. Thus the Lord had written down Jerusalem, never intending that its name or memorial should be blotted out; but now the stile is turned, and the name Jerusalem is no longer to be found.—Burder.

Ver. 15. And it came to pass, when Jezebel heard that Naboth was stoned, and was dead, that Jezebel said to Ahab, Arise, take possession of the vineyard of Naboth the Jezreelite, which he refused to give thee for money: for Naboth is not alive, but dead.

As Naboth, according to verse 10, was executed as a blasphemer and a traitor, his property did not go to his relations, but to the king. Even now, in the Turkish empire, and in Persia, the property of great men who are executed, falls to the public treasury, or the governors of the province seize upon it. The chans now enrich themselves with the confiscated property of criminals, and other fines, which formerly fell to the royal treasury, says Gmelin, in his *Travels through Persia and Northern Persia.*—Burder.

Ver. 19. Thus saith the Lord, In the place where dogs licked the blood of Naboth shall dogs lick thy blood, even thine.

There is a great dispute among the learned, as to the accomplishment of this prophecy. At the first it was no doubt intended to be literally fulfilled, but upon Ahab's repentance, (as we find below,) the punishment was transferred from him to his son Jehoram, in whom it was actually accomplished; for his dead body was cast into the portion of the field of Naboth the Jezreelite, for the dogs to devour, 2 Kings ix. 25. Since Ahab's blood therefore was licked by dogs, not at Jezreel, but at Samaria, it seems necessary that we should understand the Hebrew word, which our translation renders, *in the place where,* not as denoting the place, but the manner in which the thing was done; and so the sense of the passage will be, that as dogs licked, or in like manner, as dogs licked Naboth's blood, even so shall they lick thine, observe what I say, even thine.—Stackhouse.

Ver. 23. And of Jezebel also spake the Lord, saying, The dogs shall eat Jezebel by the wall of Jezreel.

This, to an English ear, sounds very surprising; that during the time of a single meal, so many dogs should be on the spot, ready to devour, and should so speedily despatch this business, in the very midst of a royal city, close under the royal gateway, and where a considerable train of people had so lately passed, and, no doubt, many were continually passing: this, to an English reader, appears extremely unaccountable; but we find it well accounted for by Mr. Bruce, whose information the reader will receive with due allowance for the different manners and ideas of countries; after which, this rapid devouring of Jezebel will not appear so extraordinary as it has hitherto done. "The bodies of those killed by the sword *were hewn to pieces, and scattered about the streets, being denied burial.* I was miserable, and almost driven to despair, at *seeing my hunting-dogs* twice let loose by the carelessness of my servants, *bringing into the courtyard the heads and arms of slaughtered men,* and which I could no way prevent, but by the destruction of the dogs themselves: the quantity of carrion, and the stench of it, brought down the hyenas in hundreds from the neighbouring mountains; and as few people in Gondar go out after it is dark, they enjoyed the streets to themselves, and seemed ready to dispute the possession of the city with the inhabitants. *Often, when I went home late from the palace,* and it was this time the king chose chiefly for conversation, *though I had but to pass the corner of the market-place* BEFORE THE PALACE, had lanterns with me, and was surrounded with armed men, I heard them grunting by twos and threes, so near me as to be afraid they would take some opportunity of seizing me by the leg. A pistol would have frightened them, and made them speedily run, and I constantly carried two loaded at my girdle; but the discharging a pistol in the night would have alarmed every one that heard it in the town, and it was not now the time to add any thing to people's fears. I at last scarcely ever went out, and nothing occupied my thoughts but how to escape from this bloody country, by way of Sennaar, and how I could best exert my power and influence over Yasine, at Ras el Feel, to pave my way, by assisting me to pass the desert, into Atbara. The king, missing me at the palace, and hearing I had not been at Ras Michael's, began to inquire who had been with me? Ayto Confu soon found Yasine, who informed him of the whole matter. Upon this I was sent for to the palace, where I found the king, without anybody but menial servants. He immediately remarked, that I looked very ill, which, indeed, I found to be the case, as I had scarcely ate or slept since I saw him last, or even for some days before. He asked me, in a condoling tone, what ailed me? That besides looking sick, I seemed as if something had ruffled me, and put me out of humour. I told him, that what he observed was true: that coming *across the market-place,* I had seen Za Mariam, the Ras's doorkeeper, with three men bound, one of whom he fell *a-hacking to pieces* in my presence, and, upon seeing me running across the place, stopping my nose, he called me to stay till he should come and despatch the other two, for he wanted to speak with me, as if he had been engaged about ordinary business; that the soldiers, in consideration of his haste, immediately fell upon the other two, whose cries were still remaining in my ears; that the hyenas, at night, would scarcely let me pass in the streets, when I returned *from the palace; and the dogs fled into my house to eat pieces of human carcasses at their leisure.*" (Travels, vol. iv., page 81, &c.)

Without supposing that Jezreel was pestered with hyenas, like Gondar, though that is not incredible, we may now easily admit of a sufficiency of dogs, accustomed to carnage, which had pulled the body of Jezebel to pieces, and had devoured it before the palace gate, or had withdrawn with parts of it to their hiding-places. But perhaps the mention of the head, hands, and feet, being left on the spot, indicates that it had *not* been removed by the dogs, but was eaten where it fell (as those parts adjoined the members most likely to be removed,) so that the prophecy of Elijah was literally fulfilled: "In the portion of Jezreel, shall dogs eat Jezebel." This account illustrates also the readiness of the dogs to lick the blood of Ahab, 1 Kings xxii. 38, in perfect conformity to which is the expression of the prophet Jeremiah, xv. 3, "I will appoint over them .... *the sword to slay, and the dogs to tear,* and the fowls of the heaven, and the beasts of the earth, [the hyenas of Mr. Bruce, perhaps,] to devour and destroy." Mr. Bruce's account also explains the mode of execution adopted by the prophet Samuel, with regard to Agag, king of the Amalekites, whom Samuel thus addresses:—"In like manner [literally, *in like procedure as—i. e.* in the same identical mode of execution] as thy sword has made women barren, so shall thy mother be rendered barren [childless] among women." 1 Sam. xv. 33. If these words do not imply that Agag had ripped up pregnant women, they at least imply that he had *hewed* many prisoners to death! for we find that "Samuel caused Agag to be *hewed in pieces* before the face of the Lord [probably not before the residence of Saul, but before the tabernacle, &c.] in Gilgal," directing that very same mode of punishment (hitherto, we suppose, unadopted in Israel) to be used towards him, which he had formerly used towards others. The character of the prophet Samuel has been vilified for cruelty on account of this history, with how little reason let the reader now judge; and compare a similar retributive act of justice on Adonibezek, Judges i. 7. —Taylor in Calmet.

Ver. 27. And it came to pass, when Ahab heard those words, that he rent his clothes, and put sackcloth upon his flesh, and fasted, and lay in sackcloth, and went softly.

See the man who goes into the presence of a superior; he takes off his sandals, and walks SOFTLY—he has a timid air, and you cannot hear his foot tread on the ground. When a dutiful son goes to his father, or a devotee into the presence of a sacred personage, he walks in the same way. Has a proud, boasting man, been humbled, the people say, "Ah! aha! he can now walk *mitha-vāka,*" i. e. softly. "What! the proud Mutto walk softly; whoever expected that?"—Roberts.

Going softly seems to have been one of the many expressions of mourning commonly used among the eastern nations. That it was in use among the Jews appears from the case of Ahab; and by mistake it has been confounded with walking barefoot. It seems to have been a very slow, solemn manner of walking, well adapted to the state of mourners labouring under great sorrow and dejection of mind.—Burder.

CHAPTER XXII.

Ver. 11. And Zedekiah the son of Chenaanah made him horns of iron; and he said, Thus saith the Lord, With these shalt thou push the Syrians, until thou have consumed them.

The Indian soldier wears a horn of steel on the front of his helmet, directly over the forehead. In Abyssinia the headdress of the provincial governors, according to Mr. Bruce, consists of a large broad fillet bound upon their forehead, and tied behind their head. In the middle of this rises a horn, or conical piece of silver, gilt, about four inches long, much in the shape of our common candle extinguishers. This is called *kirn,* a slight corruption of the Hebrew word *keren,* a horn, and is only worn in reviews, or parades after victory. The crooked manner in which they hold the neck when this ornament is on their forehead, for fear it should fall forward, seems to agree with what the Psalmist calls speaking with a stiff neck: "Lift not your horn on high; speak not with a stiff neck;" for it perfectly shows the meaning of speaking in this attitude, when the horn is held exact like the horn of a unicorn. An allusion is made to this custom in another passage: "But my horn shalt thou exalt like the horn of a unicorn." To raise the horn was to clothe one with authority, or to do him honour; to lower it, cut it off, or take it away, to deprive one of power, or to treat him with disrespect. Such were the "horns of iron" which Zedekiah made for himself, when he presumed, in the name of Jehovah, to flatter his prince with the promise of victory over his enemies: "Thus saith the Lord, with these" military insignia "shalt thou push the Syrians until thou hast consumed them." They were military ornaments, the symbols of strength, and courage, and power.—PAXTON.

Ver. 16. And the king said unto him, How many times shall I adjure thee that thou tell me nothing but *that which is* true in the name of the LORD?

In England, this solemn appeal is never made but in cases of extremity; but in the East, the most trifling circumstance will induce a person to say, *Unni-ăni-uddukerain*, "By thy oath;" or, "I impose it upon thee."—ROBERTS.

Ver. 25. And Micaiah said, Behold, thou shalt see in that day, when thou shalt go into an inner chamber to hide thyself.

"In one of the halls of the seraglio at Constantinople," says De la Motraye, "the eunuch made us pass by *several little chambers, with doors shut, like the cells of monks or nuns*, as far as I could judge by one that another eunuch opened, which was the only one I saw; and by the outside of others. Asan Firally Bashaw, being summoned by his friends, came out of a little house near the towers, where he had been long hidden in his harem, which, had it been suspected by the mufti, he had not denied his *fetfa* to the emperor, for seizing his person, even there. The harems are sanctuaries, as sacred and inviolable for persons pursued by justice for any crime, debt, &c. as the Roman Catholic churches in Italy, Spain, Portugal, &c. Though the grand seignior's power over his creatures is such, that he may send some of his eunuchs even there to apprehend those who resist his will. The harems of the Greeks are almost as sacred as those of the Turks; so that the officers of justice dare not enter without being sure that a man is there, contrary to the law: and if they should go in and not find what they look for, the women may punish, and even kill them, without being molested for any infringement of the law: on the contrary, the relations would have a right to make reprisals, and demand satisfaction for such violence."

Those who have not seen the cells of monks, or nuns, in foreign countries, may conceive of a long gallery, or other spacious apartment, as a large hall, &c. into which the doors of the cells open: these cells consist of one room to each person, but frequently of two rooms, one of which is used for sleeping in; the other for less retired purposes, conversation, &c. Agreeably to this, it appears, that in the East also, we must first pass through a long hall, or gallery, before we can enter the peculiar abode of any particular woman of the harem. We may first apply this mode of dwelling to a circumstance threatened by the prophet Micaiah, to his opponent Zedekiah, 1 Kings xxii. 25, "Thou shalt go into an inner chamber to hide thyself." Our translators have put in the margin, "from chamber to chamber." The Hebrew is, (חדר ב חדר *cheder be cheder*,) "chamber *within* chamber," which exactly agrees with the description extracted; but it is new to consider this threat as predicting that Zedekiah should fly for shelter to a harem, [as we find Assan Firally Bashaw had done;] that his fear should render him, as it were, effeminate, and that he should seek refuge where it was not usual for a man to seek it; where the "officers of justice," nor even those of conquerors, usually penetrated. There is an additional disgrace, a *sting* in these words, if this be the intention of the speaker, stronger than what has hitherto been noticed in them. Is not something similar related of Benhadad, 1 Kings xx. 30, "He fled," and was so overcome with fear, that he hid himself in "a chamber within chamber?" As it is very characteristic of braggarts and drunkards (see verses 16, 18, &c.) to be mentally overwhelmed when in adversity, may we not suppose that Benhadad was now concealed in the harem? Following circumstances do not militate against this supposition. That the word *cheder* means a woman's chamber, appears from Judges xv. 1, where Samson says, "I will go to my wife into *her chamber*," (החדרה.)—TAYLOR IN CALMET.

Ver. 43. And he walked in all the ways of Asa his father; he turned not aside from it, doing *that which was* right in the eyes of the LORD: nevertheless the high places were not taken away; *for* the people offered and burnt incense yet in the high places.

Many of old worshipped upon hills and on the tops of high mountains; imagining that they thereby obtained a nearer communication with heaven. Strabo says that the Persians always performed their worship upon hills. Some nations, instead of an image, worshipped the hill as the deity. In Japan most of their temples are at this day upon eminences; and often upon the ascent of high mountains, commanding fine views, with groves and rivulets of clear water: for they say, that the gods are extremely delighted with such high and pleasant spots. (Kæmpfer's *Japan.*) This practice, in early times, was almost universal; and every mountain was esteemed holy. The people who prosecuted this method of worship enjoyed a soothing infatuation, which flattered the gloom of superstition. The eminences to which they retired were lonely and silent, and seemed to be happily circumstanced for contemplation and prayer. They who frequented them were raised above the lower world, and fancied that they were brought into the vicinity of the powers of the air, and of the deity who resided in the higher regions. But the chief excellence for which they were frequented was, that they were looked upon as the peculiar places where God delivered his oracles.—BURDER.

Ver. 48. Jehoshaphat made ships of Tharshish to go to Ophir for gold; but they went not: for the ships were broken at Ezion-geber.

"Suez, which was the Arsinoe of the ancients, is situated at the top of the Red Sea: it stands surrounded by the desert, and is a shabby, ill-built place; the ships anchor a league from the town, to which the channel that leads is very narrow, and has only nine or ten feet depth of water; for which reason, the large ships that are built here must be towed down to the road, without mast, guns, or any thing in them; there are eight of them lying here, which have not been to Juddah this year; one of them is at least twelve hundred tons burden, being as lofty as a hundred gun ship, though not longer than a frigate; so that you may judge of the good proportions they observe in the construction of their ships; the timber of which they are all built is brought from Syria by water, to Cairo, and from thence on camels. This fleet sails for Juddah every year, before the Hadge; stays there two or three months, and returns loaded with coffee: this is so material an article in the diet of a mussulman, that the prayers and wishes of them all are offered up for its safety: and I believe, next to the loss of their country, the loss of their coffee would be most severely felt by them. The greatest part of it is sent to Constantinople, and other parts of Turkey, but a small quantity going to France and Italy." (Major Rooke, p. 73.)—BURDER.

THE SECOND BOOK OF KINGS.

CHAPTER I.

Ver. 2. And Ahaziah fell down through a lattice in his upper chamber that *was* in Samaria, and was sick: and he sent messengers, and said unto them, Go, inquire of Baal-zebub, the god of Ekron, whether I shall recover of this disease.

In the eastern countries the roofs of the houses were flat, and surrounded with a battlement, to prevent falling from them, because it was a customary thing for people to walk upon them, in order to take the air. Now in this battlement we may suppose that there were some wooden lattices for people to look through, of equal height with the parapet wall, and that Ahaziah negligently leaning on it, as it was rotten and infirm it broke down, and let him fall into the court, or garden, belonging to his house. Or there is another way wherein he might fall. In these flat roofs there was generally an opening, which served instead of a sky light to the house below, and this opening might be done over with lattice-work, which the king, as he was carelessly walking, might chance to step upon and slip through. Nor is there any absurdity in supposing such lattice-work in a king's palace, when the world was not arrived to that height of art and curiosity that we find in it now.—STACKHOUSE.

Ver. 3. *Is it* not because *there is* not a God in Israel, *that* ye go to inquire of Baal-zebub, the god of Ekron?

We, perhaps, may be a good deal surprised to find, that the *driving away of flies* should be thought by the inhabitants of the country about Ekron so important, that they should give a name to the idol they worshipped, expressive of that property, (Baal-zebub, *lord of the fly;*) more especially when this was not the only quality ascribed to him, but it was supposed the power of predicting such momentous matters as the continuance of the life of great princes, or their approaching death, did also belong to him; but possibly a passage in Vinisauf may lessen this astonishment. Vinisauf, speaking of the army under our Richard the First, a little before he left the Holy Land, and describing them as marching on the plain not far from the seacoast, towards a place called Ybelin, which belonged to the knights hospitalers of St. John of Jerusalem, pretty near Hebron, says, "The army stopping a while there, rejoicing in the hope of speedily setting out for Jerusalem, were assailed by a most minute kind of fly, flying about like sparks, which they called *cincinnellæ*. With these the whole neighbouring region round about was filled. These most wretchedly infested the pilgrims, piercing with great smartness the hands, necks, throats, foreheads, and faces, and every part that was uncovered, a most violent burning tumour following the punctures made by them, so that all that they stung looked like lepers." He adds, "that they could hardly guard themselves from this most troublesome vexation, by covering their heads and necks with veils." What these fireflies were, and whether they shone in the dark, and for that reason are compared to sparks flying about, or whether they were compared to them on the account of the burning heat they occasioned, as well as a swelling in the flesh of all they wounded, I shall not take upon me to determine. I would only observe, Richard and his people met with them in that part of the country, which seemed to be of the country which was not very far from Ekron, and which seemed to be of much the same general nature—a plain not far from the seacoast.

Can we wonder, after this recital, that those poor heathen who lived in and about Ekron, derived much consolation from the supposed power of the idol they worshipped, to drive away the cincinnellæ of that country, which were so extremely vexatious to these pilgrims of the 12th century, and occasioned them so much pain. Lord of the fly, lord of these cincinnellæ, must have appeared to them a very pleasing, a very important title.

I will only add, that Sandys, in his travels in the same country, but more to the northward, speaks of the air appearing as if full of *sparkles of fire*, borne to and fro with the wind, after much rain and a thunderstorm, which appearance of sparkles of fire he attributes to infinite swarms of flies that shone like glow-worms; but he gives not the least intimation of their being incommoded by them. What this difference was owing to, it is quite beside the design of these papers to inquire; whether its being about two months earlier in the year, more to the northward, or immediately after much rain and a thunderstorm, was a cause of the innoxiousness of these animals when Sandys travelled, and even whether the appearance Sandys speaks of, was really owing to insects, or to any effect of electricity, I leave to others to determine.—HARMER.

Ver. 4. Now, therefore, thus saith the LORD, Thou shalt not come down from that bed on which thou art gone up, but shalt surely die. And Elijah departed.

This expression may be illustrated by what Shaw says of the Moorish houses in Barbary, (Travels, p. 209,) where, after having observed that their chambers are spacious, of the same length with the square court on the sides of which they are built, he adds, "at one end of each chamber there is a little gallery *raised* three, four, or five feet *above the floor*, with a balustrade in the front of it, *with a few steps* likewise *leading up to it.* Here they place their beds; a situation frequently alluded to in the holy scriptures, which may likewise illustrate the circumstance of Hezekiah's *turning his face, when he prayed, towards the wall*, (i. e. from his attendants,) 2 Kings xx. 2, that the fervency of his devotion might be the less taken notice of and observed. The like is related of Ahab, (1 Kings xxi. 4,) though probably he did thus, not upon a religious account, but in order to conceal from his attendants the anguish he was in for his late disappointment."—BURDER.

Ver. 8. And they answered him, *He was* a hairy man, and girt with a girdle of leather about his loins. And he said, It *is* Elijah the Tishbite.

See on Matt. 3. 4.

Ver. 15. And the angel of the LORD said unto Elijah, Go down with him; be not afraid of him. And he arose, and went down with him unto the king.

See on 1 Sam. 17. 51.

Ver. 16. Therefore thou shalt not come down off that bed on which thou art gone up, but shalt surely die.

At one end of each chamber is a little gallery, raised three or four feet above the floor, with a balustrade in front, to which they go up by a few steps. Here they place their beds; a situation frequently alluded to in the holy scriptures. Thus Jacob addressed his undutiful son, in his last benediction: "Thou wentest up to thy father's bed,—he went up to my couch." The allusion is again involved in the declaration of Elijah to the king of Samaria: "Now, therefore, thus saith the Lord, Thou shalt not come down from that bed on which thou art gone up, but shalt surely die." And the Psalmist sware unto the Lord, and vowed unto the mighty God of Jacob, "Surely I will not come into the tabernacle of my house, nor go up into my bed,—until I find out a place for the Lord." This arrangement may likewise illustrate the circumstance of Hezekiah's "turning his face to the wall, when he prayed," that the greatness of his sorrow, and the fervour of his devotion, might, as much as possible, be concealed from his attendants. The same thing is related of Ahab, although we have no reason to think it was upon a religious account, but in order to conceal from those about him the anguish he felt for his late disappointment; or, perhaps, by so great a show of sorrow, to provoke them to devise some means to gratify his wishes: "And he laid him down upon his bed, and turned away his face, and would eat no bread."—PAXTON.

CHAPTER II.

Ver. 3. And the sons of the prophets that *were* at Bethel came forth to Elisha, and said unto him, Knowest thou that the LORD will take away thy master from thy head to-day? And he said, Yea, I know *it;* hold ye your peace.

The expression in the text is, "Knowest thou, that the Lord will take away thy master from thy head to-day?" where the sons of the prophets allude to their manner of sitting in their school: for the scholars used to sit below their masters' feet, and the masters above over their heads, when they taught them: and therefore the sense of the words is, that God would deprive Elisha of his master Elijah's instructions, viz. by a sudden death. For it does not appear that they had any notion of his translation; so far from this, that they desired leave to send out some to seek for him, "if peradventure the spirit of the Lord had taken him up, and cast him upon some mountain, or into some valley," ver. 16.—STACKHOUSE.

Ver. 11. And it came to pass, as they still went on, and talked, that, behold, *there appeared* a chariot of fire, and horses of fire, and parted them both asunder; and Elijah went up by a whirlwind into heaven.

The Hindoos believe their supreme god Siva sends his angels, with a green chariot, to fetch the souls of those who are devoted to him; that there are occasionally horses, but at other times none. "The holy king *Tirru-Sangu* (i. e. divine chank) was taken to heaven, body and soul, without the pain of dying." When a man, as a heathen, is very regular in his devotions; or when he reproves others for vice, or neglect of duty, it is often scornfully asked, "What! are you expecting the green chariot to be sent for you?" meaning, "Do you, by your devotions, expect to go to heaven in the chariot of Siva without the pain of dying?" Does a man act with great injustice, the person who finds him out asks, "Will you get the green chariot for this?" Has a heathen embraced Christianity, he is asked the same question. "Charity, charity," says the beggar at your door, "and the green chariot will be sent for you."—ROBERTS.

Ver. 12. And Elisha saw *it*, and he cried, My father, my father! the chariot of Israel, and the horsemen thereof. And he saw him no more: and he took hold of his own clothes, and rent them in two pieces.

The words of Elisha upon this occasion are, "My father, my father!" (so they called their masters and instructers,) "the chariot of Israel, and the horsemen thereof." The expression alludes to the form of the chariot and horses that he had just then beheld, and seems to imply, "That Elijah, by his example, and counsel, and prayers, and power with God, did more for the defence and preservation of Israel, than all their chariots and horses, and other warlike provisions:" unless we may suppose, that this was an abrupt speech, which Elisha, in the consternation he was in, left unfinished, and so the sacred history has recorded it.—STACKHOUSE.

Ver. 19. And the men of the city said unto Elisha, Behold, I pray thee, the situation of this city *is* pleasant, as my lord seeth: but the water *is* naught, and the ground barren.

Margin, "causing to miscarry." If the latter reading is allowed to be more just than the former, we must entertain a different idea of the situation of Jericho than the textual translation suggests. There are actually at this time cities where animal life of certain kinds pines, and decays, and dies; and where that posterity which should replace such loss is either not conceived; or, if conceived, is not brought to the birth; or if brought to the birth, is fatal in delivery to both mother and offspring. An instance of this kind occurs in Don Ulloa's Voyage to South America. He says of the climate of Porto Bello, that "it destroys the vigour of nature, and often untimely cuts the thread of life." And of Sennaar, Mr. Bruce says, that "no horse, mule, ass, or any beast of burden, will breed or even live at Sennaar, or many miles about it. Poultry does not live there; neither dog nor cat, sheep nor bullock, can be preserved a season there. They must go all, every half year, to the sands. Though every possible care be taken of them, they die in every place where the fat earth is about the town, during the first season of the rains." He further mentions, that the situation is equally unfavourable to most trees.—BURDER.

Ver. 20. And he said, Bring me a new cruise, and put salt therein. And they brought *it* to him.

The Hebrew, *tjelachit* (צלחית) is used to denote a vessel of some capacity; a vessel to be turned upside down, in order that the inside may be thoroughly wiped, (2 Kings xxi. 13;) "I will wipe Jerusalem, as a man wipeth a dish, turning it upside down." This implies, at least, that the opening of such a dish be not narrow but wide; that the dish itself be of a certain depth; yet that the hand may readily reach to the bottom of it, and there may freely move, so as to wipe it thoroughly, &c. This vessel was capable also of bearing the fire, and of standing conveniently over a fire; for we read, 2 Chron. xxxv. 13, "The priests, &c. boiled parts of the holy offerings in pans (*tjelachit*,) and distributed them speedily among the people." Meaning, perhaps, that this was not the very kind of boiler which they would have chosen, had time permitted a choice; but that haste, and multiplicity of business, made them use whatever first came to hand, that was competent to the service. This application of these vessels, however, shows that they must have been of considerable capacity and depth; as a very narrow or a very small dish, would not have answered the purpose required. [Or, was this speedy distribution of these viands, because they were best eaten hot?] A kind of dish or pan, which appears to answer these descriptions, is represented in the French work, entitled Estampes du Levant, in the hands of a confectioner of the grand seignior's seraglio, who is carrying a deep dish, full of heated viands, (recently taken off the fire,) upon which he has put a cover, in order that those viands may retain their heat and flavour. His being described on the plate as a confectioner, leads to the supposition that what he carries are delicacies; to this agrees his desire of preserving their heat: and the shape of the vessel is evidently calculated for standing, &c. over a fire. Moreover, from its form it may easily be rested on its side, for the purpose of being thoroughly wiped; and a dish used to contain delicacies, is most likely to receive such attention; for the comparison in the text referred to, evidently implies some assiduity and exertion to wipe from the dish every particle inconsistent with complete cleanliness. This dish, we suppose, is of earth, or china;—that is, of porcelain, rather than of metal.

We are now prepared to see the import of Elisha's direction to the men of Jericho, (2 Kings ii. 20.) "Bring me a new *tjelachit*"—one of the vessels used in your cookery—in those parts of your cookery which you esteem the most delicate: a culinary vessel, but of the superior kind: "and put salt therein," what you constantly mingle in your food, what readily mixes with water: and this shall be a sign to you, that in your future use of this stream, you shall find it salubrious, and fit for daily service in preparing, or accompanying, your daily sustenance. There is a striking picture of sloth, sketched out very simply, but very strongly, by the sagacious Solomon, (Prov. xix. 24,) repeated almost *verbatim*, chap. xxvi. 15:

> A slothful man hideth his hand in the *tjelachit:*
> But will not re-bring it to his mouth.
>
> A slothful man hideth his hand in the *tjelachit:*—but
> It grieveth him to bring it again to his mouth.

Meaning, he sees a dish, deep and capacious, filled with confectionary, sweetmeats, &c. whatever his appetite can desire in respect to relish and flavour; of this he is greedy. Thus excited, he thrusts his hand—his right hand—deep into the dish, loads it with delicacies; but, alas! the labour of lifting it up to his mouth is too great, too excessive, too fatiguing: he therefore does not enjoy or taste what is before him, though his appetite be so far allured as to desire, and his hand be so far exerted as to grasp. [This is the customary mode of conveying food to the mouth in the East, where knives and forks are not in use.] He suffers the viands to become cold, and thereby to lose their flavour; while he debates the important movement of his hand to his mouth, if he does not rather totally forego the enjoyment, as demanding too vast an action! Surely this picture of sloth is greatly heightened by this notion of the *tjelachit.* It seems to be sufficiently striking, that two words, rendered by our translators *lap*, or *bosom*, (Prov. xvi. 33, *chik*, and the word before us,) should both signify vases, or vessels. The first denotes, the lot-vase, used for containing the lot-pebbles, &c. to be drawn out by the hand: the other a dish for meat; neither of them referring to any part of the person, as our version seems to imply; which reads,

> A slothful man hideth his hand in his bosom,
> And will not bring it to his mouth again.

The powerful picture of sloth, painted by Solomon, gives occasion to enlarge somewhat further on the manner of eating among the Arabs; a manner that seems sufficiently rude to us, but which those who practise it insist is more natural and convenient, and not less cleanly than our own. "Extending their forefinger and thumb, (of the right hand always—the left hand is reserved for less honourable uses,) they say," observes D'Arvieux, "God made this fork before you made your steel ones." Mr. Jackson says, "The Moors are, for the most part, more cleanly in their persons than in their garments. They wash their hands before every meal, which, as they use no knives or forks, they eat with their fingers: half a dozen persons sit round a large bowl of cuscasoe, and, after the usual ejaculation (Bismillah!) 'In the name of God!' each person puts his hand to the bowl, and taking up the food, throws it, by a dexterous jerk, into his mouth, without suffering his fingers to touch his lips. However repugnant this may be to our ideas of cleanliness, yet the hand being always washed, and never touching the mouth in the act of eating, these people are by no means so dirty as Europeans have sometimes hastily imagined. They have no chairs or tables in their houses, but sit crosslegged on carpets and cushions; and at meals, the dish or bowl of provisions is placed on the floor." (Account of Morocco, p. 155.)

That a thorough sluggard should practise this "dexterous jerk of the hand," is not likely to have entered into the contemplation of the royal sage, in the passages illustrated above: and to say truth, the latter observation seems to be couched in terms much stronger than the former: "The sluggard musters up just strength enough to plunge his hand into the bowl; but this mighty effort exhausts him, he finds his weariness (נלאה) too great, too excessive, to bring it up to his mouth, loaded though it be with the delicacies of the table." There is a force in the word rendered *hide* or *plunge*, which should not be disregarded.—The sluggard buries deeply his hand:—it being customary with such characters to grasp at all, and more than all, which they can hold. Perhaps the action of a less polite class than that principally alluded to by Mr. Jackson, may best illustrate this reflection. We shall therefore add the following from Major Rooke's Travels in Arabia: "On my first going on board, I sat down with the Noquedah and his officers to supper, the floor being both our tables and chairs, on which we seated ourselves in a circle, with a large bowl of rice in the middle, and some fish and dates before each person: here I likewise found that knives and forks were useless instruments in eating, and that nature had accommodated us with what answered the same purpose: we plunged our hands into the bowl, rolled up a handful of rice into a ball, and conveyed it to our mouths in that form; our repast was short, and to that succeeded coffee and washing; and on their parts prayer, in which they were very frequent and fervent."—Taylor in Calmet.

Ver. 23. And he went up from thence unto Bethel: and as he was going up by the way, there came forth little children out of the city, and mocked him, and said unto him, Go up, thou bald-head; go up, thou bald-head.

Some suppose this alludes to the head being uncovered. I was not a little astonished in the East, when I first heard a man called a bald-head, who had a large quantity of hair on his head: and I found, upon inquiry, it was an epithet of CONTEMPT! A man who has killed himself is called "a bald-headed suicide!" A stupid fellow, "a bald-headed dunce." Of those who are powerless, "What can those bald-heads do?" Hence the epithet has often been applied to the missionaries. Is a man told his wife does not manage domestic matters well, he replies, as if in contempt of himself, "What can a bald-head do? must he not have a wife of the same kind?" Let a merchant, or any other person, who is going on business, meet a man who is REALLY bald, and he will assuredly refuse to attend to the business; and pronounce, if he dare, some imprecations on the object of his hatred. Sometimes he will repeat the proverb, "Go, thou bald-head, pilferer of a small fish, and sucker of bones cast away by the goldsmith." Call a man a *mottiyan*, i. e. bald-head, (which you may do, though he have much hair,) and then abuse, or sticks or stones, will be sure to be your portion. Thus the epithet implies great scorn, and is given to those who are WEAK OR MEAN.—Roberts.

Ver. 23. And he went up from thence unto Bethel. and as he was going up by the way, there came forth little children out of the city, and mocked him, and said unto him, Go up, thou bald-head; go up, thou bald-head. 24. And he turned back, and looked on them, and cursed them in the name of the Lord. And there came forth two she-bears out of the wood, and tare forty and two children of them.

Bethel, it is well known, was one of the cities where Jeroboam had set up a golden calf, a place strangely addicted to idolatry, and whose inhabitants had no small aversion to Elisha, as being the servant and successor of one, who had been a professed enemy to their wicked worship, and himself no less an opposer of it. It is reasonable to suppose, therefore, that the children (if they were children, for the word *naarim* may signify *grown youths* as well) who mocked Elisha, were excited and encouraged thereunto by their parents; and therefore the judgment was just, in God's punishing the wickedness of these parents by the death of their children, who, though they suffered in this life, had the happiness to be rescued from the danger of an idolatrous education, which might have been of fatal tendency both to their present and future state. In the mean time it must be acknowledged, that the insolence of these mockers (whether we suppose them children or youths) was very provoking, forasmuch as they ridiculed, not only a man whose very age commanded reverence, but a prophet likewise, whose character, in all ages, was accounted sacred, nay, and even God himself, whose honour was struck at in the reproaches against his servant, and that too in one of his most glorious and wonderful works, his assumption of Elijah into heaven: For, "Go up, thou bald-head, go up, thou bald-head," (besides the bitterness of the contempt expressed in the repetition of the words,) shows that they made a mere jest of any such translation; and therefore, in banter, they bid Elijah go up, whither, as he pretended, his friend and master was gone before. These provocations, one would think, were enough to draw an imprecation from the prophet; but this imprecation did not proceed from any passion or private resentment of his own, but merely from the command and commission of his God; who, for the terror and caution of other profane persons and idolaters, as well as for the maintenance of the honour and authority of his prophets, "confirmed the word which had gone out of his servant's mouth."

The like is to be said of the destruction which Elijah called down from heaven upon the two captains and their companies, who came to apprehend him—that he did this, not out of any hasty passion or revenge, but purely in obedience to the Holy Spirit, wherewith he was animated, and in zeal for the honour and glory of God, which in the person of his prophet, were grossly abused.—STACKHOUSE.

Ver. 34. And there came forth two she-bears out of the wood, and tare forty and two children of them.

These furious animals were she-bears, which, it is probable, had been just deprived of their young; and now following the impulse of their outraged feelings, they rushed from the wood to revenge the loss. But it is evident their native ferocity was overruled and directed by divine providence, to execute the dreadful sentence pronounced by the prophet in his name. They must, therefore, be considered as the ministers of God, the Judge of all the earth, commissioned to punish the idolatrous inhabitants of Bethel and their profligate offspring, who probably acted on this occasion with their concurrence, if not by their command. He punished in a similar way the heathen colonies planted by the king of Assyria in the cities of Samaria, after the expulsion of the ten tribes: "They feared not the Lord; therefore the Lord sent lions among them, which slew some of them." When he punished the youths of Bethel, (for so the phrase *little children* signifies in Hebrew,) by directing against them the rage of the she-bears, he only did what Moses had long before predicted, and left on record for their warning: "And if ye walk contrary unto me, and will not hearken unto me, I will bring seven times more plagues upon you, according to your sins. I will also send wild beasts among you, which shall rob you of your children." Bethel had been long the principal seat of idolatry, and its attendant vices; and to all their aggravated crimes, its inhabitants now added rude and impious mockery of a person whom they knew to be a prophet of the Lord, reviling with blasphemous tongues the Lord God of Elijah, and his now glorified servant. Baldness was reckoned a very great deformity in the East; and to be reproached with it, one of the grossest insults an Oriental could receive. Cesar, who was bald, could not bear to hear it mentioned in jest. It is one of the marks of disgrace which Homer fixes upon Thersites, that he had only a few straggling hairs on his pyramidal head. Their crime, therefore, justly merited the severest punishment.—PAXTON.

CHAPTER III.

Ver. 4. And Mesha king of Moab was a sheep-master, and rendered unto the king of Israel a hundred thousand lambs, and a hundred thousand rams, with the wool.

This was a prodigious number indeed; but then we are to consider that these countries abound with sheep, insomuch that Solomon offered a hundred and twenty thousand at the dedication of the temple, 2 Chron. vii. 5, and the Reubenites drove from the Hagarens a hundred and fifty thousand, 1 Chron. v. 7. For, as Bochart observes, their sheep frequently brought forth two at a time, and sometimes twice a year. The same learned man remarks, that in ancient times, when people's riches consisted in cattle, this was the only way of paying tribute. It is observed by others likewise, that this great number of cattle was not a tribute, which the Moabites were obliged to pay the Israelites every year, but on some special occasion only, upon the accession of every new king, for instance, when they were obliged to express their homage in this manner, to make satisfaction for some damages that the Israelites should at any time suffer from their invasions or revolts.—STACKHOUSE.

Ver. 11. And one of the king of Israel's servants answered and said, Here *is* Elisha the son of Shaphat, which poured water on the hands of Elijah.

We read, Elisha "went after Elijah, and ministered unto him;" which simply means he was his servant. The people of the East use their fingers in eating, instead of a knife and fork, or spoon; and consequently after, (as well as before,) they are obliged to wash their hands. The master, having finished his meal, calls a servant to pour water on his hands. The domestic then comes with a little brass vessel filled with water, and pours it on the hands and fingers till he hears the word *potham*, enough.—ROBERTS.

There is a description of Elisha the prophet, by a part of his office when servant to Elijah, which appears rather strange to us. "Is there not here a prophet of the Lord?" says King Jehoshaphat; he is answered, "Here is Elisha ben Shaphat, *who poured water on the hands of Elijah*," (2 Kings iii. 11,) *i. e.* who was his servant and constant attendant. So Pitts tells us: "The table being removed, before they rise (from the ground whereon they sit,) a slave, or servant, who stands attending on them with a cup of water to give them drink, steps into the middle with a basin, or copper pot of water, something like a coffee-pot, and a little soap, *and lets the water run upon their hands* one after another, in order as they sit." Such service it appears Elisha performed for Elijah: what shall we say then to the remarkable action of our Lord, "who poured water into a basin, and washed his disciples' feet," after supper? Was he indeed among them *as one who serveth?* On this subject, says D'Ohsson, "Ablution, *Abdesth*, consists in washing the hands, feet, face, and a part of the head; the law mentions them by the term—'the three parts consecrated to ablution.'.... The mussulman is generally seated on the edge of a sofa, with a pewter or copper vessel lined with tin placed before him upon a round piece of red cloth, to prevent the carpet or mat from being wet: a servant, kneeling on the ground, pours out water for his master; another holds a cloth destined for these purifications. The person who purifies himself begins by baring his arms as far as the elbow. As he washes his hands, mouth, nostrils, face, arms, &c., he repeats the proper prayers.... It is probable that Mohammed followed on this subject the book of Leviticus." It is well known that we have an officer among ourselves, who, at the coronation, and formerly at all public festivals, held a basin of water for the king to wash his hands in, after dinner; but it is not equally well known, that Cardinal Wolsey, one time, when the Duke of Buckingham held the basin for Henry VIII., after the king had washed, put his own hand into the basin: the duke resenting this intrusion, let some of the water fall on the habit of the cardinal, who never forgave the action, but brought the duke to the block, in consequence of his resentment.—TAYLOR IN CALMET.

Ver. 15. But now bring me a minstrel. And it came to pass, when the minstrel played, that the hand of the LORD came upon him.

The music of great men in civil life, has been sometimes directed to persons of a sacred character, as an expression of respect, in the East; perhaps the playing of the minstrel before the prophet Elisha is to be understood, in part, at least, in something of the same manner. When Dr. Richard Chandler was at Athens, the archbishop of that city was upon ill terms with its Vaiwode, and the Greeks in general siding with the Vaiwode, the archbishop was obliged to withdraw for a time; but some time after, when Chandler and his fellow-travellers were at Corinth, they were informed that the archbishop was returned to Athens; that the Bey or Vaiwode had received him kindly, and ordered his musicians to attend him at his palace; and that a complete revolution had happened in his favour. Here we see a civil magistrate, who had been displeased with a great ecclesiastic, sent his musicians to play at his archiepiscopal palace, in honour of him to whom this magistrate was now reconciled. Elisha might require that a like honour should be done to him, and through him to the God whom he served, who had been sadly neglected and affronted in former times by the king of Israel. The propriety of it will appear in a still stronger light, if we should suppose, that Elisha commanded the minstrel to sing, along with his music, a hymn to JEHOVAH, setting forth his being a God that gave rain, that preserved such as were ready to perish, the giver of victory, and whose power was neither limited to his temple, nor to the Jewish country sacred to him, but equally operative in every place. The coming of the spirit of prophecy upon Elisha, enabling him to declare a speedy copious fall of rain in that neighbourhood, and a complete victory over their enemies, immediately upon the submissive compliance of this idolatrous prince with the requisition of the prophet, and such a hymn in praise of the God of Israel, seems to me full as natural an interpretation, as the supposing he desired the minstrel to come in order to play some soft composing tune, to calm his ruffled spirits, and to qualify him for the reception of the influences of the spirit of prophecy. Was a warm and pungent zeal against the idolatries of Jehoram a disqualifying disposition of soul? and if it were, was mere music the happiest mode of inviting the divine influences? Yet after this manner, I think, it has been commonly explained. Singing was, and is, so frequently joined with the sound of musical instruments in the East, that I apprehend no one will think it strange, that I suppose the minstrel sung as well as played in the presence of Elisha: and when it is recollected that their songs are very frequently extemporaneous, it is natural to suppose the prophet required something to be sung, suitable both to his character and to the occasion.—HARMER.

Ver. 16. And he said, Thus saith the LORD, Make this valley full of ditches: 17. For thus saith the LORD, Ye shall not see wind, neither shall ye see rain; yet that valley shall be filled with water, that ye may drink, both ye, and your cattle, and your beasts.

A shower of rain in the East, is often preceded by a whirlwind, which darkens the sky with immense clouds of sand from the loose surface of the desert. To this common phenomenon, the prophet alludes, in his direction to the king of Israel, who was marching with his army against Moab, and was ready to perish in the wilderness for want of water: "Thus saith the Lord, Make this valley full of ditches. For thus saith the Lord, Ye shall not see wind, neither shall ye see rain; yet that valley shall be filled with water, that ye may drink, both ye, and your cattle, and your beasts." If a squall had not commonly preceded rain, the prophet would not have said, Ye shall not see wind.—PAXTON.

Ver. 19. And ye shall smite every fenced city, and every choice city, and shall fell every good tree, and stop all wells of water, and mar every good piece of land with stones.

Commentators take no pains, that I know of, to account for that part of the punishment of the king of Moab's rebellion, *Ye shall mar every good piece of land with stones;* though it does not appear very easy to conceive how this was to be done to any purpose, and indeed without giving as much trouble, or more, to Israel, to gather these stones, and carry them on their lands, as to the Moabites to gather them up again, and carry them off. I would therefore propose it to the learned to consider, whether we may not understand this of Israel's doing that nationally, and as victors, which was done by private persons very frequently in these countries in ancient times, by way of revenge, and which is mentioned in some of the old Roman laws, I think, cited by Egmont and Heyman, who, speaking of the contentions and vindictive temper of the Arabs, tell us, they were ignorant, however, whether they still retained the method of revenge formerly common among them, and which is called σκοπελισμος, mentioned in *Lib. ff. Digest. de extraord. criminib.* which contains the following account. *In provincia Arabiâ*, &c. That is, "in the province of Arabia, there is a crime called σκοπελισμος, or fixing of stones; it being a frequent practice among them, to place stones in the grounds of those with whom they are at variance as a warning, that any person who dares to till that field, should infallibly be slain, by the contrivance of those who placed the stones there." This malicious practice, they add, is thought to have had its origin in Arabia Petræa. If the Israelites, as victors, who could prescribe what laws they thought proper to the conquered, placed such stones in the best grounds of the Moabites, as interdicting them from tillage, on pain of their owners being destroyed, they without much trouble effectually marred such fields as long as their power over Moab lasted, which had before this continued some time, and by the suppression of this rebellion might be supposed to continue long. As it was an ancient practice in these countries, might it not be supposed to be as ancient as the times of Elisha, and that he referred to it? Perhaps *the time to cast away stones*, and *the time to gather stones together*, mentioned by the royal preacher, Eccles. iii. 5, is to be understood in like manner, of giving to nations with which there had been contests, the marks of perfect reconciliation, or continuing upon them some tokens of displeasure and resentment. If we suppose the latter part of the verse is exegetical of the former, which the learned know is very common in the Hebrew poetry, it will better agree with this explanation, than with that which supposes, that the *casting away of stones*, means the *demolishing of houses, and the gathering them together*, the *collecting them for building;* since the casting away of stones answers to embracing, in the latter part of the verse, not to the refraining from embracing. It may be supposed indeed that a transposition might be intended, such a one as appears in the eighth verse; but it is to be observed, that the eighth verse finishes this catalogue of different seasons, and there is no transposition in the other particulars. To which may be added, that this explanation makes the casting away of stones, and gathering them together, of the fifth verse, precisely the same thing with the breaking down and building up of the third: the supposing a greater variety of thought here will be no dishonour to the royal poet.—HARMER.

Ver. 27. Then he took his eldest son, that should have reigned in his stead, and offered him *for* a burnt-offering upon the wall. And there was great indignation against Israel: And they departed from him, and returned to *their own* land.

In great distress, several persons, like the king of Moab, have offered their own children upon their altars. Eusebius and Lactantius mention several nations who used these sacrifices. Cesar says of the Gauls, that when they were afflicted with grievous diseases, or in time of war, or great danger, they either offered men for sacrifices, or vowed they would offer them. For they imagined God would not be appeased, unless the life of a man were rendered for the life of a man.—BURDER.

CHAPTER IV.

Ver. 1. Now there cried a certain woman of the wives of the sons of the prophets unto Elisha, saying, Thy servant my husband is dead; and thou knowest that thy servant did fear the LORD: and the creditor is come to take unto him my two sons to be bondmen.

This was a case in which the Hebrews had such power over their children, that they might sell them to pay what they owed; and the creditor might force them to it. Huet thinks that from the Jews this custom was propagated to the Athenians, and from them to the Romans.—BURDER.

The Jewish law looked upon children as the proper goods of their parents, who had power to sell them for seven years, as their creditors had to compel them to do it, in order to pay their debts; and from the Jews this custom was propagated to the Athenians, and from them to the Romans. The Romans indeed had the most absolute control over their children. By the decree of Romulus they could imprison, beat, kill, or sell them for slaves; but Numa Pompilius first moderated this, and the emperor Diocletian made a law, that no free persons should be sold upon account of debt. The ancient Athenians had the like jurisdiction over their children, but Solon reformed this cruel custom; as indeed it seemed a little hard, that the children of a poor man, who have no manner of inheritance left them, should be compelled into slavery, in order to pay their deceased father's debts; and yet this was the custom, as appears from this passage, wherein the prophet does not pretend to reprove the creditor, but only puts the woman in a method to pay him.—STACKHOUSE.

Ver. 10. Let us make a little chamber, I pray thee, on the wall; and let us set for him there a bed, and a table, and a stool, and a candlestick; and it shall be when he cometh to us, that he shall turn in thither.

To most of these houses a smaller one is annexed, which sometimes rises one story higher than the house; and at other times it consists of one or two rooms only, and a terrace; while others that are built, as they frequently are, over the porch or gateway, have, if we except the ground-floor, which they want, all the conveniences that belong to the house itself. They communicate with the gallery of the house by a door, and by another door, which opens immediately from a privy stair, with the porch or street, without giving the least disturbance to the house. In these back-houses, as they may be called, strangers are usually lodged and entertained; and to them likewise the men are wont to retire from the hurry and noise of their families, to be more at leisure for meditation and amusement; and at other times, they are converted into wardrobes and magazines. This annexed building is in the holy scriptures named (עליה) *aliah;* and we have reason to believe, that the little chamber which the Shunamite built for the prophet Elisha, whither, as the text informs us, he retired at his pleasure, without breaking in upon the private affairs of the family, or being in his turn interrupted by them in his devotions, was a structure of this kind. It is thus described by the Shunamite herself: "Let us make a little chamber, I pray thee, on the wall; and let us set for him there a bed, and a table, and a stool, and a candlestick; and it shall be, that when he cometh to us, that he shall turn in thither. The internal communication of this chamber with the Shunamite's house, may be inferred, as well from its being built upon the wall which enclosed her dwelling, as from her having so free access to it, and at the second invitation, standing in the door, while the prophet announced to her the birth of a son.—PAXTON.

They did not then among the ancients sit universally as the modern inhabitants of the East now do, on the ground or floor, on some mat or carpet; they sometimes sat on thrones, or seats more or less like our chairs, often raised so high as to require a footstool. But it was considered as a piece of splendour, and offered as a mark of particular respect. It was doubtless for this reason that a seat of this kind was placed, along with some other furniture, in the chamber which the devout Shunamitess prepared for the prophet Elisha, 2 Kings iv. 10, which our version has very unhappily translated a *stool*, by which we mean the least honourable kind of seat in an apartment; whereas the original word meant to express her respect for the prophet by the kind of seat she prepared for him. The word is כסא *kissa*, the same that is commonly translated *throne*. The candlestick is, in like manner, to be considered as a piece of furniture, suitable to a room that was magnificently fitted up, according to the mode of those times, a light being kept burning all night long in such apartments. So a lamp was kept burning all night, in the apartment in which Dr. Richard Chandler slept, in the house of a Jew, who was vice-consul for the English nation, at the place where he first landed, when he proposed to visit the curious ruins of Asia Minor. Further, we are told by De la Roque, in the account given of some French gentlemen's going to Arabia Felix, page 43, 44, that they found only mats in the house of the captain of the port of Aden, where they were honourably received, which were to serve them for beds, chairs, and tables: so in the evening they brought them tapers without candlesticks, the want of which they were to supply as well as they could, which was but indifferently.—HARMER.

Ver. 20. And when he had taken him, and brought him to his mother, he sat on her knees till noon, and *then* died.

The heat, in eastern countries, is often so excessive, as to prove fatal to many people. To this cause is to be attributed the death of the child at Shunem, in the days of Elisha. Egmont and Heyman (vol. i. p. 333) found the air about Jericho extremely hot, and say that it destroyed several persons the year before they were there. The army of King Baldwin IV. suffered considerably from this circumstance near Tiberias. The heat at the time was so unusually great, that as many died by that as by the sword. After the battle, in their return to their former encampment, a certain ecclesiastic, of some distinction in the church and in the army, not being able to bear the vehemence of the heat, was carried in a litter, but expired under mount Tabor.—(Harmer.) The child of the Shunamite here spoken of, had gone to the reapers in the field, (v. 12,) where he suddenly complained of headache, (v. 19,) and soon after died. Probably he had a sun-stroke, which was very natural in the great heat which prevails in those countries at harvest-time. Monconys, speaking of himself, says, "Towards evening, the sun had struck with such force on my head, that I was seized with a violent fever, and obliged to go to bed." Werli Von Zember relates the same of himself and his companions. "After we had been obliged to remain a long time in this court, exposed to the heat of the sun, we almost all became ill, with dreadful headache, giddiness, and fever, so that some even lost their senses." Von Stammer says, "When we came into the desert, between the mountains, I was seized wtih a very severe inflammatory fever: I was unable to remain any longer on the camel, but was forced to lie down on the ground, and became so ill, that they scarcely thought I was alive."—ROSENMULLER.

Ver. 22. And she called unto her husband, and said, Send me, I pray thee, one of the young men, and one of the asses, that I may run to the man of God, and come again.

The saddle ass retaining the characteristic perverseness of his kind, is apt to become restiff under his rider, which, in cases that require haste, renders it necessary to accelerate his speed by means of the goad. This, according to Pococke, is commonly done for persons of rank by a servant on foot. This method of travelling seems to have been quite common in Palestine; for the Shunamite's husband expressed neither surprise nor hesitation, when she asked for "one of the young men, and one of the asses, that she might run to the man of God." The acknowledged inability of the ass to carry both the servant and his mistress, the custom of having an attendant, whose business it was to drive the animal forward, and the eager impatience of the bereaved mother, which required the utmost speed, sufficiently prove that she rode the ass herself, while the servant attended her on foot, or mounted perhaps on a camel, which persons in his condition often used on a journey. "And she said to her servant, Drive, (or lead,) and go forward; slack not riding for me, except I bid thee." Put him to the utmost speed, without regarding the inconveniences I may suffer. The pronoun *thy*, it has been thought, is very improperly supplied in our translation, as it leads one to suppose that the servant himself was the rider. But although no mention is made of the circumstance, it is not perfectly clear that the servant was not mounted on this occasion. The phrase, cease not to ride, (לרכב) or cease not riding, naturally suggests that he was mounted. The ass which the Shunamite saddled, was a strong animal, as the name given him by the inspired writer imports; and if we may believe Maillet, the asses in Egypt and Syria have nothing of that indolence and heaviness which are natural to ours; therefore, if the servant was not furnished with a camel, or was not a running footman by profession, of which we have no proof, the ass must have soon left him far behind, and rendered his services of no use. When the inspired writer says the Shunamite *saddled her ass*, he uses a phrase which often occurs in the sacred writings, and seems to comprehend any requisite for the convenience of the rider and the proper management of the animal.—PAXTON.

Ver. 23. And he said, Wherefore wilt thou go to him to-day? *it is* neither new moon nor sabbath. And she said, *It shall be* well.

Peter Della Vallé assures us, that it is now customary in Arabia to begin their journeys at the new moon. When the Shunamite proposed going to Elisha, her husband dissuaded her by observing that it was neither new moon nor sabbath.—Burder.

Ver. 24. Then she saddled an ass, and said to her servant, Drive, and go forward; slack not *thy* riding for me, except I bid thee.

See on Judg. 10. 4.

Where travellers are not so numerous as in caravans, their appearance differs a good deal from that of those who journey among us. To see a person mounted and attended by a servant on foot, would seem odd to us; and it would be much more so to see that servant driving the beast before him, or goading it along: yet these are eastern modes. So Dr. Pococke, in his account of Egypt, tells us that the man, the husband, I suppose he means, always leads the lady's ass there; and if she has a servant, he goes on one side: but the ass-driver follows the man, goads on the beast, and when he is to turn, directs his head with a pole. The Shunamite, when she went to the prophet, did not desire so much attendance, only requesting her husband to send her an ass, and its driver, to whom she said, "Drive, and go forward, slack not thy riding for me, except I bid thee." 2 Kings iv. 24. It appears from the eastern manner of the women's riding on asses, that the word is rightly translated *drive*, rather than *lead;* and this account of Dr. Pococke will also explain why she did not desire two asses, one for herself, and the other for the servant that attended her. Solomon might refer to the same, when he says, "I have seen servants upon horses, and princes walking as servants upon the earth," Eccl. x. 7. My reader, however, will meet with a more exact illustration of this passage in its proper place.—Harmer.

Ver. 29. Then he said to Gehazi, Gird up thy loins, and take my staff in thy hand, and go thy way: if thou meet any man, salute him not; and if any salute thee, answer him not again: and lay my staff upon the face of the child.

The rod, or staff, in the scriptures, is mentioned as an emblem of authority over inanimate nature, over man, and the diseases to which he was subject, and also as an instrument of correction for the wicked. The Lord commanded Moses, "Take thy rod, and stretch out thy hand upon the waters of Egypt, upon their streams, upon their rivers, and upon their ponds, and upon all their pools of water, that they may become blood." The magicians of the heathen king had their rods also, by which they performed many wonderful things. I see no reason to doubt that the staff of Elisha was of the same nature, and for the same purposes, as the "rod of God," which did such wonders in the hands of Moses. Gehazi, though he had the emblem of his master's office, could not perform the miracle: and no wonder; for the moment before he received the command from Elisha, he showed his evil disposition to the mother of the dead child; for when she caught the prophet "by the feet," to state her case, he went "near to thrust her away."

The *orou-mulle-pirambu* (*i. e.* a cane with one knot) is believed to possess miraculous power, whether in the hand of a magician or a private individual. It is about the size of the middle finger, and must have only one knot in its whole length. "A man bitten by a serpent will be assuredly cured, if the cane or rod be placed upon him: nay, should he be dead, it will restore him to life!" "Yes, sir, the man who has such a stick need fear neither serpents nor evil spirits." A native gentleman known to me has the staff of his umbrella made of one of these rods, and great satisfaction and comfort has he in this his constant companion. "The sun cannot smite him by day, neither the moon by night; the serpents and wild beasts move off swiftly; and the evil spirits dare not come near to him."—Roberts.

This command to salute no one, naturally calls to mind that which Jesus gave to the seventy disciples. Luke x. 4, *Salute no one by the way.* It is explained by the custom of the East. Serious and taciturn as the natives of the East usually are, they grow talkative when they meet an acquaintance and salute him. This custom has come from Asia with the Arabs, and spread over the north coast of Africa. A modern traveller relates the reciprocal salutations with which those are received who return with the caravans. "People go a great way to meet them; as soon as they are perceived, the questioning and salutation begin, and continue with the repetition of the same phrases: 'How do you do? God be praised that you are come in peace! God give you peace! How fares it with you?' The higher the rank of the person returning home, the longer does the salutation last."—Burder.

Elisha's enjoining Gehazi not to salute any that he met, or to return the salutation of such, evidently expresses the haste he would have him make to recover the child, and bring him back to life. For the salutations of the East often take up a long time. "The manner of salutation, as now practised by the people of Egypt, is not less ancient. The ordinary way of saluting people, when at a distance, is bringing the hand down to the knees, and then carrying it to the stomach. Marking their devotedness to a person by holding down the hand; as they do their affection by their after raising it up to their heart. When they come close together afterward, they take each other by the hand in token of friendship. What is very pleasant, is to see the countrypeople reciprocally clapping each other's hands very smartly, twenty or thirty times together, in meeting, without saying any thing more than *Salamat aiche halcom;* that is to say, *How do you do? I wish you good health.* It this form of complimenting must be acknowledged to be simple, it must be admitted to be very affectionate. Perhaps it marks out a better disposition of heart than all the studied phrases which are in use among us, and which politeness almost always makes use of at the expense of sincerity. After this first compliment many other friendly questions are asked, about the health of the family, mentioning each of the children distinctly, whose names they know," &c. If the forms of salutation among the ancient Jewish peasants took up as much time as those of the modern Egyptians that belong to that rank of life, it is no wonder the prophet commanded his servant to abstain from saluting those he might meet with, when sent to recover the child of the Shunamitess to life: they that have attributed this order to haste have done right; but they ought to have shown the tediousness of eastern compliments.—Harmer.

Salutations at meeting, are not less common in the East than in the countries of Europe; but are generally confined to those of their own nation, or religious party. When the Arabs salute each other, it is generally in these terms: *Salum aleikum*, peace be with you; laying, as they utter the words, the right hand on the heart. The answer is, *Aleikum essalum*, with you be peace; to which aged people are inclined to add, "and the mercy and blessing of God." The Mohammedans of Egypt and Syria never salute a Christian in these terms; they content themselves with saying to them, "Good-day to you," or, "Friend, how do you do?" Niebuhr's statement is confirmed by Mr. Bruce, who says, that some Arabs, to whom he gave the salam, or salutation of peace, either made no reply, or expressed their astonishment at his impudence in using such freedom. Thus it appears, that the Orientals have two kinds of salutations; one for strangers, and the other for their own countrymen, or persons of their own religious profession. The Jews in the days of our Lord, seem to have generally observed the same custom; they would not address the usual compliment of "Peace be to you," to either heathens or publicans; the publicans of the Jewish nations would use it to their countrymen who were publicans, but not to heathens; though the more rigid Jews refused to do it either to publicans or heathens. Our Lord required his disciples to lay aside the moroseness of Jews, and cherish a benevolent disposition towards all around them: "If ye salute your brethren only, what do ye more than others? Do not even the publicans so?" They were bound by the same authority, to embrace their brethren in Christ with a special affection, yet they were to look upon every man as a brother, to feel a sincere and cordial interest in his welfare, and to express, at meeting, their benevolence, in language corresponding with the feelings of their hearts. This precept is not inconsistent with the charge which the prophet Elisha gave to his servant Gehazi, not to salute any man he met, nor return his salutation; for he wished him to make all the haste in his power to restore he child of the Shunamite, who had laid him under so many obligations. The manners of the country rendered Elisha's precautions particularly proper and necessary, as the salutations of the East often take up a long time.—PAXTON.

Ver. 39. And one went out into the field to gather herbs, and found a wild vine, and gathered thereof wild gourds his lapful, and came and shred *them* into the pot of pottage: for they knew *them* not.

Their common pottage in the East is made by cutting their meat into little pieces, and boiling them with rice, flour, and parsley, all which is afterward poured into a proper vessel. This in their language is called Shoorba. Parsley is used in this Shoorba, and a great many other herbs, in their cookery. These are not always gathered out of gardens, even by those that live in a more settled way than the Arabs: for Russel, after having given a long account of the garden stuff at Aleppo, tells us, that besides those from culture, the fields afford bugloss, mallow, asparagus, which they use as potherbs, besides some others which they use in salads. This is the more extraordinary, as they have such a number of gardens about Aleppo, and will take off all wonder from the story of one's going into the fields, to gather herbs, to put into the pottage of the sons of the prophets, 2 Kings iv. 39, in a time when indeed Ahab, and doubtless some others, had gardens of herbs; but it is not to be supposed things were so brought under culture as in later times.—HARMER.

Ver. 39. And one went out into the field to gather herbs, and found a wild vine, and gathered thereof wild gourds his lapful, and came and shred *them* into the pot of pottage: for they knew *them* not. 40. So they poured out for the men to eat: and it came to pass, as they were eating of the pottage, that they cried out and said, O *thou* man of God, *there is* death in the pot: and they could not eat *thereof*.

In the vales near Jordan, in the neighbourhood of Jericho, not far from the Dead Sea, is found, growing in great abundance, the vine of Sodom, a plant, from the fields around that devoted city, which produces grapes as bitter as gall, and wine as deadly as the poison of a serpent. This deleterious fruit is mentioned by Moses in terms which fully justify the assertion: "For their vine is of the vine of Sodom, and of the fields of Gomorrah; their grapes are grapes of gall, their clusters are bitter, their wine is the poison of dragons, and the cruel venom of asps." It is probably the wild vine, a species of gourd, which produces the *coloquintida*, a fruit so excessively bitter that it cannot be eaten; and when given in medicine, proves a purgative so powerful, as to be frequently followed by excoriation of the vessels, and hemorrhage. It seems therefore to have been early, and not without reason, considered as poisonous. It was of this wild vine the sons of the prophets ate; and its instantaneous effect, together with their knowledge of its violent action, easily accounts for their alarm. Another species of wild vine, but of a milder character, which grows in Palestine, near the highways and hedges, is the *Labrusca*. Its fruit is a very small grape, which becomes black when ripe; but often it does not ripen at all. These are the wild grapes to which the prophet compares the inhabitants of Jerusalem, and men of Judah: "And he looked that it should bring forth grapes, and it brought forth wild grapes." They are also the sour grapes to which another inspired prophet alludes, when he predicts the destroying judgments that were coming upon his rebellious people: "In those days they shall say no more, The fathers have eaten a sour grape, and the children's teeth are set on edge.—Every man that eateth the sour grape, his teeth shall be set on edge."—PAXTON.

Ver. 42. And there came a man from Baal-shalisha, and brought the man of God bread of the first-fruits, twenty loaves of barley, and full ears of corn in the husk thereof: and he said, Give unto the people, that they may eat.

See on 1 Kings 14. 3.

The margin has, instead of in the husk, "in his scrip or garment." I think the marginal reading is better than the text. In what was the man to carry the ears of corn? In what may be seen every day—"in his scrip or garment." In the mantle (like a scarf) the natives carry many things: thus the petty merchant takes some of his ware, and the traveller his rice.—ROBERTS.

CHAPTER V.

Ver. 6. And he brought the letter to the king of Israel, saying, Now, when this letter is come unto thee, behold, I have *therewith* sent Naaman my servant to thee, that thou mayest recover him of his leprosy.

Schultens observes that, "the right understanding of this passage depends on the custom of expelling lepers, and other infectious persons, from camps or cities, and reproachfully driving them into solitary places; and that when these persons were cleansed and readmitted into cities or camps, they were said to be *recollecti*, *gathered again* from their leprosy, and again received into that society from which they had been cut off."—BURDER.

Ver. 11. But Naaman was wroth, and went away, and said, Behold, I thought, He will surely come out to me, and stand and call on the name of the LORD his God, and strike his hand over the place, and recover the leper.

Naaman thought that the prophet would effect his cure sooner and more certainly if he touched him with his hand, and, as it were, invigorated him by an effusion of his healing power. Then, as in later times, those who effected such miraculous cures were accustomed to touch the patient. Thus, Jan Mocquet says, "when the sick were brought to the sheik of the Arabian Santons, (religious,) he touched either their right arm or foot, or stroked their breast and forehead, after money had been offered him." Among all nations superstition considers the touch as the principal requisite of a miraculous cure. Hans Egede, in his *Greenland Mission*, says, "A Greenland man and woman requested me to blow upon their sick child, or to lay my hands upon it: they hoped that it would recover. Many more sick Greenlanders begged the same favour from me, because they considered me as a prophet, whom they believed able to cure the sick in a supernatural manner."—ROSENMULLER.

When they consulted a prophet, the eastern modes required a present; and they might think it was right rather to present him with eatables than other things, because it frequently happened that they were detained there some time, waiting the answer of GOD, during which time hospitality would require the prophet to ask them to take some repast with him. And as the prophet would naturally treat them with some regard to their quality, they doubtless did then, as the Egyptians do now, proportion their presents to their avowed rank and number of attendants. The present of Jeroboam's wife was that of a woman in affluent circumstances, though it by no means determined her to be a princess. That made to the prophet Samuel, was the present of a person that expected to be treated like a man in low life; how great then must be his surprise, first to be treated with distinguished honour in a large company, and then to be anointed king over Israel!

But though this seems to have been the original ground of presenting common eatables to persons who were visited at their own houses, I would by no means be understood to affirm they have always kept to this, and presented eatables when they expected to stay with them and take some repast, and other things when they did not. Accuracy is not to be expected in such matters: the observation, however, naturally accounts for the rise of this sort of presents. In other cases, the presents that anciently were, and of late have wont to be made to personages eminent for study and piety, were large sums of money, or vestments: so the present that a Syrian nobleman would have made to an Israelitish prophet, with whom he did not expect to stay any time, or indeed to enter in his house, "Behold, I thought, He will certainly come out to me, and stand, and call on the name of the Lord his God, and strike his hand over the place, and recover the leper," consisted of ten talents of silver, and six thousand pieces of gold, and ten changes of raiment. It is needless to mention the pecuniary gratifications that have been given to men of learning in the East in later times; but as to vestments, D'Herbelot tells us, that Bokhteri, an illustrious poet of Cufah, in the ninth century, had so many presents made him in the course of his life, that at his death he was found possessed of a hundred complete suits of clothes, two hundred shirts, and five hundred turbans.—HARMER.

Ver. 9. So Naaman came with his horses and with his chariot, and stood at the door of the house of Elisha. 10. And Elisha sent a messenger unto him, saying, Go and wash in Jordan seven times, and thy flesh shall come again to thee, and thou shalt be clean.

Elisha's not appearing to receive the Syrian general, is ascribed by some to the retired course of life which the prophets led; but then, why did he see him, and enter into conversation with him, when he returned from his cure? I should rather think, that it was not misbecoming the prophet, upon this occasion, to take some state upon him, and to support the character and dignity of a prophet of the most high God; especially, since this might be a means to raise the honour of his religion and ministry, and to give Naaman a righter idea of his miraculous cure, when he found that it was neither by the prayer nor presence of the prophet, but by the divine power and goodness, that it was effected.—STACKHOUSE.

Ver. 18. In this thing the LORD pardon thy servant, *that* when my master goeth into the house of Rimmon to worship there, and he leaneth on my hand, and I bow myself in the house of Rimmon; when I bow down myself in the house of Rimmon, the LORD pardon thy servant in this thing.

It is amusing to see full-grown men, as they walk along the road, like schoolboys at home, leaning on each other's hands. Those who are weak, or sick, lean on another's shoulder. It is also a mark of friendship to lean on the shoulder of a companion.—ROBERTS.

Ver. 21. So Gehazi followed after Naaman. And when Naaman saw *him* running after him, he lighted down from the chariot to meet him, and said, *Is* all well?

The *alighting* of those that ride is considered in the East as an expression of *deep respect;* so Dr. Pococke tells us, that they are wont to descend from their asses in Egypt, when they come near some tombs there, and that Christians and Jews are obliged to submit to this. So Hasselquist tells Linnæus, in one of his letters to him, that Christians were obliged to alight from their asses in Egypt, when they met with commanders of the soldiers there. This he complains of as a bitter indignity; but they that received the compliment, without doubt, required it as a most pleasing piece of respect. Achsah's and Abigail's alighting, were without doubt then intended as expressions of reverence: but is it to be imagined, that Naaman's alighting from his chariot, when Gehazi ran after him, arose from the same principle? If it did, there was a mighty change in this haughty Syrian after his cure. That *he* should pay such a reverence to a servant of the prophet must appear very surprising, yet we can hardly think the historian would have mentioned this circumstance *so very distinctly* in any other view. Rebecca's alighting from the camel on which she rode, when Isaac came to meet her, is by no means any proof that the considering this as an expression of reverence, is a modern thing in the East; it, on the contrary, strongly reminds one of D'Arvieux's account of a bride's *throwing herself at the feet of the bridegroom* when solemnly presented to him, which obtains among the Arabs.

We met a Turk, says Dr. Richard Chandler, in his Asiatic travels, "a person of distinction, as appeared from his turban. He was on horseback with a single attendant. Our janizary and Armenians respectfully alighted, and made him a profound obeisance, the former kissing the rim of his garment." So Niebuhr tells us, that at Kahira, Grand Cairo, "the Jews and Christians, who, it may be, alighted at first through fear or respect, when a Mohammedan with a great train on horseback met them, are now obliged to pay this compliment to above thirty of the principal people of that city. When these appear in public, they always cause a domestic to go before to give notice to the Jews and Greeks, and even the Europeans that they meet with, to get off their asses as soon as possible, and they are qualified on occasion to force them with a great club, which they always carry in their hands."—HARMER.

Ver. 21. So Gehazi followed after Naaman: and when Naaman saw *him* running after him, he lighted down from the chariot to meet him, and said, *Is* all well? [Heb. margin, Is there *peace?*] 22. And he said, All *is* well.

I never read this passage without fancying a Malabar man running after the chariot, and on being met by Naaman, making a most profound bow, and uttering the word *selam, peace*—the word used on this occasion, and still in use among millions in the East.—CALLAWAY.

Ver. 27. The leprosy therefore of Naaman shall cleave unto thee, and unto thy seed for ever. And he went out from his presence a leper *as white* as snow.

This was said by Elisha to Gehazi, because he ran after Naaman, (who had been cured of his leprosy) and said, his master had sent him to take "a talent of silver, and two changes of garments," and because he actually took possession of them. There is an account in the Hindoo book, called *Seythu-Purāna*, of a leper who went to Ramiseram to bathe, in order to be cured of his complaint. He performed the required ceremonies, but the priests refused his offerings. At last a Bramin came: in the moment of temptation he took the money, and immediately the leprosy of the pilgrim took possession of his body! This complaint is believed to come in consequence of great sin, and therefore no one likes to receive any reward or present from a person infected with leprosy.

There are many children born white, though their parents are quite black. These are not lepers, but albinos; and are the same as the white negroes of Africa. To see a man of that kind almost naked, and walking among the natives, has an unpleasant effect on the mind, and leads a person to suspect that all has not been right. Their skin has generally a slight tinge of red, their hair is light, their eyes are weak; and when they walk in the sun, they hang down their heads. The natives do not consider this a disease, but a BIRTH, *i. e.* produced by the sins of a former birth. It is believed to be a great misfortune to have a child of that description, and there is reason to believe that many of them are destroyed. The parents of such an infant believe ruin will come to their family; and the poor object, if spared, has generally a miserable existence. His name, in Tamul, is *Pāndan:* and this is an epithet assigned to those, also, who are NOT white, for the purpose of making them angry. The general name for Europeans in the East is *Pranky,* (which is a corruption of the word Frank.) Hence these white Hindoos are, by way of contempt, called *Pranky!* Should a man who is going to transact important business, meet one of them on the road, it will be considered a very bad sign, and he will not enter into the transaction till another day. Should a person who is giving a feast have a relation of that description, he will invite him, but the guests will not look upon him with pleasure. Women have a great aversion to them, and yet they sometimes marry them; and if they have children, they seldom take after the father. I have only heard of two white Hindoo females; which leads me to suspect that such infants are generally destroyed at the birth; as, were they allowed to grow up, no one would marry them.—Roberts.

CHAPTER VI.

Ver. 12. And one of his servants said, None, my lord, O king: but Elisha, the prophet that *is* in Israel, telleth the king of Israel the words that thou speakest in thy bedchamber.

It is not to be doubted, but that Naaman, upon his return from Samaria, spread the fame of Elisha so much in the court of Syria, that some of the great men there might have a curiosity to make a further inquiry concerning him; and being informed by several of his miraculous works, they might thence conclude that he could tell the greatest secrets, as well as perform such works as were related of him; and that therefore, in all probability, he was the person who gave the king of Israel intelligence of all the schemes that had been attempted to entrap him. —Stackhouse.

Ver. 15. And when the servant of the man of God was risen early, and gone forth, behold, a host compassed the city, both with horses and chariots. And his servant said unto him, Alas, my master! how shall we do?
16. And he answered, Fear not; for they that *be* with us *are* more than they that *be* with them.
17. And Elisha prayed, and said, Lord, I pray thee, open his eyes, that he may see. And the Lord opened the eyes of the young man: and he saw, and, behold, the mountain *was* full of horses and chariots of fire round about Elisha.

This young man, it is supposable, had been but a little while with his master, no longer than since Gehazi's dismission, and therefore perhaps had not yet seen any great experiments of his power to work miracles; or if he had, the great and imminent danger he thought his master in, (for in all probability he had learned from the people of the town, that this vast body of men were come to apprehend him only,) might well be allowed to raise his fear, and shake his faith.

It must be allowed that angels, whether they be purely spiritual, or (as others think) clothed with some material form, cannot be seen by mortal eyes; and therefore as Elisha himself, without a peculiar vouchsafement of God, could not discern the heavenly host, which, at this time, encamped about him; so he requests of God, that, for the removal of his fears, and the confirmation of his faith, his servant might be indulged the same privilege: nor does it seem unlikely, that, from such accounts as these, that have descended by tradition, that notion among the Greeks, of a certain *mist*, which intercepts the sight of their gods from the *ken* of human eyes, might at first borrow its original.—Stackhouse.

Ver. 25. And there was a great famine in Samaria: and, behold, they besieged it, until an ass's head was *sold* for fourscore *pieces* of silver, and the fourth part of a cab of doves' dung for five *pieces* of silver.

The Tamul translation for "doves' dung," is "*doves' grain*:" which is known in the East by the name of *Kāramanne-piru*. Dr. Boothroyd translates it "a cab of vetches," which amounts to about the same thing. Bochart, Dr. Clarke, and many others, believe it to have been *pulse*. The Orientals are exceeding fond of eating leguminous grains, when parched. I have often eaten the pulse which pigeons are so fond of, and have found it very wholesome, either in puddings or soup; (Lev. xx ii. 14, Ruth ii. 14, 2 Sam. xvii. 28;) and it is surprising to see what a great distance they will travel on only that food and water. It was therefore in consequence of the famine, that this, their favourite, and generally very cheap, sustenance, was so dear. Of what use would "a cab of doves' dung" be unto them? Some say, in explanation, it was good for manure! What were they to live upon till the manure had produced the grain?—Roberts.

Among the Jews, the ass was considered as an unclean animal, because it neither divides the hoof nor chews the cud. It could neither be used as food, nor offered in sacrifice. The firstling of an ass, like those of camels, horses, and other unclean animals, was to be redeemed with the sacrifice of a lamb, or deprived of life. In cases of extreme want, however, this law was disregarded; for when the Syrian armies besieged Samaria, the inhabitants were so reduced, that "an ass's head was sold for fourscore pieces of silver." Some writers, however, contend, that the term חמור *hamor* does not signify an ass, in this passage, but is the same as חומר *homer*, a certain measure of grain. But this view of the passage cannot be admitted. We know what is meant by the head of an ass; but the head of a homer, or measure of wheat or barley, is quite unintelligible. Nor could the sacred writer say with propriety, that the city was suffering by a "great famine," while a homer of grain was sold for eighty pieces of silver; for in the next chapter he informs us, that, after the flight of the Syrians, and provisions of every kind, by the sudden return of plenty, were reduced to the lowest price, "a measure of fine flour (which is the thirtieth part of a homer) was sold for a shekel, and two measures of barley for a shekel, in the gate of Samaria." Besides, had the historian intended a measure of corn, he would not have said indefinitely, a homer was sold for eighty pieces of silver; but a homer of wheat, or of barley, or of oats, which are not of the same value. The prophet accordingly says, in the beginning of the next chapter, "a measure of fine flour shall be sold for a shekel, and two measures of barley for a shekel:" And John, in the book of Revelation; "a measure of wheat for a penny, and three measures of barley for a penny." Our translators, therefore, have taken a just view of this text, and given a correct version. It is reasonable to suppose, that the ass was not the last to suffer in the siege of Samaria. Hardly treated in times of peace and abundance, he must have been left to shift for himself in such circumstances, in a place where the hunger of the inhabitants compelled them to devour every green thing; and have rapidly sunk into a poor and wretched condition. How great must that famine have been, and how dreadful the distress to which the people were reduced, when they gave three times the price of the live animal, for that part of him which could yield them at any time only a few pounds of dry and unpalatable food, but when emaciated by famine, only a few morsels of carrion. Extreme must have been the sufferings which extinguished the powerful influence of religious principle, and natural aversion to a species of food so disagreeable and pernicious; and not only prevailed upon them to use it, but even to devour it with greediness.—Paxton.

The royal city of Samaria was so severely distressed, when a certain king of Syria besieged it, that we are told, *an ass's head then sold for fourscore pieces of silver, and the fourth part of a cab of doves' dung for five pieces:* this last article has been thought to be so unfit for food, that it has been very commonly imagined, I think, that a species of pulse was meant by that term; nevertheless, I cannot but think it much the most probable, that proper doves' dung was meant by the prophetic historian, since, though it can hardly be imagined, it was bought directly for food, it might be bought for the purpose of more speedily raising a supply of certain esculent vegetables, and in greater quantities which must have been a matter of great consequence to the Israelites, shut up so straitly in Samaria. Had the kali of the scriptures been meant, how came it to pass that the common word was not made use of? Josephus and the Septuagint suppose that proper doves' dung was meant, and the following considerations may make their sentiment appear far from improbable.

All allow that melons are a most refreshing food, in those hot countries. And Chardin says, "melons are served up at the tables of the luxurious almost all the year; but the proper season lasts four months, at which time they are eaten by the common people. They hardly eat any thing but melons and cucumbers at that time." He adds, "that during these four melon months, they are brought in such quantities to Ispahan, that he believed more were eaten in that city in one day, than in all France in a month." On the other hand, he tells us, in another volume, that they have a multitude of dove-houses in Persia, which they keep up more for their dung than any thing else. This being the substance with which they manure their melon-beds, and which makes them so good and so large. Now if melons were half so much in request in those days in Judea, as they are now in Persia, it might be natural enough to express the great scarcity of provisions there, by observing an ass's head, which, according to their law was an unclean animal, sold for fourscore pieces of silver; and a small quantity of that dung that was most useful to quicken vegetation, as well as to increase those productions of the earth which were so desirable in those hot climates, that a small quantity, I say, of that substance should, in such circumstances, be sold for five such pieces. At least it is probable thus the Septuagint and Josephus understood the passage, if we should think it incredible that melons were in very common use in the days of Joram king of Israel. Josephus, in particular, says this dung was purchased for its salt, which can hardly mean to be used, by means of some preparation, as table salt, but as containing salt proper for manuring the earth. The prophet Elisha, in that very age, put salt into a spring of water, to express the imparting to it the quality of making the land watered by it fruitful, which land had been before barren, (2 Kings ii. 19—22,) to which event Josephus could be no stranger. It has been objected to this interpretation: that if the doves' dung was for *manure*, (for this interpretation is not a new one, but wanted to be better illustrated,) that there could be no room for growing any kind of vegetable food within the walls of a royal city, when besieged; but has any one a right to take this for granted? when it is known that there is a good deal of ground unbuilt upon *now* in the royal cities of the East; that Naboth had a vineyard in Jezreel, a place of royal residence a few years before; that Samaria was a new-built city; and that in the time of distress, every void place might naturally be made use of to raise a species of food, that with due cultivation, in our climate, is brought to perfection, from the time of its sowing, in four months, and at the same time is highly refreshing. When we reflect on these things, the supposition appears not at all improbable. We do not know when the siege commenced, or how long it continued; that of Jerusalem, in the time of Zedekiah, lasted a year and a half; but the time that this dung was purchased at so dear a rate, we may believe was early in the spring, for then they begin to raise melons at Aleppo, and as they were then so oppressed with want, it is probable that it was not long after that they were delivered.

This explanation will appear less improbable, if we recollect the account already given, of the siege of Damietta, where some of the more delicate Egyptians pined to death, according to Vitriaco, though they had a sufficiency of corn, for the want of the food they were used to, pumpions, &c. The Israelites might be willing then, had their stores been more abundant than they were found to have been, to add what they could to them, and especially of such grateful eatables as melons, and such like.—Harmer.

Formerly great attention was paid to the nurturing and rearing of these birds, (pigeons,) their dung bringing in a yearly income, from the produce of one pigeon-house alone, of nearly two hundred tomauns. Among other uses to which the small remains of this manure is applied, it is laid on the melon-beds of Ispahan; and hence the great reputation of the melon of that district for its unequalled flavour. Another use of the dung in older times was to extract saltpetre, for the purpose of making gunpowder; which, two centuries ago, had only just been put into the Persian list of warlike ammunition.—Sir R. K. Porter.

The dung of pigeons is the dearest manure that the Persians use: and as they apply it almost entirely for the rearing of melons, it is probably on that account that the melons of Ispahan are so much finer than those of other cities. The revenue of a pigeon-house is about a hundred tomauns per annum; and the great value of this dung, which rears a fruit that is indispensable to the existence of the natives during the great heats of summer, will probably throw some light upon that passage in scripture, where, in the famine of Samaria, the fourth part of a cab of doves' dung was sold for five pieces of silver.—Morier.

Ver. 32. But Elisha sat in his house, and the elders sat with him: and *the king* sent a man from before him: but ere the messenger came to him, he said to the elders, See ye how this son of a murderer hath sent to take away my head? look, when the messenger cometh, shut the door, and hold him fast at the door: *is* not the sound of his master's feet behind him?

See on Prov. 16. 14.

This form of speech is used to denote the rapid approach of a person. When boys at school are making a great noise, or doing any thing which they ought not, some one will say, "I hear the sound of the master's feet." Are people preparing triumphal arches, (made of leaves,) or cleaning the rest-house of a great man, some of them keep saying, "Quick, quick, I hear the sound of his feet." "Alas, alas! how long you have been! do we not hear even the sound of the judge's feet?"—Roberts.

CHAPTER VII.

Ver. 10. So they came, and called unto the porter of the city; and they told them, saying, We came to the camp of the Syrians, and, behold, *there was* no man there, neither voice of man, but horses tied, and asses tied, and the tents as they *were*.

From the circumstances recorded concerning the flight of the Syrians, it appears to have been remarkably precipitate. That they were not altogether unprepared for a hasty departure may be inferred from comparing this passage with the following extract (from *Memoirs relative to Egypt*, p. 300.) "As soon as the Arabs are apprehensive of an attack, they separate into several small camps, at a great distance from each other, and tie their camels to the tents, so as to be able to move off at a moment's notice." Such a precaution is not probably peculiar to the modern Arabs, but might be adopted by the Syrian army. If this was the case, it shows with what great fear God filled their minds, that though prepared as usual for a quick march, they were not able to avail themselves of the advantage, but were constrained to leave every thing behind them as a prey to their enemies.—Burder.

Ver. 12. And the king arose in the night, and said unto his servants, I will now show you what the Syrians have done to us: They know that we *be* hungry, therefore are they gone out of the camp to hide themselves in the field, saying, When they come out of the city, we shall catch them alive, and get into the city.

In the history of the revolt of Ali Bey, we have an account of a transaction very similar to the stratagem supposed to have been practised by the Syrians. The pacha of Damascus having approached the Sea of Tiberias, found Sheik Daher encamped there; but the sheik deferring the engagement till the next morning, during the night divided his army into three parts, and left the camp with great fires blazing, all sorts of provisions, and a large quantity of spirituous liquors, giving strict orders not to hinder the enemy from taking possession of the camp, but to come down and attack just before the dawn of day. In the middle of the night, the pacha thought to surprise Sheik Daher, and marched in silence to the camp, which, to his great astonishment, he found entirely abandoned; and imagined the sheik had fled with so much precipitation, that he could not carry off the baggage and stores. The pacha thought proper to stop in the camp and refresh his soldiers. They soon fell to plunder, and drank so freely of the liquors, that, overcome with the fatigue of the day's march, and the fumes of the spirits, they were not long ere they sunk into a profound sleep. At that time two sheiks, who were watching the enemy, came silently to the camp, and Daher having repassed the Sea of Tiberias, meeting them, they all rushed into the camp, and fell upon the sleeping foe, eight thousand of whom they butchered on the spot; and the pacha, with the remainder of the troops, escaped with much difficulty to Damascus, leaving all their baggage in the hands of the victorious Daher.—PAXTON.

Ver. 15. And they went after them unto Jordan; and, lo, all the way *was* full of garments and vessels, which the Syrians had cast away in their haste: and the messengers returned, and told the king.

The flight of the Syrians, in the reign of Jehoram, king of Israel, was produced by a panic, which so completely unmanned them, that, says the sacred historian, "all the way was full of garments and vessels, which the Syrians had cast away in their haste." The flight of Saladin's army, which was defeated by Baldwin IV. near Gaza, in the time of the crusades, was marked with similar circumstances of consternation and terror. To flee with greater expedition, they threw away their arms and clothes, their coats of mail, their greaves, and other pieces of armour, and abandoned their baggage, and fled from their pursuers, almost in a state of complete nudity.—PAXTON.

Ver. 18. And it came to pass, as the man of God had spoken to the king, saying, Two measures of barley for a shekel, and a measure of fine flour for a shekel, shall be to-morrow, about this time, in the gate of Samaria.

In our rides we usually went out of town at the *Derwazeh Shah Abdul Azeem*, or the gate leading to the village of Shah Abdul Azeem, where a market was held every morning, particularly of horses, mules, asses, and camels. At about sunrise, the owners of the animals assemble and exhibit them for sale. But, besides, here were sellers of all sorts of goods, in temporary shops and tents; and this, perhaps, will explain the custom alluded to in 2 Kings vii. 18, of the sale of barley and flour in the gate of Samaria. (Morier.)—BURDER.

CHAPTER VIII.

Ver. 9. So Hazael went to meet him, and took a present with him, even of every good thing of Damascus, forty camels' burden, and came and stood before him, and said, Thy son Ben-hadad, king of Syria, hath sent me to thee, saying, Shall I recover of this disease?

See on Gen. 43. 25.

These animals, when not loaded beyond their strength, submit with great patience. "When they are to be loaded, they bend their knees at the voice of their driver: but if they delay doing so, they are struck with a stick, or their knees forced downward, and then, as if constrained and groaning after their way, they bend their knees, put their bellies against the ground, and remain in that posture till, after having been loaded, they are commanded to rise."—BURDER.

The Syrian prince, on this occasion, in which he felt a particular interest, no doubt sent Elisha a present corresponding with his rank and magnificence; but it can scarcely be supposed that so many camels were required to carry it, or that the king would send, as a Jewish writer supposes he did, so great a quantity of provisions to one man. The meaning of this passage certainly is, that the various articles of which the present consisted, according to the modern custom of oriental courts, were carried on a number of camels for the sake of state, and that not fewer than forty were employed in the cavalcade. That these camels were not fully laden, must be evident from this, that the common load of a Turkman's camel is eight hundred pounds weight; and consequently, thirty-two thousand pounds weight is the proper loading of forty camels; "if they were only of the Arab breed, twenty thousand pounds weight was their proper loading;" a present, as Mr. Harmer justly remarks, too enormous to be sent by any one person to another.—PAXTON.

Ver. 12. And Hazael said, Why weepeth my lord? And he answered, Because I know the evil that thou wilt do unto the children of Israel: their strongholds wilt thou set on fire, and their young men wilt thou slay with the sword, and wilt dash their children, and rip up their women with child.

This piece of cruelty has in some instances been practised on men. "Soon after Djezzer bought the Pashalik of Damascus, coming to gather the tribute of Jerusalem and the neighbourhood, he pitched his camp at the village of Yenin, overlooking the plain of Esdraelon. An Arab woman came to complain to him that one of his soldiers had drank her milk, and refused to pay her. He went always armed with a sabre, yategan, and pistols, which, when he ate, lay by his side. Taking up his yategan, 'Follow me,' he said, 'and point out the man.' She did so, and he bade her be sure, as a mistake would cost her her life. Having asked the soldier if the accusation were true, and he denying it, he ripped him up, and the milk immediately poured out of his bleeding stomach. Seeing thus that the woman was right, he gave her two sequins, and sent her away. The soldier he left dead on the ground." (Turner.) The same piece of cruelty was practised by Timour. It is said that Mohammed the Second ripped up fourteen of his pages to find a melon.—BURDER.

Ver. 15. And it came to pass on the morrow, that he took a thick cloth, and dipped *it* in water, and spread *it* on his face, so that he died; and Hazael reigned in his stead.

An English proverb says, "Give a dog an ill name, and it will hang him:" much in the spirit of this proverb has been the general treatment of the character of Hazael, who, because he calls himself "a dog," has been treated with great indignity. Certainly, Hazael can be no favourite character with any upright mind; yet perhaps it is but justice to suggest what may render his *murder* of his master, King Benhadad, by means of a cloth dipped in water, at least dubious, without calling it well-intended on his part. In reading the history, (2 Kings viii. 15,) it is nothing less than natural to suppose, that Hazael must have had, professedly at least, some fair pretence, some appearance of propriety in the action; or why did not those in attendance on their sovereign prevent his proceedings? Was Hazael the *only* person present, or in waiting on the sick king? It is by no means likely; in fact, it is scarcely supposable; but if we conceive that Hazael offered to the king either a kind of remedy usual in the disorder, which nevertheless failed to cure him; or an assistance, of which he took advantage to murder his master; then we reduce his behaviour to plausibility, and to the custom of the country in such diseases. Observe also, the text does not say expressly he *did* kill him; but "he took a thick cloth, and dipped it in water, and spread it over the king's face, (or person,) and he died." It is usually said, he was *chilled to death;* but on reading the following extracts, we shall probably admit that this is an English notion, resulting from our climate and manners, &c. applied to an eastern disease, and to a country wherein both climate and manners are essentially different. If it be said Hazael stifled the king by means of the cloth spread over his face, it might be so; but we should do well to remark, that the easterns are accustomed to sleep with their faces covered; that Hazael hardly spread it over the king's face only; that it does not appear the king was asleep; he might therefore have removed the cloth, had he thought proper; and that whatever the *cloth* was, it was certainly employed, and the whole action was managed, in a way to prevent suspicion. Let us now hear Mr. Bruce:

"This fever prevailed in Abyssinia in all low grounds and plains, in the neighbourhood of all rivers which run in valleys; it is really a malignant tertian, which, however, has so many forms and modes of intermission, that it is impossible for one not of the faculty to describe it. It is not in all places equally dangerous; but on the banks and neighbourhood of Tacazzé, it is particularly fatal. The valley where the river runs is very low and sultry, being full of large trees. It does not prevail in high grounds or mountains, or in places much exposed to the air. This fever is called NEDAD, or *burning;* it begins always with a shivering and headache, a heavy eye, and an inclination to vomit;

a violent heat follows, which leaves little intermission, and ends generally in death the *third* or *fifth* day. In the last stage of the distemper, the belly swells to an enormous size, or sometimes immediately after death, and the body, within an instant, smells most insupportably; to prevent which, they bury the corpse *immediately after the breath is out*, and often within the hour. The face has a remarkable yellow appearance, with a blackish cast, as in the last stage of a dropsy, or the atrophy. This fever begins immediately with the sunshine after the first rains; that is, while there are intervals of rain and sunshine; it ceases upon the earth being thoroughly soaked, in July and August, and begins again in September; but now, at the beginning of November, it ceases everywhere. Masuah is very unwholesome, as, indeed, is the whole coast of the Red Sea, from Suez to Babelmandel; but more especially between the tropics. Violent fevers, called there NEDAD, make the principal figure in this fatal list, and generally determine the *third* day in death. If the patient survives till the fifth day, he very often recovers, by drinking water only, and throwing a quantity of cold water upon him, even in his bed, where he is permitted to lie, without attempting to make him dry, or to change his bed, till another deluge adds to the first." (Bruce's *Travels*,) vol. iii. p. 33.

Do not these extracts render it, in some degree, probable, that Hazael, besides the thick cloth soaked in water, added other *chilling* remedies? in doing which he did no more than is customary in this disease, the *nedad;* and, if this kind of fever, or one allied to it, were Benhadad's disease, Hazael might honestly spread a refreshing covering over him. Not expecting his exaltation to royalty so instantaneously, he might be loyal as yet, though his ambition soon found opportunity to be otherwise. The circumstances of the rapid approaches of death, and of immediate burial after death, seem very favourable to Hazael's instantly seating himself on the throne: especially if Benhadad had no son, &c. of proper age to be his successor.—TAYLOR IN CALMET.

CHAPTER IX.

Ver. 2. And when thou comest thither, look out there Jehu the son of Jehoshaphat, the son of Nimshi, and go in, and make him arise up from among his brethren, and carry him to an inner chamber: 3. Then take the box of oil, and pour *it* on his head, and say, Thus saith the LORD, I have anointed thee king over Israel. Then open the door, and flee, and tarry not.

The fortified cities in Canaan, as in some other countries, were commonly strengthened with a citadel, to which the inhabitants fled when they found it impossible to defend the place. The whole inhabitants of Thebes, unable to resist the repeated and furious assaults of Abimelech, retired into one of those towers, and bid defiance to his rage: "But there was a strong tower within the city, and thither fled all the men and women, and all they of the city, and shut it to them, and gat them up to the top of the tower." The extraordinary strength of this tower, and the various means of defence which were accumulated within its narrow walls, may be inferred from the violence of Abimelech's attack, and its fatal issue: "And Abimelech came unto the tower, and fought against it, and went hard unto the door of the tower, to burn it with fire. And a certain woman cast a piece of a millstone upon Abimelech's head, and all to break his scull." The city of Shechem had a tower of the same kind, into which the people retired, when the same usurper took it, and sowed it with salt. These strong towers which were built within a fortified city, were commonly placed on an eminence, to which they ascended by a flight of steps. Such was the situation of the city of David, a strong tower, upon a high eminence at Jerusalem; and the manner of entrance, as described by the sacred writer: "But the gate of the fountain repaired Shallum, unto the stairs that go down from the city of David." It is extremely probable, that Ramoth Gilead, a frontier town belonging to the ten tribes, and in the time of Jehu in their possession, was strengthened by one of these inner towers, built on an eminence, with an approach of this nature. If this conjecture be well founded, it throws light upon a very obscure passage, where the manner in which Jehu was proclaimed king of Israel, is described. His associates were no sooner informed that the prophet had anointed him king over the ten tribes, than "they hasted and took every man his garment, and put it under him on the top of the stairs, and blew with trumpets, saying, Jehu is king." Hence the stairs were not those within the tower, by which they ascended to the top; but those by which they ascended the hill, or rising ground on which the tower stood; the top of the stair will then mean the landing-place in the area before the door of the tower, and by consequence the most public place in the whole city. As it was the custom of those days to inaugurate and proclaim their kings in the most public places, no spot can be imagined more proper for such a ceremony, than the top of the steps, that is, the most elevated part of the hill, upon which stood the castle of Ramoth Gilead, in the court of which, numbers of people might be assembled, waiting the result of a council of war which was sitting at the time, deliberating on the best method of defending the city against the Syrians, in the absence of their sovereign.—PAXTON.

Ver. 10. And the dogs shall eat Jezebel in the portion of Jezreel, and *there shall be* none to bury *her*. And he opened the door and fled.

The Abbe Poiret, in his travels through Barbary, tells us, that the severest punishment among the Arabs is to be cut to pieces and thrown to the dogs. "After this the queen of Mira, concerning whom so many surprising stories had been told of her poisoning the water by drugs and enchantments, was, notwithstanding the known partiality of this king for the fair sex, ordered to be hewn in pieces by the soldiers, and her body given to the dogs." (Bruce.)—BURDER.

Ver. 13. Then they hasted, and took every man his garment, and put *it* under him on the top of the stairs, and blew with trumpets, saying, Jehu is king.

They laid down their garments instead of carpets. "The use of carpets was common in the East in the remoter ages. The kings of Persia always walked upon carpets in their palaces. Xenophon reproaches the degenerate Persians of his time, that they placed their couches upon carpets, to repose more at their ease. The spreading of garments in the street before persons to whom it was intended to show particular honour, was an ancient and very general custom. Thus the people spread their clothes in the way before our Saviour, Matthew xxi. 8, where some also strewed branches. In the Agamemnon of Æschylus, the hypocritical Clytemnestra commands the maids to spread out carpets before her returning husband, that, on descending from his chariot, he may place his foot on a "purple-covered path." We also find this custom among the Romans. When Cato of Utica left the Macedonian army, where he had become legionary tribune, the soldiers spread their clothes in the way. (Plutarch's *Life of Cato.*) The hanging out of carpets, and strewing of flowers and branches, in solemn processions, among us, is a remnant of the ancient custom.—ROSENMULLER.

Ver. 28. And his servants carried him in a chariot to Jerusalem, and buried him in his sepulchre with his fathers in the city of David.

What does this funeral chariot, which was carried by men, mean? What we may see in the vicinity of a large town every day of our lives. This chariot, or *thandeki*, (as it is called in Tamul,) is about six feet long, three feet broad, and in the centre about four feet in height. The shape is various, and the following is more common than any other. The drapery is of white, or scarlet cloth; and the whole is covered with garlands of flowers. The servants then carry it on their shoulders to the place of sepulture, or burning.—ROBERTS. (*See Engraving.*)

Ver. 30. And when Jehu was come to Jezreel, Jezebel heard *of it;* and she painted her face,

and tired her head, and looked out at a window.
31. And as Jehu entered in at the gate, she
said, *Had* Zimri peace, who slew his master?
32. And he lifted up his face to the window,
and said, Who *is* on my side? who? And
there looked out to him two *or* three eunuchs.
33. And he said, Throw her down.

She stained her eyes with stibium or antimony. This is a custom in Asiatic countries to the present day. "The Persians differ as much from us in their notions of beauty as they do in those of taste. A large, soft, and languishing black eye, with them, constitutes the perfection of beauty. It is chiefly on this account that the women use the powder of antimony, which, although it adds to the vivacity of the eye, throws a kind of voluptuous languor over it, which makes it appear, if I may use the expression, dissolving in bliss. The Persian women have a curious custom of making their eyebrows meet; and if this charm be denied them, they paint the forehead with a kind of preparation made for that purpose." (E. S. Waring's Tour to Sheeraz.)—BURDER.

In the evening we accompanied them on shore, and took some coffee in the house of the consul, where we were introduced to the ladies of his family. We were amused by seeing his wife, a very beautiful woman, sitting crosslegged by us upon the divan of his apartment, and smoking tobacco with a pipe six feet in length; her eyelashes, as well as those of all the other women, were tinged with a black powder made of the sulphuret of antimony, and having by no means a cleanly appearance, although considered as essential an addition to the decorations of a woman of rank in Syria, as her ear-rings, or the golden cinctures of her ankles. Dark streaks were also pencilled, from the corners of her eyes, along the temples. This curious practice instantly brought to our recollections certain passages of scripture, wherein mention is made of a custom among oriental women of "*putting the eyes in painting;*" and which our English translators of the Bible, unable to reconcile with their notions of a female toilet, have rendered "*painting the face.*"—CLARKE.

The court of eastern houses is for the most part surrounded with a cloister, over which, when the house has a number of stories, a gallery is erected of the same dimensions with the cloister, having a balustrade, or else a piece of carved or latticed work, going round about, to prevent people from falling from it into the court. The doors of the enclosure round the house, as already mentioned, are made very small, to defend the family from the insolence and rapacity of Arabian plunderers; but the doors of the houses very large, for the purpose of admitting a copious stream of fresh air into their apartments. The windows which look in the street, are very high and narrow, and defended by lattice-work; as they are only intended to allow the cloistered inmate a peep of what is passing without, while she remains concealed behind the casement. This kind of window the ancient Hebrews called Arubah, and is the same term which they used to express those small openings, through which pigeons passed into the cavities of the rocks, or into those buildings which were raised for their reception. Thus the prophet demands: "Who are these that fly as a cloud, and as the doves (אל־ארבתיהם) *el arubothehem*, to their small or narrow windows." The word is derived from a root which signifies to lie in wait for the prey; and is very expressive of the concealed manner in which a person examines, through that kind of window, an external object. Irwin describes the windows in upper Egypt, as having the same form and dimensions; and says expressly, that one of the windows of the houses in which they lodged, and through which they looked into the street, more resembled a pigeon-hole, than any thing else. But the sacred writers mention another kind of window, which was large and airy: it was called (חלן) *halon*, and was large enough to admit a person of mature age being cast out of it; a punishment which that profligate woman Jezebel suffered by the command of Jehu, the authorized exterminator of her family. —PAXTON.

Dr. Shaw, after having observed that the jealousy of the people there admits only of one small latticed window into the street, the rest opening into their own courts, says, "It is during the celebration only of some *zeena*, as they call a public festival, that these houses and their latticed windows or balconies are left open. For this being a time of great liberty, revelling, and extravagance, each family is ambitious of adorning both the inside and outside of the houses with their richest furniture, while crowds of both sexes, dressed out in their best apparel, and laying aside all modesty and restraint, go in and out where they please. The account we have, 2 Kings ix. 30, of Jezebel's painting her face, and tiring her head, and looking out at a window, upon Jehu's public entrance into Jezreel, gives us a lively idea of an eastern lady at one of these zeenahs or solemnities."—HARMER.

Ver. 33. And he said, Throw her down. So they threw her down: and *some* of her blood was sprinkled on the wall, and on the horses: and he trode her under foot.

While the above particulars were relating, it was a shuddering glance that looked down from the open side of the Ketkhoda's saloon, on almost the very spot where the unhappy victims had breathed their last. It recalled to my remembrance a similar window, for similar purposes, at Erivan, where the governor of that place used to dispose of his malefactors the moment sentence was pronounced. And while listening to the hideous details of a sort of punishment so common in the East, I could not but recall similar descriptions in ancient writers on these countries, which showed how old had been the practice of taking offenders to a height, and casting them headlong, sometimes from a rock, at others, from high battlements, and often from a window which commanded a sufficient steep. We have a dreadful picture of this most tremendous mode of punishment in the second book of Kings.—SIR R. K. PORTER.

CHAPTER X.

Ver. 1. And Ahab had seventy sons in Samaria.

To those who are unaccustomed to the effects of polygamy and concubinage, this appears a very remarkable circumstance. In Homer, old King Priam is represented as having fifty sons and twelve daughters. Artaxerxes Mnemon, king of Persia, had, by his concubines, who amounted to three hundred and sixty, not less than one hundred and fifteen sons, besides three by his queen. "Muley Abdallah, who was emperor of Morocco in 1720, is said, by his four wives, and the many thousand women he had in his seraglio during his long reign, to have had seven hundred sons, able to mount a horse; but the number of his daughters is not known." (Stewart's *Journey to Mequinez.*)—BURDER.

Ver. 6. Then he wrote a letter the second time to them, saying, If ye *be* mine, and *if* ye will hearken unto my voice, take ye the heads of the men your master's sons, and come to me to Jezreel by to-morrow this time. (Now the king's sons, *being* seventy persons, *were* with the great men of the city, which brought them up.)

The rich hire a *dedeh*, or wet-nurse, for their children. If a boy, the father appoints a steady man, from the age of two years, to be his *laleh*, who, I conjecture, must stand in the same capacity as the bringers-up of children mentioned in the catastrophe of Ahab's sons. But if it be a daughter, she has a *gees sefeed*, or white head, attached to her for the same purpose as the *laleh*. (Morier.)—BURDER.

Ver. 8. And there came a messenger, and told him, saying, They have brought the heads of the king's sons. And he said, Lay ye them in two heaps at the entering in of the gate until the morning.

During this fight, ten tomauns were given for every head of the enemy that was brought to the prince: and it has been known to occur, after the combat was over, that prisoners have been put to death in cold blood, in order that the heads, which are immediately despatched to the king, and deposited in heaps at the palace-gate, might make a more considerable show.—Morier.

Arrived at the palace of the pacha, inhabited by the dey, the first object that struck our eyes were six bleeding heads, ranged along before the entrance; and as if this dreadful sight were not sufficient of itself to harrow up the soul, it was still further aggravated by the necessity of stepping over them, in order to pass into the court. They were the heads of some turbulent agas, who had dared to murmur against the dey. (Pananti's *Narrative of a Residence in Algiers.*) "The pacha of Diarbech has sent to Constantinople a circumstantial report of his expedition against the rebels of Mardin. This report has been accompanied by a thousand heads, severed from the vanquished. These sanguinary trophies have been exposed, as usual, at the gate of the seraglio. The Tartar who brought them has obtained a pelisse of honour; presents have also been sent to the pacha." (*Literary Panorama*, vol. ix. p. 289.) A pyramid of heads, of a certain number of feet diameter, is sometimes exacted in Persia; and so indifferent are the executioners to the distresses of others, that they will select a head of peculiar appearance, and long beard, to grace the summit of it. Sir J. Malcolm says, that "when Timour stormed Ispahan, it was impossible to count the slain, but an account was taken of seventy thousand heads, which were heaped in pyramids, as monuments of savage revenge." "Three weeks before our arrival at Cattaro, they (the Montenegrines) had some skirmishes with the Turks, and had brought home several of their heads, which were added to the heap before the bishop's house." (Dodwell's *Tour through Greece.*)—Burder.

Ver. 12. And he arose and departed, and came to Samaria. *And* as he *was* at the shearing-house in the way, 13. Jehu met with the brethren of Ahaziah, king of Judah, and said, Who *are* ye? And they answered, We *are* the brethren of Ahaziah; and we go down to salute the children of the king, and the children of the queen. 14. And he said, Take them alive. And they took them alive, and slew them at the pit of the shearing-house, *even* two and forty men: neither left he any of them.

Our translators suppose, that the edifice at which Jehu slew the brethren of Ahaziah, king of Judah, was destined to the sole purpose of shearing of sheep; but as I apprehend, the term in the original is ambiguous, which is accordingly literally translated in the margin, *the house of shepherd's binding*, it might be better to use some less determinate word; as the word, I am ready to believe, may signify the binding sheep for shearing, the binding up their fleeces, after those fleeces taken from the sheep beforehand were washed; or the binding the sheep for the purpose of milking. Whether it was erected for all three purposes, or if only for one of them, then for which of the three, it may be very difficult precisely to say. A pit near such a building must be useful in any of the three cases, for the affording water for the sheep that were detained there for some time, in the first and third case, to drink; and for the washing the wool in the other. If the intention of the historian had been to describe it as the place appropriated to the shearing of sheep, it would have been natural for him to have used the word that precisely expresses that operation, not such a general term as the *house of binding*. All know that sheep must be bound, or at least forcibly held, in order to be shorn; and it appears in the Travels of Dr. Richard Chandler in the Lesser Asia, that "the shepherds there, sitting at the mouth of the pen, were wont to seize on the ewes and she-goats, each by the hind leg, as they pressed forward, to milk them;" which seizing them, sufficiently shows they must be held, shackled, or somehow bound, when milked.

In another observation I have taken notice of the readiness of great men, in the East, to repose themselves, when fatigued, under the shelter of roofs of a very mean kind; the brethren, it seems, of Ahaziah anciently did the same thing. But they found no more safety in this obscure retreat, than they would have found in the palaces of either Samaria or Jezreel. The slaying them at the pit, near this place, seems to have been owing to a custom at that time, whether arising from superstition, to preserve the land from being defiled, or any other notion, does not at first sight appear; but it was, it seems, a customary thing at that time to put people to death near water, at least near where water was soon expected to flow, as appears from 1 Kings xviii. 40.—Harmer.

Ver. 15. And when he was departed thence, he lighted on Jehonadab the son of Rechab, *coming* to meet him: and he saluted him, and said to him, Is thy heart right, as my heart *is* with thy heart? And Jehonadab answered, It is. If it be, give *me* thy hand. And he gave *him* his hand; and he took him up to him into the chariot.

A very solemn method of taking an oath in the East is by joining hands, uttering at the same time a curse upon the false swearer. To this form the wise man probably alludes in that proverb: "Though hand join in hand"—though they ratify their agreement by oath—"the wicked shall not be unpunished, but the seed of the righteous shall be delivered." This form of swearing is still observed in Egypt and the vicinity; for when Mr. Bruce was at Shekh Ammer, he entreated the protection of the governor in prosecuting his journey, when the great people, who were assembled, came, and after joining hands, repeated a kind of prayer, of about two minutes long, by which they declared themselves and their children accursed, if ever they lifted up their hands against him in the tell, or field, in the desert; or in the case that he or his should fly to them for refuge, if they did not protect them at the risk of their lives, their families, and their fortunes; or, as they emphatically expressed it, to the death of the last male child among them. The inspired writer has recorded an instance of this form of swearing in the history of Jehu: "And when he was departed thence, he lighted on Jehonadab, the son of Rechab, coming to meet him, and he saluted him, and said to him, Is thy heart right, as my heart is with thy heart; and Jehonadab answered, It is. If it be, give me thy hand. And he gave him his hand, and he took him up unto him into the chariot." Another striking instance is quoted by Calmet from Ockley's history of the Saracens. Telha, just before he died, asked one of Ali's men if he belonged to the emperor of the faithful; and being informed that he did, "Give me then, said he, your hand, that I may put mine in it, and by this action renew the oath of fidelity which I have already made to Ali."—Paxton.

Deep as the reverence is with which the Orientals treat their princes, yet in some cases, a mode of treatment occurs that we are surprised at, as seeming to us of the West, too near an approach to that familiarity that takes place among equals: the taking a new elected prince by the hand, in token of acknowledging his princely character, may probably appear to us in this light. D'Herbelot, in explaining an eastern term, which, he tells us, signifies the election or auguration of a calif, the supreme head of the Mohammedans, both in civil and ecclesiastical matters, tells us, that "this ceremony consisted in stretching forth a person's hand, and taking that of him that they acknowledged for calif. This was a sort of performing homage, and swearing fealty to him." He adds, that "Khondemir, a celebrated historian, speaking of the election of Othman, the third calif after Mohammed, says, that Ali alone did not present his hand to him, and that upon that occasion Abdurahman, who had by compromise made the election, said to him, 'Ali! he who violates his word is the first person that is injured by so doing;' upon hearing of which words, Ali stretched out his hand, and acknowledged Othman as calif."

How much less solemn and expressive of reverence is this, than the manner of paying homage and swearing fealty at the coronation of our princes; to say nothing of the adoration that is practised in the Romish church, upon the election of their great ecclesiastic! It may however serve to illustrate what we read concerning Jehonadab, the head of an Arab tribe that lived in, and consequently was in some measure subject to, the kingdom of Israel. "Jehonadab came to meet Jehu, and he saluted him; and Jehu said to Jehonadab, Is thy heart right as my heart is with thy heart? and Jehonadab answered, It is. And he said, If it be, give me thy hand: and he gave him his hand, and he took him up to him into the chariot." This giving him the hand appears not to have been the expression of private friendship; but the solemn acknowledgment of him as king over Israel. Our translators seem to have supposed, by their way of expressing matters, that Jehu saluted, or blessed Jehonadab, and Bishop Patrick thought it was plain that it ought so to be understood; but I cannot but think it most natural to understand the words as signifying, that Jehonadab came to meet Jehu as then king of Israel; and to compliment him on being acknowledged king of the country in which he dwelt; not that this newly anointed prince first saluted him. This would not have been in character. So when Jacob was introduced to Pharaoh, he is said to have blessed Pharaoh, not Pharaoh Jacob, Gen. xlvii. 7. The words therefore should have been translated, with a slight variation, after some such manner as this, "He lighted on Jehonadab, the son of Rechab, coming to meet him, and he, Jehonadab, saluted him, and he, Jehu, said unto him, Is thy heart," &c.—HARMER.

CHAPTER XI.

Ver. 2. But Jehosheba, the daughter of king Joram, sister of Ahaziah, took Joash the son of Ahaziah, and stole him from among the king's sons which were slain; and they hid him, *even* him and his nurse, in the bedchamber, from Athaliah, so that he was not slain.

A bedchamber does not, according to the usage of the East, mean a lodging room, but a repository for beds. Chardin says, "In the East beds are not raised from the ground with posts, a canopy, and curtains; people lie on the ground. In the evening they spread out a mattress or two of cotton, very light, of which they have several in great houses, against they should have occasion, and a room on purpose for them." From hence it appears that it was in a chamber of beds that Joash was concealed.—HARMER.

Ver. 12. And he brought forth the king's son, and put the crown upon him, and *gave him* the testimony: and they made him king, and anointed him; and they clapped their hands, and said, God save the king.

The way by which females in the East express their joy, is by gently applying one of their hands to their mouths. This custom appears to be very ancient, and seems to be referred to in several places of scripture. Pitts, describing the joy with which the leaders of their sacred caravans are received in the several towns of Barbary through which they pass, says, "This Emir Hagge, into whatever town he comes, is received with a great deal of joy, because he is going about so religious a work. The women get upon the tops of the houses to view the parade, where they keep striking their forefingers on their lips softly as fast as they can, making a joyful noise all the while." The sacred writers suppose two different methods of expressing joy by a quick motion of the hand: the clapping of the *hands*, and that of one *hand* only, though these are confounded in our translation. The former of these methods obtained anciently, as an expression of malignant joy; but other words, which our version translates clapping the hands, signify, the applying of only one hand somewhere with softness, in testimony of a joy of a more agreeable kind. Thus in 2 Kings xi. 12, and Psalm xlvii. 1, it should be rendered in the singular, *Clap your hand*, and as the word implies gentleness, it may allude to such an application of the hand to the mouth as has now been recited.—BURDER.

Ver. 14. And when she looked, behold, the king stood by a pillar, as the manner *was*, and the princes and the trumpeters by the king; and all the people of the land rejoiced, and blew with trumpets: and Athaliah rent her clothes, and cried, Treason, treason!

The Orientals looked upon a seat by a pillar or column as a particular mark of respect. In the Iliad, Homer places Ulysses on a lofty throne, by a pillar: and in the Odyssey, he more than once alludes to the same custom. The kings of Israel were, for the same reason, placed at their coronation, or on days of public festivity, by a pillar in the house of the Lord. Joash, the king of Judah, stood by a pillar when he was admitted to the throne of his ancestors; and Josiah, one of his successors, when he made a covenant before the Lord.—PAXTON.

CHAPTER XII.

Ver. 9. But Jehoiada the priest took a chest, and bored a hole in the lid of it, and set it beside the altar, on the right side as one cometh into the house of the LORD: and the priests that kept the door put therein all the money that was brought into the house of the LORD.

See on 1 Kings 18. 33.

Ver. 10. And it was *so*, when they saw that *there was* much money in the chest, that the king's scribe and the high-priest came up, and they put up in bags, and told the money that was found in the house of the LORD.

It appears to have been usual in the East for money to be put into bags, which, being ascertained as to the exact sum deposited in each, were sealed, and probably labelled, and thus passed currently. Instances of this kind may be traced in the scriptures, at least so far as that money was thus conveyed, and also thus delivered, from superior to inferior officers, for distribution: as in the passage referred to in this article. Major Rennel in giving an abstract of the History of Tobit, says, "we find him again at Nineveh, from whence he despatches his son Tobias to Rages by way of Ecbatana, for the money. At the latter place, he marries his kinswoman Sara, and sends a messenger on to Rages. The mode of keeping and delivering the money was exactly as at present in the East. Gabriel, who kept the money in trust, 'brought forth bags, which were sealed up, and gave them to him,' and received in return the handwriting or acknowledgment which Tobias had taken care to require of his father before he left Nineveh. The money, we learn, was left in *trust*, or as a *deposite*, and not on *usury*, and, as it may be concluded, with Tobit's *seal* on the bags. In the East, in the present times, a bag of money passes (for some time at least) currently from hand to hand, under the authority of a banker's seal, without any examination of its contents."—BURDER.

CHAPTER XIII.

Ver. 7. Neither did he leave of the people to Jehoahaz but fifty horsemen, and ten chariots, and ten thousand footmen; for the king of Syria had destroyed them, and had made them like the dust by thrashing.

In modern Turkey, the custom of treading out the corn by oxen is still practised. This is a much quicker way than our method of beating out the corn with the flail, but less cleanly; for, as it is performed in the open air, upon any round level plat of ground, daubed over with cow-dung, to prevent as much as possible the earth, sand, or gravel, from rising, a great quantity of them all, notwithstanding these precautions, must unavoidably be taken up with the grain; at the same time the straw, which is their only fodder, is by this means shattered to pieces. To this circumstance the sacred historian alludes, with great force and propriety, in his brief description of the wretched state to which the kingdom of the ten tribes had been reduced by the arms of Hazael king of Syria: "Neither did he leave of the people to Jehoahaz but fifty horsemen, and ten chariots, and ten thousand footmen; for the king of Syria had destroyed them, and had made them like the dust by thrashing."—PAXTON.

Ver. 17. And he said, Open the window eastward

and he opened *it*. Then Elisha said, Shoot: and he shot. And he said, The arrow of the LORD's deliverance, and the arrow of deliverance from Syria; for thou shalt smite the Syrians in Aphek till thou have consumed *them*.

It was an ancient custom to shoot an arrow, or cast a spear, into the country which an army intended to invade. Justin says, that as soon as Alexander the Great had arrived on the coasts of Ionia, he threw a dart into the country of the Persians. The dart, spear, or arrow, thus thrown, was an emblem of the commencement of hostilities. Virgil represents Turnus as giving the signal of attack by throwing a spear.

> Ecquis erit mecum, O Juvenes, qui primus in hostem?
> En, ait, et jaculum intorquens emittit in auras.
> Principium pugnæ; et campo sese arduus infert.
>
> Who first, he cried, with me the foe will dare?
> Then hurl'd a dart, the signal of the war.—(PITT.)

Servius, in his note upon this place, shows that it was a custom to proclaim war in this way. The *pater patratus*, or chief of the Feciales, a sort of heralds, went to the confines of the enemy's country; and, after some solemnities, said, with a loud voice, "I wage war with you, for such and such reasons;" and then threw in a spear. It was then the business of the parties thus defied, or warned, to take the subject into consideration; and if they did not, within thirty days, come to some accommodation, the war was begun.—BURDER.

Ver. 21. And it came to pass, as they were burying a man, that, behold, they spied a band *of men*; and they cast the man into the sepulchre of Elisha: and when the man was let down, and touched the bones of Elisha, he revived, and stood up on his feet.

With us, the poorest people have their coffins; if the relations cannot afford them, the parish is at the expense. In the East, on the contrary, they are not at all made use of in our times: Turks and Christians, Thevenot assures us, agree in this. The ancient Jews probably buried their dead in the same manner: neither was the body of our Lord, it seems, put into a coffin: nor that of Elisha, whose bones were *touched* by the corpse that was let down a little after into his sepulchre, (2 Kings xiii. 21.) It is no objection to this account, that the widow of Nain's son is represented as carried forth to be buried in a Σορος, or *bier*, for the present inhabitants of the Levant, who are well known to lay their dead in the earth unenclosed, carry them frequently out to burial in a kind of coffin: so Russel in particular describes the bier used by the Turks at Aleppo as a kind of coffin, much in the form of ours, only the lid rises with a ledge in the middle. Christians, indeed, that same author tells us, are carried to the grave in an open bier: but as the most common kind of bier there very much resembles our coffins, that used by the people of Nain might very possibly be of the same kind, in which case the word Σορος was very proper.—HARMER.

CHAPTER XIV.

Ver. 9. And Jehoash the king of Israel sent to Amaziah king of Judah, saying, The thistle that *was* in Lebanon sent to the cedar that *was* in Lebanon, saying, Give thy daughter to my son to wife: and there passed by a wild beast that *was* in Lebanon, and trode down the thistle.

We have here another beautiful instance of the way in which the ancients conveyed instruction or reproof in parables, apologues, or riddles. Jehoash, the king of Israel, the author of the parable, compares himself to a cedar: and Amaziah, the king of Judah, to a thistle. It would no doubt be very annoying to Amaziah to be represented by a thistle! and his opponent by a cedar. Some years ago, two magistrates, who were much superior to their predecessors, in reference to the way in which they had discharged their duties, were appointed to take charge of separate districts. The natives, as usual, did not speak plainly as to their merits, but under "the similitude of a parable." One of the districts was very famous for the banyan tree, the fruit of which is only eaten by the flying fox, birds, and monkeys. The people, therefore, to show how much better their present magistrate was than the former, said, "Ah! the banyan of our country is now giving the fruit of the palmirah." Those of the other district (*where the palmirah was exceedingly plentiful*) said of their magistrate, "Have you not heard that our palmirah is now giving *mangoes?*" Some men are always known by the name of certain trees. Thus, a person who is tall, and stoops a little, is called the cocoa-nut tree, and he who has long legs and arms, is called the banyan, which spreads its arms, and lets fall its supporters to the ground. It is, therefore, not very improbable that Jehoash was known by the name of the *cedar*, and Amaziah by that of the *thistle*.—ROBERTS.

CHAPTER XV.

Ver. 28. And he did *that which was* evil in the sight of the LORD; he departed not from the sins of Jeroboam the son of Nebat, who made Israel to sin.

See on 2 Kings 2. 7.

CHAPTER XVI.

Ver. 3. But he walked in the way of the kings of Israel; yea, and made his son to pass through the fire, according to the abominations of the heathen, whom the LORD cast out from before the children of Israel.

Few things are more shocking to humanity than the custom of which such frequent mention is made in scripture, of making children, &c., pass through fire in honour of Moloch: a custom, the antiquity of which appears from its having been repeatedly forbidden by Moses, as Lev. xviii. 21, and at length, in chap. xx. 1—5, where the expressions are very strong, of "giving his seed to Moloch." This cruelty, one would hope, was confined to the strangers in Israel, and not adopted by any native Israelite; yet we afterward find the kings of Israel, themselves, practising this superstition, and making their children pass through the fire. This may be illustrated by an instance: There is a remarkable variation of terms in the history of Ahaz, who (2 Kings xvi. 3) is said to make "his son to pass through the fire, according to the abominations of the heathen," *i. e.* no doubt, in honour of Moloch—which. 2 Chron. xxviii. 3, is expressed by "he BURNED his children in the fire." Now, as the book of Chronicles is best understood, by being considered as a supplementary and explanatory history to the book of Kings, it is somewhat singular, that it uses by much the strongest word in this passage—for the import of *ibor* (יבער) is, generally, *to consume, to clear off:* so Psal. lxxxiii. 14, "as the fire *burneth* a wood," so Isaiah i. 31; and this variation of expression is further heightened, by the word son (who passed through) being singular in Kings, but plural (sons) in Chronicles. It seems very natural to ask, "If he *burned* his children in the fire, how could he leave any posterity to succeed him?" We know, that the Rabbins have histories of the manner of passing through the fires, or into caves of fire; and there is an account of an image, which received children into its arms, and let them drop into a fire beneath, amid the shouts of the multitude, the noise of drums, and other instruments, to drown the shrieks of the agonizing infant, and the horrors of the parents' mind. Waiving further allusion to that account at present, we think the following extract may afford a good idea, in what manner the passing *through*, or *over* fire, was anciently performed: the attentive reader will notice the particulars. "A still more astonishing instance of the superstition of the ancient Indians, in respect to the venerated fire, remains at this day in the grand annual festival holden in honour of Darma Rajah, and called the FEAST OF FIRE; in which, as in the ancient rites of Moloch, the devotees walk *barefoot over a glowing fire, extending forty feet*. It is called the feast of fire, because they then walk on that element. It lasts eighteen days, during which time, those that make a vow to keep it, must fast, abstain from women, lie on the bare ground, and walk on a brisk fire. The eighteenth day, they assemble, *on the sound of instruments; their heads crowned with flowers, the body bedaubed with saffron, and follow in cadence the figures of Darma Rajah, and Drobede, his wife, who are carried there in procession:* when they come to the fire, they *stir it,* to *animate its activity,* and take a little of the ashes, with which they rub their forehead, and when the gods have been *three times round it,* they walk either fast or slow, according to their zeal, over a very hot fire, extending to about forty feet in length. *Some carry their children in their arms,* and others lances, sabres, and standards. "The most fervent devotees walk *several times over the fire.* After the ceremony, the people press to collect some of the ashes to rub their foreheads with, and obtain from the devotees some of the flowers with which they were adorned, and which they carefully preserve." (Sonnerat's Travels, vol. i. 154.) The flowers, then, were not burned.

This extract is taken from Mr. Maurice's "history of Hindostan," and it accounts for several expressions used in scripture: such as causing children (very young perhaps) to pass *through* fire, as we see they are *carried over* the fire, by which means, though devoted, or consecrated, they were not destroyed; neither were they injured, except by being profaned. Nevertheless, it might, and probably did happen, that some of those who thus passed, were hurt or maimed in the passing, or if not immediately slain by the fire, might be burnt in this superstitious pilgrimage, in such a manner as to contract fatal diseases. Shall we suppose, then, that while *some* of the children of Ahaz passed safely over the fire, others were injured by it, and injured even to death? But this could not be the case with all of them; as besides Hezekiah, his successor, we read of "Maaseiah, the king's son," 2 Chron. xxviii. 7. Humanity would induce us to hope that the expression "*burned,*" should be taken in a milder sense than that of *slaying by fire;* and, perhaps, this idea may be justified, by remarking the use of it—Exod. iii. 2, 3, "the bush burned with fire, yet the bush was not consumed." The word, therefore, being capable of a milder, as well as of a stronger sense, like our English word, *to burn,* it is desirable, if fact would permit, to take it in the milder sense in this instance of Ahaz, and possibly in others. Nevertheless, as the custom of widows burning themselves to death, with the body of their deceased husbands, not only continues, but is daily practised in India, it contributes to justify the harsher construction of the word *to burn;* as the superstitious cruelty which can deprive women of life, may easily be thought guilty of equal barbarity in the case of children, [and moreover the drowning of children in the Ganges, as an act of dedication, is common.]—TAYLOR IN CALMET.

CHAPTER XVII.

Ver. 10. And they set them up images and groves in every high hill, and under every green tree: 11. And there they burnt incense in all the high places, as *did* the heathen whom the LORD carried away before them; and wrought wicked things to provoke the LORD to anger.

Thus did the wicked Jews imitate the heathen. The whole verse might be a description of the localities, and usages of MODERN heathenism. See their high hills; they are all famous for being the habitation of some deity. On the summit there is generally a rude representation, formed by nature, or the distorted imagination, into the likeness of a god. In going to the spot, images are set up in every direction, as so many sentinels and guides to the sacred arcana. See the *Ficus religiosa,* and numerous other trees, under which various symbols of idolatry may be seen. Fastened into the roots of one, we discover the trident of Siva: under another, an emblem of Ganesa: there we see a few faded flowers, a broken cocoa-nut, an altar, or the ashes of a recent fire.—ROBERTS.

Ver. 17. And they caused their sons and their daughters to pass through the fire.

The Tamul translation has "to pass or *tread on* the fire." Deut. xviii. 10. 2 Kings xxiii. 10. xxi. 6. Lev. xviii. 21. Jer. xxxii. 35. are rendered "*step over*" the fire. To begin with Lev. xviii. 21. "Thou shalt not let any of thy seed pass through the fire to Moloch; neither shalt thou profane the name of thy God: I am the Lord." The marginal references "to profane the name of thy God," are chap. xix. 12. "And ye shall not SWEAR by my name falsely, neither shalt thou profane the name of thy God." (See also chap. xx. 3. xxi. 6. and xxii. 2. 32. Ezek. xxxvi. 20.) Connected therefore, with passing through the fire, as mentioned in Lev. xviii. 21, and the marginal references, it is clear that the name of God was profaned by SWEARING. The Tamul translation of Lev. xviii. 21, for "pass through the fire," has "step over the fire," which alludes to the oath which is taken by STEPPING OVER THE FIRE. It is a solemn way of swearing to innocence, by first making a fire, and when stepping over to exclaim, "*I am not guilty.*" Hence the frequency of the question, (when a man denies an accusation,) "Will you step over the fire?" But so careful are the heathen in reference to fire, when they are *not* on their oath, that they will not step over it. See a traveller on his journey; does he come to a place where there has been a fire, he will not step over it, but walk round it, lest any evil should come upon him. I think it, therefore, probable, from the words, "profane the name of thy God," as mentioned in connexion with passing through the fire, and from the eastern CUSTOM, that the ancient idolaters did take a solemn oath of allegiance to their gods, or of their innocence of crime, by thus stepping over the fire.

But it is also a custom among these heathen to pass through, or rather to walk on, the fire. This is done sometimes in consequence of a vow, or from a wish to gain popularity, or to merit the favour of the gods. A fire is made on the ground, from twenty to thirty paces in length, and the individual walks on it barefoot, backwards and forwards, as many times as he may believe the nature of his circumstances require. Some say that these devotees put a composition on their feet, which prevents them from being much burnt; but I am of opinion this is not *often* the case. To walk on the fire is believed to be most acceptable to the cruel goddess Kāli, the wife of Vyravar, who was the prince of devils. When a man is sick, he vows, "O Kāli, mother, only cure me, and I will walk on fire in your holy presence." A father, for his deeply afflicted child, vows, "O Kāli, or, O Vyravar, only deliver him, and when he is fifteen years of age, he shall walk on fire in your divine presence."—ROBERTS.

Ver. 37. And the statutes, and the ordinances, and the law, and the commandment, which he wrote for you, ye shall observe to do for evermore; and ye shall not fear other gods.

The most prominent effect of heathenism on the minds of its votaries is FEAR; and no wonder; for how can they love deities guilty of such repeated acts of cruelty, injustice, falsehood, dishonesty, and impurity? Strange as it may appear, European descendants, as well as native Christians, are in danger of FEARING the gods of the heathen. There are so many traditions of their malignity and power, that it requires strength of mind, and, above all, faith in Jesus Christ, the conqueror of devils, to give a perfect victory over it. On this account the missionaries sent out by Denmark, more than one hundred years ago, (and some of their successors,) have not approved of the native Christians studying the heathen books and superstitions. This, however, has had an injurious effect, because it disqualified the members of the church to expose the errors of heathenism to the people, and also conveyed an idea of something like inadequacy in the Gospel of Christ to meet such a system. In view of this, the missionaries of the present day, and many of their converts, have, like Ezekiel, (chap. viii.) looked into this vile arcana; have dragged the monstrous transactions to light, exposed them to public gaze, and driven from the field of argument, the proud and learned Bramin.—ROBERTS.

CHAPTER XVIII.

Ver. 8. He smote the Philistines, *even* unto Gaza, and the borders thereof, from the tower of the watchmen to the fenced city.

See on Is. 14. 29.

Ver. 11. And the king of Assyria did carry away Israel unto Assyria, and put them in Halah and in Habor *by* the river of Gozan, and in the cities of the Medes.

For the following narrative, and the particular application of it, great commendation is due to the learned and intelligent traveller. After describing some sculptured figures which he had just seen, he says: "At a point something higher up than the rough gigantic forms just described, in a very precipitous cliff, there appeared to me a still more interesting piece of sculpture, though probably not of such deep antiquity. Even at so vast a height, the first glance showed it to have been a work of some age accomplished in the art: for all here was executed with the care and fine expression of the very best at Persepolis. I could not resist the impulse to examine it nearer than from the distance of the ground, and would have been glad of Queen Semiramis's stage of packs and fardels. To approach it at all was a business of difficulty and danger; however, after much scrambling and climbing, I at last got pretty far up the rock, and finding a ledge, placed myself on it as firmly as I could; but still I was further from the object of all this peril than I had hoped: yet my eyes being tolerably long-sighted, and my glass more so, I managed to copy the whole sculpture with considerable exactness. It contains fourteen figures, one of which is in the air. The first figure (to our left in facing the sculpture) carries a spear, and is in the full Median habit, like the leaders of the guards at Persepolis: his hair is in a similar fashion, and bound with a fillet. The second figure holds a bent bow in his left hand; he is in much the same dress, with the addition of a quiver slung at his back by a belt that crosses his right shoulder, and his wrists are adorned with bracelets. The third personage is of a stature much larger than any other in the group, a usual distinction of royalty in oriental description; and, from the air and attitude of the figure, I have no doubt he is meant to designate the king. The costume, excepting the beard not being quite so long, is precisely that of the regal dignity, exhibited in the basreliefs of Nakshi-Roustan, and Persepolis: a mixture of the pontiff-king, and the other sovereign personages. The robe being the ample vesture of the one, and the diadem the simple band of the other: a style of crown which appears to have been the most ancient badge of supremacy of either king or pontiff. But as persons of inferior rank also wore fillets, it seems the distinction between theirs and their sovereigns, consisted in the material or colour. For instance, the band or cydaris, which formed the essential part in the old Persian diadem, was composed of a twined substance of purple and white: and any person below the royal dignity presuming to wear those colours unsanctioned by the king, was guilty of a transgression of the law, deemed equal to high treason. The fillets of the priesthood were probably white or silver; and the circlets of kings, in general, simple gold. Bracelets are on the wrists of this personage, and he holds up his hand in a commanding or admonitory manner, the two forefingers being extended, and the two others doubled down in the palm: an action also common on the tombs at Persepolis, and other monuments just cited; his left hand grasps a bow of a different shape from that held by his officer, but exactly like the one on which the king leans in the basrelief on the tomb at Nakshi-Roustan. This bow, together with the left foot of the personage I am describing, rests on the body of a prostrate man, who lies on his back with outstretched arms, in the act of supplicating for mercy. This unhappy personage, and also the first in the string of nine which advance towards the king, are very much injured: however, enough remains of the almost defaced leader, when compared with the apparent condition of the succeeding eight, to show that the whole nine are captives. The hands of all are tied behind their backs, and the cord is very distinct which binds the neck of the one to the neck of the other, till the mark of bondage reaches to the last in the line. If it were also originally attached to the leader, the cord is now without trace there; his hands, however, are evidently in the same trammels as his followers. The second figure in the procession has his hair so close to his head, that it appears to have been shaven, and a kind of caul covers it from the top of the forehead to the middle of the head. He is dressed in a short tunic, reaching no further than the knee; a belt fastens it round the waist; his legs are bare. Behind this figure is a much older person, with a rather pointed beard and bushy hair, and a similar caul covers the top of his head. He too is habited in a short tunic, with something like the trouser, or booted appearance on the limbs which is seen on some of the figures at Persepolis. In addition to the binding of the hands, the preceding figure, and this, are fastened together by a rope round their necks, which runs onward, noosing all the remaining eight in one string. This last-described person has the great peculiarity attached to him, of the skirt of his garment being covered entirely with inscriptions in the arrow-headed character. Next follows one in a long vestment, with full hair, without the caul. Then another in a short, plain tunic, with trousers. Then succeeds a second long vestment. After him comes one in a short tunic, with naked legs, and, apparently, a perfectly bald head. He is followed by another in long vestments. But the ninth, and last in the group, who also is in the short tunic and trouser, has the singularity of wearing a prodigious high-pointed cap; his beard and hair are much ampler than any of his companions, and his face looks of a greater age. In the air, over the heads of the centre figures, appears the floating intelligence in his circle and car of sunbeams, so often remarked on the sculptures of Nakshi-Roustan and Persepolis.

"Above the head of each individual in this basrelief is a compartment with an inscription in the arrow-headed writing, most probably descriptive of the character and situation of each person. And immediately below the sculpture, are two lines in the same language, running the whole length of the group. Under these again, the excavation is continued to a considerable extent, containing eight deep and closely-written columns in the same character. From so much labour having been exerted on this part of the work, it excites more regret that so little progress has yet been made towards deciphering the character. The design of this sculpture appears to tally so well with the great event of the total conquest over Israel, by Salmaneser, king of Assyria, and the Medes, that I venture to suggest the possibility of this basrelief having been made to commemorate that final achievement. Certain circumstances attending the entire captivity of the ten tribes, which took place in a second attack on their nation, when considered, seem to confirm the conjecture into a strong probability. In turning from this account in the scriptures, to the sculpture on the rock, the one seemed clearly to explain the other. In the royal figure, I see Salmaneser, the son of the renowned Arbaces, followed by two appropriate leaders of the armies of his two dominions, Assyria and Media, carrying the spear and the bow. Himself rests on the great royal weapon of the East, revered from earliest time as the badge of supreme power—*Behold I do set my bow in the cloud.* Besides, he tramples on a prostrate foe; not one that is slain, but one who is a captive: this person not lying stretched out and motionless, but extending his arms in supplication. He must have been a king, for on none below that dignity would the haughty foot of an eastern monarch condescend to tread. Then we see approach nine captives, bound, as it were, in double bonds, in sign of a double offence. We may understand this accumulated transgression, on recollecting that on the first invasion of Israel, by Tiglath-pileser, he carried away only part of three tribes; and on the second by Salmaneser, he not only confirmed Hoshea on the throne, but spared the remaining people. Therefore, on this determined rebellion of king and people, he punishes the ingratitude of both, by putting both in the most abject bonds, and bringing away the whole of the ten tribes into captivity; or, at least, the principal of the nation; in the same manner, probably, as was afterward adopted by Nebuchadnezzar of Babylon, with regard to the inhabitants of Judea, *he carried away all from Jerusalem, and all the princes, and all the mighty men of valour, even ten thousand captives; and all the craftsmen and smiths; none remained, save the poorest sort of people of the land.* 2 *Kings* xxiv. 14.

"Besides, it may bear on our argument, to remark, that, including the prostrate monarch, there are precisely ten captives: who might be regarded as the representatives, or heads, of each tribe, beginning with the king, who, assuredly, would be considered as the chief of his: and ending with the aged figure at the end, whose high cap may have been an exaggerated representation of the mitre worn by the sacerdotal tribe of Levi: a just punishment of the priesthood at that time, which had debased itself by every species of idolatrous compliance with the whims, or rather wickedness of the people, in the adoption of pagan worship. Hence, having all walked in the statutes of the heathen, the Lord rejected Israel, and delivered them into the hand of the spoilers. Doubtless, the figure with the inscription on his garments, from the singularity of the appendage, must have been some noted personage in the history of the event; and besides, it seems to designate a striking peculiarity of the Jews, who were accustomed to write memorable sentences of old, in the form of phylacteries, on different parts of their raiment. What those may mean, which cover the garment of this figure, we have no means of explaining, till the diligent researches of the learned may be able to decipher the arrow-headed character, and then a full light would be thrown on the whole history, by expounding the tablets over every head. If the aerial form above were ever intended to represent the heavenly apparition of a departed king, which is the opinion of some, that of the great Arbaces might appear here with striking propriety, at the final conquest of rebellious Israel. Should the discoveries of time prove my conjecture at all right, this basrelief must be nearly two hundred years older than any which are ascribed to Cyrus, at Persepolis or Pasargadæ." (Sir R. K. Porter.)—BURDER. (*See engraving, pl. no. at the end of the volume.*)

Ver. 20. Thou sayest, (but *they are but* vain words,) *I have* counsel and strength for the war. Now, on whom dost thou trust, that thou rebellest against me?

The Hindoos say of boasting words, or those which do not proceed from the heart, they are "words of the MOUTH;" but to speak evil of a person is called a *chondu-chadi*, a hint of the LIP.—ROBERTS.

Ver. 23. Now therefore, I pray thee, give pledges to my lord the king of Assyria, and I will deliver thee two thousand horses, if thou be able on thy part to set riders upon them.

In the first periods of the Jewish history, the armies of Israel consisted all of footmen. At length Solomon raised a body of twelve thousand horse, and fourteen hundred chariots, some with two, and others with four horses; but whether that magnificent prince intended them for pomp or war, is uncertain. Infantry was also the chief strength of the Greek and Roman armies. Cavalry is not so necessary in warm climates, where the march of troops is less incommoded with bad roads; nor can they be of so much use in mountainous countries, where their movements are attended with great difficulty and hazard. The eastern potentates, however, brought immense numbers of horse into the field, and chiefly trusted to their exertions for defence or conquest. The people of Israel, who were appointed to "dwell alone," and not to mingle with the nations around them, nor imitate their policy, were expressly forbidden to maintain large bodies of cavalry; and they accordingly prospered, or were defeated, as they obeyed or transgressed this divine command; which a celebrated author observes, cannot be justified by the measures of human prudence. Even upon political reasons, says Warburton, the Jews might be justified in the disuse of cavalry, in the defence of their country, but not in conquering it from a warlike people, who abounded in horses. Here, at least, the exertion of an extraordinary providence was wonderfully conspicuous. The kings who succeeded Solomon certainly raised a body of horse for the defence of their dominions, which they recruited from the studs of Egypt, in those times equally remarkable for their vigour and beauty. But the Jewish cavalry were seldom very numerous; and under the religious kings of David's line, who made the divine law the rule of their policy, they were either disembodied altogether, or reduced to a very small number. In the reign of Hezekiah, when the country was invaded by the king of Assyria, the Jews seem to have had no force of this kind, for, said Rabshakeh, "Now, therefore, I pray thee, give pledges to my lord the king of Assyria, and I will deliver thee two thousand horses, if thou be able on thy part to set riders upon them."—PAXTON.

Ver. 28. Then Rabshakeh stood, and cried with
a loud voice in the Jews' language, and spake,
saying, Hear the word of the great king, the
king of Assyria: 29. Thus saith the king, Let
not Hezekiah deceive you; for he shall not be
able to deliver you out of his hand: 30. Neither
let Hezekiah make you trust in the LORD, saying, The LORD will surely deliver us, and this
city shall not be delivered into the hand of the
king of Assyria. 31. Hearken not to Hezekiah: for thus saith the king of Assyria, Make
an agreement with me by a present, and come
out to me, and *then* eat ye every man of his
own vine, and every one of his fig-tree, and
drink ye every one the waters of his cistern;
32. Until I come and take you away to a land
like your own land; a land of corn and wine
a land of bread and vineyards, a land of oil
olive and of honey, that ye may live and not
die: and hearken not unto Hezekiah, when he
persuadeth you, saying, The LORD will deliver us.

It must be owned that there is something extremely insolent in the speeches of Rabshakeh to Hezekiah and his loyal subjects, (2 Kings xviii.;) his boastings, both as to matter and manner, appear to have been of the most unlimited kind, and to have wanted for no amplification in the capacity of the speaker to bestow on them: he describes his master's power in the highest terms, and even beyond what fidelity, as a servant to the king of Assyria, might have required from him. Probably his speeches are recorded as being in a strain somewhat unusual, and it will not be easy to find their equal: nevertheless, the reader may be amused by the following portrait, which forms no bad companion to that of Rabshakeh: if it may not rival that in expression, it falls little short of it, and is, to say the least, an entertaining representation of eastern manners and train of thought. It should be remarked, that Rabshakeh was speaking openly, in defiance to enemies: Hyat Saib was conversing in his own residence. If, when speaking in private, he was thus eloquent, what had been his eloquence, had he been employed by his sovereign in a message of defiance?

Hyat Saib, the jemadar, or governor of Baidanore, "having exhausted his whole string of questions, he turned the discourse to another subject—no less than his great and puissant lord and master, Hyder, of whom he had endeavoured to impress me with a great, if not a terrible idea; amplifying his honour, his wealth, and the extent and opulence of his dominions; and describing to me, in the most exaggerated terms, the number of his troops, his military talents, his vast, and, according to his account, unrivalled genius; his amazing abilities in conquering and governing nations; and, above all, his amiable qualities and splendid endowments of heart, no less than understanding.

"Having thus, with equal zeal and fidelity, endeavoured to impress me with veneration for his lord and master, and for that purpose attributed to him every perfection that may be supposed to be divided among all the kings and generals that have lived since the birth of Christ, and given each their due, he turned to the English government, and endeavoured to demonstrate to me the folly and inutility of our attempting to resist his progress, which he compared to that of the sea, to a tempest, to a torrent, to a lion's pace and fury—to every thing that an eastern imagination could suggest as a figure proper to exemplify grandeur and irresistible power. He then vaunted of his sovereign's successes over the English, some of which I had not heard of before, and did not believe; and concluded by assuring me, that it was Hyder's determination to drive all Europeans from Indostan, which he averred he could not fail to do, considering the weakness of the one, and the boundless power of the other.—He expended half an hour in this manner and discourse." (Campbell's Travels to India.)—TAYLOR IN CALMET.

CHAPTER XIX.

Ver. 3. And they said unto him, Thus saith Hezekiah, This day *is* a day of trouble, and of rebuke, and blasphemy: for the children are come to the birth, and *there is* not strength to bring forth.

When a person has all but accomplished his object, when only a very slight obstacle has prevented him, it is then said, "The child came to the birth, but there was not strength to bring it forth." Some time ago, an opulent man accused another, who was also very rich, and in office, of improper conduct to the government: the matter was well investigated by competent authorities; but the accused, by his superior cunning, and by bribes, escaped, as by the "skin of his teeth;" and the people said, "Alas! the child came to the mouth, but the hand could not take it." When a person has succeeded in gaining a blessing which he has long desired, he says, "Good, good! the child is born at last." Has a person lost his lawsuit in a provincial court, he will go to the capital to make an appeal to a superior court; and should he there succeed, he will say, in writing to a friend, "Good news, good news! the child is born." When a man has been trying to gain an office, his friend meeting him on return, does not always ask, "Is the child born? or did it come to the birth?" but, "Is it a male or a female?" If he say the former, he has gained his object; if the latter, he has failed.—ROBERTS.

Ver. 7. Behold, I will send a blast upon him, and he shall hear a rumour, and shall return to his own land; and I will cause him to fall by the sword in his own land.

See on Is. 37. 36.

The destruction of Sennacherib and his army appears to have been effected by that pestilential wind called the *simoom*.

At Bagdad, October 9, 1818, Sir R. K. Porter informs us, (Travels, vol. ii. p. 229,) the master of the khan "told me, that they consider October the first month of their autumn, and feel it delightfully cool in comparison with July, August, and September; for that during forty days of the two first-named summer months, the hot wind blows from the desert, and its effects are often destructive. Its title is very appropriate, being called the samiel, or baude semoom, the pestilential wind. It does not come in continued long currents, but in gusts at different intervals, each blast lasting several minutes, and passing along with the rapidity of lightning. No one dare stir from their houses while this invisible flame is sweeping over the face of the country. Previous to its approach, the atmosphere becomes thick and suffocating, and appearing particularly dense near the horizon, gives sufficient warning of the threatened mischief. Though hostile to human life, it is so far from being prejudicial to the vegetable creation, that a continuance of the samiel tends to ripen the fruits. I inquired what became of the cattle during such a plague, and was told they were seldom touched by it. It seems strange that their lungs should be so perfectly insensible to what seems instant destruction to the breath of man; but so it is, that they are regularly driven down to water at the customary times of day, even when the blasts are at the severest. The people who attend them are obliged to plaster their own faces, and other parts of the body usually exposed to the air, with a sort of muddy clay, which, in general, protects them from its most malignant effects. The periods of the winds' blowing are generally from noon till sunset; they cease almost entirely during the night; and the direction of the gusts is always from the northeast. When it has passed over, a sulphuric, and indeed loathsome smell, like putridity, remains for a long time. The poison which occasions this smell must be deadly; for if any unfortunate traveller, too far from shelter, meet the blast, he falls immediately; and in a few minutes his flesh becomes almost black, while both it and his bones at once arrive at so extreme a state of corruption, that the smallest movement of the body would separate the one from the other."—ROBINSON.

The south wind in those arid regions blowing over an immense surface of burning sand, becomes so charged with electrical matter, as to occasion the greatest danger, and often instant death, to the unwary traveller. A Turk, who had twice performed the pilgrimage to Mecca, told Dr. Clarke that he had witnessed more than once the direful effects of this hot pestilential wind in the desert. He has known all the water dried out of their skin bottles in an instant, by its influence. The camels alone gave notice of its approach, by making a noise, and burying their mouths and nostrils in the sand. This was considered as an infallible token that the desolation was at hand; and those who imitated the camels escaped suffocation.

In some districts it commits great ravages, and at times so totally burns up all the corn, that no animal will eat a blade of it, or touch any of its grain. It has been known, even in Persia, to destroy camels and other hardy animals; its effects on the human frame are represented as inconceivably dreadful. In some instances it kills instantaneously; but in others the wretched sufferer lingers for hours, or even days, in the most excruciating torture. In those places where it is not fatal to life, it resembles the breath of a glowing furnace, destroys every symptom of vegetation, and will, even during the night, scorch the skin in the most painful manner. In the sandy desert it is often so heated as to destroy every thing, animal and vegetable, with which it comes in contact. In the inhabited country every article of furniture, of glass, and even of wood, becomes as hot as if it were exposed to a raging fire. In Hindostan, when the hot wind blows, the atmosphere for many hours of the day becomes insupportable; the heavens are like brass, and the earth like heated iron. At such times the miserable inhabitants are obliged to confine themselves in dark rooms, cooled by screens of matted grass kept continually watered. To this terrible agent the prophet alludes in his prediction of Sennacherib's overthrow: "Behold, I will send a blast upon him." The return of man to his native dust is as certain and speedy as the blasting of a tender plant by the deadly breath of the simoom: "For the wind passeth over it, and it is gone; and the place thereof shall know it no more."

Campbell, in his Travels, most significantly calls it a horrid wind, whose consuming blasts extend their ravages all the way from the extreme end of the Gulf of Cambaya up to Mosul. It carries along with it fleaks of fire, like threads of silk; instantly strikes dead those that breathe it, and consumes them inwardly to ashes; the flesh soon becoming black as a coal, and dropping off the bones. The numbers that perish by its fatal influence are sometimes very great. Thevenot states, that in the year 1665, in the month of July, four thousand people died at Bassora by that wind, in three weeks' time.

By this powerful and terrific agent, invigorated by the arm, and guided by the finger of Jehovah, was the numerous army of the proud and blaspheming Sennacherib destroyed under the walls of Libnah. In the brief statement of Isaiah it is said, "Then the angel (or, as it may be rendered, the messenger) of the Lord went forth, and smote in the camp of the Assyrians a hundred and fourscore and five thousand men." Now this angel of Jehovah is expressly called, in verse 7th of the same chapter, *ruach*, a blast or wind; which can hardly leave a doubt of the manner in which this passage is to be understood.—PAXTON.

Ver. 24. I have digged and drunk strange waters, and with the sole of my feet have I dried up all the rivers of besieged places.

The curious Vitringa admires the explanation which Grotius has given, of that watering with the foot by which Egypt was distinguished from Judea, derived from an observation made on Philo, who lived in Egypt, Philo having described a machine used by the peasants of that country for watering as wrought by the feet; which sort of watering Dr. Shaw has since understood of the gardener's putting a stop to the further flowing of the water in the rill, in which those things were planted that wanted watering, by turning the earth against it with his foot. Great respect is due to so candid and ingenious a traveller as Dr Shaw; I must however own, that I apprehend the meaning of Moses is more truly represented by Grotius than the doctor. For Moses seems to intend to represent the great labour of this way of watering by the foot, which the working that instrument really was, on which account it seems to be laid aside in Egypt since the time of Philo, and easier methods of raising the water made use of; whereas the turning the earth with the foot which Dr. Shaw speaks of, is the least part of the labour of watering. If it should be remarked, that this machine was not older than Arcihmedes, which has been supposed, I would by way of reply observe, that the more ancient Egyptian machines might be equally wrought with the foot, and were undoubtedly more laborious still, as otherwise the invention of Archimedes would not have brought them into disuse. But though I think the interpretation of Deut. xi. 10, by Grotius, is preferable to that of Dr. Shaw, I readily admit that the doctor's thought may be very naturally applied to these words of Sennacherib, to which however the doctor has not applied it; for he seems to boast that he could as easily turn the water of great rivers, and cause their old channels to become dry, as a gardener stops the water from flowing any longer in a rill by the sole of his foot.

And as the gardener stops up one rill and opens another with his mattock, to let in the water, so, says Sennacherib, I have digged and drank strange waters, that is, which did not heretofore flow in the places I have made them flow in. This is the easiest interpretation that can, I believe, be given to the word *strange*, made use of by this Assyrian prince, and makes the whole verse a reference to the eastern way of watering: I have digged channels, and drank, and caused my army to drink out of new-made rivers, into which I have conducted the waters that used to flow elsewhere, and have laid those old channels dry with the sole of my foot, with as much ease as a gardener digs channels in his garden, and directing the waters of a cistern into a new rill, with his foot stops up that in which it before ran.

In confirmation of all which, let it be remembered, that this way of watering by rills is in use in those countries from whence Sennacherib came; continued down from ancient times there, without doubt, as it is in Egypt.

The understanding those words of the Psalmist, Ps. lxv. 9, *Thou visitest the earth and waterest it, thou greatly enrichest it with the rivers of* GOD, of the watering it as by a rill of water, makes an easy and beautiful sense; the rain being to the earth in general, the same thing from GOD, that a watering rill, or little river, is to a garden from man.—HARMER.

Ver. 26. Therefore their inhabitants were of small power, they were dismayed and confounded; thy were *as* the grass of the field, and *as* the green herb, *as* the grass on the house-tops, and *as corn* blasted before it be grown up.

The Hebrew has, instead of small power, "short of hand." This figure is much used here, and is taken from a man trying to reach an object for which his arm is not long enough. When it is wished to ascertain what is a man's capacity or power, it is asked, "Is his arm long or short?" "Let me tell you, friend, Tamban will never succeed; his arm is not long enough." Of feeble people it is said, "they have short hands."—ROBERTS.

Ver. 28. Because thy rage against me and thy tumult is come up into mine ears, therefore I will put my hook in thy nose, and my bridle in thy lips, and I will turn thee back by the way by which thou camest.

A person says of his deliverer from prison or danger, "Ah! the good man took me out by his *tote*," i. e. hook. A culprit says of the officers who cannot catch him, "Their hooks are become straight." The man who cannot drag another from his secrecy, says, "My hook is not sufficient for that fellow."—ROBERTS.

The dromedary differs from the common camel, in being of a finer and rounder shape, and in having upon its back a smaller protuberance. This species (for the former seldom deviating from the beaten road, travels with its head at liberty) is governed by a bridle, which being usually fastened to a ring fixed in its nostrils, may very well illustrate the expression which the sacred writer uses concerning Sennacherib: "I will put my hook in thy nose, and my bridle in thy lips, and I will turn thee back by the way by which thou camest." These words refer at once to the absolute control of heaven, under which he acted, and the swiftness of his retreat.—PAXTON.

Ver. 35. And it came to pass that night, that the angel of the LORD went out, and smote in the camp of the Assyrians a hundred fourscore and five thousand: and when they arose early in the morning, behold, they *were* all dead corpses.

Mr. Boswell, in his Life of Dr. Johnson, informs us, that it was a subject of conversation between them, in what manner so great a multitude of Sennacherib's army was destroyed. "We are not to suppose," says the doctor, in reply, "that the angel went abroad with a sword in his hand, stabbing them one by one; but that some powerful natural agent was employed; most probably the samyel." Whether the doctor had noticed some picture in which the angel was thus employed, is uncertain; but it should seem, that this idea is common; and even Dr. Doddridge appears to have conceived of the angel, as of a person employed in slaughter; for he says, in a note on the passage (Matt. xxvi. 53) where our Lord mentions that his Father could furnish him twelve legions of angels, "How dreadfully irresistible would such an *army of angels* have been, when one of these celestial spirits was able to destroy 185,000 Assyrians at one stroke!" Without attempting to investigate the power of celestial spirits, we may endeavour to present the history of the destruction of Sennacherib's army, according to what, in all probability, was the real fact; premising that *simyel, sumiel, samyel, sumoom, simoom*, &c. are different names for the same meteor. Mr. Bruce's account of this wonderful natural phenomenon, affords some very interesting particulars. The extracts are from the quarto edition of his Travels.

"On the 16th, at half past ten, we left *El Mout*, [death.] At eleven o'clock, while we contemplated with great pleasure the rugged top of Chiggré, to which we were fast approaching, and where we were to solace ourselves with plenty of good water, Idris cried out, 'Fall upon your faces, for here is the simoom!' I saw from the southeast a haze come, in colour like the purple part of the rainbow, but not so compressed or thick. It did not occupy twenty yards in breadth, and was about twelve feet high from the ground. It was a kind of blush upon the air, and it moved very rapidly, for I scarce could turn to fall upon the ground, with my head to the northward, when I felt the heat of its current plainly upon my face. We all lay flat on the ground, as if dead, till Idris told us it was blown over. The meteor, or purple haze, which I saw, was indeed passed, but the light air that still blew was of heat to threaten suffocation. For my part, I found distinctly in my breast that I had imbibed a part of it, nor was I free of an asthmatic sensation, till I had been some months in Italy, at the baths of Poretta, near two years afterward. A universal despondency had taken possession of our people. They ceased to speak to one another, and when they did it was in whispers, by which I easily guessed that they were increasing each other's fears, by vain suggestions, calculated to sink each other's spirits still further. This phenomenon of the simoom, unexpected by us, though foreseen by Idris, caused us all to relapse into our former despondency. It still continued to blow so as to exhaust us entirely, though the blast was so weak as scarcely would have raised a leaf from the ground. At twenty minutes before five, the simoom ceased, and a comfortable and cooling breeze came by starts from the north. We had no sooner got into the plains than we felt great symptoms of the simoom, and about a quarter before twelve, our prisoner first, and then Idris, cried out, *The simoom! the simoom!* My curiosity would not suffer me to fall down without looking behind me; about due south, a little to the east, I saw the *coloured haze*, as before. It seemed now to be rather less compressed, and to have with it a shade of blue. The edges of it were not defined as those of the former; but like *a very thin smoke*, with about a yard in the middle, tinged with these colours. We all fell upon our faces, and the simoom passed with a gentle ruffling wind. It continued to blow in this manner till near three o'clock, so we were all taken ill at night, and scarcely strength was left us to load the camels. The simoom, with the wind at southeast, immediately followed the wind at north, and the usual despondency that always accompanied it. The *blue* meteor, with which it began passing over us about twelve, and the *ruffling wind* that followed it, continued till near two. Silence, and a desperate kind of indifference about life, were the immediate effects upon us; and I began, seeing the condition of my camels, to fear we were all doomed to a sandy grave, and to contemplate it with some degree of resignation. I here began to provide for the worst. I saw the fate of our camels fast approaching, and that our men grew weak in proportion: our bread, too, began to fail us, although we had plenty of camel's flesh in its stead; our water, though to all appearance we were to find it more frequently than in the beginning of our journey, was nevertheless brackish, and scarce served the purpose to quench our thirst; and above all, the dreadful simoom had perfectly exhausted our strength, and brought upon us a degree of cowardice and languor that we struggled with in vain."

The following extract is from D'Osbornville's "Essays, &c. on the East:"—"Some enlightened travellers have seriously written, that every individual who falls a victim to this infection, is immediately reduced to ashes, though apparently only asleep; and that when taken hold of to be awakened by passengers, the limbs part from the body and remain in the hand. Such travellers would evidently not have taken these tales on hearsay, if they had paid a proper attention to other facts, which they either did or ought to have heard. Experience proves, that animals, by pressing their nostrils to the earth, and men, by covering their heads in their mantles, have nothing to fear from these meteors. This demonstrates the impossibility that a poison which can only penetrate the most delicate parts of the brain or lungs, should calcine the skin, flesh, nerves, and bones. I acknowledge these accounts are had from the Arabs themselves; but their picturesque and extravagant expressions are a kind of imaginary coin, to know the true value of which, requires some practice."

Notwithstanding this remark, if the word *immediately* were exchanged for *quickly*, the purport of the account might be almost exactly justified. Our author proceeds—"I have twice had an opportunity of considering the effect of these siphons, with some attention. I shall relate simply what I have seen in the case of a merchant and two travellers, who were *struck during their sleep, and died on the spot.* I ran to see if it was possible to afford them any succour, but they were already dead; the victims of an *interior suffocating fire.* There were apparent signs of the dissolution of their fluids; a kind of serous matter issued from the nostrils, mouth, and ears; and in something more than an hour, the whole body was in the same state. However, as, according to their custom, they [the Arabs] were diligent to pay them the last duties of humanity, I cannot affirm that the putrefaction was more or less rapid than usual in that country. As to the meteor itself, it may be examined with impunity at the distance of three or four fathoms; and the country people are only afraid of being suprised by it when they are asleep; neither are such accidents very common, for these siphons are only seen during two or three months of the year; and as their approach is *felt*, the camp-guards and the people awake are always very careful to rouse those that sleep, who also have a general habit of covering their faces with mantles."

Any seeming contrariety of representation between Mr. Bruce and this traveller may be accounted for, by supposing that in different deserts, or at different times, (of the year, perhaps,) these meteors are more or less fatal; but the reader's attention is desired, particularly, to certain ideas implied in these descriptions:—1. The meteor seems like a thin smoke, *i. e.* seen by daylight, when Mr. Bruce travelled. 2. It passed with a gentle ruffling wind. 3. It was some hours in passing. 4. It affected the mind, by enfeebling the body; producing despondency and cowardice. 5. It is dangerous by being breathed. 6. It is peculiarly fatal to persons sleeping. 7. Its effects, even on those to whom it is not fatal, are debilitating and lasting. 8. It is felt; and is compared to a suffocating fire. 9. Its extent is sometimes considerable; about half a mile; sometimes more, sometimes less. 10. Colonel Campbell says, at the close of the extract from him, page 9, that "to prevent drawing it in, it is necessary first to see it, which is not always practicable." No doubt, we may safely add, *especially by night.*

These particulars respecting the nature and effects of the simoom, will illustrate, by comparison, occurrences recorded 2 Kings, chap xix., and Isaiah, chap. xxxvii.

I. "Behold, I will send a *blast* upon him," (Sennacherib.) The word rendered *blast* (רוח *ruach*) does not imply a vehement wind; but a gentle breathing, a breeze, a vapour, a reek, an exhalation; and thus agrees perfectly with the descriptions extracted above.

II. It is supposed the prophet alludes to this meteor, Isa. chap. xxx. 27, "The Lord's anger is burning, or devouring, fire;" ("burning with his anger"—"*his tongue is a devouring fire.*" Eng. Trans.) And ver. 33, "The breath of the Lord, like a stream of brimstone, doth kindle it."

III. The army of Sennacherib was destroyed *by night.* No doubt the unwarrantable pride of the king had extended also to his army, (witness the arrogance of Rabshakeh,) so that being in full security the officers and soldiers were negligent; their discipline was relaxed; the "camp-guards" were not alert; or, perhaps, they themselves were the first taken off; and those who slept *not wrapped up*, imbibed the poison plentifully. If this had been an evening of dissolute mirth, (no uncommon thing in a camp,) their joy (perhaps for a victory, or "the first night of their attacking the city," says Josephus) became, by its effects, one means of their destruction.

IV. If the Assyrians were not accustomed to the action of this meteor at home, they might little expect it; and *by night*, might little watch for, or discern it. The total number of Sennacherib's army is not mentioned: perhaps it was three or four times the number slain; that it was very great, appears from his boastings sent to Hezekiah. If the extent of the meteor was half a mile, or a mile, in passing over a camp, it might destroy many thousands of sleepers; while those on each side of its course, escaped; and these, "rising early in the morning," discovered the slaughter of their fellows around them. The destruction of Cambyses' army of 50,000 men going for Ethiopia, is, in some respects, not unlike this destruction of the Assyrians.

V. The subsequent languor, despondence, and cowardice, attending this meteor, contribute to explain the forced return of Sennacherib home; even though his army might be very numerous, notwithstanding this diminution.

Observe, it was not before Jerusalem that this event occurred, but to the south.

VI. The Babylonish Talmud affirms, that this destruction of the Assyrians was executed by lightning; and some of the Targums are quoted for saying the same thing. Josephus says, "Sennacherib, on his return from the Egyptian war, found his army which he had left under Rabshakeh, almost entirely destroyed by a judicial pestilence, which swept away, in officers and common soldiers, the first night they sat down before the city, 185,000 men."

VII. That this meteor inflicts diseases where it is not immediately fatal, Mr. Bruce himself is an instance; he also says, "though Syene, by its situation, should be healthy, the general complaint is a weakness and soreness in the eyes; generally ending in *blindness* of one or both eyes; you scarce ever see a person in the street who sees with both eyes. They say it is owing to the hot wind from the desert; and this I apprehend to be true, by the violent soreness and inflammation we were troubled with in our return home, through the great desert, to Syene."—TAYLOR IN CALMET.

CHAPTER XX.

Ver. 11. And Isaiah the prophet cried unto the LORD; and he brought the shadow ten degrees backward, by which it had gone down in the dial of Ahaz.

At the beginning of the world it is certain there was no distinction of time, but by the light and darkness, and the whole day was included in the general terms of the evening and morning. The Chaldeans, many ages after the flood, were the first who divided the day into hours; they being the first who applied themselves with any success to astrology. Sun-dials are of ancient use: but as they were of no service in cloudy weather and in the night, there was another invention of measuring the parts of time by water; but that not proving sufficiently exact, they laid it aside for another by sand. The use of dials was earlier among the Greeks than the Romans. It was above three hundred years after the building of Rome before they knew any thing of them: but yet they had divided the day and night into twenty-four hours: though they did not count the hours numerically, but from midnight to midnight, distinguishing them by particular names, as by the cock-crowing, the dawn, the midday, &c. The first sun-dial we read of among the Romans, which divided the day into hours, is mentioned by Pliny, as fixed upon the temple of Quirinus by L. Papyrius, the censor, about the twelfth year of the wars with Pyrrhus. Scipio Nasica, some years after, measured the day and night into hours from the dropping of water.—BURDER.

Ver. 13. And Hezekiah hearkened unto them, and showed them the house of his precious things, the silver, and the gold, and the spices, and the precious ointment, and *all* the house of his armour, and all that was found in his treasures: there was nothing in his house, nor in all his dominion, that Hezekiah showed them not.

The display which Hezekiah made of his treasure was to gratify the ambassadors of the king of Babylon. It appears to have been an extraordinary thing, and not done but upon this and occasions of a similar nature; such probably was the general practice. Lord Macartney informs us, that "the splendour of the emperor of China and his court, and the riches of the mandarins, surpass all that can be said of them. Their silks, porcelain, cabinets, and other furniture, make a most glittering appearance. These, however, are only exposed when they make or receive visits: for they commonly neglect themselves at home, the laws against private pomp and luxury being very severe."

Vertomannus, in his voyage to the East, describing the treasure of the king of Calicut, says, that it is esteemed so immense that it cannot be contained in two remarkably large cellars or warehouses. It consists of precious stones, plates of gold, and as much coined gold as may suffice to lade a hundred mules. They say that it was collected together by twelve kings who were before him, and that in his treasury is a coffer three spans long and two broad, full of precious stones of incalculable value. This custom for the eastern princes to amass enormous loads of treasure, merely for show and ostentation, appears to have been practised by the kings of Judea. One instance of it at least is found in the case of Hezekiah, in the passage now referred to.—BURDER.

CHAPTER XXI.

Ver. 11. Because Manasseh king of Judah hath done these abominations, *and* hath done wickedly above all that the Amorites did, which *were* before him, and hath made Judah also to sin with his idols.

Bodin informs us from Maimonides, that it was customary among the Amorites to draw their new-born children through a flame; believing that by this means they would escape many calamities; and that Maimonides himself had been an eyewitness of this superstition in some of the nurses of Egypt.—BURDER.

CHAPTER XXII.

Ver. 17. Because they have forsaken me, and have burnt incense unto other gods, that they might provoke me to anger with all the works of their hands; therefore my wrath shall be kindled against this place, and shall not be quenched.

"Ah! who can *quench* the wrath of my enemy?" "Who? O, I have done it already, for his anger is turned to water." Does a person reply to another in such a way as to increase anger, it is asked, "Will ghee (clarified butter) quench fire?" "Do not cast ghee on that man's passions." "I beseech you to try to make peace for me." "Peace for you! can I quench his wrath?"—ROBERTS.

CHAPTER XXIII.

Ver. 3. And the king stood by a pillar, and made a covenant before the LORD, to walk after the LORD, and to keep his commandments and his testimonies and his statutes, with all *their* heart and all *their* soul, to perform the words of this covenant that were written in this book: and all the people stood to the covenant.

See on 2 Kings 11. 14.

Ver. 7. And he brake down the houses of the Sodomites, that *were* by the house of the LORD, where the women wove hangings for the grove.

Very large hangings are used in the temples, some of which are fastened to the roof, others used as screens, and others to cover the sacred cars. On them are painted the actions of the gods, as described in the books Râmyanum and the Scanda Purâna; and there are portrayed things of the most indecent nature.—ROBERTS.

In the history of Schemselouhar and the prince of Persia, (Arabian Nights' Entertainment,) when the former was told that the calif was coming to visit her, she ordered the paintings on silk, which were in the garden, to be taken down. In the same manner are paintings or hangings said to be used in the passage referred to. The authority given for this custom must be allowed to be sufficient to vouch for the existence of the practice in question, to whatever animadversions the work itself may be liable in any other point of view.—BURDER.

Ver. 11. And he took away the horses that the kings of Judah had given to the sun, at the entering in of the house of the LORD, by the chamber of Nathan-melech the chamberlain, which *was* in the suburbs, and burnt the chariots of the sun with fire.

The Hindoos believe that the sun is drawn in his course by seven horses, and that the deity sits in his chariot of one wheel, which is driven by Arunan. Thus may be seen the sun and his horses represented in wood, or painted on the hangings which adorn the cars. See, then, the profligacy of the kings of Judah: they gave horses and chariots to the sun as a sign of their attachment to that system of idolatry, and to procure those blessings which are believed to be dispensed by the gods; for it must be observed, that such gifts to the deities and their temples are only for the fulfilment of some vow for favours received, or for those which are earnestly desired.—ROBERTS.

By those horses, cannot well be understood, as the greater part of modern interpreters maintain, a number of sculptured figures of gold, silver, or brass, which had been presented as votive offerings to the heathen deity. The words of the sacred historian certainly refer to living horses for he simply states, that Josiah "took away the horses that the kings of Judah had given, or dedicated to the sun:" but had the figures of horses been intended, the clause, to correspond with the common manner of the sacred writers, must have run in these terms, He took away the horses of gold, of silver, or of brass; for in this way the molten calf of Aaron, the serpent of Moses, and the lions and oxen of Solomon, are distinguished in scripture from the real animals. Nor had he distinguished in one statue the horses from the chariot; nor assigned to them a particular station between the temple and the house of Nathan-melech; because they were parts and appendages of the same general figure. Besides, the destruction of the horses was effected by one operation, and the chariots by another, which shows that they were not metallic figures: Josiah took away, or (as the verb is rendered in other parts) destroyed the horses, but he burned the chariots in the fire. These horses were given or dedicated to the sun, to be offered in sacrifice to that luminary, according to some writers; or kept in honour of Baal, or Apollo, as others imagine. The Jewish writers allege that the priests of the sun led them forth at the dawn, with great pomp, into a large area, between the temple and the house of Nathan-melech, to salute their god, as soon as he appeared above the horizon.—Paxton.

Ver. 21. And the king commanded all the people, saying, Keep the passover unto the Lord your God, as *it is* written in the book of the covenant. 22. Surely there was not holden such a passover from the days of the judges that judged Israel, nor in all the days of the kings of Israel, nor of the kings of Judah.

To those who may wonder how Jerusalem could receive such multitudes, as were obliged by the Jewish law to attend there three times a year, and as we know did sometimes actually appear in it, I would recite the account that Pitts gives of Mecca, the sacred city of the Mohammedans, and the number of people he found collected together there, for the celebration of their religious solemnities, in the close of the seventeenth century. This city, he tells us, he thought he might safely say, had not one thousand families in it of constant inhabitants, and the buildings very mean and ordinary. That four caravans arrive there every year, with great numbers of people in each, and the Mohammedans say, there meet not fewer than seventy thousand souls at these solemnities; and that though he could not think the number quite so large, yet that it is very great. How such numbers of people, with their beasts, could be lodged and entertained in such a little ragged town as Mecca, is a question he thus answers: "As for houseroom, the inhabitants do straiten themselves very much, in order at this time to make their market. And as for such as come last, after the town is filled, they pitch their tents without the town, and there abide until they remove towards home. As for provision, they all bring sufficient with them, except it be of flesh, which they may have at Mecca; but all other provisions, as butter, honey, oil, olives, rice, biscuit, &c. they bring with them as much as will last through the wilderness, forward and backward, as well as the time they stay at Mecca; and so for their camels they bring store of provender, &c. with them." The number of Jews that assembled at Jerusalem at their passover, was much greater: but had not Jerusalem been a much larger city than Mecca is, as in truth it was, yet the present Mohammedan practice of abiding under tents, and carrying their provisions and bedding with them, will easily explain how they might be accommodated. Josephus says, that in one year the number of lambs slain at the passover amounted to five hundred and fifty-six thousand five hundred, and that ten men at least ate of one lamb, and often many more, even to the number of twenty. Taking therefore the number of persons at the lowest computation, i. e. ten to one lamb, there must have been present this year at Jerusalem, not less than two million five hundred and sixty-five thousand persons!—Harmer.

Ver. 30. And his servants carried him in a chariot dead from Megiddo, and brought him to Jerusalem, and buried him in his own sepulchre. And the people of the land took Jehoahaz the son of Josiah, and anointed him, and made him king in his father's stead.

See on ch. 9. 28.

CHAPTER XXV.

Ver. 7. And they slew the sons of Zedekiah before his eyes, and put out the eyes of Zedekiah, and bound him with fetters of brass, and carried him to Babylon.

This was probably done with the intention of rendering the king incapable of ever reascending the throne. Thus it was a law in Persia down to the latest time, that no blind person could mount the throne. Hence the barbarous custom, common at the time of Chardin, and even since, of depriving the sons and male relations of a Persian king, who are not to be allowed to attain the government, of their sight. Down to the time of Abbas, who reigned in 1642, this was done, according to Chardin, only by passing a red-hot copper plate before the eyes. "But the power of vision was not so entirely destroyed, but that the person blinded still retained a glimmering; and the operation was frequently performed in so favourable a manner, that still some sight remained. During the reign of Abbas II., one of the brothers of that prince once visited his aunt and his nephew, whose palace joins the residence of the Dutch: as he expressed a wish to visit these strangers, they were informed of this, and they were invited to spend an afternoon, and take supper with them. The brother of the king brought several other blinded princes with him, and when candles were introduced, it was observed that they were aware of it. They were asked if they saw any thing. The king's brother answered in the affirmative, and added, that he could see enough to walk without a stick. This was unfortunately heard by one of the court spies, who were employed to watch all the motions of the great people. According to the custom of these people, he related it to the king in a malicious manner, and so that he could not avoid being uneasy. 'How!' cried he, 'these blind people boast they can see? I shall prevent that;' and immediately he ordered their eyes to be put out in the manner above described. This is performed by entirely putting out the eyes with the point of a dagger. The Persians," continues Chardin, "consider their policy towards the children of the royal family, as humane and laudable; since they only deprive them of their sight, and do not put them to death, as the Turks do. They say that it is allowable to deprive these princes of their sight, to secure the tranquillity of the state; but they dare not put them to death for two reasons; the first is, because the law forbids to spill innocent blood; secondly, because it might be possible that those who remained alive should die without children, and if there were no other relations, the whole legitimate family would become extinct."—Rosenmuller.

Ver. 30. And his allowance *was* a continual allowance given him of the king, a daily rate for every day, all the days of his life.

The other guests were arranged round the room, according to their respective ranks: among whom was an old man, a lineal descendant of the Seffi family, whom they called Nawab, and who took his seat next to the Ameen-ad-Dowlah. Although needy and without power, he is always treated with the greatest respect. 2 Sam. ix. 1. 7. He receives a daily *sursat*, or allowance, from the king, which makes his case resemble that of Jehoiachin, for his allowance was a continual allowance given him of the king, a daily rate, all the days of his life. 2 Kings xxv. 30. Giving to the Nawab a high rank in society, is illustrative of the precedence given to Jehoiachin, by setting his throne above the throne of the kings that were with him in Babylon.—Morier.

THE FIRST BOOK OF CHRONICLES.

CHAPTER II.

Ver. 34. Now Sheshan had no sons, but daughters: and Sheshan had a servant, an Egyptian, whose name was Jarha. 35. And Sheshan gave his daughter to Jarha his servant to wife, and she bare him Attai.

The usages of the East differ very much from those of the West, with relation to the more than kind treatment of their servants; but they perfectly agree with those that are referred to in the scriptures. How far these have been taken notice of in explaining passages of holy writ, I do not know; but I believe the gathering up together, and presenting them in one view to my reader, will be a sort of novelty.

They marry their slaves frequently to their daughters, and that when they have no male issue, and those daughters are what we call great fortunes. That Hassan of whom Maillet gives a long account in his eleventh letter, and who was kiaia of the Asaphs of Cairo, that is to say, the colonel of four or five thousand men who go under that name, was the slave of a predecessor in that office, the famous Kamel, and married his daughter: "for Kamel," says he, "according to the custom of the country, gave him one of his daughters in marriage, and left him, at his death, one part of the great riches he had amassed together in the course of a long and prosperous life." What Sheshan then did, was perhaps not so extraordinary as we may have imagined, but perfectly conformable to old eastern customs, if not to the arrangements of Moses; at least it is, we see, just the same with what is now practised.—HARMER.

CHAPTER IV.

Ver. 39. And they went to the entrance of Gedor, *even* unto the east side of the valley, to seek pasture for their flocks. 40. And they found fat pasture and good, and the land *was* wide, and quiet, and peaceable; for *they* of Ham had dwelt there of old.

Our people, who are extremely watchful over their public pastures, to guard them from intruders, and so ready to go to law with their next neighbours about their right to common, or the number of beasts they shall feed there, may think it very strange that Abraham and Lot, the Kenites and Rechabites, should have been permitted to move up and down, and feed their flocks and herds unmolested, in inhabited countries as well as in deserts.

But this ancient custom still continues in Palestine, which, depopulated as it is, probably has as many inhabitants in its towns, as it had in the days of Abraham. Nor is this peculiar to Palestine; there are many that live in Barbary, and other places, in the same manner. And as the Kenites and Rechabites lived in Palestine in tents, and pastured their cattle there without molestation, when the country was very populous, so Maillet assures us, that great numbers of these people that live in tents, come into Egypt itself to pasture their cattle, a very populous country, and indeed the Holland of the Levant. As I do not know his account has ever appeared in English, I will here give it to the reader:—

"Besides these native inhabitants of Egypt, who have fixed habitations, and compose those numerous and populous villages of which I have spoken above, there are also in that part of the country that is next the deserts, and even often in those that border on the Nile, a sort of wandering people, who dwell in tents, and change their habitation, as the want of pasture or the variety of the seasons lead them. These people are called Bedouin Arabs; and we may reckon there are above two millions of them in Egypt. Some keep on the mountains, and at a distance from the cities and villages, but always in places where it is easy for them to have water. Others pitch their tents, which are very low and poor, in the neighbourhood of places that are inhabited, where they permit them for a small recompense to feed their flocks. They even give them up some lands to cultivate for their own use, only to avoid having any misunderstanding with people, who can do a great deal of mischief without any danger of having it returned upon them. For to avoid every thing of this kind, they have nothing to do but to penetrate a day's journey into the deserts, where, by their extreme frugality, and by the knowledge they have of places of water, they can subsist several months without great difficulty. There is not a more pleasing sight in the world, than the beholding, in the months of November, December, and January, those vast meadows, where the grass, almost as high as a man, is so thick that a bullock laid in it has enough of it without rising, within his reach, to feed on for a whole day, all covered with habitations and tents, with people and herds. And indeed it is at this time of the year that the Bedouins flock into Egypt, from three or four hundred leagues distance, in order to feed their camels and horses there. The tribute which they require of them for granting this permission, they pay with the produce of some manufactures of their wool, or with some sheep, which they sell, as well as their lambs, or some young camels, which they dispose of. As to what remains, accustomed as they are to extreme frugality, they live on a little, and a very small matter is sufficient for their support. After having spent a certain space of time in the neighbourhood of the Nile, they retire into the deserts, from whence, by routes with which they are acquainted, they pass into other regions, to dwell there in like manner some months of the year, till the return of the usual season calls them back to Egypt."

We see here that they are at liberty to feed their cattle, not only in the deserts adjoining to cultivated countries, but in those countries themselves, and in those that are full of people too. The commons then of these countries are not, cannot be, appropriated to this or that village, this or that district, but lie open to all, nor have they any notion of our rights of commoning. It was so anciently in Israel, as appears by the case of the Kenites and Rechabites, as well as by that ancient constitution among the Jews, ascribed by them to Joshua, and which is the first of ten that are supposed to have been established by him, by which it was lawful to feed a flock in the woods, everywhere, without any regard to the division of the lands between the tribes, so that those of the tribe of Naphtali might feed a flock in the woods of the tribe of Judah. These usages are extremely contrary to ours; the observing therefore that they continue still in full force in the East, may be requisite to engage us to admit such suppositions, in settling the Old Testament history, as we might otherwise hardly be willing to allow.—HARMER.

CHAPTER V.

Ver. 10. And in the days of Saul they made war with the Hagarites, who fell by their hand: and they dwelt in their tents throughout all the east *land* of Gilead.

The shepherds are not the only class of people that live in tents; many Orientals forsake their villages at the approach of summer, for the more airy and refreshing shelter which they afford. This custom, which may be traced to an antiquity very remote, explains, in the most satisfactory manner, an incident in the history of Jacob. When the patriarch, in consequence of a divine admonition, had formed the resolution to return from Mesopotamia to his father's house, he sent for Rachel and Leah to his flocks, and there informed them of his design; and on their consenting to go with him, he set out upon his journey so silently, that Laban had no notice of it till the third day after his departure. It appears, however, that he carried all his effects with him, and tents for the accommodation of his family; and that Laban, who pursued him, had tents also for the use of his followers. The reason is, it was the time of sheep-shearing, when the masters and all their retainers commonly lived under tents in the open fields; and had the greater part, if not the whole of their furniture with them, on account of the entertainments which were given on these joyful occasions. Thus was Jacob equipped at once for his journey, and Laban for the pursuit. It is not more difficult to account for the intelligence not reaching Laban till the third day after Jacob's escape. Laban's flocks were in two divisions—one under the care of Jacob, the other committed to the care of Laban's sons, at the distance of three days' journey; and Jacob's own flock, under the management of his family, were, probably for the same reason, at an equal distance. Besides this, there might be other circumstances which retarded the progress of the messenger, which the sacred historian did not think it necessary to state; the fact is certain, and all the incidents of the story are natural and easy. The custom of living in tents was not confined to people in the country; persons of distinction often retired from the towns into the fields, and lived under tents during the heats of summer. Tahmasp, a Persian monarch, used to spend the winter at Casbin, and to retire in the summer three or four leagues into the country, where he lived in tents at the foot of Mount Alouvent, a place famed for its cool and pleasant retreats. His successors acted in the same manner, till the time of Abbas the Great, who removed his court to Ispahan.—PAXTON.

CHAPTER IX.

Ver. 18. (Who hitherto *waited* in the king's gate eastward:) they *were* porters in the companies of the children of Levi.

This gate was so called, because Solomon built it and the rest of the wall on that side, at an extraordinary trouble and expense, raising the foundation four hundred cubits, or seven hundred and twenty-nine feet seven inches from the bottom of the deep valley of Kidron, by means of large stones, twenty cubits, or thirty-six feet five inches long, and six cubits, or ten feet ten inches high, so as to be on an equality with the rest of the surface. When Captain Light visited Jerusalem, in 1814, some of these large stones seem to have been remaining, for when describing the Turkish aga's house, which is built on the spot where the house of Pontius Pilate formerly stood, he says, "what attracted my observation most, were three or four layers of immense stones, apparently of the ancient town, forming part of the walls of the palace." The ancients delighted in building with these large kinds of stones, for in the ruins which we have of ancient buildings, they are often to be found of great magnitude. Mr. Wood, in his *Ruins of Palmyra and Balbec*, states, "that the stones which compose the sloping wall of the latter are enormous; some are from twenty-eight to thirty-five feet long, and nine feet high. There are three of the following dimensions: fifty-eight feet high, and twelve thick; they are of white granite, with large shining flakes like gypsum."

At Bagdad, the gate Al Talism is "now bricked up, in honour of its having been entered in triumph by the Sultan Murad, after his having recovered Bagdad from the Persians, and the weak grasp of the unworthy son of the great Abbas. In consequence of this signal event, the portal was instantly closed on the victor having marched through, and from that day has never been reopened. This custom of shutting up any passage that has been peculiarly honoured, that it may not be profaned by vulgar footsteps, appears to have prevailed very generally over the East. I found an instance of it at Ispahan, where the Ali Copi gate is, in like manner, held sacred for a similar reason." (Sir R. K. Porter.)—BURDER.

CHAPTER X.

Ver. 9. And when they had stripped him, they took his head, and his armour, and sent into the land of the Philistines round about to carry tidings unto their idols, and to the people.

After Saul had fallen on Mount Gilboa, his enemies "stripped him, and took off his head, and sent the tidings to their idols." When the heathen of the present day gain a victory over their enemies, they always take the tidings to their idols. There is the king, and there his general, and troops, and priests, and people, marching in triumph to the temple. Then they relate to the gods all their proceedings; how they conquered the foe, and that to them they have come to give the glory. But this practice is had recourse to, also, in the common affairs of life. A man delivered from prison, or any great emergency, always goes to his gods, to carry the joyful tidings. Hear them relate the story: "Ah! Swamy, you know Muttoo wanted to ruin me; he therefore forged a deed in my name, and tried to get my estates; but I resisted him, and it has just been decided before the court, that he is guilty. I am therefore come to praise you, O Swamy!"—ROBERTS.

CHAPTER XI.

Ver. 41. Uriah the Hittite, Zabad the son of Ahlai.

Foreigners resident in the country were permitted to serve in the Jewish armies, and they sometimes rose to a very high rank; for both Uriah and Ittai, who seemed to have held principal commands in the armies of David, were aboriginal Canaanites. But in succeeding ages, the kings of Judah, affecting to imitate the policy of the surrounding potentates, or distrusting the omnipotent protection of Jehovah, occasionally hired large bodies of foreign troops to fight their battles, who, like mercenaries of later times, after expelling the invaders, sometimes turned their arms against their employers, and ravaged the country which they came to protect.—PAXTON.

CHAPTER XII.

Ver. 8. And of the Gadites there separated themselves unto David, into the hold to the wilderness, men of might, *and* men of war *fit* for the battle, that could handle shield and buckler, whose faces *were like* the faces of lions, and *were* as swift as the roes upon the mountains.

See on 2 Sam. 2. 18.

Ver. 15. These *are* they that went over Jordan in the first month, when it had overflown all his banks; and they put to flight all *them* of the valleys, *both* towards the east and towards the west.

See on Josh. 3. 15.

Ver. 40. Moreover, they that were nigh them, *even* unto Issachar and Zebulun and Naphtali, brought bread on asses, and on camels, and on mules, and on oxen; *and* meat, meal, cakes of figs, and bunches of raisins, and wine, and oil, and oxen, and sheep abundantly: for *there was* joy in Israel.

The strong and docile ox was also taught to submit his shoulder to the heavy burden; for, at the accession of David to the throne of Israel, the people brought "bread on asses, and on camels, and on mules, and on oxen." He is less fitted, indeed, by the rotundity of his form, for this species of labour, than for those just mentioned. But although the very back of the ox, according to this elegant writer, declares that it has not been formed to receive a load, yet the concurring testimony of past ages assures us that it is not altogether unfit for that purpose. Ælian observes, that the bull submits to the bier, and carries a boy or a girl on his neck, and a woman on his back. The Roman authors mounted Bacchus on a bull, and made Europa travel in the same manner. These facts prove, that it was by no means uncommon to use the ox for burdens of every kind, and even for the saddle; a custom which Mr. Bruce avers, is still practised among some tribes. In Guzerat the oxen are perfectly white, with black horns, a skin delicately soft, and eyes rivalling those of the antelope in brilliant lustre. Those reared in the northern part of the province are noble animals, superior in size, strength, and docility; some of them travel with a hackery, a vehicle for the conveyance of women and children, from thirty to forty miles a day; and are yoked to the carriages of wealthy Hindoos in distant parts of India. In sweetness of temper and gentleness of manners they nearly resemble the elephant. Some of these oxen are valued at nearly two hundred pounds sterling.—Paxton.

CHAPTER XVII.

Ver. 16. And David the king came and sat before the Lord, and said, Who *am* I, O Lord God, and what *is* my house, that thou hast brought me hitherto?

The ceremonial of the Orientals does not end with the introduction of persons to one another, but continues during the whole visit. The most scrupulous attention is paid by all parties to the established tokens of respect; the posture of the body, the part of the room, and other circumstances, are all regulated by custom, to whose imperious dictates they have implicitly submitted from the remotest antiquity. One of the postures by which a person testifies his respect for a superior, is by sitting upon his heels, which is considered as a token of great humility. In this manner, says Dr. Pococke, resting on their hams, sat the attendants of the English consul, when he waited on the caia of the pacha of Tripoli. It was in this humble posture, probably, that David, the king of Israel, sat before the Lord in the sanctuary, when he blessed him for his gracious promise concerning his family; half sitting and half kneeling, so as to rest the body upon the heels. This entirely removes the ground of perplexity, which some expositors have felt, in their attempts to elicit a meaning from the phrase, sitting before the Lord, at once consistent with the majesty of Jehovah, and the humility of the worshipper; for this attitude expressed among the Orientals the deepest humility, and by consequence, was every way becoming a worshipper of the true God.—Paxton.

CHAPTER XVIII.

Ver. 9. Now when Tou king of Hamath heard how David had smitten all the host of Hadarezer king of Zobah, 10. He sent Hadoram his son to King David, to inquire of his welfare, and to congratulate him, because he had fought against Hadarezer, and smitten him; (for Hadarezer had war with Tou;) and *with him* all manner of vessels of gold and silver and brass.

Here, again, we have a beautiful and simple picture of eastern manners. Tou, the heathen king, sent a messenger to compliment David on his success over his enemies. Who, in the East, has not witnessed similar things? Has a man gained a case in a court of law; has he been blessed by the birth of a son; has he given his daughter in marriage; has he gained a situation under government; has he returned from a voyage or a journey, or finished a successful speculation;—then his friends and neighbours send messengers to congratulate him—to express the joy they feel in his prosperity; "so much so, that, had it come to themselves, their pleasure could not have been greater."—Roberts.

CHAPTER XXI.

Ver. 1. And Satan stood up against Israel, and provoked David to number Israel.

See on 2 Sam. 24. 1.

Ver. 5. And Joab gave the sum of the number of the people unto David. And all *they of* Israel were a thousand thousand and a hundred thousand men that drew sword: and Judah *was* four hundred threescore and ten thousand men that drew sword.

Few things in history are more surprising than the great numbers which are recorded as forming eastern armies, even the scripture accounts of the armies that invaded Judea, or were raised in Judea, often excite the wonder of their readers. To parallel these great numbers by those of other armies, is not all that is acceptable to the inquisitive; it is requisite also to show how so small a province as the Holy Land really was, could furnish such mighty armies of fighting men; with the uncertainty of the proportion of these fighting men to the whole number of the nation; in respect to which many unfounded conjectures have escaped the pens of the learned. This includes more importance than may be at first sight attached to it, because it is well known that Josephus, in narrating the same facts, often gives different numbers. In the story of Abijah, 1 Kings xv. 5, we read in some MSS. 40,000, instead of 400,000. The question is, which is wrong? since it has been concluded that both could not be right. Besides this, the answers to those who question the possibility of the Holy Land maintaining so great a population as the armies mentioned implies, have usually taken the proportion which Europe furnishes of fighting men to the mass of its inhabitants; and very erroneous conclusions (as I conceive) have been drawn from such calculations. It must be admitted, that the passages in which numbers are expressed in all ancient writings, and by parity of reason, in the scriptures, seem, more than many others, to justify suspicion of error in our present copies; and to understand them correctly requires much attention and information; especially when such numbers are very great. Having premised this, I proceed to attempt two particulars: *first*, by instances of numerous armies which *have been* occasionally raised, to show what *may* be done by despotic power, or the impulse of military glory; *secondly*, to show that the composition of Asiatic armies is such as may render credible those numbers which express their gross amount; while no just inference respecting the entire population of a country can be drawn from the numbers stated as occasionally composing its armies. As to the first particular, the accounts of the armies of Semiramis, of Darius, and of Xerxes, are in everybody's hands, but as these are not without suspicion of having been enlarged, either purposely by misreport, or accidentally by errors in copyists, I decline them; and rather submit to the reader's attention the account given by Knolles in his "History of the Turks," of the contending armies of *Bajazet* and *Tamerlane*. It is no bad specimen of the "I will" of military power, of the cares and anxieties attending on the station of command, and of the feelings of great minds on great occasions.

"So, marching on, Tamerlane at length came to Bachichich, where he staid to refresh his army eight daies, and there againe took a generall muster thereof, wherein were found (as most write) *four hundred thousand horse*, and *six hundred thousand foot*; or, as some others that were there present affirme, *three hundred thousand horsemen*, and *fiue hundred thousand foot of al nations*. Vnto whom he there gaue a generall pay, and, as his manner was, made vnto them an oration, informing them of such orders as he would haue kept, to the end they might the better obserue the same: with much other militarie discipline, whereof he was very curious with his captains. At which time, also, it was lawfull for euery common soldier to behold him with more boldness than on other daies, forasmuch as he did for that time, and such like, lay aside his imperial majestie, and shew himselfe more familiar vnto them......" Page 215.

..." *Malcozzius* hauing made true relation vnto *Baiazet*, was by him demanded 'whether of the two armies he thought bigger or stronger?' for now *Baiazet* had assembled a mightie armie of *three hundred thousand men*, or, as some report, of *three hundred thousand horsemen* and *two hundred thousand foot*. Whereunto *Malcozzius*, hauing before craued pardon, answered, 'That it could not be, but that *Tamerlane* might in reason haue the greater number, for that he was a commander of farre greater countries.' Wherewith proud *Baiazet* offended, in great choller replied, 'Out of doubt, the sight of the Tartarian hath made this coward so affraid, that he thinketh euery enemie to be two." 216...." All which *Tamerlane*, walking this night vp and down in his campe, heard, and much reioiced to see the hope that his soldiers had alreadie in general conceiued of the victorie. Who after the second watch returning vnto his pauillion, and there casting himself upon a carpet, had thought to haue slept a while; *but his cares not suffering him so to do, he then, as his manner was, called for a booke, wherein was contained the liues of his fathers and ancestors, and of other valient worthies, the which he vsed ordinarily to read, as he then did:* not as therwith vainly to deceiue the time, but to make vse thereof, by the imitation of that which was by them worthily done, and declining of such dangers as they by their rashness or ouersight fel into." Page 218..... [Vide the same kind of occupation of *Ahasuerus*, Esther vi. 1.]

..." My will is," said *Tamerlane*, " that my men come forward vnto me, as soon as they may, for I will aduance forward with *an hundred thousand footmen*, fiftie thousand vpon each of my two wings, and in the middest of them *forty thousand* of my best horsemen. My pleasure is, that after they haue tried the force of these men, that they come vnto my avauntgard, of whom I wil dispose, and *fifty thousand horse more* in three bodies, whom thou shalt command: which I wil assist with 80,000 horse, wherein shal be mine own person: hauing 100,000 footmen behind me, who shal march in two squadrons: and for my arereward I appoint 40,000 horse, and fiftie thousand footmen, who shal not march, but to my aid. And I wil make choice of 10,000 of my best horse, whom I wil send into euery place where I shal thinke needfull within my armie, for to impart my commands." (Knolles's History of the Turks, page 218.)

[It is impossible, on this occasion, not to recollect the immense army led by Napoleon Bonaparte into Russia, exceeding *six hundred thousand* troops; also the forces engaged around Leipsic, amounting (including both sides) to half a million of men. Vide LITERARY PANORAMA, for November, 1813.]

It may be said, " Such mighty empires may well be supposed to raise forces, to which the small state of Judea was incompetent;" and this may safely be admitted. But what was, in all probability, the nature and *composition* of the Jewish, as of other eastern armies, we may learn from the following relations, which contribute to strengthen the credibility of the greater numbers recorded as composing them. I shall first offer what Baron De Tott reports of the armies raised by the cham of the Crimea; and then, as still more descriptive of Asiatic armies, especially of those raised on the spur of an occasion, the remarks of M. Volney: " It may be presumed that the rustic, frugal life, which these pastoral people lead, favours population, while the wants and excesses of luxury, among polished nations, strike at its very root. In fact, it is observed, that the people are less numerous under the roofs of the Crimea, and the province of Boodjack, than in the tents of the Noguais. The best calculation we can make, is from a view of the military forces which the cham is able to assemble. We shall soon see this prince raising *three* armies at the same time; one of *a hundred thousand men*, which he commanded in person; another of *sixty thousand*, commanded by the calga; and a third of *forty thousand*, by the nooradin. He had the power of raising *double the number*, without prejudice to the necessary labours of the state.

" The invasion of New Servia, which had been determined on at Constantinople, was consented to in the assembly of the grand vassals of Tartary, and orders were expedited, throughout the provinces, for the necessary military supplies. *Three horsemen* were to be furnished by *eight families*, which number was estimated to be sufficient for the *three* armies, which were all to begin their operations at once. That of the nooradin, consisting of *forty thousand men*, had orders to repair to the Little Don; that of the calga, of *sixty thousand*, was to range the left coast of the Boristhenes, till they came beyond the Orela; and that which the cham commanded in person, of *a hundred thousand*, was to penetrate into New Servia." (De Tott.)

" *Sixty thousand men*, with them, are very far from being synonymous with *sixty thousand soldiers*, as in our armies. That of which we are now speaking affords a proof of this; it might amount, in fact, to forty thousand men, which may be classed as follows:—Five thousand Mamlouk cavalry, *which was the whole effective army;* about fifteen hundred Barbary Arabs, on foot, and no other infantry, for the Turks are acquainted with none; with them the cavalry is every thing. Besides these, each Mamlouk having in his suite *two* footmen, *armed with staves*, these would form a body of ten thousand valets, besides a number of servants and *serradgis*, or attendants on horseback, for the bey and kachefs, which may be estimated at two thousand: all the rest were sutlers, and the usual train of followers. Such was this army, as described to be in Palestine, by persons who had seen and followed it. The Asiatic armies are *mobs*, their marches ravages, their campaigns mere inroads, and their battles bloody frays. The strongest, or the most adventurous party, goes in search of the other, which not unfrequently flies without offering resistance: if they stand their ground, they engage pellmell, discharge their carbines, break their spears, and hack each other with their sabres; for they rarely have any cannon, and when they have, they are but of little service. *A panic frequently diffuses itself without cause:* one party flies, the other pursues, and shouts victory; the vanquished submits to the will of the conqueror, and the campaign often terminates without a battle." (Volney.)

It appears, by these extracts, that the numbers which compose *the gross* of Asiatic armies are very far from denoting the *true number of soldiers*, fighting men, of that army; in fact, when we deduct those whose attendance is of little advantage, it may be not very distant from truth, if we say, nine out of ten are such as, in Europe, would be forbid the army; nor is the suggestion absolutely despicable, that when we read 40, instead of 400, the true fighting corps of soldiers only are reckoned and stated. However that may be, these authorities are sufficient to justify the possibility of such numbers as scripture has recorded, being assembled for purposes of warfare; of which purposes plunder is not one of the least, in the opinion of those who usually attend a camp. It follows, also, that no conclusive estimate of the population of a kingdom can be drawn from such assemblages, under such circumstances; and therefore, that no calculation ought to be hazarded on such imperfect *data*.—TAYLOR IN CALMET.

CHAPTER XXII.

Ver. 19. Now set your heart and your soul to seek the LORD your God: arise, therefore, and build ye the sanctuary of the LORD God, to bring the ark of the covenant of the LORD, and the holy vessels of God, into the house that is to be built to the name of the LORD.

In all heathen temples, there are numerous vessels of brass, silver, and gold, which are especially *holy*. Those, however, of the highest castes, may be allowed to touch, and even borrow them for certain purposes. Thus, a native gentleman, who is going to give a feast, borrows the large caldron for the purpose of boiling the rice; should his daughter be about to be married, he has the loan of the silver salvers, plates, and even jewels; which, however, must all be purified by incense and other ceremonies when returned to the temple. " The ark" finds a striking illustration in the *keadagam* of the Hindoos,—a model of which may be seen in the house of the Royal Asiatic Society. In it are placed the idols, and other sacred symbols, which are carried on men's shoulders.—ROBERTS.

CHAPTER XXVI.

Ver. 6. Also unto Shemaiah his son were sons born, that ruled throughout the house of their father: for they were mighty men of valour.

It has been a frequent complaint among learned men, that it is commonly difficult, and oftentimes impossible, to illustrate many passages of the Jewish history, referred to in the annals of their princes, and in the predictions of their prophets, for want of profane historians of the neighbouring nations, of any great antiquity; upon which I have been ready to think, that it might not be altogether vain to compare with those more ancient transactions, events of a later date that have happened in those countries, in nearly similar circumstances, since human nature is much the same in all ages, allowing for the eccentricity that sometimes arises from some distinguishing prejudices of that particular time. The situation of the Christian kings of Jerusalem, in particular, in the twelfth century, bears, in many respects, a strong resemblance to that of the kings of Judah; and the history of the crusades may serve to throw some light on the transactions of the Jewish princes. At least the comparing them together may be amusing. It is said of King Uzziah, 1 Chron. xxvi. 6, that "he went forth and warred against the Philistines, and broke down the wall of Gath, and the wall of Jabneh, and the wall of Ashdod, and built cities about Ashdod and among the Philistines." Thus we find, in the time of the crusades, when that ancient city of the Philistines, called Ashkelon, had frequently made inroads into the territories of the kingdom of Jerusalem, the Christians built two strong castles not far from Ashkelon; and finding the usefulness of these structures, King Fulk, in the spring of the year of our Lord 1138, attended by the patriarch of Jerusalem and his other prelates, proceeded to build another castle, called Blanche Guarda, which he garrisoned with such soldiers as he could depend upon, furnishing them with arms and provisions. These watching the people of Ashkelon, often defeated their attempts, and sometimes they did not content themselves with being on the defensive, but attacked them, and did them great mischief, gaining the advantage of them. This occasioned those who claimed a right to the adjoining country, encouraged by the neighbourhood of such a strong place, to build many villages, in which many families dwelt, concerned in tilling the ground, and raising provisions for other parts of their territories. Upon this the people of Ashkelon, finding themselves encompassed round by a number of inexpugnable fortresses, began to grow very uneasy at their situation, and to apply to Egypt for help by repeated messages! Exactly in the same manner we may believe Uzziah built cities about Ashdod, that were fortified to repress the excursions of its inhabitants, and to secure to his people the fertile pastures which lay thereabout; and which pastures, I presume, the Philistines claimed, and indeed all the low land from the foot of the mountains to the sea, but to which Israel claimed a right, and of a part of which this powerful Jewish prince actually took possession, and made settlements for his people there, which he thus guarded from the Ashdodites: "He built cities about Ashdod, even among the Philistines," for so I would render the words, as the historian appears to be speaking of the same cities in both clauses. Uzziah did more than King Fulk could do, for he beat down the walls not only of Gath and Jabneh, two neighbouring cities, but of Ashdod itself, which must have cut off all thoughts of their disturbing the Jewish settlers, protected by strong fortresses, when they themselves lay open to those garrisons. Ashkelon, on the contrary, remained strongly fortified, by fortresses built by the Christians.—HARMER.

Ver. 13. And they cast lots, as well the small as the great, according to the house of their fathers, for every gate. 14. And the lot eastward fell to Shelemiah. Then for Zechariah his son (a wise counsellor) they cast lots, and his lot came out northward. 15. To Obed-edom southward; and to his sons the house of Asuppim. 16. To Shuppim and Hosah *the lot came forth* westward, with the gate Shallecheth, by the causeway of the going up, ward against ward.

Thus the gates were assigned to the different officers by lot. On the death of a parent, the whole of his fields and gardens are often divided among his children, and great disputes generally arise as to whom shall be given this or that part of the property. One says, "I will have the field to the east." "No," says another, "I will have that:" and it is not till they have quarrelled and exhausted their store of ingenuity and abuse, that they will consent to settle the matter by lot. The plan they take is as follows: they draw on the ground the cardinal points: they then write the names of the parties on separate leaves, and mix them all together: a little child is then called, and told to take one leaf and place it on any point of the compass he pleases; this being done, the leaf is opened, and to the person whose name is found therein will be given the field or garden which is in that direction. I think it therefore probable, that the lots eastward, westward, northward, and southward, which fell to Shelemiah, Zechariah, Obed-edom, and Shuppim, were drawn something in the same way.—ROBERTS.

Ver. 27. Out of the spoils won in battles did they dedicate to maintain the house of the LORD.

According to the law of Moses, the booty was to be divided equally between those who were in the battle, and those who were in the camp, whatever disparity there might be in the number of each party. The law further requires, that out of that part of the spoils which was assigned to the fighting men, the Lord's share should be separated: and for every five hundred men, oxen, sheep, &c. they were to take one for the high-priest, as being the Lord's first-fruits, and out of the other moiety belonging to the children of Israel, they were to give for every fifty men, oxen, sheep, &c. one to the Levites. Among the Greeks and Romans the plunder was brought together into one common stock, and divided afterward among the officers and soldiers, paying some respect to their rank in the distribution. Sometimes the soldiers made a reserve of the chief part of the booty, to present, by way of compliment, to their respective generals. The gods were always remembered. And the priests had sufficient influence to procure them a handsome offering, and other acceptable presents.—BURDER.

CHAPTER XXVII.

Ver. 25. And over the king's treasures *was* Azmaveth the son of Adiel: and over the storehouses in the fields, in the cities, and in the villages, and in the castles, *was* Jehonathan the son of Uzziah.

Subterranean granaries were common in the East. The following is a detailed account of those now used by the Moors:—After the harvest they used to enclose their corn in subterraneous granaries, which are pits dug in the earth, where the corn is preserved for a considerable time. This custom is very ancient, and ought to be general in all warm countries, inhabited by wandering people. To secure the corn from moisture, they line these pits with straw, in proportion as they fill them, and cover them with the same; when the granary is filled, they cover it with a stone, upon which they put some earth in a pyramidal form, to disperse the water in case of rain. Among the wealthier part, the fathers commonly fill one granary at the birth of each child, and empty it at their marriage. I have seen corn preserved in this manner during five-and-twenty years. It had lost its whiteness. When by motives of convenience, or by an imperial order, the Moors are obliged to change their habitations, not being able to carry their grain with them, they leave over these granaries a mark of stones heaped together: they have much trouble in finding them again. It is the custom now to observe the earth at the rising of the sun, when a thick vapour ascends from them: they then discover the granary, upon which the sun has a marked effect, on account of the fermentation of the corn which is shut up.—BURDER.

Ver. 28. And over the olive-trees, and the sycamore-trees that *were* in the low plains, *was* Baal-hanan the Gederite: and over the cellars of oil *was* Joash.

When our translation represents Joash as over the cellars of oil, in the time of King David, 1 Chron. xxvii. 28, they have certainly without any necessity, and perhaps improperly, substituted a particular term for a general expression. Joash was at that time, according to the sacred historian, over the treasures of oil; but whether it was kept in cellars, or in some other way, does not at all appear in the original history. The modern Greeks, according to Dr. Richard Chandler, do not keep their oil in cellars, but in large earthen jars, sunk in the ground, in areas before their houses. The custom might obtain among the Jews: as then it was needless, it must be improper to use the particular term cellars, when the original uses a word of the most general signification. It is certain they sometimes buried their oil in the earth, in order to secrete it in times of danger, on which occasion they must be supposed to choose the most unlikely places, where such concealment would be least suspected, in their fields; whether they were wont to bury it, at other times, in their courtyards, cannot be so easily ascertained.—HARMER.

The Egyptians are not the only people to whose palate the fruit of the sycamore is agreeable; Hasselquist, the Swedish traveller, found it very grateful to the taste; he describes it as soft, watery, and sweetish, with something of an aromatic flavour. The fruit of this tree comes to maturity several times in a season; according to some writers not fewer than seven times, although prolific figs, or such as are perfectly formed, ripen only once. Thus the sycamore produces a fresh crop of agreeable, and not unwholesome fruit, seven times a-year, for the use of those that dwell under its shadow; a boon which perhaps no other tree in the garden of Nature bestows on man. Nor is it a dangerous or a laborious task to gather the figs; they seem to have so little hold of the parent tree, that "if they be shaken, they shall even fall into the mouth of the eater." The disposition of the fig-tree to part with her untimely or precocious figs, is noticed by John, in the book of Revelation: "And the stars of heaven fell unto the earth, even as a fig-tree casteth her untimely figs when she is shaken of a mighty wind." This accounts for the appointment of a particular officer in the reign of David, whose sole duty it was to watch over the plantations of sycamore and olive-trees: "And over the olive-trees and the sycamore-trees that were in the low plains, was Baalhanan the Gederite." So valuable was the sycamore in the land of Canaan, during the reign of David, (from which undoubtedly may be inferred the high estimation in which it was held in every age,) that, in the commission of Baalhanan, the officer charged with its protection, it is joined with the olive, one of the most precious gifts which the God of nature has bestowed on the oriental nations. Hasselquist found the sycamore growing in great numbers in the plains and fields of Lower Egypt, which verifies the accuracy of the inspired writer; and it appears from the same traveller, that the olive delights in similar situations; for, in his journey from Jaffa to Rama, he passed through fine vales abounding with olive-trees.—PAXTON.

Ver. 30. Over the camels also *was* Obil the Ishmaelite: and over the asses *was* Jehdeiah the Meronothite.

Natural historians mention two varieties of this animal, the domestic and the wild ass; but it is to the former our attention at present is to be directed. His colour is generally a reddish brown; a circumstance to which he owes his name in the Hebrew text; for (חמור) *hamor* is derived from a verb which signifies to be red or dun. This appears to have been the predominating colour in the oriental regions; but we learn from the song of Deborah, that some asses were white, and on this account reserved for persons of high rank in the state. The term (אתון) *athon* is another name for that creature, from a root which signifies to be firm or strong; because he is equal to a greater load than any animal of the same size. To this quality Jacob alluded in his last benediction: "Issachar is a strong ass, couching down between two burdens." Or, it may refer to the stubborn temper for which he is remarkable, and the stupid insensibility which enables him to disregard the severest castigation, till he has accomplished his purpose. These qualities are beautifully described by Homer, in the 11th book of the Iliad; but the passage is too long to be quoted.

In the patriarchal ages, the breed of this animal, which we regard with so much unmerited contempt, was greatly encouraged, and constituted no inconsiderable portion of wealth among oriental shepherds. It is on this account the number of asses in the herds of Abram, and other patriarchs, is so frequently stated by Moses, in the book of Genesis. So highly were they valued in those times of primitive simplicity, that they were formed into separate droves, and committed to the management of princes, and other persons of distinction. The sacred historian informs us, that Anab, a Horite prince, did not think it unbecoming his dignity to feed the asses of Zibeon his father: and that the sons of Jacob seized the asses of Shechem and his people, and drove them away, with the sheep and the oxen. During the seven years of famine that wasted the land of Egypt, and reduced the people to the greatest distress, Joseph purchased their asses, and gave them corn to preserve them alive. When the people of Israel subdued the Midianites, they carried away "threescore and one thousand asses." In times long posterior, Saul, the son of Kish, was sent in quest of his father's asses, which had strayed from their pasture; and he was engaged in this service when the prophet Samuel received a command to anoint him king over Israel. After David's accession to the throne, and the Lord had given him rest from all his enemies, he appointed Jehdeiah the Meronothite, a prince in Israel, to superintend this part of his property. Nor was this animal unworthy of such attention and care. His humility, patience, and temperance, qualities in which he greatly excels, eminently fitted him for the service of man. His great value was soon discovered, and he was preferred even to the horse, for many domestic purposes. The sons of Jacob employed him to carry burdens of every kind; and he seems to have been the only quadruped they took with them in their repeated journeys into Egypt, to purchase corn for their households; and their descendants continued for many ages to employ him in the same manner. The fruits of the field, the produce of the vineyard, provisions and merchandise of all kinds, were carried on the backs of asses.

He was long used for the saddle in the oriental regions; and persons of high rank appeared in public, mounted on this animal. Those which the great and wealthy selected for their use, were larger and more elegant animals than the mean and unshapely creature with which we are acquainted. Dr. Russel, in his history of Aleppo, mentions a variety of the ass in Syria, much larger than the common breed; and other travellers say, that some of them in Persia are kept like horses for the saddle, which have smooth hair, carry their heads well, and are quicker in their motions than the ordinary kind, which are dressed like horses and taught to amble like them.—PAXTON.

CHAPTER XXIX.

Ver. 24. And all the princes, and the mighty men, and all the sons likewise of King David, submitted themselves unto Solomon the king.

The Hebrew has, for submitted, "Gave the hand under." To give "the hand under," is a beautiful orientalism to denote *submission*. See the man who wishes to submit to a superior; he stands at a short distance, then stooping, he keeps moving his hands to the ground, and says, "I submit, my lord." "You recollect having heard that Kandan and Chinnan had a serious quarrel?"—"Yes, I heard it."—"Well, they have settled the matter now, for Chinnan went to him last evening, and 'gave his hand under.'" "The Modeliar is no longer angry with me, because I have put down my hand to the ground." "That rebellious son has, for many years, refused to acknowledge his father's authority, but he has at last put his hand under," *i. e.* he has submitted to him—has become obedient.—ROBERTS. (*See Engraving.*)

THE SECOND BOOK OF CHRONICLES.

CHAPTER I.

Ver. 16. And Solomon had horses brought out of Egypt, and linen yarn; the king's merchants received the linen yarn at a price.

See on 1 Kings 10. 28.

CHAPTER V.

Ver. 12. Also the Levites, *which were* the singers, all of them of Asaph, of Heman, of Jeduthun, with their sons and their brethren, *being* arrayed in white linen, having cymbals and psalteries and harps, stood at the east end of the altar, and with them a hundred and twenty priests sounding with trumpets.

No person in Greece and Italy appeared at an entertainment in black, because it was a colour reserved for times of mourning, but always in white, or some other cheerful colour, which corresponded with the joyous nature of the occasion. Such were the garments of salvation in which the people of Israel celebrated their festivals, or entertained their friends. When Solomon brought up the ark of the Lord from the city of David, and placed it between the cherubim in the most holy place, the sons of Asaph, of Heman, and Jeduthun, and their brethren, who conducted the songs in the temple, stood at the east end of the altar, arrayed in vestures of fine linen, the chosen emblem of purity and joy. The few faithful witnesses that remained in Sardis, and had not defiled their garments, were promised the distinguishing honour of walking with their Saviour in white. And to encourage them in their steadfast adherence to the cause of God and truth, it is added, "He that overcometh, the same shall be clothed in white raiment." On the mount of transfiguration, the raiment of Christ became white as the light; and in the same garb of joy and gladness the angels appear at his resurrection.—Paxton.

CHAPTER VI.

Ver. 28. If there be dearth in the land, if there be pestilence, if there be blasting, or mildew, locusts, or caterpillars; if their enemies besiege them in the cities of their land; whatsoever sore or whatsoever sickness *there be.*

We are so little acquainted with the various species of destructive insects that ravage the eastern countries, that it may be thought extremely difficult to determine what kind was meant by Solomon, in his prayer at the dedication of the temple, 2 Chron. vi. 28, by the word (חסיל) *chaseel,* which our version renders *caterpillars,* and which is distinguished by him there from the locusts, which genus is so remarkable for eating up almost every green thing; but a passage of Sir John Chardin may probably illustrate that part of Solomon's address to him whom he considered as the God of universal nature. The paragraph of Solomon's prayer is this: *When heaven is shut up, and there is no rain, because they have sinned against thee; if they pray towards this place,* &c. . . . . *If there be in the land famine, if there be pestilence, blasting, mildew, locusts, or if there be caterpillars; if their enemies besiege them in the land of their cities,* &c. . . . *Then hear thou in heaven thy dwelling-place, and forgive and do,* &c. The causes of famine, reckoned up here, are want of rain, blasting, mildew, locusts, and caterpillars, according to our translation: with which may be compared the following passage of Chardin, in the second tome of his Travels: "Persia is subject to have its harvest spoiled by hail, by drought, or by insects, either locusts, or small insects, which they call *sim,* which are small white lice, which fix themselves on the foot of the stalk of corn, gnaw it, and make it die. It is rare for a year to be exempt from one or the other of these scourges, which affect the ploughed land and the gardens," &c. The enumeration by Solomon, and that of this modern writer, though not exactly alike, yet so nearly resemble each other, that one would be inclined to believe these small insects are what Solomon meant, by the word translated caterpillars in our English version.—Harmer.

CHAPTER VII.

Ver. 13. If I shut up heaven that there be no rain, or if I command the locusts to devour the land, or if I send pestilence among my people.

A term used by the sacred writers to signify the locust, is (חגב) *hagab,* which our translators render sometimes locust and sometimes grasshopper. They translate it locusts in the following passage: "If I shut up heaven that there be no more rain, or if I command the locusts (*hagab*) to devour the land, or if I send a pestilence among my people: if my people shall humble themselves and pray unto me, and seek my face, then will I hear from heaven, and will forgive their sin, and heal their land." We cannot reasonably doubt that the word, in this place, denotes the locust, for this declaration was made in answer to Solomon's prayer at the dedication of the temple, that if the heaven should be shut up, and there should be no rain; or if there should be famine, pestilence, blasting, mildew, locust, or caterpillar, then God would hear them when they spread forth their hands towards that holy place. It must also be remembered, that the grasshopper is an inoffensive animal, or noxious in a very slight degree, and therefore by no means a proper subject for deprecation in the temple. This circumstance also shows, that the Hebrew term here does not mean the cicada, as some writers have supposed; for though the noise which they make is extremely disagreeable and disturbing, as Chandler complains, it is not an insect so distressing to the Orientals, as to admit the idea that it was a subject of solemn prayer at the dedication. To disturb the slumbers of the weary traveller, or the toil-worn peasant, and to devour the fruits of the earth, and plunge the inhabitants of a country into all the horrors of famine, are evils of a very different magnitude.

Hagab is rendered grasshopper in the twelfth chapter of Ecclesiastes; and the circumstances, it must be confessed, harmonize with the character of those creatures; for it will be readily admitted that their chirping must be disagreeable to the aged and infirm, that naturally love quiet, and are commonly unable to bear much noise. But it is more probable that *hagab* denotes the locust, which is proverbially loquacious. They make a very loud, screaking, and disagreeable noise, with their wings; if one begin, others join, and the hateful concert becomes universal; a pause then ensues, and, as it were, on a signal given, it again commences; and in this manner they continue squalling for two or three hours without intermission. Mr. Harmer is of opinion, that *hagab* ought to be rendered locust in this passage too, because it becomes a burden by its depredations, and desire fails; that is, every green thing disappears, and nature puts on the semblance of universal deadness: and such is the affecting appearance of the human body in extreme old age; it resembles a tree which the locust has stripped of its leaves, has deprived of its bark, and left naked and bare, to wither in the blast, and moulder, by degrees, into the dust from whence it rose. The interpretation is ingenious; but the common meaning seems to be still more expressive, and is certainly more affecting. Some kinds of the locust are very small and light. Were the cicada not to be classed among the locust tribes, still the figure remains in all its force and beauty. The minutest of those small insects becomes a burden to extreme old age, weighed down with a load of years, and worn with toils and cares, to the verge of existence. The powers and faculties of body and mind are equally debilitated, and the relish for the enjoyments of sense, which he once felt so keenly, is extinguished for ever. Some insects live under a regular government, and, like the bee, submit to the authority of a chief; but the wise man observes, "The locusts have no king, yet they go forth by bands." How just is this remark! The head of the column, when the army is not tossed and scattered by the winds, which often happens, is directed by their voracious desire of food; and the rest follow in long succession, under the influence of the same instinct; but the devastations they commit are as methodical and complete, as if they acted under the strictest discipline.

In Barbary and Palestine, the locusts appear about the latter end of March. By the middle of April their numbers are so increased, that in the heat of the day they form themselves into large and numerous swarms, fly in the air like a succession of clouds; and, as the prophet Joel expresses it, "darken the sun." When a brisk gale happens to blow, so that these swarms are crowded by others, or thrown one upon another, the musing and intelligent traveller obtains a lively idea of the Psalmist's comparison: "I am tossed up and down like the locust." In the month of May, when the ovaries of those insects are ripe and turgid, each of these swarms begins gradually to disappear, and retire into the plains, where they deposite their eggs. These are no sooner hatched in June, than each of the broods collect themselves into a large body, sometimes extended more than a furlong on every side; and then marching directly towards the sea, they suffer nothing to escape them, eating up every thing that is green and juicy, from the tender and lowly vegetable, to the coarse leaf and bark of the vine and the pomegranate. In prosecuting their work of destruction, they keep their ranks like soldiers in order of battle, climbing as they advance, over every tree or wall that stands in their way; they enter into the very houses and bedchambers, like so many thieves. It is impossible to stop their motions, or even to alter their line of march; while the front is regardless of danger, and the rear presses on so close, that a retreat is altogether impossible. A day or two after one of these broods is in motion, others are already hatched to march and glean after them, gnawing off the very bark, and the young branches of such trees as had before escaped with the loss only of their fruit and foliage; so justly have they been compared by the prophet to a great army.—Paxton.

CHAPTER IX.

Ver. 24. And they brought every man his present, vessels of silver, and vessels of gold, and raiment, harness, and spices, horses, and mules, a rate year by year.

Presents of vestments, on the other hand, are frequently made in these countries to the great, and those that are in public stations; and they expect them. Thevenot tells us, it was a custom in Egypt, in his time, for the consuls of the European nations to send the bashaw a present of so many vests, and so many besides to some officers, both when a new bashaw came, or a new consul entered his office, as were rated at above a thousand piasters. Does not this last account remind us of the presents that were made to Solomon, by the neighbouring princes, at set times, part of which, we are expressly told, consisted of raiment? 2 Chron. ix. 24. This may be thought not very well to agree with a remark of Sir J. Chardin, mentioned under a former observation, "that vestments are not presented by inferiors to superiors; or even by an equal to an equal;" but there is really no inconsistency; vestments are not the things that are chosen by those that would make a present to the great, in common; but they may be ordered to be sent as a sort of a tribute, or a due which the superior claims.

The other things mentioned in that passage of Chronicles, vessels of silver, and vessels of gold, harness and spices, horses and mules, still continue to be thought fit presents to the great. So Russel tells us, in his account of the eastern visits, that if it is a visit of ceremony from a bashaw or a person in power, a fine horse, sometimes with furniture, or some such valuable thing, is made a present to him at his departure; and the Baron Fabricius, in his letters concerning Charles XII. of Sweden, tells us, that when he was seized at Bender, the house being set on fire, the rich presents that had been made him, consisting of tents, sabres, saddles and bridles adorned with jewels, rich housings and harnesses, to the value of 200,000 crowns, were consumed. Of the rest, the vessels of silver and the spices may be illustrated by that story of D'Herbelot concerning Akhschid, the commander of an eastern province, who is said to have purchased peace of Jezid, general of the troops of one of the califs, by sending him a present of seven hundred thousand drachms of silver in ready money; four hundred loads of saffron, which that country produced in abundance; and four hundred slaves, who each of them carried a rich turban of silk in a silver basin.—Harmer.

Presents of dresses are alluded to very frequently in the historical books of scripture, and in the earliest times: when Joseph gave to each of his brethren a change of raiment, and to Benjamin five changes of raiment, it is mentioned without particular notice, and as a customary incident, (Gen. xlv. 22, 23.) Naaman gave to Gehazi, from among the presents intended for Elisha, who declined accepting any, (as we have seen above, some persons did, on extraordinary occasions,) two changes of raiment; and even Solomon, king as he was, received raiment as presents, (2 Chron. ix. 24.) This custom is still maintained in the East: it is mentioned by all travellers; and we have merely chosen to give the following extract from De la Motraye, in preference to what might easily have been produced from others, because he notices, as a particularity, that the grand seignior gives his garment of honour *before* the wearer is admitted to his presence; but the vizier gives his honorary dresses *after* the presentation: will this apply to the parable of the wedding garment, and to the behaviour of the king, who expected to have found all his guests clad in robes of honour? (Matt. xxii. 11.) Is any thing like this management observable, Zech. iii.? Joshua being introduced to *the angel of the Lord*, not to the Lord himself, stood before the angel with filthy garments; but he ordered a handsome *caffetan* to be given him. Jonathan, son of Saul, divested himself of his robe, and his upper garment, even to his sword, his bow, and his girdle—partly intending David the greater honour, as having been apparel worn by himself; but principally, it may be conjectured, through haste and speed, he being impatient of honouring David, and covenanting for his affection. Jonathan would not stay to *send* for raiment, but instantly gave him his own. The idea of honour connected with the *caffetan*, appears also in the prodigal's father,—"*bring forth the best robe.*" We find the liberality in this kind of gifts was considerable: Ezra ii. 69, "The chief of the fathers gave one hundred priests' garments." Neh. vii. 70, "The Tirshatha gave five hundred and thirty priests' garments." This would appear sufficiently singular among us; but in the East, where to give is to honour, the gift of garments, or of any other usable commodities, is in perfect compliance with established sentiments and customs.

"The vizier entered at another door, and their excellencies rose to salute him after their manner, which was returned by a little inclining of his head; after which he sat down *on the* CORNER *of his sofa, which is the most honourable place;* then his chancellor, his kiahia, and the Chiaouz Bashaw, came and stood before him, till coffee was brought in; after which M. de Chateauneuf presented M. de Ferriol to him, as his successor, who delivered him the king his master's letters, complimenting him as from his majesty and himself, to which the vizier answered very obligingly; then they gave two dishes of coffee to their excellencies, with sweetmeats, and afterward the perfumes and sherbet; then they clothed them with CAFFETANS *of a silver brocade, with large silk flowers;* and to those that were admitted into the apartments with them, they gave *others of brocade*, almost all silk, except some slight gold or silver flowers; according to the custom usually observed towards all foreign ministers.

"Caffetans are long vests of gold or silver brocade,

flowered with silk, which the grand seignior and the vizier present to those to whom they give audience: the grand seignior *before*, and the vizier *after* audience." (De la Motraye's Travels.)—TAYLOR IN CALMET.

Ver. 28. And they brought unto Solomon horses out of Egypt, and out of all lands.

The people of Israel were, by their law, forbidden to ultiply horses; for which several reasons may be assigned. The land of Canaan, intersected in almost every direction by hills and mountains, was less adapted to the rearing of horses than other parts of Syria; but the principal reason might be, to discourage the art of war, to which mankind in all ages have shown so strong a propensity, which is so hostile to the interests of true religion, of which they were the chosen depositaries, and prevent them from relying for the defence of their country, rather on the strength of their armies, which, in the East, chiefly consisted of cavalry, than on the promised aid of Jehovah. This wise and salutary command, however, was often disregarded, even by the more pious kings of David's line, who imitated the princes around them in the number and excellence of their horses. Solomon set the first example of transgressing that precept, and of departing from the simplicity of his fathers: "For Solomon gathered together chariots and horsemen; and he had a thousand and four hundred chariots, and twelve thousand horsemen, whom he bestowed in the cities for chariots, and with the king at Jerusalem." Josephus informs us he had twenty thousand horses, which surpassed all others in beauty and swiftness. These were mounted by young men in the bloom of youth, excelling all their countrymen in stature and comeliness, with long flowing hair, habited in rich dresses of Tyrian purple, their hair powdered with gold-dust, which, by reflecting the beams of the sun, shed a dazzling splendour around their heads. It was the practice of those in the highest rank of society, in the time of Josephus, to adorn their persons in the gorgeous manner he describes; and the strong partiality which the historian cherished for his country, it is evident, induced him to transfer the extravagance of his own age to the time of Solomon. The same overweening desire to exalt the power, the riches, and the splendour of his nation, in the most brilliant epoch of her history, has prevailed upon him to contradict the page of inspiration itself, which expressly limits the number of Solomon's horses to twelve thousand. The sacred historian informs us, that these horses were purchased in Egypt, and in all the surrounding countries, by the Jewish merchants, where the fame of so great a king procured them easy access, and liberal encouragement. It is extremely probable that Solomon's stud was replenished from regions lying at a very great distance from Jerusalem; but the sacred writers particularly celebrate the breeds of Assyria, Togarmah, and Egypt. The horses of Togarmah were brought to the fairs of Tyre, and were sufficiently numerous and valuable to attract the notice of Ezekiel, who thus addresses the merchant city: "They of the house of Togarmah traded in thy fairs, with horses, and horsemen, and mules." These, in the opinion of Bochart and other geographers, were the Cappadocians, whose country has been, from time immemorial, celebrated for its superior breed of horses. The prophets of Jehovah frequently advert to the admirable qualities of the Assyrian charger. Isaiah, describing the terrible devastation which the land of Judea was doomed to suffer by the Assyrian armies, warns his people that their horses' hoofs shall be counted like flint—compact and durable as the flinty rock; qualities which, in times when the shoeing of horses was unknown, must have been of very great importance. The value of a solid hoof has not escaped the notice of Homer's muse, who celebrates, in many passages of his immortal poems, the brazen-footed horses. In the admirable instructions which Virgil communicates to the Italian husbandmen, a solid hoof is mentioned as indispensably requisite in a good breed of horses. The amazing rapidity of their movements is expressed with much beauty and force in the next clause: "Their wheels shall be like a whirlwind;" and, with equal felicity, in these words of Jeremiah: "Behold, he shall come up as clouds, and his chariots shall be as a whirlwind; his horses are swifter than eagles." The prophet Habakkuk, in describing the same quality, uses a different figure, but one equally striking: "Their horses also are swifter than the leopards, and are more fierce than the evening wolves; and their horsemen shall spread themselves, and their horsemen shall come from far; they shall fly as the eagle that hasteth to eat."—PAXTON.

CHAPTER XIII.

Ver. 5. Ought ye not to know that the LORD God of Israel gave the kingdom over Israel to David for ever, *even* to him and to his sons by a covenant of salt?

The Orientals were accustomed also to ratify their federal engagements by salt. This substance was, among the ancients, the emblem of friendship and fidelity, and therefore used in all their sacrifices and covenants. It is a sacred pledge of hospitality which they never venture to violate. Numerous instances occur of travellers in Arabia, after being plundered and stripped by the wandering tribes of the desert, claiming the protection of some civilized Arab, who, after receiving him into his tent, and giving him salt, instantly relieves his distress, and never forsakes him till he has placed him in safety. An agreement, thus ratified, is called in scripture, "a covenant of salt." The obligation which this symbol imposes on the mind of an Oriental, is well illustrated by the Baron De Tott in the following anecdote: One who was desirous of his acquaintance, promised in a short time to return. The baron had already attended him half way down the staircase, when stopping, and turning briskly to one of his domestics, Bring me directly, said he, some bread and salt. What he requested was brought; when, taking a little salt between his fingers, and putting it with a mysterious air on a bit of bread, he ate it with a devout gravity, assuring De Tott he might now rely on him.—PAXTON.

CHAPTER XVI.

Ver. 14. And they buried him in his own sepulchres, which he had made for himself in the city of David, and laid him in the bed which was filled with sweet odours and divers kinds *of spices* prepared by the apothecaries' art; and they made a very great burning for him.

A passage from Drummond's Travels ought not to be omitted here, in which he gives an account of the manner in which a large quantity of spices and perfumes was made use of, to do honour to the dead. It seems, according to a tradition that prevailed among the Turks, "An eminent prophet, who lived in Mesopotamia many ages ago, whose name was Zechariah, was beheaded by the prince of that country, on account of his virtuous opposition to some lewd scheme of his. His head he ordered to be put into a stone urn, two feet square, upon the top of which was an inscription, importing that that urn enclosed the head of that great prophet Zechariah. This urn remained in the castle of Aleppo till about eight hundred years ago, when it was removed into an old Christian church in that city, afterward turned into a mosque, which decaying, another was built near it, and the place where the head was deposited choked up by a wall." About forty years before Mr. Drummond wrote this account, which was in December, 1748, consequently about the year 1708, a zealous grand vizier, who pretended to have been admonished in a dream to remove this stone vessel into a more conspicuous place, had it removed accordingly, with many religious ceremonies, and affixed in a conspicuous part of a mosque: and in the close of all it is said, "the urn was opened, and filled with spices and perfumes, to the value of four hundred pounds." Here we see in late times honour was done to the supposed head of an eminent saint, by filling its repository with odoriferous substances. The bed of sweet spices, in which Asa was laid, seems to have been of the same kind, or something very much like it. Might not large quantities of precious perfumes, in like manner, be strewed, or designed to be strewed, about the body of our Lord? This would require large quantities. Zechariah of Mesopotamia had been dead so long, that nothing of this kind could be done with any view to preserve his head from decay, it was merely to do him honour: the spices used by the Jews in burial might be for the same purpose. —Harmer.

CHAPTER XX.

Ver. 20. And they arose early in the morning, and went forth into the wilderness of Tekoa: and as they went forth, Jehoshaphat stood and said, Hear me, O Judah, and ye inhabitants of Jerusalem; believe in the Lord your God, so shall you be established; believe his prophets, so shall ye prosper.

See on 2 Sam. 10. 9, 10.

Ver. 28. And they came to Jerusalem with psalteries and harps and trumpets, unto the house of the Lord.

See on 1 Sam. 16. 20.

CHAPTER XXI.

Ver. 20. Thirty and two years old was he when he began to reign, and he reigned in Jerusalem eight years, and departed without being desired; howbeit they buried him in the city of David, but not in the sepulchres of the kings.

The burying of persons in their cities is also an eastern manner of doing them honour. They are in common buried without the walls of their towns, as is apparent, from many places of the Old and New Testament. The ancient Jews also were thus buried; but sometimes they bury in their cities, when they do a person a distinguished honour. "Each side of the road," says the author of the History of the piratical states of Barbary, "without the gate, is crowded with sepulchres. Those of the pacha and the deys are built near the gate of Babalonet. They are between ten and twelve feet high, very curiously white-washed, and built in the form of a dome. Hali Dey, as a very eminent mark of distinction, was buried in an enclosed tomb within the city. For forty days successively his tomb was decorated with flowers, and surrounded with people, offering up prayers to God for his soul. This dey was accounted a saint, and a particular favourite of heaven, because he died a natural death; a happiness of which there are few instances since the establishment of the deys in Algiers." No comment is more lively, or more sure, than this, on those that speak of the burying of the kings of the house of David within Jerusalem; those sepulchres, and that of Huldah the prophetess, being the only ones to be found there. But it is not a perfect comment; for it is to be remembered that a peculiar holiness belonged to Jerusalem, as well as the dignity of being the royal city, but no particular sanctity is ascribed to Algiers, by those people that buried Hali Dey there.—Harmer.

CHAPTER XXII.

Ver. 11. But Jehoshabeath, the daughter of the king, took Joash the son of Ahaziah, and stole him from among the king's sons that were slain, and put him and his nurse in a bedchamber. So Jehoshabeath, the daughter of King Jehoram, the wife of Jehoiada the priest, (for she was the sister of Ahaziah,) hid him from Athaliah, so that she slew him not.

The bedchamber in the temple, in which Jehosheba hid Joash in the days of Athaliah, mentioned 2 Kings xi. 2, and 2 Chron. xxii. 11, does not seem to mean a *lodging-chamber*, but a *chamber* used as a *repository for beds*. I am indebted to Sir John Chardin for this thought, which seems to be a just one; for the original words בחדר המטות *bachadar hammittoth*, signify a *chamber of beds*, and the expression differs from that which is used when a lodging-chamber is meant. He supposes then that place is meant, where beds are kept: for in the East, and particularly in Persia and Turkey, beds are not raised from the ground with bedposts, a canopy, and curtains; people lie on the ground. In the evening they spread out a mattress or two of cotton, very light, &c. Of these they have several laid up in great houses, until they may have occasion to use them, and have a room on purpose for them. In a chamber of beds, the room used for the laying up beds, it seems Joash was secreted. Understand it how you will, it appears that people were lodged in the temple; and if any lodged there, it is to be supposed at particular times there were many, especially the relations and friends of the high-priest. Here it may be right to consult Neh. xiii. 4, 5. In the room in which beds were deposited, not a common bedchamber, it seems the young prince lay concealed. Chardin complains the Vulgar Latin translation did not rightly understand the story; nor have others represented the intention of the sacred writer perfectly, if he is to be understood after this manner.—Harmer.

CHAPTER XXIII.

Ver. 19. And he set the porters at the gates of the house of the Lord, that none *which was* unclean in any thing should enter in.

The entrance of the inner chamber of a Budhuist temple is usually low and narrow; and on each side stands a dreadful looking fellow formed of clay, and above the size of the human form, with a huge serpent in his hand, seemingly ready to lash with it whoever enters; but intended chiefly, I believe, to admonish such as come unprepared. They are styled *moorakărayo*, the usual word for *guards* or *sentinels*.—Callaway.

CHAPTER XXV.

Ver. 12. And *other* ten thousand *left* alive did the children of Judah carry away captive, and brought them unto the top of the rock, and cast them down from the top of the rock, that they all were broken in pieces.

The Greeks and Romans condemned some of their criminals to be cast down from the top of a rock. In the time of Pitts, the inhabitants of Constantine, a town of Turkey, built on the summit of a great rock, commonly executed their criminals who had been guilty of more atrocious crimes, by casting them headlong from the cliff. This punishment Amaziah, the king of Judah, inflicted on ten thousand Edomites, whom he had taken captive in war: "Other ten thousand left alive, did the children of Judah carry away captive, and brought them to the top of the rock, and cast them down from the top of the rock, and they all were broken in pieces."—Paxton.

CHAPTER XXVI.

Ver. 10. Also he built towers in the desert, and digged many wells: for he had much cattle, both in the low country and in the plains; husbandmen *also*, and vinedressers in the mountains, and in Carmel: for he loved husbandry.

The Indians build pagodas, not to be used as temples, but for the protection of their flocks, in case of any alarm. They are placed in the fields, and surrounded with good walls. Over the gates they raise high pyramids, full of pictures of their gods; and within their circuit were many little chapels, every one of which contained an idol. In these countries, the soldiers are very ill paid, and the commanders permit them to take what they can get. They therefore often seize the cattle, when the shepherds think least of it. Travellers also retire into these pagodas.—Burder.

William of Tyre describes a country not far from the Euphrates, as inhabited by Syrian and Armenian Christians, who fed great flocks and herds there, but were in subjection to the Turks, who, though few in number, yet living in strong places among them, kept them under, and received tribute from these poor peasants who inhabited the villages, and employed themselves in country business. I do not know whether this may not give us a truer view of the design of those towers that Uzziah built in the wilderness, mentioned 2 Chron. xxvi. 10, than commentators have done, who have supposed they were conveniences made for sheltering the shepherds from bad weather, or to defend them from the incursions of enemies; for they might rather be designed to keep the nations that pastured there in awe; to prevent their disputing with his servants about wells, and also to induce them quietly to pay that tribute to which the seventh and eighth verses seem to refer.—HARMER.

Ver. 15. And he made in Jerusalem engines, invented by cunning men, to be on the towers and upon the bulwarks, to shoot arrows and great stones withal: and his name spread far abroad: for he was marvellously helped till he was strong.

The batteringram was an engine with an iron head, resembling the head of a ram, with which they beat down the enemies' walls. Of this, Potter mentions three kinds; the first was plain and unartificial, being nothing but a long beam with an iron head, which the soldiers drove with main force against the wall; the second was hung with ropes to another beam, by the help of which they thrust it forward with much greater force; the third differed from the former only in being covered with a testudo, or shroud, to protect the soldiers that worked it from the darts of the enemy. The beam was sometimes no less than a hundred and twenty feet in length, and covered with iron plates, lest those who defended the walls should set it on fire; the head was armed with as many horns as they pleased. Josephus reports, that one of Vespasian's rams, the length of which was only fifty cubits, which came not up to the size of several of the Grecian rams, had a head as thick as ten men, and twenty-five horns, each of which was as thick as one man, and placed a cubit's distance from the rest; the weight, hung (as was customary) upon the hinder part, was no less than one thousand and five hundred talents; when it was removed from one place to another, it was not taken in pieces; a hundred and fifty yoke of oxen, or three hundred pair of horses and mules, laboured in drawing it; and no less than fifteen hundred men employed their utmost strength in forcing it against the walls. At other times, we find these rams driven upon wheels. Such was the formidable engine, of which the prophet warned the inhabitants of Jerusalem, and which, in the hands of the Romans, levelled at last the walls of that proud metropolis with the ground.

To this may be added, various engines for casting arrows, darts, and stones of a larger size; of which the most remarkable was the balista, which hurled stones of a size not less than millstones, with so great a violence as to dash whole houses in pieces at a blow. Such were the engines which Uzziah, the king of Judah, planted on the walls and towers of Jerusalem, to defend it against the attacks of an invading force: "And he made in Jerusalem engines, invented by cunning men, to be on the towers, and upon the bulwarks, to shoot arrows and great stones withal." Some of these inventions, however, had been in use long before; for in the reign of David, the batteringram was employed in the siege of Abel-Bethmaachah: "They cast up a bank against the city, and it stood in the trench; and all the people that were with Joab battered the wall to throw it down." These powerful engines, invented by Jewish artists, and worked by the skill and vigour of Jewish soldiers, were undoubtedly the prototypes of those which the celebrated nations of Greece and Rome afterward employed with so much success in their sieges.—PAXTON.

Ver. 23. So Uzziah slept with his fathers, and they buried him with his fathers in the field of the burial which *belonged* to the kings; for they said, He *is* a leper: and Jotham his son reigned in his stead.

The kings and princes of the oriental regions are often subjected to trial after their decease by their insulted and oppressed people, and punished according to the degree of their delinquency. While the chosen people of God were accustomed to honour in a particular manner the memory of those kings who had reigned over them with justice and clemency, they took care to stamp some mark of posthumous disgrace upon those who had left the world under their disapprobation. The sepulchres of the Jewish kings were at Jerusalem; where, in some appointed receptacle, the remains of their princes were deposited; and from the circumstance of these being the cemetery for successive rulers, it was said when one died and was buried there, that he was gathered to his fathers. But several instances occur in the history of the house of David, in which, on various accounts, they were denied the honour of being entombed with their ancestors, and were deposited in some other place in Jerusalem. To mark, perhaps, a greater degree of censure, they were taken to a small distance from Jerusalem, and laid in a private tomb. Uzziah, who had, by his presumptuous attempt to seize the office of the priesthood, which was reserved by an express law for the house of Aaron, provoked the wrath of heaven, and been punished for his temerity with a loathsome and incurable disease, "was buried with his fathers in the field of the burial which belonged to the kings; for they said, He is a leper." It was undoubtedly with a design to make a suitable impression on the mind of the reigning monarch, to guard him against the abuse of his power, and teach him respect for the feelings and sentiments of that people for whose benefit chiefly he was raised to the throne, that such a stigma was fixed upon the dust of his offending predecessors. He was, in this manner, restrained from evil, and excited to good, according as he was fearful of being execrated, or desirous of being honoured after his decease. This public mark of infamy was accordingly put on the conduct of Ahaz: "They buried him in the city, even in Jerusalem, but they brought him not into the sepulchres of the kings of Israel."—PAXTON.

CHAPTER XXVIII.

Ver. 27. And Ahaz slept with his fathers, and they buried him in the city, *even* in Jerusalem; but they brought him not into the sepulchres of the kings of Israel: and Hezekiah his son reigned in his stead.

The Israelites were accustomed to honour in a peculiar manner the memory of those kings who had reigned over them uprightly. On the contrary, some marks of posthumous disgrace followed those monarchs who left the world under the disapprobation of their people. The proper place of interment was in Jerusalem. There, in some appointed receptacle, the remains of their princes were deposited: and, from the circumstance of this being the cemetery for successive rulers, it was said, when one died and was so buried, that he was *gathered to his fathers.* Several instances occur in the history of the kings of Israel, wherein, on certain accounts, they were not thus interred with their predecessors, but in some other place in Jerusalem. So it was with Ahaz, who, though brought into the city, was not buried in the sepulchres of the kings of Israel. In some other cases, perhaps to mark out a greater degree of censure, they were taken to a small distance from Jerusalem. It is said that *Uzziah was buried with his fathers in the field of the burial which belonged to the kings; for they said, He is a leper.* (2 Chron. xxvi. 23.) It was doubtless with a design to make a suitable impression on the minds of their kings while living, that such distinctions were made after their decease. They might thus restrain them from evil or excite them to good, according as they were fearful of being execrated, or desirous of being honoured, when they were dead. The Egyptians had a custom in some measure similar to this; it was however general as to all persons, though it received very particular attention, as far as it concerned their kings. It is thus described in Franklin's *History of Ancient and Modern Egypt:* "As soon as a man was dead, he was brought to his trial. The public accuser was heard. If he proved that the deceased had led a bad life, his memory was condemned, and he was deprived of the honours of sepulture. Thus, that sage people were affected with laws which extended even beyond the grave, and every one, struck with the disgrace inflicted on the dead person, was afraid to reflect dishonour on his own memory, and that of his family. But what was singular, the sovereign himself was not exempted from this public inquest upon his death. The public peace was interested in the lives of their sovereigns in their administration, and as death terminated all their actions, it was then deemed for the public welfare, that they should suffer an impartial scrutiny by a public trial, as well as the most common subject. Even some of them were not ranked among the *honoured dead*, and consequently were deprived of public burial. The Israelites would not suffer the bodies of some of their flagitious princes to be carried into the sepulchres appropriated to their virtuous sovereigns. The custom was singular: the effect must have been powerful and influential. The most haughty despot, who might trample on laws human and divine in his life, saw, by this solemn investigation of human conduct, that at death he also would be doomed to infamy and execration."

What degree of conformity there was between the practice of the Israelites and the Egyptians, and with whom the custom first originated, may be difficult to ascertain and decide, but the conduct of the latter appears to be founded on the same principle as that of the former, and as it is more circumstantially detailed, affords us an agreeable explanation of a rite but slightly mentioned in the scriptures. —BURDER.

CHAPTER XXXII.

Ver. 3. He took counsel with his princes and his mighty men to stop the waters of the fountains, which *were* without the city; and they did help him. 4. So there was gathered much people together, who stopped all the fountains, and the brook that ran through the midst of the land, saying, Why should the kings of Assyria come and find much water?

That stream which flowed from Siloam is, I presume, the brook that Hezekiah speaks of, which in the time of the crusades was not attempted to be stopped up. What the cause of that was we are not told, but it seems the waters of some springs without the city were conveyed into Jerusalem at the time; and that Solomon in his reign had attempted to do the like, and had effected it: as to part of the water of the springs of Bethlehem, it was no wonder then that Hezekiah should think of introducing the waters of Siloam in like manner into the city, in order at once to deprive the besiegers of its waters, and benefit the inhabitants of Jerusalem by them. Probably it was done in the same manner that Solomon brought the waters of Bethlehem thither, that is, by collecting the water of the spring or springs into a subterraneous reservoir, and from thence, by a concealed aqueduct, conveying them into Jerusalem, with this difference, that Solomon took only part of the Bethlehem water, leaving the rest to flow into those celebrated pools which remain to this day; whereas Hezekiah turned all the water of Siloam into the city, absolutely stopping up the outlet into the pool, and filling it up with earth, that no trace of it might be seen by the Assyrians. Which seems indeed to be the account of the sacred writer, 2 Chron. xxxii. 30, "The same Hezekiah also stopped the upper watercourse of Gihon, (which is another name for Siloam,) and brought it straight down to the west side of the city of David." Thus our translators express it: but the original may as well be rendered, "Hezekiah stopped the upper going out (מוצא *motsa*) of the waters of Gihon, and directed them underneath, (למטה *lemattah*,) to the west of the city of David;" and so Pagninus and Arias Montanus understand the passage; he stopped up, that is, the outlet of the waters of Gihon into the open air, by which they were wont to pass into the pool of Siloam, and became a brook; and by some subterraneous contrivance directed the waters to the west side of Jerusalem.—HARMER.

Ver. 5. Also he strengthened himself, and built up all the wall that was broken, and raised *it* up to the towers, and another wall without, and repaired Millo *in* the city of David, and made darts and shields in abundance.

See on 2 Sam. 5. 9.

Ver. 8. With him *is* an arm of flesh: but with us *is* the LORD our God, to help us, and to fight our battles. And the people rested themselves upon the words of Hezekiah, king of Judah.

The margin has, for rested upon, "leaned." "I lean (from *sārukirathu*) on the words of that good man." "All people gladly lean on the words of that just judge." "Who would lean on the words of that false man?" "Alas! we leaned upon his words, and have fallen into trouble." "My husband, have I not leaned upon your words? Yes, and therefore I have not fallen."—ROBERTS.

EZRA.

CHAPTER IV.

Ver. 14. Now, because we have maintenance from *the king's* palace, and it was not meet for us to see the king's dishonour, therefore have we sent and certified the king.

Literally, "*salted with the salt of his palace.*" Some have supposed that the words refer to their receiving a stipend from the king of Persia, which was wont to be paid in salt; others suppose it expresses an acknowledgment that they were preserved by that king's protection, as flesh is preserved by salt. And many pieces of collateral learning are introduced to embellish these conceits. It is sufficient, to put an end to all these conjectures, to recite the words of a modern Persian monarch, whose court Chardin attended some time about business. "Rising in wrath against an officer, who had attempted to deceive him, he drew his sabre, fell upon him, and hewed him in pieces, at the feet of the grand vizier, who was standing, and whose favour the poor wretch courted by this deception. And looking fixedly upon him, and the other great lords that stood on each side of him, he said, with a tone of indignation, 'I have then such ungrateful servants and traitors as these *to eat my salt.* Look on this sword, it shall cut off all these perfidious heads.'" (Tome iii. p. 149.)

The Persian great men do not receive their salaries, it is well known, in salt; and the officer that was killed was under the immediate protection of the grand vizier, not the prince: our English version has given, then, the sense, though it has not literally translated the passage. It means the same thing as eating one's bread signifies here in the West, but, perhaps, with a particular energy. I beg leave to introduce one remark here, of a very different nature, that we may learn from this story, that Samuel's hewing Agag in pieces, though so abhorrent from our customs, differs very little, in many respects, from this Persian execution. Samuel was a person of high distinction in Israel: he had been their judge, or supreme governor under God; he was a prophet too; and we are ready to think his sacred hands should not have been employed in the actual shedding of blood. How strange would it be in our eyes, if we should see one of our kings cutting off the head of a traitor with his own hands; or an archbishop of Canterbury stabbing a foreign captive prince! But different countries have very different usages. Soliman, king of Persia, who hewed this unfaithful officer in pieces, reigned over a much larger and richer country than Judea, and at the same time was considered by his subjects as sacred a person as Samuel: supposed to be descended from their prophet Mohammed, to reign by a divine constitution, and to be possessed, we are assured by this writer in another place, of a kind of prophetic penetration and authority.—I have said, it appears to signify the same thing as eating one's bread, in the West, but, probably, with some particular kind of energy, marking out not merely the obligations of gratitude, but the strictest ties of fidelity. For as the letter was written not only by some of the great officers on the western side of the Euphrates, but in the name of the several colonies of people that had been transplanted thither, the Dinaites, the Apharsathchites, the Tarpelites, &c. ver. 9, 10, it is not to be supposed these tribes of people all received their food from the palace, or a stipend for their support; but with great adulation they might pretend they considered themselves as held under as strong engagements of fidelity to the kings of Persia, as if they had eaten salt in his palace.

The following story from D'Herbelot will explain this, if the views of these ancient Persians may be supposed to correspond with those of the Persians of the ninth century.

Jacoub ben Laith, the founder of a dynasty of Persian princes called the Soffarides, rising, like many other of the ancestors of the princes of the East, from a very low state to royal power, being in his first setting out in the use of arms no better than a freebooter or robber, is yet said to have maintained some regard to decency in his depredations, and never to have entirely stripped those that he robbed, always leaving them something to soften their affliction. Among other exploits that are recorded of him, he is said to "have broken into the palace of the prince of that country, and having collected a very large booty, which he was on the point of carrying away, he found his foot kicked something, which made him stumble. He imagined it might be something of value, and putting it to his mouth, the better to distinguish what it was, his tongue soon informed him it was *a lump of salt.* Upon this, according to the morality, or rather superstition of the country, where the people considered salt as *a symbol and pledge of hospitality*, he was so touched, that he left all his booty, retiring without taking away any thing with him. The next morning, the risk they had run of losing many valuable things, being perceived, great was the surprise, and strict the inquiry, what should be the occasion of their being left. At length Jacoub was found to be the person concerned, who having given an account, very sincerely, of the whole transaction to the prince, he gained his esteem so effectually, that it might be said with truth, that it was his *regard for salt* that laid the foundation of his after fortune. The prince employed him as a man of courage and genius in many enterprises, and finding him successful in all of them, he raised him, by little and little, to the chief posts among his troops, so that at that prince's death, he found himself possessed of the command in chief, and had such interest in their affections, that they preferred his interests to those of the children of the deceased prince, and he became *absolute master* of that province, from whence he afterward spread his conquests far and wide." When the Apharsathchites, the Tarpelites, and the other transplanted tribes, told Artaxerxes, the Persian monarch, that they were salted with the salt of his palace, it appears, according to these things, to mean, that they considered themselves as eating his bread, on account of being put and continued in possession of a considerable part of the Jewish country, by him and his predecessors; and that their engagements of fidelity to him were indeed as strong, as if they had eaten salt in his palace.—HARMER.

CHAPTER V.

Ver. 7. They sent a letter unto him, wherein was written thus: Unto Darius the king, all peace.

The people of the East are always very particular as to the way in which they commence a letter. Thus, they take into consideration the rank of the individual to whom they write, and keep in view also what is their object. "To you who are respected by kings." "To him who has the happiness of royalty." "To the feet of his excellency, my father, looking towards the place where he is worshipping, I write." A father to his son says, "Head of all blessings, chief of life, precious pearl." When people meet each other on the road, they say, "*Salam*, peace to you." Or, when they send a message, or ask a favour, it is always accompanied by a *salam.*—ROBERTS.

CHAPTER VI.

Ver. 2. And there was found at Achmetha, in the palace that *is* in the province of the Medes, a roll, and therein *was* a record thus written.

This passage proves the great antiquity of the custom of making copies to be deposited in the archives, of the important ordinances of the magistrates, and particularly of charters, granted either to individuals or whole communities. Thus, in an inscription on an ancient marble, quoted by Thomas Smith, it is said of a privilege granted for a separate sepulchre, "Of this inscription two copies have been made, one of which is deposited in the archives." In the same manner, elsewhere, "A copy of this inscription shall be deposited in the archives."—ROSENMULLER.

Ver. 11. Also I have made a decree, that whosoever shall alter this word, let timber be pulled down from his house, and, being set up, let him be hanged thereon.

Lud. de Dieu observes, that there is no proper construction in the words which we render, *and being set up;* he would therefore translate them, after the Seventy, "and standing, let him be beat upon it," or "whipped," as the manner was among the Persians and other nations. Among the Jews, they who were beaten, did not stand, but lay down. Deut. xxv. 2. If a greater punishment be here meant, then he makes the first words refer to the wood, and the latter to the man. "And from above, let it fall upon him:" that is, the stake being lifted up, shall be stuck into his body, and come out at his fundament. This was a cruel practice among the eastern people, and is yet continued there.—BURDER.

CHAPTER VIII.

Ver. 21. Then I proclaimed a fast there at the river of Ahava, that we might afflict ourselves before our God, to seek of him a right way for us, and for our little ones, and for all our substance.

The whole valley was covered with the tents of the pilgrims; for a very few, compared with their numbers, could find lodgings in the building. These several encampments, according to their towns or districts, were placed a little apart, each under its own special standard. Their cattle were grazing about, and the people who attended them, in their primitive eastern garbs. Women appeared, carrying in water from the brooks, and children were sporting at the tent doors. Towards evening, this pious multitude, to the number of eleven hundred at least, began their evening orisons, literally shouting their prayers, while the singing of the hymns, responded by the echoes from the mountains, was almost deafening. At intervals, during the devotion, matchlocks, muskets, and pistols, were repeatedly fired, division answering division, as if it were some concerted signal. This mixture of military and religious proceeding, produced an effect perfectly novel to a European eye, in the nineteenth century; though it might have been more than sufficiently familiar to that of a knight-companion in the thirteenth, when the crusades covered every hauberk with a pilgrim's amice. But the recollection of what country I saw these in, conjured up a very different image. I was in the land of the Medes, on the very spot to which the ten tribes were brought in captivity about two thousand years ago; and from which, in the fulness of time, the scattered remnants were collected, (after the first return, B. C. 536, by command of Cyrus,) and led back to their native land, on the decree of Artaxerxes the king, when Ezra gathered them together to the river that runneth to Ahava, and there they abode in their tents three days: and he viewed the people and the priests. And he proclaimed a fast there, that they might afflict themselves before God, to seek of him a right way for them, and for their little ones, and for their substance. And the Lord was entreated of them, and he delivered them from the hand of the enemy, and of such as lay in wait by the way. And Ezra, and those with him, came to Jerusalem. We see in this account, from the book of Ezra, chap. viii. that the wild tribes of the mountains were then regarded as banditti; and that no decrees of safe-conduct from the king would have more effect in those days, than in the present, to protect a rich caravan from ambuscade and depredation. But I must own, there are some points of observation in the encampment before me, which a little disturbed the resemblance between its holy grouping, and that which followed the really pious ordinance of the sacred scribe of Israel. The Mohammedan evening prayer over, all was noise of another description; bustle and riotous merriment, more like preparations of a fair, than a worship; showing at once the difference in spirit between the two religions. In the one, the moral law walked hand in hand with the ceremonial; and the mandate of worshipping the one God, in purity of heart, and in strictness of practice, was unvaryingly asserted in the chastisement or welfare of the people; and so we see it was acknowledged by the seemly and humble joy under pardon, with which the recalled Israelites returned to the land of their temple. But here the performance of certain rites seemed to be all in all. The preachers of the multitude holding forth, that as they advance nearer to the shrines of their pilgrimage, so in due proportion their sins depart from them; and thus every step they approach, the load becomes lighter and lighter, till the last atom flies off the moment they fall prostrate before the tomb of the prophet, or saint: and from which holy spot they rise perfectly clear, free, and often too willing to commence a new score, to be as readily wiped away.—Sir R. K. Porter.

CHAPTER IX.

Ver. 3. And when I heard this thing, I rent my garment and my mantle, and plucked off the hair of my head and of my beard, and sat down astonished.

Oriental mourners divested themselves of all ornaments, and laid aside their jewels, gold, and every thing rich and splendid in their dress. The Grecian ladies were directed in this manner to mourn the death of Achilles: "Not clothed in rich attire of gems and gold, with glittering silks or purple." This proof of humiliation and submission Jehovah required of his offending people in the wilderness: "Therefore, now put off thy ornaments from thee, that I may know what to do unto thee. And the children of Israel stripped themselves of their ornaments by the Mount Horeb." Long after the time of Moses, that rebellious nation again received a command of similar import: "Strip you, and make you bare, and gird sackcloth upon your loins."—Paxton.

Ver. 6. And said, O my God! I am ashamed and blush to lift up my face to thee, my God: for our iniquities are increased over *our* head, and our trespass is grown up unto the heavens.

"Ah, that fellow's sins are on his head: how numerous are the sins on his head. Alas! for such a head as that. Who can take them from his head? His iniquity is so great, you may see it on his head." Does a man wish to extenuate his crime, to make himself appear not so great a sinner as some suppose, he asks, "What! has my guilt grown up to heaven? no! no!" "Abominable wretch, your guilt has reached to the heavens." "Can you call that little, which has grown up to the heavens?"—Roberts.

Ver. 8. And now for a little space grace hath been *showed* from the Lord our God, to leave us a remnant to escape, and to give us a nail in his holy place, that our God may lighten our eyes, and give us a little reviving in our bondage.

See on Isa. 22. 23.

The margin has, "or a pin," that is, "a constant and sure abode." It is worthy of notice, that the Tamul translation has it, "a hut in his holy place." To "lighten" the eyes signifies to give comfort, to strengthen, to refresh. A father says to his son, when he wishes him to do any thing, "My child, make these eyes light." "O woman, enlighten my eyes, lest I be swallowed up with sorrow." "O that our eyes were clear! who will take away the darkness from my eyes?"—Roberts.

CHAPTER X.

Ver. 1. Now when Ezra had prayed, and when he had confessed, weeping and casting himself down before the house of God, there assembled unto him out of Israel a very great congregation of men, and women, and children: for the people wept very sore.

People on their arrival from England are astonished at the apparent devotion of the Hindoos, when they see them cast themselves down before their temples. Those of high rank, and in elegant attire, do not hesitate thus to prostrate themselves in the dust, before the people. How often, as you pass along, may you see a man stretched his full length on the ground, with his face IN the dust, pouring out his complaint, or making his requests unto the gods. It matters not to him who or what may be near him; he heeds not, and moves not, till his devotions are finished.—Roberts.

Ver. 9. Then all the men of Judah and Benjamin gathered themselves together unto Jerusalem within three days: it *was* the ninth month, and the twentieth *day* of the month; and all the people sat in the street of the house of God, trembling because of *this* matter, and for the great rain.

What a marked illustration we have of this passage every wet monsoon. See the people on a court-day, or when they are called to the different offices on business. The rain comes on; they have only a piece of cotton round their loins, and a small leaf, which they carry over their heads: they all run in a stooping position (as if that would save them from the rain) to the nearest tree, and there they sit in groups, huddled together, and trembling "for the great rain."—Roberts.

NEHEMIAH.

CHAPTER I.

Ver. 11. O Lord, I beseech thee, let now thine ear be attentive to the prayer of thy servant, and to the prayer of thy servants, who desire to fear thy name; and prosper, I pray thee, thy servant this day, and grant him mercy in the sight of this man: for I was the king's cupbearer.

Houbigant supposes that Nehemiah repeated this prayer, which he had often before used, now again in silence, while he administered the cup to the king in his office. The office of cupbearer was a place of great honour and advantage in the Persian court, because of the privilege which it gave him who bare it, of being daily in the king's presence, and the opportunity which he had thereby of gaining his favour, for procuring any petition he should make to him. That it was a place of great advantage seems evident by Nehemiah's gaining those immense riches which enabled him for so many years, out of his own purse only, to live in his government with great splendour and expense, without burdening the people. According to Xenophon, the cupbearer with the Persians and Medes used to take the wine out of the vessels into the cup, and pour some of it into his left hand, and drink it, that if there was any poison in it, the king might not be hurt; and then he delivered it to him upon three fingers. —Burder.

CHAPTER II.

Ver. 2. Wherefore the king said unto me, Why *is* thy countenance sad, seeing thou *art* not sick? this *is* nothing *else* but sorrow of heart.

When friends, servants, or acquaintances, have a request to make, or a secret to disclose, they walk about with a gloomy countenance, and never speak but when spoken to. Their object is to induce you to ask what is the matter, because they think you will then be disposed to listen to their complaint.—Roberts.

Ver. 7. Moreover, I said unto the king, If it please the king, let letters be given me to the governors beyond the river, that they may convey me over, till I come into Judah.

No person of consequence travels in the East without a letter, or *kattali*, *i. e.* a command from the Rasa, the governor, the collector, or officer in authority, to the different chiefs of the districts through which he may have to travel. Were it not for this, there would often be a difficulty in getting supplies, and there would generally be a great delay; the officers would be insolent and overbearing, and the purveyors would demand thrice the sum the articles were worth. The letters in question are generally in duplicate, so that one precedes the traveller, and the other is in his possession. Thus, when he arrives at the choultry or rest-house, there will always be people to receive him, who are ready to furnish him with supplies, and coolies to help him on his journey. Sometimes they declare they are in the greatest want; they cannot get rice, they have neither fish nor fowls, and are brought to the lowest ebb of misery.—Roberts.

Ver. 8. And the king granted me, according to the good hand of my God upon me.

The hand is sometimes taken in an ill sense for inflicting punishments, and sometimes in a good sense, for we extend favours to men with the hand. Thus Drusius explains Psalm lxxxviii. 5, *cut off from thy hand*, that is, fallen from thy grace and favour. Pindar thus uses *the hand of God*, for his help and aid, Θεου σὺν παλαμα, *by the hand of God*: which the scholiast interprets, by the power and help of God. Thus Nehemiah is here to be understood.—Burder.

CHAPTER IV.

Ver. 3. Now Tobiah the Ammonite *was* by him, and he said, Even that which they build, if a fox go up, he shall even break down their stone wall.

When men deride the workmanship of a mason, they say, "*Che!* why, if a dog or a jackal run against that wall, it will fall." "A wall! why, it will not keep out the jackals."—Roberts.

Ver. 14. And I looked, and rose up, and said unto the nobles, and to the rulers, and to the rest of the people, Be not ye afraid of them: remember the Lord *which is* great and terrible, and fight for your brethren, your sons and your daughters, your wives and your houses.

The ancients appear to have done more to excite the valour of their soldiers, than merely exhorting them to be courageous. This will appear in the following citation: "A circumstance which greatly tends to inflame them with heroic ardour, is the manner in which their battalions are formed. They are neither mustered nor imbodied by chance: they fight in clans, united by consanguinity, a family of warriors: their tenderest pledges are near them in the field. In the heat of the engagement, the soldier hears the shrieks of his wife, and the cries of his children. These are the darling witnesses of his conduct; the applauders of his valour, at once beloved and valued. The wounded seek their mothers and their wives: undismayed at the sight, the women count each honourable scar, and suck the gushing blood: they are even hardy enough to mix with the combatants, administering refreshment, and exhorting them to deeds of valour." (Tacitus, *De Mor. Germ.*)—Burder.

Ver. 21. So we laboured in the work: and half of them held the spears, from the rising of the morning till the stars appeared.

Thus did the people labour from the earliest dawn till the latest glimpse of evening light. "Well, Tamby, have you found your cattle?" "Found them? no! and I wandered from the rising east, till the stars appeared." "At what time do you intend to leave the temple?" "Not till the stars appear." "When do you expect the guests?" "Immediately when the stars appear."—Roberts.

CHAPTER V.

Ver. 13. Also I shook my lap, and said, So God shake out every man from his house, and from his labour, that performeth not this promise, even thus be he shaken out and emptied.

When men or women curse each other, they shake the lap, *i. e.* their cloth, or robe, and say, "It shall be so with thee." Does a man begin to shake his *sali*, or waistcloth, in the presence of another, the other will say, "Why do you shake your cloth here? go to some other place." "What! can you shake your lap here? do it not, do it not." "Yes, yes; it is all true enough; this misery has come upon me through that wretched man shaking his cloth in my presence." The natives always carry a pouch, made of the leaf of the cocoa, or other trees, in their lap; in one part of which they keep their money, and in another their areca-nut, betel leaf, and tobacco. It is amusing to see how careful they are never to have that pouch EMPTY; for they have an idea, that so long as a single coin shall be found in it, (or any of the articles alluded to,) the ATTRACTION will be so great, that the contents of the pouch will not be long without companions. See the Englishman, who wants any thing out of a pouch or bag; if he cannot soon find the article he requires, he shakes out the whole: not so the Hindoo; he will fumble and grope for an hour, rather than shake out the whole. "Do that! why, who knows how long the pouch will remain empty?" It is therefore evident, that to shake the lap conveyed with it the idea of a curse.—Roberts.

Instead of the fibula that was used by the Romans, the Arabs join together with thread, or with a wooden bodkin, the two upper corners of this garment; and after having placed them first over one of their shoulders, they then fold the rest of it about their bodies. The outer fold serves them frequently instead of an apron, in which they carry herbs, loaves, corn, and other articles, and may illustrate several allusions made to it in scripture: thus, "One of the sons of the prophets went out into the field, to gather herbs, and found a wild vine, and gathered there of wild gourds, *his lapful*." And the Psalmist offers up his prayer, that Jehovah would "render unto his neighbours sevenfold into their bosom, their reproach." The same allusion occurs in our Lord's direction to his disciples: "Give, and it shall be given unto you; good measure, pressed down, and shaken together, and running over, shall men give into your bosom." It was also the fold of this robe which Nehemiah shook before his people, as a significant emblem of the manner in which God should deal with the man who ventured to violate his oath, and promise to restore the possessions of their impoverished brethren: "Also, I shook my lap, and said, So God shake out every man from his house, and from his labour, that performeth not this promise, even thus be he shaken out and emptied." —Paxton.

He shook the dust out of the foreskirts of his garment, as a symbol of what follows. A similar rite was used in the case of peace and war, when the Roman ambassadors proposed the choice of one to the Carthaginians, as having either in their bosom to shake out. (Florus, l. ii. c. 6. Livy, l. xxi. c. 18.) "When the Roman ambassadors entered the senate of Carthage, they had their toga gathered up in their bosom. They said, We carry here peace and war: you may have which you will. The senate answered, You may give which you please. They then shook their toga, and said, We bring you war. To which all the senate answered, We cheerfully accept it."—Burder.

Ver. 14. Moreover from the time that I was appointed to be their governor in the land of Judah, from the twentieth year even unto the two and thirtieth year of Artaxerxes the king, *that is*, twelve years, I and my brethren have not eaten the bread of the governor.

Nehemiah did not eat that bread which properly belonged to him as the governor. When the Orientals say they eat the rice of a person, it denotes they are under obligations to him. People who have formerly been employed by you often come and say, "Ah, my lord, how long it is since I had the pleasure of eating your rice." Those who are in the service of the government, are said to eat the rice of the king. A servant, who is requested to injure his master, says, "No, no; have I not eaten his rice for many days?" Of a person who has been faithful to a superior, it is said, "Yes, yes; he has eaten his rice, or he would not have been so true to him."—Roberts.

Ver. 15. But the former governors that *had been* before me were chargeable unto the people, and had taken of them bread and wine, besides forty shekels of silver; yea, even their servants bare rule over the people: but so did not I, because of the fear of God.

The demanding provisions with roughness and severity by such as travel under the direction of government, or authorized by government to do it, is at this day so practised in the East, as greatly to illustrate several passages of scripture. When the Baron De Tott was sent, in 1767, to the cham of the Tartars, by the French ministry, as resident of France with that Tartar prince, he had a *mikmandar*, or conductor, given him by the pacha of Kotchim, upon his entering the Turkish territories, whose business it was to precede and prepare the way for him, as is usually done in those countries to ambassadors, and such as travel gratis, at the expense of the porte, or Turkish court. This conductor, whose name, it seems, was Ali Aga, made great use of his whip, when he came among the poor Greeks of Moldavia, to induce them to furnish out that assistance and those provisions he wanted for the baron; for though it was represented as travelling at the expense of the porte, it was really at the expense of the inhabitants of those towns or villages to which he came. The baron appears to have been greatly hurt by that mode of procedure with those poor peasants, and would rather have procured what he wanted with his money, which he thought would be sufficiently efficacious, if the command of the mikmandar should not be sufficient without the whip. The baron's account of the success of his efforts is a very droll one, which he has enlivened by throwing it into the form of dialogues between himself and the Greeks, and Ali Aga and those peasants, in which he has imitated the broken language the Greeks made use of, pretending not to understand Turkish, in order to make it more mirthful. It would be much too long for these papers, and quite unnecessary for my design, to transcribe these dialogues; it is sufficient to say, that after the jealousy of the poor oppressed Greeks of their being to be pillaged, or more heavily loaded with demands by the Turks, had prevented their voluntarily supplying the baron for his money, Ali Aga undertook the business, and upon the Moldavian's pretending not to understand the Turkish language, he knocked him down with his fist, and kept kicking him while he was rising; which brought him to complain, in good Turkish, of his beating him so, when he knew very well they were poor people, who were often in want of necessaries, and whose princes scarcely left them the air they breathed. "Pshaw! thou art joking, friend," was the reply of Ali Aga, "thou art in want of nothing, except of being well basted a little oftener; but all in good time. Proceed we to business. I must instantly have two sheep, a dozen of fowls, a dozen of pigeons, fifty pounds of bread, four oques of butter, with salt, pepper, nutmeg, cinnamon, lemons, wines, salad, and good oil of olive, all in great plenty." With tears the Moldavian replied, "I have already told you that we are poor creatures, without so much as bread to eat. Where must we get cinnamon?" The whip, it seems, was taken from under his habit, and the Moldavian beaten till he could bear it no longer, but was forced to fly, finding Ali Aga inexorable, and that these provisions must be produced; and, in fact, we are told, the quarter of an hour was not expired, within which time Ali Aga required that these things should be produced, and affirmed to the baron that they would be brought before the primate, or chief of the Moldavians of that town, who had been so severely handled, assisted by three of his countrymen; all the provisions were brought, without forgetting even the cinnamon.

May not this account be supposed to illustrate that passage of Nemehiah, chap. v. 15: *The former governors that had been before me, were chargeable unto the people, and had taken of them bread and wine, besides forty shekels of silver: yea, even their servants bare rule over the people: but so did not I, because of the fear of God.* It is evident something oppressive is meant. And that it related to the taking bread from them, or eatables in general, together with wine, perhaps sheep, fowls, pigeons, butter, fruit, and other things, when probably they were travelling, or sojourning in some place at a distance from home. And that the like imperious and unrighteous demand had, from time to time, been made upon them by the servants of these governors, whom they might have occasion to send about the country. I cannot account for the setting down the precise number of forty, when speaking of shekels, but by supposing that the word *besides*, here, אחר *acher*, should have been translated *afterward*, which it more commonly, if not more certainly, signifies; and means, that afterward they were wont to commute this demand for provisions into money, often amounting to forty shekels. It is certain it would not mean the whole annual allowance to the governor by the children of the captivity; that would have been much too small; nor could it mean what every householder was to pay annually towards the governor's support, for fifty shekels was as much as each mighty man of wealth was assessed at by Menahem, when he wanted to raise a large sum of money for the king of Assyria, and when Israel was not in so low a state as in the time of Nehemiah: it must then, surely, mean the value of that quantity of eatables and wine they might charge any town with, when single towns were charged with the support of the governor's table for a single repast, or a single day, which it is natural to suppose could only be when they thought fit to travel from place to place. This, it seems, their servants took the liberty too to require, when they were sent on a journey. And if they that belonged to the officers of the king of Persia enforced their requisitions in a manner similar to that made use of by the people belonging to the Turkish governors of provinces, when they travel on a public account among the Greeks of Moldavia, it is no wonder that Nehemiah observes, with emotion, in this passage, *Yea, even their servants bare rule over the people: but so did not I, because of the fear of God.*—HARMER.

Ver. 17. Moreover, *there were* at my table a hundred and fifty of the Jews and rulers, besides those that came unto us from among the heathen that are about us. 18. Now *that* which was prepared *for me* daily *was* one ox *and* six choice sheep; also fowls were prepared for me, and once in ten days store of all sorts of wine: yet for all this required not I the bread of the governor, because the bondage was heavy upon this people.

Nehemiah calculated the expenses of his table, not by the money he paid, but by the provisions consumed by his guests. Such is still the practice in the East. So De la Motraye informs us of the seraglio at Constantinople: "One may judge of the numbers who live in this palace, by the prodigious quantity of provisions consumed in it yearly, which some of the hattchis, or cooks, assured me amounted to more than 30,000 oxen, 20,000 calves, 60,000 sheep, 16,000 lambs, 10,000 kids, 100,000 turkeys, geese, and goslings, 200,000 fowls and chickens, 100,000 pigeons, without reckoning wild-fowl or fish, of the last of which he only named 130,000 calcam-bats, or turbots."—BURDER.

CHAPTER VI.

Ver. 5. Then sent Sanballat his servant unto me, in like manner, the fifth time, with an open letter in his hand.

A letter has its Hebrew name from the circumstance of its being rolled or folded together. The modern Arabs roll up their letters, and then flatten them to the breadth of an inch, and instead of sealing them, paste up their ends. The Persians make up their letters in a roll about six inches long, a bit of paper is fastened round it with gum, and sealed with an impression of ink. In Turkey, letters are commonly sent to persons of distinction in a bag or purse; to equals they are also enclosed, but to inferiors, or those who are held in contempt, they are sent open or unenclosed. This explains the reason of Nehemiah's observation: "Then sent Sanballat his servant unto me, with an open letter in his hand." In refusing him the mark of respect usually paid to persons of his station, and treating him contemptuously, by sending the letter without the customary appendages, when presented to persons of respectability, Sanballat offered him a deliberate insult. Had this open letter come from Geshem, who was an Arab, it might have passed unnoticed, but as it came from Sanballat, the governor had reason to expect the ceremony of enclosing it in a bag, since he was a person of distinction in the Persian court, and at that time governor of Judea.—PAXTON.

Norden tells us, that when he and his company were at Essauen, an express arrived there, despatched by an Arab prince, who brought a letter directed to the reys, (or master of their barque,) enjoining him not to set out with his barque, or carry them any farther, adding, that in a day's time he should be at Essauen, and there would give his orders relative to them. "The letter, however, according to the usage of the Turks," says this author, "was open; and as the reys was not on board, the pilot carried it to one of our fathers to read it." Sanballat's sending his servant, then, with an open letter, which is mentioned Neh. vi. 5, doth not appear an odd thing, it should seem; but if it was according to their usages, why is this circumstance complained of, as it visibly is? Why indeed is it mentioned at all? Why! because, however the sending letters open to common people may be customary in these countries, it is not according to their usages to send them so to people of distinction. So Dr. Pococke, in his account of that very country where Norden was when this letter was brought, gives us, among other things, in the 57th plate, the figure of a Turkish letter put into a satin bag, to be sent to a great man, with a paper tied to it, directed and sealed, and an ivory button tied on the wax. So Lady Montague says, the bassa of Belgrade's answer to the English ambassador, going to Constantinople, was brought to him in a purse of scarlet satin. The great emir, indeed, of the Arabs, according to D'Arvieux, was not wont to enclose his letters in these bags, any more than to have them adorned with flourishes; but that is supposed to have been owing to the unpoliteness of the Arabs; and he tells us, that when he acted as secretary to the emir, he supplied these defects, and that his doing so was highly acceptable to the emir. Had this open letter, then, come from Geshem, who was an Arab, it might have passed unnoticed; but as it was from Sanballat, the enclosing it in a handsome bag was a ceremony Nehemiah had reason to expect from him, since he was a person of distinction in the Persian court, and then governor of Judea; and the not doing it was the greatest insult, insinuating, that though Nehemiah was, according to him, preparing to assume the royal dignity, he should be so far from acknowledging him in that character, that he would not even pay him the compliment due to every person of distinction. Chardin gives us a like account of the eastern letters, adding this circumstance, that those that are unenclosed as sent to common people, are usually rolled up; in which form their paper commonly appears. A letter in the form of a small roll of paper, would appear very odd in our eyes, but it seems is very common there. If this is the true representation of the affair, commentators have given but a poor account of it. Sanballat sent him a message, says one of them, "pretending, it is likely, special respect and kindness unto him, informing him what was laid to his charge." So far Mr. Harmer.

Contrast with this open letter to Nehemiah the closed, rolled, or folded letter, sent by Sennacherib to Hezekiah, 2 Kings xix. 14. We read, verse 9, "He sent messengers to Hezekiah, saying"—"And Hezekiah received the [*sepher*] *letter* at the hand of the messenger, and read it: and Hezekiah went up into the house of the Lord, and spread it before the Lord." It was therefore folded or rolled, and no doubt enclosed in a proper envelope; and I would not be certain whether this action of taking a letter from its case is not expressed here by the word *peresh*, which signifies to divide, to separate. Consider also the passage, Isaiah xxix. 11: "And the vision shall be to you, as the word of a [*sepher*, the same as the letter spread by Hezekiah] letter that is sealed—sealed up in a bag, closely—which is given to a man of learning to read, but he says, 'It is sealed'—how should I know what information it contains? I merely can discover to whom it is directed;" while the unlearned cannot even read the address. We see such occurrences daily in the streets of London: messengers sent with letters, desire passengers to read the directions for them.—Observe, the messengers sent to Hezekiah are described as *saying*, when in fact, they say nothing, but only deliver a letter containing the message.—TAYLOR IN CALMET.

CHAPTER VI.

Ver. 10. Afterward I came unto the house of Shemaiah, the son of Delaiah, the son of Mehetabeel, who *was* shut up; and he said, Let us meet together in the house of God, within the temple; and let us shut the doors of the temple: for they will come to slay thee; yea, in the night they will come to slay thee.

By *the house of God, within the temple*, (as it is in the text, Nehem. vi. 10,) Shemaiah certainly meant the sanctuary; and to advise Nehemiah to retreat thither, he had a good pretence, because it was both a strong and a sacred place, being defended by a guard of Levites, and, by its holiness, privileged from all rude approaches; but his real design herein might be, not only to disgrace Nehemiah, and dishearten the people, when they saw their governor's cowardice, but to prepare the way likewise for the enemies' assaulting and taking the city, when there was no leader to oppose them; to give countenance to the calumny that had been spread abroad, of his affecting to be made king, because he fled upon the report of it; and perhaps, by the assistance of some other priests, that were his confederates, either to destroy him, or to secure his person until the city was betrayed into the enemies' hands.—Stackhouse.

CHAPTER VII.

Ver. 1. Now it came to pass, when the wall was built, and I had set up the doors, and the porters, and the singers, and the Levites were appointed, 2. That I gave my brother Hanani, and Hananiah the ruler of the palace, charge over Jerusalem: (for he *was* a faithful man, and feared God above many.)

Nehemiah, very likely, was now returning to Shushan, to give the king an account of the state of affairs in Judea; and therefore he took care to place such men in the city as he knew would faithfully secure it in his absence. Hanani is said to be his brother; but he chose his officers, not out of partial views to his own kindred, but because he knew that they would acquit themselves in their employment with a strict fidelity. Hanani had given proof of his zeal for God and his country, in his taking a tedious journey from Jerusalem to Shushan, to inform Nehemiah of the sad state of Jerusalem, and to implore his helping hand to relieve it, chap. i. And the reason why Nehemiah put such trust and confidence in Hananiah, was, because he was a man of conscience, and acted upon religious principles, which would keep him from those temptations to perfidiousness, which he might probably meet with in his absence, and against which a man destitute of the fear of God has no sufficient fence.—Stackhouse.

Ver. 3. And I said unto them, Let not the gates of Jerusalem be opened until the sun be hot; and while they stand by, let them shut the doors, and bar *them:* and appoint watches of the inhabitants of Jerusalem, every one in his watch, and every one *to be* over against his house.

In the hot countries of the East, they frequently travel in the night, and arrive at midnight at the place of their destination. Luke xi. 5. Mark xiii. 35. Probably they did not therefore usually shut their gates at the going down of the sun, if they did so at all through the night. Thevenot could not, however, obtain admission into Suez in the night, and was forced to wait some hours in the cold, without the walls. Doubdan, returning from the river Jordan to Jerusalem, in 1652, tells us, that when he and his companions arrived in the valley of Jehoshaphat, they were much surprised to find that the gates of the city were shut, which obliged them to lodge on the ground at the door of the sepulchre of the Blessed Virgin, to wait for the return of day, along with more than a thousand other people, who were obliged to continue there the rest of the night, as well as they. At length, about four o'clock, seeing everybody making for the city, they also set forward, with the design of entering by St. Stephen's gate; but they found it shut, and above two thousand people, who were there in waiting, without knowing the cause of all this. At first they thought it might be too early, and that it was not customary to open so soon: but an hour after a report was spread that the inhabitants had shut their gates because the peasants of the country about, had formed a design of pillaging the city in the absence of the governor and of his guards, and that as soon as he should arrive, the gates should be opened.—Burder.

Ver. 4. Now the city *was* large and great, but the people *were* few therein, and the houses *were* not built.

One reason why the bulk of the Jews (who were originally pastural, and lovers of agriculture) might rather choose to live in the country than at Jerusalem, was, because it was more suited to their genius and manner of life; but at this time their enemies were so enraged to see the walls built again, and so restless in their designs to keep the city from rising to its former splendour, that it terrified many from coming to dwell there, thinking themselves more safe in the country, where their enemies had no pretence to disturb them.—Stackhouse.

CHAPTER VIII.

Ver. 10. Then he said unto them, Go your way, eat the fat; and drink the sweet, and send portions unto them for whom nothing is prepared: for *this* day *is* holy unto our Lord: neither be ye sorry; for the joy of the Lord is your strength.

The eastern princes, and the eastern people, not only invite their friends to feasts, but it is their custom to send a portion of the banquet to those that cannot well come to it, especially their relations, and those in a state of mourning. This sending of portions to those for whom nothing was prepared, has been understood by those commentators I have consulted, to mean the poor; sending portions, however, to one another, is expressly distinguished in Esth. ix. 22, *from gifts to the poor.* There would not have been the shadow of a difficulty in this, had the historian been speaking of a private feast, but he is describing a national festival, where every one was supposed to be equally concerned: those, then, *for whom nothing was prepared*, it should seem, means those that were in a state of mourning. Mourning for private calamities being here supposed to take place of rejoicing for public concerns. But it is not only to those that are in a state of mourning that provisions are sometimes sent; others are honoured by princes in the same manner, who could not conveniently attend to the royal table, or to whom it was supposed not to be convenient. So when the grand emir found it incommoded Monsieur D'Arvieux to eat with him, he complaisantly desired him to take his own time for eating, and sent him what he liked from his kitchen, and at the time he chose. And thus, when King David would needs suppose, for secret reasons, too well known to himself, that it would be inconvenient for Uriah to continue at the royal palace, and therefore dismissed him to his own house, "there followed him a mess of meat from the king." 2 Sam. xi. 8, 10.—Harmer.

Ver. 37. And it yieldeth much increase unto the kings whom thou hast set over us because of our sins: also they have dominion over our bodies, and over our cattle, at their pleasure, and we *are* in great distress.

These people attribute all their losses and afflictions to their sins. Has a man lost his wife or child, he says, "*En-pāvatin-nemityam*, for the sake of my sins, this evil has come upon me." "Why, friend, do you live in this strange land?" "Because of my sins." No people can refer more to sin as the source of their misery, and yet none appear more anxious to commit it. "The sins of my ancestors, the sins of my ancestors, are in this habitation," says the old sinner, who wishes to escape the sight of his own.—Roberts.

CHAPTER XIII.

Ver. 15. In those days saw I in Judah *some* treading wine-presses on the sabbath, and bringing in sheaves, and lading asses; as also wine, grapes, and figs, and all *manner of* burdens, which they brought into Jerusalem on the sabbath-day: and I testified *against them* in the day wherein they sold victuals.

In peaceful times, the press in which the grapes and olives were trodden, was constructed in the vineyard: but in time of war and danger, it was removed into the nearest city. This precaution the restored captives were reduced to take for their safety, at the time they were visited by Nehemiah. In a state of great weakness themselves, without an efficient government or means of defence, they were exposed to the hostile machinations of numerous and powerful enemies. For this reason, many of the Jews brought their grapes from the vineyards, and trod them in Jerusalem, the only place of safety which the desolated country afforded. "In those days," said Nehemiah, "saw I in Judah, some treading wine-presses on the sabbath, and bringing in sheaves, and lading asses; and also wine, grapes, and figs, and all manner of burdens, which they brought into Jerusalem on the sabbath-day." Had these wine-presses been at a distance from Jerusalem, Nehemiah, who so strictly observed the precept of resting on that day, would not have seen the violation of which he complains.

Our translators, in Mr. Harmer's opinion, seem to have been guilty of an oversight in the interpretation of this verse, which plainly supposes, that sheaves of corn were brought into Jerusalem at the very time men were treading the wine-presses. This, he observes, is a strange anachronism, since the harvest there was finished in or before the third month, and the vintage was not till the seventh. But, it may be replied in favour of our translators, that by Mr. Harmer's own admission, they have at present a species of corn in the East, which is not ripe till the end of summer; which made Rauwolf say, it was the time of harvest when he arrived at Joppa, on the thirteenth of September. But if they have such a species of corn now, it is more than probable they had it then; for the customs and management of the Orientals suffer almost no alteration from the lapse of time, and change of circumstances. If this be admitted, the difficulty vanishes: and there is nothing incongruous or absurd in supposing that Nehemiah might see his countrymen bringing this late grain in sheaves from the field, to tread it out in the city, for fear of their numerous and malicious foes, who might have set upon them, had they not taken this precaution, as the Arabs frequently do on the present inhabitants, and seized the heaps on the barn-floor. Mr. Harmer translates the Hebrew term, parcels of grapes; but as the word signifies a *heap* of any thing, it may with equal propriety be rendered parcels or sheaves of corn, especially as grapes are mentioned afterward. It is true, our author makes them dried grapes, but for the word *dried* he has no authority from the original text; there is no good reason, therefore, to find fault with our translators in this instance.—PAXTON.

Though the conveniences they have in the wine countries for pressing their grapes, were frequently in peaceful times in their vineyards, yet in times of apprehension these conveniences were often in the cities themselves. Greece, to the present day, is frequently alarmed, and always under apprehension from corsairs: accordingly we find, that though the plantations of olive-trees belonging to Athens are large, and at some distance from thence, yet the mills for grinding and pressing the olives are in that town; and this, though, according to his description, the great olive-grove, or wood of these trees, as Dr. Richard Chandler calls it, watered by the Cephissus, is about three miles from the city, and has been computed as at least six miles long. The same reason that can induce men to fetch their olives from a distance into their towns, must operate more or less forcibly with regard to their grapes. This was, in particular, the state of things at the time Nehemiah visited the children of the captivity. They had many enemies about them, and those very spiteful; and they themselves were very weak. For this reason, many of them trod their grapes in Jerusalem itself: "In those days saw I in Judah some treading wine-presses on the sabbath, and bringing in sheaves, and lading asses; and also wine, grapes, and figs, and all manner of burdens, which they brought into Jerusalem on the sabbath-day." Had these wine-presses been at a distance from Jerusalem, he that so strictly observed the precept of resting that day would not have seen that violation of it. They appear, by that circumstance, as well as by the other particulars mentioned there, to have been within the walls of Jerusalem. The words of Nehemiah are to be understood as signifying, "In those days saw I in Judah some treading wine-presses on the sabbath, and bringing in parcels of grapes for that purpose in baskets, which they had laden on asses, and also jars of wine, pressed elsewhere, dried grapes and figs, and all manner of burdens of victuals, which they sold on the sabbath:" the squeezing the grapes for wine, and drying them for raisins, being, it seems, at least frequently attended to at one and the same time. So when Dr. Chandler set out from Smyrna to visit Greece, in the end of August, the vintage was just begun, "the black grapes being spread on the ground in beds, exposed to the sun to dry for raisins; while in another part, the juice was expressed for wine, a man, with feet and legs bare, treading the fruit in a kind of cistern, with a hole or vent near the bottom, and a vessel beneath it to receive the liquor." (Travels in Greece.)

If the same custom obtained in Judea then, which it seems is practised in Greece now, and that the vintage was just then finishing, Nehemiah must have been particularly galled; for it seems they finish their vintage with dancing, and therefore I presume with songs, and probably music. For speaking of the Greek dances, of which some are supposed of very remote antiquity, and of one in particular, called the crane, he says, "the peasants perform it yearly in the street of the French convent, where he and his companions lodged at that time, at the conclusion of the vintage; joining hands, and preceding their mules and their asses, which are laden with grapes in panniers, in a very curved and intricate figure; the leader waving a handkerchief, which has been imagined to denote the clew given by Ariadne;" the dance being supposed to have been invented by Theseus, upon his escape from the labyrinth.

Singing seems to have been practised by the Jews in their vineyards, and shouting when they trod the grapes, from what we read, Isaiah xvi. 10: but whether dancing too, and whether they carried their profanation of the sabbath this length, in the time of Nehemiah, we are not informed. Some may have supposed that the words of Jeremiah, ch. xxxi. 4, 5, refer to the joy expressed by the Jews in the time of vintage: "Again, I will build thee, and thou shalt be built, O virgin of Israel; thou shalt again be adorned with thy tabrets, and shalt go forth in the dances of them that make merry. Thou shalt yet plant vines upon the mountains of Samaria; the planters shall plant, and eat them as common things." Vines and dancing are here joined together.—BURDER.

Ver. 25. And I contended with them, and cursed them, and smote certain of them, and plucked off their hair, and made them swear by God, *saying*, Ye shall not give your daughters unto their sons, nor take their daughters unto your sons, or for yourselves.

In Judea, the punishment of infamy consisted chiefly in cutting off the hair of evil-doers: yet it is thought that pain was added to disgrace, and that they tore off the hair with violence, as if they were plucking a bird alive. This is the genuine signification of the Hebrew word used by Nehemiah in describing his conduct towards those Jews who had violated the law by taking strange wives: "And I contended with them, and smote certain of them, and *plucked off* their hair." This kind of punishment was common in Persia. King Artaxerxes, instead of plucking off the hair of such of his generals as had been guilty of a fault, obliged them to lay aside the tiara. The Emperor Domitian caused the hair and beard of the philosopher Apollonius to be shaved.—PAXTON.

ESTHER.

CHAPTER I.

Ver. 5. And when these days were expired, the king made a feast unto all the people that were present in Shushan the palace, both unto great and small, seven days, in the court of the garden of the king's palace; 6. *Where were* white, green, and blue *hangings*, fastened with cords of fine linen and purple to silver rings and pillars of marble: the beds *were of* gold and silver, upon a pavement of red, and blue, and white, and black marble.

In the houses of the fashionable and the gay, the lower part of the walls is adorned with rich hangings of velvet or damask, tinged with the liveliest colours, suspended on hooks, or taken down at pleasure. A correct idea of their richness and splendour may be formed from the description which the inspired writer has given of the hangings in the royal garden at Shushan, the ancient capital of Persia: "Where were white, green, and blue hangings, fastened with cords of fine linen and purple to silver rings and pillars of marble." The upper part of the walls is adorned with the most ingenious wreathings and devices, in stucco and fret-work. The ceiling is generally of wainscot, painted with great art, or else thrown into a variety of panels, with gilded mouldings. In the days of Jeremiah the prophet, when the profusion and luxury of all ranks in Judea were at their height, their chambers were ceiled with fragrant and costly wood, and painted with the richest colours. Of this extravagance, the indignant seer loudly complains: "Wo unto him that saith, I will build me a wide house and large chambers, and cutteth him out windows: and it is ceiled with cedar, and painted with vermilion." The floors of these splendid apartments were laid with painted tiles, or slabs of the most beautiful marble. A pavement of this kind is mentioned in the book of Esther: at the sumptuous entertainment which Ahasuerus made for the princes and nobles of his vast empire, "the beds," or couches, upon which they reclined, "were of gold and silver, upon a pavement of red, and blue, and white, and black marble." Plaster of terrace is often used for the same purpose; and the floor is always covered with carpets, which are, for the most part, of the richest materials. Upon these carpets, a range of narrow beds, or mattresses, is often placed along the sides of the wall, with velvet or damask bolsters, for the greater ease and convenience of the company. To these luxurious indulgences the prophets occasionally seem to allude: Ezekiel was commanded to pronounce a "wo to the women that sew pillows to all arm-holes;" and Amos denounces the judgments of his God against them "that lie upon beds of ivory, and stretch themselves upon their couches, and eat the lambs out of the flock, and the calves out of the midst of the stall."—Paxton.

To give some idea of the grandeur of this feast, we may remark, that in eastern countries their houses are built round a court, in which, upon extraordinary occasions, company is entertained, being strewed with mats and carpets. And as the court lies open to the sky, it is usual, in the summer, to have it sheltered from the heat of the sun, by a large awning or veil, which being extended upon ropes reaching across the court, from one side of the top of the house to the other, may be folded or unfolded at pleasure. The Psalmist seems to allude to some covering of this kind, Ps. 104. 2: "Who stretchest out the heavens like a curtain." Is. 40. 2. (Shaw's Travels, p. 247.) Now the Persian king entertained the whole city of Shushan, great and small, for seven days together, in the court of the garden of the king's palace. In that garden we must suppose a very spacious area, probably containing many acres, curiously paved, and having lofty columns of marble, erected in rows at proper distances; to the tops of those columns were fixed rings of silver, through which they drew purple cords of fine linen, across from row to row, and from pillar to pillar; and over those cords they spread large sheets of delicate calico, possibly painted with blue, which would make a very splendid and beautiful sky over all the court, and a delightful shade to all the guests. Instead of mats and carpets, they had beds, or couches, of gold and silver, to sit upon, and were served with wine in vessels of gold. This is probably the idea we are to entertain of the furniture of this gorgeous banquet.—Taylor's Concordance.

Dr. Russel does not represent the pavement of the courts as all mosaic work, and equally adorned, but he tells us, that it is usually that part that lies between the fountain and the arched alcove on the south side, that is thus beautified, supposing that there is but one alcove in a court; however, it should seem in some other parts of the East, there are several of these alcoves opening into the court. Maundrell, who calls them *duans*, in his account of the houses of Damascus, says expressly, that they have generally several on all sides of the court, "being placed at such different points, that at one or other of them you may always have either the shade or the sun, which you please." Are not these alcoves, or duans, of which, according to this, there might be several in the court of the palace of Ahasuerus, what the sacred writer means by the beds adorned with silver and gold? Esth. i. 6. I shall elsewhere show, that the bed where Esther was sitting, and on which Haman threw himself, must more resemble the modern oriental duans, or divans, than the beds on which the Romans reclined at their entertainments; and consequently it is more natural to understand those beds of these alcoves, or duans, richly adorned with gold and silver, while on the lower variegated pavements carpets were also laid, for the reception of those that could not find a place in these duans; on which pavements, Dr. Shaw tells us, they are wont, in Barbary, when much company is to be entertained, to strew mats and carpets.—Harmer.

Ver. 9. Also Vashti the queen made a feast for the women *in* the royal house which *belonged* to King Ahasuerus.

The women are not permitted to associate with the other sex at an eastern banquet; but they are allowed to entertain one another in their own apartments. When Ahasuerus, the king of Persia, treated all the people of his capital with a splendid feast, Vashti, the queen, we are informed, "made a banquet for the women in the royal house, which belonged to King Ahasuerus. This, observes Chardin, is the custom of all the East; the women have their feasts at the same time, but apart from the men. And Maillet informs us, in his letters, that the same custom is observed in Egypt. This is undoubtedly the reason that the prophet distinctly mentions "the voice of the bridegroom, and the voice of the bride;" he means that the noise of nuptial mirth was heard in different apartments. The personal voices of the newly married pair cannot be understood, but the noisy mirth which a marriage feast commonly excites; for in Syria, and probably in all the surrounding countries, the bride is condemned to absolute silence, and fixed by remorseless etiquette to the spot where she has been seated. When the banquet was finished, and the guests had removed, the poor came in and ate up the fragments, so that nothing was lost. This custom will account for the command to the servants, in the parable of the supper, "Go out quickly into the streets and lanes of the city, and bring in hither the poor, and the maimed, and the halt, and the blind. And the servant said, Lord, it is done as thou hast commanded, and yet there is room. And the lord said unto the servant, Go out into the highways, and hedges, and compel them to come in, that my house may be filled." These poor and destitute persons were called to the entertainment only before the time when, according to the custom of the country, they were expected to attend.—PAXTON.

Females, in the East, never have their feasts in the same room as the men, because it would be highly indecorous towards their LORDS, and they would not be able to go to those lengths of merriment, as when alone. On meeting, they embrace, and SMELL each other; and after they are seated, comes the betel-leaf, the chunam, and the areca-nuts. Have their LORDS given them any new jewels or robes; they are soon mentioned, as a proof of the favour they are in; and after they have finished their food, shroots and scandal become the order of the day.—ROBERTS.

It may be taken as a general rule, that wherever our translators have inserted a number of words in *italic*, they have been embarrassed to make sense of the passage; and some have been inclined to think, that in proportion to the number of words inserted, is the probability of their having missed the true import of the place. Without adopting this notion, we may venture to ask the reader, whether he has been satisfied with the ideas communicated in the first chapter of Esther?—"The king made a feast to all the people that were present at Shushan, the palace; both unto great and small, seven days, in the court of the garden of the king's palace; where were white, green, and blue hangings, fastened with cords of fine linen, and purple, to silver rings and pillars of marble; the beds were of gold, and silver, upon a pavement of red, and blue, and white, and black marble." What are we to understand by all this? hangings fastened to silver rings, to pillars of marble? cords made of fine linen? beds of gold and silver, laid on the pavement? &c. Commentators give very little information on this passage: and it is much better to trust at once to ourselves, than to transcribe their conjectures.

The first thing observable is the canopy covering the court: it was of white canvass, (*carpas*, כרפס:) the braces of it were blue, (ותכלת אחוז) that is, the cords, &c. used to support this canopy, and to keep it in its place, properly extended, &c. over head. Secondly, in the court below were pavilions, platforms, or railed divisions [the word *chebeli* (חבלי) signifies the railed deck of a ship] of linen [or, hung with linen] and of aragaman, [calico? fine cotton?] upon railings of silver pillars—smaller pillars (*galili*, גלילי) silvered over, and columns of white marble; and the divan cushions were embroidered with gold and silver: these were placed upon mustabys of porphyry (red marble) and white marble, and round-spotted marble, and marble with wandering, irregular veins. To justify this description, we shall first consider the canopy; the reader will judge of its probability and use by the following quotations:—

"Among the ruins remaining at Persepolis, is a court, containing many lofty pillars: one may even presume that these columns did not support any architrave, as Sir John Chardin has observed, but we may venture to suppose, that a covering of tapestry, or linen, was drawn over them, to intercept the perpendicular projection of the sunbeams. It is also probable that the tract of ground where most of the columns stand, was originally a court before the palace, like that which was before the king's house at Susa, mentioned Esther, chap. v. and through which a flow of fresh air was admitted into the apartments."—(Le Bruyn.) This idea of Le Bruyn, formed almost on the spot, supports our suggestion of a canopy covering the court. It is confirmed also by the custom of India. We have been told by a gentleman from whom we requested information on this subject, that "at the festival of Durma Rajah, in Calcutta, the great court of a very large house is overspread with a covering made of canvass, lined with calico; and this lining is ornamented with broad stripes, of various colours, in which (in India, observe) green predominates. On occasion of this festival, which is held only once in three years, the master of the house gives wine and cake, and other refreshments, to the English gentlemen and ladies who wish to see the ceremonies; he also gives payment, as well as hospitality, to those who perform them." That such a covering would be necessary in hot climates we may easily suppose; nor is the supposition enfeebled by remarking, that the coliseum, or Flavian amphitheatre, at Rome, has still remaining on its walls the marks of the masts, or scaffoldings, which were erected when that immense area was covered with an awning, as it was during the shows exhibited there to the Roman public. The word rendered *brace* (אחוז) signifies *to catch, to lay hold of, to connect;* it may be thought that these braces went from side to side of the house; were fastened to proper projections, high in the sides of the building; and, passing under the white canvass, blue braces must have had an ornamental effect. In the lower part of the court the preparations consisted in what may be called a railed platform on a mustaby: what these were the reader will understand, by an extract from Dr. Russel's History of Aleppo.

"Part of the principal court is planted with trees, and flowering shrubs; the rest is paved. At the south end is a square basin of water, with *jetsd'eaux*, and close to it, upon a stone mustaby, is built a small pavilion: or the mustaby being only railed in, an open divan is occasionally formed on it. [Note, a mustaby is a stone platform, raised about two or three feet above the pavement of the court.] This being some steps higher than the basin, a small fountain is usually placed in the middle of the divan, the mosaic pavement round which being constantly wetted by the *jet d'eau*, displays a variety of splendid colours, and the water, as it runs to the basin through marble channels, which are rough at bottom, produces a pleasing murmur. Where the size of the court admits of a larger shrubbery, temporary divans are placed in the grove, or arbours are formed of slight latticed frames, covered by the vine, the rose, or the jasmine; the rose shooting to a most luxuriant height, when in full flower, is elegantly picturesque. Facing the basin, on the south side of the court, is a wide, lofty, arched alcove, about eighteen inches higher than the pavement, and entirely open to the court. It is painted in the same manner as the apartments, but the roof is finished in plain or gilt stucco; and the floor round a small fountain is paved with marble of sundry colours, with a *jet d'eau* in the middle. A large divan is here prepared, but being intended for the summer, chints and Cairo mats are employed instead of cloth, velvet, and carpets. It is called, by way of distinction, The Divan, and by its north aspect, and a sloping painted shed projecting over the arch, being protected from the sun, it offers a delicious situation in the hot months. The sound, not less than the sight, of the *jetsd'eaux*, is extremely refreshing; and if there be a breath of air stirring, it arrives scented by the Arabian jasmine, the henna, and other fragrant plants, growing in the shrubbery, or ranged in pots round the basin. There is usually on each side of the alcove a small room, or cabinet, neatly fitted up, and serving for retirement. These rooms are called *kubbe*, whence probably the Spaniards derived their *al coba*, which is rendered by some other nations in Europe, *alcove*." In another part Dr. Russel gives a print of a mustaby, with sundry musicians sitting on it, on which he observes, "The front of the stone mustaby is fitted with marble of different colours. Part of the court is paved in mosaic, in the manner represented in the print." This print "shows, in miniature, the inner court of a great house. The doors of the kaah, and part of the cupola, appear in front; on the side, the high arched alcove, or divan, with the shed above; the marble facing of the mustaby, the mosaic pavement between that and the basin, and the fountain playing."

This account of Dr. Russel's harmonizes perfectly with the history in Esther, and we have only to imagine that the railings, or smaller pillars of the divan, on the mustaby in the palace of Ahasuerus, were of silver, (silver-gilt,) while the larger, called *columns*, placed at the corners, or elsewhere, were of marble; the flat part of the mustaby also being overspread with carpets, &c. on which, next the railings, were cushions richly embroidered, for the purpose of being leaned against. These things, mentioned in the scripture narration, if placed according to the doctor's account, enable us to comprehend the whole of the Bible description, and justify every word in it. That the last three words describe three different kinds of marble, of which the mustaby of Ahasuerus was composed, is evident from the signification of their roots. And as to the linen which was appended to the railings, with its accompanying *aragaman*, we may ask, if this word signifies *purple*, what was the subject of it, silk, worsted, or cotton? Was it the chints of Dr. Russel? or was it of the diaper kind, that is, figured linen? or was it calico? which, on the whole, we think it was.—Taylor in Calmet.

Ver. 11. To bring Vashti the queen before the king, with the crown royal, to show the people and the princes her beauty: for she *was* fair to look on.

The Persians, on festival occasions, used to produce their women in public. To this purpose Herodotus relates a story of seven Persians being sent to Amyntas, a Grecian prince, who received them hospitably, and gave them a splendid entertainment. When, after the entertainment, they began to drink, one of the Persians thus addressed Amyntas: "Prince of Macedonia, it is a custom with us Persians, whenever we have a public entertainment, to introduce our concubines and young wives." On this principle Ahasuerus gave command to bring his queen Vashti into the public assembly.—Burder.

Ver. 12. But the queen Vashti refused to come at the king's commandment by *his* chamberlains: therefore was the king very wroth, and his anger burned in him.

When a person is speaking to you, on almost any subject, he keeps saying every moment, "Be not angry, my lord;" or, "Let not your anger burn." Judah said to Joseph, "Let not thine anger burn." "Go not near that man; his anger is on fire." "Well, well, what is the matter with that fellow?" "Not much; some one has put the torch to his anger." "Go, throw some water on that fire, or it will not soon be out."—Roberts.

CHAPTER II.

Ver. 9. And the maiden pleased him, and she obtained kindness of him; and he speedily gave her her things for purification, with such things as belonged to her, and seven maidens, *which were* meet to be given her, out of the king's house: and he preferred her and her maids unto the best *place* of the house of the women.

After these presents followed eleven caroches (coaches) full of young maidens, slaues to serue the bride: these caroches were couered and shut, and either of them attended by eunuchs, Moores: after these followed twenty-eight virgins' slaues, attired in cloth of gold, and accompanied by twenty-eight blacke eunuchs all on horsebacke, and richly clad. After which were seen two hundred and forty mules, loaden with tents of tapestrie, cloath of gold, sattin, veluet, with the ground of gold, with many cushions, which are the chaires the ladies of Turkie use, with many other rich and sumptuous moueables. (Knolles's History of the Turks.)—Burder.

Ver. 11. And Mordecai walked every day before the court of the women's house, to know how Esther did, and what should become of her.

The apartments of the women are counted sacred and inviolable, over all the East; it is even a crime to inquire what passes within the walls of the harem, or house of the women. Hence, it is extremely difficult to be informed of the transactions in those sequestered habitations; and a man, says Chardin, may walk a hundred days, one after another, by the house where the women are, and yet know no more what is done there than at the farther end of Tartary. This sufficiently explains the reason of Mordecai's conduct, who "walked every day before the court of the women's house, to know how Esther did, and what should become of her."—Paxton.

CHAPTER III.

Ver. 7. In the first month, (that *is* the month Nisan,) in the twelfth year of King Ahasuerus, they cast Pur, that *is*, the lot, before Haman, from day to day, and from month to month, *to* the twelfth *month*, that *is* the month Adar.

It was customary in the East, by casting lots into an urn, to inquire what days would be fortunate, and what not, to undertake any business in. According to this superstitious practice, Haman endeavoured to find out what time in the year was most favourable to the Jews, and what most unlucky. First he inquired what month was most unfortunate, and found the month Adar, which was the last month in the year, answerable to our February. There was no festival during this month, nor was it sanctified by any peculiar rites. Then he inquired the day, and found the thirteenth day was not auspicious to them, ver. 13. Some think there were as many lots as there were days in the year, and for every day he drew a lot; but found none to his mind, till he came to the last month of all, and to the middle of it. Now this whole business was governed by providence, by which these lots were directed, and not by the Persian gods, to fall in the last month of the year; whereby almost a whole year intervened between the design and its execution, and gave time for Mordecai to acquaint Esther with it, and for her to intercede with the king for the reversing, or suspending his decree, and disappointing the conspiracy.—Patrick.

Ver. 10. And the king took his ring from his hand, and gave *it* unto Haman the son of Hammedatha the Agagite, the Jews' enemy.

This he did both as a token of affection and honour. With the Persians, for a king to give a ring to any one, was a token and bond of the greatest love and friendship imaginable. It may be this was given to Haman to seal with it the letters that were or should be written, giving orders for the destruction of the Jews. Among the Romans, in aftertimes, when any one was put into the equestrian order, a ring was given to him, for originally none but knights were allowed to wear them. It was sometimes used in appointing a successor in the kingdom: as when Alexander was dying, he took his ring from off his finger, and gave it to Perdiccas, by which it was understood that he was to succeed him.—Burder.

CHAPTER V.

Ver. 6. And the king said unto Esther at the banquet of wine, What *is* thy petition? and it shall be granted thee: and what *is* thy request? even to the half of the kingdom it shall be performed.

The time of drinking wine in the East, is at the beginning, not at the close of entertainments, as it is with us. Sir John Chardin has corrected an error of a French commentator, as to this point, in his manuscript note on Esther v. 6. It seems the commentator had supposed the banquet of wine meant the *dessert*, because this is our custom in the West; but he observes, "that the eastern people, on the contrary, drink and discourse before eating, and that after the rest is served up, the feast is quickly over, they eating very fast, and every one presently withdrawing. They conduct matters thus at the royal table, and at those of their great men." Dr. Castell, in his Lexicon, seems to have been guilty of the same fault, by a quotation annexed to that note.

Chardin's account agrees with that of Olearius, who tells us, that when the ambassadors he attended were at the Persian court, "at a solemn entertainment, the floor of the hall was covered with a cotton cloth, which was covered with all sorts of fruits and sweetmeats, in basins of gold. That with them was served up excellent Shiras wine. That after an hour's time, the sweetmeats were removed, to make way for the more substantial part of the entertainment, such as rice, boiled and roasted mutton, fowl, game, &c. That after having been at table an hour and a half, warm water was brought, in a ewer of gold, for washing; and grace being said, they began to retire without speaking a word, according to the custom of the country, as also did the ambassadors soon after." This is Olearius's account, in short: by which it appears, that wine was brought first; that the time of that part of the entertainment was double to the other; and that immediately after eating they withdrew. This was the practice of the modern court of Persia, and probably might be so in the days of Ahasuerus. Unluckily, Diodati and Dr. Castell did not attend to this circumstance, in speaking of the banquet of wine prepared by Queen Esther.—HARMER.

Ver. 9. Then went Haman forth that day joyful and with a glad heart: but when Haman saw Mordecai in the king's gate, that he stood not up, nor moved for him, he was full of indignation against Mordecai.

This is, indeed, a graphic sketch of eastern manners. The colours are so lively and so fresh, that they might have been but the work of yesterday. See the native gentleman, at the head of his courtly train: he moves along in pompous guise, and all who see him arise from their seats, take off their sandals, and humbly move in reverence to him. To some he gives a graceful wave of the hand; to others not a word nor a look. Should there be one who neither stands up nor moves to him, his name and place of abode will be inquired after, and the first opportunity eagerly embraced to glut his revenge. The case of Muttoo-Chadde-Appa, modeliar of the Dutch governor Van de Graaff's gate, is illustrative of this disposition. A Moorman of high bearing and great riches had purchased the rent of the pearl fishery of the bay of Ondachy, and, in consequence, was a person of great influence among the people. The proud modeliar was one day passing along the road, where was seated on his carpet the renter of the pearl fishery. He arose not, moved not to him, when passing by, and the modeliar's soul was fired with indignation. He forthwith resolved upon his ruin, and, by deeply-formed intrigues, too well succeeded. The rent was taken from the Moorman; the money he had advanced to the headmen, the officers, the boatmen, the divers, and others, was lost; his estates were sold; and, to make up the deficiency, he himself was disposed of by auction for four hundred and twenty-five rix-dollars, and the modeliar became the purchaser.—ROBERTS.

Ver. 12. Haman said moreover, Yea, Esther the queen did let no man come in with the king unto the banquet that she had prepared but myself; and to-morrow am I invited unto her also with the king.

The kings of Persia very seldom admitted a subject to their table. Athenæus mentions it as a peculiar honour, which no Grecian enjoyed before or after, that Artaxerxes condescended to invite Timogoras, the Cretan, to dine even at the table where his relations ate; and to send sometimes a part of what was served up at his own; which some persons looked upon as a diminution of his majesty, and a prostitution of their national honour. Plutarch, in his life of Artaxerxes, tells us, that none but the king's mother, and his real wife, were permitted to sit at his table; and he therefore mentions it as a condescension in that prince, that he sometimes invited his brothers. Haman, the prime minister of Ahasuerus, had therefore some reason to value himself upon the invitation which he received, to dine with the king: "Haman said, moreover, Yea, Esther the queen let no man come in with the king, into the banquet which she had prepared, but myself; and to morrow am I invited unto her also with the king." The same ambitious minister received another mark of great distinction from his master: "The king took his ring from his hand, and gave it unto Haman." This he did, both as a token of affection and honour; for when the king of Persia gives a ring to any one, it is a token and bond of the greatest love and friendship. "Here also," says Mr. Forbes, "we see an exact description of the mode of conferring honour on the favourite of a sovereign, a princely dress, a horse, and a ring; these are now the usual presents to foreign ambassadors, and between one Indian prince and another.—PAXTON.

CHAPTER VI.

Ver. 1. On that night could not the king sleep; and he commanded to bring the book of records of the Chronicles; and they were read before the king.

That which was practised in the court of Ahasuerus, in the passage now referred to, appears to have been customary in the Ottoman porte. "It was likewise found in the records of the empire, that the last war with Russia had occasioned the fitting out of a hundred and fifty galliots, intended to penetrate into the sea of Azoph: and the particulars mentioned in the account of the expenses not specifying the motives of this armament, it was forgotten that the ports of Azoph and Taganrag stood for nothing in the present war; the building of the galliots was ordered, and carried on with the greatest despatch." (Baron De Tott.)

"The king has near his person an officer, who is meant to be his historiographer; he is also keeper of his seal, and is obliged to make a journal of the king's actions, good or bad, without comment of his own upon them. This, when the king dies, or at least soon after, is delivered to the council, who read it over, and erase every thing false in it, while they supply every material fact that may have been omitted, whether purposely or not." (Bruce.)—BURDER.

Ver. 7. And Haman answered the king, For the man whom the king delighteth to honour, 8. Let the royal apparel be brought which the king *useth* to wear, and the horse that the king rideth upon, and the crown royal which is set upon his head: 9. And let this apparel and horse be delivered to the hand of one of the king's most noble princes, that they may array the man *withal* whom the king delighteth to honour, and bring him on horseback through the street of the city, and proclaim before him, Thus shall it be done to the man whom the king delighteth to honour.

See on Matt. 11. 21.

Pitts gives an account of a cavalcade at Algiers, upon a person's turning Mohammedan, which is designed to do him, as well as their law, honour. "The apostate is to get on horseback, on a stately steed, with a rich saddle and fine trappings; he is also richly habited, and hath a turban on his head, but nothing of this is to be called his own; only there are given him about two or three yards of broadcloth, which is laid before him on the saddle. The horse, with him on his back, is led all round the city, which he is several hours in doing. The apostate is attended with drums and other music, and twenty or thirty sergeants. These march in order, on each side of the horse, with naked swords in their hands. The crier goes before, with a loud voice giving thanks to God for the proselyte that is made." The conformity of custom in the instance now cited, and the passage alluded to in Esther, must appear remarkable.—BURDER.

Herodotus relates, that the kings of Persia had horses peculiar to themselves, that were brought from Armenia, and were remarkable for their beauty. If the same law prevailed in Persia as did in Judea, no man might ride on the king's horse, any more than sit on his throne, or hold his sceptre. This clearly discovers the extent of Haman's ambition, when he proposed to bring "the royal apparel which the king used to wear, and the horse that the king rode upon, and the crown which is set upon his head." The crown royal was not to be set on the head of the man, but on the head of the horse; this interpretation is allowed by Aben Ezra, by the Targum, and by the Syriac version. No mention is afterward made of the crown, as set upon the head of Mordecai, nor would Haman have dared to advise what, by the laws of Persia, could not be granted. But it was usual to put the crown royal on the head of a horse led in state; and this we are assured is a custom in Persia, as it is with the Ethiopians, to this day; from them it passed into Italy; for the horses which the Romans yoked in their triumphal chariots were adorned with crowns.—PAXTON.

Very few English readers are sufficiently aware of the importance attached to the donation of robes of honour in the East. They mark the degree of estimation in which the party bestowing them holds the party receiving them; and sometimes the conferring or the withholding of them leads to very serious negotiation, and misunderstandings. "The prince of Shiraz," says Mr. Morier, "went in his greatest state to Kalaat Poushan, there to meet and to be invested with the dress of honour, which was sent him by the king, on the festival of No-Rouz. Although the day of the festival had long elapsed, yet the ceremony did not take place until this time, as the astrologers did not announce a day sufficiently fortunate for the performance of an act of so much consequence as this is looked upon to be throughout Persia. All the circumstances attendant upon the reception of a Kalaat being the great criterions by which the public may judge of the degree of influence which the receiver has at court, every intrigue is exerted during the preparation of the Kalaat, that it may be as indicative of the royal favour as possible. The person who is the bearer of it, the expressions used in the firman, which announces its having been conferred, the nature of the Kalaat itself, are all circumstances that are examined and discussed by the Persian public. A common Kalaat consists of a *caba*, or coat; a *kummer-bund*, or zone; a *gouch-peech*, or shawl for the head:—when it is intended to be more distinguishing, a sword or a dagger is added. To persons of distinction, rich furs are given, such as a *catabee*, or a *coordee;* but when the Kalaat is complete, it consists exactly of the same articles as the present which Cyrus made to Syennesis, namely, a horse with a golden bridle, ἵππον χρυσοχάλινον; a golden chain, στρεῶτον χρυσοῦν; a golden sword, ἀκινάκην χρυσοῦν; besides the dress, the στολὴν Περσικὴν, which is complete in all its parts. Such, or nearly such, was the Kalaat which the prince went out to meet; and consequently he gave as much publicity to it as he could devise.... The prince himself was conspicuous at a distance, by a parasol being borne over his head, which, to this day, is a privilege allowed only to royalty, and is exemplified by the sculptures at Persepolis, where the principal personage is frequently designated by a parasol carried over him.... The road, about three miles, was strewn with roses, and watered; both of which are modes of doing honour to persons of distinction; and, at very frequent intervals, glass vases, filled with sugar, were broken under his horses' feet. The treading upon sugar is symbolical, in their estimation, of prosperity; the scattering of flowers was a ceremony performed in honour of Alexander, on his entry into Babylon, and has perhaps some affinity to the custom of cutting down branches off the trees, and strewing them in the way, as was practised on our Saviour's entry into Jerusalem, Mark xi. 5. The other circumstance, 'the spreading of garments in the way,' is used in the scriptures as announcing royalty."

In another passage, Mr. Morier observes, that the Persian plenipotentiary to the signature of a treaty with Russia, "at first was at a loss how to make himself equal in personal distinctions (and numerous titles) to the Russian negotiator; but recollecting that, previous to his departure, his sovereign had honoured him by a present of one of his swords, and of a dagger set with precious stones, to wear which is a peculiar distinction in Persia; and besides, had clothed him with one of his own shawl robes, a distinction of still greater value, he therefore designated himself in the preamble of the treaty as endowed with the special gifts of the monarch, lord of the dagger set in jewels, of the sword adorned with gems, and of *the shawl coat already worn.* This may appear ridiculous to us, but it will be remembered that the bestowing of dresses as a mark of honour among eastern nations, is one of the most ancient customs recorded both in sacred and profane history. We may learn how great was the distinction of giving a coat already worn, by what is recorded of Jonathan's love for David: 'And Jonathan stripped himself of the robe that was upon him, and gave it to David, and his garments, even to his sword, and to his bow, and to his girdle,' (1 Sam. xviii. 4;) and also in the history of Mordecai, we read, 'For the man whom the king delighteth to honour, let the royal apparel be brought which the king used to wear,' &c. Esther v. 7, 8."

The reader will be pleased with these additional circumstances and authorities: but, perhaps, he will do well to consider the sword, the bow, and the girdle of Jonathan, as *military* appendages, and as peculiarly referring to the *military* exploits of David. The history of Mordecai having taken place in Persia, every custom of that country, by which it may be illustrated, is the more strictly appropriate and acceptable.—TAYLOR IN CALMET.

CHAPTER VII.

Ver. 7. And the king arising from the banquet of wine in his wrath, *went* into the palace-garden: and Haman stood up to make request for his life to Esther the queen; for he saw that there was evil determined against him by the king.

"When the king of Persia," says Tavernier, "orders a person to be executed, and then rises, and goes into a woman's apartment, it is a sign that no mercy is to be hoped for." But even the sudden rising of the king in anger, was the same as if he had pronounced the sentence of death. Olearius relates an instance of it, which occurred when he was in Persia. Schah Sefi once felt himself offended by unseasonable jokes, which one of his favourites allowed himself in his presence. The king immediately rose and retired, upon which the favourite saw that his life was forfeited. He went home in confusion, and in a few hours afterward the king sent for his head.—ROSENMULLER.

Ver. 8. Then the king returned out of the palace-garden into the place of the banquet of wine; and Haman was fallen upon the bed whereon Esther *was.* Then said the king, Will he force the queen also before me in the house? As the word went out of the king's mouth, they covered Haman's face.

The majesty of the kings of Persia did not allow malefactors to look at them. As soon as Haman was so considered, his face was covered. Some curious correspondent examples are collected together in Poole's Synopsis, in loc. From Pococke we find the custom still continues. Speaking of the artifice by which an Egyptian bey was taken off, he says, "A man being brought before him like a malefactor just taken, with his hands behind him as if tied, and a napkin put over his head, as malefactors commonly have, when he came into his presence, suddenly shot him dead."—BURDER.

CHAPTER VIII.

Ver. 10. And he wrote in the king Ahasuerus' name, and sealed *it* with the king's ring; and sent letters by posts on horseback, *and* riders on mules, camels, *and* young dromedaries.

See on Job 9. 25.

Ver. 15. And Mordecai went out from the presence of the king in royal apparel of blue and white, and with a great crown of gold, and with a garment of fine linen and purple: and the city of Shushan rejoiced and was glad.

See on Dan. 5. 29.

CHAPTER IX.

Ver. 19. Therefore the Jews of the villages, that dwelt in the unwalled towns, made the fourteenth day of the month Adar *a day of* gladness and feasting, and a good day, and of sending portions one to another.

See on Nehem. 8. 10.

On the first of the Hindoo month of July, also on the first day of the new moon of their October, the people send portions of cakes, preserves, fruits, oil, and clothes, one to another.—ROBERTS.

The eastern princes and people not only invite their friends to feasts, but "it is their custom to send a portion of the banquet to those that cannot well come to it, especially their relations, and those in a state of mourning." (Chardin.) Thus when the grand emir found it incommoded M. D'Arvieux to eat with him, he desired him to take his own time for eating, and sent him from his kitchen, what he liked, and at the time he chose.

This was the name, after the Babylonish captivity, of the twelfth month, nearly answering to our February, O. S. and perhaps so called from the richness or exuberance of the earth in plants and flowers at that season, in the warm eastern countries. "As February advances, the fields, which were partly green before, now, by the springing up of the latter grain, become entirely covered with an agreeable verdure; and though the trees continue in their leafless state till the end of this month, or the beginning of March, yet the almond, when latest, being in blossom before the middle of February, and quickly succeeded by the apricot, peach, &c. gives the gardens an agreeable appearance. The spring now becomes extremely pleasant." (Russel's Nat. Hist. of Aleppo.)—BURDER.

Ver. 26. Wherefore they called these days Purim, after the name of Pur.

This festival was to be kept two days successively, the fourteenth and fifteenth of the month Adar, ver. 21. On both days of the feast the modern Jews read over the Megillah, or book of Esther, in their synagogues. The copy there read must not be printed, but written on vellum, in the form of a roll; and the names of the ten sons of Haman are written on it in a peculiar manner, being ranged, they say, like so many bodies hanged on a gibbet. The reader must pronounce all these names in one breath. Whenever Haman's name is pronounced, they make a terrible noise in the synagogue: some drum with their feet on the floor, and the boys have mallets, with which to knock and make a noise. They prepare themselves for their carnival by a previous fast, which should continue three days, in imitation of Esther's, Esther iv. 16, but they have mostly reduced it to one day.—JENNINGS.

CHAPTER X.

Ver. 3. For Mordecai the Jew *was* next unto the king Ahasuerus, and great among the Jews, and accepted of the multitude of his brethren, seeking the wealth of his people, and speaking peace to all his seed.

Sir John Malcolm tells us, that the sepulchre of Esther and Mordecai stands near the centre of the city of Hamadan. It is a square building, terminated by a dome, with an inscription in Hebrew upon it, translated and sent to him by Sir Gore Ouseley, late ambassador to the court of Persia. It is as follows: "Thursday, fifteenth of the month Adar, in the year 4474 from the creation of the world, was finished the building of this temple, over the graves of Mordecai and Esther, by the hands of the good-hearted brothers, Elias and Samuel, the sons of the deceased Ishmael of Kashan."

A more particular and recent account of this tomb will be found in the following extract: "This tomb is regarded by all the Jews, who yet exist in the empire, as a place of particular sanctity; and pilgrimages are still made to it at certain seasons of the year, in the same spirit of holy penitence with which, in former times, they turned their eyes towards Jerusalem. Being desirous of visiting a place, which Christians cannot view without reverence, I sent to request that favour of the priest, under whose care it is preserved. He came to me immediately on my message, and seemed pleased with the respect manifested towards the ancient people of his nation, in the manner with which I asked to be admitted to their shrine. I accompanied the priest through the town, over much ruin and rubbish, to an enclosed piece of ground, rather more elevated than any in its immediate vicinity. In the centre was the Jewish tomb; a square building of brick, of a mosque-like form, with a rather elongated dome at the top; the whole seems in a very decaying state; falling fast to the mouldered condition of some wall fragments around, which, in former times, had been connected with, and extended the consequence of the sacred enclosure. The door that admitted us into the tomb is in the ancient sepulchral fashion of the country, very small; consisting of a single stone of great thickness, and turning on its own pivots from one side. Its key is always in possession of the head of the Jews, resident at Hamadan; and doubtless has been so preserved, from the time of the holy pair's interment, when the grateful sons of the captivity, whose lives they had rescued from universal massacre, first erected a monument over the remains of their benefactors, and obeyed the ordinance of gratitude, in making the anniversary of their preservation, a lasting memorial of heaven's mercy, and the just faith of Esther and Mordecai. 'So God remembered his people, and justified his inheritance. Therefore those days shall be unto them, in the month Adar, the fourteenth and fifteenth day of the same month, and with an assembly, and joy, and with gladness before God, according to the generation for ever among his people.' Esth. x. 12, 13. The pilgrimage yet kept up, is a continuation of this appointed assembling. And thus having existed from the time of the event, such a memorial becomes an evidence to the fact, more convincing, perhaps, than even written testimony; it seems a kind of eyewitness. The original structure, it is said, was destroyed at the sacking of the place, by Timour; and soon after that catastrophe, when the country became a little settled, the present unobtrusive building was raised on the original spot. Certain devout Jews of the city stood at the expense; and about a hundred and fifty years ago, (nearly five hundred after its re-erection,) it was fully repaired by a rabbi of the name of Ismael. On passing through the little portal, which we did in an almost doubled position, we entered a small arched chamber, in which are seen the graves of several rabbis: probably, one may cover the remains of the pious Ismael; and, not unlikely, the others may contain the bodies of the first rebuilders, after the sacrilegious destruction by Timour. Having trod lightly by their graves, a second door of such very confined dimensions presented itself at the end of this vestibule, that we were constrained to enter it on our hands and knees, and then standing up, we found ourselves in a larger chamber, to which appertained the dome. Immediately under its concave, stand two sarcophagi, made of a very dark wood, carved with great intricacy of pattern, and richness of twisted ornament, with a line of inscription in Hebrew, running round the upper ledge of each. Many other inscriptions, in the same language, are cut on the walls, while one of the oldest antiquity, engraved on a slab of white marble, is let into the wall itself. The priest assured me it had been rescued from the ruins of the first edifice, at its demolition by the Tartars; and, with the sarcophagi themselves, was preserved on the same consecrated spot." (Sir R. K. Porter.)—BURDER.

JOB.

CHAPTER I.

Ver. 3. His substance also was seven thousand sheep, and three thousand camels, and five hundred yoke of oxen, and five hundred she-asses, and a very great household; so that this man was the greatest of all the men of the east.

It is remarkable that in this passage female asses only are enumerated; the reason is, because in them great part of their wealth consisted; the males being few, and not held in equal estimation. We find that the former were chosen for riding by the natives of these parts: and the ass of Balaam is distinguished as a female. They were probably led to this choice from convenience; for, where the country was so little fertile, no other animal could subsist so easily as this: and there was another superior advantage in the female; that whoever traversed these wilds upon a she-ass, if he could but find for it sufficient browse and water, was sure to be rewarded with a more pleasing and nutritious beverage.—BRYANT.

Ver. 4. And his sons went and feasted *in their* houses every one his day; and sent and called for their three sisters, to eat and to drink with them.

Literally, "were wont and held a banquet-house;" which is not exactly an English idiom. The original phrase literally signifies, "a banquet-house," or "open house for feasting;" and hence Tyndal renders it, "made bankettes;" which is not perfectly literal, but far less paraphrastic than our common rendering, "went and feasted *in their* houses." —GOOD.

Ver. 5. And it was so, when the days of *their* feasting were gone about, that Job sent and sanctified them, and rose up early in the morning, and offered burnt-offerings *according* to the number of them all: for Job said, It may be that my sons have sinned, and cursed God in their hearts. Thus did Job continually.

The feasting continued till they had been at each other's house in turn. Something like this is practised by the Chinese, who have their co-fraternities, which they call the brotherhood of the month; this consists of thirty, according to the number of days therein, and in a circle they go every day to eat at one another's houses by turns. If one man have not conveniences to receive the fraternity in his own house, he may provide for it at another; and there are many public-houses very well provided for this purpose.—BURDER.

Ver. 7. And the LORD said unto Satan, Whence comest thou? Then Satan answered the LORD, and said, From going to and fro in the earth, and walking up and down in it.

In our common version, "From going to and fro;" but this is not the exact meaning of the Hebrew שוט; which, as is well observed by Schultens, imports not so much the act of going forward and backward, as of making a circuit or circumference; of going round about. It is hence justly rendered in the Spanish, "*De* CERCAR *por la tierra,*" "From encircling or encompassing the earth:" to which is added, in the Chaldaic paraphrase, "to examine into the works of the sons of man." The Hebrew verb שוט is still in general use among Arabic writers, and, in every instance, implies the same idea of gyration, or circumambulation.—GOOD.

Ver. 10. Hast thou not made a hedge about him, and about his house, and about all that he hath on every side? Thou hast blessed the work of his hands, and his substance is increased in the land.

It is said of a man who cannot be injured, "Why attempt to hurt him? is there not a hedge about him?" "You cannot get at the fellow, he has a strong hedge about him." "Yes, yes; the modeliar has become his hedge."—ROBERTS.

To give the original verb the full force of its meaning, it should be derived from the science of engineering, and rendered, "Hast thou not raised a *palisado* about him?" The Hebrew verb שכת implies, to fence with sharp spikes, palisades, or thorns; and hence the substantive שכים is used for spikes, palisades, or thorns themselves. The Arabian writers employ the same term, and even the same idiom, still more frequently than the Hebrews. In the Arabic version of the passage before us, the metaphor is varied still further; but the observations thus offered will render the variation not difficult of comprehension: thus, instead of being interpreted as above, "Hast thou not made a *fence* about him?" it is translated in the Arabic copy, "*Hast thou not protected him with thy hand?*" The Syriac runs to the same effect, while the Chaldee paraphrast translates, "Hast thou not overcovered him with thy *word?*"

In the latter clause of this verse, the words, "increased in the land," are, in the Hebrew, "overflowed the land." Our common version merely gives the sense of the original, without the figure, whose force and elegance render it highly worthy of being retained. The Hebrew (פרץ) *peraz* does not simply mean *to increase*, but *to burst* or *break forth* as a torrent; and hence to *overflow* or exundate its boundaries. The word is used in the same rendering in many parts of the Bible, in which it cannot be otherwise translated. The following instance may suffice, from the standard English text, 2 Sam. v. 20: "The Lord *hath broken forth* upon mine enemies before me, as the breach of waters: therefore he called the name of that place *Baal*-PERAZIM." The Arabians employ, to this hour, the very same term to express the mouth or embouchure, the most rapid and irresistible part of a stream, in proof of which, Golius, with much pertinency, brings the following couplet from Gjan hari, the whole of which is highly applicable, and where the word *mouth*, in the second line, is in the original expressed by this very term:—

> "His rushing wealth o'erflowed him with its heaps:
> So, at its *mouth*, the mad Euphrates sweeps."

Dr. Stock has caught something of the idea, though it is not so clearly expressed as it might have been:

> "And his possessions *burst out* through the land."

So the versions of Junius and Tremellius, and Piscator, "*Et pecus ejus in multitudinem eruperit in terra*"—"And his cattle, for multitude, have burst forth through the land." מקנה *substance* or *possession*, is often used for *cattle*, as the earliest substance or possession. So *cattle*, among ourselves, is said by the etymologists to be derived from *capitalia*.—GOOD.

Ver. 12. And the LORD said unto Satan, Behold, all that he hath *is* in thy power; only upon himself put not forth thine hand. So Satan went forth from the presence of the LORD.

The subject proposed by the writer of the ensuing poem is the trial and triumph of the integrity of Job; a character of whose origin no certain documents have descended to us, but who, at the period in question, was chief magistrate, or emir, as we should style him in the present day, of the city of Uz; powerful and prosperous beyond all the sons of the East, and whose virtue and piety were as eminently distinguished as his rank. Of the four characters introduced into the poem, as his friends, Eliphaz, Bildad, Zophar, and Elihu, the first three are denominated, in all the Greek translations of the poem, kings of the respective cities or districts to which their names are prefixed; and the last is particularized, in the Chaldee paraphrase, as a relation of Abraham, and was probably, therefore, a descendant of Buz, the second son of Nahor, the brother of Abraham, as conjectured by Bochart. There are some critics, however, and of great distinction for learning and piety, who, in opposition to these biographical remarks, contend that the whole of the poem, as well in its characters as in its structure, is fabulous. Such especially is the opinion of Professor Michaelis, whose chief arguments are derived from the nature of the exordium, in which Satan appears as the accuser of Job; from the temptations and sufferings permitted by the great Governor of the world to befall an upright character; from the roundness of the numbers by which the patriarch's possessions are described, as seven thousand, three thousand, one thousand, and five hundred; and from the years he is said to have lived after his recovery from disease. It may perhaps be thought to demand a more subjugating force than is lodged in these arguments, to transmute into fable what has uniformly been regarded as fact, both in Europe and Asia, for perhaps upwards of four thousand years; which appears to have descended as fact, in a regular stream of belief, in the very country which forms the scene of the history, from the supposed time of its occurrence to the present day; the chief character in which is represented as having had an actual existence, and is often associated with real characters, as Noah, Abraham, Ismael, Isaac, Jacob, and Solomon, in various parts of the book which is there held most sacred, and which, so far as it is derived from national history or tradition, is entitled to minute attention; and (which should seem long since to have settled the question definitely) a character which, precisely in the same manner, is associated with real characters in the authoritative pages of the Old Testament. "It is altogether incredible," observes M. Michaelis, "that such a conversation ever took place between the Almighty and Satan, who is supposed to return with *news* from the terrestrial regions." But why should such a conversation be supposed incredible? The attempt at wit in this passage is somewhat out of place; for the interrogation of the Almighty, "Hast thou fixed thy view upon my servant Job, a perfect and upright MAN?" instead of aiming at the acquisition of news, is intended as a severe and most appropriate sarcasm upon the fallen spirit. "Hast THOU, who, with superior faculties and a more comprehensive knowledge of my will, hast not continued perfect and upright, fixed thy view upon a subordinate being, far weaker and less informed than thyself, who has continued so?" The attendance of the apostate at the tribunal of the Almighty is plainly designed to show us, that good and evil angels are equally amenable to him, and equally subject to his authority;—a doctrine common to every part of the Jewish and Christian scriptures, and, except in the mythology of the Parsees, recognised by perhaps every ancient system of religion whatever. The part assigned to Satan in the present work is that expressly assigned to him in the case of Adam and Eve in the garden of Eden, and of our Saviour in the wilderness; and which is assigned to him generally, in regard to mankind at large, by all the Evangelists and Apostles, whose writings have reached us, both in their strictest historical narratives, and closest argumentative inductions. And, hence, the argument which should induce us to regard the present passage as fabulous, should induce us to regard all the rest in the same light, which are imbued with the same doctrine;—a view of the subject which would sweep into nothingness a much larger portion of the Bible than I am confident M. Michaelis would choose to part with. The other arguments are comparatively of small moment. We want not fable to tell us that good and upright men may occasionally become the victims of accumulated calamities; for it is a living fact, which, in the mystery of providence, is perpetually occurring in every country: while as to the roundness of the numbers by which the patriarch's possessions are described, nothing could have been more ungraceful or superfluous than for the poet to have descended to units, had even the literal numeration demanded it. And, although he is stated to have lived a hundred and forty years after his restoration to prosperity, and in an era in which the duration of man did not perhaps much exceed that of the present day, it should be recollected, that in his person, as well as in his property, he was specially gifted by the Almighty: that, from various passages, he seems to have been younger than all the interlocutors, except Elihu, and much younger than one or two of them; that his longevity is particularly remarked, as though of more than usual extent; and that, even in the present age of the world, we have well-authenticated instances of persons having lived, in different parts of the globe, to the age of a hundred and fifty, a hundred and sixty, and even a hundred and seventy years.

It is not necessary for the historical truth of the book of Job, that its language should be a direct transcript of that actually employed by the different characters introduced into it; for in such case we should scarcely have a single book of real history in the world. The Iliad, Shah Nameh, and the Lusiad, must at once drop all pretensions to such a description; and even the pages of Sallust and Cesar, of Rollin and Hume, must stand upon very questionable authority. It is enough that the real sentiment be given, and the general style copied: and this, in truth, is all that is aimed at, not only in our best reports of parliamentary speeches, but, in many instances, (which indeed is much more to the purpose,) by the writers of the New Testament, in their quotations from the Old. The general scope and moral of the ensuing poem, namely, that the troubles and affliction of the good man are, for the most part, designed as tests of his virtue and integrity, out of which he will at length emerge with additional splendour and happiness, are common to eastern poets, and not uncommon to those of Greece. The Odyssey is expressly constructed upon such a basis; and, like the poem before us, has every appearance of being founded upon real history, and calls in to its aid the machinery of a sublime and supernatural agency. But in various respects the poem of Job stands alone and unrivalled. In addition to every corporeal suffering and privation which it is possible for man to endure, it carries forward the trial, in a manner, and to an extent which has never been attempted elsewhere, into the keenest faculties and sensations of the mind; and mixes the bitterest taunts and accusations of friendship, with the agonies of family bereavement and despair. The body of other poems consists chiefly of incidents; that of the present poem of colloquy or argument, in which the general train of reasoning is so well sustained, its matter so important, its language so ornamented, the doctrines it develops so sublime, its transitions from passion to passion so varied and abrupt, that the want of incidents is not felt, and the attention is still riveted, as by enchantment. In other poems, the supernatural agency is fictitious, and often incongruous: here the whole is solid reality, supported, in its grand outline by the concurrent testimony of every other part of the scriptures; an agency not obtrusively introduced, but demanded by the magnitude of the occasion; and as much more exalted and magnificent than every other kind of similar interference, as it is more veritable and solemn. The suffering hero is sublimely called forth to the performance of his part, in the presence of men and of angels; each becomes interested, and equally interested, in his conduct; the Almighty assents to the trial, and for a period withdraws his divine aid; the malice of Satan is in its full career of activity; hell hopes, earth trembles, and every good spirit is suspended with awful anxiety. The wreck of his substance is in vain; the wreck of his family is in vain; the scalding sores of a corroding leprosy are in vain; the artillery of insults, reproaches, and railing, poured forth from the mouth of bosom friends, are in vain. Though at times put in some degree off his guard, the holy sufferer is never completely overpowered. He sustains the shock without yielding: he still holds fast his integrity. Thus terminates the trial of faith:—Satan is confounded; fidelity triumphs; and the Almighty, with a magnificence well worthy of the occasion, unveils his resplendent tribunal, and crowns the afflicted champion with his applause.

This poem has been generally supposed to possess a dramatic character, either of a more or a less perfect degree; but, in order to give it such a pretension, it has uniformly been found necessary to strip it of its magnificent exordium and close, which are unquestionably narrative; and even then the dramatic cast is so singularly interrupted by the appearance of the historian himself, at the commencement of every speech, to inform us of the name of the person who is about to take up the argument, that many critics, and among the rest Bishop Lowth, are doubtful of the propriety of referring it to this department of poetry, though they do not know where else to give it a place. In the present writer's view of the subject, it is a regular Hebrew epic; and, were it necessary to enter so minutely into the question, it might easily be proved to possess all the more prominent features of an epic, as collected and laid down by Aristotle himself; such as unity, completion, and grandeur in its action; loftiness in its sentiments and language; multitude and variety in the passions which it develops. Even the characters, though not numerous, are discriminated, and well supported; the milder and more modest temper of Eliphaz is well contrasted with the forward and unrestrained violence of Bildad; the terseness and brevity of Zophar with the pent-up and overflowing fulness of Elihu; while in Job himself we perceive a dignity of mind that nothing can humiliate, a firmness that nothing can subdue, still habitually disclosing themselves, amidst the mingled tumult of hope, fear, rage, tenderness, triumph, and despair, with which he is alternately distracted. I throw out this hint, however, not with a view of ascribing any additional merit to the poem itself, but merely to observe, so far as a single fact is possessed of authority, that mental taste, or the internal discernment of real beauty, is the same in all ages and nations; and that the rules of the Greek critic are deduced from a principle of universal impulse and operation.

Nothing can have been more unfortunate for this most excellent composition, than its division into chapters, and especially such a division as that in common use; in which not only the unity of the general subject, but, in many instances, that of a single paragraph, or even of a single clause, is completely broken in upon and destroyed. The natural division, and that which was unquestionably intended by its author, is into *six* parts, or books; for in this order it still continues to run, notwithstanding all the confusion it has encountered by sub-arrangements. These six parts are, An opening or exordium, containing the introductory history and decree concerning Job;—three distinct series of arguments, in each of which the speakers are regularly allotted their respective turns;—the summing up of the controversy;—and the close or catastrophe, consisting of the suffering hero's grand and glorious acquittal, and restoration to prosperity and happiness.—GOOD.

Ver. 14. And there came a messenger unto Job, and said, The oxen were ploughing, and the asses feeding beside them.

Heb. "She-asses." In our common version, which seems borrowed from Tyndal, *asses:* yet why the sex, which is so expressly mentioned in the original and the Septuagint, and is copied into every version with which I am acquainted, excepting these two, should be here suppressed, I know not. Female asses, on account of their milk, were much more highly esteemed, at all times, in the East, than males, a few of which only appear to have been kept for continuing the breed; and hence, perhaps, they are not noticed in ver. 3 of this chapter, which gives us a catalogue of the patriarch's live-stock. She-asses, moreover, on account of their milk, were generally preferred for travelling. The ass of Balaam is expressly declared to have been female, Numb. xxii. 21; as is that of Abraham, Gen. xxii. 3.—GOOD.

Ver. 15. And the Sabeans fell *upon them*, and took them away; yea, they have slain the servants with the edge of the sword; and I only am escaped alone to tell thee.

Heb. "And the Sabean rushed forth"—a poetic expression for "the Sabeans," or "Sabean tribe." The Syriac version gives us, "a band or company rushed forth," the word Sabean being omitted. Saba, or Sheba, was a town or city of Arabia Deserta; and the Sabeans and Chaldeans were wont to wander in distinct bands or hordes, upon predatory excursions, over the whole of the border country, and perhaps, at times, as far as from the banks of the Euphrates to the outskirts of Egypt. The Bedouin Arabs of the present day present us with the best specimens of these parties of irregular plunderers. Both are equally entitled to the appellation of Kedarines; the root of which, in Arabic as well as in Hebrew, implies *assault, incursion, tumult*; and both either have employed, or still continue to employ, as a covering for their tents, a coarse brown hair cloth, obtained from their dark-coloured and shaggy goats: whence the fair bride of Solomon, in the song of songs,—

"*Brown* am I, but comely, O ye daughters of Jerusalem!
As the tents of Kedar."——GOOD.

Ver. 20. Then Job arose, and rent his mantle, and shaved his head, and fell down upon the ground, and worshipped.

These are two of the actions by which great distress or agony of mind has, in all ages, been accustomed to be expressed in the East. In addition to these, sometimes the hair of the beard was also shaven or plucked off, as was done by Ezra, on his arrival at Jerusalem, on finding that the Hebrews, instead of keeping themselves a distinct and holy people, after their return from captivity, had intermixed with the nations around them, and plunged into all their abominations and idolatries. Ezra ix. 3. And sometimes, instead of shaving the hair of the head, the mourner, in the fulness of his humiliation and self-abasement, threw the dust, in which he sat, all over him, and purposely covered his hair with it. See Job ii. 12. After shaving the head, when this sign of distress was adopted, a vow was occasionally offered to the Almighty, in the hope of obtaining deliverance. This seems to have been a frequent custom with St. Paul, who did both, as well at Cenchrea as at Jerusalem, and in both places probably on this very account. See Acts xviii. 18. and xxi. 24.—GOOD.

CHAPTER II.

Ver. 4. And Satan answered the LORD, and said, Skin for skin; yea, all that a man hath will he give for his life.

The Arabs set the exploits of their chiefs in the dialogue form, like the book of Job. The Cingalese often spend hours at night in reciting alternately the exploits of Budhu, and of their gods and devils. I have often been disturbed by them. This passage, imperfectly explained by most commentators, is, by Mr. Robinson, set in so clear a light, that the reader will be better satisfied with a quotation, than an abridgment. "Before the invention of money, trade used to be carried on by barter, that is, by exchanging one commodity for another. The man who had been hunting in the woods for wild beasts, would carry their skins to market, and exchange them with the armourer for so many bows and arrows. As these traffickers were liable to be robbed, they sometimes agreed to give a party of men a share for defending them; and skins were a very ancient tribute. With them they redeemed their own shares of property and their lives. It is to one or both of these customs, that the text alludes, as a proverb. Imagine one of these primitive fairs. A multitude of people from all parts, of different tribes and languages, in a broad field, all overspread with various commodities to be exchanged. Imagine this fair to be held after a good hunting season, and a bad harvest. The skinners are numerous, and clothing cheap. Wheat, the *staff* of life, is scarce, and the whole fair dread a famine. How many skins this year will a man give for this necessary article, without which, he and his family must inevitably die? Why, each would add to the heap, and put 'skin upon skin, for all' the skins 'that a man hath, will he give for his life.' Imagine the wheat growers, of whom Job was one, carrying home the skins, which they had taken for wheat. Imagine the party engaged to protect them, raising the tribute, and threatening if it were not paid, to put them to death. What proportion of skins would these merchants give, in this case of necessity? *Skin upon* skin, all the skins that they have, will they give for their lives. The proverb then means, that we should save our lives at any price."—CALLAWAY.

Ver. 7. So went Satan forth from the presence of the LORD, and smote Job with sore biles, from the sole of his foot unto his crown.

Respectable people have the greatest possible dread and disgust at biles, and all cutaneous diseases. Here, then, we see the princely Job the victim of a loathsome disorder, sitting among the ashes and broken earthen vessels, the impure refuse of the kitchen and other places. See the poor neglected object who is labouring under similar diseases at this day, from the head to the foot; he is covered with scales and blotches, around his loins is a scanty rag, he wanders from one lonely place to another, and when he sees you, stretches out a hand towards you, and another to his sores, and piteously implores help!—ROBERTS.

Ver. 7. So went Satan forth from the presence of the LORD, and smote Job with sore biles, from the sole of his foot unto his crown. 8. And he took him a potsherd to scrape himself withal; and he sat down among the ashes.

A remarkable disease mentioned in the scriptures is that which was inflicted on Job, and of which he so feelingly complains in several parts of his book. Commentators have differed as to its peculiar nature; but the best informed have fixed upon *elephantiasis*, as a disease well known in eastern countries, and corresponding with the hints which Job gives of it in his conversations with his friends. The following is an abridgment of what is said of it by Dr. Heberden and Michaelis. It begins with a sudden eruption of tubercles or tumours of different sizes, of a red colour, attended with great heat and itching, on different parts of the body, and a degree of fever, by which the skin acquires a remarkably shining appearance: but when the fever abates, the tubercles become either indolent knots, or in some degree scirrhous, and of a livid or copper colour; and after some months they degenerate into fetid ulcers. As the disease advances, the features of the face swell, the hair of the eyebrows falls off, the voice becomes hoarse, the breath exceedingly offensive, the skin of the body is unusually loose, wrinkled, rough, destitute of hairs, and overspread with tumours, and often with ulcers, or else with a thick, moist, scabby crust, upon those which have begun to dry up; and the legs are sometimes emaciated and ulcerated, sometimes affected with tumours, without ulceration, and sometimes swelled like posts, and indurated, having very thin scales, apparently much finer than those in leprosy, only not so white; while the soles of the feet, being thicker than the rest of the skin, feel peculiarly pained by the tumours and ulcers. Such is the state of those afflicted with elephantiasis; nor have they even intermissions of ease by refreshing rest; for as their days are rendered wretched by the distension of the skin by tumours, and a succession of burning, ill-conditioned ulcers, so their nights are tormented by perpetual restlessness or frightful dreams. The accuser of the brethren, therefore, evidently showed his sagacity and malice, when he selected this as the most likely means to provoke Job to impatience. But having described the leading features of the disease, let us next attend to the hints that are given us in the book of Job, and see whether the one corresponds with the other. In ch. ii. 7, 8, we are told, that "Satan smote Job with sore biles, from the sole of his foot even to his crown; and that he took a potsherd to scrape himself." This is evidently descriptive of elephantiasis, in its most active and rapid state, when the body is covered with tumours, which break into ulcers, and the skin becomes scaly. In ch. vi. 4, Job complains, that "the arrows of the Almighty were within him, and that the poison thereof drank up his spirit;" thereby comparing the pain he felt to that experienced from poisoned arrows; while the infection of the disease, like the influence of poison, spreads itself over the whole frame. It was formerly mentioned as an attendant on elephantiasis, that the patient could obtain no refreshing sleep, but was tormented with restlessness and frightful dreams. Accordingly, Job, in ch. vii. 3, 4, 13, 14, 15, complains in the following mournful manner: "I am made to possess months of vanity, and wearisome nights are appointed to me. When I lie down, I say, When shall I arise, and the night be gone? and I am full of tossings to and fro unto the dawning of the day.—When I say, My bed shall comfort me, my couch shall ease my complaint; then thou scarest me with dreams, and terrifiest me through visions: so that my soul chooseth strangling, and death rather than my life." The itchiness of ill-conditioned ulcers has often been ascribed to animalculæ, and their stench is intolerable. Accordingly, Job says, in ch. vii. 5, "My flesh is clothed with worms and clods of dust: my skin is broken, and become loathsome." It was said that the tumours and ulcers were peculiarly painful on the soles of the feet, from the thickness of the skin in those parts; and to that he refers in ch. xiii. 27, where he says, "Thou settest a print upon the heels of my feet;" literally, "Thou imprintest thyself, that is, thy wrath, on the soles of my feet." It was noticed that the skin in elephantiasis, when the disease hath become general, is loose, rough, and wrinkled; and Job, ch. xvi. 8, complains of this very thing, that "his skin was filled with wrinkles." An offensive breath was noticed as another evil under which the patient laboured; and this was the case with Job, for he complains, in ch. xvii. 1, that "his breath was corrupt; that his days were extinct; and that the grave was ready for him," as for a putrid carcass: adding in verse 44th, "I have said to corruption, Thou art my father; and to the worm, thou art my mother and my sister." The only other notice we have of the disease is in ch. xxx. 17, 30, where we hear him complaining that his bones were pierced with acute pain in the night season; and that his sinews, by their starting, gave him no rest; that his skin was black upon him; and his bones were burnt up with heat; all which accord well with the disease in question, when it hath taken possession of the system, and hath filled the body with livid, copper-coloured, scirrhous tumours, or black corrupted ulcers. Upon the whole, then, it appears probable, that the disease with which Job was afflicted was elephantiasis.—BROWN.

Ver. 8. And he took him a potsherd to scrape himself withal; and he sat down among the ashes.

This self-abasement appears to have been common among the Hebrews, as well as the Arabians or Idumæans, and was so probably among other oriental nations of high antiquity, in cases of deep and severe affliction. The coarsest dress, as of hair or sackcloth, was worn on such occasions; and the vilest and most humiliating situation, as a dust or cinder-heap, surrounded by potsherds and other household refuse, made choice of to sit in. It may easily be conjectured what considerable quantities of potsherds, or fragments of pottery, must have been collected in the dust-heaps above referred to, from a recollection, that in the earlier ages of the world, when the art of metallurgy was but in its infancy, almost all the domestic utensils employed for every purpose were of pottery alone. Pottery may hence be fairly supposed the oldest of the mechanical inventions: and on this account the Hebrew term here made use of, (חרש, a *potter*, *pottery*, or *potsherds*,) became afterward extended to signify wares of every other kind, or their fabricators, and hence artisans in general, whether in brass, iron, wood, or stone. The same word also, when used in the signification of a potsherd, a fragment or splinter of pottery, was also employed to import a sharp instrument in general, as a *rasp*, *scraper*, or *scalpel*, a sense in which it has to this day descended to the Arabs; for the Arabic word, (identically, as to letters, the same as the Hebrew חרש,) as a verb, implies to *scrape* or *rasp* with an edged tool, (the *purpose* to which the חרש or *shard*, was directed in the text;) and, as a substantive, a *scab*, or sharp and morbid incrustation of the skin—the *object* to which it was applied. —GOOD.

Ver. 9. Then said his wife unto him, Dost thou still retain thine integrity? Curse God, and die.

Some suppose this ought to be, bless God and die; but Job would not have reproved his wife for such advice, except she meant it ironically. It is a fact, that when the heathen have to pass through much suffering, they often ask, "Shall we make an offering to the gods for this?" *i. e.* Shall we offer our devotions, our gratitude, for afflictions? Job was a servant of the true God, but his wife might have been a heathen; and then the advice, in its most literal acceptation, would be perfectly in character. Nothing is more common than for the heathen, under certain circumstances, to curse their gods. Hear the man who has made expensive offerings to his deity, in hope of gaining some great blessing, and who has been disappointed, and he will pour out all his imprecations on the god whose good offices have (as he believes) been prevented by some superior deity. A man in reduced circumstances says, "Yes, yes; my god has lost his eyes; they are put out; he cannot look after my affairs." "Yes," said an extremely rich devotee (V. Chetty) of the supreme god Siva, after he had lost his property, "shall I serve him any more? What! make offerings to him? No, no; he is the lowest of all gods." With these facts before us, it is not difficult to believe that Job's wife actually meant what she said.—ROBERTS.

Ver. 10. But he said unto her, Thou speakest as one of the foolish women speaketh. What! shall we receive good at the hand of God, and shall we not receive evil? In all this did not Job sin with his lips.

It is not easy to know to whom Job alludes by "the foolish women;" but in all parts of the East, females are spoken of as being much inferior to man in wisdom; and nearly all their sages have proudly descanted on the ignorance of women. In the Hindoo book called the *Kurral*, it is said, "All women are ignorant." In other works it is said, "Ignorance is a woman's jewel." "Female wisdom is from the evil one." "The feminine qualities are four: ignorance, fear, shame, and impunity." "To a woman disclose not a secret." "Talk not to me in that way; it is all female wisdom."—ROBERTS.

Sanctius thinks that Job refers to the Idumean women, who, like other heathens, when their gods did not please them, or they could not obtain of them what they desired, would reproach and cast them away, and throw them into the fire, or the water, as the Persians are said to do.—BURDER.

Ver. 11. Now when Job's three friends heard of all this evil that was come upon him, they came every one from his own place; Eliphaz the Temanite, and Bildad the Shuhite, and Zophar the Naamathite: for they had made an appointment together to come to mourn with him, and to comfort him.

Has a man fallen into some great calamity, his friends immediately go to his house to comfort him. Thus, to the house of mourning for the dead may be seen numbers of people going daily, studying to find out some source of comfort for their afflicted friend. "Whither are you going?" "As a comforter to my friend in sorrow." "How great is his distress! he will not listen to the voice of the comforters."—ROBERTS.

Ver. 12. And when they lifted up their eyes afar off, and knew him not, they lifted up their voice and wept; and they rent every one his mantle, and sprinkled dust upon their heads towards heaven.

See on Josh. 7. 6.

Ver. 13. So they sat down with him upon the ground seven days and seven nights, and none spake a word unto him: for they saw that *his* grief was very great.

Those who go to sympathize with the afflicted, are often *silent* for hours together. As there were *seven days* for mourning in the scriptures, so here; and the seventh is always the greatest. The chief mourner, during the whole of these days, will never speak, except when it is absolutely necessary. When a visiter comes in, he simply looks and bows down his head.—ROBERTS.

CHAPTER III.

Ver. 1. After this opened Job his mouth, and cursed his day.

It is to be observed, says Mr. Blackwell, (Inquiry into the Life of Homer,) that the Turks, Arabians, and Indians, and in general most of the inhabitants of the East, are a solitary kind of people; they speak but seldom, and never long without emotion. Speaking is a matter of moment among such people, as we may gather from their usual introductions: for, before they deliver their thoughts, they give notice by saying, *I will open my mouth*, as here; that is, unloose their tongue. It is thus in Homer, Hesiod, and Orpheus; and thus also *Virgil:*

————finem dedit ore loquendi.

He made an end of speaking with his mouth.—BURDER.

Ver. 3. Let the day perish wherein I was born, and the night *in which* it was said, There is a man-child conceived.

Dr. Boothroyd prefers, "Perish the day in which I was *born;* the night it was said, Lo! a man child." Dr. A. Clarke thinks the word conceive "should be taken in the sense of being *born;*" and the Tamul translation takes the same view. When a male child is born, the midwife goes outside the house, and says aloud three times, "*A male child, a male child, a male child is born!*"—ROBERTS.

Ver. 12. Why did the knees prevent me? or why the breasts that I should suck.

This is not to be understood of the mother; but either of the midwife, who received the new-born infant into her lap, or of the father, as it was usual for him to take the child upon his knees as soon as it was born, Gen. l. 23. This custom obtained among the Greeks and Romans. Hence the goddess Levana had her name, causing the father in this way to own the child.—GILL.

Ver. 14. With kings and counsellors of the earth, which built desolate places for themselves.

This description is intended as a contrast to that contained in the two ensuing lines; and the same sort of contrast is admirably continued throughout the entire passage. The grave is the common receptacle of all; of the patriotic princes who have restored to their ancient magnificence the ruins of former cities, and fixed their palaces in them; and of the sordid accumulators of wealth, which they have not spirit to make use of; of the wicked, who have never ceased from troubling, and of those who have been wearied and worn out by their vexations; of the high and the low, the slave and his task-master, the servant and his lord. This idea has not, in general, been attended to, and hence the passage has not been clearly understood. Our common rendering, "Which built desolate places for themselves," is hardly explicit, though it is literally consonant with most of the versions. Schultens, not adverting to the antithesis intended to subsist between the fourteenth and fifteenth verses, imagines he perceives in the passage a metaphorical reference to the massy pyramids or sepulchres of the Egyptian monarchs, of which several have descended to our own day; and this idea has also been generally followed. But the conception is too recondite, and far less impressive, as it appears to me, than that now offered. The images and phraseology of this poem, as I have already had occasion to observe, were often copied by the boldest writers of the Jewish people; by King David, Isaiah, Jeremiah, and Ezekiel; and the smallest attention to their respective compositions will show us that the idea here communicated soon became proverbial; and that "the restorer of ruined wastes," or "of ancient ruins," was not only a phrase in general acceptation, but regarded as a character of universal veneration and esteem. Thus Isai. lviii. 12:—

> And thy descendants shall rebuild the ancient waste.
> The foundations *prostrate* for many ages shalt thou raise up:
> And thou shalt be called The repairer of ruins,
> The restorer of paths to walk in.

So Ezek. xxxvi. 33:—

> And I will also cause you to dwell in the cities;
> And the ruined wastes shall be rebuilt.

It is useless to quote further: the parallel passages are almost innumerable.—GOOD.

Ver. 21. Which long for death, but it *cometh* not; and dig for it more than for hid treasures.

We are constantly hearing of treasures which have been or are about to be discovered. Sometimes you may see a large space of ground, which has been completely turned up, or an old foundation, or ruin, entirely demolished, in hopes of finding the hidden gold. A man has found a small coin, has heard a tradition, or has had a dream, and off he goes to his toil. Perhaps he has been *seen* on the spot, or he has consulted a soothsayer; the report gets out; and then come the needy, the old, and the young, a motley group, all full of anxiety, to join in the spoil. Some have iron instruments, others have sticks, and some their fingers to scratch up the ground. At last some of them begin to look at each other with considerable suspicion, as if all were not right, and each seems to wish he had not come on so foolish an errand, and then steal off as quietly as they can. I once knew a deep tank made completely dry, (by immense labour,) in the hope of finding great treasures, which were said to have been cast in during the ancient wars. Passing near, one day, when they had nearly finished their work, and their hopes had considerably moderated, I went up to the sanguine owner, (whose face immediately began to show its chagrin,) and inquired, "Why are you taking so much trouble to empty that tank?" He replied, *as calmly as he could*, "We are merely cleaning it out." Poor man! I believe he found nothing but stones and bones, and a few copper coins. "Dig for it more than for hid treasures," finds a practical illustration in the East, and is a figure of common use in the language.—ROBERTS.

CHAPTER IV.

Ver. 2. *If* we assay to commune with thee, wilt thou be grieved? but who can withhold himself from speaking?

The term נסה, "to essay or attempt," is peculiarly expressive in the Hebrew, and is derived from the sense of smell exercised by hounds and other animals, in essaying or exploring the track of the prey they are in pursuit of. It is still used among the Arabs for a pleasant smell or odour. Eliphaz means to insinuate his desire to select the very mildest reply he could possibly meet with upon a minute research, such as, while it answered the purpose of exposing the fallacy of the patriarch's reasoning, should hurt his feelings as little as possible.—GOOD.

Ver. 6. *Is* not *this* thy fear, thy confidence, the uprightness of thy ways, and thy hope?

The clew to the genuine sense of this passage will be obtained by a slight transposition of the latter hemistich: "Is not this fear of thine, thy confidence; and the uprightness of thy ways, thy hope?" Job had before affirmed, chap. iii. 25, 26, "The thing which I greatly feared is come upon me, and that which I was afraid of is come unto me. I was not in safety, neither had I rest, neither was I quiet; yet trouble came;" *i. e.* I was continually exercised by a godly fear, a holy misgiving; I did not dare to cherish a sentiment of carnal security; even in the height of my prosperity, I was deeply sensible of my exposure to calamity, and lived habitually under a trembling anticipation of its approach. To this Eliphaz alludes; *q. d.* Here is something for which it is hard to account. "Behold, thou hast instructed many, and thou hast strengthened the weak hands. Thy words have upholden him that was falling, and thou hast strengthened the feeble knees. But now it is come upon thee, and thou faintest; it toucheth thee, and thou art troubled." How is this? Why is thy practice so much at variance with thy precepts? If thou art the man thou claimest to be; if thou hast been governed, as thou allegest, by a prevailing fear of God, and hast never indulged a feeling of self-sufficient security, why is not this thy fear a source of humble confidence to thee in the day of distress? and why does not the recollection of the unimpeachable integrity and uprightness of thy ways, serve as an anchor of hope, amid the tossings of a tried and troubled spirit? This surely were to have been expected from one of thy character. A heart conscious of innocence could not but sustain itself in such a trial; it would be entirely contrary to the analogy of the divine dispensations to suppose that such a one would be the victim of overwhelming judgments; for "remember, I pray thee, who ever perished being innocent? or when were the righteous cast off?" This interpretation makes the whole address of Eliphaz consistent, coherent, and clear, though founded upon the fallacy, that men are invariably dealt with in this world according to their desert.—BUSH.

Ver. 9. By the blast of God they perish, and by the breath of his nostrils are they consumed.

When people are angry, they distend their nostrils and blow with great force: the action may be taken from some animals, which, when angry, blow violently through their noses. Of a man who is much given to anger, it is said, "That fellow is always blowing through his nose." "You may blow through your nose for a thousand years, it will never injure me." "Go not near the breath of his nostrils, he will injure you."—ROBERTS.

Ver. 15. Then a spirit passed before my face; the hair of my flesh stood up.

This refers to the great fear of Job; but the same effect is often ascribed to great joy. Thus, in Hindoo books, in describing the ecstasy of gods or men, it is often said, "The hair of their flesh stood erect." A father says to his long absent child, "My son, not having seen your lotus face for so long, my hair stands up with joy."—ROBERTS.

Ver. 19. How much less *on* them that dwell in houses of clay, whose foundation *is* in the dust, *which* are crushed before the moth?

It is probable that this means a moth-worm, which is one state of the creature alluded to. It is first enclosed in an egg, from whence it issues a worm, and after a time becomes a complete insect, or moth. The following extracts from Niebuhr may throw light on this passage, that man is crushed by so feeble a thing as a worm:—"A disease very common in Yemen is the attack of the Guiney-worm, or the *Vena-Medinensis*, as it is called by the physicians of Europe. This disease is supposed to be occasioned by the use of the putrid waters, which people are obliged to drink in several parts of Yemen; and for this reason the Arabians always pass water, with the nature of which they are unacquainted, through a linen cloth, before drinking it. Where one unfortunately swallows any of the eggs of this insect, no immediate consequence follows; but after a considerable time, the worm begins to show itself through the skin. Our physician, Mr. Cramer, was, within a few days of his death, attacked by five of these worms at once, although this was more than five months after we had left Arabia. In the isle of Karek I saw a French officer named Le Page, who, after a long and difficult journey performed on foot, and in an Indian dress, between Pondicherry and Surat, through the heart of India, was busy extracting a worm out of his body. He supposed that he had got it by drinking bad water in the country of the Mahrattas. This disorder is not dangerous if the person affected can extract the worm without breaking it. With this view it is rolled on a small bit of wood as it comes out of the skin. It is slender as a thread, and two or three feet long. It gives no pain as it makes its way out of the body, unless what may be occasioned by the care which must be taken of it for some weeks. If unluckily it be broken, it then returns into the body, and the most disagreeable consequences ensue, palsy, a gangrene, and sometimes death."—BURDER.

CHAPTER V.

Ver. 5. Whose harvest the hungry eateth up, and taketh it even out of the thorns, and the robber swalloweth up their substance.

This seems a manifest allusion to the half-starved Arabs of the desert, who were always ready for plunder, as their descendants are to this day. Such starvelings are thus described by Volney: "These men are smaller, leaner, and blacker, than any of the Bedouins yet known; their wasted legs had only tendons without calves; their belly was glued to their back. In general, the Bedouins are small, lean, and swarthy, more so, however, in the bosom of the desert, than on the borders of the cultivated country. They are ordinarily about five feet two inches high. They seldom have more than about six ounces of food for the whole day. Six or seven dates, soaked in melted butter, a little milk, or curd, serve a man for twenty-four hours; and he seems happy when he can add a small portion of coarse flour, or a little ball of rice. Their camels also, which are their chief support, are remarkably meager, living on the meanest and most scanty provision. Nature has given it a small head, without ears, at the end of a long neck, without flesh: she has taken from its legs and thighs every muscle not immediately requisite for motion; and, in short, has bestowed on its withered body only the vessels and tendons necessary to connect its frame together; she has furnished it with a strong jaw, that it may grind the hardest aliments; and lest it should consume too much, she has straitened its stomach, and obliged it to chew the cud." —BURDER.

Ver. 7. Yet man is born unto trouble, as the sparks fly upward.

Hebrew, "Sons of the burning coal." The word SON, among the Hindoos, is applied to man, and all kinds of animal life. Men of ignoble parentage are called sons of the *koddekal*, i. e. the mechanics. When animals, reptiles, or insects, are troublesome, they are called *passăsinudia maggal*, sons of the devil; or *vease-maggal*, sons of the prostitute, or of the treacherous ones. See the ploughman, at his occupation; should the bullocks prove restive, he immediately vociferates the epithets alluded to. Listen to the almost breathless cowherd, who is running after some of his refractory kine, to bring them to the fold, and he abuses them in the most coarse and indelicate language. The man also, who, for the first time, discovers the white ants destroying his property, bawls out with all his might, "Ah! *vease-maggal*, sons of the prostitute."—ROBERTS.

Ver. 21. Thou shalt be hid from the scourge of the tongue: neither shalt thou be afraid of destruction when it cometh.

Dr. A. Clarke says, "the Targum refers this to the incantations of Balaam: from the injury by the tongue of Balaam thou shalt be hidden." The people live in great fear of the scourge of the tongue, and that independent of an incantation, because they believe the tongues of some men have the power of inflicting a dreadful curse on any object which has incurred their displeasure. Thus, many of the evils of life are believed to come from *nă-vooru*, the curse or the scourge of the tongue. "Have you heard what Kandan's tongue has done for Muttoo?" "No! what has happened?" "Why, some time ago, Kandan promised on his next voyage to bring Muttoo a cargo of rice, but he did not keep his word; Kandan, therefore, became very angry, and said, 'I shall not be surprised at hearing of thy vessel being wrecked.' Muttoo again sailed, without caring for Kandan's tongue; but lo! his vessel has been knocked to pieces on the rocks, and I saw him this morning on his way home, beating his head, and exclaiming, 'Ah! this *nă-vooru, nă-vooru*, this evil tongue, this evil tongue, my vessel has gone to pieces on the rocks." But the tongues of some men are believed to possess malignant power, not only in imprecations, but also in their *blessings* and *praises*. 'The other day, when I and some others were sitting with our friend the doctor, one of his daughters came to speak to her father; as she was delivering her message, one of the party exclaimed, 'What a beautiful set of teeth!' and from that moment they began to decay.' "Alas! alas! poor old Murager purchased a fine milch cow yesterday, and was driving her along the road this morning, on his way home, when, behold, a fellow met them and said, 'Ah, what large teats!' The cow broke from the string, she rushed to the hedge, and a stake ran through her udder." "Ah, what a miserable man is Valen! a few days ago, as his wife was nursing the infant, he said, 'How comely art thou, my fawn!' when immediately a cancer made its appearance in her breast, from which she can never recover." —ROBERTS.

Ver. 23. For thou shalt be in league with the stones of the field; and the beasts of the field shall be at peace with thee.

See on 2 Kings 3. 19.

In a country where wild beasts are so numerous and so fierce, and where the natives have so few means of defence, can it be a matter of surprise that people on a journey are always under the influence of great fear? The father says to his son, when he is about to depart, "Fear not; the beasts will be thy friends." The dealer in charms says, when giving one of his potent spells, "Be not afraid, young man; this shall make the cruel beasts respect thee."—ROBERTS.

Ver. 25. Thou shalt know also that thy seed *shall be* great, and thine offspring as the grass of the earth.

When a priest, or an aged person, blesses a young couple, he says, "Your children shall be as the grass, *arruga-pillu*, (Agrostis Linearis.) Yes; you shall twine and bind yourselves together like the grass."—ROBERTS.

Ver. 26. Thou shalt come to *thy* grave in a full age, like as a shock of corn cometh in his season.

Literally, "in dried up," or, "shrivelled age;" and hence the term here employed, (כלח) is applied by the Arabians to designate the *winter* season, in which every thing is corrugated or shrivelled. On which account some commentators propose, that the text should be rendered "in the *winter* of life;" poetically, indeed, but not thoroughly consistent with the metaphor of a shock of corn: which, in close congruity with the emblematic picture of winter, at its season of maturity, is *dried up* and *contracted*, and thus far offers an equal similitude of ripe old age; but which forcibly increases the similitude by the well known fact, that, like ripe old age also, it must be committed to the earth in order to spring to newness of life; for, in both cases, "the seed which thou sowest shall not quicken, except it die." Tyndal has given the passage thus: "In a fayre age lyke as the corn sheewes are broughte into the barne in due season:" whence Sandys,

> "Then, full of days, like weighty shocks of corn,
> In season reaped, shalt to thy grave be borne."

Nor very differently Schultens, notwithstanding that he admits that the Hebrew (אכח) in itself implies "congestion, accumulation, or heaping together." "*Intrabis* in decrepitâ senectute ad tumulum," "Thou shalt *enter* into the tomb in decrepit age;" meaning, as a shock of corn *enters* into the barn.—GOOD.

Great is the desire of the men of the East to see a good old age. Thus the beggars, when relieved, often bless you, and say, "Ah! my lord, may you live a thousand years." "Live, live, till the shakings of age."—ROBERTS.

CHAPTER VI.

Ver. 2. Oh that my grief were thoroughly weighed, and my calamity laid in the balances together!

"Ah! my lord, could you weigh my poverty, I am sure you would relieve me." "The sorrows of that man's soul, who can weigh them?" "Alas! if my sorrows could be weighed, then would pity be shown unto me."—ROBERTS.

Ver. 4. For the arrows of the Almighty *are* within me, the poison whereof drinketh up my spirit: the terrors of God do set themselves in array against me.

The practice of using poisoned arrows is universal among the interior nations of Southern Africa, to whom the gospel has not reached. The strongest of all the poisons used is that which has been discovered by the most uncivilized of all the nations, the wild Bushmen; a wound from which is attended with great pain and thirst, while the poison is working throughout the system, and attended with great depression. I brought some of the poison with me to England, to see if any antidote against it could be discovered. It has exactly the appearance of black wax, and is found deposited in sheltered corners of rocks, but how it came there is yet unknown. A medical gentleman, who had devoted much attention to the different kinds of known poisons, after delivering some lectures in London on that particular subject, heard of the Bushman poison, and applied to me to furnish him with some of it, that he might analyze it, and endeavour to find out an antidote. I rejoiced that the matter had fallen into such good hands, and immediately forwarded it by post. I received different letters, containing various experiments, but all had failed. I remember the first trial he made of the power of the poison was, by wetting the point of a needle, and, after dipping it into the powder, pricking a bird with it, which died almost immediately. The same experiment was made on a second bird, while some antidote was immediately applied to counteract the effects of the poison. After a short time it also died. Various antidotes were tried in the same way, but all proved equally ineffectual.—CAMPBELL.

Ver. 6. Can that which is unsavoury be eaten without salt? or is there *any* taste in the white of an egg.

The eastern people often make use of bread, with nothing more than salt, or some such trifling addition, such as summer-savory dried and powdered. This, Russel says, is done by many at Aleppo. The Septuagint translation of this passage seems to refer to the same practice, when it renders the first part of the verse, "will bread be eaten without salt?"—BURDER.

Ver. 12. *Is* my strength the strength of stones? or *is* my flesh of brass?

Is a servant ordered to do a thing for which he has not strength; to undergo great hardships; he asks, "Is my strength as iron? Am I a stone?"—ROBERTS.

Ver. 15. My brethren have dealt deceitfully as a brook, *and* as the stream of brooks they pass away; 16. Which are blackish by reason of the ice, *and* wherein the snow is hid; 17. What time they wax warm they vanish: when it is hot, they are consumed out of their place.

The phrase in this place is a strict orientalism, "My brethren have acted (or played) the flood with me:" and the proverbial form is at least as common now among the Arabians, as it could be when the present poem was composed. Fairly explained, nothing can be more apposite, nothing more exquisite, than the image before us, and the whole of its description. Arabia has but few rivers; Proper Arabia perhaps none; for what in this last country are called rivers, are mere torrents, which descend from the mountains during the rains, and for a short period afterward. A few rivers are found in Yemen, or the southern province; and the Tigris and Euphrates, as touching its northern limits in their passage along Irak Arabi, have occasionally been laid claim to by Arabian geographers. Even the Astam of Najd, or Neged, the province of Sandy Arabia, though laid down as a considerable river in the maps, is a mere brook. Hence the country is chiefly watered and fertilized by exudations of its dry channels, an overflow of which is uniformly regarded as a great treasure and blessing; the inhabitants in the neighbourhood hail its appearance, and prepare to enrich themselves out of its stores, by admitting it into their tanks or reservoirs. But it often happens, that the blessing is converted to a curse; that the torrent rushes with so much abruptness and rapidity, as to carry every thing before it; and that, exhausted by its own violence, its duration is as brief as its stream is rapid, allowing them scarcely time to slake their own thirst, or, at least, to fill their domestic utensils. Fair and specious, therefore, as is its first appearance, it is in the end full of deceit and cruel disappointment: "Et viatores (says Dr. Lowth, upon the passage before us) per Arabæ deserta errantes sitique confectos perfide destituunt," Præl. xii. p. 110—it promises comfort, but overwhelms with mortification. Such (says Job) are the companions who come to visit me in my affliction; they affect to console me, but they redouble my distress.—GOOD.

In desert parts of Africa it has afforded much joy to fall in with a brook of water, especially when running in the direction of the journey, expecting it would prove a valuable companion. Perhaps before it accompanied us two miles, it became invisible by sinking into the sand; but two miles farther along, it would re-appear and run as before, and raise hopes of its continuance; but after running a few hundred yards, would finally sink into the sand, not again to rise. In both cases it raised hopes which were not realized; of course it deceived. Perhaps it is to such brooks that Job refers in the 15th verse. There are many in Africa, which are described in verse 17, which run in the winter, or rainy season; but the return of the hot season completely dries them up, which prove often great disappointments to stranger travellers.—CAMPBELL.

Ver. 18. The paths of their way are turned aside; they go to nothing, and perish.

Rendered by Schultens and Reiske, "into the desert, the empty space, or land of nothing;" but the former is the more forcible rendering. The torrent progressively evaporating and branching into fresh outlets, becomes at length itself nothing. The original means equally "nothing," and "a desert," or place of nothing. It is usually rendered in the former signification. I have already observed that the latter is preferred by Reiske and Schultens; but either will answer.

The whole description is directly coincident with a very valuable article inserted by Major Colebrooke, in the seventh volume of Asiatic Researches, and entitled, "On the Course of the Ganges through Bengal." He observes, that the occasional obstructions which the rivers of Bengal meet with, on the return of their periodical flux, produce not unfrequently some very extraordinary alterations in the course and bending of their respective beds, and hence, some equally extraordinary changes in the general face of the country. While some villages that, in common, are scarcely visited by a river, even at its utmost rise, are overflowed and suddenly swept away; others, actually seated on the banks of an arm, and that used to be regularly inundated, are totally deserted, and the inhabitants have to travel over many miles to obtain water. He adds, that the Ganges has evinced changes of this nature, in a greater degree than any other Indian stream; and that even since the survey of Major Rennel, in 1764, it has deviated in its course not less than two miles and a half; whence several of the villages which figure in his map are no longer to be found in the situations assigned them; while islands of considerable magnitude, now inhabited and cultivated, have started into being where the river then rolled its deepest waters.—GOOD.

Ver. 28. Now, therefore, be content: look upon me: for *it is* evident unto you if I lie.

When a person is accused of uttering a falsehood, he says, "Look in my face, and you will soon see I am innocent." "My face will tell you the truth." When the countenance does not indicate guilt, it is said, "Ah! his face does not say so." "The man's face does not contain the witness of guilt."—ROBERTS.

CHAPTER VII.

Ver. 2. As a servant earnestly desireth the shadow,

and as a hireling looketh for *the reward of* his work.

The people of the East measure time by the length of their shadow. Hence, if you ask a man what o'clock it is, he immediately goes in the sun, stands erect, then looking where his shadow terminates, he measures the length with his feet, and tells you nearly the time. Thus they earnestly desire THE shadow which indicates the time for leaving their work. A person wishing to leave his toil, says, "How long my shadow is in coming." "Why did you not come sooner?" "Because I waited for my shadow."—ROBERTS.

Ver. 2. As a servant earnestly desireth the shadow, and as a hireling looketh for *the reward of* his work; 3. So am I made to possess months of vanity, and wearisome nights are appointed to me.

The expression, when fairly rendered from the original, is peculiarly forcible: "So much worse is my destiny than that of the bondsman and the hireling, that, while they pant and look early for the night-shade, as the close of their trouble, even the night is not free from troubles to myself."—GOOD.

Ver. 10. He shall return no more to his house, neither shall his place know him any *more.*

Inanimate objects are often spoken of as if they knew their owners. A man who has sold his field, says, "That will not *know* me any more." Does a field not produce good crops, it is said, "That field doth not know its owner." Has a man been long absent from his home, he asks, when entering the door, "Ah! do you know me?" Does he, after this, walk through his garden and grounds, the servants say, "Ah! how pleased these are to see you!" Has a person been unfortunate at sea, it is said, "The sea does not *know* him."—ROBERTS.

Ver. 12. *Am* I a sea, or a whale, that thou settest a watch over me?

Some suppose this alludes to the sea overflowing its banks. But the Orientals also believe that the sea is the dwelling-place of many of their spiritual enemies. Hence they have a deity to watch the shore, whose name is Kali. Numerous enemies, also, are compared to the sea, and wicked chiefs who oppress the people, to *timingalam*, i. e. a whale. "Ah! that whale, who can escape him?"—ROBERTS.

Crocodiles are very terrible to the inhabitants of Egypt; when therefore they appear, they watch them with great attention, and take proper precautions to secure them, so that they should not be able to avoid the deadly weapons afterward used to kill them. To these watchings, and those deadly after-assaults, I apprehend Job refers, when he says, *am I a whale,* (but a *crocodile* no doubt is what is meant there,) *that thou settest a watch over me?* "Different methods," says Maillet, "are used to take crocodiles, and some of them very singular; the most common is to dig deep ditches along the Nile, which are covered with straw, and into which the crocodile may probably tumble. Sometimes they take them with hooks, which are baited with a quarter of a pig, or with bacon, of which they are very fond. Some hide themselves in the places which they know to be frequented by this creature, and lay snares for him."—BURDER.

Ver. 19. How long wilt thou not depart from me, nor let me alone till I swallow down my spittle?

This is a proverb among the Arabians to the present day, by which they understand, Give me leave to rest after my fatigue. This is the favour which Job complains is not granted to him. There are two instances which illustrate the passage (quoted by Schultens) in Harris's Narratives, entitled the Assembly. One is of a person, who, when eagerly pressed to give an account of his travels, answered with impatience, "Let me swallow down my spittle, for my journey hath fatigued me." The other instance is of a quick return made to one who used that proverb, "Suffer me," said the person importuned, "to swallow down my spittle:" to which his friend replied, "You may if you please swallow down even Tigris and Euphrates;" that is, take what time you please.—BURDER.

CHAPTER VIII.

Ver. 11. Can the rush grow up without mire? can the flag grow without water?

The reed grows in immense numbers on the banks and in the streams of the Nile. Extensive woods of the canes *Phragmit* and *Calama magrostes,* which rise to the height of twelve yards, cover the marshes in the neighbourhood of Suez. The stems are conveyed all over Egypt and Arabia, and are employed by the Orientals in constructing the flat terraces of their habitations. Calmet thinks it probable that this extensive region of canes gave name to the Red Sea, which, in those times, entirely inundated the marshes on its borders. Jam Suph is a sea that produces canes; and as the Arabs denote two sorts of canes by the general name *buz,* the surname being added afterward, Moses, the sacred historian, following the same ancient denominations, did not attend to the specifical niceties of botanology. This same leader of the people, underwent the first dangers of his life in a cradle made of the reeds donax or hagni. This information induced Calmet to conclude, that in these reeds, which covered the banks of the Nile, we have what our translation renders the flags, (suph,) in which Moses was concealed in his trunk, or ark of bulrushes, goma. The remarkable height to which they grow, and their vast abundance, lead to the persuasion, that in some thick tuft of them, the future prophet of Israel was concealed. It appears also, from the interrogation of Job, that the *goma* cannot reach its full stature without an abundant supply of water: "Can the rush—goma, rather the tall strong cane or reed—grow up without water?" This plant, therefore, being a tall reed, is with great propriety associated with the kanah, or cane: "In the habitation of dragons, where each lay, shall be grass, with *canes and reeds.*"—PAXTON.

Ver. 12. While it *is* yet in his greenness, *and* not cut down, it withereth before any *other* herb.

The application of this beautiful similitude is easy, and its moral exquisitely correct and pertinent. As the most succulent plants are dependant upon foreign support for a continuance of that succulence, and in the midst of their vigour are sooner parched up than plants of less humidity; so the most prosperous sinner does not derive his prosperity from himself, and is often destroyed in the highday of his enjoyments, more signally and abruptly than those who are less favoured, and appear to stand less securely.—GOOD.

CHAPTER IX.

Ver. 18. He will not suffer me to take my breath, but filleth me with bitterness.

Of a cruel master it is said, "When his servants stop to take their breath, he abuses them." "The man grudges me my breath." "What! can I work without taking my breath?" "The toil is always upon me: I have not time for breathing."—ROBERTS.

Ver. 25. Now my days are swifter than a post: they flee away, they see no good.

"Ah! my days are like an arrow." "What is my time? 'tis like the wind." "'Tis like cotton spread in the strong wind." "See that falling leaf; that is life." "'Tis but as a snap of the finger." "Am I not like a flower?" "Yes; it is a stream." "A *neer-mulle,* i. e. a bubble! how softly it glides along! how beautiful its colours! but how soon it disappears."—ROBERTS.

The common pace of travelling in the East is very slow. Camels go little more than two miles an hour. Those who carried messages in haste moved very differently. Dromedaries, a sort of camel, which is exceedingly swift, are used for this purpose; and Lady M. W. Montague asserts, that they far outrun the swiftest horses. There are also messengers who run on foot, and who sometimes go a hundred and fifty miles in less than twenty-four hours; with what energy then might Job say, "My days are swifter than a post." Instead of passing away with a slowness of motion like that of a caravan, my days of prosperity have disappeared with a swiftness like that of a messenger carrying despatches.—BURDER.

Ver. 26. They are passed away as the swift ships; as the eagle *that* hasteth to the prey.

"The swift ships." Many interpretations have been given of this expression. The author of the Fragments annexed to Calmet's Dictionary, observes, that if it can be rendered supposable that any animal, or class of animals, may be metaphorically called ships, it is the dromedary, well known to Job. The eastern writers apply the term to camels and dromedaries. "The whole caravan being now assembled, consists of a thousand horses, mules, and asses, and of five hundred camels: these are the ships of Arabia; their seas are the deserts." (Sandy's Travels.) "What enables the shepherd to perform the long and tiresome journeys across Africa, is the camel, emphatically called by the Arabs, the ship of the desert: he seems to have been created for this very trade." (Bruce's Travels.) Of the dromedary, which is a kind of camel, Mr. Morgan (*History of Algiers*) says, "I saw one perfectly white all over, belonging to Lella Oumane, princess of that noble Arab Neja, named Heyl ben Ali, upon which she put a very great value, never sending it abroad but upon some extraordinary occasion, when the greatest expedition was required: having others, inferior in swiftness, for more ordinary messages. They say that one of these Aasharies will, in one night, and through a level country, traverse as much ground as any single horse can perform in ten, which is no exaggeration of the matter, since many have affirmed to me, that it makes nothing of holding its rapid pace, which is a most violent hard trot, for four-and-twenty hours on a stretch, without showing the least sign of weariness or inclination to bait; and that then having swallowed a ball or two of a sort of paste made up of barley-meal, and, may be, a little powder of dry dates among it, with a bowl of water, or camel's milk, if to be had, and which the courier seldom forgets to be provided with in skins, as well for the sustenance of himself as of his pegasus, the indefatigable animal will seem as fresh as at first setting out, and ready to continue running at the same scarcely credible rate, for as many hours longer, and so on from one extremity of the African desert to the other, provided its rider could hold out without sleep, and other refreshments." The following extracts from Arabic poetry, translated by Sir W. Jones, speak the same language:—

"Even now she (the camel) has a spirit so brisk, that she flies with the rein, like a dun cloud driven by the wind, after it has discharged its shower.

"Long is her neck; and when she raises it with celerity, it resembles the stern of a ship, floating aloft on the billowy Tigris.

"Ah, the vehicles which bore away my fair one, on the morning when the tribe of Malee departed, and their camels were traversing the banks of Deda, resembled large ships.

"Sailing from Aduli, or vessels of (the merchant) Ibn Yamin, which the mariner now turns obliquely, and now steers in a direct course:

"Ships which cleave the foaming waves with their prows, as a boy at play divides with his hand the collected earth."—BURDER.

CHAPTER X.

Ver. 10. Hast thou not poured me out as milk, and curdled me like cheese?

Much philological learning has been brought to the explanation of this passage. In the preceding verse, Job is speaking of his DEATH. "Wilt thou bring me unto dust again?" But what has the pouring out of milk to do with death? The people of the East pour milk upon their heads after performing the funeral obsequies. Has a father a profligate son, one he never expects to reclaim, he says, in reference to him, "Ah! I have poured milk upon my head," *i. e.* "I have done with him; he is as one dead to me." "And curdled me like cheese." The cheese of the East is little better than curds: and these also are used at the funeral ceremonies.—ROBERTS.

CHAPTER XII.

Ver. 2. No doubt but ye *are* the people, and wisdom shall die with you.

The people of the East take great pleasure in irony, and some of their satirical sayings are very cutting. When a sage intimates that he has superior wisdom, or when he is disposed to rally another for his meager attainments, he says, "Yes, yes; you are the man!" "Your wisdom is like the sea." "You found it in dreams." "When you die, whither will wisdom go?" "You have ALL wisdom!" "When gone, alas! what will become of wisdom?" "O the Nyāni! O the philosopher!"—ROBERTS.

Ver. 4. I am *as* one mocked of his neighbour, who calleth upon God, and he answereth him: the just upright *man is* laughed to scorn.

Though Job, in his distress, cried unto the Lord, his neighbours mocked him, and laughed him to scorn; showing their own impiety, and belief that God would not answer him. Sometimes, when a heathen (who is supposed to be *forsaken of the gods*) performs a penance or religious austerity, others will mock him, and say, "Fast for me also; yes, perform the poosy for me, and you shall have all you want." Should a man, who is suffering under the punishment due to his crimes, cry to the gods for help, those who are near reply, (*for the gods,*) "Yes, we are here; what do you want? we will help you." "When the gods come, tell them I am gone home; I could not remain any longer." Thus was the just, the upright Job, laughed to scorn when he called upon God.—ROBERTS.

Ver. 5. He that is ready to slip with *his* feet *is as* a lamp despised in the thought of him that is at ease.

The critics are by no means agreed on the import of this passage; and, to say truth, we cannot flatter ourselves with a complete removal of its uncertainty. However, the attempt to explain it is honourable, even though it fail. To us it seems to suggest a comparison between the superabundant splendours of the interior of a wealthy man's dwelling, and the dark, dismal, night-wandering of a wayworn traveller. To add a lamp, however brightly burning, to what Mr. Good calls "the sunshine of the prosperous," were to render that lamp a contempt, a ridicule, whereas the man who stays amid mire and clay, in outer darkness, would rejoice to profit by its lustre. A travelling lamp, though its light be vivid, would be laughed at amid the various elegant illuminations in the interior of a house fitted up with great taste by a man of fashion: nevertheless, however awkward, coarse, and clumsy, it may be, the man who is falling into a quagmire would be extremely thankful for its assistance. This acceptation of the sentiment demands no dislocation of any word in the text: but, whether it completely dissipates the obscurity of the passage, the reader must judge.—TAYLOR IN CALMET.

D'Oyley and Mant quote from Caryl and Poole as follows: "A despised lamp is of the same signification with a smoking firebrand; which last is a proverb for that which is almost spent, and therefore despised and thrown away as useless." In view of these observations, it is worthy of notice, that of a man who is much despised, or who is very contemptible, it is said, "That fellow is like the half-consumed firebrand of the funeral pile." Job, by his enemies, was counted as a despised lamp. When a person is sick unto death, it is said, "His lamp is going out." After death, "His lamp has gone out." When a person is indisposed, should a lamp give a dim light, the people of the house will become much alarmed, as they think it a bad sign. A lamp, therefore, which burns dimly, (as did that of Job,) will be lightly esteemed.—ROBERTS.

Ver. 20. He removeth away the speech of the trusty, and taketh away the understanding of the aged.

The term זקנים seems, in this present place, to imply something more than "of the aged," as it is commonly rendered; and rather intimates, "the aged officially convened in public council;" whence it is rendered "*senators*," by Schultens and Dr. Stock: but *elders*, or *eldermen*, is a more general term, and hence more extensively appropriate, as well as more consonant with what ought ever to be the unaffected simplicity of biblical language. Though the term *senators* includes the idea of age, it includes it more remotely. In Gen. l. 7, we have a similar use of the term elders: for we are told, that "when Joseph went up into the land of Canaan to bury his father, with him went all the servants of Pharaoh, the *elders of his* house, and all the *elders of the land* of Egypt;" in other words, the chief officers of state, the privy counsellors, and the entire senate or body of legislators, chosen from the land or people.—GOOD.

Ver. 22. He discovereth deep things out of darkness, and bringeth out to light the shadow of death.

The author of the poem discovers a great partiality for this figure: the reader can scarcely fail to recollect its occurrence in ch. x. 21, 22. In the present instance, however, it appears to be used in a different sense, and to allude, in characteristic imagery, to the dark and recondite plots, the deep and desperate designs, of traitors and conspirators, or other state-villains: for it should be observed, that the entire passage has a reference to the machinery of a regular and political government; and that its general drift is to imprint upon the mind of the hearer the important doctrine, that the whole of the constituent principles of such a government, its officers and institutions, its monarch and princes, its privy-counsellors, judges, and ministers of state; its chieftains, public orators, and assembly of elders; its nobles, or men of hereditary rank; and its stout, robust peasantry, as we should express it in the present day; nay, the deep, designing villains that plot in secret its destruction,—that the nations themselves, and the heads or sovereigns of the nations, are all and equally in the hands of the Almighty; that, with him, human pomp is poverty, human excellence turpitude, human judgment error, human wisdom folly, human dignities contempt, human strength weakness.—GOOD.

CHAPTER XIII.

Ver. 15. Though he slay me, yet will I trust in him: but I will maintain mine own ways before him.

When a master chastises an affectionate slave, or tells him to leave his service, he says, "My lord, though you slay me, yet will I trust in you." Does a husband beat his wife, she exclaims, "My husband, though you kill me, I will not let you go." "Kill me, my lord, if you please, but I will not leave you: I trust in you." "Oh! beat me not; do I not trust in you?" "What an affectionate wife that is: though her husband cut her to pieces, yet she trusts in him." "The fellow is always beating her, yet she confides in him." —ROBERTS.

Ver. 24. Wherefore hidest thou thy face, and holdest me for thine enemy?

Job, in his distress, makes this pathetic inquiry of the Lord. Should a great man become displeased with a person to whom he has been previously kind, he will, when he sees him approaching, avert his face, or conceal it with his hand, which shows at once what is the state of the case. The poor man then mourns, and complains, and asks, "Ah! why does he hide his face?" The wife says to her offended husband, "Why do you hide your face?" The son to his father, "Hide not your face from your son."—ROBERTS.

Ver. 26. For thou writest bitter things against me.

"Ah! the things that man has written against me to the judge, are all *kassapu*, all bitter." "Oh! that is a bitter, bitter fault." "Who will make this bitterness sweet?"—ROBERTS.

Ver. 27. Thou puttest my feet also in the stocks, and lookest narrowly unto all my paths; thou settest a print upon the heels of my feet.

The punishment of the stocks has been common in the East from the most remote antiquity, as is seen in all their records. But whether the stocks were formerly like clogs, or as those of the present day, it is impossible to say. Those now in use differ from those in England, as the unfortunate culprit has to lie with his back on the ground, having his feet fast in one pair, and his hands in another. Thus, all he can do is to writhe his body; his arms and legs being so fast, that he cannot possibly move them. A man placed in great difficulty, says, "Alas! I am now in the stocks." "I have put my boy in the *tulungu*," i. e. stocks; which means, he is confined, or sent to school. To a young man of roving habits, it is said, "You must have your feet in the stocks," *i. e.* get married. "Alas! alas! I am now in the stocks; the guards are around my path, and a seal is put upon my feet."—ROBERTS. (*See Engraving.*)

CHAPTER XIV.

Ver. 4. Who can bring a clean *thing* out of an unclean? not one.

The following are common sayings:—"Who can turn a black crow into a white crane?" "Who can make the bitter fruit sweet?" "Who can make straight the tail of the dog?" "If you give the serpent sweet things, will his poison depart?"—ROBERTS.

Ver. 7. For there is hope of a tree, if it be cut down, that it will sprout again, and that the tender branch thereof will not cease.

Trees here appear to be more tenacious of life than in England. See them blown down; yet from the roots fresh shoots spring up. See them sometimes at such an angle (through storms) that their branches nearly touch the ground, and yet they keep that position, and continue to bear fruit. Those trees, also, which have actually been cut down, after a few showers, soon begin to send forth the "tender branch." The plantain-tree, after it has borne fruit *once*, is cut down; but from its roots another springs up, which, in its turn, also gives fruit, and is then cut down, to make way for another. Thus, in reference to this tree, it may be truly said, Cut it down, but "the tender branch thereof will not cease."—ROBERTS.

Ver. 17. My transgression *is* sealed up in a bag, and thou sewest up mine iniquity.

The money that is collected together in the treasures of eastern princes is told up in certain equal sums, *put into bags, and sealed.*—(Chardin.) These are what in some parts of the Levant are called *purses*, where they reckon great expenses by so many purses. The money collected in the temple in the time of Joash, for its reparation, seems, in like manner, to have been told up in bags of equal value to each other, and probably delivered sealed to those who paid the workmen, (2 Kings xii. 10.) If Job alludes to this custom, it should seem that he considered his offences as reckoned by God to be very numerous, as well as not suffered to be lost in inattention, since they are only considerable sums which are thus kept.—HARMER.

Ver. 19. The waters wear the stones: thou washest away the things which grow *out* of the dust of the earth; and thou destroyest the hope of man.

Is a man found fault with because he makes slow progress in his undertaking, he says, "Never mind; the water which runs so softly, will, in time, wear away the stones." —ROBERTS.

CHAPTER XV.

Ver. 7. *Art* thou the first man *that* was born? or wast thou made before the hills?

When a majority of people agree on any subject, should an individual pertinaciously oppose them, it will be asked, "What! were you born before all others?" "Yes, yes; he is the first man: no wonder he has so much wisdom!" "Salam to the *first!* man."—ROBERTS.

Hebrew, "Wast thou born first of mankind?" Such appears to me the true rendering, though it is given differently by different commentators, and will admit of various significations; the word אדם (*Adam*) being either a proper name, or an appellative for mankind at large; whence some of the oldest versions render the passage, "Wast thou born before Adam?" while the generality, and in my opinion more correctly, give us, "An primus homo natus es?" "Art thou the first-born of men?" or, "Wast thou born first of mankind?"—GOOD.

Ver. 26. He runneth upon him, *even* on *his* neck, upon the thick bosses of his bucklers.

Wrestlers, before they began their combats, were rubbed all over in a rough manner, and afterward anointed with oil, in order to increase the strength and flexibility of their limbs. But as this unction, in making the skin too slippery, rendered it difficult for them to take hold of each other, they remedied that inconvenience, sometimes by rolling themselves in the dust of the Palæstra, sometimes by throwing fine sand upon each other, kept for that purpose in Xystæ, or porticoes of the Gymnasia. Thus prepared, they began their combat. They were matched two against two, and sometimes several couples contended at the same time. In this combat, the whole aim and design of the wrestlers was to throw their adversary upon the ground. Both strength and art were employed to this purpose; they seized each other by the arms, drew forward, pushed backward, used many distortions and twistings of the body; locking their limbs in each other's, seizing by the neck or throat, pressing in their arms, struggling, plying on all sides, lifting from the ground, dashing their heads together like rams, and twisting one another's necks. In this manner, the athletæ wrestled standing, the combat ending with the fall of one of the competitors. To this combat the words of Eliphaz seem to apply: "For he stretcheth out his hand against God" like a wrestler, challenging his antagonist to the contest, "and strengthening himself," rather vaunteth himself, stands up haughtily, and boasts of his prowess in the full view of "the Almighty," throwing abroad his arms, clapping his hands together, springing into the middle of the ring, and taking his station there in the adjusted attitude of defiance. "He runneth upon him, even on his neck," or with his neck stretched out, furiously dashing his head against the other; and this he does, even when he perceives that his adversary is covered with defensive armour, upon which he can make no impression: "he runneth upon the thick bosses of his bucklers."—PAXTON.

Ver. 33. He shall shake off his unripe grape as the vine, and shall cast off his flower as the olive.

It would be a valuable acquisition to the learned world, if observations made in Judea itself, or rather, in this case, in the land of Uz, were communicated to us relating to the natural causes which occasion, from time to time, a disappointment of their hopes from their vineyards and olive plantations; and the effects of a violently sultry southeast wind on their most useful or remarkable vegetables. I very much question, however, whether the words of Eliphaz, in the book of Job, xv. 33, refer to any blasting of the vine by natural causes; they seem rather to express the violently taking away the unripe grapes by the wild Arabs, of which I have given an account in the preceding volume. It is certain the word בסר *biser*, translated here *unripe grape*, is used to express those grapes that were so far advanced in growth as to be eaten, though not properly ripened, as appears from Jeremiah xxxi. 29, and Ezek. xviii. 2; and the verb יחמס *yachmas*, translated here *shake off*, signifies removing by violence, consequently cannot be meant of any thing done in the natural course of things, but by a human hand; and if so, may as well be applied to the depredations of the Arabs, as the impetuosity or deleterious quality of any wind, the energy of poetry making use of a verb active instead of its passive.

It may not be amiss, before I close, just to take notice, that the vulgar Latin translation was so little apprehensive that grapes, when grown to any considerable size, were wont to drop, that its authors, or correctors, have rendered the words after this manner: "Lædetur quasi vinea in *primo flore* botrus ejus," that is, "his cluster shall be injured as a vine when it first comes into flower;" intimating, that if any damage is done to the vine at all by an intemperate season, they supposed it would be upon its first flowering. How arduous is the business of translating a foreign poem into English verse! A multitude of circumstances must be attended to by such a translator, when he finds himself obliged, as he often does, to vary the expressions a little, on account of his verse; and, for want of full information as to particular points, he must frequently fail. Mistakes of this kind demand great candour.—HARMER.

A north or northeast wind frequently proves injurious to the olive-trees in Greece, by destroying the blossom. Dr. Chandler says, "We ate under an olive-tree, then laden with pale yellow flowers: a strong breeze from the sea scattered the bloom and incommoded us, but the spot afforded no shelter more eligible." In another place, he observes, "The olive-groves are now, as anciently, a principal source of the riches of Athens. The mills for pressing and grinding the olives are in the town; the oil is deposited in large earthen jars, sunk in the ground, in the areas before the houses. The crops had failed five years successively, when we arrived; the cause assigned was a northerly wind, called Greco-Tramontane, which destroyed the flower. The fruit is set in about a fortnight, when the apprehension from this unpropitious quarter ceases. The bloom in the following year was unhurt, and we had the pleasure of leaving the Athenians happy in the prospect of a plentiful harvest."—BURDER.

CHAPTER XVI.

Ver. 3. Shall vain words have an end? or what imboldeneth thee that thou answerest?

The Hebrew has, "words of *wind*." "His promise! it is only wind." "His words are all wind." "The wind has taken away his words." "Breath, breath; all breath!"—ROBERTS.

Ver. 4. I also could speak as ye *do:* if your soul were in my soul's stead, I could heap up words against you, and shake my head at you.

The whole of this passage is rendered unintelligible, in its usual mode of translating, by attributing a conditional instead of a future tense to it: "I also *could* speak, &c." or, "But I *could* speak,"—instead of, "But I *will* speak," or "talk on."—GOOD.

Ver. 9. He teareth *me* in his wrath who hateth me: he gnasheth upon me with his teeth; mine enemy sharpeneth his eyes upon me.

"Has not the cruel man been sharpening his eyes upon me?" "His eyes are like arrows: they pierce my life." "Truly, his cutting eyes are always upon me." "Yes, yes; the eyes of the serpent."—ROBERTS.

Ver. 10. They have gaped upon me with their mouth; they have smitten me upon the cheek reproachfully; they have gathered themselves together against me.

Here is another living picture of eastern manners. See the exasperated man; he opens his mouth like a wild beast, shows his teeth, then suddenly snaps them together. Again he pretends to make another snatch, and growls like a tiger. Should he not dare to come near, he moves his hand, as if striking you on the cheek, and says, "I will beat thy *kannan*, i. e. cheek, thou low-caste fellow."—ROBERTS.

From the following extracts, this treatment appears to have been considered very injurious. "Davagé was deeply incensed: nor could I do more than induce him to come to the factory on business while I was there; Mr. Pringle having, in one of his fits, struck him on the cheek with the sole of his slipper, the deepest insult that can be offered to an Asiatic; among whom it is considered as a mark of disrespect to touch even the sole of the foot." (Lord Valentia.) "In the Mahratta camp, belonging to Scindia, his prime minister, Surjee Rao, was murdered in the open bazar: his mistresses were, as usual, stripped of all they possessed; and his favourite one was sent for to court, and severely beaten in the presence of Scindia's wife, who added to the indignity, by giving her several blows herself with a slipper." (Broughton.) "When the vazir declared himself unable to procure the money, Fathh Ali Shah reproached him for his crimes, struck him on the face, and with the high wooden heel of a slipper, always iron-bound, beat out several of his teeth." (Sir W. Ouseley.)

The Hindoo, religiously abstaining from animal food and intoxicating liquors, becomes thereby of so very mild a temper, that he can bear almost any thing without emotion, except slippering; that is, a stroke with the sole of a slipper or sandal, after a person has taken it off his foot and spit on it; this is dreaded above all affronts, and considered as no less ignominious than spitting in the face, or bespattering with dirt, among Europeans.—Burder.

CHAPTER XVII.

Ver. 1. My breath is corrupt, my days are extinct, the graves *are ready* for me.

A man far advanced in years, or one who is in deep affliction, says, "The place of burning is near to me, and the wood is laid together for my funeral pile." "How are you, my friend?" "How am I? I will tell you. Go, order them to get the wood together to burn this body." A father sometimes says of his wicked sons, "Yes, I know they desire my death; they have been preparing for the funeral; they are ready to wash me: the bier is at hand, and the wood is prepared." "Why do you all look so anxious? I am not ready for the washing."—Roberts.

Ver. 3. Lay down now, put me in a surety with thee; who *is* he *that* will strike hands with me?

See on Prov. 6. 1.

The difficulty in this passage has resulted, in the first place, from the abruptness of the transition; and, secondly, from its being, in its common construction, very improperly separated from the preceding verse, and applied to the Almighty instead of to Eliphaz, the last speaker, to whom Job is peculiarly addressing himself. The fair interpretation is, "But if there be any meaning in what ye say—if ye do not revile my character, but believe me to be the oppressor and the hypocrite ye assert—come on: I will still venture to stake myself against any of you. Will any of you venture to stake me against yourselves? Who is he that will strike hands with me? that will dare to measure his deserts with my own? and appeal to the Almighty, in proof that he is a juster man than I am?" It is an *argumentum ad hominem*, of peculiar force and appropriation, admirably calculated to confound and silence the persons to whom it is addressed. The custom of staking one thing against another is of very early origin, and found in the rudest and simplest modes of social life; hence the pastorals of Theocritus, as well as of Virgil, abound with references to this practice.—Good.

Ver. 9. The righteous also shall hold on his way, and he that hath clean hands shall be stronger and stronger.

The idea here suggested is that of purity and holiness. Porphyry observes, that in the Leontian mysteries the initiated had their hands washed with honey, instead of water, to intimate that they were to keep their hands pure from all wickedness and mischief; honey being of a cleansing nature, and preserving other things from corruption.—Burder.

Ver. 14. I have said to corruption, Thou *art* my father: to the worm, *Thou art* my mother and my sister.

Those who retire from the world to spend their lives in a desert place, for the purpose of performing religious austerities, often exclaim to the beasts, "Yes; you are my relations, you are my parents; these are my companions and friends."—Roberts.

Ver. 16. They shall go down to the bars of the pit, when *our* rest together *is* in the dust.

Literally, to the *limbs*—"the grasping limbs," "the tremendous claws or talons" of the grave. The imagery is peculiarly bold, and true to the general character under which the grave is presented to us in the figurative language of sacred poetry,—as a monster, ever greedy to devour, with horrid jaws wide gaping for his prey; and, in the passage before us, with limbs in unison with his jaws, and ready to seize hold of the victims allotted to him, with a strength and violence from which none can extricate themselves. The common rendering of *fulcra, vectes*, or *bars*, as of a prison, is as unnecessary a departure from the proper figure, as it is from the primary meaning of the original term.—Good.

CHAPTER XVIII.

Ver. 2. How long *will it be ere* you make an end of words?

The commentators are not agreed to whom the opening of this speech is addressed. Being in the plural number, it cannot, according to the common forms of Hebrew colloquy, be addressed to Job alone. Le Clerc, however, attempts to prove, that, under particular circumstances, such a form may be admitted, and especially when particular respect is intended. Other interpreters conceive that it is addressed to Job and Eliphaz, to whom Job had been just replying. But the greater number concur in supposing that it relates to the family or domestics of Job, in conjunction with himself, who, it may be conceived, were present, and at least tacitly approving his rebukes: "*Tu cum tuâ familiâ*," is the explanation of Reiske. It is more probable that it applies to the interlocutors generally.—Good.

Ver. 4. He teareth himself in his anger: shall the earth be forsaken for thee? and shall the rock be removed out of his place?

"Foolish man, why are you so angry? Will your anger pull down the mountain, or take a single hair from the head of your enemy?" "This evil is only felt in your own heart and house: it is your own destruction."—Roberts.

Ver. 5. Yea, the light of the wicked shall be put out, and the spark of his fire shall not shine. 6. The light shall be dark in his tabernacle, and his candle shall be put out with him.

See on 1 Kings 11. 26.

Ver. 8. For he is cast into a net by his own feet, and he walketh upon a snare.

The original implies a snare with pieces of wood, or other substance, put crosswise, or bar-wise, so as to sustain the deceitful covering of turf, or other soil, put over it to hide the mischief it conceals. The term is used Exod. xxvii. 4, to express a *grating*, or *net-work of brass*. The same kind of snare or pitfall is still frequently employed throughout India, in elephant-hunting.—Good.

Ver. 15. It shall dwell in his tabernacle, because *it is* none of his: brimstone shall be scattered upon his habitation.

A very singular method of expressing sorrow among the ancients, was by burning brimstone in the house of the deceased. Livy mentions this practice as general among the Romans; and some commentators think it is referred to in these words of Bildad: "Brimstone shall be scattered upon his habitation." The idea corresponds with the design of the speaker, which is to describe the miserable end of the hypocrite.—Paxton.

Ver. 16. His roots shall be dried up beneath, and above shall his branch be cut off.

Man is often described as a tree, and his destruction by the cutting off of the branches. "Alas! alas! he is like a tree whose branches have been struck by the lightning." "He is a tree killed by the shepherds;" which alludes to the practice (in dry weather, when the grass is burned up) of climbing the trees to lop off the branches and leaves for the use of the flocks and cattle. "His branches and shoots are destroyed;" which means, himself and family. "I know all his branches and bunches;" meaning all his connexions. (See on Luke xxiii. 31.)—ROBERTS.

Ver. 17. His remembrance shall perish from the earth, and he shall have no name in the street.

"What kind of a man is Rāmar?" "I will tell you: his name is in every street;" which means, he is a person of great fame. "Ah! my lord, only grant me this favour, and your name shall be in every street." "Who does not wish his name to be in the streets?" "Wretch, where is thy name? What dog of the street will acknowledge thee?" "From generation to generation shall his name be in the streets." "Where is thy name written in stone? No: it is written in water."—ROBERTS.

Ver. 19. He shall neither have son nor nephew among his people, nor any remaining in his dwellings.

Heb. "Among his sojournings"—from גור "to sojourn," or "dwell for a short and uncertain period," as in travelling. The idea is peculiarly expressive and forcible: not only among his own people, and in his own settled habitation, shall his name, his memory, his family, be extinguished; but no asylum, no refuge, shall be afforded them in distant countries, and among strangers, with whom he had casually sojourned, and where his memory might be supposed to call forth the hospitalities of friendship. The Jewish history affords innumerable instances of persons compelled to fly from their native homes, and seek an asylum in the bosom of strangers, to whom they were only casually, or even altogether unknown: and, without ranging further, the history of Moses himself, the probable writer of the poem, furnishes us with a memorable example.—GOOD.

The original word for dwellings, Schultens says, signifies a territory of refuge for strangers. The great men among the Arabs called their respective districts by this name, because they took under their protection all defenceless and necessitous persons who fled thither; they prided themselves in having a great number of these clients or dependants. This was an ancient custom in Arabia, and continues to the present day. The Arabian poets frequently refer to it.—BURDER.

CHAPTER XIX.

Ver. 3. These ten times have ye reproached me: you are not ashamed *that* you make yourselves strange to me.

See on Gen. 31. 7, 8.

Ver. 6. Know now that God hath overthrown me, and hath compassed me with his net.

The allusion here may be to an ancient mode of combat practised among the Persians, Goths, and Romans. The custom among the Romans was this: one of the combatants was armed with a sword and shield, the other with a trident and net; the net he endeavoured to cast over the head of his adversary, in which, when he succeeded, the entangled person was soon pulled down by a noose, that fastened round his neck, and then despatched. The person who carried the net and trident was called Retiarius, and the other, who carried the sword and shield, Secutor, or the pursuer, because, when the Retiarius missed his throw, he was obliged to run about the ground till he got his net in order for a second throw, while the Secutor followed him, to prevent, and despatch him. The Persians used a running loop, which horsemen endeavoured to cast over the heads of their enemies, that they might pull them off their horses. The Goths used a hoop fastened to a pole. (Olaus Magnus.) "In the old Mexican paintings, we find warriors almost naked, with their bodies wrapped in a net of large meshes, which they throw over the heads of their enemy." (Humboldt.)—BURDER.

Ver. 16. I called my servant, and he gave *me* no answer: I entreated him with my mouth.

When a man becomes reduced in the world, his slaves no longer obey him: he calls, but they answer not; he looks, and they laugh at him.

Hence the verse—

Kandālum, Paysār
Alitālum, Vārār
Kavi-Kavi-Endār.

"Though I call, he comes not; though he sees, he answers not; or, I am engaged, engaged, says he."—ROBERTS.

Ver. 17. My breath is strange to my wife, though I entreated for the children's *sake* of mine own body.

It is not often that husbands, in these regions, condescend to *entreat* their wives, but they are sometimes (as when sick or in any way dependant) obliged to humble themselves. He then says, "My wife's breath is not now as mine." "For the sake of your children listen to my words." Nothing is more provoking to a woman than to say she has the breath of a man.—ROBERTS.

Ver. 20. My bone cleaveth to my skin and to my flesh, and I am escaped with the skin of my teeth.

I suppose the above words have given rise to the old English saying, "He has escaped with the skin of his teeth;" which denotes he has had great difficulty in avoiding the danger. But have the *teeth* any skin? It was formerly a custom among the heathen kings to knock out the teeth of their prisoners, or those who had offended them; and to this practice the Psalmist seems to allude: "Thou hast broken the teeth of the ungodly;" and, "Break their teeth, O God! in their mouth." Those who had been thus treated said, "We have escaped with the *murasu*," i. e. *the gums of our teeth.* When a man is angry with another, he says, "Take care; I will knock thy teeth out. Thou shalt only have thy gums left." "What!" asks the person thus threatened, "am I thy slave, to have my teeth knocked out?" But the teeth are always spoken of as being very valuable; and by them the people often estimate the worth of any blessing. "Ah! the king might have granted me that favour; his teeth would not have fallen out on that account." "Would his gums have been left, if he had told me that secret?" "Yes, yes, take care, or you will lose your pearls," (teeth.) "See the miserable man; the sickness has left him his gums only."—ROBERTS.

There is scarcely any verse in the whole poem that has more puzzled the commentators, and excited a greater variety of renderings, than this. The word *skin* is here repeated from the preceding line, for the sake of an iteration; in which figure no poets have more largely indulged than the Asiatics, whether ancient or modern. It is a word of extensive meaning, and implies generally, *cuticle, peel, integument, skin;* and in the present place more particularly, *the gums*, which are the proper *integuments* of the teeth, the substance in which they are first produced, and which, through life, affords a nutritious covering to their base. It may also be rendered *film*, although I do not think this the direct sense of the term in the present passage; it rather implies *integuments* generally, and has been preferred by the original writer to any other term expressive of the same meaning, on account, as I have already observed, of the iteration hereby produced.—GOOD.

In the celebrated inscription on the pillar at Delhi, called the Lāt of Feeroz Shah, is the following passage, exhibiting a similar hyperbole in different terms: "Blades of grass are perceived between thine adversary's teeth." (*Asiatic Researches.*) The author of the Fragments subjoined to Calmet's Dictionary, thus paraphrases the passage: "My upper row of teeth stands out so far as to adhere to my upper lip, that being so shrivelled and dried up, as to sink upon my teeth, which closely press it." He observes, if our translation be right, it may receive some illustration from the following instances of those who did not escape with the skin of their teeth. "Prithwinarayan issued an order to Suruparatana, his brother, to put to death some of the principal inhabitants of the town of Cirtipur, and to cut off the noses and lips of every one, even the infants who were not found in the arms of their mothers; ordering, at the same time, all the noses and lips that had been cut off to be preserved, that he might ascertain how many souls there were, and to change the name of the town to Naskatapir, which signifies, the town of cut noses. The order was carried into execution with every mark of horror and cruelty, none escaping but those who could play on wind instruments: many put an end to their lives in despair; others came in great bodies to us in search of medicines; and it was most shocking to see so many living people with their teeth and noses resembling the sculls of the deceased." (Asiatic Res.)—Burder.

Ver. 23. O that my words were now written! oh that they were printed in a book! 24. That they were graven with an iron pen and lead in the rock for ever!

The most ancient way of writing was upon the leaves of the palm-tree. Afterward they made use of the inner bark of a tree for this purpose; which inner bark being in Latin called *liber*, the Greek βιβλος, from hence, a book, hath ever since, in the Latin language, been called *liber*, and in the Greek, βιβλος, because their books anciently consisted of leaves made of such inner barks. The Chinese still make use of such inner barks, or rinds of trees, to write upon, as some of their books brought into Europe plainly show. Another way made use of among the Greeks and Romans, and which was as ancient as Homer, (for he makes mention of it in his poems,) was to write on tables of wood, covered over with wax. On these they wrote with a bodkin, or stile of iron, with which they engraved their letters on the wax; and hence it is that the different ways of men's writings or compositions are called different styles. This way was mostly made use of in the writing of letters or epistles; hence such epistles are in Latin called *tabellæ*, and the carriers of them *tabellarii*. When their epistles were thus written, they tied the tables together with a thread or string, setting their seal upon the knot, and so sent them to the party to whom they were directed, who, cutting the string, opened and read them. It is observable also, that anciently they wrote their public records on volumes or rolls of lead, and their private matters on fine linen and wax. The former of these customs we trace in Job's wish, "O that my words were now written! O that they were printed in a book! that they were graven with an iron pen and lead in the rock for ever!" There is a way of writing in the East, which is designed to fix words on the memory, but the writing is not designed to continue. The children in Barbary that are sent to school, make no use of paper, Dr. Shaw tells us, but each boy writes on a smooth, thin board, slightly daubed over with whiting, which may be wiped off or renewed at pleasure. There are few that retain what they have learned in their youth; doubtless things were often wiped out of the memory of the Arabs in the days of Job, as well as out of their writing-tables. Job therefore says, "O that they were written in a book," from whence they should not be blotted out! But books were liable to injuries, and for this reason he wishes his words might be even *graven in a rock*, the most lasting way of all. Thus the distinction between *writing* and *writing in a book*, becomes perfectly sensible, and the gradation appears in its beauty, which is lost in our translation, where the word *printed* is introduced, which, besides its impropriety, conveys no idea of the meaning of Job, records that are designed to last long not being distinguished from less durable papers by being printed.—Burder.

The word *rock*, which our translators have made use of, seems to me to be more just than that used by Schultens. It is certain that the word צור *tzur*, which is in the original, signifies in other places of the book of Job, a rock; and never there, or anywhere else in the scriptures, that I am aware of, and I have with some care examined the point, does it signify a small sepulchral stone, or monumental pillar. On the other hand, I am sure the words that are used for this purpose, when the sacred writers speak of the sepulchral stone on Rachel's grave; of the pillar erected by Absalom to keep up his memory; and of that monument which marked out the place where the prophet was buried that prophesied against the altar of Jeroboam, and which continued to the days of Josiah; are different. Nor can the using this term appear strange, if we consider the extreme antiquity of the book of Job; since it is easy to imagine, that the first inscriptions on stones were engraved on some places of the rocks, which were accidently smoothed, and made pretty even. And, in fact, we find some that are very ancient, engraved on the natural rock, and what is remarkable, in Arabia, where it is supposed Job lived. This is one of the most curious observations in that account of the prefetto of Egypt, which was published by the late bishop of Clogher; and is, in my apprehension, an exquisite confirmation of our translation, though there is reason to think neither the writer nor editor of that journal thought of this passage, and so consequently claims a place in this collection.

The prefetto, speaking in his journal of his disengaging himself at length from the mountains of Faran, says, "they came to a large plain, surrounded however with high hills, at the foot of which we reposed ourselves in our tents, at about half an hour after ten. These hills are called *Gebel el Mokatab*, that is, the *Written Mountains*: for, as soon as we had parted from the mountains of Faran, we passed by several others for an hour together, engraved with ancient unknown characters, which were cut in the hard marble rock, so high as to be in many places at twelve or fourteen feet distance from the ground: and though we had in our company persons who were acquainted with the Arabic, Greek, Hebrew, Syriac, Coptic, Latin, Armenian, Turkish, English, Illyrican, German, and Bohemian languages, yet none of them had any knowledge of these characters; which have nevertheless been cut into the hard rock, with the greatest industry, in a place where there is neither water, nor any thing to be gotten to eat. It is probable, therefore, these unknown characters contain some very secret mysteries, and that they were engraved either by the Chaldeans, or some other persons long before the coming of Christ."

The curious bishop of Clogher, who most laudably made very generous proposals to the Antiquarian Society, to engage them to try to decipher these inscriptions, was ready to imagine they are the ancient Hebrew characters, which the Israelites, having learned to write at the time of giving the law, diverted themselves with engraving on these mountains, during their abode in the wilderness. There are still in Arabia several inscriptions in the natural rock; and this way of writing is very durable, for these engravings have, it seems, outlived the knowledge of the characters made use of; the practice was, for the same reason, very ancient as well as durable; and if these letters are not so ancient as the days of Moses, which the Bishop of Clogher supposes, yet these inscriptions might very well be the continuation of a practice in use in the days of Job, and may therefore be thought to be referred to in these words of his, *O that they were graven . . . . in the rock for ever!*—Harmer.

Ver. 23. O that my words were now written! oh that they were printed in a book! 24. That they were graven with an iron pen and lead in the rock for ever! 25. For I know *that* my Redeemer liveth, and *that* he shall stand at the latter *day* upon the earth: 26. And *though*, after my skin, *worms* destroy this *body*, yet in my flesh shall I see God: 27. Whom I shall see for myself, and mine eyes shall behold, and not another; *though* my reins be consumed within me.

It has been the fashion with a class of interpreters and divines, pleased perhaps to associate their own with the celebrated names of Grotius, Le Clerc, and Warburton, to explode from this passage any reference to a future life, or the expectation of the Messiah; and no slight contempt has been expressed for the credulity and mental servitude (very candidly taken for granted) of those who entertain the belief of such a reference. This has, however, been the opinion of the greater number of scripture critics, ancient and modern, popish and protestant. The usual objections against this interpretation are, that no vestiges appear in the book of Job, of any acquaintance with the doctrine of a future life; that it would be very extraordinary if there really existed in the mind of the composer of this book, any knowledge of the Redeemer to come, that such a glorious hope should show itself nowhere but in this single passage; that we cannot reconcile such an avowal with the despondency which appears to have prevailed in the mind of Job; and that the terms employed do not necessarily import more than the persuasion of a deliverance, by divine goodness, from the present calamity, and a restoration to health and happiness, in the present life. To these reasonings we reply,

1. Admitting that there is no intimation of the doctrine of immortality and a future judgment, or of the expectation of a Messiah, in any other part of this book, the consequence does not follow. It should be recollected that, in a poetical book, the matter is disposed considerably according to the taste and choice of the writer; and that a more vivid impression might be made, by presenting a capital circumstance, with its brightness and force collected into one point, than would be produced if it were dispersed through the general composition. The whole texture of this passage, introduced with the most impassioned wish for attention and perpetual remembrance, and sustained in the sublimest style of utterance, is evidently thus contrived to interest and impress in the highest degree.

Those of our objectors who ascribe the date of the poem to the period of the captivity, cannot refuse to admit that the writer possessed whatever knowledge the Jewish nation had with respect to a Messiah and a future state. The writings of Moses and the former prophets, and the greater part of the works of the latter prophets, and the books grouped with the Psalms, were, at this time, the accredited scriptures of the Jews; and few will be so hardy as to affirm, that no intimations occur in those writings of the doctrines which constituted the hope and consolation of Israel. On this (in my opinion, untenable) hypothesis, it would appear highly credible that some very distinct reference to those doctrines would enter materially into the structure of the work.

2. The alleged inconsistency between these expressions of triumphant confidence, as we understand them, and the gloominess and despondency generally prevalent in the speeches of Job, presses equally on our opponents, who confine the passage to the expectation of restored prosperity in the present life. It lies even more against them, for Job, not only before, but in his very last speech, *evidently despaired of a restoration to temporal felicity*. His property might, indeed, by some wonderful, though almost incredible reverse of God's providence, be retrieved; or, at least, equivalent comforts in that class of things might be obtained: but his children were destroyed; they could not live again: and his own disorder, probably the dreadful oriental leprosy, was incurable and fatal. Yet, between this hopeless condition as to earthly enjoyments, and a vigorous aspiration of the mind after spiritual and immortal blessings, there is no inconsistency. A man must have little judgment, little taste, and less moral sensibility, who does not perceive in these alternations of faith and diffidence, despair and hope, a picture exquisitely just and touching, of the human mind, under the influence of the most agitating conflict between religious principle resting on the belief of invisible existences, and, on the other hand, the dictates of sense, the pressure of misery, and the violence of temptations.

3. But we are not disposed to grant either of the assumptions before mentioned. We have better evidence than the *dicta* of German anti-supernaturalists, or the opinions of English refiners upon theology, that the patriarchs from whom the tradition of divine truths had descended to Job, "confessed that they were strangers and pilgrims on the earth, and desired a better country, that is, a heavenly." Nor is it credible that the promise of a Messiah was totally unknown to the true worshippers of Jehovah in Arabia, allied to the family of Abraham, and in the habit of reverentially cherishing the remains of primeval truth. And, besides the possession of the patriarchal religion, what is there to prevent any but a deist from conceiving that God might INSPIRE his faithful and afflicted servant with the knowledge and the joyful confidence which he expresses? Is not such a supposition consonant with all the known scheme and principles of the divine dispensations? Was not the occasion worthy of the interposition? Has it not always been the faith of the Jewish and of the Christian church, that the *ultimate sentiments* which it is the design of the book of Job to support and illustrate, and which, in the sequel of the book, receive the stamp of divine approbation, form a part of the body of REVEALED TRUTH? There are also many passages in the book which may be rationally urged as recognitions of a future state.

4. The bare assertion that the terms of the passage do not import so much as is usually attributed to them, may be fairly enough met by asserting the contrary. To the unlearned reader, as well as to the critical scholar, the means of judging for himself are industriously presented, in the close version given above, and in the remarks and references subjoined. The words are as plain as in any instance the language of prophecy can be expected to be. It appears to me strictly rational, probable, and in harmony with the great plan of a progressive revelation, to regard this remarkable passage as dictated by the SPIRIT of prophecy, who, "in many portions, and in many modes, spake to the fathers." Let me also entreat the reader's most impartial consideration, whether the sense here maintained is not required, even necessitated, by the words, taken in their fair meaning and connexion; and whether the affixing of a lower interpretation does not oblige those who take this course, to put a manifest force upon the phrases, and upon the marks of pre-eminent importance with which the sacred author has signalized them.

After employing the utmost force and beauty of language to stamp importance upon the words which he was about to utter, and to ensure for them a never-dying attention, the patriarch protests his confidence that the LIVING GOD, the eternal, independent, and unchanging One, would be his VINDICATOR from injustice, and his REDEEMER from all his sorrows; and would restore him from the state of death, to a new life of supreme happiness in the favour and enjoyment of God.

It is not necessary to suppose that Job understood the full import and extent of what he was "moved by the Holy Spirit to speak." The general belief on the divine testimony of a future Saviour from sin and its consequent evils, would place him on a level with other saints, in his own and many succeeding ages, who "died in faith, not receiving the promises" in their *clearest* development, "but SEEING THEM AFAR OFF." Even when those promises had received many accessions of successive revelations, the Jewish prophets did not apprehend the exact design and meaning of their own predictions; for "they inquired and searched diligently—what or what kind of time, the Spirit of Christ which was in them did signify." Our inquiry is, therefore, not so much what the patriarch actually understood, as what the Author of inspiration intended; since it was "not unto themselves, but unto us," that the patriarchs and prophets "ministered those things." "No prophecy of scripture is of self-solution;" but is made gradually plainer by new communications from the same omniscient source, and by the light of events.

Upon this principle, it is proper for us to compare the language of this passage, with the character and declarations of HIM to whom "all the prophets gave witness." He, in the fulness of the times, was manifested, as the REDEEMER from sin and death, the FIRST and the LAST, and the LIVING ONE, the RESURRECTION and the LIFE; who, in the appointed season, "is coming with the clouds, and every eye shall see him; whose voice the dead shall hear, and hearing, shall live."

If, then, the evidence which we can attain in this case, be sufficient to satisfy an impartial judgment, that the passage before us was "given by inspiration of God," as a prophecy of the second coming of the only Redeemer and Judge of mankind; it is no less evidence in point to our present investigation, on the PERSON of the Great Deliverer, than if it directly regarded his first advent:—and it unequivocally designates Him by the highest titles and attributes of Deity. Upon the hypothesis of those who regard the book of Job as a divine parable, all doctrinal and practical conclusions from it are strengthened, rather than rendered weak or precarious.—J. P. SMITH.

Ver. 24. That they were graven with an iron pen and lead in the rock for ever!

This probably refers to the ancient practice of writing on stone (by means of an iron instrument) those events which were to be conveyed to posterity. The fact, also, o lead being used, may allude to the fixing of the stone by means of that metal. In all parts of the East are to be found records thus written, many of which have never been deciphered, as they are in the languages not now understood. It is proverbial to say, "The words of the wise are written on stone." "Learning for the young is like a writing in stone."—ROBERTS.

Ver. 26. And *though*, after my skin, *worms* destroy this *body*, yet in my flesh shall I see God.

Though worms be not in the original, I believe the translators have acted wisely in supplying the word for the text. Dr. Mason Good translates it, "After the *disease* hath destroyed." But the opinion of the Orientals, as expressed in their ancient writings, and also in those of the present day, is, that worms do exist in the skin, and in all parts of the body, and that they principally cause its destruction. They say the *life* is first destroyed by them, and afterward the body. A man who is very ill, often exclaims, "Ah! my body is but a nest for worms; they have paths in all parts of my frame." "Ah! these worms are continually eating my flesh." In the ancient medical work called *Kurru-Nâtich-Sooteram*, written by the celebrated *Agattiyăr*, it is said, "The human body contains eighteen kinds of worms:—1. the skin; 2. the flesh; 3. the bones; 4. the blood; 5. (producing) wind; 6. the excrement; 7. the urine; 8. intestines; 9. σπερμα; 10. abscess; 11. sores (generally;) 12. leprosy; 13. itch; 14. cancer; 15. mouth; 16. teeth; 17. scull; and 18. the hair." Is it not a fact that the medical men of England have only of late years discovered that animalcules exist in some of these parts alluded to? and perhaps they may do well also to inquire, whether old Agattiyăr be not correct in some of his other opinions.—ROBERTS.

Ver. 28. But ye should say, Why persecute we him? seeing the root of the matter is found in me.

"What is the ROOT of his conversation?" "Is his root right?" "We cannot find out his root?" "Ah! he has a good root."—ROBERTS.

CHAPTER XX.

Ver. 16. He shall suck the poison of asps: the viper's tongue shall slay him.

In a country where serpents lurk in every path, and where such numbers of people lose their lives from their bite, can it be a matter of wonder that they are greatly afraid of them, and that their language abounds with figures taken from the destructive power of that reptile? Some modern writers have asserted, that there are very few of them which have poisonous qualities. It is said that some travellers take occasional journeys of several months into Italy, Greece, and Egypt, that they may have an opportunity of writing a book "for the gratification of their friends;" and that it is necessary to contradict, or alter a little, the descriptions of their predecessors, in order to find a sale, or to ensure a modicum of popularity. There may be something like scandal in these observations; but I am quite sure they are not without force in reference to some who have favoured the world with their sketches of the East. To say there are many serpents whose bite is not FATAL, is correct; but to assert that there are many whose bite is not poisonous, is nonsense. Perhaps the most harmless of all the tribe is the rat-snake; but its bite always produces giddiness in the head, and a great degree of deadness in the part where the wound has been inflicted. Apologizing for this digression, I observe, that when a man is enraged with another, and yet dare not make a personal attack upon him, he says, "The viper shall bite thee." "From whom art thou? the race of vipers?" "Yes, yes; the poison of the *puddeyan-pâmbo*, i. e. the beaver-serpent, is in thy mouth." "What! serpent, art thou going to bite me? *Chee, Chee!* I will break thy teeth."—ROBERTS.

Ver. 17. He shall not see the rivers, the floods, the brooks of honey and butter.

See on chap. 29. 6.

Is a man about to leave his native place, to reside in another country in hope of becoming rich, people say to him, "We suppose there are rivers of ghee, and honey and milk, in the town where you are going to live!"—ROBERTS.

In these cool countries we have no idea of butter so liquid as described in these words; it appears among us in a more solid form. But as the plentiful flowing of honey, when pressed from the comb, may be compared to a little river, as it runs into the vessels in which it is to be kept, so, as they manage matters, butter is equally fluid, and may be described in the same way: "A great quantity of butter is made in Barbary, which, after it is *boiled* with salt, they put into jars, and preserve for use." (Shaw.) Streams of butter then, poured, when clarified, into jars to be preserved, might as naturally be compared to rivers, as streams of honey flowing upon pressure into other jars in which it was kept.—BURDER.

Ver. 23. *When* he is about to fill his belly, *God* shall cast the fury of his wrath upon him, and shall rain *it* upon him while he is eating.

A man in the East does not, as in England, say he has eaten plentifully, or he has not taken any thing to eat; but he has well filled his belly, or, "to his belly there is nothing." Thus, the beggar at your door stoops a little, then puts his hands on the abdomen, and exclaims, "My lord, for my belly nothing, for my belly nothing!"—ROBERTS.

CHAPTER XXI.

Ver. 15. What *is* the Almighty, that we should serve him? and what profit should we have, if we pray unto him?

The heathen sometimes ask us, "Why should we pray to your God? is there any thing to be gained by it? When we go to our own temples, we have often fruit given to us; but when we come to yours, nothing is offered: give us something, and we will pray to him." On one of these occasions, a bystander repeated a favourite proverb, "Do you ask for pay when requested to eat sugarcane?" which silenced the jester.—ROBERTS.

Ver. 16. Lo, their good *is* not in their hand: the counsel of the wicked is far from me.

There has been a difficulty of great magnitude supposed in the present and several of the ensuing verses. Reiske, in order to explain it, has recourse to his usual method; and while he changes the divison of the letters in the first member of the verse before us, in order so far to obtain an explanation, he transfers the ensuing six verses, from 17 to 22 inclusively, to a place between verses 31 and 32. Other commentators, with less hardihood, suppose a dialogue to be held between the speaker and some imaginary respondent, and have attempted to mark out, by inverted commas, the passages that belong to the respective disputants. There is no necessity for any such expedients: the general drift of the argument is clear: "The righteous, I admit, are generally rewarded with temporal prosperity; but do not, on this account alone, accuse me of hypocrisy and all wickedness, because I am at present a sufferer; for the wicked themselves, in the mysteries of providence, are occasionally allowed to partake of an equal prosperity; they live in happiness, and die in quiet, even while they abjure the Almighty, and laugh at those who serve him. Do not however mistake me—far be it from me to become an advocate for the wicked—I know the slipperiness of their foundation, and that more generally they suffer for their iniquity in the present world, as well in their own persons as in their posterity; I am only anxious to prove that your grand argument is fallacious; that no conclusion can be drawn from the actual prosperity or misery of man, as to the moral rectitude or turpitude of his heart; and that, with a wisdom which it is impossible for mortals to fathom, the Almighty not unfrequently allots a similar *external* fate, both to the righteous and the wicked."—GOOD.

Ver. 17. How oft is the candle of the wicked put

Eastern Posture of Submission.—1 Chron. 29: 24.

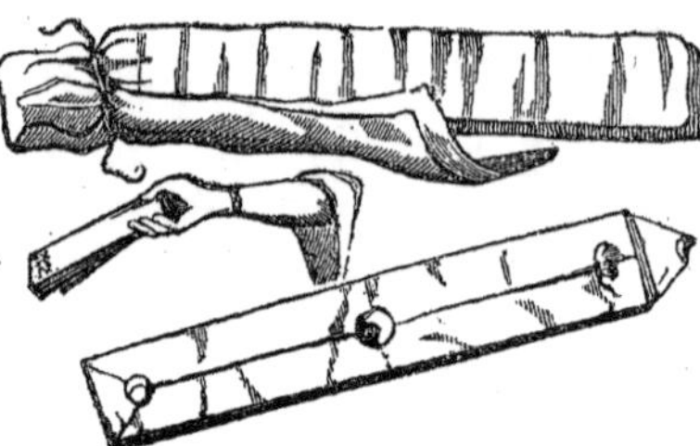

Eastern Letters.—Ezra 4: 7, 8. Neh. 6: 5.

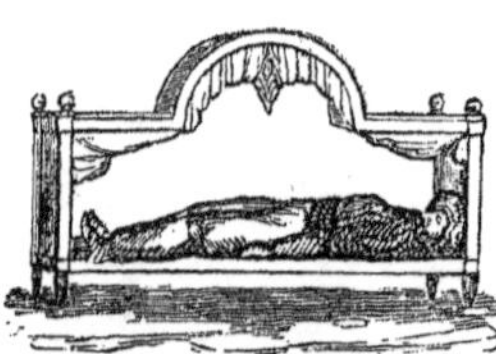

Funeral Chariot of the East.—2 Kings 9: 28.

Eastern mode of Punishment.—Job 13: 27.

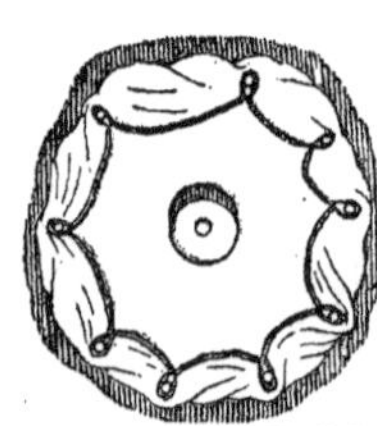

Kneading Troughs.—Ex. 12: 34.

Captivity.—2 Kings 17: 6.

Coney.—Ps. 104: 18, &c.

Ibex or Rock Goat.—Psalm 104: 18.

Wild Ass.—Job 39: 5—8.

out? and *how oft* cometh their destruction upon them? *God* distributeth sorrows in his anger.

See on 1 Kings 11. 26.

Ver. 24. His breasts are full of milk, and his bones are moistened with marrow.

When the mother dies before she has suckled her child, its life has been sometimes preserved by the milk of its father's breast. This curious fact was not unknown to Aristotle, who says, they that have a small quantity of milk, yield it in abundance when their breasts are sucked; that women who are past age, by being often sucked, and even males, have yielded milk in sufficient quantity to nourish an infant. Humboldt declares, in his Personal Narrative, that he saw a man, an inhabitant of Arenas, a village not far from Cumana, Francisco Lozano, who suckled a child with his own milk. "The mother having fallen sick, the father, to quiet the infant, took it into his bed, and pressed it to his bosom. Lozano, then thirty-two years of age, had never remarked till that day that he had milk; but the irritation of the nipple, sucked by the child, caused the accumulation of that liquid. The milk was thick and very sweet. The father, astonished at the increased size of his breast, suckled his child two or three times a-day, during five months. We saw the certificate which had been drawn up on the spot to attest this remarkable fact, eyewitnesses of which are still living, (1799.) They assured us, that during this suckling, the child had no other nourishment than the milk of his father. Lozano, who was not at Arenas during our journey in the missions, came to us at Cumana. He was accompanied by his son, who was then thirteen or fourteen years of age. Mr. Bonpland examined with attention the father's breast, and found it wrinkled like those of women who have given suck." The existence of milk in the breast of a male was known so early as the days of Job: "His breasts are full of milk, and his bones are moistened with marrow."—PAXTON.

The margin has, for breasts, "*milkpails.*" Of a man who is very rich, it is common to say, "His *chattles* (vessels) are full of milk." But of a good king or governor it is said, "He nourishes like the king whose breasts are full of milk." "Yes; he so rules, that the hearts of the goddess of the earth are full of milk."—ROBERTS.

Ver. 32. Yet shall he be brought to the grave, and shall remain in the tomb. 33. The clods of the valley shall be sweet unto him, and every man shall draw after him, as *there are* innumerable before him.

How came Job to speak of the clods of the valley, when describing magnificence of burial? I should suppose, in answer to this question, that Job is to be understood, not as intending to mark out the wonted places of their interment, but the manner of ornamenting their sepulchres; planting flowers, and odoriferous herbs or shrubs, on or about their graves: "Clods like those of a valley or torrent, verdant and flowery, shall surround him, and be pleasing to him." The liveliness of eastern poetry here representing the dead, as having the same perceptions as if they were alive in their sepulchres: "He shall watch in the heap of earth, or stones, that cover him," for such the margin of our translation tells us, is the more exact import of the Hebrew: "The clods around him, like those in some pleasant valley, or on the border of some torrent, shall be sweet unto him."—HARMER.

CHAPTER XXII.

Ver. 6. For thou hast taken a pledge from thy brother for naught, and stripped the naked of their clothing.

This *proverbial* form of speech is used when a man drags from another that which is his *last* resource. "Why do you take this tax from the naked?" "What! take a cloth from the naked? Is there no shame?" How often, also, do we see a man seize another by the cloth on the public road, and swear if he will not instantly pay his debt, he shall be left naked.—ROBERTS.

Ver. 7. Thou hast not given water to the weary to drink, and thou hast withholden bread from the hungry.

It is one of the thirty-two charities of the Hindoos, "to have water ready for the traveller to drink." Hence, on the public roads, in front of the houses of charitable people, may be seen vessels filled with water, for the use of all who pass that way. ' But respectable men do not drink there: they go inside, and say, "*Conjum-taneer*," a little water; and it is given to them.—ROBERTS.

Ver. 20. Whereas our substance is not cut down: but the remnant of them the fire consumeth.

There can be little doubt that the reference is to the cities of Sodom and Gomorrah: and as all men are often spoken of as constituting one family or community, so the abandoned inhabitants of these cities are poetically represented as descendants or remnants of the wicked that perished in the flood.—GOOD.

CHAPTER XXIII.

Ver. 11. My foot hath held his steps: his way have I kept, and not declined.

When a man follows another in a path so closely as almost to touch the feet of him who goes before, it is said, "His feet hath laid hold of his steps," intimating that the men are so near to each other, that the feet of him who follows, like unto the fingers of a man's hands, seize the feet of him who goes before. Thus the devoted disciple of a gooroo, or the man who closely pursues another, is said to take hold of the steps of him who goes before. Perhaps the figure may be taken from the great adroitness that the natives of the East have in seizing hold of any thing with their toes! See a man walking along the road: he sees something on the ground, which he wishes to pick up; but he does not stoop, as an Englishman. No! he takes it up between his first and second toes. Look at tailors, shoemakers, or sailors: when they want to twist a cord, they do not tie it to a nail, or ask another person to take hold. No; they make one end fast to the great toe, and perform the other operation with the hands. But the most remarkable illustration of this practice was in the case of Alypulle, the Kandian chief, who was beheaded near Kandy. When he arrived at the place where he was to be executed, he looked around for some time for a small shrub; and on seeing one, he seized it with his toes, in order to be firm while the executioner did his office.—ROBERTS.

CHAPTER XXIV.

Ver. 3. They drive away the ass of the fatherless; they take the widow's ox for a pledge.

How various and important are the services which this humble creature renders to his master! He serves him for riding, for bearing his burdens, drawing the plough, treading in the grain into the flooded soil, turning the millstone; and to all these services the female adds the nutritious beverage of her milk. To the poor man, therefore, a single ass might prove an invaluable treasure. In many cases, it was the principal means of support to himself and his family; a circumstance which accounts for the energetic language respecting this animal, in some passages of scripture. To "drive away the ass of the fatherless," Job denounces as a deed of atrocity, which none but a proud and unfeeling oppressor could be guilty of perpetrating.—PAXTON.

Ver. 5. Behold, *as* wild asses in the desert, go they forth to their work, rising betimes for a prey: the wilderness *yieldeth* food for them *and* for *their* children.

See on Gen. 16. 12.

The passage refers, evidently, not to the proud and haughty tyrants themselves, but to the oppressed and needy wretches, the Bedouins and other plundering tribes, whom their extortion and violence had driven from society, and compelled in a body to seek for subsistence by public robbery and pillage. In this sense the description is admirably forcible and characteristic.—GOOD.

Ver. 8. They are wet with the showers of the mountains, and embrace the rock for want of a shelter.

This exactly agrees with what Niebuhr says of the modern wandering Arabs near Mount Sinai: "Those who cannot afford a tent spread out a cloth upon four or six stakes; and others spread their cloth near a tree, or endeavour to shelter themselves from the heat and the rain in the cavities of the rocks."—Burder.

Ver. 9. They pluck the fatherless from the breast, and take a pledge of the poor.

It used to be said of the cruel king of Kandy, that he would not allow the infant to suck its mother's breast. Of a wicked woman it is said, "She will not allow her own child to suck her." "O the savage husband! he snatches the child from his wife's breast."—Roberts.

Ver. 16. In the dark they dig through houses, *which* they had marked for themselves in the daytime: they know not the light.

The short duration of mud-walled buildings is not the only objection to the use of unburnt brick; for in windy weather the streets are incommoded with dust, and with mire in time of rain. At Damascus, when a violent rain happens to fall, the whole city, by the washing of the houses, becomes as it were a quagmire. So great is the quantity of dust and mire which sometimes accumulates in the streets of an eastern city, that the prophet Zechariah borrows a figure from it, of great force and significancy in the ear of an Oriental, to denote the immense riches of Tyre: "Tyrus did build herself a strong hold, and heaped up silver as the dust, and fine gold as the mire of the streets." The beauty of the figure is lost if we attempt to judge of it by the state of an occidental city in modern times; but it will not be easy to conceive one more strikingly appropriate, if the streets of an eastern city, choked with mire, or suffocated with dust, are considered. Dr. Shaw directs the attention of his readers to the same circumstance, the dissolution of oriental buildings upon a shower, and supposes it may illustrate what Ezekiel observes respecting untempered mortar. When that traveller was at Tozer, in the month of December, they had a small drizzling shower, which continued for the space of two hours; and so little provision was made against accidents of this kind, that several of the houses, which, as usual, were built only with palm branches, mud, and tiles baked in the sun, fell down by imbibing the moisture of the shower. Nay, provided the drops had been either larger, or the shower of a longer continuance, he was persuaded the whole city would have dissolved and dropped to pieces. In his opinion, the phrase "untempered mortar" refers to the square pieces of clay of which the wall is constructed; but on looking at the text, it is evident that it refers to the plaster which is used in the East for covering the walls after they are built. The words of the prophet are: "And one built up a wall, and lo, others daubed it with untempered mortar.—Lo, when the wall is fallen, shall it not be said unto you, Where is the daubing wherewith ye have daubed it?" The view which Chardin gives of this text is, therefore, to be preferred. According to that intelligent traveller, the mud walls fall down in consequence of the rain dissolving the plaster. This plaster hinders the water from penetrating the bricks; but when it has been soaked with wet, the wind cracks it, by which means the rain, in some succeeding shower, gets between and dissolves the whole mass. To this external coating of plaster, the prophet certainly refers, and not to the bricks, of which the wall is constructed; for these, however tempered, never can be supposed to resist the action of violent rains. The ruinous effect of stormy winds and heavy rains upon such frail structures, is well described in the thirteenth verse, and exactly corresponds with the accounts of modern travellers: "Therefore, thus saith the Lord God, I will even rend it with a stormy wind in my fury; and there shall be an overflowing shower in mine anger, and great hailstones in my fury to consume it. So will I break down the wall that ye have daubed with untempered mortar, and bring it down to the ground, so that the foundation thereof shall be discovered, and it shall fall, and ye shall be consumed in the midst thereof: and ye shall know that I am the Lord." The same allusion is involved in the prediction of Amos, where he denounces the judgments of God against a profligate and refractory people: "For, behold, the Lord commandeth, and he will smite the great house with breaches, and the little house with clefts." The palaces of the great and the cottages of the poor, seem to have been constructed of the same fragile material; for they were affected by the storm and the tempest in the same manner, and when the cup of iniquity is full, are dissolved by the same shower.—Paxton.

Nearly all the houses in the East are made of unburnt bricks, so that there is very little difficulty in making a hole sufficiently large to admit the human body. No wonder, then, that this is the general way of robbing houses. Thus, in the morning, when the inmates awake, they see daylight through a hole in the wall, and immediately know what has been done.—Roberts.

Ver. 18. He *is* swift as the waters; their portion is cursed in the earth: he beholdeth not the way of the vineyards.

From this verse to the end of ver. 24, it is agreed by all the translators, that there is much difficulty and perplexity. "Non nimium, (says Le Clerc,) quam hac periodo se obscurius quicquam in sanctis scripturis"—"There is hardly any passage in the holy scriptures more obscure than the present:" and Schultens fully concurs in the observation. Hence there are no two interpreters, perhaps, who have translated it in precisely the same way, or understood it in the same manner. By many the text has been suspected to be erroneous in several instances; and a sense has been attempted to be extorted by pretended amendments of it. Reiske, here, as on all other occasions, is by far the boldest emendator; there is scarcely a verse into which he has not introduced some alteration, and in some verses an alteration amounting to nearly half the original text. It would be in vain to investigate these numerous renderings, of which no one appears to me to be more perspicuous than another, or to propose a clearer sense than that contained in our common version, obscure and in many parts unintelligible as it is allowed to be. Without dwelling, therefore, upon the misconceptions of my predecessors, I shall at once offer to the reader's attention, with much diffidence, a new interpretation of this contested passage, founded upon a different view of the writers' general scope and intention: and in doing this, while I adhere to the original text, without any amendment, the reader will find, I trust, that I shall be able to extract a very obvious meaning from it, even by such strict and literal rendering. What is the grand point of controversy between the pious patriarch and his too severe companions? I have been compelled to advert to it on various occasions, and especially in the note on chap. xxi. 16, which contains the patriarch's preceding reply. Job is, from first to last, accused by his friends of being an enormous transgressor, because it had pleased the Almighty to visit him with a severe affliction: and when he at first denied his being such a transgressor, he was immediately taxed with gross and open hypocrisy. He defends himself, in several of his subsequent answers, from this cruel and unfounded charge, and ably and completely refutes the very ground of the argument, by observing, in chap. xxi. that although it be true that the righteous are often, and for the most part, rewarded sooner or later, in this life, with prosperity, and the wicked punished as they deserve; yet that, in the mystery of providence, the rule by no means holds universally; for that the wicked also are often allowed to be prosperous, even to the latest period of their existence, and the upright to endure an uninterrupted series of pain and affliction. In chapter xxii. the original charge is again, however, advanced against the patriarch by Eliphaz, who once more advises him to repent of his misdeeds, in order that he might be restored to his former prosperity, and ascribes his vindication of himself to a spirit of obstinacy and rebellion. In the chapter before us, Job reverts to the argument so forcibly opened in his preceding reply: and in enlarging upon it, observes not only that the conduct of providence is inscrutable to us in regard to its dealings with the righteous and the wicked, but in regard to all the different classes of mankind, all the different modes of life they pursue, and all the different events that accompany them. In every scene we behold evil, moral or physical, permitted; in the retirement of the country, and in the crowded city; by sea and by land: it commences in the womb itself, and accompanies man through every stage of his being. We know nothing of the laws of providence; the Almighty often appears to be labouring in vain; and vice and virtue, the righteous and the wicked, to be almost equally, and almost promiscuously, the subject of prosperity and of affliction. The corollary is clear and unanswerable: "How absurd, then, is it to accuse me of being more a sinner than the rest of mankind, from the mere circumstance of my being a severer sufferer than others."—GOOD.

Ver. 19. Drought and heat consume the snow-waters; *so doth* the grave *those which* have sinned.

Literally, "ransack or plunder them." The reference is to those dikes, tanks, or reservoirs of water, which, in eastern countries, are always carefully filled during the periodical exudations of the large rivers, as the Nile, Indus, and Ganges, and preserved to fertilize the soil by occasional irrigations through the rest of the year, and without which there can be no harvest. So Isa. xxxvi. 16:—

Make ye peace with me, and come out to me,
And eat ye, every one of his vine, and every one of his fig-tree;
And drink ye, every one, of the waters of his own cistern, (*tank.*)

And Jeremiah, still more at large:—

And their nobles sent their little ones to the waters;
They came to the pits, (*tanks*)—they found no water;
They returned with their vessels empty;
They were ashamed and confounded, and covered their heads.
Behold! chapt was the ground, for there had been no rain on the earth;
The ploughmen were ashamed, they covered their heads.

These exudations were uniformly ascribed, and with great reason, to heavy periodical rains, and sudden thawings of the immense masses of snow deposited in the colder months on the summits of the loftier mountains, and especially of that vast and winding chain of rocks which, under the name of Caucasus and Imaus, runs, in almost every direction, from the eastern verge of Europe to the southern extremity of India. The two physical evils here adverted to, therefore, are among the severest scourges ever inflicted upon man—the failure of the vintage and of the harvest.—GOOD.

Ver. 21. He evil entreateth the barren *that* beareth not, and doeth not good to the widow.

It is considered to be very disgraceful for a married woman not to have children; and the evil treatment they receive from their own husbands and others is most shameful. Nothing can be more common than for a poor woman of that description, when she has given offence to another, to be addressed by the term *malady*, i. e. barren. "Go, barren one, get out of my sight." "*Chee!* she cannot have a child."—ROBERTS.

Ver. 24. They are exalted for a little while, but are gone and brought low; they are taken out of the way as all *other*, and cut off as the tops of the ears of corn.

Wicked men and tyrants may be prosperous for a season, but they will eventually be like the long stubble, having had the ears lopped off. This alludes to the custom, in the East, *of taking off the ears of the corn*, and leaving the straw, as before, standing on the ground. The grain called *kurrakan* is gathered by simply taking off the ears; and rice, where the water still remains in the fields, is gathered in the same way. The proud oppressor, then, in the end, shall be like the long straw standing in its place, having "the ears" cut off, and carried away.—ROBERTS.

CHAPTER XXVI.

Ver. 5. Dead *things* are formed from under the waters, and the inhabitants thereof.

What possible sense can be elicited from this passage, as thus rendered? The original for "dead things," (rephaim,) properly signifies the *mighty dead*, and is a common denomination of the *dead giants* who died before the flood. The *spirits* of these men are frequently alluded to in the scriptures, in accordance with the popular modes of belief, as incarcerated in the bowels or cavernous recesses of the earth, having been ingulfed in the waters of the deluge. Here the speaker is descanting, in a sublime and somewhat poetic manner, upon the ubiquity and omnipotence of God. Though seated upon the circle of the heavens, yet his eye penetrates, and his presence visits the profoundest abysses of the globe, and the spirits of the mighty dead, the tenants of these gloomy mansions, quail and quake before him. The true import of the original word rendered "formed" is, to *tremble, shake, quake, be put in commotion.* It is, therefore, in fact, but saying, that the regions of the dead are perfectly exposed to the omniscient survey of Jehovah, and that the despairing spirits of those who perished under the overwhelming mass of waters in the days of Noah, perpetually quake under the consciousness of his present ire. The ensuing verse is in a similar strain: "Hell (hades, the invisible world) is naked before him, and destruction hath no covering." A kindred figurative mode of representation occurs in Isaiah, ch. xiv. 6, where the approach of the once-dreaded king of Babylon to the dreary mansions of the dead, is spoken of as exciting commotion among the silent occupants of that nether world. "Hell from beneath is moved for thee to meet thee at thy coming; it stirreth up the *dead* (rephaim, *the mighty dead*) for thee, even all the chief ones of the earth." We suppose that the New Testament contains two distinct allusions to the subject of the present passage in Job, if not to the passage itself; the first is James ii. 19, "Thou believest there is one God; thou doest well; *the devils also believe, and tremble.*" Here the original word for *devils* (daimonia, *demons*) is, as Campbell has shown, the New Testament term for *spirits of dead men*, especially such as were deified and worshipped after death, the heroes or demigods of antiquity. This view of the subject brings the two passages into very near accordance with each other. The import of both is, that the spirits of these mighty dead tremble in awe before the most high God. The other occurs 1 Pet. iii. 19, 20, "By which also he went and preached unto the spirits in prison, which sometime were disobedient, when once the long-suffering of God waited in the days of Noah, while the ark was a preparing, wherein few, that is to say, eight souls, were saved by water." Christ, speaking by his spirit through Noah, and perhaps other good men living before the flood, preached to those ancient sinners, "which were of old, men of renown," but whose spirits, from their having proved disobedient and incorrigible, are now confined in the gloomy abodes of the under world, as in a prison from which there is no escape.—BUSH.

CHAPTER XXVII.

Ver. 8. For what *is* the hope of the hypocrite, though he hath gained, when God taketh away his soul?

The argument now entered upon is admirably forcible, and in point; it opposes the adverse party with their own weapons. "You accuse me of hypocrisy and of all wickedness, and you accuse me of thus acting from a love of gain. How absurd and irrational such a motive! what hope of prosperity can the wicked man indulge? what hope that God should grant him tranquillity?" Ver 11, "I will teach you his lot by the hand of God himself. Ye yourselves know it, and have seen it." Ver. 13, "Behold! this is the portion of the wicked man," &c.—GOOD.

Ver. 15. Those that remain of him shall be buried in death; and his widows shall not weep.

Nothing can be bolder, nothing more highly imbued with the spirit of oriental poetry, than the entire couplet: "No sepulchre, no funeral dirge: corruption alone shall be his tomb; his own household shall not bewail him; not even the affectionate females of his harem, his bereft wives and concubines; those of his own rank, who brought with them a dowry upon marriage, and those selected on account of their personal charms, and who were married without dowries." No honourable man was ever interred, in ancient times, and in eastern nations, without the solemnity of public mourners in long procession, loud lamentations, and metrical dirges. But it is probable that the writer, in the present place, more immediately alludes to those shrieks of domestic grief, which are so often to be met with in every quarter of the house, and especially among the females, upon the death of its master; and which is admirably described in the Iliad, upon the fall of Hector. The passage, however, has not been understood by any of the commentators or translators who have concurred in regarding שרידיו as meaning the *remains of his house*, instead of the *remains of his person;* and hence our common version, "*those that remain of him*," instead of literally, "*his remains*." Equally erroneous the common version, "shall be buried in death;" in which מות, here rendered *death*, means also "mortality," "corruption," "pestilence;" *i. e.* "corruption alone shall be his tomb, or covering," as just explained above. Reiske, not knowing how to explain this expression upon the common interpretation, suspects, as usual, an error in the reading, and proposes a choice of three amendments; neither of which, however, it is necessary to particularize.—GOOD.

Ver. 16. Though he heap up silver as the dust, and prepare raiment as the clay.

According to D'Herbelot, Bokteri, an illustrious poet of Cufah, in the ninth century, had so many presents made him in the course of his life, that when he died he was found possessed of a hundred complete suits of clothes, two hundred shirts, and five hundred turbans. This anecdote proves how frequently presents of this kind are made to persons of consideration in the Levant; and at the same time furnishes a beautiful illustration of that passage in the book of Job, where the afflicted patriarch describes the treasures of the East, in his time, as consisting of clothes and money: "Though he heap up silver as the dust, and prepare raiment as the clay; he may prepare it, but the just shall put it on, and the innocent shall divide the silver." —PAXTON.

Ver. 18. He buildeth his house as a moth, and as a booth *that* the keeper maketh.

Feeble in its structure and materials, short in its duration, and equally incapable of resisting a thunderstorm or shower of rain. So ch. viii. 14:—

"Thus shall his support rot away,
And the BUILDING OF THE SPIDER be his reliance."

The genus phalæna, or moth, is divided into plant-moths and cloth-moths; and the latter have been generally supposed to be those immediately alluded to in the present place. I have some doubt of this, but the question is not of consequence; the house or building referred to is, assuredly, that provided by the insect in its larvæ or caterpillar state, as a temporary residence during its wonderful change from a chrysalis to a winged or perfect insect. The slightness of this habitation is well known to every one who has attended to the curious operation of the silkworm, or the tribes indigenous to the plants of our own country, as the emperor-moth, tiger-moth, poplar, or willow-moth, &c. Of these, some construct a solitary dwelling; while others, as the brown-tail-moth, are gregarious, vast numbers residing together under one common web, marshalled with the most exact regularity. The web of the cloth-moth is formed of the very substance of the cloth on which it reposes, devoured for this purpose, and afterward worked into a tubular case, with open extremities; and generally approaching to the colour of the cloth by which the moth-worm is nourished.—GOOD.

The moth forms her cell in the woollen garment; a frail structure, which is soon destroyed by the devouring energy of the builder. Day after day she consumes the stuff in which her dwelling is placed, till both are involved in one common ruin, and reduced to nothing. Such, in the estimation of Job, is the prosperity of a wicked man: "He buildeth his house as a moth, and as a booth that the keeper maketh." The term which that afflicted patriarch uses in this passage, signifies a moth, and also the constellation Arcturus. Some interpreters accordingly render the words: "the wicked man shall build his house like Arcturus; shall raise, for his accommodation and pleasure, a splendid and magnificent abode, bright as the stars of Arcturus in the shining vault of heaven; but it shall speedily rush into ruin, like a temporary booth, where the keeper of a vineyard watches his property for a little while till the vintage is gathered." But this interpretation by no means accords with the design of the speaker; for it introduces an antithesis into the text, instead of the conjunction, which Job evidently meant, and separates the two comparisons of the same thing, as if they referred to different objects. Hence the common version, which unquestionably expresses the true sense of the clause, is to be preferred: "The wicked man, like the moth, builds his house at the expense of another. He expels his neighbours from their possessions, that he may join house to house, and lay field to field, till there be no place for others to inhabit, except as dependants on his forbearance or bounty, that he may dwell alone, as the sole proprietor, in the midst of the earth." The idea of Job is thus expressed by another prophet: "They covet fields, and take them by violence; and houses, and take them away; so they oppress a man and his house, even a man and his heritage." But his unrighteous acquisitions shall be of short continuance; they shall moulder insensibly away, returning to the lawful owner, or passing into the possession of others.—PAXTON.

Strictly, the mothworm, as it proceeds from the egg before it is changed into the chrysalis, aurelia, or nymph, (Nature Displayed, vol. i. p. 18,) so called from its corroding and destroying the texture of cloth. Job xiii. 28. Isaiah l. 9. li. 8. "The young moth upon leaving the egg, which a papilio has lodged upon a piece of stuff, or a skin well dressed, and commodious for her purpose, immediately finds a habitation and food in the nap of the stuff, or hair of the skin. It gnaws and lives upon the nap, and likewise builds with it its apartment, accommodated both with a front door and a back one; the whole is well fastened to the ground of the stuff, with several cords and a little glue. The moth sometimes thrusts her head out of one opening, and sometimes out of the other, and perpetually devours and demolishes all about her; and when she has cleared the place about her, she draws out all the stakes of this tent, after which she carries it to some little distance, and then fixes it with her slender cords in a new situation. In this manner she continues to live at our expense till she is satiated with her food, at which period she is first transformed into a nymph, and then changes into a papilio, or moth."—BURDER.

Ver. 19. The rich man shall lie down, but he shall not be gathered: he openeth his eyes, and he *is* not.

The heathen had a conceit that the souls of such persons as had not had the due rites of burial paid them, were not admitted into hades, but were forced to wander a hundred years, a parcel of vagabond ghosts, about the banks of the Styx. Hence we find the ghost of Patroclus supplicating Achilles to give him his funeral rites: "Bury me," says he, "that I may pass as soon as possible through the gates of hades." So speaks Palinurus, in *Virgil:* "Throw upon me some earth, that at last I may obtain rest in death, in quiet habitations." Here the self-conceited philosopher smiles at the rite of sprinkling the body three times with dust; but this, although misunderstood, and tinged with the fabulous, was borrowed from the Hebrew nation. *To gather* denotes, as to the dead, the bringing of their souls to Paradise. Although this cannot be effected by mortals, yet they expressed the benevolent wish that the thing might be. On the other hand, Job says of the rich man, *he shall lie down, but he shall not be gathered.* In the ages which followed, the performance of this rite was termed *sealing.* Of this we have a bright instance in the second book of Esdras: "Wheresoever thou findest the dead, seal them, and bury them;" that is, express the benevolent prayer which is in use among the Jews to this day: "May he be in the bundle of life, may his portion be in Paradise, and also in that future world which is reserved for the righteous." It would also appear, that in this act of *sealing* a corpse, they either wrote upon the head with ink, or simply made the form with the finger, (*Le-hovah.*) This at bottom could make no difference in the state of the deceased, but it expressed their desire that such a person might be among those *who are written unto life.* From a passage in Isaiah, it appears that persons were in use to mark with indelible ink on the hand, the words *Le-hovah*, the contracted form of this sentence, *I am the Lord's.* This agrees with what Rabbi Simeon says, "The perfectly just are sealed, and in the moment of death are conveyed to Paradise." This sealing St. Paul applies, as far as wishes can go, to Onesiphorus: "May the Lord grant to Onesiphorus, that he may obtain mercy of the Lord in that day!" "As many," says the same apostle, "as walk according to this rule, peace be on them, and upon the Israel of God!" (Gal. vi. 16.)

Such being marked in death with the expression, *belonging to the Lord*, explains this sentence, "the foundation of the Lord standeth sure, having this *seal*, the Lord knoweth them that *are his*." "Hurt not the earth, nor the trees," says the angel in the book of Revelation, "until we have sealed the servants of our God in their foreheads." This seal, we are told, is their father's name: that is, *Le-hovah, the Lord's*, alluding to the Old Testament form. This name Christ says he himself writes, and by doing so, acts the part of the *Kedosh-Israel*, opening where none can shut. This sealing, then, is taking them off by death, and placing them in his father's house; for after they are so sealed, we find them before the throne, *hungering and thirsting no more*, and the Lamb in the midst of them, and leading them forth into pastures.—BURDER.

Ver. 23. *Men* shall clap their hands at him, and shall hiss him out of his place.

See on 2 Sam. 2. 15.

The present female way of expressing joy in the East, by gently applying one of their hands to their mouths, seems to have obtained in the times of remote antiquity, and to be meant in several places of scripture. What their present custom is, appears in the following passage of Pitts, describing the joy with which the leaders of their sacred caravans are received, in the several towns of Barbary through which they pass: "This emir Hagge, into whatsoever town he comes, is received with a great deal of joy, because he is going about so religious a work; and it is, who can have the favour and honour of kissing his hand, or but his garment! He goes attended in much pomp, with flags, kettle-drums, &c. and loud acclamations do, as it were, rend the skies; nay, the very women get upon the tops of the houses to view the parade, or fine show, where they keep striking their fore fingers on their lips, as fast as they can, making a joyful noise all the while, which sounds somewhat like yow, yow, yow, hundreds of times." Others have given us nearly the same account. This seems to me to be referred to in some passages of scripture; and that the sacred writers suppose two different methods of expressing joy by a quick motion of the hand, which is lost in our translation; for I suppose the clapping of the hands in the plural, is a very distinct thing from the clapping the hand in the singular, though our translators have confounded them together. The striking one hand against the other with some smartness, which we mean by the term *clapping of the hands*, might, and I believe did, obtain anciently, as an expression of joy; not unfrequently, if not always, of the malignant kind; so the prophet Jeremiah says of Jerusalem, when it was destroyed, "All that pass by, clap their hands at thee; they hiss and wag their head at the daughter of Jerusalem, saying, Is this the city that men call the perfection of beauty, the joy of the whole earth?" Lam. ii. 15. In like manner Job, after describing the sudden destruction of the wicked, says, "Men shall clap their hands at him, and shall hiss him out of his place," Job xxvii. 23.—HARMER.

CHAPTER XXVIII.

Ver. 4. The flood breaketh out from the inhabitant; *even the waters* forgotten of the foot: they are dried up, they are gone away from men.

The mighty flood which man had dammed up, by joining together MOUNTAINS and HILLS, and thus forming an immense basin, had broken down by its weight the gigantic MOUND; had rolled "away from men," and gone in the desert places. The waters of the lake are now "forgotten of the foot, they are dried up;" for the feet of men in walking there think of them no more.—ROBERTS.

Mr. Parkhurst considers this chapter as relating to mineralogy, and renders these words, "a torrent bursteth forth from the rubbish unexpectedly; by the foot they are drawn off, by man they are removed." As an explanation, he adds the following extract from Mr. Hutchinson: "It is hardly credible how great a quantity of water will be sometimes flung upon miners, when they come to break up strata of stone, that have in them many of these cracks, that are so small that they are scarcely discernible. These are indeed the natural conveyances of water, and when once they are opened, it runs incessantly. I have observed such an eruption of water in vast quantity out of stone, that, excepting those cracks, is much too dense and close to let any humidity pass." "The vast profusion of water that sometimes ensues the breaking up of the strata in coal-pits, is well known to those who are in the least conversant in that affair: and what amazing quantities are drawn off from deep mines, either by drains or levels, or raised by engines, is also well known; nay, in digging common wells and ponds, in places where there are no springs above ground, it frequently happens that such a glut of water issues forth as to endanger the lives of the workmen."—BURDER.

Ver. 6. The stones of it *are* the place of sapphires; and it hath dust of gold.

The STONES which form and bind together the MOUNDS and hills are taken from the exact places where sapphires are found. For Jameson informs us, that "the geognostic situation of the sapphire is in alluvial soil, in the vicinity of rocks, belonging to the secondary flœtz trap formation, and imbedded in gneiss." In reference to its geographic situation, the same writer says, it is found particularly beautiful in Asia, in the Capelan mountains, in Persia, and the Island of Ceylon. Dr. Davy states, that "the sapphire occurs in considerable abundance in the granitic alluvion of Matura and Saffragam," (in Ceylon.) Thus, the STONES of which the MOUND is formed, are the true geognostic situation where the sapphire is found; and there can be no doubt that the workmen, in hewing and detaching the masses fom the rocks, and in joining them to the mountains, did, by this secondary kind of mining, often find the precious sapphire. "And it hath dust of gold." The same mineralogist states, (and it is a well known fact,) "that in Asia the sand of many rivers affords gold," and it is washed down in great quantities from the mountains on the coast of Sumatra, where it is afterward found in the beds of rivers.—ROBERTS.

Ver. 10. He cutteth out rivers among the rocks; and his eye seeth every precious thing.

In our commor version, "he cutteth out rivers;" in one or two others, "canals." The exact meaning is, the *hollows* that are delved by miners in a metallic bed or mountain, often serving as passages to the central chamber. By cleaving such openings as these, the metallurgist may truly be stated, which he could not be in the usual rendering of "cutting out rivers," "to discover every precious gem."—GOOD.

Savary informs us, the canal Bahr Joseph "must have cost immense sums, being in MANY parts CUT THROUGH the ROCK!" Bishop Heber also states that the lake of Ajmeer is formed "by damming up the gore of an extensive valley, and conveying different small rills into it!" Thus, in making his rivers and rivulets through the rocks, in order to convey the water to its destined place, he at the same time sees "every precious thing:" because his work lies in the geognostic situation of those valuable gems.—ROBERTS.

Ver. 11. He bindeth the floods from overflowing; and *the thing that is* hid bringeth he forth to light.

According to Reiske, "E fonticulo compellit in unum alveum,"—"He driveth them from their spring into a common reservoir." According to the more general interpretation, "He bindeth the flood from overflowing." The sense has not been fairly understood. Every one acquainted with mining knows, that, at different depths from the surface, the shaft, or aperture, is so apt to be overflowed with water from surrounding springs, that it is impossible to work it till the water is drawn off; the machinery to accomplish which is sometimes one of the most serious expenses incidental to working a mine. It is to the restraint of these waters, so perpetually *oozing* or *weeping* through every pore, that the writer alludes in the present passage.—GOOD.

CHAPTER XXIX.

Ver. 2. Oh that I were as *in* months past, as *in* the days *when* God preserved me; 3. When his candle shined upon my head, *and when* by his light I walked *through* darkness.

The winter in Canaan is extremely wet and cold. In the time of the crusades, many of the troops perished through want of provisions, intenseness of the cold, and the heaviness of the winter rains. Fulcherius, who was in the retinue of the prince of Antioch, in his journey to Jerusalem, and saw many of both sexes die, besides numbers of their cattle, says, they were kept wet for four or five days together, by the continual rains. So great is the quantity of rain which occasionally falls, and so intense the cold, that the elements seem to conspire the ruin of every living creature that is exposed to their fury. It is agreed by all those who have written on the subject, that all the winter months in Palestine are rainy; and by consequence, that Judea is not one of those regions where it only rains at the equinoxes. The Hebrew word horeph, accordingly, which we translate winter, in Mr. Harmer's opinion, seems rather to mean precisely the wet season. "O that I were as in months past," says Job, "as in the days when God preserved me, as I was in the days of my winter!" In the days of his moist time, when, as he expresses it, "my root was spread out by the waters, and the dew lay all night upon my branch: my glory was fresh in me." Not in the days of his disgrace then, the days in which he was stripped of his ornaments, as an herb of its leaves and flowers in the winter; but like a plant, in the latter part of the rainy season, before the violent heats come on, which scorch and burn up every green thing. But the term horeph, from the verb haraph, to strip, literally means the stripping season; and signifies that part of the year which strips vegetables of their flowers, fruit, and leaves, and consequently, the earth of its beauty. It is opposed to *kaitz*, from *koutz*, to awake, or quicken, the quickening or awakening season, and includes both autumn and winter. Is it probable that the cold and rainy season of winter would be an object of desire to Job, when "the heavens are filled with clouds, when the earth swims to rain, and all nature wears a lowering countenance?" It is more natural to render the phrase, in the days of his autumn, which in those climates is a delightful season; for then the heats are abated, the earth is moistened with dew, or refreshed with the first showers of the latter rain, and the various fruits of the earth, to use the beautiful language of inspiration, are ready to drop into the mouth of the eater; or, the fields and trees being stripped of their produce, are heaped on its board. The afflicted patriarch certainly referred to the end of harvest, in allusion to which he might say, with strict propriety, "my root was spread out by the waters, and the dew lay all night upon my branches; my glory was fresh in me."—PAXTON.

The slaughter of Saul filled his camp with terror and mourning: before that, it is probable, his tent might sometimes be distinguished by lights; at least these illuminations are now used in those countries to do honour to princes, and must not here be forgotten. So the tent of the bey of Girge, Norden tells us, was distinguished from the other tents in that encampment, by forty lanterns suspended before it in form of checker-work. So Thevenot, describing the reception of the new bashaw of Egypt under tents, near Cairo, says there were two great trees, on which two hundred lamps hung, at the gate of the little enclosure which surrounded his pavilions, which were lighted in the nighttime; and that there was the same before the tents of the principal officers, as in the caravan of Mecca. In the East, it is *now* a customary thing; if it was the same anciently, perhaps the words of Job might refer to it, ch. xxix. 2, 3: "Oh that it were with me as in months past, as in the days when God preserved me; when his candle shined upon my head," when I returned prosperous from expeditions against the enemies of my tribe, and had my tent adorned with lamps, "and I passed through the night by the light of it."—HARMER.

Ver. 4. As I was in the days of my youth, when the secret of God *was* upon my tabernacle.

Job was reverting to the time of his prosperity, as is seen in the preceding verse, "when his candle shined upon my head, and when by his light I walked through darkness;" "when my children were about me, when I washed my steps with butter." The Psalmist also is speaking of the prosperity of those who fear the Lord. To say the secret of the king is with such a person, is a strong way of describing the intimacy which exists between them. "Take care how you accuse him to the great man, because his secret is with him." "Alas! alas! his secret is no longer with me; his lamp no longer shines in my heart."—ROBERTS.

Ver. 6. When I washed my steps with butter, and the rock poured me out rivers of oil.

Bottles of goat-skin, with the hairy side inwards, receive the milk of their flocks: and when they wish to make butter, they put the cream into a goat-skin, prepared in the same manner, which they suspend in their tents, and then pressing it to and fro, in one uniform direction, quickly produce a separation of the unctuous from the wheyey part of the fluid. In the Levant, they tread upon the skin with their feet, which produces the same effect. The last method of separating the butter from the milk, perhaps may throw light upon a passage in Job, of some difficulty: "When I washed my steps with butter, and the rock poured me out rivers of oil." Commentators have observed, what must be obvious to every reader, that the afflicted patriarch meant to say, he once possessed great abundance of these products; but they have not been able to account for the manner of his expression. The way of a great personage was sometimes swept, sometimes strewed with flowers, sometimes watered; but never, as far as we know, moistened with butter. The feet were sometimes anointed with oil, in which odoriferous substances had been infused; but to them, butter was never applied. It is more natural to suppose, that these words of Job referred to the method of churning their milk, by treading upon large skins full of cream, with their bare feet. It conveys a still more lively idea of the exuberant plenty which Job once possessed, if this method was adopted when they had large quantities of milk to churn. A variety of practice very similar to this appears to have prevailed in the ancient vineyards. When a small quantity of grapes was to be pressed, it seems to have been done with the hand; for Pharaoh's butler dreamed that he took the grapes and pressed them in this manner into his master's cup. This, it must be admitted, was only a visionary scene; but we must suppose it corresponded with general custom. So, when they meant to churn a small quantity of cream, they suspended it in a skin, from the roof of the tent; and the female part of the family conducted the process. But when the quantity was very large, as it must have been in the extensive dairies of the patriarchs, who possessed such immense flocks and herds, it was put into a number of skins, and churned by the feet of men. This Mr. Harmer considers as no improbable account, and by no means an unnatural explanation of the phrase, "I washed my steps with butter;" and in the present state of our knowledge, perhaps a more satisfactory one cannot be given. Greece, indeed, lies at a great distance from the land of Uz, and the age when Job flourished is far removed from our times; but as a skin is still the churning vessel used by the Arabs in the Holy Land, as well as in Barbary, and consequently, as their customs admit of little or no variation, the use of skins in churning must belong to a very remote antiquity. And the same reason that might induce the more opulent Greeks, in the time of Chandler, to tread their cream, rather than swing it in the tent, or between two poles, as the Arabs generally do, might also induce the richer proprietors in Asia, who possessed such numerous flocks, to adopt the same custom. The expression, it must be allowed, is highly figurative, but not more so than many others, in which the oriental muse delights. The term washing, when used poetically, is not surely confined to cleansing the feet, by some purifying fluid; for dipping the feet in the blood of the slain, the Psalmist calls washing the feet. Hence, to plunge them into cream or butter, or to sprinkle them profusely with it, may be called washing them in butter, with equal propriety; and walking in it, washing the steps.

The butter is carried to market in the same goat-skins in which it is churned. In consequence of this mode of management, it becomes necessary to melt and strain it, in order to separate the impurities; a process by which it acquires a certain rancid taste, disagreeable, for the most part, to strangers, though not to the natives. To this custom of melting the butter, in order to clarify it, Zophar seems to allude, in his description of the state and portion of a wicked man: "He shall not see the rivers, the floods, the brooks of honey and butter." As the flowing of honey from the comb into the vessels in which it is to be kept, may, by a bold figure, be compared to a little river; so may clarified butter, when poured into the jars in which it is preserved for use. The wicked man, says Zophar, shall not see the rivulets, much less the rivers, still less the torrents of honey and butter, (as the clause ought to be rendered,) which the righteous may hope to possess. In our excellent translation, the beauty of the climax in this instance is lost; for instead of continuing to rise, it sinks in the close, ending with brook, after mentioning rivers and torrents; but in the original it is equally striking and well conducted.—PAXTON.

These are figurative expressions to denote great prosperity. "The man is so rich, he washes himself with *ney*," i. e. clarified butter. "Oh, the charitable man, milk and honey accompany his feet." So great was the profusion, "the honey caused the feet to slip," (in the paths,) the creepers danced, the trees nodded their heads, and milk, from the dwellings of the cattle, flowed in streams through the streets. (Scanda Purāna.)—ROBERTS.

Ver. 7. When I went out to the gate, through the city, *when* I prepared my seat in the street.

This intimates that Job was a judge among his people, as the courts of justice in former times were kept in such situations. Who has not seen a great man or a saint thus having his seat prepared in the street? There he goes under a shady tree, or under a veranda, or in a rest-house, with his servant following him, having a mat or a tiger's skin, or that of some other animal under his arm. The seat is prepared, and the crosslegged sage sits to hear and answer questions.—ROBERTS.

Chardin says, it is the custom of Asia not to go into the shops, which are very small, but to sit down in seats prepared for the purpose on the outside, on which cushions are laid for persons of distinction; and he adds, that people of quality cause carpets and cushions to be carried wherever they please, that they may repose themselves upon them more agreeably. To a custom of this kind Job seems to refer in his mournful retrospect of departed prosperity: "When I went out to the gate through the city, when I prepared my seat in the street." This patriarch was a prince and a judge among his people, and was, therefore, entitled to take his seat in the gate, which was the ordinary place of hearing causes in the East, attended by a retinue of servants, with carpets and cushions for his accommodation, according to his rank, and the office he sustained.—PAXTON.

Numbers of the Southern Arabs assemble in their markets by way of amusement, and consequently, for conversation: the same custom appears anciently to have obtained, in places of the East, less remote from us than Yemen.

"Notwithstanding this external gravity," says Niebuhr, "the Arabs love a great deal of company; accordingly, one sees them assiduously assembling in the public coffeehouses, and, above all, running to fairs, in which no country, perhaps, more abounds than Yemen; since there is scarcely a village of any consideration to be found, which has not a weekly fair. When the villages are at some distance from each other, their inhabitants assemble on the appointed day in the open fields. Some come hither to buy or to sell; others, who are mechanics of various professions, employ sometimes the whole week in going from one little borough to another, in order to work at these fairs; and finally, many propose to themselves to pass away the time there more agreeably than at home. From this taste of the Arabs for society, and especially of those of Yemen, it is easy to infer that they are more civilized than it may be imagined." Michaelis, the great promoter of Niebuhr's expedition into the East, has taken notice of this passage in his extract from this work, saying, "The public places are, to this day, in Yemen, the places of diversion, and thus serve two uses; just as the gates of cities, which anciently were made their public places, as we are told in the Bible, Gen. xix. 1. Job xxix. 7. Ps. lxix. 14," &c.—HARMER.

Ver. 8. The young men saw me, and hid themselves: and the aged arose, *and* stood up.
9. The princes refrained talking, and laid *their* hand on their mouth.

What a graphic scene is this! When a man of rank passes a crowd, the young people and children conceal themselves behind their seniors, and the aged always arise from their seats. See the man in a court of justice, who is listening to the address of the judge, and his hand is placed on his mouth. To place the hand on the mouth also denotes astonishment; and Major Laing says, when he was at Toma, in Africa, a woman was so much surprised at the sight of a white man, that she "did not stir a muscle till the whole had passed, when she gave a loud halloo of astonishment, and covered her mouth with both her hands." —ROBERTS.

This is a most elegant description, and exhibits most correctly that great reverence and respect which was paid, even by the old and decrepit, to the holy man in passing along the streets, or when he sat in public. They not only rose, which in men so old and infirm was a great mark of distinction; but they stood; they continued to do it, though even the attempt was so difficult.—LOWTH.

When the easterns wish to be silent, they place their hand upon their mouth, to express their intentions by action, and their sentiments by attitude. Many instances of this practice are to be found. "In one of the subterranean vaults in Egypt, where the mummies lie buried, they found in the coffin an embalmed body of a woman, before which was placed a figure of wood, representing a youth on his knees, laying a finger on his mouth, and holding in his other hand a sort of chafingdish, which was placed on his head, and in which, without doubt, had been some perfumes." (Maillet.)

"On our taking possession of Rosetta, at an entertainment which was given, a young Greek came up to me, kissed my shoulder, and with his finger on his lips, without uttering a single syllable, slipped privately into my hand a nosegay which he had brought me: this simple demonstration completely unfolded all his sensations, and was expressive of his political situation, his fears, and his hopes." (Denon.)—BURDER.

Ver. 14. I put on righteousness, and it clothed me: my judgment *was* as a robe and a diadem.

See on Is. 28. 5.

Or turban. This consists of a cap and a sash of fine linen or silk, wound round the bottom of it. This is the usual headdress of the Turks, Persians, Arabs, and other eastern nations. Dr. Shaw says, "The Moors and Turks, with some of the principal Arabs, wear upon the head a small hemispherical cap of scarlet cloth. The turban, as they call a long narrow web of linen, silk, or muslin, is folded round the bottom of these caps, and very properly distinguishes, by the number and fashion of these folds, the several orders and degrees of soldiers, and sometimes of citizens, one from another."—BURDER.

Ver. 15. I was eyes to the blind, and feet *was* I to the lame.

The man who bestows great charities, is said to be the eyes of the blind, and the feet of the cripples. "True, my lord, I am blind; but you are my eyes." "Ah! sir, shall I not love my eyes?" "O king," says the lame man, "are you not my staff?" "Alas! alas! our eyes have gone," say the blind, when their benefactor is dead. But when a person confides in the wisdom of another, he says, "He is my eyes." "I have two good eyes in the temple."—ROBERTS.

Ver. 19. My root *was* spread out by the waters, and the dew lay all night upon my branch.

"The precious water of the Cephissus is the property of the waivode only during the season of watering the olive-wood: for the remaining months the owners of the gardens, in a proportion settled by long usage, divert the stream into their grounds, for one, two, or three hours in a week or fortnight, according to the bargain at which they have hired or purchased their land. The instant that the stream is turned into the required channel, a public inspector, who is called Dragaris-too-nen, and is always in attendance, turns his hourglass, and the gardener also measures the time in the same manner; other Greeks frequently being present to prevent collusion, and cut off the rivulet immediately at the expiration of the stipulated hour."—(Hobhouse.)

It is well known that in the hot eastern countries, where it rarely rains during the summer months, the copious dews which fall there during the night, contribute greatly to the nourishment of vegetables in general. "This dew," says Hasselquist, speaking of the excessively hot weather in Egypt, "is particularly serviceable to the trees, which would otherwise never be able to resist this heat; but with this assistance they thrive well, and blossom and ripen their fruit."—Burder.

Ver. 20. My glory *was* fresh in me, and my bow was renewed in my hand.

This figure is much used in their poetry. "The bow is bent in his hand." "See the strong bow; it is bent to kill thee."—Roberts.

Ver. 22. After my words they spake not again; and my speech dropped upon them.

Of a man who speaks with great euphony, it is said, "His words come, *tule tule yāka*," i. e. drop by drop.—Roberts.

CHAPTER XXX.

Ver. 2. Yea, whereto *might* the strength of their hands *profit* me, in whom old age was perished?

The Tamul translation has this, "as the strength of the hands being gone by old age." Of a man who has become weak in consequence of age, it is said, "Ah! by reason of old age, the strength of his hands has departed from him." "It is true he is an old man, but the strength of his hand has not perished." But this mode of expression also refers to a man's circumstances. Thus, when a person has lost his property, it is said, "the strength of his hands has gone." "Poor man! he has not any strength in his hands."—Roberts.

Ver. 3. For want and famine *they were* solitary; fleeing into the wilderness in former time desolate and waste: 4. Who cut up mallows by the bushes, and juniper-roots *for* their meat.

This describes the ignoble state of the parents of those children by whom Job was now held in derision. In the book called Sinthā Manni, there is an account of some princesses, who once had their rice, like jasmine flowers, given them on golden plates; but now they had to go with potsherds, to beg for the leaves from the hedges for their daily food. A rich man brought to poverty, sometimes asks, "What care I? Can I not go into the desert, and live on roots and leaves?" It is a fact, that numbers do thus live, especially the Vedahs, and those who have retired from men.—Roberts.

Ver. 6. To dwell in the cliffs of the valleys, *in* caves of the earth, and *in* the rocks.

The oriental shepherd and his family sometimes take up their abode in caves, with which the country, particularly about Askelon, abounds. These caverns are often so capacious as to admit the master and his whole property. In times of imminent danger, the people forsake their towns and villages, and retire with their wives and children, their flocks and herds, into these dark recesses, which have been from time immemorial the refuge of the oppressed. It was in these hiding-places that Baldwin I., king of Jerusalem, in the barbarous age of the crusades, found the inhabitants of many villages, with their flocks and their herds, who had favoured the cause of his enemies, and fled at his approach. In Egypt, such excavations appear to have been the settled abodes of a numerous and peaceful population. Dr. Richardson entered several mountain defiles, on his way to Nubia, where he found "a number of excavations extremely well executed, covered with sculpture, and painted in the most brilliant colours; likewise a number of pits sunk perpendicularly into the rock, all of which have been used as burying-places, and many of them still contain handsome mummy cases, made of wood and stone, beautifully painted in a variety of colours, and covered with curious devices." But besides these, "high up in the front, along the base of the mountain, and over the rocky flat, all the way from Medina Thabou, there are innumerable excavations, many of them large and beautifully formed, painted, and sculptured with many curious devices, illustrative of ancient customs. In one place above Medina Thabou, the doors into these excavations are so numerous and so contiguous, that they resemble a row of houses in a village. They have a long piazza in front, and a large apartment within; and a long shaft running back into the rock. They rise in tiers above each other, according to the different elevations of the mountain. They have evidently been dwellinghouses, and, from the shady piazza in front, the spectator enjoys the most delightful view that can possibly be obtained of the plain of Thebes." In Hindostan, too, the fainting inhabitants are forced to escape from the severe fervours of an eastern noon, into vast artificial caverns, and into grottoes of the most refreshing coolness, which the great and the wealthy cause to be constructed in their gardens.—Paxton.

Ver. 16. And now my soul is poured out upon me: the days of affliction have taken hold upon me.

"Why are you so dejected, my friend?" "Because the *kettakālam*, i. e. the ruinous time, has caught me."—Roberts.

Ver. 20. I cry unto thee, and thou dost not hear me: I stand up, and thou regardest me *not*.

It is extremely mortifying, when a man stands up, not to be noticed. A native gentleman had a case which he wished to bring before the notice of the king of Tanjore, and asked my advice how to act. I recommended him to go to the capital, and wait upon his majesty. On his return, he informed me he had not stated his case to the king; and, upon my blaming him, he asked, "What could I do? I went to a place where I knew he would have to pass; and when he came near, I stood up; but he regarded me not." —Roberts.

Ver. 22. Thou liftest me up to the wind; thou causest me to ride *upon it*, and dissolvest my substance.

This figure is probably taken from the custom of an angry man, who takes any light substance and throws it into the wind, saying to his antagonist, "Thus shall it be with thee."—Roberts.

There is a remarkable figurative representation in Job, chap. xxx. 22, thus rendered in our translation: "Thou liftest me up to the wind; thou causest me to ride *upon it*, and dissolvest my substance." Possibly after we have examined the phraseology of this passage, its force may be further evident, and it may receive additional illustration. "Thou dost raise me up on high, into the air, by the agency—of—upon—the wind; thou dost make me to ride on it, as on a chariot, or other vehicle; and dost dissolve—disperse—dissipate—my whole—entire—my all: all that I ever was: all that I ever possessed." Such is the power of the original.

This might perhaps be referred to a vapour raised by the wind, which, after being borne about among the clouds, is dissolved, and falls in dew: but, (1.) the wind which raises it, seems rather to describe a storm, and during storms dew does not perceptibly rise. (2.) The current of wind, which, like a chariot, bears away the subject of its power, is a vehement, powerful, rapid blast; as we say, a *high* wind; and does not agree with the formation, &c. of dew, which is a tranquil, deliberate process. (3.) The word (מגג) *megeg*, is applied to express the melting of a solid body; as of the earth with rain, Psalm lxv. 10; of the hills, through intense heat, Nahum i. 5; so Amos ix. 13. Mr. Scott has rendered the passage—

> Roused by Almighty force a furious storm—
> Upcaught me, whirl'd me on its eddying gust,
> Then dash'd me down, and shatter'd me to dust.

Under these considerations, we presume to think the reader will agree with us in referring it to a sandstorm: possibly such as we have noticed in the former number; or, much rather, such as is described by the following information, which the reader will not be displeased to peruse, as it stands high among the most picturesque and most terrific descriptions of the kind to be met with. It is from Mr. Bruce.

"On the 14th, at seven in the morning, we left Assa Nagga, our course being due north. At one o'clock we alighted among some acacia-trees, at Waadi el Halboub, having gone twenty-one miles. We were here at once surprised and terrified by a sight surely one of the most magnificent in the world. In that vast expanse of desert, from W. and to N. W. of us, we saw a number of prodigious *pillars of sand*, at different distances, at times *moving with great celerity*, at others stalking on with a majestic slowness; at intervals we thought they were coming in a very few minutes to overwhelm us; and small quantities of sand did actually more than once reach us. Again they would retreat so as to be almost out of sight, *their tops reaching to the very clouds*. There the tops often separated from the bodies: and these, once disjoined, *dispersed in the air*, and did not appear more. Sometimes they were broken near the middle, as if struck with a large cannon shot. About noon they began to advance with considerable swiftness upon us, the wind being very strong at north. Eleven of them ranged alongside of us about the distance of three miles. The greatest diameter of the largest appeared to me at that distance as if it would measure ten feet. They retired from us with a wind at S. E. leaving an impression upon my mind to which I can give no name, though surely one ingredient in it was fear, with a considerable deal of wonder and astonishment. It was in vain to think of flying; the swiftest horse, or fastest sailing ship, could be of no use to carry us out of this danger, and the full persuasion of this riveted me as if to the spot, where I stood, and let the camels gain on me so much in my state of lameness, that it was with some difficulty I could overtake them.

"The whole of our company were much disheartened, (except Idris,) and imagined that they were advancing into whirlwinds of moving sand, from which they should never be able to extricate themselves; but before four o'clock in the afternoon, these phantoms of the plain had all of them fallen to the ground, and disappeared. In the evening we came to Waadi Dimokea, where we passed the night, much disheartened, and our fear more increased, when we found, upon wakening in the morning, that one side was perfectly buried in the sand that the wind had blown above us in the night. The sun shining through the pillars, which were thicker, and contained more sand apparently than any of the preceding days, seemed to give those nearest us an appearance as if spotted with stars of gold. I do not think at any time they seemed to be nearer than two miles. The most remarkable circumstance was, that the sand seemed to keep in that vast circular space surrounded by the Nile on our left, in going round by Chaigie towards Dongola, and seldom was observed much to the eastward of a meridian passing along the Nile through the Magiran, before it takes that turn; whereas the simoom was always on the opposite side of our course, coming upon us from the southeast. The same appearance of moving pillars of sand presented themselves to us this day in form and disposition like those we had seen at Waadi Halboub, only they seemed to be more in number, and less in size. They came several times in a direction close upon us; that is, I believe, within less than two miles. They began, immediately after sunrise, like a thick wood, and almost darkened the sun: his rays shining through them for near an hour, gave them an appearance of pillars of fire."

If my conjecture be admissible, we now see a magnificence in this imagery, not apparent before: we see how Job's dignity might be exalted in the air; might rise to great grandeur, importance, and even terror, in the sight of beholders; might ride upon the wind, which bears it about, causing it to advance, or to recede; and, after all, the wind diminishing, might disperse, dissipate, melt, scatter this pillar of sand, into the undistinguished level of the desert. This comparison seems to be precisely adapted to the mind of an Arab, who must have seen, or have been informed of similar phenomena in the countries around him.—TAYLOR IN CALMET.

Ver. 23. For I know *that* thou wilt bring me *to* death, and *to* the house appointed for all living.

Those expressions in which the grave is described as *the house appointed for all living;* the *long home* of man; and *the everlasting habitation;* are capable of much illustration from antiquity. Montfaucon says, "We observed in the fifth volume of our Antiquity a tomb styled *quietorium*, a resting-place. *Quiescere*, to rest, is often said of the dead in epitaphs. Thus we find in an ancient writer, a man speaking of his master, who had been long dead and buried, *cujus ossa bene quiescant;* may his bones rest in peace. We have an instance of the like kind in an inscription in Gruter, (p. 696,) and in another, (p. 594,) *fecit sibi requietorium*, he made himself a resting-place. This resting-place is called frequently, too, an *eternal house*. In his lifetime he built himself an eternal house, says one epitaph. He made himself an eternal house with his patrimony, says another. He thought it better (says another) to build himself an eternal house, than to desire his heirs to do it. They thought it a misfortune when the bones and ashes of the dead were removed from their place, as imagining the dead suffered something by the removal of their bones. This notion occasioned all those precautions used for the safety of their tombs, and the curses they laid on those who removed them."—BURDER.

Ver. 25. Did not I weep for him that was in trouble? was *not* my soul grieved for the poor?

Hebrew, "Should I not then weep for the ruthless day?" The meaning of the preceding verse having been generally misunderstood, that of the present, and, indeed, of the greater part of the remainder of the chapter, which follows concatenately, has been misunderstood also. The exquisite pathos of this interrogative must wind itself into the heart of every reader. The expression, "for the ruthless day," is peculiarly forcible in the original, לקשה יום, "for the stern, rigid, immoveable, pitiless, or inexorable day." In the latter clause of this verse, we may understand the Hebrew to signify, "for the rock," not "for the poor," as given by all the translators. The term indeed (אביון) admits of both these senses; but the latter is obviously the true sense in the present place; and for want of attending to this circumstance, the meaning of the passage has been utterly lost: "Should not my soul pine for the marble tomb, or sepulchral rock," in which it was usual to deposite the bodies of all those of higher rank and condition in life; "for the ROCK OR STONY RECESS of darkness and death-shade," as mentioned in ch. xxviii. 3, in which the same term is used, and rendered by every one in the sense now offered.—GOOD.

Ver. 27. My bowels boiled, and rested not; the days of affliction prevented me.

People in great distress often say, "My belly, my belly is on fire." "Who will take away this fire?" In cursing each other, "Wretch! thou shalt soon have a fire in thy belly." "Now they are beginning to *errikuther*," i. e. burn. "Ashes! ashes! thou art all ashes!"—ROBERTS.

Ver. 29. I am a brother to dragons, and a companion to owls.

See on Mic. 1. 8.

Dr. Boothroyd prefers, "A brother am I to sea-monsters." Dr. Harris says, the original is variously rendered; dragons, serpents, sea-monsters, and whales. The Tamul tranlation has it, "I am a brother to the *malli-pāmbu*," i. e. the rock snake, or *boa constrictor;* and wherever the term dragon occurs, (in that translation,) it is rendered in the same way. Some of these serpents are of immense size, and possess great muscular power. If they once get folded round the body of an animal, it is impossible for it to escape. A gentleman of my acquaintance, when on a shooting excursion, heard a sudden scream; he ran to the spot, and saw a beautiful deer in the embrace of one of these serpents: he took his rifle, and put a ball through its head; its folds instantly became loose, and the deer was set at liberty, but died soon after. He brought the reptile home, and it measured eighteen feet. I know not what induced the translators thus to render it by the name of that monster, except they have taken the idea from the prophets Micah and Jeremiah: "I will make a wailing like the dragons," and, "they snuffed up wind like dragons;" as the *malli-pāmbu* is said to make a dreadful wailing in the night, and when in want of prey, to inhale the wind for food. The sacred writers also describe it as loving to dwell in desert places, which is another feature of its character.—ROBERTS.

When the ancient Hebrews observed the dragons erect, and with expanded jaws fetching a deep inspiration, they interpreted the circumstance as if these animals, with their eyes lifted up to heaven, complained to their Maker of their miserable condition, that, hated by all creatures, and confined to the burning and steril deserts, they dragged out a tedious and miserable existence. It was perhaps to some idea of this kind that Job referred, when, bemoaning the hardness of his lot, he complained: "I am a brother to dragons, and a companion of owls." He was unable to associate with mankind; cut off from the comforts of life, and doomed to wear out the rest of his days in poverty and wretchedness. The prophet Micah has the same allusion, in the day of his adversity, to the habits of that reptile: "I will make a wailing like the dragons, and mourning as the owls." He may refer also to its hissing, which Ælian says is so loud that it alarms and terrifies every creature within hearing.—PAXTON.

Ver. 31. My harp also is *turned* to mourning, and my organ into the voice of them that weep.

The people of the East are very fond of the *yāl*, or guitar, also of the *kinaru*, or harp. When a person is in trouble, his instrument is also considered to be in sorrow. Many stories are told of the fascinating powers of the ancient musicians. "There was once a man who neglected all his affairs for the sake of his instrument: at which his wife became much dissatisfied, and asked him, in a taunting way, 'Will you ever gain a tusked elephant and a kingdom by your harp?' He was displeased with her, and said, 'I will.' He then went to the king of Kandy, and on his harp asked his majesty for a tusked elephant and a kingdom. The king was so delighted, that he gave him the elephant and the province of Jaffna. The musician then returned, and founded the town of *Yāl-Pānam*," i. e. the harp and the songster; or, as some render it, the harp-town, which we call Jaffna.—ROBERTS.

CHAPTER XXXI.

Ver. 1. I made a covenant with mine eyes; why then should I think upon a maid?

Has a man a strong desire to go on a pilgrimage to a distant temple, and should his friends remonstrate with him, he will say, "I have made a *udam-puddiki*," (i. e. a covenant with my eyes;) "I must go." Does a father reprove his son for improper conduct, he replies, "What can I do? She has made a covenant with my eyes." "My friend, let us have your opinion on this subject."—"I will not." "Why?"—"Because I have made a covenant with my mouth."—ROBERTS.

In Barbary, when the ladies appear in public, they always fold themselves up so closely in their hykes, that even without their veils one can discover very little of their faces. But in the summer months, when they retire to their country-seats, they walk abroad with less caution; though even then, on the approach of a stranger, they always drop their veils, as Rebecca did on the approach of Isaac. But although they are so closely wrapped up, that those who look at them cannot even see their hands, still less their face, yet it is reckoned indecent in a man to fix his eyes upon them; he must let them pass without seeming at all to observe them. In allusion to this rigorous custom, Job says, "I made a covenant with mine eyes; why then should I think upon a maid?" When a lady of distinction, says Hanway, travels on horseback, she is not only veiled, but has generally a servant, who runs or rides before her, to clear the way; and on such occasions, the men, even in the market-places, always turn their backs till the women are passed, it being thought the highest ill manners to look at them.—PAXTON.

Ver. 17. Or have eaten my morsel myself alone, and the fatherless hath not eaten thereof.

It is a very customary, and a very desirable thing in the East, to eat under the shade of trees; and this situation the inhabitants seem to prefer, to taking their repasts in their tents or dwellings: so De la Roque tells us, (p. 203,) "We did not arrive at the foot of the mountain till after sunset, and it was almost night when we entered the plain; but as it was full of villages, mostly inhabited by Maronites, we entered into the first we came to, to pass the night there. It was the priest of the place who wished to receive us; he gave us a supper under the trees, before his little dwelling. As we were at table, there came by a stranger, wearing a white turban, who, after having saluted the company, sat himself down to the table, without ceremony; ate with us during some time, and then went away, repeating several times the name of God. They told us it was some traveller, who, no doubt, stood in need of refreshment, and who had profited by the opportunity, according to the custom of the East, which is to exercise hospitality at all times, and towards all persons."

The reader will be pleased to see the ancient hospitality of the East still maintained, and even a stranger profiting by an opportunity of supplying his wants. It reminds us of the guests of Abraham, (Gen. chap. xviii.,) of the conduct of Job, (chap. xxxi. 17,) and especially, perhaps, of that frankness with which the apostles of Christ were to enter into a man's house after a salutation, and there to continue "eating and drinking such things as were set before them," Luke x. 7. Such behaviour would be considered as extremely intrusive, and indeed insupportable, among ourselves; but the maxims of the East would qualify that, as they do many other customs, by local proprieties, on which we are incompetent to determine.—TAYLOR IN CALMET.

Ver. 22. *Then* let mine arm fall from my shoulder-blade, and mine arm be broken from the bone.

It is said, "If I have done as you say, may these legs be broken." "Yes, let these eyes be blind, if I have seen the thing you mention." "May this body wither and faint, if I am guilty of that crime." "If I uttered that expression, then let the worms eat out this tongue."—ROBERTS.

Ver. 26. If I beheld the sun when it shined, or the moon walking *in* brightness, 27. And my heart hath been secretly enticed, or my mouth hath kissed my hand: 28. This also *were* an iniquity *to be punished by* the judge: for I should have denied the God *that is* above.

To kiss the hand and place it on the head, is a token of respect less revolting to our minds, than some of those which have been mentioned. An Oriental pays his respects to a person of superior station, by kissing his hand, and putting it to his forehead; but if the superior be of a condescending temper, he will snatch away his hand, as soon as the other has touched it; then the inferior puts his own fingers to his lips, and afterward to his forehead. It seems, according to Pitts, to be a common practice among the Mohammedans, that when they cannot kiss the hand of a superior, they kiss their own, and put it to their forehead; thus also they venerate an unseen being, whom they cannot touch. But the custom existed long before the age of Mohammed; for in the same way the ancient idolaters worshipped their distant or unseen deities. "If," said Job, "I beheld the sun when it shined, or the moon walking in brightness, and my heart hath been secretly enticed, and my mouth hath kissed my hand, this also were an iniquity to be punished by the judge; for I should have denied the God that is above." Had the afflicted man done this, in the case to which he refers, it would have been an idolatrous action, although it is exactly agreeable to the civil expressions of respect which obtained in his country, and over all the East.—PAXTON.

Ver. 32. The stranger did not lodge in the street; *but* I opened my doors to the traveller.

No people can be more kind and hospitable to travellers of their own caste, than those of the East; and even men of the lower grades have always places to go to. See the stranger enter the premises; he looks at the master and says, *parathease*, i. e. a pilgrim, and he is allowed to take up his abode for the night. For his entertainment, he has to repeat the *puthenam*, news of his country and journey, or any legend of olden time.—ROBERTS.

Ver. 35. Oh that one would hear me! behold, my desire *is that* the Almighty would answer me, and *that* mine adversary had written a book: 36. Surely I would take it upon my shoulder, *and* bind it *as* a crown to me.

This refers to accusations against the innocent Job. A man charged of a crime which he has not committed, says, "If I am guilty, I will carry it on my head." "I am sure you have done this deed."—"I?" "Yes."—"Then will I wear it on my head." "That fellow wears his crimes on his head," *i. e.* he is not ashamed of them. The head is reckoned superior to all other parts of the body.—ROBERTS.

The business of book-making, it is to be presumed, had made but little progress in the days of Job, and it is not easy to see how such a performance, on the part of Job's adversary, as the writing a book, could have afforded any peculiar gratification to the afflicted man's feelings. In modern times, when such an enterprise is of all others the most hazardous, it might perhaps be a very appropriate expression of ill-will, to wish that an adversary had engaged in a publishing speculation. But in the case of Job and his maligners, we must seek for a different explication; for even had the trade of authorship been as common and as perilous in those days as it now is, we cannot but consider Job too good a man to have given vent to so bad a wish. From the context, we learn that the pious sufferer was aggrieved by the *vagueness* of the charges preferred against him by his harsh-judging comforters. They dealt in loose generalities, affording him no opportunity to vindicate himself by answering to a specific accusation. In the words cited, he utters the earnest wish that a definite form were given to the injurious imputations of his false friends. He would fain be summoned to a formal trial; he would have *the charges booked* against him, that he might know what were the aspersions which were to be wiped from his character. Such an accusation, thus definitely written, he would bear about publicly and conspicuously, that he might publicly and conspicuously confute it; he would bear it as an ornament, convinced it would, in the end, by his triumphant disproval of it, redound to the still higher honour of his innocence. That the Heb. *sepher*, *book*, may without violence be thus interpreted, is clear from Deut. xxiv. 1: "Let him write a *bill of divorcement*, (sepher,) and give it in her hand, and send her out of his house." In the present connexion it is tantamount to a *bill of endictment*.—BUSH.

From the following extract it appears what is the customary kind of homage which, in the East, is paid not only to sovereignty, but to communications of the sovereign's will, whether by word or letter: "When the mogul, by letters, sends his commands to any of his governors, these papers are entertained with as much respect as if himself were present; for the governor, having intelligence that such letters are coming near him, himself, with other inferior officers, rides forth to meet the *patamar*, or messenger, that brings them, and as soon as he sees those letters, he alights from his horse, falls down on the earth, and takes them from the messenger, *and lays them on his head, whereon he binds them fast:* then retiring to his place of public meeting, he reads and answers them." (Sir Thomas Roe.)—BURDER.

When Soliman ascended the throne, "the letter which was to be presented to the new monarch was delivered to the general of the slaves, contained in a purse of cloth of gold, drawn together with strings of twisted gold and silk, with tassels of the same. The general threw himself at his majesty's feet, bowing to the very ground; then rising upon his knees, he drew out of the bosom of his garment the bag containing the letter which the assembly had sent to the new monarch. Presently he opened the bag, took out the letter, kissed it, laid it to his forehead, presented it to his majesty, and then rose up." To such a custom Job evidently refers in these words: "Oh that mine adversary had written a book: surely I would take it upon my shoulder, and bind it as a crown to me," or, on my head.—PAXTON.

Ver. 38. If my land cry against me, or that the furrows likewise thereof complain.

Does a man through idleness or meanness neglect to cultivate, or water, or manure his fields and gardens, those who pass that way say, "Ah! these fields have good reason to complain against the owner." "Sir, if you defraud these fields, will they not defraud you?" "The fellow who robs his own lands, will he not rob you?" "These fields are in great sorrow, through the neglect of their owner."—ROBERTS.

Ver. 39. If I have eaten the fruits thereof without money, or have caused the owners thereof to lose their life.

Was not Job the OWNER of the land? Does he not say in the preceding verse MY land? How then could he have caused the owners to lose their life? Dr. Boothroyd has it, "or have grieved the soul of its MANAGERS." Coverdale has it, "grieved any of the PLOUGHMEN." The Tamul has the same idea: "If I have eaten the fruits thereof without paying for the labour, or have afflicted the soul of the *cultivators*." Great landowners in the East do not generally cultivate their own fields: they employ men, who find all the labour, and have a certain part of the produce for their remuneration. The cultivator, if defrauded, will say, "The furrows I have made bear witness against him; they complain." Job therefore means, if the fields could complain for want of proper culture, or if he had afflicted the tiller, or eaten the produce without rewarding him for his toils, then "let thistles grow instead of wheat and cockle instead of barley."—ROBERTS.

CHAPTER XXXII.

Ver. 5. When Elihu saw that *there was* no answer in the mouth of *these* three men, then his wrath was kindled.

When men are completely confounded, when they have not a word to say in reply, it is said, "in their *vayila*, i. e. mouth, there is no answer."—ROBERTS.

Ver. 21. Let me not, I pray you, accept any man's person; neither let me give flattering titles unto man.

The Hebrew word here used signifies to surname, or more properly to call a person by a name which does not strictly belong to him, and that generally in compliment or flattery. Mr. Scott on this passage informs us from Pococke, that "the Arabs make court to their superiors by carefully avoiding to address them by their proper names, instead of which, they salute them with some title or epithet expressive of respect."—BURDER.

CHAPTER XXXIII.

Ver. 6. Behold, I *am* according to thy wish in God's stead; I also am formed out of the clay.

"The body and the herb, which come from the clay, will also return to it." "The body must return to the dust, why then trouble yourself? Will it exist for an immeasurable period?"—ROBERTS.

Ver. 16. Then he openeth the ears of men, and sealeth their instruction.

It is usual to say, "I will open that fellow's ears. I will take away the covering." "Ah! will you not open your ears?"—ROBERTS.

Ver. 24. Then he is gracious unto him, and saith, Deliver him from going down to the pit; I have found a ransom.

A species of capital punishment which serves to illustrate the sacred text, is the pit into which the condemned persons were precipitated. The Athenians, and particularly the tribe Hippothoontis, frequently condemned offenders to the pit. It was a dark, noisome hole, and had sharp spikes at the top, that no criminal might escape; and others at the bottom, to pierce and torment those unhappy persons that were cast in. Similar to this place was the Lacedemonian Καιαδας, into which Aristomenes, the Messenian, being cast, made his escape in a very surprising manner. This mode of punishment is of great antiquity; for the speakers in the book of Job make several allusions to it. Thus, in the speech of Elihu: "He keepeth back his soul from the pit, and his life from perishing by the sword."—"Then is he gracious unto him, and saith, Deliver him from going down to the pit; I have found a ransom."—"He will deliver his soul from going down into the pit, and his life shall see the light." The allusions in the book of Psalms are numerous and interesting; thus the Psalmist prays, "Be not silent to me; lest if thou be silent to me, I become like them that go down into the pit."—"Let them be cast into deep pits, that they rise not up again." The following allusion occurs in the prophecies of Isaiah: "The captive exile hasteneth, that he may be loosed, and that he should not die in the pit, nor that his bread should fail."—PAXTON.

CHAPTER XXXIV.

Ver. 7. What man *is* like Job, *who* drinketh up scorning like water?

Of a man who does not care for contempt or hatred, it is said, "He drinks up their hatred like water." When a man is every way superior to his enemies, "Ah! he drinks them up like water." "He is a man of wonderful talents, for he drinks up science as water." Thus, Elihu wished to show that Job had hardened himself, and was insensible to scorn, for he had swallowed it as water.—ROBERTS.

CHAPTER XXXVI.

Ver. 3. I will fetch my knowledge from afar, and will ascribe righteousness to my Maker.

There is something in our nature which places superior importance on any thing which comes from afar. When a man has to contend with a person who is very learned, should a friend express a doubt as to the result, or advise him to take great care, he will say, "Fear not, *veggutooratila*, from very far I will fetch my arguments." "The arguments which are afar off, shall now be brought near." "Well, sir, since you press me, I will fetch my knowledge from afar."—ROBERTS.

CHAPTER XXXVII.

Ver. 6. For he saith to the snow, Be thou *on* the earth; likewise to the small rain, and to the great rain of his strength.

In the East Indies the commencement and the breaking of the monsoons are generally very severe; the rain descends in the most astonishing torrents. In a few hours the inhabitants find themselves in a liquid plain. The high and the low grounds are equally covered, and exhibit the appearance of an immense lake, and surrounded by thick darkness, which prevents them from distinguishing a single object, except such as the vivid glare of lightning displays in horrible forms. In the winter months the mountain floods swell the small rivers of India in a wonderful manner. Within a few hours they often rise twenty or thirty feet above their usual height, and run with astonishing rapidity; and the larger rivers, before gentle and pellucid, are then furious and destructive, sweeping away whole villages, with their inhabitants and cattle, while tigers and other furious animals from the wilds join the general wreck, and unite their horrid voices with the cries of old men and helpless women, and the shrieks of their expiring children, in its passage to the ocean. It is in such a scene that the beauty of Elihu's speech to Job, in which he mentions "the great rain of his strength," are properly understood. Even in the milder climate of Judea, the rains pour down three or four days and nights together, as vehemently as if they would drown the country, sweeping away in their furious course the produce of the field, and the soil on which it grew, the flocks and herds, and human dwellings, with their hapless inmates, in one promiscuous ruin. Far different are the feelings awakened in the mind, by the sight of a majestic, pure, and quiet river, on whose verdant pastures the flocks repose, or drink, without alarm or danger, of its flowing waters. So full of majesty and gentleness, neither alarming the fears, endangering the safety, nor encouraging the carelessness of genuine Christians, are the consolations of true religion. So the Psalmist felt, when he selected the loveliest image in the natural world to convey an idea of the rich and ample provision which the divine bounty has made for man: "He maketh me to lie down in green pastures; he leadeth me beside the still waters."—PAXTON.

Ver. 7. He sealeth up the hand of every man, that all men may know his work.

Has a man something in his hand which he does not wish to show to another, he says, "My hand is sealed." Of a gentleman who is very benevolent, it is said, "His hand is sealed for charity only." "Please, sir, give me this."—"What! is my hand sealed to give to all?" "What secret was that which Tamban told you last evening?"—"I cannot answer; my mouth is sealed." "That man never forgets an injury."—"No, no, he seals it in his mind." A husband who has full confidence in his wife, says, "I have sealed her." Canticles iv. 12. To seal a person, therefore, is to secure him, and prevent others from injuring him.—ROBERTS.

CHAPTER XXXVIII.

Ver. 3. Gird up now thy loins like a man; for I will demand of thee, and answer thou me.

"Well, Tamby, you have a difficult task before you: gird up your loins." "Come, help me to gird this *sāli*, i. e. mantle, or shawl, round my loins; I have a long way to run." "Poor fellow! he soon gave it up; his loins were not well girded."—ROBERTS.

Ver. 14. It is turned as clay *to* the seal; and they stand as a garment.

The birds pillage the granary of Joseph extremely, where the corn of Egypt is deposited that is paid as a tax to the grand seignior, for it is quite uncovered at the top, there being little or no rain in that country; its doors however are kept carefully sealed, but its inspectors do not make use of wax upon this occasion, but put their seal upon a handful of clay, with which they cover the lock of the door. This serves instead of wax; and it is visible, things of the greatest value might be safely sealed up in the same manner. Had Junius known this circumstance, or had he at least reflected on it, he would not perhaps have explained Job xxxviii. 14, *It is turned as clay to the seal*, of the potters adorning clay with various paintings, or various embossings; especially had he considered, that the productions of the wheel of the potter, in the age and the country of Job, were, in all probability, very clumsy, unadorned things, since even still in Egypt, the ancient source of arts, the ewer, which is made, according to Norden, very clumsy, is one of the best pieces of earthenware that they have there, all the art of the potter, in that country, consisting in an ability to make some vile pots or dishes, without varnish.—HARMER.

Ver. 16. Hast thou entered into the springs of the sea? or hast thou walked in the search of the depth?

To a vain boasting fellow it is said, "Yes, yes; the

sea is only knee-deep to thee." "It is all true; thou hast measured the sea."—ROBERTS.

Ver. 34. Canst thou lift up thy voice to the clouds,
that abundance of waters may cover thee?
35. Canst thou send lightnings, that they may
go, and say unto thee, Here we *are?*

This probably refers to thunder, and its effects in producing rain. It is said, "Why, fellow, are you making such a noise? Are you going to shake the clouds? Is it rain you are going to produce?" "What is all this noise about? Is it rain you want?" "Cease, cease your roaring; the rain will not come." "Listen to that elephant, rain is coming."—ROBERTS.

Ver. 39. Wilt thou hunt the prey for the lions? or fill the appetite of the young lions?

To a man who is boasting of the speed of his foot, or his prowess, it is said, "Yes, there is no doubt thou wilt hunt the prey for the tiger." When a person does a favour for a cruel man, it is asked, "What! give food to the tiger?" "O yes; give milk to the serpent." "Here comes the sportsman; he has been hunting prey for the tiger."—ROBERTS.

CHAPTER XXXIX.

Ver. 1. Knowest thou the time when the wild goats of the rock bring forth? *or* canst thou mark when the hinds do calve?

It is well known that the hind goes with young eight months, and brings forth her fawn in the beginning of autumn. Why then does Jehovah address these interrogations to Job: "Knowest thou the time when the wild goats of the rock bring forth? Or canst thou mark when the hinds do calve? Canst thou number the months that they fulfil? Or knowest thou the time when they bring forth?" Could Job be ignorant of circumstances which were obvious to all the shepherds in the East, who had numerous opportunities of observing the habits and manners of these creatures? It is obvious that Jehovah could not refer to the mere speculative knowledge of these facts, but to that which is proper to himself, by which he not only knows, but also directs and governs all things. This is confirmed by the use of the verb (שמר) *shamar*, which signifies to observe, to keep, or to guard: Knowest thou the time when the wild goats bring forth, the parturition of the hinds dost thou guard? Without the protecting care of God, who upholds all his works by the word of his power, the whole race of these timid creatures would soon be destroyed by the violence of wild beasts, or the arts of the hunter. It is with great propriety, says one of the ancients, that Jehovah demands, "The birth of the hinds dost thou guard?" for, since this animal is always in flight, and with fear and terror always leaping and skipping about, she could never bring her young to maturity without such a special protection. The providence of God, therefore, is equally conspicuous in the preservation of the mother and the fawn; both are the objects of his compassion and tender care; and consequently, that afflicted man had no reason to charge his Maker with unkindness, who condescends to watch over the goats and the hinds.—PAXTON.

Ver. 3. They bow themselves, they bring forth
their young ones, they cast out their sorrows.
4. Their young ones are in good liking, they
grow up with corn; they go forth, and return
not unto them.

The hind has no sooner brought forth her fawn, than the pain she suffered is forgotten: "They bow themselves" to bring forth their young ones, "they cast out their sorrows." These words must forcibly remind the reader of the maternal pains and joys of a higher order of beings: "A woman, when she is in travail, hath sorrow, because her hour is come: but as soon as she is delivered of the child, she remembereth no more the anguish, for joy that a man is born into the world." It is added, "Their young ones are in good liking, they grow up with corn; they go forth, and return not unto them." Though they are brought forth in sorrow, and have no human owner to provide for their wants, and to guard them from danger, yet, after being suckled a while, they become vigorous and active, and shift for themselves in the open fields. They grow up with corn, says our translation; but the fawn is not commonly fed in the cornfield, because it lives in the deserts, and frequents those places which are far remote from the cultivated field. Besides, in Arabia, where Job flourished, the harvest is reaped in the months of March and April, long before the hinds bring forth their young. The fawn, therefore, does not thrive with corn, but with the few shrubs and hardy plants which grow in the wilderness or open country. But the inspired writer has committed no mistake; the original phrase is capable of another translation, which perfectly corresponds with the condition of that animal, in those parts of the world. In Chaldee, the word (בבר) *babar*, or (בברא) *babara*, is evidently the same as the Hebrew (בהוץ) *bahouts*. Thus in Laban's address to Jacob, when he arrived in Padanaram, "Why standest thou without," the Hebrew word is (בהוץ) *bahouts;* and in Jonathan and Onkelos it is (בברא) *babara*. The same remark applies to a text in the book of Exodus: "If he rise again and walk abroad upon his staff;" in Hebrew (בהוץ) *bahouts;* in Chaldee, (בברא) *babara*. Hence, the phrase may be translated, They grow up without, or in the open field. Many other instances might be specified, but these are sufficient to establish the justice of the remark. Even the Hebrew phrase itself is translated by Schultens, "in the open field," which is indisputably the sense of the passage under consideration. Thus, when the fawn is calved, it grows up in the desert, under the watchful providence of God; it soon forsakes the spot where it was brought forth, and suckled by the dam, and returns no more.—PAXTON.

Ver. 5. Who hath sent out the wild ass free? or
who hath loosed the bands of the wild ass?
6. Whose house I have made the wilderness,
and the barren land his dwellings. 7. He
scorneth the multitude of the city, neither regardeth he the crying of the driver. 8. The
range of the mountains *is* his pasture, and he
searcheth after every green thing.

This animal was called *ονος αγριος*, among the Greeks, and *onager* by the Romans. Some natural historians consider it as a different species from the tame and domestic ass; but others, among whom is the celebrated Buffon, affirm, that it differs from its unhappy relation only in those particulars which are the proper effects of independence and liberty. Although more elegantly shaped, the general form of its body is the same; but in temper and manners it is extremely dissimilar. Intended to fill a higher place in the kingdom of nature, than its abject and enslaved brother, it exhibits endowments which, in all ages, have commanded the admiration of every observer. Animated by an unconquerable love of liberty, this high-spirited animal submits his neck with great reluctance to the yoke of man; extremely jealous of the least restraint, he shuns the inhabited country, and steadily rejects all the delicacies it has to offer. His chosen haunt is the solitary and inhospitable desert, where he roves at his ease, exulting in the possession of unrestrained freedom. These are not accidental nor acquired traits in his character; but instincts, implanted by the hand of his Maker, that are neither to be extinguished nor modified by length of time, nor change of circumstances. To this wild and untameable temper, Jehovah himself condescends to direct the attention of Job, when he answered him out of the whirlwind, and said: "Who hath sent out the wild ass free? or who hath loosed the bands of the wild ass? whose house I have made the wilderness, and the barren land his dwellings. He scorneth the multitude of the city, neither regardeth he the crying of the driver. The range of the mountains is his pasture, and he searcheth after every green thing."

The proper name of this animal in the Hebrew language, is (פרא) *para*, a term which, according to some writers, is expressive of its extreme suspicion. It is employed by Moses to denote the wild and untractable disposition of Ishmael and his descendants; and by Zophar, to characterize a vain, self-righteous, and obstinate person. In accordance with this idea, the noun furnishes a verb in the Hiphil form, which signifies to act as wildly as the onager. Others derive the noun from a Chaldee verb, which signifies to run with great swiftness; and every writer, ancient and modern, who has treated of this animal, has attested the wonderful celerity with which it flies over the desert. According to Leo Africanus, the wild ass yields only to the horses of Barbary; and Xenophon avers, in his Anabasis, that it outruns the fleetest horses. It has feet like the whirlwind, says Oppian; Ælian asserts, that it seems as if it were carried forward by wings like a bird.

These testimonies are confirmed by Professor Gmelin, who saw numerous troops of them in the deserts of Great Tartary, and says, The onagers are animals adapted to running, and of such swiftness, that the best horses cannot equal them. Relying on its extraordinary powers, it frequently mocks the pursuit of the hunter; and in the striking description of its Creator, "Scorneth the multitude of the city," that invade its retreats, and seek its destruction. It laughs (as the original term properly signifies) at their numbers and their speed, and seems to take a malicious pleasure in disappointing their hopes. Xenophon states, that the onagers in Mesopotamia, when pursued on horseback, will stop suddenly in the midst of their career, till the hunters approach, and then dart away with surprising velocity; and again stop, as if inviting them to make another effort to overtake them, but immediately dart away again like an arrow shot from a bow: indeed, it would be impossible for men to take them, without the assistance of art. "We gave chase," says Mr. Morier, "to two wild asses, but which had so much the speed of our horses, that when they had got at some distance, they stood still and looked behind at us, snorting with their noses in the air, as if in contempt of our endeavours to catch them." The hunters, however, often lie in wait for them at the ponds of brackish water, to which they resort to drink; or take them alive by means of concealed pits, half filled with plants and branches of trees, to lessen the creature's fall. At other times the chase is continued by relays of fresh horses, which the hunters mount as the others are exhausted, till the strength of the animal is so completely worn out, that it can be easily overtaken.

The wild ass, unsocial in his temper, and impatient of restraint, frequents the solitary wilderness, and the vast inhospitable desert, the salt marsh, and the mountain range. This is the scene adapted to his nature and instincts, and his proper domain allotted to him by the author of his being. We are not left to infer this fact from the manners and habits of the animal; Jehovah himself has attested it in these terms: "Whose house I have made the wilderness, and the barren land his dwellings." He who made the wild ass free, and loosed his hands, provides a habitation for him in the desert, where the voice of man is not heard, nor a human dwelling meets his eye. But every desert is not equally to his liking; it is the barren or salt land in which he delights. So grateful is salt to his taste, that he uniformly prefers brackish water to fresh, and selects for his food those plants that are impregnated with saline particles, or that have bitter juices. He therefore retires from the cultivated or fertile regions, not merely to be free from the domination of man, but to enjoy the pasture which is agreeable to his instincts. "The multitude," or the abundance of the city, "he despises for the salt or bitter leaf on the sandy waste."

Into such a state of desolation and sterility was the inheritance of God's ancient people reduced, by the arms of Nebuchadnezzar: "Upon the land of my people shall come up thorns and briers, yea, upon all the houses of joy in the joyous city: because the palaces shall be forsaken, the multitude of the city shall be left, the forts and towers shall be dens for ever, a joy of wild asses, a pasture of flocks." A more affecting picture can scarcely be conceived; the depopulated fields and ruined cities of a country once flowing with milk and honey, were to become the favourite haunts of those shy creatures "for ever," or during the long period of seventy years. "Until the spirit" should be poured upon them from on high, from the beginning to the end of the captivity, a tedious and irksome period to the unhappy captives, were the wild asses to stray through their barren fields, and repose in their deserted houses, undisturbed by the presence of man. But the pride and barbarity of their oppressor were soon visited with corresponding punishment. He was deprived of reason, which he had so greatly abused, and by the violence of his disorder, "driven from the sons of men, and his heart was made like the beasts; and his dwelling was with the wild asses," in the salt land and frightful desert. He seems to have been divested of every thing human but the form; irrational and sensual, he was guided solely by his animal propensities. Nor was he longer able to distinguish what was becoming or agreeable, even to the animal nature of man; every desire and appetite was become so brutish, that he felt no wish to associate with beings of his own kind, but lived with the beasts, and fed in their pasture.

Some respectable writers have considered the *onager* as a solitary creature, refusing to associate even with those of his own species, because he shuns the presence of man, and frequents the most frightful solitudes. But this hasty opinion is completely refuted by the testimony of modern travellers, the nomadic hordes of Tartary, and the trading companies of Bukharia. From their accounts we learn that the wild asses are still very numerous in the deserts of Great Tartary, and come annually in great herds, which spread themselves in the mountainous deserts to the north and east of Lake Aral. Here they pass the summer, and assemble in the autumn by hundreds, and even by thousands, in order to return in company to their former retreats in the mountains of Northern Asia. The gregarious character of the wild ass is not in reality contradicted by the prophet in these words: "For they are gone up to Assyria, a wild ass alone by himself: Ephraim hath hired lovers." In this passage he describes the perverse and untractable dispositions of Ephraim, and the certain destruction to which their obstinacy exposed them. A wild ass alone, they were by their foolish conduct ready to become a prey to the destroyer. But it is rather the king of Assyria, than the ten tribes, whom he compares to that animal. Instead of trusting in the Lord their God, they courted the favour, and solicited the protection of that ambitious and artful monarch, who, like "a wild ass alone," consulted only his own selfish inclinations, and aimed at his own aggrandizement. This ill-advised measure, from which they promised themselves so much advantage, he declares, would certainly hasten this catastrophe, which they sought to avoid. They should find, when too late, that they had been the dupes of his deceitful policy, and the victims of his unprincipled ambition. The wild ass, like almost every creature that inhabits the barren wilderness, is reduced to subsist on coarse and scanty fare. The sweets of unbounded liberty are counterbalanced by the unremitting labour which is necessary to procure him a precarious subsistence. In those salt and dreary wastes, which providence has allotted for his residence, very few plants are to be found, and those, from the heat of the climate and the nature of the soil, are stinted in their growth, and bitter to the taste: "They see not when good cometh;" for they grow in the parched places in the wilderness, "in a salt land, and not inhabited." In such inhospitable regions, the wild ass is compelled to traverse a great extent of country, to scour the plains, and range over the mountains, in order to find here and there a few blades of coarse, withered grass, and browse the tops of the few stunted shrubs which languish in those sandy wilds. Such are the allusions involved in these words: "The range of the mountains is his pasture, and he searcheth after every green thing."

Every natural historian has recorded the extreme wildness of this animal. He is so jealous of his liberty, that on the slightest alarm, or the first appearance of danger, he flies with amazing swiftness into the desert. His senses are so acute, that it is impossible to approach him in the open country. But in spite of all his vigilance, the hunter often encloses him in his toils, and leads him away into captivity. Even in this unhappy state, he never submits his neck to the yoke of man without a determined resistance. "Sent out free" by Him that made him, he is tenacious of his independence, and opposes, to the extraordinary methods which his captors are forced to employ, the most savage obstinacy; and for the most part, he baffles all their endeavours to tame him; still he "scorneth the multitude of the city, neither regards he the crying of the driver." On the authority of this text, Chrysostom says, "this animal is strong and untameable; man can never subdue him, whatever efforts he may make for that purpose." But Varro affirms, on the contrary, that "the wild ass is fit for labour; that he is easily tamed; and that when he is once tamed, he never resumes his original wildness." The words of Jehovah certainly give no countenance to the opinion of the Greek father; they only intimate, that it is extremely difficult to subdue the high spirit and stubborn temper of this animal; for the apostle James declares, that "every kind of beast is tamed, and hath been tamed of mankind;" and great numbers of them are actually broken to the yoke in Persia, and some other countries. But it appears from the statement of Professor Gmelin, that the Persians tame the young *onagers;* and the reason probably is, that they seldom or never succeed in rendering a full grown *onager* serviceable to man.

Not more untameable and indocile is the wild ass, in the mind of Zophar, than the human kind, in their present degenerate state: "Vain man would be wise, though man be born like a wild ass's colt." Empty, self-conceited man, still aspires to equal God in wisdom and knowledge; still fondly supposes himself qualified to sit in judgment on the divine proceedings, and to take the exclusive management of his own affairs, although the wild ass's colt is not more rude, indocile, and untractable. Nor is this an acquired habit: he is born a wild ass's colt, and therefore, by nature equally impatient of salutary restraint, equally wilful in consulting his own inclinations. And this defect in his character, no created arm is able to subdue; it yields only to the sanctifying influences of the Holy Spirit, who makes him willing in the day of effectual calling, by a display of almighty power.—PAXTON.

Ver. 13. *Gavest thou* the goodly wings unto the peacocks? or wings and feathers unto the ostrich?

These birds are exceedingly numerous in the East; and it gives a kind of enchantment to a morning scene, to see flocks of them together, spreading their beautiful plumage in the rays of the sun. They proudly stalk along, and then run with great speed, particularly if they get sight of a serpent; and the reptile must wind along in his best style, or he will soon become the prey of the lordly bird. A husband sometimes says to his wife, "Come hither, my beautiful peacock. Had they not their beauty from you?" This bird is sacred to Scandan.—ROBERTS.

Ver. 13. *Gavest thou* the goodly wings unto the peacocks? or wings and feathers unto the ostrich? 14. Which leaveth her eggs in the earth, and warmeth them in the dust, 15. And forgetteth that the foot may crush them, or that the wild beast may break them. 16. She is hardened against her young ones, as though *they were* not hers: her labour is in vain without fear; 17. Because God hath deprived her of wisdom, neither hath he imparted to her understanding. 18. What time she lifteth up herself on high, she scorneth the horse and his rider.

The ostrich is by far the largest among the winged tribes, and seems to be the connecting link between the quadruped and the fowl. She is not to be classed with the former, because she is furnished with a kind of wings, which, if they cannot raise her from the ground, greatly accelerate her flight; not with the latter, for "the feathers which grow out of her small wings, are all unwoven and decomposed, and their beards consist of long hairs detached from one another, and do not form a compact body to strike the air with advantage; which is the principal office for which the feathers of the wing are intended." Those of the tail have also the same structure, and, by consequence, cannot oppose to the air a suitable resistance. They can neither expand nor close, as circumstances require, nor take different inclinations; and what is not a little remarkable, all the feathers which cover the body exhibit the same conformation. The ostrich has not, like the greater part of other birds, feathers of various kinds, some soft and downy, which are next the skin; and others of a more firm and compact consistence, which cover the former; and others still longer and of greater strength, and on which the movements of the animal depend. All her feathers are of one kind, all of them bearded with detached hairs or filaments, without consistence and reciprocal adherence; in one word, they are of no utility in flying, or in directing the flight. Besides the peculiar structure of her wings, she is pressed down to the earth by her enormous size. Buffon calculates the weight of a living ostrich, in middling condition, at no less than sixty-five or eighty pounds; which would require an immense power in the wings and motive muscles of these members, to raise and support in the air so ponderous a mass. Thus by her excessive weight and the loose texture of her feathers, she is condemned, like a quadruped, laboriously to run upon the surface of the earth, without being ever able to mount up into the air. But although incapable of raising herself from the ground, she is admirably fitted for running. The greater part of her body is covered with hair, rather than feathers; her head and her sides have little or no hair; and her legs, which are very thick and muscular, and in which her principal force resides, are in like manner almost naked; her large sinewy and plump feet, which have only two toes, resemble considerably the feet of a camel; her wings, armed with two spikes, like those of a porcupine, are rather a kind of arms than wings, which are given her for defence.

These characteristic features throw great light on a part of the description which Jehovah himself has condescended to give of this animal in the book of Job. It begins with this interrogation: "Gavest thou wings and feathers unto the ostrich?" Dr. Shaw translates it: "The wing of the ostrich is expanded; the very feathers and plumage of the stork." According to Buffon, the ostrich is covered with feathers alternately white and black, and sometimes gray by the mixture of these two colours. They are shortest, says the author, on the lower part of the neck, the rest of which is entirely naked; they become longer on the back and the belly; and are longest at the extremity of the tail and the wings; but he denies that any of them have been found with red, green, blue, or yellow plumes. This assertion, however, is not quite correct; for if credit is due to Dr. Shaw, "when the ostrich is full grown, the neck, particularly of the male, which before was almost naked, is now very beautifully covered with red feathers. The plumage, likewise, upon the shoulders, the back, and some parts of the wings, from being hitherto of a dark grayish colour, becomes now as black as jet, while some of the feathers retain an exquisite whiteness. They are, as described in the thirteenth verse, the very feathers and plumage of the stork; that is, they consist of such black and white feathers as the stork, called from thence πελαργος, is known to have. But the belly, the thighs, and the breast do not partake of this covering, being usually naked; and when touched are of the same warmth as the flesh of the quadrupeds.

The ostrich, though she inhabits the sandy deserts, where she is exposed to few interruptions, is extremely vigilant and shy. She betakes herself to flight on the first alarm, and traverses the waste with so great agility and swiftness, that the Arab is never able to overtake her, even when he is mounted upon his horse of Family. The fact is thus stated by Jehovah: "What time she lifteth up herself on high, she scorneth the horse and his rider." She affords him only an opportunity of admiring at a distance the extraordinary agility and stateliness of her motions, the richness of her plumage, and the great propriety of ascribing to her "an expanded quivering wing." Nothing certainly can be more beautiful and entertaining than such a sight; the wings, by their continual though unwearied vibrations, serving her at once for sails and oars, while her feet, no less assisting in conveying her out of sight, are equally insensible of fatigue. Her surprising swiftness is confirmed by the writer of a voyage to Senegal, who says, "She sets off at a hard gallop; but after being excited a little, she expands her wings, as if to catch the wind, and abandons herself to a speed so great that she seems not to touch the ground." "I am persuaded," continues that writer, "she would leave far behind the swiftest English courser." Buffon also admits that the ostrich runs faster than the horse. These unexceptionable testimonies completely vindicate the assertion of the inspired writer. But as it is on horseback the Arab pursues and takes her, it is necessary to explain how he accomplishes his purpose, and show its consistency with the sacred writings. "When the Arab rouses an ostrich," says Buffon, "he follows her at a distance, without pressing her too hard, but sufficiently to prevent her from taking food, yet not to determine her to escape by a prompt flight." Here the celebrated naturalist fairly admits that she has it in her power to escape if she were sufficiently alarmed. "It is the more easy," continues our author, "to follow her in this manner, because she does not proceed in a straight line, and because she describes almost always in her course a circle more or less extended." The Arabs, then, have it in their power to direct their pursuit in a concentric interior circle, and by consequence straighter; and to follow her always at a just distance, by passing over much less ground than she. When they have thus fatigued and starved her for a day or two, they take their opportunity, rush in upon her at full speed, leading her always as much as possible against the wind, and kill her with their clubs, to prevent her blood from spoiling the beautiful whiteness of her feathers. In this account of Buffon, the highest modern authority in matters of this kind, nothing occurs to contradict the assertion of the inspired writer; while he distinctly admits that she runs faster than the fleetest horses, and could not be taken but by artful management.

She constructs her humble nest in the bare ground, excavating the sand with her feet. It is hollow in the middle, and fortified on all sides by a circular mound of some height, for the purpose of preventing the rain from flowing into the nest and wetting her young. From the most accurate accounts which Dr. Shaw could obtain from his conductors, as well as from Arabs of different places, it appears that the ostrich lays from thirty to fifty eggs. Ælian mentions more than eighty; but Shaw never heard of so great a number. The first egg is deposited in the centre; the rest are placed as conveniently as possible round about it. In this manner, she is said to lay, deposite, or trust "her eggs in the earth, and to warm them in the sand, and forgetteth (as they are not placed like those of some other birds upon trees, or in the clefts of rocks, &c.) that the foot (of the traveller) may crush them, or that the wild beast may break them." She seems in a great measure insensible to the tender feelings which so powerfully operate in the greater part of other animals. This assertion, indeed, Buffon seems inclined to controvert: "As soon," says that writer, "as the young ostriches are hatched, they are in a condition to walk, and even to run and seek their food; so that in the torrid zone, where they find the degree of heat which they require, and the food which is proper to them, they are emancipated at their birth, and abandoned by their mother, of whose care they have no need. But in countries less warm, for example, at the Cape of Good Hope, the mother watches over her young as long as her assistance is necessary, and on all occasions her cares are proportioned to their wants."

This account Buffon takes from Leo Africanus and Kolbè, to whom he refers; in which it is admitted, that the mother abandons her offspring as soon as they are hatched, although it is alleged, not for want of affection, but because her cares are not necessary. But this is to suppose that they are not like other young creatures, all of which require more or less attention from their parents, for some time after their birth; an anomaly which cannot be admitted but on the most convincing evidence. Let us now hear the account of Dr. Shaw, who travelled in the native country of the ostrich, and borrowed his information from the Arabs, who were well acquainted with all her habits and dispositions: "Upon the least distant noise, or trivial occasion, she forsakes her eggs or her young ones, to which, perhaps, she never returns; or, if she does, it may be too late either to restore life to the one, or to preserve the lives of the other." Agreeably to this account, the Arabs meet sometimes with whole nests of these eggs undisturbed; some of which are sweet and good; others are addle and corrupted; others again have their young ones of different growths, according to the time, it may be presumed, they have been forsaken by the dam. They oftener meet a few of the little ones, no bigger than well-grown pullets, half starved, straggling and moaning about, like so many distressed orphans, for their mother. And in this manner, the ostrich may be said, as in verse sixteenth, "to be hardened against her young ones, as though they were not hers; her labour (in hatching and attending them so far) being in vain without fear," or the least concern of what becomes of them afterward. This want of affection is also recorded by Jeremiah, in his Lamentations: "The daughter of my people is cruel, like the ostriches in the wilderness."

In her private capacity the ostrich is not less inconsiderate and foolish, particularly in the choice of food, which is often highly detrimental and pernicious to her; for she swallows every thing greedily and indiscriminately, whether it be pieces of rags, leather, wood, stone, or iron. When Dr. Shaw was at Oran he saw one of these birds swallow, without any seeming uneasiness or inconveniency, several leaden bullets, as they were thrown upon the floor, scorching hot from the mould; the inward coats of the œsophagus and stomach being, in his opinion, probably better stocked with glands and juices, than in other animals with shorter necks. They are particularly fond of their own excrement, which they greedily eat up as soon as it is voided; no less fond are they of the dung of hens and other poultry. It seems as if their optic, as well as their olfactory nerves, were less adequate and conducive to their safety and preservation, than in other creatures. The divine Providence in this, no less than in other respects, "having deprived them of wisdom, neither hath it imparted to them understanding." This part of her character is fully admitted by Buffon, who describes it in nearly the same terms.

The ostrich was aptly called by the ancients a lover of the deserts. Shy and timorous in no common degree, she retires from the cultivated field, where she is disturbed by the Arabian shepherds and husbandmen, into the deepest recesses of the Sahara. In those dreary and arid wastes, which are scarcely ever refreshed with a shower, she is reduced to subsist on a few tufts of coarse grass, which here and there languish on their surface, or a few other solitary plants, equally destitute of nourishment, and, in the Psalmist's phrase, even "withered before they are grown up." To this dry and parched food, may perhaps be added, the great variety of land snails which occasionally cover the leaves and stalks of these herbs, and which may afford her some refreshment. Nor is it improbable that she sometimes regales herself on lizards and serpents, together with insects and reptiles of various kinds. Still, however, considering the voracity and size of this camel bird, it is wonderful how the little ones should be nourished and brought up; and especially, how those of fuller growth, and much better qualified to look out for themselves, are able to subsist.—Paxton.

Ver. 16. She is hardened against her young ones, as though *they were* not hers: her labour is in vain without fear.

Mr. Vansittart, in his Observations on Select Places of the Old Testament, proposes the following translation of this verse: "She hath hardened her young ones for that which is not hers; her labour is for another without discrimination." To justify this version he adduces these extracts from modern travellers: "We pursued our journey next morning: in the course of the day I amused myself by firing my piece to start game. A female ostrich rose from her nest, which was the largest I had seen, containing thirty-two eggs: twelve more being distributed at some distance, in a little cavity by itself. I could not conceive that one female could cover so many; they were of an unequal size, and on examination I found that nine of them were much less than the rest. This peculiarity interested me, and I ordered the oxen to be unyoked at about a quarter of a league distance from the nest. I then concealed myself in a thicket, from whence I could overlook the place, and yet remain within gunshot. I had not watched long before the female returned and sat on the eggs. During the rest of the day which I passed in the thicket, three more came to the same nest, covering it alternately; each continued sitting for the space of a quarter of an hour, and then gave place to another, who, while waiting, sat close by the side of her it was to succeed, a circumstance that made me conjecture, that in cold or rainy nights they sit by pairs, or perhaps more. The sun was almost down; the male bird approached: these, equally with the female, assist in hatching the eggs. I instantly shot him: but the report of my gun scared the others, who in their flight broke several of them. I now drew nearer, and saw with regret that the young ostriches were just ready to quit the shells, being perfectly covered with down. This peculiarity of female ostriches assisting each other for the incubation of the same nest, is, I think, calculated to awaken the attention of the naturalists: and not being a general rule, proves that circumstances sometimes determine the actions of these creatures, regulate their customs, and strengthen their natural instinct, by giving them a knowledge not generally bestowed. For is it not probable that they may associate to be the more powerful, and better able to defend their young?

"An ostrich starting before me at the distance of twenty paces, I thought it might be sitting, and hastened to the spot from whence she rose, where I found eleven eggs, quite warm, and four others at a distance of two or three feet from the nest. I called to my companions, who broke one of the warm eggs, in which was a young ostrich, perfectly formed, about the size of a chicken just hatched. I thought these quite spoiled, but found my people entertained a very different opinion of the matter, every one being eager to come in for his share. Amiroo in the mean time caught up the four outward ones, assuring me that I should find them excellent. In the sequel, I learned from this African, what the rest of my Hottentots, and even naturalists themselves, were unacquainted with, since none that I recollect have ever mentioned it: the ostrich ever places near her nest a certain number of eggs, proportioned to those she intends to sit on; these remaining separate and uncovered, continue good a long while, being designed by the providential mother for the first nourishment of her young. Experience has convinced me of the truth of this observation, for I never met with an ostrich's nest without finding eggs disposed in this manner, at a small distance from it." (Vaillant's Travels.)

"Among the very few polygamous birds that are found in a state of nature, the ostrich is one. The male, distinguished by its glossy black feathers from the dusky gray female, is generally seen with two or three, and frequently as many as five, of the latter. These females lay their eggs in one nest, to the number of ten or twelve each, which they hatch altogether, the male taking his turn of sitting on them among the rest. Between sixty and seventy eggs have been found in one nest: and if incubation has begun, a few are most commonly lying round the sides of the hole, having been thrown out by the birds on finding the nest to contain more than it could conveniently hold." (Barrow.) Ælian says, of the female ostrich, "She separates the unproductive eggs, and sits only on the good ones, from which the brood is produced; and the others she uses for food for her young." These accounts render obvious the propriety of the new-proposed translation. Because by the four mother birds having the same nest in common, and intermixing their eggs, they would likewise, when the eggs were hatched, have their young intermixed and in common; so that the parents not being able to discern their own particular young, would expend their affection equally on the whole brood, and consequently on the young of another bird equally as her own: thus she would be taking to herself the young of others instead of her own; so that in this respect she might be said to harden her own young, by taking the young of another, and dividing her affection upon them. In this sense she might be called cruel as to her own young, though she would at the same time be affectionate also.—BURDER.

Ver. 26. Doth the hawk fly by thy wisdom, *and* stretch her wings towards the south?

It is considered an exceedingly fortunate thing to see a hawk or a kite flying in circles from left to right, towards the south. When the south wind blows, those birds may be seen making their way in circles towards that quarter; but when they return they fly in a direct line.—ROBERTS.

The hawk is distinguished by the swiftness of her flight, and the rapid motion of her wings in flying. But as it is the first of these which naturally fixes the attention of an observer, the Hebrews, according to their invariable custom, selected it as the reason of the name by which she is known in their language; they call her (נץ) *nets*, from the verb *natsa*, to fly. She was reckoned by many of the ancients the swiftest of the feathered race. In Homer, the descent of Apollo from heaven is compared to her flight: "From the mountains of Ida he descended like a swift hawk, the destroyer of pigeons, that is the swiftest of birds." In the thirteenth book, Ajax tells Hector the day should come when he would wish to have horses swifter than hawks, to carry him back to the city. Among the Egyptians the hawk was the symbol of the winds; a sure proof that they contemplated with great admiration the rapidity of her motions. For the same reason, according to some writers, she was consecrated to the sun, which she resembles in the surprising swiftness of her career, and the faculty with which she moves through the boundless regions of the sky. This custom of consecrating the hawk to Apollo, the Greeks borrowed from the Egyptians, among whom no animal was so sacred as the ibis and the hawk. So great was their veneration for these animals, that if any person killed one of them, with or without design, he was punished with death; while for the destruction of any other animal, he was only subjected to an arbitrary fine. This bird, so highly venerated among the heathen, was pronounced unclean by the Jewish lawgiver; it was to be an abomination to the people of Israel; its flesh was not to be eaten, nor its carcass touched with impunity. The reason of this law may probably be found in her dispositions and qualities; she is a bird of prey, and, by consequence, cruel in her temper, and gross in her manners. Her mode of living, too, may probably impart a disagreeable taste and flavour to the flesh, and render it, particularly in a warm climate, improper for the table. Nor do we know that it was ever relished by any people, although the pressure of necessitous circumstances may have occasionally reconciled individuals to use it for food. Her daring spirit, her thirst of blood, the surprising rapidity of her flight, and her perseverance in the chase, soon pointed her out to the hunter as a valuable assistant; but even he willingly resigns her carcass to be meat to the beasts of the field.

Of this bird Jehovah demands, "Doth the hawk fly by thy wisdom, and stretch her wings towards the south?" Jerome, and several other interpreters, render the words, By thy prudence doth the hawk renew her plumage, having expanded her wings towards the south? because the verb (אבר) *abar*, in the future of the Hiphil, seems to be formed from the noun (אבר) *aber*, or (אברה) *abrah*, which signifies a feather. This law, by which the eagle, the hawk, and other birds, annually shed their feathers, was not contrived by the wisdom of man; although it appears he is able, by certain managements, to accelerate the moulting season, as well as the renovation of the plumage. But, as means and remedies derive all their efficacy from God, and depend for success only upon his co-operation, it may still be demanded, Doth the hawk renew her plumage by thy wisdom, expanding her wings towards the south? It is said, by an ancient writer on this passage, that humid and warm places are favourable to this change, and are therefore diligently sought for by hawkers, with the view of promoting the moulting of their falcons. When the south wind blows, the wild hawks, instructed by their instinctive sagacity, expand their wings till their limbs become heated; and by this means the old plumage is relaxed, and the moulting facilitated. But when the south wind refuses its aid, they expand their wings to the rays of the sun, and shaking them violently, produce a tepid gale for themselves; and thus their bodies being heated, and their pores opened, the old feathers more easily fall off, and new ones grow up in their place. But it is more probable that these words refer, not to the annual renovation of the plumage, but to the long and persevering flight of the hawk towards the south, on the approach of winter. Her migration is not conducted by the wisdom and prudence of man; but by the superintending and upholding providence of the only wise God. The words of Jehovah cannot be understood as referring to the falconer's art; for we have no evidence that the hawk was employed in hunting, till many ages after the times in which the patriarchs flourished. Besides, if the divine challenge referred to that amusement, the direction of her flight could not be confined to the south; for she pursues the game to every quarter of heaven. The renowned Chrysostom, on this passage, inquires why Jehovah has made no mention of sheep and oxen, and other animals of the same kind, but only of useless creatures, which seem to have been formed for no beneficial or important purposes. But is it to be supposed that God, who is wonderful in counsel, and excellent in working, has made any part of his works in vain? We may not be able to discover, after the most careful investigation, the end which the Almighty had in view, when he created some of his works; but shall we presume on this account to pronounce them useless or insignificant? So far from being a useless bird, the hawk, in some cases, brings the most important and effectual assistance to the hunter. It has already been observed, that the antelope, which seems rather to fly than to run, leaves the swiftest dog far behind, and could never be overtaken without the help of the falcon. The hawk, then, is not the useless and insignificant creature which the Greek father represents her; on the contrary, she has conferred benefits on mankind of no inconsiderable value.—PAXTON.

CHAPTER XL.

Ver. 15. Behold now behemoth, which I made with thee; he eateth grass as an ox.

Behemoth is an amphibious animal, whose real character is involved in much obscurity. The greater part of modern writers have thought that behemoth is the elephant, and leviathan the whale; this indisputably the largest of the aquatic, and that the largest of terrestrial animals. But their sentiments are liable to objections so numerous and weighty, that we are compelled, after the most careful investigation, to refer these names to very different animals. Bochart is of opinion, that the sacred writers refer, under these terms, to the crocodile and the hippopotamus: and he is probably correct. He follows Beza and Diodati in supposing the leviathan to be the crocodile of the Nile; and from this he infers, that the behemoth is the hippopotamus, an inhabitant of the same river. In the book of Job, the Almighty, after describing a number of terrestrial animals in a continued series, commences a new description in the fortieth chapter, in which we find leviathan, which is allowed by all to be an aquatic animal, joined with behemoth; therefore, to preserve the appointed order undisturbed, the latter must also be an aquatic animal. They are, besides, very similar in several respects: both are quadrupeds of enormous size—fierce in their dispositions—amphibious in their nature—both of them inhabitants of the Nile. Nor does the name, behemoth, ill agree with the hippopotamus; for the Hebrew term behema, may denote any beast, especially if it be of a superior size, as the hippopotamus is acknowledged to be. Aristotle gives him the size of an ass; Herodotus affirms that in stature he is equal to the largest ox; Diodorus makes his height not less than five cubits, or above seven feet and a half; Tatius calls him, on account of his prodigious strength, the Egyptian elephant. The Arabian authors quoted by Bochart, say that the behema, the same as the behemoth, is a four-footed animal, although he lives in the water. But were it admitted that behema by itself is always applied to land animals, yet behemoth may signify the hippopotamus with sufficient propriety, because that animal yields to very few in bulk and stature; it is amphibious, and resembles in many particulars terrestrial animals. No aquatic animal, indeed, so much resembles the beasts of the field; hence the hippopotamus alone, of all aquatic animals, is called, by way of excellence, behema, or, in the Egyptian dialect, behemoth; for behemoth is not a plural, but a singular noun, with an Egyptian termination, like Thoth, Paoth, Phamenoth, the names of Egyptian months, which are all in the singular number.

The description of behemoth is introduced with these words: "Behold now behemoth, which I made with thee; he eateth grass as an ox." The Almighty did not need to fetch the arguments of his mighty power from a distance; the Nile, which rolled its ample waters through regions bordering on Arabia, the native country of Job, contained the hippopotamus, one of the most surprising effects of creating power and goodness. Such seems to be the meaning of the command, "Behold now behemoth, which I have made with thee," or in thy neighbourhood. The particle *im* often signifies, near or hard by: thus, in the book of Joshua, the city of Ai is said to be *im* Bethaven, near Bethaven; and, in the book of Judges, the Danites were, *im* beth Micah, near the house of Micah. But as the propriety of the translation cannot reasonably be disputed, it is needless to multiply examples. The Almighty proceeds: "he eateth grass like an ox." The ox and the elephant are equally beasts of burden; it is therefore by no means wonderful that they live on the same kind of food; but that the hippopotamus, an aquatic animal, which lives for the most part in the bottom of the Nile, should eat grass like an ox, is a singular phenomenon, well entitled to our consideration. Nor is it without design he is compared to the ox; for, he not only associates with him in the same pastures, but also bears a considerable resemblance to him in the size and stature of his body, and in the form of his head and feet.—PAXTON.

Ver. 16. Lo now, his strength *is* in his loins, and his force *is* in the navel of his belly.

The loins are the seat of strength in every animal; hence, in the language of scripture, to strengthen the loins denotes an augmentation of power. A very decisive instance occurs in the second chapter of Nahum: "Make thy loins strong;" fortify thy power mightily. The same idea is involved in the prayer of the Psalmist, that the power which the wicked had so greatly abused, might be diminished, till it became consistent with the peace and safety of others, or entirely taken away: "Make their loins continually to shake." The last clause, "His force is in the navel of his belly," cannot well be reconciled with the statements of ancient writers, that the belly of the elephant is the most tender and vulnerable part of his body. This is a fact so generally known, so fully authenticated, that in war the hostile spear is usually directed to the navel of that formidable animal, where the most deadly wound may be inflicted. We learn from Pliny, that when the rhinoceros attacks the elephant, he likewise aims his furious thrust at the same part of the body. The same powerful instinct which directs the horn of the rhinoceros, leads the gnat, if the Talmudical writers may be credited, to the navel of the elephant, which it enters, and torments him with excruciating pains. But it is not to be supposed that the inspired writer would place the strength of that animal in the softest and most defenceless part of his frame, because it is not consistent with the truth of natural history. But the navel and belly of the hippopotamus are like the rest of his body, protected by an impenetrable skin, of so great solidity and thickness, that it is said to be formed into spears, and other missile weapons. Diodorus asserts that the hippopotamus has a skin nearly the strongest of all animals; and Ptolemy says hyperbolically, that the robbers in India have a skin like the hippopotamus, which no arrow can pierce. Zeringhi declares that a musket ball can make no impression on the dried skin of that animal, nor can any weapon pierce it, till it has been long steeped in water.—PAXTON.

Ver. 17. He moveth his tail like a cedar; the sinews of his stones are wrapped together.

Many writers, among whom are Caryl and Schultens, in order to support their hypothesis, that behemoth is the elephant, venture to contradict the uniform sense of the term *zanab*, which, in our translation, is properly rendered the tail, and make it signify the proboscis or trunk of that animal. *Zanab*, in Parkhurst, signifies the extremity or hindermost part of a thing, as the tail of an animal, or the end of a firebrand almost extinguished; and hence, as a verb in a primitive sense, to cut off the extremity or hindermost part. Yet in opposition to the constant meaning of this word in scripture, these writers turn it into the snout or trunk of the elephant, to make it agree with their favourite hypothesis. But if *zanab* be suffered to retain its usual meaning, it furnishes a strong presumption, that the hippopotamus is intended in the text under consideration, and not the elephant, whose tail, like that of the hog, is small, weak, and inconsiderable. It is, according to Buffon, but two feet and a half or three feet long, and pretty slender; but the tail of the hippopotamus, he observes from Zeringhi, does not resemble that of a hog, but rather that of a tortoise, only that it is incomparably thicker. The tail of the hippopotamus, Scheuchzer observes, although short, is thick, and may be compared to the cedar for its tapering, conical shape, its smoothness, thickness, and strength. But although it is thick, short, and very firm, yet he moves and twists it at pleasure; which, in the sacred text, is considered as a proof of his prodigious strength.

"The sinews of his stones," continues the sacred writer, "are wrapped together." Bochart renders the words, The sinews of his thighs are interwoven or twisted together.

From this short, but emphatical clause, we may certainly infer, that behemoth is one of the most powerful animals on the face of our globe. Such undoubtedly is the hippopotamus, if we may believe the accounts of Dampier, who declares he has known him set one tooth in the gunnel of a boat, and another at the distance of more than four feet, and there bite a hole through the plank, and sink the boat; and when he had done, he went away shaking his ears. On another occasion he saw him in the wash of the shore, when the sea tossed in a boat, with fourteen hogsheads of water in her, and left it dry upon his back; and another surge came and fetched the boat off, without the beast receiving any perceptible injury. Dampier and his crew made several shots at him, but to no purpose, for the bullets glanced from his sides as from a wall of adamant.—Paxton.

Ver. 18. His bones *are as* strong pieces of brass; his bones *are* like bars of iron.

The idea of his prodigious strength is increased by the account given of his bones, which are compared to strong pieces of brass, and bars of iron. Such figures are commonly employed by the sacred writers, to express great hardness and strength, of which a striking example occurs in the prophecies of Micah: "Arise and thresh, O daughter of Zion; for I will make thy horn iron, and I will make thy hoofs brass: and thou shalt beat in pieces many people." So hard and strong are the bones of the hippopotamus. The cutting, and particularly the canine teeth of the lower jaw, says Buffon, are very long, and so hard and strong, that they strike fire with steel; a circumstance which probably gave rise to the fable of the ancients, that the hippopotamus vomited fire. The substance of the canine teeth is so white, so fine, and so hard, that it is preferable to ivory for making artificial teeth. "His bones are like bars of iron;" and such, in the description of Buffon, are the bones of this animal. The cutting teeth, says that celebrated naturalist, especially those of the under jaw, are very long, cylindrical, and chamfered. The canine teeth are also long, crooked, prismatic, and sharp like the tusks of the wild boar. The largest of the cutting and canine teeth are twelve, and sometimes sixteen inches long, and each of them weighs from twelve to thirteen pounds.—Paxton.

Ver. 19. He *is* the chief of the ways of God: he that made him can make his sword to approach *unto him.*

It is added, "he is the chief of the ways of God: he that made him can make his sword to approach unto him." The phrase in the first clause, is evidently hyperbolical, and signifies merely, that he is one of the noblest animals which the almighty Creator produced. In size, the hippopotamus is inferior only to the elephant. The male, which Zeringhi brought from the Nile to Italy, was sixteen feet nine inches long, from the extremity of the muzzle to the origin of the tail; fifteen feet in circumference, and six feet and a half high; and the legs were about two feet ten inches long. The head was three feet and a half in length, and eight feet and a half in circumference. The opening of the mouth was two feet four inches, and the largest teeth were more than a foot long. Thus his prodigious strength; his impenetrable skin; the vast opening of his mouth, and his portentous voracity; the whiteness and hardness of his teeth; his manner of life, spent with equal ease in the sea, on the land, or at the bottom of the Nile,—equally claim our admiration, and entitle him to be considered as the chief of the ways of God. Nor is he less remarkable for his sagacity; of which two instances are recorded by Pliny. After he has gorged himself with corn, and begins to return with a distended belly to the deep, with averted steps he traces a great many paths, lest his pursuers, following the lines of one plain track, should overtake and destroy him while he is unable to resist. The second instance is not less remarkable: When he has become fat with too much indulgence, he reduces his obesity by copious bleedings. For this purpose, he searches for newly cut reeds, or sharp pointed rocks, and rubs himself against them, till he make a sufficient aperture for the blood to flow. To promote the discharge, it is said, he agitates his body; and when he thinks he has lost a sufficient quantity, he closes the wound by rolling himself in the mud. Hence, Pliny calls him the discoverer of the art of blood-letting; and the master of the healing art: and Ammianus, the most sagacious of all animals destitute of reason.

"He that made him can make his sword approach unto him:" or, as the words may be rendered, He who made him, has applied to him his sharp, crooked sword; of which the meaning seems to be, He has furnished his mouth with long teeth, somewhat bent, sharp, and protruded, with which, as with a crooked sword or sickle, he reaps and masticates the grass and corn on which he feeds. But if behemoth be understood of the elephant, how can it be said with any correctness, that he is provided with a crooked sword for reaping his food. The shortness of his neck prevents him from reaching the ground with his mouth, and using his teeth for collecting herbage. This operation is performed by his trunk, which receives the food, and conveys it into his mouth. His teeth are perfectly inefficient, except for mastication; and as for his trunk, it has no resemblance to any sharp instrument; on this account the ancients never gave it the name of a sword or sickle, but called it a hand; a name which it may receive with great propriety. A very learned interpreter, perceiving the inconvenience of this exposition, if behemoth mean the elephant, prefers our translation: "He that made him can make his sword approach unto him:" that is, He alone that made him can take away his life. But whether we apply the words to the elephant, or the hippopotamus, the sense is equally inadmissible, for both these animals are frequently destroyed without the immediate interference of God. Besides, to apply the sword to any one, and to take away his life with it, are not exactly the same; nor does this view agree with the whole series of the context, while the interpretation given by Bochart perfectly accords with it, and connects the verse with the rest of the narrative: He who made him, has furnished him with a sickle, or crooked sword, to reap and collect his food.—Paxton.

Ver. 20. Surely the mountains bring him forth food, where all the beasts of the field play.

This is considered as a very strong argument in favour of the elephant, an animal which, it is well known, browses upon the mountains; while, fully assured of his mild and forbearing temper, all the beasts of the field sport around him in peace and security. But the text applies with equal, and even with more propriety, to the hippopotamus; for it seems to indicate something remarkable in the circumstance, that such an animal should seek his food in peace, on the hills and mountains which skirt his habitation. But surely it is not strange, that the elephant, a creature which always lives on the land, and whose disposition leads him to eat grass like an ox, should be found on such a pasture. The hippopotamus, on the contrary, lives for the most part in the water, and walks on the bottom, as in the open air; yet he seeks his food more frequently on the land, where he devours sugarcanes, rushes, millet, rice, roots, and vegetables of every kind, in immense quantities, and ravages, far and wide, the cultivated fields. Not content with laying waste the plains, he proceeds in the night to the hills and mountains, and renews his depredations. Tatius asserts that he is the most voracious of all animals, so that he devours the standing corn of a whole field for nourishment. Natural historians give the same account of the morse, an animal which in many respects resembles the hippopotamus, and inhabits the large rivers of Russia, which roll their waters into the Frozen Ocean. He is about the size of an ox, with very short legs; his breast is higher and broader than the other parts of the body; he has two large and long tusks, resembling ivory in whiteness, and of equal value. When he is inclined to sleep, he forsakes the ocean, and, in companies, retires to the mountains. Around the hippopotamus, the beasts of the field may sport in safety; for although he feeds on fishes, crocodiles, and even cadaverous flesh, he is not known to prey on other animals. It is not even difficult to drive him away from the cultivated fields, for he is more timid on land than in the water. His only resource in danger, is to plunge into the deep, and travel under it a great way, before he ventures again to appear. The Indians, according to Dampier, are accustomed to throw him a part of their fish when he comes near their canoes, and then he passes on without doing them any harm. The same voyager relates an anecdote, which remarkably displays the mildness of his disposition; as their boat lay near the shore, he went under her, and with his back lifted her out of the water, and overset her, with six men on board, but did them no personal injury. These facts prove, at once, his incredible strength, and his habitual gentleness."—PAXTON.

Ver. 21. He lieth under the shady trees, in the covert of the reeds and fens. 22. The shady trees cover him *with* their shadow; the willows of the brook compass him about.

When satiated with food, he reposes "under the shady trees in the covert of the reed and fens." The elephant, it is admitted, delights in the shade, but very seldom lies down to sleep, as the sacred writer asserts of behemoth; nor is he known to frequent the reeds which cover the marsh, and skirt the border of the lake. But the reeds are the chosen haunt of the hippopotamus; they supply him with a grateful food, and screen him during his repose from the burning heat of the sun. In this part of his history, ancient and modern authors harmoniously accord. Marcellinus observes, that he reposes among the tall reeds, where they grow thickest in the mire. They are his covert, his food, and his medicine. Hence the prayer of David, Rebuke the company of the spearmen, or, as it may be translated, the wild beast of the reed, which has been supposed to refer to the hippopotamus, as the symbol of the Egyptian people and government; and this is the more probable, as he mentions the bulls and the calves, which that degenerate race honoured with idolatrous reverence. The circumstance of his making his bed among the thick reeds of the marsh, naturally suggests his relation to the Nile, whose banks are richly clothed with that plant; this is confirmed by many Egyptian representations, in which he is joined with the crocodile. Kimchi, and other writers, who contend that the elephant is meant in this description, unable to reconcile the clause under consideration to their theory, are compelled to throw it into the form of an interrogation: Does he lie under the holy trees in the covert of the reeds and fens? that is, he by no means lies in such places. But they did not perceive that this solution of the difficulty is destructive to their own theory; for the elephant does lie under the shady trees, or takes his repose standing under their covert. Besides, to throw the clause into the form of an interrogation, is to break the texture of the description, and to mar its beauty; and if such liberties with the sacred text were admitted, nothing is so plain or express in the word of God, which may not be eluded. The only other remark necessary to be made is, that the words of the sacred writer are confirmed by the testimony of Buffon, who says the hippopotamus, besides his usual cry, which has a great resemblance to that of the elephant, or to the stammering and indistinct sounds uttered by deaf persons when asleep, makes a kind of snorting noise, which betrays him at a distance. To prevent the danger arising from this circumstance, he generally lies among the reeds that grow upon marshy grounds, and which it is difficult to approach: there "the shady trees cover him with their shadow; the willows of the brook compass him about."—PAXTON.

Ver. 23. Behold, he drinketh up a river, *and* hasteth not: he trusteth that he can draw up Jordan into his mouth.

Behemoth, which before was feeding upon the mountains, or sleeping under the shade of the reeds and the willows, is in the next verse introduced quenching his thirst at the river: "Behold, he drinketh up a river, and hasteth not: he trusteth he can draw up Jordan into his mouth." Bochart gives a different translation: "Behold, let a river come upon him, he will not fear; he is safe though Jordan break forth upon his mouth." This version, it must be allowed, agrees perfectly with what natural historians say of the hippopotamus, that he walks deliberately into the deepest floods, and pursues his journey with the same fearless composure as in the open air, along the bottom of the torrent, or the channel of the sea. He remains a long time under water. Dampier has seen him descend to the bottom of three fathoms water, and remain there more than half an hour before he returned to the surface.—PAXTON.

Ver. 24. He taketh it with his eyes: *his* nose pierceth through snares.

The inspired writer thus concludes his description: "he taketh it with his eyes: his nose pierceth through snares." Bochart renders the words, Who shall take him in his sight, and perforate his nose with hooks? that is, Who shall come before him, and attack him with open violence? It is found extremely difficult to subdue him in fair combat; and therefore the Egyptians have recourse to stratagem. They watch near the banks of the Nile, till he leave the river to feed in the adjacent fields; they then make a large ditch in the way by which he passed, and cover it with thin planks, earth, and herbage. Passing without suspicion on his return to the flood, over the deceitful covering, he falls into the ditch, and is immediately despatched by the hunters, who rush from their ambush, and pour their shot into his head. From this review, the fair and necessary conclusion seems to be, that behemoth is not the elephant, but the hippopotamus of the Nile.—PAXTON.

CHAPTER XLI.

Ver. 1. Canst thou draw out leviathan with a hook? or his tongue with a cord *which* thou lettest down?

From this passage Hasselquist observes, that the leviathan "means a crocodile, by that which happens daily, and without doubt happened in Job's time, in the river Nile; to wit, that this voracious animal, far from being *drawn up by a hook*, bites off and destroys all fishing-tackle of this kind, which is thrown out in the river. I found, in one that I opened, *two hooks*, which it had swallowed, one sticking in the stomach, and the other in a part of the thick membrane which covers the palate."—BURDER.

The term leviathan is properly the same as *tannin*, which in our scripture is translated dragon. The royal Psalmist uses them as convertible terms, in the seventy-fourth Psalm, where he celebrates the mighty power of God in these lofty strains: "Thou brakest the heads of the dragons (*tannin*) in the waters; thou brakest the heads of leviathan in pieces, and gavest him to be meat to the people inhabiting the wilderness." He has been followed by the prophet in a passage where he foretels the deliverance of the church, from her cruel and implacable enemies: "In that day, the Lord, with his sore, and great, and strong sword, shall punish leviathan, the piercing serpent, even leviathan, that crooked serpent; and he shall slay the dragon that is in the sea." Kimchi distinguishes leviathan and *tannin*, by their magnitude alone. Leviathan, says he, is that enormous serpent or dragon. Hence, leviathan is a sinuous animal, which coils itself up like a dragon; and is described by the prophet as the oblique, tortuous, or crooked serpent. But as the word *tannin* is often used to denote the whale, and other marine animals; so, the term leviathan is, in scripture, sometimes employed to denote the same creatures. An example of this use of the term occurs in David's description of the sea: "There go the ships, there is that leviathan whom thou hast made to play therein." It is not however certain, that the term is ever used in this general sense; for it will be shown, that the creature to which it properly belongs, often infests the sea near the mouth of the great rivers of Africa and the East. Every part of the sublime description which Jehovah has given of leviathan in the book of Job, exactly corresponds with the natural history of the crocodile, which lives equally in the sea and in the river. That terrible animal bears a striking resemblance to the dragon or serpent. He has the shape of our asp; his legs are so short, that, like the serpent, he seems to go upon his belly. His feet are armed with claws, his back-bone is firmly jointed, and his tail a most formidable weapon; his whole formation is calculated for strength. Let us now hear Jehovah himself describe the leviathan, and we shall find that it exactly corresponds with the character and habits of the crocodile: "Canst thou draw out leviathan with a hook; or his tongue with a cord which thou lettest down?" He is of too great magnitude to be drawn out of the water like a fish. The second clause manifestly refers to the impossibility of drawing out his tongue, on account of its adhering throughout to his under jaw. It is besides short, thin, and broad, and by consequence, cannot be drawn out to his lips, like the tongue of any other animal.—PAXTON.

Ver. 2. Canst thou put a hook into his nose? or bore his jaw through with a thorn?

He is too powerful and fierce to be treated like a small fish: the elephant may submit to such indignities, but the crocodile scorns the dominion of man.—PAXTON.

The Hebrew word which is translated thorn, signifies rather an iron ring, fixed in the jaw. Bruce, speaking of the manner of fishing in the Nile, says, when a fisherman has caught a fish, he draws it on shore, and puts a strong iron ring into its jaw. "To this ring is fastened a rope, by which the fish is attached to the shore, which he then throws again into the water. Those who want fish go to the fisherman, as to a fish-market, and purchase them alive. We likewise bought a couple, and the fisherman showed us ten or twelve, fastened in a similar manner."—ROSENMULLER.

Ver. 3. Will he make many supplications unto thee? will he speak soft *words* unto thee?

An elegant prosopopœia, which expresses, with great force and beauty, the difficulty with which he is overcome. —PAXTON.

Ver. 4. Will he make a covenant with thee? wilt thou take him for a servant for ever?

As the vanquished are wont to redeem their life with the loss of their liberty. This question seems to intimate, that attempts have been made to tame the crocodile, but they have uniformly proved abortive. If this allusion is involved in the words, it is a certain proof that the whale is not intended; for, while attempts have actually been made to tame the crocodile, none have ever been made to domesticate the whale.—PAXTON.

Ver. 5. Wilt thou play with him as *with* a bird? wilt thou bind him for thy maidens?

"Wilt thou play with him as with a bird? or wilt thou bind him for thy maidens?" It cannot be: he is a truculent animal, and particularly hostile to children of both sexes, that, by approaching the banks of the Nile without sufficient circumspection, fall a prey to this vigilant devourer. He will even rush upon a full grown person, and drag him in a moment to the bottom of the stream. Maximus Tyrius mentions an Egyptian woman, who brought up a young crocodile, of the same age with her son, and permitted them to live together in the most familiar manner. The crocodile was gentle and harmless during his early youth, but his natural disposition gradually unfolded as he advanced to maturity, till at last he seized upon his unsuspecting associate, and devoured him. Ancient authors record many instances of crocodiles entering the houses of the inhabitants near the Nile, and destroying their children. These are sufficient to justify the interrogation of the Almighty, and to show that the terrible animal in question never can be completely tamed, nor safely trusted. —PAXTON.

Ver. 6. Shall thy companions make a banquet of him? shall they part him among the merchants?

If leviathan be the whale, both the one and the other are done every year; in some parts of the world, every day. The inhabitants of some regions feast on the blubber of the whale, and lay up the remainder for winter provisions. Cetaceous fishes are sought by "the merchants" at great expense, and constitute no inconsiderable portion of their wealth. But the fishermen neither rejoice when the crocodile is taken, except for the death of a devouring monster, nor feast upon his flesh; they do not cut up his carcass, nor expose him to sale, with the view of increasing their riches.—PAXTON.

Ver. 7. Canst thou fill his skin with barbed irons? or his head with fish-spears?

If leviathan, in this sublime expostulation, signified the whale, the answer might be given in the affirmative; for that prodigious creature has been often compelled to yield to the harpoon; his skin has been filled with barbed irons, and his head with fish spears: nor is the capture of the whale attended with much difficulty. But the crocodile is said to defy the arm of the harpooner, and the point of his spear; and in attacking him, the assailant has to encounter both great difficulty and imminent danger.—PAXTON.

Ver. 8. Lay thy hand upon him, remember the battle, do no more.

So great a horror shall seize thee, that thou shalt think rather of flight than combat, and the very touch of his skin shall convince thee, that it will not yield to thy stroke.—PAXTON.

Ver. 9. Behold, the hope of him is in vain: shall not *one* be cast down even at the sight of him?

If leviathan cannot be taken by these means, the hope of subduing him is utterly vain; none may expect to prevail against him; his very presence fills the stoutest heart with terror. It cannot however be denied, that the crocodile is often taken and destroyed; but the remark equally applies to the whale; and consequently, if the words of Jehovah describe a creature which is too powerful and too fierce to be vanquished, neither the one nor the other can be understood. But it were absurd to suppose, that any creature on the earth, or in the sea, is either invulnerable or unconquerable. The sacred writer says expressly, that every creature may be tamed by the industry of man. The language of Jehovah, therefore, only means, that the man who attacks the leviathan, must not hope for an easy conquest; and the experience of all ages attests the truth of the assertion. In size, he is very inferior to the whale; yet he sometimes extends to the length of thirty feet; and according to some ancient writers of great name, to forty or fifty. His strength is so great, that with one stroke of his tail he is said to cast the strongest animals to the ground; so that, to hunt the crocodile has always been reckoned one of the boldest and most perilous undertakings. In the time of Diodorus, the Nile and its adjacent lakes swarmed with crocodiles: yet very few were taken, and those not with hooks, but with iron nets. How difficult an undertaking this was, may be inferred from the coin which Augustus, the Roman emperor, caused to be struck, when he had completed the reduction of Egypt, on which was exhibited the figure of a crocodile, bound with a chain to a palm-tree, with this remarkable inscription, *Nemo antea relegavit.* These words certainly insinuate that in the experience of the ancients, to chain the crocodile was an achievement of the utmost difficulty. If the crocodiles which inhabit the Nile, are not, as modern travellers maintain, so fierce and dangerous as the ancients represent them, it must be owing to a number of adventitious circumstances; for in other parts of the world they are as ferocious as ever. It ought to be remembered, that Jehovah describes the general character of the species, which are admitted by writers of undoubted credit, to be the most fierce and savage of all animals. Plutarch asserts in express terms, that no creature is so ferocious; and in another part of his works, that it is an animal extremely averse to society, and the most atrocious of all the monsters which the rivers, the lakes, or the seas, produce.—PAXTON.

Ver. 10. None *is so* fierce that dare stir him up; who then is able to stand before me?

When the crocodile is satiated with prey, he leaves the deeps to repose on the banks of the river, or on the shore of the sea. At such a time, none are so bold as to disturb his slumbers, or provoke his vengeance; or if any one, disregarding the dictates of prudence, or eager to display his intrepidity, ventures in such circumstances to attack him, it is at the imminent hazard of his life, and is for the most part attended with fatal consequences. Diodorus assigns this as the reason that he was worshipped by the

Egyptians, that their enemies, for fear of him, durst not cross the river to attack them.—PAXTON.

Ver. 11. Who hath prevented me, that I should repay *him? whatsoever is* under the whole heaven is mine. 12. I will not conceal his parts, nor his power, nor his comely proportion. 13. Who can discover the face of his garment? *or* who can come *to him* with his double bridle?

These clauses, although teeming with important instruction, and, considering the authority with which they are clothed, entitled to deep attention, contribute nothing to the object of this review; we therefore proceed to the twelfth verse. "I will not conceal his parts, nor his power, nor his comely proportion." These are admirably displayed in the following particulars: "Who can discover the face of his garment, or come to him with a double bridle?" The crocodile never casts his skin, like the greater part of serpents, which he so nearly resembles, but retains it to the end of his life. The horse is a most powerful and spirited animal, yet he suffers a bit to be put into his mouth, and submits to the control of man; but the crocodile spurns his dominion, and parts with his freedom only with his life. Some interpreters propose a different version, which is equally characteristic of that animal: "Who shall venture within the reach of his jaws, which, when extended, have the appearance of a double bridle?"—PAXTON.

Ver. 14. Who can open the doors of his face? his teeth *are* terrible round about.

The doors of his face are his immense jaws, which he opens with a great and horrible hiatus. This feature of the crocodile has been mentioned by all naturalists. On the land his motions are slow, but in the river he springs eagerly on his prey, and either knocks it down with his tail, or opens a wide mouth for its destruction, armed with numerous sharp teeth of various lengths, with which, like the shark, he sometimes severs the human body at a single bite. Peter Martyr saw one, whose mouth was seven feet in width. Tatius affirms, that in seizing the prey, he becomes all mouth: and Albert, that the opening of his mouth extends as far back as his ears. Leo Africanus and Scaliger affirm, that he can receive within his mouth a young heifer. The vast capacity of his jaws is attested also by Martial, in the following lines:

"Cum comparata rictibus tuis ora
Nileacus habeas crocodilus angusta."

"His teeth are terrible round about:" or, in every respect, calculated to inspire the beholder with terror. They are sixty in number, and larger than the proportion of his body seems to require. Some of them project from his mouth like the tusks of a boar; others are serrated and connected like the teeth of a comb; hence, the bite is very retentive, and not less difficult to cure than the wound inflicted by the teeth of a mad dog. All the ancients agree, that his bite is most tenacious and horrible.—PAXTON.

Ver. 15. *His* scales *are his* pride, shut up together *as with* a close seal. 16. One is so near to another, that no air can come between them. 17. They are joined one to another, they stick together, that they cannot be sundered.

In these remarkable words is described the closeness of his scales, which, cohering to one another like the plates of a shield, cover his whole back. Those writers who make leviathan signify the whale, find themselves involved by this part of the description in an inextricable difficulty, for the whale has not a scale upon its body. This single circumstance, indeed, ought to determine the question: the whale it cannot be, for that immense animal has a smooth skin; and the history of nature furnishes no other to which the description of Jehovah will apply, but the crocodile, whose back is covered with impenetrable scales. One writer endeavours to get quit of the difficulty, by supposing that the text includes a comparison, and paraphrases it in this manner: leviathan is as safe from the assault of man, as if his body were defended with the strongest and broadest scales. But this mode of interpretation cannot be too severely reprobated; because it makes the sacred text say any thing which may suit the taste or the purpose of a writer. The words of Jehovah are express, the back of leviathan is covered with numerous, strong, and closely connected scales, under the protection of which, he fears no assailant, he shrinks from no danger. Nor is it consistent with truth, that a whale, which has no scales, is as strongly defended against the point of a spear, as if he were covered with this natural shield; for if his prodigious frame were defended by the broadest, the strongest, and the closest scales, the capture, if at all practicable, would be as arduous and difficult, as it is now easy. Abandoning this feeble and inadmissible argument, Caryl and others contend, that some cetaceous fishes are covered with scales, quoting in support of their assertion, a passage from Arrian, that he had heard Nearchus say, that the latter had heard certain mariners say, that they had seen cast upon the seashore, a monstrous fish, of fifty cubits long, which had scales all over, of a cubit thick. On this ridiculous story, it is needless to make any remark; to state is to refute it: or, if refutation be deemed necessary, it is sufficient to say, that although hundreds of cetaceous fishes are caught every year, both in the North and in the South Sea, not so much as one has been found sheathed in scales, since the days of Nearchus.—PAXTON.

"The back of the crocodile," says Thevenot, "is covered with scales, resembling a door studded with large nails, and so hard that it cannot be pierced with a halberd." Bertram says, that the whole back of the crocodile is covered with horny flakes, or scales, which no musket-ball can pierce.—BURDER.

Ver. 18. By his neesings a light doth shine, and his eyes *are* like the eyelids of the morning.

It seems to be generally admitted, that the crocodile turns his face to the sun when he goes to sleep on the banks of the river; and in this position becomes so heated, that the breath, driven forcibly through his nostrils, issues with so much impetuosity, that it resembles a stream of light. A similar expression is used concerning the war-horse, in the thirty-ninth chapter, which may give us a clearer idea of the brightness which issues from the nostrils of this animal: "The glory of his nostrils is terrible." Provoked by the sound of the trumpet, and the sight of armed men, a white fume streams from his expanded nostrils; which the Spirit of inspiration calls his glory, and common authors compare to fire. Thus, Silius Italicus, *Frenoque teneri impatiens crebras expirat naribus ignes;* and Claudian, *Ignescunt patulæ nares.* In the same manner are we to understand the words of Jehovah concerning the crocodile. The heat of that scaly monster, basking in the scorching beams of a vertical sun, together with the force with which the breath is emitted from the nostrils, produces the same luminous appearance round his nose, as plays around that of the high-mettled charger on the day of battle. The next clause possesses very great poetical beauty: "His eyes are like the eyelids of the morning:" like the brightening dawn of day. The learned Bochart mentions a curious coincidence between this striking figure, and the sentiments of the Egyptians. Among that people, the eyes of the crocodile is the hieroglyphic for the dawn; because they first arrest the attention, as the terrible animal approaches the surface of the deep; or because they are dim, and command a very limited field of vision under the water, but recover their brilliancy and acuteness as soon as he returns to the open air. Such is the appearance of the solar orb at his rising; he seems to emerge from the waves of the sea with a dim and faded lustre, but which increases every moment as he advances towards the meridian. But how it can be asserted of the whale, that his eyes are like the eyelids of the morning, it is not easy to conjecture. His eyes, which are not much larger than those of an ox, are buried beneath a ponderous eyelid, and imbedded in fat. Hence, blinder than a mole, he wanders almost at random in the mighty waters, equally unable to avoid being left by the retreating surge upon the strand, or dashed against the pointed rocks. —PAXTON.

Ver. 19. Out of his mouth go burning lamps, *and* sparks of fire leap out. 20. Out of his nostrils goeth smoke, as *out* of a seething-pot or caldron. 21. His breath kindleth coals, and a flame goeth out of his mouth.

Tatius gives a similar account of the hippopotamus: His nostrils are very broad, and emit an ignited smoke, as from a furnace of fire. The very same remark is made by Eustathius: He has a broad nose, expiring an ignited smoke as out of a furnace. These two animals live in the same element, and have the same mode of respiration. The longer they continue under water without breathing, they respire the more quickly when they begin to emerge. As the torrent rushes along with greater impetuosity, when the obstacle which opposed its progress is removed; so their breath, long repressed, effervesces and breaks out with so much violence, that they seem to vomit flame from their mouth and nostrils. The whale, it must be admitted, being of much larger size than the crocodile, breathes with a proportionate vehemence; it does not, however, vomit fire, but spouts water to an immense height in the air. The language of the inspired writer is highly figurative and hyperbolical, painting, in the most vivid colours, the heat and force with which the breath of the crocodile rushes from his expanded nostrils.—PAXTON.

Ver. 22. In his neck remaineth strength, and sorrow is turned into joy before him.

The whale has no neck, and by consequence cannot be the leviathan: like other fishes, his head is joined to his shoulders; while the crocodile is formed like a serpent, with a neck and shoulders, which enable him to move, to raise, or turn back his head, when he seizes his prey. "Sorrow is turned into joy before him;" what afflicts, alarms, or depresses other animals, animates his courage and activity. Or the words may be rendered, Sorrow dances before him; which may denote, that he spreads terror and destruction wherever he comes; for he immediately rushes upon those that happen to meet his eye, and although they may be so fortunate as to escape, still they reckon it an ill omen to have fallen in the way of that fierce and savage destroyer. Thus terror marches before him, as a herald before his sovereign, to proclaim his approach, and prepare his way.—PAXTON.

Ver. 23. The flakes of his flesh are joined together: they are firm in themselves; they cannot be moved. 24. His heart is as firm as a stone; yea, as hard as a piece of the nether *millstone.*

As the scales of leviathan present a coat of mail nearly impenetrable to the attacks of his enemies; so his flesh, or, as it is rendered by some, the prominent parts of his body, are like molten brass, the particles of which adhere so closely, that they cannot be separated. The very reverse of what Job affirmed of himself, may be asserted of the crocodile; his strength is the strength of stones, and his flesh is formed of brass; the very refuse, the vilest parts of his flesh, (for so the word signifies,) are firm, and strong, and joined; or, as the Septuagint translates it, glued together, that they cannot be moved. But if the refuse of his flesh be so firm and hard, how great must be the strength which belongs to the nobler parts of his frame? This question is answered in the next verse: "His heart is as firm as a stone; yea, as hard as a piece of the nether millstone." In all creatures, the heart is extremely firm and compact; in the leviathan it is firm as a stone; and to give us the highest idea of its hardness, Jehovah compares it to the nether millstone, which, having the principal part of the work to perform, is required to be peculiarly hard and solid. Some writers imagine, that the Almighty refers, not so much to the natural hardness of the heart, as to the cruel temper of the animal, or to his fearless intrepidity; he feels no pity, he fears no danger, he is insensible to external impressions as the hardest stone.—PAXTON.

Ver. 25. When he raiseth up himself, the mighty are afraid: by reason of breakings they purify themselves.

They feel a secret horror shoot through the whole soul; they become as it were incapable of reflection, and know not whither to turn, when they see the monster emerging from the deep, thirsting for blood, and displaying the terrors of his opening jaws. The stoutest heart is humbled, and, like the mariners in the ship with Jonah, when they despaired of life, they cry every one to his God, and promise to break off their sins by righteousness.—PAXTON.

Ver. 26. The sword of him that layeth at him cannot hold; the spear, the dart, nor the habergeon. 27. He esteemeth iron as a straw, *and* brass as rotten wood. 28. The arrow cannot make him flee: sling-stones are turned with him into stubble. 29. Darts are counted as stubble: he laugheth at the shaking of a spear.

In this glowing description, it is plainly the design of the Almighty to show, that the skin of the crocodile is impenetrable to these offensive weapons; or else, that regardless of danger, he scorns the wounds they inflict, and with fearless impetuosity seizes on his prey. This entirely accords with the accounts which natural historians give of that animal. Peter Martyr asserts that his skin is so hard it cannot be pierced with arrows; and according to other writers, he can be wounded only in the belly. But it is well known, that the whale is vulnerable in every part, and is commonly struck with the harpoon on the back, where the crocodile is defended by an impenetrable buckler of large, extremely hard, and closely compacted scales. On this armour of proof, the edge of the sword is blunted, and its point is broken; the spear falls harmless to the ground, and the dart rebounds from his impenetrable covering. But the habergeon, the coat of mail which the combatant puts on for his own defence, shall not save him from the devouring jaws of the monster; for he esteemeth iron as straw, and brass as rotten wood, which yield to the slightest touch, and crumble into dust before the smallest force. A shower of arrows makes no impression upon him; and the blow of a stone, slung by the most powerful hand, is no more to him than the stroke of a feather, or bit of stubble. Nor do the more dangerous weapons which the warrior hurls from his military engines, depress his courage, or interrupt his assault; for he laughs at the shaking of a spear, he regards it not, when, in token of defiance it is brandished before him.—PAXTON.

Ver. 30. Sharp stones *are* under him: he spreadeth sharp-pointed things upon the mire.

What is extremely incommodious, or even painful to other creatures, occasions no uneasiness to him. Criminals were punished among the ancients, by being compelled to lie on sharp stones; but so insensible is he to pain, that he can stretch his enormous bulk upon them without inconvenience: "Sharp stones are under him; he spreadeth sharp-pointed things upon the mire." Such a place of repose is his choice, not his punishment. Or the words may refer to the scales of leviathan, which are hard and sharp as a potsherd; and to his skin, which resembles a board set with sharp stones, or iron spikes. So rough is the skin of the crocodile, so hard are his scales, and so high and pointed the protuberances which rise on his back, that a more apt similitude could not be chosen than the *tribula*, or sharp thrashing instrument with iron teeth, to represent in the liveliest manner, the appearance of this terrible animal, as he lies reposing in the mud of the Nile.—PAXTON.

Ver. 31. He maketh the deep to boil like a pot: he maketh the sea like a pot of ointment.

Having described his general appearance, in which we have discovered almost every circumstance fitted to strike the mind with terror, and the impression which his emerging from the deep, and approaching the land, produce in the mind of a beholder, the inspired writer goes on to state the astonishing effects of his return to the water: "He makes the deep to boil like a pot; he makes the sea like a pot of ointment." The first clause exhibits the natural effect of a large body plunging suddenly into deep water; the second brings into view another circumstance, which beautifully expresses the violent agitation of the gulf into which the leviathan precipitates himself: "He maketh the sea to boil like a pot of ointment." The sudden and violent displacing of the waters, makes the sea resemble a large caldron furiously boiling over a strong fire; or the ascending water, being mixed with sand and mud from the bottom, excited by the violent agitation, resembles in colour, and in the smoothness of its swell, a pot of ointment; than which, more striking figures can scarcely be presented to the mind. It is the opinion of ancient writers, that the crocodile exhales from his body an odour like musk, with which he perfumes the pool where he gambols; and they assign this as the reason that the turbulence of the gulf which receives him, is compared to the boiling of a pot of ointment. But admitting what so many have asserted, that the crocodile diffuses a fragrant odour around him, it can hardly be supposed that the quantity exhaled can be so great as to warrant such a comparison. The inspired writer seems to allude, not to the ointment or its fragrance, but to the boiling of the pot in which spices are decocting, an operation which probably requires a very brisk ebullition.

Those who maintain that leviathan is the whale, demand how the crocodile, which inhabits the river, can make the sea boil? But the difficulty admits of an easy solution; the word sea, both in Hebrew and English, is often used in a restricted sense for any large expanse of water. The Jewish and Arabian writers, agreeably to this sense, frequently speak of the Nile, and its adjacent lakes, as a sea, and with great propriety, for the river itself is broad and deep, and at a certain season of the year, it overflows its banks, and covers the whole surface of Lower Egypt. The lakes which have been formed by the inundations, are of considerable depth and extent, and swarm with crocodiles; these may be called seas, with as much propriety as the sacred writers of the New Testament call the lake of Sodom the Salt Sea, and the lake of Tiberias the Sea of Galilee. The royal Psalmist, it must be admitted, mentions the sea in the proper sense of the term, as the haunt of leviathan: "So is this great and wide sea, wherein are things creeping innumerable; both small and great beasts. There go the ships: there is that leviathan whom thou hast made to play therein." But as the sea is, in that passage, opposed to the earth, it may comprehend the whole body of waters which surround and intersect the dry land, and by consequence, the proper habitation of the crocodile. This solution, however, is by no means necessary to establish the claims of this animal to the scripture title of leviathan, for it has been fully ascertained, by modern travellers, that he actually frequents the sea, although he generally prefers those rivers which are subject to annual inundations. Crocodiles, or aligators, are very common on the coast and in the deep rivers of Jamaica, though they prefer the banks of such rivers as, in consequence of frequent or periodical overflowing, are covered with mud, in which they find abundance of testaceous fish, worms, and frogs, for food. In South America, they chiefly frequent marshy lakes, and drowned savannas; but in North America, they infest both the salt parts of the rivers near the sea, the fresh currents above the reach of the tide, and the lakes both of salt and fresh water. The slimy banks of these rivers within the range of the tide, are covered by thick forests of mangrove-trees, in the entangled thickets of which the crocodiles conceal themselves, and lie in wait for their prey. According to Pinto, they abound on the coast of New Guinea; and Dampier found several on the shores of Timor, an island in the South Sea. The hippopotamus is a powerful adversary to the crocodile, and so much the more dangerous, that it is able to pursue him to the very bottom of the gulf. They are so numerous in the bay of Vincent Pinçon, and the lakes which communicate with it, as to obstruct, by their numbers, the piraguas and canoes which navigate those waters. When De la Borde was sailing along the eastern shore of South America in a canoe, and wishing to enter a small river, he found its mouth occupied by about a dozen large crocodiles. These testimonies prove, beyond a doubt, that the crocodile frequents the mouths of rivers and the bays of the sea, as well as the fresh-water stream and lake; and by consequence, the Psalmist might, in perfect agreement with the habits of that animal, represent him as playing in the great and wide sea, while the ships pursue their way to the desired haven.—Paxton.

Ver. 32. He maketh a path to shine after him; *one* would think the deep *to be* hoary.

He swims with so much force and violence near the surface of the water, that his path may be easily traced by the deep furrow which he leaves behind him, and the whitening foam he excites. The same appearances attend the motion of the dolphin: but the long withdrawing furrow, and the hoary foam, are not confined to the sea; they are likewise to be seen in the river and in the lake; and by consequence, may characterize, with sufficient propriety, the motion of the crocodile in the Nile and its adjacent lakes.—Paxton.

Ver. 33. Upon earth there is not his like, who is made without fear.

This clause Bochart renders, There is not his like upon the dust, (which is certainly the true meaning of the phrase, *al aphar;*) because, the crocodile is rather to be classed among reptiles than quadrupeds. His feet are so short, that he rather seems to creep than walk, so that he may, with great propriety, be reckoned among "the creeping things of the earth." But he differs from reptiles in this, that while they are in danger of being trampled upon, and bruised by the foot of the passenger, he is liable to no such accident. It cannot be said, in strictness of speech, that he is made without fear, for he is known to fly from the bold and resolute attack of an enemy; but the expression may be understood hyperbolically, as denoting a very high degree of intrepidity. The words of the inspired writer, however, are capable of another version, which at once removes the difficulty, and corresponds with the real character of the animal: He is so made, that he cannot be bruised; he cannot be crushed like a serpent, or trampled under the feet of his pursuer.—Paxton.

Ver. 34. He beholdeth all high *things:* he *is* a king over all the children of pride.

"He beholdeth all high things;" or, as it may be translated, he despiseth all that is high; "he is a king over all the children of pride." No creature is so large, so strong, so courageous, if we can believe the oriental writers, but he regards it with indifference or contempt. Men, women, and particularly children, who incautiously approach his haunts, become a prey to his devouring maw. The camel, the horse, the ox, and other portly quadrupeds, which fall in his way, he fiercely attacks, and forthwith devours. He will even venture to encounter, and not always without success, the elephant and the tiger, when they come to drink in the stream. His first attempt is to strike them down to the ground, or break their legs with his tail, in which he generally succeeds: he then drags them to the bottom of the river; or if they are animals of a moderate size, he swallows them up entire, without taking the trouble of putting them to death. The alligator, says Forbes, sometimes basks in the sunbeams on the banks of the river, but oftener floats on its surface: there concealing his head and feet, he appears like the rough trunk of a tree both in shape and colour: by this deception, dogs and other animals fearlessly approach, and are suddenly plunged to the bottom by their insidious foe. Even the royal tiger, when he quits his covert and comes to drink at the stream, becomes his prey. From this description, it appears that no animal is more terrible than the crocodile; no creature in form, in temper, in strength, and in habits, so nearly resembles leviathan, as described by Jehovah himself, in the book of Job, and consequently none has equally powerful claims to the name. This conclusion is greatly strengthened by several allusions to the leviathan in other parts of scripture. In the prophecies of Isaiah, he is called "the piercing serpent," or dragon: and that the prophet under that symbol refers to the king of Egypt, appears from these words: "And it shall come to pass on that day, that the Lord shall beat off from the channel of the river unto the stream of Egypt, and ye shall be gathered one by one." The prophet Ezekiel gives to Pharaoh the name of the great dragon, or leviathan: "Speak and say, thus sayeth the Lord God: Behold, I am against thee, Pharaoh king of Egypt, the great dragon that lieth in the midst of his rivers: which has said, My river is mine own, and I have made it for myself." But it would certainly be very preposterous to give the name of the elephant to the king of Egypt, which is neither a native of that country, nor ever known to visit the banks of the Nile. In allusion to the destruction of Pharaoh and his army in the Red Sea, the Psalmist sings: "Thou didst divide the sea by thy strength; thou brakest the heads of the dragons in the water; thou brakest the heads of leviathan in pieces, and gavest him to be meat to the people inhabiting the wilderness." But why should Pharaoh and his people be compared so frequently, and with so much emphasis, to the great dragon or leviathan, but because some remarkable, some terrible creature, infests their valley, to which that name properly applies? But no formidable beast of prey, except the crocodile, distinguishes Egypt from the surrounding regions; and since this creature is universally allowed to be extremely strong, cruel, and destructive, we must conclude it is no other than the leviathan of the inspired writers. The inhabitants of Egypt regarded the crocodile as the most powerful defender of their country, and the Nile as the source of all their pleasures and sociable enjoyments, and elevated both to the rank of deities. This accounts for the singular language of the prophet Ezekiel, and the boast which he puts into the mouth of Pharaoh: "My river is mine own, and I have made it for myself."—PAXTON.

CHAPTER XLII.

Ver. 10. And the LORD turned the captivity of Job, when he prayed for his friends; also the LORD gave Job twice as much as he had before.

Our idea of captivity seems to be principally confined to prisoners of war; but in the East, adversity, great adversity, and many other troubles, are spoken of in the same way. Thus, a man formerly in great prosperity, speaks of his present state as if he were in prison. "I am now a captive." "Yes, I am a slave." If again elevated, "his captivity is changed."—ROBERTS.

Ver. 11. Then came there unto him all his brethren, and all his sisters, and all they that had been of his acquaintance before, and did eat bread with him in his house; and they bemoaned him, and comforted him over all the evil that the LORD had brought upon him: every man also gave him a piece of money, and every one an ear-ring of gold.

The custom alluded to of relations and friends giving relief to a person in distress, is practised in the East at this day. When a man has suffered a great loss by an accident, by want of skill, or by the roguery of another, he goes to his brothers and sisters, and all his acquaintances, and describes his misfortunes. He then mentions a day when he will give a feast, and invites them all to partake of it. At the time appointed they come, arrayed in their best robes, each having money, ear-rings, finger-rings, or other gifts suited to the condition of the person in distress. The individual himself meets them at the gate, gives them a hearty welcome, the music strikes up, and the guests are ushered into the apartments prepared for the feast. When they have finished their repast, and are about to retire, they each approach the object of their commiseration, and present their donations, and best wishes for future prosperity. A rich merchant in North Ceylon, named Siva Sangu Chetty, was suddenly reduced to poverty; but by this plan he was restored to his former prosperity. Two money brokers, also, who were sent to these parts by their employer, (who lived on the opposite continent,) lost one thousand rix-dollars, belonging to their master; they therefore called those of their caste, profession, and country, to partake of a feast, at which time the whole of their loss was made up. When a young man puts on the ear-rings or turban for the first time, a feast of the same description, and for the same purpose, is given, to enable him to meet the expense of the rings, and to assist him in future pursuits of life. When a young woman also becomes marriageable, the female relations and acquaintances are called to perform the same service, in order to enable her to purchase jewels, or to furnish a marriage portion. In having recourse to this custom, there is nothing that is considered mean; for parents who are respectable and wealthy often do the same thing. Here, then, we have another simple and interesting illustration of a most praiseworthy usage of the days of ancient Job.—ROBERTS.

Ver. 14. And he called the name of the first Jemima; and the name of the second, Kezia; and the name of the third, Keren-happuch.

To vary names by substituting a word similar in sound, is very prevalent in the East. The following extract from Sir Thomas Roe, is a striking example of this circumstance. "They speak very much in honour of Moses, whom they call *Moosa calim Alla*, Moses the publisher of the mind of God: so of Abraham, whom they call *Ibrahim carim Alla*, Abraham the honoured, or the friend, of God: so of Ishmael, whom they call *Ismal*, the sacrifice of God: so of Jacob, whom they call *Acob*, the blessing of God: so of Joseph, whom they call *Eesoff*, the betrayed for God: so of David, whom they call *Dahood*, the lover and praiser of God: so of Solomon, whom they call *Selymon*, the wisdom of God: all expressed in short Arabian words, which they sing in ditties, unto their particular remembrance. Many men are called by these names: others are called Mahmud, or Chaan, which signifies the moon; or Frista, which signifies a star. And they call their women by the names of spices or odours; or of pearls or precious stones; or else by other names of pretty or pleasing signification. So Job called his daughters."—BURDER.

Ver. 15. And in all the land were no women found *so* fair as the daughters of Job: and their father gave them inheritance among their brethren.

In the scriptures the word fair may sometimes refer to the form of the features, as well as the colour of the skin: but great value is attached to a woman of a light complexion. Hence our English females are greatly admired in the East, and instances have occurred where great exertions have been made to gain the hand of a fair daughter of Britain. The acme of perfection in a Hindoo lady is to be of the colour of gold!—ROBERTS.

THE BOOK OF PSALMS.

PSALM I.

Ver. 3. And he shall be like a tree planted by the rivers of water, that bringeth forth his fruit in his season: his leaf also shall not wither; and whatsoever he doeth shall prosper.

Dr. Boothroyd has it, "Like a tree planted by water streams;" and Dr. A. Clarke says, "The streams or divisions of waters." This probably alludes to the artificial streams which run from the lakes or wells: by the side of these may be seen trees, at all seasons covered with luxuriant verdure, blossoms, or fruit, because the root is deriving continual nourishment from the stream; while at a distance, where no water is, may be seen dwarfish and unhealthy trees, with scarcely a leaf to shake in the winds of heaven. —Roberts.

We see no reason to suppose, with many commentators, that allusion is had to any particular species of tree, as, for example, the palm, the olive, or the pomegranate, each of which has been conceived to be intended, from its peculiar adaptedness to represent the permanent and prolific nature of the good man's happiness. It is indeed said of the righteous, Ps. xcii. 12, that "he shall flourish like the *palm-tree;* he shall grow like a *cedar* in Lebanon;" but it will answer all the demands of the passage to understand it of *any* tree advantageously situated, and evincing a vigorous and thrifty growth. In the arid climes of the East, the trees, unless sustained by artificial irrigation, are apt to lose their verdure during the sultriness of the summer months—a fact which affords an interesting clew to the imagery here employed. Although the word "rivers" is adopted in our authorized translation, yet it is by no means an adequate representative of the original. פלגי the term thus rendered, from פלג *to divide, to sunder, to split,* properly signifies *divisions, partitions, sections;* i. e. branching cuts, trenches, or water-courses, issuing either from a large body of water, as a lake, a pond, a river, Ps. xlvi. 4; or from a well or fountain-head, Prov. v. 16. Job xxvi. 6; and alludes to the methods still practised among the oriental nations, of conveying water to gardens and orchards. This was by means of canals or rivulets flowing in artificial channels, called פלגים *divisions;* i. e. *cuts* or *trenches,* which distributed the water in all directions. The whole land of Egypt was anciently sluiced in this manner, by innumerable canals and water-courses, designed to convey the fertilizing waters of the Nile over every part of the valley through which it ran. Maundrell (Trav. p. 122) speaks of a similar mode of irrigation in the neighbourhood of Damascus: "The gardens are thick set with fruit trees of all kinds, kept fresh and verdant by the waters of the Barady. This river, as soon as it issues out of the cleft of the mountain before mentioned, into the plain, is immediately divided into three streams, of which the middlemost and largest runs directly to Damascus, through a large open field called the Ager Damascenus, and is distributed to all the cisterns and fountains in the city. The other two, which I take to be the work of art, are drawn round, the one to the right, the other to the left, on the borders of the gardens, into which they are let out, as they pass, *by little rivulets,* and so dispersed all over the vast wood; insomuch that there is not a garden, but has a fine, quick stream running through it." The same traveller describing, p. 89, the orange garden of the emir of Beyroot, observes, that "it contains a large quadrangular plot of ground divided into sixteen lesser squares, four in a row, with walks between them. The walks are shaded with orange-trees of a large spreading size. Every one of these sixteen lesser squares in the garden was bordered with stone; and in the stone-work were troughs, very artificially contrived, for conveying the water all over the garden; there being little outlets cut at every tree for the stream, as it passed by, to flow out and water it." A striking allusion to trees cultivated in this manner occurs Ezek. xxxi. 3, 4: "Behold, the Assyrian was a cedar in Lebanon, with fair branches and with a shadowing shroud, and of a high stature, and his top was among the thick boughs. The *waters* made him great, the *deep* set him up on high, with her *rivers running round about his plants, and sent out her little rivers unto all the trees of the field.*" So Eccl. ii. 6, "I made me pools of water *to water therewith the wood that bringeth forth trees.*" To the same purpose, Prov. xxi. 1, "The king's heart is in the hand of the Lord, as the *rivers of waters,* (פלגי־מים *divisions of waters;*) he turneth it whithersoever he will;" i. e. as these fertilizing rivulets, the work of art, are conducted forward and backward, to the right hand or the left, diverted or stopped at the will of him who manages them, so is the heart of kings, and, by parity of reasoning, of the rich and mighty of the earth, swayed at the sovereign disposal of the Lord of all creatures. He, by the course of his providence, and by the inward promptings of his Spirit, can turn the enriching tide of their bounty in any direction he sees fit, whether to bless the poor with bread, or to supply the means of salvation to the destitute.—Bush.

Ver. 4. The ungodly *are* not so: but *are* like the chaff which the wind driveth away.

We must recollect here, that in the East the thrashing-floors are places in the open air, (Gen. l. 10,) on which the corn is not thrashed, as with us, but beaten out by means of a sledge, in such a manner that the straw is at the same time cut very small. "When the straw is cut small enough, they put fresh corn in the place, and afterward separate the corn from the cut-straw, by throwing it in the air with a wooden shovel, for the wind drives the straw a little farther, so that only the pure corn falls to the ground." (Thevenot.)—Rosenmuller.

PSALM II.

Ver. 1. Why do the heathen rage, and the people imagine a vain thing?

The Hebrew word which Luther has translated heathen, (*gojim,*) signifies, in fact, people in general; but it is used in the Old Testament, for the most part, and by the later (and even modern) Jews, exclusively of other nations who are not Jews, and that with a contemptuous and odious secondary meaning. Other nations, also, have similar names for foreigners, and for such as are not of their religious faith. Thus the Greeks and Romans called them Barbarians, that is, properly, inhabitants of the desert. The Arabs called them Adschem, by which they mean, first, their neighbours the Persians, and then all foreigners in general. The Mohammedans call all the people of the earth, who do not believe the pretended divine mission of Mohammed, Kuffar in the plural, Kafar in the singular, and by a corrupted pronunciation, Gaur, (Giavur,) which signifies unbelievers and infidels. Hence the name Kaffers, which the inhabitants of the southeastern coast of Africa received from the Mohammedan Arabs.—Rosenmuller.

Ver. 9. Thou shalt break them with a rod of iron; thou shalt dash them in pieces like a potter's vessel.

"Begone! wretch," says the infuriated man, "or I will dash thee to pieces as a *kuddam,*" i. e. an earthen vessel.—Roberts.

The rod, in remote antiquity, was a wooden staff, not much shorter than the height of a man, with golden studs or nails, or sometimes ornamented at the top with a round knob, such as are seen in the hands of the Persian kings, on the monuments of Persepolis. Justin says, "that at the time of the rape of the Sabine virgins, the kings, as insignia of their dignity, bore, instead of the diadem, long staves, which the Greeks called sceptres." Hence it may be conceived how, in Homer, kings made use of the sceptre to strike with. The sceptre, as well as throne, is often used as a symbol of government. Hence in Ps. xlv. 6, *a right sceptre* is the emblem of a just government. And in the above passage it is said of the king celebrated in this Psalm, that he would break his enemies with *a rod of iron*, by which his dominion is represented as terrible and destructive over those who oppose him. The sense is, that he will conquer them with irresistible power. A similar picture is given of the Messiah in Num. xxiv. 17. "There shall come a star out of Jacob, and a sceptre shall rise out of Israel, and shall smite the corners (according to Luther, the 'princes') of Moab."—Rosenmuller.

PSALM V.

Ver. 7. But as for me, I will come *into* thy house in the multitude of thy mercy; *and* in thy fear will I worship towards thy holy temple.

It is very natural that people, when praying, should turn the face towards the quarter where the place dedicated to the Divinity is situated, and which is considered as his abode. Hence the Jews prayed with their faces turned towards the temple, (1 Kings viii. 38, 44, 48;) and those residing out of Jerusalem, turned it towards that point of the heavens in which Jerusalem lay. Dan. vi. 10. Thus the Mohammedans, when praying, always turn their faces towards Mecca. "Kebla," says Bjornstahl, "signifies, in Arabic, the point towards which all true Mussulmen turn their faces when praying; whether in the open air or in their temples, where it is always marked by a niche, in which not only the iman stands, but also some finely written copies of the Koran are lying. This point is always towards Mecca; for there stands the Caaba, or quadrangular house, said to have been first built by Abraham and Ishmael, and which is the great sanctuary of the Mohammedans, for the sake of which such great pilgrimages are annually undertaken to Mecca, and thence to Medina, where Mohammed is buried."—Rosenmuller.

Ver. 12. For thou, Lord, wilt bless the righteous; with favour wilt thou compass him as *with* a shield.

A shield is a defensive piece of armour, and is used to ward off the blows that are aimed at the person who wears it. In this passage of the Psalmist it is spoken of in a different sense. It is to be used by a divine power for the preservation of the people of God: and, connected with their safety, they are to be honoured and exalted: and both their preservation and exaltation are to be so complete, that they are said to be compassed about with the favour of God as with a shield, in the same manner as a person completely covered with, or elevated upon, a large broad shield. This interpretation of the words is paralleled by a practice which, subsequent to the age of the Psalmist, obtained among the Romans, of which the following instances may be selected: "Brinno was placed on a shield, according to the custom of the nation, and being carried in triumph on the shoulders of the men, was declared commander-in-chief." The shields of the ancients, as a scholiast observes upon the Iliad, ii. 389, were so large as almost to cover a whole man, and hollowed, so that they in a manner enclosed the body in front. Hence Homer speaks of the surrounding shield. Tyrtæus, in the second of his hymns, still extant, says, "The warrior stands in the contest firm upon both feet; the hollow of the spacious shield covering below his sides and thighs, and his breast and shoulders above."—Burder.

PSALM VI.

Title—To the chief Musician on Neginoth upon Sheminith. A Psalm of David.

This superscription is in Luther, "*upon eight strings.*" I can hardly think that a musical instrument of eight strings is meant here, as the Hebrew word (*scheminith*) does not appear among the musical instruments mentioned in the Old Testament. The meaning of the Hebrew word is, *octave;* and in 1 Chron. xv. 21, where the singers of the temple are enumerated, it stands after a word which properly signifies *virgins*, (*alamoth*,) and may therefore signify a treble part, which was sung by women. "Might not this," says Forkal, "have signified among the Hebrews nearly the same that 'virgin air' signified among the German poets, called master-singers in the middle ages?"—Rosenmuller.

Ver. 2. Have mercy upon me, O Lord; for I *am* weak: O Lord, heal me; for my bones are vexed.

Dr. Boothroyd translates, "For my bones are troubled." The object of the expression appears to be, to show that the trouble has taken fast hold, it is deeply seated, my bones are its resting-place. The Hindoos, in extreme grief or joy, say, "our bones are melted;" *i. e.* like boiling lead, they are completely dissolved.—Roberts.

Ver. 8. Depart from me, all ye workers of iniquity: for the Lord hath heard the voice of my weeping.

Silent grief is not much known in the East: hence, when the people speak of sorrow, they say its voice. "Have I not heard the voice of his lamentation?"—Roberts.

PSALM VII.

Ver. 12. If he turn not, he will whet his sword; he hath bent his bow, and made it ready.

The Hebrew word signifies literally, "that he hath trodden on his bow," that is, to bend it. Arrian, in his Account of India, says, "Such of their warriors as combat on foot, carry a bow which is as long as a man. When they want to bend it, they set it upon the ground, and tread on it with the left foot, while they draw on the string."—Rosenmuller.

Ver. 13. He hath also prepared for him the instruments of death; he ordaineth his arrows against the persecutors.

This sentence may be rendered more accurately, "he makes his arrows burning." The image is deduced from such fiery arrows as are described by Ammianus Marcellinus. They consisted of a hollowed reed, to the lower part of which, under the point or barb, was fastened a round receptacle, made of iron, for combustible materials, so that such an arrow had the form of a distaff. The reed, as the above author says, was filled with burning naptha; and when the arrow was shot from a slack bow, (for if discharged from a tight bow the fire went out,) it struck the enemies' ranks and remained infixed, the flame consuming whatever it met with; water poured on it increased its violence; there was no other means to extinguish it but by throwing earth upon it. Similar darts or arrows, which were twined round with tar and pitch, and set fire to, are described by Livy, as having been made use of by the inhabitants of the city of Saguntum, when besieged by the Romans. An allusion to such arrows is also made in Ephesians vi. 16.—Rosenmuller.

Ver. 14. Behold, he travaileth with iniquity, and hath conceived mischief, and brought forth falsehood.

Dr. Boothroyd translates this, "Lo, the wicked hath conceived iniquity, and is big with mischief; but an abortion shall he bring forth:" which certainly corresponds better with the order of the figure of the text. "What induces that man to come so much to this place? depend upon it, he is preparing some plans."—"Yes, I am of opinion his womb has conceived something." Does the person begin to disclose his purposes, it is said, "Ah! it is this you have been conceiving the last few days." But when he puts his plans into practice, "Yes, he is now in parturition"

"Well! how has the matter ended?"—"Ended! he has brought forth *poykul*," i. e. lies.—ROBERTS.

PSALM VIII.

Ver. 6. Thou madest him to have dominion over the works of thy hands: thou hast put all *things* under his feet.

This is a common figure of speech to denote the superiority of one man over another; hence the worshippers of the gods often say in their devotions, "We put your feet upon our heads." "Truly, the feet of Siva are upon my head." "My *Gooroo*, my *Gooroo*, have I not put your feet upon my head?" "My lord, believe not that man; your feet have always been upon my head." "Ah! a mighty king was he; all things were under his feet."—ROBERTS.

PSALM IX.

Ver. 14. That I may show forth all thy praise in the gates of the daughter of Zion: I will rejoice in thy salvation.

That is, in Jerusalem, meaning in the temple itself. The "gates of the daughter of Zion" are opposed to the "gates of death," mentioned in the preceding verse. Zion is the general name of the mountain, on whose irregular eminences the city of Jerusalem was built. But in a more limited sense, the name of Zion was given to the highest of those eminences, on which, besides a part of the city, the palace of David, and several public buildings, were built. This Mount Zion was joined on the south side by means of a bridge, with the mountain or hill of Moriah, which was entirely occupied by the extensive buildings of the temple. In the Old Testament, we are often to understand by Zion and Jerusalem, the national sanctuary, the temple particularly, where, as in the above passage, the adoration of God, and the thanksgivings to be publicly offered him, are spoken of. Zion or Jerusalem is called *daughter*, because the Hebrews used to figure cities, communities, and states, under the images of women, and the inhabitants as children. Thus, the *daughter of Tyre*, the *daughter of Babylon*, for the city of Tyre and the city of Babylon. Even now, the head of the government of Tunis, in Barbary, is called Dey, or Day, that is, as D'Arvieux observes, mother's brother; because the republic is considered as the mother, the citizens as her children, and the Turkish sultan as the consort of the republic.—ROSENMULLER.

Ver. 15. The heathen are sunk down in the pit *that* they made: in the net which they hid is their own foot taken.

This image is taken from the catching of wild beasts, by means of strong ropes or nets. Lichtenstein, in speaking of the hunting of the Koofsa, (Kaffers,) says, "They catch much game by means of nets; in the woody districts, they often make low hedges, miles in length, between which they leave openings; in these openings, through which the game tries to escape, they conceal snares, which are placed so ingeniously that the animals are caught in them by the leg, and cannot extricate themselves." Also lions and elephants are caught in this manner; the latter, when they have been brought by means of fire, or by tame elephants, to a narrow place, where they cannot turn back, are caught by throwing ropes round their legs.

Ropes and nooses are meant by the figurative expression, *snares of death*, 2 Sam. xxii. 6, which the people of the ancient world used, both in the chase and in war. The word is sometimes rendered *net*, as in this passage. Arrian, in his Treatise on Hunting, relates, that Cyrus met with wild asses in the plains of Arabia, which were so swift, that none of his horsemen were able to catch them. Yet the young Lybians, even boys of eight years of age, or not much older, had pursued them, mounted on their horses, without saddle or bridle, till they threw a noose over them, and thus took them. He gives instructions to pursue stags with trained horses and dogs, till they can be either shot with arrows, or taken alive by throwing a noose over them. These are the strong snares which Pollux means, when he speaks of the wild asses, and they are also the same as those in which Habis, the natural son of an ancient Spanish king, was taken. He was exposed when a child, and suckled by a hind: having grown up among the stags, he had attained their swiftness, so that he fled with them over the mountains, and traversed forests, till he was at length caught in a noose. In the same manner Ulloa saw the Guasos (one of the aboriginal Peruvian nations) catch with their nooses (the Spanish lazo) the most active and cautious man as easily as the wild bull. Some English pirates once approaching their shore, and thinking to drive off the Guasos with their firearms, the latter threw their nooses towards the vessels, and so pulled on shore those who had not fallen down at first sight; one who was caught escaped with his life, notwithstanding he had been thus violently drawn from the boat to the shore, the noose having caught him over the shoulder on the one side, and the arm on the other; but it was some time before he was able to recover his strength. In the same manner the Sagarthian horsemen in the Persian army used their nooses in war.—(Herodotus.) These people, who, according to Stephanus, lived on the Caspian Sea, had no other arms than a noose and a dagger, to kill with the one the enemy whom they had caught with the other. The same is related by Pausanias, of the Sauromati.—ROSENMULLER.

PSALM X.

Ver. 5. His ways are always grievous: thy judgments *are* far above out of his sight: *as for* all his enemies, he puffeth at them.

Of a proud and powerful man, it is said, "He puffs away his foes;" *i. e.* they are so contemptible, so light, that like a flake of cotton, he puffs them from his presence. Great is the contempt which is shown by puffing through the mouth and blowing through the nostrils.—ROBERTS.

Ver. 15. Break thou the arm of the wicked and the evil *man:* seek out his wickedness *till* thou find none.

This member is often selected as an object for imprecations. "Ah! the *kallan*, the thief, his hand shall be torn off for that." "Evil one, thou wilt lose thy hand for this violence." But the hand or arm is also selected as an object for blessings. "My son, (says the father,) may the gods keep thy hands and thy feet."—ROBERTS.

PSALM XI.

Ver. 6. Upon the wicked he shall rain snares, fire, and brimstone, and a horrible tempest: *this shall be* the portion of their cup.

The gods are described as doing this upon their enemies; and magicians, in cursing each other, or those who are the objects of their ire, say, the fiery rain shall descend upon them.—ROBERTS.

PSALM XIV.

Ver. 4. Have all the workers of iniquity no knowledge? who eat up my people *as* they eat bread, and call not upon the LORD.

"Wicked one, the fiends shall eat thee." "That vile king eats the people as he does his rice." "Go not near that fellow, he will eat thee." But, strange as it may appear, relations say of those of their friends who are dead, they have EATEN them. Thus, a son, in speaking of his deceased parent, says, "Alas! alas! I have eaten my father." "My child, my child!" says the bereaved mother, "have I eaten you?" The figure conveys extreme grief, and an intimation that the melancholy event has been occasioned by the sins or faults of the survivors. In cursing a married man, it is common to say, "Yes, thou wilt soon have to eat thy good wife." And to a poor widow, "Wretch! hast thou not eaten thy husband?"—ROBERTS.

PSALM XVI.

Ver. 4. Their sorrows shall be multiplied *that* hasten *after* another *god:* their drink-offerings of blood will I not offer, nor take up their names into my lips.

This refers to the custom of many heathen people, to drink the wine of the sacrifice mixed with blood, particularly when they bound themselves by dreadful oaths, and to the performance of fearful deeds. This drink was called by the Romans *vinum assiratum*, because *assir*, according to Festus, signifies blood in the ancient Latin language. In this manner, as Sallust relates, Catiline took the oaths with his accomplices. "It was said at the time that Catiline, after making a speech, calling on the accomplices of his crime to take an oath, presented them with human blood mixed with wine, in cups; and when every one had drank of it, after pronouncing an imprecation, as is customary in solemn sacrifices, explained his plan." In a similar manner, Silius Italicus makes the Carthaginian Hannibal swear, an instance which is particularly suitable to illustrate the above passage, because the Carthaginians were of Phenician or Canaanite origin. When the prophet Zechariah describes the conversion of the Philistines, he makes Jehovah say, (x. 7.) "And I will take away his blood out of his mouth, and his abominations from between his teeth; but he that remaineth, even he, shall be for our God." The drinking of blood at sacrifices was prohibited to the Israelites upon pain of death.—ROSENMULLER.

Ver. 7. I will bless the LORD, who hath given me counsel; my reins also instruct me in the night-seasons.

Night is the time for the chief joys and sorrows of the Hindoos, and it is then they are principally engaged in the worship of their gods; because they believe praise is more acceptable to them then, than at any other period. It is believed, also, that the senses have more power in the night; that then is the time for thought and instruction; hence they profess to derive much of their wisdom at that season. The Psalmist says, "Thou hast visited me in the night;" and the heathen priests always pretend to have their communications with the gods "when deep sleep falleth on man." See them at their bloody sacrifices, they are nearly always held at the same time, and what with the sickly glare of lamps, the din of drums, the shrill sound of trumpets, the anxious features of the votaries, the ferocious scowl of the sacrificer, the bloody knife, and the bleeding victim, all wind up the mind to a high pitch of horror, and excite our contempt for the deities and demons to whom night is the time of offering and praise.—ROBERTS.

PSALM XVII.

Ver. 2. Let my sentence come forth from thy presence; let thine eyes behold the things that are equal.

David, in his integrity, thus cried to the Almighty, and so people in the East, who are innocent, when pleading in court, say, "Let us have YOUR sentence;" *i. e.* in contradiction of that of their enemies. "See, my lord, the things that are right." "Justice! justice!"—ROBERTS.

Ver. 10. They are enclosed in their own fat: with their mouth they speak proudly.

To say a man is fat, often means he is very proud. Of one who speaks pompously, it is said, "What can we do? *tassi-kul-lap-inâl*," i. e. from the fat of his flesh he declares himself. "Oh! the fat of his mouth; how largely he talks!" "Take care, fellow, or I will restrain the fat of thy mouth." "From the intoxication of his blood he thus talks to you."—ROBERTS.

Ver. 11. They have now compassed us in our steps; they have set their eyes bowing down to the earth.

A man who has people watching him to find out a cause for accusation to the king, or great men, says, "Yes, they are around my legs and my feet; their eyes are always open; they are ever watching my *suvadu*," i. e. steps; *i. e.* they are looking for the impress, or footsteps, in the earth. For this purpose, the eyes of the enemies of David were "bowing down to the earth."—ROBERTS.

PSALM XVIII.

Ver. 2. The LORD *is* my rock, and my fortress, and my deliverer; my God, my strength, in whom I will trust; my buckler, and the horn of my salvation, *and* my high tower.

See on Eph. 6. 16.

That is, my strong, mighty deliverer. The image is taken from the bull, whose strength and defensive weapon lie in his horns. Hence a horn is the symbol of strength. Jer. xlviii. 25, says, "The horn of Moab is cut off;" that is, his power is weakened. Micah iv. 13, says, "Arise and thrash, O daughter of Zion; for I will make thy horn iron, and I will make thy foot brass; and thou shalt beat in pieces many people." Ps. cxxxii. 17, "There will I make the horn of David to bud: I have adorned a lamp for mine anointed;" translated by Luther, "will make him strong and mighty." The Greeks and Romans made use of the same image. The former said of a bold and valiant man, "He has horns." Horace says of wine, that it revived the hope of the afflicted, and gave the poor "horns," that is, courage and strength.—ROSENMULLER.

The most extraordinary oriental costume which I have yet seen, is the head-dress worn by many females at Deir el Kamr, and in all the adjacent region of Mount Lebanon. In the cities on the seacoast it is not so frequently seen. It is called Tantoor, and is set on the forehead, projecting like a straight horn. It is from fifteen to twenty inches long; in its thickness gradually diminishing; having its diameter at one extremity about four inches, at the other about two. It is hollow, otherwise the weight would be insupportable to the stiffest neck; and it is tinselled over, so as to give it a silvery appearance. The end with the larger diameter rests on the forehead, where it is strapped to, by one strap passing behind the head, and another passing under the chin: the horn itself protrudes straight forward, inclining upward, at an angle of about twenty or thirty degrees. Over the further extremity they throw the veil, which thus serves the double purpose of modesty and shade.

I could hear no account of the origin of this unicorn costume. In its style it differs materially from the horns described by Bruce in Abyssinia, and by other travellers, which have been considered as illustrating those passages in scripture, "Lift not up your horn on high.—Thy horn hast thou exalted," &c. For here it is the females that wear it; and not the men, as in Abyssinia: it has no appearance of strength, nor indeed, to me, of beauty; although, doubtless, among the females of Mount Lebanon, there may be as much vanity in their mode of adjusting and bearing this article of dress, as is to be found at any European toilet. Some, indeed, though very few, wear this monstrous ornament protruding from one side of the face, instead of the front: but I could obtain no satisfactory account of this heretical fashion, any more than of the orthodox position of the Tantoor. It is not worn by the Druse women only. The servant of the house where I lived at Deir el Kamr wore one: so also did a young woman, whose marriage I there witnessed: several, likewise, of the virgins, that were her fellows, and bore her company, wore this head-dress; all these were Christians. Hanna Doomani told me that it is used chiefly by the lower orders: at least that those who have been brought up at Damascus, or at the principal cities, would not think of wearing it. In other words, probably, it is the true ancient female mountaineer's costume; but what is its degree of antiquity, it may be difficult to discover.—JOWETT.

Ver. 5. The sorrows of hell compassed me about; the snares of death prevented me.

The margin has, for *sorrows*, "cords." (2 Sam. xxii. 6. Prov. xiii. 14, and xiv. 27.) Dr. Boothroyd translates, "The cords of hades enclosed me; the snares of death were laid for me." The Psalmist says in another place, He "shall rain snares" upon the wicked. From the parallel texts in Samuel and Proverbs, it is evident that DEATH, by the ancients, in figure at least, was PERSONIFIED and described as having SNARES, with which to catch the bodies of men. The Hindoo *Yama*, "the catcher of the souls of men," bears some resemblance to the Charon and Minos of the Egyptians and Grecians. *Yama* rides on a buffalo, has a large SNARE in his hand, and is every way a most hideous looking monster. In his anxiety to fill his caves with mortals, he was often involved in great disputes with the gods and others; as in the case of Marcander, who was a favourite of the supreme Siva. He had already cast his SNARE upon him, and was about to drag him to the lower regions, when the deity appeared, and compelled him to relinquish his prey. When people are in the article of death, they are said to be caught in the SNARE of Yama. (See Matt. xxiii. 33.)—ROBERTS.

Ver. 33. He maketh my feet like hinds' *feet*, and setteth me upon my high places.

The allusions to this animal in the sacred volume, though not numerous, are of considerable importance. Its name in Hebrew, (איל) *ail*, is considered by Dr. Shaw as a generic word, including all the species of the deer kind; whether they are distinguished by round horns, as the stag; or by flat ones, as the fallow-deer; or by the smallness of the branches, as the roe. The term originally signified aid or assistance; and, in the progress of language, by a natural and easy transition, came to denote an animal furnished with the means of defence, but limited to horned animals, particularly the stag and the hind. This creature seems to resemble the goat, in being remarkably sure-footed, and delighting in elevated situations.

The royal Psalmist alludes to both circumstances in one of his triumphant odes: "He maketh my feet like hinds' feet, and setteth me upon my high places." He might also refer, in the first clause, to the uncommon solidity and hardness of its hoof, which Virgil compares to brass, which enables it to tread, with ease, the pointed rocks. It may seem, from the words of David, that the female possesses a surer foot and a harder hoof than the male, for he ascribes to himself the feet of the hind; but since natural historians have not remarked any difference between them, it is probable he was led to the choice from some other cause, which it may not be easy to discover. The prophet Habakkuk, in the close of his prayer, has the same allusion, and nearly in the same words: "He will make my feet like hinds' feet, and he will make me to walk upon my high places." While the Psalmist contents himself with referring merely to the firmness and security of his position, "he setteth me upon my high places," the prophet encourages himself with the persuasion, that his God would conduct him through every danger, with the same ease and safety as the hind walks among the cliffs of the rock.—PAXTON.

PSALM XIX.

Ver. 4. Their line is gone out through all the earth, and their words to the end of the world. In them hath he set a tabernacle for the sun; 5. Which *is* as a bridegroom coming out of his chamber, *and* rejoiceth as a strong man to run a race.

The espousals by money, or a written instrument, were performed by the man and woman under a tent or canopy erected for that purpose. Into this chamber the bridegroom was accustomed to go with his bride, that he might talk with her more familiarly; which was considered as a ceremony of confirmation to the wedlock. While he was there, no person was allowed to enter; his friends and attendants waited for him at the door, with torches and lamps in their hands; and when he came out, he was received by all that were present with great joy and acclamation. To this ancient custom, the Psalmist alludes in his magnificent description of the heavens: "In them he set a tabernacle for the sun; which is as a bridegroom coming out of his chamber, and rejoices as a strong man to run a race."—PAXTON.

Ver. 10. More to be desired *are they* than gold, yea, than much fine gold; sweeter also than honey and the honey-comb.

There is no difference made among us, between the delicacy of honey in the comb, and after its separation from it. We may therefore be at a loss to enter into the energy of that expression, "Sweeter than honey, and the honeycomb," Ps. xix. 10; or, to express it with the same emphasis as our translation does the preceding clause, "Sweeter than honey, yea, than the honeycomb," which last, it should seem, from the turn of thought of the Psalmist, is as much to be preferred to honey, as the finest gold is to that of a more impure nature.

But this will appear in a more easy light, if the diet and the relish of the present Moors of West Barbary be thought to resemble those of the times of the Psalmist: for a paper published first in the Philosophical Transactions, and after that by Dr. Halley, in the *Miscellanea Curiosa*, informs us, that they esteem honey a wholesome breakfast, "and the most delicious that which is in the comb, with the young bees in it, before they come out of their cases, while they still look milkwhite, and resemble, being taking out, gentles, such as fishers use: these I have often ate of, but they seemed insipid to my palate, and sometimes I found they gave me the heartburn."—HARMER.

PSALM XX.

Ver. 5. We will rejoice in thy salvation, and in the name of our God we will set up *our* banners: the LORD fulfil all thy petitions.

In all religious as well as warlike processions, the people carry banners. Hence on the pinnacles of their sacred cars, on the domes or gateways of their temples, and on the roof of a new house, may be seen the banner of the caste or sect floating in the air. Siva, the supreme, also is described as having a banner in the celestial world.

When a person makes a solemn vow to go on a pilgrimage, to perform a penance, or to bathe in holy water; or when a man has a dispute in a court of law, or in any other way; or when a disobedient son has resolved to act as he pleases; it is said, "Why try to move him from his purpose? *tussil-katti*, he has tied up, and stands by his banner:" which implies, he must and will abide by his purpose. —ROBERTS.

The banners formerly so much used were a part of military equipage, borne in times of war to assemble, direct, distinguish, and encourage the troops. They might possibly be used for other purposes also. Occasions of joy, splendid processions, and especially a royal habitation, might severally be distinguished in this way. The words of the Psalmist may perhaps be wholly figurative: but if they should be literally understood, the allusion of erecting a banner in the name of the Lord, acknowledging his glory, and imploring his favour, might be justified from an existing practice. Certain it is, that we find this custom prevalent on this very principle, in other places, into which it might originally have been introduced from Judea. Thus Mr. Turner says, "I was told that it was a custom with the soobah to ascend the hill every month, when he sets up a white flag, and performs some religious ceremonies, to conciliate the favour of a dewta, or invisible being, the genius of the place, who is said to hover about the summit, dispensing at his will good and evil to every thing around him." (Turner's Travels.)—BURDER.

PSALM XXII.

Title—To the chief Musician upon Aijeleth Shahar, (Hind of the Morning.) A Psalm of David.

Many curious observations have been made on the titles of the Psalms, but attended with the greatest uncertainty. Later eastern customs, respecting the titles of books and poems, may perhaps give a little more certainty to these matters; but great precision must not be expected. D'Herbelot tells us, that a Persian metaphysical and mystic poem was called a *Rose Bush*. A collection of moral essays, the *Garden of Anemonies*. Another eastern book, the *Lion of the Forest*. That Scherfeddin al Baussiri called a poem of his, written in praise of his Arabian prophet, who, he affirmed, had cured him of a paralytic disorder in his sleep, the *Habit of a Derveesh;* and because he is celebrated there for having given sight to a blind person, this poem is also entitled by its author, the *Bright Star*.

The ancient Jewish taste may reasonably be supposed to have been of the same kind. Agreeable to which is the explanation some learned men have given, of David's commanding the *bow* to be taught the children of Israel, 2 Sam. i. 18, which they apprehended did not relate to the use of that weapon in war, but to the hymn which he composed on occasion of the death of Saul and Jonathan, and from which he entitled this elegy, as they think, the *Bow.* The twenty-second Psalm might, in like manner, be called the *Hind of the Morning;* the fifty-sixth, the *Dove dumb in distant places;* the sixtieth, the *Lily of the Testimony;* the eightieth, the *Lilies of the Testimony*, in the plural; and the forty-fifth, simply the *Lilies.*

It is sufficiently evident, I should think, that these terms do not denote certain musical instruments. For if they did, why do the more common names of the timbre, the harp, the psaltery, and the trumpet, with which psalms were sung, Ps. lxxxi. 2, 3, never appear in those titles?

Do they signify certain tunes? It ought not however to be imagined that these tunes are so called from their bearing some resemblance to the noises made by the things mentioned in the titles, for lilies are *silent*, if this supposition should otherwise have been allowed with respect to the Hind of the Morning. Nor does the fifty-sixth Psalm speak of the *mourning* of the dove, but of its *dumbness.* If they signify *tunes* at all, they must signify the tunes to which such songs or hymns were sung, as were distinguished by these names: and so the inquiry will terminate in this point, whether the Psalms to which these titles are affixed were called by these names; or whether they were some other psalms, or songs, to the tune of which these were to be sung. And as we do not find the bow referred to, nor the same name twice made use of, so far as our lights reach, it seems most probable that these are the names of those very Psalms to which they are prefixed.

The forty-second Psalm, it may be thought, might very well have been entitled the *Hind of the Morning*, because, as that panted after the water brooks, so panted the soul of the Psalmist after God; but the twenty-second Psalm, it is certain, might equally well be distinguished by this title, *Dogs have compassed me*, the *assembly of the wicked have enclosed me:* and as the Psalmist, in the forty-second Psalm, rather chose to compare himself to a *hart*, than a *hind*, the twenty-second Psalm much better answers this title, in which he speaks of his hunted soul in the feminine gender: *Deliver my soul from the sword, my darling* (which in the original is feminine) *from the power of the dog.* Every one that reflects on the circumstances of David, at the time to which the fifty-sixth Psalm refers, and considers the oriental taste, will not wonder to see that Psalm entitled the *Dove dumb in distant places;* nor are *lilies* more improper to be made the title of other Psalms, with proper distinctions, than a *Garden of Anemonies* to be the name of a collection of moral discourses.—HARMER.

Ver. 6. But I *am* a worm, and no man; a reproach of men, and despised of the people.

When a man complains and abhors himself, he asks, "What am I? a worm! a worm!" "Ah! the proud man; he regarded me as a worm: well should I like to say to him, we are ALL worms." "Worm, crawl out of my presence."—ROBERTS.

Ver. 7. All they that see me laugh me to scorn; they shoot out the lip, they shake the head.

Ainsworth has this—"All they that see me, doe skoff at mee: they make-a-mow with the lip, they wag the head." It is exceedingly contemptuous to protrude the lower lip; and, generally speaking, it is only done to those of a mean condition. Those who cannot grant a favour, or who have not the power to perform something they have been requested to do, "shoot out the lip." To shake the head is a favourite way of giving the negative, and is also a mark of disdain.—ROBERTS.

Ver. 10. I was cast upon thee from the womb.

"What!" asks the old slave, "will you dismiss me now? Have I not been cast upon you from the *ketpum?*" womb.—ROBERTS.

Ver. 12. Many bulls have compassed me: strong *bulls* of Bashan have beset me round,

Bishop Horne says, the latter verse, if literally translated, runs thus: "Rebuke the wild beast of the reeds, the congregation of the mighty among the calves of the nations, skipping or exulting with pieces of silver." Wicked men, or those who have much bodily strength, who insult and domineer over the weak, and all "lewd fellows of the baser sort," are called *mādukul*, i. e. bulls. "Of what country are you the bull?" People of docile dispositions—those who live at peace with their neighbours—are called cows or calves: hence when violent men injure them, it is said, "See those bulls how they are oppressing the calves; look at them, they are always butting the cows." "Why has this mad bull of Point Pedro come hither? Go, bull, go, graze in thy own pastures." David, therefore, prayed that the Lord would rebuke the bulls who thus troubled his people.—ROBERTS.

The strength of the bull is too remarkable to require description; and his courage and fierceness are so great, that he ventures at times to combat the lion himself. Nor is he more celebrated for these qualities, than for his disposition to unite with those of his own kind, against their common enemy. For these reasons he has been chosen by the Spirit of inspiration, to symbolize the powerful, fierce, and implacable enemies of our blessed Redeemer; who, forgetting their personal animosities, combined against his precious life, and succeeded in procuring his crucifixion: "Many bulls have compassed me: strong bulls of Bashan have beset me round." Nor can we conceive a more striking and appropriate symbol of a fierce and ruthless warrior; an instance of which occurs in that supplication of David: "Rebuke the company of the spearmen, the multitude of the bulls, with the calves of the people, till every one submit himself with pieces of silver." In the sublime description of Isaiah, which seems to refer to some great revolutions, which are to be effected in times long posterior to the age in which he flourished; probably in these last days, antecedent to the millennial state of the church; the complete destruction of her strong and cruel enemies is thus foretold: "And the unicorns shall come down with them, and the bullocks with the bulls, and their land shall be soaked with blood, and their dust made fat with fatness."—PAXTON.

Ver. 16. For dogs have compassed me; the assembly of the wicked have enclosed me: they pierced my hands and my feet.

"The dog," says Poiret, "loses in Barbary, as in the East in general, a part of those social qualities which make him the friend of man. He is no longer that domestic, mild, insinuating animal, faithfully attached to his master, and ever ready to defend him, even at the expense of his life. Among the Arabs he is cruel, blood-thirsty, always hungry, and never satisfied. His look is savage, his physiognomy ignoble, and his appearance disagreeable. The Moors grant him, indeed, a corner of their tent; but this is all. They never caress him, never throw him any thing to eat. To this treatment, in my opinion, must the indifference of the dogs towards their master be ascribed. Very often they have not even any master. They choose a tent as a place of refuge; they are suffered to remain there, and no further notice is taken of them. Refuse, carrion, filth, every thing is good enough for them, if they can but appease their hunger. They are lean, emaciated, and have scarcely any belly. Among themselves they seldom bite each other; but they unite against the stranger who approaches the Arab tents, furiously attack him, and would tear him to pieces if he did not seek safety in flight from this starved troop. If any person were unable to defend himself, or had the misfortune to fall, he would be in danger of being devoured, for these dogs are very greedy after human flesh." D'Arvieux also observes, that the Bedouin Arabs keep a great number of dogs, which run about in and out of the camp, begin to bark at the least noise they hear, and answer each other. "These dogs," says he, "are not accustomed to see people walking about late at night, and I believe that they would tear any one in pieces who should venture to approach the camp." "In Morocco," says Höst, "there are dogs in abundance, and as the greater part of the Moors have scarcely enough to live on for themselves, much less to feed dogs, they suffer them to lie about the streets so starved that they can hardly hang together, and almost devoured by fleas and vermin. But these dogs, which do not move during the daytime, though they are frequently trodden on, are so insupportable in the night, not only on account of their barking, bellowing, and cries, but also because they are so savage and sleep so little, that nobody is able to go through the streets without a watchman."

"During all the long tour through this dreary and melancholy city, (Alexandria, in Egypt,) Europe and its liveliness was pictured to me only by the bustle and by the activity of the sparrows. I here no longer recognised the dog, that friend of man, the attached and faithful companion, the lively and honest courtier; he is here a gloomy egotist, unknown to the host under whose roof he dwells, cut off from human intercourse, without being less of a slave; he does not know him whose house he protects, and devours his corpse without repugnance. The following circumstance will fully paint his character. In the evening of the day on which I arrived at Alexandria, I went to our ship to supply myself with clean linen. It was eleven o'clock at night when I came again on shore, and I was half a league from my quarters. I was obliged to go through a city taken only that morning by storm, and in which I did not know a street. No reward could induce my man to quit his boat and accompany me. I undertook the journey alone, and went over the burying-ground, in spite of the manes, as I was best acquainted with this road. At the first habitations of the living, I was attacked by whole troops of furious dogs, who made their attacks from the doors, from the streets, and the roofs; and the barking resounded from house to house, from one family to another. I soon, however, observed that the war declared against me was not grounded on any coalition; for as soon as I had quitted the territory of the attackers, they were driven away by the others, who received me on their frontiers. The darkness was only lightened by the stars, and by the constant glimmer of the nights in this climate. Not to lose this advantage, to avoid the barking of the dogs, and to take a road which I knew could not lead me astray, I left the streets, and resolved to go along the beach; but walls and timber-yards, which extended to the sea, blocked up the way. After having waded through the water to escape from the dogs, and climbed over walls where the sea was too deep, exhausted by anxiety and fatigue, and quite wet, I reached one of our sentinels about midnight, in the conviction that the dog is the most dreadful among the Egyptian plagues." (Denon.)—ROSENMULLER.

Ver. 21. Save me from the lion's mouth: for thou hast heard me from the horns of the unicorns.

Those who are in great trouble from the power or cruelty of others, often cry out to their gods—"Ah! save me from the tusk of the elephant! From the mouth of the tiger, and the tusks of the boar, deliver me—deliver me!" "Who will save me from the horn of the *kāndam?*" This animal is now extinct in these regions, and it is not easy to determine what it was: the word in the *Sathur-Agarāthe* is rendered jungle-cow, but it was probably the rhinoceros; and Dr. Boothroyd translates, "from the horns of the rhinoceros, defend me."—ROBERTS.

PSALM XXIII.

Ver. 1. The LORD *is* my shepherd; I shall not want. 2. He maketh me to lie down in green pastures: he leadeth me beside the still waters.

In this figure the Psalmist had in his view a shepherd leading his flock into luxuriant fields, and causing them to quench their thirst and repose by gentle streams. In a tropical clime, a tranquil stream and a green pasture are peculiarly pleasing to the eye. Hence many eastern allegories are taken from such scenes. "Never, never will I forget my God: he has brought me into a plenteous pasturage, and folded me near an abundance of water." "Why does he like this country?"—"Because he has good *grazing.*" "Tamban has left his master, because there was not much grass." "Much grass! why the bull was never satisfied." "Well, friend, whither are you going? in search of grass and water?"—"Yes; the fat one has become lean, because his grass has withered and his water failed."—ROBERTS.

The patriarchs wandered with their cattle among the towns and villages of Canaan, and fed them even in the most populous districts without molestation. And it is a remarkable fact, that the Kenites and Rechabites lived in Palestine under tents, and fed their cattle wherever they could find pasture, when the country was crowded with inhabitants, long after it had been divided by lot among the tribes. The Bedouin Arabs claim the same privilege in those countries to this day, which, depopulated as they are, probably contain as many inhabitants in their towns and villages, as in the days of Abraham. Nor is this custom peculiar to Palestine; in Barbary and other places, they live in the same manner. Great numbers of Arabian shepherds come into Egypt itself, in the months of November, December, and January, from three or four hundred leagues distance, to feed their camels and their horses. After having spent some time in the neighbourhood of the Nile, they retire into the deserts, from whence, by routes with which they are acquainted, they pass into other regions to dwell there, in like manner, some months of the year, till the return of the usual season recalls them to the vale of Egypt. To this custom of leading the flocks from one country and region to another, the royal Psalmist alludes in that beautiful pastoral: "The Lord is my shepherd; I shall not want. He maketh me to lie down in green pastures; he leadeth me beside the still waters. He restoreth my soul; he leadeth me in the paths of righteousness, for his name's sake." We are taught by the prophet to look for the same blessings from the vigilant care and tenderness of Messiah: "They shall feed in the ways, and their pastures shall be in all high places. They shall not hunger nor thirst; neither shall the heat nor sun smite them; for he that hath mercy on them, shall lead them; even by the springs of water shall he guide them, and I will make all my mountains a way, and my highways shall be exalted." The conduct of the eastern shepherd in leading his flock to the green pastures, and the still waters, is clearly alluded to by John, in the book of Revelation: "For the Lamb which is in the midst of the throne, shall feed them, and lead them unto living fountains of waters; and God shall wipe away all tears from their eyes."—PAXTON.

Ver. 4. Yea, though I walk through the valley of the shadow of death, I will fear no evil: for thou *art* with me; thy rod and thy staff they comfort me.

"He was indeed a good king; by his sceptre and *umbrella* he comforted his subjects." By the staff or sceptre he gently governed and protected his people; and by his *umbrella* he defended them from the fierce rays of the sun. "Yes; by these are we instructed, guided, supported, and defended; what have we to fear? great is our safety and confidence." "You are now becoming an old man, and your children are young, what will become of them after your death?"—"Ah! friend, is there not a staff in the hand of God?" "Truly, my wife and children have gone; they have reclined in the place of burning, but my staff is still with me." "See the wicked one, he has not a staff left."—ROBERTS.

In the bag or scrip, which is mentioned by Samuel as a part of the shepherd's furniture, his provisions, and other necessaries, are carried. He bears in his hand a staff of considerable length, with which he keeps his cattle in order, and numbers them when they return from the field. To this instrument the Psalmist refers in that beautiful and affecting passage, where he addresses Jehovah as the shepherd of his soul: "Yea, though I walk through the valley of the shadow of death, I will fear no evil: for thou art with me; thy rod and thy staff they comfort me."—PAXTON.

Ver. 5. Thou preparest a table before me in the presence of mine enemies: thou anointest my head with oil; my cup runneth over.

In Hindostan, when a person of rank and opulence receives a guest, whom he wishes to distinguish by peculiar marks of regard, he pours upon his hands and arms, in the presence of the whole company, a delightful odoriferous perfume, puts a golden cup into his hand, and pours wine into it till it run over; assuring him at the same time, that it is to him a great pleasure to receive him into his house, and that he shall find under his roof every comfort which he could bestow. The reference to this custom, which at one time was probably general throughout the East, in the twenty-third Psalm, is at once beautiful and striking: "Thou preparest a table before me in the presence of mine enemies; thou anointest my head with oil, my cup runneth over." The Lord had early received the Psalmist into favour; raised him to the highest honours, from a very humble condition; and, what was infinitely better, he set before him the inestimable blessings of redeeming love, prepared him by a copious unction of the holy Spirit to enjoy them, and welcomed him in the most honourable manner, by putting the cup of salvation into his hand, in the presence of all his people, and pouring into it with unsparing liberality, the wine of heavenly consolation.—Paxton.

On all joyful occasions the people of the East anoint the head with oil. Hence, at their marriages, and other festive times, the young and old may be seen with their long black tresses neatly tied on the crown of the head, shining and smooth, like polished ebony. The Psalmist, therefore, rejoicing in God as his protector, says, "Thou anointest my head with oil." It is an act of great respect to pour perfumed oil on the head of a distinguished guest; hence the woman in the gospel manifested her respect for the Saviour by pouring "precious ointment" on his head.—Roberts.

In the East, the people frequently anoint their visiters with some very fragrant perfume; and give them a cup or a glass of some choice wine, which they are careful to fill till it runs over. The first was designed to show their love and respect; the latter to imply that while they remained there, they should have an abundance of every thing. To something of this kind the Psalmist probably alludes in this passage.—Burder.

PSALM XXIV.

Ver. 7. Lift up your heads, O ye gates; and be ye lift up, ye everlasting doors; and the King of glory shall come in.

See on Prov. 17. 19.

PSALM XXV.

Ver. 15. Mine eyes *are* ever towards the Lord; for he shall pluck my feet out of the net.

"Those who delight in fowling, do not spring the game with dogs, as we do; but, shading themselves with an oblong piece of canvass, stretched over a couple of reeds or sticks, like a door, they walk with it through the several brakes and avenues, where they expect to find game. The canvass is usually spotted, or painted with the figure of a leopard, and perforated near the top in a few places, for the fowler to look through, and observe what passes before him. The partridge, and other gregarious birds, when the canvass approaches, will covey together, although they were feeding before at some distance from one another. The woodcock, quail, and other birds, which do not commonly feed in flocks, will, at sight of the extended canvass, stand still and look with astonishment, which gives the sportsman an opportunity of coming very near them; and then resting the canvass upon the ground, and directing the muzzle of his piece through one of the holes, he will sometimes shoot a whole covey at a time. The Arabs have another, but a more laborious method of catching these birds; for observing that they become languid and fatigued, after they have been hastily put up two or three times, they immediately run in upon them, and knock them down with their bludgeons. They are likewise well acquainted with that method of catching partridges called tunnelling; and to make the capture the greater, they will sometimes place behind the net a cage with some tame ones within, which, by their perpetual chirping and calling, quickly bring down the coveys which are within hearing, and by that means destroy great numbers of them. To hunt the jackal, which greatly abounds in that country, they sometimes use a leopard which has been trained to hunting from his youth. The hunter keeps the animal before him on his horse, and when he meets with a jackal, the leopard leaps down, and creeps along till he thinks himself within reach of the prey, when he leaps upon it with incredible agility, throwing himself seventeen or eighteen feet at a time." These statements illustrate the force and propriety of those passages of holy writ, which allude to the arts and implements of the hunter and the fowler, by which the timid victim is taken ere it is aware; or the bold is compelled by main force, or by deadly wounds, to submit to his more cunning or powerful adversary. It is not without reason the Psalmist rejoiced that the snare was broken, and his soul had escaped as a bird from the snare of the fowler; and that God had brought his feet out of the net.—Paxton.

PSALM XXVII.

Ver. 6. And now shall my head be lifted up above mine enemies round about me: therefore will I offer in his tabernacle sacrifices of joy; I will sing, yea, I will sing praises unto the Lord.

"The Modeliar is now fixed in his situation."—"Is he?" —"Yes, yes, he is on the mountain, and is like unto it." "Who will take me out of this mud, and place me upon the mountain?"—Roberts.

PSALM XXVIII.

Ver. 1. Unto thee will I cry, O Lord, my rock; be not silent to me: lest, *if* thou be silent to me, I become like them that go down into the pit.

See on Job 33. 18, 24.

Ver. 2. Hear the voice of my supplications, when I cry unto thee, when I lift up my hands towards thy holy oracle.

See on Ps. 44. 20.

PSALM XXIX.

Ver. 5. The voice of the Lord breaketh the cedars; yea, the Lord breaketh the cedars of Lebanon.

See on Deut. 3. 25.

Ver. 9. The voice of the Lord maketh the hinds to calve, and discovereth the forests: and in his temple doth every one speak of *his* glory.

Ainsworth translates, "Jehovah maketh the hinds tremblingly to travel." The thunder of the East is far more terrific than that of England. The explosion is so sudden and so vast, that the earth literally trembles under its power: fierce animals rush into the covert, and birds fly affrighted to the shade. Then it is the people say, "Ah! this will cause the womb to tremble." "This thunder will make the pains to come." "I fear there will be a falling this day."—Roberts.

It seems to be generally admitted, that the hind brings forth her young with great difficulty; and, so much appears to be suggested in the third verse of the same chapter: "They bow themselves, they bring forth their young ones, they cast out their sorrows." But if Pliny, and other natural historians, are worthy of credit, divine providence has been graciously pleased to provide certain herbs, which greatly facilitate the birth; and by an unerring instinct, he directs the hind to feed upon them, when the time of gestation draws towards a close. Whatever be in this assertion, we know from higher authority, that providence does promote the parturition of the hind, by awakening her fears and agitating her frame by the rolling thunder: "The voice of Jehovah, (a common Hebrew phrase, denoting thunder,) maketh the hinds to calve." Nor ought we to wonder that so timorous a creature as the hind should be so much affected by that awfully imposing sound, when some of the proudest men that ever existed, have been made to tremble. Augustus, the Roman emperor, according to Suetonius, was so terrified when it thundered, that he wrapped a seal-skin round his body, with the view of defending it from the lightning, and concealed himself in some secret corner till the tempest ceased. The tyrant Caligula, who sometimes affected to threaten Jupiter himself, covered his head, or hid himself under a bed; and Horace confesses, he was reclaimed from atheism by the terror of thunder and lightning.—PAXTON.

PSALM XXX.

Title—A Psalm *and* Song *at* the dedication of the house of David.

It was common, when any person had finished a house, and entered into it, to celebrate it with great rejoicing, and keep a festival, to which his friends were invited, and to perform some religious ceremonies, to secure the protection of heaven. Thus, when the second temple was finished, the priests and Levites, and the rest of the captivity, kept the dedication of the house of God with joy, and offered numerous sacrifices, Ezra vi. 16. We read in the New Testament of the feast of the dedication, appointed by Judas Maccabæus, in memory of the purification and restoration of the temple of Jerusalem, after it had been defiled and laid in ruins by Antiochus Epiphanes; and celebrated annually, to the time of its destruction by Titus, by solemn sacrifices, music, songs, and hymns to the praise of God; and feasts, and every thing that could give the people pleasure, for eight days successively. (Josephus.) This was customary even among private persons. The Romans also dedicated their temples and their theatres. So also they acted with respect to their statues, palaces, and houses.—CHANDLER.

Ver. 1. I will extol thee, O LORD; for thou hast lifted me up, and hast not made my foes to rejoice over me.

"Thou hast lifted me up." The verb is used, in its original meaning, to denote *the reciprocating motion of the buckets of a well*, one descending as the other rises, and *vice versa;* and is here applied, with admirable propriety, to point out the various reciprocations and changes of David's fortunes, as described in this psalm, as to prosperity and adversity; and particularly, that gracious reverse of his afflicted condition, which he now celebrates, God having raised him up to great honour and prosperity; for having built his palace, "he perceived that the Lord had established him king over Israel, and that he had exalted his kingdom, for his people Israel's sake."—CHANDLER.

Ver. 5. For his anger *endureth but* a moment; in his favour *is* life: weeping may endure for a night, but joy *cometh* in the morning.

The Tamul method of expressing a moment is to move the hand once round the head, and give a snap of the finger. Thus they say of any thing which endures but a short time, "It is only as the snap of the fingers." The people of the East have nearly all their festivities in the night; they say it is the sorrowful time, and therefore adopt this plan to make it pass more pleasantly away. To those who are in difficulties or sorrow; to widows, orphans, and strangers, "night is the time to weep;" hence in passing through the village may be heard people crying aloud to their *departed* friends, or bitterly lamenting their own condition. They have, however, some very pleasing and philosophical sayings on the uncertainty of the sorrows and joys of life. In the book *Scanda-Purāna*, it is written, "The wise, when pleasure comes, do not greatly rejoice; and in sorrow they yield not to distress; for they judge that pleasure and pain are incident to life. The indigent become wealthy, and the wealthy indigent; and inferiors are exalted. Can wealth or poverty, pleasure or pain, be regarded as permanent to the soul? The phases of the moon remain not in one state; they diminish and increase: so your afflictions will one day terminate."—ROBERTS.

Ver. 9. What profit *is there* in my blood, when I go down to the pit? Shall the dust praise thee? shall it declare thy truth?

"When I go down to the pit, what fruit will there be in my body?" "Ah! he has fallen into the pit," *i. e.* he is dead. Of those whose bodies have been burned, it is said, they are all *sāmbal*, i. e. all ashes. "Where is your father?"—"Alas! my lord, he is ashes."—ROBERTS.

PSALM XXXI.

Ver. 2. Bow down thine ear to me; deliver me speedily; be thou my strong rock, for a house of defence to save me.

"My lord, have you not always assisted me? As a mountain and a fortress have you been to me." When a man of rank dies, it is said, "that *konam* (bastion or fortress) has fallen."—ROBERTS.

Ver. 8. And hast not shut me up into the hand of the enemy: thou hast set my feet in a large room.

Dr. Boothroyd translates this, "hast set my foot in a wider place." Many figures in the English language are unquestionably borrowed from the scriptures, among which may be, "he is in his hands;" for he is in his power. When Zedekiah ordered Ebed-melech to draw Jeremiah out of the dungeon, he was directed to take thirty men *with him;* but the margin has it, "*in thy hand!*" In eastern language, therefore, to be in the hands of a person, signifies to be in his possession or power. But David was not given into the hand of his enemy, and his feet were at liberty in a large place, so that he could walk whithersoever he pleased. In another verse, he says, "Thou hast enlarged me;" he was increased and at liberty: and again, in speaking of his enemies, and the misery he suffered, he says, "He brought me forth into a large place;" so that his feet were at liberty. The feet (as well as the hands) are sometimes taken for the *whole* man: thus, the Lord "will keep the feet of his saints," finds an illustration here. "Have I not had a protector through this journey?"—"Yes, the gods have kept my feet." "Well, have you heard from your son?"—"Yes; he has arrived in safety, and has written to me, saying, he will return next month, if the gods keep his feet." A man who is embarrassed in his circumstances, says, "My feet are in shackles." "Who will refresh my feet?" "Who will give liberty to my feet?"—ROBERTS.

Ver. 12. I am forgotten as a dead man out of mind: I am like a broken vessel.

"Yes," says the man who is reduced to poverty, "I am now a corpse to all my former friends." "What is a man without money? A *naddukera-savvam*," *a walking corpse!* "I am now a broken *chatte*," a potsherd. "Truly, I am like the *tam-bat tam*," the drum with its head broken. "I am of no use; no one enjoys me."—ROBERTS.

PSALM XXXII.

Ver. 4. My moisture is turned into the drought of summer. Selah.

The fields of Canaan are refreshed with frequent and copious rains, while some of the neighbouring countries are scarcely ever moistened with a shower. In the winter months, the rain falls indiscriminately, but seldom in the summer. Soon after the heats commence, the grass withers, the flower fades, every green thing is dried up by the roots, and the fields, so lately clothed with the richest verdure, and adorned with the loveliest flowers, are converted into a brown and arid wilderness. To the uniform withered appearance of the fields during the reign of an eastern summer, and not to any particular year of drought, the Psalmist refers in these plaintive terms: "My moisture is turned into the drought of summer." When conviction slept, and conscience was silent, the soul of David resembled a field refreshed by the genial showers of heaven; but the moment God in anger entered into judgment with him, and set his sins in order before his face, his courage failed, his beauty was turned into corruption, and his strength into weakness; "the commandment came, sin revived, and he died."—PAXTON.

In England and the neighbouring countries it is common for rain to fall in all months of the year. But it is not so in the Levant. Egypt has scarce any rain at all, and Dr

Shaw affirms that it is as uncommon in what they call at Algiers the Desert, which is the most southern part of that country. These, however, are peculiar cases. Rain indiscriminately in the winter months, and *none at all* in the summer, is what is most common in the East. Jacobus de Vitriaco assures us it is thus in Judea; for he observes that "lightning and thunder are wont, in the western countries, to be in the summer, but happen in the Holy Land in winter. In the summer it seldom or never rains there: but in winter, though the returns of rain are not so frequent, after they begin to fall, they pour down for three or four days and nights together, as vehemently as if they would drown the country." The withered appearance of an eastern summer, which is very dry, is doubtless what the Psalmist refers to when he says, "my moisture is turned into the drought of summer." The reference is not to any particular year of drought, but to what commonly occurs.—HARMER.

Ver. 7. Thou *art* my hiding-place; thou shalt preserve me from trouble; thou shalt compass me about with songs of deliverance. Selah.

We see in the case of David, and many others, that they often had to conceal themselves in caves, mountains, and desert places, from the pursuit of their enemies. In countries like these, where the police is imperfect, where population is so scattered, and where it is so easy to sustain life, it can be no wonder that offenders and injured men often conceal themselves for months and years from the vigilance of their pursuers. It is an every-day occurrence to hear of men thus hiding themselves. Has a person to account for his conduct, or to appear in a court of justice, he packs up his valuables, and makes a start into the jungle, or to some distant country. Perhaps he prowls about the skirts of a forest, and occasionally visits his family in the night. See him on his way, he walks so softly that the most delicate-eared animal cannot detect him; he looks in every direction; puts his ears near the ground, and listens for any sound; again he proceeds, sometimes crawling, sometimes walking, till he has reached his hiding-place. But the natives themselves are famous for assisting each other to elude the search of their pursuers; and often, as did Jonathan and Ahimaaz, they conceal themselves in the well! Sometimes an offender will run to a man of rank who is at enmity with his foe, and say, "My lord, you must be my hiding-place against that wicked man, who has committed so many crimes against you." "Ah! the good man, he was my hiding-place."—ROBERTS.

PSALM XXXIV.

Ver. 8. O taste and see that the LORD *is* good: blessed *is* the man *that* trusteth in him.

"I have *russe-pārtain*," i. e. *tasted* and seen the holy man. "The Modeliar is a good man; I have tasted of him many times." "Tamby, have you been to see the collector?"—"No, I am afraid of him."—"Fear not; I have tasted of him, and he is very sweet." "Do you pretend to know me?"—"Yes, I know you well; many times have I tasted of you, and have proved you to be all bitterness." A wife says of a good husband, "I have tasted him, and he is very sweet." Does a father chastise his child, he asks, "Do you now taste me? Am I sweet or sour? When you commit such things, I shall always be sour to you." Of a good and absent child, he says, "My son, my son! when will you return, that I may again taste your sweetness."—ROBERTS.

Ver. 20. He keepeth all his bones: not one of them is broken.

A curious opinion of the Jews is, that wherever their bodies may be buried, it is only in their own promised land that the resurrection can take place; and, therefore, they who are interred in any other part of the world must take their way to Palestine under ground; and this will be an operation of dreadful toil and pain, although clefts and caverns will be opened for them by the Almighty. Whether it arose from this superstition, or from that love for the land of their fathers, which, in the Jews, is connected with the strongest feelings of faith and hope, certain it is, that many have directed their remains to be sent there. "We were fraughted with wool," says an old traveller, "from Constantinople to Sidon, in which sacks, as most certainly was told to me, were many Jews' bones put into little chests, but unknown to any of the ship. The Jews, our merchants, told me of them at my return from Jerusalem to Saphet, but earnestly entreated me not to tell it, for fear of preventing them another time." Sometimes a wealthy Jew has been known to import earth from Jerusalem wherewith to line his grave. (Quarterly Review.)—BURDER.

PSALM XXXV.

Ver. 5. Let them be as chaff before the wind: and let the angel of the LORD chase *them.*

"Begone! fellow; contend not with my brother or me: thou art as chaff before the wind!" "Not a word, or soon wilt thou be as cotton before the wind!"—ROBERTS.

Ver. 21. Yea, they opened their mouth wide against me, *and* said, Aha, aha! our eye hath seen *it.*

Dr. Boothroyd, "They open wide their mouth against me, and say, Aha! aha! our eye seeth WHAT WE WISHED." See that rude fellow, who has triumphed over another; he distends his mouth to the utmost, then claps his hands, and bawls out, "*Agā! agā!* I have seen, I have seen." So provoking is this exclamation, that a man, though *vanquished*, will often commence another attack. An officer who has lost his situation is sure to have this salutation from those he has injured. Has a man been foiled in argument, has he failed in some feat he promised to perform, has he in any way made himself ridiculous, the people open their mouths, and shout aloud, saying, "*Agā!* finished, finished, fallen, fallen." Then they laugh, and clap their hands, till the poor fellow gets out of their sight.—ROBERTS.

PSALM XXXVI.

Ver. 11. Let not the foot of pride come against me, and let not the hand of the wicked remove me.

Here we have another instance of the feet and hands being used for the whole man. Our Saviour said of the man: "The HAND of him that betrayeth me." Of a sick person to whom the physician will not administer any more medicine, it will be said, *paregāri-kivuttān*, "The hand of the doctor has forsaken him." A servant is under the hand of his master. The foot of pride probably alludes to the custom of the conqueror trampling upon the vanquished: for in the next verse it is said, "The workers of iniquity are fallen: they are cast down, and shall not be able to rise."—ROBERTS.

PSALM XXXVII.

Ver. 6. And he shall bring forth thy righteousness as the light, and thy judgment as the noonday.

"Righteousness and the light are but one." "His righteousness is as the light." "Yes, he is indeed a wise judge, his decision is as the noonday." "What an erroneous judgment is this! my case was as powerful and clear as the sun in his zenith."—ROBERTS.

Ver. 35. I have seen the wicked in great power, and spreading himself like a green bay-tree.

The margin has, instead of green bay-tree, "a tree that groweth in his own soil." Ainsworth, "I have seen the wicked daunting terrible, and spreading himself bare, as a green self-growing laurel." A truly wicked man is compared to a tamarind-tree, whose wood is exceedingly hard, and whose fruit is sour. "That *passāsu*, i. e. fiend, is like the *marutha-marram*," (*Terminalia-Alate.*) This tree resists the most powerful storms; it never loses its leaves, and is sacred to Vyraver, the prince of devils. I have seen some that would measure from thirty to forty feet in circumference. The tamarind-tree at Port Pedro, under which Baldeus preached, measures thirty feet.—ROBERTS.

PSALM XXXIX.

Ver. 5. Behold, thou hast made my days *as* a hand-breadth, and mine age *is* as nothing before thee: verily every man at his best state *is* altogether vanity. Selah.

"What are the days of man? Only four fingers." "My son has gone, and has only had a life of four fingers." "You have had much pleasure?"—"Not so; it has only been the breadth of four fingers." "Is he a great landowner?"—"Yes, he has about the breadth of four fingers." "I am told that the hatred betwixt those people is daily decreasing?"—"Yes; that which is left is about four fingers in breadth."—ROBERTS.

Ver. 10. Remove thy stroke away from me: I am consumed by the blow of thy hand. 11. When thou with rebukes dost correct man for iniquity, thou makest his beauty to consume away like a moth: surely every man *is* vanity. Selah.

See on Job 4. 9.

The moths of the East are very large and beautiful, but short-lived. After a few showers these splendid insects may be seen fluttering in every breeze; but the dry weather and their numerous enemies soon consign them to the common lot. Thus the beauty of man consumes away like that of this gay rover, dressed in his robes of purple, and scarlet, and green.—ROBERTS.

PSALM XL.

Ver. 6. Sacrifice and offering thou didst not desire; mine ears hast thou opened: burnt-offering and sin-offering hast thou not required.

Ainsworth, "Mine ears hast thou digged open." In scripture phrase, the Lord is said to speak IN the ears of his people. Those young heathen who are above ten years of age, and under twenty, have the *ubbatheasum* whispered *in* their ears, which is believed to have a very sacred effect.—ROBERTS.

Ver. 7. Then said I, Lo, I come: in the volume of the book *it is* written of me.

I have elsewhere observed, that the oriental books and letters, which are wont both of them to be rolled up, are usually wrapped in a covering of an elegant kind: I would here add, that they have sometimes words on these coverings, which have a general notion of what is contained in them; which management obtained in much elder times, and might possibly be in use when some of the Psalms were written. Sir John Chardin, describing the manner of dismissing the ambassadors and envoys that were at the court of the Persian monarch, when he was there, after mentioning the presents that were made them, goes on to inform us, "that the letters to the crowned heads were sealed; that for the cardinal patron was open: that for the pope was formed so as to be larger than the rest; it was enclosed in a bag of very rich brocade, and sealed at the ends, which had fringes hanging down the bag half way. The seal was applied to the place where the knot was on both sides, upon red wax, of the diameter of a piece of fifteen sols, and very thick. Upon the middle of one of the sides of the bag were written these two Persian words, *Hamel Fasel*, which signify, excellent or precious writing." After which he goes on to explain the reasons that occasion the Persian prince to treat the popes with such distinguished honour, which it would be of no use to consider here. The remark I would make relates to the inscription on the outside of the rich bag enclosing these despatches, and which, in few words, expressed the general nature of what was contained in the roll within: it was a royal writing. This practice of writing on the outside of the case of a letter, or book rolled up, seems to be at least as ancient as the time of Chrysostom, according to a note of Lambert Bos on the 40th Psalm. Chrysostom, we are told there, remarks, that they call a wrapper the Κεφαλις, which is the word the Septuagint translators make use of to express the Hebrew word מגלה *megillath*, which we translate *volume:* "In the volume of the book it is written of me." Chrysostom seems to suppose there was written in or on the sacred volume, a word or words which signified the coming of the Messiah. But Chrysostom would hardly have thought of such an interpretation, had it not been frequently done at Constantinople in his time, or by the more eastern princes that had business to transact with the Greek emperors; or been known to have been before those times practised among the Jews.—HARMER.

PSALM XLI.

Ver. 9. Yea, mine own familiar friend in whom I trusted, which did eat of my bread, hath lifted *his* heel against me.

"The man who has eaten my rice has now become a traitor; yes, he has cut my *kuthe-kāl*," i. e. heel.—ROBERTS.

To eat of the same bread has been reckoned in every age a sure pledge of inviolable friendship. Pythagoras commanded his disciples not to break bread, because, say they, the bond of friendship is not to be broken; and all friends should assemble round the same cake. A cake of bread, observes Curtius, was the most sacred pledge of amity among the Macedonians. Nothing was reckoned baser, in the East, than to offer violence to those at whose table they had been entertained. Æschines, in his oration against Demosthenes, reproaches him especially because he had accused him, though they had eaten at the same table, and joined in the same sacred ceremonies. In perfect harmony with these views and feelings, which seem to have been derived from a very remote antiquity, the holy Psalmist complains of Ahithophel: "Yea, mine own familiar friend, in whom I trusted, who did eat of my bread, hath lifted up his heel against me." And a greater than David, in reference to Judas Iscariot: "I speak not of you all: I know whom I have chosen; but that the scripture may be fulfilled, he that eateth bread with me hath lifted up his heel against me." The traitor had lived for more than three years in the relations of peace and amity with his Lord: he had been called in the apostolic office, and had been admitted to the same familiar intercourse with his divine Master, as the other disciples had enjoyed. These invaluable privileges greatly aggravated his crime; but his eating bread at his Master's table, while he was plotting against his life, was the crowning point of his enormous wickedness.—PAXTON.

PSALM XLII.

Ver. 1. As the hart panteth after the water-brooks, so panteth my soul after thee, O God.

In the East, where streams are not common, and where the deer are so often chased by their savage co-tenants of the forest and the glade, no wonder that they are often driven from their favourite haunts to the parched grounds. After this, their thirst becomes excessive, but they dare not return to the water, lest they should again meet the enemy. When the good Rāmar and his people went through the thirsty wilderness, it is written, "As the deer cried for water, so did they." "In going through the desert yesterday, my thirst was so great, I cried out like the deer for water."—ROBERTS.

Ver. 7. Deep calleth unto deep at the noise of thy water-spouts: all thy waves and thy billows are gone over me.

A water-spout at sea is a splendid sight; in shape it resembles a funnel, with the tube pointing to the water. In 1819, a large one burst near our ship, which caused considerable alarm to all on board. We were near to it before we were aware, and the captain ordered the guns to be loaded and discharged, to cause it to break. Happily for us, it burst at some distance; but the *noise* the water made in rushing *from* the *water-spout*, and again in dashing *into the sea*, strongly reminded me of this expression, "Deep calleth unto deep at the noise of thy water-spouts." ROBERTS.

Natural philosophers often make mention of water-spouts, which are most surprising appearances; but hardly any of the commentators, that I have observed, speak of them, though our translators have used the term, Psalm xlii. 7, and the Psalmist seems to be directly describing those phenomena, and painting a storm at sea. And none of them, I think, take notice of the frequency of water-spouts on the Jewish coasts, and consequently that it was natural for a Jewish poet to mention them, in the description of a violent and dangerous storm.

That this however is the fact, we learn from Dr. Shaw, who tells us, that water-spouts are more frequently near the capes of Latikea, Greego, and Carmel, than in any other part of the Mediterranean. These are all places on the coast of Syria, and the last of them everybody knows in Judea, it being a place rendered famous by the prayers of the prophet Elijah. The Jews then could not be ignorant of what frequently happened on their coasts, and David must have known of these dangers of the sea, if he had not actually seen some of them, as Dr. Shaw did. Strange then! since this is the case, that commentators should speak of these water-spouts as only meaning vehement rains; or that any should imagine that he compares his afflictions to the pouring of water through the spouts of a house, as Bythner seems to do in his Lyra, when they have nothing to do with a storm at sea, which the Psalmist is evidently describing.

Others have remarked that these spouts are often seen in the Mediterranean, but I do not remember to have seen it anywhere remarked, before I read Dr. Shaw, that they are more frequent on the Syrian and Jewish coasts, than any other part of this sea; and as the doctor has not applied the observation to the explaining any part of scripture, I thought it was right to take notice of it in these papers, and as it belongs to the natural history of Judea, it comes into this chapter.—HARMER.

Ver. 11. Why art thou cast down, O my soul? and why art thou disquieted within me? Hope thou in God; for I shall yet praise him, *who is* the health of my countenance, and my God.

Ainsworth, "the salvations of my face." "Oh! Siva, are you not the salvation of my face?" says the prostrate devotee. "To whom shall I make known my distress? are not you the salvation of my face?" "Alas! alas! the salvation of my face has departed." "The blossoming on my face is now withered and gone," says the widow, lamenting over the corpse of her husband.—ROBERTS.

PSALM XLIV.

Ver. 20. If we have forgotten the name of our God, or stretched out our hands to a strange god.

The stretching out the hand towards an object of devotion, or a holy place, was an ancient usage among Jews and heathens both, and it continues in the East to this time, which continuance I do not remember to have seen remarked. "If," says the Psalmist, "we have forgotten the name of our God, or stretched out our hands to a strange god: shall not God search this out?" Ps. xliv. 20, 21. "Ethiopia shall soon stretch out her hands unto God," Ps. lxviii. 31. "Hear the voice of my supplications, when I cry unto thee: when I lift up my hand towards thy holy oracle," Psalm xxviii. 2.

That this attitude in prayer has continued among the eastern people, appears by the following passages from Pitts, in his account of the religion and manners of the Mohammedans. Speaking of the Algerines throwing wax candles and pots of oil overboard, as a present to some marabbot, or Mohammedan saint, Pitts goes on, and says, "When this is done, they all together hold up their hands, begging the marabbot's blessing, and a prosperous voyage." This they do in common, it seems, when in the Straits' mouth; "and if at any time they happen to be in a very great strait or distress, as being chased, or in a storm, they will gather money, and do likewise." In the same page he tells us, the "marabbots have generally a little neat room built over their graves, resembling in figure their mosques or churches, which is very nicely cleaned, and well looked after." And in the succeeding page he tells us, "Many people there are, who will scarcely pass by any of them without lifting up their hands, and saying some short prayer." He mentions the same devotion again as practised towards a saint that lies buried on the shore of the Red Sea.

In like manner, he tells us, that at quitting the *beet*, or holy house at Mecca, to which they make devout pilgrimages, "they hold up their hands towards the *beet*, making earnest petitions; and then keep going backward till they come to the abovesaid farewell gate. All the way as they retreat, they continue petitioning, holding up their hands, with their eyes fixed on the *beet*, until they are out of sight of it: and so go to their lodgings weeping."—HARMER.

PSALM XLV.

Ver. 1. My heart is enditing a good matter: I speak of the things which I have made touching the King; my tongue *is* the pen of a ready writer.

This Psalm is a poetical composition, in the form of an epithalamium, or song of congratulation, upon the marriage of a great king, to be sung to music at the wedding-feast. The topics are such as were the usual groundwork of such gratulatory odes with the poets of antiquity: they all fall under two general heads, the praises of the bridegroom, and the praises of the bride. The bridegroom is praised for the comeliness of his person, and the urbanity of his address, for his military exploits, for the extent of his conquests, for the upright administration of his government, for the magnificence of his court. The bride is celebrated for her high birth, for the beauty of her person, the richness of her dress, and her numerous train of blooming bridemaids. It is foretold that the marriage will be fruitful, and that the sons of the great king will be sovereigns of the whole earth. In this general structure of the poem, we find nothing but the common topics and the common arrangement of every wedding-song: but when we recollect that the relation between the Saviour and his church is represented in the writings both of the Old and New Testament, under the image of the relation of a husband to his wife, that it is a favourite image with all the ancient prophets, when they would set forth the loving-kindness of God for the church, or the church's dutiful return of love to him; while, on the contrary, the idolatry of the church, in her apostacies, is represented as the adultery of a married woman; that this image has been consecrated to this signification by our Lord's own use of it, who describes God in the act of settling the church in her final state of peace and perfection, as a king making a marriage for his son;—the conjecture that will naturally arise upon the recollection of these circumstances will be, that this epithalamium, preserved among the sacred writings of the ancient Jewish church, celebrates no common marriage, but the great mystical wedding, that Christ is the bridegroom, and the spouse his church. And this was the unanimous opinion of all antiquity, without exception even of the Jewish expositors. For although, with the veil of ignorance and prejudice upon their understandings and their hearts, they discern not the completion of this or of any of their prophecies in the Son of Mary, yet they allow, that this is one of the prophecies which relate to the Messiah and Messiah's people; and none of them ever dreamed of an application of it to the marriage of any earthly prince.

It is the more extraordinary, that there should have arisen in the Christian church, in later ages, expositors of great name and authority, and, indeed, of great learning, who have maintained, that the immediate subject of the psalm is the marriage of Solomon with Pharaoh's daughter, and can discover only a distant reference to Christ and the church, as typified by the Jewish king and his Egyptian bride. But read this psalm, and tell me if you can anywhere find King Solomon. We find, indeed, passages which may be applicable to Solomon, but not more applicable to him than to many other earthly kings; such as comeliness of person and urbanity of address, mentioned in the second verse. These might be qualities, for any thing that we know to the contrary, belonging to Solomon; I say, for any thing that we know to the contrary, for in these particulars the sacred history gives no information. We read of Solomon's learning, and of his wisdom, and of the admirable sagacity and integrity of his judicial decisions: but we read not at all, as far as I recollect, of the extraordinary comeliness of his person, or the affability of his speech. And if he possessed these qualities, they are no more than other monarchs have possessed, in a degree not to be surpassed by Solomon. Splendour and stateliness of dress, twice mentioned in this psalm, were not peculiar to Solomon, but belong to every great and opulent monarch. Other circumstances might be mentioned, applicable, indeed, to Solomon, but no otherwise than as generally applicable to every king. But the circumstances which are characteristic of the king who is the hero of this poem, are every one of them utterly inapplicable to Solomon, insomuch, that not one of them can be ascribed to him, without contradicting the history of his reign. The hero of this poem is a warrior, who girds his sword upon his thigh, rides in pursuit of flying foes, makes havoc among them with his sharp arrows, and reigns at last by conquest over his vanquished enemies. Now Solomon was no warrior: he enjoyed a long reign of forty years of uninterrupted peace. He retained, indeed, the sovereignty of the countries which his father had conquered, but he made no new conquests of his own. "He had dominion over all the region west of the Euphrates, over all the kings on this side of the river, (they were his vassals,) and he had peace on all sides round about him. And Judah and Israel dwelt safely, every man under his vine, and under his fig-tree, from Dan even to Beersheba, all the days of Solomon." If Solomon ever girded a sword upon his thigh, it must have been merely for state; if he had a quiver of sharp arrows, he could have had no use for them but in hunting. And it was with great good judgment, that upon the revision of our English Bible, in the reign of James the First, the Calvinistic argument of this psalm, as it stood in Queen Elizabeth's Bible, was expunged, and that other substituted which we now read in our Bible of the larger size, in these words: "The majesty and grace of Christ's kingdom; the duty of the church, and the benefits thereof;" which, indeed, contain a most exact summary of the whole doctrine of the psalm. And the particulars of this, it is my intention in future discourses to expound.

The psalm takes its beginning in a plain, unaffected manner, with a verse briefly declarative of the importance of the subject, the author's extraordinary knowledge of it, and the manner in which it will be treated:—

"My heart is enditing a good matter;"

or rather,

"My heart labours with a goodly theme:"

for the word "enditing" answers but poorly, as our translators themselves appear from their margin to have been well aware, to the emphasis of the original, which expresses, that the mind of the prophet was excited and heated, boiling over, as it were, with his subject, and eager to give utterance to its great conceptions. "A good matter," or "a goodly theme," denotes a subject of the highest interest and importance:—

"My heart labours with a goodly theme:
I address my performance to the King;"

that is, as hath been abundantly explained, to the great King Messiah:—

"My tongue is the pen of a ready writer;"

that is, of a well-instructed writer, a writer prepared and ready, by a perfect knowledge of the subject he undertakes to treat.

But with what sense and meaning is it, that the Psalmist compares his "tongue" to the "pen" of such a writer? It is to intimate, as I apprehend, that what he is about to deliver is no written composition, but an extemporaneous effusion, without any premeditation of his own, upon the immediate impulse and suggestion of the Holy Spirit: that what will fall, however, in that manner, from his "tongue," for the coherence and importance of the matter, for the correct propriety of the expression, and for the orderly arrangement of the parts, will in no degree fall short of the most laboured production of the "pen" of any writer, the best prepared by previous study of his subject; inasmuch as the Spirit of God inspires his thoughts, and prompts his utterance. After this brief preface, declaring that his subject is Messiah, chiefly in his kingly character; that he cannot contain the thoughts which are rising in his mind; that he speaks not from himself, or from previous study, but from inspiration at the moment, he plunges at once into the subject he had propounded, addressing the King Messiah, as if he were actually standing in the royal presence. And in this same strain, indeed, the whole song proceeds; as referring to a scene present to the prophet's eye, or to things which he saw doing.—HORSLEY.

Ver. 2. Thou art fairer than the children of men; grace is poured into thy lips: therefore God hath blessed thee for ever.

We have no account in the gospels of our Saviour's person. Some writers of an early age (but none so early as to have seen him) speak of it as wanting dignity, and of his physiognomy as unpleasing. It would be difficult, I believe, to find any better foundation for this strange notion, than an injudicious interpretation of certain prophecies, in a literal meaning, which represent the humiliation which the Son of God was to undergo, by clothing his divinity with flesh, in images taken from personal deformity. But from what is recorded in the gospels, of the ease with which our Saviour mixed in what, in the modern style, we should call good company; of the respectful attention shown to him, beyond any thing his reputed birth or fortune might demand; and the manner in which his discourses, either of severe reproof or gentle admonition, were received, we may reasonably conclude, that he had a dignity of exterior appearance, remarkably corresponding with that authority of speech, which, upon some occasions, impressed even his enemies with awe, and with that dignified mildness, which seems to have been his more natural and usual tone, and drew the applause and admiration of all who heard him. External feature, however, is generally the impression of the mind upon the body, and words are but the echo of the thoughts; and, in prophecy, more is usually meant than meets the ear in the first sound, and most obvious sense of the terms employed. Beauty and grace of speech are certainly used in this text as figures of much higher qualities, which were conspicuous in our Lord, and in him alone of all the sons of men. That image of God in which Adam was created, in our Lord appeared perfect and entire; in the unspotted innocency of his life, the sanctity of his manners, and his perfect obedience to the law of God; in the vast powers of his mind, intellectual and moral: intellectual, in his comprehension of all knowledge; moral, in his power of resisting all the allurements of vice, and of encountering all the difficulties of virtue and religion, despising hardship and shame, enduring pain and death. This was the beauty with which he was adorned beyond the sons of men. In him, the beauty of the divine image was refulgent in its original perfection; in all the sons of Adam, obscured and marred, in a degree to be scarce discernible; the will depraved, the imagination debauched, the reason weak, the passions rampant! This deformity is not externally visible, nor the spiritual beauty which is its opposite: but, could the eye be turned upon the internal man, we should see the hideous shape of a will at enmity with God; a heart disregarding his law, insensible of his goodness, fearless of his wrath, swelling with the passions of ambition, avarice, vain-glory, lust. Yet this is the picture of the unregenerated man, by the depravity consequent upon the fall, born in iniquity, and conceived in sin. Christ, on the contrary, by the mysterious manner of his conception, was born without spot of sin; he grew up and lived full of grace and truth, perfectly sanctified in flesh and spirit. With this beauty he was "adorned beyond the sons of men."—HORSLEY.

Ver. 3. Gird thy sword upon *thy* thigh, O *most* Mighty, with thy glory and thy majesty.

From the commendation of the comeliness of the king's person, and the graciousness of his speech, the Psalmist, in the same figurative style, passes to the topic of his prowess as a warrior, under which character our Lord is perpetually described in the prophecies. The enemies he had to engage are the wicked passions of men, the devil in his wiles and machinations, and the persecuting powers of the world. The warfare is continued through the whole of the period I have mentioned, commencing upon our Lord's ascension, at which time he is represented, in the Revelation, as going forth upon a "white horse, with a crown upon his head, and a bow in his hand, conquering and to conquer." The Psalmist, in imagery almost the same, accosts him as a warlike prince preparing to take the field; describes his weapons, and the magnificence of his armour, and promises him victory and universal dominion.

This verse, I fear, must be but ill understood by the English reader. The words, "O most Mighty!" very weakly render the original, which is a single word, one of the titles of Christ, in its literal sense expressive of might and valour. But the great difficulty which, in my apprehension, must perplex the English reader, lies in the exhortation, to gird on glory and majesty together with the sword. The things have no obvious connexion; and how are majesty and glory, in any sense which the words may bear in our language, to be girt on upon the person? The truth is, that, in the Hebrew language, these words have a great variety and latitude of meaning; and either these very words, or their synonymes, are used in other places for splendid dress, and for robes of state; and being things to be girt on, they must here denote some part of the warrior's dress. They signify such sort of armour, of costly materials and exquisite workmanship, as was worn by the greatest generals, and by kings when they led their armies in person, and was contrived for ornament as well as safety. The whole verse might be intelligibly and yet faithfully rendered, in these words:—

"Warrior! gird thy sword upon thy thigh;
Buckle on thy refulgent, dazzling armour."—HORSLEY.

Ver. 4. And in thy majesty ride prosperously, because of truth, and meekness, *and* righteousness; and thy right hand shall teach thee terrible things.

That is, take aim with thy bow and arrow at the enemy; be prosperous, or successful in the aim taken; ride on in pursuit of the flying foe, in the cause of religious truth, evangelical humility, and righteousness.

"And thy right hand shall teach thee terrible things;"

rather,

"And thy own right hand shall show thee wonderful things."

In these words, the Saviour, effecting every thing by his own power, is represented under the image of a great champion in the field, who is prompted by his own courage, and a reliance on his own strength and skill, to attempt what might seem impracticable; singly to attack whole squadrons of the enemy; to cut his way through their embattled troops; to scale their ramparts and their walls, and at last achieve what seems a wonder to himself, when the fray is over, when he is at leisure to survey the bulwarks he has demolished, and the many carcasses his single arm has stretched upon the plain. Such great things he will be able to effect.

It yet remains to be more fully explained, what is meant in the Psalmist's detail of the Messiah's war, by those "wonders" which "his own right hand was to show him:"

"Thy own right hand shall show thee wonders."

Our public translation has it, "terrible things." But the notion of terror is not of necessity included in the sense of the original word, as it is used by the sacred writers: it is sometimes, indeed, applied by them to frightful things: but it is also applied, with great latitude, to things extraordinary in their kind; grand, admirable, amazing, awful; although they should not be frightful. We have no right, therefore, to take it in the strict sense of "frightful," unless something in the context points to that meaning, which is not the case in this passage. And, accordingly, instead of "terrible," we find, in some of the oldest English Bibles, the better chosen word, "wonderful."

Now the "wonderful things" which Messiah's "own right hand" showed him, I take to be the overthrow of the pagan superstition, in the Roman empire, and other great kingdoms of the world, by the mere preaching of the gospel, seconded by the exemplary lives and the miracles of the first preachers, and by the patient endurance of imprisonment, torture, and death, for the sake of Christ. It was, indeed, a wonderful thing, wrought by Christ's single arm, when his religion prevailed over the whole system of idolatry, supported as it was by the authority of sovereigns, by the learning of philosophers, and most of all, by the inveterate prejudices of the vulgar, attached to their false gods by the gratification which their very worship afforded to the sensual passions, and by the natural partiality of mankind in favour of any system, however absurd and corrupt, sanctioned by a long antiquity. It was a wonderful thing, when the devil's kingdom, with much of its invisible power, lost at once the whole of its external pomp and splendour; when silence being imposed on his oracles, and spells and enchantments divested of their power, the idolatrous worship which by those engines of deceit had been universally established, and for ages supported, notwithstanding the antiquity of its institutions, and the bewitching gayety and magnificence of its festivals, fell into neglect; when its cruel and lascivious rites, so long holden in superstitious veneration, on a sudden became the objects of a just and general abhorrence; when the unfrequented temples, spoiled of their immense treasures, sunk in ruins, and the images, stripped of their gorgeous robes and costly jewels, were thrown into the Tiber, or into the common receptacles of filth and ordure. It was a wonderful thing, when the minds of all men took a sudden turn; kings became the nursing fathers of the church, statesmen courted her alliance, philosophy embraced her faith, and even the sword was justly drawn in her defence. These were the "wonderful things" effected by Christ's right hand; and in these, this part of the Psalmist's prophecy has received its accomplishment. Less than this his words cannot mean; and to more than this they cannot with any certainty be extended: since these things satisfy all that is of necessity involved in his expressions.—HORSLEY.

Ver. 5. Thine arrows *are* sharp in the heart of the King's enemies; *whereby* the people fall under thee.

The war in which the Psalmist represents the Saviour as engaged, is very different from the wars which the princes of this world wage with one another: it is not for the destruction of the lives of men, but for the preservation of their souls. This prophetic text of the Psalmist relates only to that spiritual war which Christ wages with the enemies of man, for man's deliverance; to the war arising from that enmity which was originally put between the seed of the serpent and the woman's seed. The offensive weapons in this war of charity, according to the Psalmist, are of two sorts, a sword and arrows. The common military sword is a heavy massive weapon, for close engagement: wielded by a strong and skilful arm, it stabs and cuts, opens dreadful gashes where it falls, severs limbs, lops the head, or cleaves the body. The arrow is a light missile weapon, which, in ancient times, was used to annoy the enemy at a distance, and particularly when put to flight. It comes whizzing through the air unseen, and, when it hits, so small is the wound, and so swift the passage of the weapon, that it is scarcely felt, till it fixes its sharp point in the very heart.

Now both these weapons, the sword and the arrow, are emblems of one and the same thing; which is no other than the word of God, in its different effects, and different manners of operation on the minds of men, represented under these two different images.

The word of God may be divided, indeed, into two parts, the word of reproof, commination, and terror; and the word of persuasion, promise, and hope. The former holds up to the sinner the picture of himself; sets forth the turpitude of sin, the holiness of God, God's hatred of unrighteousness; and alarms the conscience with the danger of a state of enmity with God, and with denunciations of implacable wrath and endless punishment.

The second, the word of persuasion, promise, and hope sets before the penitent the riches of God's mercy, displayed in the scheme of man's redemption; points to the cross, where man's guilt was expiated; bids the contrite sinner rely on the Redeemer's intercession; offers the daily supply of grace to confirm him in his resolutions, and assist him in his efforts to conform himself to the precepts and example of the Saviour, and promises victory and glory to them that persevere: thus turning despondency into hope, and fear into love.

The first, the word of terror, is the sword girt upon Messiah's thigh; the second, the word of persuasion, is the arrow shot from his bow.

For the sense of the first metaphor, we have the authority of the sacred writers themselves. "The sword of the Spirit," says St. Paul to the Ephesians, "is the word of God." And in the Epistle to the Hebrews, the full signification of the figure is opened, and the propriety of the application shown: "For the word of God," says the inspired author, "is quick and powerful, (rather, lively and energetic,) and sharper than any two-edged sword, and piercing to the parting of soul and spirit, and to the joints and marrow;"—that is, as the soldier's sword of steel cuts through all the exterior integuments of skin and muscle, to the bone, and even through the hard substance of the bone itself, to the very marrow, and divides the ligaments which keep the joints of the body together; so this spiritual sword of God's awful word penetrates the inmost recesses of the human mind, pierces to the very line of separation, as it were, of the sensitive and the intelligent principle, lops off the animal part, divides the joints where reason and passion are united, sets the intellect free to exert its powers, kills sin in our members, opens passages for grace to enter and enrich the marrow of the soul, and thus delivers the man from his body of death. Such are the effects for which the powerful word of terror is compared to a two-edged sword.

The comparison of the word of promise to the arrow is more easily understood, being more familiar, and analogous to those figures of speech which run through all languages, by which, whatever makes a quick and smart impression on the moral feelings, is represented under the image of a pointed missile weapon; as when we speak of "the thrilling darts of harmony," or, "the shafts of eloquence." The Psalmist speaks of these arrows of God's word, as sticking in "the hearts of the King's enemies," that is, of the King Messiah; for he, you will remember, is the only King in question. His enemies, in the highest sense of the word, are those who are avowedly leagued with the apostate faction; atheists, deists, idolaters, heretics, perverse disputers, those who, in any manner of set design, oppose the gospel; who resist the truth by argument, or encounter it with ridicule; who explain it away by sophisticated interpretations, or endeavour to crush it by the force of persecution. Of such hardened enemies there is no hope, till they have been hacked and hewed, belaboured, and all but slain (in the strong language of one of the ancient prophets) by the heavy sword of the word of terror. But, in a lower sense, all are enemies till they hear of Christ, and the terms of his peace are offered to them. Many such are wrought upon by mild admonition, and receive in their hearts the arrows of the word of persuasion. Such, no doubt, were many of those Jews who were pricked to the heart by St. Peter's first sermon, on the day of Pentecost: and even those worse enemies, if they can be brought to their feeling by the ghastly wounds and gashes of the terrific sword of the word of threatening, may afterward be pierced by the arrow, and carry about in their hearts its barbed point. And by the joint effect of these two weapons, the sword and the arrow, the word of terror and the word of persuasion, "peoples," says the Psalmist, that is, whole kingdoms and nations in a mass, "shall fall under thee;" shall forsake their ancient superstitions, renounce their idols, and submit themselves to Christ.

So much for the offensive weapons, the sword and the arrows. But the defensive armour demands our attention: for it has its use, no doubt, in the Messiah's war. His person, you will remember, is clad, in the third verse, "with refulgent, dazzling armour." This may be understood of whatever is admirable and amiable in the external form and appearance of the Christian religion. First, the character of Jesus himself; his piety towards God, his philanthropy towards man; his meekness, humility, ready forgiveness of injuries, patience, endurance of pain and death. Secondly, the same light of good works shining, in a less degree, in the lives of his disciples, particularly the apostles and blessed martyrs. Thirdly, whatever is decent and seemly in the government, the discipline, and the rites of the church. All these things, as they tend to draw the admiration, and conciliate the good-will of men, and mitigate the malice of the persecutor, are aptly represented under the image of the Messiah's defensive armour, and had a principal share in making "peoples fall under him."—Horsley.

Ver. 6. Thy throne, O God, *is* for ever and ever the sceptre of thy kingdom *is* a right sceptre. 7. Thou lovest righteousness, and hatest wickedness: therefore God, thy God, hath anointed thee with the oil of gladness above thy fellows.

It was before shown, how inapplicable this address is to Solomon; and it is obvious, that it is equally inapplicable to any earthly monarch: for of no throne but God's can it be affirmed with truth, that it is for ever and ever; of no king, but of God and of his Christ, it can be said, that he loves righteousness with a perfect love, and hates wickedness with a perfect hate; of no sceptre, but the sceptre of God and of his Christ, that it is a straight sceptre. The sceptre has been, from the earliest ages, a badge of royalty. It was originally nothing more than a straight slender rod, studded sometimes for ornament with little nails of gold. It was an emblem of the perfect integrity of the monarch in the exercise of his power, both by himself and by his ministers, inflexibly adhering to the straight line of right and justice, as a mason or carpenter to his rule. The perfection of the emblem consisted in the straightness of the stick; for every thing else was ornament. The straightness, therefore, ascribed by the Psalmist to Messiah's sceptre, is to be understood of the invariable justice of the administration of his government. Now, certainly there have been many kings, both in ancient and in modern times, to whom the praise is due of a cordial regard in general to righteousness, and of a settled principle of dislike to wickedness; many who, in the exercise of their authority, and the measure of their government, have been generally directed by that just sense of right and wrong: but yet kings are not exempt from the frailties of human nature; the very best of them are, at least, in an equal degree with other good men, liable to the surprises of the passions, and the seductions of temptation; insomuch that that predominant love of righteousness and hatred of iniquity, maintaining an absolute ascendency in the mind, in all times, and upon all occasions, which the Psalmist attributes to his heavenly King, has belonged to none that ever wore an earthly crown: much less is the perfect straightness of the sceptre, a perfect conformity to the rule of right, to be found in the practice and execution of the governments of the world.

But the kingdom of the God-man is in this place intended. This is evident from what is said in the seventh verse: "God, even thine own God, hath anointed thee with the oil of gladness above thy fellows;" that is, God hath advanced thee to a state of bliss and glory above all those whom thou hast vouchsafed to call thy fellows. It is said too, that the love of righteousness, and hatred of wickedness, is the cause that God hath so anointed him, who yet, in the sixth verse, is himself addressed as God. It is manifest, that these things can be said only of that person in whom the Godhead and the manhood are united; in whom the human nature is the subject of the unction, and the elevation to the mediatorial kingdom is the reward of the man Jesus: for, in his divine nature, Christ, being equal with the Father, is incapable of any exaltation. Thus, the unction with the oil of gladness, and the elevation above his fellows, characterize the manhood; and the perpetual stability of the throne, and the unsullied justice of the government, declare the Godhead. It is therefore with the greatest propriety that the text is applied to Christ, in the Epistle to the Hebrews, and made an argument of his divinity; not by any forced accommodation of words which, in the mind of the author, related to another subject, but according to the true intent and purpose of the Psalmist, and the literal sense, and only consistent exposition of his words.—Horsley.

Ver. 8. All thy garments *smell* of myrrh, and aloes, *and* cassia, out of the ivory palaces, whereby they have made thee glad.

The holy Psalmist having seated the King Messiah on his everlasting throne, proceeds to the magnificence of his court, as it appeared on the wedding-day; in which, the thing that first strikes him, and fixes his attention, is the majesty and splendour of the king's own dress, which, indeed, is described by the single circumstance of the profusion of rich perfumes with which it was scented. But this, by inference, implies every thing else of elegance and costly ornament: for among the nations of the East, in ancient times, perfume was considered as the finishing of the dress of persons of condition, when they appeared in public; and modern manners give us no conception of the costliness of the materials employed in the composition of their odours, their care and nicety in the preparation of them, and the quantity in which they were used. The high-priest of the Jews was not sprinkled with a few scanty drops of the perfume of the sanctuary; but his person was so bedewed with it, that it literally ran down from his beard to the skirts of his garment. The high-priest of the Jews, in his robes of office, was in this, as I shall presently explain, and in every circumstance, the living type of our great High-priest. The Psalmist describes the fragrance of Messiah's garments to be such, as if the aromatic woods had been the very substance out of which the robes were made:—

"Thy garments are all myrrh, aloes, and cassia."

The sequel of this verse is somewhat obscure in the original, by reason of the ambiguity of one little word, which different interpreters have taken differently. I shall give what, in my judgment, is the literal rendering of the passage, and trust I shall not find it difficult to make the meaning of it very clear.

"Thy garments are all myrrh, aloes, and cassia,
Excelling the palaces of ivory,
Excelling those which delight thee."

Ivory was highly valued and admired among the Jews, and other eastern nations of antiquity, for the purity of its white, the delicate smoothness of the surface, and the durability of the substance; being not liable to tarnish or rust like metals, or, like wood, to rot or to be worm-eaten. Hence, it was a favourite ornament in the furniture of the houses and palaces of great men; and all such ornamental furniture was plentifully perfumed. The Psalmist, therefore, says, that the fragrance of the King's garments far exceeded any thing that met the nostrils of the visiters in the stateliest and best-furnished palaces. But this is not all: he says, besides, that these perfumes of the royal garments "excel those which delight thee." To understand this, we must recollect that there were two very exquisite perfumes used in the symbolical service of the temple, both made of the richest spices, mixed in certain proportions, and by a process directed by the law. The one was used to anoint every article of the furniture of the sanctuary, and the robes and persons of the priests. The composition of it was not to be imitated, nor was it to be applied to the person of any but a consecrated priest, upon pain of death. Some, indeed, of the kings of David's line were anointed with it: but when this was done, it was by the special direction of a prophet, and it was to intimate, as I apprehend, the relation of that royal house to the eternal priesthood, to to be instituted in due season in that family. The other was a compound of other ingredients, which made the incense that was burnt upon the golden altar as a grateful odour to the Lord. This, too, was most holy, and to attempt to make the like for private use was a capital offence.

Now the perfumed garments of the Psalmist's King denote the very same thing which was typified under the law by the perfumed garments of the high-priest; the Psalmist's King being, indeed, the real person of whom the high-priest, in every particular of his office, his services, and his dress, was the type. The perfumed garments were typical: first, of the graces and virtues of the Redeemer himself in his human character; secondly, of whatever is refreshing, encouraging, consoling, and cheering, in the external ministration of the word; and, thirdly, of the internal comforts of the Holy Spirit. But the incense fumed upon the golden altar was typical of a far inferior, though of a precious and holy thing; namely, of whatever is pleasing to God in the faith, the devotions, and the good works of the saints. Now the Psalmist says, that the fragrance breathing from the garments of the King far excels, not only the sweetest odours of any earthly monarch's palace, but that it surpasses those spiritual odours of sanctity in which the King himself delights. The consolations which the faithful, under all their sufferings, receive from him, in the example of his holy life, the ministration of the word and sacraments, and the succours of the Spirit, are far beyond the proportion of any thing they have to offer in return to him, in their praises, their prayers, and their good lives, notwithstanding in these their services he condescends to take delight. This is the doctrine of this highly mystic text, that the value of all our best works of faith and obedience, even in our own eyes, must sink into nothing, when they are contrasted with the exuberant mercy of God extended to us through Christ.—Horsley.

Ver. 9. Kings' daughters *were* among thy honourable women: upon thy right hand did stand the queen in gold of Ophir.

It will be observed that the word "women," in the Bibles of the larger size, is printed in that character which is used to distinguish the words which have been inserted by the translators, to make the sense perspicuous to the English reader, without any thing expressly corresponding in the original. Omitting the word "women," our translators might have given the verse, according to their conceptions of the preceding word, which describes the women, thus:—

"Kings' daughters are among thy honourables;"

that is, among the persons appointed to services of honour. But the original word, thus expressed by "honourable women," or, by "honourables," is indeed applied to whatever is rare and valued in its kind, and, for that reason, to illustrious persons, ennobled and distinguished by marks of royal favour: and in this sense, it certainly is figuratively applicable to the persons whom I shall show to be intended here. But the primary meaning of the word is, "bright, sparkling;" and it is particularly applied to brilliant gems, or precious stones. Sparkling is, in all languages, figuratively applied to female beauty; and the imagery of the original would be better preserved, though the sense would be much the same, if the passage were thus rendered:—

"Kings' daughters are among the bright beauties of thy court."

The beauty certainly is mystic; the beauty of evangelical sanctity and innocence.

But who and what are the kings' daughters, the lustre of whose beauty adorns the great monarch's court? "Kings' daughters," in the general language of holy writ, are the kingdoms and peoples which they govern, of which, in common speech, they are called fathers. The expression may be so taken here; and then the sense will be, that the greatest kingdoms and empires of the world, converted to the faith of Christ, and shining in the beauty of the good works of true holiness, will be united, at the season of the wedding, to Messiah's kingdom. But, inasmuch as Messiah's kingdom is not one of the kingdoms of the world, and that secular kingdoms will never be immediately, and in their secular capacity, vassals of his kingdom, I rather think, that the kings' daughters mentioned here, are the various national churches, fostered for many ages by the piety of Christian princes, and now brought to the perfection of beauty, by the judgments which shall have purged every one of them of all things that offend: for they may well be called "kings' daughters," of whom kings and queens are called, in the prophetic language, the fathers and the mothers. From these, the Psalmist turns our attention to another lady, distinguished above them all, by her title, her place, and the superlative richness of her robes.

"Kings' daughters are among the bright beauties of thy court;
At thy right hand the consort has her station,
In standard gold of Ophir."

Some expositors have imagined, that the consort is an emblem of the church catholic in her totality; the kings' daughters, typical of the several particular churches, of which that one universal is composed. But the queen consort here, is unquestionably the Hebrew church; the church of the natural Israel, reunited, by her conversion, to her husband, and advanced to the high prerogative of the mother church of Christendom; and the kings' daughters are the churches which had been gathered out of the Gentiles, in the interval between the expulsion of his wife, and the taking of her home again; that is, between the dispersion of the Jews by the Romans, and their restoration. The restoration of the Hebrew church to the rights of a wife, to the situation of the queen consort in Messiah's kingdom upon earth, is the constant strain of prophecy. To prove this, by citing all the passages to that purpose, would be to transcribe whole chapters of some of the prophets, and innumerable detached passages from almost all. I shall produce only the latter part of the second chapter of Hosea. In that chapter, Jehovah, after discarding the incontinent wife, and threatening terrible severity of punishment, adds, that nevertheless the time should come, when she should again address her offended lord, by the endearing name of husband. "And I will betroth thee to myself for ever. Yes; I will betroth thee to myself, with justice, and with righteousness, and with exuberant kindness, and with tender love. Yes; with faithfulness, to myself I will betroth thee." These promises are made to the woman that had been discarded, and cannot be understood of mercies to be extended to any other. The prophet Isaiah speaks to the same effect, and describes the Gentile converts as becoming, upon the reunion, children of the pardoned wife. And I must not omit to mention, that St. Paul, in his Epistle to the Romans, to clear up the mystery of God's dealing with the Jews, tells us, that "blindness is, in part only, happened unto Israel, till the time shall arrive for the fulness of the Gentiles to come in; and then all Israel shall be saved; for the gifts and callings of God are without repentance." To expound these predictions of the ancient prophets, and this declaration of the apostle, of any thing but the restoration of the natural Israel, is to introduce ambiguity and equivocation into the plainest oracles of God.

The standard gold upon the queen's robe, denotes the treasures of which the church is the depositary; the written word, and the dispensation of grace, and forgiveness of sins, by the due administration of the sacraments.—Horsley.

Ver. 10. Hearken, O daughter, and consider, and incline thine ear; forget also thine own people, and thy father's house; 11. So shall the King greatly desire thy beauty; for he *is* thy Lord, and worship thou him.

If a princess from a distant land, taken in marriage by a great king, were admonished to forget her own people and her father's house, the purport of the advice would easily be understood to be, that she should divest herself of all attachment to the customs of her native country, and to the style of her father's court, and learn to speak the language, and assume the dress, the manners, and the taste of her husband's people. The "father's house," and "own people," which the Psalmist advises the queen consort to forget, is the ancient Jewish religion in its external form, the ceremonies of the temple service, the sacrifices and the typical purgations of the Levitical priesthood. Not that she is to forget God's gracious promises to Abraham, nor the covenant with her forefathers, (the benefit of which she will enjoy to the end of time,) nor the many wonderful deliverances that were wrought for them; nor is she to forget the history of her nation, preserved in the scriptures of the Old Testament; nor the predictions of Moses and her prophets, the full accomplishment of which she will at this time experience; and historically, she is never to forget even the ceremonial law; for the Levitical rites were nothing less than the gospel itself in hieroglyphics; and, rightly understood, they afford the most complete demonstration of the coherence of revelation with itself, in all its different stages, and the best evidence of its truth; showing that it has been the same in substance, in all ages, differing only in external form, in the rites of worship, and in the manner of teaching. But practically, the rites of their ancient worship are to be forgotten, that is, laid aside: for they never were of any other importance than in reference to the gospel, as the shadow is of no value but as it resembles the substance. Practically, therefore, the restored Hebrew church is to abandon her ancient Jewish rites, and become mere and pure Christian; and thus she will secure the conjugal affections of her husband, and render the beauty of her person perfect in his eyes. And this she is bound to do; for her royal husband is indeed her Lord: Moses was no more than his servant; the prophets after Moses, servants in a lower rank than he. But the authority of Christ, the husband, is paramount over all; he is entitled to her unreserved obedience; he is indeed her God, entitled to her adoration.—Horsley.

Ver. 12. And the daughter of Tyre *shall be there* with a gift; *even* the rich among the people shall entreat thy favour.

This submission of the consort to her wedded lord, will set her high in the esteem of the churches of the Gentiles. The "daughter of Tyre," according to the principles of interpretation we have laid down, must be a church established, either literally at Tyre, or in some country held forth under the image of Tyre. Ancient Tyre was famous for her commerce, her wealth, her excellence in the fine arts, her luxury, the profligate debauched manners of her people, and the grossness of her idolatry. The "daughter of Tyre" appearing before the queen consort "with a gift," is a figurative prediction, that churches will be established, under the protection of the government, in countries which had been distinguished for profligacy, dissipated manners, and irreligion. It is intimated in the next line, that some of these churches will be rich; that is, rich in spiritual riches, which are the only riches of a church, in the mystic language of prophecy; rich in the holy lives of their members, in the truth of their creeds, and the purity of their external forms of worship, and in God's favour.—Horsley.

Ver. 13. The King's daughter *is* all glorious within; her clothing *is* of wrought gold.

From this address to the queen, the Psalmist, in the present verse, returns to the description of the great scene lying in vision before him.

"The King's daughter is all glorious within."

In this line, the same person that has hitherto been represented as the King's wife, seems to be called his daughter. This, however, is a matter upon which commentators have been much divided. Some have imagined that a new personage is introduced; that the King's wife is, as I have all along maintained, the figure of the Hebrew church; but that this "daughter of the King" is the Christian church in general, composed of Jews and Gentiles indiscriminately, considered as the daughter of the King Messiah by his Hebrew queen. This was Martin Luther's notion. Others have thought that the wife is the Hebrew church by itself, and the daughter, the church of the Gentiles by itself. But neither of these explanations are perfectly consistent with the imagery of this psalm. Far to be preferred is the exposition of the late learned and pious Bishop Horne, who rejects the notion of the introduction of a new personage, and observes, "that the connexion between Christ and his spouse unites in itself every relation and every affection." She is, therefore, daughter, wife, and sister, all in one. The same seems to have been the notion of a learned Dominican of the seventeenth century, who remarks, that the Empress Julia, in the legends of some ancient coins, is called the daughter of Augustus, whose wife she was.

But, with much general reverence for the opinions of these learned commentators, I am persuaded that the stops have been misplaced in the Hebrew manuscripts, by the Jewish critics, upon the last revision of the text; that translators have been misled by their false division of the text, and expositors misled by translators. The stops being rightly placed, the Hebrew words give this sense:—

"She is all glorious"—

She, the consort of whom we have been speaking, is glorious in every respect—

"Daughter of a king!"

That is, she is a princess born; (by which title she is saluted in the Canticles;) she is glorious, therefore, for her high birth. She is, indeed, of high and heavenly extraction! She may say of herself, collectively, what the apostle has taught her sons to say individually, "Of his own will begat he us, with the word of his truth." Accordingly, in the Apocalypse, the bride, the Lamb's wife, is "the holy Jerusalem, descending out of heaven, from God."

The Psalmist goes on:—

> "Her inner garment is bespangled with gold;
> Her upper garment is embroidered with the needle."

These two lines require little comment. The spangles of gold upon the consort's inner garment, are the same thing with the standard gold of Ophir, of the ninth verse; the invaluable treasure with which the church is endowed, with the custody and distribution of which she is intrusted. The embroidery of her upper garment is, whatever there is of beauty in her external form, her discipline and her rites. —HORSLEY.

Ver. 14. She shall be brought unto the King in raiment of needle-work: the virgins her companions that follow her shall be brought unto thee. 15. With gladness and rejoicing *shall* they *be* brought: they shall enter into the King's palace.

Our public translation has simply, "She is brought;" but the original word implies, the pomp and conduct of a public procession. The greatest caution is requisite in attempting to interpret, in the detail of circumstances, the predictions of things yet remote. We may venture, however, to apply this conducting of the queen to the palace of her lord, to some remarkable assistance which the Israelites will receive from the Christian nations of the Gentile race, in their resettlement in the Holy Land; which seems to be mentioned under the very same image by the prophet Isaiah, at the end of the eighteenth chapter, and by the prophet Zephaniah, chap. iii. 10, and is clearly the subject of more explicit prophecies. "Thus saith Jehovah," speaking to Zion, in the prophet Isaiah, "Behold, I will lift up my hand to the Gentiles, and set up my standard to the peoples; and they shall bring thy sons in their arms, and thy daughters shall be carried upon their shoulders." And in another place, "They" (the Gentiles mentioned in the preceding verse) "shall bring all your brethren, for an offering unto Jehovah, out of all nations, upon horses, and in chariots, and in litters, and upon mules, and upon swift beasts, to my holy mountain Jerusalem."

But the Psalmist is struck with the appearance of a very remarkable band, described in the next verse, which makes a part in this procession:—

> "She is conducted in procession to the King,
> Virgins follow her, her companions,
> Coming unto thee;
> They are conducted in procession, with festivity and rejoicing;
> They enter the palace of the King."

These virgins seem to be different persons from the kings' daughters of the ninth verse. Those "kings' daughters" were already distinguished ladies of the monarch's own court: these virgins are introduced to it by the queen: they follow her as part of her retinue; and are introduced as her companions. The former represent, as we conceive, the churches of Gentile origin, formed and established in the period of the wife's disgrace: these virgins we take to be new churches, formed among nations, not sooner called to the knowledge of the gospel, and the faith in Christ, at the very season of the restoration of Israel, in whose conversion the restored Hebrew church may have a principal share. This is that fulness of the Gentiles of which St. Paul speaks as coincident in time with the recovery of the Jews, and, in a great degree, the effect of their conversion. "Have they stumbled that they should fall?" saith the apostle, speaking of the natural Israel; "God forbid: but rather, through their fall, salvation is come unto the Gentiles, for to provoke them to emulation. Now, if the fall of them be the riches of the world, and their loss the riches of the Gentiles, how much more their fulness? For if the casting away of them be the reconciling of the world, what shall the receiving of them be, but life from the dead?" In these texts, the apostle clearly lays out this order of the business, in the conversion of the whole world to Christ: First, the rejection of the unbelieving Jews: then, the first call of the Gentiles: the recovery of the Jews, after a long season of obstinacy and blindness, at last provoked to emulation, brought to a right understanding of God's dispensations, by that very call which hitherto has been one of their stumbling-blocks: and lastly, in consequence of the conversion of the Jews, a prodigious influx from the Gentile nations yet unconverted, and immersed in the darkness and corruptions of idolatry; which make little less than two thirds, not of the civilized, but of the inhabited world. The churches of this new conversion seem to be the virgins, the queen's bridemaids, in the nuptial procession.—HORSLEY.

Ver. 16. Instead of thy fathers shall be thy children, whom thou mayest make princes in all the earth. 17. I will make thy name to be remembered in all generations; therefore shall the people praise thee for ever and ever.

In the next verse (the sixteenth) the Psalmist again addresses the queen:—

> "Thy children shall be in the place of thy fathers;
> Thou shalt make them princes in all the earth."

Thy children shall be what thy fathers were, God's peculiar people; and shall hold a distinguished rank and character in the earth.

The Psalmist closes his divine song with a distich setting forth the design, and predicting the effect, of his own performance:—

> "I will perpetuate the remembrance of thy name to all generations.
> Insomuch that the peoples shall praise thee for ever."

By enditing this marriage-song, he hoped to be the means of celebrating the Redeemer's name from age to age, and of inciting the nations of the world to join in his praise. The event has not disappointed the holy prophet's expectation. His composition has been the delight of the congregations of the faithful for little less than three thousand years. For one thousand and forty, it was a means of keeping alive in the synagogue the hope of the Redeemer to come: for eighteen hundred since, it has been the means of perpetuating in Christian congregations the grateful remembrance of what has been done, anxious attention to what is doing, and of the cheering hope of the second coming of our Lord, who surely cometh to turn away ungodliness from Jacob, and to set up a standard to the nations which yet sit in darkness and the shadow of death. "He that witnesseth these things, saith, Behold, I come quickly. And the Spirit saith, Come; and the bride saith, Come; and let every one that heareth say, Amen. Even so. Come, Lord Jesus!"—HORSLEY.

PSALM XLVI.

Ver. 5. God *is* in the midst of her; she shall not be moved: God shall help her, *and that* right early.

The Hebrew has, instead of early, "when the morning appeareth." Ainsworth, "God will help it at the looking forth of the morning." A person in perplexity says, "Yes, I hope the *morning* will soon come; then will my friends help me." "When the daylight shall appear, many will be ready to assist me." "Ah! when will the morning come? How long has been this night of adversity!"—ROBERTS.

PSALM XLVII.

Ver. 1. O clap your hands, all ye people, shout unto God with the voice of triumph.

See on Lam. 2. 15.

PSALM XLVIII.

Ver. 6. Fear took hold upon them there, *and* pain, as of a woman in travail.

"His pain not great? it was equal to that of a woman in travail." "Alas! alas! this is like the agony of the womb." "Nothing but the womb knows trouble like this."—ROBERTS.

PSALM LI.

Ver. 7. Purge me with hyssop, and I shall be clean: wash me, and I shall be whiter than snow.

Hyssop, a name, derived from the Hebrew *esobh*, and like many other names of plants, passed from the eastern into the Greek, and from this into most European languages, signifies the plant called in German, wohlgemuth, (*i. e.* pleasant,) probably on account of its aromatic smell, and also marjoram, but called by botanists *origanum creticum.* Rauwolf found this plant on the Mount of Olives, and between Ramah and Joppa.—ROSENMULLER.

PSALM LV.

Ver. 6. And I said, Oh that I had wings like a dove! *for then* would I flee away, and be at rest.

The Hindoos have a science called *Aagiya-Kannam*, which teaches the art of FLYING! and numbers in every age have tried to acquire it. Those who wish to attain a blessing which is afar off, or who desire to escape from trouble, often exclaim, "Oh! that I had learned the *Aagiya-Kannam;* then should I gain the desire of my heart." "Could I but fly, these things would not be so."—ROBERTS.

Ver. 7. Lo, *then* would I wander far off, *and* remain in the wilderness. Selah.

The classical bards of Greece and Rome make frequent allusions to the surprising rapidity of the dove, and adorn their lines with many beautiful figures from the manner in which she flies. Sophocles compares the speed with which she cleaves the ethereal clouds, to the impetuous rapidity of the whirlwind; and Euripides, the furious impetuosity of the Bacchanals rushing upon Pentheus, to the celerity of her motions. And Kimchi gives it as the reason why the Psalmist prefers the dove to other birds, that while they become weary with flying, and alight upon a rock or a tree to recruit their strength, and are taken, the dove, when she is fatigued, alternately rests one wing and flies with the other, and by this means escapes from the swiftest pursuers. The Orientals knew well how to avail themselves of her impetuous wing on various occasions. It is a curious fact, that she was long employed in those countries as a courier, to carry tidings of importance between distant cities. Ælian asserts, that Taurosthenes communicated to his father at Ægina, by a carrier pigeon, the news of his success in the Olympic games, on the very same. day in which he obtained the prize. The Romans, it appears from Pliny, often employed doves in the same service; for Brutus, during the siege of Mutina, sent letters tied to their feet, into the camp of the consuls. This remarkable custom has descended to modern times; Volney informs us, that in Turkey the use of carrier pigeons has been laid aside, only for the last thirty or forty years, because the Curd robbers killed the birds, and carried off their despatches.—PAXTON.

Ver. 17. Evening, and morning, and at noon, will I pray, and cry aloud; and he shall hear my voice.

The frequency and the particular seasons of prayer are circumstances chiefly connected with the situation and disposition of such as habituate themselves to this exercise. But from a singular conformity of practice in persons remote both as to age and place, it appears probable that some idea must have obtained generally, that it was expedient and acceptable to pray three times every day. Such was the practice of David, and also of Daniel, (see ch. vi. 10,) and as a parallel, though, as far as connected with an idolatrous system, a different case, we are informed that "it is an invariable rule with the Bramins to perform their devotions three times every day: at sunrise, at noon, and at sunset." (Maurice.)—BURDER.

Ver. 21. *The words* of his mouth were smoother than butter, but war *was* in his heart: his words were softer than oil, yet *were* they drawn swords.

See on Cant. 3. 8.

PSALM LVI.

Ver. 8. Thou tellest my wanderings: put thou my tears into thy bottle: *are they* not in thy book?

The lachrymatories used in Greece and Rome are, I believe, unknown to the Hindoos. A person in distress, as he weeps, says, "Ah! Lord, take care of these tears, let them not run in vain." "Alas! my husband, why beat me? my tears are known to God."—ROBERTS.

The custom of putting tears into the *ampulla* or *urnæ lacrymales*, so well known among the Romans, seems to have been more anciently in use in Asia, and particularly among the Hebrews. These lachrymal urns were of different materials, some of glass, some of earth, and of various forms and shapes. One went about to each person in the company at the height of his grief with a piece of cotton in his hand, with which he carefully collects the falling tears, and which he then squeezes into the bottle, preserving them with the greatest care. This was no difficult matter; for Homer says the tears of Telemachus, when he heard of his father, dropped on the ground. They were placed on the sepulchres of the deceased as a memorial of the affection and sorrow of their surviving relations and friends. It will be difficult to account, on any other supposition, for the following expressions of the Psalmist: "Put thou my tears into thy bottle." If this view be admitted, the meaning will be: "Let my distress, and the tears I shed in consequence of it, be ever before thee."—PAXTON.

PSALM LVII.

Ver. 4. My soul *is* among lions; *and* I lie *even among* them that are set on fire, *even* the sons of men, whose teeth *are* spears and arrows, and their tongue a sharp sword.

The arrows were usually made of light wood, with a head of brass or iron, which was commonly barbed. Sometimes they were armed with two, three, or four hooks. The heads of arrows were sometimes dipped in poison. Horace mentions the *venenatæ agittæ*, the poisoned arrows of the ancient Moors in Africa. They were used by many other nations in different parts of the world; and if we believe the reports of modern travellers, these cruel weapons are not yet laid aside by some barbarous tribes. The negroes in the countries of Bornou and Soudan fight with poisoned arrows; the arrow is short, and made of iron; the smallest scratch with it causes the body to swell, and is infallibly mortal, unless counteracted by an antidote known among the natives. Everywhere, the poison used for this inhuman purpose was of the deadliest kind; and the slightest wound was followed by almost instant death. From this statement it will appear, that arrows were by no means contemptible instruments of destruction, although they are not to be compared with the tremendous inventions of modern warfare. We are not therefore to be surprised that sc many striking allusions to the arrow, and the trodden bow, occur in the loftier strains of the inspired writers. The bitter words of the wicked are called "their arrows;" "their teeth are spears and arrows;" and the man that beareth false witness against his neighbour, is "a sharp arrow." But in these comparisons there is perhaps a literal meaning, which supposes a connexion between the mouth and the arrow. The circumstance related by Mr. Park might possibly have its parallel in the conduct of the ancients; and if it had, clearly accounts for such figures as have been quoted. "Each of the negroes took from his quiver a handful of arrows, and putting two between his teeth, and one in his bow, waved to us with his hand to keep at a distance." Some are of opinion, that "the fiery darts," concerning which the apostle Paul warned his Ephesian converts, allude to the poisoned arrows, or javelins, which were so frequently used in those times; others contend, that the allusion is made to those missile weapons, which were sometimes employed by the ancients in battles and sieges, to scatter fire in the ranks, or among the dwellings of their enemies. "These were the πυρφορα βελη of Arrian, and the πυρφοροι οιστοι of Thucydides, the heads of which were surrounded with combustible matter, and set on fire, when they were launched against the hostile army."—PAXTON.

Ver. 8. Awake up, my glory; awake psaltery and harp; I *myself* will awake early.

Dr. Boothroyd has this, "Awake, my glory! awake, lyre

and harp!" The Orientals often speak to inanimate objects as if they had intelligence. Thus, a strolling musician, before he begins to play in your presence, says, "Arise, arise, my harp, before this great king! play sweetly in his hearing, and well shalt thou be rewarded." A person who has sold an article, says to it, when being carried away, "Go, thou, go." The Prophet says, "Awake, oh sword!" "When two heroes were preparing for a duel, one of them found a difficulty in drawing his sword from the scabbard; at which his antagonist asked, 'What! is thy sword afraid?'—'No,' replied the other, 'it is only hungry for thy blood.'"—ROBERTS.

PSALM LVIII.

Ver. 3. The wicked are estranged from the womb; they go astray as soon as they be born, speaking lies. 4. Their poison *is* like the poison of a serpent; *they are* like the deaf adder *that* stoppeth her ear.

"Do you ask whence he had this disposition? I will tell you; it was from the womb." "Expect him not to change; he had it in the womb." The figure of the wicked going astray as soon as they are born, seems to be taken from the disposition and power of a young serpent soon after its birth. The youngest serpent can convey poison to any thing it bites; and the suffering in all cases is great, though the bite is seldom fatal. Put a stick near the reptile, whose age does not amount to many days, and he will immediately snap at it. The young of the tiger and alligator are equally fierce in their earliest habits.—ROBERTS.

Several of the serpent tribe are believed to be deaf, or very dull of hearing. Perhaps that which is called the *puddeyan*, the beaver serpent, is more so than any other. I have several times been close upon them, but they did not offer to get out of the way. They lurk in the path, and the victim bitten by them will expire a few minutes after the bite. "Talk not to him: he is as the deaf serpent, he will not hear." "Truly, I am a deaf serpent, and may soon bite you." "Young man, if you repeat the *ubbatheasum*, which the priest has whispered in your ear, your next birth will be that of a deaf serpent."—ROBERTS.

Ver. 4. Their poison *is* like the poison of a serpent; *they are* like the deaf adder *that* stoppeth her ear.

"It appears, says Chardin, that all the teeth of a serpent are not venomous, because those that charm them will cause their serpents to bite them till they draw blood, and yet the wound will not swell. Adders will swell at the sound of a flute, raising themselves up on one half of their body, turning the other part about, and beating proper time; being wonderfully delighted with music, and following the instrument. Its head, before round and long like an eel, it spreads out broad and flat, like a fan. Adders and serpents twist themselves round the neck and naked body of young children, belonging to those that charm them. At Surat, an Armenian seeing one of them make an adder bite his flesh, without receiving any injury, said, I can do that; and causing himself to be wounded in the hand, he died in less than two hours." A serpent's possessing a musical ear, its keeping time in its motions with the harmony, its altering the shape of its head, are circumstances which, if true, are very wonderful.—HARMER.

Ver. 5. Which will not hearken to the voice of charmers, charming never so wisely.

Whether any man ever possessed the power to enchant or charm adders and serpents; or whether those who pretended to do so profited only by popular credulity, it is certain that a favourable opinion of magical power once existed. Numerous testimonies to this purpose may be collected from ancient writers. Modern travellers also afford their evidence. Mr. Browne, in his Travels in Africa, thus describes the charmers of serpents. Romeili is an open place of an irregular form, where feats of juggling are performed. The charmers of serpents seem also worthy of remark, their powers seem extraordinary. The serpent most common at Khaira is of the viper class, and

undoubtedly poisonous. If one of them enter a house, the charmer is sent for, who uses a certain form of words. I have seen three serpents enticed out of the cabin of a ship lying near the shore. The operator handled them, and then put them into a bag. At other times I have seen the serpents twist round the bodies of these psylli in all directions, without having had their fangs extracted or broken, and without doing them any injury.—BURDER.

Ver. 5. Which will not hearken to the voice of charmers, charming never so wisely. 6. Break their teeth, O God, in their mouth; break out the great teeth of the young lions, O LORD.

See on Eccl. x. 11.

The *kuravan*, or serpent charmer, may be found in every village, and some who have gained great fame actually live by the art. Occasionally they travel about the district, to exhibit their skill. In a basket they have several serpents, which they place on the ground. The kuravan then commences playing on his instrument, and to talk to the reptiles, at which they creep out, and begin to mantle about with their heads erect, and their hoods distended. After this, he puts his arm to them, which they affect to bite, and sometimes leave the marks of their teeth.

From close observation I am convinced that all these serpents thus exhibited have their poisonous FANGS extracted, and the Psalmist seems to have had his eyes on that when he says, "Break their teeth." Living animals have been repeatedly offered to the man for his serpents to bite, but he would never allow it; because he knew no harm would ensue.

It is, however, granted, that some of these men may believe in the power of their charms, and there can be no doubt that serpents in their wild state are affected by the influence of music. One of these men once went to a friend of mine (in the civil service) with his serpents, and charmed them before him. After some time the gentleman said, "I have a cobracapella in a cage, can you charm him?" "Oh! yes," said the charmer. The serpent was let out of the cage, and the man began his incantations and charms; the reptile fastened on his arm, and he was dead before the night.

The following is said to be a most potent charm for all poisonous serpents:—*Suttellām, pande, keere, soolave, akarudan, vārān, orou, vattami, kiddantha, pāmba, valliya, vuttakal, vāya;* which means, "Oh! serpent, thou who art coiled in the path, get out of my way; for around thee are the mongoos, the porcupine, and the kite in his circles is ready to take thee." The mongoos is in shape and size much like the English weasel. The porcupine is also a great enemy of the serpent. The kite, before he pounces on his prey, flies round in circles, and then drops like a stone; he seizes the reptile with his talons just behind the head, carries it up in the air, and bills it in the head till it expires.

But there are also charmers for bears, tigers, elephants, and other fierce animals. A party having to go through forests or deserts to a distant country, generally contrive to have some one among them possessed of that art. A servant of mine joined himself to a company who were going from Batticaloa to Colombo. There was a magician, who walked in front, who had acquired great fame as a charmer of serpents and other wild animals. After a few days they saw a large elephant, and the charmer said, "Fear not." But the animal continued to approach; and my servant thought it expedient to decamp and climb a tree. The others, also, began to retire; but the old man remained on the spot, repeating his charms. At last the elephant took him in his proboscis, and laid him gently on the ground; then lopped off the charmer's head, arms, and legs, and crushed the lifeless body flat on the earth.

By the power of charms the magicians pretend to have influence over ghosts, beasts, fire, wind, and water.—ROBERTS.

Ver. 8. As a snail *which* melteth, let *every one of them* pass away; *like* the untimely birth of a woman, *that* they may not see the sun.

The snail is, in the Hebrew scriptures, called שבלול *sabbelul*, which the learned Bochart derives from שבל, a *path*, because the snail marks out his path with his slime, and so is called שבלול, the path-maker; or, from ישב, to *lodge* ב *in*, and לול, a *winding shell*, cochlea, the well-known habitation which this animal carries about with him. Parkhurst is of opinion, that a better account of the name may be deduced from the peculiar manner in which snails *thrust themselves forward* in moving, and from the force with which they adhere to any substance on which they light. The wise Author of nature, having refused them feet and claws to creep and climb, has compensated them in a way more commodious for their state of life, by the broad skin along each side of the belly, and the undulating motion observable there. By the latter, they creep; by the former, assisted by the glutinous slime emitted from their body, they adhere firmly and securely to all kinds of superficies, partly by the tenacity of their slime, and partly by the pressure of the atmosphere. Thus, the snail wastes herself by her own motion, every undulation leaving some of her moisture behind; and in the same manner, the actions of wicked men prove their destruction. They may, like the snail, carry their defence along with them, and retire into it on every appearance of danger; they may confidently trust in their own resources, and banish far away the fear of evil; but the principles of ruin are at work within them, and although the progress may be slow, the result is certain. The holy Psalmist, guided by the spirit of inspiration, prayed, "As a snail which melteth, let every one of them pass away;" and Jehovah answered, "The wicked shall be turned into hell, and all the nations that forget God."—Paxton.

Ver. 9. Before your pots can feel the thorns, he shall take them away as with a whirlwind, both living, and in *his* wrath.

The Arabs heat stone pitchers by kindling fires in them, and then daub the outside with dough, which is thus baked. "They kindle a fire in a large stone pitcher, and when it is hot they mix the meal in water, as we do to make paste, and daub it with the hollow of their hands upon the outside of the pitcher, and this soft pappy dough spreads and is baked in an instant; the heat of the pitcher having dried up all its moisture, the bread comes off in small thin slices, like one of our wafers." (D'Arvieux.)—Burder.

PSALM LIX.

Ver. 14. And at evening let them return, *and* let them make a noise like a dog, and go round about the city.

Many cities in Syria, and other parts of the East, are crowded with dogs, which belong to no particular person, and by consequence, have none to feed them, but get their food in the streets, and about the markets. Dogs also abound in all the Indian towns and villages, and are numerous, noisy, and troublesome, especially to travellers. Like those in Syria, they have no respective owner, generally subsist upon charity, and are never destroyed. They frequently hunt in large packs, like the jackals, which they resemble in many other respects. These allusions are clearly involved in the prayer of the royal Psalmist for deliverance from his enemies: "And at evening let them return; and let them make a noise like a dog, and go round about the city. Let them wander up and down for meat, and grudge, if they be not satisfied."—Paxton.

Ver. 15. Let them wander up and down for meat, and grudge, if they be not satisfied.

The great external purity which is so studiously attended to by the modern eastern people, as well as the ancient, produces some odd circumstances with respect to their dogs. They do not suffer them in their houses, and even with care avoid their touching them in the streets, which would be considered as a defilement. One would imagine then, that under these circumstances, as they do not appear by any means to be necessary in their cities, however important they may be to those that feed flocks, there should be very few of these creatures found in those places; they are notwithstanding there in great numbers, and crowd their streets. They do not appear to belong to particular persons, as our dogs do, nor to be fed distinctly by such as might claim some interest in them, but get their food as they can. At the same time they consider it as right to take some care of them, and the charitable people among them frequently give money every week, or month, to butchers and bakers, to feed them at stated times, and some leave legacies at their deaths, for the same purpose. This is Le Bruyn's account. Thevenot and Maillet mention something of the same sort.

In like manner, dogs seem to have been looked upon among the Jews in a disagreeable light, yet they had them in considerable numbers in their cities, Ps. lix. 14. They were not, however, shut up in their houses or courts, Ps. lix. 6, 14; but seem to have been forced to seek their food where they could find it, Ps. lix. 15; to which I may add, that some care of them seems to be indirectly enjoined to the Jews, Exod. xxii. 31; circumstances that seem to be more illustrated by these travellers into the East, than by any commentators that I know of.—Harmer.

PSALM LX.

Ver. 3. Thou hast showed thy people hard things; thou hast made us to drink the wine of astonishment. 4. Thou hast given a banner to them that fear thee, that it may be displayed because of the truth. Selah.

Albertus Aquensis tells us, that when Jerusalem was taken in 1099, about three hundred Saracens got upon the roof of a very lofty building, and earnestly begged for quarter, but could not be induced by any promises of safety to come down, until they had received the banner of Tancred, one of the chiefs of the crusade army, as a pledge of life. It did not indeed avail them, as that historian observes; for their behaviour occasioned such indignation, that they were destroyed to a man. The event showed the faithlessness of these zealots, whom no solemnities could bind; but the Saracens surrendering themselves upon the delivery of a standard to them, proves in what a strong light they looked upon the giving them a banner, since it induced them to trust it, when they would not trust any promises. Perhaps the delivery of a banner was anciently esteemed, in like manner, an obligation to protect, and that the Psalmist might consider it in this light, when, upon a victory gained over the Syrians and Edomites, after the public affairs of Israel had been in a bad state, he says, *Thou hast showed thy people hard things*, &c. *Thou hast given a banner to them that fear thee.* Though thou didst for a time give up thine Israel into the hands of their enemies, thou hast now given them an assurance of thy having received them under thy protection. When the Psalmist is represented as saying, *Thou hast given a banner to them that fear thee, that it may be displayed*, it may be questioned whether it is rightly translated, since it is most probable they used anciently only a spear, properly ornamented, to distinguish it from a common one, as this same Albertus tells us, that a very long spear, covered all over with silver, to which another writer of those crusade wars adds a ball of gold on the top, was the standard of the Egyptian princes at that time, and carried before their armies. *Thou hast given a banner*, נס *nes*, an ensign, or a standard, *to them that fear thee, that it may be lifted up*, may perhaps be a better version; or rather, *that they may lift it up to themselves*, or encourage themselves with the confident persuasion that they are under the protection of God *because of the truth*, thy word of promise, which is an assurance of protection, like the giving me and my people a banner, the surest of pledges.—Harmer.

Ver. 4. Thou hast given a banner to them that fear thee, that it may be displayed because of the truth. Selah.

Has a person gained a signal triumph over his enemy by the assistance of another, he then says of the latter, "He has given me a victorious *kuddi*," banner. "Yes," say the conquerors, "we have gained a victorious banner"—Roberts.

PSALM LXII.

Ver. 3. How long will ye imagine mischief against a man? ye shall be slain all of you:

as a bowing wall *shall ye be, and as* a tottering fence.

Dr. Boothroyd, "like a tottering wall." In consequence of heavy rains and floods, and unsound foundations, it is VERY common to see walls much out of perpendicular, and some of them so much so, that it might be thought scarcely possible for them to stand. "Poor old Râman is very ill, I hear."—"Yes, the wall is bowing." "Begone, thou low caste; thou art a *kutte-chivver*," i. e. a ruined wall. "By the oppression of the head man the people of that village are like a ruined wall."—ROBERTS.

PSALM LXIII.

Ver. 10. They shall fall by the sword; they shall be a portion for foxes.

The jackal is here probably referred to. In India, the disgusting sight of jackals devouring human bodies, may be seen every day. So ravenous are these animals, that they frequently steal infants as they lie by the breast of the mother; and sick persons, who lie friendless in the street, or by the side of the Ganges, are sometimes devoured alive by these animals in the night. Persons in a state of intoxication have thus been devoured as they lay in the streets of Calcutta. (Ward.)—BURDER.

PSALM LXV.

Ver. 1. Praise waiteth for thee, O God, in Zion; and unto thee shall the vow be performed.

Margin, "is silent." Ainsworth, "Prayse silent wayteth for thee, O God." The people of the East are much given to meditation and silent praise, and sometimes they may be seen for hours so completely absorbed, as to be insensible to all surrounding objects. "Oh! Swamy, have you not heard my silent praises?" Among the devotees are to be found the silent praises of Siva. "My lord, only grant me this favour, and you will HEAR even my SILENT praises."—ROBERTS.

Ver. 13. The pastures are clothed with flocks; the valleys also are covered over with corn: they shout for joy, they also sing.

People in passing fields or gardens, after a fine rain, say, "Ah! how these fields and trees are laughing to-day." "Yes, you may well laugh; this is a fine time for you." "How nicely these flowers are laughing together."—ROBERTS.

PSALM LXVIII.

Ver. 9. Thou, O God, didst send a plentiful rain, whereby thou didst confirm thine inheritance, when it was weary.

I have taken notice of the traces of rain found in the desert between the Nile and the Red Sea; and I would here remark, that rain sometimes is found to fall in that part of the desert which lies on the eastern side of the Red Sea, where Israel wandered so many years, which circumstance is referred to in the scripture, and therefore claims some attention among the other observations contained in these papers.

Pitts, in his return to Egypt from Mecca, which he visited on a religious account, found rain in this desert. His words are as follows: "We travelled through a certain valley, which is called by the name of *Attash el Wait*, i. e. the river of the fire, the vale being so excessively hot, that the very water in their goat skins has sometimes been dried up with the gloomy, scorching heat. But we had the happiness to pass through it when it rained, so that the fervent heat was much allayed thereby; which the hagges looked on as a great blessing, and did not a little praise God for it." This naturally reminds us of a passage in the 68th Psalm, ver. 9: "Thou, O God, didst send a plentiful rain, whereby thou didst confirm thine inheritance, when it was weary;" speaking of God's going before his people when they came out of Egypt, and entered upon their sojourning in this wilderness. The Mohammedan pilgrims that were with Pitts, do not seem to have wanted water to drink, but the fall of rain, it seems, was highly acceptable to them, on account of cooling the air in a place where, from its situation, it was frequently wont to be extremely hot.

One of the first things that occurs to a reflecting mind upon reading this passage of the Psalmist, is, an inquiry whether this rain was miraculous, or a common exertion of the power of the God of nature, though under the direction of a gracious providence. It seems now, from this account of Mr. Pitts, to have been the last, and not contrary to the common course of things in that wilderness.

No mention is made of this merciful shower in the books of Moses, so far as I remember; but as we are told in the Psalm, immediately after, of the fleeing of kings, if the circumstances referred to here are ranged in exact order, it must have been before the Amalekites set upon Israel in Rephidim; but there can be no dependance upon that, especially as mention is made of Sinai in a preceding verse, and in the outset of the description of God's marching before his people through the wilderness.—HARMER.

Ver. 13. Though ye have lain among the pots, *yet shall ye be as* the wings of a dove covered with silver, and her feathers with yellow gold.

The dove is universally admitted to be one of the most beautiful objects in nature. The brilliancy of her plumage, the splendour of her eye, the innocence of her look, the excellence of her dispositions, and the purity of her manners, have been the theme of admiration and praise in every age. To the snowy whiteness of her wings, and the rich golden hues which adorn her neck, the inspired Psalmist alludes in these elegant strains: "Though ye have lain among the pots, yet ye shall be as the wings of a dove covered with silver, and her feathers with yellow gold." These bold figures do not seldom occur in the classical poets of antiquity. Virgil celebrates the *argenteus anser*, the silver-coloured goose; Ovid, the crow, which once rivalled the dove in whiteness; Lucretius, the changeful hues of her neck, which she turns to the sunbeam, as if conscious of its unrivalled beauty. Mr. Harmer is of opinion, that the holy Psalmist alludes, not to an animal adorned merely by the hand of nature, but to the doves that were consecrated to the Syrian deities, and ornamented with trinkets of gold; and agreeably to this view, he interprets the passage, "Israel is to me as a consecrated dove; and though your circumstances have made you rather appear like a poor dove, blackened by taking up its abode in a smoky hole of the rock; yet shall ye become beautiful and glorious as a Syrian silver-coloured pigeon, on whom some ornament of gold is put." But this view makes the Holy Ghost speak with some approbation, or at least without censure, of a heathenish rite, and even to borrow from it a figure to illustrate the effects of divine favour among his chosen people. No other instance of this kind occurs in the sacred scriptures, and therefore it cannot be admitted here without much stronger evidence than that respectable writer has produced. It is much more natural to suppose, that the Psalmist alludes to party-coloured doves, with white wings, and the rest of their feathers of a bright brown. Buffon mentions a species of turtle-dove in the bay of Campeachy, which is entirely brown, while others are of a snowy white; and both Ælian and Homer mention a dove of a red, or deep yellow colour, resembling gold. To these varieties the sacred writer might refer; and the more effectually to represent the blissful effects of divine favour, might combine the beauties of each into one picture.—PAXTON.

In Asia Minor, according to Chandler, the dove lodges in the holes of the rock; and Dr. Shaw mentions a city in Africa, which derives its name from the great number of wild pigeons which breed in the adjoining cliffs. It is not uncommon for shepherds and fishermen, to seek for shelter in the spacious caverns of that country, from the severity of the weather, and to kindle fires in them, to warm their shivering limbs, and dress their victuals; in consequence of which, the doves which happen to build their nests on their shelves, must be frequently smutted, and their plumage soiled. Some have conjectured, that the royal Psalmist may allude to this scene, in which he had perhaps acted a part, while he tended his father's flocks, in that singular promise, "Though ye have lain among the pots, yet shall ye be as the wings of a dove covered with silver, and her feathers with yellow gold." The people of Israel, who had long bent their necks to the galling yoke of Egypt, and groaned under the most cruel oppression, may not unfitly be compared to a dove in the fissure of a rock, which had been terrified by the intrusion of strangers, and polluted by the smoke of their fires, which ascended to the roof of the cavern, and penetrated into the most remote and secret corner; or by the smut of the pots, which they had set over these fires for culinary purposes, among which she fluttered in her haste to escape. The dove issues from the cave of the shepherds, black and dirty, her heart dejected, and her feathers in disorder; but, having washed herself in the running stream, and trimmed her plumage, she gradually recovers the serenity of her disposition, the purity of her colour, and the elegance of her appearance. So did the people of Israel more than once escape by the favour of Jehovah, from a low and despised condition, and gradually rise to great prosperity and splendour. In Egypt, they laboured in the brick-kilns, and in all the services of the field—a poor, enslaved, and oppressed people; and after their settlement in the land of promise, they were often reduced to a state of extreme distress; but in their misery they cried to the Lord, and he heard and delivered them from all their calamities; he subdued the surrounding nations to their sway; he poured the accumulated riches of ancient kings into their treasury; he made them the terror or the admiration of the East. But the holy Psalmist may have a prospective reference to the deliverance which the Gentile nations were to obtain, from the basest and most despicable condition, the worshipping of wood and stone, the gratifying of the vilest lusts, and their advancement to the service of Christ, and the practice of universal holiness and virtue. His words are not less applicable to the deliverance of the church, from the distresses in which she may be at any time involved, and the restoration of individual believers from a state of spiritual decline. On these joyous occasions, the people of God shake off their fears and their sorrows, and resume their wonted serenity, peace, and joy; they worship God in the beauty of holiness; they press forward with renovated vigour to the promised inheritance; they are as a dove, the most beautiful of the species, whose wings rival silver in whiteness, and the feathers of whose neck, the yellow radiance of gold.—Ibid.

The Hebrew word may refer to those fire-ranges or rows of stones on which the caldrons or pots were placed for boiling, probably something like, but more durable in their structure, than those which Niebuhr says are used by the wandering Arabs. "Their fireplace is soon constructed; they only set their pots upon several separate stones, or over a hole digged in the earth." Lying among these, denotes the most abject slavery; for this seems to have been the place of rest allotted to the vilest slaves. So old Laertes, grieving for the loss of his son, is described in Homer, as in the winter, sleeping where the slaves did, in the ashes near the fire.—Burder.

Ver. 14. When the Almighty scattered kings in it, it was *white* as snow in Salmon.

Perhaps in allusion to the bones of the slaughtered foe, which were scattered about, and lay bleaching on the summit of Salmon.—B.

Ver. 15. The hill of God *is as* the hill of Bashan; a high hill, *as* the hill of Bashan.

The Hebrew word is plural, and means a mountain of eminences, or backs. This may, perhaps, be a title peculiarly applicable to Bashan. The mountain with teeth, might be a name given it, from the appearance of the face of it, studded over with small hills. Monserrat, in Spain, is an instance of a mountain deriving its name from its shape; as it is Mons Serratas, or a mountain whose craggy cliffs have, at a distance, the resemblance of the teeth of a saw. The Sierra Morena, in Spain, is named from its shape and colour.—Burder.

Ver. 21. But God shall wound the head of his enemies, *and* the hairy scalp of such a one as goeth on still in his trespasses.

This language, in the East, is equivalent to saying, "I will kill you." "The king will soon break the *uche* (the scalp) of that fellow." "Tamban's *uche* is broken, he died last week." "Under the scalp is the royal wind, which is the last to depart after death." "With those who are *buried*, it remains three days in its place: but when the body is *burned*, it immediately takes its departure, which is a great advantage."—Roberts.

Ver. 25. The singers went before, the players on instruments *followed* after; among *them were* the damsels playing with timbrels.

This, no doubt, is a description of a religious procession in the time of David. In the sacred and domestic processions of the Hindoos they observe the same order, and have the same class of people in attendance. See them taking their god to exhibit to the people, or to remove some calamity; he is put into his car or tabernacle, and the whole is placed on men's shoulders. As they move along, the men and women precede, and sing his praises; then follow the musicians, who play with all their might in honour of the god, and for the enjoyment of the people.—Roberts.

Ver. 30. Rebuke the company of spearmen, the multitude of the bulls, with the calves of the people, *till every one* submit himself with pieces of silver: scatter thou the people *that* delight in war.

Literally, *rebuke the beast of the reeds*, or canes. This in all probability means the wild-boar, which is considered as destructive to the people of Israel, Psalm lxxx. 13. That wild-boars abound in marshes, fens, and reedy places, appears from Le Bruyn, who says, "we were in a large plain full of canals, marshes, and bullrushes. This part of the country is infested by a vast number of wild-boars, that march in troops, and destroy all the seeds and fruits of the earth, and pursue their ravages as far as the entrance into the villages. The inhabitants, in order to remedy this mischief, set fire to the rushes which afford them a retreat, and destroyed above fifty in that manner: but those that escaped the flames spread themselves all round in such a manner, that the people themselves were obliged to have recourse to flight, and have never disturbed them since for fear of drawing upon themselves some greater calamity. They assured me that some of these creatures were as large as cows."—Burder.

Ver. 31. Princes shall come out of Egypt; Ethiopia shall soon stretch out her hands unto God.

See on Ps. 44. 20.

PSALM LXIX.

Ver. 9. For the zeal of thy house hath eaten me up; and the reproaches of them that reproached thee are fallen upon me.

He who is zealous in his religion, or ardent in his attachments, is said to be eaten up. "Old Muttoo has determined to leave his home for ever; he is to walk barefoot to the Ganges for the salvation of his soul: his zeal has eaten him up."—Roberts.

Ver. 14. Deliver me out of the mire, and let me not stink: let me be delivered from them that hate me, and out of the deep waters.

"Ah! this *chearu*, this *chearu*," (this mud, this mud,) says the man who is in trouble, "who will pull me out?" "I am like the bullock, with his legs fast in the mud; the more I struggle, the faster I am."—Roberts.

Ver. 21. They gave me also gall for my meat; and in my thirst they gave me vinegar to drink.

The refreshing quality of vinegar cannot be doubted; but a royal personage had reason to complain of his treatment in having this only presented to him to quench his thirst, when it was only made use of by the meanest people. Pitts tells us, that the food that he and the rest had when first taken by the Algerines, was generally only five or six spoonfuls of vinegar, half a spoonful of oil, a few olives, with a small quantity of black biscuit, and a pint of water, a day. The juice of lemons is what those of higher life now use, and probably among the higher orders the juice of pomegranates might be used, to produce a grateful acidity.—Harmer.

Ver. 31. *This* also shall please the Lord better than an ox *or* bullock that hath horns and hoofs.

Dr. Boothroyd, "For this will be more acceptable to Jehovah than a full-horned and a full-hoofed steer." Buffaloes, which are offered in sacrifice, must always be full grown, and must have their horns and hoofs of a particular size and shape. Those without horns are offered to devils. Thus, it is difficult and expensive to procure a victim of the right kind. The writer of this psalm is supposed to have been a captive in Babylon, and consequently poor, and otherwise unable to bring an acceptable sacrifice to the Lord; but he rejoiced to know that he "heareth the poor, and despiseth not his prisoners;" and that, by praising "the name of God with a song," and by magnifying him with thanksgiving, would be more acceptable than the most *perfect* victim offered to him in sacrifice.—Roberts.

PSALM LXXI.

Ver. 11. Saying, God hath forsaken him; persecute and take him: for *there is* none to deliver *him*.

When a respectable man, in the service of his sovereign, or superior, falls into disgrace; when rich men become poor, or servants lose the favour of their masters; then a horde of accusers, who did not before dare to show their faces, come forward with the most fearful stories of the wickedness of the fallen man. Formerly they were ever flattering and cringing at his feet; but now they are the most brutal and bold of his enemies.—Roberts.

PSALM LXXII.

Ver. 5. They shall fear thee as long as the sun and moon endure, throughout all generations.

At the time appointed for the commencement of the new year, which, among the Singalese, is always in April, the king sat on his throne in state, surrounded by his chiefs, and the event was announced to the people by the discharge of jingalls. At the hour appointed for the second ceremony, young women of certain families, with lighted tapers in their hands, and a silver dish containing undressed rice, and turmeric water, stood at a little distance from the king, and when he directed his face to the southeast, with imbal leaves under his feet, and nuga leaves in his hand, and applied the medicinal juice to his head and body, they thrice exclaimed, Increase of age to our sovereign of five thousand years! increase of age as long as the sun and moon last! increase of age as long as heaven and earth exist! By the chiefs and people of consequence, this part of the ceremony was performed in a manner as nearly similar as possible. (Davy's Account of Ceylon.)—Burder.

Ver. 9. They that dwell in the wilderness shall bow before him; and his enemies shall lick the dust.

This is a very favourite way of threatening among the Hindoos. The half frantic man says to his foe, "Yes, thou shalt soon eat the earth;" which means his mouth will soon be open to receive it, *as in death*. "Soon, soon wilt thou have *man*," i. e. earth, "in thy mouth." In time of great scarcity, it is said, "The people are now eating earth; the cruel, cruel king, did nothing but put earth in the mouths of his subjects."—Roberts.

In Mr. Hugh Boyd's account of his embassy to the king of Candy, in Ceylon, there is a paragraph which singularly illustrates this part of the Psalm; and shows the adulation and obsequious reverence with which an eastern monarch is approached. Describing his introduction to the king, he says, "The removal of the curtain was the signal of our obeisances. Mine, by stipulation, was to be only kneeling. My companions immediately began the performance of theirs, which were in the most perfect degree of eastern humiliation. They almost literally licked the dust; prostrating themselves with their faces almost close to the stone floor, and throwing out their arms and legs; then rising on their knees, they repeated in a very loud voice a certain form of words of the most extravagant meaning that can be conceived:—that the head of the king of kings might reach beyond the sun; that he might live a thousand years," &c. Compare this with the passage of scripture now referred to. "He shall have dominion also from sea to sea, and from the river unto the ends of the earth. They that dwell in the wilderness shall bow before him, and his enemies shall lick the dust," i. e. the wild unconquered Arabians shall be brought to abject submission. This is beautifully emblematic of the triumph of Christ over those nations and individuals, whom it appeared impossible for the Gospel to subdue. "The kings of Tarshish and of the Isles shall bring presents; the kings of Sheba and Seba shall offer gifts. Yea, all kings shall fall down before him; all nations shall serve him."—Burder.

Ver. 16. There shall be a handful of corn in the earth upon the top of the mountains; the fruit thereof shall shake like Lebanon: and *they* of the city shall flourish like grass of the earth.

The rapidity with which grass grows in the East is the idea here referred to. "When the ground there hath been destitute of rain nine months together, and looks all of it like the barren sand in the deserts of Arabia, where there is not one spire of green grass to be found, within a few days after those fat enriching showers begin to fall, the face of the earth there (as it were by a new resurrection) is so revived, and, as it were, so renewed, as that it is presently covered all over with a pure green mantle. (Sir Thomas Roe.)—Burder.

PSALM LXXIV.

Ver. 11. Why withdrawest thou thy hand, even thy right hand? pluck *it* out of thy bosom.

The word which we translate bosom does not always, in eastern language, mean the breast; but OFTEN the lap, or that part of the body where the long robe folds round the loins. Thus, in the folds of the garment, in front of the body, the Orientals keep their little valuables, and there, when they are perfectly at ease, they place their hands. Sternhold and Hopkins, who translated from the original text, have the same idea:—

"Why dost thou draw thy hand aback,
And hide it in thy lap?"

To a king, whose enemies have invaded his territories, and are ravaging his kingdom, it will be said, should he not make any exertions to repel them, "Why does your majesty keep your hands in your *maddeyila*, (bosom?) Take your sword, your heroism thence." When two men go to a magistrate to complain of each other, perhaps one says, "He has beaten me severely, my lord." Then the other replies, "It is true, I did strike him, but these wounds on my body show he did not keep his hands in his bosom." "Complain not to me, fellow, for want of food; do I not see you always with your hands in your bosom?" "He has been cursing me in the most fearful way, but I told him to put the imprecations in his own bosom."

"Thy right hand," which is the hand of honour. Hence, "the right hand of the Most High." The Hindoos have a right-hand caste, and when they take a solemn oath they lift up that hand to heaven.

The whole of the right side of a man is believed to be more honourable than the left, and all its members are said to be *larger* and *stronger*; and, to give more dignity to it, they call it the *ānpackham*, i. e. the male side; whereas the other is called the female. This idea, also, is followed up in reference to their great deity, Siva; his right side is called male, and the other the female; which notion also applies to the Jupiter of western antiquity, as he was said to be male and also female.—Roberts.

Ver. 13. Thou didst divide the sea by thy strength: thou brakest the heads of the dragons in the waters. 14. Thou brakest the heads of leviathan in pieces, *and* gavest him *to be* meat to the people inhabiting the wilderness.

See on Job 41. 1, &c.

Ver. 19. O deliver not the soul of thy turtle-dove unto the multitude *of the wicked;* forget not the congregation of thy poor for ever.

It has already been observed, that the turtle-dove never admits a second mate, but lingers out her life in sorrowful widowhood. To this remarkable circumstance, these words of David are by many thought to refer: "O deliver not the soul of thy turtle-dove unto the multitude of the wicked; forget not the congregation of thy poor for ever." As the turtle cleaves to her mate with unshaken fidelity, so these interpreters say, had Israel adhered to their God. But it is well known that God's ancient people were a stiff-necked and rebellious race, equally fickle and perfidious, and discovering on almost every occasion a most violent and unreasonable inclination to the worship of heathen deities. It is, therefore, more natural to suppose, that the holy Psalmist, by this term, alludes to the weak and helpless state of his people, that like the turtle had neither power nor inclination to resist their numerous enemies. The dove is a harmless and simple creature, equally destitute of skill and courage for the combat; and the turtle is the smallest of the family. She is therefore a most proper emblem of the national imbecility into which the people of Israel had sunk, in consequence of their numerous iniquities, with which they had long provoked the God of their fathers. They who were the terror of surrounding nations, while they feared the Lord and kept his commandments, whom God himself instructed in the art of war, and led to certain victory, had by their folly become the scorn of their neighbours, and an easy prey to every invader.—Paxton.

Sometimes those that have no tents, shelter themselves from the inclemency of the night air, in holes and caverns which they find in their rocky hills, where they can kindle fires to warm themselves, as well as to dress their provisions; to which may be added, that *doves* also, in those countries, frequently haunt such places, as well as some other birds. Dr. Richard Chandler, in his travels in Asia Minor, has both taken notice of the doves there lodging in holes of the rocks; and of the shepherds and fishermen being wont to make use of such retreats, and of their kindling fires in them, by which practice those doves must be frequently very much smutted, and their feathers dirtied. And I have been sometimes ready to imagine, that an attention to these circumstances may afford as easy and natural an account as any that has been given of that association of such very different things as *doves* and *smoky places*, which we meet with in the 68th Psalm. It is certain the people of Israel are compared to a dove, in the book of Psalms; "O deliver not the soul of thy turtle-dove unto the multitude of the wicked; forget not the congregation of thy poor for ever," Ps. lxxiv. 19; and the same image appears to have been made use of, in this 68th Psalm. If it was made use of, it was not unnatural to compare Israel, who had been in a very afflicted state in Egypt, to a dove making its abode in the hollow of a rock, which had been smutted by the fires shepherds had made in it for the heating their milk, or other culinary purposes; which led them to make such little heaps of stones, on which they might set their pots, having a hollow under them, in which they put the fuel, according to the eastern mode, of which I have given an account elsewhere, and which little buildings are meant by the word here translated *pots*.

This image might very properly be made use of to express any kind of affliction Israel might have suffered, when they are compared as a body of people to a dove; and certainly not less so, when they had been forced to work without remission in the brick-kilns of Egypt. For so the sense will be something like this: O my people! though ye have been like a dove in a hole of a rock, that hath been blackened by the fires of the shepherds for the boiling their pots; yet on this joyous occasion did you appear as the most beautiful of that species, whose wings are like silver, and the more muscular parts, from whence the strength of the wings are derived, like the splendour of gold.—Harmer.

PSALM LXXV.

Ver. 4. I said unto the fools, Deal not foolishly; and to the wicked, Lift not up the horn: 5. Lift not up your horn on high: speak *not with* a stiff neck.

This passage will receive some illustration from Bruce's remarks in his Travels to discover the source of the Nile, where, speaking of the head-dress of the governors of the provinces of Abyssinia, he represents it as consisting of a large broad fillet bound upon their forehead, and tied behind their head. In the middle of this was a horn, or a conical piece of silver gilt, about four inches long, much in the shape of our common candle extinguishers. This is called kirn, or horn, and is only worn in reviews, or parades after victory. The crooked manner in which they hold the neck, when this ornament is on their forehead, for fear it should fall forward, seems to agree with what the Psalmist calls *speaking with a stiff neck*, for it perfectly shows the meaning of speaking with a stiff neck, when you hold the horn on high, or erect, like the horn of a unicorn.—Burder.

Mr. Munroe, speaking of the females in a Maronite village, in Mount Lebanon, observes: "But the most remarkable peculiarities of their dress, are the immense silver ear-rings hanging forward upon the neck, and the *tantoura*, or 'horn,' which supports the veil. This latter ornament varies in form, material, and position, according to the dignity, taste, and circumstances of the wearer. They are of gold, silver gilt, or silver, and sometimes of wood. The former are either plain or figured in low relief, and occasionally set with jewels; but the length and position of them is that upon which the traveller looks with the greatest interest, as illustrating and explaining a familiar expression of scripture. The young, the rich, and the vain, wear the *tantoura* of great length, standing straight up from the top of the forehead; whereas the humble, the poor, and the aged, place it upon the side of the head, much shorter, and spreading at the end like a trumpet. I do not mean to say, that these distinctions are universal, but I was told that they are very general, and thus the 'exalted horn' still remains a mark of power and confidence, as it was in the days of Israel's glory."—(Summer Ramble in Syria, 1833.)—B.

"We stopped for the night at the village of Barook, chiefly inhabited by Druses, many of whom are said to have adopted the creed of their Maronite neighbours. Our tent was placed close to the house of the principal vender of small wares, round which an arrival soon attracted a crowd, but far superior in appearance and civility to the inhabitants of any district we had previously seen. Most of the men wore clean white turbans, and the women were wrapped in blue veils, beneath which a *tantoor*, that invariable article of Druse luxury, which is worn day and night, made a conspicuous figure. This we had now an opportunity of examining, for our host, accompanied by his wife, came to our tent, attracted by the novelty of tea, which they both drank, when well sweetened, with apparent satisfaction. The lady, in return, satisfied our curiosity by taking off her *tantoor*, which was of silver, rudely enclosed with flowers, stars, and other devices. In length it was, perhaps, something more than a foot: but in shape had little resemblance to a horn, being a mere hollow tube, increasing in size from the diameter of an inch and a half at one extremity, to three inches at the other, where it terminated like the mouth of a trumpet. If the smaller end was closed, it might serve for a drinking-cup; and in Germany glasses of the same form and size are occasionally used. This strange ornament, placed on a cushion, is securely fixed to the upper part of the forehead by two silk cords, which, after surrounding the head, hang behind nearly to the ground, terminating in large tassels, which among the better classes are capped with silver."—(Hogg's Visit to Damascus, Jerusalem, &c., 1833.)—B.

A man of lofty bearing is said to carry his horn very high. To him who is proudly interfering with the affairs of another it will be said, "Why show your *kombu* (horn) here?" "What! are you a horn for me?" "See that fellow, what a fine horn he has; he will make the people run." "Truly, my lord, you have a great horn." "Chinnan has lost his money, ay, and his hornship too." "Alas! alas! I am like the deer, whose horns have fallen off."—ROBERTS.

Ver. 8. For in the hand of the LORD *there is* a cup, and the wine is red; it is full of mixture, and he poureth out of the same: but the dregs thereof, all the wicked of the earth shall wring *them* out, *and* drink *them*.

Red wine, in particular, is more esteemed in the East than white. And we are told in the travels of Olearius, that it is customary with the Armenian Christians in Persia to put Brazil wood, or saffron, into their wine, to give it a higher colour, when the wine is not so red as they like, they making no account of white wine. He mentions the same thing also in another place. These accounts of their putting Brazil wood or saffron into their wines, to give them a deeper red, seem to discover an energy in the Hebrew word אדם *adam*, which is used Prov. xxiii. 31, that I never remarked anywhere. It is of the conjugation called Hithpahel, יתאדם *yithaddam*, which, according to grammarians, denotes an action that turns upon the agent itself: it is not always, it may be accurately observed; but in this case it should seem that it ought to be taken according to the strictness of grammar, and that it intimates the wine's making itself redder by something put into it: *Look not on the wine when it maketh itself red.* It appears, indeed, from Is. lxiii. 2, that some of the wines about Judea were naturally red; but so Olearius supposed those wines to be which he met with in Persia, only more deeply tinged by art; and this colouring it, apparently is to make it more pleasing and tempting to the eye.

There are two other places relating to wine, in which our translators have used the term red; but the original word חמר *chemer* differs from that in Proverbs, and I should therefore imagine intended another idea; what that might be, may, perhaps, appear in the sequel. The word, it is certain, sometimes signifies what is made thick or turbid; so it expresses the thickening water with mud, Ps. lxxvi. 3. May it not then signify the thickening wine with its lees? It seems plainly to do so in one of the passages: "In the hand of the Lord is a cup, and the wine is red, *or turbid:* it is full of mixture, and he poureth out the same: but the dregs thereof, all the wicked of the earth shall wring them out, and drink them," Ps. lxxv. 8. The turbidness of wine makes it very inebriating, and consequently expressive of the disorder affliction brings on the mind; thus, Thevenot, I remember, tells us the wine of Shiras, in Persia, is full of lees, and therefore very heady; to remedy which, they filtrate it through a cloth, and then it is very clear, and free from fumes.—HARMER.

The punishments which Jehovah inflicts upon the wicked, are compared to a cupfull of fermenting wine, mixed with intoxicating herbs, of which all those to whom it is given must drink the dregs or sediment. The same image is found, not only frequently in other places in the Old Testament, but also very often in the Arabian poets. Thus Taabbata Scharran, in a passage of an Arabic Anthology, by Alb. Schultens: "To those of the tribe of Hodail, we gave the cup of death, whose dregs were confusion, shame, and reproach." Another poet says: "A cup such as they gave us, we gave to them." When Calif Almansor had his valiant, though dreaded general, Abre-Moslem, murdered, he repeated the following verse, in which he addressed the corpse: "A cup such as he gave, gave I him, bitterer to the taste than wormwood." (Elmacin.)—BURDER.

PSALM LXXVI.

Ver. 11. Vow, and pay unto the LORD your God: let all that be round about him bring presents unto him that ought to be feared.

Taxes in Persia are commonly levied under the form of presents to the monarch. The usual presents are those made annually by all governors of provinces and districts, chiefs of tribes, ministers, and all others invested with high office, at the feast of the vernal equinox. These gifts are regulated by the nature of the office, and the wealth of the individual, and consist of the best of the produce of every part of the kingdom. Sometimes a large sum of money is given, which is always the most acceptable present. Allusive to this custom is that command in relation to Messiah: "Let all that are round about him bring presents unto him that ought to be feared." Besides these ordinary presents, extraordinary largesses, of a less defined nature, but which are also of very considerable amount, are expected. Of this kind were, in the opinion of some writers, the presents which the enemies of Saul refused to bring, at his accession to the throne of Israel: "But the children of Belial said, How shall this man save us? And they despised him, and brought him no presents. But he held his peace."—PAXTON.

PSALM LXXVII.

Ver. 2. In the day of my trouble I sought the LORD: my sore ran in the night, and ceased not: my soul refused to be comforted.

The margin has, instead of sore, "*hand.*" Ainsworth, "In the day of my distress I sought the Lord: my hand by night reached out and ceased not." Dr. Boothroyd, "In the day of my distress I seek Jehovah: by night, my hand, without ceasing, is stretched out unto him." Dr. A. Clarke says, "My hand was stretched out," *i. e.* in prayer. The Tamul translation, "My hands, in the night, were spread out, and ceased not." "Ah!" says the sorrowful mother, over her afflicted child, "all night long were my hands spread out to the gods on thy behalf." In that position do they sometimes hold their hands for the night together. Some devotees do this with their right hand throughout the whole of their lives, till the arm becomes quite stiff.—ROBERTS.

Ver. 10. And I said, this *is* my infirmity: *but I will remember* the years of the right hand of the Most High.

Dr. Boothroyd, "Then I said, this is the time of my sorrow; but the right hand of the Most High can change it." I have shown that superior honour is given to the RIGHT hand. It is that with which men fight: the "sword arm," consequently protection, or deliverance, comes from that. David was in great distress; but, he asks, has "God forgotten to be gracious?" To this his heart replied, No! and he determined to believe in the *right hand* of the Most High, which had often delivered and defended him in days past, and which could again change all his circumstances. The *right hand* is that which dispenses gifts; no Hindoo would offer a present with his *left hand.* A miser is said to have two left hands! "Never, never shall I forget the right hand of that good man: he always relieved my wants." "Ah! the ungrateful wretch, how many years have I helped him! he has forgotten my right hand." "Yes, poor fellow, he has lost all his property; he cannot now use his right hand." "My children, my children," says the aged father, "how many years have I supported you? Surely you will never forget the right hand of your father."—ROBERTS.

PSALM LXXVIII.

Ver. 21. Therefore the LORD heard *this*, and was wroth: so a fire was kindled against Jacob, and anger also came up against Israel.

The first supply of quails was followed by no visible judgment from heaven; for although they were guilty of murmuring against the Lord, he spared them in his love and in his pity; but they provoked him on this occasion, by their indecent desire of good living; by loathing the manna, which was provided for them by his distinguishing kindness; by regretting the provisions which they had enjoyed in Goshen; and by denying the divine power and goodness, which they had already experienced in supplying them with quails, soon after they came out of Egypt, and of which they had every day the most substantial proofs, in giving them bread from heaven. Incensed by this undutiful conduct, Jehovah unequivocally notified his righteous displeasure, before he granted their demands: "Ye shall eat it a whole month, until it come out at your nostrils, and it be loathsome unto you; because that ye have despised the Lord which is among you, and have wept before him, saying, Why came we forth out of Egypt?" These words are a proof, that he had heard the murmurings of his people with great indignation. When, therefore, the month was completed, and while the flesh with which they had gorged themselves was yet in their mouth, "the wrath of the Lord was kindled against the people, and the Lord smote the people with a very great plague." Various are the views which interpreters have given of this judgment; but their opinion seems entitled to the preference, who suppose it was a fire from heaven, by which some of the people were consumed. Their undutiful murmurings were punished in this manner, a very short time before: "And when the people complained, it displeased the Lord; and the Lord heard it, and his anger was kindled; and the fire of the Lord burnt among them, and consumed them that were in the uttermost parts of the camp." Bochart, indeed, considers this brief statement as a summary view of the scene which is more minutely described in the rest of the chapter. The same place, he thinks, is called Taberah, from the conflagration, and Kibroth-hataavah, "because there they buried the people that lusted." But this opinion seems to rest upon no solid foundation; no trace of a more brief, and then of a more extended narrative, can be discovered in the passage. The sacred writer plainly describes two different calamities, of which the first was indisputably by fire, which renders it not improbable that the second was also produced by the same devouring element. This probability is greatly increased by the words of David, in his sublime description of this very judgment: "Therefore, the Lord heard, and was wroth; so a fire was kindled against Jacob, and anger also came up against Israel; because they believed not God, nor trusted in his salvation." An instance of similar perverseness is recorded of this people, soon after they came out of Egypt. But, although they were perhaps equally blameable, they were not subjected to the same punishment; for, in this instance, Jehovah bestowed upon them a supply of quails that evening; and the day after, he rained manna from heaven around their tents. He had a right to punish them for their iniquity; but he graciously turned away his anger, and yielded to their importunities. And for this forbearance, several reasons may be assigned. If any fall a second time into the sins which had already been forgiven, he is more guilty than before; because he both insults the justice, and tramples on the grace and mercy of God. Besides, in this instance, the people of Israel murmured against their leaders, because they were pressed by famine, and in want of all the necessaries of life. But in the desert of Paran, bread from heaven descended in daily showers around their encampment, in sufficient quantity to satisfy the whole congregation; they lived on angel's food; they were satiated with the bread of heaven; and by consequence, the flesh which they demanded with so great eagerness and importunity, was not required to supply their necessity, but to gratify their lustful desires. When they murmured against Moses and Aaron in the wilderness of Sin, they had but lately come out of Egypt—they were still in a rude and untutored state, for the law was not yet given; but in Paran they rebelled, after long and various experience of the divine care and goodness, after the law was given, and after they had been instructed by many sufferings, in the evil nature and bitter consequences of sin; their conduct, therefore, was much more criminal, and deservedly subjected them to severe castigation.—PAXTON.

Ver. 25. Man did eat angels' food: he sent them meat to the full. 26. He caused an east wind to blow in the heaven; and by his power he brought in the south wind. 27. He rained flesh also upon them as dust, and feathered fowls like as the sand of the sea.

See on Ex. 16. 12, 13.

On this passage it has been asked, How can these winds blow together, and at the same time bring up the quails from the sea into the desert? The Seventy interpreters, and the Vulgate, found it so difficult to give a satisfactory answer to these queries, that they were induced to render the first clause, "He removed the east wind from the heaven;" as if the removal of one wind was necessarily succeeded by another. But this version cannot be admitted, because the Psalmist clearly intends to represent the east and the south winds, as the joint instruments of divine goodness, which, by their united force, collected and brought up the quails from the sea. If the Psalmist had meant to express the removing of the east wind, he must have used the phrase, (מן השמים) *from the heaven;* but instead of this, he uses the words, (בשמים) *in or into the heavens,* which convey an idea quite the reverse. Our version, therefore, gives the true sense of the sacred text: He caused an east wind to blow in the heaven; that is, he introduced it for the very purpose of bringing the quails into the camp. To this may be added, that in the whole of this Psalm, as often in the other poetical books of the Hebrews, the two hemistiches are almost parallel, and mutually explain each other. From whence it follows, that (יסע) *yasah* in this text, has nearly the same meaning as its parallel verb, (וינהג) *vainhag,* which signifies to introduce. This is accordingly the sense which all interpreters, ancient and modern, have adopted, except the Septuagint and the Vulgate.

From this statement it appears, that the royal Psalmist in this passage means to excite, not to remove the east wind; to introduce, not to expel it from the heavens. But to understand the matter clearly, let it be remembered, that the people of Israel were at that time in the wilderness of Paran; at the distance of three days' journey from Sinai, directly north from the extremity of the Arabian gulf; and by consequence, from Theman, the country from whence the south wind blows, whose name it commonly bears, in the Hebrew text, which brought the quails into the camp of Israel. The same region is named (קדים) *kadim,* that is, the east; because it lay towards the southeast; and was denominated sometimes by the one name, and sometimes by the other. Although the cardinal winds are reckoned four in number, which are again subdivided into many more; yet the ancient philosophers, and particularly Aristotle and Theophrastus, distributed them into two, the north and the south. The westerly winds they included in the north, because they are colder; and the easterly winds in the south, because they are attended by a greater degree of heat. But, since the east wind was anciently comprehended in the south, the east and the south may be used in this text as synonymous; and by consequence, the east is the same, or nearly the same, as the south wind. Nor is it in this text alone, that the sacred writers ascribe to the east, what might seem to be the proper effects of the south wind; the same thing may be observed in every part of scripture. It burns up the fruits of the earth; it blasts the vines, and other fruit-bearing trees; it drove back the Red Sea, and opened a passage to the people of God; it dries up the fountains of water; and by its irresistible violence, it dashes the ships of Tharshish in pieces; and, in fine, scatters destruction among the dwellings of wicked men, and sweeps them from the face of the earth, into the silent mansions of the grave. The prophet Isaiah on this account, calls it a rough wind; and Jonah feelingly describes the vehemence with which it beat upon his head till he fainted, and wished in himself to die. The Greek interpreters uniformly render it the south wind; and Theodoret regards these two winds as nearly the same. Although, therefore, the phrase (רוח הקדים) *ruah hakadim,* properly and precisely speaking, denotes the east wind; yet, because the east and the south winds resemble each other in many particulars, the Hebrews, in the opinion of Bochart and other learned writers, appear to have used these names promiscuously; which is the reason that (קדים) *kadim* is, in every part of the Greek version, and particularly in the text under review, rendered the south wind. Thus the same wind seems to have been intended by both these terms, the south or African wind, which, from the interior of Egypt, wafted the quails into the desert, and scattered them round the tents of Israel.

This difficulty admits of other solutions equally natural and easy. The inspired writer may be understood to mean the southeast wind, which might bring the quails as well from the east as from the south; or, that both the east and the south winds were employed on that occasion, the first to scatter about the tents of Israel the congregated flocks, which the last had swept into the desert; or, in order to secure a complete supply for so great a multitude, to gather at the same time from the east and the south, the widely dispersed troops of these birds, which, in distant regions of the sky, were pursuing their annual journey from their winter quarters, to the more temperate latitudes.

It is indeed objected by some writers, that the west wind, rather than the east, ought to blow, in order to produce the effect recorded by Moses; and that, according to Pliny and Aristotle, the quails do not trust themselves to the sky when the humid and boisterous south wind blows; and for this reason, the winds blowing from the north and west, are distinguished by the name of ornithian, because they are favourable to the migratory tribes. But no miracle is involved in this circumstance; for these ancient authors only mean, that the quails pursue their journey with greater difficulty, and are more easily taken when the south wind blows; while, according to the observation of others, these birds of passage were brought back in the spring, by the south winds, which are the most proper for conducting them from the banks of the Nile and the shores of the Red Sea, into the wilderness of Paran.—Paxton.

Ver. 31. The wrath of God came upon them, and slew the fattest of them, and smote down the chosen *men* of Israel.

See on Ps. 22. 12.

Ver. 45. He sent divers sorts of flies among them, which devoured them; and frogs, which destroyed them.

See on Ex. 8. 4.

Ver. 47. He destroyed their vines with hail, and their sycamore-trees with frost.

The land of Egypt never produced a sufficient quantity of wine to supply the wants of its inhabitants: but still it contained many vines, although it could not boast of extensive and loaded vineyards. The vines of Egypt are conjoined by the Psalmist, with the sycamores, in his triumphant song on the plagues which desolated that country, and procured the liberation of his ancestors: "He destroyed their vines with hail, and their sycamore-trees with frost." This was to the people of Egypt a very serious loss; for the grape has been in all ages a principal part of the viands, with which they treated their friends. Norden was entertained with coffee and grapes by the aga of Essauen: and when Maillet resided in that country, the natives used the young leaves of their vines even more than the fruit. A principal article of their diet consist in minced meat, which they wrap up in small parcels in vine leaves, and laying thus one leaf upon another, they season it according to the custom of their country, and make of it one of the most delicate dishes presented on their tables. The remainder of the vintage they convert into wine, of so delicious a taste and flavour, that it was carried to Rome in the days of her pride and luxury, and esteemed by epicures the third in the number of their most esteemed wines. The use of wine being prohibited by the Mohammedan law, very little is manufactured at present; but it seems, in ancient times, to have been produced in much greater abundance. In the reign of the Pharaohs, it was certainly made in considerable quantities for the use of the court, who probably could procure no such wine from other countries, nor were they acquainted with such liquors as the great now drink in Egypt; and consequently the loss of their vines, as the sacred writer insinuates, must have been considerable.

The grapes of Egypt are said to be much smaller than those which grow in the land of Canaan. Dandini, though an Italian, seems to have been surprised at the extraordinary size of the grapes produced in the vineyards of Lebanon. They are as large as prunes, and as may be inferred from the richness and flavour of the wines for which the mountains of Lebanon have been renowned from time immemorial, of the most delicious taste. To the size and flavour of these grapes, brought by the spies to the camp in the wilderness, the Italian traveller, little versed, it should seem, in the history of the Old Testament, imputes the ardour with which the people of Israel prosecuted the conquest of Palestine. The magnificent cluster which the spies brought from Eshcol, was certainly fitted, in no common degree, to stimulate the parched armies of Israel to deeds of heroic valour; but their kindling spirit was effectually damped by the report of the spies, who were intimidated by the robust and martial appearance of the Canaanites, the strength of their cities, and the gigantic stature of the sons of Anak.

The grapes produced in the land of Egypt, although very delicious, are extremely small; but those which grow in the vineyards of Cœlo Syria and Palestine, swell to a surprising bigness. The famous bunch of Eshcol required the strength of two men to bear it. This difference sufficiently accounts for the surprise and pleasure which the people of Israel manifested, when they first beheld, in the barren and sandy desert, the fruits which grew in their future inheritance. The extraordinary size of the grapes of Canaan, is confirmed by the authority of a modern traveller. In traversing the country about Bethlehem, Doubdan found a most delightful valley full of aromatic herbs and rose bushes, and planted with vines, which he supposed were of the choicest kind: it was actually the valley of Eshcol, from whence the spies carried that prodigious bunch of grapes to Moses, of which we read in the book of Numbers. That writer, it is true, saw no such cluster, for he did not visit that fruitful spot in the time of the vintage; but the monks assured him, they still found some, even in the present neglected state of the country, which weighed ten or twelve pounds.

The vineyards of Canaan produce grapes of different kinds; some of them are red, and some white, but the greater part are black. To the juice of the red grape, the sacred writers make frequent allusions: "Wherefore art thou red in thine apparel, and thy garments like him that treadeth in the wine fat?" "In that day, sing ye unto her a vineyard of red wine: I the Lord do keep it." It is, therefore, with strict propriety, the inspired writer calls it "the blood of the grape," a phrase which seems intended to indicate the colour of the juice, or the wine produced from it: "Thou didst drink the pure blood of the grape."

The sycamore forms the middle link in the vegetable kingdom, between the fig and the mulberry; and partakes, according to some natural historians, of the nature of both. This is the reason the Greeks call it συκαμορος,—a name compounded of συκος, a fig-tree, and μορος, a mulberry. It resembles the fig-tree in the shape and size of its fruit; which grows neither in clusters, nor at the end of the branches, but by a very singular law, sticking to the trunk of the tree. Its taste is much like that of the wild fig, and pretty agreeable: Pliny says the fruit is very sweet.

It may seem strange that so inferior a tree as the sycamore should be classed by the Psalmist with the choicest vines, in his ode on the plagues of Egypt: "He destroyed their vines with hail, and their sycamore-trees with frost." Many other trees, it may be supposed, might be of much greater consequence to them; and in particular, the date, which, on account of its fruit, the modern Egyptians hold in the highest estimation. But it ought to be remembered, that several trees which are now found in Egypt, and highly valued, might not then be introduced. Very few trees at present in Egypt, are supposed to be natives of the country. If this idea be just, the sycamore and the vine might, at that early period, be in reality the most valuable trees in that kingdom. But, admitting that the sycamore was, in respect of intrinsic properties or general utility, much inferior to some other trees which they possessed, accidental circumstances might give it an importance to which it had originally no claim. The shade of this umbrageous tree is so grateful to the inhabitants of those warm latitudes, that they plant it along the side of the ways near their villages; and as a full-grown sycamore branches out to so great a distance, that it forms a canopy for a circle of forty paces in diameter, a single row of trees on one side of the way is sufficient. It is often seen stretching its arms over the houses, to screen the fainting inhabitant from the glowing heats of the summer. This was a benefit so important to them, that it obtained a place in the divine promise: "They shall sit every man under his vine and under his fig-tree;" and to show at once the certainty of the promise, and the value of the favour, it is repeated by another inspired prophet: "Ye shall call every man his neighbour under his vine and under his fig-tree." Now, it appears from the most authentic records, that the ancient Egyptian coffins, intended to preserve to many generations the bodies of departed relatives; the little square boxes which were placed at the feet of the mummies, enclosing the instruments and utensils in miniature, which belonged to the trade and occupation of the deceased; the figures and instruments of wood found in the catacombs,—are all made of sycamore wood, which, though spongy and porous to appearance, has continued entire and uncorrupted for at least three thousand years. The innumerable barks which ply on the river and over all the vale, in the time of the inundation, are also fabricated of sycamore wood. But besides the various important uses to which the wood was applied, the sycamore produces a species of fig, upon which the people almost entirely subsist, thinking themselves well regaled, when they have a piece of bread, a couple of sycamore figs, and a pitcher filled with water from the Nile.—PAXTON.

Ver. 63. The fire consumed their young men; and their maidens were not given to marriage.

This is described as one of the effects of God's anger upon Israel. In Hindoo families, sometimes, the marriage of daughters is delayed; this is, however, always considered as a great calamity and disgrace. If a person sees girls more than twelve years of age unmarried in a family, he says, "How is it, that that Bramin can sit at home, and eat his food with comfort, when his daughters, at such an age, remain unmarried?" (Ward.)—BURDER.

Ver. 64. Their priests fell by the sword; and their widows made no lamentation.

When the cholera swept off such multitudes, the cities from every house had a fearful effect on the passers by; but, after some time, though the scourge remained, the people ceased to lament, asking, "Why should we mourn? the *Amma*," i. e. the goddess, "is at her play." Thus, instead of the shrieks and howls so common on such occasions, scarcely a sigh or a whisper was heard from the survivers.—ROBERTS.

Ver. 66. And he smote his enemies in the hinder parts; he put them to a perpetual reproach.

Dr. Boothroyd, "And smote his enemies in the hinder parts, and he put them to perpetual disgrace." Some commentators think this alludes "to the emerods inflicted on the Philistines;" but the figure is used in reference to those who are conquered, and who consequently show their backs when running away. "I will make that fellow show his back," means, "I will cause him to run from me." It is also considered exceedingly disgraceful to be beaten on that part.—ROBERTS.

PSALM LXXIX.

Ver. 2. The dead bodies of thy servants have they given *to be* meat unto the fowls of the heaven, the flesh of thy saints unto the beasts of the earth. 3. Their blood have they shed like water round about Jerusalem; and *there was* none to bury *them*.

See on 1 Sam. 31. 9.

Criminals were at other times executed in public; and then commonly without the city. To such executions without the gate, the Psalmist undoubtedly refers in this complaint: "The dead bodies of thy saints have they given to be meat unto the fowls of the heaven, the flesh of thy saints unto the beasts of the earth. Their blood have they shed like water round about Jerusalem; and there was none to bury them." The last clause admits of two senses. 1st. There was no friend or relations left to bury them. 2d. None were allowed to perform this last office. The despotism of eastern princes often proceeds to a degree of extravagance which is apt to fill the mind with astonishment and horror. It has been thought, from time immemorial, highly criminal to bury those who had lost their lives by the hand of an executioner, without permission. In Morocco, no person dares to bury the body of a malefactor without an order from the emperor; and Windus, who visited that country, speaking of a man who was sawed in two, informs us, that "his body must have remained to be eaten by the dogs, if the emperor had not pardoned him; an extravagant custom to pardon a man after he is dead; but unless he does so, no person dares bury the body." To such a degree of savage barbarity it is probable the enemies of God's people carried their opposition, that no person dared to bury the dead bodies of their innocent victims. —PAXTON.

Ver. 11. Let the sighing of the prisoner come before thee; according to the greatness of thy power preserve thou those that are appointed to die.

To illustrate the miserable condition of an oriental prisoner, Chardin relates a story of a very great Armenian merchant, who for some reason was thrown into prison. So long as he bribed the jailer with large donations, he was treated with the greatest kindness and attention; but upon the party who sued the Armenian presenting a considerable sum, first to the judge and afterward to the jailer, the prisoner first experienced a change of treatment. His privileges were retrenched; he was then closely confined; then treated with such inhumanity, as not to be permitted to drink but once in twenty-four hours, and this in the hottest time of the year; and no person was suffered to see him but the servants of the prison; at length he was thrown into a dungeon, where he was in a quarter of an hour brought to the point, which all this severe usage was intended to gain. After such a relation, we cannot be surprised to find the sacred writers placing so strong an emphasis on "the sighing of the prisoner," and speaking of its coming before God, and the necessity of almighty power being exerted for his deliverance.—PAXTON.

PSALM LXXX.

Ver. 4. O LORD God of hosts, how long wilt thou be angry against the prayer of thy people.

Hebrew, "wilt thou smoke?" Ainsworth, "Jehovah, God of hosts; how long wilt thou smoke against the prayer of thy people?" Of an *angry* man, it is said, "He is continually *smoking*." "My friend, why do you smoke so to-day?" "This smoke drives me away; I cannot bear it." "How many days is this smoke to remain in my house?" "What care I for the smoke? It does not hurt me."—ROBERTS.

Ver. 5. Thou feedest them with the bread of tears; and givest them tears to drink in great measure.

When a master or a father is angry, he says to his children or servants, "Yes, in future you shall have rice, and the water of your eyes to eat." "You shall have the water of your eyes in abundance to drink." "Alas! alas! I am ever drinking tears."—ROBERTS.

Ver. 13. The boar out of the wood doth waste it, and the wild beast of the field doth devour it.

See on 2 Sam. 18. 8.

Wild hogs are exceedingly numerous and destructive in the East: hence a fine garden will in one night be completely destroyed. The herd is generally led by old boars, that go along with great speed and fierceness. Should there be a fence, they will go round till they find a weak place, and then they all rush in. In travelling, sometimes a large patch of grass may be seen completely torn up, which has been done by the wild hog for the sake of the roots. These animals are also very ferocious, as they will not hesitate to attack either man or beast, when placed in circumstances of difficulty. One of them once ran at a friend of mine, when travelling in his palanquin; but the creature, not calculating well as to the speed of the coolies, only just struck the pole with his tusk; but the hole he left behind in the hard wood was nearly half an inch deep.—ROBERTS.

Under the beautiful allegory of a vine, the royal Psalmist describes the rise and fall of the Jewish commonwealth, in this address to Jehovah: "Thou hast brought a vine out of Egypt, thou hast cast out the heathen and planted it.

Thou preparedst a room before it, and didst cause it to take deep root, and it filled the land. The hills were covered with the shadow of it, and the boughs thereof were like the goodly cedars. She sent out her boughs unto the sea, and her branches unto the river. Why hast thou then broken down her hedges, so that all they that pass by the way, do pluck her? The boar out of the wood doth waste it, and the wild beast of the field doth devour it." This terrible animal is both fierce and cruel, and so swift that few of the savage tribes can outstrip him in running. His chief abode, says Forbes, is in the forests and jungles; but when the grain is nearly ripe, he commits great ravages in the fields and sugar plantations. The powers that subverted the Jewish nation, are compared to the wild boar and the wild beast of the field, by which the vine is wasted and devoured; and no figure could be more happily chosen. That ferocious and destructive animal, not satisfied with devouring the fruit, lacerates and breaks with his sharp and powerful tusks the branches of the vine, or with his snout digs it up by the roots, pollutes it with his touch, or tramples it under his feet. In Egypt, according to Herodotus and other writers, the labours of this ferocious animal are rendered useful to man. When the Nile has retired within his proper channel, the husbandman scatters his grain upon the irrigated soil, and sends out a number of swine, that partly by treading it with their feet, partly by digging it with their snout, immediately turn it up, and by this means cover the seed. But in every other part of the world, the hog is odious to the husbandman. It was an established custom among the Greeks and Romans, to offer a hog in sacrifice to Ceres, at the beginning of harvest, and another to Bacchus, before they began to gather the vintage; because that animal is equally hostile to the growing corn and the loaded vineyard. From these examples it is quite evident that the prophet meant to describe, under the figure of a wild boar, the cruel and implacable enemies of the church. And it is extremely probable, that he alluded to some more remarkable adversary, as Sennacherib, the king of Assyria, or Nebuchadnezzar, the king of Babylon; both of whom were not less ferocious and destructive than the savage by which they were symbolized.—Paxton.

Ver. 17. Let thy hand be upon the man of thy right hand, upon the son of man *whom* thou madest strong for thyself.

If we would understand the genuine import of this phrase, we must attend to a custom which obtained in Judea and other eastern countries. At meals the master of the feast placed the person whom he loved best on his right hand, as a token of love and respect: and as they sat on couches, in the intervals between the dishes, when the master leaned upon his left elbow, the man at his right hand, leaning also on his, would naturally repose his head on the master's bosom; while at the same time the master laid his right hand on the favourite's shoulder or side, in testimony of his favourable regard. See also John xxi. 20. (Pirie.)—Burder.

PSALM LXXXI.

Ver. 2. Take a psalm, and bring hither the timbrel, the pleasant harp with the psaltery.

By timbrels are meant the hand-instruments, still used in the East, and called *diff*, the same name which stands here in the Hebrew text. By the Hebrew word *kinnor*, here translated harp, we are probably to understand a stringed instrument, a kind of guitar, similar to those called by the Arabs, *tambura*. Josephus says, that this instrument had ten strings, and was played with a plectrum; in more ancient times, however, it appears to have been played with the fingers, as we may infer from 1 Sam. xvi. 23. xviii. 16. xix. 9. It is almost always mentioned in the Old Testament on occasions of cheerful entertainments and rejoicings. The name of the third instrument, näbel, mentioned in the text, and here translated psaltery, has also been preserved in the Greek and Latin languages, nabla, nablium. As the Hebrew word signifies a leathern bottle, it has been conjectured that the sounding-board was of that shape. But St. Jerome and Isidore say that the instrument resembled a Greek delta inverted, ∇. This leads us to conjecture that näbel was that kind of lyre so frequently found on ancient monuments, and in statues of Apollo. A similar stringed instrument is still usual in the East. Niebuhr has given a description and drawing of one in his Travels, vol. i. p. 179. He saw it in the hand of the barbari, who came from Dongola to Cairo, and call it in their language *kussir*, whereas the Arabs call it, like other foreign stringed instruments, *tambra*. "The belly of it is like a wooden dish, with a small hole below, and having a skin stretched over it, which is higher in the middle than on the sides. Two sticks, which are united at the top by a third, go obliquely through the skin. Five catgut strings lie over it, supported by a bridge. There are no pegs to this instrument, but each string is tuned by having some linen wound with it round the transverse stick. It is played in two different ways, namely, either pinched with the fingers, or by passing a piece of leather, which hangs at the side, over the strings; and my barbari danced as he played." According to the observation of one Rabbi Simeon, quoted by Rabbi Salomon Jarchi, in his commentary on the above passage in the Psalms, kinnor differed from näbel only in number of strings and pegs.—Rosenmuller.

Ver. 10. I *am* the Lord thy God, which brought thee out of the land of Egypt: open thy mouth wide, and I will fill it.

"My friend, you tell me you are in great distress: take my advice: go to the king, and *open your mouth wide*." "I went to the great man and opened my mouth, but he has not given me any thing." "I opened my mouth to him, and have gained all I wanted." "Why open your mouth there? it will be all in vain." Does a person not wish to be troubled, he says to the applicant, "Do not say Ah, ah! here;" which means, do not open your mouth, because that word *cannot* be pronounced without opening the mouth.—Roberts.

Ver. 16. He should have fed them also with the finest of the wheat: and with honey out of the rock should I have satisfied thee.

The soil, both of the maritime and inland parts of Syria and Phenicia, is of a light loamy nature, and easily cultivated. Syria may be considered as a country consisting of three long strips of land, exhibiting different qualities: one extending along the Mediterranean, forming a warm humid valley, the salubrity of which is doubtful, but which is extremely fertile; the other, which forms its frontier, is a hilly, rugged soil, but more salubrious; the third, lying beyond the eastern hills, combines the drought of the latter, with the heat of the former. We have seen by what a happy combination of climate and soil this province unites in a small compass the advantages and productions of different zones, insomuch that the God of nature seems to have designed it for one of the most agreeable habitations of this continent. The soil is a fine mould, without stones, and almost without even the smallest pebble. Volney himself, who furnishes the particulars of this statement, is compelled to admit, that what is said of its actual fertility, exactly corresponds with the idea given of it in the Hebrew scriptures. Wherever wheat is sown, if the rains do not fail, it repays the cultivator with profusion, and grows to the height of a man. The Mount of Olives, near Jerusalem, and several other districts in Judea and Galilee, are covered with olive plantations, whose fruit is equal to any produced in the Levant. The fig-trees in the neighbourhood of Joppa, are equally beautiful and productive as the olive. Were the Holy Land as well inhabited and cultivated as formerly, Dr. Shaw declares it would still be more fruitful than the very best part of Syria or Phenicia; for the soil itself is generally much richer, and all things considered, yields a preferable crop. Thus, the cotton, which is gathered in the plains of Rama, Esdraelon, and Zabulon, is in greater esteem, according to that excellent writer, than what is cultivated near Sidon and Tripoli; neither is it possible for pulse, wheat, or grain of any kind, to be richer or better tasted, than what is commonly sold at Jerusalem. The barrenness, or scarcity rather, of which some authors may either ignorantly or maliciously complain, does not proceed, in the opinion of Dr. Shaw, from the incapacity or natural unfruitfulness of the country, bu from the want of inhabitants, and from the great aversion to labour and industry in those few by whom it is possessed. The perpetual discords and depredations among the petty princes who share this fine country, greatly obstruct the operations of the husbandman, who must have small encouragement to sow, when it is quite uncertain who shall gather in the harvest. It is in other respects a fertile country, and still capable of affording to its neighbours the like ample supplies of corn and oil, which it is known to have done in the days of Solomon, who gave yearly to Hiram twenty thousand measures of wheat for food to his household, and twenty measures of pure oil.

The parts about Jerusalem particularly, being rocky and mountainous, have been therefore supposed to be barren and unfruitful: yet, granting this conclusion, which is however far from being just, a country is not to be characterized from one single district of it, but from the whole. And besides, the blessing which was given to Judah was not of the same kind with the blessing of Asher or of Issachar, that "his bread should be fat or his land pleasant," but that "his eyes should be red with wine, and his teeth should be white with milk." In the estimation of the Jewish lawgiver, milk and honey (the chief dainties and subsistence of the earlier ages, as they still continue to be of the Bedouin Arabs) are the glory of all lands; these productions are either actually enjoyed in the lot of Judah, or at least, might be obtained by proper care and application. The abundance of wine alone is wanting at present; yet the acknowledged goodness of that little, which is still made at Jerusalem and Hebron, clearly proves, that these barren rocks, as they are called, would yield a much greater quantity, if the abstemious Turk and Arab would permit the vine to be further propagated and improved.

Wild honey, which formed a part of the food of John the Baptist in the wilderness, may indicate to us the great plenty of it in those deserts; and, that consequently taking the hint from nature, and enticing the bees into hives and larger colonies, it might be produced in much greater quantity. Josephus accordingly calls Jericho the honey-bearing country. The great abundance of wild honey is often mentioned in scripture; a memorable instance of which occurs in the first book of Samuel: "And all they of the land came to a wood, and there was honey upon the ground; and when the people were come to the wood, behold the honey dropped." This circumstance perfectly accords with the view which Moses gave of the promised land, in the song with which he closed his long and eventful career: "He made him to suck honey out of the rock, and oil out of the flinty rock." That good land preserved its character in the time of David, who thus celebrates the distinguishing bounty of God to his chosen people: "He would have fed them also with the finest of the wheat, and with honey out of the rock would I have satisfied thee." In these holy strains, the sacred poet availed himself of the most valuable products of Canaan, to lead the faith and hope of his nation to bounties of a higher order, of greater price, and more urgent necessity, than any which the soil even of that favoured region, stimulated and sustained as it certainly was by the special blessing of heaven, produced, —the bounties of sovereign and redeeming mercy, purchased with the blood, and imparted by the spirit of the Son of God.—Paxton.

PSALM LXXXIV.

Ver. 1. How amiable *are* thy tabernacles, O Lord of hosts! 2. My soul longeth, yea, even fainteth, for the courts of the Lord; my heart and my flesh crieth out for the living God.

The first part of the Psalm cannot be better illustrated (let there be no misinterpretation of our meaning) than by the example of those who go in pilgrimage to Mecca. As their enthusiasm increases in proportion as they advance through the desert to the holy place; as they are used to be ravished when they behold the shining towers of the Kaaba, so does the journey to Jerusalem proceed with increasing longing spirit and joy through the scorched valleys. They become as it were a well of water, for already at Baca they behold the face of Jehovah.—Rosenmuller.

A parallel instance of pious enthusiasm is exhibited in Dr. Clarke's account of his approach to the Holy City, (Travels in the Holy Land, p. 144.) "At three P. M. we again mounted our horses, and proceeded on our route. No sensation of fatigue or heat could counterbalance the eagerness and zeal which animated all our party, in the approach to Jerusalem; every individual pressed forward, hoping first to announce the joyful intelligence of its appearance. We passed some insignificant ruins, either of ancient buildings or of modern villages; but had they been of more importance, they would have excited little notice at the time, so earnestly bent was every mind towards the main object of interest and curiosity. At length, after about two hours had been passed in this state of anxiety and suspense, ascending a hill towards the south, 'Hagiopolis!' exclaimed a Greek in the van of our cavalcade: and instantly throwing himself from his horse, was seen bareheaded, upon his knees, facing the prospect he surveyed. Suddenly the sight burst upon us all. Who shall describe it? The effect produced was that of total silence throughout the whole company. Many of the party, by an immediate impulse, took off their hats, as if entering a church, without being sensible of so doing. The Greeks and Catholics shed torrents of tears; and presently beginning to cross themselves with unfeigned devotion, asked if they might be permitted to take off the covering from their feet, and proceed, barefooted, to the Holy Sepulchre. We had not been prepared for the grandeur of the spectacle, which the city alone exhibited. Instead of a wretched and ruined town, by some described as the desolated remnant of Jerusalem, we beheld, as it were, a flourishing and steady metropolis; presenting a magnificent assemblage of domes, towers, palaces, churches, and monasteries; all of which, glittering in the sun's rays, shone with inconceivable splendour. As we drew nearer, our whole attention was engrossed by its noble and interesting appearance. The lofty hills whereby it is surrounded give to the city itself an appearance of elevation inferior to that which it really possesses."—B.

Ver. 3. Yea, the sparrow hath found a house, and the swallow a nest for herself, where she may lay her young, *even* thine altars, O Lord of hosts, my King, and my God.

The ibis was so venerated in Egypt, as to be an allowed inmate in sacred structures. Something of the same kind occurs also in Persia. "Within a mosque at Oudjicun, lies interred the son of a king, called Schah-Zadeh-Imam Dgiafer, whom they reckon a saint: the dome is rough cast over; before the mosque there is a court, well planted with many high plane-trees, on which we saw a great many storks that haunt thereabout all the year round." (Thevenot.)

By the altars of Jehovah we are to understand the temple. The words probably refer to the custom of several nations of antiquity, that birds which build their nests on the temples, or within the limits of them, were not suffered to be driven away, much less killed, but found a secure and uninterrupted dwelling. Hence, when Aristodikus disturbed the birds'-nests of the temple of Kumæ, and took the young from them, a voice, according to a tradition preserved by Herodotus, is said to have spoken these words from the interior of the temple: "Most villanous of men, how darest thou do such a thing? to drive away such as seek refuge in my temple?" The Athenians were so enraged at Atarbes, who had killed a sparrow which built on the temple of Æsculapius, that they killed him. Among the Arabs, who are more closely related to the Hebrews, birds which have built their nests on the temple of Mecca were inviolable from the earliest times. In the very ancient poem of a Dschorhamidish prince, published by A. Schultens, in which he laments that his tribe had been deprived of the protection of the sanctuary of Mecca, it is said,

> We lament the house, whose dove
> Was never suffered to be hurt,
> She remained there secure; in it also
> The sparrow built its nest.

Another ancient Arabian poet, Nabega, the Dhobianit, swears "by the sanctuary which affords shelter to the birds which seek it there." Niebuhr says: "I will observe, that among the Mohammedans, not only is the Kaaba a refuge for pigeons, but also on the mosques over the graves of Ali and Hossein, on the Dsjamea, or chief mosque at Helle and in other cities, they are equally undisturbed."—ROSENMULLER.

The term in this passage is connected with the proper name of the swallow; and therefore cannot be understood as the common name of the feathered race, but like the other, must denote a particular species of bird, which, by the general suffrage of interpreters, is the sparrow. This idea is confirmed by the plaintive description of David, according to which, that little bird, under the direction of instinct alone, provides a habitation for herself, in the abodes of men, where she rears her young, and enjoys the sweets of repose. Some of these birds the Psalmist had probably seen constructing their nests, and propagating their kind, in the buildings near the altar, or in the courts of the temple; and piously longs to revisit a scene so dear to his heart. The altar is here by a synecdoche of a part for the whole, to be understood of the tabernacle, among the rafters of which the sparrow and the swallow were allowed to nestle; or rather, for the buildings which surrounded the sacred edifice, where the priests and their assistants had their ordinary residence. Even these exterior buildings were extremely desirable to the exiled monarch, because of their vicinity to the splendid symbols of the divine presence, and the instruments of his worship. The holy Psalmist sometimes wished for the wings of a dove, to waft him into the desert from the cruel oppression of his enemies; but on this occasion, when he is compelled to flee for his life into the wilderness, he longs for the enjoyment of a sparrow, which flew unobserved into the courts of the tabernacle, and flitted among the beams without interruption.—PAXTON.

Ver. 6. *Who* passing through the valley of Baca, make it a well: the rain also filleth the pools.

The words, Who passing through the valley of Baca, make it a pool: the rain also filleth the pools,—are, in the margin, Who passing through the valley of mulberry-trees. The Seventy, in Chronicles, render it pear-trees; in which they are followed by Aquila and the Vulgate. Some think Baca, in the eighty-fourth Psalm, is the name of a rivulet, which burst out of the earth, at the foot of a mountain, with a plaintive murmur, from which it derived its name. But it is more probable that Baca is the name of some shrub or tree. Those who translate it the mulberry-tree, to illustrate the passage in the Psalm, pretend it grows best in the dry ground; but this seems to be unfounded. Marinus imagines, that Baca signifies the mulberry-tree, because the fruit of the mulberry exudes a juice resembling trees. Parkhurst rather thinks that Baca means a kind of large shrub, which the Arabs likewise call Baca, and which probably was so named from its distilling an odoriferous gum. For Baca with an *aleph*, seems to be related to Bacah with a *hay*, which signifies to ooze, to distil in small quantities, to weep or shed tears. This idea perfectly corresponds with the description which Celsius has given of this valley. It is not, according to him, a place abounding with fountains and pools of water, but rugged and embarrassed with bushes and stones, which could not be passed through without labour and suffering; a striking emblem of that vale of thorns and tears, through which all believers must pass to the heavenly Jerusalem.

The great uncertainty among interpreters concerning the real meaning of the term Becaim, has induced Mr. Harmer to hazard a conjecture, that the tree meant in this passage is the weeping-willow. But this plant is not found in a dry sandy vale, where the thirsty traveller is compelled to dig for water, and to form cisterns in the earth, to receive the rain of heaven. In such a situation, we expect to find the pungent aromatic shrub distilling its fragrant gum; not the weeping-willow, the favourite situation of which is the watery plain, or the margin of the brook.—PAXTON.

Ver. 7. They go from strength to strength; *every one of them* in Zion appeareth before God.

The scarcity of water in the East makes travellers particularly careful to take up their lodgings as much as possible near some river or fountain. D'Herbelot informs us, that the Mohammedans have dug wells in the deserts, for the accommodation of those who go in pilgrimage to Mecca. To conveniences perhaps of this kind, made, or renewed, by the devout Israelites in the valley of Baca, to facilitate their going up to Jerusalem, the Psalmist may refer in these words. Hence also there appears less of accident than we commonly think of, in Jacob's lodging on the banks of Jabbok, and the men of David awaiting for him by the brook Besor, when they could not hold out with him in his march.—HARMER.

In this Psalm are described the journeys of the Israelites to their feasts at Jerusalem, from the distant parts of the country. It mentions their digging wells in the valley of Baca, which, in the rainy season, were filled with excellent water, and became a great convenience to succeeding travellers. In reference to them, the travellers are said to have gone from strength to strength till they arrived at Mount Zion, in Jerusalem, to appear before God there, which was the object of their journey. When a weary traveller arrives at a well in the wilderness, his strength is nearly gone, but on drinking of its water he is revived and strengthened for another stage; and, on falling in with another well, he receives fresh vigour for again proceeding on his journey. So that going from strength to strength may literally mean from well to well; though some understand by this, going from company to company.—CAMPBELL.

Ver. 10. For a day in thy courts *is* better than a thousand. I had rather be a door-keeper in the house of my God, than to dwell in the tents of wickedness.

Ainsworth, "I have chosen to *sit* at the threshold, in the house of my God." And Dr. Boothroyd, "*Abide*, or *sit*, at the threshold." I believe the word door-keeper does not convey the proper meaning of the words, "*to sit at the threshold*;" because the preference of the Psalmist was evidently given to a very HUMBLE situation, whereas that of a door-keeper, in eastern estimation, is truly respectable and confidential. The gods are always represented as having door-keepers, who were of great dignity and power, as they also fought against other deities. In the heathen temples there are images near the entrance, called *kāval-kāran*, i. e. guards or door-keepers. Kings and great men also have officers, whose business it is to stand at the door, or gate, as keepers of the entrance. The most dignified native of Ceylon is the Maha Modeliar of the governor's gate, to whom all others must make obeisance. The word door-keeper, therefore, does not convey the idea of humility, but of honour.

The marginal reading, however, "to sit at the threshold," at once strikes an eastern mind as a situation of deep humility. See the poor heathen devotee, he goes and sits near the threshold of his temple. Look at the beggar, he sits, or prostrates himself at the threshold of the door or gate, till he shall have gained his suit. "I am in great trouble; I will go and lie down at the door of the temple." "Friend, you appear to be very ill."—"Yes!" "Then go and prostrate yourself at the threshold of the temple!" "Muttoo, I can get you the situation of a Peon; will you accept of it?"—"Excuse me, sir, I pray you; I had better lie at your threshold than do that." "Go, do that! it is far better for me to lie at the threshold as a common beggar." I think, therefore, the Psalmist refers to the attitude of a beggar, a suppliant at the threshold of the house of the Lord, as being preferable to the splendid dwellings of the wicked.—ROBERTS.

PSALM LXXXV.

Ver. 10. Mercy and truth are met together; righteousness and peace have kissed *each other*.

Dr. Boothroyd, "Righteousness and peace have embraced." In the Hindoo book called Iraku-Vangesham, it is said, the "lotus flowers were kissing each other." When the branches of two separate trees meet, in consequence of strong winds, it is said, "they kiss each other." When a young palmirah-tree, which grows near the parent stock, begins to move, (by the wind,) the people say, "Ah! the mother is kissing the daughter." A woman says of the ornaments around her neck, "Yes, these embrace my neck." Has a female put on the nose-ring, it is, it is said, kissing her. The idea, therefore, is truly oriental, and shows the intimate union of righteousness and peace.—ROBERTS.

PSALM LXXXVII.

Ver. 2. The LORD loveth the gates of Zion more than all the dwellings of Jacob.

"Truly, I love the *gates* of Chinna Amma more than the gates of Pun-Amma." "No, no; he does not love the gates of that woman; he will never marry her." "He is angry with my gates; he will not pass them." "Love his gates! ay, for a good reason; he gets plenty of help from them."—ROBERTS.

Ver. 7. As well the singers as the players on instruments *shall be there:* all my springs are in thee.

A man of great charities is said to have many springs: "His heart is like the springs of a well." "Where are my springs, my lord; are they not in you?" Tears also are spoken of as coming from springs in the body; thus the mother of Rāmar said to him, in consequence of great sorrow, "The waters of my eyes have dried up the springs of affection."—ROBERTS.

PSALM LXXXIX.

Ver. 9. Thou rulest the raging of the sea: when the waves thereof arise, thou stillest them. 10. Thou hast broken Rahab in pieces, as one that is slain: thou hast scattered thine enemies with thy strong arm. 11. The heavens *are* thine, the earth also *is* thine: *as for* the world, and the fulness thereof, thou hast founded them.

See on Eph. 6. 16.

Ver. 12. The north and the south thou hast created them: Tabor and Hermon shall rejoice in thy name.

The northeast part of Lebanon, adjoining to the Holy Land, is in scripture distinguished by the name of Hermon; and is, by consequence, mentioned as the northern boundary of the country beyond Jordan, and more particularly of the kingdom of Og, or of the half tribe of Manasseh, on the east of that river. But, besides this Mount Hermon, in the northern border of the country beyond Jordan, we read of another mountain of the same name, lying within the land of Canaan, on the west of the river Jordan, not far from Mount Tabor. To this mountain the holy Psalmist is thought to refer in these words: "The north and the south thou hast created them: Tabor and Hermon shall rejoice in thy name;" and in the following passage: "As the dew of Hermon, and as the dew that descends upon the mountains of Sion."—PAXTON.

Ver. 14. Justice and judgment *are* the habitation of thy throne: mercy and truth shall go before thy face.

Dr. Boothroyd, "Are the basis of thy throne." The Hebrew, "the establishment of thy throne." "What was the foundation of his throne?" "Justice! Truly righteousness is the *atle-vāram*, foundation or basis, of all his ways."—ROBERTS.

Ver. 25. I will set his hand also in the sea, and his right hand in the rivers.

The meaning is: he shall reign from the Mediterranean Sea to the Euphrates. This is figuratively expressed thus: his right hand shall extend to the sea, or his left to the Euphrates. A similar expression was used, according to Curtius, by the Scythian ambassadors to Alexander. "If," said they, "the gods had given thee a body as great as thy mind, the whole world would not be able to contain thee; thou wouldst reach with one hand to the east, and with the other to the west."—ROSENMULLER.

PSALM XC.

Ver. 4. For a thousand years in thy sight *are but* as yesterday when it is past, and *as* a watch in the night.

It is evident in the scriptures, that besides these cares, they had watchmen who used to patrol in their streets: and it is natural to suppose, that they were these people that gave them notice how the seasons of the night passed away. I am indebted for this thought to Sir John Chardin. He observes, in a note on Ps. xc. 4, that as the people of the East have no clocks, the several parts of the day and of the night, which are eight in all, are given notice of. In the Indies, the parts of the night are made known as well by instruments of music, in great cities, as by the rounds of the watchmen, who with cries and small drums, give them notice that a fourth part of the night is passed. Now as these cries awaked those who had slept all that quarter part of the night, it appeared to them but as a moment. There are sixty of these people in the Indies, by day, and as many by night; that is, fifteen for each division.

It is apparent the ancient Jews knew how the night passed away, which must probably be by some public notice given them: but whether it was by simply publishing at the close of each watch, what watch was then ended; or whether they made use of any instruments of music in this business, may not be easily determinable; and still less what measures of time the watchmen made use of.—HARMER.

Ver. 5. Thou carriest them away as with a flood; they are *as* a sleep: in the morning *they are* like grass *which* groweth up. 6. In the morning it flourisheth, and groweth up; in the evening it is cut down, and withereth.

In temperate latitudes, the fields are generally covered with durable verdure; but in Asia, gramineous plants of all kinds are extremely perishable. The wonderful rapidity of their growth is celebrated by every traveller into the East. Sir Thomas Roe says, that when the ground has been destitute of rain nine months together, and looks all of it like the barren sand in the desert of Arabia, where there is not one spire of green grass to be found, within a few days after those fat enriching showers begin to fall, the face of the earth there (as it were by a new resurrection) is so revived, and throughout so renewed, as that it is presently covered all over with a pure green mantle. Dr. Russel, in the same admiring terms, describes the springing of the earth as a resurrection of vegetable nature. Vegetation is so extremely quick in Hindostan, that, as fast as the water rises, the plants of rice grow before it, so that the ear is never immersed. To the powerful influence of the rain upon the face of oriental nature, Moses compares, with singular beauty and force, the effect which the lessons of heavenly wisdom produce in the human mind: "My doctrine shall drop as the rain, my speech shall distil as the dew, as the small rain upon the tender herb, and as the showers upon the grass." Even the dews, which are most copious in those regions, produce a change so beneficial and sudden, that Solomon compares to their energy, the influence of royal favour, which, in oriental courts, frequently raises in one day a person from the lowest condition, to the highest ranks of life: The king's "favour is as a dew upon the grass." But such extraordinary quickness of growth is incompatible with strength and permanence; the feeble and sickly blade yields as quickly to the burning heat, and vanishes away. To this rapid change the Psalmist compares the short-lived prosperity of wicked men: his own evanescent comforts; the swift progress of his days, and of time in general. So soon are the powers of nature exhausted, that the grass does not always come to maturity, even in the best soils; in the language of ancient prophecy, "it is blasted before it be grown up."—PAXTON.

Ver. 9. For all our days are passed away in thy wrath; we spend our years as a tale *that is told.*

"This year has been to me as a fabulous story: like the repetition of a dream, my days pass away. The beginning of life is as the dew-drop upon the tender herb: in ten moons it assumes its shape, and is brought forth; it lies down, crawls, prattles, walks, and becomes acquainted with science. At sixteen he is a man; goes forth in the pride of his youth, gets a wife, and becomes the father of children. The husk of his rice he refuses to part with, and his wish is to enjoy all. He thinks by living cheaply, by refusing to support charities, or to dispense favours, he is of all men the most happy. He is regardless of the writing on his forehead, (fate,) and is like the lamp which shineth, and ceaseth to shine; pour in oil, and there will be light; take it away, and there will be darkness. In old age come the rheumatics, the jaundice, and an enlarged belly; the eyes are filled with rheums, and the phlegm comes forth. His body becomes dry, his back bends, his wife and children abhor him, and in visions he sees the deathly car and horse. The place of burning says, 'Come, come;' and his family say, 'Go, go.' His strength is gone, his speech falters, his eyeballs roll, and his living soul is taken away. The people then talk of his good and evil deeds, and ask, 'Is this life?' The funeral rites follow; the music sounds forth, and the DYING carry the DEAD to its place of burning." Thus sung the devoted *Aruna-Kiriyār.* —ROBERTS.

Ver. 14. O satisfy us early with thy mercy, that we may rejoice and be glad all our days.

Ainsworth, "Satisfie us in the morning with thy mercie." Afflictions and sorrows are spoken of as the "night of life;" and the deliverance from them, as the "morning of joy." "Yes, the night has been long and gloomy, but the morning has at last come." "Ah! morning, morning, when wilt thou come?"—ROBERTS.

PSALM XCI.

Ver. 1. He that dwelleth in the secret place of the Most High, shall abide under the shadow of the Almighty.

To say a person is under the SHADOW of a great man, means, he is under his PROTECTION. "Oh, my lord, all the people are against me; they are pursuing me as the tiger: let me come under your *unnel*," i. e. SHADOW. "Ay, ay, the fellow is safe enough, now he has crept under the SHADOW of the king." "Begone, miscreant, thou shalt not creep under my shadow." "Many years have I been under the shadow of my father; how shall I now leave it?" "Gone, for ever gone, is the shadow of my days!" says the lamenting widow. —ROBERTS.

Ver. 5. Thou shalt not be afraid for the terror by night, *nor* for the arrow *that* flieth by day. 6. *Nor* for the pestilence *that* walketh in darkness, *nor* for the destruction *that* wasteth at noonday.

When the cholera rages, no one will go out while the sun is at its zenith, because it is believed that the demon of the pestilence is then actively engaged. "The hot exhalations of noonday are the chariots of the fiends." The demons of darkness are said to have the most power at midnight.—ROBERTS.

The arrow, in this passage, means the pestilence. The Arabs thus denote it: "I desired to remove to a less contagious air. I received from Solyman, the emperor, this message: that the emperor wondered what I meant, in desiring to remove my habitation. Is not the pestilence God's arrow, which will always hit his mark. If God would visit me herewith, how could I avoid it. 'Is not the plague,' said he, 'in my own palace; and yet I do not think of removing.'" (Busbequius.)

We find the same opinion expressed in Smith's Remarks on the Turks. "What," say they, "is not the plague the dart of Almighty God, and can we escape the blow he levels at us. Is not his hand steady to hit the persons he aims at? Can we run out of his sight, and beyond his power?" So Herbert, (p. 99,) speaking of Curroon, says, "that year his empire was so wounded with God's arrows of plague, pestilence, and famine, as this thousand years before was never so terrible."—BURDER.

Ver. 13. Thou shalt tread upon the lion and adder: the young lion and the dragon shalt thou trample under foot.

"Thou shalt tread upon the lion." This expression denotes the subjection of the lion, and the fiercest beasts, to the power of man. His superiority is indisputable. Eastern monarch have on particular occasions displayed their grandeur by exhibiting lions in a tame condition. When a Greek ambassador was introduced to the Calif Moctader, "among the other spectacles of rare and stupendous luxury, a hundred lions were brought out, with a keeper to each lion." This embassy was received at Bagdad, A. H. 305. A. D. 917. When Mr. Bell, of Antermony, accompanied the Russian ambassador to the audience of the unfortunate Shah Hussein, of Persia, two lions were introduced, to denote the power of the king over the fiercest animals.—BURDER.

The adder was known to the ancient Hebrews under various names.—It is the opinion of some interpreters, that the word שחל *sachal,* which in some parts of scripture denotes a lion, in others means an adder, or some other kind of serpent. Thus, in the ninety-first Psalm, they render it the basilisk: "Thou shalt tread upon the adder and the basilisk, the young lion and the dragon thou shalt trample under foot." Indeed, all the ancient expositors agree, that some species of serpent is meant, although they cannot determine what particular serpent the sacred writer had in his eye. The learned Bochart thinks it extremely probable, that the holy Psalmist in this verse treats of serpents only; and by consequence, that both the terms (שחל) *sachal* and (כפיר) *chephir,* mean some kind of snakes, as well as (פתן) *phethan* and (תנין) *tannin,* because the coherence of the verse is by this view better preserved, than by mingling lions and serpents together, as our translators and other interpreters have commonly done. The union of lions, adders, and dragons, is not natural; nor is it easy to imagine what can be meant by treading upon the lion, and trampling the young lion under foot; for it is not possible in walking to tread upon the lion, as upon the adder, the basilisk, and other serpents.

As the term (שחל) *sachal,* when applied to wild beasts, denotes a black lion; so in the present application, it means the black adder. Many serpents are of a black colour, but some of them are much blacker than others. The sachal, therefore, denotes the black snake, the colour of which is intensely deep.

Another name which the adder bears in scripture is (עכשוב) *achsub.* It occurs in the following description of wicked men: "They have sharpened their tongues like a serpent: adders' poison is under their lips." The Chaldee renders it the poison of a spider; but the most common interpretation is that which our translators have adopted. Some, however, contend that the asp is intended; and in support of their opinion, quote the authority of many Greek and Latin interpreters, and what must be decisive with every Christian, the suffrage of an inspired apostle, who gives this version of the Hebrew text: "The poison of asps is under their lips." The name in Hebrew is derived from an Arabic verb, which signifies to coil up; which perfectly corresponds with the nature of this animal, for, in preparing to strike, it contracts itself into a spiral form, and raises its horrid head from the middle of the orb. It assumes the same form when it goes to *sleep,* coiling its body into a number of circles, with its head in the centre. This is the reason that in Greek, Ασπις denotes a shield, as well as a serpent. Now, the Grecian shields are circular, as we learn from Virgil, but whether the name of the shield (Ασπις) was derived from the serpent, or the name of the serpent from the form of the shield, it is of no consequence to determine.—PAXTON.

PSALM XCII.

Ver. 10. But my horn shalt thou exalt like *the horn of* a unicorn: I shall be anointed with fresh oil.

Montanus has, instead of FRESH oil, given the literal meaning of the original, *virido oleo,* with GREEN oil. Ainsworth also says, "fresh or green oile.' Calmet, "As the plants imparted somewhat of their colour, as well as of their fragrance, hence the expression GREEN oil." Harmer, "I shall be anointed with GREEN oil." Some of these writers think the term GREEN, as it is in the original, means "precious fragrant oil;" others, literally green in COLOUR; and others, FRESH or NEWLY made oil. But I think it will appear to mean COLD DRAWN oil, that which has been expressed or squeezed from the nut or fruit *without the process of boiling*. The Orientals prefer this kind for anointing themselves to all others; it is considered the most precious, the most pure and efficacious. Nearly all the medicinal oils are thus extracted; and because they cannot gain so much by this method as by the boiling process, oils so drawn are very dear. Hence their name for the article also thus prepared is *patche*, i. e. GREEN oil! But this term in eastern phraseology is applied to other things, which are *unboiled* or *raw*; thus unboiled water is called *patche*, green water: *patche-pāl*, also, green milk, means that which has not been boiled, and the butter made from it is called green butter; and uncooked meat, or yams, go by the same name. I think, therefore, the Psalmist alludes to that valuable article which is called GREEN oil, on account of its being expressed from the nut, or fruit, without the process of boiling.—ROBERTS.

The virgin-oil (l'ogleo virgineo) is made as well from green and unripe, as from ripe fruit; but with the difference, that no hot water, or very little, is used, in the pressing: by which the berries are less affected, and less of the acrid or crude elements extracted from them. In this manner less oil is obtained, but it is whiter, more pleasant, and justly preferred to every other sort. The ancients called it green oil, probably on account of its being extracted from green and unripe berries. This explains a passage in Suetonius, which says, "that Julius Cesar, out of politeness, ate old and spoiled oil, instead of green, not to give the person who had invited him any ground to complain of his want of politeness, or his inattention. Some commentators on the Bible reasonably suppose that this green oil is spoken of as being the best, when the Psalmist expresses the happiness with which God had blessed him: *I am anointed with green oil.* (Keyssler.)—BURDER.

Mr. Bruce, after having given it as his opinion that the reem of scripture is the rhinoceros, says, "the derivation of this word, both in the Hebrew and in the Ethiopic, seems to be from erectness, or standing straight. This is certainly no particular quality in the animal itself, which is not more, or even so much erect, as many other quadrupeds, for in its knees it is rather crooked; but it is from the circumstance and manner in which *his horn is placed*. The horns of other animals are inclined to some degree of parallelism with the nose or os frontis. The horn of the rhinoceros alone is erect and perpendicular to this bone, on which it stands at right angles, thereby possessing a greater purchase, or power, as a lever, than any horn could possibly have in any other position. "This situation of the horn is very happily alluded to in the sacred writings: *my horn shalt thou exalt like the horn of a unicorn;* and the horn here alluded to is not wholly figurative, as I have already taken notice in the course of my history, but was really an ornament worn by great men in the days of victory, preferment, or rejoicing, when they were anointed with new, sweet, or fresh oil, a circumstance which David joins with that of erecting the horn."

The term for unicorn, in the Hebrew text, is (רים) *rim*, or (ראם) *reem;* and is derived from a verb, which signifies to be exalted or lifted up. This term, which in Hebrew signifies only height, is rendered by the Greek interpreters μονοκερος, and by the Latins unicornis; both which answer to our English word unicorn. Jerome and others, doubtful to what animal it belongs, render it sometimes rhinoceros, and sometimes unicorn. It is evident from the sacred scriptures, that the reem is an animal of considerable height, and of great strength. Thus Balaam reluctantly declared concerning Israel: "God brought them out of Egypt; he hath as it were the strength of (a reem) a unicorn." So great in the estimation of that reluctant seer, was the strength of the reem, that he repeats the eulogium in the very same words in the next chapter. From the grateful ascriptions of David, we learn that it is a horned animal: "But my horn shalt thou exalt like the horn of a unicorn." And Moses, in his benediction of Joseph, states a most important fact, that it has two horns; the words are: His horns are like the horns of (ראם a *reem*, in the singular number) a unicorn. Some interpreters, determined to support the claims of the unicorn to the honour of a place in the sacred volume, contend, that in this instance the singular, by an enallage or change of number, is put for the plural. But this is a gratuitous assertion; and besides, if admitted, would greatly diminish the force and propriety of the comparison. The two sons of Joseph, Ephraim and Manasseh, had been adopted into the family of Jacob, and appointed the founders of two distinct tribes, whose descendants in the times of Moses were become numerous and respectable in the congregation. These were the two horns with which Joseph was to attack and subdue his enemies; and by consequence, propriety required an allusion to a creature, not with one, but with two horns.

In the book of Job, the reem is represented as a very fierce and intractable animal, which, although possessed of sufficient strength to labour, sternly and pertinaciously refuses to bend his neck to the yoke: "Will the unicorn (in Hebrew the reem) be willing to serve thee, or abide by thy crib? Canst thou bind the reem with his band in the furrow, or will he harrow the valleys after thee? Wilt thou trust him because his strength is great? Or wilt thou leave thy labour to him? Wilt thou believe him that he will bring home thy seed, and gather it into thy barn?" So far from being disposed to submit to the dominion of man, he is extremely hostile and dangerous. Little inferior to the lion himself in strength and fury, he is sometimes associated in scripture with that destroyer. "Save me," cried our Lord to his Father, "save me from the lion's mouth: for thou hast heard me from the horns of (ראמים) the unicorns." In the prophecies of Isaiah, it is united with other powerful animals, to symbolize the great leaders and princes of the hostile nations, that laid waste his native land: "And the unicorns shall come down with them, and the bullocks with the bulls: and their land shall be soaked with blood, and their dust made fat with fatness." Such are the general characters of the reem, as delineated in the sacred volume: but besides these, several hints are given, which seem to point out, with no little certainty, the genus under which the reem ought to be classed. In that sublime composition, where the Psalmist assigns the reasons why God is to be honoured, he joins the calf with the young reem, and ascribes to them the same kind of movement: "He maketh them also to skip like a calf; Lebanon and Sirion like a young (reem, or) unicorn." The prophet Isaiah, in a passage already quoted, classes him with the bullocks and the bulls; and Moses assigns him the same station, furnishes him with horns, and makes him push like a bullock. If these circumstances are duly considered, no doubt will remain that he is nearly allied to the creatures with which he is associated.

These observations will enable us to examine with more success the various interpretations of the original name proposed by different expositors. Our translators, following the Greek fathers, consider the reem as a creature with one horn; and, agreeably to this idea, render it unicorn. But this interpretation is encumbered with insuperable difficulties. The unicorn is a creature totally unknown in those countries where the scriptures were written, and the patriarchs sojourned. But is it probable, that God himself, in his expostulation with Job, would take an illustration of considerable length, from a creature with which the afflicted man was altogether unacquainted; and mention this unknown animal in the midst of those with which he was quite familiar? Nor is it to be supposed, that Moses, David, and the prophets, would so frequently speak of an animal unknown in Egypt and Palestine, and the surrounding countries; least of all, that they would borrow their comparisons from it, familiarly mention its great strength, and describe its habits and dispositions. Aware of this objection, and at loss how to elude its force, some writers, on the authority of Pliny, remove the native land of the unicorn to India. But this will be found of no advantage to their cause; for still the objection returns with nearly undiminished force; how could the sacred writers borrow their illustrations from a creature with which, even on this supposition, they were so little acquainted? They make no mention of the elephant, a creature not less powerful and fierce than the unicorn, renowned for its docility, and the various important services which it renders to man; and numerous in Africa, and many countries of Asia. Of this noble animal, the people of Israel seem to have had no knowledge at all, except what they derived from t··

trade in ivory, which they carried on during the reign of Solomon to some extent. But if the elephant, which abounded in countries much nearer the Holy Land than India, whose teeth formed an article of commerce among the ancient Israelites, was so little known to them; it cannot be supposed that they had any knowledge of an animal which was proper to India.

But we have in reality no proof that such an animal ever existed in any part of the world. It must be admitted, that both Pliny and Ælian have described the unicorn in their writings; but these eminent authors borrowed their statements from Ctesias, a writer of little respectability. Had the unicorn existed in any part of the East, it must have been discovered and brought to Rome by those whom the Romans employed to explore the remotest countries, with the express view of collecting the rarest animals they contained, in order to be exhibited at the public shows. The tiger, the rhinoceros, and other animals, natives of regions which the Roman eagles never visited, were often exhibited in the amphitheatre, before the proud oppressors of the world. So numerous and diversified were the animals produced on the arena at their public entertainments, that Aristides, in his encomium of Rome, declared, "All things meet here, whatsoever is bred or made; and whatsoever is not seen here, is to be reckoned among those things which are not, nor ever were." But although these shows continued for many ages, not a single unicorn was ever exhibited at Rome; a strong proof that no such animal existed. In modern times, the remotest countries in Asia have been traversed, in almost every direction, by intelligent and inquisitive travellers; but no animal of this kind has been discovered; nor has the least information been obtained concerning the unicorn, among the natives. From these facts it may be safely concluded, that the unicorn exists only in the imagination of vain and credulous writers, and by consequence, cannot be the reem of the sacred scriptures.

The rhinoceros, on the contrary, was often exhibited in the amphitheatre at Rome; and has been frequently seen by modern travellers. No doubt, therefore, can be entertained concerning the reality of its existence: but the character of the reem, given in the scriptures, will not apply to this animal. The reem, it is evident, was equally well known to Moses and the prophets, and the people whom they addressed, as the bullocks and the bulls with which they are mentioned. But the rhinoceros inhabits the southern parts of Africa, and the remotest parts of the East, beyond the Ganges; and by consequence, could be still less known to the people of Israel than the elephant, which is not once mentioned in the sacred volume.

Besides, the reem has large horns; for, says the Psalmist, "My horn shalt thou exalt like the horn of a unicorn;" but the rhinoceros has seldom more than one, and that of a small size, not exalted like the horn of a reem, but turned back towards the forehead. Nor will the use to which the reem applies his horns, correspond with the manners of the rhinoceros: the former pushes with his horns, which must therefore be placed on his forehead; but the horn of the latter, which is placed on his nose, and bent backwards, is not formed for pushing, but for ripping up the trunks or bodies of the more soft and succulent trees, and reducing them into a kind of laths, which constitute a part of the animal's food.

It is the opinion of others, that the reem is a species of wild bull; which they have endeavoured to establish by several plausible arguments. In many places of scripture, say they, the ox and the reem are joined together, as animals of the same family; in others, the latter is represented as a strong and fierce animal, with large and very strong horns, greatly addicted to push, and by consequence, an enemy much to be dreaded. The reem, therefore, cannot be the buffalo, because his horns being turned inward, are unfit for the combat; but either the bison, or the urus. It is rather supposed, however, that the urus is the reem of the Hebrews, because the bison, though a very fierce and obstinate animal, may be subdued by the art of man, and at length entirely domesticated. But as to the urus, Cesar says expressly, that they cannot be tamed and rendered useful to mankind, not even their young ones excepted; they are therefore taken in pits and destroyed. Pliny thus describes the urus: He is of a size little inferior to the elephant; in appearance, colour, and figure, he resembles the bull; his strength and velocity are great; and he neither spares man nor beast that comes in his way.

These arguments have considerable weight; but they are liable to the same objections which these very writers have urged with so much force against the claims of the unicorn and the rhinoceros. It is by no means probable that the sacred writers would make so many allusions to animals, with which the people whom they addressed were utterly unacquainted; would speak so familiarly about them; would borrow their figures and illustrations, from their form, dispositions, and manners; or that Jehovah himself would converse with Job so long about a creature which was unknown to the people of those countries. The urus skulked from the remotest times in the deep recesses of the Hircanian forest; and was quite unknown to the Romans before the time of Cesar. Neither the urus nor the bison, according to Pliny, were to be found in Greece; and the former has been considered by some authors as a native of Germany. It is even admitted by Boetius, who strenuously maintains the claims of the urus, that he can find no writer who says that these wild oxen are produced in Syria and Palestine. Aben Ezra, on the contrary, asserts, in his commentary on the prophecies of Hosea, that no wild bull is to be found in Judea, and the surrounding countries. It is not sufficient to say, that these varieties of the bovine family, may have existed there in the times of Moses and the prophets, for a mere conjecture proves nothing. If they existed once, why do they not exist now, as well as the wild goat, the hart, and the antelope? Why is not a single trace of them to be found in the warmer climates of Greece and Asia? Pliny indeed states, that the Indian forests abounded with wild oxen; but it will not follow, that the urus was known to the Jews, because it was discovered in the forests of India, the regions of Scythia, or the more remote wilds of Africa. But the truth is, we have no proof that he meant to speak of the urus or the bison; he only mentions wild oxen in general; from which no certain argument can be drawn in support of the opinion which Boetius and others maintain.—Paxton.

Bochart, and after him, Rosenmuller and others, regard the *reem* of the Hebrews as a species of antelope, the *rim* of the Arabs, and the *oryx* or *leucoryx* of the Greeks. The argument of most weight in Bochart's mind, seems to be the fact, that *rim*, in Arabic, which is equivalent to *reem* in Hebrew, is thus used for a species of white gazelle or antelope, (Niebuhr, Descr. of Arab. p. xxxviii. Germ. ed.) which would seem to be very probably the *leucoryx*. But then the other characteristics of these animals by no means correspond to those of the *reem*, which is everywhere described as a fierce, intractable animal, acting on the offensive, and attacking even men of its own accord. Now, however wild and untameable many species of antelopes may be, they are universally described as a shy and retiring animal, always flying from pursuit, and avoiding even the approach of man. In opposition to this, Bochart and Rosenmuller produce a passage of Martial, where he gives to the oryx the epithet *fierce*, (saevus oryx, Epigr. xiii. 95,) and another from Oppian, where he says, "There is a beast, with pointed horns, familiar to the woods, the savage oryx, most terrible to other beasts." (Cyneget. ii. 445.) Now all these epithets and descriptions, even allowing nothing for poetical amplification, are perfectly applicable to the stag of our forests and of Asia; they imply no more than that the oryx, when hard pushed, will turn upon its pursuers, and defend himself with fury. Yet no one would hence draw the conclusion, that it was characteristic of the stag to act on the offensive; nor can such a conclusion be drawn with better reason in regard to the oryx.—The *oryx* of Pliny and other ancient writers, is understood to be the *antelope oryx* of zoologists; the *gazella Indica* of Ray, the *capra gazella* of the Syst. Nat., the *Egyptian antelope* of Pennant, and the *pasan* of Buffon. It is about the size of a fallow deer, having straight, slender, annulated horns, which taper to a point; the horns are about three feet long, the points sharp, and about fourteen inches asunder; the body and sides are of a reddish ash colour; the face is white, with a black spot at the base of the horns, and another on the middle of the face. It is a native of Asia and Africa.—The *leucoryx*, which some suppose to be the oryx of Oppian, is in general similar to the animal above described, except that the body is of a milk-white colour. It inhabits the neighbourhood of Bassora, on the Persian gulf.

Most obviously neither of these animals answer the description of the Hebrew *reem*. The fact that the Arabs apply the word *rim* to this class of animals, has probably its origin in the same cause, which also leads them to apply to the races of deer and antelopes, in general, the epithet *wild oxen*. (See Schultens, Comm. in Job xxxix. 3.)

Other writers have supposed the *reem* of the Hebrews to be the *urus, bison*, or wild ox, described by Cesar, which is understood to be the same animal as the American buffalo. The characteristics of this animal accord well with those attributed to the *reem;* but there is no evidence that the bison existed in Palestine, or was known to the Hebrews. A more obvious supposition, therefore, is that of Schultens, De Wette, Gesenius, and others, that under the *reem* we are to understand the buffalo of the eastern continent, the *bos bubalus* of Linnæus, which differs from the bison, or American buffalo, chiefly in the shape of the horns and the absence of the dewlap. This animal is indigenous, originally in the hotter parts of Asia and Africa, but also in Persia, Abyssinia, and Egypt; and is now also naturalized in Italy and southern Europe. As, therefore, it existed in the countries all around Palestine, there is every reason to suppose that it was also found in that country, or at least in the regions east of the Jordan, and south of the Dead Sea, as Bashan and Idumea.

The oriental buffalo appears to be so closely allied to our common ox, that without an attentive examination it might be easily mistaken for a variety of that animal. In point of size it is rather superior to the ox; and upon an accurate inspection, it is observed to differ in the shape and magnitude of the head, the latter being larger than in the ox. But it is chiefly by the structure of the horns that the buffalo is distinguished, these being of a shape and curvature altogether different from those of the ox. They are of gigantic size in proportion to the bulk of the animal, and of a compressed form, with a sharp exterior edge; for a considerable length from their base these horns are straight, and then bend slightly upward; the prevailing colour of them is dusky, or nearly black. The buffalo has no dewlap; his tail is small, and destitute of vertebræ near the extremity; his ears are long and pointed. This animal has the appearance of uncommon strength. The bulk of his body, and prodigious muscular limbs, denote his force at the first view. His aspect is ferocious and malignant; at the same time that his physiognomy is strongly marked with features of stupidity. His head is of a ponderous size; his eyes diminutive; and what serves to render his visage still more savage, are the tufts of frizzled hair which hang down from his cheeks and the lower part of his muzzle.

This animal, although originally a native of the hotter parts of India and Africa, is now completely naturalized to the climate of the south of Europe. Mr. Pennant supposes the *wild bulls* of Aristotle to have been buffaloes, and Gmelin and other distinguished naturalists are of the same opinion. Gmelin also supposes the *Bos Indicus* of Pliny to have been the same animal. Buffon, however, endeavours to show, that the buffalo of modern times was unknown to the Greeks and Romans, and that it was first transported from its native countries, the warmer regions of Africa and the Indies, to be naturalized in Italy, not earlier than the seventh century.

The buffalo grows in some countries to an extremely large size. The buffaloes of Abyssinia grow to twice the size of our largest oxen, and are called elephant bulls. Mr. Pennant mentions a pair of horns in the British Museum, which are six feet and a half long, and the hollow of which will hold five quarts. Father Lobo affirms that some of the horns of the buffaloes in Abyssinia will hold ten quarts; and Dillon saw some in India that were ten feet long. They are sometimes wrinkled, but generally smooth. The distance between the points of the two horns is usually five feet.

Wild buffaloes occur in many parts of Africa and India, where they live in great troops in the forests, and are regarded as excessively fierce and dangerous animals. In all these particulars they coincide with the buffaloes of America. The hunting of them is a favourite, but very dangerous pursuit; the hunters never venture in any numbers to oppose these ferocious animals face to face; but conceal themselves in the thickets, or in the branches of the trees; whence they attack the buffaloes as they pass along.

In Egypt, as also in Southern Europe, the buffalo has been partially domesticated. In Egypt especially, it is much cultivated, where, according to Sonnini, it yields plenty of excellent milk, from which butter and various kinds of cheese are made.

"The buffalo," says Sonnini, "is an acquisition of the modern Egyptians, with which their ancestors were unacquainted. It was brought over from Persia into their country, where the species is at present universally spread, and is very much propagated. It is even more numerous than the common ox, and is there equally domestic, though but recently domesticated; as is easily distinguished by the constantly uniform colour of the hair, and still more by a remnant of ferocity and intractability of disposition, and a wild and lowering aspect, the characters of all half-tamed animals. The buffaloes of Egypt, however, are not near so wild, nor so much to be feared, as those of other countries. They there partake of the gentleness of other domestic animals, and only retain a few sudden and occasional caprices. They are so fond of water, that I have seen them continue in it a whole day. It often happens that the water which is fetched from the Nile, near its banks, has contracted their musky smell."

These animals multiply more readily than the common ox; they breed in the fourth year, producing young for two years together, and remaining steril the third; and they commonly cease breeding after their twelfth year. Their term of life is much the same as that of the common ox. They are more robust than the common ox, better capable of bearing fatigue, and, generally speaking, less liable to distempers. They are therefore employed to advantage in different kinds of labour. Buffaloes are made to draw heavy loads, and are commonly guided by means of a ring passed through the nose. In its habits the buffalo is much less cleanly than the ox, and delights to wallow in the mud. His voice is deeper, more uncouth and hideous, than that of the bull. The milk is said by some authors to be not so good as that of the cow, but more plentiful; Buffon, on the contrary, asserts that it is far superior to cow's milk. The skin and horns are of more value than all the rest of the animal; the latter are of a fine grain, strong, and bear a good polish, and are therefore in much esteem with cutlers and other artisans.

Italy is the country where buffaloes are, at present, most common perhaps in a domesticated state. They are used more particularly in the Pontine marshes, and those in the district of Sienna, where the fatal nature of the climate acts unfavourably on common cattle, but affects the buffaloes less. The Spaniards also have paid attention to them; and indeed the cultivation of this useful animal seems to be pretty general in all the countries bordering on the Mediterranean Sea, both in Europe and Africa. Niebuhr remarks, that he saw buffaloes not only in Egypt, but also at Bombay, Surat, on the Euphrates, Tigris, Orontes, at Scanderoon, &c. and indeed in almost all marshy regions, and near large rivers. He does not remember any in Arabia, there being perhaps in that country too little water for this animal. (Descr. of Arabia, p. 165, Germ. edit.)

We have been thus particular in describing the buffalo of Asia, in order to show that it possesses, in its wild state, all the characteristics attributed to the Hebrew *reem*. All the evidence goes to show that it has been domesticated only at a comparatively recent period; and that the Hebrews therefore were probably acquainted with it only as a wild, savage, ferocious animal, resembling the ox; and it was not improbably often intended by them under the epithet, *bulls of Bashan*. The appropriateness of the foregoing description to the Hebrew *reem* will be apparent, on a closer inspection of the passages where this animal is mentioned.

In Deut. xxxiii. 17, and Ps. xcii. 10, the comparison is with his horns; which requires no further illustration after what is said above. In Numb. xxiii. 22, xxiv. 8, it is said, "he hath as it were the *strength* of a *reem;*" this is certainly most appropriate, if we adopt here the word *strength*, as the proper translation. But the Hebrew word here rendered *strength*, means strictly, *rapidity of motion, speed*, combined, if you please, with *force*. In this sense also, it is not less descriptive of the buffalo, which runs with great speed and violence when excited; as is often the case in regard to whole herds, which then rush blindly forwards with tremendous power. (See the account of Major Long's expedition to the Rocky Mountains.) In three other passages, the *reem* is closely coupled with the common ox, or with the employment of the latter. In Ps. xxix. 6, it is said, "He maketh them also to skip like a calf; Lebanon and Sirion like a young *reem*;" where the young of the *reem* stands in parallelism with the calf, so that we should naturally expect a great similarity between them. Isa. xxxiv. 7, "And the *reemim* shall come down with them, and the bullocks with the bulls," &c. Here, in verse 6, it is said that the Lord has a great sacrifice in Bozrah; and the idea in verse 7 is, according to the LXX and Gesenius, that the *reemim* shall *come down*, i. e. shall make part of this sacrifice, as also the bullocks, old and young, of the land of Edom, so that their "land shall be soaked with blood," &c. The other passage is Job xxix. 9—12, "Will the *reem* be willing to serve thee, or abide by the crib? Canst thou bind the *reem* with his band in the furrow, or will he harrow the valleys after thee? Wilt thou trust him because his strength is great, or wilt thou leave thy labour to him? Wilt thou believe him, that he will bring home thy seed, and gather it into thy barn?" Here Job is asked, whether he would dare to intrust to the *reem* such and such labours as were usually performed by oxen. Nothing can be more appropriate to the wild buffalo than this language; and we have seen above that the Hebrews probably knew it only in a wild state. The only other passage where the *reem* is mentioned is Ps. xxii. 21, and this requires a more extended notice. The Psalmist in deep distress says in verse 12, "Many bulls (פרים) have compassed me, strong bulls of Bashan have beset me round. They gaped upon me with their mouths, as a ravening and roaring lion. For dogs have compassed me," &c. Here it will be observed that three animals are mentioned as besetting the writer, bulls of Bashan, lions, dogs. The Psalmist proceeds to speak of his deliverance; verse 20, "Deliver my soul [me] from the sword, my darling [me] from the power of the dog. Save me from the lion's mouth; for thou hast heard [and saved] me from the horns of the *reemim*." Here also it will be seen are three animals, corresponding to the three before mentioned as besetting him, but ranged in an inverted order, viz. the dog, the lion, and the *reem*, in place of the bulls of Bashan; that is, from the whole structure of the poem, and the fact that these animals and no others are alluded to, the inference is almost irresistible, that the *reemim* of verse 21 are the *pârim* of verse 12, the bulls of Bashan, as has been already suggested above. At least we may infer that the *reem* was an animal not so unlike those bulls, but that it might with propriety be interchanged with them in poetic parallelism; a circumstance most appropriately true of the wild buffalo, and of him only.

From all these considerations, and from the fact that the buffalo must have been far better known in western Asia than either the rhinoceros or the oryx, (even if the description of the *reem* suited these animals in other respects,) we feel justified in assuming the *taurus bubalus*, or wild buffalo, to be the *reem* of the Hebrew scriptures, and the *unicorn* of the English version.

The principal difficulty in the way of this assumption, is the fact that the LXX have usually translated the Hebrew *reem* by μονόκερως, *unicorn, one-horn.* It must, however, be borne in mind, that these translators lived many centuries after the Hebrew scriptures were written, and not long indeed before the birth of Christ; they lived, too, in Egypt, where it is not impossible that the buffalo had in their age begun to be domesticated. In such circumstances, and being unacquainted with the animal in his fierce and savage state, they may have thought that the allusions to the *reem* were not fully answered by the half-domesticated animal before them, and they may, therefore, have felt themselves at liberty to insert the name of some animal which seemed to them more appropriate. That they did often take such liberties, is well known. An instance occurs in the very passage of Isaiah above quoted, ch. xxxiv. 7, where the Hebrew is ופרים עם אבירים, "and the bullocks with the bulls," i. e. the bulls with the strong ones, or, according to Gesenius, "the bulls both young and old:" this the LXX translates, καὶ οἱ κριοὶ καὶ οἱ ταῦροι, "and the rams (or wethers) and the bulls,"—certainly a *quid pro quo* not less striking than that of putting *unicorn* for *buffalo.*

That the LXX, in using the word *monoceros*, (unicorn, one-horn,) did not understand by it the *rhinoceros*, would seem obvious; both because the latter always had its appropriate and peculiar name in Greek, (ῥινόκερως, *rhinoceros, nose-horn*,) taken from the position of its horn upon the snout; and also from the circumstance so much insisted on above in the extracts from Mr. Bruce, that the rhinoceros of that part of Africa adjacent to Egypt actually has *two* horns. They appear rather to have had in mind the half-fabulous unicorn, described by Pliny, but lost sight of by all subsequent naturalists; although imperfect hints and accounts of a similar animal have been given by travellers in Africa and India, in different centuries, and entirely independent of each other. The interesting nature of the subject renders it proper to exhibit here all the evidence which exists in respect to such an animal; especially as it is nowhere brought together in the English language, or at least in no such form as to render it generally accessible.

The figure of the unicorn, in various attitudes, is depicted, according to Niebuhr, on almost all the stair-cases found among the ruins of Persepolis. One of these figures is given in vol. ii. plate xxiii. of Niebuhr's Travels; and also in vol. i. p. 594, 595, of the Travels of Sir R. K. Porter. The latter traveller supposes it to be the representation of a bull with a single horn. Pliny, in speaking of the wild beasts of India, says with regard to the animal in question: *Asperrimam autem feram monocerotem, reliquo corpore equo similem, capite cervo, pedibus elephanti, cauda apro, mugitu gravi, uno cornu nigro media fronte cubitorum duum eminente. Hanc feram vivam negant capi.* (Hist. Nat. vii. 21.) "The unicorn is an exceeding fierce animal, resembling a horse as to the rest of its body, but having the head like a stag, the feet like an elephant, and the tail like a wild boar: its roaring is loud, and it has a black horn of about two cubits projecting from the middle of its forehead." These seem to be the chief ancient notices of the existence of the animal in question.

In 1530, Ludivico de Bartema, a Roman patrician, travelled to Egypt, Arabia, and India; and having assumed the character of a Mussulman, he was able to visit Mecca with the Hadj, or great caravan of pilgrims. In his account of the curiosities of this city, in Ramusio's Collection of Travels, (Racotta di Viaggi, Venet. 1563, p. 163,) he says: "On the other side of the Caaba is a walled court, in which we saw two unicorns, which were pointed out to us as a rarity; and they are indeed truly remarkable. The larger of the two is built like a three-year-old colt, and has a horn upon the forehead about three ells long. The other unicorn was smaller, like a yearling foal, and has a horn perhaps four spans long.—This animal has the colour of a yellowish brown horse, a head like a stag, a neck not very long, with a thin mane; the legs are small and slender, like those of a hind or roe; the hoofs of the forefeet are divided, and resemble the hoofs of a goat. These two animals were sent to the sultan of Mecca, as a rarity of great value, and very seldom found, by a king of Ethiopia, who wished to secure, by this present, the good will of the sultan of Mecca."

Don Juan Gabriel, a Portuguese colonel, who lived several years in Abyssinia, assures us, that in the region of Agamos, in the Abyssinian province of Damota, he had seen an animal of the form and size of a middle-sized horse, of a dark chestnut-brown colour, and with a whitish horn, about five spans long, upon the forehead; the mane and tail were black, and the legs short and slender. Several other Portuguese, who were placed in confinement upon a high mountain in the district of Namna, by the Abyssinian king, Adamas Saghedo, related that they had seen, at the foot of the mountain, several unicorns feeding. (Ludolf's Hist. Æthiop. lib. i. c. 10. n. 80, seq.) These accounts are confirmed by Father Lobo, who lived for a long time as a missionary in Abyssinia. He adds, that the unicorn is extremely shy, and escapes from closer observation by a speedy flight into the forests; for which reason there is no exact description of him. (Voyage histor. d'Abyssinie, Amst. 1728, vol. i. p. 83, 291.) All these accounts are certainly not applicable to the rhinoceros; although it is singular that Mr. Bruce speaks only of the latter animal as not uncommon in Abyssinia, and makes apparently no allusion to the above accounts.

In more recent times we find further traces of the animal in question in Southern Africa. Dr. Sparrmann, the Swedish naturalist, who visited the Cape of Good Hope and the adjacent regions, in the years 1772–1776, gives, in his travels, the following account: Jacob Knock, an observing peasant on Hippopotamus river, who had travelled over the greater part of Southern Africa, found on the face of a perpendicular rock a drawing made by the Hottentots, representing a quadruped with one horn. The Hottentots told him that the animal there represented was very like the horse on which he rode, but had a straight horn upon the forehead. They added, that these one-horned animals were rare, that they ran with great rapidity, and were also very fierce. They also described the manner of hunting them. "It is not probable," Dr. Sparrmann remarks, "that the savages wholly invented this story, and that too so very circumstantially; still less can we suppose, that they should have received and retained, merely from history or tradition, the remembrance of such an animal. These regions are very seldom visited; and the creature might, therefore, long remain unknown. That an animal so rare should not be better known to the modern world, proves nothing against its existence. The greater part of Africa is still among the *terræ incognitæ*. Even the *giraffe* has been again discovered only within comparatively a few years. So also the *gnu*, which, till recently, was held to be a fable of the ancients."

A somewhat more definite account of a similar animal is contained in the Transactions of the Zealand Academy of Sciences at Flushing. (Pt. xv. Middelb. 1792. Præf. p. lvi.) The account was transmitted to the society in 1791, from the Cape of Good Hope, by Mr. Henry Cloete. It states that a bastard Hottentot, Gerrit Slinger by name, related, that while engaged several years before with a party, in pursuit of the savage Bushmen, they had got sight of nine strange animals, which they followed on horseback, and shot one of them. This animal resembled a horse, and was of a light-gray colour, with white stripes under the lower jaw. It had a single horn, directly in front, as long as one's arm, and at the base about as thick. Towards the middle the horn was somewhat flattened, but had a sharp point; it was not attached to the bone of the forehead, but fixed only in the skin. The head was like that of the horse, and the size also about the same. The hoofs were round, like those of a horse, but divided below like those of oxen. This remarkable animal was shot between the so-called Table Mountain and Hippopotamus river, about sixteen days' journey on horse-back from Cambedo, which would be about a month's journey in ox-wagons from Capetown. Mr. Cloete mentions, that several different natives and Hottentots testify to the existence of a similar animal with one horn, of which they profess to have seen drawings by hundreds, made by the Bushmen on rocks and stones. He supposes that it would not be difficult to obtain one of these animals, if desired. His letter is dated at the Cape, April 8, 1791. (See thus far Rosenmuller's Altes u. neues Morgenland, ii. p. 269, seq. Leipz. 1818.)

Such appear to have been the latest accounts of the animal in question, when it was again suddenly brought into notice as existing in the elevated regions of central India. The Quarterly Review for Oct. 1820, (vol. xxiv. p. 120,) in a notice of Frazier's tour through the Himalaya Mountains, goes on to remark as follows: "We have no doubt that a little time will bring to light many objects of natural history peculiar to the elevated regions of Central Asia, and hitherto unknown in the animal, vegetable, and mineral kingdoms, particularly in the two former. This is an opinion which we have long entertained; but we are led to the expression of it on the present occasion, by having been favoured with the perusal of a most interesting communication from Major Latter, commanding in the rajah of Sikkim's territories, in the hilly country east of Nepaul, addressed to Adjutant-general Nicol, and transmitted by him to the Marquis of Hastings. This important paper explicitly states that the unicorn, so long considered as a fabulous animal, actually exists at this moment in the interior of Thibet, where it is well known to the inhabitants. 'This,'—we copy from the Major's letter—'is a very curious fact, and it may be necessary to mention how the circumstance became known to me. In a Thibetian manuscript, containing the names of different animals, which I procured the other day from the hills, the *unicorn* is classed under the head of those whose hoofs are divided: it is called the one-horned *tso'po*. Upon inquiring what kind of animal it was, to our astonishment, the person who brought the manuscript described exactly the unicorn of the ancients; saying, that it was a native of the interior of Thibet, about the size of a *tattoo*, [a horse from twelve to thirteen hands high,] fierce and extremely wild; seldom, if ever, caught alive, but frequently shot: and that the flesh was used for food.'—'The person,' Major Latter adds, 'who gave me this information, has repeatedly seen these animals, and eaten the flesh of them. They go together in herds, like our wild buffaloes, and are very frequently to be met with on the borders of the great desert, about a month's journey from Lassa, in that part of the country inhabited by the wandering Tartars.'

"This communication is accompanied by a drawing made by the messenger from recollection. It bears some resemblance to a horse, but has cloven hoofs, a long curved horn growing out of the forehead, and a boar-shaped tail, like that of the *fera monoceros* described by Pliny. From its herding together, as the unicorn of the scriptures is said to do, as well as from the rest of the description, it is evident that it cannot be the rhinoceros, which is a solitary animal; besides, Major Latter states, that in the Thibetian manuscript the rhinoceros is described under the name of *servo*, and classed with the elephant; 'neither,' says he, 'is it the wild horse, (well known in Thibet,) for that has also a different name, and is classed in the manuscript with the animals which have the hoof's undivided.'—'I have written,' he subjoins, 'to the Sachia Lama, requesting him to procure me a perfect skin of the animal, with the head, horn, and hoofs; but it will be a long time before I can get it down, for they are not to be met with nearer than a month's journey from Lassa.'"

As a sequel to this account, we find the following paragraph in the Calcutta Government Gazette, August, 1821: "Major Latter has obtained the horn of a young unicorn from the Sachia Lama, which is now before us. It is twenty inches in length; at the root it is four inches and a half in circumference, and tapers to a point; it is black, rather flat at the sides, and has fifteen rings, but they are only prominent on one side; it is nearly straight. Major Latter expects to obtain the head of the animal, with the hoofs and the skin, very shortly, which will afford positive proof of the form and character of the *tso'po*, or Thibet unicorn."

Such are the latest accounts which have reached us of this animal; and although their credibility cannot well be contested, and the coincidence of the description with that of Pliny is so striking, yet it is singular that in the lapse of more than ten years, (1832,) nothing further should have been heard on a subject so interesting.—But whatever may be the fact as to the existence of this animal, the adoption of it by the LXX, as being the Hebrew *reem*, cannot well be correct; both for the reasons already adduced above, and also from the circumstance, that the *reem* was evidently an animal frequent and well known in the countries where the scenes of the Bible are laid; while the unicorn, at all events, is and was an animal of exceeding rarity.—ROBINSON IN CALMET.

Ver. 12. The righteous shall flourish like the palm-tree; he shall grow like a cedar in Lebanon.

The palm-tree is very common in Judea, and in the surrounding regions. The Hebrews call it (תמר) *tamar*, and the Greeks φοινιξ, *phenix*. The finest-palm trees grow about Jericho and Engeddi; they also flourish in great numbers along the banks of Jordan, and towards Scythopolis. Jericho is by way of distinction called "the city of palm-trees." It seems indeed to have been recognised as the common symbol of the Holy Land; for Judea is represented on several coins of Vespasian, by a disconsolate woman sitting under a palm-tree; and in like manner, upon the Greek coin of his son Titus, struck on a similar occasion, we see a shield suspended on a palm-tree, with a victory writing upon it. The same tree is delineated upon a medal of Domitian, as an emblem of Neapolis or Naplosa, the ancient Sichem; and upon a medal of Trajan, it is the symbol of Sepphoris, the metropolis of Galilee. From these facts it may be presumed that the palm-tree was formerly much cultivated in Palestine. Several of them still grow in the neighbourhood of Jericho, which abounds with water, where the climate is warm, and the soil sandy; a situation in which they delight, and where they rise to full maturity. But at Jerusalem, Sichem, and other places to the northward, two or three of them are rarely seen together; and even these, as their fruit seldom or never comes to maturity, are of no further service than, like the palm-tree of Deborah, to shade the dwellings of the parched inhabitants, or to supply them with branches at the solemn festival. The present condition and quality of palm-trees in Canaan, leads us to conclude, that they never at any time were either very numerous or fruitful in that country. The opinion that Phenice is the same with a country of date-trees, does not appear probable; for if such a valuable plant had ever been cultivated in Palestine with success, it would have been cultivated down to the present times, as in Egypt and in Barbary. In these countries the traveller meets with large plantations of palm-trees on the seacoast, as well as in the interior; although those only which grow in the sandy deserts of Sahara, and the regions of Getulia, and the Jereeda, bring their fruit to perfection. They are propagated chiefly from young shoots taken from the roots of full-grown trees; which, if well transplanted and taken care of, will yield their fruit in the sixth or seventh year; while those which are raised immediately from the kernel, will not bear till about their sixteenth year. This method of raising the φοῖνιξ, or palm, and particularly the circumstance, that when the old trunk dies, young shoots are never wanting to succeed it, may have given occasion to the well-known fable of the *phenix*, which perishes in a flame of her own kindling; while a young one springs from her ashes, to continue the race.

The palm-tree arrives at its greatest vigour about thirty years after being transplanted, and continues in full strength and beauty for seventy years longer, producing yearly fifteen or twenty clusters of dates, each of them weighing fifteen or twenty pounds. After this period it begins gradually to decline, and usually falls about the latter end of its second century. "Cui placet curas agere seculorum," says Palladius, "depalmis cogitet conserendis." It requires no other culture and attendance than to be well watered once in four or five days, and to have a few of the lower boughs lopped off when they begin to droop or wither. These, whose stumps or pollices, in being thus gradually left upon the trunk, serve, like so many rounds of a ladder, to climb up the tree, either to fecundate or to lop it, or to gather the fruit, are quickly supplied with others, which gradually hang down from the crown or top, contributing both to the regular and uniform growth of this tall, knotless, and beautiful tree, and to its perpetual and delightful verdure.

It is usual with persons of better station, to entertain their guests on days of joyous festivity with the honey of the palm-tree. This they procure by cutting off the head or crown of one of the more vigorous plants, and scooping the top of the trunk into the shape of a basin, where the sap in ascending lodges itself, at the rate of three or four quarts a day, during the first week or fortnight; after which the quantity daily diminishes, and at the end of six weeks or two months the juices are entirely consumed, the tree becomes dry, and serves only for timber or fire-wood. This liquor, which has a more luscious sweetness than honey, is of the consistence of a thin syrup, but quickly grows tart and ropy, acquiring an intoxicating quality, and giving by distillation an agreeable spirit—the Aaraky of the natives, and the palm-wine of the natural historian.

The palm is one of the most beautiful trees in the vegetable kingdom; it is upright, lofty, verdant, and embowering. It grows by the brook or well of living water; and resisting every attempt to press or bend it downward, shoots directly towards heaven. For this reason, perhaps, it was regarded by the ancients as peculiarly sacred, and therefore most frequently used in adorning their temples. The chosen symbol of constancy, fruitfulness, patience, and victory; the more it is oppressed, the more it flourishes, the higher it grows, and the stronger and broader the top expands. To this majestic and useful tree the child of God is compared in the holy scriptures, with singular elegance and propriety. Adorned with the beauties of holiness, and rich in the mercies of the covenant, fruitful in good works, and reposing all his thoughts in heaven, precious in the sight of God, and lovely in the view of every rational being capable of forming a just estimate of his character, he may well be said to flourish like the palm-tree, and to grow like a cedar in Lebanon. "Planted in the house of the Lord, he shall flourish in the courts of our God. He shall still bring forth fruit in old age; he shall be fat and flourishing; to show that the Lord is upright; that he is his rock; and there is no unrighteousness in him."—PAXTON.

"The wicked spring as the grass, but good men endure like the palm-tree, and bear much fruit." "A grateful man is like the palmirah-tree; for small attentions he gives much fruit."—ROBERTS.

Ver. 13. Those that be planted in the house of the LORD shall flourish in the courts of our God.

The being planted in the house of God, or in its courts, may allude to an ancient custom, still used in the East, of planting trees in the courtyard of a house. Plaisted, in his Journal from Busserah to Aleppo, informs us, that the people of Aleppo plant a cypress-tree in the courtyard of their houses. Dr. Fryer, in his new account of the East Indies and Persia, describes a nabob's apartments as encompassing in the middle a verdant quadrangle of trees and plants. It is also observable, that the Jews, though forbidden to plant trees in the temple, planted them in their proseuchae, which were, in some sort, houses of God. —BURDER.

Ver. 14. They shall still bring forth fruit in old age; they shall be fat and flourishing.

The Hebrew, instead of flourishing, has, "GREEN!" Ainsworth, "shall be fat and green." Of a very old man who has retained his strength, the Hindoos say, "he is a GREEN veteran." "See that *patche-killaven*, (green old man,) how strong he is." "My friend, if you act in this way, you will never be a green old man." A man who has been long noted for roguery is called a *patche-kallan*, a green rogue; and a well-known utterer of falsehoods, a green liar. "Ah! my lord!" says the relieved mendicant, "in your old age you will be fat and flourishing;" or, "You will be a green old man."—ROBERTS.

PSALM CI.

Ver. 3. I will set no wicked thing before mine eyes: I hate the work of them that turn aside; *it* shall not cleave to me.

Pleasure or displeasure, approbation or abhorrence, may be known by the look, or the cast of the eye. What we are pleased and delighted with attracts and fixes the eye. What we dislike or hate, we turn away from the sight of; and when the Psalmist resolves that *he would not fix his eyes upon any evil thing*, he means, he would never give it the least countenance or encouragement, but treat it with displeasure, as what he hated, and was determined to punish. For he adds, "I hate the work of them that turn aside." Mr. Schultens hath shown in his commentary on Prov. vii. 25, that שטה hath a much stronger and more significant meaning than that of mere *turning aside;* and that it is used of an unruly horse, that champs upon the bit through his fiery impatience; and when applied to a bad man, denotes one impatient of all restraint, of unbridled passions, and who is headstrong and ungovernable in the gratification of them, trampling on all the obligations of religion and virtue. Such as these are the deserved objects of the hatred of all good men, whose criminal deviations and presumptuous crimes they detest; none of which *shall cleave to them;* they will not harbour the love of or inclination to them, nor habitually commit them, nor encourage the practice of them.—CHANDLER.

PSALM CII.

Ver. 3. For my days are consumed like smoke, and my bones are burned as a hearth.

A person believing himself to be near death, says, in the bitterness of his soul, "Alas! my days have passed away like smoke; my bones are as a firebrand."—ROBERTS.

Ver. 6. I am like a pelican of the wilderness; I am like an owl of the desert.

The pelican is another bird of the desert, to which the sacred writers sometimes allude. Its Hebrew name is kaath, literally, the vomiter from the Hebrew verb kaath, to vomit. The reason assigned for this name by the ancients is, that it discharges the shells it had swallowed, after they have been opened by the heat of its belly, in order to pick out the fish, which form its principal food. This fact, says Bochart, is so generally attested by the writers of antiquity, that it cannot be called in question; and then cites a great number of authorities in its support. But with all deference to this learned writer, it may be justly doubted, if this bird really takes the shell-fish on which it feeds into its stomach, in the first instance; it is more probable that it deposites them in the bag or pouch under its lower chap, which serves not only as a net to catch, but also as a repository for its food. In feeding its young ones, (whether this bag is loaded with water or more solid food,) the pelican squeezes the contents of it into their mouths, by strongly compressing it upon its breast with its bill; an action which may well justify the propriety of the name which it received from the ancient Hebrews. To the same habit, it is probable, may be traced the traditionary report, that the pelican, in feeding her young, pierces her own breast, and nourishes them with her blood.

Dr. Shaw contends, that kaath cannot mean the pelican, because the royal Psalmist describes it as a bird of the wilderness, where that fowl must necessarily starve, because its large webbed feet, and capacious pouch, with the manner of catching its food, which can only be in the water, show it to be entirely a water-fowl. But this objection proceeds on the supposition, that the deserts which it frequents contain no water, which is a mistake; for Ptolemy places three lakes in the interior parts of Marmorica, which is extremely desolate; and Moses informs us, that the people of Israel met with the waters of Mara, and the fountains of Elim, in the barren sands of Arabia. Besides, it is well known that a water-fowl often retires to a great distance from her favourite haunts; and this is confirmed by a fact, which Parkhurst states from the writings of Isidore, that the pelican inhabits the solitudes of the Nile. This far-famed river, as we know from the travels of Mr. Bruce, rolls its flood through an immense and frightful desert, where water-fowls of different kinds undoubtedly find a secure retreat. Mr. Bruce himself sprang a duck in the burning wilderness, at a considerable distance from its banks, which immediately winged her flight towards it; a clear proof of her being familiarly acquainted with its course. From this circumstance we may infer, that the pelican is no stranger to the most desert and inhospitable borders of the Nile. It also appears from Damir, the Arabian naturalist quoted by Bochart, that the pelican, like the duck which Bruce found in the desert of Senaar, does not always remain in the water, but sometimes retires from it to a great distance; and indeed its monstrous pouch, which, according to Edwards, in his natural history of birds, is capable of receiving twice the size of a man's head, seems to be given it for this very reason, that it might not want food for itself and its young ones, when at a distance from the water.

Bochart is of opinion, that kaath, in some passages of scripture, is intended to express the bittern, which differs from the pelican, by his own admission, only in the form of the bill. Thus the holy Psalmist complains, "I am like a pelican (bittern) of the wilderness; I am like an owl of the desert." The clear and consistent exposition of this passage, he contends, requires the word kaath to be rendered bittern; because the sacred writer compares himself to the bittern and the owl, or more properly the ostrich, on account of his groaning. It is therefore natural to conclude, that both these animals have a mournful cry. Many reasons have been advanced, to prove that the chos, rendered in our translation the owl, is in reality the female ostrich; of which this is one, that it has a most hideous voice, resembling, in a very remarkable manner, the lamentations of a human being in deep affliction. That the Psalmist may be consistent with himself, the same thing must be asserted of the kaath, which it would be difficult to admit, if that term signified only the pelican; for natural historians observe a profound silence in relation to the voice of that bird. But if the name kaath is common to the bittern and the pelican, the difficulty vanishes, for the former has a clear voice. All the ancient natural historians agree, that the bittern, by inserting its bill in the mud of the marsh, or plunging it under water, utters a most disagreeable cry, like the roaring of a bull, or the sound of distant thunder.

But the opinion of that celebrated writer, in this instance, rests upon a false, or at least an uncertain foundation. The afflicted Psalmist seems to refer, not so much to the plaintive voice of these birds, as to their lonely situation in the wilderness. One of the first and most common effects of pungent sorrow, is the desire of solitude; and on this occasion the royal Psalmist, oppressed with grief, seems to have become weary of society, and like the pelican, or the female ostrich, to have contracted a relish for deep retirement. Besides, as our author allows, that the pelican and the bittern differ only in the form of the bill, the translation for which he contends is of no real importance; and it is certainly a good rule to admit of no change in a received translation, unless it can be shown, that the new term or phrase expresses the meaning of the original with greater justness, propriety, or elegance.

The bird of night, which, like the ostrich, delights in the desert and solitary place, is distinguished by several names in the sacred writings. In the book of Psalms, it is mentioned under the name *kous*, which is evidently derived from the verb *kasah, to hide;* because the owl constantly hides herself in the daytime, and comes abroad in the evening. The Seventy, Theodotion, Aquila, and other interpreters, render it νυκτικοραξ, in English, the horned owl. The learned Bochart suspected that *kous* might denote the *onocrotalus*, thus named from its monstrous cap or bag under the lower chap. It must be admitted, that *kous* might properly enough be given as a name to that bird, from this extraordinary circumstance in its form; but after the most diligent inquiry, the writer has not been able to discover any difference between the pelican of the ancients, and the *onocrotalus;* and as *kaath* is mentioned in the same contexts with *kous*, and rendered in the ancient versions either the pelican or *onocrotalus*, *kous*, in his opinion, must have a different meaning. This idea receives no little confirmation from a passage in the hundred and second Psalm, where *kous* is followed in construction by *haraboth*, and signifies *kous*, not of the desert, as we render it, but of the desolate or ruined buildings; which exactly corresponds with the habits of the owl; but does not seem so applicable to the *onocrotalus*, or pelican. Buffon calls the horned owl the eagle of the night, and the sovereign of that tribe of birds which shun the light of day, and never fly but in the evening, or after it is dark. But, as a description of it is connected with the illustration of no passage of scripture, it falls not within the design of this work. The voice of the horned owl is said to be frightful, and is often heard resounding in the silence of night; which is the season of his activity, when he flies abroad in search of his prey. He inhabits the lonely rocks or deserted towers on the sides of the mountains; he seldom descends into the plain, and never willingly perches upon trees. The dreary and frightful note of the owl sounding along the desert, and alarming or terrifying the birds that are reposing in their nests, represents, in a very striking manner, the deep and lonely afflictions of the royal Psalmist, and the affecting complaints which his distresses wrung from his bosom.

Yansuph is another term which our translators render the owl; it occurs only three times in the sacred volume, and is derived from the verb *nashaph*, to blow, or from *nesheph*, the twilight or the dawn. It is supposed to denote a species of owl, which flies about in the twilight; and is the same as the twilight bird. But of this interpretation Parkhurst disapproves, contending, that since the yansuph is clearly mentioned by Moses among the water-fowls, and the Seventy have in two passages rendered it by ibis, it should seem to mean some kind of water-fowl, resembling the bird of that name; and from its derivation, remarkable for its blowing. And of such birds, he says, the most eminent seems to be the bittern, which, in the north of England, is called the mire-drum, from the noise it makes, which may be heard a long way off. But the opinion of Bochart, that it denotes the owl, is more probable; because the owl delights in the silent desert, where little or no water is to be found; while the ibis is an aquatic bird, whose instincts lead it to the lake, or running stream. In the thirty-fourth chapter of Isaiah, the *yansuph* is mentioned as frequenting the desolated land of Edom, which, according to Dr. Shaw, is remarkably destitute of water, and by consequence, quite improper for the abode of a water-fowl, which feeds on fish. It is admitted that the *kaath*, or pelican, another water-fowl, is mentioned in the same text with *yansuph;* that all the larger water-fowls are extremely shy; that they sometimes build their nests in retired places, a long way from the water where they seek their food; and that even the common heron will come at least twelve or fourteen miles, and perhaps much farther, from her usual residence, to the lakes and streams which abound with fish. But no argument can be founded on the arrangements of scripture, in matters of this kind; because the inspired writers do not always observe a strict order, or scientific classification. It ought also to be remembered, that in the passage quoted from Isaiah, the *yansuph* is connected with the raven, which is not an aquatic bird. The owl and the raven are associated with greater propriety in scenes of desolation, to which they have been assigned by the common suffrage of mankind, and accordingly regarded as inauspicious birds, and objects of fear and aversion:—

"Foedaque fit volucris venturi nuntia luctus
Ignavus bubo dirum mortalibus omen."—*Ovid.*

The presence of the owl and the raven, two hateful birds, in company with the cormorant and the bittern, greatly heighten the general effect of the picture delineated by the prophet: "But the cormorant and the bittern shall possess it; the owl also and the raven shall dwell in it; and he shall stretch out upon it the line of confusion, and the stones of emptiness."—PAXTON.

Ver. 7. I watch, and am as a sparrow alone upon the house-top.

Brookes says of this bird, "It usually sits alone on the tops of old buildings and roofs of churches, singing very sweetly, especially in the morning; and is an oriental bird." —BURDER.

The sparrow has been considered by some interpreters as a solitary moping bird, which loves to dwell on the house-top alone; and so timid, that she endeavours to conceal herself in the darkest corners, and passes the night in sleepless anxiety. Hence they translate the words of the Psalmist: "I watch, and am as a sparrow alone upon the house-top." But her character and manners by no means agree with their description. She is a pert, loquacious, bustling creature, which, instead of courting the dark and solitary corner, is commonly found chirping and fluttering about in the crowd. The term in this text, therefore, must be understood in its general sense, and probably refers to some variety of the owl. Jerome renders it, I was as a solitary bird on the roof. The Hebrew text contains nothing which can with propriety suggest the sparrow, or any similar bird; and indeed, nothing seems to be more remote from the mind of David: all the circumstances seem to indicate some bird of the night; for the Psalmist, bending under a load of severe affliction, shuns the society of men, and mingles his unceasing groans and lamentations with the mournful hootings of those solitary birds which disturb the lonely desert. "By reason of the voice of my groaning, my bones cleave to my skin; I am like a pelican of the wilderness; I am like an owl of the desert." He then proceeds with his comparison: "I watch, and am as a bird upon the house-top alone;" I watch, that is, I have spent a sleepless night: or, as it is paraphrased in the Chaldee, I have watched the whole night long, without once closing my eyes. Every part of this description directs our attention to some nocturnal bird, which hates the light, and comes forth from its hiding-place when the shadows of evening fall, to hunt the prey, and from the top of some ruined tower, to tell its joys or its sorrows to a slumbering world. But, with what propriety can the sparrow be called a solitary bird, when it is gregarious, and, so far from loving solitude, builds her nest in the roofs of our dwellings? Natural historians mention two kinds of this bird, one domestic, and the other wild. But the wild sparrow does not repair for shelter, like her relative, mentioned by David, to the human dwelling; she never takes her station on the house-top, but seeks a home in her native woods. If the allusion, therefore, be made to the sparrow, it must be to the domestic, not to the wild species. It is in vain to argue, that the domestic sparrow may be called solitary, when she is deprived of her mate; for she does not, like the turtle, when she loses her spouse, remain in a state of inconsolable widowhood, but accepts, without reluctance, the first companion that solicits her affections. Hence the Psalmist undoubtedly refers to some species of the owl, whose dreary note and solitary dispositions, are celebrated by almost every poet of antiquity.—PAXTON.

Ver. 11. My days *are* like a shadow that declineth; and I am withered like grass.

"My days are like the declining shadow," says the old man: "my shadow is fast declining:" *siyanthu, siyanthu,* declining, declining. "I am withered." Indran, the king of heaven, said of himself and others, They were *withered* by the mandates of Sooran. "Alas! his face and heart are withered." "My heart is withered, I cannot eat my food." "Sorrow, not age, has withered my face." "Alas! how soon this blossom has withered."—ROBERTS.

Ver. 26. They shall perish, but thou shall endure; yea, all of them shall wax old like a garment; as a vesture shalt thou change them, and they shall be changed.

It is reckoned in the East, according to Dr. Pococke, a mark of respect often to change their garments, in the time of a visit for a night or two. He expresses himself, however, with obscurity and some uncertainty; but it is made certain by the accounts of other travellers, that it is a matter of state and magnificence. So Thevenot tells us, that when he saw the grand seignior go to the new mosque, he was clad in a satin doliman of a flesh colour, and a vest of almost the same colour; but when he had said his prayers, then he changed his vest, and put on one of a particular kind of green. At another time he went to the mosque in a vest of crimson velvet, but returned in one of a fired satin. To this frequent change of vestments among the great, possibly the Psalmist alludes, when, speaking of the Lord of all, he says, The heavens, unchangeable as they are, when compared with the productions of the earth, shall perish, while he shall remain; yea, they shall be laid aside, in comparison of his immortality, as soon as a garment grows old; or rather, this change which they shall undergo, shall come on more speedily, with respect to his eternity, than the laying aside of a vestment which kings and princes change often in a day. The changing of clothes is a piece of eastern magnificence: how wonderfully sublime, then, in this view, is this representation of the grandeur of God, "Thou shalt change these heavens as a prince changes his vesture."—HARMER.

PSALM CIII.

Ver. 15. *As for* man, his days *are* as grass; as a flower of the field, so he flourisheth.

See on 2 Kings 19. 7.

Ver. 16. For the wind passeth over it, and it is gone; and the place thereof shall know it no more.

See on Est. 1. 5, 6.

PSALM CIV.

Ver. 2. Who coverest *thyself* with light as *with* a garment; who stretchest out the heavens like a curtain.

It is usual in the summer season, and upon all occasions when a large company is to be received, to have the court of the house (which is the middle of an open square) sheltered from the heat of the weather by an umbrella or veil, which, being expanded upon ropes from one side of the parapet-wall to the other, may be folded or unfolded at pleasure. The Psalmist seems to allude to some covering of this kind in that beautiful expression of "stretching out the heavens like a curtain."—SHAW.

Ver. 10. He sendeth the springs in o the valleys, *which* run among the hills. 11. They give drink to every beast of the field: the wild asses quench their thirst.

See on Job 39. 5.

Ver. 17. Where the birds make their nests: *as for* the stork, the fir-trees *are* her house.

This bird has long been celebrated for her amiable and pious disposition, in which she has no rival among the feathered race. Her Hebrew name is *chasida*, which signifies pious or benign; to the honour of which, her character and habits, as described by the pen of antiquity, prove her to be fully entitled. Her kind, benevolent temper, she discovers in feeding her parents in the time of incubation, when they have not leisure to seek their food, or when they have become old, and unable to provide for themselves. This attention of the stork to her parents is confirmed by the united voice of antiquity; and we find nothing in the scriptures to invalidate the testimony. She was classed by the Jewish lawgiver among the unclean birds, probably because she feeds on serpents, and other venomous animals, and rears her young by means of the same species of food. In the challenge which the Almighty addressed to Job, the wings and feathers of the ostrich are compared with those of the stork: "Gavest thou the goodly wings unto the peacocks, or wings and feathers unto the ostrich;" or, as it is rendered by the learned Bochart, and after him by Dr. Shaw, "the plumage of the stork." Natural historians inform us, that the wings are tipped with black, and a part of the head and thighs are adorned with feathers of the same colour; the rest of the body is white. Albert says, the stork has black wings, the tail and other parts white; while Turner asserts, that the wings are white, spotted with black. From these different accounts, it is evident that the feathers of the stork are black and white, and not always disposed in the same manner. She constructs her nest with admirable skill, of dry twigs from the forest, and coarse grass from the marsh; but wisely yielding to circumstances, she does not confine herself to one situation. At one time she selects for her dwelling the pinnacle of a deserted tower, or the canal of an ancient aqueduct; at another, the roof of a church or dwelling-house. She frequently retires from the noise and bustle of the town, into the circumjacent fields; but she never builds her nest on the ground. She chooses the highest tree of the forest for her dwelling; but always prefers the fir, when it is equally suitable to her purpose. This fact is clearly stated by the Psalmist, in his meditation on the power of God: "As for the stork, the fir-trees are her house." In another passage, the Psalmist calls the nest of the sparrow her house: "Yea, the sparrow hath found a house, and the swallow a nest for herself, where she may lay her young." But the term house is not used in these passages, merely by a figure of speech; if the description of ancient writers be true, it is in every respect the most proper and expressive that can be selected. The stork chooses the site of her dwelling with much care and intelligence; she combines her materials with great art, and prosecutes her plan with surprising exactness. After the structure is finished, she examines it on all sides, tries its firmness and solidity, supplies any defect she may discover, and with admirable industry, reduces with her bill an unsightly projection, or ill-adjusted twig, till it perfectly corresponds with her instinctive conception of safety, neatness, and comfort.

The inspired writer alludes to this bird, with an air of constant and intimate acquaintance: "As for the stork, the fir-tree is her house." We learn from the narrative of Doubdan, that the fields between Cana and Nazareth are covered with numerous flocks of them, each flock containing, according to his computation, more than a thousand. In some parts, the ground is entirely whitened by them; and on the wing they darken the air like a congeries of clouds. At the approach of evening, they retire to roost on the trees. The inhabitants carefully abstain from hurting them, on account of their important services in clearing the country of venomous animals. The annual migration of this bird did not escape the notice of the prophet Jeremiah, who employs it with powerful effect for the purpose of exposing the stupidity of God's ancient people: "Yea, the stork in the heaven knoweth her appointed time, and the turtle, the crane, and the swallow, observe the time of their coming; but my people know not the judgment of the Lord." They know, with unerring precision, the time when it is necessary for them to remove from one place to another, and the region whither they are to bend their flight; but the people of God, that received many special revelations from heaven, and enjoyed the continual instructions of his prophets, had become so depraved, that they neither understood the meaning of mercies nor judgments; they knew not how to accommodate themselves to either, nor to answer the design of heaven in such dispensations; they knew not the signs of their times, nor what they ought to do. The stork, that had neither instructer to guide her, nor reason to reflect, and judgment to determine, what was proper to be done, found no difficulty in discerning the precise time of her departure and return.—PAXTON.

Ver. 18. The high hills *are* a refuge for the wild goats, *and* the rocks for the conies.

The wild goat, or ibex, belongs to the same species with the domestic goat, and exhibits nearly the same character and dispositions. His Hebrew name, *yaala*, from a verb which signifies to ascend, indicates one of the strongest habits implanted in his nature, to scale the loftiest pinnacle of the rock, and the highest ridge of the mountains. He takes his station on the edge of the steep, and seems to delight in gazing on the gulf below, or surveying the immense void before him. Those frightful precipices which are inaccessible to man, and other animals, where the most adventurous hunter dares not follow him, are his favourite haunts. He sleeps on their brow; he sports on their smallest projections, secure from the attack of his enemies. These facts were observed by the shepherds of the East, recorded by the pen of inspiration, and celebrated in the songs of Zion: "The high hills are a refuge for the wild goats." In the expostulation which Jehovah addressed to Job, they are called "the wild goats of the rock;" because it is the place which the Creator has appointed for their proper abode, and to which he has adapted all their dispositions and habits. The dreary and frightful precipices, which frown over the Dead Sea, towards the wilderness of Engedi, the inspired historian of David's life calls emphatically "the rocks of the wild goats," as if accessible only to those animals.

The ibex is distinguished by the size of his horns. No creature, says Gesner, has horns so large as those of the mountain goat, for they reach from his head as far as his buttocks. Long before his time, Pliny remarked, that the ibex is a creature of wonderful swiftness, although its head is loaded with vast horns. According to Scaliger, the horns of an elderly goat are sometimes eighteen pounds weight, and marked by twenty-four circular prominences, the indications of as many years. The horns of the ibex, according to the Chaldee interpreter, are mentioned by the prophet among the valuable commodities which enriched the merchants of Tyre, in the days of her prosperity: "The men of Dedan were thy merchants; many isles were the merchandise of thy hand; they brought thee for a present, horns of ivory and ebony." It is certain that the horns of this animal were greatly esteemed among the ancients, on account of the various useful purposes to which they were converted. The Cretan archers had them manufactured into bows; and the votaries of Bacchus, into large cups, one of which, says Ælian, could easily hold three measures. The conjecture of Bochart is therefore extremely probable, that the ἴξαλος of Homer, is the ibex of the Latins; for he calls it a wild goat, says that it was taken among the rocks and had horns of sixteen palms, of which the bow of Pandarus was fabricated. We may conclude from the wisdom and goodness of God, which shine conspicuously in all his works, that the enormous horns of the ibex are not a useless encumbrance, but, in some respects, necessary to its safety and comfort. The Arabian writers aver, that when it sees the hunter approach the top of the rock, where it happens to have taken its station, and has no other way of escape, turning on its back, it throws itself down the precipice, at once defended by its long bending horns from the projections of the rock, and saved from being dashed in pieces, or even hurt by the fall. The opinion of Pliny is more worthy of credit, that the horns of the ibex serve as a poise to its body in its perilous excursions among the precipitous rocks, or when it attempts to leap from one crag to another. The feats which it is said to perform among the Alpine summits, are almost incredible; one fact, however, seems to be certain, that in bounding from one height to another, it far surpasses all the other varieties of the species. To hunt the ibex has been justly reckoned a most perilous enterprise, which frequently terminates in the hunter's destruction. These facts place in a very strong light the extreme dangers which at one time compelled David to seek a refuge from the pursuit of his infatuated father-in-law, among the rocks of the wild goats; and, at the same time, the bitter and implacable spirit which prompted Saul to follow him in places so full of peril.

The Hebrew name of the cony is derived from a verb which signifies to hide, and seems to indicate a creature of a timid and harmless disposition. Unable to avoid or encounter the various dangers to which it would be exposed in the plain, it seeks a shelter among the rocks, in the fissures of which it hides itself from the pursuit of its enemies. This circumstance is attested by the sacred writer, in one of the songs of Zion: "The high hills are a refuge for the wild goats, and the rocks for the (שפנים) shaphans." The choice which the shaphan makes of the rock for the place of its abode, is mentioned by Solomon as a proof of sagacity: "The shaphans are but a feeble folk, yet make they their houses in the rocks." It is evident from these words also, that the shaphan is a gregarious animal, although they afford us no hint from which the numbers which constitute their little communities may be inferred. To what particular animal the name shaphan really belongs, has been much disputed among the learned. In our version it is rendered by the word cony or rabbit; in which our translators have followed the greater part of modern interpreters. Several circumstances seem to favour this interpretation; it is twice connected in the law of Moses with the hare, as if it were a kindred animal; the noun in the plural is rendered hare by the Seventy, in which they have been followed by many ancient interpreters of great name: the meaning of shaphan seems to correspond with the timidity of the rabbit; and it is certain that the Rabbinical writers formerly interpreted the original word in this manner. Besides, the rabbit is a gregarious animal, of a diminutive size, and found in great numbers in the plain of Jericho. But these facts are not sufficient to establish the point for which they are brought forward; for, instead of seeking a habitation in the fissures of the rocks, the rabbit delights to burrow in the sandy downs. Sometimes, indeed, he digs a receptacle for himself in rocky eminences, where the openings are filled with earth, but he generally prefers a dwelling in the sand, a situation for which he is evidently formed by nature. The words of David clearly show, that the instincts and habits of the shaphan, as naturally and constantly lead him to the rocks for shelter, as those of his associate impel him to rove among the mountains. He does not allude to an occasional residence, but to a fixed and permanent abode; not to the wanderings of a few, but to the habitual choice of a whole species. But the rabbit as uniformly seeks the sandy plain, as the wild goat the summit of the mountain. The shaphan, according to Solomon, discovers great wisdom and sagacity in retiring from the plain country, to the natural fastness which the almighty Creator has provided for its reception; but it is no mark of wisdom in the rabbit, that he forsakes occasionally the sandy plain, which he is naturally formed to occupy, and retires to the rocks, which are so little suited to his habits and manners. This is an act of rashness or folly, not of wisdom. The wise man is also noting the sagacity of a whole species, not of a rambling individual; but the species is to be found on the plain, not among the rocks. Nor is the rabbit a feeble creature; he runs with considerable swiftness; and he is provided with the means of digging his burrow, which he employs with so great energy, particularly when alarmed by the approach of danger, that he buries himself in the sand with surprising rapidity. To exert his strength, according to existing circumstances, is all the sagacity which he discovers; and this, it must be admitted, is not peculiar to him, but common to the hare, the hedgehog, and many other animals. He betrays no foresight, except in preparing his dwelling, and he is never known to supply the want of strength by any contrivance. The shaphan, as described both by David and Solomon, exhibits a very different character, and therefore cannot be the same animal.

But if we apply these characters to the *daman* Israel, or, as Mr. Bruce calls it, the *ashkoko*, the identity of this animal with the shaphan of the scriptures will instantly appear: "The daman is a harmless creature, of the same size and quality with the rabbit, and with the like incurvating posture and disposition of the fore-teeth. But it is of a browner colour, with smaller eyes, and a head more pointed, like the marmot's; the forefeet likewise are short, and the hinder are nearly as long in proportion as those of the jerboa. Though this animal is known sometimes to burrow in the ground, yet he is so much attached to the rock, that he is seldom or never seen on the ground, or from among large stones in the mouth of caves, where he fixes his constant residence. He is gregarious, as the wise man intimates, and lives in families; he is a native of Judea, Palestine, and Arabia, and consequently, must have been familiar to Solomon, and other inspired writers. The royal Psalmist, in a passage already quoted, describes him with great propriety, and joins him with other animals, which were perfectly known in that country. Solomon favours us with a more detailed account of his character: "There be four things which are little upon the earth, but they are exceeding wise; the sephanim are a feeble folk, yet make they their houses in the rocks." This exactly corresponds with the character which natural historians give us of the daman Israel, which they represent as equally feeble in body and temper. The toes of his forefeet very much resemble the fingers of the human hand; his feet are perfectly round, very pulpy or fleshy, liable to be excoriated or hurt, and of a soft fleshy substance. They are quite inadequate to dig holes in the ground, much more to force their way into the hard rock. Unable or afraid to stand upright on his feet, he steals along every moment as it were apprehensive of danger, his belly almost close to the ground, advancing a few steps at a time, and then pausing, as if afraid or uncertain whether he should proceed. His whole appearance and behaviour indicate a mild, feeble, and timid disposition; which is confirmed by the ease with which he is tamed. Conscious as it were of his total inability to dig in the ground, or to mingle with the sterner beasts of the field, he builds his house on rocks, more inaccessible than those to which the cony retires, and in which he resides in greater safety, not by exertions of strength, for he has it not, but by his own sagacity and judgment. Solomon has therefore justly characterized him as "a feeble animal, but exceeding wise."

The Arabian writers confound the daman Israel with the jerboa, which seems to be a species of rat. It ruminates, builds its house on the rocks, or digs its abode in the ground, but always in some high and rocky place, where it may be safe from the influx of waters, and the foot of the wild beast. If we may believe the Arabic writer quoted by Bochart, these diminutive animals discover no little sagacity in the conduct of public affairs, particularly in appointing a leader, whose business it is to give them notice on the approach of danger, and who in case of neglect is punished with death, and succeeded by another more attentive to their safety. Mr. Bruce, on the contrary, contends with great earnestness, that the habits of the jerboa are quite different from those which Solomon ascribes to the shaphan; he asserts, that the jerboa always digs his habitation in the smoother places of the desert, especially where the soil is fixed gravel; for in that chiefly he burrows, dividing his hole below into many mansions. He is not gregarious, like the shaphan, nor is he distinguished for his feebleness, which he supplies by his wisdom. Although, therefore, he ruminates in common with some other animals, and abounds in Judea, he cannot be the shaphan of the scripture. Hence, it is probable, that the Arabian writers improperly confounded the daman Israel, or shaphan, and the jerboa; and it may be considered as nearly certain, that the shaphan of Solomon is not the rabbit, but the daman Israel, which, though bearing some resemblance to it, is an animal of a different species.—PAXTON.

Ver. 20. Thou makest darkness, and it is night, wherein all the beasts of the forest do creep *forth*.

Immediately after landing, we hired horses to conduct us to Fanskog, ten miles and a half, where we arrived at so neat an inn, and were withal so subdued by want of sleep and fatigue, that we rested for a few hours, writing our journals without candles half an hour after midnight, by a light that could not be called twilight; it was rather the glare of noon, being reflected so strongly from the walls and houses, that it was painful to our eyes, and we began already to perceive, what we never felt before, that darkness is one of those benevolent gifts of Providence, the value of which, as conducive to repose, we only become sensible of, when it ceases altogether to return. There were no shutters to the windows, and the continual blaze which surrounded us, we could gladly have dispensed with, had it been possible. When we closed our eyes, they seemed to be still open; we even bound on them our handkerchiefs; but a remaining impression of brightness, like a shining light, wearied and oppressed them. To this inconvenience we were afterward more exposed, and although use rendered us somewhat less affected by it, it was an evil of which we all complained, and we hailed the returning gloom of autumn as a comfort and a blessing.—Clarke.

PSALM CV.

Ver. 26. He sent Moses his servant, and Aaron whom he had chosen.

Calmet says the word *servant*, among the Hebrews, "generally signifies a slave:" and Dr. A. Clarke says, (on Rom. i. 1, "Paul a servant of Jesus Christ,") the word δουλος, which we translate servant, properly means a slave, one who is the entire property of his master, and is used here by the apostle with great propriety. In eastern language the word used as expressive of the relationship of men to their deities is slave. "I am the *adumi*," i. e. SLAVE, "of the supreme Siva." "I am the devoted slave of Vishnoo." Hindoo saints are always called the *slaves* of the gods. The term servant is applied to one who is at liberty to dispose of himself, in serving different masters: but not so a slave, he is the property of his owner; from him he receives protection and support, and he is not at liberty to serve another master; hence it is that the native Christians, in praying to the true God, and our Saviour Jesus Christ, always speak of themselves as slaves; they are not their own, but "bought with a price."—Roberts.

Ver. 30. The land brought forth frogs in abundance, in the chambers of their kings.

It is not difficult for an Englishman in an eastern wet monsoon, to form a tolerable idea of that plague of Egypt, in which the frogs were in the "houses, bedchambers, beds, and kneading-troughs," of the Egyptians. In the season alluded to, myriads of them send forth their constant croak in every direction, and a man not possessed of overmuch patience, becomes as petulant as was the licentious god, and is ready to exclaim,

"Croak, croak, indeed I shall choke
If you pester and bore my ears any more
With your croak, croak, croak."

A new-comer, on seeing them leap about the rooms, becomes disgusted, and forthwith begins an attack upon them, but the next evening will bring a return of his active visiters. It may appear almost incredible, but in one evening we killed upwards of forty of these guests in the Jaffna Mission House. They had principally concealed themselves in a small tunnel connected with the bathing-room, and their noise had become almost insupportable. I have been amused when a man has been making a speech which has not given pleasure to his audience, to hear another person ask, "What has that fellow been croaking about, like a frog of the wet monsoon?" The natives also do us the honour of saying, that our singing, in parts, is very much like the notes of the large and small frogs. The bass singers, say they, resemble the croak of the bull-frogs, and the other parts the notes of the small fry.—Roberts.

PSALM CVII.

Ver. 5. Hungry and thirsty, their soul fainted in them.

Many perish, victims of the most horrible thirst. It is then that the value of a cup of water is really felt; he that has a zenzabia of it is the richest of all: in such a case, there is no distinction; if the master has none, the servant will not give it to him; for very few are the instances where a man will voluntarily lose his life to save that of another, particularly in a caravan in the desert, where people are strangers to each other. What a situation for a man, though a rich one, perhaps the owner of all the caravans! He is dying for a cup of water; no one gives it to him; he offers all he possesses; no one hears him; they are all dying, though by walking a few hours farther they might be saved. The camels are lying down, and cannot be made to rise; no one has strength to walk; only he that has a glass of that precious liquid lives to walk a mile farther, and perhaps dies too. If the voyages on seas are dangerous, so are those in the deserts. At sea, the provisions very often fail; in the desert, it is worse. At sea, storms are met with; in the desert there cannot be a greater storm than to find a dry well. At sea, one meets pirates; we escape, we surrender, or die; in the desert they rob the traveller of all his property and water. They let him live, perhaps, but what a life! to die the most barbarous and agonizing death. In short, to be thirsty in a desert, without water, exposed to the burning sun, without shelter, and no hopes of finding either, is the most terrible situation that a man can be placed in, and I believe that it is one of the greatest sufferings that a human being can sustain. The eyes grow inflamed, the tongue and lips swell, a hollow sound is heard in the ears, which brings on deafness, and the brains appear to grow thick and inflamed. All these feelings arise from the want of a little water. In the midst of all this misery, the deceitful mirages appear before the traveller, at no great distance, something like a lake or river of clear fresh water. The deception of this phenomenon is well known, but it does not fail to invite the longing traveller towards that element, and to put him in remembrance of the happiness of being on such a spot. If perchance a traveller is not undeceived, he hastens his pace to reach it sooner: the more he advances towards it, the more it goes from him, till at last it vanishes entirely, and the deluded passenger often asks where is the water he saw at no great distance. He can scarcely believe that he was so deceived; he protests that he saw the waves running before the wind, and the reflection of the high rocks in the water. (Belzoni.)—Burder.

Ver. 16. For he hath broken the gates of brass, and cut the bars of iron in sunder.

See on Acts 12. 10.

PSALM CIX.

Ver. 9. Let his children be fatherless, and his wife a widow. 10. Let his children be continually vagabonds, and beg: let them seek *their bread* also out of their desolate places.

Listen to two married men who are quarrelling, you will hear the one accost the other, "Thy family will soon come to destruction." "And what will become of thine?" rejoins the other: "I will tell thee; thy wife will soon take off her *thāli*," which means she will be a widow, as the *thāli* is the marriage jewel, which must be taken off on the death of a husband. "Yes, thy children will soon be beggars; I shall see them at *my door*."—Roberts.

Ver. 23. I am gone like the shadow when it declineth: I am tossed up and down as the locust.

See on 2 Chron. 7. 13.

Dr. Shaw, speaking of the swarms of locusts, which he saw near Algiers, in 1724 and 1725, says, "when the wind blew briskly, so that these swarms were crowded by others, we had a lively idea of that comparison of the Psalmist, of being *tossed up and down as the locust*."—Burder.

PSALM CX.

Ver. 1. The Lord said unto my Lord, Sit thou at my right hand, until I make thine enemies thy footstool.

The host always places a distinguished guest on his right hand, because that side is considered more honourable than the other. Hence the rank known by the name of *valangkiyar*, right-hand caste, is very superior to the *idungkiyar*, or left-hand caste.—Roberts.

PSALM CXII.

Ver. 10. The wicked shall see *it*, and be grieved; he shall gnash with his teeth, and melt away; the desire of the wicked shall perish.

An enraged man snaps his teeth together, as if about to bite the object of his anger. Thus, in the book *Rāmyanum*, the giant *Rāvanan* is described as in his fury gnashing together his "thirty-two teeth!" "Look at the beast, how he gnashes his teeth." "Go near that fellow."—"Not I, indeed, he will only gnash his teeth."—Roberts.

PSALM CXIII.

Ver. 9. He maketh the barren woman to keep house, *to be* a joyful mother of children.

Should a married woman, who has long been considered steril, become a mother, her joy, and that of her husband and friends, is most extravagant. "They called her *Malady*," *i. e.* barren, "but she has given us some good fruit." "My neighbours pointed at me, and said, *Malady*: but what will they say now?" A man who manifests great delight, is said to be like the barren woman, who has borne a child. Of any thing which is exceedingly valuable, it is said, "This is as precious as the son of the barren woman," *i. e.* of her who had long been reputed barren.—Roberts.

PSALM CXIX.

Ver. 82. Mine eyes fail for thy word, saying, When wilt thou comfort me?

Has a mother promised to visit her son or daughter, and should she not be able to go, the son or daughter will say, "Alas! my mother promised to come to me; how long have I been looking for her? but a speck has grown upon my eye." "I cannot see, my eyes have failed me;" *i. e.* by looking so intensely for her coming.—Roberts.

Ver. 83. For I am become like a bottle in the smoke; *yet* do I not forget thy statutes.

Bottles are made of the skins of goats, sheep, and other animals; and there are several articles preserved in them, in the same way as the English keep hogs' lard in bladders. Some kinds of medicinal oil, assafœtida, honey, a kind of treacle, and other drugs, are kept for a great length of time, by hanging the bottles in the smoke, which soon causes them to become black and shrivelled. The Psalmist was ready to faint for the salvation of the Lord: his eyes had failed in looking for His blessing, and anxiety had made him like unto a skin bottle, shrivelled and blackened in the smoke.—Roberts.

Cups and drinking vessels of gold and silver were doubtless used in the courts of princes. (1 Kings x. 21.) But in the Arab tents leathern bottles, as well as pitchers, were used. These of course were smoky habitations. To this latter circumstance, and the contrast between the drinking utensils, the Psalmist alludes: "My appearance in my present state is as different from what it was when I dwelt at court, as the furniture of a palace differs from that of a poor Arab's tent."—Harmer.

The eastern bottle is made of a goat or kid skin, stripped off, without opening the belly; the apertures made by cutting off the tail and legs are sewed up, and when filled, it is tied about the neck. The Arabs and Persians never go a journey without a small leathern bottle of water hanging by their side like a scrip. These skin bottles preserve their water, milk, and other liquids, in a fresher state than any other vessels they can use. The people of the East, indeed, put into them every thing they mean to carry to a distance, whether dry or liquid, and very rarely make use of boxes and pots, unless to preserve such things as are liable to be broken. They enclose these leathern bottles in woollen sacks, because their beasts of carriage often fall down under their load, or cast it down on the sandy desert. This method of transporting the necessaries of life has another advantage; the skin bottles preserve them fresher; defend them against the ants, and other insects, which cannot penetrate the skin; and prevent the dust, of which immense quantities are constantly moving about, in the arid regions of Asia, and so fine, that no coffer is impenetrable to it, from reaching them. It is for these reasons that provisions of every kind are enclosed in vessels made of the skins of these animals. The conjecture, therefore, is highly probable, that not only the balm and the honey, which are somewhat liquid, but also the nuts and almonds, which were sent as a present to Joseph from Canaan, were enclosed in little vessels of kid skin, that they might be preserved fresh; and to defend them against injuries, from the restiveness of the camels or asses, or other accidents, the whole were enclosed in woollen sacks. This custom has descended to the present times; for fruits and provisions of every kind are still commonly packed up in skins, by the inhabitants of Syria.

To those goat-skin vessels the Psalmist refers in this complaint: "I am become as a bottle in the smoke." My appearance in the state of my exile is as different from what it was when I dwelt at court, as are the gold and silver vessels of a palace, from the smoky skin bottle of a poor Arab's tent, where I am now compelled to reside. Not less emphatical is the lamentation of the prophet, that the precious sons of Zion, comparable to fine gold, or to vessels fabricated of that precious metal, were considered as no better than earthen pitchers, the work of the potter. The holy Psalmist compares himself to a bottle in the smoke; which is a convertible phrase with a bottle in the tent of an Arab; because, when fires are lighted in it, the smoke instantly fills every part, and greatly incommodes the tenant. Nor will this appear surprising, when it is considered that an Arabian tent has no aperture but the door, from which the smoke can escape. The inspired writer, therefore, seems to allude both to the meanness of a skin bottle, and to its blackness, from the smoke of the tent in which it is placed. And a most natural image it was for him to use, driven from the vessels of silver and gold in the palace of Saul, to quench his thirst with the wandering Arabs, from a smutted bottle of goat-skin. These bottles are liable to be rent, when old or much used, and at the same time capable of being repaired. In the book of Joshua we are informed, the Gibeonites "took wine bottles, old and rent, and bound up." This is perfectly according to the custom of the East; and the manner in which they mend their old and rent bottles is various. Sometimes they set in a piece; sometimes they gather up the wounded place in the manner of a purse; sometimes they put in a round flat piece of wood, and by that means stop the hole.—Paxton.

Ver. 103. How sweet are thy words unto my taste! *yea, sweeter* than honey to my mouth.

An affectionate wife often says, "My husband, your words are sweeter to me than honey; yes, they are sweeter than the sugarcane." "Alas! my husband is gone," says the widow; "how sweet were his words! honey dropped from his mouth; his words were ambrosia."—Roberts.

Ver. 136. Rivers of water run down mine eyes, because they keep not thy law.

This figure occurs in the poem called *Veerale-vudu-toothe*. "Rivers of tears run down the face of that mother bereft of her children," is a saying in common use. "The water of her eyes runs like a river."—Roberts.

PSALM CXX.

Ver. 4. Sharp arrows of the mighty, with coals of juniper.

"Coals of juniper;" more properly, like the glowing of coals of broom. The Hebrew word *rothem*, here translated juniper, means a shrub of the genista or broom species, the Spartium junceum of Linnæus, which grows in the south of France and in Spain, where it has retained its Arabic name, roterna. It is a moderate shrub, with thin branches, and white flowers, that grows in the deserts. Forskal found it frequently in the sandy heaths about Suez. The caravans use it for fuel. When the Psalmist compares the tongue of the slanderer with the glowing of the coals of broom, he doubtless alludes to the severe pain caused by touching those coals, which continue to glow for a very long time.—Rosenmuller.

PSALM CXXI.

Ver. 5. The Lord *is* thy keeper; the Lord *is* thy shade upon thy right hand.

An umbrella is a very ancient, as well as honourable defence against the pernicious effects of the scorching beams of the sun, in those sultry countries; may we not then suppose this is that kind of shade the Psalmist refers to in the 121st Psalm? ver. 5, "The Lord is thy keeper; the Lord is thy shade upon thy right hand." "The sun shall not smite thee by day, nor the moon by night."

Niebuhr, who visited the southern part of Arabia, gives us the following account of a solemn procession of the Iman that resides at Sana, who is a great prince in that part of Arabia, and considered as a holy personage, being descended from Mohammed, their great prophet. "It is well known that the sultan at Constantinople goes every Friday to the mosque, if his health will at all admit of it. The Iman of Sana observes also this religious practice, with vast pomp. We only saw him in his return, because this was represented to us as the most curious part of the solemnity, on account of the long circuit he then takes, and the great number of his attendants, after their having performed their devotions in other mosques...... The Iman was preceded by some hundreds of soldiers. He, and each of the princes of his numerous family, caused a *mdalla*, or large umbrella, to be carried by his side, and it is a privilege which, in this country, is appropriated to princes of the blood, just as the sultan of Constantinople permits none but his vizier to have his kaik, or gondola, covered behind, to keep him from the heat of the sun. They say that in the other provinces of Yemen, the independent lords, such, for example, as the sheiks of Jafâ, and those of Haschid u Bekil, the scherif of Abu Arisch, and many others, cause these *mdallas*, in like manner, to be carried for their use, as a mark of their independence. Besides the princes, the Iman had in his train at least six hundred lords of the most distinguished rank, as well ecclesiastics as seculars, and those of the military line, many of them mounted on superb horses, and a great multitude of people attended him on foot. On each side of the Iman was carried a flag, different from ours, in that each of them was surmounted with a little silver vessel like a censer. It is said that within some charms were put, to which they attributed a power of making the Iman invincible. Many other standards were unfurled with the same censer-like vessels, but without any regularity. In one word, the whole train was numerous, and in some measure magnificent, but no order seemingly was observed."

It appears by the carvings at Persepolis, umbrellas were very anciently used by the eastern princes; charms, we have reason to believe, were at least as ancient: may we not, with some degree of probability, suppose then this 121st Psalm refers to these umbrellas, where the response made, probably, by the ministers of the sanctuary, to the declaration of the king, in the two first verses, reminded him that Jehovah would be to him all that heathen princes hoped for, as to defence and honour, from their royal umbrellas and their sacred charms, but hoped for in vain, as to them? "The Lord shall be thy shade on thy right hand. The sun shall not smite thee by day nor the moon by night."—Harmer.

Ver. 6. The sun shall not smite thee by day, nor the moon by night.

A meridian summer's sun in England gives but a faint idea of the power of this luminary in the East; and yet, even in this temperate climate, who has not been inconvenienced when exposed to his rays? But how much greater is his effect in India! Sometimes "a stroke of the sun" smites man and beast with *instant* death. The moon has also a pernicious effect upon those who sleep in its beams: and fish, having been exposed to them for one night, becomes most injurious to those who eat it: hence our English seamen, when sailing in tropical climes, always take care to place their fish out of "the sight of the moon."—Roberts.

The very severe cold of the nights in the East was ascribed by the ancients to the influence of the moon, which they also supposed to be the origin of the dew. Macrobius says "that the nurses used to cover their sucklings against the moon, that they might not, as damp wood which bends in the heat, get crooked limbs from the superabundance of moisture. It is also well known," continues he, "that he who has slept in the moonlight is heavy when he awakes, and as if deprived of his senses, and, as it were, oppressed by the weight of the dampness which is spread over his whole body." The same opinion of the injurious effects of the light of the moon upon the human body, still prevailed in the East Indies in later times. Iwrgen Anderson, in his Description of the East, says, "One must here (in Batavia) take great care not to sleep in the beams of the moon uncovered. I have seen many people whose neck has become crooked, so that they look more to the side than forward. I will not decide whether it is to be ascribed to the moon, as people imagine here." In some of the southern parts of Europe the same opinions are entertained of the pernicious influence of the moonbeams. An English gentleman walking in the evening in the garden of a Portuguese nobleman at Lisbon, was most seriously admonished by the owner to put on his hat, to protect him from the moonbeams. The fishermen in Sicily are said to cover, during the night, the fish which they expose to dry on the sea-shore, alleging that the beams of the moon cause them to putrefy.—Rosenmuller.

PSALM CXXII.

Ver. 2. Our feet shall stand within thy gates, O Jerusalem.

I think, so far as the sense is concerned, it does not matter whether this be read in the past, present, or future tense; for, in my opinion, the arguments on that subject are of little importance. I believe it to be a declaration of affection for Jerusalem, in which the feet, as the instruments of going to the holy place, were in eastern style naturally associated. The devout Hindoo, when absent from the sacred city of Sedambarum, often exclaims, "Ah! Sedambarum, my feet are ever walking in thee." "Ah! *Siva-stalham*, are not my feet in thee?" A man who has long been absent from his favourite temple, says, on his return, "My feet once more tread this holy place."—Roberts.

PSALM CXXIII.

Ver. 2. Behold, as the eyes of servants *look* unto the hand of their masters, *and* as the eyes of a maiden unto the hand of her mistress; so our eyes *wait* upon the Lord our God, until that he have mercy upon us.

The hand is looked at as the member by which a superior gives protection or dispenses favours; and if this Psalm be, as some suppose, a complaint of the captives in Babylon, it may refer to the hand as the instrument of deliverance. A man in trouble says, "I will look at the hand of my friend." "I looked at the hand of my mistress, and have been comforted." A father, on returning from a journey, says, "My children will look to my hands," i. e. for a present. Of a troublesome person it is said, "He is always looking at my hands." A slave of a cruel master says to his god, "Ah! Swamy, why am I appointed to look at his hands?"—Roberts.

The Easterns direct their servants very generally by signs—even in matters of consequence. The Cingalese intimate their wish for a person to approach, by bending the finger with the point towards the person wanted, as if to seize him—quite in the opposite direction to the English way of beckoning. To depart is signified by a side nod; and a frown by a front one.—Callaway.

The servants or slaves in the East attend their masters or mistresses with the profoundest respect. Maundrell observes, that the servants in Turkey stand round their master and his guests with the profoundest respect, silence, and order, imaginable. Pococke says, that at a visit in Egypt, every thing is done with the greatest decency, and the most profound silence, the slaves or servants standing at the bottom of the room, with their hands joined before them, watching with the utmost attention every motion of their master, who commands them by signs. De La Motraye says, that the eastern ladies are waited on "even at the least wink of the eye, or motion of the fingers, and that in a manner not perceptible to strangers." The Baron De Tott relates a remarkable instance of the authority attending this mode of commanding, and of the use of significant motions. "The customary ceremonies on these occasions were over, and Racub (the new vizier) continued to discourse familiarly with the ambassador, when the *muzar aga* (or high provost) coming into the hall, and approaching the pacha, whispered something in his ear, and we observed that all the answer he received from him was a slight horizontal motion with his hand, after which the vizier instantly resuming an agreeable smile, continued the conversation for some time longer: we then left the hall of audience, and came to the foot of the great staircase, where we remounted our horses: here, nine heads, cut off, and placed in a row on the outside of the first gate, completely explained the *sign*, which the vizier had made use of in our presence." Hence we discover the propriety of the *actions* performed by the prophets. Ezekiel was a sign to the people in not mourning for the dead, (chap. xxiv.) in his removing into captivity, and digging through the wall, (chap. xii.) Such conduct was perfectly well understood, and was very significant.—BURDER.

PSALM CXXIV.

Ver. 7. Our soul is escaped as a bird out of the snare of the fowlers: the snare is broken, and we are escaped.

A man who has narrowly escaped danger says, "My life is like that of the bird which has escaped from the snare." The life of a man is often compared to that of a bird. Thus, of him whose spirit has departed, it is said, "Ah! the bird has left its nest; it has gone away." "As the unhatched bird must first burst from the shell before it can fly, so must this soul burst from its body."—ROBERTS.

PSALM CXXV.

Ver. 2. *As* the mountains *are* round about Jerusalem, so the LORD *is* round about his people from henceforth, even for ever.

The description which Volney gives of his approach to Jerusalem, furnishes no contemptible illustration of this verse; and as it is pleasant to compel an avowed infidel to illustrate and confirm the religion of Christ, which he detests, I shall subjoin his account. "Two days' journey south of Nablous, following the direction of the mountains, which gradually become more rocky and barren, we arrive at a town, which, like many others already mentioned, presents a striking example of the vicissitude of human affairs: when we behold its walls levelled, its ditches filled up, and all its buildings embarrassed with ruins, we scarcely can believe we view that celebrated metropolis, which formerly baffled the efforts of the most powerful empires, and for a time resisted the efforts of Rome herself; though by a whimsical change of fortune, its ruins now receive her homage and reverence: in a word, we with difficulty recognise Jerusalem. Nor is our astonishment less, to think of its ancient greatness, when we consider its situation amidst a rugged soil, destitute of water, and surrounded by dry channels of torrents and steep heights. Distant from every great road, it seems neither to have been calculated for a considerable mart of commerce, nor the centre of a great consumption. It however overcame every obstacle, and may be adduced as a proof of what popular opinion may effect, in the hands of an able legislator, or when favoured by happy circumstances." The proud unbeliever had found a shorter and easier road to his conclusion, in the volume of inspiration; and particularly in the passages quoted above, from the Psalms of David, who refers the singular prosperity of Jerusalem to the peculiar favour of Heaven. This was the real source of her greatness, and it was this alone, and not the natural strength of her situation, nor the skill and valour of her defenders, which enabled her so long to baffle the designs of her enemies.—PAXTON.

PSALM CXXVI.

Ver. 2. Then was our mouth filled with laughter, and our tongue with singing; then said they among the heathen, The LORD hath done great things for them.

"See that happy man; his mouth is always full of laughing, his tongue is always singing; he is ever showing his teeth."—ROBERTS.

Ver. 4. Turn again our captivity, O LORD, as the streams in the south.

This image is taken from the *torrents* in the deserts to the south of Judea; in Idumea, Arabia Petræa, &c., a mountainous country. These torrents were constantly dried up in the summer, (Job vi. 17, 18,) and as constantly *returned* after the rainy season, and filled again their deserted channels. The point of the comparison seems to be the *return* and renewal of these (not *rivers*, but) *torrents*, which yearly leave their beds dry, but fill them again; as the Jews had left their country desolate, but now flowed again into it.—BP. HORNE.

Ver. 5. They that sow in tears shall reap in joy. 6. He that goeth forth and weepeth, bearing precious seed, shall, doubtless, come again with rejoicing, bringing his sheaves *with him*.

See on Ezek. 25. 4.

These figures are taken from agricultural pursuits; the seed, being well watered, will produce a plenteous harvest. The Jews in their captivity had been sowing good seed, had watered it with their tears, and the time was now come for them to reap with joy, and to return with their sheaves rejoicing. It is proverbial to say to a boy who weeps because he must go to school, or because he cannot easily acquire his lesson, "My child, the plants of science require the water of the eyes." "If you sow with tears, the profit will appear in your own hands."—ROBERTS.

The writer of the account of the ruins of Balbec, speaking of the valley in which it stood, observes, that it has very little wood; and adds, "though shade be so essential an article of oriental luxury, yet few plantations of trees are seen in Turkey, the inhabitants being discouraged from labours, which produce such distant and precarious enjoyment, in a country where even the annual fruits of their industry are uncertain. In Palestine we have often seen the husbandman sowing, accompanied by an armed friend, to prevent his being *robbed of the seed*." The Israelites that returned from Babylon upon the proclamation of Cyrus, were in similar circumstances to husbandmen sowing their corn amidst enemies and robbers. The rebuilding of their towns and their temple resembled a time of sowing; but they had reason to fear that the neighbouring nations would defeat these efforts. (Nehem. iv. 7.) In opposition to this apprehension the Psalmist expresses his hope, perhaps *predicts*, that there would be a happy issue of these beginnings, to re-people their country.—HARMER.

PSALM CXXVII.

Ver. 4. As arrows *are* in the hand of a mighty man: so *are* children of the youth. 5. Happy *is* the man that hath his quiver full of them: they shall not be ashamed, but they shall speak with the enemies in the gate.

The margin has, instead of *speak*, "*subdue* the enemies in the gate." In ancient books, and also among the learned, (in common conversation,) sons are spoken of as the arrows of their fathers. To have a numerous male progeny is considered a great advantage; and people are afraid of offending such a family, lest the arrows should be sent at them. "What a fine fellow is the son of Kandan! he is like an arrow in the hand of a hero."—ROBERTS.

The Orientals are accustomed to call brave and valiant sons the "arrows" and "darts" of their parents, because they are able to defend them. "To sharpen arrows," "to make sharp arrows," is among them, to get brave and valiant sons. Merrick mentions a similar Chinese mode of expression. "When a son is born in a family, it is customary to hang up bows and arrows before the house, as a sign that the family has acquired a defender."—ROSENMULLER.

PSALM CXXVIII.

Ver. 3. Thy wife *shall be* as a fruitful vine by the sides of thy house: thy children like olive-plants round about thy table.

The people are exceedingly fond of having their houses covered with different kinds of vines; hence may be seen various creepers thus trained, bearing an abundance of fruit. Many interesting figures, therefore, are taken from plants which are thus SUSTAINED. A priest in blessing a married couple, often says, "Ah! may you be like the trees *Cama-Valley* and *Cat-Pagga-Tharu!*" These are said to grow in the celestial world, and are joined together: the *Cama-Valley*, being parasitical, cannot live without the other.—ROBERTS.

The natives of those countries are careful to decorate their habitations with the choicest products of the vegetable kingdom. The quadrangular court in front of their houses, is adorned with spreading trees, aromatic shrubs, and fragrant flowers, which are continually refreshed by the crystal waters of a fountain playing in the middle. To increase the beauty of the scene they cover the stairs which lead to the upper apartments with vines, and have often a lattice-work of wood raised against the dead walls, upon which climbs a vine, or other mantling shrub. This pleasing custom justifies Doddridge in supposing the occasion of our Lord's comparing himself to a vine, might be his standing near a window, or in some court by the side of the house, where the sight of a vine creeping upon the staircase or the wall might suggest this beautiful simile. This kind of ornament seems to have been very common in Judea, and may be traced to a very remote antiquity. From the familiar manner in which the Psalmist alludes to it, we may suppose it was one of the decorations about the royal palace: "Thy wife shall be as a fruitful vine by the sides of thy house; thy children like olive-plants round about the table. Behold, that thus shall the man be blessed that feareth the Lord." Kimchi, a celebrated Jewish writer, explains the psalm in the same way; and observes, that a wife is compared to a vine, because that alone of all trees can be planted in a house. In confirmation of Kimchi's remark, Dr. Russel says, "It is generally true, if fruit-bearing trees be intended, as the vine is almost the only fruit-tree which is planted in the houses; pomegranates are another."—PAXTON.

PSALM CXXIX.

Ver. 3. The ploughers ploughed upon my back; they made long their furrows.

"The enemies of Israel cut their backs, as the ploughers cut the soil." (Dr. Boothroyd.) When a man is in much trouble through oppressors, he says, "How they plough me and turn me up! All are now ploughing me. Begone! have you not already turned me up?" "Alas! alas! my enemies, nay, my children, are now ploughing me."—ROBERTS.

Ver. 6. Let them be as the grass *upon* the house-tops, which withereth afore it groweth up; 7. Wherewith the mower filleth not his hand, nor he that bindeth sheaves, his bosom.

See on Ruth 2. 4, 5.

The tops of the houses in Judea were flat, and so grass grew upon them, being covered with plaster of terrace. As it was but small and weak, and, being on high, was exposed to the scorching sun, it was soon withered. (Shaw.) Menochius says, that he saw such roofs in the island of Corsica, flat, and having earth upon them, on which grass grew of its own accord; but being burnt up in summer time by the sun, soon withered. But what Olaus Magnus relates is extraordinary. He says, that in the northern Gothic countries they feed their cattle from the tops of houses, especially in a time of siege; that their houses are built of stone, high and large, and covered with rafters of fir and bark of birch: on this is laid grass-earth, cut out of the fields four-square, and sowed with barley or oats, so that their roofs look like green meadows: and that what is sown, and the grass that grows thereon, may not wither before plucked up, they very diligently water it. Maundrell says, that these words allude to the custom of plucking up corn from the roots by handfuls, leaving the most fruitful fields as naked as if nothing had ever grown in them; and that this is done, that they may not lose any of the straw, which is generally very short, and necessary for the sustenance of their cattle, no hay being made in that country.—BURDER.

In the morning the master of the house laid in a stock of earth, which was carried and spread evenly on the top of the house, which is flat. The whole roof is thus formed of mere earth, laid on and rolled hard and flat. On the top of every house is a large stone roller, for the purpose of hardening and flattening this layer of rude soil, so that the rain may not penetrate; but upon this surface, as may be supposed, grass and weeds grow freely. It is to such grass that the Psalmist alludes, as useless and bad.—JOWITT.

The reapers in Palestine and Syria make use of the sickle, in cutting down their crops, and according to the present custom in this country, "fill their hand" with the corn, and those who bind up the sheaves, their "bosom." When the crop is thin and short, which is generally the case in light soils, and with their imperfect cultivation, it is not reaped with the sickle, but plucked up by the root with the hand. By this mode of reaping they leave the most fruitful fields as naked as if nothing had ever grown on them; and as no hay is made in the East, this is done, that they may not lose any of the straw, which is necessary for the sustenance of their cattle. The practice of reaping with the hand is perhaps involved in these words of the Psalmist, to which reference has already been made: "Let them be as the grass upon the house-tops, which withereth afore it groweth up; wherewith the mower filleth not his hand, nor he that bindeth sheaves, his bosom." The tops of the houses in Judea are flat, and being covered with plaster of terrace, are frequently grown over with grass. As it is but small and weak, and from its elevation exposed to the scorching sun, it is soon withered. To prevent this, they pluck it up for the use of their cattle, with the hand. A more beautiful and striking figure, to display the weak and evanescent condition of wicked men, cannot easily be conceived. They are every moment exposed to the judgments of God, like the grass on the house-top, which is tossed by the breeze, and scorched by the sun, and to the grasp of Omnipotence, which, weak and defenceless as they are, they can neither avoid nor resist. The sudden destruction of the wicked is described by the same writer, under another figure not less remarkable for its force and propriety: "I have seen the wicked in great power, and spreading himself like a green bay-tree. Yet he passed away, and, lo, he was not; yea, I sought him, but he could not be found."—PAXTON.

"Ah! that wretched family shall soon be as withered grass." "Go, vile one, for soon wilt thou be as parched grass."—ROBERTS.

PSALM CXXXII.

Ver. 9. Let thy priests be clothed with righteousness; and let thy saints shout for joy.

"See that excellent man; he wears the garments of justice and charity."—ROBERTS.

Ver. 17. There will I make the horn of David to bud: I have ordained a lamp for mine anointed.

"Yes, that man will flourish; already his horn has begun to appear—it is growing."—ROBERTS.

Ver. 18. His enemies will I clothe with shame; but upon himself shall his crown flourish.

This idea seems to be taken from the nature of the ancient crowns bestowed upon conquerors. From the earliest periods of history the laurel, olive, and ivy, furnished crowns to adorn the heads of heroes, who had conquered in the field of battle, gained the prize in the race, or performed some other important service to the public. These were the dear-bought rewards of the most heroic exploits of antiquity. This sets the propriety of the phrase in full view. The idea of a crown of gold and jewels flourishing, is at least unnatural: whereas flourishing is natural to laurels and oaks. These were put upon the heads of the victors in full verdure. (Pirie.)—BURDER.

PSALM CXXXIII.

Ver. 3. As the dew of Hermon, *and as the dew* that descended upon the mountains of Zion: for there the LORD commanded the blessing, *even* life for evermore.

See on Ps. 89. 12.

A great difficulty occurs in the comparison which the Psalmist makes to the dew of Hermon, that fell on the hill of Zion; which might easily be interpreted, if it had been observed, that the clouds which lay on Hermon, being brought by the north winds to Jerusalem, caused the dews to fall plentifully on the hill of Zion. But there is a Shihon mentioned in the tribe of Issachar, (Josh. xix. 19,) which may be the Zion spoken of by Eusebius and Saint Jerome, as near Mount Tabor; and there might be a hill there of that name, on which the dew of the other Hermon might fall, that was to the east of Esdraelon. However, as there is no certainty that Mount Hermon in that part is even mentioned in scripture, so I should rather think it to be spoken of this famous mountain, and that Tabor and Hermon are joined together, as rejoicing in the name of God, not on account of their being near to one another, but because they are two of the highest hills in all Palestine. So that if any one considers this beautiful piece of eloquence of the Psalmist, and that Hermon is elsewhere actually called Zion, (Deut. iv. 48,) he will doubtless be satisfied, that the most natural interpretation of the Psalmist would be to suppose, though the whole might be called both Hermon and Zion, yet that the highest summit of this mountain was in particular called Hermon, and that a lower part of it had the name of Zion; on which supposition, the dew falling from the top of it down to the lower parts, might well be compared in every respect to *the precious ointment upon the head that ran down unto the beard, even unto Aaron's beard, and went down to the skirts of his clothing*, and that both of them in this sense are very proper emblems of the blessings of unity and friendship, which diffuse themselves throughout the whole society. (Pococke.)—BURDER.

When Maundrell was in the neighbourhood of Mount Hermon, he remarked, "We were instructed by experience, what the Psalmist means by the dew of Hermon, our tents being as wet with it as if it had rained all night." In Arabia, says Dr. Shaw, the dew often wets the traveller who has no covering but the heavens, to the skin; but no sooner is the sun risen, and the atmosphere a little heated, than the mists are quickly dispersed, and the copious moisture which the dews communicated to the sands would be entirely evaporated.—PAXTON.

PSALM CXXXV.

Ver. 7. He causeth the vapours to ascend from the ends of the earth: he maketh lightnings for the rain: he bringeth the wind out of his treasures.

In Syria, lightnings are frequent in the autumnal months. Seldom a night passes without a great deal of lightning in the northwest, but without thunder; but when it appears in the west or southwest points, it is a sure sign of approaching rain, and is often attended with thunder. It has been observed already, that a squall of wind and clouds of dust, are the usual forerunners of the first rains. To these natural phenomena, the sacred writers frequently allude; and in the precise order which has been marked in the preceding observations. The royal Psalmist, in a very beautiful strain, ascribes them to the immediate agency of heaven: "He causeth the vapours to ascend from the ends of the earth: he maketh lightnings for the rain: he bringeth the wind out of his treasures." The cisterns of the clouds are replenished by exhalations from every part of the globe; and, when they are ready to open and pour out their refreshing showers on the parched ground, the glad tidings are announced by the rapid lightning, and the precious treasure is scattered over the fields by the attendant winds; and that the sweet singer of Israel looked through nature with an accurate, discriminating eye, is confirmed by the concurring testimony of all ages.—PAXTON.

Russel says, that at Aleppo a night seldom passes without lightning in the northwest quarter, but not attended with thunder. When it appears in the west or southwest points, it is a sure sign of the approaching rain; this lightning is often followed by thunder. Thus "God maketh the lightnings for the rain; and when he uttereth his voice, there is a multitude of waters in the heavens;" and as these refreshing showers are preceded by squalls of wind, "he bringeth forth the wind out of his treasure," Jer. li. 16.—HARMER.

PSALM CXXXVII.

Ver. 1. By the rivers of Babylon there we sat down; yea, we wept, when we remembered Zion.

See on Lam. 2. 10.

Ver. 5. If I forget thee, O Jerusalem, let my right hand forget *her cunning*.

In the Hindoo book, *Scanda-Purāna*, it is written, "Singā-Muggam, on seeing that his heart throbbed, the tears flowed, and his hands and feet forgot their cunning." "Yes; if I lose thee, if I forget thee, it will be like the losing, like the forgetting of these eyes and arms."—ROBERTS.

The last words mean, may my right hand forget, refuse to perform its service; namely, cease to move, be benumbed. A similar, and, as it appears, proverbial expression, is found in an old Arabian poem, in De Sacy's Chrestom Arab: "No, never have I done any thing that could displease thee; if this is not true, may my hand be unable to lift my scourge;" that is, may it be lamed.—ROSENMULLER.

PSALM CXXXVIII.

Ver. 6. Though the LORD *be* high, yet hath he respect unto the lowly: but the proud he knoweth afar off.

This is truly oriental: "*Nān avari veggu tooratila arrika-rain*, i. e. I know him afar off. Let him be at a great distance; allow him to conduct his plans with the greatest secrecy; yet, I compass his path, I am close to him. You pretend to describe the fellow to me: I know him well; there is no need to go near to him, for I can recognise him at the greatest distance. See how he carries his head; look at his gait; who can mistake his proud bearing?" "How does your brother conduct himself?"—"I cannot tell, for he knows me afar off."—ROBERTS.

PSALM CXL.

Ver. 4. Keep me, O LORD, from the hand of the wicked; preserve me from the violent man; who have purposed to overthrow my goings.

See on Ps. 91. 13.

PSALM CXLI.

Ver. 5. Let the righteous smite me; *it shall be* a kindness: and let him reprove me; *it shall be* an excellent oil, *which* shall not break my head: for yet my prayer also *shall be* in their calamities.

Certain oils are said to have a most salutary effect on the head; hence in fevers, or any other complaints which affect the head, the medical men always recommend oil. I have known people who were deranged, cured in a very short time by nothing more than the application of a peculiar kind of oil to the head. There are, however, other kinds, which are believed (when thus applied) to produce delirium. Thus the reproofs of the righteous were compared to excellent oil, which produced a most salutary effect on the head. So common is this practice of anointing the head, that all who can afford it do it every week. But strange as it may appear, the crown of the head is the place selected for chastisement. Thus owners of slaves, or husbands, or schoolmasters, beat the heads of the offenders with their knuckles. Should an urchin come late to school, or forget his lesson, the pedagogue says to some of the other boys, "Go, beat his head." "Begone, fellow! or I will beat thy head." Should a man be thus chastised by an *inferior*, he quotes the old proverb—"If my head is to be beaten, let it be done with the fingers that have rings on;" meaning a man of rank. "Yes, yes; let a holy man smite my head: and what of that? it is an excellent oil." "My master has been beating my head, but it has been good oil for me."—ROBERTS.

Ver. 6. When their judges are overthrown in stony places, they shall hear my words; for they are sweet.

Ainsworth, "Their judges are thrown down by the rock sides." In 2 Chronicles xxv. 12, it is recorded that the children of Judah took ten thousand captives, "and brought them unto the top of the rock, and cast them down from the top of the rock, that they were all broken in pieces." It was a custom in all parts of the East thus to despatch criminals, by casting them down a precipice; the Tarpeian rock affords a similar instance. But who were these judges? probably those "men that work iniquity," as mentioned in the 4th verse. In the 5th verse he speaks of the salutary nature of the reproofs of the RIGHTEOUS, but in the 7th he seems to refer to the cruel results of having UNRIGHTEOUS judges; for in consequence of their SMITINGS he says, "Our bones are scattered at the grave's mouth, as when one cutteth and cleaveth wood;" *i. e.* their bones were like the fragments and chips scattered on the earth, left by the hewers of wood. Therefore these judges were to be "overthrown in stony places."—ROBERTS.

Ver. 7. Our bones are scattered at the grave's mouth, as when one cutteth and cleaveth *wood* upon the earth.

A remarkable expression of the Psalmist David, Psalm cxli. 7, appears to have much poetical heightening in it, which even its author, in all probability, did not mean should be accepted *literally;* while, nevertheless, it might be susceptible of a literal acceptation, and is sometimes a fact.—The Psalmist says, "Our bones are scattered at the grave's mouth, as when one cutteth and cleaveth *wood* upon the earth." This seems to be strong eastern painting, and almost figurative language; but that it may be strictly true, the following extract demonstrates: "At five o'clock we left *Garigana*, our journey being still to the eastward of north; and at a quarter past six in the evening arrived at the village of that name, *whose inhabitants had all perished with hunger the year before; their wretched bones being all unburied, and scattered upon the surface of the ground, where the village formerly stood. We encamped among the bones of the dead; no space could be found free from them;* and on the 23d, at six in the morning, full of horror at this miserable spectacle, we set out for Teawa; this was the seventh day from Ras El Feel. After an hour's travelling, we came to a small river, which still had water standing in some considerable pools, although its banks were destitute of any kind of shade." (Bruce.) The reading of this account thrills us with horror; what then must have been the sufferings of the ancient Jews at such a sight?—when to have no burial was reckoned among the greatest calamities; when their land was thought to be polluted, in which the dead (even criminals) were in any manner exposed to view; and to whom the very touch of a dead body, or part of it, or of any thing that had touched a dead body, was esteemed a defilement, and required a ceremonial ablution?—TAYLOR IN CALMET.

PSALM CXLII.

Ver. 7. Bring my soul out of prison, that I may praise thy name; the righteous shall compass me about; for thou shalt deal bountifully with me.

These people speak of afflictions, difficulties, and sorrows, as so many prisons. "*Iyo intha marryil eppo vuttu pome?*" i. e. "Alas! when will this imprisonment go?" exclaims the man in his difficulties.—ROBERTS.

PSALM CXLIV.

Ver. 12. That our sons *may be* as plants grown up in their youth; *that* our daughters *may be* as corner-stones, polished *after* the similitude of a palace.

Of a man who has a hopeful and beautiful family, it is said, "His sons are like shoots, (springing up from the parent stock,) and his daughters are like carved work and precious stones."—ROBERTS.

Ver. 13. *That* our garners *may be* full, affording all manner of store; *that* our sheep may bring forth thousands and ten thousands in our streets.

The surprising fecundity of the sheep has been celebrated by writers of every class. It has not escaped the notice of the royal Psalmist, who, in a beautiful ascription of praise to the living and the true God, entreats, that the sheep of his chosen people might "bring forth thousands and ten thousands in their streets." In another song of Zion, he represents, by a very elegant metaphor, the numerous flocks, covering like a garment the face of the field: "The pastures are clothed with flocks; the valleys also are covered over with corn; they shout for joy, they also sing." The bold figure is fully warranted by the prodigious numbers of sheep which whitened the extensive pastures of Syria and Canaan. In that part of Arabia which borders on Judea, the patriarch Job possessed at first seven thousand, and after the return of his prosperity, fourteen thousand sheep; and Mesha, the king of Moab, paid the king of Israel "a yearly tribute of a hundred thousand lambs, and an equal number of rams with the wool." In the war which the tribe of Reuben waged with the Hagarites, the former drove away "two hundred and fifty thousand sheep." At the dedication of the temple, Solomon offered in sacrifice "a hundred and twenty thousand sheep." At the feast of the passover, Josiah, the king of Judah, "gave to the people, of the flock, lambs and kids, all for the passover-offerings, for all that were present, to the number of thirty thousand, and three thousand bullocks; these were of the king's substance." The ewe brings forth her young commonly once a year, and in more ungenial climes, seldom more than one lamb at a time. But in the oriental regions, twin lambs are as frequent as they are rare in other places; which accounts in a satisfactory manner for the prodigious numbers which the Syrian shepherd led to the mountains. This uncommon fruitfulness seems to be intimated by Solomon in his address to the spouse: "Thy teeth are like a flock of sheep that are even shorn, which came up from the washing; whereof every one beareth twins, and none is barren among them."—PAXTON.

PSALM CXLVIII.

Ver. 9. Mountains, and all hills; fruitful trees, and all cedars: 10. Beasts, and all cattle; creeping things, and flying fowl: 11. Kings of the earth, and all people; princes, and all judges of the earth: 12. Both young men and maidens; old men and children: 13. Let them praise the name of the LORD: for his name alone is excellent; his glory *is* above the earth and heaven.

Those who are unacquainted with oriental literature, sometimes affect to smile at the addresses which are made in scripture to animate and inanimate nature. "How ridiculous," say they, "to talk about the mountains skipping like rams, and the little hills like lambs!" but they know not that this is according to the figurative and luxuriant genius of the people of the East. The proprietor of lands, forests, orchards, and gardens, often exclaims, when walking among them in time of drought, "Ah! trees, plants, and flowers, tanks and cattle, birds and fish, and all living creatures, sing praises to the gods, and rain shall be given to you."—ROBERTS.

PSALM CXLIX.

Ver. 5. Let the saints be joyful in glory: let them sing aloud upon their beds.

After the troops were assembled, a public sacrifice was offered upon the national altar, which was succeeded by a martial feast prepared for the whole army; and to confirm their purpose and inflame their courage, a hymn to Jehovah closed the festival. The hundred and forty-ninth psalm, was, in the opinion of Doddridge, composed on such an occasion; it was sung when David's army was marching out to war against the remains of the devoted nations of Canaan, and first went up in solemn procession to the house of God, there, as it were, to consecrate the arms he put into their hands. On that occasion, the devout monarch called on his associates in arms (ver. 5) "to sing aloud upon their beds," that is, the couches upon which they reclined at the banquet attending their sacrifices, which gives a clear and important sense to a very obscure and difficult passage. To these military sacrifices and banquets the people were summoned by the sound of two silver trumpets of a cubit long, according to Josephus, but, like ours, wider at bottom. These were blown by two priests, as the law of Moses required; and they were sounded in a particular manner, that the people might know the meaning of the summons. Then the anointed for the war, going from one battalion to another, exhorted the soldiers in the Hebrew language, no other being allowed on that occasion, to fight valiantly for their country, and for the cities of their God. Officers were appointed to give notice, that those whose business it was should make sufficient provision for the army, before they marched; and every tenth man was appointed for this purpose. This arrangement was made by a resolution of the tribes, recorded in the book of Judges: "And we will take ten men of a hundred throughout all the tribes of Israel, and a hundred of a thousand, and a thousand out of ten thousand, to fetch victual for the people, that they may do, when they come to Gibeah of Benjamin, according to all the folly that they have wrought in Israel." Mr. Harmer contends, that "these men were not intended so much to collect food for the use of their companions in that expedition, as to dress it, to serve it up, and to wait upon them in eating it." But although the difference is not very material, the supposition that the tenth part of the army was to forage for the rest is more natural, and at the same time more agreeable to the literal meaning of the text, which signifies to hunt the prey.—PAXTON.

PSALM CL.

Ver. 3. Praise him with the sound of the trumpet: praise him with the psaltery and harp. 4. Praise him with the timbrel and dance: praise him with stringed instruments and organs. 5. Praise him with the loud cymbals: praise him upon the high-sounding cymbals.

Instruments of music were used in the worship of the Most High God: and the Hindoos, in singing praises, and performing religious ceremonies to their deities, always have the same accompaniments. Thus the trumpet and the "high-sounding cymbals," the timbrels, (which correspond partly with the tambarine,) the harp, כנור *kinnor*, (also called *kinnora* in Tamul,) is a stringed instrument, played with the fingers: and may be heard in all their temples at the time of service. The devotee engaged in making offerings often exclaims, "Praise him, O ye musicians! praise him; praise the Swamy:" and great is their enthusiasm; their eyes, their heads, their tongues, their hands, their legs, are all engaged. At a marriage, or when a great man gives a feast, the guests go to the players on instruments, and say, "Praise the noble host, praise the bride and the groom; praise aloud, O cymbals! give forth the voice, ye trumpets; strike up the harp and the timbrel; praise him in the song, serve him, serve him."—ROBERTS.

Ver. 5. Praise him with the loud cymbals: praise him upon the high-sounding cymbals.

The Hebrew word, which is here translated cymbal, signifies rather, metal plates or basins. In the above passage, a larger and smaller kind are probably meant, both of which are still customary in the East. The latter are metal plates, castanets, such as the oriental female dancers take two on each hand, over one finger and the thumb. For military music, they have large plates of the same form. And these are those which are here called "high-sounding cymbals."—BURDER.

THE BOOK OF PROVERBS.

CHAPTER I.

Ver. 1. The proverbs of Solomon, the son of David, king of Israel.

In those periods of remote antiquity, which may with the utmost propriety be styled the infancies of societies and nations, the usual, if not the only mode of instruction, was by detached aphorisms or proverbs. Human wisdom was then indeed in a rude and unfinished state: it was not digested, methodized, or reduced to order and connexion. Those who by genius and reflection, exercised in the school of experience, had accumulated a stock of knowledge, were desirous of reducing it into the most compendious form, and comprised in a few maxims those observations which they apprehended most essential to human happiness. This mode of instruction was, in truth, more likely than any other to prove efficacious with men in a rude stage of society; for it professed not to dispute, but to command; not to persuade, but to compel: it conducted them, not by a circuit of argument, but led immediately to the approbation and practice of integrity and virtue. That it might not, however, be altogether destitute of allurement, and lest it should disgust by an appearance of roughness and severity, some degree of ornament became necessary; and the instructers of mankind added to their precepts the graces of harmony, and illuminated them with metaphors, comparisons, allusions, and the other embellishments of style. This manner, which with other nations prevailed only during the first periods of civilization, with the Hebrews continued to be a favourite style to the latest ages of their literature.—LOWTH.

Ver. 6. To understand a proverb, and the interpretation; the words of the wise, and their dark sayings.

The people of the East look upon the acquirements of antiquity as being every way superior to those of modern times: thus their noblest works of art and their sciences are indebted to antiquity for their invention and perfection. Instead, therefore, of their minds being enlightened and excited by the splendid productions of modern genius, they are ever reverting to the wisdom of their forefathers, and sighing over the loss of many of their occult sciences. We, on the other hand, by contemplating the imposing achievements of the present age, are in danger of looking with contempt on antiquity, and of pursuing with thoughtless avidity the novelties and speculations of modern inventions.

Solomon could repeat "three thousand proverbs, and his songs were a thousand and five;" and many of the philosophers of the present age in the East have scarcely any other wisdom. Listen to two men engaged in argument: should he who is on the point of being foiled, quote an apposite proverb against his antagonist, an advantage is considered as having been gained, which scarcely any thing can counteract. See a man who is pondering over some difficulty: his reason cannot decide as to the course he ought to pursue, when, perhaps, some one repeats a *pallamulle*, i. e. an old saying: the whole of his doubts are at once removed, and he starts with vigour in the prescribed course.

"Young man, talk not to me with INFANT wisdom, what are the sayings of the ancients! you ought to obey your parents. Listen! 'The father and the mother are the first deities a child has to acknowledge.' Is it not said, 'Children who obey willingly are as ambrosia to the gods?'" "Were you my friend, you would not act thus; because, as the proverb says, 'True friends have but one soul in two bodies.'" "I am told you have been trying to ruin me; 'but will the moon be injured by the barking of a dog?'" "You have become proud, and conduct yourself like the upstart who must 'carry his silk umbrella to keep off the sun at midnight!'" "You talk about your hopes of some coming good: what say the ancients? 'EXPECTATION is the midday dream of life.'" "Cease to be indolent, for, as our fathers said, 'Idleness is the rust of the mind.'" "That you have been guilty of many crimes I cannot doubt, as the proverb says, 'Will there be smoke without fire?' Your wife has, I fear, led you astray, but she will be your ruin: what said the men of antiquity? 'As is the affection of a file for the iron, of a parasitical plant for the tree which supports it; so is the affection of a violent woman for her husband: she is like *Yama*, (the deity of death,) who eats and destroys without appearing to do so.'" With these specimens, the English reader may form a tolerable idea of the importance which is attached to proverbs.—ROBERTS.

Ver. 19. So *are* the ways of every one that is greedy of gain; *which* taketh away the life of the owners thereof.

The words rendered "greedy of gain," denote one who cuts or clips off every scrap of money he possibly can. In the times of Abraham and Moses, and long after, they used to weigh their silver, and, no doubt, to cut and clip off pieces of it, to make weight in their dealings with each other, as is practised by some nations, particularly the Chinese, to this day.—BURDER.

Ver. 26. I also will laugh at your calamity; I will mock when your fear cometh; 27. When your fear cometh as desolation, and your destruction cometh as a whirlwind; when distress and anguish cometh upon you.

According to Savary, the south wind, which blows in Egypt from February to May, fills the atmosphere with a subtile dust, which impedes respiration, and brings with it pernicious vapours. Sometimes it appears only in the shape of an impetuous whirlwind, which passes rapidly, and is fatal to the traveller, surprised in the middle of the deserts. Torrents of burning sand roll before it, the firmament is enveloped in a thick veil, and the sun appears of the colour of blood. It is therefore with strict propriety that the sacred writers distinguish from all others the whirlwinds of the south, and with peculiar force and beauty, compare the sudden approach of calamity to their impetuous and destructive career. "I also will laugh at your calamity; I will mock when your fear cometh: when your fear cometh as desolation, and your destruction cometh as a whirlwind: when distress and anguish cometh upon you." Whole caravans have been overwhelmed in a moment, by the immense quantity of sand which it puts in motion. The Arab who conducted Mr. Bruce through the frightful deserts of Senaar, pointed out to him a spot among some sandy hillocks, where the ground seemed to be more elevated than the rest, where one of the largest caravans which ever came out of Egypt was covered with sand, to the number of several thousand camels. This awful phenomenon Addison has well described in the following lines, which he puts into the mouth of Syphax, a Numidian prince:—

"So where our wide Numidian states extend,
Sudden the impetuous hurricanes descend,
Wheel through the air, in circling eddies play,
Tear up the sands, and sweep whole plains away.
The helpless traveller, with wild surprise,
Sees the dry desert all around him rise,
And, smothered in the dusty whirlwind, dies."—PAXTON.

CHAPTER III.

Ver. 8. It shall be health to thy navel, and marrow to thy bones.

The navel of an infant is often very clumsily managed in the East: hence it is no uncommon thing to see that part greatly enlarged, and diseased. The fear of the Lord, therefore, would be as medicine and health to the navel, causing it to grow and prosper. Strange as it may appear, the navel is often spoken of as a criterion of prosperity; and Solomon appears to have had the same idea, for he mentions this health of the navel as being the result of trusting in the Lord, and of acknowledging Him in all our ways. He says in the next verse, "Honour the Lord with thy substance, and with the first-fruits of all thine increase: so shall thy barns be filled with plenty, and thy presses shall burst out with new wine." And this reference to the navel, as being connected with earthly prosperity, is common at this day. Has a person arisen from poverty to affluence, it is said, "His navel has grown much larger." Should he insult the man from whom he has derived his prosperity, the latter will ask, "Who made your navel to grow?"—ROBERTS.

Medicines in the East are chiefly applied externally, and in particular to the stomach and belly. This comparison, Chardin says, is drawn from the plasters, ointments, oils, and frictions, which are made use of in the East upon the belly and stomach in most maladies; they being ignorant in the villages, of the art of making decoctions and potions, and the proper doses of such things.—HARMER.

CHAPTER IV.

Ver. 13. Take fast hold of instruction; let *her* not go: keep her; for she *is* thy life.

It is said of the fixed will or purpose of those who take fast hold of learning or any other thing, "Ah! they are like the hand of the monkey in the shell of the cocoa-nut; it will not let go the rice."

"On the banks of a broad river there was once a very large herd of monkeys, which greatly injured the fields and gardens of the inhabitants. Several consultations were held as to the best way of getting rid of those troublesome marauders: to take their lives was altogether contrary to their religious prejudices of the people; and to take them in traps was almost impossible, as the monkeys never approached any place without well examining the ground. At last it was determined to procure a sufficient number of cocoa-nuts; to make in each a small hole, and fill them with rice. These were strewed on the ground, and the people retired to watch the success of their plan. The offenders soon went to the place, and seeing the rice (their favourite food) in the nuts, they began to eat the few grains scattered about on the ground: but these only exciting their appetite, they each thrust a HAND through the small hole into the nut, which was soon clasped full of rice. The HAND now became so enlarged that it could not be withdrawn without losing its booty: to leave such a dainty was more than the monkey could consent to: the people therefore came forward, and soon seized their foes, as the cocoa-nut attached to the hand prevented them from getting quickly out of the way. They were, therefore, all made prisoners, and ferried across the river, and left to seek their food in the wilderness." "Take fast hold of instruction; let her not go; keep her; for she is thy life."—ROBERTS.

CHAPTER V.

Ver. 18. Let thy fountain be blessed; and rejoice with the wife of thy youth. 19. *Let her be as* the loving hind and pleasant roe; let her breasts satisfy thee at all times, and be thou ravished always with her love.

The hind is celebrated for affection to her mate; hence a man, in speaking of his wife, often calls her by that name. "My hind, my hind! where is my hind?" "Alas! my hind has fallen; the arrow has pierced her life."—ROBERTS.

The hind of loves, and the roe of grace, in the language of the ancient Hebrews, mean, the amiable hind and the lovely roe. These creatures, it is generally admitted, in the whole form of their bodies, and in all their dispositions and manners, are wonderfully pleasing. The ancients were particularly delighted with them; they kept them in their houses; they fed them at their tables with the greatest care; they washed, and combed, and adorned them with garlands of flowers, and chains of gold or silver. The hind seems to have been admitted to all those privileges, except that of reposing with her master on the same couch, which must have been rendered inconvenient by the largeness of her size. If these things are duly considered, the charge of the wise man will not appear so singular; to the ear of an Oriental it was quite intelligible, and perfectly proper. Let a man tenderly love his spouse; relax in her company from the severer duties of life; take pleasure in her innocent and amiable conversation; and in fine, treat her with all the kindness, and admit her to all the familiarity, which the beauty of her form, the excellence of her dispositions, and the nearness of her relation, entitle her to expect. —PAXTON.

The Orientals still compare a beautiful woman to a hind, or the gazelle, which resembles the roe. "When the Arabs wish to describe the beauty of a woman, they say, that she has the eyes of a gazelle. All their songs, in which they celebrate their mistresses, speak of nothing but gazelle eyes, and they need only compare them to this animal, to describe, in one word, a perfect beauty. The gazelle is in fact a very pretty animal; it has something innocently timid about it, not unlike the modesty and bashfulness of a young girl." (D'Arvieux.) Sparrmann says of the Cape or African gazelle, which is very nearly related to that of Palestine, "This animal is, perhaps, the most beautiful of all gazelles, and is particularly distinguished, as the gazelle in general, for its fiery and beautiful eyes: hence, in some parts of the East, it is properly considered as the greatest praise which can be bestowed on the beauty of a woman, to say, Thy eyes are like the eyes of a gazelle."—ROSENMULLER.

Ver. 19. *Let her be as* the loving hind and pleasant roe; let her breasts satisfy thee at all times, and be thou ravished always with her love.

See on 2 Sam. 2. 18.

CHAPTER VI.

Ver. 1. My son, if thou be surety for thy friend, *if* thou hast stricken thy hand with a stranger, 2. Thou art snared with the words of thy mouth.

It was at first reckoned sufficient if the covenant was made in the presence of all the people; but in process of time, the ceremony of striking hands was introduced at the conclusion of a bargain, which has maintained its ground among the customs of civilized nations down to the present time. To strike hands with another was the emblem of agreement among the Greeks under the walls of Troy; for Nestor complains, in a public assembly of the chiefs, that the Trojans had violated the engagements which they had sanctioned by libations of wine, and giving their right hands. And in another passage, Agamemnon protests that the agreement which the Trojans had ratified by the blood of lambs, libations of wine, and their right hands, could not in any way be set aside. The Roman faith was plighted in the same way; for in Virgil, when Dido marked from her watch-towers the Trojan fleet setting forward with balanced sails, she exclaimed, Is this the honour, the faith? "En dextra fidesque?" The wise man alludes often to this mode of ratifying a bargain, which shows it was in general practice among the people: "My son, if thou be surety for thy friend, if thou hast stricken thy hand with a stranger, thou art snared with the words of thy mouth." Traces of this custom may be discovered in ages long anterior to that in which Solomon flourished; for Job, in his solemn appeal to God from the tribunal of men, thus expresses himself: "Lay down now, put me in surety with thee; who is he that will strike hands with me?"—PAXTON.

Ver. 5. Deliver thyself as a roe from the hand *of the hunter*, and as a bird from the hand of the fowler.

Does a man complain of his numerous enemies, it will be said, "Leap away, friend, as the deer from the snare." "Fly off, fly off, as the bird from the fowler." "Go slyly to the place; and then, should you see the snare, fly away like a bird."—ROBERTS.

Before dogs were so generally employed, the hunters were obliged to make use of nets and snares, to entangle the game. When the antelope finds itself enclosed in the toils, terror lends it additional strength and activity; it strains every nerve, with vigorous and incessant exertion, to break the snare, and escape before the pursuer arrives. And such is the conduct which the wise man recommends to him who has rashly engaged to be surety for his neighbour: "Deliver thyself as (an antelope) from the hand of the hunter, and as a bird from the hand of the fowler." The snare is spread, the adversary is at hand, instantly exert all thy powers to obtain a discharge of the obligation; a moment's hesitation may involve thee and thy family in irretrievable ruin.—PAXTON.

Ver. 6. Go to the ant, thou sluggard; consider her ways, and be wise.

The name of this minute insect in Hebrew is (נמלה) *nemala*, from a root which signifies to cut down; perhaps because the God of nature has taught it to divide or cut off the top of the grain, which it lays up in its subterraneous cells for the winter, to prevent their germination. This operation is attested by numerous ancient writers, among whom we observe the celebrated names of Pliny and Plutarch. It is at least certain, that the ant cuts off the tops of growing corn, that it may seize upon the grain; which may perhaps be the true reason of its Hebrew name. The allusions to this little animal in the sacred writings, although not numerous, are by no means unimportant. The wisest of men refers us to the bright example of its foresight and activity: "Go to the ant, thou sluggard; consider her ways, and be wise: which having no guide, overseer, or ruler, provideth her meat in the summer, and gathereth her food in the harvest." Their uniform care and promptitude in improving every moment as it passes; the admirable order in which they proceed to the scene of action; the perfect harmony which reigns in their bands; the eagerness which they discover in running to the assistance of the weak or the fatigued; the readiness with which those that have no burden yield the way to their fellows that bend under their loads, or when the grain happens to be too heavy, cut it in two, and take the half upon their own shoulders; furnish a striking example of industry, benevolence, and concord, to the human family. Nor should the skill and vigour which they display in digging under ground, in building their houses, and in constructing their cells, in filling their granaries with corn for the winter, in forming channels for carrying off the rain, in bringing forth their hidden stores which are in danger of spoiling by the moisture, and exposing them to the sun and air, be passed over in silence. These, and many other operations, clearly show how instructive a teacher is the ant, even to men of understanding; and how much reason Solomon had to hold up its shining example to their imitation.

We find another allusion to the ant near the close of the same book: "The ants are a people not strong, yet they prepare their meat in the summer." It is, according to the royal preacher, one of those things which are little upon the earth, but exceeding wise. The superior wisdom of the ant has been recognised by many writers. Horace, in the passage from which the preceding quotation is taken, praises its sagacity; Virgil celebrates its foresight, in providing for the wants and infirmities of old age, while it is young and vigorous:

——"atque inopi metuens formica senectæ."

And we learn from Hesiod, that among the earliest Greeks it was called Idris; that is, wise, because it foresaw the coming storm, and the inauspicious day, and collected her store. Aristotle observes, that some of those animals which have no blood, possess more intelligence and sagacity than some that have blood; among which are the bees and the ants. Cicero believed that the ant is not only furnished with senses, but also with mind, reason, and memory: "In formica non modo sensus sed etiam mens, ratio, memoriæ." Some authors go so far as to prefer the ant to man himself, on account of the vigorous intelligence and sagacity which they display in all their operations. Although this opinion is justly chargeable with extravagance, yet it must be admitted, that the union of so many noble qualities in so small a corpuscle, is one of the most remarkable phenomena in the works of nature. This is admitted by Solomon himself: "The ants are a people not strong, yet they prepare their meat in the summer." He calls them a people, because they are gregarious; living in a state of society, though without any king or leader to maintain order and superintend their affairs. The term people is frequently applied to them by ancient writers. Ælian says, in a passage already quoted, that the ants which ascend the stalks of growing corn, throw down the spikes which they have bit off, τω δημω, τω κατω, to the people, that is, the ants below. Apuleius, describing the manner in which the ants convoke an assembly of the nations, says, that when the signal is given, Ruunt aliæ superque aliæ sepedum populorum undæ. The wise man adds, they are not strong; that is, they are feeble insects; nor is it possible that great strength can reside in so minute a creature. Hence the Arabians say contemptuously of a man that has become weak and infirm, "he is feebler than the ant."—PAXTON.

Ver. 13. He winketh with his eyes, he speaketh with his feet, he teacheth with his fingers

See on Matt. 6. 3.

It should be remembered, that when people are in their houses, they do not wear sandals; consequently their feet and toes are exposed. When guests wish to speak with each other, so as not to be observed by the host, they convey their meaning by the feet and toes. Does a person wish to leave a room in company with another, he lifts up one of his feet; and should the other refuse, he also lifts up a foot, and then suddenly puts it down on the ground.

"He teacheth with his fingers." When merchants wish to make a bargain in the presence of others, without making known their terms, they sit on the ground, have a piece of cloth thrown over the lap, and then put each a hand under, and thus speak with the fingers! When the Bramins convey religious mysteries to their disciples, they teach with their fingers, having the hands concealed in the folds of their robes.—ROBERTS.

Ver. 27. Can a man take fire in his bosom, and his clothes not be burnt?

When an individual denies a crime of which he has been accused, it will be asked, "Will you put fire in your bosom?" "I am innocent, I am innocent; in proof of which I will put fire in my bosom." Does a man boast he will do that which is impossible, another will say, "He is going to put fire in his bosom without being burned."—ROBERTS.

Ver. 34. For jealousy *is* the rage of a man; therefore he will not spare in the day of vengeance.

Jealousy is very common and powerful among the people of the East; and is frequently carried to an extent, of which we have no example in European countries. "Whoever, in Persia, has the misfortune to see, or the imprudence to look at, the wife of a man of rank, were it but as she travels on the road, and at ever so great a distance, is sure to be severely beaten by her eunuchs, and, perhaps, put to death; and to meet any of the king's concubines is such a capital crime, that, on a certain occasion, when the favourite queen happened, during the chase, to be overtaken by a storm, and under the necessity of taking refuge in a hamlet, not one of the people would let her majesty in, that they might not have the misfortune of seeing her." (Michaelis.)—BURDER.

CHAPTER VII.

Ver. 10. And, behold, there met him a woman, *with* the attire of a harlot, and subtle of heart.

Females of that class are generally dressed in scarlet; have their robes wound tightly round their bodies; their eyelids and finger nails are painted or stained; and they wear numerous ornaments. (2 Kings ix. 30.) See on Isa. iii. 16, and following verses.—ROBERTS.

Ver. 11. She *is* loud and stubborn; her feet abide not in her house.

In ancient Greece, the women were strictly confined within their lodgings, especially virgins and widows; of whom the former, as having less experience in the world, were more closely watched. Their apartment was commonly well guarded with locks and bolts; and sometimes they were so straitly confined, that they could not pass from one part to another without permission. New-married women were almost under as strict a confinement as virgins; but when once they had brought forth a child, they commonly enjoyed greater liberty. This indulgence, however, was entirely owing to the kindness of their husbands; for those who were jealous or morose, kept their wives in perpetual imprisonment. But how gentle and kind soever husbands might be, it was considered as very indecent for women to go abroad. A Jewess was not so much confined; but still it was deemed improper for her to appear much in public; for in Hebrew she is called (עלמה) *almah*, from a verb which signifies to hide or conceal, because she was seldom or never permitted to mingle in promiscuous company. The married women, though less restrained, were still expected to keep at home, and occupy their time in the management of their household. In the book of Proverbs, the wise man states it as a mark of a dissolute woman, that "her feet abide not in her house:" while "every wise woman," by her industrious and prudent conduct, "buildeth her house." "She looketh well to the ways of her household, and eateth not the bread of idleness."—PAXTON.

Ver. 16. I have decked my bed with coverings of tapestry, with carved *works*, with fine linen of Egypt.

We are not to suppose that all beds were alike; no doubt, when King David wanted warmth, his attendants would put both mattresses below, and coverlets above, to procure it for him. Neither are we to understand, when a bed is the subject of boasting, that it consisted merely of the *krabbaton*, or *oresh*. In Pro. vii. 16, the harlot vaunts of her bed, as highly ornamented "with tapestry-work—with brocade I have brocaded—bedecked—my *oresh;* the covering to my duan (rather the *makass*) is fine linen of Egypt, embossed with embroidery." This description may be much illustrated by the account which Baron De Tott gives of a bed, in which he was expected to sleep, and in which he might have slept, had not European habit incapacitated him from that enjoyment: "The time for taking our repose was now come, and we were conducted into another large room, in the middle of which was a kind of bed, *without bedstead or curtains*. Though the coverlet and pillows exceeded in magnificence the richness of the sofa, which likewise ornamented the apartment, I foresaw that I could expect but little rest on this bed, and had the curiosity to examine its make in a more particular manner. *Fifteen mattresses of quilted cotton, about three inches thick, placed one upon another*, formed the ground-work, and were covered by a sheet of Indian linen, sewed on the last mattress. A coverlet of *green* satin, adorned with *gold, embroidered in embossed work*, was, in like manner, fastened to the sheets, the ends of which, turned in, were sewed down alternately. Two large pillows of crimson satin, *covered with the like embroidery, in which there was no want of gold or spangles*, rested on two cushions of the sofa, brought near to serve for a back, and intended to support our heads. The taking of the pillows entirely away would have been a good resource, if we had had any bolster; and the expedient of turning the other side upward having only served to show they were embroidered in the same manner on the bottom, we at last determined to lay our handkerchiefs over them, which, however, did not prevent our being very sensible of the embossed ornaments underneath."

Here we have (1.) many mattresses of quilted cotton: (2.) a sheet of Indian linen; (*query*, muslin, or the fine linen of Egypt?) (3.) a coverlet of green satin, embossed: (4.) two large pillows, embossed also: (5.) two cushions from the sofa, to form a back. So that we see an eastern bed may be an article of furniture sufficiently complicated.

This description, compared with a note of De La Motraye, (p. 172,) leads to the supposition, that somewhat like what he informs us is called MAKASS, *i. e.* a brocaded covering for show, is what the harlot boasts of, as being the upper covering to her *minder*, or *oresh*. "On a rich sofa," says he, "was a *false covering* of plain *green* silk, for the same reason as that in the hall; but I lifted it up, while the two eunuchs who were with us had their backs turned, and I found that the MAKASS of the minders was a *very rich brocade, with a gold ground, and flowered with silk of several colours, and the cushions of green velvet also, grounded with gold, and flowered like them.*" *Note.* "The *minders* have two covers, one of which is called MAKASS, *for ornament:* and the other to preserve that, especially when they are rich, as these were." This was in the seraglio at Constantinople.

It is perfectly in character for the harlot, who (Pro. ix. 14) "sits on a kind of throne at her door," and who in this passage boasts of all her showy embellishments, to mention whatever is gaudy, even to the tinsel bedeckings of her room, her furniture, and her makasses, assuming nothing less than regal dignity in words and description: though her apartment be the way to hell; and the alcove containing her bed be the very lurking chamber of death.—TAYLOR IN CALMET.

Ver. 27. Her house *is* the way to hell, going down to the chambers of death.

See on Is. 22. 16.

CHAPTER IX.

Ver. 1. Wisdom hath built her house, she hath hewn out her seven pillars: 2. She hath killed her beasts; she hath mingled her wine; she hath also furnished her table: 3. She hath sent forth her maidens: she crieth upon the highest places of the city, 4. Whoso *is* simple, let him turn in hither: *as for* him that wanteth understanding, she saith to him, 5. Come, eat of my bread, and drink of the wine *which* I have mingled.

Hasselquist takes notice of what appears to us an old custom in Egypt, which he supposes is very ancient, though he does not apply it to the illustration of any passage of scripture; it seems, however, to be referred to by Solomon in the book of Proverbs. He saw, he says, a number of women, who went about inviting people to a banquet, in a singular, and, without doubt, very ancient manner. They were about ten or twelve, covered with black veils, as is customary in that country. They were preceded by four eunuchs: after them, and on the side, were Moors with their usual walking staves. As they were walking, they all joined in making a noise, which he was told signified their joy, but which he could not find resembled a joyful or pleasing song. The sound was so singular, as that he found himself at a loss to give an idea of it to those that never heard it. It was shrill, but had a particular quavering, which they learnt by long practice. The passage in Proverbs, which seems to allude to this practice, is the beginning of the ninth chapter: "Wisdom hath killed her beasts; she hath mingled her wine; she hath also furnished her table; she hath sent forth her maidens: she crieth upon the highest places of the city, Whoso is simple, let him turn in hither: as for him that wanteth understanding, she saith to him, Come, eat of my bread, and drink of the wine which I have mingled."

Here the reader observes, that the invitation is supposed to be made by more than one person; that they were of the female sex that were employed in the service; and that the invitation is supposed not to have been, as among us, a private message, but open to the notice of all. Whether it was with a singing tone of voice, as now in Egypt, does not, determinately at least, appear by the word here made use of, and which is translated *crieth: She crieth*, by her maidens, *upon the highest places of the city*. It may not be improper to add, that though the eastern people now eat out of the dishes oftentimes, which are brought in singly, and follow one another with great rapidity, not out of plates, yet many lesser appendages are placed round about the table by way of preparation, which seems to be what is meant by the expression, *she also hath furnished her table*, in one word, *all things were then ready*, and the more ditant kinds of preparation had been followed by the nearer, till every thing was ready, so as that the repast might immediately begin. The cattle were killed, the jars of wine emptied into drinking vessels, and the little attendants on the great dishes placed on the table.—HARMER.

Ver. 14. For she sitteth at the door of her house, on a seat in the high places of the city.

The custom of sitting at their doors, in the most alluring pomp that comes within their reach, is still an eastern practice. "These women," says Pitts, speaking of the ladies of pleasure at Grand Cairo, "used to sit at the door, or walk in the streets unveiled. They are commonly very rich in their clothes, some having their shifts and drawers of silk, &c. These courtesans, or ladies of pleasure, as well as other women, have broad velvet caps on their heads, beautified with abundance of pearls, and other costly and gaudy ornaments, &c. These madams go along the streets smoking their pipes of four or five feet long; and when they sit at their doors, a man can scarce pass by but they will endeavour to decoy him in."—BURDER.

CHAPTER X.

Ver. 11. The mouth of a righteous *man is* a well of life: but violence covereth the mouth of the wicked.

"The language of a holy man is like a well with good springs: thousands may be refreshed there." "The words of a bad man are like the springs of the sea; though very strong, they are not sweet." "Violence covereth the mouth of the wicked." To cover the mouth is the sign of sorrow: thus, they who act violently will sooner or later reap the fruits thereof. They will have to cover their mouth in token of sorrow for the past, and in anticipation of the future.—ROBERTS.

CHAPTER XI.

Ver. 1. A false balance *is* abomination to the LORD: but a just weight *is* his delight.

Great severity has been frequently exercised in the punishment of those who were detected in the kind of fraud here referred to. "A police-officer observing one morning a female, not a native, carrying a large piece of cheese, inquired where she had purchased it; being ignorant of the vender's name, she conducted him to his shop, and the magistrate, suspecting the quantity to be deficient in weight, placed it in the scales, and found his suspicion verified: whereupon he straightway ordered his attendants to cut from the most fleshy part of the delinquent's person what would be equivalent to the just measure: the order was instantly executed, and the sufferer bled to death." (Joliffe.) —BURDER.

Ver. 21. *Though* hand *join* in hand, the wicked shall not be unpunished: but the seed of the righteous shall be delivered.

See on 2 Kings 10. 15

To join hands was anciently, and still continues in the East, a solemn method of taking an oath, and making an engagement. This circumstance is probably alluded to in these words of Solomon; its present existence is clearly ascertained by what Mr. Bruce (Trav. vol. i. p. 199) relates: "I was so enraged at the traitorous part which Hassan had acted, that, at parting, I could not help saying to Ibrahim—Now, shekh, I have done every thing you have desired, without ever expecting fee or reward; the only thing I now ask you, and it is probably the last, is, that you avenge me upon this Hassan, who is every day in your power. Upon this *he gave me his hand*, saying, he shall not die in his bed, or I shall never see old age."—BURDER.

The expression, *though hand join in hand*, may bear a slight correction, conformable both to the original Hebrew, and also to the custom actually prevailing in Syria. The original יד ליד simply signifies, *hand to hand*. And this is the custom of persons in the East, when they greet each other, or strike hands, in token of friendship and agreement. They touch their right hands respectively; and then raise them up to their lips and forehead. This is the universal eastern courtesy; the English version, and the devices grounded upon it, give the idea of *hand clasped in hand*, which is European, rather than oriental. The sense, therefore, is, *Though hand meet hand*—intimating that heart assents to heart in the perpetration of wickedness—*yet shall not the wicked go unpunished*.—JOWETT.

There is a remarkable passage (Proverbs xi. 21) thus rendered by our translators: "*Though* hand *join* in hand, the wicked shall not be unpunished; but the seed of the righteous shall be delivered:" *i. e.* though they make many associations, and oaths, and join hands among themselves, (as formed part of the ceremony of swearing among these shepherds of Suakem,) yet they shall not be punished." But Michaelis proposes another sense of these words, "hand in hand"—my hand in your hand, *i. e.* as a token of swearing, "the wicked shall not go unpunished."—TAYLOR IN CALMET.

Ver. 22. *As* a jewel of gold in a swine's snout, *so is* a fair woman which is without discretion.

Nearly all the females of the East wear a jewel of gold in their nostrils, or in the septum of the nose; and some of them are exceedingly beautiful, and of great value. The oriental lady looks with as much pleasure on the gem which ADORNS her nose, as any of her sex in England do upon those which deck their ears. But as is that splendid jewel in the snout of a swine, so is beauty in a woman without discretion. She may have the ornament, her mien may be graceful, and her person attractive; but without the matchless jewel of virtue, she is like the swine with a gem in her nose, wallowing in the mire. "The most beautiful ornament of a woman is virtue," Tamul proverb. —ROBERTS.

This proverb is manifestly an allusion to the custom of wearing nose-jewels, or rings set with jewels, hanging from the nostrils, as ear-rings from the ears, by holes bored to receive them. This fashion, however strange it may appear to us, was formerly, and is still, common in many parts of the East, among women of all ranks. Paul Lucas, speaking of a village, or clan of wandering people, a little on this side of the Euphrates, says, "The women almost all of them travel on foot; I saw none handsome among them. They have almost all of them the nose bored, and wear in it a great ring, which makes them still more deformed." But in regard to this custom, better authority cannot be produced than that of Pietro della Valle, in the account which he gives of Signora Maani Gioerida, his own wife. The description of her dress, as to the ornamental parts of it, with which he introduces the mention of this particular, will give us some notion of the taste of the eastern ladies for finery. "The ornaments of gold, and of jewels, for the head, for the neck, for the arms, for the legs, and for the feet, (for they wear rings even on their toes,) are indeed, unlike those of the Turks, carried to great excess, but not of great value: as turquoises, small rubies, emeralds, carbuncles, garnets, pearls, and the like. My spouse dresses herself with all of them, according to their fashion, with exception however of certain ugly rings, of very large size, set with jewels, which, in truth very absurdly, it is the custom to wear fastened to one of their nostrils, like buffaloes; an ancient custom however in the East, which, as we find in the holy scriptures, prevailed among the Hebrew ladies, even in the time of Solomon. These nose-rings, in complaisance to me, she has left off; but I have not yet been able to prevail with her cousin and her sisters to do the same. So fond are they of an old custom, be it ever so absurd, who have been long habituated to it." To this account may be subjoined the observation made by Chardin, as cited in Harmer: "It is the custom in almost all the East for the women to wear rings in their noses, in the left nostril, which is bored low down in the middle. These rings are of gold, and have commonly two pearls and one ruby between, placed in the ring. I never saw a girl or young woman in Arabia, or in all Persia, who did not wear a ring after this manner in her nostril."— BURDER.

Ver. 26. He that withholdeth corn, the people shall curse him: but blessing *shall be* upon the head of him that selleth *it*.

Mirza Ahady, in conjunction with the prince's mother

was believed to have monopolized all the corn of the country; and he had no sooner reached Shiraz than he raised its price, which, of course, produced a correspondent advance in that of bread. Ventre affamé n'a point d'oreilles,—the people became outrageous in their misery. As is usual in all public calamities in the East, they commenced by shutting their shops in the bazar. They then resorted to the house of the sheikh-el-islam, the head of the law, requiring him to issue a *fetwah*, which might make it lawful to kill Mirza Ahady, and one or two more, whom they knew to be his coadjutors in oppressing them. They then appeared in a body before the gate of the prince's palace, where they expressed their grievances in a tumultuous way, and demanded that Mirza Ahady should be delivered up to them. Mohammed Zeky Khan, our former mehmander, was sent out by the prince to appease them, accompanied by Mirza Bauker, the chief baker of the city, who was one of those whose life had been denounced. As soon as the latter appeared, he was overwhelmed with insults and reproaches: but he managed to pacify them, by saying, What crime have I committed? Mirza Ahady is the man to abuse; if he sells corn at extravagant prices, bread must rise in consequence. In the meantime, Mirza Ahady had secreted himself from the fury of the mob; but being countenanced by the prince's mother, and, consequently, by the prince himself, he let the storm rage, and solaced himself by making fresh plans for raising more money. The price of bread was lowered for a few days, until the commotion should cease: and, as it was necessary that some satisfaction should be given to the people, all the bakers of the town were collected together, and publicly bastinadoed on the soles of their feet." (Morier.) "We are told of the fate of one person in whose house an immense quantity of grain was found: a stake was fixed in the centre of his granary, to which he was bound, and left to perish from hunger amidst that abundance which he had refused to share with his fellow-citizens." (Malcolm.)—BURDER.

Ver. 29. He that troubleth his own house shall inherit the wind: and the fool *shall be* servant to the wise of heart.

This form of expression is still used in India. "I understand Kandan will give a large dowry with his daughter; she will, therefore, be a good bargain for your son." —"You are correct, my friend; she is to inherit the wind." "I once had extensive lands for my portion; but now I inherit the wind." "I know you would like to have hold of my property: but you may take the wind."—ROBERTS.

CHAPTER XII.

Ver. 10. A righteous *man* regardeth the life of his beast: but the tender mercies of the wicked *are* cruel.

"During my stay at Surat, I rode out most evenings with our worthy chief, and, among other uncommon sights to a stranger, I took notice that many trees had jars hanging to several of the boughs; on inquiring, I was told that they were filled with water every evening, by men hired on purpose by the Gentoos, in order to supply the birds with drink. This account excited a desire of visiting the banyan hospital, as I had heard much of their benevolence to all kinds of animals that were either sick, lame, or infirm, through age or accident. On my arrival, there were presented to my view many horses, cows, and oxen, in one apartment; in another, dogs, sheep, goats, and monkeys, with clean straw for them to repose on. Above-stairs were depositories for seeds of many sorts, and flat broad dishes for water, for the use of those birds and insects which might chance to come into the apartment through the windows, which were latticed, with apertures large enough to admit small birds to enter. I was told by the attendants, that each apartment was cleaned every morning, the beasts fed and littered once a day, the seeds above-stairs winnowed, the dishes washed, and clean water put in them daily." (Parson's Travels in Asia.) Thevenot describes a banyan hospital, where he saw a number of sick oxen, camels, and horses, and many invalids of the feathered race. "Animals deemed incurable," he says, "were maintained there for life; those that recovered were sold to Hindoos exclusively."—BURDER.

Ver. 27. The slothful *man* roasteth not that which he took in hunting; but the substance of a diligent man *is* precious.

There is something particular in the word (חרך) *charak*, used in this passage of Solomon; it is not the word that is commonly used for *roasting*, but it signifies rather *singing*, as appears from Dan. iii. 27. No author, I think, gives us an account what this should mean, understood in this sense. Besides wild-boars, antelopes, and hares, which are particularly mentioned by D'Arvieux, when he speaks of the Arabs as diverting themselves with hunting in the Holy Land, Dr. Shaw tells us, all kinds of game are found in great plenty in that country: but I do not remember an account of any thing being prepared for food by *singing*, that is taken either in hunting or hawking, except hares, which I have indeed somewhere read of as dressed, in the East, after this manner: a hole being dug in the ground, and the earth scooped out of it laid all round its edge, the brushwood with which it is filled is set on fire, the hare is thrown unskinned into the hole, and afterward covered with heated earth that was laid round about it, where it continues till it is thought to be done enough, and then being brought to table, sprinkled with salt, is found to be very agreeable food.—HARMER.

CHAPTER XV.

Ver. 17. Better *is* a dinner of herbs where love is, than a stalled ox, and hatred therewith.

This passage is rendered by the Septuagint, as if they understood it of the forced accommodation of travellers, which Arabs and conquered people were obliged to submit to. It was not unusual for travellers to eat at the expense of those who were not pleased with entertaining them; and to use a kind of force, which produced hatred. Dr. Shaw notices this circumstance. Speaking of Barbary, he says, "In this country, the Arabs and other inhabitants are obliged, either by long custom, by the particular tenure of their lands, or from fear and compulsion, to give the Spahees, and their company, the Moquanah, as they call it, which is such a sufficient quantity of provisions, for ourselves, together with straw and barley for our mules and horses. Besides a bowl of milk, and a basket of figs, raisins, or dates, which, upon our arrival, were presented to us, to stay our appetites, the master of the tent where we lodged fetched us from his flock, according to the number of our company, a kid or a goat, a lamb or a sheep, half of which was immediately seethed by his wife, and served up with cuscasooe; the rest was made Kab-ab, *i. e.* cut into pieces, and roasted, which we reserved for our breakfast or dinner the next day." In the next page he says, "when we were entertained in a courteous manner, (for the Arabs will sometimes supply us with nothing till it is extorted by force,) the author used to give the master of the tent a knife, a couple of flints, or a small quantity of English gunpowder," &c. To prevent such parties from living at free charges upon them, the Arabs take care to pitch in woods, valleys, or places the least conspicuous, and that in consequence they found it difficult often to discover them.—BURDER.

Ver. 19. The way of the slothful *man is* as a hedge of thorns: but the way of the righteous *is* made plain.

The oriental gardens were either open plantations, or enclosures defended by walls or hedges. Rauwolf found, about Tripoli, many gardens and vineyards enclosed for the most part with hedges, and separated by shady walks. Some fences in the Holy Land, in later times, are not less beautiful than our living fences of white thorn, and perfectly answer the description of ancient Jewish prophets, who inform us, that the hedges in their times consisted of thorns, and that the spikes of these thorny plants were exceedingly sharp. Doubdan found a very fruitful vineyard, full of olives, fig-trees, and vines, about eight miles south-west from Bethlehem, enclosed with a hedge; and that part of it adjoining to the road, strongly formed of thorns and rose-bushes, intermingled with pomegranate-trees of surpassing beauty and fragrance. A hedge composed of rose-bushes and wild pomegranate-shrubs, then in full flower, mingled with other thorny plants, adorned in the varied livery of spring, must have made at once a strong and beautiful fence. The wild pomegranate-tree, the species probably used in fencing, is much more prickly than the other variety; and when mingled with other thorny bushes, of which they have several kinds in Palestine, some whose prickles are very long and sharp, must form a hedge very difficult to penetrate. These facts illustrate the beauty and force of several passages in the sacred volume: thus, in the Proverbs of Solomon, "The way of the slothful man is as a hedge of thorns;" it is obstructed with difficulties, which the sloth and indolence of his temper represent as galling or insuperable; but which a moderate share of resolution and perseverance would easily remove or surmount.—PAXTON.

Hasselquist says, that he saw the plantain-tree, the vine, the peach, and the mulberry-tree, all four made use of in Egypt to hedge about a garden: now these are all unarmed plants. This consideration throws a great energy into the words of Solomon: *The way of the slothful man is a hedge of thorns.* It appears as difficult to him, not only as breaking through a *hedge*, but even through a *thorn fence:* and also into that threatening of God to Israel: *Behold, I will hedge up the way with thorns,* Hosea ii. 6. —BURDER.

CHAPTER XVI.

Ver. 11. A just weight and balance *are* the LORD'S; all the weights of the bag *are* his work.

The Jews were required to be exact in their weights and measures, that the poor might not be defrauded. Hesychius remarks upon this point, as a reason for such great care, that what the possession of a field or house is to a wealthy man, that the measure of corn, or wine, or the weight of bread, is to the poor, who have daily need of such things for the support of life. "The Jewish doctors assert, that it was a constitution of their wise men, for the preventing of all frauds in these matters, that no weights, balances, or measures, should be made of any metal, as of iron, lead, tin, (which were liable to rust, or might be bent, or easily impaired,) but of marble, stone, or glass, which were less subject to be abused: and therefore the scripture, speaking of the justice of God's judgments, observes, (according to the *Vulgate*,) that *they are weighed with all the stones in the bag*." (Lewis.)—BURDER.

Ver. 14. The wrath of a king *is as* messengers of death; but a wise man will pacify it.

Executions in the East are often very prompt and arbitrary. In many cases the suspicion is no sooner entertained, or the cause of offence given, than the fatal order is issued; the messenger of death hurries to the unsuspecting victim, shows his warrant, and executes his orders that instant in silence and solitude. Instances of this kind are continually occurring in the Turkish and Persian histories. "When the enemies of a great man among the Turks have gained influence enough over the prince to procure a warrant for his death, a capidgi (the name of the officer who executes these orders) is sent to him, who shows him the order he has received to carry back his head; the other takes the warrant of the grand seignior, kisses it, puts it on his head in token of respect, and then having performed his ablutions, and said his prayers, freely resigns his life. The capidgi having strangled him, cuts off his head, and brings it to Constantinople. The grand seignior's order is implicitly obeyed; the servants of the victim never attempt to hinder the executioner, although these capidgis come very often with few or no attendants." It appears from the writings of Chardin, that the nobility and grandees of Persia are put to death in a manner equally silent, hasty, and unobstructed. Such executions were not uncommon among the Jews under the government of their kings. Solomon sent Benaiah as his capidgi, or executioner, to put Adonijah, a prince of his own family, to death; and Joab, the commander-in-chief of the forces in the reign of his father. A capidgi likewise beheaded John the Baptist in the prison, and carried his head to the court of Herod. To such silent and hasty executioners the royal preacher seems to refer in that proverb, "The wrath of a king is as messengers of death; but a wise man will pacify it;" his displeasure exposes the unhappy offender to immediate death, and may fill the unsuspecting bosom with terror and dismay, like the appearance of a capidgi; but by wise and prudent conduct, a man may sometimes escape the danger.

From the dreadful promptitude with which Benaiah executed the commands of Solomon on Adonijah and Joab, it may be concluded that the executioner of the court was as little ceremonious, and the ancient Jews nearly as passive, as the Turks or Persians. The prophet Elisha is the only person on the inspired record, who ventured to resist the bloody mandate of the sovereign; the incident is recorded in these terms: "But Elisha sat in his house, and the elders sat with him; and the king sent a man from before him; but ere the messenger came to him, he said to the elders, See how this son of a murderer has sent to take away my head? Look when the messenger cometh; shut the door, and hold him fast at the door—is not the sound of his master's feet behind him?" But if such mandates had not been too common among the Jews, and in general submitted to without resistance, Jehoram had scarcely ventured to despatch a single messenger to take away the life of so eminent a person as Elisha.—PAXTON.

Ver. 15. In the light of the king's countenance *is* life; and his favour *is* as a cloud of the latter rain.

Poets often speak of the generosity of the great, as the clouds full of rain, but the uncharitable are like the clouds without rain. "O the benevolent man! he is like the fruitful rain; ever giving, but never receiving."—ROBERTS.

The former and latter rains is a phrase quite familiar to every reader of the scriptures. The distinction which it announces is founded in nature, and is of great importance in those parts of the world. At Aleppo, the drought of summer commonly terminates in September, by some heavy showers, which occasionally continue some days; after which, there is an interval of fine weather, of between twenty and thirty days, when the showers return, which are called the second rains. The first rains fall between the twenty-sixth of September and the sixth of October: but it is later in Judea; the former rain, descending in Palestine about the beginning of November. The seasons in the East are exceedingly regular, yet it is not to be supposed that they admit of no variation; the descent of the first and second rain occasionally varies a whole month. But the first and second rains of Syria, mentioned by Russel, do not seem to correspond with the former and latter rains of the holy scriptures. This is the opinion of Jerome, who lived long in Palestine: nor do the natural historians of those countries take any notice of the first and second rains in autumn; but uniformly speak of the former and latter rains. It is therefore of some importance to inquire, what are the times of the year when these rains descend. Here it may be proper to observe, that rain in the vernal season, is represented by oriental writers as of great advantage. The more wet the spring, the later the harvest, and the more plentiful the crop. In Barbary, the vernal rains are indispensably requisite to secure the hopes of the husbandman. If the latter rains fall as usual in the middle of April, he reckons his crop secure; but extremely doubtful if they happen to fail. This accounts well for the great value which Solomon sets upon them: "In the light of the king's countenance is life, and his favour is as a cloud of the latter rain." To this may be added, that the words translated the former and latter rains, are not expressive of first and second; and by consequence, do not refer to the rains mentioned by Russel, but mark a distinction of much greater importance. They must therefore be the same as the vernal rains, which are universally allowed to be of the utmost consequence in those regions.

The time of the first rains is differently stated by modern travellers. According to Dr. Shaw, the first autumnal rains usually fall about the eleventh of November; from a manuscript journal of travels in those countries, Mr. Harmer found that the rain fell in the Holy Land on the second of November; and he was assured by the historian of the revolt of Ali Bey, who lived some years in Palestine that the rains begin to fall there about the eighteenth day of September; at first they descend in slight showers, but as the season advances, they become very copious and heavy, though never continual.

Dr. Shaw seems to suppose, that the Arabs of Barbary do not begin to break up their grounds till the first rains of autumn fall; while the author of the history of Ali Bey's revolt supposes that they sometimes plough their land before the descent of the rain, because the soil is then light, and easily worked. This statement contains nothing incredible; grain will remain long in the earth unhurt, and vegetate as soon as the descending showers communicate sufficient moisture. The oriental husbandman may cultivate his field, as is often done in other countries, in expectation of rain; a circumstance to which Solomon seems to refer: "He that observeth the wind shall not sow, and he that regardeth the clouds shall not reap." If they never sowed in the East but when the soil was moistened with rain, they could have no reason to observe whether the wind threatened rain or promised fair weather; but if the seed was cast into the ground previous to the descent of the rain, they might naturally enough be induced to wait till they observed the signs of its approach. The rainy season in the beginning of winter, by the concurring testimony of travellers, is commonly introduced by a gale of wind from the northeast. In Syria, the winds are variable in November, and the two succeeding months; seldom strong, but more inclined to the north and east, than any of the other quarters. They continue to blow nearly in the same direction, till about the end of February, when they begin to blow hard westerly. The weather in April is in general fair and clear; seldom dark or cloudy, except when it rains, which it does in hard thundershowers, as in the last month, but not so often. When light northerly or easterly breezes happen to blow, they have commonly a few close, hazy days; but the westerly winds are generally fresh.—PAXTON.

CHAPTER XVII.

Ver. 12. Let a bear, robbed of her whelps, meet a man, rather than a fool in his folly.

The furious passions of the female bear never mount so high, nor burn so fiercely, as when she happens to be deprived of her young. When she returns to her den, and misses the objects of her love and care, she becomes almost frantic with rage. Disregarding every consideration of danger to herself, she attacks, with intense ferocity, every animal that comes in her way, "and in the bitterness of her heart, will dare to attack even a band of armed men." The Russians of Kamschatka never venture to fire on a young bear when the mother is near; for if the cub drop, she becomes enraged to a degree little short of madness; and if she get sight of the enemy, will only quit her revenge with her life. "A more desperate attempt, therefore, can scarcely be performed, than to carry off her young in her absence. The moment she returns, and misses them, her passions are inflamed; her scent enables her to track the plunderer; and unless he has reached some place of safety before the infuriated animal overtake him, his only safety is in dropping one of the cubs, and continuing to flee; for the mother, attentive to its safety, carries it home to her den, before she renews the pursuit."

These statements furnish an admirable illustration of a passage in the counsel of Hushai to Absalom, in which he represents the danger of attacking David and his followers with so small a force as twelve thousand chosen men, when their tried courage was inflamed, and their spirits were imbittered by the variety and severity of their sufferings, and when their caution, matured by long and extensive experience in the art of war, and sharpened by the novelty and peril of their circumstances, would certainly lead them to anticipate, and take measures to defeat the attempt. "Hushai said unto Absalom, The counsel that Ahithophel hath given, is not good at this time; for (said Hushai) thou knowest thy father and his men, that they be mighty men, and they be chafed in their minds as a bear robbed of her whelps in the field." The frantic rage of the female bear, when she has lost her young, gives wonderful energy to the proverb of Solomon: "Let a bear, robbed of her whelps, meet a man, rather than a fool in his folly." Dreadful as it is to meet a bear in such circumstances, it is yet more dangerous to meet a "fool in his folly," a furious and revengeful man, under the influence of his impetuous passions, and his heart determined on their immediate gratification. Naturally stubborn and cruel as the bear, and equally devoted to his lusts as she is to her young, he pursues them with equal fury and eagerness. It is possible to escape the vengeance of a bereaved bear, by surrendering part of the litter, and diverting part of her pursuit; but no consideration of interest or duty, no partial gratifications, can arrest his furious career, or divert his attention. Reason, degraded and enslaved, lends all her remaning wisdom and energy to passion, and renders the fool more cruel and mischievous than the bear, in proportion as she is superior to instinct.—PAXTON.

Ver. 18. A man void of understanding striketh hands, *and* becometh surety in the presence of his friend.

See on ch. 6. 1.

The Hindoo proverb says, "*Munidār muneruka-kaduvār*," i. e. "He who stands BEFORE may have to pay." This, therefore, is the idea of a surety; he stands BEFORE the debtor, and covenants with the creditor for the payment of the money: he, therefore, who stands before, is literally betwixt the contending parties. In this respect "was Jesus made a surety" for us: he stood BEFORE, and became our μεσιτης, or Mediator.

The melancholy instances of ruin, in consequence of becoming surety for others, are exceedingly numerous in the East. Against this they have many proverbs, and fearful examples; but nothing seems to give them wisdom. Nearly all the government monopolies, both among native and European rulers, are let to the highest bidders: thus, the privilege of searching for precious stones in certain districts, of taking up the chiar root, salt rents, fishing for chanks, or pearls, is confined to those who pay a fixed sum to government. As the whole of the money cannot be advanced till a part of the produce shall be sold, SURETIES have to be accountable for the amount. But as such speculations are generally entered into, in order to better a reduced fortune, an extravagant price is often paid, and ruin is the consequence, both to the principal and his surety. This practice of suretyship, however, is also COMMON in the most TRIFLING affairs of life: "*Parrellutha-vonum*, i. e. Sign your name," is asked for to every petty agreement. In every legal court or magistrate's office may be seen, now and then, a trio entering, thus to become responsible for the engagements of another. The cause of all this SURETYSHIP is probably the bad faith which so commonly prevails among the heathen.—ROBERTS.

Ver. 19. He that exalteth his gate seeketh destruction.

The general style of buildings in the East, seems to have continued from the remotest ages down to the present times, without alteration or any attempt at improvement. Large doors, spacious chambers, marble pavements, cloistered courts, with fountains sometimes playing in the midst, are certainly conveniences well adapted to the circumstances of these hotter climates. All the windows of their dwellings, if we except a small latticed window or balcony which sometimes looks into the street, open into their respective courts or quadrangles; an arrangement probably dictated by the jealousy which unceasingly disturbs the repose of an oriental householder. It is only during the celebration of some public festival, that these houses, and their latticed windows, or balconies, are left open. The streets of an oriental city, the better to shade the inhabitants from the sun, are commonly narrow, with sometimes a range of shops on each side. People of the same trade occupy the same street. Both in Persia and in Turkey the trades are carried on in separate bazars, in which their shops are extended adjacent to each other on both sides of the building. The remark equally applies to Damascus and other cities in the Lesser Asia. The entrance from the streets into one of the principal houses, is through a porch or gateway, with benches on each side, where the master of the family receives visits, and despatches business; few persons, not even the nearest relations, having further admission, except upon extraordinary occasions. The door of the porch by which a person enters the court, is very small; sometimes not above three feet high. The design of such low and inconvenient doors is, to prevent the Arabs from riding into the houses to plunder them; for these freebooters, who are almost centaurs, seldom think of dismounting in their excursions; and therefore the peaceable inhabitants find such small entrances the easiest and most effectual way of preventing their violence. To this singular practice the royal preacher may be supposed to refer: "He that exalteth his gate, seeketh destruction." It can hardly be supposed that Solomon mentioned the loftiness of the gate, rather than other circumstances of magnificence in a building, as the wideness of the house, the airiness of the rooms, the cedar ceilings, and the vermilion paintings, which the prophet Jeremiah specifies as pieces of grandeur, without some particular meaning. But if bands of Arabs had taken the advantage of large doors to enter into houses in his territories, or in the surrounding kingdoms, the apothegm possesses a singular propriety and force. We have the more reason to believe that Solomon had his eye on the insolence of the Arabs in riding into the houses of those they meant to plunder, because the practice seems not to have been unusual in other countries; and is not now peculiar to those plunderers. The Armenian merchants at Julfa, the suburb of Ispahan, in which they reside, find it necessary to make the front door of their houses in general small, partly to hinder the Persians, who treat them with great rigour and insolence, from entering them on horseback, and partly to prevent them from observing the magnificent furniture within. But the habitation of a man in power is known by his gate, which is generally elevated in proportion to the vanity of its owner. A lofty gate is one of the insignia of royalty; and it must have been the same in ancient times. The gates of Jerusalem, of Zion, and other places, are often mentioned in the scripture with the same notions of grandeur annexed to them: thus the Psalmist addresses the gates of Zion: "Lift up your heads, O ye gates; even lift them up, ye everlasting doors: and the king of glory shall come in."—Paxton.

The Arabs are accustomed to ride into the houses of those they design to harass. To prevent this, Thevenot tells us that the door of the house in which the French merchants lived at Rama was not three feet high, and that all the doors of that town are equally low. Agreeably to this account, the Abbé Mariti, speaking of his admission into a monastery near Jerusalem, says, "the passage is so low that it will scarcely admit a horse; and it is shut by a gate of iron, strongly secured in the inside. As soon as we entered, it was again made fast with various bolts and bars of iron: a precaution extremely necessary in a desert place, exposed to the incursions and insolent attacks of the Arabs." To *exalt the gate*, would consequently be to court destruction.—Burder.

CHAPTER XVIII.

Ver. 10. The name of the Lord *is* a strong tower; the righteous runneth into it, and is safe.

Men of wealth are called towers. Thus, when such a person dies, it is said, "The *pellata-koburam*, i. e. strong tower, has fallen." "I am going to my *koburam*," says the man who is going to his powerful friend.—Roberts.

Ver. 16. A man's gift maketh room for him, and bringeth him before great men.

See on 1 Sam. 9. 7.

Ver. 18. The lot causeth contentions to cease and parteth between the mighty.

In nearly all cases where reason cannot decide, or where the right of several claimants to one article has to be settled, recourse is had to the lot, which "causeth contentions to cease." Though an Englishman might not like to have a wife assigned to him in such a way, yet many a one in the East has no other guide in that important acquisition.

Perhaps a young man is either so accomplished, or so respectable, or so rich, that many fathers aspire to the honour of calling him son-in-law. Their daughters are said to be beautiful, wealthy, and of a good family: what is he to do? The name of each young lady is written on a separate piece of olah; and then all are mixed together. The youth and his friends then go to the front of the temple; and being seated, a person who is passing by at the time is called, and requested to take one of the pieces of olah, on which a lady's name is inscribed, and place it near the anxious candidate. This being done, it is opened, and she whose name is written there, becomes his wife!

Are two men inclined to marry two sisters, a dispute often arises as to whom the youngest shall be given. To cause the "contentions to cease," recourse is again had to the lot. The names of the sisters and the disputants are written on separate pieces of olah, and taken to a sacred place: those of the men being put on one side, and the females on the other. A person then, who is unacquainted with the matter, takes a piece of olah from each side, and the couple whose names are thus joined together become man and wife. But sometimes a wealthy father cannot decide betwixt two young men who are candidates for the hand of his daughter: "what can he do? he must settle his doubts by lot." Not long ago, the son of a medical man, and another youth, applied for the daughter of Sedambara-Suppiyan, the rich merchant. The old gentleman caused two "holy writings" to be drawn up, the names of the lovers were inscribed thereon: the son of Kandan, the doctor, was drawn forth, and the young lady became his wife. Three Bramins, also, who were brothers, each ardently desired the hand of one female; and, after many disputes, it was settled by lot, which "causeth contentions to cease;" and the youngest of the three gained the prize.

But medical men are also sometimes selected in the same way. One person tells the afflicted individual such a doctor has far more skill than the rest: another says, "He! what is he but a cow-doctor? how many has he killed! Send for such a person, he will soon cure you." A third says, "I know the man for you; he had his knowledge from the gods; send for him." The poor patient at last says, "Select me one by lot;" and as is the name, so is the doctor. But another thing has to be settled; the medical gentleman intimates that there are two kinds of medicine which appear to him to be equally good, and therefore the lot is again to decide which is best. "The lot causeth contentions to cease."—Roberts.

Ver. 19. A brother offended *is harder to be won* than a strong city; and *their* contentions *are* like the bars of a castle.

See on Acts 12. 10.

CHAPTER XIX.

Ver. 12. The king's wrath *is* as the roaring of a lion: but his favour *is* as dew upon the grass.

"The favour of my friend is as the refreshing dew." "The favours of that good man are continually dropping upon us." "He bathes me with his favours."—Roberts.

Ver. 13. The contentions of a wife *are* a continual dropping.

See on ch. 21. 9.

The allusion in this passage is generally thought to be to an old and decayed house, through which the rain continually drops, rendering it highly disagreeable to inhabit. Durell supposes that the allusion is to the "dropping of the eaves of a house, or any continued gentle falling of water, than which nothing is more apt to be tiresome and distracting." Mr. Harmer thinks that it refers to the arbours made of the boughs of trees upon the house-tops, in which the inhabitants of those sultry regions were accustomed to sleep in summer. "Egmont and Heyman tell us that at Caipha, at the foot of Mount Carmel, the houses are small and flat-roofed, where, during the summer, the inhabitants sleep in arbours made of the boughs of trees." Again, "Dr. Pococke tells us, in like manner, that when he was at Tiberias, in Galilee, he was entertained by the sheik's steward, and that they supped upon the top of the house for coolness, according to their custom, and lodged there likewise in a sort of closet, about eight feet square, of a wicker-work, plastered round towards the bottom, but without any door." "However pleasant," says Mr. Harmer, "these arbours and these wicker-work closets may be in the dry part of the year, they must be very disagreeable in the wet and they that should then lodge in them *would be exposed to a continual dropping*. To such circumstances probably it is that Solomon alludes, when he says, 'It is better to dwell in the corner of the house-top, than with a brawling woman in a wide house.' A corner covered with boughs or rushes, and made into a little arbour, in which they used to sleep in summer, but which must have been a very incommodious place to have made an entire dwelling. To the same allusion belong those other expressions that speak of the contentions of a wife being like a continual dropping. Put together they amount to this, that it is better to have no other habitation than an arbour on the house-top, and be there exposed to the wet of winter, which is oftentimes of several days' continuance, than to dwell in a wide house with a brawling woman, for her contentions are a continual dropping, and, wide as the house may be, you will not be able to avoid them or get out of their reach."—BUSH.

Ver. 24. A slothful *man* hideth his hand in *his* bosom, and will not so much as bring it to his mouth again.

Many of the Arabs, and other eastern people, use no spoon in eating their victuals; they dip their hands into the milk, which is placed before them in a wooden bowl, and lift it to their mouth in their palm. Le Bruin observed five or six Arabs eating milk together, on the side of the Nile, as he was going up that river to Cairo; and D'Arvieux says they eat their pottage in the same way. Is it not reasonable to suppose, says Harmer, that the same usage obtained anciently among the Jews; and that Solomon refers to it when he says, "A slothful man hides his hand in the dish, and will not so much as bring it to his mouth again?" Our translators render it the bosom; but the word every where signifies a pot or dish. The meaning, therefore, according to Harmer, is, "the slothful man having lifted up his hand full of milk or pottage to his mouth, will not do it a second time; no, though it be actually dipped into the milk or pottage, he will not submit to the fatigue of lifting it again from thence to his mouth." But as it is rather a caricature to represent the sluggard as so excessively indolent or lazy, that he will rather let his hand lie in the dish among the milk or pottage, than lift it to his mouth a second time, the explanation of Dr. Russel is to be preferred: "The Arabs, in eating, do not thrust their whole hand into the dish, but only their thumb and two first fingers, with which they take up the morsel, and that in a moderate quantity at a time. I take, therefore, the sense to be, that the slothful man, instead of taking up a moderate mouthful, thrusts his hand into the pillaw, or such like, and takes a handful at a time, in order to avoid the trouble of returning frequently to the dish." According to this view, the slothful man endeavours by one effort to save himself the trouble of continued exertion. It seems to have been adopted by the Arabs, as much for the sake of despatch as from necessity; for D'Arvieux says, a man would eat upon very unequal terms with a spoon, among those that, instead of them, use the palms of their hands. This mode of drinking was used by three hundred men of Gideon's army: "And the number of them that lapped, putting their hands to their mouth, were three hundred men; but all the rest of the people bowed down upon their knees to drink water." Three hundred men, immediately on their coming to the water, drank of it in the quickest manner they could, by lifting it in their palms, and lapping it like a dog, that they might be ready, without delay, to follow their leader to the battle: the rest took up water in pitchers, or some kind of vessel, and bending down upon their heels and knees, or with their knees placed upright before them, either of which might be called bowing their knees to drink, they handed these drinking-vessels slowly from one to another, as at an ordinary meal; an act which procured their dismission. The Hottentot manner of drinking water from a pool, or stream, seems exactly to coincide with the mode adopted by the three hundred, and gives a very clear idea of it: They throw it up with their right hand into their mouth, seldom bringing the hand nearer than the distance of a foot from the mouth, and so quickly, that however thirsty, they are soon satisfied. Mr. Campbell, who had an opportunity of seeing this operation, when travelling among that people, frequently tried to imitate it, but without success.—PAXTON.

CHAPTER XX.

Ver. 4. The sluggard will not plough by reason of the cold; *therefore* shall he beg in harvest, and *have* nothing.

Margin, winter. "They begin to plough about the latter end of September, and sow their earliest wheat about the middle of October. The frosts are never severe enough to prevent their ploughing all the winter."—BURDER.

Ver. 10. Divers weights, *and* divers measures, both of them *are* alike abomination to the LORD.

Here we have a true view of the way in which nearly all travelling merchants deal with their customers. See that Mohammedan pedler with his BAGS over his shoulder: the one contains his merchandise, the other his DECEITFUL WEIGHTS. He comes to your door, throws his bags on the ground, and is willing either to buy or to sell. Have you any old silver, gold, jewels, precious stones, iron, or lead, he is ready to be your customer; but he only *buys* with his own weights, which are much heavier than the standard. Should YOU, however, require to purchase any articles, then he has other weights by which he SELLS; and you may often see him fumbling for a considerable time in the BAG before he can find those which are less in weight than the regular standard.—ROBERTS.

Ver. 29. The glory of young men *is* their strength: and the beauty of old men *is* the gray head.

Should a youth despise the advice of a gray-headed man, the latter will point to his hairs. When young men presume to give advice to the aged, they say, "Look at our gray hairs." Do old people commit things unworthy of their years, the young ask, "Why have you these gray hairs?" intimating they ought to be the emblem of wisdom.—ROBERTS.

CHAPTER XXI.

Ver. 1. The king's heart *is* in the hand of the LORD, *as* the rivers of water; he turneth it whithersoever he will.

See on Ps. 1. 3.

Ver. 4. A high look, and a proud heart, *and* the ploughing of the wicked, *is* sin.

The margin has, instead of *ploughing, light*: "The light of the wicked." The Tamul translation has, the *lamp* of the wicked. In eastern language, as well as in the scriptures, the word *lamp* is often used to denote the *life* of man: but in this passage it means the PROSPERITY of the wicked. "Look at Valen, how brightly does his lamp burn in these days!"—"Yes, his lamp has now a thousand faces." Thus the haughty eyes, the proud hearts, and the PROSPERITY of the wicked, were alike sinful before God. The lamp (*i. e.* prosperity) of the wicked is sin.—ROBERTS.

Ver. 8. The way of man is froward and strange: but *as for* the pure, his work *is* right.

This passage, according to the common interpretation, is very obscure. The original Hebrew words are used to signify a man *laden* with *guilt* and *crimes*, and that his way is (not *froward* and *strange*, as in our translation, but) *unsteady*, or *continually varying*; in which expression there is a most beautiful allusion to a beast which is so *overburdened* that he cannot keep in the straight road, but is continually tottering and staggering, first to the right hand, and then to the left.—PARKHURST.

Ver. 9. *It is* better to dwell in a corner of the house-top, than with a brawling woman in a wide house.

See on ch. 19. 13.

How pleasant soever the arbour, or wicker-closet, upon the roof, may be during the burning heats of summer, it must be very disagreeable in the rainy season. They who lodge in either at that time, must be exposed continually to the storm beating in upon them from every quarter. In allusion, perhaps, to this uncomfortable situation, Solomon observes: "It is better to dwell in a corner of the house-top, than with a brawling woman in a wide house;" in a corner formed with boughs or rushes into a little arbour, which, although cool and pleasant in the dry and sultry months of summer, is a cold and cheerless lodge when the earth is drenched with rain, or covered with snow. The royal preacher, in another proverb, compares the contentions of a wife to the continual dropping of an arbour, placed upon the house-top, in the rainy season, than which it is not easy to conceive any thing more disagreeable: "The contentions of a wife are a continual dropping;" an incessant and unavoidable cause of uneasiness or vexation. Instructed probably by his own feelings, harassed and goaded, as was meet, by the daily quarrels of his seraglio, he returns in a succeeding apothegm to the subject: "A continual dropping in a very rainy day, and a contentious woman, are alike." It appears from these proverbs, that the booths were generally constructed in the corner, where two walls met, for greater safety; for, on the middle of the roof, they had been too much exposed to the storm. This is confirmed by Dr. Russel, who remarks, in a manuscript note, that these booths in Syria are often placed near the walls; so minutely correct are even the most incidental observations of the inspired writers.—PAXTON.

The termagants of the East are certainly not inferior to those of their own sex in any part of the world: in some respects, the females are perhaps more timid and retired than those of Europe; but let them once go beyond the prescribed bounds, and let their powers be brought fairly into action, and they are complete furies. Has any one caused a woman's child to cry, does a neighbour intimate that she is not what she ought to be, or that some of her friends are no better than they should be, the whoop is immediately sounded, and the brawl begins. She commences her abuse in her best and highest tone of voice: vociferates all the scandal she can think of, and all she can INVENT. Sometimes she runs up to her antagonist, as if about to knock her down: again she retires, apparently to go home; but, no! she thinks of something more which ought not to be lost, and again returns to the contest. At intervals (merely to vary the scene) she throws up dust in the air, and curses her opponent, her husband, and her children. Should the poor woman not have been blessed with a progeny, that will not be overlooked, and a thousand highly provoking and indecent allusions will be made. See her fiery eyes, her dishevelled hair, her uplifted hand, and she is more like a fury from another region, than a human being.

An eastern sage says, "Should one woman scold, the whole earth will shake; should two commence, the sign Pisces will fall; if three join in the brawl, the sea will dry up; but if four try their powers, what will become of the world?" In the *Scanda Purana* it is said, "It is better for any one to fall into hell, than to perform the duties of a householder with a woman who will not respect her husband's word. Is there any other disease, any other *Yamā*, than spending life with such a woman?"

One of their philosophers describes some of the defects in young females which ought to deter any man from marrying them. "Those who love to be at the house of other people, who are great sleepers, who love dancing and other sports, who are wounded by the arrows of Cama, (Cupid,) who love before their fathers betroth them, who have voices like thunder, who have tender, or rolling, or cat eyes, who have coarse hair, who are older than yourself, who are full of smiles, who are very athletic, who are caught in the hell of useless and strange religions, who despise the *gooroo*, and call the gods' statues; have nothing to do with them." Solomon says, in another place, "The contentions of a wife are a continual dropping;" and the Tamul proverb has it, "She is like the thunder of the rain, and is ever dropping." —ROBERTS.

This expression the LXX render εν οικω κοινω. The Vulgate, "in domo communi," in a common house; that is, in a house common or shared out to several families. Dr. Shaw says, that "the general method of building, both in Barbary and the Levant, seems to have continued the same from the earliest ages down to this time, without the least alteration or improvement: large doors, spacious chambers, &c. The court is for the most part surrounded with a cloister, over which, when the house has one or more stories, there is a gallery erected. From the cloisters or galleries we are conducted into large spacious chambers of the same length with the court, but seldom or never communicating with one another. One of them frequently serves a whole family; particularly when a father indulges his married children to live with him; or when several persons join in the rent of the same house."—BURDER.

CHAPTER XXII.

Ver. 13. The slothful *man* saith, *There is* a lion without, I shall be slain in the streets.

The sluggard is fond of sleep; and, to excuse his sloth fulness, he makes use of the pretence, when he is to go out of his house in the morning dawn, and to follow his business, that he might fall a prey to one of the wild beasts which prowl about during the night. When it becomes dark, the people of the East shut themselves up in their houses for fear of the wild beasts. Thus Alvarez, in his account of Ethiopia, says, that "in Abyssinia, as soon as night sets in, nobody is to be seen abroad for fear of wild beasts, of which the country is full."—ROSENMULLER.

Ver. 14. The mouth of strange women *is a* deep pit: he that is abhorred of the LORD shall fall therein.

Maundrell, describing the passage out of the jurisdiction of the Bashaw of Aleppo into that of him of Tripoli, tells us, the road was rocky and uneven, but attended with variety. "Sometimes it led us under the cool shade of thick trees: sometimes through narrow valleys, watered with fresh murmuring torrents: and then for a good while together upon the brink of a precipice. And in all places it treated us with the prospect of plants and flowers of divers kinds; as myrtles, oleanders, cyclamens, &c. Having spent about two hours in this manner, we descended into a low valley; at the bottom of which is a fissure into the earth, of a great depth; but withal so narrow, that it is not discernible to the eye till you arrive just upon it, though to the ear a notice of it is given at a great distance, by reason of the noise of a stream running down into it from the hills. We could not guess it to be less than thirty yards deep. But it is so narrow, that a small arch, not four yards over, lands you on its other side. They call it *the sheik's wife*; a name given to it from a woman of that quality, who fell into it, and, I need not add, perished." May not Solomon refer to some such dangerous place as this, when he says, "The mouth of a strange woman is a deep pit: he that is abhorred of the Lord shall fall therein," Prov. xxvii. 14; and, "A whore is a deep ditch; and a strange woman is a narrow pit," Prov. xxiii. 27. The flowery pleasures of the place, where this fatal pit was, make the allusion still more striking. How agreeable to sense the path that led to this *chamber of death!*—HARMER.

Ver. 26. Be not thou *one* of them that strike hands, *or* of them that are sureties for debts.

See on ch. 6. 1.

CHAPTER XXIII.

Ver. 3. Be not desirous of his dainties; for they *are* deceitful meat.

See on Gen. 27. 4.

Ver. 5. Wilt thou set thine eyes upon that which is not? for *riches* certainly make themselves wings; they fly away, as an eagle towards heaven.

A husband who complains of the extravagance of his family, says, "How is it that wings grow on all my property? not many days ago I purchased a large quantity of *paddy*, but it has taken the wing and flown away. The next time I buy any thing, I will look well after the wings." "You ask me to give you money, and I would, if I possessed any."—"Possessed any! why! have wings grown on your silver and gold?" "Alas! alas! I no sooner get things into the house, than wings grow on hem, and they fly away. Last week I began to clip wings; but they have soon grown again."—Roberts.

Ver. 6. Eat thou not the bread of *him that hath* an evil eye, neither desire thou his dainty meats: 7. For as he thinketh in his heart, so *is* he: Eat and drink, saith he to thee; but his heart *is* not with thee. 8. The morsel *which* thou hast eaten shalt thou vomit up, and lose thy sweet words.

Whether the same ideas are to be attached to the expression "evil eye," as used by Solomon, and as understood by the Egyptians, may not be easily ascertained, though perhaps worthy of consideration. Pococke says of the Egyptians, that "they have a great notion of the magic art, have books about it, and think there is much virtue in talismans and charms; but particularly are strongly possessed with an opinion of the evil eye. When a child is commended, except you give it some blessing, if they are not very well assured of your good will, they use charms against the evil eye; and particularly when they think any ill success attends them on account of an evil eye, they throw salt into the fire."—Burder.

Many references are made in the scriptures to an evil eye. Sometimes they mean anger or envy; but in the passage cited an allusion appears to be made to the malignant influence of an evil eye: "The morsel which thou hast eaten shalt thou vomit up." The *kan-nuru*, evil-eye, of some people is believed to have a most baneful effect upon whatsoever it shall be fixed. Those who are reputed to have such eyes are always avoided, and none but near relations will invite them to a feast. "Your cattle, your wives, your children, your orchards, your fields, are all in danger from that fellow's eyes. The other day he passed my garden, cast his eye upon my lime-tree, and the fruit has since fallen to the ground. Ay, and worse than that, he caught a look at my child's face, and a large abscess has since appeared."

To prevent such eyes from doing any injury to their children, many parents (both Mohammedan and Hindoo) adorn them with numerous jewels and jackets of varied colours, to attract the eye from the person to the ornaments. —Roberts.

Ver. 20. Be not among wine-bibbers; among riotous eaters of flesh.

The Arabs are described by Shaw, as very abstemious. They rarely diminish their flocks by using them for food, but live chiefly upon bread, milk, butter, dates, or what they receive in exchange for their wool. Their frugality is in many instances the effect of narrow circumstances; and shows with what propriety Solomon describes an expensive way of living by their *frequent eating of flesh*.—Burder.

Ver. 27. For a whore *is* a deep ditch; and a strange woman *is* a narrow pit.

See on ch. 22. 14.

Ver. 30. They that tarry long at the wine, they that go to seek mixed wine.

Dandini informs us that it was the practice of tipplers not merely to tarry long over the bottle, but over the wine cask. "The goodness of the wine of Candia renders the Candiots great drinkers, and it often happens, that two or three great drinkers will sit down together at the foot of a cask, from whence they wil. not depart till they have emptied it." See also Isaiah v. 11.—Burder.

Ver. 31. Look not thou upon the wine when it is red, when it giveth his colour in the cup, *when* it moveth it elf aright.

Red wines were most esteemed in the East. So much was the red colou admired, that when it was too white they gave it a deeper tinge by mixing it with saffron or Brazil wood. By extracting the colouring matter of such ingredients, the wine may be said to make itself redder; a circumstance which, in Mr. Harmer's opinion, Solomon means to express in that proverb, "Look not on the wine when it is red, when it giveth his colour in the cup, when it moveth itself aright." The verb is in the Hebrew Middle Voice, or Hithpahel conjugation, which denotes an action that turns upon the agent itself, and in this instance imparts great energy to the warning.—Paxton.

CHAPTER XXIV.

Ver. 11. If thou forbear to deliver *them that are* drawn unto death, and *those that are* ready to be slain.

It was allowed among the Jews, that if any person could offer any thing in favour of a prisoner after sentence was passed, he might be heard before execution was done: and therefore it was usual, as the Mishna shows, that when a man was led to execution, a crier went before him and proclaimed, "This man is now going to be executed for such a crime, and such and such are witnesses against him; whoever knows him to be innocent, let him come forth, and make it appear."—Doddridge.

Ver. 26. *Every man* shall kiss *his* lips that giveth a right answer.

The rescripts of authority used to be kissed whether they were believed to be just or not; and the letters of people of figure were treated in this manner; but it is possible these words may refer to another custom, which D'Arvieux gives an account of in his description of the Arabs of Mount Carmel, who, when they present any petition to their emir for a favour, offer their billets to him with their right hands, after having first kissed the papers. The Hebrew manner of expression is short; *every lip shall kiss, one maketh to return a right answer*, that is, every one shall be ready to present the state of his case, kissing it as he delivers it, when there is a judge whose decisions are celebrated for being equitable.—Harmer.

Ver. 31. And lo, it was all grown over with thorns, *and* nettles had covered the face thereof, and the stone wall thereof was broken down.

Stone walls were frequently used for the preservation of vineyards, as well as living fences. Van Egmont and Heyman, describing the country about Saphet, a celebrated city of Galilee, tell us, "the country round it is finely improved, the declivity being covered with vines supported by low walls."—Harmer.

CHAPTER XXV.

Ver. 7. For better *it is* that it be said unto thee, Come up hither, than that thou shouldst be put lower in the presence of the prince whom thine eyes have seen.

In an eastern feast or ceremony, nothing can exceed the particularity which is observed in reference to the rank and consequent precedence of the guests. Excepting where kings or members of the royal family are present, the floor and seats are always of an equal height; but the upper part of a room is most respectable, and there the most dignified individual will be placed. Should, however, an inferior presume to occupy that situation, he will soon be told to go to a lower station. There are also rooms assigned to different guests, in reference to their rank or caste, and none but their peers can remain in the place. I was once present at the marriage feast of a person of high caste: the ceremonies were finished, and the festivities had commenced; but just before the supper was announced, it was discovered that one of the guests was not quite equal in rank to those in the same apartment. A hint was therefore given to him, but he refused to leave the place: the host was then called; but, as the guest was scarcely a grade lower than the rest, he felt unwilling to put him out. The remainder, therefore, consisting of the first men in the town, immediately arose and left the house —Roberts.

Ver. 11. A word fitly spoken *is like* apples of gold in pictures of silver.

Some suppose this alludes to fruit served up in filigree-work: but I believe it does not refer to real fruit, but to representations and ornaments in solid gold. The Vulgate has, instead of pictures, "*in lectis argenteis*," "in silver beds." The Tamul translation has, in place of pictures of silver, *velle-tattam*, i. e. salvers or trays of silver. The Rev. T. H. Horne, "Apples of GOLD in net-work of silver." In the 6th and 7th verses, directions are given as to the way a person ought to conduct himself in the presence of a king: and words fitly spoken are compared, in their effect on the mind, to apples of gold, in salvers of silver, when presented as tributes or presents to the mighty. When eastern princes visit each other, or when men of rank have to go into their presence, they often send silver trays, on which are gold ornaments, as presents to the king, to propitiate him in their favour. Thus, when the governor-general, and the native sovereigns, visit each other, it is said, they distributed so many TRAYS of jewels, or other articles of great value. Golden ornaments, whether in the shape of fruit or any other thing, when placed on highly-polished silver salvers, or in net-work of the same metal, have a very beautiful appearance to the eye, and are highly acceptable and gratifying to him who receives them. As, then, apples or jewels of gold are in "salvers," or "beds," or "net-work" of silver, to the feelings of the receiver, so are words fitly spoken, when addressed to the mind of him who is prepared to receive them. To confirm this explanation, the next verse is very apposite: "As an ear-ring of gold, and an ornament of fine gold, so is a wise reprover upon an obedient ear." The EFFECT, then, of a wise reproof on an obedient ear, is equal to that produced by the presents of ear-rings of gold, or ornaments of fine gold.—ROBERTS.

Ver. 13. As the cold of snow in the time of harvest, *so is* a faithful messenger to them that send him; for he refresheth the soul of his masters.

The custom of cooling wines with snow, was usual among the eastern nations, and was derived from the Asiatics and Greeks to the Romans. The snow of Lebanon was celebrated, in the time of D'Vitriaco, for its refrigerating power in tempering their wine: "All summer, and especially in the sultry dog-days, and the month of August, snow of an extreme cold nature, is carried from Mount Libanus, two or three days' journey, that, being mixed with wine, it may make it cold as ice. The snow is kept from melting by the heat of the sun, or the warmth of the air, by being covered up with straw." To this custom, the wise man seems to allude in that proverb: "As the cold of snow in the time of harvest; so is a faithful servant to them that send him, for he refreshes the soul of his masters." The royal preacher could not speak of a fall of snow in the time of harvest, as pleasant and refreshing; it must, on the contrary, have been very incommoding, as we actually find it in this country; he must therefore be understood to mean liquids cooled by snow. The sense then will be: As the mixing of snow with wine, in the sultry time of harvest, is pleasing and refreshing; so a successful messenger revives the spirit of his master who sent him, and who was greatly depressed from an apprehension of his failure.—PAXTON.

Ver. 14. Whoso boasteth himself of a false gift, *is like* clouds and wind without rain.

See on 2 Kings 3. 16, 17.

Ver. 17. Withdraw thy foot from thy neighbour's house, lest he be weary of thee, and *so* hate thee.

"The premises are in grief through him who so often visits them."—Tamul Proverb. "The man, who though lost in the dark, and yet refuses to go to the house of him who will not treat him with respect, is worth ten millions of pieces of gold."—ROBERTS.

Ver. 19. Confidence in an unfaithful man in time of trouble, *is like* a broken tooth, and a foot out of joint.

The eastern saying, "To put confidence in an unfaithful man, is like trying to cross a river on a horse made of clay," is quoted for the same purpose.—ROBERTS.

Ver. 23. The north wind driveth away rain; *so doth* an angry countenance a backbiting tongue.

Our translators were at a loss how to render Prov. xxv. 23: they could not tell whether Solomon spoke of the *north wind* as driving away rain, or *bringing it forth*, and therefore put one sense in the text, and the other in the margin. I have observed nothing decisive as to this point in the books of travels which I have perused, and indeed very little more relating to the winds, excepting the violent heat they sometimes bring with them in these countries. At Aleppo, "the coldest winds in the winter are those that blow from between the northwest and the east, and the nearer they approach to the last-mentioned point, the colder they are during the winter, and part of the spring. But from the beginning of May to the end of September, the winds blowing from the very same points, bring with them a degree and kind of heat which one would imagine came out of an oven, and which, when it blows hard, will affect metals within the houses, such as locks of room-doors, nearly as much as if they had been exposed to the rays of the sun; yet it is remarkable that water kept in jars is much cooler at this time than when a cool westerly wind blows. In these seasons, the only remedy is to shut all the doors and windows, for though these winds do not kill as the *sammiel*, which are much of the same nature, do in the desert, yet they are extremely troublesome, causing a languor and difficulty of respiration to most people," &c.—HARMER.

Ver. 27. *It is* not good to eat much honey; so *for men* to search their own glory *is not* glory.

Delicious as honey is to an eastern palate, it has been thought sometimes to have produced terrible effects. So Sanutus tells us, that the English that attended Edward I. into the Holy Land, died in great numbers, as they marched, in June, to demolish a place, which he ascribes to the excessive heat, and their intemperate eating of fruits and honey. This, perhaps, may give us the thought of Solomon when he says, "It is not good to eat much honey." He had before, in the same chapter, mentioned that an excess in eating honey occasioned sickness and vomiting; but, if it was thought sometimes to produce deadly effects, there is a greater energy in the instruction.—HARMER.

CHAPTER XXVI.

Ver. 3. A whip for the horse, a bridle for the ass, and a rod for the fool's back.

According to our notions, we should rather say, "A bridle for the horse, and a whip for the ass." But it should be remembered that the eastern asses, particularly those of the Arabian breed, are much larger, more beautiful, and better goers, than those in our cold northerly countries. "In Arabia," says Nicholson, "we meet with two kinds of asses. The small and sluggish kind are as little esteemed in the East as in Europe. But there are some of a species large and spirited, which appeared to me more convenient for travelling than the horses, and which are very dear." Such, no doubt, there are evidently in Palestine, and as the modern Arabs take pains in training them to a pleasant pace, there is the highest probability that something of the kind was practised among the ancient Israelites; since from numerous passages of the Old Testament it appears that *asses* were the beasts on which that people, and even their great men, usually rode. Their asses, therefore, being active and well broke, would need only a *bridle* to guide them; whereas their horses, being scarce, and probably often caught wild, and badly broke, would be much less manageable, and frequently require the correction of the *whip*."—PARKHURST.

In the East, the horse was taught only two motions, to walk in state, or to push forward in full career; a bridle was therefore unnecessary, and seldom used, except for mere ornament; the voice, or the hand of his master, was sufficient to direct his way, or to stop his course. While the ass reluctantly submits to the control of the bridle, he presents his back with stupid insensibility to the rod. This instrument of correction is, therefore, reserved for the fool, and is necessary to subdue the vicious propensities of his heart, and turn him from the error of his way. The ancient Israelites preferred the young ass for the saddle. It is on this account the sacred writers so frequently mention riding on young asses and on ass colts. They must have found them, from experience, like the young of all animals, more tractable, lively, and active, than their parents, and, by consequence, better adapted to this employment. Buffon remarked particularly of the young ass, that it is a gay, nimble, and gentle animal, "and therefore to be preferred for riding to the same animal when become lazy and stubborn through age." "Indeed, the Hebrew name of the young ass, עיר," from a root which signifies to rouse or excite, "is expressive of its character for sprightliness and activity." On public and solemn occasions, they adorned the asses which they rode, with rich and splendid trappings. "In this manner," says an excellent writer of Essays on Sacred Zoology, "the magistrates, in the time of the Judges, appear to have rode in state. They proceeded to the gate of their city, where they sat to hear causes, in slow procession, mounted on asses superbly caparisoned with white cloth, which covered the greater part of the animal's body. It is thus that we must interpret the words of Deborah: 'Speak, ye that ride on white asses,' on asses caparisoned with coverings made of white woollen cloth, 'ye that sit in judgment, and walk,' or march in state, 'by the way.' The colour is not that of the animal, but of his *hiran*, or covering, for the ass is commonly dun, and not white."

No doubt can be entertained in relation to the existence of the custom alluded to in this quotation. It prevails among the Arabs to the present day; but it appears rather unnatural to ascribe the colour of a covering to the creature that wears it. We do not call a man white or black, because he happens to be dressed in vestments of white or black cloth; neither did the Hebrews. The expression naturally suggests the colour of the animal itself, not of its trappings; and the only point to be ascertained is, whether the ass is found of a white colour. Buffon informs us, that the colour of the ass is not dun, but flaxen, and the belly of a silvery white. In many instances, the silvery white predominates; for Cartwright, who travelled into the East, affirms, that he beheld, on the banks of the Euphrates, great droves of wild beasts, among which were many wild asses, all white. Oppian describes the wild ass, as having a coat of silvery white; and the one which Professor Gmelin brought from Tartary, was of the same colour. White asses, according to Morier, come from Arabia; their scarcity makes them valuable, and gives them consequence. The men of the law count it a dignity, and suited to their character, to ride on asses of this colour. As the Hebrews always appeared in white garments at their public festivals, and on days of rejoicing, or when the courts of justice were held; so they naturally preferred white asses, because the colour suited the occasion, and because asses of this colour being more rare and costly, were more coveted by the great and the wealthy. The same view is taken of this question by Lewis, who says, the asses in Judea "were commonly of a red colour; and therefore white asses were highly valued, and used by persons of superior note and quality." In this passage he clearly speaks of the colour of the animals themselves, not of their coverings.—PAXTON.

Ver. 11. As a dog returneth to his vomit; *so* a fool returneth to his folly.

"See the fellow," it is said, "he has repeatedly suffered for his folly; how often has he been corrected! and yet, like the dog, he eats up the food he has vomited." "Yes, he is ever washing his legs, and ever running into the mud." "You fool; because you fell nine times, must you fall again?"—ROBERTS.

Ver. 14. *As* the door turneth upon his hinges, so *doth* the slothful upon his bed.

The doors of the ancients did not turn on hinges, but on pivots thus constructed: the upright of the moveable door next the wall had, at each extremity, a copper case sunk into it, with a projecting point on the inside, to take the better hold of the wood-work. This case was generally of a cylindric form; but there have been found some square ones, from which there sprang on each side iron straps, serving to bind together and strengthen the boards with which the door was constructed hollow. (Winckelman's Herculaneum.)—BURDER.

Ver. 17. He that passeth by, *and* meddleth with strife *belonging* not to him, *is like* one that taketh a dog by the ears.

"Why meddle with that matter?" "Will a rat seize a cat by the ears?" "I will break thy bones, thou low caste." —"No doubt about that; I suppose in the same way as the rat which seized my cat last night: begone, or I will give thee a bite."—ROBERTS.

Ver. 25. When he speaketh fair, believe him not: for *there are* seven abominations in his heart.

The number seven is often used to denote MANY. "If we have rain, we shall have a crop of seven years." "My friend, I came to see you seven times, but the servants always said *teen-tingarăr*," i. e. he is eating. "I will never speak to that fellow again; he has treated me with contempt these seven times." "You stupid ass, I have told you seven times." "The wind is fair, and the dhony is ready for sea."—"I cannot believe you; I have already been on board seven times."—ROBERTS.

CHAPTER XXVII.

Ver. 6. Faithful *are* the wounds of a friend; but the kisses of an enemy *are* deceitful.

"Begone! wretch: you cannot deceive me. I am more afraid of your smiles, than the reproaches of my friend. I know the serpent—get out of my way." "Ah!" says the stranger, "the trees of my own village are better to me than the friends of this place."—ROBERTS.

Ver. 9. Ointment and perfume rejoice the heart; so *doth* the sweetness of a man's friend by hearty counsel.

At the close of a visit in the East, it is common to sprinkle rose, or some other sweet-scented water, on the guests, and to perfume them with aloe-wood, which is brought last, and serves for a sign that it is time for a stranger to take leave. It is thus described by M. Savary: "Towards the conclusion of a visit among persons of distinction in Egypt, a slave, holding in his hand a silver plate, on which are burning precious essences, approaches the face of the visiters, each of whom in his turn perfumes his beard. They then pour rose-water on his head and hands. This is the last ceremony, after which it is usual to withdraw." As to the method of using the aloe-wood, Maundrell says, they have for this purpose a small silver chafingdish, covered with a lid full of holes, and fixed upon a handsome plate. In this they put some fresh coals, and upon them a piece of lignum aloes, and then shutting it up, the smoke immediately ascends with a grateful odour through the cover. Probably to such a custom, so calculated to refresh and exhilarate, the words of Solomon have an allusion.—BURDER.

Great numbers of authors take notice of this part of Eastern complaisance, but some are much more particular and distinct than others. Maundrell, for instance, who gives a most entertaining account of the ceremony of burning odours under the chin, does not mention any thing of the sprinkling sweet-scented waters; however, many other writers do, and Dr. Pococke has given us the figure of the vessel they make use of upon this occasion, in his first volume. They are both then used in the East, but if one is spoken of more than the other, it is, I think, the perfuming persons with odoriferous smoke. The scriptures, in like manner, speak of perfumes as used anciently for civil purposes, as well as sacred, though they do not mention particulars. "Ointment and perfumes rejoice the heart," Prov. xxvii. 9. Perhaps this word, perfume, comprehends in its meaning, the waters distilled from roses, and odoriferous flowers, whose scents in the East, at least in Egypt, if Maillet may be admitted to be a judge, are much higher and more exquisitely grateful, than with us; but if those distillations should be thought not to have been known so early, the burning fragrant things, and the making a sweet smoke with them, we are sure, they were acquainted with, and to that way of perfuming, Solomon at least refers. But a passage in Daniel makes it requisite to enter more minutely into this affair, and as at the same time it mentions some other eastern forms of doing honour, which I have already taken notice of, but to all which in this case objections have been made, I will make my remarks upon it in a distinct article, which I will place immediately after this, and show how easy that little collection of oriental compliments may be accounted for, as well as explain more at large this particular affair of burning odours merely as a civil expression of respect.—Harmer.

Ver. 15. A continual dropping in a very rainy day, and a contentious woman, are alike.

See on ch. 21. 9.

Ver. 19. As in water, face *answereth* to face; so the heart of man to man.

The Hindoos do not appear to have had mirrors made of silvered glass, until they became acquainted with Europeans; but they had them of burnished metal and other articles. Many even at this day pour water into a vessel which they use for the same purpose. "His friendship for me is like my body and its shadow in the sun, which never separate."—Roberts.

Ver. 22. Though thou shouldst bray a fool in a mortar among wheat with a pestle, *yet* will not his foolishness depart from him.

Pounding in a mortar is a punishment still used among the Turks. The ulemats, or body of lawyers, in Turkey, are by law secured in two important privileges—they cannot lose their goods by confiscation, nor can they be put to death except by the pestle and mortar. The guards of the towers who suffered Prince Coreskie to escape from prison, were, some of them, empaled, and others pounded or beaten to pieces in great mortars of iron, by order of the Turkish government. This dreadful punishment appears to have been occasionally imposed by the Jewish rulers, for Solomon clearly alludes to it in one of his Proverbs: "Though thou shouldst bray a fool in a mortar among wheat with a pestle, yet will not his foolishness depart from him."—Paxton.

Dr. Boothroyd says, "that is, no correction, however severe, will cure him." Large mortars are used in the East for the purpose of separating the rice from the husk. When a considerable quantity has to be prepared, the mortar is placed outside the door, and two women, with each a pestle of five feet long, begin the work. They strike in rotation, as blacksmiths do on the anvil.

Cruel as it is, this is a punishment of the state; the poor victim is thrust into the mortar, and beaten with the pestle. The late king of Kandy compelled one of the wives of his rebellious chiefs thus to beat her own infant to death. Hence the saying, "Though you beat that loose woman in a mortar, she will not leave her ways;" which means, though you chastise her ever so much, she will never improve.—Roberts.

There is a remarkable passage, Prov. xxvii. 22, "Though thou shouldst bray a fool in a mortar among wheat with a pestle, yet will not his foolishness depart from him." The mode of punishment referred to in this passage, has been made a subject of inquiry, by a correspondent of the Gentleman's Magazine, who signs R. W., [conjectured to be Richard Winter, a very respectable minister among the dissenters.] In answer to his inquiries, another correspondent assured him there *were no traces of any such custom* in the East. But, besides what probability arises in the affirmative, from the proverbial manner of speech adopted by Solomon, the allusion may be strengthened, and the existence of such a punishment may be proved by positive testimony. None who are well informed, can willingly allow that any mode of expression in scripture is beyond elucidation, or can consent that the full import of a simile, adopted by an inspired writer, should be contracted or diminished.

"Fanaticism has enacted, in Turkey, in favour of the ulemats, [or body of lawyers,] that their goods shall never be confiscated, nor themselves put to death, *but by being bruised in a mortar*. The honour of being treated in so distinguished a manner, may not, perhaps, be sensibly felt by every one; examples are rare;—yet the insolence of the Mufti irritated Sultan Osman to such a degree, that he ordered *the mortars to be replaced*, which, having been long neglected, had been thrown down, and almost covered with earth. This order alone produced a surprising effect; the body of ulemats, justly terrified, submitted." (Baron De Tott.)

"The Mohammedans consider this office as so important, and entitled to such reverence, that the person of a pacha, who acquits himself well in it, becomes inviolable, even by the sultan; it is no longer permitted to shed his blood. But the divan has invented a method of satisfying its vengeance on those who are protected by this privilege, without departing from the literal expression of the law, *by ordering them to be pounded in a mortar*, of which there have been various instances." (Volney.)—Taylor in Calmet.

I have a drawing by a Cingalese, of the treatment received by the family of Elypola, one of Raja Singha's ministers, in 1814, and which led to his dethronement. In the first part of the picture the king is represented sitting in his palace, with one of his queens having her face in the opposite direction. Elypola is prostrate before him, with his wife and five children behind, guarded by a sentinel. In the second division, one executioner is ripping open one of the children, and another holding up the reeking head of the next, just cut off, and ready to drop it into a mortar. Next, the unhappy mother appears with the pestle lifted in her hands, to bray the head of her infant. It appears from the published accounts of this inhuman business, that the poor woman let fall the pestle once, and fainted away. Lastly, three children appear on a precipice with bound hands, and fastened to a large stone, intended to sink them in the pond, into which an executioner behind is about to precipitate them.—Calloway.

Ver. 25. The hay appeareth, and the tender grass showeth itself, and herbs of the mountains are gathered.

There is a gross impropriety in our version of Proverbs xxvii. 25, "The hay appeareth, and the tender *grass* showeth itself, and *herbs* of the mountains are gathered." Now, certainly, if the *tender grass* is but just beginning to show itself, the hay, which is grass cut and dried, after it has arrived at maturity, ought by no means to be associated with it, still less to precede it. And this leads us to notice, that none of the dictionaries, &c. which we have seen, give what seems to be the accurate import of this word, which we apprehend means, the first shoots, the rising—just budding—spires of grass. So in the present passage (נלה חציר *galeh chajir*) *the tender risings of the grass are in motion; and the buddings of grass* (grass in its early state, as is the peculiar import of דשא *desha*) *appear; and the tufts of grass*, proceeding from the same root, *collect themselves* together, and, by their union, begin *to clothe the mountain* tops with a pleasing verdure." Surely, the beautiful progress of vegetation, as described in this passage, must appear to every man of taste too poetical to be lost; but what must it be to an eastern beholder! to one whose imagination is exalted by a poetic spirit; one who has lately witnessed all-surrounding sterility, a grassless waste!—Taylor in Calmet.

Ver. 27. And *thou shalt have* goats' milk enough for thy food, for the food of thy household, and *for* the maintenance of thy maidens.

Milk is a great part of the diet of the eastern people. Their goats furnish them with some part of it, and Russel tells us are chiefly kept for that purpose; that they yield it in no inconsiderable quantity; and that it is sweet, and well-tasted. This at Aleppo is, however, chiefly from the beginning of April to September; they being generally supplied the other part of the year with cows' milk, such as it is: for the cows being commonly kept at the gardens, and fed with the refuse, the milk generally tastes so strong of garlic or cabbage-leaves, as to be very disagreeable. This circumstance sufficiently points out how far preferable the milk of goats must have been.—HARMER.

CHAPTER XXVIII.

Ver. 3. A poor man that oppresseth the poor *is like* a sweeping rain, which leaveth no food.

To feel the force of this passage a person should see the rains which sometimes fall in the East. For many months together we are occasionally without a single drop of rain, and then it comes down as if the heavens were breaking up, and the earth were about to be dissolved. The ground, which had become cracked by the drought, suddenly swells; the foundations of houses sink, or partially remove from their places; men and beasts flee for shelter; vegetables, trees, blossoms, fruits, are destroyed; and when the waters go off, there is scarcely any thing left for the food of man or beast. The torrents which fell on the continent of India and North Ceylon, in May, 1827, were a fearful illustration of the "sweeping rain which leaveth no food."—ROBERTS.

Ver. 15. *As* a roaring lion, and a ranging bear; *so is* a wicked ruler over the poor people.

The bear is occasionally found in company with the lion, in the writings of the Old Testament; and if the savage ferocity of his disposition be duly considered, certainly forms a proper associate for that destroyer. "There came a lion and a bear," said the son of Jesse, "and took a lamb out of the flock;" and Solomon unites them, to constitute the symbol of a wicked magistrate: "As a roaring lion, and a ranging bear, so is a wicked ruler over the poor people." The savage, which in these texts is associated with the lion, is the brown or red bear. Natural historians mention two other species, the white and black, the dispositions and habits of which are entirely different. The white bear differs in shape from the others, is an inhabitant of the polar regions, and feeds "on the bodies of seals, whales, and other monsters of the deep." It is properly a sea bear, and must have been totally unknown to the inspired writers, who lived so far remote from those dreary and desolate shores which it frequents. The black and the brown bears are considered by many as only varieties of the same species; but their temper and manners are so different, that Buffon, and other respectable writers, contend, that they ought to be regarded as specifically different. The brown or red bear is both a larger animal than the black, and a beast of prey that in strength and ferocity scarcely yields to the lion himself; while the black bear chiefly subsists on roots, fruits, and vegetables, and is never known to prey upon other animals. This species uniformly flies from the presence of men, and never attacks them but in self-defence; but the red bear is a bold, and extremely mischievous animal, which will attack a man with equal indifference as a lamb or a fawn. The black bear also confines himself to the more temperate northern latitudes, never ascending to the arctic circle, nor descending lower than the Alps, where it is sometimes found; but the brown bear accommodates himself to every clime, and is to be found in every desert, or uncultivated country, on the face of our globe. He ranges the Scythian wilds as far as the shores of the frozen ocean; he infests the boundless forests of America; he traverses the burning wastes of Lybia and Numidia, countries of Africa, which supplied the ancient Romans with bears to be exhibited at their public spectacles; he prowls on the glowing sands of Arabia; he lounges on the banks of the Nile, and on the shores of the Red Sea; he inhabits the wilderness adjoining to the Holy Land. Hence, the black bear must have been unknown to the inhabitants of Canaan; while the red bear infested their country, prowled around their flocks, and watched near their dwellings, affording them but too many opportunities of studying his character, and too much reason to remember his manners.

A particular description of this animal is to be found in every work on natural history; our concern is only with those traits in his character, which serve to illustrate the sacred writings. His external appearance is unusually rugged and savage; his limbs are strong and thick; his forefeet somewhat resemble the human hand; his hair is shaggy and coarse, and his whole aspect dull and heavy. His motions are as awkward as his shape is clumsy; but under this forbidding exterior he conceals a considerable degree of alertness and cunning. If hunger compel him to attack a man, or one of the larger animals, he watches the moment when his adversary is off his guard. In pursuit of his prey, he swims with ease the broad and rapid stream, and climbs the highest tree in the forest. Many beasts of prey surpass him in running; yet his speed is so great, that a man on foot can seldom escape. Hence, the danger to which a person is exposed from his pursuit, is extreme; he can scarcely hope to save himself by flight; the interposing river can give him no security; and the loftiest tree in the forest is commonly the chosen dwelling of his pursuer, which, so far from affording a safe retreat, only ensures his destruction. The danger of the victim, which the bear has marked for destruction, is increased by his natural sagacity, the keenness of his eye, and the excellence of his other senses, particularly his sense of smelling, which Buffon conjectures, from the peculiar structure of the organ, to be perhaps more exquisite than that of any other animal. Nor can any hope be rationally entertained from the forbearance or generosity of his temper; to these, or any other amiable quality, his rugged and savage heart is an entire stranger. His anger, which is easily excited, is at once capricious and intense. A dark and sullen scowl, which on his forbidding countenance never relaxes into a look of satisfaction, indicates the settled moroseness of his disposition; and his voice, which is a deep murmur, or rather growl, often accompanied with a grinding of the teeth, betrays the discontent which reigns within. It is therefore with justice that the inspired writers uniformly number him among the most ferocious and dangerous tenants of the forest, and associate his name and manner with the sorest judgments which afflict mankind.—PAXTON.

CHAPTER XXX.

Ver. 4. Who hath ascended up into heaven, or descended? who hath gathered the wind in his fists? who hath bound the waters in a garment? who hath established all the ends of the earth? what *is* his name, and what *is* his son's name, if thou canst tell?

"Yes, you are full of confidence, you are quite sure, you know all about it: have you just returned from the heavens?" "Truly, he has just finished his journey from above: listen, listen, to this divine messenger." "Our friend is about to do wonderful things, he has already caught the wind; he has seized it with his hand."—ROBERTS.

Ver. 10. Accuse not a servant unto his master, lest he curse thee, and thou be found guilty.

Whatever crimes your servants commit, no one will tell you of them, except those who wish to gain your favour. But let them once fall, then people in every direction come to expose their villany.—ROBERTS.

Ver. 15. The horse-leech hath two daughters, *crying*, Give, give.

This creature is only once mentioned in the holy scriptures. It was known to the ancient Hebrews under the name (עלוקה) *aluka*, from the verb *alak*, which, in Arabic, signifies to adhere, stick close, or hang fast. The reason of the Hebrew name is evident; the leech sticks fast to the skin: and in several languages, its pertinacious adhesion is become proverbial. Horace celebrates it in this line—

"Non missura cutem, nisi plena cruoris hirudo."

An ancient author calls it the black reptile of the marsh, because it is commonly found in marshy places. Its cruelty and thirst of blood, are noted by many writers, and, indeed, are too prominent qualities in this creature to be overlooked.

"——jam ego me vertam in hirudinem
Atque eorum exsugebo sanguinem."—*Plaut. in Epidico*, Act ii.

Long before the time of that ancient Roman, the royal preacher introduced it in one of his Proverbs, to illustrate the cruel and insatiable cupidity of worldly men: "The horse-leech hath two daughters, crying, Give, give." Several questions have been proposed in relation to this text; whether, for example, it is to be literally understood; and what the royal preacher means by its two daughters. Bochart contends, that it cannot be literally understood, first, because its introduction into that proverb would be quite improper; second, because the horse-leech has no daughters, being generated of putrid matter in the bottom of the marsh. In answer to these reasons, it may be observed, that if it be connected with the preceding verse, the introduction is quite proper, and highly emphatical; indeed, we can scarcely conceive any thing more forcible and beautiful than the comparison. To the second objection, it is sufficient to reply, that Bochart has merely asserted the formation of the horse-leech from putrid mire; but the absurdity of equivocal generation has already been considered. Mercer supposes, that the two daughters of the horse-leech are the forks of her tongue, by which she inflicts the wound; but this exposition is inadmissible, because she is destitute of that member, and acts merely by suction. Bochart, supposing that the clause where it is introduced, cannot with propriety be connected with any part of the context, considers it, of course, as independent; and admitting the derivation of *aluka* from *alak*, to hang or be appended, interprets the term as denoting the termination of human life, appended as it were to the purpose of God, limiting the term of our mortal existence; and by consequence, that her two daughters are death and the grave, or, should these be thought nearly synonymous, the grave, where the body returns to its dust, and the world of spirits, where the soul takes up its abode. But with all deference to such high authority, this interpretation appears very forced and unnatural. The common interpretation seems, in every respect, entitled to the preference. Solomon, having in the preceding verses mentioned those that devoured the property of the poor, as the worst of all the generations he had specified, proceeds in the fifteenth verse to state and illustrate the insatiable cupidity with which they prosecuted their schemes of rapine and plunder.—As the horse-leech hath two daughters, cruelty and thirst of blood, which cannot be satisfied; so, the oppressor of the poor has two dispositions, cruelty and avarice, which never say they have enough, but continually demand additional gratifications.—PAXTON.

Ver. 17. The eye *that* mocketh at *his* father, and despiseth to obey *his* mother, the ravens of the valley shall pick it out, and the young eagles shall eat it.

In the East, in consequence of the superstitions of heathenism, numerous human bodies are exposed to become the prey of birds and wild beasts; and it is worthy of being recorded, that the EYE is the first part selected by the former, as their favourite portion. It is, however, considered to be a great misfortune to be left without sepulchral rites; and it is no uncommon imprecation to hear, "Ah! the crows shall one day pick out thy EYES." "Yes, the lizards shall lay their eggs in thy SOCKETS."—ROBERTS.

Solomon appears to give a distinct character to some of the ravens in Palestine, when he says, "The eye that mocketh at his father, and despiseth to obey his mother, the ravens of the valley shall pick it out, and the young eagles shall eat it." The wise man, in this passage, may allude to a species of raven, which prefers the valley for her habitation to the clefts of the rock; or he may perhaps refer to some sequestered valley in the Land of Promise, much frequented by these birds, which derived its name from that circumstance; or, as the rocky precipice where the raven loves to build her nest, often overhangs the torrent, (which the original word, נחל *nahal*, also signifies,) and the lofty tree, which is equally acceptable, rises on its banks, the royal preacher might, by that phrase, merely intend the ravens which prefer such situations. Bochart conjectures, that the valley alluded to was Tophet, in the neighbourhood of Jerusalem, which the prophet Jeremiah calls the valley of the dead bodies; because the dead bodies of criminals were cast into it, where they remained without burial, till they were devoured by flocks of ravens, which collected for that purpose from the circumjacent country. If this conjecture be right, the meaning of Solomon will be this: He who is guilty of so great a crime, shall be subjected to an infamous punishment; and shall be cast into the valley of dead bodies, and shall find no grave, but the devouring maw of the impure and voracious raven. It was a common punishment in the East, (and one which the Orientals dreaded above all others,) to expose in the open fields the bodies of evil-doers that had suffered by the laws of their offended country, to be devoured by the beasts of the field, and the fowls of heaven. Hence, in Aristophanes, an old man deprecates the punishment of being exposed to the ridicule of women, or given as a banquet to the ravens; and Horace, in his sixteenth epistle to Quintius, represents it as the last degree of degradation, to be devoured by these hateful birds.

"—— non pasces in cruce corvos."

The wise man insinuates, that the raven makes his first and keenest attack on the eye; which perfectly corresponds with his habits, for he always begins his banquet with that part of the body. Isidore says of him, "Primo in cadaveribus oculum petit:" and Epictetus, 'Οι μεν κορακες των τετελευτηκοτων τους οφθαλμους λυμαινονται: the ravens devour the eyes of the dead. Many other testimonies might be adduced; but these are sufficient to justify the allusion in the proverb.—PAXTON.

Ver. 25. The ants *are* a people not strong, yet they prepare their meat in the summer.

See on ch. 6. 6.

Ver. 26. The conies *are but* a feeble folk, yet make they their houses in the rocks.

See on Ps. 104. 18.

Ver. 27. The locusts have no king, yet go they forth all of them by bands.

See on 2 Chron. 7. 13.

Ver. 33. Surely the churning of milk bringeth forth butter, and the wringing of the nose bringeth forth blood; so the forcing of wrath bringeth forth strife.

The ancient way of making butter in Arabia and Palestine, was probably nearly the same as is still practised by the Bedouin Arabs and Moors in Barbary, and which is thus described by Dr. Shaw: "Their method of making butter is by putting the milk or cream in a goat's-skin turned inside out, which they suspend from one side of the tent to the other, and then pressing it to and fro in one uniform direction, they quickly occasion the separation of the unctuous and wheyey parts." So "the butter of the Moors in the empire of Morocco, which is bad, is made of all the milk as it comes from the cow, by putting it into a skin and shaking it till the butter separates from it." (Stewart's Journey to Mequinez.) And what is more to the purpose, as relating to what is still practised in Palestine, Hasselquist, speaking of an encampment of the Arabs, which he found not far from Tiberias, at the foot of the mountain or hill where Christ preached his sermon, says, "they make butter in a leathern bag hung on three poles, erected for the purpose, in the form of a cone, and drawn to and fro by two women."—BURDER.

The following is a description given by Thevenot of the manner of making butter at Damascus, which he, however, expressly assures us, is the same all over the East. "They tie a stick with both ends to the hind-feet of a goat's-skin, which serves instead of a leathern bag, that is, each end of the stick to one foot, and the same with the forefeet, that these sticks may serve as handles; they then put the milk into this bag, close it carefully, shake it about, holding by the two sticks; after a time, add some water, and then shake it as before, till butter comes."—ROSENMULLER.

CHAPTER XXXI.

Ver. 18. She perceiveth that her merchandise *is* good: her candle goeth not out by night.

To give a modern instance of a similar kind—Monsieur De Guys, in his Sentimental Journey through Greece, says, "embroidery is the constant employment of the Greek women. Those who follow it for a living are employed in it from morning to night, as are also their daughters and slaves. This is a picture of the industrious wife, painted after nature by Virgil, in the eighth book of his Æneid:—

'Night was now sliding in her middle course:
The first repose was finish'd; when the dame,
Who by her distaff's slender art subsists,
Wakes the spread embers and the sleeping fire,
Night adding to her work: and calls her maids
To their long tasks, by lighted tapers urg'd.'

I have a living portrait of the same kind constantly before my eyes. The lamp of a pretty neighbour of mine, who follows that trade, is always lighted before day, and her young assistants are all at work betimes in the morning."—BURDER.

Ver. 24. She maketh fine linen, and selleth *it;* and delivereth girdles unto the merchant.

Herodotus, it seems, thought the Egyptian women's carrying on commerce was a curiosity that deserved to be inserted in his history; it can hardly then be thought an impropriety to take notice of this circumstance in a collection of papers tending to illustrate the scriptures, and especially in a country where the women indeed spin, but the men not only buy and sell, but weave, and do almost every thing else relating to manufactures. The commerce mentioned by Herodotus is lost, according to Maillet, from among the women of Egypt in general, being only retained by the Arabs of that country who live in the mountains. The Arabian historians say, that the women used to deal in buying and selling of things woven of silk, gold, and silver, of pure silk, of cotton, of cotton and thread, or simple linen cloth, whether made in the country or imported; the men in wheat, barley, rice, and other productions of the earth. Maillet, in giving an account of the alteration in this respect in Egypt, affirms that this usage still continues among the Arabs to this day, who live in the mountains; and consequently he must be understood to affirm, that the things that are woven among the Arabs and sold, are sold by the women, who are indeed the persons that weave the men's hykes in Barbary, according to Dr. Shaw, and doubtless weave in Egypt.—HARMER.

ECCLESIASTES, OR THE PREACHER.

CHAPTER II.

Ver. 4. I made me great works; I built me houses; I planted me vineyards; 5. I made me gardens and orchards, and I planted trees in them of all *kind of* fruits; 6. I made me pools of water, to water therewith the wood that bringeth forth trees.

The following account of these reservoirs will evince at what an immense expense and labour they were constructed. Solomon's cisterns "are seated in a valley, and are three in number, each occupying a different level, and placed in a right line with each other, so that the waters of the one may descend into the next below it. Their figures are quadrangular: the first, or southern one, being about three hundred feet long; the second, four hundred; and the third, five hundred; the breadth of each being about two hundred feet. They are all lined with masonry, and descended to by narrow flights of steps, at one of the corners; the whole depth, when emtpy, not exceeding twenty or thirty feet. They were, at the present moment, all dry; but though they may be considered useful works in so barren and destitute a country as Judea, yet they are hardly to be reckoned among the splendid monuments of a luxurious sovereign's wealth or power, since there are many of the Hebrew tanks in Bombay, the works of private individuals, in a mere commercial settlement, which are much more elegant in their design, and more expensive in their construction, than any of these. Near these reservoirs there are two small fountains, of whose waters we drank, and thought them good. These are said to have originally supplied the cisterns through subterranean aqueducts; but they are now fallen into decay from neglect, and merely serve as a watering-place for cattle, and a washing-stream for the females of the neighbouring country." (Buckingham.)

"After a slight repast, we took leave of our hosts, and set out in a southern direction to examine the Piscine, said to have been constructed by Solomon. The royal preacher has been imagined to allude to these, among other instances of his splendour and magnificence, in the passage where he is arguing for the insufficiency of worldly pursuits to procure happiness, Eccl. ii. 6. They are three in number, placed nearly in a direct line above each other, like the locks of a canal. By this arrangement, the surplus of the first flows into the second, which is again discharged into the third: from thence a constant supply of living water is carried along the sides of the hill to Bethlehem and Jerusalem. The figure of these cisterns is rectangular, and they are all nearly of the same width, but of considerable difference in length, the third being almost half as large again as the first. They are still in a certain state of preservation, and with a slight expense might be perfectly restored. The source from whence they are supplied is about a furlong distant; the spring rises several feet below the surface, the aperture of which is secured by a door, so contrived, that it may be impenetrably closed on any sudden danger of the water being contaminated." (Jolliffe's Letters.)—BURDER.

At about an hour's distance to the south of Bethlehem, are the pools of Solomon. They are three in number, of an oblong figure, and are supported by abutments. The antiquity of their appearance entitles them, Dr. Richardson thinks, to be considered as the work of the Jewish monarch: "like every thing Jewish," he says, "they are more remarkable for strength than for beauty." They are situated at the south end of a small valley, and are so disposed on the sloping ground, that the waters of the uppermost may descend into the second, and those of the second into the third. That on the west is nearest the source of the spring, and is about 480 feet long; the second is about 600 feet in length, and the third about 660; the breadth of all three being nearly the same, about 270 feet. They are lined with a thick coat of plaster, and are capable of containing a great quantity of water, which they discharge into a small aqueduct that conveys it to Jerusalem. This aqueduct is built on a foundation of stone: the water runs through round earthen pipes, about ten inches in diameter, which are cased with two stones, hewn out so as to fit them, and they are covered over with rough stones, well cemented together. The whole is so much sunk into the ground on the side of the hills round which it is carried, that in many places nothing is to be seen of it. In time of war, however, this aqueduct could be of no service to Jerusalem, as the communication could be easily cut off. The fountain which supplies these pools is at about the distance of 140 paces from them. "This," says Maundrell, "the friars will have to be that sealed fountain to which the holy spouse is compared, Cant. iv. 12." And he represents it to have been by no means difficult to seal up these springs, as they rise under ground, and have no other avenue than a little hole, "like to the mouth of a narrow well." "Through this hole you descend directly down, but not without some difficulty, for about four yards; and then arrive in a vaulted room fifteen paces long and eight broad. Joining to this is another room of the same fashion, but somewhat less. Both these rooms are covered with handsome stone arches, very ancient, and perhaps the work of Solomon himself. You find here four places at which the water rises. From these separate sources it is conveyed by little rivulets into a kind of basin, and from thence is carried by a large subterraneous passage down into the pools. In the way, before it arrives at the pools, there is an aqueduct of brick pipes, which receives part of the stream, and carries it by many turnings and windings to Jerusalem. Below the pools, here runs down a narrow rocky valley, enclosed on both sides with high mountains. This the friars will have to be 'the enclosed garden' alluded to in the same place of the Canticles. As to the pools, it is probable enough they may be the same with Solomon's; there not being the like store of excellent spring-water to be met with anywhere else throughout Palestine. But, for the gardens, one may safely affirm, that if Solomon made them in the rocky ground which is now assigned for them, he demonstrated greater power and wealth in finishing his design, than wisdom in choosing the place for it."—Modern Traveller.

It were very desirable to convey some idea, though imperfect, of the nature and arrangement of the gardens annexed to royal palaces, in the East; for which this would be a proper place. But to bring the subject within a moderate compass is not easy; and every situation has peculiarities, which do not admit of illustration by comparison, or of application to our present purpose. The gardens of the seraglio at Constantinople command an extensive sea view, and are constructed accordingly. Dr. E. D. Clarke and M. Pouqueville agree that they are far from magnificent, as Europeans estimate magnificence; and may rather be thought wildernesses than gardens. They abound in fruit-tress, in treillages, in fountains, and in kiosques. Their other ornaments are but meager; and their flowers, which should constitute the chief distinction of a garden, especially of an imperial garden, are but ordinary. In fact, those gentlemen rather apologize to their readers for anticipated disappointment. "I promise," says Dr. Clarke, "to conduct my readers, not only within the retirement of the seraglio, but into the harem itself, and the most secluded haunts of the Turkish sovereign. Would only I could also promise a degree of satisfaction, in this respect adequate to their desire of information."

Chardin has given plates of several Persian gardens; and from what he says—which is confirmed by Mr. Morier—coolness and shade beneath wide-spreading trees, water, and verdure, are the governing powers of a Persian paradise. It might be so, anciently, at Jerusalem; nevertheless, we are still left in uncertainty as to what might characterize the ancient city of David, his palace, and his gardens. We may safely infer that they were extensive, since his demesne occupied the whole area of Mount Zion: they afforded a variety of heights, since the mount was far from level: it rose, also, much above Mount Moriah, on which stood the city of Jerusalem, and consequently commanded distinct views of that city and its environs. The various heights afforded situations for buildings of different descriptions; private kiosques adorned with the utmost magnificence and skill, (under Solomon,) dwellings for the inmates, the guards, the attendants, the harem, and for foreign curiosities also; for specimens of natural history, birds, beasts, &c. Nor was the extent of Mount Zion a rock; for Dr. Clarke states expressly, "If this be indeed Mount Zion, the prophecy concerning it, (Micah iii. 12,) that the plough should pass over it, has been fulfilled to the letter; for such labours were actually going on when we arrived." Here was therefore a space (or spaces) of arable land; and this, after so many revolutions of the surface, and so great intermixture of unproductive ruins, derived from the buildings and fortifications upon it, and around it. In its original state, we need not doubt but that it would admit, not only of the growth of shrubs, but of trees; "the thick gloom of cypresses and domes," which, as Dr. Clarke observes, of Constantinople, distinguish the most beautiful part of that city. How greatly such combinations must have contributed to the general aspect of the Hebrew metropolis, surrounded by barren mountains, we can be at no loss to conceive: and with these royal embellishments we may connect those which were "planted in the house of the Lord," Psalm xcii. 13. Mr. Rich says, very justly, "We should form a very incorrect notion of the residence of an eastern monarch, if we imagined it was one building which in its decay would leave a single mound, or mass of ruins. Such establishments always consist of a fortified enclosure, the area of which is occupied by many buildings of various kinds, without symmetry or general design, and with large vacant spaces between them."—Taylor in Calmet.

CHAPTER III.

Ver. 5. A time to cast away stones, and a time to gather stones together: a time to embrace, and a time to refrain from embracing.

See on 2 Kings 3. 19.

Ver. 7. A time to rend, and a time to sew; a time to keep silence, and a time to speak.

New clothes were thought very necessary for the solemnization of a stated eastern festival. Commentators have taken notice, that the *rending* mentioned by Solomon, Eccles. iii. 7, refers to the oriental modes of expressing sorrow; but they seem to think, that the *sewing* signifies nothing more than the terminating, perhaps nothing more than the abating, of affliction. Maimonides is quoted on this occasion, as saying, He that mourns for a father, &c., let him stitch up the rent of his garment at the end of thirty days, but never let him sow it up well. As the other cases, however, are as directly opposite as possible, is it not more probable, that a season of joy is here meant, in contrast to a time of bitter grief, than merely of some abatement of distress? And that by *a time of sewing*, is meant a time of making up new vestments, rather than a slight tacking together the places of their clothes, which were torn in the paroxysm of their grief?

Thus, when Jacob supposed he had lost his son Joseph, he *rent his clothes*, for grief, Gen. xxxvii. 34; while the time of preparing for the circumcision of the son of Ishmael, the bashaw of Egypt, when Maillet lived there, must have been a time of great sewing; for the rejoicing on that occasion lasted, it seems, "ten days, and on the first day of the ceremony the whole household of the bashaw appeared in new clothes, and were very richly dressed. Two vests of different-coloured satin had been given to every one of his domestics, one of English cloth, with breeches of the same, and a lining of fur of a Moscovite fox. The meanest slave was dressed after this sort with a turban, of which the cap was of velvet, or English cloth, and the other part adorned with gold. The pages had large breeches of green velvet, and short vests of gold brocade. Those of higher rank were more richly dressed; and there was not one of them but changed his dress two or three times during the solemnity. Ibrahim, the young lord that was to be circumcised, appeared on the morning of the first day, clothed in a half vest of white cloth, lined with a rich fur, over a doliman of Venetian cloth of gold, and over this half vest he wore a robe of fire-coloured camlet, lined with a green tabby. This vest, or quiriqui, was embroidered with pearls of a large size, and fastened before with a clasp of large diamonds. Through all the time the solemnity lasted, Ibrahim changed his dress three or four times a day, and never wore the same thing twice, excepting the quiriqui, with its pearls; which he put on three or four times." I need not go on with Maillet's account; it is sufficiently evident that the time of preparing for this rejoicing was a time of *sewing*.—Harmer.

CHAPTER IV.

Ver. 11. Again, if two lie together, then they have heat: but how can one be warm *alone?*

In the oriental regions the oppressive heat requires the members of the same family, in general, to occupy each a separate bed. This, according to Maillet, is the custom in Egypt; where, not only the master and the mistress of the family sleep in different beds in the same apartment, but also their female slaves, though several lodge in the same chamber, have each a separate mattress. Yet Solomon seems to intimate that a different custom prevailed in Canaan, and one which the extreme heat of the climate seems positively to forbid: "If two lie together, then they have heat, but how can one be warm alone?" Mr. Harmer endeavours to solve the difficulty, by supposing that two might sometimes occupy one bed for medicinal purposes. It is certain that, in the case of David, it was thought a very efficacious method of recalling the vital warmth when it was almost extinguished. But it is probable that the royal preacher alluded rather to the nipping cold of a Syrian winter, when the earth is bound with frost and covered with snow, than to the chilling rigours of extreme old age. The cold winter is very severe during the night in that country. Even in the daytime it is so keen, that Jehoiakim, the king of Judah, had a fire burning before him on the hearth, when he cut the scroll in which the prophecies of Jeremiah were written, and committed it to the flames. This accounts, in the most satisfactory manner, for the remark of Solomon; for nothing surely can be more natural than for two to sleep under the same canopy during the severe cold of a wintry night. The same desire of comfort, one would think, which induces them to separate in the summer, will incline them, at least occasionally, to cherish the vital heat by a nearer approximation than sleeping in the same room. It is usual, through the East, for a whole family to sleep in the same apartment, especially in the lower ranks of life, laying their beds on the ground. To this custom our Lord alludes in the parable: "He from within shall answer and say, Trouble me not; the door is now shut, and my children are now with me in bed;" that is, my whole family are now a-bed in the same room with me: "I cannot arise to give thee."—PAXTON.

CHAPTER V.

Ver. 6. Suffer not thy mouth to cause thy flesh to sin; neither say thou before the angel, that it *was* an error: wherefore should God be angry at thy voice, and destroy the work of thy hands?

"Let not thy mouth weakly excuse thee to no purpose; and do not say before the messenger, (who may be sent to inquire of thee what thou hast vowed,) it was a mistake." As the priests kept a servant to levy their share out of the offerings of the people, (1 Sam. ii. 13—16,) and as they were greatly concerned in seeing the vows punctually paid, it is probable that they kept messengers to go and summon those whom they knew to have vowed any thing, for the purpose of enforcing the payment of it. An employment which we find in aftertimes in the synagogues, without knowing when it began, might be the same, for the most part, with that which is here alluded to. The Jews, who scrupled to touch money on the sabbath-day, used to bind themselves on that day to an officer, sent by the rulers of the synagogue, to give such sum for alms; and that officer received it from them the next day. This conjecture is the more probable, as that officer, who was the chagan or minister of the synagogue, is sometimes styled the messenger of the synagogue. (Desvæux.)—BURDER.

Ver. 12. The sleep of a labouring man *is* sweet, whether he eat little or much: but the abundance of the rich will not suffer him to sleep.

In many parts of the East there are not any banks, or public offices, in which the affluent can deposite their riches; consequently the property has to be kept in the house, or concealed in some secret place. Under these circumstances, it is no wonder that a man having great wealth should live in constant dread of having it stolen. There are those who have large treasures concealed in their houses, or gardens, or fields, and the fact being known they are closely watched, whenever they pay special attention to any particular object, or place. The late king of Kandy, after he was taken prisoner, and on his voyage to Madras, was much concerned about some of his concealed treasures, and yet he would not tell where they were. So great is the anxiety of some, arising from the jewels and gold they keep in their frail houses, that they literally watch a great part of the night, and sleep in the day, that their golden deity may not be taken from them.

I knew a man who had nearly all his wealth in gold pagodas, which he kept in a large chest in his bedroom: neither in body nor in mind did he ever wander far from the precious treasure; his abundance hindered him from sleeping; and for a time it seemed as if it would hinder him from dying; for when that fatal moment came, he several times, when apparently gone, again opened his eyes, and again gave ANOTHER look at the chest; and one of the LAST offices of his hands was to make an attempt to feel for the key under his pillow!—ROBERTS.

CHAPTER VI.

Ver. 7. All the labour of man *is* for his mouth, and yet the appetite is not filled.

"My friend," says the sage, to the diligent and successful merchant, "why are you so anxious to have riches? Know you not that all this exertion is for the support of one single span of the belly?" "Tamby, you and your people work very hard; why do you do so?" The man will look at you for a moment, and then putting his fingers on his navel, say, "It is all for the belly."—ROBERTS.

CHAPTER VII.

Ver. 6. For as the crackling of thorns under a pot, so *is* the laughter of the fool. This also *is* vanity.

Cow-dung dried was the fuel commonly used for firing, but this was remarkably slow in burning. On this account the Arabs would frequently threaten to burn a person with cow-dung, as a lingering death. When this was used it was generally under their pots. This fuel is a very striking contrast to thorns and furze, and things of that kind, which would doubtless be speedily consumed, with the crackling noise alluded to in this passage. Probably it is this contrast which gives us the energy of the comparison.—HARMER.

Ver. 10. Say not thou, What is *the cause* that the former days were better than these? for thou dost not inquire wisely concerning this.

The Hindoos have four ages, which nearly correspond with the golden, silver, brazen, and iron ages of the western heathen. In the first age, called *Kretha*, they say the corn sprang up spontaneously, and required no attention; in the second, named *Treatha*, the justice of kings and the blessings of the righteous caused it to grow; in the third, called *Tuvara*, rain produced it; but in this, the fourth age, called *Kally*, many works have to be done to cause it to grow. "Our fathers," say they, "had three harvests in the year: the trees also gave an abundance of fruit. Where is now the cheapness of provisions? the abundance of fish? the fruitful flocks? the rivers of milk? the plenty of water? Where the pleasures? Where the docility of animals? Where the righteousness, the truth, and affection? Where the riches, the peace, the plenty? Where the mighty men? Where the chaste and beautiful mothers, with their fifteen or sixteen children? Alas! alas! they are all fled."—ROBERTS.

Ver. 13. Consider the work of God: for who can make *that* straight which he hath made crooked?

"My lord, it is of no use trying to reform that fellow: his ways are crooked: should you by force make him a little straight, he will relapse into his former state." "If you make straight the tail of the dog, will it remain so?"—ROBERTS.

Ver. 25. I applied my heart to know, and to search, and to seek out wisdom, and the reason *of things*, and to know the wickedness of folly, even of foolishness *and* madness.

The margin has, instead of applied, "I and my heart compassed," *i. e.* encircled, went round it. According to Dr. Adam Clarke, "I made a circuit;—I circumscribed the ground I was to traverse: and all within my circuit I was determined to know."—In English we say, "I *studied* the subject," but in eastern idiom, it is, "I went ROUND it." "Have you studied grammar?"—"Yes, *sutte sutte*," round and round. "That man is well acquainted with magic, for to my knowledge he has been round and round it: nay more, I am told he has COMPASSED ALL the sciences."—ROBERTS.

Ver. 26. And I find more bitter than death the woman whose heart *is* snares and nets, *and* her hands *as* bands: whoso pleaseth God shall escape from her; but the sinner shall be taken by her.

The following insidious mode of robbery gives a very lively comment upon these words of Solomon: "The most cunning robbers in the world are in this country. They use a certain slip with a running noose, which they cast with so much sleight about a man's neck when they are within reach of him, that they never fail, so that they strangle him in a trice. They have another curious trick also to catch travellers. They send out a handsome woman upon the road, who, with her hair dishevelled, seems to be all in tears, sighing and complaining of some misfortune which she pretends has befallen her. Now, as she takes the same way as the traveller goes, he easily falls into conversation with her, and finding her beautiful, offers her his assistance, which she accepts: but he hath no sooner taken her up on horseback behind him, but she throws the snare about his neck, and strangles him, or at least stuns him, until the robbers who lie hid come running in to her assistance, and complete what she hath begun." (Thevenot.)—BURDER.

CHAPTER IX.

Ver. 8. Let thy garments be always white; and let thy head lack no ointment.

This comparison loses all its force in Europe, but in India, where white cotton is the dress of all the inhabitants, and where the beauty of garments consists, not in their shape, but in their being clean and white, the exhortation becomes strikingly proper. A Hindoo catechist addressing a native Christian on the necessity of correctness of conduct, said, See how welcome a person is whose garments are clean and white. Such let our conduct be, and then, though we have lost caste, such will be our reception. (Ward.)—BURDER.

Ver. 12. For man also knoweth not his time: as the fishes that are taken in an evil net, and as the birds *that are* caught in the snare; so *are* the sons of men snared in an evil time, when it falleth suddenly upon them.

"Alas! alas! trouble has come suddenly upon me; I am caught as fishes in the net." "We are all of us to be caught as fishes in the net."—ROBERTS.

CHAPTER X.

Ver. 7. I have seen servants upon horses, and princes walking as servants upon the earth.

See on 1 Kings 10. 8.

In all ages and nations, we read or hear of complaints against those who have arisen from obscurity to respectability or rank in the state. It is not so modern as some suppose for servants and inferiors to imitate their superiors; and though some would like to see a return of the "good old times!" when a man's vest and jerkin would have to be regulated by his rank, such things are doubtless best left to themselves. The Hindoos are most tenacious in their adherence to caste, and should any one, through property or circumstances, be elevated in society, he will always be looked upon with secret contempt. Their proverb is, "He who once walked on the ground, is now in his palanquin; and he who was in his palanquin, is now on the ground."—ROBERTS.

Persons of rank and opulence, in those countries, are now distinguished from their inferiors, by riding on horseback when they go abroad; while those of meaner station, and Christians of every rank, the consuls of Christian powers excepted, are obliged to content themselves with the ass or the mule. A Turkish grandee, proud of his exclusive privilege, moves on horseback with a very slow and stately pace. To the honour of riding upon horses, and the stately manner in which the oriental nobles proceed through the streets, with a number of servants walking before them, the wise man seems to allude, in his account of the disorders which occasionally prevail in society: "I have seen servants upon horses, and princes walking as servants upon the earth."—PAXTON.

Ver. 8. He that diggeth a pit shall fall into it; and whoso breaketh a hedge, a serpent shall bite him.

Other enclosures have fences of loose stones, or mud walls, some of them very low, which often furnish a retreat to venomous reptiles. To this circumstance the royal preacher alludes, in his observations of wisdom and folly: "He that diggeth a pit, shall fall into it: and whoso breaketh a hedge, a serpent shall bite him." The term which our translators render hedge in this passage, they might with more propriety have rendered wall, as they had done in another part of the writings of Solomon: "I went by the field of the slothful, and by the vineyard of the man void of understanding; and lo, it was all grown over with thorns, and nettles had covered the face thereof, and the stone wall thereof was broken down."—PAXTON.

Ver. 11. Surely the serpent will bite without enchantment; and a babbler is no better.

The incantation of serpents is one of the most curious and interesting facts in natural history. This wonderful art, which sooths the wrath, and disarms the fury of the deadliest snake, and renders it obedient to the charmer's voice, is not an invention of modern times; for we discover manifest traces of it in the remotest antiquity. It is asserted, that Orpheus, who probably flourished soon after letters were introduced into Greece, knew how to still the hissing of the approaching snake, and to extinguish the poison of the creeping serpent. The Argonauts are said to have subdued by the power of song the terrible dragon that guarded the golden fleece: Ηδειη ενοπη θελξαι τερας. Ovid ascribes the same effect to the soporific influence of certain herbs, and magic sentences. But it seems to have been the general persuasion of the ancients, that the principal power of the charmer lay in the sweetness of his music. Pliny says accordingly, that serpents were drawn from their lurking-places by the power of music. Serpents, says Augustine, are supposed to hear and understand the words of the Marsi; so that, by their incantations, these reptiles, for the most part, sally forth from their holes.

The wonderful effect which music produces on the serpent tribes, is confirmed by the testimony of several respectable moderns. Adders swell at the sound of a flute, raising themselves upon the one half of their body, turning themselves round, beating proper time, and following the instrument. Their head, naturally round and long like an eel, becomes broad and flat like a fan. The tame serpents, many of which the Orientals keep in their houses, are known to leave their holes in hot weather, at the sound of a musical instrument, and run upon the performer. Dr. Shaw had an opportunity of seeing a number of serpents keep exact time with the dervishes in their circulatory dances, running over their heads and arms, turning when they turned, and stopping when they stopped. The rattle-snake acknowledges the power of music as much as any of his family; of which the following instance is a decisive proof: When Chateaubriand was in Canada, a snake of that species entered their encampment; a young Canadian, one of the party, who could play on the flute, to divert his associates, advanced against the serpent with his new species of weapon. "On the approach of his enemy, the haughty reptile coiled himself into a spiral line, flattened his head, inflated his cheeks, contracted his lips, displayed his envenomed fangs and his bloody throat; his double tongue glowed like two flames of fire; his eyes were burning coals; his body, swollen with rage, rose and fell like the bellows of a forge; his dilated skin assumed a dull and scaly appearance; and his tail, which sounded the denunciation of death, vibrated with so great rapidity, as to resemble a light vapour. The Canadian now began to play upon his flute, the serpent started with surprise, and drew back his head. In proportion as he was struck with the magic effect, his eyes lost their fierceness, the oscillations of his tail became slower, and the sound which it emitted became weaker, and gradually died away. Less perpendicular upon their spiral line, the rings of the fascinated serpent were by degrees expanded, and sunk one after another upon the ground, in concentric circles. The shades of azure, green, white, and gold, recovered their brilliancy on his quivering skin, and slightly turning his head, he remained motionless, in the attitude of attention and pleasure. At this moment, the Canadian advanced a few steps, producing with his flute sweet and simple notes. The reptile, inclining his variegated neck, opened a passage with his head through the high grass, and began to creep after the musician, stopping when he stopped, and beginning to follow him again, as soon as he moved forward." In this manner he was led out of their camp, attended by a great number of spectators, both savages and Europeans, who could scarcely believe their eyes, when they beheld this wonderful effect of harmony. The assembly unanimously decreed that the serpent which had so highly entertained them should be permitted to escape. Many of them are carried in baskets through Hindostan, and procure a maintenance for a set of people who play a few simple notes on the flute, with which the snakes seem much delighted, and keep time by a graceful motion of the head, erecting about half their length from the ground, and following the music with gentle curves, like the undulating lines of a swan's neck.

The serpent most common at Cairo, belongs to the viper class, and is undoubtedly poisonous. If one of them enter a house, the charmer is sent for, who uses a certain form of words. By this means, Mr. Brown saw three serpents enticed out of the cabin of a ship lying near the shore. The operator handled them, and put them into a bag. At other times, he saw the fascinated reptiles twist round the bodies of these charmers in all directions, without having had their fangs extracted, or broken, and without doing them any harm. Adders and serpents will twist themselves round the neck and naked bodies of young children belonging to the charmers, and suffer them to escape unhurt. But if any person who is ignorant of the art happens to approach them, their destructive powers immediately revive. At Surat, an Armenian seeing one of these charmers make an adder bite him, without receiving any other injury than the mere incision, boasted he could do the same; and causing himself to be wounded in the hand, died in less than two hours.

While the creature is under the influence of the charm, they sometimes break out the tooth which conveys the poison, and render it quite harmless: for the poison is contained in a bag, at the bottom of the fangs, which lie flat in the mouth, and are erected only when the serpent intends to bite. The bag, upon being pressed, discharges the poison through a hole or groove in the fang, formed to receive it, into the wound, which is at the same instant inflicted by the tooth. That all the teeth are not venomous, is evident from this circumstance, that the charmers will cause their serpents to bite them, till they draw blood, and yet the hand will not swell.

But on some serpents, these charms seem to have no power; and it appears from scripture, that the adder sometimes takes precautions to prevent the fascination which he sees preparing for him; "for the deaf adder shutteth her ear, and will not hear the voice of the most skilful charmer." The method is said to be this: the reptile lays one ear close to the ground, and with his tail covers the other, that he cannot hear the sound of the music; or he repels the incantation by hissing violently. The same allusion is involved in the words of Solomon: "Surely the serpent will bite without enchantment, and a babbler is no better." The threatening of the prophet Jeremiah proceeds upon the same fact: "I will send serpents (cockatrices) among you, which will not be charmed, and they shall bite you." In all these quotations, the sacred writers, while they take it for granted that many serpents are disarmed by charming, plainly admit, that the powers of the charmer are in vain exerted upon others. To account for this exception, it has been alleged, that in some serpents the sense of hearing is very imperfect, while the power of vision is exceedingly acute; but the most intelligent natural historians maintain, that the very reverse is true. In the serpent tribes, the sense of hearing is much more acute than the sense of vision. Pliny observes, that the serpent is much more frequently roused by the ear than by sight: "Jam primum hebetes oculos huic malo dedit, eosque non in fronte ex adverso cernere sed in temporibus: itaque excitatur, sed sæpius auditu quam visu." In this part of his work, the ancient naturalist discourses not concerning any particular species, but the whole class of serpents, asserting of them all, that nature has compensated the dulness of their sight, by the acuteness of their hearing. Unable to resist the force of truth, others maintain, that the adder is deaf, not by nature, but by design; for the Psalmist says, she shutteth her ear, and will not hear the voice of the charmer. But the phrase perhaps means no more than this, that some adders are of a temper so stubborn, that the various arts of the charmer make no impression; they are like creatures destitute of hearing, or whose ears are so completely obstructed, that no sounds can enter. The same phrase is used in other parts of scripture to signify a hard and obdurate heart: "Whoso stoppeth his ears at the cry of the poor, he also shall cry himself, but shall not be heard." It is used in the same sense by the prophet: "That stoppeth his ears from hearing of blood, and shutteth his eyes from seeing evil." The righteous man remains as unmoved by the cruel and sanguinary counsels of the wicked, as if he had stopped his ears. In the same manner, the stubborn or infuriated aspic, as little regards the power of song, as if her sense of hearing were obstructed or destroyed.

If the serpent repel the charm, or is deaf to the song, the charmer, it is believed, exposes himself to great danger, the whole force of the incantation falling upon the head of its author, against whom the exasperated animal directs its deadliest rage. But which of the serpent tribes have the power to repel the incantations of the charmer, or inject a poison which his art is unable to counteract, no ancient Greek writer has been able to discover, or has thought proper to mention. Ælian states, indeed, that the bite of an aspic admits of no remedy, the powers of medicine, and the arts of the charmer, being equally unavailing. But their omission has been amply supplied by the Arabian philosophers quoted by Bochart, our principal guide in this part of the work. These clear and accurate writers divide serpents into three classes. In the first, the force of the poison is so intense, that the sufferer does not survive their attack longer than three hours, nor does the wound admit of any cure, for they belong to the class of deaf or stridulous serpents, which are either not affected by music and other charms, or which, by their loud and furious hissing, defeat the purpose of the charmer. The only remedy, in this case, is instantaneous amputation, or searing the wound with a hot iron, which extinguishes the virus, or prevents it from reaching the sanguiferous system. In this class they place the regulus, the basilisk, and the various kinds of asps, with all those the poison of which is in the highest degree of intensity. This doctrine seems to correspond with the view which the Psalmist and the prophet give us in the passages already quoted, of the adder and cockatrice, or basilisk. It is certain, however, from the authentic statements of different travellers, that some of those serpents, as the aspic and the basilisk, which the Arabians place on the list of deaf and untameable snakes, whose bite admits of no remedy, have been frequently subjected to the power of the charmer; nor is it necessary to refer the words of the inspired writers to this subject, for they nowhere recognise the classification adopted by the Arabian philosophers. The only legitimate conclusion to be drawn from their words, is, that the power of the charmer often fails, whether he try to fascinate the aspic, basilisk, or any other kind of serpent. In order to vindicate the sacred writers, it is not necessary to suppose, with the Arabians, that some species of serpents exist, which the charmer endeavours in vain to fascinate; for in operating upon the same species, the success of his incantations may be various.—PAXTON.

Ver. 16. Wo to thee, O land, when thy king *is* a child, and thy princes eat in the morning!

It is considered to be most gross, most disgraceful, and ruinous, to eat EARLY in the morning: of such a one it is said, "Ah! that fellow was born with his belly."—"The beast eats on his bed!"—"Before the water awakes, that creature begins to take his food," which alludes to the notion that water in the well sleeps in the night. "He only eats and sleeps *pandy-pole*," i. e. as a pig.—"How can we prosper? he no sooner awakes than he cries, *teen! teen!*" food! food!—Roberts.

Ver. 16. Wo to thee, O land, when thy king *is* a child, and thy princes eat in the morning! 17. Blessed *art* thou, O land, when thy king *is* the son of nobles, and thy princes eat in due season, for strength, and not for drunkenness!

Dr. Russel tells us of the eastern people, that "as soon as they get up in the morning, they breakfast on fried eggs, cheese, honey, leban," &c.

We are not to suppose that when Solomon says, "Wo to thee, O land, when thy king is a child, and thy princes eat in the morning," Eccles. x. 16, that he means absolutely all kinds of eating; but feasting, the indulging themselves such length of time in eating, and drinking proportionably of wine, so as improperly to abridge the hours that should be employed in affairs of government, and perhaps to disqualify themselves for a cool and dispassionate judgment of matters.

This is confirmed by the following words, "Blessed art thou, O land, when thy king is the son of nobles, and thy princes eat in due season, for strength, and not for drunkenness," ver. 17. They may with propriety eat in a morning, bread, honey, milk, fruit, which, in summer, is a common breakfast with them, but it would be wrong then to drink wine as freely as in the close of the day.

Wine being forbidden the Mohammedans by their religion, and only drank by the more licentious among them, in a more private manner, it is not to be expected to appear at their breakfasts; but it is used by others, who are not under such restraints, in the morning, as well as in their other repasts.

So Dr. Chandler tells us, in his Travels in Asia Minor: "In this country, on account of the heat, it is usual to rise with the dawn. About daybreak we received from the French consul, a Greek, with a respectable beard, a present of grapes, the clusters large and rich, with other fruits, all fresh gathered. We had, besides, bread and coffee for breakfast, and good wines, particularly one sort, of an exquisite flavour, called muscadel." If they drank then wine at all in a morning, it ought to be, according to the royal preacher, in small quantities, for strength, not for drunkenness.

The eastern people, Arabians and Turks both, are observed to eat very fast, and, in common, without drinking; but when they feast and drink wine, they begin with fruit and sweatmeats, and drinking wine, and they sit long at table: Wo to the land whose princes so eat in a morning, eating after this manner a great variety of things, and slowly, as they do when feasting, and prolonging the time with wine. So the prophet Isaiah, in like manner, says, ch. v. 11, "Wo unto them that rise up early in the morning, that they may follow strong drink, that continue until night, until wine inflame them." Such appears to be the view of Solomon here.

If great men will indulge themselves in the pleasures of the table and of wine, it certainly should be in the evening, when public business is finished.—Harmer.

Ver. 20. Curse not the king, no, not in thy thought; and curse not the rich in thy bedchamber; for a bird of the air shall carry the voice, and that which hath wings shall tell the matter.

The manner of sending advice by pigeons was this: They took doves, which had a very young and unfledged brood, and carried them on horseback to the place from whence they wished them to return, taking care to let them have a full view. When any advices were received, the correspondent tied a billet to the pigeon's foot, or under the wing, and let her loose. The bird, impatient to see her young, flew off with the utmost impetuosity, and soon arrived at the place of her destination. These pigeons have been known to travel from Alexandretta to Aleppo, a distance of seventy miles, in six hours, and in two days from Bagdad; and when taught, they never fail, unless it be very dark, in which case they usually send two, for fear of mistake. The poets of Greece and Rome, often allude to these winged couriers, and their surprising industry. Anacreon's dove, which he celebrates in his ninth ode, was employed to carry her master's letters; and her fidelity and despatch are eulogized in these lines:

Εγω δε Ανακρεοντι, &c.

"In such things, I minister to Anacreon; and now see what letters I bring him."

It is more than probable, that to this singular custom Solomon alludes in the following passage: "Curse not the king, no, not in thy thought; and curse not the rich in thy bedchamber; for a bird of the air shall carry the voice, and they which have wings shall tell the matter." The remote antiquity of the age in which the wise man flourished, is no valid objection; for the customs and usages of Orientals, are almost as permanent as the soil on which they tread. Averse to change, and content, for the most part, with what their fathers have taught them, they transmit the lessons they have received, and the customs they have learned, with little alteration, from one generation to another. The pigeon was employed in carrying messages, and bearing intelligence, long before the coming of Christ, as we know from the odes of Anacreon and other classics; and the custom seems to have been very general, and quite familiar. When, therefore, the character of those nations, and the stability of their customs, are duly considered, it will not be reckoned extravagant to say, Solomon, in this text, must have had his eye on the carrier pigeon.—Paxton.

CHAPTER XI.

Ver. 1. Cast thy bread upon the waters: for thou shalt find it after many days.

I believe Dr. Adam Clarke is right in supposing that this alludes to the sowing of rice. The Tamul translation has it, "Cast thy food upon the waters, and the profit thereof shall be found after many days." Rice fields are so made as to receive and retain the rains of the wet monsoon, or to be watered from the tanks or artificial lakes. The rice prospers the most when the ground, at the time of sowing, is in the state of mud, or covered with a little water. In some lands, the water is allowed FIRST to overflow the whole, and then the roots are just stuck into the mud, leaving the blades to float on the surface. In reaping-time, as the water often remains, the farmer simply lops off the ears. See on Job xxiv. 24.—Roberts.

The Arabs have a very similar proverb, "Do good, throw bread into the water, it will one day be repaid thee." The Turks have borrowed it from the Arabs, with a slight alteration, according to which, it is as follows: "Do good throw bread into the water; even if the fish does not know, yet the Creator knows it." The meaning of the Hebrew, as well as of the Arabic and Turkish proverb, is, "Distribute thy bread to all poor people, whether known or unknown to thee; throw thy bread even into the water, regardless whether it swims, and who may derive advantage from it, whether men or fish; for even this charity, bestowed at a venture, God will repay thee sooner or later."—Rosenmuller.

Ver. 9. Rejoice, O young man, in thy youth, and let thy heart cheer thee in the days of thy youth, and walk in the ways of thy heart, and in the sight of thine eyes: but know thou, that for all these *things* God will bring thee into judgment.

Herodotus, speaking of the Egyptians, says, that "at the entertainments of the rich, just as the company are about to rise from the repast, a small coffin is carried round, containing a perfect representation of a dead body; it is in size sometimes of one, but never of more than two cubits, and as it is shown to the guests in rotation, the bearer exclaims, Cast your eyes on this figure; after death you yourself will resemble it; drink, then, and be happy."—Burder.

CHAPTER XII.

Ver. 4. And the doors shall be shut in the streets, when the sound of the grinding is low; and he shall rise up at the voice of the bird; and all the daughters of music shall be brought low.

It is to the first crowing of the house-cock in the morning, which is before daybreak, that Solomon probably alludes. This well describes the readiness of the restless old man to quit his uneasy bed, since it was much earlier than the usual time of rising. In the East, it was common to all, the young and the healthy, as well as the aged, to rise with the dawn.

The people in the East bake every day, and usually grind their corn as they want it. The grinding is the first work in the morning. This grinding with their mills makes a considerable noise, or rather, as Sir John Chardin says, "the songs of those who work them." May not this help to explain the meaning of this passage, in which the royal preacher, describing the infirmities of old age, among other weaknesses, says, *the doors shall be shut in the streets, when the sound of the grinding is low?* that is, the feeble old man shall not be able to rise from his bed early in the morning to attend that necessary employment of grinding corn, consequently his doors shall be shut; neither will the noise of their songs, which are usual at that employment, be heard, or when it is heard, it will be only in a low, feeble tone.—BURDER.

Ver. 5. Also *when* they shall be afraid of *that which is* high, and fears *shall be* in the way, and the almond-tree shall flourish, and the grasshopper shall be a burden, and desire shall fail; because man goeth to his long home, and the mourners go about the streets.

See on Jer. 1. 11, 12.

Ver. 11. The words of the wise *are* as goads, and as nails fastened *by* the masters of assemblies, *which* are given from one shepherd.

It is said, "The words of that judge are quite certain; they are like the driven nails." "I have heard all he has to say, and the effect on my mind is like a nail driven home." "What a speaker! all his words are nails; who will draw them out again?"—ROBERTS.

THE SONG OF SOLOMON.

CHAPTER I.

Ver. 5. I *am* black, but comely, O ye daughters of Jerusalem; as the tents of Kedar, as the curtains of Solomon.

Entertainments are frequently given in the country under tents, which, by the variety of their colours, and the peculiar manner in which they are sometimes pitched, make a very pleasant appearance. To this agreeable custom the spouse probably alludes, in that description of her person: "I am black, but comely, O ye daughters of Jerusalem; as the tents of Kedar, as the curtains of Solomon." The seeming contradiction in the first clause, is easily obviated. The Arabs generally make use of tents covered with black hair-cloth; the other nations around them live in booths, or huts, constructed of reeds and boughs, or other materials, or in tents of different colours. In Palestine, the Turcomans live in tents of white linen cloth; while the Turks, in their encampments, prefer green or red, which have a very pleasing effect in the eye of the traveller. It is only the Arabian tents, or the tents of Kedar, which are uniformly black, or striped. This is the reason the spouse compares herself, not to tents in general, which are of different colours, but to those of Kedar, which are all covered with black hair-cloth, and have therefore a disagreeable appearance. These tents are stretched on three or four pickets, only five or six feet high, which gives them a very flat appearance: at a distance, one of these camps seems only like a number of black spots.

To be black, but comely, involves no contradiction; for it is certain that the face may be discoloured by the sun, to the influence of which the spouse positively ascribes her sable hue, and yet possess an exquisite gracefulness. The Arab women, whom Mr. Wood saw among the ruins of Palmyra, were well shaped, and, although very swarthy, yet had good features. Zenobia, the celebrated queen of that renowned city, was reckoned eminently beautiful; and the description we have of her person answers to that character; her complexion of a dark brown, (the necessary effect of her way of life in that burning climate;) her eyes black and sparkling, and of an uncommon fire; her countenance animated and sprightly in a very high degree; her person graceful and genteel beyond imagination; her teeth white as pearl; her voice clear and strong. Such is the picture which historians have drawn of the beautiful and unfortunate Zenobia; from whence it appears, that a person may be both black and comely; and by consequence, that the description of Solomon, which certainly refers to the moral and religious state and character of the genuine worshipper of Jehovah, is neither incongruous nor exaggerated, but perfectly agreeable to nature. In this case, however, the duskiness of complexion was not natural, but the consequence of exposure to the rays of the sun; for the spouse anticipates the surprise which the daughters of Jerusalem would feel when they beheld her countenance: "Look not upon me, because I am black, because the sun hath looked upon me." Females of distinction in Palestine, and even in Mesopotamia, are not only beautiful and well-shaped, but, in consequence of being always kept from the rays of the sun, are very fair. This fact is attested by D'Arvieux, who was favoured with a sight of several Arabian ladies of high rank. It is not unworthy of notice, that the scripture bears the same testimony concerning the complexion of Sarah, of Rebecca, and of Rachel; they were "beautiful and well-favoured." But the women in general are extremely brown and swarthy in the complexion; although there are not a few of exquisite beauty in these torrid regions, especially among those who are less exposed to the heat of the sun. It is on this account that the prophet Jeremiah, when he would describe a beautiful women, represents her as one that keeps at home: because those who are desirous to preserve their beauty, go very little abroad The spouse proceeds, "As the tents of Kedar, as the curtains of Solomon." By the last clause may be understood those splendid tents, to which the great monarch, who, by his own confession, denied himself no earthly pleasure, retired in the heats of summer, or when he wished to entertain his nobles and courtiers, or sought the amusement of the chase. Some are of opinion, these curtains refer to the sumptuous hangings which surrounded the bed of the Israelitish king: and their idea receives some countenance from a manuscript note of Dr. Russel's, which states, that moscheto curtains are sometimes suspended over the beds in Syria and Palestine. But since it is common in Hebrew poetry to express nearly the same thought in the second parallel line as in the first; and since it is equally common in scripture to put a part for the whole,—it is more natural to suppose, that the tents of Solomon are actually meant in this passage; and as we are sure they were extremely magnificent, they might, with great propriety, be introduced here, on account of their beauty.—Paxton.

Ver. 7. Tell me, O thou whom my soul loveth, where thou feedest, where thou makest *thy flock* to rest at noon: for why should I be as one that turneth aside by the flocks of thy companions?

Before noon, the shepherds and their flocks may be seen slowly moving towards some shady banyan, or other tree, where they recline during the heat of the day. The sheep sleep, or lazily chew the cud; and the shepherds plat pouches, mats, or baskets, or in dreamy musings while away their time.—Roberts.

Ver. 9. I have compared thee, O my love, to a company of horses in Pharaoh's chariots.

This appears a very coarse compliment to a mere English reader, arising from the difference of our manners; but the horse is an animal in very high estimation in the East. The Arabians are extravagantly fond of their horses, and caress them as if they were their children. D'Arvieux gives a diverting account of the affectionate caresses an Arab used to give a mare which belonged to him. He had sold it to a merchant at Rama, and when he came to see it, (which he frequently did,) he would weep over it, kiss its eyes, and when he departed, go backwards, bidding it adieu in the most tender manner. The horses of Egypt are so remarkable for stateliness and beauty, as to be sent as presents of great value to the sublime porte; and it appears from sacred history, that they were in no less esteem formerly among the kings of Syria, and of the Hittites, as well as Solomon himself, who bought his horses at 150 shekels, which (at Dean Prideaux's calculation of three shillings the shekel) is £22. 10*s.* each, a very considerable price at which to purchase twelve thousand horses together. The qualities which form the beauty of these horses, are tallness, proportionable corpulency, and stateliness of manner; the same qualities which they admire in their women, particularly *corpulency*, which is known to be one of the most esteemed characters of beauty in the East. Niebuhr says, "as plumpness is thought a beauty in the East, the women, in order to obtain this beauty, swallow, every morning and every evening, three of these insects, (a species of *tenebriones*,) fried in butter." Upon this principle is founded the compliment of Solomon; and it is remarkable that the elegant Theocritus, in his epithalamium for the celebrated queen Helen, whom he described as *plump* and *large*, uses exactly the same image, comparing her to *the horse in the chariots of Thessaly*.—Burder.

Ver. 10. Thy cheeks are comely with rows *of jewels*, thy neck with chains *of gold*.

Olearius observes, in his description of the dress of the Persian women, "around the cheeks and chin they have one or two rows of pearls or jewels, so that the whole face is adorned with pearls or jewels. I am aware that this is a very ancient eastern custom; for already in Solomon's song it is said, "thy cheeks are comely with rows of jewels," &c. All these Persian court ladies had over their curled locks, instead of pearls, two long and thick cords of woven and beaten gold, hanging down from the crown of the head over the face on both sides; this ornament, because it is worn at court, is quite usual among the Persian women, and does not become them ill, in their black hair." (Della Valla.) Rauwolf gives a similar description of the head-dress of the Arabian women in the desert of Mesopotamia: "When they wish to adorn themselves, they have their trinkets, such as balls of marble, and yellow agate, glass beads of divers colours, longish pieces of metal strung upon a thread, hanging pendent upon their temples, nearly a span in length."—Rosenmuller.

Ver. 12. While the King *sitteth* at his table, my spikenard sendeth forth the smell thereof.

See on Mark 14. 3, 5.

Ver. 13. A bundle of myrrh *is* my well-beloved unto me; he shall lie all night betwixt my breasts.

The eastern women, among other ornaments, used little perfume-boxes, or vessels filled with perfumes, to smell at. These were worn suspended from the neck, and hanging down on the breast. This circumstance is alluded to in the *bundle of myrrh*. These *olfactoriola*, or smelling-boxes, (as the Vulgate rightly denominates them,) are still in use among the Persian women, to whose necklaces, which fall below the bosom, is fastened a large box of sweets; some of these boxes are as big as one's hand; the common ones are of gold, the others are covered with jewels. They are all bored through, and filled with a black paste very light, made of musk and amber, but of very strong smell.—Burder.

Ver. 14. My beloved *is* unto me *as* a cluster of camphire in the vineyards of Engedi.

"A cluster of camphire." This is the al-hennah, or cyprus. It is here mentioned as a perfume, and its clusters are noticed. This beautiful odoriferous plant, if it is not annually cut and kept low, grows ten or twelve feet high, putting out its little flowers in clusters, which yield a most grateful smell, like camphire, and may, therefore, be alluded to, Cant. i. 14. Its plants after they are dried and powdered, are disposed of to good advantage in all the markets of this kingdom, of Tunis. For with this all the African ladies, that can purchase it, tinge their lips, hair, hands, and feet; rendering them thereby of a tawny, saffron colour, which, with them, is reckoned a great beauty. Russel mentions the same practice of dying their feet and hands with hennah, as general among all sects and conditions at Aleppo. Hasselquist assures us he saw the nails of some mummies tinged with the al-hennah, which proves the antiquity of the practice. And as this plant does not appear to be a native of Palestine, but of India and Egypt, and seems mentioned, Cant. i. 14, as a curiosity growing in the vineyards of Engedi, it is probable that the Jews might be acquainted with its use as a die or tinge before they had experienced its odoriferous quality, and might, from the former circumstance, give it its name. See more concerning the hennah, or al-hennah, in Harmer's Outlines of a New Commentary on Solomon's Song, p. 218, &c.—Burder.

CHAPTER II.

Ver. 1. I *am* the rose of Sharon *and* the lily of the valleys.

In the East this flower is extremely fragrant, and has always been much admired. In what esteem it was held by the ancient Greeks, may be seen in the Odes of Anacreon, and the comparisons in Ecclus. 24. 14. 18. L. 8, show that the Jews were likewise much delighted with it. "In no country of the world does the rose grow in such perfection as in Persia; in no country is it so cultivated and prized by the natives. Their gardens and courts are crowded with its plants, their rooms ornamented with vases, filled with its gathered bunches, and every bath strewn with the full-blown flowers, plucked from the ever-replenished stems. Even the humblest individual, who pays a piece of copper money for a few whifs of a kelioun, feels a double enjoyment when he finds it stuck with a bud from his dear native tree." (Sir R. K. Porter.)—Burder.

Ver. 3. As the apple-tree among the trees of the wood, so *is* my beloved among the sons. I sat down under his shadow with great delight, and his fruit *was* sweet to my taste.

In Canaan, and the circumjacent regions, the apple-tree

is of no value; and, therefore, seems by no means entitled to the praise with which it is honoured by the spirit of inspiration. The inhabitants of Palestine and Egypt import their apples from Damascus, the produce of their own orchards being almost unfit for use. The tree then, to which the spouse compares her Lord in the Song of Solomon, whose shade was so refreshing, and whose fruit was so delicious, so comforting, so restorative, could not be the apple-tree, whose fruit can hardly be eaten; nor could the apple-tree, which the prophet mentions with the vine, the fig, the palm, and the pomegranate, which furnished the hungry with a grateful repast, the failure of which was considered as a public calamity, be really of that species: "The vine is dried up, the fig-tree languisheth, the pomegranate-tree, the palm-tree, also the apple-tree, even all the trees of the field, are withered; because joy is withered away from the sons of men." M. Forskall says, the apple-tree is extremely rare, and is named *tyffah* by the inhabitants of Palestine. In deference to his authority, the editor of Calmet, with every disposition to render the original term by the *citron*, is inclined to revert again to the apple. But if, as Forskall admits, the apple-tree is extremely rare, it cannot, with propriety, be classed with the vine, and other fruit-bearing trees, that are extremely common in Palestine and Syria. And if it grow 'with difficulty in hot countries," and required even the 'assiduous attention" of such a monarch as Solomon, before it could be raised and propagated, an inspired writer certainly would not number it among the "trees of the field," which, as the phrase clearly implies, can live and thrive without the fostering care of man.

The citron is a large and beautiful tree, always green, perfuming the air with its exquisite odour, and extending a deep and refreshing shade over the panting inhabitants of the torrid regions. Well, then, might the spouse exclaim: "As the citron-tree among the trees of the wood; so is my beloved among the sons. I sat down under his shadow with great delight, and his fruit was sweet to my taste." A more beautiful object can hardly be conceived, than a large and spreading citron, loaded with gold-coloured apples, and clothed with leaves of the richest green. Maundrell preferred the orange garden, or citron grove, at Beroot, the palace of the Emir Facardine, on the coast of Syria, to every thing else he met with there, although it was only a large quadrangular plot of ground, divided into sixteen smaller squares: but the walks were so shaded with orange-trees, of a large spreading size, and so richly adorned with fruit, that he thought nothing could be more perfect in its kind, or, had it been duly cultivated, could have been more delightful. When it is recollected that the difference between citron and orange-trees is not very discernible, excepting by the fruit, both of which, however, have the same golden colour, this passage of Maundrell's may serve as a comment on the words of Solomon, quoted in the beginning of the section.—PAXTON.

Shade, according to Mr. Wood, in his description of the ruins of Balbec, is an essential article in oriental luxury. The greatest people seek these refreshments, as well as the meaner. So Dr. Pococke found the patriarch of the Maronites, (who was one of their greatest families,) and a bishop, sitting under a tree. Any tree that is thick and spreading doth for them; but it must certainly be an addition to their enjoying of themselves, when the tree is of a fragrant nature, as well as shady, which the *citron-tree* is. Travellers there, we find in their accounts, have made use of plane-trees, walnut-trees, &c., and Egmont and Heyman were entertained with coffee at Mount Sinai, under the orange-trees of the garden of that place.

The people of those countries not only frequently sit under shady trees, and take collations under them, but sometimes the fruit of those trees under which they sit, is shaken down upon them, as an agreeableness. So Dr. Pococke tells us, when he was at Sidon, he was entertained in a garden, in the shade of some *apricot-trees*, and the fruit of them was shaken upon him. He speaks of it indeed as if it was done as a great proof of their abundance, but it seems rather to have been designed as an agreeable addition to the entertainment.—HARMER.

Ver. 5. Stay me with flagons, comfort me with apples; for I *am* sick of love.

Dr. Boothroyd:—"Support me with cordials; support me with citrons: for still I languish with love." Dr. A. Clarke:—"The versions in general understand some kind of ointments or perfumes by the first term," *i. e.* flagons. "Comfort me with apples:" they had not apples, as we in England; it is, therefore, probable that the citron or the orange (both of which are believed to be good for the complaint alluded to) is the fruit meant. "I am sick of love." Is it not amusing to see parents and physicians treating this affection as a DISEASE of a very serious nature? It is called the *Cāma-Cāchal*, i. e. Cupid's fever, which is said to be produced by a wound inflicted by one of his five arrows. When a young man or woman becomes languid, looks thin, refuses food, seeks retirement, and neglects duties, the father and mother hold grave consultations; they apply to the medical man, and he furnishes them with medicines, which are forthwith to be administered, to relieve the poor patient.

I believe the "versions in general" are right in supposing "ointments or perfumes" are meant, instead of flagons, because they are still considered to be most efficacious in removing the COMPLAINT. Thus, when the fever is most distressing, the sufferer is washed with rose-water, rubbed with perfumed oils, and the dust of sandal wood. The margin has, instead of comfort, "straw me with apples;" which probably means the citrons were to be put near to him, as it is believed they imbibe the heat, and consequently lessen the fever. It is also thought to be highly beneficial for the young sufferer to sleep on the tender leaves of the plantain-tree, (*banana*,) or the lotus flowers; and if, in addition, strings of pearls are tied to different parts of the body, there is reason to hope the patient will do well.—ROBERTS.

Ver. 7. I charge you, O ye daughters of Jerusalem, by the roes, and by the hinds of the field, that ye stir not up, nor awake *my* love, till he please.

See on 2 Sam. 2. 18.

Here again the custom illustrates the passage; it would be considered barbarous in the extreme to awake a person out of his sleep. How often, in going to the house of a native, you are saluted with "*Nittera-kulla-karār*," i. e. "He sleeps." Ask them to arouse him: the reply is, "*Koodātha*," i. e. "I cannot." Indeed, to request such a thing shows at once that you are griffin, or new-comer. "Only think of that ignorant Englishman: he went to the house of our chief, and being told he was asleep, he said he must see him, and actually made such a noise as to awake him; and then laughed at what he had done."—ROBERTS.

The antelope, like the hind, with which it is so frequently associated in scripture, is a timid creature, extremely jealous and watchful, sleeps little, is easily disturbed, takes alarm on the slightest occasion; and the moment its fears are awakened, it flies, or seems rather to disappear, from the sight of the intruder. Soft and cautious is the step which interrupts not the light slumbers of this gentle and suspicious creature. It is probable, from some hints in the sacred volume, that the shepherd in the eastern desert, sometimes wished to beguile the tedious moments, by contemplating the beautiful form of the sleeping antelope. But this was a gratification he could not hope to enjoy, unless he approached it with the utmost care, and maintained a profound silence. When, therefore, an Oriental charged his companion by the antelope, not to disturb the repose of another, he intimated, by a most expressive and beautiful allusion, the necessity of using the greatest circumspection. This statement imparts a great degree of clearness and energy, to the solemn adjuration which the spouse twice addresses to the daughters of Jerusalem, when she charged them not to disturb the repose of her beloved: "I charge you, O ye daughters of Jerusalem, by the roes, (the antelopes,) and by the hinds of the field, that ye stir not up, nor awake my love, till he please." In this language, which is pastoral, and equally beautiful and significant, the spouse delicately intimates her anxiety to detain her Lord, that she may enjoy the happiness of contemplating his glory; her deep sense of the evil nature and bitter consequences of sin; her apprehension, lest her companions, the members of her family, should by some rash and unholy deed provoke him to depart; and how reasonable it was, that they who coveted the society of that beautiful creature, and were accustomed to watch over its slumbers in guarded silence, should be equally cautious not to disturb the communion which she then enjoyed with her Saviour.—PAXTON.

Ver. 8. The voice of my beloved! behold, he cometh leaping upon the mountains, skipping upon the hills.

See on Ps. 18. 33.

Ver. 8. The voice of my beloved! behold, he cometh leaping upon the mountains, skipping upon the hills. 9. My beloved is like a roe, or a young hart: behold, he standeth behind our wall, he looketh forth at the window, showing himself through the lattice.

Mr. Harmer thinks this means the green wall, as it were, of a kiosque, or eastern arbour, which is thus described by Lady M. W. Montague: "In the midst of the garden is the kiosque, that is, a large room, commonly beautified with a fine fountain in the midst of it. It is raised nine or ten steps, and enclosed with gilded lattices, round which vines, jessamines, and honeysuckles, make a sort of green wall; large trees are planted round this place, which is the scene of their greatest pleasures."—BURDER.

In the Song of Solomon, the spouse more than once compares her beloved to the antelope, particularly alluding to the wonderful elasticity of its limbs, and the velocity with which, by a few leaps, it scales the loftiest precipice, or oounds from one cliff to another. Waiting with eager expectation his promised coming, she hears him at last speaking peace and comfort to her soul; and instantly describes him as hastening, in the ardour of his love, to her relief, and surmounting with ease every obstruction in his way.—PAXTON.

Dr. Russel observes, that the two species of antelopes about Aleppo, in Syria, "are so extremely fleet, that the greyhounds, though very good, can seldom take them, without the assistance of a falcon, unless in soft, deep ground." The following occurrence proves the strong attachment which some of the Arabs cherish for these animals: "A little Arab girl brought a young antelope to sell, which was bought by a Greek merchant, whose tent was next to me, for half a piaster. She had bored both ears, into each of which she had inserted two small pieces of red silk riband. She told the purchaser, that as it could run about and lap milk, he might be able to rear it up; and that she should not have sold it, but that she wanted money to buy a riband, which her mother could not afford her: then almost smothering the little animal with kisses, she delivered it, with tears in her eyes, and ran away. The merchant ordered it to be killed and dressed for supper. In the close of the evening, the girl came to take her last farewell of her little pet, knowing that we were to decamp at daybreak. When she was told that it was killed, she seemed much surprised, saying that it was impossible that anybody could be so cruel as to kill such a pretty creature. On its being shown to her, with its throat cut, she burst into tears, threw the money in the man's face, and ran away crying." (Parson's Travels.)—BURDER.

Ver. 10. My beloved spake, and said unto me, Rise up, my love, my fair one, and come away. 11. For, lo, the winter is past, the rain is over *and* gone.

The Orientals distinguish their winter into two parts, or rather the depth of winter, from the commencement and termination of the season, by the severity of the cold. This, which lasts about forty days, they call Murbania. To this rigorous part of the season, the wise man seems to refer, in that beautiful passage of the Song: "Rise up, my love, my fair one, and come away. For, lo, the winter is past, the rain is over and gone; the flowers appear on the earth: the time of the singing of birds is come; and the voice of the turtle is heard in our land." If we explain this text by the natural phenomena, these words, "the rain is over and gone," cannot be considered as an exposition of the preceding clause, "for, lo, the winter is past;" and as denoting, that the moist part of the year was entirely gone, along with which, Dr. Russel assures us, all rural delights abandon the plains of Syria: but the meaning is, that the Murbania, the depth of winter, is past and over, and the weather become agreeably warm; the rain has just ceased, and consequently, has left the sure and agreeable prospect of undisturbed and pleasant serenity, for several days. It had been no inducement to the spouse to quit her apartments with the view of enjoying the pleasures of the country, to be told, that the rainy season had completely terminated, and the intense heats of summer, under which almost any plant and flower sickens and fades away, had commenced. —PAXTON.

Ver. 12. The flowers appear on the earth; the time of the singing of *birds* is come, and the voice of the turtle is heard in our land.

The inhabitants of the great towns of Syria, during the pleasant weather in winter, frequently leave their homes, and give entertainments to their friends under tents, pitched in the country for that purpose. In April, and part of May, they retire to the gardens; and in the heat of summer, receive their guests in the summer-houses, or under the shade of the trees. The same custom seems, from the invitation of the bridegroom, to have prevailed in the land of Canaan in the time of Solomon. The inhabitants of Aleppo make their excursion very early in the season; and the cold weather is not supposed by Solomon to have ceased long before, since it is distinctly mentioned. In Syria, the narcissus flowers during the whole of the Murbania; hyacinths and violets, at latest, before it is quite over. Therefore, when Solomon says the flowers appear on the earth, he does not mean the time when the earliest flowers disclose their bloom, but when the verdant turf is thickly studded with all the rich, the gay, and the diversified profusion of an oriental spring. This delightful season is ushered in at Aleppo about the middle of February, by the appearance of a small cranes-bill on the bank of the river, which meanders through its extensive gardens; and a few days after, so rapid is the progress of vegetation, all the beauty of spring is displayed: about the same time, the birds renew their songs. When Thevenot visited Jordan, on the sixteenth of April, he found the little woods on the margin of the river, filled with nightingales in full chorus. This is rather earlier than at Aleppo, where they do not appear till nearly the end of the month. These facts illustrate the strict propriety of Solomon's description, every circumstance of which is accurately copied from nature.—PAXTON.

Ver. 14. O my dove, *that art* in the clefts of the rock, in the secret *places* of the stairs, let me see thy countenance, let me hear thy voice; for sweet *is* thy voice, and thy countenance *is* comely.

See on Ps. 68. 13.

The Tamul translation has, instead of "countenance," "form:" "Thy form is comely." Dr. Boothroyd says, "stairs" is certainly improper; but may there not be here an allusion to the ancient custom of building towers in the East, for the purpose of accommodating doves? I have seen one which had stairs inside, (probably to enable a person to ascend and watch for the approach of strangers;) on the outside were numerous holes, in regular order, where the doves concealed themselves, and brought up their young. It is common to call a female by the name of dove, but it refers more to secrecy than beauty. The mother of Rāmar said it was necessary for him to go to the desert, but she did not mention the reason to her husband; upon which he said, by way of persuading her to tell him, "Oh! my dove, am I a stranger?"—ROBERTS.

The phrase, which we render the secret places of the stairs, may, with more propriety, be translated, the secret crevices of the precipitous rocks; for the original term signifies a place so high and steep, that it cannot be approached but by ladders. So closely pursued were the people of Israel, and so unable to resist the assault of their enemies, that, like the timid dove, they fled to the fastnesses of the mountains, and the holes of the rocks.—PAXTON.

Ver. 15. Take us the foxes, the little foxes, that spoil the vines; for our vines *have* tender grapes.

Foxes are observed by many authors to be fond of grapes, and to make great havoc in vineyards. Aristophanes (in his Equites) compares soldiers to foxes, who spoil whole countries, as the others do vineyards. Galen (in his book of Aliments) tells us, that hunters did not scruple to eat the flesh of foxes in autumn, when they were grown fat with feeding on grapes.—BURDER.

CHAPTER III.

Ver. 5. I charge you, O ye daughters of Jerusalem, by the roes, and by the hinds of the field, that ye stir not up, nor awake *my* love till he please.

See on ch. 2. 7.

Ver. 6. Who *is* this that cometh out of the wilderness like pillars of smoke, perfumed with myrrh and frankincense, with all powders of the merchant?

The use of perfumes at eastern marriages is common; and upon great occasions very profuse. Not only are the garments scented till, in the Psalmist's language, they smell of myrrh, aloes, and cassia; it is also customary for virgins to meet, and lead the procession, with silver gilt pots of perfumes; and sometimes aromatics are burned in the windows of all the houses in the streets through which the procession is to pass, till the air becomes loaded with fragrant odours. In allusion to this practice it is demanded, "Who is this that cometh out of the wilderness like pillars of smoke, perfumed with myrrh and frankincense?" So liberally were these rich perfumes burned on this occasion, that a pillar of smoke ascended from the censers, so high, that it could be seen at a considerable distance; and the perfume was so rich, as to equal in value and fragrance all the powders of the merchant. The custom of burning perfumes on these occasions still continues in the East; for Lady Mary Wortley Montague, describing the reception of a young Turkish bride at the bagnio, says, "Two virgins met her at the door; two others filled silver gilt pots with perfumes, and began the procession, the rest following in pairs, to the number of thirty. In this order they marched round the three rooms of the bagnio." And Maillet informs us, that when the ambassadors of an eastern monarch, sent to propose marriage to an Egyptian queen, made their entrance into the capital of that kingdom, the streets through which they passed were strewed with flowers, and precious odours burning in the windows, from very early in the morning, embalmed the air.—PAXTON.

Ver. 11. Go forth, O ye daughters of Zion, and behold King Solomon with the crown wherewith his mother crowned him in the day of his espousals, and in the day of the gladness of his heart.

Such a ceremony as this was customary among the Jews at their marriages. Maillet informs us the crowns were made of different materials. Describing the custom, as practised by the members of the Greek church, who now live in Egypt, he says, "that the parties to be married are placed opposite to a reading-desk, upon which the book of the gospels is placed, and upon the book two crowns, which are made of such materials as people choose, of flowers, of cloth, or of tinsel. There he (the priest) continues his benedictions and prayers, into which he introduces all the patriarchs of the Old Testament. He after that places these crowns, the one on the head of the bridegroom, the other on that of the bride, and covers them both with a veil." After some other ceremonies, the priest concludes the whole by taking off their crowns, and dismissing them with prayers.—BURDER.

CHAPTER IV.

Ver. 9. Thou hast ravished my heart, my sister, *my* spouse; thou hast ravished my heart with one of thine eyes, with one chain of thy neck.

There is a singularity in this imagery, which has much perplexed the critics; and perhaps it is not possible to ascertain the meaning of the poet beyond a doubt. Supposing the royal bridegroom to have had a *profile*, or side view of his bride, in the present instance, only one eye, or one side of her necklace, would be observable; yet this charms and overpowers him. Tertullian mentions a custom in the East, of women unveiling only one eye in conversation, while they keep the other covered: and Niebuhr mentions a like custom in some parts of Arabia. This brings us to nearly the same interpretation as the above. (Williams.)—BURDER.

Ver. 12. A garden enclosed *is* my sister, my spouse; a spring shut up, a fountain sealed.

This morning we went to see some remarkable places in the neighbourhood of Bethlehem. The first place that we directed our course to, was those famous fountains, pools, and gardens, about an hour and a quarter distant from Bethlehem, southward, said to have been the contrivance and delight of King Solomon. To these works and places of pleasure, that great prince is supposed to allude, Eccl. ii. 5, 6, where, among the other instances of his magnificence, he reckons up his gardens, and vineyards, and pools. As for the pools, they are three in number, lying in a row above each other, being so disposed that the waters of the uppermost may descend into the second, and those of the second into the third. Their figure is quadrangular; the breadth is the same in all, amounting to about ninety paces; in their length there is some difference between them, the first being about one hundred and sixty paces long, the second two hundred, the third two hundred and twenty. They are all lined with wall, and plastered, and contain a great depth of water. Close by the pools is a pleasant castle of a modern structure; and at about the distance of one hundred and forty paces from them is a fountain, from which, principally, they derive their waters. This the friars will have to be that *sealed fountain*, to which the holy spouse is compared, Cant. iv. 12, and, in confirmation of this opinion, they pretend a tradition, that King Solomon shut up these springs, and kept the door of them sealed with his signet, to the end that he might preserve the waters for his own drinking, in their natural freshness and purity. Nor was it difficult thus to secure them, they rising under ground, and having no avenue to them but by a little hole, like to the mouth of a narrow well. Through this hole you descend directly down, but not without some difficulty, for about four yards, and then arrive in a vaulted room, fifteen paces long, and eight broad. Joining to this is another room, of the same fashion, but somewhat less. Both these rooms are covered with handsome stone arches, very ancient, and perhaps the work of Solomon himself. Below the pools here runs down a narrow rocky valley, enclosed on both sides with high mountains. This the friars will have to be the *enclosed garden* alluded to in the same place of the Canticles before cited. What truth there may be in this conjecture, I cannot absolutely pronounce. As to the pools, it is probable enough they may be the same with Solomon's; there not being the like store of excellent spring-water to be met with anywhere else throughout all Palestine. (Maundrell.)—BURDER.

Féirouz, a vizier, having divorced his wife Chemsennissa, on suspicion of criminal conversation with the sultan, the brothers of Chemsennissa applying for redress to their judge, "My lord," said they, "we had rented to Féirouz a most delightful garden, a terrestrial paradise; he took possession of it, encompassed with high walls, and planted with the most beautiful trees, that bloomed with flowers and fruit. He has broken down the walls, plucked the tender flowers, devoured the finest fruit, and would now restore to us this garden, robbed of every thing that contributed to render it delicious, when we gave him admission to it." Féirouz, in his defence, and the sultan in his attention to Chemsennissa's innocence, still carry on the same allegory of the garden, as may be seen in the author.—BURDER.

Ver. 16. Awake, O north wind, and come, thou

south; blow upon my garden, *that* the spices thereof may flow out. Let my beloved come into his garden, and eat his pleasant fruits.

The suffocating heats wafted on the wings of the south wind from the glowing sands of the desert, are felt more or less in all the oriental regions; and even in Italy itself, although far distant from the terrible wastes of the neighbouring continents, where they produce a general languor, and difficulty of respiration. A wind so fatal or injurious to the people of the East, must be to them an object of alarm or dismay. Yet, in the Song of Solomon, its pestilential blast is invited by the spouse to come and blow upon her garden, and waft its fragrance to her beloved. If the south winds in Judea are as oppressive as they are in Barbary and Egypt, and as the winds from the desert are at Aleppo, (which, according to Russel, are of the same nature as the south winds in Canaan;) or if they are only very hot, as Le Bruin certainly found them in October, would the spouse have desired the north wind to depart, as Bochart renders it, and the south wind to blow? The supposition cannot be admitted. An inspired writer never departs from the strictest truth and propriety in the use of figures, according to the rules of oriental composition; and therefore a meaning directly opposite must be the true one, to correspond with the physical character of that wind. The nature of the prayer also requires a different version; for is it to be supposed that the spouse, in the same breath, would desire two directly opposite winds to blow upon her garden? It now remains to inquire, if the original text will admit of another version; and it must be evident, that the only difficulty lies in the term which we render, Come thou. Now the verb *bo*, signifies both to come and to depart; literally, to remove from one place to another. In this sense of going or departing, it is used in the prophecies of Jonah twice in one verse: "He found a ship (baa) going to Tarshish; so he paid the fare thereof, and went down into it (labo) to go with them." It occurs again in this sense in the book of Ruth, and is so rendered in our translation: "He went (vayabo) to lie down at the end of the heap of corn." The going down or departure of the sun, is expressed by a derivative of the same verb in the book of Deuteronomy: "Are they not on the other side Jordan, by the way where the sun *goeth down?*" Joshua uses it in the same sense: "Unto the great sea, (Mebo,) towards the going down of the sun, shall be your coast." The passage, then, under consideration, may be rendered in this manner, putting the address to the south wind in a parenthesis: Arise, O north wind, (retire, thou south,) blow upon my garden, let the spices thereof flow forth, that my beloved may come into his garden, and eat his pleasant fruits.

This conclusion, were any confirmation necessary to establish so plain a truth, is verified by the testimony of Le Bruin, already quoted, who, in the course of his travels in Palestine, found, from experience, that it produced an oppressive heat, not the gentle and inviting warmth which Sanctius supposed. No traveller, so far as the writer has been able to discover, gives a favourable account of the south wind; consequently, it cannot be an object of desire; the view therefore which Harmer first gave of this text, is, in every respect, entitled to the preference: "Awake, O north wind, (depart, thou south,) blow upon my garden, that the spices thereof may flow out."—PAXTON.

CHAPTER V.

Ver. 2. I sleep, but my heart waketh: *it is* the voice of my beloved that knocketh, *saying*, Open to me, my sister, my love, my dove, my undefiled: for my head is filled with dew, *and* my locks with the drops of the night.

See on ch. 6. 9.

Ver. 4. My beloved put in his hand by the hole *of the door*, and my bowels were moved for him.

In the capital of Egypt, also, all their locks and keys are of wood; they have none of iron, not even for their city gates, which may with ease be opened without a key. The keys, or bits of timber, with little pieces of wire, lift up other pieces of wire that are in the lock, and enter into certain little holes, out of which the ends of the wires that are in the key have just expelled the corresponding wires, upon which the gate is opened. But to accomplish this, a key is not necessary; the Egyptian lock is so imperfectly made, that one may without difficulty open it with his finger, armed with a little soft paste. The locks in Canaan, at one time, do not seem to have been made with greater art, if Solomon allude to the ease with which they were frequently opened without a key: "My beloved put in his hand by the hole of the door, and my bowels were moved for him."—PAXTON.

Ver. 5. I rose up to open to my beloved; and my hands dropped *with* myrrh, and my fingers *with* sweet-smelling-myrrh, upon the handles of the lock.

When the spouse rose from her bed to open to her beloved, her hand dropped myrrh, (balsam,) and her fingers sweet-smelling myrrh, on the handles of the lock. In this remark, she seems to allude rather to a liquid than a powder; for the word rendered dropped, signifies to distil as the heavens or the clouds do rain, or as the mountains are said to distil new wine from the vines planted there, or as the inverted cups of lilies shed their roscid or honey drops. The same term is figuratively applied to words or discourse, which are said to distil as the dew, and drop as the rain; but still the allusion is to some liquid. As a noun, it is the name of stacte, or myrrh, distilling from the tree of its own accord, without incision. Again, the word rendered sweet-smelling signifies passing off, distilling, or trickling down; and, therefore, in its present connexion, more naturally refers to a fluid than to a dry powder. If these observations be just, it will not be difficult to ascertain the real sense of the passage.

When the spouse rose from her bed, to open the door of her apartment, she hastily prepared to receive her beloved, by washing herself with myrrh and water; or, according to an established custom in the East, by anointing her head with liquid essence of balsam: a part of which, in either case, might remain on her hands and fingers, and from them trickle down on the handles of the lock.—PAXTON.

Ver. 7. The watchmen that went about the city found me, they smote me, they wounded me; the keepers of the walls took away my veil from me.

See on Ezek. 33. 2.

They plucked off her veil, in order to discover who she was. It is well known that the eunuchs, in the eastern countries, are at present authorized to treat the females under their charge in this manner.—BURDER.

Ver. 10. My beloved *is* white and ruddy, the chiefest among ten thousand.

In our translation, the church represents her Saviour as the standard-bearer in the armies of the living God. "My beloved is white and ruddy, the chiefest among ten thousand;" or, according to the margin, a standard-bearer among ten thousand. These phrases are made synonymous, on the groundless supposition that a standard-bearer is the chief of the company; for among the modern Orientals, a standard-bearer is not the chief, more than among the nations of Europe. He is, on the contrary, the lowest commissioned officer in the corps who bears the colours. This, however, seems to be merely a mistake of our translators, in rendering the phrase *dagul meribabah*. If we understand by the word *dagul*, such a flag as is carried at the head of our troops, then, as the Hebrew participle is the pahul, which has a passive, and not an active sense, it must signify one before whom a standard is borne; not the person who lifts up and displays it, but him in whose honour the standard is displayed. It was not a mark of superior dignity in the East to display the standard, but it was a mark of dignity and honour to have the standard carried before one; and the same idea seems to be entertained in other parts of the world. The passage then, is rightly translated thus: My beloved is white and ruddy, and honourable, as one before whom, or around whom, ten thousand standards are borne.

The compliment is returned by her Lord in these words: "Thou art beautiful, O my love, as Tirzah, comely as Jerusalem, terrible as an army with banners;" and again, "Who is she that looketh forth as the morning, fair as the moon, clear as the sun, terrible as an army with banners?" Mr. Harmer imagines that these texts refer to a marriage procession, surrounded with flambeaux. But what is terrible in a company of women, even although "dressed in rich attire, surrounded with nuptial flambeaux," blazing ever so fiercely? Besides, his view sinks the last member of the comparison, and, indeed, seems to throw over it an air of ridicule: Who is this that looketh forth as the morning, fair as the moon, clear as the sun, and dazzling, like a bride lighted home with flambeaux? The common translation certainly sustains much better the dignity of the last clause, while it gives the genuine meaning of (אים) *aim*, which, in every passage of scripture where it occurs, signifies either terrible, or the tumult and confusion of mind which terror produces.—PAXTON.

Ver. 12. His eyes *are* as *the eyes* of doves by the rivers of water, washed with milk, *and* fitly set.

Hebrew, for fitly set, "sitting in fulness;" that is, "fitly placed, and set as a precious stone in the foil of a ring." "See that youth, what a beautiful eye he has! it is like a sapphire set in silver;" which means, the metal represents the white and the blue, the other part of the eye. The eyes of their more sacred idols are made of precious stones. "Washed with milk." Though people thus wash themselves after a funeral, the custom is also spoken of by way of figure, as a matter of great joy. "Oh! yes, they are a happy pair; they wash themselves with milk." "The joy is as great as being bathed in milk." But some do thus actually wash their bodies three or four times a month, and the effect is said to be cooling and pleasing. I suppose, however, it arises as much from an idea of luxury, as any other cause. The residence of the god Vishnoo is said to be surrounded by a SEA OF MILK, which may also be another reason to induce the devotee thus to bathe himself.—ROBERTS.

The eyes of a dove, always brilliant and lovely, kindle with peculiar delight by the side of a crystal brook, for this is her favourite haunt; here she loves to wash and to quench her thirst. But the inspired writer seems to intimate, that not satisfied with a single rivulet, she delights especially in those places which are watered with numerous streams, whose full flowing tide approaches the height of the banks, and offers her an easy and abundant supply. They seem as if they were washed with milk, from their shining whiteness; and fitly, rather fully set, like a gem set in gold, neither too prominent nor too depressed, but so formed as with nice adaptation to fill up the socket.—PAXTON.

Ver. 15. His legs *are as* pillars of marble set upon sockets of fine gold; his countenance *is* as Lebanon, excellent as the cedars.

"His thighs are as pillars of marble, fixed upon pedestals of fine gold;" alluding to his sandals bound on his feet with golden ribands; or, perhaps, expressive of the feet themselves, as being of a redder tincture than the legs and thighs. The Asiatics used to die their feet of a deep red colour. Thus the lover in Gitagovinda says, O damsel, shall I die red with the juice of alactaca, those beautiful feet, which will make the full-blown land lotos blush with shame? (Sir W. Jones.)—BURDER.

CHAPTER VI.

Ver. 4. Thou *art* beautiful, O my love, as Tirzah; comely as Jerusalem; terrible as *an army* with banners.

This and the next chapter give an idea of what were the notions of beauty in the bride; she was like the city of Tirzah, belonging to the tribe of Ephraim. A handsome Hindoo female is compared to the sacred city of Seedambaram. The following, also, are signs of beauty in an eastern woman: her skin is the colour of gold; her hands, nails, and soles of the feet, are of a reddish hue; her limbs must be smooth, and her gait like the stately swan. Her feet are small, like the beautiful lotus; her waist is slender as the lightning; her arms are short, and her fingers resemble the five petals of the kāntha flower; her breasts are like the young cocoa-nut, and her neck is as the trunk of the areca-tree. Her mouth is like the ambal flower, and her lips as coral; her teeth are like beautiful pearls; her nose is high, and lifted up, like that of the chameleon, (when raised to snuff the wind;) her eyes are like the sting of a wasp, and the karungu-vally flower; her brows are like the bow, and nicely separated; and her hair is as the black cloud.—ROBERTS.

Ver. 9. My dove, my undefiled, is *but* one: she *is* the *only* one of her mother, she *is* the choice *one* of her that bare her.

The conjugal chastity of the dove has been celebrated by every writer, who has described or alluded to her character. She admits but of one mate; she never forsakes him till death puts an end to their union; and never abandons of her own accord, the nest which their united labour has provided. Ælian, and other ancient writers, affirm, that the turtle and the wood-pigeon punish adultery with death. The black pigeon, when her mate dies, obstinately rejects the embraces of another, and continues in a widowed state for life. Hence, among the Egyptians, a black pigeon was the symbol of a widow who declined to enter again into the marriage relation. This fact was so well known, or at least so generally admitted among the ancients, that Tertullian endeavours to establish the doctrine of monogamy by the example of that bird. These facts have been transferred by later authors to the widowed turtle, which, deaf to the solicitations of another mate, continues, in mournful strains, to deplore her loss, till death puts a period to her sorrows. These facts unfold the true reason, that the church is by Solomon so frequently compared to the dove.—PAXTON.

Ver. 11. I went down into the garden of nuts, to see the fruits of the valley, *and* to see whether the vine flourished, *and* the pomegranates budded.

See on ch. 7. 11, 12.

CHAPTER VII.

Ver. 1. How beautiful are thy feet with shoes, O prince's daughter! the joints of thy thighs *are* like jewels, the work of the hands of a cunning workman.

The word rendered *joints* means the concealed dress, or drawers, which are still worn by the Moorish and Turkish women of rank. Lady M. W. Montague, in describing her Turkish dress, says, "the first part of my dress is a pair of drawers, very full, that reaches down to my shoes, and conceals the legs more modestly than your petticoats; they are of a thin, rose-coloured damask, brocaded with flowers." —BURDER.

Ver. 3. Thy two breasts *are* like two young roes *that are* twins.

See on ch. 2. 8.

Ver. 4. Thy neck *is* as a tower of ivory; thine eyes *like* the fish-pools in Heshbon, by the gate of Bathrabbim; thy nose *is* as the tower of Lebanon, which looketh towards Damascus.

Whatever is majestic and comely in the human countenance; whatever commands the reverence, and excites the love of the beholder,—Lebanon, and its towering cedars, are employed by the sacred writers to express. In the commendation of the church, the countenance of her Lord is as Lebanon, excellent as the cedars: while in the eulogium which he pronounces on his beloved, one feature of her countenance is compared to the highest peak of that mountain, to the Sannin, which rises, with majestic grandeur, above the tallest cedars that adorn its summits: "Thy nose is as the tower of Lebanon, which looketh towards Damascus." Calmet imagines, with no small degree of probability, that the sacred writer alludes to an elegant tower of white marble, which, in his days, crowned the summit of a lofty precipice, at the foot of which the river Barrady foams, about the distance of two miles from Damascus. When Maundrell visited the place, he found a small structure, like a sheik's sepulchre, erected on the highest point of the precipice, where it had probably stood. From this elevated station, which forms a part of Lebanon, the traveller enjoyed the most perfect view of the city. So charming was the landscape, so rich and diversified the scenery, that he confessedly found it no easy matter to tear himself away from the paradise of delights which bloomed at his feet. Nor was a very late traveller less delighted with this most enchanting prospect.—PAXTON.

Ver. 5. Thy head upon thee *is* like Carmel, and the hair of thy head like purple; the King *is* held in the galleries.

The only remarkable mountain on the western border of Canaan, is Carmel, which lies on the seacoast, at the south end of the tribe of Asher, and is frequently mentioned in the sacred writings. On this mountain, which is very rocky, and about two thousand feet in height, the prophet Elijah fixed his residence: and the monks of the Greek church, who have a convent upon it, show the inquisitive stranger the grotto, neatly cut out in the solid rock, where, at a distance from the tumult of the world, the venerable seer reposed. At the distance of a league are two fountains, which they pretend the prophet, by his miraculous powers, made to spring out of the earth; and lower down, towards the foot of the mountain, is the cave where he instructed the people. It is an excavation in the rock, cut very smooth, both above and below, of about twenty paces in length, fifteen in breadth, and very high; and Thevenot, who paid a visit to the monks of Mount Carmel, pronounces it one of the finest grottoes that can be seen. The beautiful shape and towering height of Carmel, furnish Solomon with a striking simile, expressive of the loveliness and majesty of the church in the eyes of her Redeemer: "Thy head upon thee is like Carmel, and the hair of thy head like purple; the King is held in the galleries." The mountain itself is nothing but rock. The monks, however, have with great labour covered some parts of it with soil, on which they cultivate flowers and fruits of various kinds; but the fields around have been celebrated in all ages for the extent of their pastures, and the richness of their verdure. So great was the fertility of this region, that, in the language of the sacred writers, the name, Carmel, is often equivalent to a fruitful field. This was undoubtedly the reason that the covetous and churlish Nabal chose it for the range of his numerous flocks and herds. —PAXTON.

Ver. 8. I said, I will go up to the palm-tree, I will take hold of the boughs thereof; now also thy breasts shall be as clusters of the vine, and the smell of thy nose like apples.

See on ch. 2. 3.

Ver. 11. Come, my beloved, let us go forth into the field; let us lodge in the village. 12. Let us get up early to the vineyards; let us see if the vine flourish, *whether* the tender grape appear, *and* the pomegranates bud forth: there will I give thee my loves.

In the gardens around Aleppo, commodious villas are built, for the use of the inhabitants, to which they retire during the oppressive heats of summer. Here, amid the wild and almost impervious thickets of pomegranate, and other fruit-bearing trees, the languid native and exhausted traveller find a delightful retreat from the scorching beams of the sun. A similar custom of retiring into the country, and taking shelter in the gardens, at that season, appears to have been followed in Palestine, in ages very remote.

The exquisite pleasure which an Oriental feels, while he reclines under the deep shade of the pomegranate, the apple, and other fruitful trees, in the Syrian gardens, which, uniting their branches over his head, defend him from the glowing firmament, is well described by Russel. "Revived by the freshening breeze, the purling of the brooks, and the verdure of the groves, his ear will catch the melody of the nightingale, delightful beyond what is heard in England; with conscious gratitude to heaven, he will recline on the simple mat, and bless the hospitable shelter. Beyond the limits of the gardens, hardly a vestige of verdure remains the fields are turned into a parched and naked waste." In Persia, Mr. Martyn found the heat of the external air quite intolerable. In spite of every precaution, the moisture of the body being soon quite exhausted, he grew restless, and thought he should have lost his senses, and concluded, that though he might hold out a day or two, death was inevitable. Not only the actual enjoyment of shade and water diffuses the sweetest pleasure through the panting bosom of an Oriental, but what is almost inconceivable to the native of a northern clime, even the very idea, the simple recurrence of these gratifications to the mind, conveys a lively satisfaction, and a renovating energy to his heart, when ready to fail him in the midst of the burning desert. "He who smiles at the pleasure we received," says Lichtenstein, "from only being reminded of shade, or thinks this observation trivial, must feel the force of an African sun, to have an idea of the value of shade and water."—PAXTON.

CHAPTER VIII.

Ver. 2. I would lead thee, *and* bring thee into my mother's house, *who* would instruct me: I would cause thee to drink of spiced wine of the juice of my pomegranate.

The fragrant odour of the wines produced in the vineyards of Lebanon, seems chiefly to have attracted the notice of our translators. This quality is either factitious or natural. The Orientals, not satisfied with the fragrance emitted by the essential oil of the grape, frequently put spices into their wines, to increase their flavour. To this practice Solomon alludes in these words: "I would cause thee to drink of spiced wine of the juice of my pomegranate." But Savary, in his Letters on Greece, affirms, that various kinds of naturally perfumed wines, are produced in Crete and some of the neighbouring islands: and the wine of Lebanon, to which the sacred writer alludes, was probably of the same species.—PAXTON.

Ver. 6. Set me as a seal upon thy heart, as a seal upon thine arm: for love *is* strong as death; jealousy *is* cruel as the grave: the coals thereof *are* coals of fire, *which hath* a most vehement flame.

When a husband is going to a distant country, the wife says to him, "Ah! place me as a seal upon thy heart," *i. e.* let me be impressed on thy affections, as the seal leaves its impression upon the wax. "Let not your arms embrace another; let me only be sealed there:" "for love is strong as death, jealousy is cruel as the grave."—ROBERTS.

This alludes to jewels, having the name or portrait of the beloved person engraved on it, and worn next the heart, or on the arm. In the pictures of the eastern princesses and heroines, there is sometimes a large square jewel on the forepart of the arm, a little below the shoulder. "When all the persons had assembled in the divan, every one remained sitting or standing in his place without moving, till in about half an hour came two kapudschis, one of whom carried the imperial signet-ring, and presented it to the grand vizier, who arose from his sofa, and received the signet-ring with a kind of bow, kissed it, put it on his hand, took it off again, and put it in the bag in which it had been before, and placed both in a pocket at the left side of his kaftan, as it were upon his heart." (Schultz.) —ROSENMULLER.

Ver. 14. Make haste, my beloved, and be thou like to a roe, or to a young hart, upon the mountains of spices.

See on ch. 2. 8, 9.

ISAIAH.

CHAPTER I.

Ver. 3. The ox knoweth his owner, and the ass his master's crib: *but* Israel doth not know, my people doth not consider.

"Ah! my children, my cows and my sheep know me well; but you cease to acknowledge me." "Alas! alas! my cattle know me better than my wife; I will go and live with them, for their love is sincere to me. I will not remain any longer in such a family; henceforth the affectionate cattle shall be my companions, they shall be my children."—ROBERTS.

Ver. 8. And the daughter of Zion is left as a cottage in a vineyard, as a lodge in a garden of cucumbers, as a besieged city.

This was a little temporary hut, covered with boughs, straw, turf, or the like materials, for a shelter from the heat by day, and the cold and dews by night, for the watchman that kept the garden, or vineyard, during the short season while the fruit was ripening, (Job xxvii. 18,) and presently removed when it had served that purpose. The eastern people were probably obliged to have such a constant watch to defend the fruit from the jackals. "The jackal," says Hasselquist, "is a species of mustela, which is very common in Palestine, especially during the vintage, and often destroys whole vineyards, and gardens of cucumbers."—BURDER.

Ver. 9. Except the LORD of hosts had left unto us a very small remnant, we should have been as Sodom, *and* we should have been like unto Gomorrah.

See on Job 4. 9.

Ver. 18. Though your sins be as scarlet, they shall be as white as snow; though they be red like crimson, they shall be as wool.

This, by many, is believed to refer to the strength of the colour, and to the difficulty of discharging it: and though I do not presume to contradict that opinion, it may perhaps be suggested to have an additional meaning. Dr. Adam Clarke says, "Some copies have (כשנים) *ke-shanim*, like crimson garments."

The iniquities of Israel had become very great. In the 10th verse the rulers are addressed as if of Sodom and Gomorrah; and in the 21st, it is said the faithful city had become a HARLOT. In the 29th, "They shall be ashamed of the oaks which ye have desired, and ye shall be confounded for the gardens that ye have chosen." Is it not certain that these references to Sodom, to a harlot, and the gardens, allude to the wickedness, the idolatry, and the union which Israel had formed with the heathen? For what purposes were the gardens or groves used, of which the frequenters were to be ashamed? No doubt, for the same as those in the East at the present day. The courtesans of the temples receive those in the groves, who are ashamed to go to their houses. Those wretched females are called *Soli-killikal*, i. e. parrots of the GROVE. "The wicked youth is always gathering flowers in the grove." "Thou hideous wretch! no one will marry thee; thou art not fit for the grove." (See on chap. lxvi. 17.)

Scarlet, or crimson, was the favourite colour of the ancient heathen prostitutes. (Jer. iv. 30.) "And when thou art spoiled, what wilt thou do? Though thou clothest thyself with CRIMSON, though thou deckest thee with ornaments of gold, though thou rentest thy face with painting, in vain shalt thou make thyself fair; thy lovers will despise thee." This is an exact description of the dress, and other modes of allurement, used by a female of the same character, at this day. (Rev. xvii. 4.) "The woman was arrayed in purple and SCARLET colour, and decked with gold and precious stones and pearls; having a golden cup in her hand, full of abominations and filthiness of her fornication: And upon her forehead was a name written, Mystery, Babylon the Great, the Mother of HARLOTS and Abominations of the Earth." In that most vivid description of Ezekiel (chap. xxii.) of the idolatries of Samaria and Jerusalem, they are represented as TWO HARLOTS, and there such disclosures are made as convey a most frightful picture of the depravity of the people. "She increased her whoredoms: for when she saw men portrayed upon the wall, the IMAGES of the Chaldeans portrayed with VERMILION." Her paramours, also, were "exceeding in DIED attire upon their heads." The SACRED prostitutes of the temple always have their garments of scarlet, crimson, or vermilion.—ROBERTS.

Ver. 22. Thy silver is become dross, thy wine mixed with water.

This is an image used for the adulteration of wine with more propriety than may at first appear, if what Thevenot says of the people of the Levant of late times, were true of them formerly. "They never mingle water with their wine to drink, but drink by itself what water they think proper for abating the strength of the wine." It is remarkable, that whereas the Greeks and Latins, by *mixed wine*, always understood wine diluted and lowered with water, the Hebrews, on the contrary, generally mean by it, wine made stronger and more inebriating, by the addition of higher and more powerful ingredients, such as honey, spices, defrutum, (or wine inspissated by boiling it down to two thirds, or one half of the quantity,) myrrh, mandragora, opiates, and other strong drugs. Such were the exhilarating, or rather stupifying ingredients, which Helen mixed in the bowl, together with the wine, for her guests oppressed with grief, to raise their spirits, the composition of which she had learned in Egypt. Such was the *spiced wine* mentioned Solomon's Song viii. 2; and how much the eastern people, to this day, deal in artificial liquors of prodigious strength, the use of wine being forbidden, may be seen in a curious chapter of Kempfer, upon that subject.—LOWTH.

Ver. 25. And I will turn my hand upon thee, and purely purge away thy dross, and take away all thy tin.

The propriety of the denunciation will appear from the following circumstance: "Silver, of all the metals, suffers most from an admixture of tin, a very small quantity serving to make that metal as brittle as glass; and, what is worse, being with difficulty separated from it again. The very vapour of tin has the same effect as the metal itself, on silver, gold, and copper, rendering them brittle." (New and Complete Dictionary of Arts, art. Tin.)—BURDER.

Ver. 29. For they shall be ashamed of the oaks which ye have desired, and ye shall be confounded for the gardens that ye have chosen.

In the language of the Hebrews, every place where plants and trees were cultivated with greater care than in the open field, was called a garden. The idea of such an enclosure was certainly borrowed from the garden of Eden, which the bountiful Creator planted for the reception of his favourite creature. The garden of Hesperides, in eastern fables, was protected by an enormous serpent; and the gardens of Adonis, among the Greeks, may be traced to the same origin; for the terms "*horti Adonides*," the gardens of Adonis, were used by the ancients to signify gardens of pleasure, which corresponds with the name of Paradise, or the garden of Eden, as *horti Adonis* answers to the garden of the Lord. Besides, the gardens of primitive nations were commonly, if not in every instance, devoted to religious purposes. In these shady retreats were celebrated, for a long succession of ages, the rites of pagan superstition. Thus, Jehovah calls the apostate Jews, "a people that provoked me continually to anger to my face, that sacrificeth in gardens." And in a preceding chapter, the prophet threatens them in the name of the Lord: "They shall be ashamed of the oaks which ye have desired, and ye shall be confounded for the gardens which ye have chosen." The inspired writer not only mentions these gardens, but also makes a clear allusion to the tree of life, or rather of knowledge, both of which were placed in the midst of Paradise.—PAXTON.

Ver. 30. For ye shall be as an oak whose leaf fadeth, and as a garden that hath no water.

See on Ps. 1. 3.

In the hotter parts of the eastern countries, a constant supply of water is so absolutely necessary for the cultivation, and even for the preservation and existence of a garden, that should it want water but for a few days, every thing in it would be burnt up with the heat, and totally destroyed. There is therefore no garden whatever in those countries, but what has such a certain supply, either from some neighbouring river, or from a reservoir of water collected from springs, or filled with rain-water in the proper season, in sufficient quantity to afford ample provision for the rest of the year.—BURDER.

CHAPTER II.

Ver. 4. And he shall judge among the nations, and shall rebuke many people; and they shall beat their swords into ploughshares, and their spears into pruning-hooks: nation shall not lift up sword against nation, neither shall they learn war any more.

See on Joel 3. 10.

Ver. 8. Their land also is full of idols; they worship the work of their own hands, that which their own fingers have made.

This is a true and literal description of India: the traveller cannot proceed a MILE, through an inhabited country, without seeing idols and vestiges of idolatry in every direction. See their vessels, their implements of husbandry, their houses, their furniture, their ornaments, their sacred trees, their DOMESTIC and public temples; and they all declare that the land is full of idols.—ROBERTS.

Ver. 13. And upon all the cedars of Lebanon, *that are* high and lifted up, and upon all the oaks of Bashan.

See on Deut. 3. 25.

Ver. 20. In that day a man shall cast his idols of silver, and his idols of gold, which they made *each one* for himself to worship, to the moles, and to the bats.

This, no doubt, refers to the total destruction of idolatry. "To the bats," (*V[illegible]nāls*,) those of the smaller species; as the larger are eaten by the Hindoos, and were also used as an article of food by the Assyrians. The East may be termed the country of bats; they hang by hundreds and thousands in caves, ruins, and under the roofs of large buildings. To enter such places, especially after rain, is MOST offensive. I have lived in rooms where it was sickening to remain, on account of the smell produced by those creatures, and whence it was almost impossible to expel them. What from the appearance of the creature, its sunken diminutive eye, its short legs, (with which it cannot walk,) its leather-like wings, its half-hairy, oily skin, its offensive ordure ever and anon dropping on the ground, its time for food and sport, darkness, "when evil spirits also range abroad," makes it one of the most disgusting creatures to the people of the East. No wonder, then, that its name is used by the Hindoos (as by the prophet) for an epithet of contempt. When a house ceases to please the inhabitants, on account of being haunted, they say, (and also do,) give it to the *bats*. "Alas! alas! my wife and children are dead; my houses, my buildings, are all given to the bats." "The bats are now the possessors of the once splendid mansions of royalty." People ask, when passing a tenantless house, "Why is this habitation given to the bats?" "Go, miscreant, go, or I will give thee to the bats." "The old magician has been swearing we shall all be given to the bats."—ROBERTS.

The bat is a winged quadruped, the link which connects the four-footed animal and the bird. It is a most deformed and hideous creature, which uniformly endeavours to shun the light of day, as if conscious of its disgusting aspect, and fixes its abode in the horrid cavern, or the ruined habitation. The great, or Ternat bat, belongs to the East, and was not altogether unknown to the ancients. It is noted for its cruelty, voracity, and filthiness. It is more mischievous than any other species of bat; but it carries on the work of destruction by open force, both during the night and day. It kills poultry and small birds; attacks men, and often wounds them in the face. This unsightly animal, says Forbes, fixes its dwelling among owls and noxious reptiles in the desolate tower, or lonely, unfrequented mausoleum, which it seldom or never leaves, except in the dusk of evening. In the East, where they grow to an enormous size, their stench is so intolerable that it is impossible to remain many seconds to examine the place. Into the vault or trench of the mole, and those dismal abodes frequented by the Ternat bats, which man can scarcely endure to visit, the idolater, terrified by the destructive judgments of a just and righteous God, shall cast his idols of silver, and his idols of gold, which he made for himself to worship; regardless of their intrinsic value, ashamed of the trust he reposed in them, and distracted by the terrors of the Almighty, he shall cast them in desperation and scorn out of his sight, that, freed from the useless encumbrance, he may escape for his life. "In that day a man shall cast his idols of silver, and his idols of gold, which they made each one for himself to worship, to the moles, and to the bats." Instead of building magnificent temples for their reception, where nothing to offend the senses is permitted to enter; instead of watching over them with scrupulous care, devoting their days, their riches, and all they possess, to their service, instead of adoring them with insensate prostrations and offerings, they shall cast them to creatures so vile or dangerous, into places so dismal and loathsome, as to preclude the possibility of returning to their idolatrous practices. Or to cast their idols to the moles and the bats, may signify the utter destruction of these objects of worship. When the Greeks said, Βαλλ' ες κορακας, cast him to the ravens, the meaning was, cast him to destruction: and this prophecy may refer to a proverbial expression among the Jews of similar import.—PAXTON.

CHAPTER III.

Ver. 15. What mean ye *that* ye beat my people to pieces, and grind the faces of the poor? saith the LORD God of hosts.

"Ah! my lord, do not thus crush my face: alas! alas! my nose and other features will soon be rubbed away. Is my face to be made quite flat with grinding? My heart is squeezed, my heart is squeezed. That head man has been grinding the faces of all his people."—ROBERTS.

Ver. 16. Moreover, the LORD saith, Because the daughters of Zion are haughty, and walk with stretched-forth necks and wanton eyes, walking, and mincing *as* they go, and making a tinkling with their feet.

In this, and the next eight verses, we have an accurate description of the ornaments and manners of a Hindoo dancing girl. These females are given by their parents, when they are about seven years of age, to the temples, for the purposes of being taught to sing the praises of the gods; of dancing before them, during some of their services, or when taken out in procession; and to be given to the embraces of the priests and people. Near the temples and the topes, *i. e.* groves, are houses built for their accommodation, and there they are allowed to receive their paramours. When they become too old for the duties of their profession, their business is to train the young ones for their diabolical services and pleasures.

"Walk with stretched-forth necks." When the females dance, they stretch forth their necks, and hold them awry, as if their heads were about to fall off their shoulders. "And wanton eyes." The margin, "deceiving with their eyes." As the votaries glide along, they roll their eyes, (which are painted,) and cast wanton glances on those around. "Walking and mincing;" margin, "tripping nicely." Some parts of the dance consist of a tripping or mincing step, which they call *tatte-latte.* The left foot is put first, and the inside of the right keeps following the heel of the former. "Making a tinkling with their feet." This sound is made by the ornaments which are worn round their ankles. The first is a large silver curb, like that which is attached to a bridle; the second is of the same kind, but surrounded by a great number of small BELLS; the third resembles a bracelet; and the fourth is a convex hoop, about two inches deep.—ROBERTS.

Ver. 18. In that day the LORD will take away the bravery of *their* tinkling ornaments *about their feet*, and *their* cauls, and *their* round tires like the moon.

After the hair is platted and perfumed, the eastern ladies proceed to dress their heads, by tying above the lock into which they collect it, a triangular piece of linen, adorned with various figures in needle-work. This, among persons of better fashion, is covered with a *sarmah*, as they call it, which is made in the same triangular shape, of thin flexible plates of gold or silver, carefully cut through, and engraven in imitation of lace, and might therefore answer to (השהרנים) *hasheharnim*, the moon-like ornament mentioned by the prophet in his description of the toilet of a Jewish lady. A handkerchief of crape, gauze, silk, or painted linen, bound close over the sarmah, and falling afterward carelessly upon the favourite lock of hair, completes the head-dress of the Moorish ladies. The kerchief is adjusted in the morning, and worn through the whole of the day: in this respect it differs from the veil, which is assumed as often as they go abroad, and laid aside when they return home. So elegant is this part of dress in the esteem of the Orientals, that it is worn by females of every age, to heighten their personal charms. In Persia, the prophet Ezekiel informs us, the kerchief was used by women of loose character, for the purpose of seduction; for so we understand that passage in his writings, "Wo to the women that sew pillows to all arm-holes, and make kerchiefs upon the head of every stature to hunt souls." The oriental ladies delighted in ornamenting their dress with devices of embroidery and needle-work; but it was chiefly about the neck they displayed their taste and ingenuity. To such decorations the sacred writers often allude, which clearly shows how greatly they were valued, and how much they were used. Nor were they confined to the female sex; they seem to have been equally coveted by the males; and a garment of needle-work was frequently reserved, as the most acceptable part of the spoil, for the stern and ruthless warrior. The mother of Sisera, in the fondness of her heart, allotted to her son the robe curiously wrought with vivid colours on the neck: "To Sisera, a prey of divers colours, a prey of divers colours of needle-work, of divers colours of needlework on both sides, meet for the necks of them that take the spoil."—PAXTON.

"Tinkling ornaments," *i. e.* those which have been described. "Cauls;" margin, "net-works." The caul is a strap, or girdle, about four inches long, which is placed on the top of the head, and which extends to the brow in a line with the nose. The one I have examined is made of gold, and has many joints; it contains forty-five rubies, and nine pearls, which give it a net-work appearance.

"Round tires like the moon." The shape of an ornament like the crescent moon is a great favourite in all parts of the East. In Judges viii. 21, it is said that Gideon "took away the ornaments that were on the camels' necks:" but in the Septuagint, the word *ornaments*, is rendered, *like the moon;* so also in the margin of the English Bible. The crescent is worn by Pārvati and Siva, from whom proceed the LINGAM, and the principal impurities of the system. No dancing girl is in full dress without her round tires like the moon.—ROBERTS.

Ver. 19. The chains, and the bracelets, and the mufflers.

These consist, first, of one most beautifully worked, with a pendent ornament for the neck; there is also a profusion of others, which go round the same part, and rest on the bosom. In making curious chains, the goldsmiths of England do not surpass those of the East. The Trichinopoly chains are greatly valued by the fair of our own country. The "bracelets" are large ornaments for the wrists, in which are sometimes enclosed small BELLS. The mufflers are, so far as I can judge, not for the face, but for the breasts.—ROBERTS.

Ver. 20. The bonnets, and the ornaments of the legs, and the head-bands, and the tablets, and the ear-rings.

Besides ornamental rings in the nose and the ears, they wore others round the legs, which made a tinkling as they went. This custom has also descended to the present times; for Rauwolf met with a number of Arabian women on the Euphrates, whose ankles and wrists were adorned with rings, sometimes a good many together, which moving up and down as they walked, made a great noise. Chardin attests the existence of the same custom in Persia, in Arabia, and in very hot countries, where they commonly go without stockings, but ascribes the tinkling sound to little bells fastened to those rings. In the East Indies, golden bells adorned the feet and ankles of the ladies from the earliest times; they placed them in the flowing tresses of their hair; they suspended them round their necks, and to the golden rings which they wore on their fingers, to announce their superior rank, and exact the homage which they had a right to expect from the lower orders; and from the banks of the Indus, it is probable the custom was introduced into the other countries of Asia. The Arabian females in Palestine and Syria, delight in the same ornaments, and, according to the statements of Dr. Clarke, seem to claim the honour of leading the fashion. "Their bodies are covered with a long blue shift; upon their heads they wear two handkerchiefs; one as a hood, and the other bound over it, as a fillet across the temples. Just above the right nostril, they place a small button, sometimes studded with pearl, a piece of glass, or any other glittering substance; this is fastened by a plug, thrust through the cartilage of the nose. Sometimes they have the cartilaginous separation between the nostrils bored for a ring, as large as those ordinarily used in Europe for hanging curtains; and this pendant in the upper lip covers the mouth; so that, in order to eat, it is necessary to raise it. Their faces, hands, and arms, are tattooed, and covered with hideous scars; their eyelashes and eyes being always painted, or rather dirtied, with some dingy black or blue powder. Their lips are died of a deep and dusky blue, as if they had been eating blackberries. Their teeth are jet black; their nails and fingers brick red; their wrists, as well as their ankles, are laden with large metal cinctures, studded with sharp pyramidical knobs and bits of glass. Very ponderous rings are also placed in their ears."—PAXTON.

Ver. 22. The changeable suits of apparel, and the mantles, and the wimples, and the crisping-pins.

The eastern ladies take great pride in having many changes of apparel, because their fashions NEVER alter. Thus, the rich brocades worn by their grandmothers, are equally fashionable for themselves. "The mantles." A loose robe, which is gracefully crossed on the bosom. "Wimples." Probably the fine muslin which is sometimes thrown over the head and body. "Crisping-pins." This has been translated, the "little purses," or CLASPS! When the dancing girl is in full dress, half her long hair is folded in a knot on the top of the head, and the other half hangs down her back in three tails. To keep these from unbraiding, a small *clasp*, or gold hoop, curiously worked, is placed at the end of each tail.—ROBERTS.

Ver. 24. And it shall come to pass, *that* instead of sweet smell, there shall be stink; and instead of a girdle, a rent; and instead of well-set hair, baldness; and instead of a stomacher, a girding of sackcloth; *and* burning instead of beauty.

"Sweet smell." No one ever enters a company without being well perfumed; and in addition to various scents and oils, they are adorned with numerous garlands, made of the most odoriferous flowers. "A girdle." Probably that which goes round the waist, which serves to keep the garments from falling, while the girls are dancing. It is sometimes made of silver. "Well-set hair." No ladies pay more attention to the dressing of the hair than do these; for as they never wear caps, they take great delight in this, their natural ornament. "Baldness," in a woman, makes her most contemptible; and formerly, to shave their head was a most degrading punishment. "Stomacher." I once saw a dress beautifully plaited and stiffened for the front, but I do not think it common. Here, then, we have a strong proof of the accurate observations of Isaiah in reference to the Jewish ladies; he had seen their motions, and enumerated their ornaments; and here we have a most melancholy picture of the fallen state of "the daughters of Zion."—ROBERTS.

The persons of the Assyrian ladies are elegantly clothed and scented with the richest oils and perfumes; and it appears from the sacred scriptures, that the Jewish females did not yield to them in the elegance of their dress, the beauty of their ornaments, and the fragrance of their essences. So pleasing to the Redeemer is the exercise of divine grace in the heart and conduct of a true believer: "How much better is thy love than wine, and the smell of thine ointments than all spices? The smell of thy garments is like the smell of Lebanon." When a queen was to be chosen by the king of Persia instead of Vashti, the virgins collected at Susana, the capital, underwent a purification of twelve months' duration, to wit, "six months with oil of myrrh, and six months with sweet odours." The general use of such precious oils and fragrant perfumes among the ancient Romans, particularly among ladies of rank and fashion, may be inferred from these words of Virgil:—

"Ambrosiæque comæ divinum vertice odorem
Spiravere: pedes vestis fluxit ad imos."—*Æn.* lib. i. l. 403.

"From her head the ambrosial locks breathed divine fragrance; her robe hung waving down to the ground." In the remote age of Homer, the Greeks had already learnt the lavish use of such perfumes; for, in describing Juno's dress, he represents her pouring ambrosia and other perfumes all over her body. Hence, to an eastern lady, no punishment could be more severe, none more mortifying to her delicacy, than a diseased and loathsome habit of body, instead of a beautiful skin, softened and made agreeable with all that art could devise, and all that nature, so prodigal in those countries of rich perfumes, could supply. Such was the punishment which God threatened to send upon the haughty daughters of Zion, in the days of Isaiah: "And it shall come to pass, that instead of perfume there shall be ill savour; and instead of a girdle, a rent; and instead of well-set hair, baldness; and instead of a stomacher, a girding of sackcloth; and a sun-burnt skin instead of beauty."

The description which Pietro della Valle gives of his own wife, an Assyrian lady, born in Mesopotamia, and educated at Bagdad, whom he married in that country, will enable the reader to form a pretty distinct idea of the appearance and ornaments of an oriental lady in full dress. "Her eyelashes, which are long, and according to the custom of the East, dressed with stibulum, (as we often read in the holy scriptures of the Hebrew women of old, and in Xenophon of Astyages, the grandfather of Cyrus, and the Medes of that line,) give a dark, and, at the same time, a majestic shade to the eyes. The ornaments of gold and of jewels for the head, for the neck, for the arms, for the legs, and for the feet, (for they wear rings even on their toes,) are, indeed, unlike those of the Turks, carried to great excess, but not of great value: for in Bagdad, jewels of high price either are not to be had, or are not used; and they wear such only as are of little value, as turquoises, small rubies, emeralds, carbuncles, garnets, pearls, and the like. My spouse dresses herself with all of them, according to their fashion; with exception, however, of certain ugly rings, of very large size, set with jewels, which, in truth very absurdly, it is the custom to wear fastened to one of their nostrils, like buffaloes; an ancient custom, however, in the East, which, as we find in the holy scriptures, prevailed among the Hebrew ladies, even in the time of Solomon. These nose-rings, in compliance to me, she has left off; but I have not yet been able to prevail with her cousin, and her sisters, to do the same; so fond are they of an old custom, be it ever so absurd, who have been long habituated to it."—PAXTON.

Ver. 26. And her gates shall lament and mourn: and she, *being* desolate, shall sit upon the ground.

Sitting on the ground was a posture that denoted mourning and deep distress. Lam. ii. 10. "We find Judea on several coins of Vespasian and Titus in a posture that denotes sorrow and captivity—sitting on the ground. The Romans might have an eye on the customs of the Jewish nation, as well as those of their own country, in the several marks of sorrow they have set on this figure. The Psalmist describes the Jews lamenting their captivity, in the same pensive posture: 'By the waters of Babylon we sat down, and wept when we remembered thee, O Zion.' But what is more remarkable, we find Judea represented as a woman in sorrow sitting on the ground, in a passage of the prophet that foretels the very captivity recorded on this medal." (Addison.)—BURDER.

CHAPTER V.

Ver. 1. Now will I sing to my well-beloved a song of my beloved touching his vineyard. My well-beloved hath a vineyard in a very fruitful hill: 2. And he fenced it, and gathered out the stones thereof, and planted it with the choicest vine, and built a tower in the midst of it, and also made a wine-press therein: and he looked that it should bring forth grapes, and it brought forth wild grapes.

The wine-press, constructed for expressing the juice of the grapes, does not seem to be a moveable implement in the East; and our Lord, in the parable of the vineyard, says expressly, that it was formed by digging. Chardin found the wine-press in Persia was made after the same manner; as it was a hollow place dug in the ground, and lined with mason-work. Besides this, they had what the Romans called *lacus*, the lake, a large open place or vessel, which, by a conduit or spout, received the must from the wine-press. In very hot countries it was perhaps necessary, or at least convenient, to have the lake under ground, or in a cave hewed out of the rock for coolness, that the heat might not cause too great a fermentation, and sour the must. To these circumstances the prophet Isaiah distinctly refers, in the beginning of the fifth chapter: "My well-beloved has a vineyard in a very fruitful hill: and he fenced it, and gathered out the stones thereof, and planted it with the choicest vine, and built a tower in the midst of it, and also made a wine-press therein: and he looked that it should bring forth grapes, and it brought forth wild grapes." The tower which the prophet mentions, and which our Lord also introduces into one of his parables, is generally explained by commentators, as designed for the keepers of the vineyard to watch and defend the fruits. But for this purpose it was usual to make a little temporary hut, called in the first chapter, not a tower, but a cottage, which might answer for the short season while the grapes were ripening, and was afterward removed. The tower, therefore, according to Lowth, means a building of a more permanent nature and use; the farm of the vineyard, as we may call it, containing all the offices and implements, and the whole apparatus necessary for cultivating the vineyard and making the wine. To this image in the allegory, the situation, the manner of building, the use, and the whole service of the temple, exactly answered. They have still such towers for pleasure or use, in their gardens, in the oriental regions; for Marcus Sanutus, as quoted by Harmer, informs us, that in the thirteenth century the inhabitants of Ptolemais beat down the towers of their gardens to the ground, and removed the stones of them, together with those of their burying-places, on the approach of the Tartars. The gardens of Damascus are furnished with the same kind of edifices. In most of the gardens near Aleppo, summer-houses are built for the reception of the public. In others, at a greater distance, are tolerable commodious villas, to which the Franks resort in the spring, as the natives do in the summer. "To a tower, or building of this kind, it is to be supposed," says Russel, "our Lord refers in the parable; for it is scarcely to be imagined that he is speaking of the slight and unexpensive buildings in a vineyard, which, indeed, are sometimes so slight as to consist only of four poles, with a floor on the top of them, to which they ascend by a ladder: but rather of those elegant turrets erected in gardens, where the eastern people of fortune spend some considerable part of their time." But this excellent writer expressly admits that in all the orchards near Aleppo, a small square watch-house is built for the accommodation of the watchmen in the fruit season, or, in their stead, temporary bowers are constructed of wood, and thatched with green reeds and branches. Small and detached square towers for the accommodation of the watchmen appointed to guard the vineyards, are still to be met with in Judea. It is more probably to the substantial watch-tower that the Saviour alludes, than either to the offices of the vineyard, or the commodious summer-house. —PAXTON.

Ver. 2. And built a tower in the midst of it, and made a wine-press therein.

See on 2 Kings 4. 39.

Lowth, "And he hewed out also a lake therein." By this expression we are to understand, not the wine-press itself, but what the Romans called lacus, the lake, the large open place, or vessel, which by a conduit or spout received the must from the wine-press. In very hot countries it was perhaps necessary, or at least very convenient, to have the lake under ground, or in a cave hewn out of the side of a rock, for coolness, that the heat might not cause too great a fermentation, and sour the wine. The wine-presses in Persia, Chardin says, are formed by making hollow places in the ground, lined with mason's work.—BURDER.

Ver. 11. Wo unto them that rise up early in the morning, *that* they may follow strong drink; that continue until night, *till* wine inflame them!

The Persians, when they commit a debauch, arise betimes, and esteem the morning as the best time for beginning to drink wine, by which means they carry on their excess till night.—MORIER.

Ver. 18. Wo unto them that draw iniquity with cords of vanity, and sin as it were with a cart-rope!

See on Isa. 66. 20.

Ver. 26. And he will lift up an ensign to the nations from far, and will hiss unto them from the end of the earth: and, behold, they shall come with speed swiftly.

The metaphor is taken from the practice of those that keep bees, who draw them out of their hives into the fields, and lead them back again, by a hiss or a whistle.—LOWTH.

Ver. 28. Whose arrows *are* sharp, and all their bows bent, their horses' hoofs shall be counted like flint, and their wheels like whirlwind.

The shoeing of horses with iron plates nailed to the hoof, is quite a modern practice, and was unknown to the ancients, as appears from the silence of the Greek and Roman writers, especially those that treat of horse-medicine, who could not have passed over a matter so obvious, and of such importance, that now the whole science takes its name from it, being called by us farriery. The horse-shoes of leather and of iron, which are mentioned; the silver and the gold shoes, with which Nero and Poppea shod their mules, used occasionally to preserve the hoofs of delicate cattle, or for vanity, were of a very different kind; they enclosed the whole hoof, as in a case, or as a shoe does a man's foot, and were bound, or tied on. For this reason the strength, firmness, and solidity of a horse's hoof, was of much greater importance with them than with us, and was esteemed one of the first praises of a fine horse. For want of this artificial defence to the foot, which our horses have, Amos, vi. 12, speaks of it as a thing as much impracticable to make horses run upon a hard rock, as to plough up the same rock with oxen. These circumstances must be taken into consideration, in order to give us a full notion of the propriety and force of the image by which the prophet sets forth the strength and excellence of the Babylonish cavalry, which made a great part of the strength of the Assyrian army.—LOWTH.

CHAPTER VI.

Ver. 11. Then said I, LORD, how long? And he answered, Until the cities be wasted without inhabitant, and the houses without man, and the land be utterly desolate.

A public edict of the Emperor Adrian rendered it a capital crime for a Jew to set a foot in Jerusalem, and prohibited them from viewing it even at a distance. Heathens, Christians, and Mohammedans, have alternately possessed Judea; it has been the prey of the Saracens; the descendants of Ishmael have often overrun it; the children of Israel have alone been denied the possession of it, though thither they ever wish to return; and though it forms the only spot on earth where the ordinances of their religion can be observed. And, amid all the revolutions of states, and the extinction of many nations, in so long a period, the Jews alone have not only ever been aliens in the land of their fathers, but whenever any of them have been permitted, at any period since the time of their dispersion, to sojourn there, they have experienced even more contumelious treatment than elsewhere. Benjamin of Tudela, who travelled in the twelfth century through great part of Europe and of Asia, found the Jews everywhere oppressed, *particularly in the Holy Land.* And to this day (while the Jews who reside in Palestine, or who resort thither in old age, that their bones may not be laid in a foreign land, are alike ill-treated and abused by Greeks, Armenians, and Europeans) the haughty deportment of the despotic Turkish soldier, and the abject state of the poor and helpless Jews, are painted to the life by the prophet.—KEITH.

Ver. 13. But yet in it *shall be* a tenth, and *it* shall return, and shall be eaten: as a teil-tree, and as an oak, whose substance *is* in them when they cast *their leaves*, *so* the holy seed *shall be* the substance thereof.

Though the cities be waste, and the land be desolate, it is not from the poverty of the soil that the fields are abandoned by the plough, nor from any diminution of its ancient and natural fertility, that the land has rested for so many generations. Judea was not forced only by artificial means, or from local and temporary causes, into a luxuriant cultivation, such as a barren country might have been, concerning which it would not have needed a prophet to tell, that if once devastated and abandoned it would ultimately and permanently revert into its original sterility. Phenicia at all times held a far different rank among the richest countries of the world: and it was not a bleak and steril portion of the earth, nor a land which even many ages of desolation and neglect could empoverish, that God gave in possession and by covenant to the seed of Abraham. No longer cultivated as a garden, but left like a wilderness, Judea is indeed greatly changed from what it was; all that human ingenuity and labour did devise, erect, or cultivate, men have laid waste and desolate; all the "plenteous goods" with which it was enriched, adorned, and blessed, have fallen like seared and withered leaves, when their greenness is gone; and, stripped of its "ancient splendour," it is left as *an oak whose leaf fadeth*:—but its inherent sources of fertility are not dried up; the natural richness of the soil is unblighted: *the substance is in it*, strong as that of the teil-tree or the solid oak, which retain their substance when they cast their leaves. And as the leafless oak waits throughout winter for the genial warmth of returning spring, to be clothed with renewed foliage, so the once glorious land of Judea is yet full of latent vigour, or of vegetative power strong as ever, ready to shoot forth, even "better than at the beginning," whenever the sun of heaven shall shine on it again, and the "holy seed" be prepared for being finally "the substance thereof." The *substance that is in it*—which alone has here to be proved—is, in few words, thus described by an enemy: "The land in the plains is *fat and loamy*, and exhibits every sign of the *greatest fecundity*. Were nature assisted by art, the fruits of the most distant countries might be produced within the distance of twenty leagues." "Galilee," says Malte Brun, "would be a paradise, were it inhabited by an industrious people, under an enlightened government. Vine stocks are to be seen here a foot and a half in diameter."—KEITH.

CHAPTER VII.

Ver. 18. And it shall come to pass in that day, *that* the LORD shall hiss for the fly that *is* in the uttermost part of the rivers of Egypt, and for the bee that *is* in the land of Assyria.

Some writers have contended that bees are destitute of the sense of hearing; but their opinion is entirely without foundation. This will appear, if any proof were necessary, from the following prediction: "And it shall come to pass in that day, that the Lord shall hiss for the fly that is in the uttermost part of the rivers of Egypt; and for the bee that is in the land of Assyria." The allusion which this text involves, is the practice of calling out the bees from their hives, by a hissing, or whistling sound, to their labour in the fields, and summoning them again to return, when the heavens begin to lower, or the shadows of evening to fall. In this manner, Jehovah threatens to rouse the enemies of Judah, and lead them to the prey. However widely scattered, or far remote from the scene of action, they should hear his voice, and with as much promptitude as the bee, that has been taught to recognise the signal of its owner, and obey his call, they should assemble their forces; and although weak and insignificant as a swarm of bees in the estimation of a proud and infatuated people, they should come, with irresistible might, and take possession of the rich and beautiful region which had been abandoned by its terrified inhabitants.—PAXTON.

This insect is called Zimb; it has not been described by any naturalist. It is, in size, very little larger than a bee, of a thicker proportion, and his wings, which are broader than those of a bee, placed separate, like those of a fly: they are of pure gauze, without colour or spot upon them; the head is large, the upper jaw or lip is sharp, and has at the end of it a strong pointed hair, of about a quarter of an inch long; the lower jaw has two of these pointed hairs; and this pencil of hairs, when joined together, makes a resistance to the finger, nearly equal to that of a strong hog's bristle; its legs are serrated in the inside, and the whole covered with brown hair or down. As soon as this plague appears, and their buzzing is heard, all the cattle forsake their food, and run wildly about the plain, till they die, worn out with fatigue, fright, and hunger. No remedy remains, but to leave the black earth, and hasten down to the sands of Atbara; and there they remain, while the rains last, this cruel enemy never daring to pursue them farther. Though his size be immense, as is his strength, and his body covered with a thick skin, defended with strong hair, yet, even the camel is not capable to sustain the violent punctures the fly makes with his pointed proboscis. He must lose no time in removing to the sands of Atbara; for, when once attacked by this fly, his body, head, and legs, break out into large bosses, which swell, break, and putrefy, to the certain destruction of the creature. Even the elephant and rhinoceros, who, by reason of their enormous bulk, and the vast quantity of food and water they daily need, cannot shift to desert and dry places, as the season may require, are obliged to roll themselves in mud and mire, which, when dry, coats them over like armour, and enables them to stand their ground against this winged assassin: yet I have found some of these tubercles upon almost every elephant and rhinoceros that I have seen, and attribute them to this cause. All the inhabitants of the sea-coast of Melinda, down to Cape Gardefan, to Saba, and the south coast of the Red Sea, are obliged to put themselves in motion, and remove to the next sand, in the beginning of the rainy season, to prevent all their stock of cattle from being destroyed. This is not a partial emigration; the inhabitants of all the countries, from the mountains of Abyssinia northward, to the confluence of the Nile, and Astaboras, are once a-year obliged to change their abode, and seek protection on the sands of Beja; nor is there any alternative, or means of avoiding this, though a hostile band were in their way, capable of spoiling them of half their substance. This fly has no sting, though he seems to me to be rather of the bee kind; but his motion is more rapid and sudden than that of the bee, and resembles that of the gad-fly in England. There is something particular in the sound or buzzing of this insect; it is a jarring noise, together with a humming, which induces me to believe it proceeds, at least in part, from a vibration made with the three hairs at his snout. (Bruce.)—BURDER.

Ver. 20. In the same day shall the LORD shave with a razor that is hired, *namely*, by them beyond the river, by the king of Assyria, the head, and the hair of the feet: and it shall also consume the beard.

By reading what is written on 2 Kings ii. 23, a better view will be gained of the contempt attached to those who were bald, and of the term, as being expressive of the most complete weakness and destitution. To tell a man you will SHAVE him, is as much as to say you will ruin him—entirely overthrow him. "Our king has SHAVED all his enemies," means, he has punished them; reduced them to the most abject condition; so that they have not a single vestige of power in their possession. "What, fellow! didst thou say thou wouldst SHAVE me?" "I will give thy bones to the crows and the jackals. Begone, bald-head, get out of my way." The punishment to be inflicted on the Jews was very great: they were to be SHAVED on the head, the beard, and "the hair of the feet." The latter expression alludes to a most disgusting practice, common in all parts of the East. Calmet says, "The Hebrews modestly express by feet those parts which decency forbids to name: 'the water of the feet;' 'to cover the feet;' 'the hair of the feet.'" Thus the Lord was about to SHAVE the Jews by a razor which they themselves had HIRED!—ROBERTS.

CHAPTER VIII.

Ver. 6. Forasmuch as this people refuseth the waters of Shiloah that go softly, and rejoice in Rezin and Remaliah's son; 7. Now therefore, behold, the LORD bringeth up upon them the waters of the river, strong and many, *even* the king of Assyria, and all his glory: and he shall come up over all his channels, and go over all his banks.

The gentle waters of Shiloah, a small fountain and brook just without Jerusalem, which supplied a pool within the city for the use of the inhabitants, are an apt emblem of the state of the kingdom and house of David, much reduced in its apparent strength, yet supported by the blessing of God; and are finely contrasted with the waters of the Euphrates, great, rapid, and impetuous; the image of the Babylonian empire, which God threatens to bring down like a mighty flood upon all these apostates of both kingdoms, as a punishment for their manifold iniquities.—BURDER.

Ver. 14. And he shall be for a sanctuary; but for a stone of stumbling, and for a rock of offence, to both houses of Israel: for a gin and for a snare to the inhabitants of Jerusalem.

The idea appears to be taken from a stone, or a block of wood, being thrown in the path of travellers, over which they fall. "Well, friend, did the king grant you your request?"—"No, no; there was a *Udaru-Katti*, (from the verb *Udarukuthu*, to stumble, and *katti*, a block,) a stumbling-block in the way." "Just as Valen was attaining the object of his wishes, that old stumbling-block, the Modeliar, laid down in the way, and the poor fellow stumbled, and fell." "Why are you so dejected this morning?"—"Because I have had a severe fall over that stumbling-block, my profligate son."—ROBERTS.

CHAPTER IX.

Ver. 3. Thou hast multiplied the nation, *and* not increased the joy: they joy before thee according to the joy in harvest, *and* as *men* rejoice when they divide the spoil.

"Kandan's wife has at length borne her husband a son, and all the relations are rejoicing together, like unto the joy of harvest." "Are you happy in your new situation?"—"Yes; my *santosham*, my happiness, is greater than that of the time of harvest." "Listen to the birds, how merry they are; can they be taking in their harvest?"—ROBERTS.

Ver. 6. For unto us a Child is born, unto us a Son is given; and the government shall be upon his shoulder: and his name shall be called Wonderful, Counsellor, The mighty God, The everlasting Father, The Prince of Peace.

It is common in the East to describe any quality of a person by calling him *the father of the quality*. D'Herbelot, speaking of a very eminent physician, says, he did such admirable cures, that he was surnamed Aboul Berekiat, the *father of benedictions*. The original words of this title of Christ, may be rendered, *the father of that which is everlasting*: Christ, therefore, as the head and introducer of an everlasting dispensation, never to give place to another, was very naturally, in the eastern style, called the *father of eternity*.—HARMER.

The phrase, "shall be called," refers not so much to the appellation by which the promised child should be known, as to the nature by which he should be distinguished. It is remarkable that the original word, (pela,) here rendered "wonderful," is elsewhere rendered "secret." Thus Judg. xiii. 17, 18, "And Manoah said unto the angel of the Lord, What is thy name, that when thy sayings come to pass, we may do thee honour? And the angel of the Lord said unto him, Why askest thou thus after my name, seeing it is secret, (pala?") Here the angel evidently appropriates one of the distinguishing titles of the promised Messiah, thus identifying his real character, and while ostensibly refusing to make known his name, does in fact impart one of the most significant and sublime of all his designations. —BUSH.

Ver. 10. The bricks are fallen down, but we will build with hewn stones; the sycamores are cut down, but we will change *them into* cedars.

The houses of the lower orders in Egypt are in like manner constructed of unburnt bricks, or square pieces of clay, baked in the sun, and only one story high; but those of the higher classes, of stone, are generally two, and sometimes three stories high. These facts are at once a short and lively comment on the words of the prophet: "All the people shall know, even Ephraim, and the inhabitants of Samaria, that say, in the pride and stoutness of heart, The bricks are fallen down, but we will build with hewn stones; the sycamores are cut down, but we will change them into cedars." Bricks dried in the sun, are poor materials for building, compared with hewn stone, which, in Egypt, is almost equal to marble, and forms a strong contrast between the splendid palace and mud-walled cabin. And if, as is probable, the houses of the higher orders in Israel were built with the same species of costly and beautiful stone, the contrast stated by the prophet places the vaunting of his wealthier countrymen in a very strong light. The boastful extravagance of that people is still further displayed by the next figure: "The sycamores are cut down, but we will change them into cedars;" the forests of sycamore, the wood of which we have been accustomed to employ in building, are cut down by the enemy, but instead of them we will import cedars, of whose fragrant and beautiful wood we will construct and adorn our habitations. The sycamore grew in abundance in the low country of Judea, and was not much esteemed; but the cedar was highly valued; it was brought at a great expense, and with much labour, from the distant and rugged summits of Lebanon, to beautify the dwellings of the great, the palaces of kings, and the temple of Jehovah. It was therefore an extravagant boast, which betrayed the pride and vanity of their depraved hearts, that all the warnings, threatenings, and judgments of the living God, were insufficient to subdue or restrain.—PAXTON.

CHAPTER X.

Ver. 1. Wo unto them that decree unrighteous decrees, and that write grievousness *which* they have prescribed.

The manner of making eastern decrees differs from ours: they are first written, and then the magistrate authenticates them, or annuls them. This, I remember, is the Arab manner, according to D'Arvieux. When an Arab wanted a favour of the emir, the way was to apply to the secretary, who drew up a decree according to the request of the party; if the emir granted the favour, he printed his seal upon it; if not, he returned it torn to the petitioner. Sir J. Chardin confirms this account, and applies it, with great propriety, to the illustration of a passage which I never thought of when I read over D'Arvieux. After citing Is. x. 1, *Wo unto them that decree unrighteous decrees, and to the writers that write grievousness*, for so our translators have rendered the latter part of the verse in the margin, much more agreeably than in the body of the version, Sir John goes on, "The manner of making the royal acts and ordinances hath a relation to this: they are always drawn up according to the request; the first minister, or he whose office it is, writes on the side of it, 'according to the king's will,' and from thence it is sent to the secretary of state, who draws up the order in form."

They that consult Vitringa upon the passage, will find that commentators have been perplexed about the latter part of this wo: every one sees the propriety of denouncing evil on those that decree unrighteous judgments; but it is not very clear why they are threatened that write them; it certainly would be wrong to punish the clerks of our courts, that have no other concern in unjust decrees, than barely writing them down, according to the duty of their place, as mere amanuenses. But according to the eastern mode, we find he that writes or draws up the order at first, is deeply concerned in the injustice, since he expresses matters as he pleases, and is the source of the mischief; the superior only passes or rejects it. He indeed is guilty if he passes an unjust order, because he ought to have rejected it; but a great deal of the guilt unquestionably comes upon him who first draws the order, and who makes it more or less oppressive to others, just as he pleases, or rather, according to the present that is made him by the party that solicits the order. For it appears from D'Arvieux, that the secretary of the emir drew up no order without a present, which was wont to be proportionate to the favour asked; and that he was very oppressive in his demands.

In this view of things the words of the prophet are very clear, and easy to be understood; and Sir John Chardin, by his acquaintance with the East, proves a much better interpreter than the most learned western commentators, even celebrated rabbies themselves: for according to Vitringa, Rabbi David Kimchi supposes the judges themselves were the writers the prophet meant, and so called, because they caused others to write unjust determinations: though Vitringa admits, that such an interpretation does not well agree with the conjugation of the Hebrew word.—HARMER.

Ver. 13. For he saith, By the strength of my hand I have done *it*, and by my wisdom; for I am prudent: and I have removed the bounds of the people, and have robbed their treasures, and I have put down the inhabitants like a valiant *man:* 14. And my hand hath found, as a nest, the riches of the people: and as one gathereth eggs *that are* left, have I gathered all the earth; and there was none that moved the wing, or opened the mouth, or peeped.

These are the sentiments and boastings of Sennacherib, a proud Assyrian monarch, who viewed and treated cities just as we in Africa viewed and treated ostrich nests, when they fell in our way: we seized the eggs as if they had been our own, because we had found them, and because there was no power that could prevent us. So did Sennacherib seize and plunder cities with as little compunction as we seized the eggs of the absent ostrich; never thinking of the misery for life which he thereby brought on many peaceable families, who had done nothing to injure or offend him.—Campbell.

Ver. 19. And the rest of the trees of his forest shall be few, that a child may write them.

Volney remarks, in a note, that there are but four or five of those trees, which deserve any notice; and in a note, it may be added, from the words of Isaiah, "the rest of the trees of his forest shall be few, that a child may write them," ch. x. 19. Could not the infidel write a brief note, or state a minute fact, without illustrating a prophecy? Maundrell, who visited Lebanon in the end of the seventeenth century, and to whose accuracy in other matters all subsequent travellers who refer to him bear witness, describes some of the cedars near the top of the mountain as "very old, and of a prodigious bulk, and others younger, of a smaller size." Of the former he could reckon up only sixteen. He measured the largest, and found it above twelve yards in girth. Such trees, however few in number, show that the *cedars of Lebanon* had once been no vain boast. But after the lapse of more than a century, not a single tree of such dimensions is now to be seen. Of those which now remain, as visited by Captains Irby and Mangles, there are about fifty in the whole, on a single small eminence, from which spot the cedars are the only trees to be seen in Lebanon.—Keith.

Ver. 32. As yet shall he remain at Nob that day: he shall shake his hand *against* the mount of the daughter of Zion, the hill of Jerusalem.

This is a part of the description of the march of Sennacherib against Jerusalem. When he arrives near the city, he lifts up his hand and shakes it, to denote that he will soon inflict signal punishment upon it. How often may this significant motion of the hand be seen; it is done by lifting it up to the height of the head, and then moving it backward and forward in a cutting direction. Thus, when men are at so great a distance as to be scarcely able to hear each other's voice, they have this convenient way of making known their threatenings. Sometimes, when brawlers have separated, and apparently finished their quarrel, one of them will turn round and bawl out with all his might, and then shake his hand in token of what he will still do.—Roberts.

CHAPTER XI.

Ver. 4. But with righteousness shall he judge the poor, and reprove with equity for the meek of the earth: and he shall smite the earth with the rod of his mouth, and with the breath of his lips shall he slay the wicked.

The application of this figure in the East refers rather to angry expressions, than to a judicial sentence. "The mouth of that man burns up his neighbours and friends." "His mouth! it has set on fire all the people."—Roberts.

Ver. 6 The wolf also shall dwell with the lamb, and the leopard shall lie down with the kid; and the calf, and the young lion, and the fatling together; and a little child shall lead them. 7. And the cow and the bear shall feed; their young ones shall lie down together: and the lion shall eat straw like the ox. 8. And the suckling child shall play on the hole of the asp, and the weaned child shall put his hand on the cockatrice-den. 9. They shall not hurt nor destroy in all my holy mountain: for the earth shall be full of the knowledge of the Lord, as the waters cover the sea.

See on Job 20. 14.

CHAPTER XIII.

Ver. 7. Therefore shall all hands be faint, and every man's heart shall melt.

This figure appears to be taken from the melting of wax, or metals. "My heart, my mind, melts for him; I am dissolved by his love." "Alas! alas! my bowels are melting within me."—Roberts.

Ver. 8. And they shall be afraid: pangs and sorrows shall take hold of them; they shall be in pain as a woman that travaileth; they shall be amazed one at another; their faces *shall be as* flames.

Great pains are often spoken of as the anguish of parturition. "Ah! my lord, I am very ill; my pains are like those of a woman when bringing forth her first-born." "Has it come to this? am I to bring forth like a woman?" "He cries like the woman in her agony." "Yes, my friend; as the pains of a female in child-bearing are produced by sin; so your present sufferings are produced by the sins of a former birth."—Roberts.

Ver. 14. And it shall be as the chased roe, (antelope,) and as a sheep that no man taketh up: they shall every man turn to his own people, and flee every one into his own land.

See on 2 Sam. 2. 10.

To hunt the antelope is a favourite amusement in the East; but which, from its extraordinary swiftness, is attended with great difficulty. On the first alarm, it flies like an arrow from the bow, and leaves the best mounted hunter, and the fleetest dog, far behind. The sportsman is obliged to call in the aid of the falcon, trained to the work, to seize on the animal, and impede its motions, to give the dogs time to overtake it. Dr. Russel thus describes the chase of the antelope: "They permit horsemen, without dogs, if they advance gently, to approach near, and do not seem much to regard a caravan that passes within a little distance; but the moment they take the alarm, they bound away, casting from time to time a look behind: and if they find themselves pursued, they lay their horns backward, almost close on the shoulders, and flee with incredible swiftness. When dogs appear, they instantly take alarm; for which reason the sportsmen endeavour to steal upon the antelope unawares, to get as near as possible before slipping the dogs; and then, pushing on at full speed, they throw off the falcon, which, being taught to strike or fix upon the cheek of the game, retards its course by repeated attacks, till the greyhounds have time to get up."—Burder.

Ver. 18. *Their* bows also shall dash the young men to pieces; and they shall have no pity on the fruit of the womb; their eye shall not spare children.

See on 2 Sam. 22. 35.

Both Herodotus and Xenophon mention that the Persians used large bows; and the latter says particularly, that their bows were three cubits long. They were celebrated for their archers, Jer. xlix. 35. Probably their neighbours and allies, the Medes, dealt much in the same sort of arms. In Psalm xviii. 34, and Job xx. 24, mention is made of a bow of brass. If the Persian bows were of metal, we may easily conceive that with a metalline bow of three cubits' length, and proportionably strong, the soldiers might dash and slay the young men, the weaker and unresisting part of the inhabitants, in the general carnage on taking the city.—LOWTH.

Ver. 19. And Babylon, the glory of kingdoms, the beauty of the Chaldees' excellency, shall be as when God overthrew Sodom and Gomorrah.
20. It shall never be inhabited, neither shall it be dwelt in from generation to generation; neither shall the Arabian pitch tent there, neither shall the shepherds make their fold there.

From Rauwolf's testimony it appears that in the sixteenth century, "there was not a house to be seen." And now the eye wanders over a *barren desert*, in which the ruins are nearly the only indication that it had ever been inhabited." "It is impossible," adds Major Keppel, "to behold this scene, and not to be reminded how exactly the predictions of Isaiah and Jeremiah have been fulfilled, even in the appearance Babylon was doomed to present, that *she should never be inhabited;* that 'the Arabian should not pitch his tent there;' that she should 'become heaps;' that her cities should be a 'desolation, a dry wilderness.'" "Babylon is spurned alike by the heel of the Ottomans, the Israelites, and the sons of Ishmael. It is a *tenantless* and desolate metropolis."—(Mignan.)

Neither shall the Arabian pitch his tent there, neither shall the shepherds make their fold there. It was prophesied of Ammon, that it should be a stable for camels and a couching-place for flocks; and of Philistia, that it should be cottages for shepherds, and a pasture for flocks. But Babylon was to be visited with a far greater desolation, and to become unfit or unsuiting even for such a purpose. And that neither a tent would be pitched there, even by an Arab, nor a fold made by a shepherd, implies the last degree of solitude and desolation. "It is common in these parts for shepherds to make use of ruined edifices to shelter their flocks in." (Mignan.) But Babylon is an exception. Instead of taking the bricks *from thence*, the shepherd might with facility erect a defence from wild beasts, and make a fold for his flock amid the heaps of Babylon: and the Arab, who fearlessly traverses it by day, might pitch his tent by night. But neither the one nor the other could now be persuaded to remain a single night among the ruins. The superstitious dread of evil spirits, far more than the natural terror of the wild beasts, effectually prevents them. Captain Mignan was accompanied by six *Arabs*, completely armed, but he "could not induce them to remain towards night, from the apprehension of evil spirits. It is impossible to eradicate this idea from the minds of these people, who are very deeply imbued with superstition." And when the sun sunk behind the Mujelibé, and the moon would have still lighted his way among the ruins, it was with infinite regret that he obeyed "*the summons of his guides.*" "*All the people of the country* assert that it is extremely dangerous to *approach* this mound after nightfall, on account of the multitude of evil spirits by which it is haunted."—KEITH.

The scriptures, in describing the ruined state into which some celebrated cities were to be reduced, represent them not unfrequently, (Jer. xlix. 18,) as to be so desolated, that no shepherds with flocks should haunt them; which supposes they were to be found on the remains of others.

This is a proper representation of complete destruction. For in the East it is common for shepherds to make use of remaining ruins to shelter their flocks from the heat of the middle of the day, and from the dangers of the night. So Dr. Chandler, after mentioning the exquisite remains of a temple of Apollo, in Asia Minor, which were such as that it was impossible, perhaps, to conceive greater beauty and majesty of ruin, goes on, "At evening a large flock of goats, returning to the fold, their bells tinkling, spread over the heap, climbing to browse on the shrubs and trees growing between the huge stones." Another passage of the same writer, shows that they make use of ruins also to guard their flocks from the noon-tide heat. Speaking of Aiasaluck, generally understood to be the ancient Ephesus, and certainly near the site of that old city, and at least its successor, he says, "A herd of goats was driven to it for shelter from the sun at noon; and a noisy flight of crows from the quarries seemed to insult its silence. We heard the partridge call in the area of the theatre and of the stadium. The glorious pomp of its heathen worship is no longer remembered; and Christianity, which was there nursed by apostles, and fostered by general councils, until it increased to fulness of stature, barely lingers on in an existence hardly visible."

This description is very gloomy and melancholy; however, the usefulness of these ruins is such, for the habitation of those that tend flocks, that it often prevents a place from being quite desolate, and continues it among inhabited places, though miserably ruinated. Such is the state of Ephesus: it is described by Chandler, as making a very gloomy and melancholy appearance, but as not absolutely without people. "Our horses," says he, "were disposed among the walls and rubbish, with their saddles on; and a mat was spread for us on the ground. We sat here, in the open air, while supper was preparing; when, suddenly, fires began to blaze up among the bushes, and we saw the villagers collected about them in savage groups, or passing to and fro with lighted brands for torches. The flames, with the stars and a pale moon, afforded us a dim prospect of ruin and desolation. A shrill owl, called cucuvaia, from its note, with a nighthawk, flitted near us; and a jackal cried mournfully, as if forsaken by his companions on the mountain."—BURDER.

Ver. 21. But wild beasts of the desert shall lie there; and their houses shall be full of doleful creatures; and owls shall dwell there, and satyrs shall dance there.

See on ch. 34. 13.

"Yes; the wretch is now punished for his crimes, and those of his father; dogs and devils are now dwelling in his habitation." The owl, whose native name is ANTHI, is one of the most ominous birds of the East. Let him only alight upon the house of a Hindoo, and begin his dismal screech, and all the inmates will be seized with great consternation. Some one will instantly run out and make a noise with his areca-nut cutter, or some other instrument, to affright it away. I recollect one of these creatures once flew into the house of a lady when she was in the pains of parturition: the native servants became greatly alarmed, and run to me, lamenting the fearful omen. I had it driven from the house; and notwithstanding the malignant influence of the feathered visiter, and the qualms of the domestics, all things went on well. On another occasion, I shot one of them which had troubled us on the roof, night by night: but as he was only wounded in the wing, I took him into the house, with the intention of keeping him: but the servants were so uncomfortable, and complained so much at having such a "BEAST" in the house, I was obliged to send him away. From these statements it will be seen what ideas would be attached to the OWLS dwelling in the houses of Babylon.—ROBERTS.

"There are many dens of wild beasts in various parts. There are quantities of porcupine quills, (kephud.) And while the lower excavations are often pools of water, in most of the cavities are numbers of bats and *owls*. These souterrains, (caverns,) over which the chambers of majesty may have been spread, are now the refuge of jackals and other savage animals. The mouths of their entrances are strewed with the bones of sheep and *goats;* and the loathsome smell that issues from most of them is sufficient warning not to proceed into the den." (Buckingham.) The king of the forest now ranges over the site of that Babylon which Nebuchadnezzar built for his own glory. And the temple of Belus, the greatest work of man, is now like unto a natural den of lions. "Two or three majestic lions" were seen upon its heights, by Sir Robert Ker Porter, as he was approaching it; and "the broad prints of their feet were left plain in the clayey soil." Major Keppel saw there a similar foot-print of a lion. It is also the unmolested retreat of jackals, hyenas, and other noxious animals. Wild beasts are "numerous" at the *Mujelibé*, as well as on *Birs Nimrood.* "The mound was full of large holes; we entered some of them, and found them strewed with carcasses and skeletons of animals recently killed. The ordure of wild beasts was so strong, that prudence got the better of curiosity, for we had no doubt as to the savage nature of the inhabitants. Our guides, indeed, told us that all the ruins abounded in lions and other wild beasts; so literally has the divine prediction been fulfilled, that wild beasts of the desert should lie there, and their houses be full of doleful creatures; that the wild beasts of the island should cry in their desolate houses." (Keppel.)—KEITH.

Ver. 22. And the wild beasts of the island shall cry in their desolate houses, and dragons in *their* pleasant palaces; and her time *is* near to come, and her days shall not be prolonged.

Europeans are often astonished, in walking through a town or village, to see so many DESOLATE houses, and frequently come to improper conclusions, from an idea that the place had once a greater number of inhabitants. At half an hour's notice, families may be seen to leave their dwellings, never to enter them more. Hence, in almost every direction, may be seen buildings with roofs half fallen in; with timbers hanging in various positions; shutters and doors flapping in the wind, or walls half-levelled to the ground. Various are the reasons for which the superstitious idolater will leave his dwelling: should one of the family die on the fifth day of the new or waning moon, the place must be forsaken for six months; or should the Cobra Capella (serpent) enter the house at the times alluded to, the people must forthwith leave the house. Does an OWL alight on the roof for two SUCCESSIVE nights, the inmates will take their departure; but if for ONE only, then, by the performance of certain ceremonies, the evils may be averted. Are evil spirits believed to visit the dwelling? are the children often sick? are the former as well as the present occupiers unfortunate? then will they never rest till they have gained another habitation. Sometimes, however, they call for the *sāstre*, i. e. magician, to inquire if he can find out the cause of their troubles; when perhaps he says, the walls are too high, or too much in this or that direction; and then may be seen master, servants, children, carpenters, and masons, all busily employed in making the prescribed alterations. But another reason for the desolation in houses is, that a father sometimes leaves the dwelling to two or three of his sons; and then, when the necessary repairs have to be made, one will not do this, another will not do that, till the whole tumbles to the ground.—ROBERTS.

CHAPTER XIV.

Ver. 8. Yea, the fir-trees rejoice at thee, *and* the cedars of Lebanon, *saying*, Since thou art laid down, no feller is come up against us.

As we passed through the extensive forest of fir-trees situated between Deir el Kamr and Ainep, we had already heard, at some distance, the stroke of one solitary axe, resounding from hill to hill. On reaching the spot, we found a peasant, whose labour had been so far successful, that he had felled his tree and lopped the branches. He was now hewing it in the middle, so as to balance the two halves upon his camel, which stood patiently by him, waiting for his load. In the days of Hiram, king of Tyre, and subsequently under the kings of Babylon, this romantic solitude was not so peaceful: that most poetic image in Isaiah, who makes these very trees vocal, exulting in the downfall of the destroyer of nations, seems now to be almost realized anew—*Yea, the fir-trees rejoice at thee, and the cedars of Lebanon, saying, Since thou art laid down, no feller is come up against us.*—JOWETT.

Ver. 9. Hell from beneath is moved for thee to meet *thee* at thy coming: it stirreth up the dead for thee, *even* all the chief ones of the earth; it hath raised up from their thrones all the kings of the nations.

The sepulchres of the Hebrews, at least those of respectable persons, and those which hereditarily belonged to the principal families, were extensive caves, or vaults, excavated from the native rock by art and manual labour. The roofs of them in general were arched: and some were so spacious as to be supported by colonnades. All round the sides were cells for the reception of the sarcophagi; these were properly ornamented with sculpture, and each was placed in its proper cell. The cave or sepulchre admitted no light, being closed by a great stone, which was rolled to the mouth of the narrow passage or entrance. Many of these receptacles are still extant in Judea: two in particular are more magnificent than all the rest, and are supposed to be the sepulchres of the kings. One of these is in Jerusalem, and contains twenty-four cells; the other, containing twice that number, is in a place without the city.—BURDER.

Ver. 16. They that see thee shall narrowly look upon thee, *and* consider thee, *saying*, *Is* this the man that made the earth to tremble, that did shake kingdoms?

Narrowly to look on and to consider even the view of the Mujelibé, is to see what the palace of Babylon, in which kings, proud as "Lucifer," boasted of exalting themselves above the stars of God, has now become, and how, cut down to the ground, it is *broken in pieces.* "On pacing over the loose stones, and fragments of brick-work which lay scattered through the immense fabric, and surveying the sublimity of the ruins," says Captain Mignan, "I naturally recurred to the time when these walls stood proudly in their original splendour,—when the halls were the scenes of festive magnificence, and when they resounded to the voices of those whom death has long since swept from the earth. This very pile was once the seat of luxury and vice; now abandoned to decay, and exhibiting a melancholy instance of the retribution of Heaven. It stands alone;—the solitary habitation of the goatherd marks not the forsaken site." —KEITH.

Ver. 19. But thou art cast out of thy grave like an abominable branch, *and as* the raiment of those that are slain, thrust through with a sword, that go down to the stones of the pit; as a carcass trodden under feet.

Rather like the abominable tree, meaning that on which criminals were executed. This, in the Roman law, is denominated infelix arbor; and Maimonides tells us, that the Jews used to bury it with the criminal who suffered on it, as involved equally with him in the malediction of their law.—BURDER.

"Several deep excavations have been made in different places into the sides of the Mujelibé; some probably by the wearing of the seasons; but many others have been dug by the rapacity of the Turks, tearing up its bowels in search of hidden treasure,"—*as if the palace of Babylon were cast out of its grave.* "Several *penetrate very far* into the body of the structure," till it has become *as the raiment of those that are slain, thrust through with a sword.* "And some, it is likely, have never yet been explored, the *wild beasts of the desert* literally keeping guard over them." (Keppel.) "The mound was full of large holes"—*thrust through.* Near to the Mujelibé, on the supposed site of the hanging gardens which were situated within the walls of the palace, "the ruins are so *perforated* in consequence of the digging for bricks, that the original design is entirely lost. All that could favour any conjecture of gardens built on terraces are two *subterranean* passages. There can be no doubt that both *passages* are of vast extent: they are lined with bricks laid in with bitumen, and *covered over with large masses of stone.* This is nearly the only place where stone is observable." Arches built upon arches raised the hanging-gardens from terrace to terrace, till the highest was on a level with the top of the city walls. Now they *are cast out like an abominable branch*—and *subterranean* passages are disclosed—*down to the stones of the pit.* "*As a carcass trodden under feet.*" The streets of Babylon were parallel, crossed by others at right angles, and abounded with houses three and four stories high; and none can now traverse the site of Babylon, or find any other path, without *treading them under foot.* The traveller directs his course to the highest mounds; and there are none, whether temples or palaces, that are not *trodden on.* The Mujelibé "rises in a steep ascent, *over which* the passengers can only go up by the winding paths *worn* by frequent visits to the ruined edifice."—KEITH.

Ver. 23. I will also make it a possession for the bittern, and pools of water: and I will sweep it with the besom of destruction, saith the LORD of hosts.

What was he going to sweep? The devoted city of Babylon. The word BESOM is often used, as a figure, to denote the way in which people are swept from the earth. Thus, when the cholera morbus began to rage, it was said, "Alas! alas! it is sweeping us away as with a BESOM." "How is the cholera in your village?"—"It has come like besoms." When the people made offerings and sacrifices to the demons who were believed to produce the disease, the magician, who was believed to be the devil's agent, sometimes said, "Make such and such offerings, or I will sweep you away with a besom." In the Hindoo calendar, or almanac, where predictions are given respecting certain months of the year, it is often said, "The year is not good, it brings a besom."—ROBERTS.

Ver. 29. Rejoice not thou, whole Palestina, because the rod of him that smote thee is broken: for out of the serpent's root shall come forth a cockatrice, and his fruit *shall be* a fiery flying serpent.

In Egypt and other oriental countries, a serpent was the common symbol of a powerful monarch; it was embroidered on the robes of princes, and blazoned on their diadem, to signify their absolute power and invincible might, and that, as the wound inflicted by the basilisk is incurable, so the fatal effects of their displeasure were neither to be avoided nor endured. These are the allusions involved in the address of the prophet, to the irreconcilable enemies of his nation.—PAXTON.

Ver. 31. Howl, O gate; cry, O city: thou, whole Palestina, *art* dissolved: for there shall come from the north a smoke, and none *shall be* alone in his appointed times.

This may be in allusion to smoke arising from distant conflagrations, caused by an advancing desolating army, the sight of which would greatly alarm the inhabitants of Palestina. I have seen the smoke from mountains, whose grass and bushes were on fire, at the distance of forty or fifty miles. Or it may refer to clouds of sand or dust raised by troops rapidly advancing to attack them. By this means I have observed the advance of travelling parties, long before they reached us, from the cloud of sand raised by the movement of the oxen. Game is also frequently discovered by the same means.—CAMPBELL.

CHAPTER XV.

Ver. 1. The burden of Moab. Because in the night Ar of Moab is laid waste, *and* brought to silence; because in the night Kir of Moab is laid waste, *and* brought to silence.

See on Jer. 49. 1—28.

CHAPTER XVI.

Ver. 2. For it shall be, *that* as a wandering bird cast out of the nest, *so* the daughters of Moab shall be at the fords of Arnon.

The figure appears to be taken from a young bird being thrown out of the nest before it is able to fly, and which consequently wanders about for a place of refuge. "Well, Tamban, what has become of your profligate son?"—"I know not, my friend, because I have turned him out of the nest." "Why, my boy, have you come to this distant country?"—"Because my relations turned me out of the nest." "Alas for me! alas for me!" says the bereaved mother; "my young one has taken to the wing; it has flown from the nest." "I have only one left in the nest; shall I not take care of it?" "I should like to get into that nest;" says the young man who wishes to marry into a high and rich family. "Ah! my lord, dismiss me not from your service: to whom shall I go for employment? I have many children, who will be sufferers if I leave you: who will throw a stone at the nestlings? who will put fire to the lair of the young cubs of the jungle? Ah! my lord, turn me not away; I shall be like a bird wandering from its nest."—ROBERTS.

CHAPTER XVII.

Ver. 6. Yet gleaning-grapes shall be left in it, as the shaking of an olive-tree, two *or* three berries in the top of the uppermost bough, four *or* five in the outmost fruitful branches thereof, saith the LORD God of Israel.

The vintager cuts down the grapes from the vine with a sharp hook or sickle; but the olive was sometimes beaten off the tree, and sometimes shaken. The former method is mentioned by Moses, in one of his precepts: "When thou beatest thine olive-tree, thou shalt not go over the boughs again; it shall be for the stranger, for the fatherless, and for the widow." The latter is marked by the prophet Isaiah: "Yet gleaning grapes shall be left in it, as the shaking of an olive-tree; two or three berries in the top of the uppermost bough, four or five in the outmost fruitful branches thereof, saith the Lord God of Israel." It occurs again in a denunciation of divine judgments, by the same prophet: "When thus it shall be in the midst of the land among the people, there shall be as the shaking of an olive-tree, and as the gleaning grapes, when the vintage is done." The conjecture of Harmer, on these quotations, in which the shaking of the olive-tree is connected with the gleaning of grapes, is not improbable, "that the shaking of the olive-tree does not indicate an improvement made in after times on the original mode of gathering them; or different methods of procedure by different people, in the same age and country, who possessed olive-yards; but rather expressed the difference between the gathering of the main crop by the owners, and the way in which the poor collected the few olive-berries that were left, and which, by the law of Moses, they were permitted to take."

The custom of beating the olive with long poles, to make the fruit fall, is still followed in some parts of Italy. This foolish method, besides hurting the plant, and spoiling many branches that would bear the year following, makes the ripe and unripe fruit fall indiscriminately, and bruises a great deal of both kinds, by which they become rancid in the heaps, and give an ill-flavoured oil. Such is the statement of the Abbot Fortis, in his account of Dalmatia; we are not then to wonder, that in the time of Moses, when the art of cultivation was in so simple and unimproved a state, beating should have been the common way of gathering olives by the owners, who were disposed to leave, we may suppose, as few as possible, and were forbidden by their law to go over the branches a second time. But shaking them appears to have been sufficient, when they had hung till they were fully ripe; and was therefore practised by the poor, or by strangers, who were either not provided with such long poles as the owners possessed, or did not find them necessary. Indeed, it is not improbable, that the owners were well aware of the injury done to the olive-trees by beating, although they practised it, because it was the most effectual way of gathering the fruit with which they were acquainted; and might therefore prohibit the poor and the stranger to collect the gleanings in that manner: they were on that account reduced to the necessity of shaking the olive-berries from the tree, how ineffectual soever might be the method, or remain without them. The main crop, then, seems to have been taken from the olive by beating, and the gleanings uniformly by shaking. Under this conviction, Dr. Lowth has, with great judgment, translated the sixth verse of the seventeenth chapter of Isaiah: A gleaning shall be left in it, as in the shaking of the olive-tree.—PAXTON.

CHAPTER XVIII.

Ver. 2. That sendeth ambassadors by the sea, even in vessels of bulrushes upon the waters, *saying*, Go, ye swift messengers, to a nation scattered and peeled, to a people terrible from their beginning hitherto; a nation meted out and trodden down, whose land the rivers have spoiled!

"In order to pass along the Nile, the inhabitants have recourse to the contrivance of a float, made of large earthen pitchers, tied closely together, and covered with leaves of palm-trees. The man that conducts it, has commonly in his mouth a cord, with which he fishes, as he passes on." (Norden.) Egmont and Heyman saw some small floats, used by the Egyptian fishermen, consisting of bundles of reeds, floated by calabashes. "My palanquin bearers now found no difficulty in fording the stream of the Dahder; the last time I crossed, it was with some danger on a raft placed over earthen pots, a contrivance well known in modern Egypt, where they make a float of earthen pots, tied together, covered with a platform of palm-leaves, which will bear a considerable weight, and is conducted without difficulty." (Forbes.)—BURDER.

Ver. 6. They shall be left together unto the fowls of the mountains, and to the beasts of the earth: and the fowls shall summer upon them, and all the beasts of the earth shall winter upon them.

See on 1 Sam. 13. 18.

CHAPTER XXI.

Ver. 5. Prepare the table, watch in the watch-tower, eat, drink: arise, ye princes, *and* anoint the shield.

The ancient warrior did not yield to the moderns in keeping his armour in good order. The inspired writer often speaks of furbishing the spear, and making bright the arrows; and the manner in which he expresses himself in relation to this part of the soldier's duty, proves that it was generally and carefully performed. But they were particularly attentive to their shields, which they took care frequently to scour, polish, and anoint with oil. The oriental soldier seems to have gloried in the dazzling lustre of his shield, which he so highly valued, and upon which he engraved his name and warlike exploits. To produce the desired brightness, and preserve it undiminished, he had recourse to frequent unction; which is the reason of the prophet's invitation: "Arise, ye princes, and anoint the shield." As this was done to improve its polish and brightness, so it was covered with a case, when it was not in use, to preserve it from becoming rusty. This is the reason the prophet says, "Kir uncovered the shield." The words of David, already quoted, from his lamentation over Saul and Jonathan, may refer to this practice of anointing the shield, rather than anointing the king: "The shield of the mighty is vilely cast away, the shield of Saul, as though it had not been anointed with oil:" the word *he* being a supplement, the version now given is perfectly agreeable to the original text.—PAXTON.

Strange as it may appear, the Hindoos make offerings to their weapons of war, and to those used in hunting. Fishermen offer incense to the bag in which they carry their fish, and also to the net; thus, while the incense is burning, they hold the different implements in the smoke. They also, when able, sacrifice a sheep or a fowl, which is said to make the ceremony more acceptable to Varuna, the god of the sea. Should the tackle thus consecrated not prove successful, they conclude some part of the ceremony has not been properly performed, and therefore must be repeated. But in addition to this, they often call for their magicians to bless the waters, and to intercede for prosperity. Nor is this sacrificing to implements and weapons confined to fishermen, hunters, and warriors, for even artisans do the same thing to their tools; as also do students and scholars to their books. Thus, at the feast called *nava-rātere*, i. e. the nine nights, carpenters, masons, goldsmiths, weavers, and all other tradesmen, may be seen offering to their tools. Ask them a reason, and they say the incense and ceremonies are acceptable to *Sarusa-pathi*, the beautiful goddess of Brama.—ROBERTS.

Ver. 9. And, behold, here cometh a chariot of men, *with* a couple of horsemen. And he answered and said, Babylon is fallen, is fallen; and all the graven images of her gods he hath broken unto the ground.

This is a prophecy, and yet speaks as if the event to which it relates had been already accomplished. In Jeremiah, also, li. 8, it is said, "Babylon is suddenly fallen and destroyed." David says, "Thou hast smitten all mine enemies." Dr. A. Clarke says, "That is, thou wilt smite!" He speaks in full confidence of God's interference, and knows that he shall as surely have the victory, as if he had it already. In these selections the PAST tense is used instead of the FUTURE. He who came from Edom, with died garments from Bozrah, is made to say, "I will stain all my raiment." Dr. A. Clarke has, "And I have stained." In this instance, therefore, the FUTURE is used for the PAST, Ps. lxix:—"Let their table become a snare before them; and that which should have been for their welfare, let it become a trap. Let their eyes be darkened, that they see not; and make their loins continually to shake. Pour out thine indignation upon them, and let thy wrathful anger take hold of them. Let their habitation be desolate; and let none dwell in their tents." Dr. Boothroyd renders these imprecations in the future, because he believes the whole to refer to judgments that SHOULD fall on the enemy. Dr. A. Clarke says, "The execrations here, and in the following verses, should be read in the FUTURE tense, because they are PREDICTIVE, and not in the IMPERATIVE mood, as if they were the offspring of the Psalmist's resentment." It is common in eastern speech, in order to show the CERTAINTY of any thing which SHALL be done, to speak of it as having been ALREADY accomplished. Thus the Psalmist, in speaking of the iniquities of bad men as having already received their reward, evidently alludes to the CERTAINTY of future punishment. It is therefore of the first importance to know in what tense the verb is meant, as that alone will give a true view of the intention of the writer. In the Tamul language the PAST tense is often elegantly used for the FUTURE: thus, in the *Nan-nool* (the Native Grammar) this distinction is beautifully illustrated. Does a note require to be taken to another place in a very short time, the messenger, on being charged not to loiter on the way, replies, "*Nan vanthu vuttain*," i. e. "I have already RETURNED:" whereas he has not taken a single step of his journey. "My friend," asks the priest, "when do you intend to go to the sacred place and perform your vows?" "*Nan poye van-thain*," i. e. "I have been and returned," which means he is going immediately. "Carpenter, if you are not quick in finishing that car, the gods will be angry with you."—"My lord, the work is already done;" when perhaps some months will have to elapse before the work can be finished. But they also use the PAST for the FUTURE, to denote CERTANTY as well as SPEED. 'Do the ants begin to run about with their eggs in their mouth, it is said, "*mally-pay-yattu*," it has rained, though a single drop has not fallen on the ground. The meaning is, the sign is so CERTAIN, that all doubt is removed. "Why does that man go to the village? Does he not know the cholera is sweeping as a besom? Alas! alas! *avvon-chetu ponān;* he is already dead;" which means, he will certainly die. Should the friends of a young man inquire whether he may go to sea, the soothsayer says, (if the signs are unfavourable,) "He is already drowned." But the FUTURE is also used instead of the past, as in the case of the deliverer from Bozrah: "I will stain," for "I have stained." Should a man refuse to obey an officer, and inquire, "Where is the order of the king?" the reply is, "He WILL command," which strongly intimates it has been done, and that other consequences will follow. (1 Sam. iii. 13.) See margin, 1 Kings iii. 13; also vi. 1; and xv. 25. 2 Kings viii. 16. Dan. ii. 28; also iii. 29; for all of which see marginal readings. See Dr. A. Clarke on Matt. iii. 17; also xxvi. 28, blood is shed, for WILL be shed.—ROBERTS.

Ver. 11. The burden of Dumah. He calleth to me out of Seir, Watchman, what of the night? watchman, what of the night?

The Orientals employed watchmen to patrol the city during the night, to suppress any disorders in the streets, or to guard the walls against the attempts of a foreign enemy. To this custom Solomon refers in these words: "The watchmen that went about the city found me, they smote me, they wounded me; the keepers of the wall took away my veil from me." This custom may be traced to a very remote antiquity; so early as the departure of Israel from the land of Egypt, the morning watch is mentioned, certainly indicating the time when the watchmen were commonly relieved. In Persia, the watchmen were obliged to indemnify those who were robbed in the streets; which accounts for the vigilance and severity which they display in the discharge of their office, and illustrates the character of watchman given to Ezekiel, who lived in that country, and the duties he was required to perform. If the wicked perished in his iniquities without warning, the prophet was to be accountable for his blood; but if he duly pointed out his danger, he delivered his own soul. These terms, therefore, were neither harsh nor severe; they were the common appointments of watchmen in Persia. They were also charged to announce the progress of the night to the slumbering city: "The burden of Dumah: he calls to me out of Seir, Watchman, what of the night? watchman, what of the night? The watchman said, The morning cometh, and also the night." This is confirmed by an observation of Chardin, upon these words of Moses: "For a thousand years in thy sight are but as yesterday when it is past, and as a watch in the night;" that as the people of the East have no clocks, the several parts of the day and of the night, which are eight in all, are announced. In the Indies, the parts of the night are made known, as well by instruments of music, in great cities, as by the rounds of the watchmen, who, with cries and small drums, give them notice that a fourth part of the night is past. Now, as these cries awaked those who had slept all that quarter part of the night, it appeared to them but as a moment. There are sixty of these people in the Indies by day, and as many by night; that is, fifteen for each division. It is evident the ancient Jews knew, by means of some public notice, how the night-watches passed away; but, whether they simply announced the termination of the watch, or made use of trumpets, or other sonorous instruments, in making the proclamation, it may not be easy to determine; and still less what kind of chronometers the watchmen used. The probability is, that the watches were announced with the sound of a trumpet; for the prophet Ezekiel makes it a part of the watchman's duty, at least in time of war, to blow the trumpet, and warn the people.—PAXTON.

CHAPTER XXII.

Ver. 1. The burden of the valley of vision. What aileth thee now, that thou art wholly gone up to the house-tops?

The houses in the East were in ancient times as they are still, generally, built in one and the same uniform manner. The roof or top of the house is always flat, covered with broad stones, or a strong plaster of terrace, and guarded on every side with a low parapet-wall. The terrace is frequented as much as any part of the house. On this, as the season favours, they walk, they eat, they sleep, they transact business, they perform their devotions. The house is built with a court within, into which chiefly the windows open; those that open to the street are so obstructed with lattice-work, that no one either without or within can see through them. Whenever, therefore, any thing is to be seen or heard in the streets, every one immediately goes up to the house-top to satisfy his curiosity. In the same manner, when any one had occasion to make any thing public, the readiest and most effectual way of doing it, was to proclaim it from the house-tops to the people in the streets. —LOWTH.

Ver. 8. And he discovered the covering of Judah, and thou didst look in that day to the armour of the house of the forest.

The editor of the Fragments subjoined to Calmet's Dictionary of the Bible, thus renders and explains this passage: He rolled up, turned back, the covering of Judah, as the covering veils, hanging at the door of a house or tent, are rolled up, for more convenient passage, and did look, inspect carefully, the arms and weapons of the house of the forest. The ideas contained in this interpretation are aptly expressed in the following extract from Frazer's History of Kouli Khan: "Nadir Shah, having taken Delhi, ordered Sirbullind Khan to attend the Towpehi Bashi, the master of the ordnance; and the Nissikchi Bachi, head regulator, commissary of seizures, who had each two hundred horse, to seize all the king's and the omra's ordnance, the treasury, jewels, toishik-khanna, (the arsenal,) and all the other implements and arms that belonged to the emperor, and the deceased omras; and to send to Mahommed Shah, the captive emperor, his son, Sultan Ahmed, and Malika al Zumani, (the queen of the times,) the empress. Nadir Shah took away the ordnance, effects, and treasure." May not such a conduct in a conqueror justify the allusion supposed to be intended in this representation of the prophet; for what is this but rolling back what covered the privacy of the conquered state, and prying into the house of its armoury.—BURDER.

Ver. 16. What hast thou here, and whom hast thou here, that thou hast hewed thee out a sepulchre here, *as* he that hewed him out a sepulchre on high, *and* that graveth a habitation for himself in a rock?

The Orientals bury without the walls of their cities, unless when they wish to bestow a distinguishing mark of honour upon the deceased. For this reason, the sepulchres of David and his family, and the tomb of Huldah the prophetess, were within the city of Jerusalem; and perhaps the only ones to be found there. The sepulchres of the Hebrews, that were able to afford the necessary expense, were extensive caves or vaults, excavated in the native rock, by the art and exertions of man. The roofs were generally arched; and some were so spacious as to be supported by colonnades. All round the sides were cells for the reception of the sarcophagi; these were ornamented with appropriate sculpture, and each was placed in its proper cell. The cave or sepulchre admitted no light, being closed by a great stone which was rolled to the mouth, by the narrow passage or entrance. Many of these receptacles are still extant in Judea; two in particular are more magnificent than all the rest, and for that reason supposed to be the sepulchres of the kings. One of these is in Jerusalem, and contains twenty-four cells; the other, containing twice that number, is without the city. "You are to form to yourself," says Lowth, speaking of these sepulchres, "an idea of an immense subterraneous vault, a vast gloomy cavern, all round the sides of which are cells to receive the dead bodies; here the deceased monarchs lie in a distinguished sort of state, suitable to their former rank, each on his own couch, with his arms beside him, his sword at his head, and the bodies of his chiefs and companions round about him."

"Whoever," says Maundrell, "was buried there, this is certain, that the place itself discovers so great an expense, both of labour and of treasure, that we may well suppose it to have been the work of kings. You approach it at the east side through an entrance cut out of the natural rock, which admits you into an open court of about forty paces square, cut down into the rock, with which it is encompassed instead of walls. On the south side of the court, is a portico, nine paces long, and four broad, hewn likewise out of the rock. This has a kind of architrave running along its front, adorned with sculpture of fruits and flowers, still discernible, but by time much defaced. At the end of the portico on the left hand, you descend to the passage into the sepulchres. Passing through it, you arrive in a large apartment about seven or eight yards square, cut out of the natural rock. Its sides and ceiling are so exactly square, and its angles so just, that no architect with levels and plummets could build a room more regular; and the whole is so firm and entire, that it may be called a chamber hollowed out of one piece of marble. From this room you pass into six more, one within another, all of the same fabric as the first. Of these the two innermost are deeper than the rest, having a second descent of about six or seven steps into them. In every one of these rooms, except the first, were coffins of stone placed in niches in the sides of the chambers. They had been at first covered with handsome lids, and carved with garlands; but now most of them are broken to pieces by sacrilegious hands. The sides and ceilings of the rooms were also drooping with the moist damps condensed upon them; to remedy which nuisance, and to preserve these chambers of the dead polite and clean, there was in each room a small channel cut in the floor, which served to drain the drops that fell constantly into it.

To these sepulchres, and their interior chambers, one within another, the wise man, by a bold and striking figure, compares the dwelling of a lewd woman: "Her house is the way to *hades;*" her first or outer chamber is like the open court that leads to the tomb, "going down to the chambers of death;" her private apartments, like the separate recesses of a sepulchre, are the receptacles of loathsome corruption; and he calls them, in allusion to the solidity of the rock in which they are hewn, the "long home," (בית עלם) *beth olam*, the house of ages. The higher such sepulchres were cut in the rock, or the more conspicuously they were situated, the greater was supposed to be the honour of reposing there. "Hezekiah was buried in the chiefest," says our translation; rather, in the highest part "of the sepulchres of the sons of David," to do him the more honour. The vanity of Shebna, which so much displeased the Lord, was discovered in preparing for himself a sepulchre in the face of some lofty rock: "What hast thou here, and whom hast thou here, that thou hast hewed thee out a sepulchre here, as he that heweth him out a sepulchre on high, and that graveth a habitation for him in a rock." Several modern travellers mention some monuments still remaining in Persia of great antiquity, which gave them a clear idea of Shebna's pompous design for his sepulchre. They consist of several tombs, each of them hewn in a high rock near the top; the front of the rock to the valley below, being the outside of the sepulchre, is adorned with carved work in relief. Some of these sepulchres are about thirty feet in the perpendicular from the valley. Diodorus Siculus mentions these ancient monuments, and calls them the sepulchres of the kings of Persia. The tombs of Telmissus, in the island of Rhodes, which Dr. Clarke visited, furnish a still more remarkable commentary on this text. They "are of two kinds; the first are sepulchres hewn in the face of perpendicular rocks. Wherever the side of a mountain presented an almost inaccessible steep, there the ancient workmen seem to have bestowed their principal labour. In such situations are seen excavated chambers, worked with such marvellous art, as to exhibit open façades, porticoes with Ionic columns, gates and doors beautifully sculptured, in which are carved the representation of an embossed iron work, bolts and hinges of one stone.

"The other kind of tomb is the true Grecian soros, the sarcophagus of the Romans. Of this sort there are several, but of a size and grandeur far exceeding any thing of the kind elsewhere, standing in some instances upon the craggy pinnacles of lofty precipitous rocks. Each consists of a single stone, others of still larger size, of more than one stone. Some consist of two masses of stone, one for the body, or chest of the soros, and the other for its operculum; and to increase the wonder excited by the skill and labour manifested in their construction, they have been almost miraculously raised to the surrounding heights, and there left standing upon the projections and crags of the rocks, which the casualties of nature presented for their reception. At Macri, the tombs are cut out of the solid rock, in the precipices towards the sea. Some of them have a kind of portico, with pillars in front. In these they were almost plain. The hewn stone was as smooth as if the artist had been employed upon wood, or any other soft substance. They most nearly resemble book-cases, with glass doors. A small rectangular opening, scarcely large enough to pass through, admits a stranger to the interior of these tombs; where is found a square chamber, with one or more receptacles for dead bodies, shaped like baths, upon the sides of the apartment, and neatly chiselled in the body of the rock. The mouths of these sepulchres had been originally closed by square slabs of stone, exactly adapted to grooves cut for their reception; and so nicely adjusted, that when the work was finished, the place of entrance might not be observed. Of similar construction were the sepulchres of the Jews in Palestine, and particularly that in which our Lord was buried. Many of these have the appearance of being inaccessible; but by dint of climbing from rock to rock, at the risk of a dangerous fall, it is possible to ascend even to the highest. They are fronted with rude pillars, which are integral parts of the solid rock. Some of them are twenty feet high. The mouths of these sepulchres are closed with beautiful sculptured imitations of brazen or iron doors, with hinges, knobs, and bars."

This intelligent traveller visited a range of tombs of the same kind on the borders of the lake of Tiberias, hewn by the earliest inhabitants of Galilee, in the rocks which face the water. They were deserted in the time of our Saviour, and had become the resort of wretched men, afflicted by diseases, and made outcasts of society; for these tombs are particularly alluded to in the account of a cure performed upon a maniac in the country of the Gadarenes. The tombs at Naplose, the ancient Sichem, where Joseph, Joshua, and others, were buried, are also hewn out of the solid rock, and durable as the hills in which they are excavated. Constituting integral parts of mountains, and chiselled with a degree of labour not to be conceived from mere description, these monuments suffer no change from the lapse of ages; they have defied, and will defy, the attacks of time, and continue as perfect at this hour, as they were in the first moment of their completion.—Paxton.

Ver. 17. Behold, the Lord will carry thee away with a mighty captivity, and will surely cover thee.

To be covered is a sign of mourning, of degradation, and inferiority. People in great sorrow cover their faces with their robes; thus may be seen the weeping mother and sorrow-struck father: they cover themselves from the sight of others, to conceal their dejection and tears. But when people are ashamed, also, they cover their heads and faces. For a man to say he will cover another, intimates superiority, and shows that he will put him to confusion. "Yes, the man who was brought up and nourished by the Modeliar, is now greater than his benefactor, for he covers him." "Look at that parasitical banyan tree; when it first began to grow on the other tree, it was a very small plant, but it has been allowed to flourish, and now it covers the parent stock." Thus, those who were to be carried into captivity, were to be covered, in token of their sorrow, degradation, and inferiority.—Roberts.

Ver. 22. And the key of the house of David will I lay upon his shoulder: so he shall open, and none shall shut; and he shall shut, and none shall open.

How much was I delighted when I first saw the people, especially the Moors, going along the streets with each his key on his shoulder. The handle is generally made of brass, (though sometimes of silver,) and is often nicely worked in a device of filigree. The way it is carried, is to have the corner of a kerchief tied to the ring; the key is then placed on the shoulder, and the kerchief hangs down in front. At other times they have a bunch of large keys, and then they have half on one side of the shoudler, and half on the other. For a man thus to march along with a large key on his shoulder, shows at once that he is a person of consequence. "Râman is in great favour with the Modeliar, for he now carries the key." "Whose key have you got on your shoulder?" "I shall carry my key on my own shoulder." The key of the house of David was to be on the shoulder of Eliakim, who was a type of him who had the "government" "upon his shoulder;" "the mighty God, the everlasting Father, the Prince of Peace."—Roberts.

Ver. 23. And I will fasten him *as* a nail in a sure place; and he shall be for a glorious throne to his father's house.

When a man in power has given a situation to another, it is said of the favoured individual, "He is fastened as a nail." "Yes, his situation is fixed, he will not be moved." "What! has Tamban lost his glory? I thought he had been fastened as a nail."—Roberts.

The Orientals, in fitting up their houses, were by no means inattentive to the comfort and satisfaction arising from order and method. Their furniture was scanty and plain; but they were careful to arrange the few household utensils they needed, so as not to encumber the apartments to which they belonged. Their devices for this purpose, which, like every part of the structure, bore the character of remarkable simplicity, may not correspond with our ideas of neatness and propriety; but they accorded with their taste, and sufficiently answered their design. One of these consisted in a set of spikes, nails, or large pegs, fixed in the walls of the house, upon which they hung up the moveables and utensils in common use, that belonged to the room. These nails they do not drive into the walls with a hammer or mallet, but fix them there when the house is building; for if the walls are of brick, they are too hard, or if they consist of clay, too soft and mouldering, to admit the action of the hammer. The spikes, which are so contrived as to strengthen the walls, by binding the parts together, as well as to serve for convenience, are large, with square heads like dice, and bent at the ends so as to make them cramp-irons. They commonly place them at the windows and doors, in order to hang upon them, when they choose, veils and curtains, although they place them in other parts of the room, to hang up other things of various kinds. The care with which they fixed these nails, may be inferred, as well from the important purposes they were meant to serve, as from the promise of the Lord to Eliakim: "And I will fasten him as a nail in a sure place." Pins and nails, Dr. Russel observes, in a manuscript note, are seldom used (at Aleppo) for hanging clothes or other articles upon, which are usually laid one over the other, on a chest, or particular kind of chair. This intelligent writer does not refuse that they are occasionally used in modern times; and it is evident from the words of the prophet, that it was common in his time to suspend upon them the utensils belonging to the apartment: "Will men take a pin of it to hang any vessel thereon?" The word used in Isaiah for a nail of this sort, is the same which denotes the stake, or large pin of iron, which fastened down to the ground the cords of their tents. These nails, therefore, were of necessary and common use, and of no small importance in all their apartments; and if they seem to us mean and insignificant, it is because they are unknown to us, and inconsistent with our notions of propriety, and because we have no name for them but what conveys to our ear a low and contemptible idea. It is evident from the frequent allusions in scripture to these instruments, that they were not regarded with contempt or indifference by the natives of Palestine. "Grace has been showed from the Lord our God," said Ezra, "to leave us a remnant to escape, and to give us a nail in his holy place;" or, as explained in the margin, a constant and sure abode. The dignity and propriety of the metaphor appears from the use which the prophet Zechariah makes of it: "Out of him cometh forth the corner, out of him the nail, out of him the battle bow, out of him every oppressor together." The whole frame of government, both in church and state, which the chosen people of God enjoyed, was the contrivance of his wisdom, and the gift of his bounty: the foundations upon which it rested; the bonds which kept the several parts together; its means of defence; its officers and executors, were all the fruits of distinguishing goodness; even the oppressors of his people were a rod of correction in the hand of Jehovah, to convince them of sin, and restore them to his service.—PAXTON.

CHAPTER XXIV.

Ver. 5. The earth also is defiled under the inhabitants thereof, because they have transgressed the laws, changed the ordinance, broken the everlasting covenant.

These expressive words, while they declare the cause of the judgments and desolation, denote also the great depravity of those who were to inhabit the land of Judea, during the time of its desolation, and while its ancient inhabitants were to be "scattered abroad." And although the ignorance of those who dwell therein may be pitied, their degeneracy will not be denied. The ferocity of the Turks, the predatory habits of the Arabs, the abject state of the few poor Jews who are suffered to dwell in the land of their fathers, the base superstitions of the different Christian sects; the frequent contentions that subsist among such a mingled and diversified people, and the gross ignorance and great depravity that prevail throughout the whole, have all sadly changed and stained the moral aspect of that country, which, from sacred remembrances, is denominated the Holy Land; have converted that region, where alone in all the world, and during many ages, the only living and true God was worshipped; and where alone the pattern of perfect virtue was ever exhibited to human view, or in the human form, into one of the most degraded countries of the globe, and in appropriate terms, may well be said to have *defiled the land.* And it has been defiled throughout many an age. The Father of mercies afflicteth not willingly, nor grieves the children of men. Sin is ever the precursor of the actual judgments of Heaven. It was on account of their idolatry and wickedness that the ten tribes were earliest plucked from off the land of Israel. The blood of Jesus, according to their prayer, and the full measure of their iniquity, according to their doings, was upon the Jews and upon their children. Before they were extirpated from that land which their iniquities had defiled, it was drenched with the blood of more than a million of their race. Judea afterward had a partial and temporary respite from desolation, when Christian churches were established there. But in that land, the nursery of Christianity, the seeds of its corruption, or perversion, began soon to appear. The moral power of religion decayed, the worship of images prevailed, and the nominal disciples of a pure faith "broke the everlasting covenant." The doctrine of Mohammed, the Koran, or the sword, was the scourge and the cure of idolatry; but all the native impurities of the Mohammedan creed succeeded to a grossly corrupted form of Christianity. Since that period, hordes of Saracens, Egyptians, Fatimites, Tartars, Mamelukes, Turks, (a combination of names of unmatched barbarism, at least in modem times,) have, for the space of twelve hundred years, *defiled the land* of the children of Israel with iniquity and with blood. And in very truth the prophecy savours not in the least of hyperbole: *the worst of the heathen shall possess their houses, and the holy places shall be defiled.* Omer, on the first conquest of Jerusalem by the Mohammedans, erected a mosque on the site of the temple of Solomon; and, jealous as the God of Israel is, that his glory be not given to another, the unseemly, and violent, and bloody contentions among Christian sects, around the very sepulchre of the Author of the faith which they dishonour, bear not a feebler testimony in the present day, than the preceding fact bore, at so remote a period, to the truth of this prediction. The phrensied zeal of crusading Christians could not expel the heathen from Judea, though Europe then poured like a torrent upon Asia. But the defilement of the land, no less than that of the holy places, is not yet cleansed away. And Judea is still defiled to this hour, not only by oppressive rulers, but by an unprincipled and a lawless people. "The barbarism of Syria," says Volney, "is complete." "I have often reflected," says Burckhardt, in describing the dishonest conduct of a Greek priest in the hauran, (but in words that admit of too general an application,) "that if the English penal laws were suddenly promulgated in this country, there is scarcely any man in business, or who has money-dealings with others, who would not be liable to transportation before the end of the first six months. Under the name of Christianity, every degrading superstition and profane rite, equally remote from the enlightened tenets of the gospel, and the dignity of human nature, are professed and tolerated. The pure gospel of Christ, everywhere the herald of civilization and of science, is almost as little known in the Holy Land, as in California or New Holland. A series of legendary traditions, mingled with remains of Judaism, and the wretched fantasies of illiterate ascetics, may now and then exhibit a glimmering of heavenly light; but if we seek for the effects of Christianity in the Land of Canaan, we must look for that period when the desert shall blossom as the rose, and the wilderness become a fruitful field."-KEITH.

Ver. 6. Therefore hath the curse devoured the earth, and they that dwell therein are desolate: therefore the inhabitants of the earth are burned, and few men left.

"The government of the Turks in Syria is a pure military despotism, that is, the bulk of the inhabitants are subject to the caprices of a faction of armed men, who dispose of every thing according to their interest and fancy. In each government the pacha is an absolute despot. In the villages, the inhabitants, limited to the mere necessaries of life, have no arts but those without which they cannot subsist. There is no safety without the towns, nor security within their precincts." (Volney.) "Few men left." While their character is thus depraved, and their condition miserable, their number is also small indeed, as the inhabitants of so extensive and fertile a region. After estimating the number of inhabitants in Syria in general, Volney remarks, "So feeble a population in so excellent a country, may well excite our *astonishment;* but this will be increased, if we compare the present number of inhabitants with that of ancient times. We are informed by the philosophical geographer, Strabo, that the territories of Yanmia and Yoppa, in Palestine alone, were formerly so populous as to bring forty thousand armed men into the field. At present they could scarcely furnish three thousand. From the accounts we have of Judea, in the time of Titus, which are to be esteemed tolerably accurate, that country must have contained four millions of inhabitants. If we go still further back into antiquity, we shall find the same populousness among the Philistines, the Phenicians, and in the kingdoms of Samaria and Damascus." Though the ancient population of the land of Israel be estimated at the lowest computation, and the existing population be rated at the highest, yet that country does not now contain a tenth part of the number of inhabitants which it plentifully supported, exclusively from their industry, and from the rich resources of its own luxuriant soil, for many successive centuries; and how could it possibly have been imagined that this identical land would ever yield so scanty a subsistence to he desolate dwellers therein, and that there would be so *few men left?*—Keith.

Ver. 13. When thus it shall be in the midst of the land among the people, *there shall be* as the shaking of an olive-tree, *and* as the gleaning-grapes when the vintage is done.

See on ch. 17. 6.

CHAPTER XXV.

Ver. 6. And in this mountain shall the Lord of hosts make unto all people a feast of fat things, a feast of wines on the lees; of fat things full of marrow, of wines on the lees well refined.

See on ch. 51. 17.

In the East they keep their wine in jugs, from which they have no method of drawing it off fine: it is therefore commonly somewhat thick and turbid, by the lees with which it is mixed: to remedy this inconvenience they filtrate or strain it through a cloth, and to this custom, as prevailing in his time, the prophet here plainly alludes.—Burder.

Ver. 10. For in this mountain shall the hand of the Lord rest, and Moab shall be trodden down under him, even as straw is trodden down for the dunghill.

See on ch. 28. 26—28.

Dr. A. Clarke has, "for the dunghill," "under the wheels of the car." This may allude to their ancient cars of war, under which Moab was to be crushed, or under her own heathen cars, in which the gods were taken out in procession. To spread forth the hands, as a person when swimming, may refer to the involuntary stretching forth of the limbs, when the body was crushed with the weight of the car; or to the custom of those who, when they go before the car in procession, prostrate themselves on the ground, and spread out their hands and legs as if swimming; till they have measured the full distance the car has to go, by throwing themselves on the earth at the length of every six feet, and by motions as if in the act of swimming. The whole of this is done as a penance for sin, or in compliance with a vow made in sickness or despair.—Roberts.

CHAPTER XXVI.

Ver. 19. Thy dead *men* shall live, *together with* my dead body shall they arise. Awake and sing, ye that dwell in dust: for thy dew *is as* the dew of herbs, and the earth shall cast out the dead.

As they sometimes plant herbs and flowers about the graves of the dead, so Dr. Addison observed, that the Jews of Barbary adorned the graves of their dead in a less lasting manner, with green boughs brought thither from time to time; might not this practice originate from the doctrine of the resurrection? perhaps from that well known passage of a prophet: "Thy dead men shall live, together with my dead body shall they arise. Awake and sing, ye that dwell in dust: for thy dew is as the dew of herbs, and the earth shall cast out the dead." Is. xxvi. 19. Or if it was practised still earlier, might not this passage have reference to that custom? It is admitted, that the practice obtained among those that entertained no expectation of a resurrection, but in the language of St. Paul sorrowed as people that had no such hope. The ancient Greeks practised this decking the graves of their dead, but it might notwithstanding originate from that doctrine, and be adopted by those of a different belief, as having something in it softening the horrors of viewing their relatives immersed in the dust; and might be thought to be agreeable by those that entered into medical considerations, as correcting those ill-scented and noxious exhalations that might arise in those burial places, to which their women, more especially, were frequently induced to go, to express their attachment to the departed. Maillet supposes the modern Egyptians lay leaves and herbs on the graves of their friends, from a notion that this was a consolation to the dead, and believed to be refreshing to them from their shade. The women there, according to him, go, "at least two days in the week, to pray and weep at the sepulchres of the dead; and the custom then is to throw upon the tombs a sort of herb which the Arabs call *rihan*, and which is our sweet basil. They cover them also with the leaves of the palm-tree." If they use any other plants for this purpose in Egypt, he has neglected to mention them.—Harmer.

CHAPTER XXVII.

Ver. 10. Yet the defenced city *shall be* desolate, *and* the habitation forsaken, and left like a wilderness: there shall the calf feed, and there shall he lie down, and consume the branches thereof.

Josephus describes Galilee, of which he was the governor, as "full of plantations of trees of all sorts, the soil universally rich and fruitful, and all, without the exception of a single part, cultivated by the inhabitants. Moreover," he adds, "the cities lie here very thick, and there are very many villages, which are so full of people, by the richness of their soil, that the very least of them contained above fifteen thousand inhabitants." Such was Galilee, at the commencement of the Christian era, several centuries after the prophecy was delivered; but now "the plain of Esdraelon and all the other parts of Galilee which afford *pasture*, are occupied by Arab tribes, around whose brown tents the sheep and *lambs* gambol to the sound of the reed, which at nightfall calls them home." The calf feeds and lies down amid the ruins of the cities, and consumes, without hinderance, the branches of the trees; and, however changed may be the condition of the inhabitants, *the lambs feed after their manner*, and, while the land mourns, and the merry-hearted sigh, they gambol to the sound of the reed. The precise and comple contrast between the ancient and existing state of Palestine, as separately described by Jewish and Roman historians and by modern travellers, is so strikingly exemplified in their opposite descriptions, that, in reference to whatever constituted the beauty and the glory of the country, or the happiness of the people, an entire change is manifest, even in minute circumstances. The universal richness and fruitfulness of the soil of Galilee, together with its being "full of plantations of all sorts of trees," are represented by Josephus as "inviting the most slothful to take pains in its cultivation." And the other provinces of the Holy Land are also described by him as "having abundance of trees, full of autumnal fruit, both that which grows wild, and that which is the effect of cultivation." Tacitus relates, that, besides all the fruits of Italy, the palm and balsam-tree flourished in the fertile soil of Judea. And he records the great carefulness with which, when the circulation of the juices seemed to call for it, they gently made an incision in the branches of the balsam, with a shell, or pointed stone, not venturing to apply a knife. No sign of such art or care is now to be seen throughout the land. The balm-tree has disappeared where long it flourished; and hardier plants have perished from other causes than the want of due care in their cultivation. And instead of relating how the growth of a delicate tree is promoted, and the medicinal liquor at the same time extracted from its branches, by a nicety or perfectibility of art worthy of the notice of a Tacitus, a different task has fallen to the lot of the traveller from a far land, who describes the customs of those who now dwell where such arts were practised. "The olive-trees (near Arimathea) are daily perishing through age, the *ravages* of contending factions, and even *from secret mischief*. The Mamelukes having cut down all the olive-trees, for the pleasure they take in destroying, or to make *fires*, Yafahas has lost its greatest convenience." Instead of "abundance of trees" being still the effect of cultivation, such, on the other hand, has been the effect of these ravages, that many places in Palestine are now "absolutely destitute of fuel." Yet in this devastation, and in all its progress, may be read the literal fulfilment of the prophecy, which not only described the desolate cities of Judea as a pasture of flocks, and as places for the calf to feed and lie down, and consume the branches thereof; but which, with equal truth, also declared, "when the boughs thereof are withered, they shall be broken off; the women come and set them on fire."—KEITH.

CHAPTER XXVIII.

Ver. 1. Wo to the crown of pride, to the drunkards of Ephraim, whose glorious beauty *is* a fading flower, which *are* on the head of the fat valleys of them that are overcome with wine!

The city of Sebaste, the ancient Samaria, beautifully situated on the top of a round hill, and surrounded immediately with a rich valley and a circle of other hills beyond it, suggested the idea of a chaplet, or wreath of flowers, worn upon their heads on occasions of festivity; expressed by the proud crown and the fading flower of the drunkards. That this custom of wearing chaplets in their banquets prevailed among the Jews, as well as among the Greeks and Romans, appears from Wisdom ii. 7, 8.—LOWTH.

Ver. 15. Because ye have said, We have made a covenant with death, and with hell are we at agreement; when the overflowing scourge shall pass through, it shall not come unto us; for we have made lies our refuge, and under falsehood have we hid ourselves.

Of those who have often had a narrow escape from death, it is said, "Those fellows have entered into an agreement with death." "They have made a friendship; death injure them! *chee, chee*, they understand each other."—ROBERTS.

Ver. 25. When he hath made plain the face thereof, doth he not cast abroad the fitches, and scatter the cummin, and cast in the principal wheat, and the appointed barley, and the rye, in their place?

See on ch. 32. 20.

Ver. 26. For his God doth instruct him to discretion, *and* doth teach him. 27. For the fitches are not thrashed with a thrashing instrument, neither is a cart-wheel turned about upon the cummin; but the fitches are beaten out with a staff, and the cummin with a rod.

28. Bread-*corn* is bruised; because he will not ever be thrashing it, nor break *it with* the wheel of his cart, nor bruise it *with* his horsemen.

The method of thrashing out the grain, varied according to the species. Isaiah mentions four different instruments, the flail, the drag, the wain, and the feet of the ox. The staff, or flail, was used for the smaller seeds, which were too tender to be treated in the other methods. The drag consisted of a sort of strong planks, made rough at the bottom with hard stones or iron; it was drawn by oxen, or horses, over the corn sheaves spread on the floor, the driver sitting upon it. The wain, or cart, was much like the former, but had wheels, with iron teeth or edges like a saw. From the statement of different authors, it would seem that the axle was armed with iron teeth, or serrated wheels throughout. Niebuhr gives a description and print of such a machine, used at present in Egypt for the same purpose; it moves upon three rollers, armed with iron teeth or wheels to cut the straw. In Syria, they make use of the drag, constructed in the very same manner as before described. This not only forced out the grain, but also cut the straw in pieces, which is used in this state over all the East as fodder for the cattle. Virgil also mentions the slow rolling wains of the Eleusinian mother, the planks and sleds for pressing out the corn, and harrows of unwieldy weight. The Israelitish farmer, endowed with discretion from above, made use of all these instruments in separating from the chaff the various produce of his fields: "For his God doth instruct him to discretion, and doth teach him. For the fitches are not thrashed with a thrashing instrument, neither is a cart-wheel turned about upon the cummin; but the fitches are beaten out with a staff, and the cummin with a rod. Bread-corn is bruised: because he will not ever be thrashing it, nor break it with the wheel of his cart, nor bruise it with his horsemen. This also cometh forth from the Lord of hosts, who is wonderful in counsel and excellent in working." In the early periods of the Jewish commonwealth, however, these various methods, adapted to the different kinds of grain, were unknown; the husbandman employed the staff, or flail, in thrashing all his crop. When the angel of the Lord appeared to Gideon, he found him thrashing wheat by the wine-press with a staff, for so the original term (חובט) signifies; and after Ruth had gleaned in the field till the evening, she beat out with a staff (ותחבט) what she had gleaned. The Seventy render the verb in both passages, by the Greek word *ραβδιζειν*, to beat with a rod; but the natural sagacity of the human mind, directed by the finger of God, at last invented the other more efficacious implements, to which Isaiah so frequently refers in the course of his writings. He compares Moab, in the day of their overthrow, to straw which is trodden down under the wain: and he promises to furnish his oppressed people with the same powerful instrument, which we translate a new sharp thrashing instrument having teeth, that they may thrash the mountains, and beat them small, and make the hills as chaff; or dropping the metaphor, he promises them complete victory over their numerous and powerful enemies, who should be given by the Lord of hosts as driven stubble to their bow, and swept away before the armies of Israel as chaff before the whirlwinds of the south.—PAXTON.

As in different parts of the holy scriptures there are frequent allusions to the *sowing of rice*, *watering the grounds*, *thrashing*, or what the prophet Isaiah, xxviii. 28, terms, *breaking it with the wheel of the cart;* or, *bringing the wheel over it*, Prov. xx. 26, it may not be improper to conclude these remarks with a short account of the sowing, cultivation, thrashing, and preservation of rice, taken from the travels of Mr. Sonnini, a writer worthy of the utmost credit in every thing that concerns the natural history and antiquities of Egypt.

"Rice is sown in Lower Egypt from the month of March to that of May. During the inundation of the Nile, the fields are covered by its waters; and in order to detain them there as long as possible, small dikes, or a sort of raised embankments, are thrown up, round each field, to prevent them from running off. Trenches serve to convey thither a fresh supply; for, in order to make the plant thrive, its roots must be constantly watered. The ground is so moistened, that in some places a person sinks in half way up to his chin. Rice is nearly six months before it comes to maturity; and it is generally cut down by the middle of November. In Egypt the use of the *flail* is unknown. To separate the grain from the straw, the inhabitants prepare with a mixture of earth and pigeon's dung, spacious floors, well beat, and very clean. The rice is spread thereon in thick layers. They then have a sort of cart, formed of two pieces of wood joined together by two cross-pieces: it is almost in the shape of sledges which serve for the conveyance of burdens in the streets of our cities. Between the longer sides of this sledge are fixed transversely three rows of small wheels, made of solid iron, and narrowed off towards their circumference. On the forepart, a very high and very wide seat is clumsily constructed. A man sitting there drives two oxen, which are harnessed to the machine, and the whole moves on slowly, and always in a circular direction, over every part of the heap of rice, until there remains no more grain in the straw. When it is thus beat, it is spread in the air to be dried. In order to turn it over, several men walk abreast, and each of them, with his foot, makes a furrow in the layer of grain, so that in a few moments the whole mass is moved, and that part which was underneath is again exposed to the air.

"The dried rice is carried to the mill, where it is stripped of its chaff or husk. This mill consists of a wheel turned by oxen, and which sets several levers in motion: at their extremity is an iron cylinder, near a foot long, and hollowed out underneath. They beat in troughs which contain the grain. At the side of each trough there constantly stands a man, whose business is to place the rice under the cylinders. He must not suffer his attention to be diverted; for he would run a risk of having his hand crushed. After this operation, the rice is taken out of the mill, and sifted in the open air; which is done by filling a small sieve with as much grain as a man can lift; this he raises above his head, and gently spills the rice, turning his face to the wind, which blows away the small chaff or dust. This cleaned rice is put a second time in the mill, in order to bleach it. It is afterward mixed up in troughs with some salt, which contributes very much to its whiteness, and principally to its preservation; it has then undergone its whole preparatory process, and in this state it is sold."—Harmer.

CHAPTER XXIX.

Ver. 1. Wo to Ariel, to Ariel, the city *where* David dwelt! add ye year to year; let them kill sacrifices.

The numbers that assembled at Jerusalem must of course consume great quantities of provision. The consumption of flesh also must there have been much larger, in proportion to the number of the people, than elsewhere; because in the East they live in common very much on vegetables, farinacious food, oil, honey, &c.; but at Jerusalem vast quantities of flesh were consumed in the sacred feasts, as well as burnt upon the altar. Perhaps this circumstance will best explain the holy city's being called *Ariel*, or the *Lion of God*, Isaiah xxix. 1: an appellation which has occasioned a variety of speculation among the learned. Vitringa, in his celebrated commentary on Isaiah, supposes that David, according to the eastern custom, was called the Lion of God, and so this city was called by this name from him; a resolution by no means natural. The Arabs, indeed, in later ages, have often called their great men by this honourable term; D'Herbelot, I think, somewhere tells us, that Ali, Mohammed's son-in-law, was so called; and I am sure he affirms, that Mohammed gave this title to Hamzah, his uncle. It will be readily allowed that this was comformable to the taste of much more ancient times. "The modern Persians will have it," says D'Herbelot, in his account of Shiraz, a city of that country, "that this name was given to it, because this city consumes and devours like a lion, which is called *Sheer* in Persian, all that is brought to it, by which they express the multitude, and it may be the good appetite, of its inhabitants."

The prophet then pronounces wo to Zion, perhaps as too ready to trust to the number of its inhabitants and sojourners, which may be insinuated by this term which he uses, *Ariel*.—Harmer.

Ver. 3. And I will camp against thee round about, and will lay siege against thee with a mount, and I will raise forts against thee.

Moveable towers of wood were usually placed upon the mount, which were driven on wheels fixed within the bottom planks, to secure them from the enemy. Their size was not always the same, but proportioned to the towers of the city they besieged. the front was usually covered with tiles, and in later times the sides were likewise guarded with the same materials; their tops were covered with raw hides, and other things, to preserve them from fire balls and missive weapons; they were formed into several stories, which were able to carry both soldiers and several kinds of engines." All these modes of attack were practised in the days of Isaiah, who threatens Jerusalem with a siege conducted according to this method: "And I will encamp against thee round about, and will lay siege against thee with a mount; and I will raise forts against thee." The prophet Ezekiel repeats the prediction in almost the same words, adding only the name of the engine which was to be employed in battering down the walls: "Thou also, son of man, take thee a tile, and lay it before thee, and portray upon it the city, even Jerusalem; and lay siege against it, and cast a mount against it; set the camp also against it; and set battering rams against it round about."—Paxton.

Ver. 8. It shall even be as when a hungry *man* dreameth, and, behold, he eateth; but he awaketh, and his soul is empty: or as when a thirsty *man* dreameth, and, behold, he drinketh; but he awaketh, and, behold, *he is* faint, and his soul hath appetite: so shall the multitude of all the nations be that fight against Mount Zion.

As the simile of the prophet is drawn from nature, an extract which describes the actual occurrence of such a circumstance will be agreeable. "The scarcity of water was greater here at Bubaker than at Benown. Day and night the wells were crowded with cattle lowing, and fighting with each other to come at the trough. Excessive thirst made many of them furious: others being too weak to contend for the water, endeavoured to quench their thirst by devouring the black mud from the gutters near the wells; which they did with great avidity, though it was commonly fatal to them. This great scarcity of water was felt by all the people of the camp; and by none more than myself. I begged water from the negro slaves that attended the camp, but with very indifferent success: for though I let no opportunity slip, and was very urgent in my solicitations both to the Moors and to the negroes, I was but ill supplied, and frequently passed the night in the situation of Tantalus. No sooner had I shut my eyes, than fancy would convey me to the streams and rivers of my native land; there, as I wandered along the verdant bank, I surveyed the clear stream with transport, and hastened to swallow the delightful draught; but, alas! disappointment awakened me, and I found myself a lonely captive, perishing of thirst amid the wilds of Africa." (Park.)—Burder.

Ver. 17. *Is* it not yet a very little while, and Lebanon shall be turned into a fruitful field, and the fruitful field shall be esteemed as a forest?

The storms and tempests which, gathering on the highest peak of Lebanon, burst on the plains and valleys below, are often very severe. When De la Valle was travelling in the neighbourhood of that mountain, in the end of April, a wind blew from its summits so vehement and cold, with so great a profusion of snow, that though he and his company "were in a manner buried in their quilted coverlets, yet it was sensibly felt, and proved very disagreeable." It is not therefore without reason that Lebanon, or the white mountain, as the term signifies, is the name by which that lofty chain is distinguished; and that the sacred writers so frequently refer to the snow and the gelid waters of Lebanon. They sometimes allude to it as a wild and desolate region; and certainly no part of the earth is more dreary and barren than the Sannin, the region of perpetual snow. On that naked summit, the seat of storm and tempest, where the principles of vegetation are extinguished, the art and industry of man can make no impression; nothing but the creating power of God himself, can produce a favourable alteration. Thus, predicting a wonderful change, such as results from the signal manifestations of the divine favour to individuals or the church, the prophet demands, "Is it not yet a very little while, and Lebanon shall be turned into a fruitful field?" The contrast in this promise, between the naked, snowy, and tempestuous summits of Lebanon, and a field beautiful and enriched with the fairest and most useful productions of nature, expresses, with great force, the difference which the smiles of Heaven produce in the most wretched and hopeless circumstances of an individual or a nation.—PAXTON.

CHAPTER XXX.

Ver. 14. And he shall break it as the breaking of the potter's vessel that is broken in pieces; he shall not spare: so that there shall not be found in the bursting of it a sherd to take fire from the hearth, or to take water *withal* out of the pit.

This solemn threatening refers to the Jews for their wicked reliance "in the shadow of Egypt:" they were to be reduced to the greatest straits for thus trusting in the heathen. It is proverbial to say of those who have been robbed, and left in destitute circumstances, "They have not even a potsherd, not a broken *chatty* in their possession." To appreciate this idea, it must be remembered that nearly all their cooking utensils, all their domestic vessels, are made of earthenware; so that not to have a potsherd, a fragment left, shows the greatest misery. Even Job, in all his poverty and wretchedness, was not so destitute, for he had "a potsherd to scrape himself withal."—"A sherd to take fire from the hearth." This allusion may be seen illustrated every morning in the East. Should the good woman's fire have been extinguished in the night, she takes a potsherd in the morning, and goes to her neighbour for a little fire to rekindle her own; and as she goes along, she may be seen every now and then blowing the burning ember, lest it should go out. They were not to have a sherd, out of which they could drink a little water. Not having pumps, they are obliged to have something to take water from the well or tank. Of a very poor country, it is said, "In those parts there is not a sherd out of which you can drink a little water." "The wretchedness of the people is so great, they have not a sherd with which to take water from the tank."—ROBERTS.

Ver. 24. The oxen likewise, and the young asses that ear the ground, shall eat clean provender which hath been winnowed with the shovel and with the fan.

See on 1 Kings 4. 24.

Those who form their opinion of the latter article by an English FAN, will entertain a very erroneous notion. That of the East is made of the fibrous part of the palmirah or cocoa-tree leaves, and measures about a yard each way. Thus may be seen the farmer wafting away the chaff from the corn, having the round part of the fan in his hand: and thus may be seen the females in the morning, tossing in the husk from their rice. (See on Jer. xv. 7.)—ROBERTS.

In these words, the prophet foretels a season of great plenty, when the cattle shall be fed with corn better in quality, separated from the chaff, and (as the term rendered *clean* in our version, properly signifies) acidulated, in order to render it more grateful to their taste. The evangelist clearly refers to the practice, which was common in every part of Syria, of ploughing with the ass, when he calls him, ὑποζύγιον, a creature subject to the yoke. In rice-grounds, which require to be flooded, the ass was employed to prepare them for the seed, by treading them with his feet. It is to this method of preparing the ground, that Chardin supposes the prophet to allude when he says, "Blessed are ye that sow beside all waters, that send forth thither the feet of the ox and the ass." They shall be blessed under the future reign of the promised Messiah. In times anterior to his appearing, their country was to be made a desolation; briers and thorns were to encumber their fields; their sumptuous dwellings were to be cast down; their cities and strongholds levelled with the dust. But when Messiah commences his reign, times of unequalled prosperity shall begin their career. The goodness of Jehovah shall descend in fertilizing showers, to irrigate their fields, and to swell the streams which the skill and industry of the husbandman conducts among his plantations, or with which he covers his rice-grounds. Secure from the ruinous incursions of aliens, and in the sure hope of an abundant harvest, he shall scatter his rice on the face of the superincumbent water, and tread it into the miry soil with "the feet of the ox and the ass." Prosperous and happy himself, he will consider it his duty, and feel it his delight, "to do good and to communicate,"—to succour the widow and the fatherless, to open his doors to the stranger, to diffuse around him the light of truth, and to swell, by the diligent and prudent use of all the means that Providence has brought within his reach, the sum of human enjoyment.—PAXTON.

Ver. 29. Ye shall have a song, as in the night *when* a holy solemnity is kept; and gladness of heart, as when one goeth with a pipe to come into the mountain of the LORD, to the mighty One of Israel.

Music is considered far more enchanting at night than at any other period; "it gives cheerfulness to darkness, and pleasure to the heart." Their favourite proverb is, "the DAY SONG is like the flower of the gourd," *i. e.* devoid of smell. Nothing is more common than for adults to sing themselves to sleep: thus, as they recline, they beat a tabret and chant the praises of their gods, till through heaviness they can scarcely articulate a word. At other times the mother or wife gently taps the instrument, and in soft tones lulls the individual to repose. In the night, should they not be able to sleep, they have again recourse to the same charm, and not until they shall have fairly gone off in fresh slumbers, will their companions have any rest. Hence, in passing through a village or town at midnight, may be heard people at their nightly song, to grace the festive scene, to beguile away their time, to charm their fears, or to procure refreshing sleep. The Jews then were to be delivered from the proud Assyrian's yoke, and again to have their pleasant song in the night.—ROBERTS.

CHAPTER XXXII.

Ver. 2. And a man shall be as a hiding-place from the wind, and a covert from the tempest; as rivers of water in a dry place; as the shadow of a great rock in a weary land.

"Ah! that benevolent man, he has long been my shelter from the wind; he is a river to the dry country."—ROBERTS.

Well does the traveller remember a day in the wilds of Africa, where the country was chiefly covered with burning sand; when scorched with the powerful rays of an almost vertical sun, the thermometer in the shade standing at 100°.—He remembers long looking hither and thither for something that would afford protection from the almost insupportable heat, and where the least motion of air felt like flame coming against the face. At length he espied a huge loose rock leaning against the front of a small cliff which faced the sun. At once he fled for refuge underneath its inviting shade. The coolness emitted from this rocky canopy he found exquisitely exhilarating. The wild beasts of the desert were all fled to their dens, and the feathered songsters were all roosting among the thickest foliage they could find of the evergreen-trees. The whole creation around seemed to groan, as if their vigour had been entirely exhausted. A small river was providentially at hand, to the side of which, after a while, he ventured, and sipped a little of its cooling water, which tasted better than the best burgundy, or the finest old hock, in the world. During all this enjoyment, the above apropos text was the interesting subject of the traveller's meditation; though the allusion, as a figure, must fall infinitely short of that which is meant to be prefigured by it.—CAMPBELL.

The shadow of a great projecting rock is the most refreshing that is possible in a hot country, not only as most perfectly excluding the rays of the sun, but also having in itself a natural coolness, which it reflects and communicates to every thing about it.—LOWTH.

Ver. 13. Upon the land of my people shall come up thorns *and* briers, yea, upon all the houses of joy in the joyous city: 14. Because the palaces shall be forsaken; the multitude of the city shall be left; the forts and towers shall be for dens for ever, a joy of wild asses, a pasture of flocks.

See on Job 39. 5.

Ver. 20. Blessed *are* ye that sow beside all waters, that send forth *thither* the feet of the ox and the ass.

See on ch. 30. 24.

The various kinds of grain, which they commonly sow in the Holy Land, are frequently mentioned in the sacred volume; and the correctness of the statement is attested by modern historians. Oats are not cultivated near Aleppo; but Dr. Russel observed some fields of them about Antioch, and on the seacoast. The horses are fed universally with barley; but lucern is also cultivated for their use, in the spring. The earliest wheat is sown about the middle of October; other grain, among which are barley, rye, and Indian millet, continue to be sown till the end of January; and barley, even so late as the end of February. The Persian harrow consists of a large rake, which is fastened to a pole, and drawn by oxen. In Hindostan, it is like an ordinary rake with three or four teeth, and is drawn by two oxen. Similar to this was probably the Syrian harrow. But in Palestine, the harrow is seldom used, the grain being covered by repassing the plough along the edge of the furrow; and in places where the soil is sandy, they first sow, and then plough the seed into the ground. It appears, from the prophecies of Isaiah, that besides the more valuable kinds of grain, several aromatic seeds were sown; as the sesamum, coriander, and cummin. These the Orientals sprinkled upon their bread, to give it a more agreeable flavour. Rice is trodden into the ground by the feet of oxen; a practice seemingly alluded to by the prophet, in these words: "Blessed are ye that sow beside all waters, that send forth thither the feet of the ox and the ass." This, according to Chardin, answers exactly the manner of planting rice: for they sow it upon the waters; and before sowing, while the earth is covered with water, they cause the ground to be trodden by oxen, horses, and asses, to prepare it for receiving the seed. As they sow the rice on the water, so they transplant in the water; for the roots of this plant must be kept continually moist, to bring the rice to maturity.

Two bushels and a half of wheat or barley are sufficient to sow as much ground as a pair of beeves will plough in one day; which is, a little more or less, equal to one of our acres. Dr. Shaw could never learn that Barbary afforded yearly more than one crop; one bushel yielding ordinarily from eight to twelve, though some districts may perhaps afford a much greater increase, for it is common to see one grain produce ten or fifteen stalks. Even some grains of the Murwany wheat, which he brought with him to Oxford, and sowed in the physic garden, threw out each of them fifty. But Muzeratty, one of the kaleefas, or viceroys of the province of Tlemsan, brought once with him to Algiers, a root that yielded fourscore, telling Dr. Shaw and his party, that in consequence of a dispute concerning the respective fruitfulness of Egypt and Barbary, the Emir Hadge, or prince of the western pilgrims, sent once to the bashaw of Cairo, one that yielded sixscore. Pliny mentions some that bore three or four hundred. It likewise happens, that one of these stalks will sometimes bear two ears, while each of these ears will as often shoot out into a number of lesser ones, affording by that means a most plentiful increase. And may not these large prolific ears, when seven are said to come up upon one stalk, explain what is mentioned of the seven fruitful years in Egypt, that the earth brought *them* forth by handfuls?—PAXTON.

The emigrants that went from England some years ago to the colony of the Cape of Good Hope, were chiefly located in a district called Albany, on the confines of Caffraria. Many of them were ruined by not literally attending to the contents of this text. They were not sufficiently aware of the indispensable necessity of water, or at least moisture under ground, to render fields at all productive in a hot and dry climate. They ploughed land, and dug a deep ditch round each field, as they were accustomed to do in England; with the mould dug from it they formed a mud wall, which made all look very pretty and farmer-like. Dutch boors from a distance came to see what they were about. They told them their fields were too far from the river; that unless they could lead water upon them, they must not expect to have any harvest. Looking at the neat ditch that surrounded the field, they inquired what this was for? For defence, was the reply. "Yes," said the boors, "it will defend your field from receiving any moisture from the surrounding ground;" and, shaking their heads, said "That is a bad defence." From the high ideas they had of their own superior knowledge of agriculture, they only smiled at the remarks made by the African farmers. The rainy season came, when the grain sprang up, and made rapid progress while that season lasted; but lo, the sun returned from its northern circuit, dispelled the clouds, and darted forth its unimpeded fiery rays, which soon caused the surface of the ground to become as hard as a brick, consequently the grain withered and died, and cleanness of teeth, for want of bread, was in all their hamlets that season! But had there been plenty of water to lead over their fields, the crops would probably have been most abundant. The expression, "sending forth the feet of the ox and the ass," seems to refer to the practice said still to prevail in the East, where these animals are employed to tread the thin mud when saturated with water, to fit it for receiving the seed. Should there be a river there, a fountain here, and a pool elsewhere, it is far wiser to have the fields near, than at a distance from any of these. Sometimes God gives peculiarly happy spiritual seasons to countries, or districts in countries, causing the river of life abundantly to flow, and streams from it extensively to spread its influence; then the wise husbandman will hasten to scatter his seed, in cities, towns, villages, hamlets, and among individual families, in expectation of a rich harvest, from the well watering of the garden of plants.—CAMPBELL.

CHAPTER XXXIII.

Ver. 11. Ye shall conceive chaff; ye shall bring forth stubble: your breath *as* fire shall devour you.

When married females quarrel, they often say, "Yes, thy womb shall give children, but they shall all be as chaff." "Yes, barren one, you may have a child, but it will be blind and dumb." "True, true, you will bring forth a *pāmbu-vethe*," i. e. a generation of serpents.—ROBERTS.

Ver. 21. But there the glorious LORD *will be* unto us a place of broad rivers *and* streams; wherein shall go no galley with oars, neither shall gallant ship pass thereby.

In such a highly cultivated country as England, and where great drought is almost unknown, we have not an opportunity to observe the fertilizing influence of a broad river; but in South Africa, where almost no human means are employed for improving the land, the benign influence of rivers is most evident. The Great, or Orange River, is a remarkable instance of this. I travelled on its banks, at one time, for five or six weeks; when, for several hundred miles, I found both sides of it delightfully covered with trees of various kinds, all in health and vigour, and abundance of the richest verdure; but all the country beyond the reach of its influence was complete desert. Every thing appeared struggling for mere existence; so that we might be said to have had the wilderness on one side, and a kind of paradise on the other.—CAMPBELL.

CHAPTER XXXIV.

Ver. 7. And the unicorns shall come down with them, and the bullocks with the bulls; and their land shall be soaked with blood, and their dust made fat with fatness.

See on Ps. 22. 12, 15.

CHAPTER XXXV.

Ver. 6. Then shall the lame *man* leap as a hart, and the tongue of the dumb shall sing: for in the wilderness shall waters break out, and streams in the desert.

See on Ps. 18. 33.

Lameness and dumbness are the uniform effects of long walking in a desert; the sand and gravel produce the former, fatigue the latter. In such cases some of us have walked hours together without uttering a sentence; and all walked as if crippled, from the sand and gravel getting into the shoes; but the sight of water, especially if unexpected, unloosed every tongue, and gave agility to every limb; men, oxen, goats, sheep, and dogs, ran with speed and expressions of joy to the refreshing element.—CAMPBELL.

Ver. 7. And the parched ground shall become a pool, and the thirsty land springs of water: in the habitation of dragons, where each lay, *shall be* grass, with reeds and rushes.

Instead of the *parched ground*, Bp. Lowth translates it, the *glowing sand shall become a pool*, and says in a note, that the word is Arabic as well as Hebrew, expressing in both languages the same thing, the glowing sandy plain, which in the hot countries at a distance has the appearance of water. It occurs in the Koran, (cap. xxiv.) "But as to the unbelievers, their works are like a vapour in a plain which the thirsty traveller thinketh to be water, until, when he cometh thereto, he findeth it to be nothing." Mr. Sale's note on this place is, the Arabic word *serab* signifies that false appearance, which in the eastern countries is often seen in sandy plains about noon, resembling a large lake of water in motion, and is occasioned by the reverberation of the sunbeams. It sometimes tempts thirsty travellers out of their way, but deceives them when they come near, either going forward, (for it always appears at the same distance,) or quite vanishes.—BURDER.

CHAPTER XXXVII.

Ver. 24. By thy servants hast thou reproached the LORD, and hast said, By the multitude of my chariots am I come up to the height of the mountains, to the sides of Lebanon; and I will cut down the tall cedars thereof, *and* the choice fir-trees thereof: and I will enter into the height of his border, *and* the forest of his Carmel.

At six o'clock we again set forward, and passing near the church, the priest, a venerable old man, with a flowing beard, was standing on the threshold, and courteously saluted us. Our road, somewhat better than yesterday, continued gradually to rise, and we were now fairly within that long elevated chain which has borne, from the earliest ages, the name of Lebanon. We had felt a great anxiety to see the celebrated cedars, which are supposed to be the remains of the ancient forests that once entirely clothed these heights. Hitherto we had been allured forward by our guides, with the promise of soon reaching them, but we now discovered that we had been purposely deceived, and ought to have taken another road, in which case the village of Eden, in their immediate vicinity, would have afforded us a more commodious halting-place. After leaving Balbec, and approaching Lebanon, towering walnut-trees, either singly or in groups, and a rich carpet of verdure, the offspring of numerous streams, give to this charming district the air of an English park, majestically bounded with snow-tipped mountains. At Deir el Akmaar the ascent begins—winding among dwarf oaks, hawthorns, and a great variety of shrubs and flowers. After some hours of laborious toil, a loaded horse slipped near the edge of a precipice, and must inevitably have perished, if a servant, with great presence of mind, had not cut the girths, and saved the animal, at the expense of most of the stores, and the whole of the crockery. Vain were the lamentations over fragments of plates and glasses, broken bottles, and spilt brandy and wine, in an impoverished country, where nothing that contributes to comfort can be replaced. Seven hours were spent in attaining the summit of the mountain after leaving the village. The view on both sides was splendid.—A deep bed of snow had now to be crossed, and the horses sunk or slipped at every moment. To ride was impracticable, and to walk dangerous, for the melting snow penetrated our boots, and our feet were nearly frozen. An hour and a half brought us to the cedars. Seven of the most ancient still remain. They are considered to be coeval with Solomon, and therefore held sacred. Rude altars have been erected near them, and an annual Christian festival is held, when worship is performed beneath their venerable branches. Other cedars, varying in age and size, form around them a protecting grove. We reckoned every tree with scrupulous care. Many, indeed, have sprung up from ancient roots, but enumerating all that present independent trunks, including the patriarchal trees, they amount to three hundred and forty-three. At a quarter of an hour from the cedars is the village of Beesharry, a lovely, romantic spot, on the brink of a deep glen.—HOGG.

Ver. 27. Therefore their inhabitants *were* of small power, they were dismayed and confounded: they were *as* the grass of the field, and *as* the green herb: *as* the grass on the house-tops, and *as corn* blasted before it be grown up.

See on Ruth 2. 4.

Ver. 29. Because thy rage against me, and thy tumult, is come up into mine ears; therefore will I put my hook in thy nose, and my bridle in thy lips, and I will turn thee back by the way by which thou camest.

It is usual in the East to fasten an iron ring in the nose of their camels and buffaloes, to which they tie a rope, by means of which they manage these beasts. God is here speaking of Sennacherib, king of Assyria, under the image of a furious refractory beast, and accordingly, in allusion to this circumstance, says, *I will put my hook in thy nose.*—BURDER.

CHAPTER XXXVIII.

Ver. 12. Mine age is departed, and is removed from me as a shepherd's tent: I have cut off like a weaver my life: he will cut me off with pining sickness: from day *even* to night wilt thou make an end of me.

Hezekiah makes use of a simile, in that hymn of his which Isaiah has preserved, that appeared, many years ago, very perplexing to a gentleman of good sense and learning, who resided in one of the most noted towns of the kingdom for weaving. He could not conceive, why the cutting short the life of that prince, should be compared to a weaver's cutting off a piece from his loom when he had finished it, and he and everybody that saw it in that state expected it as a thing of course. He consulted those that were acquainted with the manufactory, but could gain no satisfaction. Perhaps it may appear more easy to the mind, if the simile is understood to refer to the weaving of a carpet, filled with flowers and other ingenious devices: just as a weaver, after having wrought many decorations into a piece of carpeting, suddenly cuts it off, while the figures were rising into view as fresh and as beautiful as ever, and the spectator is expecting the weaver would proceed in his work; so, after a variety of pleasing and amusing transactions in the course of my life, suddenly and unexpectedly it seemed to me that it was come to its period, and was just going to be cut off. Unexpectedness must certainly be intended here.—HARMER.

The shepherds of the East are often obliged to remove their flocks to distant places to find pasturage; hence their habitations are exceedingly light, in order to be the more easily removed. The "lodge in a garden of cucumbers," and the frail resting-place of the shepherd, greatly resemble each other.—ROBERTS.

Ver. 14. Like a crane *or* a swallow, so did I chatter: I did mourn as a dove: mine eyes fail *with looking* upward: O Lord, I am oppressed; undertake for me.

No bird is more noisy than the crane; and none utters a harsher note. The prophet, however, applies the verb (צפצף) *tsaphtsaph*, which signifies to chatter, to the loud and screaming cry of this bird; for which Mr. Harmer professes himself unable to account. "The word tsaphtsaph," says he, "translated chatter, appears to signify the low, melancholy, interrupted voice of the complaining sick, rather than a chattering noise, if we consult the other places in which it is used: as for the chattering of the crane, it seems quite inexplicable." But the difficulty had not, perhaps, appeared so great, if this respectable writer had observed that the connective vau is wanting in the original text, which may be thus considered: "As a crane, a swallow, so did I chatter." The two nouns are not, therefore, necessarily connected with the verb tsaphtsaph, but admit the insertion of another verb suitable to the nature of the first nominative. The ellipsis may be supplied in this manner: "As a crane, so did I scream, as a swallow, so did I chatter." Such a supplement is not, in this instance, forced and unnatural; for it is evidently the design of Hezekiah to say, that he expressed his grief after the manner of these two birds, and therefore suitably to each; and he uses the verb tsaphtsaph, which properly corresponds only with the last noun, to indicate this design, leaving the reader to supply the verb which corresponds with the other. It is also perfectly agreeable to the manners of the East, where sorrow is expressed sometimes in a low interrupted voice, and anon in loud continued exclamations. The afflicted monarch, therefore, expressed his extreme grief after the manner of the Orientals, in loud screams like the crane, or in low interrupted murmurings like the swallow. According to some writers, the verb under consideration signifies the note of any bird, and by consequence may with equal propriety be employed to denote the loud scream of the crane, or the melancholy twitter of the swallow; if this be so, the difficulty admits of an easy solution.—Paxton.

Ver. 17. Behold, for peace I had great bitterness: but thou hast in love to my soul *delivered it* from the pit of corruption: for thou hast cast all my sins behind thy back.

Jeroboam preferred "molten images" to the true God, and therefore the Lord said unto him by Ahijah, thou "hast cast me behind thy back." The Levites said of the children of Israel, they "rebelled against thee, and cast thy law behind their backs." The Lord said of the wicked cities of Samaria and Jerusalem, "Thou hast forgotten me, and cast me behind thy back." This metaphor, to cast behind the back, is in common use, and has sometimes a very offensive signification. The expression is used to denote the most complete and contemptuous rejection of a person or thing. "The king has cast his minister behind his back," *i. e.* fully removed him, treated him with sovereign contempt. "Alas! alas! he has thrown my petition behind his back; all my efforts are defeated." "Yes, man, I have forgiven you; all your crimes are behind my back; but take care not to offend me again."—Roberts.

CHAPTER XL.

Ver. 3. The voice of him that crieth in the wilderness, Prepare ye the way of the Lord, make straight in the desert a highway for our God. 4. Every valley shall be exalted, and every mountain and hill shall be made low: and the crooked shall be made straight, and the rough places plain.

When a great prince in the East sets out on a journey, it is usual to send a party of men before him, to clear the way. The state of those countries in every age, where roads are almost unknown, and from the want of cultivation in many parts overgrown with brambles, and other thorny plants, which renders travelling, especially with a large retinue, very incommodious, requires this precaution. The emperor of Hindostan, in his progress through his dominions, as described in the narrative of Sir Thomas Roe's embassy to the court of Delhi, was preceded by a very great company, sent before him to cut up the trees and bushes, to level and smooth the road, and prepare their place of encampment. Balin, who swayed the imperial sceptre of India, had five hundred chosen men, in rich livery, with their drawn sabres, who ran before him, proclaiming his approach, and clearing the way. Nor was this honour reserved exclusively for the reigning emperor; it was often shown to persons of royal birth. When an Indian princess made a visit to her father, the roads were directed to be repaired, and made clear for her journey; fruit-trees were planted, water-vessels placed in the road-side, and great illuminations prepared for the occasion. Mr. Bruce gives nearly the same account of a journey, which the king of Abyssinia made through a part of his dominions. The chief magistrate of every district through which he had to pass, was, by his office, obliged to have the roads cleared, levelled, and smoothed; and he mentions, that a magistrate of one of the districts having failed in this part of his duty, was, together with his son, immediately put to death on the spot, where a thorn happened to catch the garment, and interrupt for a moment the progress of his majesty. This custom is easily recognised in that beautiful prediction: "The voice of him that crieth in the wilderness, Prepare ye the way of the Lord, make straight in the desert a highway for our God. Every valley shall be exalted, and every mountain and hill shall be brought low; and the crooked shall be made straight, and the rough places plain; and the glory of the Lord shall be revealed, and all flesh shall see it together, for the mouth of the Lord hath spoken it." We shall be able, perhaps, to form a more clear and precise idea, from the account which Diodorus gives of the marches of Semiramis, the celebrated queen of Babylon, into Media and Persia. In her march to Ecbatane, says the historian, she came to the Zarcean mountain, which extending many furlongs, and being full of craggy precipices and deep hollows, could not be passed without taking a great compass. Being therefore desirous of leaving an everlasting memorial of herself, as well as of shortening the way, she ordered the precipices to be digged down, and the hollows to be filled up; and at a great expense she made a shorter and more expeditious road; which to this day is called from her, the road of Semiramis. Afterward she went into Persia, and all the other countries of Asia subjected to her dominion; and wherever she went, she ordered the mountains and the precipices to be levelled, raised causeys in the plain country, and at a great expense made the ways passable. Whatever may be in this story, the following statement is entitled to the fullest credit: "All eastern potentates have their precursors and a number of pioneers to clear the road, by removing obstacles, and filling up the ravines, and the hollow ways in their route. In the days of Mogul splendour, the emperor caused the hills and mountains to be levelled, and the valleys to be filled up for his convenience. This beautifully illustrates the figurative language in the approach of the Prince of Peace, when every valley shall be exalted, and every mountain and hill shall be made low, and the crooked shall be made straight, and the rough places plain."—Paxton.

Ver. 11. He shall feed his flock like a shepherd: he shall gather the lambs with his arm, and carry *them* in his bosom, *and* shall gently lead those that are with young.

See on Ezek. 25. 5.

One of the great delights in travelling through a pastoral country, is to see and feel the force of the beautiful imagery in the scriptures, borrowed from pastoral life. All day long the shepherd attends his flock, leading them into "green pastures" near fountains of water, and chooses a convenient place for them to "rest at noon." At night he drives them near his tent, and if there is danger, encloses them in the fold. They know his voice and follow him. When travelling, he tenderly watches over them, *and carries such as are exhausted in his arms.* Such a shepherd is the Lord Jesus Christ. See John x.—Rev. R. Anderson's Tour through Greece.

The shepherds of antiquity were "an abomination unto

the Egyptians," and so they are among the Hindoos; and as the Egyptians would not eat with the Hebrews, so neither will the various castes of India eat with their shepherds. The pastoral office in the East is far more responsible than in England, and it is only by looking at it in its various relations and peculiarities, as it exists there, that we gain a correct view of many passages of scripture. Flocks at home are generally in fine fields, surrounded by hedges or fences; but there they are generally in the wilderness, and were it not for the shepherds, would go astray, and be exposed to the wild beasts. As the sons of Jacob had to go to a great distance to feed their flocks, so still they are often absent for one and two months together, in the place where there is plenty of pasturage. In their removals, it is an interesting sight to see the shepherds carrying the lambs in their bosoms, and also to witness how gently they "lead those that are with young." Another interesting fact is the relationship which exists betwixt the pastor and his flock; for being so much together, they acquire a friendly feeling: hence the sheep "know his voice, and a stranger will they not follow." Does he wish to remove to another place, he goes to such a distance as that they can hear his voice, and then he imitates the noise made by a sheep, and immediately they may be seen bounding along to the spot where he is. Thus "he goeth before them, and the sheep follow him, for they know his voice." But another way of leading a flock, especially where there are goats, is to take the branch of a tree, and keep showing it to them, which causes them to run along more cheerfully. He also calleth "his own sheep by name," and it is interesting to notice how appropriate the names are to the animals. Thus, should a sheep or a cow have a bad temper, (or any other failing,) it will be called the angry one, the malicious, or sulky, or wandering one; the killer of her young, the fiend; the mad one, the jumper, the limper, the dwarf, the barren, the fruitful, the short, the fat, the long, the tricky one. The cows also are named after some of their goddesses, particularly after the wives of Siva, Vishnoo, and Scandan; thus Lechymy, Pārvati, and Valle, may be heard in every herd. To bulls are given the names of men and devils; as, Vyraven, Pulliār, Māthan, &c. Before the sun shall have gained his meridian, the shepherds seek out a shady place, where they may make their flocks "to rest at noon." As the shepherd who mounted the throne of Israel carried his sling and his stone, so these generally have the same missiles by which they correct the wanderers, and keep off their foes: hence the dog is scarcely ever used in the tending or guiding of flocks. As was Jacob, so here the shepherds are often remunerated in kind, and therefore have not any other wages, (except now and then a little cloth or rice;) hence, often, a certain number of the rams are given as pay, and to this also the patriarch may allude: "The rams of thy flocks have I not eaten." In most of these particulars we see illustrations of Him who "is the Shepherd, the Stone of Israel," who laid prostrate the "roaring lion" of hell, and who keeps us in safety, so that the foe cannot pluck us out of his hand.—ROBERTS.

Ver. 12. Who hath measured the waters in the hollow of his hand, and meted out heaven with the span, and comprehended the dust of the earth in a measure, and weighed the mountains in scales, and the hills in a balance?

Here we have a vivid illustration of the dignified and gorgeous imagery of the East. "What man can take up the waters of the unknown dark ocean in his hands?" "Whose fingers are long enough to span the arch of heaven?" "Who can bring together all the dust of the earth in a measure?" "Who can weigh the hills and mountains in scales?" These figures largely show the insignificance of man.—ROBERTS.

Ver. 16. And Lebanon *is* not sufficient to burn, nor the beasts thereof sufficient for a burnt-offering.

The stupendous size, the extensive range, and great elevation of Libanus; its towering summits, capped with perpetual snow, or crowned with fragrant cedars; its olive plantations; its vineyards, producing the most delicious wines; its clear fountains and cold-flowing brooks; its fertile vales and odoriferous shrubberies,—combine to form in Scripture language, "the glory of Lebanon." But that glory, liable to change, has, by the unanimous consent of modern travellers, suffered a sensible decline. The extensive forests of cedar, which adorned and perfumed the summits and declivities of those mountains, have almost disappeared. Only a small number of these "trees of God, planted by his almighty hand," which, according to the usual import of the phrase, signally displayed the divine power, wisdom, and goodness, now remain. Their countless number in the days of Solomon, and their prodigious bulk, must be recollected, in order to feel the force of that sublime declaration of the prophet: "Lebanon is not sufficient to burn, nor the beasts thereof sufficient for a burnt-offering."—PAXTON.

Ver. 24. Yea, they shall not be planted: yea, they shall not be sown: yea, their stock shall not take root in the earth: and he shall also blow upon them, and they shall wither, and the whirlwind shall take them away as stubble.

Whirlwinds occasionally sweep along the country in an extremely frightful manner, carrying away in their vortex, sand, branches, and stubble, and raising them to an immense height in the air. Very striking is the allusion which the prophet makes to this phenomenon: "He shall also blow upon them, and they shall wither, and the whirlwind shall take them away as stubble." With equal force and beauty, the Psalmist refers to the rotatory action of the whirlwind, which frequently impels a bit of straw, over the waste, like a wheel set in rapid motion: "O my God; make them like a wheel, as the stubble before the wind." Sometimes it comes from no particular point, but moves about in every direction. Mr. Bruce, in his journey through the desert of Senaar, had the singular felicity to contemplate this wonderful phenomenon in all its terrific majesty, without injury, although with considerable danger and alarm. In that vast expanse of desert, from west and to northwest of him, he saw a number of prodigious pillars of sand at different distances, moving at times with great celerity, at others, stalking on with majestic slowness; at intervals he thought they were coming in a very few minutes to overwhelm him and his companions. Again they would retreat so as to be almost out of sight, their tops reaching to the very clouds. There the tops often separated from the bodies; and these, once disjoined, dispersed in the air, and appeared no more. Sometimes they were broken near the middle, as if struck with a large cannon-shot. About noon they began to advance with considerable swiftness upon them, the wind being very strong at north. Eleven of these awful visiters ranged alongside of them about the distance of three miles. The greatest diameter of the largest appeared to him, at that distance, as if it would measure ten feet. They retired from them with a wind at southeast, leaving an impression upon the mind of our intrepid traveller to which he could give no name, though he candidly admits that one ingredient in it was fear, with a considerable deal of wonder and astonishment. He declares it was in vain to think of flying; the swiftest horse, or fastest sailing ship, could be of no use to carry them out of this danger; and the full persuasion of this riveted him to the spot where he stood. Next day they were gratified with a similar display of moving pillars, in form and disposition like those already described, only they seemed to be more in number and less in size. They came several times in a direction close upon them; that is, according to Mr. Bruce's computation, within less than two miles. They became, immediately after sunrise, like a thick wood, and almost darkened the sun; his rays shining through them for near an hour, gave them an appearance of pillars of fire. At another time they were terrified by an army (as it seemed) of these sand pillars, whose march was constantly south; a number of which seemed once to be coming directly upon them; and though they were little nearer than two miles, a considerable quantity of sand fell around them. On the twenty-first of November, about eight in the morning, he had a view of the desert to the westward as before, and the sands had already begun to rise in immense twisted pillars, which darkened the heav ens, and moved over the desert with more magnificence than ever. The sun shining through the pillars, which were thicker, and contained more sand apparently than any of the preceding days, seemed to give those nearest them an appearance as if spotted with stars of gold. A little before twelve, the wind at north ceased, and a considerable quantity of fine sand rained upon them for an hour afterward. To this species of rain, Moses was no stranger; he had seen it, and felt its effects in the sandy deserts of Arabia, and he places it among the curses that were, in future ages, to punish the rebellion of his people; "The Lord shall make the rain of thy land powder and dust: from heaven shall it come down upon thee, until thou be destroyed."—Paxton.

CHAPTER XLI.

Ver. 15. Behold, I will make thee a new sharp thrashing instrument having teeth: thou shalt thrash the mountains, and beat *them* small, and shalt make the hills as chaff.

The manner of thrashing corn in the East differs essentially from the method practised in western countries. It has been fully described by travellers, from whose writings such extracts are here made, and connected together, as will convey a tolerable idea of this subject. In Isaiah xxviii. 27, 28, four methods of thrashing are mentioned, as effected by different instruments: the flail, the drag, the wain, and the treading of the cattle. The staff, or flail, was used for the *infirmiora semina*, says Hieron, the grain that was too tender to be treated in the other methods. The drag consisted of a sort of frame of strong planks, made rough at the bottom with hard stones or iron; it was drawn by horses or oxen over the corn-sheaves spread on the floor, the driver sitting upon it. The wain was much like the former, but had wheels with iron teeth, or edges like a saw. The axle was armed with iron teeth, or serrated wheels throughout: it moves upon three rollers, armed with iron teeth or wheels, to cut the straw. In Syria they make use of the drag, constructed in the very same manner as above described. This not only forced out the grain, but cut the straw in pieces for fodder for the cattle, for in the eastern countries they have no hay. The last method is well known from the law of Moses, which forbids the ox to be muzzled when he treadeth out the corn. Deut. xxv. 4. (Lowth.) "In thrashing their corn, the Arabians lay the sheaves down in a certain order, and then lead over them two oxen, dragging a large stone. This mode of separating the ears from the straw is not unlike that of Egypt." (Niebuhr.) "They use oxen, as the ancients did, to beat out their corn, by trampling upon the sheaves, and dragging after them a clumsy machine. This machine is not, as in Arabia, a stone cylinder, nor a plank with sharp stones, as in Syria, but a sort of sledge, consisting of three rollers, fitted with irons, which turn upon axles. A farmer chooses out a level spot in his fields, and has his corn carried thither in sheaves, upon asses or dromedaries. Two oxen are then yoked in a sledge, a driver gets upon it, and drives them backwards and forwards (rather in a circle) upon the sheaves, and fresh oxen succeed in the yoke from time to time. By this operation the chaff is very much cut down; the whole is then winnowed, and the pure grain thus separated. This mode of thrashing out the corn is tedious and inconvenient: it destroys the chaff, and injures the quality of the grain." (Ibid.) In another place, Niebuhr tells us that "two parcels or layers of corn are thrashed out in a day; and they move each of them as many as eight times with a wooden fork of five prongs, which they call *meddre*. Afterward they throw the straw into the middle of the ring, where it forms a heap, which grows bigger and bigger; when the first layer is thrashed, they replace the straw in the ring, and thrash it as before. Thus the straw becomes every time smaller, till at last it resembles chopped straw. After this, with the fork just described, they cast the whole some yards from thence, and against the wind, which driving back the straw, the corn and the ears not thrashed out fall apart from it, and make another heap. A man collects the clods of dirt, and other impurities, to which any corn adheres, and throws them into a sieve. They afterward place in a ring the heaps, in which a good many entire ears are still found, and drive over them for four or five hours together a dozen couple of oxen, joined two and two, till by absolute trampling they have separated the grains, which they throw into the air with a shovel to cleanse them."

"The Moors and Arabs continue to tread out their corn after the primitive custom of the East. Instead of beeves, they frequently make use of mules and horses, by tying in the like manner by the neck three or four of them together, and whipping them afterward round about the nedders, (as they call the thrashing floors, the *Lybicæ areæ* of Horace,) where the sheaves lie open and expanded in the same manner as they are placed and prepared with us for thrashing. This, indeed, is a much quicker way than ours, but less cleanly; for, as it is performed in the open air, (Hos. xiii. 3,) upon any round level plat of ground, daubed over with cow's dung, to prevent as much as possible the earth, sand, or gravel, from rising, a great quantity of them all, notwithstanding this precaution, must unavoidably be taken up with the grain; at the same time the straw, which is their only fodder, is hereby shattered *to pieces*, a circumstance very pertinently alluded to 2 Kings xiii. 7, where the king of Syria is said to have made the Israelites like dust by thrashing." (Shaw.)—Burder.

Ver. 18. I will open rivers in high places, and fountains in the midst of the valleys; I will make the wilderness a pool of water, and the dry land springs of water.

A most important pastoral duty in the eastern regions, is to provide water for the flock. The living fountain and the flowing stream, generally furnish a sure and abundant supply; but these are seldom to be found in the burning desert, where the oriental shepherd is often compelled to feed his cattle. In such circumstances, happy is he who finds a pool where his flocks may quench their thirst. Often, as he pursues his journey, a broad expanse of water, clear as crystal, seems to open to his view; and faint and weary under the fierce sunbeam, he gazes on the unexpected relief with ineffable delight, and fondly anticipates a speedy termination to his present distress. He sees the foremost camels enter the lake, and the water dashed about by their feet. He quickens his pace, and hastens to the spot; but to his utter disappointment the vision disappears, and nothing remains but the dry and thirsty wilderness. To such deceitful appearances, the prophet opposes, with admirable effect, the real pool, the overflowing fountain, and the running stream; the appropriate symbols of those substantial blessings of grace and mercy, that were laid up in store for the church of Christ in the last days: "And the parched ground (or the scorching heat) shall become a pool, and the thirsty land springs of water." "I will open rivers in high places, and fountains in the midst of the valleys; I will make the wilderness a pool of water."—Paxton.

Ver. 19. I will plant in the wilderness the cedar, the shittah-tree, and the myrtle, and the oil-tree; I will set in the desert the fir-tree, *and* the pine, and the box-tree together.

See on Ex. 25. 10.

CHAPTER XLII.

Ver. 2. He shall not cry, nor lift up, nor cause his voice to be heard in the street.

When two or more people go along the streets, they speak in such a loud voice, that all who pass may hear. Has a person gained or lost a cause in a court of justice, he vociferates his story again and again to his companions, as he goes along the road. This practice may have arisen from the custom of the superior walking the first, which makes it necessary for him to speak in a loud voice, that those who are in the rear may hear his observations. Men of a boisterous temper, who wish to raise a clamour, or those who are leaders in any exploit, always bawl aloud when they talk to their companions, as they go along the road.—Roberts.

Ver. 11. Let the wilderness and the cities thereof lift up *their voice*, the villages *that* Kedar doth inhabit: let the inhabitants of the rock sing, let them shout from the top of the mountains.

"By *desert*, or *wilderness*, the reader is not always to understand a country altogether barren and unfruitful, but such only as is rarely or never sown or cultivated; which, though it yields no crops of corn or fruit, yet affords herbage, more or less, for the grazing of cattle, with fountains or rills of water, though more sparingly interspersed than in other places." (Shaw.) Agreeable to this account, we find that Nabal, who was possessed of three thousand sheep, and a thousand goats, dwelt in the wilderness, 1 Sam. xxv. 2. This it would have been impossible for him to have done, had there not been sufficient pasturage for his flocks and herds.—BURDER.

Not satisfied with cultivating the rich plains and fertile valleys of his native land, the Jewish farmer reduced the barren rocks and rugged mountains under his domain, and compelled them to minister to his necessities. For this purpose he covered them with earth; or, where this was impracticable, he constructed walls of loose stones, in parallel rows along their sides, to support the mould, and prevent it from being washed down by the rains. On these circular plots of excellent soil, which gradually rose one above another, from the base to the very summits of the mountains, he raised abundant crops of corn and other esculent vegetables; or, where the declivity was too rocky, he planted the vine and the olive, which delight in such situations, and which rewarded his toil with the most picturesque scenery, and the richest products. Thus, the places where only the wild goat wandered and the eagle screamed, which appeared to be doomed to perpetual nakedness and sterility, were converted by the bold and persevering industry of the Syrian husbandman into corn-fields and gardens, vineyards and olive plantations, the manifest traces of which, in all the mountains of Palestine, remain to this day. The inhabitants of that "good land," literally sang from the top of the rock when it flowed with the blood of the grape, and poured them out "rivers of oil."—PAXTON.

Ver. 14. I have long time holden my peace; I have been still, *and* refrained myself: *now* will I cry like a travailing woman; I will destroy and devour at once.

The words *devour*, *swallow*, or *sup*, as used by Isaiah, and Habakkuk, evidently allude to the same thing. Jehovah had refrained himself, but now he was about to come forth and utterly destroy his enemies. When a king wishes to convey an idea that he will completely destroy his foes, he says, I will MULLUNGA-VAIN, *i. e.*, "swallow them up." Habakkuk says of the Chaldeans, "Their faces shall sup up, as the East wind." Of a man who has a savage face, it is said, "He has a MULLUNGERA-MUGGAM, a devouring face." "Look at that fellow's face, you may see he could swallow you." But the Chaldeans are compared to the destructive EAST wind; and it is a fact, that the same wind is spoken of in similar terms in all parts of the East. Its name is ALLIKKERA-KATTU, *i. e.*, the destroying wind, and so sure as it shall blow for any length of time, will vegetation be destroyed. How this is produced is, perhaps, among the inexplicable mysteries of nature. Its destructive qualities on vegetable nature in England are well known, and yet it would appear that not one time in a thousand can it blow in an uninterrupted current from the distant East, because there are always, so far as I have been able to observe, counter currents. Another fact is, that, however far east you may travel, it is still the same wind which brings destruction. The allusion, therefore, in Genesis, (and other places,) is illustrated by the continued malignity of that wind.—ROBERTS.

Ver. 19. Who *is* blind, but my servant; or deaf, as my messenger *that* I sent? who *is* blind as *he that is* perfect, and blind as the LORD's servant?

I think we are to understand this as alluding to the AGENT employed by the Lord, *i. e.*, he was so absorbed with his message as to be blind and deaf to all other attractions. When the Yogee affects to deliver a message from the gods, or when he speaks of futurity, he is as one who is blind and deaf; and so insensible is he to external things, that whatever sights may pass before his vision, and whatever sounds may fall upon his ear, he appears to be altogether insensible to their power. The people say he is so full of the deity as to be unconscious of passing scenes.—ROBERTS.

CHAPTER XLIII.

Ver. 19. Behold, I will do a new thing: now it shall spring forth; shall ye not know it? I will even make a way in the wilderness, *and* rivers in the desert.

From Lattakoo to Kurree-chane, which is about three hundred miles, might, when I travelled it, be justly called a wilderness, for there was not a single mile of any visible path or road. The ruts made by the wheels of my wagons on going up the country, were so visible, that on returning I was delighted to find natives travelling with loaded oxen along those ruts: and as other natives would probably do the same, it would soon become a beaten visible highway, which most likely was the manner of the formation of all original roads.

A visible road in a wilderness saves much trouble and anxiety to travellers, even when they have travelled over the same ground before. In general they must be guided by landmarks such as hill, clumps of trees, fords, &c.; but in plains or across forests, where no hills can be seen, they must often be puzzled what course to follow. But where there is a visible path, however bad, travellers are relieved from all this trouble, anxiety, and uncertainty, as if they constantly heard a voice behind them saying, "This is the way, walk ye in it."

In a heathen land the inhabitants are ignorant of the way to true happiness either here or hereafter; but when gospel light enters, publishing what the Son of God has done and suffered for sinners, then a highway may be said to be in that land, which, by the blessing of God, will greatly increase the comfort of the population.—CAMPBELL.

Ver. 24. Thou hast brought me no sweet cane with money, neither hast thou filled me with the fat of thy sacrifices; but thou hast made me to serve with thy sins, thou hast wearied me with thine iniquities.

See on Jer. 6, 20.

Dr. Boothroyd has "sweet reed." Tamal, "sweet bark!" This probably means cinnamon, as we know that "sweet bark" was used by Moses in the service of the sanctuary: and it is in connexion with the sacrifices of the Most High that it is here mentioned by the prophet.—ROBERTS.

On approaching and entering first the city of Mashow, and afterward that of Kurree-chane, the two highest up towns which I visited in Africa, various of the inhabitants who, like all the rest of their countrymen, had never seen wagons or white men before, were charmed with the sight, and, as a proof of it, they presented me with pieces of sugar, or sweet cane, about a foot in length, and in such numbers, that the bottom of that part of the wagon where I sat was covered with sweet cane. It was an act of kindness. This occurrence explained to me this passage in Isaiah, where God is evidently charging his ancient people with want of affection, or unkindness: which expression they would understand, having probably the same custom which I found in Africa, which the Hebrews may have learned while they resided in Africa, viz., in Egypt.—CAMPBELL.

CHAPTER XLIV.

Ver. 3. For I will pour water upon him that is thirsty, and floods upon the dry ground; I will pour my Spirit upon thy seed, and my blessing upon thine offspring.

This probably alludes to the way in which people bathe. They do not in general, as in England, plunge into a stream or river, but go near a well or tank: and then, with a little vessel, pour water on their heads and bodies.

See the man who is weary, he calls for his neighbour, or servant, or wife, to accompany him to the well; he then takes off his clothes, (except a small strip round his loins,) sits on his hams, and the individual who assists begins to "POUR WATER" upon him, till he be refreshed, and exclaims, POTHAM, *i. e.* sufficient. In this way his body is invigorated, his *thirst quenched*, and he is made ready for his food.—ROBERTS.

Ver. 4. And they shall spring up *as* among the grass, as willows by the water-courses.

In many parts of South Africa, no trees are to be found but near rivers. The trees are of various kinds; the most plentiful was the lovely mimosa; but willows, when there were any, always stood in front of the others, on the very margin of the water, which was truly a river of life to them. Like those in Isaiah's days, they required much water—could not prosper without it, therefore near it they were alone found;—a loud call, by a silent example, to Christians to live near the throne of grace, word of grace, and ordinances of grace, if they wish to grow in wisdom, knowledge, faith, and holiness.—CAMPBELL.

Ver. 5. One shall say, I *am* the LORD's; and another shall call *himself* by the name of Jacob; and another shall subscribe *with* his hand unto the LORD, and surname *himself* by the name of Israel.

This is an allusion to the marks which were made by punctures, rendered indelible by fire or by staining, upon the hand, or some other part of the body, signifying the state or character of the person, and to whom he belonged. The slave was marked with the name of his master; the soldier of his commander; the idolater with the name or ensign of his god; and the Christians seem to have imitated this practice by what Procopius says upon this place of *Isaiah.* "Many marked their wrists or their arms with the sign of the cross, or with the name of Christ." (Lowth.) To this explanation I shall subjoin the following extract from Dr. Doddridge's Sermons to Young People, p. 79, both as it corroborates and still further elucidates this transaction. "Some very celebrated translators and critics understand the words which we render, *subscribe with his hand unto the Lord*, in a sense a little different from that which our English version has given them. They would rather render them, *another shall write upon his hand, I am the Lord's;* and they suppose it refers to a custom which formerly prevailed in the East, of stamping the name of the general on the soldier, or that of the master on the slave. As this name was sometimes borne on the forehead, so at other times on the hand; and it is certain that several scriptures, which may easily be recollected, are to be explained as alluding to this: Rev. iii. 12. vii. 2, 3. xiii. 16, 17. Now from hence it seems to have grown into a custom among some idolatrous nations, when solemnly devoting themselves to the service of any deity, to be initiated into it by receiving some marks in their flesh, which might never wear out. This interpretation the original will certainly bear; and it here makes a very strong and beautiful sense, since every true Christian has a sacred and indelible character upon him, which shall never be erased. But if we retain our own version it will come to nearly the same, and evidently refers to a practice which was sometimes used among the Jews, (Nehem. ix. 38. x. 29,) and which is indeed exceedingly natural, of obliging themselves to the service of God, by setting their hands to some written articles, emphatically expressing such a resolution."—BURDER.

Ver. 18. They have not known nor understood: for he hath shut their eyes, that they cannot see; *and* their hearts, that they cannot understand.

The Orientals, in some cases, deprive the criminal of the light of day, by sealing up his eyes. A son of the great Mogul was actually suffering this punishment when Sir Thomas Roe visited the court of Delhi. The hapless youth was cast into prison, and deprived of the light by some adhesive plaster put upon his eyes, for the space of three years; after which the seal was taken away, that he might with freedom enjoy the light; but he was still detained in prison. Other princes have been treated in a different manner, to prevent them from conspiring against the reigning monarch, or meddling with affairs of state: they have been compelled to swallow opium, and other stupifying drugs, to weaken or benumb their faculties, and render them unfit for business. Influenced by such absurd and cruel policy, Shah Abbas, the celebrated Persian monarch, who died in 1629, ordered a certain quantity of opium to be given every day to his grandson, who was to be his successor, to stupify him, and prevent him from disturbing his government. Such are probably the circumstances alluded to by the prophet: "They have not known, nor understood; for he hath shut their eyes that they cannot see; and their hearts that they cannot understand." The verb (טח) tah, rendered in our version, to shut, signifies to overlay, to cover over the surface; thus the king of Israel prepared three thousand talents of gold, and seven thousand talents of refined silver (טח) to overlay the walls of the temple. But it generally signifies to overspread, or daub over, as with mortar or plaster, of which Parkhurst quotes a number of examples; a sense which entirely corresponds with the manner in which the eyes of a criminal are sealed up in some parts of the East. The practice of sealing up the eyes, and stupifying a criminal with drugs, seems to have been contemplated by the same prophet in another passage of his book: "Make the heart of this people fat, and make their ears heavy, and shut their eyes, lest they see with their eyes, and hear with their ears, and understand with their heart, and convert and be healed."—PAXTON.

Ver. 20. He feedeth on ashes: a deceived heart hath turned him aside, that he cannot deliver his soul, nor say, *Is there* not a lie in my right hand?

"That wicked fellow has now to eat dust or ashes." "Begone, wretch! for soon wilt thou have to feed on dust." The man who is accused of a great crime, takes dust, or ashes, in his mouth, and thus swears that he is innocent. The idea seems to be, if I am guilty, may my mouth soon be filled with earth as in death. "A lie in my right hand." "The right hand is the abode of truth." The idols are often made with the RIGHT hand lifted up, to show that they are truth; and men thus swear, by lifting up the RIGHT hand. In the ninth and twentieth verses (inclusive) of this chapter, we have an admirable disquisition on the absurdity of idolatry; and neither can the maker of idols nor their worshippers say, there is "not a lie in my *right hand.*"—ROBERTS.

CHAPTER XLV.

Ver. 2. I will go before thee, and make the crooked places straight; I will break in pieces the gates of brass, and cut in sunder the bars of iron.

See on Acts 12. 10.

Ver. 3. And I will give thee the treasures of darkness, and hidden riches of secret places, that thou mayest know that I the LORD which call *thee* by thy name, *am* the God of Israel.

As treasures are frequently hidden under ground in the East, by those that are apprehensive of revolutions; so the finding them is one great object, in their apprehension, of sorcery. We are told by travellers into the East, that they have met with great difficulties very often, from a notion universally disseminated among them, that all Europeans are magicians, and that their visits to those eastern countries are not to satisfy curiosity, but to find out, and get possession of those vast treasures they believe to be buried there in great quantities. These representations are very common; but Sir J. Chardin gives us a more particular and amusing account of affairs of this kind. "It is common in the Indies, for those sorcerers that accompany conquerors, everywhere to point out the place where treasures are hid. Thus at Surat, when Siragi came thither, there were people who, with a stick striking on the ground, or against walls, found out those that had been hollowed or dug up, and ordered such places to be opened." He then intimates, that something of this nature had happened to him in Mingrelia.

Among the various contradictions that agitate the human breast, this appears to be a remarkable one: they firmly believe the power of magicians to discover hidden treasures, and yet they continue to hide them. Dr. Perry has given us an account of some mighty treasures hidden in the ground by some of the principal people of the Turkish empire, which upon a revolution were discovered by domestics, privy to the secret. D'Herbelot has given us accounts of treasures concealed in the same manner, some of them of great princes, discovered by accidents extremely remarkable; but this account of Chardin's, of conquerors pretending to find out hidden treasures by means of sorcerers, is very extraordinary. As, however, people of this cast have made great pretences to mighty things in all ages, and were not unfrequently confided in by princes, there is reason to believe they pretended sometimes, by their art, to discover treasures anciently to princes, of which they had gained intelligence by other methods; and as God opposed his prophets, at various times, to pretended sorcerers, it is not unlikely that the prophet Isaiah points at some such prophetic discoveries in those remarkable words, Is. xlv. 3: "And I will give thee the treasures of darkness, and hidden riches of secret places, that thou mayest know, that I the Lord which call thee by thy name, am the God of Israel." I will give them, by enabling some prophet of mine to tell thee where they are concealed. Such a supposition throws a great energy into those words.—HARMER.

Ver. 10. Wo unto him that saith unto *his* father, What begettest thou? or to the woman, What hast thou brought forth?

Dr. Boothroyd has, "to a mother, what dost thou bring forth?" Unnatural as is this language, yet children often use it to their parents. Listen to a son who has been chided by his father for bad conduct—"Why did you beget me? Did I ask you? Why reprove me for evil? Whose fault is it? Had you not begotten me, should I have been here?" The father replies, "Alas! for the day in which I became thy parent." The mother says, "Why did I bear this dog? Have I given birth to a monkey? Yes! I am the mother of this ass."—ROBERTS.

CHAPTER XLVI.

Ver. 3. Hearken unto me, O house of Jacob, and all the remnant of the house of Israel, which are borne *by me* from the belly, which are carried from the womb.

"True, this fiendish son was borne from my belly. Ten long moons did I carry him in my womb." "Is it for this I have carried him so long in my womb? My fate! my fate! alas! my fate!"—ROBERTS.

CHAPTER XLVII.

Ver. 1. Come down, and sit in the dust, O virgin daughter of Babylon, sit on the ground: *there is* no throne, O daughter of the Chaldeans: for thou shalt no more be called tender and delicate. 7. And thou saidst, I shall be a lady for ever: *so* that thou didst not lay these *things* to thy heart, neither didst remember the latter end of it.

See on Ezek. 13. 18.

Ver. 2. Take the millstones, and grind meal: uncover thy locks, make bare the leg, uncover the thigh, pass over the rivers.

To grind flour in the East is the work of servants or slaves, and to make it by pounding with a pestle and mortar is the office of female servants or slaves. There being but few bridges, those who are in a low condition are obliged to ford the rivers; hence may be seen large companies going to the opposite banks, who have been obliged to "make bare the leg" and to "uncover the thigh." Thus were the "tender and delicate" daughters of Babylon, who had been nurtured on a throne, to be reduced to the condition of menials, and to cross the rivers as people of the lowest degree.—ROBERTS.

Ver. 14. Behold, they shall be as stubble; the fire shall burn them; they shall not deliver themselves from the power of the flame: *there shall* not *be* a coal to warm at, *nor* fire to sit before it.

It is very usual in the East to burn the stubble and the grass, in order to destroy the vermin. Thus Hanway, speaking of the inhabitants of the deserts of Tartary, says, "that they arrived in the desert in the first winter month, and that the inhabitants who live nearest to it, often manure tracts of land by burning the grass, which grows very high." The words of our Saviour also allude to this, when he says, "Wherefore if God so clothe the grass of the field, which to-day is, and to-morrow is cast into the oven." Matt. vi. 30.—ROSENMULLER.

CHAPTER XLIX.

Ver. 9. That thou mayest say to the prisoners, Go forth; to them that *are* in darkness, Show yourselves. They shall feed in the ways, and their pastures *shall be* in all high places. 10. They shall not hunger nor thirst, neither shall the heat nor sun smite them: for he that hath mercy on them shall lead them, even by the springs of water shall he guide them. 11. And I will make all my mountains a way, and my highways shall be exalted.

See on Ps. 23. 1—3.

Ver. 15. Can a woman forget her sucking child, that she should not have compassion on the son of her womb? yea, they may forget, yet will I not forget thee.

This question is asked when a person doubts of finding mercy, where there is every reason to expect it. Does an individual express surprise at seeing a mother pay attention to an infant which is deformed, or supposed to be possessed by a devil; it is asked, Can a woman forget her sucking child? Is a woman in great haste to return home, it is inquired, "What, have you a sucking child in the house? The cub of the monkey is as dear to its dam, as gold is to us."—ROBERTS.

Ver. 16. Behold, I have graven thee upon the palms of *my* hands; thy walls *are* continually before me.

It is common to make punctures on the arms and wrists, in memory of visiting any holy place, or to represent the deity to whom the individual is consecrated: thus, a god, a temple, a peacock, or some indecent object, is described; but I never saw or heard of any thing of the kind being engraved on the PALMS of the HANDS. The palms of the hands are, however, believed to have written on them the *fate* of the individual; and, from this, it is common to say, in reference to men or things, they are written on the palms of his hands. "I wonder why Râman has taken Seethe for his wife?" "Why wonder? She was written on the palms of his hands." "Fear not," says the old soothsayer, looking into the hands of the anxious youth, "she is written here, thou shalt have her." "Alas! alas! the old deceiver told me her name was written on my palms, but she has gone, and the writing is erased." "Give up that pursuit? Never! it is written on the palms of my hands." "Ah! my friend, you have long since forgotten me." "Forgotten you! Never, for your walls are ever before me." "Ah! my father, I am now in the distant country, but your walls are always in my sight." "Ah! when shall I again visit

my favourite temple; the walls are continually before me."
—Roberts.

This is an allusion to the eastern custom of tracing out on their hands, not the names, but the sketches of certain eminent cities or places, and then rubbing them with the powder of the hennah or cypress, and thereby making the marks perpetual. This custom Maundrell thus describes: "The next morning nothing extraordinary passed, which gave many of the pilgrims leisure to have their arms marked with the usual ensigns of Jerusalem. The artists, who undertake the operation, do it in this manner: they have stamps in wood of any figure that you desire, which they first print off upon your arm, with powder or charcoal; then taking two very fine needles tied close together, and dipping them often, like a pen, in certain ink, compounded, as I was informed, of gunpowder and ox gall, they make with them small punctures all along the lines of the figure which they have printed, and then washing the part in wine, conclude the work. These punctures they make with great quickness and dexterity, and with scarce any smart, seldom piercing so deep as to draw blood.—Burder.

Ver. 22. Thus saith the Lord God, Behold, I will lift up my hand to the Gentiles, and set up my standard to the people: and they shall bring thy sons in *their* arms, and thy daughters shall be carried upon *their* shoulders.

It is a custom, in many parts of the East, to carry their children astride upon the hip, with the arm around the body. In the kingdom of Algiers, when the slaves take the children out, the boys ride upon their shoulders; and in a religious procession, which Symes had an opportunity of seeing at Ava, the capital of the Burman empire, the first personages of rank that passed by, were three children borne astride on men's shoulders. It is evident from these facts, that the oriental children are carried sometimes the one way, sometimes the other. Nor was the custom in reality different in Judea, though the prophet expresses himself in these terms: "They shall bring thy sons in their arms, and thy daughters shall be carried upon their shoulders; for according to Dr. Russel, the children able to support themselves, are usually carried astride on the shoulder; but in infancy they are carried in the arms, or awkwardly on one haunch. Dandini tells us, that on horseback the Asiatics "carry their young children upon their shoulders with great dexterity. These children hold by the head of him who carries them, whether he be on horseback or on foot, and do not hinder him from walking, nor doing what he pleases." "This augments the import of the passage in Isaiah, who speaks of the Gentiles bringing children thus; so that distance is no objection to this mode of conveyance, since they may thus be brought on horseback from 'among the peoples,' however remote."—Paxton.

Children of both sexes are carried on the shoulders. Thus may be seen the father carrying his son, the little fellow being astride on the shoulder, having, with his hands, hold of his father's head. Girls, however, sit on the shoulder, as if on a chair, their legs hanging in front, while they also with their hands lay hold of the head. In going to, or returning from, heathen festivals, thousands of parents and their children may be thus seen marching along with joy. In this way shall the Gentiles bring their sons and their daughters to Jehovah: kings shall then be "nursing fathers," and queens "nursing mothers."—Roberts.

Ver. 23. And kings shall be thy nursing fathers, and their queens thy nursing mothers: they shall bow down to thee with *their* face towards the earth, and lick up the dust of thy feet; and thou shalt know that I *am* the Lord: for they shall not be ashamed that wait for me.

The accomplishment of this prediction is often the subject of the prayers of Christians. They regard it as one of the illustrious features of the times of the millennium, that kings and potentates shall, as foster-fathers, take the church under their special protection and patronage, and instead of opposing and oppressing it, exercise towards it all the kind and tutelary offices of a devoted nurse or mother towards the children of her care. In this view of the passage, it has perhaps been forgotten that the prophetic scriptures are not lacking in intimations, that in that bright and blissful period, the ancient institutions of the world will be so modified, and the different fabrics of government, civil and ecclesiastical, so revolutionized, that it is, to say the least, doubtful whether there will then be any such rulers as *kings* and *queens* to bestow their regal regards upon the spouse of Christ. At any rate, it is certain that the text will not then be applied, as it now is, as authorizing *a religious establishment subject to the control of a civil power*, or in other words, as sanctioning *the union of church and state*. To the abetters of this pernicious alliance, the present passage has ever been a "pillar of strength" in the way of proof. Let us endeavour, then, to collect the true sense of the prediction from its various connexions. It may be remarked, that the prophecy of which it forms a part, abounds with metaphor; as for instance, v. 22, "the lifting up of the Lord's hand;" "the setting up of his standard to the Gentiles and people;" "their bringing Zion's sons in their arms, and carrying her daughters upon their shoulders:" and v. 23, "the kings and queens of the Gentiles bowing down to the church, with their faces towards the earth, and licking up the dust of her feet." Here is scarce an expression but is highly figurative, and shall we suppose that in the phrase "kings nursing fathers" there is nothing of the same character? For what is the office of the nurse? Is it not to nourish the child? But do kings, as human rulers, in the true sense, nourish the church? Do they afford to it that spiritual pabulum on which it lives and thrives? Do they administer the word and sacraments? Is not this the peculiar and distinguishing office of the ministry of the gospel, set apart to this very work, and acting as the only pastors, i. e. *feeders*, of the flock of Christ? Is not this the office which they claim as their privilege, which the New Testament gives them, and with which neither kings nor magistrates are to intermeddle? It is easy enough to understand how kings are nursing fathers to the subjects of the nations over which they rule; and as it is the duty of their subjects to regard them in this character, so it is their duty to act towards their subjects consistently with this designation, especially in protecting them in the peaceful enjoyment of their natural and civil rights. But it is not so easy to perceive how kings and queens, *as such*, are nurses to any but their people, in the capacity of subjects. If indeed the nations of Christendom be churches, then the king of the nation is the king of the church, and so is the nurse of the church. But this is not the kind of church spoken of in the New Testament, nor does the prophetical promise in question speak of any such church. It is evident then, that it is at best only in a metaphorical sense that the words of the promise legitimately hold good. What that sense is precisely, when stripped of its figurative dress, we shall endeavour to show in the sequel.

At present, we call attention to the immediate connexion of the words under review. They are introduced as an answer to the question, v. 21, (following the promise of a numerous church upon the rejection of the Jews, v. 19, 20.) "Then shalt thou say in thy heart, Who hath begotten me these, seeing I lost my children, and am desolate, a captive, and removing to and fro? And who hath brought up these? Behold, I was left alone; these, where had they been?" Upon the rejection of the Jews, it is supposed to be matter of wonder, from whence so many children should still be found clustering about this bereaved and desolate mother. From the New Testament narrative, we learn the difficulty there was in regard to this, in the minds of the Apostles, and the early Jewish believers, and how astonishing it was to them, when it came to pass. The prophecy may be considered as expressing, in a striking manner, the perplexed ruminations of the church in regard to an event so strange and mysterious. It was a problem she knew not how to solve. "Who brought up these? Where had they been?" This is her anxious interrogatory, and the Lord answers, "The kings of the Gentiles shall be thy nursing fathers, and their queens thy nursing mothers;" i. e. they *shall have been* such; when this multitude is gathered in, they *shall have been* reared and brought up as the subjects and servants of worldly kings, who little thought of the service they were rendering to the church. They were unconsciously acting the part of nurses to those who were destined in the purpose of God to be the children of Zion just as the teachers of a literary seminary are often unwittingly employed in training their pupils for higher service in the church of God, when subsequently his grace subdues their hearts, and makes them his devoted servants. In this sense, how large a portion of the colleges in our land are *nurseries* of the church? In like manner, it is here predicted that earthly governments shall be *nurseries* for the spiritual dominion of Jesus Christ. Out of *their* subjects shall *his* subjects be gathered. The agency of kings and queens and all worldly potentates in *nursing* the people of their rule shall be so controlled by a directing providence, as to be made subservient to the measureless enlargement of his kingdom. This is the grand drift of the prophecy before us. It speaks not of the defence or upholding of the church by the powers of the earth, or the bestowing of worldly possessions and distinctions upon it. Rich and satisfied in the covenant, favour, and spiritual glory of her Head and Husband, what can she ask or expect at the hands of earthly princes? What can *they* do for her sublime interest, of whom it is said, "They shall bow down *to thee* with their faces towards the earth, and lick up the dust of thy feet." The Zion of our God has boons to bestow upon worldly sovereigns, but none to ask of them. Thus interpreted, the passage is throughout consistent. The answer is suitable to the question, and both, to the scope of the prophecy, which is, to pre-intimate the calling of the Gentiles, and the increase of the church, upon the casting away of the Jews, by the bringing of the elect of all nations into that new Jerusalem which is from above, and is the mother of them all.—BUSH.

Thus were those who had been enemies to Jehovah to bow down and acknowledge his majesty. They were to "lick up the dust," which is a figurative expression to denote submission and adoration. "Boasting vain fellow! the king your friend! he your companion! You will not have even the dust of his feet given you for food." "The minister give you that office! he will not give you the dust of his feet." "Alas! alas! for me, I expected his favour; I depended on his word; but I have not gained the dust of his feet." "I will not remain longer in this country; I will leave you, and go to reside with the king." "With the king! Why, the dust of his feet will not be given you for a reward." "Could I but see that holy man! I would eat the dust of his feet." So great then is to be the humility and veneration of kings and queens, in reference to the Most High, that they will bow down before him, and lick up the dust of his feet.—ROBERTS.

CHAPTER L.

Ver. 2. Wherefore, when I came, *was there* no man? when I called, *was there* none to answer? Is my hand shortened at all, that it cannot redeem? or have I no power to deliver? behold, at my rebuke I dry up the sea, I make the rivers a wilderness: their fish stinketh, because *there is* no water, and dieth for thirst.

The Krooman (or Koorooman) river, in Africa, which is a considerable stream, used to run in an oblique direction across the great southern Zahara desert, till it emptied itself into the Great Orange River. Now it sinks out of sight into the sand almost immediately on entering the desert, only a few miles after the junction of the Macklareen river with its waters. As a proof that it had once run in the desert, I travelled ten or fifteen miles on its hard dry channel along which it had run after entering the desert, having a steep bank on both sides, beyond which there was nothing but deep sand. The aged natives told me that in their young days there was a considerable river in that channel, and sometimes rose so high that it could not be crossed for a long time. They first blamed the Matslaroo people for drying it up by means of witchcraft, but afterward acknowledged it must have been done by the hand of God.—CAMPBELL.

Ver. 6. I gave my back to the smiters, and my cheeks to them that plucked off the hair: I hid not my face from shame and spitting.

Mr. Hanway has recorded a scene differing little, if at all, from that alluded to by the prophet. "A prisoner was brought, who had two large logs of wood fitted to the small of his leg, and riveted together; there was also a heavy triangular collar of wood about his neck. The general asked me, if that man had taken my goods. I told him, I did not remember to have seen him before. He was questioned some time, and at length ordered to be beaten with sticks, which was performed by two soldiers with such severity as if they meant to kill him. The soldiers were then ordered to spit in his face, an indignity of great antiquity in the East. This, and the cutting off beards, which I shall have occasion to mention, brought to my mind the sufferings recorded in the prophetical history of our Saviour. Isaiah l. 6. "Sadoc Aga sent prisoner to Astrabad—his beard was cut off; his face was rubbed with dirt, and his eyes cut out. Upon his speaking in pathetic terms with that emotion natural to a daring spirit, the general ordered him to be struck across the mouth to silence him; which was done with such violence that the blood issued forth." —BURDER.

CHAPTER LI.

Ver. 6. Lift up your eyes to the heavens, and look upon the earth beneath; for the heavens shall vanish away like smoke, and the earth shall wax old like a garment, and they that dwell therein shall die in like manner: but my salvation shall be for ever, and my righteousness shall not be abolished. 7. Hearken unto me, ye that know righteousness, the people in whose heart *is* my law; fear ye not the reproach of men, neither be ye afraid of their revilings.

See on Job 4. 9.

Ver. 8. For the moth shall eat them up like a garment, and the worm shall eat them like wool: but my righteousness shall be for ever, and my salvation from generation to generation.

As the fashions of the garments of the Orientals never change, they have large stores of them; but they have no little difficulty in preserving them from moths: which circumstance may have occasioned their profuse use of perfumes.—ROBERTS.

Ver. 11. Therefore the redeemed of the LORD shall return, and come with singing unto Zion; and everlasting joy *shall be* upon their head: they shall obtain gladness and joy; *and* sorrow and mourning shall flee away.

Is there not here an allusion to the custom so common in the East, of singing upon a journey, particularly with a view to quicken the pace of the camels? "We should not have passed this plain so rapidly, but for the common custom of the Arabs of urging on their camels by singing: the effect is very extraordinary: this musical excitement increases their pace at least one fourth. First one camel-driver sings a verse, then the others answer in chorus. It reminded me somewhat of the Venetian gondoliers. I often asked the camel-drivers to sing, not only to hasten our progress, but also for the pleasure of hearing their simple melodies. Some of their best songs possess a plaintive sweetness that is almost as touching as the most exquisite European airs. The words are often beautiful, generally simple and natural, being improvisatory effusions. The following is a very imperfect specimen. One takes up the song:—'Ah, when shall I see my family again? the rain has fallen and made a canal between me and my home. Oh, shall I never see it more?' The reply to this and similar verses was always made by the chorus, in words such as these:—'Oh, what pleasure, what delight, to see my family again; when I see my father, mother, brothers, sisters, I will hoist a flag on the head of my camel for joy.'" (Hoskins' Trav. in Ethiopia, p. 26.)—BUSH.

In describing the order of the caravans, Pitts informs us, "that some of the camels have bells about their necks, and some about their legs, like those which our carriers put about their fore-horses' necks, which, together with the servants (who belong to the camels and travel on foot) singing all night, make a pleasant noise, and the journey passes away delightfully." This circumstance is explanatory of the singing of the Israelites in their return to Jerusalem.—HARMER.

Ver. 14. The captive exile hasteneth that he may be loosed, and that he should not die in the pit, nor that his bread should fail.

See on Job 33. 18, 24.

Ver. 17. Awake, awake, stand up, O Jerusalem, which hast drunk at the hand of the LORD the cup of his fury; thou hast drunken the dregs of the cup of trembling, *and* wrung *them* out.

Artificial liquors, or mixed wines, were very common in ancient Italy, and the Levant. The Romans lined their vessels with odorous gums, to give their wines a warm bitter flavour; and it is said, that several nations of modern times communicate to their wines a favourite relish by similar means. In Greece this is accomplished by infusing the cones of the pine in the wine vats. Hasselquist says they use the sweet-scented violet in their sherbet, which they make of violet sugar dissolved in water; the grandees sometimes add ambergris, as the highest luxury and indulgence of their appetite. The prophet Isaiah mentions a mixture of wine and water; but it is evident from the context, that he means to express by that phrase the degenerate state of his nation; and consequently, we cannot infer from it, the use of diluted wine in those countries. It is observed by Thevenot, that the people of the Levant never mingle water with their wine at meals, but drink by itself what water they think proper, for abating the strength of the wine. While the Greeks and Romans by mixed wine always understood wine diluted and lowered with water, the Hebrews, on the contrary, meant by it wine made stronger, and more inebriating, by the addition of powerful ingredients, as honey, spices, defrutum, or wine inspissated, by boiling it down to two thirds or one half of the quantity, myrrh, opiates, and other strong drugs. The Greeks were no strangers to perfumed and medicated wines; for in Homer, the far-famed Helen mixed a number of stupifying ingredients in the bowl, to exhilarate the spirits of her guests that were oppressed with grief; the composition of which, the poet says, she learnt in Egypt. Of the same kind was the spiced wine mentioned in the Song of Solomon; and to this day, such wines are eagerly sought by the people of Syria and Palestine. The drunkards in Israel preferred these medicated wines to all others: "Who hath wo?" said the wise man, "who hath contentions? who hath sorrow? who hath babbling? who hath wounds without cause? who hath redness of eyes? They that tarry long at the wine; they that go to seek mixed wine." Nor were the manners of that people more correct in the days of Isaiah; for he was directed to pronounce a "wo unto them that rose up early in the morning, that they might follow *strong drink*; that continued until night, till wine inflamed them." This ancient custom furnished the holy Psalmist with a highly poetical and sublime image of divine wrath: "For in the hand of the Lord . . . a cup; and the wine is red; it is full of mixture." The prophet Isaiah uses the same figure in one of his exhortations: "Awake, awake, stand up, O Jerusalem, which hast drunk at the hand of the *Lord* the cup of his fury; thou hast drunken the dregs of the cup of trembling, and wrung them out." The worshippers of the beast and his image, are threatened with the same fearful punishment: "The same shall drink of the wine of the wrath of God, which is poured out without mixture into the cup of his indignation." The Jews sometimes acidulated their wine with the juice of the pomegranate; a custom to which the spouse thus alludes. "I would cause thee to drink of spiced wine, of the juice of my pomegranate;" or of wine mixed with the juice of that fruit. Prepared in this way, it proves a cooling and refreshing draught in the heat of summer, and by consequence, highly acceptable to an Oriental.—PAXTON.

Ver. 20. Thy sons have fainted, they lie at the head of all the streets, as a wild bull in a net: they are full of the fury of the LORD, the rebuke of thy God.

What a graphic picture we have here of an eastern city or town in time of famine! See the squalid objects: in their despair, they rush forth, throw themselves down in the streets, and there remain till they die, or are relieved. They have scarcely a rag left to defend them from the heat of the sun, or the dew of the night; and they court death as a blessing. Ask them why they lie there, they reply, to die: tell them to get out of the way, and they answer not again; and so great is their indifference, that many of them would literally be crushed to death, rather than make the least effort to preserve life.—ROBERTS.

CHAPTER LII.

Ver. 1. Awake, awake; put on thy strength, O Zion; put on thy beautiful garments, O Jerusalem, the holy city: for henceforth there shall no more come unto thee the uncircumcised and the unclean.

Jerusalem had long been afflicted by her foes, but the time of her deliverance was at hand, and in token of that she was to deck herself in her glorious attire. At the time of famine, sickness, or sorrow, the people clothe themselves in their meanest apparel, and their ornaments are laid aside: but on the return of prosperity, they array themselves in their most "beautiful garments."—ROBERTS.

Ver. 2. Shake thyself from the dust; arise, *and* sit down, O Jerusalem: loose thyself from the bands of thy neck, O captive daughter of Zion.

See the poor prisoners; see mothers bereft of their children, or wives of their husbands; they roll themselves in the dust, and there make their bitter lamentations. The holy city had figuratively been in the dust, but she was now to arise, to take the shackles from her neck, and to sit down in the place prepared for her.—ROBERTS.

Ver. 2. Shake thyself from the dust; arise, *and* sit down, O Jerusalem: loose thyself from the bands of thy neck, O captive daughter of Zion.
10. The LORD hath made bare his holy arm in the eyes of all the nations; and all the ends of the earth shall see the salvation of our God.

The use of the oriental dress, which I now wear, brings to the mind various scriptural illustrations, of which I will only mention two. The figure in Isaiah lii. 10, "The Lord hath made bare his holy arm," is most lively: for the loose sleeve of the Arab shirt, as well as that of the outer garment, leaves the arm so completely free, that, in an instant, the left hand passing up the right arm, makes it bare; and this is done when a person, a soldier, for example, about to strike with the sword, intends to give his right arm full play. The image represents Jehovah as suddenly prepared to inflict some tremendous, yet righteous judgment, so effectual, "that all the ends of the world shall see the salvation of God."

The other point illustrated occurs in the second verse of the same chapter, where the sense of the last expression is, to an Oriental, extremely natural: "Shake thyself from the dust, arise, sit down, O Jerusalem." It is no uncommon thing to see an individual, or a group of persons, even when very well-dressed, sitting with their feet drawn under them, upon the bare earth, passing whole hours in idle conversation. Europeans would require a chair; but the natives here prefer the ground. In the heat of summer and autumn, it is pleasant to them to while away their time in this manner, under the shade of a tree. Richly-adorned females, as well as men, may often be seen thus amusing themselves. As may naturally be expected, with whatever care they may, at first sitting down, choose their place, yet the flowing dress by degrees gathers up the dust; as this occurs, they, from time to time, arise, adjust themselves, shake off the dust, and then sit down again. The captive daughter of Zion, therefore, brought down to the dust of suffering and oppression, is commanded to arise and shake herself from that dust; and then, with grace, and dignity, and composure, and security, to *sit down;* to take, as it were, again, her seat and her rank, amid the company of the nations of the earth, which had before afflicted her, and trampled her to the earth.

It may be proper to notice, that Bishop Lowth gives another rendering, "Arise, ascend thy lofty seat," and quotes eastern customs, to justify the version: but I see no necessity for the alteration, although to English ears it may sound more appropriate. A person of rank in the East often sits down upon the ground, with his attendants about him.—JOWETT.

Ver. 7. How beautiful upon the mountains are the feet of him that bringeth good tidings, that publisheth peace; that bringeth good tidings of good, that publisheth salvation; that saith unto Zion, Thy God reigneth!

Small feet are considered beautiful in all parts of the East. The feet of kings and holy people are spoken of in preference to the other parts of the body. His majesty of the Burmese empire is always mentioned as the "golden feet." "My messenger will soon return, he will bring me good tidings; his feet will be glorious." "Ah! when will the feet of my priest return this way; how glorious is their place!" "Are you in health?" asks the holy man. "Yes; by the glory of your feet," is the reply. "Ah! Swamy, it is a happy circumstance for me that your feet have entered my house."—ROBERTS.

Ver. 8. Thy watchmen shall lift up the voice; with the voice together shall they sing: for they shall see eye to eye, when the LORD shall bring again Zion.

The phrase, "see eye to eye," is that which we propose to explain, and the preceding verse should be read in order to show more clearly the connexion. The whole passage is a prediction of gospel times; it points to the proclamation of the joyful and welcome tidings which constituted the burden of our Saviour's preaching, and that of his apostles. In the poetical style of the East, the watchmen are represented as standing upon their watch-tower, or post of observation, and stretching their vision to the utmost point of the horizon, as if in eager expectation of the appearance of a news-bearing messenger. On a sudden the wished-for object appears in sight, on the summit of the distant mountain, speeding his rapid way to the city, while the watchmen, anticipating the tenor of his tidings, burst forth in a shout of gratulation and triumph. "Thy watchmen shall lift up the voice; with the voice together shall they sing." The imagery strikingly represents the expectant attitude and heedful vigilance of the believing part of the teachers and pastors of the nation of Israel on the eve of the Messiah's manifestation. The reason of the outbreak of their holy joy is immediately given: "For they shall see eye to eye, when the Lord shall bring again Zion," i. e. they shall have a clear and unclouded discernment of the actual execution of the divine purposes. As faithful watchmen, intent upon their duty, and earnestly looking out for the signs of promise, they shall be favoured with a clear, distinct, luminous perception of the objects of their gaze, in which they shall be honourably distinguished from a class of watchmen spoken of by the same prophet, ch. lvi. 10, of whom it is said, "His watchmen are *blind;*" instead of seeing clearly, they see nothing. That this is the genuine force of the expression, "they shall see eye to eye," is to be inferred from the parallel usage, Num. xiv. 14, "For they have heard that thou, Lord, art among this people, that thou, Lord, art seen *face to face,*" (Heb. eye to eye;) i. e. in the most open, evident manner. Of equivalent import are the expressions, Ex. xxx. 11, "And the Lord spake unto Moses *face to face,* as a man speaketh unto his friend." Num. xii. 8, "With him will I speak *mouth to mouth,* even apparently, and not in dark speeches;" where the latter part of the verse is exegetical of the former. We conclude, therefore, that the words do not in their primary and most legitimate sense imply a perfect unanimity of religious or doctrinal belief in the watchmen, or spiritual guides, of the Christian church. At the same time, though not expressly taught in this passage, it is but reasonable to expect, that in proportion as the prosperity of the church advances, truth will be more clearly discerned, and there will be a constant approximation among the pious, to a uniform standard of theological faith.—BUSH.

Ver. 10. The LORD hath made bare his holy arm in the eyes of all the nations.

The right arm or shoulder is always alluded to as the place of strength: with that the warrior wields his sword, and slays his foes. The metaphor appears to allude to a man who is preparing for the battle: he takes the robe from his right arm, that being thus uncovered, "made bare," it may the more easily perform its office. "Tell your boasting master to get ready his army, for our king has shown his shoulder," *i. e.* uncovered it. "Alas! I have heard that the mighty sovereign of the neighbouring kingdom has pointed to his shoulder," *i. e.* he is ready to come against us. See two men disputing; should one of them point to his right arm and shoulder, the other will immediately fall into a rage, as he knows it amounts to a challenge, and says, in effect, "I am thy superior." Thus may be seen men at a distance, when defying each other, slapping each his right hand or shoulder. Jehovah, in reference to the nations of the earth, "hath made bare his holy arm." "And all the ends of the earth shall see the salvation of our God."—ROBERTS.

Ver. 15. So shall he sprinkle many nations; the kings shall shut their mouths at him; for *that* which had not been told them shall they see, and *that* which they had not heard shall they consider.

At an eastern feast a person stands near the entrance with a silver vessel, which is full of rose-water, or some other perfumed liquid, with which he sprinkles the guests as they approach, as if from a watering-pan. The object is to show they are now the king's, or the great man's guests: they are in his favour and under his protection. So shall the eternal Son of God sprinkle many nations, and admit them into his presence in token of their purification, and of his protection and favour. The kings of the earth shall no longer rebel against him; but "shall shut their mouths" to denote their submission and respect.—ROBERTS.

When the company were ready to separate, a servant entered and sprinkled them profusely with rose-water, as a valedictory mark of his master's regard. In some places, this was done at the beginning of the entertainment, and was considered as a cordial welcome. Mr. Bruce informs us, that when he rose to take his leave of an eastern family, he "was presently wet to the skin, by deluges of orange-flower water." "The first time," says Niebuhr, "we were received with all the eastern ceremonies, (it was at Rosetta, at a Greek merchant's house,) there was one of our company who was excessively surprised, when a domestic placed himself before him, and threw water over him, as well on his face, as over his clothes." It appears from the testimony of both these authors, that this is the customary mode of showing respect and kindness to a guest in the East. The prophet Isaiah seems to refer to this custom, in a passage where he describes the character and functions of the Messiah: "So shall he sprinkle many nations, the kings shall shut their mouths at him."—PAXTON.

CHAPTER LIII.

Ver. 1. Who hath believed our report; and to whom is the arm of the LORD revealed?

In these parts of the world, the fashion is in a state of almost daily fluctuation, and different fashions are not unfrequently seen contending for the superiority; but in the East, where the people are by no means given to change, the form of their garments continues nearly the same from one age to another. The greater part of their clothes are long and flowing, loosely cast about the body, consisting only of a large piece of cloth, in the cutting and sewing of which, very little art or industry is employed. They have more dignity and gracefulness than ours, and are better adapted to the burning climates of Asia. From the simplicity of their form, and their loose adaptation to the body, the same clothes might be worn with equal ease and convenience by many different persons. The clothes of those Philistines whom Samson slew at Ashkelon, required no altering to fit his companions; nor the robe of Jonathan to answer his friend. The arts of weaving and fulling seemed to have been distinct occupations in Israel, from a very remote period, in consequence of the various and skilful operations which were necessary to bring their stuffs to a suitable degree of perfection; but when the weaver and the fuller had finished their part, the labour was nearly at an end; no distinct artisan was necessary to make them into clothes; every family seems to have made their own. Sometimes, however, this part of the work was performed in the loom; for they had the art of weaving robes, with sleeves all of one piece: of this kind was the coat which our Saviour wore during his abode with men. These loose dresses, when the arm is lifted up, expose its whole length. To this circumstance the prophet Isaiah refers. "To whom is the arm of the Lord revealed"—uncovered—Who observes that he is about to exert the arm of his power?—PAXTON.

Ver. 7. He was oppressed, and he was afflicted; yet he opened not his mouth: he is brought as a lamb to the slaughter, and as a sheep before her shearers is dumb, so he opened not his mouth.

This image was designed by the prophet to represent the meek, uncomplaining manner in which Christ stood before his judge, and submitted even to death for the salvation of mankind. Philo-Judæus, a philosopher and a Jew, born and bred in Egypt, and well acquainted with their customs, has a passage, by which it appears that the figurative language of Isaiah was founded upon the practice of the eastern shepherds. "Woolly rams, laden with thick fleeces, in spring season, being ordered by their shepherd, stand without moving, and silently stooping a little, put themselves into his hand, to have their wool shorn; being accustomed, as cities are, to pay their yearly tribute to man, their king by nature."—BURDER.

CHAPTER LIV.

Ver. 2. Enlarge the place of thy tent, and let them stretch forth the curtains of thy habitation: spare not, lengthen thy cords, and strengthen thy stakes.

In Africa, when we expected an increase of hearers, the Hottentots moved the pins all round, a yard or a yard and a half, farther from the tent, towards which they stretched the canvass, and fastened it, which considerably increased the room inside.—CAMPBELL.

Ver. 11. O thou afflicted, tossed with tempest, *and* not comforted, behold, I will lay thy stones with fair colours, and lay thy foundations with sapphires. 12. And I will make thy windows of agates, and thy gates of carbuncles, and all thy borders of pleasant stones.

This figurative way of speaking is in exact keeping with the eastern notions of magnificence: thus the abodes of the gods, or distant kings, are described as having pillars of red coral; rooms made of crystal; ruby doors; thrones of the nine precious stones; walls of gold, surrounded by emerald rivers. Such passages, therefore, are not to be received literally, but as being indicative of great splendour and unrivalled prosperity.—ROBERTS.

Many of the oriental buildings, however, have displayed unrivalled magnificence and splendour. The walls, columns, floors, and minarets of the mosques, were of the choicest marble, granite, and porphyry, inlaid with agates and precious stones. The ornamental parts were of gold and silver, or consisted of the most elegant borders, with festoons of fruit and flowers, in their natural colours, composed entirely of agates, cornelians, turquoises, lapis-lazuli, and other valuable gems. The hangings and carpets were of the richest manufacture: and the splendid edifice was illumined with chandeliers of massive gold. "How forcibly," says Forbes, "do these remind us of the truth and beauty of the metaphorical language in the sacred page, promising sublime and spiritual joys, in allusion to these subjects in eastern palaces!"—PAXTON.

CHAPTER LV.

Ver. 12. For ye shall go out with joy, and be led forth with peace: the mountains and the hills shall break forth before you into singing, and all the trees of the field shall clap *their* hands. 13. Instead of the thorn shall come up the fir-tree, and instead of the brier shall come up the myrtle-tree: and it shall be to the LORD for a name, and for an everlasting sign, *that* shall not be cut off.

Here we have another specimen of the fervid and splendid imagery of eastern language. Some people affect to despise the hyperboles, the parables, and high-toned allusions of such a style; but they ought to recollect they arise as much from the climate, the genius, and customs of the people, as do our more plain and sober effusions from opposite circumstances. When the god Rāmar was going to the desert, it was said to him, "The trees will watch for you; they will say, He is come, he is come; and the white flowers will clap their hands. The leaves, as they shake, will say, Come, come; and the thorny places will be changed into gardens of flowers."—ROBERTS.

CHAPTER LVI.

Ver. 3. Neither let the son of the stranger, that hath joined himself to the LORD, speak, saying, The LORD hath utterly separated me from his people: neither let the eunuch say, Behold, I *am* a dry tree.

People without posterity, of both sexes, are called dry trees; which, strictly speaking, means they are dead, having neither sap, nor leaves, nor fruit.—ROBERTS.

CHAPTER LVII.

Ver. 6. Among the smooth *stones* of the stream *is* thy portion; they, they *are* thy lot; even to them hast thou poured a drink-offering, thou hast offered a meat-offering. Should I receive comfort in these?

This refers to stones made smooth by oil poured on them, as was frequently done by the heathen. Theophrastus has marked this as one strong feature in the character of the superstitious man: "Passing by the anointed stones in the streets, he takes out his vial of oil, and pours it on them; and having fallen on his knees, and made his adorations, he departs."—LOWTH.

CHAPTER LVIII.

Ver. 5. Is it such a fast that I have chosen? a day for a man to afflict his soul? *is it* to bow down his head as a bulrush, and to spread sackcloth and ashes *under him?* wilt thou call this a fast, and an acceptable day to the LORD?

The eastern people spread mats or small carpets under them when they pray, and even suppose it unlawful to pray on the bare ground; is it not natural to suppose the Jews had something under them when they prayed, and that this was a piece of sackcloth in times of peculiar humiliation? When they wore sackcloth in the day, it is not perhaps natural to suppose they slept in fine linen; but I should suppose some passages of scripture, which, in our translation, speak of lying in sackcloth, are rather to be understood of lying prostrate before God on sackcloth, than taking their repose on that coarse and harsh kind of stuff.

The learned and exact Vitringa makes no remark on

this kind on that passage of Isaiah, "Is it such a fast that I have chosen? a day for a man to afflict his soul? is it to bow down his head as a bulrush, and to spread sackcloth and ashes under him?" He only quotes what is said of Ahab, 1 Kings xxi. 27, and the Jews in Shushan, Esther iv. 2, as of a similar nature, and seems to understand this piece of humiliation before God of lodging on sackcloth. But, surely, it must be much more natural to understand the solemnity of prostration on sackcloth before God, which follows the mention of hanging down the head, used in kneeling, or in standing as suppliants before him, rather than of sleeping in sackcloth, the night before or the night after the day of fasting. It seems to me, in like manner, to express the humiliation of Ahab with more energy, than as commonly understood: "And it came to pass, when Ahab heard those words, that he rent his clothes, and put sackcloth upon his flesh, and fasted, and prostrated himself on sackcloth," &c. The like may be said of the lying of the Jews in Shushan in sackcloth.

A passage in Josephus strongly confirms this, in which he describes the deep concern of the Jews for the danger of Herod Agrippa, after having been stricken suddenly with a violent disorder in the theatre of Cesarea. Upon the news of his danger, "immediately the multitude, with their wives and children, sitting upon sackcloth, according to their country rites, prayed for the king: all places were filled with wailing and lamentation: while the king, who lay in an upper room, beholding the people thus below falling prostrate on the ground, could not himself refrain from tears." Antiq. lib. xix. cap. 8, § 2, p. 951. Here we see the sitting on sackcloth, resting on their hams, in prayer, and falling prostrate at times on the sackcloth, was a Jewish observance in times of humiliation and distress.—HARMER.

Ver. 9. Then shalt thou call, and the LORD shall answer; thou shalt cry, and he shall say, Here I *am*. If thou take away from the midst of thee the yoke, the putting forth of the finger, and speaking vanity.

This chapter commences with, "Cry aloud, spare not, lift up thy voice like a trumpet, and show my people their transgression, and the house of Jacob their sins." After this, the people are severely reproved for their hypocrisy, "ye fast for strife and debate, and smite with the fist of wickedness;" and then they are exhorted to cease from their oppressions, "to undo the heavy burdens, and to let the oppressed go free, and that ye break every yoke." It appears they were tyrants under the garb of sanctity, and in contempt for the injured, they took delight in "putting forth of the finger, and speaking vanity." See that boasting tyrant, when addressing his humbled antagonist, he scowls and storms "like the raging sea," and then lifts up the fore-finger of the right hand to the height of his head, and moves it up and down, to show that punishment of a still higher nature shall be the award of the victim of his wrath.—ROBERTS.

Ver. 10. And *if* thou draw out thy soul to the hungry, and satisfy the afflicted soul; then shall thy light rise in obscurity, and thy darkness *be* as the noonday.

Has a person in reference to temporal circumstances been in great difficulty, has he been delivered, then is he compared to a man in a dark place who suddenly finds a light, which enables him to walk with pleasure and safety in his appointed way. "True, true, I was in darkness, but the light has come; it shines around me; there is no shade."—ROBERTS.

Ver. 11. And the LORD shall guide thee continually, and satisfy thy soul in drought, and make fat thy bones: and thou shalt be like a watered garden, and like a spring of water, whose waters fail not.

In a hot climate where showers seldom fall, except in what is called the rainy season, the difference between a well and ill watered garden is most striking. I remember some gardens in Africa where they could lead no water up them; the plants were all stunted, sickly, or others completely gone, only the hole left where the faded plant had been. The sight was unpleasant, and caused gloom to appear in every countenance: they were pictures of desolation. But in other gardens, to which the owners could bring daily supplies of water from an everflowing fountain, causing it to traverse the garden, every plant had a green, healthy appearance, loaded with fruit, in different stages towards maturity, with fragrant scent proceeding from beds of lovely flowers; and all this produced by the virtue God hath put into the single article of water.—CAMPBELL.

CHAPTER LIX.

Ver. 4. None calleth for justice, nor *any* pleadeth for truth: they trust in vanity, and speak lies; they conceive mischief, and bring forth iniquity.

See on Ps. 14. 29.

Ver. 5. They hatch cockatrices' eggs, and weave the spider's web: he that eateth of their eggs dieth, and that which is crushed breaketh out into a viper.

See on ch. 11. 8.

The margin has, instead of *cockatrice*, "*or adders*." So far as the strength of the poison is concerned, I believe there is scarcely any difference betwixt the oviparous and the viviparous serpents. The eggs of the former are generally deposited in heaps of stones, in old walls, or holes in dry places; and under some circumstances, (like those of the large lizard,) are soft and yielding to the touch. The pliability of the shell MAY be the result of being newly laid, as I have seen some shells as hard as those of other eggs. It is said of the plans of a decidedly wicked and talented man, "That wretch! he hatches serpents' eggs." "Beware of the fellow, his eggs are nearly hatched." "Ah! my friend, touch not that affair, meddle not with that matter; there is a serpent in the shell." "Interfere not, interfere not, young serpents are coming forth." "I have been long absent from my home, and on my return I thought that I should have much enjoyment, but on opening a basket to procure some cakes, I found they were all serpents," meaning, instead of pleasure, he had found pain on his return. "I touch it! No, no; the last time I did so the shell broke, and a young serpent gave me a bite, which has poisoned my whole frame."—ROBERTS.

Ver. 11. We roar all like bears, and mourn sore like doves: we look for judgment, but *there is* none; for salvation, *but* it is far off from us.

In parturition those animals are said to make a tremendous noise: hence people in poignant sorrow say, "We roar like bears." "Heard you not the widow's cry last night? the noise was like that of a she-bear." "What is the fellow roaring about? he is like a she-bear."—ROBERTS.

Ver. 15. Yea, truth faileth; and he *that* departeth from evil maketh himself a prey: and the LORD saw *it*, and it displeased him that *there was* no judgment.

In the preceding verses, the wickedness of the abandoned Jews is strongly portrayed; and when they began to confess their sins and repent, as in the ninth and fourteenth verses inclusive, they were by some, as in the margin, "accounted mad," in consequence of their change of views and conduct. It is an amusing fact, that when the heathen become very attentive to the directions of their own religion when they rigidly perform the prescribed austerities; "when they sell themselves to the gods, and appear like men of another world," they are "accounted mad" by their neighbours. On the other hand, should a man begin to deride the national faith; should he never go near the temples, and laugh at idols and outward ceremonies, the people again exclaim, "The fellow is mad!" But, above all, should a person embrace Christianity, the general story is, the poor fellow has gone mad. "Have you heard Supplyan has become a Christian?"—"No; but I have heard he has become a madman."—ROBERTS.

CHAPTER LX.

Ver. 6. The multitude of camels shall cover thee, the dromedaries of Midian and Ephah; all they from Sheba shall come: they shall bring gold and incense; and they shall show forth the praises of the LORD.

That species of camel called the dromedary, is chiefly remarkable for its prodigious swiftness; the Arabs affirming, that it will run over as much ground in one day, as one of their best horses will perform in eight or ten. If this be true, the prophet had reason to call it the "swift dromedary;" and the messengers of Esther acted wisely, in choosing this animal to carry their important despatches to the distant provinces of that immense empire. Dr. Shaw had frequent opportunities, in his travels, of verifying the wonderful accounts of the Arabs in relation to the swiftness of this creature. The sheik who conducted the party to Mount Sinai, rode a camel of this kind, and would frequently divert them with a display of its abilities; he would depart from their caravan, reconnoitre another just in view, and return to them again in less than a quarter of an hour.—PAXTON.

Ver. 7. All the flocks of Kedar shall be gathered together unto thee, the rams of Nebaioth shall minister unto thee: they shall come up with acceptance on mine altar, and I will glorify the house of my glory.

Here we have unquestionably another metaphor, to illustrate the prosperity and influence of the church among the heathen. I think, therefore, it is trifling with the text, to suppose it alludes to a *literal* possession of the "rams of Nebaioth," "the flocks of Kedar," or the "dromedaries of Midian." I believe it refers to the *people* of those countries, who are spoken of in the passage, under the names of the animals for which their localities were most famous. This mode of speech is perfectly oriental, and may often be heard in common conversation. Thus, for instance, the district of Mulliteevo is famous for its numerous buffaloes; hence the people of that place, when they go to another town, are often, by way of pleasantry, called buffaloes. The district of Poonareen abounds with the wild hog; and it excites a smile to call one of its inhabitants the *pandy*, i. e. pig of Poonareen. The islands opposite North Ceylon are noted for shells, and when the islanders come to the towns, it is asked, should a person wish to have a little merriment at their expense, "Why do these shells of the islands come hither?" Batticotta is celebrated for having numerous men who are expert in digging tanks: hence all the people, as circumstances may require, are humorously called OTTAR, *i. e.* diggers. I think, therefore, the figure is descriptive of the glory of the church in the acquisition of the PEOPLE of Midian, Ephah; of Sheba, of Kedar, and Nebaioth.—ROBERTS.

Ver. 8. Who *are* these *that* fly as a cloud, and as the doves to their windows.

In this passage, he beheld in vision the captive Israelites, liberated by the decree, and encouraged by the invitation of Cyrus, returning with the greatest alacrity to the land of their fathers; and exulting at the sight, he cries out with surprise and pleasure, "Who are these that fly as doves to their windows?" The prophet apparently supposes, that in his time, buildings for the reception of doves were very common. And this is by no means improbable; for, when Maundrell visited Palestine, dove-cots were numerous in some parts of the country. In the neighbourhood of Ispahan are many pigeon-houses built for the sole purpose of collecting pigeons' dung for manure. The extraordinary flights of pigeons which alight upon one of those buildings, furnish a good illustration of the prophet's vision. Their great numbers and the compactness of their mass, literally look like a cloud at a distance, and obscure the sun in their passage. In some parts of Egypt are numerous whitened dove-cots on the tops of the houses. The dove flies more swiftly when she returns to the windows of these cots, than when she leaves them; because she hastens to revisit her young which she had left, and to distribute among them the food which she had collected. A similar passage occurs in Hosea: "They shall tremble as a dove out of Egypt; and as a dove out of the land of Assyria; and I will place them in their houses, saith the Lord." They shall fly with trepidation; or, like a dove trembling for its young, or alarmed for its own safety, which puts forth its utmost speed. Phrases of this kind are not uncommon in the sacred writings; thus, when Samuel came to Bethlehem, the elders of the town trembled at his coming; that is, they ran out with trepidation to meet him. A similar phrase occurs in the third chapter of Hosea: "They shall fear to the Lord and his goodness;" that is, they shall run with trepidation to the Lord and his goodness in the latter days. These verbs (חרד) harad and (פחד) phahad, which are nearly synonymous, according to some Jewish writers, mean only to return with haste. Thus, Aben Ezra, on the last quotation from the prophecies of Hosea: "They shall return with haste to the Lord and his goodness."—PAXTON.

Ver. 11. Therefore thy gates shall be open continually; they shall not be shut day nor night; that *men* may bring unto thee the forces of the Gentiles, and *that* their kings *may be* brought.

Dr. Boothroyd says, "That they may bring to thee the wealth of the nations." Of a wealthy man who is continually adding to his stores, it is said, "His gates neither day nor night, AKO-RAT-TIRAM, are closed." Also it is said of a charitable king, "His gates are always open." So in those days of glorious accession to the church, "Her doors shall be open continually, and day and night shall the Gentiles be gathered into her pale."—ROBERTS.

Ver. 14. The sons also of them that afflicted thee shall come bending unto thee; and all they that despised thee shall bow themselves down at the soles of thy feet; and they shall call thee, The city of the LORD, The Zion of the Holy One of Israel.

"Come bending unto thee." Who in the East has not seen the humble suppliant come BENDING to ask forgiveness or to entreat a favour? See him go stooping along, with his hands spread out, till he come near his superior, and then, as in the next words, he bows himself down at his feet.—ROBERTS.

CHAPTER LXI.

Ver. 3. To appoint unto them that mourn in Zion, to give unto them beauty for ashes, the oil of joy for mourning, the garment of praise for the spirit of heaviness: that they might be called Trees of Righteousness, The Planting of the LORD, that he might be glorified.

Perfumed oils are very expensive, and are believed to possess MANY virtues. Except for medicinal purposes, they are used only on joyous occasions. "My friend, why are you so dejected? the gods shall give you PARE-MALATIYALUM," *i. e.* precious or odoriferous ointment.—ROBERTS.

Ver. 10. I will greatly rejoice in the LORD, my soul shall be joyful in my God; for he hath clothed me with the garments of salvation, he hath covered me with the robe of righteousness, as a bridegroom decketh *himself* with ornaments, and as a bride adorneth *herself* with her jewels.

It would be considered unfortunate in the extreme for a bride to be married without having on numerous jewels: hence the poorest females, those who have not a farthing in the world, may be seen on such occasions literally covered with jewels. The plan is this:—the neighbours and friends of the poor girl lend their ornaments in order to make a splendid show; and I have not known an instance (except when lost) of their not being returned; which may be considered a remarkable fact among people who are not *very* famed for honesty. But the bridegroom also has numerous ear-rings, neck-rings, chains, breastplates, and finger-rings. "I will greatly rejoice ——— as a bridegroom." "You appear to be very happy, Chinnan?"—"Indeed I am happy; and it is like the joy of a *kalle-yānum*," i. e. marriage. "Ah! my heart has a wedding to-day," says the man who is in great pleasure. "Have you heard of the joy of old Kandan?" "No, why; is he so happy?" "Because his daughter has *kālmāre-poltāl*," i. e. literally, changed her legs; meaning, she has got married. "Happy man should I have been if my daughter had not changed her legs," says the father whose daughter has been unfortunately married. —ROBERTS.

CHAPTER LXII.

Ver. 4. Thou shalt no more be termed Forsaken: neither shall thy land any more be termed Desolate: but thou shalt be called Hephzibah, and thy land Beulah: for the LORD delighteth in thee, and thy land shall be married.

The margin has for *Beulah, married.* A sovereign is spoken of as being married to his dominions: they mutually depend upon each other. When a king takes possessions from another, he is said to be married to them. Thus in that day shall God's people, and their inheritance, be married to the Lord.—ROBERTS.

Ver. 5. For *as* a young man marrieth a virgin, *so* shall thy sons marry thee: and *as* the bridegroom rejoiceth over the bride, *so* shall thy God rejoice over thee.

In general, no youth marries a WIDOW: such a thing I scarcely ever heard of, nor will it ever be, except under some extraordinary circumstance, as in the case of a queen, princess, or great heiress. Even widowers also, if possible, always marry virgins.—ROBERTS.

Ver. 6. I have set watchmen upon thy walls, O Jerusalem, *which* shall never hold their peace day nor night: ye that make mention of the LORD, keep not silence.

The image in this place is taken from the temple service, in which there was appointed a constant watch day and night by the Levites. Now the watches in the East, even to this day, are performed by a loud cry from time to time by the watchmen, to mark the time, and that very frequently, and in order to show that they themselves are constantly attentive to their duty. "The watchmen in the camp of the caravans go their rounds, crying one after another, *God is one, he is merciful;* and often add, *take heed to yourselves.*" (Tavernier.) The reader will observe in this extract how mention is made of the name of God by the watchmen.— —BURDER.

Ver. 10. Go through, go through the gates; prepare ye the way of the people; cast up, cast up the highway; gather out the stones; lift up a standard for the people.

The situation of Babylon, on the river Euphrates, must have made causeways necessary to those that had occasion to go thither or come from thence, as marks set up must have been very requisite to those that had to pass through the deserts, that lay between Chaldea and Palestine: to both which conveniences Isaiah seems to refer, as well as to some other circumstances attending eastern travelling, in that passage in which he prophetically describes the return of Israel from Babylon. The passage I mean is in the close of the 62d chapter: "Go through, go through the gates; prepare ye the way of the people, cast up, cast up the highway; gather out the stones; lift up a standard for the people. Behold, the LORD hath proclaimed unto the end of the world, Say ye to the daughter of Zion, Behold, thy salvation cometh."

Irwin, speaking of his passing through the deserts on the eastern side of the Nile, in his going from Upper Egypt to Cairo, tells us, "that after leaving a certain valley which he mentions, their road lay over level ground. As it would be next to an impossibility to find the way over these stony flats, where the heavy foot of a camel leaves no impression, the different bands of robbers, wild Arabs he means, who frequent that desert, have heaped up stones at unequal distances, for their direction through this desert. We have derived great assistance from the robbers in this respect, who are our guides when the marks either fail, or are unintelligible to us." After which he remarks, that if it be considered, that this road to Cairo is seldom trodden, it is no wonder that those persons they had with them, as conductors, were frequently at a loss to determine their way through this desert. The learned know very well, that there are many great deserts in various parts of the East, and in particular a great desert between Babylon and Judea; and as Judea was, in the time of the captivity, an abandoned country, at least as to a great part of it, and the road through that desert might have been much neglected, is it not reasonable to suppose, that the piling up heaps of stones might actually be of considerable importance, to facilitate the return of Israel into their own country? And if not, is it not natural to suppose the difficulties in the way of their return might be represented by want of such works? And consequently, that that clause should be rendered, not *gather out the stones*, but *throw ye up heaps of stones*, that you may be directed in your march through the most difficult and dangerous places where you are to pass. It is certain the word סקלו *sakkeloo*, that is used here is, confessedly, in every other place but one, Is. v. 2, used to signify the throwing stones at a person, after which they were wont to cover them with a heap of them, as a memorial of what was done; see particularly the account of the punishment of Achan, Josh. vii. 25, 26; now it must appear somewhat strange, that the same word should signify gathering stones up in order to take them away, and also, on the contrary, to cover over a person or a spot with them, thrown up on a heap. And especially when the stoning the ways, that is, pouring down heaps of stone, at proper distances, to direct travellers in danger of mistaking their way, is so natural a thought in this passage; while we find few or no traces of the gathering stones out of an eastern road, to make journeying more pleasant to the traveller.—HARMER.

CHAPTER LXIII.

Ver. 1. Who *is* this that cometh from Edom, with died garments from Bozrah? this *that is* glorious in his apparel, travelling in the greatness of his strength? I that speak in righteousness, mighty to save. 2. Wherefore *art thou* red in thine apparel, and thy garments like him that treadeth in the wine-fat? 3. I have trodden the wine-press alone; and of the people, *there was* none with me: for I will tread them in mine anger, and trample them in my fury; and their blood shall be sprinkled upon my garments, and I will stain all my raiment.

The treading of grapes and olives is a custom to which frequent reference is made by the inspired writers. The glorious Redeemer of the church appeared in a vision to the prophet, in the garb and mien of a mighty conqueror returning in triumph from the field of battle, and drew from him this admiring interrogation: "Who is this that cometh from Edom, with died garments from Bozrah? this that is glorious in his apparel, travelling in the greatness of his strength?" To which the Saviour answers: "I that speak in righteousness, mighty to save." The prophet resumes: "Wherefore art thou red in thine apparel, and thy garments like him that treadeth in the wine-fat?" And Jehovah Jesus replies: "I have trodden the wine-press alone; and of the people, there was none with me; for I will tread them in mine anger, and trample them in my fury; and their blood shall be sprinkled upon my garments, and I will stain all my raiment." As the raiment of the treader was sprinkled with the blood of the grapes, so were the garments of the Redeemer, with the blood of his enemies, that were as effectually and easily crushed by his almighty power, as are the clusters of the vine when fully ripe, beneath the feet of the treader. The same figure is employed in the book of Revelation, to express the decisive and fearful destruction which awaits the man of sin and his coadjutors, that refuse to turn from the error of their way: "And another angel came out from the altar, which had power over fire; and cried with a loud cry to him that had the sharp sickle, saying, Thrust in thy sharp sickle, and gather the clusters of the vine of the earth, and cast it into the great wine-press of the wrath of God. And the wine-press was trodden without the city, and blood came out of the wine-press, even unto the horses' bridles, by the space of a thousand and six hundred furlongs." The new wines in some places, are always poured into casks that had been kept for ages, and after remaining on the old lees of former years, are drawn off for use, which adds greatly to the quality of the wine. To this practice the words of the prophet evidently refer; "And in this mountain shall the Lord of hosts make unto all people a feast of fat things, a feast of wines on the lees, of fat things full of marrow, of wines on the lees well refined."—Paxton.

The manner of pressing grapes is as follows: having placed them in a hogshead, a man with naked feet gets in and treads the grapes: in about half an hour's time, the juice is forced out: he then turns the lowest grapes uppermost, and treads them for about a quarter of an hour longer: this is sufficient to squeeze the good juice out of them, for an additional pressure would even crush the unripe grapes, and give the whole a disagreeable flavour.—Burder.

Ver. 13. That led them through the deep, as a horse in the wilderness, *that* they should not stumble? 14. As a beast goeth down into the valley, the Spirit of the Lord causeth him to rest; so didst thou lead thy people, to make thyself a glorious name.

The prophet Isaiah makes an allusion to the horse, which is apt, from the difference of our manners and feelings, to leave an unfavourable impression upon the mind; it occurs in the sixty-third chapter, and runs in these terms: "That led them through the deep, as a horse in the wilderness, that they should not stumble. As a beast goeth down into the valley, the Spirit of the Lord caused him to rest: so didst thou lead thy people, to make thyself a glorious name." If these words be understood as merely referring to the unobstructed course of a single horse in the plain, and the descent of a beast into the valley to repose,—the allusion, more especially considering the general beauty and sublimity which characterize the style of Isaiah, seems rather flat and mean; and this is the more surprising, when it is considered, that the prophet is here describing a scene by which the Lord acquired to himself a glorious name, and which, by consequence, demanded no common strength or magnificence of thought. Nor does it appear for what reason, in order to rest, a herd should descend into a valley; for the hills must be equally pleasing and comfortable places of repose as the vales. We shall find it in the manners of the Arabian, to which the simile refers; and a very little attention is necessary to convince a dispassionate inquirer, that the image is most lively and magnificent.

The original Hebrew term (סוס) *sous*, in the singular number, denotes both a single horse, and a body of cavalry. In the same manner we use the word horse, to express a single animal of that species, and at other times, the horsemen of an army. In the book of Exodus, *sous* denotes the horsemen of Pharaoh's army who pursued after the tribes of Israel. But if it denote the horse of an Egyptian army, it may, with equal propriety, denote the horse or cavalry of an Arabian tribe. Now, Arabian horses are remarkable for the surprising swiftness with which they escape the hottest pursuit of their enemies. In two hours after an alarm is given, the Arabs strike their tents, and with their families, and their whole property, plunge into the deepest recesses of their sandy deserts, which the boldest and most exasperated enemy dares not invade. In the time of De la Roque, the great emir of Mount Carmel had a mare which he valued at more than five thousand crowns. The Arabians, it seems, prefer the female to the male because it is more gentle, silent, and able to endure fatigue, hunger, and thirst; qualities in which, they have found from experience, the former excels the latter. The mare which the emir or prince of Carmel rode, had carried him three days and three nights together, without eating or drinking, and by this means effectually saved him from the pursuit of his enemies. This account entirely removes the apparent meanness of the prophetic representation, and imparts a liveliness and dignity to the description. At the moment when Pharaoh and his army thought the people of Israel were completely in their power, shut in by the sea and the mountains, that they could not escape,—like the Arab horsemen, they decamped, and through the sea marched into the desert, whither their enemies were unable to follow. If the Arabian horses are not so sure-footed as the mule, which Dr. Shaw affirms, it will account for the next clause in the same verse: "As a horse in the wilderness, they should not stumble." The departure of Israel from the land of Egypt was sudden, and their movements were rapid, like those of an Arab, whom his enemy has surprised in his camp; yet no misfortune befell them in their retreat, as at times overtakes the swiftest and surest-footed horses. The next verse may be explained by the same custom: "As a beast or herd goeth down into the valley, so the Spirit of the Lord caused him to rest." The Arab, decamping at the first alarm, marches off with his flocks and herds, his wife and children, into the burning deserts. This he does, not from choice, but for safety; and by consequence, how proper and agreeable soever the hills may be for pasturage, in times of alarm or danger, the deep sequestered valley must be far more desirable. The custom of the Arabs in Barbary, stated by Dr. Shaw, finely illustrates this figure. About the middle of the afternoon, his party began to look out for the encampment of some Arabian horde, who, to prevent such numerous parties as his from living at free charges upon them, take care to pitch in woods, valleys, or places the least conspicuous. And he confesses, that if they had not discovered their flocks, the smoke of their tents, or heard the barking of their dogs, they had either not found the encampment at all, or with extreme difficulty.—Paxton.

CHAPTER LXIV.

Ver. 5. Thou meetest him that rejoiceth and worketh righteousness; *those that* remember thee in thy ways: behold, thou art wroth; for we have sinned: in those is continuance, and we shall be saved.

Does a man expect a guest for whom he has a great regard, he goes forth to meet him. Not to do so would show a great deficiency in affection and etiquette.—Roberts.

CHAPTER LXV.

Ver. 3. A people that provoketh me to anger continually to my face; that sacrificeth in gardens, and burneth incense upon altars of brick.

See on ch. 1. 29.

Ver. 4. Which remain among the graves, and lodge in the monuments; which eat swine's flesh, and broth of abominable *things is in* their vessels; 5. Which say, Stand by thyself, come not near to me; for I am holier than thou. These *are* a smoke in my nose, a fire that burneth all the day.

"Come not near to me, for I am holier than thou." Here we have another instance of the glaring wickedness of the Jews, in their imitation of the heathen devotees, who resembled the Hindoo Yogees. Those men are so isolated by their superstition and penances, that they hold but little intercourse with the rest of mankind. They wander about in the dark in the place of burning the dead, or "among the graves;" there they affect to hold converse with evil and other spirits; and there they pretend to receive intimations respecting the destinies of others. They will eat things which are religiously clean or unclean; they neither wash their bodies, nor comb their hair, nor cut their nails, nor wear clothes. They are counted to be *most holy*, among the people, and are looked upon as beings of another world. —Roberts.

Ver. 22. For as the days of the tree *are* the days of my people.

The people of the East have a particular desire for long life; hence one of their best and most acceptable wishes is, "May you live a thousand years." "May you live as long as the *aali-tree*," i. e. the banyan or ficus indica. I never saw a tree of that description dead, except when struck by lightning. And to cut one down would, in the estimation of a Hindoo, be almost as great a sin as the taking of life. I do not think this tree will die of itself, because it continues to let fall its own supporters, and will march over acres of land if not interrupted. Under its gigantic branches the beasts of the forests screen themselves from the heat of the sun; and under its sacred shade may be seen the most valued temples of the Hindoos.—Roberts.

CHAPTER LXVI.

Ver. 12. For thus saith the Lord, Behold, I will extend peace to her like a river, and the glory of the Gentiles like a flowing stream: then shall ye suck, ye shall be borne upon *her* sides, and be dandled upon *her* knees. 13. As one whom his mother comforteth, so will I comfort you; and ye shall be comforted in Jerusalem.

The native females of South Africa, when at home, literally carry about their children on their side, putting one leg of the child behind, and the other before her, and resting on the upper part of the hip. The child clings to her side, and from the prolongation of her breasts, the mother can conveniently suckle it, without moving it from its place. When I saw this done, it had always a very affectionate appearance. When they travel, or are fleeing from an enemy, they carry their children on their back, under their cloak, their heads only being visible. The females in the South Sea Islands have the same custom. Whether that part of the passage has an allusion to a similar practice existing among Jewish females, I know not; but this I know, that on witnessing the African custom, I thought of the above text, which refers to a peaceful and prosperous period, when God should act in the kindest manner towards his ransomed people. To me, when I saw it, it had the appearance of peace, security, and affection.—Campbell.

Ver. 17. They that sanctify themselves, and purify themselves in the gardens, behind one *tree* in the midst, eating swine's flesh, and the abomination, and the mouse, shall be consumed together, saith the Lord.

Not only sacred groves in general, but the centres of such groves in special, were, as the Abbé Banier has observed, made use of for temples by the first and most ancient heathens. Some one tree in the centre of each such grove was usually had in more eminent and special veneration, being made the penetrale or more sacred place, which, doubtless, they intended as the anti-symbol of the tree of life, and of the knowledge of good and evil, in the midst of the garden of Eden. To this strange abuse alludes that prophetic censure of some, who sanctified and purified themselves with the waters of their sacred fountains and rivers in the gardens or groves, behind one tree in the midst.—Burder.

Ver. 20. And they shall bring all your brethren *for* an offering unto the Lord, out of all nations, upon horses, and in chariots, and in litters, and upon mules, and upon swift beasts, to my holy mountain Jerusalem, saith the Lord, as the children of Israel bring an offering in a clean vessel into the house of the Lord.

The editor of the Ruins of Palmyra tells us, that the caravan they formed, to go to that place, consisted of about two hundred persons, and about the same number of beasts of carriage, which were an odd mixture of horses, camels, mules, and asses; but there is no account of any vehicle drawn on wheels in that expedition; nor do we find an account of such things in other eastern journeys. There are, however, some vehicles among them used for the sick, or for persons of high distinction. So Pitts observes, in his account of his return from Mecca, that at the head of each division some great gentleman or officer was carried in a thing like a horse-litter, borne by two camels, one before and another behind, which was covered all over with searcloth, and over that again with green broadcloth, and set forth very handsomely. If he had a wife attending him, she was carried in another. This is apparently a mark of distinction. There is another eastern vehicle used in their journeys, which Thevenot calls a coune. He tells us, the counes are hampers, like cradles, carried upon camels' backs, one on each side, having a back, head, and sides, like the great chairs sick people sit in. A man rides in each of these counes, and over them they lay a covering, which keeps them both from the rain and sun, leaving, as it were, a window before and behind upon the camel's back. The riding in these is also, according to Maillet, a mark of distinction; for, speaking of the pilgrimage to Mecca, he says ladies of any figure have litters; others are carried sitting in chairs, made like covered cages, hanging on both sides of a camel; and as for ordinary women, they are mounted on camels without such conveniences, after the manner of the Arab women, and cover themselves from sight, and the heat of the sun, as well as they can, with their veils. These are the vehicles which are in present use in the Levant. Coaches, on the other hand, Dr. Russel assures us, are not in use at Aleppo; nor do we meet with any account of their commonly using them in any other part of the East: but one would imagine, that if ever such conveniences as coaches had been in use, they would not have been laid aside in countries where ease and elegance are so much consulted.

As the caravans of the returning Israelites are described by the prophet, as composed, like Mr. Dawkin's to Palmyra, of horses and mules, and swift beasts; so are we to understand, I imagine, the other terms of the litters and counes, rather than of coaches, which the margin mentions; or of covered wagons, which some Dutch commentators suppose one of the words may signify, unluckily transferring the customs of their own country to the East; or of chariots, in our common sense of the word. For though our translators have given us the word *chariot*, in many passages of scripture, those wheel-vehicles which those writers speak of, and which our version renders chariots, seem to have been mere warlike machines; nor do we ever read of ladies riding in them. On the other hand, a word derived from the same original is made use of for a seat any how moved, such as the mercy-seat, 1 Chron. xxxviii. 18, where our translators have used the word chariot, but which was no more of a chariot, in the common sense of the word, than a litter is; it is made use of also for that sort of seat mentioned Lev. xv. 9, which they have rendered saddle, but which seems to mean a litter, or a coune. In these vehicles many of the Israelites were to be conducted, according to the prophet, not on the account of sickness, but to mark out the eminence of those Jews, and to express the great respect their conductors should have for them.—Harmer.

JEREMIAH.

CHAPTER I.

Ver. 11. Moreover, the word of the LORD came unto me, saying, Jeremiah, what seest thou? And I said, I see a rod of an almond-tree. 12. Then said the LORD unto me, Thou hast well seen: for I will hasten my word to perform it.

The almond-tree, so frequently mentioned in the sacred writings, was called by the Hebrews *shakad*, from a verb which signifies to awake, or watch; because it is the first tree which feels the genial influences of the sun, after the withering rigours of winter. It flowers in the month of January, and in the warm southern latitudes brings its fruit to maturity in March. To the forwardness of the almond, the Lord seems to refer in the vision with which he favoured his servant Jeremiah: "The word of the Lord came unto me, saying, Jeremiah, what seest thou? And I said, I see a rod of an almond-tree. Then said the Lord unto me, Thou hast well seen; for I will hasten my word to perform it;" or rather, "I am hastening, or watching over my word to fulfil it." In this manner it is rendered by the Seventy, εγρηγορα εγω επι: and by the Vulgate, Vigilabo ego super verbum meum. This is the first vision with which the prophet was honoured; and his attention is roused by a very significant emblem of that severe correction with which the Most High was hastening to visit his people for their iniquity; and from the species of tree to which the rod belonged, he is warned of its near approach. The idea which the appearance of the almond rod suggested to his mind, is confirmed by the exposition of God himself: "I am watching over, or on account of my word, to fulfil it;" and this double mode of instruction, first by emblem, and then by exposition, was certainly intended to make a deeper impression on the mind, both of Jeremiah and the people to whom he was sent. It is probable, that the rods which the princes of Israel bore, were scions of the almond-tree, at once the ensign of their office, and the emblem of their vigilance. Such, we know from the testimony of scripture, was the rod of Aaron; which renders it exceedingly probable that the rods of the other chiefs were from the same tree: "And Moses spake unto the children of Israel, and every one of their princes gave him a rod apiece, for each prince, according to their fathers' houses, twelve rods; and the rod of Aaron was among their rods . . . and behold the rod of Aaron, for the house of Levi, was budded, and brought forth buds, and bloomed blossoms, and yielded almonds." The almond rod of Aaron, in the opinion of Parkhurst, which was withered and dead, and by the miraculous power of God made to bud and blossom, and bring forth almonds, was a very proper emblem of him who first arose from the grave; and as the light and warmth of the vernal sun seems first to affect the same symbolical tree, it was with great propriety that the bowls of the golden candlestick were shaped like almonds. The hoary head is beautifully compared by Solomon to the almond-tree, covered in the earliest days of spring with its snow-white flowers, before a single leaf has budded: "The almond-tree shall flourish, and the grasshopper shall be a burden, and desire shall fail." Man has existed in this world but a few days, when old age begins to appear; sheds its snows upon his head; prematurely nips his hopes, darkens his earthly prospects, and hurries him into the grave.—PAXTON.

Ver. 13. And the word of the LORD came unto me the second time, saying, What seest thou? And I said, I see a seething-pot, and the face thereof *is* towards the north. 14. Then the LORD said unto me, Out of the north an evil shall break forth upon all the inhabitants of the land.

To compensate in some measure for the scarcity of fuel, the Orientals endeavour to consume as little as possible in preparing their victuals. For this purpose they make a hole in their dwellings, about a foot and a half deep, in which they put their earthen pots, with the meat in them, closed up, about the half above the middle; three fourth parts they lay about with stones, and the fourth part is left open, through which they fling in their dried dung, and any other combustible substances they can procure, which burn immediately, and produce so great a heat, that the pot becomes as hot as if it stood over a strong fire of coals; so that they boil their meat with greater expedition and much less fuel, than it can be done upon the hearth. The hole in which the pot is set, has an aperture on one side, for the purpose of receiving the fuel, which seems to be what Jeremiah calls the face of the pot: "I see," said the prophet, "a pot, and the face thereof is towards the north;" intimating that the fuel to heat it was to be brought from that quarter. This emblematical prediction was fulfilled when Nebuchadnezzar, whose dominions lay to the north of Palestine, led his armies against Jerusalem, and overturned the thrones of the house of David.—PAXTON.

CHAPTER II.

Ver. 6. Neither said they, Where *is* the LORD that brought us up out of the land of Egypt, that led us through the wilderness; through a land of deserts, and of pits; through a land of drought, and of the shadow of death; through a land that no man passed through, and where no man dwelt?

The account that Mr. Irwin has given of that part of this wilderness which lies on the western side of the Red Sea, through the northern part of which Israel actually passed, very much corresponds with this description, and may serve to illustrate it. When it is described as a land without water, we are not to suppose it is absolutely without springs, but only that water is very scarce there. Irwin accordingly found it so. On the first day after his setting out, having only travelled five miles, they filled thirty water-skins from the river Nile, but which he thought might prove little enough for their wants, before they reached the next watering-place They travelled, according to their computation, fifty-four miles farther, before they found, three days after, a spring, at which they could procure a fresh supply; and this was a new discovery to their guides, and for which they were indebted to a very particular accident. It was not till the following day, that they arrived at the valley where their guides expected to water their camels, and where accordingly they replenished the few skins that were then empty: the spring was seventy-nine miles from the place from whence they set out. The next spring of water which they met with was, according to their reckoning, one hundred and seventy-four miles distant from the last, and not met with till the seventh day after, and was, therefore, viewed with extreme pleasure. "At nine o'clock we came suddenly upon a well, which is situated among some broken ground. The sight of a spring of water was inexpressibly agreeable to our eyes, which had so long been strangers to so refreshing an object." The next day they found another, which "gushed from a rock, and threw itself with some violence into a basin, which it had hollowed for itself below. We had no occasion for a fresh supply; but could not help lingering a few minutes to admire a sight, so pretty in itself, and so bewitching to our eyes, which had of late been strangers to bubbling founts and limpid streams."

We must here mention the smallness of the quantity of water one of these four springs afforded, which Irwin met with in the desert, or at least the difficulty of watering their beasts at it. "We lost," says this writer, "the greatest part of the day at this spring. Though our skins were presently filled, the camels were yet to drink. As the camels could not go to the well, a hole was sunk in the earth below the surface of the spring, over which a skin was spread, to retain the water which flowed into it. At this but two camels could drink at a time; and it was six hours before our camels, which amounted to forty-eight in all, were watered. Each camel, therefore, by this calculation, takes a quarter of an hour to quench his enormous thirst; and to water a common caravan of four hundred camels, at such a place as this, would require two days and two nights. A most unforeseen and inconceivable delay to an uninformed traveller!" If we are to give this part of the prophet's description of that wilderness a popular explanation, and not take it in the most rigorous sense, we ought, undoubtedly, to put the same kind of construction on the two last clauses of it. *A land that no man passed through, and where no man dwelt:* a land, that is not usually passed, and where hardly any man dwelt. So Irwin describes the desert of Thebaïs as "unknown even to the inhabitants of the country; and which, except in the instances I have recited, has not been traversed for this century past by any but the outcasts of humankind." Such a wilderness might very well be said not to be passed through, when only two or three companies travelled in it in the compass of a hundred years, and that on account of extreme danger, at that particular time, attending the common route. He actually calls it, "a road seldom or never trodden." As to its being inhabited, Irwin travelled, by his estimation, above 300 miles in this desert, from Ghinnah to the towns on the Nile, without meeting with a single town, village, or house. They were even extremely alarmed at seeing the fresh tracks of a camel's feet, which made a strong impression on a soft soil, and which the Arabs with them thought were not more than a day old; and they could not comprehend what business could bring any but Arab freebooters into that waste.

When the prophet describes this wilderness, according to our version, as *the land of the shadow of death*, his meaning has been differently understood by different people. Some have supposed it to mean a place where there were no comforts or conveniences of life; but this seems too general, and to explain it as a particular and distinct member of the description, pointing out some quality different from the other circumstances mentioned by *Jeremiah*, seems to be a more just, as it is undoubtedly a more lively way of interpreting the prophet. Others have accordingly understood this clause as signifying, it was the habitation of venomous serpents, or destroying beasts; some as endangering those that passed through it, as being surrounded by the hostile tribes of Arabs; some as being overshadowed by trees of a deleterious quality. They might better have introduced the whirlwinds of those southern deserts than the last particular, which winds, taking up the sand in great quantities, darken the air, and prove fatal to the traveller. This last would be giving great beauty and energy to the expression, (the shadow of death,) since these clouds of dust, literally speaking, overshadow those that have the misfortune to be then passing through those deserts, and must at the same time give men the utmost terror of being overwhelmed by them, and not unfrequently do in fact prove deadly.

Another clause, *a land of pits*, is also a part of the prophet's description. Irwin affords a good comment on this part of our translation: in one place he says, "The path winded round the side of the mountain, and to our left, a horrid chasm, some hundred fathoms deep, presented itself to our view. It is surprising no accident befell the loaded camels." In another, "On each side of us were perpendicular steeps some hundred fathoms deep. On every part is such a wild confusion of hanging precipices, disjointed rocks, and hideous chasms, that we might well cry out with the poet, 'Chaos is come again.' Omnipotent Father! to thee we trust for our deliverance from the perils that surround us. *It was through this wilderness that thou didst lead thy chosen people.* It was here thou didst manifest thy signal protection, in snatching them from the jaws of destruction which opened upon every side." And in the next page, "At two o'clock we came suddenly upon a dreadful chasm in the road, which appears to have been the effect of an earthquake. It is about three hundred yards long, one hundred yards wide, and as many deep; and what is a curiosity, in the middle of the gulf, a single column of stone raises its head to the surface of the earth. The rudeness of the work, and the astonishing length of the stone, announce it to be a lusus naturæ, though the robbers declared to us, that beneath the column there lies a prodigious sum of money; and added, with a grave face, they have a tradition, that none but a Christian's hand can remove the stone to come at it. We rounded the gulf, which was called Somah, and leaving it behind us, we entered a valley where we found a very craggy road." The first clause in this passage, *through a land of deserts*, is the most obscure and difficult to ascertain. Instead of travelling in the night, as he had proposed, to avoid the burning heat of the sun, he says, "At seven o'clock we halted for the night. The Arabs tell us, that the roads are too rugged and dangerous to travel over in the dark." Under the next day, "we reached the foot of a prodigious high mountain, which we cannot ascend in the dark." The following day he tells us, "by six o'clock we had accoutred our camels, and leading them in our hands, began to ascend the mountain on foot; as we mounted the steep, we frequently blessed ourselves that we were not riding, as the path was so narrow, the least false step must have sent the beast down the bordering precipice." Under another day he remarks, that the greatest part of that day's journey was "over a succession of hills and dales, where the road was so intricate and broken, that nothing but a camel could get over it. The appearance of the road is so frightful in many places, that we do not wonder why our people have hitherto laid by in the night." (Harmer.)

"After we had passed the salt desert, we came to the Malek-el-moat-dereh, or the valley of the angel of death. This extraordinary appellation, and the peculiar nature of the whole of this tract of land, broken into deep ravines, without water, of a dreariness without example, will, perhaps, be found forcibly to illustrate Jer. ii. 6." (Morier.)—BURDER.

Ver. 13. For my people have committed two evils; they have forsaken me, the fountain of living waters, *and* hewed them out cisterns, broken cisterns, that can hold no water.

In eastern language, "living water" signifies springing water, that which bubbles up. The people had forsaken Jehovah, the never-failing spring, for the small quantity which could be contained in a cistern; nay, in broken cisterns, which would let out the water as fast as they received it. When people forsake a good situation for that which is bad, it is said, "Yes; the stork which lived on the borders of the lake, where there was a never-failing supply of water, and constant food, has gone to dwell on the brink of a well," *i. e.* where there is no fish, and where the water cannot be had.—ROBERTS.

Ver. 18. And now, what hast thou to do in the way of Egypt, to drink the waters of Sihor? or what hast thou to do in the way of Assyria, to drink the waters of the river?

The Euphrates is always muddy, and the water, consequently, not good to drink, unless it has stood an hour or two in earthen vessels, for the sand and impurities to settle, which at times lie half a finger thick at the bottom of the vessel. Hence it was not without reason that the Lord said to the Israelites, by the prophet Jeremiah, "What hast thou to do in the way of Assyria, to drink the waters of the river!" (Euphrates.) For this reason we find in the houses of the city and villages, particularly those lying on the Great River, many large earthen vessels holding a pailful or two, which they fill from the Euphrates, and do not use till the impurities have settled at the bottom, unless they are very thirsty, and then they drink through their pocket-handkerchiefs." (Rauwolf.)—ROSENMULLER.

Ver. 25. Withhold thy foot from being unshod,

and thy throat from thirst: but thou saidst, There is no hope: no; for I have loved strangers, and after them will I go.

See on Ruth 4. 7.

Ver. 37. Yea, thou shalt go forth from him, and thy hands upon thy head: for the Lord hath rejected thy confidences, and thou shalt not prosper in them.

See on Matt. 11. 21.

Impenitent Jerusalem was to be punished for revolting against God; and, as a token of her misery, she was to go forth with her "hands on her head." Tamar "laid her hand on her head," as a sign of her degradation and sorrow. When people are in great distress, they put their hands on their head, the fingers being clasped on the top of the crown. Should a man who is plunged into wretchedness meet a friend, he immediately puts his hands on his head, to illustrate his circumstances. When a person hears of the death of a relation or friend, he forthwith clasps his hands on his head. When boys have been punished at school, they run home with their hands on the same place. Parents are much displeased and alarmed, when they see their children with their hands in that position; because they look upon it not merely as a sign of grief, but as an emblem of bad fortune. Thus of those who had trusted in Egypt and Assyria, it was said, "Thou shalt be ashamed" of them: and they were to go forth with their hands on their head, in token of their degradation and misery.—Roberts.

CHAPTER III.

Ver. 2. Lift up thine eyes unto the high places, and see where thou hast not been lain with: in the ways hast thou sat for them, as the Arabian in the wilderness; and thou hast polluted the land with thy whoredoms, and with thy wickedness.

Every one knows the general intention of the prophet, but Chardin has given so strong and lively a description of the eagerness that attends their looking out for prey, that I am persuaded my readers will be pleased with it. "Thus the Arabs wait for caravans with the most violent avidity, looking about them on all sides, raising themselves up on their horses, running here and there to see if they cannot perceive any smoke, or dust, or tracks on the ground, or any other marks of people passing along."—Harmer.

CHAPTER IV.

Ver. 13. Behold, he shall come up as clouds, and his chariots *shall be* as a whirlwind: his horses are swifter than eagles. Wo unto us! for we are spoiled.

See on Isa. 66. 20.

Ver. 17. As keepers of a field are they against her round about; because she hath been rebellious against me, saith the Lord.

In Arabia, and probably in other parts of the East, instead of a solitary watchman in the middle of the plantation, they place guards at certain distances round the whole field, increasing or diminishing their numbers according to the supposed danger. This custom furnishes a clear and easy explanation of a passage in the prophecies of Jeremiah, where he solemnly warns his people of their approaching calamities: "As keepers of a field, are they against her round about; because she hath been rebellious against me, saith the Lord."—Paxton.

Fields in the East have not fences to keep off cattle and other marauders, but only low embankments; hence, were there not keepers, they would be exposed to all kinds of depredations. These men wander about the ridges, or spend their time in platting baskets or pouches for areca-nuts and betel leaf; or tend a few sheep. At night they sleep in a small stall, about six feet by four, which stands on four legs, and is thatched with leaves. The whole affair is so light, that it can be removed in its complete state to any other part, by two men; or be taken to pieces in a few minutes, and removed and put together, by one man. The frail fabric illustrates the "lodge in a garden of cucumbers."—Roberts.

Ver. 30. And *when* thou *art* spoiled, what wilt thou do? Though thou clothest thyself with crimson, though thou deckest thee with ornaments of gold, though thou rendest thy face with painting, in vain shalt thou make thyself fair; *thy* lovers will despise thee, they will seek thy life.

The Hebrew has, instead of face, "eyes." This is a minute description of an eastern courtesan. In Ezekiel xxiii. 40, similar language is used: "For whom thou didst wash thyself, paintedst thine eyes, and deckedst thyself with ornaments, and satest upon a stately bed." Jezebel also "painted her face, and tired her head, and looked out at a window." She was the patroness of a most impure system, and the term "whoredoms," as applied to her, may be safely used in the most obvious sense. The females alluded to adorn themselves with those ornaments which have been described in the 3d chapter of Isaiah; and having bathed, they rub their bodies with saffron, to make themselves fair; and then put on their crimson robes. One kind of paint with which they teint their eyelids is made of a nut called *kaduki*, which is first burned to a powder, then mixed with castor-oil; after which it is set on fire, and that which drops from it is the paint referred to. Another kind is made of the juice of limes, indigo, and saffron. In these allusions we see again the hateful and loathsome state of Jerusalem.—Roberts.

Several authors, and Lady M. W. Montague in particular, have taken notice of the custom that has obtained from time immemorial among the eastern women, of tinging the eyes with a powder, which, at a distance, or by candle-light, adds very much to the blackness of them. The ancients call the mineral substance, with which this was done, *stibium*, that is, *antimony*; but Dr. Shaw tells us, it is a rich *lead ore*, which, according to the description of naturalists, looks very much like antimony. Those that are unacquainted with that substance may form a tolerable idea of it, by being told it is not very unlike the black-lead of which pencils are made, that are in everybody's hands. Pietro Della Valle, giving a description of his wife, an Assyrian lady, born in Mesopotamia, and educated at Bagdad, whom he married in that country, says, "her eyelashes, which are long, and, according to the custom of the East, dressed with stibium, as we often read in the holy scriptures of the Hebrew women of old, and in Xenophon, of Astyages, the grandfather of Cyrus, and of the Medes of that time, give a dark and at the same time majestic shade to the eyes." "Great eyes," says Sandys, speaking of the Turkish women, "they have in principal repute; and of those the blacker they be the more amiable; insomuch that they put between the eyelids and the eye a certain black powder, with a fine long pencil, made of a mineral brought from the kingdom of Fez, and called *alchole*, which by the not disagreeable staining of the lids doth better set forth the whiteness of the eye; and though it be troublesome for a time, yet it comforteth the sight, and repelleth ill humours." Dr. Shaw furnishes us with the following remarks on this subject. "But none of these ladies take themselves to be completely dressed, till they have tinged the hair and edges of their eyelids with the powder of lead-ore. Now as this operation is performed by dipping first into the powder a small wooden bodkin of the thickness of a quill, and then drawing it afterward through the eyelids, over the ball of the eye, we shall have a lively image of what the prophet (Jer. iv. 30) may be supposed to mean by *rending the eyes with painting*. The sooty colour, which is in this manner communicated to the eyes, is thought to add a wonderful gracefulness to persons of all complexions. The practice of it, no doubt, is of great antiquity; for besides the instance already taken notice of, we find that when Jezebel is said (2 Kings ix. 30,) *to have painted her face*, the original words are, *she adjusted her eyes with the powder of lead-ore*."—Burder.

CHAPTER V.

Ver. 6. Wherefore a lion out of the forest shall slay them, *and* a wolf of the evenings shall spoil them, a leopard shall watch over their cities: every one that goeth out thence shall be torn in pieces; because their transgressions are many, *and* their backslidings are increased.

The lion prowls about in the day, which I have often witnessed in Africa; but the habits of the wolf are different, as it seldom makes its appearance before sunset, after which it comes forth, like other thieves of the night, in search of prey. I never, when moving about in Africa, saw more than one wolf stalking about in daylight, and that was in a most forsaken part, where, to a great extent, the land was absolutely paved with flag-stones, the same as the side pavements in our streets; but when night came, they were constantly howling and hovering around our encampment. The habit of the leopard, also, is to be slumbering in concealment during the day; but the darkness rouses him, and he comes forth seeking what he may devour. It is of the tiger species, and rather smaller. The wolves and leopards should have the boldness to prowl about their cities, as the wild beasts did about our wagons in the wilderness, so that it should be most hazardous for man or beast to venture outside their walls.—CAMPBELL.

The rapacious character of the wolf was familiarly known to the ancients, for both the Greek and Latin poets frequently mention it. In the first book of the Georgics, Virgil says, this office was given to the wolf by Jupiter, to hunt the prey. The rapacious wolf, is a phrase which often occurs in the odes of Horace; and Ovid, in one of his Elegies, sings, how the wolf, rapacious and greedy of blood, when pressed by famine, plunders the unguarded fold: his ravenous temper prompts him to destructive and sanguinary depredations. He issues forth in the night, traverses the country, and not only kills what is sufficient to satisfy his hunger, but, everywhere, unless deterred by the barking of dogs or the vociferation of the shepherds, destroys a whole flock; he roams about the cottages, kills all the animals which have been left without, digs the earth under the doors, enters with a dreadful ferocity, and puts every living creature to death, before he chooses to depart, and carry off his prey. When these inroads happen to be fruitless, he returns to the woods, searches about with avidity, follows the track of wild beasts, and pursues them in the hope that they may be stopped and seized by some other wolf, and that he may be a partaker of the spoil. "To appease hunger," says Buffon, "he swallows indiscriminately every thing he can find, corrupted flesh, bones, hair, skins half tanned and covered with lime;" and Pliny avers, that he devours the earth on which he treads, to satisfy his voracious appetite. When his hunger is extreme, he loses the idea of fear; he attacks women and children, and even sometimes darts upon men; till, becoming perfectly furious by excessive exertions, he generally falls a sacrifice to pure rage and distraction. He has been accordingly joined with the lion in executing punishment upon wicked men; and it is evident from his character and habits, that he is well adapted to the work of judgment: "The great men," said Jeremiah, "have altogether broken the yoke, and burst the bonds; wherefore a lion out of the forest shall slay them, and a wolf of the evenings shall spoil them." The rapacious and cruel conduct of the princes of Israel, is compared by Ezekiel to the mischievous inroads of the same animal: "Her princes in the midst thereof, are like wolves ravening the prey, to shed blood, to destroy souls, to get dishonest gain." The disposition of the wolf to attack the weaker animals, especially those which are under the protection of man, is alluded to by our Lord in the parable of the hireling shepherd: "The wolf catches them and scatters the flock;" and the apostle Paul, in his address to the elders of Ephesus, gives the name of this insidious and cruel animal, to the false teachers who disturbed the peace, and perverted the faith of their people: "I know this, that after my departing, shall grievous wolves enter in among you, not sparing the flock." Ovid gives him the same character in his fable of Lycaon.—PAXTON.

Ver. 8. They were *as* fed horses in the morning: every one neighed after his neighbour's wife.

The same term is used in the East to denote a similar thing. It is said, "Listen to that evil man, he is always neighing." "O that wicked one, he is like the horse in his phrensy." "The men of that family are all neighers." Heathenism is ever true to itself; impurity is its inseparable companion.—ROBERTS.

CHAPTER VI.

Ver. 1. O ye children of Benjamin, gather yourselves to flee out of the midst of Jerusalem, and blow the trumpet in Tekoa, and set up a sign of fire in Beth-haccerem: for evil appeareth out of the north, and great destruction.

The methods by which the besieged in time of war endeavoured to defend themselves and their families were various. When the enemy approached, they gave notice to their confederates to hasten their assistance. In the day, this was done by raising a great smoke; in the night, by fires or lighted torches. If the flaming torch was intended to announce the arrival of friends, it was held still; but on the approach of an enemy, it was waved backwards and forwards, an apt emblem of the destructive tumults of war. In allusion to this practice, the prophet Jeremiah calls to the people of Benjamin and Judah; "Gather yourselves to flee out of the midst of Jerusalem, and blow the trumpet in Tekoah, and set up a sign of fire in Beth-haccerem; for evil approaches out of the north, and great destruction."—PAXTON.

In Beth-haccerem there might possibly be a very high tower. Kimchi observes that the word signifies a high tower, for the keepers of the vines to watch in. If it were so, it was a very proper place to set up the sign of fire in, to give notice to all the surrounding country. It was usual with the Persians, Grecians, and Romans, to signify in the night by signs of fire, and by burning torches, either the approach of an enemy, or succour from friends. The former was done by shaking and moving their torches; the latter by holding them still.—BURDER.

Ver. 2. I have likened the daughter of Zion to a comely and delicate *woman*.

A passage of D'Arvieux will account for that surprise, which he supposes the daughters of Jerusalem would notwithstanding feel, upon seeing the swarthiness of the person which Solomon had chosen for his spouse, as it shows the attention usually paid by the great men of the East to the complexion of their wives, as well as the great tanning power of the sun in Palestine. "The princesses, and the other Arab ladies, whom they showed me from a private place of the tent, appeared to me beautiful and well-shaped; one may judge by these, and by what they told me of them, that the rest are no less so; they are very fair, because they are always kept from the sun. The women in common are extremely sunburnt, besides the brown and swarthy colour which they naturally have," &c. Naturally, he says, though this most permanent swarthiness must arise from the same cause with that temporary tanning he speaks of, or otherwise the Arab princesses would have been swarthy, though not sunburnt, being natives of the country, which yet, he affirms, they were not.

It is on this account, without doubt, that the prophet Jeremiah, when he would describe a comely woman, describes her by the character of one that dwelleth at home. The delicate, and those that are solicitous to preserve their beauty, go very little abroad: it seems it was so anciently, and therefore the prophet uses a term to express a woman of beauty, which would not be very applicable to many British fine ladies.—HARMER.

Ver. 20. To what purpose cometh there to me incense from Sheba, and the sweet cane from a far country? your burnt-offerings *are* not acceptable, nor your sacrifices sweet unto me.

The sweet-smelling reed grows in the deserts of Arabia. It is gathered near Jambo, a port town of Arabia Petrea, from whence it is brought into Egypt. Pliny says it is common to India and Syria. This plant was probably among the number of those which the queen of Sheba presented to Solomon; and what seems to confirm the opinion is, that it is still very much esteemed by the Arabs on account of its fragrance.

It is likely the sweet cane of Jeremiah, who calls it prime, or *excellent*, and associates it with incense from Sheba. "To what purpose cometh there to me incense from Sheba, and the sweet cane from a far country?" And, in allusion to the same plant, Isaiah complains in the name of Jehovah, "Thou hast bought me no sweet cane with money." In the book of Exodus, it is called "sweet calamus," and is said to come "from a far country;" which agrees with the declaration of ancient writers, that the best is brought from India.—PAXTON.

Ver. 24. We have heard the fame thereof; our hands wax feeble: anguish hath taken hold of us, *and* pain as of a woman in travail.

When a person is hungry, or weary, or when he hears bad news, it is said, "His hands have become weak." "His hands have turned cold."—ROBERTS.

CHAPTER VII.

Ver. 34. Then will I cause to cease from the cities of Judah, and from the streets of Jerusalem, the voice of mirth, and the voice of gladness, the voice of the bridegroom, and the voice of the bride; for the land shall be desolate.

It was the custom in the East, even in modern times, to conduct the bride and bridegroom through the streets, with the loudest demonstrations of joy. Rauwolf found this custom also prevalent in Aleppo. "When a Turkish woman is going to be married, and the bridegroom is conducted to her house, their relations and friends, who are invited to the wedding, as they go along through the streets cry with such a loud voice, which they gradually raise as they advance, that they can be heard from one street to the other." When the prophet paints a period of public distress, he says among other things, "The voice of the bride and the bridegroom shall no longer be heard." Thus, in Persia, no marriages are celebrated during Lent, (the month of Ramadan,) and the solemnities of mourning in memory of Hossein; because every thing must then be still and mournful. (Olearius.)—ROSENMULLER.

CHAPTER VIII.

Ver. 7. Yea, the stork in the heaven knoweth her appointed times; and the turtle, and the crane, and the swallow, observe the time of their coming: but my people know not the judgment of the LORD.

See on Ps. 104. 17.

Some interpreters imagine, that by the phrase, "the stork in the heaven," the prophet means to distinguish between the manner of her departure, and that of other migrating birds. The storks collect in immense numbers, and darken the air with their wide-extended squadrons, as they wing their flight to other climes; while many other birds of passage come and go in a more private and concealed manner. But, if this was the prophet's design, he ought not to have introduced the crane, or our translators should have found another sense for the term which he uses; for the crane is seen pursuing her annual journey through the heavens equally as the stork, and in numbers sufficient to engage the public attention. When Dr. Chandler was in Asia, about the end of August, he saw cranes flying in vast caravans, passing high in the air, from Thrace as he supposed, on their way to Egypt. But, in the end of March, he saw them in the Lesser Asia, busily engaged in picking up reptiles, or building their nests. Some of them, he assures us, built their nests in the ruins of an old fortress; and that the return of the crane, and the beginning of the bees to work, are considered there as a sure sign that the winter is past.

The first clause of that verse then, equally suits the stork and the crane; and by consequence, the conjecture of these interpreters is unfounded. It is more natural to suppose, that the prophet alludes to the impression which the atmosphere makes upon these birds, and the hint which instinct immediately suggests, that the time of their migration is come. As soon as they feel the cold season approaching, or tepid airs beginning to soften the rigours of winter, in the open firmament of heaven, where they love to range, they perceive the necessity of making preparations for their departure, or their return. The state of the weather is the only monitor they need to prepare for their journey, —their own feelings, the only guides to direct their long and adventurous wanderings.

But it is most probable that the prophet by these words, "in the heaven," which by the structure of the clause he seems to apply exclusively to the stork, as a peculiar trait in her character, intends to express both the astonishing rapidity of her flight, when she starts for distant regions, and the amazing height to which she soars. She is beyond almost any other, a bird "in the heaven," journeying on the very margin of ether, far above the range of the human eye.

From the union of the stork and the crane in the same passage, from the similarity of their form and habits of life, Harmer thinks it by no means improbable, that the Hebrew word *hasida* signifies both these, and, in one word, the whole class of birds that come under the prophet's description. But that respectable writer has no foundation for his opinion; the stork and the crane, although they resemble each other in several particulars, belong to different families, and are distinguished in Hebrew by different names.

The return of these birds to the south, marked the approach of winter, and the time for the mariner to lay up his frail bark; for the ancients never ventured to sea during that stormy season. Stillingfleet has given a quotation from Aristophanes, which is quite appropriate. The crane points out the time for sowing, when she flies with her warning notes to Egypt; she bids the sailor hang up his rudder and take his rest, and every prudent man provide himself with winter garments. On the other hand, the flight of these birds towards the north, proclaimed the approach of spring. The prophet accordingly mentions the times appointed for the stork in the plural number, which is probably used to express both the time of her coming and of her departure.

No doubt is entertained about the meaning of the second term; it is universally allowed to denote the turtle; and as the voice of the turtle and the song of the nightingale are coincident, it seems to be the prophet's intention to mark out the coming of a bird later in the spring than the *hasida*, for, according to Chardin, the nightingale begins to be heard some days later than the appearance of the stork, and marks out the beginning of spring, as the stork indicates the termination of winter.—PAXTON.

Should a husband be fond of roving from his house, and remaining in other places, his wife says, "The storks know their time and place, but my husband does not know." "In the rain neither the Koku nor other birds will depart from their nestlings: but my husband is always leaving us." "Ah! my wicked son! would that he, as the stork, knew his appointed time and place!"—ROBERTS.

Ver. 17. For behold, I will send serpents, cockatrices, among you, which *will* not *be* charmed, and they shall bite you, saith the LORD.

See on Eccl. 10. 11. Ps. 58. 5, 6. and Is. 11. 8.

The East Indian jugglers ascribe it to the power of a certain root that they touch venomous serpents without danger, and are able to do with them whatever they please. This is confirmed by one of the best-informed and most judicious observers, Mr. Kaempfer, a German physician, who practised his profession from the year 1682, for twelve years, in several countries in Asia. In his instructive work, written in Latin, in which he has recorded the greater part of his observations, a separate chapter is dedicated to the arts of the East India charmers of serpents, the substance of which we will add here.

"Among the arts of the Indian jugglers and mountebanks, the most remarkable is, that they make one of the most venomous serpents, the Naja, called by the Portuguese Cobra de Cabello, dance. This serpent, so dangerous to man, infuses, by its bite, a most deadly poison into the wound. Those who are bit by it are immediately seized with fits and oppression, and expire in convulsions, unless speedy assistance is given; at least they hardly escape mortification, in the injured part, and the cure of which is difficult, if antidotes are applied too late. This serpent, which belongs to the class of vipers, is from three to four feet long, and of a middling thickness; its skin is scaly, and beautifully striped, rough, dark brown, and belly white. When provoked, this viper has the peculiar property of puffing up the skin on both sides of the neck, and extending it like a fillet, which, on the reverse side, shows like a pair of spectacles, distinctly marked with a white colour, the circles of which are visible in the skin, which is spread round the head: thus, with its body raised, and extended jaws, displaying two rows of sharp teeth, it darts upon the enemy with surprising swiftness. That this formidable animal should be brought, by singing, to make, before spectators, movements resembling a dance, is incredible to those who hear it, and an agreeable and astonishing sight to those that witness it. But if we examine this serpent dance more closely, and learn how these animals are taught, we shall find every thing very natural: I will first describe the dance, as it is called.

"A charmer of serpents, who intends to display his art, before he does any thing, takes a piece of a certain root, of which he always carries some in the scarf which he wears round his waist, in his right hand, which he closes firmly; this root, according to his declaration, defends him against all attacks from serpents, so that he can do any thing with them without being endangered: upon this, he throws the serpent upon the ground out of the vessel in which he carries it about, and gently irritates it with a stick, or with the clinched fist in which he holds this root. The provoked animal, resting on the point of its tail, raises up its whole body, and darts upon the fist, which he holds out to him, with extended jaws, from which the hissing tongue is protruded, and with flaming eyes. The charmer now begins his song, at the same time moving his fist backward and forward, up and down, according to the time. The serpent, with its eyes constantly directed towards the fist, imitates its movements with its head and whole body, so that without quitting its place, and resting on its tail, it extends its head two spans long, and moves to and fro, together with the body, in beautiful undulations, which is called dancing: this, however, does not last longer than half a quarter of an hour; for, exhausted by the erect position, and movements to the time, the serpent throws itself upon the ground and escapes: to avoid this, the charmer breaks off his song a little before, when the serpent lays itself quietly upon the ground, and suffers itself to be brought back to its receptacle.

"The question now is, how it is effected, that the serpent follows the motion of the hand which is held before it? whether by the secret power of the root held in it? or by the song of the charmer? These people, indeed, affirm that this effect is produced by both. The root, say they, causes the serpent to do no harm, and the song makes it dance. They, therefore, bring this root to the spectators to purchase, and do not much like to let any one approach a dancing serpent without having previously secured himself with it; but that others may not be able to discover what root it is, they cut them only in very small pieces, which in taste and external appearance resemble the sarsaparilla, but are only a little stronger. But we must not believe that the root makes the serpent harmless, and that the song makes it dance. I threw two pieces of the root, which I had purchased for a trifle from a charmer, to a serpent which was quietly lying on the ground after the dance was finished; but it did not cause it to move, nor did it show any sign of aversion. But no person of sense in our days, probably, can believe that serpents are so charmed by the song, that they dance; and David, in the well-known passage in the Psalms, does not appear to say this. In short, according to my conviction, it is only fear, by which this species of serpents, which is more docile than any other, is taught to follow the motions of its master's hand, which is held before it, and so makes movements with its body resembling a dance. I myself saw how a Hindoo of the Bramin tribe, who lived in a suburb of Nagapatam, instructed such a serpent to dance in a few days, by means of a stick and a basin, which he held before it: they are rendered harmless by employing the poison-bags at the root of the canine teeth of the upper jaw, which is done by provoking them, and making them bite a cloth, or some other soft and warm body, and repeating this for some days successively."—Burder.

Ver. 20. The harvest is past, the summer is ended, and we are not saved.

Has a man lost a good situation, it is said, "His harvest is past." Is a person amassing much money, it is said, "He is gathering in his harvest."—Roberts.

CHAPTER IX.

Ver. 1. Oh that my head were waters, and mine eyes a fountain of tears, that I might weep day and night for the slain of the daughter of my people!

The marginal reading intimates the head was exhausted, the fountain was dry. People in prospect of great misery, ask, "Have we waters in our heads for that grief?" "That my sorrows may not dry up, these eyes are always weeping."—Roberts.

Ver. 2. Oh that I had in the wilderness a lodging-place of wayfaring men, that I might leave my people, and go from them! for they *be* all adulterers, an assembly of treacherous men.

People in the East, on their journeys to other towns or countries, are obliged to travel through the most lonely wilds. Hence the native sovereigns, or opulent men, erect what are called rest-houses, or choultries, where the travellers or pilgrims reside for the night. It is in the wilderness where the devotees and ascetics live retired from men: there, either for life, or for a short period, they perform their austerities, and live in cynical contempt of man. When a father is angry with his family, he often exclaims, "If I had but a shade in the wilderness, then should I be happy: I will become a pilgrim, and leave you." Nor is this mere empty declamation to alarm his family; for numbers in every town and village thus leave their homes, and are never heard of more. There are, however, many who remain absent for a few months or years, and then return. Under these circumstances, it is no wonder, when a father or husband threatens his family he will retire to the *kātu*, i. e. wilderness, that they become greatly alarmed. But men who have been reduced in their circumstances become so mortified, that they also retire from their homes, and wander about all their future lives as pilgrims. "Alas! alas! I will retire to the jungle, and live with wild beasts," says the broken-hearted widow.

"Oh for a lodge in some vast wilderness,
Some boundless contiguity of shade." (Cowper.)—Roberts.

Ver. 8. Their tongue *is as* an arrow shot out; it speaketh deceit: *one* speaketh peaceably to his neighbour with his mouth, but in heart he layeth his wait.

The circumstance related by Mr. Mungo Park, in the following extract, might possibly have its parallel in the conduct of the ancients; and if it had, clearly accounts for such figures as that used by the prophet: "Each of the negroes took from his quiver a handful of arrows, and putting two between his teeth, and one in his bow, waved to us with his hand to keep at a distance." (Travels in Africa.)—Burder.

Ver. 17. Thus saith the Lord of hosts, Consider ye and call for the mourning women, that they may come; and send for cunning *women*, that they may come: 18. And let them make haste, and take up a wailing for us, that our eyes may run down with tears, and our eyelids gush out with waters.

The custom of hiring women to weep at funerals, who

were called by the Romans præficæ, has been preserved in the East to this day. J. H. Mayer, one of the latest travellers who visited Egypt and Syria in 1812 and 1813, makes the following observations. "I here found the mourning women, who are several times spoken of in the Bible, and of whom I could not form a proper notion. This ancient custom has been retained here to this day. I have often seen the ceremony, but most clearly and nearest here, in Medini, an Egyptian village. Fifteen or twenty women, dressed in dark, with a black or dark-blue handkerchief round their heads, assemble before the house of the deceased; one of them beats a talourine, the others move in a circle, keeping time to the instrument, singing at the same time the praises of the deceased; in the space of a minute they clasp their hands twenty or thirty times together before their face, and then let them drop to the knee. The constant violent motion changes the ceremony into a dance; every moment a piercing cry, almost like a whistle, is heard from one of the attendants. The mourning continues seven days, during which the nearest female relation, accompanied by mourning women, visit the grave of the deceased, and as they march along, alternately utter this shrill and piercing cry."—Rosenmuller.

Immediately after death the people of the house begin to make a great lamentation: they speak of the virtues of the deceased, and address the body in very touching language. The female relations come together, and beat their breasts. Their long hair is soon dishevelled: they sit down on the floor around the corpse, put their arms on each others' shoulders, and in a kind of mournful recitative bewail the loss of their friend.

I have sometimes been not a little affected to hear their exclamations. See the wife bending over the dead body of her husband; listen to her lamentations:—"Ah, how many years have we been married, and lived happily together? never were we separated, but now! Alas, my king, my kingdom, my master, my wealth, my eyes, my body, my soul, my god. Shall I make an offering to Brama, because thou art taken away? Now will your enemies rejoice, because your are gone. Did the gods call for you? are you in Siva's mount? Though I saw you die, I am still alive. When shall I again see the light of your beautiful countenance? O when again shall I behold his noble mien? how can I look upon that face which was once like the full-blown lotus, but now withered and dry. When shall I again see his graceful bearing in the palanquin. Alas! my name is now the *widow*. When will my aged father again say to you, son-in-law? Do the eyes which saw the splendour of my bridal day witness this deadly scene? In future, by whom will these children be defended? When I am sick, who will go for the far-famed doctor? When my children cry, to whom shall I complain? When they are hungry, to whom will they say, father? Ah! my children, my children, you must now forget that pleasant word."

Hear the daughter over her father.—"My father, had I not my existence from you? Who had me constantly in his arms, lest I should fall? Who would not eat except I was with him? Who fed me with rice and milk? When I was dejected, who purchased me bracelets? Who purchased the beautiful jewel for my forehead? O! my god, you never could bear to look in my withered face. Who will now train my brothers? Who procured me the tali? (husband.) To whom shall I go when my husband is angry? Under whose shade shall my husband and children now go? To whom will my children now say, grandfather? In whose face will my mother now look? Alas! my father, my father, you have left us alone."

Listen to the son over his father:—"From infancy to manhood you have tenderly nursed me. Who has given me learning? Who has taught me to conduct myself with discretion? Who caused me to be selected by many? Who would not eat if I had the headache? Who would not allow me to be fatigued by walking? Who gave me the beautiful palanquin? Who loved to see his son happy? Whose eyes shone like diamonds on his son? Who taught me to prepare the fields? who taught me agriculture? Ah! my father, I thought you would have lived to partake of the fruits of the trees I had planted. Alas! alas! I shall now be called the fatherless son."

Hear the aged father over the body of his son:—"My son, my son, art thou gone? What! am I left in my old age? My lion, my arrow, my blood, my body, my soul, my third eye! gone, gone, gone. Ah! who was so near to his mother? To whom will she now say, son? What! gone without assisting us in our old age? Ah! what will thy betrothed do? I hoped thou wouldst have lived to see our death. Who will now perform the funeral rites for us? Who will light up the pile? Who will perform the annual ceremonies? To the bats, to the bats, my house is now given."

The daughter over the body of her mother says, "Alas! what shall I do in future? We are like chickens, whose mother is killed. Motherless children are beaten on the head. We are like the honeycomb hanging on the trees, at which a stone has been thrown: all, all are scattered." She says to the females who are coming to mourn over her mother, "I am the worm which has to eat a dead body. Though you should give me a large vessel full of water, it will not quench my thirst so well as a *few drops* from the hand of my mother! My mother has gone, and left us for the streets. Who lulled me to repose? Who bathed me near the well? Who fed me with milk? Ah! my father also is dead. Why have you gone without seeing the splendour of my bridal day? Did you not promise to deck me for the festive scene? What! am I to be alone that day? Ah! my mother, how shall I know how to conduct myself? When I am married, should my husband use me ill, to whom shall I go? Who will now teach me to manage household affairs? Ah! there is nothing like a mother! How many pains, how many difficulties, have you had with me? What have I done for you? Alas! alas! had you been long sick, I might have done something for you. Ah! you told me disobedience would be my ruin. You are gone: why did I not obey you? My fate, my fate! my mother, my mother! will you not look at me? Are you asleep? You told us you should die before our father. My mother, will you not again let me hear your voice? When I am in pain, who will say, fear not, fear not? I thought you would have lived to see the marriage of my daughter. Come hither, my infant, look at your grandmother. Was I not nursed at those breasts? You said to my father, when you were dying, 'Love my children.' You said to my husband, 'Cherish my daughter.' Ah! did you not bless us all? My mother, my mother, that name I will not repeat again."

The son says to the mourning women, "Ah! was she not the best of mothers? Did she not conceal my faults? Can I forget her joy when she put the bracelets on my wrists. O! how she did kiss and praise me, when I had learned the alphabet. She was always restless while I was at school, and when I had to return, she was always looking out for me. How often she used to say, 'My son, my son, come and eat;' but now, who will call me?" Then, taking the hand of his deceased mother into his own, he asks, "and are the worms to feed on this hand which has fed me?" Then, embracing her feet, "Ah! these will never more move about this house. When my great days are come, in whose face shall I look? Who will rejoice in my joy? When I go to the distant country, who will be constantly saying, 'Return, return?' Ah! how did she rejoice on my wedding day. Who will now help and comfort my wife? If she did not see me every moment, she was continually saying, 'My son, my son.' Must I now apply the torch to her funeral pile? Alas! alas! I am too young for that. What! have the servants of the funeral house been anxious to get their money? Could they not have waited a few years? What do those bearers want? Have you come to take away my mother?" Then, lying on the bier by her side, he says, "Take me also. Alas! alas! is the hour come? I must now forget you. Your name must never again be in my mouth. I must now perform the annual ceremony. O life, life! the bubble, the bubble!"

Listen to the affectionate brother over the body of his sister:—"Were we not a pair? why are we separated? Of what use am I alone? Where is now my shade? I will now be a wanderer. How often did I bring you the fragrant lotus? but your face was more beautiful than that flower. Did I not procure you jewels? Who gained you the bridegroom? Have I not been preparing to make a splendid show on your nuptial day? Alas! all is vanity. How fatal is this for your betrothed. For whose sins have you been taken away? You have vanished like the goddess Lechimy. In what birth shall we again see you?

How many suiters waited for you? You have poured fire into my bowels: my senses have gone, and I wander about like an evil spirit. Instead of the marriage ceremonies, we are now attending to those of your funeral. I may get another mother, for my father can marry again: I may acquire children; but a sister, never, never. Ah! give me one look: let your lotus-like face open once—one smile. Is this your marriage ceremony? I thought one thing, but fate thought another. You have escaped like lightning: the house is now full of darkness. When I go to the distant town, who will give me her commissions? To whom shall we give your clothes and jewels? My sister, I have to put the torch to your funeral pile. You said, 'Brother, we will never part; we will live together in one house:' but you are gone. I refused to give you to the youth in the far country; but now whither have you gone? To whom shall I now say, I am hungry? Alas! alas! my father planted cocoa, mango, and jack trees in YOUR name, but you have not lived to eat the fruit thereof. I have been to tell them you are gone. Alas! I see her clothes: take them away. Of what use is that palanquin now? Who used to come jumping on the road to meet me? If I have so much sorrow, what must have been that of your mother for ten long moons? Whose evil eye has been upon you? Who aimed the blow? Will there ever again be sorrow like this? My belly smokes. Ah, my sister, your gait, your speech, your beauty, all gone: the flower is withered—the flower is withered. Call for the bier; call for the musicians."

Husbands who love their wives are exceedingly pathetic in their exclamations: they review the scenes of their youth, and speak of their tried and sincere affection. The children she has borne are also alluded to; and, to use an orientalism, the man is plunged into a sea of grief. "What, the apple of my eye gone? My swan, my parrot, my deer, my Lechimy? Her colour was like gold, her gait like the stately swan, her waist was like lightning, her teeth were like pearls, her eyes like the kiyal fish, (oval,) her eyebrows like the bow, and her countenance like the full-grown lotus. Yes, she has gone, the mother of my children. No more welcome, no more smiles in the evening when I return. All the world to me is now as the place of burning. Get ready the wood for my pile. O! my wife, my wife, listen to the voice of thy husband."—ROBERTS.

CHAPTER X.

Ver. 5. They *are* upright as the palm-tree, but speak not; they must needs be borne, because they cannot go. Be not afraid of them; for they cannot do evil, neither also *is it* in them to do good.

From the first clause, it is evident that he alluded also to the shape of their gods. Before the art of carving was carried to perfection, the ancients made their images all of a thickness, straight, having their hands hanging down and close to their sides, the legs joined together, the eyes shut, with a very perpendicular attitude, and not unlike to the body of a palm-tree; such are the figures of those antique Egyptian statues that still remain. The famous Greek architect and sculptor Dædalus, set their legs at liberty, opened their eyes, and gave them a freer and easier attitude. But according to some interpreters, and particularly Mr. Parkhurst, the inspired writer sometimes gives it a more honourable application; selecting it to be the symbol of our blessed Redeemer, who himself bore our sins in his own body on the tree. The voice of antiquity ascribes to the palm, the singular quality of resisting a very great weight hung upon it, and of even bending in the contrary direction, to counterbalance the pressure. Of this circumstance, Xenophon takes notice in his Cyropedia; *και δη πιεζομενοι οι φοινικες ὑπο βαρους ανω κυρτουνται*; "and indeed, palm-trees when loaded with any weight, rise upward, and bend the contrary way." The same observation was made by Plutarch. It has been already observed, that the Hebrew name of the palm-tree is Thamar; and in the Old Testament, we meet with a place in Canaan called Baalthamar, in honour, it is probable, of Baal or the sun, for many ages the object of universal veneration among the Orientals; and who had been worshipped there by the Canaanites under this attribute, as supporting the immense pressure of the celestial fluid on all sides, and sustaining the various parts and operations of universal nature in their respective situations and courses. The symbol of this support, stolen and perverted as usual from the sacred ritual, appears to have been a palm-tree, which was also the symbol of support among the Greeks and Egyptians. With how much greater propriety is it the appointed symbol of him who sustained the inconceivable pressure of divine wrath for his people, and was so far from being utterly depressed under such a load of sin and punishment, that he successfully endured all that the law and justice of his Father demanded, rose victorious over death and the grave; and shall for ever, as these interpreters suppose, "flourish like the palm-tree, and grow or spread abroad like the cedar in Lebanon!" Hence in the outer temple, (the symbol of Jehovah incarnate,) palm-trees were engraved on the walls and doors between the coupled cherubs. And for this reason, the prophetess Deborah is supposed to have fixed her dwelling under a palm-tree, emblematically to express her trust, not in the idolatrous Ashtaroth or Blessers, at that time the abomination of Israel, but in the promised Messiah, who was to be made perfect through sufferings. At the feast of tabernacles, the people of Israel were to take branches of palm-trees; at once to typify Jehovah's dwelling in our nature, and the spiritual support which, by this means, all true believers derive from him; and also, to ascribe to him as the Creator and Preserver of all things, in opposition to Baal or the sun, the honour of sustaining the operations of nature in producing and ripening the fruits of the earth. The feast of tabernacles was also the feast of ingathering; and every person in the least acquainted with the customs of oriental nations knows, that the palm was among idolaters the chosen symbol of the sun, and consecrated to that luminary; and that the temples erected to his honour through all the regions of the East, were surrounded with groves of palm-trees, whose leaf, resembling in shape the solar beam, and maintaining a perpetual verdure, might continually remind the adoring suppliants of the quickening influence and sustaining energy of their favourite deity.—PAXTON.

CHAPTER XII.

Ver. 2. Thou hast planted them; yea, they have taken root: they grow; yea, they bring forth fruit: thou *art* near in their mouth, and far from their reins.

Does a man who has been elevated in society by another, cease to respect his patron; it is said, "Ah, my lord, the tree which you planted has taken root:—in his mouth you are near; but in his heart you are afar off."—ROBERTS.

Ver. 8. My heritage is unto me as a lion in the forest; it crieth out against me: therefore have I hated it. 9. My heritage *is* unto me *as* a speckled bird; the birds round about *are* against her; come ye, assemble all the beasts of the field, come to devour.

See on 1 Sam. 13. 18.

Ver. 9. My heritage *is* unto me *as* a speckled bird, the birds round about *are* against her; come ye, assemble all the beasts of the field, come to devour.

Dr. Boothroyd, "Ravenous birds." The context confirms this rendering, and also the marginal reading, "talons." Considering the NUMEROUS birds of prey in the East, it is no wonder that there are so many allusions in the scriptures to their ravenous propensities. Of a ferocious man it is said, "That fellow is in every place with his talons." "What! wretch, have you come hither to snatch with your talons?" "Alas! alas! how many has this disease snatched away in its talons?" "True, true even my own children have now got talons."—ROBERTS.

Ver. 10. Many pastors have destroyed my vineyard, they have trodden my portion under foot, they have made my pleasant portion a desolate wilderness.

Besides successive invasions by foreign nations, and the systematic spoliation exercised by a despotic government, other causes have conspired to perpetuate the desolation of Judea, and to render abortive the substance that is in it. Among these has chiefly to be numbered its being literally *trodden under foot by many pastors.* Volney devotes a chapter, fifty pages in length, to a description, as he entitles it, "Of the *pastoral*, or *wandering* tribes of Syria," chiefly of the Bedouin Arabs, by whom especially Judea is incessantly traversed. "The pachalics of Aleppo and Damascus may be computed to contain about thirty thousand wandering Turkmen, (Turcomans.) All their property consists in cattle." In the same pachalics, the number of the Curds "exceed twenty thousand tents and huts," or an equal number of armed men. "The Curds are almost everywhere looked upon as robbers. Like the Turkmen, these Curds are *pastors* and *wanderers.* A third wandering people in Syria are the Bedouin Arabs." "It often happens that even individuals turn *robbers*, in order to withdraw themselves from the laws, or from tyranny, unite and form a little camp, which maintain themselves by arms, and, increasing, become new hordes and new tribes. We may pronounce, that in cultivable countries the wandering life originates in the injustice or want of policy of the government; and that the sedentary and the cultivating state is that to which mankind is most naturally inclined." "It is evident that agriculture must be very precarious in such a country, and that, under a government like that of the Turks, it is safer to lead a wandering life than to choose a settled habitation, and rely for subsistence on agriculture." "The Turkmen, the Curds, and the Bedouins, have *no fixed habitations*, but keep *perpetually wandering* with their tents and *herds*, in limited districts of which they look upon themselves as the proprietors. The Arabs spread over the whole frontier of Syria, and even the plains of Palestine."—Thus, contrary to their natural inclination, the peasants, often forced to abandon a settled life, and pastoral tribes in great numbers, or *many*, and without fixed habitations, divide the country, as it were, by mutual consent, and apportion it in limited districts among themselves by an assumed right of property, and the Arabs, subdivided also into different tribes, spread over the plains of Palestine, "wandering perpetually," as if on very purpose to *tread it down.*—What could be more unlikely or unnatural in such a land! yet what more strikingly and strictly true! or how else could the effect of the vision have been seen! Many *pastors* have destroyed my vineyard; they have *trodden* my portion *under foot.*—KEITH.

CHAPTER XIII.

Ver. 4. Take the girdle that thou hast got, which *is* upon thy loins, and arise, go to Euphrates, and hide it there in a hole of the rock.

The girdle of the Orientals is sometimes made of silver or gold, or embroidered silk, or highly died muslin. Its uses are, to keep the lower garments fast to the loins, to strengthen the body, and to command respect. Chiefs have numerous folds of muslin round that part, and they march along with great pomp, thus enlarged in their size. That, therefore, which was of so much use, and which indicated the dignity of the wearer, was to be marred, typifying the degradation of the Jews in their approaching captivity. The Hindoos have a custom of burying certain articles by the side of a tank or river, in order to inflict or prefigure evil in reference to certain obnoxious individuals who are thus placed under the ban. Thus eggs, human hair, thread, a ball of saffron, or a little of the earth on which the devoted person has had his feet, are BURIED in the situations alluded to.—ROBERTS.

Ver. 4. Take the girdle that thou hast got, which *is* upon thy loins, and arise, go to Euphrates, and hide it there in a hole of the rock. 5. So I went, and hid it by Euphrates, as the LORD commanded me. 6. And it came to pass after many days, that the LORD said unto me, Arise, go to Euphrates, and take the girdle from thence, which I commanded thee to hide there. 7. Then I went to Euphrates, and digged, and took the girdle from the place where I had hid it; and, behold, the girdle was marred, it was profitable for nothing.

See on ch. 32. 13, 14.

Ver. 18. Say unto the king and to the queen, Humble yourselves, sit down; for your principalities shall come down, *even* the crown of your glory.

The margin has instead of "principalities," "or head tires." This again alludes to the threatened judgments which were to befall the people and their rulers. Dr. Boothroyd has, instead of "principalities," "the diadem of your glory." Of a proud man who treats another with contempt it is said, "Ah! his turban will soon fall." "Yes, imperious upstart! thy head-dress will soon come down." "Have you heard of the proud wife of Kandan?"—"No." "Her head ornaments have fallen; she is humbled." "Ah," says the bereaved father, over the dead body of his son, "my crown is fallen! my crown is fallen." When men quarrel, it is common for the one to say to the other, "I will beat thee till thy turban fall." When they fight, the great object of the combatants is to pull off each other's turban or head-dress; because it shows that the individual is then disgraced and humbled. The feelings of a man who has his turban knocked off his head, are probably something like those which are produced by the knocking off of a man's wig. For the turban to FALL off the head by ACCIDENT is considered to be a very bad omen. Jehoiakim and his queen were to have their "head tires" brought down; they were to be humbled on account of their sins.—ROBERTS.

Ver. 23. Can the Ethiopian change his skin, or the leopard his spots? *then* may ye also do good, that are accustomed to do evil.

See on ch. 5. 6.

CHAPTER XIV.

Ver. 2. Judah mourneth, and the gates thereof languish; they are black unto the ground; and the cry of Jerusalem is gone up.

"Have you heard that the wife of Muttoo and all the children have died of the cholera? Alas, the poor old man is left alone, and the *gates* are in sorrow—even they pity him."—ROBERTS.

Ver. 3. And their nobles have sent their little ones to the waters: they came to the pits, *and* found no water; they returned with their vessels empty; they were ashamed and confounded, and covered their heads. 4. Because the ground is chapt, for there was no rain in the earth, the ploughmen were ashamed, they covered their heads.

See on Matt. 11. 21.

Ver. 4. Because the ground is chapt, for there was no rain in the earth, the ploughmen were ashamed, they covered their heads.

The description that Sir J. Chardin gives us of the state of these countries, with respect to the cracking of the earth, before the autumnal rains fell, is so lively a comment on Jer. xiv. 4, that I beg leave to introduce it here as a distinct observation. The lands of the East, he says, which the great dryness there causes to crack, are the ground of this figure, which is certainly extremely beautiful; for these dry lands have chinks too deep for a person to see to the bottom of: this may be observed in the Indies more than anywhere, a little before the rains fall, and wherever the lands are rich and hard. The prophet's speaking of ploughmen, shows that he is speaking of the autumnal state of those countries; and if the cracks are so deep from the common dryness of their summers, what must they be when the rains are withheld beyond the usual time, which is the case Jeremiah is referring to.—HARMER.

This refers to a drought which was to take place in Judah. At such times, in the East, the ground is "chapt;" large fissures meet your eye in every direction, and the husbandmen are then ashamed and put to confusion: they know not what to do: to plough the land under such circumstances is of no use; and, therefore, they are obliged to wait till it shall rain. Thus, should the rains be later than usual, the people are daily looking for them, and after one night's fall, the farmers may be seen in every direction working in their fields with the greatest glee, in the full hope of soon casting in the seed.—ROBERTS.

Ver. 5. Yea, the hind also calved in the field, and forsook *it*, because there was no grass.

Some ancient writers allege, that the hind bestows much pains in rearing and instructing her young. She carefully hides her fawn in the thicket, or among the long grass, and corrects it with her foot, when it discovers an inclination prematurely to leave its covert. When it has acquired sufficient strength, she teaches it to run, and to bound from one rock to another; till, conscious of its ability to provide for itself, it bends its rapid course into the boundless waste, and from that moment, loses the recollection of its parent and her tender care. But affectionate as is the hind to her young one, and attentive to its safety and instruction, circumstances occur at times, which diminish, which even extinguish the benignity of her nature, and render her insensible to the sufferings of her own offspring. The slightness of her connexion with guilty man, and her distance from his dwelling, do not prevent her from sharing in the calamities to which all sublunary natures are subjected on account of his sin. The grievous famine which dims the fine eye of the wild ass, and compels her to take refuge on the summits of the mountains, where, sucking in the cooling breeze instead of water, which is no longer to be found, she lingers out a few miserable days, hardens the gentle and affectionate heart of the hind, so that she forsakes her fawn in the open field, because there is no grass, without making a single effort to preserve its existence. She forsakes it when it is newly calved, when her natural affection is commonly strongest, and when it needs most her fostering care; she forsakes it in the desert, where it must soon perish of hunger: deaf to its cries, and indifferent to its sufferings, she leaves it in search of somewhat to prolong her own wretched existence. At such a failure of the kindest affections in the heart of a loving hind, we shall not be surprised, when the dreadful effects of severe famine on the human mind are considered. The prediction of Moses was completely fulfilled: "Thou shalt eat the fruit of thine own body, the flesh of thy sons, and of thy daughters, which the Lord thy God hath given thee, in the siege, and in the straitness, wherewith thine enemies shall distress thee."—"The tender and delicate woman among you, which would not adventure to set the sole of her foot upon the ground, for delicateness and tenderness, her eye shall be evil towards the husband of her bosom, and towards her son, and towards her daughter, and towards the young one that cometh out from between her feet, and towards her children which she shall bear; for she shall eat them for want of all things, secretly, in the siege and straitness."—PAXTON.

Ver. 16. And the people to whom they prophesy shall be cast out in the streets of Jerusalem, because of the famine and the sword; and they shall have none to bury them, their wives, nor their sons, nor their daughters; for I will pour their wickedness upon them.

See on Job 39. 5.

Ver. 22. Are there *any* among the vanities of the Gentiles that can cause rain? or can the heavens give showers? *Art* not thou he, O LORD our God: therefore we will wait upon thee; for thou hast made all these *things*.

There are persons among the South African nations who pretend to have power to bring rain in time of drought, and who are called rain-makers. A nation seldom employs their own rain-maker, but generally thinks those at a distance have more power to produce it than those at home. A rain-maker, from high up the country, once travelled with my party for a few weeks. I asked him seriously, if he really believed that he had power to bring rain when he pleased? His reply was, that "he could not say he had, but he used means to bring it;" such as rolling great stones down the sides of mountains, to draw down the clouds. A rain-maker at Lattakoo who was unsuccessful, first said it was because he had not got sufficient presents of cattle. He then desired them first to bring him a live baboon; hundreds tried but could not catch one. He next demanded a live owl, but they could not find one. No rain coming they called him rogue, impostor, &c. and ordered him away.—CAMPBELL.

CHAPTER XV.

Ver. 3. And I will appoint over them four kinds saith the LORD; the sword to slay, and the dogs to tear, and the fowls of the heaven, and the beasts of the earth, to devour and destroy.

An oriental enemy, as in former ages, cuts down the trees of the country which he invades, destroys the villages, and burns all the corn and provender which he cannot carry off: the surrounding plain, deprived of its verdure, is covered with putrid carcasses and burning ashes; the hot wind wafting its fetid odours, and dispersing the ashes among the tents, renders his encampment extremely disagreeable. During the night the hyenas, jackals, and wild beasts of various kinds, allured by the scent, prowl over the field with a horrid noise; and as soon as the morning dawns, a multitude of vultures, kites, and birds of prey, are seen asserting their claim to a share of the dead. Such was the scene which Forbes contemplated on the plains of Hindostan; "and it was to me," says that writer, "a scene replete with horrid novelty, realizing the prophet's denunciation: 'I will appoint over them four kinds, saith the Lord; the sword to slay, and the dogs to tear, and the fowls of the heaven, and the beasts of the earth, to devour and destroy.'"—PAXTON.

Ver. 7. And I will fan them with a fan in the gates of the land; I will bereave *them* of children, I will destroy my people, *since* they return not from their ways. 8. Their widows are increased to me above the sand of the seas: I have brought upon them, against the mother of the young men, a spoiler at noonday; I have caused *him* to fall upon it suddenly, and terrors upon the city.

When the cholera or any other pestilence rages, it is said, "Alas! this sickness has fanned the people away." "Truly they have been suddenly fanned from the earth." See on Isa. xxx. 24.—ROBERTS.

Ver. 9. She that hath borne seven languisheth; she hath given up the ghost; her sun is gone down while *it was* yet day; she hath been ashamed and confounded: and the residue of them will I deliver to the sword before their enemies, saith the LORD.

Of a person who is dead, it is said, "He is set," and of one dying, "He is setting." Should a beautiful young man or woman be reduced by sickness, it is said, "He is like the evening, which is occupying the place of the morning!"—ROBERTS.

Ver. 18. Why is my pain perpetual, and my wound incurable, *which* refuseth to be healed? wilt thou be altogether unto me as a liar, *and as* waters *that* fail?

"Waters that fail." Heb. "Waters that are not to be trusted," i. e. such as are delusive, such as disappoint expectation. That which Mr. Harmer proposes simply as a query, may be stated as a very probable suggestion, viz. that in these words the prophet alludes to the phenomenon of the *mirage*, so frequently mentioned by eastern travellers. "There is," says Chardin, "a vapour or splendour, in the plains of the desert, formed by the repercussion of the rays from the sand, that appears like a vast lake. Travellers afflicted with thirst are drawn on by such appearances, but coming near find themselves mistaken; it seems to draw back as they advance, or quite vanishes."—"To the southeast, at a distance of four or five miles, we noticed on the yellow sands two black masses, but whether they were the bodies of dead camels, the temporary hair-tents of wandering Bedouins, or any other objects, magnified by the refraction which is so strongly produced in the horizon of the desert, we had no means of ascertaining. With the exception of these masses, all the eastern range of vision presented only one unbroken waste of sand, till its visible horizon ended in the illusive appearance of a lake, thus formed by the heat of a midday sun on a nitrous soil, giving to the parched desert the semblance of water, and reflecting its scanty shrubs upon the view, like a line of extensive forests; but in no direction was either a natural hill, a mountain, or other interruption to the level line of the plain, to be seen." (Buckingham's Travels in Mesopotamia.) "We have suffered very much from the fatigue of this day's journey, and have still five days' march through this waterless desert. The only object to interest us, and relieve the weariness of mind and body, has been the *mirage*, so often described. Some travellers state that this phenomenon has deceived them repeatedly. This I am surprised at, since its peculiar appearance, joined to its occurrence in a desert where the traveller is too forcibly impressed with the recollection that no lakes or standing pools exist, would appear to me to prevent the possibility, that he who has once seen it, can be a second time deceived. Still, this does not diminish the beauty of the phenomenon:—to see amid burning sands and barren hills, an apparently beautiful lake, perfectly calm and unruffled by any breeze, reflecting in its bosom the surrounding rocks, is, indeed, an interesting and wonderful spectacle; but it is a tantalizing sight, traversing the desert on foot, always with a scanty supply of water, and often, owing to their great imprudence, wholly destitute of it." (Hoskins' Travels in Ethiopia.)—Bush.

CHAPTER XVI.

Ver. 5. For thus saith the Lord, Enter not into the house of mourning, neither go to lament nor bemoan them: for I have taken away my peace from this people, saith the Lord, *even* loving-kindness and mercies.

See on 1 Kings 18. 28.

Ver. 6. Both the great and the small shall die in this land: they shall not be buried, neither shall *men* lament for them, nor cut themselves, nor make themselves bald for them.

The cutting off the hair in mourning for the dead, is an eastern, as well as a Grecian custom; and appears to have obtained in the East in the prophetic times, as well as in later ages. That it was practised among the Arabs, in the seventh century, appears by a passage of D'Herbelot. Khaled ben Valid ben Mogaïrah, who was one of the bravest of the Arabs in the time of Mohammed, and surnamed by him, after Khaled had embraced the new religion he introduced into the world, the "sword of God," died under the califate of Omar, in the city of Emessa, in Syria; and he adds, that there was not a female of the house of Mogaïrah, who was his grandfather, either matron or maiden, who caused not her hair to be cut off at his burial. How the hair that was cut off was disposed of, does not appear in D'Herbelot. Among the ancient Greeks, it was sometimes laid upon the dead body; sometimes cast into the funeral pile; sometimes placed upon the grave. Under this variation of management among the Greeks, it would have been an agreeable additional circumstance to have been told, how the females of the house of Mogaïrah disposed of their hair. We are equally ignorant of the manner in which the ancient Jews disposed of theirs, when they cut it off in bewailing the dead. But that they cut it off, upon such occasions, is evident from a passage of the prophet Jeremiah, ch. xvi. 6. "Both the great and the small shall die in this land: they shall not be buried, neither shall men lament for them, nor cut themselves, nor make themselves bald for them." The words do not seem determinately to mean, that those of the male sex only were wont to cut themselves, or make themselves bald for the dead; but that there should be no cutting of the flesh made at all for them, no baldness, leaving it uncertain which sex had been wont to make use of these rites of mourning, who should then omit them. So the interlineary translation of Montanus understands the words.

Both practices seem to have been forbidden by the law of Moses; the soft and impressible temper of the female sex might, it may be imagined, engage them sooner to deviate from the precept, than the firmer disposition of the other. So here we see they were the *females* of the family of Mogaïrah that cut off their hair at the burial of Khaled; not a word of the men. And accordingly we find among the modern Mohammedans, the outward expressions at least of mourning are much stronger among the women than the men: the nearest male relations, Dr. Russel tells us, describing their way of carrying a corpse to be buried, immediately follow it, "and the women close the procession, with dreadful shrieks, while the men all the way are singing prayers out of the Koran. The women go to the tomb every Monday or Thursday, and carry some flowers or green leaves to dress it with. They make a show of grief, often expostulating heavily with the dead person, 'Why he should leave them, when they had done every thing in their power to make life agreeable to him.' This however, by the men, is looked upon as a kind of impiety; and, if overheard, they are chid severely for it: and, I must say, the men generally set them a good example in this respect, by a patient acquiescence in the loss of their nearest relations, and indeed show a firm and steady fortitude under every kind of misfortune."—Harmer.

Ver. 7. Neither shall *men* tear *themselves* for them in mourning, to comfort them for the dead; neither shall *men* give them the cup of consolation to drink for their father or for their mother. 8. Thou shalt not also go into the house of feasting, to sit with them to eat and to drink.

The making a kind of funeral feast was also a method of honouring the dead, used anciently in these countries, and is continued down to these times. The references of commentators here have been, in common, to the Greek and Roman usages; but as it must be more pleasing to learn eastern customs of this kind, I will set down what Sir J. Chardin has given us an account of in one of his manuscripts; and the rather, as some particulars are new to me. "The oriental Christians still make banquets of this kind, (speaking of the ancient Jewish feasts of mourning, mentioned Jer. xvi. 6, 7, and elsewhere,) by a custom derived from the Jews; and I have been many times present at them, among the Armenians in Persia. The 7th verse speaks of those provisions which are wont to be sent to the house of the deceased, and of those healths that are drunk to the survivers of the family, wishing that the dead may have been the victim for the sins of the family. The same, with respect to eating, is practised among the Moors. Where we find the word *comforting* made use of, we are to understand it as signifying the performing these offices." In like manner he explains the *bread of men*, mentioned Ezek. xxiv. 17, as signifying, "the bread of others; the bread sent to mourners; the bread that the neighbours, relations, and friends sent."—Harmer.

D'Oyley and Mant say, "Friends were wont to come, after the funeral was over, to comfort those who had buried the dead, and send in provisions to make a feast, it being supposed that they themselves were so sorrowful as not to be able to think of their necessary food." After the corpse has been consumed on the funeral pile or buried, the relations of the deceased prepare and send a fine kind of gruel (made of the Palmirah killunga) to the funeral house. At the anniversary of a funeral, the relations of the deceased meet to eat together, and give food to the poor. Hence great numbers on these occasions get plenty of provisions. —Roberts.

CHAPTER XVII.

Ver. 6. For he shall be like the heath in the desert, and shall not see when good cometh; but shall inhabit the parched places in the wilderness, *in* a salt land, and not inhabited.

Nothing can be more desolate and solitary than the salt plains of the East. Not a shrub, not a tree, to cheer the eye; even birds and beasts seem affrighted at the scene. What with the silence of these solitudes, the absence of shade, of water, of vegetable and animal life, the traveller moves on with renewed speed to escape from such dreary wastes. Idolatrous Judah had trusted in idols: her sin was written "with a pen of iron;" it could not be erased; and for thus trusting in them, and in man, she was to dwell in "the parched places," the "salt land," which was "not inhabited."—Roberts.

Ver. 8. For he shall be as a tree planted by the waters, and *that* spreadeth out her roots by the river, and shall not see when heat cometh, but her leaf shall be green; and shall not be careful in the year of drought, neither shall cease from yielding fruit.

See on Ps. 1. 3.

To appreciate the beauty of this allusion, it is necessary to think of a parched desert, where there is scarcely a green leaf to relieve the eye. In the midst of that waste is perhaps a tank, a well, or a stream, and near to the water's edge will be seen plants, and shrubs, and trees covered with the most beautiful foliage. So shall be the man who puts his trust in Jehovah.—Roberts.

Ver. 11. *As* the partridge sitteth *on eggs*, and hatcheth *them* not; *so* he that getteth riches, and not by right, shall leave them in the midst of his days, and at his end shall be a fool.

See on 1 Sam. 26. 20.

Ver. 13. O Lord, the hope of Israel, all that forsake thee shall be ashamed, *and* they that depart from me shall be written in the earth, because they have forsaken the Lord, the fountain of living waters.

Dr. Pococke represents the Coptis, who are used by the great men of Egypt for keeping their accounts, &c. as making use of a sort of pasteboard for that purpose, from which the writing is wiped off from time to time with a wet sponge, the pieces of pasteboard being used as slate. Peter Della Valle observed a more inartificial way still of writing short-lived memorandums in India, where he beheld children writing their lessons with their fingers on the ground, the pavement being for that purpose strewed all over with very fine sand. When the pavement was full, they put the writings out: and, if need were, strewed new sand, from a little heap they had before them wherewith to write farther. One would be tempted to think the prophet Jeremiah had this way of writing in view, when he says of them that depart from God, "they shall be written in the earth," ch. xvii. 13. Certainly it means in general, "soon be blotted out and forgotten," as is apparent from Psalm lxix. 28, Ezek. xiii. 9. Dr. Bell's plan of teaching a number of pupils to read at the same time, was taken from what he saw practised in the East; and this is the plan which Mr Lancaster has since greatly improved and extended. The plan of writing on *sand* is still in use in the East.—Clarke in Harmer.

CHAPTER XVIII.

Ver. 3. Then I went down to the potter's house and behold, he wrought a work on the wheels.

The original word means *stones* rather than *wheels*. Dr. Blayney, in a note on this passage, says, "the appellation will appear very proper, if we consider this machine as consisting of a pair of circular stones, placed one upon another like millstones, of which the lower was immoveable, but the upper one turned upon the foot of a spindle, or axis, and had motion communicated to it by the feet of the potter sitting at his work, as may be learned from Ecclus. xxxviii. 29. Upon the top of this upper stone, which was flat, the clay was placed, which the potter, having given the stone the due velocity, formed into shape with his hands."—Burder.

Ver. 6. O house of Israel, cannot I do with you as this potter? saith the Lord. Behold, as the clay *is* in the potter's hand, so *are* ye in my hand, O house of Israel.

It is said of an obedient son, "He is like wax; you may shape him any way you please; you may send him hither and thither, this way or that way, all will be right."—Roberts.

Ver. 14. Will *a man* leave the snow of Lebanon *which cometh* from the rock of the field? *or* shall the cold flowing waters that come from another place be forsaken?

Tacitus, Hist. lib. v. cap. 6. Præcipuum montium Libanum erigit, mirum dictu, tantos inter ardores opacum fidumque nivibus. "Of the mountains of Judea, Libanus is the chief; and, what is surprising, notwithstanding the extreme heat of the climate, is shaded with trees, and perpetually covered with snow." Whether this of Tacitus be strictly true may be doubted. The author of the Universal History informs us, that "Rauwolf, who visited the cedars of Libanus, about mid-summer, complains of the rigour of the cold and snows here. Radzeville, who was here in June, about five years after him, talks of the snow that never melts away from the mountains. Other travellers speak to the same purpose; among whom our Maundrell represents the cedars as growing among the snow; but he was there in the month of May. From all this he might have formed a judgment that the cedars stand always in the midst of the snow: but we are assured of the contrary by another traveller, (La Roque,) according to whom the snows here begin to melt in April, and are no more to be seen after July; nor is, says he, any at all left but in such clifts of the mountains as the sun cannot come at; that the snow begins not to fall again till December; and that he himself, when he was there, saw no snow at all; and it is probable he speaks nothing but the truth."—Burder.

Ver. 17. I will scatter them as with an east wind before the enemy; I will show them the back, and not the face, in the day of their calamity.

Nothing exasperates a person more, when he goes to see another, than for the individual thus visited to arise and turn his back to the visiter. To see a man thus erect with his back towards another has a striking effect on the mind. In the face of the man thus insulted is chagrin and confusion; in the other, contempt and triumph. After a pause, the figure who shows his back moves forward, leaving the other to indulge in spleen and imprecations.—Roberts.

CHAPTER XX.

Ver. 15. Cursed *be* the man who brought tidings to my father, saying, A man-child is born unto thee; making him very glad.

I have already noticed the great anxiety of the people of

the East to have male children. At the time of parturition the husband awaits in an adjoining room or the garden; and so soon as the affair shall be over, should the little stranger be a son, the midwife rushes outside, and beats the thatch on the roof three times, and exclaims aloud, "A male child! a male child! a male child is born!" Should the infant be a female, not a word is said, and the father knows what is the state of the case. When a person conducts himself in an unmanly way, the people ask, "Did they beat the roof for you? Was it not said to your father, A male child is born?"—ROBERTS.

CHAPTER XXII.

Ver. 13. Wo unto him that buildeth his house by unrighteousness, and his chambers by wrong; *that* useth his neighbour's service without wages, and giveth him not for his work.

Upper chambers. The principal rooms anciently in Judea were those above, as they are to this day at Aleppo; the ground-floor being chiefly made use of for their horses and servants. Busbequius, speaking of the house he had hired at Constantinople, says, "Pars superior, sola habitatur; pars inferior equorum stabulationi destinata est. The upper part is alone inhabited; the lower is allotted for the horses' stabling." "At Prevesa the houses are all of wood, for the most part with only a ground-floor, and where there is one story, the communication to it is by a ladder or wooden steps on the outside, sheltered, however, by the overhanging eaves of the roof. In this case the horses and cattle occupy the lower chamber, or it is converted into a warehouse, and the family live on the floor above, in which there are seldom more than two rooms." (Hobhouse.) "In Greece, the wealthiest among them, the papas, have houses with two rooms raised on a second floor, the lower part being divided into a stable, cowhouse, and cellar (Dodwell.)—BURDER.

Ver. 24. *As* I live, saith the LORD, though Coniah the son of Jehoiakim, king of Judah, were the signet upon my right hand, yet would I pluck thee thence.

The SIGNET is always worn on the little finger of the right hand. Things which are dear are spoken of as that ornament. "O my child, you are as my signet." "We are like the ring-seal, and the impression;" meaning, the child resembles the father. "Never will I see him more; were he my signet, I would throw him away." "I do that! rather would I throw away my ring-seal."—ROBERTS.

CHAPTER XXIII.

Ver. 25. I have heard what the prophets said, that prophesy lies in my name, saying, I have dreamed, I have dreamed.

Exactly in the same way do the heathen priests and devotees impose on the people at this day. Have they some profitable speculation which requires the sanction of the gods, they affect to have had a visit from them, and they generally manage to relate some secret transaction (as a proof) which the individual concerned supposed was only known to himself.—ROBERTS.

CHAPTER XXIV.

Ver. 6. For I will set mine eyes upon them for good, and I will bring them again to this land: and I will build them, and not pull *them* down; and I will plant them, and not pluck *them* up.

The eye is spoken of as the source, and also as the cause, of a blessing. Thus, has a person been sick, and is he asked, how did you recover? he replies, "The gods fixed their eyes upon me." Does a man promise a favour, he says, "I will place my eyes upon you." Does he refuse, he says, "I will not put my eyes on you."—ROBERTS.

CHAPTER XXV.

Ver. 10. Moreover, I will take from them the voice of mirth, and the voice of gladness, the voice of the bridegroom, and the voice of the bride, the sound of the millstones, and the light of the candle.

"In the East they grind their corn at break of day. When one goes out in a morning, he hears everywhere the noise of the mill, and this noise often awakens people." (Chardin.) He supposes also that songs are made use of when they are grinding. It is very possible then, that when the sacred writers speak of the noise of the millstones, they may mean the noise of the songs of those who worked them. This earliness of grinding makes the going of Rechab and Baanah to fetch wheat the day before from the palace, to be distributed to the soldiers under them, very natural. (2 Sam. iv. 2—7.) They are female slaves who are generally employed at these handmills. It is extremely laborious, and esteemed the lowest employment in the house. (Harmer.) Mr. Park observed this custom in the interior parts of Africa, when he was invited into a hut by some female natives, in order to shelter him from the inclemency of a very rainy night. While thus employed, one of the females sung a song, the rest joining in a sort of chorus.

The houses of Egypt are never without lights. Maillet assures us, (Lett. ix. p. 10,) they burn lamps not only all the night long, but in all the inhabited apartments of a house; and that the custom is so well established, that the poorest people would rather retrench part of their food than neglect it. This remark will elucidate several passages of scripture. In the words above referred to, Jeremiah makes the taking away of the light of the *candle* and total destruction the same thing. Job describes the destruction of a family among the Arabs, and the rendering one of their habitations desolate, after the same manner: "How oft is the candle of the wicked put out, and how oft cometh their destruction upon them!" Job xviii. 5. xxi. 17. On the other hand, when God promises to give David a lamp always in Jerusalem, (1 Kings xi. 36,) considered in this point of view, it is an assurance that his house should never become desolate.—BURDER.

The people of the East who can afford it, have always a lamp burning in their room the whole of the night. It is one of their greatest comforts; because, should they not be able to sleep, they can then look about them, and amuse themselves. "Evil spirits are kept away, as they do not like the light!" Lechemy, the beautiful goddess, also takes pleasure in seeing the rooms lighted up. But that which is of the MOST importance is, the light keeps off the serpents and other poisonous reptiles.—ROBERTS.

Ver. 15. For thus saith the Lord God of Israel unto me, Take the wine-cup of this fury at my hand, and cause all the nations to whom I send thee, to drink it. 16. And they shall drink, and be moved, and be mad, because of the sword that I will send among them.

See on Mark 15. 2, 3.

Ver. 16. And they shall drink, and be moved, and be mad, because of the sword that I will send among them.

"This is an allusion to those intoxicating draughts which used to be given to malefactors just before their execution, to take away their senses. Immediately before the execution began, says the Talmud, they gave the condemned a quantity of frankincense in a cup of wine, to stupify him, and render him insensible of his pain. The compassionate ladies of Jerusalem generally provided this draught at their own cost. The foundation of this custom was the command of Solomon, Prov. xxxi. 6. "Give strong drink to him that is ready to perish, and wine to those that be of heavy hearts."—LEWIS.

Ver. 38. He hath forsaken his covert, as the lion: for their land is desolate, because of the fierceness of the oppressor, and because of his fierce anger.

See on Isa. 38. 14.

CHAPTER XXVI.

Ver. 18. Micah the Morasthite prophesied in the days of Hezekiah king of Judah, and spake to all the people of Judah, saying, Thus saith the LORD of hosts, Zion shall be ploughed *like* a field, and Jerusalem shall become heaps, and the mountain of the house as the high places of the forest.

See on Mic. 3. 12.

CHAPTER XXXI.

Ver. 15. Thus saith the LORD, A voice was heard in Ramah, a lamentation, *and* bitter weeping; Rachel weeping for her children, refused to be comforted for her children, because they *were* not.

From Le Bruyn's Voyage in Syria we learn, that "the women go in companies, on certain days, out of the towns to the tombs of their relations, in order to weep there; and when they are arrived, they display very deep expressions of grief. While I was at Ramah, I saw a very great company of these weeping women, who went out of the town. I followed them, and after having observed the place they visited adjacent to their sepulchres, in order to make their usual lamentations, I seated myself on an elevated spot. They first went and placed themselves on their sepulchres, and wept there; where, after having remained about half an hour, some of them rose up, and formed a ring, holding each other by the hand, as is done in some country-dances. Quickly two of them quitted the others, and placed themselves in the centre of the ring; where they made so much noise in screaming, and in clapping their hands, as, together with their various contortions, might have subjected them to the suspicion of madness. After that they returned, and seated themselves to weep again, till they gradually withdrew to their homes. The dresses they wore were such as they generally used, white, or any other colour; but when they rose up to form a circle together, they put on a black veil over the upper parts of their persons."—BURDER.

Ver. 18. I have surely heard Ephraim bemoaning himself *thus:* Thou hast chastised me, and I was chastised, as a bullock unaccustomed *to the yoke:* turn thou me, and I shall be turned; for thou *art* the LORD my God.

The simile is a most apt one. I had frequent opportunities of witnessing the conduct of oxen when for the first time put into the yoke to assist in dragging the wagons. On observing an ox that had been in the yoke for seven or eight hundred miles beginning to get weak, or his hoofs to be worn down to the quick, by treading on the sharp gravel, a fresh ox was put into the yoke in his place. When the selection fell on an ox I had received as a present from some African king, of course one completely unaccustomed to the yoke, such generally made a strenuous struggle for liberty,—repeatedly breaking the yoke, and attempting to make its escape. At other times such bullocks lay down upon their sides or backs, and remained so in defiance of the Hottentots, though two or three of them would be lashing them with their ponderous whips. Sometimes, from pity to the animal, I would interfere, and beg them to be less cruel. "Cruel!" they would say, "it is *mercy*, for if we do not conquer him now, he will require to be so beaten all his life." Some oxen would seem convinced of the folly of opposing the will of the Hottentots by the end of the first day; some about the middle of the second; while some would continue the struggle to the third; after which they would go on as willingly and quietly as any of their neighbour oxen. They seemed convinced that their resisting was fruitless as kicking against the pricks, or sharp pointed iron, which they could not injure, but that every kick they gave only injured themselves.—CAMPBELL.

Ver. 19. Surely after that I was turned, I repented; and after that I was instructed, I smote upon *my* thigh: I was ashamed, yea, even confounded, because I did bear the reproach of my youth.

It appears to have been the custom, when a person was in sorrow, to smite his thigh. Is it not interesting to know that the people of the East, when in similar circumstances, do the same thing at this day? See the bereaved father; he smites his right thigh, and cries aloud, "*Iyo! Iyo!*" alas! alas!—ROBERTS.

Ver. 28. And it shall come to pass, *that* like as I have watched over them, to pluck up, and to break down, and to throw down, and to destroy, and to afflict; so will I watch over them, to build, and to plant, saith the LORD.

See on ch. 5. 6.

Ver. 29. In those days they shall say no more, The fathers have eaten a sour grape, and the children's teeth are set on edge. 30. But every one shall die for his own iniquity: every man that eateth the sour grape, his teeth shall be set on edge.

See on Gen. 49. 11.

CHAPTER XXXII.

Ver. 11. So I took the evidence of the purchase, *both* that which was sealed *according* to the law and custom, and that which was open.

The double evidences of Jeremiah's purchase, which are mentioned ch. xxxii. 11, seems a strange management in their civil concerns; yet something of the like kind obtains still among them. Both the writings were in the hands of Jeremiah, and at his disposal, verse 14; for what purpose then were duplicates made? To those that are unacquainted with the eastern usages, it must appear a question of some difficulty.

"The open or unsealed writing," says an eminent commentator, "was either a copy of the sealed deed, or else a certificate of the witnesses, in whose presence the deed of purchase was signed and sealed."—(Lowth.) But it still recurs, of what use was a copy that was to be buried in the same earthen vessel, and run exactly the same risks with the original? If by a certificate is meant a deed of the witnesses, by which they attested the contract of Jeremiah and Hananeel, and the original deed of purchase had no witnesses at all, then it is natural to ask, why were they made separate writings? and much more, why was one sealed, and not the other?

Sir J. Chardin's account of modern managements, which he thinks illustrates this ancient story, is, "that after a contract is made, it is kept by the party himself, not the notary; and they cause a copy to be made, signed by the notary alone, which is shown upon proper occasions, and never exhibit the other." According to this account, the two books were the same, the one sealed up with solemnity, and not to be used on common occasions; that which was open, the same writing, to be perused at pleasure, and made use of upon all occasions. The sealed one answered to a record with us; the other a writing for common use.—HARMER.

Ver. 13. And I charged Baruch before them, saying, 14. Thus saith the LORD of hosts, the God of Israel, Take these evidences, this evidence of the purchase, both which is sealed, and this evidence which is open, and put them in an earthen vessel, that they may continue many days.

Whatever materials the ancient Jews wrote upon, they were liable to be easily destroyed by the dampness when hidden in the earth. It was therefore thought requisite to enclose them in something that might keep them from the damp, lest they should decay and be rendered useless. In those days of roughness, when war knew not the softenings of later times, men were wont to bury in the earth every part of their property that could be concealed after that manner, not only silver and gold, but wheat, barley, oil, and honey; vestments and writings too. For that I apprehend was the occasion of Jeremiah's ordering, that the writings he delivered to Baruch, mentioned in his thirty-second chapter, should be put into an earthen vessel.—HARMER.

CHAPTER XXXIII.

Ver. 13. In the cities of the mountains, in the cities of the vale, and in the cities of the south, and in the land of Benjamin, and in the places about Jerusalem, and in the cities of Judah, shall the flocks pass again under the hands of him that telleth *them*, saith the LORD.

See on Ps. 23. 4.

It was the custom of more accurate or severe masters, to number their flocks in the morning when they went out to pasture, and again in the evening when they returned to the fold. But the most indulgent masters seem to have always numbered their flocks in the evening; a fact clearly attested by Virgil in the close of his sixth Eclogue:

"Cogere donec oves stabulis numerumque referre
Jussit, et invito processit vesper Olympo."

"Till vesper warned the shepherds to pen their sheep in the folds and recount their number; and advanced on the sky, full loth to lose the song." Agreeably to this custom, the prophet Jeremiah is directed by the Spirit of God to promise, "The flocks shall pass again under the hands of him that telleth them, saith the Lord." The reference of these words to the rod of the shepherd numbering his flock, when they return from the pasture, appears from the verse immediately preceding: "Thus saith the Lord of hosts, again in this place, which is desolate, without man and without beast, and in all the cities thereof, shall be an habitation of shepherds, causing their flocks to lie down."—PAXTON.

CHAPTER XXXIV.

Ver. 3. And thou shalt not escape out of his hand, but shalt surely be taken, and delivered into his hand; and thine eyes shall behold the eyes of the king of Babylon, and he shall speak with thee mouth to mouth, and thou shalt go to Babylon.

To say, your eyes shall see the eyes of another, implies pleasure or pain. Thus, to comfort one who greatly desires to see another, but who fears he shall not have that pleasure, it is said, "Fear not, your eyes shall see his eyes." But, should a person have committed some crime, it is said to him, in order to make him afraid, "Yes; your eyes shall see his eyes," *i. e.* of the person who has been injured, and who has power to inflict punishment.—ROBERTS.

CHAPTER XXXVI.

Ver. 22. Now the king sat in the winter-house in the ninth month: and *there was a fire* on the hearth burning before him.

In Palestine, and the surrounding regions, the coldness of the night in all the seasons of the year, is often very inconvenient. The king of Judah is described by the prophet, as sitting in his winter-house in the ninth month, corresponding to the latter end of November and part of December, with a fire burning on the hearth before him. This answers to the state of the weather at Aleppo, where, as Russel informs us, the most delicate people make no fires till the end of November. The Europeans, resident in Syria, he observes in a note, continue them till March; the people of the country, seldom longer than February; but fires are occasionally made in the wet seasons, not only in March, but in April also, and would be acceptable, at the gardens, sometimes even in May. Dr. Pococke, in his journey to Jerusalem, being conducted by an Arab to his tent, found his wife and family warming themselves by the fire on the seventeenth of March; and on the eighth of May, he was treated with a fire to warm him, by the governor of Galilee. The nights in that season are often very cold; and of this the inhabitants are rendered more sensible by the heats of the day. In May and June, and even in July, travellers very often put on fires in the evening. This statement clearly discovers the reason, that the people who went to Gethsemane to apprehend our Lord, kindled a fire of coals, to warm themselves at the time of the passover, which happened in the spring. But it is not only in elevated situations, as that on which the city of Jerusalem stands, that the cold of the night is so piercing; the traveller has to encounter its severity on the low-lying plains, by the seaside, and in the sandy deserts, where, during the day, beneath the scorching sunbeam, he could scarcely breathe. The severe cold of the morning compelled Mr. Doubdan to remain some hours at Joppa, in a poor Greek hovel, before he could set out for Rama. At ancient Tyre his condition was still more distressing. On the sixteenth of May, he found the heat near that once-renowned mar of nations so great, that though he and his party took their repast on the grass, under a large tree, by the side of a small river, yet he complains, "they were burnt up alive." After attempting in vain to prosecute their voyage, night overtook them at the ruins of Tyre. Near those ruins, they were obliged to pass a considerable part of the night, not without suffering greatly from the cold, which was as violent and sharp as the heat of the day had been intense. Our traveller acknowledges, that he shook, as in the depth of winter, more than two or three full hours.—PAXTON.

The "hearth" here mentioned was in all probability the *tandoor* of the East, of which so full an account is given in Smith and Dwight's Travels in Armenia.—"What attracted our attention most this stormy day, was the apparatus for warming us. It was the species of oven called *tannoor*, common throughout Armenia, and also in Syria, but converted here for purposes of warmth into what is called a *tandoor*. A cylindrical hole is sunk about three feet in the ground in some part of the room, with a flue entering it at the bottom to convey a current of air to the fire which heats it. For the emission of smoke no other provision is made than the open sky-light in the terrace. When used for baking bread, the dough, being flattened to the thickness of common pasteboard, perhaps a foot and a half long by a foot broad, is stuck to its smooth sides by means of a cushion upon which it is first spread. It indicates, by cleaving off, when it is done, and being then packed down in the family chest, it lasts at least a month in the winter and ten days in the summer. Such is the only bread known in the villages of Armenia; and even the cities of Eriván and Tebriz offer no other variety than a species perhaps only twice as thick, and so long that it might almost be sold by the yard. To bake it, the bottom of a large oven is covered with pebbles, (except one corner where a fire is kept constantly burning,) and upon them, when heated, the sheets of dough are spread. The convenience of such thin bread, where knives and forks are not used, and spoons are rare, is that a piece of it doubled enables you to take hold of a mouthful of meat more delicately than with your bare fingers; or, when properly folded, helps you to convey a spoonful safely to your mouth to be eaten with the spoon itself. When needed for purposes of warmth, the tannoor is easily transformed into a tandoor. A round stone is laid upon the mouth of the oven, when well heated, to stop the draught; a square frame about a foot in height is then placed above it; and a thick coverlet, spread over the whole, lies upon the ground around it, to confine the warmth. The family squat upon the floor, and warm themselves by extending their legs and hands into the heated air beneath it, while the frame holds, as occasion requires, their lamp or their food. Its economy is evidently great. So full of crevices are the houses, that an open fireplace must consume a great quantity of fuel, and then almost fail of warming even the air in its immediate vicinity. The tandoor, heated once, or at the most twice, in twenty-four hours by a small quantity of fuel, keeps one spot continually warm for the relief of all numb fingers and frozen toes."—BUSH.

Ver. 30. Therefore thus saith the LORD of Jehoiakim king of Judah: He shall have none to sit upon the throne of David: and his dead body shall be cast out in the day to the heat, and in the night to the frost.

It may not be improper here to remark upon the wisdom and goodness of God displayed in the temperature of an oriental sky. The excessive heats of the day, which are sometimes incommodious, even in the depth of winter, are compensated and rendered consistent with animal and vegetable life, by a corresponding degree of coolness in the night. The patriarch Jacob takes notice of this fact, in his expostulation with Laban: "By day the heat consumed me, and the frost by night." Mr. Bruce, in like manner, frequently remarks in his journey through the deserts of Senaar, where the heat of the day was almost insupportable, that the coldness of the night was very great. When Rauwolf travelled on the Euphrates, he was wont to wrap himself up in a frieze coat in the nighttime, to defend himself from the frost and dew, which, he observes, are very frequent and violent there. Thevenot traversed the very fields where Jacob tended the flocks of Laban; and he found the heats of the day so intense, that although he wore upon his head a large black handkerchief after the manner of the Orientals when they travel, yet, his forehead was frequently so scorched, as to swell exceedingly, and actually to suffer excoriation; his hands being more exposed to the burning sun, were continually parched; and he learned from experience, to sympathize with the toil-worn shepherd of the East. In Europe, the days and nights resemble each other, with respect to the qualities of heat and cold; but if credit be due to the representations of Chardin, it is quite otherwise in oriental climates. In the Lower Asia, particularly, the day is always hot; and as soon as the sun is fifteen degrees above the horizon, no cold is felt in the depth of winter itself: on the contrary, the nights are as cold as at Paris in the month of March. It is for this reason, that in Turkey and Persia they always used furred habits in the country, such only being sufficient to resist the cold of the night. Chardin travelled in Arabia and Mesopotamia, the scene of Jacob's adventures, both in winter and in summer, and attested on his return the truth of what the patriarch asserted, that he was scorched with heat in the day, and stiffened with cold in the night. This difference in the state of the air in twenty-four hours, is in some places extremely great, and according to that respectable traveller, not conceivable by those who have not seen it; one would imagine, they had passed in a moment from the violent heats of summer to the depth of winter. Thus it has pleased a beneficent Deity to temper the heat of the day by the coolness of the night, without which, the greatest part of the East would be a parched and steril desert, equally destitute of vegetable and animal life. This account is confirmed by a modern traveller. When Campbell was passing through Mesopotamia, he sometimes lay at night out in the open air, rather than enter a town; on which occasions, he says, "I found the weather as piercing cold, as it was distressfully hot in the daytime." The same difference between the days and nights, has been observed on the Syrian bank of the Euphrates; the mornings are cold, and the days intensely hot. This difference is distinctly marked in these words of the prophet: "Therefore, thus saith the Lord of Jehoiakim, king of Judah: he shall have none to sit upon the throne of David; and his dead body shall be cast out in the day to the heat, and in the night to the frost." So just and accurate are the numerous allusions of scripture to the natural state of the oriental regions; and so necessary it is to study with care the natural history of those celebrated and interesting countries, to enable us to ascertain with clearness and precision, the meaning, or to discern the beauty and force of numerous passages of the sacred volume.—PAXTON.

CHAPTER XXXVII.

Ver. 15. Wherefore the princes were wroth with Jeremiah, and smote him, and put him in prison in the house of Jonathan the scribe: for they had made that the prison.

The treatment of those that are shut up in the eastern prisons differs from our usages, but serves to illustrate several passages of scripture. Chardin relates several circumstances concerning their prisons, which are curious, and should not be omitted. In the first place, he tells us that the eastern prisons are not public buildings erected for that purpose; but a part of the house in which their criminal judges dwell. As the governor and provost of a town, or the captain of the watch, imprisoned such as are accused in their own houses, they set apart a canton of it for that purpose, when they are put into these offices, and choose for the jailer the most proper person they can find of their domestics.

Sir John supposes the prison in which Joseph, together with the chief butler and chief baker of Pharaoh, was put, was in Potiphar's own house. But I would apply this account to the illustration of another passage of scripture: "Wherefore," it is said, Jer. xxxvii. 15, "the princes were wroth with Jeremiah, and smote him, and put him in prison in the house of Jonathan the scribe; for they had made that the prison." Here we see a dwelling-house was made a prison; and the house of an eminent person, for it was the house of a scribe, which title marks out a person of quality: it is certain it does so in some places of Jeremiah, particularly ch. xxxvi. 12, "Then he went down into the king's house into the scribe's chamber, and lo, all the princes sat there, even Elishama the scribe, and Delaiah," &c. The making the house of Jonathan the prison, would not now, in the East, be doing him any dishonour, or occasion the looking upon him in a mean light; it would rather mark out the placing him in an office of importance. It is probable it was so anciently, and that his house became a prison, when Jonathan was made the royal scribe, and became, like the chamber of Elishama, one of the prisons of the people.—HARMER.

Ver. 21. Then Zedekiah the king commanded that they should commit Jeremiah into the court of the prison, and that they should give him daily a piece of bread out of the bakers' street, until all the bread in the city were spent. Thus Jeremiah remained in the court of the prison.

In primitive times, an oven was designed only to serve a single family, and to bake for them no more than the bread of one day; a custom which still continues in some places of the East; but the increase of population in the cities, higher degrees of refinement, or other causes in the progress of time, suggested the establishment of public bakehouses. They seem to have been introduced into Judea long before the captivity; for the prophet Jeremiah speaks of "the bakers' street," in the most familiar manner, as a place well known. This, however, might be only a temporary establishment, to supply the wants of the soldiers assembled from other places, to defend Jerusalem. If they received a daily allowance of bread, as is the practice still in some eastern countries, from the royal bakehouses, the order of the king to give the prophet daily a piece of bread, out of the street where they were erected, in the same manner as the defenders of the city, was perfectly natural. The custom alluded to still maintains its ground at Algiers, where the unmarried soldiers receive every day from the public bakehouses a certain number of loaves. Pitts indeed asserts, that the Algerines have public bakehouses for the accommodation of the whole city. The women prepare their dough at home, and the bakers send their boys about the streets, to give notice of their being ready to receive and carry it to the bakehouses. They bake their cakes every day, or every other day, and give the boy who brings the bread home, a piece or little cake for the baking, which is sold by the baker. Small as the eastern loaves are, it appears from this account, that they give a piece of one only to the baker, as a reward for his trouble. This will perhaps illustrate Ezekiel's account of the false prophets receiving pieces of bread by way of gratuities: "And will ye pollute me among my people, for handfuls of barley, and pieces of bread?" These are compensations still used in the East, but of the meanest kind, and for services of the lowest sort.—PAXTON.

The bazars at Ispahan are very extensive, and it is possible to walk under cover in them for two or three miles together. The trades are here collected in separate bodies which make it very convenient to purchasers; and, indeed we may from analogy suppose the same to have been the case from the most ancient times, when we consider the command of Zedekiah to feed Jeremiah from the bakers' street.—MORIER.

CHAPTER XXXVIII.

Ver. 6. Then took they Jeremiah, and cast him into the dungeon of Malchiah the son of Hammelech, that *was* in the court of the prison: and they let down Jeremiah with cords. And in the dungeon *there was* no water, but mire: so Jeremiah sunk in the mire.

There were two prisons in Jerusalem; of which one was called the king's prison, which had a lofty tower that overlooked the royal palace, with a spacious court before it, where state prisoners were confined. The other was designed to secure debtors and other inferior offenders: and in both these the prisoners were supported by the public, on bread and water. Suspected persons were sometimes confined under the custody of state officers, in their own houses; or rather a part of the house which was occupied by the great officers of state, was occasionally converted into a prison. This seems to be a natural conclusion from the statement of the prophet Jeremiah, in which he gives an account of his imprisonment: "Wherefore, the princes were wroth with Jeremiah, and smote him, and put him in prison, in the house of Jonathan the scribe; for they had made that the prison." This custom, so different from the manners of our country, has descended to modern times; for when Chardin visited the East, their prisons were not public buildings erected for that purpose, but, as in the days of the prophet, a part of the house in which their criminal judges reside. "As the governor, or provost of a town," says our traveller, "or the captain of the watch, imprison such as are accused, in their own houses, they set apart a canton of them for that purpose, when they are put into these offices, and choose for the jailer, the most proper person they can find of their domestics." The royal prison in Jerusalem, and especially the dungeon, into which the prisoner was let down naked, seems to have been a most dreadful place. The latter cannot be better described, than in the words of Jeremiah himself, who for his faithfulness to God and his country, in a most degenerate age, had to encounter all its horrors: "Then took they Jeremiah, and cast him into the dungeon that was in the court of the prison; and they let him down with cords; and in the dungeon there was no water, but mire; and his feet sunk in the mire." A discretionary power was given to the keeper, to treat his prisoners as he pleased; all that was expected of him being only to produce them when required. If he kept them in safe custody, he might treat them well or ill as he chose; he might put them in irons or not; shut them up close, or indulge them with greater liberty; admit their friends and acquaintances to visit them, or suffer no person to see them. The most worthless characters, the most atrocious criminals, if they can bribe the jailer and his servants with large fees, shall be lodged in his own apartment, and have the best accommodation it can afford; but if he be the enemy of those committed to his charge, or have received larger presents from their persecutors, he will treat them in the most barbarous manner.—Paxton.

Ver. 7. Now when Ebed-melech the Ethiopian, one of the eunuchs which was in the king's house, heard that they had put Jeremiah in the dungeon: the king then sitting in the gate of Benjamin.

The possession of black eunuchs is not very common in the Levant; they are hardly anywhere to be found, except in the palaces of the sovereign or of the branches of the royal family. When the Baron De Tott's wife and mother-in-law were permitted to visit Asma Sultana, daughter of the Emperor Achmet, and sister of the reigning prince, he tells us, that "at the opening of the third gate of her palace, several black eunuchs presented themselves, who, with each a white staff in his hand, preceded the visiters, leading them to a spacious apartment, called the chamber of strangers." He adds, that to have such attendants is a piece of great state, as the richest people have not more than one or two of them.—Harmer.

CHAPTER XXXIX.

Ver. 6. Then the king of Babylon slew the sons of Zedekiah in Riblah before his eyes: also the king of Babylon slew all the nobles of Judah. 7. Moreover, he put out Zedekiah's eyes, and bound him with chains, to carry him to Babylon.

By an inhuman custom, which is still retained in the East, the eyes of captives taken in war are not only put out but sometimes literally scooped or dug out of their sockets. This dreadful calamity Samson had to endure, from the unrelenting vengeance of his enemies. In a posterior age, Zedekiah, the last king of Judah and Benjamin, after being compelled to behold the violent death of his sons and nobility, had his eyes put out, and was carried in chains to Babylon. The barbarous custom long survived the decline and fall of the Babylonian empire, for by the testimony of Mr. Maurice, in his History of Hindostan, the captive princes of that country were often treated in this manner, by their more fortunate rivals; a red-hot iron was passed over their eyes, which effectually deprived them of sight, and at the same time of their title and ability to reign.—Paxton.

CHAPTER XLI.

Ver. 5. That there came certain from Shechem, from Shiloh, and from Samaria, *even* fourscore men, having their beards shaven, and their clothes rent, and having cut themselves, with offerings and incense in their hand, to bring *them* to the house of the Lord.

See on 1 Kings 18. 28.

Ver. 8. But ten men were found among them that said unto Ishmael, Slay us not: for we have treasures in the field, of wheat, and of barley, and of oil, and of honey. So he forbare, and slew them not among their brethren.

See on Job 27. 18.

This refers to stores they had concealed, as is clear from the mentioning of "the oil and honey." During the time of the Kandian war many prisoners received lenient treatment, because of the assurance that they had treasures hid in the field, and that they should be the property of their keepers. In some cases there can be no doubt there were large sums thus acquired by certain individuals.—Roberts.

CHAPTER XLII.

Ver. 2. And said unto Jeremiah the prophet, Let, we beseech thee, our supplication be accepted before thee, and pray for us unto the Lord thy God, *even* for all this remnant; (for we are left *but* a few of many, as thine eyes do behold us.)

The margin has this, "Let our supplication fall before thee." "O my lord," says the suppliant, "let my prayers be prostrate at your feet." "O forget not my requests, but let them ever surround your feet." "Allow my supplications to lie before you." "Ah! give but a small place for my prayers." "At your feet, my lord, at your feet, my lord, are all my requests."—Roberts.

CHAPTER XLIII.

Ver. 9. Take great stones in thy hand, and hide them in the clay in the brick-kiln, which *is* at the entry of Pharaoh's house in Tahpanhes, in the sight of the men of Judah.

If their bricks, in those hot and dry countries, are in general only dried in the sun, not burnt, there is some reason to be doubtful whether the Hebrew word מלבן *malben* signifies a brick-kiln, as multitudes besides our translators have supposed. The bricks used in the construction of the Egyptian canals, must have been well burnt: those dried in the sun could have lasted no time. But bricks for this use could not have been often wanted. They were not necessary for the building those treasure cities which are mentioned Exod. i. 11. One of the pyramids is built with sun-dried bricks, which Sir J. Chardin tells us are *durable*, as well as accommodated to the temperature of the air there; which last circumstance is, I presume, the reason they are in such common use in these very hot countries. There must then be many places used in the East for the making bricks, where there are no kilns at all; and such a place, I apprehend, the word מלבן *malben* signifies; and it should seem to be the perpetual association of a kiln, and of the places where bricks are made, with us in the West, that has occasioned the word to be translated *brick-kiln*. The interpretation I have given best suits Jer. xliii. 9. The smoke of the brick-kiln, in the neighbourhood of a royal Egyptian palace, would not have agreed very well with the eastern cleanliness and perfumes.—HARMER.

Ver. 12. And I will kindle a fire in the houses of the gods of Egypt; and he shall burn them, and carry them away captives: and he shall array himself with the land of Egypt, as a shepherd putteth on his garment: and he shall go forth from thence in peace.

The deserts that lie between Egypt and Syria are at this day terribly infested by the wild Arabs. "In travelling along the seacoast of Syria, and from Suez to Mount Sinai," says Dr. Shaw, "we were in little or no danger of being robbed or insulted; in the Holy Land, and upon the isthmus between Egypt and the Red Sea, our conductors cannot be too numerous." He then goes on to inform us, that when he went from Ramah to Jerusalem, though the pilgrims themselves were more than six thousand, and were escorted by four bands of Turkish infantry, exclusive of three or four hundred spahees, (cavalry,) yet were they most barbarously insulted and beaten by the Arabs.

This may lead us, perhaps, to the true sense of the preceding words, "And he shall array himself with the land of Egypt, as a shepherd putteth on his garment." It signifies, that just as a person appearing to be a shepherd, passed unmolested in common by the wild Arabs; so Nebuchadnezzar, by his subduing Egypt, shall induce the Arab tribes to suffer him to go out of that country unmolested, the possession of Egypt being to him what a shepherd's garment was to a single person: for though, upon occasion, the Arabs are not afraid to affront the most powerful princes, it is not to be imagined that conquest and power have no effect upon them. *They that dwell in the wilderness*, (says the Psalmist, referring to these Arabs,) *shall bow before him*, whom he has described immediately before, *he having dominion from sea to sea, and from the river to the ends of the earth*, and which he unquestionably supposes was the great inducement to that submission.

Thus the Arab that was charged with the care of conducting Dr. Pococke to Jerusalem, after secreting him for some time in his tent, when he took him out into the fields, to walk there, put on him his striped garment; apparently for his security, and that he might pass for an Arab. So D'Arvieux, when he was sent by the consul of Sidon to the camp of the grand emir, equipped himself for the greater security exactly like an Arab, and accordingly passed unmolested, and unquestioned.—BURDER.

CHAPTER XLIV.

Ver. 17. But we will certainly do whatsoever thing goeth forth out of our own mouth, to burn incense unto the queen of heaven, and to pour out drink-offerings unto her, as we have done, we, and our fathers, our kings, and our princes, in the cities of Judah, and in the streets of Jerusalem: for *then* had we plenty of victuals, and were well, and saw no evil.

When the new moon is first seen, the people present their hands in the same form of adoration, and take off the turban, as they do to other gods. If a person have a favourite son or wife, or any friend with whom he thinks himself fortunate, he will call for one of them on that night, and, after looking at the new moon, will steadfastly look at the face of the individual. But if there be no person of that description present, he will look at his white cloth, or a piece of gold.—ROBERTS.

CHAPTER XLVI.

Ver. 4. Harness the horses; and get up, ye horsemen, and stand forth with *your* helmets; furbish the spears, *and* put on the brigandines.

A piece of defensive armour used in early times, was the breastplate or corslet: with this Goliath was accoutred; but in our version the original term is rendered a coat of mail; and in the inspired account of the Jewish armour, it is translated habergeon. It was between the joints of this harness (for so we render it in that passage) that Ahab received his mortal wound by an arrow shot at a venture. To this species of armour the prophet Isaiah alludes, where the same Hebrew word is used as in the preceding texts, but is here rendered breastplate; and in the prophecies of Jeremiah it is translated brigandine. From the use of these various terms, in translating the Hebrew term (שריון) *shirion*, it seems to have covered both the back and breast of the warrior, but was probably intended chiefly for the defence of the latter, and, by consequence, took its name from that circumstance.—PAXTON.

Ver. 11. Go up into Gilead and take balm, O virgin, the daughter of Egypt: in vain shalt thou use many medicines; *for* thou shalt not be cured.

Physicians in England would be perfectly astonished at the numerous kinds of medicine which are administered to a patient. The people themselves are unwilling to take one kind for long together, and I have known a sick woman swallow ten different sorts in one day. Should a patient, when about to take his medicine, scatter or spill the least quantity, nothing will induce him to take the rest; it is a bad omen; he must have the nostrum changed.—ROBERTS.

Ver. 25. The LORD of hosts, the God of Israel, saith, Behold, I will punish the multitude of No, and Pharaoh, and Egypt, with their gods, and their kings; even Pharaoh, and *all* them that trust in him.

No, or No-Amon, or Amon of No, (Jer. xlvi. 25, marginal reading,) was the metropolis of Upper Egypt, by the Greek geographers termed Thebes, a city eminently distinguished for the worship of Jupiter, who by the Egyptians was called Amon or Ammon; hence the city received the appellation of Diospolis, or the city of Jupiter. The grandeur of ancient Thebes must now be traced in the four small towns or hamlets of Luxor, Karnak, Medinet-Abou, and Gournou. Karnak is regarded by the most accurate modern travellers as the principal site of Diospolis; and the Egyptians seem to have called forth all the resources of wealth, and all the efforts of art, in order to render it worthy of their supreme divinity.

The great temple at Karnak has twelve principal entrances; each of which is composed of several propyla and colossal gateways, besides other buildings attached to them, in themselves larger than most other temples. One of the propyla is entirely of granite, adorned with the most finished hieroglyphics. On each side of many of them there have been colossal statues of basalt and granite, from twenty to thirty feet in height, some of which are in the attitude of sitting, while others are standing erect. A double range of colossal sphinxes extends across the plain from the temple at Luxor, (a distance of nearly two miles,) which terminates at Karnak in a most magnificent gateway, fifty feet in height, which still remains unimpaired. From this gateway the great temple was approached by an avenue of fifty lofty columns, one of which only now remains, leading to a vast propylon in front of the portico. The interior of this portico presents a *coup d'œil*, which surpasses any other that is to be found among the remains of Egyptian architecture. Twelve columns, sixty feet high, and of a beautiful order, form an avenue through the centre of the building, like the nave of a Gothic cathedral, and they are flanked on each side by sixty smaller ones, ranged in six rows, which are seen through the intervals in endless perspective. The walls are covered with bas-reliefs of a similar character with those found in the other ancient Egyptian temples.

In an open space beyond the portico there were four obelisks, two only of which are now standing. One of these, according to Capt. C. F. Head, has a base of eight feet square, and rises to a height of eighty feet, and is formed of a single block of granite. The hieroglyphics, which are beautifully wrought, are supposed to record the succession of Pharaohs who reigned over Egypt. From the most ancient rulers of the land to the Ptolemies, almost every king, except the Persian, has his name recorded in this temple. But it was said, "the sceptre of Egypt shall depart away," (Zech. x. 11;) and, as if in direct fulfilment of the prophecy, the portion of the rocky tables that was to have been occupied by the names of others of its royal line, has been shattered, and (it has been conjectured) by no human hand.

The most interesting of the sculptured ornaments in this temple, Capt. Head states, are on the northwest, where there are battle scenes, with innumerable figures of military combatants using bows and arrows, spears and bucklers, of prostrate enemies, of war chariots and horses. The fiery action and elegant shape of the steeds are remarkable. On the exterior walls of the southwest corner of the portico, are depicted other victories, which are conjectured to be those of the Egyptians over the Jews.

The field of ruins at Karnak is about a mile in diameter. Dr. Richardson conjectures that the whole of this space was once, in the prouder days of Thebes, consecrated entirely to the use of the temple. There are evidences of walls considerably beyond this, which probably enlarged the city in its greatest extent; but, after the seat of government had been withdrawn, the capital removed to another spot, and the trade transferred to another mart, the inhabitants narrowed the circuit of their walls, and placed their houses within the lines of the sacred confines.

Such is the mass of disjointed fragments collected together in these magnificent relics of ancient art, that more than human power would appear to have caused the overthrow of the strongholds of superstition. Some have imagined that the ruin was caused by the instantaneous concussion of an earthquake. Whether this conjecture be well founded or erroneous, the divine predictions against Egypt have been literally accomplished. "The land of Egypt" has been made "desolate and waste;" "judgments" have been executed "in No," whose "multitude" has been "cut off;" and No IS RENT ASUNDER. (Ezek. xxix. 9. xxx. 14, 15, 16.)—HORNE.

CHAPTER XLVII.

Ver. 5. Baldness is come upon Gaza: Ashkelon is cut off *with* the remnant of their valley: how long wilt thou cut thyself?

See on 1 Kings 18. 28.

The land of the Philistines was to be destroyed. It partakes of the general desolation common to it with Judea, and other neighbouring states. While ruins are to be found in all Syria, they are particularly abundant along the seacoast, which formed, on the south, the realm of the Philistines. But its aspect presents some existing peculiarities, which travellers fail not to, particularize, and which, in reference both to the state of the country, and the fate of its different cities, the prophets failed not to discriminate as justly as if their description had been drawn both with all the accuracy which ocular observation and all the certainty which authenticated history could give. And the authority so often quoted may here be again appealed to. Volney, (though, like one who in ancient times was instrumental to the fulfilment of a special prediction, "he meant not so, neither did his heart think so,") from the manner in which he generalizes his observations, and marks the peculiar features of the different districts of Syria, with greater acuteness and perspicuity than any other traveller whatever, is the ever-ready purveyor of evidence in all the cases which came within the range of his topographical description of the wide field of prophecy—while, at the same time, from his known, open and zealous hostility to the Christian cause, his testimony is alike decisive and unquestionable: and the vindication of the truth of the following predictions may safely be committed to this redoubted champion of infidelity.

"The seacoasts shall be dwellings and cottages for shepherds, and folds for flocks. The remnant of the Philistines shall perish. Baldness is come upon Gaza; it shall be forsaken. The king shall perish from Gaza. I will cut off the inhabitants from Ashdod. Ashkelon shall be a desolation, it shall be cut off with the remnant of the valley; it shall not be inhabited." "In the plain between Ramla and Gaza" (the very plain of the Philistines along the seacoast) "we met with a number of villages badly built, of dried mud, and which, like the inhabitants, exhibit every mark of poverty and wretchedness. The houses, on a nearer view, are only so many huts (cottages) sometimes detached, at others ranged in the form of cells round a courtyard, enclosed by a mud wall. In winter, they and their cattle may be said to live together, the part of the dwelling allotted to themselves being only raised two feet above that in which they lodge their beasts"—(*dwellings and cottages for shepherds, and folds for flocks.*) "Except the environs of these villages, all the rest of the country is a *desert*, and abandoned to the Bedouin Arabs, who feed their flocks on it." *The remnant* shall perish; the land of the Philistines shall be destroyed, that there shall be no inhabitant, and the *seacoasts* shall be dwellings and cottages for shepherds, and folds for flocks.

"The ruins of white marble sometimes found at Gaza prove that it was formerly the abode of luxury and opulence. It has shared in the general destruction; and, notwithstanding its proud title of the capital of Palestine, it is now no more than a defenceless village," (*baldness has come upon it,*) "peopled by, at most, only two thousand inhabitants." *It is forsaken and bereaved of its king.* "The seacoast, by which it was formerly washed, is every day removing farther from the *deserted ruins* of Ashkelon." *It shall be a desolation. Ashkelon shall not be inhabited.* "Amid the various successive ruins, those of Edzoud, (Ashdod,) so powerful under the Philistines, are now remarkable for their scorpions." *The inhabitants shall be cut off from Ashdod.* Although the Christian traveller must yield the palm to Volney, as the topographer of prophecy, and although supplementary evidence be not requisite, yet a place is here willingly given to the following just observations.

"Ashkelon was one of the proudest satrapies of the lords of the Philistines; now there is not an inhabitant within its walls; and the prophecy of Zechariah is fulfilled. 'The king shall perish from Gaza, and Ashkelon shall not be inhabited.' When the prophecy was uttered, both cities were in an equally flourishing condition; and nothing but the prescience of Heaven could pronounce on which of the two, and in what manner, the vial of its wrath should be poured out. Gaza is truly without a king. The lofty towers of Ashkelon lie scattered on the ground, and the ruins within its walls do not shelter a human being. How is the wrath of man made to praise his Creator! Hath he not said, and shall he not do it? The oracle was delivered by the mouth of the prophet more than five hundred years before the Christian era, and we beheld its accomplishment eighteen hundred years after that event." Cogent and just as the reasoning is, the facts stated by Volney give wider scope for an irresistible argument. The fate of one city is not only distinguished from that of another; but the varied aspect of the country itself, the dwellings and cottages for shepherds in one part, and that very region named, the rest of the land destroyed and uninhabited, a desert, and abandoned to the flocks of the wandering Arabs; Gaza, bereaved of a king, a defenceless village, destitute of all its fortifications; Ashkelon, a desolation, and without an inhabitant; the inhabitants also cut off from Ashdod, as reptiles tenanted it instead of men—form in each instance a specific prediction, and a recorded fact, and present such a view of the existing state of Philistia as renders it difficult to determine, from the strictest accordance that prevails between both, whether the inspired penman or the defamer of scripture give the more vivid description. Nor is there any obscurity whatever in any one of the circumstances, or in any part of the proof. The coincidence is too glaring, even for wilful blindness not to discern; and to all the least versed in general history the priority of the predictions to the events is equally obvious. And such was the natural fertility of the country, and such was the strength and celebrity of the cities, that no conjecture possessing the least shadow of plausibility can be formed in what manner any of these events could possibly have been thought of, even for many centuries after the "vision and prophecy" were sealed. After that period Gaza defied the power of Alexander the Great, and withstood for two months a hard-pressed siege. The army with which he soon afterward overthrew the Persian empire having there, as well as at Tyre, been checked or delayed in the first flush of conquest, and he himself having been twice wounded in desperate attempts to storm the city, the proud and enraged king of Macedon, with all the cruelty of a brutish heart, and boasting of himself as a second Achilles, dragged at his chariot-wheels the intrepid general who had defended it, twice around the walls of Gaza. Ashkelon was no less celebrated for the excellence of its wines than for the strength of its fortifications. And of Ashdod it is related by an eminent ancient historian, not only that it was a great city, but that it withstood the longest siege recorded in history, (it may also be said either of prior or of later date,) having been besieged for the space of twenty-nine years by Psymatticus, king of Egypt. Strabo, after the commencement of the Christian era, classes its citizens among the chief inhabitants of Syria. Each of these cities, Gaza, Ashkelon, and Ashdod, was the See of a Bishop from the days of Constantine to the invasion of the Saracens. And, as a decisive proof of their existence as cities long subsequent to the delivery of the predictions, it may further be remarked, that different coins of each of these very cities are extant, and are copied and described in several accounts of ancient coins. The once princely magnificence of Gaza is still attested by the "ruins of white marble;" and the house of the present aga is composed of fragments of ancient columns, cornices, &c.; and in the courtyard, and immured in the wall, are shafts and capitals of granite columns.

In short, *cottages for shepherds, and folds for flocks*, partially scattered along the *seacoast*, are now truly the best substitutes for populous cities that the once powerful realm of Philistia can produce; and the *remnant* of that land which gave titles and grandeur to the lords of the Philistines *is destroyed*. *Gaza*, the chief of its satrapies, "the abode of luxury and opulence," now *bereaved of its king, and bald* of all its fortifications, is the defenceless residence of a subsidiary ruler of a devastated province; and, in kindred degradation, ornaments of its once splendid edifices are now bedded in a wall that forms an enclosure for beasts. A handful of men could now take unobstructed possession of that place, where a strong city opposed the entrance, and defied, for a time, the power of the conqueror of the world. The walls, the dwellings, and the people of *Ashkelon*, have all perished: and though its name was in the time of the crusades shouted in triumph throughout every land in Europe, it is now literally *without an inhabitant*. And *Ashdod*, which withstood a siege treble the duration of that of Troy, and thus outrivalled far the boast of Alexander at Gaza, has, in verification of "the word of God, which is sharper than any two-edged sword," been *cut off*, and has fallen before it to nothing.

There is yet another city which was noted by the prophets, the very want of any information respecting which, and the absence of its name from several modern maps of Palestine, while the sites of other ruined cities are marked, are really the best confirmation of the truth of the prophecy that could possibly be given. *Ekron shall be rooted up.* It is rooted up. It was one of the chief cities of the Philistines; but though Gaza still subsists, and while Ashkelon and Ashdod retain their names in their ruins, the very name of Ekron is missing. The wonderful contrast in each particular, whether in respect to the land or to the cities of the Philistines, is the exact counterpart of the literal prediction; and having the testimony of Volney to all the facts, and also indisputable evidence of the great priority of the predictions to the events, what more complete or clearer proof could there be that each and all of them emanated from the prescience of Heaven?—KEITH.

CHAPTER XLVIII.

Ver. 1. Against Moab thus saith the LORD of
hosts, the God of Israel, Wo unto Nebo! for it
is spoiled; Kiriath-Aim is confounded *and*
taken; Misgab is confounded and dismayed.
2. *There shall be* no more praise of Moab: in
Heshbon they have devised evil against it;
come, and let us cut it off from *being* a nation:
also thou shalt be cut down, O Madmen; the
sword shall pursue thee.

The land of Moab lay to the east and southeast of Judea, and bordered on the east, northeast, and partly on the south, by the Dead Sea. Its early history is nearly analogous to that of Ammon; and the soil, though perhaps more diversified, is, in many places where the desert and plains of salt have not encroached on its borders, of equal fertility. There are manifest and abundant vestiges of its ancient greatness. "The whole of the plains are covered with the sites of towns, on every eminence or spot convenient for the construction of one. And as the land is capable of rich cultivation, there can be no doubt that the country now so deserted once presented a continued picture of plenty and fertility." The form of fields is still visible; and there are the remains of Roman highways, which in some places are completely paved, and on which there are milestones of the times of Trajan, Marcus Aurelius, and Severus, with the number of the miles legible upon them. Wherever any spot is cultivated, the corn is luxuriant: and the riches of the soil cannot perhaps be more clearly illustrated than by the fact, that one grain of Heshbon wheat exceeds in dimensions two of the ordinary sort, and more than double the number of grains grow on the stalk. The frequency, and almost, in many instances, the close vicinity of the sites of the ancient towns, "prove that the population of the country was formerly proportioned to its natural fertility." Such evidence may surely suffice to prove, that the country was well cultivated and peopled at a period so long posterior to the date of the predictions, that no cause less than supernatural could have existed at the time when they were delivered, which could have authorized the assertion, with the least probability or apparent possibility of its truth, that Moab would ever have been reduced to that state of great and permanent desolation in which it has continued for so many ages, and which vindicates and ratifies to this hour the truth of the scriptural prophecies.

And the cities of Moab have all disappeared. Their place, together with the adjoining part of Idumea, is characterized, in the map of Volney's Travels, by the *ruins of towns*. His information respecting these ruins was derived from some of the wandering Arabs; and its accuracy has been fully corroborated by the testimony of different European travellers of high respectability and undoubted veracity, who have since visited this devastated region. The whole country abounds with ruins. And Burckhardt, who encountered many difficulties in so desolate and dangerous a land, thus records the brief history of a few of them: "The ruins of Eleale, Heshbon, Meon, Medaba, Dibon, Aroer, still subsist to illustrate the history of the Beni Israel." And it might with equal truth have been added, that they still subsist to confirm the inspiration of the Jewish scripture, or to prove that the seers of Israel were the prophets of God, for the desolation of each of these very cities was the theme of a prediction. Every thing worthy of observation respecting them has been detailed, not only in Burckhardt's Travels in Syria, but also by Seetzen, and, more recently, by Captains Irby and Mangles, who, along with Mr. Banks and Mr. Legh, visited this deserted district. The predicted judgment has fallen with such truth upon these cities, and upon all the cities of the land of Moab far and near, and they are so utterly *broken down*, that even the prying curiosity of such indefatigable travellers could discover among a multiplicity of ruins only a few remains so entire as to be worthy of particular notice. The subjoined description is drawn from their united testimony.—Among the ruins of El Aal (Eleale) are a number of large cisterns, fragments of buildings, and foundations of houses. At Heshban (Heshbon) are the ruins of a large ancient town, together with the remains of a temple, and some edifices. A few broken shafts of columns are still standing; and there are a number of deep wells cut in the rock. The ruins of *Medaba* are about two miles in circumference. There are many remains of the walls of private houses constructed with blocks of silex, but not a single edifice is standing. The chief object of interest is an immense tank or cistern of hewn stones, "which, as there is no stream at Medaba," Burckhardt remarks, "might still be of use to the Bedouins, were the surrounding ground cleared of the rubbish to allow the water to flow into it; *but such an undertaking is far beyond the views of the wandering Arabs.*" There is also the foundation of a temple built with large stones, and apparently of great antiquity, with two columns near it. The ruins of *Diban* (Dibon) situated in the midst of a fine plain, are of considerable extent, but present nothing of interest. The neighbouring hot wells, and the similarity of the name, identify the ruins of Myoun with *Meon*, or Beth Meon of scripture. Of this ancient city, as well as of Araayr (Aroer,) nothing is now remarkable but what is common to them with all the cities of Moab—their entire desolation. The extent of the ruins of *Rabba* (Rabbath Moab,) formerly the residence of the kings of Moab, sufficiently proves its ancient importance, though no other object can be particularized among the ruins except the remains of a palace or temple, some of the walls of which are still standing; a gate belonging to another building; and an insulated altar. There are many remains of private buildings, but none entire. There being no springs on the spot, the town had two birkets, the largest of which is cut entirely out of the rocky ground, together with many cisterns. Mount *Nebo* was completely barren when Burckhardt passed over it, and the site of the ancient city had not been ascertained. *Nebo is spoiled.*

While the ruins of all these cities still retain their ancient names, and are the most conspicuous amid the wide scene of general desolation, and while each of them was in like manner particularized in the visions of the prophet, they yet formed but a small number of the cities of Moab: and the rest are also, in similar verification of the prophecies, *desolate, without any to dwell therein.* None of the ancient cities of Moab now exist as tenanted by men. Kerek, which neither bears any resemblance in name to any of the cities of Moab which are mentioned as existing in the time of the Israelites, nor possesses any monuments which denote a very remote antiquity, is the only nominal town in the whole country, and in the words of Seetzen, who visited it, "in its present ruined state it can only be called a hamlet:" "and the houses have only one floor." But the most populous and fertile province in Europe (especially any situated in the interior of a country like Moab) is not covered so thickly with towns as Moab is plentiful in ruins, deserted and desolate though now it be. Burckhardt enumerates about *fifty* ruined sites within its boundaries, many of them extensive. In general they are a *broken down* and undistinguishable mass of ruins; and many of them have not been closely inspected. But, in some instances, there are the remains of temples, sepulchral monuments, the ruins of edifices constructed of very large stones, in one of which buildings "some of the stones are twenty feet in length, and so broad that one constitutes the thickness of the wall;" traces of hanging gardens; entire columns lying on the ground, three feet in diameter, and fragments of smaller columns; and many cisterns cut of the rock.—When the towns of Moab existed in their prime, and were at ease,—when arrogance, and haughtiness, and pride prevailed among them—the desolation and total desertion and abandonment of them all must have utterly surpassed all human conception. And that such numerous cities—which subsisted for many ages—which were diversified in their sites, some of them being built on eminences, and naturally strong; others on plains, and surrounded by the richest soil; some situated in valleys by the side of a plentiful stream; and others where art supplied the deficiencies of nature, and where immense cisterns were excavated out of the rock—and which exhibit in their ruins many monuments of ancient prosperity, and many remains easily convertible into present utility—should have all fled away,—all met the same indiscriminate fate—and be all *desolate, without any to dwell therein,* notwithstanding all these ancient assurances of their permanent durability, and their existing facilities and inducements for being the habitations of men—is a matter of just wonder in the present day,—and had any other people been the possessors of Moab, the fact would either have been totally impossible or unaccountable. Trying as this test of the truth of prophecy is—*that is the word of God, and not of erring man, which can so well and so triumphantly abide it. They shall cry of Moab, How is it broken down!*—Keith.

Ver. 8. And the spoiler shall come upon every city, and no city shall escape; the valley also shall perish, and the plain shall be destroyed, as the Lord hath spoken.

Moab has often been a field of contest between the Arab and Turks; and although the former have retained possession of it, both have mutually reduced it to desolation The different tribes of Arabs who traverse it, not only bear a permanent and habitual hostility to Christians and to Turks, but one tribe is often at variance and at war with another; and the regular cultivation of the soil, or the improvement of those natural advantages of which the country is so full, is a matter either never thought of, or that cannot be realized. Property is there the creature of power, and not of law: and possession forms no security when plunder is the preferable right. Hence the extensive plains, where they are not partially covered with wood, present a barren aspect, which is only relieved at intervals by a few clusters of wild fig-trees, that show how the richest gifts of nature degenerate when unaided by the industry of man. And instead of the profusion which the plains must have exhibited in every quarter, nothing but "patches of the best soil in the territory are now cultivated by the Arabs;" and these only "whenever they have the prospect of being able to secure the harvest against the incursions of enemies." The Arab herds now roam at freedom over the valleys and the plains; and "the many vestiges of field enclosures" form not any obstruction; they wander undisturbed around the tents of their masters, over the face of the country; and while *the valley is perished, and the plain destroyed, the cities also of Aroer are forsaken; they are for the flocks which lie down, and none make them afraid.* The strong contrast between the ancient and the actual state of Moab is exemplified in the condition of the inhabitants as well as of the land; and the coincidence between the prediction and the fact is as striking in the one case as in the other.—Keith.

Ver. 11. Moab hath been at ease from his youth, and he hath settled on his lees, and hath not been emptied from vessel to vessel, neither hath he gone into captivity: therefore his taste remained in him, and his scent is not changed.

They frequently pour wine from vessel to vessel in the East: for when they begin one, they are obliged immediately to empty it into smaller vessels, or into bottles, or it would grow sour. From the *jars*, says Dr. Russel, in which the wine ferments, it is drawn off into *demyans*, which contain perhaps twenty quart bottles; and from those into bottles for use: but as these bottles are generally not well washed, the wine is often sour. The more careful use pint bottles, or half-pint bottles, and cover the surface with a little sweet oil.—Burder.

Ver. 12. Therefore, behold, the days come, saith the Lord, that I will send unto him wanderers, that shall cause him to wander, and shall empty his vessels, and break their bottles.

The Bedouin (wandering) Arabs are now the chief and almost the only inhabitants of a country once studded with cities. Traversing the country, and fixing their tents for a short time in one place, and then decamping to another, depasturing every part successively, and despoiling the whole land of its natural produce, they *are wanderers who have come up against it, and who keep it in a state of perpetual desolation.* They lead a wandering life; and the only regularity they know or practice is to act upon a systematic scheme of spoliation. They prevent any from forming a fixed settlement who are inclined to attempt it; for although the fruitfulness of the soil would abundantly repay the labour of settlers, and render migration wholly unnecessary, even if the population were increased more than tenfold, yet the Bedouins forcibly deprive them of the means of subsistence, compel them to search for it elsewhere, and, in the words of the prediction, literally *cause them to wander*. "It may be remarked generally of the Bedouins," says Burckhardt, in describing their extortions in this very country, "that wherever they are the masters of the cultivators, the latter are soon reduced to beggary by their unceasing demands."—KEITH.

Ver. 27. For was not Israel a derision unto thee? was he found among thieves? for since thou spakest of him, thou skippedst for joy.

See on 1 Kings 18. 28.

Ver. 28. O ye that dwell in Moab, leave the cities, and dwell in the rock, and be like the dove *that* maketh her nest in the sides of the hole's mouth.

Where art intervenes not, pigeons build in those hollow places nature provides for them. A certain city in Africa is called Hamam-et, from the wild pigeons that copiously breed in the adjoining cliffs; and in a curious paper relating to Mount Ætna, (Phil. Trans. vol. lx.) which mentions a number of subterraneous caverns there, one is noticed as being called by the peasants, La Spelonca della Palomba, from the wild pigeons building their nests therein. (Sol. Song ii. 14.) Though Ætna is a burning mountain, yet the cold in these caverns is excessive: this shows that pigeons delight in cool retreats, and explains the reason why they resort to mountains which are known to be very cold even in those hot countries. The words of the Psalmist, *flee as a bird to your mountain*, without doubt refer to the flying of doves thither when frightened by the fowler. Dove-houses, however, are very common in the East. Of Kefteen, a large village, Maundrell says, there are more dove-cots than other houses. In the southern part of Egypt, the tops of their habitations are always terminated by a pigeon-house. Isaiah lx. 8.—HARMER.

In a general description of the condition of the inhabitants of that extensive desert which now occupies the place of these ancient flourishing states, Volney, in plain but unmeant illustration of this prediction, remarks, that the "wretched peasants live in perpetual dread of losing the fruit of their labours: and no sooner have they gathered in their harvest, than they hasten to secrete it in private places, and retire among the rocks which border on the Dead Sea." Towards the opposite extremity of the land of Moab, and at a little distance from its borders, Seetzen relates, that "there are many families living in caverns;" and he actually designates them "the inhabitants of the rocks." And at the distance of a few miles from the ruined site of Heshbon, there are many artificial caves in a large range of perpendicular cliffs—in some of which are chambers and small sleeping apartments. While the cities are desolate, without any to dwell therein, the rocks are tenanted. But whether flocks lie down in the former without any to make them afraid, or whether men are to be found dwelling in the latter, and are like the dove that maketh her nest in the sides of the hole's mouth—the wonderful transition, in either case, and the close accordance, in both, of the fact to the prediction, assuredly mark it in characters that may be visible to the purblind mind, as the word of that God before whom the darkness of futurity is as light, and without whom a sparrow cannot fall unto the ground. And although chargeable with the impropriety of being somewhat out of place, it may not be here altogether improper to remark, that, demonstrative as all these clear predictions and coincident facts are of the inspiration of the scriptures, it cannot but be gratifying to every lover of his kind, when he contemplates that desolation caused by many sins and fraught with many miseries, which the wickedness of man has wrought, and which the prescience of God revealed, to know that all these prophecies, while they mingle the voice of wailing with that of denunciation, are the word of that God who, although he suffers not iniquity to pass unpunished, overrules evil for good, and makes the wrath of man to praise him, and who in the midst of judgment can remember mercy. And reasoning merely from the "uniform experience" (to borrow a term and draw an argument from Hume) of the truth of the prophecies already fulfilled, the unprejudiced mind will at once perceive the full force of the proof derived from experience, and acknowledge that it would be a rejection of the authority of reason as well as of revelation to mistrust the truth of that prophetic affirmation of resuscitating and redeeming import, respecting Ammon and Moab, which is the last of the series, and which alone now awaits futurity to stamp it with the brilliant and crowning zeal of its testimony. "I will bring again the captivity of Moab in the latter days, saith the Lord. I will bring again the captivity of the children of Ammon, saith the Lord. The remnant of my people shall possess them. They shall build the old wastes, they shall raise up the former desolations, and they shall repair the waste cities, the desolations of many generations."—KEITH.

Ver. 37. For every head *shall be* bald, and every beard clipped: upon all the hands *shall be* cuttings, and upon the loins sackcloth.

The relations of the deceased often testify their sorrow in a more serious and affecting manner, by cutting and slashing their naked arms with daggers. To this absurd and barbarous custom, the prophet thus alludes: "For every head shall be bald, and every beard clipped; upon all hands shall be cuttings, and upon the loins sackcloth." And again, "Both the great and the small shall die in the land; they shall not be buried, neither shall men lament for them, nor cut themselves." It seems to have been very common in Egypt, and among the people of Israel, before the age of Moses, else he had not forbidden it by an express law: "Ye are the children of the Lord your God; ye shall not cut yourselves, nor make any baldness between your eyes for the dead." Mr. Harmer refers to this custom, the "wounds in the hands" of the prophet, which he had given himself, in token of affection to a person.—PAXTON.

"We find Arabs," La Roque tells us from D'Arvieux, "who have their arms scarred by the gashes of a knife, which they sometimes give themselves, to mark out to their mistresses what their rigour and the violence of love make them suffer." From this extract we learn what particular part of the body received these *cuttings*. The scripture frequently speaks of them in a more general manner.—HARMER.

Ver. 40. For thus saith the LORD, Behold, he shall fly as an eagle, and shall spread his wings over Moab.

See on Ezek. 17. 8.

CHAPTER XLIX.

Ver. 3. Howl, O Heshbon: for Ai is spoiled: cry, ye daughters of Rabbah, gird ye with sackcloth; lament, and run to and fro by the hedges: for their king shall go into captivity, *and* his priests and his princes together.

The places of burial in the East are without their cities, as well as their gardens, and consequently their going to them must often be by their garden walls, (not *hedges.*) The ancient warriors of distinction, who were slain in battle, were carried to the sepulchres of their fathers; and the people often went to weep over the graves of those whom they would honour. These observations put together sufficiently account for this passage.—HARMER.

Ver. 7. Concerning Edom, thus saith the LORD of hosts, *Is* wisdom no more in Teman? is counsel perished from the prudent? is their wisdom vanished?

Compare with this Obad. v. 8, "shall I not in that day, saith the Lord, even destroy the wise men out of Edom, and understanding out of the Mount of Esau?" Fallen and despised as now it is, Edom, did not the prescription of many ages abrogate its right, might lay claim to the title of having been the first seat of learning, as well as the centre of commerce. Sir Isaac Newton, who was no mean master in chronology, and no incompetent judge to give a decision in regard to the rise and first progress of literature, considers Edom as the nursery of the arts and sciences, and adduces evidence to that effect from profane as well as from sacred history. "The Egyptians," he remarks, "*having learned the skill of the Edomites*, began now to observe the position of the stars, and the length of the solar year, for enabling them to know the position of the stars at any time, and to sail by them at all times without sight of the shore, and this gave a beginning to astronomy and navigation." It seems that letters, and astronomy, and the trade of carpenters, were invented by the merchants of the Red Sea, and that they were propagated from Arabia Petræa into Egypt, Chaldea, Syria, Asia Minor, and Europe. While the philosopher may thus think of Edom with respect, neither the admirer of genius, the man of feeling, nor the child of devotion will, even to this day, seek from any land a richer treasure of plaintive poetry, of impassioned eloquence, and of fervid piety, than Edom has bequeathed to the world in the book of Job. It exhibits to us, in language the most pathetic and sublime, all that a man could feel, in the outward pangs of his body and the inner writhings of his mind, of the frailties of his frame, and of the dissolution of his earthly comforts and endearments; all that mortal can discern, by meditating on the ways and contemplating the works of God, of the omniscience and omnipotence of the Most High, and of the inscrutable dispensations of his providence; all *that* knowledge which could first tell, in written word, of Arcturus, and Orion, and the Pleiades; and all that devotedness of soul, and immortality of hope, which, with patience that faltered not even when the heart was bruised and almost broken, and the body covered over with distress, could say, "Though he slay me, yet will I trust in him." But if the question now be asked, *Is* understanding perished out of Edom? the answer, like every response of the prophetic word, may be briefly given: It is. The minds of the Bedouins are as uncultivated as the deserts they traverse. Practical wisdom is, in general, the first that man learns, and the last that he retains. And the simple but significant fact, already alluded to, that the clearing away of a little rubbish, merely "to allow the water to flow" into an ancient cistern, in order to render it useful to themselves, "is an undertaking far beyond the views of the wandering Arabs," shows that *understanding is* indeed *perished from among them*. They view the indestructible works of former ages, not only with wonder, but with superstitious regard, and consider them as the work of genii. They look upon a European traveller as a magician and believe that, having seen any spot where they imagine that treasures are deposited, he can afterward command the guardian of the treasure to set the whole before him. In Teman, which yet maintains a precarious existence, the inhabitants possess the desire without the means of knowledge. The Koran is their only study, and contains the sum of their wisdom. And, although he was but a "miserable comforter," and was overmastered in argument by a kinsman stricken with affliction, yet no *Temanite* can now discourse with either the wisdom or the pathos of *Eliphaz* of old. *Wisdom is no more in Teman, and understanding has perished out of the Mount of Esau.*

While there is thus subsisting evidence and proof that the ancient inhabitants of Edom were renowned for wisdom as well as for power, and while desolation has spread so widely over it, that it can scarcely be said to be inhabited by man, there still are tenants who hold possession of it, to whom it was abandoned by man, and to whom it was decreed by a voice more than mortal. And insignificant and minute as it may possibly appear to those who reject the light of revelation, or to the unreflecting mind, (that will use no measuring-line of truth which stretches beyond that which inches out its own shallow thoughts, and wherewith, rejecting all other aid, it tries, by the superficial touch of ridicule alone, to sound the unfathomable depths of infinite wisdom,) yet the following scripture, mingled with other words already verified as the voice of inspiration, and voluntarily involving its title to credibility in the appended appeal to fact and challenge to investigation, may, in conjunction with kindred proofs, yet tell to man—if hearing he will hear, and show him, if seeing he will see—the verity of the divine word, and the infallibility of the divine judgments; and, not without the aid of the rightful and unbiased exercise of reason, may give understanding to the skeptic, that he may be converted, and that he may be healed by Him whose word is ever truth.

"But the cormorant and the bittern shall possess it, (Idumea;) the owl also, and the raven shall dwell in it. It shall be a habitation for dragons, and a court for owls: the wild beasts of the desert shall also meet with the wild beasts of the island, and the satyr (the hairy or rough creature) shall cry to his fellow; the screech owl also shall rest there, and find for herself a place of rest; there shall the great owl make her nest, and lay, and hatch, and gather under her shadow; there shall the vultures also be gathered every one with her mate. Seek ye out of the book of the Lord and read; no one of these shall fail, none shall want her mate; for my mouth it hath commanded, and his spirit it hath gathered them. And he hath cast the lot for them, and his hand hath divided it unto them by line: they shall possess it for ever; from generation to generation shall they dwell therein." Isa. xxxiv. 11, 13—17. "I laid the mountains of Esau and his heritage waste for the dragons of the wilderness." Mal. i. 3.

Such is the precision of the prophecies, so remote are they from all ambiguity of meaning, and so distinct are the events which they detail, that it is almost unnecessary to remark, that the different animals here enumerated were not all in the same manner, or in the same degree, to be possessors of Edom. Some of them were to rest, to meet, to be gathered there: the owl and the raven were to dwell in it, and it was to be a habitation for dragons; while of the cormorant and bittern, it is emphatically said, that they were to possess it. And is it not somewhat beyond a mere fortuitous coincidence, imperfect as the information is respecting Edom, that, in "seeking out" proof concerning these animals and whether none of them do fail, the most decisive evidence should, in the first instance, be unconsciously communicated from the boundaries of Edom, of the one which is first noted in the prediction, and which was to possess the land? It will at once be conceded, that in whatever country any particular animal is unknown, no proper translation of its name can there be given; and that for the purpose of designating or identifying it, reference must be had to the original name, and to the natural history of the country in which it is known. And, without any ambiguity or perplexity arising from the translation of the word, or any need of tracing it through any other languages to ascertain its import, the identical word of the original, with scarcely the slightest variation (and that only the want of the final vowel in the Hebrew word, vowels in that language being often supplied in the enunciation, or by points,) is, from the affinity of the Hebrew and Arabic, used on the very spot by the Arabs, to denote the very bird which may literally be said to possess the land. While in the last inhabited village of Moab, and close upon the borders of Edom, Burckhardt noted the animals which frequented the neighbouring territory, in which he distinctly specifies Shera, the land of the Edomites; and he relates that the bird katta is "met with in immense numbers. They fly in such large flocks that the Arab boys often kill two or three of them at a time, merely by throwing a stick among them." If any objector be here inclined to say, that it is not to be wondered at that any particular bird should be found in any given country, that it might continue to remain for a term of ages, and that such a surmise would not exceed the natural probabilities of the case, the fact may be freely admitted as applicable, perhaps, to most countries of the globe. But whoever, elsewhere, saw any wild bird in any country, in flocks so immensely numerous, that two or three of them could be killed by the single throw of a stick from the hand of a boy; and that this could be stated, not as a forcible, and perhaps false, illustration to denote their number, nor as a wonderful chance or unusual incident, but as a fact of frequent occurrence? Whoever, elsewhere, heard of such a fact, not as happening merely on a sea rock, the resort of myriads of birds, on their temporary resting-place, when exhausted in their flight, but in an extensive country, their permanent abode? Or if, among the manifold discoveries of travellers in modern times, it were really related that such occupants of a country are to be found, or that a corresponding fact exists in any other region of the earth which was once tenanted by man, who can also "find" in the records of a high antiquity the prediction that declared it? Of what country now inhabited could the same fact be now with certainty foretold; and where is the seer who can discern the vision, fix on the spot over the world's surface, and select, from the whole winged tribe, the name of the first in order and the greatest in number of the future and chief possessors of the land?

Of the bittern (kephud) as a joint possessor with the katta of Idumea, evidence has not been given, or ascertained;—but numerous as the facts have been which modern discoveries have consigned over to the service of revelation, that word of truth which fears no investigation can appeal to other facts, unknown to history and still undiscovered—but registered in prophecy, and there long since revealed.

The owl also and the raven (or crow) shall dwell in it.—The owl and raven do dwell in it. Captain Mangles relates, that while he and his fellow-travellers were examining the ruins and contemplating the sublime scenery of Petra, "the screaming of the eagles, hawks, and owls, who were soaring above their heads in considerable numbers, seemingly annoyed at any one approaching their lonely habitation, added much to the singularity of the scene." The fields of Tafyle, situated in the immediate vicinity of Edom, are, according to the observation of Burckhardt, frequented by an immense number of crows. "I expected," says Seetzen, (alluding to his purposed tour through Idumea, and to the information he had received from the Arabs,) "to make several discoveries in mineralogy, as well as in the animals and vegetables of the country, on the manna of the desert, the ravens," &c.

It shall be a habitation for dragons, (serpents.) I laid his heritage waste for the dragons of the wilderness.—The evidence, though derived from testimony, and not from personal observation, of two travellers of so contrary characters and views as Shaw and Volney, is so accordant and apposite, that it may well be sustained in lieu of more direct proof. The former represents the land of Edom, and the wilderness of which it now forms part, as abounding with a variety of lizards and vipers, which are very dangerous and troublesome. And the narrative given by Volney, already quoted, is equally decisive as to the fact. The Arabs, in general, avoid the ruins of the cities of Idumea, "on account of *the enormous scorpions with which they swarm.*" Its cities, thus deserted by man, and abandoned to their undisturbed and hereditary possession, Edom may justly be called *the inheritance of dragons.*

The wild beasts of the desert shall also meet with the wild beasts of the island, (or of the borders of the sea.) Instead of these words of the English version, Parkhurst renders the former the *ravenous birds hunting the wilderness.* This interpretation was given long before the fact to which it refers was made known. But it has now been ascertained (and without any allusion, on the other hand, to the prediction) that eagles, hawks, and ravens, all ravenous birds, are common in Edom, and *do not fail* to illustrate the prediction as thus translated. But when animals from different regions are said to meet, the prophecy, thus implying that some of them at least did not properly pertain to the country, would seem to require some further verification. And of all the wonderful circumstances attached to the history, or pertaining to the fate, of Edom, there is one which is not to be ranked among the least in singularity, that bears no remote application to the prefixed prophecy, and that ought not, perhaps, to pass here unnoted. It is recorded in an ancient chronicle, that the Emperor Decius caused fierce lions and lionesses to be transported from (the deserts of) Africa to the borders of Palestine and Arabia, in order that, propagating there, they might act as an annoyance and a barrier to the barbarous Saracens: between Arabia and Palestine lies the doomed execrated land of Edom. And may it not thus be added, that a cause so unnatural and unforeseen would greatly tend to the destruction of the flocks, and to the desolation of all the adjoining territory,—and seem to be as if the king of the forest was to take possession of it for his subjects? And may it not be even literally said *that the wild beasts of the desert meet there with the wild beasts of the borders of the sea?*

The satyr shall dwell there.—The satyr is entirely a fabulous animal. The word (soir) literally means *a rough, hairy one;* and, like a synonymous word in both the Greek and Latin languages which has the same signification, has been translated both by lexicographers and commentators *the goat.* Parkhurst says, that in this sense he would understand this very passage; and Lowth distinctly asserts, without assigning to it any other meaning, that "the word originally signifies *goat.*" Such respectable and well-known authorities have been cited, because their decision must have rested on criticism alone, as it was impossible that their minds could have been biased by any knowledge of the fact in reference to Edom. It was their province, and that of others, to illustrate its meaning—it was Burckhardt's, however unconsciously, to bear, from ocular observation, witness to its truth. "In all the Wadys south of the Modjel and El Asha," (pointing to Edom,) "large herds of mountain goats are met with. They pasture in flocks of forty and fifty together."—*They dwell there.*

But the evidence respecting all the animals specified in the prophecy, as the future possessors of Edom, is not yet complete, and is difficult to be ascertained. And, in words that seem to indicate this very difficulty, it is still reserved for future travellers,—perhaps some unconscious Volney,—to disclose the facts; and for future inquirers, whether Christian or infidel, to seek out of the book of the Lord and read; and to "find that no one of these do fail." Yet, recent as the disclosure of any information respecting them has been, and offered, as it now for the first time is, for the consideration of every candid mind, the positive terms and singleness of object of the prophecies themselves, and the undesigned and decisive evidence, are surely enough to show how greatly these several specific predictions and their respective facts exceed all possibility of their being the word or the work of man; and how clearly there may be discovered in them all, if sight itself be conviction, the credentials of inspiration, and the operation of His hands,—to whose prescience futurity is open,—to whose power all nature is subservient,—and "whose mouth it hath commanded, and whose spirit it hath gathered them."

Noted as Edom was for its terribleness, and possessed of a capital city, from which even a feeble people could not easily have been dislodged, there scarcely could have been a question, even among its enemies, to what *people* that country would eventually belong. And it never could have been thought of by any native of another land, as the Jewish prophets were, nor by any uninspired mortal whatever, that a kingdom which had previously subsisted so long, (and in which princes ceased not to reign, commerce to flourish, and "a people of great opulence" to dwell for more than six hundred years thereafter,) would be finally extinct, that all its cities would be for ever desolate, and though it could have boasted more than any other land of indestructible habitations for men, that their *habitations* would be *desolate;* and that certain *wild animals,* mentioned by name, would in different manners and degrees possess the country from generation to generation.

There shall not be any remaining of the house of Esau. Edom shall be cut off for ever. The aliens of Judah ever look with wistful eyes to the land of their fathers; but no Edomite is now to be found to dispute the right of any animal to the possession of it, or to banish the owl from the temples and palaces of Edom. But the house of Esau did remain, and existed in great power, till after the commencement of the Christian era, a period far too remote from the date of the prediction for their subsequent history to have been foreseen by man. The Idumeans were soon after mingled with the Nabatheans. And in the third century their language was disused, and their very name, as designating any people, had utterly perished; and their country itself, having become an outcast from Syria, among whose kingdoms it had long been numbered, was united to Arabia Petræa. Though the descendants of the twin-born Esau and Jacob have met a diametrically opposite fate, the fact is no less marvellous and undisputed, than the prediction in each case is alike obvious and true. While the posterity of Jacob have been "dispersed in every country under heaven," and are "scattered among all nations," and have ever remained distinct from them all, and while it is also declared that "a full end will never be made of them," the Edomites, though they existed as a nation for more than seventeen hundred years, *have,* as a period of nearly equal duration has proved, *been cut off for ever;* and while Jews are in every land, *there is not any remaining* on any spot of earth *of the house of Esau.*

Idumea, in aid of a neighbouring state, did send forth, on a sudden, an army of twenty thousand armed men,—it contained at least eighteen towns, for centuries after the

Christian era,—successive kings and princes reigned in Petra,—and magnificent palaces and temples, whose empty chambers and naked walls of wonderful architecture still strike the traveller with amazement, were constructed there, at a period unquestionably far remote from the time when it was given to the prophets of Israel to tell, that the house of Esau was to be cut off for ever, that there would be no kingdom there, and that wild animals would possess Edom for a heritage. And so despised is Edom, and the memory of its greatness lost, that there is no record of antiquity that can so clearly show us what once it was in the days of its power, as we can now read in the page of prophecy its existing desolation. But in that place where kings kept their court, and where nobles assembled, where manifest proofs of ancient opulence are concentrated, where princely habitations, retaining their external grandeur, but bereft of all their splendour, still look as if "fresh from the chisel,"—even there no man dwells; it is given by lot to birds, and beasts, and reptiles; it is a "court for owls," and scarcely are they ever frayed from their "lonely habitation" by the tread of a solitary traveller from a far distant land, among deserted dwellings and desolated ruins.

Hidden as the history and state of Edom has been for ages, every recent disclosure, being an echo of the prophecies, amply corroborates the truth, that the word of the Lord does not return unto him void, but ever fulfils the purpose for which he hath sent it. But the whole of its work is not yet wrought in Edom, which has further testimony in store: and while the evidence is not yet complete, so neither is the time of the final judgments on the land yet fully come. Judea, Ammon, and Moab, according to the word of prophecy, shall revive from their desolation, and the wild animals who have conjoined their depredations with those of barbarous men, in perpetuating the desolation of these countries, shall find a refuge and undisturbed possession in Edom, when, the year of recompenses for the controversy of Zion being past, it shall be divided unto them by line, when they shall possess it for ever, and from generation to generation shall dwell therein. But without looking into futurity, a retrospect may here warrant, before leaving the subject, a concluding clause.

That man is a bold *believer*, and must with whatever reluctance forego the name of *skeptic*, who possesses such redundant credulity as to think that all the predictions respecting Edom, and all others recorded in Scripture, and realized by facts, were the mere haphazard results of fortuitous conjectures. And he who thus, without reflecting how incongruous it is to "strain at a gnat and swallow a camel," can deliberately, and with an unruffled mind, place such an opinion among the articles of his faith, may indeed be pitied by those who know in whom they have believed, but, if he forfeit not thereby all right of ever appealing to reason, must at least renounce all title to stigmatize, in others, even the most preposterous belief. Or if such, after all, must needs be his philosophical creed, and his rational conviction! what can hinder him from believing also that other chance words—such as truly marked the fate of Edom, but more numerous and clear, and which, were he to "seek out and read," he would find in the selfsame "book of the Lord"—may also prove equally true to the spirit, if not to the letter, against all the enemies of the gospel, whether hypocrites or unbelievers? May not his belief in the latter instance be strengthened by the experience that many averments of Scripture, in respect to times then future, and to facts then unknown, have already proved true? And may he not here find some analogy, at least, on which to rest his faith, whereas the conviction which, in the former case, he so readily cherishes is totally destitute of any resemblance whatever to warrant the possibility of its truth? Or is this indeed the sum of his boasted wisdom, to hold to the conviction of the fallacy of all the coming judgments denounced in Scripture, till "experience," personal though it should be, prove them to be as true as the past, and a compulsory and unchangeable but unredeeming faith be grafted on despair? Or if less proof can possibly suffice, let him timely read, and examine, and disprove also, all the credentials of revelation, before he account the believer credulous, or the unbeliever wise; or else let him abandon the thought that the unrepentant iniquity and wilful perversity of man and an evil heart of unbelief (all proof derided, all offered mercy rejected, all meetness for an inheritance among them that are sanctified unattained, and all warning lost) shall not finally forbid that Edom stand alone—the seared and blasted monument of the judgments of Heaven.

A word may here be spoken even to the wise. Were any of the sons of men to be uninstructed in the fear of the Lord, which is the beginning of wisdom, and in the knowledge of his word, which maketh wise unto salvation, and to be thus ignorant of the truths and precepts of the gospel, which should all tell upon every deed done in the body; what in such a case—if all their superior knowledge were unaccompanied by religious principles—would all mechanical and physical sciences eventually prove but the same, in kind, as the wisdom of the wise men of Edom? And were they to perfect in astronomy, navigation, and mechanics what, according to Sir Isaac Newton, the Edomites began, what would the moulding of matter to their will avail them, as moral and accountable beings, if their own hearts were not conformed to the Divine will? and what would all their labour be at last but strength spent for naught? For were they to raise column above column, and again to hew a city out of the cliffs of the rock, let but such another word of that God whom they seek not to know go forth against it, and all their mechanical ingenuity and labour would just end in forming—that which Petra is, and which Rome itself is destined to be—"a cage of every unclean and hateful bird." The experiment has already been made; it may well and wisely be trusted to as much as those which mortals make; and it is set before us that, instead of provoking the Lord to far worse than its repetition in personal judgments against ourselves, we may be warned by the spirit of prophecy, which is the testimony of Jesus, to hear and obey the words of Him—"even of Jesus, who delivereth from the wrath to come." For how much greater than any degradation to which hewn but unfeeling rocks can be reduced, is that of a soul, which while in the body might have been formed anew after the image of an all holy God, and made meet for beholding His face in glory, passing from spiritual darkness into a spiritual state, where all knowledge of earthly things shall cease to be power—where all the riches of this world shall cease to be gain—where the want of religious principles and of Christian virtues shall leave the soul naked, as the bare and empty dwellings in the clefts of the rocks—where the thoughts of worldly wisdom, to which it was inured before, shall haunt it still, and be more unworthy and hateful occupants of the immortal spirit than are the owls amid the palaces of Edom—and where all those sinful passions which rested on the things that were seen shall be like unto the scorpions which hold Edom as their heritage for ever, and which none can now scare away from among the wild vines that are there intwined around the broken altars where false gods were worshipped!—Keith.

Ver. 8. Flee ye, turn back, dwell deep, O inhabitants of Dedan; for I will bring the calamity of Esau upon him, the time *that* I will visit him.

When the Arabs have drawn upon themselves the resentment of the more fixed inhabitants of those countries, and think themselves unable to stand against them, they withdraw into the depths of the great wilderness, where none can follow them. Thus also very expressly M. Savary; (tom. ii. p. 8,) "always on their guard against tyranny, on the least discontent that is given them, they pack up their tents, load their camels with them, ravage the flat country, and, loaded with plunder, *plunge* into the burning sands, whither none can pursue them, and where they alone can dwell." Is it not then most probable that the *dwelling deep*, mentioned in these words, means their plunging far into the deserts, rather than going into deep caves and dens, as has been most commonly supposed? This explanation is also strongly confirmed by verse 30. *Flee, get you far off, dwell deep.*—Harmer.

The phrase to "dwell deep," in relation to the fixed inhabitants of that city, and the kingdom of which it was the capital, must therefore refer to the caverns in Galilee and the neighbourhood, in whose capacious recesses they were accustomed to take refuge in time of war. Or, if it signify to dwell far remote from the threatened danger, the many other caverns beyond Damascus, towards Arabia, which the prophet might allude to, were at a sufficient distance to justify his language. Nor is it inconsistent with the manners of the Arabians, as Harmer supposes, to retire into caves and dens of the earth for shelter; for the Bedouins in the neighbourhood of Aleppo, who encamp near the gates in the spring, inhabit grottoes in the winter. And Mohammed mentions an Arabian tribe, that hewed houses out of the mountains for their security. To these caverns, both the wandering Arabs and the fixed inhabitants, certainly retreated in time of danger; although the more common practice of the former, was to retire into the depth of their terrible deserts, where no enemy could disturb their repose.—PAXTON.

Ver. 16. Thy terribleness hath deceived thee, *and* the pride of thy heart, O thou that dwellest in the clefts of the rock, that holdest the height of the hill: though thou shouldst make thy nest as high as the eagle, I will bring thee down from thence, saith the LORD.

In this beautiful passage, the prophet strictly adheres to the truth of history. Esau subdued the original inhabitants of Mount Hor, and seized on its savage and romantic precipices. His descendants covered the sides of their mountains "with an endless variety of excavated tombs and private dwellings, worked out in all the symmetry and regularity of art, with colonnades and pediments, and ranges of corridors, adhering to the perpendicular surface." On the inaccessible cliffs which, in some places, rise to the height of seven hundred feet, and the barren and craggy precipices which enclose the ruins of Petra, the capital of the Nebatæi, a once powerful but now forgotten people, the eagle builds his nest, and screams for the safety of his young, when the unwelcome traveller approaches his lonely habitation.—PAXTON.

Ver. 17. Also Edom shall be a desolation; every one that goeth by it shall be astonished, and shall hiss at all the plagues thereof. 18. As in the overthrow of Sodom and Gomorrah, and the neighbour *cities* thereof, saith the LORD, no man shall abide there, neither shall a son of man dwell in it.

Judea, Ammon, and Moab exhibit so abundantly the remains and the means of an exuberant fertility, that the wonder arises in the reflecting mind, how the barbarity of man could have so effectually counteracted for so "many generations" the prodigality of nature. But such is Edom's desolation, that the first sentiment of *astonishment* on the contemplation of it is, how a wide-extended region, now diversified by the strongest features of desert wildness, could ever have been adorned with cities, or tenanted for ages by a powerful and opulent people. Its present aspect would belie its ancient history, were not that history corroborated by "the many vestiges of former cultivation," by the remains of walls and paved roads, and by the ruins of cities still existing in this ruined country. The total cessation of its commerce—the artificial irrigation of its valleys wholly neglected—the destruction of all the cities, and the continued spoliation of the country by the Arabs while aught remained that they could destroy—the permanent exposure, for ages, of the soil, unsheltered by its ancient groves, and unprotected by any covering from the scorching rays of the sun—the unobstructed encroachments of the desert, and of the drifted sands from *the borders of the Red Sea*, the consequent absorption of the water of the springs and streamlets during summer, are causes which have all combined their baneful operation in rendering Edom *most desolate, the desolation of desolations.* Volney's account is sufficiently descriptive of the desolation which now reigns over Idumea; and the information which Seetzen derived at Jerusalem respecting it is of similar import. He was told, that "at the distance of two days' journey and a half from Hebron, he would find considerable ruins of the ancient city of Abde, and that for all the rest of the journey he would see *no place of habitation;* he would meet only with a few tribes of wandering Arabs." From the borders of Edom, Captains Irby and Mangles beheld a boundless extent of desert view, which they had hardly ever seen equalled for singularity and grandeur. And the following extract, descriptive of what Burckhardt actually witnessed in the different parts of Edom, cannot be more graphically abbreviated than in the words of the prophet. Of its eastern boundary, and of the adjoining part of Arabia Petræa, strictly so called, Burckhardt writes—"It might with truth be called Petræa, not only on account of its rocky mountains, but also of the elevated plain already described, which is so much covered with stones, especially flints, that it may with great propriety be called a stony desert, although susceptible of culture; in many places it is overgrown with wild herbs, and must once have been thickly inhabited; for the traces of many towns and villages are met with on both sides of the Hadj road, between Maan and Akaba, as well as between Maan and the Plains of Hauran, in which direction are also many springs. At present all this country is a desert, and Maan (Teman) is the only inhabited place in it." *I will stretch out my hand against thee, O Mount Seir, and will make thee most desolate. I will stretch out my hand upon Edom, and will make it desolate from Teman.*

In the interior of Idumea, where the ruins of some of its ancient cities are still visible, and in the extensive valley which reaches from the Red to the Dead Sea—the appearance of which must now be totally and sadly changed from what it was—"the whole plain presented to the view an expanse of shifting sands, whose surface was broken by innumerable undulations and low hills. The same appears to have been brought from *the shores of the Red Sea* by the southern winds; and the Arabs told me that the valleys continue to present the same appearance beyond the latitude of Wady Mousa. In some parts of the valley the sand is very deep, and there is not the slightest appearance of a road, or of any work of human art. A few trees grow among the sand-hills, but the depth of sand precludes *all vegetation* of herbage." *If grape-gatherers come to thee, would they not leave some gleaning grapes? if thieves by night, they will destroy till they have enough; but I have made Esau* BARE. *Edom shall be a desolate wilderness.* "On ascending the western plain, on a higher level than that of Arabia, we had before us an immense expanse of dreary country, entirely covered with black flints, with here and there some hilly chain rising from the plain." *I will stretch out upon Idumea the line of confusion, and the stones of emptiness.*

Of the remains of ancient cities still exposed to view in different places throughout Idumea, Burckhardt describes "the ruins of a large town, of which nothing remains but broken walls and heaps of stones; the ruins of an ancient city, consisting of large heaps of hewn blocks of silicious stone; the extensive ruins of Gherandel, Arindela, an ancient town of Palestina Tertia." "The following ruined places are situated in *Djebel Shera* (Mount Seir) to the S. and S. W. of Wady Mousa,—Kalaab, Djirba, Basta, Eyl, Ferdakh, Anyk, Bir el Beytar, Shemakh, and Syk. Of the towns laid down in D'Anville's map, Thoana excepted, no *traces* remain." *I will lay thy cities waste, and thou shalt be desolate. O Mount Seir, I will make thee perpetual desolations; and thy cities shall not return.*

While the cities of Idumea, in general, are thus most desolate; and while the ruins themselves are as indiscriminate as they are undefined in the prediction, (there being nothing discoverable, as there was nothing foretold, but their excessive desolation, and that they shall not return,) there is one striking exception to this promiscuous desolation, which is alike singled out by the inspired prophet and by the scientific traveller.

Burckhardt gives a description, of no ordinary interest, of the site of an ancient city which he visited, the ruins of which, not only attest its ancient splendour, but they "are entitled to rank among the most curious remains of ancient art." Though the city be desolate, the monuments of its opulence and power are durable. These are—a channel on each side of the river for conveying the water to the city—numerous tombs—above two hundred and fifty sepulchres, or excavations—many mausoleums, one in particular, of colossal dimensions in perfect preservation, and a work of immense labour, containing a chamber sixteen paces square and above twenty-five feet in height, with a colonnade in front thirty-five feet high, crowned with a pediment highly ornamented, &c.; two large truncated pyramids, and a theatre with all its benches capable of containing about three thousand spectators, ALL *cut out of the rock*. In some places these sepulchres are excavated one over the other, and the side of the mountain is so perpendicular, that *it seems impossible to approach the uppermost*, no path whatever being visible. "The ground is covered with heaps of hewn stones, foundations of buildings, fragments of columns, and vestiges of paved streets, all clearly indicating that a large city once existed here. On the left bank of the river is a rising ground, extending westward for nearly three quarters of a mile, entirely covered with similar remains. On the right bank, where the ground is more elevated, ruins of the same description are to be seen. There are also the remains of a palace and of several temples. In the eastern *cliff* there are upwards of fifty separate sepulchres close to each other." These are not the symbols of a feeble race, nor of a people that were to perish utterly. But a judgment was denounced against the strongholds of Edom. The prophetic threatening has not proved an empty boast, and could not have been the word of an uninspired mortal. "I will make thee small among the heathen; thy terribleness hath deceived thee and the pride of thy heart, O thou that dwellest in the clefts of the rock, that holdest the height of the hill; though thou shouldst make thy nest as high as the eagle, I will bring thee down from thence, saith the Lord: also Edom shall be a desolation."

These descriptions, given by the prophet and by the observer, are so analogous, and the precise locality of the scene, from its peculiar and characteristic features, so identified—and yet the application of the prophecy to the fact so remote from the thoughts or view of Burckhardt as to be altogether overlooked—that his single delineation of the ruins of the chief (and assuredly the strongest and best-fortified) city of Edom was deemed in the first edition of this treatise, and in the terms of the preceding paragraph, an illustration of the prophecy alike adequate and legitimate. And though deprecating any allusion whatever of a personal nature, and earnest for the elucidation of the truth, the author yet trusts that he may here be permitted to disclaim the credit of having been the first to assign to the prediction its wonderful and appropriate fulfilment; and it is with no slight gratification that he is now enabled to adduce higher evidence than any opinion of his own, and to state, that the selfsame prophecy has been applied by others—with the Bible in their hands, and with the very scene before them—to the selfsame spot. Yet it may be added, that this coincident application of the prophecy, without any collusion, and without the possibility, at the time, of any interchange of sentiment, affords, at least, a strong presumptive evidence of the accuracy of the application, and of the truth of the prophecy; and it may well lead to some reflection in the mind of any reader, if skepticism has not barred every avenue against conviction.

On entering the pass which conducts to the theatre of Petra, Captains Irby and Mangles remark:—"The ruins of the city here burst on the view in their full grandeur, shut in on the opposite side by barren craggy precipices, from which numerous ravines and valleys branch out in all directions; the sides of the mountains covered with an endless variety of excavated tombs and private dwellings, (*O thou that dwellest in the clefts of* THE ROCK, &c. Jer. xlix. 16,) presented altogether the most singular scene we ever beheld." In still further confirmation of the identity of the site, and the accuracy of the application, it may be added, in the words of Dr. Vincent, that "the name of this capital, in all the various languages in which it occurs, implies a rock, and as such it is described in the scriptures, in Strabo, and Al Edrissi." And in a note he enumerates among the various names having all the same signification—Sela, a rock, (the very word here used in the original,) Petra, a rock, the Greek name, and The Rock, pre-eminently—expressly referring to this passage of scripture.

Captains Irby and Mangles having, together with Mr. Bankes and Mr. Legh, spent two days in diligently examining them, give a more particular detail of the ruins of Petra than Burckhardt's account supplied; and the more full the description, the more precise and wonderful does the prophecy appear. Near the spot where they awaited the decision of the Arabs, "the high land was covered upon both its sides, and on its summits, with lines and solid masses of dry wall. The former appeared to be traces of ancient cultivation, the solid ruin seemed to be only the remains of towers for watching in harvest and vintage time. The whole neighbourhood of the spot bears similar traces of former industry, all which seem to indicate the vicinity of a great metropolis." A narrow and circuitous defile, surrounded on each side by precipitous or perpendicular rocks, varying from four hundred to seven hundred feet in altitude, and forming, for two miles, "a sort of subterranean passage," opens on the east the way to the ruins of Petra. The rocks or rather hills, then diverge on either side, and leave an oblong space, where once stood the metropolis of Edom, deceived by its terribleness, where now lies a waste of ruins, encircled on every side, save on the northeast alone, by stupendous cliffs, which still show how the pride and labour of art tried there to vie with the sublimity of nature. Along the borders of these cliffs, detached masses of rock, numerous and lofty, have been wrought into sepulchres, the interior of which is excavated into chambers, while the exterior has been cut from the live rock into the forms of towers, with pilasters, and successive bands of frieze and entablature, wings, recesses, figures of animals, and columns.

Yet, numerous as these are, they form but a part of "the vast necroplis of Petra." "Tombs present themselves, not only in every avenue to the city, and upon every precipice that surrounds it, but even intermixed almost promiscuously with its public and domestic edifices; the natural features of the defile grew more and more imposing at every step, and the excavations and sculpture more frequent on both sides, till it presented at last a continued street of tombs." The base of the cliffs wrought out in all the symmetry and regularity of art, with colonnades, and pedestals, and ranges of corridors adhering to the perpendicular surface; flights of steps chiselled out of the rock; grottoes in great numbers, "which are certainly not sepulchral;" some excavated residences of large dimensions, (in one of which is a single chamber sixty feet in length, and of a breadth proportioned;) many other dwellings of inferior note, particularly abundant in one defile leading to the city, the steep sides of which contain a sort of excavated suburb, accessible by flights of steps; niches, sometimes thirty feet in excavated height, with altars for votive offerings, or with pyramids, columns, or obelisks; a bridge across a chasm now apparently inaccessible; some small pyramids hewn out of the rock on the summit of the heights; horizontal grooves, for the conveyance of water, cut in the face of the rock, and even across the architectural fronts of some of the excavations; and, in short, "the rocks hollowed out into innumerable chambers of different dimensions, whose entrances are variously, richly, and often fantastically decorated with every imaginable order of architecture"—all united, not only form one of the most singular scenes that the eye of man ever looked upon, or the imagination painted—a group of wonders perhaps unparalleled in their kind—but also give indubitable proof, both that in the land of Edom there was a city where human ingenuity, and energy, and power must have been exerted for many ages, and to so great a degree as to have well entitled it to be noted for its strength or *terribleness*, and that the description given of it by the prophets of Israel was as strictly literal as the prediction respecting it is true. "The barren state of the country, together with the desolate condition of the city, without a single human being living near it, seem," in the words of those who were spectators of the scene, "strongly to verify the judgment denounced against it." "O thou who dwellest in the clefts of the rock, &c.—also Edom shall be a desolation," &c.

Of all the ruins of Petra, the mausoleums and sepulchres are among the most remarkable, and they give the clearest indication of ancient and long-continued royalty, and of courtly grandeur. Their immense number corroborates the accounts given of their successive kings and princes by Moses and Strabo; though a period of eighteen hundred years intervened between the dates of their respective records concerning them. The structure of the sepulchres also shows that many of them are of a more recent date. "Great," says Burckhardt, "must have been the opulence of a city which could dedicate such monuments to the memory of its rulers." But the long line of the kings and of the nobles of Idumea has for ages been cut off; they are without any representative now, without any memorial
the multitude and the magnificence of their unvisite
chres. "They shall call the nobles thereof to th
(or rather, they shall call, or summon, the no

EDOM.—Jer. 49:17. Page 512.

but there shall be no kingdom there, and all her princes shall be nothing."

Amid the mausoleums and sepulchres, the remains of temples or palaces, and the multiplicity of tombs, which all form, as it were, the grave of Idumea, where its ancient splendour is interred, there are edifices, the Roman and Grecian architecture of which decides that they were *built long* posterior to the era of the prophets.—KEITH.

Ver. 19. Behold, he shall come up like a lion from the swelling of Jordan against the habitation of the strong: but I will suddenly make him run away from her; and who *is* a chosen *man, that* I may appoint over her? for who *is* like me? and who will appoint me the time? and who *is* that shepherd that will stand before me?

See on Josh. 3. 15.

CHAPTER L.

Ver. 2. Declare ye among the nations, and publish, and set up a standard; publish, *and* conceal not: say, Babylon is taken, Bel is confounded, Merodach is broken in pieces; her idols are confounded, her images are broken in pieces.

As it was generally believed that the divinity abandoned any figure or image which was mutilated or broken, this prophetic declaration may be considered as asserting the destruction of the idols. Such a sentiment still prevails among the heathen. Dr. Buchanan, who visited many Indian provinces at the commencement of the seventeenth century, mentions that a Polygar chief, about two hundred and fifty years before, had been directed by the god Ganesa to search for treasures under a certain image, and to erect temples and reservoirs with whatever money he should find. "The treasures were accordingly found, and applied as directed; the image from under which the treasures had been taken was shown to me, and I was surprised at finding it lying at one of the gates quite neglected. On asking the reason why the people allowed their benefactor to remain in such a plight, he informed me, that the finger of the image having been broken, the divinity had deserted it: for no mutilated image is considered as habitable by a god." —BURDER.

Merodach was a name, or a title, common to the princes and kings of Babylon, of which, in the brief scriptural references to their history, two instances are recorded, viz. Merodach-baladan, the son of Baladan, King of Babylon, who exercised the office of government, and Evil-Merodach, who lived in the days of Jeremiah. From Merodach being here associated with Bel, or the temple of Belus, and from the similarity of their judgments—the one *bowed down* and *confounded*, and the other *broken in pieces*—it may reasonably be inferred that some other famous Babylonian building is here also denoted; while, at the same time, from the express identity of the name with that of the kings of Babylon, and even with Evil-Merodach, then residing there, it may with equal reason be inferred that, under the name of Merodach, the palace is spoken of by the prophet. And next to the idolatrous temple, as the seat of false worship which corrupted and destroyed the nations, it may well be imagined that the royal residence of the despot who made the earth to tremble and oppressed the people of Israel, would be selected as the marked object of the righteous judgments of God. And secondary only to the Birs Nimrood in the greatness of its ruins is the Mujelibé, or Makloube, generally understood and described by travellers as the remains of the chief palace of Babylon.

The palace of the King of Babylon almost vied with the great temple of their god. And there is now some controversy, in which of the principal mountainous heaps the one or the other lies buried. But the *utter desolation* of both leaves no room for any debate on the question,—which of the twain is *bowed down and confounded*, and which of them is *broken in pieces*. The two palaces, or castles, of Babylon were strongly fortified. And the larger was surrounded by three walls of great extent. When the city was suddenly taken by Demetrius, he seized on one of the castles by surprise, and displaced its garrison by seven thousand of his own troops, whom he stationed within it. Of the other he could not make himself master. Their extent and strength, at a period of three hundred years after the delivery of the prophecy, are thus sufficiently demonstrated. The solidity of the structure of the greater as well as of the lesser palace, might have warranted the belief of its unbroken durability for ages.—And never was there a building whose splendour and magnificence were in greater contrast to its present desolation. The vestiges of the walls which surrounded it are still to be seen, and serve with other circumstances to identify it with the Mujelibé, as the name Merodach is identified with the palace. *It is broken in pieces*, and hence its name Mujelibé, signifying overturned, or turned upside down. Its circumference is about half a mile; its height one hundred and forty feet. But it is "a mass of confusion, none of its members being distinguishable." The existence of chambers, passages, and cellars, of different forms and sizes, and built of different materials, has been fully ascertained. It is the receptacle of wild beasts, and full of doleful creatures; wild beasts cry in the desolate houses, and *dragons in the pleasant palaces*—"venomous reptiles being very numerous throughout the ruins." "All the sides are worn into furrows by the weather, and in some places where several channels of rain have united together, these furrows are of great depth, and penetrate a considerable way into the mound." "The *sides* of the ruin exhibit *hollows* worn partly by the weather." *It is brought down to the grave, to the sides of the* PIT.—KEITH.

Ver. 8. Remove out of the midst of Babylon, and go forth out of the land of the Chaldeans, and be as the he-goats before the flocks.

From this passage it appears that it was customary with the ancient Israelites to have he-goats among their flocks of sheep, and that in travelling the goats went foremost. The same judicious custom exists in South Africa to this day The goat possesses much more fortitude than the sheep, and is more forward in advancing through difficulties, especially in crossing rivers; and the sheep, who are not fond of such exploits, implicitly follow them. While travelling in Africa, I was obliged to have a small flock of sheep, to secure food when game was scarce; and as instigators to bold and rapid travelling, I was necessitated always to have a few goats in the flock. They always took the lead, especially in crossing rivers, one of which, the Great Orange River, was about a quarter of a mile across, and there the goats behaved nobly. Had they been rational creatures I should have returned them public thanks. The goats, always taking the lead among the sheep, seem as if sensible of possessing superior mental powers.—CAMPBELL.

Ver. 38. A drought *is* upon her waters; and they shall be dried up: for it *is* the land of graven images, and they are mad upon *their* idols.

Fully to understand this passage, a person must see the phrensy of the heathen when they get a sight of their idols. Thus, when the gods are taken out in procession, the multitudes shout, and the priests mutter and rave. The gestures are all distorted, and the devotees are affected with alternate sorrow or joy.—ROBERTS.

CHAPTER LI.

Ver. 13. O thou that dwellest upon many waters, abundant in treasures, thine end is come, *and* the measure of thy covetousness.

On taking Babylon suddenly and by surprise, Cyrus became immediately possessed of *the treasures of darkness, and hidden riches of secret places*. On his first publicly appearing in Babylon, all the officers of his army, both of the Persians and allies, according to his command, wore very splendid robes, those belonging to the superior officers being of various colours, all of the finest and brightest die, and richly embroidered with gold and silver; and thus the *hidden riches of secret places* were openly displayed. And when the treasures of Babylon became the spoil of another great king, Alexander gave six *minæ* (about 15*l.*) to *each* Macedonian horseman, to each Macedonian soldier and foreign horseman two *minæ*, (5*l*.) and to every other man in his army a donation equal to two months' pay. Demetrius ordered his soldiers to plunder the land of Babylon for *their own use*.—But it is not in these instances alone that Chaldea has been a spoil, and that *all* who spoil her have been *satisfied*. It was the abundance of her treasures which brought successive spoliators. Many nations came from afar, and though they *returned to their own country*, (as in formerly besieging Babylon, so in continuing to despoil the land of Chaldea,) *none returned in vain*. From the richness of the country, new treasures were speedily stored up, till again *the sword came upon them, and they were robbed*. The prey of the Persians and of the Greeks for nearly two centuries after the death of Alexander, Chaldea became afterward the prey chiefly of the Parthians, from the north, for an equal period, till a greater nation, the Romans, *came from the coasts of the earth* to pillage it. To be restrained from dominion and from plunder was the exciting cause, and often the shameless plea, of the anger and fierce wrath of these famed, but cruel, conquerors of the world. Yet, within the provinces of their empire, it was their practice, on the submission of the inhabitants, to protect and not to destroy. But Chaldea, from its extreme distance, never having yielded permanently to their yoke, and the limits of their empire having been fixed by Hadrian on the western side of the Euphrates, or on the very borders of Chaldea, that hapless country obtained not their protection, though repeatedly the scene of ruthless spoliation by the Romans. The authority of Gibbon, in elucidation of Scripture, cannot be here distrusted, any more than that of heathen historians. To use his words, "a hundred thousand captives, and a *rich booty*, rewarded the fatigues of the Roman soldiers," when Ctesiphon was taken, in the second century, by the generals of Marcus. Even Julian, who, in the fourth century, was forced to raise the siege of Ctesiphon, came not in vain to Chaldea, and failed not to take of it a spoil; nor, though an apostate, did he fail to verify by his acts the truth which he denied. After having given Perisador to the flames, "the plentiful magazines of corn, of arms, and of splendid furniture, were partly distributed among the troops, and partly reserved for the public service; the *useless stores* were destroyed by fire, or thrown into the stream of the Euphrates." (Gibbon.) Having also rewarded his army with a hundred pieces of silver to each soldier, he thus stimulated them (when still dissatisfied) to fight for greater spoil—"Riches are the object of your desires? those riches are in the hands of the Persians, and the *spoils* of this fruitful country are proposed as the prize of your valour and discipline." The enemy being defeated after an arduous conflict, "the *spoil* was such as might be expected from the riches and luxury of an oriental camp; *large quantities of silver and gold*, splendid arms and trappings, and beds and tables of massy silver." (Ibid.)

When the Romans under Heraclius ravaged Chaldea, "though much of the treasure had been removed from Destagered, and much had been expended, the *remaining wealth* appears to have *exceeded their hopes*, and even to have SATIATED their avarice." While the deeds of Julian and the words of Gibbon show how Chaldea was *spoiled*—how a *sword* continued to be on her *treasures*—and how, *year after year*, and age after age, there was *rumour on rumour* and *violence in her land*—more full illustrations remain to be given of the truth of the same prophetic word. And as a painter of great power may cope with another by drawing as closely to the life as he, though the features be different, so Gibbon's description of the sack of Ctesiphon, as previously he had described the sack and conflagration of Seleucia, (cities each of which may aptly be called "the daughter of Babylon," having been, like it, the capital of Chaldea,) is written as if, by the most graphic representation of facts, he had been aspiring to rival Volney as an illustrator of scripture prophecy. "The capital was taken by assault; and the disorderly resistance of the people gave a keener edge to the *sabres* of the Moslems, who shouted with religious transport, 'This is the white palace of Chosroes; this is the promise of the apostle of God.' The naked *robbers* of the desert were suddenly *enriched* beyond the measure of their hope or knowledge. Each chamber revealed a new *treasure*, *secreted* with art, or ostentatiously displayed; the *gold* and *silver*, the various wardrobes and precious furniture, surpassed (says Abulfeda) the estimate of fancy or numbers; and another historian defines the untold and almost infinite mass by the fabulous computation of three thousand of thousands of thousands of pieces of gold. One of the apartments of the palace was decorated with a carpet of silk sixty cubits in length and as many in breadth, (90 feet;) a paradise, or garden, was depicted on the ground; the flowers, fruits, and shrubs, were imitated by the figures of the *gold* embroidery, and the colours of the *precious stones*: and the ample square was encircled by a variegated and verdant border. The rigid Omar *divided the prize* among his brethren of Medina; the picture was destroyed; but such was the intrinsic value of the materials, that the share of Ali alone was sold for 20,000 drachms. A mule that carried away the tiara and cuirass, the belt and bracelets of Chosroes, was overtaken by the pursuers; the gorgeous trophy was presented to the commander of the faithful, and the gravest of the companions condescended to smile when they beheld the white beard, hairy arms, and uncouth figure of the veteran, who was invested with the *spoil* of the great king."

Recent evidence is not wanting to show that, wherever a *treasure* is to be found, a sword, in the hand of a *fierce* enemy, is upon it, and spoliation has not ceased in the land of Chaldea. "On the west of Hilleh, there are two towns which, in the eyes of the Persians and all the Shiites, are rendered sacred by the memory of two of the greatest martyrs of that sect. These are Meshed Ali and Meshed Housien, lately filled with riches, accumulated by the devotion of the Persians, but carried off by the ferocious Wahabees to the middle of their deserts."

And after the incessant spoliation of ages, now that *the end is come* of the treasures of Chaldea, the earth itself fails not to disclose its *hidden treasures*, so as to testify, that they once were *abundant*. In proof of this an instance may be given. At the ruins of Hoomania, near to those of Ctesiphon, pieces of silver having (on the 5th of March, 1812) been accidentally discovered, edging out of the bank of the Tigris; "on examination there were found and brought away," by persons sent for that purpose by the pacha of Bagdad's officers, "between six and seven hundred ingots of silver, each measuring from one to one and a half feet in length; and an earthen jar, containing upwards of two thousand Athenian coins, all of silver. Many were purchased at the time by the late Mr. Rich, formerly the East India Company's resident at Bagdad, and are now in his valuable collection, since bought by government, and deposited in the British Museum." Amid the ruins of Ctesiphon "the natives often pick up coins of gold, silver, and copper, for which they always find a ready sale in Bagdad. Indeed, some of the wealthy Turks and Armenians, who are collecting for several French and German consuls, hire people to go and search for coins, medals, and antique gems; and I am assured they never return to their employers empty-handed," as if *all who spoil Chaldea shall be satisfied, till even the ruins be spoiled unto the uttermost*.—Keith.

Ver. 25. Behold, I *am* against thee, O destroying mountain, saith the Lord, which destroyest all the earth; and I will stretch out my hand upon thee, and roll thee down from the rocks, and will make thee a burnt mountain.

On the summit of the hill are "immense fragments of brick-work of no determinate figures, tumbled together, and converted into solid vitrified masses." "Some of these huge fragments measured twelve feet in height, by twenty-four in circumference; and from the circumstance of the standing brick-work having remained in a perfect state, the change exhibited in these is only accountable from their having been exposed to the *fiercest fire*, or *rather scathed by lightning*." "They are completely molten—a strong presumption that fire was used in the destruction of the tower, which, in parts, resembles what the scriptures prophesied it should become, 'a burnt mountain.' In the denunciation respecting Babylon, fire is particularly mentioned as an agent against it. To this Jeremiah evidently alludes, when he says that it should be 'as when God overthrew Sodom and Gomorrah,' on which cities, it is said, 'the Lord rained brimstone and fire.'—'Her high gates shall be burned with fire, and the people shall labour in vain, and the folk in the fire, and they shall be weary.'" "In many of these immense unshapen masses might be traced the gradual effects of the consuming power, which had produced so remarkable an appearance; exhibiting parts burnt to that variegated dark hue, seen in the vitrified matter lying about in glass manufactories; while, through the whole of these awful testimonies of the fire (whatever fire it was!) which, doubtless, hurled them from their original elevation," (*I will roll thee down from the rocks,*) "the regular lines of the cement are visible, and so hardened in common with the bricks, that when the masses are struck they ring like glass. On examining the base of the standing wall, contiguous to these huge transmuted substances, it is found tolerably free from any similar changes—in short, quite in its original state; hence," continues Sir Robert Ker Porter, "I draw the conclusion, that the consuming power acted from above, and that the scattered ruin fell from some higher point than the summit of the present standing fragment. The heat of the fire which produced such amazing effects must have burned with the force of the strongest furnace; and from the general appearance of the cleft in the wall, and these vitrified masses, I should be induced to attribute the catastrophe to lightning from heaven. Ruins by the explosion of any combustible matter would have exhibited very different appearances."

"The falling masses bear evident proof of the operation of fire having been continued on them, as well after they were broken down as before, since every part of their surface has been so equally exposed to it, that many of them have acquired a rounded form, and in none can the place of separation from its adjoining one be traced by any appearance of superior freshness, or any exemption from the influence of the destroying flame."

The high gates of the temple of Belus, which were standing in the time of Herodotus, have been *burnt with fire;* the vitrified masses which fell when *Bel bowed down* rest on the top of its stupendous ruins. "The hand of the Lord has been stretched upon it; it has been rolled down from the rocks, and has been made a burnt mountain,"—of which it was further prophesied, "They shall not take of thee a stone for a corner, nor a stone for foundations, but thou shalt be desolate for ever, saith the Lord." The old wastes of Zion shall be built; its former desolations shall be raised up: and Jerusalem shall be inhabited again in her own place, even in Jerusalem. But it shall not be with Bel as with Zion, nor with Babylon as with Jerusalem. For as the "heaps of rubbish impregnated with nitre" which cover the site of Babylon "cannot be cultivated," so the vitrified masses on the summit of Birs Nimrood cannot be rebuilt. Though still they be of the hardest substance, and indestructible by the elements, and though once they formed the highest pinnacles of Belus, yet, incapable of being hewn into any regular form, they neither are nor can now be taken *for a corner or for foundations.* And the bricks on the solid fragments of wall, which rest on the summit, though neither scathed nor molten, are so firmly cemented, that, according to Mr. Rich, "it is nearly impossible to detach any of them whole," or, as Captain Mignan still more forcibly states, "they are so firmly cemented, that it is utterly impossible to detach any of them." "My most violent attempts," says Sir Robert Ker Porter, "could not separate them." And Mr. Buckingham, in assigning reasons for lessening the wonder at the total disappearance of the walls at this distant period, and speaking of the Birs Nimrood generally, observes, "that the burnt bricks (the only ones sought after) which are found in the Mujelibé, the Kasr, and the Birs Nimrood, the only three *great monuments* in which there are any traces of their having been used, are so difficult, in the two last indeed so impossible, to be extracted whole, from the tenacity of the cement in which they are laid, that they could never have been resorted to while any considerable portion of the walls existed to furnish an easier supply: even now, though some portion of the mounds on the eastern bank of the river," (the Birs is on the western side,) "are occasionally dug into for bricks, they are not extracted without a comparatively great expense, and very few of them whole, in proportion to the great number of fragments that come up with them." Around the tower there is not a single whole brick to be seen.

These united testimonies, given without allusion to the prediction, afford a better than any conjectural commentary, such as previously was given without reference to these facts. While of Babylon, in general, it is said, that it would be *taken from thence;* and while, in many places, *nothing is left,* yet of the *burnt mountain,* which forms an accumulation of ruins enough in magnitude to build a city, men do not take a stone for foundations, nor a stone for a corner. Having undergone the action of the fiercest fire, and being completely molten, the masses on the summit of Bel, on which the hand of the Lord has been stretched, cannot be reduced into any other form or substance, nor built up again by the hand of man. And the tower of Babel, afterward the temple of Belus, which witnessed the first dispersion of mankind, shall itself be witnessed by the latest generation, even as now it stands, *desolate for ever,*—an indestructible monument of human pride and folly, and of Divine judgment and truth. The greatest of the ruins, as one of the edifices of Babylon, is rolled down into a vast, indiscriminate, cloven, confounded, useless, and blasted mass, from which fragments might be hurled with as little injury to the ruined heap, as from a bare and rocky mountain's side. Such is the triumph of the word of the living God over the proudest of the temples of Baal.—KEITH.

Ver. 27. Set ye up a standard in the land, blow the trumpet among the nations, prepare the nations against her, call together against her the kingdoms of Ararat, Minni, and Ashchenaz; appoint a captain against her; cause the horses to come up as the rough caterpillars.

Some think locusts are meant, instead of caterpillars; and one reason assigned is, that they "have the appearance of horses and horsemen." Others translate, "bristled locusts." There are bristled caterpillars in the East, which at certain seasons are extremely numerous and annoying. They creep along in troops like soldiers, are covered with stiff hairs or bristles, which are so painful to the touch, and so powerful in their effects, as not to be entirely removed for many days. Should one be swallowed, it will cause death: hence people, at the particular season when they are numerous, are very cautious in examining their water vessels, lest any should have fallen in. In the year 1826, a family at Manipy had to arise early in the morning to go to their work, and they therefore prepared their rice the evening before. They were up before daylight, and took their food: in the course of a short time they were all ill, and some of them died during the day. The rice chatty was examined, and there were found the remains of the *micutty*, the rough caterpillar. Dr. Hawkesworth says, of those he saw in the West Indies, "their bodies were thick set with hairs, and they were ranging on the leaves side by side, like files of soldiers, to the number of twenty or thirty together. When we touched them, we found their bodies had the qualities of nettles."—ROBERTS.

Ver. 36. Therefore thus saith the LORD, Behold, I will plead thy cause, and take vengeance for thee; and I will dry up her sea, and make her springs dry. 37. And Babylon shall become heaps, a dwelling-place for dragons, an astonishment, and a hissing, without an inhabitant.

On the one side, near to the site of Opis, "the country all around appears to be one wide desert of sandy and barren soil, thinly scattered over with brushwood and tufts of reedy grass." On the other, between Bussorah and Bagdad, "immediately on either bank of the Tigris, is the *untrodden desert.* The absence of all cultivation,—the steril, arid, and wild character of the whole scene, formed a contrast to the rich and delightful accounts delineated in scripture. The natives, in travelling over these pathless deserts, are compelled to explore their way by the stars." "The face of the country is open and flat, presenting to the eye one vast level plain, where nothing is to be seen but here and there a herd of half-wild camels. This immense tract is very rarely diversified with any trees of moderate growth, but is an immense wild, bounded only by the horizon." In the intermediate region, "the whole extent from the foot of the wall of Bagdad is a barren waste, without a blade of vegetation of any description; on leaving the gates, the traveller has before him the prospect of a bare *desert,*—a flat and barren country." "The whole country between Bagdad and Hillah is a perfectly flat and (with the excep tion of a few spots as you approach the latter place) *uncultivated waste.* That it was at some former period in a far different state, is evident from the number of canals by which it is traversed, now *dry* and neglected; and the quantity of heaps of earth covered with fragments of brick and broken tiles, which are seen in every direction,—the indisputable traces of former population. At present the only inhabitants of the tract are the Sobeide Arabs. Around, as far as the eye can reach, is a *trackless desert.*" "The abundance of the country has vanished as clean away as if the 'besom of desolation' had swept it from north to south; the whole land, from the outskirts of Babylon to the farthest stretch of sight, lying a melancholy waste. *Not a habitable spot* appears for countless miles." *The land of Babylon is desolate, without an inhabitant.* The Arabs traverse it; and every man met with in the desert is looked on as an enemy. Wild beasts have now their home in the land of Chaldea; but the traveller is less afraid of them,—even of the lion,—than of "the wilder animal, the desert Arab." The country is frequently "totally impassable." "Those splendid accounts of the Babylonian lands yielding crops of grain two or three hundred-fold, compared with the modern face of the country, afford a remarkable proof of the *singular desolation* to which it has been subjected. The canals at present can only be traced by their decayed banks."

"The soil of this desert," says Captain Mignan, who traversed it on foot, and who, in a single day, crossed forty water-courses, "consists of a hard clay, mixed with sand, which at noon became so heated with the sun's rays that I found it too hot to walk over it with any degree of comfort. Those who have crossed those desert wilds are already acquainted with their dreary tediousness even on horseback; what it is on foot they can easily imagine." Where astronomers first calculated eclipses, the natives, as in the deserts of Africa, or as the mariner without a compass on the pathless ocean, can now direct their course only by the stars, over the pathless desert of Chaldea. Where cultivation reached its utmost height, and where two hundred-fold was stated as the common produce, there is now one wide and uncultivated waste; and *the sower and reaper are cut off from the land of Babylon.* Where abundant stores and treasures were laid up, and annually renewed and increased, *fanners* have *fanned,* and *spoilers* have *spoiled* them till they have *emptied* the land. Where labourers, shaded by palm-trees a hundred feet high, irrigated the fields till all was plentifully watered from numerous canals, the wanderer, without an object on which to fix his eye, but "stinted and short-lived shrubs," can scarcely set his foot without pain, after the noonday heat, on the "arid and parched ground," in plodding his weary way through a desert, a dry land, and a wilderness. Where there were crowded thoroughfares, from city to city, there is now "silence and solitude;" for the ancient cities of Chaldea are desolations,—where no man dwelleth, neither doth any son of man pass thereby.—Keith.

Ver. 42. The sea is come up upon Babylon: she is covered with the multitude of the waves thereof.

This metaphor is in common use to show the overwhelming power of an enemy. "Tippoo Saib went down upon his foes, like the sea he swept them all away." "True, true, the British troops went like the sea upon Bhurtpore, the forts have been carried away."—Roberts.

Ver. 58. Thus saith the Lord of hosts, The broad walls of Babylon shall be utterly broken, and her high gates shall be burnt with fire; and the people shall labour in vain, and the folk in the fire, and they shall be weary.

They were so broad, that, as ancient historians relate, six chariots could be driven on them abreast; or a chariot and four horses might pass and turn. They existed as walls for more than a thousand years after the prophecy was delivered; and long after the sentence of utter destruction had gone forth against them, they were numbered among "the seven wonders of the world." And what can be more wonderful now, or what could have been more inconceivable by man, when Babylon was in its strength and glory, than that the broad walls of Babylon should be so utterly broken that it cannot be determined with certainty that even the slightest vestige of them exists.

"All accounts agree," says Mr. Rich, "in the height of the walls, which was fifty cubits, having been reduced to these dimensions from the prodigious height of three hundred and fifty feet" (formerly stated, by the lowest computation of the length of the cubit, at three hundred feet,) "by Darius Hystaspes, after the rebellion of the town, in order to render it less defensible. I have not been fortunate enough to discover the *least trace* of them in *any part* of the ruins at Hillah; which is rather an unaccountable circumstance, considering that they survived the final ruin of the town, long after which they served as an enclosure for a park; in which comparatively perfect state St. Jerome informs us they remained in his time."

In the sixteenth century they were seen for the last time by any European traveller, (so far as the author has been able to trace,) before they were finally so utterly broken as totally to disappear. And it is interesting to mark both the time and the manner in which the walls of Babylon, like the city of which they were the impregnable yet unavailing defence, were brought down to the grave, to be seen no more.

"The meanwhile," as Rauwolf describes them, "when we were lodged there, I considered and viewed this ascent, and found that there were two behind one another," (Herodotus states that there was both an inner, or inferior, and outer wall,) "distinguished by a ditch, and extending themselves like unto two parallel *walls* a great way about, and that they were open in some places, where one might go through like gates; wherefore I believe that they were the wall of the old town that went about them; and that the places where they were open have been anciently the gates (whereof there were one hundred) of that town. And this the rather because I saw in some places under the sand (wherewith the two ascents were *almost covered*) the *old wall* plainly appear."

The cities of Seleucia, Ctesiphon, Destagered, Kufa, and anciently many others in the vicinity, together with the more modern towns of Mesched Ali, Mesched Hussein, and Hillah, "with towns, villages, and caravansaries without number," have, in all probability, been chiefly built out of the walls of Babylon. Like the city, the walls have been *taken from thence,* till none of them are *left.* The rains of many hundred years, and the waters coming upon them annually by the overflowing of the Euphrates, have also, in all likelihood, washed down the dust and rubbish from the broken and dilapidated walls into the ditch from which they were originally taken, till at last the sand of the parched desert has smoothed them into a plain, and added the place where they stood to the wilderness, so that the *broad walls of Babylon are utterly broken.* And now, as the subjoined evidence, supplementary of what has already been adduced, fully proves,—it may verily be said that the loftiest walls ever built by man, as well as the "greatest city on which the sun ever shone," which these walls surrounded, and the most fertile of countries, of which Babylon the great was the capital and the glory,—have all been *swept by the Lord of Hosts with the besom of destruction.*

A chapter of sixty pages in length, of Mr. Buckingham's Travels in Mesopotamia, is entitled, "Search after the walls of Babylon." After a long and fruitless search, he discovered on the eastern boundary of the ruins, on the *summit* of an *oval mound* from seventy to eighty feet in height, and from three to four hundred feet in circumference, "a mass of solid wall, about thirty feet in length, by twelve or fifteen in thickness, yet evidently once of much greater dimensions each way, the work being, in its present state, *broken* and incomplete *in every part;*" and this heap of ruin and fragment of wall he conjectured to be a part—the only part, if such it be, that can be discovered—of the walls of Babylon, *so utterly* are *they broken.* Beyond this there is not even a pretension to the discovery of any part of them.

Captain Frederick, of whose journey it was the "principal object to search for the remains of the wall and ditch that had compassed Babylon," states, that "neither of these have been seen by any modern traveller. All my inquiries among the Arabs," he adds, "on this subject, completely failed in producing the smallest effect. Within the space of twenty-one miles in length along the banks of the Euphrates, and twelve miles across it in breadth, I was unable o perceive any thing that could admit of my imagining that either a wall or a ditch had existed within this extensive area. If any remains do exist of the walls, they must have been of greater circumference than is allowed by modern geographers. I may possibly have been deceived; but I spared no pains to prevent it. I never was employed in riding and walking less than eight hours for six successive days, and upwards of twelve on the seventh."

Major Keppel relates that he and the party who accompanied him, "in common with other travellers, had totally failed in discovering any trace of the city walls;" and he adds, "the Divine predictions against Babylon have been so literally fulfilled in the appearance of the ruins, that I am disposed to give the fullest signification to the words of Jeremiah,—*the broad walls of Babylon shall be utterly broken.*"

Babylon shall be an astonishment.—Every one that goeth by Babylon shall be astonished. It is impossible to think on what Babylon was, and to be an eyewitness of what it is, without *astonishment.* On first entering its ruins, Sir Robert Ker Porter thus expresses his feelings: "I could not but feel an indescribable awe in thus passing, as it were, into the gates of fallen Babylon."—"I cannot portray," says Captain Mignan, "the overpowering sensation of reverential awe that possessed my mind while contemplating the extent and magnitude of ruin and devastation on every side."

How is the hammer of the whole earth cut asunder! How is Babylon become a desolation among the nations! —The following interesting description has lately been given from the spot. "After speaking of the ruined embankment, divided and subdivided again and again, like a sort of tangled network, over the apparently interminable ground—of large and wide-spreading morasses—of ancient foundations—and of chains of undulating heaps—Sir Robert Ker Porter emphatically adds:—"The whole view was particularly solemn. The majestic stream of the Euphrates, wandering in solitude, like a pilgrim monarch through the silent ruins of his devastated kingdom, still appeared a noble river, under all the disadvantages of its desert-tracked course. Its banks were hoary with reeds; and the gray osier willows were yet there on which the captives of Israel hung up their harps, and while Jerusalem was not, refused to be comforted. But how is the rest of the scene changed since then! At that time those broken hills were palaces —those long undulating mounds, streets—this vast solitude filled with the busy subjects of the proud daughter of the East.—Now, wasted with misery, her *habitations are not to be found*—and for herself, *the worm is spread over her.*"

From palaces converted into broken hills;—from streets to long lines of heaps;—from the throne of the world to sitting in the dust; from the hum of mighty Babylon to the death-like silence that rests upon the grave to which it is brought down;—from the great storehouse of the world, where treasures were gathered from every quarter, and the prison-house of the captive Jews, where, not loosed to return homewards, they served in a hard bondage, to Babylon the spoil of many nations, itself taken from thence, and nothing left; —from a vast metropolis, the place of palaces and the glory of kingdoms, whither multitudes ever flowed, to a dreaded and shunned spot not inhabited nor dwelt in from generation to generation, where even the Arabian, though the son of the desert, pitches not his tent, and where the shepherds make not their folds;—from the treasures of darkness, and hidden riches of secret places, to the taking away of bricks, and to an uncovered nakedness;—from making the earth to tremble, and shaking kingdoms, to being cast out of the grave like an abominable branch;—from the many nations and great kings from the coasts of the earth that have so often come up against Babylon, to the workmen that still cast her up as heaps and add to the number of pools in the ruins;—from the immense artificial lake, many miles in circumference, by means of which the annual rising of the Euphrates was regulated and restrained, to these pools of water, a few yards round, dug by the workmen, and filled by the river;—from the first and greatest of temples to a burnt mountain desolate for ever; from the golden image, forty feet in height, which stood on the top of the temple of Belus, to all the graven images of her gods, that are broken unto the ground and mingled with the dust;—from the splendid and luxuriant festivals of Babylonian monarchs, the noise of the viols, the pomp of Belshazzar's feast, and the godless revelry of a thousand lords drinking out of the golden vessels that had been taken from Zion, to the cry of wild beasts, the creeping of doleful creatures of which their desolate houses and pleasant palaces are full, the nestling of owls in cavities, the dancing of wild goats on the ruinous mound as on a rock, and the dwelling-place of dragons and of venomous reptiles;—from arch upon arch, and terrace upon terrace, till the hanging gardens of Babylon rose like a mountain, down to the stones of the pit now disclosed to view;—from the palaces of princes who sat on the mount of the congregation, and thought in the pride of their hearts to exalt themselves above the stars of God, to heaps cut down to the ground, perforated as the raiment of those that are slain, and as a carcass trodden under feet;—from the broad walls of Babylon, in all their height, as Cyrus camped against them round about, seeking in vain a single point where congregated nations could scale the walls or force an opening, to the untraceable spot on which they stood, where there is nothing left to turn aside, or impede in their course, the worms that cover it;—and finally, from Babylon the great, the wonder of the world, to fallen Babylon, the astonishment of all who go by it;—in extremes like these, whatever changes they involve, and by whatever instrumentality they may have been wrought out, there is not to this hour, in this most marvellous history of Babylon, a single fact that may not most appropriately be ranked under a prediction, and that does not tally entirely with its express and precise fulfilment, while at the same time they all united show, as may now be seen,—reading the judgments to the very letter, and looking to the facts as they are,—the destruction which has come from the Almighty upon Babylon.

Has not every purpose of the Lord been performed against Babylon? And having so clear illustrations of the facts before us, what mortal shall give a negative answer to the questions, subjoined by their omniscient Author to these very prophecies?—"Who hath declared this from ancient time? Who hath told it from that time? Have not I, the Lord? and there is no god beside me;—declaring the end from the beginning, and from ancient times the things that are not yet done—saying, my counsel shall stand, and I will do all my pleasure." Is it possible that there can be any attestation of the truth of prophecy, if it be not witnessed here? Is there any spot on earth which has undergone a more complete transformation? "The records of the human race," it has been said with truth, "do not present a contrast more striking than that between the primeval magnificence of Babylon and its long desolation." Its ruins have of late been carefully and scrupulously examined by different natives of Britain, of unimpeached veracity, and the result of every research is a more striking demonstration of the literal accomplishment of every prediction. How few spots are there on earth of which we have so clear and faithful a picture as prophecy gave of fallen Babylon, at a time when no spot on earth resembled it less than its present desolate solitary site! Or could any prophecies respecting any single place have been more precise, or wonderful, or numerous, or true,—or more gradually accomplished throughout many generations? And when they look at what Babylon was, and what it is, and perceive the minute realization of them all—may not nations learn wisdom, may not tyrants tremble, and may not skeptics think?—Keith.

Ver. 62. Then shalt thou say, O Lord, thou hast spoken against this place, to cut it off, that none shall remain in it, neither man nor beast, but that it shall be desolate for ever.

The course of the Tigris through Babylonia, instead of being adorned, as of old, with cities and towns, is marked with the sites of "ancient ruins." Sitace, Sabata, Narisa, Fuchera, Sendia "no longer exist." A succession of longitudinal mounds, crossed at right angles by others, mark the supposed site of Artemita, or Destagered. Its once luxuriant gardens are covered with grass; and a higher mound distinguishes "the royal residence" from the ancient streets. Extensive ridges and mounds, (near to Houmania,) varying in height and extent, are seen branching in every direction. A wall, with sixteen bastions, is the only memorial of Apollonia. The once magnificent Seleucia is now a scene of desolation. There is not a single entire building, but the country is strewed for miles with fragments of decayed buildings. "As far," says Major Keppel, "as the eye could reach, the horizon presented a broken line of mounds; the whole of this place was a desert flat." On the opposite bank of the Tigris, where Ctesiphon its rival stood, besides fragments of walls and broken masses of brick-work, and remains of vast structures encumbered with heaps of earth, there is one magnificent monument of antiquity, "in a remarkably perfect state of preservation," "a large and noble file of building, the front of which presents to view a wall three hundred feet in length, adorned with four rows of arched recesses, with a central arch, in span eighty-six feet, and above a hundred feet high, supported by walls sixteen feet thick, and leading to a hall which extends to the depth of one hundred and fifty-six feet," the width of the building. A great part of the back wall, and of the roof, is broken down; but that which remains "still appears much larger than Westminster Abbey." It is supposed to have been the lofty palace of Chosroes; but there desolation now reigns. "On the site of Ctesiphon, the smallest insect under heaven would not find a single blade of grass wherein to hide itself, nor one drop of water to allay its thirst." In the rear of the palace, and attached to it, are mounds two miles in circumference, indicating the utter desolation of buildings formed to minister to luxury. But, in the words of Captain Mignan, "such is the extent of the irregular mounds and hillocks that overspread the site of these renowned cities, that it would occupy some months to take the bearings and dimensions of each with accuracy."

While the ancient *cities of Chaldea* are thus *desolate*, the sites of others cannot be discovered, or have not been visited, as none pass thereby; the more modern cities, which flourished under the empire of califs, are "all in ruins." The second Bagdad has not indeed yet shared the fate of the first. And Hillah—a town of comparatively modern date, near to the site of Babylon, but in the gardens of which there is not the least vestige of ruins—yet exists. But the former, "ransacked by massacre, devastation, and oppression, during several hundred years," has been "gradually reduced from being a rich and powerful city to a state of comparative poverty, and the feeblest means of defence." And of the inhabitants of the latter, about eight or ten thousand, it is said that "if any thing could identify the modern inhabitants of Hillah as the descendants of the ancient Babylonians, it would be their extreme profligacy, for which they are notorious even among their immoral neighbours." They give no sign of repentance and reformation to warrant the hope that judgment, so long continued upon others, will cease from them; or that they are the people that shall escape. Twenty years have not passed since towns in Chaldea have been ravaged and pillaged by the Wahabees; and so lately as 1823, the town of Sheereban "was sacked and ruined by the Coords," and reduced to desolation. Indications of ruined cities, whether of a remote or more recent period, abound throughout the land. The process of destruction is still completing. Gardens which studded the banks of the Tigris have very recently disappeared, and mingled with the desert,—and concerning the *cities* also *of Chaldea* the word is true that they *are desolations*. For "the whole country is strewed over with the debris of Grecian, Roman, and Arabian towns, confounded in the same mass of rubbish."

But while these lie in indiscriminate ruins, the chief of the cities of Chaldea, the first in name and in power that ever existed in the world, bears many a defined mark of the judgments of heaven. The progressive and predicted decline of Babylon the great, till it ceased to be a city, has already been briefly detailed. About the beginning of the Christian era, a small portion of it was inhabited, and the far greater part was cultivated. It diminished as Seleucia increased, and the latter became the greater city. In the second century nothing but the walls remained. It became gradually a great desert; and, in the fourth century, its walls, repaired for that purpose, formed an enclosure for wild beasts, and Babylon was converted into a field for the chase—a hunting-place for the pastime of the Persian monarchs. The name and the remnant were cut off from Babylon; and there is a blank, during the interval of many ages, in the history of its mutilated remains and of its mouldering decay. It remained long in the possession of the Saracens; and abundant evidence has since been given, that every feature of its prophesied desolation is now distinctly visible—for the most ancient historians bore not a clearer testimony to facts confirmatory of the prophecies relative to its first siege and capture by Cyrus, than the latest travellers bear to the fulfilment of those which refer to its final and permanent ruin. The identity of its site has been completely established. And the truth of every general and of every particular prediction is now so clearly demonstrated, that a simple exhibition of the facts precludes the possibility of any cavil, and supersedes the necessity of any reasoning on the subject.

It is not merely the general desolation of Babylon,—however much that alone would have surpassed all human foresight,—which the Lord declared by the mouth of his prophets. In their *vision*, they saw not more clearly, nor defined more precisely, the future history of Babylon, from the height of its glory to the oblivion of its name, than they saw and depicted *fallen Babylon* as now it lies, and as, in the nineteenth century of the Christian era, it has, for the first time, been fully described. And now when *an end has come upon Babylon*, after a long succession of ages has wrought out its utter desolation, both the pen and the pencil of travellers, who have traversed and inspected its ruins, must be combined, in order to delineate what the word of God, by the prophets, told from the beginning that that end would be.

Truth ever scorns the discordant and encumbering aid of error: but to diverge in the least from the most precise facts would here weaken and destroy the argument; for the predictions correspond not closely with any thing, except alone with the express and literal reality. To swerve from it, is, in the same degree, to vary from them: and any misrepresentation would be no less hurtful than iniquitous. But the actual fact renders any exaggeration impossible, and any fiction poor. Fancy could not have feigned a contrast more complete, nor a destruction greater, than that which has come from the Almighty upon Babylon. And though the greatest city on which the sun ever shone be now a *desolate wilderness*, there is scarcely any spot on earth more clearly defined—and none could be more accurately delineated by the hands of a draftsman—than the scene of Babylon's desolation is set before us in the very words of the prophets; and no words could now be chosen like unto these, which, for two thousand five hundred years, have been its "burden"—the burden which now it bears.

Such is the multiplicity of prophecies and the accumulation of facts, that the very abundance of evidence increases the difficulty of arranging, in a condensed form, and thus appropriating its specific fulfilment to each precise and separate prediction, and many of them may be viewed connectedly. All who have visited Babylon concur in acknowledging or testifying that the desolation is exactly such as was foretold. They, in general, apply the more prominent predictions; and, in minute details, they sometimes unconsciously adopt, without any allusion or reference, the very words of inspiration.

Babylon is wholly desolate. It has become heaps—it is cut down to the ground—brought down to the grave—trodden on—uninhabited—its foundations fallen—its walls thrown down, and utterly broken—its loftiest edifices rolled down from the rocks—the golden city has ceased—the worms are spread under it, and the worms cover it, &c. There the Arabian pitches not his tent; there the shepherds make not their folds; but wild beasts of the desert lie there, and their houses are full of doleful creatures, and owls dwell there, &c. It is a possession for the bittern, and a dwelling-place for dragons; a wilderness, a dry land, and a desert; a burnt mountain; pools of water; spoiled, empty, nothing left, utterly destroyed; every one that goeth by is astonished, &c.

Babylon shall become heaps. Babylon, the glory of kingdoms, is now the greatest of ruins. Immense tumuli of temples, palaces, and human habitations of every description, are everywhere seen, and from long and varied lines of ruins, which, in some places, rather resemble natural hills than *mounds* which cover the remains of great and splendid edifices. Those buildings which were once the labour of slaves and the pride of kings, are now misshapen heaps of rubbish. "The whole face of the country is covered with vestiges of building, in some places consisting o brick walls surprisingly fresh, in others, merely a *vast succession of mounds* of rubbish, of such indeterminate figures, variety, and extent, as to involve the person who should have formed any theory in inextricable confusion." Long mounds, running from north to south, are crossed by others from east to west; and are only distinguished by their form, direction, and number, from the decayed banks of canals. The greater part of the mounds are certainly the remains of buildings, originally disposed in streets, and crossing each other at right angles. The more distinct and prominent of these "heaps" are double, or lie in parallel lines, each exceeding twenty feet in height, and are intersected by cross passages, in such a manner as to place beyond a doubt the fact of their being rows of houses or streets fallen to decay. Such was the form of the streets of Babylon, leading towards the gates; and such are now the lines of heaps—"There are also, in some places, two hollow channels, and three mounds, running parallel to each other for a considerable distance, the central mound being, in such cases, a broader and flatter mass than the other two, as if there had been two streets going parallel to each other, the central range of houses which divided them being twice the size of the others, from their being double residences, with a front and door of entrance to face each avenue." "Irregular hillocks and mounds, *formed over* masses of ruins, present at every step memorials of the past."

From the temple of Belus and the two royal palaces, to the streets of the city and single dwellings, all have *become heaps;* and the only difference or gradation now is, from the vast and solid masses of ruins which look like mountains, to the slight mound that is scarcely elevated above the plain. *Babylon is fallen,* literally FALLEN to such a degree that those who stand on its site and look on numerous parallel mounds, with a hollow space between, are sometimes at a loss to distinguish between the remains of a street or a canal, or to tell where the crowds frequented or where the waters flowed. *Babylon is fallen,* till its ruins cannot fall lower than they lie. *It is cut down to the ground. Her foundations are fallen;* and the ruins rest not on them. Its palaces, temples, streets, and houses, lie "*buried* in shapeless heaps." And "the view of Babylon," as taken from the spot, is truly a picture of utter desolation, presenting its *heaps* to the eye, and showing how, as if literally buried under them, *Babylon is brought down to the grave.*

Cast her up as heaps. Mr. Rich, in describing a grand heap of ruins, the shape of which is nearly a square of seven hundred yards in length and breadth, states that the workmen pierce into it in every direction, in search of bricks, "hollowing out deep ravines and pits, and *throwing up* the rubbish *in heaps* on the surface." "The summit of the Kasr" (supposed to have been the lesser palace) is in like manner "covered with *heaps of rubbish.*"

Let nothing of her be left. Vast heaps constitute *all that now remains* of ancient Babylon. All its grandeur is departed; all its treasures have been spoiled; all its excellence has utterly vanished; the very heaps are searched for bricks, when nothing else can be found; even these are *not left* wherever they can be taken away, and Babylon has for ages been "a quarry above ground," ready to the hand of every successive despoiler. Without the most remote allusion to this prophecy, Captain Mignan describes a mound attached to the palace ninety yards in breath by half that in height, the whole of which is deeply furrowed, in the same manner as the generality of the mounds. "The ground is extremely soft, and tiresome to walk over, and appears *completely exhausted* of all its building materials: *nothing now is left* save one towering hill, the earth of which is mixed with *fragments* of broken brick, red varnished pottery, tile, bitumen, mortar, glass, shells, and pieces of mother-of-pearl"—worthless fragments, of no value to the poorest. *From thence shall she be taken—let nothing of her be left.* One traveller, towards the end of the last century, passed over the site of ancient Babylon, without being conscious of having traversed it.

While the workmen *cast her up as heaps* in piling up the rubbish while excavating for brick, that they may *take* them *from thence,* and that *nothing be left;* they labour more than trebly in the fulfilment of prophecy, for the numerous and deep excavations form *pools of water,* on the overflowing of the Euphrates, and, annually filled, they are not dried up throughout the year. Deep cavities are also formed by the Arabs, when digging for hidden treasure. The ground is sometimes covered with *pools of water* in the hollows." *Sit on the dust, sit on the ground, O daughter of the Chaldeans.* The *surface* of the mounds, which form all that remains of Babylon, consists of decomposed buildings reduced to dust; and over all the ancient streets and habitations there is literally nothing but the dust of the ground on which to sit. *Thy nakedness shall be uncovered.* "Our path," says Captain Mignan, "lay through the great mass of ruined heaps on the site of 'shrunken Babylon.' And I am perfectly incapable of conveying an adequate idea of the dreary, lonely nakedness that appeared before me."—KEITH.

CHAPTER LII.

Ver. 21. And *concerning* the pillars, the height of one pillar *was* eighteen cubits, and a fillet of twelve cubits did compass it; and the thickness thereof *was* four fingers: *it was* hollow.

In the same way do the people of the East speak of any thing which is less in measure than a SPAN. "What height are your pepper vines?"—"About two fingers." "When the rice becomes five fingers in height we shall want more rain." That which is less than a finger is spoken of as a grain of rice; the next gradation is an *ellu,* i. e. gingelly seed; the next is a mustard seed; and the last an *anu,* i. e an atom.—ROBERTS.

BIRS NIMROOD.—Is. 46: 1. Jer. 50: 2, and 51: 61, 62.
"I will roll thee down from the rocks and make thee a burnt mountain."

LAMENTATIONS OF JEREMIAH.

CHAPTER I.

Ver. 1. How doth the city sit solitary *that was* full of people! *how* is she become as a widow! she *that was* great among the nations, *and* princess among the provinces, *how* is she become tributary!

Jerusalem had been sacked by a ruthless foe, and her sons had been carried off to Babylon. "As a widow." When a husband dies, the solitary widow takes off her marriage jewels, and other ornaments; *her head is shaved!* and she sits down in the dust to bewail her lamentable condition. In the book Scanda Purāna, it is said, after the splendid city of Kupera had been plundered by the cruel Assurs, "the city deprived of its riches by the pillage of the Assurs, resembled the WIDOW!" Jerusalem became as a widow in her loneliness bemoaning her departed lord.—ROBERTS.

Ver. 3. Judah is gone into captivity, because of affliction, and because of great servitude; she dwelleth among the heathen, she findeth no rest: all her persecutors overlook her between the straits.

It was the practice with those who hunted wild beasts to drive them, if possible, into some *strait* and *narrow* passage, that they might more effectually take them, as in such a situation an escape could hardly be effected. It is to this circumstance that the prophet alludes in these words.—BURDER.

Ver. 11. All her people sigh, they seek bread; they have given their pleasant things for meat to relieve the soul: see, O LORD, and consider; for I am become vile.

What a melancholy picture have we here! the captives, it appears, had been allowed, or they had concealed, some of their "pleasant things," their jewels, and were now obliged to part with them for food. What a view we also have here of the cruelty of the vile Babylonians! The people of the East retain their little valuables, such as jewels and rich robes, to the last extremity. To part with that, which has, perhaps, been a kind of heir-loom in the family, is like parting with life. Have they sold the last wreck of their other property; are they on the verge of death; the emaciated members of the family are called together, and some one undertakes the heart-rending task of proposing such a bracelet, or armlet, or anklet, or ear-ring, or the pendant of the forehead, to be sold. For a moment all are silent, till the mother or daughters burst into tears, and then the contending feelings of hunger, and love for their "pleasant things," alternately prevail. In general the conclusion is, to pledge, and not to sell, their much-loved ornaments; but such is the rapacity of those who have money, and such the extreme penury of those who have once fallen, they seldom regain them. Numbers give their jewels to others to keep for them, and never see them more. I recollect a person came to the mission house, and brought a large casket of jewels for me to keep in our iron chest. The valuable gems were shown to me one by one; but I declined receiving them, because I had heard that the person was greatly indebted to the government, and was led to suspect the object was to defraud the creditor. They were then taken to another person, who received them,—decamped to a distant part of the country, and the whole of the property was lost, both to the individual and the creditors.—ROBERTS.

Ver. 17. Zion spreadeth forth her hands, *and there is* none to comfort her: the LORD hath commanded concerning Jacob, *that* his adversaries *should be* round about him: Jerusalem is as a menstruous woman among them.

What a graphic view we have here of a person in distress! See that poor widow looking at the dead body of her husband, as the people take it from the house: she spreads forth her hands to their utmost extent, and piteously bewails her condition. The last allusion in the *verse* is very common.—ROBERTS.

CHAPTER II.

Ver. 1. How hath the LORD covered the daughter of Zion with a cloud in his anger, *and* cast down from heaven unto the earth the beauty of Israel, and remembered not his footstool in the day of his anger.

Those who are in favour with the king, or those who obey him, are called his footstool. But the figure is also used in a degrading sense. Thus, do two men quarrel, one says to the other, "I will make thee my footstool." "Ah! my lord, be not angry with me, how long have I been your footstool?" "I be that fellow's footstool! Never! Was he not footstool to my father?"—ROBERTS.

Ver. 15. All that pass by clap *their* hands at thee; they hiss and wag their head at the daughter of Jerusalem, *saying, Is* this the city that *men* call The perfection of beauty, The joy of the whole earth?

See on Job 27. 23.

The vulgar, the low triumph of a victorious party, in the East, is extremely galling; there is nothing like moderation or forbearance in the victors. No, they have recourse to every contemptuous and brutal method to degrade their fallen foe. Has one party triumphed over another in a court of law, or in some personal conflict, the conquerors shout loud, "Aha! aha! fallen, fallen;" and then go close to the vanquished, and "clap their hands."—ROBERTS.

Oriental females express their respect for persons of high rank, by gently applying one of their hands to their mouths; a custom which seems to have existed from time immemorial. In some of the towns of Barbary, the leaders of the sacred caravans are received with loud acclamations, and every expression of the warmest regard. The women view the parade from the tops of the houses, and testify their satisfaction by striking their four fingers on their lips as fast as they can, all the while making a joyful noise. The sacred writers perhaps allude to this custom, in those passages where clapping the hand in the singular number is mentioned. Striking one hand smartly upon the other, which we call clapping the hands, was also used to express joy, in the same manner as among ourselves; but in the East it appears to have been generally employed to denote a malignant satisfaction, a triumphant or insulting joy. In this way, the enemies of Jerusalem expressed their satisfaction, at the fall of that great and powerful city.—PAXTON.

CHAPTER III.

Ver. 7. He hath hedged me about, that I cannot get out: he hath made my chain heavy.

This figure is taken from a prisoner having a heavy chain to drag as he goes along. Husbands sometimes speak of their wives as a chain. Thus, is a man invited to a distant country; he asks in reply, "How can I come? my wife has made my chain heavy." "My husband, my husband, you shall not go; my weeping shall make your chain heavy." A man in great trouble asks, Who will break this *sangale?* i. e. chain. "My chain, my chain, who will break this chain?" "Have you heard Varavar's chain is broken? He is dead! Who will make another chain for him?"—ROBERTS.

Ver. 15. He hath filled me with bitterness, he hath made me drunken with wormwood.

"Wicked, wicked son," says the disappointed mother, "I expected to have had pleasure from thee, but thou hast given me *kasapu*," i. e. bitterness. "Shall I go to his house to live on bitterness?" "Who can make this bitterness sweet?"—ROBERTS.

CHAPTER IV.

Ver. 5. They that did feed delicately are desolate in the streets; they that were brought up in scarlet embrace dunghills.

In preparing their victuals, the Orientals are, from the extreme scarcity of wood in many countries, reduced to use cow-dung for fuel. At Aleppo, the inhabitants use wood and charcoal in their rooms, but heat their baths with cow-dung, the parings of fruit, and other things of a similar kind, which they employ people to gather for that purpose. In Egypt, according to Pitts, the scarcity of wood is so great, that at Cairo they commonly heat their ovens with horse or cow dung, or dirt of the streets; what wood they have being brought from the shores of the Black Sea, and sold by weight. Chardin attests the same fact; "The eastern people always use cow-dung for baking, boiling a pot, and dressing all kinds of victuals that are easily cooked, especially in countries that have but little wood;" and Dr. Russel remarks, in a note, that "the Arabs carefully collect the dung of the sheep and camel, as well as that of the cow; and that the dung, offals, and other matters, used in the bagnios, after having been new gathered in the streets, are carried out of the city, and laid in great heaps to dry, where they become very offensive. They are intolerably disagreeable, while drying, in the town adjoining to the bagnios; and are so at all times when it rains, though they be stacked, pressed hard together, and thatched at top." These statements exhibit, in a very strong light, the extreme misery of the Jews, who escaped from the devouring sword of Nebuchadnezzar: "They that feed delicately, are desolate in the streets; they that were brought up in scarlet, embrace dunghills." To embrace dunghills, is a species of wretchedness, perhaps unknown to us in the history of modern warfare; but it presents a dreadful and appalling image, when the circumstances to which it alludes are recollected. What can be imagined more distressing to those who lived delicately, than to wander without food in the streets? What more disgusting and terrible to those who had been clothed in rich and splendid garments, than to be forced, by the destruction of their palaces, to seek shelter among stacks of dung, the filth and stench of which it is almost impossible to endure. The dunghill, it appears from holy writ, is one of the common retreats of the mendicant, which imparts an exquisite force and beauty to a passage in the song of Hannah: "He raiseth up the poor out of the dust, and lifteth the beggar from the dunghill, to set them among princes, and to make them inherit the throne of glory." The change in the circumstances of that excellent woman, she reckoned as great (and it was to her not less unexpected) as the elevation of a poor despised beggar, from a nauseous and polluting dunghill, rendered tenfold more fetid by the intense heat of an oriental sun, to one of the highest and most splendid stations on earth.—PAXTON.

Ver. 7. Her Nazarites were purer than snow, they were whiter than milk, they were more ruddy in body than rubies, their polishing *was* of sapphire: 8. Their visage is blacker than a coal; they are not known in the streets: their skin cleaveth to their bones; it is withered, it is become like a stick.

I leave it to physicians and naturalists to determine, with minute exactness, what effect extreme hunger produces on the body, particularly as to *colour*. It is sufficient for me to remark, that the modern inhabitants of the East suppose it occasions an approach to *blackness*, as the ancient Jews also did. "Her Nazarites," says the prophet, complaining of the dreadful want of food, just before Jerusalem was taken by Nebuchadnezzar, "her Nazarites were purer than snow, they were whiter than milk, they were more ruddy in body than rubies, their polishing was of sapphire. Their visage is blacker than a coal: they are not known in the streets: their skin cleaveth to their bones; it is withered, it is become like a stick." Lam. iv. 7, 8. The like is said, ch. v. 10: "Our skin was black like an oven, because of the terrible famine."

The same representation of its effects still obtains in those countries. So Sir John Chardin tells, that the common people of Persia, to express the sufferings of Hossein, a grandson of their prophet Mohammed, and one of their most illustrious saints, who fled into the deserts before his victorious enemies, that pursued him ten days together, and at length overtook him, ready to die with heat, thirst, and fatigue, and slew him with a multitude of wounds, in memory of which they annually observe ten days with great solemnity; I say, he tells us, that the common people then, to express what he suffered, "appear entirely naked, excepting the parts modesty requires to be covered, and *blackened* all over; while others are stained with blood; others run about the streets, beating two flint-stones against each other, their tongues hanging out of their mouths like people quite exhausted, and behaving like persons in despair, crying with all their might, Hossein, &c. Those that coloured themselves *black*, intended to represent the extremity of thirst and heat which Hossein had suffered, which was so great, they say, *that he turned black*, and his tongue swelled out of his mouth. Those that were covered with *blood*, intended to represent his being so terribly wounded, as that all his blood had issued from his veins before he died."

Here we see thirst, want of food, and fatigue, are supposed to make a human body look black. They are now supposed to do so; as they were supposed anciently to have that effect.—HARMER.

CHAPTER V.

Ver. 4. We have drunken our water for money; our wood is sold unto us.

See on Num. 20. 19.

That numbers of the Israelites had no wood growing on their own lands, for their burning, must be imagined from the openness of their country. It is certain, the eastern villages now have oftentimes little or none on their premises: so Russel says, that inconsiderable as the stream that runs at Aleppo, and the gardens about it, may appear, they, however, contain almost the only trees that are to be met with for twenty or thirty miles round, "for the villages are destitute of trees," and most of them only supplied with what rainwater they can save in cisterns. D'Arvieux gives us to understand, that several of the present villages of the Holy Land are in the same situation; for, observing that the Arabs burn cow-dung in their encampments, he adds, that all the villagers, who live in places where there is a scarcity of wood, take great care to provide themselves with sufficient quantities of this kind of fuel. This is a circumstance I have elsewhere taken notice of. The Holy Land appears, by the last observations, to have been as little wooded anciently as at present; nevertheless, the Israelites seem to have burnt wood very commonly, and without buying it too, from what the prophet says, Lam. v. 4. "We have drunken our water for money, our wood is sold to us." Had they been wont to buy their fuel, they would not have complained of it as such a hardship.

The true account of it seems to be this: The woods of the land of Israel being from very ancient times common, the people of the villages, which, like those about Aleppo, had no trees growing in them, supplied themselves with fuel out of these wooded places, of which there were many anciently, and several that still remain. This liberty of taking wood *in common*, the Jews suppose to have been a constitution of Joshua, of which they give us ten; the first, giving liberty to an Israelite to feed his flock in the woods of any tribe: the second, that it should be free to take wood in the fields any where. But though this was the ancient custom in Judea, it was not so in the country into which they were carried captives; or if this text of Jeremiah respects those that continued in their own country for a while under Gedaliah, as the ninth verse insinuates, it signifies, that their conquerors possessed themselves of these woods, and would allow no fuel to be cut down without leave, and that leave was not to be obtained without money. It is certain, that presently after the return from the captivity, timber was not to be cut without leave, Neh. ii. 8.—HARMER.

Ver. 12. Princes are hanged up by their hand: the faces of elders were not honoured.

No punishment is more common than this in the East, especially for slaves and refractory children. Thus, has a master an obstinate slave; has he committed some great offence with his hands; several men are called, who tie the offender's hands, and hoist him to the roof, till he beg for forgiveness. Schoolboys, who are in the habit of playing truant, are also thus punished. To tell a man you will hang him by the hands, is extremely provoking. See, then, the lamentable condition of the princes in Babylon, they were "hanged up by their hands," as common slaves. —ROBERTS.

Ver. 16. The crown is fallen *from* our head: wo unto us, that we have sinned.

Has a man lost his property, his honour, his beauty, or his happiness, he says, "My crown has fallen;" does a father or grandfather reprove his sons for bad conduct, he asks, "Has my crown fallen?"—ROBERTS.

EZEKIEL.

CHAPTER I.

Ver. 1. Now it came to pass in the thirtieth year, in the fourth *month*, in the fifth *day* of the month, as I *was* among the captives by the river of Chebar, *that* the heavens were opened, and I saw visions of God.

The prophet Ezekiel holds a conspicuous place among the writers of the Old Testament, although, from the highly figurative style of his predictions, a greater degree of obscurity has been supposed to attach to this book, than perhaps to any other, except the Revelations, in the whole sacred canon. This remark applies peculiarly to the first and tenth chapters of the book, which contain the description of a remarkable emblematical vision, presented, indeed, under some variations of aspect in each, but in its general features manifestly the same. These chapters, together with the nine last, are said to have been reckoned so sacredly obscure by the ancient Jews, that they abstained from reading them till they were thirty years of age. The mystery appears to have been but little abated by time, as the great mass of commentators still speak of the unpenetrated veil of symbolical darkness in which the prophet's meaning is wrapped, and the common readers of scripture reiterate the lamentation; although doubtless every portion of the inspired writings is just as luminous and intelligible as infinite Wisdom saw best it should be; and it is a feature of revelation worthy of that Wisdom, that it is adapted to every stage of progress and attainment in spiritual knowledge. While in some parts, and those the most important, it levels itself to the capacity of a child, in others it gives scope to the intellect of an angel.

Most of the earlier predictions of the book of Ezekiel, have respect to the remnant of the nation left in Judea, and to the further judgments impending over them, such as the siege and sacking of Jerusalem—the destruction of the Temple—the slaughter of a large portion of its inhabitants —and the abduction of the remainder into a foreign land. The date of the first chapter is about six years prior to the occurrence of these events, and the vision which it contains was undoubtedly designed TO EXHIBIT A VISIBLE SYMBOL OF THE DIVINE GLORY WHICH DWELT AMONG THAT NATION. The tokens of Jehovah's presence constituted the distinguishing honour of Israel, and its departure from among them would consequently form the essence of their national calamities, and swell them indefinitely beyond all similar disasters which could possibly befall any other people. Plain intimations of the abandonment of the Holy City by the emblems of the Lord's glory, are interspersed through several ensuing chapters, till we come to the tenth, where the same splendid image is again brought to view, *and is now exhibited in the act of forsaking its ancient dwelling-place.* The first chapter describes what their treasure was; the tenth, the loss of it. Together with this, the latter contains several additional particulars in the description of the vision, which are all-important to its explication. By keeping in mind this general view of the contents of these chapters, the reader will find himself assisted in giving that significancy to each, which he was probably before at a loss to discover. It may be here remarked, that the symbol of the Divine glory described by Ezekiel was not designed as a mere *temporary* emblem, adapted only to that occasion, but that it is a *permanent one*, of which we have repeated intimations in the scriptures. It is from this fact, chiefly, that it derives its importance as an object of investigation.—BUSH.

Ver. 7. And their feet *were* straight feet; and the sole of their feet *was* like the sole of a calf's foot; and they sparkled like the colour of burnished brass.

Heb. "their feet was a straight foot." By foot here is meant the lower part of the legs, including the ankles. As the human foot is formed, motion of the body in any particular direction requires the foot to be turned in that direction. The form here mentioned precludes that necessity, which is doubtless the reason of its being assigned them.—BUSH.

Ver. 9. Their wings *were* joined one to another; they turned not when they went; they went every one straight forward. 10. As for the likeness of their faces, they four had the face of a man, and the face of a lion on the right side; and they four had the face of an ox on the left side; they four also had the face of an eagle.

The reader must imagine such a relative position of the living creatures, preserving the form of a square, that to the eye of a spectator the different faces would be presented as here described, for the prophet could not see the four faces of each at once. Suppose two of the living creatures on a right line in front, and two on each side of the line, equidistant from it, and the faces can be easily arranged so as to conform to the description.—BUSH.

Ver. 12. And they went every one straight forward: whither the spirit was to go, they went; *and* they turned not when they went.

One design of their having four faces was, that they might go directly forward towards either of the four cardinal points without turning their bodies.—BUSH.

Ver. 16. The appearance of the wheels and their work *was* like unto the colour of a beryl; and they four had one likeness: and their appearance and their work *was* as it were a wheel in the middle of a wheel. 17. When they went, they went upon their four sides; *and* they turned not when they went.

From all that we can gather of the form of these wheels, they appear to have been *spherical*, or each composed of two of equal size, and inserted, the rim of the one into that of the other at right-angles, and so consisting of four equal parts or half circles. They were accordingly adapted to run either forward or backward, to the right hand or the left, without any lateral turning; and by this means, their motion corresponded with that of the four faces of the living creatures to which they were attached. "When they went upon their four sides, they turned not as they went;" Heb. "When they went, they went upon the quarter-part of their fourfoldness," i. e. upon, or in the direction of, one of the four vertical semicircles into which they were divided, and which looked towards the four points of the compass. When it is said—"they turned not"—it is not to be understood that they had not a revolving or rotary motion, but that they, like the faces, never forsook a straight forward course.—BUSH.

Ver. 19. And when the living creatures went, the wheels went by them; and when the living creatures were lifted up from the earth, the wheels were lifted up. 20. Whithersoever the spirit was to go, they went, thither *was their* spirit to go; and the wheels were lifted up over against them: for the spirit of the living creature *was* in the wheels.

These circumstances are doubtless dwelt upon with peculiar emphasis, in order to show the intimacy of relation and harmony of action subsisting between the living creatures and the wheels, or more properly between the things symbolically represented by them.—BUSH.

Ver. 22. And the likeness of the firmament upon the heads of the living creatures *was* as the colour of the terrible crystal, stretched forth over their heads above.

Heb. "As for the likeness upon the heads of the living creatures, *it was that of* an expansion stretched over their heads above, like the aspect of the terrible crystal." This expansion was a splendid level pavement or flooring, of a crystal clearness, and resting upon the heads of the living creatures, as the temple lavers rested upon the four cornerstays, or "undersetters," of their bases. The resemblance to the crystal was not in colour, but in transparency, for the colour was like that of a sapphire stone or the cerulean azure of the real firmament of heaven. This is evident from v. 26, and also from Ex. xxiv. 9, 10, containing an evident allusion to this vision, and perhaps the germ of it. "Then went up Moses and Aaron, Nadab and Abihu, and seventy of the elders of Israel; and they saw the God of Israel; and there was under his feet as it were a paved-work of a sapphire-stone, and, as it were, the body of heaven in its clearness."—BUSH.

Ver. 23. And under the firmament *were* their wings straight, the one towards the other: every one had two, which covered on this side, and every one had two, which covered on that side, their bodies.

The wings therefore of the whole four being in contact with each other, formed a kind of curtain beneath the incumbent pavement, and thus completed the resemblance to the Temple Bases, and forming in fact a magnificent living chariot.—BUSH.

Ver. 24. And when they went, I heard the noise of their wings, like the noise of great waters, as the voice of the Almighty, the voice of speech, as the noise of a host: when they stood, they let down their wings.

Heb. "And there was a voice—in their standing they let down their wings." The design of the prophet seems to be, to show the perfect obsequiousness of the living creatures to the word of command emanating from the throne above, and directing their movements. When the word was given to move, their wings were at once expanded, the resounding din was heard, and the glorious vehicle, instinct with life, rolled on in amazing majesty. Again, when the counter mandate was heard, they in an instant stayed themselves in mid career, and relaxed their wings.—BUSH.

Ver. 27. And I saw as the colour of amber, as the appearance of fire round about within it; from the appearance of his loins even upward, and from the appearance of his loins even downward, I saw as it were the appearance of fire, and it had brightness round about.

There is a studied indistinctness in the image here described, yet it is plain that a *human form* is intended to be shadowed forth, and that too in connexion with the splendour of fire—a usual accompaniment of the visible manifestations of the Deity. There is little room to doubt, therefore, that in the august occupant of the throne, we are to recognise the Son of God, the true God of Israel, anticipating, in this emblematic manner, his manifestation in the flesh, and his future exaltation as King of Zion, riding forth in the chariot of the Gospel.

Such was the vision presented to the view of the prophet of the captivity. A more magnificent conception can scarcely be framed by the mind of man. Indeed if we except the Apocalyptic disclosures of "the holy city, the new Jerusalem, coming down from God out of heaven, prepared as a bride adorned for her husband," we know of nothing of this nature in the whole compass of revelation to be compared with it. Let the reader bring before his mind's eye the four living creatures of majestic size—so posited, and with their wings so expanded and in contact, as to form a hollow square—the whole four raised above the earth, and resting upon an equal number of spherical wheels compounded like the equator and meridian circles of the globe—their heads, with the quaternion of faces, made the supporters of a broad lucid pavement, clear as crystal, and having the hue of the ethereal vault—and this splendid firmament surmounted by the visible Divine Glory, controlling the movements of the living chariot—let him imagine this rolling throne moving onward with the noise of mighty thunderings, or of many waters, even "as the voice of the Almighty God when he speaketh," while fiery splendours and a bright rainbow surround the Majesty above, and the light of lamps, burning coals, and lightnings, glow amid the living creatures, and he cannot but feel, that the ordinary creations of human genius, whether of poets or painters, present nothing worthy to be placed by the side of it.—BUSH.

CHAPTER II.

Ver. 6. And thou, son of man, be not afraid of them, neither be afraid of their words, though briers and thorns *be* with thee, and thou dost dwell among scorpions: be not afraid of their words, nor be dismayed at their looks, though they *be* a rebellious house.

The scorpion is one of the most loathsome objects in nature. It resembles a small lobster; its head appears to be joined and continued to the breast; it has two eyes in the middle of its head, and two towards the extremity, between which come, as it were, two arms, which are divided into two parts, like the claws of a lobster. It has eight legs proceeding from its breast, every one of which is divided into six parts, covered with hair, and armed with talons or claws. The belly is divided into seven rings, from the last of which the tail proceeds, which is divided into seven little heads, of which the last is furnished with a sting. In some are observed six eyes, and in others eight may be perceived. The tail is long, and formed after the manner of a string of beads, tied end to end, one to another; the last bigger than the others, and somewhat longer; to the end of which, are sometimes two stings, which are hollow, and filled with a cold poison, which it injects into the wound it inflicts. It is of a blackish colour, and moves sidewise like a crab. Darting with great force at the object of its fury, it fixes violently with its snout, and by its feet, on the persons which it seizes, and cannot be disengaged without difficulty.

[About the middle of July, the waters had risen to the proper height in the basin of the Nilometer. Orders were immediately sent to the sub-governor, to open the kalidge with all the customary pomp which, from time immemorial, has ushered in this festival. The pacha had bad news from the Morea, and did not attend, but all his court was there; the defterdar flinging paras among the multitude, bands of music playing all night on the banks of the canal, and some pieces of artillery firing at intervals. I went there at night, for the festival commences the preceding evening; the Nile was covered with decorated boats, splendidly illuminated, and all the beauty of Cairo was collected, either on the banks of the river or in the gaudy boats; it was altogether different from a Turkish festival, there was no gravity, every body laughed and talked; the ladies enjoyed their liberty, and I fear, that night, too many of them abused it.

It was impossible, however, to observe so much gayety and good-humour, "in a country which may better be called the grave, than the mother of her children," without feeling pleasure. I was in high spirits, when suddenly I perceived something biting my leg; I put down my hand, and discovered a scorpion, the first I had seen in Egypt. The pain was hardly perceptible; but I felt rather uncomfortable about the consequences, and expressed my alarm to an old Arab who sat near me; he very good-naturedly led me to a coffee-house, and without asking my consent to doctor me, he proceeded to boil a small quantity of olive-oil, then took a bit of his own old turban, dipped it in the oil, and applied it, hotter than I could well bear, to the bite. I let him have his way; for, in such cases, I think the people of the country are better judges of remedies than a college of doctors. I was right in thinking so, for I suffered no inconvenience whatever from the accident.—Madden.]

To the northward of mount Atlas, the scorpion is not very hurtful, for the sting being only attended with a slight fever, the application of a little Venice treacle quickly assuages the pain. But the scorpion of Getulia, and most other parts of the Sahara, as it is larger, and of a darker complexion, so its venom is proportionably malignant, and frequently attended with death." In Syria it does not seem to be deadly, but occasions much inconvenience and suffering to the inhabitants. Whole companies are suddenly affected with vomitings, which is supposed to be produced by the poisonous matter which exudes from the skin of the scorpion, as it crawls over their kitchen utensils or provisions. Nor is it possible almost to avoid the danger; it is never at rest during the summer months, and so malicious is its disposition, that it may be seen continually flourishing its tail in which the sting is lodged, and striking at every object within its reach. So mischievous and hateful is this creature, that the sacred writers use it in a figurative sense for wicked, malicious, and crafty men. Such was the house of Israel to the prophet Ezekiel: "Thou dwellest," said Jehovah to his servant, "among scorpions." No animal in the creation seems endued with a nature so irascible. When taken, they exert their utmost rage against the glass which contains them; will attempt to sting a stick, when put near them; will sting animals confined with them, without provocation; are the cruelest enemies to each other. Maupertuis put a hundred together in the same glass; instantly they vented their rage in mutual destruction, universal carnage! in a few days only fourteen remained, which had killed and devoured all the others. It is even asserted, that when in extremity or despair, the scorpion will destroy itself; he stings himself on the back of the head, and instantly expires. Surely Moses with great propriety mentions scorpions among the dangers of the wilderness; and no situation can be conceived more hazardous than that of Ezekiel, who is said to dwell among scorpions; nor could a fitter contrast be selected by our Lord: "Will a father give a scorpion to his child instead of an egg?" Jesus invested his disciples with power to tread on serpents and scorpions; by which may be denoted, power and authority to counteract and baffle every kind of agent which the devil employs to vex and injure the church. The disciples of Antichrist, who, by their poisonous doctrines, injure or destroy the souls of men, are likewise compared to these dangerous animals: "And there came out of the smoke locusts upon the earth: and unto them was given power as the scorpions of the earth have power."—PAXTON.

CHAPTER IV.

Ver. 1. Thou also, son of man, take thee a tile, and lay it before thee, and portray upon it the city, *even* Jerusalem.

The tile was probably an undried one.—Lord Cornwallis got a good idea of Bangalore from a Bramin, who acted as spy, and drew a plan of the place with great accuracy in a short time in moist clay.—CALLAWAY.

Ver. 1. Thou also, son of man, take thee a tile, and lay it before thee, and portray upon it the city, *even* Jerusalem: 2. And lay siege against it, and build a fort against it, and cast a mount against it; set the camp also against it, and set *battering*-rams against it round about.

See on Is. 29. 3.

When the Hebrews were besieged by their enemies, they erected engines on their towers and bulwarks, to shoot arrows and hurl stones; and when they sat down before a place with the view of besieging it, they dug trenches; they drew lines of circumvallation; they built forts and made ramparts; they cast up mounts on every side, and planted battering rams upon them, to breach the walls, and open a way into the city. These engines, it is probable, bore some resemblance to the balistæ and catapultæ of the Romans, which were employed for throwing stones and arrows, and were, in reality, the mortars and carcasses of antiquity. Josephus asserts, that Uzziah the king of Judah taught his soldiers to march in battalia, after the manner of the Macedonian phalanx, arming them with swords, targets, and corslets of brass, with arrows and darts. He also provided a great number of engines to batter cities, and to shoot stones and darts, besides hooks of different forms, and other instruments of a similar kind.

Calmet describes "an engine used for throwing very heavy stones, by means of a strong bow, whose circular arms are tightly held by two vertical beams, nearly upright; the cord of the bow is drawn back by means of a windlass, placed between two beams also, behind the former, but uniting with them at top; in the centre is an arm, capable of swinging backward and forward; round this arm the bowstring passes; at the bottom of this arm is placed the stone, in a kind of seat. The bowstring being drawn backward, by the power of the windlass drawing the moving arm, the rope is suddenly let go from this arm by a kind of cock, when the bowstring, recovering its natural situation, with all its power violently swings forwards the moving arm, and with it the stone, thereby projecting the stone with great force and velocity."

"Another machine for throwing stones, consists of two arms of a bow, which are strengthened by coils of rope, sinews, or hair, (women's hair was reckoned the best for the purpose.) These arms being drawn backward as tight as possible, by a windlass placed at some distance behind the machine, the string of the bow is attached to a kind of cock, and the stone to be discharged being placed immediately before it, on touching the cock, the violent effort of the bow threw of the stone to a great distance." The arms of this bow were of iron; which was the same as the *balistæ* of the Romans.

"Besides these kind of instruments that were extremely powerful, others off smaller size, and inferior powers, were constructed for the purpose of being carried about: these were somewhat like our ancient cross-bows; and the bow-string was drawn back by various contrivances, often merely by strength of arm, or by reducing the board that carried the arrow to its station backwards, by pressing it against the ground."—PAXTON.

Ver. 4. Lie thou also upon thy left side, and lay the iniquity of the house of Israel upon it: *according* to the number of the days that thou shalt lie upon it thou shalt bear their iniquity.

It is more than probable something is alluded to here which we cannot understand. When a person is sick, he will not lie on his RIGHT side, because that would be a bad omen: should he in his agony, or when asleep, turn on that side, his attendants will immediately again place him on the *left side*. After people have taken their food, they generally sleep a little, but they are careful to repose on the left side, "because the food digests better." It is impossible to say what is the origin of this practice: it may have arisen from the circumstance that the RIGHT side "is of the masculine gender," and the left feminine, as is the case with the supreme Siva. Females are directed to recline on the right side, and many curious stories are told, in reference to them, which are not worth repeating.—ROBERTS.

Ver. 9. Take thou also unto thee wheat, and barley, and beans, and lentiles, and millet, and fitches, and put them in one vessel, and make thee bread thereof, *according* to the number of the days that thou shalt lie upon thy side; three hundred and ninety days shalt thou eat thereof.

This word (millet) occurs more than once in the sacred volume: Ezekiel calls it *duchan* or *dochan;* and Calmet thinks it is probably the holcus durra, which forms a principal food among the Orientals. Its Latin name, millet, is supposed to be derived from mille, that is, a thousand grains, in allusion to its extraordinary fruitfulness. It requires a light sandy soil; is sown late, and gathered in about the middle of October; while the wheat and the barley are reaped by the end of May, just before the drought of a Syrian summer comes on. The worldly man is accustomed to regard such different management as the fruit of human observation and sagacity; but the inspired prophet ascribes it with equal truth and energy to the suggestion of divine wisdom and goodness: "For his God doth instruct him to discretion, and doth teach him." It is made into bread, with camel's milk, oil, butter, and other unctuous substances, and is almost the only food eaten by the common people of Arabia Felix. Niebuhr found it so disagreeable, that he would willingly have preferred plain barley bread. This is certainly the reason that it was appointed to the prophet Ezekiel, as a part of his hard fare. But Rauwolf seems to have been of a different mind, or not so difficult to please; of this grain, says he, they bake very well-tasted bread and cakes, and some of them are rolled very thin, and laid together after the manner of a letter; they are about four inches broad, six long, and two thick, and of an ashen colour. The grain, however, is greatly inferior to wheat or barley, and by consequence must form a very inferior species of bread.—PAXTON.

Ver. 15. Then he said unto me, Lo, I have given thee cow's dung for man's dung, and thou shalt prepare thy bread therewith.

In some places, firewood being very scarce, the people gather cow-dung, make it into cakes, and dry it in the sun, after which it is ready for fuel. Those who are accustomed to have their food prepared in this way, prefer it to any other: they tell you it is sweeter and more holy, as the fuel comes from their sacred animal. The other allusion in this verse, and in chap. iv. 12, is often made use of when people are angry with each other. Has some one stolen a person's fuel, he says in his rage, "Ah! that wretch shall get ready his food" as described in iv. 12. Does a wife ask her husband for firewood, he will (should he be angry) reply to her as above.—ROBERTS.

In consequence of the want of wood, camel's dung is used in the East for fuel. Shaw, in the preface to his Travels, where he gives a detailed description of the mode of travelling in the East, says, that in consequence of the scarcity of wood, when they wanted to bake or boil any thing, the camel's dung which had been left by a preceding caravan was their usual fuel, which, after having been exposed to the sun during three days, easily catches fire, and burns like charcoal. The following quotation from D'Arvieux serves still better to illustrate the text in which the prophet is commanded to bake bread, or rather thin cakes of bread, upon cow-dung. "The second sort of bread is baked under ashes, or between two lumps of dried and lighted cow-dung. This produces a slow fire, by which the dough is baked by degrees; this bread is as thick as our cakes. The crumb is good if eaten the same day, but the crust is black and burnt, and has a smoky taste from the fire in which the bread is baked. A person must be accustomed to the mode of life of the Bedouins, and very hungry, who can have any relish for it." We will also add what Niebuhr says, in his description of Arabia. "The Arabs of the desert make use of an iron plate to bake their bread-cakes; or they lay a round lump of dough in hot coals of wood or camel's dung, and cover them entirely with it, till the bread in their opinion is quite done, when they take the ashes from it, and eat it warm." —ROSENMULLER.

CHAPTER V.

Ver. 16. When I shall send upon them the evil arrows of famine, which shall be for *their* destruction, *and* which I will send to destroy you: and I will increase the famine upon you, and will break your staff of bread. 17. So will I send upon you famine, and evil beasts, and they shall bereave thee; and pestilence and blood shall pass through thee; and I will bring the sword upon thee. I the LORD have spoken it.

See on Ps. 91. 5, 6.

CHAPTER VI.

Ver. 14. So will I stretch out my hand upon them, and make the land desolate, yea, more desolate than the wilderness *towards* Diblath, in all their habitations; and they shall know that I *am* the LORD.

"The land shall be utterly spoiled,—I will make the land more desolate than the wilderness." "The *temples* are thrown down; the palaces demolished; the ports filled up; the towns destroyed; and the earth, stripped of inhabitants, seems a dreary burying-place." (Volney.) "Good God!" exclaims the same writer, "from whence proceed such melancholy revolutions? For what cause is the fortune of these countries so *strikingly changed?* Why are so many cities destroyed? Why is not that ancient population reproduced and perpetuated?" "I wandered over the country, I traversed the provinces; I enumerated the kingdoms of Damascus and Idumea, of Jerusalem and Samaria. This Syria, SAID *I to myself*, now almost depopulated, then contained a hundred flourishing cities, and abounded with towns, villages, and hamlets. What are become of so many productions of the hands of man? What are become of those ages of abundance and of life?" &c. Seeking to be wise, men become fools when they trust to their own vain imaginations, and will not look to that word of God which is as able to confound the wise, as to give understanding to the simple. These words, from the lips of a great advocate of infidelity, proclaim the certainty of the truth which he was too blind or bigoted to see. For not more unintentionally or unconsciously do *many* illiterate Arab *pastors* or herdsmen verify one prediction, while they literally *tread* Palestine *under foot*, than Volney, the academician, himself verifies another, while, speaking in his own name, and the spokesman also of others, he thus confirms the unerring truth of God's holy word, by what he *said*, as well as by describing what he saw.

It is no "secret malediction," spoken of by Volney, which God has pronounced against Judea. It is the curse of a broken covenant that rests upon the land; the consequences of the iniquities of the people, not of those only who have been plucked from off it and scattered throughout the world, but of those also that dwell therein. The ruins of empires originated, not from the regard which mortals paid to revealed religion, but from causes diametrically the reverse. The desolations are not of Divine appointment, but only as they have followed the violations of the laws of God, or have arisen from thence. And none other curses have come upon the land than those that are written in the Book. The character and condition of the people are not less definitely marked than the features of the land that has been smitten with a curse because of their iniquities. And when the unbeliever asks, Wherefore hath the Lord done this unto the land? the same word which foretold that the question would be put, supplies an answer and assigns the cause. —KEITH.

CHAPTER VII.

Ver. 10. Behold the day, behold, it is come; the morning is gone forth; the rod hath blossomed; pride hath budded. 11. Violence is risen up into a rod of wickedness: none of them *shall remain*, nor of their multitude, nor of any of theirs; neither *shall there be* wailing for them.

This alludes to the punishment of the children of Israel; and Jehovah, through his servant, addresses the people in eastern language: "The morning is gone forth." Their wickedness, their violence, had grown into a rod to punish them. The idea is implied in the Tamul translation also. "Yes, wretch, the rod has long been growing for thee, 'tis now ready, they may now cut it." "True, true, the man's past crimes are as so many rods for him."—ROBERTS.

Ver. 16. But they that escape of them shall escape, and shall be on the mountains like doves of the valleys, all of them mourning, every one for his iniquity.

This is a most strikingly apt simile to all who have heard the sound made by the turtle-dove. In the woods of Africa I have often listened to the sound of the turtle-dove's apparent mourning and lamentations, uttered incessantly for hours together—indeed, without a moment's intermission. In a calm, still morning, when every thing in the wilderness is at rest, no sound can be more plaintive, pitiful, and melancholy. It would cause gloom to arise in the most sprightly mind,—it rivets the ear to it,—the attention is irresistibly arrested.—CAMPBELL.

Ver. 21. And I will give it into the hands of the strangers for a prey, and to the wicked of the earth for a spoil; and they shall pollute it. 22. My face will I turn also from them, and they shall pollute my secret *place*: for the robbers shall enter into it, and defile it.

Instead of abiding under a settled and enlightened government, Judea has been the scene of frequent invasions, "which have introduced a succession of foreign nations, (des peuples *etrangers*.")" "When the Ottomans took Syria from the Mamelouks, they considered it as the *spoil* of a vanquished enemy. According to this law, the life and *property* of the vanquished belong to the conqueror. The government is far from disapproving of a system of *robbery* and plunder which it finds so profitable." (Volney.)—KEITH.

CHAPTER VIII.

Ver. 7. And he brought me to the door of the court; and when I looked, behold, a hole in the wall.

Caves, and other similar subterraneous recesses, consecrated to the worship of the sun, were very generally, if not universally, in request among nations where that superstition was practised. The mountains of Chusistan at this day abound with stupendous excavations of this sort. Allusive to this kind of cavern temple, and this species of devotion, are these words of Ezekiel. The prophet in a vision beholds, and in the most sublime manner stigmatizes the horrible idolatrous abominations which the Israelites had borrowed from their Asiatic neighbours of Chaldea, Egypt, and Persia. "And he brought me, says the prophet, to the door of the court; and when I looked, behold, a hole in the wall. Then said he unto me, son of man, dig now in the wall; and, when I had digged in the wall, behold a door. And he said unto me, Go in, (that is, into this cavern temple,) and behold the wicked abominations that they do there. So I went in, and saw, and behold, every form of creeping things, and abominable beasts, and all the idols of the house of Israel, were portrayed upon the wall round about." In this subterraneous temple were seventy men of the ancients of the house of Israel, and their employment was of a nature very nearly similar to that of the priests in Salsette. "They stood with every man his censer in his hand, and a thick cloud of incense went up. Then said he unto me, Son of man, hast thou seen what the ancients of Israel do in the dark, every man in the chambers of his imagery?" In Egypt, to the particular idolatry of which country, it is plain, from his mentioning every form of creeping thing and abominable beasts, the prophet in this place alludes, these dark secluded recesses were called mystic cells, and in them were celebrated the secret mysteries of Isis and Osiris, represented by the quadrupeds sacred to those deities. (Maurice.)—BURDER.

Ver. 17. Then he said unto me, Hast thou seen *this*, O Son of man? Is it a light thing to the house of Judah that they commit the abominations which they commit here? for they have filled the land with violence, and have returned to provoke me to anger; and, lo, they put the branch to their nose.

This last expression undoubtedly alludes to some particular ceremony belonging to their idolatrous worship. Mr. Lowth (on the prophets) says, the words may refer to a custom among the idolaters of dedicating a branch of laurel, or some other tree, to the honour of the sun, and carrying it in their hands at the time of their worship. Lewis observes, that the most reasonable exposition is, that the worshipper, with a wand in his hand, would touch the idol, and then apply the stick to his nose and mouth, in token of worship and adoration.—BURDER.

CHAPTER IX.

Ver. 2. And, behold, six men came from the way of the higher gate, which lieth towards the north, and every man a slaughter-weapon in his hand; and one man among them *was* clothed with linen, with a writer's inkhorn by his side; and they went in, and stood beside the brazen altar.

See on Matt. 10. 9.

As they use not wax in sealing up doors, but clay, so they use ink, not wax, in sealing their writings in the East. So D'Arvieux tells us, that "the Arabs of the desert, when they want a favour of their emir, get his secretary to write an order agreeable to their desire, as if the favour was granted: this they carry to the prince, who, after having read it, sets his seal to it with ink, if he grants it; if not, he returns the petitioner his paper torn, and dismisses him." In another place he informs us, that "these papers are without date, and have only the emir's flourish or cipher at the bottom, signifying, *The poor, the abject Mehemet, son of Turabeye.*" Two things appear in these passages. The one, that the Arab seals have no figure engraven on them, but a simple inscription, formed, with some art, into a kind of cipher; the other, that when they seal, they do not make an impression on wax, but stamp letters of ink on the paper.

The modern inhabitants of Egypt appear to make use of ink in their sealing, as well as the Arabs of the desert, who may be supposed not to have such conveniences as those that live in such a place as Egypt: for Dr. Pococke says, that "they make the impression of their name with their seal, generally of carnelian, which they wear on their finger, and which is blacked when they have occasion to seal with it." This may serve to show us, that there is a closer connexion between the vision of St. John, Rev. vii. 2, and that of Ezekiel, ch. ix. 2, than commentators appear to have apprehended. They must be joined, I imagine, to have a complete view of either. St. John saw an angel with the seal of the living God, and therewith multitudes were sealed in their foreheads; but to understand what sort of a mark was made there, you must have recourse to the inkhorn of Ezekiel. On the other hand, Ezekiel saw a person equipped with an inkhorn, who was to mark the servants of God on their foreheads, that is, with ink, but how the ink was to be applied is not expressed; nor was there any need that it should, if in those times ink was applied with a seal being in the one case plainly supposed; as in the Apocalypse, the mention of a seal made it needless to take any notice of an inkhorn by his side.

This position of the inkhorn of Ezekiel's writer may appear somewhat odd to a European reader, but the custom of placing it by the side continues in the East to this day. Olearius, who takes notice of a way that they have of thickening their ink with a sort of paste they make, or with sticks of Indian ink, which is the best paste of all, a circumstance favourable to their sealing with ink, observes, that the Persians carried about with them, by means of their girdles, a dagger, a knife, a handkerchief, and their money; and those that follow the profession of writing out books, their inkhorn, their penknife, their whetstone to sharpen it, their letters, and every thing the Moscovites were wont in his time to put in their boots, which served them instead of pockets. The Persians, in carrying their inkhorns after this manner, seem to have retained a custom as ancient as the days of Ezekiel; while the Muscovites, whose garb was very much in the eastern taste in the days of Olearius, and who had many oriental customs among them, carried their inkhorns and their papers in a very different manner. Whether some such variations might cause the Egyptian translators of the Septuagint version to render the words, "a girdle of sapphire, or embroidery, on the loins," I will not take upon me to affirm; but I do not imagine our Dr. Castell would have adopted this sentiment in his Lexicon, had he been aware of this eastern custom: for with great propriety is the word קסת *keseth* mentioned in this chapter three times, if it signified an *inkhorn*, the requisite instrument for sealing those devout mourners; but no account can be given why this קסת should be mentioned so often, if it only signified an "embroidered girdle." As to the other point relating to the Arab seals; their having no figures upon them, only an inscription, it is to be thought that those of the Jews were in like manner without any images, since they were as scrupulous as the Mohammedans can be; and from hence it will appear, that it was extremely natural for St. Paul to make a seal and an inscription equivalent terms, in 2 Tim. ii. 19; "The foundation of God standeth sure, having his seal," this inscription, "the Lord knoweth those that are his; and let every one that nameth the name of Christ depart from iniquity."—Harmer.

Ver. 4. And the Lord said unto him, Go through the midst of the city, through the midst of Jerusalem, and set a mark upon the foreheads of the men that sigh, and that cry, for all the abominations that be done in the midst thereof.

Mr. Maurice, speaking of the religious rites of the Hindoos, says, before they can enter the great pagoda, an "indispensable ceremony takes place, which can only be performed by the hand of a bramin; and that is, the impressing of their foreheads with the *tiluk*, or mark of different colours, as they may belong either to the sect of Veeshnu, or Seeva. If the temple be that of Veeshnu, their foreheads are marked with a longitudinal line, and the colour used is vermilion. If it be the temple of Seeva, they are marked with a parallel line, and the colour used is turmeric, or saffron. But these two grand sects being again subdivided into numerous classes, both the size and the shape of the *tiluk* are varied in proportion to their superior or inferior rank. In regard to the *tiluk*, I must observe, that it was a custom of very ancient date in Asia, to mark their servants in the forehead. It is alluded to in these words of Ezekiel, where the Almighty commands his angels to "go through the midst of the city, and set a mark on the foreheads of the men who sigh for the abominations committed in the midst thereof." The same idea occurs also in Rev. vii. 3.—Burder.

CHAPTER XII.

Ver. 3. Therefore, thou son of man, prepare the
stuff for removing, and remove by day in their
sight; and thou shalt remove from thy place to
another place in their sight: it may be they
will consider, though they *be* a rebellious house.
4. Then shalt thou bring forth thy stuff by day
in their sight, as stuff for removing: and thou
shalt go forth at even in their sight, as they that
go forth into captivity. 5. Dig thou through
the wall in their sight, and carry out thereby:
6. In their sight shalt thou bear *it* upon *thy*
shoulders, *and* carry *it* forth in the twilight:
thou shalt cover thy face, that thou see not the
ground; for I have set thee *for* a sign unto the
house of Israel. 7. And I did so as I was
commanded: I brought forth my stuff by day,
as stuff for captivity, and in the even I digged
through the wall with my hand; I brought *it*
forth in the twilight, *and* I bare *it* upon *my*
shoulder in their sight.

When they travel to distant places, they are wont to send off their baggage to some place of rendezvous some time before they set out. The account that an ingenious commentator, whose expositions are generally joined to Bishop Patrick's, gives of a paragraph of the prophet Ezekiel, ought to be taken notice of here: it is, in a few words, this, "that the prophet was to get the goods together, to pack them up openly, and at noonday, that all might see, and take notice of it; that he was to get forth at even, as men do that would go off by stealth: that he was to dig through the wall, to show that Zedekiah should make his escape by the same means; that what the prophet was commanded to carry out in the twilight, must be something differen from the goods he removed in the daytime, and therefore must mean provision for his present subsistence; and that he was to cover his face, so as not to see the ground, as Zedekiah should do, that he might not be discovered."

Sir John Chardin, on the contrary, supposes, there was nothing unusual, nothing very particular, in the two first of the abovementioned circumstances. His manuscript notes on this passage of Ezekiel are to the following purport. "This is as they do in the caravans: they carry out their baggage in the daytime, and the caravan loads in the evening, for in the morning it is too hot to set out on a journey for that day, and they cannot well see in the night. However, this depends on the length of their journeys; for when they are too short to take up a whole night, they load in the night, in order to arrive at their journey's end early in the morning, it being a greater inconvenience to arrive at an unknown place in the night, than to set out on a journey then. As to his digging through the wall, he says Ezekiel is speaking, without doubt, of the walls of the caravansary. These walls, in the East, being mostly of earth, mud, or clay, they may easily be bored through."

I cannot, I own, entirely adopt either of these accounts: Ezekiel's collecting together his goods, does not look like a person's flying in a hurry, and by stealth; and consequently his going forth in the evening, in consequence of this preparation, cannot be construed as designed to signify a stealing away. These managements rather mark out the distance of the way they were going: going into captivity in a very far country. The going into captivity had not privacy attending it; and accordingly, the sending their goods to a common rendezvous beforehand, and setting out in an evening, are known to be eastern usages.

On the other hand, I should not imagine it was the wall of a caravansary, or of any place like a caravansary, but the wall of the place where Ezekiel was, either of his own dwelling, or of the town in which he then resided: a management designed to mark out the flight of Zedekiah; as the two first circumstances were intended to shadow out the carrying Israel openly, and avowedly, into captivity.

Ezekiel was, I apprehend, to do two things: to imitate the going of the people into captivity, and the hurrying flight of the king: two very distinct things. The mournful, but composed collecting together all they had for a transmigration, and leading them perhaps on asses, being as remote as could be from the hurrying and secret management of one making a private breach in a wall, and going off precipitately, with a few of his most valuable effects on his shoulder, which were, I should think, what Ezekiel was to carry, when he squeezed through the aperture in the wall, not provisions. Nor am I sure the prophet's covering his face was designed for concealment: it might be to express Zedekiah's distress. David, it is certain, had his head covered when he fled from Absalom, at a time when he intended no concealment; and when Zedekiah fled, it was in the night, and consequently such a concealment not wanted; not to say, it would have been embarrassing to him in his flight, not to be able to see the ground. The prophet mentions the digging through the wall, after mentioning his preparation for removing as into captivity; but it is necessary for us to suppose these emblematical actions of the prophet are ranged just as he performed them.—Harmer.

CHAPTER XIII.

Ver. 4. O Israel, thy prophets are like the foxes in the deserts.

When game fails him, or when the sword has ceased to supply his wants, the fox devours with equal greediness, honey, fruits, and particularly grapes. In allusion to his eager desire for the fruit of the vine, it is said in the Song of Solomon, "Take us the foxes, the little foxes, that spoil the vines, for our vines have tender grapes." In scripture, the church is often compared to a vineyard; her members to the vines with which it is stored; and by consequence, the grapes may signify all the fruits of righteousness, which those mystical vines produce. The foxes that spoil these vines, must therefore mean false teachers, who corrupt the purity of the doctrine, obscure the simplicity of worship, overturn the beauty of appointed order, break the unity of believers, and extinguish the life and vigour of Christian practice. These words of Ezekiel may be understood in the same sense: "O Jerusalem! thy prophets, (or as the context clearly proves,) thy flattering teachers, are as foxes in the deserts;" and this name they receive, because, with vulpine subtlety, they speak lies in hypocrisy. Such teachers the apostle calls "wolves in sheep's clothing," deceitful workers, who, by their cunning, subvert whole houses; and whose word, like the tooth of a fox upon the vine, eats as a canker.—Paxton.

In this passage, Dr. Boothroyd, instead of foxes, translates "jackals," and I think it by far the best rendering. These animals are exceedingly numerous in the East, and are remarkably cunning and voracious. I suppose the reason why they are called the lion's provider is, because they yell so much when they have scent of prey, that the noble beast hearing the sound, goes to the spot and satisfies his hunger. They often hunt in packs, and I have had from twenty to thirty following me (taking care to conceal themselves in the low jungle) for an hour together. They will not, *in general*, dare to attack man: but, let him be helpless or dead, and they have no hesitation. Thus our graveyards are often disturbed by these animals; and, after they have once tasted of human flesh, they (as well as many other creatures) are said to prefer it to any other. Their cunning is proverbial: thus, a man of plots and schemes is called a *nareyan*, i. e. a jackal. "Ah! only give that fellow a tai., and he will make a capital jackal." "Begone, low caste, or I will give thee to jackals."—Roberts.

Ver. 11. Say unto them which daub *it* with untempered *mortar*, that it shall fall: there shall be an overflowing shower; and ye, O great hailstones, shall fall; and a stormy wind shall rend *it*.

In countries destitute of coal, bricks are only either sun-dried or very slightly burnt with bushes and branches of trees, laid over them and set on fire. Such are ready to moulder if exposed to moisture, and entirely to melt away if exposed to heavy rain dashing against them. To prevent such a catastrophe, all the houses in the Cape colony are daubed or plastered over with fine mortar, made from ground seashells. Should only a small hole remain unnoticed in the plaster, powerful rain will get into it, and probably soon be the destruction of the whole building. Well do I remember one deluge of rain that turned a new house of three floors absolutely into a mass of rubbish, and brought down the gable of a parish church, besides injuring many other buildings.—Campbell.

Ver. 18. And say, Thus saith the Lord God, Wo to the *women* that sew pillows to all arm-holes, and make kerchiefs upon the head of every stature, to hunt souls! Will ye hunt the souls of my people, and will ye save the souls alive *that come* unto you?

The margin has, instead of "arm-holes," "elbows." The marginal reading is undoubtedly the best. Rich people have a great variety of pillows and bolsters to support themselves in various positions when they wish to take their ease. Some are long and round, and are stuffed till they are quite hard; whilst others are short and soft, to suit the convenience. The verse refers to females of a loose character, and Parkhurst is right when he says, "These false prophetesses decoyed men into their gardens, where probably some impure rites of worship were performed." The pillows were used for the vilest purposes and the kerchiefs were used as an affectation of shame.—Roberts.

In Barbary and the Levant they "always cover the floors of their houses with carpets; and along the sides of the wall or floor, a range of narrow beds or mattresses is often placed upon these carpets; and, for their further ease and convenience, several velvet or damask bolsters are placed upon these carpets or mattresses—indulgences that seem to be alluded to by the *stretching of themselves upon couches*, and by the sewing of pillows to arm-holes." (Shaw.) But Lady M. W. Montague's description of a Turkish lady's apartment throws still more light on this passage. She says, "The rooms are all spread with Persian carpets, and raised at one end of them, about two feet. This is the sofa, which is laid with a richer sort of carpet, and all round it, a sort of couch, raised half a foot, covered with rich silk, according to the fancy or magnificence of the owner. Round about this are placed, standing against the walls, two rows of cushions, the first very large, and the rest little ones. The seats are so convenient and easy, that I believe I shall never endure chairs again as long as I live." And in another place she thus describes the fair Fatima: "On a sofa raised three steps, and covered with fine Persian carpets, sat the kahya's lady, leaning on cushions of white satin embroidered. She ordered cushions to be given me, and took care to place me in the corner, which is the place of honour."—Burder.

Ver. 19. And will ye pollute me among my people for handfuls of barley, and for pieces of bread, to slay the souls that should not die, and to save the souls alive that should not live, by your lying to my people that hear *your* lies?

See on Jer. 37. 21.

At Algiers they have public bakehouses for the people in common, so that the women only prepare the dough at home, it being the business of other persons to bake it. Boys are sent about the streets to give notice when they are ready to bake bread; "upon this the women within come and knock at the inside of the door, which the boy hearing makes towards the house. The women open the door a very little way, and hiding their faces, deliver the cakes to him, which, when baked, he brings to the door again, and the women receive them in the same manner as they gave them." This is done almost every day, and they give the boy a *piece*, or *little cake*, for the baking, which the baker sells. (Pitts.) This illustrates the account of the false prophetesses receiving as gratuities *pieces of bread:* they are compensations still used in the East, but are compensations of the meanest kind, and for services of the lowest sort.—HARMER.

CHAPTER XV.

Ver. 3. Shall wood be taken thereof to do any work? or will *men* take a pin of it to hang any vessel thereon

See on Isa. 22. 23.

CHAPTER XVI.

Ver. 4. And *as for* thy nativity, in the day thou wast born, thy navel was not cut, neither wast thou washed in water to supple *thee:* thou wast not salted at all, nor swaddled at all.

It was an ancient custom to salt the bodies of new-born infants. It is probable that they only sprinkled them with salt, or washed them with salt-water, which they imagined would dry up all superfluous humours. Galen says, "Sale modico inspersο, cutis infantis densior, solidiorque redditur;" that is, a little salt being sprinkled upon the infant, its skin is rendered more dense and solid. It is said that the inhabitants of Tartary still continue the practice of salting their children as soon as they are born.—BURDER.

Ver. 10. I clothed thee also with broidered work, and shod thee with badgers' skin, and girded thee about with fine linen, and I covered thee with silk.

See on Ex. 25. 5.

Ver. 18. And tookest thy broidered garments, and coveredst them: and thou hast set mine oil and mine incense before them. 19. My meat also which I gave thee, fine flour, and oil, and honey, *wherewith* I fed thee, thou hast even set it before them for a sweet savour: and *thus* it was, saith the Lord GOD.

The burning of perfumes is now practised in the East in times of feasting and joy; and there is reason to believe that the same usage obtained anciently in those countries. Niebuhr mentions a Mohammedan festival, "after which every one returned home, feasted, chewed kaad, burnt fragrant substances in his house, stretched himself at length on his sofa, and lighted his kiddre, or long pipe, with the greatest satisfaction."—HARMER.

CHAPTER XVII.

Ver. 3. And say, Thus saith the Lord GOD, A great eagle with great wings, long-winged, full of feathers, which had divers colours, came unto Lebanon, and took the highest branch of the cedar.

The eagle is the strongest, the fiercest, and the most rapacious of the feathered race. He dwells alone in the desert, and on the summits of the highest mountains; and suffers no bird to come with impunity within the range of his flight. His eye is dark and piercing, his beak and talons are hooked and formidable, and his cry is the terror of every wing. His figure answers to his nature; independently of his arms, he has a robust and compact body, and very powerful limbs and wings; his bones are hard, his flesh is firm, his feathers are coarse, his attitude is fierce and erect, his motions are lively, and his flight is extremely rapid. Such is the golden eagle, as described by the most accurate observers of nature. To this noble bird the prophet Ezekiel evidently refers, in his parable to the house of Israel: "A great eagle, with great wings, long-winged, full of feathers, which had divers colours, came unto Lebanon, and took the highest branch of the cedar." In this parable, a strict regard to physical truth is discovered, in another respect, for the eagle is known to have a predilection for cedars, which are the loftiest trees in the forest, and therefore more suited to his daring temper than any other. La Roque found a number of large eagle's feathers scattered on the ground beneath the lofty cedars which still crown the summits of Lebanon, on the highest branches of which, that fierce destroyer occasionally perches.—PAXTON.

Ver. 7. There was also another great eagle with great wings and many feathers; and, behold, this vine did bend her roots towards him, and shot forth her branches towards him, that he might water it by the furrows of her plantation.

The reason of the figure must be obvious to every reader: the erect and majestic mien of the eagle, point him out as the intended sovereign of the feathered race; he is, therefore, the fit emblem of superior excellence, and of regal majesty and power. Xenophon, and other ancient historians, inform us, that the golden eagle with extended wings, was the ensign of the Persian monarchs, long before it was adopted by the Romans; and it is very probable that the Persians borrowed the symbol from the ancient Assyrians, in whose banners it waved, till imperial Babylon bowed her head to the yoke of Cyrus. If this conjecture be well founded, it discovers the reason why the sacred writers, in describing the victorious march of the Assyrian armies, allude so frequently to the expanded eagle. Referring still to the Babylonian monarch, the prophet Hosea proclaimed in the ears of Israel, the measure of whose iniquities was nearly full: "He shall come as an eagle against the house of the Lord." Jeremiah predicted a similar calamity to the posterity of Lot: "For thus saith the Lord, Behold, he shall fly as an eagle, and shall spread his wings over Moab:" and the same figure is employed to denote the sudden destruction which overtook the house of Esau: "Behold, he shall come up and fly as the eagle, and spread his wings over Bozrah." The words of these inspired prophets were not suffered to fall to the ground; they received a full accomplishment in the irresistible impetuosity and complete success with which the Babylonian monarchs, and particularly Nebuchadnezzar, pursued their plans of conquest. Ezekiel denominates him with striking propriety, "a great eagle with great wings;" because he was the most powerful monarch of his time, and led into the field more numerous and better appointed armies, (which the prophet calls by a beautiful figure, his wings,) than perhaps the world had ever seen.—PAXTON.

CHAPTER XIX.

Ver. 8. Then the nations set against him on every side from the provinces, and spread their net over him: he was taken in their pit.

The manner in which this is done, Xenophon describes at considerable length: They dig a large circular pit, and at night introduce into it a goat, which they bind to a stake or pillar of earth at the bottom, and then enclose the pit with a hedge of branches, that it cannot be seen, leaving no entrance. The savage beast hearing in the night the voice of the goat, prowls round the hedge, and finding no opening, leaps over, and is taken. When the hunter proposes to catch him in the toils, he stretches a series of nets in a semicircular form, by means of long poles fixed in the ground; three men are placed in ambush, among the nets; one in the middle, and one at each extremity. The toils being disposed in this manner, some wave flaming torches; others make a noise by beating their shields, knowing that lions are not less terrified by loud sounds than by fire. The men on foot and horseback, skilfully combining their movements and raising a mighty bustle and clamour, rush in upon them, and impel them towards the nets, till, intimidated by the shouts of the hunters and the glare of the torches, they approach the snares of their own accord, and are entangled in the folds.—Paxton.

Ver. 11. And she had strong rods for the sceptres of them that bare rule, and her stature was exalted among the thick branches, and she appeared in her height with the multitude of her branches.

The allusion here is evidently to the sceptres of the ancients, which were no other than walking-sticks, cut from the stems or branches of trees, and decorated with gold, or studded with golden nails. Thus Achilles is introduced as swearing by a sceptre, which being cut from the trunk of a tree on the mountains, and stripped of its bark and leaves, should never more produce leaves and branches, or sprout again. Such a one the Grecian judges carried in heir hands. See Homer, Il. i. 234.—Burder.

CHAPTER XXI.

Ver. 14. Thou, therefore, son of man, prophesy, and smite *thy* hands together, and let the sword be doubled the third time, the sword of the slain: it *is* tho sword of the great *men that are* slain, which entereth into their privy chambers.

"Smite thy hands together." To smite the hands together, in the East, amounts to an oath! In the 17th verse, the Lord says, in reference to Jerusalem, "I will also smite my hands together, and I will cause my fury to rest: I the Lord have said." By the solemn smiting of hands it was shown the word had gone forth, and would not be recalled. When a priest delivers a message to the people, when he relates any thing which he professes to have received from the gods, he smites his hands together, and says, "true."

Does a Pandārum, or other kind of religious mendicant, consider himself to be insulted, he smites his hands against the individuals, and pronounces his imprecations upon them, crying aloud, "True, true, it will all come upon you." Should a person, when speaking of any thing which is certain to happen, be doubted by others, he will immediately smite his hands. "Have you heard that Muttoo has been killed by a tiger?"—"No! nor do I believe it." The relater will then (if true) smite together his hands, which at once confirms the fact. "Those men cannot escape for any great length of time, because the king has smitten his hands;" meaning, he has sworn to have them taken. Jehovah did smite His hands together against Jerusalem.—Roberts.

Ver. 21. For the king of Babylon stood at the parting of the way, at the head of the two ways, to use divination; he made *his* arrows bright, he consulted with images, he looked in the liver.

Heb. "mother of the way." It is a common thing among the people of the East to denominate a man the *father* of a thing for which he is remarkable. It appears also that both people and places may in like manner be called the *mother* of such things for which they are particularly noticed. Thus Niebuhr tells us, that the Arabs call a woman that sells butter *omm es subbet*, the *mother* of butter. He also says, that there is a place between Basra and Zobier, where an ass happened to fall down, and throw the wheat with which the creature was loaded into some water, on which account that place is called to this day, *the mother of wheat.*

In like manner, in the Bibliotheque Orientale of D'Herbelot, *omm alketab*, or *the mother of books*, signifies the book of the divine decrees; and at other times the first chapter of the Koran. The *mother of the throat* is the name of an imaginary being (a fairy) who is supposed to bring on and cure that disorder in the throat, which we call the quinsy. In the same collection we are told, that the acacia, or Egyptian thorn is called by the Arabians the *mother of satyrs*, because these imaginary inhabitants of the forests and deserts were supposed to naunt under them. After this we shall not at all wonder when we read of Nebuchadnezzar's standing in the *mother of the way*, a remarkable place in the road, where he was to determine whether he would go to Jerusalem, or to some other place, one branch of the road pointing to Jerusalem, the other leading to a different town.

"He made his arrows bright." This was for the purpose of divination. Jerome on this passage says, that "the manner of divining by arrows was thus: They wrote on several arrows the names of the cities they intended to make war against, and then putting them promiscuously all together into a quiver, they caused them to be drawn out in the manner of lots, and that city whose name was on the arrow first drawn out, was the first they assaulted." A method of this sort of divination, different from the former, is worth noticing. Della Valle says, "I saw at Aleppo a Mohammedan, who caused two persons to sit upon the ground, one opposite to the other, and gave them four arrows into their hands, which both of them held with theii points downward, and as it were in two right lines united one to the other. Then, a question being put to him about any business, he fell to murmur his enchantments, and thereby caused the said four arrows of their own accord to unite their points together in the midst, (though he that held them stirred not his hand,) and, according to the future event of the matter, those of the right side were placed over those of the left, or on the contrary." This practice the writer refers to diabolical influence.

The method of divination practised by some of the idolatrous Arabs, but which is prohibited by the Koran, is too singular to be unnoticed. "The arrows used by them for this purpose were like those with which they cast lots, being without heads or feathers, and were kept in the temple of some idol, in whose presence they were consulted. Seven such arrows were kept at the temple of Mecca: but generally in divination they make use of three only, on one of which was written, my Lord hath commanded me; on another, my Lord hath forbidden me; and the third was blank. If the first was drawn, they looked on it as an approbation of the enterprise in question; if the second, they made a contrary conclusion; but if the third happened to be drawn, they mixed them, and drew over again, till a decisive answer was given by one of the others. These divining arrows were generally consulted before any thing of moment was undertaken, as when a man was about to marry, or about to go a journey, or the like."—Burder.

CHAPTER XXII.

Ver. 12. In thee have they taken gifts to shed blood; thou hast taken usury and increase, and thou hast greedily gained of thy neighbours by extortion, and hast forgotten me, saith the Lord God.

There is surely no part of the world worse than the East for usury and extortion. A rich man will think nothing of demanding twenty per cent. for his precious loan. Does a person wish to buy or sell an article; does he want to avoid any office or duty, or to gain a situation, or place any person under an obligation; he cannot think of doing the one or the other, without giving himself into the hands of the extortioner.—Roberts.

Ver. 30. And I sought for a man among them that should make up the hedge, and stand in the gap before me for the land, that I should not destroy it; but I found none.

A man having lost all his children, and in complaining of his forlorn condition, says, "Alas! I have not any one to stand in the gate; my enemies can now enter when they please to tear and devour me." "In the gate, in the gate, no one stands."—Roberts.

CHAPTER XXIII.

Ver. 5. And Aholah played the harlot when she was mine; and she doted on her lovers, on the

Assyrians *her* neighbours, 6. *Which were* clothed with blue, captains and rulers, all of them desirable young men, horsemen riding upon horses.

Blue was a sky colour in great esteem among the Jews, and other oriental nations. The robe of the ephod, in the gorgeous dress of the high priest, was made all of blue; it was a prominent colour in the sumptuous hangings of the tabernacle; and the whole people of Israel were required to put a fringe of blue upon the border of their garments, and on the fringe a riband of the same colour. The palace of Ahasuerus, the king of Persia, was furnished with curtains of this colour, on a pavement of red, and blue, and white marble; a proof it was not less esteemed in Persia, than on the Jordan. And from Ezekiel we learn, that the Assyrian nobles were habited in robes of this colour: "She doted on the Assyrians her neighbours, which were clothed with blue, captains and rulers, all of them desirable young men." It is one of the most remarkable vicissitudes in the customs of the East, that this beautiful colour, for many ages associated in their minds with every thing splendid, elegant, and rich, should have gradually sunk in public estimation, till it became connected with the ideas of meanness and vulgarity, and confined to the dress of the poor and the needy. In modern times, the whole dress of an Arabian female of low station, consists of drawers, and a very large shift, both of blue linen, ornamented with some needle-work of a different colour. And if credit may be given to Thevenot, the Arabs between Egypt and Mount Sinai, who lead a most wretched life, are clothed in a long blue shirt, To solve this difficulty, Mr. Harmer supposes that "the art of dying blue, was discovered in countries more to the east or south than Tyre; and that the die was by no means become common in the days of Ezekiel, though some that were employed in the construction of the tabernacle, and some of the Tyrians in the time of Solomon, seem to have possessed the art of dying with blue. These blue cloths were manufactured in remote countries; and to them that wore scarcely any thing but woollens and linens of the natural colour, these blue calicoes formed very magnificent vestments. It does not appear, however, that the Jews ever wore garments wholly of this colour; and perhaps they abstained from it as sacred and mysterious, than which none was more used about the tabernacle and the temple, in the curtains, veils, and vestments, belonging to these sacred edifices."—PAXTON.

Ver. 14. And that she increased her whoredoms: for when she saw men portrayed upon the wall, the images of the Chaldeans portrayed with vermilion.

The nature of those images, and the practices, may be seen from the context, and the portraying was of the colour of VERMILION. In the Hindoo temples and vestibules, figures of the most revolting descriptions are portrayed on the walls: there the sexes are painted in such a way as few men of discretion would dare to describe. In some temples there are stone figures in such positions as hell itself could only have suggested: and, recollect, these are the places where men, women, and children, assemble for WORSHIP.—ROBERTS.

CHAPTER XXIV.

Ver. 3. And utter a parable unto the rebellious house, and say unto them, Thus saith the Lord GOD, Set on a pot, set *it* on, and also pour water into it: 4. Gather the pieces thereof into it, *even* every good piece, the thigh, and the shoulder; fill *it* with the choice bones. 5. Take the choice of the flock, and burn also the bones under it, *and* make it boil well, and let him seethe the bones of it therein.

The following account of a royal Arab camel feast, will afford some illustration of the parable contained in this chapter: "Before midday a carpet being spread in the middle of the tent our dinner was brought in, being served up in large wooden bowls between two men; and truly to my apprehension load enough for them. Of these great platters there were about fifty or sixty in number, perhaps more, with a great many little ones; I mean, such as one man was able to bring in, strewed here and there among them, and placed for a border or garnish round about the table. In the middle was one of a larger size than all the rest, in which were the camel's bones, and a thin broth in which they were boiled. The other greater ones seemed all filled with one and the same sort of provision, a kind of plumbbroth, made of rice and the fleshy part of the camel, with currants and spices, being of a somewhat darker colour than what is made in our country." (Philosophical Transactions Abridged.) The Hebrew word translated *burn*, should have been rendered, as in the margin, *heap*. The meaning cannot be that the bones were to be burnt under the caldron, but that they were to be heaped up in it; for it is said, "let them seethe the bones of it therein." With this interpretation the Septuagint translation of the passage agrees: and viewed in this light, the object is ascertained by the foregoing extract.—BURDER.

Ver. 17. Forbear to cry, make no mourning for the dead, bind the tire of thy head upon thee, and put on thy shoes upon thy feet, and cover not *thy* lips, and eat not the bread of men.

The time of mourning for the dead was longer or shorter, according to the dignity of the person. Among the modern Jews, the usual time is seven days, during which they shut themselves up in their houses; or if some extraordinary occasion forces them to appear in public, it is without shoes, as a token they have lost a dear friend. This explains the reason that when Ezekiel was commanded to abstain from the rites of mourning, he was directed to put his shoes on his feet.

To cover the lips was a very ancient sign of mourning; and it continues to be practised among the Jews of Barbary to this day. When they return from the grave to the house of the deceased, the chief mourner receives them with his jaws tied up with a linen cloth, in imitation of the manner in which the face of the dead is covered; and by this the mourner is said to testify that he was ready to die for his friend. Muffled in this way, the mourner goes for seven days, during which the rest of his friends come twice every twenty-four hours to pray with him. This allusion is perhaps involved in the charge which Ezekiel received when his wife died, to abstain from the customary forms of mourning: "Forbear to cry, make no mourning for the dead; bind the tire of thy head upon thee, and put on thy shoes upon thy feet, and *cover not thy lips*, and eat not the bread of men." The law of Moses required a leper to have his clothes rent, his head bare, and a covering upon his upper lip, because he was considered as a dead man, "of whom the flesh is half consumed when he cometh out of his mother's womb."—PAXTON.

This refers to mourning for the dead, and the prophet was forbidden to use any symbol of sorrow on the death of his wife. At a funeral ceremony the tires and turbans are taken off, and the sandals are laid aside. Thus nobles, who wear the most costly turbans, are seen walking with their heads uncovered, and those who had on beautiful sandals are barefoot. But the prophet was to PUT ON his tire and sandals, to indicate he was *not* mourning for the dead. —ROBERTS.

CHAPTER XXV.

Ver. 2. Son of man, set thy face against the Ammonites, and prophesy against them.

It was prophesied concerning Ammon, "Son of man, set thy face against the Ammonites, and prophesy against them. I will make Rabbah of the Ammonites a stable for camels and a couching-place for flocks. Behold, I will stretch out my hand upon thee, and deliver thee for a spoil to the heathen; I will cut thee off from the people, and cause thee to perish out of the countries; I will destroy thee. The Ammonites shall not be remembered among the nations. Rabbah (the chief city) of the Ammonites shall be a desolate heap. Ammon shall be a perpetual desolation."

"Ammon was to be delivered to be a spoil to the heathen

—to be destroyed, and to be a perpetual desolation." "All this country, formerly so populous and flourishing, is now changed into a vast desert." Ruins are seen in every direction. The country is divided between the Turks and the Arabs, but chiefly possessed by the latter. The extortions of the one and the depredations of the other, keep it in *perpetual desolation*, and make it *a spoil to the heathen*. "The far greater part of the country is uninhabited, being abandoned to the wandering Arabs, and the towns and villages are in a state of total ruin." "At every step are to be found the vestiges of ancient cities, the remains of many temples, public edifices, and Greek churches." The cities are desolate. "Many of the ruins present no object of any interest. They consist of a few walls of dwelling-houses, heaps of stones, the foundations of some public edifices, and a few cisterns filled up; there is nothing entire, but it appears that the mode of building was very solid, all the remains being formed of large stones. In the vicinity of Ammon there is a fertile plain interspersed with low hills, which, for the greater part, are covered with ruins."

While the country is thus despoiled and desolate, there are valleys and tracts throughout it, which "are covered with a fine coat of verdant pasture, and are places of resort to the Bedouins, where they pasture their camels and their sheep." "The whole way we traversed," says Seetzen, "we saw villages in ruins, and met numbers of Arabs with their *camels*," &c. Mr. Buckingham describes a building among the ruins of Ammon, "the masonry of which was evidently constructed of materials gathered from the ruins of other and older buildings on the spot. On entering it at the south end," he adds, "we came to an open square court, with arched recesses on each side, the sides nearly facing the cardinal points. The recesses into the northern and southern walls were originally open passages, and had arched doorways facing each other—but the first of these was found wholly closed up, and the last was partially filled up, leaving only a narrow passage, just sufficient for the entrance of one man and the goats, which the Arab keepers drive in here occasionally for shelter during the night." He relates that he lay down among "flocks of sheep and goats," close beside the ruins of Ammon;—and particularly remarks that, during the night, he was almost entirely prevented from sleeping by the "bleating of flocks." So literally true is it, although Seetzen, and Burckhardt, and Buckingham, who relate the facts, make no reference or allusion whatever to any of the prophecies, and travelled for a different object than the elucidation of the scriptures,—that "the chief city of the Ammonites is a stable for camels, and a couching-place for flocks."

"The Ammonites shall not be remembered among the nations." While the Jews, who were long their hereditary enemies, continue as distinct a people as ever, though dispersed among all nations, no trace of the Ammonites remains; none are now designated by their name, nor do any claim descent from them. They did exist, however, long after the time when the eventual annihilation of their race was foretold, for they retained their name, and continued a great multitude, until the second century of the Christian era. "Yet they are cut off from the people. Ammon has perished out of the countries; it is destroyed." No people is attached to its soil—none regard it as their country and adopt its name; and the Ammonites are not remembered among the nations.

Rabbah (Rabbah Ammon, the chief city of Ammon) *shall be a desolate heap*. Situated, as it was, on each side of the borders of a plentiful stream; encircled by a fruitful region; strong by nature and fortified by art; nothing could have justified the suspicion, or warranted the conjecture in the mind of an uninspired mortal, that the royal city of Ammon, whatever disasters might possibly befall it in the fate of war or change of masters, would ever undergo so total a transmutation as to become a desolate heap. But although, in addition to such tokens of its continuance as a city, more than a thousand years had given uninterrupted experience of its stability, ere the prophets of Israel denounced its fate; yet a period of equal length has now marked it out, as it exists to this day, a desolate heap—a perpetual or permanent desolation. Its ancient name is still preserved by the Arabs, and its site is now "covered with the ruins of private buildings; nothing of them remaining except the foundations, and some of the doorposts. The buildings, exposed to the atmosphere, are all in decay," so that they may be said literally to form a desolate heap. The public edifices, which once strengthened or adorned the city, after a long resistance to decay, are now also desolate; and the remains of the most entire among them, subjected as they are to the abuse and spoliation of the wild Arabs, can be adapted to no better object than *a stable for camels*. Yet these broken walls and ruined palaces, which attest the ancient splendour of Ammon, can now be made subservient, by means of a single act of reflection, or simple process of reason, to a far nobler purpose than the most magnificent edifices on earth can be, when they are contemplated as monuments on which the historic and prophetic truth of scripture is blended in one bright inscription. A minute detail of them may not therefore be uninteresting.

Seetzen (whose indefatigable ardour led him, in defiance of danger, the first to explore the countries which lie east of the Jordan, and east and south of the Dead Sea, or the territories of Ammon, Moab, and Edom) justly characterizes Ammon as "once the residence of many kings—an ancient town, which flourished long before the Greeks and Romans, and even before the Hebrews;" and he briefly enumerates those remains of ancient greatness and splendour which are most distinguishable amid its ruins. "Although this town has been destroyed and deserted for many ages, I still found there some remarkable ruins, which attest its ancient splendour. Such as, 1st, A square building, very highly ornamented, which has been perhaps a mausoleum. 2d, The ruins of a large palace. 3d, A magnificent amphitheatre of immense size, and well preserved, with a peristyle of Corinthian pillars without pedestals. 4th, A temple with a great number of columns. 5th, The ruins of a large church, perhaps the see of a bishop in the time of the Greek emperors. 6th, The remains of a temple with columns set in a circular form, and which are of an extraordinary size. 7th, The remains of the ancient wall, with many other edifices." Burckhardt, who afterward visited the spot, describes it with greater minuteness. He gives a plan of the ruins; and particularly noted the ruins of many temples, of a spacious church, a curved wall, a high arched bridge, the banks and bed of the river still partially paved; a large theatre, with successive tiers of apartments excavated in the rocky side of a hill; Corinthian columns fifteen feet high; the castle, a very extensive building, the walls of which are thick, and denote a remote antiquity; many cisterns and vaults; and a plain covered with the decayed ruins of private buildings;—monuments of ancient splendour standing amid a *desolate heap*.—Keith.

Ver. 4. Behold, therefore, I will deliver thee to the men of the East for a possession, and they shall set their palaces in thee, and make their dwellings in thee: they shall eat thy fruit, and they shall drink thy milk.

The seed-time is attended with considerable danger to the husbandmen, in Palestine and Syria; for although the more peaceful Arabs apply themselves to agriculture, to supply their families with grain, many of the same wandering race choose rather to procure the corn which they want by violence, than by tillage. So precarious are the fruits of the earth in Palestine, that the former is often seen sowing, accompanied by an armed friend, to prevent his being robbed of the seed. These vexations, and often desolating incursions, are described by the prophet in the following remarkable terms, when he denounced the judgments of God against the descendants of Ammon: "Behold, therefore, I will deliver thee to the men of the East for a possession, and they shall set their palaces in thee, and make their dwellings in thee: they shall eat thy fruit, and they shall drink thy milk." The practice of robbing the sower in the field, seems to have been very ancient: and is perhaps alluded to by the Psalmist, when he encourages the righteous man, to persevere in working out his salvation, in spite of the dangers to which he is exposed, by the complete success, which in due time shall assuredly crown his endeavours. "They that sow in tears," on account of the danger from the lurking and unfeeling Arabian, "shall reap in joy." He that goeth forth and weepeth, bearing precious seed, shall doubtless come again with rejoicing, bringing his sheaves with him." It is much more natural to suppose that these verses refer to such acts of violence, than to imagine, with all the commentators who have turned their attention to this circumstance, that they allude to the anxiety of a husbandman, who sows his corn in a time of great scarcity, and is afraid his hopes may be disappointed by the failure of the succeeding harvest. We nowhere read, that such fearful anticipations ever produced weeping and lamentation, although the Orientals are very prone to violent expressions of grief. But, if we refer the passage to the danger which the farmer in those parts of the world often incurred, of losing his precious seed, the hope of his future subsistence, and even his life, in attempting to defend it, we have an adequate cause for his tears and lamentations. The passage contains a beautiful picture of the success which, by the blessing of God, attended the efforts of his chosen people, to return from their captivity to the land of their fathers; and holds out a powerful encouragement to believers in Christ, to persevere in their heavenly course, notwithstanding the numerous and severe trials of this present life; for in due time, they shall certainly enter into the rest which remains for the people of God.—PAXTON.

Ver. 5. And I will make Rabbah a stable for camels, and the Ammonites a couching-place for flocks; and ye shall know that I *am* the LORD.

The Syrian shepherds were exposed, with their flocks, to all the vicissitudes of the seasons. It was indeed impossible to erect buildings capacious enough to receive the countless numbers of cattle, which constituted the wealth of those pastoral princes. Their servants were, therefore, compelled to watch the flocks night and day. The flocks of Libya "often graze both night and day, and for a whole month together, and repair into long deserts, without any shelter, so wide the plain extends." The Mesopotamian shepherd was reduced to the same incessant labour, chilled by the piercing cold of the morning, and scorched by the succeeding heats of a flaming sun, the opposite action of which often swells and chafes his lips and face. Jacob complains, "Thus I was; in the day, the drought consumed me, and the frost by night; and my sleep departed from mine eyes." In times long posterior to the age when Jacob flourished, the angels who descended to announce the birth of our Lord, found the shepherds to whom they were sent, keeping watch over their flocks by night. To prevent them from wandering, they shut them up in a fold formed of hurdles, and took their station on the outside, to defend them from the attacks of wild beasts, or bands of robbers, that infested the country, and preyed upon the property of the peaceful and industrious inhabitants.

When the prophet Ezekiel threatened the Ammonites, that Rabbah, their capital, should become a stable for camels, we are not to imagine that the Arabian shepherds were careful to provide such coverts for these more tender animals. Chardin says, that as they feed them on the ground, and do not litter them, they never think of erecting such buildings for their reception. The same fact is admitted by Dr. Shaw, when he makes a supposition that the cattle of these countries would be much more numerous than they are, if they had some little shelter in winter. The only shelter to which they have recourse, is the desolate ruin; and to this circumstance the prophet Ezekiel most probably alluded, when he described Rabbah as about to become a stable for camels, or, as the original term may be rendered with equal propriety, a place of camels, where they screen themselves from the rays of a burning sun, and feed on the nettles, and other plants, which spring up among the mouldering walls of ruined habitations. The same term is rendered in the twenty-third psalm, pastures; and perhaps all that the prophet means is only this, that Rabbah should be so completely destroyed, that camels should feed on the place where it stood; and if this was his meaning, it has been long since realized, for the last remains of that proud city have entirely disappeared. The greatest skill and vigilance, and even tender care, are required in the management of such immense flocks as wander on the Syrian plains. Their prodigious numbers compel the keepers to remove them too frequently in search of fresh pastures, which proves very destructive to the young that have not strength to follow. This circumstance displays the energy of Jacob's apology to his brother Esau, for not attending him as he requested: "The flocks and herds with young are with me; and if men should over-drive them one day, all the flocks would die." It illustrates also another passage in the prophecies of Isaiah: "He shall feed his flock like a shepherd; he shall gather the lambs with his arm, and carry them in his bosom, and shall gently lead those that are with young:" a beautiful image, expressing with great force and elegance, the tender and unceasing attention of the shepherd to his flock.—PAXTON.

CHAPTER XXVI.

Ver. 3. Therefore thus saith the Lord GOD, Behold, I *am* against thee, O Tyrus, and will cause many nations to come up against thee, as the sea causeth his waves to come up. 4. And they shall destroy the walls of Tyrus, and break down her towers: I will also scrape her dust from her, and make her like the top of a rock. 5. It shall be *a place for* the spreading of nets in the midst of the sea: for I have spoken *it*, saith the Lord GOD; and it shall become a spoil to the nations.

This history of the city is most affecting, and it has been said with much force, that "the noble dust of Alexander, traced by the imagination till found stopping a beer-barrel, would scarcely afford a stronger contrast of grandeur and abasement than Tyre, at the period of being besieged by that conqueror, and the modern town of Tsour erected on its ashes." It was probably a colony of the Sidonians, as it is called "the daughter of Sidon." From its present name appears to have been taken the general name of Syria. Its first mention is in Joshua, where it is called "the strong city Tyre." At an early period it became the mistress of the seas; traded even to Britain, and planted colonies in different parts of the Mediterranean, among which Carthage became the most celebrated.

The history of Tyre is more especially interesting to the Christian, from its connexion with prophecy, and from the striking eloquence with which inspiration has described the majesty of its brighter days, and the impressive circumstances of its destruction. It was also referred to by our Saviour, when he pronounced wo upon the inhabitants of Chorazin and Bethsaida, because they had seen his mighty works and repented not. Her merchants were princes, her traffickers the honourable of the earth. She heaped up silver as dust, and fine gold as the mire of the streets. The boards of her ships were of the fir-trees of Senir, her masts of the cedars of Lebanon, her oars of the oaks of Bashan, her benches of the ivory of Chittim, her sails of fine linen, broidered work from Egypt, and her awnings were of purple. Her heart was lifted up, and she said, I am a god, I sit in the seat of God, in the midst of the seas. Such is the description given in sacred writ of the pride and magnificence of ancient Tyre. Now, in the language of the same authority, the noise of her songs is ceased, and the voice of her harps is no more heard: her walls are broken down, her pleasant houses are no more, she is made like the top of a rock, a place to spread nets upon: she is built no more.

The Saracens and Turks were the unconscious instruments who carried these prophecies into their fulfilment: they utterly destroyed Sidon and Tyre, that they might not afford further refuge to the crusaders. There were two harbours, formed by the island; one towards the north, and the other towards the south; and there was a passage between the island and the shore from the one to the other. The island is represented by Pliny as having been four miles in circumference, but the peninsula upon which the present town is situated, is of much less extent. It would therefore appear that it is built for the most part upon the mole thrown up by Alexander, including a small portion of the original island. There is thus enough of the rock left in existence for the fishers to spread their nets upon, while the principal area, once mantled with palaces and alive with a busy population, has been swept into "the midst of the waters," and can be built no more. The disappearance of the island has caused the destruction of the harbours; and as all protection to shipping is now taken away, Tyre can never again rise to eminence as "the mart of nations."

There are still two small rocks in the sea, to which the island probably extended; and as the fishermen's boats can approach them in calm weather, they seem to invite the spreading of nets upon their surface. I and my companions sailed over the present harbour in a small boat, to examine the columns that may clearly be seen under the water on a fine day, but the sea was too rough to allow us to discover many of them. The present town is walled, and is of very modern date. The space inside is in a great measure open, and the houses are mean. The governor's residence is the only respectable building. There are many columns near the small harbour, and others on the opposite side of the peninsula, but there is no ruin of ancient date, the plan of which can be traced. We saw in a garden a granite column of one block, that measured 30 feet in length, and the diameter was in proportion. The eastern end of the cathedral is still standing. We ascended to the top of the ruin by a spiral staircase, and from thence had a view of the town. The burial-ground is near. From this situation the houses had a singular appearance, as the roofs are all flat, and were then verdant with a rich covering of grass. Upon the plain there are the remains of an extensive aqueduct. The mole appears like a mere collection of sand, but beneath there may be some construction of more enduring materials.

"Is this your joyous city, whose antiquity is of ancient days? Who hath taken this counsel against Tyre? The Lord of Hosts hath purposed it, to stain the pride of all glory, and to bring into contempt all the honourable of the earth."—Isa. xxiii. 7—9. The stirring scenes of a seaport exhibit a picture of more constant excitement than can ever be presented by any other place. The arrival and discharge of ships; the cries of the captains as they direct their ready mariners; the songs of the boatmen, the dash of the oars, and the roll of the sea; the solitary female, whose eye catches every speck that appears white in the horizon, and never leaves it till one after another of its inmates have been carefully numbered, that perchance she may discover among them the father of her disconsolate children; the faltering step of the aged sailor, whose battles have been fought, and whose victories have been won; the tears of those who are bidding farewell, and the rapture of those who are greeting the arrival of a long-absent friend; the anxious assemblies of the merchants, either speaking of traffic, or proclaiming their good fortune, or lamenting the loss of some fair ship in a destructive gale; the reckless merriment of the seamen, as they enjoy upon land a little respite from their constant toils:—all these, and a thousand other scenes of noise, and joyousness, and wealth, have been exhibited upon these shores. They have passed away, like the feverish dream of a disturbed sleep. Ships may be seen, but at a distance; no merchant of the earth ever enters the name of Tyre upon his books, and where thousands once assembled in pomp and pride, and there was beauty, and splendour, and dominion, I could discover only a few children amusing themselves at play, and a party of Turks sitting in gravity, and sipping their favourite coffee.—Hardy.

The desolate appearance of Soor from the sea,—a straggling, repulsive village of low scattered dwellings, with a few squalid inhabitants loitering on the beach—is in gloomy contrast with the gorgeous descriptions of insular Tyre, before Alexander effected its destruction by the daring expedient of uniting it with the continent.

The present peninsula, once the site of this splendid city, anciently estimated at three miles in circumference, but apparently of somewhat less extent, is now a dreary waste, distinguished only by hillocks and furrows; and the memorable isthmus, then so laboriously constructed, has become less conspicuous from the augmentation of its width, by the gradual accumulation of sand. Its once vaunted port is now so effectually choked, that only small boats can approach the shore, although, amidst the waves, the foundations are still visible of the massive walls that formed its fortified boundaries, leaving only a narrow entrance secured by a chain. Near the landing-place, a few tolerable houses face the sea, and similar ones are sparingly distributed in other directions. An insignificant bazar offers few temptations even to those who seek ordinary commodities, and the diverging streets are little more than circuitous alleys, capriciously winding between high walls, as if concealment alone afforded security. Here and there a low door opens into an orchard or paddock, but more frequently into a small court, surrounded with miserable hovels, evidently the abodes of abject poverty. Occasionally an unclosed door exhibits a court of larger dimensions, where a few rude implements of husbandry, and the less meager looks of better-clad occupants, betoken a state somewhat approaching to comfort and ease. Little cultivation, however, is perceptible near the town—of commercial activity there is no sign—listless groups fill every vacant space—and fishermen no longer "spread their nets" on the shore. Hence it becomes difficult to conjecture how a population, scarcely removed from indigence, can here subsist, notwithstanding the temperate habits of the East, which demand little more than a morning and evening repast of fresh baked cakes, sometimes eaten with a sort of pottage made of lentils, onions, &c, and sometimes merely with a draught of water, or a little fruit.

Relentless desolation seems to brood over this devoted region. Fragments of clustered columns and broken walls, at the southeast extremity of the town—the only visible remains of the structures even of the middle ages—perhaps mark the site of the magnificent metropolitan church, once the conspicuous ornament of Christian Tyre. In that splendid edifice of rich gothic architecture, distinguished by three spacious naves, and two lofty towers, where councils were held and princes and prelates assembled, the bones of the Emperor Frederic Barbarossa were deposited in a sumptuous sepulchre. Every trace of the mausoleum of Origen, raised in the third century, and still existing in the twelfth, has now disappeared. Broken shafts thrown into a narrow creek awkwardly serve the purpose of a bridge; others piled in the sea, form a barrier against hostile approach. A few columns of marble, of granite, and of porphyry, lie unheeded round a small cove, now the only landing-place, while mounds of sand, thinly strewn with architectural fragments, alone point out the ancient circuit of the town. And is this all that remains to tell the tale of ancient Tyre—the early seat of civilization—the empress of the waves? Could this dreary coast have poured forth dauntless navigators to explore distant regions;—this cheerless waste, could it ever have been the patrimony of "merchant-princes?" Could this little territory have been the emporium of the commerce of the world?—Hogg.

Ver. 4. And they shall destroy the walls of Tyrus, and break down her towers: I will also scrape her dust from her, and make her like the top of a rock. 12. And they shall make a spoil of thy riches, and make a prey of thy merchandise; and they shall break down thy walls, and destroy thy pleasant houses: and they shall lay thy stones, and thy timber, and thy dust, in the midst of the water.

One of the most singular events in history was the manner in which the siege of Tyre was conducted by Alexander the Great. Irritated that a single city should alone oppose his victorious march, enraged at the murder of some of his soldiers, and fearful for his fame,—even his army's despairing of success could not deter him from the siege. And Tyre was taken in a manner, the success of which was more wonderful than the design was daring; for it was surrounded by a wall one hundred and fifty feet in height, and situated on an island half a mile distant from the shore. A mound was formed from the continent to the island; and the ruins of old Tyre, two hundred and forty years after its demolition, afforded ready materials for the purpose. Such was the work, that the attempts at first defeated the power of an Alexander. The enemy consumed and the storm destroyed it. But its remains, buried beneath the water, formed a barrier which rendered successful his renewed efforts. A vast mass of additional matter was requisite The soil and the very rubbish were gathered and heaped. And the mighty conqueror, who afterward failed in raising again any of the ruins of Babylon, cast those of Tyre into the sea, and took her very dust from off her. He left not the remnant of a ruin—and the site of *ancient* Tyre is now unknown.—Keith.

Ver. 14. And I will make thee like the top of a

EGYPT—RUINED TEMPLES.—Ex. 30:6—13. Page 535.

rock; thou shalt be *a place* to spread nets upon; thou shalt be built no more: for I the LORD have spoken *it*, saith the Lord GOD.

Passing by Tyre from curiosity only, I came to be a mournful witness of the truth of that prophecy, "that Tyre, the queen of nations, should be a rock for fishers to dry their nets on." Two wretched fishermen, with miserable nets, having just given over their occupation, with very little success, I engaged them, at the expense of their nets, to drag in those places where they said shellfish might be caught, in hopes to have brought out one of the famous *purple* fish. I did not succeed; but in this I was, I believe, as lucky as the old fishers had ever been. The purple fish at Tyre seems to have been only a concealment of their knowledge of *cochineal*, as, if the whole city of Tyre applied to nothing else but fishing, they would not have coloured twenty yards of cloth in a year.—BRUCE.

CHAPTER XXVII.

Ver. 11. The men of Arvad, with thine army, *were* upon thy walls round about, and the Gammadims were in thy towers: they hanged their shields upon thy walls round about; they have made thy beauty perfect.

The eastern soldiers in times of peace are disposed of about the walls of places, and particularly in the towers, and at the gates. Niebuhr tells us, that the foot-soldiers of the imam of Yemem have very little to do in times of peace, any more than the cavalry: some of them mount guard at the dela's, or governor's; they are also employed at the gates and upon the towers. Van Egmont and Heyman give a similar account. Sandys, speaking of the decorations of one of the gates of the imperial seraglio in Constantinople, tells us, that it is hung with shields and cimeters. Through this gate people pass to the divan, where justice is administered; and these are the ornaments of this public passage.—HARMER.

Ver. 13. Javan, Tubal, and Meshech, they *were* thy merchants: they traded the persons of men and vessels of brass in thy market.

The domestic utensils of the Orientals are nearly always brass: and to these they often refer, as a sign of property. "He is a rich man; his house is full of brass vessels." "Begone! fellow, I have more brass in my house than would purchase all thy property." "The miserable man has not a brass dish in his house."—ROBERTS.

CHAPTER XXVIII.

Ver. 14. Thou *art* the anointed cherub that covereth; and I have set thee *so:* thou wast upon the holy mountain of God; thou hast walked up and down in the midst of the stones of fire.

This has been considered as a very obscure epithet to apply to the prince of Tyre, and great difficulties have occurred in explaining the meaning of the expression. It has been apprehended by some critics to be an allusion to the posture of the cherubic figures that were over the ark, (Exod. xxv. 20,) and by others to signify the protection which this prince afforded to different neighbouring states. But the first of these interpretations is set aside by considering that the prophet evidently refers to a *living* cherub, not the posture of the image of one made of gold, or of an olive-tree. As to the other construction, it is inadmissible, because it does not appear from the prophecies that Tyre was remarkable for defending its neighbours, but rather the contrary. Mr. Harmer proposes a new, and probably a just elucidation of this passage. He observes that *takhtdar* is a Persian word, which properly signifies a precious carpet, which is made use of for covering the throne of the kings of Persia; and that this word is also used as an epithet by which the Persians describe their princes, on account of their being possessed of this throne. The prophet Ezekiel may with the same view give this appellation to the prince of Tyre. Such an application of it is certainly no more than strictly reconcilable to the eastern taste. This explanation also answers to the rest of the imagery used in this passage.—BURDER.

Ver. 24. And there shall be no more a pricking brier unto the house of Israel, nor *any* grieving thorn of all *that are* round about them, that despised them; and they shall know that I *am* the Lord GOD.

Enemies are often compared to thorns and thistles. "Ah! how this thorn goads me," says the man of his foe. When a man's adversaries are dead, he says, "This is now a desert without thorns." "Ah! as our father is dead, we are to our enemies like a jungle without thorns."—ROBERTS.

CHAPTER XXIX.

Ver. 3. Speak, and say, Thus saith the Lord GOD, Behold, I *am* against thee, Pharaoh king of Egypt, the great dragon that lieth in the midst of his rivers, which hath said, My river *is* mine own, and I have made *it* for myself.

See on ch. 32. 2.

Ver. 18. Son of man, Nebuchadnezzar king of Babylon caused his army to serve a great service against Tyrus: every head *was* made bald, and every shoulder *was* peeled: yet had he no wages, nor his army, for Tyrus, for the service that he had served against it.

What an illustration of this passage we have in those who have not been accustomed to carry the palanquin! During the first day the skin is literally peeled off. To prevent the pole from galling the shoulder, the coolies have cushions, or a piece of the plantain-tree, put under the pole. The shoulders of those who assisted at the siege against Tyre, were PEELED by hard labour.—ROBERTS.

CHAPTER XXX.

Ver. 6. Thus saith the LORD, They also that uphold Egypt shall fall; and the pride of her power shall come down: from the tower of Syene shall they fall in it by the sword, saith the Lord GOD. 7. And they shall be desolate in the midst of the countries *that are* desolate, and her cities shall be in the midst of the cities *that are* wasted. 12. And I will make the rivers dry, and sell the land into the hand of the wicked: and I will make the land waste, and all that is therein, by the hand of strangers; I the LORD have spoken *it.* 13. Thus saith the Lord GOD, I will also destroy the idols, and I will cause *their* images to cease out of Noph; and there shall be no more a prince of the land of Egypt: and I will put a fear in the land of Egypt.

Egypt was one of the most ancient and one of the mightiest of kingdoms, and the researches of the traveller are still directed to explore the unparalleled memorials of its power. No nation, whether of ancient or of modern times, has ever erected such great and durable monuments. While the vestiges of other ancient monarchies can hardly be found amid the mouldering ruins of their cities, those artificial mountains, visible at the distance of thirty miles, the pyramids of Egypt, without a record of their date, have withstood, unimpaired, all the ravages of time. The dynasty of Egypt takes precedence, in antiquity, of every other. No country ever produced so long a catalogue of kings. The learning of the Egyptians was proverbial. The number of their cities, and the population of their country, as recorded by ancient historians, almost surpass credibility. Nature and are united in rendering it a most fertile region. It was called the granary of the world. It was divided into several kingdoms, and their power often extended over many of the surrounding countries Yet the knowledge of all its greatness and glory deterred not the Jewish prophets from declaring, that Egypt would become "a base kingdom, and never exalt itself any more among the nations." And the *literal* fulfilment of every prophecy affords as clear a demonstration as can possibly be given, that each and all of them are the dictates of inspiration.

Egypt became entirely subject to the Persians about three hundred and fifty years previous to the Christian era. It was afterward subdued by the Macedonians, and was governed by the Ptolemies for the space of two hundred and ninety-four years; until about thirty years before Christ, it became a province of the Roman empire. It continued long in subjection to the Romans—tributary first to Rome, and afterward to Constantinople. It was transferred, A. D. 641, to the dominion of the Saracens. In 1250 the Mamelukes deposed their rulers, and usurped the command of Egypt. A mode of government the most singular and surprising that ever existed on earth was established and maintained. Each successive ruler was raised to supreme authority, from being a *stranger* and a slave. No son of the former ruler—no native of Egypt succeeded to the sovereignty; but a chief was chosen from among a new race of imported slaves. When Egypt became tributary to the Turks in 1517, the Mamelukes retained much of their power, and every pacha was an oppressor and a stranger. During all these ages, every attempt to emancipate the country, or to create a prince of the land of Egypt, has proved abortive, and has often been fatal to the aspirant. Though the facts relative to Egypt form too prominent a feature in the history of the world to admit of contradiction or doubt, yet the description of the fate of that country, and of the form of its government, shall be left to the testimony of those whose authority no infidel will question, and whom no man can accuse of adapting their descriptions to the predictions of the event. Gibbon and Volney are again our witnesses of the facts:—

"Such is the state of Egypt. Deprived twenty-three centuries ago of her natural proprietors, she has seen her fertile fields successively a prey to the Persians, the Macedonians, the Romans, the Greeks, the Arabs, the Georgians, and, at length, the race of Tartars, distinguished by the name of Ottoman Turks. The Mamelukes, purchased as slaves, and introduced as soldiers, soon usurped the power and elected a leader. If their first establishment was a singular event, their continuance is not less extraordinary. They are replaced by slaves *brought from their original country*. The system of oppression is methodical. Every thing the traveller sees or hears reminds him he is in the country of slavery and tyranny." "A more unjust and absurb constitution cannot be devised than that which condemns the natives of a country to perpetual servitude, under the arbitrary dominion of strangers and slaves. Yet such has been the state of Egypt above five hundred years. The most illustrious sultans of the Baharite and Borgite dynasties were themselves promoted from the Tartar and Circassian bands; and the four-and-twenty beys, or military chiefs, have ever been succeeded, not by their sons, but by their servants." These are the words of Volney and of Gibbon: and what did the ancient prophets foretel? "I will lay the land waste, and all that is therein, by the hands of strangers. I the Lord have spoken it. And there shall be no more a prince of the land of Egypt. The sceptre of Egypt shall depart away." The prophecy adds:—"They shall be a base kingdom—it shall be the basest of kingdoms." After the lapse of two thousand and four hundred years from the date of this prophecy, a scoffer at religion, but an eyewitness of the facts, thus describes the selfsame spot: "In Egypt there is no middle class, neither nobility, clergy, merchants, landholders. A universal air of misery, manifest in all the traveller meets, points out to him the rapacity of oppression, and the distrust attendant upon slavery. The profound ignorance of the inhabitants equally prevents them from perceiving the causes of their evils, or applying the necessary remedies. Ignorance, diffused through every class, extends its effects to every species of moral and physical knowledge. Nothing is talked of but intestine troubles, the public misery, pecuniary extortions, bastinadoes, and murders. Justice herself puts to death without formality." (Volney.) Other travellers describe the most execrable vices as common, and represent the moral character of the people as corrupted to the core. As a token of the desolation of the country, mud-walled cottages are now the only habitations where the ruins of temples and palaces abound. Egypt is surrounded by the dominions of the Turks and of the Arabs; and the prophecy is literally true which marked it in the midst of desolation:—"They shall be desolate in the midst of the countries that are desolate, and her cities shall be in the midst of the cities that are wasted." The systematic oppression, extortion, and plunder, which have so long prevailed, and the price paid for his authority and power by every Turkish pacha, have rendered the country "desolate of that whereof it was full," and still show, both how "it has been wasted by the hands of strangers," and how "it has been sold into the hand of the wicked."

Can any words be more free from ambiguity, or could any events be more wonderful in their nature, or more unlikely or impossible to have been foreseen by man, than these prophecies concerning Egypt? The long line of its kings commenced with the first ages of the world, and, while it was yet unbroken, its final termination was revealed. The very attempt once made by infidels to show, from the recorded number of its monarchs and the durations of their reigns, that Egypt was a kingdom previous to the Mosaic era of the deluge, places the wonderful nature of these predictions respecting it in the most striking view. And the previous experience of two thousand years, during which period Egypt had never been without a prince of its own, seemed to preclude the possibility of those predicted events which the experience of the last two thousand years has amply verified. Though it had often tyrannised over Judea and the neighbouring nations, the Jewish prophets foretold that its own sceptre would depart away; and that that country of kings (for the number of its contemporary as well as successive monarchs may warrant the appellation) would never have a prince of its own: and that it would be laid waste by the hands of strangers. They foretold that it should be a base kingdom—the basest of kingdoms—that it should be desolate itself and surrounded by desolation—and that it should never exalt itself any more among the nations. They described its ignominious subjection and unparalleled baseness, notwithstanding that its past and present degeneracy bears not a more remote resemblance to the former greatness and pride of its power, than the frailty of its mud-walled fabric now bears to the stability of its imperishable pyramids. Such prophecies, accomplished in such a manner, prove, without a comment, that they must be the revelation of the omniscient Ruler of the universe.—KEITH.

CHAPTER XXXII.

Ver. 2. Son of man, take up a lamentation for Pharaoh king of Egypt, and say unto him, Thou art like a young lion of the nations, and thou *art* as a whale in the seas; and thou camest forth with thy rivers, and troubledst the waters with thy feet, and fouledst their rivers.

Nothing is more common, in the East, than the comparing princes to *lions*, or better known to those that are acquainted with their writings; but the comparing them to *crocodiles*, if possessed of *naval* power, or strong by a *watery* situation, has hardly ever been mentioned. D'Herbelot, however, cites an eastern poet, who, celebrating the prowess of Gelaleddin, surnamed Mankberni, and Khovarezme Shah, a most valiant Persian prince, said, "He was dreadful as a lion in the field, and not less terrible in the water than a crocodile."

The power of the ancient kings of Egypt seems to be represented after the same manner, by the prophet Ezekiel, ch. xxix. 3, "Behold, I am against thee, Pharaoh king of Egypt, the great dragon (*the great crocodile*) that lieth in the midst of his rivers, which hath said, My river is mine own, and I have made it myself." In his 32d chapter, 2d verse, the same prophet makes use of both the similes, I think, of the panegyrist of Gelaleddin: "Take up a lamentation for Pharaoh king of Egypt, and say unto him, Thou art like a young lion of the nations, and thou art as a whale (*a crocodile*) in the seas: and thou camest forth with (or from) thy rivers, and troubledst the waters with thy feet, and fouledst their rivers."

It is very odd in our translators, to render the original word תנים *taneem*, *whale*, and at the same time talk of *feet;* nor indeed are rivers the abode of the whale; its bulk is too great to admit of that: the term dragon, which is thrown into the margin, is the preferable version; which word in our language, as the Hebrew word in the original, is, I think, *generic*, and includes the several species of oviparous quadrupeds, if not those of the serpentine kind. A crocodile is, without doubt, the creature the prophet means; and the comparison seems to point out the power of Egyptian kings of antiquity: they were mighty by sea as well as by land.—HARMER.

Ver. 3. Thus saith the Lord GOD, I will, therefore, spread out my net over thee with a company of many people; and they shall bring thee up in my tent.

Herodotus relates that in his time they had in Egypt many and various ways of taking the crocodile. Brookes says, "The manner of taking the crocodile in Siam is by throwing three or four nets across a river at proper distances from each other; that so if he break through the first, he may be caught by one of the others."—BURDER.

When a person has been caught by the stratagem of another, it is said, "He is caught in his net." "He is like a deer caught in the net." Has a man escaped: "The fellow has broken the net." "Catch him in your net! will you catch the lightning?"—ROBERTS.

Ver. 27. And they shall not lie with the mighty *that are* fallen of the uncircumcised, which are gone down to hell with their weapons of war; and they have laid their swords under their heads; but their iniquities shall be upon their bones, though *they were* the terror of the mighty in the land of the living.

The ancients, in every part of the world, were accustomed to inter their warriors in complete armour. We are informed by Chardin, that the Mingrelian soldier sleeps with his sword under his head, and his arms by his side; and he is buried in the same manner, his arms being placed in the same position. The allusion of Ezekiel to this ancient custom is extremely clear.—PAXTON.

CHAPTER XXXIII.

Ver. 30. Also, thou son of man, the children of thy people still are talking against thee by the walls, and in the doors of the houses, and speak one to another, every one to his brother, saying, Come, I pray you, and hear what is the word that cometh forth from the LORD.

In those frequent intervals of returning warmth, which relieve the severity of an oriental winter, the people of the East enjoy the conversation of their friends; the poorer class in the open air sauntering about, and sitting under the walls of their houses; people of rank and fashion in the porches or gateways, where the master of a family receives visits, and transacts business—few persons, not even the nearest relations, being admitted into their apartments, except upon extraordinary occasions.

To these circumstances the prophet Ezekiel seems to refer in the following passage: "Also, thou son of man, the children of thy people are still talking against (or rather concerning) thee by the walls, and in the doors of the houses, and speak one to another, every one to his brother, saying, Come, I pray you, and hear what is the word that cometh forth from the Lord." Our translators render the original word *beha*, against thee; the Septuagint, περι σου, of or concerning thee. This is the more singular, as the same particle is rendered in other parts of scripture, of or concerning: thus, in the eighty-seventh Psalm, "Glorious things are spoken of thee, O city of the Lord." The following words incontestably prove they were not speaking against Ezekiel, but in his favour: "And they come unto thee as the people cometh: and they sit before thee as my people; and they hear thy words, but they will not do them; for with their mouth they show much love; but their heart goeth after their covetousness." But if "their mouth showed much love," they did not speak against the prophet, but in his commendation. These conversations respecting the prophet were held in winter; for it was the tenth month, answering to the latter end of December, or beginning of January, when the Orientals sit under the walls for the benefit of the sun, or in the porches or gateways of their houses.

As the Copts in Egypt commonly spend their holydays in conversing with one another under the walls of their habitation, so Mr. Harmer is of opinion, that these words of Ezekiel may refer to such times. And if so, he asks, will they not show that the Israelites observed their sabbaths in the captivity? And that so early as the time of the first destruction of Jerusalem, they used to assemble on those days, to hear if the prophets had received any messages from the Lord in that week, and to receive those advices which their calamitous circumstances made peculiarly seasonable? It is very probable that the Jews in those early times assembled to hear the instructions of the prophets, and for the public worship of their God, so far as their painful circumstances might permit; but the words of Ezekiel under consideration, appear to be of a more general character, referring as well to the public meetings of the synagogue, as to the private parties and conversations of the people.—PAXTON.

Severe as sometimes the cold weather is in the East, Russel observes, that even in the depth of that season, when the sun is out, and there is no wind, it is warm, nay, sometimes almost hot, in the open air; and Pococke informs us, that the people there enjoy it, for the Copts spend their holydays in sauntering about, and sitting under their walls in winter, and under shady trees in summer. This doubtless is to be understood of the poorer sort, who have no places more proper for conversation with their friends; the better houses having porches with benches on each side, where the master of the family receives visits, and despatches business. These circumstances greatly illustrate the words of Ezekiel, "Also, thou son of man, the children of thy people are still talking against thee, or rather, concerning thee, by the walls and in the doors of the houses," &c.—HARMER.

Ver. 32. And, lo, thou *art* unto them as a very lovely song of one that hath a pleasant voice, and can play well on an instrument: for they hear thy words, but they do them not.

"Gone! gone!" says the bereaved admirer; "she was indeed like a sweet voice to my ear." "I hear not the sweet song." "Where is my music?" "The song of the night! the song of the night! has left me."—ROBERTS.

CHAPTER XXXIV.

Ver. 6. My sheep wandered through all the mountains, and upon every high hill: yea, my flock was scattered upon all the face of the earth, and none did search or seek *after them.*

When travelling in wilderness parts of the world, cattle are, on various accounts, apt to wander or to be scattered, and require attentive shepherds to watch their motions. Should the grass near the encampment of the traveller not suit their taste, or be scarce, they will gradually move to a greater and greater distance, till bushes or clumps of trees are between them and the wagons; then, perhaps, having the scent of water, or that of better grass, they will move off at great speed. The distant roar of a lion also will so alarm them that they will start off like furious or frantic animals.

I remember halting for a night about a hundred miles beyond Lattakoo. Knowing that lions were numerous in that part, all the oxen were made fast by ropes to the wagons. During the night lions had roared within hearing of the oxen, when all, no doubt, had through terror endeavoured to break loose from their fastenings, but only three had succeeded, which having fled, were pursued by two lions, and one of them caught, and almost entirely devoured by those two voracious animals. After they had fairly killed the one, they pursued the other two for upwards of two miles, when they gave up the chase, and returned to feast on the one they had secured. All this we knew from the foot-marks they had left on the ground. In the morning the Hottentots were sent in search of the other two, which they found feeding several miles off.

The Jewish shepherds were condemned for not searching for the scattered sheep. When men are fatigued by travelling, they become lazy and indolent and feel indisposed to set off in search of strayed oxen many miles distant; yet I never noticed our Hottentots unwilling to go in search of strayed oxen, however fatigued they might be, and rarely did they return without finding them, though, in some instances, they had to trace their foot-marks for upwards of twenty miles.—CAMPBELL.

Ver. 25. And I will make with them a covenant
of peace, and will cause the evil beasts to cease
out of the land; and they shall dwell safely in
the wilderness, and sleep in the woods.

The oriental shepherds, when unprovided with tents, erect huts or booths of loose stones, covered with reeds and boughs. Pococke found, in the neighbourhood of Acre, some open huts, made of boughs raised about three feet from the ground, inhabited by Arabs. In such booths many of the people of Israel were obliged to take shelter in the wilderness, from the want of a sufficient number of tents, the remembrance of which they were commanded to preserve by a solemn festival. But even these meaner and more inconvenient habitations are not always within the reach of an Arabian shepherd; he is often obliged to take refuge under the projecting rock, and to sleep in the open air. A grove or woodland occasionally furnishes a most agreeable retreat. The description which Chandler has left us of one of these stations, is so strikingly picturesque, that it must be given in his own words: "About two in the morning, our whole attention was fixed by the barking of dogs, which, as we advanced, became exceedingly furious. Deceived by the light of the moon, we now fancied we could see a village; and were much mortified to find only a station of poor goatherds, without even a shed, and nothing for our horses to eat. They were lying, wrapped in their thick capotes or loose coats, by some glimmering embers, among the bushes in a dale, under a spreading tree by the fold. They received us hospitably, heaping on fresh fuel, and producing sour curds and coarse bread, which they toasted for us on the coals. We made a scanty meal, sitting on the ground, lighted by the fire and by the moon; after which, sleep suddenly overpowered me. On waking, I found my two companions by my side, sharing in the comfortable cover of the janizary's cloak, which he had carefully spread over us. I was now much struck with the wild appearance of the spot. The tree was hung with rustic utensils; the she-goats in a pen, sneezed, and bleated, and rustled to and fro; the shrubs by which our horses stood, were leafless, and the earth bare; a black caldron with milk, was simmering over the fire; and a figure, more than gaunt or savage, close by us, struggling on the ground with a kid, whose ears he had slit, and was endeavouring to cauterize with a red-hot iron." This description forms a striking comment on a passage in Ezekiel, in which God condescends to give this promise to his people: "I will make with them a covenant of peace, and will cause the evil beasts to cease out of the land; and they shall dwell safely in the wilderness, and sleep in the woods." No reasonable doubt can be entertained that they were often exposed in the same manner, while tending their flocks; and in great danger, when their country, from the thinness of the population, or other causes, happened to be overrun with beasts of prey. They are accordingly cheered with the sure prospect of those ravenous animals being exterminated, and every woodland becoming a place of safety to the slumbering shepherd.—PAXTON.

CHAPTER XXXV.

Ver. 1. Moreover, the word of the LORD came
unto me, saying, 2. Son of man, set thy face
against Mount Seir, and prophesy against it,
3. And say unto it, Thus saith the Lord GOD,
Behold, O Mount Seir, I *am* against thee, and
I will stretch out my hand against thee, and I
will make thee most desolate. 7. Thus will I
make Mount Seir most desolate, and cut off
from it him that passeth out, and him that returneth.

There is a prediction which, being peculiarly remarkable as applicable to Idumea, and bearing reference to a circumstance explanatory of the difficulty of access to any knowledge respecting it, is entitled, in the first instance, to notice, "None shall pass through it for ever and ever." Isaiah xxxiv. 10. "I will cut off from Mount Seir him that passeth out and him that returneth." Ezek. xxxv. 7. The ancient greatness of Idumea must, in no small degree, have resulted from its commerce. Bordering with Arabia on the east, and Egypt on the southwest, and forming from north to south the most direct and most commodious channel of communication between Jerusalem and her dependencies on the Red Sea, as well as between Syria and India, (through the continuous valleys of El Ghor and El Arabia, which terminated on the one extremity at the borders of Judea, and on the other at Elath and Esiongaber on the Elanitic Gulf of the Red Sea,) Idumea may be said to have formed the emporium of the commerce of the East. A Roman road passed directly through Idumea, from Jerusalem to Akaba, and another from Akaba to Moab; and when these roads were made, at a time long posterior to the date of the predictions, the conception could not have been formed, or held credible by man, that the period would ever arrive when none would pass through it. Above seven hundred years after the date of the prophecy, Strabo relates, that "many Romans and other foreigners" were found at Petra by his friend Athenodorus, the philosopher, who visited it. The prediction is yet more surprising, when viewed in conjunction with another, which implies that travellers would *pass by* Idumea,—every one that goeth by shall be astonished. And the hadj routes (routes of the pilgrims) from Damascus and from Cairo to Mecca, the one on the east, and the other towards the south of Idumea, along the whole of its extent, go by it, or touch partially on its borders, without passing through it. The truth of the prophecy (though hemmed in thus by apparent impossibilities and contradictions, and with extreme probability of its fallacy in every view that could have been visible to man) may yet be tried.

The words of the prediction might well be understood as merely implying that Idumea would cease to be a thoroughfare for the commerce of the nations which adjoined it, and that its "highly-frequented marts" would be forsaken as centres of intercourse and traffic; and easy would have been the task of demonstrating its truth in this limited sense, which skepticism itself ought not to be unwilling to authorize. But the fact to which it refers forbids that the prophecy should be limited to a general interpretation, and demands that it be literally understood and applied. The fact itself being of a negative nature, requires a more minute investigation and detail than any matter of observation or discovery that is proveable at once by a simple description. And instead of merely citing authorities in affirmation of it, evidence, as remarkable as the prediction, and at once the most undesigned and conclusive, shall be largely adduced to establish its truth.

The remark of Volney, who passed at a distance to the *west* of Idumea, and who received his information from the Arabs in that quarter, "that it had not been visited by any traveller," will not be unobserved by the attentive reader. Soon after Burckhardt had entered, on the *north-east*, the territories of the Edomites, the boundary of which he distinctly marks, he says, that "he was without protection in the midst of a desert, where no traveller had ever been before seen." It was then "that for the first time he had ever felt fear during his travels in the desert, and his route thither was the most dangerous he had ever travelled." Mr. Joliffe, who visited the northern shore of the Dead Sea, in alluding to the country south of its opposite extremity, describes it as "one of the wildest and most dangerous divisions of Arabia," and says, that any research in that quarter was impracticable. Sir Frederick Henniker, in his Notes dated from Mount Sinai, on the *south* of Idumea, unconsciously concentrates striking evidence in verification of the prediction, while he states a fact that would seem, at first sight, to militate against it. "Seetzen, on a vessel of paper pasted against the wall, notifies his having penetrated the country in a direct line between the Dead Sea and Mount Sinai," (through Idumea,) "*a route never before accomplished.* This was the more interesting to me, as I had previously determined to attempt the same, it being the *shortest* way to Jerusalem. The Cavalier Frediani, whom I met in Egypt, would have persuaded me that it was impracticable, and that he, having had the same intention himself, after having been detained in hope five weeks, was compelled to relinquish his design. While I was yet ruminating over this scrap of paper, the superior paid me a morning visit; he also said it was *impossible;* but at length promised to search for guides. I had already endeavoured to persuade those who had accompanied me from Tor, but they also talked of dangers, and declined." Guides were found, who, after resisting for a while his entreaties and bribes, agreed to conduct him by the desired route; but, unable to overcome their fears, deceived him, and led him towards the Mediterranean coast, through the desert of Gaza.

There yet remains a detail of the complication of difficulties which, in another direction still, the nearest to Judea, and apparently the most accessible, the traveller has to encounter in reaching that desolate region which once formed the kingdom of Idumea,—difficulties that it may safely be said are scarcely to be met with in any other part of Asia, or even in any other quarter of the world where no natural obstructions intervene. "To give an idea," say Captains Irby and Mangles, "of the difficulties which the Turkish government supposed there would be for an Englishman to go to Kerek and Wady Mousa, it is necessary to say, that when Mr. Banks applied at Constantinople to have these places inserted in his firman, they returned for answer, "that they knew of none such within the grand seignior's dominions; but as he and Mr. Frere, the British minister, pressed the affair very much, they at length referred him to the pacha of Damascus, who (equally averse to have any thing to do with the business) passed him on to the governor of Jerusalem." The governor of Jerusalem, "having tried all he could to dissuade them from the undertaking," referred him in like manner to the governor of Jaffa, who not only "evaded the affair altogether," but endeavoured to put a stop to their journey. Though frustrated in every attempt to obtain any protection or assistance from the public authorities, and also warned of the danger that awaited them from "Arabs of a most savage and treacherous race," these adventurous travellers, intent on visiting the ruins of Petra, having provided themselves with horses and arms, and Arab dresses, and being eleven in number, including servants and two guides, "determined to proceed to try their fortune with the sheikh of Hebron." He at first expressed compliance with their wishes, but being soon "alarmed at his own determination," refused them the least aid or protection. Repeated offers of money to guides met a decided refusal; and they procured no means of facilitating their journey. The peculiar difficulty, not only of *passing through* Idumea, (which they never attempted,) but even of entering within its borders, and the greater hazard of travelling thither than in any other direction, are still further illustrated by the acquiescence of an Arab tribe afterward to accompany and protect them to Kerek, at a reasonable rate, and by their positive refusal, upon any terms or stipulation whatever, to conduct them to a spot that lay within the boundaries of Edom. "We offered five hundred piastres if they would conduct us to Wady Mousa, but nothing could induce them to consent. They said they would not go if we would give them five thousand piastres," (forty times the sum for which they had agreed to accompany them to Kerek, although the distance was not nearly double,) "observing that money was of no use to a man if he lost his life." Having afterward obtained the protection of an intrepid Arab chief, with his followers, and having advanced to the borders of Edom, their further progress was suddenly opposed in the most threatening and determined manner. And in the whole course of their travels, which extended to about three thousand miles, in Thrace, Asia Minor, Cyprus, the desert, Egypt, and in Syria, in different longitudinal and lateral directions, from one extremity to the other, they found nowhere such a barrier to their progress, except in a previous abortive attempt to reach Petra from another quarter; and though they were never better prepared for encountering it, they never elsewhere experienced so formidable an opposition. The sheikh of Wady Mousa and his people swore that they would not suffer them to go forward, and "that they should neither drink of their water, *nor pass into their territory.*" The Arab chief who had espoused their cause also took an oath, "by the faith of a true Mussulman," that they should drink of the water of Wady Mousa, and go whithersoever he pleased to carry them. "Thus," it is remarked, "were both the rival chiefs oppositely pledged in their resolutions respecting us."

Several days were passed in entreaties, artifices, and mutual menaces, which were all equally unavailing.—The determination and perseverance of the one party of Arabs was equalled by the resistance and obstinacy of the other. Both were constantly acquiring an accession of strength, and actively preparing for combat. The travellers, thus finding all the dangers and difficulties of which they had been forewarned fully realized, "could not but compare their case to that of the Israelites under Moses, *when Edom refused to give them a passage through his country.*" "They offered even to abandon their object rather than proceed to extremities," and endanger the lives of many others, as well as their own; and they were told that they were fortunate in the protection of the chief who accompanied them, otherwise they never would have returned. The hostile Arabs, who defied them and their protectors to approach, having abandoned their camps, and having concentrated their forces, and possessed themselves of the passes and heights, sent messengers with a renewal of oaths and protestations *against entering their territory;* announced that they were fully prepared to maintain their purpose—that war "was positively determined on as the only alternative of the travellers not being permitted to see what they desired:" and their sheikh vowed that "if they *passed through* his lands, they should be shot like so many dogs." Abou Raschid, the firm and fearless chief who had pledged his honour and his oath in guarantee for the advance of the travellers, and whose obstinate resolution nothing could exceed, his arguments, artifices, and falsehoods having all failed, despatched messengers to the camps under his influence, rejected alike all compromise with the opposing Arabs, and all remonstrances on the part of his adherents and dependants, (who thought that the travellers were doomed to destruction by their rashness,) and resolved to achieve by force what he had sworn to accomplish. "The camp assumed a very warlike appearance; the spears stuck in the sand, the saddled horses before the tents, with the arms hanging up within, altogether had an imposing effect. The travellers, however, were at last permitted to proceed in peace: but a brief space were allowed them for inspecting the ruins, and they could plainly distinguish the opposing party of Arabs, in great numbers, watching them from the heights. Abou Raschid was then dismayed, "he was never at his ease, and constantly urged them to depart." Nothing could obtain an extension of the time allotted them, and they returned, leaving much unexplored, and even unable by any means or possibility to penetrate a little farther, in order to visit a large temple which they could clearly discern. Through Idumea they did not pass.

Thus Volney, Burckhardt, Joliffe, Henniker, and Captains Irby and Mangles, not only give their personal testimony of the truth of the fact which corroborates the prediction, but also adduce a variety of circumstances, which all conspire in giving superfluity of proof that Idumea, which was long resorted to from every quarter, is so beset on every side with dangers to the traveller, that *none pass through it.* Even the Arabs of the neighbouring regions whose home is the desert, and whose occupation is wandering, are afraid to enter it, or to conduct any within its borders. Yet amid all this manifold testimony to its truth, there is not, in any single instance, the most distant allusion to the prediction; and the evidence is as unsuspicious and undesigned, as it is copious and complete.

"I will make thee small among the nations; thou art greatly despised." Though the border of wickedness, and the retreat of a horde of thieves, who are distinguished as peculiarly savage even among the wild Arabs, and thus an object of dread, as well as of astonishment, to those who pass thereby, yet, contrasted with what it was, or reckoned among the nations, Edom is small indeed. Within almost all its boundary, it may be said that none *abide,* or have any fixed permanent residence; and instead of the superb structures, the works of various ages, which long adorned its cities, the huts of the Arabs, where even huts they have, are mere mud-hovels, of "mean and ragged appearance," which, in general, are deserted on the least alarm. But, miserable habitations as these are, they scarcely seem to exist anywhere throughout Edom, but on a single point of its borders; and wherever the Arabs otherwise wander in search of spots for pasturage for their cattle, (found in hollows, or near to springs after the winter rains,) tents are their only covering. Those which pertain to the more powerful tribes are sometimes both numerous and large; yet, though they form at least but a frail dwelling, many of them are "very low and small." Near to the ruins of Petra, Burckhardt passed an encampment of Bedouin tents, most of which were "the smallest he had ever seen, about four feet high, and ten in length;" and towards the southwest border of Edom he met with a few wanderers, who had no tents with them, and whose only shelter from the burning rays of the sun and the *heavy dews of night* was the scanty branches of the talk-trees. The subsistence of the Bedouins is often as precarious as their habitations are mean; the flocks they tend, or which they pillage from more fertile regions, are their only possessions; and in that land where commerce long concentrated its wealth, and through which the treasures of Ophir passed, the picking of gum arabic from thorny branches is now the poor occupation, the only semblance of industry, practised by the wild and wandering tenants of a desert. Edom is *small among the nations;* and how *greatly is it despised*, when the public authorities at Constantinople deny any knowledge of it!—KEITH.

Ver. 15. As thou didst rejoice at the inheritance of the house of Israel, because it was desolate, so will I do unto thee: thou shalt be desolate, O Mount Seir, and all Idumea, *even* all of it; and they shall know that I *am* the LORD.

Idumea was situated to the south of Judea and of Moab; it bordered on the east with Arabia Petrea, under which name it was included in the latter part of its history, and it extended southward to the eastern gulf of the Red Sea. A single extract from the Travels of Volney will be found to be equally illustrative of the prophecy and of the fact. "This country *has not been visited by any traveller*, but it well merits such an attention; for from the reports of the Arabs of Bakir, and the inhabitants of Gaza, who frequently go to Maan and Karak, on the road of the pilgrims, there are, to the southeast of the lake Asphaltites, (Dead Sea,) *within three days' journey*, upwards of thirty ruined towns *absolutely deserted*. Several of them have large edifices, with columns that may have belonged to the ancient temples, or at least to Greek churches. The Arabs sometimes make use of them to fold the cattle in; but in general avoid them on account of the enormous scorpions with which they swarm. We cannot be surprised at these traces of ancient population, when we recollect that this was the country of the Nabatheans, the most powerful of the Arabs, and of the *Idumeans*, who, at the *time of the destruction of Jerusalem*, were almost as numerous as the Jews, as appears from Josephus, who informs us, that on the first rumour of the march of Titus against Jerusalem, thirty thousand Idumeans instantly assembled, and threw themselves into that city for its defence. It appears that, besides the advantages of being under a tolerably good government, these districts enjoyed a considerable share of the commerce of Arabia and India, which increased their industry and population. We know that as far back as the time of Solomon, the cities of Astioum Gaber (Esion Gaber) and Ailah (Eloth) were highly-frequented marts. These towns were situated on the adjacent gulf of the Red Sea, where we still find the latter yet retaining its name, and perhaps the former in that of El Akaba, or the end (of the sea.) These two places are in the hands of the Bedouins, who, being destitute of a navy and commerce, do not inhabit them. But the pilgrims report that there is at El Akaba a wretched fort. The Idumeans, from whom the Jews only took their ports at intervals, must have found in them a great source of wealth and population. It even appears that the Idumeans rivalled the Tyrians, who also possessed a town, the name of which is unknown, on the coast of Hedjaz, in the desert of Tih, and the city of Faran, and, without doubt, El-Tor, which served it by way of port. From this place the caravans might reach Palestine and Judea (through Idumea) in eight or ten days. This route, which is longer than that from Suez to Cairo, is infinitely shorter than that from Aleppo to Bassorah." Evidence which must have been undesigned, which cannot be suspected of partiality, and which no illustration can strengthen, and no ingenuity pervert, is thus borne to the truth of the most wonderful prophecies. That the Idumeans were a populous and powerful nation long posterior to the delivery of the prophecies; that they possessed a tolerably good government, (even in the estimation of Volney;) that Idumea contained many cities; that these cities are now absolutely deserted, and that their ruins swarms with enormous scorpions; that it was a commercial nation, and possessed highly-frequented marts; that it forms a shorter route than an ordinary one to India, and yet that it had not been visited by any traveller, are facts all recorded, or proved to a wish, by this able but unconscious commentator.

A greater contrast cannot be imagined than the ancient and present state of Idumea. It was a kingdom previous to Israel, having been governed first by dukes or princes, afterward by eight successive kings, and again by dukes, before there reigned any king over the children of Israel. Its fertility and early cultivation are implied, not only in the blessings of Esau, whose dwelling was to be the fatness of the earth, and of the dew of heaven from above, but also in the condition proposed by Moses to the Edomites, when he solicited a passage for the Israelites through their borders, "that they would not pass through the fields nor through the vineyards;" and also in the great wealth, especially in the multitudes of flocks and herds, recorded as possessed by an individual inhabitant of that country, at a period, in all probability, even more remote. The Idumeans were, without doubt, both an opulent and a powerful people. They often contended with the Israelites, and entered into a league with their other enemies against them. In the reign of David they were indeed subdued and greatly oppressed, and many of them even dispersed throughout the neighbouring countries, particularly Phenicia and Egypt. But during the decline of the kingdom of Judah, and for many years previous to its extinction, they encroached upon the territories of the Jews, and extended their dominion over the southwestern part of Judea. Though no excellence whatever be now attached to its name, which exists only in past history, Idumea, including perhaps Judea, was then not without the praise of the first of Roman poets:

Primus Idumeas referam tibi, Mantua, palmas.
Virg. Georg. lib. iii. l. 12.

And of Lucan, (Phars. lib. iii.)

Arbustis palmarum dives Idume.

But Idumea, as a kingdom, can lay claim to a higher renown than either the abundance of its flocks or the excellence of its palm-trees. The celebrated city of Petra (so named by the Greeks, and so worthy of the name, on account both of its rocky vicinity and its numerous dwellings excavated from the rocks) was situated within the patrimonial territory of the Edomites. There is distinct and positive evidence that it was a city of Edom, and the metropolis of the Nabatheans, whom Strabo expressly identifies with the Idumeans—possessors of the same country, and subject to the same laws. "Petra," to use the words of Dr. Vincent, by whom the state of its ancient commerce was described before its ruins were discovered, "is the capital of Edom or Seir, the Idumea or Arabia Petræa of the Greeks, the Nabatea, considered both by geographers, historians, and poets, as the source of all the precious commodities of the East." "The caravans, in all ages, from Minea in the interior of Arabia, and from Gerrha on the Gulf of Persia, from Hadramaut on the ocean, and some even from Sabea or Yemen, appear to have pointed to Petra as a common centre; and from Petra the trade seems to have again branched out in every direction to Egypt, Palestine, and Syria, through Arsinoe, Gaza, Tyre, Jerusalem, Damascus, and a variety of subordinate routes that all terminated on the Mediterranean. There is every proof that is requisite to show that the Tyrians and Sidonians were the first merchants who introduced the produce of India to all the nations which encircled the Mediterranean so is there the strongest evidence to prove that the Tyrians obtained all their commodities from Arabia. But if Arabia was the centre of this commerce, Petra was the point to which all the Arabians tended from the three sides of their vast peninsula." At a period subsequent to the commencement of the Christian era, there always reigned at Petra, according to Strabo, a king of the royal lineage, with whom a prince was associated in the government. It was a place of great strength in the time of the Romans. Pompey marched against it, but desisted from the attack; and Trajan afterward besieged it. It was a metropolitan see, to which several bishopricks were attached in the time of the Greek emperors, and Idumea was included in the third Palestine—*Palestina tertia sive salutaris.* But the ancient state of Idumea cannot in the present day be so clearly ascertained from the records respecting it which can be gleaned from history, whether sacred or profane, as by the wonderful and imperishable remains of its capital city, and by "the traces of many towns and villages," which indisputably show that it must once have been thickly inhabited. It not only can admit of no dispute that the country and cities of Idumea subsisted in a very different state from that absolute desolation in which, long prior to the period of its reality, it was represented in the prophetic vision; but there are prophecies regarding it that have yet a prospective view, and which refer to the time when "the children of Israel shall possess their possessions," or to "the year of recompenses for the controversy of Zion." But, dangerous as it is to explore the land of Idumea and difficult to ascertain those existing facts and precise circumstances which form the strongest features of its desolate aspect, (and that ought to be the subject of scientific as well as of religious inquiry,) enough has been discovered to show that the sentence against it, though fulfilled by the agency of nature and of man, is precisely such as was first recorded in the annals of inspiration.—KEITH.

CHAPTER XXXVII.

Ver. 16. Moreover, thou son of man, take thee one stick, and write upon it, For Judah, and for the children of Israel his companions: then take another stick, and write upon it, For Joseph, the stick of Ephraim, and *for* all the house of Israel his companions.

The original manner of communicating ideas by letters, among the ancient Britons, was by cutting the letters upon sticks, which were most commonly squared, and sometimes formed into three sides. The squares were used for general subjects, and for stanzas of four lines in poetry: the trilateral ones were adapted to trides, and for a peculiar kind of ancient metre, called triban, or triplet, and englyn milwyr, or the warrior's verse. Several sticks with writing upon them were put together, forming a kind of frame, which was called peithynen, or elucidator; and was so constructed, that each stick might be turned for the facility of reading, the end of each running out alternately on both sides of the frame. (*See engraving, at the end of the volume.*)

A continuation of this mode of writing may be found in the Runic or log almanacs of the northern states of Europe, in which the engraving on square pieces of wood has been continued to so late a period as the sixteenth century. The Scythians also conveyed their ideas by marking or cutting certain figures and a variety of lines, upon splinters or billets of wood. Aulus Gellius (lib. ii. c. 12) says, that the ancient laws of Solon, preserved at Athens, were cut in tablets of wood.

At Umea, in Sweden, a person whom Dr. Clarke visited, "produced several ancient Runic staves, such as are known in Sweden under the name of Runic almanacs, or Runic calendars. They were all of wood, about three feet and a half long, shaped like the straight swords represented in churches upon the brazen sepulchre-plates of our Saxon ancestors. The blades were on each side engraved with Runic characters, and signs, like hieroglyphics, extending their whole length. The signs were explained to us as those of the months, and the characters denoted the weeks and days. The Runic staves which had been given to us, were afterward exhibited at Morvana, and in the different places through which we passed, in the hope of procuring more. We afterward saw others; but they were always rare, and considered more as curious antiquities than things in actual use: although the inhabitants were well acquainted with them, and were often able to explain the meaning of the characters upon them, and the purpose for which these instruments were made, especially in this part of Sweden. We saw one of more elaborate workmanship, where the Runic characters had been very elegantly engraved upon a stick, like a physician's cane: but this last seemed to be of a more modern date. In every instance, it was evident, from some of the marks upon them, that their first owners were Christians: the different lines and characters denoting the fasts and festivals, golden numbers, dominical letter, epact, &c. But the custom of thus preserving written records upon rods or sticks is of the highest antiquity. There is an allusion to this custom in Ezekiel, xxxvii. 16—20, where mention is made of something very similar to the Runic staff." Nearly nine centuries before the age of Ezekiel's prophecy, Moses used rods in the same manner. Numbers xvii. 2, 3. We may now see how satisfactorily the use to which these written rods were in after-ages applied, is illustrated by the Runic staves, which have generally the form of a sword or sceptre, being the ensigns of office and dignity borne in the hands by the priests, the elders, and princes of the people. The recurved rods of the priests among the Greeks, and the crosier of a modern bishop, had the same origin.—BURDER.

CHAPTER XXXVIII.

Ver. 11. And thou shalt say, I will go up to the land of unwalled villages; I will go to them that are at rest, that dwell safely, all of them dwelling without walls, and having neither bars nor gates.

The Orientals were attentive to safety, not less than to convenience and pleasure. To secure their dwellings from the depredations of hostile tribes, that scoured their country in all directions in quest of plunder, they were forced to surround them with lofty walls. This mode of defence seems to have been adopted at a very remote period; for the spies whom Moses sent into Canaan to view the country, reported that the cities were great, and walled up to heaven. The height of these walls, which by a bold oriental figure, dictated by the pusillanimous fears of the spies, are said to reach up to heaven, must have appeared to the people of Israel, unaccustomed as they were to warfare of that kind, and totally unprovided with the means necessary for besieging fortified places, a very serious obstacle to the accomplishment of their wishes. But the magnitude of it may be illustrated with the greatest advantage, from the accounts which modern travellers have given us of the present inhabitants of those deserts, who are much in the same circumstances as the people of Israel were when they came out of Egypt, whose attacks are effectually repelled by the lofty walls of one or two Christian monasteries.

The great monastery of Mount Sinai, Thevenot says, is well built of good freestone, with very high smooth walls; on the east side there is a window, by which those that were within drew up the pilgrims into the monastery with a basket, which they let down by a rope that runs by a pulley, to be seen above at the window, and the pilgrims went into it one by one, and so were hoisted up. These walls are so high that they cannot be scaled, and without cannon that place cannot be taken.

The monastery of St. Anthony, in Egypt, says Maillet, is a vast enclosure, with good walls, raised so high as to secure this place from the insults of the Arabs. There is no entrance into it but by a pulley, by means of which people are hoisted up on high, and so conveyed into the monastery. No warlike apparatus which the Arabian freebooters possess, are sufficient for the reduction of these fortified places. The Israelites, not better provided for besieging strongholds, hastily concluded that the walled cities of Canaan, of which they heard such discouraging accounts, must oppose an insurmountable barrier to their progress. It is not to be supposed that the descendants of Canaan, like the timid monks of Sinai, walled up their gates on the approach of danger, and permitted none to enter the place, but by means of a pulley; but if their gates had not been well secured, the precaution of raising their wall so high had been in vain.—PAXTON.

CHAPTER XXXIX.

Ver. 11. And it shall come to pass at that day, *that* I will give unto Gog a place there of graves in Israel, the valley of the passengers on the east of the sea; and it shall stop the *noses* of the passengers: and there shall they bury Gog, and all his multitude; and they shall call *it*, The valley of Hamon-gog.

This refers to the dreadful stench which should arise from the dead bodies of Gog. The Tamul translation has it, "cause to STOP the noses." The moment people smell any thing offensive, they immediately press the nostrils together with their fingers. They say of a bad smell, It has STOPPED my nose; which means the nose is so full of that, it is not sensible of any other smell. The figure is much used in reference to the decayed oysters at the pearl fishery. —ROBERTS.

CHAPTER XLIV.

Ver. 2. Then said the LORD unto me, This gate shall be shut, it shall not be opened, and no man shall enter in by it; because the LORD, the God of Israel, hath entered in by it, therefore it shall be shut.

Among other instances of the extreme distance, and profound awe, with which eastern majesty is treated, one that is mentioned by Sir John Chardin, in his account of Persia, appears very strange to us, yet may afford a lively comment on a passage of the prophet Ezekiel. Sir John tells us, "It is a common custom in Persia, that when a great man has built a palace, he treats the king and his grandees in it for several days. Then the great gate of it is open: but when these festivities are over, they shut it up, never more to be opened." He adds, "I have heard that the same thing is practised in Japan." It seems surprising to us, that great and magnificent houses within should have only small entrances into them, which no one would suppose would lead into such beautiful edifices: but such, he observes, is the common custom there: making no magnificent entrance into their houses at all; or if they do, shutting them up after a little time, and making use of some small entrance near the great one, or it may be, in some very different part of the building.—HARMER.

DANIEL.

CHAPTER I.

Ver. 2. And the LORD gave Jehoiakim king of Judah into his hand, with part of the vessels of the house of God, which he carried into the land of Shinar, to the house of his god; and he brought the vessels into the treasure-house of his god.

In all heathen temples there is a place for the sacred jewels and other treasures. The ornaments of the idols are sometimes of GREAT value. I have seen the small crown, breastplate, and necklaces of one idol, worth more than 400*l*.—ROBERTS.

Ver. 3. And the king spake unto Ashpenaz the master of his eunuchs, that he should bring *certain* of the children of Israel, and of the king's seed, and of the princes; 4. Children in whom *was* no blemish, but well-favoured, and skilful in all wisdom, and cunning in knowledge, and understanding science, and such as *had* ability in them to stand in the king's palace, and whom they might teach the learning and the tongue of the Chaldeans.

The master of the black eunuchs is still one of the most important officers at the court of the Turkish emperor, the arrangement of which is, for the most part, formed after the household of the ancient Persian emperors. He is called Kislar-Aga, that is, overseer of the girls, and is the chief of the black eunuchs who guard the harem or residence of the women. "The Kislar-Aga, by his place, enjoys a powerful influence in affairs, but particularly in those of the court, for which reason the other agas bring concerns before him. His consideration and influence over the emperor is almost always secure." (Von Hammer.)—ROSENMULLER.

Curtius says, that in all barbarous or uncivilized countries, the stateliness of the body is held in great veneration: nor do they think any capable of great services or actions, to whom nature has not vouchsafed to give a beautiful form and aspect. It has always been the custom of the eastern nations to choose such for their principal officers, or to wait on princes and great personages. Sir Paul Ricaut observes, "that the youths that are designed for the great offices of the Turkish empire, must be of admirable features and looks, well-shaped in their bodies, and without any defects of nature: for it is conceived that a corrupt and sordid soul can scarce inhabit in a serene and ingenuous aspect; and I have observed not only in the seraglio, but also in the courts of great men, their personal attendants have been of comely lusty youths, well habited, deporting themselves with singular modesty and respect in the presence of their masters; so that when a pacha aga spahi travels, he is always attended with a comely equipage, followed by flourishing youths, well clothed and mounted, in great numbers."—BURDER.

Ver. 8. But Daniel purposed in his heart that he would not defile himself with the portion of the king's meat, nor with the wine which he drank: therefore he requested of the prince of the eunuchs that he might not defile himself.

It was the custom of most nations, before their meals, to make an oblation of some part of what they ate and drank to their gods, as a thankful acknowledgment that every thing which they enjoyed was their gift. These oblations were called *libamina* among the Romans, so that every entertainment had something in it of the nature of a sacrifice. This practice generally prevailing, made Daniel and his friends look upon the provisions coming from the king's table as no better than meats offered to idols, and, by being so offered, to be accounted unclean or polluted.—BURDER.

Ver. 15. And at the end of ten days their countenances appeared fairer and fatter in flesh than all the children which did eat the portion of the king's meat.

It is probable that there was nothing extraordinary or out of the common way in this circumstance. Sir J. Chardin observes, "I have remarked this, that the countenances of the Kechichs are in fact more rosy and smooth than those of others, and that these people who fast much, I mean the Armenians and the Greeks, are notwithstanding very beautiful, sparkling with health, with a clear and lively countenance."—HARMER.

CHAPTER II.

Ver. 4. Then spake the Chaldeans to the king in Syriac, O king, live for ever: tell thy servants the dream, and we will show the interpretation.

These words are not addressed to the ears of royalty MERELY. Has a man been greatly favoured by another, he says, "Ah! may you never die." "So good a man ought never to die." "May you live for ever." "Will death come to such a man as this?" "Live, live, for ever."—ROBERTS.

Ver. 31. Thou, O king, sawest, and, behold, a great image. This great image, whose brightness *was* excellent, stood before thee, and the form thereof *was* terrible. 32. This image's head *was* of fine gold, his breast and his arms of silver, his belly and his thighs of brass. 33. His legs of iron, his feet part of iron and part of clay.

There is usually an obvious and striking congruity in the prophetic and parabolic imagery of the scriptures. In the present case there would seem to be an exception; for who can conceive of the manner in which iron and clay could be made to combine in the same mass? In respect to the other materials, the gold, the silver, the brass, they are sufficiently homogeneous in their nature to allow of being united in the manner supposed in the vision. But how a soft yielding substance like clay could form a constituent part of the same image, and that too of the very base and pediment upon which it rested, is by no means obvious. We see not therefore why the definition given to the original Chaldaic word by Cocceius, Buxtorf, Gesenius, Simonis, Gibbs, and others, viz. *potter's ware*, or *burnt baked clay*, is not decidedly to be preferred. And of the original phrase subsequently occurring, "miry clay," v. 41, 42. The first of these lexicographers says expressly, "Nonigitur lutum vel limum notat, sed opus coctum ex limo, vel limum excoctum," *it does not therefore signify clay or mud, in its soft state, but something formed by baking from clay.* This interpretation gives consistency to the whole imagery, and, if needs be, can be abundantly confirmed from the frequent use of the same term by the Chaldee Targums.—BUSH.

Ver. 46. Then the king Nebuchadnezzar fell upon his face, and worshipped Daniel, and commanded that they should offer an oblation and sweet odours unto him.

Odoriferous ointments and perfumes were often presented by the great as a particular mark of distinction. The king of Babylon treated the prophet Daniel with the richest perfumes, after he had predicted the future destinies of his empire, as a distinguished proof of his esteem and admiration: "Then the king Nebuchadnezzar fell upon his face, and worshipped Daniel, and commanded that they should offer an oblation and sweet odours unto him." This passage Mr. Harmer considers as exceedingly difficult; and he labours hard to prove that the king meant nothing more than civil respect. "Nebuchadnezzar, in all this matter, appeared to have considered Daniel merely as a prophet: his words strongly express this, Your God is a God of gods; and had it been otherwise, a person so zealous as Daniel, who risked his life, rather than neglect his homage to his God, and had the courage to pray to him with his windows open towards Jerusalem, contrary to the king's command, would undoubtedly, like Paul and Barnabas, have rejected these odours." This view completely vindicates the prophet from the charge of conniving at the idolatry of the king; but it is not necessary to his defence. The conduct of Nebuchadnezzar, it is allowed, admits of a favourable construction; but, at the same time, it is scarcely possible to avoid the suspicion that he was, on this memorable occasion, guilty of idolatrous veneration. The verb *Sagad, he worshipped*, so far as the writer has been able to trace it, both in Hebrew and Chaldee, expresses the homage which is rendered to a god, and is, perhaps, universally applied to the worship of false deities in the sacred scriptures. If this remark be just, it is greatly to be suspected that Nebuchadnezzar, who had few, or no correct religious principles, to restrain the sudden movements of his impetuous passions, did intend, on that occasion, to honour Daniel as a god, or, which is not materially different, to worship the divinity in the prophet. But it may be demanded, how then is Daniel to be vindicated? Shall we suppose that a prophet of the Lord, a man highly favoured and distinguished for his eminent holiness, would suffer idolatry to be practised in his presence, more especially when he himself was the object of it, without expressing his disapprobation? To this objection, the following answer is offered: The sacred writers, studious of extreme brevity, often pass over many incidents in the scenes which they describe. Daniel, therefore, might actually reject the intended honour, although it is not mentioned in the record. This silence of the historian will not prove that it was not done, while there are certain circumstances in the narrative which go far to prove that the prophet did reject the homage of Nebuchadnezzar. In the 28th verse of the second chapter, he solemnly declares before the king and the whole court, that "it is the God of heaven that revealeth secrets, and makes known to the king Nebuchadnezzar what shall be in the latter days;" and the 30th verse, "But as for me, this secret is not revealed to me for any wisdom that I have more than any living." When these faithful declarations are considered, it is not to be supposed that Daniel neglected to remind the king that religious worship is due to God alone; and that such a testimony was given at the time, is intimated with considerable clearness in the confession of the king himself, verse 47th, which seems to refer to something the prophet had just said to him: "The king answered unto Daniel, and said, Of a truth it is, that your God is a God of gods, and a Lord of kings, and a Revealer of secrets, seeing thou couldst reveal this secret." The character of Daniel, therefore, is not affected by the misconduct of his sovereign, in paying him divine honours.—PAXTON.

CHAPTER III.

Ver. 6. And whoso falleth not down and worshippeth, shall the same hour be cast into the midst of a burning fiery furnace.

This mode of putting to death was not unusual in the East in more modern times. Chardin, in his Travels, after speaking of the most common modes of punishing with death, says, "But there is still a particular way of putting to death such as have transgressed in civil affairs, either by causing a dearth, or by selling above the tax by a false weight, or who have committed themselves in any other manner. The cooks are put upon a spit and roasted over a slow fire, bakers are thrown into a hot oven. During the dearth in 1668, I saw such ovens heated on the royal square in Ispahan, to terrify the bakers, and deter them from deriving advantage from the general distress."—ROSENMULLER.

Ver. 25. He answered and said, Lo, I see four men loose, walking in the midst of the fire, and they have no hurt; and the form of the fourth is like the Son of God.

Professor Eichorn has manifested a strong inclination to expel the prophet Daniel from the sacred writings. As the difficulties which attend some representations in this prophet, [" fires which do not burn; and an image strangely disproportioned," are especially selected,] are among the professor's principal reasons, we could wish, before see

.ence were passed on the delinquent, that not only what we have just noticed in relation to his animals, but also the following hints in relation to some of his other subjects, were duly weighed, and accurately understood. The story of the three Hebrews in the fiery furnace would be much more within our comprehension, if we knew the true form of what is denominated a *furnace;* it is usually conceived of, as being somewhat like our tile-kilns, a solid, enclosed, brick building, with an aperture only for entrance, or, at most, with a door-way below, and a vent above for the flame, smoke, &c. But the circumstances of the story do not warrant an edifice of this construction; for it appears that Nebuchadnezzar, still seated on his throne, saw the persons in the fire. Now this he could not do, *through* the solid wall of such a building; neither could the flame, issuing from a narrow orifice, *easily* slay those men who threw in the Hebrews, the solid wall being *between* them and the fire. Either, then, the opening to this furnace, if it were a solid edifice, was large enough to admit of full view into it; or we must seek some other construction for it. We may carry this idea somewhat further, and infer the propriety of supposing Nebuchadnezzar to see *throughout* the structure; by consequence, the building had no covering; but was, at most, an enclosure of fire; or, an area surrounded by a wall, within which the fire raged.—TAYLOR IN CALMET.

CHAPTER IV.

Ver. 25. That they shall drive thee from men, and thy dwelling shall be with the beasts of the field, and they shall make thee to eat grass as oxen, and they shall wet thee with the dew of heaven, and seven times shall pass over thee, till thou know that the Most High ruleth in the kingdom of men, and giveth it to whomsoever he will.

This was one of the miseries of Nebuchadnezzar, and a much greater one than the people in England imagine. Think of the state of the body and pores after being twelve hours in a blazing sun, and then think on such a dew falling as will saturate all the clothes; and a tolerable view is gained of the great reverse, and the effect it must have on the human frame. Of a wretched man it is said, " The sun falls on his head by day, and the dew by night." "He is scorched by the sun, and made wet by the dew."—ROBERTS.

Ver. 29. At the end of twelve months he walked in the palace of the kingdom of Babylon.

See on 1 Sam 9. 25, 26.

The custom of walking upon the roof in the cool of the day, to inhale the refreshing breeze, and to survey the surrounding scenery, may serve to explain a scripture incident of considerable interest, which does not appear to have been generally understood. It is thus recorded in the prophecies of Daniel: "At the end of twelve months, he (Nebuchadnezzar) walked in the palace of the kingdom of Babylon." The true sense of the original is, "he walked upon the palace;" but this interpretation our translators have placed in the margin, as more doubtful than the other. If Nebuchadnezzar walked in some apartment of his palace, it is not easy to account for the proud and rapturous exclamation which suddenly burst from his mouth; we can see no proper excitement, no adequate cause; but if we suppose him walking upon the roof of his palace, which proudly rose above the surrounding habitations, and surveying the vast extent, the magnificence, and the splendour of that great city, the mistress of the world—its walls of prodigious height and thickness—its hanging gardens, reputed one of the most astonishing efforts of art and power—its glittering palaces; the Euphrates rolling his majestic flood through the middle of the place, shut in on both sides by strong bulwarks and doors of brass; it was quite natural for such a man to feel elated with the sight, and indulge his pride and arrogance in the manner described by the prophet.—PAXTON.

CHAPTER V.

Ver. 12. Forasmuch as an excellent spirit, and knowledge, and understanding, interpreting of dreams, and showing of hard sentences, and dissolving of doubts, were found in the same Daniel, whom the king named Belteshazzar: now let Daniel be called, and he will show the interpretation.

The margin (Chald.) has, instead of "doubts," "knots." A very difficult subject is called a *mudiche*, a knot! Thus the explaining of a riddle is called "untying the knot." Of a talented man it is said, "Ah! he is very clever, he can tie or untie any knot." Of a dream, it is asked, "Who can loose this knot?" Of any mysteries, or of deep plans, it is asked, "Ah! who can untie these knots?" "How difficult that passage was, but he soon unravelled the knot."—ROBERTS.

In the copy of a patent given to Sir John Chardin by the king of Persia, we find it is addressed "To the lords of lords, who have the presence of a lion, the aspect of Deston, the princes who have the stature of Tahem-ten-ten, who seem to be in the time of Ardevon, the regents who carry the majesty of Ferribours, the conquerors of kingdoms, superintendents that *unloose all manner of knots*, and who are under the ascendant of Mercury," &c.—BURDER.

Ver. 21. And he was driven from the sons of men; and his heart was made like the beasts, and his dwelling *was* with the wild asses: they fed him with grass like oxen, and his body was wet with the dew of heaven; till he knew that the most high God ruled in the kingdom of men, and *that* he appointeth over it whomsoever he will.

See on Job 39. 5.

Ver. 27. TEKEL; Thou art weighed in the balances, and art found wanting.

This striking form of speech is much used in the East at this day. Thus, should two men be disputing respecting the moral character of a third person, one will say, "I know the fellow well; I have weighed him, and he is found wanting." "He found wanting! you are much lighter than he." "What! miscreant, do you wish to weigh against me?" "Thou art but as one part in a thousand." "Begone! fellow, or I will soon weigh thee." "Yes, yes, there is no doubt about it: you have weighed me; I am much lighter than you." "What kind of times are these? the slaves are weighing their masters." "Yes, the low castes have become very clever, they are weighing their superiors." "What! woman, do you call in question the authority of your husband: are YOU qualified to weigh him?" "The judge has been weighing the prisoners, and they are all wanting."—ROBERTS.

From the following extract it will appear that there is an allusion in these words, which will justify a literal interpretation of them. "The first of September, (which was the late mogul's birthday,) he, retaining an ancient yearly custom, was, in the presence of his chief grandees, weighed in a balance: the ceremony was performed within his house, or tent, in a fair spacious room, whereinto none were admitted but by special leave. The scales in which he was thus weighed were plated with gold; and so was the beam, on which they hung by great chains, made likewise of that most precious metal. The king sitting in one of them, was weighed first against silver coin, which immediately afterward was distributed among the poor; then was he weighed against gold; after that against jewels, (as they say,) but I observed (being there present with my lord ambassador) that he was weighed against three several things, laid in silken bags on the contrary scale. When I saw him in the balance, I thought on Belshazzar, who was found too light. By his weight (of which his physicians yearly keep an exact account) they presume to guess of the present estate of his body, of which they speak flatteringly, however they think it to be." (Sir Thomas Roe.)—BURDER.

Ver. 29. Then commanded Belshazzar, and they clothed Daniel with scarlet, and *put* a chain of gold about his neck, and made a proclamation concerning him, that he should be the third ruler in the kingdom.

This was designed to honour Daniel, and certainly was, according to the custom of the East, a ceremony highly expressive of dignity. To come out from the presence of a superior in a garment different from that in which the person went in, was significant of approbation and promotion. Whether it was the precise intention of this clothing to declare Daniel's investiture with the dignity of the third ruler of the kingdom, or whether it was an honorary distinction, unconnected with his advancement, cannot be absolutely decided, because caffetans, or robes, are at this day put on people with both views.—Burder.

CHAPTER VI.

Ver. 18. Then the king went to his palace, and passed the night fasting: neither were instruments of music brought before him; and his sleep went from him.

See on Ezra 9. 3.

Ver. 23. Then was the king exceeding glad for him, and commanded that they should take Daniel up out of the den. So Daniel was taken up out of the den, and no manner of hurt was found upon him, because he believed in his God.

The Orientals have an idea, that in whatever a man believes, whether in reference to the existence or nonexistence of evil or danger in regard to himself, that so will his condition be regulated. In walking once with a learned Bramin, through a grove of cocoa-trees, I inquired, Why are you not afraid of those nuts falling on your head, and killing you on the spot? "Because I have only to believe they will not fall, and all is safe," was his reply.—Roberts.

CHAPTER VII.

Ver. 2. Daniel spake and said, I saw in my vision by night, and, behold, the four winds of the heaven strove upon the great sea.

The whirlwind, it appears from the sacred writings, comes from different points of the compass. The prophet Ezekiel speaks of one that came from the north; and although it appeared to him in vision, it was according to the course of nature; for we learn from other sources of information, that it sometimes arises in that quarter. William of Tyre records an instance of a violent whirlwind from the north, in the time of the crusades, which enveloped two hostile armies in an immense cloud of dust, and compelled them for a while to suspend the work of destruction. When that enterprising traveller, Mr. Parke, was traversing the Sahara, or Great Desert, in his way to the Niger, destitute of provisions and water, his throat pained with thirst, and his strength nearly exhausted, he heard a wind sounding from the east, and instinctively opened his parched mouth to receive the precious drops of rain which he confidently expected, but it was instantly filled with sand drifted from the desert. So immense was the quantity raised into the air, and wafted upon the wings of the wind, and so great the velocity with which it flew, that he was compelled to turn his face to the west to prevent suffocation, and continue motionless till it passed. In Persia, violent currents of air are sometimes seen impelling the clouds in different directions, whose concussion produces an awful noise, like the rushing of a great body of water. As the cloud approaches the earth, the sound becomes still more alarming: for nothing, says Mr. Morier, can be more awful. To this natural phenomenon, the strife of the four winds in the vision of Daniel is perhaps allusive.—Paxton.

Ver. 5. And, behold, another beast, a second, like to a bear, and it raised up itself on one side, and *it had* three ribs in the mouth of it between the teeth of it: and they said thus unto it, Arise, devour much flesh.

It has been satisfactorily proved by the best writers on the subject, that the vision refers to the four great monarchies, the Babylonian, the Medo-Persian, the Macedonian or Grecian, and the Roman; and that the second beast, which was like to a bear, symbolizes the empire of the Medes and Persians. All the four monarchies are represented by beasts of prey, to intimate their agreement in the general character of fierceness and rapacity; and by beasts of different species, to intimate the existence of important differences in their character and mode of operation. The Babylonish empire is symbolized by a lion with eagle's wings, because it was the first and noblest kingdom upon earth; it was strong and fierce as a lion; it was swift and rapid in its movements, as a lion with eagle's wings; rising in a few years, under the conduct of Nebuchadnezzar, to the highest pinnacle of power and greatness. The third kingdom is represented by another beast, "like a leopard, which had upon the back of it four wings of a fowl; the beast had also four heads; and dominion was given unto it." This is the Grecian monarchy; the distinguishing characters of which, are great variety of disposition and manners, undaunted boldness, and rapidity of conquest, never before or since exemplified in the history of nations. The fourth beast was so great and horrible, that no adequate name could be found for it; this nondescript was the symbol of the Roman empire, which differed from all others in the form of its government, in strength, in power, in greatness, in length of duration, and in extent of dominion. The Persian monarchy, symbolized by the bear, has also certain specific differences, which are to be learned from the natural history of that animal. Cruel and rapacious as the others, the bear is inferior in strength and courage to the lion, and, although slower in its motions, more uniform in its appearance, and steady in its purpose, than the leopard. Such was the empire of the Medes and Persians: weaker and less warlike than the Babylonian, whose symbol is the lion; but less various in its principles of government, in the forms which it assumed, in the customs and manners of the nations which composed it, and less rapid in its conquests, than the Macedonian, symbolized by the spotted leopard, one of the most rapid and impetuous animals that traverse the desert. But if the bear is inferior to the lion and the leopard in strength, in courage, and in swiftness, it surpasses them in ferocious cruelty and insatiable voracity; it thirsts for blood and riots in carnage; and such was the empire of the Medes and Persians. They are stigmatized by ancient historians as the greatest robbers and spoilers that ever oppressed the nations. The symbol of this all-devouring people is accordingly represented as having "three ribs in the mouth of it, between the teeth of it," in the very act of devouring three weaker animals which it has seized, that is, of oppressing the kingdoms of Babylon, Lydia, and Egypt, which it conquered. And besides, to denote its rapaciousness and cruelty, it is added in the vision, "they said thus unto it, Arise, devour much flesh."

The fourth empire is symbolized by "a dreadful and terrible beast," for which the prophet found no name in the kingdom of nature. It resembled the fabulous monsters, which poetic imagination sometimes delights to portray; for, in the book of Revelation, John describes it as compounded of the three which preceded it: "The beast which I saw was like unto a leopard, and his feet was as the feet of a bear, and his mouth as the mouth of a lion." It possessed all the qualities which render beasts of prey a terror to man and other animals; the swiftness and cunning of the leopard, the ferocity of the bear, and the boldness and strength of the lion. The Roman empire, which it symbolized, resembled no state of society known among men; it displayed, in its character and proceedings, the vigour and courage of the Babylonians, the various policy and alacrity of the Greeks, and the unchanging firmness of the Medes and Persians; qualities which have been equally conspicuous in the Papal state of that empire.—Paxton.

Ver. 15. I Daniel was grieved in my spirit in the midst of *my* body, and the visions of my head troubled me.

Margin, (Chald.) "sheath;" this is a very curious expression, when applied to such a subject, but it is perfectly natural. When a person has swooned, the people say, "His life has gone into its URI," *i. e.* SHEATH, meaning some particular place into which the life is supposed to retire and conceal itself from the sight. Has a man been wounded by a serpent, and should he appear to be dead, it is often said, "Fear not, his life has merely gone into its SHEATH." When a person's eyes are much sunken by sickness, the people say, "Alas! his eyes have gone into their sheath." "Well, my friend, when did you arrive?" "I came just as the sun was going into its sheath," *i. e.* going down. "I am happy to hear that the king hath put his anger and his sword into the sheath."—ROBERTS.

CHAPTER VIII.

Ver. 5. And as I was considering, behold, a he-goat came from the west, on the face of the whole earth, and touched not the ground: and the goat *had* a notable horn between his eyes.

It is very well known that in former times Macedon, and the adjacent countries, particularly Thrace, abounded with goats; insomuch that they were made symbols, and are to be found on many of the coins that were struck by different towns in those parts of Greece. But not only many of the individual towns in Macedon and Thrace employed this type, but the kingdom itself of Macedon, which is the oldest in Europe of which we have any regular and connected history, was represented also by a goat with this particularity, that it had but one horn. The custom of representing the type and power of a country under the form of a horned animal, is not peculiar to Macedon. Persia was represented by a ram. Ammianus Marcellinus acquaints us, that the king of Persia, when at the head of his army, wore a ram's head, made of gold and set with precious stones, instead of a diadem. The relation of these emblems to Macedon and Persia is strongly confirmed by the vision of Daniel recorded in this chapter, and which from these accounts receives no inconsiderable share of illustration. An ancient bronze figure of a goat with one horn, dug up in Asia Minor, was lately inspected by the society of antiquaries in London. The original use of it probably was to be affixed to the top of a military standard, in the same manner as the Roman eagle. This supposition is somewhat supported by what is related of Caranus, that he ordered goats to be carried before the standards of his army.—BURDER.

CHAPTER XI.

Ver. 2. And now will I show thee the truth. Behold, there shall stand up yet three kings in Persia; and the fourth shall be far richer than *they* all: and by his strength through his riches he shall stir up all against the realm of Grecia. 3. And a mighty king shall stand up, that shall rule with great dominion, and do according to his will.

Soon after the death of Alexander the Great, his kingdom was divided towards the four winds of heaven, but not to his posterity; four of his captains, Ptolemy, Antigonus, Lysimachus, and Cassander, reigned over Egypt, Syria, Thrace, and Greece. The kingdoms of Egypt and of Syria became afterward the most powerful: they subsisted as independent monarchies for a longer period than the other two; and, as they were more immediately connected with the land of Judea, which was often reduced to their dominion, they form the subject of the succeeding predictions. Bishop Newton gives even a more copious illustration of the historical facts, which verify the whole of this prophecy, than that which had previously been given by his illustrious predecessor of the same name—who has rendered that name immortal. He quotes or refers to authorities in every instance: and his dissertation on that part of the prophecy which relates to the kingdoms of Syria and Egypt is wound up in these emphatic words: "It may be proper to stop here, and reflect a little how particular and circumstantial this prophecy is concerning the kingdoms of Egypt and Syria, from the death of Alexander to the time of Antiochus Epiphanes. There is not so complete and regular a series of their kings—there is not so concise and comprehensive an account of their affairs to be found in any author of these times. The prophecy is really more perfect than any history. No one historian hath related so many circumstances, and in such exact order of time, as the prophet hath foretold them; so that it was necessary to have recourse to several authors, Greek and Roman, Jewish and Christian, and to collect here something from one, and to collect there something from another, for better explaining and illustrating the great variety of particulars contained in this prophecy." So close is the coincidence between the prophetic and the real history of the kings of Egypt and of Syria, that Porphyry, one of the earliest opponents of Christianity, laboured to prove its extreme accuracy, and alleged from thence that the events must have preceded the prediction. The same argument is equally necessary at the present hour to disprove the subsequent parts of the same prophecy—though none can urge it now. The last of those facts to which it refers, the accomplishment of which is already past, are unfolded with equal precision and truth as the first—and the fulfilment of the whole is yet incomplete. The more clearly that the event corresponds to the prediction, instead of being an evidence against the truth, the more conclusive is the demonstration that it is the word of Him who hath the times and the seasons in his own power.

The subject of the prophecy is represented in these words:—"I am come to make thee understand what shall befall thy people in the latter days; for the vision is for many days." And that which is noted in the scripture of truth terminates not with the reign of Antiochus. At that very time the Romans extended their conquests towards the East. Macedonia, the seat of the empire of Alexander the Great, became a province of the Roman empire. And the prophecy, faithfully tracing the transition of power, ceases to prolong the history of the kings of Egypt and of Syria, and becomes immediately descriptive of the progress of the Roman arms. The very term (*shall stand up*) which previously marked the commencement of the Persian and of the Macedonian power, is here repeated, and denotes the commencement of a third era, or a new power. The word in the original is the same in each. And "arms (an epithet sufficiently characteristic of the extensive military power of the Romans) shall stand up, and they shall pollute the sanctuary of strength, and shall take away the daily sacrifice, and they shall place the abomination that maketh desolate." All these things, deeply affecting the Jewish state, the Romans did—and they finally rendered the country of Judea "desolate of its old inhabitants." The propagation of Christianity—the succeeding important event—is thus represented:—"The people that do know their God shall be strong and do exploits. And they that understand among the people shall instruct many." The persecutions which they suffered are as significantly described:—"Yet they shall fall by the sword and by flame, by captivity and by spoil many days. Now, when they shall fall, they shall be holpen with a little help, and many shall cleave to them with flatteries." And such was Constantine's conversion and the effect which it produced. No other government but that of the Romans *stood up*—but the mode of that government was changed. After the days of Constantine, Christianity became gradually more and more corrupted. Previous to that period there had existed no system of dominion analogous to that which afterward prevailed. The greatest oppressors had never extended their pretensions beyond human power, nor usurped a spiritual tyranny. But, in contradiction to every other, the next succeeding form of government, unparalleled in its nature, in the annals of despotism or of delusion, is thus characterized by the prophet:—"And the king (the ruling power signifying any government, state, or potentate) shall do according to his will; and he shall exalt himself and magnify himself above every god, and shall speak marvellous things against the God of gods, and shall prosper till the indignation be accomplished." This description is suited to the history of the eastern or western churches—to the government under the Grecian emperors at Constantinople, or of the popes at Rome. The extent of the Roman empire might justify its application to the latter; but the connexion of the prophecy, as referable to local events, tends to limit it to the former. In either case it is descriptive of that mode of government which prospered so long in the East and in the West—and which consisted in the impious usurpation of spiritual authority—in the blasphemous assumption of those attributes which are exclusively divine, and in exalting itself above the laws of God and man. But instead, perhaps, of being confined exclusively to either, it may have been intended to represent, as it does characterize, the spiritual tyranny, and the substitution of the commandments of men for the will of God, which oppressed Christendom for ages, and hid from men the word of God. The prevalence of superstition, the prohibition or discouragement of marriage, and the worship of saints, as characteristic of the same period and of the same power, are thus prophetically described:—"Neither shall he regard the God of his fathers, nor the desire of women, or matrimony, neither shall he regard any god. But in his estate shall he honour the God of forces—*Mahuzzim*," protectors or guardians, a term so applicable to the worship of saints, and to the confidence which was reposed in them, that expressions exactly synonymous are often used by many ancient writers in honour of them—of which Mede and Sir Isaac Newton have adduced a multiplicity of instances. Mahuzzim were the *tutelary saints* of the Greek and Romish churches. The subserviency, which long existed, of spiritual power to temporal aggrandizement, is also noted in the prophecy: "and he shall cause them to rule over many, and shall divide the land for gain." And that the principal teachers and propagators of the worship of *Mahuzzim*—"the bishops, priests, and monks, and religious orders, have been honoured, and reverenced, and esteemed in former ages; that their authority and jurisdiction have extended over the purses and consciences of men; that they have been enriched with noble buildings and large endowments, and have had the choicest of the lands appropriated for church-lands; are points of such notoriety, that they require no proof, and will admit of no denial."

Having thus described the antichristian power, which prospered so long and prevailed so widely, the prophecy next delineates, in less obscure terms, the manner in which that power was to be humbled and overthrown, and introduces a more particular definition of the rise, extent, and fall of that kingdom, which was to oppress and supplant it in the latter days. "And at the time of the end shall the king of the south push at him." The Saracens extended their conquests over great part of Asia and of Europe: they penetrated the dominions of the Grecian empire, and partially subdued, though they could not entirely subvert it, nor obtain possession of Constantinople, the capital city. The prediction, however brief, significantly represents their warfare, which was desultory, and their conquest, which was incomplete. And Arabia is situated to the south of Palestine. The Turks, the next and last invaders of the Grecian empire, were of Scythian extraction, and came from the north. And while a single expression identifies the Saracen invasion—the irruption of the Turks, being of a more fatal character and more permanent in its effects, is fully described. Every part of the description is most faithful to the facts. Their local situation, the impetuosity of their attack, the organization of their armies, and the success of their arms, form the first part of the prediction respecting them. "And the king of the north shall come against him like a whirlwind, with chariots and with horsemen, and with many ships; and he shall enter into the countries, and shall overflow and pass over." Although the Grecian empire withstood the predatory warfare of the Saracens, it gave way before the overwhelming forces of the Turks, whose progress was tracked with destruction, and whose coming was indeed like a whirlwind. Chariots and horsemen were to be the distinguishing marks of their armies, though armies, in general, contain the greatest proportion of foot-soldiers. And, in describing their first invasion of the Grecian territory, Gibbon relates, that "the myriads of Turkish horse overspread a frontier of six hundred miles from Tauris to Arzeroum, and the blood of one hundred and thirty thousand Christians was a grateful sacrifice to the Arabian prophet. The Turkish armies at first consisted so exclusively of horsemen, that the stoutest of the youths of the captive Christians were afterward taken and trained as a band of infantry, and called janizaries, (yengi cheri,) or new soldiers." In apparent contradiction to the nature of their army, they were also to possess many ships. And Gibbon again relates, that "a fleet of two hundred ships was constructed by the hands of the captive Greeks." But no direct evidence is necessary to prove that many ships must have been requisite for the capture of so many islands, and the destruction of the Venetian naval power, which was once the most celebrated in Europe. "The words, *shall enter into the countries, and overflow and pass over*, give us an exact idea of their *overflowing* the western parts of Asia, and then passing over into Egypt."

"He shall enter also into the glorious land, and many countries shall be overthrown." This expression, "the glorious land," occurs in the previous part of the prophecy, (v. 16,) and, in both cases, it evidently means the land of Israel; and such the Syriac translation renders it. The Holy Land formed part of the first conquest of the Turks. And *many countries shall be overthrown*. The limits of the Turkish empire embraced the ancient kingdoms of Babylon, Macedon, Thrace, Epirus, Greece, &c. and the many countries over which they ruled. The whole of Syria was also included, with partial exceptions. These very exceptions are specified in the prophecy, though these territories partially intersect the Turkish dominions, and divide one portion of them from another, forming a singular contrast to the general continuity of kingdoms. And, while every particular prediction respecting these separate states has been fully verified, their escaping out of the hands of the Turks has been no less marvellously fulfilled. "But these shall escape out of his hand, even Edom and Moab, and the chief of the children of Ammon." Mede, Sir Isaac and Bishop Newton, in applying this prophecy to the Turkish empire, could only express, in general terms, that the Arabs possessed these countries, and exacted tribute from the Turks for permitting their caravans to pass through them. But recent travellers, among whom Volney has to be numbered, have unconsciously given the most satisfactory information, demonstrative of the truth of all the minutiæ of the prediction. Volney describes these countries in part—Burckhardt traversed them all—and they have since been visited by other travellers. Edom and Moab are in possession of the Bedouin (or wandering) Arabs. The Turks have often attempted in vain to subjugate them. The partial escape of Ammon from their dominion is not less discriminating than just. For although that territory lies in the immediate vicinity of the pachalic of Damascus, to which part of it is subjected,—though it be extremely fertile by nature,—though its situation and its soil have thus presented, for several centuries, the strongest temptation to Turkish rapacity,—though they have often attempted to subdue it,—yet no fact could have been more explicitly detailed, or more incidentally communicated, than that the inhabitants of the greater part of that country, particularly what adjoins the ancient, but now desolate city of Ammon, "live in a state of complete independence of the Turks."

"He shall stretch forth his hand also upon the countries." How significantly do these words represent the vast extent of the Turkish empire, which alone has stretched its dominion over many countries of Asia, of Europe, and of Africa? Ill-fated Egypt was not to escape from subjection to such a master. "And the land of Egypt shall not escape; but he shall have power over the treasures of gold and of silver, and over all the precious things of Egypt." The Turks have drained Egypt of its wealth, of its gold and of its silver, and of its precious things: and such power have they exercised over them, that the kingdom of the Pharaohs, the land where everlasting pyramids were built, despoiled to the utmost, is now one of the poorest, as it has long been the basest, of kingdoms. "The Libyans and Ethiopians shall be at his steps." These form the extremities of the Turkish empire, and were partially subject to its power. "After the conquest of Egypt, the terror of Selim's victories," says the historian, "spreading wide, the kings of Africa, bordering upon Cyrenaica, sent their ambassadors with offers to become his tributaries. Other more remote nations also towards Ethiopia were easily induced to join in amity with the Turks." Exclusive of Egypt, they still retain the nominal power over other countries of Africa. Such is the prophetic description of the rise and extent of that power which was to possess Judea in the latter days; and it is a precise delineation of the rise and extent of the Turkish empire, to which Judea has been subject for centuries.—KEITH.

HOSEA.

CHAPTER III.

Ver. 2. So I bought her to me for fifteen *pieces* of silver, and *for* a homer of barley, and a half homer of barley.

Sir J. Chardin observed in the East, that in their contracts for their temporary wives, which are known to be frequent there, which contracts are made before the kady, there is always the formality of a measure of corn mentioned, over and above the sum of money that is stipulated. I do not know of any thing that should occasion this formality of late days in the East; it may then possibly be very ancient, as it is apparent this sort of wife is: if it be, it will perhaps account for Hosea's purchasing a woman of this sort for fifteen pieces of silver, and a certain quantity of barley.—Harmer.

CHAPTER IV.

Ver. 12. My people ask counsel at their stocks, and their staff declareth unto them: for the spirit of whoredoms hath caused *them* to err, and they have gone a whoring from under their God.

The method of divination alluded to by the prophet in these words, is supposed to have been thus performed: The person consulting measured his staff by spans, or by the length of his finger, saying, as he measured, "I will go, or, I will not go; I will do such a thing, or, I will not do it;" and as the last span fell out, so he determined. Cyril and Theophylact, however, give a different account of the matter. They say that it was performed by erecting two sticks, after which they murmured forth a certain charm, and then, according as the sticks fell, backward or forward, towards the right or left, they gave advice in any affair.—Burder.

CHAPTER V.

Ver. 12. Therefore *will* I *be* unto Ephraim as a moth, and to the house of Judah as rottenness.

See on Job 4. 9. and 27. 18.

CHAPTER VI.

Ver. 4. O Ephraim, what shall I do unto thee? O Judah, what shall I do unto thee? for your goodness *is* as a morning cloud, and as the early dew it goeth away.

"Early dew." "What, is this prosperity? what, this pleasure? Ah! what are my riches, and what my glory? Alas! 'tis like the dew, which flies off at the sight of the morning sun." "My son, my son, be not too confident; for life is like the dew."—Roberts.

Dr. Shaw, speaking of Arabia Petræa, says, "The dews of the night, as we had the heavens only for our covering, would (in the night) frequently wet us to the skin: but no sooner was the sun risen, and the atmosphere a little heated, than the mists were quickly dispersed, and the copious moisture, which the dews had communicated to the sands, would be entirely evaporated."—Burder.

Ver. 9. And as troops of robbers wait for a man, *so* the company of priests murder in the way by consent: for they commit lewdness.

The margin has, instead of "consent," "shoulder." The Hindoos for the same thing say, "with one hand." Thus, those people with "one hand" have gone to the judge, *i. e.* with one consent. "Those wretches with one hand are doing evil." "If the coolies do their duty with one hand, the work will soon be finished." "Why have they not accomplished their object? because they did not go about it with one hand."—Roberts.

CHAPTER VII.

Ver. 16. They return, *but* not to the Most High; they are like a deceitful bow: their princes shall fall by the sword for the rage of their tongue. This *shall be* their derision in the land of Egypt.

The strings of African bows are all made of the entrails of animals, a kind of catgut. Moist weather renders it so soft, that they cannot shoot with it: should they try it, the string would either instantly break, or it would stretch to such a length that it could not impel the arrow. In consequence of this being the case, I have heard the remark made in Africa, that the safest time to travel among the wild Bushmen is in wet weather, for then they cannot shoot you. Were people using such bows for defence, and unacquainted with this effect of moisture, in a time of danger to seize their bow for self-defence, they would be grievously deceived, by finding them useless when most needed. They would thus prove deceitful bows.—Campbell.

CHAPTER VIII.

Ver. 8. Israel is swallowed up: now shall they be among the Gentiles as a vessel wherein *is* no pleasure.

I believe this refers to an earthen vessel, and not to one made of skin. People often compare each other to an uppu-panum, *i. e.* literally, a salt vessel; because after it has contained salt it is most fragile, the least thing will break it to pieces. "What are you, sir? an *uppu-panum*," a salt vessel. "Look at that poor salt vessel; if you touch him he will fall to pieces."—Roberts.

Ver. 9. For they are gone up to Assyria, a wild ass alone by himself: Ephraim hath hired lovers.

See on Job 39. 5—8.

CHAPTER IX.

Ver. 10. I found Israel like grapes in the wilderness; I saw your fathers as the first ripe in the fig-tree at her first time: *but* they went to Baal-peor and separated themselves unto *that* shame; and *their* abominations were according as they loved.

In Barbary, and no doubt in the hotter climate of Judea, after mild winters, some of the more forward trees will now and then yield a few ripe figs, six weeks or more before the full season. Such is probably the allusion in this place. (Shaw.)—Burder.

CHAPTER X.

Ver. 7. *As for* Samaria, her king is cut off as the foam upon the water.

"Those sons of fiends are now gone as the *neer-molle*," *i. e.* the bubble. "Alas! my race is cut off: it has disappeared like the bubble." "Yes, those people were only bubbles; they have all gone."—Roberts.

Ver. 8. The high places also of Aven, the sin of Israel, shall be destroyed: the thorn and the thistle shall come up on their altars, and they shall say to the mountains, Cover us; and to the hills, Fall on us.

Has a man by fraud gained possession of another person's land, then the imprecation is uttered, "Thorns and thistles shall ever grow there!" "He get rice from his land! Never! he will have thorns and thistles." "Yes, yes, the rice shall be as thorns in his bowels."—ROBERTS.

Ver. 12. Sow to yourselves in righteousness, reap in mercy; break up your fallow ground: for *it is* time to seek the LORD, till he come and rain righteousness upon you.

It is said of a good king, "What a blessing is he to the land; he is always RAINING justice upon us." "You talk to me about the MERIT of remaining with such a master: he is always RAINING blessings upon him." A son after the decease of his father, asks, "Where is now the RAIN of love? alas! I am withered and dry." The figure is also used sarcastically, "Yes, indeed you are a very good friend, you are always RAINING favours upon me."—ROBERTS.

CHAPTER XI.

Ver. 2. *As* they called them, so they went from them: they sacrificed unto Baalim, and burnt incense to graven images.

We read frequently of graven images, and of molten images, and the words are become so familiar, as names of idolatrous images, that although they are not well chosen to express the Hebrew names, it seems not advisable to change them for others, that might more exactly correspond with the original. The graven image was not a thing wrought in metal by the tool of the workman we should now call an engraver; nor was the molten image an image made of metal, or any other substance melted and shaped in a mould. In fact, the graven image and the molten image are the same thing, under different names. The images of the ancient idolaters were first cut out of wood by the carpenter, as is very evident from the prophet Isaiah. This figure of wood was overlaid with plates either of gold or silver, or sometimes perhaps of an inferior metal; and in this finished state it was called a graven image, (*i. e.* a carved image,) in reference to the inner solid figure of wood, and a molten (*i. e.* an overlaid, or covered) image, in reference to the outer metalline case or covering. Sometimes both epithets are applied to it at once. "I will cut off the graven and molten image." (Nahum i. 14.) Again, 'What profiteth the graven and molten image?" (Hab. ii. 18.) The English word *molten* conveys a notion of melting, or fusion. But this is not the case with the Hebrew word for which it is given. The Hebrew signifies, generally, to overspread, or cover all over, in whatever manner, according to the different subject, the overspreading or covering be effected; whether by pouring forth a substance in fusion, or by spreading a cloth over or before, or by hammering on metalline plates. It is on account of this metalline case, that we find a founder employed to make a graven image, (Judges xvii. 3;) and that we read in Isaiah xl. 19, of a workman *that melteth a graven image;* and in another place (chap. xliv.) we find the question, "Who hath molten a graven image?" In these two passages the words should be *overlayeth,* and *overlaid.*—HORSLEY.

Ver. 4. I drew them with cords of a man, with bands of love; and I was to them as they that take off the yoke on their jaws, and I laid meat unto them.

Here we have another figure to show the affection of Jehovah for backsliding Israel. An affectionate wife says of a good husband, "He has bound me with the cords of love." "Ah! woman, have you not drawn me with the cords of love?" "True, true, I was once drawn by the cords of love, but they are now all broken."—ROBERTS.

It is very probable that these words refer to the custom of raising the yoke forward to cool the neck of the labouring beast.—BURDER.

Ver. 11. They shall tremble as a bird out of Egypt, and as a dove out of the land of Assyria: and I will place them in their houses, saith the LORD.

See on Is. 60. 8.

CHAPTER XII.

Ver. 1. Ephraim feedeth on wind, and followeth after the east wind: he daily increaseth lies and desolation; and they do make a covenant with the Assyrians, and oil is carried into Egypt.

Syria is a land in which olives abound, and particularly that part of it which the people of Israel inhabited. This explains the reason why the Jews, when they wished to court the favour of their neighbours, the Egyptians, sent them a present of oil. The prophet thus upbraids his degenerate nation for the servility and folly of their conduct: "Ephraim feedeth on wind, and followeth after the east wind; he daily increaseth lies and desolation: and they do make a covenant with the Assyrians, and oil is carried into Egypt." The Israelites, in the decline of their national glory, carried the produce of their olive-plantations into Egypt, as a tribute to their ancient oppressors, or as a present to conciliate their favour, and obtain their assistance, in the sanguinary wars which they were often compelled to wage with the neighbouring states.

Oil is now presented in the East, to be burnt in honour of the dead, whom they reverence with a religious kind of homage. Mr. Harmer thinks it most natural to suppose, that the prophet Hosea refers to a similar practice, when he upbraids the Israelites with carrying oil into Egypt. They did not carry it thither in the way of lawful commerce; for they carried it to Tyre without reproof, to barter it for other goods. It was not sent as a present to the king of Egypt; for the Jewish people endeavoured to gain the friendship of foreign potentates with gold and silver. It was not exacted as a tribute; for when the king of Egypt dethroned Jehoahaz the king of Judah, and imposed a fine upon the people, he did not appoint them to pay so much oil, but so much silver and gold. But if they burnt oil in those early times in honour of their idols, and their departed friends, and the Jews sent it into Egypt with that intention, it is no wonder the prophet so severely reproaches them for their conduct. Oil is in modern times very often presented to the objects of religious veneration in Barbary and Egypt. The Algerines, according to Pitts, when they are in the mouth of the straits, throw a bundle of wax candles, together with a pot of oil, overboard, as a present to the marabot or saint who lies entombed there, on the Barbary shore, near the sea.—PAXTON.

CHAPTER XIV.

Ver. 5. I will be as the dew unto Israel: he shall grow as the lily, and cast forth his roots as Lebanon.

The earth, while it supplies the various plants which grow upon it, is supplied for that purpose very much by the dew, which is full of oleaginous particles. "The dews seem to be the richest present the atmosphere gives to the earth; having, when putrefied in a vessel, a black sediment like mud at the bottom; this seems to cause the darkish colour to the upper part of the ground; and the sulphur which is found in the dew may be the chief ingredient of the cement of the earth, sulphur being very glutinous, as nitre is dissolvent. Dew has both these." (Tull's Husbandry.) A lively comment this upon the promise in this passage, "I will be as the dew unto Israel."—BURDER.

A priest, or aged man, in blessing a newly married couple, often says, "Ah! may your roots shoot forth like the ARUGAPILLU," (*Agrostis Linearis.*) This beautiful grass puts forth NUMEROUS roots, and is highly valued for the feeding of cattle.—ROBERTS.

Ver. 5. I will be as the dew unto Israel: he shall grow as the lily, and cast forth his roots as Lebanon. 6. His branches shall spread, and his beauty shall be as the olive-tree, and his smell as Lebanon. 7. They that dwell under his shadow shall return; they shall revive *as* the corn, and grow as the vine: the scent thereof *shall be* as the wine of Lebanon.

Le Bruyn concludes his description of Lebanon, with an account of the cedar-apples, or the fruit which these celebrated trees produce. He cut one of them in two, and found that the smell within exactly resembled turpentine. They exuded a juice from small oval grains, with which a great many small cavities are filled, which also resembles turpentine, both in smell and in clamminess. These cedar-apples must be classed with the scented fruits of the oriental regions; and have perhaps contributed greatly to the fragrance for which the sacred writers so frequently celebrate the mountains of Lebanon.—PAXTON.

Not only both the great and small cedars of Lebanon have a fragrant smell, but Maundrell found the great rupture in that mountain, which "runs at least seven hours' travel directly up into it, and is on both sides exceedingly steep and high, clothed with fragrant greens from top to bottom, and everywhere refreshed with fountains, falling down from the rocks in pleasant cascades, the ingenious works of nature. These streams all uniting at the bottom, make a full and rapid torrent, whose agreeable murmuring is heard all over the place, and adds no small pleasure to it."—BURDER.

The approach to Lebanon is adorned with olive-plantations, vineyards, and luxuriant fields; and its lower regions, besides the olive and the vine, are beautified with the myrtle, the styrax, and other odoriferous shrubs: and the perfume which exhales from these plants, is increased by the fragrance of the cedars which crown its summits, or garnish its declivities. The great rupture which runs a long way up into the mountain, and is on both sides exceedingly steep and high, is clothed from the top to the bottom with fragrant evergreens, and everywhere refreshed with streams, descending from the rocks in beautiful cascades, the work of divine wisdom and goodness. These cool and limpid streams uniting at the bottom, form a large and rapid torrent, whose agreeable murmur is heard over all the place, and adds greatly to the pleasure of that romantic scene. The fragrant odours wafted from the aromatic plants of this noble mountain, have not been overlooked by the sacred writers. The eulogium which Christ pronounces on the graces of the church, contains the following direct reference: "The smell of thy garments is like the smell of Lebanon;" and the prophet Hosea, in his glowing description of the future prosperity of Israel, converts the assertion of Solomon into a promise: "His branches shall spread, and his beauty shall be as the olive-tree, and his smell as Lebanon."

The richness and flavour of the wines produced in its vineyards, have been celebrated by travellers in all ages. Rauwolf declares, that the wine which he drank at Canobin, a Greek monastery on mount Libanus, far surpassed any he had ever tasted. His testimony is corroborated by Le Bruyn, who pronounces the wines of Canobin better and more delicate than are to be found anywhere else in the world. They are red, of a beautiful colour, and so oily, that they adhere to the glass; these are so excellent, that our traveller thought he never tasted any kind of drink more delicious. The wines produced on other parts of the mountain, although in much greater abundance, are not nearly so good. To the delicious wines of Canobin, the prophet Hosea certainly refers in this promise: "They that dwell under his shadow shall return; they shall revive as the corn, and grow as the vine: the scent thereof shall be as the wine of Lebanon."

De la Roque, who also visited Canobin, entirely agrees with these travellers in their account of the superior quality of its wines; and expresses his full conviction, that the reputation of the wines of Lebanon mentioned by the prophet, is well founded. Volney asserts, indeed, that he found the wines of Lebanon of a very inferior quality; this may be true, and yet the testimony of these respectable travellers perfectly correct. He might not be presented with the most exquisite wine of Canobin, which has deservedly obtained so high a character; or the vintage of that year might be inferior. But whatever might be the reason, no doubt can be entertained concerning the accuracy of other equally credible witnesses, who, from their own experience, and with one voice, attest the unrivalled excellence of the wine of Lebanon. These travellers admit, that the neighbourhood of Canobin produces wines of inferior quality; but, when the wine of Lebanon is mentioned by way of eminence, the best is undoubtedly meant.

In striking allusion to the scenery and productions of that mountain, it is promised in the sixth verse: "His branch shall spead, and his beauty shall be as the olive-tree, and his smell (or his memorial, as the original term signifies) as Lebanon." His branches shall spread like the mighty arms of the cedar, every one of which is equal in size to a tree; his beauty shall be as the olive-tree, which is generally admitted to be one of the most beautiful productions of nature; and his smell, his very memorial, shall be as the wine of Lebanon, which delights the taste, and the very recollection of which excites the commendation of those that have drank it, long after the banquet is over. The meaning of these glowing figures undoubtedly is, that the righteous man shall prosper by the distinguishing favour of Heaven; shall become excellent, and useful, and highly respected while he lives; and after his death, his memory shall be blessed and embalmed in the affectionate recollection of the church, for the benefit of many who had not the opportunity of profiting by his example.—PAXTON.

JOEL.

CHAPTER I.

Ver. 6. For a nation is come up upon my land, strong, and without number, whose teeth *are* the teeth of a lion, and he hath the cheek teeth of a great lion. 7. He hath laid my vine waste, and barked my fig-tree; he hath made it clean bare, and cast *it* away; the branches thereof are made white.

So valuable is the fig-tree in the land of Canaan, and so high is the estimation in which it is held, that to bark and kill it, is reckoned among the severest judgments which God inflicted upon his offending people. The prophet alludes in these words to the destructive progress of the locust, which, with insatiable greediness, devours the leaves and bark of every tree on which it lights, till not the smallest portion of rind is left, even on the slenderest twig, to convey the sap from the root, and leaves it white and withering in the sun, for ever incapable of answering the hopes of the husbandman. Such were the people of Israel, delivered by Jehovah, for their numerous and inveterate transgressions, into the hands of their cruel and implacable enemies.—Paxton.

The skin of a man is sometimes spoken of as the bark of a tree. Thus it is said of those who have been severely flogged, "Their backs are like the margossa-tree stripped of its bark:" which alludes to the custom of taking off the bark of that tree for medical purposes.—Roberts.

Ver. 13. Gird yourselves, and lament, ye priests; howl, ye ministers of the altar; come, lie all night in sackcloth, ye ministers of my God: for the meat-offering and the drink-offering is withholden from the house of your God.

See on Is. 20. 3.

Ver. 17. The seed is rotten under their clods, the garners are laid desolate, the barns are broken down; for the corn is withered.

Dr. Shaw informs us, that "in Barbary, after the grain is winnowed, they lodge it in *mattamores* or *subterraneous magazines*, two or three hundred of which are sometimes together, the smallest holding four hundred bushels." And Dr. Russel says, that "about Aleppo, in Syria, their granaries are even at this day subterraneous grottoes, the entry to which is by a small hole or opening like a well, often in the highway; and as they are commonly left open when empty, they make it not a little dangerous riding near the villages in the night."—Burder.

Ver. 19. O Lord, to thee will I cry: for the fire hath devoured the pastures of the wilderness, and the flame hath burnt all the trees of the field.

There are doubtless different methods for felling timber, practised by various nations. In more rude and uncivilized times, and even still among people of that description, we may expect to find the most simple, and perhaps, as they may appear to us, inconvenient contrivances adopted. Prior to the invention of suitable implements, such means as would any way effect this purpose would certainly be resorted to. We must not be surprised then to find that formerly, and in the present day, trees were felled by the operation of fire. Thus Niebuhr says, "we cannot help condemning the unskilful expedient which these highlanders employ for felling trees: they set fire to the root, and keep it burning till the tree falls of itself." Mr. Bruce mentions whole forests, whose underwood and vegetation are thus consumed. Possibly this custom may be alluded to in Zech. xii. 6: "I will make the governors of Judah like a hearth of fire among the wood, and like a torch of fire in a sheaf, and they shall devour all the people round about." Such fires may be kindled either from design or accident. In such instances, as obtaining the timber is the object, these fires are purposely lighted, and would be so managed as to do as little damage as possible, though some injury must certainly result from this method of felling trees. Strange as it may seem, we learn from Turner's Embassy to Thibet, that there "the only method of felling timber in practice, I was informed, is by fire. In the trees marked out for this purpose, vegetation is destroyed by burning their trunks half through; being left in that state to dry; in the ensuing year the fire is again applied, and they are burnt till they fall." An allusion to something of this kind the prophet Joel certainly has in these words. Perhaps it may be rather to a general undesigned devastation by fire, than to any contrivance for procuring the timber.—Burder.

CHAPTER II.

Ver. 4. The appearance of them *is* as the appearance of horses; and as horsemen, so shall they run. 5. Like the noise of chariots on the tops of mountains shall they leap, like the noise of a flame of fire that devoureth the stubble, as a strong people set in battle array. 6. Before their face the people shall be much pained; all faces shall gather blackness. 7. They shall run like mighty men; they shall climb the wall like men of war; and they shall march every one on his ways, and they shall not break their ranks.

I never saw such an exhibition of the helplessness of man, as I have seen to-day. While we were sitting at dinner, a person came into the house, quite pale, and told us that the locusts were coming. Every face gathered darkness. I went to the door—I looked above, and all round, and saw nothing. "Look to the ground," was the reply, when I asked where they were. I looked to the ground, and there I saw a stream of young locusts without wings, covering the ground at the entrance of the village. The stream was about five hundred feet broad, and covering the ground, and moving at the rate of two miles an hour. In a few minutes they covered the garden wall, some inches deep, and the water was immediately let into the channel, into which it flows to water the garden. They swim with the greatest ease over standing water, but the stream carried them away, and after floating in it about a hundred paces, they were drowned. All hands were now at work to keep them from the gardens, and to keep them from crossing the streams. To examine the phenomenon more nearly, I walked about a mile and a half from the village, following the course of the stream. Here I found the stream extending a mile in breadth, and, like a thousand rivulets, all flowing into one common channel. It appeared as if the dust under my feet was forming into life, and as if God, when he has a controversy with a people, could raise the very dust of the earth on which they tread in arms against them. Men can conquer the tiger, the elephant, the lion, and all the wild beasts of the desert; he can turn the course of the mighty rivers, he can elude the violence of the tempest, and chain the wind to his car; he can raise the waters into clouds, and by the means of steam, create a power that is yet beyond human measurement; he can play with the lightnings of heaven, and arrest the thunders of heaven; but he is nothing before an army of locusts. Such a scene as I have seen this afternoon would fill England with more consternation than the terrific cholera. One of the people here informs us, that he had seen a stream that continued ten days and nights flowing upon his place. During that time every person in the place was at work, to preserve his garden; as to the cornfields, they were obliged to give them up. They continued to the fifth day defending their gardens; on the evening of the fifth day, the locusts were between five and ten feet deep, and the mass by this time became terrible, and literally fell in pieces over the garden walls.—CAMPBELL.

In some regions of the East, the whole earth is at times covered with locusts for the space of several leagues, often to the depth of four, sometimes of six or seven inches. Their approach, which causes a noise like the rushing of a torrent, darkens the horizon, and so enormous is their multitude, it hides the light of the sun, and casts an awful gloom, like that of an eclipse, over the field. Major Moore, when at Poonah, had the opportunity of seeing an immense army of these animals which ravaged the Mahratta country, and was supposed to have come from Arabia. "The column they composed," says he, "extended five hundred miles; and so compact was it when on the wing, that like an eclipse, it completely hid the sun, so that no shadow was cast by any object;" and some lofty tombs distant from his residence not two hundred yards, were rendered quite invisible. The noise they make in browsing on the trees and herbage may be heard at a great distance, and resembles the rattling of hail, or the noise of an army foraging in secret. The inhabitants of Syria have observed that locusts are always bred by too mild winters, and that they constantly come from the deserts of Arabia. When they breed, which is in the month of October, they make a hole in the ground with their tails, and having laid three hundred eggs in it, and covered them with their feet, expire; for they never live above six months and a half. Neither rains nor frost, however long and severe, can destroy their eggs; they continue till spring, and, hatched by the heat of the sun, the young locusts issue from the earth about the middle of April.

From the circumstance of their young ones issuing from the ground, they are called גב, *gob* or *gobai*, from an Arabic verb, which signifies to rise out of the earth. Another name is גזם *gazam*, from the root *gazaz*, to cut off, or to spoil; and more destructive and insatiable spoilers were never let loose to desolate the earth. Pliny calls them a scourge in the hand of an incensed Deity. Wherever their innumerable bands direct their march, the verdure of the country, though it resembled before the paradise of God, almost instantaneously disappears. The trees and plants, stripped of their leaves, and reduced to their naked boughs and stems, cause the dreary image of winter to succeed in an instant to the rich scenery of spring; and the whole country puts on the appearance of being burnt. Fire itself devours not so fast; nor is a vestige of vegetation to be found when they again take their flight to produce similar disasters. In a few hours they eat up every green thing, and consign the miserable inhabitants of the desolated regions to inevitable famine. Many years are not sufficient to repair the desolation which these destructive insects produce. When they first appear on the frontiers of the cultivated lands, the husbandmen, if sufficiently numerous, sometimes divert the storm by their gestures and their cries, or they strive to repulse them by raising large clouds of smoke, but frequently their herbs and wet straw fail them; they then dig a variety of pits and trenches, all over their fields and gardens, which they fill with water, or with heath, stubble, and other combustible matter, which they set on fire upon the approach of the enemy. These methods of stopping their march are of great antiquity, for Homer familiarly refers to them as practised in his time. But they are all to no purpose, for the trenches are quickly filled, and the fires extinguished, by infinite swarms succeeding one another; and forming a bed on their fields of six or seven inches in thickness. Fire itself is not more active than these devourers; and not a trace of vegetation is to be discovered, when the cloud has resumed its flight. But the two most powerful destroyers of these insects, is the south, or southeasterly winds, and the bird called the *samarmar*. These birds, which greatly resemble the woodpecker, follow them in large flocks, greedily devour them, and besides, kill as many as they can; they are, therefore, much respected by the peasants, and no person is ever allowed to destroy them. The southerly winds waft them over the Mediterranean, where they perish in so great quantities, that when their carcasses are cast on the shore, they infect the air for several days to a considerable distance. In a state of putrefaction, the stench emitted from their bodies is scarcely to be endured; the traveller, who crushes them below the wheels of his wagon, or the feet of his horses, is reduced to the necessity of washing his nose with vinegar, and holding his handkerchief, dipped in it, continually to his nostrils.

One of the most grievous calamities ever inflicted by the locust, happened to the regions of Africa, in the time of the Romans, and fell with peculiar weight on those parts which were subject to their empire. Scarcely recovered from the miseries of the last Punic war, Africa was doomed to suffer, about one hundred and twenty-three years before the birth of Christ, another desolation, as terrible as it was unprecedented. An immense number of locusts covered the whole country, consumed every plant and every blade of grass in the field, without sparing the roots, and the leaves of the trees, with the tendrils upon which they grew. These being exhausted, they penetrated with their teeth the bark, however bitter, and even corroded the dry and solid timber. After they had accomplished this terrible destruction, a sudden blast of wind dispersed them into different portions, and after tossing them awhile in the air, plunged their innumerable hosts into the sea. But the deadly scourge was not then at an end; the raging billows threw up enormous heaps of their dead and corrupted bodies upon that long-extended coast, which produced a most insupportable and poisonous stench. This soon brought on a pestilence, which affected every species of animals; so that birds, and sheep, and cattle, and even the wild beasts of the field, perished in great numbers; and their carcasses, being soon rendered putrid by the foulness of the air, added greatly to the general corruption. The destruction of the human species was horrible; in Numidia, where at that time Micipsa was king, eighty thousand persons died; and in that part of the seacoast which bordered upon the reigon of Carthage and Utica, two hundred thousand are said to have been carried off by this pestilence. When Le Bruyn was at Rama he was informed that the locusts were once so destructive there, that in the space of two hours they ate up all the herbage round the town; and in the garden belonging to the house in which he lodged, they ate the very stalks of the artichoke down to the ground.

This statement will show, that the locust is one of the most terrible instruments in the hand of incensed Heaven; it will discover the reason that the inspired writers, in denouncing his judgments, so frequently allude to this insect, and threaten the sinner with its vengeance; it accounts, in the most satisfactory manner, for the figures which the prophets borrow, when they describe the march of cruel and destructive armies, from the character and habits of this creature. The narratives of Volney, Thevenot, and other travellers, who have seen and described the innumerable swarms of the locusts, and their wasteful ravages, fully confirm the glowing description of Joel and other inspired prophets, quoted in the beginning of this article. "A nation," says Joel, "has come up upon my land, strong and without number. He has laid my vine waste, and barked my fig-tree; he has made it clean bare, and cast it away; the branches thereof are made white—the vine is dried up, and the fig-tree languishes, the pomegranate-tree, the palm-tree also, and the apple-tree, even all the trees of the field, are withered; because joy is withered away from the sons of men." "A day of darkness and of gloominess, a day of clouds and thick darkness. A fire devoureth before them, and behind them a flame burneth. They march every one in his ways; they do not break their ranks, neither does one thrust another. The land is as the garden of Eden before them, and behind them a desolate wilderness." "They shall run up the wall; they shall climb up upon the houses; they shall enter into the windows like a thief. The earth shall quake before them; the heavens shall tremble, the sun and the moon shall be darkened, and the stars shall

PETRA—TRIUMPHAL ARCH.—Joel 3:19. Page 554.

withdraw their shining." The same allusion is involved in these words of Nahum, concerning the fall of the Assyrian empire: "Thy crowned are as the locusts; and thy captains as the great grasshoppers, which camp in the hedges in the cold day, but when the sun ariseth, they flee away, and their place is not known." Bochart and other writers, who are best acquainted with the eastern countries, mention a great variety of locusts, which vindicates the language of the prophet: "Thy captains are as the great grasshoppers." The next clause is attended with some difficulty. Mr. Lowth, in his comment, supposes that these insects flee away to avoid the heat of the sun; and it has been queried, whether the phrase *cold day*, does not mean the night. But it is well known that the heat of the sun, instead of compelling the locusts to retire, quickens them into life and activity; and the words *cold day*, we believe, are never used in scripture, nor by any writer of value, to signify the night. The prophet evidently refers, not to their flight during the heat of the day, but to the time of their total departure; for he does not speak of their moving from one field to another, but of their leaving the country which they have invaded, so completely that the place of their retreat is not known.

The day of cold cannot mean the depth of winter, for they do not make their appearance in Palestine at that season; and although in Arabia, from whence Fulcherius supposes they come, thickets are found in some places, and it has been imagined that the locusts lie concealed in them during the winter, which may be thought to be their camping in the hedges in the cold day; yet it is to be observed, that the word translated hedges, properly signifies, not living fences, but stone walls, and therefore cannot with propriety be applied to thickets. But if the locust appears in the months of April and May, the phrase "cold day" may seem to be improperly chosen. This difficulty, which may be thought a considerable one, arises entirely from our translation. The original term, (קרה) *karah*, denotes both cold and cooling; and the difficulty vanishes when the latter is introduced, and the words are translated, the day of cooling, or the time when the Orientals open their windows with the view of refrigerating their houses, or to retreat from the oppressive heats which commence in the months of April and May, to the cooling shades of their gardens. A derivative of this term is employed by the sacred historian, to denote the refrigeratory or summer parlour, which Eglon, the king of Moab, occupied, when Ehud presented the tribute of his nation.—Paxton.

Ver. 6. Before their face the people shall be much pained; all faces shall gather blackness.

The margin has, for "blackness," "pot." The Tamul translation has, "All faces shall wither, or shrivel." Thus of a man in great poverty it is said, "His face is shrivelled." It is very provoking to tell a person his face is like the kare-chatte, *i. e.* the earthen vessel in which the rice is boiled. The "pot" may allude to such a utensil, in being made black with the smoke.—Roberts.

We have an expression, Joel ii. 6, "Before their approach [of the locusts] the people shall be much pained; *all faces shall gather blackness*," which is also adopted by the prophet Nahum, ii. 10: "the heart melteth, the knees smite together, much pain is in all loins, and the *faces of them all gather blackness*." This phrase, which sounds uncouth to an English ear, is elucidated by the following history from Ockley's History of the Saracens, (vol. ii. p. 319,) which we the rather introduce, as Mr. Harmer has referred this *blackness* to the effect of hunger and thirst; and Calmet, in his Dictionary, under the article obscure, has referred it to a bedaubing of the face with soot, &c. a proceeding not very consistent with the hurry of flight, or the terror of distress. "Kumeil, the son of Ziyad, was a man of fine wit. One day Hejage made him come before him, and reproached him, because in such a garden, and before such and such persons, whom he named to him, he had made a great many imprecations against him, saying, *the Lord blacken his face*, that is, *fill him with shame and confusion;* and wished that his neck was cut off, and his blood shed." The reader will observe how perfectly this explanation agrees with the sense of the passages quoted above: to gather blackness, then, is equivalent to suffering extreme confusion, and being overwhelmed with shame, or with terror and dismay.

In justice to Kumeil, we ought not to omit the ready turn of wit which saved his life. "It is true," said he, "I did say such words in such a garden; but then I was under a vine-arbour, and was looking on a bunch of grapes that was not yet ripe: and I wished it might be turned black soon, that they might be cut off, and be made wine of." We see, in this instance, as says the sagacious moralist, that "with the well-advised is wisdom:" and "the tongue of the wise is health;" that is, preservation and safety.—Taylor in Calmet.

Ver. 8. Neither shall one thrust another, they shall walk every one in his path: and *when* they fall upon the sword, they shall not be wounded.

Dr. Shaw, speaking of locusts, says, "Those which I saw were much bigger than our grasshoppers: no sooner were any of them hatched, than they collected themselves into a body of about two hundred yards square, which marching forward, climbed over trees and houses, and ate up every thing in their way. The inhabitants made large fires on the approach of them, but to no purpose; for the fires were quickly put out by infinite swarms succeeding one another; while the front seemed regardless of danger; and the rear pressed on so close, that retreat was impossible."—Burder.

Ver. 23. Be glad then, ye children of Zion, and rejoice in the Lord your God: for he hath given you the former rain moderately, and he will cause to come down for you the rain, the former rain, and the latter rain in the first *month*.

See on Prov. 16. 15.

Ver. 23. Be glad then, ye children of Zion, and rejoice in the Lord your God: for he hath given you the former rain moderately, and he will cause to come down for you the rain, the former rain, and the latter rain in the first *month*. 24. And the floors shall be full of wheat, and the fats shall overflow with wine and oil.

In southern climates, rain comes at particular seasons, which are generally termed the rainy seasons. The rain seldom continues to fall long at one time even then, but rather falls in what may be called thunder-showers, and in torrents. If the ground happens to be hard, which it generally is, such a short, though plentiful fall of rain, does little service to the land, as it runs off immediately, not having time to soften and sink into the ground; afterward the powerful heat of the sun, soon breaking forth from behind the clouds, draws up the little damp that has been left, which soon rehardens the surface of the ground, and renders it as impervious as before, so that succeeding showers are rendered almost useless; but rain falling moderately, as promised in the text, gradually penetrates the ground, and prepares it to retain future showers, which process produces fertility.—Campbell.

CHAPTER III.

Ver. 1. For, behold, in those days, and in that time, when I shall bring again the captivity of Judah and Jerusalem, 2. I will also gather all nations, and will bring them down into the valley of Jehoshaphat, and will plead with them there for my people, and *for* my heritage Israel, whom they have scattered among the nations, and parted my land.

Those spiritualizing Jews, Christians, and Mohammedans, who wrest this passage, like a thousand others of the scriptures, from a literal to a mystical sense, insist on its applying to the resurrection of the dead on the last great day. From this belief the modern Jews, whose fathers are thought, by some of the most learned, to have had no idea of a resurrection, or a future state, have their bones deposited in the valley of Jehoshaphat. From the same hope the Mohammedans have left a stone jutting out of the eastern wall of Jerusalem, for the accommodation of their prophet, who, they insist, is to sit on it here, and call the whole world from below to judgment. And a late traveller, with the staff of a Christian pilgrim, after summoning up all the images of desolation which the place presents, but without once thinking of the contemptible size of this theatre for so grand a display, says, one might say that the trumpet of judgment had already sounded, and that the dead were about to rise in the valley of Jehoshaphat. (Chateaubriand.) —BUCKINGHAM.

Ver. 3. And they have cast lots for my people: and have given a boy for a harlot, and sold a girl for wine, that they might drink.

Morgan, in his history of Algiers, gives us such an account of the unfortunate expedition of the emperor Charles the Fifth against that city, so far resembling a passage of the prophet Joel, as to induce me to transcribe it into these papers.

That author tells us, that besides vast multitudes that were butchered by the Moors and the Arabs, a great number were made captives, mostly by the Turks and citizens of Algiers; and some of them, in order to turn this misfortune into a most bitter, taunting, and contemptuous jest, parted with their new-made slaves for an onion apiece. "Often have I heard," says he, "Turks and Africans upbraiding Europeans with this disaster, saying, scornfully, to such as have seemed to hold their heads somewhat loftily, 'What! have you forgot the time when a Christian at Algiers was scarce worth an onion?' The treatment of the Jewish people by the heathen nations, which the prophet Joel has described, was, in like manner, contemptuous and bitterly sarcastic: "They have cast lots for my people, and have given a boy for a harlot, and sold a girl for wine, that they might drink." Joel iii. 3.

They that know the large sums that are wont to be paid, in the East, for young slaves of either sex, must be sensible that the prophet designs, in these words, to point out the extreme contempt in which these heathen nations held the Jewish people.

Considered as slaves are in the East, they are sometimes purchased at a very low price. Joel complains of the contemptuous cheapness in which the Israelites were held by those who made them captives. "They cast lots for my people, and have given a boy for a harlot, and sold a girl for wine, that they might drink." On this passage Chardin remarks, that, "the Tartars, Turks, and Cossacks, sell the children sometimes as cheap, which they take. Not only has this been done in Asia, where examples of it are frequent; our Europe has seen such desolations. When the Tartars came into Poland they carried off all they were able. I went thither some years after. Many persons of the court assured me that the Tartars, perceiving that they would no more redeem those that they had carried off, sold them for a crown, and that they had purchased them for that sum. In Mingrelia they sell them for provisions, and for wine."—HARMER.

Ver. 10. Beat your ploughshares into swords, and your pruning-hooks into spears: let the weak say, I *am* strong.

The Syrian plough, which was probably used in all the regions around, is a very simple frame, and commonly so light, that a man of moderate strength might carry it in one hand. Volney states that in Syria it is often nothing else than the branch of a tree, cut below a bifurcation, and used without wheels. It is drawn by asses and cows, seldom by oxen. And Dr. Russel informs us, the ploughing of Syria is performed often by a little cow, at most with two, and sometimes only by an ass. In Persia it is for the most part drawn by one ox only, and not unfrequently even by an ass, although it is more ponderous than in Palestine. With such an imperfect instrument the Syrian husbandman can do little more than scratch the surface of his field, or clear away the stones or weeds that encumber it, and prevent the seed from reaching the soil. The ploughshare is a "piece of iron, broad, but not large, which tips the end of the shaft." So much does it resemble the short sword used by the ancient warriors, that it may, with very little trouble, be converted into that deadly weapon; and when the work of destruction is over, reduced again to its former shape, and applied to the purpose of agriculture. In allusion to the first operation, the prophet Joel summons the nations to leave their peaceful employments in the cultivated field, and buckle on their armour: "Beat your ploughshares into swords, and your pruning-hooks into spears." This beautiful image the prophet Isaiah has reversed, and applied to the establishment of that profound and lasting peace which is to bless the church of Christ in the latter days: "And they shall beat their swords into ploughshares, and their spears into pruning-hooks; nation shall not lift up sword against nation, neither shall they learn war any more."—PAXTON.

An hour and a half beyond the bridge we gained the road from Jaffa to Ramleh. The country had now become generally cultivated, the husbandry good, the crops and fallows clean. Upon a space of ten or twelve acres I observed fourteen ploughs at work; and so simple and light is the construction of these implements, that the husbandman, when returning from his labour in the evening, takes his plough home upon his shoulder, and carries it to the field again in the morning. The share is of wood, and armed only at the end with a tooth, or point of iron. The beam is very slender, as well as the rude handle by which it is directed.—MUNROE'S SUMMER RAMBLE IN SYRIA.

Ver. 19. Egypt shall be a desolation, and Edom shall be a desolate wilderness, for the violence *against* the children of Judah, because they have shed innocent blood in their land.

Of the striking scene delineated in the engraving, the enterprising traveller, who has contributed it, must speak for himself: "Our conductor preceded us, calling our attention to some large slabs, traces of an ancient pavement, by which the labour of man had converted this abrupt and wild ravine into a magnificent avenue. After many windings in the midst of this almost subterranean street, (so near do the summits of the rocks above approach each other,) we were arrested by a prospect which it were vain to attempt to describe. Our view is taken from the entry of the ravine. Two Arabs, with their camels, are seen in the foreground, advancing towards the city of Selah or Petra, the magnificent ruins of which, seen in the distance, fully exemplify the prophetic denunciation—'Edom shall be a desolation.' (Joel iii. 19.) A grand triumphal arch raised at this spot, such as the ancients were accustomed to construct at the approaches of cities, boldly connects together these two great walls of rocks. The impression produced by it is very imposing, at the moment the traveller enters this kind of covered way."

The novel disposition of this triumphal arch led M. de Laborde at first to think that it might have served both as a passage from one side of the rocks to another, and also as a channel for conveying part of the waters of an aqueduct, which was carried along the ravine. He ascended by a steep opening encumbered with rocks; but after reaching the summit with difficulty, he found nothing which could authorize the supposition that this arch was destined for any other use than that of adorning the approaches to the capital of Arabia Petræa.—HORNE.

[*See Jer.* 49. 15—17. *Mal.* 1. 4, *and the engravings there. See also the* COMPREHENSIVE COMMENTARY, *and some additional views of this city, in that work.*]

PETRA—RUINS OF THE CITY.—Joel 3:19. Page 554.

AMOS.

CHAPTER I.

Ver. 2. And he said, The Lord will roar from Zion, and utter his voice from Jerusalem; and the habitations of the shepherds shall mourn, and the top of Carmel shall wither.

See on ch. 9. 2, 3.

Ver. 5. I will break also the bar of Damascus, and cut off the inhabitant from the plain of the Aven, and him that holdeth the sceptre from house of Eden: and the people of Syria shall go into captivity unto Kir, saith the LORD.

Rather more than a century ago, Mr. Maundrell visited the mountains of Lebanon. Having proceeded about half an hour through the olive-yards of Sidon, he and his party came to the foot of Mount Libanus. They had an easy ascent for two hours, after which it grew more steep and difficult; in about an hour and a half more, they came to a fountain of water, where they encamped for the night. Next day, after ascending for three hours, they reached the highest ridge of the mountain, where the snow lay by the side of the road. They began immediately to descend on the other side, and in two hours came to a small village, where a fine brook, gushing at once from the side of the mountain, rushes down into the valley below, and after flowing about two leagues, loses itself in the river Letane. The valley is called Bocat, and seems to be the same with the Bicah-Aven of the prophet: "I will break also the bar of Damascus, and cut off the inhabitant from the plain (rather the vale) of Aven, and him that holdeth the sceptre from the house of Eden." The neighbourhood of Damascus, and particularly a place near it, which, in the time of Maundrell, still bore the name of Eden, render his conjecture extremely probable. It might also have the name of Aven, which signifies vanity, from the idolatrous worship of Baal practised at Balbec or Heliopolis, which is situated in this valley.—PAXTON.

Ver. 13. Thus saith the LORD, For three transgressions of the children of Ammon, and for four, I will not turn away *the punishment* thereof; because they have ripped up the women with child, of Gilead, that they might enlarge their border.

Margin, for "ripped," "divided the mountains." It was common in the ancient wars thus to treat women, but in general the Orientals are very kind to their wives in the state alluded to. Nay, even to animals in that condition, they are very tender: a man to beat his cow when with calf, would be called a great sinner; and to kill a goat or a sheep when with young, is altogether out of the question. The Hindoo hunters will not destroy wild animals when in that state. The term in the margin is applied to that condition. "In the tenth moon the child fell from the mountain."—ROBERTS.

CHAPTER II.

Ver. 1. Thus saith the LORD, For three transgressions of Moab, and for four, I will not turn away *the punishment* thereof; because he burnt the bones of the king of Edom into lime.

"To plaster the walls of his house with it," as the Chaldee paraphrase explains the text, which was a cruel insulting of the dead. A piece of barbarity resembling this is told by Sir Paul Rycaut, that the wall of the city of Philadelphia was made of the bones of the besieged, by the prince who took it by storm.—BURDER.

Ver. 6. Thus saith the LORD, for three transgressions of Israel, and for four, I will not turn away *the punishment* thereof; because they sold the righteous for silver, and the poor for a pair of shoes.

The shoes, or rather SANDALS, have the least honour of any thing which is worn by man, because they belong to the feet, and are comparatively of little value. Nothing is more disgraceful than to be beaten with the sandals: thus when one man intends to exasperate another, he begins to take off a sandal, as if going to strike him. To spit in the face is not a greater indignity than this. When a person wishes to insult another in reference to the price of any article, he says, "I will give you my sandals for it." "That fellow is not worth the value of my sandals." "Who are you, sir? you are not worthy to carry my sandals;" which alludes to the custom of a rich man always having a servant with him to carry his sandals; *i. e.* when he chooses to walk barefoot. "Over Edom will I cast out my shoe:" so contemptible and so easy was it to be conquered.—ROBERTS.

Ver. 7. That pant after the dust of the earth on the head of the poor, and turn aside the way of the meek; and a man and his father will go in unto the *same* maid, to profane my holy name.

Who were those that thus oppressed the poor, who sold them for a pair of shoes, and panted "after the dust of the earth?" They were the judges and the princes of the people. The Tamul translation has it, "To the injury of the poor they eagerly took the dust of the earth;" literally, they gnawed the earth as a dog does a bone. "Dust of the earth." What does this mean? I believe it alludes to the lands of the poor, of which they had been deprived by the judges and princes. Nothing is more common in eastern language than for a man to call his fields and gardens his MAN; *i. e.* his dust, his earth. "That man has gnawed away my dust or sand." "Ah! the fellow! by degrees he has taken away all that poor man's earth." "The cruel wretch! he is ever trying to take away the dust of the poor." In consequence of there not being fences in the East, landowners often encroach on each other's possessions. On the latter part of the verse and the next to it, I dare not write. The heathenism, the devilism, described by Amos, is still the same. Who did these things? *the princes, the judges, and the people of Judah.*—ROBERTS.

Ver. 8. And they lay *themselves* down upon clothes laid to pledge by every altar, and they drink the wine of the condemned *in* the house of their god.

It was found advantageous, both for ease and health, to have a carpet or some soft and thick cloth spread on the ground for those to sit upon who dwelt in tents: subsequently, those who lived in houses used them too. When they held their idolatrous feasts in the temples dedicated to the gods, they sat upon the ground, but not on the bare earth, or the marble pavement of those temples, but upon something soft and dry spread under them, brought for the purpose. The clothes mentioned by the prophet may mean the coverings of the body for the night, as well as for the day. "When it was dark, three coverlets, richly embroidered, were taken from a press in the room which we occupied, and delivered, one to each of us; the carpet or sofa, and a cushion, serving, with this addition, instead of a bed." (Chandler's Travels in Asia Minor.) Such carpets or embroidered coverlets would neither be an improper pledge for money, (Exod. xxii. 26, 27,) nor disgrace the pomp of a heathen temple. It may not be amiss to consider why the circumstance of clothes being taken to pledge, is mentioned here. Attending an idolatrous feast must have been undoubtedly wrong in these Israelites: but of what consequence was it to remark, that some of them seated themselves on carpets that had been put into their hands by way of pledge? It may be answered, that it might be galling to those that had been obliged to pledge these valuable pieces of furniture secretly, to have them thus publicly exposed; that it may insinuate that these idolatrous zealots detained them, when they ought to have been restored, (Ezek. xviii. 7, 12, 16. xxx. 15;) and that they subjected them to be injured, in the tumult of an extravagant and riotous banquet in a heathen temple; to which may be added, that they might belong to some of their countrymen who abhorred those idols, and might consider them as dishonoured, and even dreadfully polluted, by being so employed.

With respect to the last of these circumstances but one, (the being injured in extravagant and riotous banqueting,) I would remark, that they are accustomed, in their common repasts, to take great care that their carpets are not soiled, by spreading something over them; but in public solemnities they affect great carelessness about them, as a mark of their respect and profound regard. (Russel.) Thus De la Valle, describing the reception the Armenians of Ispahan gave the king of Persia, in one of their best houses, when he had a mind to attend at the celebration of their Epiphany, says, after the ceremonies were over, he was conducted to the house of Chogia Sefer, a little before deceased, where his three sons and his brother had prepared every thing for his reception: "All the floor of the house, and all the walks of the garden, from the gate next the street to the most remote apartments, were covered with carpets of brocatel, of cloth of gold, and other precious manufactures, which were for the most part spoiled, by being trampled upon by the feet of those that had been abroad in the rain, and their shoes very dirty: their custom being, not to put them off at the entering into a house, but only at the door of the apartments, and the places where they would sit down."—BURDER.

CHAPTER III.

Ver. 2. You only have I known of all the families of the earth: therefore I will punish you for all your iniquities.

In eastern language, to say you know a person, means you APPROVE of him. Thus, should a man be well acquainted with two brothers, and should he not approve of one of them, he will say, "I do not know him." But of him he loves, he says, "Ah! I know him well." Jehovah had known, *i. e.* approved of Israel, but because of their abominations he had determined to punish them.—ROBERTS.

Ver. 12. Thus saith the LORD, As the shepherd taketh out of the mouth of the lion two legs, or a piece of an ear; so shall the children of Israel be taken out that dwell in Samaria in the corner of a bed, and in Damascus *in* a couch.

Two kinds of goats wander in the pastures of Syria and Canaan; one that differs little from the common sort in Britain; the other remarkable for the largeness of its ears. The size of this variety is somewhat larger than ours; but their ears are often a foot long, and broad in proportion. The Syrians keep them chiefly for their milk, of which they yield a considerable quantity. The present race of goats in the vicinity of Jerusalem, are of this broad-eared species. To this kind of goat, so different from the common breed, it is probable the prophet refers: "As the shepherd taketh out of the mouth of the lion two legs, or a piece of an ear, so shall the children of Israel be taken out, that dwell in Samaria and in Damascus." It is indeed the intention of the prophet to express how few of his people escaped from the overthrow of their country, and were settled in foreign parts; but it would have been hardly natural to suppose, that a shepherd would exert himself to make a lion quit a piece of an ear, only of a common goat; it must therefore be supposed to refer to the long-eared kind. Rauwolf observed goats on the mountains around Jerusalem, with pendent ears almost two feet long.—PAXTON.

Sitting in the corner is a stately attitude, and is expressive of superiority. Russel says, "the divans at Aleppo are formed in the following manner. Across the upper end, and along the sides of the room, is fixed a wooden platform, four feet broad and six inches high; upon this are laid cotton mattresses exactly of the same breadth, and over these a cover of broadcloth, trimmed with gold lace and fringes, hanging over to the ground. A number of large oblong cushions stuffed hard with cotton, and faced with flowered velvet, are then ranged in the platform close to the wall. The two upper *corners* of the divan are furnished also with softer cushions, half the size of the others, which are laid upon a square fine mattress, spread over those of cloth, both being faced with brocade. The corners in this manner distinguished are held to be the places of honour, and a great man never offers to resign them to persons of inferior rank." Mr. Antes, among other observations made on the manners and customs of the Egyptians, from 1770 to 1782, says, on his being carried before one of the beys of Egypt, in about half an hour the bey arrived, with all his men, and lighted flambeaux before him; he alighted, and went up stairs into a room, *sat down in a corner*, and all his people placed themselves in a circle round him.—HARMER.

An attendant came forward to usher us into the august presence of the ruler of Egypt. We proceeded into a large room, lighted by numerous windows, on every side except that by which we entered. The pacha was standing up, but when he perceived us approach, he hastily took his accustomed seat in the *corner* with great alertness. Round three sides of the room was a broad scarlet divan, supplied with cushions of gold brocade resting against the walls. *The corners were distinguished as places of honour* by a square of crimson and gold silk, with a cushion of the same colour and materials at the back of each.—HOGG'S VISIT TO DAMASCUS.

Ver. 15. And I will smite the winter-house with the summer-house; and the houses of ivory shall perish, and the great houses shall have an end, saith the LORD.

In the writings of Jeremiah and Amos, a distinction is made between winter and summer-houses. Russel thinks they may refer to different apartments in the same house; but if the customs of Barbary resemble those of Palestine in this respect, it is better to understand them of different houses. The hills and valleys round about Algiers, according to Dr. Shaw, are all over beautified with gardens and country-seats, whither the inhabitants of better fashion retire during the heat of the summer season. They are little white houses, shaded with a variety of fruitful trees and evergreens, which, besides the shade and retirement, afford a gay and delightful prospect towards the sea. The gardens are all of them well stocked with melons, fruit, and pot herbs of all kinds; and (what is chiefly regarded in these hot climates) each of them enjoys a great command of water. In Persia most of the summer-houses are slightly constructed and divided into three pavilions at a considerable distance from each other, with canals, fountains, and flower gardens in the intermediate spaces: while the winter-houses, or palaces in cities, are built of strong masonry, and ornamented at great expense; and palaces, villas, and mosques, are often named after their principal embellishments. Thus at Barocke and Ahmedabad are the ivory and silver mosques. This account furnishes an easy exposition of a passage in the prophecies of Amos: "I will smite the winter-house," the palaces of the great in fortified towns, "with the summer-house," the small houses of pleasure, used in the summer, to which any foe can have access; "and the houses of ivory shall perish; and the great houses shall have an end, saith the Lord," those that are distinguished by their amplitude and richness, built as they are in their strongest places, yet all of them shall perish like their country-seats, by the irresistible stroke of almighty power.—PAXTON.

CHAPTER IV.

Ver. 2. The Lord GOD hath sworn by his holiness, that, lo, the days shall come upon you, that he will take you away with hooks, and your posterity with fish-hooks.

I am at a loss to know why there is a distinction betwixt "HOOKS" and "FISH-HOOKS." I think it fanciful to explain it by saying it means "two modes of fishing." The Tamul translation has, instead of "HOOKS," *kuradu*, i. e. pincers, and it ought to be known that these were formerly much used in punishments. In the Hindoo hells this instrument is spoken of as being used to torture the inhabitants. A man in his rage says, "I will tear thee with pincers." "Alas! alas! I have been dragged away with pincers." "Ah! the severity of these troubles—they are like pincers." But it is said that HOOKS also were formerly used to stick into criminals when taken to the place of execution; and there is nothing very doubtful about this, because devotees often have large HOOKS fastened into their flesh, by which they are hoisted up on a long pole. "Your posterity with fish-hooks:" this figure is used in the East to show how people DRAW each other to any given place. Thus, does a man wish to have a large party at some feast or ceremony he is going to make, he persuades a man to say he will honour him with his company; and then he says to others, you are invited to meet such an illustrious guest, which causes numbers to come to the occasion. The man of rank in that case is called the fish-hook; because, through him, the guests are CAUGHT.—ROBERTS.

Ver. 9. I have smitten you with blasting and mildew: when your gardens, and your vineyards, and your fig-trees, and your olive-trees increased, the palmer-worm devoured *them:* yet have ye not returned unto me, saith the LORD.

Abp. Newcome says, that this means the unwholesome effluvia on the subsiding of the Nile, which causes some peculiarly malignant diseases in this country. Maillet says, that "the air is bad in those parts, where, when the inundations of the Nile have been very great, this river, in retiring to its channel, leaves marshy places, which infect the country round about. The dew is also very dangerous in Egypt." —BURDER.

CHAPTER VI.

Ver. 4. That lie upon beds of ivory, and stretch themselves upon their couches, and eat the lambs out of the flock, and the calves out of the midst of the stall.

Amos reckons *fat lambs* among the delicacies of the Israelites; and it seems these creatures are in the East extremely delicious. Sir John Chardin, in his manuscript note to Amos vi. 4, expresses himself in very strong terms on the deliciousness of these animals in the East. He tells us, that there, in many places, lambs are spoken of as a sort of food excessively delicious. That one must have eaten of them in several places of Persia, Media, and Mesopotamia, and of their kids, to form a conception of the moisture, taste, delicacy, and fat of this animal; and as the eastern people are no friends of game, nor of fish, nor fowls, their most delicious food is the lamb and the kid. This observation illustrates those passages that speak of kids as used by them for delicious repasts, and presents; as well as those others that speak of the feasting on lambs. It also gives great energy to our apprehensions of what is meant, when the Psalmist talks of *marrow and fatness.*—HARMER.

Ivory is so plentiful in the East, it is no wonder that the sovereigns had their beds made principally of that article. But why is there a distinction made in reference to BEDS and COUCHES? I believe the latter word refers to the swinging cot, as the Tamul translation also implies. In the houses of the voluptuous these cots are always found, and many are the stories in ancient books of kings and queens who were swinging together in their cots. When a man affects great delicacy as to the place where he sleeps, it is common to say, "You had better have a swinging cot."—ROBERTS.

Ver. 9. And it shall come to pass, if there remain ten men in one house, that they shall die. 10. And a man's uncle shall take him up, and he that burneth him, to bring out the bones out of the house, and shall say unto him that *is* by the sides of the house, *Is there* yet *any* with thee? and he shall say, No. Then shall he say, Hold thy tongue; for we may not make mention of the name of the LORD.

These verses and the context refer to the mortality which should result from the pestilence and famine, (in consequence of the sins of the people;) and to the BURNING of the bodies. The number "TEN" probably refers to MANY, as that is a common expression in the East to denote many. I believe the whole alludes to the custom of burning human bodies, and to that of gathering up the half-calcined bones, and to the putting them into an earthen vessel, and then to the carrying back these fragments to the house or into some OUT-BUILDING, where they are kept till conveyed to a sacred place. In India this is done by a son or a near relation; but in case there is not one near akin, then any person who is going to the place (as to the Ganges) can take the fragments of bones, and thus perform the last rites. Dr. Boothroyd takes the same view as to the PLACE where the bones have to be kept till they are removed, because he translates, "a side-room of the house." "Hold thy tongue," finds a forcible illustration in chap. viii. 3, where it is mentioned that there were "dead in every place;" and where it is said, they were to "cast them forth with silence." When the cholera or any other pestilence has carried off MANY of the people, the relations cease to weep or speak; they ask, "What is the use of wailing?" it is over, "hold thy tongue."—ROBERTS.

Ver. 11. For, behold, the LORD commandeth, and he will smite the great house with breaches, and the little house with clefts.

See on Ezek. 13. 11.

Chardin, speaking concerning the rains, says, "they are the rains which cause the walls to fall, which are built of clay, the mortar-plastering dissolving. This plastering hinders the water form penetrating the bricks; but when the plastering has been soaked with wet, the wind cracks it, and occasions the rain in some succeeding showers to get between and dissolve every thing." This account illustrates the words of the prophet in a very happy manner, as the houses were mostly built of these fragile materials.—HARMER.

CHAPTER VII.

Ver. 1. Thus hath the Lord GOD showed unto me; and, behold, he formed grasshoppers in the beginning of the shooting up of the latter growth; and, lo, *it was* the latter growth after the king's mowings.

See on Prov. 27. 25.

As they seldom make any hay in the East, the word rendered "mowing," should rather have been, "feedings." There is reason to conjecture, from the following passage of La Roque, that the time of the king's feedings was the month of March, or thereabouts: "The Arabs," he tells us, from the papers of D'Arvieux, "turn their horses out to grass in the month of March, when the grass is pretty well grown; they then take care to have their mares covered, and they eat grass at no other time in the whole year, any more than hay: they never give them any straw but to heat them, when they have been some time without discovering an inclination to drink; they live wholly upon barley." The Arab horses are all designed for riding and war; so, there is reason to believe, were those of the kings of Israel: and if the present usages of the Arabs prevailed anciently, they were turned out early in the spring, in the month of March, and at other times were nourished with barley. These things seem to determine the time of the king's feedings to March, of the shooting up of the latter growth of April.—Burder.

Ver. 14. Then answered Amos, and said to Amaziah, I *was* no prophet, neither *was* I a prophet's son; but I *was* a herdman, and a gatherer of sycamore fruit.

The sycamore buds in the latter end of March, and the prolific fruit ripens in the beginning of June. Pliny and other natural historians allege, that it continues immature till it is rubbed with iron combs, after which it ripens in four days. Is it not an operation of this kind to which the prophet Amos refers, in the text which we translate, "I was a gatherer of sycamore fruit?" The Septuagint seems to refer it to something done to the fruit, to hasten its maturity; probably to the action of the iron comb, without an application of which the figs cannot be eaten, because of their intolerable bitterness. Parkhurst renders the phrase, a scraper of sycamore fruit; which he contends, from the united testimony of natural historians, is the true meaning of the original term. The business of Amos, then, before his appointment to the prophetical office, was to scrape or wound the fruit of the sycamore-tree, to hasten its maturity and prepare it for use. Simon renders it a cultivator of sycamore fruit, which is perhaps the preferable meaning; for it appears that the cultivation of this fig required a variety of operations, all of which it is reasonable to suppose, were performed by the same persons. To render the tree fruitful, they scarified the bark, through which a kind of milky liquor continually distilled. This, it is said, causes a little bough to be formed without leaves, having upon it sometimes six or seven figs. They are hollow, without grains, and contain a little yellow matter, which is generally a nest of grubs. At their extremity, a sort of water collects, which, as it prevents them from ripening, must be let out. Amos, it is probable, was employed in these various operations; which has induced Simon and others to render the words, not a gatherer of sycamore fruit, but a dresser of the sycamore-tree; which includes all the culture and attendance it requires.

The sycamore is a large spreading tree, sometimes shooting up to a considerable height, and so thick, that three men can hardly grasp the trunk; according to Hasselquist, the stem is often fifty feet thick. This unfolds the reason why Zaccheus climbed up into a sycamore-tree, to get a sight of his Redeemer. The incident also furnishes a proof that the sycamore was still common in Palestine; for this tree stood to protect the traveller by the side of the highway.—Paxton.

CHAPTER IX.

Ver. 2. Though they dig into hell, thence shall my hand take them; though they climb up to heaven, thence will I bring them down. 3. And though they hide themselves in the top of Carmel, I will search and take them out thence; and though they be hid from my sight in the bottom of the sea, thence will I command the serpent, and he hall bite them.

Carmel was one of the barriers of the promised land, which Sennacherib boasted he would scale with the multitude of his horses and his chariots: "I will enter into the lodgings of his borders, and into the forest of his Carmel." Ungrateful as the soil of this mountain is, the wild vines and olive-trees that are still found among the brambles which encumber its declivities, prove that the hand of industry has not laboured among the rocks of Carmel in vain. So well adapted were the sides of this mountain to the cultivation of the vine, that the kings of Judah covered every improvable spot with vineyards and plantations of olives. Its deep and entangled forests, its savage rocks and lofty summit, have been in all ages the favourite retreat of the guilty or the oppressed. The fastnesses of this rugged mountain are so difficult of access, that the prophet Amos classes them with the deeps of hell, the height of heaven, and the bottom of the sea. The church, in her most affluent state, is compared to a fugitive lurking in the deep recesses of this mountain: "Feed thy people with thy rod, the flock of thy heritage which dwell solitarily in the midst of Carmel." Lebanon raises to heaven a summit of naked and barren rocks, covered for the greater part of the year with snow: but the top of Carmel, how naked and steril soever its present condition, seems to have been clothed with verdure in the days of Amos, which seldom was known to fade: "And he said, The Lord will roar from Zion, and utter his voice from Jerusalem, and the habitation of the shepherds shall mourn, and the top of Carmel shall wither."—Paxton.

The wind was high when we left Acre, and blew the sand about with such violence that we had great difficulty in making our way. The bay to the southward extends to Mount Carmel, and we were three hours in skirting its shore. We first forded the river Belus, the sand of which has been much used in the making of glass, and then came to "that ancient river, the river Kishon," immortalized in the song of Deborah and Barak, over which we were ferried by a Jewish boatman. The saddles are never taken off the horses in these countries during a journey, either by day or night. They were now taken from the animals that they might not be wet in crossing the river, and the backs of the poor creatures had been so chafed by them, that I felt unwilling to mount mine again. After passing some sepulchres in the rocks we entered the town of Hypha, and were detained some time by the guard, until one of our party waited on the governor, and obtained our release. There were several brass cannon upon the walls, all ready for action. The vessels have here better shelter than at Acre, but the water is shallow. This town is nearly at the foot of Mount Carmel, which extends about 30 miles in a southeastern direction from the sea, in nearly an equal ridge, and at an elevation of about 1600 feet. It is often referred to in scripture, and was once covered with trees, but it is now nearly bare, and "the excellency of Carmel" has withered before the curse of Heaven. It was the usual residence of the prophets Elijah and Elisha. The place where the false prophets of Baal were discomfited and slain was towards the other extremity, nearer Jezreel, to which Ahab retired; and at some point near which it is approached by the Kishon. We may stand at the top of Carmel, as did Gehazi, and look towards the sea, but alas! there is now no "little cloud like a man's hand;" still there is the promise of a shower, and in due time the streams of divine mercy will again fall upon this thirsty land, and men shall again liken themselves in their prosperity to "the excellency of Carmel and Sharon." Near the point that overlooks the sea there is a monastery of Carmelite friars. It was destroyed a few years ago by Abdullah Pacha, that he might convert the materials to his own use, and though he was ordered to rebuild it at his own expense by the sultan, when a proper representation of the circumstances had been made to his court, no attention was ever paid to the mandate. The monks are now rebuilding it themselves in a very splendid manner, and one of the fraternity is the architect. At a lower elevation on the same point, is a palace recently erected by the pacha. There is a small building near the sea, said to cover the cave in which Elisha dwelt, but as the door was locked we could not gain admittance.—Hardy.

Ver. 6. *It is* he that buildeth his stories in the heaven, and hath founded his troop in the earth; he that calleth for the waters of the sea, and poureth them out upon the face of the earth: The Lord *is* his name.

See on Jer. 22. 13.

The chief rooms of the house of Aleppo at this day are those above, the ground-floor being chiefly made use of for their horses and servants. Perhaps the prophet referred to this circumstance, when he spoke of the heavens of God's chambers, the most noble and splendid apartments of the palace of God, where his presence is chiefly manifested, and the collection of its offices, its numerous little mean divisions, of this earth.—Harmer.

Ver. 3. Behold, the days come, saith the Lord,

that the ploughman shall overtake the reaper, and the treader of grapes him that soweth seed; and the mountains shall drop sweet wine, and all the hills shall melt.

The Arabs commit depredations of every description. They strip the trees of their fruit even in its unripe state, as well as seize on the seed and corn of the husbandman. Maillet ascribes the alteration for the worse, that is found in the wine of a province in Egypt, to the precipitation with which they now gather the grapes. This was done to save them from the Arabs, "who frequently made excursions into it, especially in the season in which the fruits begin to ripen. It is to save them from these depredations that the inhabitants of the country gather them before they come to maturity." It is this circumstance that must explain this passage of the prophet: "Behold, the days come, saith the Lord, that the ploughman shall overtake the reaper, and the treader of grapes him that soweth seed; and the mountains shall drop sweet wine, and all the hills shall melt:" that is, the days shall come when the grapes shall not be gathered, as they were before, in a state of immaturity, for fear of Arabs or other destroying nations, but they shall be suffered to hang till the time of ploughing; so perfect shall be the security of these times.—Harmer.

JONAH.

CHAPTER I.

Ver. 2. Arise, go to Nineveh, that great city, and cry against it; for their wickedness is come up before me.

See on Nah. 2. 8—11.

Ashur, probably imitating the policy of his dangerous competitor, built four cities for the accommodation and defence of his descendants; the first of which was Nineveh, the capital of his kingdom. This powerful city stood on the east side of the Tigris, nor far from the river Lycus, one of its tributary streams; but on which side of the Lycus it lay, cannot now be discovered. The prediction of Nahum, that Nineveh should be so completely destroyed that future ages should search in vain for the spot which it once covered, has been fulfilled in all its extent: "With an overflowing flood, he will make an utter end of the place thereof." Ancient geographers inform us of another city of this name, which stood on the Euphrates, and was probably built by Nimrod in honour of his son. But Nineveh, so frequently mentioned in scripture, lay near the Tigris; and to this last the following observations refer. Strabo affirms that Nineveh was larger than Babylon itself; an assertion confirmed by Diodorus, who makes that city 60 miles in compass, while Strabo makes Babylon only about 48. It is therefore with justice that the inspired writer calls Nineveh "an exceeding great city of three days' journey." This account some interpreters refer not to the length, but to the compass of the city; allowing twenty miles for a day's journey, which accords with the common estimation of those times. But the phrase, "Jonah began to enter into the city a day's journey," seems rather to intimate, that the measure of three days' journey is to be understood of the length, not of the compass of Nineveh. Hence it may be easily supposed, that agreeably to the statement of the prophet, it contained "more than sixscore thousand persons that could not discern between their right hand and their left hand;" for, supposing this to be understood of infants under two years old, these generally, as Bochart observes, make at least the fifth part of the city. If this proportion be just, the inhabitants of Nineveh would not be more than six hundred thousand; which is not more than Seleucia contained in the days of Pliny, and not so many as has been numbered in the capital of the British empire.—Paxton.

Ver. 5. Then the mariners were afraid, and cried every man unto his god, and cast forth the wares, that *were* in the ship into the sea, to lighten *it* of them: but Jonah was gone down into the sides of the ship; and he lay, and was fast asleep.

Here again *we* are at home, (to speak royally:) never was there a more natural description of the conduct of a heathen crew, in a storm, than this. No sooner does danger come, than one begins to beat his head, and cry aloud, Siva, Siva; another piteously shrieks, and beats his breast, and says, Vishnoo; and a third strikes his thigh, and shouts with all his might, Varuna. Thus do they cry to their gods, instead of doing their duty. More than once have I been in these circumstances, and never can I forget the horror and helplessness of the poor idolaters.—Roberts.

Ver. 7. And they said every one to his fellow, Come, and let us cast lots, that we may know for whose cause this evil *is* upon us. So they cast lots, and the lot fell upon Jonah. 15. So they took up Jonah, and cast him forth into the sea; and the sea ceased from her raging. 16. Then the men feared the Lord exceedingly, and offered a sacrifice unto the Lord, and made vows.

In a storm, the heathen mariners always conclude that there is some one on board who has committed a great crime, and they begin to inquire, "Who is the sinner?" Some time ago, a number of native vessels left the roads of Negapatam, at the same hour, for Point Pedro, in the Island of Ceylon: they had not been long at sea before it was perceived that one of them could not make any way; she rolled, and pitched, and veered about in every direction; but the other vessels went on beautifully before the wind. The captain and his crew began to look at the passengers, and, at last, fixed their eyes upon a poor woman, who was crouched in a corner of the hold; they inquired into her condition, and found she was in a state of impurity: "Let down the canoe," was the order, "and take this woman ashore:" in vain she remonstrated, she was compelled to enter, and was soon landed on the beach. "After this, the vessel sailed as well as any other!" When the storm rages, they make vows to their gods; one will go on a pilgrimage to some holy place, another will perform a penance, and a third will make a valuable present to his favourite temple. "Offered a sacrifice:" this is generally done when they get safe to shore, but I have been on board when they have offered cocoa-nuts and other articles with the greatest earnestness. To interfere with them is not always prudent; because, were it not from the hope they have from such offerings, they would cease to work the vessel.—Roberts.

CHAPTER III.

Ver. 4. And Jonah began to enter into the city a day's journey; and he cried, and said, Yet forty days, and Nineveh shall be overthrown.

See on Nah. 1. 8.

CHAPTER IV.

Ver. 5. So Jonah went out of the city, and sat on the east side of the city, and there made him a booth, and sat under it in the shadow, till he might see what would become of the city. 6. And the Lord GOD prepared a gourd, and made *it* to come up over Jonah, that it might be a shadow over his head, to deliver him from his grief. So Jonah was exceeding glad of the gourd. 7. But God prepared a worm, when the morning rose the next day, and it smote the gourd that it withered. 8. And it came to pass, when the sun did arise, that God prepared a vehement east wind: and the sun beat upon the head of Jonah, that he fainted, and wished in himself to die, and said, *It is* better for me to die than to live.

The gourd produces leaves and branches resembling those of the garden cucumber. Its fruit is shaped like an orange, of a light white substance when the rind is taken off, and so bitter that it has been called *the gall of the earth.* It is not eatable; but is a very fit vessel for flagons, being light, capacious, and smooth, frequently a foot and a half in diameter.

The gourd of Jonah is generally allowed to be the *elkeroa* or *ricinus*, a plant well known in the East; "it grows very high, and projects many branches and large leaves. In a short time it reaches a considerable height: its stem is thick, channelled, distinguished by many knots, hollow within, branchy at top, of a sea-green colour: its leaves are large, cut into seven or more divisions, pointed and edged, of a bright, blackish, shining-green. Those nearest the top are the largest; its flowers are ranged on their stem like a thyrsus: they are of a deep-red, and stand three together.

With this description agrees the account in the prophet, of its rising over his head to shelter it; for this plant rises eight or nine feet, and is remarkably rapid in withering, when decayed or gathered.

The gourd which defended the prophet is said to have been prepared by the Lord. We have no reason to conclude from this expression, that the Almighty created it for the special purpose; he only appointed and promoted its growth in that particular spot, raising its stem and expanding its branches and leaves according to the ordinary laws of nature, till it formed a most refreshing shade over the place where the angry seer waited the fulfilment of his prediction. "We may conceive of it," says Calmet, "as an extraordinary one of its kind, remarkably rapid in growth, remarkably hard in its stem, remarkably vigorous in its branches, and remarkable for the extensive spread of its leaves, and the deep gloom of their shadow; and after a certain duration, remarkable for a sudden withering and uselessness to the impatient prophet.

The worm which struck the gourd has been considered rather as a maggot than a worm. It was, no doubt, of the species appropriate to the plant; but of what particular species is uncertain. Like the gourd, it was also prepared by Jehovah, to indicate its extraordinary size and vigour; that it acted by his commission; and that the effect of its operations was so rapid and decisive, as clearly to discover the presence of divine energy.—PAXTON.

Ver. 6. And the Lord GOD prepared a gourd, and made *it* to come up over Jonah, that it might be a shadow over his head, to deliver him from his grief. So Jonah was exceeding glad of the gourd.

The margin has, instead of "gourd," "Kikajon, or Palmecrist!" Dr. Clarke asks, "But what was the Kikajon? the best judges say the racinus or Palma-Christi, from which we get what is vulgarly called castor-oil." The Tamul translation has, instead of "gourd," Amanaku, *i. e.* the Palma-Christi! It is believed, also, the verb is in the preterperfect tense, HAD prepared, which may be another instance of the verb as illustrated under Isa. xxi. 9. The Palma-Christi is most abundant in the East, and I have had it in my own garden to the height of fourteen feet. The growth is very rapid: v. 7, "God prepared a worm when the morning rose the next day, and it smote the gourd that it withered," *i. e.* the Palma-Christi till it withered. This tree, in the course of a VERY short period, produces the "rough caterpillar," respecting which, I have written under Jer. li. 27, and in one night (where the caterpillers are abundant) will they strip the tree of its leaves, and thus take away the shade. But there is another worm in the East, called the *kuruttu-pullu*, i. e. blind worm, SAID to be produced by the dew; it begins its devastations at what is called the cabbage part of the palm, and soon destroys the tree: v. 8, "God prepared a vehement east wind." I have already written on that parching, life-destroying wind. But the margin has it, or "SILENT," which probably means CALM. Thus when there is a lull of an easterly wind, and the sun pours his fierce rays on the head of the poor traveller, it seems as if life must depart: birds and beasts pant; there is the silence of death, and nature seems ready to expire.—ROBERTS.

"It was early in the evening, when the pointed turrets of the city of *Mosul* opened on our view, and communicated no very unpleasant sensations to my heart. I found myself on scripture-ground, and could not help feeling some portion of the pride of the traveller, when I reflected that I was now within sight of NINEVEH, renowned in holy writ. The city is seated in a very barren sandy plain, on the banks of the river Tigris, embellished with the united gifts of Pomona, Ceres, and Flora. The external view of the town is much in its favour, being encompassed with stately walls of solid stone, over which the steeples or minarets, and other lofty buildings, are seen with increased effect. Here I saw a caravan encamped, halting on its march from the Gulf of Persia to Armenia; and it certainly made a most noble appearance, filling the eye with a multitude of grand objects, all uniting to form one magnificent whole. But though the outside be so beautiful, the inside is most detestable: the heat is so intense, that in the middle of the day there is no stirring out, and even *at night the walls of the houses are so heated by the day's sun, as to produce a disagreeable heat to the body, at a foot, or even a yard distance from them.* However, I entered it with spirits, because I considered it as the last stage of the worst part of my pilgrimage. But, alas! I was disappointed in my expectation; for the TIGRIS *was dried up by the intensity of the heat, and an unusual long drought*, and I was obliged to take the matter with a patient shrug, and accommodate my mind to a journey on horseback, which, though not so long as that I had already made, was likely to be equally dangerous; and which, therefore, demanded a full exertion of fortitude and resolution.

"It was still the hot season of the year, and we were to travel through that country, over which the horrid wind I have before mentioned sweeps its consuming blasts: it is called by the Turks *samiel*, is mentioned by holy Job under the name of the east wind, and extends its ravages all the way from the extreme end of the Gulf of Cambaya, up to Mosul; it carries along with it fleaks of fire, like threads of silk; instantly strikes dead those that breathe it, and consumes them inwardly to ashes; the flesh soon becoming black as a coal, and dropping off the bones. Philosophers consider it as a kind of electric fire, proceeding from the sulphureous or nitrous exhalations which are kindled by the agitation of the winds. The only possible means of escape from its fatal effects, is to fall flat on the ground, and thereby prevent the drawing it in: to do this, however, it is necessary first to see it, which is not always practicable. Besides this, *the ordinary heat of the climate is extremely dangerous to the blood and lungs, and even to the skin, which it blisters and peels from the flesh*, affecting the eyes so much, that travellers are obliged to wear a transparent covering over them to keep the heat off."

These accounts, from Col. Campbell's Travels, illustrate the history of JONAH, his behaviour and his sufferings, in the same parts. The colonel reports that the heat is extreme, both by day and night, in the town; that the Tigris was dried up by the intensity of the heat; that the heat blisters the skin, &c. "Now Jonah went out of the city, and sat on the east side of the city, till he might see what would become of the city," (iv. 5,) to which he had prophesied destruction in forty days' time, (iii. 4.) Jonah could not expect the destruction of the city until about, or after, the expiration of the forty days' respite allowed to it; so long then, at least, he waited in this burning climate. But, as he *knew God to be slow to anger*, (iv. 2,) he might wait some days, or even some weeks, after the expiration of the appointed time; so that although he was sent on his message, and had delivered it *before the great heats came on*, yet, to satisfy his curiosity, he endured them. Thus circumstanced, he constructed for himself a shelter from the sun; and doubtless, when the קיקיון KIKIUM, (*gourd*, English translation,) or kind of palm, rose in addition to his booth, at once ornamenting, filling, and shadowing it, to complete his shelter, he might well *rejoice over the gourd with exceeding great joy*. [Might not this plant, growing chiefly by night, Heb. "which a son of night was, and (as) a son of night perished," be some time in rising for that purpose? See Kikajon, Jonah, and Fragment, No. lxxviii.] This plant, during a time, perhaps during a great part of the forty days, or several weeks succeeding, afforded him shelter; then, while in full vigour, without apparent decay, he left it well overnight, and in the morning it was shrunk, faded, and gone: so that at sunrise, when the morning should be cool, Jonah, examining his plant, was struck by the scarcely-moving *aura* of an east wind, vehemently hot; no wonder, then, he fainted, and wished to die, when the only part of the day in which he could hope for coolness, was thus suffocating. What Jonah must have endured from the heat, Colonel Campbell's account may assist us to conceive. We may observe, further, how aptly this plant was a SIGN of Nineveh, its history, and its fate: it was a time in coming to perfection, and it was a time in a perfect state: so that city was long before it was mistress of the countries around it, and it held that dignity for a time; but, at about forty years after Jonah's prophecy, (prophetic days, for years, as some have supposed,) the worm (insurrection and rebellion) smote the plant; and the king of Nineveh (Sardanapalus) burnt himself, with his treasures, &c., in his palace. A fate very appropriately prefigured by the *kikium* of Jonah! The expectation of coolness in the morning, may be justified from the following extract, in which we find the colonel, like Jonah, reposing under trees in the heat of the day. "From Latikea to Aleppo, mounted on a mule, I travelled along, well pleased with the fruitful appearance of the country; and delighted with the serenity of the air. We were, as well as I can now recollect, near ten days on the road; during which time, we *travelled only in the morning early*, and in the heat of the day we reposed under the shade of trees."—TAYLOR IN CALMET.

Ver. 11. And should not I spare Nineveh, that great city, wherein are more than sixscore thousand persons that cannot discern between their right hand and their left hand; and *also* much cattle?

See on Nah. 1. 8.

MICAH.

CHAPTER I.

Ver. 7. And all the graven images thereof shall be beaten to pieces, and all the hires thereof shall be burnt with the fire, and all the idols thereof will I lay desolate: for she gathered *it* of the hire of a harlot, and they shall return to the hire of a harlot.

Here again we have unalloyed and rampant heathenism: the "sacred" courtesans of the temple give a part of their hire towards the repairing and beautifying of the building; and also to purchase idols, or carry on the festivals. At the annual festival of Scandan, which continues twenty-four days, the females alluded to defray the expenses of the last day from the proceeds of their own wickedness.—ROBERTS.

Ver. 8. Therefore I will wail and howl, I will go stripped and naked: I will make a wailing like the dragons, and mourning as the owls.

Or, "ostriches." It is affirmed by travellers of good credit, that ostriches make a fearful, screeching, lamentable noise. "During the lonesome part of the night, they often make a very doleful and hideous noise. I have often heard them groan, as if they were in the greatest agonies: an action beautifully alluded to by the prophet Micah." (Shaw.) —BURDER.

Ver. 16. Make thee bald, and poll thee for thy delicate children; enlarge thy baldness as the eagle; for they are gone into captivity from thee.

Mr. Bruce has given us an account of an eagle, known in Ethiopia only by the name nisser, eagle; but by him called the golden eagle; by the vulgar, abou duch'n, father long-beard, from the tuft of hair under his chin. He is a very large bird. "A forked brush of strong hair, divided at the point into two, proceeded from the cavity of his lower jaw, at the beginning of his throat. He had the smallest eye I ever remember to have seen in a large bird, the aperture being scarcely half an inch. The crown of his head was bare or bald, so was the front where the bill and scull joined." This is the bird alluded to by the prophet.—BURDER.

CHAPTER II.

Ver. 2. And they covet fields, and take *them* by violence; and houses, and take *them* away: so they oppress a man and his house, even a man and his heritage.

See on Job 27. 18.

CHAPTER III.

Ver. 12. Therefore shall Zion for your sake be ploughed *as* a field; and Jerusalem shall become heaps; and the mountain of the house as the high places of the forest.

We had been to examine the hill, which now bears the name of Zion; it is situated on the south side of Jerusalem, part of it being excluded by the wall of the present city, which passes over the top of the mount. If this be indeed Mount Zion, the prophecy concerning it, that the plough should pass over it, has been fulfilled to the letter; for such labours were actually going on when we arrived.—CLARKE.

CHAPTER IV.

Ver. 4. But they shall sit every man under his vine, and under his fig-tree; and none shall make *them* afraid: for the mouth of the LORD of hosts hath spoken *it*.

See on Ps. 88. 47.

The people of the East have great pleasure in sitting or lounging under their tamarind or mango-trees in the grove. Thus, in the heat of the day, they while away their time in playing with their children, in taking up the fruit, or smoking their much-loved shroot.—ROBERTS.

This expression most probably alludes to the delightful eastern arbours, which were partly composed of vines; and the agreeable retreat which was enjoyed under them might also be found under their fig-trees. Norden expressly speaks of *vine arbours* as common in the Egyptian gardens, (vol. i. p. 71,) and the Prænestine pavement, in Dr. Shaw, gives us the figure of an ancient one.—BURDER.

Ver. 5. For all people will walk every one in the name of his god, and we will walk in the name of the LORD our God for ever and ever.

Nothing more arrests the notice of a stranger, on entering Sinde, than the severe attention of the people to the forms of religion, as enjoined by the prophet of Arabia. In all places, the meanest and poorest of mankind may be seen, at the appointed hours, turned towards Mecca, offering up their prayers. I have observed a boatman quit the laborious duty of dragging the vessel against the stream, and retire to the shore, wet and covered with mud, to perform his genuflexions. In the smallest villages the sound of the "mowuzzun," or crier, summoning true believers to prayers, may be heard, and the Mohammedans within reach of the sonorous sound suspend, for the moment, their employment, that they may add their "Amen" to the solemn sentence when concluded. The effect is pleasing and impressive; but, as has often happened in other countries at a like stage of civilization, the moral qualities of the people do not keep pace with this fervency of devotion.—BURNES.

CHAPTER VI.

Ver. 7. Will the LORD be pleased with thousands of rams, *or* with ten thousands of rivers of oil? shall I give my first-born *for* my transgression, the fruit of my body *for* the sin of my soul?

Allusions are often made in the scriptures to the value of oil; and to appreciate them, it should be recollected, that oil ONLY is used to light the houses, and also, for anointing the body, and MANY medicinal purposes. "Have you heard of the charity of Venäse? Why, he has given a RIVER of oil to the temple; and Muttoo has given a RIVER of ghee." "Milk! why that farmer has RIVERS of it; and the Modeliar has a SEA."—ROBERTS.

Ver. 15. Thou shalt sow, but thou shalt not reap; thou shalt tread the olives, but thou shalt not anoint thee with oil; and sweet wine, but shalt not drink wine.

See on Ps. 37. 35; Deut. 33. 24; and Is. 63. 1—3.

CHAPTER VII.

Ver. 1. Wo is me! for I am as when they have gathered the summer-fruits, as the grape-gleanings of the vintage: *there is* no cluster to eat: my soul desired the first ripe fruit.

The expression here made use of by the prophet may probably be understood by the assistance of a remark which Sir John Chardin has made upon this passage. He informs us, that the Persians and Turks are not only fond of almonds, plumbs, and melons in a mature state, but that they are remarkable for eating them before they are ripe. As soon as ever they approach to that state, they make use of them, the great dryness and temperature of the air preventing flatulencies.—HARMER.

Ver. 3. That they may do evil with both hands earnestly, the prince asketh, and the judge *asketh* for a reward; and the great *man* he uttereth his mischievous desire: so they wrap it up.

We have seen that to do a thing with ONE hand, signifies earnestness and oneness of consent. Whenever a person has to receive a thing from a superior, he must put out BOTH hands; for not to do so, would be a mark of great disrespect. "Alas! I went to that man with both hands, (*i. e.* held them out to him,) but he turned me away." "The greedy wretch eats with both hands," meaning, he is a glutton; because all respectable and decent people eat with the right hand ONLY.—ROBERTS.

Ver. 14. Feed thy people with thy rod, the flock of thy heritage, which dwell solitarily *in* the wood, in the midst of Carmel: let them feed *in* Bashan and Gilead, as in the days of old.

See on Am. 9. 10.

Ver. 19. He will turn again, he will have compassion upon us: he will subdue our iniquities; and thou wilt cast all their sins into the depths of the sea.

When a devotee believes the guilt of his transgressions has been removed, whether by prayers or austerities, he says, "My sins have all fallen into the sea."—ROBERTS.

NAHUM.

CHAPTER I.

Ver. 8. But with an over-running flood he will make an utter end of the place thereof, and darkness shall pursue his enemies.

To a brief record of the creation of the antediluvian world, and of the dispersion and the different settlements of mankind after the deluge, the scriptures of the Old Testament add a full and particular history of the Hebrews for the space of fifteen hundred years, from the days of Abraham to the era of the last of the prophets. While the historical part of scripture thus traces, from its origin, the history of the world, the prophecies give a prospective view which reaches to its end. And it is remarkable that profane history, emerging from fable, becomes clear and authentic about the very period when sacred history terminates, and when the fulfilment of these prophecies commences, which refer to other nations besides the Jews.

Nineveh, the capital of Assyria, was for a long time an extensive and populous city. Its walls are said, by heathen historians, to have been a hundred feet in height, sixty miles in compass, and to have been defended by fifteen hundred towers, each two hundred feet high. Although it formed the subject of some of the earliest of the prophecies, and was the very first which met its predicted fate, yet a heathen historian, in describing its capture and destruction, repeatedly refers to an ancient prediction respecting it. Diodorus Siculus relates, that the king of Assyria, after the complete discomfiture of his army, confided in an old prophecy, that Nineveh would not be taken unless the river should become the enemy of the city; that after an ineffectual siege of two years, the river, swollen with long-continued and tempestuous torrents, inundated part of the city, and threw down the wall for the space of twenty furlongs; and that the king, deeming the prediction accomplished, despaired of his safety, and erected an immense funeral pile, on which he heaped his wealth, and with which himself, his household, and palace, were consumed. The book of Nahum was avowedly prophetic of the destruction of Nineveh: and it is there foretold, "that the gates of the river shall be opened, and the palace shall be dissolved." "Nineveh of old, like a pool of water—with an overflowing flood he will make an utter end of the place thereof." The historian describes the facts by which the other predictions of the prophet were as literally fulfilled. He relates that the king of Assyria, elated with his former victories, and ignorant of the revolt of the Bactrians, had abandoned himself to scandalous inaction; had appointed a time of festivity, and supplied his soldiers with abundance of wine; and that the general of the enemy, apprized by deserters of their negligence and drunkenness, attacked the Assyrian army while the whole of them were fearlessly giving way to indulgence, destroyed a great part of them, and drove the rest into the city. The words of the prophet were hereby verified: "While they be folden together as thorns, and while they are drunken as drunkards, they shall be devoured as stubble full dry." The prophet promised much spoil to the enemy: "Take the spoil of silver, take the spoil of gold; for there is no end of the store and glory out of all the pleasant furniture." And the historian affirms, that many talents of gold and silver, preserved from the fire, were carried to Ecbatana. According to Nahum, the city was not only to be destroyed by an overflowing flood, but the fire also was to devour it; and, as Diodorus relates, partly by water, partly by fire, it was destroyed.

The utter and perpetual destruction and desolation of Nineveh were foretold:—"The Lord will make an utter end of the place thereof. Affliction shall not rise up the second time. She is empty, void, and waste. The Lord will stretch out his hand against the north, and destroy Assyria, and will make Nineveh a desolation, and dry like a wilderness. How is she become a desolation, a place for beasts to lie down in!" In the second century, Lucian, a native of a city on the banks of the Euphrates, testified that Nineveh was utterly perished; that there was no vestige of it remaining; and that none could tell where once it was situated. This testimony of Lucian, and the lapse of many ages during which the place was not known where it stood, render it at least somewhat doubtful whether the remains of an ancient city, opposite to Mosul, which have been described as such by travellers, be indeed those of ancient Nineveh. It is, perhaps, probable that they are the remains of the city which succeeded Nineveh, or of a Persian city of the same name, which was built on the banks of the Tigris by the Persians subsequently to the year 230 of the Christian era, and demolished by the Saracens in 632. In contrasting the then existing great and increasing population, and the accumulating wealth of the proud inhabitants of the mighty Nineveh, with the utter ruin that awaited it, —the word of God (before whom all the inhabitants of the earth are as grasshoppers) by Nahum was—"Make thyself many as the canker-worm, make thyself many as the locusts. Thou hast multiplied thy merchants above the stars of heaven: the canker-worm spoileth, and flyeth away. Thy crowned are as the locusts, and thy captains as the great grasshoppers, which camp in the hedges in the cold day: but when the sun riseth, they flee away; and their place is not known where they are," or were. Whether these words imply that even the site of Nineveh would in future ages be uncertain or unknown; or, as they rather seem to intimate, that every vestige of the palaces of its monarchs, of the greatest of its nobles, and of the wealth of its numerous merchants, would wholly disappear; the truth of the prediction cannot be invalidated under either interpretation. The avowed ignorance respecting Nineveh, and the oblivion which passed over it, for many an age, conjoined with the meagerness of evidence to identify it, still prove that the place was long unknown where it stood, and that, even now, it can scarcely with certainty be determined. And if the only spot that bears its name, or that can be said to be the place where it was, be indeed the site of one of the most extensive of cities on which the sun ever shone, and which continued for many centuries to be the capital of Assyria—the "principal mounds," few in number, which "show neither bricks, stones, nor other materials of building, but are in many places overgrown with grass, and resemble the mounds left by intrenchments and fortifications of ancient Roman camps," and the *appearances* of other mounds and ruins less marked than even these, extending for ten miles, and widely spread, and seeming to be "the wreck of former buildings," show that Nineveh is left without one monument of royalty, without any token whatever of its splendour or wealth; that their place is not known where they were; and that it is indeed a desolation—"empty, void, and waste," its very ruins perished, and less than the wreck of what it was. "Such an *utter ruin*," in every view, "has been made of it; and such is the truth of the divine predictions."—Keith.

CHAPTER II.

Ver. 7. And Huzzab shall be led away captive, she shall be brought up, and her maids shall lead *her* as with the voice of doves, tabering upon their breasts.

See on Is. 5. 12.

When D'Arvieux was in the camp of the great emir, his princess was visited by other Arab princesses. The last that came, whose visit alone he describes, was mounted, he says, on a camel, covered with a carpet, and decked with flowers; a dozen women marched in a row before her, holding the camel's halter with one hand; they sung the praises of their mistress, and songs which expressed joy, and the happiness of being in the service of such a beautiful and amiable lady. Those which went first, and were more distinct from her person, came in their turn to the head of the camel, and took hold of the halter, which place, as being the post of honour, they quitted to others, when the princess had gone a few paces. The emir's wife sent her women to meet her, to whom the halter was entirely quitted, out of respect, her own women putting themselves behind the camel. In this order they marched to the tent, where they alighted. They then all sung together the beauty, birth, and good qualities of this princess. This account illustrates those words of the prophet, wherein he speaks of the presenting of the queen of Nineveh, or Nineveh itself, under the figure of a queen, to her conqueror. He describes her as led by the maids, with the voice of doves, that is, with the voice of mourning; their usual songs of joy, with which they used to lead her along, as the Arab women did their princess, being turned into lamentations.—HARMER.

CHAPTER III.

Ver. 14. Draw the waters for the siege, fortify thy strongholds: go into clay, and tread the mortar, make strong the brick-kiln.

See on Is. 41. 25.

Ver. 17. Thy crowned *are* as the locusts, and thy captains as the great grasshoppers, which camp in the hedges in the cold day; *but* when the sun ariseth they flee away, and their place is not known where they *are.*

"The operation of the female locust in laying her eggs is highly interesting. She chooses a piece of light earth, well protected by a bush or hedge, where she makes a hole for herself, so deep that her head just appears above it; she here deposites an oblong substance, exactly the shape of her own body, which contains a considerable number of eggs, arranged in neat order, in rows against each other, which remain buried in the ground most carefully, and artificially protected from the cold of winter." (Pliny.) "The eggs are brought into life by the heat of the sun. If the heats commence early, the locusts early gain strength, and it is then that their depredations are most feared, because they commence them before the corn has had time to ripen, and they attack the stem when it is still tender. I conjecture that camping in the hedges in the cold day may be explained by the eggs being deposited during the winter: and when the sun ariseth they flee away, may also be illustrated by the flying away of the insect, as soon as it had felt the sun's influence." (Morier.)—BURDER.

HABAKKUK.

CHAPTER I.

Ver. 8. Their horses also are swifter than the leopards, and are more fierce than the evening wolves: and their horseman shall spread themselves, and their horsemen shall come from far; they shall fly as the eagle *that* hasteth to eat.

The Baron De Tott, in his entertaining work, has given us an account of the manner in which an army of modern Tartars conducted themselves, which serves greatly to illustrate this passage: "These particulars," says the baron, "informed the cham or prince, and the generals, what their real position was; and it was decided that a third of the army, composed of volunteers, and commanded by a sultan and several mirzas, should pass the river at midnight, divide into several columns, subdivide successively, and thus overspread New Servia, burn the villages, corn, and fodder, and carry off the inhabitants of the country. The rest of the army, in order to follow the plan concerted, marched till they came to the beaten track in the snow made by the detachment. This we followed, till we arrived at the place where it divides into seven branches, to the left of which we constantly kept, observing never to mingle or confuse ourselves with any of the subdivisions which we successively found; and some of which were only small paths, traced by one or two horsemen. Flocks were found frozen to death on the plain, and twenty columns of smoke, already rising in the horizon, completed the horrors of the scene, and announced the fires which had laid waste New Servia." The difficulties which have attended the explanation of this prediction are thus happily removed, and the propriety of the expression fully established.—PAXTON.

Ver. 10. And they shall scoff at the kings, and the princes *shall be* a scorn unto them: they shall deride every stronghold; for they shall heap dust, and take it.

Another contrivance which the besiegers employed, was the *agger* or mount, which they raise so high as to equal, if not exceed, the top of the besieged walls: the sides were supported with bricks or stones, or secured with strong rafters to hinder it from falling; the forepart only remained bare, because it was to be advanced by degrees nearer the city. The pile itself consisted of all sorts of materials, as earth, timber, boughs, stones; into the middle were cast also wickers, and twigs of trees to fasten, and, as it were, cement the other parts. The prophet Habakkuk manifestly refers to the mount, in that prediction where he describes the desolating march of the Chaldeans, and the success of their arms.—PAXTON.

CHAPTER II.

Ver. 2. And the LORD answered me, and said, Write the vision, and make *it* plain upon tables, that he may run that readeth it.

Writing-tables were used in and before the time of Homer; for he speaks of writing very pernicious things upon a two-leaved table. They were made of wood, consisted of two, three, or five leaves, and were covered with wax; on this impressions were easily made, continued long, and were very legible. It was a custom among the Romans for the public affairs of every year to be committed to writing by the *pontifex maximus*, or high-priest, and published on a table. They were exposed to public view, so that the people might have an opportunity of being acquainted with them. It was also usual to hang up laws approved and recorded on tables of brass in their market-places, and in their temples, that they might be seen and read. In like manner the Jewish prophets used to write, and expose their prophecies publicly on tables, either in their own houses, or in the temple, that every one that passed by might read them. —BURDER.

Ver. 11. For the stone shall cry out of the wall, and the beam out of the timber shall answer it.

The margin has, instead of "answer it," "or witness against." When a man denies what he has solemnly promised, the person who complains of his perfidy, says, "The place where you stood shall witness against you." "A beautiful princess was once enjoying herself in a fragrant grove, when a noble prince passed that way; she became enamoured of his person, and he solemnly promised to return and marry her. When he left her, she wept bitterly, and said, 'Ah! should he not return, this tali-tree (*pandanus odoratissima*) shall WITNESS against him. Yes, the birds shall be my witnesses.'"—ROBERTS.

Ver. 17. For the violence of Lebanon shall cover thee, and the spoil of beasts, *which* make them afraid, because of men's blood, and for the violence of the land, of the city, and of all that dwell therein.

The lofty summits of Lebanon were the chosen haunts of various beasts of prey; the print of whose feet Maundrell and his party observed in the snow. But they are not confined to these situations: a recent traveller continued descending several hours, through varied scenery, presenting at every turn some new feature, distinguished either by its picturesque beauty or awful sublimity. On arriving at one of the lower swells, which form the base of the mountain, he and his party broke rather abruptly into a deep and thick forest. As they traversed the bocage, the howlings of wild animals were distinctly heard from the recesses. To these savage tenants of the desert, the prophet Habakkuk seems to allude. The violence of Lebanon is a beautiful and energetic expression, denoting the ferocious animals that roam on its mountains, and lodge in its thickets; and that, occasionally descending into the plain in quest of prey, ravage the fold or seize upon the unwary villager. —PAXTON.

CHAPTER III.

Ver. 4. And *his* brightness was as the light; he had horns *coming* out of his hand; and there *was* the hiding of his power.

See on Ps. 92. 10.

Ver. 9. Thy bow was made quite naked, *according* to the oaths of the tribes, *even thy* word. Selah. Thou didst cleave the earth with rivers.

The oriental bows, according to Chardin, were usually carried in a case hung to their girdles; it was sometimes of cloth, but more commonly of leather. The expression in these words of the prophet must consequently be understood of the bow when out of the case.—HARMER.

Ver. 19. The LORD God *is* my strength, and he will make my feet like hinds' *feet*, and he will make me to walk upon my high places. To the chief singer on my stringed instruments.

See on Ps. 18. 33.

ZEPHANIAH.

CHAPTER I.

Ver. 8. And it shall come to pass in the day of the LORD's sacrifice, that I will punish the princes, and the king's children, and all such as are clothed with strange apparel. 9. In the same day also will I punish all those that leap on the threshold, which fill their masters' houses with violence and deceit.

"Those that wear strange apparel." These are words that in this connexion seem to mean only the rich that were conscious of such power and influence as to dare in time of oppression and danger, to avow their riches, and who therefore were not afraid to wear the precious manufactures of strange countries, though they were neither magistrates, nor yet of royal descent. A great number of attendants is a modern piece of oriental magnificence; as I shall hereafter have occasion to remark it appears to have been so anciently, Eccles. v. 11; these servants, now, it is most certain, frequently attend their master on horseback, richly attired, sometimes to the number of twenty-five or thirty: if they did so anciently, with a number of servants attending great men, who are represented by this very prophet as at that time in common terrible oppressors, ch. iii. 3, they may be naturally supposed to ride into people's houses, and having gained admission by deceit, to force from them by violence considerable contributions: for this riding into houses is not now only practised by the Arabs; it consequently might be practised by others, too, anciently. It is not now peculiar to the Arabs, for Le Bruyn, after describing the magnificent furniture of several of the Armenian merchants at Julfa, that suburb of Ispahan in which they live, tells us, that the front door of the greatest part of these houses is very small, partly to hinder the Persians from entering into them on horseback, and partly that they may less observe the magnificence within. To which ought to be added, what he elsewhere observes, that these Armenians are treated with great rigour and insolence by the Persians. If this text refers to a violence of this sort, they are the thresholds of the oppressed over which they leaped, not the thresholds of the oppressive masters, which some have supposed, when they returned laden with spoil.—HARMER.

Ver. 12. And it shall come to pass at that time, *that* I will search Jerusalem with candles, and punish the men that are settled on their lees: that say in their heart, The LORD will not do good, neither will he do evil.

The margin has, in place of "settled," "curdled or thickened." The Tamul translation has this, "dregs stirred up," *i. e.* sediment shaken together well thickened. Of people who are in great straits, of those who are a strange compound of good and evil, of things which are difficult to understand, it is said, "Ah! this is all *kullumbin-vandal*," i. e. stirred up dregs. This appears to have been the state of the Jews, and they wanted to show that the Lord would neither do good nor evil; that in him was not any distinct character; and that he would not regard them in their thickened and mixed condition; that though they were joined to the heathen, it was not of any consequence. "I will search Jerusalem with candles;" thus were they mistaken in their false hopes. Does a man declare his innocence of any crime, the accusers say, "We will search thee with lamps." "Yes, yes, I will look into that affair with lamps." "What! have your lamps gone out? You see I am not guilty."—ROBERTS.

CHAPTER II.

Ver. 4. For Gaza shall be forsaken, and Ashkelon a desolation; they shall drive out Ashdod at the noonday, and Ekron shall be rooted up.

The city of Ashkelon or Ascalon, was one of the five principalities of the ancient Philistines: it is situated on the coast of the Mediterranean Sea, between Azotus, or Ashdod, and Gaza. Ashkelon is mentioned in Judg. i. 18, as having been taken by the tribe of Judah; afterward it fell successively under the dominion of the Assyrians, Persians, Macedonians, and Romans. This city had a temple dedicated to Venus Urania, which was destroyed by the Scythians, six hundred and thirty years before the Christian era; another dedicated to Derceto, a tutelary deity of the Philistines; and another consecrated to Apollo, of which Herod, the grandfather of Herod the Great, was priest: the latter was born here, and from this circumstance he has sometimes been called the Ascalonite. In the early ages of Christianity, Ascalon was a bishop's see. During the crusades it was a place of considerable importance; but having been repeatedly captured and recaptured by the Saracens, it was finally reduced to a heap of ruins. Though it was one of the chief maritime cities of Phenicia, at present it does not exhibit the least vestige of a port.

"The position of Ashkelon is strong: the walls are built on the top of a ridge of rock that winds round the town in a semicircular direction, and terminates at each end in the sea. The foundations remain all the way round; the walls are of great thickness, and in some places of considerable height, and flanked with towers at different distances. Patches of the wall preserve their original elevation; but in general it is ruined throughout, and the materials lie scattered around the foundation, or rolled down the hill on either side. The ground falls within the walls, in the same manner that it does without: the town was situated in the hollow, so that no part of it could be seen from the outside of the walls. Numerous small ruined houses still remain, with small gardens interspersed among them. In the highest part of the town are the remains of a Christian convent close upon the sea, with a well of excellent water beside it. The sea beats strongly against the bank on which the convent stands; and six prostrate columns of gray granite, half covered with the waves, attest the effects of its encroachments. There is no bay or harbour for shipping; but a small harbour, advancing a little way into the town towards its eastern extremity, seems to have been formed for the accommodation of such small craft as were used in the better days of the city." The water, seen in the foreground of our view, is the result of the overflowing of a torrent during the rainy season, the channel of which is dry at other times.

Ashkelon was one of the proudest satrapies of the Philistines: *now* there is not an inhabitant within its walls; and the predictions of Jeremiah, Amos, Zephaniah, and Zechariah, have been literally fulfilled:—"Ashkelon is cut off with the remnant of *their* valley." (Jer. xlvii. 5.) He "that holdeth the sceptre" has been cut off "from Ashkelon." (Amos i. 8.) "Gaza shall be forsaken, and Ashkelon a desolation." (Zeph. ii. 4.) "The king shall perish from Gaza, and Ashkelon shall not be inhabited." (Zech. ix. 5.) At the time the two last-cited predictions were uttered, both these satrapies of the Philistines were in a flourishing condition; each the capital of its own petty state: "and nothing but the prescience of heaven could pronounce on which of the two, and in what manner, the vial of his wrath should thus be poured out." Gaza is still a large and respectable town, but truly without a king: the walls of Ashkelon are broken down, its lofty towers lie scattered on the ground, and the houses are lying in ruins without a human inhabitant to occupy them, or to build them up. "How is the wrath of man made to praise his Creator! Hath He said, and shall He not do it? The oracle was delivered by the prophet (Zechariah) more than five hundred years before the Christian era, and we behold its accomplishment eighteen hundred years after that event, and see with our eyes that the king has perished from Gaza, and that Ashkelon is not inhabited; and were there no others on which the mind could confidently rest, from the fulfilment of this one prophecy even the most skeptical may be assured, that all that is predicted in the sacred volume shall come to pass."—HORNE.

Ver. 6. And the seacoast shall be dwellings, *and* cottages for shepherds, and folds for flocks.

Archbishop Newcome has remarked, that many manuscripts and three editions have a single letter in one of these words more than appears in the common editions; which, instead of cherith, gives us a word which signifies *caves;* and he thus renders the words: *and the seacoast shall be sheep-cotes; caves for shepherds, and folds for flocks.* This translation will appear perfectly correct, if it be considered that the mountains bordering on the Syrian coast are remarkable for the number of caves in them. In the history of the crusades it is particularly mentioned that a number of persons retired with their wives and children, their flocks and herds, into subterraneous caves, to find shelter from the enemy.—HARMER.

Ver. 7. And the coast shall be for the remnant of the house of Judah; they shall feed thereupon: in the houses of Ashkelon shall they lie down in the evening: for the LORD their God shall visit them, and turn away their captivity.

An extract from Dr. Chandler's Travels furnishes a very lively comment on these words: "Our horses were disposed among the walls and rubbish, (of Ephesus,) with their saddles on; and a mat was spread for us on the ground. We sat here in the open air while supper was preparing; when suddenly fires began to blaze up among the bushes, and we saw the villagers collected about them in savage groups, or passing to and fro, with lighted brands for torches. The flames, with the stars and a pale moon, afforded us a dim prospect of ruin and desolation. A shrill owl, called cucuvaia from its note, with a nighthawk, flitted near us; and a jackal cried mournfully, as if forsaken by his companions on the mountain."—BURDER.

Ver. 9. Therefore, *as* I live saith the LORD of hosts, the God of Israel, Surely Moab shall be as Sodom, and the children of Ammon as Gomorrah, *even* the breeding of nettles, and saltpits, and a perpetual desolation: the residue of my people shall spoil them, and the remnant of my people shall possess them.

See on Jer. 17. 5, 6.

Ver. 14. And flocks shall lie down in the midst of her, all the beasts of the nations: both the cormorant and the bittern shall lodge in the upper lintels of it; *their* voice shall sing in the windows; desolation *shall be* in the thresholds: for he shall uncover the cedar-work.

Margin, "knobs or chapiters." Chardin, describing the magnificent pillars that he found at Persepolis, tells us, that the storks (birds respected by the Persians) make their nests on the tops of these columns with great boldness, and are in no danger of being dispossessed.—BURDER.

ASKELON.—Zeph. 2:4. Page 566.

ZECHARIAH.

CHAPTER I.

Ver. 8. I saw by night, and behold a man riding upon a red horse, and he stood among the myrtle-trees that *were* in the bottom: and behind him *were there* red horses, speckled, and white.

The word here translated red signifies blood-red, not any kind of bright bay, or other colour usual among horses. But the custom of painting or dying animals for riding, whether asses or horses, explains the nature of this description. Tavernier, speaking of a city which he visited, says, "five hundred paces from the gate of the city we met a young man of a good family, for he was attended by two servants, and rode upon an ass, the hinder part of which was painted red." And Mungo Park informs us, that the Moorish sovereign Ali, always rode upon a milk-white horse, with its tail died red. See also Zech. vi. 2. Rev. vi. 4.—BURDER.

CHAPTER II.

Ver. 4. And said unto him, Run, speak to this young man, saying, Jerusalem shall be inhabited *as* towns without walls for the multitude of men and cattle therein: 5. For I, saith the LORD, will be unto her a wall of fire round about, and will be the glory in the midst of her.

The promise of God's being to Jerusalem, or his church, a *wall of fire*, seems to be spoken in allusion to the manner in which travellers in desert parts of the earth defend themselves in the nighttime from the attacks of ferocious animals. They place fires in various directions around their encampment. This was our constant practice in the wilds of Africa, when timber to burn could be obtained. While the fires kept burning, we were in perfect safety, as no undomesticated animal, however ferocious, will approach near to fire. Something in its brightness seems to give alarm.—CAMPBELL.

CHAPTER III.

Ver. 2. And the LORD said unto Satan, The LORD rebuke thee, O Satan; even the LORD that hath chosen Jerusalem rebuke thee: *is* not this a brand plucked out of the fire?

When a man has had a VERY narrow escape from danger or from death, he is called a firebrand! Thus, when the cholera rages, should only one in a family escape, he is named "the firebrand." When a person talks of selling his property in consequence of not having an heir, people say, "Sell it not, there will be yet a firebrand to inherit it." "Alas! alas! my relations are all dead, I am a firebrand."—ROBERTS.

Ver. 3. Now Joshua was clothed with filthy garments, and stood before the angel.

It was usual, especially among the Romans, when a man was charged with a capital crime, and during his arraignment, to let down his hair, suffer his beard to grow long, to wear filthy ragged garments, and appear in a very dirty and sordid habit; on account of which they were called *sordidati*. When the person accused was brought into court to be tried, even his near relations, friends, and acquaintances, before the court voted, appeared with dishevelled hair, and clothed with garments foul and out of fashion, weeping, crying, and deprecating punishment. The accused sometimes appeared before the judges clothed in black, and his head covered with dust. In allusion to this ancient custom, the prophet Zechariah represents Joshua, the high-priest, when he appeared before the Lord, and Satan stood at his right hand to accuse him, as clothed with filthy garments. After the cause was carefully examined, and all parties impartially heard, the public crier, by command of the presiding magistrate, ordered the judges to bring in their verdict.—PAXTON.

Ver. 10. In that day, saith the LORD of hosts, shall ye call every man his neighbour under the vine and under the fig-tree.

See on Ps. 78. 47, and 1 Kings 1. 9.

The oriental banquet, in consequence of the intense heat, is often spread upon the verdant turf, beneath the shade of a tree, where the streaming rivulet supplies the company with wholesome water, and excites a gentle breeze to cool their burning temples. The vine and the fig, it appears from the faithful page of inspiration, are preferred on such joyous occasions.—PAXTON.

CHAPTER IV.

Ver. 10. For who hath despised the day of small things? for they shall rejoice, and shall see the plummet in the hand of Zerubbabel *with* those seven; they *are* the eyes of the LORD, which run to and fro through the whole earth.

The margin has, instead of "they shall rejoice," "or since the seven eyes of the Lord shall." (iii. 9, "Seven eyes.") Dr. Boothroyd says, these eyes represent "the perfect oversight and providence of God," which I doubt not is the true meaning. It is a curious fact that the sun which shines seven times in the course of the week, is spoken of as the "seven eyes" of the deity, because there is an eye for each day. Thus, the Sunday, the "first eye" of God shines, and so on through the rest of the days. In the 9th verse mention is made of laying the foundation stone of a temple for Jehovah, and again in the 10th verse it is asked, "Who hath despised the day of small things?" saying it is ONLY the foundation, this is a small beginning: fear not, for the "seven eyes" of the Lord are over the work. His good providence shall accomplish the whole, because he has an eye for each day of the week. Has a man suffered a great evil, has an antagonist triumphed over another, either in a court of justice or any other way, he says, in talking about his misfortunes, "God has lost his eyes, or I should not have fallen into this trouble." "Well, friend, how is this? I hear you have gained the day."—"True, true, the eyes of God were upon me." Should there not have been rain for some time, the people say, "God has no eyes in these days," *i. e.* he does not take care of us. In the book *Neethe-veanpā* it is said, "To all there are two eyes; to the learned there are three; to the giver of alms there are SEVEN eyes, (alluding to each day;) but to those who through penance have received gracious gifts, there are innumerable eyes."—ROBERTS.

CHAPTER V.

Ver. 9. Then lifted I up mine eyes, and looked, and, behold, there came out two women, and the wind *was* in their wings; (for they had wings like the wings of a stork;) and they lifted up the ephah between the earth and the heaven.

In the vision of which these words are a part, the prophe

beheld in fearful perspective, the future calamities of his nation. The ephah represented the measure of iniquity which the Jews were fast filling up by their increasing enormities. The woman whom he saw sitting in the midst of the ephah, signified the Jewish nation in their degenerate state; this woman the angel calls wickedness, the abstract being put for the concrete, the wicked people of the Jews, to whom God was about to render according to their works. Into the ephah the woman is thrust down, and a talent of lead cast upon the mouth of it, to keep her a close prisoner; denoting that the condemned sinner who has filled up the measure of his iniquity, can neither escape from the curse of God, nor endure the misery which it inflicts. The ephah containing this mystical woman, he now sees carried away into a far country; that is, the nation of the Jews overthrown, their civil and religious polity extinguished, their temple burned, their priests slain, and the poor remains of their people scattered over the face of all the earth. This great and terrible destruction is accomplished by the Roman emperors, Vespasian and Titus, symbolized by "two women who had wings like a stork," which are sufficiently powerful to waft that bird to a very distant country. These symbolical women lifted up the ephah between the earth and the heaven; which was fulfilled when the Roman armies, with a rapidity resembling the flight of a bird of passage, came up against the Jews, now ripe for destruction, and swept them from the land of their fathers into regions far remote, from which they were not, as in the first captivity, to return after seventy years, but to remain in a state of depression and suffering for many generations. Under the curse of incensed heaven they still remain, and must do so, till the fulness of the Gentiles be come in, and then all Israel shall be saved.—PAXTON.

CHAPTER VIII.

Ver. 7. Thus saith the LORD of hosts, Behold, I will save my people from the east country, and from the west country.

The margin has, instead of "west country," "country of the going down of the sun." The form in the margin is exceedingly common; thus people do not always say, We are to go to the east or west, but "to the side where is the going down," or "to the side where is the ascending place." "In what direction are you going?"—"To the place of the going down."—ROBERTS.

Ver. 16. These *are* the things that ye shall do, Speak ye every man the truth to his neighbour; execute the judgment of truth and peace in your gates.

It appears from the above, and other passages of scripture, that the kings of Israel distributed justice, or sat in judgment to decide causes that might be brought before them, at the gate,—that the gate of the city was the place where these causes came before them, and where they pronounced their decision;—that the king held his councils at the gate, or where the elders or chiefs met the king, to consider the affairs of the nation;—and that, in fact, all their principal assemblies were held at the gates of the city. This Jewish custom still exists high in the interior of South Africa. While in Kurreechane, a city about twelve or thirteen hundred miles up from the Cape of Good Hope, I was told that a cause was going to be brought before the king. Being anxious to witness it, I was led in haste to the gate, where I saw the king sit down at the right side of it, with his secretary on his right hand, and the prosecutor, or complainer, on his left, who stated his case across to the secretary. During his narrating his case, the king was looking about as if not attending to what was said, but I saw from his eye that he was attending to what, for form's sake, was addressed to the secretary. When the party had finished what he had to say, the secretary repeated the whole to the king, as if he had been entirely ignorant of the matter. The king immediately gave judgment.—CAMPBELL.

CHAPTER X.

Ver. 4. Out of him came forth the corner, out of him the nail, out of him the battle-bow, out of him every oppressor together.

See on Is. 22. 23.

CHAPTER XI.

Ver. 1. Open thy doors, O Lebanon, that the fire may devour thy cedars.

See on Ps. 72. 16.

Ver. 1. Open thy doors, O Lebanon, that the fire may devour thy cedars. 2. Howl, fir-tree, for the cedar is fallen; because all the mighty are spoiled: howl, O ye oaks of Bashan; for the forest of the vintage is come down.

The mountainous range of Lebanon was celebrated for the extent of its forests, and particularly for the size and excellence of its cedars. The ascent from the village of Eden, or Aden, near Tripoli, to the spot where the cedars grow, is inconsiderable. This distance is computed by Captains Irby and Mangles to be about five miles, allowing for the windings of the road, which is very rugged, and passes over hill and dale. These far-famed trees are situated on a small eminence in a valley at the foot of the highest part of the mountain: the land on the mountain's side has a steril aspect, and the trees are remarkable by being altogether in one clump. By the natives they are called Arsilebân. There are, in fact, two generations of trees; the oldest are large and massy, four, five, or even seven trunks springing from one base; they rear their heads to an enormous height, spreading their branches afar; and they are not found in any other part of Lebanon, though young trees are occasionally met with.

The ancient cedars—those which superstition has consecrated as holy, and which are the chief object of the traveller's curiosity, have been gradually diminishing in number for the last three centuries. In 1550, Belloni found them to be twenty-eight in number; Rauwolf, in 1575, counted twenty-four; Dandini, in 1600, and Thevenot, about fifty years after, enumerated twenty-three, which Maundrell, in 1697, states were reduced to sixteen. Dr. Pococke, in 1738, found fifteen standing, and one which had been recently blown down. Burckhardt, in 1810, counted eleven or twelve; twenty-five others were very large ones, about fifty of middling size, and more than three hundred smaller and young ones. Lastly, in 1818, Dr. Richardson found that the old cedars, "the glory of Lebanon," were no more than seven in number. In the course of another century, it is probable that not a vestige of them will remain, and the predictions of the prophets will then be most literally fulfilled:—"Lebanon is ashamed and hewn down. The high ones of stature shall be hewn down: Lebanon shall fall mightily." (Isa. xxxiii. 9; x. 33, 34.) "Upon the mountains and in all the valleys his branches are fallen; to the end that none of all the trees by the water exalt themselves for their height, neither shoot up the top among the thick boughs." (Ezek. xxxi. 12, 14.) "Open thy doors, O Lebanon, that the fire may destroy thy cedars. The cedar is fallen; the forest of the vintage is come down." (Zech. xi. 1, 2.)

The trunks of the old trees are covered with the names of travellers and other persons who have visited them, some of which go as far back as 1640. These trunks are described by Burckhardt as seeming to be quite dead; their wood is of a gray teint. Maundrell, in 1697, measured one, which he found to be twelve yards and six inches in girth, and thirty-seven yards in the spread of its boughs: at above five or six yards from the ground it was divided into five limbs, each of which was equal to a great tree. Forty-one years afterward, (viz. 1738,) Dr. Pococke measured one which had the roundest body, though not the largest, and found it twenty-four feet in circumference; another, with a sort of triple body and of a triangular figure, measured twelve feet on each side. In 1818, Dr. Richardson measured one, which he afterward discovered was not the largest in the clump, and found it to be thirty-two feet in circumference. Finally, in 1824, Mr. Madox rested under the branches of a cedar, which measured twenty-seven feet in circumference, a little way from the ground: after which he measured the largest of the trees now standing, which he found to be thirty-nine or forty feet in circumference: it has three very large stems, and seven large branches, with various smaller ones.

The cedars of Lebanon are frequently mentioned in the sacred writings. Besides their uncommon size and beauty of shape and foliage, (which must be borne in mind in order to enter fully into the meaning of the sacred writers,) they send forth a fragrant odour, which seems to be intended by "the smell of Lebanon." (Hos. xiv. 6. Sol. Song iv. 11.) Its timber was used in the erection of the first and second temple at Jerusalem, as well as of the palace of Solomon; and in the last-mentioned edifice, so much cedar-wood appears to have been used, that it was called "the house of the forest of Lebanon." (1 Kings vii. 2; x. 19.) The Tyrians used it in ship-building, (Ezek. xxvii. 5, 6.)—HORNE.

[*See engraving of the* CEDARS OF LEBANON, *in the* COMPREHENSIVE COMMENTARY.]

Ver. 7. And I will feed the flock of slaughter, *even* you, O poor of the flock. And I took unto me two staves; the one I called Beauty, and the other I called Bands: and I fed the flock.

Written obligations were cancelled in different ways; one was by blotting or drawing a line across them, and another by striking them through with a nail; in both cases the bond was rendered useless, and ceased to be valid. These customs the apostle applies to the death of Christ in his epistle to the Colossians: "Blotting out the handwriting of ordinances that was against us, which was contrary to us, and took it out of the way, nailing it to the cross." A rod was sometimes broken, as a sign that the covenant into which they had entered was nullified. A trace of this ancient custom is still discernible in our own country: the lord steward of England, when he resigns his commission, breaks his wand of office, to denote the termination of his power. Agreeably to this practice, the prophet Zechariah broke the staves of Beauty and Bands, the symbols of God's covenant with ancient Israel, to show them, that in consequence of their numerous and long-continued iniquities, he withdrew his distinguishing favour, and no longer acknowledged them as his peculiar people. This is the exposition given by the prophet himself: "And I took my staff, even Beauty, and cut it asunder, that I might break my covenant which I had made with all the people; and it was broken in that day. Then I cut asunder my other staff, even Bands, that I might break the brotherhood between Judah and Israel."—PAXTON.

CHAPTER XII.

Ver. 6. In that day will I make the governors of Judah like a hearth of fire among the wood, and like a torch of fire in a sheaf; and they shall devour all the people round about, on the right hand and on the left: and Jerusalem shall be inhabited again in her own place, *even* in Jerusalem.

See on Joel 1. 19.

CHAPTER XIII.

Ver. 4. And it shall come to pass in that day, *that* the prophets shall be ashamed every one of his vision, when he hath prophesied: neither shall they wear a rough garment to deceive.

See on Is. 20. 3.

Ver. 6. And *one* shall say unto him, What *are* these wounds in thy hands? Then he shall answer, *Those* with which I was wounded *in* the house of my friends.

See on Lev. 19. 36.

Ver. 9. And I will bring the third part through the fire, and will refine them as silver is refined, and will try them as gold is tried.

The people of the East try the QUALITY of gold by the TOUCH. Thus, they have a small stone on which they first rub a needle of KNOWN quality: they then take the article they wish to try, and rub it near to the mark left by the other, and by comparing the two, they judge of the value of that which they "try." In those regions there are not any MARKS by which we can judge of the STANDARD, except in the way alluded to. Under such circumstances, there cannot be any wonder that there is much which is NOT "fine gold;" and such is the skill of some of the goldsmiths, they often deceive the most practised eye. The grand secret of ALCHYMY, by which other metals could be transmuted into gold, has never been FULLY divulged, but multitudes believe that certain individuals have this knowledge. Nor was that invaluable acquirement confined to Hindoos; for "Diocletian caused a diligent inquiry to be made for all the ancient books which treated of the admirable art of making gold and silver, and without pity committed them to the flames, apprehensive, as we are assured, lest the opulence of the Egyptians should inspire them with confidence to rebel against the empire." "The conquest of Egypt by the Arabs diffused that vain science over the globe."

Numbers in the East waste their entire property in trying to acquire this wonderful secret. Not long ago a party of the "gold-makers," having heard of a very charitable man, went to him and said they had heard of his good deeds, and in order to enable him to be more benevolent, they offered, at a trifling expense, to make him a large quantity of gold. The kind-hearted creature was delighted at the thought, and furnished the required materials, among which, it must be observed, was a considerable quantity of gold. The time came for making the precious metal, and the whole was cast into the crucible, the impostors taking care to put in an extra quantity of gold. When it was nearly ready, the alchymists threw in some stalks of an unknown plant, and pronounced certain incantations: after which the contents were turned out, and there the astonished man saw a great deal more gold than he had advanced. Such an opportunity was not to be lost; he therefore begged them to make him a much larger quantity, and after some objections the knaves consented, taking good care immediately to decamp with the whole amount. An ARMENIAN gentleman, who died at the age of 82, as is recorded in the Madras Gazette of July 22, 1830, had expended the whole of his property, amounting to 30,000 pagodas, in search of the philosopher's stone, but left the world a beggar.

"With crucible and furnace, bursting on his trunk,
His last remains of blissful fervour sunk."—ROBERTS.

CHAPTER XIV.

Ver. 18. And if the family of Egypt go not up and come not, that *have* no *rain*, there shall be the plague wherewith the LORD will smite the heathen that come not up to keep the feast of tabernacles.

See on 1 Kings 17. 1.

Ver. 20. In that day shall there be upon the bells of the horses, HOLINESS UNTO THE LORD; and the pots in the LORD'S house shall be like the bowls before the altar.

The finest breed of Arabian horses is in this country, and has furnished us with those we make use of for the turf. They are here chiefly articles of luxury, used only in war, or for parade. The governor has a large stud opposite the house where I live, which affords me much pleasure, as I pay them frequent visits. They are small, but finely shaped and extremely active. Of this I had an opportunity of judging yesterday, when the cavalry had a field-day in the great square, which, from the mode of exercise, called to my mind the idea of our ancient tilts and tournaments. The horses were sumptuously caparisoned, being adorned with gold and silver trappings, *bells hung round their necks*, and rich housings. The riders were in handsome Turkish dresses, with white turbans, and the whole formed to me a new and pleasing spectacle. (Rooke's Travels to the Coast of Arabia Felix.)—BURDER.

MALACHI.

CHAPTER I.

Ver. 1. The burden of the word of the LORD to Israel by Malachi.

The prophecy is here called "burden," a term which frequently occurs elsewhere, and which is usually understood as equivalent to "burdensome prophecy," or such as denounced heavy and grievous things. But from the following passage of Jeremiah, it would seem that that interpretation does not universally hold: "And as for the prophet, and the priest, and the people, that shall say, The burden of the Lord, I will even punish that man and his house. Thus shall ye say every one to his neighbour, and every one to his brother, What hath the Lord answered? and, What hath the Lord spoken? And the burden of the Lord shall he mention no more: for every man's word shall be his burden; for ye have perverted the words of the living God, of the Lord of hosts our God. Thus shalt thou say to the prophet, What hath the Lord answered thee? and, What hath the Lord spoken? But since ye say, The burden of the Lord; therefore thus saith the Lord, Because you say this word, The burden of the Lord, and I have sent unto you, saying, Ye shall not say, The burden of the Lord." (Jer. xxiii. 34—38.) This has evidently the air of a prohibition against taking the word in that unfavourable sense. The original term *massa*, from a root signifying to *bear*, *carry*, *take up*, is of doubtful import, and sometimes signifies *a burden*, and sometimes what was *borne*, *carried*, or *delivered* from one to another, whether a thing or a word, and so was used for a prophecy or message from God, or other speech or doctrine. The Jews, therefore, regarding the messages received from God, and delivered to them by the prophets, as things grievous and burdensome, called the word thus spoken, *a burden*, by way of reproach, meaning that it always portended evil, and never good, or in other words, a calamitous prophecy. But God, seeing the wickedness of their hearts, charges them with perverting his word, and forbids them any more so to abuse it. We infer that the term does not originally and exclusively imply a grievous and heavy burden, but simply a message, whether its import were joyous or afflictive. This is confirmed by Zech. xii. 1, where it is prefixed to the promise of good things.—BUSH.

Ver. 4. Whereas Edom saith, We are impoverished, but we will return and build the desolate places; thus saith the LORD of hosts, They shall build, but I will throw down; and they shall call them, The border of wickedness, and, The people against whom the LORD hath indignation for ever.

See on Jer. 49. 15—17, and Joel 3. 19.

Astonishment, for which language can scarcely find utterance, is the sentiment expressed by every traveller who has been able to explore the magnificent ruins of the once proud metropolis of Idumea or Edom. A narrow and circuitous defile, surrounded on each side by lofty and precipitous or perpendicular rocks, forms the approach to the desolate yet magnificent scene delineated in our engraving. The ruins of the city here burst upon the view in their full grandeur, shut in on the opposite side by barren craggy precipices, from which numerous ravines and valleys branch out in all directions; the sides of the mountains, covered with an endless variety of excavated tombs and private dwellings, present altogether the most singular scene that can well be conceived. In further confirmation of the identity of the site, and the accuracy of the application of the prophecy of Jeremiah, it may be added, that the name of this capital, in all the various languages in which it occurs, implies A ROCK.

The theatre, which is seen on the left of our view, is the first object which presents itself to the traveller on entering PETRA from the eastward. Captains Irby and Mangles state that it was entirely hewn out of the live rock. The scene was unfortunately built, and not excavated. Fragments of columns are strewed on the ground in front. This theatre is surrounded by sepulchres. Every avenue leading to it is full of them; and it may be safely affirmed, that one hundred of the largest dimensions are visible from it. Indeed, throughout almost every quarter of this metropolis, the depositories of the dead must have presented themselves constantly to the eyes of the inhabitants, and have almost outnumbered the inhabitants of the living. There is a long line of them, not far from the theatre, at such an angle as not to be comprehended from the view of it, but which must have formed a principal object for the city itself.

"The largest of the sepulchres had originally three stories, of which the lowest presented four portals, with large columns set between them; and the second and third, a row of eighteen Ionic columns each, attached to the façade: the live rock being insufficient for the total elevation, a part of the story was grafted on in masonry, and is for the most part fallen away. The four portals of the basement open into as many chambers, but all sepulchral, and without any communication between them. In one were three recesses, which seem to have been ornamented with marble or some other extraneous material.

"Of all the ruins of PETRA, the mausoleums and sepulchres are among the most remarkable; and they give the clearest indication of ancient and long-continued royalty and of courtly grandeur. Their immense number corroborates the accounts given of their successive kings and princes by Moses and Strabo, though a period of eighteen hundred years intervened between the dates of their respective records concerning them. The structure of the sepulchres also shows that many of them are of a more recent date. Great must have been the opulence of a city which could dedicate such monuments to the memory of its rulers. But the long line of the kings and nobles of Idumea has for ages been cut off: they are without any representative now, without any memorial but the multitude and magnificence of their unvisited sepulchres. 'No more shall they boast of the renown of the kingdom; and all her princes shall utterly fail.' (Bp. Lowth's translation of Isa. xxxiv. 12.)

"Amid the mausoleums and sepulchres, the remains of temples or palaces, and the multiplicity of tombs,—which all form, as it were, the grave of Idumea, where its ancient splendour is interred,—there are edifices, the Greek and Roman architecture of which decides that they were *built* long posterior to the era of the prophets."—"They shall *build*, but I will throw down." (Mal. i. 4.)—HORNE.

Ver. 7. Ye offer polluted bread upon my altar; and ye say, Wherein have we polluted thee? In that ye say, The table of the LORD *is* contemptible.

"In that ye say." They said, in effect, that the altar of Jehovah was vile and contemptible, by offering on it torn, blind, lame, and sick victims.—NEWCOMB.

Ver. 8. And if ye offer the blind for sacrifice, *is it* not evil? and if ye offer the lame and sick, *is it* not evil? offer it now unto thy governor; will he be pleased with thee, or accept thy person? saith the LORD of hosts.

Though things of very little value are sometimes offered as presents, those to whom presents are made do not think themselves always obliged graciously to accept every thing that is brought, or even to dissemble their dislike; they frequently reject the present, and refuse the favour sought. The behaviour of an aga in Egypt to Dr. Pococke, demonstrates this; as does also this passage of Capt. Norden: "The cashef of Esna was encamped in this place. He made us come ashore. I waited immediately upon him, with some small presents. He received me very civilly, and ordered coffee to be served me. But he refused absolutely what I offered him as a present, and let me know by the interpreter, that in the places from whence we were come, we had given things of greater value, and that we ought not to show less respect to him." Something of the like nature appears in many other passages in travels.

If a present was not somewhat proportionate to the quality of the person applied to, the circumstances of him that offered it, and the value of the favour asked, it was rejected. Lambs and sheep were often given as presents. So the cashef I have been speaking of, made Norden and his company a present the next day of two very fat sheep, together with a great basket of bread. The reys, or boatmen, that had carried them up the Nile, we are told, in like manner, came to see them three days before, and made them a present of an excellent sheep, together with a basket of Easter bread. Perhaps we may be ready to imagine presents of this kind were only made to travellers that wanted provisions; but this would be a mistake. Sir John Chardin, in his MS. expressly tells us, "it is the custom of the East for poor people, and especially those that live in the country, to make presents to their lords of lambs and sheep, as an offering, tribute, or succession. Presents to men, like offerings to God, expiate offences." So D'Arvieux mentions lambs among the things offered to him as presents, when he officiated as secretary to the great emir of the Arabs. The Jewish people were in a low state in the time of Malachi, and almost entirely engaged in country business.

How energetic, if we assemble these circumstances together, is the expostulation of the prophet! "If ye offer the blind for sacrifice, is it not evil? And if ye offer the lame and the sick, is it not evil? Offer it now unto thy governor, will he be pleased with thee, or accept thy person?" Mal. i. 8. When they made presents of lambs or sheep, they brought those that were very fat: would a Jewish governor have accepted one that was blind, and consequently half starved? or pining with lameness or sickness?—HARMER.

Ver. 13. Ye said also, Behold, what a weariness *is it!* and ye have snuffed at it, saith the LORD of hosts: and ye brought *that which was* torn, and the lame, and the sick; thus ye brought an offering: should I accept this of your hand? saith the LORD.

The margin has, instead of "and ye have snuffed at it," "or whereas ye might have blown it away." The marginal reading is, I doubt not, the best. The Jews had complained of the "WEARINESS" of their duties: they were tired of making offerings, and those they did offer were "polluted," or "lame," or "blind;" whereas, instead of those duties being burdensome, they were so LIGHT that they might have BLOWN them away. Does a person complain of his numerous labours or duties, another will ask, "What are they? why, a breath will blow them away." "Alas! I have many things to attend to."—"Fy on you for talking so; if you BLOW on them they will go."—ROBERTS.

CHAPTER II.

Ver. 3. Behold, I will corrupt your seed, and spread dung upon your faces, *even* the dung of your solemn feasts, and *one* shall take you away with it.

In the 11th verse of this chapter, allusion is again made to the *heathenism* of Judah: they had "married the daughter of a strange god." "Dung upon your faces." What can this refer to? Probably to the custom of the IDOLATERS, of spreading the ashes of COW-DUNG on their FACES, and to the marginal reference of Deut. xxix. 17, "dungy gods," on which see the remarks.—ROBERTS.

Ver. 12. The LORD will cut off the man that doeth this, the master and the scholar, out of the tabernacles of Jacob, and him that offereth an offering unto the LORD of hosts.

"The master and the scholar." This should rather be rendered, "the watchman and the answerer," as Arias Montanus has it, *vigilantem et respondentem.* The true explanation is probably to be brought from the temple service, in which there was appointed a constant watch, day and night, by the Levites; and among them this seems to have belonged particularly to the singers, 1 Chron. ix. 33. Now the watches in the East are, to this day, performed by a loud cry from time to time, by the watchmen, one after another, to mark the hour, and that very frequently, in order to show that they are constantly attentive to their duty. Tavernier remarks, that "the watchmen in the camps go their rounds, crying one after another, "God is one, He is merciful;" and often add, "Take heed to yourselves." The hundred and thirty-fourth Psalm gives us an example of the temple-watch. The whole Psalm is nothing more than the alternate cry of the two different divisions of the watch. The allusion is similar in the passage before us. (See Lowth on Is. lxii. 6.)—BUSH.

Ver. 14. Yet ye say, Wherefore? Because the LORD hath been witness between thee and the wife of thy youth, against whom thou hast dealt treacherously: yet *is* she thy companion, and the wife of thy covenant. 15. And did not he make one? Yet had he the residue of the Spirit. And wherefore one? That he might seek a godly seed. Therefore take heed to your spirit, and let none deal treacherously against the wife of his youth.

"And did not he make one?" This, Madan contends, (Thelypthora, vol. 1, p. 135,) should be rendered, "and did not one make?" The mass of commentators, he remarks, misled by translators, understand the words as signifying that in the beginning God made but *one woman;* He had the residue of the spirit, i. e. of power, and therefore could have made more women for Adam, if he had seen fit. To this interpretation he objects, that the original word אחד cannot signify *one woman,* inasmuch as it is not of the feminine, but of the masculine gender. Besides which, to read it in this manner requires an unnatural transposition of the words. He prefers, therefore, the rendering, "Did not *one* make?" as v. 10, "Have we not all *one* Father? Did not *one* God create us? Did not *one,* or *The one,* make both you and your Jewish wives? Did he not form both of you *naturally* of the same seed of Abraham, and *spiritually* by the same holy dispensation and ordinances? And he hath (or, hath he not) the residue of the spirit? i. e. Hath he not the same *power* he ever had? Is his hand shortened at all so that he cannot complete your restoration if he pleases, or punish you still more severely if ye continue disobedient to his will? And wherefore one? What did he seek? A godly seed; or, Heb. *a seed of God,* a holy seed. Therefore take heed to your spirit, i. e. to your temper, your affections. Curb your irregular passions, and let none deal treacherously against the wife of his youth, by putting her away, and taking these idolatresses; for I the Lord hate putting away."

The consideration of the relation in which they stood to Jehovah; he their common Father, they his professing children; was one argument against their separating. Another was, that as the Lord sought a *godly seed* in their offspring, by their being devoted to him in their earliest infancy, then brought up in the nurture and admonition of the Lord, this design would be defeated by their taking idolatrous women, who, instead of devoting the children to Jehovah, would be apt to bring them up to the worship of their idols, and an *ungodly seed* would be the consequence. Lastly, he had forbidden *divorce* from the beginning, for he hateth putting away at any rate; but how much more to see his own professing daughters put away, that his own professing sons might marry the daughters of a strange god. This was indeed doing an abominable thing, which God hated.—BUSH.

CHAPTER III.

Ver. 14. Ye have said, It *is* vain to serve God: and what profit *is it* that we have kept his ordinance, and that we have walked mournfully before the LORD of hosts?

The margin, for "mournfully," has, "in black." Here we have another instance of the base ingratitude of the people: "It is vain to serve God."—"In black." "My friend, why has your face become so black?" "Alas! my sorrow, my sorrow; therefore my face is full of blackness." "Yes, my sorrows are chased away, like dew before the sun, and my face no longer gathers blackness."—ROBERTS.

CHAPTER IV.

Ver. 2. But unto you that fear my name shall the Sun of righteousness arise with healing in his wings; and ye shall go forth and grow up as calves of the stall.

The late Mr. Robinson, of Cambridge, called upon a friend just as he had received a letter from his son, who was surgeon on board a vessel then lying off Smyrna. The son mentioned to his father, that every morning about sunrise a fresh gale of air blew from the sea across the land, and from its wholesomeness and utility in clearing the infected air, this wind is always called the Doctor. "Now," says Mr. Robinson, "it strikes me that the prophet Malachi, who lived in that quarter of the world, might allude to this circumstance, when he says, The Sun of righteousness shall arise with *healing in his wings*. The Psalmist mentions the *wings of the wind*, and it appears to me that this salubrious breeze, which attends the rising of the sun, may be properly enough considered as the wings of the sun, which contain such healing influences, rather than the beams of the sun, as the passage has been commonly understood."—BURDER.

Ver. 3. And ye shall tread down the wicked; for they shall be ashes under the soles of your feet, in the day that I shall do *this*, saith the LORD of hosts.

See on Is. 41. 25.

One sort of mortar made in the East is composed of one part of sand, two of wood-ashes, and three of lime, wel mixed together, and beaten for three days and nights incessantly with wooden mallets. (Shaw.) Chardin mentions this circumstance, and applies it to this passage of the prophet, supposing there is an allusion in these words to the making of mortar in the East, with ashes collected from their baths. Some learned men have supposed the wicked here are compared to ashes, because the prophet had been speaking of their destruction under the notion of burning, ver. 1; but the sacred writers do not always keep close to those figures which they first propose; the paragraph of Malachi is a proof of this assertion, and if they had, he would not have spoken of treading on the wicked like ashes if it had not been customary in these times to tread ashes which it seems was done to make mortar.—HARMER.

END OF THE OLD TESTAMENT.

GENERAL VIEW OF PETRA FROM THE NORTH-EAST.—Mal 1: 4. Jer 49.

NAZARETH.—Matt. 2:23. Page 576

THE

NEW TESTAMENT.

THE GOSPEL ACCORDING TO MATTHEW.

CHAPTER I.

Ver. 18. Now the birth of Jesus Christ was on this wise: When as his mother Mary was espoused to Joseph, before they came together, she was found with child of the Holy Ghost.

Espousing or betrothing was a solemn promise of marriage made by two persons, each to the other, at such a distance of time as they agreed upon. The manner of performing this espousal was either by a writing, or by a piece of silver given to the bride, or by cohabitation. The writing that was prepared on these occasions ran in this form: "On such a day of such a month, in such a year, A, the son of A, has said to B, the daughter of B, be thou my spouse according to the law of Moses and the Israelites, and I will give thee, for the portion of thy virginity, the sum of two hundred zuzim, as it is ordained by the law. And the said B has consented to become his spouse upon these conditions, which the said A has promised to perform upon the day of marriage. To this the said A obliges himself: and for this he engages all his goods, even as far as the cloak which he wears upon his shoulder. Moreover, he promises to perform all that is intended in contracts of marriage in favour of the Israelitish women. Witnesses, A, B, C." The promise by a piece of silver, and without writing, was made before witnesses, when the young man said to his mistress, "Receive this piece of silver, as a pledge that you shall become my spouse." The engagement by cohabitation, according to the rabbins, was allowed by the law, but it had been wisely forbidden by the ancients, because of the abuses that might happen, and to prevent the inconvenience of clandestine marriages. After such espousal was made, (which was generally when the parties were young,) the woman continued with her parents several months, if not some years, before she was brought home and her marriage consummated.—Calmet.

CHAPTER II.

Ver. 1. Now when Jesus was born in Bethlehem of Judea in the days of Herod the king, behold, there came wise men from the east to Jerusalem.

There is no traveller in Palestine, of any nation, whatever may be his creed, who does not visit Bethlehem, where "Jesus was born in the days of Herod the king." (Matt. ii. 1.) Though now reduced to a village, anciently it was a city, (Ruth iii. 11. iv. 1,) and was fortified by Rehoboam. (2 Chron. xi. 6.) In Matt. ii. 1, 5, it is called Bethlehem of Judea, in order to distinguish it from another town of the same name, which had been allotted to the tribe of Zebulun. In Luke ii. 4, it is termed the "city of David," because David was born and educated there.

Two roads lead from Jerusalem to Bethlehem: the shortest, which is most used, passes over ground extremely rocky and barren, diversified only by some cultivated patches, bearing a scanty crop of grain, and by banks of wild flowers, which grow in great profusion. This town, or rather village, is pleasantly situated about six miles southwest of Jerusalem, on the brow of a steep hill, in a very fertile soil, which only wants cultivation to render it what the name, "Bethlehem," imports,—*a house of bread.* At the further extremity, like a citadel, stands the convent of Saint Giovanni, which contains the Church of the Nativity. A star is introduced into our view, in order to guide the reader's eye to this spot. This convent is divided among the Greek, Roman, and Armenian Christians, to each of whom are assigned separate portions, as well for lodging as for places of worship; but on certain days they may all perform their devotions at the altars which are erected over the most memorable spots within these sacred walls. This convent is entered through a door strongly bound with iron, so low as to oblige the party entering to stoop considerably, and too narrow to allow more than one person to pass at a time. This leads into the Church of the Nativity, which was erected by the Empress Helena, on the site of a temple of Adonis, which was built here by the Emperor Hadrian, in his hatred against all who professed the Christian name and faith.

About a mile to the northeast of Bethlehem is a deep valley, in which Dr. Clarke imagined that he halted at the identical fountain or well, for the delicious water of which David longed. (2 Sam. xxiii. 15—18.) Here, according to tradition, is the field where the shepherds kept watch by night, when the angels announced to them the birth of our Lord. (Luke ii. 8—11.) When this spot was visited by Mr. Carne, two fine and venerable trees stood in the centre; and the earth around it was thickly covered with flowers: he represents it as "so sweet and romantic a spot, that it would be painful to doubt its identity."

Bethlehem is now a poor village, with a population of about three hundred inhabitants, most of whom are Christians. Their number was dreadfully reduced by the plague in the year 1832; and though this village is only a few miles distant from Jerusalem, the mortality is generally much greater here than in the metropolis of the Holy Land. The Bethlehemites are represented by all travellers as a bold and fierce race, of whom both Turks and Arabs stand in awe. The greater part of them gain their livelihood by making beads, carving mother-of-pearl shells with sacred subjects, and other trinkets, which are highly valued and eagerly purchased by the devout visiters. The monks of Bethlehem claim the exclusive privilege of marking the limbs and bodies of such pilgrims as choose to submit to the operation, with crosses, stars, and monograms, by means of gunpowder;—an operation this, which is always painful, and sometimes dangerous. This practice is very ancient; it is noticed by Virgil (Æneid. lib. iv. v. 146) and by Pomponius Mela, (lib. xxi.) Dr. Clarke remarks, that there rarely exists an instance among the minor popular superstitions of the Greek and Roman churches, but its origin may be found in more remote antiquity, and very often among the religious customs of the heathen nations.—HORNE.

Ver. 11. And when they were come into the house, they saw the young child with Mary his mother, and fell down, and worshipped him: and when they had opened their treasures, they presented unto them gifts; gold, and frankincense, and myrrh.

The birth of a son is always a time of great festivity in the East; hence the relations come together, to congratulate the happy parents, and to present their *gifts* to the little stranger. Some bring the silver anklets; others, the bracelets, or ear-rings, or silver cord for the loins. Others, however, take gold, and a variety of needful articles. The wise men did not make presents as a matter of charity, but to show their *affection* and *respect*. When the infant son of a king is shown, the people make their *obeisance* to him.—ROBERTS.

Ver. 18. In Rama was there a voice heard, lamentation, and weeping, and great mourning, Rachel weeping *for* her children, and would not be comforted, because they are not.

See on ch. 9. 23.

Ver. 23. And he came and dwelt in a city called Nazareth: that it might be fulfilled which was spoken by the prophets, He shall be called a Nazarene.

Nassara, the Nazareth of the scriptures, is called by Maundrell an inconsiderable village; by Brown, a pleasant one, with a respectable convent; and in Dr. Clarke's visit was said to have so declined, under the oppressive tyranny of Djezzar's government, as to seem destined to maintain its ancient reputation, since now, as of old, one might ask, with equal reason, *Can there any good thing come out of Nazareth?* John i. 46. This town, or village, is situated in a deep valley, not on the top of a hill, as has been erroneously stated, but rather on the side of a hill, nearer its base than its summit, facing to the southeast, and having above it the rocky eminence which we had passed over in approaching it. The fixed inhabitants are estimated at about two thousand, five hundred of whom are Catholic Christians, about three hundred Maronites, and two hundred Mohammedans; the rest being schismatic Greeks. These are all Arabs of the country, and notwithstanding the small circle in which their opposing faiths meet, it is said to their honour, that they live together in mutual forbearance and tranquillity. The private dwellings of the town, to the number of about two hundred and fifty, are built of stone, which is a material always at hand: they are flat-roofed, being in general only of one story, but are sufficiently spacious and commodious for the accommodation of a numerous poor family. The streets are steep, from the inclination of the hill on which they stand; narrow, from custom; and dirty, from the looseness of the soil. Of the public buildings, the mosque is the most conspicuous from without, and is, indeed, a neat edifice; it has six arches on one of its sides, for we could see no more of it, as it is enclosed within a wall of good masonry, and furnished with a plain whitened thin arch, surrounded by a gallery, and surmounted by the crescent: the whole rising from the centre of the town, as if to announce the triumph of its dominion to those approaching it from afar. The Greeks have their church on the southeast edge of the town, at the foot of the hill; the Maronites theirs in front of the Franciscan convent. The church is built over a grotto, held sacred from a belief of its being the scene of the angels announcing to Mary her favour with God, and her conception and bearing of the Saviour. On entering it we passed over a white marble pavement, ornamented in the centre with a device in Mosaic, and descended by a flight of marble steps into a grotto, beneath the body of the church. In the first compartment of this subterraneous sanctuary, we were told had stood the mass which constitutes the famous chapel of Loretto, in Italy; and the friars assured us, with all possible solemnity, that the angels appointed to the task took out this mass from the rock, and flew with it, first to Dalmatia and afterward to Loretto, where it now stands: and that in measuring the mass itself, and the place from which it had been taken, they had found them to correspond in every respect, neither the one by the voyage, nor the other by age, having lost or altered any part of its size or shape. Proceeding farther in, we were shown a second grotto, or a continuation of the first, with two red granite pillars, of about two feet in diameter, at its entrance, and were told that one marked the spot where the angel stood when he appeared to Mary, exclaiming, *Hail, thou that art highly favoured, the Lord is with thee: blessed art thou among women.* Luke i. 28. The pillar on the right is still perfect, but that on the left has a piece of its shaft broken out, leaving a space of about a foot and a half between the upper and under fragment; the latter of those continuing still to be supported by being firmly imbedded in the rock above, offers to the eyes of believing visiters, according to the expression of the friars, a standing miracle of the care which Christ takes of his church, as they insist on its being supported by the hand of God alone. The grotto here, though small, and about eight feet in height, remains still in its original roughness, the roof being slightly arched. In the outer compartment, from whence the chapel of Loretto is said to have been taken, the roof, as well as the sides, have been reshaped, and plastered, and ornamented, so that the original dimensions no longer remain. Within, however, all is left in its first rude state, to perpetuate to future ages the interesting fact which it is thought to record. Passing onward from hence, and ascending through narrow passages, over steps cut out of the rock, and turning a little to the right, we came to a chamber which the friars called La Cucina della Santa Madona; they here showed us the chimney of the hearth on which Mary warmed the food for Jesus, while yet a helpless infant, and where she baked the cakes for her husband's supper, when he returned from the labours of the day. This was an apartment of the house, as they observed, in which the Son of God lived so many years in subjection to man; as it is believed by all that he was brought up from childhood to manhood in Nazareth. The fact of Joseph and Mary having resided in this house, and used the very room in which we stood, as their kitchen, has nothing at all of improbability in it: and as excavated dwellings, in the side of a steep hill like this, would be more secure, and even more comfortable, than fabricated ones, it is quite as probable that this might have really been the residence of the holy family, as of any other. The synagogue in which Jesus read and expounded the prophet Esaias on the sabbath, is shown here within the town, while the precipice from which the exasperated people would have hurled him, is pointed out at a place more than a mile distant, to the southward, and on the other side of the vale.—BUCKINGHAM.

CHAPTER III.

Ver. 4. And the same John had his raiment of camel's hair, and a leathern girdle about his loins; and his meat was locusts and wild honey.

See on Mark 1. 6.

His raiment was not made of the fine hair of that animal, whereof an elegant kind of cloth is made, which is thence called camlet, (in imitation of which, though made of wool, is the English camlet,) but of the long and shaggy hair of camels, which is in the East manufactured into a coarse stuff, anciently worn by monks and anchorites. It is only when understood in this way, that the words suit the description here given of John's manner of life.—CAMPBELL.

The girdle is an indispensable article in the dress of an Oriental; it has various uses; but the principal one is to tuck up their long flowing vestments, that they may not incommode them in their work, or on a journey. The Jews, according to some writers, wore a double girdle, one of greater breadth, with which they girded their tunic when they prepared for active exertions: the other they wore under their shirt, around their loins. This under-girdle they reckon necessary to distinguish between the heart, and the less honourable parts of the human frame. The upper girdle was sometimes made of leather, the material of which the girdle of John the Baptist was made; but it was more commonly fabricated of worsted, often very artfully woven into a variety of figures, and made to fold several times about the body; one end of which being doubled back, and sewn along the edges, serves them for a purse, agreeably to the acceptation of ζωνη in the scriptures, which is translated purse in several places of the New Testament.—PAXTON.

The dress of John greatly resembled that of the interior nations of South Africa, only substituting a skin cloak for one of camel's hair; and his food that of the wild Bushmen during the locust season. Locusts resemble gigantic grasshoppers furnished with wings. When they come, like innumerable armies, they certainly destroy all vegetation; but their carcasses are sufficient for the support of human life. The wild Bushmen kill millions of them, which they gather together, dry them in the sun, and then grind them into powder, which they mix up with wild honey, or what the bees deposite upon rocks, trees, and bushes, and on this compound live a part of the year; so that the locusts, which are the greatest scourge of more civilized people, are considered as welcome visiters by the wild Bushmen, who hail their approach. Indeed, the crocus and locust seasons are called their harvests; thus showing that what is a judgment to one nation is a mercy to another.—CAMPBELL.

Ver. 11. I indeed baptize you with water unto repentance: but he that cometh after me is mightier than I, whose shoes I am not worthy to bear: he shall baptize you with the Holy Ghost, and *with* fire.

The custom of loosing the sandals from off the feet of an eastern worshipper was ancient and indispensable. It is also commonly observed in visits to great men. The sandals or slippers are pulled off at the door, and either left there, or given to a servant to bear. The person to bear them means an inferior domestic, or attendant upon a man of high rank, to take care of, and return them to him again. This was the work of servants among the Jews: and it was reckoned so servile, that it was thought too mean for a scholar or a disciple to do. The Jews say, "all services which a servant does for his master a disciple does for his master, except unloosing his shoes." John thought it was too great an honour for him to do that for Christ, which was thought too mean for a disciple to do for a wise man. —GILL.

A respectable man *never* goes out without his servant or attendant; thus, he has always some one to talk with, and to do any thing he may require. When the ground is smooth, or where there is soft grass to walk on, the sandals are taken off, and the servant carries them in his hand. The devoted, the humble John, did not consider himself worthy to bear the sandals of his divine Master.—ROBERTS.

Ver. 12. Whose fan *is* in his hand, and he will thoroughly purge his floor, and gather his wheat into the garner; but will burn up the chaff with unquenchable fire.

There is, in what the Baptist here declares, an evident allusion to the custom of burning the chaff after winnowing, that it might not be blown back again, and so be mingled with the wheat. There was danger, lest, after they had been separated, the chaff should be blown again among the wheat by the changing of the wind. To prevent this they put fire to it at the windward side, which *crept* on and never gave over till it had consumed all the chaff. In this sense it was an *unquenchable fire*. See also Psalm lxxxiii. 13, 14. Isaiah v. 24.—BURDER.

After the grain is trodden out, they winnow it by throwing it up against the wind with a shovel—the το πτυον of the gospels according to Matthew and Luke, there rendered a fan, which is too cumbersome a machine to be intended by the evangelist. The text should rather run, whose shovel or fork, the οργανον οδοντικον, (which is a portable instrument,) is in his hand, agreeably to the practice recorded by Isaiah, who mentions both the shovel and the fan: "The oxen likewise, and the young asses that ear the ground, shall eat clean provender, which hath been winnowed with the shovel and with the fan."

After the grain is winnowed, they lodge it in subterraneous magazines, as was formerly the custom of other nations; two or three hundred of these receptacles are sometimes to be found together, the smallest holding four hundred bushels. These grottoes are dug in the form of an oven, gradually enlarging towards the bottom, with one round opening at top; and this being close shut when the magazine is full, is covered over with earth, so as to remain perfectly concealed from an enemy. These magazines are sometimes discovered in the midst of a ploughed field; sometimes on the verge, and even in the middle of the highway. The same kind of granaries are used in Palestine as in Syria. Le Bruyn speaks of a number of deep pits at Rama, which he was told were designed for corn: and Rauwolf, of three very large vaults at Joppa, where the inhabitants laid up their corn, when he was in that country. The treasures in the field, consisting of wheat and of barley, of oil and of honey, which were offered to Ishmael, as a ransom for the lives of his captives, were undoubtedly laid up in the same kind of repositories. In dangerous and unsettled times like those of Jeremiah, it is quite common, even at present, for the Arabs to secure their corn and other effects, which they cannot carry along with them, in deep pits or subterraneous grottoes. Sir John Chardin, in a note upon this very passage of the prophet, says, "The eastern people in many places hide their corn in these concealments." To these various customs the Baptist alludes in his solemn warning to the multitudes concerning Christ: "Whose fan (rather whose shovel) is in his hand, and he will thoroughly purge his floor, and gather his wheat into the garner; but the chaff will he burn with unquenchable fire." And our Lord himself, in his parable of the good seed: "Gather ye together first the tares, and bind them in bundles to burn them; but gather the wheat into my barn."—PAXTON.

Ver. 16. And Jesus, when he was baptized, went up straightway out of the water: and lo, the heavens were opened unto him, and he saw the Spirit of God descending like a dove, and lighting upon him.

Many have supposed, that the third person of the trinity, on this occasion, assumed the real figure of a dove; but the sacred writer seems to refer, not to the shape, but to the manner in which the dove descends from the sky. Had it related to the shape or form, it would not have been ὡσει περιστεραν, as a dove; but ὡσει περιστερας, as of a dove. In this manner, the likeness of fire is expressed by the same evangelist, in the Acts of the Apostles: "There appeared cloven tongues (ὡσει πυρος) as of fire." The meaning of the clause therefore is, that as a dove hovers on the wing, and overshadows the place upon which she intends to perch, so did the Holy Spirit, in the form of a luminous cloud, like the Shechinah which rested on the tabernacle, gradually descend, hovering, and overshadowing the Saviour as he came up from the water. This exposition refutes another opinion, which was entertained by many of the ancients, that it was a real dove which alighted upon the head of our Lord; for if the sacred writer describes only the manner of descending, neither the form nor the real presence of a dove can be admitted. But although the evangelist alludes only to the manner in which that bird descends from the wing, he clearly recognises her as the chosen emblem of the Holy Spirit, the messenger of peace and joy to sinful and miserable men.—PAXTON.

CHAPTER IV.

Ver. 1. Then was Jesus led up of the Spirit into the wilderness to be tempted of the devil.

In sacred language, a mountainous, or less fruitful tract, where the towns and villages are thinly scattered, and single habitations few and far between, is distinguished by the name of the wilderness. The forerunner of our Lord resided in the wilderness of Judah till he commenced his public ministry. We are informed, in the book of Genesis, that Ishmael settled in the wilderness of Paran; and in the first book of Samuel, that David took refuge from the persecution of Saul in the same desert, where it appears the numerous flocks of Nabal the Carmelite were pastured. Such places, therefore, were not absolute deserts, but thinly peopled, or less fertile districts. But this remark will scarcely apply to the wilderness where our Lord was tempted of the devil. It is a most miserable, dry, and barren solitude, "consisting of high rocky mountains, so torn and disordered, as if the earth had here suffered some great convulsion, in which its very bowels had been turned outward." A more dismal and solitary place can scarcely be found in the whole earth. About one hour's journey from the foot of the mountains which environ this wilderness, rises the lofty Quarantania, which Maundrell was told is the mountain into which the devil carried our blessed Saviour, that he might show him all the kingdoms and glory of the world. It is, as the evangelist styles it, "an exceeding high mountain," and in its ascent both difficult and dangerous. It has a small chapel at the top, and another about half way up, founded on a prominent part of the rock. Near the latter are several caves and holes in the sides of the mountain, occupied formerly by hermits, and even in present times the resort of religious devotees, who repair to these lonely cells to keep their lent, in imitation of our Lord's fasting in the wilderness forty days.—Paxton.

Ver. 23. And Jesus went about all Galilee, teaching in their synagogues, and preaching the gospel of the kingdom, and healing all manner of sickness, and all manner of disease among the people.

The scribes ordinarily taught in the synagogues: but it was not confined to them, as it appears that Christ did the same. It has been questioned by what right Christ and his apostles, who had no public character among the Jews, taught in their synagogues. In answer to this Dr. Lightfoot observes, that though this liberty was not allowed to any illiterate person or mechanic, but to the learned only, they granted it to prophets and workers of miracles, and such as set up for heads and leaders of new sects, in order that they might inform themselves of their dogmata, and not condemn them unheard and unknown. Under these characters Christ and his apostles were admitted to this privilege.—Jennings.

Ver. 24. And his fame went throughout all Syria: and they brought unto him all sick people that were taken with divers diseases and torments, and those which were possessed with devils, and those which were lunatic, and those that had the palsy, and he healed them. 25. And there followed him great multitudes of people, from Galilee, and *from* Decapolis, and *from* Jerusalem, and *from* Judea, and *from* beyond Jordan.

The news that a foreign hakeem or doctor, was passing through the country, very soon was spread abroad; and at every halt our camp was thronged with the sick, not only of the village near to which we were encamped, but of all the surrounding villages. Many came several days' journey to consult our doctor, and were brought to him in spite of every difficulty and inconvenience; some came on asses, bolstered up with cushions, and supported by their relations; others on camels, whose rough pace must have been torture to any one in sickness. It may be conceived what a misfortune sickness must be in a country where there is no medical relief, nor even a wheeled conveyance to seek relief when it is at hand. The greatest credit is due to the medical gentlemen, who were attached, not only to our embassy, but to all preceding embassies, for the charity and humanity with which they relieved the wants of these poor people: they not only distributed their medicines gratis, but they as gratuitously bestowed their skill, their time, and their zeal, for which, it is grievous to say, in very few instances did they meet with corresponding gratitude."—Morier.

CHAPTER V.

Ver. 1. And seeing the multitudes, he went up into a mountain: and when he was set, his disciples came unto him.

We left our route to visit the elevated mount, where it is believed that Christ preached to his disciples that memorable sermon, concentrating the sum and substance of every Christian virtue. Having attained the highest point of it, a view was presented which, for its grandeur, independently of the interest excited by the different objects contained in it, has no parallel in the Holy Land.

From this situation we perceived that the plain, over which we had been so long riding, was itself very elevated. Far beneath appeared other plains, one lower than the other, in that regular gradation, concerning which observations were recently made, and extending to the surface of the Sea of Tiberias, or Sea of Galilee. This immense lake, almost equal in the grandeur of its appearance to that of Geneva, spreads its waters over all the lower territory, extending from the northeast towards the southwest, and then bearing east of us. Its eastern shore presents a sublime scene of mountains, extending towards the north and south, and seeming to close in at either extremity, both towards Chorazin, where the Jordan enters, and the Aulon or *Campus Magnus*, through which it flows to the Dead Sea. The cultivated plains reaching to its borders, which we beheld at an amazing depth below our view, resembled, by the various hues their different produce exhibited, the motley pattern of a vast carpet. To the north appeared snowy summits, towering beyond a series of intervening mountains, with unspeakable greatness. We considered them as the summits of Libanus; but the Arabs belonging to our caravan called the principal eminence Jebel el Sieh, saying it was near Damascus: probably, therefore, a part of the chain of Libanus. This summit was so lofty, that the snow entirely covered the upper part of it; not lying in patches, as I have seen it during summer, upon the tops of very elevated mountains, (for instance, that of Ben Nevis, in Scotland,) but investing all the higher part with that perfect white and smooth velvet-like appearance which snow only exhibits when it is very deep; a striking spectacle in such a climate, where the beholder, seeking protection from a burning sun, almost considers the firmament to be on fire. The elevated plains upon the mountainous territory, beyond the northern extremity of the lake, are called by a name, in Arabic, which signifies *The Wilderness*. To the southwest, at the distance of only twelve miles, we beheld Mount Tabor, having a conical form, and standing quite insular, upon the northern side of the plain of Esdraelon. The mountain whence this superb view was presented, consists entirely of limestone; the prevailing constituent of all the mountains in Greece, Asia Minor, Syria, Phenicia, and Palestine.

As we rode towards the Sea of Tiberias, the guides pointed to a sloping spot from the heights upon our right, whence we had descended, as the place where the miracle was accomplished by which our Saviour fed the multitude: it is therefore called *The Multiplication of Bread;* as the mount above, where the sermon was preached to the disciples, is called *The Mountain of Beatitudes*, from the expressions used in the beginning of that discourse. This part of the Holy Land is very full of wild animals. Antelopes are in great number. We had the pleasure of seeing these beautiful quadrupeds in their natural state, feeding among the thistles and tall herbage of these plains, and bounding before us occasionally as we disturbed them. The lake now continued in view upon our left. The wind rendered its surface rough, and called to mind the situation of our Saviour's disciples, when, in one of the small vessels which traverse these waters, they were tossed in a storm, and saw Jesus, in the fourth watch of the night, walking to them upon the waves, Matt. xiv. 24. Often as this subject has been painted, combining a number of circumstances adapted for the representation of sublimity, no artist has been aware of the uncommon grandeur of the scenery, memorable on account of the transaction. The lake of Gennesareth is surrounded by objects well calculated to heighten the solemn impression made by such a picture; and, independent of the local feelings likely to be excited in its contemplation, affords one of the most striking prospects in the Holy Land. It is by comparison alone that any due conception of the appearance it presents can be conveyed to the minds of those who have not seen it: and, speaking of it comparatively, it may be described as longer and finer than any of our Cumberland and Westmoreland lakes, although, perhaps, it yields in majesty to the stupendous features of Loch Lomond, in Scotland. It does not possess the vastness of the lake of Geneva, although it much resembles it in particular points of view. The lake of Locarno, in Italy, comes nearest to it in point of picturesque beauty, although it is destitute of any thing similar to the islands by which that majestic piece of water is adorned. It is inferior in magnitude, and, perhaps, in the height of its surrounding mountains, to the lake Asphaltites; but its broad and extended surface, covering the bottom of a profound valley, environed by lofty and precipitous eminences, added to the impression of a certain reverential awe under which every Christian pilgrim approaches it, give it a character of dignity unparalleled by any similar scenery. —CLARKE.

Sitting was the proper posture of masters or teachers. The form in which the master and his disciples sat, is thus described by Maimonides: "The master sits at the head, or in the chief place, and the disciples before him in a circuit, like a crown; so that they all see the master, and hear his words. The master may not sit upon a seat, and the scholars upon the ground; but either all upon the earth, or upon seats. Indeed from the beginning, or formerly, the master used to sit, and the disciples to stand; but before the destruction of the second temple, all used to teach their disciples sitting."—BURDER.

Ver. 2. And he opened his mouth and taught them.

Some have made impertinent observations respecting this mode of expression; he *opened* his mouth. When the Hindoos speak of a king, or a priest, or the gods, as giving instructions or commands, they use the same form of speech. But the word which is used to denote the opening of a door, or of any thing which requires to be unfolded, is *never* applied to the opening of the mouth of a beautiful or dignified speaker. For of that action in him, they say, his mouth *mallara-kurrathu*, i. e. *blossomed;* the flower unfolded itself: and there were its fair teints, and promised fruits. So the Redeemer *opened* his mouth, and taught them, saying.—ROBERTS.

Ver. 13. Ye are the salt of the earth: but if the salt have lost his savour, wherewith shall it be salted? it is thenceforth good for nothing, but to be cast out, and to be trodden under foot of men.

Our Lord's supposition of the salt losing its savour is illustrated by Mr. Maundrell, who tells us, that in the Valley of Salt near Gebul, and about four hours' journey from Aleppo, there is a small precipice, occasioned by the continual taking away of the salt. "In this," says he, "you may see how the veins of it lie. I broke a piece of it, of which the part was exposed to the rain, sun, and air, though it had the sparks and particles of salt, yet had perfectly lost its savour. The innermost, which had been connected to the rock, retained its savour, as I found by proof."—BURDER.

Ver. 18. For verily I say unto you, Till heaven and earth pass, one jot or one tittle shall in no wise pass from the law, till all be fulfilled.

It has been thought that this refers to one of those ducts, dashes, or corners of letters, which distinguish one letter from another, and nearly resemble each other. Other persons have apprehended that it refers to one of those little strokes in the tops of letters, which the Jews call crowns or spikes, in which they imagined great mysteries were contained. There were some persons among them who made it their business to search into the meaning of every letter, and of every one of these little horns or pricks that were upon the top of them. To this custom Christ is here supposed to refer.—BURDER.

Ver. 29. And if thy right eye offend thee, pluck it out, and cast *it* from thee: for it is profitable for thee that one of thy members should perish, and not *that* thy whole body should be cast into hell.

This *metaphor* is in common use to this day; hence people say of any thing which is valuable, "It is like my *vallutha-kan*," i. e. right eye! "Yes, yes, that child is the *right eye* of his father." "I can never give up that lady; she is my *right* eye." "That fellow forsake his sins! never; they are his right eye." "True, true; I will pull out my right eye." —ROBERTS.

Ver. 36. Neither shalt thou swear by thy head, because thou canst not make one hair white or black.

It was very common among the Orientals to swear by the head or the life of the king. Joseph, improperly yielding to the fashion of the country, swore by the life of Pharaoh; and this oath is still used in various regions of the East. According to Mr. Hanway, the most sacred oath among the Persians is by the head of the king: and Thevenot asserts, that to swear by the king's head is, in Persia, more authentic, and of greater credit, than if they swore by all that is most sacred in heaven and upon earth. In the time of our Lord, it seems to have been a common practice among the Jews to swear by this form; for, said he to the multitudes, "Neither shalt thou swear by thy head, because thou canst not make one hair white or black."—PAXTON.

Ver. 40. And if any man will sue thee at the law, and take away thy coat, let him have *thy* cloak also.

The laws of Moses prohibited the taking or keeping in pledge certain indispensable articles, such as,

1. "The upper garment of the poor, which served him also by night for a blanket," Exod. xxii. 25, 26. Deut. xxiv. 12, 13. If taken as a pledge, it was to be restored to him before sunset; "for," says Moses, or rather God by Moses, "it is his only covering, in which he inwraps his naked body. Under what, then, shall he sleep? If he cries for it unto me, I will hearken unto him; for I am merciful." The better to understand this law, we must know, that the upper garment of the Israelites (*simla* שמלה) was a large square piece of cloth, which they threw loosely over them, and which by the poor was also used for a blanket or coverlet to their beds. Dr. Shaw, in his travels through Barbary, has given the best description of it, under its modern Arabic name, *hyke*. It might be laid aside in the daytime, and, in fact, in walking it was so troublesome, that labouring people preferred being clear of it, and were then, what the ancients so often call *naked*. When they had to walk, they tucked it together, and hung it over their shoulder. By night it was indispensable to the poor man for a covering: at least, it was at the risk of his health, and even his life, by exposure to the cold, if he wanted it: for in southern climates the nights, particularly in the summer, are extremely cold.

It appears, however, that the above-quoted law of Moses concerning the upper garment had, by a very strange misconstruction, in process of time, given a handle to the exercise of a claim in the highest degree absurd. It is merely of pledge that Moses speaks; and the natural meaning of the law is that no one would leave his *under* garment in pledge, and go naked from the presence of his creditor with what he had borrowed; while, on the other hand, there might be frequent cases where a man, to the great detriment of his health, having pledged his *upper* garment, must lie all night without a covering. He, therefore, enacted the law in favour of the latter, and did not think it necessary to say a word about the former. But when the Jews came to regulate their procedure solely by the letter of his law, as *that* made no mention of the under garment, so in the time of Christ, we find cruel creditors claiming the under garment of their debtors; but, at the same time, quite conscientiously leaving with them the upper one, which Moses had expressly privileged. This I infer from a pas sage in the sermon on the mount, which though in itself obscure, receives great light from a comparison with Exod. xxii. 25, 26, and from the conjecture above stated, upon it: "Whoever will go to law with thee, and take thy (χιτωνα) *under* garment, let him have thy (ιματιον) *upper* one also." Matt. v. 40. If a man went to law with another, and was determined to accept of nothing else in payment but the very shirt off his back, he must have conceived that he could urge a legal right to it, or at least the resemblance of one; or that else his complaint, instead of being admitted by any court, would, without their once citing his adversary, be dismissed as futile. We must suppose a court to be incredibly corrupt and imprudent, if we can doubt this. Now, that a person, to whom I am nothing indebted, should urge a claim to my under garment, is what I can scarcely comprehend. The case, therefore, which Christ puts, is most probably this: "I have borrowed from some one, and as I cannot pay, my hard-hearted creditor, with the help of the law, means to strip me of my clothes. To my upper garment he can put in no claim, because it is privileged by Moses; and therefore he directs his attack against my under garment, which I wear over my naked body. Here, on the one hand, the *summum jus*, as it is called, is, no doubt, in favour of my creditor; but, on the other, perhaps the highest equity, and even humanity itself, pleads for me." In this case, the admonition of Jesus is to this effect: "So far should it be from your desire to act unjustly, or manifest exasperation, and vow revenge against a cruel creditor, that, if your under garment does not suffice to pay him, you ought to give him even the upper one, although he could not get it by any judicial decree."—MICHAELIS.

Ver. 41. And whosoever shall compel thee to go a mile, go with him twain.

Our Lord in this passage refers to the *angari*, or Persian messengers, who had the royal authority for pressing horses, ships, and even men, to assist them in the business on which they were employed. In the modern government of Persia there are officers not unlike the ancient angari, called *chappars*, who serve to carry despatches between the court and the provinces. When a chappar sets out, the master of the horse furnishes him with a single horse, and when that is weary, he dismounts the first man he meets, and takes his horse. There is no pardon for a traveller who should refuse to let a chapper have his horse, nor for any other who should deny him the best horse in his stable. (Hanway.)—BURDER.

CHAPTER VI.

Ver. 3. But when thou doest alms, let not thy left hand know what thy right hand doeth.

The *right* hand always dispenses gifts, because "it is more honourable than the other;" the left hand, therefore, was to be unacquainted with the charities of the other, *i. e.* there was to be no ostentation; to be perfect secrecy. The Hindoos say of things which are not to be revealed, "The left ear is not to hear that which went into the right, nor the right to be acquainted with that which was heard by the left."—ROBERTS.

The manner in which the Samaritan priest desired me, on parting, to express our mutual good-will, was by an action, than which there is not one more common in all the Levant. He put the forefinger of his right hand parallel to that of his left, and then rapidly rubbed them together, while I was expected to do the same, repeating the words, *sui, sui;* that is, "right, right;" or, in common acceptation, "together, together." It is in this manner that persons express their consent on all occasions; on concluding a bargain, on engaging to bear one another company, and on every kind of friendly agreement or good understanding.

May not this serve to explain the phrase in Matt. vi. 3: "Let not thy left hand know what thy right hand doeth?" that is, "Let not thy heart consent to its own good thoughts, with a sinful self-applause." So much is said in the Old Testament of speaking with the eyes, hands, and even feet, that it is scarcely understood by Englishmen. They should see the expressive and innumerable gesticulations of foreigners when they converse: many a question is answered, and many a significant remark conveyed, by even children, who learn this language much sooner than their mother-tongue. Perhaps the expression of Solomon, that the wicked man *speaketh with his feet*, (Prov. vi. 13,) may appear more natural, when it is considered that the mode of sitting on the ground in the East brings the feet into view, nearly in the same direct line as the hands; the whole body crouching down together, and the hands, in fact, often resting upon the feet.—JOWETT.

Ver. 5. And when thou prayest, thou shalt not be as the hypocrites *are:* for they love to pray standing in the synagogues, and in the corners of the streets, that they may be seen of men. Verily I say unto you, They have their reward.

False religion has ever been fond of *show;* hence its devotees have assumed a greater appearance of sanctity to make up the deficiency of real worth. Pehaps few systems are so replete with the *show* of religion as Hindooism. Its votaries may be seen in every street with uplifted hands, or bespattered bodies; there they are standing before every temple, making their prostrations or repeating their prayers. Nor are the Mohammedans, with all their boasting, a whit the better. See them when the sun is going down, spreading their garments on the ground, on which they are about to kneel, and say their prayers. They bow down to the earth, and touch it with their forehead; and then arise, putting their hands above their heads, with the fingers pointing to the clouds; and now they bring them lower, in a supplicating position, and all the time keep muttering their prayers; again they kneel, and again touch the earth with their forehead, and all this, without paying any apparent attention to those who pass that way.—ROBERTS.

Such a practice as here intimated by our Lord was probably common at that time with those who were fond of ostentation in their devotions, and who wished to engage the attention of others. It is evident that the practice was not confined to one place, since it may be traced in different nations. We have an instance of it related by Aaron Hill, in his Travels: "Such Turks as at the common hours of prayer are on the road, or so employed as not to find convenience to attend the mosques, are still obliged to execute that duty: nor are they ever known to fail, whatever business they are then about, but pray immediately when the hour alarms them, in that very place they chance to stand on: insomuch that when a janizary, whom you have to guard you up and down the city, hears the notice which is given him from the steeples, he will turn about, stand still, and beckon with his hand, to tell his charge he must have patience for a while; when, taking out his handkerchief, he spreads it on the ground, sits cross-legged thereupon, and says his prayers, though in the *open market*, which having ended, he leaps briskly up, salutes the person whom he undertook to convey, and renews his journey with the mild expression of *ghell, johnnum, ghell*, or, come, dear, follow me." It may be proper to add, that such a practice as this is general throughout the East.—BURDER.

Ver. 19. Lay not up for yourselves treasures upon earth, where moth and rust doth corrupt, and where thieves break through and steal.

"At Pondicherry," says Bartolomeo, "I met with an incident which excited my astonishment. I had put my effects into a chest which stood in my apartment, and being one day desirous of taking out a book, in order to amuse myself with reading, as soon as I opened the chest, I discovered in it an innumerable multitude of what are improperly called white-ants. The appellation, termites, from the Latin systematic name, termes, is better. There are various kinds of them, but only in warm countries, which are all equally destructive, and occasion great devastations, not only in sugar-plantations, but also among furniture and clothes in habitations. When I examined the different articles in the chest, I observed that these little animals had perforated my shirts in a thousand places, and gnawed to pieces my books, my girdle, my amice, and my shoes. They were moving in columns, each behind the other; and each carried away in its mouth a fragment of my effects which were more than half destroyed." (Bartolomeo.)—CRITICA BIBLICA.

Ver. 20. But lay up for yourselves treasures in heaven, where neither moth nor rust doth corrupt, and where thieves do not break through nor steal.

See on Job 27. 18.

Ver. 26. Behold the fowls of the air: for they sow not, neither do they reap, nor gather into barns; yet your heavenly Father feedeth them. Are ye not much better than they?

Does a person who has lost his situation complain, from a fear of the future; it is said to him, by way of comfort, "Look at the birds and beasts, have they any situations? Do they sow or reap? Who sustains the frog in the stone? or the germ in the egg? or the fetus in the womb? or the worm which the wasp encloses in its house of clay? Does not the Lord support all these? and will he not help you?" —ROBERTS.

Ver. 27. Which of you by taking thought can add one cubit unto his stature?

This form of speech is sometimes used to humble those of high pretensions; thus, a man of low caste, who has become rich, and who assumes authority over his better-born, though poor neighbours, will be asked, "What! has your money made you a cubit higher?" *i. e.* in the scale of being. Is a man ambitious of raising in society; a person who wishes to annoy him, puts his finger on his elbow, and, showing that part to the tip of the middle finger, asks, "Friend, will you ever rise thus much, (a cubit,) after all your cares?" "Yes, yes, the low-caste thinks himself a cubit taller, because he has got the favour of the king."—ROBERTS.

Ver. 28. And why take ye thought for raiment? Consider the lilies of the field how they grow; they toil not, neither do they spin.

The lily of the field sometimes appears with unrivalled magnificence. This remark is justified by the following statement of Mr. Salt, Voyage to Abyssinia: "At a few miles from Adowa, we discovered a new and beautiful species of amaryllis, which bore from ten to twelve spikes of bloom on each stem, as large as those of the bella-donna, springing from one common receptacle. The general colour of the corolla was white, and every petal was marked with a single streak of bright purple down the middle; the flower was sweet scented, and its smell, though much more powerful, resembled that of the lily of the valley. This superb plant excited the admiration of the whole party; and it brought immediately to my recollection the beautiful comparison used on a particular occasion by our Saviour: "I say unto you, that Solomon, in all his glory, was not arrayed like one of these."—BURDER.

Ver. 30. Wherefore, if God so clothe the grass of the field, which to-day is, and to-morrow is cast into the oven, *shall he* not much more *clothe* you, O ye of little faith?

The scarcity of fuel in the East obliges the inhabitants to use, by turns, every kind of combustible matter. The withered stalks of herbs and flowers, the tendrils of the vine, the small branches of myrtle, rosemary, and other plants, are all used in heating their ovens and bagnios. We can easily recognise this practice in these words of our Lord: "Consider the lilies of the field how they grow; they toil not, neither do they spin; and yet I say unto you, that Solomon, in all his glory, was not arrayed like one of these. Wherefore, if God so clothe the grass of the field, which to-day is, and to-morrow is cast into the oven, shall he not much more clothe you, O ye of little faith?" The grass of the field in this passage, evidently includes the lilies of which our Lord had just been speaking; and by consequence herbs in general; and in this extensive sense the word χορτος is not unfrequently taken.—PAXTON.

CHAPTER VII.

Ver. 3. And why beholdest thou the mote that is in thy brother's eye, but considerest not the beam that is thine own eye?

See on ch. 23. 24.

Ver. 6. Give not that which is holy unto the dogs, neither cast ye your pearls before swine, lest they trample them under their feet, and turn again and rend you.

Similar language is used to those who speak on subjects of a highly sacred nature before people of gross minds. "What, are silk tassels to be tied to the broom? Will you give a beautiful flower to a monkey? Who would cast rubies into a heap of rubbish? What, are you giving ambrosia to a dog?"—ROBERTS.

Ver. 9. Or what man is there of you, whom if his son ask bread, will he give him a stone?

"What father, when his son asks for sugar-cane, will give him the poison-fruit? If he asks a fish, will he give him a serpent?" This may allude to the eel, which is so much like the serpent. Some have said, on the parallel passage in Luke: "If he shall ask an egg, will he offer him a scorpion?"—"This expression is used, because the white scorpion is *like* an egg." They might as well have said, it is like a whale.—ROBERTS.

Ver. 18. A good tree cannot bring forth evil fruit, neither *can* a corrupt tree bring forth good fruit.

When people converse on the good qualities of an obedient son, it is asked, "Will the seed of the watermelon produce the fruit of the bitter *pavatta-kotti?*"—meaning, the father is good, and *therefore* the son is the same. A profligate son always leads the people to suspect the father or grandfather was not what he ought to have been. "You talk to me about that family: I know them well; the tree is bad, and the fruit is the same."—ROBERTS.

Ver. 26. And every one that heareth these sayings of mine, and doeth them not, shall be likened unto a foolish man, which built his house upon the sand.

The fishermen of Bengal build their huts in the dry season on the beds of sand, from which the river has retired. When the rains set in, which they often do very suddenly, accompanied with violent northwest winds, the water pours down in torrents from the mountains. In one night multitudes of these huts are frequently swept away, and the place where they stood is the next morning undiscoverable. (Ward's View of the Hindoos.)

"It so happened, that we were to witness one of the greatest calamities that have occurred in Egypt in the recollection of any one living. The Nile rose this season three feet and a half above the highest mark left by the former inundation, with uncommon rapidity, and carried off several villages, and some hundreds of their inhabitants. I never saw any picture that could give a more correct idea of a deluge than the valley of the Nile in this season. The Arabs had expected an extraordinary inundation this year, in consequence of the scarcity of water in the preceding season; but they did not apprehend it would rise to such a height. They generally erect fences of earth and reeds around their villages, to keep the water from their houses; but the force of this inundation baffled all their efforts. Their cottages being built of earth, could not stand one instant against the current; and no sooner did the water reach them, than it levelled them with the ground. The rapid stream carried off all that was before it; men, women, children, cattle, corn, every thing was washed away in an instant, and left the place where the village stood without any thing to indicate that there had ever been a house on the spot." (Belzoni.)—BURDER.

Ver. 27. And the rain descended, and the floods came, and the winds blew, and beat upon that house; and it fell: and great was the fall of it.

The rains, and floods, and winds of an eastern monsoon, give a striking illustration of the above passage. When people in those regions speak of the strength of a house, it is not by saying it will last so many years, but, "It will outstand the rains: it will not be injured by the floods." Houses built of the best materials and having deep foundations, in a few years often yield to the rains of a monsoon. At first, a small crack appears in some angle, which gradually becomes larger, till the whole building tumbles to the ground. And who can wonder at this, when he considers the state of the earth? For several months there is not a drop of rain, and the burning sun has loosened the ground; when at once the torrents descend, the chapped earth suddenly swells, and the foundations are moved by the change. The house founded upon a rock can alone stand the rains and floods of a wet monsoon.—ROBERTS.

Ver. 29. For he taught them as *one* having authority, and not as the scribes.

When the scribes delivered any thing to the people, they used to say, "Our rabbins, or our wise men, say so." Such as were on the side of Hillel made use of his name, and those who were on the side of Shammai made use of his. Scarcely ever would they venture to say any thing as of themselves. But Christ spake boldly, of himself, and did not go about to support his doctrine by the testimony of the elders.—GILL.

CHAPTER VIII.

Ver. 20. And Jesus saith unto him, The foxes have holes, and the birds of the air *have* nests; but the Son of man hath not where to lay *his* head.

Listen to that poor man who is stating his case to a rich man; he pathetically laments his forlorn condition, and says, "Ah! sir, even the birds have their nests, but I have not so much as they."—ROBERTS.

Ver. 28. And when he was come to the other side, into the country of the Gergesenes, there met him two possessed with devils, coming out of the tombs, exceeding fierce, so that no man might pass by that way.

"As I was not induced to accept the offers made me to remain at Tiberias, I left it early the following morning, the 11th of September, coasted the lake, and trod the ground celebrated for the miracle of the unclean spirit driven by our Saviour among the swine. The tombs still exist in the form of caverns, on the sides of the hills that rise from the shore of the lake; and from their wild appearance may well be considered the habitation of men exceeding fierce, possessed by a devil: they extend at a distance for more than a mile from the present town." (Light's Travels in Egypt.) "From this tomb we went to a still more perfect one, which was entirely cleared out, and now used as a private dwelling. Though the females of the family were within, we were allowed to enter, and descended by a flight of three steps, there being either a cistern or a deep sepulchre on the right of this descent. The portals and architrave were here perfectly exposed; the ornaments of the latter were a wreath and open flowers; the door also was divided by a studded bar, and panelled, and the ring of the knocker remained, though the knocker itself had been broken off, the door, which was of the same size and thickness as those described, traversed easily on its hinges, and we were permitted to open and close it at pleasure. The tomb was about eight feet in height, on the inside, as there was the descent of a steep step from the stone threshold to the floor. Its size was about twelve paces square; but as no light was received into it except by the door, we could not see whether there was an inner chamber, as in some of the others. A perfect sarcophagus still remained within, and this was now used by the family as a chest for corn and other provisions: so that this violated sepulchre of the dead had thus become a secure, a cool, and a convenient retreat to the living of a different race." (Buckingham.) These burying-grounds frequently afford shelter to the weary traveller when overtaken by the night; and their recesses are also a hiding-place for thieves and murderers, who sally out from thence to commit their nocturnal depredations. (Forbes.)—BURDER.

CHAPTER IX.

Ver. 9. And as Jesus passed forth from thence, he saw a man named Matthew, sitting at the receipt of custom: and he saith unto him, Follow me. And he arose and followed him.

The publicans had houses or booths built for them at the foot of bridges, at the mouth of rivers, and by the seashore, where they took toll of passengers that went to and fro. Hence we read of the tickets or seals of the publicans, which, when a man had paid toll on one side of a river, were given him by the publican to show to him that sat on the other side, that it might appear he had paid. On these were written two great letters, larger than those in common use.—GILL.

Arriving at Persepolis, Mr. Morier observes, "here is a station of rahdars, or toll-gatherers, appointed to levy a toll upon kafilehs, or caravans of merchants; and who, in general, exercise their office with so much brutality and extortion as to be execrated by all travellers. The collections of the toll are farmed, consequently extortion ensues; and, as most of the rahdars receive no other emolument than what they can exact over and above the prescribed dues from the traveller, their insolence is accounted for, and a cause sufficiently powerful is given for their insolence on the one hand, and the detestation in which they are held on the other. Baj-gah means the place of tribute: it may also be rendered the receipt of custom; and, perhaps, it was from a place like this that our Saviour called Matthew to follow him."—BURDER.

Ver. 15. And Jesus said unto them, Can the children of the bride-chamber mourn, as long as the bridegroom is with them? but the days will come, when the bridegroom shall be taken from them, and then shall they fast.

Does a man look sorry when he ought to rejoice, has he become rich, has he been greatly honoured, has a dear friend come to see him, has he become the father of a *male* child, and does he still appear dejected, it is asked, "What, do people weep in the house of marriage? Is it a funeral or a wedding you are going to celebrate?" Does a person go to cheer his friend, he says, on entering the house, "I am come this day to the house of marriage."—ROBERTS.

Ver. 17. Neither do men put new wine into old bottles: else the bottles break, and the wine runneth out, and the bottles perish: but they put new wine into new bottles, and both are preserved.

The eastern bottle, called *turunthe*, is made of the raw hide of an animal, consequently, when any fermenting liquor is put into it, the skin being comparatively green, distends itself to the swelling of the liquor. But, should the bottle have been previously stretched by the same process, then it must burst if put to a *second* trial, because it cannot yield to the *new* pressure of fermentation.—ROBERTS.

Ver. 20. And behold, a woman which was diseased with an issue of blood twelve years, came behind *him*, and touched the hem of his garment.

The Jewish mantle or upper garment was considered as consisting of four quarters, called in the oriental idiom wings. Every wing contained one corner, whereat was suspended a tuft of threads or strings, which they called κρασπεδον. Numb. xv. 37. Deut. xxii. 12. What are there called fringes are those strings, and the four quarters of the vesture are the four corners. As in the first of the passages above referred to, they are mentioned as serving to make them remember the commandments of the Lord to do them, there was conceived to be a special sacredness in them, which must have probably led the woman to think of touching that part of his garment, rather than any other. CAMPBELL.

Ver. 23. And when Jesus came into the ruler's house, and saw the minstrels and the people making a noise.

In Egypt, the lower class of people call in women, who play on the tabour, and whose business it is, like the hired mourners in other countries, to sing elegiac airs to the sound of that instrument, which they accompany with the most frightful distortions of their limbs. These women attend the corpse to the grave, intermixed with the female relations and friends of the deceased, who commonly have their hair in the utmost disorder, their heads covered with dust, their faces daubed with indigo, or at least rubbed with mud, and howling like maniacs. Such were the minstrels whom our Lord found in the house of Jairus, making so great a noise round the bed on which the dead body of his daughter lay. The noise and tumult of these retained mourners, and the other attendants, appear to have begun immediately after the person expired. "The moment," says Chardin, "any one returns from a long journey, or dies, his family burst into cries that may be heard twenty doors off; and this is renewed at different times, and continues many days, according to the vigour of the passions. Especially are these cries long and frightful in the case of death, for the mourning is right down despair, and an image of hell."

The longest and most violent acts of mourning are when they wash the body; when they perfume it; when they carry it out to be interred. During this violent outcry, the greater part even of the relations do not shed a single tear. While the funeral procession moves forward, with the violent wailings of the females, the male attendants engage in devout singing. It is evident that this sort of mourning and lamentation was a kind of art among the Jews: "Wailing shall be in the streets; and they shall call such as are skilful of lamentation to wail." Mourners are hired at the obsequies of Hindoos and Mohammedans, as in former times. To the dreadful noise and tumult of the hired mourners, the following passage of Jeremiah indisputably refers, and shows the custom to be derived from a very remote antiquity: "Call for the mourning women that they may come; and send for cunning women, that they may come, and let them make haste, and take up a wailing for us, that our eyes may run down with tears, and our eyelids gush out with waters."—PAXTON.

CHAPTER X.

Ver. 9. Provide neither gold, nor silver, nor brass in your purses.

Clothed as the eastern people were with long robes, girdles were indispensably necessary to bind together their flowing vestments. They were worn about the waist, and properly confined their loose garments. These girdles, ζωνια, were so contrived as to be used for purses; and they are still so worn in the East. Dr. Shaw, speaking of the dress of the Arabs in Barbary, says, "The girdles of these people are usually of worsted, very artfully woven into a variety of figures, and made to wrap several times about their bodies. One end of them being doubled and sewed along the edges, serves them for a purse, agreeable to the acceptation of the word ζωνη in the holy scripture." The Roman soldiers used in like manner to carry their money in their girdles. Whence in Horace, *qui zonam perdidit*, means one who had lost his purse. And in Aulus Gellius, C. Gracchus is introduced, saying, those girdles which I carried out full of money, when I went from Rome, I have at my return from the province brought home empty.—BURDER.

Ver. 10 Nor scrip for *your* journey, neither two coats, neither shoes, nor yet staves: (for the workman is worthy of his meat.)

Though the hospitality of the Arabs be general, and not confined to the superior classes, yet we are not to suppose that it admits of imposition, or is without proper bounds. Of this we have a manifest instance in the directions of our Lord to the apostles, Matt. x. 11. To send a couple of hearty men with appetites good, and rendered even keen, by the effect of travelling—to send two such to a family, barely able to meet its own necessities—having no provision of bread—or sustenance for a day beforehand, were to press upon indigence beyond the dictates of prudence, or the permission of Christian charity. Our Lord, therefore, commands his messengers—"Into whatsoever city or town ye enter, inquire who in it is worthy; and there abide till ye go thence." "Worthy," ἄξιος, this has no reference to moral worthiness; our Lord means *suitable;* to whom your additional board for a few days will be no inconvenience—substantial man. And this is exactly the import of the same directions, given Luke x. 5, 6: "Into whatever *oikia*—house-establishment on a respectable scale—residence affording accommodation for strangers, (the *hospitalia* of the Latins,) ye enter, in the same *oikia* remain: go not from *oikia* to *oikia*, in search of superior accommodations; though it may happen that after you have been in a town some days, you may hear of a more wealthy individual, who could entertain you better. No; in the same house remain, eating and drinking such things as they give;—whatever is set before you." The same inference is deduced from the advice of the apostle John to the lady Electa, (2 Epistle 10.) "If there come any to you, and bring not this doctrine, receive him not into your *oikia*." She was, therefore, a person of respectability, if not of rank; mistress of a household establishment, on a scale proper for the exercise of Christian benevolence in a convenient and suitable manner—of liberal heart, and of equally liberal powers.

Whoever has well considered the difficulties to which travellers in the East are often exposed to procure supplies, or even sufficient provisions to make a meal, will perceive the propriety of these directions. Although it was one sign of the Messiah's advent, that to the poor the gospel was preached, yet it was not the Messiah's purpose to add to the difficulties of any man's situation. He supposes that a family-man, a housekeeper, might be without bread, obliged to borrow from a friend, to meet the wants of a single traveller, (Luke xi. 5, "I have nothing to set before him,") no uncommon case; but, if this were occasioned by real penury, the rights of hospitality, however congenial to the manners of the people, or to the feelings of the individual, and however urgent, must be waived.—TAYLOR IN CALMET.

Ver. 12. And when ye come into a house, salute it.

When the priests or pandārams go into a house, they sometimes sing a verse of blessing; at other times the priest stretches out his right hand, and says aloud, "*āservātham,*" i. e. blessing.—ROBERTS.

Ver. 25. It is enough for the disciple that he be as his master, and the servant as his lord: if they have called the master of the house Beelzebub, how much more *shall they call* them of his household?

It is supposed that this idol was the same with Baal-zebub, the fly-god, worshipped at Ekron, (2 Kings i. 2,) and who had his name changed afterward by the Jews to Baal-zebul, the dung-god: a title expressive of the utmost contempt. Among the Jews it was held, in a manner, for a matter of religion to reproach idols, and to give them odious names: and among the ignominious ones bestowed upon them, the general and common one was zebul, dung, or a dunghill. Many names of evil spirits, or devils, occur in the Talmud. Among all the devils, they esteemed him the worst, the prince of the rest, who ruled over idols, and by whom oracles and miracles were given forth among the heathen. This demon they called Baal-zebul.—BURDER.

Ver. 42. And whosoever shall give to drink unto

one of these little ones, a cup of cold *water* only, in the name of a disciple, verily, I say unto you, he shall in no wise lose his reward.

In the eastern countries, a cup of water was a considerable object. In India, the Hindoos go sometimes a great way to fetch it, and then boil it, that it may do the less hurt to travellers when they are hot; and after that, they stand from morning till night in some great road, where there is neither pit nor rivulet, and offer it in honour of their god, to be drank by all passengers. This necessary work of charity, in these hot countries, seems to have been practised by the more pious and humane Jews. (Asiatic Miscellany.)—Burder.

CHAPTER XI.

Ver. 8. But what went ye out for to see? A man clothed in soft raiment? Behold, they that wear soft *clothing* are in king's houses.

Persons devoted to a life of austerity, commonly wore a dress of coarse materials. John the Baptist, we are told in the sacred volume, was clothed in a garment of camel's hair, with a broad leathern girdle about his loins. It is a circumstance worthy of notice, that the finest and most elegant shawls, which constitute so essential a part of the Turkish dress, and are worn by persons in the highest ranks of life, are fabricated of camel's hair. These unquestionably belong to the "soft raiment" worn by the residents in the palaces of eastern kings. But it is evident that the inspired writer intends, by the remark on the dress of John, to direct our attention to the meanness of his attire. "What went ye out for to see? a man clothed in soft raiment? Behold, they that are in king's houses wear soft clothing;" but the garments of John were of a very different kind. It is, indeed, sufficiently apparent, that the inhabitants of the wilderness, where John spent his days before he entered upon his ministry, and other thinly settled districts, manufactured a stuff, in colour and texture somewhat resembling our coarse hair-cloths, of the hair which fell from their camels, for their own immediate use, of which the raiment of that venerable prophet consisted. In the same manner, the Tartars of modern times work up their camel's hair into a kind of felt, which serves as a covering to their tents, although their way of life is the very reverse of easy and pompous. Like the austere herald of the Saviour, the modern dervises wear garments of the same texture, which they, too, gird about their loins with great leathern girdles. Elijah, the Tishbite, seems to have worn a habit of camel's hair, equally mean and coarse; for he is represented in our translation as a "hairy man," which perhaps ought to be referred to his dress, and not to his person.—Paxton.

Ver. 16. But whereunto shall I liken this generation? It is like unto children sitting in the markets, and calling unto their fellows.

It was the custom of children among the Jews, in their sports, to imitate what they saw done by others upon great occasions, and particularly the customs in festivities, wherein the musician beginning a tune on his instrument, the company danced to his pipe. So also in funerals, wherein the women beginning the mournful song, (as the *præfacæ* of the Romans,) the rest followed lamenting and beating their breasts. These things the children acted and personated in the streets in play, and the rest not following the leader as usual, gave occasion to this speech: "We have piped unto you, and ye have not danced; we have mourned unto you, and ye have not lamented."—Burder.

Ver. 16. But whereunto shall I liken this generation? It is like unto children sitting in the markets, and calling unto their fellows, 17. And saying, We have piped unto you, and ye have not danced; we have mourned unto you, and ye have not lamented.

The funeral procession was attended by professional mourners, eminently skilled in the art of lamentation, whom the friends and relations of the deceased hired, to assist them in expressing their sorrow. They began the ceremony with the stridulous voices of old women, who strove, by their doleful modulations, to extort grief from those that were present. The children in the streets through which they passed, often suspended their sports, to imitate the sounds, and joined with equal sincerity in the lamentations. —Paxton.

CHAPTER XII.

Ver. 27. And if I by Beelzebub cast out devils, by whom do your children cast *them* out? therefore they shall be your judges.

The universal opinion in the East is, that devils have the power to enter into and take possession of men, in the same sense as we understand it to have been the case, as described by the sacred writers. I have often seen the poor objects who were believed to be under demoniacal influence, and certainly, in some instances, I found it no easy matter to account for their conduct on natural principles. I have seen them writhe and tear themselves in the most frantic manner; they burst asunder the cords with which they were bound, and fell on the ground as if dead. At one time they are silent, and again most vociferous; they dash with fury among the people, and loudly pronounce their imprecations. But no sooner does the exorcist come forward, than the victim becomes the subject of new emotions; he stares, talks incoherently, sighs, and falls on the ground; and in the course of an hour is as calm as any who are around him. Those men who profess to eject devils are frightful-looking creatures, and are seldom associated with, except in the discharge of their official duties. It is a fact, that they affect to eject the evil spirits by their *prince of devils.* Females are much more subject to those affections than men; and *Friday* is the day of all others on which they are most liable to be attacked. I am fully of opinion that nearly all their *possessions* would be removed by medicine, or by arguments of a more *tangible* nature. Not long ago, a young female was said to be under the influence of an evil spirit, but the father, being an *unbeliever*, took a large broom and began to beat his daughter in the most unmerciful manner. After some time the *spirit* cried aloud, "*Do not beat me, do not beat me,*" and took its departure! There is a fiend called *poothani*, which is said to take great delight in entering little children; but the herb called *pa-maruta* is then administered with great success!—Roberts.

Ver. 42. The queen of the south shall rise up in the judgment with this generation, and shall condemn it: for she came from the uttermost parts of the earth to hear the wisdom of Solomon; and behold, a greater than Solomon *is* here.

This is spoken in allusion to a custom among the Jews and Romans, which was, for the witnesses to *rise* from their seats when they accused criminals, or gave any evidence against them.—Burder.

CHAPTER XIII.

Ver. 25. But while men slept, his enemy came and sowed tares among the wheat and went his way.

Strange as it may appear, this is still literally done in the East. See that lurking villain, watching for the time when his neighbour shall *plough* his field; he carefully marks the period when the work has been finished, and goes in the night following, and casts in what the natives call the *pandinellu*, i. e. pig paddy; this being of rapid growth, springs up before the good seed, and scatters itself before the other can be reaped, so that the poor owner of the field will be for years before he can get rid of the troublesome weed. But there is another noisome plant which these wretches cast into the ground of those they hate, called *perũm-pirandi*, which is more destructive to vegetation than any other plant. Has a man purchased a field out of the hands of another, the offended person says, "I will plant the *perum-pirandi* in his grounds."—Roberts.

Ver 31. Another parable put he forth unto them, saying, The kingdom of heaven is like to a grain of mustard-seed, which a man took, and sowed in his field: 32. Which indeed is the least of all seeds: but when it is grown, it is the greatest among herbs, and becometh a tree, so that the birds of the air come and lodge in the branches thereof.

The account which our Lord gave of the mustard-tree, recorded in the gospel of Matthew, has often excited the ridicule of unbelievers, or incurred their pointed condemnation: "The kingdom of heaven is like to a grain of mustard seed, which a man took and sowed in his field; which indeed is the least of all seeds, but when it is grown, it is the greatest among herbs, and becomes a tree, so that the birds of the air come and lodge in the branches of it." We behold no such mustard-trees in this country, say the enemies of revelation, therefore the description of Christ must be erroneous. But the consequence will not follow, till it is proved that no such trees exist in any part of the world. This parable of the mustard-tree was delivered in a public assembly, every individual of which was well acquainted with it; many of them were the avowed enemies of our Lord, and would have gladly seized the opportunity of exposing him to the scorn of the multitude, if he had committed any mistake. The silent acquiescence of the scribes and Pharisees affords an irrefragable proof that his description is perfectly correct. They knew that the same account of that plant more than once occurs in the writings of their fathers. In the Babylonish Talmud, a Jewish rabbi writes, that a certain man of Sichem had bequeathed him by his father three boughs of mustard: one of which broken off from the rest yielded nine kabs of seed, and the wood of it was sufficient to cover the potter's house. Another rabbi, in the Jerusalem Talmud, says, he had a stem of mustard in his garden, into which he could climb as into a fig-tree. After making every reasonable allowance for the hyperbolical terms in which these Talmudical writers indulged, they certainly referred to real appearances in nature; and no man will pretend that it was any part of their design to justify the Saviour's description. But the birds of the air might certainly lodge with ease among the branches of a tree that was sufficiently strong to sustain the weight of a man. The fact asserted by our Lord is stated in the clearest terms by a Spanish historian, who says, that in the province of Chili, in South America, the mustard grows to the size of a tree, and the birds lodge under its shade, and build their nests in its branches.—PAXTON.

Ver. 44. Again, The kingdom of heaven is like unto treasure hid in a field; the which when a man hath found, he hideth, and for joy thereof goeth and selleth all that he hath, and buyeth that field.

No practice was more common than that of hiding treasures in a field or garden, because the people had not any place of safety in which to deposite their riches, and because their rapacious rulers were sure to find some pretext for accusation against them, in order to get their money. Hence men of great property affected poverty, and walked about in mean apparel, in order to deceive their neighbours, and hence came the practice of hiding their treasures in the earth. In the book of fate, called *Sagā-Thevan Sasterām*, the following question occurs many times: "Will the buried things be found?" There can be no doubt that there are immense treasures buried in the East at this day. Not long ago a toddy drawer ascended a palmirah-tree to lop off the upper branches, when one of them in falling stuck in the ground. On taking out that branch, he saw something yellow; he looked, and found an earthern vessel full of gold coins and other articles. I rescued three of the coins from the crucible of the goldsmith, and what was my surprise to find on one of them, in ancient *Greek* characters, *konob-obryza*. About two years ago an immense hoard was found at Putlam, which must have been buried for severa. ages.—ROBERTS.

Ver. 55. Is not this the carpenter's son? is not his mother called Mary? and his brethren, James, and Joses, and Simon, and Judas?

See on Mark 6. 3.

CHAPTER XIV.

Ver. 7. Whereupon he promised with an oath to give her whatsoever she would ask.

In the East it is customary for public dancers, at festivals in great houses, to solicit from the company they have been entertaining, such rewards as the spectators may choose to bestow. These usually are small pieces of money, which the donor sticks on the face of the performer. A favourite dancer will have her face covered with such presents. "Shah Abbas, being one day drunk, gave a woman that danced much to his satisfaction, the fairest hhan in all Ispahan, which was not yet finished, but wanted little. This hhan yielded a great revenue to the king, to whom it belonged, in chamber-rents. The nazar having put him in mind of it next morning, took the freedom to tell him that it was unjustifiable prodigality; so the king ordered to give her a hundred tomans, with which she was forced to be contented." (Thevenot.)—BURDER.

Ver. 26. And when the disciples saw him walking on the sea, they were troubled, saying, It is a spirit; and they cried out for fear.

The Hindoos have to do with so many demons, gods, and demigods, it is no wonder they live in constant dread of their power. There is not a hamlet without a *tree*, or some secret place, in which evil spirits are not believed to dwell. Hence the people live in constant fear of those sprites of darkness, and nothing but the most pressing necessity will induce a man to go abroad after the sun has gone down. See the unhappy wight who is obliged to go out in the dark; he repeats his incantations and *touches* his amulets, he seizes a firebrand to keep off the foes, and begins his journey. He goes on with gentle step, he listens, and again repeats his prayers; should he hear the rustling of a leaf, or the moaning of some living animal, he gives himself up for lost. Has he worked himself up into a state of artificial courage, he begins to sing and bawl aloud, "to keep his spirits up." But, after all his efforts, his heart will not beat with its wonted ease till he shall have gained a place of safety. I was once sitting, after sunset, under a large banyan-tree, (*ficus religiosa*,) when a native soldier passed that way. He saw me in the shade, and immediately began to cry aloud, and *beat his breast*, and ran off in the greatest consternation. That man had conducted himself bravely in the Kandian war, but his courage fled when in the presence of a supposed spirit. On another occasion, having to go to some islands to distribute tracts, and having determined when to return, I directed my servant to bring my pony to a certain point of land, where I intended to disembark. Accordingly, when I had finished my work, I returned in a little canoe, and saw my pony and the boy in the distance. But the sun having gone down, the unfortunate fellow, seeing us indistinctly, thought we were *spirits*: he mounted the pony and galloped off with all speed, leaving me to my meditations on a desolate beach. "They were troubled, saying, It is a spirit."—ROBERTS.

CHAPTER XV.

Ver. 2. Why do thy disciples transgress the tradition of the elders? for they wash not their hands when they eat bread.

No Hindoo of good caste will eat till he has washed his hands. Thus, however numerous a company may be, the guests never commence eating till they have performed that necessary ablution.—ROBERTS.

Ver. 4. For God commanded, saying, Honour thy father and mother: and he that curseth father or mother, let him die the death. 5. But ye say, Whosoever shall say to *his* father or *his* mother, *It is* a gift, by whatsoever thou mightest be profited by me: 6. And honour not his father or his mother, *he shall be free*. Thus have ye made the commandment of God of none effect by your tradition.

By the term *cursing*, we are here to understand, not only what may be peculiarly so termed, that is, *imprecating* evil on a parent, but probably *all rude and reproachful language* used towards him; at least, the Hebrew word קלל, (to which I cannot find any German term altogether equivalent; and the Latin, *maledicere*, which more nearly resembles it, has rather a wider range of signification,) would seem to comprehend as much, according to the common usage of the language. An example of this crime, and, indeed, one altogether in point, is given by Christ, in Matt. xv. 4—6, or Mark vii. 9—12, where he upbraids the Pharisees with their giving, from their deference to human traditions and doctrines, such an exposition of the divine law, as converted an action, which, by the law of Moses, would have been punished with death, into a vow, both obligatory and acceptable in the sight of God. It seems that it was then not uncommon for an undutiful and degenerate son, who wanted to be rid of the burden of supporting his parents, and, in his wrath, to turn them adrift upon the wide world, to say to his father or mother, "Korban, or, Be that Korban (consecrated) which I should appropriate to thy support; that is, Every thing wherewith I might ever aid or serve thee, and, of course, every thing, which I ought to devote to thy relief in the days of helpless old age, I here vow unto God." A most abominable vow indeed! and which God would, unquestionably, as little approve or accept, as he would a vow to commit adultery or sodomy. And yet some of the Pharisees pronounced on such vows this strange decision; that they were absolutely obligatory, and that the son who uttered such words, was bound to abstain from contributing, in the smallest article, to the behoof of his parents; because every thing that should have been so appropriated, had become consecrated to God, and could no longer be applied to their use, without sacrilege and a breach of his vow. But on this exposition, Christ not only remarked, that it abrogated the fifth commandment, but he likewise added, as a counter-doctrine, that Moses, their own legislator, had expressly declared, that *the man who cursed father or mother deserved to die*. Now, it is impossible for a man to curse his parents more effectually, than by a vow like this, when he interprets it with such rigour, as to preclude him from doing any thing in future for their benefit. It is not imprecating upon them a curse in the common style of curses, which but evaporate into air, because neither the *devil*, nor the *lightning*, are wont to be so obsequious as to obey our wishes every time we call upon the one to *take*, or the other to *strike dead*, our adversaries: but it is fulfilling the curse, and making it to all intents and purposes effectual.—MICHAELIS.

Ver. 28. Then Jesus answered and said unto her, O woman, great *is* thy faith! be it unto thee even as thou wilt. And her daughter was made whole from that very hour.

The sex, on all common occasions, are always addressed with this distinctive appellation. Thus people in going along the road, should they have to speak to a female, say, *manushe*, i. e. woman, hear me. The term sometimes is expressive of affection; but, generally, it is intended to convey an intimation of weakness and contempt.—ROBERTS.

CHAPTER XVI.

Ver. 19. And I will give unto thee the keys of the kingdom of heaven: and whatsoever thou shalt bind on earth, shall be bound in heaven; and whatsoever thou shalt loose on earth, shall be loosed in heaven.

As stewards of a great family, especially of the royal household, bore a key, probably a golden one, in token of their office, the phrase of giving a person the key naturally grew into an expression of raising him to great power. (Comp. Is. xxii. 22, with Rev. iii. 7.) This was with peculiar propriety applicable to the stewards of the mysteries of God. (1 Cor. iv. 1.) Peter's opening of the kingdom of heaven, as being the first that preached it both to the Jews and to the Gentiles, may be considered as an illustration of this promise; but it is more fully explained by the power of binding and loosing afterward mentioned. —BURDER.

CHAPTER XVII.

Ver. 1. And after six days Jesus taketh Peter, James, and John his brother, and bringeth them up into a high mountain apart, 2. And was transfigured before them: and his face did shine as the sun, and his raiment was white as the light.

Mount Tabor, or Thabor, as it is sometimes called, is a calcareous mountain of a conical form, entirely detached from any neighbouring mountain: it stands on one side of the great plain of Esdraelon. The sides are rugged and precipitous, and covered to the summit with the most beautiful shrubs and flowers. Here Barak was encamped when, at the suggestion of the prophetess Deborah, he descended with ten thousand men, and discomfited the host of Sisera. (Judg. iv. 6, &c.) And, long afterward, Hosea reproached the princes of Israel and the priests of the golden calves, with having "been a snare in Mizpeh and a net spread upon Tabor," (Hos. v. 1,) doubtless referring to the altars and idols which were here set up; and on this "high mountain apart" the transfiguration of Jesus Christ is generally believed to have taken place. (Matt. xvii. 1, 2.) Tabor is computed to be about a mile in height. To a person standing at its foot, it appears to terminate in a point: but, on reaching the top, he is agreeably surprised to find an oval plain, about a quarter of a mile in its greatest length, covered with a bed of fertile soil on the west, and having on its eastern side a mass of ruins, apparently the vestiges of churches, grottoes, and strong walls, all decidedly of some antiquity, and a few appearing to be the works of a very remote age. The Hon. Capt. Fitzmaurice, who visited this mountain in February, 1833, states that he saw the ruins of a very ancient church, built over the spot where the transfiguration is supposed to have taken place.

The prospects from the summit of Mount Tabor are singularly delightful and extensive. On the northwest, says Mr. Buckingham, (whose graphic description has been confirmed by subsequent travellers,) "we had a view of the Mediterranean Sea, whose blue surface filled up an open space left by a downward bend in the outline of the western hills: to the west-northwest a small portion of its waters were seen; and on the west, again, the slender line of the distant horizon was just perceptible over the range of land near the seacoast. From the west to the south, the plain of Esdraelon extended over a vast space, being bounded on the south by a range of hills generally considered to be Hermon, whose dews are poetically celebrated, (Psal. cxxxiii. 3,) and having in the same direction, nearer the foot of Tabor, the springs of Ain-el-Sherar, which send a perceptible stream through its centre, and form the brook Kishon of antiquity. From the southeast to the east is the plain of Galilee, being almost a continuation of Esdraelon, and, like it, appearing to be highly cultivated. Beneath the range of Hermon is seated Endor, famed for the witch who raised the ghost of Samuel, (1 Sam. xxviii.) and Nain, equally celebrated as the place at which Jesus raised to life the only son of a widow, and restored him to his afflicted parent. The range which bounds the eastern view is thought to be the 'mountains of Gilboa,' so fatal to Saul, (1 Sam. xxxi.) The Sea of Tiberias, or Lake of Gennesareth, is clearly discovered towards the northeast, and somewhat further in this direction is pointed out the village of Saphet, anciently named Bethulia, the city alluded to by Jesus Christ in his divine sermon on the mount, from which it is also very conspicuous.

"The rest of this glorious panorama comprehends the sublime 'Mount of Beatitudes,' upon which that memorable sermon was delivered, together with the route to Damascus, and, lastly, Mount Lebanon, towering in the background in prodigious grandeur, the summit of which is covered with perpetual snow."—HORNE.

CHAPTER XVIII.

Ver. 6. But whoso shall offend one of these little

ones which believe in me, it were better for him that a millstone were hanged about his neck, and *that* he were drowned in the depth of the sea.

It was a favourite punishment in ancient times, to tie a large stone round the neck of a criminal, and then to cast him into the sea or deep waters. Thus, Appe-Murte, a man of rank, was destroyed in this way, for changing his religion, Budhism, for Hindooism. The punishment is called *sala-paruchy*. The millstones in the East are not more than twenty inches in diameter, and three inches thick, so that there would not be that difficulty which some have supposed in thus despatching criminals. It is common, when a person is much oppressed, to say, "I had rather have a stone tied round about my neck, and be thrown into the sea, than thus suffer." A wife says to her husband, "Rather than beat me thus, tie a stone round my neck, and throw me into the tank."—ROBERTS.

Ver. 10. Take heed that ye despise not one of these little ones: for I say unto you, That in heaven their angels do always behold the face of my Father which is in heaven.

Why is the fact of the angels constantly beholding the face of God in heaven, a reason for not despising one of Christ's little ones? On this point the commentators, for the most part, leave the reader no more enlightened than they found him. We suppose the true answer to be, that a posture of strict attention, a look of wistful, intense, and obsequious regard, directed to the eye, the countenance, or the hand of a superior, is characteristic of a dutiful servant, of one intent upon the performance of his master's commands. It is a posture indicative at once of an anxious wish to know, and a cordial readiness to execute, the will of a lord or ruler. This is apparent from the following instances of scripture usage:—1 Kings i. 20, "And then, my lord, O king, *the eyes of all Israel are upon thee*, that thou shouldst tell them who shall sit on the throne of my lord the king after him." Ps. cxxiii. 2, "Behold, as *the eyes of servants look unto the hand of their masters*, and as the eyes of a maiden unto the hand of her mistress; so our eyes wait upon the Lord our God." Our Saviour accordingly would intimate that such was the attitude of the angels in heaven, who are ministering spirits to the heirs of salvation. Acting as a tutelary cohort to the sons of the kingdom, they were always on the alert to undertake their cause. For this purpose they stood obedient to the beck and bidding of their heavenly master. Like devoted servants ready to take their orders from a bare look, a glance of the eye, or a turn of the head, so these guardian spirits were incessantly on the watch, to learn when and where they should be sent, with the speed of the wind, to avenge the wrongs and injuries of God's chosen. Seeing then such a prompt and powerful custody is provided for the little ones of Christ, it must be dangerous to despise them, whether in word or deed.—BUSH.

Ver. 21. Then came Peter to him, and said, Lord, how oft shall my brother sin against me, and I forgive him? till seven times?

This number is in common use, to show a thing has been *often* done. "Have I not told you *seven* times to fetch water and wash my feet?" "Seven times have I been to the temple, but still my requests are not granted." "Seven times have I requested the father to give me the hand of his daughter, but he refused me: and, therefore, will not ask him again." "Have I not forgiven you *seven* times, and how shall I forgive you again?"—ROBERTS.

Ver. 34. And his lord was wroth, and delivered him to the tormentors, till he should pay all that was due unto him.

The word βασανιστης properly denotes examiner, particularly one who has it in charge to examine by torture. Hence it came to signify jailer, for on such in those days this charge commonly devolved. They were not only allowed, but even commanded, to treat the wretches in their custody with every kind of cruelty, in order to extort payment from them, in case they had concealed any of their effects; or, if they had nothing, to wrest the sum owed from the compassion of their relations and friends, who, to release an unhappy person for whom they had a regard from such extreme misery, might be induced to pay the debt; for, let it be observed, that the person of the insolvent debtor was absolutely in the power of the creditor, and at his disposal.—CAMPBELL.

CHAPTER XIX.

Ver. 6. Wherefore they are no more twain, but one flesh. What, therefore, God hath joined together, let no man put asunder.

Of a happy couple it is said, "They have *one* life and *one* body." If they are not happy, "Ah! they are like the *knife* and the *victim*." "They are like the *dog* and the *cat*, or the *crow* and the *bow*, or the *kite* and the *serpent*."—ROBERTS.

Ver. 24. And again I say unto you, It is easier for a camel to go through the eye of a needle, than for a rich man to enter into the kingdom of God.

This *metaphor* finds a parallel in the proverb which is quoted to show the *difficulty* of accomplishing any thing. "Just as soon will an elephant pass through the spout of a kettle." "Ah! the old sinner, he finds it no easy thing to die; his life is lingering, lingering; it *cannot* escape; it is like the elephant trying to get through the spout of a kettle."—ROBERTS.

To pass a camel through the eye of a needle, was a proverbial expression among the nations of high antiquity, denoting a difficulty which neither the art nor the power of man can surmount. Our Lord condescends to employ it in his discourse to the disciples, to show how extremely difficult it is for a rich man to forsake all for the cause of God and truth, and obtain the blessings of salvation: "I say unto you, it is easier for a camel to go through the eye of a needle, than for a rich man to enter into the kingdom of God." Many expositors, however, are of opinion, that the allusion is not to the animal of that name, but to the cable by which an anchor is made fast to the ship; and for camel, they read camil, from which our word cable is supposed to be descended. It is not perhaps easy to determine which of these ought to be preferred; and some interpreters of considerable note have accordingly adopted both views. The more common signification of the term, however, seems rather to countenance the first view. The Talmudical writers had a similar proverb concerning him who proposed to accomplish an impossibility, which they couched in the following terms: "Thou art perchance from the city of Pomboditha, where they send an elephant through the eye of a needle." Another Hebrew adage, mentioned by the learned Buxtorf, bears a striking resemblance to this: They neither show one a golden palm, nor an elephant which enters through the eye of a needle. Both these proverbial expressions were intended to express either a thing extremely difficult, or altogether impracticable to human power; but our Lord, instead of the elephant, took the camel, as being an animal better known to the Jews. The striking analogy, however, between a cable and a thread which is wont to be passed through the eye of a needle would incline us to embrace the second view. By the Hebrew term (גמל) *gamel*, and the Greek word (καμηλος) *kamilos*, the Syrians, the Helenistis Jews, and the Arabians, all understood a ship's cable: and hence, the Assyrians and Arabians contended that the word must be so interpreted in the proverb under consideration. The Talmudical writers also have a similar adage, which is quoted by Buxtorf: "The departure of the soul from the body is difficult as the passing of a cable through a small aperture."—PAXTON.

CHAPTER XX.

Ver. 6. And about the eleventh hour he went out, and found others standing idle, and saith unto them, Why stand ye here all the day idle?

7. They say unto him, Because no man hath hired us. He saith unto them, Go ye also into the vineyard; and whatsoever is right, *that* shall ye receive.

The most conspicuous building in Hamadan is the Mesjid Jumah, a large mosque now falling into decay, and before it a maidan or square, which serves as a market-place. Here we observed every morning before the sun rose, that a numerous band of peasants were collected with spades in their hands, waiting, as they informed us, to be hired for the day to work in the surrounding fields. This custom, which I have never seen in any other part of Asia, forcibly struck me as a most happy illustration of our Saviour's parable of the labourers in the vineyard in the 20th chapter of Matthew, particularly when passing by the same place late in the day, we still found others standing idle, and remembered his words, "Why stand ye here all the day idle?" as most applicable to their situation: for in putting the very same question to them, they answered us, "Because no man hath hired us."—MORIER.

Ver. 11. And when they had received *it*, they murmured against the good man of the house.

Pay a man ever so liberally, he will still *murmur;* he looks at the money and then at your face, and says, "PO-THATHU," *i. e.* not sufficient. He tells you a long story about what he has done and suffered, about the great expense he has been at to oblige you, and he entreats you for a little more. I ask any Englishman who has been in India, if he ever met with a Hindoo who was not at ALL times ready to MURMUR?—ROBERTS.

Ver. 16. So the last shall be first, and the first last: for many be called, but few chosen.

The Jews never spake of levying troops, but of choosing them; because all the males, from twenty years old and upwards, being liable to serve, they had always a great many more than they wanted. In allusion to the general muster of the people, and the selection of a certain number for the service of their country, our Lord observes, "Many are called, but few chosen." The great mass of the people were called together by sound of trumpet, and on passing in review before the officers, those were chosen who were deemed most fit for service. This is the reason the Hebrews usually called their soldiers young men, and *bahurim*, chosen. But no man, who felt a disposition to serve his country, was rejected; though an Israelite was not chosen, he might volunteer his services, and was then enrolled.—PAXTON.

CHAPTER XXI.

Ver. 5. Tell ye the daughter of Sion, Behold, thy king cometh unto thee, meek, and sitting upon an ass, and a colt the foal of an ass.

See on Is. 30. 24.

Ver. 7. And brought the ass, and the colt, and put on them their clothes, and they set *him* thereon.

In later times also it was customary in those countries to make riding more convenient in this manner. Tucher, who made a pilgrimage to the holy sepulchre in the last half of the fifteenth century, gives the following advice to a person who intends travelling in Palestine: "Have a coat made at Venice of double cloth: it is very convenient in the Holy Land. You spread it upon the ass, and ride on it."—ROSENMULLER.

Ver. 8. And a very great multitude spread their garments in the way; others cut down branches from the trees, and strewed them in the way.

It was a common practice in the East, and one which, on certain great and joyful occasions, has been practised in other countries, to strew flowers and branches of trees in the way of conquerors and renowned princes. Herodotus states, that people went before Xerxes passing over the Hellespont, and burnt all manner of perfumes on the bridges, and strewed the way with myrtles. So did those Jews who believed Christ to be the promised Messiah, and the king of Israel; they cut down branches of the trees, and strewed them in the way. Sometimes the whole road which leads to the capitol of an eastern monarch, for several miles, is covered with rich silks over which he rides into the city. Agreeably to this custom, the multitudes spread their garments in the way when the Saviour rode in triumph into Jerusalem.—PAXTON.

Campbell is right, "Spread their MANTLES in the way." The people of the East have a robe which corresponds with the mantle of an English lady. Its name is SALVI, and how often may it be seen spread on the ground where men of rank have to walk! I was not a little surprised soon after my arrival in the East, when going to visit a native gentleman, to find the path through the garden covered with white garments. I hesitated, but was told it was for "my respect." I must walk ON them to show I accepted the honour.—ROBERTS.

Ver. 12. And Jesus went into the temple of God, and cast out all them that sold and bought in the temple, and overthrew the tables of the money-changers, and the seats of them that sold doves.

The money-changers were such persons as supplied the Jews, who came from distant parts of Judea, and other parts of the Roman empire, with money, to be received back at their respective homes, or which they had paid before they began their journey. Perhaps also they exchanged foreign coins for those current at Jerusalem. The Talmud and Maimonides inform us that the half-shekel paid yearly to the temple by all the Jews, (Exod. xxx. 15,) was collected there with great exactness in the month Adar, and that on changing the shekels and other money into half-shekels for that purpose, the money-changers exacted a small stated fee, or payment, called kolbon. It was the tables on which they trafficked for this unholy gain which Christ overturned.—HAMMOND.

CHAPTER XXII.

Ver. 2. The kingdom of heaven is like unto a certain king, which made a marriage for his son.

The hospitality of the present day, in the East, exactly resembles that of the remotest antiquity. The parable of the "great supper" is in those countries literally realized. And such was the hospitality of ancient Greece and Rome. When a person provided an entertainment for his friends or neighbours, he sent round a number of servants to invite the guests; these were called vocatores by the Romans, and κλητωρες by the Greeks. The day when the entertainment is to be given is fixed some considerable time before; and in the evening of the day appointed, a messenger comes to bid the guests to the feast. The custom is thus introduced in Luke: "A certain man made a great supper, and bade many; and sent his servant at supper time, to say to them that were bidden, Come, for all things are now ready." They were not now asked for the first time; but had already accepted the invitation, when the day was appointed, and were therefore already pledged to attend at the hour when they might be summoned. They were not taken unprepared, and could not in consistency and decency plead any prior engagement. They could not now refuse, without violating their word and insulting the master of the feast, and therefore justly subjected themselves to punishment. The terms of the parable exactly accord with established custom, and contain nothing of the harshness to which infidels object.—PAXTON.

Ver. 4. Again he sent forth other servants, saying, Tell them which are bidden, Behold, I have prepared my dinner; my oxen and *my* fatlings *are* killed, and all things *are* ready: come unto the marriage.

The following extract gives us an interesting account of a Persian dinner: "On the ground before us was spread the sofra, a fine chints cloth, which perfectly intrenched our legs, and which is used so long unchanged, that the accumulated fragments of former meals collect into a musty paste, and emit no very savoury smell; but the Persians are content, for they say that changing the sofra brings ill luck. A tray was then placed before each guest; on these trays were three fine China bowls, which were filled with sherbets, two made of sweet liquors, and one of a most exquisite species of lemonade. There were, besides, fruits ready cut, plates with elegant little arrangements of sweetmeats and confectionary, and smaller cups, of sweet sherbet; the whole of which were placed most symmetrically, and were quite inviting, even by their appearance. In the vases of sherbet were spoons made of the pear-tree, with very deep bowls, and worked so delicately, that the long handle just slightly bent when it was carried to the mouth. The pillaws succeeded, three of which were placed before each two guests; one of plain rice, called the chillo, one made of mutton, with raisins and almonds; the other of a fowl, and rich spices and plums. To this were added various dishes, with rich sauce. Their cooking, indeed, is mostly composed of sweets. The business of eating was a pleasure to the Persians, but it was misery to us. They comfortably advanced their chins close to the dishes, and commodiously scooped the rice or other victuals into their mouths with three fingers and the thumb of their right hand; but in vain did we attempt to approach the dish: our tight-kneed breeches, and all the ligaments and buttons of our dress, forbid us; and we were forced to manage as well as we could, fragments of meat and rice falling through our fingers all around us." (Morier.)—BURDER.

Ver. 9. Go ye therefore into the highways, and, as many as ye shall find, bid to the marriage.

It is as common in the East for a rich man to give a feast to the poor, and the maimed, and the blind, as it is in England for a nobleman to entertain men of his own degree. Thus, does he wish to gain some temporal or spiritual blessing, he orders his head servant to prepare a feast for one or two hundred poor guests. Messengers are then despatched into the streets and lanes to inform the indigent, that on such a day rice and curry will be given to all who are there at the appointed time. Long before the hour the visiters may be seen bending their steps towards the house of the RASA, or king: there goes the old man, who is scarcely able to move his palsied limbs, he talks to himself about better days; and there the despised widow moves with a hesitating step; there the *sanyāsi* or *pandārum* boldly brushes along and scowls upon all who offer the least impediment to his progress; there objects suffering under every possible disease of our nature congregate together, without a single kindred association, excepting the one which occupies their expectations. The food is ready, the guests sit in rows on the grass, (Luke ix. 14,) and the servants begin to hand out the portions in order. Such is the hunger of some that they cannot stay to let the mess get cool, and thus have to suffer the consequences of their impatience; others, upon whom disease or age has made a fatal inroad, can scarcely taste the provision; some are of *high caste*, who growl as they eat, at those of lower grades, for having presumed to come near them; and others, on account of the high blood which flows in their veins, are allowed to take a portion to their homes. What a motley scene is that, and what a strange contrariety in their talk; some are bawling out for *more food*, though they are already *gorged* to the full: others are talking about *another* feast which is to be given in such a village, and others who have got a sight of the host, are loudly applauding his princely generosity. He is delighted to hear their flattery; it all falls sweetly on his feelings, for the higher the tone, the greater the relish. He has gained his object, *taramum*, i. e. charity has been attended to; he has been exhilarated with adulation, he has got a "*name in the street*," (Job xviii. 17,) and the gods have been propitiated.—ROBERTS.

Ver. 11. And when the king came in to see the guests, he saw there a man which had not on a wedding garment.

"The Persians, in circumstances of grief or joy, visit each other with great attention, which is a tribute of duty always expected from persons of inferior condition, especially if they be dependant. The guests are ushered into a large room, and served with coffee and tobacco. After some time *the master of the house enters*, and his visiters, rising to receive him, continue standing till he has passed through the whole company and paid his respects to each: he then takes his seat, and by signs permits them to be also seated." (Goldsmith's Geography.) In the parable now referred to, the circumstances of which may reasonably be supposed conformable to existing customs, it is evidently implied that the guests were collected together previous to the appearance of the king, who *came in to see the guests.* So also in Luke xiv. 10, in a similar parable, it is said, "when thou art bidden, go and sit down in the lowest *room;* that *when he that bade thee cometh*, he may say unto thee, Go up higher." This unquestionably confirms the application of the Persian ceremony to the parable first cited. It may just be further observed, that in the last-mentioned passage it seems as if it had then been the prevailing practice for the master of the house "to pass through the guests, and pay his respects to each of them," as was certainly the case in Persia.

The following extract will show the importance of having a suitable garment for a marriage feast, and the offence taken against those who refuse it when presented as a gift: "The next day, Dec. 3, the king sent to invite the ambassadors to dine with him once more. The Mehemander told them, it was the custom that they should wear over their own clothes the best of those garments which the king had sent them. The ambassadors at first made some scruple of that compliance: but when they were told that it was a custom observed by all ambassadors, and that no doubt the king would take it very ill at their hands if they presented themselves before him without the marks of his liberality, they at last resolved to do it; and, after their example, all the rest of the retinue." (Abassador's Travels.)—BURDER.

CHAPTER XXIII.

Ver. 6. And love the uppermost rooms at feasts, and the chief seats in the synagogues.

See on Luke 14. 8—11.

At their feasts matters were commonly ordered thus: three couches were set in the form of the Greek letter Π. The table was placed in the middle, the lower end whereof was left open to give access to servants for setting and removing the dishes, and serving the guests. The other three sides were enclosed by the couches, whence it got the name of triclinium. The middle couch, which lay along the upper end of the table, and was therefore accounted the most honourable place, and that which the Pharisees are said particularly to have affected, was distinguished by the name πρωτοκλισια.—CAMPBELL.

Ver. 7. And greetings in the markets, and to be called of men, Rabbi, Rabbi. 8. But be not ye called Rabbi; for one is your Master, *even* Christ, and all ye are brethren.

This title (rabbi) began first to be assumed by men of learning about the time of the birth of Christ. Simeon, the son of Hillel, who succeeded his father as president of the Sanhedrim, was the first Jewish rabbi. The title was generally conferred with a great deal of ceremony. When a person had gone through the schools, and was thought worthy of the degree of rabbi, he was first placed in a chair, a little raised above the company; then were delivered to him a key and a table-book; the key as a symbol of the power and authority conferred upon him to teach others, and the table-book as a symbol of his diligence in his studies. The key he afterward wore as a badge of honour, and when he died it was buried with him. On this occasion also, the imposition of hands by the delegates of the sanhedrim was practised. (Alting.) —BURDER.

Ver. 16. Wo unto you, *ye* blind guides! which

say, Whosoever shall swear by the temple, it is nothing: but whosoever shall swear by the gold of the temple, he is a debtor.

With respect to oaths, there came a doctrine into vogue among the Jews, in the time of Christ, which made such a nice distinction between what *was* and what *was not* an oath, that illiterate people were really incapable of comprehending it, or indeed forming any idea of it: and thus a Jew had it in his power to be guilty of the grossest treachery to his neighbour, even when the latter thought he had heard him swear *by all that was sacred*. Who could suppose, for instance, that a Jew did not speak seriously, when he swore *by the temple*. Yet by this doctrine, such an oath was a mere nothing, *because the stones of the temple were not consecrated*. I do not mean to describe this morality by passages from the writings of the rabbins, both because sufficient collections of these have already been made by others, and because they are not only too extensive, but also too modern for my purpose, as I have principally to do with it as it stood in the time of Christ. I rather choose to take what the Jewish moralists of his day taught, from his own mouth, and to accompany their doctrine with his refutation. The reader who wishes to see passages from the rabbins, may either consult learned commentators on Matt. v. 33—37. xxiii. 16—22, or peruse what Wetstein has collected from them, in whose New Testament he will find a pretty copious collection of such passages.

Christ himself, then, in Matt. xxiii. 16—22, mentions some specimens of their doctrine, which he finds it necessary to controvert. The Pharisees, whom he censured, were in the way of saying, "If a man swear by the temple, he is not bound by that oath; but if he swear by the gold of the temple, he is bound." This was a very paradoxical distinction; and no one who heard their oaths could possibly divine it, unless he happened to be initiated into the whole villany of the business. One would naturally entertain the very same idea concerning it, which Christ expresses in his refutation of it, viz. that "the temple which consecrates the gold is of greater account, and belongs more immediately to God, than the gold." But the foundation of the refined distinction made by the Pharisees was, that the gold was sanctified, but not the materials of the edifice. Again, the Pharisees said, "If a man swear by the altar, it is no oath; but if he swear by the offering, he is bound;" because, forsooth, the offering was consecrated, but the stones of the altar, nothing more than common stones. But to this doctrine, Jesus, with equal reason, makes the following objection: that "the altar which sanctifies the offering is greater than the offering;" and he founds it on this unanswerable argument: "If I appear to swear, and use the language of an oath, my words, though perhaps otherwise equivocal, must be understood in the sense which they generally have in oaths. Thus, if I merely mention *heaven*, that word may have various meanings; it may mean *heaven*, in the *physical* sense of the term, that is, either the *blue atmosphere* which we behold, or that *unknown matter* which fills the remote regions of space above us, and which the ancients called *ether;* but neither of these is God. When, however, I swear *by heaven*, every one understands me as regarding heaven in its relation towards God, as his dwelling-place, or as his throne; and thinks I forbear pronouncing the name of God, merely from reverential awe, and that, in naming the throne of God, I include the idea of him who sitteth upon it; so that if my words are to be explained honestly and grammatically, I have really sworn *by God*. In like manner, if a man swear *by the temple*, that is not swearing by the stones or other materials of which the temple is composed, but *by the God* who dwelleth *in* the temple: and thus also, he who swears *by the altar*, is *not* to understand the bare stones, *as such*, but as they form an altar, and have offerings made upon them; so that he swears *by the altar and what is upon it*: an oath no less solemn and binding, than that most awful oath which is taken amid a sacrifice, by passing between the dismembered pieces of the victim." A most rational exposition; without which we can never, in any compact, be sure of understanding our neighbour's words; not even though he name the name of God in his oath, and swear without any mental reservation whatever; for the *syllables*, perhaps, might still be susceptible of another signification! —MICHAELIS.

Ver. 24. *Ye* blind guides! which strain at a gnat, and swallow a camel.

In these words, he charges them with being extremely scrupulous about very small matters, while they betrayed a glaring and criminal negligence about things of great importance. But as the Pharisees could not literally swallow down a camel, Cajetan supposes a corruption in the text; and maintains that our Lord did not mention a camel, but a larger species of fly, which might actually be swallowed in drinking. Without admitting this, he contends the words contain no proper antithesis. But as all the ancient versions of this text harmonize with the Greek, a corruption cannot be admitted. Nor is the objection of any importance; for, does not our Lord say, "Why beholdest thou the mote that is in thy brother's eye, and considerest not the beam that is thine own eye?" Is it usual then for a beam to be in the eye? Our Lord, who knows all things, knew that a camel cannot be swallowed; but on this very account the proverb was proper; because, while the Pharisees were extremely precise in little things, they readily perpetrated crimes, which, like the camel, were of enormous magnitude. The design of our Lord was, not to teach that a camel could be swallowed, but that the minutiæ of the law in which they displayed such scrupulous accuracy, as the tithing of mint, anise, and cummin, were as much inferior to the weightier matters of the law, as a gnat is inferior to a camel.—PAXTON.

Ver. 27. Wo unto you, scribes and Pharisees, hypocrites! for ye are like unto whited sepulchres, which indeed appear beautiful outward, but are within full of dead *men's* bones, and of all uncleanness. 28. Even so ye also outwardly appear righteous unto men, but within ye are full of hypocrisy and iniquity. 29. Wo unto you, scribes and Pharisees, hypocrites! because ye build the tombs of the prophets, and garnish the sepulchres of the righteous.

The tombs of the lower orders are constructed of stone, at a small distance from their cities and villages, where a great extent of ground is allotted for that purpose. Each family has a particular portion of it walled in like a garden, where the bones of their ancestors have remained for many generations; for, in these enclosures, the graves are all distinct and separate, having each of them a stone placed upright both at the head and feet, inscribed with the name of the person who lies there interred; while the intermediate space is either planted with flowers, bordered round with stone, or paved all over with tiles. The graves of more wealthy citizens are further distinguished by some square chambers, or cupolas, that are built over them. The sepulchres of the Jews were made so large, that persons might go into them. The rule for making them is this: he that sells ground to his neighbour, to make a burying-place, must make a court at the mouth of the cave, six feet by six, according to the bier and those that bury. It was into this court that the women, who visited the sepulchre of our Lord, entered. Here they could look into the sepulchre, and the several graves in it, and see every thing within. The words of the sacred historian are: "And entering into the sepulchre, they saw a young man, sitting on the right side, clothed in a long white garment, and they were affrighted."

These different sorts of tombs and sepulchres, with the very walls likewise of the enclosures, are constantly kept clean, whitewashed, and beautified; and by consequence, continue to this day to be an excellent comment upon that expression of our Saviour's: "Ye are like unto whited sepulchres, which indeed appear beautiful outward, but are within full of dead men's bones and rottenness.—Wo unto you, scribes and Pharisees, hypocrites! because ye build the tombs of the prophets, and garnish the sepulchres of the righteous." It was in one of these chambers, or cupolas, which were built over the sepulchre, that the demoniacs, mentioned in the eighth chapter of Matthew, probably had their dwelling.—PAXTON.

Ver. 37. O Jerusalem, Jerusalem, *thou* that kill-est the prophets, and stonest them which are sent unto thee: how often would I have gathered thy children together, even as a hen gathereth her chickens under *her* wings, and ye would not!

The Psalmist says, "Hide me under the shadow of thy wings." "The children of men put their trust under the shadow of thy wings." The word WING primarily signifies PROTECTION, and *not comfort*, as some have supposed. They appear to have gained that idea from the comfort which chickens have under the wing of the hen. In the East, hawks, kites, and other birds of prey, are continually on the wing; hence it is difficult to rear chickens, because at every moment they are in danger of being pounced on and carried off. Hence the eye of the mother is continually looking up to watch the foes, and no sooner does she see them skimming along, than she gives a scream, and the brood for PROTECTION run UNDER her WINGS.—ROBERTS.

CHAPTER XXIV.

Ver. 17. Let him which is on the house-top not come down to take any thing out of his house.

"It was not possible to view this country without calling to mind the wonderful events that have occurred in it at various periods from the earliest times: more particularly the sacred life and history of our Redeemer pressed foremost on our minds. One thing struck me in the form of the houses in the town now under our view, which served to corroborate the account of former travellers in this country explaining several passages of scripture, particularly the following: In Matt. xxiv. 17, our blessed Saviour, in describing the distresses which shortly would overwhelm the land of Judea, tells his disciples, 'when the abomination of desolation is seen standing in the holy place, let him who is on the house-top not come down to take any thing out of his house, but fly,' &c. The houses in this country are all flat-roofed, and communicate with each other: a person there might proceed to the city walls and escape into the country, without coming down into the street." (Willyams's Voyage up the Mediterranean.) Mr. Harmer endeavours to illustrate this passage, by referring to the eastern custom of the staircase being on the outside of the house: but Mr. Willyams's representation seems to afford a more complete elucidation of the text.—BURDER.

Ver. 18. Neither let him which is in the field return back to take his clothes.

The oriental husbandman is compelled, by the extreme heat of the climate, to prosecute his labours in the field almost in a state of nudity. The ardour with which the farmer urged his labour, even under the milder sky of Italy, required the same precaution. "Plough naked, and sow naked," said Virgil; "winter is an inactive time for the hind."

Aurelius Victor informs us, that the Roman messengers, who were sent to Cincinnatus, from Atenutius, the consul, whom he had delivered from a siege, found him ploughing naked, beyond the Tiber. But the truth is, neither the Syrian nor Italian husbandman pursued his labours in the field entirely naked, but only stripped off his upper garments. An Oriental was said to be naked when these were laid aside. This enables us to understand the meaning of the charge which our Lord gave his disciples: "Neither let him who is in the field return back to take his clothes." The Israelitish peasant when he proceeded to his work in the field, was accustomed to strip off his upper garments, and leave them behind in the house, and to resume them when his task was finished.—PAXTON.

Ver. 28. For wheresoever the carcass is, there will the eagles be gathered together.

It has often appeared to me that the sight and scent of birds of prey in the East are keener than those of the same species in England. Any garbage thrown from the kitchen, or in the wilderness, will soon attract these winged scavengers. Should there be a dead elephant or any other beast in the jungle, vast numbers of ravenous birds and animals hasten to the spot. The eagles, kites, and crows, begin to tear at the carcass and attack each other, and the jackals snap at their feathered rivals; thus, though there is enough for all, they each try to hinder the other from eating. There can be no doubt that birds of prey are very useful in the East, as they carry off the putrid matter which would otherwise infect the air. Hence Europeans do not often destroy such birds, and in the city of Calcutta there is a law to protect them from being injured.—ROBERTS.

Ver. 41. Two *women shall be* grinding at the mill; the one shall be taken, and the other left.

See on Ex. 11. 5.

CHAPTER XXV.

Ver. 4. But the wise took oil in their vessels with their lamps.

Sir John Chardin informs us, that in many parts of the East, and in particular in the Indies, instead of torches and flambeaux, they carry a pot of oil in one hand, and a lamp full of oily rags in the other. This seems to be a very happy illustration of this part of the parable. He observes, elsewhere, that they seldom make use of candles in the East, especially among the great; candles casting but little light, and they sitting at a considerable distance from them. Ezek. i. 18, represents the light of lamps accordingly as very lively.—HARMER.

Ver. 6. And at midnight there was a cry made, Behold, the bridegroom cometh; go ye out to meet him.

An eastern wedding is always celebrated in the *night;* for though the *fortunate* hour for performing some parts of the ceremony may be in the *day*, yet the festivities of the scene will not take place till *night*. When the bridegroom goes forth to the house of the bride, or when he returns to his own habitation or to that of his father, he is always accompanied by numerous friends and dependants, who carry lamps and torches. When he approaches either house the inmates rush out to meet him, and greet him with their best wishes and congratulations. The path is covered with "*garments*," and lamps like fire flies sparkle in every direction.—ROBERTS.

A similar custom is observed among the Hindoos. The husband and wife, on the day of their marriage, being both in the same palanquin, go about seven or eight o'clock at night, accompanied with all their kindred and friends; the trumpets and drums go before them; and they are lighted by a number of flambeaux; immediately before the palanquin walk many women, whose business it is to sing verses, in which they wish them all manner of prosperity. They march in this equipage through the streets for the space of some hours, after which they return to their own house, where the domestics are in waiting. The whole house is illuminated with small lamps; and many of those flambeaux already mentioned are kept ready for their arrival, besides those which accompany them, and are carried before the palanquin. These flambeaux are composed of many pieces of old linen, squeezed hard against one another in a round figure, and thrust down into a mould of copper. The persons that hold them in one hand, have in the other a bottle of the same metal with the copper mould, which is full of oil, which they take care to pour out from time to time upon the linen, which otherwise gives no light.—PAXTON.

Ver. 7. Then all those virgins arose, and trimmed their lamps.

The nuptial lamps, probably, were highly decorated, the trimming was to prepare them for burning. The following account of the celebration of a wedding taken from the Zendavesta, may throw some light on this place. "The day appointed for the marriage, about five o'clock in the evening, the bridegroom comes to the house of the bride, where the mobed, or priest, pronounces, for the first time, the nuptial benediction: he then brings her to his own house, gives her some refreshment, and afterward the assembly of our relatives and friends reconduct her to her father's house. When she arrives, the mobed repeats the nuptial benediction, which is generally done about midnight; immediately after, the bride, accompanied with a part of her attending troop, the rest having returned to their own houses, is reconducted to the house of her husband, where she generally arrives about three o'clock in the morning. Nothing can be more brilliant than these nuptial ceremonies in India: sometimes the assembly consists of not less than 2000 persons, all richly dressed with gold and silver tissue; the friends and relatives of the bride, encompassed with their domestics, are all mounted on horses richly harnessed. The goods, wardrobe, and even the bed of the bride, are carried in triumph. The husband, richly mounted and magnificently dressed, is accompanied by his friends and relatives; and the friends of the bride following him in covered carriages. At intervals, during the procession, guns and rockets are fired, and the spectacle is rendered grand beyond description by a prodigious number of lighted torches, and by the sound of a multitude of musical instruments."—BURDER.

Ver. 10. And while they went to buy, the bridegroom came; and they that were ready went in with him to the marriage: and the door was shut.

At a marriage, the procession of which I saw some years ago, the bridegroom came from a distance, and the bride lived at Serampore, to which place the bridegroom was to come by water. After waiting two or three hours, at length, near midnight, it was announced, as if in the very words of scripture, Behold, the bridegroom cometh, go ye out to meet him. All the persons employed now lighted their lamps, and ran with them in their hands to fill up their stations in the procession; some of them had lost their lights, and were unprepared, but it was then too late to seek them, and the cavalcade moved forward to the house of the bride, at which place the company entered a large and splendidly illuminated area, before the house, covered with an awning, where a great multitude of friends, dressed in their best apparel, were seated upon mats. The bridegroom was carried in the arms of a friend, and placed on a superb seat in the midst of the company, where he sat a short time, and then went into the house, the door of which was immediately shut, and guarded by Sepoys. I and others expostulated with the door-keepers, but in vain." (Ward's View of the Hindoos.)—BURDER.

Ver. 36. Naked, and ye clothed me: I was sick, and ye visited me: I was in prison, and ye came unto me.

It is more easy in the East to visit imprisoned friends than it is in Europe. Thus Rauwolf tells us, that he was allowed at Tripolis, in Syria, to visit his confined friends as often as he liked. "After we had gone through small and low doors into the prisons in which they were confined, their keepers always willingly let me in and out; sometimes I even remained in the prison with them during the night."—ROSENMULLER.

CHAPTER XXVI.

Ver. 18. And he said, Go into the city to such a man, and say unto him, The Master saith, My time is at hand; I will keep the passover at thy house with my disciples.

When a man believes himself to be near death, he says, "Go tell the priest I am going on my journey, my time is at hand." When dead, it is said of him, "His time has gone, he has fallen."—ROBERTS.

Ver. 23. And he answered and said, He that dippeth *his* hand with me in the dish, the same shall betray me.

See on John 13. 23.

The practice which was most revolting to me was this: when the master of the house found in the dish any dainty morsel, he took it out with his fingers, and applied it to my mouth. This was true Syrian courtesy and hospitality; and, had I been sufficiently well-bred, my mouth would have opened to receive it. On my pointing to my plate, however, he had the goodness to deposite the choice morsel there. I would not have noticed so trivial a circumstance, if it did not exactly illustrate what the Evangelists record of the Last Supper.—JOWETT.

Ver. 30. And when they had sung a hymn, they went out into the Mount of Olives.

This was the *Hallel* which the Jews were obliged to sing on the night of the passover. It consisted of six psalms, the hundred and thirteenth, and the five following ones. This they did not sing all at once, but in parts. Just before the drinking of the second cup and eating of the lamb they sung the first part; and on mixing the fourth and last cup they sung the remainder; and said over it what they call the blessing of the song, which was Psalm cxlv. 10. They might, if they would, mix a fifth cup, and say over it the *Great Hallel*, which was Psalm cxxxvi. but they were not obliged to.—GILL.

Ver. 34. Jesus said unto him, Verily I say unto thee, That this night, before the cock crow, thou shalt deny me thrice.

See on Mark 14. 30.

Ver. 69. Now Peter sat without in the palace: and a damsel came unto him, saying, Thou also wast with Jesus of Galilee.

The Greek words are more accurately translated by, "Peter sat without in the court." This court (αὐλή) in which Peter was at the fire in the palace of the high-priest, was, according to the usual old and oriental mode of building, the inner part of the house enclosed on all sides, which was not roofed, but was in the open air.—BURDER.

CHAPTER XXVII.

Ver. 2. And when they had bound him, they led *him* away, and delivered him to Pontius Pilate the governor.

The Street of Grief, or Dolorous Way, derives its appellation from its being the supposed site of the street through which the chief priests and elders of the Jews, after binding Jesus Christ, led him away and delivered him to Pontius Pilate. (Mat. xxvii. 2.) It proceeds from the gate of Saint Stephen up to an archway, which appears to have been at one time called "the Gate of Judgment," because malefactors were anciently conducted through it to the place of execution. This archway is exhibited in the annexed engraving. At the period of the crucifixion, this gate stood in the western wall of Jerusalem: but now it is in the centre of the city. The wall above the archway is supposed to have formed a part of the house of Pilate; and the central window is reputed to have been the place whence our Saviour was shown unto the people.

The "Street of Grief" rises with a gradual ascent, becoming narrower towards Calvary, where it terminates. It is difficult to pass along it, owing to the stones being broken up, and it is completely out of order.—HORNE.

[*See* COMPREHENSIVE COMMENTARY, *on Ps.* 122. 3, *and the engraving there of an* ARCHED STREET *in Jerusalem.*

Ver. 7. And they took counsel, and bought with them the potters' field, to bury strangers in.

It lay immediately without the wall of the city, on the southeast corner, about a mile from the Temple. "On the west side of the valley of Hinnom, is the place anciently called the potters' field, and afterward the field of blood, but now campo sancto. It is only a small piece of ground, about thirty yards long, and fifteen broad; one half of which is taken up by a square fabric, built for a charnel-house, that is twelve yards high. Into this building dead bodies are let down from the top, there being five holes left open for that purpose, through which they may be seen under several degrees of decay." (Maundrell.)

Why a potters' field should be preferred to any other as

ROCK-HEWN TOMB, Petra. Job 3: 14. Jer. 49: 10, 16, 20.

TOMB called 'of the Kings,' Jerusalem. 2 Chr. 21: 20. 32: 33.

ARCHED STREET, Jerusalem: note, Ps. 122: 3. p. 112.

a burial-place, may be conjectured from the following extract, as in all probability the same causes which prevented its being convertible to arable or pasture ground, must have existed in an equal degree in Palestine. A burial-ground was one of the few purposes to which it could have been applied.

"We travelled eleven hours this day, and the last six without once halting. The ground over which we travelled seemed strewed over with small pieces of green earthenware, which was so plenty that many bushels could be gathered in the space of a mile. I inquired into the occasion of it: the information which we received from our sheik and others in the caravan, was, that in former ages the greatest part of this plain was inhabited by potters, as the soil abounded then, as it does at present, with clay fit for their use: that they moved their works from place to place, as they consumed the clay, or it suited their convenience. They now make at Bagdad such kinds of earthenware, with a green glazing on it. When the sun shines it appears like green glass, which is very hurtful to the sight. They cannot plough this ground, as it would cut the feet of both men and oxen." (Parsons' Travels in Asia.)—BURDER.

Ver. 26. Then released he Barabbas unto them: and when he had scourged Jesus, he delivered *him* to be crucified. 29. And when they had platted a crown of thorns, they put *it* upon his head, and a reed in his right hand: and they bowed the knee before him, and mocked him, saying, Hail, King of the Jews!

Mohammed Zemaun Khan was carried before the king. When he had reached the camp, the king ordered Mohammed Khan, chief of his camel artillery, to put a mock-crown upon the rebel's head, bazubends or armlets on his arms, a sword by his side, to mount him upon an ass, with his face towards the tail; then to parade him throughout the camp, and to exclaim, This is he who wanted to be the king. After this was over, and the people had mocked and insulted him, he was led before the king, who called for his looties, and ordered them to turn him into ridicule, by making him dance and make antics against his will: he then ordered, that whoever chose might spit in his face. After this he received the bastinado on the soles of his feet, which was administered by the chiefs of the Cagar tribe, and some time after he had his eyes put out.—MORIER.

Ver. 29. And when they had platted a crown of thorns, they put *it* upon his head, and a reed in his right hand: and they bowed the knee before him, and mocked him, saying, Hail, King of the Jews!

Among other circumstances of suffering and ignominy, which accompanied the death of Christ, it is said that they platted "a crown of thorns, and put it upon his head." Hasselquist says: "The naba or nabka of the Arabians is in all probability the tree which afforded the crown of thorns put on the head of Christ: it grows very commonly in the East. This plant was very fit for the purpose, for it has many small and sharp spines, which are well adapted to give pain; the crown might be easily made of these soft, round, and pliant branches; and what in my opinion seems to be the greatest proof is, that the leaves much resemble those of ivy, as they are of a very deep green. Perhaps the enemies of Christ would have a plant somewhat resembling that with which emperors and generals were used to be crowned, that there might be calumny even in the punishment."—BURDER.

Ver. 31. And after that they had mocked him, they took the robe off from him, and put his own raiment on him, and led him away to crucify *him*.

Crucifixion was a very common mode of inflicting the punishment of death among several ancient nations, namely, among the Egyptians, Carthaginians, Persians, Greeks, and Romans. The cross consisted of a long pole, and a short transverse beam, both of which, as the ancients affirm, were united in the form of a Greek and Roman T; a little piece of the perpendicular beam, however, generally projected at the top, to which the writing, containing the cause of the punishment, was affixed. In the middle of the perpendicular poles there was a wooden plug, which projected like a horn, on which the person crucified rode or rested, that the weight of the body might not tear the hands loose. The cross was erected on the place of execution, and fastened in the ground; it was generally not high, and the feet of the criminal were scarcely four feet above the ground. The person condemned was raised up, quite naked, upon the projecting plug, or pulled up with cords; his hands were first tied with cords to the transverse beam, and then nailed on with strong iron nails. Cicero against Verres calls crucifixion the most cruel and horrid punishment; and in another place, a punishment which must be far, not only from the body of a Roman citizen, but also from his eyes, and even his thoughts. It was, therefore, properly designed among the Romans only for such as had been guilty of murder, highway robbery, rebellion against the government, and violation of the public tranquillity. A learned physician, George Gottlieb Richter, has proved in a treatise dedicated to this subject, that the tortures of crucifixion must have been indeed indescribable. Even the unnatural constrained situation of the body, with the arms stretched upward, sometimes for days together, must have been an inexpressible torment, especially as not the slightest motion or convulsion could take place without causing excruciating pain over the whole body, particularly in the pierced limbs, and on the back, mangled by previous scourging. Besides this, the nails were driven through the hands, and sometimes through the feet, exactly in places where irritable nerves and sinews meet, which were partly injured and partly forcibly compressed, by which the most acute pains must have been excited, and constantly increased. As the wounded parts were always exposed to the air, they became inflamed. The same also probably occurred in many other parts, where the circulation of the juices was impeded by the violent tension of the whole body. As the blood, too, which is impelled from the left ventricle of the heart through the veins into all parts of the body, did not find room enough in the wounded and violently extended extremities, it must flow back to the head, which was free, unnaturally extend and oppress the arteries, and thus cause constantly increasing headache. On account of the impediment of the circulation of the blood in the external parts, the left ventricle of the heart could not entirely discharge itself of all the blood, and, consequently, not receive all the blood which comes from the right ventricle; hence the blood in the lungs had no free vent, by which a dreadful oppression was occasioned; under such constantly increasing tortures, the person crucified lived generally three days, sometimes even longer. Hence Pilate did not credit the account that Jesus had expired so soon, and, therefore, questioned the centurion who had kept watch at the cross. —ROSENMULLER.

Ver. 48. And straightway one of them ran, and took a sponge, and filled *it* with vinegar, and put *it* on a reed, and gave him to drink.

What most tormented crucified persons was, dreadful thirst, which must naturally be occasioned by the heat of the wounds or fever. Out of a spirit of humanity, one of the soldiers keeping watch, gave Jesus, at his request, a sponge dipped in vinegar. It is probable that they gave Jesus such vinegar as they had standing there for their usual drink. An example, in more modern times, of giving, in the East, a sponge dipped in vinegar, to such as were to be executed by slow torture, in order to refresh them, is mentioned by Heberer, in his Description of his Slavery in Egypt. "When this Greek had hung upon the hook beyond the third day in much pain, one of the keepers was at last prevailed upon, by the presents of his friends, secretly to give him poison upon a sponge, under the appearance of refreshing him a little with vinegar."—BURDER.

Ver. 51. And, behold, the vail of the temple was rent in twain, from the top to the bottom; and the earth did quake, and the rocks rent.

"About one yard and a half distance from the hole in which the foot of the cross was fixed, is seen that memorable cleft in the rock, said to have been made by the earthquake which happened at the suffering of the God of Nature, when the rocks rent, and the very graves were opened. This cleft, as to what now appears of it, is about a span wide, at its upper part, and two deep, after which it closes; but it opens again below, (as you may see in another chapel contiguous to the side of Calvary,) and runs down to an unknown depth in the earth. That this rent was made by the earthquake that happened at our Lord's passion, there is only tradition to prove; but that it is a natural and genuine breach, and not counterfeited by any art, the sense and reason of every one that sees it may convince him; for the sides of it fit like two tallies to each other; and yet it runs in such intricate windings as could not well be counterfeited by art, nor arrived at by any instruments." (Maundrell.) "The far end of this chapel, called the Chapel of St. John, is confined with the foot of Calvary, where, on the left side of the altar, there is a cleft in the rock: the insides do testify that art had no hand therein, each side to the other being answerably rugged, and these were inaccessible to the workmen: that before spoken of, in the chapel below, is a part of this, which reacheth, as they say, to the centre." (Sandys.)—Burder.

Ver. 60. And laid it in his own new tomb, which he had hewn out in the rock: and he rolled a great stone to the door of the sepulchre, and departed.

The sepulchres were not only made in rocks, but had doors to go in and out at; these doors were fastened with a large and broad stone rolled against them. It was at the shutting up of the sepulchre with this stone that mourning began: and after it was shut with this sepulchral stone, it was not lawful to open it.—Burder.

CHAPTER XXVIII.

Ver. 6. He is not here; for he is risen, as he said. Come, see the place where the Lord lay.

The Church of the Holy Sepulchre, with the *Sepulchre* itself, is a prominent object of attention to the devout pilgrim. The *Holy Sepulchre*, in which, according to ancient tradition, the body of the Redeemer was deposited by Nicodemus, after he had taken it down from the cross, (John xix. 39—42,) stands a little north of the centre of this church, and is covered by a small oblong quadrilateral building of marble, crowned with a tiny cupola standing upon pillars, and divided into three compartments. Over the entrance to this edifice, the reader will observe a temporary covering of canvass extended by means of cords, the object of which is to prevent the voice of the preacher, who lectures from the door of the Sepulchre during Passion-week, from being dissipated in the dome above and rendered inaudible. The first compartment is an antechamber, which may contain six or eight persons: here the pilgrims put off their shoes from their feet, before they enter upon the holy ground within; where, occupying half of the second part of the building, is "the place where the Lord lay." (Matt. xxviii. 6.) The third compartment is a small chapel appropriated to the Copts, which is entered from behind, and which has no internal communication with the others.

Dr. E. D. Clarke, the traveller, (whose skepticism concerning some of the sacred antiquities of Jerusalem was as great as his credulity in others,) was of opinion that the spot now shown as the site of the sepulchre, was not the place of Christ's interment, from the variance of its present appearance with the accounts in the Gospel. His reasons for disbelief are as follows:—1. The tomb of Christ was in a garden without the walls of Jerusalem: the structure which at present bears its name is in the heart of, at least, the modern city; and Dr. Clarke is unwilling to believe that the ancient limits can have been so much circumscribed to the north as to exclude its site. 2. Further, the original sepulchre was undoubtedly a cave: the present offers no such appearance, being an insulated pile, constructed or cased with distinct slabs of marble.

Bishop Heber, however, in his elaborate critique on Dr. Clarke's Travels, has shown that these arguments are inconclusive. For,—

1. One of the Discourses of Cyril, patriarch of Jerusalem, incidentally proves two facts; viz., first, that the sepulchre, as we now see it, *was* without the ancient wall; and, secondly, that before it was ornamented by the Emperess Helena, (with whom he was contemporary,) it was a simple cave in the rock.

2. Further, that the present sepulchre, defaced and altered as it is, may really be "the place where the Lord lay," is likely from the following circumstances: "Forty yards, or thereabouts," says Bishop Heber, "from the upper end of the sepulchre, the natural rock is visible: and in the place which the priests call Calvary, it is at least as high as the top of the sepulchre itself. The rock then *may* have extended as far as the present entrance; and though the entrance itself is hewn into form, and cased with marble, the adytum yet offers proof that it is not factitious. It is a trapezium of seven feet by six, neither at right angles to its own entrance, nor to the aisle of the church which conducts to it, and in no respect conformable to the external plan of the tomb. This last is arranged in a workmanlike manner, with its frontal immediately opposite the principal nave, and in the same style with the rest of the church. It is shaped something like a horseshoe, and its walls, measured from this outer horseshoe to the inner trapezium, vary from five to eight feet in thickness, a sufficient space to admit of no inconsiderable density of rock between the outer and inner coating of marble. This, however, does not apply to the antechamber, of which the frontal, at least, is probably factitious; and where that indenture in the marble is found which induced Dr. Clarke to believe that the whole thickness of the wall was composed of the same costly substance. Now these circumstances afford, we apprehend, no inconsiderable grounds for supposing, with Pococke, that it is indeed a grotto above ground: the irregularity of the shape; the difference between the external and internal plan; the thickness of the walls, so needless, if they are throughout of masonry, all favour this opinion; nor is the task ascribed to Helena's workmen, of insulating this rock from that which is still preserved a few yards distant, at all incredible, when we consider that the labour, while it pleased the taste of their employer, furnished at the same time materials for her intended cathedral."

3. Although the Church of the Holy Sepulchre has been burnt down since Dr. Clarke's visit, yet the "rock-built sepulchre of the Messiah, being of all others the least liable to injury, has remained in spite of the devouring element."

The *Holy Sepulchre* is a sarcophagus of white marble, destitute of ornament, and slightly tinged with blue; 6 ft. 1¼ in. long, 3 ft. 0¾ in. broad, and 2 ft. 1¼ in. deep, measured on the outside. It is but indifferently polished, and appears as if it had at one time been exposed to the pelting of the storm and the changes of the seasons, by which it has been considerably disintegrated. Over it are suspended twelve massy splendid silver lamps, the gifts of monarchs and princes: these are kept continually burning, in honour of the twelve apostles. The sarcophagus occupies about one half of the sepulchral chamber, and extends from one end of it to the other. A space, not exceeding three feet wide, in front of it, is all that remains for the reception of visiters, so that not more than three or four persons can be conveniently admitted at a time. Over the sarcophagus is a large painting, representing Christ bursting the bonds of the tomb, and his triumphant ascent out of the grave on the morning of the resurrection. A Greek or Latin priest always stands here with a silver vase of incense, which he waves over the pilgrims.—Horne.

THE GOSPEL ACCORDING TO MARK.

CHAPTER I.

Ver. 3. The voice of one crying in the wilderness, Prepare ye the way of the Lord, make his paths straight.

When a man of rank has to pass through a town or village, a messenger is despatched to tell the people to *prepare* the way, and to await his orders. Hence may be seen some sweeping the road, others who "spread their garments in the way," and some who are cutting "down branches from the trees" (Matt. xxi. 8) to form arches and festoons where the great man has to pass.—ROBERTS.

Ver. 6. And John was clothed with camel's hair, and with a girdle of a skin about his loins; and he did eat locusts and wild honey.

The Jews were allowed to eat locusts, and when sprinkled with salt, and fried, they are not unlike our fresh water cray fish. The Acridophagi must have preferred them to almost every other species of food, since they derived their name from their eating locusts. We learn from the valuable work of Dr. Russel, that the Arabs salt and eat them as a delicacy. Locusts were accordingly the common food of John, the precursor of Christ, while he remained in the wilderness. In feeding on that insect, the Baptist submitted to no uncommon privation, and practised no savage rigour, like many of the hermits who inhabited the deserts; but merely followed the abstemious mode of living to which the people were accustomed, in the less frequented parts of the country. The food upon which he subsisted in the wilderness appears to be particularly mentioned, merely to show that he fared as the poorest of men, and that his manner of living corresponded with the meanness of his dress. Much unnecessary pains have been taken by some squeamish writers, to prove that the locusts which John used for food, were the fruit of a certain tree, and not the carcass of the insects distinguished by that name; but a little inquiry will fully clear up this matter, and show, that however disgusting the idea of that kind of meat may appear to us, the Orientals entertain a different opinion. Many nations in the East, as the Indians of the Bashee islands, the Tonquinese, and the inhabitants of Madagascar, make no scruple to eat these insects, of which they have innumerable swarms, and prefer them to the finest fish. The ancients affirm, that in Africa, Syria, Persia, and almost throughout Asia, the people commonly eat these creatures. Clenard, in a letter from Fez, in 1541, assures us, that he saw wagon loads of locusts brought into that city for food. Kirstenius, in his notes on Matthew, says, he was informed by his Arabic master, that he had often seen them on the river Jordan; that they were of the same form with ours, but larger; that the inhabitants pluck off their wings and feet, and hang the rest at their necks till they grow warm and ferment; and then they eat them, and think them very good food. A monk, who had travelled into Egypt, asserts, that he had eaten of these locusts, and that in the country they subsisted on them four months in the year. In Bushire, they are used by the lowest peasantry as food. The Arabs feed on them to this day, and prepare them for use in the following manner: They grind them to flour in their handmills, or powder them in stone mortars. This flour they mix with water to the consistency of dough, and make thin cakes of it, which they bake like other bread on a heated girdle; and this, observes Hasselquist, serves instead of bread to support life for want of something better. At other times they boil them in water, and afterward stew them with butter, and make a sort of fricassee, which has no bad taste.—PAXTON.

Ver. 10. And straightway coming up out of the water, he saw the heavens opened, and the Spirit like a dove descending upon him.

See on Matt. 3. 11.

CHAPTER II.

Ver. 3. And they come unto him, bringing one sick of the palsy, which was borne of four.
4. And when they could not come nigh unto him for the press, they uncovered the roof where he was; and when they had broken *it* up, they let down the bed wherein the sick of the palsy lay.

Among other pretended difficulties and absurdities relating to this fact, it has been urged, that, as the uncovering, or breaking up of the roof, as mentioned by Mark, or the letting a person down through it, as recorded by Luke, supposes the breaking up of tiles, spars, rafters, &c., "so," says the infidel, "it was well if Jesus, and his disciples, escaped with only a broken pate, by the falling of the tiles, and if the rest were not smothered with dust." But if the construction of an oriental dwelling be recollected, we shall find nothing in the conduct of these men either absurd in itself, or hazardous to others. Dr. Shaw contends, that no violence was offered to the roof, and that the bearers only carried the paralytic up to the top of the house, either by forcing their way through the crowd up the staircase, or else by conveying him over some of the neighbouring terraces, and these, after they had drawn away the στέγη, or veil, let him down along the side of the roof (through the opening, or *impluvium*) into the midst of the court before Jesus. But this ingenious explanation is encumbered with several important difficulties. The natural and obvious idea which the text suggests to the mind is, that the roof of the house was actually opened, and the paralytic let down through the tiling, or roof, into the upper apartment, where Jesus was sitting; while an elaborate process of criticism is necessary to elicit the sense of the learned author: this is a circumstance strongly in favour of the common exposition. Besides, he has produced no proof that στέγη ever signifies a veil, for which the sacred writers, in particular, employ other words, as Καλυμμα, Καταπετασμα; but its usual meaning is the roof, or flat terrace of a house, and, by an easy transition, the house itself. Nor has he assigned a sufficient reason for the use of the strong term εξορυξαντὲς, by which he is evidently embarrassed. He endeavours, in the first place, to get quit of it altogether, by observing that it is omitted in the Cambridge manuscript, and not regarded in the Syriac, and some other versions. But conscious it could neither be expunged, nor disregarded upon such authority, he thinks "it may be considered as further explanatory of απεστέγασαν; or, as in the Persian version, referred either to the letting down of the bed, or, preparatory thereto, to the making holes in it for the cords to pass through." But the word cannot, with propriety, be considered as a further explanation of απεστέγασαν; for it has quite a different meaning; it signifies to dig out, to break up, or pluck out, and always involves the idea of force and violence; but no violence, and but very little exertion was necessary, to fold back the veil, which was expanded by cords over the court. Nor can it be referred to the removal of other obstructions, for when the veil was removed, no further obstruction remained. It cannot, in this place, signify to tie the four corners of the bed or bedstead with cords, for it bears no such meaning in any other part of the holy scriptures, or in any classic author; and since it is more naturally constructed with στέγη than with κραββατον, it ought to be referred to the former. Pearce, in his Miracles of Jesus Vindicated, offers another solution; according to him, they opened the trap-door, which used to be on the top of the houses in Judea, and which lying even with the roof, was a part of it when it was let down and shut. But with regard to this exposition, Parkhurst justly observes, that the most natural interpretation of αποστεγαζειν, is to unroof, break up the roof, and that the verb is twice used by Strabo, as cited by Elsner and Wetstein, in this sense; which also best agrees with the following word εξορυξαντες. The history, as recorded by the evangelists Mark and Luke, seems to be this; Jesus, after some days absence, returned to Capernaum, and to the house where he used to dwell. And when it was reported that he was there, the people crowded to the square court, about which the house was built, in such numbers that there was no room for them, even though they filled the porch. The men who carried the paralytic, endeavoured to bring him into the court among the crowd; but, finding this impossible, they went up the staircase which led from the porch (or possibly came from the terrace of a neighbouring house) to the flat roof of the house, over the upper room in which Jesus was, Και εξορυξαντες; and having forced up as much both of the tiles or plaster, and of the boards on which they were laid, as was necessary for the purpose, they let down the paralytic's mattress, δια των κεραμων, through the tiles or roof, into the midst of the room before Jesus. This operation, under the careful management of these men, who must have been anxious not to incommode the Saviour and his auditory, could be attended with no danger. The tiles or plaster might be removed to another part of the flat roof, and the boards likewise, as they were broken up; and as for the spars, they might be sufficiently wide to admit the narrow couch of the sick man, without moving any of them from their places. It may be even inferred from the silence of the two evangelists, that the company suffered not the least inconvenience; and the infidel can produce the testimony of no writer in support of his insinuations. But though we were unable to remove the objection, or silence the ridicule of the unbeliever, it is in every respect better to abide by the natural and obvious sense of the passage. Many of the oriental princes and nobles have a favourite upper chamber to which they retire from the fatigues of state and the hurry of business. To such a retired apartment the Saviour and his disciples withdrew to celebrate the passover before he suffered.—PAXTON.

Ver. 16. And when the scribes and Pharisees saw him eat with publicans and sinners, they said unto his disciples, How is it that he eateth and drinketh with publicans and sinners.

At this period there were in the Roman empire two classes of men, who might be called publicans, (*publicani*, τελῶναι.) First, such as farmed the revenues of whole provinces. These were generally Roman knights, frequently highly respected men, as may be inferred from the picture which Cicero draws of some of them in his speeches for the Manilian law and for Plancus. These were properly called publicani, but they are not mentioned in the Evangelists. They likewise did not collect the taxes themselves; they employed for this purpose their freedmen and slaves, to whom they gave as assistants as many natives as was requisite. These sub tax-gatherers were indeed also called publicans, (*publicani*, τελῶναι;) but their proper Latin name was portitores. Their places were united with great temptations; for as they had farmed the taxes for a fixed sum, they tried to press as much as possible from individual persons. Besides this, gathering the taxes for a foreign power, is undoubtedly a detested employment in every country, and among the natives generally only people of the meanest rank, and of a low way of thinking, lend themselves to it. Among the Jews, the ill-will towards people of this class was increased by pride and zeal for the independence of the nation; and such of their countrymen as suffered themselves to be employed in gathering taxes for heathens, they considered as apostates to their religion. Publicans and sinners were among their synonymous names.—ROSENMULLER.

CHAPTER V.

Ver. 38. And he cometh to the house of the ruler of the synagogue, and seeth the tumult, and them that wept and wailed greatly.

See on Gen. 45. 2.

CHAPTER VI.

Ver. 3. Is not this the carpenter, the son of Mary the brother of James and Joses, and of Juda, and Simon? and are not his sisters here with us? And they were offended at him.

It was a common practice, in almost every country, to distinguish a person from others of the same name, by giving him a surname derived from the trade or occupation of his parent. The English language furnishes us with examples of this in the surnames of Baker, Taylor, Carpenter, and the like; and what is still more to the point, it is at this day the custom in some of the oriental nations, and particularly among the Arabs, to distinguish any learned and illustrious man, who may chance to be born of parents who follow a particular trade or art, by giving him the name of such trade or art as a surname, although he may never have followed it himself. Thus, if a man of learning happen to be descended from a dier or a tailor, they call him the tailor's son or the dier's son, or frequently omitting the word son, simply the dier or the tailor. According to this custom, the remark of the Jews, in which our Saviour is termed the carpenter, may be considered as referring merely to the occupation of his reputed father: and that τεκτων ought to be understood in this place as meaning nothing more than ὁ του τεκτονος υἱός, the son of the carpenter. This explanation of the term is supported by the authority of another evangelist, who resolves it by this very phrase." (Mosheim.)—PAXTON.

Ver. 8. And commanded them that they should take nothing for *their* journey, save a staff only; no scrip, no bread, no money in *their* purse.

See on Mat. 10. 9.

Ver. 11. And whosoever shall not receive you, nor hear you, when ye depart thence, shake off the dust under your feet for a testimony against them. Verily I say unto you, It shall be more tolerable for Sodom and Gomorrah, in the day of judgment, than for that city.

When a person is made angry by another, he says, "I will shake thee off as I do the dust from my sandals." "I have washed my feet; never more shall they tread that place."—ROBERTS.

Ver. 13. And they cast out many devils, and anointed with oil many that were sick, and healed *them*.

The people of the East give a decided preference to *external* applications; hence when they are directed to "eat" or "drink" medicine, they ask, can they not have something to apply outside? For almost every complaint a man will smear his body with bruised leaves, or saffron, or ashes of certain woods, or OILS; and he professes to derive more benefit from them than from those medicines which are taken internally: at all events, he knows they cannot do him so much harm. It ought to be observed, that they do not attach any miraculous effects to the being "anointed with oil."—ROBERTS.

Ver. 21. And when a convenient day was come, that Herod, on his birthday, made a supper to his lords, high captains, and chief *estates* of Galilee.

The Orientals have nearly all their great feasts in the evening: thus, to give a *supper* is far more common than a dinner. Those evening festivals have a very imposing effect: what with the torches and lamps, the splendid dresses jewels, processions, the bowers, the flowers, and the music, a kind of enchantment takes hold of the feelings, and the mind is half bewildered in the scenes.—ROBERTS.

CHAPTER IX.

Ver. 41. For whosoever shall give you a cup of water to drink, in my name, because ye belong to Christ, verily I say unto you, He shall not lose his reward.

In the sacred scriptures, bread and water are commonly mentioned as the chief supports of human life; and to provide a sufficient quantity of water, to prepare it for use, and to deal it out to the thirsty, are still among the principal cares of an oriental householder. To furnish travellers with water is, even in present times, reckoned of so great importance, that many of the eastern philanthropists have been at considerable expense to procure them that enjoyment. The nature of the climate, and the general aspect of the oriental regions, require numerous fountains to excite and sustain the languid powers of vegetation; and the sun, burning with intense heat in a cloudless sky, demands for the fainting inhabitants the verdure, shade, and coolness, which vegetation produces. Hence fountains of living water are met with in the towns and villages, in the fields and gardens, and by the sides of the roads and of the beaten tracks on the mountains; and a cup of cold water from these wells, is no contemptible present.

In Arabia, equal attention is paid by the wealthy and benevolent to the refreshment of the traveller. On one of the mountains of Arabia, Niebuhr found three little reservoirs, which are always kept full of fine water for the use of passengers. These reservoirs, which are about two feet and a half square, and from five to seven feet high, are round, or pointed at the top, of mason's work, having only a small opening in one of the sides, by which they pour water into them. Sometimes he found, near these places of Arab refreshment, a piece of a ground shell, or a little scoop of wood for lifting the water.

The same attention to the comfort of travellers, is manifested in Egypt, where public buildings are set apart in some of their cities, the business of whose inhabitants is to supply the passenger with water free of expense. Some of these houses make a very handsome appearance; and the persons appointed to wait on the passengers, are required to have some vessels of copper, curiously tinned and filled with water, always ready on the wingow next the street. Some of the Mohammedan villagers in Palestine, not far from Nazareth, brought Mr. Buckingham and his party bread and water, while on horseback, without even being solicited to do so; and when they halted to accept it, both compliments and blessings were mutually interchanged.* Hence a cup of cold water is a present in the East of much value, though there are some other refreshments of a superior quality. When Sisera asked a little water to drink, Jael brought him milk, which she thought he would naturally prefer; and in the book of Proverbs, the mother of Lemuel instructed him to give strong drink to him that is ready to perish, and wine to those that were of heavy heart. Still, however, the value of a cup of water, though to be numbered among the simplest presents the traveller can receive, is of great value in those countries. If this be duly considered, the declaration of our Lord, "Whosoever shall give you a cup of water to drink, in my name, because ye belong to Christ, verily I say unto you, He shall not lose his reward," is of greater importance than we are apt at first sight to imagine. The general thought is plain to every reader, That no service performed to a disciple of Christ, out of love to his master, although comparatively small, shall remain unrewarded; but the inhabitants of more temperate climates are sometimes ready to think that the instance which our Lord mentions, is rather insignificant. It certainly would not appear so now to an inhabitant of the East, nor did it then, we have reason to believe, appear so to them who heard the Saviour's declaration. But the words of Christ evidently contain more than this; they lead up our thoughts to the character of him for whose sake the cup of water is given. An act of benevolence, how small soever, is certainly pleasing in the sight of God, so far as it proceeds from proper motives, is performed in the appointed manner, and directed to the proper end, and particularly if it be connected with the name of his own Son. But to give a cup of water to a disciple in the name of Christ, and because he belongs to him, must signify, that it is given in honour of Christ; and this is the particular reason of the reward which the remunerative justice of God bestows. An article in the Asiastic Miscellany, quoted by Dr. Clarke in his edition of Harmer, will set this in a very clear light. In India, the Hindoos go sometimes a great way to fetch water, and then boil it, that it may not be hurtful to travellers who are hot; and after this, stand from morning till night in some great road, where there is neither pit nor rivulet, and offer it in honour of their gods, to be drunk by the passengers. Such necessary works of charity in these hot countries, seem to have been practised among the more pious and humane Jews; and our Lord assures them, that if they do this in his name, they shall not lose their reward. This one circumstance, Dr. Clarke justly remarks, of the Hindoos offering the water to the fatigued passengers, in honour of their gods, is a better illustration of our Lord's words, than all the collections of Mr. Harmer on the subject.—PAXTON.

* "In this, as in most of the other villages, is a hut with a large jar of water in it, by the road-side, for travellers. When there are no houses, this jar is generally placed under a fine-tree." (Waddington's Travels in Ethiopia, p. 35.)—B.

CHAPTER X.

Ver. 46. And they came to Jericho: and as he went out of Jericho with his disciples, and a great number of people, blind Bartimeus, the son of Timeus, sat by the highway-side, begging.

Here again the picture is teeming with life. See that blind man seated under a shady tree "by the highway side," he has occupied the place from infancy. The travellers who are accustomed to pass that way always expect to see the blind beggar; and were he not there they would have a sense of discomfort, and anxiously inquire after the cause. So soon as he hears the sound of a footstep he begins to cry aloud, "*The blind! the blind! remember the blind!*" He knows almost every man's voice, and has always some question to ask in reference to the family at home. Should a stranger be passing, he inquires, *Ath-ār*, i. e. Who is that? Those who cannot walk are carried to their wonted place, as was the man who was "laid daily at the gate of the temple, which is called Beautiful, to ask alms of them that entered into the temple." Some cripples are carried about in a basket by two men, who have a share of the alms. Sometimes they have tremendous quarrels, as the bearers take too great a share of the money or provisions, which induces the lame man to use his tongue: they, however, generally get the victory by threatening to leave the poor fellow to get home as well as he can. Some of the blind mendicants have not the patience to remain in one place: hence they get a person to lead them, and here again they have a constant source of quarrel in the suspicions of the one and the rogueries of the other. The guide falls into a passion, and abuses the beggar, tells him he is cursed of the gods, and pretends to take his departure; the blind man retorts, and calls him a *low caste*, a *servant* of beggars, and tells him he shall not hav any more of his rice. They both having expended al their hard words, become a little calmer; and after a few expostulations, once more approximate, and trudge off in pursuit of their calling.—ROBERTS.

CHAPTER XII.

Ver. 1. And he began to speak unto them by parables. A *certain* man planted a vineyard and set a hedge about *it*, and digged *a place for* the wine-fat, and built a tower, and let it out to husbandmen, and went into a far country

I was particularly struck with the appearance of several small and detached square towers in the midst of vinelands, said by our guide to be used as watch-towers, from which watchmen looked out to guard the produce of the lands themselves even in the present day.—BUCKINGHAM.

CHAPTER XIII.

Ver. 15. And let him that is on the house-top not go down into the house, neither enter *therein*, to take any thing out of his house.

See on Matt. 24. 17.

When the houses were not contiguous, the staircase, according to the description of some travellers, was conducted along the outside of the house; but when they were built close together, it was placed in the porch, or at the entrance into the court, and continued through one corner of the gallery, or another, to the top of the house. For the sake of greater privacy, and to prevent the domestic animals from daubing the terrace, and by that means spoiling the water which falls from thence into the cisterns below the court, a door was hung on the top of the stair, and kept constantly shut. This door, like most others to be met with in those countries, is hung, not with hinges, but by having the jamb formed at each end into an axletree or pivot; of which the uppermost, which is the longest, is to be received into a correspondent socket in the lintel, while the other falls into a similar cavity in the threshold. Doors with hinges of the same kind are still to be seen in the East. The stone door, so much admired by Mr. Maundrell, is exactly of this fashion, and very common in most places. "The staircase is uniformly so contrived, that a person may go up or come down by it, without entering into any of the offices or apartments; and by consequence, without disturbing the family, or interfering with the business of the house. In allusion to this method of building, our Lord commands his disciples, when the Roman armies entered Judea, to "flee to the mountains;" and adds, "Let him that is on the house-top not go down into the house, neither enter therein, to take any thing out of his house." They were commanded to flee from the top of the house to the mountains, without entering the house; which was impossible to be done, if the stairs had not been conducted along the outside of it, by which they could escape.—PAXTON.

Ver. 35. Watch ye, th⸗⸗fore: for ye know not when the master of the house cometh, at even, or at midnight, or at the cock-crowing, or in the morning.

See on ch. 14. 30.

CHAPTER XIV.

Ver. 3. And being in Bethany, in the house of Simon the leper, as he sat at meat, there came a woman, having an alabaster box of ointment of spikenard, very precious; and she brake the box, and poured *it* on his head.

While the entertainment was going on, the master of the family, to show his respect for the company, and to prevent the hurtful consequences of indulgence, caused the servants in attendance to anoint their heads with precious unguents, and perfume the room by burning myrrh, frankincense, and other odours. Hence the act of Mary, in anointing the head of her Lord, as he sat at meat in the house of Simon, was agreeable to the established custom of the country, and she did no more on that occasion than what the rules of politeness required from his entertainer. It was at once a signal testimony of her veneration for the Saviour, and a pointed reproof to Simon for his disrespectful omission. "As Jesus sat at meat, there came a woman, having an alabaster box of ointment of spikenard, (or liquid nard, according to the margin,) very precious, and she brake the box and poured it on his head." The balsam was contained in a box of alabaster, whose mouth was stopped with cotton, upon which melted wax was poured so as effectually to exclude the air. When Mary approached to anoint her Lord, she broke the cement which secured the stopple, not the box itself, for this was quite unnecessary; and we know that in the language of the East, the opening of a vessel, by breaking the cement that secured it, was called breaking the vessel.—PAXTON.

Ver. 30. And Jesus saith unto him, Verily I say unto thee, That this day, *even* in this night, before the cock crow twice, thou shalt deny me thrice.

The cock-crowing was, properly, the time which intervened between midnight and the morning; which is evident from the words of the evangelist just quoted. Availing themselves of this circumstance, the Romans divided their day and night into various parts, which they distinguished by appropriate names. Midnight was the point at which their day commenced and terminated; then followed, what they called the inclination of midnight; after that, the cock-crowing; then the conticinium, or time of silence, when all was still; this was followed by the dawn, which ushered in the morning; and this in its turn was succeeded by the noonday. The Greek term which denotes the cock-crowing, is often used in the plural number, because that wakeful bird announces more than once the approach of light. He begins to chant at midnight; and again raises his warning voice, between midnight and the dawn; which, on this account, is often called the second cock-crowing. Thus Juvenal:

> "Quod tamen ad cantum galli facit ille secundi,
> Proximus ante diem caupo sciet."—(Sat. ix. l. 106.)

The second cock-crowing corresponds with the fourth watch of the night; for, says Ammianus, he ascended Mount Casius, from whence, at the second crowing of the cock, the rising sun might be first descried. But, according to Pliny, from the towering height of Mount Casius, the sun might be seen at the fourth watch, ascending through the shades of night. But, although the cock crows twice in the night, yet, when any thing is said to be done at the time of the cock-crowing, without stating whether it is the first or the second, it must always be understood of the last, which is by way of distinction called the cock-crowing, either because the warning is more loud and cheerful, or because it is more useful to mankind, as it rouses them from their slumbers to the active scenes of life; or, in fine, because the time of the first warning is called by another name, the middle of the night. Thus, the evangelist Mark agrees with the uninspired writers of antiquity, in placing the time of the second crowing between the hour of midnight and the morning. And Isidore, as quoted by Bochart, says, it was called the cock-crowing, because then the cock announced the approach of day. Hence it is evident he meant the time of the second crowing. Horace also refers to the same hour in these lines:

> "Agricolum laudat juris legumque peritus
> Sub galli cantum consultor ubi ostia pulsat."—(Sat. i. l. 10.)

It appears from these, and many other testimonies, which the learned reader will find in Bochart, that the same time was now called simply, the cock-crowing; and now more expressly, the second cock-crowing: from whence it has been justly thought, that Mark may be easily reconciled with the other evangelists, in relation to the time when the apostle Peter thrice denied his Lord. According to Mark, the Saviour informed his presumptuous disciple, "Before the cock crow twice, thou shalt deny me thrice." As the Saviour had foretold, the cock crew after the first, and a second time after the third denial; but according to the other evangelists, the cock did not crow before he denied him the third time. The words of Christ, according to Matthew, are these: "Verily I say unto thee, that this night before the cock crow, thou shalt deny me thrice." In Luke: "I tell thee, Peter, the cock shall not crow this day, before that thou shalt thrice deny that thou knowest me." In John: "Wilt thou lay down thy life for my sake? Verily, verily, I say unto thee, the cock shall not crow, till thou hast denied me thrice." But it is no difficult task to reconcile these different accounts; for the prediction clearly refers to the time of the second crowing, before when, according to all the four evangelists, Peter had thrice denied his Master. These phrases, The cock shall not crow, or, Before the cock shall crow, are the same as if he had said, Before the time of the cock-crowing, or the cock shall not give that loud and cheerful alarm, from which the time called emphatically the cock-crowing (αλεκτοροφωνια) is dated, before thou shalt deny me thrice. No doubt can reasonably be entertained, that Mark, who was the disciple of Peter, recorded the very words of Christ, as he received them from the apostle. But it was sufficient for the others to mention the principal fact, that Christ not only foresaw and predicted the threefold denial of Peter, but also fixed the time when it should happen, before the second crowing. The words of our Lord are certainly to be understood of the second, because this only was simply called the cock-crowing; yet Mark expressly asserts it, and declares also, that the first denial of Peter preceded the first cock-crowing. Here it may be objected, that between the first and second crowing, the fourth part of the night commonly intervenes; which at that time was nearly three hours; for in Judea, at the time of the year when our Lord was crucified, the nights are more than eleven hours in length; but between the first and second denial of Peter, scarcely the half of that time could have elapsed. This appears from the narrative of the evangelist Luke, in which it is stated, that when the terrified apostle had first denied his Lord to the maid, as he sat by the fire, "A little after, another saw him, and said, Thou art also of them. And Peter said, Man, I am not;" which was the second denial. "And about the space of one hour after, another confidently affirmed, saying, Of a truth, this fellow also was with him; for he is a Galilean." "And Peter denied the third time, and immediately the cock crew." To this objection it may be sufficient to reply, that the statement of the evangelist is extremely brief; and while Peter endeavoured to clear himself of the charge, many words might pass on both sides, which are not put on record, and the discussion be protracted through a great part of the night. Nor will it follow from the phrase which Luke uses, *after a little while*, that no time, or only a very short interval passed, between the first and second denial; for the apostle John, in his gospel, mentions many incidents which happened in that time; and the third denial, which Luke says happened about the space of one hour after the second denial, is in Matthew and Mark said to have taken place "a little after." Hence, this phrase may denote a much longer space of time than is commonly supposed. Besides, Luke does not say, that the third denial happened precisely at the distance of one hour, but about the space of one hour, which might therefore be considerably more. In fine, although the fourth part of the night commonly intervenes between the first and second crowing, it is not always the case; for it is well known, that these birds do not always crow at stated times. Some cock, therefore, after the third denial of Peter, might anticipate the usual time of announcing the approach of morning, by one hour. It may be objected again, when Peter denied his Lord, the scribes, the priests, and the elders, were met in the house of Caiaphas, and sitting in judgment on the Saviour; while the apostle waited the issue, among the servants in the hall. But it is not likely that the council would prolong their sitting through so great a part of the night. Who can believe, that so many persons of the first rank among the Jews, would spend almost the whole night on the judgment-seat, when the cause for which they were assembled could, with equal convenience, be referred to another time? But this objection is urged in vain; for the fact, that they actually did so, is certain. This will appear, when it is considered how many things were done that night, before the apostle denied his Lord the third time. When the evening was come, that is, at the setting of the sun, our Lord celebrated the passover with his disciples; he then washed their feet, and addressed them on the occasion. After finishing this discourse, he instituted the supper; then he reproved his disciples for their contentions with one another about the supremacy. When he had finished this reproof, he sung a hymn, which, according to the Talmudical writers, consisted of a number of psalms. This act of devotion being ended, he went out to the mount of Olives,—came to the garden of Gethsemane—withdrew from his disciples to pray—and after praying an hour, he returned to the disciples, whom he found asleep, and reproved them for their unseasonable indulgence; this he did a second, and a third time. In the meantime, Judas arrived with a numerous party, and apprehended him; and led him away, first to Annas, and then to Caiaphas, in whose house, the scribes, the priests, and the elders were assembled. Into the hall of judgment, Peter with difficulty obtained admission; and, being recognised as one of his followers, denied his Lord. Christ was placed at the bar, and interrogated by Caiaphas; this being done, Peter denied his Master a second time, and again in the space of an hour. It will appear to every reflecting and candid mind, that these transactions must have occupied the greater part of the night. The despatch which the high-priest and his council made, indeed would seem quite extraordinary, if we did not consider that the passover, their most solemn festival, was just ready to commence, and that the worst passions of their depraved hearts were now in a state of high excitement against the Redeemer.—PAXTON.

Ver. 35. And he went forward a little, and fell on the ground, and prayed, that, if it were possible, the hour might pass from him.

How often are we reminded of this by the way in which the heathen worship their gods! they fall prostrate before the temples and repeat their prayers. In our own chapels and school rooms, natives sometimes prostrate themselves at the time of prayer.—ROBERTS.

Ver. 51. And there followed him a certain young man, having a linen cloth cast about *his* naked *body:* and the young men laid hold on him.
52. And he left the linen cloth, and fled from them naked.

See on Judg. 14. 12.

Pococke observes, in describing the dresses of the people of Egypt, that "it is almost a general custom among the Arabs and Mohammedan natives of the country, to wear a large blanket, either white or brown, and in summer a blue and white cotton sheet, which the Christians constantly use in the country: putting one corner before, over the left shoulder, they bring it behind, and under the right arm, and so over their bodies, throwing it behind over the left shoulder, and so the right arm is left bare for action. When it is hot, and they are on horseback, they let it fall down on the saddle round them: and about Faiume, I particularly observed, that young people especially, and the poorer sort, had *nothing on whatever* but this blanket; and it is probable the young man was clothed in this manner, who followed our Saviour when he was taken, having a linen cloth cast about his naked body; and when the young men laid hold on him, he left the linen cloth, and fled from them naked."—BURDER.

CHAPTER XV.

Ver. 11. But the chief priests moved the people, that he should rather release Barabbas unto them.

Another mode of capital punishment, to which the inspired writers refer, is crucifixion. It was used in Greece, but not so frequently as at Rome. It consisted of two beams, one of which was placed across the other, in a form nearly resembling the letter T, but with this difference, that the transverse beam was fixed a little below the top of the straight one. When a person was crucified, he was nailed to the cross as it lay upon the ground, his feet to the upright, and his hands to each side of the transverse beam; it was then erected, and the foot of it thrust with violence into a hole prepared in the ground to receive it. By this means, the body, whose whole weight hung upon the nails which went through the hands and feet, was completely disjointed, and the sufferer expired by slow and agonizing torments. This kind of death, the most cruel, shameful, and accursed that could be devised, was used by the Romans only for slaves, and the basest of the people. The malefactors were crucified naked, that is, without their upper garments: for it does not appear they were stripped of all their clothes, and we know that an Oriental was said to be naked, when he had parted with his upper garments, which were loosely bound about him with a girdle.—PAXTON.

THE GOSPEL ACCORDING TO LUKE.

CHAPTER I.

Ver. 78. Through the tender mercy of our God; whereby the day-spring from on high hath visited us.

A king's minister once said of the daughter of Pānde-yan, after she had been in great trouble on account of the danger in which her husband had been placed, "She had seen the great ocean of darkness, but now she saw the rising sun, the day-spring appeared."—Roberts.

CHAPTER II.

Ver. 4. And Joseph also went up from Galilee, out of the city of Nazareth into Judea, unto the city of David, which is called Bethlehem, (because he was of the house and lineage of David,) 5. To be taxed with Mary his espoused wife, being great with child.

A Jewish virgin legally betrothed, was considered as a lawful wife; and by consequence, could not be put away without a bill of divorce. And if she proved unfaithful to her betrothed husband, she was punished as an adulteress; and her seducer incurred the same punishment as if he had polluted the wife of his neighbour. This is the reason that the angel addressed Joseph, the betrothed husband of Mary, in these terms: "Joseph, thou son of David, fear not to take unto thee Mary thy wife; for that which is conceived in her is of the Holy Ghost." The evangelist Luke gives her the same title: "And Joseph also went up from Galilee unto Bethlehem, to be taxed, with Mary his espoused wife."—Paxton.

Ver. 7. And she brought forth her first-born son, and wrapped him in swaddling-clothes, and laid him in a manger; because there was no room for them in the inn.

It will be proper here to give a full and explicit account of the inns or caravansaries of the East, in which travellers are accommodated. They are not all alike, some being simply places of rest, by the side of a fountain if possible, and at a proper distance on the road. Many of these places are nothing more than naked walls; others have an attendant, who subsists either by some charitable donation, or the benevolence of passengers; others are more considerable establishments, where families reside, and take care of them, and furnish the necessary provisions.

"Caravansaries were originally intended for, and are now pretty generally applied to the accommodation of strangers and travellers, though, like every other good institution, sometimes perverted to the purposes of private emolument, or public job. They are built at proper distances through the roads of the Turkish dominions, and afford to the indigent or weary traveller an asylum from the inclemency of the weather: are in general built of the most solid and durable materials, have commonly one story above the ground-floor, the lower of which is arched, and serves for warehouses to store goods, for lodgings, and for stables, while the upper is used merely for lodgings; besides which they are always accommodated with a fountain, and have cooks-shops and other conveniences to supply the wants of lodgers. In Aleppo, the caravansaries are almost exclusively occupied by merchants, to whom they are, like other houses, rented." (Campbell.)

The poverty of the eastern inns appears from the following extract. "There are no inns anywhere; but the cities, and commonly the villages, have a large building called a *khan*, or *caravansary*, which serves as an asylum for all travellers. These houses of reception are always built without the precincts of towns, and consist of four wings round a square court, which serve by way of enclosure for the beasts of burden. The lodgings are cells, where you find nothing but bare walls, dust, and sometimes scorpions. The keeper of this *khan* gives the traveller the key and a mat, and he provides himself the rest; he must therefore carry with him his bed, his kitchen utensils, and even his provisions, for frequently not even bread is to be found in the villages. On this account the Orientals contrive their equipage in the most simple and portable form. The baggage of a man, who wishes to be completely provided, consists in of carpet, a mattress, a blanket, two saucepans with lids contained within each other, two dishes, two plates, and a coffee-pot, all of copper well tinned; a small wooden box for salt and pepper; a round leathern table, which he suspends from the saddle of his horse; small leathern bottles or bags for oil, melted butter, water, and brandy, (if the traveller be a Christian,) a pipe, a tinder-box, a cup of cocoa-nut, some rice, dried raisins, dates, Cyprus-cheese, and above all, coffee-berries, with a roaster and wooden mortar to pound them." (Volney.)

"The caravansaries are the eastern inns, far different from ours; for they are neither so convenient nor handsome: they are built square, much like cloisters, being usually but one story high, for it is rare to see one of two stories. A wide gate brings you into the court, and in the midst of the building, in the front; and upon the right and left hand, there is a hall for persons of the best quality to keep together. On each side of the hall are lodgings for every man by himself. These lodgings are raised all along the court, two or three steps high, just behind which are the stables, where many times it is as good lying as in the chambers. Right against the head of every horse there is a niche with a window into the lodging-chamber, out of which every man may see that his horse is looked after. These niches are usually so large that three men may lie in them, and here the servants usually dress their victuals." (Tavernier.)—Burder.

The following graphic sketch will afford the reader a still more correct idea of an eastern inn, or caravansary. "After descending for about two hours, we met with an isolated khan, (inn,) beneath magnificent plantains, on the edge of a fountain. It will be proper to describe, once for all, what is called a khan in Syria, as well as in every other eastern country; it is a hut, the walls of which are of ill-joined uncemented stones, affording no protection from wind or rain; these stones are generally blackened by the smoke of the hearth, which continually filters through the open spaces. The walls are about seven or eight feet high, and covered over with pieces of rough wood retaining its bark and largest branches; the whole is shaded with dry fagots, answering the purpose of a roof. The inside is unpaved, and is, according to the season of the year, a bed of dust or of mud. One or two stakes support the roof of leaves, and the traveller's cloak and arms are suspended thereon. In one corner is a small hearth raised upon a few rough stones; a charcoal fire is constantly burning upon this hearth, and one or two copper coffee-pots are always full of thick farinaceous coffee, the habitual refreshment and only want of the Turks and Arabs. There are in general two rooms similar to the one I have described. One or two Arabs are authorized, in return for the tribute they pay to the pacha, to do the honours of the dwelling, and to sell coffee and barley-flour cakes to the caravans. When the traveller reaches the door of these khans, he alights from his horse or camel, and removes the straw mats or damask carpets which are to serve him for a bed; they are spread in a corner of the smoking-room; he sits down, calls for coffee, lights his pipe, and waits until his slaves have collected some dry wood to prepare his repast. This repast usually consists of two or three cakes, half-baked on a heated pebble, and of some slices of hashed mutton, which is boiled with rice in a copper pot. It rarely happens that rice or mutton can be procured in the khan; the traveller must then be satisfied with the cakes and the excellent fresh water which is always found in the neighbourhood of khans. The servants, the slaves, the moukres, (camel-leaders,) and the horses, remain round the khan in the open air. There is generally in the neighbourhood some noted and long-standing tree, which serves as a beacon to the caravan; this is mostly an immense sycamore fig-tree, such as I have never seen in Europe; it is of the size of the largest oaks, and grows to an older age. Its trunk sometimes measures thirty or forty feet in circumference, and is often larger; its branches, which begin to spread at an elevation of fifteen or twenty feet from the ground, at first extend in a horizontal direction, to an immense distance; the upper branches then group themselves in narrower cones, and resemble from afar our beech-trees. The shadow of those trees, which Providence seems to have scattered here and there, as an hospitable cloud over the burning soil of the desert, extends to a great distance from the trunk; and it is not unusual to see perhaps sixty camels and horses, and as many Arabs, encamped, during the heat of the day, under the shadow of one of these trees. In this, however, as in every thing else, it is painful to notice the indifference of eastern people and of their government. These plantains, which should be preserved with care, as inns provided by nature for the wants of the caravan, are left to the stupid improvidence of those who benefit by their shade; the Arabs light their fires at the foot of the sycamore, and the trunks of most of these splendid trees are blackened and hollowed by the flames of Arab hearths. Our little caravan settled itself under one of those majestic sycamores, and we passed the night wrapped up in our cloaks, and stretched on a straw mat in a corner of the khan. (De Lamartine's Pilgrimage.)—B.

Ver. 25. And, behold, there was a man in Jerusalem, whose name *was* Simeon; and the same man *was* just and devout, waiting for the consolation of Israel; and the Holy Ghost was upon him.

The Jews often used to style the expected Messiah, *the consolation;* and, *may I never see the consolation* was a common form of swearing among them.—GILL.

Ver. 44. But they, supposing him to have been in the company, went a day's journey; and they sought him among *their* kinsfolk and acquaintance.

We are assisted in our view of this subject by the large companies which go to and return from the heathen festivals. Ten or twenty thousand sometimes come together to one ceremony, and it is almost impossible for friends and relations to keep together; hence, in going home, though they cannot find each other in the way, they do not give themselves any trouble, as they consider it to be a matter of *course* to be thus separated.—ROBERTS.

As at the three great festivals all the men who were able were obliged, and many women chose, at least at the passover, to attend the celebration at Jerusalem, they used, for their greater security against the attacks of robbers on the road, to travel in large companies. All who came, not only from the same city, but from the same canton or district, made one company. They carried necessaries along with them, and tents for their lodging at night. Sometimes, in hot weather, they travelled all night, and rested in the day. This is nearly the manner of travelling in the East to this hour. Such companies they now call caravans; and in several places have got houses fitted up for their reception, called caravansaries. This account of their manner of travelling furnishes a ready answer to the question, How could Joseph and Mary make a day's journey, without discovering before night that Jesus was not in the company? In the daytime we may reasonably presume that the travellers would, as occasion, business, or inclination led them, mingle with different parties of their friends or acquaintance; but that in the evening, when they were about to encamp, every one would join the family to which he belonged. As Jesus did not appear when it was growing late, his parents first sought him where they supposed he would most probably be, among his relations and acquaintance; and not finding him, returned to Jerusalem.—CAMPBELL.

CHAPTER III.

Ver. 22. And the Holy Ghost descended in a bodily shape like a dove upon him; and a voice came from heaven, which said, Thou art my beloved Son; in thee I am well pleased.

See on Mat. 3. 16.

CHAPTER IV.

Ver. 1. And Jesus, being full of the Holy Ghost, returned from Jordan, and was led by the spirit into the wilderness.

Mr. Maundrell, in his travels in the Holy Land, saw the place which was the scene of Christ's temptations, and thus describes it: "From this place (the Fountain of the Apostles) you proceed in an intricate way among hills and valleys interchangeably, all of a very barren aspect at present, but discovering evident signs of the labour of the husbandman in ancient times. After some hours' travel in this sort of road, you arrive at the mountainous desert into which our blessed Saviour was led by the spirit to be tempted by the devil. A most miserable dry barren place it is, consisting of high rocky mountains, so torn and disordered as if the earth had suffered some great convulsion, in which its very bowels had been turned outward."—BURDER.

Ver. 16. And he came to Nazareth, where he had been brought up: and, as his custom was, he went into the synagogue on the sabbath-day, and stood up for to read.

The custom of reading the scriptures publicly was an appointment of Moses, according to the Jews. It was also usual to stand at reading the law and the prophets. Some parts of the Old Testament were allowed to be read sitting or standing; as particularly, the book of Esther. Common Israelites, as well as priests and Levites, were allowed to read the scriptures publicly. Every sabbath-day seven persons read; a priest, a Levite, and five Israelites. And it is said to be a known custom to this day, that even an unlearned priest reads before the greatest wise man in Israel. —GILL.

Ver. 20. And he closed the book, and he gave *it* again to the minister, and sat down. And the eyes of all them that were in the synagogue were fastened on him.

The third part of the synagogue service was expounding the scriptures and preaching to the people. The posture in which this was performed, whether in the synagogue or in other places, was sitting. Accordingly, when our Saviour had read the haphtaroth in the synagogue at Nazareth, of which he was a member, having been brought up in that city, instead of retiring to his place, he sat down in the desk or pulpit; and it is said that the eyes of all that were present were fastened upon him, as they perceived by his posture that he was going to preach to them. And when Paul and Barnabas went into the synagogue at Antioch, and sat down, thereby intimating their desire to speak to the people if they might be permitted, the rulers of the synagogue sent to them, and gave them leave. Acts xiii. 14, 15 —BURDER.

Ver. 23. And he said unto them, Ye will surely say unto me this proverb, Physician, heal thyself: whatsoever we have heard done in Capernaum, do also here in thy country.

In the same way do the people recriminate on each other. "You teach me to reform my life! go, reform your own."

"Doctor, go heal yourself, and you shall then heal me." "Yes, yes, the fellow can cure all but his own wife and himself."—Roberts.

Ver. 29. And rose up, and thrust him out of the city, and led him unto the brow of the hill whereon their city was built, that they might cast him down headlong.

The Mount of Precipitation, as it is now called, is about a mile and a half distant from Nazareth, according to Dr. Richardson, but two miles according to the observations made by Mr. Buckingham and the Rev. W. Jowett; though Dr. E. D. Clarke maintains that the words of the evangelist explicitly prove the situation of the ancient city to have been precisely that which is occupied by the modern village. Mr. Jowett, however, has (we conceive) clearly shown that the Mount of Precipitation could not be immediately contiguous to Nazareth. This village, it will be observed, is situated in a little sloping vale or dell on the side, and nearly extends to the foot of a hill, which, though not very lofty, is rather steep and overhanging.

"The eye naturally wanders over its summit, in quest of some point from which it might probably be, that the men of this place endeavoured to cast our Saviour down, (Luke iv. 29;) but in vain: no rock adapted to such an object appears. At the foot of the hill is a modest simple plain, surrounded by low hills, reaching in length nearly a mile: in breadth, near the city, a hundred and fifty yards; but farther on, about four hundred yards. On this plain there are a few olive-trees and fig-trees, sufficient, or rather scarcely sufficient, to make the spot picturesque. Then follows a ravine, which gradually grows deeper and narrower, till, after walking about another mile, you find yourself in an immense chasm with steep rocks on either side, from whence you behold, as it were beneath your feet, and before you, the noble Plain of Esdraelon. Nothing can be finer than the apparently immeasurable prospect of this plain, bounded to the south by the mountains of Samaria. The elevation of the hills on which the spectator stands in this ravine is very great; and the whole scene, when we saw it, was clothed in the most rich mountain-blue colour that can be conceived. At this spot, on the right hand of the ravine, is shown the rock to which the men of Nazareth are supposed to have conducted our Lord, for the purpose of throwing him down. With the Testament in our hands, we endeavoured to examine the probabilities of the spot: and I confess there is nothing in it which excites a scruple of incredulity in my mind. The rock here is perpendicular for about fifty feet, down which space it would be easy to hurl a person who should be unawares brought to the summit; and his perishing would be a very certain consequence. That the spot might be at a considerable distance from the city is an idea not inconsistent with St. Luke's account; for the expression 'thrusting' Jesus 'out of the city, and leading him to the brow of the hill on which their city was built,' gives fair scope for imagining, that, in their rage and debate, the Nazarenes might, without originally intending his murder, press upon him for a considerable distance after they had quitted the synagogue. The distance, as already noticed, from modern Nazareth to this spot is scarcely two miles—a space which, in the fury of persecution, might soon be passed over. Or should this appear too considerable, it is by no means certain but that Nazareth may at that time have extended through the principal part of the plain, which lies before the modern town: in this case, the distance passed over might not exceed a mile. It remains only to note the expression—'the brow of the hill, on which their city was built:' this, according to the modern aspect of the spot, would seem to be the hill north of the town, on the lower slope of which the town is built; but I apprehend the word 'hill' to have in this, as it has in very many other passages of scripture, a much larger sense; denoting sometimes a range of mountains, and in some instances a whole mountainous district. In all these cases the singular word 'Hill,' 'Gebel,' is used, according to the idiom of the language of this country. Thus, 'Gebel Carmel,' or Mount Carmel, is a range of mountains: 'Gebel Libnan,' or Mount Lebanon, is a mountainous district of more than fifty miles in length: 'Gebel ez-Zeitun,' the Mount of Olives, is certainly a considerable tract of mountainous country. And thus any person, coming from Jerusalem and entering on the Plain of Esdraelon, would, if asking the name of that bold line of mountains which bounds the north side of the plain, be informed that it was 'Gebel Nasra,' the Hill of Nazareth; though, in English, we should call them the Mountains of Nazareth. Now the spot shown as illustrating Luke iv. 29, is, in fact, on the very brow of this lofty ridge of mountains; in comparison of which, the hill upon which the modern town is built is but a gentle eminence."

This intelligent traveller, therefore, concludes that this mountain may be the real scene where our Divine Prophet, Jesus, experienced so great a dishonour from the men of his own country and of his own kindred. In a valley near Nazareth is a fountain which bears the name of the Virgin Mary, and where the women are seen passing to and fro with pitchers on their heads as in days of old. It is justly remarked that, if there be a spot throughout the Holy Land which was more particularly honoured by the presence of Mary, we may consider this to be the place; because the situation of a copious spring is not liable to change, and because the custom of repairing thither to draw water has been continued among the female inhabitants of Nazareth from the earliest period of its history.—Horne.

We went out to see the hill from which the inhabitants of Nazareth were for throwing down Christ when he preached to them. This is a high stony mountain, situated some gun-shots from Nazareth, consisting of the limestone common here, and full of fine plants. On its top, towards the south, is a steep rock, which is said to be the spot for which the hill is famous: it is terrible to behold, and proper enough to take away the life of a person thrown from it.—Hasselquist.

CHAPTER V.

Ver. 5. And Simon answering, said unto him, Master, we have toiled all the night, and have taken nothing: nevertheless, at thy word I will let down the net.

In general, the fishermen of the East prefer the night to any other time for fishing. Before the sun has gone down they push off their canoes, or *catta-marams*, each carrying a lighted torch, and, in the course of a few hours, may be seen out at sea, or on the rivers, like an illuminated city. They swing the lights about over the sides of the boat, which the fish no sooner see than they come to the place, and then the men cast in the hook or the spear, as circumstances may require. They have many amusing sayings about the folly of the fish in being thus attracted by the glare of a torch.—Roberts.

Ver. 19. And when they could not find by what *way* they might bring him in because of the multitude, they went upon the house-top, and let him down through the tiling, with *his* couch, into the midst before Jesus.

From the gate of the porch, one is conducted into the quadrangular court, which, being exposed to the weather, is paved with stone, in order to carry off the water in the rainy season. The principal design of this quadrangle is, to give light to the house, and admit the fresh air into the apartments; it is also the place where the master of the house entertains his company, which are seldom or never honoured with admission into the inner apartments. This open space bears a striking resemblance to the *impluvium* or *cava ædium* of the Romans, which was also an uncovered area, from whence the chambers were lighted. For the accommodation of the guests, the pavement is covered with mats or carpets; and as it is secured against all interruption from the street, is well adapted to public entertainments. It is called, says Dr. Shaw, the middle of the house, and literally answers to the *το μεσον* of the Evangelist, into which the man afflicted with the palsy was let down through the ceiling, with his couch, before Jesus. Hence, he conjectures that our Lord was at this time instructing the people in the court of one of these houses; and it is by no means improbable that the quadrangle was to him and his apostles a favourite situation, while they were engaged in disclosing the mysteries of redemption. To defend the company from the scorching sunbeam, or "windy storm and tempest," a veil was expanded upon ropes from the one side of the parapet wall to the other, which might be folded or unfolded at pleasure. The Psalmist seems to allude either to the tents of the Bedouins, or to some covering of this kind, in that beautiful expression of spreading out the heavens like a veil or curtain. We have the same allusion in the sublime strains of Isaiah: "It is he that sitteth upon the circle of the earth, and the inhabitants thereof are as grasshoppers; that stretcheth out the heavens as a curtain, and spreadeth them out as a tent to dwell in."—PAXTON.

CHAPTER VI.

Ver. 38. Give, and it shall be given unto you; good measure, pressed down, and shaken together, and running over, shall men give into your bosom. For with the same measure that ye mete withal, it shall be measured to you again.

Instead of the fibula that was used by the Romans, the Arabs join together with thread, or with a wooden bodkin, the two upper corners of this garment; and after having placed them first over one of their shoulders, they then fold the rest of it about their bodies. The outer fold serves them frequently instead of an apron, in which they carry herbs, loaves, corn, and other articles, and may illustrate several allusions made to it in scripture: thus, "One of the sons of the prophets went out into the field to gather herbs, and found a wild vine, and gathered there of wild gourds, *his lap full.*" And the Psalmist offers up his prayer, that Jehovah would "render unto his neighbours sevenfold into their bosom, their reproach." The same allusion occurs in our Lord's direction to his disciples: "Give, and it shall be given unto you; good measure, pressed down, and shaken together, and running over, shall men give into your bosom." It was also the fold of this robe which Nehemiah shook before his people, as a significant emblem of the manner in which God should deal with the man who ventured to violate his oath and promise, to restore the possessions of their impoverished brethren: "Also, I shook my lap, and said, So God shake out every man from his house, and from his labour, that performeth not this promise, even thus be he shaken out, and emptied." —PAXTON.

Ver. 48. He is like a man which built a house, and digged deep, and laid the foundation on a rock: and, when the flood arose, the stream beat vehemently upon that house, and could not shake it: for it was founded upon a rock.

In the rainy season, the clouds pour down their treasures at certain intervals with great violence, for three or four days together. Such abundant and violent rains, in a mountainous country like Judea, by washing away the soil, must often be attended with very serious consequences to the dwellings of the inhabitants, which happen to be placed within the reach of the rapid inundation. At Aleppo, the violent rains often wash down stone walls; and Dr. Russel mentions a remarkable instance of a hamlet with a fig garden, in the Castravan mountains, being suddenly removed by the swelling waters to a great distance. It was to an event of this kind, which is by no means uncommon in those regions, that our Lord refers.—PAXTON.

CHAPTER VII.

Ver. 3. And when he heard of Jesus, he sent unto him the elders of the Jews, beseeching him that he would come and heal his servant.

This is the oriental way of making an inquiry or a propitiation. Does a man wish to know something about another, he will not go himself, because that might injure him in his future operations; he calls for two or three confidential friends, states what he wants to ascertain, and tells them how to proceed. They perhaps first go to some neighbour to gain all the information they can, and then go to the man himself, but do not at once tell him their errand: no, no, they TRY the ground, and make sure of their object, before they disclose their purposes. Should they, however, be in doubt, they have the adroitness to conceal their plans; and if asked what they want, they simply reply "CHUMA," *i. e.* nothing; they only came to say SALAM, "had not seen the honoured individual for a long time, and therefore wished to set their eyes on him." When a person desires to gain a favour, as did the centurion, he sends an elder, a respectable person, to state his case, and there is generally an understanding that the messenger, if he succeed, shall share in the benefit. If flattery, humiliations, and importunities can do any thing, he is sure to gain the point.—ROBERTS.

Ver. 36. And one of the Pharisees desired him that he would eat with him, and he went into the Pharisee's house, and sat down to meat.

The tables of the ancient Jews were constructed of three distinct parts, or separate tables, making but one in the whole. One was placed at the upper end crossways, and the two others joined to its ends, one on each side, so as to leave an open space between, by which the attendants could readily wait at all the three. Round these tables were placed, not *seats,* but *beds,* one to each table; each of these beds was called *clinium,* and three of these being united to surround the three tables made the *triclinium.* At the end of each clinium was a footstool for the convenience of mounting up to it. These beds were formed of mattresses, and were supported on frames of wood, often highly ornamented. Each guest reclined on his left elbow, using principally his right hand, which was therefore kept at liberty. The feet of the person reclining being towards the external edge of the bed, were much more readily reached by any body passing than any other part.

The Jews, before they sit down to table, carefully wash their hands; they consider this ceremony as essential. After meals, they wash them again. When they sit down to table, the master of the house, or chief person in the company, taking bread, breaks it, but does not divide it; then putting his hand to it he recites this blessing: Blessed be thou, O Lord, our God, the king of the world, who producest the bread of the earth. Those present answer, Amen. Having distributed the bread among the guests, he takes the vessel of the wine in his right hand, saying, Blessed art thou, O Lord, our God, king of the world, who hast produced the fruit of the vine. They then repeat the 23d psalm. They take care that after meals there shall be a piece of bread remaining on the table. The master of the house orders a glass to be washed, fills it with wine, and elevating it, says, Let us bless him of whose benefits we have been partaking; the rest answer, Blessed be he who has heaped his favours on us, and by his goodness has now fed us. Then he recites a pretty long prayer, wherein he thanks God for his many benefits vouchsafed to Israel; beseeches him to pity Jerusalem and his temple; to restore the throne of David; to send Elijah and the Messiah, and to deliver them out of their long captivity. They all answer, Amen. They recite Psalm xxiv. 9, 10. Then giving the glass with the little wine in it to be drank round, he takes what is left, and the table is cleared. These are the ceremonies of the modern Jews.—CALMET.

Ver. 38. And stood at his feet behind *him* weeping, and began to wash his feet with tears, and did wipe *them* with the hairs of her head, and kissed his feet, and anointed *them* with the ointment.

During my travels, I was in the custom of having a lancet always about me, in case of accidents, and when I took this out of my pocket-book, put it into his hands, and told him it was for himself, he looked at me, and at it, with his mouth open, as if he hardly comprehended the possibility of my parting with such a jewel. But when I repeated the words, It is yours, he threw himself on the ground, kissed my knees and my feet, and wept with a joy that stifled his expression of thanks.—SIR R. K. PORTER.

Ver. 44. And he turned to the woman, and said unto Simon, Seest thou this woman? I entered into thy house, thou gavest me no water for my feet: but she hath washed my feet with tears, and wiped *them* with the hairs of her head.

The first ceremony after the guests arrived at the house of entertainment, was the salutation performed by the master of the house, or one appointed in his place. Among the Greeks, this was sometimes done by embracing with arms around; but the most common salutation was by the conjunction of their right hands, the right hand being reckoned a pledge of fidelity and friendship. Sometimes they kissed the lips, hands, knees, or feet, as the person deserved more or less respect. The Jews welcomed a stranger to their house in the same way; for our Lord complains to Simon, that he had given him no kiss; had welcomed him to his table with none of the accustomed tokens of respect.—PAXTON.

Ver. 45. Thou gavest me no kiss; but this woman, since the time I came in, hath not ceased to kiss my feet.

See that poor woman whose husband has committed some crime, for which he is to be taken to the magistrate; she rushes to the injured individual, she casts herself down and begins to kiss his feet; she touches them with her nose, her eyes, her ears, and forehead, her long hair is dishevelled, and she beseeches the *feet* of the offended man to forgive her husband. "Ah! my lord, the gods will then forgive you." "My husband will in future be your slave, my children will love you, the people will praise you; forgive, forgive, my lord." (See on John xii. 3.)—ROBERTS.

CHAPTER IX.

Ver. 59. And he said unto another, Follow me. But he said, Lord, suffer me first to go and bury my father.

It is considered exceedingly desirable for children to be with their parents when they die; they then hear their last requests and commands, and also can perform the funeral rites in such a way as none but themselves can do. It is just before death, also, that the father mentions his property; especially that part which he has concealed in his house, gardens, or fields. It is, therefore, a very common saying, "When I have buried my father, I will do this or that." Should a young man be requested to do that which is not agreeable to his father, he says, "Let me first perform the funeral rites, and then I will do it."—ROBERTS.

Ver. 62. And Jesus said unto him, No man having put his hand to the plough, and looking back, is fit for the kingdom of God.

The plough used in Syria is so light and simple in its construction, that the husbandman is under the necessity of guiding it with great care, bending over it, and loading it with his own weight, else the share would glide along the surface without making any incision. His mind should be wholly intent on his work, at once to press the plough into the ground, and direct it in a straight line. "Let the ploughman," said Hesiod, "attend to his charge, and look before him; not turn aside to look on his associates, but make straight furrows, and have his mind attentive to his work." And Pliny: "Unless the ploughman stoop forward" to press his plough into the soil, and conduct it properly, "he will turn it aside." To such careful and incessant exertion our Lord alludes in that declaration: "No man having put his hand to the plough, and looking back, is fit for the kingdom of heaven."—PAXTON.

CHAPTER X.

Ver. 4. Carry neither purse, nor scrip, nor shoes: and salute no man by the way.

The object of this instruction was to prevent their being hindered by unnecessary delay in their journey. It was not designed to prevent the usual and proper civilities which were practised among the people, but to avoid the impediments occasioned by form and ceremony: and this was the more necessary, since it was a maxim with the Jews, *prevent every man with a salutation.* How persons might thus be prevented and hindered will clearly appear in the following extract. "The more noble and educated the man, the oftener did he repeat his questions. A well-dressed young man attracted my particular attention, as an adept in the perseverance and redundancy of salutation. Accosting an Arab of Augila, he gave him his hand, and detained him a considerable time with his civilities: when the Arab being obliged to advance with greater speed to come up again with his companions, the youth of Fezzan thought he should appear deficient in good manners if he quitted him so soon. For near half a mile he kept running by his horse, while all his conversation was, How dost thou fare? well, how art thou thyself? praised be God, thou art arrived in peace! God grant thee peace! how dost thou do? &c."—HORNEMAN.

Our Lord commanded his disciples to salute no man by the way. It is not to be supposed, that he would require his followers to violate or neglect an innocent custom, still less one of his own precepts; he only directed them to make the best use of their time in executing his work. This precaution was rendered necessary by the length of time which their tedious forms of salutation required. They begin their salutations at a considerable distance, by bringing the hand down to the knees, and then carrying it to the stomach. They express their devotedness to a person, by holding down the hand; as they do their affection by raising it afterward to the heart. When they come close together, they take each other by the hand in token of friendship. The countrypeople at meeting, clap each other's hands very smartly twenty or thirty times together, without saying any thing more than, How do ye do? I wish you good health. After this first compliment, many other friendly questions about the health of the family, mentioning each of the children distinctly, whose names they know. To avoid this useless waste of time, rather than to indicate the meanness in which the disciples were to appear, as Mr. Harmer conjectures, our Lord commanded them to avoid the customary salutations of those whom they might happen to meet by the way.—PAXTON.

Ver. 19. Behold, I give unto you power to tread on serpents and scorpions, and over all the power of the enemy; and nothing shall by any means hurt you.

See on Ezek. 2. 6.

Ver. 30. And Jesus answering, said, A certain *man* went down from Jerusalem to Jericho, and fell among thieves, which stripped him of his raiment, and wounded *him*, and departed, leaving *him* half dead.

This is thus illustrated by a recent traveller who "went down from Jerusalem to Jericho," under the protection of a tribe of Arabian shepherds, and the conduct of two of their number. "After going through the pass, we descended again into deeper valleys, travelling sometimes on the edges of cliffs and precipices, which threatened destruction on the slightest false step. The scenery all around us was grand and awful, notwithstanding the forbidding aspect of the barren rocks that everywhere met our view; but it was that sort of grandeur which excited fear and terror, rather than admiration."

"The whole of this road from Jerusalem to the Jordan, is held to be the most dangerous about Palestine, and, indeed, in this portion of it, the very aspect of the scenery is sufficient, on the one hand, to tempt to robbery and murder, and on the other, to occasion a dread of it on those who pass that way. It was partly to prevent any accident happening to us in this early stage of our journey, and partly, perhaps, to calm our fears on that score, that a messenger had been despatched by our guides to an encampment of their tribe near, desiring them to send an escort to meet us at this place. We were met here accordingly, by a band of about twenty persons on foot, all armed with matchlocks, and presenting the most ferocious and robber-like appearance that could be imagined. The effect of this was heightened by the shouts which they sent forth from hill to hill, and which were re-echoed through all the valleys, while the bold projecting crags of rock, the dark shadows in which every thing lay buried below, the towering height of the cliffs above, and the forbidding desolation which everywhere reigned around, presented a picture that was quite in harmony throughout all its parts.

"It made us feel most forcibly the propriety of its being chosen as the scene of the delightful tale of compassion which we had before so often admired for its doctrine, independently of its local beauty. One must be amid these wild and gloomy solitudes, surrounded by an armed band, and feel the impatience of the traveller who rushes on to catch a new view at every pass and turn; one must be alarmed at the very tramp of the horses' hoofs rebounding through the caverned rocks, and at the savage shouts of the footmen, scarcely less loud than the echoing thunder produced by the discharge of their pieces in the valleys;—one must witness all this upon the spot, before the full force and beauty of the admirable story of the good Samaritan can be perceived. Here, pillage, wounds, death, would be accompanied with double terror, from the frightful aspect of every thing around. Here the unfeeling act of passing by a fellow-creature in distress, as the priest and Levite are said to have done, strikes one with horror, as an act almost more than inhuman. And here, too, the compassion of the good Samaritan is doubly virtuous, from the purity of the motive which must have led to it, in a spot where no eyes were fixed on him to draw forth the performance of any duty, and from the bravery which were necessary to admit of a man's exposing himself by such delay, to the risk of a similar fate to that from which he was endeavouring to rescue his fellow-creature."—PAXTON.

CHAPTER XI.

Ver. 5. And he said unto them, Which of you shall have a friend, and shall go unto him at midnight, and say unto him, Friend, lend me three loaves; 6. For a friend of mine in his journey is come to me, and I have nothing to set before him?

The eastern journeys are often performed in the night, on account of the great heat of the day. This is the time in which the caravans chiefly travel: the circumstance therefore of the arrival of a friend at midnight is very probable.—HARMER.

Ver. 7. And he from within shall answer and say, Trouble me not: the door is now shut, and my children are with me in bed; I cannot rise and give thee.

See on Eccl. 4. 17.

Maillet informs us that it is common in Egypt for each person to sleep in a separate bed. Even the husband and the wife lie in two distinct beds in the same apartment. Their female slaves also, though several lodge in the same chamber, yet have each a separate mattress. Sir John Chardin also observes, that it is usual for a whole family to sleep in the same room, especially those in lower life, laying their beds on the ground. From these circumstances we learn the precise meaning of the reply now referred to: "He from within shall answer and say, Trouble me not: the door is now shut, and my children are with me in bed; I cannot rise and give thee:" it signifies that they were all in bed in the same apartment, not in the same bed.—BURDER.

Ver. 47. Wo unto you! for ye build the sepulchres of the prophets, and your fathers killed them.

We visited what are called the sepulchres of the prophets, close to the spot where we had halted. We descended through a circular hole into an excavated cavern of some extent, cut with winding passes, and forming a kind of subterraneous labyrinth. The superincumbent mass was supported by portions of the rock, left in the form of walls and irregular pillars, apparently once stuccoed; and from the niches still remaining visible in many places, we had no doubt of its having once been appropriated to sepulture: but whether any, or which of the prophets were interred here, even tradition does not suggest, beyond the name which it bestows on the place.—BUCKINGHAM.

CHAPTER XII.

Ver. 35. Let your loins be girded about, and *your* lights burning.

They who travel on foot are obliged to fasten their garments at a greater height from their feet than they do at other times. This is what is understood by girding up their loins. Chardin observes, that "all persons who travel on foot always gather up their vest, by which they walk more commodiously, having the leg and knee unburdened and disembarrassed by the vest, which they are not when that hangs over them." After this manner he supposes the Israelites were prepared for their going out of Egypt, when they ate the first passover. (Exod. xii. 11.)—HARMER.

Ver. 55. And when *ye see* the south wind blow, ye say, There will be heat; and it cometh to pass.

This circumstance accords perfectly with the relations of travellers into Syria, Egypt, and several parts of the East. When the south wind begins to blow, the sky becomes dark and heavy, the air gray and thick, and the whole atmosphere assumes a most alarming aspect. The heat produced by these southern winds has been compared to that of a large oven at the moment of drawing out the bread; and to that of a flame blown upon the face of a person standing near the fire which excites it. (Thevenot.)—BURDER.

CHAPTER XIII.

Ver. 7. Then said he unto the dresser of his vineyard, Behold, these three years I come seeking fruit on this fig-tree, and find none: cut it down; why cumbereth it the ground?

This similitude, by which Jesus illustrates the patience and forbearance of God towards sinners, is founded, it is true, in the experience of all countries, and we find in it nothing difficult or unintelligible. But our Saviour probably alluded to a certain custom of eastern gardeners, mentioned by an Arabian writer, Ibn-al-Uardi, in his work on geography and natural history, called Pearls of Wonderful Things. In the tenth chapter of this work, which treats of some curiosities of the vegetable kingdom, of which the Swedish author, Charles Aurivillius, in a Dissertation, published in Upsal, in 1752, has given in Arabic and Latin that part which relates to the cultivation of the palm-tree, we find the following observations. Among the diseases to which the palm-tree is subject, is barrenness. But this may be removed by the following means: "You take an axe, and go to the tree with a friend, to whom you say, 'I will hew this palm down, because it is unfruitful.' The latter replies, 'Do not do it, it will certainly bear fruit this year.' But the former says, 'It cannot be otherwise,' and strikes the trunk three times with the back of the axe. The other prevents him, and says, 'For God's sake, do not do it; you will certainly have fruit from it this year; have patience with it, and do not be precipitate; if it bears no fruit, then hew it down.' It will then certainly be fruitful this year, and bear fruit in abundance."—BURDER.

Ver. 32. And he said unto them, Go ye, and tell that fox, Behold, I cast out devils, and I do cures to-day and to-morrow, and the third *day* I shall be perfected.

At Nice, in Asia, at night, "I heard a mighty noise, as if it had been of men, who jeered and mocked us. I asked what was the matter. I was answered, it was only the howling of certain beasts, which the Turks call ciacals, or jackals. They are a sort of wolves, somewhat bigger than foxes, but less than common wolves; yet as greedy and devouring as the most ravenous wolves, or foxes, of all.

They go in flocks, and seldom hurt man or beast; but get their food by craft and stealth, more than by open force. Thence it is that the Turks call subtle and crafty persons, especially the Asiatics, by the metaphorical name of ciacals. Their manner is to enter tents, or houses, in the nighttime; what is eatable they eat; gnaw leather, shoes, boots; are as cunning as they are thievish: but in this they are very ridiculous, that they discover themselves by the noise they make; for while they are busy in the house, devouring their prey, if any one of their herd without doors chance to howl, they all set up a howling likewise." (Busbequius.) —BURDER.

CHAPTER XIV.

Ver. 8. When thou art bidden of any *man* to a wedding, sit not down in the highest room, lest a more honourable man than thou be bidden of him; 9. And he that bade thee and him come and say to thee, Give this man place; and thou begin with shame to take the lowest room. 10. But when thou art bidden, go and sit down in the lowest room; that when he that bade thee cometh, he may say unto thee, Friend, go up higher: then shalt thou have worship in the presence of them that sit at meat with thee. 11. For whosoever exalteth himself shall be abased; and he that humbleth himself shall be exalted.

See on Mark 9. 39.

When a Persian comes into an assembly, and has saluted the house, he then measures with his eye the degree of rank to which he holds himself entitled; he straightway wedges himself into the line of guests, without offering any apology for the general disturbance which he produces. It often happens that persons take a higher seat than that to which they are entitled. The Persian scribes are remarkable for their arrogance in this respect, in which they seem to bear a striking resemblance to the Jews of the same profession in the days of our Lord. The master of the entertainment has, however, the privilege of placing any one as high in the rank of the assembly as he may choose. And Mr. Morier saw an instance of it at a public entertainment to which he was invited. When the assembly was nearly full, the governor of Kashan, a man of humble mien, although of considerable rank, came in and seated himself at the lowest place; when the master of the house, after numerous expressions of welcome, pointed with his hand to an upper seat in the assembly, to which he desired him to move, and which he accordingly did. These circumstances furnish a beautiful and striking illustration of the parable which our Lord uttered when he saw how those that were invited, chose the highest places. —PAXTON.

Ver. 16. Then said he unto him, A certain man made a great supper, and bade many: 17. And sent his servant at supper-time to say to them that were bidden, Come, for all things are now ready.

See on Matt. 22. 2, 3.

Ver. 19. And another said, I have bought five yoke of oxen, and I go to prove them: I pray thee have me excused.

This was not such a trifling affair as some have supposed, for it should be remembered it is with oxen only the Orientals perform all their agricultural labours. Such a thing as a horse in a plough or cart, among the natives, I never saw. A bullock unaccustomed to the yoke is of no use; they therefore take the greatest precaution in making such purchases, and they will never close the bargain till they have PROVED them in the field. Nor will the good man trust to his own judgment, he will have his neighbours and friends to assist him. The animals will be tried in ploughing softly, deeply, strongly, and they will be put on all the required paces, and then sent home. When he who wishes to purchase is fully satisfied, he will fix a day for settling the amount and for fetching the animals away.—ROBERTS.

Ver. 21. So that servant came, and showed his lord these things. Then the master of the house, being angry, said to his servant, Go out quickly into the streets and lanes of the city, and bring in hither the poor, and the maimed, and the halt, and the blind.

While the higher orders in the East commonly affect so much state, and maintain so great a distance from their inferiors, they sometimes lay aside their solemn and awful reserve, and stoop to acts of condescension, which are unknown in these parts of the world. It is not an uncommon thing to admit the poor to their tables, when they give a public entertainment. Pococke was present at a great feast in Egypt, where every one, as he had done eating, got up, washed his hands, took a draught of water, and retired to make way for others; and so on in a continual succession, till the poor came in and ate up all. "For the Arabs," he says, "never set by any thing that is brought to table, so that when they kill a sheep, they dress it all, call in their neighbours and the poor, and finish every thing." The same writer, in another passage, mentions a circumstance which is still more remarkable, that an Arab prince will often dine in the street before his door, and call to all that pass, even to beggars, in the usual expression of Bismillah, that is, in the name of God, who come and sit down to meat, and when they have done, retire with the usual form of returning thanks. Hence, in the parable of the great supper, our Lord describes a scene which corresponded with existing customs. When the guests, whom the master of the house had invited to the entertainment, refused to come, he "said to his servants, go out quickly into the streets and lanes of the city, and bring in hither the poor and the maimed, and the halt and the blind. And the servant said, Lord, it is done as thou hast commanded, and yet there is room. And the lord said unto the servant, Go out into the highways and hedges, and compel them to come in, that my house may be filled."—PAXTON.

CHAPTER XV.

Ver. 16. And he would fain have filled his belly with the husks that the swine did eat: and no man gave unto him.

That κερατιον answers to *siliqua*, and signifies a husk or pod, wherein the seeds of some plants, especially those of the leguminous tribe, are contained, is evident. Both the Greek and Latin terms signify the fruit of the carob-tree, a tree very common in the Levant, and in the southern parts of Europe, as Spain and Italy. This fruit still continues to be used for the same purpose, the feeding of swine. It is also called St. John's bread, from the opinion that the Baptist used it in the wilderness. Miller says it is mealy, and has a sweetish taste, and that it is eaten by the poorer sort, for it grows in the common hedges, and is of little account.—CAMPBELL.

Ver. 20. And he arose and came to his father. But when he was yet a great way off, his father saw him and had compassion, and ran, and fell on his neck, and kissed him.

The Orientals vary their salutation according to the rank of the persons whom they address. The common method of expressing good-will, is by laying the right hand on the bosom, and inclining their bodies a little; but when they salute a person of rank, they bow almost to the ground, and kiss the hem of his garment. The two Greek noblemen at Scio, who introduced the travellers Egmont and Heyman to the cham of Tartary, kissed his robe at their entrance, and took leave of him with the same ceremony. Sandys was present when the grand seignior himself paid his people the usual compliment, by riding in great state through the streets of Constantinople. He saluted the multitude as he moved along, having the right hand constantly on his breast, bowing first to the one side, and then to the other, when the people with a low and respectful voice wished him all happiness and prosperity. Dr. Shaw's account of the Arabian compliment, or common salutation, Peace be unto you, agrees with these statements; but he observes further, that inferiors, out of deference and respect, kiss the feet, the knees, or the garments of their superiors. They frequently kiss the hand also; but this last seems not to be regarded as a token of equal submission with the others; for D'Arvieux observes, that the women who wait on the Arabian princesses, kiss their hands when they do them the favour not to suffer them to kiss their feet, or the border of their robe.

All these forms of salutation appear to have been in general use in the days of our Lord, for he represents a servant as falling down at the feet of his master, when he had a favour to ask; and an inferior servant, as paying the same compliment to the first, who belonged, it would seem, to a higher class: "The servant, therefore, fell down and worshipped him, saying, Lord, have patience with me and I will pay thee all." "And his fellow-servant fell down at his feet, and besought him, saying, Have patience with me and I will pay thee all." When Jairus solicited the Saviour to go and heal his daughter, he fell down at his feet: the apostle Peter, on another occasion, seems to have fallen down at his knees, in the same manner as the modern Arabs fall down at the knees of a superior. The woman who was afflicted with an issue of blood, touched the hem of his garment; and the Syrophenician woman fell down at his feet. In Persia, the salutation among intimate friends is made by inclining the neck over each other's necks, and then inclining the cheek to cheek; which Mr. Morier thinks is most likely the falling upon the neck and kissing, so frequently mentioned in scripture.—PAXTON.

Ver. 25. Now his elder son was in the field: and as he came and drew nigh to the house, he heard music and dancing.

To express the joy which the return of the prodigal afforded his father, *music and dancing* was provided as a part of the entertainment. This expression does not however denote the dancing of the family and guests, but that of a company of persons hired on this occasion for that very purpose. Such a practice prevailed in some places to express peculiar honour to a friend, or joy upon any special occasion. Major Rooke, in his travels from India through Arabia Felix, relates an occurrence which will illustrate this part of the parable. "Hadje Cassim, who is a Turk, and one of the richest merchants in Cairo, had interceded on my behalf with Ibrahim Bey, at the instance of his son, who had been on a pilgrimage to Mecca, and came from Judda in the same ship with me. The father, in celebration of his son's return, gave a most magnificent fete on the evening of the day of my captivity, and as soon as I was released, sent to invite me to partake of it, and I accordingly went. His company was very numerous, consisting of three or four hundred Turks, who were all sitting on sofas and benches, smoking their long pipes. The room in which they were assembled was a spacious and lofty hall, in the centre of which was a band of music, composed of five Turkish instruments, and some vocal performers as there were no ladies in the assembly, you may suppose it was not the most lively party in the world, but being new to me, was for that reason entertaining."—BURDER.

CHAPTER XVI.

Ver. 3. Then the steward said within himself, What shall I do, for my lord taketh away from me the stewardship? I cannot dig; to beg I am ashamed.

How often are we reminded of this passage by beggars when we tell them to work. They can scarcely believe their ears; and the religious mendicants, who swarm in every part of the East, look upon you with the most sovereign contempt when you give them such advice. "I work! why, I never have done such a thing; I am not able." "Surely, my lord, you are not in earnest; you are joking with me."—ROBERTS.

Ver. 19. There was a certain rich man, which was clothed in purple and fine linen, and fared sumptuously every day.

This view will enable the reader to form a correct judgment of the streets of the city of Jerusalem, which (it will be seen) are partly open and partly covered. The apartment, which stands over the archway in the distance, forms part of what is called "the house of the rich man," who is mentioned in the narrative of St. Luke, (xvi. 19—31.) It is one of the best in Jerusalem. The fountain, which is a prominent feature in our engraving, is executed in bold relief; although of Saracenic workmanship, it is conjectured by Mr. Catherwood to be derived from the style of architecture introduced by the crusaders. In common with the other fountains in Jerusalem, this fountain is supplied from the pools of Solomon, which lie a few miles to the southwest of Bethlehem. The water is conducted through a small aqueduct, partly under, and partly above ground: it is of excellent quality, but the supply is not sufficiently copious for the consumption of the inhabitants, who make up the deficiency from the water supplied by the cisterns which are filled by the periodical rains.—HORNE.

[*See engraving, and see also* COMPREHENSIVE COMMENTARY *on Ps.* 122. 3, *and the engraving there.*]

Ver. 22. And it came to pass, that the beggar died, and was carried by the angels into Abraham's bosom: the rich man also died, and was buried.

How offensive to good taste, and to the FIGURE of the text, is the notion of some painters, who represent Lazarus in heaven as reposing in the bosom of the patriarch. Such attempts have a tendency to lessen that veneration and awe which we owe to subjects of so sacred a nature. This world is the legitimate field for the painter, but let him not presume to desecrate with his pencil the scenes beyond. A beloved son, though at a distance, is still said to be in the BOSOM of his parents. "The king is indeed very fond of that man, he keeps him in his bosom." "Yes, the servant is a great favourite with his master, he has a place in his bosom." "Why, Muttoo, do you never intend to allow your son to go out of your bosom?" The ideas implied by the term bosom are intense affection, security, and comfort. But objects of endearment are sometimes spoken of as being in the HEAD. "He not fond of his wife! he keeps her in his head." "My husband, you are ever in my head." "Yes, beloved, you are in my eye; my eye is your resting-place."—ROBERTS.

CHAPTER XVII.

Ver. 6. And the Lord said, If ye had faith as a grain of mustard seed, ye might say unto this sycamine-tree, Be thou plucked up by the root and be thou planted in the sea; and it should obey you.

The sycamore buds late in the spring, about the latter end of March, and is therefore called by the ancients, *arborum sapientissima*, the wisest of trees, because it thus avoids the nipping frosts to which many others are exposed. It strikes its large diverging roots deep into the soil; and on this account our Lord alludes to it as the most difficult to be rooted up and transferred to another situation: "If ye had faith as a grain of mustard seed, ye might say unto this sycamine-tree, be thou plucked up by the root, and be thou planted in the sea, and it should obey you." The extreme difficulty with which this tree is transferred from its native spot to another situation, gives to the words of our Lord a peculiar force and beauty. The stronger and more diverging the root of a tree, the more difficult it must be to pluck it up, and insert it again so as to make it strike root and grow; but far more difficult still to plant it in the sea, where the soil is so far below the surface, and where the restless billows are continually tossing it from one side to another; yet, says our Lord, a task no less difficult than this to be accomplished, can the man of genuine faith perform with a word; for with God nothing is impossible, nothing difficult or laborious.—PAXTON.

CHAPTER XVIII.

Ver. 5. Yet, because this widow troubleth me, I will avenge her, lest by her continual coming she weary me.

The word ὑπωπιάζειν, *to weary*, properly signifies *to beat on the face*, and particularly under the eye, so as to make the parts black and blue. Here it has a metaphorical meaning, and signifies to give great pain, such as arises from severe beating. The meaning therefore is, that the uneasy feelings which this widow raised in the judge's breast, by the moving representation which she gave of her distress, affected him to such a degree that he could not bear it, but to get rid of them resolved to do her justice. The passage understood in this sense has a peculiar advantage, as it throws a beautiful light on our Lord's argument, and lays a proper foundation for the conclusion which it contains. —MACKNIGHT.

CHAPTER XIX.

Ver. 5. And when Jesus came to the place, he looked up, and saw him, and said unto him, Zaccheus, make haste, and come down; for to-day I must abide at thy house.

Zaccheus did not appear to have seen our Saviour before, but he would not be surprised when it was said, "I must abide at thy house." Hospitality may almost be called a sacred rite in all parts of the East; and, were it not so, what would become of travellers and pilgrims? In general there are no places for public entertainment, for the rest-houses and choultries are seldom more than open places to shelter passengers from the sun and rain. View the stranger passing through a village, he sees a respectable house, and having found out the master, he stands before him, and puts out his right hand, and says, *paratheasi*, i. e. a pilgrim or traveller: he is then requested to be seated, and is asked, whence he came, and whither he is going? His temporal wants are supplied, and when inclined he pursues his journey.—ROBERTS.

Ver. 40. And he answered and said unto them, I tell you, that, if these should hold their peace, the stones would immediately cry out.

Has a man been greatly favoured by another, he says, "Ah! if I ever forget him the stones will cause me to stumble." "I cease to recollect his goodness! then will the stones make me to stumble and die." The idea appears to be, they will arise up and cause him to fall.—ROBERTS.

CHAPTER XX.

Ver. 18 Whosoever shall fall upon that stone shall be broken; but on whomsoever it shall fall, it will grind him to powder.

Here is an allusion to the two different ways of stoning among the Jews, the former by throwing a person down upon a great stone, and the other by letting a stone fall upon him.—WHITBY.

CHAPTER XXI.

Ver. 18. But there shall not a hair of your head perish.

"Well, friend, have you heard that Chinnan has gone to the judge to complain against you?" "Let him go, not a hair of this head will be spoiled by that." "I advise you to take care, for the Vedan has sworn to ruin you." "He! the jackal cannot pull out a single hair." "What care I for thy anger? thou canst not pull out one hair." "He injure my son! let him touch a single hair."—ROBERTS.

CHAPTER XXII.

Ver. 34. And he said, I tell thee, Peter, the cock shall not crow this day, before that thou shalt thrice deny that thou knowest me.

See on Mark 14. 30.

Ver. 48. But Jesus said unto him, Judas, betrayest thou the Son of Man with a kiss?

See on 2 Sam. 20. 9.

Ver. 64. And when they had blindfolded him, they struck him on the face, and asked him, saying, Prophesy: Who is it that smote thee?

This usage of Christ refers to that sport so ordinary among children, called μυινδα, in which it is the manner first to blindfold, then to strike, then to ask who gave the blow, and not to let the person go till he named the right man who had struck him. It was used on this occasion to reproach our blessed Lord, and expose him to ridicule. —HAMMOND.

CHAPTER XXIII.

Ver. 31. For if they do these things in a green tree, what shall be done in the dry?

The venerable Mr. Wesley has caught the idea when he says on this passage, "The Jews compare a good man to a green tree, and a bad man to a dead one." Thus still an abandoned character, a decided profligate, is called a PATTA-MARAM, *i. e.* a dried or a dead tree. "Why water that tree?" "Your money, your influence is all wasted there: cease, cease to attend to that dead tree." "The tree is dead, there are no leaves, it will never more give blossoms or fruit, it is only fit for the fire." A spendthrift or one who has been unfortunate says, "I am a *pattamaram*, I have been struck by the lightning." A good man is compared to a TALITA-MARAM, *i. e.* a tree which has "spreading *shady* branches." People may repose there during the heat of the day: they have defence and comfort. Jesus was the "green tree" under whom the Jews might have reposed. If, then, they did such things to the "green tree," what would be done to themselves, the dry, the leafless trees of the desert? The lightnings of heaven did strike them; the Roman eagles did pounce on them; thousands were cut to the ground, and thousands went as slaves to the land of the conquerors.—ROBERTS.

Ver. 48. And all the people that came together to that sight, beholding the things which were done, smote their breasts, and returned.

Grief is often far more violent in the East than in England. The frantic mother, bereaved of her son, or the wife bereft of her husband, BEATS her BREAST as if she intended to burst a passage to her vitals. I have sometimes been amazed at the blows which in their agony they thus inflict upon themselves. "Alas! alas! that *amma* (i. e lady) will never cease to beat her breasts."—ROBERTS.

THE GOSPEL ACCORDING TO JOHN.

CHAPTER I.

Ver. 15. John bare witness of him, and cried, saying, This was he of whom I spake, He that cometh after me, is preferred before me: for he was before me.

Before we reached Mayar, we were met by Mirza Abdul Cossim, a confidential officer of the governor of Ispahan, by a hakeem or doctor, one of the learned of the city, and by several other men of respectability. These deputations were called Peeshwaz, openers of the way, and are one of the principal modes among the Persians of doing honour to their guests. The more distinguished the persons sent, and the greater the distance to which they go, so much more considerable is the honour.—MORIER.

Ver. 32. And John bare record, saying, I saw the Spirit descending from heaven like a dove, and it abode upon him.

See on Matt. 3. 16.

Ver. 42. And he brought him to Jesus. And when Jesus beheld him, he said, Thou art Simon the Son of Jona: thou shalt be called Cephas, which is, by interpretation, A stone.

Names were frequently given to preserve the remembrance of particular circumstances. And, as will appear in the following extract, frequently as contrasts to the character and condition of those on whom they were imposed: "Among the people of the house, who attended us here, was a hhabshi, or Abyssinian slave, an old man, of hideous deformity, entitled Almas, or the diamond. And I observed that at Shiraz, Fassa, and other towns, the African slaves were distinguished by flowery names or epithets, in proportion to their natural ugliness or offensive smell. Thus, I have known Yasmin, the jessamine; Sumbul, the hyacinth; Jauher, the jewel; and Makbul, the pleasing, or agreeable." (Sir W. Ouseley.)—BURDER.

Ver. 48. Nathanael saith unto him, Whence knowest thou me? Jesus answered and said unto him, Before that Philip called thee, when thou wast under the fig-tree, I saw thee.

The oriental garden displays little method, beauty, or design; the whole being commonly no more than a confused medley of fruit-trees, with beds of esculent plants, and even plots of wheat and barley sometimes interspersed. The garden belonging to the governor of Eleus, a Turkish town, on the western border of the Hellespont, which Dr. Chandler visited, consisted only of a very small spot of ground, walled in, and containing only two vines, a fig and a pomegranate-tree, and a well of excellent water. And it would seem, the garden of an ancient Israelite could not boast of greater variety; for the grape, the fig, and the pomegranate, are almost the only fruits which it produced. This fact may perhaps give us some insight into the reason of the sudden and irresistible conviction which flashed on the mind of Nathaniel, when the Saviour said to him, "When thou wast under the fig-tree I saw thee." The good man seems to have been engaged in devotional exercises, in a small retired garden, walled in, and concealed from the scrutinizing eyes of men. The place was so small, that he was perfectly certain that no man but himself was there; and so completely defended, that none could break through, or look over the fence; and by consequence, that no eye was upon him, but the all-seeing eye of God; and, therefore, since Christ saw him there, Nathaniel knew he could be no other than the Son of God, and the promised Messiah.—PAXTON.

Ver. 50. Jesus answered and said unto him, Because I said unto thee, I saw thee under the fig-tree, believest thou? thou shalt see greater things than these.

On account of the thick-spreading branches and broad leaves of the fig-tree, which, in warm eastern countries, grows much larger and stronger than with us, it was very suitable for the purpose of overshadowing those who sat under it. Hasselquist, in his Journey from Nazareth to Tiberias, says, "We refreshed ourselves in the shade of a fig-tree, under which was a well, where a shepherd and his herd had their rendezvous, but without either tent or hut."—BURDER.

CHAPTER II.

Ver. 6. And there were set there six water-pots of stone, after the manner of the purifying of the Jews, containing two or three firkins apiece.

Cana still exists, and was visited a few years ago by Dr. Clarke and his fellow-travellers, who breakfasted there as they passed through it in their way from Nazareth to Tiberias. He says, "it is worthy of note, that walking among the ruins of a church, we saw large massy stone pots, answering the description given of the ancient vessels of the country, not preserved nor exhibited as relics, but lying about, disregarded by the present inhabitants as antiquities with whose original use they were unacquainted. From their appearance, and the number of them, it was quite evident that a practice of keeping water in large stone pots, each holding from eighteen to twenty-seven gallons, was once common in the country."—BURDER.

Ver. 10. And saith unto him, Every man at the beginning doth set forth good wine; and when men have well drunk, then that which is worse: *but* thou hast kept the good wine until now.

The Abbe Mariti, speaking of the age of the wines of Cyprus, says, "the oldest wines used in commerce do not exceed eight or ten years. It is not true, as has been reported, that there is some of it a hundred years old; but it is certain that at the birth of a son or a daughter, the father causes a jar filled with wine to be buried in the earth, having first taken the precaution to seal it hermetically; in this manner it may be kept till these children marry. It is then placed on the table before the bride and bridegroom, and is distributed among their relations, and the other guests invited to the wedding." If such a custom prevailed formerly, it throws great significancy into the assertion of *good wine* being first brought out upon such an occasion; and if this supposition is admitted, tends to increase the greatness of the miracle, that notwithstanding what had been drank at first was peculiarly excellent, yet that which Christ by his divine power produced as an after supply, was found to be of a superior quality.—BURDER.

CHAPTER III.

Ver. 8. The wind bloweth where it listeth, and thou hearest the sound thereof, but canst not tell whence it cometh, and whither it goeth: so is every one that is born of the Spirit.

When a man is unhappy because he does not understand

his circumstances, when things come upon him which cannot be accounted for by himself or by others, it is asked, "Do you know whence cometh the wind?" "You say you know not how this matter will end: do you know in what quarter the present wind will blow the next moment?" —ROBERTS.

Ver. 29. He that hath the bride is the bridegroom: but the friend of the bridegroom, which standeth and heareth him, rejoiceth greatly because of the bridegroom's voice. This my joy therefore is fulfilled.

Among the Jews, in their rites of espousals, there is frequent mention of a place where, under a covering, it was usual for the bridegroom to discourse familiarly but privately with his spouse, whereby their affections might be more knit to one another, in order to marriage, which however were not supposed to be so till the bridegroom came cheerfully out of the *chuppah*, or covered place. To this David refers, (Psalm xix. 5,) when he speaks of the sun, "which is a bridegroom coming out of his chamber, and rejoiceth as a strong man to run a race." It is affirmed that this custom is still observed among the Jews in Germany; either before the synagogues in a square place covered over, or where there is no synagogue, they throw a garment over the bridegroom and the bride for that purpose. While this intercourse is carrying on, the friend of the bridegroom stands at the door to hearken; and when he hears the bridegroom speak joyfully, (which is an intimation that all is well,) he rejoices himself, and communicates the intelligence to the people assembled, for their satisfaction.—HAMMOND.

CHAPTER IV.

Ver. 5. Then cometh he to a city of Samaria, which is called Sychar, near to the parcel of ground that Jacob gave to his son Joseph. 6. Now Jacob's well was there. Jesus, therefore, being wearied with *his* journey, sat thus on the well: *and* it was about the sixth hour.

"At one third of an hour from Naplosa, we came to Jacob's well, famous not only on account of its author, but much more for that memorable conference which our blessed Saviour here had with the woman of Samaria. If it should be questioned whether this be the very well that it is pretended for or not, seeing it may be suspected to stand too remote from Sychar for women to come so far to draw water, it is answered, that probably the city extended farther this way in former times than it does now, as may be conjectured from some pieces of a very thick wall still to be seen not far from hence. Over the well there stood formerly a large church, erected by that great and devout patroness of the Holy Land, the Empress Helena; but of this the voracity of time, assisted by the hands of the Turks, has left nothing but a few foundations remaining: the well is covered at present with an old stone vault, into which you are let down through a very straight hole; and then removing a broad flat stone, you discover the mouth of the well itself. It is dug in a firm rock, and contains about three yards in diameter, and thirty-five in depth, five of which we found full of water." (Maundrell.)

"The principal object of veneration is Jacob's well, over which a church was formerly erected. This is situated at a small distance from the town, in the road to Jerusalem, and has been visited by pilgrims of all ages; but particularly since the Christian era, as the place where our Saviour revealed himself to the woman of Samaria. This spot is so distinctly marked by the evangelist, and so little liable to uncertainty, from the circumstance of the well itself, and the features of the country, that if no tradition existed for its identity, the site of it could hardly be mistaken. Perhaps no Christian scholar ever attentively read the fourth chapter of St. John without being struck with the numerous internal evidences of truth which crowd upon the mind in its perusal: within so small a compass, it is impossible to find in other writings so many sources of reflection and of interest. Independently of its importance as a theological document, it concentrates so much information, that a volume might be filled with the illustration it reflects on the history of the Jews, and on the geography of their country. All that can be gathered on these subjects from Josephus seems but as a comment to illustrate this chapter. The journey of our Lord from Judea into Galilee; the cause of it; his passage through the territory of Samaria; his approach to the metropolis of this country; its name; his arrival at the Amorite field, which terminates the narrow valley of Sichem; the ancient custom of halting at a well; the female employment of drawing water; the disciples sent into the city for food, by which its situation out of the town is obviously implied; the question of the woman referring to existing prejudices, which separated the Jews from the Samaritans; the depth of the well; the oriental allusion contained in the expression, *living water;* the history of the well, and the customs thereby illustrated; the worship upon Mount Gerizim; all these occur within the space of twenty verses; and if to these be added what has already been referred to in the remainder of the same chapter, we shall, perhaps, consider it as a record, which, in the words of him who sent it, we may *lift up our eyes, and look upon, for it is white already to harvest.*" (Clarke.)

"In inquiring for the Bir-el-Yakoab, or Jacob's well, we were told by everybody that this was in the town; which not corresponding with the described place of the well we were desirous of seeing, led to further explanation; and, at length, by telling the story attached to it, we found it was known here only by the name of Ber Samarea, or the well of Samaria. Procuring a Christian boy to accompany us, we went out by the eastern gate; and passing through a continuation of the same valley in which Nablous stands, thickly covered with olive-trees, we reached the end of it in about a quarter of an hour on foot, the pass opening into a round and more extensive vale, and the mountains east of the Jordan being in sight. On the right were some Mohammedan buildings; on the sides, at the foot of Mount Gerizim, either mosques or tombs, now called mahmoodeea, and said to stand over Joseph's sepulchre. On the left, at the foot of Mount Ebal, were several well-hewn grottoes in the rocks; some with arched, and others with square doors; most probably ancient sepulchres without the old city of Sichem, or Sychar. These grottoes were called here khallat rowgh-ban; but we had no time to examine them. From hence, in another half of an hour, we reach the well of Samaria; it stands at the commencement of the round vale, which is thought to have been the parcel of ground bought by Jacob for a hundred pieces of money, which, like the narrow valley west of Nablous, is rich and fertile. Over this well stood anciently a large building, erected by St. Helena; of which there are now no other remains than some shafts of granite pillars, all the rest lying in one undistinguished heap of ruins. The mouth of the well itself had an arched or vaulted building over it; and the only passage down to it at this moment is by a small hole in the roof, scarcely large enough for a moderate sized person to work himself down through. We lighted a taper here; and taking off my large Turkish clothes, I did not then get down without bruising myself against the sides; nor was I at all rewarded for such an inconvenience by the sight below. Landing on a heap of dirt and rubbish, we saw a large, flat, oblong stone, which lay almost on its edge, across the mouth of the well, and left barely space enough to see that there was an opening below. We could not ascertain its diameter; but, by the time of a stone's descent, it was evident that it was of considerable depth, as well as that it was perfectly dry at this season, the fall of the stones giving forth a dead and hard sound. Not far from the well of Samaria is the bir-yusef, over which is a modern building; and it is said to be, even at this day, frequented for water from Nablous. The well of Samaria might also have been so, therefore, from Sychar, although that city is said not to have extended further east than the present town; and, indeed, it is no uncommon thing in Syria, as I myself have often witnessed, for water to be brought from a much greater distance. It is highly probable, therefore, that this is the identical well at which the interesting conference between Jesus and the woman of Samaria really happened." (Buckingham.)—BURDER.

Ver. 6. Now Jacob's well was there. Jesus, therefore, being wearied with *his* journey, sat thus on the well: *and* it was about the sixth hour.

The learned have been greatly divided in their opinions concerning the true meaning of the particle ουτως in John iv. 6, which is rendered *thus*, in our version: JESUS, *therefore, being wearied with his journey, sat* THUS *on the well: and it was about the sixth hour;* which everybody knows with the Jews meant *noon.* But an attention to the usages of the East, and of antiquity, might, I think, ascertain its meaning with a good deal of exactness. Our version of the word *thus*, gives no determinate idea. We know, on the contrary, what is meant by the translation of a celebrated writer, who renders the word by the English term *immediately*, but that translation, I think by no means the happiest he has given us. It conveys the idea of extreme weariness: but nothing in the after part of the narration leads to such an interpretation; nor can I conceive for what imaginable purpose the circumstance of his immediately throwing himself down near the well, before the woman came up, and which, consequently, it is to be supposed she knew nothing of, is mentioned by the evangelist. Not to say that the passage cited in proof of this interpretation, Acts xx. 11, which, instead of *so he departed*, he thought signified the immediateness of his departure, by no means gives satisfaction. It is not so expressed in his own translation of that passage, nor does it appear so to signify. The simple meaning, I apprehend, of the particle is, that JESUS, being wearied with his journey, sat down by the well, like a person so wearied, as to design to take some repose and refreshment there: to which St. John adds, it was about the sixth hour. If this be just, the translation should have been something like this: "JESUS therefore being wearied with his journey, sat down accordingly, or like such a one, by the well. It was about the sixth hour."

The particle certainly expresses *conformity* to an account to be given after; so John xxi. 1, JESUS *showed himself again to his disciples at the sea of Tiberias; and* ON THIS WISE *he himself*, referring to the account about to be given. And sometimes it signifies *conformity* to an account that had been *before* given: so John xi. 47, 48, *What do we? for this man doth many miracles. If we let him* THUS *alone*, after this manner doing many miracles, *all men will believe on him.* So ch. viii. 59, *Then took they up stones to cast at him: but* JESUS *hid himself, and went out of the temple, going through the midst of them, and so passed by:* passed by, by hiding himself after this manner. After this latter manner it is to be understood, I think, here: JESUS being wearied with his journey, sat down like a weary person by the side of the well, and in that attitude the woman found him, preparing to take some repose and repast. The disciples, it is said, ver. 8, were *gone away into the city to buy meat;* but it does not at all follow from thence that they all went, nor is it so probable that they did, leaving him alone; but that, on the contrary, some of them stayed with him, making such preparations as indicated a design in them to eat bread there.—HARMER.

Ver. 9. Then saith the woman of Samaria unto him, How is it that thou, being a Jew, askest drink of me, which am a woman of Samaria? (for the Jews have no dealings with the Samaritans.)

In Atleet, on the road from Nablous to Jerusalem, passing out of a gateway similar to the other, at the opposite extremity of the wall, we crossed a marsh, and remounting, were proceeding on our way, when some women were discovered drawing water at a well near the track, and the day being hot, I desired my servant to ask if they would give me some to drink; but they refused the indulgence, one of them exclaiming, "Shall I give water to a Christian, and make my pitcher filthy, so that I can use it no more for ever?" This happened within the precincts of Samaria, and was a proof how little change the spirit of the people has undergone within the last eighteen centuries. These women were young and handsome, with full, dignified, and stately figures: a dark-coloured fillet bound the head, and passing under the chin, left the face entirely covered.—MUNROE'S SUMMER RAMBLE IN SYRIA.

Ver. 11. The woman saith unto him, Sir, thou hast nothing to draw with, and the well is deep: from whence then hast thou that living water?

See on Gen. 24. 20.

In those dry countries they find themselves obliged to carry with them great leathern bottles of water, which they refill from time to time, as they have opportunity; but what is very extraordinary, in order to be able to do this, they, in many places, are obliged to carry lines and buckets with them. So Thevenot, in giving an account of what he provided for his journey from Egypt to Jerusalem, tells us, he did not forget "leathern buckets to draw water with." Rauwolf goes further, for he gives us to understand, that the wells of inhabited countries there, as well as in deserts, have oftentimes no implements for drawing of water, but what those bring with them that come thither: for speaking of the well or cistern at Bethlehem, he says, it is a good rich cistern, deep and wide; for which reason, "the people that go to dip water are provided with small leathern buckets and a line, as is usual in these countries; and so the merchants that go in caravans through great deserts into far countries, provide themselves also with these, because in these countries you find more cisterns or wells than springs that lie high." In how easy a light does this place the Samaritan woman's talking of the depth of Jacob's well, and her remarking that she did not observe that our Lord had any thing to draw with, though he spoke of presenting her with water.

Wells and cisterns differ from each other, in that the first are supplied with water by springs, the other by rain: both are to be found in considerable numbers in Judea, and are, according to Rauwolf, more numerous in these countries than springs that lie high, than fountains and brooks that are of running water. Some of these have been made for the use of the people that dwell in their neighbourhood, some for travellers, and especially those that travel for devotion. Thevenot found two, made a little before his time for the use of travellers, by Turks of distinction, in the desert between Cairo and Gaza. And from a history D'Herbelot has given us, it appears that the Mohammedans have dug wells in the deserts, for the accommodation of those that go in pilgrimage to Mecca, their sacred city, where the distance between such places as Nature had made pleasant for them to stop, and take up water at, were too great: for he tell us, that Gianabi, a famous Mohammedan rebel, filled up with sand all the wells that had been dug in the road to Mecca for the benefit of the pilgrims.—HARMER.

CHAPTER V.

Ver. 2. Now there is at Jerusalem, by the sheep-*market*, a pool, which is called in the Hebrew tongue, Bethesda, having five porches

This was the name of a pool, or rather bath of water, having five porticoes: and so called from the miraculous cures performed there. They still show you "the pool of Bethesda, contiguous on one side to St. Stephen's gate, on the other to the area of the temple." Maundrell says it is a hundred and twenty paces long, forty broad, and at least eight deep: at its west end may be discovered some old arches, which are now dammed up. "A little above, we entered the city at the gate of St. Stephen, where, on each side, a lion retrograde doth stand, called, in time past, the port of the valley and of the flock, for that the cattle came in at this gate, which were to be sacrificed in the temple, and were sold in the market adjoining. On the left hand is a stone bridge, which passeth at the east end of the north wall into the court of the temple of Solomon; the head to the pool of Bethesda, underneath which it (the water) had a conveyance, called also probaticum, for that the sacrifices were therein washed ere delivered to the priests. Now it is a great square profundity, green and uneven at the bottom, into which a barren spring doth drill between the stones of the northward wall, and stealeth away almost undiscovered. The place is for a good depth hewn out of the rock; confined above on the north side with a steep wall, on the west with high buildings, perhaps a part of the castle of Antonia, where are two doors to descend by, now all that are, half choked with rubbish; and on the south with the wall of the court of the temple." (Sandys.) — BURDER.

Ver. 13. And he that was healed wist not who it was: for Jesus had conveyed himself away, a multitude being in *that* place.

Doddridge translates the word *slipped away*, and observes from Casaubon, that it is an elegant metaphor borrowed from swimming; it well expresses the easy unobserved manner in which Jesus as it were *glided* through them, while, like a stream of water, they opened before him, and immediately closed again leaving no trace of the way he had taken.—BURDER.

Ver. 35. He was a burning and a shining light; and ye were willing for a season to rejoice in his light.

This character of John the Baptist is perfectly conformable to the mode of expression adopted by the Jews. It was usual with them to call any person who was celebrated for knowledge, a candle. Thus they say that Shuah, the father-in-law of Judah, (Gen. xxxviii. 2,) was the candle or light of the place where he lived, because he was one of the most famous men in the city, enlightening their eyes; hence they call a rabbin, the candle of the law, and the lamp of light. —LIGHTFOOT.

CHAPTER VI.

Ver. 1. After these things Jesus went over the sea of Galilee, which is *the sea* of Tiberias.

The present town of Tabareeah, as it is now called, is in form of an irregular crescent, and is enclosed towards the land by a wall flanked with circular towers: it lies nearly north and south along the western edge of the lake, and has its eastern front opposed to the water, on the brink of which it stands, as some of the houses there are almost washed by the sea. The whole does not appear a mile in circuit, and cannot contain more than six hundred separate dwellings, from the manner in which they are placed. There are two gates visible from without; one near the southern, and the other in the western wall, the latter of which is in one of the round towers, and is the only one now open. There are appearances also of the tower having been surrounded by a ditch, but this is now filled up by cultivable soil. The interior presents but few objects of interest besides the ordinary habitations, which are, in general, small and mean. There is a mosque, with a dome and minaret, now frequented; and another with an octangular tower, now in ruins. The former of these is not far from the gate of entrance; the latter is nearer to the beach. There are also two synagogues of the Jews near the centre of the town, both of them inferior to that of Jerusalem, though similar in design; and one Christian place of worship, called the house of Peter, near the northern quarter, close to the water's edge. The last, which has been thought by some to be the oldest place of Christian worship now extant in Palestine, is a vaulted room about thirty feet by fifteen, and perhaps fifteen in height; it stands nearly east and west, having its door of entrance at the western front, and its altar immediately opposite in a shallow recess. Over the door is one small window, and on each side four others, all arched and open. The masonry of the edifice is of an ordinary kind; the pavement within is similar to that used for streets in this country; and the whole is devoid of sculpture or other ornament, as far as I could perceive. In a court without the house of Peter, I observed, however, a block of stone, on which were the figures of two goats, and two lions or tigers, coarsely executed; but whether this ever belonged to the building itself, no one could inform me. During my visit to this church, morning mass was performed by the abuna, at whose house we had lodged; the congregation consisted of only eleven persons, young and old; and the furniture and decorations of the altar and the priest were exceedingly scanty and poor. This edifice is thought by the people here to have been the very house which Peter inhabited at the time of his being called from his boat to follow Christ. It was evidently constructed, however, for a place of worship, and probably at a period much posterior to the time of the apostle whose name it bears, though it might have been erected on the spot which tradition has marked as the site of his more humble habitation: from hence, they say, too, it was, that the boat pushed off into the lake when the miraculous draught of fishes was taken. Besides the public buildings already specified are the house of the aga, on the rising ground near the northern quarter of the town; a small but good bazar, and two or three coffee sheds. The ordinary dwellings of the inhabitants are such as are commonly seen in eastern villages; but are marked by a peculiarity, which I witnessed here for the first time. On the terrace of almost every house stands a small square enclosure of reeds, loosely covered with leaves: these I learnt were resorted to by the heads of families to sleep in during the summer months, when the heat of the nights is intolerable, from the low situation of the town, and the unfrequency of cooling breezes. The whole population of Tabareeah does not exceed two thousand souls, according to the opinion of the best-informed residents. Provisions are not abundant, and therefore generally dear; and fish, when occasionally taken by a line from the shore, are sold to the aga, or to some of the rich Jews, at an exorbitant price.—BUCKINGHAM.

Ver. 1. After these things Jesus went over the sea of Galilee, which is *the sea* of Tiberias. 2. And a great multitude followed him, because they saw his miracles which he did on them that were diseased. 3. And Jesus went up into a mountain, and there he sat with his disciples.

Tiberias, one of the principal cities of Galilee, was erected by the tetrarch Herod Antipas, who gave it this appellation in honour of the Emperor Tiberius. It was this Herod who beheaded John the Baptist, (Matt. xiv. 3—11,) and who sought the life of Christ himself, (Luke xiii. 31.) He probably resided in Tiberias, which may be the reason why the Saviour never visited this place. It was situated near the Sea of Galilee, on a plain of singular fertility, which was greatly increased by assiduous cultivation. Josephus describes this region as a perfect paradise, blessed with a delicious temperature, and producing the fruits of every climate under heaven, not at stated periods merely, but in endless succession throughout the year. The neglect of agriculture in modern times has, of course, made it less productive; but the mildness of the climate, and the richness of the soil, are still extolled by travellers. When the Romans made war upon the Jews, Tiberias surrendered without waiting for a siege: on this account the Jews remained unmolested; and after the destruction of Jerusalem, this city became eminent for its academy, over which a succession of Jewish doctors presided until the fourth century. In the early ages of Christianity, Tiberias was an episcopal see; in the seventh century it was taken by the Saracens under the Calif Omar; and though it passed into the hands of the Christians during the crusades, the Mohammedans regained the possession of it towards the close of the fourteenth century. Widely scattered ruins of walls and other buildings, as well as fragments of columns, indicate the ancient extent of Tiberias. The stone of these ruins is described by the Rev. William Jowett as being "very black, so that there is nothing about them of the splendour of antiquity,—nothing but an air of mourning and desolation. In this circumstance they differ so greatly from the magnificent antiquities of Egypt and Greece, as to leave the most sombre impression on the fancy: they are perfectly funereal."

The modern town of Tiberias, which is delineated in our engraving, is by the natives called Tabaria, or Tabareeah; it occupies part of the site of the ancient city, and is situated at a short distance to the east from the Sea of Galilee. It is surrounded with walls and towers, which at first view are very imposing; on a nearer approach, however, their insignificance is apparent. A few cannon would put them down in an instant, though to an assault from the natives they would present, probably, a very long and effectual resistance. One fourth of the space within the walls is stated by Dr. Richardson to be unoccupied by house or building; and many parts of the town are in a ruined and filthy condition. The population has been computed at one thousand five hundred, or two thousand persons;

TIBERIAS AND SEA OF GALILEE.—John 6:1, 2. Page 612.

eighty houses are occupied by Christians, and one hundred and fifty by Turks, but the largest portion (amounting to two hundred) is tenanted by Jews of all nations, who come here to spend the rest of their days. On the north side of the town, not far from the lake, there is a Greek church, the architecture of which exhibits much of the character of those sacred edifices which were erected by the Empress Helena: it is said to occupy the identical spot on which stood the house of the apostle Peter, who, previously to his becoming a disciple of Jesus Christ, had been a fisherman on the lake.

To the south of Tiberias lie the celebrated hot baths, the water of which contains a strong solution of muriate of soda, (common salt,) with a considerable intermixture of iron and sulphur; it emits a powerful sulphureous smell. A thermometer placed in different spots where the water gushes out, rose to the various heights of 131, 132, 138, and 139 degrees of Fahrenheit; in the bath, where it cools after standing some time, its temperature was 110. An humble building is erected over the bath, containing mean apartments, on one side for men, on the other for women: it is much frequented as a cure for almost every complaint, particularly by the Jews, who have a great veneration for a Roman sepulchre excavated in a cliff near the spot, which they imagine to be the tomb of Jacob. About a mile from the town, and exactly in front of the lake, is a chain of rocks, in which are distinctly seen cavities or grottoes that have resisted the ravages of time. These are uniformly represented to travellers as the places referred to in the gospel history, which were the resort of miserable and fierce demoniacs, upon one of whom Jesus Christ wrought a miraculous and instantaneous cure: (Matt. viii. 28. Mark v. 2, 3. Luke viii. 37.)

The Sea of Galilee, which is seen in the background of our engraving, derives its name from its situation on the eastern borders of the province of Galilee; it was anciently called the Sea of Chinnereth, or Chinneroth, (Numb. xxxiv. 11. Josh. xii. 3,) from its vicinity to the town of that name. In 1 Mac. xi. 67, it is called the Water of Gennesar, and in Luke v. 1, the Lake of Gennesaret, from the neighbouring land of that name. Its most common appellation is the Sea of Tiberias, from the contiguous town of Tiberias, which has been described in the preceding paragraphs.

This capacious lake is from twelve to fifteen miles in length, and from six to nine miles in breadth; along the shore its depth varies, and in some parts it may be sixty feet. The water is perfectly fresh, and it is used by the inhabitants of Tiberias to drink, and for every culinary purpose. The waters of the northern part of this lake abound with delicious fish. It is remarkable that there is not a single boat of any description on the Sea of Tiberias at present, although it is evident from the gospel history that it was much navigated in the time of Jesus Christ. The fish are caught partly by the fishermen going into the water up to their waist, and throwing in a hand-net, and partly with casting-nets from the beach; the consequence is, that a very small quantity only is taken in comparison of what might be obtained if boats were employed. This accounts for the circumstance of fish being so dear at Tiberias, as to be sold at the same price per pound as meat. Viewed from a height, the water looks, amid the surrounding mountains, like an immense reservoir; and from the northern part being covered with volcanic remains, it has been conjectured that this lake was at one period the crater of a volcano. It has been compared by travellers to Loch Lomond, in Scotland; and, like the Lake of Windermere, in Westmoreland, it is often greatly agitated by winds. A strong current marks the passage of the Jordan through this lake; and when this is opposed by contrary winds, which blow here with the force of a hurricane from the southeast, sweeping into the lake from the mountains, a boisterous sea is instantly raised, which the small vessels of the country (such as were anciently in use) were ill qualified to resist. Such a tempest is described in Matt. viii. 24—26, which was miraculously calmed by Jesus Christ with a word. The broad and extended surface of this lake, "covering the bottom of a profound valley, surrounded by lofty and precipitous eminences, when added to the impression under which every Christian pilgrim approaches, gives to it a character of unparalleled dignity."—HORNE.

CHAPTER VII.

Ver. 3. His brethren, therefore, said unto him, Depart hence, and go into Judea, that thy disciples also may see the works that thou doest.

In eastern language it is common to apply the word brother or sister to those relations who have no right to it in England. Thus, cousins are called "brothers;" *i. e.* the sons of brothers are called brothers; but a daughter, though she would be called sister by her cousins, yet her children would not be addressed in the same way, but "*machăn*," i. e. cousin, would be their proper title. The name sister, which Abraham gave to his wife, is still given to the same degree of relationship. Gen. xx. 12. "She is the daughter of my father, but not the daughter of my mother."—ROBERTS.

Ver. 38. He that believeth on me, as the scripture hath said, out of his belly shall flow rivers of living water.

It is said of divine sages, of great *gooroos*, "Ah! in their heads are kept the rivers of life, or life-giving rivers." The figure in reference to them is, I doubt not, taken from Siva, as the Ganges is said to flow from his head.—ROBERTS.

CHAPTER IX.

Ver. 2. And his disciples asked him, saying, Master, who did sin, this man, or his parents, that he was born blind?

The Hindoos and Ceylonese very commonly attribute their misfortunes to the transgressions of a former state of existence. I remember being rather struck with the seriousness of a cripple, who attributed his condition to the unknown fault of his former life. His conjecture was, that he had broken the leg of a fowl. Offerings are made with a view to an honourable or happy birth at the nex transmigration.—CALLAWAY.

Ver. 7. And said unto him, Go, wash in the pool of Siloam, (which is, by interpretation, Sent.) He went his way, therefore, and washed, and came seeing.

The following description of the fountain of Siloam is from the journal of Messrs. Fisk and King, under date of April 28, 1823. (Missionary Herald, 1824, p. 66.) "Near the southeast corner of the city, at the foot of Zion and Moriah, is the pool of Siloah, (Neh. 3. 15,) whose waters flow with a gentle murmur from under the holy mountain of Zion, or rather from under Ophel, having Zion on the west, and Moriah on the north. The very fountain issues from a rock, twenty or thirty feet below the surface of the ground, to which we descended by two flights of steps. Here it flows out without a single murmur, and appears clear as crystal. From this place it winds its way several rods under the mountain, then makes its appearance with gentle gurgling, and, forming a beautiful rill, takes its way down into the valley, towards the southeast. We drank of the water both at the fountain and from the stream, and found it soft, of a sweetish taste, and pleasant. The fountain is called in scripture the 'pool of Siloam.' It was to this that the blind man went and washed, and came seeing."—BUSH.

CHAPTER X.

Ver. 1. Verily, verily, I say unto you, He that entereth not by the door into the sheepfold, but climbeth up some other way, the same is a thief and a robber.

In summer, the flocks were enclosed in folds, to which allusion is frequently made in the sacred volume. The fold of Polyphemus, the far-famed Sicilian shepherd, was a spacious cave, where his cattle, his sheep, and goats reposed. In Persia the shepherds frequently drive their flocks into caverns at night, and enclose them by heaping up walls of loose stones. But the more common sheepfold was an enclosure in the manner of a building, and constructed of stone and hurdles, or fenced with reeds. It had a large door, or entrance, for admitting the flock, which was closed with hurdles; and to facilitate the tithing, which was done in the fold, they struck out a little door, so small, that two lambs could not escape together. To this entrance, which is still used in the East, our Lord alludes in this declaration: "He that entereth not by the door into the sheepfold, but climbeth up some other way, the same is a thief and a robber."—PAXTON.

Ver. 3. To him the porter openeth: and the sheep hear his voice: and he calleth his own sheep by name, and leadeth them out. 4. And when he putteth forth his own sheep, he goeth before them, and the sheep follow him: for they know his voice. 5. And a stranger will they not follow, but will flee from him: for they know not the voice of strangers.

See on Is. 40. 11.

Having had my attention directed last night to the words, "The sheep hear his voice, and he calleth his own sheep by name," I asked my man if it was usual in Greece to give names to the sheep. He informed me that it was, and that the sheep obeyed the shepherd when he called them by their names. This morning I had an opportunity of verifying the truth of this remark. Passing by a flock of sheep, I asked the shepherd the same question which I had put to my servant, and he gave me the same answer. I then bade him to call one of his sheep. He did so, and it instantly left its pasturage and its companions, and ran up to the hand of the shepherd with signs of pleasure, and with a prompt obedience. It is also true of the sheep in this country, *that a stranger they will not follow, but will flee from him, for they know not the voice of strangers.* The shepherd told me that many of his sheep were still wild; that they had not yet learned their names; but that by teaching they would all learn them.—HARTLEY'S JOURNAL OF A TOUR IN GREECE.

Ver. 5. And a stranger will they not follow, but will flee from him: for they know not the voice of strangers.

The oriental shepherd marches before his flock to the field, with his rod in his hand and his dog by his side; and they are so perfectly disciplined, that they follow him wherever he chooses to lead them. To facilitate the management of his charge, he gives names to his sheep, which answer to them, as dogs and horses answer to theirs in these parts of the world. The shepherds of Egypt select a ram to lead the flock, and suspend a bell from his neck that they may follow him with greater ease and certainty.—PAXTON.

Ver. 11. I am the good shepherd: the good shepherd giveth his life for the sheep. 12. But he that is a hireling, and not the shepherd, whose own the sheep are not, seeth the wolf coming, and leaveth the sheep, and fleeth: and the wolf catcheth them and scattereth the sheep. 13. The hireling fleeth, because he is a hireling, and careth not for the sheep.

Being wakeful at night, I occasionlly heard noises from the hills, which our attendants said proceeded from *wolves.* The watchful shepherds shouted, and the sheep probably escaped. I was forcibly reminded of the "good shepherd;" were the flock near our tent to be forsaken by the shepherd for a single night, it would be scattered and devoured.—REV. R. ANDERSON'S TOUR IN GREECE.

CHAPTER XI.

Ver. 1. Now a certain *man* was sick, *named* Lazarus, of Bethany, the town of Mary and her sister Martha.

Bethany is a miserable village, containing between forty and fifty wretched stone huts, and inhabited solely by Arabs. It stands on a rocky mountain, well cultivated, and producing olive and fig-trees, vines, beans, and corn, which, over the whole country, are now ready for harvest. The tomb supposed to be that of Lazarus is a cave in the rock, to which we descended by twenty-six rude steps. At the bottom of these, in a small chamber, we saw a smal door in the ground; we descended by two large steps, and stooping through a low passage, about five feet long, entered the tomb, which is not hewed out of the rock, but built with large stones, and arched: I found it to be seven feet four inches, by eight feet two inches and a half, and ten feet high: it is in its original rude state, and belongs to the Catholics, who say mass in it occasionally. In the tomb are two small windows, opening to holes in the rock.—TURNER.

Ver. 17. Then when Jesus came, he found that he had *lain* in the grave four days already.

It was customary among the Jews to go to the sepulchres of their deceased friends, and visit them for three days, for so long they supposed that their spirits hovered about them; but when once they perceived that their visage began to change, as it would in three days in these countries, all hopes of a return to life were then at an end. After a revolution of humours, which in seventy-two hours is completed, the body tends naturally to putrefaction; and therefore Martha had reason to say, that her brother's body (which appears by the context to have been laid in the sepulchre the same day that he died) would now on the fourth day become offensive.—STACKHOUSE.

Ver. 19. And many of the Jews came to Martha and Mary, to comfort them concerning their brother.

The general time of mourning for deceased relations, both among Jews and Gentiles, was seven days. During these days of mourning their friends and neighbours visited them, in order that by their presence and conversation they might assist them in bearing their loss. Many therefore in so populous a part of the country must have been going to and coming from the sisters, while the days of their mourning for Lazarus lasted. The concourse too would be the greater as it was the time of the passover. Besides, a vast multitude now attended Jesus on his journey. This great miracle therefore must have had many witnesses.—MACKNIGHT.

Ver. 31. The Jews then which were with her in the house, and comforted her, when they saw Mary, that she rose up hastily, and went out, followed her, saying, She goeth unto the grave to weep there.

Authors that speak of the eastern people's visiting the tombs of their relations, almost always attribute this to the women; the men, however, sometimes visit them too, though not so frequently as the other sex, who are more susceptible of the tender emotions of grief, and think that propriety requires it of them; whereas the men commonly think that such strong expressions of sorrow would misbecome them. We find that some male friends came from Jerusalem to condole with Mary and Martha on account of the death of their brother Lazarus, who, when they supposed that her rising up and going out of the house was with a view to repair to his grave to weep, "followed her, saying, She goeth unto the grave to weep there." It is no wonder that they thought her rising up in haste was to go to the grave to weep, for Chardin informs us, that the mourning in the East does not consist in wearing black clothes, which they call an infernal dress, but in great outcries, in sitting motionless, in being slightly dressed in a brown or pale habit, in refusing to take any nourishment for eight days running, as if they were determined to live no longer. Her starting up then with a sudden motion, who, it was expected, would have sat still without stirring at all, and her going out of the house, made them conclude that it must be to go to the grave to weep there, though, according to the modern Persian ceremonial, it wanted five or six days of the usual time for going to weep at the grave: but the Jews possibly might repair thither sooner than the Persians do.—HARMER.

Ver. 38. Jesus, therefore, again groaning in himself, cometh to the grave. It was a cave, and a stone lay upon it. 39. Jesus said, Take ye away the stone. Martha, the sister of him that was dead, said unto him, Lord, by this time he stinketh; for he hath been *dead* four days.

The Jewish tombs, like those of Macri, have entrances, which were originally closed with a large and broad stone rolled to the door, which it was not lawful, in the opinion of a Jew, to displace. They were adorned with inscriptions and emblematical devices, alluding to particular transactions in the lives of the persons that lie there entombed. Thus the place where the dust of Joshua reposed, was called Timnath-heres, because the image of the sun was engraved on his sepulchre, in memory of his arresting that luminary in his career, till he had gained a complete victory over the confederate kings. Such significant devices were common in the East. Cicero says, the tomb of Archimedes was distinguished by the figure of a sphere and a cylinder.—PAXTON.

Ver. 44. And he that was dead came forth, bound hand and foot with grave-clothes: and his face was bound about with a napkin. Jesus saith unto them, Loose him, and let him go.

As the Jews did not make use of coffins, they placed their dead separately in niches, or little cells, cut into the sides of the caves, or rooms, which they had hewed out of the rock. This form of the Jewish sepulchre suggests an easy solution of a difficulty in the resurrection of Lazarus. The sacred historian states, that when our Lord cried with a loud voice, "Lazarus, come forth, he that was dead came forth, bound hand and foot with grave-clothes." Upon this circumstance, the enemies of revelation seize with avidity, and demand with an air of triumph, How he should come out of a grave, who was bound hand and foot with grave-clothes? But the answer is easy: the evangelist does not mean that Lazarus walked out of the sepulchre, but only that he sat up, then putting his legs over the edge of his niche or cell, slid down and stood upright upon the floor; all which he might easily do, notwithstanding his arms were bound close to his body, and his legs were tied straight together, by means of the shroud and rollers with which he was swathed. Hence, when he was come forth, Jesus ordered his relations to loose him and let him go; a circumstance plainly importing the historian's admission that Lazarus could not walk till he was unbound.—PAXTON.

[This interpretation, though plausible and ingenious, does not well accord with the letter of the text. From this it is not easy to avoid the impression, that in some way he came forth from the inner part to the outer opening of the cave, enveloped in his grave-clothes. As to the impossibility of his walking when thus impeded, we may safely admit, that if his limbs were thus entirely confined, he was conveyed to the door of the cave, by the same Almighty power by which he was raised from the dead.—BUSH.]

CHAPTER XIII.

Ver. 18. I speak not of you all; I know whom I have chosen: but, that the scripture may be fulfilled, He that eateth bread with me hath lift up his heel against me.

See on Ps. 41. 9.

Ver. 38. Jesus answered him, Wilt thou lay down thy life for my sake? Verily, verily, I say unto thee, The cock shall not crow, till thou hast denied me thrice.

See on Mark 14. 30.

It is very common for people to regulate their time in the night by the crowing of the cock: thus, "I did not leave the temple till the *Sâma-koli*," i. e. midnight cock. "I left my home at the *Vudeya-koli*," i. e. the morning cock. The people attach a high value to those birds which crow with the greatest regularity; and some of them keep the time with astonishing precision.—ROBERTS.

CHAPTER XVII.

Ver. 5. And now, O Father, glorify thou me with thine own self, with the glory which I had with thee before the world was.

Our Lord is undoubtedly here praying to be glorified with his *mediatorial* glory. But this was not the glory which he had with the Father before the world was, for prior to the creation he did not exist as mediator, and therefore could not enjoy a mediator's glory. Consequently the phrase, "which I had with thee before the world was," probably means, "which I had in the divine purpose, which thou didst ordain and destine that I *should* have in the ages to come." By a similar diction, Christ is termed "the Lamb slain from the foundation of the world." But he was not *actually* slain from the foundation of the world, but only in the divine purpose. So here, Christ prays to be put in possession of that honour and glory which the Father from eternity had decreed should redound to him, in virtue of his assuming the office of Messiah, and being constituted Head and Lord of the New Testament dispensation. At this glory he looks, not with a retrospective, but with an anticipative eye.—BUSH.

CHAPTER XVIII.

Ver. 3. Judas then, having received a band *of men* and officers from the chief priests and Pharisees, cometh thither with lanterns, and torches, and weapons.

Norden, among other particulars, has given some account of the lamps and lanterns that they make use of commonly at Cairo. "The lamp is of the palm-tree wood, of the height of twenty-three inches, and made in a very gross manner. The glass, that hangs in the middle, is half filled with water and has oil on the top, about three fingers in depth. The wick is preserved dry at the bottom of the glass, where they have contrived a place for it, and ascends through a pipe. These lamps do not give much light, yet they are very commodious, because they are transported easily from one place to another. With regard to the lanterns, they have pretty nearly the figure of a cage, and are made of reeds. It is a collection of five or six glasses, like to that of the lamp which has been just described. They suspend them by cords in the middle of the streets, when there is any great festival at Cairo, and they put painted paper in the place of the reeds."

Were these the lanterns that those who came to take Jesus made use of? or were they such lamps as these that Christ referred to in the parable of the virgins? or are we rather to suppose that these lanterns are appropriated to the Egyptian illuminations, and that Pococke's account of the lanterns of this country will give us a better idea of those that were anciently made use of at Jerusalem? Speaking of the travelling of the people of Egypt, he says, "by night they rarely make use of tents, but lie in the open air, having large lanterns made like a pocket paper lantern, the bottom and top being of copper tinned over, and instead of paper they are made with linen, which is extended by hoops of wire, so that when it is put together it serves as a candlestick, &c. and they have a contrivance to hang it up abroad by means of three staves."—HARMER.

CHAPTER XIX.

Ver. 2. And the soldiers platted a crown of thorns, and put *it* on his head, and they put on him a purple robe.

There still exists a plant in Palestine, known among botanists by the name of the "Thorn of Christ," supposed to be the shrub which afforded the crown worn by the Saviour at his crucifixion. It has many small sharp prickles, well adapted to give pain; and as the leaves greatly resemble those of ivy, it is not improbable that the enemies of Messiah chose it, from its similarity to a plant with which emperors and generals were accustomed to be crowned; and thence, that there might be calumny, insult, and derision, meditated in the very act of punishment,

"The mockery of reed and robe, and crown
Of platted thorns upon his temple pressed."—RUSSEL.

Ver. 5. Then came Jesus forth, wearing the crown of thorns, and the purple robe. And *Pilate* saith unto them, Behold the man!

On quitting the church we proceeded to the Mount of Olives; our road lay through the Via-dolorosa, so called from its having been the passage by which Christ was conducted from the place of his imprisonment to Mount Calvary. The outer walls of what was once the residence of Pilate, are comprehended in this street. The original entrance to the palace is blocked up, and the present access is at one of the angles of the court. The portal was formerly in the centre, and approached by a flight of steps, which were removed some centuries ago to Rome, and are now in a small chapel near the church of San Giovanni di Laterano. Very little of this structure is still extant; but the Franciscan monks imagine they have actually traced out the dungeon in which our Saviour was incarcerated, as well as the hall where Cesar's officer proceeded to give judgment. The place where the Messiah was scourged is now a ruined court, on the opposite side of the street; and not far from thence, but in a direction nearer to Mount Calvary, is the arch which the Latin friars designate "Il arco d'ecce homo," from the expression of Pilate, as recorded by St. John xix. 5; upon an eminence between the pillars which support the curvature, the Roman governor exhibited this illustrious victim to his deluded countrymen. Between this place and the scene of his crucifixion, Christ is said to have fainted under the weight of the cross. Tradition relates, that he sunk beneath its pressure three times; and the different stages are supposed to have been actually noted; they are severally designated by two columns, and an indenture in the wall.—JOLLIFFE.

Ver. 23. Then the soldiers, when they had crucified Jesus, took his garments, and made four parts, to every soldier a part, and also *his* coat: now the coat was without seam, woven from the top throughout.

The dress of the Arabs, in this part of the Holy Land, and indeed throughout all Syria, is simple and uniform; it consists of a blue shirt, descending below the knees, the legs and feet being exposed, or the latter sometimes covered with the ancient cothurnus, or buskin. A cloak is worn of very coarse and heavy camel's-hair cloth, almost universally decorated with broad black and white stripes, passing vertically down the back; this is of one square piece, with holes for the arms; it has a seam down the back; made without this seam, it is considered of greater value. Here, then, we perhaps behold the form and materials of our Saviour's garment, for which the soldiers cast lots, being "without seam, woven from the top throughout." It was the most ancient dress of the inhabitants of this country.—CLARKE.

Ver. 39. And there came also Nicodemus, (which at the first came to Jesus by night,) and brought a mixture of myrrh and aloes, about a hundred pound *weight*.

The Old Testament historian entirely justifies the account which the evangelist gives of the quantity of spices with which the sacred body of Christ was swathed. The Jews object to the quantity used on that occasion, as unnecessarily profuse, and even incredible; but it appears from their own writings, that spices were used at such times in great abundance. In the Talmud, it is said, that no less than eighty pounds of spices were consumed at the funeral of Rabbi Gamaliel the elder. And at the funeral of Herod, if we may believe the account of their most celebrated historian, the procession was followed by five hundred of his domestics carrying spices. Why then should it be reckoned incredible that Nicodemus brought of myrrh and aloes about a hundred pounds weight, to embalm the body of Jesus?—PAXTON.

CHAPTER XXI.

Ver. 5. Then Jesus saith unto them, Children, have ye any meat? They answered him, No.

Thus did the risen Saviour address himself to his disciples. In this way, also, do spiritual guides, and men of learning, and aged men, address their disciples or dependants. In the Scanda Purana, it is said, "Sooran asked Kāsipan what he should do? to which he replied, *Children*, I will mention one thing as a security for you, which is, to perform glorious austerity." Again, in the same work, "Thus proceeding, Singu Măggam, who was to him as his own life, following Velly, took him into his hall, and seated him, and heartily welcomed him with good words, and asked, *Children*, what are you come for?"—ROBERTS.

Ver. 7. Therefore that disciple whom Jesus loved, saith unto Peter, It is the Lord. Now, when Simon Peter heard that it was the Lord, he girt *his* fisher's coat *unto him*, (for he was naked,) and did cast himself into the sea.

The fishermen in the East, when engaged in their vocation, are generally naked, excepting a small strip of cloth round their loins; so that, without any inconvenience, they can cast themselves into the sea.—ROBERTS.

Ver. 18. Verily, verily, I say unto thee, When thou wast young, thou girdedst thyself, and walkedst whither thou wouldst: but when thou shalt be old, thou shalt stretch forth thy hands, and another shall gird thee, and carry *thee* whither thou wouldst not.

It was customary in the ancient combats for the vanquished person to stretch out his hands to the conqueror, signifying that he declined the battle, yielded the victory, and submitted to the direction of the victor. So, Turnus in Virgil:

——— "Vicisti et victum tendere palmas
Ausonii videre."—Æn. lib. xii. l. 936.

"You have overcome, and the Ausonians have seen thy vanquished foe stretch forth his suppliant hands." To this custom our Lord alludes in his prediction to Peter: "When thou shalt be old, thou shalt stretch forth thy hands, and another shall gird thee." The aged apostle was to stretch out his hands as a token of submission to that power under which he would fall and perish.—PAXTON.

THE ACTS OF THE APOSTLES.

CHAPTER I.

Ver. 26. And they gave forth their lots: and the lot fell upon Matthias; and he was numbered with the eleven apostles.

The account which Grotius gives of the manner in which lots were cast, seems very probable and satisfactory. He says, they put their lots into two urns, one of which contained the names of Joseph and Matthias, and the other a blank, and the word apostle. In drawing these out of the urns, the blank came up with the name of Joseph, and the lot on which was written the word *apostle* came up with the name of Matthias. This being in answer to their prayers, they concluded that Matthias was the man whom the Lord had chosen to the apostleship.—BURDER.

CHAPTER IV.

Ver. 1. And, as they spake unto the people, the priests, and the captain of the temple, and the Sadducees, came upon them.

There was a garrison placed in the tower of Antonia, for the guard of the temple. This tower stood in the northeast corner of the wall, which parted the mountain of the house from the city. It was built by Hyrcanus the Asmonean, the high-priest. There he himself dwelt, and there he laid up the holy garments of the priesthood, whenever he put them off, having finished the service of the temple. Herod repaired this tower at a great expense, and named it Antonia, in honour of Antony. It was used as the depository of the priest's garments, till the removal of Archelaus from his kingdom, and the confiscation of his estate. The tower then came into the hands of the Romans, and was kept as a garrison by them. The high-priest's garments were then kept there under their power, till Vitellius restored them to the Jews. The captain here spoken off was the commander of the company who had the keeping of the castle.—LIGHTFOOT.

Ver. 34. Neither was there any among them that lacked: for as many as were possessors of lands or houses, sold them, and brought the prices of the things that were sold, 35. And laid *them* down at the apostles' feet: and distribution was made unto every man according as he had need.

When a person takes a present or an offering to a priest, or a spiritual guide, or to a distinguished scholar, he does not give it into the hands of his superior, but places it at his *feet*. It is called the *pātha-kāniki*, i. e. the feet-offering. Ananias and Sapphira also brought a part of the price of the land, "and laid it at the apostles' *feet*."—ROBERTS.

CHAPTER V.

Ver. 6. And the young men arose, wound him up, and carried *him* out, and buried *him*.

The bier used by the Turks at Aleppo, says Russel, is a kind of coffin, much in the form of ours, only the lid rises with a ledge in the middle. Christians, according to the same author, are carried to the grave in an open bier of the same kind as that used by the people of Nain. But the Jews seem to have conveyed their dead bodies to their funerals without any support, as may be inferred from the history of Ananias and his wife Sapphira: "And the young men arose, wound him up, and carried him out and buried him." With equal despatch they carried forth Sapphira, and buried her by her husband. No hint is given of a bier in either case.—PAXTON.

CHAPTER VIII.

Ver. 40. But Philip was found at Azotus; and, passing through, he preached in all the cities, till he came to Cesarea.

The present state of Azotus is thus described by Dr. Wittman:—"Pursuing our route through a delightful country, we came to Ashdod, called by the Greeks Azotus, and under that name mentioned in the Acts of the Apostles, a town of great antiquity, provided with two small entrance gates. In passing through this place we saw several fragments of columns, capitals, cornices, &c., of marble. Towards the centre is a handsome mosque, with a minaret. By the Arab inhabitants Ashdod is called Mezdel. Two miles to the south, on a hill, is a ruin, having in its centre a lofty column still standing entire. The delightful verdure of the surrounding plains, together with a great abundance of fine old olive-trees, rendered the scene charmingly picturesque. In the villages, tobacco, fruits, and vegetables are cultivated abundantly by the inhabitants; and the fertile and extensive plains yield an ample produce of corn. At this time the wheat was just coming into ear, the harvest taking place so early as towards the latter end of April or beginning of May."—BURDER.

CHAPTER IX.

Ver. 5. And he said, Who art thou, Lord? And the Lord said, I am Jesus whom thou persecutest: *it is* hard for thee to kick against the pricks.

See on Judg. 3. 31.

Ver. 11. And the Lord *said* unto him, Arise, and go into the street which is called Straight, and inquire in the house of Judas, for *one* called Saul of Tarsus: for, behold, he prayeth.

Tarsus, the place of Saul's nativity, was at that time the most celebrated school in the world, and, for polite literature, far surpassed Athens and Alexandria. Strabo, who lived in that age, gives the following account of it: "The inhabitants of this place cherish such a passion for philosophy, and all the various branches of polite letters, that they have greatly excelled Athens and Alexandria, and every other place in which there are schools and academies for philosophy and erudition. But Tarsus differs in this, that those who here devote themselves to the study of literature, are all natives of that country: there are not many from foreign parts who reside here. Nor do the natives of the country continue here for life, but they go abroad to finish their studies, and when they have perfected themselves they choose to live in other places. There are but few who return home." He also says, that "Rome can best witness the great number of learned men, the natives of this city; for it is full of literati from Tarsus and Alexandria."—BURDER.

Ver. 34. And Peter said unto him, Eneas, Jesus Christ maketh thee whole: arise, and make thy bed. And he arose immediately.

Mattresses, or something of that kind, were used for sleeping upon. The Israelites formerly lay upon carpets. (Amos ii. 8.) Russel says the "beds consist of a mattress laid on the floor, and over this a sheet, (in winter a carpet, or some such woollen covering,) the other sheet being sewed to the quilt. A divan cushion often serves for a pillow and bolster." They do not now keep their beds made; the mattresses are rolled up, carried away, and placed in cupboards till they are wanted at night. Hence we learn the propriety of our Lord's address to the paralytic, "Arise, take up thy bed, and walk."—HARMER.

Ver. 36. Now there was at Joppa a certain disciple named Tabitha, which, by interpretation, is called Dorcas: this woman was full of good works and alms-deeds which she did.

It was common not only among the Arabs, but also among the Greeks, to give their females the names of agreeable animals. Tabitha appears to have been a word used in the Syriac, which being interpreted is Dorcas; that is, an antelope, an animal remarkable for beautiful eyes. On this account it might have been given to the person here designated by it. (Parkhurst.)—BURDER.

CHAPTER X.

Ver. 23. Then called he them in, and lodged *them*. And on the morrow Peter went away with them, and certain brethren from Joppa accompanied him.

The people of the East have a general propensity for associates in all their transactions and all their journeys. Has a man from a distant village some business to do with you, he does not, as an Englishman would, come alone; he brings a large company of his neighbours and friends. Go, ask any of them, why have you come? the reply is, (pointing at the same time at the man of business,) "I came because he did." It is often surprising to see people at a great distance from their homes, having no other reason than "we came with him." See the man going to a court of justice, he is accompanied by a large band of his acquaintances, who canvass all the probabilities of the case, and who have a salvo for every exigency. Perhaps a love of show is one motive; but the desire to have witnesses of what has been said or done, and to have help at hand in case of any emergency, are other reasons for their love of company. The Oriental is like the granivorous animals of his native deserts, who are all, more or less, gregarious in their habits; and, as it is, so it was in the most remote antiquity. The Psalmist says of those who were travelling to the temple at Jerusalem, "they go from strength to strength;" but the margin has it, "from company to company." Thus did they stretch on, from one party to another, till they each appeared before God in his earthly "Zion." In the conduct, therefore, of Peter and his six companions, in the arrangement of our Divine Master in sending forth his disciples "by two and two," and in very numerous passages of scripture, we see the simplicity, caution, and affection of those concerned. —ROBERTS.

Ver. 25. And, as Peter was coming in, Cornelius met him, and fell down at his feet, and worshipped *him*. 26. But Peter took him up, saying, Stand up; I myself also am a man.

Mr. Harmer contends, that Cornelius the centurion, when he fell down at the feet of the apostle Peter and worshipped him, did not intend to pay him divine honours, but merely to salute him with a reverence esteemed the lowest and most submissive in the ceremonious East. He allows there was something extraordinary in the behaviour of Cornelius, but no mixture of idolatry. But it is to be feared the verdict which this respectable writer pronounces for the excellent Roman, is too favourable. The apostles did not at other times refuse the common tokens of respect and civility from those around them; and if the act of Cornelius meant no more, the refusal cannot be accounted for, upon the common principles of human nature. But the words of the evangelist ought to decide the question; he says expressly that Cornelius worshipped him; τροσεκυνησεν, the term which Luke and other inspired writers commonly use to express the homage which is due only to the Supreme Being. This term, it is admitted, is often employed by writers, both sacred and profane, to denote merely civil respect; but it cannot with propriety be so understood here, because the reason which the apostle assigned for his refusal, derives all its propriety and force from religious worship: "Stand up; I myself also am a man." But surely it is not inconsistent with the character of a man to receive an extraordinary token of respect from another. Mr. Harmer thinks the conduct of the apostle John, in throwing himself at the feet of the angel, is to be viewed in a somewhat different light. "John did nothing at all," says our author, "but what was conformable to the usages of his own country, when the people of it designed innocently to express great reverence and gratitude." But if the apostle meant only to express, by his prostration, the ordinary feelings of civil respect, why did the angel refuse it; and that because he was one of his fellow-servants? That it was actually more than civil respect—that it was really divine honours which John meant in the tumult of his feelings, or from a mistaken view of the angel's character, to pay, is quite evident from the charge which the celestial messenger gave him, to render unto God the homage which he intended at this time for him. But surely God is not the proper object of civil respect, but of religious adoration; and therefore, it must have been the latter which John intended. Though he was a Jew by descent, an enemy to all idolatry, and a zealous preacher against it, still he was but a man of like passions with others; and although under the supernatural influence of the Divine Spirit as an apostle, he was not infallible as a Christian, and by consequence he was liable, highly favoured as he certainly was, to deviate from the path of duty; and had he not at this time done a very improper thing, the angel had not reproved him, nor used terms so expressive of his abhorrence: "See thou do it not; for I am thy fellow-servant, and of thy brethren the prophets, and of them which keep the sayings of this book; worship God." That his conduct on this memorable occasion had at least a mixture of idolatry, is evident from the command he receives, to reserve such homage for God alone, to whom it is due.—PAXTON.

CHAPTER XII.

Ver. 10. When they were past the first and the second ward, they came unto the iron gate that leadeth unto the city; which opened to them of his own accord: and they went out, and passed on through one street; and forthwith the angel departed from him.

One method of securing the gates of fortified places, among the ancients, was to cover them with thick plates of iron; a custom which is still used in the East, and seems to be of great antiquity. We learn from Pitts that Algiers has five gates, and some of these have two, some three other gates within them, and some of them plated all over with thick iron. The place where the apostle was imprisoned, seems to have been secured in the same manner; for, says the inspired historian, "When they were past the first and second ward, they came unto the iron gate that leadeth into the city, which opened to them of its own accord." Pococke, speaking of a bridge not far from Antioch, called the iron bridge, says, there are two towers belonging to it, the gates of which are covered with iron plates, which he supposes is the reason of the name it bears. Some of their gates are plated over with brass; such are the enormous gates of the principal mosque at Damascus, formerly the church of John the Baptist. To gates like these, the Psalmist probably refers in these words: "He hath broken the gates of brass;" and the prophet, in that remarkable passage, where God promises to go before Cyrus his anointed, and "break in pieces the gates of brass, and cut in sunder the bars of iron."

But the locks and keys which secure these iron and brazen doors, by a singular custom, the very reverse of what prevails in the West, are of wood. The bolts of these wooden locks, which are also of wood, are made hollow within, which they unlock with wooden keys, about a span long, and about the thickness of a thumb. Into this key they drive a number of short nails, or strong wires, in such an order and distance, that they exactly fit others within the lock, and so turn them as they please. The locks and keys which shut the doors and gates in countries adjacent to Syria, are fabricated of the same materials, and in the same form. But those cities which were fortified with more than ordinary care, had sometimes bars of brass, or iron. In describing the superior and almost impregnable strength of Babylon, which Cyrus was chosen by the Almighty to subdue, the prophet particularly mentions the gates of brass and bars of iron. According to this view, the emphasis of the following passage is much greater perhaps than is commonly apprehended: "A brother offended is harder to be won than a strong city; and their contentions are like the bars of a castle," that are extremely difficult to be removed, both on account of their size, and of the strong and durable materials of which they are made.—PAXTON.

Ver. 21. And upon a set day, Herod, arrayed in royal apparel, sat upon his throne, and made an oration unto them.

Josephus gives the following account of this matter, but omitting to make any mention of the Tyrians and Sidonians on the occasion: "In the third year of Herod's being king of all Judea, he exhibited shows to the people in honour of the emperor; and he appeared in the theatre at Cesarea, dressed in a robe made all of silver tissue, of admirable workmanship. As the sun was then rising, the rays of it coming on his robe, made it shine so bright, that the people cried out, Forgive us, if we have hitherto reverenced you only as a man, but from this time we shall acknowledge you to be something superior to what is mortal. The king did not reprove them, nor reject this blasphemous flattery; and, before he went out of the theatre, he was seized with pains in his bowels, so as to cry out, I, whom you called your god, am now going to die! From thence he was carried to his palace immediately, and in the space of five days he died of those pains which he first felt in the theatre, in the fifty-fourth year of his age, after he had reigned four years over Iturea and Abilene, and three more over all Judea." "The king generally appoints for the reception of ambassadors such an hour as, according to the season, or the intended room of audience, will best enable him to display in full sunshine the brilliancy of his jewels. The title of bright, or resplendent, was added to the name of one sovereign, because his regal ornaments, glittering in the sun's rays on a solemn festival, so dazzled the eyes of all beholders, that they scarcely could bear the effulgence: and some knew not which was the monarch, and which the great luminary of day. Thus Theophylact relates, that the Persian king Hormisdas, sitting on his throne, astonished all spectators by the blazing glories of his jewels. Jemshid, having triumphed over the blacks, and the dives or demons, caused immense quantities of jewels, obtained as spoils from the enemy, to be piled upon his throne, so that all might behold them; as the sun shone through the windows on those jewels and the gold, his whole palace was illuminated by their reflected brilliancy. He caused his throne to be placed in such a manner, facing the east, that when the rising sun beamed on his splendid crown, the multitude exclaimed, This is the dawn of a new day." (Sir W. Ouseley.)—BURDER.

CHAPTER XIII.

Ver. 14. But, when they departed from Perga, they came to Antioch in Pisidia, and went into the synagogue on the Sabbath-day, and sat down.

If we had not seen the aqueduct, the quantity of immense squared blocks of stone and sculptured fragments, which we saw all the way to the khan, would have convinced us at once that we were on the site of a great city. We felt convinced that we had attained the great object of our journey, and were really on the spot consecrated by the labours and persecution of the apostles Paul and Barnabas. Leaving the town, and going on the north side of it, in the direction of the aqueduct, we were soon upon an elevated plateau, accurately described by Strabo by the name of λοφος. The quantity of ancient pottery, independently of the ruins, told us at once that we were upon the emplacement of the city of Antioch. The superb members of a temple, which, from the *thyrsus* on many of them, evidently belonged to Bacchus, was the first thing we saw. Passing on, a long and immense building, constructed with prodigious stones, and standing east and west, made me entertain a hope that it might be a church—a church of Antioch? It was so; the ground-plan, with the circular end for the bema, all remaining! Willingly would I have remained hours in the midst of a temple—perhaps one of the very earliest consecrated to the Saviour; but we were obliged to hasten on.

The next thing that attracted our notice were two large magnificent arches, a souterrain running far beneath the hill, and supporting the platform of a superb temple. A high wall of immense stones, without cement, next occurred, part probably of the gate of the city, and near it the ground-plan of another building. From hence ran a wall, at least its ruins, along towards the aqueduct, crowning the brow of the hill, and abruptly terminating where the hill became so precipitous as to require no defence. The remains of the aqueduct, of which twenty-one arches are perfect, are the most splendid I ever beheld: the stones, without cement, of the same massy dimensions as in the wall. The view, when near the aqueduct, was enchanting, and well entitled Antioch to its rank of capital of the province of Pisidia. In the valley on the left, groves of poplars and weeping willows seemed to sing the song of the Psalmist, "We hanged our harps upon the willows," &c. mourning, as at Babylon, for the melancholy fate of this once great Christian city. Not a Christian now resides in it, except a single Greek in the khan. Not a church, nor any priest to officiate, where Paul and Barnabas, and their successors, converted the thousands of idolaters to the true faith!

Behind the valley in the east rises a rugged mountain, part of the Paroreia; and in front of the place where I sat is the emplacement of the city, where once stood the synagogue, and the mansions that hospitably received the apostles, and those of their persecutors who drove them from the city—all now levelled to the ground! Behind the city, in the middle distance, is seen the modern city or town of Yalabatz, the houses intermixed with poplars and other trees, in autumnal colouring, and so numerous as to resemble a grove rather than a city. Beyond is a plain, bounded by the heights of Taurus, under which appeared a lake, probably of Eyerdir. On the right, in the middle distance also, the plain bounded by mountains, and these overtopped by the rugged Alpine peaks of Mount Taurus, covered with snow. In the foreground, the aqueduct, with the plains and groves of Yalabatz appearing through its arches. Behind us rose an amphitheatre of round low hills, backed by mountains, naked and lofty. Reserving a fuller examination for the morrow, we returned to our khan, seeing in our way an inscription on a fountain, which with the others we shall notice hereafter.—ARUNDELL.

Ver. 15. And after the reading of the law and the prophets, the rulers of the synagogue sent unto them, saying, *Ye* men *and* brethren, if ye have any word of exhortation for the people, say on.

The custom of reading the law, the Jews say, existed a hundred and seventy years before the time of Christ. The division of it into sections is ascribed to Ezra. The five books of Moses, here called the law, contained fifty-three sections, so that by reading one on each sabbath, and two in one day, they read through the whole in the course of a year, finishing at the feast of tabernacles, which they called "the rejoicing of the law." When Antiochus Epiphanes burnt the book of the law, and forbid the reading of it, the Jews in the room of it selected some passages out of the prophets, which they thought came nearest in words and sense to the sections of the law, and read them in their stead; but when the law was restored again, they still continued the reading of the prophetic sections; and the section for the day was called the dismission, because usually the people were dismissed upon it, unless any one stood up and expounded the word of God to them. This is the reason of the message sent to the apostles, "Ye men and brethren, if ye have any word of exhortation for the people, say on."—GILL.

CHAPTER XIV.

Ver. 13. Then the priest of Jupiter, which was before their city, brought oxen and garlands unto the gates, and would have done sacrifice with the people.

When the gods are taken out in procession, their necks are adorned with garlands; the priests also wear them at the same time. On all festive occasions men and women have on their sweet-scented garlands, and the smell of some of them is so strong as to be offensive to an Englishman. Does a man of rank offer to adorn you with a garland, it is a sign of his respect, and must not be refused. In the latter part of 1832 I visited the celebrated pagoda of Ramiseram, (the temple of Rāmar:) so soon as I arrived within a short distance of the gates, a number of dancing girls, priests, and others, came to meet us with *garlands;* they first did me the honour of putting one around my neck, and then presented others for Mrs. Roberts and the children.—ROBERTS.

CHAPTER XVI.

Ver. 11. Therefore, loosing from Troas, we came with a straight course to Samothracia, and the next *day* to Neapolis.

The view of the ancient Sichem, now called Napolose, otherwise Neapolis, and Napoleos, surprised us, as we had not expected to find a city of such magnitude in the road to Jerusalem. It seems to be the metropolis of a very rich and extensive country, abounding with provisions, and all the necessary articles of life, in much greater profusion than the town of Acre. White bread was exposed for sale in the streets, of a quality superior to any that is to be found elsewhere throughout the Levant. The governor of Napolose received and regaled us with all the magnificence of an eastern sovereign; refreshments of every kind known in the country, were set before us: and, when we supposed the list to be exhausted, to our very great astonishment a most sumptuous dinner was brought in. Nothing seemed to gratify our host more, than that any of his guests should eat heartily; and, to do him justice, every individual of the party ought to have possessed the appetite of ten hungry pilgrims, to satisfy his wishes in this respect.

There is nothing in the Holy Land finer than a view of Napolose, from the heights around it. As the traveller descends towards it from the hills, it appears luxuriantly imbosomed in the most delightful and fragrant bowers; half concealed by rich gardens, and by stately trees collected into groves, all around the bold and beautiful valley in which it stands. Trade seems to flourish among its inhabitants. Their principal employment is in making soap; but the manufactures of the town supply a very widely extended neighbourhood, and they are exported to a great distance upon camels. In the morning after our arrival, we met caravans coming from Grand Cairo; and noticed others reposing in the large olive plantations near the gates.—CLARKE.

Ver. 13. And on the Sabbath we went out of the city by a river side, where prayer was wont to be made; and we sat down, and spake unto the women which resorted *thither.*

The Jewish proseuchæ were places of prayer, in some circumstances similar to, in others different from, their synagogues; the latter were generally in cities, and were covered places; whereas for the most part the proseuchæ were out of the cities, on the banks of rivers, having no covering, except, perhaps, the shade of some trees, or covered galleries. Their vicinity to water was for the convenience of those frequent washings and ablutions which were introduced among them.—BURDER.

Ver. 22. And the multitude rose up together against them; and the magistrates rent off their clothes, and commanded to beat *them.*

It was usual for the Roman magistrates to command the lictors to rend open the clothes of the criminal, that he might the more easily be beaten with rods. No care was taken of the garments on these occasions: but they were suddenly and with violence rent open. Thus were Paul and Silas treated in this instance.—BURDER.

Ver. 24. Who, having received such a charge, thrust them into the inner prison, and made their feet fast in the stocks.

It is generally supposed that these stocks were the cippi, or large pieces of wood used among the Romans, which not only loaded the legs of prisoners, but sometimes distended them in a very painful manner; so that it is highly probable the situation of Paul and Silas here might be made more painful than that of an offender sitting in the stocks, as used among us, especially if (as is very possible) they lay with their bare backs, so lately scourged, on the hard or dirty ground; which renders their joyful frame, expressed by songs of praise, so much the more remarkable. Beza explains it of the numellæ, in which both the feet and the neck were fastened, in the most uneasy posture that can well be imagined.—PAXTON.

CHAPTER XVIII.

Ver. 3. And because he was of the same craft, he abode with them, and wrought: (for by their occupation they were tent-makers.)

It was a received custom among the Jews for every man, of what rank or quality soever, to learn some trade or handicraft; one of their proverbial expressions is, that whoever teaches not his son a trade, teaches him to be a thief. In those hot countries, where tents (which were commonly made of skins, or leather sewed together, to keep out the violence of the weather) were used not only by soldiers, but by travellers, and others whose business required them to be abroad, a tent-maker was no mean or unprofitable employment. This custom, so generally practised by the Jews, was adopted also by other nations in the East. Sir Paul Rycaut observes, that the grand seignior, to whom he was ambassador, was taught to make wooden spoons. The intention of this usage was not merely amusement, but to furnish the person so instructed with some method of obtaining their living, should they ever be reduced to want and poverty.—BURDER.

Ver. 6. And when they opposed themselves, and blasphemed, he shook *his* raiment, and said unto them, Your blood *be* upon your own heads: I *am* clean: from henceforth I will go unto the Gentiles.

"The shaking of his coat, a very common act in Turkey, is, no doubt, an act of the same kind and import as that of St. Paul, who, when the Jews opposed themselves and blasphemed, shook his raiment." (Morier.) "Our Tchochodar Ibrahim, at sight of this people, immediately grasped his carbine, and shaking the hem of his pelisse, made signs to us to be upon our guard." (Clarke.) This is a sign of caution universal among the Turks.—BURDER.

Ver. 19. And he came to Ephesus, and left them there: but he himself entered into the synagogue, and reasoned with the Jews.

Ephesus was a celebrated city on the western coast of Asia Minor, situated between Smyrna and Miletus, on the sides and at the foot of a range of mountains which overlooked a fine plain, watered and fertilized by the river Caÿster. Among other splendid edifices which adorned this metropolis of Ionia was the magnificent temple of Diana, which was two hundred and twenty years in building, and was reckoned one of the seven wonders of the world. This edifice having been burnt by the incendiary Herostratus, B. C. 356, in the foolish hope of immortalizing his name, it was afterward rebuilt with increased splendour at the common expense of the Grecian states of Asia Minor. The remains of ancient Ephesus have been discovered by learned modern travellers at the Turkish village of Ayasaluk. The ruins delineated in our engraving comprise all that is supposed now to exist of this far-famed structure, which in the time of St. Paul had lost nothing of its magnificence. Here was preserved a wooden statue of Diana, which the credulous Ephesians were taught to believe had fallen from heaven, (Acts xix. 35,) and of this temple small silver mod-

EPHESUS.—Acts 18:19. Page 620.

els were made, and sold to devotees. (Acts. xix. 24.) Nero is said to have plundered this temple of many votive images and great sums of gold and silver. This edifice appears to have remained entire in the second century; though the worship of Diana diminished and sunk into insignificance, in proportion to the extension of Christianity. At a later period "the temple of the great goddess Diana, whom Asia and all the world" worshipped, (Acts xix. 27,) was again destroyed by the Goths and other barbarians; and time has so completed the havoc made by the hand of man, that this mighty fabric has almost entirely disappeared.

During three years' residence in this city, (Acts xx. 31,) the great apostle of the Gentiles was enabled, with divine assistance, to establish the faith of Christ, and to found a flourishing Christian church. Of his great care of the Ephesian community strong proof is extant in the affecting charge which he gave to the elders, whom he had convened at Miletus on his return from Macedonia, (Acts xx. 16—38;) and still more in the epistle which he addressed to them from Rome. Ecclesiastical history represents Timothy to have been the first bishop of Ephesus, but there is greater evidence that the apostle John resided here towards the close of his life: here, also, he is supposed to have written his Gospel, and to have finally ended his life. Besides the ruins which are delineated in our engraving, widely scattered and noble remains attest the splendour of the theatre mentioned in Acts xix. 31, the elevated situation of which on Mount Prion accounts for the ease with which an immense multitude was collected, the loud shouts of whose voices, being reverberated from Mount Corrissus, would not a little augment the uproar caused by the populace rushing into the theatre.

The Ephesian church is the first of the "apocalyptic churches" addressed by the apostle John in the name of Jesus Christ. "His charge against her is declension in religious fervour, (Rev. ii. 4;) and his threat, in consequence, (ii. 5,) is a total extinction of her ecclesiastical brightness. After a protracted struggle with the sword of Rome and the sophisms of the Gnostics, Ephesus at last gave way. The incipient indifference, censured by the warning voice of the prophet, increased to a total forgetfulness; till at length the threatenings of the Apocalypse were fulfilled; and Ephesus sunk with the general overthrow of the Greek empire, in the fourteenth century." The plough has passed over this once celebrated city: and in March, 1826, when it was visited by the Rev. Messrs. Arundell and Hartley, green corn was growing in all directions amid the forsaken ruins: and one solitary individual only was found, who bore the name of Christ, instead of its once flourishing church. Where assembled thousands once exclaimed, "Great is Diana of the Ephesians!" the eagle now yells, and the jackal moans. The sea having retired from the scene of desolation, a pestilential morass, covered with mud and rushes, has succeeded to the waters, which brought up the ships laden with merchandise from every country. The surrounding country, however, is both fertile and healthy: and the adjacent hills would furnish many delightful situations for villages, if the difficulties were removed which are thrown in the way of the industrious cultivator by a despotic government, oppressive agas, and wandering banditti.—Horne.

CHAPTER XIX.

Ver. 11. And God wrought special miracles by the hands of Paul: 12. So that from his body were brought unto the sick handkerchiefs or aprons, and the diseases departed from them, and the evil spirits went out of them.

At a short distance, near the road-side, we saw the burial-place of a Persian saint, enclosed by very rude walls. Close to it grew a small bush, upon the branches of which were tied a variety of rags and remnants of garments. The Persians conceive that these rags, from their vicinity to the saint, acquire peculiar preservative virtues against sickness; and substituting others, they take bits away, and tying them about their persons, use them as talismans. May not this custom have some distant reference to Acts xix. 11, 12?—Morier.

Ver. 28. And when they heard *these sayings*, they were full of wrath, and cried out, saying, Great *is* Diana of the Ephesians.

The temple of Diana, at Ephesus, always has been admired as one of the noblest pieces of architecture that the world has ever produced. It was four hundred and twenty-five Roman feet long, two hundred and twenty broad, and supported by one hundred and twenty-seven columns of marble, sixty, or as some say, seventy feet high, twenty-seven of which were beautifully carved. This temple, which was at least two hundred years in building, was burnt by one Herostratus, with no other view than to perpetuate his memory: however, it was rebuilt, and the last temple was not inferior, either in riches or beauty, to the former; being adorned by the works of the most famous statuaries of Greece. This latter temple was, according to Trebellius, plundered and burnt by the Scythians, when they broke into Asia Minor, in the reign of Gallienus, about the middle of the third century. The cry of the Ephesian populace was a usual form of praise among the Gentiles, when they magnified their gods, for their beneficent and illustrious deeds. In Aristides, a similar passage occurs: "There was a great cry, both of those who were present, and of those who were coming, shouting in that well-known form of praise, Great is Æsculapius." (Sir R. K. Porter.)—Burder.

CHAPTER XX.

Ver. 7. And upon the first *day* of the week, when the disciples came together to break bread, Paul preached unto them, ready to depart on the morrow; and continued his speech until midnight.

Bishop Pearce, in his note on this passage, says, "In the Jewish way of speaking, *to break bread* is the same as to make a meal: and the meal here meant seems to have been one of those which was called *αγαπαι*, *love-feasts*. Such of the heathen as were converted to Christianity were obliged to abstain from meats offered to idols, and these were the main support of the poor in the heathen cities. The Christians therefore, who were rich, seem very early to have begun the custom of those αγαπαι, love-feasts, which they made on every first day of the week, chiefly for the benefit of the poorer Christians, who, by being such, had lost the benefit, which they used to have for their support, of eating part of the heathen sacrifices. It was towards the latter end of these feasts, or immediately after them, that the Christians used to take bread and wine in remembrance of Jesus Christ, which, from what attended it, was called the eucharist, or holy communion.—Burder.

Ver. 9. And there sat in a window a certain young man named Eutychus, being fallen into a deep sleep; and, as Paul was long preaching, he sunk down with sleep, and fell down from the third loft, and was taken up dead.

Chardin informs us, that the eastern windows are very large, and even with the floor. It is no wonder Eutychus might fall out if the lattice was not well fastened, or if it was decayed, when, sunk into a deep sleep, he leaned with all his weight against it.—Harmer.

Ver. 17. And from Miletus he sent to Ephesus, and called the elders of the church.

The present state of this city is thus given by Dr. Chandler: "Miletus is a very mean place, but still is called Palat, or Palatia, the palaces. The principal relic of its former magnificence is a ruined theatre, which is visible afar off, and was a most capacious edifice, measuring 457 feet long. The external face of this vast fabric is marble. On the side of the theatre next the river, is an inscription, in mean characters, rudely cut, in which the city Miletus is mentioned seven times. This is a monument of heretical Christianity. One Basilides, who lived in the second century, was the founder of an absurd sect, called Basilidians and Gnostics, the original proprietors of the many gems, with strange devices and inscriptions, intended to be worn as amulets or charms, with which the cabinet of the curious now abound. One of the idle tenets was, that the appellative Jehovah possessed signal virtue and efficacy. They expressed it by the seven Greek vowels, which they transposed into a variety of combinations. This superstition appears to have prevailed in no small degree at Miletus. In this remain the mysterious name is frequently repeated, and the deity six times invoked: Holy Jehovah, preserve the town of the Milesians, and all the inhabitants! The archangels, also, are summoned to be their guardians, and the whole city is made the author of these supplications; from which, thus engraved, it expected, as may be presumed, to derive lasting prosperity, and a kind of talismanical protection. The whole site of the town, to a great extent, is spread with rubbish, and overrun with thickets. The vestiges of the heathen city are pieces of wall, broken arches, and a few scattered pedestals and inscriptions, a square marble urn, and many wells. One of the pedestals has belonged to a statue of the Emperor Hadrian, who was a friend to the Milesians, as appears from the titles of saviour and benefactor given him. Another supported the statute of the Emperor Severus, and has a long inscription, with this curious preamble: 'The senate and people of the city of the Milesians, the first settled in Ionia, and the mother of many and great cities, both in Pontus and Egypt, and various other parts of the world.' From the number of forsaken mosques, it is evident that Mohammedanism has flourished in its turn at Miletus. The history of this place, after the declension of the Greek empire, is very imperfect. The whole region has undergone frequent ravages from the Turks, while possessed of the interior country, and intent on extending their conquests westward to the shore. One sultan, in 1175, sent twenty thousand men, with orders to lay waste the Roman provinces, and bring him sea-water, sand, and an oar. All the cities on the Meander, and on the coast, were then ruined; Miletus was again destroyed towards the end of the thirteenth century, by the conquering Othman."—BURDER.

CHAPTER XXI.

Ver. 11. And when he was come unto us, he took Paul's girdle, and bound his own hands and feet, and said, Thus saith the Holy Ghost, So shall the Jews at Jerusalem bind the man that owneth this girdle, and shall deliver *him* into the hands of the Gentiles.

This was significant of what was to occur to the apostle. Does a person wish to dissuade another from some project, he acts in such a way as to show what will be the nature of the difficulties or dangers. Thus, should he doubt his personal safety or fear disgrace, he puts off his sandals, to intimate he will die or be beaten with them. Or he takes off his turban, unfolds it, and ties it around his neck, or gropes as if in the dark, to intimate the difficulty.—ROBERTS.

Ver. 21. And they are informed of thee, that thou teachest all the Jews which are among the Gentiles to forsake Moses, saying, that they ought not to circumcise *their* children, neither to walk after the customs.

In every part of the world man is too often the slave of custom; but in all the old countries of the East, where innovations have not been made, the people are most tenaciously wedded to their customs. Ask, Why do you act thus? the reply is, "It is a *custom.*" Their implements of agriculture, their modes of sowing and reaping, their houses, their furniture, their domestic utensils, their vehicles, their vessels in which they put to sea, their modes of living, and their treatment of the various diseases, are all regulated by the *customs* of their fathers. Offer them better implements, and better plans for their proceedings, they reply, "We cannot leave our *customs:* your plans are good for yourselves, ours are good for ourselves: we cannot alter."—ROBERTS.

Ver. 40. And when he had given him license, Paul stood on the stairs, and beckoned with the hand unto the people. And when there was made a great silence, he spake unto *them* in the Hebrew tongue.

The object of Paul in beckoning with his hand was to obtain silence. See that man who has to address a crowd, and who wishes for silence, he does not begin to bawl out, Silence, that would be an affront to them; he lifts up his hand to its extreme height, and begins to beckon with it, *i. e.* to move it backward and forward; and then the people say to each other, "*pasâthe, pasâthe,*" i. e. be silent, be silent.—ROBERTS.

CHAPTER XXII.

Ver. 3. I am, verily, a man *which am* a Jew, born in Tarsus, *a city* in Cilicia, yet brought up in this city at the feet of Gamaliel, *and* taught according to the perfect manner of the law of the fathers, and was zealous towards God, as ye all are this day.

This form of expression is only used in reference to great saints or great teachers. "He had his holiness at the feet of the *gooroo*, or his learning at the feet of the philosopher."—ROBERTS.

With respect to the schools among the Jews it should be observed, that, besides the common schools in which children were taught to read the law, they had also academies, in which their doctors gave comments on the law, and taught the traditions to their pupils. Of this sort were the two famous schools of Hillel and Sammai, and the school of Gamaliel, who was St. Paul's tutor. In these seminaries the tutor's chair is said to have been so much raised above the level of the floor, on which the pupils sat, that his feet were even with their heads. Hence St. Paul says, that he was brought up at the feet of Gamaliel.—BURDER.

Ver. 22. And they gave him audience unto this word, and *then* lifted up their voices, and said, Away with such a *fellow* from the earth; for it is not fit that he should live. 23. And as they cried out, and cast off *their* clothes, and threw dust into the air, 24. The chief captain commanded him to be brought into the castle, and bade that he should be examined by scourging; that he might know wherefore they cried so against him.

A great similarity appears between the conduct of the Jews on this occasion, and the behaviour of the peasants in Persia, when they go to court to complain of the governors, whose oppressions they can no longer endure. "They carry their complaints against their governors by companies, consisting of several hundreds, and sometimes of a thousand; they repair to that gate of the palace nearest to which their prince is most likely to be, where they set themselves to make the most horrid cries, tearing their garments, and throwing dust into the air, at the same time demanding justice. The king, upon hearing these cries, sends to know the occasion of them: the people deliver their complaints in writing, upon which he lets them know that he will commit the cognizance of the affair to such a one as he names; in consequence of this, justice is usually obtained."—PAXTON.

Ver. 25. And as they bound him with thongs, Paul said unto the centurion that stood by, Is it lawful for you to scourge a man that is a Roman, and uncondemned?

Scourging was a very common punishment among the Jews. It was inflicted in two ways; with thongs or whips made of ropes or straps of leather; or with rods, twigs, or branches of some tree. The offender was stripped from his shoulders to his middle, and tied by his arms to a low pillar, that his back might be more fully exposed to the lash of the executioner, who stood behind him upon a stone, to have more power over him, and scourged him both on the back and breast, in open court, before the face of his judges. Among the Arabians, the prisoner is placed upright on the ground, with his hands and feet bound together, while the executioner stands before him, and with a short stick strikes him with a smart motion on the outside of his knees. The pain which these strokes produce is exquisitely severe, and which no constitution can support for any length of time. The Romans often inflicted the punishment of the scourge; the instruments employed were sticks or staves, rods, and whips or lashes. The first were almost peculiar to the camp; the last were reserved for slaves, while rods were applied to citizens, till they were removed by the Porcian law.—Paxton.

CHAPTER XXIII.

Ver. 2. And the high-priest Ananias commanded them that stood by him, to smite him on the mouth.

The Persians smote the criminals who attempted to speak in their own defence with a shoe, the heel of which was shod with iron; which is quite characteristic of the eastern manners, as described in the sacred volume. The shoe was also considered as vile, and never allowed to enter sacred or respected places; and to be smitten with it is to be subjected to the last ignominy. Paul was smitten on the mouth by the orders of Ananias: and the warmth with which the apostle resented the injury, shows his deep sense of the dishonour: "Then said Paul unto him, God shall smite thee, thou whited wall: for sittest thou to judge me after the law, and commandest me to be smitten contrary to law?"—Paxton.

"Call the Ferashes," exclaimed the king, "and beat these rogues till they die." The Ferashes came, and beat them violently; and when they attempted to say any thing in their own defence, they smote them on the mouth with a shoe, the heel of which was shod with iron. (Morier.) The shoe was always considered as vile, and never allowed to enter sacred or respected places; and to be smitten with it, is to be subjected to the last ignominy. "As soon as the ambassador came in, he punished the principal offenders by causing them to be beaten before him; and those who had spoken their minds a little too unreservedly, he smote upon the mouth with a shoe, which in their idiom they call kufsh khorden, eating shoe." "By far the greatest of all indignities, and the most insupportable, is to be hit with a shoe, or one of the pandoufles, which the Hindoos commonly wear on their feet. To receive a kick from any foot, with a slipper on it, is an injury of so unpardonable a nature, that a man would suffer exclusion from his caste who could submit to it without receiving some adequate satisfaction. Even to threaten one with the stroke of a slipper is held to be criminal, and to call for animadversion." (Dubois' Description of the People of India.)—Burder.

CHAPTER XXVII.

Ver. 40. And when they had taken up the anchors, they committed *themselves* unto the sea, and loosed the rudder-bands, and hoisted up the mainsail to the wind, and made towards shore.

Bishop Pococke, in his travels, has explained very particularly the *rudder-bands* mentioned by St. Luke, Acts xxvii. 40, and my plan excludes that account from these papers; but Sir John Chardin has mentioned some other things relating to this ship of St. Paul, which ought not to be omitted.

First, the eastern people, he tells us, "are wont to leave their skiffs in the sea, fastened to the stern of their vessels." The skiff of this Egyptian ship was towed along, it seems, after the same manner, v. 16, *We had much work to come by the boat.*

Secondly, They never, according to him, hoist it into the vessel, it always remains in the water, fastened to the ship. He therefore must suppose the *taking it up*, ην αραντες, mentioned ver. 17, does not mean hoisting it up into the vessel, as several interpreters have imagined, but drawing it up close to the stern of the ship; and the word χαλασαντων, which we translate, in the thirteenth verse, *letting down into the sea*, must mean letting it go farther from the ship into the sea.

Thirdly, He supposes this ship was like "a large modern Egyptian saique, of three hundred and twenty tons, and capable of carrying from twenty-four to thirty guns."

Fourthly, These saiques, he tells us, "always carry their anchors at the stern, and never their prow," contrarily to our managements; the anchors of St. Paul's ship were, in like manner, *cast out of the stern*, ver. 29.

Fifthly, They carry their anchors at some distance from the ship, "by means of the skiff, in such a manner as always to have one anchor on one side, and the other on the other side, so that the vessel may be between them, lest the cables should be entangled with each other." To St. Paul's ship there were four anchors, two on each side.

All these several particulars are contained, though not distinctly proposed, in his remarks on the vessel in which St. Paul was shipwrecked: the curious will probably consider them. If the mode of navigating eastern ships had been attended to, it is possible the jocular and lively remarks of some indevout sailors, bordering on profaneness, would never have been made upon this part of the narration of St. Luke; and some clauses would have been differently translated from what we find them in our version.—Harmer.

CHAPTER XXVIII.

Ver. 3. And when Paul had gathered a bundle of sticks, and laid *them* on the fire, there came a viper out of the heat, and fastened on his hand. 4. And when the barbarians saw the *venomous* beast hang on his hand, they said among themselves, No doubt this man is a murderer, whom, though he hath escaped the sea, yet vengeance suffereth not to live. 5. And he shook off the beast into the fire, and felt no harm. 6. Howbeit, they looked when he should have swollen, or fallen down dead suddenly: but after they had looked a great while, and saw no harm come to him, they changed their minds, and said that he was a god.

The certain and speedy destruction which follows the bite of this creature, clearly proves the seasonable interposition of Almighty power for the preservation of the apostle Paul. Exasperated by the heat of the fire, the deadly reptile, leaping from the bushwood where it had concealed itself, fixed the canine teeth, which convey the poison into the wound which they had made, in his hand. Death must have been the consequence, had not the power of his God, which long before shut the lions' mouths, that they might not hurt the prophet, neutralized the viper's deadly poison, and miraculously preserved the valuable life of his servant. The supernatural agency of God is clearly taught in these words of the historian: "He shook off the beast into the fire, and felt no harm;" for he who had been wounded by a viper, could not be said to have been exempt from all harm. The disposition of the enraged reptile to take its full revenge, is intimated by the word καθαπτειν, to fasten and twine itself about the hand of Paul. Some interpreters render the term to seize upon, others to hang from the hand, and others to bite; but according to Bochart, it properly signifies to bind or intwine, a sense which seems entitled to the preference; for, when a serpent fastens on its prey, it endeavours uniformly to strangle the victim by winding round its body. The viper on this memorable occasion exhibited every symptom of rage, and put forth all its powers; the deliverance of Paul, therefore, was not accidental, nor the effect of his own exertion, but of the mighty power of that Master whom he served, whose voice even the deadly viper is compelled to obey. This conclusion was in effect drawn by the barbarians themselves; for when "they had looked a great while, and saw no harm come to him, they changed their minds, and said that he was a god:" they did not hesitate to attribute his preservation to divine power; they only mistook his real character, not the true nature of that agency which was able to render the bite of the viper harmless.

This was to them a singular and most unexpected occurrence, for they looked when he should have swollen and fallen down dead suddenly. We are informed by natural historians, that under the action of this dreadful poison, the whole body swells to an extraordinary size, and in about seven hours death relieves the hopeless and agonized sufferer from his torments. These barbarians, it would seem, had been taught by their own experience, or the testimony of others, that the poison of this creature proves fatal in a much shorter time, for they waited some time in the confident expectation of seeing Paul suddenly expire. They knew, perhaps, what has been fully ascertained, that the bite of this animal is more pernicious, according to the place of its abode, the aliment on which it feeds, its age, the heat of the season when the wound is inflicted, and the degree of provocation it has received. On this occasion, it must have been exceedingly provoked; and the high state of excitement in which the Melitese saw it fastened upon the hand of the stranger, was, perhaps, the true and the only reason which induced them to believe the poison would produce a sudden effect.—PAXTON.

ROMANS.

CHAPTER III.

Ver. 13. Their throat *is* an open sepulchre; with their tongues they have used deceit; the poison of asps *is* under their lips.

Of a deceitful man, of one who speaks in smooth language, it is said, "Ah! at the tip of his tongue is ambrosia, but under it is poison."—ROBERTS.

CHAPTER VII.

Ver. 24. O wretched man that I am! who shall deliver me from the body of this death?

"Wretched man that I am!" "Do I often cry out, in such a circumstance, with no better supports and incitements than the law can give, 'Who shall rescue me, miserable captive as I am, from the body of this death?' from this continual burden which I carry about with me; and which is cumbersome and odious as a DEAD CARCASS tied to a living body, to be dragged along with it wherever it goes?" Thus are the words paraphrased by Dr. Doddrige, to which he subjoins this note: "It is well known that some ancient writers mention this as a cruelty practised by some tyrants on miserable captives who fell into their hands; and a more forcible and expressive image of the case represented cannot surely enter into the mind of man." That such a cruelty was once practised is certain from Virgil:

"Quid memorem infandas cædes? quid facta tyranni!" &c.

"Why should I mention his unutterable barbarities? Or, why the tyrant's horrid deeds? May the gods recompense them on his own head and on his race. Nay, he even bound to the living the bodies of the dead, joining together hands to hands, and face to face, a horrid kind of torture: and them, pining away with gore and putrefaction in this loathed embrace, he thus destroyed with lingering death." —BURDER.

CHAPTER XI.

Ver. 24. For if thou wert cut out of the olive-tree which is wild by nature, and wert grafted contrary to nature into a good olive-tree; how much more shall these, which be the natural *branches*, be grafted into their own olive-tree.

This practice is so far contrary to nature, that it is not usual for a branch of a wild olive-tree to be grafted in a good olive-tree, though a branch of the good is frequently grafted into the wild. Pliny says this latter was frequently practised in Africa. And Kolben tells us, that "long ago, some garden olive slips were carried to the Cape from Holland, and grafted on the stocks of the wild olives at Constantia, a seat so called in the Capian colony." Theophrastus takes notice of both the abovementioned modes of graftiny olives.—BURDER.

CHAPTER XII.

Ver. 13. Distributing to the necessity of saints; given to hospitality.

Hospitality has always been highly esteemed by civilized nations. It has been exercised from the earliest ages of the world. The Old Testament affords numerous instances of its being practised in the most free and liberal manner. In the New Testament it is also recommended and enforced. The primitive Christians were so ready in the discharge of this duty, that even the heathens admired them for it. Hospitable as they were to all strangers, they were particularly so to those who were of their own faith and communion. In Homer and the ancient Greek writers, we see what respect they had for their guests. From these instances we turn with satisfaction to view the kind and friendly disposition of less polished people. Modern travellers often mention the pleasing reception they met with from those among whom they made a temporary residence. Volney, speaking of the Druzes, says, "whoever presents himself at their door in the quality of a suppliant or passenger, is sure of being entertained with lodging and food in the most generous and unaffected manner. I have often seen the lowest peasants give the last morsel of bread they had in their houses to the hungry traveller. When they have once contracted with their guest the sacred engagement of bread and salt, no subsequent event can make them violate it." "An engagement with a stranger is sometimes accepted as an excuse for not obeying the summons of a great man, when no other apology, hardly even that of indisposition, would be admitted." (Russel.)

The Hindoos extend their hospitality sometimes to enemies, saying, "the tree does not withdraw its shade even from the wood-cutter."—BURDER.

CHAPTER XIII.

Ver. 4. For he is the minister of God to thee for good. But if thou do that which is evil, be afraid; for he beareth not the sword in vain: for he is the minister of God, a revenger to *execute* wrath upon him that doeth evil.

This is spoken agreeably to the notions and customs of the Romans at the time when the apostle wrote. Thus Suetonius says, (in Vitell. cap. 15,) that Vitellius gave up his dagger, which he had taken from his side, to the attending consul, thus surrendering the authority of life and death over the citizens. So the kings of Great Britain are not only at their inauguration solemnly girt with the sword of state, but this is afterward carried before them on public occasions, as a sword is likewise before some inferior magistrates among us.—BURDER.

Ver. 14. But put ye on the Lord Jesus Christ,

and make not provision for the flesh, to *fulfil* the lusts *thereof*.

"To be clothed with a person" is a Greek phrase, signifying to assume the interests of another, to enter into his views, to imitate him, to be wholly on his side. Chrysostom particularly mentions this as a common expression, O δεινα τον δεινα ενεδυσατο, *Such a one hath put on such a one.* So Dionysius Halicarnassus, speaking of Appius and the rest of the decemviri, says, ουκετι μετριαζοντες αλλα τον Ταρκυνιον ικεινον ενδυομενοι—*They were no longer the servants of Tarquin, but they clothed themselves with him.* Eusebius, in his Life of Constantine, says of his sons, they put on their father. The mode of speech is taken from stage-players, who assume the name and garments of the person whose character they represent.—BURDER.

CHAPTER XIV.

Ver. 2. For one believeth that he may eat all things; another, who is weak, eateth herbs.

Thousands of Hindoos never (to their knowledge) taste of any thing which has had animal life; and to eat an egg would be as repugnant to their feelings as to eat flesh, because it contains the germ of life. They live on herbs, roots, fruit, grain, milk, butter, and honey. They appear to be as strong and as healthy as those who live on flesh, and they avoid the "sin" of taking life. They believe that all who take life for the purpose of food will assuredly go to one of the seven hells. It has a distressing effect on their minds to show them, through a microscope, the animalcules which exist in the water they drink: for they are convinced by this they must often destroy life.—ROBERTS.

CHAPTER XVI.

Ver. 16. Salute one another with a holy kiss. The churches of Christ salute you.

Saluting one another on the face, in token of respect and friendship, was an ancient and common custom among both Jews and Gentiles; and was continued for some time among the primitive Christians in their religious assemblies, and particularly at the end of their prayers, before the celebration of the Lord's Supper, to testify their mutual love. It was therefore called the holy kiss, to distinguish it from that which was merely of the civil kind. By this symbol they showed that Christians, as such, were equal; because among the Persians and other eastern nations, equals kissed each other on the cheek, but inferiors kissed only the hand of a superior.—BURDER.

THE FIRST EPISTLE OF PAUL, THE APOSTLE, TO THE CORINTHIANS.

CHAPTER I.

Ver. 28. And base things of the world, and things which are despised, hath God chosen, *yea*, and things which are not, to bring to naught things that are.

"All things which are not." The venerable Mr. Wesley says, "The Jews frequently called the Gentiles '*them that are not*,' in such supreme contempt did they hold them." When a man of rank among the Hindoos speaks of low-caste persons, of notorious profligates, or of those whom he despises, he calls them *allā-tha-varkul*, i. e. *those who are not.* The term does not refer to life or existence, but to a quality or disposition, and is applied to those who are vile and abominable in all things. "My son, my son, go not among them *who are not.*" "Alas! alas! those people are all *allā-thā-varkul.*" When wicked men prosper, it is said, "This is the time for those *who are not.*" "Have you heard that those *who are not* are now acting righteously?" Vulgar and indecent expressions are also called "words that are not." To address men in the phrase "*are not*," is provoking beyond measure; their eyes will soon brighten, and their tongue and hands begin to move at the individual who thus insults them. The Lord did select the "base things of the world, and things which are despised hath God chosen, yea, and *things which are not*, to bring to naught hings that are."—ROBERTS.

CHAPTER IV.

Ver. 9. For I think that God hath set forth us the apostles last, as it were appointed to death: for we are made a spectacle unto the world, and to angels, and to men.

In the word εσχατους, *last*, which the apostle here uses, there is a reference to the Roman custom of bringing forth those persons on the theatre in the after part of the day, to fight either with each other, or with wild beasts, who were appointed to certain death, and had not that poor chance of escaping which those brought forth in the morning had. Such kind of spectacles were so common in all the provinces, that it is no wonder we should find such an allusion here. The words απεδειξεν, *exhibited*, and Θεατρον, *a spectacle on the theatre*, have in this connexion a beautiful propriety. The whole passage is indeed full of high eloquence, and finely adapted to move their compassion in favour of those who were so generously expiring, and sacrificing themselves for the public good.—DODDRIDGE.

CHAPTER V.

Ver. 6. Your glorying *is* not good. Know ye not, that a little leaven leaveneth the whole lump?

This is said of the man who corrupts others; also of a bad servant; "the more sour the leaven, the better the bread." When a mother has to administer nauseous medicine, she says, "My child, take it; do you not know the more sour the leaven, the better the bread?" Meaning, because the potion or powder is offensive, it will produce better effects.—ROBERTS.

CHAPTER IX.

Ver. 7. Who goeth a warfare at any time at his own charges? who planteth a vineyard, and eateth not of the fruit thereof? or who feedeth a flock, and eateth not of the milk of the flock?

The wages of the shepherds in the East do not consist of ready money, but in a part of the milk of the flocks which they tend. Thus Spon says of the shepherds in modern Greece, "These shepherds are poor Albanians, who feed the cattle, and live in huts built of rushes; they have a tenth part of the milk, and of the lambs, which is their whole wages: the cattle belong to the Turks." The shepherds in Ethiopia, also, according to Alvares, have no pay except the milk and butter which they obtain from the cows, and on which they and their families subsist.—Rosenmuller.

Ver. 24. Know ye not, that they which run in a race, run all, but one receiveth the prize? So run, that ye may obtain.

Games and combats were instituted by the ancients in honour of their gods; and were celebrated with that view by the most polished and enlightened nations of antiquity. The most renowned heroes, legislators, and statesmen, did not think it unbecoming their character and dignity to mingle with the combatants, or contend in the race; they even reckoned it glorious to share in the exercises, and meritorious to carry away the prize. The victors were crowned with a wreath of laurel in presence of their country; they were celebrated in the rapturous effusions of their poets; they were admired, and almost adored by the innumerable multitudes which flocked to the games from every part of Greece, and many of the adjacent countries. They returned to their own homes in a triumphal chariot, and made their entrance into their native city, not through the gates which admitted the vulgar throng, but through a breach in the walls, which were broken down to give them admission; and at the same time to express the persuasion of their fellow-citizens, that walls are of small use to a city defended by men of such tried courage and ability. Hence the surprising ardour which animated all the states of Greece to imitate the ancient heroes, and encircle their brows with wreaths, which rendered them still more the objects of admiration or envy to succeeding times, than the victories they had gained, or the laws they had enacted. But the institutors of those games and combats had higher and nobler objects in view than veneration for the mighty dead, or the gratification of ambition or vanity; it was their design to prepare the youth for the profession of arms; to confirm their health; to improve their strength, their vigour, and activity; to inure them to fatigue; and to render them intrepid in close fight, where, in the infancy of the art of war, muscular force commonly decided the victory.

This statement accounts for the striking allusions which the apostle Paul makes in his epistles to these celebrated exercises. Such references were calculated to touch the heart of a Greek, and of every one familiarly acquainted with them, in the liveliest manner, as well as to place before the eye of his mind the most glowing and correct images of spiritual and divine things. No passages in the nervous and eloquent epistles from the pen of Paul, have been more admired by critics and expositors, even in modern times, than those into which some allusion to these agonistic exercises is introduced; and, perhaps, none are calculated to leave a deeper impression on the Christian's mind, or excite a stronger and more salutary influence on his actions.—Paxton.

Ver. 25. And every man that striveth for the mastery is temperate in all things. Now they *do it* to obtain a corruptible crown; but we an incorruptible.

The honours and rewards granted to the victors were of several kinds. They were animated in their course by the rapturous applauses of the countless multitudes that lined the stadium, and waited the issue of the contest with eager anxiety; and their success was instantly followed by reiterated and long-continued plaudits; but these were only a prelude to the appointed rewards, which, though of little value in themselves, were accounted the highest honour to which a mortal could aspire. These consisted of different wreaths of wild olive, pine, parsley, or laurel, according to the different places where the games were celebrated. After the judges had passed sentence, a public herald proclaimed the name of the victor; one of the judges put the crown upon his head, and a branch of palm into his right hand, which he carried as a token of victorious courage and perseverance. As he might be victor more than once in the same games, and sometimes on the same day, he might also receive several crowns and palms. When the victor had received his reward, a herald, preceded by a trumpet, conducted him through the stadium, and proclaimed aloud his name and country; while the delighted multitudes, at the sight of him, redoubled their acclamations and applauses.

The crown, in the Olympic games, was of wild olive; in the Pythian, of laurel; in the Isthmian or Corinthian, of pine-tree; and in the Nemæan, of smallage or parsley. Now, most of these were evergreens; yet they would soon grow dry, and crumble into dust. Elsnor produces many passages, in which the contenders in these exercises are rallied by the Grecian wits, on account of the extraordinary pains they took for such trifling rewards; and Plato has a celebrated passage, which greatly resembles that of the apostle, but by no means equals it in force and beauty: "Now they do it to obtain a corruptible crown, but we an incorruptible." The Christian is called to fight the good fight of faith, and to lay hold of eternal life; and to this he is more powerfully stimulated by considering that the ancient athletæ took all their care and pains only for the sake of obtaining a garland of flowers, or a wreath of laurel, which quickly fades and perishes, possesses little intrinsic value, and only serves to nourish their pride and vanity, without imparting any solid advantage to themselves or others; but that which is placed in the view of the spiritual combatants, to animate their exertions, and reward their labours, is no less than a crown of glory which never decays: "a crown of infinite worth and duration; an inheritance incorruptible, undefiled, and that fadeth not away, reserved in heaven for them." More than conquerors through him that loved them, and washed from their sins in his own blood; they, too, carry palms in their right hands, the appropriate emblems of victory, hardly contested, and fairly won. "After this I beheld, and, lo, a great multitude, which no man could number, of all nations and kindreds, and people, and tongues, stood before the throne, and before the Lamb, clothed in white robes, and palms in their hands." But the victory sometimes remained doubtful, in consequence of which a number of competitors appeared before the judges, and claimed the prize; and sometimes a combatant, by dishonourable management, endeavoured to gain the victory. The candidates, who were rejected on such occasions by the judge of the games, as not having fairly merited the prize, were called by the Greeks αδοκιμοι, or disapproved, and which we render *cast away*, in a passage already quoted from Paul's first epistle to the Corinthians: "But I keep under my body, and bring it into subjection, lest that by any means, when I have preached to others, I myself should be (αδοκιμος) a cast-away," rejected by the Judge of all the earth, and disappointed of my expected crown.—Paxton.

Ver. 26. I therefore so run, not as uncertainly; so fight I, not as one that beateth the air.

In order to attain the greater agility and dexterity, it was usual for those who intended to box in the games, to exercise their arms with the gauntlet on, when they had no antagonist near them, and this was called σκιομαχια, in which a man would of course beat the air. In the foot-race, the runners, of whatever number they were, ranged themselves in a line, after having drawn lots for their places. While they waited the signal to start, they practised, by way of prelude, various motions to awaken their activity, and to keep their limbs pliable, and in a right temper. They kept themselves breathing by small leaps, and making little excursions, which were a kind of trial of their speed and agility; in such exercises, they might be said with great propriety to *run uncertainly*, towards no particular point, and with no direct or immediate view to the prize. Both these allusions occur in the declaration of the apostle: "I therefore so run, not as uncertainly; so fight I, not as one that beateth the air." He did not engage in his Christian course as one doubtful in himself whether, in pursuing the path of duty, he should have the honour of being crowned at last or not; as they are, who know that one only receives the prize; nor did he exercise himself unto godliness, like boxers or wrestlers, who sometimes fight in jest, or merely to prepare for the combat, or to display their strength and agility, while they had no resistance to encounter, no enemy to subdue, no reward to merit; but he pressed on, fully persuaded that, by the grace of God, he should obtain an incorruptible crown from the hands of his Redeemer.—PAXTON.

Ver. 27. But I keep under my body, and bring *it* into subjection: lest that by any means, when I have preached to others, I myself should be a cast-away.

See on ver. 25.

Like the Grecian combatants, the Christian must be wellborn—born, "not of corruptible seed, but of incorruptible, by the word of the Lord, which liveth and abideth for ever;" he must be free—"a citizen with the saints, and of the household of faith;" he must "abstain from fleshly lusts," and "walk in all the statutes and commandments of the Lord, blameless." Such was Paul; and in this manner he endeavoured to act: "But I keep under my body, and bring it into subjection: lest that by any means, when I have preached to others, I myself should be a cast-away." The latter part of this verse Doddridge renders, "Lest after having served as a herald, I should be disapproved;" and says in a note, "I thought it of importance to retain the primitive sense of these gymnastic expressions." It is well known to those who are at all acquainted with the original, that the word *κηρύξας*, means to discharge the office of a herald, whose business it was to proclaim the conditions of the games, and display the prizes, to awaken the emulation and resolution of those who were to contend in them. But the apostle intimates, that there was this peculiar circumstance attending the Christian contest—that the person who proclaimed its laws and rewards to others, was also to engage himself; and that there would be a peculiar infamy and misery in his miscarrying. *Αδοκιμος*, which we render *cast-away*, signifies one who is disapproved by the judge of the games, as not having fairly deserved the prize.—PAXTON.

CHAPTER X.

Ver. 25. Whatsoever is sold in the shambles, *that* eat, asking no questions for conscience' sake: 28. But if any man say unto you, This is offered in sacrifice unto idols, eat not for his sake that showed it, and for conscience' sake: for the earth *is* the Lord's, and the fulness thereof.

These verses refer to articles of food which had been presented to the idols, and were afterward sent to the shambles to be sold. The heathen make large presents to the temples of grain, fruit, milk, and other eatables, and therefore the priests send what they do not require to the market to be sold. The fruit called plantain (banana) may be known as having been offered to idols by having a small piece pinched off one end; and the other articles have generally some sign by which they may be known. It is however impossible at all times to ascertain the fact, and I doubt not that most Englishmen have at one time or another eaten things which have been offered to idols.

The apostle is very particular in his directions to the Christian converts, (v. 27:) "If any of them that believe not bid you to a feast, and ye be disposed to go, whatsoever is set before you, eat, asking no questions for conscience' sake." We see the converts were not forbidden to go to a feast, *i. e.* a family, *not a religious* festival; but the phrase, "If ye be disposed to go," shows there were doubts and hesitations as to whether they ought to go. The moment they found the food had been offered to idols they were to "*eat not.*"—ROBERTS.

CHAPTER XI.

Ver. 5. But every woman that prayeth or prophesieth with *her* head uncovered, dishonoureth her head: for that is even all one as if she were shaven.

It is still customary to this day in the East, when you accidentally meet a woman in her house, that she instantly covers herself up, and even runs away, and will not appear before a man; nay, even if a person lives among them as a physician, and eventually has free access to their rooms, he has yet great trouble to get a sight of their faces, unless they have a defect there; nay, he can scarcely ask it of them, though in diseases much may be perceived and judged of by the countenance. Now, as in these countries modesty requires that women should cover themselves, even when at home, before all men, and particularly before young people, it would have been extremely improper, if, when speaking publicly in the congregation, they had exposed themselves to everybody's view.—ROSENMÜLLER.

Ver. 10. For this cause ought the woman to have power on *her* head, because of the angels.

The head-dress of the women is simple: their hair is drawn behind the head, and divided into several tresses: the beauty of this head-dress consists in the thickness, and in the length of these tresses, which should fall even down to the heels, in default of which they lengthen them with tresses of silk. The ends of these tresses they decorate with pearls, and jewels, or ornaments of gold, or silver. The head is covered *under* the veil, or kerchief, (*couvre chef,*) only by the end of a small *bandeau*, shaped into a triangle. this *bandeau*, which is of various colours, is thin and light. The *bandelette* is embroidered by the needle, or covered with jewellery, according to the quality of the wearer. This is, in my opinion, the ancient *tiara*, or *diadem*, of the queens of Persia; only married women wear it; and it is the mark by which it is known that they are under subjection, (*c'est là la marque à laquelle on reconnoit qu'elles sont sous* PUISSANCE—*power.*) The girls have little *caps*, instead of this kerchief, or tiara; they wear no veil at home, but let two tresses of their hair fall under their cheeks. The caps of girls of superior rank are tied with a row of pearls. Girls are not shut up in Persia till they attain the age of six or seven years; before that age they go out of the seraglio, sometimes with their father, so that they may then be seen. I have seen some wonderfully pretty. They show the neck and bosom; and more beautiful cannot be seen.—CHARDIN.

The wearing of a veil by a married woman was a token of her being under power. The Hebrew name of the veil signifies dependence; great importance was attached to this part of dress in the East. "All the women of Persia are pleasantly apparelled; when they are abroad in the streets, all, both rich and poor, are covered with a great veil, or sheet of very fine white cloth, of which one half, like a forehead cloth, comes down to the eyes, and, going over the head, reaches down to the heels, and the other half muffles up the face below the eyes, and being fastened with a pin to the left side of the head, falls down to their very shoes, even covering their hands, with which they hold that cloth by the two sides, so that, except the eyes, they are covered all over with it. Within doors they have their faces and breasts uncovered; but the Armenian women, in their houses, have always one half of their faces covered with a cloth, that goes athwart their noses, and hangs over their chins and breasts, except the maids of that nation, who, within doors, cover only the chin, until they are married."—THEVENOT.

Ver. 14. Doth not even nature itself teach you, that if a man have long hair it is a shame unto him?

See on 1 Pet. 3. 3.

Ver. 15. But if a woman have long hair, it is a glory to her: for *her* hair is given her for a covering.

The eastern ladies are remarkable for the length, and the great number of the tresses of their hair. The men there, on the contrary, wear very little hair on their heads. Lady M. W. Montague thus speaks concerning the hair of the women: "Their hair hangs at full length behind, divided into tresses, braided with pearl or riband, which is always in great quantity. I never saw in my life so many fine heads of hair. In one lady's I have counted one hundred and ten of these tresses, all natural; but it must be owned that every kind of beauty is more common here than with us." The men there, on the contrary, shave all the hair off their heads, excepting one lock; and those that wear hair are thought effeminate. Both these particulars are mentioned by Chardin, who says, they are agreeable to the custom of the East: the men are shaved, the women nourish their hair with great fondness, which they lengthen, by tresses and tufts of silk, down to the heels. The young men who wear their hair in the East, are looked upon as effeminate and infamous.—HARMER.

CHAPTER XIV.

Ver. 7. And even things without life giving sound, whether pipe or harp, except they give a distinction in the sounds, how shall it be known what is piped or harped? 8. For if the trumpet give an uncertain sound, who shall prepare himself to the battle?

The words of St. Paul, in 1 Cor. xiv. 7, will appear with the greatest energy, if we consider them as signifying, that for want of a due distinction of sounds, those by whom a procession according to the usages of the East should pass, might be at a loss to know whether they should join them with expressions of gratulation, or in words of lamentation. Irwin has given an instance of such a joining in the latter case, where, speaking of the singing in a funeral procession, that went by his house, he says, "There was an Arabian merchant on a visit to us, when the funeral went by; and though in company with strangers, he was not ashamed to run to the window, and to join audibly in the devotions of the train." If a pipe was designed to regulate the expressions that were to be made use of, if it gives an uncertain sound, and sometimes seemed to announce a triumph or a wedding, and sometimes a procession on account of the dead, how should a bystander know how to behave himself? "Even things without life give sound, whether pipe or harp; except they give a distinction in the sounds, how shall a man know what is piped or harped?" How shall a man know what the music is designed to produce, congratulation, or condolence? This is a much stronger sense than the supposing, if the sounds were irregular, the apostle meant it was impossible to tell what dance was intended. In truth, such an explanation would not well agree with the extemporaneousness of eastern dances, for the hearer of the music might in that case know what was to be done, and all that would follow from it would be, that if the music was irregular, so would the dance be.—HARMER.

CHAPTER XV.

Ver. 24. Then *cometh* the end, when he shall have delivered up the kingdom to God, even the Father; when he shall have put down all rule, and all authority, and power.

If the opinion of the eminent critic, Storr, may be admitted, that the kingdom here said to be delivered up to the Father is *not* the kingdom of Christ, but the rule and dominion of all adverse powers—an opinion rendered very probable by the following words: "when he shall have *put down* (Gr. done away, abolished) all rule and all authority and power," and ver. 25, "till he hath put all *enemies* under his feet"—then is the passage of identical import with Rev. xi. 15, referring to precisely the same period: "And the seventh angel sounded; and there were great voices in heaven, saying, The kingdoms of the world are become the kingdoms of our Lord and of his Christ; and he shall reign for ever and ever." It is, therefore, we conceive, but a peculiar mode of denoting the *transfer, the making over* of the kingdoms of this world from their former despotic and antichristian rulers to the sovereignty of Jesus Christ, the appointed heir and head of all things, whose kingdom is to be everlasting. If this interpretation be correct, we are prepared to advance a step farther, and suggest that the phrase, *he shall have delivered up*, (Greek, *parado*,) be understood as an instance of the idiom in which the verb is used without any personal nominative, but has reference to the *purpose of God as expressed in the scriptures;* so that the passage may be read, "Then cometh the end, (i. e. not the close, the final winding up, but the perfect development, expansion, completion, consummation of the divine plans, in regard to this world,) when the prophetic announcements of the scriptures require the delivering up (i. e. the making over) of all adverse dominion into the hands of the Messiah, to whose supremacy we are taught to expect that every thing will finally be made subject."—BUSH.

Ver. 32. If after the manner of men I have fought with beasts at Ephesus, what advantageth it me, if the dead rise not? let us eat and drink; for to-morrow we die.

The barbarous custom of making men combat with wild beasts has prevailed in the East down to the most modern times. Jurgen Andersen, who visited the states of the great mogul in 1646, gives an account in his Travels, of such a combat with animals, which he witnessed at Agra, the residence of the great mogul. His description affords a lively image of those bloody spectacles in which ancient Rome took so much pleasure, and to which the above words of the apostle refer. Alamardan-Chan, the governor of Cashmire, who sat among the chans, stood up, and exclaimed, "It is the will and desire of the great mogul, Schah Choram, that if there are any valiant heroes who will show their bravery by combating with wild beasts, armed with shield and sword, let them come forward: if they conquer, the mogul will load them with great favour, and clothe their countenance with gladness." Upon this three persons advanced, and offered to undertake the combat. Alamardan-Chan again cried aloud, "None should have any other weapon than a shield and a sword, and whosoever has a breastplate under his clothes, should lay it aside and fight honourably." Hereupon a powerful lion was let into the garden, and one of the three men abovementioned advanced against him; the lion, on seeing his enemy, ran violently up to him; the man however defended himself bravely, and kept off the lion for a good while, till his arms grew tired; the lion then seized the shield with one paw, and with the other his antagonist's right arm, so that he was not able to use his weapon; the latter, seeing his life in danger, took with his left hand his Indian dagger, which he had sticking in his girdle, and thrust it as far as possible into the lion's mouth; the lion then let him go; the man however was not idle, but cut the lion almost through with one stroke, and after that entirely to pieces. Upon this victory, the common people began to shout, and call out, "Thank God, he has conquered." But the mogul said, smiling, to this conqueror, "Thou art a brave warrior, and hast fought admirably! But did I not command to fight honourably only with shield and sword? But, like a thief, thou hast stolen the life of the lion with thy dagger." And immediately he ordered two men to rip up his belly, and to place him upon an elephant, and, as an example to others, to lead him about, which was done on the spot. Soon after a tiger was let loose; against which a tall, powerful man, advanced with an air of defiance, as if he would cut the tiger up. The tiger, however, was far too sagacious and active, for, in the first attack, he seized the combatant by the neck, tore his throat, and then his whole body in pieces. This enraged another good fellow, but little, and of mean appearance, from whom one would not have expected it: he rushed forward like one mad, and the tiger on his part undauntedly flew at his enemy; but the man at the first attack cut off his two forepaws, so that he fell, and the man cut his body to pieces. Upon this the king cried, "What is your name?" He answered, "My name is Geyby." Soon after one of the king's servants came and brought him a piece of gold brocade, and said, "Geyby, receive the robe of honour with which the mogul presents you." He took the garment with great reverence, kissed it three times, pressing it each time to his eyes and breast, then held it up, and in silence put up a prayer for the health of the mogul; and when he had concluded it, he cried, "May God let him become as great as Tamerlane, from whom he is descended. May he live seven hundred years, and his house continue to eternity!" Upon this he was summoned by a chamberlain to go from the garden up to the king, and when he came to the entrance, he was received by two chans, who conducted him between them to kiss the mogul's feet. And when he was going to retire, the king said to him, "Praised be thou, Geyby-Chan, for thy valiant deeds, and this name shalt thou keep to eternity. I am your gracious master, and thou art my slave."—ROSENMULLER.

CHAPTER XVI.

Ver. 9. For a great door and effectual is opened unto me, and *there are* many adversaries.

The chariot races were the most renowned of all the exercises used in the games of the ancients, and those from which the victors derived the greatest honour; but the writer can find only one or two allusions to them in the sacred volume, and those involved in some uncertainty. One occurs in Paul's first epistle to the Corinthians, where he informs them of his great success in collecting a church at Ephesus: "But I will tarry at Ephesus until pentecost; for a great door and effectual is opened unto me, and there are many adversaries." The inspired writer, it is thought, alludes here to the door of the circus, which was opened to let out the chariots when the races were to begin; and by the word αντικειμενοι, which is translated *adversaries*, but which Doddridge renders *opposers*, means the same with antagonists, with whom he was to contend as in a course. This opposition rendered his presence more necessary to preserve those that were already converted, and to increase the number, if God should bless his ministry. Accordingly a celebrated church was planted at Ephesus; and so far as we can learn from the tenor of his epistle, there was less to reprove and correct among them than in most of the other churches to which he wrote.—PAXTON.

Ver. 22. If any man love not the Lord Jesus Christ, let him be anathema, maran-atha.

The expression used by the apostle, "Let him be *anathema, maran-atha*," is so remarkable, that it has attracted general notice. It is usually understood to be a Syriac exclamation, signifying, "Let him be accursed, when the Lord comes." It certainly was not now, for the first time, used as a new kind of cursing by the apostle, but was the application of a current mode of speech, to the purpose he had in contemplation. Perhaps, therefore, by inspecting the manners of the East, we may illustrate the import of this singular passage: the nearest approach to it that I have been able to discover, is in the following extract from Mr. Bruce; and though, perhaps, this does not come up to the full power of the apostle's meaning, yet, probably, it gives the idea which was commonly attached to the phrase among the public. Mr. Bruce had been forced by a pretended saint, in Egypt, to take him on board his vessel, as if to carry him to a certain place—whereas Mr. B. meant no such thing; but, having set him on shore at some little distance from whence he came, "we slacked our vessel down the stream a few yards, filling our sails and stretching away. On seeing this, our saint fell into a desperate passion, cursing, blaspheming, and stamping with his feet; at every word crying 'SHAR ULLAH!' *i. e.* 'MAY GOD SEND, AND DO JUSTICE!' This appears to be the strongest execration this passionate Arab could use, *q. d.* 'To punish you adequately is out of my power: I remit you to the vengeance of God.' Is not this the import of *anathema, maran-atha?*"—TAYLOR IN CALMET.

THE SECOND EPISTLE OF PAUL, THE APOSTLE, TO THE CORINTHIANS.

CHAPTER III.

Ver. 11. For if that which is done away *was* glorious, much more that which remaineth *is* glorious.

This verse, as any who consults the original will see, is undoubtedly susceptible of a much improved rendering. An exact translation would not vary essentially from the following:—"For if that which was done away, (was done away) by glory; much more that which remaineth, (remaineth) in glory." That is, since that which was done away, was done away by means of a greater glory and splendour, then certainly that which remains must remain glorious. The reasoning of the apostle may be illustrated thus: If the light of the stars, which vanishes at the rising of the sun, was done away by the superior light and brightness of the sun; much more shall the light of the sun, having thus eclipsed that of the stars, remain glorious. So since the glory of the gospel has availed to abolish that of the law, the gospel is hereby evinced to be superlatively great, and that of the law will never be able to equal it.—BUSH.

CHAPTER IV.

Ver. 7. But we have this treasure in earthen vessels, that the excellency of the power may be of God, and not of us.

Cups of the most beautiful appearance, and ornamented in the most costly manner, are formed out of the nautilus. Such drinking-vessels are frequent in China. Perhaps to such beautiful vessels as these, containing the most costly liquor, the apostle alludes when he speaks of earthen vessels, literally vessels made of shell.—BURDER.

In a Cingalese pottery, I have seen hundreds of erathen vessels for hoarding money in. They are nearly round, and in size something less than the two fists. They have no opening but a small hole, like that in a till to slip in a coin; and are said to be mostly bought up by children, to hide the profit of their play in, and other such sums.—CALLAWAY.

CHAPTER VI.

Ver. 14. Be ye not unequally yoked together with unbelievers: for what fellowship hath righteousness with unrighteousness? and what communion hath light with darkness?

See on Deut. 22. 10.

CHAPTER X.

Ver. 14. For we stretch not ourselves beyond *our measure*, as though we reached not unto you; for we are come as far as to you also in *preaching* the gospel of Christ.

Within the measure and determinate limits of the stadium, the athletæ were bound to contend for the prize, which they forfeited without hope of recovery, if they deviated ever so little from the appointed course. In allusion to this inviolable arrangement, the apostle tells the Corinthians, "We will not boast of things without our measure, but according to the measure of the rule which God hath distributed to us, a measure to reach even unto you. For we stretch not ourselves beyond our measure, as though we reached not unto you; for we are come as far as unto you also, in preaching the gospel of Christ." It may help very much to understand this and the following verses, if, with Hammond, we consider the terms used in them as *agonistical*. In this view of them, the measure of the rule alludes to the path marked out, and bounded by a white line, for racers in the Isthmian games, celebrated among the Corinthians; and so the apostle represents his works in preaching the gospel as his spiritual race, and the province to which he was appointed as the compass or stage of ground, which God had distributed or measured out for him to run in. Accordingly, "to boast without his measure," and to stretch himself beyond his measure, refer to one that ran beyond or out of his line. "We are come as far as to you," alludes to him that came foremost to the goal; and "in another man's line," signifies in the province that was marked out for somebody else, in allusion to the line by which the race was bounded, each of the racers having the path which he ought to run chalked out to him, and if one stepped over into the other's path he extended himself over his line.—PAXTON.

CHAPTER XI.

Ver. 19. For ye suffer fools gladly, seeing ye *yourselves* are wise.

The Orientals pay a particular respect to lunatics. "The Arabs," says Poiret, "show a kind of reverence to lunatics according to the principles of their religion. They look upon them as saints, as beings endowed with peculiar privileges, and favoured by Heaven. I met such a man in the duar (villages of the Bedouin Arabs) of Ali Bey. He was quite naked, went into all the tents, and showed himself to the women, without the men being offended at it. It would be considered as a criminal action to send away such a man, or to treat him ill. He could eat where he pleased; nothing was denied him. Ali Bey himself bore his freedoms and importunities with a degree of indulgence that astonished me." Lempriere says, that in Morocco insane persons form a peculiar class of saints. The Moors believe that such men are under the especial protection of God. They consequently find everywhere compassion and support. To treat their excesses with rigour is thought to be as criminal as to lay hands on the person of the emperor. The consequence of this ill-judged humanity is, that worthless vagabonds feign lunacy, and commit the greatest crimes, no one venturing to hinder them. A lunatic of this description went about without restraint in Morocco, who, under the appearance of being immersed in his devotions, strangled with his rosary several persons who came too near him. Stephen Schultz relates a story of a Franciscan monk, who, being pursued by the populace in the streets of Alexandria, saved himself by feigning madness, dancing and playing strange antics, so that he not only escaped the shower of stones that threatened his life, but was treated with the greatest respect. Œdmann applies these observations to illustrate the words of the apostle in the above passage. Paul's adversaries in Corinth, endeavoured to lessen the reputation he enjoyed, by extolling their own merits. He therefore found it necessary to compare his merits with those which these people assumed. Such self-praise he declares to be folly: but as it was extorted from him, he requests them to judge favourably, or at least to grant him the indulgence which they afford to a man whose mental faculties were deranged. "You are accustomed," says he, "to treat mental weakness with indulgence, to give proof of your own understanding. You disregard it, when such an idiot in his madness treats you as slaves, consumes what is yours, or appropriates to himself what belongs to you; or is proud and fancies himself above you; nay, even if he strikes you in the face. This indulgence you will not refuse me, now that I have been compelled to be guilty of the weakness of speaking in my own praise."

The above account of the opinion entertained of lunatics by the Orientals, serves to illustrate what is said of David, I Sam. xxi. 10, when, to escape the pursuit of Saul, he fled to Achish, king of the Philistines, but was discovered; then he feigned himself mad, and thus saved his life.—ROSENMÜLLER.

CHAPTER XII

Ver. 2. I knew a man in Christ above fourteen years ago, (whether in the body, I cannot tell; or whether out of the body, I cannot tell: God knoweth;) such a one caught up to the third heaven.

Macknight says, "That the apostle speaks of himself here is evident from verses 6 and 7." This is the eastern way in which a man *modestly* speaks of himself. Has an individual performed a great exploit which he does not like to mention in plain terms as having been done by himself, he simply says, in relating the affair, "I know the man who did it." *Nān-arevain*, i. e. I know. Do people express their pleasure or surprise in the presence of a person at some work which has been accomplished by himself, and should they inquire, "who is the man," he will say, "I know him:" he will not say he is the man, because some would perhaps not be disposed to believe him; and the slight intimation conveyed in the terms, *I know him*, is quite sufficient to convince others he is the fortunate individual. Should a person receive a favour from an unknown hand, he will make many inquiries; and when he thinks he has found him out, he will go to him and talk on the subject, and then, should he be right, the individual will say, "I know him." But in this way also the people praise themselves, by saying, "I know a man who performed such a penance: I am acquainted with one who gave such gifts to the temples: I know one who performed an extraordinary fast, or went on such a dangerous pilgrimage."—ROBERTS.

Ver. 7. And lest I should be exalted above measure through the abundance of the revelations, there was given to me a thorn in the flesh, the messenger of Satan to buffet me, lest I should be exalted above measure.

The following communication from a Mr. Stephen, in a letter to Mrs. Hannah More, presents an interpretation of this passage, so highly ingenious and plausible, that it is well entitled to a place in the present work:—

"When are we to have our new or improved views of St. Paul? With such a subject, and such an artist, we may reasonably be impatient for the exhibition. Does it fall within the plan or general character of the work to notice the thorn in the flesh, the messenger of Satan, and to give any conjecture as to the infirmity alluded to? I have an interpretation of this, which, as far as my reading, or that of Wilberforce's and some others, goes, is original, and yet it is admitted by them to be as probable, or more so, than any other of the many conjectures they have seen. For my own part, I hold it almost demonstrably the true solution. St. Paul's infirmity was one well known in hot climates, a chronical ophthalmia. Hence he was what is called *blear-eyed*, and was often, perhaps, obliged to wear a shade. It made his personal presence mean, it was a visible infirmity in his flesh, it hindered his usefulness, and therefore he besought the Lord anxiously that it might depart from him: but was answered, 'My grace is sufficient for thee.' It made it for the most part painful and difficult for him to write. Hence he generally employed an amanuensis, and regarded it as a great matter when he used his own pen. 'You see how long a letter I have written to you with mine own hand.'—'The salutation of me, Paul, written with mine own hand.' It is thought that he might abstain from writing to save his strength or time; why then did he work at tent-making? A man who maintained himself by that sedentary labour, might as well have been at his desk, for we cannot suppose that the wages of a journeyman tent-maker were greater than those of an amanuensis. It exposed him to contempt and derision among strangers, and therefore he gives praise to the Galatians, that when he preached the gospel to them at the first through infirmity of the flesh, his temptation, which was in 'his flesh, they despised not.' That the infirmity was of a bodily kind seems to me quite indisputable. Doddridge, and a.. the best commentators, take that aside. It is literally so described; and the calling it a 'messenger of Satan' is perfectly consistent with its being a bodily disease. Satan, in fifty places, is represented as the immediate author of corporal defects and maladies. The passages cited show it was something visible to others. How could a temptation to a particular sin be so unless it was complied with? It would be derogatory to the character of the apostle, and even of an Antinomian tendency, to suppose this to have been the case. The Galatians *ought* to have despised him, if in preaching the gospel he had exhibited before them the strength of a temptation by the commission of open sin. They would have deserved no praise for not despising, but the reverse;—i. e. for not despising the temptation, if but for the visible sin, which was its evidence. In short, I am astonished how many pious and judicious commentators should think this 'thorn in the flesh' a thorn in the conscience.

"If it was bodily, it was also some bodily infirmity of an unsightly appearance, making his '*person*' or aspect '*mean*,' and exposing him to contempt. How shall we find a more probable hypothesis to suit those and the other preconceptions? He was not lame—witness his great bodily activity.

"Doddridge supposes that the view he had of celestial glories might have effected his nervous system, so as to occasion stammering in his speech, and some ridiculous distortion in his countenance. (Exposition, 2 Cor. xii. 7.) But it is at least equally probable that those heavenly visions, or the supernatural light which blinded him at his conversion, might have left a weakness and disease in the organs immediately affected. It is notorious, that after a severe inflammation in the eyes, they are extremely liable for a long time, or through life, to a return of the complaint. It may be even presumed from analogy, that unless the miracle which restored Paul to sight removed also a natural secondary effect of the temporary injury the organs had received, there must have been a predisposition afterward to the complaint which I suppose him to have had. Now that frugality in the use of means which has been observed even in the miraculous works of God, may be supposed to have permitted that predisposition to remain, it being designed that the apostle, for his humiliation and the exercise of his faith and patience, should have a permanent infirmity of the flesh to struggle with in future life.

"The choice of the metaphor by which St. Paul describes his infirmity, also weighs much with me; indeed it first excited my conjecture. The pain of ophthalmia, when severe, exactly resembles the prick of a thorn or pin. I once had it very severely indeed in the West Indies. It made me blind in a manner for about three weeks, and during that time, if a ray of light by any means broke into my darkened chamber, it was like a thorn or pin run into my eye, and so I often described it. I felt also the subsequent effect for years, which I suppose to have been experienced by St. Paul,—a predisposition to inflammation in the eyes, which extreme care and timely applications prevented from recurring.

"I see a further possible source of this idea in his mind, in the fact that thorns in *the eyes* are figuratively used in different parts of scripture to signify troubles and temptations, (see Numbers xxxiii. 55, and Joshua xxiii. 13.) Now if this metaphor had an affinity with the actual bodily sensations of the apostle, it was natural he should think of and use it; but as natural that he should vary it into the more general term *flesh*, that he might not confound the proper with the metaphorical sense, and be understood to mean that a thorn actually thrust into his eye had produced the disease.

"This may be thought perhaps too refined. But the strongest argument of all remains, and appears to me nearly, if not quite, decisive. It rests upon Galatians iv. 15. After praising them in the preceding verse for not despising his fleshly infirmity, (whatever that was,) he here subjoins, *I bear you record, that if it had been possible, ye would have plucked out your own eyes, and have given them to me.* How natural this context on my hypothesis! How little so on any other! Was it a moral infirmity, a temptation shown by its fruits? It might then have *pardon*, it might have charitable and respectful *indulgence*, in consideration of the great and good qualities which were seen in the same character; but it could not give rise to such glowing affection, such ardour of sympathetic kindness, as these words import. Again, was it a bodily infirmity affecting some other member than the eyes? how extremely unnatural this expression of the sympathy which it produced. Let us take, for instance, Doddridge's conjecture, 'You saw my paralytic distortions in my *mouth* and *cheeks*, you heard my stammering *tongue*, when I first preached the gospel to you; but you despised not those infirmities. On the contrary, you would, if it had been possible, have plucked out your own *eyes* and given them to me.' Suppose lameness, or some sharp internal disease, (as others have supposed, notwithstanding the visible character of the infirmity,) and the incongruity is not much, if at all, less. But if the apostle was speaking of his diseased eyes, which made his aspect unsightly, and prevented perhaps much of the natural effect of his preaching, to which they nevertheless respectfully listened, and with affectionate sympathy did all they could for his comfort and relief, how natural, how appropriate this grateful close of the encomium! Such was your generous and tender sympathy, that I verily believe if you could have removed those sufferings of mine, and that obstacle to my more perfect usefulness, by taking the infirmity in my stead, by plucking out your own sound eyes, and transferring them to my use, you would have been willing to do so.

"If parental fondness for a supposed discovery of my own does not deceive me, these reasons, when taken together, are nearly conclusive. The point to be sure, after all, is of no great importance; but if Mrs. H. More thinks it worth her while to notice the guesses on this subject at all, here is what I suppose to be a new one, for her consideration." (Memoirs of Mrs. Hannah More, vol. ii. p. 224.)—B

THE EPISTLE OF PAUL, THE APOSTLE, TO THE GALATIANS.

CHAPTER II.

Ver. 9. And when James, Cephas, and John, who seemed to be pillars, perceived the grace that was given unto me, they gave to me and Barnabas the right hands of fellowship; that we *should go* unto the heathen, and they unto the circumcision.

"Pillars," *i. e.* "the principal supporters and defenders of the gospel." It is said of those who have done much to support a temple, or who are zealous in its religious ceremonies, "They are the pillars of black stone belonging to the temple."—Roberts.

CHAPTER III.

Ver. 24. Wherefore the law was our schoolmaster *to bring us* unto Christ, that we might be justified by faith.

The Hindoos have some books which they call schoolmaster, *etāsāriyan*, or rather *schoolmaster-book*, meaning, they will teach science without the help of a master. When a man who was formerly in poverty has learned how to procure a comfortable living, he says, "Ah! my adversity was my *teacher;* it has guided me into this."—Roberts.

CHAPTER IV.

Ver. 15. Where is then the blessedness ye spake of? for I bear you record, that if *it had been* possible, ye would have plucked out your own eyes, and have given them to me.

"Ah! how great was her love for him; had he asked her, she would have given him her own eyes." "Dearer, dearer than my own eyes."—Roberts.

CHAPTER VI.

Ver. 7. Be not deceived; God is not mocked: for whatsoever a man soweth, that shall he also reap.

The Tamul proverb on this subject is, "*virtti-aruppān,*" i. e. he reaps what he sowed. "Ah! the wretch, he cast in cruelties, and is now reaping them." "Yes, yes, he has a large harvest; his lies have produced fruit." "Go, go to thy harvest, fiend."—Roberts.

THE EPISTLE OF PAUL, THE APOSTLE, TO THE EPHESIANS.

CHAPTER II.

Ver. 14. For he is our peace, who hath made both one, and hath broken down the middle wall of partition *between us.*

Some think that this refers to the ancient manner of living among the Gentiles, who always endeavoured to reside in some place by themselves, and to have a river or a wall between them and their heathen neighbours. Some others refer it to that partition-wall in the temple, which separated the court of the Gentiles from that into which the Jews entered, and on which was written, that no alien might go into it, it being, says Josephus, a sanction of Antiochus, that no foreigner should enter within the enclosure of the temple.—Burder.

CHAPTER IV.

Ver. 8. Wherefore he saith, When he ascended up on high, he led captivity captive, and gave gifts unto men.

The highest military honour which could be obtained in the Roman state, was a triumph, or solemn procession, in which a victorious general and his army advanced through the city, to the capitol. He set out from the Campus Martius, and proceeded along the Via Triumphalis, and from thence through the most public places of the city. The streets were strewed with flowers, and the altars smoked with incense. First went a numerous band of music, singing and playing triumphal songs; next were led the oxen to be sacrificed, having their horns gilt, and their heads adorned with fillets and garlands; then in carriages were brought the spoils taken from the enemy; also golden crowns sent by the allied and tributary states. The titles of the vanquished nations were inscribed on wooden frames; and images or representations of the conquered countries and cities were exhibited. The captive leaders followed in chains, with their children and attendants; after the captives came the lictors, having their faces wreathed with laurel, followed by a great company of musicians and dancers, dressed like satyrs, and wearing crowns of gold; in the midst of whom was a pantomime, clothed in a female garb, whose business it was, with his looks and gestures, to insult the vanquished; a long train of persons followed, carrying perfumes; after them came the general, dressed in purple, embroidered with gold, with a crown of laurel on his head, a branch of laurel in his right hand, and in his left an ivory sceptre, with an eagle on the top, his face painted with vermilion, and a golden ball hanging from his neck on his breast; he stood upright in a gilded chariot, adorned with ivory, and drawn by four white horses, attended by his relations, and a great crowd of citizens, all in white. His children rode in the chariot along with him, his lieutenants and military tribunes commonly by his side. After the general followed the consuls and senators on foot; the whole procession was closed by the victorious army drawn up in order, crowned with laurel, and decorated with the gifts which they had received for their valour, singing their own and their general's praises. The triumphal procession was not confined to the Romans; the Greeks had a similar custom, for the conquerors used to make a procession through the middle of their city, crowned with garlands, repeating hymns and songs, and brandishing their spears; the captives followed in chains, and all their spoils were exposed to public view.

The great apostle of the Gentiles alludes to these splendid triumphal scenes, in his epistle to the Ephesians, where he mentions the glorious ascension of his Redeemer into heaven: "When he ascended up on high, he led captivity captive, and gave gifts unto men." These words are a quotation from the sixty-eighth Psalm, where David, in Spirit, describes the ascension of Messiah, in very glowing colours: "The chariots of God are twenty thousand, even thousands of angels; the Lord is among them, as in Sinai, in the holy place. Thou hast ascended on high, thou hast led captivity captive," or an immense number of captives; "thou hast received gifts for men, yea, for the rebellious also; that the Lord God might dwell among them. Blessed be the Lord, who daily loadeth us with his benefits, even the God of our salvation; Selah." Knowing the deep impression which such an allusion is calculated to make on the mind of a people familiarly acquainted with triumphal scenes, the apostle returns to it in his epistle to the Colossians, which was written about the same time: "Having spoiled principalities and powers, he made a show of them openly, triumphing over them in it." After obtaining a complete victory over all his enemies, he ascended in splendour and triumph into his Father's presence on the clouds of heaven, the chariots of the Most High, thousands of holy angels attending in his train; he led the devil and all his angels, together with sin, the world, and death, as his spoils of war, and captives in chains, and exposed them to open contempt and shame, in the view of all his angelic attendants, triumphing like a glorious conqueror over them, in virtue of his cross, upon which he made complete satisfaction for sin, and by his own strength, without the assistance of any creature, destroyed him that had the power of death, that is, the devil. And as mighty princes are accustomed to scatter largesses among the people, and reward their companions in arms with a liberal hand, when, laden with the spoils of vanquished nations, they returned in triumph to their capital; so the Conqueror of death and hell, when he ascended far above all heavens, and sat down in the midst of the throne, shed forth in vast abundance the choicest blessings of the Spirit upon people of every tongue and of every nation.—PAXTON.

Ver. 26. Be ye angry and sin not; let not the sun go down upon your wrath.

One of the apartments in the houses of some rich men is appropriated to a very curious purpose, viz. when any members of the family are angry, they shut themselves up in this room, called krodhagarû, the room of anger, or of the angry. When any individual is gone into this room, the master of the family goes and persuades him or her to come out. (Ward's View of the Hindoos.)—BURDER.

CHAPTER VI.

Ver. 14. Stand, therefore, having your loins girt about with truth, and having on the breastplate of righteousness.

The breastplate is frequently mentioned in the sacred volume. It was properly a half corslet, defending the breast, as its name imports, but leaving the back exposed to the enemy. Breastplates were not always formed of the same materials; some were made of line or hemp twisted into small cords, and close set together; but these were more frequently used in hunting than in war. The most approved breastplates were made of brass, iron, or other metals, which were sometimes so admirably hardened as to resist the greatest force. Plutarch reports, that Zoilus, an artificer, having made a present of two iron brigandines to Demetrius Poliorcetes, for an experiment of their hardness, caused an arrow to be shot out of an engine called catapulta, placed about twenty-six paces off, which was so far from piercing the iron, that it scarcely rased or made the least impression upon it. These facts may serve to display the inestimable value of "the breastplate of righteousness," which the apostle recommends to the hearers of the gospel: a piece of spiritual armour which the fiery darts of the devil cannot pierce. The scales of brass, which composed the breastplate of the ancient warrior, often reflected the light so as to dazzle the eyes of his antagonist, and strike him with terror.

The military girdle was another piece of defensive armour; it surrounded the other accoutrements; the sword was suspended in it, as in modern times in the soldier's belt; and it was necessary to gird the clothes and armour of the combatant together. This was so essential to a warrior, that among the Greeks, ζωννυσθαι, to gird, came to be a general name for putting on armour. Homer thus introduces Agamemnon commanding the Grecians to arm:

Ατρειδης δε βοησεν, ιδε ζωννυσθαι ανωγεν.—*Iliad*, lib. ix.

"Atrides strait commands them all to arm, or gird themselves." We learn from Plutarch, that the Romans had the same custom; and it prevailed also among the Persians, for Herodotus relates, that Xerxes having reached Abdera, when he fled from Athens, and thinking himself out of danger, λυειν την ζωνην, loosed his girdle, that is, put off his armour. The same phrases occur in many parts of the sacred volume, the military belt being not less necessary to the Hebrew soldier, on account of his loose and flowing dress. To gird and to arm, are therefore synonymous terms in scripture; for those who are said to be able to put on armour, are, according to the Hebrew and Septuagint, girt with a girdle; from whence came the expression of girding to the battle. This was the species of girdle which Jonathan bestowed on David, as one of the pledges of his entire love and friendship. He stripped himself, not only of his wearing apparel, but what a warrior valued at a much higher price, his military habiliments also, his sword, his bow, and his girdle, and gave them to David.

The girdle is mentioned by the apostle, in his particular description of the Christian armour, addressed to the church at Ephesus: "Stand, therefore, having your loins girt about with truth." As warriors are accustomed to gird themselves with a broad belt to keep up their long garments, to bind them and their armour close together, and to fortify their loins, that they may be stronger, and more fitted for the labours and fatigues of war; so must believers encompass themselves with sincerity and uprightness of heart, and with truth and honesty of conversation, that righteousness may be the girdle of their loins, and faithfulness the girdle of their reins, that they may be steady, active, and resolute in every spiritual encounter.—PAXTON.

Ver. 15. And your feet shod with the preparation of the gospel of peace.

The legs of the Grecian warrior were defended with greaves of brass, copper, or other metals. Potter thinks it is probable that this piece of armour was at first either peculiar to the Grecians, or at least more generally used by them than any other nations; because we find them so perpetually called by the poet (ευκνημιδες Αχαιοι) the well-greaved Achaians. But they seem to have been equally common among the warriors of Canaan, and other eastern countries. When Goliath appeared in complete armour, and challenged the armies of Israel to furnish a man able to contend with him in single combat, he wore greaves of brass upon his legs. This piece of armour is also recommended by the apostle, in these words: "And your feet shod with the preparation of the gospel of peace." The soldier is wont to wear greaves of brass, or a sort of strong boots, to guard his feet and legs against briers and thorns, the iron spikes which the enemy scatters in his way, and the sharp pointed stones which retard his march; so must the heart and life of the Christian be disengaged from worldly thoughts, affections, and pursuits, that would hinder him in his heavenly course; and be filled with holy resolutions, by divine grace, to hold on his way, in spite of every hardship and danger, fortified against the many snares and temptations that beset him in his progress, and prepared for the assault, from what enemy or quarter soever it may come.

The feet were protected with shoes of stout, well-prepared leather, plated or spiked on the sole, to prevent the combatant from slipping. Moses seems, at least according to our translation, to have had some allusion to shoes of this kind, in his farewell address to the tribes: "Thy shoes shall be iron and brass, and as thy days, so shall thy strength be." And the apostle Paul, in his description of the spiritual armour: "Having the feet shod with the preparation of the gospel of peace." "Not iron," says Calmet, "not steel; but patient investigation, calm inquiry, assiduous, laborious, lasting; if not rather with firm footing in the gospel of peace."—PAXTON.

Ver. 16. Above all, taking the shield of faith, wherewith ye shall be able to quench all the fiery darts of the wicked.

See on Ps. 57. 4.

The Hebrew soldiers used two kinds of shields, the (צנה) *tsinna*, and the (מגן) *magen*. From the middle of the tsinna rose a large boss, surmounted by a dagger, or sharp pointed protuberance, which was extremely useful in repelling missive weapons, and bearing down their enemy when they came to close fight. A shield of this construction was partly a defensive and partly an offensive weapon. Martial seems to allude to the tsinna in this line:

"In turbam incideris, cunctos umbone repellet."

"Should you get into a crowd, your slave with his boss would repel them all." The ancient bucklers generally covered the whole body; for Virgil represents the troops as standing close covered under their bucklers:

—"clypeique sub orbe teguntur."—*Æn.* lib. ii. l. 227.

And in Tyrtæus, the mighty buckler covered the thighs, legs, and breast, belly, and shoulders too. The *magen* was a short buckler intended merely for defence, and of great service in the warfare of those days. To these must be added the (סוחרה) *sihara*, or round shield; and these three differed from one another, nearly as the *scutum*, *clypeus*, and *parma*, among the Romans. The *tsinna* was double the weight of the *magen*, and was carried by the infantry; the others, as being more light and manageable, were reserved for the cavalry. These different shields were also used by the Greeks. The great apostle of the Gentiles earnestly recommends this weapon, among others, to the use of the churches under the present dispensation: "Above all, taking the shield of faith, wherewith ye shall be able to quench all the fiery darts of the wicked."—PAXTON.

Ver. 17. And take the helmet of salvation, and the sword of the Spirit, which is the word of God.

The first piece of defensive armour entitled to our notice, is the helmet, which protected the head. This has been used from the remotest ages by almost every nation of a martial spirit. The champion of the Philistines had a helmet of brass upon his head, as had also the king of Israel, who commanded the armies of the living God. This martial cap was also worn by the Persians and Ethiopians in the day of battle. The Grecian helmets were very often made of the skins of beasts; but the helmet of the Jewish warrior seems to have been uniformly made of brass or iron; and to this sort of casque only, the sacred writer seems to refer. In allusion to this piece of defensive armour, Paul directs the believer to put on for a helmet the hope of salvation, which secures the head in every contest, till, through him that loved him, he gain a complete victory over all his enemies. That well-grounded hope of eternal life which is attended with ineffable satisfaction, and never disappoints the soul, like a helmet of brass, shall guard it against fear and danger, enable it patiently to endure every hardship, and fortify it against the most furious and threatening attacks of Satan and all his confederates. Such adversaries, this solid hope is not less calculated to strike with dismay, than was the helmet of an ancient warrior in the day of battle his mortal foes, by its dazzling brightness, its horrific devices of gorgons and chimeras, and its nodding plumes which overlooked the dreadful cone.—PAXTON.

THE EPISTLE OF PAUL, THE APOSTLE, TO THE PHILIPPIANS.

CHAPTER I.

Ver. 7. Even as it is meet for me to think this of you all, because I have you in my heart; inasmuch as both in my bonds, and in the defence and confirmation of the gospel, ye all are partakers of my grace.

This peculiar expression intimates, not only that the apostle cherished for the Philippians the most sincere and ardent affection, but that they were ever in his recollection, and that he was thus animated to promote, in every possible way, their spiritual benefit and prosperity. If not strictly similar, the following instance may be considered as nearly approaching to this phraseology: "The old man followed us, with his women, to a distance from the village, and, at parting, recommended me to his relations. 'He is your brother,' he said to his son: 'and there,' opening his son's waistcoat, and putting his hand upon his bosom, 'There let him be placed.' A way of recommendation much in use in the Arabian desert likewise." (Burckhardt.)—BURDER.

CHAPTER II.

Ver. 15. That ye may be blameless and harmless, the sons of God, without rebuke, in the midst of a crooked and perverse nation, among whom ye shine as lights in the world.

This metaphor has an allusion to the buildings which we call *light-houses*, the most illustrious of which was raised in the island of Pharos, when Ptolemy Philadelphus built that celebrated tower, on which a bright flame was always kept burning in the night, that mariners might perfectly see their way, and be in no danger of suffering shipwreck. Some of these light-houses were constructed in the form of human figures. The colossus at Rhodes held in one hand a flame which enlightened the whole port. These lights were also sometimes moveable, and were used to direct the marches of the caravans in the night. Pitts thus describes them: "They are somewhat like iron stoves, into which they put short dry wood, which some of the camels are loaded with. Every cotter hath one of these poles belonging to it, some of which have ten, some twelve of these lights on their tops, and they are likewise of different figures, one perhaps oval, another triangular, or like an N or M, &c. so that every one knows by them his respective cotter. They are carried in the front, and set up in the place where the caravan is to pitch, before that comes up, at some distance from one another." The meaning of the passage from these representations is obvious. "Ye shine as elevated lights in the dark world about you," that ye may direct those that sail on this dangerous sea, and secure them from suffering shipwreck, or guide those who travel through this desert in their way to the city of rest.—BURDER.

CHAPTER III.

Ver. 2. Beware of dogs, beware of evil-workers, beware of the concision.

The champion of Gath inquired of David, "Am I a dog?" And David, when pursued by the infatuated and cruel Saul, asked, "After whom dost thou pursue? after a dead dog?" The term NI, *i. e.* dog, is an expression of sovereign contempt for the faithless, the ignoble, and the outcasts. "Never more will I go to the house of that dog." "You call me a dog! then (running at him) I will bite thee." "Here, dog, are some bones for thee." "Yes, yes, he will be a dog in the next birth."—ROBERTS.

Ver. 14. I press towards the mark, for the prize of the high calling of God in Christ Jesus.

The most remarkable parts of the stadium, were its entrance, middle, and extremity. The entrance was marked at first only by a line drawn on the sand, from side to side of the stadium. To prevent any unfair advantage being taken by the more vigilant or alert candidates, a cord was at length stretched in front of the horses or men that were to run; and sometimes the space was railed in with wood. The opening of this barrier was the signal for the racers to start. The middle of the stadium was remarkable, only by the circumstance of having the prizes allotted to the victors set up there. From this custom, Chrysostom draws a fine comparison: "As the judges, in the races and other games, expose in the midst of the stadium, to the view of the champions, the crowns which they were to receive; in like manner, the Lord, by the mouth of his prophets, has placed the prizes in the midst of the course, which he designs for those who have the courage to contend for them."

At the extremity of the stadium was a goal, where the foot-races ended; but in those of chariots and horses, they were to run several times round it without stopping, and afterward conclude the race, by regaining the other extremity of the lists from whence they started. It is therefore to the foot-race the apostle alludes, when he speaks of the race set before the Christian, which was a straight course, to be run only once, and not, as in the other, several times without stopping.

According to some writers, it was at the goal, and not in the middle of the course, that the prizes were exhibited; and they were placed in a very conspicuous situation, that the competitors might be animated by having them always in their sight. This accords with the view which the apostle gives of the Christian life: "Brethren, I count not myself to have apprehended; but this one thing I do, forgetting those things which are behind, and reaching forth unto those things which are before, I press towards the mark for the prize of the high calling of God in Christ Jesus." L'Enfant thinks the apostle here compares our Lord to those who stood at the elevated place at the end of the course, calling the racers by their names, and encouraging them by holding out the crown, to exert themselves with vigour.—PAXTON.

Ver. 19. Whose end *is* destruction, whose god *is their* belly, and *whose* glory *is* in their shame, who mind earthly things.

When a pandārum is reproved and told to serve the gods, he exclaims, "What! is not the belly the god?" "I will tell you all about him, his god is in his belly." "Belly, belly, nothing to the belly," bawls the beggar at your door. —ROBERTS.

CHAPTER IV.

Ver. 3. And I entreat thee also, true yoke-fellow, help those women which laboured with me in the gospel, with Clement also, and *with* other my fellow-labourers, whose names *are* in the book of life.

This expression refers to the custom of those cities which had registers containing the names of all the citizens, from which the names of infamous persons were erased. Agreeably to this we read of names being blotted out of God's book, Rev. iii. 5. Those citizens who were orderly and obedient were continued on the roll, from whence they could easily obtain their title to all the immunities and privileges common to all the members of the city; and to be excluded from these was both disgraceful and injurious.—BURDER.

THE EPISTLE OF PAUL, THE APOSTLE, TO THE COLOSSIANS.

CHAPTER II.

Ver. 14. Blotting out the handwriting of ordinances that was against us, which was contrary to us, and took it out of the way, nailing it to his cross.

See on Zech. 11. 7.

The handwriting, χειρόγραφον, signifies a bill or bond whereby a person binds himself to some payment or duty, and which stands in force against him till the obligation is discharged. In these words the apostle alludes to the different methods by which bonds formerly were cancelled: one was by blotting or crossing them out with a pen, and another was by striking a nail through them. In either of these cases the bond was rendered useless, and ceased to be valid. These circumstances the apostle applies to the death of Christ.—BURDER.

Ver. 15. *And* having spoiled principalities and powers, he made a show of them openly, triumphing over them in it.

The most grand and magnificent procession the ancients ever beheld was a Roman triumph. After a decisive battle gained, the most illustrious captives in war, with their wives and children, were led in fetters before the general's chariot, through the public streets of Rome, scaffolds being everywhere erected, and the public places crowded to behold the sight. It was also accompanied by vast numbers of wagons, full of rich furniture, statues, pictures, plate, vases, and vests, of which they had stripped houses and palaces; carts loaded with the arms they had taken from the enemy; the coin of the empires they had conquered and enslaved: these preceded the triumphal car. The temples were all thrown open, and adorned with garlands; they were filled with clouds of incense and perfume. The spectators were clothed in white garments. Whole hecatombs of victims were slain, and the most sumptuous entertainments were given. The captives, after being publicly exposed, were generally imprisoned and put to death, or sold for slaves.—BURDER.

THE FIRST EPISTLE OF PAUL, THE APOSTLE, TO THE THESSALONIANS.

CHAPTER IV.

Ver. 17. Then we, which are alive *and* remain, shall be caught up together with them in the clouds, to meet the Lord in the air; and so shall we ever be with the Lord.

See on 2 Tim. 4. 7, 8.

CHAPTER V.

Ver. 8. But let us, who are of the day, be sober, putting on the breastplate of faith and love; and for a helmet, the hope of salvation.

See on Eph. 6. 17.

Ver. 17. Pray without ceasing.

We learn from church history that an ancient sect, called Euchitæ, gathered from this and similar passages, that it was the duty of Christians to pray literally *without ceasing*, making prayer the whole means of salvation and the whole business of the Christian life. A slight acquaintance with the idiom of the original languages of the scriptures, will enable us to correct this as well as many other errors which have, at different times, crept into both the practical and speculative theology of the church. It may be laid down as a canon of philological interpretation, that adverbs of time expressing perpetuity, sometimes denote only frequency or regularity at stated times and seasons. This will abundantly appear from the following examples: Ex. xxvii. 20, "To cause the lamp to burn *always*." (Hebrew, *tamid.*) That this is not to be taken strictly, but merely as equivalent to, "from evening to morning," appears from the ensuing verse: "Aaron and his sons shall order it *from evening to morning*." That the lamp of the tabernacle did not burn during the day, is evident from 1 Sam. iii. 3: "Ere the lamp of God *went out* in the temple of the Lord." Again, it is said, Ex. xxviii. 30, "And thou shalt put in the breastplate of judgment, the Urim and the Thummim; and they shall be upon Aaron's heart, when he goeth in before the Lord; and Aaron shall bear the judgment of the children of Israel upon his heart before the Lord *continually*;" i. e. whenever he went into the inner place of the sanctuary, as is clear from the preceding clause, by which the word "continually" is to be limited. So 2 Sam. ix. 7, David says to Mephibosheth, "Thou shalt eat bread at my table *continually*;" i. e. at the stated hours of meals. In like manner, "to pray without ceasing," is, to pray constantly, morning and evening, at the stated hours of prayer. In this precept, the apostle seems to have had reference to the injunction of the Mosaic law, Ex. xxix. 38, 42: "Now this is that which you shall offer upon the altar: two lambs of the first year, day by day, *continually*. The one lamb you shall offer in the morning, and the other lamb you shall offer in the evening. This shall be a *continual* burnt-offering throughout your generations." At those stated hours of sacrifice, viz. at nine o'clock in the morning, and at three in the afternoon, the devout Jews used either to go up to the temple to pray, or to pray in their own houses. This duty the apostle would have the Christian disciples still observe; and the word here used, (adialeiptoes, *without ceasing, continually*,) is applied to their praying statedly, morning and evening. The same rule of interpretation will throw light upon numerous other passages of scripture, which are frequently misapprehended by the English reader, such as David's saying that he would "dwell in the house of the Lord *for ever*;" that he would "bless the Lord *at all times*;" that he would "meditate in his law *day and night*." So Luke ii. 37, it is said of Anna the prophetess, that "she *departed not from the temple*, but served God with fasting and prayers *night and day*;" by which is implied, not that she took up her permanent abode at the temple, but regularly resorted thither, at stated times, and was uncommonly assiduous in her devotions. Compare with this, Acts xxvi. 7: "Unto which promise our twelve tribes, instantly *serving God day and night*, hope to come." This is in accordance with our Saviour's direction, Luke xviii. 1, "That men ought *always to pray*, and not to faint;" i. e. that they should continue in the regular discharge of this duty every day at the appointed times; and that they should not desist, though their prayers should not be immediately granted. According to the same usage, from the apostles going up to the temple at the stated hours of prayer, they are said to have been "*continually* in the temple, blessing and praising God." To this circumstance of the temple-worship there is a beautiful allusion, Rev. iv. 8, where, concerning the four living creatures, it is said, "They rest not *day nor night*, (or at the morning and evening sacrifices,) saying, Holy, holy, holy, Lord God Almighty, which was, and is, and is to come." In the same sense, Cornelius is said (Acts x. 2) to have "prayed to God *always*." And through Christ we are said to "offer unto God the sacrifice of praise *continually*." And, finally, in this sense of the words are we to understand all such passages as the following, in which the apostle speaks of the *unremittingness* of his prayers and praises to God on the behalf of Christians. Rom. i. 9: "For God is my witness that, *without ceasing*, I make mention of you always in my prayers." Col. i. 3: "Praying *always* for you." 1 Thes. i. 2, 3: "We give thanks to God *always* for you all, making mention of you in our prayers; remembering, *without ceasing*, your work of faith." 2 Tim. i. 3: "I thank God, whom I serve from my forefathers with pure conscience, that, *without ceasing*, I have remembrance of thee in my prayers *night and day*."—BUSH.

THE FIRST EPISTLE OF PAUL, THE APOSTLE, TO TIMOTHY.

CHAPTER II.

Ver. 9. In like manner also, that women adorn themselves in modest apparel, with shame-facedness and sobriety; not with broidered hair, or gold, or pearls, or costly array.

See on 1 Pet. 3. 3.

CHAPTER VI.

Ver. 7. For we brought nothing into *this* world, *and it is* certain we can carry nothing out.

"My friend, why are you so anxious after this world? How much did you bring into it? How much will you take out?" "Ah! my son, be charitable to all; recollect, you brought nothing into the world, and be assured you will take nothing out." "That wretch would like to carry his money and lands into the other world." "Tamby, did you bring these fields into the world with you? No; and they will remain when you are gone."—ROBERTS.

THE SECOND EPISTLE OF PAUL, THE APOSTLE, TO TIMOTHY.

CHAPTER II.

Ver. 5. And if a man also strive for masteries, *yet* is he not crowned, except he strive lawfully.

Those who were designed for the profession of athletæ, or combatants, frequented from their earliest years the academies maintained for that purpose at the public expense. In these places they were exercised under the direction of different masters, who employed the most effectual methods to inure their bodies for the fatigues of the public games, and to form them for the combats. The regimen to which they submitted was very hard and severe. At first they had no other nourishment than dried figs, nuts, soft cheese, and a gross heavy sort of bread called μαζα; they were absolutely forbid the use of wine, and enjoined continence.

When they proposed to contend in the Olympian games, they were obliged to repair to the public gymnasium at Elis, ten months before the solemnity, where they prepared themselves by continual exercises. No man that had omitted to present himself at the appointed time, was allowed to put in for any of the prizes; nor were the accustomed rewards of victory given to such persons, if by any means they insinuated themselves, and overcame their antagonists; nor would any apology, though seemingly ever so reasonable, serve to excuse their absence. No person that was himself a notorious criminal, or nearly related to one, was permitted to contend. Further, to prevent underhand dealings, if any person was convicted of bribing his adversary, a severe fine was laid upon him; nor was this alone thought a sufficient guard against unfair contracts and unjust practices, but the contenders were obliged to swear they had spent ten whole months in preparatory exercises; and besides all this, they, their fathers, and their brethren, took a solemn oath, that they would not by any sinister or unlawful means endeavour to stop the fair and just proceedings of the games. The spiritual contest, in which all true Christians aim at obtaining a heavenly crown, has its rules also, devised and enacted by infinite wisdom and goodness, which require implicit and exact submission, which neither yield to times nor circumstances, but maintain their supreme authority, from age to age, uninterrupted and unimpaired. The combatant who violates these rules forfeits the prize, and is driven from the field with indelible disgrace, and consigned to everlasting wo. Hence the great apostle of the Gentiles exhorts his son Timothy strictly to observe the precepts of the divine law, the rule of his conduct in the hand of the Mediator, without which he can no more hope to obtain the approbation of God, and the possession of the heavenly crown, than a combatant in the public games of Greece, who disregards the established rules, can hope to receive from the hands of his judge the promised reward: "And if a man also strive for masteries, yet is he not crowned, except he strive lawfully," or according to the established laws of the games.—PAXTON.

Ver. 19. Nevertheless, the foundation of God standeth sure, having this seal, The Lord knoweth them that are his. And, Let every one that nameth the name of Christ, depart from iniquity.

See on Ezek. 9. 4.

CHAPTER IV.

Ver. 6 For I am now ready to be offered, and the time of my departure is at hand.

This is an allusion to that universal custom of the world of pouring wine or oil on the head of the victim immediately before it was slain: the apostle's emphatical word signifies, wine is just now pouring on my head, I am just going to be sacrificed to pagan rage and superstition.—BLACKWALL.

Ver. 7. I have fought a good fight, I have finished *my* course, I have kept the faith: 8. Henceforth there is laid up for me a crown of righteousness, which the Lord, the righteous Judge, shall give me at that day: and not to me only, but unto all them also that love his appearing.

The officers and soldiers also, were rewarded according to their merit. Among the Romans, the noblest reward which a soldier could receive, was the civic crown, given to him who had saved the life of a citizen, made of oak leaves, and, by order of the general, presented by the person who had been saved to his preserver, whom he ever after respected as a parent. Alluding to this high distinction, the apostle says to his son Timothy: "I have fought a good fight—henceforth there is laid up for me a crown of righteousness, which the Lord, the righteous Judge, shall give me at that day; and not to me only, but unto all them also that love his appearing." And lest any one should imagine that the Christian's crown is perishable in its nature, and soon fades away, like a crown of oak leaves, the apostle Peter assures the faithful soldier of Christ, that his crown is infinitely more valuable and lasting: "Ye shall receive a crown of glory that fadeth not away." And this account is confirmed by James: "Blessed is the man that endureth temptation, for when he is tried, he shall receive the crown of life, which the Lord hath promised to them that fear him."

The military crowns were conferred by the general in presence of the army; and such as received them, after a public eulogium on their valour, were placed next his person. The Christian also receives his unmerited reward from the hand of the Captain of his salvation: "Be thou faithful unto death, and I will give thee a crown of life." And like the brave veteran of ancient times, he is promoted to a place near his Lord: "To him that overcometh, will I grant to sit with me in my throne, even as I also overcame, and am set down with my Father on his throne." The saints must all appear before the judgment-seat of Christ, who will produce the proofs of their fidelity before assembled worlds, to justify the sentence he is about to pronounce. Holy angels will applaud the justice of the proceeding, and condemned spirits and reprobate men will have nothing to object; then, while he pronounces a sentence which at once eulogizes their conduct, and announces their honourable acquittal, "Well done, good and faithful servants, enter ye into the joy of your Lord;" he will set upon their heads a crown of purest gold, put a palm of victory into their right hand, clothe them in robes of celestial brightness, and place them around his throne: "And so shall they be for ever with the Lord."—PAXTON.

THE EPISTLE OF PAUL TO TITUS.

CHAPTER II.

Ver. 5. *To be* discreet, chaste, keepers at home, good, obedient to their own husbands, that the word of God be not blasphemed.

Jealousy is so common and powerful among the people of the East, that their wives are very much confined to their houses. Russel informs us, that "the Turks of Aleppo being very jealous, keep their women as much at home as they can, so that it is but seldom that they are allowed to visit each other. Necessity, however, obliges the husbands to suffer them to go often to the bagnio, and Mondays and Thursdays are a sort of licensed days for them to visit the tombs of their deceased relations, which furnishes them with an opportunity of walking abroad in the gardens or fields; they have so contrived that almost every Thursday in the spring bears the name of some particular sheik, (or saint,) whose tomb they must visit on that day. (Their cemeteries and gardens are out of their cities in common.) By this means the greatest part of the Turkish women of the city get abroad to breathe the fresh air at such seasons, unless confined (as is not uncommon) to their houses by order of the bashaw, and so deprived even of that little freedom which custom had procured them from their husbands." The prohibitions of the bashaws are designed, or pretended to be designed at least, to prevent the breach of chastity, for which these liberties of going abroad might be supposed to afford an opportunity. For the same reason it may be apprehended that St. Paul joins the being *chaste and keepers at home* together.—HARMER.

CHAPTER III.

Ver. 12. When I shall send Artemas unto thee, or Tychicus, be diligent to come unto me to Nicopolis: for I have determined there to winter.

Concerning the annals of Nicopolis, only a few trifling memorials are to be gleaned from the works of historians. How soon it enjoyed the light of Christianity is not precisely known, but that it was honoured early with the presence of that great champion of the faith, St. Paul, we may infer from his intention expressed to Titus, of spending the winter there, on his return from Macedonia; from whence it is extremely probable that he had many Nicopolitan converts already established. Its reign of splendour was but short, for it soon experienced those bitter reverses of fortune, which all the other unhappy provinces endured in the decline of the Roman empire. The city mentioned by St. Paul could not possibly have been (according to the surmise of some critics) Nicopolis on the Danube, or that of Thrace, for these were both built by Trajan. (Hughes's Travels in Sicily.)—BURDER.

THE EPISTLE OF PAUL, THE APOSTLE, TO THE HEBREWS.

CHAPTER I.

Ver. 8. But unto the Son *he saith*, Thy throne, O God, *is* for ever and ever; a sceptre of righteousness *is* the sceptre of thy kingdom.

The apostle here cites a passage from the 45th Psalm, in which the Psalmist, and not the Most High, is the speaker. Consequently this is not an address of the Father to the Son, as might be thought from our present translation. "He saith," should properly be rendered, according to a common idiom, "it is said," or, if a nominative be supplied, "the scripture saith, thy throne, O God," &c. The same remark is applicable to the same expression, ver. 7: "And of the angels he saith, (it is said,) Who maketh his angels spirits, and his ministers a flame of fire." A similar phraseology occurs, 1 Cor. vii. 16: "What, know ye not that he which is joined to a harlot is one body? for two, saith he, (i. e. it is said in the scriptures,) shall be one flesh." Rom. xv. 10: "And again he saith, (again it is said,) Rejoice, ye Gentiles, with his people." James iv. 6: "Wherefore he saith, (it is said,) God resisteth the proud, but giveth grace unto the humble." It may also be remarked, that the true rendering of the preposition (*pros*) in this passage, and in fact the whole context, is not "to," but "of," "in respect to," "concerning;" "of, or as to, the Son, it is said," &c. This import of the original is so common and so obviously pertinent to the text in this connexion, that it will be unnecessary to attempt to establish it by an array of parallel passages.—Bush.

CHAPTER VI.

Ver. 8. But that which beareth thorns and briers *is* rejected, and *is* nigh unto cursing; whose end *is* to be burned.

The land, which, notwithstanding the most careful cultivation, produces nothing but thorns and briers, or noxious weeds of different kinds, is rejected, or given up as unimproveable; its briers, thorns, and brushwood burnt down; and then left to be pastured on by the beasts of the field. This seems to be the custom in husbandry, to which the apostle alludes. The nature of the case prevents us from supposing that he refers to burning in order to further fertilization. This practice has been common from very early ages.

> Sæpe etiam steriles incendere profuit agros,
> Atque levem stipulam crepitantibus urere flammis.
> (Virgil, Geor. i. ver. 84.)
>
> Long practice has a sure improvement found,
> With kindled fires to burn the barren ground;
> When the light stubble to the flames resigned,
> Is driven along, and crackles in the wind.
> (Dryden.)—Burder.

Ver. 20. Whither the forerunner is for us entered, *even* Jesus, made a high-priest for ever after the order of Melchisedec.

"The forerunner." The metaphorical allusion here is to the person who carries the anchor in a boat within the pier head, because there is not water sufficient to take the ship in.—Burder.

CHAPTER XI.

Ver. 35. Women received their dead raised to life again: and others were tortured, not accepting deliverance; that they might obtain a better resurrection.

The ancients sometimes exposed criminals to a particular species of torture, by means of a tympanum or drum, on which they were extended in the most violent manner, and then beaten with clubs, which must have been attended with exquisite pain. To this mode of punishment, Doddridge is of opinion the apostle alludes in his epistle to the Hebrews, where he describes the sufferings of ancient believers: "Others were tortured, not accepting deliverance;" because the word ετυμπανισθησαν, tortured, is not a general term, but one which signifies the specific torture of the tympanum. It is, however, generally understood by interpreters, not as a mode of punishment distinct from others, but as a general term for all kinds of capital punishment and violent death; but the opinion of Doddridge ought to be preferred, because the original word possesses a specific character; and the passage viewed in that light is precise and impressive.—Paxton.

Ver. 37. They were stoned, they were sawn asunder, were tempted, were slain with the sword; they wandered about in sheep-skins and goat-skins, being destitute, afflicted, tormented.

The epistle to the Hebrews describes some of the ancient sufferers for piety and virtue, as driven out from the society of their countrymen, and wandering about, like miserable outcasts, in deserts and mountains, with no better vestments than sheep-skins and goat-skins; referring, probably, to some in the beginning of the opposition made by the Maccabee family, to the attempts of the Syrian princes to force the Jewish people to abandon the religion of their forefathers, and unite with the heathens in their idolatrous customs. It may be acceptable to the reader to learn, that there are numbers of such miserable outcasts from common society, in that very country, to this day: not indeed on a religious account, for they are all Mohammedans; but from national prejudices, and distinctions arising from that source.

Doubdan frequently met with such in his peregrinations in that country. He sometimes calls them Moors, by which, I apprehend, is meant the descendants from the old natives of that country, who inhabited it before the Turks, a branch of the Tartars, overran these parts of Asia. Some of the Arabs he met with are not described as in more elegant circumstances: these are another eastern nation, who are attached to the living in tents, and will by no means be induced to dwell in more fixed habitations, and commonly dwell in deserts, and very retired places.

Upon leaving Jerusalem, in order to embark at Joppa, they halted some little time on a short plain, not far from the Holy City, to give time to the caravan to assemble, with which they were to travel: while waiting there, he says, "We saw six Bedouins pass along;" he means these wandering Arabs; "who had no other clothing than a sheep-skin on their shoulders, and a rag about their loins, emaciated and burnt up with the heat, of a horrible aspect, their eyes fiery, and each with a great club. These people are Arabs, and the greatest robbers in all the country."

He describes some of the Moors in the neighbourhood of Bethlehem, who live in the village where the shepherds dwelt to whom the angel of the Lord appeared, according to the tradition of the country, in much the same manner. He says, "it is a poor hamlet, of twenty or twenty-five hovels." That he was informed "its inhabitants are some of the poorest and most miserable people of the country. That they saw some who looked like true savages, almost entirely naked, sunburnt, black as a coal, and shining with the grease and oil with which they rub themselves, horrid in their countenances, with a surly voice, with which they keep mumbling, and terrify those that are not accustomed to meet them. More especially when, upon their going to visit a certain place to which their devotion led them, they saw four poor miserable Moors running to them across the fields, huge, frightful creatures, all of them naked and sunburnt, two armed with bows and arrows, the other two with cudgels, threatening to use them with severity, if they did not give them money."

The same scenery is exhibited in other places, and represents, I imagine, excepting the violence, an accurate picture of those poor persecuted Hebrews, who wandered about in sheep-skins and goat-skins, destitute of many of the comforts of life, emaciated, tormented with the burning heat of the sun, and afflicted with many other bitternesses in that wild and rough state.—HARMER.

Ver. 38. (Of whom the world was not worthy;) they wandered in deserts, and *in* mountains, and *in* dens, and caves of the earth. 39. And these all, having obtained a good report through faith, received not the promise.

Such places were frequently used as habitations. "In returning to Achmetchet, we stopped to water our horses in the steppes or plains, where the dwellings were entirely subterranean. Not a house was to be seen, but there were some holes as entrances in the ground, through one of which we descended to a cave, rendered almost suffocating by the heat of a stove for dressing the victuals of its poor owners. The wall, floor, and roof, were all of the natural soil." (Clarke.) "At eleven, we arrived on the plain and a better road, but being excessively hot, and seeing a village with many low houses, or rather huts, we struck out of our path, and arrived there about noon, when, instead of houses, we found them to be caverns, dug in the earth, and vaulted, with only the upper part appearing above ground. The people received us kindly; both men and horses descended into one of the caverns, and immediately felt such a comfortable coolness as was extremely delightful. The cavern which we were now in was more than one hundred feet in length, and near forty wide, entirely vaulted the whole way, and very lofty. It was divided into apartments on each side, in some of which were grain, in others flour, in others oil, all in very large jars, buried half way in the earth: in other divisions were roosts for poultry; in others cows were kept; in some, goats and sheep; and some served as places to sleep in. The middle part was kept clear as a passage to each room or division." (Parsons.)—BURDER.

CHAPTER XII.

Ver. 1. Wherefore, seeing we also are compassed about with so great a cloud of witnesses, let us lay aside every weight, and the sin which doth so easily beset *us*, and let us run with patience the race that is set before us.

The athletæ took care to disencumber their bodies of every article of clothing which could in any manner hinder or incommode them. The pugilists at first used a belt, with an apron or scarf fastened to it, for their more decent appearance in the combats; but one of the combatants happening to lose the victory by this covering's falling off, modesty was in future sacrificed to convenience, and the apron was laid aside. In the foot-race they were anxious to carry as little weight as possible, and uniformly stripped themselves of all such clothes as, by their weight, length, or otherwise, might entangle or retard them in the course. The Christian, also, must "lay aside every weight, and the sin which doth so easily beset" him: in the exercise of faith and self-denial, he must "cast off the works of darkness," lay aside all malice and guile, hypocrisies, and envyings, and evil speakings, inordinate affections, and worldly cares, and whatever else might obstruct his holy profession, damp his spirits, and hinder his progress in the paths of righteousness.

The olympic games generally opened with races, and were celebrated at first with no other exercise. The lists or course where the athletæ exercised themselves in running, was at first but one stadium in length, or about six hundred feet; and from this measure it took its name, and was called the stadium, whatever might be its extent. This, in the language of Paul, speaking of the Christians' course, was "the race which was set before them," determined by public authority and carefully measured. On each side of the stadium and its extremity, ran an ascent or kind of terrace, covered with seats and benches, upon which the spectators were seated, an innumerable multitude collected from all parts of Greece, to which the apostle thus alludes in his figurative description of the Christian life: "Seeing we are compassed about with so great a cloud of witnesses, let us lay aside every weight."—PAXTON.

Ver. 4. Ye have not yet resisted unto blood, striving against sin.

The exercise of boxing was sometimes performed by combatants, having in their hands balls of stone or lead. At first their hands and arms were naked and unguarded, but afterward surrounded with thongs of leather, called cestus, which were used both as defensive arms, and to annoy the enemy, being filled with plummets of lead and iron, to add force to the blows.

This was one of the rudest and most dangerous of the gymnastic combats, because the antagonists ran the hazard either of being disabled, or losing their lives. They sometimes fell down dead or dying upon the sand; or they quitted the fight with a countenance so disfigured, that it was not easy to know themselves; carrying away with them the sad marks of their vigorous resistance, as bruises and contusions in the face, the loss of an eye, their teeth knocked out, their jaws broken, or some more considerable fracture. It is to this rude and dangerous exercise the apostle refers in his reasoning with the Hebrew converts: "Ye have not yet resisted unto blood, striving against sin." The contest in which they were engaged with their adversaries, had been severe and of long continuance; they had sustained no small loss of liberty and property, which they cheerfully resigned for the sake of Christ, in hope of a better inheritance in heaven; they were in danger of becoming weary and faint in their minds, from the length of the contest; but though their antagonists had often tried to defeat and foil them, they had not been permitted to shed their blood, or take away their lives, as they did to many of the saints in preceding ages. The combatant in the public games, who gave up the contest before he had lost a drop of his blood, merely because he had received a few contusions, or been roughly handled by his opponent, would have been infallibly branded with infamy. Not less shameful, and infinitely more dangerous, it would have been for any of these Hebrews to flinch from their duty, or desist from their Christian course, on account of the slighter difficulties and losses they had met with in striving against sin.—PAXTON.

Ver. 6. For whom the Lord loveth he chasteneth, and scourgeth every son whom he receiveth.

It is said, in the East, of a truly good father, when he is obliged to punish his son,—

"*Adikam, oru ki;*
Anikam, oru ki."

One hand, chastises;
One hand, embraces.

Showing, that though he is obliged to inflict punishment with one hand, yet in his heart he embraces him with the other.—ROBERTS.

THE GENERAL EPISTLE OF JAMES.

CHAPTER II.

Ver. 2. For if there come unto your assembly a man with a gold ring, in goodly apparel, and there come in also a poor man, in vile raiment.

By the assembly here mentioned we are not to understand a congregation convened for public worship, as is commonly represented, but a court of judicature, in which men are too apt to favour the cause of the rich against the poor. The phrase, *sit thou under my footstool*, naturally refers to courts of justice, where the judge is commonly exalted upon a higher seat than the rest of the people. The apostle also says, that such a respect of persons as he here speaks of is contrary to the law, and that those who are guilty of it, *are convinced of the law as transgressors.* Now there was no divine law against distinction of places in worshipping assemblies, into those which were more or less honourable; this must therefore refer to the law of partiality in judgment. "Ye shall do no unrighteousness in judgment; thou shalt not respect the person of the poor, nor honour the person of the mighty." Levit. xix. 15. The Talmudists say it was a rule, that when a poor man and a rich man pleaded together in judgment, the rich should not be bid to sit down, and the poor to stand; but either both shall sit, or both shall stand. To this rule or custom the apostle seems to refer, when he insinuates a charge against them of saying to the rich man, "Sit thou here in a good place, and to the poor, Stand thou there."—Jennings.

"A man with a gold ring." By this circumstance the apostle describes a rich man. Among the Romans, those of the senatorial and equestrian orders were distinguished from the common people by wearing a gold ring. In time the use of them became promiscuous. The ancients used to wear but one.—Burder.

CHAPTER III.

Ver. 6. And the tongue *is* a fire, a world of iniquity: so is the tongue among our members, that it defileth the whole body, and setteth on fire the course of nature; and it is set on fire of hell.

The original is very beautiful, and is an allusion to a wheel catching fire, as not unfrequently happens, by its rapid motion, spreading its flames around, and at last involving the whole machine in destruction. The true version is, It setteth on fire the wheel of human life, and thus finally destroyeth the whole body. The original word for course, Τρόχος, signifies a wheel.—Burder.

CHAPTER IV.

Ver. 13. Go to now, ye that say, To-day, or tomorrow, we will go into such a city, and continue there a year, and buy, and sell, and get gain.

The merchants of the East have ever been famous for their trading peregrinations; and often are we reminded of the "company of Ishmaelites (who) came from Gilead, with their camels bearing spicery, and balm, and myrrh, going to carry it down to Egypt." See the young adventurer; he has received a certain sum from his father, and goes to another town, where he has relations or friends, and he *cautiously* commences his business; he never loses sight of frugality; and should he, in the course of a few years, have gained a competency, he *returns* to his native place, there to husband out his days. But should he not prosper, he goes to another town, for his affairs are so arranged in reference to rents and other matters, he finds no difficulty in removing. But another trader will not thus settle; he carries in two or three bags various spices, (which are needed by every family,) and gums, and drugs, or cloth and silk, and muslins, or jewels, or precious stones, and after a year or so he returns with the proceeds of his journey.—Roberts.

Ver. 15. For that ye *ought* to say, If the Lord will, we shall live, and do this, or that.

It was a custom among the Jews to begin all things with God. They undertook nothing without this holy and devout parenthesis, *If God will.* They otherwise expressed it, *if the name please;* or, *if the name determine so.* The phrase was so common that they abbreviated it, using a letter for a word. But this was not peculiar to the Jews; it was common with all the eastern people. Few books are written in Arabic, but they begin with the word *bismillah—in the name of God.* With the Greeks the expression is, συν Θεω: with the Latins, *Deo volente.*—Burder.

CHAPTER V.

Ver. 7. Be patient, therefore, brethren, unto the coming of the Lord. Behold, the husbandman waiteth for the precious fruit of the earth, and hath long patience for it, until he receive the early and latter rain.

In our climate, where it rains at all times of the year, we have no notion of "early and latter rain;" but nothing is more natural than this division in a climate like that of Palestine, where in the summer months it seldom or never rains. It was not till after the autumnal equinox, about the seed-time, when the Jews began their civil year, that the autumnal or winter rains set in; and these they called the early rains; the latter rain was that which fell in March and April, towards harvest time. "The rain," says Korte, "which falls in October, November, and December, is called the early rain, and that which comes in March and April, the latter rain. Respecting this latter rain, it is to be observed, that about the time of the greatest heat, there are many years when it rains only a few hours, or half a day, or at the outside two or three days successively. This rain is extremely propitious to the standing nellu, (rice, resembling our barley,) which is beginning to ripen, and needs nothing more than such a good wetting, to make the grain fuller and more solid, and to mature it. This rain, therefore, which comes in the hot season, is very different from the rain in the rainy season, and is very favourable to the standing corn. In the rainy season, at the end of the year, as soon as it begins to rain copiously, and the ground is thereby softened, and rendered fit for the plough, the farmer loses no time to commence his operations and sow his grain."—Rosenmuller.

Ver. 14. Is any sick among you? let him call for the elders of the church; and let them pray over him, anointing him with oil in the name of the Lord.

"In Yemen, the anointing of the body is believed to strengthen and protect it from the heat of the sun, by which the inhabitants of this province, as they wear so little clothing, are very liable to suffer. Oil, by closing up the pores of the skin, is supposed to prevent that too copious transpiration which enfeebles the frame; perhaps, too, these Arabians think a glistening skin a beauty. When the intense heat comes in, they always anoint their bodies with oil. At Sana, all the Jews, and many of the Mohammedans, have their bodies anointed whenever they find themselves indisposed." (Niebuhr.) That in some degree explains the direction of the apostle James, the meaning of which will be, to do that solemnly for the purpose of healing, which was often done medicinally; and accordingly we find Solomon, in many places of his Proverbs, speaking of administering ointment, which rejoices the heart, which may be a healing medicine to the navel, &c.—Burder.

THE FIRST EPISTLE GENERAL OF PETER.

CHAPTER I.

Ver. 4. To an inheritance incorruptible, and undefiled, and that fadeth not away, reserved in heaven for you.

See on 1 Cor. 9. 25.

CHAPTER III.

Ver. 3. Whose adorning, let it not be that outward *adorning* of platting the hair, and of wearing of gold, or of putting on of apparel.

The eastern females wear their hair, which the prophet emphatically calls the "instrument of their pride," very long, and divided into a great number of tresses. In Barbary, the ladies all affect to have their hair hang down to the ground, which, after they have collected into one lock, they bind and plat with ribands; a piece of finery which the apostle marks with disapprobation: "Whose adorning, let it not be that outward adorning of platting the hair, and of wearing of gold, or of putting on of apparel." Not that he condemns in absolute terms all regard to neatness and elegance in dress and appearance, but only an undue attention to these things; his meaning plainly is: "Whose adorning, let it not chiefly consist in that outward adorning of platting the hair, but rather let it be the hidden man of the heart, in that which is not corruptible, even the ornament of a meek and quiet spirit, which is, in the sight of God, of great price." The way in which the apostle uses the negative particle in this text, is a decisive proof that this is his true meaning; it extends to every member of the sentence; and by consequence, if it prohibit the platting of hair, it equally prohibits the putting on of apparel. But it never could be his design to forbid women to wear clothes, or to be decently and neatly dressed; therefore, the negative must have only a comparative sense, instructing us in the propriety and necessity of attending more to the dispositions of the mind, than to the adorning of the body. And as one inspired writer cannot, in reality, contradict another, the command of Paul must be explained in the same way, not as an absolute, but comparative prohibition: "In like manner, that women adorn themselves in modest apparel, with shamefacedness and sobriety, not with," or, according to this view, rather than with "broidered hair, or gold, or pearls, or costly array." Where nature has been less liberal in its ornaments, the defect is supplied by art, and foreign is procured to be interwoven with the natural hair. The males, on the contrary, shave all the hair of their heads, excepting one lock; and those who wear their hair are stigmatized as effeminate. The apostle's remark on this subject, corresponds entirely with the custom of the East, as well as with the original design of the Creator: "Does not even nature itself teach you, that if a man have long hair, it is a shame unto him? But if a woman have long hair, it is a glory to her; for her hair is given her for a covering." The men in the East, Chardin observes, are shaved; the women nourish their hair with great fondness, which they lengthen by tresses, and tufts of silk, down to the heels.—Paxton.

THE SECOND EPISTLE GENERAL OF PETER.

CHAPTER III.

Ver. 12. Looking for and hasting unto the coming of the day of God, wherein the heavens being on fire shall be dissolved, and the elements shall melt with fervent heat.

The word "unto" has here been supplied without authority. The original (*speudontas teen parousian*) exhibits no preposition, and properly requires a transitive rendering, viz. *accelerating, or hastening on, the coming*, &c. Thus understood, the words convey the very interesting and solemn intimation, that Christians are not only earnestly to *expect* the great day of God, the day of the restitution of all things, but by their devoted lives and a pre-eminent sanctity of spirit, they are to be instrumental in *expediting* its approach. According to their conduct, as marked by all manner of holy conversation and godliness, or the reverse, will be the speediness or the tardiness of its arrival.—Bush.

SMYRNA.—Rev. 2. 8 Page 643.

THE GENERAL EPISTLE OF JUDE.

Ver. 4. For there are certain men crept in unawares, who were before of old ordained to this condemnation; ungodly men, turning the grace of our God into lasciviousness, and denying the only Lord God, and our Lord Jesus Christ.

Those who were summoned before the courts of justice were said to be προγεγραμμενοι εις κρισιν, because they were cited to appear, by posting up their names in some public place; and the judgment of the court was published or declared in writing. Such persons the Romans called proscriptos, or proscribed, that is, whose names were posted up in writing, in some public place, as persons doomed to die, with a reward offered to any that should kill them. These are the terms which the apostle Jude applies to the ungodly, who had crept unawares into the church: they were before of old, προγεγραμμενοι, ordained to this condemnation; persons who must not only give an account of their crimes to God, but are proscribed or destined to the punishment which they deserve. In Persia, malefactors were not allowed to look on the king; this was the reason, that as soon as Haman was considered a criminal they covered his face. From Pococke we find the custom still continues, for speaking of the artifice by which an Egyptian bey was taken off, he says, "A man being brought before him like a malefactor just taken, with his hands behind him as if tied, and a napkin put over his head, as malefactors commonly have, when he came into his presence, suddenly shot him dead."—Paxton.

THE REVELATION OF JOHN THE DIVINE.

CHAPTER I.

Ver. 9. I John, who also am your brother, and companion in tribulation, and in the kingdom and patience of Jesus Christ, was in the isle that is called Patmos, for the word of God, and for the testimony of Jesus Christ.

Patmos has an excellent harbour, and the town, being situated on the loftiest part of the island, makes a pretty appearance on entering. The houses, being constructed of a white freestone, have a peculiarly neat aspect. It has been calculated that the town has an elevation of nearly five hundred feet above the level of the sea. In its centre is a large convent dedicated to St. John the Evangelist, who was banished to this island. Here he wrote his Revelation. We saw, in walking to the summit of the hill, the grotto in which he is said to have composed them. The convent has a resident bishop, with a considerable number of monks, and is a college for the education of young men of the Greek persuasion. In those parts of the island which the inhabitants are able to cultivate, we saw several small fields, or patches of corn, banked up with stones to prevent the soil from being washed away by the rains. It appeared, however, to be capable of producing but an inconsiderable quantity of grain. The inhabitants procure sheep and cattle from the neighbouring islands. The town contains about two hundred houses. The women are to the men in proportion of five to one. (Wittman.)—Burder.

CHAPTER II.

Ver. 1. Unto the angel of the church of Ephesus write; These things saith he that holdeth the seven stars in his right hand, who walketh in the midst of the seven golden candlesticks.

See on Acts 18. 19.

Ver. 8. And unto the angel of the church in Smyrna write; These things saith the first and the last, which was dead, and is alive.

Smyrna, situated at the extremity of a beautiful bay on the coast of Asia Minor, was one of the principal cities of the ancient region of Ionia: its early history is involved in some obscurity. According to the geographer Strabo, it derived its name from an Amazon, so called, who, having conquered Ephesus, had in the first instance transmitted her appellation to that city. The Ephesians afterward founded the town to which it has since been appropriated. Herodotus, however, states that Smyrna originally belonged to the Æolians, who received into the city some Colophonian exiles. These subsequently taking advantage of a festival held without the town, to which festival the Smyrnæans resorted in great numbers, shut the gates and became masters of the place. From that time Smyrna ceased to be an Æolian city, but was received into the Ionian confederacy. Of all the different cities which laid claim to the honour of being the birth-place of Homer, Smyrna seems to assert her claim to that distinction with the greatest zeal and plausibility.

Though the Smyrnæans successfully resisted the attacks of Gyges, king of Lydia, they were subjugated by his descendant, Alyattes; and in consequence of this event the city sunk into decay, and was deserted for the space of four hundred years. Alexander proposed to rebuild it; which design was carried into effect by Antigonus and Lysimachus, the latter of whom completed the new city; the streets of which are said to have been remarkably handsome, being well paved, and drawn at right angles. Numerous fine porticoes, temples, theatres, and a public library, with the splendid and lofty acropolis, rendered it one of the most beautiful cities of Ionia. Various grants and privileges were conferred upon the Smyrnæans by the Roman senate, for the part which they had taken during the wars with Antiochus and Mithridates. Under the Roman emperors, Smyrna flourished greatly; and its schools of eloquence and philosophy were held in considerable repute. Under the Greek emperors Smyrna experienced great vicissitudes. Having been taken by Tzachas, a Turkish chief, towards the close of the eleventh century, it was nearly destroyed by a Greek fleet under the command of John Ducas: the Emperor Comnenus subsequently restored it, but it again suffered very severely from a siege which it sustained against the forces of Tamerlane. Not long after this event it fell into the hands of the Turks, in whose possession it has remained ever since.

Modern Smyrna, by the Turks called Ismir, is beautifully situated at the foot of a lofty mountain, that stretches along the shore to a great extent, and has upon its summit the castellated building seen on the right of our engraving, which looks towards the bay. From this elevation the prospect is truly grand; and this is perhaps the finest port in Asia, as a large fleet might ride in it, and vessels receive and discharge their cargoes close to the shore. Upon this mountain was founded one of those churches which became the peculiar care of the apostle John, who addressed to its angel (presiding minister or bishop) the solemn admonitions in Rev. ii. 8—11. This church is dedicated to Polycarp, the first bishop of Smyrna, who suffered martyrdom here A. D. 166, being committed to the flames. The population is commonly estimated at 100,000 or 110,000; but the Rev. John Hartley, who was here in the year 1825, is of opinion that it is greatly overcharged. He thinks that Smyrna does not contain many more than 75,000 inhabitants; of whom about 45,000 are Turks, 10,000 Greeks, 8000 Armenians, 8000 Jews, and less than 1000 Europeans of different nations. The English residents may be upwards of one hundred: they dwell in the British factory, which is very extensive, and is enclosed with gates. The streets are narrow, and many of the houses, which are built of clay, are low; most of them have roofs of pantiles, some of which are flat, while others are gaudily painted. There are twenty mosques: the Greeks have three churches; the Armenians, one; the Latins, two; and the Protestants, two: the Jews have eight synagogues. Frank street, where the Europeans reside, and in which many sign-boards are exhibited, is by far the best street in Smyrna: by the English it has been named Bond street; but the Turks call it Ghul Mahala, or the Rose Quarter.

Smyrna has been subject to several awful visitations. In 1743 it was destroyed by fire, and in 1750 by an earthquake; in 1752, 1758, and 1760, it was depopulated by plague; fire again consumed almost the whole of it in 1763, 1769, and 1778; and in 1814 there were 40,000 persons cut off by the plague. Earthquakes and the plague, indeed, are the great calamities of this place: the condition of the Christians residing here (which is not the most secure under the Turkish government) is said to be better than in that of any other of the sites of the seven churches mentioned in the Apocalypse, as if the promise was still in some measure made good to Smyrna:—"Fear none of those things which thou shalt suffer...... Be thou faithful unto death, and I will give thee a crown of life." (Rev. ii. 10.)—HORNE.

Ver. 12. And to the angel of the church in Pergamos write; These things saith he which hath the sharp sword with two edges.

Pergamos, or Pergamus, was the ancient metropolis of Mysia, and the residence of the Attalian kings, who collected here a noble library, containing two hundred thousand volumes, which was afterward transported to Egypt by Cleopatra, and added to the library at Alexandria. It is situated on the right bank of the river Caïcus, about sixty miles to the north of Smyrna.

Against the church at Pergamus was adduced the charge of partial instability; but to its wavering faith was promised the all-powerful protection of God. (Rev. ii. 12—17.) The errors of Balaam and of the Nicolaitans have been purged away; Pergamus has been preserved from the destroyer; and three thousand Christians, out of a population of fourteen or fifteen thousand inhabitants, now cherish the rites of their holy religion in the same spot where it was planted by the Apostle Paul; though the poor Greeks are restricted to one small and mean church, under the Acropolis, or citadel of the ancient city, where the hymn of praise to their Redeemer is whispered, rather than sung, for fear of offending the fanatical Turks.

Numerous ancient ruins of a fortress, a theatre, and a naumachia, attest the magnificence of this once royal city. The modern town of Bergamo is seen through the magnificent arch on the right of our engraving. It lies partly on the slope of the hill, and partly in the plain. On the summit of the hill, upon the left, is the Acropolis, on which is a castle nearly covering its whole summit, including about eight acres, together with some remains of a heathen temple. A neighbouring cemetery has, for ages, been supplied with marble embellishments from the theatre, which are collected in great profusion to ornament the graves, near to which, if not on that site itself, was once placed the celebrated temple of Æsculapius, which, among other privileges, had that of an asylum. Here also are massive ruins of the church of Agios Theologos, conjectured to be one of those which the Emperor Theodosius caused to be erected. There is another ancient church in the town, that of Saint Sophia, which, about thirty years since, was desecrated by being converted into a Turkish mosque. The scenery from the Acropolis is grand, but sad. The fine plain before Pergamus, which seems ready to start into fertility at a touch, is sparingly cultivated, except on the very edges of the town; but that touch is wanting. The unrestrained flood-courses of the Caïcus and its tributary streams have cut the plain into broad sandy veins.

In 1828, when this place was visited by Mr. Macfarlane, a collection, in a Greek school, of about fifty volumes, in Romaic, or modern Greek, was called "the library," and represented the ancient store of two hundred thousand volumes, which had been formed by the munificent monarchs of Pergamus: and a dirty little Italian quack, ignorant and insolent, was head practitioner of medicine in the city which gave birth to Galen, and of which Æsculapius was the tutelary divinity. The town was as dull as the grave, except during the night, when, as it happened to be the Ramazan of the Turks, there was some stir among the Mohammedan portion of the inhabitants.—HORNE.

Ver. 17. He that hath an ear, let him hear what the Spirit saith unto the churches; To him that overcometh will I give to eat of the hidden manna, and will give him a white stone, and in the stone a new name written, which no man knoweth, saving he that receiveth *it*.

It was a custom among the ancients to give their votes by white or black stones; with these they condemned the guilty, with those acquitted the innocent. In allusion to this ancient custom, our Lord promises to give the spiritual conqueror "a white stone; and in the stone a new name written, which no man knoweth, saving he that receiveth it;" the white stone of absolution or approbation, and inseparably connected with it, a new name of dignity and honour, even that of a child of God and heir of glory, which is known only to himself, or the inhabitants of that world to which he shall be admitted, and who have already received it. When sentence of condemnation was pronounced, if the case was capital, the witnesses put their hands on the head of the criminal, and said, Thy blood be upon thine own head. To this custom the Jews alluded, when they cried out at the trial of Christ, "His blood be on us, and on our children." Then was the malefactor led to execution, and none were allowed openly to lament his misfortune. His hands were secured with cords, and his feet with fetters; a custom which furnished David with an affecting allusion, in his lamentation over the dust of Abner: "Thy hands were not bound, nor thy feet put in fetters."—PAXTON.

CHAPTER III.

Ver. 1. And unto the angel of the church in Sardis write; These things saith he that hath the seven Spirits of God, and the seven stars: I know thy works, that thou hast a name, that thou livest, and art dead.

Sardis, or Sardes, the capital of the country of Lydia, in Asia, was a city of great antiquity, the founder of which is not certainly known. It was situated in a fertile plain, at the foot of the northern slope of Mount Tmolus; which rears its majestic head in the background of our engraving, and commands an extensive view over the circumjacent country. The river Pactolus, (now an insignificant brook,) which

PERGAMUS.—Rev. 2:12. Page 644.

is also seen in our view, flowed through the forum. To the south of the plain, on which Sardis was erected, stood the temple of Cybele, the fabled mother of the gods, according to pagan mythology: it was a very ancient and magnificent edifice, constructed of white marble. Of this temple the two noble columns which are delineated in the foreground of our engraving, together with a few mutilated fragments of other columns scattered on the sward or sunk in it, are all that now remain: these columns are buried nearly to the half of their height in the soil, which has accumulated in the valley since their erection, most probably by the destruction of the continually crumbling eminence, on which stood the acropolis or citadel. The columns which have been destroyed have been blown up by gunpowder, reduced to blocks, and sold to masons and cutters of tombstones: and as other materials are wanted, the two columns which are yet standing in all probability will be blasted in the same manner; and the traveller, who may hereafter visit this spot, will vainly seek for a vestige of the Sardeian temple of Cybele.

After experiencing various fortunes, Sardis became a great and flourishing city in the reign of Crœsus, king of Lydia, by the fame of whose riches and hospitality men of talents and learning were attracted thither. On the overthrow of this monarch by Cyrus, B. C. 545, Sardis continued to be the chief town of the Persian dominions in this part of Asia. On the revolt excited by Aristagoras and Histiæus, the Ionians, with the aid of an Athenian force, surprised this city, except the citadel, which was defended by a numerous Persian garrison. Though burnt to the ground on this occasion, Sardis was again rebuilt; and, soon after the defeat of the Persians at the battle of the Granicus, it surrendered to Alexander the Great, who commanded that the Lydians should regain their liberty, and resume their ancient laws and usages. During the reigns of the Greek sovereigns in Asia, this city sustained numerous reverses; and from Antiochus, the last king of Syria, it passed into the possession of the Romans, having surrendered to the two Scipios, B. C. 187. Sardis was indebted to the Emperor Tiberius for its restoration, after a disastrous earthquake, which had reduced it to a heap of ruins.

We have no information in the New Testament at what time Christianity was planted at Sardis; but probably it was not till after Saint Paul had founded the church at Ephesus; and there can be little doubt that the metropolis of Lydia is included in St. Luke's declaration, that "all they which dwelt in Asia heard the word of the Lord Jesus, both Jews and Greeks," (Acts xix. 10,) and also in the salutation of "all the churches of Asia," (1 Cor. xvi. 19.) This is rendered manifest by the book of Revelation, where Sardis is expressly named among the seven churches of that province. When the warning voice was addressed "Unto the angel" or bishop "of the church in Sardis," it was evidently in a declining state. (Rev. iii. 1—5.) Subsequently, this city became the seat of a bishoprick; and ecclesiastical history mentions more than one council as having been held here.

Sardis continued to be a flourishing city, through the Roman emperors, to the close of the Byzantine dynasty. In the eleventh century the Turks took possession of it, and, two centuries later, it was nearly destroyed by Tamerlane. This once-celebrated capital of the Lydian kings is now reduced to a wretched village called Sart, consisting of a few mud huts occupied by Turkish herdsmen, and erected in the midst of extensive ruins; among which Lieut. Col. Leake observed the remains of a large Christian church.

"If" (says the Rev. Mr. Arundell, who visited this place in 1833) "I should be asked what impresses the mind most strongly on beholding Sardis, I should reply, its indescribable *solitude*, like the darkness in Egypt,—darkness that could be felt. So the deep solitude of the spot, once the 'Lady of kingdoms,' produces a corresponding feeling of *desolate abandonment* in the mind, which can never be forgotten. Connect this feeling with the message in the Apocalypse to the church of Sardis:—'Thou hast a name that thou livest, and art dead . . . . . I will come on thee as a thief, and thou shalt not know at what hour I will come upon thee.' (Rev. iii. 1, 3.) And then look around and ask, 'Where are the churches, where are the Christians of Sardis?' The tumuli beyond the Hermus reply, 'All dead,' suffering the infliction of the threatened judgments of God."—HORNE.

Ver. 7. And to the angel of the church in Philadelphia write; These things saith he that is holy, he that is true, he that hath the key of David, he that openeth, and no man shutteth; and shutteth, and no man openeth.

Philadelphia was a very considerable city of Lydia, in Asia Minor, which derived its name from its founder, Attalus Philadelphus, brother of Eumenes, king of Pergamus. It stands in the plain of the Hermus, about midway between that river and the determination of Mount Tmolus. Besides the Hermus, which divides the plain, numerous brooks and rills give beauty, verdure, and fertility, to the neighbourhood; which, however, is but little cultivated.

This city has, at various times, suffered greatly from earthquakes. Tacitus mentions it among the towns restored by Tiberius after a more than ordinary calamity of this kind. (Annal. lib. ii. c. 47.) Not long before the date of the apocalyptic epistle, (Rev. iii. 7—13,) Philadelphia had suffered so much from earthquakes, that it had been in a great measure deserted by its inhabitants, which may, in some degree, account for the poverty of its church, as described in that epistle. "Philadelphia appears to have resisted the attacks of the Turks, in 1312, with more success than other cities. At a distance from the sea, forgotten by the emperor, encompassed on all sides by the Turks, her valiant citizens defended their religion and freedom above fourscore years, and at length capitulated with the proudest of the Ottomans, (Bajazet,) in 1390. Among the Greek colonies and churches of Asia, Philadelphia is still erect—a column in a scene of ruins." Whatever may be lost of the spirit of Christianity, there is still the form of a Christian church in this city, which is now called Allah-Shehr, or the City of God, by the Turks, and which possesses a few remains of heathen antiquity.

Philadelphia is now a considerable town, spreading over the slopes of three or four hills. Many remains of the walls, which once encompassed it, are now standing, but with large gaps: the materials of its fortifications are small stones with strong cement. The Rev. Mr. Arundell (by whom our view is sketched) is of opinion that these walls are not much older than the last days of the lower empire, if indeed they are so ancient. He describes the passage through the streets as being filthy in the extreme; though the view of the place, as the traveller approaches it, is very beautiful. The prospect from the hill is magnificent: highly cultivated gardens and vineyards lie on the back sides of the town, and before it is one of the richest and most extensive plains in Asia.

Philadelphia contains about three hundred houses occupied by Greeks, and nearly three thousand which are inhabited by Turks. There are twenty-five churches, in five only of which divine service is performed once every week: in the larger number it is celebrated but once a year. A solitary fragment is shown as the remains of the church of the Apocalypse, dedicated to St. John.—HORNE.

Ver. 14. And unto the angel of the church of the Laodiceans, write; These things saith the Amen, the faithful and true Witness, the beginning of the creation of God.

Laodicea was one of the largest cities in the province of Phrygia Magna, at the commencement of the Christian æra; though, originally, it was an inconsiderable place. This increase was chiefly owing to the fertility of its surrounding soil, and to the munificent bequests and donations of various opulent individuals. Its earlier name was Diospolis; but after it had been enlarged by Antiochus II. king of Syria, it was called Laodicea, in honour of his consort Laodice. Situated on a volcanic eminence, this city was frequently exposed to earthquakes, in common with the surrounding towns and villages. Its inhabitants derived great profit from the sale of the fine wools produced by their flocks, which fed in the adjacent plains.

In the early age of Christianity, Laodicea possessed a flourishing church, St. Paul's zeal for which is attested by the mention which he makes of it in his Epistle to the Colossians:—"I would that ye knew what great conflict I have for you, and for them at Laodicea, and for as many as have not seen my face in the flesh." (ii. 1.) And, "when this epistle is read among you, cause that it be read also in the church of the Laodiceans; and that ye likewise read the epistle from Laodicea." (iv. 16.) From the mention here made of the epistle from Laodicea, it has been conjectured that the Apostle had written a special letter to the converts in that city, which is now lost; but it is with more probability supposed that he refers to another of his epistles, either that to the Ephesians, or the first Epistle to Timothy.

The book of the Revelation of St. John contains a severe rebuke of the Laodiceans for their lukewarmness and worldly-mindedness, and threatens them with that ruin which has been so completely accomplished. (Rev. iii. 14—19.) In our engraving several arches of a once magnificent aqueduct are seen; and the remains of an amphitheatre and other edifices attest the ancient splendour and extent of Laodicea. Inscribed altars, columns, friezes, and cornices, are dispersed among the houses and burying-grounds. The doom of the church at Laodicea seems to have been more severe and terrible than that of the other apocalyptic churches. Not a single Christian is said to reside at Laodicea, which is even more solitary than Ephesus. The latter city has a prospect of a rolling sea or a whitening sail to enliven its decay; the former sits in widowed loneliness. Its temples are desolate, and the stately edifices of ancient Laodicea are now peopled by wolves and jackals. The prayers of the Mohammedan mosque are the only prayers heard near the yet splendid ruins of the city, on which the prophetic denunciation seems to have been fully executed in its utter rejection as a church.—HORNE.

CHAPTER IV.

Ver. 10. The four and twenty elders fall down before him that sat on the throne, and worship him that liveth for ever and ever, and cast their crowns before the throne.

This short expedition was brought to a close by the personal submission of Abool Fyze Khan, who, attended by all his court, proceeded to the tents of Nadir Shah, and laid his crown, and other ensigns of royalty, at the feet of the conqueror, who assigned him an honourable place in his assembly, and in a few days afterward restored him to his throne.—MALCOLM'S HISTORY OF PERSIA.

CHAPTER VII.

Ver. 2. And I saw another angel ascending from the east, having the seal of the living God: and he cried with a loud voice to the four angels, to whom it was given to hurt the earth and the sea.

See on Ezek. 9. 2.

Ver. 3. Saying, Hurt not the earth, neither the sea, nor the trees, till we have sealed the servants of our God in their foreheads.

See on ch. 13. 16.

Ver. 9. After this, I beheld, and lo, a great multitude, which no man could number, of all nations, and kindreds, and people, and tongues, stood before the throne, and before the Lamb, clothed with white robes, and palms in their hands.

See on John 12. 13, 14, and 1 Cor. 9. 25.

Ver. 13. And one of the elders answered, saying unto me, What are these which are arrayed in white robes? and whence came they? 14. And I said unto him, Sir, thou knowest. And he said to me, These are they which came out of great tribulation, and have washed their robes, and made them white in the blood of the Lamb.

In order to mark with absolute precision the meaning of the original in the latter clause, the preposition "in" should be translated "by." It is not the purport of the passage, to intimate that the robes of the Martyrs and Confessors here spoken of, were actually *died in the blood* of the Lamb, as Joseph's coat was in that of the wild beast slain by his brethren for the purpose; for this would have made them *red*, not *white*, at least unless we allow the words to do the greatest violence to metaphorical congruity. But the sacred writers are not apt to outrage propriety and congruity in this manner. In the present case, the idea doubtless is, that it was *by* the blood of Christ, by suffering unto death for his name's sake, by shedding their blood for his cause, which he graciously accounted as the shedding of his own, that they had been enabled to make their raiment white, or, in other words, had become entitled to be arrayed, by way of reward, in the white robes of salvation. Their own sufferings, in connexion with the merits of the Saviour's blood, had been the means of conferring this honour upon them. The blood of the Lamb was rather the medium *by* which, than the fountain *in* which, their garments had been thus blanched into the lustrous and pearly whiteness of the vesture of the risen, rewarded, and beatified saints.—BUSH.

Ver. 17. For the Lamb, which is in the midst of the throne, shall feed them, and shall lead them unto living fountains of waters, and God shall wipe away all tears from their eyes.

See on Ps. 23. 1—3.

CHAPTER VIII.

Ver. 4. And the smoke of the incense *which came* with the prayers of the saints, ascending up before God, out of the angel's hand.

There is a pagan rite, mentioned by C. Dampier, as practised by the nobility of Tonquin, which greatly illustrates this passage. When they pray with their families, the prayer is written upon a paper; and being recited by a proper officer, is thrown into a fire of coals, where, probably, incense or some other perfume is thrown at the same time, so that the prayer ascends up with the smoke.—DAUBUZ.

CHAPTER IX.

Ver. 1. And the fifth angel sounded, and I saw a star fall from heaven unto the earth; and to him was given the key of the bottomless pit. 2. And he opened the bottomless pit; and there arose a smoke out of the pit, as the smoke of a great furnace; and the sun and the air were darkened by reason of the smoke of the pit.

Commentators at the present day are almost universally agreed in regarding the fifth trumpet as symbolizing and predicting the appearance of the Arabian impostor, his spurious religion, and his Saracen followers. But as it is by no means evident how Mohammed himself can properly be represented as "a star falling from heaven," the usual symbol of an apostate Christian teacher, or of a number of them, we apprehend the design of the Holy Spirit in this imagery to be, to teach us that *Mohammedanism is to be considered as the fruit or product of a Christian heresy.* The star *had* fallen before the time of the false prophet, in the person of Arius, and other gross heretics; and as the consequence of their apostacy from the truth, the providence of God so ordered it, that the desolating delusion of Mohammedanism should arise and overspread some of the fairest portions of the Church. This view of the arch-imposture of Islamism has been taken by some very able writers of modren times, particularly by Mr. Whitaker, in his "Origin of Arianism." The grand heresies, therefore, of the Christian church, previous to the time of Mohammed, seem to be here personified in the fallen star, and represented as being instrumental in introducing this master-plague of error and superstition into the world. The poetical machinery of the vision is supposed to be taken from the sacred oracular caves of the ancient Pagans, which were often thought to communicate with the sea, or the great abyss, and which were specially valued, when (like that at Delphi) they emitted an intoxicating vapour: it is used, therefore, with singular propriety in foretelling the rise of a religious imposture. There may possibly be an allusion also to the cave of Hera, whither the prophet was wont to retire for the purpose of excogitating his system, and from which it really emanated. The opening of the bottomless pit, therefore, and the letting out the vapour and smoke of the infernal regions, aptly represents the wicked and diabolical system of religion, the dense and noxious fumes of the corrupt theology which he broached, and by means of which so large a portion of Christendom was finally obscured and involved in darkness. The preternatural darkening of the sun foreshows the eclipse of the true religion; and that of the air prefigures the uncontrolled dominion of the powers of darkness. As a striking coincidence with the signs here predicted, it is worthy of note, that a remarkable comet immediately preceded the birth of Mohammed; and that an eclipse of the sun, of extraordinary degree and duration, attended the first announcement of his pretended mission.—BUSH.

Ver. 3. And there came out of the smoke locusts upon the earth; and unto them was given power, as the scorpions of the earth have power.

Arabia has long been noted for giving birth to prodigious swarms of locusts, which often overspread and lay waste the neighbouring countries; and it is remarkable, that in a genuine Arabian romance, the locust is introduced as the national emblem of the Ishmaelites. The symbol, therefore, of the locusts issuing out of the smoke strikingly represents the armies of the Saracens, the martial followers of the prophet, first engendered, as it were, amid the fumes of his religion, and then marching forth, at his command, to conquer and to proselyte the world. The pages of history must be consulted to learn the devastations of those hosts of destructive Saracens, which, under the guidance of Mohammed and his successors, alighted upon and wasted the apocalyptic earth. Yet, notwithstanding the phantasms that came forth from the pit of the abyss bore a general resemblance to locusts, they were marked by several peculiarities, by which they were more perfectly adapted to typify the people designed to be thus shadowed out. These we shall consider as we proceed.—BUSH.

Ver. 4. And it was commanded them that they should not hurt the grass of the earth, neither any green thing, neither any tree; but only those men which have not the seal of God in their foreheads.

By the command that they should not hurt the grass, nor the trees, but *men* only, it is evident that these were not natural, but symbolical locusts; and also that they were under providential control. The same thing appears from other attributes assigned them, which plainly belong to the *objects signified*, and not to the *sign;* as the human face, the woman's hair, the golden crowns, the iron breastplates. But it is very common in the symbolic diction of prophecy, to find the *literal* and the *allegorical* sense intermixed, and that even in the same passage. We are thus furnished with a clew to the real meaning of the symbols. By the precept here given, the emblematic locusts were required to act in a manner perfectly dissimilar to the ravages of natural locusts: and yet how faithfully the command was obeyed, may be inferred from the following very remarkable injunction of the Calif Abubeker to Yezid, upon setting out on the expedition against Syria, the *first* undertaking of the Saracens in the way of foreign conquest. It can scarcely be doubted, that these instructions have been preserved, under the providence of God, for the express purpose of furnishing an illustration of this prophetic text. "Remember," said Abubeker, "that you are always in the presence of God, on the verge of death, in the assurance of judgment, and the hope of paradise. When you fight the battles of the Lord, acquit yourselves like men, without turning your backs; but let not your victory be stained with the blood of women or children. *Destroy no palm-trees, nor burn any fields of corn. Cut down no fruit-trees; nor do any mischief to cattle, only such as you kill to eat.* When you make any covenant, stand to it, and be as good as your word. As you go on, you will find some religious persons, who live retired in monasteries, and propose to themselves to serve God that way: let them alone, and neither kill them, nor destroy their monasteries. And you will find another sort of people, that belong to the synagogue of Satan, who have shaven crowns: be sure you cleave their sculls, and give them no quarter till they either turn Mohammedans, or pay tribute." It has accordingly been noticed, that those parts of the Roman empire which were left untouched by these Saracen hordes, were those in which, as it appears from history, the remnant of the true church of God was still found residing: they were only to hurt the men who had not the mark of God on their foreheads.—BUSH.

Ver. 5. And to them it was given that they should not kill them, but that they should be tormented five months: and their torment *was* as the torment of a scorpion, when he striketh a man.

Mr. Gibbon's undesigned commentary on these words will show how the commission was fulfilled. "The fair option of friendship or submission, or a battle, was proposed to the enemies of Mohammed. If they professed the creed of Islam, they were admitted to all the temporal and spiritual benefits of his primitive disciples, and marched under the same banners, to extend the religion they had embraced. The clemency of the prophet was decided by his interests; yet he seldom trampled on a prostrate enemy, and he seemed to promise, that on the payment of a tribute, the least guilty of his unbelieving subjects might be indulged in their worship." The period assigned for the power of the locusts, in this prediction, is "five months." Prophecy has its peculiar mode of computing time. A day for the most part stands for a year. Five months, therefore, of thirty days each, amount, in the computation of prophecy, to one hundred and fifty years. As five literal months is the utmost term of the duration of the natural plague of the locusts, so the prophetic five months accurately denote the period of the main conquests of the Saracen empire, computing from the appearance of Mohammed to the foundation of Bagdad. "Read," says Bishop Newton, "the history of the Saracens, and you will find that their greatest exploits were performed, and their greatest conquests made, within the space of five prophetic months, or one hundred and fifty years,—between the year 612, when Mohammed opened the bottomless pit, and began publicly to teach and propagate his imposture; and the year 762, when Almansor built Bagdad, and called it the City of Peace." The comparison of the locusts' torments to that of the scorpion will be considered subsequently.—BUSH.

Ver. 6. And in those days shall men seek death, and shall not find it; and shall desire to die, and death shall flee from them.

This prediction has usually been considered as awfully expressive of the hopeless sufferings and despair of eastern Christendom, under the lawless insults, violences, and oppressions, systematically practised by their Saracen masters. We would not deny that this may have been alluded to; yet, as it would seem that men desirous of escaping suffering by death, might easily, in a thousand ways, have accomplished their object, it may be suggested, whether the Saracens themselves are not the persons here referred to, as coveting death in battle, from a view to the honour and the rewards of such a decease. The following passage from the Koran, is worthy of special note in this connexion. "Moreover, ye did sometimes wish for death, before that ye met it." On these words Sale remarks, in a note, "that several of Mohammed's followers, who were not present at Beder, wished for an opportunity of obtaining, in another action, the like honour as those had gained who fell martyrs in that event." The import of the language, therefore, may be, that God should give to the Moslem hosts such an uninterrupted tide of conquests, they should so uniformly come off victorious in their engagements, and that with such inconsiderable losses, that numbers, in the height of their enthusiasm, should pant in vain for the glorious privilege of dying in the field of battle.—BUSH.

Ver. 7. And the shapes of the locusts *were* like

unto horses prepared unto battle; and on their heads *were* as it were crowns like gold, and their faces *were* as the faces of men.

"Arabia," says Gibbon, "is, in the opinion of naturalists, the native country of the horse." The horsemanship of the Arabs has ever been an object of admiration. "The martial youth, under the banner of the emir, is ever on horseback, and in the field, to practise the exercise of the bow, the javelin, and the cimeter." In correspondence, therefore, with the hieroglyphic of the prophet, the strength of the Saracens consisted very much in their numerous cavalry, and the unrivalled speed of the Arabian coursers forms the most striking possible emblem of the rapid career of the Saracen armies.

"And on their heads were as it were crowns like gold, and their faces were as the faces of men."—"Make a point," says a precept of Mohammed, "of wearing *turbans;* because it is the way of angels." The turban, accordingly, has ever been the distinctive head-dress of the Arabs, and their boast has been, that they wore, as their common attire, those ornaments which among other people are the peculiar badges of royalty. The notice of the "faces of men" seems to be intended merely to afford a clew to the meaning of the emblem; to intimate, that not natural locusts, but human beings, were depicted under this symbol.—BUSH.

The Mamalukes wearing their beards long and rough, with grave and stern countenances, having strong and able bodies, used such cunning in all their fights and battles, that after they had given the first charge with their lances, they would by-and-by, with wonderful activity, use their bows and arrows, casting their targets behind them; and forthwith the horseman's mace, or crooked cimeter, as the manner of the battle or place required. Their horses were strong and courageous, in make and swiftness much like unto the Spanish jennets: and that which is of many hardly believed, so docile, that at certain signs or speeches of the rider, they would with their teeth reach him up from the ground a lance, an arrow, or such like thing; and as if they had known the enemy, run upon him with open mouth, and lash at him with their heels, and had by nature and custom learned not to be afraid of any thing. These courageous horses were commonly furnished with silver bridles, gilt trappings, rich saddles, their necks and breast armed with plates of iron: the horseman himself was commonly content with a coat of mail, or a breastplate of iron. The chief and wealthiest of them used head-pieces: the rest a linen covering of the head, curiously folded into many wreaths, wherewith they thought themselves safe enough against any handy strokes; the common soldiers used thrumbed caps, but so thick that no sword could pierce them.—KNOLLES.

Ver. 8. And they had hair as the hair of women, and their teeth were as *the teeth* of lions.
9. And they had breastplates, as it were breastplates of iron; and the sound of their wings *was* as the sound of chariots of many horses running to battle.

The Arabs, as Pliny testifies, wore their beards, or rather mustaches, as men, while their hair, like that of women, was flowing or platted. The "teeth like those of lions," has reference to the weapons and implements of war; and the "breastplates of iron," to the armour made use of by the Saracen troops in their expeditions. The "sound of their wings as the sound of chariots of many horses running to battle," is but a part of the same expressive imagery denoting warlike scenes and preparations.—BUSH.

Ver. 10. And they had tails like unto scorpions; and there were stings in their tails: and their power *was* to hurt men five months.

The interpretation of the symbols of the Apocalypse must be sought for in the Old Testament. From the following words of Isaiah (ch. ix. 14, 15) it appears that the tail of a beast denotes the false doctrines or the superstitions which he maintains: "Therefore the Lord will cut off from Israel head and tail, branch and rush, in one day. The ancient and honourable, he is the head; and *the prophet that teacheth lies, he is the tail.*" The emblem, therefore, strikingly represents the infliction of spiritual wounds by the propagation of poisonous and deadly errors and heresies. And nothing is more evident from the page of history, than that the Moslem followers of Mohammed have scattered, like scorpions, the venom of their doctrines behind them; and whether conquering or conquered, have succeeded in palming a new creed upon those with whom they have had to do. By this symbol, then, we are plainly taught, that the plague of the allegorical locusts consisted not only in the ravages of war, but in the successful propagation of a false religion, of which the doctrines should be as deleterious in a spiritual point of view, as the sting of a scorpion in a natural. In like manner, when it is said (ch. xii. 3, 4) of the "great red dragon having seven heads and ten horns, that his tail drew the third part of the stars of heaven, and did cast them to the earth," the explication is, that the antichristian power shadowed out by this formidable monster should be permitted to instil the most pernicious errors into the minds of the professed ministers of the truth, and thus bring about their entire defection from Christianity.—BUSH.

Ver. 11. And they had a king over them, *which is* the angel of the bottomless pit, whose name in the Hebrew tongue *is* Abaddon, but in the Greek tongue, he hath *his* name Apollyon.

Both these terms signify *destroyer.* Since the locusts are at once secular conquerors and the propagators of a false religion, their king must stand to them in the double relation of a temporal and spiritual head. Such accordingly were Mohammed and the Califs his successors, who must be viewed as jointly constituting the locust-king Abaddon; for in the usual language of prophecy, a king denotes, not any single individual, but a dynasty or kingdom. The chief of the locusts, when they first issued from the pit of the abyss, was Mohammed himself; but during the allotted period of the wo which they occasioned, the reigning destroyer was, of course, the reigning Calif. If, therefore, we were to suppose *the genius of Mohammedanism* under the Califs to be personified, and this symbolical personage to be designated by the most appropriate title, Abaddon, the destroyer, would be the appellation. As the portion of the prophecy thus far considered, has reference to the origin of Mohammed's imposture, and to the rise, progress, and conquests of the Saracens, its earliest abetters and propagators, so the remaining part announces the commencement and career of the Turkish power, the principal of its later supporters.—BUSH.

Ver. 13. And the sixth angel sounded, and I heard a voice from the four horns of the golden altar, which is before God.

It is impossible, from the train of events, and from the quarter of the world in which we are directed to look for the irruption of these prodigious multitudes of horsemen, to mistake to whom the prophecy refers. The four angels who are described as bound in the regions bordering on the river Euphrates, not *in* the river itself, are the four contemporary sultanies or dynasties, into which the empire of the Seljukian Turks was divided towards the close of the eleventh century: Persia, Kerman, Syria, and Rhoum. These sultanies, from different causes, were long restrained from extending their conquests beyond wha may be geographically termed the Euphratean regions, but towards the close of the thirteenth century, the four angels on the river Euphrates were loosed in the persons of their existing representatives, the united Ottoman and Seljukian Turks. Gibbon, the historian of the Decline and Fall of the Roman Empire, must of necessity be the guide to any English commentator on this part of the prophetic history. The following is his testimony as to the immense number of the Turkish cavalry: "As the subject nations marched under the standard of the Turks, *their cavalry, both men and horses, were proudly computed by millions.* On this occasion, *the myriads of the Turkish horse* overspread a

frontier of six hundred miles from Taurus to Erzeroum."
BUSH.

Ver. 17. And thus I saw the horses in the vision, and them that sat on them, having breastplates of fire, and of jacinth and brimstone: and the heads of the horses *were* as the heads of lions; and out of their mouths issued fire, and smoke, and brimstone. 18. By these three was the third part of men killed, by the fire, and by the smoke, and by the brimstone, which issued out of their mouths.

These prophetic characteristics of the Euphratean warriors accord in the most perfect manner with the description which history gives of the Turks. They brought immense armies into the field, chiefly composed of horse, and from their first appearance on the great political stage of nations, their costume has been peculiarly distinguished by the colours of scarlet, blue, and yellow, which are here denoted by the terms "fire," "jacinth," and "brimstone." Rycaut's "Present State of the Ottoman Empire," published towards the close of the seventeenth century, will satisfy the reader on this point.

"And the heads of the horses were as the heads of lions, and out of their mouths issued fire, and smoke, and brimstone." We have here a symbol which is not elsewhere to be met with in the scriptures. The prophetic horses are represented as vomiting out of their mouths "fire, and smoke, and brimstone," by which, it is added, "the third part of men was killed." Mede, Newton, Faber, and most other eminent expositors of the Revelation, agree in supposing that the flashes of fire attended by smoke and brimstone, which seemed to proceed from the mouths of the horses, were in reality *the flashes of artillery*. The Turks were among the first who turned to account the European invention of gunpowder in carrying on their wars. Cannon, the most deadly engine of modern warfare, were employed by Mohammed II. in his wars against the Greek empire; and it is said that he was indebted to his heavy ordnance for the reduction of Constantinople. The prophet, therefore, is to be considered as depicting the visionary scene of a field of battle, in which the cavalry and artillery are so mingled together, that while flashes of fire and dense clouds of smoke issued from the cannon, the horses' heads alone would be dimly discerned through the sulphureous mist, and would seem to the eye of the spectator to belch forth the smoky flames from their own mouths. As the design of this striking imagery is to describe the *appearances* rather than the *reality* of things, the prophet employs an expression, "in the vision," or rather "in vision," i. e. *apparently as it seemed*, which evidently conveys the idea that the phantasm of a battle scene was presented to the imagination. We may now see how far history confirms this interpretation: "Among the implements of destruction," says Mr. Gibbon, "he (Mohammed II.) studied with peculiar care the recent and tremendous discovery of the Latins; and his *artillery* surpassed whatever had yet appeared in the world." "The Ottoman *artillery* thundered on all sides, and the camp and city, the Greeks and Turks, *were involved in a cloud of smoke*, which could only be dispelled by the final deliverance or destruction of the Roman empire." "The great cannon of Mohammed *has been separately an important and visible object in the history of the times*. But that enormous engine, which required, it is said, seventy yoke of oxen and two thousand men to draw it, was flanked by two fellows almost of equal magnitude: the long order of *Turkish artillery* was pointed against the wall; fourteen batteries thundered at once on the most accessible places; and of one of these it is ambiguously expressed, that it was mounted with a hundred and thirty guns, or that it discharged a hundred and thirty bullets."—BUSH.

Ver. 19. For their power is in their mouth, and in their tails: for their tails *were* like unto serpents, and had heads, and with them they do hurt.

The emblematic import of the tail of a beast we have already considered. The imagery in the present symbol is slightly different from that of the Saracen locusts, which had the tails of scorpions; but the import is the same. Here the tails of the horses terminated in a serpent's head; and it is not a little remarkable, that the Turks have been in the habit, from the earliest periods of their history, of tying a knot in the extremity of the long flowing tails of their horses, when preparing for war; so that their resemblance to serpents with swelling heads must have been singularly striking. Striking too is the fact, that so slight a circumstance should have been adverted to by the historian so often quoted, who thought as little of being an organ to illustrate the predictions of scripture, as the Turks themselves did of being the agents to fulfil them. Speaking of Alp Arslan, the first Turkish invader of the Roman empire, he says, "With his own hands *he tied up his horse's tail*, and declared that if he were vanquished, that spot should be the place of his burial." The scope of the hieroglyphic here employed is to predict the propagation of a deadly imposture by the instrumentality of the same warlike power which should achieve such prodigious conquests. The event has corresponded with the prophecy. Like the Saracens of the first wo, the Turks were not merely secular conquerors. They were animated with all the wild fanaticism of a false religion; they professed and propagated the same theological system as their Arabian predecessors; they injured by their doctrines no less than by their conquests; and wherever they established their dominion, the Koran triumphed over the gospel. Thus writes Mr. Gibbon: "The whole body of the nation embraced the religion of Mohammed." "Twenty-five years after the death of Basil, his successors were suddenly assaulted by an unknown race of barbarians, who united *the Scythian valour* with the *fanaticism of new converts*."

Sufficient proof has now been afforded, if we mistake not, that the appearance of the Arabian prophet in the world, and the rise, progress, and results of his imposture, are clearly foretold in the sacred volume. Indeed, it would not be easy to specify any admitted subject of prophecy, upon which history and Providence have thrown a stronger or clearer light, than that which we have been considering. Interpreters have been justly struck at the surprising exactness of the delineations, and their perfect accordance with the details of history. "The prophetic truths," says Dr. Zouch, "comprised in the ninth chapter of the Apocalypse, are, of themselves, sufficient to stamp the mark of divinity upon that book. When I compare them with the page of history, I am filled with amazement. The Saracens, a people which did not exist in the time of John, and the Turks, a nation then utterly unknown, are there described in language the most appropriate and distinct." If, then, the considerations commonly adduced to account for the rise, progress, and reign of Mohammedanism, appear to be inadequate,—if the human causes usually quoted to explain the astonishing success of Mohammedan imposture still seem to us to leave many of the phenomena inexplicable, and the greatest revolution in the world connected with the history of the Church, stands forth an unsolved problem,—why should we hesitate to ascribe it directly to the determinate will and counsel of the Most High, and thus find a clew to all the mysteries connected with it? Why should we be anxious to escape the recognition of a Divine interference in the rise of this arch-heresy? If we have been correct in our interpretation of the preceding predictions of Daniel and John, the Mohammedan delusion is as real and as prominent a subject of prophecy, as any in the whole compass of the Bible. Now, to insist upon the operation of merely human causes in the production of an event which is truly a subject of prophecy, is in fact to take the government of the world out of the hands of God. And this principle pushed to the extreme will inevitably lower and impugn the sure word of prophecy; for it makes God the predicter of events over which, at the same time, he has no special superintendence or control. Such a principle cannot stand the least examination. When Daniel foretels the fortunes of the four great empires; or when Isaiah speaks of Cyrus by name, as one who should accomplish certain great purposes of the Infinite Mind, is it to be supposed, that the events predicted were to happen exclusive of Providential agency? As easily and as justly then we may acknowledge a special pre-ordainment in the case of

Mohammed, whose still more formidable dominion and more lasting and more fatal agency in the affairs of men, are equally the theme of unquestionable predictions. No admission of this nature militates with the free agency of man, or at all affects the moral character of his actions. The mere fact that an event is foreknown or foretold by the Deity, neither takes away nor weakens the accountability of the agents concerned. Of this, the whole scripture is full of proofs. But the reflecting reader will desire no further confirmation of so plain a position.—BUSH.

CHAPTER X.

Ver. 5. And the angel, which I saw stand upon the sea, and upon the earth, lifted up his hand to heaven, 6. And sware by him that liveth for ever and ever, who created heaven, and the things that therein are, and the earth, and the things that therein are, and the sea, and the things which are therein, that there should be time no longer: 7. But in the days of the voice of the seventh angel, when he shall begin to sound, the mystery of God should be finished, as he hath declared to his servants the prophets.

The solemn asseveration of the angel here cited is very frequently misunderstood. It contains no intimation of the actual and absolute cessation of time, for in the part of the prophecy in which it is introduced, the spirit of inspiration is not speaking of the end of the world, the winding up of all sublunary concerns, or of any thing pertaining to it, but of the ushering *into* the world of a state of triumph and glory. The object of the angel is simply to announce beforehand that this grand event shall take place, *without longer delay*, under the seventh trumpet. A translation that should give the exact scope of the original, would, disregarding the present punctuation, read thus: "that there should be delay no longer, than unto the days of the voice of the seventh angel," &c. The original word for 'time' (*chronos*) is in several instances in the sacred writings used in the sense of *delay*, as is also the verb *chronizo*, formed directly from it, as Matt. xxiv. 48, "And if that evil servant shall say in his heart, My Lord *delayeth* (chronizei) his coming." That the Greek *alla, but*, is used in the sense of *except, than, unless*, &c. is expressly shown by Schleusner, in his N. T. Lexicon. The conclusion therefore may be safely rested in, that the burden of the angel's oath in this place is not that time, considered in itself, should then end, but that the consummation of a certain great event, called the "finishing of the mystery of God," should not be deferred any longer than to the period of the seventh trumpet. What this event is, is clearly intimated Rev. xi. 15, "And the seventh angel sounded; and there were great voices in heaven, saying, The kingdoms of this world are become the kingdoms of our Lord and his Christ; and he shall reign for ever and ever." But this is an event which is certainly to take place during the course of time, and not after its close.—BUSH.

CHAPTER XIII.

Ver. 16. And he causeth all, both small and great, rich and poor, free and bond, to receive a mark in their right hand, or in their foreheads.

It was a general custom in the East to brand their slaves in the forehead, as being the most exposed; sometimes in other parts of the body. The common way of stigmatizing was by burning the member with a red-hot iron, marked with certain letters, till a fair impression was made, and then pouring ink into the furrows, that the inscription might be more conspicuous. Slaves were often branded with marks, or letters, as a punishment of their offences; but the most common design of these marks was to distinguish them if they should desert their masters. For the same reason, it was common to brand their soldiers, but with this difference, that while slaves were marked in the hand, with the name, or some peculiar character belonging to their masters; soldiers were marked in the hand with the name or character of their general. In the same manner, it was the custom to stigmatize the worshippers and votaries of some false gods. Lucian affirms, that the worshippers of the Syrian goddess, were all branded with certain marks, some in the palms of their hands, and others in their necks. To this practice may be traced the custom, which became so prevalent among the Syrians, thus to stigmatize themselves; and Theodoret is of opinion, that the Jews were forbidden to brand their bodies with stigmata, because the idolaters, by that ceremony, used to consecrate themselves to their false deities. The marks employed on these occasions were various. Sometimes they contained the name of the god; sometimes his particular ensign, as the thunderbolt of Jupiter, the trident of Neptune, the ivy of Bacchus: or they marked themselves with some mystical number, which described the name of the god. Thus the sun, who was denoted by the number DC VIII, is said to have been represented by the two numeral letters XH. These three ways of stigmatizing, are all expressed by the apostle John in the book of Revelation: "And he causeth all, both small and great, rich and poor, free and bond, to receive a mark in their right hand or in their foreheads; and that no man might buy or sell, save he that had the mark or the name of the beast, or the number of his name." The followers of the beast received a mark in their right hand, because they ranged themselves under his banners, ready to support his interests, and extend his dominions with fire and sword; they bore the name of their general, the bishop of Rome, Λατεινος, and the number of his name, which is 666. But they also received the mark of slaves on their foreheads, to denote that they were his absolute property, whom he arrogated a right to dispose of according to his pleasure; who could neither buy nor sell, live with comfort, nor die in peace, without his permission. But they were not only soldiers and slaves; they were also devotees, that regarded and acknowledged him as a god, and even exalted him above all that is called God and is worshipped; in token of which they received a mark in the palm of their hands, or in their foreheads. The practice of marking the soldier and the devotee, although of great antiquity, may be traced to one origin, to a custom still more ancient, of marking a slave with some peculiar stigma, to prevent him from deserting his master's service, or rendering his discovery and restoration certain and easy. To this custom the prophet Ezekiel refers: "Go through the midst of the city, through the midst of Jerusalem, and set a mark upon the foreheads of the men that sigh, and that cry for all the abominations that be done in the midst thereof." Another instance may be mentioned from the Revelation: "Hurt not the earth, neither the sea, nor the trees, till we have sealed the servants of our God in their foreheads." In both instances, it is the symbol of protection and security both to the persons and privileges of the people of God.—PAXTON.

CHAPTER XXI.

Ver. 19. And the foundations of the wall of the city *were* garnished with all manner of precious stones. The first foundation *was* jasper; the second, sapphire; the third, a chalcedony; the fourth, an emerald.

This is not only a description of what must be exceedingly beautiful in its appearance, but is moreover manifestly corresponding with the mode of building among the ancient Romans, who, it is well known, constructed their walls from the bottom to the top with *alternate layers*, or rows of bricks, and of white stone, and sometimes of black flints. Each of these layers was always of a considerable thickness, or breadth; and while their different colours formed a beautiful appearance to the eye, and were a most elegant kind of ornament, this mode of placing materials of different dimensions and substance in alternate rows greatly strengthened the work.—KING.

INDEX.

PATMOS

www.ingramcontent.com/pod-product-compliance
Lightning Source LLC
LaVergne TN
LVHW021048110826
845150LV00001B/15

* 9 7 8 1 4 2 5 5 6 8 5 1 1 *